# RAND McNALLY

S0-CFA-659

# Chicago & Vicinity
# 6-County

## StreetFinder®

## Contents

**Chicago and Cook County**
Detailed Street Maps 10-95
Street Index 97-144

**DuPage County**
Detailed Street Maps 4-35
Street Index 37-59

**Kane County**
Detailed Street Maps 4-51
Street Index 52-64

**Lake County**
Detailed Street Maps 4-51
Street Index 53-77

**McHenry County**
Detailed Street Maps 4-51
Street Index 52-64

**Will County**
Detailed Street Maps 4-77
Street Index 79-96

Photo credit: Buckingham Fountain / Chicago Office of Tourism

PageFinder™ Map U.S. Patent No. 5,419,586.

Information included in this publication has been checked for accuracy
prior to publication. Since changes do occur, the publisher cannot be
responsible for any variations from the information printed.

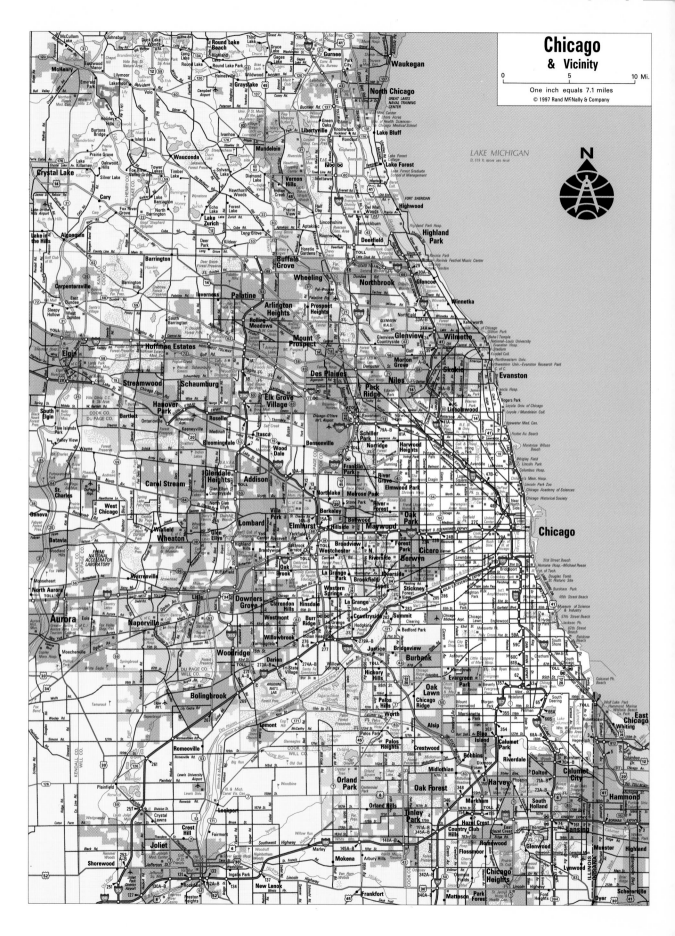

**Chicago & Vicinity**

0    5    10 Mi.

One inch equals 7.1 miles

© 1997 Rand McNally & Company

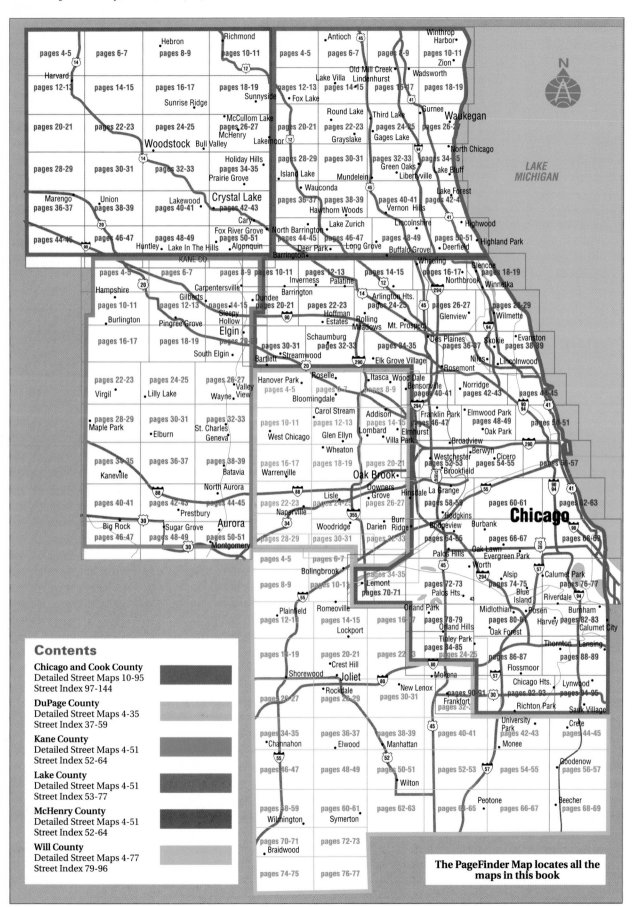

## Contents

The PageFinder Map locates all the maps in this book

This StreetFinder is the comprehensive, easy-to-use atlas of streets in the entire Chicago 6-County area. Featuring the **PageFinder™ Map** *(illustrated at right)*, the exclusive fold-out page is designed for quick map and page location. Also included are 336 pages of full-color maps, an index of 57,160 street names, and Quick Reference Guides to each of the six collar counties of Chicago.

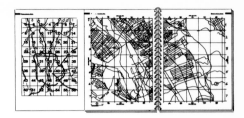

PageFinder Map

## Using the StreetFinder

### PageFinder Map

Located on the following page, the PageFinder Map folds out for reference when using the book *(as shown in the above illustration)*.

The PageFinder Map is a grid showing page numbers for all the maps in the StreetFinder. The Chicago area is divided by the grid beginning in the northwest area of the map. Maps proceed in rows according to the grid from west to east.

### Example of Use

As an example of typical StreetFinder use, open the PageFinder Map to the left of the book. Assume you want to know which page McCullom Lake is on. You can quickly identify which map page you need. As shown on the open PageFinder Map, McCullom Lake is on page 26 of the McHenry section of this book. Using the PageFinder Map you can get around the Chicago area as well as the StreetFinder with ease.

### StreetFinder Maps

Each map page contains a letter-number grid. This letter-number system provides coordinates that allow you to quickly find streets and places listed in the index. The letter number system is based on miles from point zero at State and Madison streets in downtown Chicago. For example, central McHenry has coordinates of 33W-33N, 33 miles north and west of State and Madison. This universal grid/index system applies to the entire Chicago area. The map pages also include a reference at the edges to adjoining maps. Look for neighboring areas by referring to "See page..." notations.

### StreetFinder Index

Each county section of the book lists the street name; the direction in which it runs; the coordinates of the grid square in which the name of the street can be found; and the appropriate page number. In cases where a street runs through several grid squares within the same community, the Street Index will list the coordinates of the grid squares located at the outermost boundaries of the community. The page number will be for the westernmost or southernmost map page that contains the street.

### Use Maps or Index

Locate your destination by either using the PageFinder Map or by consulting the index.

## Map Legend

| | |
|---|---|
| Free/Toll Expressway | |
| U.S. or State Route | |
| Through Road | |
| Other Street | |
| Interstate | (95) |
| U.S. | (1) |
| State | (7) |
| Point of Interest | |
| Cemetery | |
| Park | |
| Forest Preserve | |
| Golf Course or Country Club | |
| School | |
| Church | |
| Zip Code | 60622 |

0 ——————— ½ ——————— 1

**1 inch = 1/2 mile**

### Zip Code Map Index

| | | |
|---|---|---|
| Chicago & Cook County | Cook County | Pg. 96 |
| DuPage County | DuPage County | Pg. 36 |
| Kane County | DuPage County | Pg. 64 |
| Lake County | Lake County | Pg. 52 |
| McHenry County | Lake County | Pg. 80 |

# RAND McNALLY

# Chicago &
# Cook County

## StreetFinder®

page **Contents**

A    Using the StreetFinder

B    PageFinder Map

C    Vicinity Map

1    Contents

2    Downtown Chicago Map

4    Quick Reference Guide

9    Chicago Block Number System

10    StreetFinder Maps

97    StreetFinder Index

Photo credit: Chicago Skyline by Peter J. Schulz / Chicago Office of Tourism

## CHICAGO DOWNTOWN STREET INDEX

### Downtown Chicago

**Points of Interest**

- Tourist info
- Hospital
- Police
- Theatre
- Bank
- Post Office
- Shopping
- Hotel
- Restaurant
- Parking
- Church

N

0   0.1   0.2   0.3   0.4 km
0      0.1      0.2      0.3 mi

## CHICAGO DOWNTOWN POINTS OF INTEREST

## Cook County Municipal Offices

| | Location | Page |
|---|---|---|
| Alsip Village | 5W-14S | 74 |
| 4500 123rd St; 385-6902 | | |
| Arlington Heights Village Hall | 17W-14N | 24, 25 |
| 33 S Arlington Heights Rd; 253-2340 | | |
| Barrington Village Hall | 25W-18N | 12 |
| 206 S. Hough; 381-2141 | | |
| Barrington Hills Village Hall | 28W-16N | 11 |
| 112 Algonquin Rd; 428-1200 | | |
| Bartlett Village Hall | 29W-8N | 30, 31 |
| 228 Main St; 837-0800 | | |
| Bedford Park Village Hall | 9W-7S | 60 |
| 6701 Archer Rd.; 458-2067 | | |
| Blue Island City Hall | 3W-15S | 75 |
| 13051 Greenwood Ave; 597-8600 | | |
| Broadview Village Hall | 11W-0S | 47 |
| 1600 Roosevelt Rd; 681-3600 | | |
| Burbank City Hall | 8W-9S | 65 |
| 6530 W 79th; 559-5500 | | |
| Burr Ridge Village Hall | 15W-8S | 58 |
| 220 75th; 325-0420 | | |
| Calumet City City Hall | 4E-17S | 83 |
| 204 Pulaski Rd; 891-8100 | | |
| Calumet Park Village Offices | 1W-14S | 76 |
| 12409 Throop; 388-0850 | | |
| Chicago City Hall | 0W-0N | 51 |
| 121 N. LaSalle Ave; 744-5000 | | |
| Chicago Heights City Hall | 1W-25S | 93 |
| 1601 Chicago Rd; 756-5317 | | |
| Chicago Ridge Village Hall | 7W-12S | 66 |
| 10655 S Oak Ave; 425-7700 | | |
| Cicero Town Offices | 6W-2S | 55 |
| 4936 25th Pl; 656-3600 | | |
| Country Club Hill City Hall | 4W-21S | 87 |
| 3700 W 175th Pl; 798-2616 | | |
| Countryside City Hall | 12W-5S | 58 |
| Des Plaines City Hall | 13W-11N | 26 |
| 1420 Miner; 391-5300 | | |
| East Hazel Crest Village Hall | 1W-20S | 88 |
| 17223 Throop; 798-0213 | | |
| Elk Grove Village Hall | 19W-8N | 33 |
| 901 Wellington Ave; 439-3900 | | |
| Elmwood Park Village Hall | 9W-3N | 41 |
| 11 Conti Pkwy; 452-7302 | | |
| Evanston Civic Center | 2W-12N | 29 |
| 2100 Ridge Ave; 328-2100 | | |
| Evergreen Park Village Hall | 4W-10S | 66, 67 |
| 9418 Kedzie Ave; 422-1551 | | |
| Flossmoor Village Hall | 3W-23S | 87 |
| 2800 Flossmoor Rd; 798-2300 | | |

| | Location | Page |
|---|---|---|
| Forest Park Village Hall | 9W-0S | 48 |
| 517 Des Plaines Ave; 366-2323 | | |
| Franklin Park Village Hall | 11W-3N | 41 |
| 9554 Belmont; 671-4800 | | |
| Glencoe Village Ctr | 6W-17N | 18, 19 |
| 325 Hazel; 835-4111 | | |
| Glenview Village Hall | 8W-13N | 27 |
| 1225 Waukegan Rd; 724-1700 | | |
| Glenwood Village Hall | 0E-22S | 88 |
| 13 S Rebecca; 758-5150 | | |
| Golf Village Hall | 8W-12N | 27 |
| 1 Briar Rd; 998-8852 | | |
| Hanover Park Village Hall | 27W-8N | 31 |
| 2121 Lake; 837-3800 | | |
| Hazel Crest Municipal Ctr | 3W-20S | 87 |
| 3000 W 170th Pl; 335-9600 | | |
| Hoffman Estates Village Hall | 24W-12N | 22 |
| 1200 N Gannon Dr; 882-9100 | | |
| Hometown City Hall | 5W-10S | 66 |
| 4331 SW Hwy; 424-7500 | | |
| Homewood Village Hall | 2W-21S | 87 |
| 2020 Chestnut Rd; 798-3000 | | |
| Lansing Mayor & Clerks Office | 3E-21S | 89 |
| 18200 Chicago Ave; 895-7200 | | |
| Lynwood Village Office | 2E-24S | 95 |
| 20636 Torrence Ave; 758-6101 | | |
| Lyons Village Hall | 9W-4S | 54 |
| 7801 Ogden Ave; 447-8886 | | |
| Markham City Hall | 3W-19S | 81 |
| 16313 Kedzie Ave; 331-4905 | | |
| Maywood Village Hall | 10W-0N | 47 |
| 115 S 5th Ave; 344-1200 | | |
| Merrionette Park Village Hall | 3W-13S | 75 |
| 3165 115th St.; 396-3180 | | |
| Midlothian Village Hall | 4W-17S | 81 |
| 14801 Pulaski Rd; 389-0200 | | |
| Morton Grove Village Hall | 7W-10N | 37 |
| 6101 Capulina Ave; 965-4100 | | |
| Niles Village Admin Bldg | 9W-9N | 37 |
| 7601 Milwaukee Ave; 967-6100 | | |
| Norridge Village Offices | 9W-5N | 41 |
| 4020 Olcott Ave; 453-0800 | | |
| Northbrook Village Hall | 10W-17N | 17 |
| 1225 Cedar Lane; 272-5050 | | |
| Northfield Village Hall | 6W-15N | 18, 19 |
| 361 Happ Rd; 446-9200 | | |
| North Riverside Village Hall | 10W-2S | 53 |
| 2400 Desplaines Ave; 447-4211 | | |
| Oak Forest City Hall | 7W-18S | 80 |
| 15440 Central Ave; 687-4050 | | |
| Oak Lawn Village Hall | 6W-10S | 66 |
| 5252 Dumke Dr; 636-4400 | | |

| | Location | Page |
|---|---|---|
| Oak Park Village Hall | 8W-0N | 48 |
| 1 Village Hall Plaza; 383-6400 | | |
| Orland Park Village Hall | 12W-17S | 78 |
| 14415 Beacon Ave; 349-5400 | | |
| Park Forest Village Hall | 3W-26S | 92 |
| 200 Forest Blvd; 748-1112 | | |
| Park Ridge City Hall | 10W-8N | 36, 37 |
| 505 Park Pl; 399-5200 | | |
| Phoenix Village Hall | 0W-18S | 82 |
| 15240 Vincennes Rd; 331-2636 | | |
| Posen Village Hall | 3W-17S | 81 |
| 2440 W 147th; 385-0139 | | |
| Richton Park Village Hall | 5W-27S | 91 |
| 4455 Sauk Tr; 841-2200 | | |
| Riverdale Village Hall | 0W-16S | 82 |
| 325 W 142d; 841-2200 | | |
| River Forest Village Hall | 9W-0N | 48 |
| 400 Park Ave; 366-5481 | | |
| River Grove Village Hall | 10W-3N | 42 |
| 2601 Thatcher Ave; 453-8000 | | |
| Robbins Village Hall | 4W-16S | 75 |
| 3329 137th; 385-8940 | | |
| Rolling Meadows City Hall | 20W-13N | 23 |
| 3600 Kirchoff Rd; 394-8500 | | |
| Schaumburg Municipal Bldg | 22W-10N | 32, 33 |
| 101 S Schaumburg Ct; 894-4500 | | |
| Schiller Park Village Hall | 12W-5N | 40, 41 |
| 9526 Irving Park Rd; 678-2550 | | |
| Skokie Village Hall | 6W-9N | 38 |
| 5127 Oakton; 673-0500 | | |
| South Chicago Heights Village Hall | 1W-26S | 93 |
| 2729 Jackson Ave; 755-1880 | | |
| South Holland Village Hall | 0E-19S | 82 |
| 16226 Wausau Ave; 333-0572 | | |
| Steger Village Hall | 1W-27S | 93 |
| 35 W 34th; 754-3395 | | |
| Streamwood Village Hall | 28W-9N | 31 |
| 401 Irving Park Rd; 837-0200 | | |
| Tinley Park Village Hall | 8W-20S | 85,86 |
| 17355 68th Ct; 532-7700 | | |
| Westchester Village Hall | 12W-0S | 46,47 |
| 10240 Roosevelt Rd; 345-0020 | | |
| Wheeling Village Hall | 14W-18N | 16 |
| 255 W Dundee Rd; 459-2600 | | |
| Wilmette Village Hall | 3W-13N | 29 |
| 1200 Wilmette Ave; 251-2700 | | |

## Colleges & Universities

| | Location | Page |
|---|---|---|
| American Islamic Col | 0W-5N | 45 |
| Brisk Rabbinical Col | 3W-7N | 39 |
| Catholic Theological Union | 2E-5S | 63 |
| Chicago Baptist Institute | 0E-5S | 62 |
| Chicago Col of Osteopathic Medicine | 1E-5S | 62, 63 |
| Chicago Natural Col of Naprapathy | 5W-4N | 44 |
| Chicago State Univ | 0E-11S | 68 |
| Chicago Theological Sem | 1E-6S | 62, 63 |
| Christ Sem- Seminex | 1E-5S | 62, 63 |
| City Col of Chicago-Kennedy-King | 0W-7S | 62 |
| City Col of Chicago-Richard J Daley Col | 5W-8S | 60 |
| City Col of Chicago-Truman Col | 1W-5N | 45 |
| City Col of Chicago-Malcolm X Col | 2W-0S | 50 |
| City Col of Chicago-Olive-Harvey | 1E-11S | 68 |
| City Col of Chicago-Wright Col | 7W-4N | 42, 43 |
| Columbia Col | 0E-0S | 51 |
| Concordia Col | 9W-1N | 48 |
| Cortez W Peters Bus Col | 2W-11S | 67 |
| DePaul Univ | 1W-2N | 51 |
| DePaul Univ-Lincoln Park | 1W-2N | 51 |
| DeVry Inst of Tech | 3W-4N | 44 |
| Garrett Evangelical Theological Sem | 2W-12N | 29 |
| Harper College NE Ctr | 13W-15N | 16 |
| Hebrew Theological Col | 6W-8N | 38 |
| Ill Col of Optometry | 0E-3S | 57 |
| Ill Inst of Technology | 0E-3S | 57 |
| Kendall Col | 2W-12N | 29 |
| Loyola Univ | 1W-8N | 39 |
| Loyola Univ-Downtown | 0E-1N | 51 |
| Lutheran School of Theology at Chicago | 1E-5S | 62, 63 |
| McCormick Theological Sem | 1E-6S | 62, 63 |
| Meadville-Lombard Theological School | 1E-6S | 62, 63 |
| Moody Bible Inst | 0W-1N | 51 |
| Moraine Valley Col | 11W-12S | 65 |
| Morton Jr Col | 6W-3S | 55 |
| Mundelein Col | 1W-8N | 39 |
| National Col | 2W-13N | 29 |
| North Park Col & Theological Seminary | 4W-6N | 38, 44 |
| Northeastern Ill Univ | 4W-6N | 38, 44 |
| Northwestern Bus Col | 6W-6N | 43 |
| Northwestern Univ | 2W-12N | 29 |
| Northwestern Univ-Chicago | 0E-0N | 51 |
| Oakton Comm Col | 12W-12N | 26 |
| Prairie State Col | 1W-23S | 88 |
| Roosevelt Univ | 0E-0S | 51 |
| Rosary Col | 9W-1N | 48 |
| St Augustine Col | 1W-6N | 45 |
| St Xavier Col | 4W-11S | 66, 67 |
| Seabury-Western Theological Sem | 2W-12N | 29 |
| Thornton Comm Col | 0W-18S | 82 |
| Triton Col | 10W-2N | 47, 48 |
| Univ of Chicago | 1E-6S | 62, 63 |
| Univ of Illinois at Chicago | 1W-0S | 51 |
| Vander Cook Col of Music | 0E-3S | 57 |
| Willam Rainey Harper Col | 22W-13N | 23 |

## Forest Preserves

*Forest preserves may cover an extensive area.*
*Only one set of map coordinates is given for each page*
*of the StreetFinder on which a particular woods or*
*preserve may be found.*

| | Location | Page |
|---|---|---|
| Algonquin Woods | 12W-9N | 35, 36 |
| Allison Woods | 12W-15N | 16, 26 |
| Bachelor Grove Woods | 8W-16S | 73, 79 |
| Beaubien Woods | 1E-15S | 76, 77 |
| Black Partridge FP | 20W-13S | 70 |
| Bunker Hill Woods | 8W-8N | 37 |
| Burnham Woods | 4E-16S | 83 |
| Calumet Grove | 2W-16S | 75 |
| Che-che-pin-qua Woods | 10W-4N | 41, 42 |
| Chipilly Woods FP | 8W-17N | 18 |
| Chippewa Woods | 11W-8N | 36 |
| Clayton F Smith Woods | 7W-8N | 37, 38 |
| Crabtree Nature Center | 27W-16N | 11 |
| Dam No 1 Woods | 13W-17N | 16 |
| Dam No 2 Woods | 11,12W-13N | 26 |
| Dam No 4 Woods | 11W-8N | 36 |
| Dan Ryan Woods | 2W-10S | 67 |
| Deer Grove FP | 21W-18N | 12, 13 |
| Edgebrook Woods | 6W-7N | 37 |
| Eggers Woods | 4E-13S | 77 |
| Forest Preserves | 7W-17N | 18 |
| | 7W-21S | 86 |
| | 10W-1S | 53 |
| | 13W-12N | 26 |
| | 12W-11N | 26 |
| | 12W-2S | 52 |
| | 9W-0N | 48 |
| Fullerton Woods East | 10W-2N | 48 |
| Fullerton Woods West | 10W-2N | 48 |
| GAR Woods | 10W-0N | 47, 48 |
| Golf Corner Driving Range FP | 13W-12N | 26 |
| Harms Woods | 7W-12N | 28 |
| Indian Road Woods | 6W-7N | 38 |
| Iroquois Woods | 12W-9N | 36 |
| Kickapoo Meadows | 1W-16S | 82 |
| La Bagh Woods | 5W-6N | 43 |
| Lansing Woods | 2, 3E-22S | 89 |
| Linne Woods | 7W-11N | 27, 28 |
| Linne Woods West | 8W-11N | 27, 28 |
| Lion Woods | 13W-11N | 26 |
| Miami Woods | 8W-10N | 37 |
| Midlothian Meadow | 5W-18S | 81, 82 |
| Miller Meadows | 10W-1S | 54 |
| Ned Brown FP | 19W-11N, | |
| | 18W-10N | 33, 34 |
| Paul Douglas FP | 24W-13N | 22 |
| Palos Hills Forest Preserve | 14W-13S | 71, 72 |

| | Location | Page |
|---|---|---|
| Poplar Creek FP | 27W-12N, | |
| | 30W-11N | 21, 30, 31 |
| Potawatomi Woods | 13W-18N | 16 |
| Rubio Woods | 7W-16S | 74 |
| St Paul Woods | 8W-10N | 37 |
| Sauk Trail Woods | 2W-27S | 93 |
| Schuth's Grove | 10W-1S | 53 |
| Seymour Simon Preserve | 10, 11W-4N | 41 |
| Somme Woods FP | 9W-18N | 18 |
| Spring Creek Valley FP | 29W-15N | 20, 21 |
| Spring Valley Nature Sanct | 22W-10N | 33 |
| Sunset Ridge Woods FP | 8W-17N | 18 |
| Tampier Slough FP | 14, 15W-15S | 71 |
| Thatcher Woods | 10W-1N | 47, 48 |
| Thatcher Woods Glen | 10W-0N | 47, 48 |
| Thomas Jefferson Woods | 10W-0N | 47, 48 |
| Tinley Creek Woods | 8W-16S | 73 |
| Whistler Woods | 0W-15S | 76 |
| William N. Erikson FP | 7W-18N | 18 |
| Yankee Woods | 7W-19S | 80 |

## Country Clubs & Golf Courses

| | Location | Page |
|---|---|---|
| Anetsberger GC | 9W-16N | 18 |
| Arlington Lakes GC | 18, 19W-12N | 24 |
| Bartlett Hills G&CC | 29W-8N | 30, 31 |
| Beverly CC | 3W-9S | 67 |
| Billy Caldwell GC | 6W-7N | 37, 38 |
| Bryn Mawr CC | 5W8N | 38 |
| Burnham Woods GC | 4E-16S | 83 |
| Calumet CC | 2W-20S | 87 |
| Cherry Hill CC | 4W-22S | 87 |
| Chicago Heights CC | 2W-24, 25S | 93, 94 |
| Chick Evans GC | 7W-11N | 27, 28 |
| Cog Hill CC | 16, 17W-13S | 71 |
| Columbus Park GC | 7W-0S | 48, 49 |
| Edgebrook GC | 7W-7N | 37, 38 |
| Edgewood Valley CC | 13W-8S | 58 |
| Evanston GC | 5W-10N | 28, 38 |
| Evergreen Park GC | 3W-10S | 67 |
| Flossmoor CC | 2W-23S | 87 |
| Fresh Meadow G&CC | 14W-1S | 52 |
| Glencoe GC | 7W-18N | 18 |
| Gleneagles CC | 16W-14S | 71 |
| Glenview GC | 7W-12N | 27, 28 |
| Glenview NAS GC | 9, 10W-13N | 27 |
| Glenwoodie CC | 0E-23S | 88 |
| Golden Acres CC | 23W-10, 11N | 32 |
| Golden Acres CC | 8W-18N | 18 |
| Hickory Hills GC | 10W-11S | 65 |
| Highland Woods GC | 22, 23W-13N | 22, 23 |
| Hilldale CC | 25W-12N | 22 |
| Idlewild CC | 2W- 22, 23S | 87 |

| | Location | Page |
|---|---|---|
| Indian Boundary GC | 10W-4N | 41 |
| Indian Hill GC | 4, 5W-14N | 28, 29 |
| Inverness GC | 23W-16N | 12, 13 |
| Jackson Park GC | 2E-7S | 63 |
| Joe Louis GC | 1W-15S | 75, 76 |
| La Grange CC | 13W-5S | 58 |
| Lake Shore CC | 6W-18N | 18, 19 |
| Lakewood CC | 3E-26S | 95 |
| Marquette Park GC | 4W-7S | 61 |
| Midlothian CC | 6W-17S | 80 |
| Mission Hills CC | 12W-16N | 16 |
| Mt Prospect GC | 16W-12N | 25 |
| North Shore CC | 7, 8W-13N | 27, 28 |
| Northwestern GC | 7W-11N | 27, 28 |
| Oak Park CC | 10W-2N | 47 |
| Old Orchard CC | 15W-14N | 25 |
| Olympia Fields CC | 3W-24S | 92, 93 |
| Palatine Hills GC | 21W-17N | 13 |
| Palos CC | 11W-15S | 72, 73 |
| Park Ridge CC | 10W-9N | 36 |
| Peter N. Jans GC | 2,3W-12,13N | 29 |
| Poplar Creek GC | 26W-12N | 31, 32 |
| Poplar Lake GC | 26W-12N | 31, 32 |
| Ravisloe CC | 2, 3W-21S | 87 |
| Ridge CC | 3W-12S | 67 |
| Ridgemoor CC | 8W-5N | 42 |
| River Forest GC | 15W-4N | 40 |
| River Oaks GC | 2E-19S | 83 |
| Riverside GC | 10W-2S | 53 |
| Robert A Black GC | 2W-8N | 39 |
| Rob Roy GC | 14W-14N | 25 |
| Rolling Green CC | 16W-14N | 25 |
| Rolling Knolls GC | 31W-11N | 30 |
| Sheridan Shore Yacht Club | 2W-13N | 29 |
| Silver Lake CC | 10W-17S | 79 |
| Skokie CC | 6W-17N | 18 |
| Skokie Playfield GC | 6W-15, 16N | 18, 19 |
| South Shore GC | 3E-7S | 63 |
| Sportsman's CC | 11, 12W-17N | 16 |
| Sunset Ridge CC | 8W-16N | 18 |
| Thunderbird CC | 24W-18N | 12 |
| Valley-Lo Sports Club GC | 8W-14N | 27 |
| Villa Olivia G & CC | 30, 31W-9N | 30 |
| Walnut Hills CC | 10W-11S | 65 |
| Waveland Ave. GC | 0W-5N | 45 |
| Westgate Valley CC | 8W-15S | 73, 74 |
| Westmore-land CC | 5W-12, 13N | 28, 29 |
| Wilmette GC | 6, 7W-14N | 28 |

## Hospitals

| | Location | Page |
|---|---|---|
| Alexian Brothers Medical Ctr | 19W-8N | 33 |
| Augustana Hosp | 0W-2N | 45, 51 |

| | Location | Page |
|---|---|---|
| Belmont Comm Hosp | 5W-4N | 44 |
| Bethany Methodist Hosp | 2W-6N | 45 |
| Bethany Hosp | 4W-0S | 50 |
| Bethesda Hosp | 3W-9N | 39 |
| Central Comm Hosp | 2W-6S | 61 |
| Charter Barclay Hosp | 1W-5N | 45 |
| Chicago Lakeshore Hosp | 1W-6N | 45 |
| Chicago-Read Mental Health Center | 8W-5N | 42 |
| Childrens Mem Hosp | 0W-2N | 45, 51 |
| Christ Hosp & Medical Ctr | 5W-10S | 66 |
| Columbus Hosp | 0W-3N | 45 |
| Cook County Hosp | 2W-0S | 50 |
| Edgewater Hosp | 2W-7N | 39 |
| Elizabeth Hosp | 2W-1N | 50 |
| Evanston Hosp | 2W-13N | 29 |
| Forest Hosp | 12W-11N | 26 |
| Frank Cuneo Mem Hosp | 1W-5N | 45 |
| Franklin Blvd Comm Hosp | 4W-0N | 50 |
| Glenbrook Hosp | 11W-14N | 26 |
| Gottlieb Mem Hosp | 10W-2N | 47 |
| Grant Hosp | 0W-2N | 51 |
| Hartgrove Hosp | 4W-0N | 50 |
| Holy Cross Hosp | 3W-7S | 61 |
| Holy Family Hosp | 13W-12N | 26 |
| Hospital of Englewood | 1W-6S | 61, 62 |
| Humana Hosp Hoffman Ests | 26W-12N | 22 |
| Hyde Park Comm Hosp | 1E-6S | 63 |
| Ill Masonic Med Ctr | 1W-3N | 45 |
| Ill State Psychiatric Inst | 2W-0S | 50 |
| Ingalls Memorial Hosp | 1W-18S | 81, 82 |
| Jackson Park Hosp | 2E-8S | 63 |
| La Rabida Children's Hosp & Res Ctr | 0W-1S | 63 |
| Lakeside Comm Hosp | 0W-1S | 57 |
| Lincoln West Medical Ctr | 3W-5N | 44 |
| Little Company of Mary Hosp | 3W-10S | 67 |
| Loretto Hosp | 7W-0S | 48, 49 |
| Loyola Univ Med Ctr | 10W-0S | 47 |
| Lutheran General Hosp | 11W-10N | 36 |
| MacNeal Hosp | 8W-3S | 54 |
| Martha Washington Hosp | 2W-5N | 44, 45 |
| Mary Thompson Hosp | 2W-0N | 50 |
| Mercy Hosp & Med Ctr | 0E-2S | 57 |
| Michael Reese Hosp & Med Ctr | 0E-2S | 57 |
| Northwest Community Hosp | 18W-13N | 24 |
| Northwest Hosp | 7W-4N | 42, 43 |
| Northwest Mem Hosp | 0E-0N | 51 |
| Norwegian American Hosp | 3W-1N | 50 |
| Oak Forest Hosp | 5W-19S | 80, 81 |
| Oak Park Hosp | 8W-0S | 47 |
| Old Orchard Hosp | 5W-12N | 28 |
| Olympia Fields Osteopathic Medical Ctr | 4W-24S | 92 |

| | Location | Page |
|---|---|---|
| Palos Comm Hosp | 8W-14S | 73 |
| Provident Med Ctr | 0E-5S | 62 |
| Ravenswood Hosp Med Ctr | 2W-5N | 45 |
| Rehab Institute of Chicago | 0E-0N | 51 |
| Resurrection Hosp | 9W-7N | 37 |
| Riveredge Hosp | 10W-0S | 47 |
| Roseland Comm Hosp | 0W-13S | 76 |
| Rush Presbyterian-St Lukes Med Ctr | 2W-0S | 50 |
| St Annes Hosp | 6W-1N | 49 |
| St Annes Hosp West | 13W-1N | 46 |
| St Anthony Hosp | 3W-1S | 56 |
| St Bernard Hosp | 0W-7S | 62 |
| St Frances X Cabrini Hosp | 1W-0S | 51 |
| St Francis Hosp | 2W-9N | 39 |
| St Francis Hosp | 2W-15S | 75 |
| St James Hosp | 1W-25S | 93 |
| St Joseph Hosp | 0W-3N | 45 |
| St Mary of Nazareth Hosp Ctr | 2W-1N | 50 |
| Schwab Rehab Ctr | 3W-1S | 56 |
| Sheridan Road Hosp | 1W-7N | 39 |
| Shriners Hosp for Crippled Children | 8W-2N | 48 |
| Skokie Valley Hosp | 5W-12N | 28, 29 |
| South Chicago Comm Hosp | 2E-10S | 69 |
| South Shore Hosp | 2E-9S | 69 |
| South Suburban Hosp | 4W-21S | 87 |
| Swedish Covenant Hosp | 3W-6N | 44 |
| Thorek Hosp & Med Ctr | 0W-5N | 45 |
| Tinley Park Mental Health Ctr | 9W-21S | 85 |
| Univ of Chicago Hosps & Clins | 1E-6S | 62, 63 |
| Univ of Ill Hosp | 2W-0S | 50 |
| VA Hosp (Hines) | 10W-1S | 53 |
| VA Lakeside Med Ctr | 0E-0N | 51 |
| VA West Side Med Ctr | 2W-0S | 50 |
| Walther Memorial Hosp | 4W-1N | 50 |
| Weiss Mem Hosp | 0W-5N | 45 |
| Westlake Comm Hosp | 11W-0N | 47 |
| West Suburban Hosp Med Ctr | 7W-0N | 51, 52 |
| Woodlawn Hosp | 1E-6S | 62, 63 |

## Shopping Centers

| | Location | Page |
|---|---|---|
| Brickyard SC | 8W-3N | 42 |
| Canterbury SC | 3W-19S | 81 |
| Deerbrook SC | 10W-18N | 17 |
| Dunbrook SC | 10W-18N | 17 |
| Edens Plaza SC | 6W-14N | 28 |
| Evergreen Plaza SC | 3W-11S | 67 |
| Flossmoor Commons East SC | 4W-23S | 87 |
| Flossmoor Commons West SC | 4W-23S | 87 |
| Ford City SC | 5W-8S | 60 |
| Forest Park Mall | 9W-0S | 48 |
| Four Flags SC | 10W-11N | 27 |
| French Vill SC | 4W-21S | 87 |

| | Location | Page |
|---|---|---|
| Golf Mill SC | 10W-11N | 36, 47 |
| Golf Rose SC | 23W-11N | 32 |
| Golfview SC | 8W-12N | 27, 28 |
| Greenlake SC | 11W-12N | 26 |
| Grenoble Sq SC | 4W21S | 87 |
| Grove Mall SC | 19W-8N | 33 |
| Highland Plaza SC | 4W-20S | 87 |
| Hillside Mall SC | 13W-0S | 46 |
| Hillside Mall SC | 28W-10N | 31 |
| Hoffman Plaza SC | 23W-11N | 32 |
| Lake Cook Plaza SC | 10W-18N | 17 |
| Lincoln Mall SC | 5W-25S | 91 |
| Market Place SC | 15W-11N | 25 |
| Matteson Town Ctr SC | 6W-25S | 91 |
| McDade SC | 10W-11N | 27 |
| Meadow Plaza SC | 9W-17N | 17 |
| Millbrook SC | 10W-11N | 27 |
| Mt Prospect SC | 14W-13N | 25 |
| Northbrook Court SC | 9W-18N | 18 |
| Northbrook Shop Plaza SC | 9W-17N | 18 |
| Northpoint SC | 17W-16N | 14, |
| North Riverside Park Mall SC | 9W-2S | 53 |
| Norwood SC | 3W-26S | 93 |
| Oak Park Mall | 8W-0N | 48 |
| Old Orchard SC | 6W-12N | 28 |
| Orland Court SC | 11W-18S | 78, 79 |
| Orland Sq SC | 11W-17S | 78, 79 |
| Palwaukee SC | 13W-15N | 16 |
| Park & Shop SC | 18W-10N | 34 |
| Park Plaza SC | 25W-8N | 32 |
| Plaza SC | 3W-27S | 92, 93 |
| Plaza-del-Prado SC | 10W-15N | 17 |
| Prospect Heights SC | 15W-14, 15N | 15, 25 |
| Randhurst SC | 15W-14N | 25 |
| River Oaks SC | 3E-19S | 83 |
| River Oaks West SC | 2E-19S | 83 |
| Sanders Court SC | 12W-17N | 16 |
| Sauk Trail SC | 4W-27S | 92 |
| Shoppers Walk | 10W-11N | 27 |
| Stonebridge SC | 3W-21S | 87 |
| Streamwood SC | 28W-10N | 31 |
| Town-N-Country Mall SC | 17W-15N | 14 |
| Town Sq. SC | 23W-10N | 32 |
| Tradewinds SC | 26W-9N | 31 |
| Venture SC | 10W-12N | 27 |
| Weathersfield Commons SC | 25W-10N | 32 |
| White Plains SC | 11W-17N | 16, 17 |
| Wiseway Plaza SC | 25W-9N | 32 |
| Woodfield Commons SC | 21W-11N | 33 |
| Woodland Hts SC | 28W-9N | 31 |

## Getting Around Chicago

For the most part, streets in Chicago lie in a grid pattern, with the city center at the intersection of State and Madison Streets in downtown Chicago. Madison Street, running east and west, and State Street, running north and south, are the base lines from which all block and house numbers are determined.

Generally, block numbers in Chicago ascend in all directions by multiples of 100. Chicago street names and block numbers may not extend into neighboring suburbs. Here is a list of the major streets in Chicago along with their distance from the baseline in both miles and block numbers:

| North of Madison Street | | Block No. |
|---|---|---|
| Chicago Ave | 1 mile | 800 |
| North Ave | 2 miles | 1600 |
| Fullerton Ave | 3 miles | 2400 |
| Belmont Ave | 4 miles | 3200 |
| Irving Park Rd | 5 miles | 4000 |
| Lawrence Ave | 6 miles | 4800 |
| Bryn Mawr Ave | 7 miles | 5600 |
| Devon Ave | 8 miles | 6400 |
| Touhy Ave | 9 miles | 7200 |
| Howard St | 9 1/2 miles | 7600 |

| South of Madison Street | | |
|---|---|---|
| Roosevelt Rd | 1 mile | 1200 |
| Cermak Rd | 2 miles | 2200 |
| 31st St | 3 miles | 3100 |
| Pershing Rd | 4 miles | 3900 |
| 47th St | 5 miles | 4700 |
| 55th St | 6 miles | 5500 |
| 63rd St | 7 miles | 6300 |
| 71st St | 8 miles | 7100 |
| 79th St | 9 miles | 7900 |
| 87th St | 10 miles | 8700 |
| 95th St | 11 miles | 9500 |

| West of State Street | | |
|---|---|---|
| Halsted St | 1 mile | 800 |
| Ashland Ave | 2 miles | 1600 |
| Western Ave | 3 miles | 2400 |
| Kedzie Ave | 4 miles | 3200 |
| Pulaski Rd | 5 miles | 4000 |
| Cicero Ave | 6 miles | 4800 |
| Central Ave | 7 miles | 5600 |
| Narragansett Ave | 8 miles | 6400 |
| Harlem Ave | 9 miles | 7200 |

| East of State Street | | |
|---|---|---|
| South Park Ave | 1/2 mile | 400 |
| Cottage Grove Ave | 1 miles | 800 |
| Woodlawn Ave | 1 1/2 miles | 1200 |
| Stony Island Ave | 2 miles | 1600 |
| Jeffrey Ave | 2 1/2 miles | 2000 |
| Yates Ave | 3 miles | 2400 |
| Brandon Ave | 4 miles | 3200 |

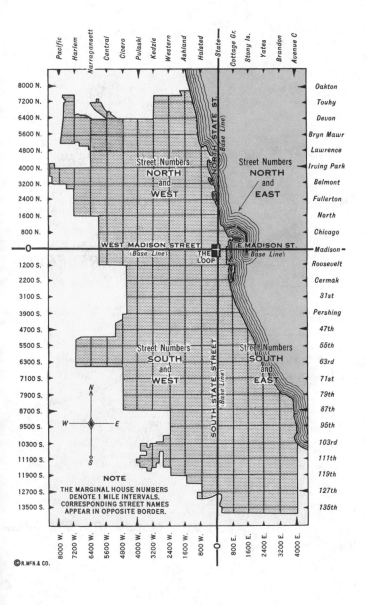

SEE McHENRY COUNTY PAGES 50-51

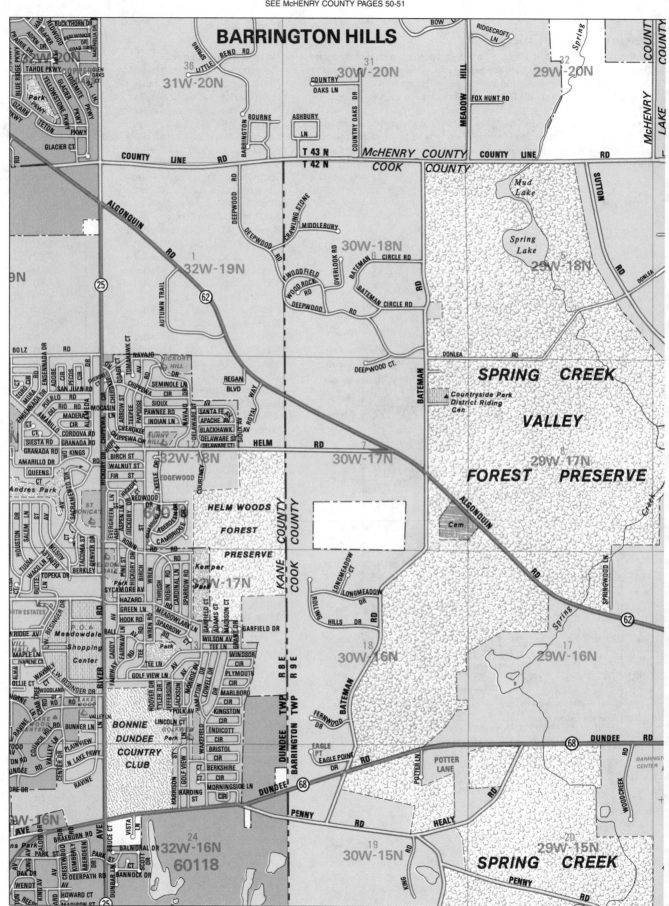

# BARRINGTON HILLS

SEE PAGES 20-21

SEE LAKE COUNTY PAGES 44-45

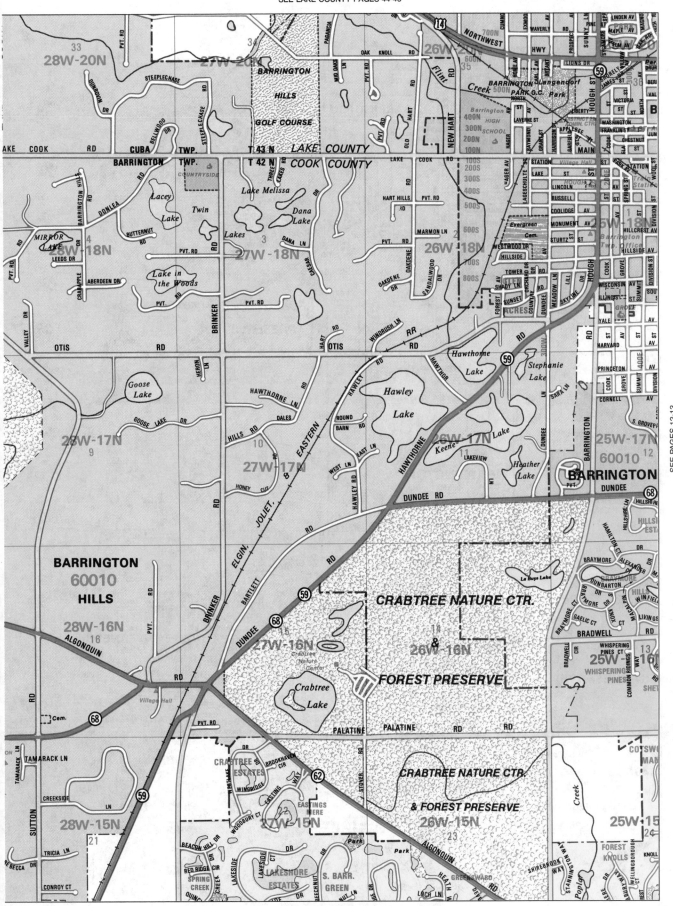

SEE PAGES 12-13

SEE LAKE COUNTY PAGES 44-45

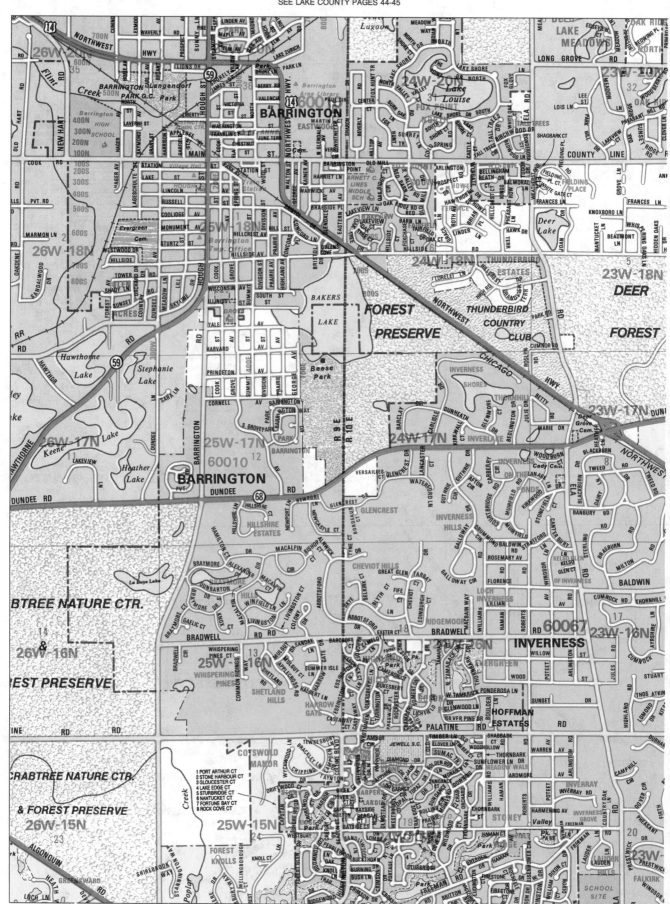

SEE PAGES 10-11

SEE PAGES 22-23

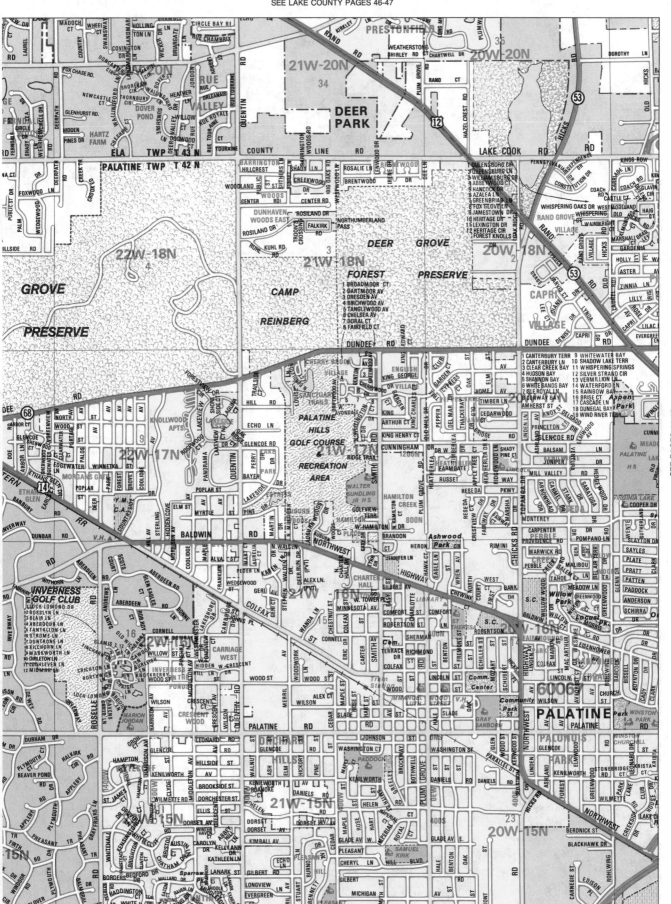

SEE LAKE COUNTY PAGES 46-47

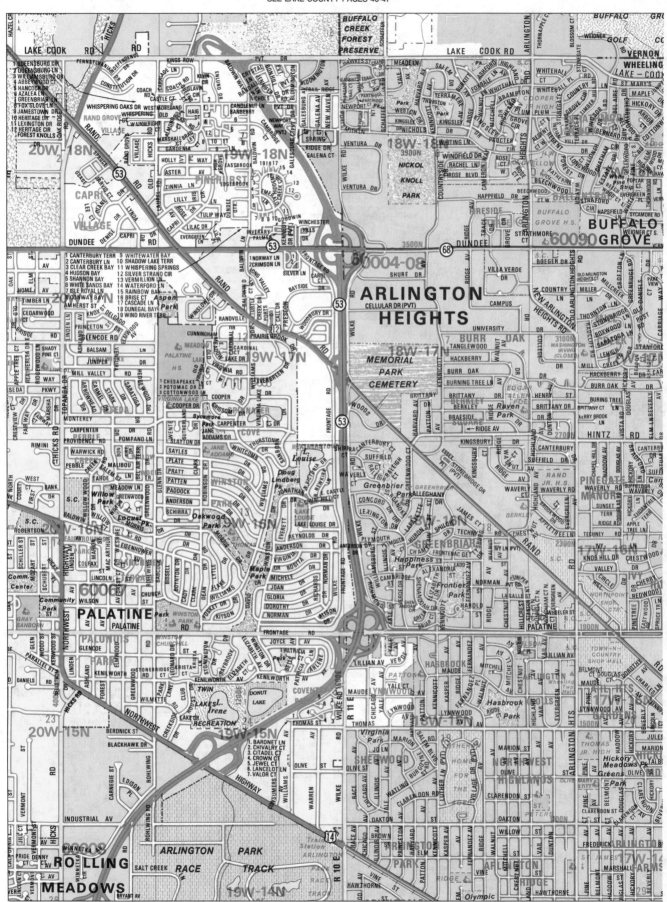

SEE LAKE COUNTY PAGES 48-49

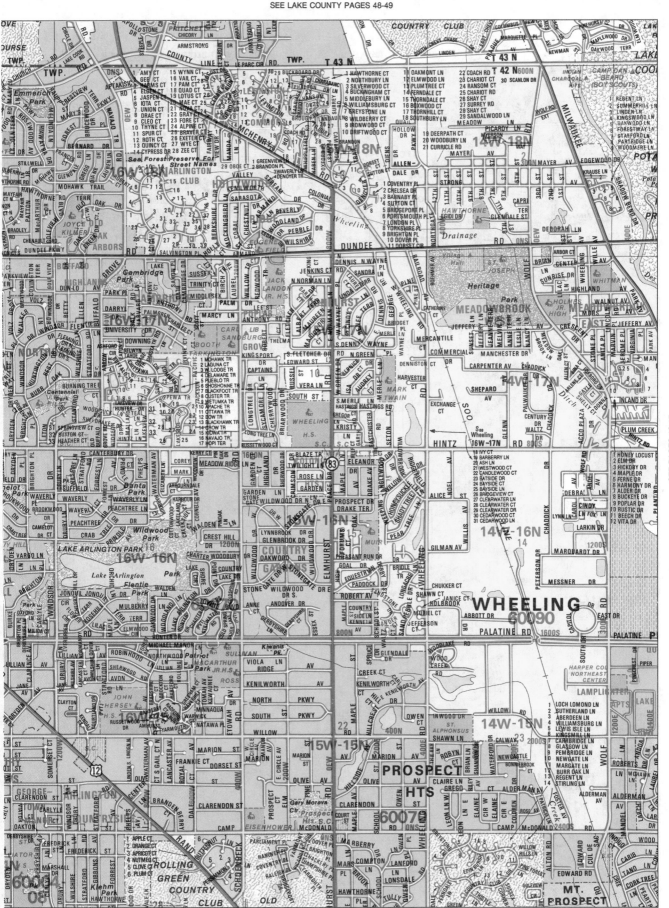

SEE PAGES 16-17

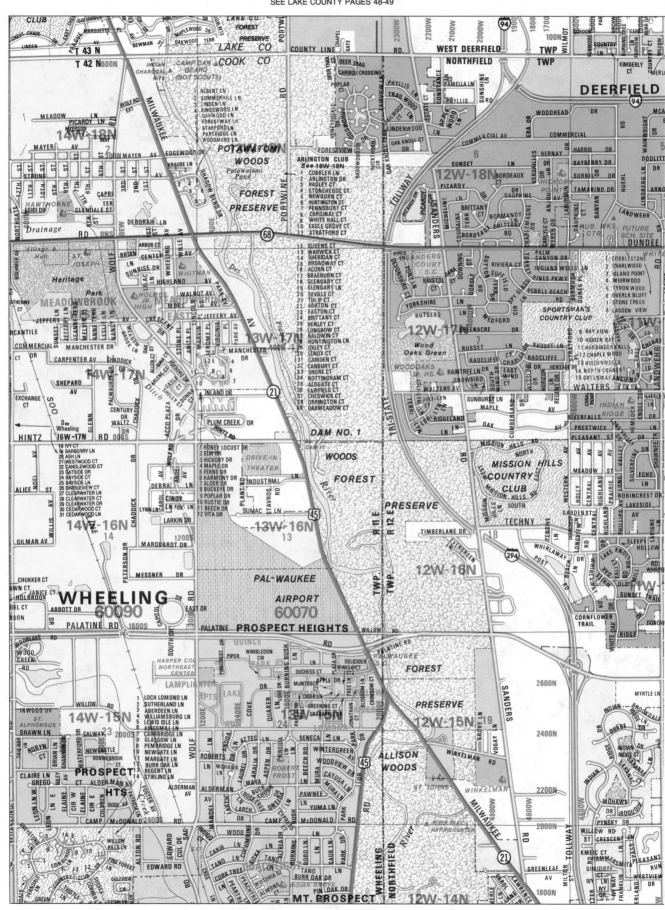

SEE LAKE COUNTY PAGES 50-51

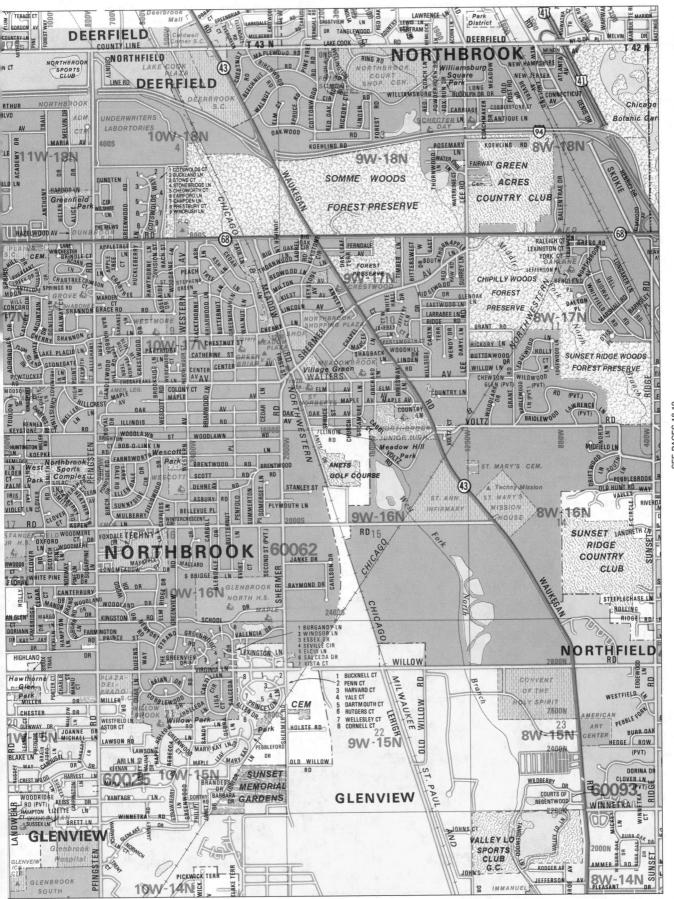

SEE PAGES 18-19

SEE LAKE COUNTY PAGES 50-51

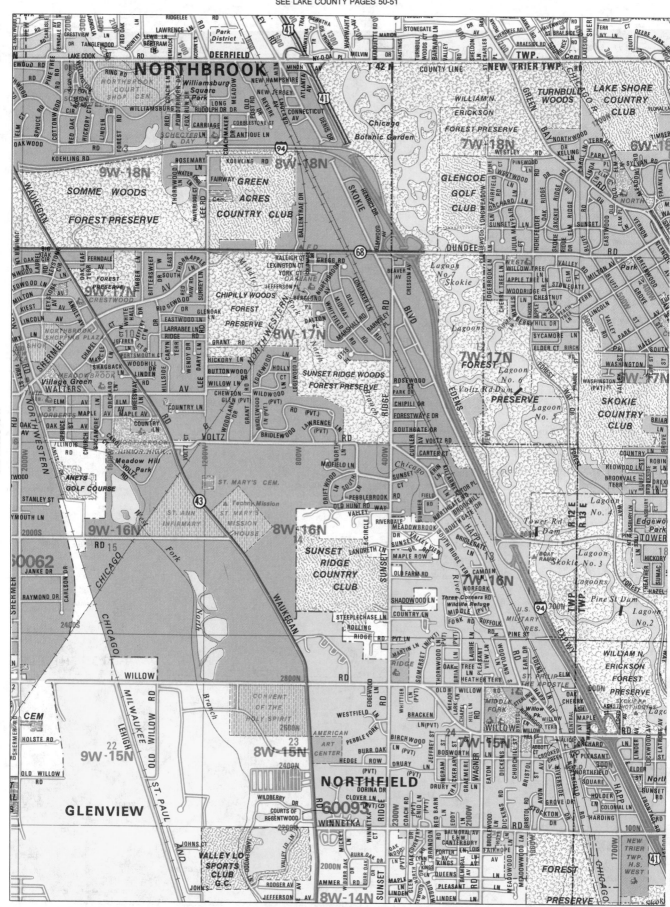

SEE PAGES 16-17

SEE PAGES 28-29

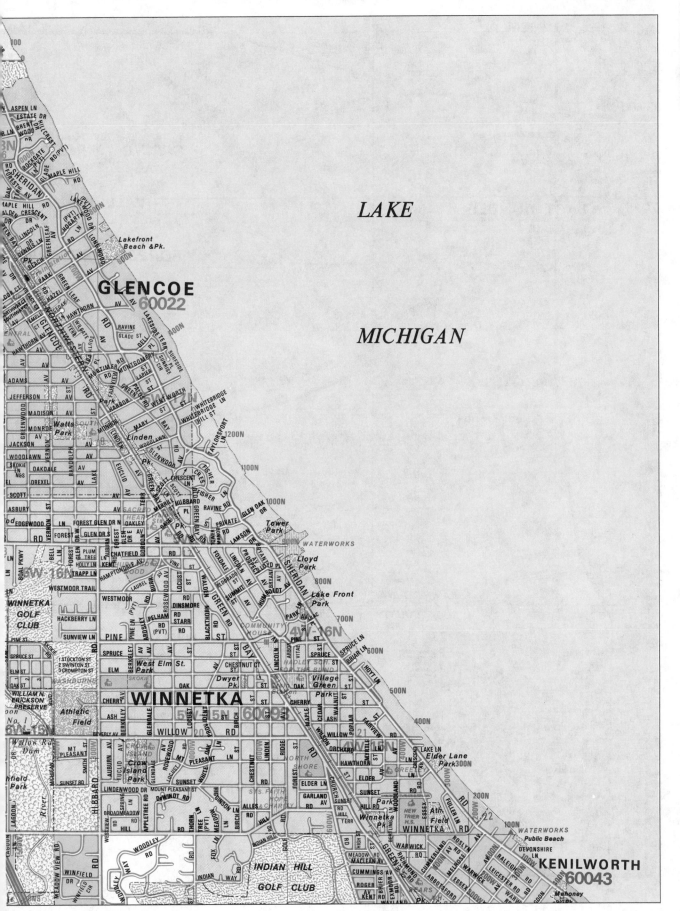

LAKE

MICHIGAN

GLENCOE 60022

WINNETKA 60093

KENILWORTH 60043

SEE PAGES 28-29

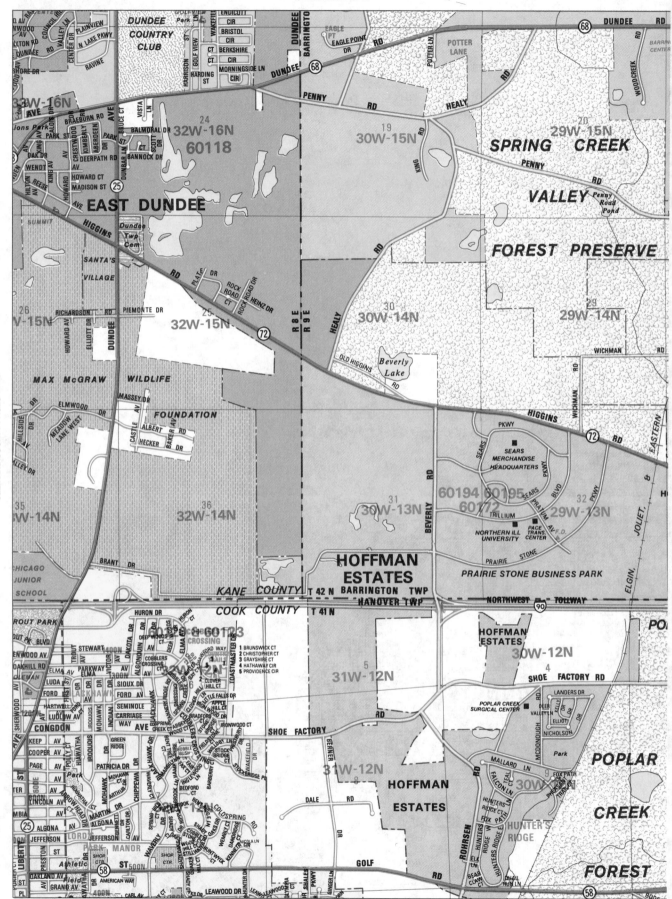

SEE PAGES 10-11

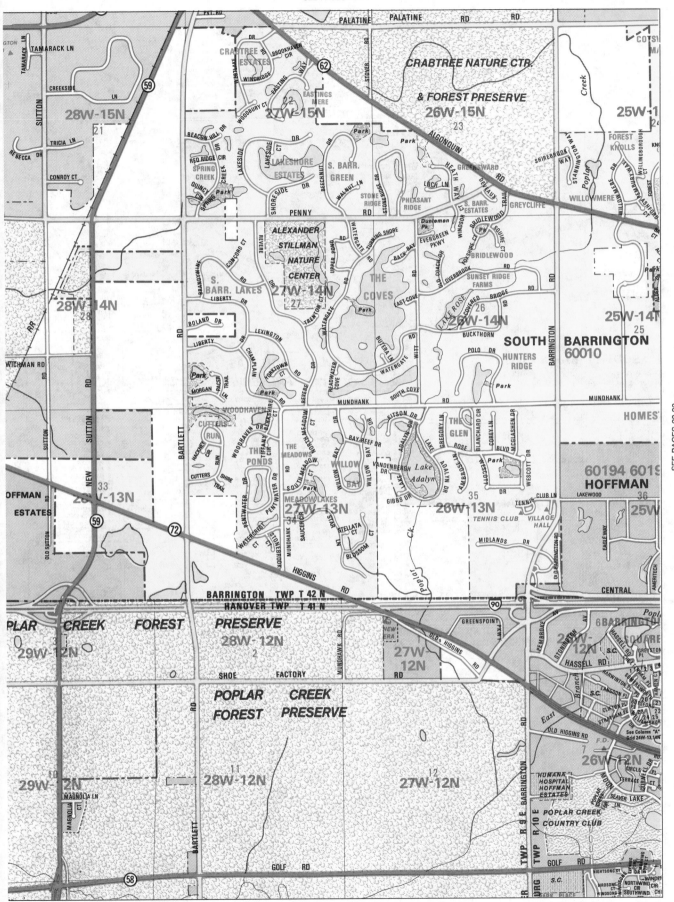

SEE PAGES 22-23

SEE PAGES 12-13

SEE PAGES 20-21

COTSWOLD MANOR

1 PORT ARTHUR CT
2 STONE HARBOUR CT
3 GLOUCESTER CT
4 LAKE EDGE CT
5 STURBRIDGE CT
6 NANTUCKET CT
7 FORTUNE BAY CT
8 ROCK COVE CT

25W-15N

FOREST KNOLLS

PRESERVE

25W-14N

SOUTH BARRINGTON 60010

HUNTERS RIDGE

HOMESTEAD

60194 60195 60172
HOFFMAN ESTATES
25W-13N

PAUL DOUGLAS
FOREST PRESERVE

SOUTH BARRINGTON

24W-14N

**COLUMN "A"**
SEE GRID 25,26W-12N
1. HOLBROOK LN.
2. CARDIGAN PL.
3. BRIGHTON LN.
4. OXFORD LN.
5. KETTERING RD.
6. GEORGETOWN LN.
7. ERIE LN.
8. DUNMORE PL.
9. FRANKLIN PL.
10. RALEIGH LN.
11. STOCKTON DR.
12. HASTINGS DR.
13. HANCOCK DR.
14. MARQUETTE LN.
15. LIBERTY PL.
16. RALEIGH LN.
17. BAYBERRY LN.
18. GARDEN TERR.
19. SUDBURY DR.
20. WHITINGHAM LN.
21. DANBURY PL.
22. SUTHERLAND PL.
23. SMETHWICK LN.
24. GRANTHAM PL.
25. WELLINGTON PL.

**COLUMN "B"**
SEE GRID 26W-11N
1. MIDDLEBURY CT.
2. SANDHURST CT.
3. OAK KNOLL CT.
4. BOXWOOD CT.
5. DRIFTWOOD CT.
6. IRONWOOD CT.
7. DOGWOOD CT.
8. BIRCHWOOD CT.
9. ARROWOOD CT.
10. SANDALWOOD CT.
11. WHITEHALL CT.
12. CLARIDGE CT.
13. OAK MEADOW CT.
14. OAKMONT CT.
15. PLUM TREE CT.
16. SOUTHBURY CT.
17. WOODBURY CT.
18. GREYSTONE CT.
19. WARWICK CT.
20. FERNWOOD CT.
21. SIEVERWOOD CT.
22. LEXINGTON CT.

**COLUMN "C"**
SEE GRID 26W-11N
1. ANDOVER CT.
2. DENTON CT.
3. HUNTLY CT.
4. SHAW CT.
5. NEWTON CT.
6. RAMSEY CIR.
7. HYDE CT.
8. KENDALL CT.
9. BURGESS CT.
10. CLAYTON CT.
11. ACADEMY CT.
12. MANOR CT.
13. BRYN MAWR CT.
14. BRITTANY CT.
15. CARDINAL CT.
16. DORCHESTER CT.
17. DEERFIELD CT.
18. EAGLE CT.
19. FLOWER CT.
20. GLENVIEW CT.
21. OXHILL CT.
22. PALACE CT.
23. OLD KINGS CT.
24. ONYX CT.
25. LIBERTY CT.
26. LEAR CT.
27. KAVALIER CT.
28. KNOLLWOOD CT.
29. HAMILTON CIR.
30. HAMILTON PL.

**COLUMN "D"**
SEE GRID 24W-9N
1. FISKEVILLE LN.
2. DANVERS CT.
3. STONINGTON CT.
4. SWANSEA CT.
5. WOONSOCKET CT.
6. TAUNTON CT.
7. BELMONT CT.
8. MATFIELD CT.
9. GROTON CT.
10. RUSKIN CT.
11. HOLLISTON CT.
12. WALPOLE LN.
13. SUDBURY CT.
14. GLASTONBURY LN.
15. SAYLESVILLE LN.
16. SHANNOCK LN.
17. MOHEGAN LN.

**COLUMN "E"**
SEE GRID 25W-11N
1. HASTINGS CT.
2. FINCHLEY CT.
3. RICHMOND CT.
4. CARNABY CT.
5. DUNBAR CT.
6. BISHOP CT.
7. ANGUS CT.
8. CARLISLE CT.
9. MANSFIELD CT.
10. FENWICK CT.
11. HANLEY CT.
12. LARGO CT.
13. BROMLEY CT.
14. CARDIFF CT.
15. DURSFORD CT.
16. LANCASHIRE CT.
17. STOCKBRIDGE CT.
18. CLARENDON SPRINGS CT.

HIGHLAND WOODS GOLF COURSE

60172 60193-95

SCHAUMBURG

POPLAR CREEK COUNTRY CLUB

HUMANA HOSPITAL HOFFMAN ESTATES

HILLDALE COUNTRY CLUB

60010

SEE PAGES 32-33

Binny's
302 W. Golf

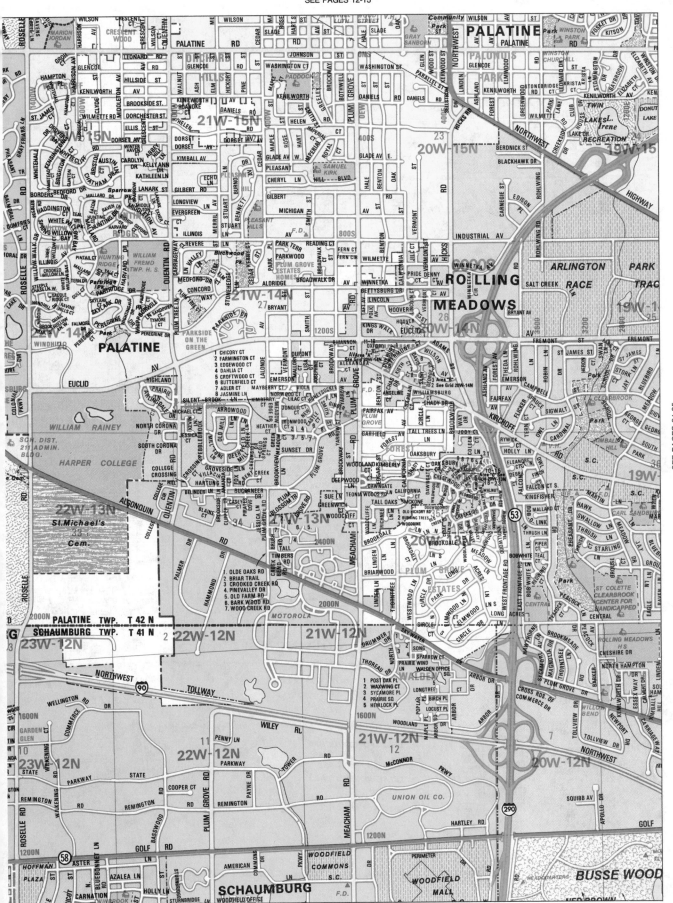

SEE PAGES 24-25

SEE PAGES 14-15

SEE PAGES 22-23

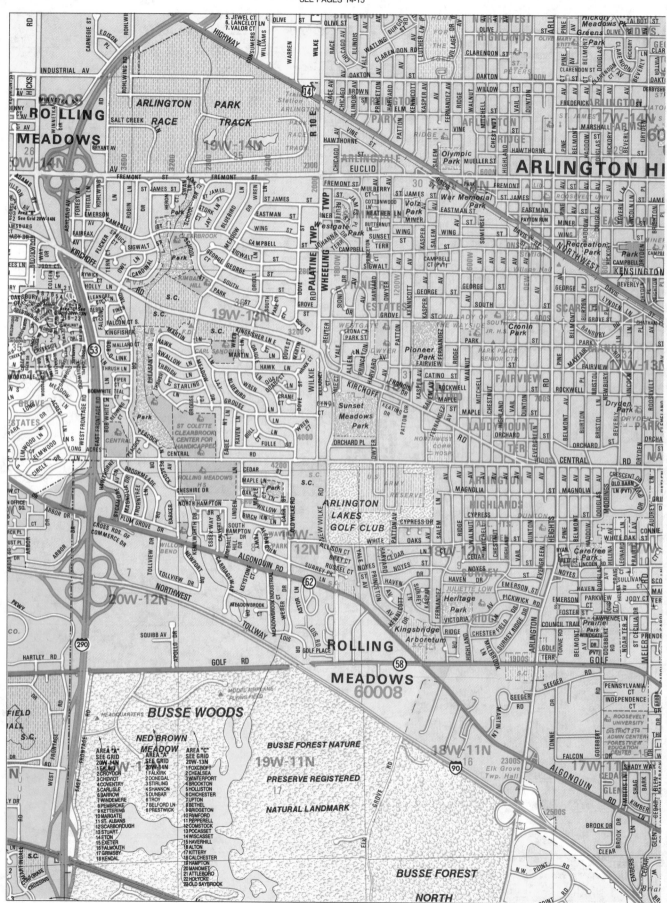

SEE PAGES 14-15

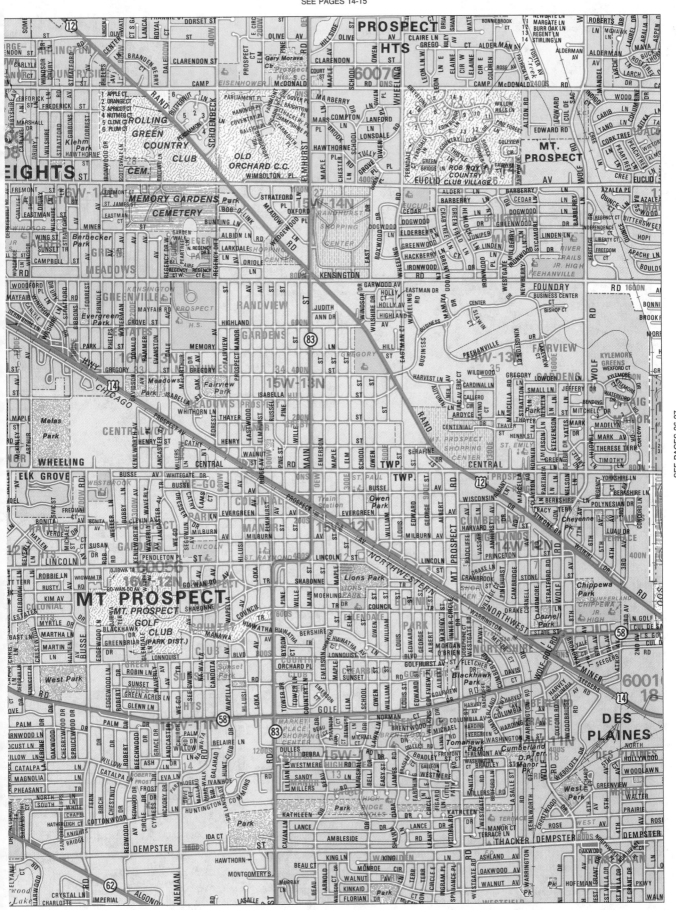

SEE PAGES 26-27

SEE PAGES 16-17

SEE PAGES 24-25

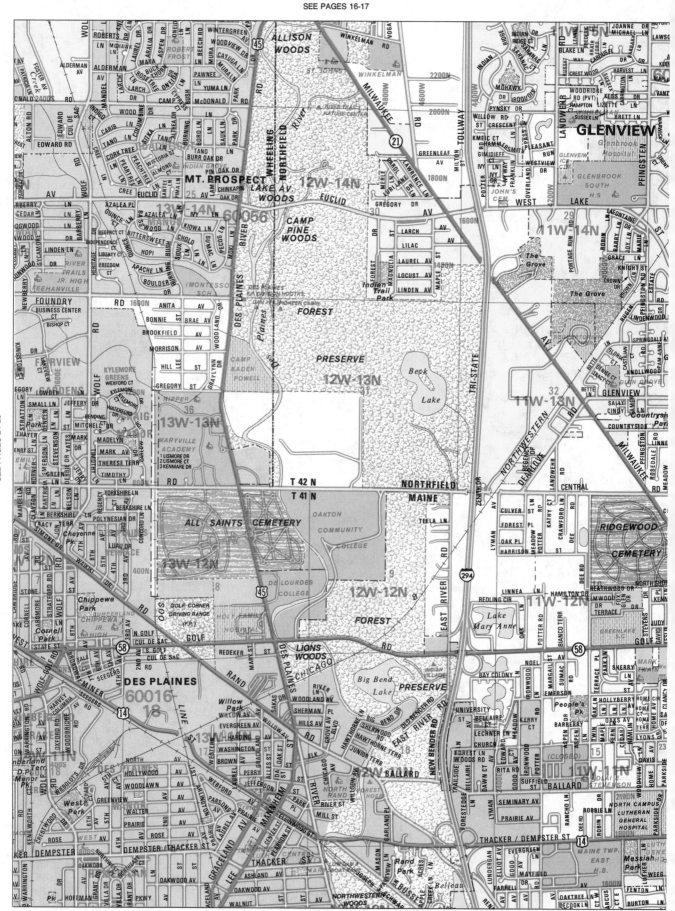

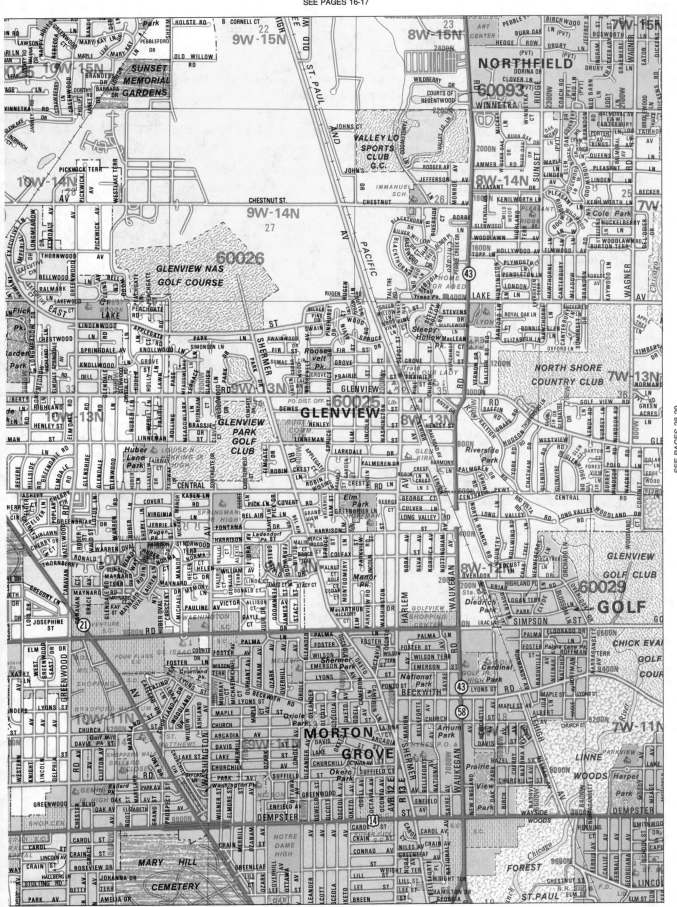

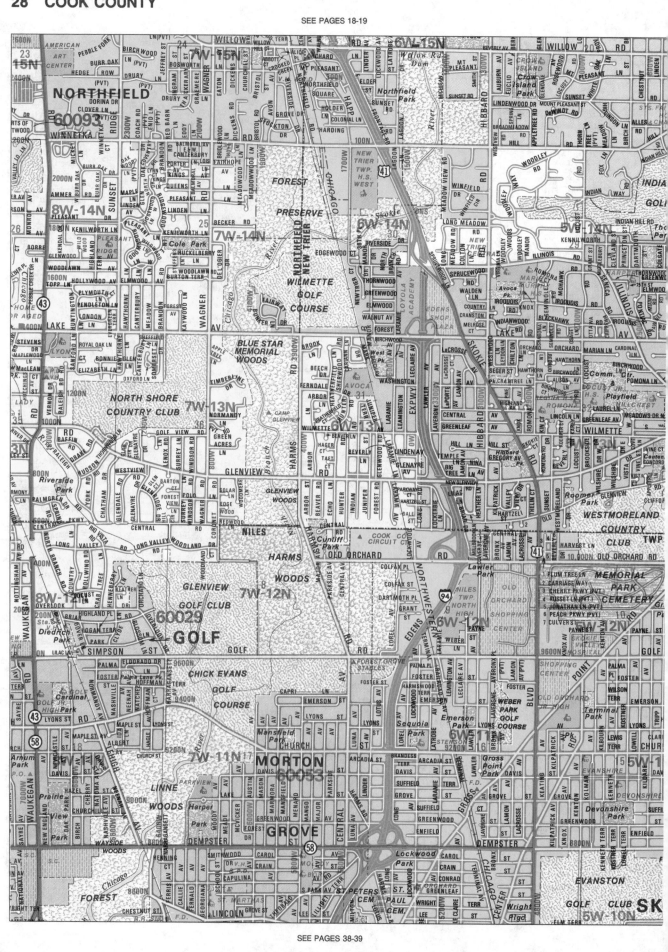

SEE PAGES 18-19

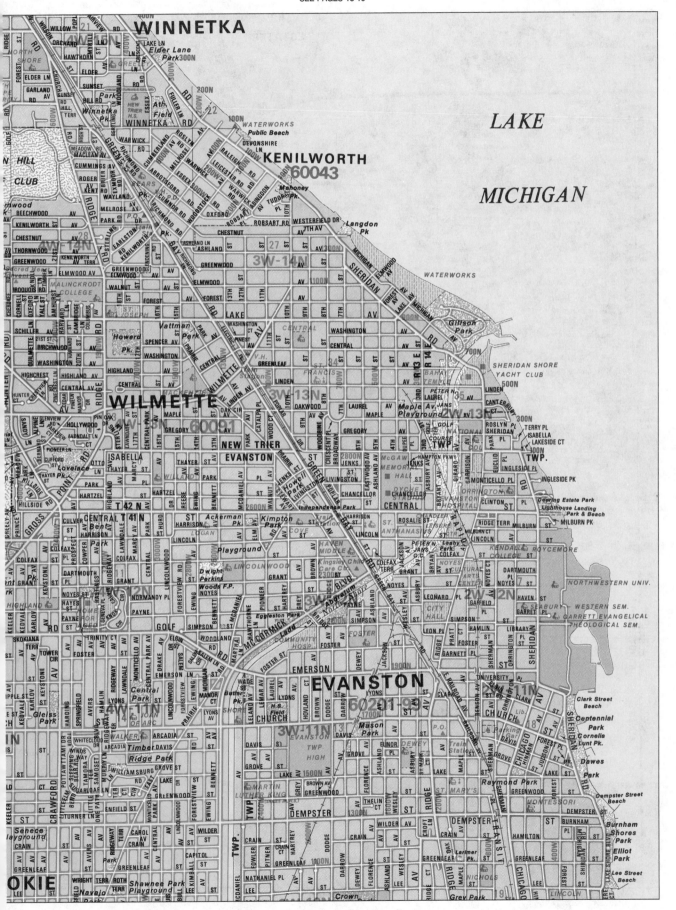

SEE PAGES 20-21

SEE KANE COUNTY PAGES 20-21

SEE DU PAGE COUNTY PAGES 4-5

SEE PAGES 20-21

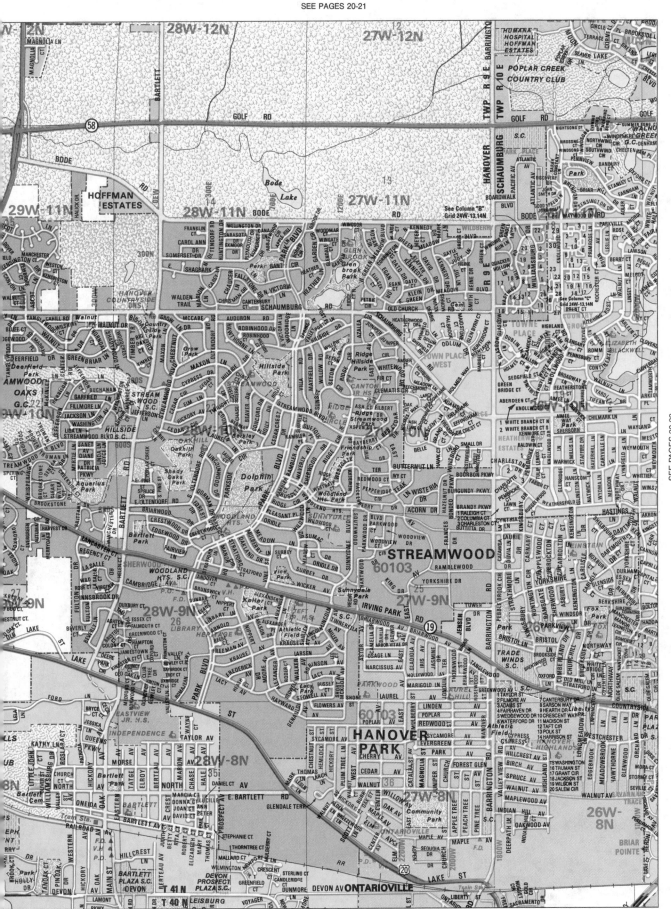

SEE PAGES 32-33

**STREAMWOOD**
60103

**HANOVER PARK**

60103

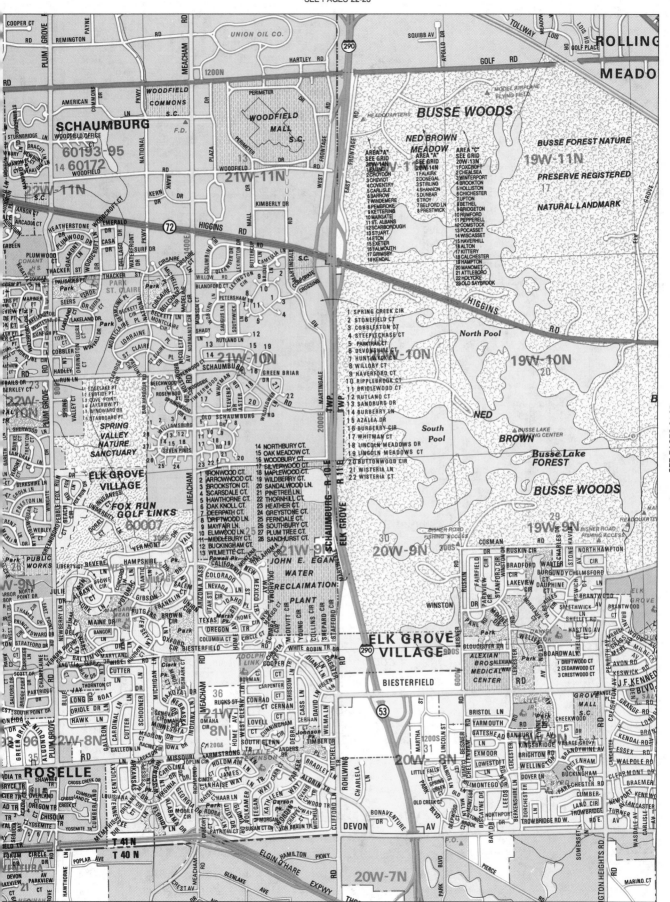

SEE PAGES 24-25

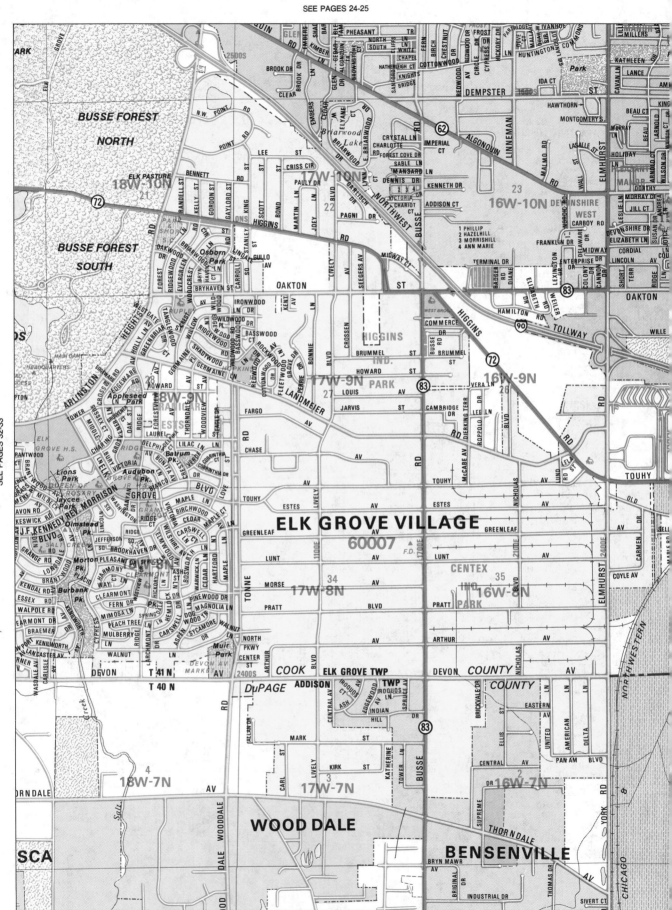

SEE PAGES 32-33

**ELK GROVE VILLAGE**

60007

**WOOD DALE**

**BENSENVILLE**

SEE DU PAGE COUNTY PAGES 8-9

SEE PAGES 24-25

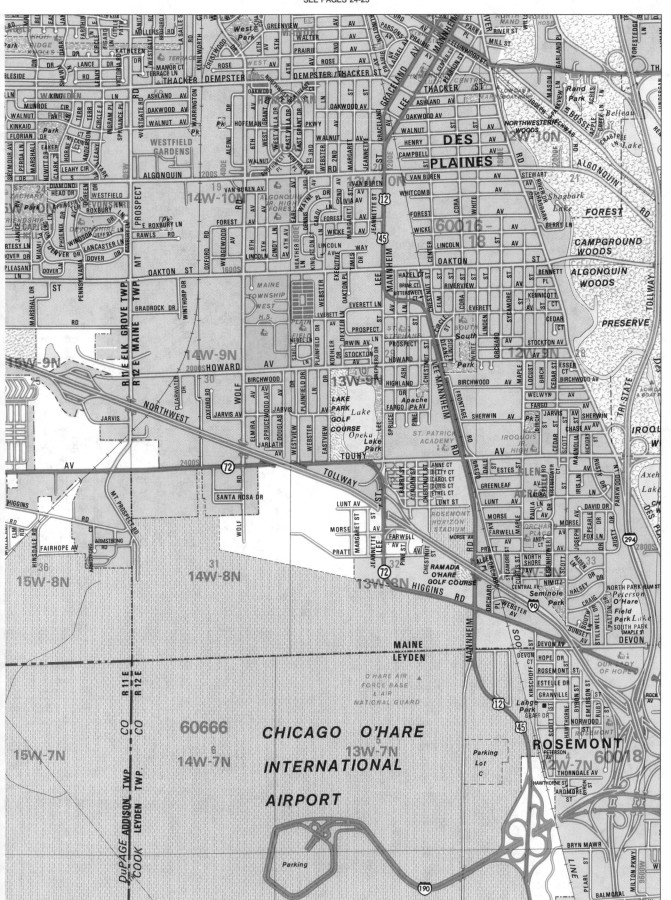

SEE PAGES 36-37

SEE PAGES 40-41

SEE PAGES 26-27

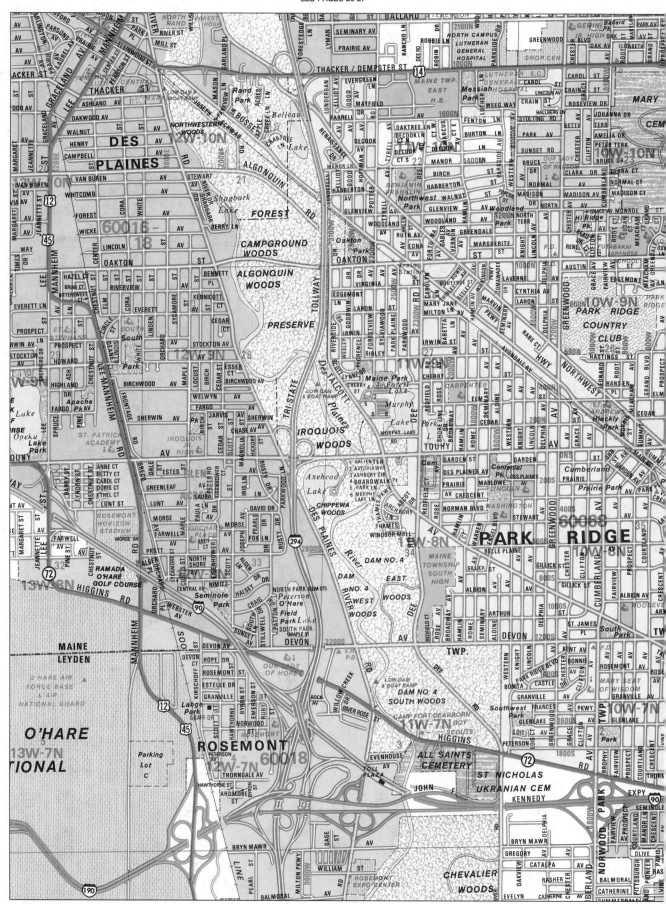

SEE PAGES 26-27

SEE PAGES 38-39

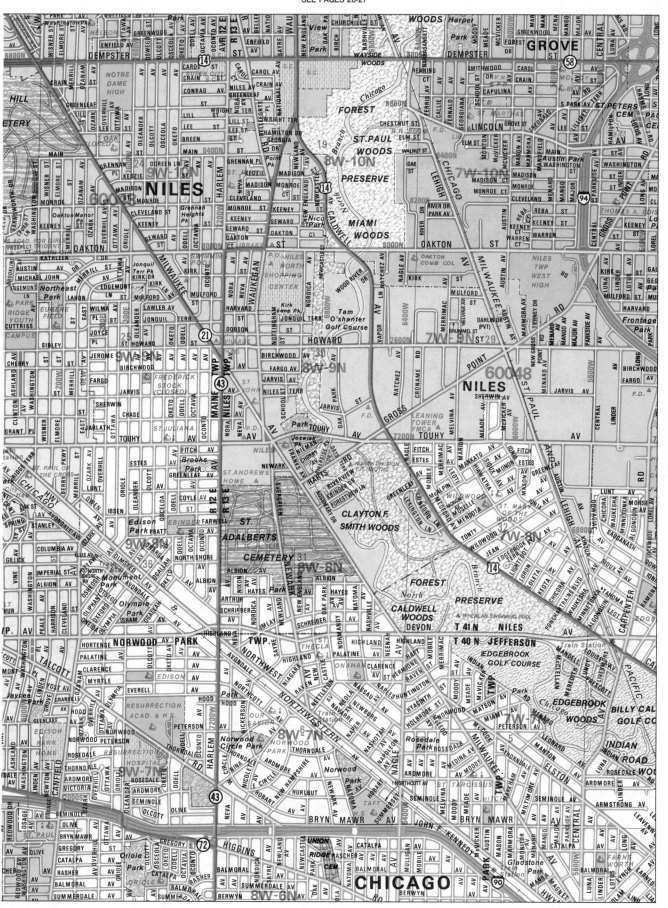

SEE PAGES 42-43

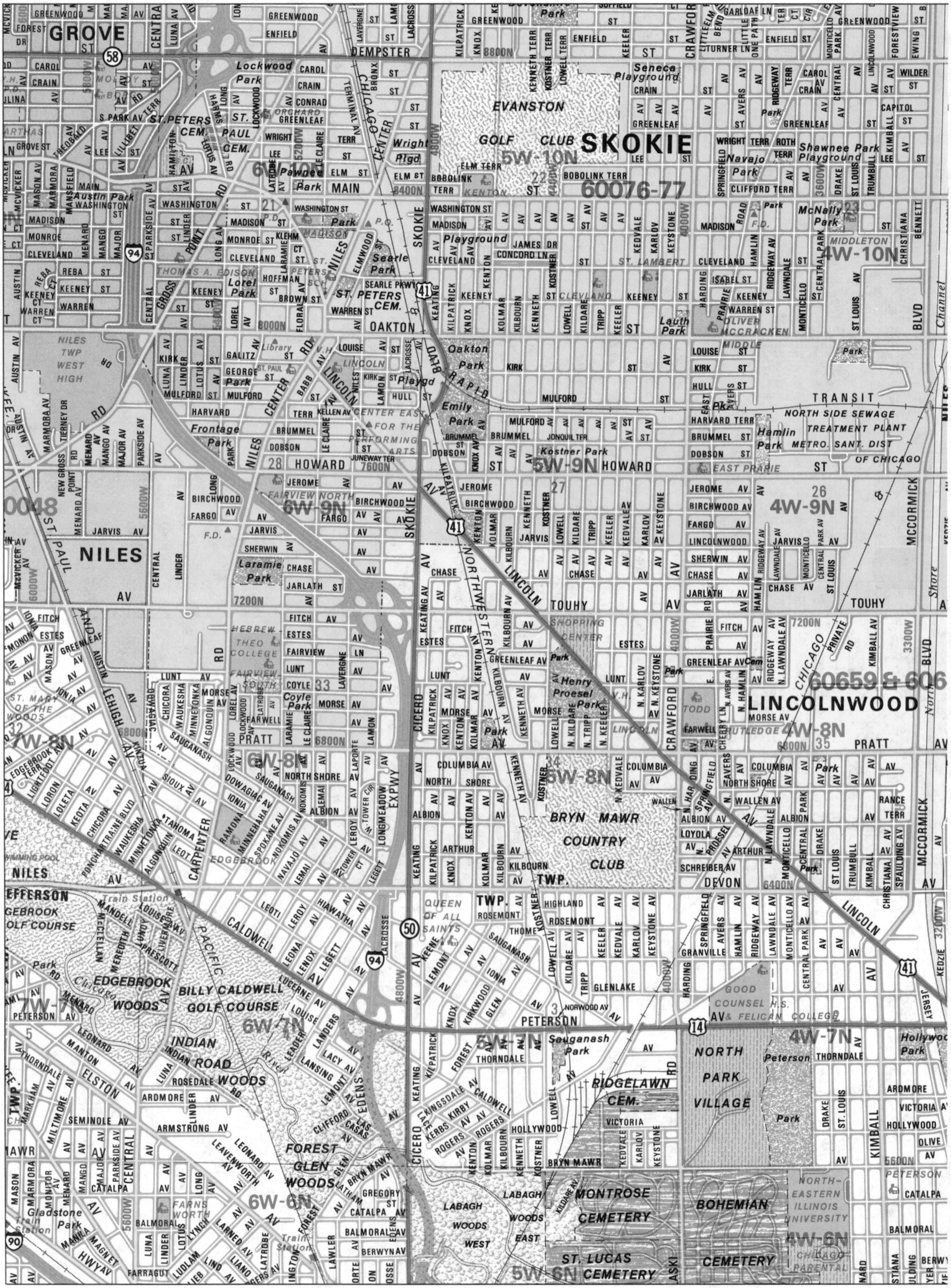

SEE PAGES 36-37

SEE PAGES 44-45

GROVE ST

SKOKIE

60076-77

EVANSTON GOLF CLUB

5W-10N

4W-10N

NILES

5W-9N

6W-9N

4W-9N

LINCOLNWOOD

60659 & 606

4W-8N

6W-8N

5W-8N

7W-8N

BRYN MAWR COUNTY CLUB

NILES

6W-7N

4W-7N

5W-7N

EDGEBROOK WOODS

BILLY CALDWELL GOLF COURSE

INDIAN ROAD WOODS

FOREST GLEN WOODS

NORTH PARK VILLAGE

RIDGELAWN CEM.

6W-6N

5W-6N

4W-6N

MONTROSE CEMETERY

BOHEMIAN CEMETERY

ST. LUCAS CEMETERY

NORTH-EASTERN ILLINOIS UNIVERSITY

Hollywood Park

NORTH SIDE SEWAGE TREATMENT PLANT METRO. SANT. DIST. OF CHICAGO

HEBREW THEO COLLEGE

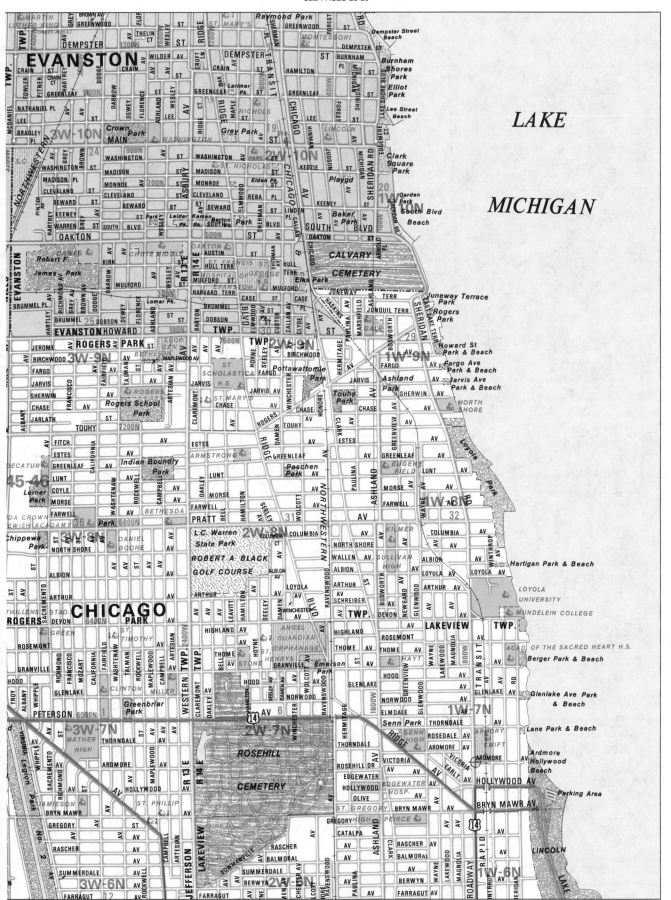

SEE PAGES 34-35

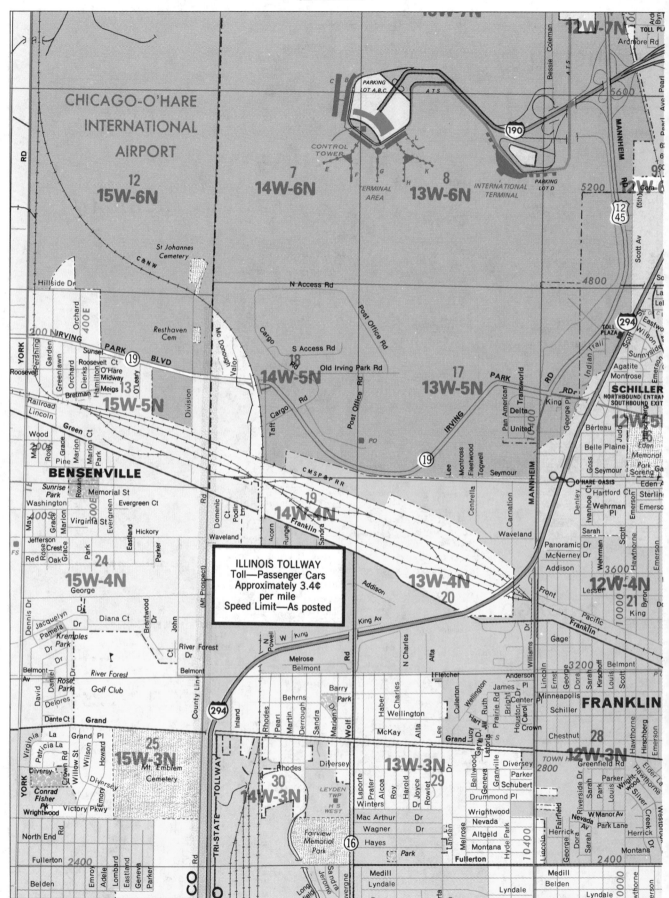

CHICAGO-O'HARE
INTERNATIONAL
AIRPORT

12
**15W-6N**

7
**14W-6N**

**13W-6N**

CONTROL
TOWER

TERMINAL
AREA

INTERNATIONAL
TERMINAL

PARKING
LOT D

**12W-7N**

**12W-6**

St Johannes
Cemetery

Resthaven
Cem

18

14W-5N

17
**13W-5N**

13
**15W-5N**

BENSENVILLE

19
14W-4N

13W-4N

**12W-4N**

ILLINOIS TOLLWAY
Toll—Passenger Cars
Approximately 3.4¢
per mile
Speed Limit—As posted

24
**15W-4N**

20

21

River Forest
Golf Club

FRANKLIN

25
**15W-3N**

30
14W-3N

28
**12W-3N**

13W-3N
29

LEYDEN
TWP
H S
WEST

Fairview
Memorial
Park

16

SCHILLER
NORTHBOUND ENTRAN
SOUTHBOUND EXIT

O'Hare OASIS

SEE PAGES 36-37

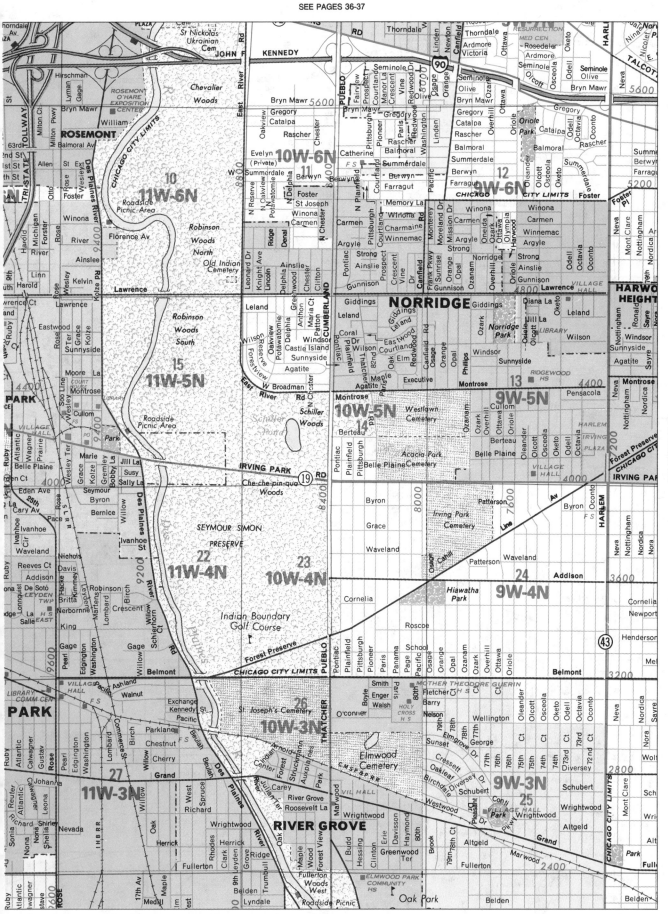

SEE PAGES 42-43

NORRIDGE

HARWOOD HEIGHTS

RIVER GROVE

ELMWOOD PARK

SEYMOUR SIMON PRESERVE

Indian Boundary Golf Course

Forest Preserve

CHICAGO CITY LIMITS

IRVING PARK RD

Schiller Woods

Oakview Potawatomie

St. Joseph's Cemetery

Elmwood Cemetery

Irving Park Cemetery

Acacia Park Cemetery

Belle Plaine Cemetery

Westlawn Cemetery

Norridge Park

Union Ridge Cemetery

Ridgemoor Country Club

CHICAGO-READ MENTAL HEALTH CENTER

Mt. Olive Cemetery

Mt. Isaiah Cem.

Rosemont Cem.

Mt. Mayriv Cemetery

THE BRICKYARD

Riis Park

Steinmetz HS

Shabbona Park

Bell Park

Sayre Park

Forest Preserve

Oak Park Country Club

Elmwood Woods West

Roadside Picnic Area

HOLY CROSS HS

MOTHER THEODORE GUERIN HS

WRIGHT JR COLL

TAFT HS

RIDGEWOOD HS

ELMWOOD PARK COMMUNITY HS

SHRINERS HOSP FOR CRIPPLED CHILDREN

10W-6N  9W-6N  8W-6N

10W-5N  9W-5N  8W-5N

10W-4N  9W-4N

10W-3N  9W-3N  8W-3N

HARLEM

NARRAGANSETT

NAGLE

CUMBERLAND

THATCHER

PUEBLO

Des Plaines River

East River Rd

SEE PAGES 40-41

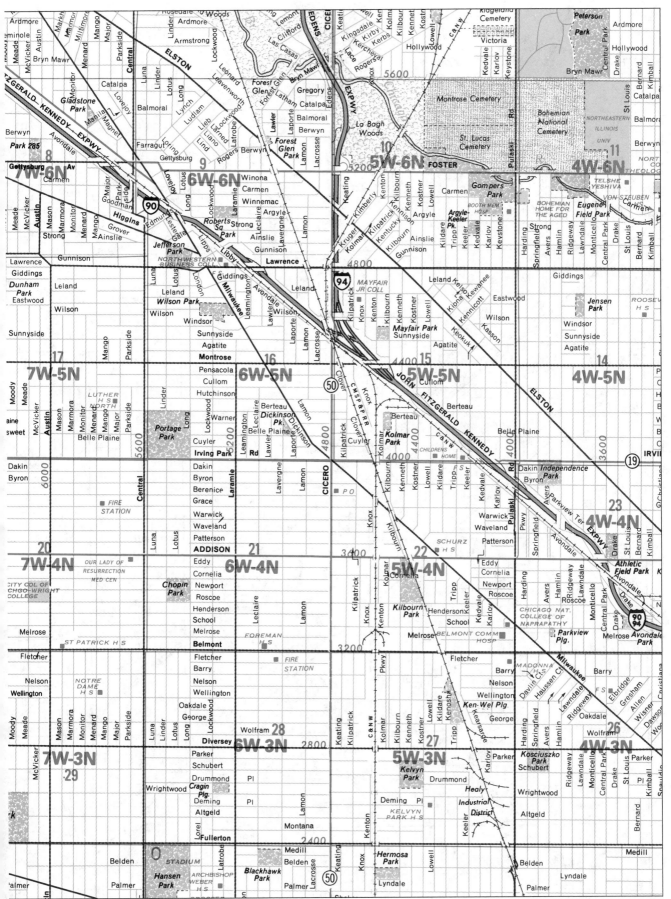

SEE PAGES 38-39

SEE PAGES 42-43

5600

Victoria
Hollywood
Bryn Mawr
Park
Hollywood
Victoria
Legion Park

Montrose Cemetery
Bohemian National Cemetery
St. Lucas Cemetery
La Bagh Woods
Forest Glen Park
NORTHEASTERN ILLINOIS UNIV
NORTH PARK COL & THEOLOGICAL SEM

5200
**10  5W-6N  FOSTER**
R
**11  4W-6N**
**12  3W-6N  FOSTER**

SWEDISH COVENANT HOSP

**6N**
Winona
Carmen
Winnemac
Argyle
Ainslie
Gunnison
Gompers Park
Argyle-Keeler Pk.
BOOTH MEM HOSP
BOHEMIAN HOME FOR THE AGED
Eugene Field Park
TELSHE YESHIVA
VON STEUBEN
Kiwanis Plg Park
River Park
Ronan Park
Gross Plg.

Lawrence
4800
Lawrence
Lawrence
LAWRENCE HALL ORPHANAGE

**94**
MAYFAIR JR COLL
Leland
Kildare Kilbora Kewanee
Eastwood
Wilson
Jensen Park
ROOSEVELT H S
Leland
Eastwood
Wilson
Ravenswood Manor Park
Jacob Park
Eastwood
Sunken Gardens P
LINCOLN W HOSPITA

Mayfair Park
Sunnyside
Windsor
Sunnyside
Agatite
Buffalo Park

4400
**16  6W-5N**
**15  5W-5N**
**14  4W-5N**
**13  3W-5N**

**50**
C M S P & R R
JOHN FITZGERALD KENNEDY
ELSTON
Pensacola
Cullom
Hutchinson
Berteau
Warner
Belle Plaine
Cuyler
Horner Park

Dickinson Pk.
Berteau
Belle Plaine
Kolmar Park
C & N W
CHILDRENS HOME

**19  IRVING PARK  ROAD**

Dakin
Byron
Independence Park
Byron
California Park
Revere Dak Park
Berenic
POST OFFICE
Bradley Pl

**21  6W-4N**
**22  5W-4N**
**23  4W-4N**
**24  3W-4N**

SCHURZ H S
Warwick
Waveland
Patterson
Athletic Field Park
Kedzie Ave Industrial District
GORDON TECH. H.S.
ADDISON
Waveland
LANE TE H.S

Eddy
Cornelia
Newport
Roscoe
Kilbourn Park
CHICAGO NAT. COLLEGE OF NAPRAPATHY
Parkview Plg.
Kedzie Ave Industrial District
Eddy
Cornelia
Roscoe
Henderson
Brands Park
DE VRY INST OF TEC

Melrose
BELMONT COMM HOSP
Parkview Park
Melrose
Avondale Park
School
Melrose

Fletcher
Irene
Belmont
Fletcher

FIRE STATION
3200
FOREMAN H S
MADONNA H CTS
Milwaukee
Barry
Nelson
Wellington
Barry
Nelson
Wellington

Barry
Nelson
Wellington
Ken-Wel Plg
George
Davlin Ct Haussen Ct
Oakdale
Wolfram
Logan Square
George

Wolfram
**28  6W-3N**
2800
**27  5W-3N**
**26  4W-3N**
**25  3W-3N**
Diversey
LOGAN

Kosciuszko Park
Schubert
Kelvyn Park
Healy
Drummond
Logan Square
Schubert

Deming Pl
KELVYN PARK H S
Industrial District
Wrightwood
Altgeld
Linden Pl
Altgeld
Willets

2400
Montana
Medill
Belden
Blackhawk Park
Hermosa Park
Lyndale
Belden
Lyndale
Palmer
Shakespeare
Medill
Belden
Lyndale
Palmer
Haas Plg
Medill
Belde
Lynda
Park

**50**
**34**
KEDZIE
Palmer Sq
**PALMER BLVD**
St Georges Ct Pringiville
Julia Ct

SEE PAGES 50-51

SEE PAGES 40-41

SEE DU PAGE COUNTY PAGES 14-15

DU PAGE CO

COOK CO

TRI-STATE

**NORTHLAKE**

**STONE PARK**

**ELMHURST**

**BERKELEY**

**HILLSIDE**

**BELL**

Fairview Memorial Park

Crestview Park

Elm Lawn Cemetery

Arlington Cemetery

Elmhurst Memorial Hospital

East End Park

Golden Meadows Park

LEYDEN COMM HOSP

Eisenhower Park

Butterfield Park

Wild Meadows Pk

Cernan Park

Gladstone Park

Mr Carmel Cemetery

Proviso West HS

FOREST PRESERVE No. 1

Slavish Cem

Queen of Heaven Cemetery

Glen Oak Cemetery

Oakridge Cemetery

WESTBOUND ENTRANCE

SOUTHBOUND ENTRANCE NORTHBOUND EXIT

NORTHBOUND ENT SOUTHBOUND EXIT

DWIGHT D. EISENHOWER EXPWY

EAST-WEST TOLLWAY

15W-2N

14W-2N

13W-2N

12W

15W-1N

14W-1N

13W-1N

12W-1N

15W-0N

14W-0N

13W-0N

12W

15W-0S

14W-0S

13W-0S

12W

NORTH

LAKE

ROOSEVELT

Fullerton

Wrightwood

Victory Pkwy

North End Rd

Belden

Crestview

Michigan
Kenilworth
Indiana
Willow
Armitage

Romans

Mac Arthur Dr
Wagner Dr
Hayes

Wrightwood
Nevada
Altgeld
Montana

Medill
Lyndale
Dewey
Palmer
Dickens
Major Dr
Village Dr

Bernice
Whitehall

Armitage
Whittier

Golfview Dr
Franklin Dr
West Dr
Westward Ho Dr

Morse
Le Moyne

Soffel

Bohlander
Murray Dr
Hawthorne

Randolph
Cypress

Eisenhower Park

Washington

Prospect
Locust
Madison

Van Buren
Harrison

Harrison

Congress

Adams
Jackson

Darmstadt

Lexington

Concord

Harvard

Duncan

Fillmore

SEE PAGES 52-53

SEE PAGES 40-41

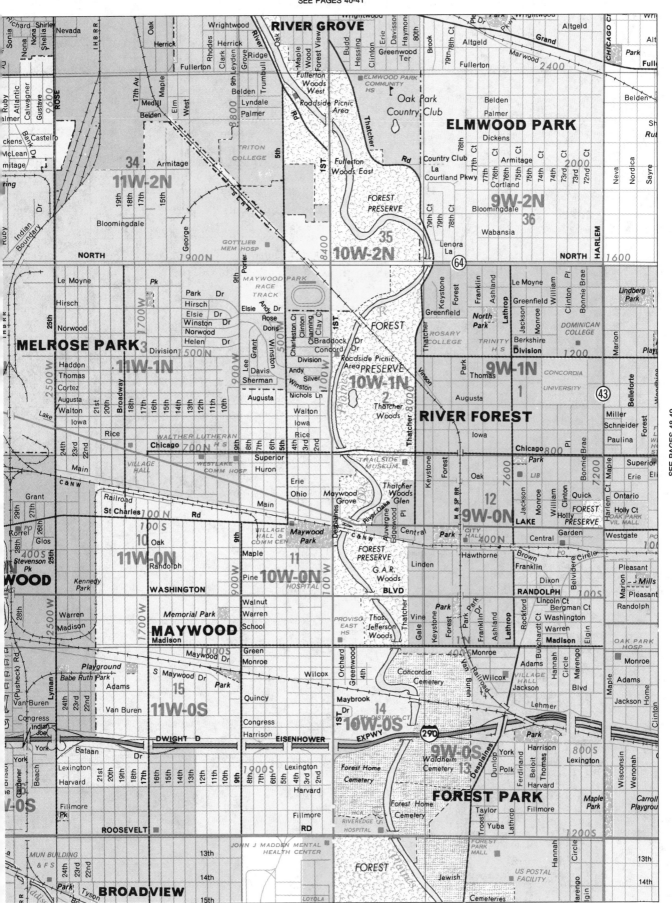

SEE PAGES 48-49

SEE PAGES 42-43

SEE PAGES 46-47

# RIVER GROVE

# ELMWOOD PARK

**9W-2N**
36

**10W-2N**
35

**8W-2N**
31

**7W-2N**
32

Riis Park

Oak Park Country Club

ELMWOOD PARK COMMUNITY HS

Fullerton Woods West

Roadside Picnic Area

TRITON COLLEGE

Fullerton Woods East

FOREST PRESERVE

Sayre Park

SHRINERS HOSP FOR CRIPPLED CHILDREN

Rutherford Park

Amundsen Park

MAYWOOD RACE TRACK

**10W-1N**

**9W-1N**
1

**8W-1N**
6

ROSARY COLLEGE

TRINITY HS

DOMINICAN COLLEGE

CONCORDIA UNIVERSITY

Lindberg Park

Field Playground

Taylor Park

Andersen Playground

Thatcher Woods

# RIVER FOREST

TRAILSIDE MUSEUM

Thatcher Woods Glen

Maywood Grove

FRANK LLOYD WRIGHT HOME STUDIO

# OAK PARK

OAK PARK & RIVER FOREST HS

WEST SUBURBAN HOSPITAL MEDICAL CENTER

Stevenson Plg

**10W-0N**
11

**9W-0N**
12

**8W-0N**
7

VILLAGE HALL & COMM CEN

Maywood Park

FOREST PRESERVE G.A.R. Woods

Scoville Park

Ridgeland Common Park

Mills Park

PROVISO EAST HS

Thos. Jefferson Woods

RANDOLPH

WASHINGTON

OAK PARK HOSP

FENWICK HS

VILLAGE HALL

Concordia Cemetery

VILLAGE HALL

Fox Park

Longfellow Park

**10W-0S**
14

**9W-0S**
13

**8W-0S**
18

EISENHOWER EXPWY

Waldheim Cemetery

Forest Home Cemetery

Rehm Park

Barrie Park

Carroll Playground

Euclid Square

ROOSEVELT

# FOREST PARK

HCA RIVEREDGE HOSPITAL

FOREST PARK MALL

US POSTAL FACILITY

JOHN J MADDEN MENTAL HEALTH CENTER

HINES

LOYOLA

SEE PAGES 54-55

SEE PAGES 42-43

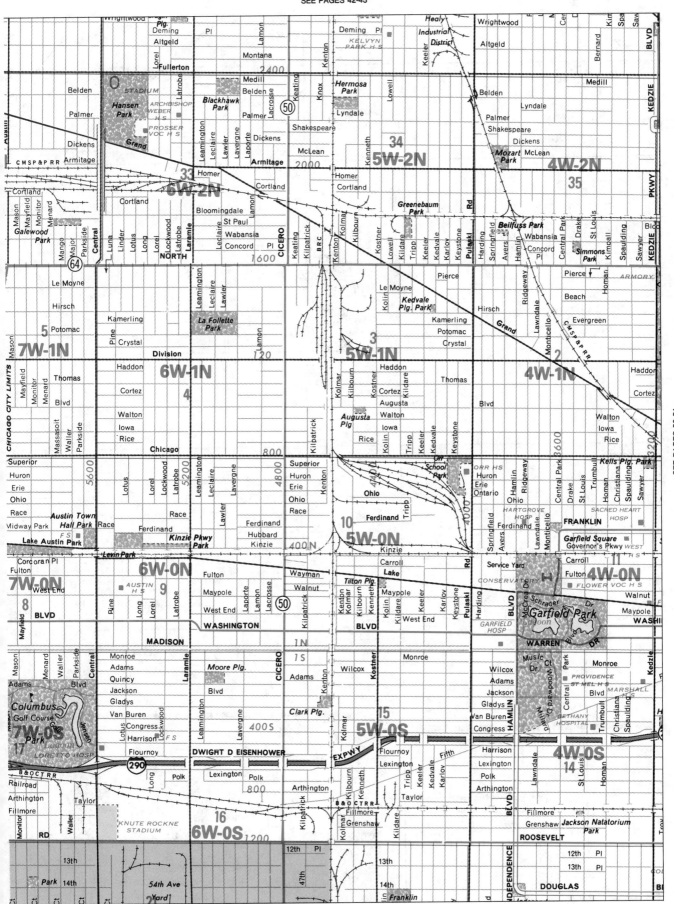

SEE PAGES 50-51

SEE PAGES 48-49

Industrial District

Keeler · Bernard · Altgeld · Willets · Altgeld · Fairfield · Washtenaw · Rockwell · Maplewood · Campbell · Artesian · Montana · Wrightwood

BLVD · Linden Pl · Albany · Fullerton

Medill · Belden · Lyndale · Palmer · Shakespeare · Dickens

90 94 · Winchester · Wolcott · Honore · Medill

Senior Citizens Mem Pk.

Belden · Lyndale · Belden · Lyndale · Palmer · Charleston · Claremont · Webster · Dickens

Mozart Park · McLean · PALMER BLVD · Dickens · Haas Plg · Holstein Park

Mozart Park · 4W-2N · 35 · Armitage · McLean · 3W-2N · 36 · Shakespeare · Dickens · McLean · 2W-2N · 31

Homer · Cortland · Moffat · Homer · Cortland · Moffat · Cortland

Greenebaum Park · Bellfuss Park · Wabansia · Concord Pl · Simmons Park · Bloomingdale · Churchill · Walsh Plg

Kildare · Tripp · Keeler · Kedvale · Karlov · Keystone · Pulaski · Harding · Springfield · Avers · Hamlin · Central Park · Drake · St Louis · Kimball · Spaulding · Sawyer · KEDZIE · Troy · Albany · Whipple · HUMBOLDT · Richmond · Mozart · California · Fairfield · Washtenaw · Talman · Rockwell · Campbell · Artesian · WESTERN · Bell · Damen · Winchester · Wolcott · Honore · Wood · Hermitage · Paulina · Marshfield · Ashland

St Paul · Wabansia · Canton · Concord Pl · 1600

Pierce · Beach · ARMORY · NORTH · 64 · Le Moyne · Maplewood Plg. Park · Pierce · Le Moyne · Julian · Beach · Bauwans

Kedvale Plg. Park · Hirsch · Humboldt Park · St Elizabeth's Hosp · Hirsch · Schiller · Wicker Park · Josephinum HS

Kamerling · Grand · Evergreen · Potomac · Crystal · Clemente · Evergreen · Crystal

Potomac · Crystal · Division · 1200

4W-1N · Thomas · Haddon · 3W-1N · Clemente HS · 2W-1N · Haddon

Norwegian-American Hosp · Thomas · St Mary of Nazareth Med Center · Augusta · 6 · Cortez

Cortez · Walton · Iowa · Rice · Walton · Iowa · Rice · Wells HS · Blvd · Rice · Pearson · Commercial Club Plg.

Chicago · 800

Orr School Park · Orr HS · Huron · Erie · Ontario · Ohio · Kells Plg Park · Superior · Huron · Smith Park · Erie · Ohio · Lee Pl

Hartgrove Hosp · Sacred Heart Hosp · Ferdinand · Hubbard · Anson Pl · Hart · Hartland Ct · Hermitage · Ontario

FRANKLIN · BLVD · Grand · Race · Kinzie

Garfield Square · Governor's Pkwy · WEST · Sacramento Square · 12 · 3W-0N · C&NW · Carroll · Fulton · Walnut

Service Yard · CONSERVATORY · 4W-0N · FLOWER VOC HS · Walnut · Maypole · Lake · 7 · 2W-0N · Maypole · SPALDING HS

Garfield Park · WASHINGTON · WARREN · BLVD · Union Park

Garfield Hosp · WARREN · Madison · MARION ADULT ED & CAREER TRAINING

Monroe · Music Ct · Monroe · Providence · St Mel HS · Marshall HS · Wilcox · Armory Park · Monroe · Wilcox · 1N · 1S · Touhy-Herbert Park · Arcade · Young Park

Wilcox · Adams · Jackson · Gladys · Van Buren · Congress · Adams · Jackson · Gladys · Van Buren · United Center · City Col of Chgo Malcolm X Col

Horan Plg · Bethany Hospital · Crane HS · 400S · Cregier Voc HS · DWIGHT D

290 · Congress · Altgeld · Harrison · 13 · Flournoy · 2W-0S · 18 · Rush Presbyterian St Lukes Med Center · Cook Co Hosp

4W-0S · 14 · Harrison · Lexington · Polk · Arthington · 3W-0S · Flournoy · Lexington · Polk · Arthington · Taylor · 800 · Univ of Illinois Hospital · VA West Side Med Center · Garibaldi Plg

Fillmore · Grenshaw · Jackson Natatorium Park · Grenshaw · 1200 · Fillmore · Taylor

ROOSEVELT · RD · Cook Co Juvenile Court · Chicago Lighthouse for the Blind · Washburne

12th Pl · 13th Pl · Collins HS · Burkhardt · Schwab Rehabilitation Center · 13th · Hastings

DOUGLAS · BLVD · Douglas · 14th · 14th Pl · Hastings

Independence Square · INDEPENDENCE · DOUGLAS · Douglas Lagoon · 15th

SEE PAGES 44-45

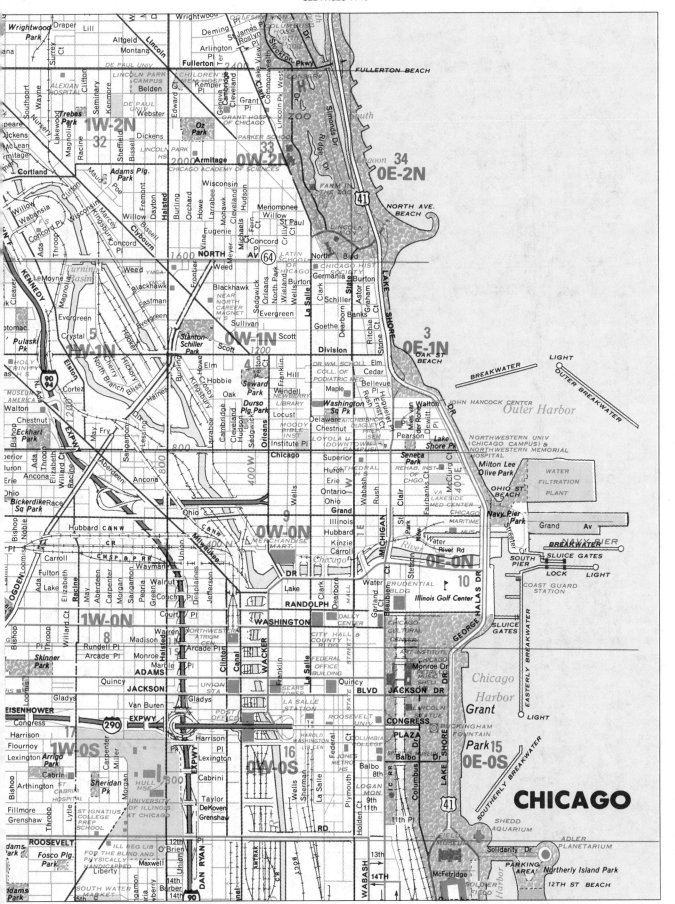

CHICAGO

SEE PAGES 46-47

SEE DU PAGE COUNTY PAGES 20-21

WESTCHESTER

OAK BROOK

LA GRANGE PARK

LA GRANGE

WESTERN SPRINGS

Mt Carmel Cemetery

Queen of Heaven Cemetery

Slavish Cem

Dickens

Fresh Meadow Golf Course

Glen Oak Cemetery

Oakridge Cemetery

Immaculate Heart of Mary HS

St Joseph HS

Immanuel Lutheran Cem

Community Park

Forest Preserve

Brezina Woods

Mannheim Woods

Pine Tree Timber

Meadow Lark Golf Course

FOREST PRESERVE

Bemis Woods North

Bemis Woods South

Salt Creek Forest Preserve

La Grange Park Woods

Possum Hollow Wood

Robert Crown Ctr. for Health Ed. & Mus.

Burr Oak

Graue Mill & Mus.

Duncan Field

Spinning Wheel

Hinsdale Hosp

Lyons Twp HS North

Lyons Twp HS South

TRI-STATE TOLLWAY

EAST-WEST TOLLWAY

I-294

CERMAK RD

OGDEN

13W-0S
12W-0S
15W-1S
14W-1S
13W-1S
12W-1S
15W-2S
14W-2S
13W-2S
12W-2S
15W-3S
14W-3S
13W-3S
12W-3S
15W-4S
14W-4S
13W-4S
12W-4S

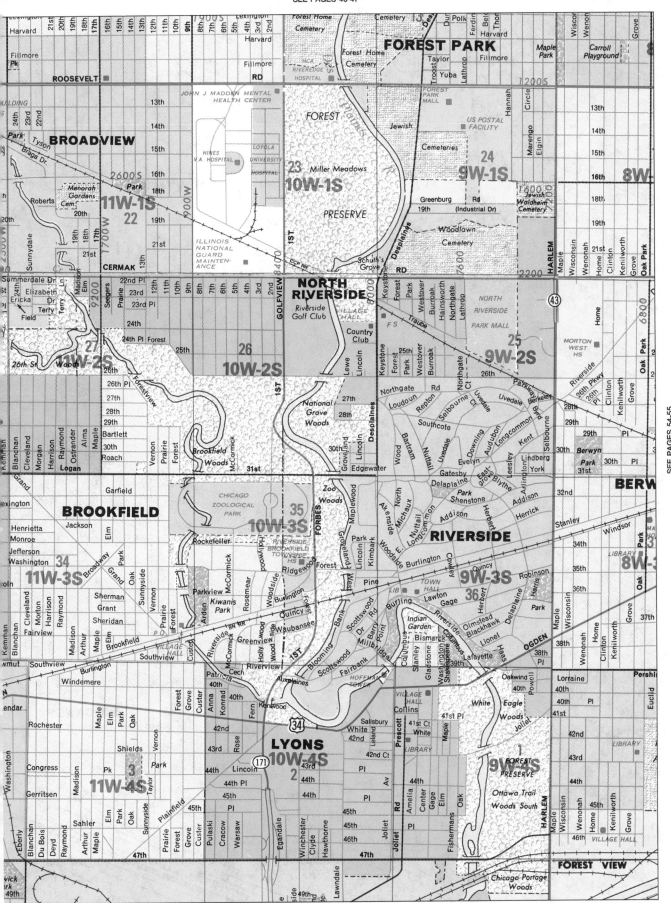

SEE PAGES 48-49

**FOREST PARK**

8W-0S

18

Harvard

Barrie Park | Garfield | Railroad | Arthington | Fillmore

Cemetery | Harvard

Fillmore | Forest Home Cemetery

HCA RIVEREDGE HOSPITAL

Taylor | Troost | Yuba | Lathrop | Fillmore

Maple Park | Carroll Playground | Fillmore | Euclid Square | ROOSEVELT | Monitor | RD

MENTAL H CENTER

FOREST

13th | 14th | 15th | 16th | 18th | 19th

FOREST PARK MALL

US POSTAL FACILITY

19

8W-1S | FS | LIBRARY | 7W-1S

LOYOLA UNIVERSITY HOSPITAL

23 | 10W-1S | Miller Meadows

24 | 9W-1S

**BERWYN**

61st | 61st | 60th | 20 | Warren C | 18th

PRESERVE

Cemeteries | Jewish Waldheim Cemetery

Greenburg Rd | 19th (Industrial Dr)

East

19th | 19th | 59th | 58th

Woodlawn Cemetery

21st | Maple | Wisconsin | Wenonah | Home | Clinton | Kenilworth | Grove | Oak Park | Euclid | Wesley | Clarence | Scoville | Gunderson | Elmwood | Ridgeland | Highland | Harvey | Lombard | Pk

**NORTH RIVERSIDE**

Schuth's Grove | Keystone | Forest Park | Westover | Hainsworth | Northgate | Lathrop

NORTH RIVERSIDE PARK MALL

43 | 23rd | PO | 30 | 8W-2S

Riverside Golf Club | VILLAGE HALL

Country Club

FS | Traube

24th | 25th | 26th | Home | Riverside | Oak Park | Clinton | Kenilworth | Grove | Euclid | Wesley | Clarence | Scoville | Gunderson | Elmwood | Ridgeland | Cuyler | Highland | Harvey | Lombard | BLVD | MORTON EAST HS

26 | 0W-2S

MORTON WEST HS

25 | 9W-2S | 7W-2S

Lewe | Lincoln | 25th | Forest Park | Westover | Burroak | 26th | Parkway Blvd | Berkeley | 26th Pkwy | 28th | CITY HALL | 26th Pl | 27th | 29 | Pk | 59th | 58th

National Grove Woods | 27th | Northgate Rd | Loudoun | Repton | Selbourne | Uvedale | Uvedale | 28th | 29th | Janura Park | 27th Pl | 28th | 28th Pl | 61st | 60th | AUSTIN | 59th | 58th

28th | Southcote | Downing | Audubon | Longcommon | Kent | Selbourne | 29th Pl | CCP RR | 29th

30th | Wood | Bartram | Nuttall | Uvedale | Evelyn | Leesley | Lindberg | 30th Berwyn Park | 30th Pl | BN RR | 31st

31st | Groveland | Lincoln | Edgewater | Gatesby | Eaglgrove | Blythe | York | 31st | Park | 32nd | 32nd | Edgewood | OGDEN

Zoo Woods | Maplewood | Delaplaine | Arlington | Addison | 32nd | Stanley | Fairfield | 33rd | Park

35 | 0W-3S | North | Michaux | Park | Shenstone | Addison | Herbert | Herrick | 33rd | MACNEAL HOSP | Sinclair | 33rd | 32

RIVER BROOK TOWNSHIP HS | Akenside | Nuttall | Longcommon | **RIVERSIDE** | 31 | 8W-3S | Windsor | LIBRARY | Ct | Av | 7W-3S

Ridgewood | Forest | E. Kimbark | Burlington | Cowley | Quincy | 34th | 35th | Oak | 35th | Ct

Rosemear | Woodside | Pine | 9W-3S | Robinson | 36th | 36th

Burlington | LIB | TOWN HALL | Lawton | Gage | Harris | Wisconsin | Grove | 37th | Ridgeland | Highland | Harvey | Lombard | 61st | 60th | Austin | 59th | 58th | Pershing

Quincy | Scottswood | Burling | Herbert | Delaplaine | Park | Maple | 38th | Wenonah | Home | Clinton | Kenilworth | VILLAGE HALL

Greenview | Bank | Dr | Barry | Indian Garden | Olmstead | Blackhawk | Lionel | Lafayette | **OGDEN** | Lorraine | Pershing | 40th | Euclid | Wesley | Clarence | 40th

Riverview | Blooming | Scottswood | Fairbank | Millbridge | Columbus | Stanley | Washington | Shakespeare | Haas | 38th | 40th | Pl

Desplaines | HOFFMAN TOWER | Gladstone | Bismarck | Oakwind | Powell | 41st

VILLAGE HALL | Collins | White | 40th | Eagle Woods | White | Joliet | 41st | 42nd | 41st | STICKNEY

34 | Salisbury | 41st Ct | White | 42nd | LIBRARY | 42nd | Mount Auburn Cem | 42nd

**LYONS** | 10W-4S | Leland | Maple | 43rd | LIBRARY | 43rd | Scoville | Gunderson | Elmwood | 7W-4S

171 | 2 | 43rd | PL | 1 | 9W-4S | FOREST PRESERVE | 44th | 6 | 8W-4S

Lincoln | 44th | 44th | 44th | Ottawa Trail Woods South | 45th | Wenonah | Home | Kenilworth | Grove | East | 5

45th | PL | 45th | 46th | HARLEM | Wisconsin | VILLAGE HALL

47th | Fishermans | 47th | **FOREST VIEW** | Canal Bank | Rd | 51st

Chicago Portage Woods | **STEVENSON EXPWY**

SEE PAGES 52-53

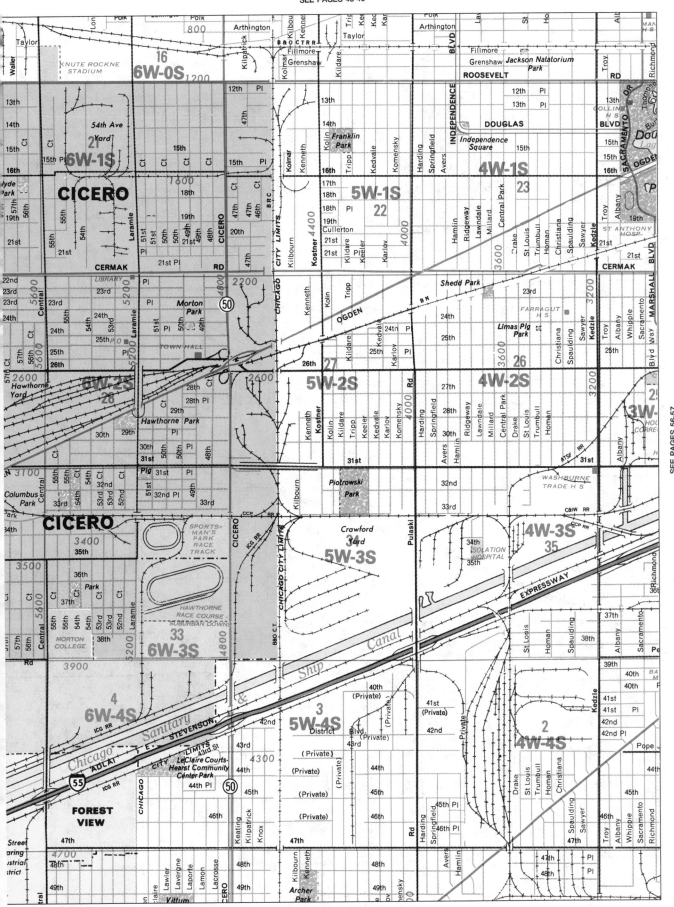

Lexington
Polk
Arthington
Taylor
MANLEY HS
Alban
Maple
Campbell 800
Claremont
Oakley
Bell
Bowler
Lea
VA WEST SIDE MED CENTER
COOK CO HOSP
UNIV. OF ILLINOIS HOSPITAL
Hermita
Paulina
Marshfield
Laflin
Bishop
Lexington
Arrigo Park
Cabrini
Garibaldi Plg.
Arthington
ST CABRINI HOSPITAL
Sheri Pk

Fillmore
Grenshaw
Jackson Natatorium Park
ROOSEVELT
RD
Troy
Richmond
Francisco
Mozart
Fairfield
Washtenaw
Grenshaw 1200
Fillmore
ILL ST. PSYCH. INST.
Taylor
Fillmore
Grenshaw
Throop
Lytle
ST IGNATE COLLEGE PREP SCHOOL

12th Pl
13th Pl
DOUGLAS
Independence Square
15th
Thompson Dr
Burkhardt Dr
Collins HS
13th
12th Pl
13th
14th
Talman
BLVD
COOK CO JUVENILE COURT
CHICAGO LIGHTHOUSE FOR THE BLIND
Washburne
13th
Hastings
14th
15th
Addams Park
Fosco Plg. Park
ROOSEVELT
FOR THE PHYSICALLY HANDICA
Liber

4W-1S
23
DOUGLAS BLVD
Douglas Lagdn
SCHWAB REHABILITATION CENTER
13th Pl
14th
15th
16th
Ogden
MT SINAI HOSP. MED CENTER OF CHICAGO
1600
19
2W-1S
B&OCT RR
C&NW
+16th
17th
18th
Addams Park
SOUTH W MARKET
15th
1W-1S
20
18th Pl
19th Pl

Hamlin
Ridgeway
Lawndale
Millard
Central Park
Drake
St Louis
Trumbull
Homan
Christiana
Spaulding
Sawyer
Kedzie
3600
Troy
Albany
ST ANTHONY HOSP.
19th
21st
Park
24
3W-1S
19th
Cullerton
21st
WESTERN
Oakley
Leavitt
Hoyne
Damen 2000
Harrison Park
18th Pl
19th
21st
21st
Wolcott
Wood
Paulina
1600
Blue Island
Ada
Cullerton
Pl
May
Racine 200
Dvorak Park
18th Pl
19th Pl
Carpenter
Miller

CERMAK
4300
MARSHALL BLVD 3200
California
Fairfield
Washtenaw
Rockwell
2200
RD
2400
22nd Pl
23rd
23rd
24th
Bell
Leavitt
Winchester
Barrett Plg
Seeley
JUAREZ HS
23rd
ASHLAND
Laflin
Loomis
Stetson Canal
Samson Canal
Throop
29
1W-2S

Shedd Park
23rd
FARRAGUT HS
Limas Plg Park
Christiana
Spaulding
Sawyer
Kedzie
3600
Troy
Albany
Whipple
Sacramento
24TH BLVD
Francisco
Luther
Washtenaw
Plg Park
24th
25th
26th
Oakley
Coulter
Blue Island
Hoyne
BN
Eleanor
Fuller
Crowell
Bonfield
Farrell
Hillock
25th
1W-2S

26
4W-2S
3200
CRIMINAL COURT
25
3W-2S 2800
HOUSE OF CORRECTIONS
HOSPITAL
CALIFORNIA BLVD 2600
31ST BLVD
Artesian
31st
27th
28th
30
2W-2S
Hoyne
Wolcott
Wood
1600
31st St
Bonaparte
Arch
Haynes
Lloyd
Lyman
Bosley Plg

ATSF RR
CP RR
C&IW RR
31st
WASHBURNE TRADE HS
Albany
3100
AT&SF RY
31st St
I-55
32nd
31st Pl
Robin
S. Fork
S. Fork Chicago River
31st
32nd
32nd
Racine
Wilson Plg
1W-3S
32

34th
ISOLATION HOSPITAL
35th
4W-3S
35
EXPRESSWAY
Richmond
Mozart
36
3W-3S
Maplewood
B&O C.T.
34th Pl
35th
36th
ICG RR
Claremont
Oakley
Leavitt
Hamilton
Bross
33rd
34th
35th
Hoyne Plg
Seeley
Damen
Winchester
Wolcott
3500
34th
33rd Pl Plg Park
Justine
Paulina
Marshfield
Laflin Pl
Jasper Pl
Loomis Pl
Iron
May
Chicago River
36th
Moran

37th
St Louis
Homan
Spaulding
Albany
Sacramento
Francisco
California
Washtenaw
Rockwell
Campbell
McKINLEY Park
POOL
Pershing Rd
36th
37th
38th
Hoyne
Seeley
Damen
Winchester
Wolcott
Wood
Hermitage
37th Pl
38th
2W-3S
31
US ARMY ADMIN CEN
38th

39th
40th
BALZEKAS MUSEUM
ARCHER
Kelly Park
Brighton Pl
Montgomery
40th
40th Pl
3900
41st
Oakley
Damen Ave
Viaduct
St. No. 1
St. No. 4 St. No. 2
St. No. 3
Exchange
INTERNA
AMPHITH

41st
Kedzie 3200
42nd
42nd Pl
KELLY HS
Pope John Paul II
2
4W-4S
3W-4S
1
Kelly Park
41st Pl
42nd
43rd 6
2W-4S
42nd
43rd
44th
5
1W-4
43rd
Private
Drake
St Louis
Trumbull
Homan
Christiana
Spaulding
Sawyer
44th
45th
46th
47th
Troy
Albany
Whipple
Sacramento
Richmond
Francisco
Mozart
Fairfield
Washtenaw
Talman
Rockwell
45th Pl
46th
WESTERN
Wolcott
Honore
Wood
Hermitage
Paulina
Marshfield
Davis Sq Park
ASHLAND
Justine
McDowell
45th
Packers
44th
47th

47th Pl
48th
4700
47th Pl
48th Pl
ST JOSEPH HS
Laflin
Bishop
Loomis
Throop
1200
ay
47th

SEE PAGES 54-55

SEE PAGES 50-51

# CHICAGO

SHEDD AQUARIUM

ADLER PLANETARIUM

Solidarity Dr

Parking Area

Northerly Island Park

12TH ST BEACH

McFetridge

SOLDIER FIELD

Burnham

NORTHERLY ISLAND

Waldron Dr

Park Parking Area

CHICAGO MERRILL C MEIGS FIELD

McCORMICK PLACE NORTH

23RD ST VIADUCT

McCORMICK PLACE CONVENTION COMPLEX

PARKING AREA

0E-0S

0E-1S

0W-0S

0W-1S

Mercy Hosp & Med Center

Williams Park

Dunbar Park

Humana Hospital Michael Reese

DUNBAR HS

0E-2S

0W-2S

McGuane Park

31ST ST BEACH

Lake Meadows Park

VANDER COOK COLLEGE OF MUSIC

ILLINOIS INSTITUTE OF TECHNOLOGY

ILLINOIS COLLEGE OF OPTOMETRY DE LA SALLE INSTITUTE

Armour Sq Park

Groveland Pk

Woodland Pk

Douglas Mon Park

Douglas Tomb St Mem

0W-3S

0E-3S

1E-3S

Comiskey Park (WHITE SOX)

Stateway Gardens Park

Anderson Park

PHILLIPS HS

Madden Park

Oakland Park

Browning

Donovan Pig

De Saible

Wentworth Gardens Park

OAKWOOD

Oakland Crescent

Oakenwald

LAKE SHORE Park

Taylor-Lauridsen Pig Park

Bowen

MARTIN L. KING, JR. H.S.

0W-4S

0E-4S

1E-4S

Fuller Park

Taylor Park

TILDEN H S

SEE PAGES 62-63

SEE DU PAGE COUNTY PAGES 26-27

WESTERN SPRINGS

LA GRANGE

13W-4S

13W-5S

12W-5S

14W-5S

14W-6S

13W-6S

12W-6S

COUNTRYSIDE

INDIAN HEAD PARK

HODGKINS

14W-7S

13W-7S

12W-7S

BURR RIDGE

14W-8S

13W-8S

12W-8S

13W-9S

12W-9S

LYONS TWP H S SOUTH

LA GRANGE MEM HOSP

La Grange Country Club

SUBURBAN HOSP

CO SANITARIUM

Legge Memorial Park

Par Three Golf Club

Timber Trails Country Club

Maple Crest G C

1. Indian Head Tr
2. Indian Head Ct
3. Elmwood Dr
4. Elmwood Square
5. Elmwood Ct
6. Westwood Ct
7. Westwood Square
8. Heatherwood Ct
9. Arrowhead

10. Tanglewood Ct
11. Stratford Pl
12. Hawthorne Sq
13. Natona Ln

Sundown Meadow

FOREST PRESERVE

Cantigny Woods North

Cantigny Woods South

ADLAI E. STEVENSON EXPWY

TRI-STATE TOLLWAY

Theodore Stone Forest

Hodgkins Park

La Grange Cemetery

Weeping Willow

Edgewood Valley CC
1 Waterside
2 Trent
3 Northgate
4 Huntington
5 Chasemoor
6 East
7 Thornhill
8 Foxborough
9 Stone Edge
10 Southgate

1 Jewei
2 Roger
3 Sharon
4 Bill
5 Fransean
6 Oak
7 Elm
8 Walnut
9 Park

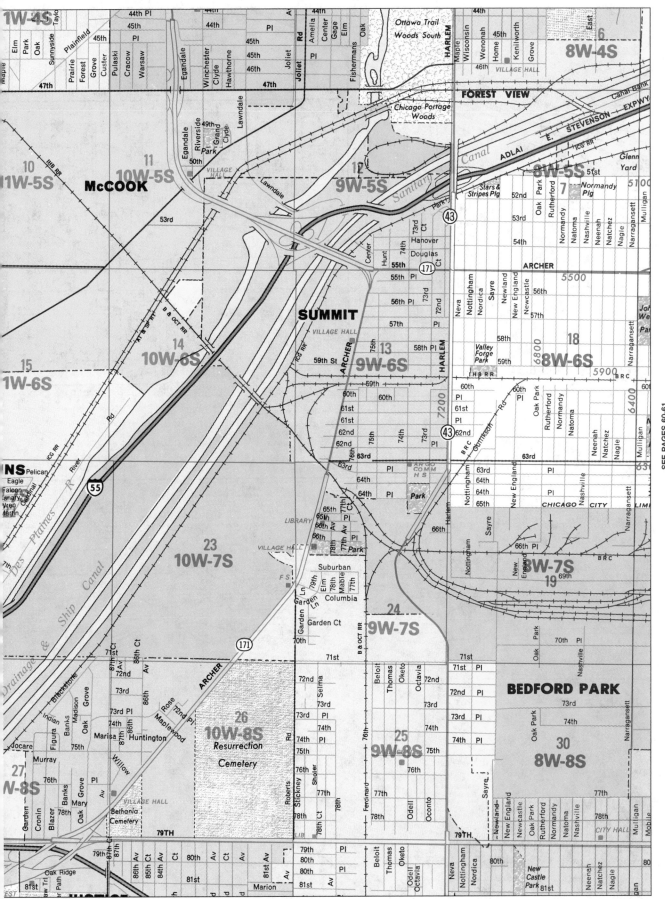

SEE PAGES 54-55

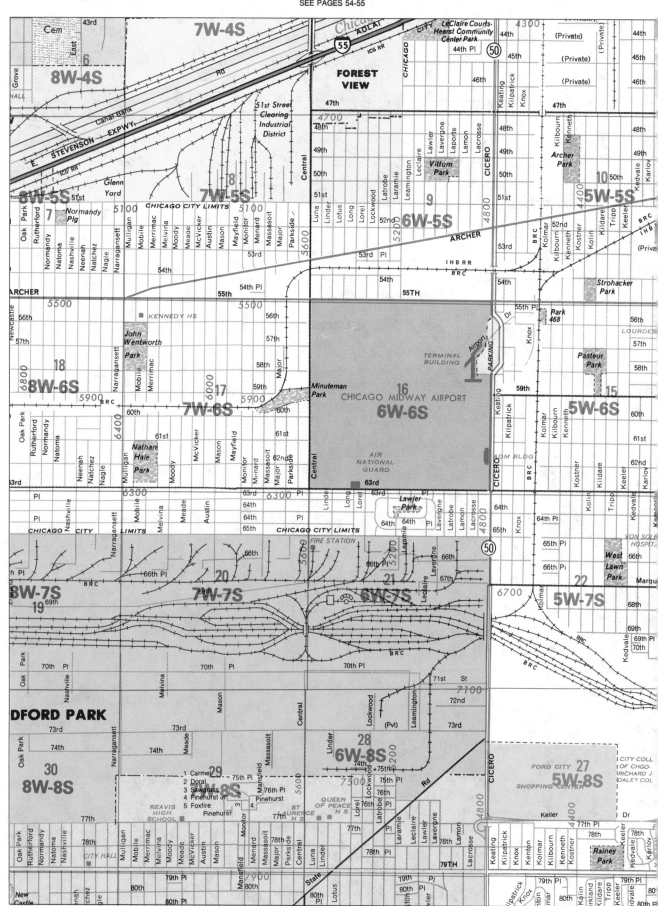

SEE PAGES 66-67

44th  **3W-4S**  1

**2W-4S**

Davis Sq Park

ASHLAND

Packers  43rd

Harding  Springfield  Rd  45th  45th Pl  46th Pl  47th

Drake  St Louis  Trumbull  Homan  Christiana  Spaulding  Sawyer

44th  45th  46th  47th

Troy  Albany  Whipple  Sacramento  Richmond  Francisco  Mozart

Fairfield  Washtenaw  Talman  Rockwell

45th  46th  46th

WESTERN

Damen  44th  45th  Wolcott  Honore  Wood  46th  Hermitage  Paulina  Marshfield

Justine  McDowell  45th

47th  4700  47th  48th

Avers  Hamlin  47th Pl  48th Pl

48th

GTWRR

48th  49th

St Joseph HS

Laflin  Bishop  Loomis  Throop Plg

CURIE HS  4000  Park 408

50th Pl  **4W-5S**  11  52nd  53rd  54th  55TH  55th Pl  56th  57th  58th Pl  14  **4W-6S**  59th

50th  (Pvt)  51st  12  52nd  53rd

St Louis  Homan  Spaulding  Trowbridge Pl  Ridgeway  Lawndale  Millard  Hamlin  Ridgeway  Lawndale  Millard

Christiana  Sawyer  Kedzie  Senka Park  Trumbull  Pl  Pl

50th  3200  51st  **3W-5S**  2800  5100  52nd  53rd  Pl  Pl  Pl  5500  56th  57th  58th  5900  59th Pl  60th Pl  61st  62nd

California  2400

54th  55TH

Washtenaw  Talman  Rockwell  Maplewood  Campbell  Artesian  Fairfield  Maplewood  Campbell  Artesian

Oakley  49th Pl  50th  Oakley Plg  51st  52nd  James  Micek Plg  53rd Pl  54th  2000  Hoyne  Seeley  Cornell Square Park  50th  51st  7  **2W-5S**  Winchester  Wolcott  Honore  Wood  Hermitage  Paulina  Marshfield  GARFIELD  1600

Damen  Ada  Throop  Elizabeth  1W

ASHLAND  Sherman Dr  Sherman Park  BLVD

RICHARDS VOC HS  GAGE PARK HS  Gage Park

Claremont  Oakley  Hamilton  Hoyne  Seeley  56th  57th  58th  18  Hermitage Plg  **2W-6S**  Lindblom Park  60th  61st  62nd  LINDBLOM HS

Laflin  Bishop  Throop  Elizabeth  56th  57th  58th  Ada  1W  1  SEE PAGES 62-63

58th  59th  59th Pl  60th  **3W-6S**  61st  62nd  63rd  13

Troy  Albany  Whipple  Sacramento  Richmond  Francisco  Mozart  WESTERN  B & O C T R R

63rd  6300  64th  65th  66th  6700  67th Pl  68th  69th  70th

HUBBARD HS  64th Pl  65th Pl  66th Pl  Rd  67th Pl  68th Pl  69th Pl  70th Pl  71st

Central  Millard  23  **4W-7S**  Mann Dr  Hollett Dr  Marquette Park  Golf Course  Redfield Dr  Kansas Dr  Rose Garden  71st Pl

California  24  **3W-7S**  Marquette  MARIA HS  HOLY CROSS HOSP

Claremont  Oakley  Bell  Hamilton  Rd  64th  65th  66th  HARPER HS  Winchester  Wolcott  Honore  19  Hermitage  **2W-7S**  67th Pl  68th Pl  69th Pl  70th  70th Pl  71st

Justine  Laflin  Bishop  Loomis  Ogden Park  Ada  1W  Throop  Elizabeth

Pulaski

Fairfield  Washtenaw  Talman  Rockwell  Maplewood  Campbell  Artesian

71st Pl  72nd  73rd  74th  2800  75th Pl  76th  77th

Avers  Ridgeway  Millard  Central  Harding  Springfield  Hamlin  Ridgeway  Lawndale

72nd  73rd  C&WIRR  Homan  Christiana  Spaulding  Sawyer  Kedzie  Louis  BRC  St  Park

Troy  Albany  Whipple  Sacramento  Richmond  Francisco  Mozart  2800

71st Pl  72nd  73rd  74th  7100  72nd  73rd  74th

Leavitt  Hoyne  Seeley  Damen  71st Pl  72nd Pl  73rd  74th  Murray Plg  **2W-8S**  N&W RY

Wolcott  Paulina  Marshfield  Wood  71st Pl  72nd  73rd

Laflin  Bishop  Ada  Throop  Elizabeth  71st Pl  72nd  Pl  73rd Pl  74th

26  **4W-8S**  Hayford  76th  Pippin  77th  78th  Myrick

75th Pl  76th  77th Pl  78th

3600  3200  Dooley Plg  Reilly  Trumbull  Park  Pl  78th

76th  **3W-8S**  25  77th  COLUMBUS

California  WESTERN  7500  2800  2400  75th  76th  77th  79TH  ST RITA HS  N&W RY

Claremont  Oakley  Hamilton  75th  76th  77th  78th  1600  30  2000  Laflin  75th Pl  Ada  Throop  29  77th  Blvd  78th  1W-8S

BOGAN HS  Bogan  79th Pl  80th

Central  Homan  79th  80th

Sacramento  cisco  fornia  htenaw  7900  pbell  sian  Loomis

79th Pl  80th

SEE PAGES 56-57

SEE PAGES 60-61

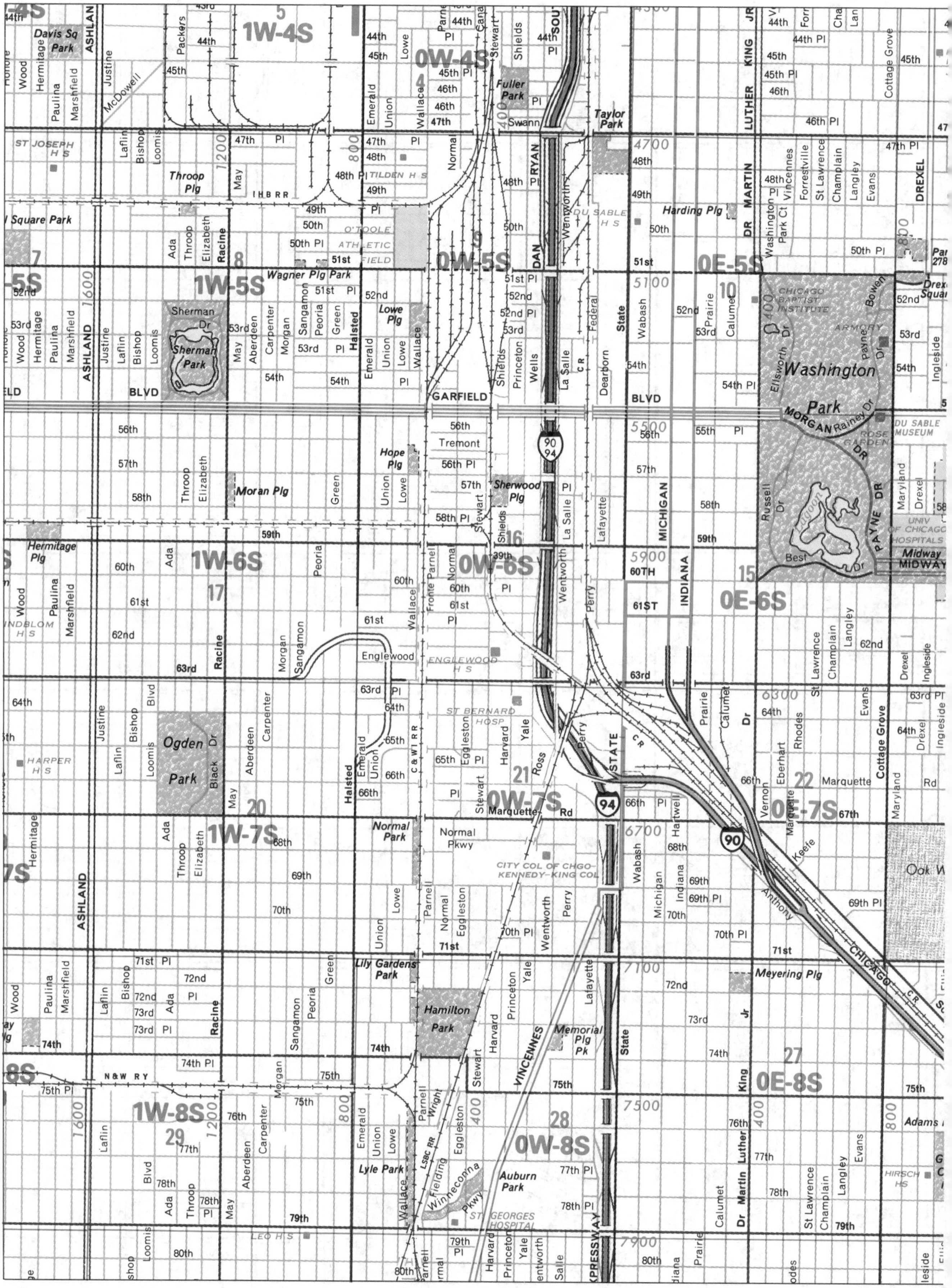

Davis Sq Park

1W-4S   0W-4S

ST JOSEPH HS

Throop Plg   TILDEN HS

Fuller Park   Taylor Park

Square Park   O'TOOLE ATHLETIC FIELD

1W-5S   0W-5S   0E-5S

Sherman Park   Wagner Plg Park   Lowe Plg

DU SABLE HS   Harding Plg

CHICAGO BAPTIST INSTITUTE

ARMORY   Washington Park

GARFIELD   BLVD

DU SABLE MUSEUM

Hope Plg   Tremont   ROSE GARDEN

Moran Plg   Sherwood Plg

UNIV OF CHICAGO HOSPITALS   Midway MIDWAY

Hermitage Plg   1W-6S   0W-6S   0E-6S

Englewood   ENGLEWOOD HS

Ogden Park   ST BERNARD HOSP

HARPER HS   1W-7S   0W-7S   0E-7S

Normal Park   CITY COL OF CHGO KENNEDY-KING COL   Oak W

Lily Gardens Park   Meyering Plg

Hamilton Park   Memorial Plg Pk

N&W RY

1W-8S   0W-8S   0E-8S

Lyle Park   Winneconna Pkwy   Auburn Park   HIRSCH HS

LEO HS   ST GEORGES HOSPITAL

SEE PAGES 68-69

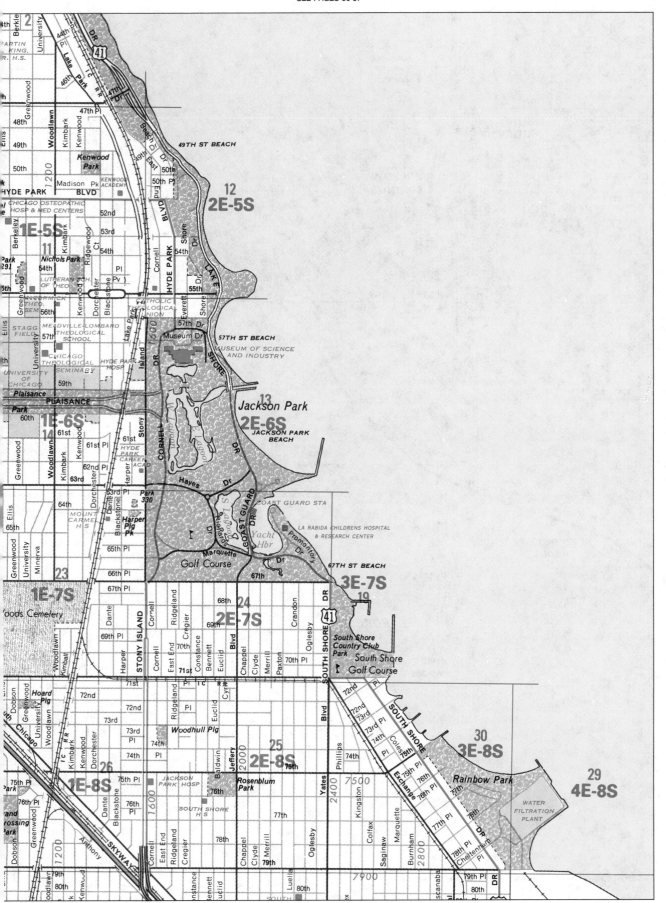

49TH ST BEACH

12
**2E-5S**

**1E-5S**

11

Nichols Park

**1E-6S**

14

Jackson Park

13
**2E-6S**

JACKSON PARK BEACH

57TH ST BEACH

MUSEUM OF SCIENCE AND INDUSTRY

COAST GUARD STA

La Rabida Childrens Hospital & Research Center

Yacht Hbr

Marquette Golf Course

67TH ST BEACH

**3E-7S**

**1E-7S**

Woods Cemetery

23

24
**2E-7S**

19

South Shore Country Club Park

South Shore Golf Course

Woodhull Plg

25
**2E-8S**

30
**3E-8S**

Rainbow Park

29
**4E-8S**

Rosenblum Park

26

**1E-8S**

WATER FILTRATION PLANT

SEE PAGES 58-59

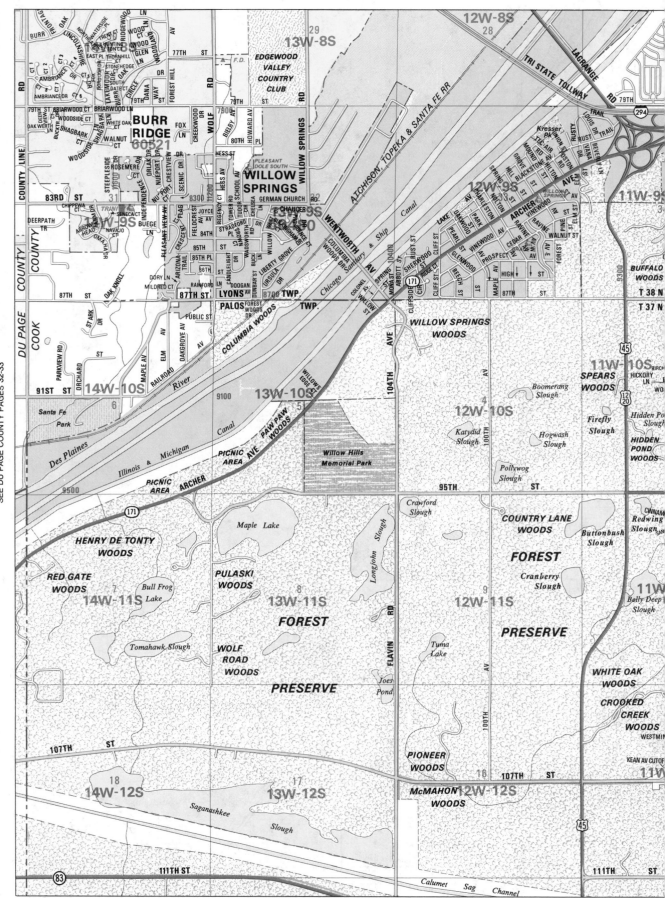

SEE PAGES 72-73

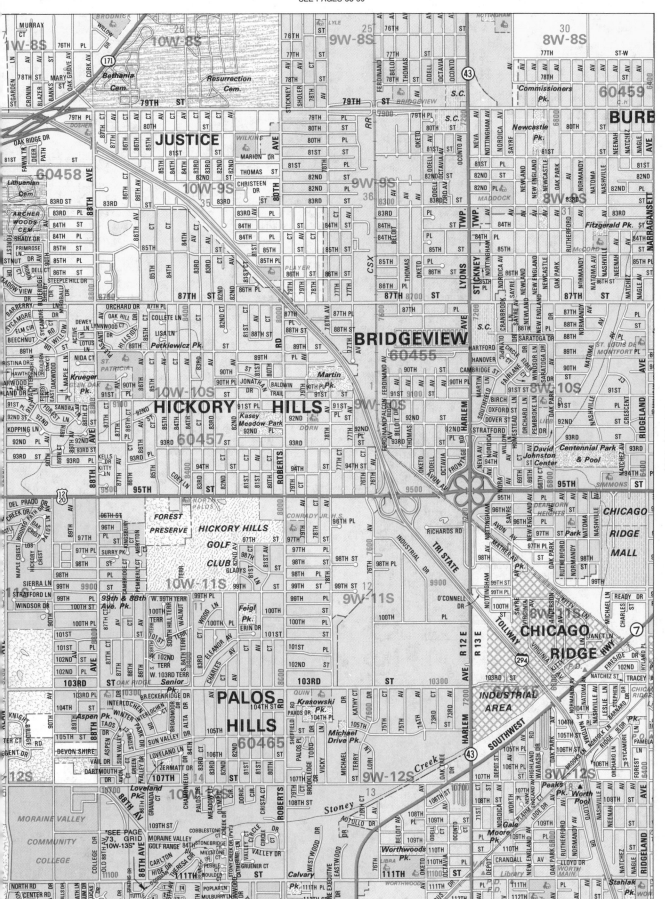

SEE PAGES 66-67

BURBANK

NARRAGANSETT AVE

STICKNEY TWP.

WORTH TWP.

HOMETOWN

OAK LAWN

CHICAGO RIDGE MALL

Ford City S. C.

Holy Sepulchre Cemetery

SOUTHWEST HWY (93RD)

60459

60453

60451

7W-8S   6W-8S   5W-8S

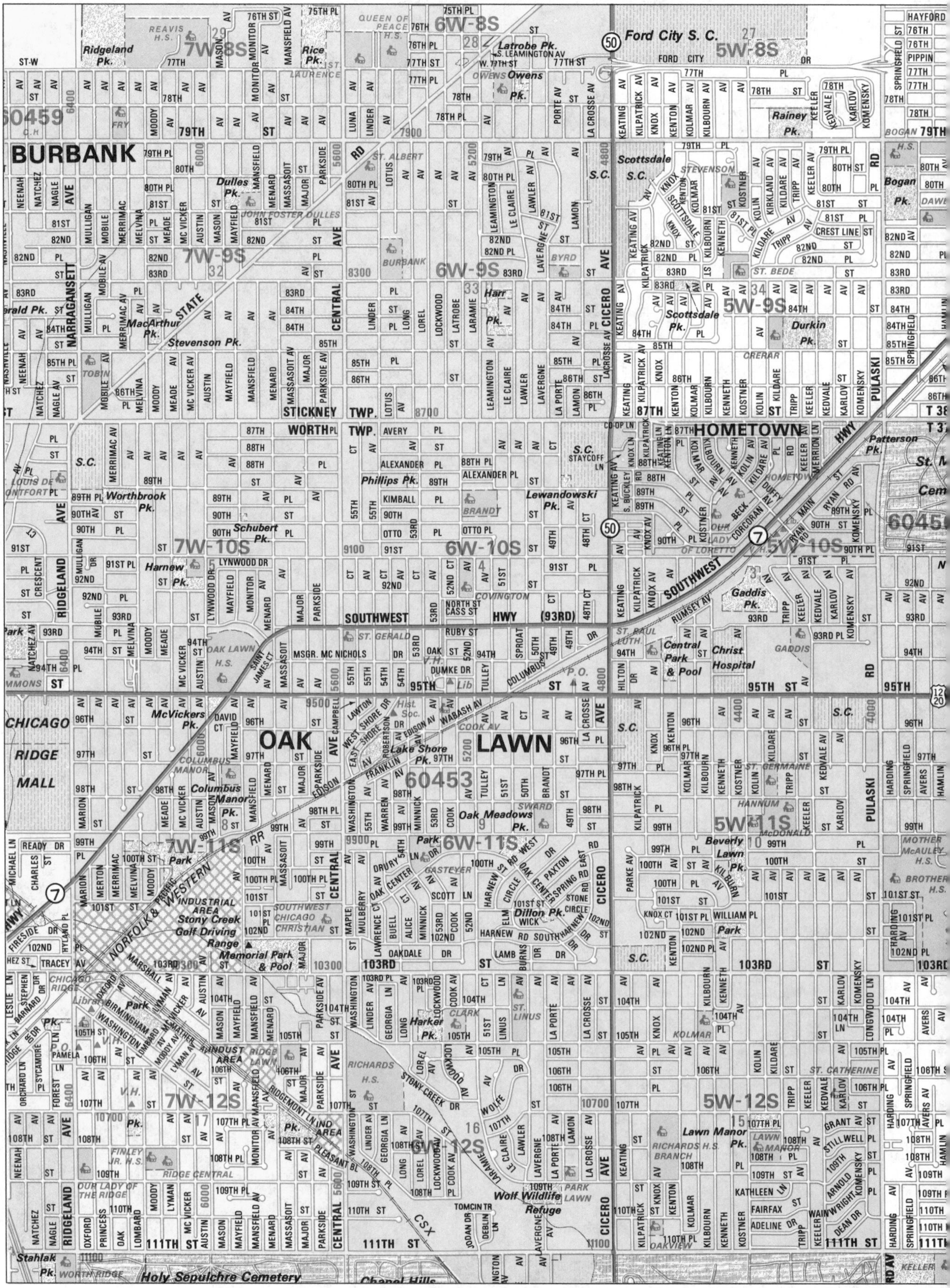

7W-9S   6W-9S   5W-9S

7W-10S   6W-10S   5W-10S

7W-11S   6W-11S   5W-11S

7W-12S   6W-12S   5W-12S

SEE PAGES 64-65

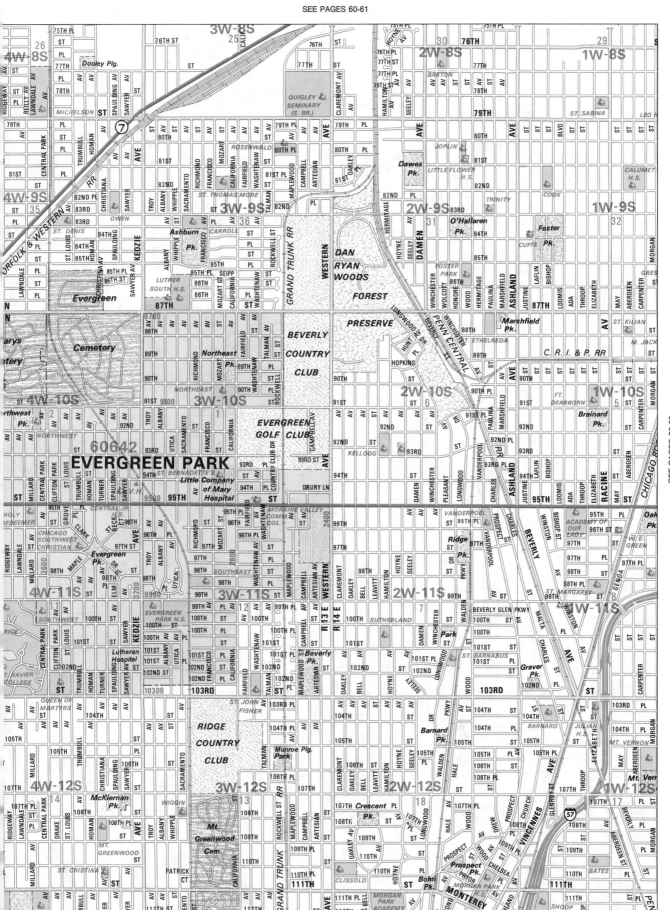

SEE PAGES 68-69

SEE PAGES 62-63

SEE PAGES 66-67

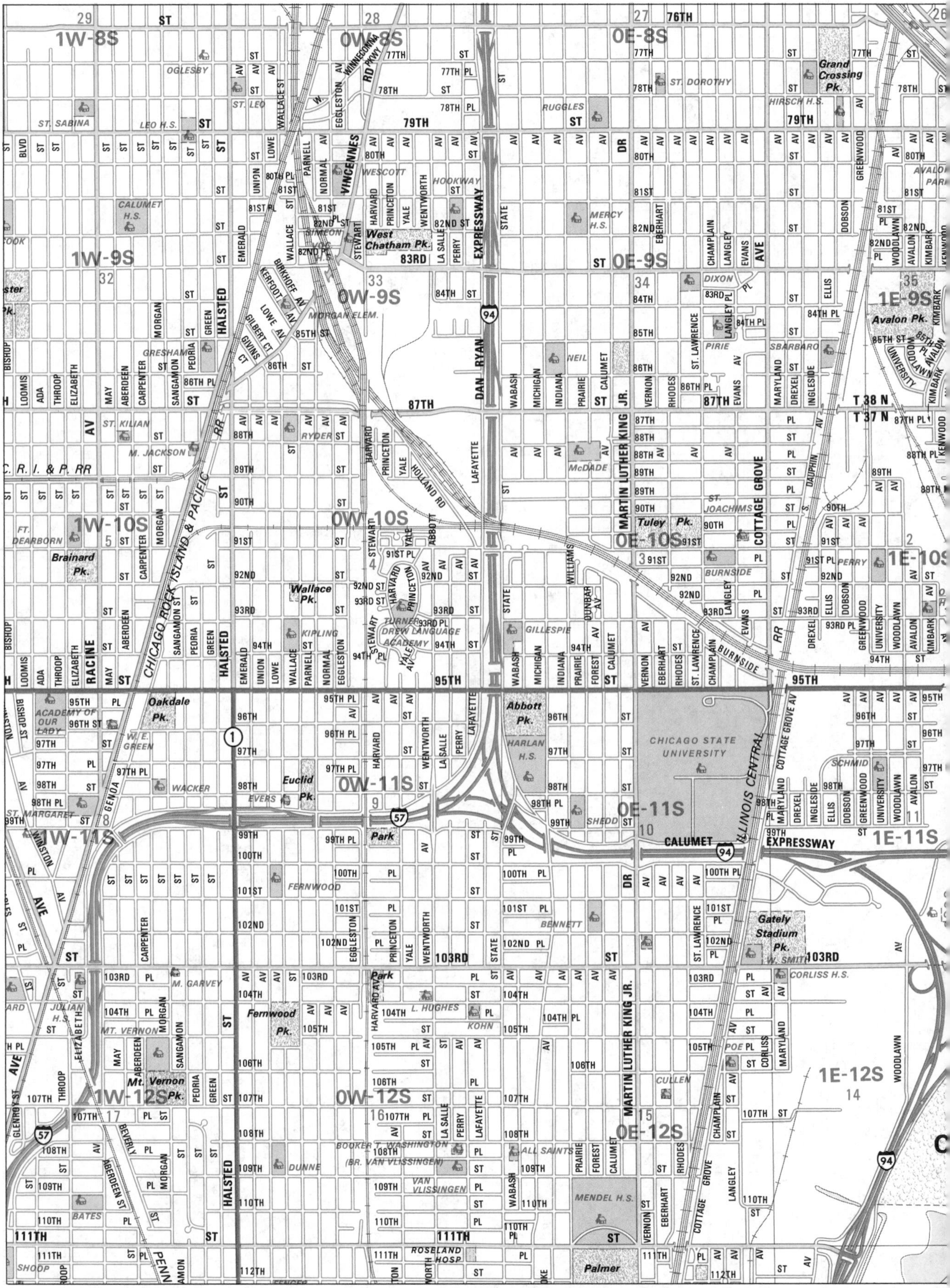


SEE PAGES 76-77

SEE PAGES 62-63

SEE PAGES 76-77

SEE DU PAGE COUNTY PAGES 34-35

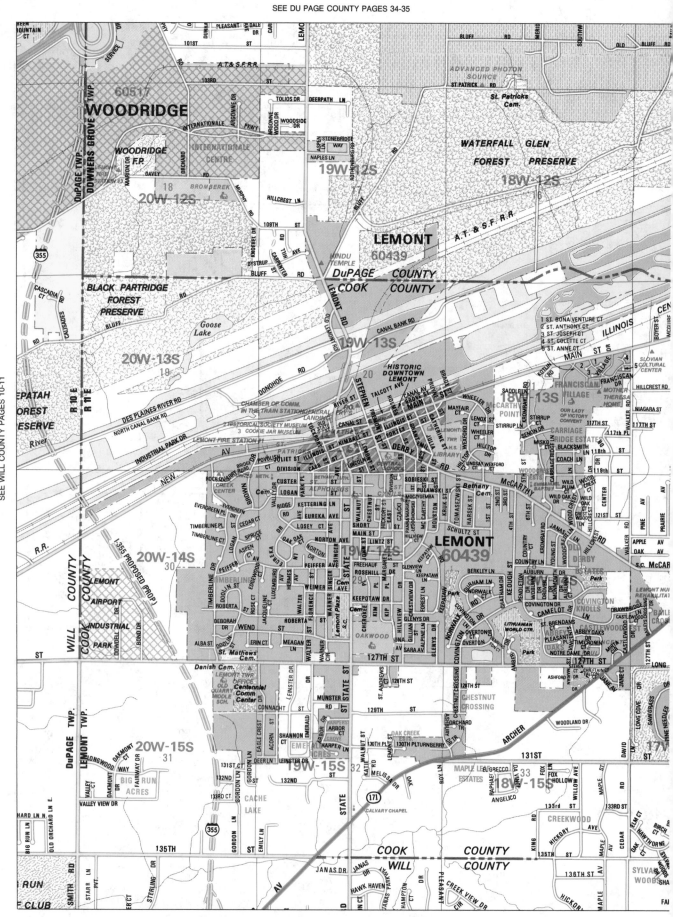

SEE WILL COUNTY PAGES 10-11

SEE WILL COUNTY PAGES 16-17

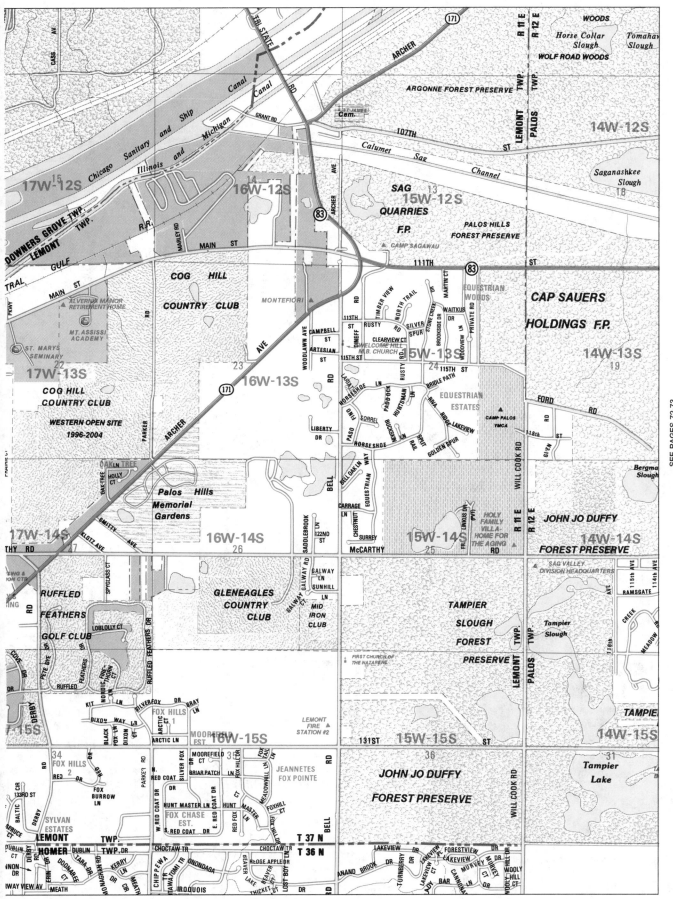

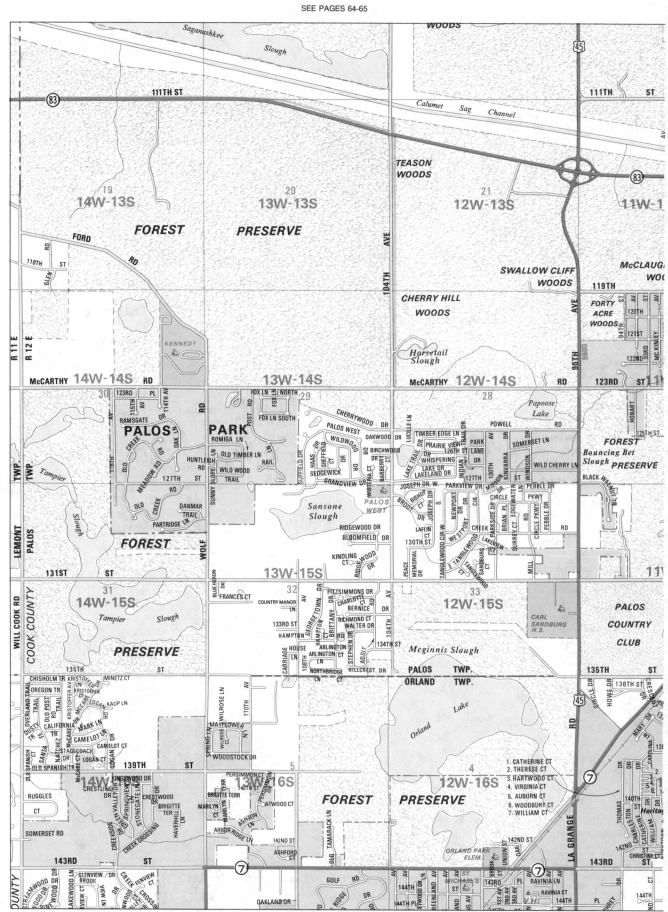

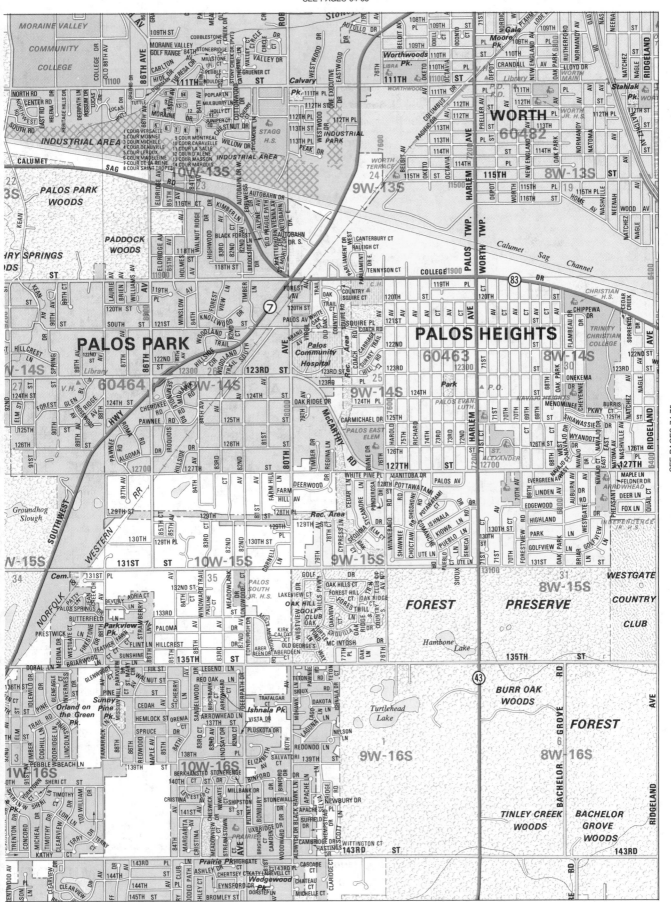

SEE PAGES 66-67

SEE PAGES 72-73

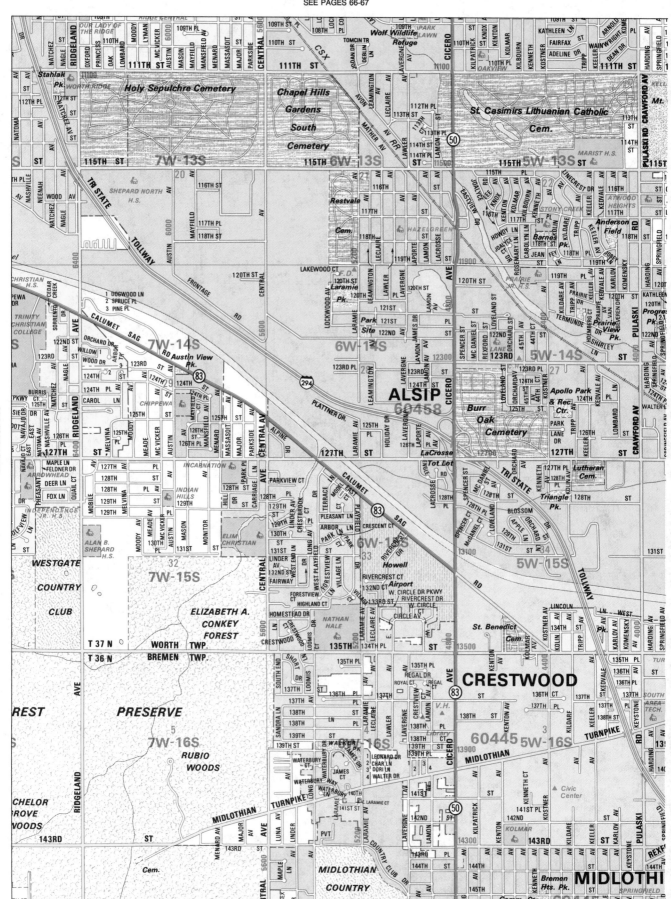

SEE PAGES 80-81

SEE PAGES 66-67

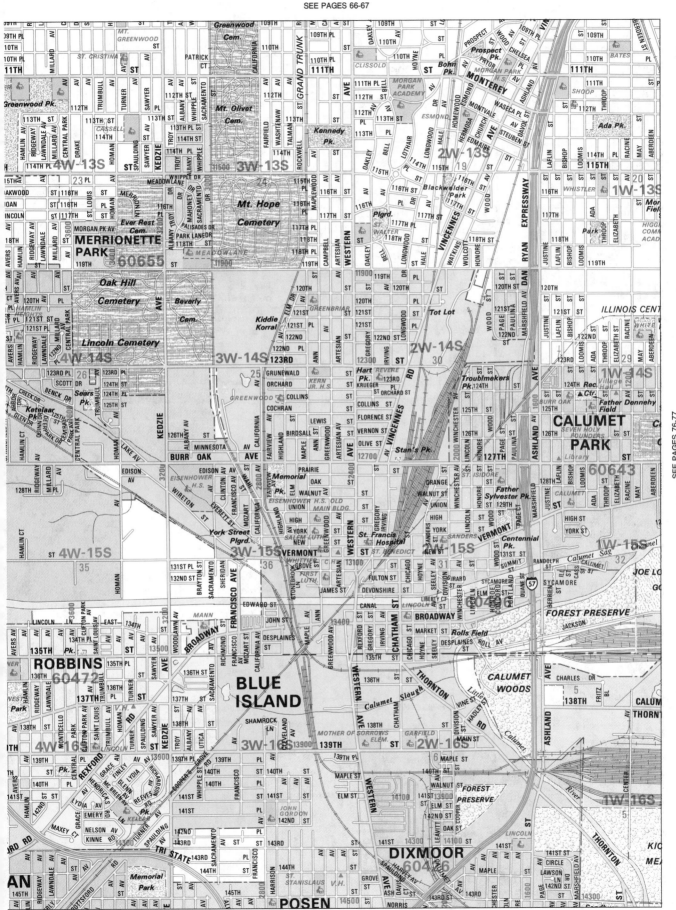

SEE PAGES 76-77

SEE PAGES 68-69

SEE PAGES 74-75

Fernwood Pk.

L. Hughes

KOHN

MT. VERNON

Mt. Vernon Pk.

1W-12S

0W-12S

0E-12S

MARTIN LUTHER KING JR.

CULLEN

1E-12S

Booker T. Washington (Br. Van Vlissingen)

DUNNE

ALL SAINTS

VAN VLISSINGEN

MENDEL H.S.

SHOOP

ROSELAND HOSP.

Palmer Pk.

1E-13S

FENGER H.S.

HOLY ROSARY

Ada Pk.

St. WILLBROD H.S.

BRENAN

St. NICHOLAS

1W-13S

0W-13S

0E-13S

WHISTLER

St. ANTHONYS

KENSINGTON

Morgan Field

Park

HIGGINS COMM. ACAD.

St. CATHERINE

SCANLAN

Kensington Pk.

St. SALAMEAS

WEST PULLMAN

Lake

Port of Chicago Lake Calumet Habor Facilities

ILLINOIS CENTRAL RR

White Park

ASSUMPTION

0E-14S

0W-14S

1W-14S

METCALFE

West Pullman Pk.

GOMPERS

JESSE OWENS MAGNET

Lion Field

CALUMET PARK

Village Hall

Father Dennehy Field

Calumet Park Pool & Tot Lot

Cedar Park Cemetery

NANSEN

Kiwanis Field

BRAYTON

Library

60643

VERMONT

CHICAGO & EASTERN ILLINOIS RR

CSX

CALUMET

HIGH ST

YORK ST

1W-15S

Calumet Sag Channel

Little Calumet River

13100

PRIVATE RDS

ALDRIDGE

130TH ST

DUBOIS

GEO. WASHINGTON CARVER PRIMARY

JOE LOUIS THE CHAMP GOLF COURSE

WHISTLER PRESERVE

0W-15S

Carver Pk.

CHARLES DR

REST PRESERVE

JACKSON

FOREST VIEW

SCHOOL ST

ACME AV

CARVER MIDDLE

0E-15S

Community Ctr. & Pool

Blue Island-Riverdale

Mohawk Pk.

Memorial Fieldhouse

Riverdale Pk.

St. MARY'S

Sunshine Pk.

CALUMET TWP.

THORNTON TWP.

PACESETTER

PATTON

St. PAUL

RIVERDALE

WASHINGTON

LINCOLN

T 37 N

T 36 N

SEE PAGES 82-83

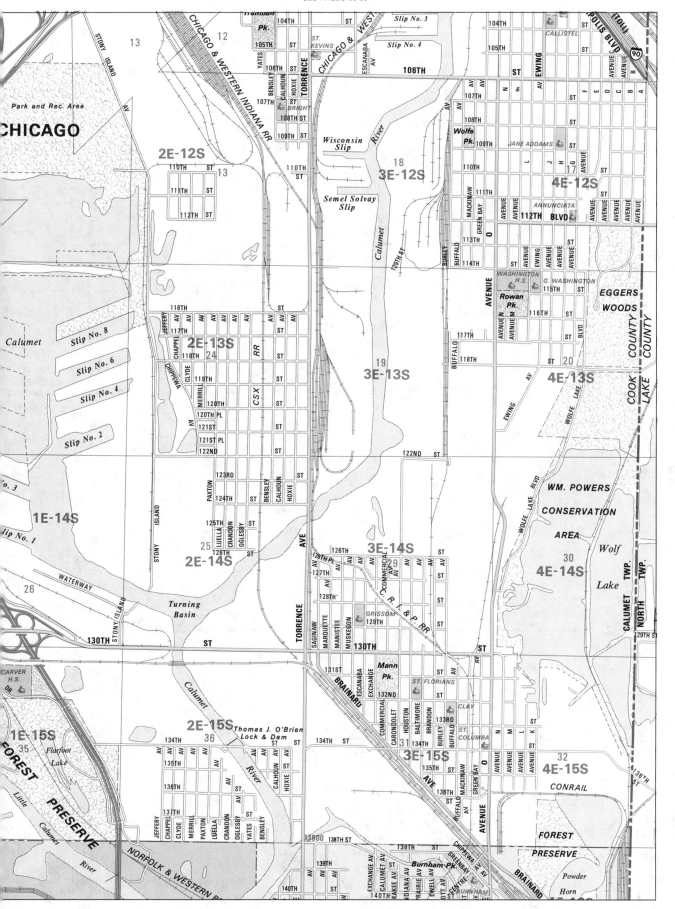

SEE PAGES 72-73

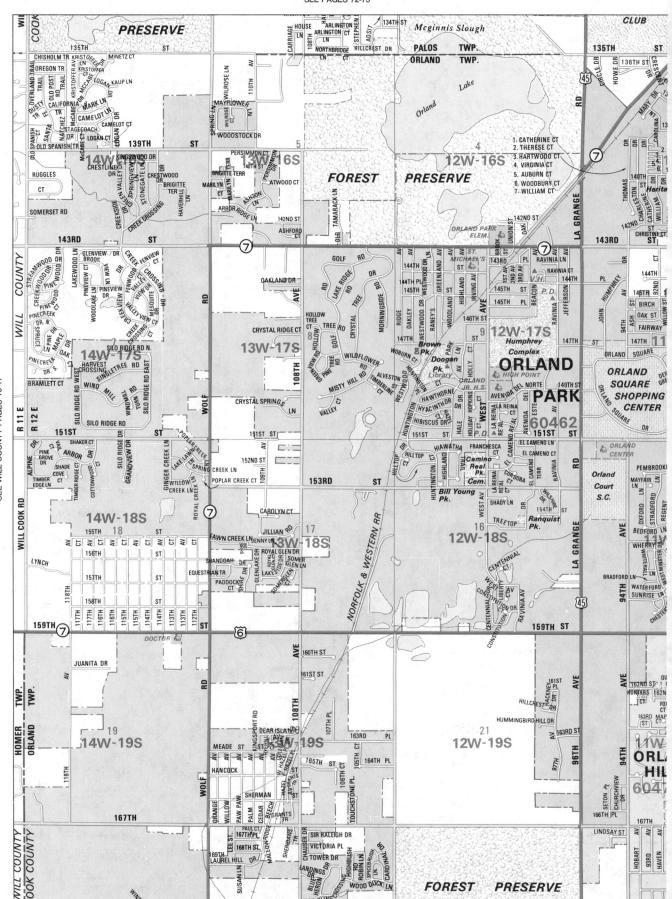

SEE PAGES 72-73

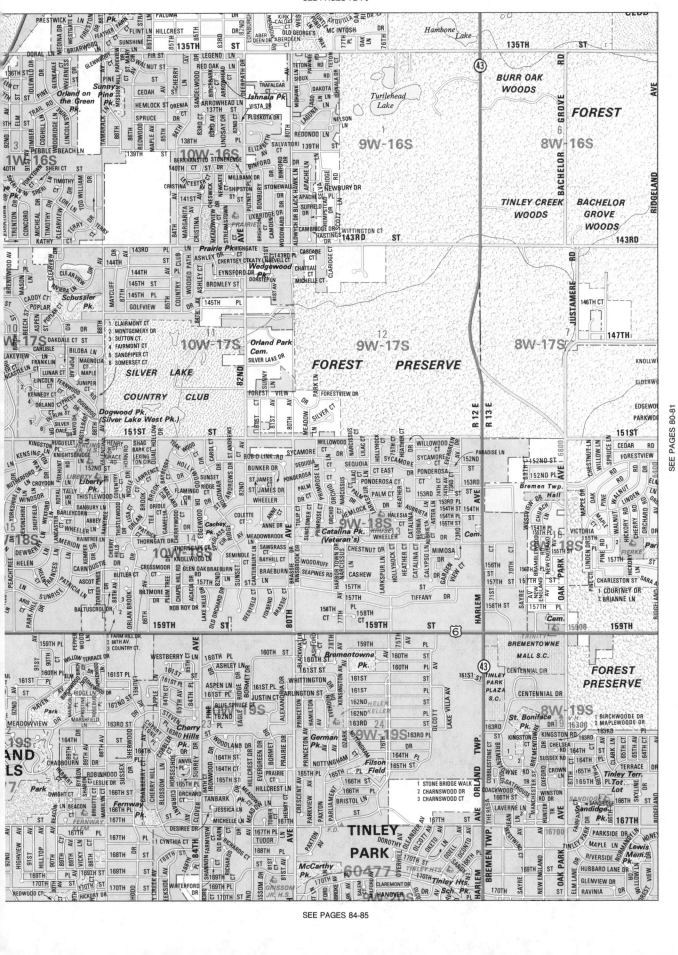

SEE PAGES 80-81

# 80 COOK COUNTY

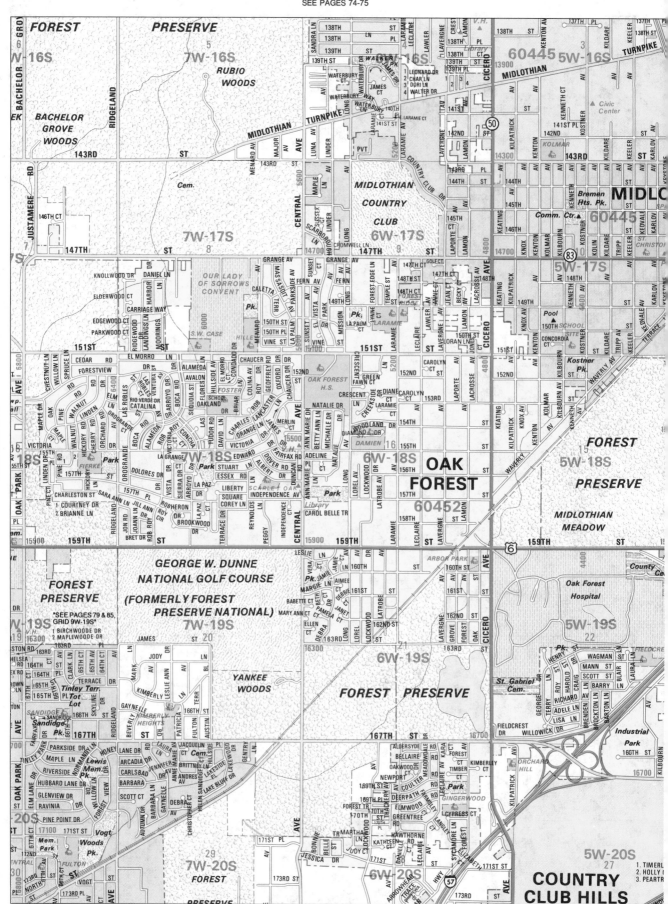

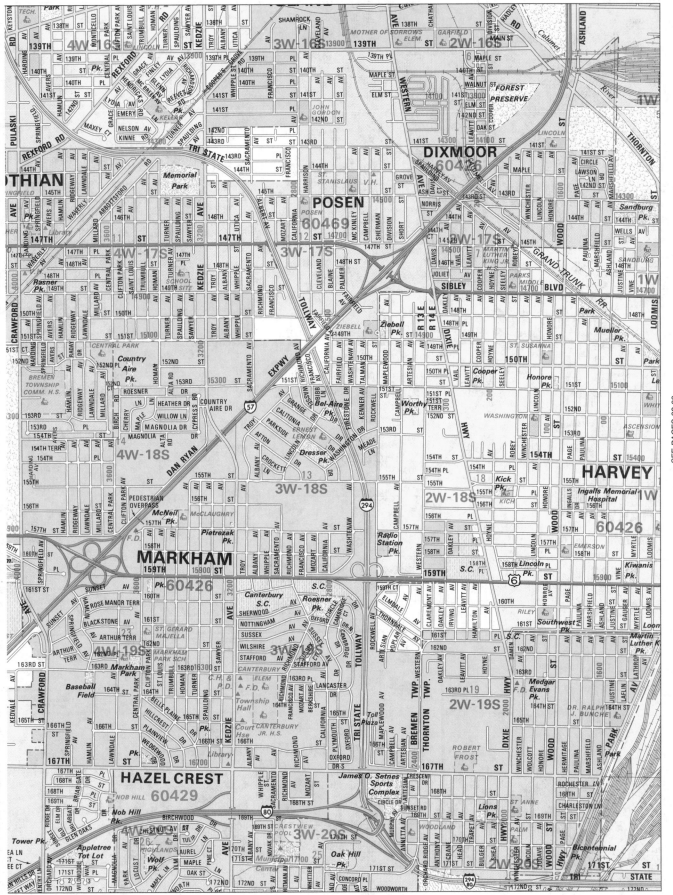

SEE PAGES 76-77

SEE PAGES 80-81

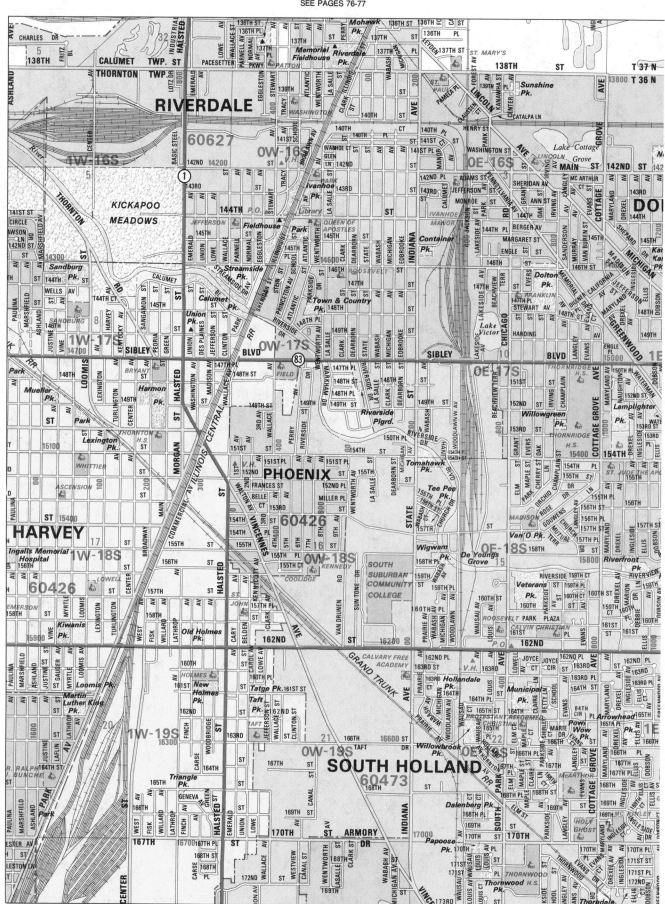

SEE PAGES 76-77

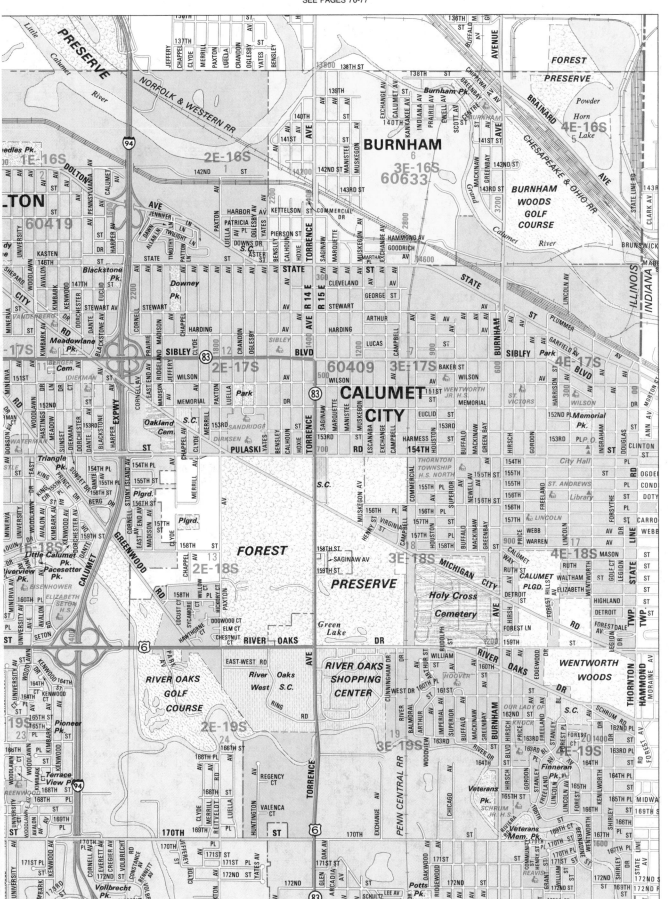

SEE PAGES 78-79

FOREST PRESERVE

12W-20S

FOREST PRESERVE

14W-20S

13W-20S

ORLAND PARK

14W-21S

13W-21S

12W-21S

COOK COUNTY
WILL COUNTY

T 36 N ORLAND TWP.
T 35 N FRANKFORT TWP.

Tinley Gardens Tot Lot

14W-22S

13W-22S

12W-22S

14W-23S 60448

MOKENA

13W-23S

12W-23S

NORMAL TOWERS INDUS PARK

Arbury Hills

SEE WILL COUNTY PAGES 22-23

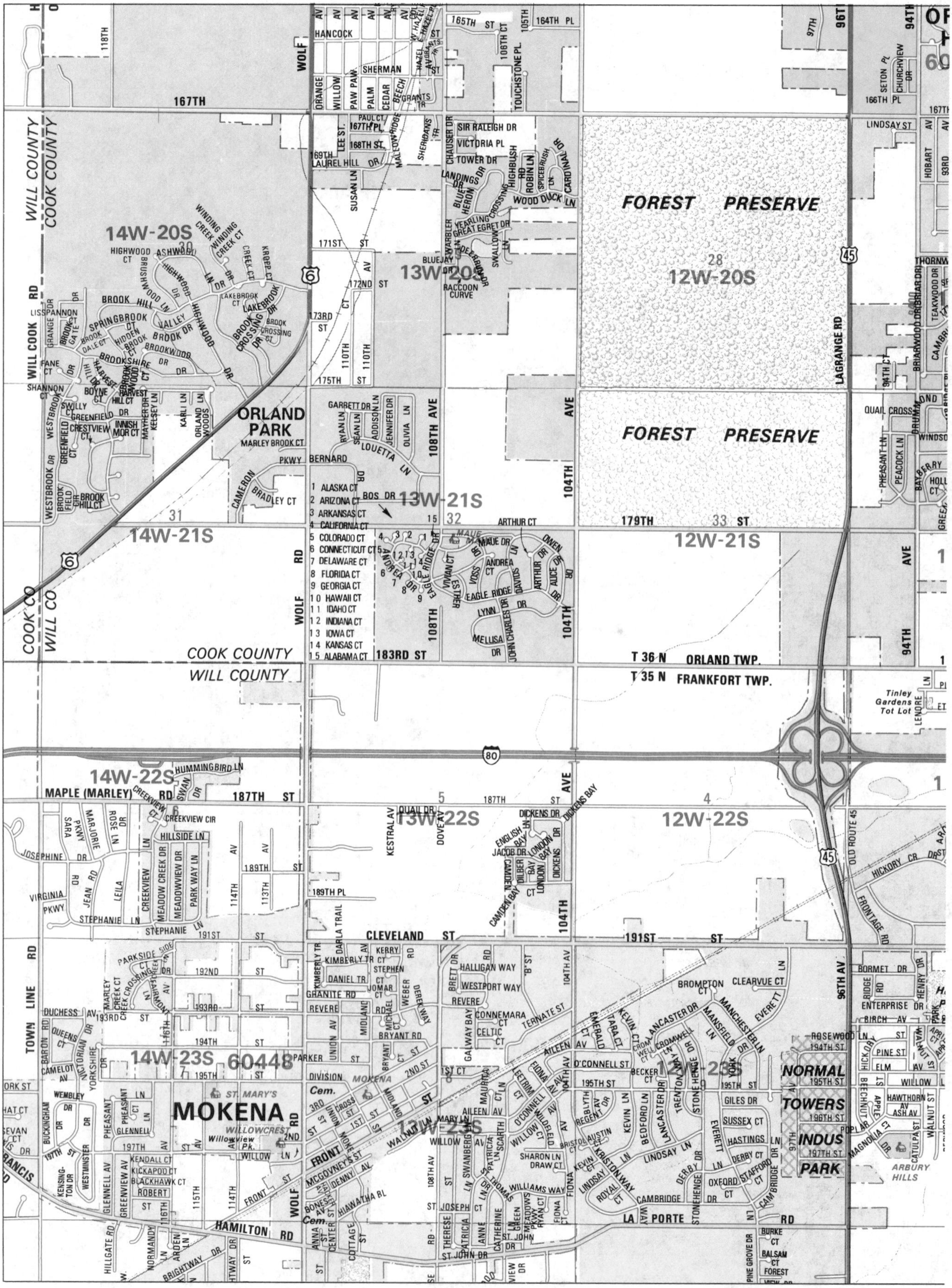

SEE PAGES 78-79

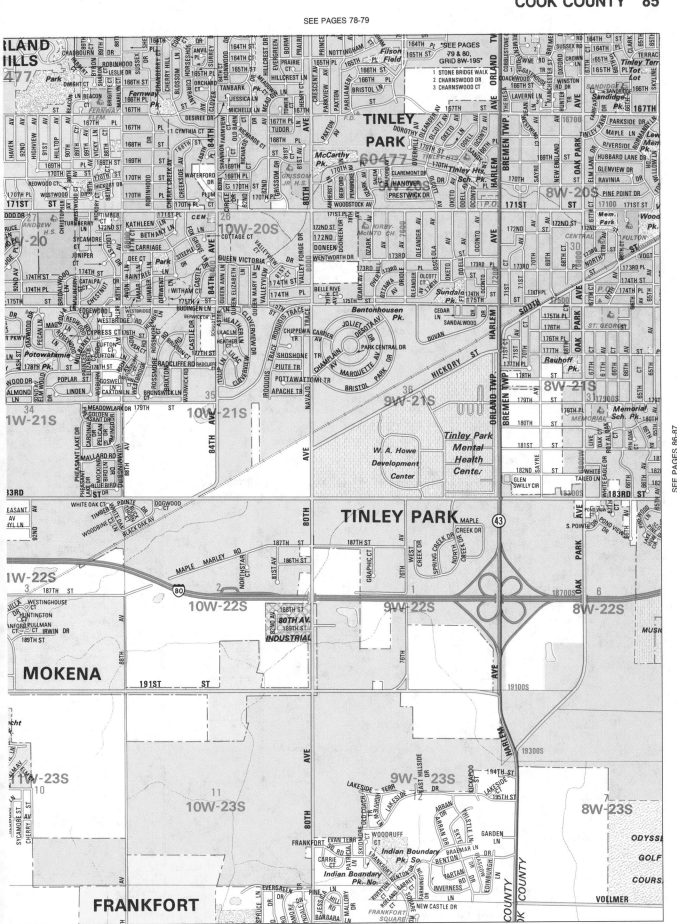

SEE PAGES 86-87

SEE PAGES 80-81

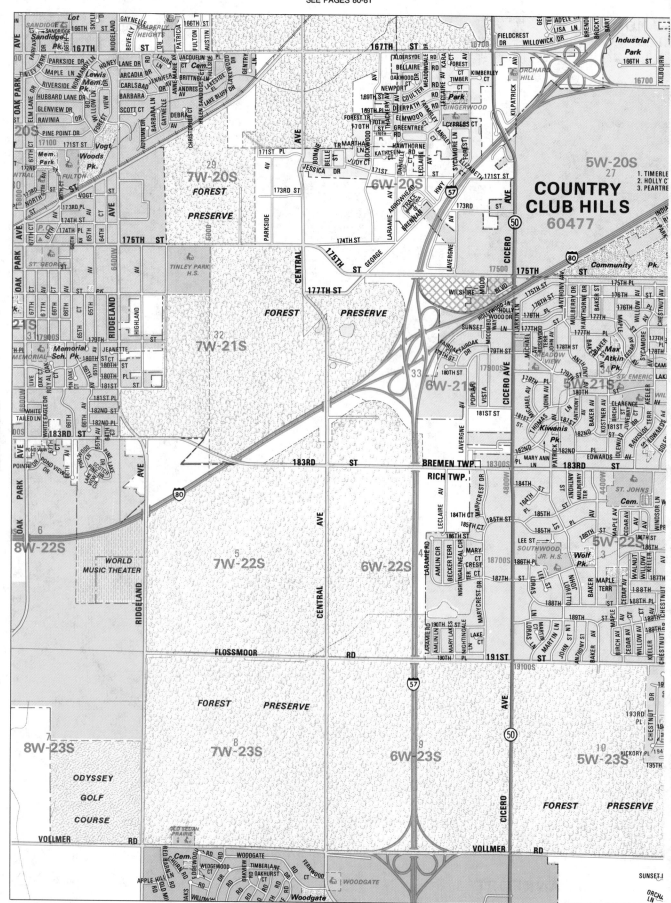

COUNTRY
CLUB HILLS
60477

SEE PAGES 84-85

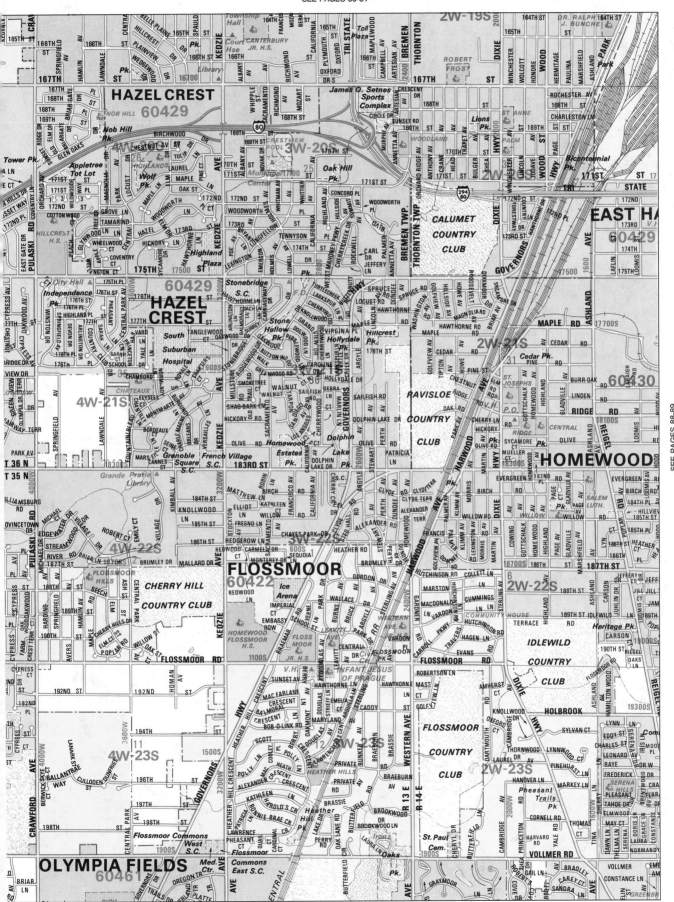

SEE PAGES 82-83

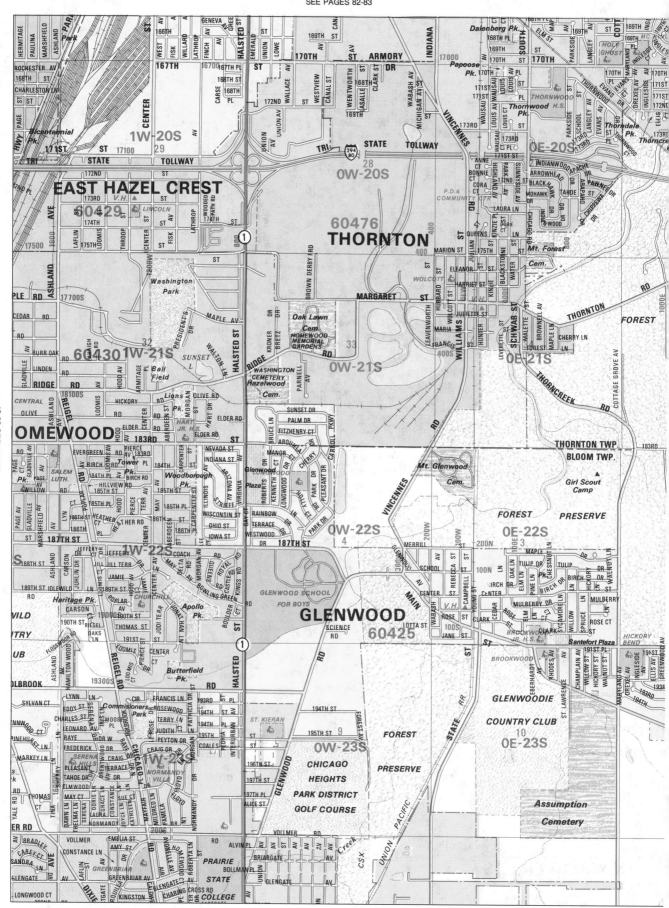

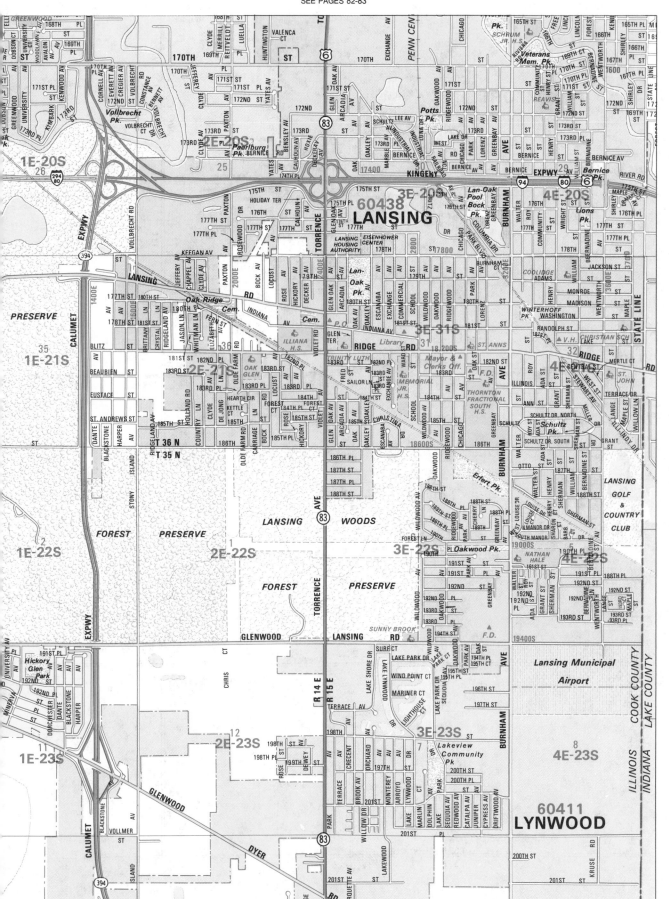

SEE PAGES 84-85

# FRANKFORT

ODYSSEY GOLF COURSE

VOLLMER

Indian Boundary Pk. So.

Indian Boundary Pk. No.

NEW CASTLE DR

SUMMIT HILL JR. H.S.

Kiwanis Pk.

Frankfort Square

Kingston

Hoffman Pk.

Community Pk.

**9W-24S**

**W-24S**

Hickory Cem.

**10W-24S**

ST. FRANCIS RD

**8W-24S**

S.C.

Brickstone Dr

Harvest Dr West

FARMHOUSE RD

WHEATFIELD DR

Green Meadow

Hunter Prairie Pk.

WELL DR

WOODLAND CT

Woodlawn Pk.

Hickory

INDIAN TRAIL

Frankfort Square

Glenshire Dr

**W-25S**

LINCOLN HWY

LIBRARY

**10W-25S**

ANN RUTLEDGE

**9W-25S**

HUNTER WOODS EST.

**8W-25S**

COVENTRY LN

Georgetown Commons

Old N. Church

Yorktown

Virginia

TIMBER R

Old Plank Road Trail
(Under development) RD

PRESTWICK COUNTRY CLUB

Pheasant Trail

HERITAGE CT

FRANKFORT TWP.

RICH TWP.

1. WILDROCK TER.
2. TULLAMORE TER.
3. BRIARBRANCH TER.
4. PLEASANT TER.
5. N. WINDMERE CIR.
6. S. WINDMERE CIR.
7. KNOLLWOOD CIR.
8. HEDGEWICK CT.
9. BURLWOOD CT.
10. CANDLEGATE CIR.
11. BRUSHWOOD DR
12. THISTLE CT.
13. HEARTSIDE RD.
14. HEATHERMEAD RD.
15. PRAIRIE RD.
16. GREEN SWARD WAY
17. HICKORY GLEN
18. CHAPPARAL TER.
19. WOODBINE TER.
20. IVYLOG TER.
21. THORNTREE TER.

BLACKTHORN

HUNTSBRIDGE

**9W-26S**

SAUK TRAIL

**11W-26S**

**10W-26S**

GLEN EAGLES CT

HIGHLAND

FRANKFORT JR. H.S.

HICKORY CREEK

**8W-26S**

LARAWAY FOREST RD SAUK TRAIL

PRESERVE

SOUTHWICK

port

**W-27S**

**10W-27S**

**9W-27S**

**8W-27S**

HARLEM

MUSTANG RD

PFEIFFER

T 35 N STEGER RD

T 34 N

WILL COUNTY / COOK COUNTY

SEE WILL COUNTY PAGES 32-33

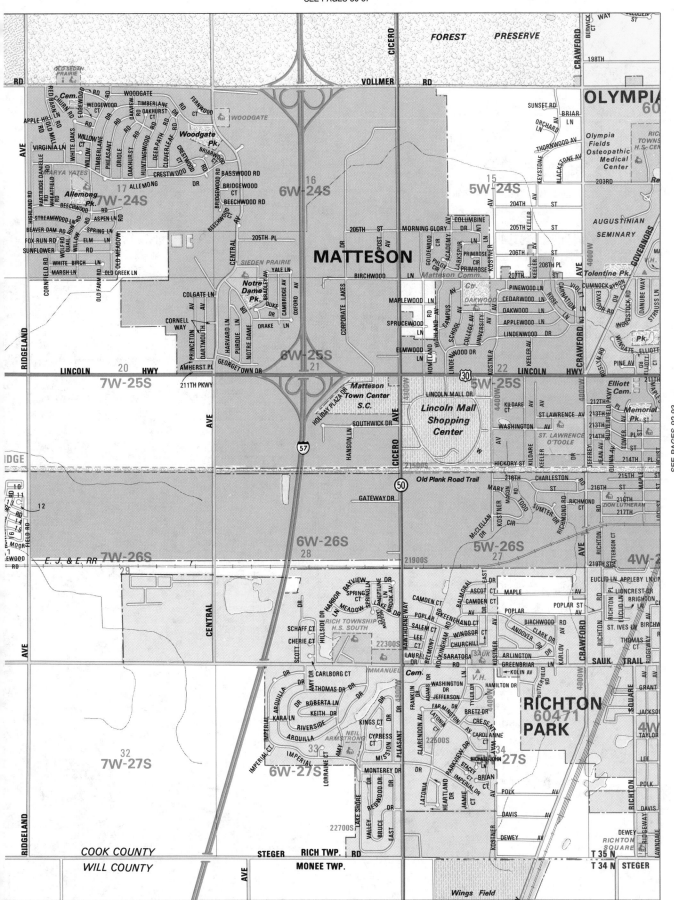

SEE PAGES 92-93

SEE PAGES 86-87

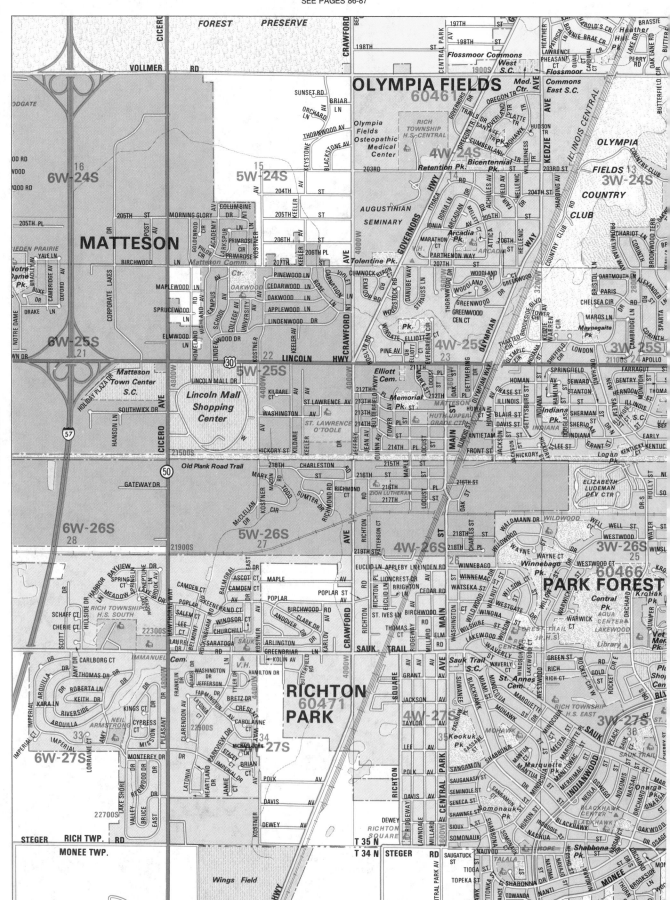

SEE PAGES 90-91

SEE WILL COUNTY PAGES 42-43

SEE PAGES 86-87

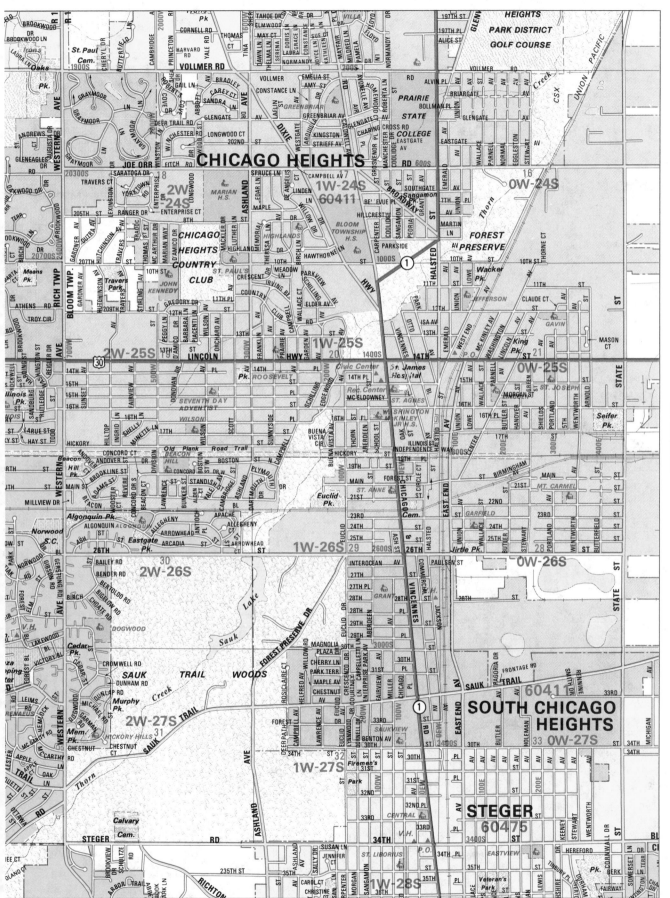

SEE PAGES 94-95

SEE WILL COUNTY PAGES 44-45

SEE PAGES 88-89

SEE PAGES 92-93

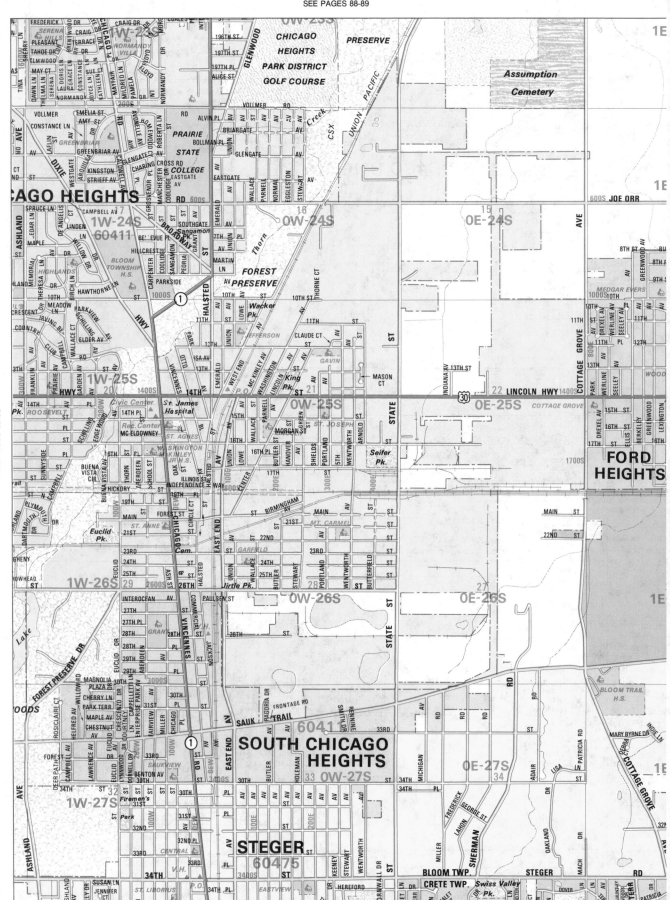

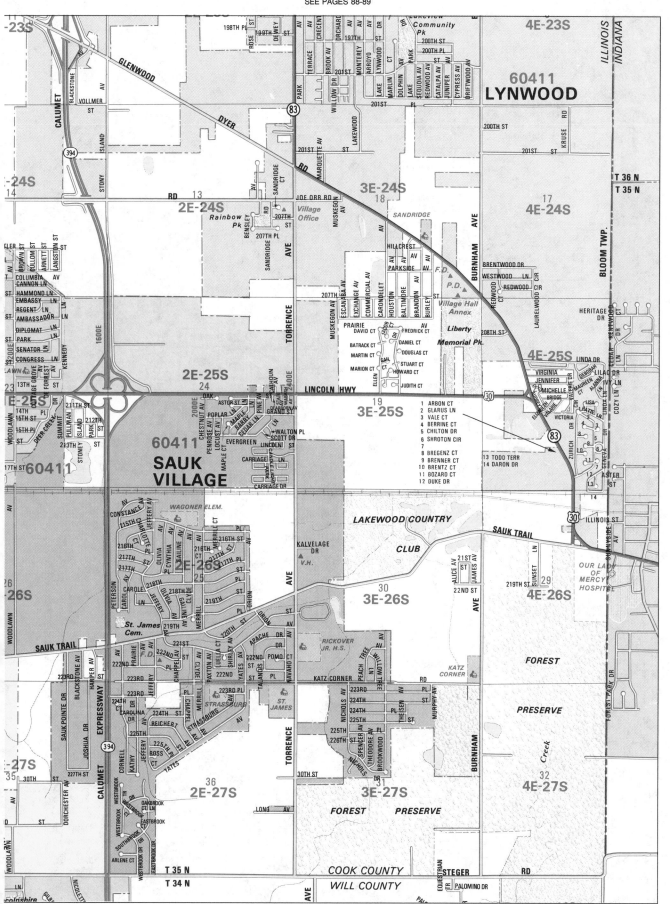

# Chicago &
# Cook County

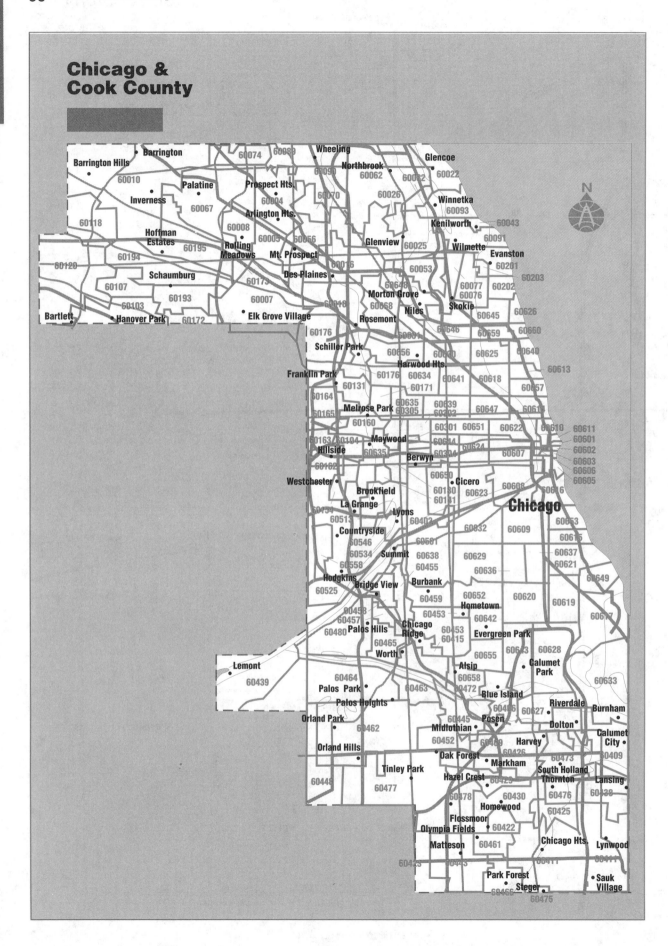

# Street Index

Grid Page

## Chicago

Abbott St. N&S ...... 0W-10S 68
Aberdeen St. N&S ... 1W-14S,1W-0N 76
Ada St. N&S 1W-14S,1W-2N 76
Adams St. E&W ... 6W-0S,0W-0S 49
Addison Dr. E&W .... 0W-4N 45
Addison St. E&W ... 9W-4N,1W-4N 42
Agatite Av. E&W ... 10W-5N,1W-5N 41
Ainslie St. E&W ... 7W-6N,1W-6N 42
Airport Dr. NE&SW.... 5W-6S 60
Albany Av. N&S ... 3W-13S,3W-9N 75
Albion Av. E&W ... 9W-8N,1W-8N 37
Aldine Av. E&W ...... 0W-4N 45
Alexander St. E&W.... 0W-2S 57
Algonquin Av. N&S.... 6W-8N 38
Allen Av. NE&SW .... 4W-3N 44
Allport St. N&S ...... 1W-1S 56
Alta Vista Ter. N&S .. 1W-4N 45
Altgeld St. E&W ... 8W-3N,1W-3N 42
Ancona St. E&W...... 1W-0N 51
Anson Pl. E&W ...... 2W-0N 50
Anthon Av. N&S .... 10W-5N 41
Anthony Av. NW&SE ... 0E-7S,1E-8S 62
Arbor Pl. E&W ........ 1W-0N 51
Arcade Pl. E&W ... 2W-0S,0W-0S 50
Arch St. NW&SE...... 1W-2S 56
Archer Av. NE&SW ... 8W-5S,0W-1S 59
Ardmore Av. E&W ... 9W-7N,1W-7N 37
Argyle St. E&W ... 8W-6N,1W-6N 42
Arlington Pl. E&W .... 0W-3N 45
Armitage Av. E&W ... 8W-2N,0W-2N 48
Armour St. N&S ...... 1W-0N 51
Armstrong Av. E&W .. 6W-7N 38
Artesian Av. N&S ... 3W-13S,3W-9N 75
Arthington St. E&W ... 7W-0S,1W-0S 48
Arthur Av. E&W ... 8W-8N,1W-8N 37
Ashland Av. N&S ... 2W-13S,2W-9N 75
Astor St. N&S ........ 0E-1N 51
Attrill St. NE&SW .... 3W-2N 50
Augusta Blvd. E&W ... 5W-1N,2W-1N 49
Austin Av. N&S ... 7W-7S,7W-6N 60
Avalon Av. N&S ... 1E-11S,1E-9S 68
Avenue A N&S ...... 4E-12S 69
Avenue B N&S ... 4E-12S,4E-11S 69
Avenue C N&S ... 4E-12S,4E-11S 69
Avenue D N&S ...... 4E-12S 69
Avenue E N&S ...... 4E-12S 69
Avenue F N&S ...... 4E-12S 69
Avenue G N&S ... 4E-12S,4E-11S 69
Avenue H N&S ... 4E-12S,4E-10S 69
Avenue J N&S ... 4E-12S,4E-10S 69
Avenue K N&S ...... 4E-15S 77
Avenue L N&S ... 4E-15S,4E-10S 77
Avenue M N&S ... 4E-15S,4E-10S 77
Avenue N N&S ... 4E-15S,4E-10S 77
Avenue O N&S ... 3E-15S,4E-10S 77
Avers St. N&S ... 4W-12S,4W-7N 67
Avondale Av. NW&SE ... 9W-8N,2W-2N 37
Balbo Dr. E&W ........ 0E-0S 51
Baldwin Av. N&S ...... 2E-8S 63
Balmoral Av. E&W ... 10W-6N,1W-6N 41
Baltimore Av. N&S ... 3E-15S,3E-10S 77
Banks St. E&W........ 0E-1N 51
Barber St. E&W ...... 0W-1S 57
Barry Av. E&W ... 8W-3N,0W-3N 42
Bauwans St. N&S .... 2W-1N 50
Beach Av. E&W ... 4W-1N,2W-1N 50
Beach Dr. NW&SE .... 2E-5S 63
Beacon St. N&S ...... 1W-5N 45
Beaubien Ct. N&S .... 0E-0N 51
Belden Av. E&W ... 8W-2N,1W-2N 48
Bell Av. N&S 2W-13S,2W-8N 75
Belle Plaine Av. E&W ... 10W-5N,1W-5N 41
Bellevue Pl. E&W...... 0E-1N 51
Belmont Av. E&W ... 9W-4N,1W-4N 42
Belmont Harbor Dr. NW&SE ... 0W-4N 45
Bennett Av. N&S ... 2E-11S,2E-7S 69
Bensley Av. N&S ... 2E-15S,3E-11S 77
Berenice Av. E&W ... 7W-4N,2W-4N 42
Berkeley Av. N&S ... 1E-5S,1E-4S 62
Bernard St. N&S ... 4W-3N,4W-7N 44
Berteau Av. E&W ... 10W-5N,1W-5N 41
Berwyn Av. E&W ... 10W-6N,1W-6N 41
Besly Ct. NW&SE .... 1W-2N 51
Bessie Coleman Dr. N&S ... 12W-7N 40
Best Dr. E&W ........ 0E-6S 62
Beverly Av. NW&SE.. 1W-11S 68
Beverly Glen Pkwy. E&W ... 2W-11S 67
Beverly St. NW&SE ... 1W-12S,2W-10S 68
Bingham St. NW&SE .. 3W-2N 50
Birchwood Av. E&W ... 9W-9N,2W-9N 37
Birkhoff Av. NW&SE .. 0W-9S 68
Bishop St. N&S ... 1W-14S,1W-1N 76
Bissell St. N&S ...... 1W-2N 51
Bittersweet Pl. E&W ... 8W-5N,0W-5N 42
Black Dr. N&S ........ 1W-7S 62
Blackhawk St. E&W ... 1W-1N,0W-1N 51
Blackstone Av. N&S ... 1E-10S,1E-5S 68
Blake St. NW&SE .... 2W-3S 56
Bliss St. NE&SW...... 1W-1N 51
Bloomingdale Av. E&W ... 8W-2N,2W-2N 48
Blue Island Av. NE&SW ... 2W-2S,1W-1S 56
Bonaparte St. NE&SW ... 1W-2S 56
Bonfield St. NW&SE .. 1W-2S 56
Bosworth Av. N&S ... 1W-1N,1W-9N 51
Boulevard Way N&S .. 3W-2S 56
Bowen Av. E&W ...... 0E-4S 57
Bowler St. NE&SW.... 2W-0S 50
Bowmanville NE&SW .. 2W-6N 45
Bradley Pl. E&W ... 3W-4N,1W-4N 44
Brainard Av. NW&SE 3E-15S 77
Brandon Av. N&S ... 3E-15S,3E-9S 77
Brayton Av. E&W .... 0W-14S 76
Brayton St. E&W .... 0W-14S 76
Brennan Av. N&S .... 2E-11S 69
Brenock Dr. N&S .... 3W-1N 50
Briar Pl. E&W ........ 0W-3N 45
Brighton Pl. NW&SE .. 3W-4S 56
Broad St. NW&SE .... 1W-2S 56
Broadway St. N&S ... 0W-3N,1W-6N 45
Brompton Av. E&W .. 0W-4N 45
Bross Av. E&W ...... 3W-3S 56
Browning Av. E&W .... 0E-3S 57
Bryn Mawr Av. E&W ... 10W-7N,1W-7N 36
Buckingham Pl. E&W .. 0W-4N 45
Buena Ter. E&W ...... 0W-5N 45
Buffalo Av. N&S ... 3E-15S,4E-9S 77
Burkhardt Dr. E&W.... 3W-1S 56
Burley Av. N&S ... 3E-15S,4E-9S 77
Burling St. N&S ... 0W-1N,0W-3N 51
Burnham Av. N&S ... 3E-9S,3E-8S 69
Burnside Av. NW&SE ... 0E-10S 68
Burton Pl. E&W ...... 0E-1N 51
Busse Av. N&S ...... 8W-6N 42
Byron St. E&W ... 10W-4N,1W-4N 41
Cabrini St. E&W ... 1W-0S,0W-0S 51
Cahill Ter. NE&SW .... 9W-4N 42
Caldwell Av. NW&SE ... 7W-8N,5W-7N 37
Calhoun Av. N&S ... 2E-15S,2E-11S 77
California Av. N&S ... 3W-12S,3W-9N 67
California Blvd. N&S .. 3W-2S 56
California Ter. E&W .. 0W-3N 45
Calumet Av. N&S ... 0E-15S,0E-1S 76
Calumet Expwy. N&S ... 0E-11S,1E-14S 68
Cambridge Av. N&S ... 0W-1N,0W-3N 51
Campbell Av. N&S ... 3W-13S,3W-9N 75
Canal St. N&S ... 0W-4S,0W-0S 57
Canalport Av. SW&NE ... 1W-1S 56
Canfield Av. N&S ... 9W-6N,9W-7N 42
Cannon Dr. NW&SE .. 0W-3N 45
Canton St. E&W ...... 2W-2N 50
Carmen Av. E&W ... 10W-6N,1W-6N 41
Carondolet Av. N&S ... 3E-15S,3E-14S 77
Carpenter Rd. N&S .. 6W-8N 38
Carpenter St. N&S ... 1W-14S,1W-0N 76
Carroll Av. E&W ... 2W-0N,0W-0N 50
Carver Dr. NW&SE .. 1E-15S 76
Castle Island Av. E&W ... 10W-5N 41
Castlewood Ter. E&W ... 1W-6N 45
Catalpa Av. E&W ... 10W-6N,1W-6N 41
Catherine Av. E&W .. 10W-6N 41
Cedar St. E&W........ 0E-1N 51
Central Av. N&S ... 6W-6S,7W-7N 60
Central Park Av. N&S ... 4W-13S,4W-7N 75
Central Park Blvd. N&S ... 4W-0S,4W-0N 50
Cermak Rd. E&W ... 3W-1S,0W-1S 56
Champlain Av. N&S ... 0E-13S,0E-4S 76
Chanay St. NE&SW .. 3W-2N 50
Chappel Av. N&S ... 2E-15S,2E-7S 77
Charles St. NW&SE ... 1W-11S,2W-10S 68
Charleston St. E&W .. 2W-2N 50
Chase Av. E&W ... 9W-9N,1W-9N 37
Chelsea Pl. NW&SE .. 2W-12S 67
Cheltenham Pl. NE&SW ... 3E-8S 63
Cherry St. NW&SE.... 1W-1N 51
Chester Av. N&S .... 10W-6N 41
Chestnut St. E&W ... 1W-1N,0W-1N 51
Chicago Av. E&W ... 6W-1N,0W-0N 49
Chicago Skyway N&S ... 0E-7S,4E-11S 62
Chicora Av. NE&SW ... 7W-8N,6W-8N 37
Chippewa N&S ...... 2E-13S 77
Christiana Av. N&S ... 4W-12S,4W-7N 67
Christina Av. N&S .... 4W-9S 67
Church St. NE&SW ... 2W-13S,1W-12S 75
Churchill St. E&W .... 2W-2N 50
Cicero Av. N&S ... 5W-8S,5W-7N 60
Claremont Av. N&S ... 2W-12S,2W-9N 67
Clarence Av. E&W ... 9W-7N,8W-7N 37
Clarendon Av. N&S .. 1W-5N 45
Clark St. N&S 0W-1S,2W-8N 57
Cleaver St. N&S ...... 1W-1N 51
Cleveland Av. N&S ... 0W-1N,0W-2N 51
Clifford Av. NE&SW .. 6W-7N 38
Clifton Av. N&S ... 1W-2N,1W-5N 51
Clinton St. N&S ... 0W-1S,0W-0N 57
Clover Av. NW&SE.... 5W-5N 43
Clybourn Av. NW&SE ... 2W-3N,1W-2N 45
Clyde Av. N&S ... 2E-15S,2E-7S 77
Coast Guard Dr. N&S .. 2E-7S 63
Coles Av. N&S .. 3E-9S,3E-8S 69
Colfax Av. N&S ... 3E-10S,3E-8S 69
Columbia Av. E&W ... 2W-8N,1W-8N 39
Columbus Av. NE&SW ... 4W-9S,3W-8S 67
Columbus Dr. N&S .... 0E-0S 51
Commercial Av. N&S ... 3E-15S,3E-9S 77
Commonwealth Av. N&S ... 0W-2N,0W-3N 51
Concord Pl. E&W ... 6W-2N,0W-2N 49
Congress Pkwy. E&W ... 6W-0S,1W-0S 49
Constance Av. N&S ... 2E-10S,2E-7S 69
Corcoran Pl. E&W .... 7W-0N 48
Corliss Av. N&S ... 0E-15S,1E-12S 76
Cornelia Av. E&W ... 10W-4N,1W-4N 41
Cornell Av. N&S ... 2E-10S,2E-5S 69
Cortez Dr. E&W ... 6W-1N,1W-1N 49
Cortland Pkwy. E&W .. 1W-2N 51
Cottage Grove Av. N&S ... 0E-14S,0E-2S 76
Couch Pl. E&W ...... 0W-0N 51
Coulter St. NE&SW .. 2W-2S 56
Court Pl. E&W........ 0W-0N 51
Courtland Av. N&S .. 10W-6N 41
Coyle Av. E&W ... 9W-8N,3W-8N 37
Craft St. NW&SE .... 1W-4N 45
Crandon Av. N&S ... 2E-15S,2E-7S 77
Cregier Av. N&S ... 2E-10S,2E-7S 69
Crestline St. E&W .... 5W-9S 66
Crilly Ct. N&S ........ 0W-2N 51
Crosby St. NW&SE .. 0W-1N 51
Crowell St. NW&SE .. 1W-2S 56
Crystal St. E&W ... 6W-1N,1W-1N 49
Cullerton St. E&W ... 5W-1S,0W-1S 55
Cullom Av. E&W ... 6W-5N,1W-5N 43
Cumberland Av. N&S ... 10W-5N,10W-6N 41
Cuyler Av. E&W ... 7W-5N,1W-5N 42
Cyril Ct. N&S.......... 2E-8S 63
Dakin St. E&W ... 8W-4N,1W-4N 42
Damen Av. N&S ... 2W-11S,2W-8N 67
Dante Av. N&S ... 1E-10S,1E-7S 68
Dauphin Av. NE&SW.. 1E-10S 68
Davlin Ct. NE&SW .... 4W-3N 44
Davol St. NE&SW.... 2W-13S 75
Dawson Av. NE&SW .. 4W-3N 44
Dayton St. N&S ... 1W-2N,1W-5N 51
DeKoven St. E&W .... 0W-0S 51
Dean St. NW&SE .... 2W-1N 50
Dearborn St. N&S ... 0W-5S,0W-1N 62
Delaware Pl. E&W .... 0W-1N 51
Delphia Av. N&S ... 10W-5N,10W-6N 41
Deming Pl. E&W ... 6W-3N,0W-3N 43
Denvir Av. N&S ...... 3W-0S 50
DesPlaines St. N&S ... 0W-1S,0W-0N 57
Devon Av. E&W ... 9W-8N,1W-8N 37
Dewitt Pl. N&S........ 0E-1N 51
Dexter Park Av. N&S.. 1W-4S 56
Dickens Av. E&W ... 8W-2N,1W-2N 48
Dickinson Av. NW&SE ... 6W-5N 43
District Blvd. E&W .... 5W-4S 55
Diversey Av. E&W ... 6W-3N,1W-3N 43
Diversey Dr. E&W .... 0W-3N 45
Diversey Pkwy. E&W.. 1W-3N 45
Division St. E&W ... 6W-1N,0W-1N 49
Dix St. NW&SE ...... 1W-1N 51
Dobson St. N&S ... 1E-15S,1E-8S 76
Dominick St. NW&SE 1W-2N 51
Dorchester Av. N&S ... 1E-10S,1E-5S 68
Doty Av. NW&SE .... 1E-15S 76
Douglas Blvd. E&W .. 4W-1S 55
Dover St. N&S........ 1W-5N 45
Dowagiac Av. NW&SE ... 6W-8N 38
Drake Av. N&S ... 4W-13S,4W-7N 75
Draper St. E&W ...... 1W-3N 45
Drew St. N&S ...... 2W-12S 67
Drexel Av. N&S ... 1E-11S,1E-6S 68
Drexel Blvd. N&S...... 1E-5S 62
Drummond Pl. E&W ... 6W-3N,0W-3N 43
Dunbar Av. N&S...... 0E-10S 68
Early Av. NW&SE .... 1W-7N 39
Cir. ........ 8W-7N 37
East End Av. N&S ... 2E-10S,2E-5S 69
East River Rd. NS&EW ... 10W-5N 41
Eastlake Ter. N&S .... 1W-9N 39
Eastman St. E&W .... 1W-1N 51
Eastwood Av. E&W ... 7W-5N,1W-5N 42
Eberhart Av. N&S ... 0E-15S,0E-7S 76
Edbrooke Av. N&S ... 0W-14S,0E-12S 76
Eddy St. E&W ... 7W-4N,1W-4N 42
Edens Expwy. N&S .. 6W-7N 38
Edens Expwy. N&S .. 6W-6N 43
Edgebrook Ter. NW&SE ... 7W-8N 37
Edgewater Av. E&W .. 2W-7N 39
Edmaire St. NW&SE 2W-13S 75
Edmunds St. NE&SW ... 6W-6N 43
Edward Ct. N&S...... 0W-2N 51
Eggleston Av. N&S ... 0W-15S,0W-7S 76
Eisenhower, Dwight Expy. E&W........ 7W-0S,1W-0S 48
Elaine Pl. N&S........ 0W-4N 45
Elbridge Av. NE&SW .. 4W-3N 44
Eleanor St. NE&SW .. 1W-2S 56
Elias Ct. NW&SE...... 1W-2S 56
Elizabeth St. N&S ... 1W-14S,1W-0N 76
Elk Grove Av. NW&SE ... 2W-1N 50
Ellen St. E&W ........ 2W-1N 50
Elliott Av. NE&SW .... 2E-9S 69
Ellis Av. E&W ........ 9W-8N 37
Ellis Av. N&S .. 1E-15S,0E-2S 76
Ellsworth Dr. N&S .... 0E-5S 62
Elm St. E&W ........ 0W-1N 51
Elmdale Av. E&W .... 1W-7N 39
Elston Av. NW&SE ... 7W-7N,1W-1N 37
Emerald Av. N&S ... 0W-14S,0W-2S 76
Emmett St. NW&SE .. 4W-3N 44
Englewood Av. E&W .. 0W-6S 62
Erie St. E&W .. 7W-0N,0W-0N 48
Ernst Ct. N&S ........ 0E-1N 51
Escanaba Av. N&S .. 3E-11S 69
Escanaba Av. N&S ... 3E-15S,3E-9S 77
Esmond St. NE&SW ... 2W-13S,2W-12S 75
Essex Av. N&S ... 3E-10S,3E-9S 69
Estes Av. E&W ... 9W-8N,1W-8N 37
Euclid Av. N&S ... 2E-10S,2E-7S 69
Eugenie St. E&W .... 0W-2N 51
Evans Av. N&S ... 0E-15S,0E-4S 76
Evelyn Ln. E&W .... 10W-6N 41
Everell Av. E&W ...... 9W-7N 37
Everett Av. N&S ...... 2E-6S 63
Evergreen Av. E&W ... 4W-1N,0W-1N 50
Ewing Av. N&S ... 4E-13S,4E-10S 77
Fairbanks Ct. N&S .... 0E-0N 51
Fairfield Av. N&S ... 3W-13S,3W-9N 75
Fargo Av. E&W ... 9W-9N,1W-9N 37
Farragut Av. E&W ... 10W-6N,1W-6N 41
Farrell St. NW&SE .... 1W-2S 56
Farrer Dr. NE&SW .... 3W-1S 56
Farwell Av. E&W ... 9W-8N,1W-8N 37
Federal St. N&S ... 0W-5S,0W-0S 62
Felton Ct. N&S ...... 0W-1N 51
Ferdinand St. E&W ... 6W-0N,2W-0N 49
Fern Ct. N&S ........ 0W-2N 51
Field Blvd. N&S ...... 0E-0N 51
Fielding Av. NE&SW .. 0W-8S 62
Fifth Av. NE&SW ... 5W-0S,3W-0S 49
Fillmore St. E&W ... 7W-0S,1W-0S 48
Fitch Av. E&W ... 9W-8N,3W-8N 37
Fleetwood St. N&S .. 13W-5N 40
Fletcher St. E&W ... 8W-3N,1W-3N 42
Flournoy St. E&W ... 6W-0S,1W-0S 49
Ford Av. NE&SW .... 0W-2S 57
Ford City Dr. E&W.... 5W-8S 60
Foreman Dr. E&W .... 4E-10S 69
Forest Av. N&S ... 0E-15S,0E-10S 76
Forest Glen Av. NE&SW ... 6W-6N,5W-7N 43
Forest Preserve Dr. NE&SW ... 10W-4N 41
Forestview Av. N&S.. 10W-5N 41
Forestville Av. N&S ... 0E-15S,0E-4S 76
Fort Dearborn Dr. N&S ... 0E-2S 57

| Street | Grid | Page |
|---|---|---|
| Foster Av. E&W | 9W-6N,1W-6N | 42 |
| Foster Pl. E&W | 8W-6N | 42 |
| Francis Pl. NE&SW | 3W-2N | 50 |
| Francisco Av. N&S | 3W-9S,3W-9N | 67 |
| Franklin Blvd. E&W | 4W-0N,3W-0N | 50 |
| Franklin St. N&S | 0W-0S,0W-1N | 51 |
| Fremont St. N&S | 1W-2N,1W-4N | 51 |
| Front Av. N&S | 0E-14S | 76 |
| Front St. N&S | 0E-13S,0E-12S | 76 |
| Fronte Av. N&S | 0W-6S | 62 |
| Frontier Av. N&S | 0W-1N | 51 |
| Fry St. E&W | 1W-1N | 51 |
| Fuller St. E&W | 1W-2S | 56 |
| Fullerton Av. E&W | 8W-3N,1W-3N | 42 |
| Fullerton Pkwy. E&W | 0W-3N | 45 |
| Fulton St. E&W | 7W-0N,1W-0N | 48 |
| Gale St. NE&SW | 6W-6N | 43 |
| Garfield Blvd. E&W | 2W-5S,0W-5S | 61 |
| Garland Ct. N&S | 0E-0N | 51 |
| Geneva Ter. N&S | 0W-2N | 51 |
| Genoa Av. NE&SW | 1W-11S,1W-10S | 68 |
| George St. E&W | 8W-3N,1W-3N | 42 |
| Germania Pl. E&W | 0E-1N | 51 |
| Gettysburg E&W | 6W-6N | 43 |
| Giddings St. E&W | 7W-5N,2W-5N | 42 |
| Gilbert Ct. N&S | 0W-9S | 68 |
| Giles Av. N&S | 0E-3S | 57 |
| Givins St. NW&SE | 0W-9S | 68 |
| Gladys Av. E&W | 6W-0S,0W-0S | 49 |
| Glenlake Av. E&W | 5W-7N,1W-7N | 38 |
| Glenroy St. N&S | 1W-12S | 68 |
| Glenwood Av. N&S | 6W-6N,1W-8N | 45 |
| Goethe St. E&W | 0W-1N | 51 |
| Gole Dr. N&S | 5W-0S | 49 |
| Goodman St. E&W | 7W-6N | 42 |
| Gordon Ter. E&W | 1W-5N | 45 |
| Governor's Pkwy. E&W | 4W-0N | 49 |
| Grace St. E&W | 10W-4N,1W-4N | 41 |
| Graham Ct. N&S | 0E-1N | 51 |
| Grand Av. E&W | 0E-0N | 51 |
| Grand Av. NW&SE | 6W-2N | 49 |
| Grant Pl. E&W | 0W-2N | 51 |
| Granville Av. E&W | 4W-7N,1W-7N | 38 |
| Gratten Av. E&W | 1W-2S | 56 |
| Green Bay Av. N&S | 3E-15S,4E-9S | 77 |
| Green St. N&S | 1W-15S,1W-0N | 76 |
| Greenleaf Av. E&W | 9W-8N,1W-8N | 37 |
| Greenview Av. N&S | 1W-1N,1W-9N | 51 |
| Greenwood Av. N&S | 1E-15S,1E-4S | 76 |
| Gregory St. E&W | 10W-6N,1W-6N | 41 |
| Gresham Av. NE&SW | 4W-3N | 44 |
| Grilly Dr. NW&SE | 4E-10S | 69 |
| Grove Av. NE&SW | 0W-2S | 57 |
| Grover St. NW&SE | 7W-6N | 42 |
| Grower Dr. N&S | 3W-1N | 50 |
| Gullikson Rd. NE&SW | 8W-6S | 59 |
| Gunnison St. E&W | 7W-6N,1W-6N | 42 |
| Haddon Av. E&W | 6W-1N,2W-1N | 49 |
| Haft St. NE&SW | 7W-7N | 37 |
| Haines St. N&S | 1W-1N | 51 |
| Halas, George Dr. N&S | 0E-0N | 51 |
| Hale Av. N&S | 2W-13S,2W-12S | 75 |
| Halsted St. N&S | 1W-14S,1W-4N | 76 |
| Hamilton Av. N&S | 2W-12S,2W-8N | 67 |
| Hamlin Av. N&S | 4W-13S,4W-7N | 75 |
| Hampden Pl. N&S | 0W-3N | 45 |
| Hanes St. NW&SE | 1W-2S | 56 |
| Harding Av. N&S | 4W-12S,4W-7N | 67 |
| Harlem Av. N&S | 9W-4N,9W-7N | 42 |
| Harper Av. N&S | 1E-10S,1E-6S | 68 |
| Harrison St. E&W | 6W-0S,0W-0S | 49 |
| Hart Av. N&S | 2W-0N | 50 |
| Hartland Ct. N&S | 2W-0N | 50 |
| Hartwell Av. N&S | 0E-7S | 62 |
| Harvard Av. N&S | 0W-12S | 68 |
| Harvard Av. N&S | 0W-14S,0W-0N | 76 |
| Haskins Av. NW&SE | 2W-9N | 39 |
| Hastings St. E&W | 2W-0S | 56 |
| Haussen Ct. NE&SW | 4W-3N | 44 |
| Hawthorne Pl. E&W | 0W-4N | 45 |
| Hayes Av. E&W | 8W-8N | 37 |
| Hayes Dr. E&W | 2E-6S | 63 |
| Hayford St. E&W | 4W-8S | 61 |
| Haynes Ct. NW&SE | 1W-2S | 56 |
| Hazel St. N&S | 1W-5N | 45 |
| Heath Av. N&S | 2W-1S | 56 |
| Henderson St. E&W | 8W-4N,1W-4N | 42 |
| Henry Ct. NE&SW | 3W-2N | 50 |
| Hermione St. NE&SW | 7W-7N | 37 |
| Hermitage Av. N&S | 2W-9S,2W-9N | 67 |
| Hermosa Av. E&W | 2W-13S,2W-12S | 75 |
| Hiawatha Av. NW&SE | 7W-8N,5W-7N | 37 |
| Hickory St. NW&SE | 1W-1N | 51 |
| Higgins Av. NW&SE | 8W-6N | 42 |
| Higgins Rd. NW&SE | 7W-6N | 43 |
| Highland Av. E&W | 8W-7N,2W-7N | 37 |
| Hill St. E&W | 0W-1N | 51 |
| Hillock Av. NE&SW | 1W-2S | 56 |
| Hirsch Dr. E&W | 7W-1N,3W-1N | 48 |
| Hobart St. E&W | 8W-7N | 37 |
| Hobbie St. E&W | 0W-1N | 51 |
| Hobson Av. NE&SW | 2W-2N | 50 |
| Hoey St. NE&SW | 1W-2S | 56 |
| Holbrook St. NE&SW | 7W-7N | 37 |
| Holden Ct. N&S | 0E-0S | 51 |
| Holland Rd. NW&SE | 0W-10S | 68 |
| Hollett Dr. N&S | 4W-7S | 61 |
| Holly Av. NW&SE | 1W-2S | 56 |
| Hollywood Av. E&W | 5W-7N,1W-7N | 38 |
| Homan Av. N&S | 4W-13S,4W-1N | 75 |
| Homer St. E&W | 6W-2N,2W-2N | 49 |
| Homewood Av. N&S | 2W-13S | 75 |
| Honore St. N&S | 2W-9S,2W-9N | 67 |
| Hood Av. E&W | 9W-7N,1W-7N | 37 |
| Hooker St. NW&SE | 1W-1N | 51 |
| Hopkins Pl. E&W | 2W-10S | 67 |
| Hortense Av. E&W | 9W-7N | 37 |
| Houston Av. N&S | 3E-15S,3E-9S | 77 |
| Howard St. E&W | 3W-9N | 39 |
| Howe St. N&S | 0W-1N,0W-2N | 51 |
| Hoxie Av. N&S | 2E-15S,2E-11S | 77 |
| Hoyne Av. N&S | 2W-12S,2W-9N | 67 |
| Hoyne Av. NS&EW | 2W-8S | 61 |
| Hubbard St. E&W | 6W-0N,0W-0N | 49 |
| Hudson Av. N&S | 0W-1N,0W-3N | 51 |
| Huguelet Pl. N&S | 0E-1N | 51 |
| Humboldt Blvd. N&S | 3W-2N | 50 |
| Humboldt Dr. N&S | 3W-1N | 50 |
| Hunt Pl. NW&SE | 2W-10S | 67 |
| Huntington St. NE&SW | 7W-7N | 37 |
| Hurlbut Av. E&W | 8W-7N | 37 |
| Huron St. E&W | 7W-0N,0W-1N | 48 |
| Hutchinson St. E&W | 6W-5N,0W-5N | 43 |
| Hyacinth St. NE&SW | 7W-7N | 37 |
| Hyde Park Blvd. E&W | 1E-5S,2E-5S | 62 |
| Ibsen St. E&W | 9W-8N | 37 |
| Illinois St. E&W | 0W-0N | 51 |
| Imlay Av. E&W | 8W-8N | 37 |
| Independence Blvd. E&W | 4W-1S,4W-0S | 55 |
| Indian Rd. NW&SE | 7W-7N,6W-7N | 37 |
| Indiana Av. N&S | 0W-14S,0E-2S | 76 |
| Indianapolis Blvd. NW&SE | 4E-11S | 69 |
| Ingleside Av. N&S | 0E-15S,1E-5S | 76 |
| Institute Pl. E&W | 0W-1N | 51 |
| Interstate 290 E&W | 7W-1W-0S | 48 |
| Interstate 55 NE&SW | 2W-3S | 56 |
| Interstate 57 N&S | 0W-11S,1W-13S | 68 |
| Interstate 90 NW&SE | 4E-11S,10W-7N | 69 |
| Interstate 90-94 N&S | 0W-6S,4W-4N | 62 |
| Interstate 94 N&S | 1E-12S,6W-7N | 68 |
| Ionia Av. N&S | 5W-7N,7W-8N | 38 |
| Iowa St. E&W | 6W-1N,2W-1N | 49 |
| Irene Av. NE&SW | 3W-4N | 44 |
| Iron St. N&S | 1W-3S | 56 |
| Irving Park Rd. E&W | 10W-5N,1W-5N | 41 |
| Isham Av. E&W | 9W-8N | 37 |
| Jackson Blvd. E&W | 0W-0S,7W-0S | 49 |
| Jackson Dr. E&W | 0E-0S | 51 |
| James St. E&W | 2W-5S | 61 |
| Janssen Av. N&S | 1W-3N,1W-6N | 45 |
| Jarlath Av. E&W | 9W-7N | 37 |
| Jarlath St. E&W | 3W-9N | 39 |
| Jarvis Av. E&W | 9W-9N,2W-9N | 37 |
| Jasper Pl. N&S | 1W-3S | 56 |
| Jean Av. NE&SW | 7W-8N | 37 |
| Jefferson St. N&S | 0W-1S,0W-0N | 57 |
| Jeffery Av. N&S | 2E-15S,2E-10S | 77 |
| Jeffery Blvd. N&S | 2E-9S,2E-7S | 69 |
| Jerome St. E&W | 9W-9N,3W-9N | 37 |
| Jersey Av. N&S | 4W-7N | 38 |
| Jessie Ct. N&S | 2W-0N | 50 |
| Jones St. NW&SE | 2W-3N | 45 |
| Jonquil Ter. E&W | 1W-9N | 39 |
| Jourdan Ct. N&S | 1W-1S | 56 |
| Julia Ct. SE&NW | 3W-2N | 50 |
| Julian St. E&W | 2W-1N | 50 |
| Juneway Ter. E&W | 2W-9N | 39 |
| Junior Ter. E&W | 0W-5N | 45 |
| Justine St. N&S | 1W-14S,1W-0N | 76 |
| Kamerling Av. N&S | 6W-1N,5W-1N | 49 |
| Kanst Dr. N&S | 3W-7S | 61 |
| Karlov Av. N&S | 5W-9S,5W-7N | 66 |
| Kasson Av. NW&SE | 5W-5N | 43 |
| Kearsarge Av. NW&SE | 5W-5N | 43 |
| Keating Av. N&S | 5W-9S,5W-7N | 66 |
| Kecte Av. NE&SW | 0E-7S | 62 |
| Kedvale Av. N&S | 5W-9S,5W-7N | 66 |
| Kedzie Av. N&S | 4W-13S,4W-7N | 75 |
| Kedzie Blvd. N&S | 4W-2N,4W-3N | 50 |
| Kedzie Pkwy. N&S | 4W-2N | 50 |
| Keeler Av. N&S | 5W-9S,5W-7N | 66 |
| Keeley St. NE&SW | 1W-2S | 56 |
| Keene Av. NE&SW | 5W-7N | 38 |
| Keller Dr. E&W | 5W-8S | 60 |
| Kelso Av. NE&SW | 5W-5N | 43 |
| Kemper Pl. E&W | 0W-2N | 51 |
| Kenmore Av. N&S | 1W-2N,1W-6N | 51 |
| Kennedy, John F. Expy. NW&SE | 10W-7N,1W-1N | 36 |
| Kenneth Av. N&S | 5W-9S,5W-7N | 66 |
| Kennicott Av. NE&SW | 5W-5N | 43 |
| Kennison Av. NW&SE | 5W-6N | 43 |
| Kenosha Av. N&S | 5W-3N | 43 |
| Kensington Av. E&W | 0E-13S | 76 |
| Kenton Av. N&S | 5W-9S,5W-7N | 66 |
| Kentucky Av. NE&SW | 5W-6N | 43 |
| Kenwood Av. N&S | 1E-10S,1E-5S | 68 |
| Keokuk Av. NE&SW | 5W-5N | 43 |
| Keota Av. NE&SW | 7W-8N | 37 |
| Kerbs Av. NE&SW | 5W-5N | 43 |
| Kercheval Av. NW&SE | 5W-7N | 38 |
| Kerfoot Av. NW&SE | 0W-9S | 68 |
| Kewanee Av. E&W | 5W-5N | 43 |
| Keystone Av. N&S | 5W-0N,5W-7N | 49 |
| Kilbourn Av. N&S | 5W-9S,5W-7N | 66 |
| Kildare Av. N&S | 5W-9S,5W-7N | 66 |
| Kilpatrick Av. N&S | 5W-9S,5W-7N | 66 |
| Kimball Av. N&S | 4W-2N,4W-7N | 50 |
| Kimbark Av. N&S | 1E-10S,1E-5S | 68 |
| Kimberly Av. NE&SW | 5W-6N | 43 |
| Kingsbury St. N&S | 1W-2N,0W-1N | 51 |
| Kingsdale Av. NE&SW | 5W-7N | 38 |
| Kingston Av. N&S | 3E-10S,3E-8S | 69 |
| Kinzie St. E&W | 6W-0N,0E-0N | 49 |
| Kinzua Av. NW&SE | 7W-8N | 37 |
| Kiona Av. NE&SW | 5W-5N | 43 |
| Kirby Av. NE&SW | 5W-7N | 38 |
| Kirkland Av. N&S | 5W-9S | 66 |
| Kirkwood Av. NE&SW | 5W-7N | 38 |
| Knox Av. N&S | 5W-9S,5W-7N | 66 |
| Kolin Av. N&S | 5W-9S,5W-1N | 66 |
| Kolmar Av. N&S | 5W-9S,5W-7N | 66 |
| Komensky Av. N&S | 5W-9S,5W-1S | 66 |
| Kostner Av. N&S | 5W-9S,5W-7N | 66 |
| Kruger Av. NE&SW | 5W-6N | 43 |
| LaCrosse Av. N&S | 6W-7S,6W-7N | 60 |
| LaSalle St. N&S | 0W-14S,0W-1N | 76 |
| Lacey Av. NW&SE | 6W-7N | 38 |
| Lafayette Av. N&S | 0W-14S,0W-6S | 76 |
| Laflin Pl. N&S | 1W-3S | 56 |
| Laflin St. N&S | 1W-14S,1W-0N | 76 |
| Lake Park Av. NW&SE | 1E-6S,0E-2S | 62 |
| Lake Shore Dr. N&S | 2E-6S,0W-6N | 63 |
| Lake Shore Dr., W. E&W | 0W-3N | 45 |
| Lake St. E&W | 7W-0N,0W-0N | 48 |
| Lakeside Pl. E&W | 1W-5N | 45 |
| Lakeview Av. N&S | 0W-3N | 45 |
| Lakewood Av. N&S | 1W-2N,1W-7N | 51 |
| Lamon Av. N&S | 6W-7S,6W-6N | 60 |
| Landers Av. NE&SW | 6W-7N | 38 |
| Landmark N&S | 2W-3N | 45 |
| Langley Av. N&S | 0E-15S,0E-4S | 76 |
| Langley Pl. N&S | 0E-9S | 68 |
| Lansing Av. NW&SE | 6W-7N | 38 |
| Laporte Av. N&S | 6W-0N,6W-6N | 49 |
| Laramie Av. N&S | 6W-5S,6W-6N | 60 |
| Larchmont Av. E&W | 2W-4N | 45 |
| Larned Av. NW&SE | 6W-6N | 43 |
| Larrabee St. N&S | 0W-1N,0W-2N | 51 |
| Las Casas Av. NW&SE | 6W-7N | 38 |
| Latham Av. NW&SE | 6W-6N | 43 |
| Latrobe Av. N&S | 6W-7S,6W-6N | 60 |
| Lavergne Av. N&S | 6W-7S,6W-6N | 60 |
| Lawler Av. N&S | 6W-5S,6W-6N | 60 |
| Lawndale Av. N&S | 4W-13S,4W-6N | 75 |
| Lawrence Av. E&W | 6W-6N,1W-6N | 43 |
| Lawrence Dr. E&W | 0W-6N | 45 |
| Le Mai Av. N&S | 6W-8N | 38 |
| Le Moyne Dr. E&W | 7W-1N,1W-1N | 48 |
| Leader Av. N&S | 6W-7N | 38 |
| Leamington Av. N&S | 6W-5S,6W-5N | 60 |
| Leavenworth Av. NW&SE | 6W-6N | 43 |
| Leavitt St. N&S | 2W-12S,2W-8N | 67 |
| Leclaire Av. N&S | 6W-5S,6W-6N | 60 |
| Lee St. N&S | 13W-5N | 40 |
| Leggett Av. NE&SW | 6W-7N | 38 |
| Lehigh Av. NW&SE | 7W-8N | 37 |
| Lehmann Ct. NW&SE | 0W-3N | 45 |
| Leland Av. E&W | 10W-5N,2W-5N | 41 |
| Lemai NE&SW | 6W-8N | 38 |
| Lemont Av. N&S | 6W-7N,5W-7N | 38 |
| Lenox Av. NE&SW | 6W-7N | 38 |
| Leona Av. NE&SW | 6W-7N | 38 |
| Leonard Av. N&S | 6W-6N,7W-7N | 43 |
| Leoti Av. NE&SW | 6W-7N,7W-8N | 38 |
| Leroy Av. NE&SW | 6W-7N | 38 |
| Lessing St. N&S | 1W-1N | 51 |
| Lester Av. NE&SW | 6W-6N | 43 |
| Lexington St. E&W | 6W-0S,0W-0S | 49 |
| Leyden Av. N&S | 0E-15S | 76 |
| Liano Av. N&S | 6W-6N | 43 |
| Libby Av. N&S | 6W-6N | 43 |
| Liberty E&W | 1W-1S | 56 |
| Lieb Av. NE&SW | 6W-6N | 43 |
| Lightfoot Av. NE&SW | 7W-8N | 37 |
| Lill Av. E&W | 1W-3N | 45 |
| Lincoln Av. NW&SE | 1W-3N,4W-7N | 45 |
| Lincoln Park West St. N&S | 0W-2N | 51 |
| Lind Av. NW&SE | 6W-6N | 43 |
| Linden Pl. E&W | 3W-3N | 44 |
| Linder Av. N&S | 6W-7S,6W-7N | 60 |
| Line Av. NE&SW | 9W-4N | 42 |
| Lipps Av. NW&SE | 6W-6N | 43 |
| Lister Av. N&S | 2W-2N | 50 |
| Lituanica Av. N&S | 1W-3S | 56 |
| Livermore Av. N&S | 6W-7N | 38 |
| Lloyd Av. NW&SE | 1W-2S | 56 |
| Lock St. NW&SE | 1W-1N | 51 |
| Lockwood Av. N&S | 6W-5S,6W-7N | 60 |
| Locust St. E&W | 0W-1N | 51 |
| Logan Blvd. E&W | 3W-3N,2W-3N | 44 |
| Loleta Av. NE&SW | 7W-8N | 37 |
| London Av. N&S | 6W-5N | 43 |
| Long Av. N&S | 6W-7S,6W-6N | 60 |
| Longwood Dr. N&S | 2W-13S,2W-10S | 75 |
| Loomis Blvd. N&S | 1W-9S,1W-7S | 68 |
| Loomis Pl. N&S | 1W-3S | 56 |
| Loomis St. N&S | 1W-14S,1W-0N | 76 |
| Lorel Av. N&S | 6W-7S,6W-3N | 60 |
| Loring Av. NW&SE | 6W-6N | 43 |
| Loron Av. NE&SW | 7W-8N | 37 |
| Lothair Av. N&S | 2W-13S | 75 |
| Lotus Av. N&S | 6W-5S,6W-6N | 60 |
| Louise Av. NW&SE | 6W-7N | 38 |
| Lovejoy Av. NW&SE | 7W-6N,6W-6N | 42 |
| Lowe Av. N&S | 0W-14S,0W-2S | 76 |
| Lowell Av. N&S | 5W-2N,5W-7N | 49 |
| Loyola Av. E&W | 2W-8N,1W-8N | 39 |
| Lucerne Av. NE&SW | 6W-7N | 38 |
| Ludlam Av. NE&SW | 6W-6N | 43 |
| Luella Av. N&S | 2E-15S,2E-7S | 77 |
| Lumber St. E&W | 1W-2S,0W-1S | 56 |
| Luna Av. N&S | 6W-5S,6W-7N | 60 |
| Lundy Av. NE&SW | 6W-7N | 38 |
| Lunt Av. E&W | 9W-8N,1W-8N | 37 |
| Luther St. NE&SW | 3W-2S | 56 |
| Lyman St. NE&SW | 1W-2S | 56 |
| Lynch Av. NE&SW | 6W-6N | 43 |
| Lyndale St. E&W | 5W-2N,3W-2N | 49 |
| Lytle St. N&S | 1W-0S | 51 |
| Mackinaw Av. N&S | 4E-15S,4E-9S | 77 |
| Madison Park E&W | 1E-5S | 62 |
| Madison St. E&W | 6W-0N,1W-0N | 49 |
| Magnet Av. NW&SE | 7W-6N | 42 |
| Magnolia Av. N&S | 1W-1N,1W-7N | 51 |
| Major Av. N&S | 7W-6S,7W-7N | 60 |
| Malden St. N&S | 1W-5N | 45 |
| Malta St. N&S | 1W-11S | 68 |
| Mandell Av. NE&SW | 7W-7N | 37 |
| Mango Av. N&S | 7W-2N,7W-6N | 48 |
| Manila Av. NE&SW | 7W-6N | 42 |
| Manistee Av. N&S | 3E-15S,3E-9S | 77 |
| Mankato Av. NE&SW | 7W-8N | 37 |
| Mann Dr. E&W | 4W-7S | 61 |
| Manor Av. NW&SE | 3W-5N | 44 |
| Manton Av. NE&SW | 7W-7N | 37 |
| Maple St. E&W | 0W-1N | 51 |
| Maplewood Av. N&S | 3W-13S,3W-9N | 67 |
| Marble Pl. E&W | 0W-0S | 51 |
| Marcey St. N&S | 1W-2N | 51 |
| Margate Ter. E&W | 1W-6N | 45 |
| Maria Ct. N&S | 10W-5N | 41 |
| Marine Dr. NW&SE | 0W-5N | 45 |
| Marion Ct. N&S | 2W-1N | 50 |
| Market St. E&W | 0E-15S | 76 |
| Markham Av. N&S | 7W-7N | 37 |
| Marmora Av. N&S | 7W-3N,7W-7N | 42 |
| Marquette Av. N&S | 3E-14S,3E-8S | 77 |
| Marquette Dr. E&W | 2E-7S | 63 |
| Marquette Rd. E&W | 5W-7S,0E-7S | 60 |
| Marshall Blvd. N&S | 3W-2S,3W-1S | 56 |
| Marshfield Av. N&S | 2W-10S,2W-9N | 67 |
| Martin Luther King Jr. Dr. N&S | 0E-12S,0E-4S | 68 |
| Mary St. NW&SE | 1W-2S | 56 |
| Maryland Av. N&S | 0E-15S,1E-6S | 76 |
| Mason Av. N&S | 7W-6S,7W-6N | 60 |
| Massasoit Av. N&S | 7W-6S,7W-1N | 60 |
| Matson Av. NE&SW | 7W-7N | 37 |
| Maud Av. NW&SE | 1W-2N | 51 |
| Mautene Ct. NE&SW | 2W-1N | 50 |
| Maxwell St. E&W | 1W-1S | 56 |
| May St. N&S | 1W-13S,1W-1N | 76 |
| Mayfield Av. N&S | 7W-6S,7W-2N | 60 |
| Maypole Av. E&W | 6W-0N,2W-0N | 49 |
| McAlpin Av. NW&SE | 7W-8N | 37 |
| McClellan Av. NW&SE | 7W-7N | 37 |
| McClurg Ct. N&S | 0E-0N | 51 |
| McCook Av. N&S | 7W-7N | 37 |
| McCormick Blvd. NE&SW | 4W-8N | 38 |
| McCrea Dr. N&S | 4W-0N | 50 |
| McDowell Av. E&W | 1W-4S | 56 |
| McFetridge Dr. E&W | 0E-1S | 57 |
| McLean Av. E&W | 5W-2N,1W-2N | 49 |
| McLeod Av. NE&SW | 7W-7N | 37 |
| McVicker Av. N&S | 7W-6S,7W-9N | 60 |
| Meade Av. N&S | 7W-7S,7W-9N | 60 |
| Medford Av. NW&SE | 7W-8N | 37 |
| Medill Av. N&S | 8W-2N,2W-2N | 48 |

**Grid | Page**

Medina Av. NE&SW .. 7W-7N 37
Melrose St. E&W
.......... 8W-4N,0W-4N 42
Melvina Av. N&S
.......... 7W-7S,7W-7N 60
Memory Ln. E&W ....10W-6N 41
Menard Av. N&S
.......... 7W-6S,7W-6N 60
Mendell St. N&S ...... 1W-2N 51
Mendota Av. N&S .... 7W-8N 37
Menomonee St. E&W 0W-2N 51
Meredith Av. N&S ... 7W-7N 37
Merrill Av. N&S
.......... 2E-15S,2E-7S 77
Merrimac Av. N&S
.......... 7W-6S,7W-8N 60
Merrion Av. N&S .... 2E-11S 69
Meyer Ct. N&S ...... 0W-2N 51
Miami Av. N&S .... 7W-7N 37
Michaels Ct. N&S ... 0W-2N 51
Michigan Av. E&W ....0E-14S 76
Michigan Av. N&S
.......... 0W-14S,0E-0N 76
Midway Park E&W .... 7W-0N 48
Midway Plaisance E&W
.......... 1E-6S 62
Mies van der Rohe Way N&S
.......... 0E-1N 51
Mildred Av. N&S .... 1W-3N 45
Millard Av. N&S
.......... 4W-13S,4W-0S 75
Miller St. NE&SW
.......... 1W-1S,1W-0S 56
Miltimore Av. N&S .... 7W-7N 37
Milwaukee Av. NW&SE
.......... 7W-7N,0W-0N 37
Minerva Av. N&S .... 1E-7S 62
Minnehaha Av. NE&SW
.......... 6W-8N 38
Minnetonka Av. NE&SW
.......... 7W-8N,6W-8N 37
Mobile Av. N&S
.......... 7W-7S,7W-8N 60
Moffat St. E&W
.......... 3W-2N,2W-2N 50
Mohawk St. N&S ...... 0W-2N 51
Monitor Av. N&S
.......... 7W-6S,7W-7N 60
Monon Av. NE&SW .. 7W-8N 37
Monroe Dr. E&W ......0E-0S 51
Monroe St. E&W
.......... 6W-0S,1W-0S 49
Mont Clare Av. N&S
.......... 8W-3N,8W-6N 42
Montana St. E&W
.......... 6W-3N,1W-3N 43
Monterey Av. NW&SE
.......... 2W-13S 75
Montgomery Av. NW&SE
.......... 3W-4S 56
Monticello Av. N&S
.......... 4W-0N,4W-6N 50
Montrose Av. E&W
.......... 10W-5N,1W-5N 41
Montrose Dr. E&W ....0W-5N 45
Montrose Harbor Dr. E&W
.......... 0W-5N 45
Montrose St. N&S .. 13W-5N 40
Montvale Av. NW&SE
.......... 2W-13S 75
Moody Av. N&S
.......... 7W-6S,7W-7N 60
Moorman St. N&S
.......... 2W-1N 50
Morgan Dr. NW&SE .. 0E-6S 62
Morgan St. N&S
.......... 1W-15S,1W-0N 76
Morse Av. E&W
.......... 6W-8N,1W-8N 38
Moselle Av. NE&SW .. 7W-8N 37
Mozart St. N&S
.......... 3W-9S,3W-7N 67
Mulligan Av. N&S
.......... 7W-6S,7W-7N 60
Museum Dr. E&W .... 2E-6S 63
Music Ct. E&W .... 4W-0S 50
Cir. ................ 4W-0S 50
Muskegon Av. N&S
.......... 3E-14S,3E-9S 77
Myrick St. N&S .... 4W-8S 61
Myrtle Av. E&W .... 9W-7N 37
Nagle Av. N&S
.......... 8W-6S,8W-8N 59
Naper Av. NE&SW .. 8W-7N 37
Naples Av. NW&SE .. 8W-7N 37
Napoleon Av. NE&SW
.......... 8W-7N 37
Narragansett Av. N&S
.......... 8W-7S,8W-5N 59
Nashotah Av. NE&SW
.......... 8W-7N 37
Nashville Av. N&S .... 8W-8N 37
Nashville Av. N&S
.......... 8W-3N,8W-6N 42
Nashville Av. N&S
.......... 8W-7S,8W-3N 59
Nashville Av. N&S
.......... 8W-7S,8W-2N 59
Nassau Av. N&S .. 8W-7N 37
Natchez Av. N&S
.......... 8W-6S,8W-6N 59
Natoma Av. N&S
.......... 8W-6S,8W-8N 59
Navajo Av. N&S .. 6W-8N 38
Navarre Av. NW&SE .. 8W-7N 37
Neenah Av. N&S
.......... 8W-6S,8W-7N 59

Nelson St. E&W
.......... 8W-3N,1W-3N 42
Neola Av. N&S
.......... 8W-6N,8W-7N 42
Nettleton Av. NE&SW
.......... 8W-7N 37
Neva Av. N&S
.......... 8W-6S,8W-8N 59
New N&S .......... 0E-0N 51
New England Av. N&S
.......... 8W-6S,8W-8N 59
New Hampshire Av. NE&SW
.......... 8W-7N 37
Newark Av. N&S
.......... 8W-7N,8W-8N 37
Newberry Av. N&S .... 1W-1S 56
Newburg Av. NW&SE
.......... 8W-7N 37
Newcastle Av. N&S
.......... 8W-6S,8W-7N 59
Neward Av. N&S .... 1W-8N 39
Newland Av. N&S
.......... 8W-6S,8W-8N 59
Newport Av. E&W
.......... 8W-4N,1W-4N 42
Niagara Av. N&S ....8W-7N 37
Nickerson Av. N&S ....8W-7N 37
Nicolet Av. N&S .. 8W-7N 37
Nina Av. NE&SW .. 8W-7N 37
Nixon Av. N&S ...... 8W-8N 37
Noble St. E&W
.......... 1W-0N,1W-1N 51
Nokomis Av. NE&SW 6W-8N 38
Nora Av. N&S .... 8W-3N 42
Nordica Av. N&S
.......... 8W-6S,8W-8N 59
Normal Av. N&S
.......... 0W-15S,0W-1S 76
Normal Pkwy. E&W .. 0W-7S 62
Normandy Av. N&S
.......... 8W-6S,8W-8N 59
North Av. E&W
.......... 6W-2N,0W-2N 49
North Blvd. E&W......0W-2N 51
North Branch St. N&S
.......... 1W-1N 51
North Park Av. N&S .. 0W-1N 51
North Shore Av. E&W
.......... 9W-8N,2W-8N 37
North Water St. E&W .. 0E-0N 51
Northcott Av. NW&SE
.......... 8W-7N 37
Northwest Hwy. NW&SE
.......... 8W-7N 37
Norwood Av. E&W
.......... 9W-7N,1W-7N 37
Nottingham Av. N&S
.......... 8W-7S,8W-6N 59
Nursery St. N&S .. 1W-2N 51
O'Brien St. E&W ....0W-1S 57
Oak Park Av. N&S
.......... 8W-6S,8W-8N 59
Oak St. E&W ...... 0W-1N 51
Oakdale Av. E&W
.......... 8W-3N,1W-3N 42
Oakdale Pl. E&W .. 2W-3N 45
Oakenwald Av. NW&SE
.......... 1E-4S 57
Oakley Av. N&S
.......... 2W-13S,2W-8N 75
Oakley Blvd. N&S
.......... 2W-0S,2W-1N 50
Oakview St. N&S
.......... 10W-5N,10W-6N 41
Oakwood Blvd. E&W .. 0E-4S 57
Oconto Av. N&S
.......... 9W-3N,9W-9N 42
Octavia Av. N&S
.......... 9W-3N,9W-9N 42
Odell Av. N&S
.......... 9W-3N,9W-9N 42
Ogallah Av. NE&SW .. 9W-8N 37
Ogden Av. NE&SW
.......... 5W-2S,1W-0N 55
Oglesby Av. N&S
.......... 2E-15S,2E-7S 77
Ohio St. E&W 7W-0N,0W-0N 48
Oketo Av. N&S
.......... 9W-3N,9W-9N 42
Olcott Av. N&S
.......... 9W-3N,9W-8N 42
Old Mannheim Rd. N&S
.......... 13W-7N 40
Oleander Av. N&S
.......... 9W-3N,9W-8N 42
Oliphant Av. NE&SW .. 9W-8N 37
Olive Av. E&W
.......... 9W-7N,2W-7N 37
Olmsted Av. NW&SE .. 9W-8N 37
Olympia Av. N&S
.......... 9W-6N,9W-8N 42
Onarga Av. NW&SE .. 9W-8N 37
Oneida Av. N&S .... 9W-8N 37
Ontario St. E&W
.......... 4W-0N,0W-0N 50
Opal Av. N&S ...... 9W-4N 42
Orange Av. N&S
.......... 9W-4N,9W-7N 42
Orchard St. N&S
.......... 0W-2N,0W-3N 51
Oriole Av. N&S
.......... 9W-4N,9W-8N 42
Orleans St. N&S ......0W-1N 51
Osage Av. N&S
.......... 9W-4N,9W-7N 42
Osceola Av. N&S
.......... 9W-3N,9W-8N 42

Oshkosh Av. NE&SW
.......... 9W-8N 37
Oswego St. N&S .... 2W-0N 50
Otsego Av. NW&SE .. 9W-8N 37
Ottawa Av. N&S
.......... 9W-4N,9W-9N 42
Otto Av. N&S ...... 12W-6N 40
Overhill Av. N&S
.......... 9W-4N,9W-8N 42
Owen Av. N&S .... 9W-8N 37
Oxford Av. NE&SW .. 9W-8N 37
Ozanam Av. N&S
.......... 9W-4N,9W-7N 42
Ozark Av. N&S
.......... 9W-4N,9W-9N 42
Pacific Av. N&S
.......... 10W-4N,10W-6N 41
Packers Av. N&S .... 1W-4S 56
Page Av. N&S .... 10W-4N 42
Palatine Av. E&W
.......... 9W-7N,8W-7N 37
Palmer Blvd. E&W .. 3W-2N 50
Palmer St. E&W
.......... 8W-2N,2W-2N 48
Panama Av. N&S .. 10W-4N 41
Paris Av. N&S
.......... 10W-4N,10W-6N 41
Park N&S .......... 0E-0N 51
Parker Av. E&W
.......... 6W-3N,4W-3N 43
Parkside Av. N&S
.......... 7W-6S,7W-7N 60
Parkview Ter. NW&SE
.......... 4W-4N 44
Parnell Av. N&S
.......... 0W-14S,0W-2S 76
Patrick Ct. E&W .. 3W-12S 67
Patterson Av. E&W
.......... 9W-4N,0W-4N 42
Patton Dr. N&S......10W-5N 41
Paulina St. N&S
.......... 2W-10S,2W-9N 67
Paxton Av. N&S
.......... 2E-15S,2E-7S 77
Payne Dr. NE&SW .... 0E-6S 62
Pearson St. E&W
.......... 2W-1N,0E-1N 50
Pensacola Av. E&W
.......... 9W-5N,1W-5N 43
Peoria St. N&S
.......... 1W-15S,1W-0N 76
Perry Av. N&S
.......... 0W-14S,0W-6S 76
Pershing Rd. E&W
.......... 3W-3S,0W-3S 56
Peterson Av. E&W
.......... 9W-7N,3W-7N 37
Phillips Av. N&S
.......... 3E-10S,3E-8S 69
Pierce Av. E&W
.......... 5W-1N,2W-1N 49
Pine Av. N&S..6W-0N,6W-1N 49
Pine Grove Av. N&S
.......... 0W-3N,0W-4N 45
Pioneer Av. N&S
.......... 10W-4N,10W-6N 41
Pippin St. E&W ...... 4W-8S 61
Pitney Ct. NW&SE .... 1W-2S 56
Pittsburgh Av. N&S
.......... 10W-4N,10W-6N 41
Plainfield Av. N&S
.......... 10W-4N,10W-5N 41
Pleasant Av. N&S ....2W-10S 67
Plymouth Ct. N&S .. 0W-0S 51
Poe St. NW&SE .... 1W-2N 51
Point St. NW&SE .... 3W-2N 50
Polk St. E&W ..6W-0S,3W-0S 49
Ponchartrain Blvd. NE&SW
.......... 7W-8N 37
Pontiac Av. N&S
.......... 10W-4N,10W-5N 41
Pope John Paul II Dr. E&W
.......... 3W-4S 56
Poplar Av. NW&SE ..1W-2S 56
Potawatomie St. N&S
.......... 10W-5N,10W-6N 41
Potomac Av. E&W
.......... 7W-1N,1W-1N 48
Prairie Av. N&S
.......... 0E-15S,0E-1S 76
Pratt Av. E&W
.......... 9W-8N,2W-8N 37
Prescott Av. NW&SE ..6W-7N 38
Princeton Av. N&S
.......... 0W-14S,0W-2S 76
Prindville Av. NE&SW ..3W-2N 50
Promontory Dr. N&S .. 2E-7S 63
Prospect Av. N&S
.......... 2W-12S,2W-11S 67
Pryor Av. NW&SE
.......... 2W-12S,2W-13S 67
Pueblo Av. N&S
.......... 10W-4N,10W-7N 41
Pulaski Rd.(Crawford) N&S
.......... 5W-9S,5W-7N 66
Quarry St. NW&SE....1W-2S 56
Quincy St. E&W
.......... 6W-0S,0W-0S 49
Quinn St. NW&SE .. 1W-2S 56
Race Av. N&S
.......... 7W-0N,1W-0N 48
Racine Av. N&S
.......... 1W-13S,1W-5N 76
Railroad Av. N&S .... 7W-0N 48
Rainey Dr. E&W ...... 0E-6S 62
Randolph St. E&W....0W-0N 51
Rascher Av. E&W
.......... 10W-6N,1W-6N 42

Rascher Av. E&W
.......... 10W-6N,9W-6N 42
Raven St. E&W
.......... 8W-7N,7W-7N 37
Ravenswood Av. N&S
.......... 2W-4N,2W-8N 45
Redfield Dr. E&W .... 4W-7S 61
Reilly Ter. N&S .... 4W-8S 61
Reserve Av. N&S
.......... 10W-5N,10W-6N 41
Reta Av. N&S ...... 1W-4N 45
Rhodes Av. N&S
.......... 0E-15S,0E-3S 76
Rice St. E&W ..6W-1N,2W-1N 49
Richards Dr. N&S......2E-7S 63
Richmond St. N&S
.......... 3W-9S,3W-7N 67
Ridge Av. NW&SE ....1W-7N 39
Ridge Blvd. NW&SE ..2W-8N 39
Ridge Dr. N&S......0W-2N 51
Ridgeland Av. N&S
.......... 2E-10S,2E-7S 69
Ridgeway Av. N&S
.......... 4W-13S,4W-7N 75
Ridgewood Ct. N&S .. 1E-5S 62
Ritchie Ct. N&S .... 0E-1N 51
River Rd. E&W ......0E-0N 51
Riverdale NW&SE .. 0E-15S 76
Robinson St. NW&SE 2W-3S 56
Rockwell St. N&S
.......... 3W-13S,3W-8N 75
Rogers Av. NE&SW
.......... 6W-6N,2W-9N 43
Roosevelt Rd. E&W
.......... 4W-0S,1W-1S 50
Root St. E&W ...... 0W-4S 57
Roscoe St. E&W
.......... 10W-4N,0W-4N 41
Rosedale Av. E&W
.......... 9W-7N,6W-7N 37
Rosehill Dr. E&W .. 2W-7N 39
Rosemont Av. E&W
.......... 5W-7N,1W-7N 38
Roslyn Pl. E&W ...... 0W-3N 45
Ross Av. N&S ...... 0W-7S 62
Rt. 19 E&W ..10W-5N,1W-5N 41
Rt. 43 N&S ....8W-6S,9W-9N 59
Rt. 50 N&S ....5W-7S,5W-7N 60
Rt. 64 E&W .. 7W-2N,0W-2N 48
Rt. 72 NW&SE ...... 10W-7N 36
Ruble St. N&S ...... 0W-1S 57
Rundell Pl. E&W .... 4W-0S 50
Rush St. N&S . 0E-0N,0E-1N 51
Russell St. N&S .... 0E-6S 62
Rutherford Av. N&S
.......... 8W-6S,8W-6N 59
Ryan, Dan Expwy. N&S
.......... 0W-15S,0W-1S 75
Sacramento Av. N&S
.......... 3W-12S,3W-7N 67
Sacramento Blvd. N&S
.......... 3W-0S,3W-0N 50
Sacramento Dr. N&S .. 3W-1S 56
Saginaw Av. N&S
.......... 3E-14S,3E-8S 77
Sangamon St. N&S
.......... 1W-15S,1W-1N 76
Sauganash Av. NW&SE
.......... 6W-8N,5W-7N 38
Sawyer Av. N&S......4W-9S 67
Sawyer Av. N&S
.......... 4W-13S,4W-6N 75
Sayre Av. N&S
.......... 8W-6S,8W-7N 59
Schiller St. E&W
.......... 2W-1N,0W-1N 50
School St. E&W
.......... 10W-4N,1W-4N 41
Schorsch St. E&W ....8W-4N 42
Schrader Dr. E&W ....8W-4N 50
Schreiber Av. E&W
.......... 8W-8N,2W-8N 37
Schubert Av. E&W
.......... 8W-3N,0W-3N 42
Scott St. E&W........0W-1N 51
Scottsdale Av. NW&SE
.......... 5W-9S 66
Sedgwick St. N&S .... 0W-1N 51
Seeley Av. N&S
.......... 2W-12S,2W-9N 67
Seipp St. E&W........3W-9S 67
Seminary Av. N&S
.......... 1W-2N,1W-4N 51
Seminole Av. N&S
.......... 9W-7N,7W-7N 37
Senour Av. N&S .. 1W-2S 56
Service Yard Dr. E&W
.......... 4W-0N 50
Shakespeare Av. E&W
.......... 8W-2N 48
Sheffield Av. N&S
.......... 1W-2N,1W-4N 51
Shelby Ct. N&S .... 1W-1S 56
Sheridan Rd. N&S
.......... 0W-3N,1W-9N 45
Sherman Av. N&S .... 0W-0S 51
Sherman Dr. E&W .. 1W-5S 62
Sherman St. N&S .... 0W-0S 51
Sherwin Av. E&W
.......... 9W-9N,1W-9N 37
Shields Av. N&S
.......... 0W-5S,0W-2S 56
Shore Dr. N&S..2E-6S,2E-5S 63
Short St. N&S .... 1W-2S 56
Simonds Dr. N&S
.......... 0W-2N,0W-6N 51
Sioux Av. NW&SE
.......... 7W-8N,6W-8N 37

Solidarity Dr. E&W .... 0E-1S 57
South Chicago Av. NW&SE
.......... 1E-8S,2E-9S 62
South Exchange Av. N&S
.......... 3E-15S,3E-8S 77
South Shore Dr. N&S
.......... 3E-9S,2E-7S 69
Southport Av. N&S
.......... 1W-2N,1W-4N 51
Spaulding Av. N&S
.......... 4W-13S,4W-6N 75
Spokane Av. NE&SW 6W-8N 38
Springfield Av. N&S
.......... 4W-12S,4W-7N 67
St. Clair St. N&S .... 0E-0N 51
St. Georges Ct. NE&SW
.......... 3W-2N 50
St. Helen Ct. NE&SW
.......... 3W-2N 50
St. James Pl. E&W....0W-3N 45
St. Joseph Av. E&W
.......... 10W-6N 41
St. Lawrence Av. N&S
.......... 0E-15S,OE-5S 76
St. Louis Av. N&S
.......... 4W-13S,4W-7N 75
St. Mary St. NE&SW ..3W-2N 50
St. Paul Av. E&W
.......... 6W-2N,0W-2N 49
Stark St. NW&SE .... 1W-2S 56
State Rt. 19 E&W
.......... 10W-5N,1W-5N 41
State Rt. 43 N&S
.......... 8W-6S,8W-4N 59
State Rt. 50 N&S
.......... 5W-7S,6W-7N 60
State Rt. 64 E&W
.......... 7W-1N,0W-1N 48
State St. N&S
.......... 0W-14S,0W-1N 76
Stave St. NW&SE .... 3W-2N 50
Stetson Av. N&S ......0E-0N 51
Steuben St. NW&SE
.......... 2W-13S 75
Stevenson Expwy. NE&SW
.......... 6W-4S 55
Stewart Av. N&S
.......... 0W-14S,0W-1S 76
Stockton Dr. N&S .. 0W-3N 45
Stone Ct. N&S ...... 0E-1N 51
Stony Island Av. N&S
.......... 2E-14S,1E-6S 77
Stratford Pl. NE&SW ..0W-4N 45
Streeter Dr. NS&EW ..0E-0N 51
Strong St. E&W
.......... 8W-6N,4W-6N 42
Sullivan St. E&W......0W-1N 51
Summerdale Av. N&S
.......... 10W-6N,2W-6N 41
Summerset Av. NE&SW
.......... 8W-7N 37
Sunnyside Av. E&W
.......... 10W-5N,2W-5N 41
Superior St. E&W
.......... 7W-0N,0W-0N 48
Surf St. E&W ...... 0W-3N 45
Surrey Ct. N&S .... 1W-3N 45
Swann St. E&W ...... 0W-4S 57
Tahoma Av. N&S .. 6W-8N 38
Talcott Av. NW&SE .. 9W-7N 37
Talman Av. N&S
.......... 3W-13S,3W-9N 75
Taylor St. E&W
.......... 7W-0S,0W-0S 48
Terra Cotta Pl. NE&SW
.......... 2W-3N 45
Thomas St. E&W
.......... 7W-1N,1W-1N 48
Thome Av. E&W
.......... 5W-7N,1W-7N 38
Thompson Dr. N&S . 3W-1S 56
Thorndale Av. E&W
.......... 9W-7N,1W-7N 37
Throop St. N&S
.......... 1W-14S,1W-2N 76
Togwell St. N&S .. 13W-5N 40
Tonty Av. NE&SW .. 7W-8N 37
Torrence Av. N&S
.......... 2E-14S,2E-11S 77
Touhy Av. E&W
.......... 9W-9N,2W-9N 37
Tremont St. E&W .... 0W-6S 62
Tripp Av. N&S
.......... 5W-9S,5W-7N 66
Troy Av. N&S
.......... 3W-13S,3W-12S 75
Troy St. N&S ..3W-9S,3W-7N 67
Trumbull Av. N&S
.......... 4W-13S,4W-0N 75
Turner Av. N&S .... 4W-13S 75
U.S. Rt. 12 N&S
.......... 2E-10S,4E-11S 69
U.S. Rt. 14 N&S
.......... 1W-6N,7W-8N 45
U.S. Rt. 20 E&W
.......... 2E-10S,4E-11S 69
U.S. Rt. 41 NW&SE
.......... 4E-11S,4W-7N 69
Union Av. N&S
.......... 0W-14S,0W-0N 76
University Av. N&S
.......... 1E-11S,1E-4S 68
Van Buren St. E&W
.......... 6W-0S,1W-0S 49
Van Vlissingen Rd. NW&SE
.......... 2E-11S 69
Vanderpool Av. N&S
.......... 2W-11S,2W-10S 67

| Street | Grid | Page |
|---|---|---|
| Vermont Av. NE&SW | 1W-15S,0W-15S | 76 |
| Vernon Av. N&S | 0E-15S,0E-3S | 76 |
| Victoria Av. E&W | 9W-7N,1W-7N | 37 |
| Vincennes Av. NW&SE | 2W-13S,0E-3S | 75 |
| Vine Av. N&S | 0W-2N | 51 |
| Virginia Av. NW&SE | 3W-5N,3W-6N | 44 |
| W. 85th Pl. E&W | 4W-8S | 61 |
| W. 86th St. E&W | 4W-8S | 61 |
| Wabansia Av. E&W | 7W-2N,2W-2N | 48 |
| Wabash Av. N&S | 0W-14S,0E-0N | 76 |
| Wacker Dr. N&S | 0W-0S,0W-0N | 51 |
| Walden Pkwy. N&S | 2W-12S,2W-11S | 67 |
| Waldron Dr. E&W | 0E-1S | 57 |
| Wallace St. N&S | 0W-8S | 68 |
| Wallace St. N&S | 0W-14S,0W-2S | 76 |
| Wallen Av. E&W | 2W-8N | 39 |
| Waller Av. N&S | 7W-0S,7W-1N | 48 |
| Walnut St. E&W | 5W-0N,0W-0N | 49 |
| Walton Dr. N&S | 4E-10S | 69 |
| Walton St. E&W | 6W-1N,1W-1N | 49 |
| Warner Av. E&W | 6W-5N,1W-5N | 43 |
| Warren Av. E&W | 0W-0N | 51 |
| Warren Blvd. E&W | 3W-0N | 50 |
| Warren Dr. E&W | 4W-0N | 50 |
| Warwick Av. E&W | 7W-4N,5W-4N | 42 |
| Waseca Pl. NW&SE | 2W-13S | 75 |
| Washburne Av. E&W | 2W-1S | 56 |
| Washington Blvd. E&W | 6W-0N,0W-0N | 49 |
| Washington Park Ct. N&S | 0E-5S | 62 |
| Washtenaw Av. N&S | 3W-13S,3W-8N | 75 |
| Water St. E&W | 0E-0N | 51 |
| Waterloo Ct. N&S | 0W-3N | 45 |
| Waterway NW&SE | 1E-14S | 76 |
| Watkins Av. NE&SW | 2W-13S | 75 |
| Waukesha Av. N&S | 6W-8N | 38 |
| Waveland Av. E&W | 10W-4N,1W-4N | 41 |
| Wayman St. E&W | 5W-0N,1W-0N | 49 |
| Wayne Av. N&S | 1W-2N,1W-8N | 51 |
| Webster Av. E&W | 2W-2N,1W-2N | 50 |
| Weed St. E&W | 1W-1N,0W-1N | 51 |
| Wellington Av. E&W | 9W-3N,1W-3N | 42 |
| Wells St. N&S | 0W-5S,0W-1N | 62 |
| Wendell St. E&W | 0W-1N | 51 |
| Wentworth Av. N&S | 0W-14S,0W-1S | 76 |
| West Broadman Av. E&W | 10W-5N | 41 |
| Cir. | 8W-7N | 37 |
| West End Av. E&W | 7W-0N | 48 |
| West Exchange Av. E&W | 1W-4S | 56 |
| Western Av. N&S | 3W-13S,3W-9N | 75 |
| Western Blvd. N&S | 2W-4S | 56 |
| Whipple St. N&S | 3W-12S,3W-7N | 67 |
| Wicker Park Av. NW&SE | 2W-1N | 50 |
| Wieland St. N&S | 0W-1N | 51 |
| Wilcox St. E&W | 5W-0S,3W-0S | 49 |
| Wildwood Av. NE&SW | 7W-8N | 37 |
| Willard Ct. N&S | 1W-0N | 51 |
| Willets Ct. NW&SE | 3W-3N | 44 |
| Williams Av. N&S | 0E-10S | 68 |
| Willow St. E&W | 2W-2N,0W-2N | 50 |
| Wilmot Av. NW&SE | 2W-2N | 50 |
| Wilson Av. E&W | 10W-5N,2W-5N | 41 |
| Wilson Dr. E&W | 0W-5N | 45 |
| Wilton Av. N&S | 1W-3N,1W-4N | 45 |
| Winchester Av. N&S | 2W-11S,2W-9N | 67 |
| Windsor Av. E&W | 10W-5N,1W-5N | 41 |
| Winnebago Av. NW&SE | 2W-2N | 50 |
| Winneconna Pkwy. NE&SW | 0W-8S | 62 |
| Winnemac Av. E&W | 8W-6N,1W-6N | 42 |
| Winona St. E&W | 10W-6N,1W-6N | 41 |
| Winston Av. N&S | 1W-11S | 68 |
| Winthrop Av. N&S | 1W-6N,1W-8N | 45 |
| Wisconsin St. E&W | 1W-2N,0W-2N | 51 |
| Wisner Av. NE&SW | 4W-3N | 44 |
| Wolcott N&S | 2W-3N | 45 |
| Wolcott Av. N&S | 2W-13S,2W-8N | 75 |
| Wolfe Lake Blvd. N&S | 4E-14S,4E-13S | 77 |
| Wolfram St. E&W | 8W-3N,1W-3N | 42 |
| Wood St. N&S | 2W-13S,2W-2N | 75 |
| Woodard St. NE&SW | 4W-3N | 44 |
| Woodlawn Av. N&S | 1E-12S,1E-5S | 68 |
| Woodward Dr. N&S | 4W-0S | 50 |
| Wright St. NE&SW | 0W-8S | 62 |
| Wrightwood Av. E&W | 8W-3N,0W-3N | 42 |
| Yale Av. N&S | 0W-14S,0W-7S | 76 |
| Yale Av. NE&SW | 0W-10S | 68 |
| Yates Av. N&S | 2E-15S,2E-11S | 77 |
| Yates Blvd. N&S | 2E-10S,2E-8S | 69 |
| 8th St. E&W | 0E-0S | 51 |
| 9th St. E&W | 0E-0S | 51 |
| 11th Pl. E&W | 0E-0S | 51 |
| 11th St. E&W | 0E-0S | 51 |
| 12th Pl. E&W | 4W-1S,0W-1S | 55 |
| 13th Pl. E&W | 4W-1S,3W-1S | 55 |
| 13th St. E&W | 5W-1S,0E-1S | 55 |
| 14th Pl. E&W | 3W-1S,2W-1S | 56 |
| 14th St. E&W | 5W-1S,0E-1S | 55 |
| 15th Pl. E&W | 3W-1S,0W-1S | 56 |
| 15th St. E&W | 4W-1S,0W-1S | 55 |
| 16th St. E&W | 5W-1S,0E-1S | 55 |
| 17th Pl. E&W | 0W-1S | 57 |
| 17th St. E&W | 5W-1S,0W-1S | 55 |
| 18th Pl. E&W | 5W-1S,1W-1S | 55 |
| 18th St. E&W | 5W-1S,0E-1S | 55 |
| 19th Pl. E&W | 1W-1S | 56 |
| 19th St. E&W | 5W-1S,0W-1S | 55 |
| 20th Pl. E&W | 1W-1S | 56 |
| 21st Pl. E&W | 5W-1S,2W-1S | 55 |
| 21st St. E&W | 5W-1S,0E-1S | 55 |
| 22nd Pl. E&W | 3W-2S,0W-2S | 56 |
| 22nd St. E&W | 1W-2S,0W-2S | 56 |
| 23rd Pl. E&W | 3W-2S,0W-2S | 56 |
| 23rd St. E&W | 4W-2S,0E-2S | 55 |
| 23rd St. Viaduct E&W | 0E-2S | 57 |
| 24th Blvd. E&W | 3W-2S | 56 |
| 24th Pl. E&W | 5W-2S,0E-2S | 55 |
| 24th St. E&W | 4W-2S,0E-2S | 55 |
| 25th Pl. E&W | 5W-2S,3W-2S | 55 |
| 25th St. E&W | 4W-2S,0E-2S | 55 |
| 26th Pl. E&W | 0W-2S | 57 |
| 26th St. E&W | 5W-2S,0E-2S | 55 |
| 27th St. E&W | 4W-2S,0E-2S | 55 |
| 28th Pl. E&W | 0W-2S | 57 |
| 28th St. E&W | 4W-2S,0E-2S | 55 |
| 29th Pl. E&W | 0E-2S | 57 |
| 29th St. E&W | 1W-2S,0E-2S | 56 |
| 30th St. E&W | 4W-2S,0W-2S | 55 |
| 31st Blvd. E&W | 3W-2S | 56 |
| 31st Pl. E&W | 2W-3S,0E-3S | 56 |
| 31st St. E&W | 5W-2S,0E-2S | 55 |
| 32nd Pl. E&W | 1W-3S,0E-3S | 56 |
| 32nd St. E&W | 4W-3S,0E-3S | 55 |
| 33rd Pl. E&W | 2W-3S,0E-3S | 56 |
| 33rd St. E&W | 4W-3S,0E-3S | 55 |
| 34th Pl. E&W | 3W-3S,1W-3S | 56 |
| 34th St. E&W | 4W-3S,0E-3S | 55 |
| 35th Pl. E&W | 3W-3S,1W-3S | 56 |
| 35th St. E&W | 4W-3S,0E-3S | 55 |
| 36th Pl. E&W | 3W-3S,0E-3S | 56 |
| 36th St. E&W | 3W-3S,0E-3S | 56 |
| 37th Pl. E&W | 3W-3S,0E-3S | 56 |
| 37th St. E&W | 2W-3S,0E-3S | 56 |
| 38th Pl. E&W | 4W-3S,0E-3S | 55 |
| 38th St. E&W | 3W-3S,0E-3S | 56 |
| 39th Pl. E&W | 3W-4S,0W-6S | 56 |
| 40th Pl. E&W | 3W-4S,0W-4S | 56 |
| 40th St. E&W | 5W-4S,1E-4S | 55 |
| 41st Pl. E&W | 3W-4S,1E-4S | 56 |
| 41st St. E&W | 4W-4S,1E-4S | 55 |
| 42nd Pl. E&W | 3W-4S,1E-4S | 56 |
| 42nd St. E&W | 5W-4S,0E-4S | 55 |
| 43rd Pl. E&W | 0W-4S | 57 |
| 43rd St. E&W | 5W-4S,1E-4S | 55 |
| 44th Pl. E&W | 6W-4S,1E-4S | 55 |
| 44th St. E&W | 5W-4S,1E-4S | 55 |
| 45th Pl. E&W | 4W-4S,0E-4S | 55 |
| 45th St. E&W | 5W-4S,1E-4S | 55 |
| 46th Pl. E&W | 4W-4S,0E-4S | 55 |
| 46th St. E&W | 6W-4S,1E-4S | 55 |
| 47th Dr. E&W | 1E-4S | 57 |
| 47th Pl. E&W | 4W-5S,1E-5S | 61 |
| 47th St. E&W | 5W-4S,1E-4S | 55 |
| 48th Pl. E&W | 4W-5S,0E-5S | 61 |
| 48th St. E&W | 6W-5S,1E-5S | 60 |
| 49th Dr. NE&SW | 2E-5S | 63 |
| 49th Pl. E&W | 2W-5S,1W-5S | 61 |
| 49th St. E&W | 5W-5S,1E-5S | 60 |
| 50th Pl. E&W | 4W-5S,2E-5S | 61 |
| 50th St. E&W | 5W-5S,2E-5S | 60 |
| 51st Pl. E&W | 2W-5S,0W-5S | 61 |
| 51st St. E&W | 5W-5S,0E-5S | 60 |
| 52nd Pl. E&W | 4W-5S,0W-5S | 61 |
| 52nd St. E&W | 8W-5S,1E-5S | 59 |
| 53rd Pl. E&W | 6W-5S,1W-5S | 60 |
| 53rd St. E&W | 8W-5S,1E-5S | 59 |
| 54th Pl. E&W | 7W-5S,1E-5S | 60 |
| 54th St. E&W | 8W-5S,2E-5S | 59 |
| 55th Pl. E&W | 5W-6S,0E-6S | 60 |
| 55th St. E&W | 7W-5S,2E-5S | 60 |
| 56th Pl. E&W | 4W-6S,0W-6S | 61 |
| 56th St. E&W | 8W-6S,1E-6S | 59 |
| 57th Dr. E&W | 2E-6S | 63 |
| 57th Pl. E&W | 4W-6S,0W-6S | 61 |
| 57th St. E&W | 8W-6S,1E-6S | 59 |
| 58th Pl. E&W | 4W-6S,0W-6S | 61 |
| 58th St. E&W | 8W-6S,1E-6S | 59 |
| 59th Pl. E&W | 4W-6S | 61 |
| 59th St. E&W | 8W-6S,1E-6S | 59 |
| 60th Pl. E&W | 8W-6S,0W-6S | 59 |
| 60th St. E&W | 8W-6S,1E-6S | 59 |
| 61st Pl. E&W | 4W-6S,1E-6S | 61 |
| 61st St. E&W | 8W-6S,1E-6S | 59 |
| 62nd Pl. E&W | 4W-6S,1E-6S | 61 |
| 62nd St. E&W | 8W-6S,0E-6S | 59 |
| 63rd Pl. E&W | 8W-7S,1E-7S | 59 |
| 63rd St. E&W | 8W-6S,1E-6S | 59 |
| 64th Pl. E&W | 8W-7S,1E-7S | 59 |
| 64th St. E&W | 8W-7S,1E-7S | 59 |
| 65th Pl. E&W | 5W-7S,1E-7S | 60 |
| 65th St. E&W | 8W-7S,1E-7S | 59 |
| 66th Pl. E&W | 5W-7S,1E-7S | 60 |
| 66th St. E&W | 5W-7S,0E-7S | 60 |
| 67th Pl. E&W | 4W-7S,1E-7S | 61 |
| 67th St. E&W | 0E-7S,2E-7S | 62 |
| 68th Pl. E&W | 4W-7S,2W-7S | 61 |
| 68th St. E&W | 5W-7S,2E-7S | 60 |
| 69th Pl. E&W | 4W-7S,1E-7S | 61 |
| 69th St. E&W | 5W-7S,2E-7S | 60 |
| 70th Pl. E&W | 4W-7S,2E-7S | 61 |
| 70th St. E&W | 5W-7S,2E-7S | 60 |
| 71st Pl. E&W | 4W-8S,1E-8S | 61 |
| 71st St. E&W | 4W-7S,2E-7S | 61 |
| 72nd Pl. E&W | 4W-8S,1E-8S | 61 |
| 72nd St. E&W | 4W-8S,3E-8S | 61 |
| 73rd Pl. E&W | 4W-8S,3E-8S | 61 |
| 73rd St. E&W | 4W-8S,3E-8S | 61 |
| 74th Pl. E&W | 1W-8S,3E-8S | 62 |
| 74th St. E&W | 4W-8S,3E-8S | 61 |
| 75th Pl. E&W | 4W-8S,3E-8S | 61 |
| 75th Pl. E&W | 2W-8S | 61 |
| 75th St. E&W | 4W-8S,3E-8S | 61 |
| 76th Pl. E&W | 4W-8S,3E-8S | 61 |
| 76th Pl. E&W | 2W-8S | 61 |
| 76th St. E&W | 4W-8S,3E-8S | 61 |
| 77th Pl. E&W | 5W-8S,3E-8S | 60 |
| 77th Pl. E&W | 2W-8S | 61 |
| 77th St. E&W | 4W-8S,3E-8S | 61 |
| 77th St. E&W | 2W-8S | 61 |
| 78th Pl. E&W | 4W-8S,3E-8S | 61 |
| 78th St. E&W | 5W-8S,3E-8S | 60 |
| 78th St. E&W | 2W-8S | 61 |
| 79th Pl. E&W | 5W-9S,4E-9S | 66 |
| 79th St. E&W | 5W-8S,2E-8S | 60 |
| 80th Pl. E&W | 5W-9S,3E-9S | 66 |
| 80th Pl. E&W | 0W-9S | 68 |
| 80th St. E&W | 5W-9S,3E-9S | 66 |
| 81st Pl. E&W | 5W-9S,3E-9S | 66 |
| 81st Pl. E&W | 0W-9S | 68 |
| 81st St. E&W | 5W-9S,3E-9S | 66 |
| 82nd Pl. E&W | 5W-9S,1E-9S | 66 |
| 82nd Pl. E&W | 0W-9S | 68 |
| 82nd St. E&W | 5W-9S,3E-9S | 66 |
| 82nd St. E&W | 0W-9S | 68 |
| 83rd Pl. E&W | 5W-9S,2E-9S | 66 |
| 83rd Pl. E&W | 0E-9S | 68 |
| 83rd St. E&W | 5W-9S,4E-9S | 66 |
| 84th Pl. E&W | 5W-9S,2E-9S | 66 |
| 84th Pl. E&W | 0E-9S | 68 |
| 84th St. E&W | 5W-9S,4E-9S | 66 |
| 85th Pl. E&W | 4W-9S,2E-9S | 67 |
| 85th St. E&W | 5W-9S,4E-9S | 66 |
| 86th Pl. E&W | 4W-9S,2E-9S | 67 |
| 86th St. E&W | 5W-9S,4E-9S | 66 |
| 86th St. E&W | 4W-9S | 67 |
| 87th Pl. E&W | 0E-10S,2E-10S | 68 |
| 87th St. E&W | 5W-9S,3E-9S | 66 |
| 88th Pl. E&W | 0E-10S,1E-10S | 68 |
| 88th St. E&W | 2W-10S,4E-10S | 67 |
| 89th Pl. E&W | 0E-10S,1E-10S | 68 |
| 89th St. E&W | 2W-10S,4E-10S | 67 |
| 90th Pl. E&W | 2W-10S,1E-10S | 67 |
| 90th St. E&W | 2W-10S,3E-10S | 67 |
| 91st Pl. E&W | 2W-10S,2E-10S | 67 |
| 91st Pl. NW&SE | 0W-10S | 68 |
| 91st St. E&W | 2W-10S,3E-10S | 67 |
| 92nd Pl. E&W | 2W-10S,2E-10S | 67 |
| 92nd St. E&W | 2W-10S,3E-10S | 67 |
| 92nd St. E&W | 0W-10S | 68 |
| 93rd Pl. E&W | 2W-10S | 67 |
| 93rd Pl. NW&SE | 0W-10S | 68 |
| 93rd St. E&W | 2W-10S,3E-10S | 67 |
| 93rd St. E&W | 0W-10S | 68 |
| 94th Pl. NW&SE | 0W-10S | 68 |
| 94th St. E&W | 2W-10S,3E-10S | 67 |
| 95th Pl. E&W | 2W-11S,2E-11S | 67 |
| 95th St. E&W | 1W-10S,3E-10S | 68 |
| 96th Pl. E&W | 0W-11S,1E-11S | 68 |
| 96th St. E&W | 2W-11S,4E-10S | 67 |
| 97th Pl. E&W | 1W-11S,3E-11S | 68 |
| 97th St. E&W | 2W-11S,4E-10S | 67 |
| 98th Pl. E&W | 1W-11S,2E-11S | 68 |
| 98th St. E&W | 2W-11S,4E-10S | 67 |
| 99th Pl. E&W | 3W-11S,0E-11S | 67 |
| 99th St. E&W | 2W-11S,4E-11S | 67 |
| 100th Blvd. E&W | 3E-11S,4E-11S | 69 |
| 100th Pl. E&W | 3W-11S,0E-11S | 67 |
| 100th St. E&W | 3W-11S,3E-11S | 67 |
| 101st Pl. E&W | 3W-11S,0E-11S | 67 |
| 101st St. E&W | 3W-11S,4E-11S | 67 |
| 102nd Pl. E&W | 3W-11S,0E-11S | 67 |
| 102nd St. E&W | 3W-11S,4E-11S | 67 |
| 103rd Pl. E&W | 3W-12S,0E-12S | 67 |
| 103rd St. E&W | 3W-11S,4E-11S | 67 |
| 104th Pl. E&W | 4W-12S,0E-12S | 67 |
| 104th St. E&W | 4W-12S,4E-11S | 67 |
| 105th Pl. E&W | 4W-12S,0E-12S | 67 |
| 105th St. E&W | 4W-12S,4E-11S | 67 |
| 106th Pl. E&W | 3W-12S,0W-12S | 67 |
| 106th St. E&W | 4W-12S,4E-11S | 67 |
| 107th Pl. E&W | 4W-12S,0W-12S | 67 |
| 107th St. E&W | 4W-12S,4E-12S | 67 |
| 108th Pl. E&W | 4W-12S,0W-12S | 67 |
| 108th St. E&W | 4W-12S,4E-12S | 67 |
| 109th Pl. E&W | 4W-12S,0W-12S | 67 |
| 109th St. E&W | 4W-12S,4E-12S | 67 |
| 110th Pl. E&W | 4W-12S,0W-12S | 67 |
| 110th St. E&W | 4W-12S,4E-12S | 67 |
| 111th Pl. E&W | 2W-13S,0E-13S | 75 |
| 111th St. E&W | 4W-12S,4E-12S | 67 |
| 112th Blvd. E&W | 4E-12S | 69 |
| 112th Pl. E&W | 4W-13S,0W-13S | 75 |
| 112th St. E&W | 3W-13S,2E-12S | 75 |
| 113th Pl. E&W | 2W-13S,0W-13S | 75 |
| 113th St. E&W | 4W-13S,4E-12S | 75 |
| 114th Pl. E&W | 4W-13S,0E-13S | 75 |
| 114th St. E&W | 5W-13S,4E-12S | 74 |
| 115th Pl. E&W | 4W-13S,0W-13S | 75 |
| 115th St. E&W | 4W-13S,4E-13S | 75 |
| 116th Pl. E&W | 4W-13S,0W-13S | 75 |
| 116th St. E&W | 4W-13S,4E-13S | 75 |
| 117th Pl. E&W | 3W-13S,0E-13S | 75 |
| 117th St. E&W | 4W-13S,4E-13S | 75 |
| 118th Pl. E&W | 3W-13S,0E-13S | 75 |
| 118th St. E&W | 4W-13S,4E-13S | 75 |
| 119th Pl. E&W | 0E-14S | 76 |
| 119th St. E&W | 3W-13S,2E-13S | 75 |
| 120th Pl. E&W | 0E-14S,2E-13S | 76 |
| 120th St. E&W | 1W-14S,2E-13S | 76 |
| 121st Pl. E&W | 0E-14S,2E-13S | 76 |
| 121st St. E&W | 1W-14S,2E-13S | 76 |
| 122nd Pl. E&W | 0E-14S | 76 |
| 122nd St. E&W | 1W-14S,3E-13S | 76 |
| 123rd St. E&W | 1W-14S,2E-14S | 76 |
| 124th Pl. E&W | 0W-14S | 76 |
| 124th St. E&W | 0W-14S,2E-14S | 76 |
| 125th Pl. E&W | 0W-14S | 76 |
| 125th St. E&W | 0W-14S,2E-14S | 76 |
| 126th Pl. E&W | 0W-14S | 76 |
| 126th St. E&W | 0W-14S,3E-14S | 76 |
| 127th Pl. E&W | 0W-15S | 76 |
| 127th St. E&W | 0W-14S,3E-14S | 76 |
| 128th Pl. E&W | 1W-15S,0W-15S | 76 |
| 128th Pl. NW&SE | 3E-14S | 77 |
| 128th St. E&W | 0W-15S,3E-14S | 76 |
| 129th Pl. E&W | 1W-15S,0W-15S | 76 |
| 129th St. E&W | 3E-14S | 77 |
| 130th Pl. (Pvt.) E&W | 0E-15S,1E-15S | 76 |
| 130th St. E&W | 0E-14S,3E-14S | 76 |
| 131st St. (Pvt.) E&W | 0E-15S,3E-15S | 76 |
| 132nd Pl. (Pvt.) E&W | 1E-15S | 76 |
| 132nd St. (Pvt.) E&W | 0E-15S,3E-15S | 76 |
| 133rd Pl. E&W | 0E-15S | 76 |
| 133rd St. (Pvt.) E&W | 0E-15S,3E-15S | 76 |
| 134th Pl. E&W | 0E-15S | 76 |
| 134th St. E&W | 0E-15S,3E-15S | 76 |
| 135th Pl. E&W | 0E-15S | 76 |
| 135th St. E&W | 0E-15S,3E-15S | 76 |
| 136th Pl. E&W | 0E-15S | 76 |
| 136th St. E&W | 0E-15S,3E-15S | 76 |
| 137th St. E&W | 0E-15S,2E-15S | 76 |
| 138th Pl. E&W | 0E-15S | 76 |
| 138th St. E&W | 3E-15S | 77 |


## Alsip


| Street | Grid | Page |
|---|---|---|
| Albany Av. N&S | 3W-14S | 75 |
| Alpine Dr. NW&SE | 6W-14S | 74 |
| Apple Ln. N&S | 5W-15S | 74 |
| Arbor Dr. NW&SE | 4W-14S | 75 |
| Austin Av. N&S | 7W-14S,7W-13S | 74 |
| Avers Av. N&S | 4W-14S | 75 |
| Avon Av. NW&SE | 6W-13S | 74 |
| Benck Dr. NW&SE | 4W-14S | 75 |
| Blossom Dr. E&W | 5W-15S | 74 |
| Carolyn Ln. N&S | 5W-13S | 74 |
| Central Av. N&S | 7W-14S,7W-13S | 74 |
| Central Park Av. N&S | 4W-14S | 75 |
| Cicero Av. N&S | 6W-14S,6W-13S | 74 |
| Creek Dr. NW&SE | 4W-14S | 75 |
| Deerpark Dr. NS&EW | 4W-14S | 75 |
| Eastview Dr. NW&SE | 5W-13S | 74 |
| Engle Rd. NS&EW | 6W-15S | 74 |
| Fey Ln. E&W | 5W-13S | 74 |
| Frontage Rd. NW&SE | 7W-14S | 74 |
| Glen Dr. NW&SE | 4W-14S | 75 |
| Hamlin Av. N&S | 4W-14S,4W-13S | 75 |
| Hamlin Ct. N&S | 4W-15S,4W-14S | 75 |
| Harding Av. N&S | 4W-14S,4W-13S | 75 |
| Holiday Dr. N&S | 6W-14S | 74 |
| Holmberg Ct. N&S | 5W-14S | 74 |
| Homan Av. N&S | 4W-15S,4W-14S | 75 |
| Howdy Ln. E&W | 5W-13S | 74 |
| Interstate 294 NW&SE | 6W-14S | 74 |
| James Dr. N&S | 6W-14S | 74 |
| Jean St. E&W | 5W-13S | 74 |
| Joalyce Ct. NE&SW | 5W-13S | 74 |
| Joalyce Dr. NW&SE | 5W-13S | 74 |
| Joan St. E&W | 4W-13S | 75 |
| Jobey Ln. NW&SE | 5W-13S | 74 |
| Karlov Av. N&S | 5W-14S,5W-13S | 74 |
| Kathleen Ct. N&S | 4W-14S | 75 |
| Kedvale Av. N&S | 5W-14S,5W-13S | 74 |
| Kedzie Av. N&S | 4W-15S,4W-14S | 75 |
| Keeler Av. N&S | 5W-14S,5W-13S | 74 |
| Kenneth Av. N&S | 5W-15S,5W-13S | 74 |
| Kenton Av. N&S | 5W-13S | 74 |
| Kilbourn Av. N&S | 5W-13S | 74 |
| Kildare Av. N&S | 5W-14S,5W-13S | 74 |
| Knox Av. N&S | 5W-13S | 74 |
| Kolin Av. N&S | 5W-15S,5W-13S | 74 |
| Kolmar Av. N&S | 5W-13S | 74 |
| Komensky Av. N&S | 5W-14S | 74 |
| Kostner Av. N&S | 5W-15S,5W-14S | 74 |
| Lacrosse Av. N&S | 6W-15S,6W-13S | 74 |
| Lake Av. NW&SE | 4W-14S | 75 |
| Lamon Av. N&S | 6W-14S,6W-13S | 74 |
| Laporte Av. N&S | 6W-14S,6W-13S | 74 |
| Laramie Av. N&S | 6W-14S,6W-14S | 74 |
| Lavergne Av. N&S | 6W-14S | 74 |
| Lawler Av. N&S | 6W-14S,6W-13S | 74 |
| Lawndale Av. N&S | 4W-14S | 75 |
| Leamington Av. N&S | 6W-14S,6W-13S | 74 |
| Leclaire Av. N&S | 6W-13S | 74 |
| Lee Rd. N&S | 5W-13S | 74 |
| Linecrest Dr. E&W | 5W-13S | 74 |
| Lockwood Av. N&S | 6W-14S | 74 |

| | Grid | Page |
|---|---|---|
| Lockwood Ct. E&W | 6W-14S | 74 |
| Lombard Ln. N&S | 5W-14S | 74 |
| Loveland Av. N&S | 5W-14S | 74 |
| Loveland St. N&S | 5W-14S | 74 |
| Mansfield Av. N&S | 7W-14S | 74 |
| Mather Av. N&S | 6W-14S | 74 |
| Mayfield Av. N&S | 7W-13S | 74 |
| Mayfield Ct. N&S | 7W-14S | 74 |
| McDaniels Ct. NE&SW | 5W-15S | 74 |
| McDaniels St. N&S | 5W-15S,5W-14S | 74 |
| Menard Av. N&S | 7W-14S | 74 |
| Millard Av. N&S | 4W-15S,4W-14S | 75 |
| Minnesota Av. E&W | 3W-14S | 75 |
| Orchard Av. N&S | 5W-15S,5W-14S | 74 |
| Orchard Ln. N&S | 5W-15S | 74 |
| Orchard St. N&S | 5W-14S | 74 |
| Park Lane Dr. N&S | 5W-14S | 74 |
| Prairie Av. N&S | 5W-14S | 74 |
| Prairie Dr. E&W | 5W-14S | 74 |
| Pulask Rd. N&S | 5W-15S,5W-13S | 74 |
| Quinn Dr. N&S | 4W-14S | 75 |
| Rexford St. N&S | 5W-14S | 74 |
| Ridgeway Av. N&S | 4W-15S,4W-14S | 75 |
| Rosemary Ln. N&S | 5W-13S | 74 |
| Rt. 50 N&S | 5W-13S | 74 |
| Scott Dr. E&W | 4W-14S | 75 |
| Shirley Ln. NW&SE | 5W-14S | 74 |
| Spencer Ct. NE&SW | 5W-15S | 74 |
| Spencer St. N&S | 5W-15S,5W-14S | 74 |
| Springfield Av. N&S | 4W-14S,4W-13S | 75 |
| Termunde Dr. NW&SE | 5W-14S | 74 |
| Tri State Tollway NW&SE | 5W-13S,5W-15S | 74 |
| Tripp Av. N&S | 5W-14S,5W-13S | 74 |
| Trumbull Av. N&S | 4W-14S | 75 |
| Van Beveren Dr. N&S | 5W-14S | 74 |
| Walter Ln. E&W | 4W-14S | 75 |
| 44th Ct. N&S | 5W-14S | 74 |
| 45th Ct. N&S | 5W-14S | 74 |
| 111th St. E&W | 6W-12S | 66 |
| 112th Pl. E&W | 6W-13S | 74 |
| 113th Ct. NE&SW | 6W-13S | 74 |
| 113th Pl. E&W | 6W-13S | 74 |
| 113th St. E&W | 6W-13S | 74 |
| 114th Pl. E&W | 6W-13S | 74 |
| 114th St. E&W | 6W-13S | 74 |
| 115th Pl. E&W | 6W-13S | 74 |
| 115th St. E&W | 7W-13S,5W-13S | 74 |
| 116th Pl. E&W | 5W-13S | 74 |
| 116th St. E&W | 7W-13S,5W-13S | 74 |
| 117th Pl. E&W | 7W-13S | 74 |
| 117th St. E&W | 6W-13S,5W-13S | 74 |
| 118th Pl. E&W | 7W-13S,5W-13S | 74 |
| 119th Pl. E&W | 5W-14S | 74 |
| 119th St. E&W | 6W-13S,4W-13S | 74 |
| 120th Pl. E&W | 7W-14S,5W-14S | 74 |
| 120th St. E&W | 7W-14S,4W-14S | 74 |
| 121st Pl. E&W | 6W-14S,4W-14S | 74 |
| 121st St. E&W | 6W-14S,4W-14S | 74 |
| 122nd St. E&W | 6W-14S,4W-14S | 74 |
| 123rd Pl. E&W | 6W-14S,4W-14S | 74 |
| 123rd St. E&W | 6W-14S,5W-14S | 74 |
| 124th Pl. E&W | 7W-14S,4W-14S | 74 |
| 124th St. E&W | 6W-14S,5W-14S | 74 |
| 125th Pl. E&W | 6W-14S | 75 |
| 125th St. E&W | 7W-14S,4W-14S | 75 |
| 125th St. NW&SE | 4W-14S | 75 |
| 126th Pl. E&W | 7W-14S,6W-14S | 74 |
| 126th St. E&W | 7W-14S,3W-14S | 74 |
| 127th Pl. E&W | 5W-15S | 74 |
| 127th St. E&W | 7W-14S,5W-14S | 74 |
| 128th Pl. E&W | 6W-15S,5W-15S | 74 |
| 128th Pl. E&W | 4W-15S | 75 |
| 128th St. E&W | 5W-15S | 74 |
| 129th St. E&W | 5W-15S | 74 |
| 131st St. E&W | 5W-15S,4W-15S | 74 |

## Arlington Heights

| | Grid | Page |
|---|---|---|
| Alexandria St. E&W | 18W-16N | 14 |
| Algonquin Rd. NW&SE | 18W-11N,17W-11N | 24 |
| Alleghany Dr. E&W | 18W-16N | 14 |
| Allen Ln. N&S | 18W-13N | 24 |
| Allison Ct. E&W | 19W-12N | 24 |
| Amhurst Ct. NW&SE | 16W-15N | 15 |
| Anderson Dr. E&W | 18W-16N | 14 |
| Appletree Ln. N&S | 17W-16N | 14 |
| Arlington Heights Rd. N&S | 18W-11N,18W-18N | 24 |
| Arthur Av. N&S | 18W-16N | 24 |
| Ashbury St. NW&SE | 16W-15N | 15 |
| Ashford Ln. E&W | 18W-18N | 14 |
| Avon Ct. E&W | 16W-15N | 15 |
| Avon St. N&S | 16W-15N | 15 |
| Banbury Rd. E&W | 17W-13N | 24 |
| Barberry Ct. E&W | 16W-15N | 15 |
| Bel Aire Dr. E&W | 16W-14N | 25 |
| Belmont Av. N&S | 17W-12N,17W-15N | 24 |
| Berkley Dr. E&W | 18W-17N | 14 |
| Best Dr. NW&SE | 17W-17N,16W-17N | 14 |
| Beverly Av. N&S | 17W-14N,17W-17N | 24 |
| Beverly Ln. N&S | 17W-13N,17W-15N | 24 |
| Bloomington Av. NE&SW | 19W-18N | 14 |
| Boeger Dr. E&W | 17W-17N | 14 |
| Bradford Ct. E&W | 17W-16N | 14 |
| Bradford Dr. N&S | 17W-16N | 14 |
| Bradshire Ct. N&S | 16W-15N | 15 |
| Braeside Dr. E&W | 17W-16N | 14 |
| Brampton Ln. E&W | 18W-18N | 14 |
| Brandenberry Ct. NW&SE | 16W-15N | 15 |
| Bray Ct. E&W | 19W-12N | 24 |
| Brett Ct. E&W | 17W-12N | 24 |
| Brighton Pl. N&S | 17W-13N,17W-17N | 24 |
| Bristol Ln. N&S | 17W-17N | 24 |
| Brittany Ct. E&W | 17W-17N | 14 |
| Brittany Dr. E&W | 18W-17N,17W-17N | 14 |
| Brockton Ct. N&S | 16W-15N | 15 |
| Brook Dr. E&W | 17W-11N | 24 |
| Brookwood Ct. N&S | 17W-16N | 14 |
| Brookwood Dr. E&W | 17W-16N | 14 |
| Brown St. E&W | 18W-14N | 24 |
| Buffalo Grove Rd. N&S | 16W-17N | 15 |
| Burgoyne Rd. N&S | 18W-16N | 14 |
| Burke N&S | 17W-16N | 14 |
| Burkitt NE&SW | 18W-18N | 14 |
| Burning Tree Ct. E&W | 17W-16N | 15 |
| Burning Tree Ln. E&W | 18W-17N,17W-17N | 14 |
| Burr Oak Dr. E&W | 18W-17N,17W-17N | 14 |
| Burton Pl. N&S | 17W-13N | 24 |
| Butternut Ln. E&W | 18W-14N | 24 |
| Cambridge St. E&W | 18W-16N | 14 |
| Camelot Ct. E&W | 17W-16N | 14 |
| Campbell St. E&W | 18W-14N,16W-14N | 14 |
| Campus Dr. NS&EW | 18W-17N | 14 |
| Canterbury Ct. E&W | 18W-16N | 14 |
| Canterbury Dr. E&W | 17W-16N,16W-16N | 14 |
| Carlyle NW&SE | 17W-13N | 24 |
| Carlyle Ct. NS&EW | 17W-15N | 14 |
| Carlyle Ln. N&S | 17W-14N | 24 |
| Carlyle Pl. N&S | 17W-16N | 14 |
| Carriage Way Dr. N&S | 17W-17N | 14 |
| Catino St. E&W | 18W-13N | 24 |
| Cedar Ct. E&W | 18W-12N | 24 |
| Cedar Glen Dr. N&S | 17W-11N | 24 |
| Cedar Ln. E&W | 18W-12N | 24 |
| Cedar St. E&W | 18W-12N | 24 |
| Central Rd. E&W | 17W-13N | 24 |
| Champlain St. NS&EW | 18W-16N | 14 |
| Chapel Hill Dr. N&S | 17W-16N | 14 |
| Charles NW&SE | 16W-15N | 14 |
| Charter Point Dr. NW&SE | 16W-16N | 15 |
| Charter Point Dr. (Pvt.) NE&SW | 16W-16N | 15 |
| Chatham Pl. NE&SW | 17W-13N | 24 |
| Cherry Hill Dr. N&S | 16W-16N | 15 |
| Cherry Ln. E&W | 17W-16N | 14 |
| Chesterfield Dr. E&W | 18W-12N | 24 |
| Chestnut Av. N&S | 18W-12N,18W-16N | 24 |
| Chicago Av. N&S | 18W-14N,18W-15N | 24 |
| Circle Hill Dr. NS&EW | 17W-16N | 14 |
| Clarence Av. N&S | 18W-18N | 14 |
| Clarendon Av. NW&SE | 17W-15N | 14 |
| Clarendon Ct. NE&SW | 17W-15N | 14 |
| Clarendon Rd. E&W | 18W-15N | 14 |
| Clarendon St. E&W | 18W-15N,17W-15N | 14 |
| Clayton Ct. E&W | 16W-15N | 15 |
| Clearbrook Dr. NS&EW | 18W-11N | 24 |
| Cleveland Av. N&S | 17W-13N | 24 |
| Coldspring Rd. (Pvt.) N&S | 16W-16N | 15 |
| College Dr. NS&EW | 18W-17N | 14 |
| Concord Dr. NS&EW | 18W-16N | 14 |
| Cottonwood Ln. E&W | 18W-14N | 24 |
| Council Trail E&W | 17W-12N | 24 |
| Country Lake Rd. E&W | 16W-16N | 15 |
| Country Ln. E&W | 17W-17N | 14 |
| Courtland Dr. (Pvt.) | 16W-15N | 15 |
| Crabtree Dr. NE&SW | 17W-16N,16W-16N | 14 |
| Crestwood Dr. E&W | 17W-16N | 14 |
| Cyndi Ct. E&W | 17W-12N,18W-12N | 24 |
| Cypress Dr. E&W | 18W-12N | 24 |
| Cypress St. E&W | 18W-12N | 24 |
| Dale Av. N&S | 16W-13N,16W-15N | 25 |
| Daniels Ct. N&S | 17W-17N | 14 |
| Davis St. NW&SE | 16W-13N,18W-14N | 25 |
| Derbyshire Av. N&S | 17W-14N | 24 |
| Derbyshire Dr. N&S | 17W-16N | 14 |
| Derbyshire Ln. NW&SE | 16W-13N,17W-16N | 25 |
| Donald Av. N&S | 16W-13N,16W-14N | 25 |
| Dorothy Av. NE&SW | 17W-15N | 14 |
| Douglas N&S | 17W-17N | 14 |
| Douglas Av. N&S | 17W-16N | 14 |
| Douglas Av. N&S | 17W-12N,17W-15N | 24 |
| Douglas Rd. N&S | 17W-16N,17W-17N | 14 |
| Dover Ct. N&S | 16W-15N | 15 |
| Dover Ln. N&S | 16W-15N | 15 |
| Drury Ln. NW&SE | 16W-13N,16W-16N | 25 |
| Dryden Av. N&S | 17W-14N,17W-15N | 24 |
| Dryden Pl. E&W | 17W-13N,17W-17N | 24 |
| Dundee Rd. E&W | 18W-18N | 14 |
| Dunhill Ct. N&S | 17W-16N | 14 |
| Dunton Av. N&S | 17W-12N,18W-17N | 24 |
| Dwyer Av. N&S | 18W-13N,18W-14N | 24 |
| Eastman St. E&W | 16W-14N | 25 |
| Eastman St. E&W | 18W-12N,16W-14N | 25 |
| Eastwood Dr. N&S | 17W-16N | 14 |
| Elizabeth Dr. NE&SW | 18W-16N | 14 |
| Elk Grove Rd. N&S | 18W-11N | 24 |
| Elm Ln. N&S | 17W-17N | 14 |
| Elm St. E&W | 18W-14N | 14 |
| Elmwood Cir. N&S | 16W-16N | 15 |
| Embers Ln. N&S | 17W-11N | 24 |
| Emerson St. E&W | 18W-12N,17W-12N | 24 |
| Essex Pl. NE&SW | 18W-16N | 14 |
| Eton Dr. E&W | 17W-17N | 14 |
| Euclid Av. E&W | 16W-14N,18W-12N | 25 |
| Evanston Av. N&S | 16W-13N,16W-14N | 25 |
| Evergreen Av. N&S | 18W-12N,18W-16N | 24 |
| Evergreen Ter. NS&EW | 16W-16N | 15 |
| Fairview St. E&W | 18W-14N,16W-14N | 25 |
| Falcon Dr. E&W | 17W-11N | 24 |
| Fernandez Av. N&S | 18W-12N,18W-16N | 24 |
| Fernandez Ct. E&W | 18W-12N | 24 |
| Fernandez Pl. N&S | 18W-15N | 14 |
| Fleming Dr., N. E&W | 16W-17N | 15 |
| Flentie Ln. E&W | 16W-17N | 15 |
| Flower Cir. NW&SE | 16W-16N | 15 |
| Forest Av. N&S | 16W-13N,16W-16N | 25 |
| Forrest Ln. N&S | 16W-16N | 15 |
| Foster St. E&W | 17W-12N | 24 |
| Foxdale Ln. E&W | 18W-18N | 14 |
| Francis Dr. E&W | 18W-13N | 24 |
| Frederick St. E&W | 18W-18N | 14 |
| Fremont Ct. N&S | 16W-14N | 25 |
| Fremont St. N&S | 16W-14N,18W-14N | 25 |
| Frontenac Dr. E&W | 18W-16N | 14 |
| Galena Ct. E&W | 18W-16N | 14 |
| Galesburg Ct. N&S | 19W-18N | 14 |
| Garden Walk E&W | 16W-14N | 25 |
| George St. E&W | 17W-13N,18W-13N | 24 |
| Gettysburg Dr. NS&EW | 18W-16N | 14 |
| Gibbons Av. N&S | 16W-13N,16W-14N | 25 |
| Goebbert Rd. N&S | 17W-11N,17W-12N | 24 |
| Golf Rd. E&W | 17W-12N | 24 |
| Golf Ter. E&W | 17W-12N | 24 |
| Green Briar Ct. NS&EW | 18W-16N | 14 |
| Greenwood Ct. N&S | 16W-15N | 15 |
| Gregory St. E&W | 16W-13N | 25 |
| Gresham Ct. NE&SW | 16W-15N | 15 |
| Grove St. E&W | 16W-13N,18W-13N | 25 |
| Hackberry Dr. NS&EW | 18W-17N,17W-17N | 14 |
| Haddow Av. N&S | 16W-13N,16W-14N | 24 |
| Happfield Dr. E&W | 18W-18N | 14 |
| Harold St. E&W | 18W-16N | 14 |
| Hartford Ct. N&S | 16W-15N | 15 |
| Harvard Av. N&S | 18W-12N,18W-18N | 24 |
| Haven Dr. E&W | 17W-12N,18W-12N | 24 |
| Haverhill Ct. NE&SW | 16W-15N | 15 |
| Hawthorne St. E&W | 18W-14N,16W-14N | 24 |
| Heather Ln. E&W | 18W-14N | 24 |
| Henry St. E&W | 17W-17N | 14 |
| Hickory Av. N&S | 17W-14N,17W-17N | 24 |
| Hickory Ln. N&S | 17W-16N | 14 |
| Highland Av. N&S | 18W-12N | 24 |
| Hintz Rd. E&W | 17W-16N | 14 |
| Hunter Dr. E&W | 16W-15N | 15 |
| Hunter Dr. NE&SW | 16W-16N | 15 |
| Huntington Dr. E&W | 17W-17N | 14 |
| Huron St. E&W | 18W-16N | 14 |
| Illinois Av. N&S | 18W-14N,18W-16N | 24 |
| Illinois Dr. NS&EW | 18W-13N | 24 |
| Independence Ct. E&W | 17W-11N | 24 |
| Interstate 90 NW&SE | 18W-11N | 24 |
| Ironwood Dr. N&S | 16W-14N | 25 |
| Ivy Ln. E&W | 17W-16N | 14 |
| Ivy Ln. (Pvt.) E&W | 18W-16N | 14 |
| James Ct. NW&SE | 18W-16N | 14 |
| Jane Av. E&W | 17W-15N | 14 |
| Jennifer Ct. NW&SE | 17W-15N | 14 |
| Jo Ln. E&W | 18W-15N | 14 |
| Johanna Ter. NE&SW | 18W-14N | 24 |
| Jonquil Ct. E&W | 16W-16N | 15 |
| Jonquil Ter. E&W | 16W-16N | 15 |
| Jules St. E&W | 17W-16N | 14 |
| Juniper Ln. NS&EW | 18W-16N | 14 |
| Kaspar Av. N&S | 18W-12N,18W-15N | 24 |
| Keating Dr. E&W | 18W-13N | 24 |
| Kendal Ct. NW&SE | 16W-16N | 15 |
| Kennicott Av. N&S | 18W-13N,18W-18N | 24 |
| Kennicott Ct. N&S | 18W-16N | 14 |
| Kensington (Foundry) E&W | 17W-14N,16W-14N | 24 |
| Kerrybrook Ln. E&W | 17W-17N | 14 |
| Kimber Ln. E&W | 17W-11N | 24 |
| Kingsbury Ct. N&S | 18W-16N | 14 |
| Kingsbury Dr. E&W | 18W-16N | 14 |
| Kingsley Dr. E&W | 18W-18N | 14 |
| Kinley Av. N&S | 17W-13N | 24 |
| Kirchoff Rd. NW&SE | 17W-13N,18W-13N | 24 |
| Knob Hill Dr. E&W | 17W-16N | 14 |
| LaSalle St. N&S | 18W-16N | 14 |
| Ladd St. E&W | 18W-16N | 14 |
| Lafayette St. N&S | 18W-16N | 14 |
| Lake Arlington Dr. NE&SW | 16W-16N | 15 |
| Lake Cook Rd. E&W | 17W-18N | 14 |
| Lake Shore Cir. NS&EW | 16W-16N | 15 |
| Lancaster Ct. N&S | 16W-15N | 15 |
| Leona Ter. E&W | 18W-13N | 24 |
| Lexington Dr. NW&SE | 16W-16N | 14 |
| Lilac Ter. E&W | 16W-16N | 15 |
| Lillian Av. E&W | 18W-15N,18W-16N | 14 |
| Lillian Ln. E&W | 16W-15N | 15 |
| Lincoln Ct. N&S | 17W-15N | 14 |
| Lincoln Ln. N&S | 17W-13N,17W-15N | 24 |
| Lincoln Rd. E&W | 17W-12N | 24 |
| Luther Ln. (Pvt.) N&S | 18W-15N | 14 |
| Lynden Ln. NW&SE | 17W-13N | 24 |
| Lynnwood Av. E&W | 18W-15N,17W-15N | 14 |
| Magnolia St. E&W | 18W-12N,17W-12N | 24 |
| Mallard Ln. N&S | 17W-12N | 14 |
| Maple Ln. N&S | 16W-16N | 15 |
| Maple St. E&W | 18W-13N,17W-13N | 24 |
| Margaret Av. NE&SW | 17W-15N | 14 |
| Marion Rd. E&W | 18W-15N | 14 |
| Marion St. E&W | 18W-15N,17W-15N | 14 |
| Marshall Dr. E&W | 16W-14N | 25 |
| Martin Ln. N&S | 18W-11N | 24 |
| Maude Av. E&W | 18W-15N,17W-15N | 14 |
| Mayfair Rd. E&W | 17W-13N,16W-13N | 24 |
| McKinley Av. N&S | 17W-13N | 24 |
| Meade Ln. E&W | 18W-18N | 14 |
| Michael Manor E&W | 16W-15N | 15 |
| Milida E&W | 17W-16N | 14 |
| Millbrook Ln. N&S | 18W-12N | 24 |
| Miner St. E&W | 18W-14N,16W-14N | 24 |
| Mitchell Av. N&S | 18W-12N,18W-15N | 24 |
| Mitchell Ct. E&W | 18W-15N | 14 |
| Mitchell Dr. N&S | 18W-15N | 14 |
| Moorings Dr. (Pvt.) NS&EW | 17W-12N | 24 |
| Mueller St. E&W | 18W-14N | 24 |
| Mulberry Ct. E&W | 18W-14N | 24 |
| Mulberry Ln. E&W | 16W-16N | 15 |
| Newbury Pl. N&S | 17W-13N | 24 |
| Newport Ct. N&S | 18W-18N | 14 |
| Newport Ln. E&W | 18W-18N | 14 |
| Newport Way (Pvt.) NW&SE | 19W-18N | 14 |
| Nichols E&W | 18W-18N | 14 |
| Normandy Ct. N&S | 16W-15N | 15 |
| Northwest Hwy. NW&SE | 18W-15N,16W-13N | 14 |
| Northwest Tollway NW&SE | 18W-11N,17W-10N | 24 |
| Northwood Ln. E&W | 16W-15N | 15 |
| Noyes St. E&W | 19W-12N,17W-12N | 24 |
| Oakton St. E&W | 18W-15N,16W-15N | 14 |
| Oakwood Dr. N&S | 16W-16N | 15 |
| Old Barn Ln. (Pvt.) E&W | 17W-12N | 24 |
| Olive St. E&W | 18W-15N,16W-15N | 14 |
| Orchard Pl. E&W | 18W-13N | 24 |
| Orchard St. E&W | 18W-13N,17W-13N | 24 |
| Orchid Ln. N&S | 16W-16N | 15 |
| Oxford Ln. E&W | 17W-16N | 14 |
| Page N&S | 17W-17N | 14 |
| Palatine Rd. E&W | 18W-16N,16W-16N | 14 |
| Par Ct. N&S | 18W-18N | 14 |
| Park Pl. NW&SE | 18W-14N | 24 |
| Park St. E&W | 18W-13N,18W-14N | 24 |
| Parkview Av. E&W | 17W-12N | 24 |
| Partridge Ct. N&S | 18W-18N | 14 |
| Partridge Ln. NE&SW | 18W-18N | 14 |
| Patton N&S | 18W-13N,18W-17N | 24 |
| Patton Cir. N&S | 18W-13N | 24 |
| Payton Run NW&SE | 18W-14N | 24 |
| Peachtree Dr. E&W | 16W-16N | 15 |
| Peachtree Ln. E&W | 16W-16N | 15 |
| Peartree Ln. N&S | 16W-14N | 25 |
| Pennsylvania Ct. E&W | 17W-11N | 24 |
| Pheasant Tr. Ct. N&S | 18W-18N | 14 |
| Pheasant Trail Dr. NE&SW | 18W-18N | 14 |
| Pheasant Trail Ln. N&S | 18W-18N | 14 |
| Phelps Av. N&S | 16W-13N,16W-16N | 25 |
| Phelps Ct. E&W | 16W-16N | 15 |
| Pickwick Rd. E&W | 18W-12N | 24 |
| Pine Av. N&S | 17W-12N,17W-15N | 24 |
| Pinetree Dr. N&S | 17W-16N | 14 |
| Plum Grove Cir. E&W | 18W-18N | 14 |
| Plymouth Ct. E&W | 18W-16N | 14 |
| Plymouth Dr. E&W | 18W-16N | 14 |
| Portsmith Ln. NS&EW | 18W-18N | 14 |
| Princeton Av. N&S | 18W-12N,18W-15N | 24 |
| Princeton Ct. N&S | 18W-14N | 24 |
| Prindle Av. N&S | 16W-13N,16W-16N | 25 |
| Proctor Cir. NW&SE | 18W-18N | 14 |
| Pvt. Rd. E&W | 18W-16N | 14 |
| Quail Ct. E&W | 18W-18N | 14 |
| Race Av. N&S | 18W-14N,18W-15N | 24 |
| Radcliff Rd. N&S | 17W-17N | 14 |
| Radford Ct. E&W | 16W-15N | 15 |

| | Grid | Page |
|---|---|---|
| Raleigh Ct. NE&SW | 18W-16N | 14 |
| Raleigh St. NW&SE | 18W-16N | 14 |
| Rammer Av. N&S | 16W-13N,16W-14N | 25 |
| Rand Rd. NW&SE | 18W-16N,17W-15N | 14 |
| Redwood Ln. E&W | 17W-16N | 14 |
| Regency Ct., E. E&W | 16W-14N | 25 |
| Regency Ct., W. E&W | 16W-14N | 25 |
| Regency Dr., E. N&S | 16W-14N | 25 |
| Regency Dr., W. N&S | 16W-14N | 25 |
| Reuter Dr. N&S | 18W-13N,18W-14N | 24 |
| Richmond St. E&W | 18W-16N | 14 |
| Ridge Av. N&S | 18W-12N,18W-18N | 24 |
| Ridge Ct. E&W | 18W-15N | 14 |
| Ridge Dr. NS&EW | 18W-12N | 24 |
| Ridge Rd. E&W | 17W-16N | 14 |
| Roanoke Dr. NW&SE | 18W-16N | 14 |
| Robinhood Ln. NW&SE | 16W-15N | 15 |
| Rockwell St. E&W | 18W-13N,16W-13N | 24 |
| Rolling Ln. N&S | 16W-15N | 15 |
| Roosevelt Av. N&S | 17W-13N | 24 |
| Rosehill Dr. E&W | 16W-16N | 15 |
| Rt. 53 N&S | 18W-15N,18W-17N | 14 |
| Rt. 58 E&W | 18W-12N,17W-12N | 24 |
| Rt. 62 NW&SE | 18W-11N,17W-11N | 24 |
| Rt. 68 E&W | 18W-17N | 14 |
| Russell Ct. E&W | 19W-12N | 24 |
| Russetwood Dr. NW&SE | 16W-15N | 15 |
| Ryan Ct. E&W | 17W-12N | 24 |
| Salem Av. N&S | 18W-13N,18W-14N | 24 |
| Salem Blvd. NW&SE | 18W-15N | 14 |
| Salem Dr. N&S | 18W-18N | 14 |
| Salem Ln. N&S | 18W-12N | 24 |
| Schaefer N&S | 18W-18N | 14 |
| Schoenbeck Rd. N&S | 16W-16N | 15 |
| Scottsvale Ln. N&S | 16W-14N | 25 |
| Seeger Rd. E&W | 18W-11N,17W-11N | 24 |
| Shady Way E&W | 17W-11N | 24 |
| Shag Bark N&S | 17W-11N | 24 |
| Shenandoah Dr. N&S | 18W-16N | 14 |
| Sherwood Rd. NW&SE | 16W-15N | 15 |
| Shiloh Dr. E&W | 18W-16N | 14 |
| Shirra Ct. E&W | 18W-16N | 14 |
| Shure Dr. E&W | 18W-17N | 14 |
| Sigwalt St. E&W | 18W-14N,17W-14N | 24 |
| Somerset Ct. N&S | 17W-18N | 14 |
| Somerset Ln. N&S | 18W-14N | 24 |
| South St. E&W | 18W-13N | 24 |
| Spring Ridge Dr. NS&EW | 19W-18N | 14 |
| Spruce Tr. N&S | 17W-16N | 14 |
| St. James Pl. N&S | 18W-14N | 24 |
| St. James St. E&W | 18W-14N,16W-14N | 24 |
| Stanford Ln. N&S | 17W-17N | 14 |
| Stanton Ct. N&S | 17W-16N | 14 |
| Stillwater Rd. NE&SW | 16W-16N | 15 |
| Stratford Rd. N&S | 16W-13N,16W-17N | 25 |
| Stuart Dr. N&S | 17W-16N,16W-16N | 14 |
| Suffield Ct. E&W | 18W-16N | 14 |
| Suffield Dr. E&W | 17W-16N,16W-16N | 14 |
| Sunset Dr. E&W | 17W-16N | 14 |
| Sunset Ter. E&W | 18W-14N | 24 |
| Sunset Tr. E&W | 16W-14N | 25 |
| Surrey Park Ln. NW&SE | 19W-12N | 24 |
| Surrey Ridge Dr. NE&SW | 18W-12N | 24 |
| Talbot St. E&W | 17W-15N | 14 |
| Tanglewood Dr. NS&EW | 17W-17N,17W-18N | 14 |
| Techny Rd. E&W | 18W-16N,17W-16N | 14 |
| Terramere Av. NS&EW | 18W-18N | 14 |
| Thomas Av. E&W | 18W-15N,17W-15N | 14 |
| Thorntree Ter. NE&SW | 17W-16N | 14 |
| Three States Blvd. N&S | 17W-17N | 14 |
| Thurston Pl. NW&SE | 18W-18N | 14 |
| Tonne Rd. N&S | 17W-11N,17W-12N | 24 |
| Towne Blvd. NW&SE | 16W-16N | 15 |
| U.S. Route 12 NW&SE | 18W-17N,16W-15N | 14 |
| U.S. Route 14 NW&SE | 18W-14N,16W-13N | 24 |
| University Dr. E&W | 18W-17N,17W-17N | 14 |
| Vail Av. N&S | 18W-12N,18W-15N | 24 |
| Valley Ln. E&W | 17W-16N | 14 |
| Vargo Ln. E&W | 17W-16N | 14 |
| Ventura Dr. NS&EW | 18W-18N | 14 |
| Verde Av. N&S | 18W-16N | 14 |
| Verde Dr. N&S | 18W-16N | 14 |
| Viator Ct. NS&EW | 17W-15N | 14 |
| Victoria Ln. E&W | 18W-12N | 24 |
| Villa Verde Dr. E&W | 18W-17N | 14 |
| Village Dr. (Pvt.) N&S | 18W-15N | 14 |
| Vine St. E&W | 18W-14N | 24 |
| Vista Rd. N&S | 17W-17N | 14 |
| Voltz Dr. NS&EW | 17W-17N | 14 |
| W. Whiting Ln. E&W | 18W-18N | 14 |
| Walden Ln. E&W | 16W-16N | 15 |
| Walker Ln. NS&EW | 17W-17N | 14 |
| Walnut NS&EW | 18W-12N,18W-18N | 24 |
| Walnut Ct. NE&SW | 18W-16N | 14 |
| Warwick Ct. E&W | 16W-15N | 15 |
| Waterman Av. N&S | 16W-13N,16W-16N | 25 |
| Watling Rd. NE&SW | 18W-15N | 14 |
| Waverly Ct. NS&EW | 16W-18N,18W-16N | 15 |
| Waverly Dr. NW&SE | 17W-16N,16W-16N | 14 |
| Waverly Pl. E&W | 17W-16N | 14 |
| Waverly Rd. E&W | 17W-16N | 14 |
| Weston Dr. E&W | 18W-18N | 14 |
| Wheeler St. E&W | 17W-16N | 14 |
| White Oak St. E&W | 18W-12N,17W-12N | 24 |
| Whitehall Dr. E&W | 18W-18N | 14 |
| Wilke Rd. N&S | 19W-18N,18W-18N | 14 |
| Wilke Rd. N&S | 19W-12N,19W-18N | 24 |
| Williamsburg St. N&S | 18W-16N | 14 |
| Willow St. E&W | 18W-14N,17W-14N | 24 |
| Wilshire Ln. NS&EW | 16W-13N,16W-17N | 25 |
| Windham Ct. N&S | 17W-16N | 14 |
| Windsor Dr. NS&EW | 16W-13N,17W-17N | 25 |
| Wing St. E&W | 18W-14N,16W-14N | 24 |
| Woodbury Dr. E&W | 16W-16N | 15 |
| Woodford Pl. E&W | 17W-13N | 24 |
| Woodland Ln. N&S | 16W-16N | 15 |
| Woodridge Ln. N&S | 17W-14N | 24 |
| Woods Dr. NS&EW | 18W-17N | 14 |
| Yale Av. N&S | 18W-13N,18W-18N | 24 |
| Yale Av. N&S | 19W-12N | 24 |
| Yale Ct. E&W | 18W-15N | 14 |
| Yarmouth Ct. NE&SW | 16W-15N | 15 |

## Barrington*
**(Also see Lake County)**

| | Grid | Page |
|---|---|---|
| Balmoral Ln. E&W | 24W-18N | 12 |
| Barrington Point E&W | 25W-18N | 12 |
| Barrington Rd. N&S | 25W-17N,25W-18N | 12 |
| Bellingham Dr. E&W | 24W-18N | 12 |
| Braeside Pl. E&W | 25W-18N | 12 |
| Bristol Dr. NW&SE | 25W-18N | 12 |
| Concord Ln. NW&SE | 25W-18N | 12 |
| Concord Pl. N&S | 25W-18N | 12 |
| Cook St. N&S | 25W-18N,25W-20N | 12 |
| Coolidge Av. E&W | 25W-18N | 12 |
| Country Dr. N&S | 26W-18N | 11 |
| Division St. N&S | 25W-18N | 12 |
| Dundee Av. N&S | 26W-18N | 11 |
| Dundee Rd. E&W | 25W-17N | 12 |
| Eastern Av. N&S | 25W-18N | 12 |
| Ela Rd. N&S | 24W-18N,24W-20N | 12 |
| Fairfield Dr. NS&EW | 24W-18N | 12 |
| Forest Av. N&S | 26W-18N | 11 |
| George Av. N&S | 25W-18N | 12 |
| Glendale Av. N&S | 25W-18N | 12 |
| Grove Av. N&S | 25W-18N,26W-18N | 12 |
| Hager Av. N&S | 26W-18N,26W-20N | 11 |
| Harriet Ln. E&W | 25W-18N | 12 |
| Heath Ct. E&W | 24W-18N | 12 |
| Highland Av. N&S | 25W-18N | 12 |
| Hill St. E&W | 25W-18N | 12 |
| Hillcrest Av. E&W | 25W-18N | 12 |
| Hillside Av. E&W | 26W-18N,25W-18N | 11 |
| Hillside Ct. N&S | 24W-18N | 12 |
| Hough St. N&S | 25W-18N | 12 |
| Illinois St. E&W | 25W-18N | 12 |
| Kainer Av. N&S | 25W-18N | 12 |
| Kings Row N&S | 24W-18N | 12 |
| Lageschulte St. N&S | 26W-18N | 11 |
| Lake St. E&W | 26W-18N,25W-18N | 11 |
| Lakewood Ct. E&W | 24W-18N | 12 |
| Lakewood Dr. NS&EW | 24W-18N | 12 |
| Lill St. N&S | 25W-18N | 12 |
| Lincoln Av. E&W | 25W-18N | 12 |
| Meadow Ln. N&S | 25W-18N | 12 |
| Monument Av. E&W | 25W-18N | 12 |
| Newport Ln. E&W | 25W-17N | 12 |
| Northwest Hwy. NW&SE | 24W-18N | 12 |
| Oak Ridge Cir. NS&EW | 24W-18N | 12 |
| Oak Ridge Rd. E&W | 24W-18N | 12 |
| Oakland Ct. NW&SE | 24W-18N | 12 |
| Oakland Dr. NS&EW | 24W-18N | 12 |
| Old Mill Ct. E&W | 24W-18N | 12 |
| Old Mill Rd. N&S | 24W-18N | 12 |
| Orchard Dr. N&S | 26W-18N | 11 |
| Park Av. NW&SE | 25W-18N | 12 |
| Park Barrington Dr. NS&EW | 25W-17N | 12 |
| Park Barrington Way NS&EW | 25W-17N | 12 |
| Park Rd. E&W | 23W-18N | 12 |
| Prairie Av. N&S | 25W-18N | 12 |
| Private Rd. (Pvt.) NS&EW | 25W-17N | 12 |
| Queens Cove E&W | 25W-18N | 12 |
| Red Barn Ln. NS&EW | 24W-18N | 12 |
| Rt. 59 N&S | 25W-18N,25W-20N | 12 |
| Rt. 68 E&W | 25W-17N | 12 |
| Russell St. E&W | 25W-18N | 12 |
| S. Grove Av. NW&SE | 25W-17N | 12 |
| Shady Ln. E&W | 26W-18N | 11 |
| Skyline Dr. NE&SW | 25W-18N | 12 |
| South St. E&W | 25W-18N | 12 |
| South Valley Rd. NW&SE | 24W-18N | 12 |
| Spring St. N&S | 25W-18N | 12 |
| Station St. E&W | 26W-18N,25W-18N | 11 |
| Sturtz St. E&W | 25W-18N | 12 |
| Summit St. N&S | 25W-18N | 12 |
| Sunset Rd. NE&SW | 26W-18N | 11 |
| Tower Rd. E&W | 26W-18N | 11 |
| Tudor Dr. N&S | 24W-18N | 12 |
| Walton St. N&S | 25W-18N | 12 |
| Warwick Av. E&W | 25W-18N | 12 |
| Westwood Dr. E&W | 26W-18N | 11 |
| Wisconsin Av. E&W | 25W-18N | 12 |
| Wool St. N&S | 25W-18N | 12 |
| Wyngate Dr. NS&EW | 24W-18N | 12 |

## Barrington Hills*
**(Also see Kane, Lake and McHenry Counties)**

| | Grid | Page |
|---|---|---|
| Aberdeen Dr. E&W | 28W-18N | 11 |
| Algonquin Rd. NW&SE | 28W-16N | 11 |
| Barrington Hills Rd. N&S | 28W-18N | 11 |
| Bartlett Rd. NE&SW | 27W-16N,26W-17N | 11 |
| Bateman Circle NS&EW | 30W-18N | 10 |
| Bateman Rd. N&S | 30W-16N,30W-18N | 10 |
| Bateman Rd. NS&EW | 30W-18N | 10 |
| Brinker Rd. N&S | 28W-16N,27W-18N | 11 |
| Butternut Rd. NS&EW | 28W-18N | 11 |
| Caesar Dr. N&S | 27W-18N | 11 |
| Conroy Ct. E&W | 28W-15N | 21 |
| Crabapple Dr. N&S | 28W-18N | 11 |
| Crawling Stone NE&SW | 30W-18N | 10 |
| Creekside Ln. NS&EW | 28W-15N | 21 |
| Dales Rd. NS&EW | 27W-17N | 11 |
| Dana Ln. E&W | 27W-18N | 11 |
| Deepwood Ct. E&W | 30W-18N | 10 |
| Deepwood Rd. NW&SE | 30W-18N | 10 |
| Donlea Rd. NE&SW | 28W-18N | 11 |
| Dundee Ln. N&S | 26W-17N,27W-16N | 10 |
| Dundee Rd. NE&SW | 30W-15N,26W-17N | 20 |
| Eagle Point Dr. NS&EW | 30W-15N | 20 |
| East Ln. NE&SW | 27W-17N | 11 |
| Far Hills Rd. NS&EW | 30W-18N | 10 |
| Fernwood Dr. E&W | 30W-16N | 10 |
| Fernwood Ln. E&W | 30W-16N | 10 |
| Goose Lake Dr. E&W | 28W-17N,27W-17N | 11 |
| Hart Hills Rd. E&W | 26W-18N | 11 |
| Harts Rd. N&S | 27W-18N | 11 |
| Hawley Rd. NE&SW | 27W-17N,26W-17N | 11 |
| Hawthorne NW&SE | 26W-17N | 11 |
| Hawthorne Ln. NW&SE | 27W-17N | 11 |
| Hawthorne Rd. NE&SW | 26W-17N | 11 |
| Healy Rd. NE&SW | 30W-15N,29W-15N | 20 |
| Helm Rd. E&W | 30W-17N | 10 |
| Heron Ln. N&S | 27W-17N | 11 |
| Hills Rd. NE&SW | 27W-17N | 11 |
| Honey Cut Rd. E&W | 27W-17N | 11 |
| King Rd. N&S | 30W-15N | 20 |
| Lakeview Ln. NS&EW | 26W-17N | 11 |
| Leeds Dr. E&W | 28W-18N | 11 |
| Long Meadow Ct. NE&SW | 30W-16N | 10 |
| Long Meadow Dr. E&W | 30W-16N | 10 |
| Marmon Ln. E&W | 26W-18N | 11 |
| Middlebury E&W | 30W-18N | 10 |
| Oakdene Rd. NS&EW | 26W-18N | 11 |
| Otis Rd. E&W | 28W-18N,26W-18N | 11 |
| Overlook Rd. NS&EW | 30W-18N | 10 |
| Palatine Rd. E&W | 26W-16N | 11 |
| Penny Rd. E&W | 30W-15N | 20 |
| Potter Ln. NW&SE | 30W-15N | 20 |
| Private Rd. E&W | 28W-18N,27W-18N | 11 |
| Private Rd. N&S | 28W-16N | 11 |
| Rebecca Dr. E&W | 28W-15N | 21 |
| Rock River Rd. N&S | 29W-21N | 56 |
| Rolling Hills Dr. NS&EW | 30W-16N | 10 |
| Round Barn Rd. E&W | 27W-17N | 11 |
| Rt. 59 NE&SW | 28W-15N,26W-17N | 21 |
| Rt. 62 NW&SE | 30W-18N,27W-16N | 10 |
| Rt. 68 E&W | 30W-15N,28W-16N | 11 |
| Sandlewood Dr. NS&EW | 26W-18N | 11 |
| Sarah Ln. NE&SW | 25W-17N | 12 |
| Springwood Ln. N&S | 29W-16N | 10 |
| Sutton Rd. NW&SE | 29W-18N | 10 |
| Sutton Rd. NW&SE | 28W-13N,29W-18N | 21 |
| Tamarack Ln. NS&EW | 28W-15N | 21 |
| Three Lakes Rd. N&S | 27W-18N | 11 |
| Tricia Ln. E&W | 28W-15N | 21 |
| Valley Dr. N&S | 28W-18N | 11 |
| West Ln. E&W | 27W-17N | 11 |
| Wichman Rd. E&W | 28W-14N | 21 |
| Wichman Rd. NS&EW | 29W-14N | 20 |
| Windrush Ln. NE&SW | 26W-18N | 11 |
| Wood Rock Rd. NE&SW | 30W-18N | 10 |
| Woodcreek Rd. N&S | 29W-15N | 20 |

## Barrington Township

| | Grid | Page |
|---|---|---|
| Algonquin Rd. NW&SE | 26W-15N | 21 |
| Bartlett Rd. N&S | 28W-13N | 21 |
| Boland Dr. E&W | 27W-14N | 21 |
| Bradwell Cir. N&S | 25W-16N | 12 |
| Cook St. N&S | 25W-17N,25W-18N | 12 |
| Division St. N&S | 25W-17N,25W-18N | 12 |
| George Av. N&S | 25W-17N,25W-18N | 12 |
| Grove Av. N&S | 27W-17N,25W-18N | 11 |
| Harvard Av. E&W | 25W-18N | 12 |
| Old Higgins Rd. NW&SE | 30W-14N | 20 |
| Palatine Rd. E&W | 26W-16N | 11 |
| Prairie Av. N&S | 25W-17N,25W-18N | 12 |
| Princeton Av. E&W | 25W-17N | 12 |
| Stover Rd. N&S | 27W-15N | 21 |
| Summit St. N&S | 25W-17N,25W-18N | 12 |
| Yale Av. E&W | 25W-18N | 12 |

## Bartlett*
**(Also see Du Page County)**

| | Grid | Page |
|---|---|---|
| Acorn Ct. E&W | 28W-8N | 31 |
| Ann Ct. E&W | 28W-8N | 31 |
| Aspen Ct. N&S | 29W-9N | 30 |
| Bartlett Av. E&W | 29W-8N,28W-8N | 30 |
| Bay Tree Dr. E&W | 29W-9N | 30 |
| Bayberry Dr. E&W | 29W-8N | 30 |
| Baytree Dr. NE&SW | 29W-9N | 30 |
| Berteau Av. N&S | 28W-8N | 31 |
| Betty Ct. N&S | 28W-8N | 31 |
| Bryce Ct. E&W | 29W-8N | 30 |
| Burton Dr. N&S | 32W-8N | 30 |
| Butler Dr. NW&SE | 32W-8N | 30 |
| Candleridge Ct. E&W | 28W-8N | 31 |
| Capalino N&S | 31W-8N | 30 |
| Cardinal Dr. N&S | 31W-9N | 30 |
| Carroll Way* E&W | 31W-8N | 30 |
| Cecil Ct. NW&SE | 29W-8N | 30 |
| Cedarfield Dr. N&S | 32W-8N | 30 |
| Chase Av. N&S | 28W-8N | 31 |
| Chestnut Ct. E&W | 29W-9N | 30 |
| Church Ct. E&W | 29W-8N | 30 |
| Cobblewood Ln. E&W | 28W-8N | 31 |
| Crab Tree Ln. NS&EW | 29W-9N | 30 |
| Crescent Ct. E&W | 28W-8N | 31 |
| Crest Av. N&S | 28W-8N | 31 |
| Crystals Ln. N&S | 30W-8N | 30 |
| Daniel Ct. N&S | 28W-8N | 31 |
| Dave Dr. N&S | 31W-8N | 30 |
| David Ct. E&W | 28W-8N | 31 |
| Deere Park Cir. NS&EW | 29W-9N | 30 |
| Devon Ave. E&W | 29W-8N,28W-8N | 30 |
| Dogleg Ln. NE&SW | 31W-9N | 30 |
| Donna Ct. E&W | 28W-8N | 31 |
| Doral Dr. NE&SW | 29W-8N,29W-9N | 30 |
| Eastern Av. N&S | 28W-8N | 31 |
| Elizabeth Ct. N&S | 28W-8N | 31 |
| Elmwood Ln. E&W | 30W-8N | 30 |
| Elroy Av. N&S | 28W-8N | 31 |
| Emil Ct. N&S | 28W-8N | 31 |
| Ford Ln. E&W | 29W-8N | 30 |
| Golfer's Ln. NE&SW | 31W-9N | 30 |
| Golfview Dr. E&W | 31W-9N,30W-9N | 30 |
| Greenfield Ct. E&W | 28W-8N | 31 |
| Hackberry Ct. E&W | 29W-9N | 30 |
| Hale Av. N&S | 28W-8N | 31 |
| Hazelnut Ct. N&S | 29W-9N | 30 |
| Helen Dr. N&S | 31W-8N | 30 |
| Hickory Av. N&S | 29W-8N | 30 |
| Hillcrest Ln. E&W | 28W-8N | 31 |
| Holly Dr. E&W | 29W-8N | 30 |
| Honey Locust Ct. E&W | 29W-9N | 30 |
| Ingalton Av. N&S | 30W-8N | 30 |
| James Dr. N&S | 31W-8N | 30 |
| Jessica Ln. E&W | 29W-8N | 30 |
| Joan Ct. E&W | 28W-8N | 31 |
| Jodi Ln. N&S | 30W-8N | 30 |
| Jones Dr. N&S | 31W-8N | 30 |
| Joseph Dr. N&S | 31W-8N | 30 |
| Judith Ct. N&S | 28W-8N | 31 |
| Kathy Ln. E&W | 29W-8N | 30 |
| Knoll Crest Dr. N&S | 31W-9N | 30 |
| Knollwood Ln. E&W | 30W-8N | 30 |
| La Costa Av. E&W | 29W-8N | 30 |
| Lake St. E&W | 29W-9N,28W-8N | 30 |
| Laurie Ln. N&S | 31W-8N | 30 |
| Lela Ln. N&S | 29W-8N | 30 |
| Little John Ct. N&S | 29W-8N | 30 |
| Lucille Ct. E&W | 28W-8N | 31 |
| Mable Ln. N&S | 31W-8N | 30 |
| Main St. N&S | 29W-8N | 30 |
| Mallard Ct. NE&SW | 28W-8N | 31 |
| Maplewood Ln. E&W | 30W-8N | 30 |
| Marcia Ct. E&W | 28W-8N | 31 |
| Marion Av. N&S | 28W-8N | 31 |
| Mary Ct. N&S | 28W-8N | 31 |
| Monarch Birch Ct. E&W | 30W-9N | 30 |
| Monarch Birch Ln. E&W | 30W-9N | 30 |
| Morse Av. E&W | 29W-8N,28W-8N | 30 |
| Mulberry Ct. N&S | 28W-8N | 31 |
| Newport Ln. N&S | 28W-8N | 31 |
| Nina Ln. NS&EW | 31W-8N | 30 |
| North Av. E&W | 29W-8N,28W-8N | 30 |
| Oak Av. N&S | 29W-8N | 30 |
| Oakbrook Ct. N&S | 29W-8N | 30 |
| Oakmont Dr. N&S | 29W-8N | 30 |
| Oakwood Dr. N&S | 29W-8N | 30 |
| Olive Pkwy. E&W | 29W-9N | 30 |
| Oliver Valley N&S | 29W-8N | 30 |
| Oneida Av. E&W | 29W-8N,28W-8N | 30 |
| Park Pl. E&W | 30W-8N | 30 |
| Patricia Ln. N&S | 29W-8N | 30 |
| Pebble Beach Ln. N&S | 29W-8N,29W-9N | 30 |
| Persimmon Ct. E&W | 30W-9N | 30 |

| | Grid | Page |
|---|---|---|
| Persimmon Ln. E&W | 30W-9N | 30 |
| Peter Ct. E&W | 28W-8N | 31 |
| Philip Dr. NE&SW | 30W-9N | 30 |
| Pinoak Dr. N&S | 29W-9N | 30 |
| Preserve Tr. E&W | 30W-8N | 30 |
| Prospect Av. N&S | 28W-7N,28W-8N | 31 |
| Queens Pkwy. E&W | 29W-9N | 30 |
| Railroad Av. E&W | 29W-8N | 30 |
| Ranier St. NE&SW | 32W-8N | 30 |
| Red Bud Ct. E&W | 29W-9N | 30 |
| Red Oak Ct. E&W | 29W-9N | 30 |
| Red Oak Dr. NW&SE | 29W-9N | 30 |
| Rich Dr. N&S | 31W-8N | 30 |
| Rich's Ln. N&S | 31W-8N | 30 |
| Rita Ct. N&S | 28W-8N | 31 |
| Robert Ct. E&W | 28W-8N | 31 |
| Rose Ln. N&S | 31W-8N | 30 |
| Roslara Ct. N&S | 29W-8N | 30 |
| Rt. 59 N&S | 30W-8N | 30 |
| Scarlet Ct. N&S | 31W-9N | 30 |
| Snow Drift Cir. E&W | 30W-9N | 30 |
| Snow Drift Ct.* E&W | 30W-9N | 30 |
| Southfield Dr.* | 32W-8N | 30 |
| Spaulding Av. E&W | 31W-9N,30W-9N | 30 |
| Spaulding Rd. | 30W-9N | 30 |
| Spitzer St. N&S | 31W-8N | 30 |
| Stephani N&S | 28W-8N | 31 |
| Sterling Ct. E&W | 28W-8N | 31 |
| Taige Av. N&S | 28W-8N | 31 |
| Tanoak Ct. N&S | 29W-8N | 30 |
| Taylor Av. E&W | 28W-8N | 31 |
| Thomas Ct. N&S | 28W-8N | 31 |
| Thorn Tree Ct. NE&SW | 28W-8N | 31 |
| Timber Ridge Dr. N&S | 29W-9N | 30 |
| Topaz Ln. NW&SE | 31W-9N | 30 |
| Trontman Dr.* E&W | 31W-8N | 30 |
| Valley N&S | 29W-8N | 30 |
| Wayne Ct. N&S | 28W-8N | 31 |
| West Bartlett Rd. E&W | 30W-8N,29W-8N | 30 |
| Western Av. N&S | 29W-9N | 30 |
| White Oak Ln. NS&EW | 29W-9N | 30 |
| Williamsburg Dr. N&S | 29W-8N | 30 |
| Wilmington Dr. NW&SE | 28W-8N | 31 |
| 1st Av. E&W | 31W-8N | 30 |
| 2nd Av. E&W | 31W-8N | 30 |
| 3rd Av. E&W | 31W-8N | 30 |
| 4th Av. E&W | 31W-8N | 30 |
| 5th Av. E&W | 31W-8N | 30 |
| 6th Av. E&W | 31W-8N | 30 |
| 7th Av. E&W | 31W-8N | 30 |
| 8th Av. E&W | 31W-8N | 30 |
| 9th Av. E&W | 31W-8N | 30 |
| 10th Av. E&W | 31W-8N | 30 |
| 11th Av. E&W | 31W-8N | 30 |
| 12th Av. E&W | 31W-8N | 30 |

**Bedford Park**

| | Grid | Page |
|---|---|---|
| Belt Cir. N&S | 8W-7S | 59 |
| Central N&S | 7W-8S | 59 |
| Harlem St. N&S | 8W-7S | 59 |
| Interstate 55 SW&NE | 11W-7S | 58 |
| Laramie N&S | 6W-7S | 60 |
| Lavergne N&S | 6W-7S | 60 |
| Leamington N&S | 6W-8S | 60 |
| Leclaire N&S | 6W-7S | 60 |
| Linder N&S | 6W-8S | 60 |
| Lockwood N&S | 6W-8S | 60 |
| Mason N&S | 7W-8S | 60 |
| Massasoit N&S | 7W-8S | 60 |
| Meade N&S | 7W-8S | 60 |
| Narragansett N&S | 8W-8S | 59 |
| Nashville Av. N&S | 8W-7S | 59 |
| New England St. N&S | 8N-7S | 59 |
| Oak Park N&S | 8W-8S | 59 |
| Rt. 171 SW&NE | 10W-7S | 59 |
| Rt. 50 N&S | 6W-7S | 60 |
| Sayre N&S | 8W-6S,8W-7S | 59 |
| 65th E&W | 9W-7S | 59 |
| 65th Pl. E&W | 9W-7S | 59 |
| 66th E&W | 9W-7S,6W-7S | 59 |
| 66th Pl. E&W | 9W-7S,6W-7S | 59 |
| 67th E&W | 6W-7S | 60 |
| 68th E&W | 8W-7S | 60 |
| 70th Pl. E&W | 8W-7S | 59 |
| 71st E&W | 11W-7S,8W-7S | 58 |
| 71st Pl. E&W | 8W-8S | 59 |
| 72nd E&W | 6W-8S | 60 |
| 72nd Pl. E&W | 8W-8S | 59 |
| 73rd E&W | 8W-8S,6W-8S | 59 |
| 73rd Pl. E&W | 8W-8S | 59 |
| 74th E&W | 8W-8S,6W-8S | 59 |
| 74th Pl. E&W | 8W-8S | 59 |
| 75th E&W | 6W-8S | 60 |
| 77th E&W | 8W-8S | 59 |
| 77th Av. N&S | 9W-7S | 59 |
| 77th Ct. N&S | 9W-7S | 59 |
| 78th Av. N&S | 9W-7S | 59 |

**Bellwood**

| | Grid | Page |
|---|---|---|
| Adams E&W | 12W-0S | 46 |
| Bellwood N&S | 12W-0S,12W-0N | 46 |

| | Grid | Page |
|---|---|---|
| Bohland N&S | 12W-0S,12W-0N | 46 |
| Butterfield Rd. E&W | 12W-0N | 46 |
| Castle Dr. E&W | 13W-0N | 46 |
| Center N&S | 13W-0N | 46 |
| Congress E&W | 12W-0S | 46 |
| Eastern N&S | 12W-0N | 46 |
| Erie E&W | 13W-0N | 46 |
| Frederick N&S | 12W-0N | 46 |
| Gladys E&W | 12W-0S | 46 |
| Glos E&W | 12W-0S | 46 |
| Grant E&W | 12W-0N | 46 |
| Jackson E&W | 12W-0S | 46 |
| Korel E&W | 12W-0N | 46 |
| Linden N&S | 12W-0S,12W-0N | 46 |
| Lyman E&W | 12W-0S | 46 |
| Madison E&W | 12W-0N | 46 |
| Marshall N&S | 12W-0N,12W-0S | 46 |
| Marshall E&W | 12W-0S | 46 |
| Miami Rd. E&W | 12W-0N | 46 |
| Monroe E&W | 12W-0S | 46 |
| Morris N&S | 12W-0N | 46 |
| Oak E&W | 12W-0N | 46 |
| Park Ct. E&W | 12W-0N | 46 |
| Pusheck Rd. N&S | 12W-0S | 46 |
| Railroad E&W | 12W-0N | 46 |
| Randolph E&W | 13W-0N | 46 |
| Rice N&S | 12W-0S,12W-0N | 46 |
| St. Charles Pl. E&W | 12W-0N | 46 |
| St. Paul E&W | 12W-0N | 46 |
| Twining E&W | 13W-0N | 46 |
| Van Buren E&W | 12W-0S | 46 |
| Warren E&W | 12W-0N | 46 |
| Wilcox E&W | 12W-0S | 46 |
| Zuelke Dr. N&S | 12W-0N | 46 |
| 22nd N&S | 11W-0S | 47 |
| 23rd N&S | 11W-0S | 47 |
| 24th N&S | 11W-0S | 47 |
| 25th N&S | 12W-0N | 46 |
| 26th N&S | 12W-0N | 46 |
| 27th N&S | 12W-0N | 46 |
| 28th N&S | 12W-0N | 46 |
| 29th N&S | 12W-0N | 46 |
| 30th N&S | 12W-0S,12W-0N | 46 |
| 31st N&S | 12W-0S,12W-0N | 46 |
| 32nd N&S | 12W-0S,12W-0N | 46 |
| 42nd N&S | 13W-0N | 46 |
| 43rd N&S | 13W-0N | 46 |
| 44th N&S | 13W-0N | 46 |
| 45th N&S | 13W-0N | 46 |
| 46th N&S | 13W-0N | 46 |
| 47th N&S | 13W-0N | 46 |
| 48th N&S | 13W-0N | 46 |
| 51st N&S | 13W-0N | 46 |
| 52nd N&S | 13W-0N | 46 |

**Berkeley**

| | Grid | Page |
|---|---|---|
| Albin Ter. E&W | 14W-0N | 46 |
| Arthur N&S | 14W-0S,14W-1N | 46 |
| Ashbel N&S | 14W-0N | 46 |
| Atwood N&S | 14W-0S,14W-0N | 46 |
| Bohlander E&W | 14W-0N | 46 |
| Burr Oak E&W | 14W-0N | 46 |
| Calvin N&S | 14W-0S | 46 |
| Chicago N&S | 14W-0N | 46 |
| Coolidge N&S | 14W-0N | 46 |
| Electric E&W | 14W-0N | 46 |
| Elm E&W | 14W-0N | 46 |
| Harding N&S | 14W-0N | 46 |
| Hawthorne E&W | 14W-0N | 46 |
| Herber N&S | 14W-0S,14W-1N | 46 |
| High N&S | 14W-0S | 46 |
| Hillside N&S | 14W-0N | 46 |
| Howard N&S | 14W-0N | 46 |
| Huron E&W | 14W-0N | 46 |
| Interstate 294 N&S | 14W-1N | 46 |
| Irving N&S | 14W-0N | 46 |
| KubaRose E&W | 14W-0N | 46 |
| Lee N&S | 13W-0N | 46 |
| Lind N&S | 14W-0N | 46 |
| Maple E&W | 14W-0N | 46 |
| McDermott E&W | 14W-1N | 46 |
| Morris N&S | 13W-0N | 46 |
| Murray Dr. E&W | 14W-1N | 46 |
| Park E&W | 14W-1N | 46 |
| Prospect E&W | 14W-0N | 46 |
| Proviso E&W | 14W-1N | 46 |
| Rhode N&S | 14W-0N | 46 |
| Ridge E&W | 14W-0N | 46 |
| School N&S | 14W-0N | 46 |
| Speechley N&S | 13W-0N | 46 |
| Spencer N&S | 14W-0N | 46 |
| St. Charles E&W | 13W-1N | 46 |
| Sunnyside Dr. N&S | 14W-0N | 46 |
| Superior E&W | 14W-0N | 46 |
| Taft N&S | 14W-0S,14W-1N | 46 |
| Victoria N&S | 14W-0N | 46 |

**Berwyn**

| | Grid | Page |
|---|---|---|
| Clarence N&S | 8W-2S,8W-1S | 54 |
| Clinton N&S | 8W-3S,8W-1S | 54 |
| Cuyler N&S | 7W-3S,7W-1S | 54 |
| East N&S | 8W-3S,8W-1S | 54 |
| Elmwood N&S | 8W-2S,8W-1S | 54 |
| Euclid N&S | 8W-2S,8W-1S | 54 |
| Fairfield N&S | 8W-3S | 54 |
| Grove N&S | 8W-3S,8W-3S | 54 |
| Gunderson N&S | 8W-2S,8W-1S | 54 |
| Harvey N&S | 7W-3S,7W-1S | 54 |
| Highland N&S | 7W-3S,7W-1S | 54 |

| | Grid | Page |
|---|---|---|
| Home N&S | 8W-3S,8W-1S | 54 |
| Kenilworth N&S | 8W-3S,8W-1S | 54 |
| Lombard N&S | 7W-3S,7W-1S | 54 |
| Maple N&S | 8W-3S,8W-1S | 54 |
| Oak Park N&S | 8W-3S,8W-1S | 54 |
| Park N&S | 7W-3S | 54 |
| Ridgeland N&S | 8W-3S,8W-1S | 54 |
| Riverside Dr. N&S | 8W-2S | 54 |
| Rt. 43 N&S | 8W-3S | 54 |
| Scoville N&S | 8W-2S,8W-1S | 54 |
| Sinclair E&W | 8W-3S | 54 |
| Stanley E&W | 8W-3S | 54 |
| Wenonah N&S | 8W-3S,8W-1S | 54 |
| Wesley N&S | 8W-2S,8W-1S | 54 |
| Windsor E&W | 8W-3S | 54 |
| Wisconsin N&S | 8W-3S,8W-1S | 54 |
| 13th E&W | 8W-1S | 54 |
| 14th E&W | 8W-1S | 54 |
| 15th E&W | 8W-1S | 54 |
| 16th E&W | 8W-1S | 54 |
| 18th E&W | 8W-1S | 54 |
| 19th E&W | 8W-1S,7W-1S | 54 |
| 21st E&W | 8W-2S | 54 |
| 23rd E&W | 8W-2S | 54 |
| 24th E&W | 8W-2S | 54 |
| 25th E&W | 8W-2S | 54 |
| 26th E&W | 8W-2S | 54 |
| 26th Pkwy. E&W | 8W-2S | 54 |
| 27th E&W | 8W-2S | 54 |
| 27th Pl. E&W | 8W-2S | 54 |
| 28th E&W | 8W-2S | 54 |
| 28th Pl. E&W | 8W-2S | 54 |
| 29th E&W | 8W-2S,7W-2S | 54 |
| 29th Pl. E&W | 8W-2S | 54 |
| 30th E&W | 8W-2S | 54 |
| 30th Pl. E&W | 8W-2S | 54 |
| 32nd E&W | 8W-3S,7W-3S | 54 |
| 33rd E&W | 8W-3S,7W-3S | 54 |
| 34th E&W | 8W-3S | 54 |
| 35th E&W | 8W-3S,7W-3S | 54 |
| 36th E&W | 8W-3S | 54 |
| 37th E&W | 8W-3S | 54 |
| 38th E&W | 8W-3S | 54 |

**Bloom Township**

| | Grid | Page |
|---|---|---|
| Alice Av. N&S | 3E-26S | 95 |
| Arnett St. N&S | 1E-24S | 94 |
| Ashland Av. N&S | 1W-27S,1W-26S | 93 |
| Audrey NW&SE | 4W-25S | 92 |
| Baltimore N&S | 3E-25S,3E-24S | 95 |
| Batrack Ct. E&W | 3E-25S | 95 |
| Blackstone Av. N&S | 1E-26S,1E-23S | 94 |
| Brandon Av. N&S | 3E-25S,3E-24S | 95 |
| Bridge E&W | 4E-25S | 95 |
| Brown St. N&S | 1E-24S | 94 |
| Burley Av. N&S | 3E-25S,3E-24S | 95 |
| Burnham Av. N&S | 3E-27S,3E-24S | 95 |
| Butler St. E&W | 1E-24S | 94 |
| Calumet Expwy. N&S | 1E-27S,1E-22S | 94 |
| Carondelet Av. N&S | 3E-25S,3E-24S | 95 |
| Chicago Av. N&S | 3E-22S | 89 |
| Chris Ct. N&S | 2E-23S | 89 |
| Columbia Av. | 1E-24S | 94 |
| Commercial Av. | 3E-25S | 95 |
| Cottage Grove Av. N&S | 0E-24S,1E-27S | 94 |
| Cullom St. N&S | 1E-24S | 94 |
| Daniel Ct. E&W | 3E-25S | 95 |
| David Ct. E&W | 3E-25S | 95 |
| Douglas Ct. E&W | 3E-25S | 95 |
| Dutra Av. NE&SW | 2W-24S | 93 |
| Elizabeth NE&SW | 4E-25S | 95 |
| Ellen Dr. N&S | 3E-25S | 95 |
| Escanaba Av. N&S | 3E-25S | 95 |
| Exchange Av. N&S | 3E-25S | 95 |
| Frederick Ct. E&W | 3E-25S | 95 |
| Gail Ct. E&W | 3E-25S | 95 |
| Glenwood Dyer Rd. NW&SE | 2E-23S,2E-24S | 89 |
| Glenwood Dyer Rd. NW&SE | 1E-23S,3E-24S | 89 |
| Glenwood Lansing Rd. N&S | 2E-22S | 89 |
| Harper N&S | 1E-26S | 94 |
| Hillcrest Av. N&S | 3E-24S | 95 |
| Houston N&S | 3E-25S,3E-24S | 95 |
| Howard Ct. N&S | 3E-25S | 95 |
| Indiana Av. N&S | 0E-26S | 95 |
| Jacob Ct. N&S | 3E-25S | 95 |
| James Av. N&S | 3E-26S | 95 |
| Jennifer E&W | 4E-25S | 95 |
| Joe Orr Rd. N&S | 1E-24S,2E-24S | 94 |
| Judith Ct. E&W | 3E-25S | 95 |
| Langston St. N&S | 1E-24S | 94 |
| Lincoln Hwy. E&W | 1E-25S | 95 |
| Long Av. N&S | 2E-27S | 95 |
| Main St. E&W | 0E-26S | 94 |
| Marion Ct. E&W | 3E-25S | 95 |
| Martin Ct. E&W | 3E-25S | 95 |
| Michelle E&W | 4E-25S | 95 |
| Muskegon Av. N&S | 3E-25S | 95 |

| | Grid | Page |
|---|---|---|
| Oakwood Av. N&S | 3E-22S | 89 |
| Park N&S | 1E-25S | 94 |
| Parkside N&S | 3E-24S | 95 |
| Prairie Av. N&S | 3E-25S | 95 |
| Pullman N&S | 1E-25S | 94 |
| Sauk Trail E&W | 2E-27S,4E-26S | 95 |
| State St. N&S | 0E-23S | 88 |
| Steger Rd. E&W | 2E-27S,4E-27S | 95 |
| Stirling Av. E&W | 2W-25S | 93 |
| Stoney Island Av. N&S | 1E-25S | 95 |
| Stony Island Av. N&S | 1E-22S | 89 |
| Stuart Ct. E&W | 3E-25S | 95 |
| Summit E&W | 1E-25S | 94 |
| Sunset Ln. N&S | 4E-26S | 95 |
| Torrence Av. N&S | 2E-27S,2E-22S | 95 |
| Travers Av. N&S | 2W-25S,2W-24S | 93 |
| Valarie NE&SW | 4E-25S | 95 |
| Valerie Dr. N&S | 4E-25S | 95 |
| Victoria Cir. NS&EW | 4E-25S | 95 |
| Virginia N&S | 4E-25S | 95 |
| Vollmer St. E&W | 1E-23S | 89 |
| 13th E&W | 0E-25S | 94 |
| 21st E&W | 3E-26S | 95 |
| 22nd St. E&W | 0E-26S | 94 |
| 22nd St. E&W | 3E-26S | 95 |
| 30th St. E&W | 1E-27S | 94 |
| 190th St. E&W | 1W-22S | 88 |
| 205th St. E&W | 2W-24S | 93 |
| 207th St. E&W | 2W-24S,3E-24S | 93 |
| 211th St. E&W | 1E-25S | 95 |
| 212th St. E&W | 1E-25S | 94 |
| 213th St. E&W | 1E-25S | 95 |
| 219th St. E&W | 4E-26S | 95 |

**Blue Island**

| | Grid | Page |
|---|---|---|
| Albany Av. N&S | 3W-14S | 75 |
| Ann St. N&S | 3W-15S,3W-14S | 75 |
| Artesian Av. N&S | 3W-15S,3W-14S | 75 |
| Ashland Av. N&S | 2W-15S | 75 |
| Berrien St. N&S | 1W-15S | 76 |
| Birdsall St. E&W | 3W-14S | 75 |
| Broadway E&W | 3W-15S,2W-15S | 75 |
| Burr Oak Av. E&W | 3W-14S | 75 |
| California Av. N&S | 3W-16S,3W-15S | 75 |
| Calumet St. N&S | 1W-15S | 76 |
| Canal St. E&W | 2W-15S | 75 |
| Chatham St. N&S | 2W-16S,2W-15S | 75 |
| Chicago St. N&S | 2W-15S | 75 |
| Cleveland Av. N&S | 3W-16S | 75 |
| Clinton Av. N&S | 3W-15S | 75 |
| Cochran St. E&W | 3W-14S | 75 |
| Collins St. E&W | 3W-14S,2W-14S | 75 |
| Concord St. N&S | 2W-15S | 75 |
| Coopers Grove Rd. NE&SW | 3W-16S | 75 |
| Dan Ryan Expressway N&S | 2W-15S | 75 |
| Des Plaines St. N&S | 3W-15S,2W-15S | 75 |
| Devonshire St. E&W | 2W-15S | 75 |
| Division St. N&S | 3W-15S,2W-15S | 75 |
| Duane St. NS&EW | 2W-15S | 75 |
| Edison Av. N&S | 4W-15S,3W-15S | 75 |
| Edward St. E&W | 3W-15S | 75 |
| Elim E&W | 2W-15S | 75 |
| Elm Dr. NE&SW | 3W-14S | 75 |
| Elm St. N&S | 3W-15S,3W-14S | 75 |
| Everett St. NW&SE | 3W-15S | 75 |
| Fairview Av. N&S | 3W-15S,3W-14S | 75 |
| Florence St. E&W | 2W-14S | 75 |
| Francisco Av. N&S | 3W-16S,3W-15S | 75 |
| Fulton St. E&W | 3W-15S | 75 |
| Girard St. E&W | 2W-15S | 75 |
| Greenwood Av. N&S | 3W-15S,3W-14S | 75 |
| Gregory St. N&S | 2W-15S,3W-15S | 75 |
| Grove St. E&W | 3W-15S,3W-14S | 75 |
| Grunewald St. E&W | 3W-14S | 75 |
| Hadley St. NE&SW | 2W-16S | 75 |
| High St. E&W | 3W-15S,3W-14S | 75 |
| Highland Av. N&S | 3W-15S,3W-14S | 75 |
| Homan Av. N&S | 4W-14S | 75 |
| Honore St. N&S | 2W-15S | 75 |
| Hoyne Av. N&S | 2W-15S | 75 |
| Interstate 57 N&S | 2W-15S | 75 |
| Irving N&S | 2W-15S,2W-14S | 75 |
| James St. E&W | 3W-15S | 75 |
| John St. E&W | 3W-15S | 75 |
| Kedzie Av. N&S | 3W-15S | 75 |
| Krueger St. E&W | 2W-14S | 75 |
| Lewis St. E&W | 3W-15S | 75 |
| Liberty St. NW&SE | 2W-15S | 75 |
| Lincoln St. N&S | 2W-15S | 75 |
| Longwood Dr. N&S | 2W-16S | 75 |
| Main St. E&W | 2W-15S | 75 |

| | Grid | Page |
|---|---|---|
| Maple Av. N&S | 3W-15S,3W-14S | 75 |
| Market St. E&W | 2W-15S | 75 |
| Minnesota St. E&W | 3W-14S | 75 |
| Mozart St. N&S | 3W-15S | 75 |
| New St. E&W | 3W-15S | 75 |
| Oak St. E&W | 3W-15S | 75 |
| Olive St. E&W | 2W-14S | 75 |
| Orange St. E&W | 2W-15S | 75 |
| Orchard St. E&W | 3W-14S,2W-14S | 75 |
| Portland St. E&W | 2W-15S | 75 |
| Prairie St. E&W | 3W-15S,2W-15S | 75 |
| Randolph St. E&W | 1W-15S | 75 |
| Rexford St. E&W | 2W-15S | 75 |
| Roll Av. E&W | 2W-15S | 75 |
| Sacramento Av. N&S | 3W-15S | 75 |
| Sanders St. E&W | 2W-15S | 75 |
| Seeley Av. N&S | 2W-15S | 75 |
| Shamrock Ln. N&S | 3W-16S | 75 |
| Stonebrook Ln. N&S | 3W-15S | 75 |
| Summit St. E&W | 3W-14S | 75 |
| Sycamore St. E&W | 1W-15S | 76 |
| Thornton Rd. NW&SE | 2W-16S | 75 |
| Union St. E&W | 3W-15S,2W-15S | 75 |
| Vermont St. E&W | 3W-15S,2W-15S | 75 |
| Vernon St. E&W | 2W-14S | 75 |
| Vincennes Rd. NE&SW | 2W-14S | 75 |
| Vine St. E&W | 2W-15S | 75 |
| Wahl St. NW&SE | 3W-15S | 75 |
| Walnut St. E&W | 3W-15S,2W-15S | 75 |
| Western Av. N&S | 3W-16S,3W-14S | 75 |
| Whipple St. N&S | 3W-16S | 75 |
| Winchester Av. N&S | 2W-15S | 75 |
| Wireton St. NW&SE | 3W-15S | 75 |
| Wood St. N&S | 2W-15S,2W-14S | 75 |
| York St. E&W | 3W-15S,2W-15S | 75 |
| 119th Pl. E&W | 2W-14S | 75 |
| 120th Pl. E&W | 2W-14S | 75 |
| 120th St. E&W | 3W-14S,2W-14S | 75 |
| 121st Pl. E&W | 3W-14S,2W-14S | 75 |
| 121st St. E&W | 3W-14S,2W-14S | 75 |
| 122nd Pl. E&W | 3W-14S | 75 |
| 122nd St. E&W | 3W-14S,2W-14S | 75 |
| 123rd Pl. E&W | 2W-14S | 75 |
| 123rd St. E&W | 3W-14S,2W-14S | 75 |
| 127th St. E&W | 3W-15S,2W-15S | 75 |
| 131st St. E&W | 2W-14S | 75 |
| 135th St. E&W | 3W-16S | 75 |
| 136th St. E&W | 2W-16S | 75 |
| 138th St. E&W | 2W-16S | 75 |
| 139th Pl. E&W | 3W-16S | 75 |
| 139th St. E&W | 3W-16S,2W-16S | 75 |
| 140th Pl. E&W | 3W-16S | 75 |
| 140th St. E&W | 2W-16S | 75 |
| 141st Pl. E&W | 3W-16S | 75 |
| 141st St. E&W | 3W-16S | 75 |

**Bremen Township**

| | Grid | Page |
|---|---|---|
| Arrowhead Trace NS&EW | 6W-20S | 86 |
| Artesian Av. N&S | 3W-19S | 81 |
| Austin Blvd. N&S | 7W-19S | 80 |
| Bachelor Grove Rd. N&S | 8W-16S | 79 |
| Beverly Av. N&S | 7W-19S | 80 |
| Bramblewood Rd. N&S | 8W-18S | 79 |
| California Av. N&S | 3W-18S,3W-17S | 81 |
| Central Av. N&S | 7W-21S,7W-20S | 86 |
| Chippewa Ct. SW&NE | 6W-20S | 86 |
| Danielle Ct. N&S | 6W-20S | 86 |
| Elmdale Av. N&S | 3W-18S,2W-18S | 81 |
| Fairfield Av. NW&SE | 3W-17S | 81 |
| Forest Av. N&S | 6W-20S | 86 |
| Francisco Av. N&S | 3W-18S,3W-17S | 81 |
| Fulton Terr. N&S | 7W-19S | 80 |
| Gaynelle Rd. NS&EW | 7W-19S | 80 |
| George Brennan Hwy. NE&SW | 6W-20S | 86 |
| Highland Av. N&S | 7W-21S | 86 |
| Interstate 57 NE&SW | 6W-21S,6W-20S | 86 |
| James St. E&W | 7W-19S | 80 |
| Jody Ln. E&W | 6W-20S | 86 |
| Justamere Rd. N&S | 8W-18S | 79 |
| Kathleen Ct. E&W | 6W-20S | 86 |
| Kilpatrick Av. N&S | 6W-20S | 86 |
| Kimberly Ln. E&W | 7W-19S | 80 |
| Lamon Av. N&S | 6W-17S | 80 |
| Laramie Av. N&S | 6W-20S | 86 |
| Laramie Rd. N&S | 6W-20S | 86 |

| | Grid | Page |
|---|---|---|
| Lavergne Av. N&S .. | 6W-21S | 86 |
| Lawndale Av. N&S .. | 4W-21S | 87 |
| Leclaire Av. N&S ... | 6W-20S | 86 |
| Leslie Ann Dr. N&S . | 7W-19S | 80 |
| Linder Av. N&S.... | 6W-16S | 74 |
| Lockwood Av. N&S ... | 6W-20S | 86 |
| Luna Av. N&S .... | 6W-16S | 74 |
| Major Av. N&S .... | 7W-16S | 74 |
| Mark Ln. N&S ..... | 7W-19S | 80 |
| Menard Av. N&S ... | 7W-16S | 74 |
| Midlothian Turnpike NE&SW | | |
| .......... 7W-16S,6W-16S | | 74 |
| New England Av. N&S | | |
| .......... 8W-18S | | 79 |
| Oak Park Av. N&S .. | 8W-18S | 79 |
| Parkside Av. N&S ... | 7W-20S | 80 |
| Patricia Av. N&S .. | 7W-19S | 80 |
| Poplar Av. N&S ... | 3W-19S | 81 |
| Richmond Av. N&S .. | 3W-18S | 81 |
| Rt. 43 N&S..8W-17S,8W-16S | | 79 |
| Sacramento Av. N&S | | |
| .......... 3W-17S,3W-16S | | 81 |
| Sayre Av. N&S .... | 8W-18S | 79 |
| Sayre Av. N&S .... | 8W-21S | 85 |
| Springfield Av. N&S . | 4W-21S | 87 |
| Thorndale Av. NW&SE | | |
| .......... 3W-18S,2W-18S | | 81 |
| 139th St. E&W ... | 6W-16S | 74 |
| 142nd Pl. E&W ... | 3W-16S | 75 |
| 143rd Pl. E&W ... | 3W-17S | 81 |
| 143rd Pl. E&W | | |
| .......... 8W-16S,3W-16S | | 79 |
| 144th St. E&W ... | 3W-17S | 81 |
| 147th Ct. E&W ... | 6W-17S | 80 |
| 147th St. E&W | | |
| .......... 8W-17S,7W-17S | | 79 |
| 150th St. E&W ... | 6W-17S | 80 |
| 151st St. E&W ... | 3W-17S | 81 |
| 155th Pl. E&W ... | 8W-18S | 79 |
| 155th St. E&W ... | 8W-18S | 79 |
| 156th Pl. E&W ... | 8W-18S | 79 |
| 157th Pl. E&W ... | 8W-18S | 79 |
| 157th St. E&W ... | 8W-18S | 79 |
| 159th St. E&W ... | 2W-18S | 81 |
| 163rd St. E&W ... | 5W-19S | 80 |
| 166th St. E&W ... | 7W-19S | 80 |
| 171st Pl. E&W ... | 6W-20S | 86 |
| 171st St. E&W ... | 6W-20S | 86 |
| 173rd St. E&W | | |
| .......... 7W-20S,6W-20S | | 86 |
| 174th St. E&W | | |
| .......... 6W-21S,6W-20S | | 86 |
| 175th St. E&W | | |
| .......... 7W-20S,6W-21S | | 86 |
| 177th St. E&W ... | 6W-21S | 86 |
| 178th St. E&W ... | 8W-21S | 85 |
| 179th St. E&W ... | 7W-21S | 86 |
| 180th St. E&W ... | 8W-21S | 85 |
| 181st St. E&W ... | 8W-21S | 85 |
| 182nd St. E&W ... | 8W-21S | 85 |
| 183rd St. E&W | | |
| .......... 7W-21S,6W-21S | | 86 |

## Bridgeview

| | Grid | Page |
|---|---|---|
| Avon Av. NW&SE.... | 9W-10S | 65 |
| Beloit Av. N&S | | |
| .......... 9W-10S,9W-8S | | 65 |
| Birch E&W ....... | 8W-10S | 65 |
| Cambridge St. E&W | | |
| .......... 9W-10S,8W-10S | | 65 |
| Circle Ct. NW&SE.... | 8W-10S | 65 |
| Columbia E&W...... | 9W-7S | 59 |
| Cranbrook Ln. N&S . | 8W-10S | 65 |
| Dover St. N&S .... | 8W-10S | 65 |
| Elder Ct. NW&SE ... | 8W-10S | 65 |
| Elm N&S ........ | 9W-7S | 59 |
| Fairlane Dr. NE&SW | 8W-10S | 65 |
| Falcon Ridge Dr. N&S | | |
| .......... 9W-10S | | 65 |
| Ferdinand Av. N&S | | |
| .......... 9W-10S,9W-8S | | 65 |
| Ferdinand Rd. N&S .. | 9W-10S | 65 |
| Frontage Rd. N&S .. | 9W-10S | 65 |
| Garden Ct. E&W ... | 9W-7S | 59 |
| Garden Ln. E&W ... | 9W-7S | 59 |
| Garden Ln. N&S ... | 9W-7S | 59 |
| Hanover Dr. N&S... | 8W-10S | 65 |
| Harlem Av. N&S | | |
| .......... 9W-10S,9W-8S | | 65 |
| Hartford E&W | | |
| .......... 9W-10S,8W-10S | | 65 |
| Homestead Ln. N&S | | |
| .......... 8W-10S | | 65 |
| Industrial Dr. NW&SE | | |
| .......... 9W-11S | | 65 |
| Mable N&S ....... | 9W-7S | 59 |
| Martin Ln. N&S.... | 8W-10S | 65 |
| Oak Park Av. N&S .. | 8W-10S | 65 |
| Oconto N&S........ | 9W-8S | 59 |
| Oconto Av. N&S | | |
| .......... 9W-9S,9W-8S | | 65 |
| Octavia Av. N&S | | |
| .......... 9W-10S,9W-8S | | 65 |
| Odell Av. N&S | | |
| .......... 9W-10S,9W-8S | | 65 |
| Oketo Av. N&S | | |
| .......... 9W-10S,9W-8S | | 65 |
| Olympic Dr. NS&EW | 8W-10S | 65 |
| Orchard Ln. N&S ... | 8W-10S | 65 |
| Oxford St. E&W ... | 8W-10S | 65 |
| Pembroke Ln. N&S .. | 9W-11S | 65 |
| Richards Rd. E&W .. | 9W-11S | 65 |
| Roberts Rd. N&S .... | 9W-8S | 59 |
| Saratoga Dr. NS&EW | | |
| .......... 8W-10S | | 65 |
| Selma N&S ....... | 9W-8S | 59 |
| Sholer Av. N&S .... | 9W-8S | 59 |

| | Grid | Page |
|---|---|---|
| Southfield Dr. NE&SW | | |
| .......... 8W-10S | | 65 |
| Stickney N&S ..... | 9W-8S | 59 |
| Stickney Av. N&S .. | 9W-8S | 59 |
| Stratford Dr. E&W . | 8W-10S | 65 |
| Suburban E&W .... | 9W-7S | 59 |
| Thomas Av. N&S | | |
| .......... 9W-10S,9W-8S | | 65 |
| Tri-State Tollway NW&SE | | |
| .......... 9W-11S,9W-10S | | 65 |
| Willow Ln. N&S... | 8W-10S | 65 |
| Windsor Ln. N&S... | 8W-10S | 65 |
| 70th E&W ....... | 9W-7S | 59 |
| 71st E&W ....... | 9W-7S | 59 |
| 72nd E&W ....... | 9W-7S | 59 |
| 73rd E&W ....... | 9W-8S | 59 |
| 73rd Av. N&S&EW .. | 9W-9S | 65 |
| 73rd Pl. E&W ..... | 9W-8S | 59 |
| 74th E&W ....... | 9W-8S | 59 |
| 74th Pl. E&W ..... | 9W-8S | 59 |
| 75th E&W ....... | 9W-8S | 59 |
| 75th St. E&W ..... | 9W-8S | 59 |
| 76th E&W ....... | 9W-8S | 59 |
| 76th St. E&W ..... | 9W-8S | 59 |
| 77th E&W ....... | 9W-8S | 59 |
| 77th Av. N&S | | |
| .......... 9W-10S,9W-9S | | 65 |
| 77th Ct. N&S ..... | 9W-9S | 65 |
| 77th Pl. E&W ..... | 9W-8S | 59 |
| 78th E&W ....... | 9W-8S | 59 |
| 78th Av. N&S .9W-9S,9W-8S | | 65 |
| 78th Ct. E&W ..... | 9W-8S | 59 |
| 78th St. E&W ..... | 9W-8S | 59 |
| 79th N&S ....... | 9W-7S | 59 |
| 79th Pl. E&W ..... | 9W-9S | 65 |
| 79th St. E&W ..... | 9W-8S | 59 |
| 80th Pl. E&W ..... | 9W-9S | 65 |
| 80th St. E&W ..... | 9W-9S | 65 |
| 81st Pl. E&W ..... | 9W-9S | 65 |
| 81st St. E&W ..... | 9W-9S | 65 |
| 82nd Pl. E&W ..... | 9W-9S | 65 |
| 82nd St. E&W ..... | 9W-9S | 65 |
| 83rd Pl. E&W ..... | 9W-9S | 65 |
| 83rd St. E&W ..... | 9W-9S | 65 |
| 84th Pl. E&W ..... | 9W-9S | 65 |
| 84th St. E&W ..... | 9W-9S | 65 |
| 85th Pl. E&W ..... | 9W-9S | 65 |
| 85th St. E&W ..... | 9W-9S | 65 |
| 86th Pl. E&W ..... | 9W-9S | 65 |
| 86th St. E&W ..... | 9W-9S | 65 |
| 87th Pl. E&W ..... | 9W-10S | 65 |
| 87th St. E&W ..... | 9W-10S | 65 |
| 88th St. E&W ..... | 9W-10S | 65 |
| 90th Pl. E&W ..... | 9W-10S | 65 |
| 90th St. E&W ..... | 9W-10S | 65 |
| 91st St. E&W ..... | 9W-10S | 65 |
| 92nd Pl. E&W ..... | 9W-10S | 65 |
| 92nd St. E&W ..... | 9W-10S | 65 |
| 93rd St. E&W ..... | 9W-10S | 65 |
| 98th Pl. E&W ..... | 9W-11S | 65 |
| 100th Pl. E&W .... | 9W-11S | 65 |

## Broadview

| | Grid | Page |
|---|---|---|
| Beach N&S........ | 12W-0S | 46 |
| Braga Dr. NW&SE .. | 11W-1S | 53 |
| Cermak E&W...... | 11W-1S | 53 |
| Elizabeth Dr. E&W . | 11W-2S | 53 |
| Ericka E&W ...... | 11W-2S | 53 |
| Field Av. N&S .... | 11W-2S | 53 |
| Fillmore E&W...... | 11W-0S | 47 |
| Gardner N&S...... | 12W-0S | 46 |
| Roberts E&W ..... | 11W-1S | 53 |
| Roosevelt Rd. E&W . | 11W-0S | 47 |
| Summerdale Dr. E&W | | |
| .......... 11W-2S | | 53 |
| Sunnydale N&S .... | 11W-2S | 53 |
| Terry Ln. E&W .... | 11W-2S | 53 |
| Tyson E&W ...... | 11W-1S | 53 |
| York E&W ....... | 12W-0S | 46 |
| 13th E&W ....... | 11W-1S | 53 |
| 13th N&S ....... | 11W-0S | 47 |
| 14th E&W ....... | 11W-1S | 53 |
| 14th N&S ....... | 11W-0S | 47 |
| 15th E&W ....... | 11W-1S | 53 |
| 15th N&S ....... | 11W-0S | 47 |
| 16th E&W ....... | 11W-1S | 53 |
| 16th N&S ....... | 11W-0S | 47 |
| 17th N&S ....... | 11W-1S | 53 |
| 18th E&W ....... | 11W-1S | 53 |
| 18th N&S ....... | 11W-1S | 53 |
| 19th E&W ....... | 11W-1S | 53 |
| 19th N&S ....... | 11W-1S | 53 |
| 20th E&W ....... | 11W-1S | 53 |
| 21st E&W ....... | 11W-1S | 53 |
| 22nd N&S ....... | 11W-1S | 53 |
| 23rd E&W ....... | 11W-1S | 53 |
| 23rd Pl. E&W ..... | 12W-2S | 52 |
| 23rd St. E&W ..... | 12W-2S | 52 |
| 24th N&S ....... | 11W-1S | 53 |
| 24th N&S ....... | 11W-1S | 53 |
| 26th N&S ....... | 12W-2S | 52 |
| 27th N&S ....... | 12W-1S | 52 |

## Brookfield

| | Grid | Page |
|---|---|---|
| Arden N&S ...... | 10W-3S | 53 |
| Arthur N&S..11W-4S,11W-3S | | 53 |
| Bartlett N&S ..... | 11W-2S | 53 |
| Blanchan N&S | | |
| .......... 11W-4S,11W-3S | | 53 |
| Broadway SW&NE .. | 11W-3S | 53 |
| Brookfield E&W.... | 11W-3S | 53 |
| Burlington E&W ... | 11W-3S | 53 |
| Cleveland N&S .... | 11W-3S | 53 |
| Congress Park E&W | | |
| .......... 11W-4S | | 53 |

| | Grid | Page |
|---|---|---|
| Custer E&W | | |
| .......... 11W-4S,11W-3S | | 53 |
| Deyd N&S ....... | 11W-4S | 53 |
| DuBois N&S ..... | 11W-4S | 53 |
| Elm N&S .... 11W-4S,11S-3S | | 53 |
| Fairview E&W ..... | 11W-2S | 53 |
| Forest N&S  11W-4S,11W-2S | | 53 |
| Forestview E&W ... | 11W-2S | 53 |
| Garfield E&W...... | 11W-3S | 53 |
| Gerritsen E&W .... | 11W-3S | 53 |
| Grand NW&SE .... | 11W-3S | 53 |
| Grant E&W ...... | 11W-3S | 53 |
| Greenview E&W ... | 10W-3S | 53 |
| Grove N&S ...... | 11W-4S | 53 |
| Harrison N&S..... | 11W-3S | 53 |
| Henrietta E&W .... | 11W-3S | 53 |
| Hollywood N&S ... | 10W-3S | 53 |
| Jackson E&W ..... | 11W-3S | 53 |
| Jefferson E&W .... | 11W-3S | 53 |
| Lexington E&W .... | 11W-3S | 53 |
| Madison N&S | | |
| .......... 11W-4S,11W-3S | | 53 |
| Maple N&S..11W-4S,11W-3S | | 53 |
| McCormick N&S ... | 10W-3S | 53 |
| Monroe E&W ..... | 11W-3S | 53 |
| Morton N&S ..... | 11W-3S | 53 |
| Oak N&S....11W-4S,11W-3S | | 53 |
| Park N&S....11W-4S,11S-3S | | 53 |
| Parkview E&W .... | 10W-3S | 53 |
| Plainfield E&W .... | 11W-4S | 53 |
| Prairie N&S ..11W-4S,11W-3S | | 53 |
| Raymond N&S | | |
| .......... 11W-4S,11W-3S | | 53 |
| Riverside N&S .... | 10W-3S | 53 |
| Riverview E&W .... | 10W-4S | 53 |
| Roach E&W ...... | 11W-3S | 53 |
| Rochester E&W ... | 11W-4S | 53 |
| Rockfeller E&W .... | 11W-3S | 53 |
| Rosemear N&S .... | 10W-3S | 53 |
| Sahler E&W ...... | 11W-4S | 53 |
| Sheridan E&W .... | 11W-3S | 53 |
| Sherman E&W .... | 11W-3S | 53 |
| Shields E&W ..... | 11W-3S | 53 |
| Southview E&W ... | 11W-3S | 53 |
| Sunnyside N&S | | |
| .......... 11W-4S,11W-3S | | 53 |
| Taylor N&S........ | 11W-4S | 53 |
| Vernon N&S | | |
| .......... 11W-4S,11W-2S | | 53 |
| Washington E&W .. | 11W-3S | 53 |
| Windemere E&W ... | 11W-4S | 53 |
| Woodside N&S .... | 10W-3S | 53 |
| 26th E&W ....... | 11W-2S | 53 |
| 26th Pl. E&W ..... | 11W-2S | 53 |
| 27th E&W ....... | 11W-2S | 53 |
| 28th E&W ....... | 11W-2S | 53 |
| 29th E&W ....... | 11W-2S | 53 |
| 30th E&W ....... | 11W-2S | 53 |
| 31st E&W ....... | 10W-2S | 53 |
| 45th E&W ....... | 11W-4S | 53 |
| 47th E&W ....... | 11W-4S | 53 |

## Buffalo Grove*
### (Also see Lake County)

| | Grid | Page |
|---|---|---|
| Anthony Ct. N&S .. | 16W-17N | 15 |
| Anthony Rd. E&W .. | 16W-17N | 15 |
| Arbor Ct. NW&SE .. | 17W-18N | 14 |
| Arlington Heights Rd. N&S | | |
| .......... 18W-18N | | 14 |
| Ashford Ct. N&S .. | 17W-17N | 14 |
| Beacon Ct. N&S.... | 17W-17N | 14 |
| Beechwood Ct., E. NW&SE | | |
| .......... 17W-18N | | 14 |
| Beechwood Rd. E&W | | |
| .......... 17W-18N | | 14 |
| Bel Aire Ct. N&S .. | 17W-18N | 14 |
| Bel Aire Rd. N&S . | 17W-18N | 14 |
| Bernard Ct. N&S .. | 17W-18N | 14 |
| Bernard Dr. | | |
| .......17W-18N,16W-18N | | 14 |
| Betty Dr. N&S .... | 16W-17N | 15 |
| Boxwood Ln. NE&SW | | |
| .......... 17W-17N | | 14 |
| Bradley Rd. E&W .. | 17W-18N | 14 |
| Brentwood Ct.... | 17W-17N | 14 |
| Brucewood Dr. N&S | | |
| .......... 16W-18N | | 15 |
| Buffalo Grove Rd. N&S | | |
| .......16W-17N,16W-20N | | 15 |
| Cambridge Dr. N&S | | |
| .......... 16W-17N | | 15 |
| Cameron Way N&S | | |
| .......... 18W-18N | | 14 |
| Carriage Way N&S . | 17W-17N | 14 |
| Charles Ct. NW&SE | | |
| .......... 16W-17N | | 15 |
| Chatham Cir. N&S .. | 17W-18N | 14 |
| Chenault Rd. E&W . | 17W-18N | 14 |
| Cherrywood Rd. N&S | | |
| .......... 17W-18N | | 14 |
| Church Rd. NE&SW | | |
| .......... 17W-18N | | 14 |
| Cottonwood Rd. N&S | | |
| .......... 17W-18N | | 14 |
| Country Ln. NE&SW | | |
| .......... 17W-18N | | 14 |
| Countryside Dr. E&W | | |
| .......... 18W-18N | | 14 |
| Covington Ter. N&S | | |
| .......... 17W-17N | | 14 |
| Crestview Ter. NW&SE | | |
| .......... 16W-18N | | 15 |
| Crofton Ln. N&S.... | 17W-17N | 14 |
| Darryl Dr. E&W .. | 16W-17N | 15 |
| Diane Dr. N&S .... | 16W-18N | 15 |
| Downing Rd. E&W . | 16W-17N | 15 |
| Dun-Lo Av. E&W . | 16W-17N | 15 |

| | Grid | Page |
|---|---|---|
| Dundee Pkwy. E&W | | |
| .......... 17W-18N | | 14 |
| Dundee Rd. E&W | | |
| .......18W-18N,17W-18N | | 14 |
| Eaton Ct. N&S .... | 16W-17N | 15 |
| Ellen Dr. N&S .... | 16W-17N | 15 |
| Elmwood Dr. NS&EW | | |
| .......... 17W-18N | | 14 |
| Estate Dr. N&S .. | 17W-18N | 14 |
| Evergreen Pl. E&W | | |
| .......... 17W-18N | | 14 |
| Forest Pl. NS&EW .. | 16W-18N | 15 |
| Forest Way Dr. N&S | | |
| .......... 17W-18N | | 14 |
| Frances Ct. NW&SE | | |
| .......... 16W-17N | | 15 |
| Glendale Rd. NS&EW | | |
| .......... 16W-18N | | 15 |
| Golfview E&W .... | 16W-18N | 15 |
| Golfview Ter. N&S | | |
| .......... 16W-18N | | 15 |
| Greenridge Rd. N&S | | |
| .......... 17W-17N | | 14 |
| Gregg Ln. N&S .. | 16W-18N | 15 |
| Grove Cir. N&S .. | 17W-18N | 14 |
| Grove Dr. N&S .. | 18W-18N | 14 |
| Hapsfield Ln. E&W . | 17W-18N | 14 |
| Harvard Ln. N&S .. | 16W-17N | 15 |
| Hawthorne Rd. E&W | | |
| .......... 17W-18N | | 14 |
| Hiawatha Dr. N&S .. | 17W-18N | 14 |
| Hickory Av. N&S .. | 17W-17N | 14 |
| Hickory Dr. NW&SE | | |
| .......... 17W-18N | | 14 |
| Indian Hill Dr E&W . | 17W-18N | 14 |
| Juniper Ct. NE&SE | 17W-18N | 14 |
| Katherine Ct. N&S . | 17W-18N | 14 |
| Lake Blvd. NS&EW | | |
| .......... 16W-17N | | 15 |
| Lauren Ln. N&S .. | 16W-18N | 15 |
| Lehigh Ln. NE&SW | | |
| .......... 17W-17N | | 14 |
| Lincoln Ter. N&S .. | 17W-18N | 14 |
| Longwood Ct. NE&SW | | |
| .......... 17W-18N | | 14 |
| Longwood Dr. NS&EW | | |
| .......... 17W-18N | | 14 |
| MacArthur Ct. E&W | | |
| .......... 17W-18N | | 14 |
| MacArthur Dr. N&S | | |
| .......... 17W-18N | | 14 |
| Maple Dr. E&W .. | 17W-18N | 14 |
| Marylu Ln. N&S .. | 17W-18N | 14 |
| Mayfair Ct., N. E&W | | |
| .......... 17W-18N | | 14 |
| Mayfair Ct., S. NW&SE | | |
| .......... 17W-18N | | 14 |
| Mayfair Ln. NS&EW | | |
| .......... 17W-18N | | 14 |
| Melinda Ln. E&W .. | 17W-18N | 14 |
| Middlesex Ct. E&W | | |
| .......... 16W-17N | | 15 |
| Mill Creek Dr. NS&EW | | |
| .......... 17W-17N | | 14 |
| Miller Ln. E&W .. | 17W-17N | 14 |
| Mohawk Ct. E&W .. | 16W-18N | 15 |
| Mohawk Tr. E&W .. | 16W-18N | 15 |
| Mulberry Ct. E&W . | 17W-18N | 14 |
| N. Greenwood Ct. N&S | | |
| .......... 17W-18N | | 14 |
| Navajo Tr. N&S .. | 16W-18N | 15 |
| Oak Creek Dr. NE&SW | | |
| .......... 16W-18N | | 15 |
| Old Oak Ct., E E&W | | |
| .......... 16W-18N | | 15 |
| Old Oak Ct., W. NE&SW | | |
| .......... 16W-18N | | 15 |
| Old Oak Dr. N&S . | 16W-18N | 15 |
| Old Post Rd. NE&SW | | |
| .......... 17W-17N | | 14 |
| Palmgren Ct. E&W . | 16W-18N | 15 |
| Park Pl. E&W .... | 17W-18N | 14 |
| Park View N&S ... | 17W-17N | 14 |
| Parkview Ter. E&W | | |
| .......... 17W-17N | | 14 |
| Patton Dr. E&W .. | 17W-18N | 14 |
| Plum Grove Cir. E&W | | |
| .......... 17W-18N | | 14 |
| Poplar Ct. E&W .. | 17W-18N | 14 |
| Rachel Ln. NS&EW | | |
| .......... 18W-18N | | 14 |
| Raupp Blvd. N&S | | |
| .......17W-18N,16W-18N | | 14 |
| Red Oak Ct. NW&SE | | |
| .......... 16W-17N | | 15 |
| Regent Ct., E. NE&SW | | |
| .......... 17W-18N | | 14 |
| Regent Ct., W. NE&SW | | |
| .......... 17W-18N | | 14 |
| Regent Dr. NS&EW | | |
| .......... 17W-18N | | 14 |
| Roberta Ct. NW&SE | | |
| .......... 16W-18N | | 15 |
| Rose Blvd. NS&EW | | |
| .......... 17W-18N | | 14 |
| Rose Ct., E. E&W . | 18W-18N | 14 |
| Rose Ct., W. E&W . | 18W-18N | 14 |
| Rosewood Av. N&S | | |
| .......... 17W-17N | | 14 |
| S. Greenwood Ct. N&S | | |
| .......... 16W-18N | | 15 |
| Saratoga Ln. N&S | | |
| .......... 17W-18N | | 14 |
| Saxon Pl. N&S .... | 16W-17N | 15 |
| Selwyn Ln. E&W .. | 17W-17N | 14 |

| | Grid | Page |
|---|---|---|
| St. Mary's Pkwy. E&W | | |
| .......17W-18N,16W-18N | | 14 |
| Stanford Ln. . | 17W-17N | 14 |
| Stillwell Dr. N&S .. | 17W-18N | 14 |
| Stonebridge Ln. E&W | | |
| .......... 17W-17N | | 14 |
| Stonegate Ct. N&S | | |
| .......... 17W-18N | | 14 |
| Stonegate Rd. NS&EW | | |
| .......... 17W-18N | | 14 |
| Straford Cir. E&W .. | 17W-18N | 14 |
| Strathmore Ct. E&W | | |
| .......... 18W-18N | | 14 |
| Sussex Ct. NS&EW | | |
| .......... 17W-18N | | 14 |
| Sycamore Rd. E&W | | |
| .......... 16W-17N | | 15 |
| Terrace Pl. N&S ... | 17W-18N | 14 |
| Thornton Ln. E&W . | 17W-17N | 14 |
| Thornwood Rd. N&S | | |
| .......... 17W-18N | | 14 |
| Timber Hill Rd. N&S | | |
| .......... 17W-18N | | 14 |
| Trace Dr. NS&EW . | 18W-18N | 14 |
| Trinity Ct. E&W .... | 16W-17N | 15 |
| University Dr. E&W | | |
| .......... 16W-17N | | 15 |
| Vernon Ct., N. E&W | | |
| .......... 17W-18N | | 14 |
| Vernon Ct., S. E&W | | |
| .......... 17W-18N | | 14 |
| Vernon Ln. N&S .. | 16W-18N | 14 |
| W. Beechwood Ct. E&W | | |
| .......... 17W-18N | | 14 |
| Weidner Ct. E&W . | 17W-18N | 14 |
| Weidner Rd. N&S .. | 17W-18N | 14 |
| White Pine Rd. N&S | | |
| .......... 17W-18N | | 14 |
| Whitehall Ct. E&W . | 17W-18N | 14 |
| Whitehall Pl. E&W . | 17W-18N | 14 |
| Windsor Dr. N&S .. | 17W-18N | 14 |

## Burbank

| | Grid | Page |
|---|---|---|
| Austin Av. N&S | | |
| .......... 7W-9S,7W-8S | | 66 |
| Carmel St. E&W ... | 7W-8S | 60 |
| Central Av. N&S | | |
| .......... 6W-9S,6W-8S | | 66 |
| Cicero Av. N&S | | |
| .......... 6W-9S,6W-8S | | 66 |
| Doral St. E&W .... | 7W-8S | 60 |
| Foxfire St. N&S ... | 7W-8S | 60 |
| Harlem Av. N&S .. | 8W-9S | 65 |
| La Crosse Av. N&S | | |
| .......... 6W-9S,6W-8S | | 66 |
| La Porte Av. N&S | | |
| .......... 6W-9S,6W-8S | | 66 |
| LaCrosse N&S..... | 6W-8S | 60 |
| Lamon Av. N&S .. | 6W-9S | 66 |
| Laramie Av. N&S | | |
| .......... 6W-9S,6W-8S | | 66 |
| Latrobe Av. N&S | | |
| .......... 6W-9S,6W-8S | | 66 |
| Lavergne Av. N&S | | |
| .......... 6W-9S,6W-8S | | 66 |
| Lawler Av. N&S | | |
| .......... 6W-9S,6W-8S | | 66 |
| Le Claire Av. N&S | | |
| .......... 6W-9S,6W-8S | | 66 |
| Leamington Av. N&S | | |
| .......... 6W-9S,6W-8S | | 66 |
| Linder Av. N&S | | |
| .......... 6W-9S,6W-8S | | 66 |
| Lockwood Av. N&S | | |
| .......... 6W-9S,6W-8S | | 66 |
| Long Av. N&S 6W-9S,6W-8S | | 66 |
| Lorel Av. N&S 6W-9S,6W-8S | | 66 |
| Lotus Av. N&S | | |
| .......... 6W-9S,6W-8S | | 66 |
| Luna Av. N&S .... | 6W-8S | 60 |
| Major Av. N&S | | |
| .......... 7W-9S,7W-8S | | 66 |
| Mansfield Av. N&S | | |
| .......... 7W-9S,7W-8S | | 66 |
| Mason Av. N&S | | |
| .......... 7W-9S,7W-8S | | 66 |
| Massasoit Av. N&S | | |
| .......... 7W-9S,7W-8S | | 66 |
| Mayfield Av. N&S | | |
| .......... 7W-9S,7W-8S | | 66 |
| McVicker Av. N&S | | |
| .......... 7W-9S,7W-8S | | 66 |
| Meade Av. N&S ... | 7W-9S | 66 |
| Melvina Av. N&S | | |
| .......... 7W-9S,7W-8S | | 66 |
| Menard Av. N&S | | |
| .......... 7W-9S,7W-8S | | 66 |
| Merrimac Av. N&S | | |
| .......... 7W-9S,7W-8S | | 66 |
| Mobile Av. N&S | | |
| .......... 7W-9S,7W-8S | | 66 |
| Monitor N&S...... | 7W-8S | 60 |
| Monitor N&S...... | 7W-8S | 60 |
| Moody Av. N&S | | |
| .......... 7W-9S,7W-8S | | 66 |
| Mulligan Av. N&S | | |
| .......... 7W-9S,7W-8S | | 66 |
| Nagle Av. N&S | | |
| .......... 8W-9S,8W-8S | | 65 |
| Narragansett Av. N&S | | |
| .......... 8W-9S,8W-8S | | 65 |
| Nashville Av. N&S | | |
| .......... 8W-9S,8W-8S | | 65 |
| Natchez Av. N&S | | |
| .......... 8W-9S,8W-8S | | 65 |
| Natoma Av. N&S | | |
| .......... 8W-9S,8W-8S | | 65 |

| | Grid | Page |
|---|---|---|
| Neenah Av. N&S | 8W-9S,8W-8S | 65 |
| Neva Av. N&S | 8W-9S | 65 |
| New England Av. N&S | 8W-9S | 65 |
| Newcastle Av. N&S | 8W-9S,8W-8S | 65 |
| Newland Av. N&S | 8W-9S,8W-8S | 65 |
| Nordica Av. N&S | 8W-9S | 65 |
| Normandy Av. N&S | 8W-9S,8W-8S | 65 |
| Nottingham Av. N&S | 8W-9S | 65 |
| Oak Park Av. N&S | 8W-9S,8W-8S | 65 |
| Parkside N&S | 7W-8S | 60 |
| Parkside Av. N&S | 7W-9S,7W-8S | 66 |
| Pinehurst St. E&W | 7W-8S | 60 |
| Rt. 43 N&S | 8W-9S | 65 |
| Rt. 50 N&S | 6W-9S,6W-8S | 66 |
| Rutherford Av. N&S | 8W-9S,8W-8S | 65 |
| Sawgrass St. E&W | 7W-8S | 60 |
| Sayre Av. N&S | 8W-9S | 65 |
| State Rd. NE&SW | 7W-9S,6W-8S | 66 |
| 75th Pl. E&W | 7W-8S,6W-8S | 60 |
| 76th E&E | 7W-8S,6W-8S | 60 |
| 76th Pl. E&W | 6W-8S | 60 |
| 76th St. E&W | 7W-8S,6W-8S | 60 |
| 77th E&W | 7W-8S | 60 |
| 77th Pl. E&W | 6W-8S | 60 |
| 77th St. E&W | 8W-8S,6W-8S | 59 |
| 78th E&W | 8W-8S,6W-8S | 59 |
| 78th Pl. E&W | 6W-8S | 60 |
| 78th St. E&W | 8W-8S,6W-8S | 59 |
| 79th E&W | 8W-8S,6W-8S | 59 |
| 79th Pl. E&W | 7W-8S,6W-8S | 60 |
| 79th St. E&W | 8W-8S,6W-8S | 59 |
| 80th Pl. E&W | 8W-9S,7W-9S | 65 |
| 80th St. E&W | 8W-9S,7W-9S | 65 |
| 81st Pl. E&W | 8W-9S,7W-9S | 65 |
| 81st St. E&W | 8W-9S,6W-9S | 65 |
| 82nd Pl. E&W | 8W-9S,6W-9S | 65 |
| 82nd St. E&W | 8W-9S,6W-9S | 65 |
| 83rd Pl. E&W | 8W-9S,6W-9S | 65 |
| 83rd St. E&W | 8W-9S,6W-9S | 65 |
| 84th Pl. E&W | 8W-9S,6W-9S | 65 |
| 84th St. E&W | 8W-9S,6W-9S | 65 |
| 85th Pl. E&W | 8W-9S,6W-9S | 65 |
| 85th St. E&W | 8W-9S,6W-9S | 65 |
| 86th Pl. E&W | 7W-9S,6W-9S | 66 |
| 86th St. E&W | 8W-9S,6W-9S | 65 |
| 87th St. E&W | 8W-9S,6W-9S | 65 |

## Burnham

| | Grid | Page |
|---|---|---|
| Bensley Av. N&S | 2E-16S | 83 |
| Brainard Av. NW&SE | 4E-16S | 83 |
| Burnham Av. N&S | 3E-16S | 83 |
| Calhoun Av. N&S | 2E-16S | 83 |
| Calumet Av. N&S | 3E-16S | 83 |
| Centre Av. NE&SW | 3E-16S | 83 |
| Chippewa Av. NW&SE | 3E-16S | 83 |
| Commercial Dr. NW&SE | 2E-16S | 83 |
| Ewell Av. N&S | 3E-16S | 83 |
| Exchange Av. N&S | 2E-16S | 83 |
| Goodrich Av. E&W | 3E-16S | 83 |
| Greenbay Av. N&S | 3E-16S | 83 |
| Hammond Av. E&W | 3E-16S | 83 |
| Hoxie Av. N&S | 2E-16S | 83 |
| Indiana Av. N&S | 3E-16S | 83 |
| Kankakee Av. N&S | 3E-16S | 83 |
| Kettelson St. E&W | 2E-16S | 83 |
| Mackinaw St. N&S | 3E-16S | 83 |
| Manistee Av. N&S | 3E-16S | 83 |
| Marquette Av. N&S | 3E-16S | 83 |
| Muskegon Av. N&S | 3E-16S | 83 |
| Pierson St. E&W | 2E-16S,3E-16S | 83 |
| Prairie Av. N&S | 3E-16S | 83 |
| Saginaw Av. N&S | 3E-16S | 83 |
| Scott Av. N&S | 3E-16S | 83 |
| State Line Rd. N&S | 4E-16S | 83 |
| State St. E&W | 2E-16S,3E-16S | 83 |
| Torrence Av. N&S | 2E-16S | 83 |
| Yates Av. N&S | 2E-16S | 83 |
| 138th St. E&W | 3E-16S | 83 |
| 139th St. E&W | 3E-16S | 83 |
| 140th St. E&W | 2E-16S,3E-16S | 83 |
| 141st St. E&W | 2E-16S,3E-16S | 83 |
| 142nd St. E&W | 3E-16S | 83 |
| 143rd St. E&W | 3E-16S | 83 |

## Burr Ridge*
**(Also see Du Page County)**

| | Grid | Page |
|---|---|---|
| Ambriance Dr. N&S | 14W-8S | 58 |
| Arbor NW&SE | 14W-8S | 58 |
| Arrowhead Farm Dr. NS&EW | 14W-9S | 64 |
| Bastern Rd. N&S | 14W-7S | 58 |
| Briarwood Ct. E&W | 14W-9S | 64 |
| Briarwood Ln. E&W | 14W-9S | 64 |
| Bridle Path E&W | 14W-7S | 58 |
| Brighton E&W | 14W-7S | 58 |
| Brighton Pl. NW&SE | 14W-7S | 58 |
| Buck Trail Dr. N&S | 14W-9S | 64 |
| Burr Oak NE&SW | 14W-8S | 58 |
| Burr Ridge N&S | 14W-8S | 58 |
| Carriage Pl. E&W | 14W-7S | 58 |
| Carriage Wy. NE&SW | 14W-7S | 58 |
| Central N&S | 14W-8S | 58 |
| Chasemoor Dr. NS&EW | 14W-8S | 58 |
| Chippewa Ct. E&W | 14W-9S | 64 |
| Cir. | 14W-8S | 58 |
| Circle Dr. NE&SW | 14W-8S | 58 |
| Commonwealth N&S | 14W-8S | 58 |
| County Line N&S | 14W-7S | 58 |
| County Line Ln. N&S | 14W-7S | 58 |
| County Line Rd. N&S | 14W-9S,14W-6S | 64 |
| Creekwood Dr. (Pvt.) N&S | 14W-9S | 64 |
| Ct. 1 N&S | 14W-8S | 58 |
| Ct. 2 N&S | 14W-8S | 58 |
| Ct. 3 N&S | 14W-8S | 58 |
| Ct. 4 NE&SW | 14W-8S | 58 |
| Ct. 5 E&W | 14W-8S | 58 |
| Ct. 6 E&W | 14W-8S | 58 |
| Ct. 7 N&S | 14W-8S | 58 |
| Ct. 8 E&W | 14W-8S | 58 |
| Dana N&S | 14W-8S | 58 |
| Dana Way N&S | 14W-8S | 58 |
| Deerview Rd. N&S | 14W-9S | 58 |
| Dougshire E&W | 14W-6S | 58 |
| Dougshire Ct. E&W | 14W-6S | 58 |
| East St. E&W | 14W-8S | 58 |
| East Trail Ln. N&S | 14W-9S | 64 |
| Erin E&W | 14W-7S | 58 |
| Fair Elms Av. N&S | 14W-8S | 58 |
| Forest Hill N&S | 14W-8S | 58 |
| Fox Borough Dr. N&S | 14W-8S | 58 |
| Fox Ln. E&W | 14W-9S | 64 |
| Frontage Rd. NE&SW | 14W-8S | 58 |
| Garywood Dr. N&S | 14W-7S,14W-6S | 58 |
| Gregford E&W | 14W-6S | 58 |
| Hampton E&W | 14W-7S | 58 |
| Hillcrest N&S | 14W-7S | 58 |
| Huntington Ct. E&W | 14W-8S | 58 |
| Laurie Ct. N&S | 14W-6S | 58 |
| Laurie Ln. N&S | 14W-6S | 58 |
| Lincolnshire N&S | 14W-8S | 58 |
| Longwood Dr. E&W | 14W-7S | 58 |
| Manor N&S | 14W-7S | 58 |
| Manor Dr. N&S | 14W-7S | 58 |
| McClintock N&S | 14W-8S | 58 |
| Navajo Ct. N&S | 14W-9S | 64 |
| Northgate Pl. NS&EW | 14W-8S | 58 |
| Oak Werth Ln. E&W | 14W-9S | 64 |
| Omaha Dr. NW&SE | 14W-9S | 64 |
| Plainfield SW&NE | 14W-7S | 58 |
| Purdie St. E&W | 14W-7S | 58 |
| Ridgewood E&W | 14W-8S | 58 |
| Ridgewood Ln. NS&EW | 14W-8S | 58 |
| Seneca Ct. NE&SW | 14W-9S | 64 |
| Shady St. NW&SE | 14W-7S | 58 |
| Shagbark Ct. E&W | 14W-9S | 64 |
| Shagbark Ln. NE&SW | 14W-9S | 64 |
| South E&W | 14W-6S | 58 |
| Southgate Ct. E&W | 14W-8S | 58 |
| St. James Ct. N&S | 14W-7S | 58 |
| Steeplechase Ln. N&S | 14W-9S | 64 |
| Steepleside Dr. N&S | 14W-9S | 64 |
| Stirrup Ln. E&W | 14W-7S | 58 |
| Stonehedge Ct. E&W | 14W-8S | 58 |
| Surrey SW&NE | 14W-7S | 58 |
| Surrey Ln. E&W | 14W-7S | 58 |
| Tartan Ridge Rd. NW&SE | 14W-6S | 58 |
| Tend St. E&W | 14W-8S | 58 |
| Thornhill Ct. E&W | 14W-8S | 58 |
| Tomlin Cir. NS&EW | 14W-6S | 58 |
| Tomlin Dr. N&S | 14W-6S | 58 |
| Tower E&W | 14W-7S | 58 |
| Trent Ct. NE&SW | 14W-9S | 64 |
| Walnut Ct. E&W | 14W-9S | 64 |
| Waterside Pl. NE&SW | 14W-9S | 64 |
| White Oak Ct. E&W | 14W-9S | 64 |
| Wolf N&S | 14W-8S | 58 |
| Wolf Rd. N&S | 14W-9S,14W-8S | 64 |
| Woodglen E&W | 14W-8S | 58 |
| Woodland Ct. E&W | 14W-8S | 58 |
| Woodland Ln. NW&SE | 14W-8S | 58 |
| Woodside Ct. E&W | 14W-9S | 64 |
| Woodside Ln. N&S | 14W-9S | 64 |
| Woodview N&S | 14W-6S | 58 |
| 63rd E&W | 14W-6S | 58 |
| 67th E&W | 14W-7S | 58 |
| 72nd St. E&W | 14W-8S | 62 |
| 73rd Pl. E&W | 14W-8S | 58 |
| 73rd St. E&W | 14W-8S | 58 |
| 74th St. E&W | 14W-8S | 58 |
| 75th St. E&W | 14W-8S | 58 |
| 77th St. E&W | 14W-8S | 64 |
| 79th St. E&W | 14W-8S | 64 |
| 83rd St. E&W | 14W-9S | 64 |

## Calumet City

| | Grid | Page |
|---|---|---|
| Allan Ln. NE&SW | 2E-16S | 83 |
| Arthur Av. E&W | 3E-17S | 83 |
| Arthur St. N&S | 3E-19S | 83 |
| Aster St. E&W | 2E-16S | 83 |
| Baker St. E&W | 3E-17S | 83 |
| Balmoral Av. N&S | 3E-19S | 83 |
| Bensley Av. N&S | 2E-17S | 83 |
| Blackstone Av. N&S | 1E-17S | 82 |
| Buffalo Av. N&S | 3E-19S,3E-17S | 83 |
| Burnham Av. N&S | 3E-19S,3E-17S | 83 |
| Calhoun Av. N&S | 2E-17S | 83 |
| Calumet Way NW&SE | 4E-18S | 83 |
| Campbell Av. N&S | 3E-18S,3E-17S | 83 |
| Chappel Av. N&S | 2E-17S | 83 |
| Chestnut Ct. E&W | 2E-18S | 83 |
| Cleveland Av. E&W | 3E-17S | 83 |
| Clyde Av. N&S | 2E-18S,2E-17S | 83 |
| Commercial Av. N&S | 3E-18S,3E-17S | 83 |
| Cornell Av. N&S | 2E-18S,2E-17S | 83 |
| Crandon Av. N&S | 2E-17S | 83 |
| Cunningham Dr. N&S | 3E-19S | 83 |
| Dante Av. N&S | 1E-17S | 82 |
| Dawn Ln. E&W | 2E-16S | 83 |
| Detriot St. E&W | 4E-18S | 83 |
| Dogwood Ct. E&W | 2E-18S | 83 |
| Dolton Av. NW&SE | 2E-16S | 83 |
| Dorchester Av. N&S | 1E-17S | 82 |
| Douglas Av. N&S | 4E-17S | 83 |
| Downs Dr. E&W | 2E-16S | 83 |
| East End Av. N&S | 2E-18S,2E-17S | 83 |
| East-West Rd. E&W | 2E-19S | 83 |
| Edgewood Dr. N&S | 4E-19S | 83 |
| Elm Ct. E&W | 2E-18S | 83 |
| Escanaba Av. N&S | 3E-17S | 83 |
| Euclid St. E&W | 3E-17S | 83 |
| Exchange Av. N&S | 3E-17S | 83 |
| Forest Av. N&S | 4E-19S | 83 |
| Forest Ct. E&W | 4E-19S | 83 |
| Forest Hills Av. N&S | 4E-18S | 83 |
| Forest Ln. E&W | 4E-18S | 83 |
| Forest Pl. N&S | 4E-19S | 83 |
| Forestdale Av. E&W | 4E-18S | 83 |
| Forsythe Av. N&S | 4E-18S,4E-17S | 83 |
| Freeland Av. N&S | 4E-19S,4E-18S | 83 |
| Garfield Av. NW&SE | 4E-17S | 83 |
| George St. E&W | 3E-17S | 83 |
| Golf Ct. N&S | 4E-18S | 83 |
| Gordon Av. N&S | 4E-19S,4E-17S | 83 |
| Green Bay Av. N&S | 3E-19S,3E-17S | 83 |
| Greenwood Rd. NW&SE | 2E-18S | 83 |
| Harbor Av. E&W | 2E-16S | 83 |
| Harding Av. E&W | 2E-17S,4E-17S | 83 |
| Harmess St. E&W | 3E-17S | 83 |
| Harrison St. N&S | 4E-17S | 83 |
| Hawthorne Ct. NE&SW | 2E-18S | 83 |
| Henry St. NE&SW | 3E-18S | 83 |
| Hickory Ct. N&S | 2E-18S | 83 |
| Highland St. E&W | 4E-18S | 83 |
| Hirsch Av. N&S | 4E-19S,4E-17S | 83 |
| Hirsch Blvd. N&S | 4E-19S | 83 |
| Houston Av. N&S | 3E-18S,3E-17S | 83 |
| Hoxie Av. N&S | 2E-17S | 83 |
| Huntington Av. N&S | 2E-19S | 83 |
| Imperial Av. N&S | 3E-19S | 83 |
| Ingram Av. N&S | 4E-17S | 83 |
| Jeffery Av. N&S | 2E-17S | 83 |
| Jennifer Ln. EW&NS | 2E-16S | 83 |
| Kenilworth Dr. N&S | 4E-19S | 83 |
| Legion Dr. N&S | 4E-18S | 83 |
| Lincoln Av. N&S | 4E-19S,4E-17S | 83 |
| Lincoln Pl. N&S | 4E-19S | 83 |
| Locust Ct. N&S | 2E-18S | 83 |
| Lucas St. E&W | 3E-17S | 83 |
| Luella Av. N&S | 2E-17S,2E-16S | 83 |
| Mackinaw Av. N&S | 3E-19S,3E-17S | 83 |
| Madison Av. N&S | 2E-18S,2E-17S | 83 |
| Manistee Av. N&S | 3E-17S | 83 |
| Marquette Av. N&S | 3E-17S | 83 |
| Mason St. E&W | 4E-18S | 83 |
| Memorial Dr. E&W | 2E-17S,4E-17S | 83 |
| Merril Av. N&S | 2E-17S | 83 |
| Michigan City Rd. NW&SE | 2E-17S,4E-18S | 83 |
| Muskegon Av. N&S | 3E-18S,3E-17S | 83 |
| Newell Av. N&S | 3E-18S | 83 |
| Oglesby Av. N&S | 2E-17S,2E-16S | 83 |
| Park Av. NW&SE | 2E-19S | 83 |
| Patricia Pl. E&W | 2E-16S | 83 |
| Patton Ln. N&S | 2E-16S | 83 |
| Paxton Av. N&S | 2E-18S,2E-16S | 83 |
| Plummer Av. NW&SE | 4E-17S | 83 |
| Prairie Av. N&S | 2E-17S | 83 |
| Price Av. N&S | 4E-19S,4E-17S | 83 |
| Pulaski Rd. E&W | 2E-17S | 83 |
| Regency Ct. E&W | 2E-19S | 83 |
| Ridgeland Av. N&S | 2E-17S | 83 |
| Ring Rd. NS&EW | 2E-19S | 83 |
| River Dr. N&S | 3E-19S | 83 |
| River Oaks Dr. NW&SE | 2E-19S,4E-19S | 83 |
| Rt. 83 NS&EW | 2E-17S | 83 |
| Rudolph St. N&S | 3E-18S | 83 |
| Ruth St. E&W | 4E-18S | 83 |
| Saginaw Av. N&S | 3E-17S | 83 |
| Schrum Rd. NW&SE | 4E-19S | 83 |
| Shirley Dr. N&S | 4E-20S,4E-19S | 89 |
| Sibley Blvd. E&W | 2E-17S,4E-17S | 83 |
| Stanley Blvd. N&S | 4E-19S | 83 |
| State Line Rd. N&S | 4E-18S | 83 |
| State St. E&W | 2E-17S,4E-17S | 83 |
| Stewart Av. E&W | 2E-17S,3E-17S | 83 |
| Superior Av. N&S | 3E-19S,3E-18S | 83 |
| Sycamore Ct. N&S | 2E-18S | 83 |
| Timothy Ln. N&S | 2E-16S | 83 |
| Torrence Av. N&S | 2E-19S,2E-17S | 83 |
| Twilight Ln. E&W | 2E-16S | 83 |
| Valenca Ct. E&W | 2E-19S | 83 |
| Virginia St. E&W | 3E-18S | 83 |
| Waltham St. E&W | 4E-18S | 83 |
| Warren Av. E&W | 4E-18S | 83 |
| Webb Av. E&W | 4E-18S | 83 |
| Wentworth Av. N&S | 4E-20S,4E-17S | 89 |
| West Dr. E&W | 3E-19S | 83 |
| William St. E&W | 3E-19S | 83 |
| Willow Ct. N&S | 2E-18S | 83 |
| Wilson Av. E&W | 2E-17S,4E-17S | 83 |
| Woodview Av. N&S | 3E-19S | 83 |
| Yates Av. N&S | 2E-17S,2E-16S | 83 |
| 142nd St. E&W | 2E-16S | 83 |
| 151st St. E&W | 3E-17S | 83 |
| 152nd Pl. E&W | 4E-17S | 83 |
| 153rd Pl. E&W | 4E-17S | 83 |
| 153rd St. E&W | 2E-17S,4E-17S | 83 |
| 154th Pl. E&W | 4E-18S | 83 |
| 154th St. E&W | 3E-17S,4E-17S | 83 |
| 155th Pl. E&W | 3E-18S,4E-18S | 83 |
| 155th St. E&W | 3E-18S,4E-18S | 83 |
| 156th Pl. E&W | 3E-18S,4E-18S | 83 |
| 156th St. E&W | 3E-18S,4E-18S | 83 |
| 157th Pl. E&W | 3E-18S | 83 |
| 157th St. E&W | 3E-18S,4E-18S | 83 |
| 158th Pl. E&W | 2E-18S | 83 |
| 158th St. E&W | 3E-18S | 83 |
| 159th St. E&W | 3E-18S,4E-18S | 83 |
| 160th Pl. E&W | 3E-19S | 83 |
| 160th St. E&W | 3E-19S | 83 |
| 161st St. E&W | 3E-19S,4E-19S | 83 |
| 162nd Pl. E&W | 4E-19S | 83 |
| 162nd St. E&W | 3E-19S,4E-19S | 83 |
| 163rd Pl. E&W | 4E-19S | 83 |
| 163rd St. E&W | 3E-19S,4E-19S | 83 |
| 164th Pl. E&W | 4E-19S | 83 |
| 164th St. E&W | 3E-19S,4E-19S | 83 |
| 165th Pl. E&W | 4E-19S | 83 |
| 165th St. E&W | 4E-19S | 83 |
| 166th Pl. E&W | 4E-19S | 83 |
| 166th St. E&W | 4E-19S | 83 |
| 167th Pl. E&W | 4E-20S | 89 |
| 167th St. E&W | 4E-19S | 83 |
| 169th St. E&W | 4E-20S | 89 |
| 170th St E&W | 2E-19S,4E-19S | 83 |

## Calumet Park

| | Grid | Page |
|---|---|---|
| Aberdeen St. N&S | 1W-15S,1W-14S | 76 |
| Ada St. N&S | 1W-15S,1W-14S | 76 |
| Ashland Av. N&S | 2W-15S,2W-14S | 75 |
| Bishop St. N&S | 1W-15S,1W-14S | 76 |
| Calumet St. E&W | 1W-15S | 75 |
| Carpenter St. N&S | 1W-15S,1W-14S | 76 |
| Cass St. N&S | 1W-15S | 75 |
| Elizabeth St. N&S | 1W-15S,1W-14S | 76 |
| Green St. N&S | 1W-14S | 76 |
| Halsted St. N&S | 1W-14S | 76 |
| High St. E&W | 1W-15S | 76 |
| Honore St. N&S | 2W-14S | 75 |
| Illinois St. N&S | 1W-15S | 75 |
| Justine St. N&S | 1W-15S,1W-14S | 76 |
| Laflin St. N&S | 1W-15S,1W-14S | 76 |
| Lincoln St. N&S | 2W-14S | 75 |
| Loomis St. N&S | 1W-15S,1W-14S | 76 |
| Marshfield Av. N&S | 2W-15S,2W-14S | 75 |
| May St. N&S | 1W-15S,1W-14S | 76 |
| Morgan St. N&S | 1W-14S | 76 |
| Page Ct. N&S | 2W-15S | 75 |
| Page St. N&S | 2W-14S | 75 |
| Paulina St. N&S | 2W-14S | 75 |
| Peoria St. N&S | 1W-14S | 76 |
| Racine Av. N&S | 1W-15S,1W-14S | 76 |
| Sangamon St. N&S | 1W-14S | 76 |
| Throop St. N&S | 1W-15S,1W-14S | 76 |
| Vermont St. E&W | 1W-15S | 76 |
| Winchester Av. N&S | 2W-14S | 75 |
| Wood St. N&S | 2W-14S | 75 |
| York St. E&W | 1W-15S | 76 |
| 119th St. E&W | 2W-14S | 75 |
| 120th St. E&W | 2W-14S | 75 |
| 121st St. E&W | 2W-14S | 75 |
| 122nd St. E&W | 2W-14S | 75 |
| 123rd St. E&W | 1W-14S | 76 |
| 124th St. E&W | 2W-14S,1W-14S | 75 |
| 125th St. E&W | 2W-14S,1W-14S | 75 |
| 126th St. E&W | 2W-14S,1W-14S | 75 |
| 127th St. E&W | 2W-14S | 75 |
| 128th St. E&W | 1W-15S | 76 |
| 129th Pl. E&W | 1W-15S | 76 |
| 129th St. E&W | 2W-15S | 75 |

## Chicago Heights

| | Grid | Page |
|---|---|---|
| Abbott Av. N&S | 2W-24S | 93 |
| Aberdeen St. N&S | 1W-25S | 93 |
| Adams St. NE&SW | 2W-26S | 93 |
| Alden Ct. N&S | 2W-26S | 93 |
| Alice St. E&W | 0W-23S | 88 |
| Alvin Pl. E&W | 0W-24S | 94 |
| Amy St. E&W | 1W-24S | 93 |
| Andover Ct. NW&SE | 2W-26S | 93 |
| Andover Dr. E&W | 2W-26S | 93 |
| Arnold St. N&S | 0W-25S | 94 |
| Arquilla Dr. N&S | 1W-24S | 93 |
| Ash St. NW&SE | 1W-26S | 93 |
| Ashland Av. N&S | 2W-25S,2W-23S | 93 |
| Avonelle Av. N&S | 1W-24S | 93 |
| Barbara Ln. N&S | 2W-25S | 93 |
| Beacon Blvd. E&W | 2W-26S | 93 |
| Beacon Ct. N&S | 2W-26S | 93 |
| Bellevue Pl. E&W | 1W-24S | 93 |
| Birch Ln. N&S | 1W-24S | 93 |
| Birmingham Av. E&W | 0W-26S | 94 |
| Bollman Pl. E&W | 0W-24S | 94 |
| Boston St., N. E&W | 2W-26S | 93 |
| Boston St., W. N&S | 2W-26S | 93 |
| Bradley Dr. E&W | 2W-24S | 93 |
| Bradoc St. N&S | 2W-24S | 93 |
| Brentwood Dr. N&S | 1W-23S | 88 |
| Briargate Av. E&W | 0W-24S | 94 |
| Broadway NW&SE | 1W-24S | 93 |
| Brookline St. E&W | 2W-26S | 93 |
| Buena Vista Av. N&S | 1W-25S | 93 |
| Buena Vista Cir. N&S | 1W-25S | 93 |
| Bunker St. N&S | 2W-26S | 93 |
| Butler St. N&S | 0W-26S,0W-25S | 94 |
| Butterfield St. N&S | 0W-26S | 94 |
| Caldwell Av. N&S | 1W-24S | 93 |
| Cambridge St. N&S | 2W-26S | 93 |
| Campbell Av. N&S | 1W-25S,1W-24S | 93 |
| Carey Ct. E&W | 2W-24S | 93 |
| Carpenter St. N&S | 1W-24S | 93 |
| Cedar Ln. N&S | 1W-24S | 93 |
| Center Av. NE&SW | 0W-25S | 94 |
| Charing Cross Rd. E&W | 1W-24S | 93 |
| Charles St. E&W | 1W-23S | 88 |
| Chicago Rd. N&S | 1W-24S,1W-23S | 93 |
| Circle Ct. N&S | 1W-26S | 93 |
| Claude Ct. N&S | 0W-25S | 94 |
| Coales St. E&W | 1W-23S | 88 |
| Concord Ct. NW&SE | 2W-26S | 93 |
| Concord Dr., S. N&S | 2W-26S | 93 |
| Concord Dr., W. E&W | 2W-26S | 93 |
| Constance Ln. N&S | 1W-24S,1W-23S | 93 |
| Coolidge St. N&S | 1W-24S | 93 |
| Cottage Grove Av. N&S | 0E-25S | 94 |
| Country Club Rd. E&W | 1W-25S | 93 |
| Craig Dr. E&W | 1W-23S | 88 |
| Crescent Dr. E&W | 1W-25S | 93 |
| D'amico Dr. N&S | 2W-25S,2W-24S | 93 |
| Dartmouth Dr. N&S | 1W-26S | 93 |
| Dawn Ln. N&S | 1W-23S | 88 |
| De Angelis Ct. N&S | 1W-24S | 93 |
| Deer Trail Rd. E&W | 2W-24S | 93 |
| Division St. N&S | 2W-26S,2W-25S | 93 |

| Street | Grid | Page |
|---|---|---|
| Dixie Hwy. NW&SE | 1W-25S,1W-24S | 93 |
| Donovan Dr. N&S | 2W-25S | 93 |
| Doris Ln. N&S | 1W-23S | 88 |
| East End Av. N&S | 0W-26S | 94 |
| Eastgate Av. | 1W-24S,0W-24S | 93 |
| Eddy St. E&W | 1W-23S | 88 |
| Edgewood Av. N&S | 1W-23S | 93 |
| Elder Av. E&W | 1W-25S | 93 |
| Elmwood Dr. E&W | 1W-23S | 88 |
| Emelia St. E&W | 1W-24S | 93 |
| Emerald Av. N&S | 0W-25S,0W-24S | 94 |
| Engleston Av. N&S | 0W-24S | 94 |
| Enterprise Ct. NW&SE | 2W-24S | 93 |
| Enterprise Dr. N&S | 2W-24S | 93 |
| Euclid Av. E&W | 1W-26S | 93 |
| Fairview Av. N&S | 2W-24S | 93 |
| Fitch Rd. E&W | 2W-24S | 93 |
| Flossmoor Rd. NE&SW | 1W-23S | 88 |
| Floyd Ln. N&S | 1W-23S | 88 |
| Forest St. E&W | 1W-26S | 93 |
| Francis Ln. E&W | 1W-23S | 88 |
| Franklin Av. N&S | 1W-25S | 93 |
| Frederick Dr. E&W | 1W-23S | 88 |
| Frontage Rd. E&W | 0W-27S | 94 |
| Gail Ln. E&W | 2W-24S | 93 |
| Garden Av. N&S | 1W-25S | 93 |
| Glengate Av. N&S | 2W-24S,0W-24S | 93 |
| Glenwood Rd. NE&SW | 0W-23S | 88 |
| Grace Ln. N&S | 1W-23S | 88 |
| Grant Av. N&S | 1W-24S | 93 |
| Green St. N&S | 0W-25S | 94 |
| Greenbriar Av. E&W | 1W-24S | 93 |
| Gregory Dr. E&W | 2W-25S | 93 |
| Grosvenor Pl. N&S | 1W-24S | 93 |
| Halsted St. N&S | 1W-26S,1W-24S | 93 |
| Hamilton Wood N&S | 1W-23S | 88 |
| Hanover St. N&S | 0W-25S | 94 |
| Hawthorne Ln. E&W | 1W-24S | 93 |
| Hickory St. E&W | 2W-25S,1W-25S | 93 |
| Highland Dr. E&W | 2W-24S | 93 |
| Hillcrest Av. E&W | 1W-24S | 93 |
| Hilltop Av. N&S | 2W-25S | 93 |
| Holbrook Cir. NS&EW | 1W-23S | 88 |
| Holbrook Rd. E&W | 1W-23S | 88 |
| Homewood Ct. N&S | 1W-24S | 93 |
| Illinois St. N&S | 1W-25S | 93 |
| Independence Way E&W | 1W-25S | 93 |
| Ingrid Ln. N&S | 2W-25S | 93 |
| Iris Ln. N&S | 1W-23S | 88 |
| Irving Blvd. E&W | 1W-25S | 93 |
| Isa Av. E&W | 1W-25S | 93 |
| Joe Orr Rd. E&W | 2W-24S,0E-24S | 93 |
| Joyce Ln. N&S | 1W-23S | 88 |
| Judith Ln. E&W | 1W-23S | 88 |
| Kathleen Ln. N&S | 1W-23S | 88 |
| Kingston Pl. E&W | 1W-24S | 93 |
| Laflin St. N&S | 1W-25S | 93 |
| Laura Ln. E&W | 1W-23S | 88 |
| Lawrence St. N&S | 2W-26S | 93 |
| Le Rose Dr. N&S | 1W-23S | 88 |
| Leonard Av. N&S | 1W-23S | 88 |
| Lexington Dr. N&S | 2W-24S | 93 |
| Lincoln Av. NE&SW | 0W-25S | 94 |
| Lincoln Hwy. E&W | 2W-25S,0E-25S | 93 |
| Linden Ln. E&W | 1W-24S | 93 |
| Longwood Ct. E&W | 2W-24S | 93 |
| Longwood Dr. N&S | 2W-24S | 93 |
| Lowe Av. N&S | 0W-25S,0W-24S | 94 |
| Luther Ln. N&S | 2W-24S | 93 |
| Lynn Ln. E&W | 1W-23S | 88 |
| Mackler Dr. N&S | 2W-24S | 93 |
| Main St. E&W | 2W-26S,0W-26S | 93 |
| Manchester Dr. N&S | 1W-24S | 93 |
| Maple Ln. E&W | 1W-24S | 93 |
| Marian Way N&S | 2W-24S | 93 |
| Martin Ln. E&W | 0W-24S | 94 |
| Mason Ct. N&S | 0W-25S | 94 |
| May Ct. E&W | 1W-23S | 88 |
| Mayfair Pl. N&S | 1W-24S,1W-23S | 93 |
| McArthur Dr. N&S | 2W-24S | 93 |
| McEldowney Pl. E&W | 1W-25S | 93 |
| McKinley Av. NE&SW | 0W-25S | 94 |
| Meadow Ln. E&W | 1W-25S | 93 |
| Memorial Dr. NS&EW | 1W-24S | 93 |
| Mildred Ln. N&S | 1W-23S | 88 |
| Millview Dr. N&S | 3W-26S | 92 |
| Minette Ln. NE&SW | 2W-25S | 93 |
| Morgan St. E&W | 0W-25S | 94 |
| Morgan St. N&S | 1W-23S | 88 |
| Normal Av. N&S | 0W-24S | 94 |
| Normandy Dr. NS&EW | 1W-23S | 88 |
| Oak St. NW&SE | 1W-25S | 93 |
| Orchard Av. N&S | 1W-25S | 93 |
| Otto Blvd. NW&SE | 1W-25S | 93 |
| Pagoria Dr. N&S | 0W-27S | 94 |
| Pamela Ln. N&S | 1W-23S | 88 |
| Park Av. NW&SE | 1W-25S | 93 |
| Parkside Av. E&W | 1W-24S | 93 |
| Parkview Av. NW&SE | 1W-25S | 93 |
| Parnell Av. N&S | 0W-25S,0W-24S | 94 |
| Patricia Dr. N&S | 1W-23S | 88 |
| Peggy Ln. N&S | 2W-25S | 93 |
| Peoria St. N&S | 1W-23S | 88 |
| Peyton Dr. E&W | 1W-23S | 88 |
| Piacenti Ln. N&S | 2W-25S | 93 |
| Pleasant Dr. E&W | 1W-23S | 88 |
| Plymouth Dr. NW&SE | 1W-26S | 93 |
| Portland Av. N&S | 0W-25S | 94 |
| Prairie Av. N&S | 1W-23S | 88 |
| Ranger Dr. E&W | 2W-24S | 93 |
| Raye Dr., E. E&W | 1W-23S | 88 |
| Raye Dr., W. E&W | 1W-23S | 88 |
| Revere St. N&S | 2W-26S | 93 |
| Roberta Ln. N&S | 1W-23S | 88 |
| Rosewood Ln. E&W | 1W-25S | 93 |
| Rt. 1 N&S | 1W-25S | 93 |
| Sandra Ln. E&W | 2W-24S | 93 |
| Sangamon St. N&S | 1W-23S | 88 |
| Saratoga Dr. E&W | 2W-24S | 93 |
| Schilling Av. N&S | 1W-24S | 93 |
| School St. N&S | 1W-25S | 93 |
| Scott Av. N&S | 2W-25S | 93 |
| Serena Dr. N&S | 1W-23S | 88 |
| Shea Dr. N&S | 2W-24S | 93 |
| Shelly Ln. N&S | 2W-25S | 93 |
| Sherry Ln. N&S | 1W-23S | 88 |
| Shields Av. N&S | 0W-25S | 94 |
| Southgate Av. E&W | 1W-24S | 93 |
| Spruce Ln. E&W | 1W-24S | 93 |
| Standish St. E&W | 2W-26S | 93 |
| State St. N&S | 0W-26S,0W-24S | 94 |
| Stewart Av. N&S | 0W-26S,0W-24S | 94 |
| Stirling Av. N&S | 2W-25S | 93 |
| Strieff Av. E&W | 1W-24S | 93 |
| Sue Ct. E&W | 1W-23S | 88 |
| Sunnyside Av. N&S | 1W-25S | 93 |
| Sunset Av. N&S | 2W-24S | 93 |
| Tahoe Dr. E&W | 1W-23S | 88 |
| Terrace Dr. E&W | 1W-23S | 88 |
| Terry Ct. E&W | 1W-23S | 88 |
| Thelma Ln. E&W | 1W-23S | 88 |
| Theresa Ln. N&S | 1W-23S | 88 |
| Thomas St. N&S | 2W-24S | 93 |
| Thorn St. N&S | 1W-25S | 93 |
| Thorne Ct. NE&SW | 0W-24S | 94 |
| Travers Ct. NE&SW | 2W-24S | 93 |
| Union Av. N&S | 0W-26S,0W-24S | 94 |
| Vincennes Av. NW&SE | 1W-25S | 93 |
| Vollmer Rd. E&W | 2W-23S,0W-23S | 87 |
| Wallace Av. N&S | 1W-25S | 93 |
| Wallace St. N&S | 0W-26S,0W-24S | 94 |
| Washington Av. NE&SW | 0W-25S | 94 |
| Wentworth Av. N&S | 0W-26S,0W-24S | 94 |
| West End Av. NE&SW | 0W-25S | 94 |
| Western Av. N&S | 2W-25S | 93 |
| Westgate Av. N&S | 1W-24S | 93 |
| Willow Dr. NW&SE | 1W-24S | 93 |
| Wilson Av. N&S | 2W-25S | 93 |
| Winchester Rd. E&W | 2W-24S | 93 |
| Winston Av. N&S | 2W-24S | 93 |
| Wood St. N&S | 2W-24S | 93 |
| Wooster Ct. N&S | 2W-26S | 93 |
| Yale Av. N&S | 2W-26S | 93 |
| Yorktown Rd. E&W | 2W-24S | 93 |
| 5th Av. N&S | 0W-25S | 94 |
| 7th Pl. E&W | 1W-24S | 94 |
| 8th St. E&W | 2W-24S | 93 |
| 10th St. E&W | 2W-25S,0W-24S | 93 |
| 11th Pl. E&W | 2W-25S | 93 |
| 11th St. E&W | 1W-25S,0W-25S | 93 |
| 12th Pl. SW&NE | 1W-25S | 93 |
| 12th St. E&W | 2W-25S,0W-25S | 93 |
| 13th St. E&W | 1W-25S,0W-25S | 93 |
| 14th Pl. E&W | 2W-25S,1W-25S | 93 |
| 14th St. E&W | 1W-25S,0W-25S | 93 |
| 15th Pl. E&W | 2W-25S,1W-25S | 93 |
| 15th St. E&W | 2W-25S,1W-25S | 93 |
| 16th Pl. E&W | 2W-25S,0W-25S | 93 |
| 16th St. E&W | 2W-25S,0W-25S | 93 |
| 16th St. E&W | 0E-25S | 94 |
| 17th St. E&W | 2W-25S,0W-25S | 93 |
| 19th Pl. E&W | 1W-26S | 93 |
| 19th St. E&W | 1W-26S | 93 |
| 21st St. E&W | 1W-25S,0W-25S | 93 |
| 22nd St. E&W | 0W-26S | 94 |
| 23rd St. E&W | 1W-26S,0W-26S | 93 |
| 24th St. E&W | 1W-26S,0W-26S | 93 |
| 25th St. E&W | 1W-26S,0W-26S | 93 |
| 26th St. E&W | 1W-26S,0W-26S | 93 |
| 28th St. E&W | 0W-26S | 94 |
| 197th Pl. E&W | 0W-23S | 88 |
| 197th St. E&W | 0W-23S | 88 |
| 202nd St. E&W | 2W-24S | 93 |
| 205th St. E&W | 2W-24S | 93 |
| 209th St. E&W | 2W-25S | 93 |

## Chicago Ridge

| Street | Grid | Page |
|---|---|---|
| Anderson Av. N&S | 8W-11S | 65 |
| Austin Av. N&S | 7W-12S | 66 |
| Avon Av. NW&SE | 8W-11S | 65 |
| Barnard Dr. NE&SW | 8W-12S | 65 |
| Birmingham Av. NW&SE | 7W-12S | 66 |
| Brooks Ln. NE&SW | 8W-12S | 65 |
| Central Av. N&S | 7W-12S | 66 |
| Charles St. N&S | 8W-12S | 65 |
| Fireside Dr. E&W | 8W-11S | 65 |
| Forest Ln. N&S | 8W-12S | 65 |
| Harlem Av. N&S | 8W-11S | 65 |
| Hyland Pl. N&S | 8W-11S | 65 |
| Interstate 294 NW&SE | 8W-11S | 65 |
| Janet Ln. E&W | 8W-11S | 65 |
| Kitty Ln. NW&SE | 8W-11S | 65 |
| Leslie Ln. N&S | 8W-12S | 65 |
| Lombard Av. N&S | 7W-12S | 66 |
| Lyman Av. N&S | 7W-12S | 66 |
| Lyman Av. NE&SW | 7W-12S | 66 |
| Major Av. N&S | 7W-12S | 66 |
| Mansfield Av. N&S | 7W-12S | 66 |
| Marshall Av. NW&SE | 7W-12S | 66 |
| Mason Av. N&S | 7W-12S | 66 |
| Massasoit Av. N&S | 7W-12S | 66 |
| Mather Av. NW&SE | 8W-11S,7W-12S | 65 |
| Mayfield Av. N&S | 7W-12S | 66 |
| McVicker Av. N&S | 7W-12S | 66 |
| Menard Av. N&S | 7W-12S | 66 |
| Michael Ln. N&S | 8W-11S | 65 |
| Monitor Av. N&S | 7W-12S | 66 |
| Moody Av. N&S | 7W-12S | 66 |
| Nashville Av. N&S | 8W-12S | 65 |
| Natchez St. N&S | 8W-11S | 65 |
| Natoma Av. N&S | 8W-11S | 65 |
| New England Av. N&S | 8W-11S | 65 |
| Norfolk Ln. N&S | 8W-11S | 65 |
| Normandy Av. N&S | 8W-12S | 65 |
| Nottingham Av. N&S | 8W-11S | 65 |
| O'Connell Dr. N&S | 8W-11S | 65 |
| Oak Av. N&S | 7W-12S | 66 |
| Oak Park Av. N&S | 8W-12S,8W-11S | 65 |
| Orchard Ln. N&S | 8W-12S | 65 |
| Oxford Av. N&S | 7W-12S | 66 |
| Pamela Ln. E&W | 8W-12S | 65 |
| Parkside Av. N&S | 7W-12S | 66 |
| Pleasant Blvd. NW&SE | 7W-12S | 66 |
| Princess Av. N&S | 7W-12S | 66 |
| Ready Dr. E&W | 8W-11S | 65 |
| Ridge Dr. NE&SW | 8W-12S | 65 |
| Ridgeland Av. N&S | 7W-12S,7W-11S | 66 |
| Ridgemont Ln. NW&SE | 7W-12S | 66 |
| Rt. 43 N&S | 8W-12S | 65 |
| Rt. 7 NE&SW | 8W-11S | 65 |
| Rutherford Av. N&S | 8W-11S | 65 |
| Sayre Av. N&S | 8W-11S | 65 |
| Southwest Hwy. NE&SW | 8W-12S,8W-11S | 65 |
| Stephen Dr. N&S | 8W-11S | 65 |
| Sycamore Dr. N&S | 8W-12S | 65 |
| Tracey Av. N&S | 8W-12S | 65 |
| Virginia Av. NW&SE | 8W-11S | 65 |
| Washington St. NW&SE | 7W-12S | 66 |
| 97th Pl. E&W | 8W-11S | 65 |
| 98th St. E&W | 8W-11S | 65 |
| 99th Pl. E&W | 8W-11S | 65 |
| 99th St. E&W | 8W-11S | 65 |
| 100th St. E&W | 8W-11S | 65 |
| 101st St. E&W | 7W-11S | 66 |
| 102nd Pl. E&W | 8W-11S | 65 |
| 103rd St. E&W | 8W-11S,7W-11S | 65 |
| 104th Pl. E&W | 8W-11S | 65 |
| 104th St. E&W | 8W-12S | 65 |
| 105th St. E&W | 8W-12S,7W-12S | 65 |
| 106th Pl. E&W | 8W-11S | 65 |
| 106th St. E&W | 8W-12S,7W-12S | 65 |
| 107th Pl. E&W | 7W-12S | 66 |
| 107th St. E&W | 8W-12S,7W-12S | 65 |
| 108th Pl. E&W | 7W-12S | 66 |
| 108th St. E&W | 7W-12S | 66 |
| 109th Pl. E&W | 7W-12S | 66 |
| 109th St. E&W | 7W-12S | 66 |
| 110th St. E&W | 7W-12S | 66 |
| 111th St. E&W | 7W-12S | 66 |

## Cicero

| Street | Grid | Page |
|---|---|---|
| Austin N&S | 7W-3S | 54 |
| Austin Blvd. N&S | 7W-2S | 54 |
| Central N&S | 7W-3S,7W-2S | 54 |
| Cermak Rd. E&W | 6W-1S | 55 |
| Cicero Av. N&S | 5W-3S,6W-1S | 54 |
| Edgewood E&W | 7W-3S | 54 |
| Laramie N&S | 6W-3S,6W-1S | 55 |
| Ogden E&W | 7W-3S | 54 |
| Park E&W | 7W-3S | 54 |
| Rt. 50 N&S | 6W-2S | 55 |
| 12th Pl. E&W | 5W-1S | 55 |
| 13th E&W | 7W-1S | 54 |
| 14th E&W | 7W-1S | 54 |
| 15th E&W | 7W-1S,6W-1S | 54 |
| 15th Pl. E&W | 7W-1S,6W-1S | 54 |
| 16th E&W | 7W-1S | 54 |
| 18th E&W | 7W-1S,6W-1S | 54 |
| 19th E&W | 7W-1S,6W-1S | 54 |
| 20th E&W | 5W-1S | 55 |
| 21st E&W | 7W-1S,6W-1S | 54 |
| 21st Pl. E&W | 6W-1S | 55 |
| 22nd E&W | 7W-2S | 54 |
| 23rd E&W | 7W-2S,6W-2S | 54 |
| 24th Pl. E&W | 6W-1S | 55 |
| 25th E&W | 6W-2S | 55 |
| 25th Pl. E&W | 6W-1S | 55 |
| 26th E&W | 6W-1S | 55 |
| 28th E&W | 6W-1S | 55 |
| 28th Pl. E&W | 6W-1S | 55 |
| 29th E&W | 6W-1S | 55 |
| 29th Pl. E&W | 6W-1S | 55 |
| 30th E&W | 6W-1S | 55 |
| 30th Pl. E&W | 6W-1S | 55 |
| 31st E&W | 7W-2S,6W-1S | 54 |
| 31st Pl. E&W | 6W-3S | 55 |
| 32nd E&W | 6W-3S | 55 |
| 32nd Pl. E&W | 6W-3S | 55 |
| 33rd E&W | 7W-3S,6W-3S | 54 |
| 34th E&W | 7W-3S | 54 |
| 35th E&W | 6W-3S | 55 |
| 36th E&W | 6W-3S | 55 |
| 37th E&W | 6W-3S | 55 |
| 38th E&W | 6W-3S | 55 |
| 46th N&S | 5W-1S | 55 |
| 47th N&S | 5W-1S | 55 |
| 47th Ct. N&S | 5W-1S | 55 |
| 48th Ct. N&S | 6W-2S,6W-1S | 55 |
| 49th N&S | 6W-3S,6W-1S | 55 |
| 49th Ct. N&S | 6W-1S | 55 |
| 50th N&S | 6W-2S,6W-1S | 55 |
| 50th Ct. N&S | 6W-3S,6W-1S | 55 |
| 51st N&S | 6W-3S,6W-1S | 55 |
| 51st Ct. N&S | 6W-1S | 55 |
| 52nd Ct. N&S | 6W-3S | 55 |
| 53rd N&S | 6W-3S,6W-2S | 55 |
| 53rd Ct. N&S | 6W-2S | 55 |
| 54th N&S | 6W-3S,6W-1S | 55 |
| 54th Ct. N&S | 6W-3S | 55 |
| 55th N&S | 6W-3S,6W-1S | 55 |
| 55th Ct. N&S | 6W-3S,6W-1S | 55 |
| 56th Ct. N&S | 7W-3S,7W-1S | 54 |
| 57th N&S | 7W-3S,7W-1S | 54 |
| 57th Ct. N&S | 7W-3S,7W-1S | 54 |
| 58th N&S | 7W-3S,7W-1S | 54 |
| 58th Ct. N&S | 7W-3S,7W-1S | 54 |
| 59th N&S | 7W-3S,7W-1S | 54 |
| 59th Ct. N&S | 7W-3S,7W-1S | 54 |
| 60th N&S | 7W-3S | 54 |
| 60th Ct. N&S | 7W-3S,7W-1S | 54 |
| 61st N&S | 7W-3S,7W-1S | 54 |
| 61st Ct. N&S | 7W-3S,7W-1S | 54 |

## Country Club Hills

| Street | Grid | Page |
|---|---|---|
| Amlin Cir. N&S | 6W-22S | 86 |
| Amlin Ln. N&S | 6W-22S | 86 |
| Anthony Av. N&S | 5W-21S | 86 |
| Anthony St. N&S | 5W-22S | 86 |
| Apple Tree Dr. N&S | 5W-20S | 87 |
| Arlington Av. N&S | 4W-21S | 87 |
| Baker Av. N&S | 5W-22S,5W-21S | 86 |
| Baker St. NE&SW | 5W-21S | 86 |
| Becker Tr. N&S | 5W-22S | 86 |
| Birch Av. N&S | 5W-22S | 86 |
| Birch St. N&S | 5W-22S | 86 |
| Brairgate Dr. N&S | 4W-20S | 87 |
| Cedar Av. N&S | 5W-22S,5W-21S | 86 |
| Cedar St. N&S | 5W-22S | 86 |
| Central Pk. Av. N&S | 4W-21S | 87 |
| Chestnut Av. N&S | 5W-21S,5W-22S | 86 |
| Chestnut Dr. N&S | 5W-23S,5W-22S | 86 |
| Cicero Av. N&S | 6W-21S,6W-20S | 86 |
| Clarence Av. N&S | 5W-21S | 86 |
| Country Club Dr. N&S | 4W-21S | 87 |
| Coventry Ln. N&S | 5W-20S | 86 |
| Crest Ct. E&S | 6W-22S | 86 |
| Cypress Av. N&S | 5W-22S,5W-21S | 86 |
| Cypress Ct. N&S | 5W-23S | 86 |
| Cypress Dr. N&S | 5W-23S,5W-22S | 86 |
| Devon Av. N&S | 5W-21S | 87 |
| East Gate Dr. N&S | 5W-20S | 87 |
| Edwards Av. N&S | 5W-20S | 86 |
| Elm Dr. N&S | 5W-23S | 86 |
| Fairoak Ct. N&S | 5W-21S | 86 |
| Fairoak Dr. E&W | 6W-21S | 86 |
| Fairway Ter. NW&SE | 5W-21S | 86 |
| Farm Crest Ter. N&S | 5W-22S | 87 |
| Frontage Rd. N&S | 6W-20S | 86 |
| Glen Oaks Ct. NW&SE | 4W-20S | 87 |
| Glen Oaks Dr. NE&SE | 4W-20S | 87 |
| Greenview Ter. N&S | 5W-21S | 87 |
| Harvard Ln. N&S | 4W-21S | 87 |
| Hawthorne Dr. N&S | 5W-21S | 86 |
| Hickory Pl. N&S | 5W-23S | 86 |
| Highland Pl. E&W | 4W-21S | 87 |
| Holly Ct.* N&S | 4W-20S | 87 |
| Hollywood Dr. E&W | 5W-21S | 86 |
| Hollywood Ln. NE&SE | 6W-21S | 86 |
| Idlewild Dr. N&S | 5W-21S | 86 |
| Indian Hills Dr. NE&SW | 5W-20S | 87 |
| Interstate 57 NE&SW | 6W-20S | 86 |
| Interstate 80 NE&SW | 5W-20S | 86 |
| John Av. N&S | 5W-21S | 86 |
| John St. N&S | 5W-22S | 86 |
| Juneway Ct. N&S | 5W-21S | 86 |
| Keeler Av. N&S | 5W-22S,5W-21S | 86 |
| Kostner Av. N&S | 5W-21S | 86 |
| Lake Ct. E&W | 6W-22S | 86 |
| Lakeview Dr. E&W | 5W-21S | 86 |
| Laramie Rd. N&S | 6W-22S | 86 |
| Larkin Ln. N&S | 5W-21S | 86 |
| Lavergne Av. N&S | 6W-20S,6W-21S | 86 |
| Laverne Av. N&S | 6W-20S | 86 |
| Lee St. N&S | 5W-22S | 86 |
| Loras Ln. N&S | 5W-22S | 86 |
| Loretto Ln. N&S | 5W-22S | 86 |
| Maple Av. N&S | 5W-22S,5W-21S | 86 |
| Maple Ter. E&W | 5W-22S | 86 |
| Martin Ct. N&S | 5W-22S | 86 |
| Martin Ln. N&S | 5W-22S | 86 |
| Mary Ann Ln. NE&SW | 5W-21S | 86 |
| Mary Ct. E&W | 6W-22S | 86 |
| Marycrest Dr. N&S | 6W-22S | 86 |
| Marylakes Dr. N&S | 6W-22S | 86 |
| Michael Av. N&S | 5W-21S | 86 |
| Mocombo Way N&S | 6W-21S | 86 |
| Mulberry Dr. N&S | 5W-21S | 86 |
| Mulberry Ter. N&S | 5W-22S | 86 |
| Neal Cir. N&S | 6W-22S | 86 |
| Nightingale Ln. N&S | 6W-22S | 86 |
| Nightingdale Ter. N&S | 6W-22S | 86 |
| Oakwood Ct. N&S | 5W-22S,5S-21S | 86 |
| Oakwood Ct. N&S | 5W-22S | 86 |
| Old Elm Dr. N&S | 4W-20S | 87 |
| Olympia Dr. N&S | 5W-21S | 86 |
| Orchard Av. N&S | 4W-20S | 87 |
| Park Ln. N&S | 5W-20S | 86 |
| Patrick Av. N&S | 5W-21S | 86 |
| Peartree Ct.* N&S | 4W-20S | 87 |
| Pheasant Ln. N&S | 4W-21S | 87 |
| Poplar N&S | 6W-21S | 86 |
| Princeton Ln. N&S | 4W-21S | 87 |
| Provincetown Dr. E&W | 5W-22S | 86 |
| Pulaski Rd. N&S | 5W-20S,5W-23S | 86 |
| Ravisloe Ter. N&S | 5W-21S | 86 |
| Rosewood Ter. N&S | 5W-21S | 86 |
| Rt. 50 N&S | 5W-22S,5W-20S | 86 |
| Russet Way NE&SW | 5W-20S | 86 |
| Sarah Ct. NW&SE | 4W-21S | 87 |
| Sarah Ln. N&S | 4W-21S | 87 |
| School Dr. E&W | 4W-21S | 86 |
| Soleri Dr. NE&SW | 5W-21S | 86 |
| Springfield Av. N&S | 4W-21S | 87 |
| Sunset Av. E&W | 6W-22S | 86 |
| Sunset Ridge Dr. N&S | 4W-20S | 87 |
| Sycamore Av. N&S | 5W-21S | 86 |
| Thomas Ln. NE&SW | 5W-21S | 86 |
| Timerlea Ct. N&S | 4W-20S | 87 |
| Timerlea Ln.* N&S | 4W-20S | 87 |
| Vista N&S | 6W-21S | 86 |
| Walnut Av. N&S | 5W-22S | 86 |
| Wildwood Way N&S | 4W-20S | 87 |
| Williamsburg Rd. E&W | 5W-22S | 87 |
| Willow Av. N&S | 5W-22S,5W-21S | 86 |
| Willow Ct. N&S | 5W-21S | 86 |
| Wilshire Blvd. N&S | 6W-21S | 86 |
| Windsor Av. N&S | 5W-22S | 86 |
| Winston Ct. NW&SE | 4W-21S | 87 |
| Winston Dr. E&W | 4W-21S | 87 |
| Yale Ln. N&S | 4W-21S | 87 |
| 19th Pl. E&W | 6W-22S | 86 |
| 167th Pl. E&W | 4W-20S | 87 |
| 167th St. E&W | 5W-19S,4W-19S | 81 |
| 168th Pl. E&W | 4W-20S | 87 |
| 168th St. E&W | 4W-20S | 87 |
| 169th St. E&W | 4W-20S | 87 |
| 171st Pl. E&W | 4W-20S | 87 |
| 171st St. E&W | 4W-20S | 87 |
| 172nd Pl. NE&SW | 5W-20S | 86 |
| 172nd St. E&W | 4W-20S | 87 |

| Street | Grid | Page |
|---|---|---|
| 173rd St. E&W | 6W-20S | 86 |
| 175th Pl E&W | 4W-21S | 87 |
| 175th Pl. E&W | 5W-21S | 86 |
| 175th St. E&W | 5W-20S,4W-21S | 86 |
| 176th St. E&W | 5W-21S | 86 |
| 176th St. E&W | 4W-21S | 87 |
| 177th Pl. E&W | 5W-21S | 86 |
| 177th St. E&W | 5W-21S,4W-21S | 86 |
| 178th Pl. E&W | 4W-21S | 87 |
| 178th St. E&W | 5W-21S | 86 |
| 179th Pl. E&W | 5W-21S | 86 |
| 179th St. E&W | 6W-21S,5W-21S | 86 |
| 180th St. E&W | 5W-21S | 86 |
| 181st St. E&W | 5W-21S | 86 |
| 182nd Pl. E&W | 5W-21S | 86 |
| 182nd St. E&W | 5W-21S | 86 |
| 183rd St. E&W | 5W-21S | 86 |
| 184th Ct. E&W | 6W-22S | 86 |
| 184th Pl. NE&SW | 5W-22S | 86 |
| 184th St. E&W | 5W-22S | 86 |
| 185th Ct. E&W | 6W-22S | 86 |
| 185th Pl. E&W | 5W-22S | 86 |
| 185th St. E&W | 6W-22S,6W-21S | 86 |
| 186th Pl. E&W | 5W-22S | 86 |
| 186th St. E&W | 5W-22S | 86 |
| 187th Pl. E&W | 5W-22S | 86 |
| 187th St. E&W | 6W-22S,5W-22S | 86 |
| 188th Pl. E&W | 5W-22S | 86 |
| 188th St. E&W | 5W-22S | 86 |
| 189th Pl. E&W | 5W-22S | 86 |
| 189th St. E&W | 5W-22S | 86 |
| 190th St. E&W | 6W-22S | 86 |
| 191st St. E&W | 6W-22S,5W-22S | 86 |
| 192nd Pl. E&W | 5W-23S | 86 |
| 192nd St. E&W | 5W-23S | 86 |
| 193rd Pl. E&W | 5W-23S | 86 |
| 194th Ct. E&W | 5W-23S | 86 |
| 194th St. E&W | 5W-23S | 86 |
| 195th St. E&W | 5W-23S | 86 |

## Countryside

| Street | Grid | Page |
|---|---|---|
| Adlai E. Stevenson Expwy. E&W | 13W-7S,12W-7S | 58 |
| Ashland N&S | 12W-6S,12W-5S | 58 |
| Barton E&W | 12W-6S | 58 |
| Bobolink E&W | 12W-5S | 58 |
| Brainard N&S | 12W-7S | 58 |
| Cantigny E&W | 13W-7S | 58 |
| Catherine N&S | 12W-6S,12W-5S | 58 |
| Constance SW&NE | 12W-7S,12W-6S | 58 |
| Crestview E&W | 13W-7S | 58 |
| Dansher N&S | 12W-5S | 58 |
| Dawn N&S | 13W-7S | 58 |
| East N&S | 12W-5S | 58 |
| Forestview E&W | 13W-7S | 58 |
| Francis Av. N&S | 12W-6S | 58 |
| Golfview N&S | 13W-7S | 58 |
| Hillsdale E&W | 13W-7S | 58 |
| Kensington N&S | 12W-6S | 58 |
| Leitch N&S | 13W-6S | 58 |
| Longview E&W | 12W-6S | 58 |
| Longview N&S | 12W-6S | 58 |
| Lorraine E&W | 12W-6S | 58 |
| Lorraine N&S | 13W-7S | 58 |
| Madison N&S | 12W-6S,12W-5S | 58 |
| Maplewood E&W | 13W-7S | 58 |
| Merry N&S | 12W-6S | 58 |
| Park N&S | 13W-6S | 58 |
| Parkside N&S | 13W-7S | 58 |
| Peck N&S | 13W-6S | 58 |
| Rose Av. N&S | 12W-6S | 58 |
| Rose Ct. N&S | 12W-6S | 58 |
| Rosemary N&S | 12W-6S | 58 |
| Staleford E&W | 13W-7S | 58 |
| Sunset N&S | 13W-7S | 58 |
| Terry E&W | 12W-6S | 58 |
| Willow Springs N&S | 13W-6S | 58 |
| 6th N&S | 12W-6S,12W-5S | 58 |
| 7th N&S | 12W-5S | 58 |
| 8th N&S | 12W-5S | 58 |
| 9th N&S | 12W-5S | 58 |
| 55th St. E&W | 12W-5S | 58 |
| 56th E&W | 12W-6S | 58 |
| 57th St. E&W | 12W-6S | 58 |
| 58th E&W | 12W-6S | 58 |
| 60th Pl. E&W | 12W-6S | 58 |
| 61st Pl. E&W | 12W-6S | 58 |
| 67th E&W | 13W-7S | 58 |
| 71st Pl. E&W | 13W-8S | 58 |
| 75th E&W | 13W-8S | 58 |

## Crestwood

| Street | Grid | Page |
|---|---|---|
| Arbor Ln. E&W | 6W-15S | 74 |
| Avers Av. N&S | 4W-16S | 75 |
| Calumet Sag Rd. NW&SE | 6W-15S,5W-15S | 74 |
| Carriage Ln. N&S | 7W-15S | 74 |
| Central Av. N&S | 7W-15S | 74 |
| Char Ln. N&S | 6W-16S | 74 |
| Cicero Av. N&S | 6W-16S,6W-15S | 74 |
| Circle Ct. E&W | 6W-15S | 74 |
| Crescent Ct. NW&SE | 6W-15S | 74 |
| Crestbrook Ct. N&S | 6W-15S | 74 |
| Crestview Ct. N&S | 6W-16S | 74 |
| Crestwood Ct. NW&SE | 6W-15S | 74 |
| Crestwood Dr. E&W | 6W-15S | 74 |
| Dori Ln. N&S | 6W-16S | 74 |
| E. Circle Av. N&S | 6W-15S | 74 |
| East Playfield Dr. N&S | 6W-15S | 74 |
| Fairway Dr. NS&EW | 6W-15S | 74 |
| Forestview Ct. E&W | 6W-15S | 74 |
| Forestview Ln. N&S | 6W-15S | 74 |
| Hamlin Av. N&S | 4W-16S | 75 |
| Harding Av. N&S | 4W-16S | 75 |
| Highland Ct. E&W | 6W-15S | 74 |
| Hill Dr. N&S | 7W-15S | 74 |
| Homestead Dr. E&W | 6W-15S | 74 |
| Interstate 294 NW&SE | 5W-16S,4W-16S | 74 |
| James Ct. E&W | 6W-16S | 74 |
| James Dr. NW&SE | 6W-16S | 74 |
| Karlov Av. N&S | 5W-16S | 74 |
| Keeler Av. N&S | 5W-16S | 74 |
| Kenneth Ct. N&S | 6W-15S | 74 |
| Kenton Av. N&S | 6W-15S,5W-16S | 74 |
| Kildare Av. N&S | 5W-16S | 74 |
| Kilpatrick Av. N&S | 5W-16S | 74 |
| Kostner Av. N&S | 5W-16S | 74 |
| Lamon Av. N&S | 6W-16S | 74 |
| Laramie Av. N&S | 6W-16S,6W-15S | 74 |
| Laramie Ct. N&S | 6W-16S | 74 |
| Lavergne Av. N&S | 6W-16S | 74 |
| Lawler Av. N&S | 6W-16S | 74 |
| LeClaire Av. N&S | 6W-15S | 74 |
| Leclaire Av. N&S | 6W-16S | 74 |
| Leonard Dr. N&S | 6W-16S | 74 |
| Linder Av. E&W | 6W-15S | 74 |
| Long Av. N&S | 6W-16S,6W-15S | 74 |
| Loomis Ct. N&S | 6W-15S | 74 |
| Loomis Ln. N&S | 6W-16S | 74 |
| Midlothian Turnpike NE&SW | 6W-16S,5W-16S | 74 |
| Model Ct. NE&SW | 6W-15S | 74 |
| Park Ct. NW&SE | 6W-15S | 74 |
| Park Ln. E&W | 6W-15S | 74 |
| Park Pl. N&S | 7W-15S | 74 |
| Parkview Ct. E&W | 6W-15S | 74 |
| Pleasant Ln. E&W | 6W-15S | 74 |
| Pulaski Rd. N&S | 5W-16S | 74 |
| Regal Ct. N&S | 6W-16S | 74 |
| Regal Dr. E&W | 6W-16S | 74 |
| Rexford Rd. NE&SW | 4W-16S | 75 |
| Rivercrest Ct. E&W | 6W-15S | 74 |
| Rivercrest Dr. SW&NE | 6W-15S | 74 |
| Royal E&W | 6W-16S | 74 |
| Rt. 50 N&S | 5W-16S | 74 |
| Sandra Ln. N&S | 6W-16S,6W-15S | 74 |
| Short Dr. N&S | 6W-16S | 74 |
| South End Ln. N&S | 6W-16S | 74 |
| Springfield Av. N&S | 4W-16S | 75 |
| Terrace Ln. N&S | 6W-15S | 74 |
| Tri State Tollway NW&SE | 5W-16S,4W-16S | 74 |
| Village Ct. NW&SE | 6W-15S | 74 |
| Village Ln. N&S | 6W-15S | 74 |
| W. Circle Av. N&S | 6W-15S | 74 |
| W. Circle Dr. Pkwy. E&W | 6W-15S | 74 |
| Walter Dr. N&S | 6W-16S | 74 |
| Waterbury Ct. E&W | 6W-16S | 74 |
| Waterbury Dr. N&S | 6W-16S | 74 |
| Waterbury Ln. E&W | 6W-16S | 74 |
| Waterbury Way E&W | 6W-16S | 74 |
| West End Ln. N&S | 6W-15S | 74 |
| West Playfield Dr. N&S | 6W-15S | 74 |
| 128th Pl. E&W | 6W-15S | 74 |
| 128th St. E&W | 7W-15S | 74 |
| 129th Pl. E&W | 6W-15S | 74 |
| 129th St. E&W | 7W-15S | 74 |
| 130th St. E&W | 6W-15S | 74 |
| 131st St. E&W | 6W-15S | 74 |
| 132nd Ct. E&W | 6W-15S | 74 |
| 132nd St. E&W | 6W-15S | 74 |
| 133rd St. E&W | 6W-15S | 74 |
| 134th Pl. E&W | 6W-15S | 74 |
| 135th Pl. E&W | 6W-16S | 74 |
| 135th St. E&W | 6W-15S,5W-15S | 74 |
| 136th Ct. E&W | 5W-16S | 74 |
| 136th Pl. E&W | 6W-16S | 74 |
| 137th Pl. E&W | 6W-16S,5W-16S | 74 |
| 137th St. E&W | 6W-16S,5W-16S | 74 |
| 138th Ct. E&W | 6W-16S | 74 |
| 138th Pl. E&W | 6W-16S | 74 |
| 138th St. E&W | 6W-16S,5W-16S | 74 |
| 139th Pl. E&W | 6W-16S | 74 |
| 139th St. E&W | 6W-16S | 74 |
| 140th Pl. E&W | 6W-16S | 74 |
| 141st St. E&W | 6W-16S,4W-16S | 74 |
| 142nd St. E&W | 6W-16S,5W-16S | 74 |
| 143rd Pl. E&W | 6W-17S | 80 |
| 143rd St. E&W | 5W-16S | 74 |

## Deerfield*

**(Also see Lake County)**

| Street | Grid | Page |
|---|---|---|
| County Line Rd. NS&EW | 10W-18N | 17 |
| Interstate 94 E&W | 11W-18N | 16 |
| Route 43 NW&SE | 10W-18N | 17 |

## Des Plaines

| Street | Grid | Page |
|---|---|---|
| Acres Ln. N&S | 12W-10N | 36 |
| Albany Ln. NE&SW | 14W-12N | 25 |
| Alden Ln. NW&SE | 12W-8N | 36 |
| Alfini Dr. NS&EW | 14W-10N | 35 |
| Alger E&W | 12W-8N | 36 |
| Algonquin Rd. E&W | 14W-10N | 35 |
| Alles St. N&S | 13W-11N | 26 |
| Ambleside Rd. E&W | 15W-11N | 25 |
| Amherst Av. N&S | 14W-12N | 25 |
| Anderson Ter. N&S | 15W-10N | 34 |
| Andrea Ln. N&S | 15W-10N | 34 |
| Andy Ct. E&W | 12W-8N | 36 |
| Anita N&S | 14W-11N | 25 |
| Applecreek Ln. N&S | 12W-10N | 36 |
| Ardmore Rd. N&S | 14W-12N | 25 |
| Arlington Av. N&S | 13W-11N | 26 |
| Armstrong Rd. NS&EW | 15W-8N | 34 |
| Arnold Ct. N&S | 15W-10N | 34 |
| Ash Ln. N&S | 13W-9N | 35 |
| Ashland Av. E&W | 14W-10N,13W-10N | 35 |
| Ballard Rd. E&W | 12W-11N | 26 |
| Beau Ct. E&W | 15W-10N,15W-11N | 34 |
| Beau Dr. N&S | 15W-10N,15W-11N | 34 |
| Bedford Ln. N&S | 14W-11N | 25 |
| Bell Dr. N&S | 15W-11N | 25 |
| Bellaire Av. N&S | 12W-11N | 26 |
| Bellaire Ct. E&W | 11W-11N | 26 |
| Bennett Ln. N&S | 15W-11N | 25 |
| Bennett Pl. E&W | 12W-9N | 36 |
| Berkshire Ct. N&S | 14W-12N | 25 |
| Berkshire Ln. E&W | 14W-12N,13W-12N | 25 |
| Berry Ln. E&W | 12W-10N | 36 |
| Big Bend Dr. NW&SE | 12W-11N | 26 |
| Birch St. N&S | 12W-9N | 36 |
| Birchwood Av. E&W | 14W-9N,12W-9N | 35 |
| Bittersweet Ct. NW&SE | 13W-9N | 35 |
| Bradley Ct. NE&SW | 15W-11N | 25 |
| Bradley St. E&W | 15W-11N,14W-11N | 25 |
| Bradrock Dr. E&W | 14W-9N | 35 |
| Brentwood Dr. E&W | 15W-11N | 25 |
| Briar Ct. E&W | 13W-9N | 35 |
| Broadway N&S | 14W-12N | 25 |
| Brown St. E&W | 13W-11N | 26 |
| Busse Hwy. NW&SE | 12W-10N | 36 |
| Cambridge Rd. N&S | 14W-12N | 25 |
| Campbell Av. E&W | 13W-10N,12W-10N | 35 |
| Carol Ln. NS&EW | 13W-10N | 35 |
| Cavan Ln. N&S | 15W-11N | 25 |
| Cedar Ct. E&W | 12W-9N | 36 |
| Cedar St. N&S | 12W-9N | 36 |
| Center St. NE&SW | 13W-10N,13W-11N | 35 |
| Central Av. E&W | 12W-8N | 36 |
| Central Rd. E&W | 14W-12N | 25 |
| Chase Av. E&W | 12W-9N | 36 |
| Chestnut St. N&S | 13W-9N | 35 |
| Chicago Av. NS&EW | 12W-11N | 26 |
| Church St. E&W | 11W-11N | 26 |
| Cindy Ln. N&S | 14W-10N | 35 |
| Circle St. NE&SW | 13W-9N | 35 |
| Clark Ln. N&S | 15W-10N | 34 |
| Clayton Ln. N&S | 14W-12N | 25 |
| Columbia Av. E&W | 14W-11N | 25 |
| Concord Ln. NS&EW | 13W-12N | 26 |
| Cora St. N&S | 12W-9N,12W-10N | 36 |
| Cordial Ln. E&W | 15W-10N | 34 |
| Cornell Av. N&S | 14W-12N | 25 |
| Courtesy Ln. E&W | 15W-10N | 34 |
| Crabtree Ln. N&S | 12W-10N | 36 |
| Craig Dr. NS&EW | 12W-8N | 36 |
| Cranbrook St. E&W | 14W-12N | 25 |
| Crestwood Dr. NS&EW | 14W-11N | 25 |
| Cumberland Pkwy. N&S | 14W-11N,14W-12N | 25 |
| Curtis St. N&S | 12W-8N | 36 |
| Dale St. N&S | 12W-8N | 36 |
| Danbury Ln. N&S | 15W-10N | 34 |
| Dara James Rd. N&S | 15W-11N | 25 |
| Daton Pl. N&S | 15W-10N | 34 |
| David Dr. E&W | 12W-8N | 36 |
| Davis Ct. E&W | 14W-11N | 25 |
| Dawn Ct. N&S | 12W-11N | 26 |
| Deane St. N&S | 13W-9N | 35 |
| Debra Dr. E&W | 15W-11N | 25 |
| Dempster St. E&W | 14W-10N,12W-10N | 35 |
| Dennis Pl. NS&EW | 13W-10N | 35 |
| Denver Dr. E&W | 15W-10N | 34 |
| Des Plaines River Rd. N&S | 12W-8N,13W-11N | 36 |
| Devon Av. E&W | 12W-8N | 36 |
| Devonshire Dr. E&W | 15W-10N | 34 |
| Dexter Ln. N&S | 13W-9N | 35 |
| Diamond Head Dr. E&W | 15W-10N | 34 |
| Doreen Dr. N&S | 15W-10N | 34 |
| Dorthy Dr. E&W | 15W-10N | 34 |
| Douglas Av. N&S | 14W-9N | 35 |
| Dover Dr. E&W | 15W-10N | 34 |
| Dover Ln. E&W | 15W-10N | 34 |
| Drake Ln. E&W | 14W-12N | 25 |
| Dulles Rd. E&W | 15W-11N | 25 |
| Eaker Pl. E&W | 15W-10N | 34 |
| Earl Av. N&S | 13W-10N | 35 |
| East Grant Dr. N&S | 13W-10N | 35 |
| East River Rd. NE&SW | 12W-11N | 26 |
| East Villa Dr. N&S | 13W-10N | 35 |
| Eastview Dr. N&S | 13W-9N | 35 |
| Easy St. N&S | 15W-11N | 25 |
| Edward Ct. N&S | 11W-11N | 26 |
| Eisenhower Ct. N&S | 12W-8N | 36 |
| Eisenhower Dr. N&S | 12W-8N | 36 |
| Elizabeth Ln. E&W | 15W-10N | 34 |
| Elk Blvd. NS&EW | 12W-11N | 26 |
| Ellinwood St. NW&SE | 13W-11N | 26 |
| Elm St. N&S | 13W-9N | 35 |
| Elmhurst Rd. N&S | 15W-10N | 34 |
| Elmira Av. N&S | 14W-9N | 35 |
| Esser Ct. E&W | 12W-9N | 36 |
| Estes Av. E&W | 12W-8N | 36 |
| Everett Av. E&W | 13W-9N,12W-9N | 35 |
| Everett Ln. E&W | 13W-9N | 35 |
| Evergreen Av. E&W | 14W-11N,13W-11N | 25 |
| Executive Way NS&EW | 13W-10N | 35 |
| Fairhope Av. E&W | 15W-8N | 34 |
| Fargo Av. E&W | 13W-9N,12W-9N | 35 |
| Farthing Ln. N&S | 15W-11N | 25 |
| Farwell Av. E&W | 12W-8N | 36 |
| Figard Ln. NS&EW | 15W-11N | 25 |
| Fletcher Dr. E&W | 14W-11N | 25 |
| Florian Dr. E&W | 15W-10N | 34 |
| Forest Av. E&W | 14W-10N,12W-10N | 35 |
| Forest Ln. E&W | 12W-11N | 26 |
| Forestedge Ln. N&S | 12W-11N | 26 |
| Fox Ln. E&W | 12W-8N | 36 |
| Fremont Av. E&W | 14W-11N | 25 |
| Fremont Ct. E&W | 15W-11N | 25 |
| Frontage Rd. N&S | 13W-9N | 35 |
| Galleon N&S | 15W-11N | 25 |
| Garland Pl. N&S | 12W-11N | 26 |
| Golf Cul De Sac, N. E&W | 13W-12N | 26 |
| Golf Cul De Sac, S. E&W | 13W-12N | 26 |
| Golf Rd. E&W | 13W-12N | 26 |
| Good Av. N&S | 11W-11N | 26 |
| Graceland Av. NE&SW | 13W-10N,13W-11N | 35 |
| Greco Av. N&S | 12W-8N | 36 |
| Greenleaf Av. E&W | 12W-8N | 36 |
| Greenview Av. E&W | 14W-11N,13W-11N | 25 |
| Gregory St. E&W | 13W-13N | 26 |
| Grove Av. N&S | 12W-11N | 26 |
| Halsey Dr. NE&SW | 12W-8N | 36 |
| Harding Av. E&W | 14W-11N,13W-11N | 25 |
| Harvard St. E&W | 14W-12N | 25 |
| Harvey Av. NS&EW | 14W-11N | 25 |
| Hawthorne Ln. N&S | 12W-11N | 26 |
| Hawthorne Ter. NW&SE | 12W-11N | 26 |
| Hazel Ct. E&W | 13W-9N | 35 |
| Heather Ln. N&S | 13W-10N | 35 |
| Henry Av. E&W | 13W-10N,12W-10N | 35 |
| Hewitt Dr. N&S | 15W-10N | 34 |
| Hickory St. N&S | 12W-9N | 36 |
| Higgins Rd. E&W | 15W-8N | 34 |
| Highland Dr. E&W | 13W-9N | 35 |
| Hills Av. E&W | 13W-11N,12W-11N | 26 |
| Hinsdale Rd. N&S | 15W-8N | 34 |
| Hoffman Pkwy. E&W | 14W-10N,13W-10N | 35 |
| Holiday Ln. E&W | 15W-10N | 34 |
| Hollywood Av. E&W | 13W-11N | 26 |
| Horne Ter. N&S | 15W-10N | 34 |
| Howard Av. E&W | 14W-9N,12W-9N | 35 |
| Ida St. N&S | 13W-11N | 26 |
| Illinois St. N&S | 13W-9N | 35 |
| Ingram Pl. N&S | 15W-10N | 34 |
| Inner Circle Dr. N&S | 14W-12N | 25 |
| Interstate 294 N&S | 12W-8N | 36 |
| Interstate 90 NW&SE | 16W-9N,12W-8N | 34 |
| Iris Ln. N&S | 12W-8N | 36 |
| Ironwood N&S | 11W-11N | 26 |
| Irwin Av. E&W | 13W-9N | 35 |
| James Rd. N&S | 15W-11N | 25 |
| Janice Av. N&S | 15W-10N | 34 |
| Jarlath Av. E&W | 14W-9N | 35 |
| Jarvis Av. E&W | 15W-9N,12W-9N | 34 |
| Jeanette St. N&S | 13W-10N | 35 |
| Jefferson St. E&W | 13W-11N | 26 |
| Jeffry Ln. E&W | 15W-10N | 34 |
| Jill Ct. E&W | 15W-10N | 34 |
| Jon Ct. N&S | 15W-11N | 25 |
| Jon Ln. N&S | 14W-12N | 25 |
| Joseph Av. N&S | 12W-8N | 36 |
| Joseph J. Schwab Rd. NW&SE | 12W-10N | 36 |
| Josephine Ct.* N&S | 14W-12N | 25 |
| Joyce N&S | 15W-10N | 34 |
| Junior Ter. NW&SE | 12W-11N | 26 |
| Kathleen Dr. E&W | 15W-11N,14W-11N | 25 |
| Kenilworth Ct. N&S | 14W-11N | 25 |
| Kennicott Ct. E&W | 12W-9N | 36 |
| Kerry Ct. E&W | 11W-11N | 26 |
| King Ln. E&W | 15W-10N | 34 |
| Kingston Ct. N&S | 13W-10N | 35 |
| Kinkaid Ct. E&W | 15W-10N | 34 |
| Koehler Dr. N&S | 13W-9N | 35 |
| Kylemore Ct. NW&SE | 13W-13N | 26 |
| Kylemore Dr. E&W | 13W-13N | 26 |
| LaSalle St. N&S | 14W-11N | 25 |
| Lancaster Ln. E&W | 15W-10N | 34 |
| Lance Dr. E&W | 15W-11N | 25 |
| Laura Ln. E&W | 12W-8N | 36 |
| Laurel Av. N&S | 13W-11N | 26 |
| Lawn Ln. N&S | 15W-11N | 25 |
| Leahy Cir., E. N&S | 15W-10N,15W-11N | 34 |
| Leahy Cir., S. E&W | 15W-10N | 34 |
| Lechner Ln. E&W | 11W-11N | 26 |
| Lee St. N&S | 13W-8N,13W-10N | 35 |
| Leslie Ln. N&S | 15W-10N | 34 |
| Lillian Ln. N&S | 15W-11N | 25 |
| Lincoln Av. E&W | 15W-10N,12W-10N | 34 |
| Linden St. N&S | 12W-9N | 36 |
| Lismore Ct. E&W | 13W-13N | 26 |
| Lismore Dr. E&W | 13W-13N | 26 |
| Little Path Rd. N&S | 15W-11N | 25 |
| Locust St. N&S | 12W-9N | 36 |
| Luau Dr. E&W | 14W-12N | 25 |
| Lunt Av. E&W | 12W-8N | 36 |
| Lyman Av. N&S | 12W-11N | 26 |
| Lynn Ct. N&S | 15W-11N | 25 |
| Madelyn Dr. NS&EW | 13W-13N | 26 |
| Magnolia St. N&S | 12W-9N | 36 |
| Mannheim Rd. N&S | 13W-9N,13W-11N | 35 |
| Manor Ct. N&S | 14W-11N | 25 |
| Maple St. N&S | 12W-8N,12W-9N | 36 |
| Marcella Rd. N&S | 14W-12N | 25 |
| Margaret St. N&S | 13W-10N | 35 |
| Marina St. N&S | 15W-12N | 25 |
| Mark Av. E&W | 13W-13N | 26 |
| Marshall Dr. N&S | 15W-9N,15W-11N | 34 |
| Mary St. N&S | 13W-12N | 26 |
| Mason Ln. N&S | 12W-10N | 36 |
| McCain Ct. E&W | 15W-10N | 34 |
| Meadow Ln. N&S | 11W-11N | 26 |
| Meyer Ct. NW&SE | 14W-11N,14W-12N | 25 |
| Miami Ln. NW&EW | 15W-10N | 34 |
| Michael Ct. E&W | 15W-11N | 25 |
| Michael Rd. E&W | 15W-11N | 25 |
| Mill St. E&W | 12W-11N | 26 |
| Millers Rd. E&W | 15W-11N,14W-11N | 25 |
| Miner (Northwest Hwy) NW&SE | 14W-11N | 25 |
| Morgan O'brien St. E&W | 14W-12N | 25 |
| Morray Ct. E&W | 15W-10N | 34 |
| Morse Av. E&W | 12W-8N | 36 |
| Mt. Prospect Rd. N&S | 15W-8N,14W-12N | 34 |
| Munroe Cir. E&W | 15W-10N | 34 |
| Murray Ln. E&W | 15W-10N | 34 |
| Nebel Ln. E&W | 13W-9N | 35 |
| Nelson Ln. N&S | 14W-12N | 25 |
| Nimitz Dr. E&W | 12W-8N | 36 |
| Norman Ct. E&W | 15W-11N | 25 |
| North Av. E&W | 13W-11N | 26 |
| North Shore Av. E&W | 12W-8N | 36 |
| Northeast Pl. NE&SW | 13W-10N | 35 |
| Northwest Hwy. NW&SE | 14W-12N | 25 |
| Northwest Pl. NW&SE | 14W-10N | 35 |
| Northwest Tollway NW&SE | 16W-9N,12W-8N | 34 |
| Oak St. N&S | 13W-11N | 26 |

| | Grid | Page |
|---|---|---|
| Oakton Pl. N&S | 13W-9N | 35 |
| Oakton St. E&W | | |
| | 15W-10N,12W-10N | 34 |
| Oakwood Av. E&W | | |
| | 14W-10N,13W-10N | 35 |
| Oakwood Ct. E&W | | |
| | 14W-10N,13W-10N | 35 |
| Olivia Av N&S | 13W-9N | 35 |
| Orchard Ct. N&S | 14W-11N | 25 |
| Orchard Pl. N&S | 12W-8N | 36 |
| Orchard St. N&S | | |
| | 12W-9N,12W-10N | 36 |
| Oxford Rd. N&S | | |
| | 14W-9N,14W-10N | 35 |
| Park Pl. NW&SE | 13W-11N | 26 |
| Parkview Ln. N&S | 12W-10N | 36 |
| Parkwood Ln. N&S | 12W-8N | 36 |
| Parsons Av. NW&SE | | |
| | 13W-11N | 26 |
| Partricia Ln. N&S | 14W-12N | 25 |
| Patton Dr. N&S | 12W-8N | 36 |
| Paula Ln. NS&EW | 12W-8N | 36 |
| Pearle St. E&W | 12W-8N | 36 |
| Pearson St. NE&SW | | |
| | 13W-10N,13W-11N | 35 |
| Pennsylvania Av. N&S | | |
| | 15W-10N | 34 |
| Perda Ln. N&S | 15W-10N | 34 |
| Perry St. E&W | 13W-11N | 26 |
| Peter Rd. N&S | 12W-8N | 36 |
| Phoenix Dr. N&S | 15W-10N | 34 |
| Pine St. N&S | 13W-9N | 35 |
| Pinehurst Dr. N&S | 14W-12N | 25 |
| Plainfield St. E&W | 13W-9N | 35 |
| Pleasant Ln. E&W | 15W-10N | 34 |
| Polynesian Dr. E&W | | |
| | 14W-12N | 25 |
| Potter Rd. N&S | 11W-11N | 26 |
| Prairie Av. NS&EW | | |
| | 13W-11N,11W-11N | 26 |
| Pratt Av. E&W | 13W-9N | 35 |
| Princeton Av. E&W | 14W-12N | 25 |
| Prospect Av. | | |
| | 13W-9N,12W-9N | 35 |
| Prospect Ln. E&W | 13W-9N | 35 |
| Radcliff Av. N&S | | |
| | 14W-11N,14W-12N | 25 |
| Rand Rd. NW&SE | 13W-11N | 26 |
| Rawls Rd. E&W | 14W-10N | 35 |
| Redeker Rd. E&W | 13W-10N | 26 |
| Regency N&S | 14W-12N | 25 |
| Ridge Ln. N&S | 15W-10N | 34 |
| Rita Rd. N&S | 11W-11N | 26 |
| River Dr. N&S | 12W-10N | 36 |
| River Ln. N&S | 12W-11N | 26 |
| River St. N&S | 12W-11N | 26 |
| Riverview Av. E&W | 13W-9N | 35 |
| Rose Av. N&S | | |
| | 14W-11N,13W-11N | 25 |
| Roxbury Ln. E. N&S | 15W-10N | 34 |
| Roxbury Ln. E. | | |
| | 14W-10N | 35 |
| Rt. 58 E&W | | |
| | 14W-11N,13W-12N | 25 |
| Rt. 72 E&W | | |
| | 14W-9N,12W-8N | 35 |
| Rt. 83 N&S | | |
| | 15W-10N,15W-11N | 34 |
| Rusty Dr. N&S | 12W-8N | 36 |
| Sakas Dr. N&S | 13W-11N | 26 |
| Sandy Ln. N&S | 14W-12N | 25 |
| Santa Rosa Dr. E&W | | |
| | 14W-8N | 35 |
| Scott St. N&S | | |
| | 12W-8N,12W-9N | 36 |
| Seegers Rd. E&W | 14W-11N | 25 |
| Seminary Av. E&W | 11W-11N | 26 |
| Seymour Av. N&S | 15W-10N | 34 |
| Shagbark Dr. N&S | 12W-10N | 36 |
| Shannon Ct. NS&EW | | |
| | 15W-11N | 25 |
| Shawn Ln. N&S | 15W-11N | 25 |
| Shepherd Dr. N&S | 13W-9N | 35 |
| Sherman Pl. E&W | | |
| | 13W-11N,12W-11N | 26 |
| Sherwin Av. E&W | 12W-9N | 36 |
| Sherwood Rd. NW&SE | | |
| | 12W-11N | 26 |
| Short Ter. N&S | 15W-10N | 34 |
| Simone Dr. NW&SE | | |
| | 14W-12N | 25 |
| South Ln. N&S | 12W-8N | 36 |
| Southeast Pl. NE&SW | | |
| | 13W-10N | 35 |
| Southwest Pl. NE&SW | | |
| | 14W-10N | 35 |
| Springfield Ter. E&W | | |
| | 15W-10N | 34 |
| Spruance Pl. N&S | 15W-10N | 34 |
| Spruce St. N&S | 13W-9N | 35 |
| Sprucewood Av. N&S | | |
| | 14W-9N | 35 |
| Stark Pl. N&S | 15W-10N | 34 |
| State St. E&W | 14W-12N | 25 |
| Stewart Av. E&W | 12W-10N | 36 |
| Stillwell Dr. N&S | 12W-8N | 36 |
| Stockton Av. E&W | | |
| | 12W-9N,13W-9N | 36 |
| Stone St. E&W | 14W-12N | 25 |
| Stratford Rd. N&S | 14W-12N | 25 |
| Suffield St. E&W | 11W-11N | 26 |
| Sunset Av. E&W | 12W-8N | 36 |
| Susan Dr. N&S | 15W-10N | 34 |
| Sycamore St. N&S | | |
| | 12W-8N,12W-9N | 36 |
| Terrace Ln. E&W | 14W-11N | 25 |
| Thacker St. E&W | | |
| | 14W-11N,13W-10N | 25 |

| | Grid | Page |
|---|---|---|
| Therese Ter. E&W | 13W-13N | 26 |
| Times Dr. N&S | 13W-10N | 35 |
| Timothy Ln. NS&EW | | |
| | 14W-13N,13W-13N | 26 |
| Touhy Av. E&W | 13W-9N | 35 |
| Tracy Ter. E&W | 14W-12N | 25 |
| Trailside Ln. N&S | 12W-11N | 26 |
| Tri-State Tollway N&S | | |
| | 12W-8N,12W-11N | 36 |
| Tures Ln. N&S | 13W-9N | 35 |
| U.S. Route 12 SE&NW | | |
| | 13W-10N,14W-12N | 35 |
| U.S. Route 14 SE&NW | | |
| | 14W-11N | 25 |
| U.S. Route 45 N&S | | |
| | 13W-10N | 35 |
| University St. E&W | 11W-11N | 26 |
| Van Buren Av. E&W | | |
| | 14W-10N,12W-10N | 35 |
| Vassar Ln. N&S | 14W-12N | 25 |
| Victoria Rd. N&S | 15W-11N | 25 |
| Village Ct. NE&SW | 14W-12N | 25 |
| Waikiki Dr. NW&SE | | |
| | 14W-12N | 25 |
| Walnut Av. E&W | | |
| | 15W-10N,12W-10N | 34 |
| Walnut Ct. N&S | | |
| | 14W-10N,13W-10N | 35 |
| Walter Av. E&W | 13W-11N | 26 |
| Warrington Rd. NW&SE | | |
| | 14W-10N,14W-12N | 35 |
| Washington Ct. E&W | | |
| | 14W-11N | 25 |
| Washington St. E&W | | |
| | 14W-11N,13W-11N | 25 |
| Wayne Dr. NS&EW | | |
| | 13W-10N | 35 |
| Webford Av. NW&SE | | |
| | 13W-10N | 26 |
| Webster Av. E&W | 12W-8N | 36 |
| Webster Ln. N&S | | |
| | 13W-9N,13W-10N | 35 |
| Wedgewood Dr. N&S | | |
| | 14W-10N | 35 |
| Welwyn Av. E&W | 12W-9N | 36 |
| West Grant Dr. N&S | | |
| | 14W-10N | 35 |
| West Villa Dr. N&S | 14W-10N | 35 |
| Western Av. N&S | 13W-11N | 26 |
| Westfield Ln. N&S | 15W-10N | 34 |
| Westgate Rd. N&S | | |
| | 14W-10N,14W-12N | 35 |
| Westmere Rd. E&W | | |
| | 15W-11N | 25 |
| Westview Dr. N&S | 13W-9N | 35 |
| Wexford St. E&W | 13W-13N | 26 |
| Whitcomb Av. E&W | | |
| | 13W-10N,12W-10N | 35 |
| White St. N&S | | |
| | 12W-9N,12W-10N | 36 |
| Wicke Av. E&W | | |
| | 13W-10N,12W-10N | 35 |
| Wiebolts Dr. NW&SE | | |
| | 14W-11N | 25 |
| Wilkins Dr. N&S | 15W-11N | 25 |
| Wille Rd. E&W | 15W-9N | 34 |
| Willow Av. E&W | 12W-11N | 26 |
| Wilson Av. N&S | 12W-11N | 26 |
| Wilson Dr. N&S | 15W-10N | 34 |
| Windsor Dr. NE&SW | | |
| | 15W-10N | 34 |
| Winthrop Dr. N&S | 14W-9N | 35 |
| Wisconsin Dr. N&S | | |
| | 14W-12N | 25 |
| Wolf Rd. N&S | | |
| | 14W-9N,13W-13N | 35 |
| Woodbridge Rd. N&S | | |
| | 14W-11N | 25 |
| Woodland Av. N&S | | |
| | 13W-11N,12W-11N | 26 |
| Woodlawn Av. E&W | | |
| | 13W-11N | 26 |
| Woods Rd. E&W | 12W-11N | 26 |
| Yale Ct. E&W | 14W-12N | 25 |
| Yorkshire Ln. E&W | | |
| | 14W-12N,13W-12N | 25 |
| 1st Av. N&S | 13W-11N | 26 |
| 2nd Av. N&S | | |
| | 13W-10N,13W-11N | 35 |
| 3rd Av. N&S | | |
| | 13W-10N,13W-11N | 35 |
| 4th Av. N&S | | |
| | 14W-10N,14W-11N | 35 |
| 5th Av. N&S | | |
| | 14W-10N,14W-12N | 35 |
| 5th Ct. NE&SW | 14W-11N | 25 |
| 6th Av. N&S | | |
| | 14W-10N,14W-11N | 35 |
| 7th Av. N&S | | |
| | 14W-11N,14W-12N | 25 |
| 8th Av. N&S | 14W-12N | 25 |

## Dixmoor

| | Grid | Page |
|---|---|---|
| Ash St. E&W | 2W-16S | 75 |
| Ashland Av. N&S | 1W-17S | 82 |
| Calumet Av. N&S | 2W-16S | 81 |
| Circle Dr. NS&EW | 2W-16S | 75 |
| Cooper Av. N&S | 2W-17S | 81 |
| Cooper St. N&S | 2W-16S | 75 |
| Dan Ryan Expressway | | |
| NE&SW | 2W-17S,2W-16S | 81 |
| Davis Av. N&S | 2W-17S | 81 |
| Davis Ct. N&S | 2W-16S | 75 |
| Elm St. E&W | 2W-16S | 75 |
| Harvey Av. NW&SE | 2W-17S | 81 |
| Honore Av. N&S | | |
| | 2W-17S,2W-16S | 81 |

| | Grid | Page |
|---|---|---|
| Hoyne Av. N&S | 2W-17S | 81 |
| Interstate 57 NE&SW | | |
| | 2W-17S,2W-16S | 81 |
| Joliet Av. E&W | 2W-17S | 81 |
| Lawson Ln. E&W | 2W-16S | 75 |
| Leavit Av. N&S | | |
| | 2W-17S,2W-16S | 81 |
| Lincoln Av. N&S | | |
| | 2W-17S,2W-16S | 81 |
| Maple St. E&W | 2W-16S | 75 |
| Marshfield Av. N&S | 1W-17S | 82 |
| Norris St. E&W | 2W-16S | 81 |
| Oak St. E&W | 2W-16S | 75 |
| Oakley Av. N&S | 2W-17S | 81 |
| Page Av. N&S | 2W-16S | 75 |
| Paulina Av. N&S | 1W-17S | 82 |
| Robey Av. N&S | | |
| | 2W-17S,2W-16S | 81 |
| Seeley Av. N&S | 2W-17S | 81 |
| Sibley Blvd. E&W | 2W-17S | 81 |
| Spaulding Av. NW&SE | | |
| | 2W-16S | 75 |
| Thornton Rd. NW&SE | | |
| | 2W-17S | 81 |
| Vail Av. N&S | 2W-17S | 81 |
| Walnut St. E&W | 2W-16S | 75 |
| Western Av. N&S | | |
| | 2W-17S,2W-16S | 81 |
| Winchester Av. N&S | | |
| | 2W-17S,2W-16S | 81 |
| Wood St. N&S | | |
| | 2W-17S,2W-16S | 81 |
| 140th St. E&W | 2W-16S | 75 |
| 141st St. E&W | 2W-16S | 75 |
| 142nd St. E&W | 2W-16S | 75 |
| 143rd St. E&W | 2W-17S | 81 |
| 144th St. E&W | 2W-17S | 81 |
| 144th St. E&W | | |
| | 2W-17S,1W-17S | 81 |
| 145th St. E&W | 2W-17S | 81 |
| 146th St. E&W | 2W-17S | 81 |

## Dolton

| | Grid | Page |
|---|---|---|
| Adams St. N&S | 0E-16S | 82 |
| Ann St. E&W | 0E-16S | 82 |
| Atlantic St. NE&SW | 0W-17S | 82 |
| Avalon Av. N&S | 1E-17S | 82 |
| Beachview Ter. N&S | 0E-17S | 82 |
| Berg Dr. E&W | 1E-18S | 82 |
| Berger Av. E&W | 0E-16S | 82 |
| Blackstone Av. N&S | 1E-17S | 82 |
| Blouin Dr. E&W | 1E-18S | 82 |
| California Av. NE&SW | | |
| | 0E-17S,1E-17S | 82 |
| Calumet Expressway N&S | | |
| | 1E-17S | 82 |
| Calumet Av. N&S | | |
| | 0E-16S,1E-16S | 82 |
| Catalpa Ln. E&W | 0E-17S | 82 |
| Center Av. N&S | 0E-16S | 82 |
| Champlain Av. N&S | 0E-17S | 82 |
| Chicago Rd. N&S | | |
| | 0E-17S,0E-16S | 82 |
| Clark St. N&S | 0W-17S | 82 |
| Claussen Ct. NE&SW | | |
| | 0E-16S | 82 |
| Cornell Av. N&S | | |
| | 2E-18S,2E-17S | 83 |
| Cottage Grove Av. N&S | | |
| | 0E-18S,0E-16S | 82 |
| Dante Av. N&S | | |
| | 1E-17S,1E-16S | 82 |
| Dearborn St. N&S | 0W-17S | 82 |
| Diekman Ct. N&S | 1E-17S | 82 |
| Dillner Pl. NE&SW | 0E-17S | 82 |
| Dobson Av. N&S | | |
| | 1E-18S,1E-16S | 82 |
| Dolton Rd. NW&SE | 1E-16S | 82 |
| Dorchester Av. N&S | | |
| | 1E-17S,1E-16S | 82 |
| Drexel Av. N&S | | |
| | 1E-18S,1E-16S | 82 |
| East End Av. N&S | 2E-18S | 83 |
| Edbrooke Av. N&S | 0W-17S | 82 |
| Ellis Av. N&S | 1E-18S,1E-16S | 82 |
| Engle Pl. E&W | 1E-17S | 82 |
| Engle St. E&W | 0E-16S | 82 |
| Euclid Av. E&W | 1E-17S | 82 |
| Evans Ct. N&S | 0E-17S | 82 |
| Evans St. N&S | 0E-17S | 82 |
| Evers St. N&S | 0E-17S | 82 |
| Forest Av. N&S | 0E-16S | 82 |
| Grant St. N&S | | |
| | 0E-17S,0E-16S | 82 |
| Greenwood Rd. NW&SE | | |
| | 0E-16S,1E-16S | 82 |
| Harding Av. E&W | 0E-17S | 82 |
| Harper Av. N&S | | |
| | 1E-17S,1E-16S | 82 |
| Hastings Dr. N&S | 1E-17S | 82 |
| Henry St. E&W | 1E-16S | 82 |
| Indiana Av. N&S | | |
| | 0W-17S,0W-16S | 82 |
| Ingleside Av. N&S | | |
| | 1E-18S,1E-16S | 82 |
| Interstate 94 N&S | 1E-16S | 82 |
| Irving Av. N&S | | |
| | 0E-17S,0E-16S | 82 |
| Jackson St. N&S | 0E-16S | 82 |
| Jefferson St. NW&SE | | |
| | 1E-16S,1E-17S | 82 |
| Kanawha St. E&W | 1E-16S | 82 |
| Kasten Dr. E&W | 1E-16S | 82 |
| Kenwood Av. N&S | | |
| | 1E-17S,1E-16S | 82 |
| Kimbark Av. N&S | | |
| | 1E-17S,1E-16S | 82 |

| | Grid | Page |
|---|---|---|
| La Salle St. N&S | 0W-17S | 82 |
| Lakeside Av. N&S | | |
| | 0E-17S,0E-16S | 82 |
| Langley Av. N&S | | |
| | 0E-17S,0E-16S | 82 |
| Lincoln Av. NW&SE | 0E-16S | 82 |
| Madison Av. N&S | 2E-18S | 83 |
| Madison St. NW&SE | 1E-17S | 82 |
| Main St. E&W | 0E-16S | 82 |
| Manor Ct. N&S | 0E-16S | 82 |
| Margaret St. N&S | 0E-16S | 82 |
| Maryland Av. N&S | | |
| | 1E-17S,1E-16S | 82 |
| Mc Arthur Ct. E&W | 0E-16S | 82 |
| Meadow Ln. N&S | 1E-17S | 82 |
| Memorial Dr. NW&SE | | |
| | 0E-17S | 82 |
| Michigan Av. N&S | 0W-17S | 82 |
| Michigan City Rd. NW&SE | | |
| | 0E-16S,2E-18S | 82 |
| Minera Av. N&S | | |
| | 1E-18S,1E-17S | 82 |
| Monroe St. E&W | 0E-16S | 82 |
| Murray Av. N&S | 0E-16S | 82 |
| Oak St. N&S | 0E-17S,0E-16S | 82 |
| Pamela Pl. NE&SW | 0E-16S | 82 |
| Park Av. N&S | 0E-16S | 82 |
| Parkside Dr. N&S | 0W-17S | 82 |
| Pennsylvania Av. N&S | | |
| | 1E-16S | 82 |
| Pennsylvania Av. NW&SE | | |
| | 0E-16S | 82 |
| Princeton Av. NE&SW | | |
| | 0W-17S | 82 |
| Riverside Dr. NW&SE | 1E-17S | 82 |
| Sanderson Av. N&S | 0E-16S | 82 |
| Shepard Dr. NW&SE | | |
| | 0E-16S,1E-16S | 82 |
| Sheridan Av. N&S | 0E-16S | 82 |
| Sheridan St. NE&SW | | |
| | 0W-17S | 82 |
| Sibley Blvd. E&W | | |
| | 0W-17S,1E-16S | 82 |
| State St. N&W | 0W-17S | 82 |
| Stein St. NE&SW | 0W-17S | 82 |
| Stewart Av. N&S | | |
| | 1E-17S,0E-16S | 82 |
| Stoney Island Av. N&S | | |
| | 2E-18S | 83 |
| Sunset Dr. N&S | | |
| | 1E-18S,1E-17S | 82 |
| University Av. N&S | | |
| | 1E-18S,1E-16S | 82 |
| Van Buren St. N&S | 0E-16S | 82 |
| Wabash Av. N&S | 0W-17S | 82 |
| Washington St. E&W | 0E-16S | 82 |
| Wentworth Av. N&S | 0W-17S | 82 |
| Woodlawn Av. N&S | | |
| | 1E-17S,1E-16S | 82 |
| 138th St. E&W | | |
| | 0E-16S,1E-16S | 82 |
| 139th Pl. E&W | 0E-16S | 82 |
| 140th Pl. NS&EW | 0E-16S | 82 |
| 141st St. E&W | 0E-16S | 82 |
| 141st St. NE&SW | 0E-16S | 82 |
| 142nd Pl. E&W | 0E-16S | 82 |
| 142nd St. E&W | | |
| | 0E-16S,1E-16S | 82 |
| 143rd St. E&W | | |
| | 0E-16S,1E-16S | 82 |
| 144th Pl. E&W | 0E-16S | 82 |
| 144th St. E&W | | |
| | 0E-16S,1E-16S | 82 |
| 145th St. E&W | | |
| | 0E-16S,1E-16S | 82 |
| 146th St. E&W | | |
| | 0E-16S,1E-16S | 82 |
| 147th Pl. E&W | 0E-17S | 82 |
| 147th St. E&W | | |
| | 0W-17S,1E-17S | 82 |
| 148th Pl. E&W | 0W-17S | 82 |
| 148th St. E&W | | |
| | 0W-17S,1E-17S | 82 |
| 149th St. E&W | | |
| | 0W-17S,1E-17S | 82 |
| 151st St. E&W | | |
| | 0E-17S,1E-17S | 82 |
| 152nd St. E&W | | |
| | 0E-17S,1E-17S | 82 |
| 153rd St. E&W | | |
| | 0E-17S,1E-17S | 82 |
| 154th Pl. E&W | | |
| | 1E-18S,2E-18S | 82 |
| 154th St. E&W | | |
| | 0E-17S,1E-17S | 82 |
| 155th Pl. E&W | 1E-18S | 82 |
| 155th St. E&W | | |
| | 1E-18S,2E-18S | 82 |
| 156th St. E&W | | |
| | 1E-18S,2E-18S | 82 |
| 157th St. E&W | 1E-18S | 82 |

## Downers Grove Township

| | Grid | Page |
|---|---|---|
| Deerpath Tr. E&W | 14W-9S | 64 |
| Maple Av. N&S | 14W-10S | 64 |
| Orchard St. NS&EW | | |
| | 14W-10S | 64 |
| Public St. N&S | 14W-10S | 64 |
| Railroad Av. (91st St.) | | |
| NE&SW | 14W-10S | 64 |
| 114th St. N&S | 14W-10S | 64 |

## East Dundee*
### (Also see Kane County)

| | Grid | Page |
|---|---|---|
| Healy Rd. NE&SW | 30W-14N | 20 |
| Higgins Rd. NW&SE | | |
| | 30W-14N | 20 |

## East Hazel Crest

| | Grid | Page |
|---|---|---|
| Ashland Av. N&S | 2W-20S | 87 |
| Center St. N&S | 1W-20S | 88 |
| Country Ln. NS&EW | | |
| | 2W-20S | 87 |
| Dixie Hwy. N&S | 2W-20S | 87 |
| Fisk Av. N&S | 1W-20S | 88 |
| Forestway Dr. NS&EW | | |
| | 2W-20S | 87 |
| Governors Hwy. N&S | | |
| | 2W-20S | 87 |
| Halsted St. N&S | 1W-20S | 88 |
| Hawthorne Dr. NE&SW | | |
| | 2W-20S | 87 |
| Laflin St. N&S | 1W-20S | 88 |
| Lathrop Av. N&S | 1W-20S | 88 |
| Loomis St. N&S | 1W-20S | 88 |
| Rt. 1 N&S | 1W-20S | 88 |
| Throop St. N&S | 1W-20S | 88 |
| Tri State Tollway E&W | | |
| | 2W-20S,1W-20S | 87 |
| Union Av. N&S | 1W-20S | 88 |
| Westview Av. N&S | 0W-20S | 88 |
| Wooded Path Rd. N&S | | |
| | 1W-20S | 88 |
| 171st St. E&W | | |
| | 2W-20S,1W-20S | 87 |
| 172nd Pl. NW&SE | 2W-20S | 87 |
| 172nd St. E&W | | |
| | 2W-20S,1W-20S | 87 |
| 173rd St. E&W | | |
| | 2W-20S,1W-20S | 87 |
| 174th St. E&W | 1W-20S | 88 |
| 175th St. E&W | 1W-20S | 88 |

## Elgin*
### (Also see Kane County)

| | Grid | Page |
|---|---|---|
| Abbeywood Ct. E&W | | |
| | 32W-12N | 20 |
| Adler Ln. NW&SE | 31W-11N | 30 |
| Alcott Ct. NW&SE | 31W-11N | 30 |
| Alder Ln. E&W | 31W-11N | 30 |
| Algona Av. E&W | 32W-12N | 20 |
| Algonquin Dr. N&S | 32W-12N | 20 |
| Allen Dr. N&S | 32W-11N | 30 |
| Allen Dr. NE&SW | 32W-11N | 30 |
| Aller St. NE&SW | 32W-10N | 30 |
| American Way E&W | | |
| | 32W-12N | 20 |
| Anderson Dr. N&S | 32W-10N | 30 |
| Anderson St. E&W | 32W-10N | 30 |
| Apple Hill Ct. E&W | 32W-12N | 20 |
| Apple Ln. NW&SE | 32W-11N | 30 |
| Arrowhead Ct. N&S | | |
| | 32W-12N | 20 |
| Arrowhead Dr. N&S | | |
| | 32W-12N | 20 |
| Arthur Dr. NS&EW | 32W-10N | 30 |
| Ash Dr. E&W | 32W-12N | 20 |
| Aspen Ct. N&S | 31W-11N | 30 |
| Barberry Ct. N&S | 32W-12S | 20 |
| Basswood Ct. E&W | | |
| | 32W-10N | 30 |
| Beaulah E&W | 32W-10N | 30 |
| Bedford Ct. E&W | 32W-12S | 20 |
| Bennett Dr. N&S | 32W-12N | 20 |
| Bent Ridge Ln. E&W | | |
| | 32W-12N | 20 |
| Bent Tree Ct. N&S | 32W-12N | 20 |
| Berkshire Ct. NW&SE | | |
| | 32W-10N | 30 |
| Beulah E&W | 32W-10N | 30 |
| Beverly Tr. N&S | 32W-10N | 30 |
| Birch Dr. E&W | 32W-11N | 30 |
| Blackhawk Dr. N&S | | |
| | 32W-12N | 20 |
| Bluff City Blvd. E&W | | |
| | 32W-10N | 30 |
| Bode Rd. E&W | | |
| | 32W-11N,31W-11N | 30 |
| Borden Cir. E&W | 31W-11N | 30 |
| Borden Ct. N&S | 31W-11N | 30 |
| Borden Dr. NS&EW | | |
| | 32W-11N,31W-11N | 30 |
| Bradford St. NE&SW | | |
| | 32W-12N | 20 |
| Brentwood Tr. NS&EW | | |
| | 31W-11N | 30 |
| Briarwood Ct. NW&SE | | |
| | 32W-11N | 30 |
| Briarwood Dr. N&S | | |
| | 31W-11N | 30 |
| Brittany Tr. NE&SW | | |
| | 31W-11N | 30 |
| Bruce Dr. NS&EW | 32W-11N | 30 |
| Brunswick Ct. N&S | | |
| | 32W-12N | 20 |
| Burns Dr. E&W | 31W-10N | 30 |
| Butler Bay Ct. E&W | | |
| | 32W-12N | 20 |
| Campus Ct. E&W | 31W-10N | 30 |
| Campus Dr. N&S | 31W-10N | 30 |
| Canterbury Ct. E&W | | |
| | 32W-12N | 20 |
| Cardinal Dr. E&W | 31W-11N | 30 |
| Carl Av. E&W | | |
| | 32W-12N,32W-11N | 20 |
| Carlton Dr. N&S | 32W-12N | 20 |
| Carlyle Ct. E&W | 31W-11N | 30 |

|  | Grid | Page |
|---|---|---|
| Carmella Ln. E&W .. | 32W-10N | 30 |
| Carriage Way E&W | | |
| .............. | 32W-12N | 20 |
| Case Ln. NE&SW .. | 32W-11N | 30 |
| Chaparral Ct. N&S .. | 31W-11N | 30 |
| Chapel Hill Dr. N&S | | |
| .............. | 31W-11N | 30 |
| Chaucer Ct. N&S . | 32W-11N | 30 |
| Chicago St. NW&SE | | |
| .............. | 32W-11N | 30 |
| Chippewa Dr. N&S.. | 32W-12N | 20 |
| Christopher Ct. NE&SW | | |
| .............. | 32W-12N | 20 |
| Cleveland Av. N&S | 32W-10N | 30 |
| Clover Hill Ct. N&S | 32W-13N | 20 |
| Cloverhill Ln. NS&EW | | |
| .............. | 32W-12N | 20 |
| Cobblers Crossing NS&EW | | |
| .............. | 32W-12N | 20 |
| Cobblers Crossing Ct. N&S | | |
| .............. | 32W-13N | 20 |
| Cobblestone Ct. NW&SE | | |
| .............. | 32W-12N | 20 |
| Coldspring Rd. NS&EW | | |
| .............. | 32W-12N | 20 |
| Coleman* Ct. N&S . | 32W-11N | 30 |
| Concord Ct. NE&SW | | |
| .............. | 31W-10N | 30 |
| Concord Dr. E&W | | |
| ...........32W-10N, | 31W-10N | 30 |
| Congdon Av. E&W . | 32W-12N | 20 |
| Congress St. E&W . | 32W-10N | 30 |
| Cookane Av. N&S .. | 32W-10N | 30 |
| Corley Ct. E&W .... | 31W-11N | 30 |
| Corley Dr. NW&SE | | |
| ....32W-11N, | 31W-11N | 30 |
| Dakota Ct. N&S .. | 32W-12N | 20 |
| Danridge Ct. N&S .. | 32W-12N | 20 |
| David N&S .... | 32W-11N | 30 |
| Deepwoods Ct. E&W | | |
| .............. | 32W-13N | 20 |
| Deepwoods Dr. N&S | | |
| .............. | 32W-12N | 20 |
| Dempster St. E&W | 32W-11N | 30 |
| Dickens Tr. NW&SE | | |
| .............. | 31W-11N | 30 |
| Dickie Av. NE&SW . | 32W-10N | 30 |
| Dogwood Ct. N&S .. | 31W-11N | 30 |
| Dover Ct. NE&SW .. | 32W-10N | 30 |
| Dover Dr. NE&SW .. | 32W-10N | 30 |
| Edgebrook Tr. NW&SE | | |
| .............. | 32W-10N | 30 |
| Eliot Tr. NW&SE.... | 31W-11N | 30 |
| Elma Av. E&W .. | 32W-12N | 20 |
| Elma Av. NS&EW .. | 32W-13N | 20 |
| Eric Cir. NW&SE ... | 31W-10N | 30 |
| Fairfax Ct. N&S .. | 32W-12S | 20 |
| Fairfax Ct. NW&SE | | |
| .............. | 32W-12S | 20 |
| Fieldstone Ct. NE&SW | | |
| .............. | 32W-12N | 20 |
| First St. N&S .. | 32W-13N | 20 |
| Ford Av. E&W.... | 32W-13N | 20 |
| Ford Ct. NE&SW .. | 32W-12N | 20 |
| Forest Av. E&W | | |
| ......32W-12N, | 32W-11N | 20 |
| Galt Blvd. N&S .. | 31W-10N | 30 |
| Gaskett Dr. E&W | | |
| .....32W-8N, | 31W-8N | 30 |
| Getty St. E&W .. | 32W-10N | 30 |
| Gifford Rd. N&S | | |
| .....32W-8N, | 32W-10N | 30 |
| Glen Ivy Dr. N&S .. | 32W-10N | 30 |
| Grand Av. E&W .. | 32W-12N | 20 |
| Grayshire Ct. N&S .. | 32W-12N | 20 |
| Green Ridge NS&EW | | |
| .............. | 32W-12N | 20 |
| Hackberry Ct. E&W | | |
| .............. | 32W-11N | 30 |
| Hampshire Ln. E&W | | |
| .............. | 32W-12N | 20 |
| Harrison St. .. | 32W-10N | 30 |
| Hastings St. E&W .. | 32W-10N | 30 |
| Hathaway Cir. NS&EW | | |
| .............. | 32W-12N | 20 |
| Hathaway Ct. N&S | 32W-12N | 20 |
| Haverman Ct. N&S . | 32W-10N | 30 |
| Hecker Ct. E&W.... | 32W-11N | 30 |
| Hecker Dr. E&W .. | 32W-11N | 30 |
| Hemlock Ct. E&W . | 32W-11N | 30 |
| Hemlock Ln. NW&SE | | |
| .............. | 32W-11N | 30 |
| Hiawatha Ct. NW&SE | | |
| .............. | 32W-12N | 20 |
| Hiawatha Dr. N&S .. | 32W-12N | 20 |
| Hiawatha St. N&S .. | 32W-12N | 20 |
| Highbury Ct. NE&SW | | |
| .............. | 32W-11N | 30 |
| Highbury Dr. E&W .. | 32W-11N | 30 |
| Hilliard Dr. N&S .. | 31W-10N | 30 |
| Hobble Bush Ln. NS&EW | | |
| .............. | 32W-11N | 30 |
| Horace Dr. NE&SW | | |
| .............. | 31W-10N | 30 |
| Houston E&W.... | 32W-10N | 30 |
| Hunt Wyck Ct. NW&SE | | |
| .............. | 32W-12N | 20 |
| Hunter Dr. NE&SW | | |
| ......32W-11N, | 32W-12N | 20 |
| Huron Ct. NE&SW... | 32W-13N | 20 |
| Huron Dr. N&S .. | 32W-12N | 20 |
| Indian Dr. N&S .. | 32W-12N | 20 |
| Inglewood Ln. NE&SW | | |
| .............. | 32W-12N | 20 |
| Inverness E&W .. | 32W-11N | 30 |
| Ironwood Ct. N&S . | 32W-12N | 20 |
| Ironwood Dr. N&S .. | 32W-12N | 20 |
| Iroquois Dr. N&S .. | 32W-12N | 20 |

|  | Grid | Page |
|---|---|---|
| Jan Marie Ln. E&W | | |
| .............. | 32W-11N | 30 |
| Jay St. E&W .. | 32W-10N | 30 |
| Jefferson Av. E&W . | 32W-12N | 20 |
| Joan Ct. E&W .. | 32W-10N | 30 |
| John Dr.* N&S .. | 32W-11N | 30 |
| Joslyn Dr. NE&SW . | 32W-11N | 30 |
| Joyce Ln. E&W .. | 32W-11N | 30 |
| Julie Ann Ln. E&W . | 32W-10N | 30 |
| Cir. .............. | 32W-12N | 20 |
| Kingsley Ct. N&S . | 32W-11N | 30 |
| Kirk Av. NE&SW... | 32W-10N | 30 |
| Kramer Av. E&W .. | 32W-10N | 30 |
| Lake St. NW&SE | | |
| ....32W-10N, | 32W-10N | 30 |
| Langtry Ct. NW&SE | | |
| .............. | 32W-11N | 30 |
| Leawood Ct. NE&SW | | |
| .............. | 31W-11N | 30 |
| Leawood Dr. E&W . | 32W-12N | 20 |
| Lehman Dr. NS&EW | | |
| .............. | 31W-10N | 30 |
| Lincolnshire Ct. N&S | | |
| .............. | 32W-11N | 30 |
| Lisa Ln. E&W .. | 32W-10N | 30 |
| Little Falls Dr. NS&EW | | |
| .............. | 32W-12N | 20 |
| Long Ford Cir. NS&EW | | |
| .............. | 31W-11N | 30 |
| Longford Ct. NE&SW | 31W-11N | 30 |
| Longford Dr. N&S .. | 31W-11N | 30 |
| Lovell Rd. N&S .... | 31W-10N | 30 |
| Lucile Av. N&S | | |
| ....32W-10N, | 32W-11N | 30 |
| Lucile Av. NS&EW .. | 32W-10N | 30 |
| Luda St. E&W .. | 32W-12N | 20 |
| Ludlow Av. E&W .. | 32W-12N | 20 |
| Mackey Ln. E&W .. | 32W-11N | 30 |
| Maple Pl. N&S .. | 32W-11N | 30 |
| Marbilynn NE&SW .. | 32W-12N | 20 |
| Mariner Ct. N&S .. | 32W-10N | 30 |
| Mariner Dr. N&S .. | 32W-10N | 30 |
| Maroon Dr. N&S .. | 32W-10N | 30 |
| Martin Dr. NE&SW .. | 32W-12N | 20 |
| Mohawk Ct. E&W .. | 32W-12N | 20 |
| Mohawk Dr. N&S .. | 32W-12N | 20 |
| Mulford Ct. NW&SE | | |
| .............. | 32W-11N | 30 |
| Mulford Dr. NS&EW | | |
| .............. | 32W-11N | 30 |
| Nancy Ann Ln. E&W | | |
| .............. | 32W-11N | 30 |
| Natoma Ct. N&S .. | 32W-10N | 30 |
| Natoma Dr. NW&SE | | |
| .............. | 32W-10N | 30 |
| Nicola Ln. N&S .... | 32W-12N | 20 |
| Oakwood Blvd. NE&SW | | |
| .............. | 32W-11N | 30 |
| Old Mill Ct. N&S .. | 32W-13N | 20 |
| Olive Ct. N&S .. | 32W-10N | 30 |
| Olive St. E&W .. | 32W-10N | 30 |
| Olympia Ct. N&S .. | 31W-11N | 30 |
| Packard Dr. N&S .. | 32W-10N | 30 |
| Parkway Av. E&W .. | 32W-13N | 20 |
| Patricia Dr. E&W .. | 32W-12N | 20 |
| Peach Tree Ct. N&S | | |
| .............. | 32W-11N | 30 |
| Peach Tree Ln. E&W | | |
| .............. | 32W-11N | 30 |
| Peck Pl. N&S .. | 32W-11N | 30 |
| Pegwood Dr. N&S .. | 32W-11N | 30 |
| Polly Ct. N&S .. | 32W-11N | 30 |
| Poplar Creek Dr. NE&SW | | |
| .............. | 32W-11N | 30 |
| Poplar View Bend NE&SW | | |
| .............. | 31W-11N | 30 |
| Prestbury Dr. NE&SW | | |
| .............. | 32W-12N | 20 |
| Price Dr. N&S .. | 32W-11N | 30 |
| Providence Cir. E&W | | |
| .............. | 32W-12N | 20 |
| Quaker Hill Ct. N&S | | |
| .............. | 32W-12N | 20 |
| Quincy Ct. E&W .. | 31W-11N | 30 |
| Radclyffe Ct. NE&SW | | |
| .............. | 32W-10N | 30 |
| Ramona Av. E&W | | |
| .............. | 32W-10N | 30 |
| Red Oak Ct. NE&SW | | |
| .............. | 32W-11N | 30 |
| Ripplebrook Ct. NE&SW | | |
| .............. | 32W-12N | 20 |
| Ripplebrook Ln. N&S | | |
| .............. | 32W-12N | 20 |
| Ripplebrook Dr. NW&SE | | |
| .............. | 32W-12S | 20 |
| Rodney Ln. E&W .. | 32W-10N | 30 |
| Rose Ln. N&S .... | 31W-9N | 30 |
| Rosewood Ct. N&S | | |
| .............. | 32W-11N | 30 |
| Rt. 19 E&W.... | 32W-10N | 30 |
| Rt. 58 E&W .. | 32W-12N | 20 |
| Sadler Av. N&S | | |
| ....32W-10N, | 32W-11N | 30 |
| Sandra Ln. E&W.... | 32W-10N | 30 |
| Saxon Ct. N&S .. | 32W-11N | 30 |
| Seal Dr. E&W | | |
| ....32W-8N, | 31W-8N | 30 |
| Sebring Dr. E&W .. | 32W-11N | 30 |
| Seminole Dr. E&W .. | 32W-12N | 20 |
| Shady Oaks Ct. NE&SW | | |
| .............. | 32W-12N | 20 |
| Shady Oaks Dr. NS&EW | | |
| .............. | 32W-12N | 20 |
| Shales Pkwy. N&S | | |
| ....31W-10N, | 31W-11N | 30 |
| Sharon Ct.* N&S .. | 32W-11N | 30 |

|  | Grid | Page |
|---|---|---|
| Shawford Way N&S | | |
| .............. | 32W-12N | 20 |
| Sheldon Dr. E&W .. | 31W-10N | 30 |
| Shiloh Ct. E&W .. | 32W-11N | 30 |
| Shiloh Ln. NS&EW .. | 32W-11N | 30 |
| Shoe Factory Rd. E&W | | |
| .............. | 32W-12N | 20 |
| Sioux Dr. E&W .. | 32W-13N | 20 |
| Sommerset Ct. N&S | | |
| .............. | 32W-12N | 20 |
| Spaulding Rd. E&W | | |
| ....32W-10N, | 31W-9N | 30 |
| Spring Creek Ct. E&W | | |
| .............. | 32W-12N | 20 |
| Spring Creek Rd. N&S | | |
| .............. | 32W-12N | 20 |
| Spring Hill Ct. N&S | 32W-12N | 20 |
| Spruce Ln. E&W .. | 32W-11N | 30 |
| Stewart Av. N&S .. | 32W-12N | 20 |
| Stillwater Rd. NE&SW | | |
| .............. | 32W-12N | 20 |
| Stockbridge Ct. N&S | | |
| .............. | 31W-11N | 30 |
| Stockbridge Pl. NW&SE | | |
| .............. | 31W-11N | 30 |
| Stonebridge Ct. NE&SW | | |
| .............. | 32W-12N | 20 |
| Stonehurst Dr. N&S | | |
| .............. | 32W-11N | 30 |
| Stratford Ct. E&W .. | 32W-11N | 30 |
| Sumac Ln. NS&EW | | |
| .............. | 31W-11N | 30 |
| Summit Av. E&W .. | 32W-12N | 20 |
| Suzzane Ct. E&W .. | 31W-11N | 30 |
| Tannery Ridge Rd. N&S | | |
| .............. | 32W-12N | 20 |
| Ted Ln. E&W .. | 32W-10N | 30 |
| Tefft Av. N&S .. | 32W-11N | 30 |
| Terrace Av. E&W .. | 32W-11N | 30 |
| Terrace Ct. E&W .. | 32W-11N | 30 |
| Thoreau Dr. N&S .. | 31W-10N | 30 |
| Thorndale Ct. NE&SW | | |
| .............. | 31W-10N | 30 |
| Thorndale Dr. NW&SE | | |
| ....32W-10N, | 31W-10N | 30 |
| Toastmaster Dr. N&S | | |
| .............. | 32W-13N | 20 |
| Tori Ln. E&W .. | 32W-10N | 30 |
| Trout Av. N&S .. | 32W-12N | 20 |
| U.S. Route 20 NW&SE | | |
| ....32W-10N, | 31W-11N | 30 |
| Varsity Dr. NE&SW | | |
| .............. | 32W-10N | 30 |
| Victor Av. N&S .. | 32W-13N | 20 |
| Victoria Av. N&S... | 32W-12N | 20 |
| Villa Av. NW&SE .. | 32W-10N | 30 |
| Village Ct. N&S .. | 32W-11N | 30 |
| Virgil Av. N&S .. | 32W-10N | 30 |
| Vivian Tr. N&S .. | 32W-10N | 30 |
| Wakefield Dr. N&S .. | 32W-12N | 20 |
| Walden Ct. E&W .. | 31W-10N | 30 |
| Waverly Ct. N&S .. | 32W-12N | 20 |
| Waverly Ct. NE&SW | | |
| .............. | 32W-11N | 30 |
| Waverly Ct., N. NE&SW | | |
| .............. | 32W-11N | 30 |
| Waverly Ct., S. NE&SW | | |
| .............. | 32W-11N | 30 |
| Waverly Dr. NE&SW | | |
| ....32W-11N, | 32W-12N | 30 |
| Wembly Ct. N&S .. | 32W-12N | 20 |
| West Bartlett Rd. E&W | | |
| ....31W-8N, | 32W-8N | 30 |
| Willard Av. N&S | | |
| ....32W-10N, | 32W-11N | 30 |
| Willoby Ln. NS&EW | | |
| .............. | 32W-12N | 20 |
| Windsor Ct. N&S . | 31W-11N | 30 |
| Woodhill Ct. N&S .. | 32W-12N | 20 |
| Woodview Cir. N&S | | |
| .............. | 32W-11N | 30 |
| Woodview Dr. N&S | | |
| .............. | 32W-11N | 30 |
| Wright Av. NE&SW | | |
| .............. | 32W-10N | 30 |
| Wynnfield Ct. NE&SW | | |
| .............. | 32W-10N | 30 |
| Yew Ct. N&S .. | 32W-11N | 30 |
| Yorkshire Ct. NW&SE | | |
| .............. | 32W-10N | 30 |

## Elk Grove Township

|  | Grid | Page |
|---|---|---|
| Crest Av. N&S .. | 18W-9N | 34 |
| Dierking Ter. E&W . | 16W-9N | 34 |
| Elizabeth Dr. N&S . | 16W-9N | 34 |
| Forestview Av. E&W | | |
| .............. | 18W-9N | 34 |
| Hamilton Rd. E&W . | 16W-9N | 34 |
| Higgins Rd. NW&SE | | |
| ....20W-10N, | 16W-9N | 33 |
| Howard St. N&S .. | 18W-9N | 34 |
| Kenneth Dr. E&W . | 16W-10N | 34 |
| Laurel St. N&S .. | 18W-9N | 34 |
| Lee Ln. N&S .. | 16W-9N | 34 |
| Lela St. N&S .. | 16W-9N | 34 |
| Lindale St. N&S .. | 17W-10N | 34 |
| Linneman Rd. N&S | 16W-10N | 34 |
| Lund Rd. N&S .. | 16W-9N | 34 |
| Malmo Rd. N&S .. | 16W-10N | 34 |
| Northwest Tollway NW&SE | | |
| .............. | 16W-9N | 34 |
| Roppolo Dr. N&S .. | 16W-9N | 34 |
| Rt. 72 NW&SE | | |
| ....20W-10N, | 15W-9N | 33 |
| Thorndale Av. E&W . | 18W-9N | 34 |
| Tonne N&S .. | 17W-12N | 24 |
| Touhy Av. E&W .. | 15W-8N | 34 |

|  | Grid | Page |
|---|---|---|
| Vera Ln. N&S .. | 16W-9N | 34 |
| Weiler Rd. N&S.... | 16W-9N | 34 |

## Elk Grove Village*
### (Also see Du Page County)

|  | Grid | Page |
|---|---|---|
| Alabama Dr. NW&SE | | |
| .............. | 21W-8N | 33 |
| Albany St. E&W .. | 22W-9N | 33 |
| Aldrin Tr. NW&SE .. | 21W-8N | 33 |
| Alexian Way E&W .. | 19W-8N | 33 |
| Anders Dr. N&S .. | 21W-8N | 33 |
| Arizona Pass N&S .. | 21W-9N | 33 |
| Arkansas Dr. N&S .. | 21W-8N | 33 |
| Armstrong Ct. NW&SE | | |
| .............. | 21W-8N | 33 |
| Armstrong Ln. E&W .. | 21W-8N | 33 |
| Arthur Av. E&W | | |
| ....17W-8N, | 16W-8N | 34 |
| Ash St. E&W .. | 18W-8N | 34 |
| Aspen Ln. N&S .. | 18W-8N | 34 |
| Atlantic Ln. E&W .. | 22W-9N | 33 |
| Avon Rd. E&W .. | 19W-8N | 33 |
| Baltimore Dr. E&W . | 22W-9N | 33 |
| Banbury Rd. E&W .. | 19W-8N | 33 |
| Bangor Rd. N&S .. | 22W-9N | 33 |
| Banyan Dr. N&S .. | 18W-8N | 34 |
| Basswood Ct. E&W | | |
| .............. | 17W-9N | 34 |
| Basswood Dr. N&S . | 17W-9N | 34 |
| Bay Dr. N&S .... | 19W-8N | 33 |
| Beisner Rd. N&S | | |
| ....20W-8N, | 20W-9N | 33 |
| Bennett Rd. E&W | | |
| ....18W-10N, | 17W-10N | 34 |
| Berkenshire Ln. N&S | | |
| .............. | 19W-8N | 33 |
| Bianco Dr. E&W .. | 18W-9N | 34 |
| Biesterfield Pkwy. E&W | | |
| .............. | 18W-8N | 34 |
| Biesterfield Rd. E&W | | |
| ....21W-9N, | 19W-8N | 33 |
| Birchwood Av. E&W | 18W-8N | 34 |
| Biscayne Dr. N&S .. | 18W-8N | 33 |
| Bismark Ct. N&S .... | 21W-8N | 33 |
| Blue Jay Cir. NS&EW | | |
| .............. | 22W-8N | 33 |
| Boardwalk Ct. E&W | 19W-8N | 33 |
| Bonaventure Dr. E&W | | |
| .............. | 20W-8N | 33 |
| Bond St. E&W .. | 17W-10N | 34 |
| Bonita Av. N&S..... | 18W-9N | 34 |
| Bonnie Ln. N&S .... | 17W-9N | 34 |
| Bordeaux Ct. NW&SE | | |
| .............. | 19W-9N | 33 |
| Borman Ct. NS&EW | 21W-8N | 33 |
| Bosworth Ln. N&S .. | 18W-8N | 34 |
| Bradford Cir. E&W .. | 19W-9N | 33 |
| Bradley Ln. NW&SE | 21W-8N | 33 |
| Braemer Dr. E&W | | |
| ....19W-8N, | 18W-8N | 33 |
| Brandywine Av. E&W | | |
| .............. | 19W-8N | 33 |
| Brantwood Av. N&S | | |
| ....19W-9N, | 18W-8N | 33 |
| Brantwood Ct. E&W | | |
| .............. | 19W-9N | 33 |
| Brantwood Pl. NW&SE | | |
| .............. | 19W-9N | 34 |
| Briarwood Ln. NW&SE | | |
| .............. | 18W-10N | 34 |
| Brighton Rd. E&W .. | 19W-8N | 33 |
| Bristol Ln. NS&EW .. | 19W-8N | 33 |
| Brookhaven Dr. E&W | | |
| .............. | 18W-8N | 34 |
| Brown Cir. NE&SW . | 21W-9N | 33 |
| Brummel St. E&W | | |
| ....17W-9N, | 16W-9N | 34 |
| Brynhaven Ct. N&S | | |
| .............. | 18W-10N | 34 |
| Brynhaven St. E&W | | |
| .............. | 18W-10N | 34 |
| Buckingham Ct. E&W | | |
| .............. | 19W-8N | 33 |
| Burgundy Ct. E&W .. | 19W-9N | 33 |
| Busse Rd. N&S...... | 16W-9N | 34 |
| California St. NS&EW | | |
| .............. | 21W-9N | 33 |
| Cambridge Dr. NW&SE | | |
| .............. | 16W-9N | 34 |
| Canyon Dr. N&S .. | 18W-9N | 34 |
| Cardinal Ln. N&S .. | 22W-8N | 33 |
| Carlisle Av. N&S | | |
| ....19W-8N, | 18W-8N | 33 |
| Carmen Dr. N&S .. | 15W-8N | 34 |
| Carolina Dr. E&W .. | 21W-8N | 33 |
| Carpenter Ct. NS&EW | | |
| .............. | 21W-8N | 33 |
| Carr Ct. N&S .. | 21W-8N | 33 |
| Carroll Sq. N&S .. | 17W-10N | 34 |
| Carswell Av. N&S .. | 18W-8N | 34 |
| Carswell Ct. N&S.... | 18W-8N | 34 |
| Carswell Dr. N&S .. | 18W-8N | 34 |
| Cass Ln. N&S .. | 21W-8N | 33 |
| Cedar Ln. NS&EW .. | 18W-8N | 34 |
| Cedarwood Ct.* NS&EW | | |
| .............. | 20W-8N | 33 |
| Center St. E&W .. | 17W-8N | 34 |
| Cernan Ct. E&W .. | 21W-8N | 33 |
| Chaffee Ct. N&S .. | 21W-8N | 33 |
| Charing Cross Rd. N&S | | |
| .............. | 18W-9N | 33 |
| Charlela Ln. N&S .. | 20W-8N | 33 |
| Charles Rd. N&S .. | 19W-9N | 33 |
| Chase Av. E&W .. | 17W-9N | 34 |
| Cheekwood Ct. N&S | | |
| .............. | 19W-8N | 33 |

|  | Grid | Page |
|---|---|---|
| Cheekwood Dr. E&W | | |
| .............. | 19W-8N | 33 |
| Chelmsford Ln. NS&EW | | |
| .............. | 19W-9N | 33 |
| Cheltenham Rd. N&S | | |
| .............. | 19W-9N | 33 |
| Chester Ln. NW&SE | | |
| .............. | 21W-8N | 33 |
| Cindy Ln. E&W .. | 21W-8N | 33 |
| Circle Ct. E&W .. | 21W-8N | 33 |
| Clearmont Dr. E&W | | |
| ....19W-8N, | 18W-8N | 33 |
| Clifford Ct. E&W .. | 21W-8N | 33 |
| Clover Hill Ct. NE&SW | | |
| .............. | 20W-8N | 33 |
| Clover Hill Ln. E&W | | |
| ....20W-8N, | 19W-8N | 33 |
| Collins Cir. N&S .. | 21W-9N | 33 |
| Colorado Ln. E&W .. | 21W-8N | 33 |
| Columbia Ct. .. | 21W-9N | 33 |
| Commerce Dr. E&W | 19W-9N | 34 |
| Concord Ln. N&S.... | 22W-9N | 33 |
| Conrad Ct. E&W .. | 21W-8N | 33 |
| Cooper Ct. NS&EW . | 21W-8N | 33 |
| Corrinthia Ct. N&S .. | 18W-9N | 34 |
| Corrinthia Dr. .. | 18W-9N | 34 |
| Cosman Rd. E&W .. | 19W-9N | 33 |
| Cottonwood Dr. N&S | | |
| .............. | 17W-9N | 34 |
| Coyle Ln. E&W .. | 15W-8N | 34 |
| Creighton Av. N&S .. | 19W-9N | 33 |
| Crest Av. NE&SW .. | 19W-9N | 34 |
| Crestwood Ct.* NS&EW | | |
| .............. | 20W-8N | 33 |
| Criss Cir. E&W .. | 17W-10N | 34 |
| Crossen Av. N&S | | |
| ....17W-9N, | 17W-10N | 34 |
| Cumberland Ln. NS&EW | | |
| .............. | 19W-8N | 33 |
| Cunningham Cir. NE&SW | | |
| .............. | 19W-8N | 33 |
| Cutter Ln. NS&EW . | 22W-9N | 33 |
| Cypress Ln. N&S .. | 18W-8N | 34 |
| Dakota Dr. E&W .. | 21W-8N | 33 |
| Dauphine Ct. E&W .. | 19W-9N | 33 |
| David Ln. N&S .. | 21W-8N | 33 |
| Debra Ln. N&S .. | 21W-8N | 33 |
| Deepwood Ct. N&S . | 20W-8N | 33 |
| Delaware Ln. NS&EW | | |
| .............. | 21W-8N | 33 |
| Delmar Cir. N&S .. | 22W-9N | 33 |
| Delphia Av. E&W .. | 18W-9N | 34 |
| Delphia St. N&S .. | 18W-9N | 34 |
| Devon Av. E&W | | |
| ....20W-8N, | 19W-8N | 33 |
| Devon Av. E&W | | |
| ....17W-8N, | 16W-8N | 34 |
| Diane Ln. NW&SE .. | 21W-8N | 33 |
| Dierking Ter. E&W .. | 16W-9N | 34 |
| Dogwood Tr. E&W .. | 18W-8N | 34 |
| Doral Ct. NE&SW.... | 22W-9N | 33 |
| Dorchester Ln. N&S . | 19W-8N | 33 |
| Dover Ln. N&S .. | 18W-9N | 33 |
| Driftwood Ct.* NS&EW | | |
| .............. | 20W-8N | 33 |
| Dupoint Cir. NE&SW | | |
| .............. | 22W-9N | 33 |
| Eagle Dr. N&S .. | 22W-8N | 33 |
| Eden Rd. NS&EW | | |
| ....19W-8N, | 18W-8N | 33 |
| Edgeware Rd. NW&SE | | |
| .............. | 18W-9N | 34 |
| Edgewood Ln. NW&SE | | |
| .............. | 18W-9N | 33 |
| Elk Grove Blvd. N&S | | |
| ....18W-8N, | 18W-8N | 33 |
| Elmhurst Rd. N&S | | |
| ....16W-8N, | 16W-9N | 34 |
| Elmwood Ln. N&S .. | 18W-8N | 34 |
| Essex Rd. E&W .. | 19W-8N | 33 |
| Estes Av. E&W | | |
| ....17W-8N, | 16W-8N | 34 |
| Evans Ct. NE&SW .. | 21W-8N | 33 |
| Evergreen Cir E&W | | |
| .............. | 18W-10N | 34 |
| Evergreen St. N&S | 18W-10N | 34 |
| Exmoor Rd. NS&EW | | |
| .............. | 19W-8N | 33 |
| Fairfield Ct. N&S .. | 19W-8N | 33 |
| Fargo Av. E&W .. | 17W-9N | 34 |
| Fern Dr. E&W .. | 18W-8N | 34 |
| Fleetwood Ln. N&S | 17W-9N | 34 |
| Florida Ln. NS&EW . | 21W-8N | 33 |
| Forest Ln. N&S .. | 18W-10N | 34 |
| Forestview Av. N&S . | 18W-10N | 34 |
| Fox Run Dr. NE&SW | | |
| .............. | 22W-9N | 33 |
| Franklin Ln. NS&EW | | |
| .............. | 21W-9N | 33 |
| Galleon Ln. NE&SW .. | 22W-9N | 33 |
| Garlisch Ct. N&S .. | 17W-10N | 34 |
| Gateshead Ln. E&W | | |
| .............. | 19W-8N | 33 |
| Gaylord St. N&S... | 18W-10N | 34 |
| Geneva Ct. E&W .. | 19W-8N | 33 |
| Georgia Dr. NW&SE | 21W-8N | 33 |
| Germaine Ln. E&W . | 18W-9N | 34 |
| Germaine Pl. N&S .. | 18W-9N | 34 |
| Gibson Dr. N&S | | |
| ....22W-9N, | 21W-8N | 33 |
| Gloria Dr. N&S .. | 21W-8N | 33 |
| Gloucester Dr. E&W | 19W-8N | 33 |
| Gordon St. N&S .. | 18W-10N | 34 |
| Grange Pl. NW&SE . | 19W-8N | 33 |
| Grange Rd. NW&SE | 19W-8N | 33 |
| Grassmere Rd. NE&SW | | |
| .............. | 19W-8N | 33 |

| | Grid | Page |
|---|---|---|

Green Briar St. E&W .................. 18W-9N 34
Greenleaf Av. E&W .................. 17W-8N,15W-8N 34
Greensboro Ct. N&S .................. 22W-9N 33
Gregory Ct. N&S .... 21W-8N 33
Grissom Tr. N&S .... 21W-8N 33
Grosvenor Ct. NE&SW .................. 18W-9N 34
Grosvenor Ln. N&S . 18W-9N 34
Grove Dr. N&S ... 17W-9N 34
Gullo Av. N&S ... 17W-10N 34
Haar Ln. E&W ...... 18W-9N 33
Haise Ct. NE&SW .. 21W-8N 33
Haise Ln. E&W ... 21W-8N 33
Hampshire Dr. NS&EW .................. 22W-9N,21W-9N 33
Harmony Ln. E&W .. 18W-8N 34
Hartford Ln. N&S .. 18W-8N 34
Hastings Av. N&S .19W-9N 33
Hawk Ln. E&W .....22W-8N 33
Helen Ln. NW&SE .. 21W-9N 33
Hemlock Ln. N&S .. 18W-8N 34
Hickory Ln. N&S .. 18W-8N 34
Higgins Rd. N&S .................. 18W-10N,17W-10N 34
Holdmair Ln. E&W .. 21W-8N 33
Holly Ln. N&S .... 18W-9N 34
Home Av. N&S .. 21W-8,9, 33
Home Cir. E&W ... 21W-9N 33
Howard St. E&W .................. 18W-9N,17W-10N 34
Hudson Ct. NW&SE 22W-9N 33
Idaho Pl. E&W .... 21W-9N 33
Indiana Ln. N&S .. 21W-8N 33
Interstate 90 SE&NE .................. 17W-10N 34
Inverness Ct. SW&NE .................. 22W-9N 33
Iowa Dr. E&W .... 21W-8N 33
Ipswich Ct. N&S .. 21W-9N 33
Ironwood Dr. E&W .17W-10N 34
Ironwood Ln. E&W 17W-10N 34
J.F. Kennedy Blvd. NE&SW .................. 19W-8N,18W-8N 33
Jackson Cir E&W .... 22W-8N 33
James Way E&W ... 21W-8N 33
Jarvis St. E&W .... 17W-9N 34
Jefferson St. E&W .. 18W-8N 34
Jersey Ln. N&S .................. 22W-9N,21W-9N 33
Joey Ln. N&S ... 17W-10N 34
Joplin Cir. NE&SW . 21W-8N 33
Judy Dr. N&S .... 21W-8N 33
Julie Dr. E&W ..... 22W-9N 33
Kathleen Way NS&EW .................. 21W-8N 33
Kelly St. N&S ... 18W-10N 34
Kendal Rd. E&W .. 18W-8N 33
Kenilworth Av. NS&EW .................. 19W-8N,18W-8N 33
Kent Av. N&S ..... 17W-10N 34
Kentucky Ln. NS&EW .................. 22W-8N 33
Keswick Rd. E&W .. 19W-8N 33
King St. N&S ... 17W-10N 34
Kingsbridge Rd. E&W .................. 19W-8N 33
Knottingham Dr. NS&EW .................. 22W-8N 33
Lakeview Cir. E&W . 19W-9N 33
Lancaster Av. NS&EW .................. 19W-8N 33
Landmeir Rd. E&W .................. 17W-9N,16W-9N 34
Larchmont Dr. N&S .. 18W-9N 34
Laurel St. E&W .... 18W-9N 34
Lee Ln. E&W ...... 18W-9N 34
Lee St. E&W ..... 17W-10N 34
Leeds Ln. N&S .... 19W-8N 33
Leicester Rd. N&S .................. 19W-8N,19W-9N 33
Lela St. NE&SW ... 16W-9N 33
Liberty Ct. E&W ... 22W-9N 33
Lilac Ln. E&W ..... 19W-9N 33
Lincoln N&S ...... 18W-8N 34
Lindale St. E&W ... 17W-10N 34
Little Falls Ct. E&W . 20W-8N 33
Long Boat Dr. E&W ..22W-8N 33
Lonsdale Rd. NS&EW .................. 19W-8N,18W-8N 33
Louis Av. E&W ... 17W-9N 34
Louisiana Dr. NW&SE .................. 22W-8N 33
Love St. N&S .................. 18W-8N,18W-9N 34
Lovell Ct. NS&EW .. 21W-8N 33
Lowestoft Ln. E&W .. 19W-8N 33
Lund Rd. N&S .... 16W-9N 34
Lunt Av. E&W .................. 17W-8N,16W-8N 34
Lynne Dr. N&S .... 19W-8N 33
Madison Ct. NW&SE .................. 18W-8N 34
Magnolia Ln. E&W .. 18W-8N 34
Maine Dr. E&W ....22W-9N 34
Maple Ct. E&W .... 18W-8N 34
Maple Ln. NS&EW .. 18W-8N 34
Martin Ln. N&S ... 17W-10N 34
Maryland Dr. E&W ..22W-9N 34
McCabe Av. N&S .. 18W-8N 34
McDevitt Cir. N&S .. 21W-9N 34
Meacham Rd. N&S .................. 21W-8N,21W-9N 33
Meegan Way NS&EW .................. 21W-8N 33

Memphis Cir. NE&SW .................. 22W-8N 33
Michigan Ln. N&S..21W-8N 33
Middlebury Ln. N&S ..18W-8N 34
Midway Ct. NW&SE .................. 17W-10N 34
Milbeck Av. NW&SE .................. 19W-8N 33
Milbeck Ct. NS&EW.19W-8N 33
Mimosa Ln. E&W .. 18W-8N 34
Minnesota Dr. NW&SE .................. 21W-8N 33
Minot Ct. N&S .... 21W-8N 33
Mississippi Ln. N&S..22W-8N 33
Missouri Dr. E&W ..21W-8N 33
Mitchell Tr. N&S .. 21W-8N 33
Mobile Ct. E&W ... 21W-8N 33
Montana Way NE&SW .................. 21W-9N 33
Montego Ct. N&S...19W-8N 33
Montego Dr. E&W . 19W-8N 33
Moore Dr. NW&SE . 19W-9N 33
Morgan Dr. NS&EW.21W-9N 33
Morse Av. E&W ... 17W-8N 34
Mulberry Ln. E&W . 18W-8N 34
N.W. Point Rd. N&S .................. 18W-10N,17W-10N 34
Nebraska Dr. N&S .. 21W-8N 33
Nerge Rd. E&W .................. 22W-8N,20W-8N 33
Nevada Ln. E&W .. 21W-9N 33
New Mexico Ct. NE&SW .................. 21W-9N 33
New Mexico Tr. N&S .................. 21W-9N 33
New York Ln. NS&EW .................. 22W-9N 33
Newberry Ln. N&S .. 22W-9N 33
Newport Av. E&W .. 19W-8N 33
Nicholas Blvd. N&S .................. 16W-8N,16W-9N 34
North Hampton Av. E&W .................. 19W-9N 33
North Pkwy. E&W . 17W-8N 34
Northampton Cir. E&W .................. 19W-9N 33
Northport Dr. E&W . 19W-8N 33
Northwest Tollway .................. 17W-10N 34
Oak St. E&W .... 18W-9N 34
Oakton St. E&W...17W-10N 34
Oakwood Dr. N&S..18W-10N 34
Oklahoma Cir. NE&SW .................. 21W-9N 33
Oklahoma Way N&S .................. 21W-9N 33
Old Creek Ct. NW&SE .................. 20W-8N 33
Old Mill Ln. NS&EW .20W-8N 33
Oregon Tr. E&W .. 21W-9N 33
Oriole Dr. E&W .... 22W-8N 33
Orleans Ct. NE&SW.22W-8N 33
Oxford Cir. NW&SE .21W-8N 33
Pagni Dr. E&W ... 17W-10N 34
Pahl Rd. NS&EW ... 19W-9N 33
Park Blvd. NS&EW . 20W-8N 33
Parkchester Rd. E&W .................. 19W-8N 33
Parker Pl. N&S .. 21W-8N 33
Parkview Cir. N&S . 19W-9N 33
Patricia Ct. E&W .. 21W-8N 33
Pauly Dr. E&W ... 17W-10N 34
Peach Tree Ln. N&S .................. 18W-8N 34
Pebble Beach Cir. NS&EW .................. 22W-9N 33
Penrith Av. N&S . 19W-8N 33
Perrie Dr. E&W ... 17W-9N 34
Pinewood Dr. E&W . 18W-8N 34
Placid Way E&W .. 18W-8N 34
Pleasant Dr. E&W . 18W-8N 34
Potomac Ln. N&S..22W-9N 33
Pratt Blvd. E&W .................. 17W-8N,16W-8N 34
Racine Cir. E&W .. 21W-8N 33
Randall St. N&S .. 18W-10N 34
Red Fox Ln. N&S...22W-9N 33
Redwood Av. E&W . 17W-9N 34
Rev. Morrison Blvd NE&SW .................. 18W-8N 34
Revere Ln. E&W .. 22W-9N 33
Richmond Ct. E&W . 21W-8N 33
Ridge Av. N&S .................. 18W-8N,18W-9N 33
Ridge Ct. E&W ... 18W-8N 34
Ridge Sq. E&W ... 18W-8N 34
Ridgewood Rd. N&S .................. 18W-10N 34
Rockwood Dr. N&S..17W-9N 34
Rohlwing Rd. N&S .................. 20W-18N,20W-19N 13
Roosa Ln. N&S ... 21W-8N 33
Roppolo Dr. N&S...16W-9N 34
Rt. 290 N&S .................. 20W-8N,20W-9N 33
Rt. 72 E&W .... 17W-10N 34
Rt. 83 N&S........17W-9N 34
Ruskin Cir. E&W .. 19W-9N 33
Ruskin Dr. NS&EW.19W-9N 33
Rutgers Ln. E&W .................. 22W-9N,21W-9N 33
Salem Ct. N&S ... 21W-9N 33
Schirra Ct. N&S .. 21W-8N 33
Schooner Ln. N&S . 22W-8N 33
Scott St. N&S .... 18W-10N 34
Seegars Av. N&S .. 17W-10N 34
Shadywood Ln. E&W .................. 18W-10N 34

Shelley Ct. N&S .... 19W-8N 33
Shelley Rd. E&W ... 19W-9N 33
Shepard Cir. N&S ... 21W-9N 33
Smethwick Ln. E&W .................. 19W-9N 33
Somerset Ln. N&S .. 19W-8N 33
South Glenn Tr. E&W .................. 17W-10N 34
Spring Creek Ct. NS&EW .................. 20W-8N 33
Springdale Ln. NS&EW .................. 18W-8N 34
Spruce Ln. N&S ... 18W-8N 34
Stafford Cir. N&S .. 21W-9N 33
Stanford Cir. N&S .. 19W-9N 33
Stanley St. N&S ... 17W-10N 34
Stone Brook Ct. E&W .................. 20W-8N 33
Stonehaven Av. N&S .................. 19W-9N 33
Stowe Cir. E&W ...22W-9N 33
Susan Ct. E&W ... 21W-8N 33
Sussex Ct. N&S .. 18W-8N 34
Sycamore Dr. E&W . 18W-8N 34
Sylvan St. E&W ... 19W-9N 33
Talbots Ln. N&S ... 20W-8N 33
Tanglewood Ct. NS&EW .................. 18W-9N 34
Tanglewood Dr. N&S .................. 18W-9N 34
Tennessee Ln. NS&EW .................. 22W-8N 33
Texas St. E&W ... 21W-9N 33
Thorndale Av. E&W . 18W-9N 34
Thornton Ct. E&W . 22W-8N 33
Timber Ln. E&W .... 21W-8N 33
Tonne Rd. N&S .................. 17W-8N,17W-9N 34
Tottenham Ln. N&S . 19W-9N 33
Touhy Av. E&W .................. 17W-8N,16W-8N 34
Tower Ln. E&W ... 18W-9N 34
Trowbridge Rd., E. NS&EW .................. 19W-9N 33
Trowbridge Rd., W. E&W .................. 19W-9N 33
Turner Av. E&W ... 19W-8N 33
Union Cir. NW&SE . 21W-9N 33
University Ln. NW&SE .................. 22W-9N 33
Utah Cir. E&W ... 21W-9N 33
Utah St. N&S.....21W-9N 33
Vera Ln. E&W ... 16W-9N 34
Verde Ln. E&W .... 16W-9N 34
Vermont Dr. E&W .................. 22W-9N,21W-9N 33
Vernon Cir. NE&SW..22W-9N 33
Versailles Cir. NS&EW .................. 19W-9N 33
Victoria Ln. E&W .................. 18W-8N,18W-9N 34
Village Grove Dr. E&W .................. 19W-8N 33
Vine Ln. N&S .....22W-9N 33
Virginia St. N&S..21W-8N 33
Volkamer Tr. NS&EW .................. 21W-8N 33
Von Braun Ct. NE&SW .................. 21W-8N 33
Von Braun Tr. N&S..21W-8N 33
Walnut Ln. E&W ... 18W-8N 34
Walpole Rd. E&W .. 19W-8N 33
Walter Av. E&W ... 18W-8N 33
Warwick Ln. N&S .. 18W-8N 34
Wasdale Av. N&S....19W-8N 33
Washington Sq. N&S .................. 18W-8N 34
Wellington Av. NS&EW .................. 20W-8N,19W-9N 33
West Gate Av. N&S . 18W-9N 34
West Glenn Tr. N&S .................. 21W-8N 33
Westview Dr. N&S . 18W-8N 33
White Robin Dr. E&W .................. 21W-8N 33
White Robin Tr. N&S .................. 21W-8N 33
White Tr. E&W ... 21W-8N 33
Wildwood Dr. N&S . 18W-8N 34
Wildwood Pl. E&W . 18W-8N 34
Wildwood Rd. N&S . 18W-8N 34
Willow Ln. E&W ... 18W-8N 34
Wilma Ln. N&S .... 21W-8N 33
Wilshire Av. N&S .. 18W-8N 34
Winston Dr. NS&EW .................. 19W-9N 33
Wisconsin Ln. N&S . 21W-8N 33
Wise Rd. E&W ....22W-9N 33
Wood Tr. NW&SE .. 21W-8N 33
Woodcrest Ln. N&S .................. 18W-10N 34
Woodview Av. N&S. 18W-9N 34
Worden Way NS&EW .................. 21W-8N 33
Yale Ct. NE&SW ... 21W-9N 33
Yarmouth Pl. E&W . 19W-9N 33
Young Cir. N&S .... 21W-9N 33

### Elmwood Park
Altgeld E&W ......9W-3N 42
Armitage E&W....9W-2N 48
Barry E&W .......9W-3N 42
Belden E&W.......9W-3N 48
Cir. ...........9W-3N 42
Bloomingdale E&W..9W-2N 48
Brook N&S .........9W-3N 42
Cortland E&W........9W-2N 48

Cortland Pkwy. E&W..9W-2N 48
Country Club Ln. E&W .................. 9W-2N 48
Cir. ...........9W-3N 42
Dickens E&W .....9W-3N 48
Diversey E&W ....9W-3N 42
Cir. ...........9W-3N 42
Fletcher E&W .....9W-3N 42
Fullerton E&W ....9W-3N 42
George E&W ......9W-3N 42
Grand E&W .......9W-3N 42
Harlem Av. N&S ...9W-2N 48
Lenora E&W ......9W-2N 48
Marwood E&W ....9W-3N 42
Nelson E&W ......9S-3N 42
North E&W .......9W-2N 48
Cir. ...........9W-3N 42
Palmer E&W ......9W-3N 42
Schubert E&W .....9W-3N 42
Cir. ...........9W-3N 42
Wabansia E&W ....9W-2N 48
Wellington E&W ...9W-3N 42
Westwood Dr. E&W .9W-3N 42
Wrightwood E&W ..9W-3N 42
72nd Ct. N&S 9W-2N,9W-3N 48
73rd E&W ....9W-2N,9W-3N 48
73rd Ct. N&S..9W-2N,9W-3N 48
74th N&S ...9W-2N,9W-3N 48
74th Ct. N&S..9W-2N,9W-3N 48
75th N&S .. 9W-2N,9W-3N 48
75th Ct. N&S..9W-2N,9W-3N 48
76th N&S ...9W-2N,9W-3N 48
76th Ct. N&S..9W-2N,9W-3N 48
77th N&S ...9W-2N,9W-3N 48
77th Ct. N&S..9W-2N,9W-3N 48
78th N&S ...9W-2N,9W-3N 48
78th Ct. N&S..9W-2N,9W-3N 48
79th N&S ...9W-2N,9W-3N 48
79th Ct. N&S ........9W-2N 48

### Evanston
Arnold Pl. N&S ...... 2W-10N 39
Ashbury Av. N&S .................. 3W-10N,2W-13N 39
Ashland Av. N&S .................. 3W-9N,3W-13N 39
Austin St. N&S ...... 2W-9N 39
Barton Av. N&S .... 2W-9N 39
Bennett Av. N&S .................. 4W-12N,4W-13N 29
Benson Av. N&S ... 2W-11N 39
Bernard St. N&S ... 4W-13N 29
Bradley Pl. E&W ... 3W-10N 39
Bridge St. NW&SE .. 3W-12N 29
Broadway N&S .... 3W-13N 29
Brown Av. N&S .................. 3W-9N,3W-12N 39
Brummel Pl. E&W ... 3W-9N 39
Brummel St. E&W .................. 3W-9N,2W-9N 39
Bryant Av. N&S .................. 2W-12N,2W-13N 29
Burnham Pl. E&W . 2W-10N 39
Callan Av. N&S .................. 2W-9N,2W-10N 39
Calvin St. E&W .... 4W-12N 29
Case Pl. E&W .... 2W-9N 39
Case St. E&W ....... 2W-9N 39
Central Park Av. N&S .................. 4W-12N 29
Central St. E&W .................. 4W-12N,3W-12N 29
Chancellor St. E&W ..3W-13N 29
Chicago Av. N&S .................. 2W-10N,2W-11N 39
Church St. E&W .................. 3W-11N,2W-11N 29
Clark St. E&W .... 2W-11N 29
Cleveland St. E&W .................. 3W-10N,2W-10N 39
Clifford St. E&W ... 4W-13N 29
Clinton Pl. E&W ... 2W-11N 29
Clyde Av. N&S......2W-9N 39
Colfax Pl. E&W .... 4W-12N 29
Colfax St. E&W .................. 4W-12N,2W-12N 29
Colfax Ter. N&S ... 3W-12N 29
Cowper Av. N&S ... 4W-12N 29
Craford Av. NW&SE 5W-13N 28
Crain St. E&W .................. 3W-10N,2W-10N 39
Croft Ln. N&S ...... 3W-10N 39
Culver St. E&W .... 4W-12N 29
Custer Av. N&S ...... 2W-9N 39
Darrow Av. N&S .................. 3W-9N,3W-11N 39
Dartmough Pl. E&W .................. 4W-12N,2W-12N 29
Davis St. E&W .................. 3W-11N,2W-11N 29
Dempster St. E&W .................. 3W-11N,2W-10N 39
Dewey Av. N&S .................. 3W-9N,3W-11N 39
Dobson St. E&W .................. 3W-9N,2W-9N 39
Dodge Av. N&S .................. 3W-9N,3W-12N 39
East Railroad Av. NW&SE .................. 2W-11N 39
Eastwood Av. N&S . 3W-13N 29
Edgemere Ct. N&S . 1W-10N 39
Elgin Rd. NW&SE ...2W-11N 29
Elinor Pl. E&W .... 2W-11N 29
Elm N&S .........3W-12N 29
Elmwood Av. N&S .................. 2W-9N,2W-10N 39

Emerson St. E&W .. 3W-11N 29
Euclid Park Pl. N&S .. 2W-13N 29
Ewing Av. N&S .................. 4W-12N,4W-13N 29
Florence Av. N&S .................. 3W-9N,3W-11N 39
Forest Av. N&S .................. 2W-10N,2W-11N 39
Forest Pl. N&S .... 2W-11N 29
Forestview Rd. N&S 4W-12N 29
Foster St E&W .................. 3W-11N,2W-11N 29
Fowler Av. N&S ... 3W-10N 39
Gaffield Pl. E&W .. 2W-11N 29
Garnett Pl. E&W ... 2W-11N 29
Garret Pl. E&W ... 2W-12N 29
Garrison Av. N&S...2W-13N 29
Geneva Pl. N&S ... 4W-12N 29
Girard Av. N&S ... 4W-13N 29
Golf Rd. E&W ..... 4W-12N 29
Grant St. E&W .................. 4W-12N,2W-12N 29
Greeley Av. N&S .. 5W-12N 28
Green Bay Rd. NW&SE .................. 3W-12N 29
Greenleaf St. E&W .................. 3W-10N,2W-10N 39
Greenwood St. E&W .................. 3W-11N,2W-11N 29
Grey Av. N&S .................. 3W-9N,3W-12N 39
Gross Point Rd. NE&SW .................. 4W-12N 29
Grove St. E&W .................. 3W-11N,2W-11N 29
Hamilton St. E&W .. 2W-10N 39
Hamlin St. E&W ... 2W-12N 29
Hampton Pkwy. N&S .................. 2W-13N 29
Harrison St. E&W .................. 4W-12N,3W-11N 29
Hartrey Av. N&S .................. 3W-9N,3W-11N 39
Hartzel St. E&W ... 4W-13N 29
Harvard Ter. E&W .. 2W-9N 39
Hastings Av. N&S...4W-12N 29
Haven St. E&W ... 2W-12N 29
Hawthorne Ln. N&S..3W-12N 29
Hayes St. E&W ... 4W-13N 29
Highland Av. N&S .. 4W-13N 29
Hillside Ln. NW&SE . 4W-13N 29
Hillside Rd. E&W .. 4W-13N 29
Hinman Av. N&S .................. 2W-10N,2W-11N 39
Hovland Ct. N&S .. 3W-11N 39
Howard St. E&W ... 3W-9N 39
Hull Ter. E&W ..... 2W-9N 39
Hurd Av. N&S .... 4W-12N 29
Ingleside Pk. E&W . 2W-13N 29
Ingleside Pl. E&W .. 2W-13N 29
Isabella E&W .................. 4W-13N,2W-13N 29
Jackson Av. N&S ... 3W-12N 29
Jenks St. NE&SW .. 3W-13N 29
Judson Av. N&S .................. 2W-10N,2W-11N 39
Kedzie St. E&W ... 2W-10N 39
Keeney St. E&W .................. 3W-10N,2W-10N 39
Kirk St. N&S ..... 3W-9N 39
Knox Cir. N&S .... 4W-12N 29
Lake Shore Blvd. N&S .................. 1W-10N 39
Lake St. E&W .................. 3W-11N,2W-11N 29
Lakeside Ct. NW&SE .................. 2W-13N 29
Laurel Av. N&S .... 3W-11N 29
Lawndale Av. N&S . 3W-11N 29
Lee St. E&W .................. 3W-10N,2W-10N 39
Leland Av. N&S ... 3W-11N 29
Lemar Av. N&S.....3W-11N 29
Leon Pl. E&W .... 2W-12N 29
Leonard Pl. E&W .. 3W-11N 29
Library Pl. E&W ... 2W-12N 29
Lincoln St. E&W .................. 4N-12N,2W-12N 29
Lincolnwood Dr. N&S .................. 4W-12N 29
Livingston St. E&W . 3W-13N 29
Lyons St. E&W .... 3W-10N 39
Madison Pl. E&W .. 3W-10N 39
Madison St. E&W .................. 3W-10N,2W-10N 39
Main St. E&W .... 3W-10N 39
Maple Av N&S .................. 3W-10N,2W-11N 39
Marcy Av. N&S .................. 4W-12N,4W-13N 29
Martha Ln. N&S ... 4W-11N 29
McCormick Blvd. NW&SE .................. 3W-11N,3W-12N 29
McDaniel Av. N&S .................. 3W-10N,4W-13N 39
Meadowlark Ln. N&S .................. 4W-13N 29
Michigan Av. N&S . 2W-10N 39
Milburn Pk. E&W ... 2W-12N 29
Milburn St. E&W ... 2W-12N 29
Monroe St. E&W .................. 3W-10N,2W-10N 39
Monticello St. E&W . 2W-13N 29
Mulford St. E&W .................. 3W-9N,3W-11N 39
Nathaniel Pl. E&W . 3W-10N 39
Normandy Pl. E&W .4W-12N 29
Noyes Ct. N&S......2W-12N 29

**Grid | Page**

Noyes St. E&W  
........4W-12N,2W-12N 29  
Oak Av. N&S........2W-10N 39  
Oakton St. E&W  
........3W-10N,1W-10N 39  
Orrington Av. N&S . 2W-11N 29  
Otto Ln. E&W...... 4W-13N 29  
Park Pl. E&W  
........4W-13N,3W-11N 29  
Payne St. E&W  
........4W-12N,3W-12N 29  
Pioneer Rd. N&S .... 3W-12N 29  
Pitner Av. N&S ...... 3W-10N 39  
Poplar St. NW&SE .. 3W-13N 29  
Prairie Av. NW&SE . 3W-13N 29  
Pratt Ct. N&S ...... 2W-11N 29  
Princeton Av. N&S .. 4W-12N 29  
Prospect Av. N&S .. 4W-12N 29  
Railroad Av. NW&SE  
............2W-11N 29  
Reba Pl. E&W ...... 2W-10N 39  
Reese Av. N&S .... 4W-13N 39  
Richmond Av. N&S...3W-9N 39  
Ridge Av. N&S  
........2W-11N,2W-10N 29  
Ridge Blvd. N&S .. 2W-10N 39  
Ridge Ct. N&S .... 2W-10N 39  
Ridge Ter. N&S .... 4W-12N 29  
Ridgeway Av. N&S . 4W-12N 29  
Rosalie St. E&W .... 3W-12N 29  
Roslyn Pl. N&S .... 2W-13N 29  
Seward St. E&W  
........3W-10N,2W-10N 39  
Sheridan Pl. E&W ... 2W-13N 29  
Sheridan Rd. N&S  
........2W-10N,2W-11N 39  
Sheridan Sq. N&S .. 1W-10N 39  
Sherman Av. N&S  
........2W-10N,2W-12N 39  
Sherman Pl. N&S ... 2W-11N 29  
Simpson St. E&W  
........4W-12N,2W-12N 29  
South Blvd. E&W  
........3W-10N,2W-10N 39  
St. Mark Ct. N&S .. 2W-11N 29  
Stewart Av. NW&SE  
............3W-13N 29  
Terry Pl. E&W ...... 3W-13N 29  
Thayer St. E&W .... 4W-13N 29  
Thelin Ct. E&W ..... 3W-11N 29  
University Pl. E&W . 2W-11N 29  
Wade St. E&W ...... 3W-11N 29  
Walnut Av. N&S .... 3W-13N 29  
Warren St. E&W .... 3W-10N 39  
Washington St. E&W  
........3W-10N,2W-10N 39  
Wesley Av. N&S  
........3W-9N,3W-12N 39  
Wilder Av. N&S .... 4W-12N 29  
Woodbine Av. N&S . 3W-13N 29  

## Evergreen Park

Albany Av. N&S  
........3W-11S,3W-10S 67  
Artesian Av. N&S .... 3W-11S 67  
Avers Av. N&S  
........4W-11S,4W-10S 67  
Beck Ct. N&S .... 4W-11S 67  
California Av. N&S  
........3W-11S,3W-10S 67  
Campbell Av. N&S . 3W-11S 67  
Central Park Av. N&S  
........4W-11S,4W-10S 67  
Clark Dr. NW&SE....4W-11S 67  
Clifton Park Av. N&S  
........4W-11S,4W-10S 67  
Country Club Dr. N&S  
............3W-10S 67  
Drury Ln. E&W .... 3W-10S 67  
Elm Pl. N&S .... 4W-11S 67  
Fairfield Av. N&S  
........3W-11S,3W-10S 67  
Francisco Av. N&S .. 3W-10S 67  
Grove Pl. N&S .... 4W-11S 67  
Hamlin Av. N&S  
........4W-11S,4W-10S 67  
Harding Av. N&S  
........4W-11S,4W-10S 67  
Homan Av. N&S  
........4W-11S,4W-10S 67  
Kedzie Av. N&S  
........4W-11S,4W-10S 67  
Lawndale Av. N&S  
........4W-11S,4W-10S 67  
Maple St. NE&SW .. 4W-11S 67  
Maplewood Av. N&S  
............3W-11S 67  
Millard Av. N&S  
........4W-11S,4W-10S 67  
Mozart St. N&S  
........3W-11S,3W-10S 67  
Pulaski Rd. N&S  
........5W-11S,5W-10S 66  
Richmond Av. N&S  
........3W-11S,3W-10S 67  
Ridgeway Av. N&S  
........4W-11S,4W-10S 67  
Rockwell St. N&S....3W-10S 67  
Sacramento Av. N&S  
........3W-11S,3W-10S 67  
Sawyer Av. N&S  
........4W-11S,4W-10S 67  
Spaulding Av. N&S  
........4W-11S,4W-10S 67  
Springfield Av. N&S  
........4W-11S,4W-10S 67  

St. Louis Av. N&S  
........4W-11S,4W-10S 67  
Talman Av. N&S .... 3W-10S 67  
Troy Av. N&S  
........3W-11S,3W-10S 67  
Trumbull Av. N&S  
........4W-11S,4W-10S 67  
Turner Av. N&S  
........4W-11S,4W-10S 67  
U.S. Route 12-20 E&W  
........4W-11S,3W-11S 67  
Utica Av. N&S  
........3W-11S,3W-10S 67  
Washtenaw Av. N&S  
........3W-11S,3W-10S 67  
Western Av. N&S  
........3W-11S,3W-10S 67  
87th St. E&W........3W-10S 67  
88th St. E&W........3W-10S 67  
89th Pl. E&W........3W-10S 67  
89th St. E&W........3W-10S 67  
90th Pl. E&W........3W-10S 67  
90th St. E&W........3W-10S 67  
91st St. E&W  
........4W-10S,3W-10S 67  
92nd St. E&W  
........4W-10S,3W-10S 67  
93rd Pl. E&W........3W-10S 67  
93rd St. E&W  
........4W-10S,3W-10S 67  
94th Pl. E&W........3W-10S 67  
94th St. E&W  
........4W-10S,3W-10S 67  
95th Pl. E&W  
........4W-11S,3W-11S 67  
95th St. E&W  
........4W-10S,3W-10S 67  
96th Pl. E&W........3W-11S 67  
96th St. E&W  
........4W-11S,3W-11S 67  
97th Pl. E&W........3W-11S 67  
97th St. E&W  
........4W-11S,3W-11S 67  
98th Pl. E&W........3W-11S 67  
98th St. E&W  
........4W-11S,3W-11S 67  
99th Pl. E&W........3W-11S 67  
99th St. E&W  
........4W-11S,3W-11S 67  
100th Pl. E&W......3W-11S 67  
100th St. E&W  
........4W-11S,3W-11S 67  
101st Pl. E&W......3W-11S 67  
101st St. E&W  
........4W-11S,3W-11S 67  
102nd Pl. E&W  
........4W-11S,3W-11S 67  
102nd St. E&W  
........4W-11S,3W-11S 67  
103rd St. E&W ...... 4W-11S 67  

## Flossmoor

Alexander Crescent E&W  
............3W-23S 87  
Amherst Ct. E&W .. 2W-23S 87  
Argyle Av. N&S......3W-22S 87  
Arquilla Av. NE&SW . 3W-23S 87  
Ash St. N&S ...... 4W-22S 87  
Avers Av. N&S ...... 4W-22S 87  
Balmoral Crescent E&W  
............3W-22S 87  
Beech St. E&W......4W-22S 87  
Berry Ln. N&S .... 3W-23S 87  
Bob-o-link Rd. E&W . 3W-23S 87  
Bonnie Brae Crescent E&W  
............3W-23S 87  
Braeburn Av. NS&EW  
............3W-23S 87  
Braemar Rd. NE&SW  
............3W-22S 87  
Brassie Av. N&S .. 3W-23S 87  
Brookwood Dr. E&W  
............3W-23S 87  
Bruce Av. N&S ...... 3W-22S 87  
Brumley Dr. E&W .. 3W-22S 87  
Bunker Av. N&S .. 3W-23S 87  
Burns Av. N&S .... 3W-22S 87  
Butterfield Cir. N&S  
........3W-24S,3W-23S 92  
Butterfield Ln. N&S . 2W-23S 87  
Butterfield Rd. N&S . 3W-23S 87  
Caddy St. E&W.... 3W-23S 87  
Cambridge Av. N&S . 2W-23S 87  
Cardinal Ct. N&S .. 3W-23S 87  
Carmel Dr. N&S .. 3W-22S 87  
Carrol Pkwy. NE&SW  
............2W-22S 87  
Central Dr. E&W .. 3W-22S 87  
Central Park Av. N&S  
........4W-23S,4W-22S 87  
Cherry Hills Dr. E&W  
............4W-22S 87  
Cheryl Dr. N&S .... 3W-23S 87  
Collett Ln. E&W .... 3W-22S 87  
Cooley Pl. E&W .... 3W-22S 87  
Cornell Rd. N&S .. 2W-22S 87  
Cummings Ln. E&W . 2W-22S 87  
Dartmouth Rd. N&S . 2W-23S 87  
Dixie Hwy. NW&SE . 2W-22S 87  
Douglas Av. N&S  
........3W-23S,3W-22S 87  
Dundee Av. N&S .. 3W-22S 87  
Elm Ct. SW&NE .... 4W-22S 87  
Elm St. N&S ...... 4W-22S 87  
Embassy Row E&W . 3W-22S 87  
Emelia Ct. E&W .... 3W-23S 87  

Evans Rd. E&W .... 2W-22S 87  
Flossmoor Rd. E&W  
........4W-22S,2W-22S 87  
Gardner Rd. N&S .. 2W-22S 87  
Golfview Ln. N&S .. 2W-23S 87  
Gordon Dr. E&W .. 2W-23S 87  
Governors Hwy. NE&SW  
........4W-23S,3W-22S 87  
Hagen Ln. E&W .... 2W-22S 87  
Hamlin Av. N&S .... 4W-22S 87  
Hanover Ln. E&W .. 2W-22S 87  
Harding Av. N&S .. 4W-22S 87  
Harold's Crescent E&W  
............3W-23S 87  
Harvard Rd. N&S .. 2W-23S 87  
Hawthorne Ln. E&W  
............3W-23S 87  
Heather Hill Crescent N&S  
............3W-23S 87  
Heather Rd. E&W .. 3W-23S 87  
Holbrook Rd. E&W . 3W-23S 87  
Hutchinson Rd. NS&EW  
............2W-22S 87  
Imperial Ct. E&W .. 2W-22S 87  
Kathleen Ln. E&W . 3W-23S 87  
Kedzie Av. N&S  
........4W-23S,4W-22S 87  
Knollwood Dr. E&W . 3W-23S 87  
Lake Dr. NE&SW .. 3W-23S 87  
Cir. ............ 3W-23S 87  
Laurel St. E&W .... 2W-23S 87  
Lawrence Crescent NE&SW  
............3W-23S 87  
Leavitt St. N&S .... 2W-23S 87  
Lynnwood Ct. E&W . 2W-23S 87  
MacDonald Ln. E&W  
............2W-22S 87  
MacFarlane Crescent E&W  
............3W-23S 87  
MacHeath Crescent E&W  
............3W-23S 87  
Maple Rd. N&S .... 4W-22S 87  
Markey Ln. E&W .. 2W-22S 87  
Marston Ln. E&W .. 2W-22S 87  
Maryland Av. N&S . 2W-22S 87  
Mast Ct. E&W .... 2W-22S 87  
Monterey Dr. E&W . 2W-22S 87  
Oak Ct. NE&SW .. 4W-22S 87  
Oak Lane Rd. E&W . 3W-23S 87  
Oak St. E&W ...... 4W-22S 87  
Oakmont Av. N&S . 3W-23S 87  
Oxford Ct. E&W .. 3W-23S 87  
Park Dr. NS&EW .. 3W-22S 87  
Patricia Ln. NE&SW . 3W-23S 87  
Perry Rd. E&W .... 3W-23S 87  
Perth Av. N&S .... 3W-22S 87  
Pheasant Ct. N&S . 3W-23S 87  
Pinehurst Ln. E&W . 2W-23S 87  
Polly Ln. E&W .... 3W-23S 87  
Poplar Rd. E&W .. 4W-22S 87  
Princeton Rd. N&S . 2W-22S 87  
Private Rd. E&W .. 3W-22S 87  
Pulaski Rd. N&S  
........4W-23S,4W-22S 87  
Quail Ct. N&S .... 3W-23S 87  
Redwood Ct. E&W . 3W-23S 87  
Redwood Ln. E&W . 3W-23S 87  
Robertson Ln. E&W . 2W-23S 87  
School St. N&S .... 3W-22S 87  
Scott Crescent E&W  
............3W-23S 87  
Springfield Av. N&S . 4W-22S 87  
Sterling Av. N&S .. 2W-22S 87  
Sterling Av. NE&SW . 3W-22S 87  
Strieff Ln. N&S .... 3W-23S 87  
Sunset Av. N&S .. 3W-23S 87  
Sylvan St. E&W .... 2W-23S 87  
Thomas Ct. E&W .. 3W-23S 87  
Thornwood Dr. E&W  
............2W-23S 87  
Tina Ln. N&S...... 3W-23S 87  
Travers Ln. N&S .. 2W-22S 87  
Vardon Ln. E&W .. 2W-22S 87  
Vardon Pl. E&W .. 3W-22S 87  
Verne Ln. N&S .... 3W-22S 87  
Vollmer Rd. E&W  
........4W-23S,2W-23S 87  
Wallace Dr. E&W .. 3W-22S 87  
Western Av. N&S .. 3W-22S 87  
Willow St. E&W .... 4W-22S 87  
Yale Rd. N&S ...... 2W-23S 87  
187th St. E&W .... 2W-22S 87  
188th St. E&W .... 4W-22S 87  
189th St. E&W .... 4W-22S 87  
190th St. E&W .... 4W-22S 87  
198th St. E&W .... 4W-22S 87  

## Ford Heights

Ambassador Ln. E&W  
............1E-25S 94  
Berkeley Av. N&S .. 1E-25S 94  
Calhoun Av. N&S .. 2E-25S 95  
Calumet Expressway  
............1E-25S 94  
Cannon Ln. E&W .. 1E-24S 94  
Columbia Av. N&S . 1E-25S 94  
Congress Ln. E&W . 1E-25S 94  
Cottage Grove Av. N&S  
........1E-25S,0E-25S 94  
DeForest Av. N&S . 1E-25S 94  
Deer Creek Dr. NE&SW  
............1E-25S 94  
Diplomat Ln. E&W . 1E-25S 94  
Drexel Av. N&S .... 1E-25S 94  
Ellis Av. N&S ...... 1E-24S 94  
Embassy Ln. E&W . 1E-25S 94  

Greenwood Av. N&S  
........1E-25S,1E-24S 94  
Hammond Ln. E&W . 1E-24S 94  
Kennedy Ln. E&W . 1E-25S 94  
Lexington Av. N&S . 1E-25S 94  
Lincoln Hwy. E&W . 1E-25S 94  
Park Av. N&S ...... 1E-25S 94  
Park Ln. E&W ...... 1E-25S 94  
Regent Ln. E&W .. 1E-25S 94  
Rt. 394 N&S ...... 1E-25S 94  
Seeley Av. N&S .. 1E-25S 94  
Senator Ln. E&W . 1E-25S 94  
U.S. Rt. 30 E&W .. 1E-25S 94  
Werline Av. N&S .. 1E-25S 94  
Woodlawn N&S .. 1E-25S 94  
8th Pl. E&W ...... 1E-24S 94  
8th St. E&W ...... 1E-24S 94  
9th St. E&W ...... 1E-24S 94  
10th Pl. E&W .... 1E-24S 94  
10th St. E&W .... 1E-24S 94  
11th Pl. E&W .... 1E-25S 94  
11th St. E&W .... 1E-25S 94  
12th St. E&W .... 1E-25S 94  
13th St. E&W .... 1E-25S 94  
14th St. E&W .... 1E-25S 94  
15th Pl. E&W .... 1E-25S 94  
15th St. E&W .... 1E-25S 94  
16th St. E&W .... 1E-25S 94  
17th St. E&W .... 1E-25S 94  

## Forest Park

Adams E&W ........ 9W-0S 48  
Beloit N&S ........ 9W-0S 48  
Belvidere N&S ...... 9W-0N 48  
Bergman Ct. E&W .. 9W-0N 48  
Brown E&W ........ 9W-0N 48  
Burchardt N&S .... 9W-0N 48  
Circle E&W .. 9W-1S,9W-0N 54  
Des Plaines N&S .. 9W-0S 48  
Dixon E&W ........ 9W-0N 48  
Dunlop N&S ........ 9W-0S 48  
Elgin N&S .. 9W-1S,9W-0N 54  
Ferdinand N&S .... 9W-0S 48  
Fillmore E&W ...... 9W-0S 48  
Franklin E&W ...... 9W-0N 48  
Hannah N&S .. 9W-1S,9W-0S 54  
Harlem N&S ........ 9W-1S 48  
Harrison E&W ...... 9W-0S 48  
Harvard E&W ...... 9W-0S 48  
Industrial Dr. E&W . 9W-1S 53  
Industrial Dr. E&W . 9W-1S 54  
Jackson Blvd. E&W . 9W-0S 48  
Lathrop N&S ...... 9W-0S 48  
Lehmer E&W ...... 9W-0S 48  
Lexington E&W .... 9W-0S 48  
Lincoln Ct. E&W .. 9W-0N 48  
Madison E&W ...... 9W-0N 48  
Marengo N&S .. 9W-1S,9W-0S 54  
Monroe E&W ...... 9W-0S 48  
Polk E&W .......... 9W-0S 48  
Railroad N&S ...... 9W-0S 48  
Randolph E&W .... 9W-0N 48  
Rockford N&S ...... 9W-0N 48  
Taylor E&W ........ 9W-0S 48  
Thomas N&S ...... 9W-0N 48  
Troost N&S ........ 9W-0S 48  
Van Buren N&S .... 9W-0S 48  
Warren E&W ...... 9W-0N 48  
Washington E&W .. 9W-0N 48  
Wilcox E&W ...... 9W-0S 48  
York E&W .......... 9W-0S 48  
Yuba E&W .......... 9W-0S 48  

## Forest View

Adlai E. Stevenson Expwy.  
E&W ........ 8W-5S 59  
Canal Bank Rd. E&W 8W-5S 59  
Canal Bank Rd. E&W 8W-5S 60  
Grove N&S ........ 8W-4S 54  
Home N&S ........ 8W-4S 54  
Interstate 55 E&W .. 6W-4S 55  
Kenilworth N&S .... 8W-4S 54  
Maple N&S ........ 8W-4S 54  
Wenonah N&S .... 8W-4S 54  
Wisconsin N&S .... 8W-4S 54  
46th St. E&W ...... 8W-4S 53  
46th St. E&W ...... 8W-4S 59  
47th E&W .......... 6W-4S 55  

## Franklin Park

Acorn N&S.......... 14W-4N 40  
Addison E&W  
........13W-4N,12W-4N 40  
Alta N&S .......... 13W-4N 40  
Anderson Pl. E&W . 13W-3N 40  
Ashland N&S ...... 11W-3N 40  
Atlantic N&S ...... 12W-4N 40  
Belden E&W ...... 11W-2N 47  
Belmont E&W  
........14W-4N,11W-4N 40  
Birch N&S .. 11W-3N,11W-4N 41  
Bright N&S ........ 13W-4N 40  
Britta E&W ........ 11W-4N 41  
Calwagner N&S .... 12W-3N 40  
Carnation N&S .... 13W-4N 40  
Carol N&S ........ 13W-4N 40  
Center Pl. E&W .... 12W-4N 40  
Centrella N&S .... 12W-4N 40  
Cherry E&W ...... 11W-4N 41  
Chestnut E&W  
........12W-3N,11W-3N 40  
Commerce St. N&S . 11W-3N 41  
Crescent E&W .... 11W-4N 41  
Crown E&W ...... 13W-4N 40  

Cullerton St. N&S .. 13W-3N 40  
Davis E&W ........ 11W-4N 41  
Des Plaines River Rd. N&S  
............11W-4N 40  
Desoto St. E&W .. 12W-4N 41  
Dodge E&W ...... 11W-4N 41  
Dora N&S .. 12W-3N,12W-4N 40  
Edgington N&S  
........11W-3N,11W-4N 41  
Elder Ln. N&S .... 12W-3N 40  
Emerson N&S  
........12W-3N,12W-4N 40  
Ernst N&S .. 12W-2N,12W-4N 46  
Exchange Pl. E&W . 11W-3N 41  
Fairfield N&S ...... 12W-3N 40  
Fletcher E&W .... 13W-3N 40  
Franklin E&W .... 12W-4N 40  
Front E&W ........ 12W-3N 40  
Gage E&W . 12W-4N,11W-4N 40  
Gary N&S ........ 11W-4N 41  
George N&S  
........12W-3N,12W-4N 40  
Grand E&W  
........13W-3N,11W-3N 40  
Greenfield Rd. E&W.12W-3N 40  
Gustav N&S ...... 12W-3N 40  
Hacke N&S ........ 11W-4N 41  
Hart E&W ........ 13W-3N 40  
Hawthorne N&S  
........12W-3N,12W-4N 40  
Herrick E&W  
........12W-3N,11W-3N 40  
Hirschberg N&S .. 12W-3N 40  
Houston Dr. N&S .. 13W-3N 40  
Iona N&S ........ 12W-4N 41  
James E&W ...... 13W-3N 40  
Jill N&S .......... 13W-3N 40  
Johanna E&W .... 12W-3N 40  
Kennedy St. E&W .. 11W-4N 41  
Kimmey N&S ...... 11W-4N 41  
King E&W .. 12W-4N,11W-4N 40  
King Av. E&W .... 11W-4N 40  
Kirshoff N&S  
........12W-3N,12W-4N 40  
LaSalle St. E&W .. 12W-4N 41  
Laidria N&S ...... 13W-3N 40  
Leona N&S ........ 12W-3N 40  
Lesser E&W ...... 12W-4N 40  
Leyden N&S ...... 11W-4N 41  
Lincoln N&S  
........12W-3N,12W-4N 40  
Lombard N&S  
........11W-3N,11W-4N 41  
Lonnquist Dr. N&S . 12W-4N 40  
Louis N&S ........ 12W-3N 40  
Lucy N&S ........ 13W-3N 40  
Mannheim N&S .... 11W-4N 40  
Maple N&S ........ 11W-2N 47  
Martens N&S ...... 11W-4N 41  
McNerney Dr. N&S . 12W-4N 40  
Medill E&W ........ 11W-2N 47  
Melrose E&W ...... 14W-4N 40  
Minneapolis E&W .. 12W-3N 40  
Montana N&S ...... 12W-3N 40  
Nerborne E&W .... 11W-4N 41  
Nevada E&W  
........12W-3N,11W-3N 40  
Nichols E&W ...... 11W-4N 41  
Nona N&S ........ 12W-3N 40  
North Charles N&S . 13W-4N 40  
North Powell N&S .. 14W-4N 40  
Oak N&S .......... 11W-3N 41  
Pacific E&W  
........12W-4N,11W-3N 40  
Park Lane E&W .. 12W-3N 40  
Parklane E&W .... 11W-4N 41  
Pearl N&S . 11W-3N,11W-4N 41  
Prairie Rd. N&S .. 13W-3N 40  
Reeves Ct. E&W .. 12W-4N 40  
Reuter N&S ...... 12W-3N 40  
Richard E&W ...... 12W-3N 40  
Riverside Dr. N&S . 12W-4N 40  
Robinson N&S .... 11W-4N 41  
Rose N&S ........ 12W-3N 40  
Rose N&S ........ 11W-2N 47  
Ruby N&S .. 12W-3N,12W-4N 40  
Runge N&S ........ 14W-4N 40  
Ruth N&S ........ 13W-3N 40  
Sandra N&S ...... 14W-4N 40  
Sarah N&S.. 12W-3N,12W-4N 40  
Schierhorn Ct. N&S . 11W-4N 41  
Schiller E&W ...... 12W-3N 40  
Scott N&S ........ 12W-3N 40  
Seymour E&W .... 13W-5N 40  
Shelia N&S ........ 12W-3N 40  
Shirley E&W ...... 12W-3N 40  
Silver Creek Dr. N&S  
............12W-3N 40  
Sonia N&S ........ 12W-3N 40  
Wagner N&S ...... 12W-3N 40  
Walnut E&W ...... 11W-3N 41  
Washington  
........11W-3N,11W-4N 41  
Waveland E&W .... 12W-4N 40  
Wehrman N&S .... 12W-4N 40  
Wellington St. NE&SW  
............13W-3N 40  
West King N&S .. 14W-4N 40  
West Manor Av. E&W  
............12W-3N 40  
Westbrook Dr. N&S . 12W-3N 40  
Williams Dr. N&S . 13W-4N 40  
Willow N&S  
........11W-3N,11W-4N 41  
Wrightwood N&S .. 12W-3N 40  
17th Av. N&S .... 11W-2N 47

## Glencoe

Grid Page

Adams Av. E&W .... 6W-17N 18
Apple Tree Ln. E&W ........ 7W-17N 18
Aspen Ln. E&W .... 6W-18N 18
Beach Rd. NW&SE ........ 6W-17N,6W-18N 18
Birch Rd. E&W ...... 7W-17N 18
Bluff Rd. N&S ...... 6W-18N 18
Bluff St. N&S ........ 6W-17N,6W-16N 18
Brentwood Dr. E&W ........ 6W-18N 18
Briar Ln. E&W ...... 6W-17N 18
Brookside Ln. N&S .. 6W-16N 18
Brookvale Ter. E&W ........ 6W-16N 18
Carol Ln. N&S ...... 6W-18N 18
Cedar Ln. NE&SW .. 6W-17N 18
Cherry Tree Ln. N&S ........ 7W-17N 18
Chestnut Ln. E&W .. 7W-17N 18
Clover Ln. NE&SW .. 7W-17N 18
Country Ln. E&W .... 6W-16N 18
Crescent Dr. E&W .. 6W-18N 18
Crescent Ln. E&W .. 5W-17N 19
Dell Pl. NE&SW ...... 5W-17N 19
Dennis Ln. NW&SE .. 6W-18N 18
Drexel Av. N&S ...... 6W-16N 18
Drexel Ln. N&S ...... 6W-16N 18
Dundee Rd. E&W .... 7W-18N 18
Eastwood Rd. N&S .. 6W-18N 18
Edens Expwy. NW&SE ........ 7W-16N 18
Edgebrook Ln. N&S .. 7W-17N 18
Elder Ct. E&W ...... 7W-17N 18
Elm Ct. NE&SW .... 6W-18N 18
Elm Pl. N&S ........ 7W-17N 18
Elm Ridge Dr. N&S .. 7W-18N 18
Estate Dr. E&W .... 6W-18N 18
Euclid Av. N&S ...... 5W-16N 19
Fairfield Rd. N&S .... 7W-18N 18
Fairview Rd. N&S .... 5W-17N 19
Forest Av. NE&SW .. 6W-18N 18
Franklin Rd. N&S .... 6W-18N 18
Glade Rd. (Pvt.) N&S ........ 6W-18N 18
Glencoe Dr. N&S ........ 6W-17N,6W-18N 18
Glencoe Rd. NW&SE ........ 6W-17N 18
Glenwood Av. NE&SW ........ 5W-16N 19
Green Bay Rd. NW&SE ........ 6W-18N,5W-17N 18
Green Leaf Av. N&S ........ 6W-17N,6W-18N 18
Greenwood Av. N&S ........ 6W-17N 18
Grove St. N&S ...... 6W-17N 18
Harbor St. NE&SW .. 5W-17N 19
Hawthorn Av. NE&SW ........ 6W-17N 18
Hazel Av. NE&SW .. 6W-17N 18
Hillcrest Dr. N&S .... 6W-18N 18
Hogarth Ln. (Pvt.) NW&SE ........ 6W-18N 18
Hohlfelder Rd. N&S .. 7W-18N 18
Ida Pl. N&S ........ 6W-17N 18
Ivy Ln. E&W ........ 6W-16N 18
Jackson Av. E&W .. 6W-17N 18
Jefferson Av. E&W .. 6W-17N 18
Julia Ct. N&S ........ 7W-18N 18
Kelling Ln. E&W .... 7W-18N 18
Knollwood Ln. E&W .. 6W-18N 18
Lake Cook Rd. E&W ........ 7W-18N 18
Lake St. N&S ...... 6W-16N 18
Lakeside Ter. N&S .. 5W-17N 19
Lakewood Dr. (Pvt.) NE&SW ........ 6W-18N 18
Lapier St. NE&SW .. 5W-17N 19
Lincoln Av. NE&SW .. 6W-17N 18
Lincoln Dr. E&W .... 6W-18N 18
Linda Ln. N&S ...... 6W-18N 18
Linden Av. NW&SE .. 5W-17N 19
Longmeadow Ln. N&S ........ 7W-18N 18
Longwood Av. N&S .. 6W-18N 18
Madison Av. E&W .. 6W-17N 18
Maple Hill Rd. E&W .. 6W-18N 18
Mary St. NE&SW .... 5W-17N 19
Mayfair Ln. N&S .... 7W-18N 18
Meadow Rd. N&S .. 6W-18N 18
Milton Av. NE&SW .. 6W-17N 18
Monroe NE&SW .... 5W-17N 19
Monroe Av. E&W .... 6W-17N 18
Montgomery St. E&W ........ 5W-17N 19
Mortimer Rd. E&W .. 5W-17N 19
North Way NE&SW .. 6W-17N 18
Northwood Dr. E&W ........ 7W-18N 18
Oak Dr. N&S ........ 7W-17N 18
Oak Ridge Dr. N&S .. 7W-18N 18
Oak Ter. N&S ...... 6W-18N 18
Oakdale Av. E&W .... 6W-16N 18
Old Elm Ln. N&S .... 6W-18N 18
Old Elm Pl. N&S .... 6W-18N 18
Orchard Ln. E&W .... 7W-18N 18
Palos Rd. NW&SE .. 5W-17N 19
Park Av. NW&SE .... 6W-17N 18
Park Pl. E&W ........ 6W-18N 18
Peach Tree Ln. NE&SW ........ 7W-17N 18
Pebblewood Ln. N&S ........ 7W-18N 18
Pine Ct. N&S ........ 7W-18N 18
Pinewood Ln. N&S .. 7W-18N 18
Prairie St. N&S ...... 7W-17N 18
Randolph St. N&S ........ 6W-16N,6W-17N 18
Ravine Glade St. E&W ........ 5W-17N 19
Redwood Ln. E&W .. 6W-16N 18
Robin Ln. E&W ...... 6W-16N 18
Rockgate Ln. (Pvt.) NW&SE ........ 6W-18N 18
Scott Av. NE&SW .. 5W-16N 19
Scott Ln. NW&SE .... 5W-16N 19
Sheridan Rd. NW&SE ........ 6W-18N 18
Skokie Ln., N. N&S .. 6W-16N 18
Skokie Ln., S. E&W .. 6W-16N 18
Skokie Ridge Dr. N&S ........ 7W-18N 18
Skokie Ridge Rd. N&S ........ 7W-18N 18
South Av. E&W ...... 6W-17N 18
South Way NE&SW .. 6W-17N 18
Stonegate Ter. NE&SW ........ 7W-17N 18
Strawberry Hill Dr. N&S ........ 7W-17N 18
Sunrise Cir. NW&SE ........ 5W-17N 19
Sunset Ln. E&W ........ 7W-18N,6W-18N 18
Surfside Pl. NW&SE 5W-17N 19
Sycamore Ln. E&W .. 7W-17N 18
Sylvan Rd. E&W .... 6W-18N 18
Temple Ct. NE&SW .. 6W-17N 18
Terrace Ct. E&W .... 6W-18N 18
Thorn Apple Ln. N&S ........ 7W-17N 18
Timber Ln. E&W .... 6W-18N 18
Tudor Ct. NE&SW .. 6W-17N 18
Valley Rd. N&S ........ 7W-17N,6W-17N 18
Valley St. N&S ...... 6W-17N 18
Vernon Av. N&S ........ 6W-16N,6W-18N 18
Village Ct. NW&SE .. 6W-17N 18
Walden Dr. E&W .... 6W-18N 18
Washington Av. E&W ........ 6W-17N 18
Washington Pl. (Pvt.) E&W ........ 6W-17N 18
Wentworth St. NE&SW ........ 5W-17N 19
Westley Rd. E&W .... 7W-18N 18
Westwood Ln. E&W 7W-18N 18
Whitebridge Hill St. NE&SW ........ 5W-17N 19
Wilgate Ter. NW&SE ........ 6W-17N 18
Willow Tree Ln. E&W ........ 7W-17N 18
Woodlawn Av. NE&SW ........ 6W-16N 18
Woodlawn St. NE&SW ........ 5W-17N 19
Woodridge Ln. E&W ........ 7W-17N 18

## Glenview

Alder Pl. E&W ...... 8W-14N 27
Alvin Ct. N&S ...... 9W-13N 27
Ammer Rd. E&W .... 8W-14N 27
Apple Tree Ln. E&W ........ 7W-13N 28
Applegate Ct. NW&SE ........ 9W-13N 27
Arbor Ln. N&S ...... 6W-13N 28
Arbor St. N&S ...... 6W-13N 28
Ardmore St. E&W .... 6W-13N 28
Ari Ln. NS&EW .... 10W-15N 17
Astor Ct. E&W .... 10W-15N 17
Baffin Rd. E&W ...... 8W-13N 27
Balmoral Av. N&S .... 7W-14N 28
Barbara Dr. E&W .. 10W-15N 17
Barbary Ln. N&S .. 11W-15N 16
Barry Ln. N&S ...... 11W-14N 26
Barton Ct. E&W .... 7W-13N 28
Basswood Cir N&S .. 8W-14N 27
Basswood Ct. NE&SW ........ 8W-14N 27
Beaver Ln. N&S .... 6W-13N 28
Beaver Rd. N&S .... 6W-13N 28
Becker Rd. E&W .... 7W-14N 28
Beech Dr. E&W ...... 6W-13N 28
Bel Air Dr. N&S ...... 9W-12N 27
Bel Air Ln. E&W .... 9W-12N 27
Bellwood Ln. N&S .. 10W-14N 27
Bette Ln. N&S ...... 11W-13N 26
Beverly Ln. E&W .... 6W-13N 28
Bianco Ter. E&W .... 9W-12N 27
Birchwood Ct. E&W .. 9W-12N 27
Blackthorn Dr. N&S .. 8W-14N 27
Blake Ln. E&W .... 11W-15N 16
Bonnie Glen Ln. E&W ........ 8W-13N,7W-13N 27
Borre Ln. N&S ...... 8W-14N 27
Braiford Ln. N&S .. 11W-15N 16
Brandess Dr. E&W .. 10W-15N 17
Brandon Rd. N&S .... 7W-14N 28
Brassie Dr. E&W .... 9W-13N 27
Brett Ln. E&W ...... 11W-14N 26
Briarhill N&S ........ 9W-12N 27
Brook Ln. E&W ...... 6W-13N 28
Brookdale Ln. NW&SE ........ 11W-15N 16
Bucknell Ct. N&S .... 9W-15N 17
Burnham Ct. N&S .... 9W-13N 27
Burr Oak Dr. E&W .. 8W-14N 27
Burton Ter. E&W .... 7W-14N 28
Button Wood Ln. NW&SE ........ 9W-13N,9W-14N 27
Canterbury Ln. N&S ........ 7W-13N,7W-14N 28
Cariann Ln. N&S .... 6W-13N 28
Carol Ln. NW&SE .. 12W-14N 26
Carousel Dr. E&W .. 11W-15N 16
Carrington Ln. N&S ........ 11W-15N 16
Castle Dr. N&S .... 11W-13N 26
Cedar Ct. E&W ...... 9W-12N 27
Cedar Wood N&S .... 9W-13N 27
Central Pkwy. E&W .. 8W-13N 27
Central Rd. E&W ........ 10W-13N,6W-13N 27
Charlie Ct. N&S .... 11W-15N 16
Chatham Dr. N&S .... 8W-13N 27
Chester Dr. E&W .. 11W-15N 16
Chesterfield St. N&S ........ 9W-13N 27
Chestnut Av. E&W .. 8W-14N 27
Church St. N&S .... 8W-13N 27
Cindy Ln. E&W .... 11W-13N 26
Clavey Ln. N&S ...... 9W-12N 27
Clearview Dr. N&S .. 10W-13N 27
Clover Ct. N&S ...... 9W-13N 27
Cir. ........ 7W-13N 28
Colfax St. E&W ...... 9W-12N 27
Collins Av. N&S .... 10W-14N 27
Cornell Ct.* N&S .... 9W-15N 17
Coronet Rd. N&S ........ 7W-12N,7W-13N 28
Country Ln. N&S .... 8W-12N 27
Covert Rd. E&W ........ 10W-12N,9W-12N 27
Crab Tree Ln. N&S .. 8W-12N 27
Crescent Ln. E&W .. 11W-14N 26
Crestwood Dr. E&W ........ 11W-15N 16
Crestwood Ln. E&W ........ 10W-13N 27
Crown Dr. N&S .... 11W-14N 26
Crown Ln. N&S .... 11W-14N 26
Crystal Ct. N&S .... 10W-13N 27
Culver Ln. E&W .... 8W-12N 27
Dale St. E&W ...... 6W-13N 28
Dartmouth Ct.* N&S 9W-15N 17
De L'ogier Dr. N&S .. 7W-14N 28
Dearlove Rd. N&S .. 11W-13N 26
Debra Ln. N&S .... 10W-15N 17
Dell Pl. E&W ...... 10W-13N 27
Denise Ct. NW&SE ........ 11W-13N 26
Depot St. N&S ...... 8W-13N 27
Dewes St. E&W .... 9W-13N 27
Dorthy Rd. E&W .... 10W-15N 17
Drake Rd. E&W .... 8W-13N 27
East Burr Oak Dr. N&S ........ 8W-14N 27
East Lake St. E&W ........ 10W-13N 27
Echo Ln. N&S ...... 6W-13N 28
Edgewood E&W .... 7W-13N 28
Elizabeth Ln. N&S .. 8W-13N 27
Elm St. N&S ........ 9W-12N,9W-13N 27
Elmdale Av. N&S .. 10W-14N 27
Elmdale Rd. NS&EW ........ 10W-13N 27
Elmgate Dr. N&S .... 9W-13N 27
Elmwood Av. E&W .. 7W-14N 28
Estate Ln. N&S .... 10W-14N 27
Evergreen Ter. N&S .. 8W-14N 27
Executive Cir. N&S ........ 10W-14N 27
Executive Ct. N&S .. 10W-14N 27
Executive Ln. N&S .. 10W-14N 27
Fairhope Av. E&W .. 7W-14N 28
Fairway Ct. E&W .. 10W-13N 27
Fairway Dr. N&S .. 10W-13N 27
Ferndale Dr. E&W .. 6W-13N 28
Fernwood Ln. N&S .. 9W-12N 27
Fir St. N&S ........ 9W-13N 27
Flora Av. N&S ...... 9W-12N 27
Fontana Dr. E&W .... 9W-12N 27
Forest Av. E&W .... 7W-14N 28
Forest Rd. N&S .... 6W-13N 28
Forestview Ln. E&W ........ 7W-13N 28
Franklin Ln. N&S .. 11W-14N 26
Frederic Ct. N&S .. 11W-15N 16
Garden Ct. N&S .... 9W-13N 27
George Ct. E&W .... 8W-12N 27
Gimidieff Ct. E&W .. 11W-14N 26
Gladish Ln. N&S .... 9W-13N 27
Glen Ct. N&S ........ 7W-13N 28
Glen Oak Dr. N&S .. 7W-14N 28
Glenayre Dr. N&S .... 7W-13N 28
Glendale Rd. N&S .. 7W-13N 28
Glenlake Dr. NE&SW ........ 10W-14N 27
Glenridge Dr. N&S .. 7W-13N 28
Glenview Rd. E&W ........ 11W-13N,7W-13N 26
Glenway Dr. E&W .. 11W-15N 16
Glenwood Av. E&W .. 8W-14N 27
Glenwood Rd. N&S ........ 10W-13N 27
Glenwood Rd. N&S .. 6W-13N 28
Gloria Ct. N&S .... 11W-13N 26
Golf Ct. E&W ...... 9W-12N 27
Golf Rd. E&W ........ 9W-12N,8W-12N 27
Golf View Ln. N&S .. 7W-13N 28
Golf View Rd. E&W .. 7W-13N 28
Grace Ln. E&W .... 11W-14N 26
Grandview Pl. E&W .. 9W-12N 27
Green Acres Ln. E&W ........ 7W-13N 28
Green Willow Ln. E&W ........ 8W-13N 27
Greenbrier Dr. E&W ........ 10W-12N 27
Greenbrier Ln. E&W .. 9W-12N 27
Greenfield Dr. N&S .. 9W-12N 27
Greenwood Av. N&S ........ 10W-14N 27
Greenwood Ct. E&W ........ 10W-15N 17
Greenwood Rd. N&S ........ 10W-15N 17
Gregory Dr. E&W .. 12W-14N 26
Grove St. E&W ........ 9W-13N,8W-13N 27
Hackberry Ct. E&W .. 6W-13N 28
Hager Ct. E&W ...... 6W-13N 28
Hammersmith E&W ........ 11W-14N 26
Happy Hollow Rd. N&S ........ 10W-15N 17
Harlem Av. N&S .... 8W-12N 27
Harmony Ln. E&W .. 8W-13N 27
Harms Rd. N&S .... 7W-13N 28
Harrison St. E&W .... 9W-12N 27
Harvard Ct.* E&W .. 9W-15N 17
Harvest Ln. E&W .. 11W-15N 16
Hawthorne Ln. N&S ........ 7W-13N,7W-14N 28
Heather Ln. E&W .... 8W-12N 27
Heatherfield Ln. N&S ........ 6W-13N 28
Henley St. E&W ........ 9W-13N,8W-13N 27
Henneberry Ln. N&S ........ 8W-12N 27
Hickory Ct. E&W .... 9W-12N 27
Highland Ln. N&S .. 10W-13N 27
Highland Ter. N&S .. 8W-14N 27
Hill Cir. N&S ........ 7W-13N 28
Hollywood Av. E&W .. 8W-14N 27
Huber Ln. N&S ........ 10W-13N,10W-12N 27
Huckelberry Ln. E&W ........ 7W-14N 28
Hudson Rd. E&W .... 8W-13N 27
Hunter Rd. N&S .... 6W-13N 28
Huntington Ln. N&S .. 8W-14N 27
Hutchings Av. N&S .. 8W-13N 27
Imperial Dr. N&S .... 10W-14N 27
Indian Rd. N&S ...... 6W-13N 28
Indian Ridge Ct. N&S ........ 11W-15N 16
Indian Ridge Dr. NS&EW ........ 11W-15N 16
Iroquois Dr. E&W .. 11W-15N 16
Ivy Dr. E&W ........ 11W-14N 26
Ivy Ln. E&W ...... 11W-14N 26
Ivy Way N&S ...... 11W-14N 26
Janet Dr. N&S ...... 10W-15N 17
Janney Rd. N&S .... 10W-15N 17
Jefferson Av. E&W .. 8W-14N 27
Jerrie Ln. E&W .... 10W-12N 27
Joanne Dr. E&W .... 11W-15N 16
John's Dr. N&S ...... 9W-14N 27
Johns Ct. E&W ...... 9W-14N 27
Joy Ln. N&S ...... 11W-14N 26
Juniper St. N&S .... 6W-13N 28
Juniper Ter. N&S .... 6W-13N 28
Karen Ln. E&W .... 10W-12N 27
Kaywood Ln. N&S .. 7W-14N 28
Keenan Ln. E&W .. 10W-15N 17
Keiss Dr. E&W .... 11W-15N 16
Kendal Dr. N&S ...... 8W-14N 27
Kenilworth Ln. E&W ........ 8W-14N,7W-14N 27
Kings Av. E&W ...... 7W-14N 28
Kings Ln. E&W ...... 7W-14N 28
Kmeic Ct. E&W .... 11W-14N 26
Knight St. E&W .... 11W-14N 26
Knollwood Ln. E&W ........ 10W-13N 27
LaFontaine Dr. NW&SE ........ 11W-14N 26
Lake Av. E&W ...... 8W-14N 27
Lakewood Ct. E&W ........ 10W-13N 27
Landwehr Rd. N&S ........ 11W-14N,11W-15N 26
Laramie Av. N&S .... 6W-13N 28
Laramie Ln. N&S .... 6W-13N 28
Larkdale Dr. E&W .. 9W-13N 27
Lawrence Ln. NW&SE ........ 12W-14N 26
Lawson Rd. E&W .. 10W-15N 17
Leaf Dr. E&W ...... 9W-13N 27
Leanne Ct. N&S .... 11W-15N 16
Lehigh Av. NW&SE .. 8W-13N 27
Lenox Rd. N&S ...... 7W-13N 28
Lexington Ln. E&W ........ 10W-15N 17
Liberty Ln. E&W .... 10W-13N 27
Limar Ln. N&S .... 10W-14N 27
Lincoln St. N&S ........ 9W-12N,9W-13N 27
Linden N&S ........ 9W-13N 27
Linden Av. E&W .... 7W-14N 28
Linden Leaf Dr. N&S ........ 9W-13N 27
Linden Ln. E&W .... 7W-14N 28
Lindenwood Ln. N&S ........ 11W-13N,10W-13N 26
Linneman St. E&W .. 9W-13N 27
Lizette Ln. E&W .... 11W-15N 16
Locust Ln. E&W .... 8W-12N 27
Lois Ln. E&W ...... 7W-14N 28
London Ln. E&W .... 8W-14N 27
Long Rd. N&S ...... 6W-13N 28
Long Valley Rd. E&W ........ 8W-12N 27
Longmeadow Dr. N&S ........ 10W-13N,10W-14N 27
Lori Dr. N&S ...... 10W-15N 17
Lotus Ln. N&S .... 10W-12N 27
Luri Lane Dr. NE&SW ........ 12W-14N 26
Lynn Ct. E&W ...... 7W-14N 28
MacArthur Dr. E&W .. 9W-12N 27
MacLean Ct. E&W .. 8W-13N 27
Malik Ct. E&W ...... 9W-12N 27
Maple Leaf Dr. E&W ........ 11W-15N 16
Maple Ln. E&W ...... 7W-14N 28
Maplewood Ln. E&W ........ 8W-13N 27
Marie Ln. N&S .... 11W-14N 26
Mark Dr. N&S ...... 6W-13N 28
Mary Ct. N&S ...... 11W-15N 16
Mary Kay Ln. E&W ........ 10W-15N 17
Meadow Ln. N&S .... 7W-14N 28
Meadowlark Ln. N&S ........ 9W-13N 27
Merle Ln. N&S .... 12W-14N 26
Michael Ln. E&W .. 11W-15N 16
Michael Manor N&S ........ 10W-12N 27
Mickey Ln. N&S .... 8W-14N 27
Miller Dr. E&W ........ 11W-15N,10W-15N 16
Mohawk Dr. E&W .. 11W-15N 16
Monroe Av. N&S .... 8W-14N 27
Montgomery Ln. N&S ........ 9W-12N 27
Mulberry Ln. E&W .. 6W-13N 28
Myrtle Ln. E&W .... 11W-15N 16
Neva Av. N&S ...... 8W-12N 27
Nora Av. N&S ...... 8W-12N 27
Nordica Av. N&S .... 8W-12N 27
Normandy Ln. E&W .. 7W-13N 28
North Branch Rd. N&S ........ 8W-12N 27
North Dr. N&S ...... 7W-14N 28
Norwich Ct. NW&SE ........ 10W-14N 27
Norwood Ter. E&W ........ 10W-12N 27
Nottingham Av. N&S ........ 8W-12N 27
Oakwood Ln. NE&SW ........ 7W-14N 28
Old Willow Rd. E&W ........ 9W-15N 17
Old Willow Rd. N&S 9W-15N 17
Osage Dr. E&W .... 11W-15N 16
Overland Pass N&S ........ 11W-14N 26
Overlook Dr. E&W .. 8W-12N 27
Oxford Ln. E&W .... 7W-13N 28
Palmgren Dr. E&W ........ 9W-13N,8W-13N 27
Pam-Anne Dr. N&S ........ 10W-13N 27
Park Dr. N&S ........ 9W-13N 27
Park Ln. N&S ...... 9W-13N 27
Parkview Rd. N&S .. 9W-12N 27
Pebble Creek Dr. N&S ........ 8W-14N 27
Pebbleford Dr. N&S ........ 10W-15N 17
Pendleton Ln. E&W .. 8W-14N 27
Penn Ct.* NE&SW .. 9W-15N 17
Pfingsten Rd. N&S ........ 11W-13N,11W-14N 26
Philipi N&S ........ 10W-15N 17
Pick Dr. N&S ........ 9W-12N 27
Pick Ln. E&W ...... 9W-12N 27
Pickwick Av. N&S .. 10W-14N 27
Pickwick Ter. E&W ........ 10W-14N 27
Pine Ct. E&W ...... 8W-13N 27
Pine St. N&S ........ 8W-13N 27
Pinehurst Dr. N&S .. 9W-13N 27
Pleasant Dr. E&W .... 8W-14N 27
Pleasant Ln. NW&SE ........ 7W-14N 28
Pleasant Run E&W 11W-14N 26
Plymouth Ct. E&W .. 8W-14N 27
Plymouth Ln. E&W .. 8W-14N 27
Polo Ln. E&W ...... 7W-13N 28
Portage Run Rd. N&S ........ 11W-14N 26
Porter Av. E&W .... 7W-14N 28
Porter Ct. N&S .... 11W-15N 16
Potter Rd. N&S .... 11W-14N 26
Prairie Lawn Rd. N&S ........ 10W-13N 27
Prairie St. E&W ........ 9W-13N,8W-13N 27
Princeton Ln. NS&EW ........ 10W-15N 17
Pvt. Rd. E&W ...... 7W-13N 28
Pynsky Dr. E&W .... 11W-15N 16
Queens Ln. E&W .... 7W-14N 28
Railroad Av. NW&SE ........ 8W-13N 27
Raleigh Rd. NW&SE ........ 8W-13N 27
Ralmark Ln. E&W .. 10W-14N 27
Rebecca Ln. N&S .. 10W-15N 17
Red Bud Ln. NE&SW ........ 8W-14N 27

| | Grid | Page |
|---|---|---|
| Ridgewood Ln., E. N&S | 7W-14N | 28 |
| Ridgewood Ln., W. N&S | 7W-14N | 28 |
| Rio Vista Rd. NW&SE | 8W-12N | 27 |
| River Dr. NW&SE | 8W-13N | 27 |
| Riverside Ct. N&S | 8W-14N | 27 |
| Robin Crest Ln. E&W | 9W-13N | 27 |
| Robin Crest Ln., N. E&W | 8W-13N | 27 |
| Robin Crest Ln., S. E&W | 8W-13N | 27 |
| Robin Ln. N&S | 11W-14N | 26 |
| Roder St. N&S | 10W-12N | 27 |
| Rogers Av. E&W | 8W-14N | 27 |
| Rolling Pass N&S | 9W-13N | 27 |
| Rollwind Rd. N&S | 8W-12N | 27 |
| Roosevelt Av. N&S | 9W-13N | 27 |
| Royal Oak Ln. E&W | 8W-13N | 27 |
| Rugen Ln. N&S | 9W-14N | 27 |
| Rugen Rd. E&W | 11W-13N,9W-14N | 26 |
| Russet Way N&S | 11W-15N | 16 |
| Rutgers Ct.* NE&SW | 9W-15N | 17 |
| Sally E&W | 10W-13N | 27 |
| Sandy Ln. E&W | 10W-15N | 17 |
| Sanford Ct. E&W | 8W-13N | 27 |
| Sanford Ln. N&S | 8W-13N | 27 |
| Saranac Ct. E&W | 11W-15N | 16 |
| Saranac Ln. N&S | 11W-15N | 16 |
| Sequoia Tr. NE&SW | 8W-14N | 27 |
| Sheffield Ln. E&W | 7W-13N | 28 |
| Shermer Rd. NW&SE | 9W-13N | 27 |
| Sherwood Rd. N&S | 6W-13N | 28 |
| Sheryl Ln. N&S | 10W-12N | 27 |
| Short Ln. N&S | 9W-12N | 27 |
| Silver Pine Dr. E&W | 9W-13N | 27 |
| Silver Willow Dr. NW&SE | 8W-14N | 27 |
| Simonsen Ln. E&W | 9W-13N | 27 |
| Sioux Trail N&S | 11W-15N | 16 |
| Sleepy Hollow Rd. NE&SW | 8W-13N | 27 |
| Solar Ln. E&W | 7W-13N | 28 |
| Somerset Dr. N&S | 7W-13N | 28 |
| Southgate Dr. N&S | 9W-13N | 27 |
| Spring Rd. N&S | 8W-13N | 27 |
| Springdale Av. NS&EW | 11W-13N,10W-13N | 26 |
| Spruce Dr. N&S | 9W-13N | 27 |
| Spruce St. N&S | 9W-12N,9W-13N | 27 |
| Steffens Ln. N&S | 7W-14N | 28 |
| Stevens Dr. E&W | 8W-13N | 27 |
| Strawberry Ln. N&S | 10W-15N | 17 |
| Sumac Cir. N&S | 9W-13N | 27 |
| Sunset Ridge Rd. N&S | 8W-14N | 27 |
| Surrey Ln. N&S | 7W-13N | 28 |
| Sussex Ln. E&W | 11W-14N | 17 |
| Sussex Ln. N&S | 11W-15N | 16 |
| Swainwood Dr. N&S | 9W-13N | 27 |
| Taft Ct. E&W | 6W-13N | 28 |
| Tall Tree Rd. N&S | 8W-14N | 27 |
| Tamer N&S | 11W-13N | 26 |
| Tanglewood Ln. NW&SE | 8W-14N | 27 |
| Terrace Ln. N&S | 9W-13N | 27 |
| Thornwood Av. N&S | 10W-14N | 27 |
| Thornwood Ln. NE&SW | 8W-13N | 27 |
| Timberline Dr. E&W | 7W-13N | 28 |
| Tinkerway N&S | 8W-13N | 27 |
| Topp Ln. E&W | 8W-14N | 27 |
| Tracy Ct. NW&SE | 11W-13N | 26 |
| Trent Ct. NW&SE | 10W-14N | 26 |
| Tri-state Tollway N&S | 11W-13N | 26 |
| Tulip Tree Ct. NE&SW | 8W-14N | 27 |
| Valley Lo Ln. N&S | 8W-14N | 27 |
| Vantage Ln. E&W | 10W-15N | 17 |
| Vernon Dr. N&S | 8W-13N | 27 |
| Virginia Ln. E&W | 10W-12N | 27 |
| Virginia Ln. N&S | 10W-15N | 17 |
| Wagner Rd. N&S | 7W-13N,7W-14N | 28 |
| Wald St. N&S | 10W-12N | 27 |
| Walnut Ct. E&W | 9W-12N | 27 |
| Warren Rd. N&S | 10W-12N | 27 |
| Washington St. N&S | 9W-12N,9W-13N | 27 |
| Waukegan Rd. N&S | 8W-12N | 27 |
| Wedgewood Dr. N&S | 9W-13N | 27 |
| Wellesley Ct.* NE&SW | 9W-15N | 17 |
| West Burr Oak Dr. N&S | 8W-14N | 27 |
| West Lake Av. E&W | 11W-14N | 26 |
| Westfield Ln. E&W | 10W-15N | 17 |
| Westlake Ter. N&S | 10W-14N | 27 |
| Westview Dr. E&W | 11W-14N | 26 |
| Westview Rd. E&W | 7W-13N | 28 |
| Wild Wood N&S | 8W-14N | 27 |
| Wildberry Dr. E&W | 8W-15N | 18 |
| Wildwood Ln. NW&SE | 7W-14N | 28 |
| Willow Ln. N&S | 11W-15N | 16 |
| Willow Rd. E&W | 11W-15N,9W-15N | 16 |
| Willow Rd. E&W | 11W-14N | 26 |
| Wilmette Av. E&W | 6W-13N | 28 |
| Windsor Rd. N&S | 7W-13N | 28 |
| Winnetka Rd. E&W | 10W-15N | 17 |
| Wissing Ln. NE&SW | 9W-13N | 27 |
| Wood Dr. E&W | 9W-13N | 27 |
| Woodland Ct. N&S | 7W-12N | 28 |
| Woodland Dr. N&S | 7W-12N | 28 |
| Woodland Rd. E&W | 7W-14N | 28 |
| Woodlawn Av. E&W | 8W-14N | 27 |
| Woodmere Ln. N&S | 7W-13N | 28 |
| Woodridge Rd. (Pvt.) E&W | 11W-15N | 16 |
| Woodview Ln. E&W | 8W-13N | 27 |
| Yale Ct.* E&W | 9W-15N | 17 |
| York Rd. N&S | 8W-13N | 27 |

## Glenwood

| | Grid | Page |
|---|---|---|
| Arizona Av. N&S | 1W-22S | 88 |
| Arquilla Dr. N&S | 0W-22S,0W-21S | 88 |
| Birch Dr. E&W | 0E-22S | 88 |
| Blackstone Av. N&S | 1E-23S | 89 |
| Bruce Ln. N&S | 0W-21S | 88 |
| Calumet Expwy. N&S | 1E-23S | 89 |
| Campbell St. N&S | 0E-22S | 88 |
| Carroll Pkwy. N&S | 0W-22S,0W-21S | 88 |
| Cedar Ln. N&S | 0W-22S | 88 |
| Center St. E&W | 0W-22S,0E-22S | 88 |
| Champlain Av. N&S | 0E-23S | 88 |
| Cherry Dr. N&S | 0W-22S | 88 |
| Chestnut Ln. N&S | 0E-22S | 88 |
| Clark St. E&W | 0E-22S | 88 |
| Coales St. E&W | 1W-23S | 88 |
| Cottage Grove Av. N&S | 0E-23S,0E-22S | 88 |
| Dante Av. N&S | 1E-23S | 89 |
| Dorchester Av. N&S | 1E-23S | 89 |
| Drexel Av. N&S | 1E-23S | 89 |
| Eberhardt Av. N&S | 0E-23S | 88 |
| Ellis Av. N&S | 1E-23S | 89 |
| Elm Ln. N&S | 0E-22S | 88 |
| Fitzhenry Ct. E&W | 0W-21S | 88 |
| Forest Av. N&S | 0W-23S | 88 |
| Gay Ct. N&S | 0E-23S | 88 |
| Glenwood Av. NW&SE | 0W-22S | 88 |
| Glenwood Dyer Rd. NW&SE | 0E-23S,1E-23S | 88 |
| Glenwood Rd. NE&SW | 0W-23S | 88 |
| Glenwood-Lansing Rd. E&W | 1E-23S | 89 |
| Greenwood Av. N&S | 1E-23S | 89 |
| Halsted St. N&S | 0W-22S | 88 |
| Harper Av. N&S | 1E-23S | 89 |
| Hickory Ln. N&S | 0E-22S | 88 |
| Hickory St. N&S | 0E-23S | 88 |
| Holly Ct. N&S | 0W-22S | 88 |
| Illinois Av. N&S | 1W-22S | 88 |
| Indiana St. E&W | 1W-22S | 88 |
| Ingleside Av. N&S | 1E-23S | 89 |
| Interurban Av. N&S | 1W-23S | 88 |
| Iowa St. E&W | 1W-22S | 88 |
| Jane St. E&W | 0E-22S | 88 |
| Kenneth Ct. N&S | 0W-22S | 88 |
| Lee Ct. N&S | 1W-22S | 88 |
| Longwood Dr. N&S | 0W-22S | 88 |
| Lotta St. E&W | 0W-22S | 88 |
| Main St. NW&SE | 0W-22S,0E-22S | 88 |
| Manor Ct. E&W | 0W-22S | 88 |
| Maple Dr. E&W | 0E-22S | 88 |
| Maryland Av. N&S | 1E-23S | 89 |
| Merril St. E&W | 0W-22S,0E-22S | 88 |
| Minerva Av. N&S | 1E-23S | 89 |
| Mulberry Ct. N&S | 0E-22S | 88 |
| Mulberry Dr. E&W | 0E-22S | 88 |
| Nevada St. E&W | 1W-22S | 88 |
| Oak Ln. N&S | 0E-22S | 88 |
| Oak St. N&S | 0W-22S | 88 |
| Ohio St. E&W | 1W-22S | 88 |
| Palm Dr. E&W | 0W-21S | 88 |
| Park Dr. N&S | 0W-22S | 88 |
| Peoria St. N&S | 1W-23S | 88 |
| Pine Ln. N&S | 0E-22S | 88 |
| Pleasant Dr. N&S | 0W-22S | 88 |
| Rainbow Dr. E&W | 0W-22S | 88 |
| Rebecca St. N&S | 0E-22S | 88 |
| Rhodes Av. N&S | 0E-23S | 88 |
| Roberts Dr. N&S | 0W-22S | 88 |
| Rose Ct. E&W | 0E-22S | 88 |
| Rose St. E&W | 0E-22S | 88 |
| Rt. 1 N&S | 0W-22S | 88 |
| School St. E&W | 0W-22S,0E-22S | 88 |
| Science Rd. E&W | 0W-22S | 88 |
| Spruce Ln. N&S | 0E-22S | 88 |
| St. Lawrence Av. N&S | 0E-23S | 88 |
| State St. N&S | 0E-23S,0E-22S | 88 |
| Strieff Ln. E&W | 1W-22S,0W-22S | 88 |
| Sunset Dr. E&W | 0W-21S | 88 |
| Sycamore Ln. N&S | 0E-22S | 88 |
| Terrace Dr. E&WN& | 0W-22S | 88 |
| Tulip Dr. E&W | 0E-22S | 88 |
| University Av. N&S | 1E-23S | 89 |
| Virginia Av. N&S | 1W-22S | 88 |
| Wabash Av. N&S | 0E-22S | 88 |
| Walnut Ln. N&S | 0E-22S | 88 |
| Walnut St. N&S | 0E-23S | 88 |
| Westwood Dr. E&W | 0W-22S | 88 |
| Willow Ln. N&S | 0E-22S | 88 |
| Willow St. N&S | 0E-23S | 88 |
| Wisconsin St. E&W | 1W-22S | 88 |
| Young St. N&S | 0E-22S | 88 |
| 183rd St. E&W | 1W-22S | 88 |
| 187th St. E&W | 0W-22S | 88 |
| 191st Pl. E&W | 0E-23S,1E-23S | 88 |
| 192nd Pl. E&W | 1E-23S | 89 |
| 192nd St. E&W | 1E-23S | 89 |
| 193rd Pl. E&W | 1W-23S,1E-23S | 88 |
| 193rd St. NW&SE | 1E-23S | 89 |
| 194th Pl. E&W | 1W-23S | 88 |
| 194th St. E&W | 1W-23S,1E-23S | 88 |
| 195th St. E&W | 1W-23S,0W-23S | 88 |
| 196th St. E&W | 0W-23S | 88 |

## Golf

| | Grid | Page |
|---|---|---|
| Blossom Ln. NW&SE | 8W-12N | 27 |
| Briar Rd. NW&SE | 8W-12N | 27 |
| Clyde Ln. N&S | 8W-12N | 27 |
| Dover Ln. NW&SE | 8W-12N | 27 |
| Highland Pl. N&S | 8W-12N | 27 |
| Lilac Ln. NW&SE | 8W-12N | 27 |
| Logan Ter. E&W | 8W-12N | 27 |
| Orchard Ln. N&S | 8W-12N | 27 |
| Overlook Dr. NW&SE | 7W-12N | 28 |
| Park Ln. E&W | 8W-12N | 27 |
| Simpson St. E&W | 8W-12N | 27 |

## Hanover Park*

**(Also see Du Page County)**

| | Grid | Page |
|---|---|---|
| Adams St. E&W | 25W-9N | 32 |
| Alden Ln. NW&SE | 27W-8N | 31 |
| Apple Tree St. N&S | 27W-8N | 31 |
| Applewood Ct. N&S | 26W-9N | 31 |
| Arbor Vitae Dr. E&W | 27W-9N | 31 |
| Asbury Cir. N&S | 26W-9N | 31 |
| Astor Av. N&S | 27W-9N | 31 |
| Bamberg Ct. NW&SE | 26W-9N | 31 |
| Barrington Rd. N&S | 27W-8N,27W-9N | 31 |
| Berkshire Ct. NW&SE | 26W-9N | 31 |
| Berkshire Dr. E&W | 26W-9N | 31 |
| Birch Av. E&W | 26W-8N | 31 |
| Bolton Way E&W | 25W-9N | 32 |
| Breezewood Ln. SE&NW | 27W-8N | 31 |
| Brentwood Ct. NE&SW | 26W-9N | 31 |
| Briar Ln. NE&SW | 27W-9N | 31 |
| Briarwood Av. NW&SE | 27W-9N | 31 |
| Briarwood St. N&S | 27W-9N | 31 |
| Bristol Ln. E&W | 26W-9N | 31 |
| Brockton Ct. N&S | 26W-9N | 31 |
| Brookside Ct. E&W | 26W-9N | 31 |
| Brookside Dr. N&S | 26W-9N | 31 |
| Burr Oak St. NE&SW | 27W-8N | 31 |
| Camelia Dr. N&S | 27W-9N | 31 |
| Canterbury Dr. E&W | 25W-9N | 32 |
| Carlisle Ct. E&W | 26W-9N | 31 |
| Carlisle Dr. N&S | 26W-9N | 31 |
| Carnaby Ct. N&S | 26W-9N | 31 |
| Carrolton Ct. N&S | 26W-9N | 31 |
| Catalpa St. N&S | 27W-8N | 31 |
| Catawba Ln. N&S | 26W-9N | 31 |
| Cedar Av. E&W | 27W-8N | 31 |
| Center Av. N&S | 27W-8N | 31 |
| Cherry Av. E&W | 27W-8N | 31 |
| Chestnut St. N&S | 27W-8N | 31 |
| Church St. N&S | 27W-8N | 31 |
| Churchill Dr. N&S | 26W-9N | 31 |
| Countryside Dr. E&W | 26W-8N | 31 |
| Coventry Ln. N&S | 26W-9N | 31 |
| Crescent Way NE&SW | 26W-9N | 31 |
| Cumberland Dr. N&S | 26W-9N | 31 |
| Cynthia Ln. E&W | 26W-9N | 31 |
| Cypress Av. E&W | 26W-8N | 31 |
| Cypress Ct. N&S | 26W-8N | 31 |
| Dahlia Dr. N&S | 27W-9N | 31 |
| Dartmouth Ct. NE&SW | 26W-9N | 31 |
| Dartmouth Ln. NS&EW | 26W-9N | 31 |
| Deerpath Ln. N&S | 26W-8N | 31 |
| Durham Ct. E&W | 26W-9N | 31 |
| East Av. N&S | 27W-8N,27W-9N | 31 |
| Edgebrook Ln. N&S | 26W-8N | 31 |
| Elm Av. NW&SE | 27W-8N | 31 |
| Elm Ct. N&S | 27W-8N | 31 |
| Essex Ct. E&W | 26W-9N | 31 |
| Evergreen Av. E&W | 27W-8N | 31 |
| Fairhaven Dr. E&W | 25W-9N | 32 |
| Farmstead Ln. N&S | 25W-9N | 32 |
| Filmore Av.* E&W | 25W-9N | 32 |
| Flower Ct. N&S | 27W-9N | 31 |
| Forest Glen E&W | 27W-8N | 31 |
| Gladiola Av. N&S | 27W-9N | 31 |
| Glendale Ter. NE&SW | 27W-8N | 31 |
| Glenside Ct. E&W | 26W-9N | 31 |
| Glenwood Ln. N&S | 26W-8N | 31 |
| Grant Cir. E&W | 25W-9N | 32 |
| Greenwood Av. E&W | 27W-9N | 31 |
| Guilford Commons E&W | 26W-9N | 31 |
| Hadom Way E&W | 25W-9N | 32 |
| Hanover St. N&S | 27W-8N,27W-9N | 31 |
| Harrison St.* E&W | 26W-9N | 31 |
| Hartman Dr. E&W | 25W-9N | 32 |
| Hartmann NW&SE | 25W-9N | 32 |
| Hastings Ln. E&W | 26W-9N | 31 |
| Hawthorne Ln. N&S | 26W-8N | 31 |
| Hearth Dr. N&S | 25W-9N | 32 |
| Hearth Dr. NE&SW | 25W-9N | 32 |
| Hemlock St. N&S | 27W-9N | 31 |
| Hickory St. N&S | 27W-8N | 31 |
| Highland St. N&S | 26W-8N | 31 |
| Hillcrest Av. E&W | 26W-8N | 31 |
| Hollywood Av. E&W | 27W-9N | 31 |
| Huntington Cir. N&S | 26W-9N | 31 |
| Indian Hill Av. E&W | 26W-8N | 31 |
| Indian Hill Ct. N&S | 26W-8N | 31 |
| Iris Av. N&S | 27W-9N | 31 |
| Irving Park Rd. NW&SE | 27W-8N | 31 |
| Jackson St.* E&W | 25W-9N | 32 |
| Jasmine Dr. N&S | 27W-9N | 31 |
| Jensen Blvd. N&S | 27W-9N | 31 |
| Jonquil Ter. N&S | 27W-9N | 31 |
| Juniper St. N&S | 27W-8N | 31 |
| Kensington Ln. N&S | 26W-9N | 31 |
| Kent Ct. NW&SE | 26W-9N | 31 |
| Kingsbury Dr. N&S | 26W-9N | 31 |
| Lake St. NW&SE | 28W-8N,27W-8N | 31 |
| Larch Ln. NE&SW | 27W-8N | 31 |
| Laurel Av. E&W | 27W-9N | 31 |
| Laurie Ln. E&W | 26W-9N | 31 |
| Leslie Ln. NW&SE | 28W-8N,27W-8N | 31 |
| Lexington Cir. E&W | 26W-9N | 31 |
| Lincoln Cir.* NW&SE | 26W-8N | 31 |
| Linden Av. E&W | 27W-8N | 31 |
| Longmeadow Ln. N&W | 26W-8N | 31 |
| Madison St.* N&S | 26W-9N | 31 |
| Madrid Ct. E&W | 26W-9N | 31 |
| Magnolia St. N&S | 27W-8N | 31 |
| Manchester Manor NW&SE | 26W-9N | 31 |
| Maple Av. NW&SE | 27W-8N | 31 |
| Maplewood Av. E&W | 26W-8N | 31 |
| Marigold Ln. E&W | 27W-9N | 31 |
| Mark Thomas Ln. E&W | 28W-8N,27W-8N | 31 |
| Meadowbrook Ln. N&S | 26W-8N | 31 |
| Mulberry St. N&S | 27W-8N,27W-9N | 31 |
| Nantucket Cove N&S | 26W-9N | 31 |
| Narcissus Av. E&W | 27W-9N | 31 |
| Northway Ct. E&W | 26W-9N | 31 |
| Northway Dr. N&S | 26W-9N | 31 |
| Oak Av. NW&SE | 27W-8N | 31 |
| Oakwood Av. E&W | 26W-8N | 31 |
| Old Mill Ln. E&W | 26W-9N | 31 |
| Olde Salem Cir. N&S | 25W-9N | 32 |
| Olde Salem Dr. NE&SW | 26W-9N | 31 |
| Olde Salem Rd. N&S | 26W-9N | 31 |
| Olivia Ln. N&S | 26W-9N | 31 |
| Orchard Ln. N&S | 26W-8N | 31 |
| Osage Ln. E&W | 27W-9N | 31 |
| Oxford Ln. E&W | 26W-9N | 31 |
| Park Av. E&W | 27W-8N | 31 |
| Parkview Dr. E&W | 26W-9N | 31 |
| Peach Tree St. N&S | 27W-8N | 31 |
| Pebblebrook Cir. N&S | 26W-9N | 31 |
| Pine Tree St. N&S | 27W-8N | 31 |
| Plum Tree Ln. N&S | 27W-8N | 31 |
| Polk St.* N&S | 26W-8N | 31 |
| Poplar Av. E&W | 27W-8N | 31 |
| Princeton Circle Dr. N&S | 26W-9N | 31 |
| Ramblewood Dr. E&W | 26W-9N | 31 |
| Ramsgate Cir. N&S | 26W-9N | 31 |
| Redwood Av. E&W | 27W-8N | 31 |
| Roosevelt Rd.* E&W | 26W-8N | 31 |
| Rosewood St. N&S | 27W-9N | 31 |
| Roxbury Ct. NW&SE | 26W-9N | 31 |
| Rt. 19 E&W | 27W-9N,26W-9N | 31 |
| Salem Cir. N&S | 26W-9N | 31 |
| Sarson Way NE&SW | 25W-9N | 32 |
| Scott Ln. NE&SW | 27W-8N | 31 |
| Sequoia Dr. E&W | 27W-8N | 31 |
| Shelbourne Ct. NW&SE | 26W-9N | 31 |
| Sherwood Cir. N&S | 26W-9N | 31 |
| Sommerset Cir. E&W | 26W-9N | 31 |
| Spruce Av. E&W | 26W-8N | 31 |
| Stratford Ln. E&W | 26W-9N | 31 |
| Strathmore Ln. N&S | 26W-9N | 31 |
| Sycamore Av. E&W | 27W-8N | 31 |
| Taft Cir.* E&W | 26W-8N | 31 |
| Tanglewood Av. NW&SE | 27W-9N | 31 |
| Taylor St.* E&W | 25W-9N | 32 |
| Tea Party Ln. N&S | 26W-9N | 31 |
| Thornwood St. N&S | 27W-9N | 31 |
| Tower Dr. E&W | 27W-9N | 31 |
| Truman St.* NW&SE | 25W-9N | 32 |
| U.S. Route 20 NW&SE | 27W-8N | 31 |
| Valley View Rd. N&S | 26W-8N | 31 |
| Walnut Av. E&W | 27W-8N,26W-8N | 31 |
| Walnut Ct. N&S | 27W-8N | 31 |
| Washington St.* E&W | 26W-9N | 31 |
| Waterford Dr. E&W | 25W-9N | 32 |
| Wedgewood Dr. E&W | 25W-9N | 32 |
| West Av. N&S | 27W-8N | 31 |
| Westchester Dr. E&W | 26W-8N | 31 |
| Weymouth Cir. NE&SW | 26W-9N,25W-9N | 31 |
| Weymouth Cir. NS&EW | 25W-9N | 32 |
| White Bridge Ct. N&S | 26W-9N | 31 |
| White Bridge Ln. E&W | 26W-9N | 31 |
| Willow Av. NW&SE | 27W-8N | 31 |
| Wilson St.* E&W | 25W-9N | 32 |
| Windsor Ln. E&W | 26W-9N | 31 |
| Wise Rd. E&W | 25W-9N | 32 |
| Yorkshire Ct. N&S | 26W-9N | 31 |
| Yorkshire Dr. E&W | 26W-9N | 31 |

## Hanover Township

| | Grid | Page |
|---|---|---|
| Adler Ln. NW&SE | 31W-11N | 30 |
| Bartlett Rd. N&S | 28W-11N,28W-12N | 31 |
| Bellingham Ln. E&W | 30W-8N | 30 |
| Berner Dr. N&S | 31W-12N | 20 |
| Beverly Rd. N&S | 31W-12N | 20 |
| Bode Rd. NW&SE | 29W-11N,27W-11N | 30 |
| Borden Dr. N&S | 31W-11N | 30 |
| Cardinal Dr. E&W | 31W-11N | 30 |
| Chapel Hill Dr. N&S | 31W-11N | 30 |
| Chestnut St. E&W | 31W-11N | 30 |
| Cheviot Ln. N&S | 30W-8N | 30 |
| Circle Dr. NW&SE | 31W-11N | 30 |
| Dale Dr. E&W | 31W-12N | 20 |
| Dale Rd. E&W | 31W-12N | 20 |
| Dennis Ln. N&S | 30W-10N | 30 |
| Douglas Rd. E&W | 30W-10N | 30 |
| Forest View Dr. NE&SW | 31W-11N,30W-11N | 30 |
| Friar Tuck Dr. NE&SW | 31W-10N | 30 |
| Gifford Rd. N&S | 32W-9N | 30 |
| Glen Echo St. N&S | 31W-11N | 30 |
| Golf Keys Rd. (Pvt.) NS&EW | 30W-9N | 30 |
| Golf Rd. E&W | 31W-12N,27W-12N | 20 |
| Golfview Dr. E&W | 30W-9N | 30 |
| Greenfeather Ln. NE&SW | 30W-10N | 30 |
| Greenwood Rd. NE&SW | 31W-10N | 30 |
| Gromer Rd. NE&SW | 30W-10N | 30 |
| Hillard Dr. NE&SW | 31W-10N | 30 |
| Hilltop Rd. NE&SW | 31W-11N,30W-11N | 30 |
| Irving Park Rd. NW&SE | 31W-10N,30W-10N | 30 |
| King Arthur Ct. NE&SW | 31W-10N | 30 |
| Lady Marion Dr. NE&SW | 31W-10N | 30 |
| Lake St. NW&SE | 31W-10N,29W-9N | 30 |
| Little John Dr. NW&SE | 31W-10N | 30 |
| Longboat Key Ln. E&W | 30W-9N | 30 |
| Magnolia Ct. N&S | 29W-12N | 20 |
| Magnolia Ln. E&W | 29W-12N | 20 |
| Mundhawk Rd. N&S | 28W-12N | 21 |
| Naperville Rd. N&S | 30W-9N | 30 |
| Northwest Tollway E&W | 31W-12N,27W-12N | 20 |
| Nottingham Ln. NW&SE | 31W-10N | 30 |
| Old Higgins Rd. NW&SE | 30W-14N,27W-12N | 20 |
| Old Lake St. NE&SW | 29W-9N | 30 |
| Philip Dr. NE&SW | 30W-9N | 30 |
| Phillippi Creek Dr. NS&EW | 30W-9N | 30 |
| Poplar Creek Dr. N&S | 32W-11N | 30 |

| | Grid | Page |
|---|---|---|
| Poplar View Bend NE&SW | 31W-11N | 30 |
| Quincey Ct. E&W | 31W-11N | 30 |
| Robinhood Dr. NW&SE | 31W-10N | 30 |
| Rohrson Rd. N&S | 31W-11N | 30 |
| Rolling Hills Av. NS&EW | 31W-11N | 30 |
| Rosewood Ct. NE&SW | 32W-11N | 30 |
| Sayer Rd. NW&SE | 30W-8N | 30 |
| Schaumburg Rd. E&W | 30W-10N | 30 |
| Sherwood Rd. NE&SW | 31W-10N | 30 |
| Shoe Factory Rd. E&W | 31W-12N,27W-12N | 20 |
| Siesta Key Ln. NW&SE | 30W-9N | 30 |
| Spaulding Rd. E&W | 30W-9N | 30 |
| Stonehurst Dr. N&S | 32W-11N | 30 |
| Sutton Rd. N&S | 30W-9N | 30 |
| Tameling Ct. N&S | 31W-8N | 30 |
| West Bartlett Rd. E&W | 32W-8N,30W-8N | 30 |
| Will Scarlet Ln. NE&SW | 31W-10N,30W-10N | 30 |
| Windsor Ct. E&W | 31W-11N | 30 |
| Wolsfeld Rd. E&W | 31W-11N | 30 |

## Harvey

| | Grid | Page |
|---|---|---|
| Artesian Av. N&S | 3W-17S | 81 |
| Ashland Av. N&S | 2W-19S,2W-17S | 82 |
| Belden Av. N&S | 0W-18S | 82 |
| Broadway Av. N&S | 1W-18S,1W-17S | 82 |
| California Av. N&S | 3W-17S | 81 |
| Calumet Blvd. E&W | 1W-17S | 82 |
| Campbell Av. N&S | 2W-18S | 81 |
| Carol Av. N&S | 0W-19S | 82 |
| Carse Av. N&S | 1W-20S,1W-19S | 88 |
| Cary Av. N&S | 0W-19S,0W-18S | 82 |
| Center Av. N&S | 1W-18S,1W-17S | 82 |
| Center St. N&S | 1W-20S,1W-19S | 88 |
| Clark Av. N&S | 0W-18S | 82 |
| Clinton St. N&S | 0W-19S,0W-17S | 82 |
| Commercial Av. NE&SW | 1W-18S | 82 |
| Cooper Av. N&S | 2W-17S | 81 |
| Des Plaines St. N&S | 0W-17S | 82 |
| Dixie Hwy. NW&SE | 2W-18S,2W-17S | 81 |
| Emerald Av. N&S | 0W-19S | 82 |
| Fairfield Av. N&S | 3W-17S | 81 |
| Finch Av. N&S | 1W-19S,1W-18S | 82 |
| Fisk Av. N&S | 1W-19S,1W-18S | 82 |
| Gauger Av. N&S | 1W-19S | 82 |
| Geneva Av. E&W | 1W-19S | 82 |
| Green St. N&S | 1W-19S,1W-17S | 82 |
| Halsted St. N&S | 1W-19S,1W-17S | 82 |
| Harvey Av. N&S | 1W-17S | 82 |
| Honore Av. N&S | 2W-19S,2W-17S | 81 |
| Hoyne Av. N&S | 2W-18S,2W-17S | 81 |
| Ingalls Dr. N&S | 1W-18S | 82 |
| Jefferson St. N&S | 0W-19S,0W-17S | 82 |
| Justine St. N&S | 1W-19S,1W-17S | 82 |
| Kennicott Av. N&S | 0W-18S | 82 |
| Kentucky Av. N&S | 1W-17S | 82 |
| Lathrop Av. N&S | 1W-19S,1W-18S | 82 |
| Leavitt Av. N&S | 2W-17S | 81 |
| Lexington Av. N&S | 1W-18S,1W-17S | 82 |
| Lincoln Av. N&S | 2W-19S,2W-17S | 81 |
| Loomis St. N&S | 1W-19S,1W-17S | 82 |
| Lowe Av. N&S | 0W-19S | 82 |
| Madison Av. N&S | 0W-17S | 82 |
| Main St. N&S | 1W-18S,1W-17S | 82 |
| Maplewood Av. N&S | 3W-17S | 81 |
| Markham Dr. N&S | 0W-17S | 82 |
| Marshfied Av. N&S | 2W-19S,2W-17S | 81 |
| Morgan St. N&S | 1W-17S | 82 |
| Myrtle Av. N&S | 1W-19S,1W-17S | 82 |
| Normal Av. N&S | 0W-17S | 82 |
| Oakley Av. N&S | 2W-17S | 81 |
| Page Av. N&S | 1W-19S,1W-17S | 82 |
| Park Av. NE&SW | 0W-17S | 82 |
| Parnell Av. N&S | 0W-17S | 82 |
| Paulina Av. N&S | 1W-19S,1W-17S | 82 |
| Peoria St. N&S | 1W-17S | 82 |
| Robey St. N&S | 2W-18S | 81 |
| Rockwell St. N&S | 2W-18S | 81 |
| Rt. 83 E&W | 0W-17S | 82 |
| Sangamon St. N&S | 1W-17S | 82 |
| Seeley Av. N&S | 2W-17S | 81 |
| Sibley Blvd. E&W | 2W-17S,0W-17S | 81 |
| Streamside Dr. NW&SE | 1W-17S,0W-17S | 82 |
| Talman Av. N&S | 3W-17S | 81 |
| Thornton Rd. NW&SE | 1W-17S | 82 |
| Turlington Av. N&S | 1W-18S,1W-17S | 82 |
| U.S. Route 6 E&W | 2W-18S | 81 |
| Union St. N&S | 0W-19S,0W-17S | 82 |
| Vail Av. N&S | 2W-17S | 81 |
| Vine Av. N&S | 1W-18S,1W-17S | 82 |
| Wallace Rd. N&S | 0W-17S | 82 |
| Wallace St. N&S | 0W-19S,0W-17S | 82 |
| Washtehaw Av. N&S | 3W-17S | 81 |
| Wells Av. E&W | 1W-17S | 82 |
| West Av. N&S | 1W-19S,1W-18S | 82 |
| Western Av. N&S | 2W-18S | 81 |
| Willard Av. N&S | 1W-19S,1W-18S | 82 |
| Winchester Av. N&S | 2W-18S,2W-17S | 81 |
| Wood St. N&S | 2W-19S,2W-17S | 81 |
| Woodbridge Av. N&S | 1W-19S,1W-18S | 82 |
| 144th Ct. E&W | 1W-17S | 82 |
| 144th St. E&W | 1W-17S | 82 |
| 145th St. E&W | 2W-17S,1W-17S | 81 |
| 146th St. E&W | 2W-17S,1W-17S | 81 |
| 147th Pl. E&W | 0W-17S | 82 |
| 148th Pl. E&W | 2W-17S | 81 |
| 148th St. E&W | 2W-17S,0W-17S | 81 |
| 149th Pl. E&W | 2W-17S | 81 |
| 149th St. E&W | 3W-17S,1W-17S | 81 |
| 150th Pl. E&W | 2W-17S | 81 |
| 150th St. E&W | 3W-17S,1W-17S | 81 |
| 151st Pl. E&W | 2W-18S | 81 |
| 151st St. E&W | 3W-17S,1W-17S | 81 |
| 151st Ter. E&W | 2W-18S | 81 |
| 152nd St. E&W | 2W-18S,1W-18S | 81 |
| 153rd St. E&W | 3W-18S,1W-18S | 81 |
| 154th Pl. E&W | 2W-18S | 81 |
| 154th St. E&W | 2W-18S,1W-18S | 81 |
| 155th Pl. E&W | 2W-18S | 81 |
| 155th St. E&W | 2W-18S,1W-18S | 81 |
| 156th Pl. E&W | 2W-18S | 81 |
| 156th St. E&W | 2W-18S,1W-18S | 81 |
| 157th Pl. E&W | 2W-18S,0W-18S | 81 |
| 157th St. E&W | 2W-18S,0W-18S | 81 |
| 158th Pl. E&W | 2W-18S | 81 |
| 158th St. E&W | 2W-18S,0W-18S | 81 |
| 159th St. E&W | 2W-18S,1W-18S | 81 |
| 160th Pl. E&W | 0W-9S | 68 |
| 160th St. E&W | 2W-19S,0W-19S | 81 |
| 161st St. E&W | 2W-19S,0W-19S | 81 |
| 162nd St. E&W | 1W-19S,0W-19S | 82 |
| 163rd St. E&W | 1W-19S,0W-19S | 82 |
| 164th St. E&W | 1W-19S,0W-19S | 82 |
| 165th St. E&W | 1W-19S,0W-19S | 82 |
| 166th St. E&W | 1W-19S,0W-9S | 82 |
| 167th Pl. E&W | 1W-20S | 88 |
| 167th St. E&W | 1W-20S,0W-20S | 88 |
| 168th Pl. E&W | 1W-20S | 88 |
| 168th St. E&W | 1W-20S | 88 |
| 171st St. E&W | 1W-20S | 88 |

## Harwood Heights

| | Grid | Page |
|---|---|---|
| Ainslie E&W | 9W-6N | 42 |
| Argyle E&W | 9W-6N | 42 |
| Carmen E&W | 9W-6N | 42 |
| Cullom E&W | 8W-5N | 42 |
| Diana Ln. E&W | 9W-5N | 42 |
| Gunnison E&W | 9W-6N,8W-5N | 42 |
| Jill Ln. E&W | 9W-5N | 42 |
| Lawrence E&W | 9W-6N,8W-5N | 42 |
| Leland E&W | 9W-5N,8W-5N | 42 |
| Nagle N&S | 8W-5N | 42 |
| Natchez N&S | 8W-5N | 42 |
| Neenan N&S | 8W-5N | 42 |
| New Castle N&S | 8W-5N | 42 |
| New England N&S | 8W-5N | 42 |
| Newland N&S | 8W-5N | 42 |
| Nora N&S | 8W-5N | 42 |
| Norwood Ct. E&W | 8W-5N | 42 |
| Oak Park N&S | 8W-5N | 42 |
| Oconto N&S | 9W-6N | 42 |
| Octavia N&S | 9W-6N | 42 |
| Odell N&S | 9W-6N | 42 |
| Oketo N&S | 9W-5N | 42 |
| Olcott N&S | 9W-5N | 42 |
| Oriole N&S | 9W-6N | 42 |
| Ronald N&S | 8W-5N | 42 |
| Rutherford N&S | 8W-5N | 42 |
| Sayre N&S | 8W-5N | 42 |
| Senior Pl. NW&SE | 8W-5N | 42 |
| Strong E&W | 9W-6N | 42 |
| Wilson E&W | 9W-5N,8W-5N | 42 |
| Winnemac E&W | 9W-6N | 42 |
| Winona E&W | 9W-6N | 42 |

## Hazel Crest

| | Grid | Page |
|---|---|---|
| Albany Av. N&S | 3W-20S | 87 |
| Annetta Av. N&S | 3W-20S | 87 |
| Anthony Av. N&S | 2W-20S | 87 |
| Apple Tree Dr. N&S | 4W-20S | 87 |
| Argyle Av. N&S | 3W-21S | 87 |
| Arlington Ln. N&S | 3W-21S | 87 |
| Artesian Av. N&S | 3W-20S | 87 |
| Balmoral Ln. N&S | 3W-21S | 87 |
| Birchwood Dr. E&W | 4W-20S | 87 |
| Bordeaux Ct. E&W | 4W-21S | 87 |
| Briar Ln. E&W | 4W-22S | 87 |
| Brumley Dr. E&W | 4W-22S | 87 |
| Bryant Ln. NW&SE | 3W-20S | 87 |
| Bulger Av. N&S | 2W-20S | 87 |
| Burgandy Ln. NW&SE | 4W-21S | 87 |
| Burr Oak Ln. N&S | 4W-20S | 87 |
| Butternut Rd. N&S | 3W-21S | 87 |
| Buttonwood Walk E&W | 3W-20S | 87 |
| California Av. N&S | 3W-20S | 87 |
| Cannes Ct. E&W | 4W-21S | 87 |
| Carl Dr. E&W | 3W-20S | 87 |
| Carraigeway Dr. N&S | 3W-21S | 87 |
| Central Park Av. N&S | 4W-20S | 87 |
| Chambord Ln. E&W | 4W-21S | 87 |
| Chantilly Ln. N&S | 4W-21S | 87 |
| Charlemagne Av. N&S | 4W-21S | 87 |
| Charleston Ln. E&W | 2W-20S | 87 |
| Charters Ct. NE&SW | 4W-21S | 87 |
| Cherry Creek Dr. NE&SW | 3W-20S | 87 |
| Cherrywood Ln. NW&SE | 3W-21S | 87 |
| Chestnut Av. E&W | 4W-20S | 87 |
| Circle Dr. E&W | 3W-20S | 87 |
| Coach Ln. E&W | 3W-21S | 87 |
| Concord Pl. E&W | 3W-20S | 87 |
| Cottonwood Ct. NW&SE | 4W-20S | 87 |
| Coventry Ct. E&W | 4W-20S | 87 |
| Crane Av. N&S | 2W-20S | 87 |
| Crescent Dr. E&W | 3W-20S | 87 |
| Dixie Hwy N&S | 2W-20S,2W-19S | 87 |
| Dogwood Ln. N&S | 3W-21S | 87 |
| Elm Dr. N&S | 4W-20S | 87 |
| Elysees Ct. N&S | 4W-21S | 87 |
| Emerson Av. N&S | 3W-20S | 87 |
| Fountainbleau Dr. NE&SW | 4W-21S | 87 |
| Glynwood Ln. E&W | 4W-20S | 87 |
| Governors Hwy. NE&SW | 2W-20S | 87 |
| Grandview Dr. N&S | 3W-21S | 87 |
| Greenwood Rd E&W | 3W-21S | 87 |
| Grove Ln. E&W | 4W-20S | 87 |
| Hawthorne Ln. E&W | 3W-21S | 87 |
| Hazel Ln. E&W | 4W-20S | 87 |
| Head Av. N&S | 2W-20S | 87 |
| Hickory Ln. E&S | 4W-20S | 87 |
| Highland Av. N&S | 3W-20S | 87 |
| Hillside Av. N&S | 3W-20S | 87 |
| Holmes Av. N&S | 3W-20S | 87 |
| Interstate 80 E&W | 4W-20S,3W-20S | 87 |
| Jeffery Ln. E&W | 3W-20S | 87 |
| Jodave Av. N&S | 2W-20S | 87 |
| Kedzie Av. N&S | 4W-21S,4W-20S | 87 |
| Kimball Av. N&S | 4W-22S | 87 |
| Knollwood Pl. E&W | 3W-21S | 87 |
| Larkspur Ln. NW&SE | 3W-21S | 87 |
| Laurel Ln. NE&SW | 4W-20S | 87 |
| Lexington Dr. E&W | 3W-20S | 87 |
| Lincoln St. N&S | 2W-20S | 87 |
| Locust Dr. N&S | 4W-20S | 87 |
| Longfellow Av. NE&SW | 3W-20S | 87 |
| Lowell Av. N&S | 3W-20S | 87 |
| Magnolia Dr. N&S | 4W-20S | 87 |
| Maple Ln. E&W | 4W-20S | 87 |
| Marseille Ln. NS&EW | 4W-21S | 87 |
| Millstone Rd. N&S | 3W-21S | 87 |
| Montmarte Av. NE&SW | 4W-21S | 87 |
| Murphy Av. N&S | 3W-20S | 87 |
| Normandy Ln. N&S | 4W-21S | 87 |
| Novak Dr. N&S | 3W-20S | 87 |
| Oak St. E&W | 4W-20S | 87 |
| Oakwood Dr. E&W | 3W-21S | 87 |
| Old Trail Rd. N&S | 3W-21S | 87 |
| Orchard Ridge Av. N&S | 2W-20S | 87 |
| Orleans Dr. N&S | 4W-21S | 87 |
| Page St. N&S | 2W-20S | 87 |
| Palmer Blvd. N&S | 3W-20S | 87 |
| Peach Grove Ln. EW&NS | 4W-20S | 87 |
| Pebblewood Ln. N&S | 3W-21S | 87 |
| Pine Ct. N&S | 4W-20S | 87 |
| Poe Av. N&S | 3W-20S | 87 |
| Pulaski Rd. N&S | 4W-22S | 87 |
| Ridgewood Dr. NE&SW | 3W-21S | 87 |
| Rochester Av. E&W | 2W-20S | 87 |
| Rockwell Av. N&S | 3W-20S | 87 |
| Royale Ln. NE&SW | 4W-21S | 87 |
| Sacramento Av. N&S | 3W-20S | 87 |
| Seine Ct. NW&SE | 4W-21S | 87 |
| Shagbark Ln. E&W | 3W-21S | 87 |
| Shea Av. N&S | 2W-20S | 87 |
| Smoketree Ct. E&W | 3W-21S | 87 |
| Stonebridge Dr. NE&SW | 3W-21S | 87 |
| Summit Av. N&S | 3W-20S | 87 |
| Sunset Rd. E&W | 3W-20S | 87 |
| Surrey Ln. N&S | 3W-21S | 87 |
| Sycamore Dr. N&S | 4W-20S | 87 |
| Tamarino Ln. E&W | 4W-20S | 87 |
| Tanglewood Ct.* N&S | 4W-21S | 87 |
| Tennyson Pl. E&W | 3W-20S | 87 |
| Trapet Av. N&S | 2W-20S | 87 |
| Tri-State Tollway E&W | 3W-20S,2W-20S | 87 |
| Tulip Dr. NE&SW | 4W-20S | 87 |
| Turtlecreek Dr. NW&SE | 3W-21S | 87 |
| Versailles Ln. N&S | 4W-21S | 87 |
| Village Dr. N&S | 4W-22S | 87 |
| Wellington Ct. E&W | 4W-20S | 87 |
| West Mahoney Pkwy. NE&SW | 3W-20S | 87 |
| Wheelwood Ct. E&W | 4W-20S | 87 |
| Whipple St. N&S | 3W-20S | 87 |
| Whitman Av. N&S | 3W-20S | 87 |
| Whittier Av. N&S | 3W-20S | 87 |
| Winchester Av. N&S | 2W-20S | 87 |
| Wood St. N&S | 2W-20S | 87 |
| Woodworth Pl. E&W | 4W-20S,3W-20S | 87 |
| 167th St. E&W | 4W-20S,1W-20S | 87 |
| 168th St. E&W | 3W-20S,2W-20S | 87 |
| 169th St. E&W | 3W-20S,2W-20S | 87 |
| 170th St. E&W | 3W-20S,2W-20S | 87 |
| 171st St. E&W | 3W-20S,2W-20S | 87 |
| 172nd Ct. E&W | 4W-20S | 87 |
| 172nd St. E&W | 3W-20S,2W-20S | 87 |
| 173rd St. E&W | 4W-20S,3W-20S | 87 |
| 174th St. E&W | 3W-20S | 87 |
| 175th St. E&W | 4W-20S,2W-20S | 87 |
| 176th St. E&W | 4W-21S | 87 |
| 177th St. E&W | 4W-21S | 87 |
| 183rd St. E&W | 4W-22S | 87 |

## Hickory Hills

| | Grid | Page |
|---|---|---|
| Active Ln. N&S | 11W-10S | 64 |
| Ash Ln. N&S | 11W-10S | 65 |
| Baldwin Trail NS&EW | 10W-10S | 65 |
| Barberry Ln. E&W | 11W-10S | 64 |
| Bath Av. N&S | 10W-12S | 65 |
| Beechnut Rd. E&W | 11W-10S | 64 |
| Birch Ln. N&S | 11W-10S | 65 |
| Blueridge Av. N&S | 11W-9S | 64 |
| Briarwood Ln. E&W | 11W-10S | 64 |
| Chestnut Dr. E&W | 11W-9S | 64 |
| Christina Dr. E&W | 11W-10S | 65 |
| Coey Ln. NW&SE | 10W-10S | 65 |
| Collette Ln. E&W | 10W-10S | 65 |
| Dell Ct. E&W | 11W-9S | 64 |
| Dewey Ln. E&W | 11W-10S | 64 |
| Elm Cir. E&W | 11W-10S | 64 |
| Forest Dr. NS&EW | 11W-9S | 64 |
| Forest Ln. NW&SE | 11W-10S | 64 |
| Forest Ln., E. N&S | 11W-10S | 64 |
| Gladys Ln. NS&SE | 10W-11S | 65 |
| Goldenoak Ct. N&S | 11W-10S | 65 |
| Hawthorn Dr. E&W | 11W-10S | 65 |
| Hickory Ln. N&S | 11W-10S | 64 |
| Hillside Dr. N&S | 10W-10S | 65 |
| Interstate 294 SE&NW | 9W-10S | 65 |
| Jonathan Dr. E&W | 10W-10S | 65 |
| Kean Av. N&S | 11W-10S,11W-9S | 64 |
| Kells Dr. E&W | 10W-10S | 65 |
| Kitty Ln. E&W | 10W-10S | 65 |
| Kopping Ln. E&W | 11W-10S | 64 |
| Lisa Ln. E&W | 10W-10S | 65 |
| Lotus Ln. E&W | 11W-10S | 64 |
| Lynnwood Dr. E&W | 10W-10S | 65 |
| Maple Ln. N&S | 11W-10S | 64 |
| Meadowview Dr. E&W | 11W-9S | 64 |
| Miroballi Dr. N&S | 11W-9S | 65 |
| Nida Ct. E&W | 11W-10S | 64 |
| Northwest Rd. NW&SE | 11W-13S | 72 |
| Oak Hill Ct. E&W | 10W-10S | 65 |
| Oakwood Dr. N&S | 11W-10S | 64 |
| Orchard Dr. E&W | 10W-10S | 65 |
| Pleasant Av. N&S | 10W-10S | 65 |
| Primrose Ln. E&W | 11W-9S | 64 |
| Roberts Rd. N&S | 10W-10S | 65 |
| Robin Ct. N&S | 11W-9S | 64 |
| Sandra Ln. E&W | 11W-10S | 64 |
| Shady Dr. E&W | 11W-9S | 64 |
| Shelby Dr. E&W | 11W-9S | 65 |
| Steeple Hill Dr. N&S | 11W-9S | 65 |
| Sycamore Ct. N&S | 11W-10S | 64 |
| Sycamore Dr. E&W | 11W-10S | 64 |
| U.S. Route 12-20 E&W | 11W-10S | 64 |
| Willow Rd. N&S | 11W-10S | 64 |
| Woodland Dr. E&W | 11W-10S | 64 |
| 76th Av. N&S | 9W-11S,0W-10S | 65 |
| 76th Ct. N&S | 9W-10S | 65 |
| 77th Av. N&S | 9W-10S | 65 |
| 77th Ct. N&S | 9W-10S | 65 |
| 78th Av. N&S | 9W-11S,9W-10S | 65 |
| 78th Ct. N&S | 9W-11S,9W-10S | 65 |
| 79th Av. N&S | 9W-11S,9W-10S | 65 |
| 79th Ct. N&S | 9W-10S | 65 |
| 80th Ct. N&S | 10W-10S | 65 |
| 81st Av. N&S | 10W-10S | 65 |
| 81st Ct. N&S | 10W-10S,10W-9S | 65 |
| 82nd Av. N&S | 10W-10S,10W-9S | 65 |
| 82nd Ct. N&S | 10W-10S,10W-9S | 65 |
| 83rd Av. N&S | 10W-10S,10W-9S | 65 |
| 83rd Ct. N&S | 10W-10S,10W-9S | 65 |
| 84th Av. N&S | 10W-10S,10W-9S | 65 |
| 84th Ct. N&S | 10W-10S,10W-9S | 65 |
| 85th Av. N&S | 10W-10S | 65 |
| 85th Ct. N&S | 10W-10S,10W-9S | 65 |
| 85th St. E&W | 10W-9S | 65 |
| 86th Av. N&S | 10W-10S,10W-9S | 65 |
| 86th Ct. N&S | 10W-10S | 65 |
| 86th Pl. E&W | 10W-9S | 65 |
| 86th St. E&W | 11W-9S | 64 |
| 87th Av. N&S | 10W-10S | 65 |
| 87th Ct. N&S | 10W-10S | 65 |
| 87th Pl. E&W | 9W-10S | 65 |
| 87th St E&W | 11W-9S,10W-9S | 64 |
| 88th Av. N&S | 11W-10S | 64 |
| 88th Ct. N&S | 11W-10S | 64 |
| 88th St. E&W | 10W-10S,9W-10S | 65 |
| 89th Av. N&S | 11W-10S | 64 |
| 89th Ct. N&S | 11W-10S | 64 |
| 89th Pl. E&W | 10W-10S,9W-10S | 65 |
| 89th St. E&W | 11W-10S,9W-10S | 64 |
| 90th Av. N&S | 11W-10S,11W-9S | 64 |
| 90th Pl. E&W | 10W-10S,9W-10S | 65 |
| 90th St. E&W | 10W-10S | 65 |
| 91st Pl. E&W | 11W-10S,9W-10S | 64 |
| 91st St. E&W | 10W-10S,9W-10S | 65 |
| 92nd Pl. E&W | 11W-10S,10W-10S | 64 |
| 92nd St. E&W | 11W-10S,9W-10S | 64 |
| 93rd Pl. E&W | 11W-10S,9W-10S | 64 |
| 93rd St. E&W | 11W-10S,9W-10S | 64 |
| 94th St. E&W | 10W-10S,9W-10S | 65 |
| 95th St. E&W | 11W-10S,9W-10S | 64 |
| 96th Pl. E&W | 9W-11S | 65 |
| 97th Pl. E&W | 9W-11S | 65 |
| 97th St. E&W | 9W-11S | 65 |
| 98th Pl. E&W | 9W-11S | 65 |
| 98th St. E&W | 9W-11S | 65 |
| 99th St. E&W | 9W-11S | 65 |
| 104th Pl. E&W | 9W-12S | 65 |

## Hillside

| | Grid | Page |
|---|---|---|
| Adams E&W | 14W-0S | 46 |
| Ashbel N&S | 14W-0S | 46 |
| Augustine NW&SE | 14W-0S,13W-0S | 46 |
| Bellwood N&S | 13W-0N | 46 |
| Broadview N&S | 13W-0N | 46 |
| Buckthorn N&S | 13W-0S | 46 |
| Center St. N&S | 13W-0S | 46 |
| Clayton Rd. E&W | 13W-0S | 46 |

| | Grid | Page |
|---|---|---|
| Clayton Rd. N&S | 13W-0S | 46 |
| Cypress Dr. E&W | 14W-0N | 46 |
| Darmstadt E&W | 14W-0S | 46 |
| Division E&W | 13W-0S | 46 |
| East N&S | 13W-0S | 46 |
| East End N&S | 14W-0N | 46 |
| Edgewater E&W | 13W-0S | 46 |
| Electric E&W | 14W-0N | 46 |
| Elm N&S | 14W-0S,14W-0N | 46 |
| Englewood N&S | 13W-0N | 46 |
| Fencl N&S | 13W-0S | 46 |
| Forest N&S | 13W-0S | 46 |
| Frontage Rd. NW&SE | 13W-0S | 46 |
| Geneva N&S | 13W-0N | 46 |
| Granville N&S | 13W-0N | 46 |
| Highridge Rd. N&S | 13W-0S | 46 |
| Hillside N&S | 14W-0S,14W-0N | 46 |
| Howard N&S | 14W-0S | 46 |
| Hyde Park N&S | 13W-0N | 46 |
| Idlewild Ln. SW&NE | 13W-0S | 46 |
| Iroquis Rd. N&S | 13W-0S | 46 |
| Irving N&S | 14W-0S,14W-0N | 46 |
| Jackson Blvd. E&W | 14W-0S | 46 |
| Jackson Blvd. SW&NE | 13W-0S | 46 |
| Laverne N&S | 14W-0S | 46 |
| Leviton N&S | 13W-0S | 46 |
| Lind N&S | 14W-0S | 46 |
| Locust E&W | 14W-0N | 46 |
| Madison E&W | 14W-0N,13W-0N | 46 |
| Maple Ln. N&W | 13W-0S | 46 |
| May E&W | 13W-0S | 46 |
| Melrose N&S | 13W-0N | 46 |
| Mueller N&S | 13W-0S | 46 |
| Oak N&S | 13W-0S | 46 |
| Oak Ridge N&S | 13W-0S | 46 |
| Orchard N&S | 13W-0S | 46 |
| Railroad Av. S. NE&SW | 13W-0S | 46 |
| Randolph E&W | 14W-0N | 46 |
| Raymond Dr. E&W | 13W-0S | 46 |
| Rose E&W | 13W-0S | 46 |
| St. Paul Ct. E&W | 14W-0N | 46 |
| Sunnyside Dr. E&W | 14W-0N | 46 |
| Taft St. N&S | 14W-0S | 46 |
| Van Buren E&W | 14W-0S | 46 |
| Vanna | 13W-0S | 46 |
| Warren E&W | 14W-0N,13W-0N | 46 |
| Washington E&W | 14W-0N | 46 |
| 49th N&S | 13W-0N | 46 |
| 50th N&S | 13W-0N | 46 |
| 51st N&S | 13W-0N | 46 |
| 52nd N&S | 13W-0N | 46 |
| 53rd N&S | 13W-0N | 46 |
| 54th N&S | 13W-0N | 46 |
| 55th N&S | 13W-0N | 46 |

## Hinsdale*
**(Also see Du Page County)**

| | Grid | Page |
|---|---|---|
| Bittersweet E&W | 14W-5S | 58 |
| Bittersweet Ln. E&W | 14W-5S | 58 |
| Bobolink E&W | 14W-4S | 52 |
| Chicago E&W | 14W-4S | 52 |
| Cleveland Dr. NW&SE | 14W-5S | 58 |
| Cleveland Rd. NW&SE | 14W-5S | 58 |
| Columbia N&S | 14W-5S | 58 |
| County Line Ct. E&W | 14W-5S | 58 |
| Dalewood NW&SE | 14W-5S | 58 |
| Flagg Ct. E&W | 15W-4S | 52 |
| Fuller Rd. E&W | 14W-4S | 45 |
| Harding N&S | 14W-5S | 58 |
| Hickory E&W | 14W-4S | 52 |
| Highland E&W | 14W-4S | 52 |
| Hill Grove E&W | 14W-4S | 52 |
| Hillcrest Av. N&S | 14W-5S | 58 |
| Hillcrest Cir. N&S | 14W-5S | 58 |
| Interstate 294 N&S | 14W-6S | 58 |
| Justina N&S | 14W-4S | 52 |
| McKinley N&S | 14W-5S | 58 |
| Mills N&S | 14W-4S | 52 |
| Minneola E&W | 14W-4S | 52 |
| Pamela E&W | 14W-5S | 58 |
| Pamela Cir. E&W | 14W-5S | 45 |
| Phillippa St. N&S | 15W-4S | 52 |
| Princeton NW&SE | 14W-5S | 58 |
| Ravine E&W | 14W-4S | 52 |
| Sharron N&S | 14W-5S | 58 |
| Springlake N&S | 14W-5S | 58 |
| Taft N&S | 14W-5S | 58 |
| Walnut E&W | 14W-4S | 52 |
| Wilson N&S | 14W-5S | 58 |
| Woodland Av. E&W | 14W-5S | 58 |
| Cir. | 14W-5S | 58 |
| Woodside E&W | 14W-5S | 58 |
| Woodside Av. E&W | 14W-4S | 45 |
| 1st E&W | 14W-5S | 58 |
| 3rd E&W | 14W-5S | 58 |
| 6th E&W | 14W-5S | 58 |
| 7th E&W | 14W-5S | 58 |
| 10th E&W | 14W-6S | 58 |

## Hodgkins

| | Grid | Page |
|---|---|---|
| Bill Rd. N&S | 12W-7S | 58 |
| Canary Rd. E&W | 11W-7S | 59 |
| Cardinal Rd. NE&SW | 11W-7S | 59 |
| Catherine Ann E&W | 11W-6S | 58 |
| Chester N&S | 11W-7S | 58 |
| Cobb E&W | 11W-7S | 58 |
| Conrad N&S | 11W-7S | 58 |
| Eagle Rd. E&W | 11W-7S | 59 |
| East N&S | 12W-7S | 58 |
| Elm Rd. N&S | 12W-7S | 58 |
| Falcon Rd. E&W | 11W-7S | 59 |
| Franbean Rd. N&S | 12W-7S | 58 |
| Jewel Rd. N&S | 12W-7S | 58 |
| Kane N&S | 11W-7S | 58 |
| Kimball N&S | 11W-7S | 58 |
| La Grange N&S | 12W-7S | 58 |
| Lenzi N&S | 11W-6S | 58 |
| Lyons E&W | 11W-7S | 58 |
| Mance Rd. E&W | 12W-7S | 58 |
| Martin Rd. E&W | 11W-7S | 59 |
| Oak Rd. N&S | 12W-7S | 58 |
| Park St. N&S | 12W-7S | 58 |
| Pelican Rd. E&W | 11W-7S | 59 |
| River Rd. NE&SW | 12W-8S | 58 |
| Roger Rd. N&S | 12W-7S | 58 |
| Santa Fe SW&NE | 12W-8S | 58 |
| Sharon Rd. N&S | 12W-7S | 58 |
| U.S. Rt. 12 N&S | 12W-7S | 58 |
| U.S. Rt. 20 N&S | 12W-7S | 58 |
| U.S. Rt. 45 N&S | 12W-7S | 58 |
| Walnut St. N&S | 12W-7S | 58 |
| Weeping Willow Pl. NS&EW | 12W-7S | 58 |
| Wenz N&S | 11W-7S | 58 |
| Wren Rd. E&W | 11W-7S | 59 |
| 67th E&W | 12W-7S | 58 |

## Hoffman Estates

| | Grid | Page |
|---|---|---|
| Abbeywood Dr. N&S | 25W-12N | 22 |
| Aberdeen Ct. E&W | 22W-11N | 33 |
| Aberdeen St. N&S | 22W-11N | 33 |
| Adler Ct. NW&SE | 25W-14N | 22 |
| Alcoa Ln. E&W | 24W-11N | 32 |
| Alder Dr. NS&EW | 25W-14N | 22 |
| Algonquin Rd. NW&SE | 25W-14N,23W-14N | 22 |
| Alhambra Ln. NE&SW | 22W-11N | 33 |
| Almond Ln. N&S | 22W-11N | 33 |
| Alpine Ln. NW&SE | 23W-11N,22W-11N | 32 |
| Amber Cir. NS&EW | 24W-15N | 22 |
| Ameritech Center Dr. NS&EW | 25W-13N | 22 |
| Amherst Ln. E&W | 24W-12N | 22 |
| Anjou Ln. NE&SW | 24W-14N | 22 |
| Apache Ln. NW&SE | 23W-11N,22W-11N | 32 |
| Apple St. NE&SW | 23W-11N | 32 |
| Apricot St. N&S | 23W-11N | 32 |
| Arbor Ct. E&W | 22W-11N | 33 |
| Arcadia Ct. E&W | 22W-11N | 33 |
| Ardwick Dr. NW&SE | 25W-12N | 22 |
| Arizona Blvd. NW&SE | 23W-11N | 32 |
| Arlington Ct. NW&SE | 22W-11N | 33 |
| Arlington St. N&S | 22W-11N | 33 |
| Arrowwood Ln. N&S | 25W-14N | 22 |
| Asbury Ln. E&W | 23W-11N | 32 |
| Ascot Ct. NE&SW | 24W-11N | 32 |
| Ash Rd. N&S | 23W-11N | 32 |
| Ashland St. N&S | 22W-11N | 33 |
| Ashley Ct. NW&SE | 24W-12N | 22 |
| Ashley Rd. N&S | 24W-12N | 22 |
| Aspen St. NE&SW | 22W-11N | 33 |
| Aster Ln. E&W | 23W-11N,22W-11N | 32 |
| Atlantic Av. NS&EW | 26W-11N | 31 |
| Audobon Ct. NW&SE | 22W-11N | 33 |
| Audobon Pl. E&W | 22W-11N | 33 |
| Audobon St. N&S | 22W-11N | 33 |
| Avondale Ln. E&W | 22W-11N | 33 |
| Azalea Ln. E&W | 23W-11N,22W-11N | 32 |
| Barberry Ct. NW&SE | 25W-14N | 22 |
| Barcroft Ct. NW&SE | 24W-16N | 12 |
| Barcroft Dr. NS&EW | 24W-16N | 12 |
| Bardwick Ct. N&S | 24W-16N | 12 |
| Barrington Rd. N&S | 27W-11N,27W-12N | 31 |
| Bartlett Rd. N&S | 28W-12N | 21 |
| Basswood St. N&S | 22W-11N | 33 |
| Batavia Ln. E&W | 23W-11N | 32 |
| Baxter Ln. E&W | 24W-11N | 32 |
| Bayberry Ln.* E&W | 24W-13N | 22 |
| Bayside Cir. NS&EW | 24W-15N | 22 |
| Bayside Ct. E&W | 24W-15N | 22 |
| Beacon Ct. NW&SE | 25W-15N | 22 |
| Bear Claw Ct. NE&SW | 30W-12N | 20 |
| Bedford Ct. NW&SE | 24W-12N | 22 |
| Bedford Rd. N&S | 24W-12N | 22 |
| Berkley Ct. N&S | 24W-11N | 32 |
| Berkley Ln. E&W | 24W-11N | 32 |
| Berkley Pl. N&S | 24W-11N | 32 |
| Bernay Ln. N&S | 24W-14N | 22 |
| Beverly Rd. N&S | 30W-13N | 20 |
| Bicek Ct. N&S | 24W-15N | 22 |
| Bicek Dr. NE&SW | 24W-15N | 22 |
| Blair Ln. E&W | 25W-12N | 22 |
| Boardwalk Blvd. E&W | 26W-11N | 31 |
| Bode Cir. N&S | 24W-11N | 32 |
| Bode Rd. NS&EW | 26W-11N,23W-11N | 31 |
| Bolleana Ct. NW&SE | 25W-14N | 22 |
| Bonnie Ln. E&W | 25W-12N | 22 |
| Bordeaux Dr. NE&SW | 24W-14N | 22 |
| Botsford Pl. E&W | 26W-12N | 21 |
| Boulder Ln. N&S | 24W-16N | 12 |
| Bradley Ln. E&W | 23W-11N | 32 |
| Briarcliff Ln. E&W | 24W-12N | 22 |
| Brigantine Ct. N&S | 24W-15N | 22 |
| Brigantine Ln. N&S | 24W-15N | 22 |
| Brigton Ln.* N&S | 24W-14N | 22 |
| Bristol Walk E&W | 25W-12N | 22 |
| Brittany Ln. N&S | 24W-14N | 22 |
| Brookside Dr. E&W | 25W-12N | 22 |
| Brookside Ln. E&W | 25W-12N | 22 |
| Buckeye Dr. N&S | 23W-11N | 32 |
| Buckingham Ct. NW&SE | 24W-11N | 32 |
| Buckthorn Dr. E&W | 24W-15N | 22 |
| Burnham Dr. NW&SE | 24W-15N | 22 |
| Burning Bush Ln. E&W | 24W-15N | 22 |
| Burr Ridge Dr. NS&EW | 25W-14N | 22 |
| Buttercreek Ct. NW&SE | 23W-11N | 32 |
| Butterfield Ct. E&W | 23W-14N | 22 |
| Caldwell Ln. E&W | 25W-12N | 22 |
| Cambridge Ln. NW&SE | 24W-12N | 22 |
| Camelot Ln. NE&SW | 24W-16N | 12 |
| Cameron Ct. NW&SE | 24W-16N | 12 |
| Campbell Ln. E&W | 25W-12N | 22 |
| Candlewood Ln. E&W | 25W-11N | 32 |
| Cape Breton Ct. E&W | 24W-15N | 22 |
| Capstan Dr. NS&EW | 25W-15N | 22 |
| Cardigan Pl.* N&S | 24W-14N | 22 |
| Carleton Rd. N&S | 24W-12N | 22 |
| Carling Rd. N&S | 24N-12N | 22 |
| Carmel Ct. NE&SW | 25W-12N | 22 |
| Carnation Ln. E&W | 23W-11N | 32 |
| Carthage Ln. E&W | 23W-11N | 32 |
| Castaway Ct. E&W | 24W-16N | 12 |
| Castaway Ln. N&S | 24W-16N | 12 |
| Castlewood Ct. E&W | 23W-14N | 22 |
| Cedar Tree Ct. E&W | 23W-11N | 32 |
| Central Rd. E&W | 25W-13N | 22 |
| Chambers Dr. N&S | 24W-16N | 12 |
| Chandler Ln. E&W | 23W-11N | 32 |
| Chanora Ct. NE&SW | 25W-14N | 22 |
| Charlemagne Dr. NE&SW | 24W-14N | 22 |
| Charleston Ln. E&W | 24W-14N,23W-14N | 22 |
| Chatsworth Ln. E&W | 25W-11N | 32 |
| Chelmsford Pl. NE&SW | 25W-12N | 22 |
| Cheltenham Pl. NW&SE | 26W-12N | 21 |
| Cherry Ct. N&S | 25W-15N | 22 |
| Chesapeake Ct. N&S | 24W-15N | 22 |
| Chesapeake Dr. E&W | 24W-15N | 22 |
| Chestnut Ln. E&W | 25W-14N | 22 |
| Chippendale Rd. NW&SE | 24W-12N | 22 |
| Circle Pl. E&W | 26W-12N | 21 |
| Claremont Rd. N&S | 24W-12N | 22 |
| Clarendon St. NE&SW | 23W-11N | 32 |
| Claridge Cir. NE&SW | 24W-11N | 32 |
| Clifton Pl. NE&SW | 26W-12N | 21 |
| Clover Ln. E&W | 24W-15N | 22 |
| Clubhouse Ln. E&W | 25W-12N | 22 |
| Cobble Hill Ct. E&W | 24W-12N | 22 |
| Cobble Hill Dr. E&W | 24W-12N | 22 |
| Cochise St. N&S | 23W-11N | 32 |
| Colgate Ct. E&W | 24W-12N | 22 |
| Colony Ct. NW&SE | 24W-14N | 22 |
| Colony Ln. NE&SW | 24W-14N | 22 |
| Concord Cove NE&SW | 23W-14N | 22 |
| Concord Ln. E&W | 24W-14N,23W-14N | 22 |
| Cooper Rd. N&S | 24W-12N | 22 |
| Cornell Cir. E&W | 26W-12N | 21 |
| Cornell Ct. E&W | 26W-12N | 21 |
| Cornell Dr. N&S | 26W-12N | 21 |
| Cornell Pl. E&W | 26W-12N | 21 |
| Cornell Ter. E&W | 26W-12N | 21 |
| Cottonwood Tr. NS&EW | 25W-15N | 22 |
| Cove Ln. N&S | 25W-15N | 22 |
| Coventry Ct. N&S | 23W-14N | 22 |
| Crab Orchard Dr. N&S | 24W-15N | 22 |
| Cranshire Ct. NW&SE | 23W-14N | 22 |
| Crescent Ct. NE&SW | 25W-12N | 22 |
| Crescent Ln. NW&SE | 25W-12N | 22 |
| Crimson Ct. NW&SE | 24W-15N | 22 |
| Crimson Dr. NS&EW | 24W-15N | 22 |
| Cumberland St. N&S | 23W-11N | 32 |
| Cypress Ct. N&S | 25W-12N | 22 |
| Danbury Pl.* E&W | 24W-13N | 22 |
| Darien Ct. NW&SE | 24W-11N | 32 |
| Darlington Cir. NS&EW | 25W-11N | 32 |
| Darlington Ct. E&W | 25W-11N | 32 |
| Decatur St. N&S | 23W-11N | 32 |
| Deer Path Ct. N&S | 24W-11N | 32 |
| Deer Valley Ln. E&W | 30W-12N | 20 |
| Dennison Rd. N&S | 24W-12N | 22 |
| Des Plaines Ln. NE&SW | 23W-11N | 32 |
| Devonshire Ln. NW&SE | 25W-12N | 22 |
| Diamond Dr. E&W | 24W-15N | 22 |
| Dixon Ct. NE&SW | 23W-15N | 22 |
| Dixon Dr. N&S | 23W-15N | 22 |
| Dogwood Ct. NE&SW | 25W-14N | 22 |
| Dogwood Dr. NW&SE | 25W-14N | 22 |
| Dorchester Ln. E&W | 25W-11N | 32 |
| Douglas Ct. E&W | 23W-11N | 32 |
| Dover Ct. E&W | 24W-15N | 22 |
| Dovington Ct. N&S | 25W-11N | 32 |
| Downing Dr. NE&SW | 24W-15N | 22 |
| Dresden Ct. NW&SE | 24W-15N | 22 |
| Dresden Dr. NE&SW | 24W-15N | 22 |
| Driftwood Ct. E&W | 25W-15N | 22 |
| Dukesbery Ct. E&W | 24W-16N | 12 |
| Dukesbery Ln. N&S | 24W-16N | 12 |
| Dunmore Pl.* E&W | 24W-13N | 22 |
| Durham Ct. NW&SE | 24W-12N | 22 |
| Durham Ln. E&W | 24W-12N | 22 |
| E. Berkley Ln. E&W | 23W-11N | 32 |
| E. Bluebonnet Ln. NW&SE | 22W-11N | 33 |
| Eagle Way N&S | 25W-13N | 22 |
| Edgefield Ln. E&W | 25W-12N | 22 |
| Edgemont Ln. E&W | 24W-12N | 22 |
| Eisenhower Cir. N&S | 24W-14N | 22 |
| Elizabeth Ct. N&S | 24W-12N | 22 |
| Elk Ln. E&W | 30W-12N | 20 |
| Elliot Dr. NS&EW | 30W-12N | 20 |
| Emory Rd. N&S | 24W-12N | 22 |
| Englewood Rd. NE&SW | 24W-12N | 22 |
| Eric Dr. NE&SW | 26W-12N | 21 |
| Erie Ln.* N&S | 24W-13N | 22 |
| Essington Ct. N&S | 24W-16N | 12 |
| Essington Ln. NE&SW | 24W-16N | 12 |
| Evanston St. N&S | 23W-11N | 32 |
| Evergreen Ln. E&W | 24W-12N | 22 |
| Exeter Ct. E&W | 24W-16N | 12 |
| Fairfield Cir. E&W | 25W-12N | 22 |
| Fairfield Ln. NS&EW | 25W-12N | 22 |
| Fairmont Rd. N&S | 25W-12N | 22 |
| Fairway Ct. N&S | 25W-12N | 22 |
| Falcon Ln. NW&SE | 30W-12N | 20 |
| Fayette E&W | 25W-12N | 22 |
| Fir Ct. N&S | 24W-15N | 22 |
| Firestone Ct. E&W | 24W-15N | 22 |
| Firestone Dr. NW&SE | 24W-15N,24W-14N | 22 |
| Firestone Ln. E&W | 24W-14N | 22 |
| Flagstaff Ln. E&W | 24W-11N,23W-11N | 32 |
| Forest Glen Dr. N&S | 25W-15N | 22 |
| Forest Park Ln. E&W | 23W-11N | 32 |
| Fortune Bay Ct. NS&EW | 25W-15N | 22 |
| Fox Path Ct. NE&SW | 30W-12N | 20 |
| Fox Path Ln. NS&EW | 30W-12N | 20 |
| Franklin Pl.* E&W | 24W-13N | 22 |
| Frederick Ct. NW&SE | 23W-12N | 22 |
| Frederick Ln. E&W | 24W-12N,23W-12N | 22 |
| Freeman Rd. NS&EW | 25W-13N,23W-15N | 22 |
| Fremont Ct. NW&SE | 24W-12N | 22 |
| Fremont Rd. NE&SW | 24W-12N | 22 |
| Gannon Ct. NW&SE | 24W-11N | 32 |
| Gannon Dr. N&S | 24W-11N,24W-12N | 32 |
| Garden Ter.* E&W | 24W-13N | 22 |
| Garnet Cir. E&W | 24W-15N | 22 |
| Gentry Rd. N&S | 24W-12N | 22 |
| Georgetown Ln.* NW&SE | 24W-13N | 22 |
| Geronimo St. NW&SE | 23W-11N | 32 |
| Glen Lake Cir. E&W | 25W-12N | 22 |
| Glen Lake Dr. E&W | 25W-12N | 22 |
| Glen Lake Pl. E&W | 25W-12N | 22 |
| Glen Lake Rd. N&S | 25W-12N | 22 |
| Glen Ln. NS&EW | 25W-12N,24W-12N | 22 |
| Glendale Ln. E&W | 24W-11N | 32 |
| Glenwood Ln. E&W | 24W-16N | 12 |
| Gloucester Ct. E&W | 25W-15N | 22 |
| Golden Rod Ln. E&W | 24W-15N | 22 |
| Golf Rd. E&W | 26W-12N,24W-12N | 21 |
| Governors Ln. N&S | 25W-12N | 22 |
| Grand Canyon Pkwy. NE&SW | 23W-11N | 32 |
| Grand Canyon St. N&S | 23W-11N | 32 |
| Grantham Pl.* NE&SW | 24W-13N | 22 |
| Greenfield Rd. N&S | 25W-12N | 22 |
| Greens Ct. NW&SE | 26W-12N | 21 |
| Greenspoint Pkwy. NS&EW | 27W-12N | 21 |
| Greystone Pl. E&W | 26W-12N | 21 |
| Grissom Ct. E&W | 23W-11N | 32 |
| Grissom Ln. E&W | 23W-11N | 32 |
| Haman Av. NE&SW | 24W-15N | 22 |
| Haman Ct. E&W | 24W-15N | 22 |
| Hampton Rd. N&S | 24W-12N | 22 |
| Hancock Dr.* NE&SW | 24W-13N | 22 |
| Harbor Cir. NS&EW | 25W-15N | 22 |
| Harrison Ln. NW&SE | 24W-15N,23W-15N | 22 |
| Harvard Ln. NW&SE | 24W-12N | 22 |
| Harwinton Pl. NW&SE | 26W-12N | 21 |
| Hassell Cir. N&S | 25W-12N | 22 |
| Hassell Ct. N&S | 25W-12N | 22 |
| Hassell Dr. N&S | 25W-12N | 22 |
| Hassell Pl. N&S | 25W-12N | 22 |
| Hassell Rd. E&W | 26W-12N,24W-12N | 21 |
| Hassell Rd. N&S | 26W-12N | 21 |
| Hastings Dr.* NW&SE | 24W-13N | 22 |
| Hawthorn Ln. NW&SE | 23W-11N,22W-11N | 32 |
| Heather Ln. NS&EW | 24W-12N | 22 |
| Heritage Dr. E&W | 24W-11N | 32 |
| Hermitage Cir. N&S | 24W-12N | 22 |
| Hermitage Ct. N&S | 24W-12N | 22 |
| Hermitage Ln. NW&SE | 24W-12N | 22 |
| Higgins Quarter Dr. N&S | 24W-11N | 32 |
| Higgins Rd. NW&SE | 30W-14N,22W-11N | 20 |
| Highland Blvd. NS&EW | 24W-12N | 22 |
| Hill Dr. E&W | 24W-11N | 32 |
| Hillcrest Blvd. NE&SW | 24W-12N,23W-12N | 22 |
| Hillcrest Ct. N&S | 24W-12N | 22 |
| Hillside Ct. NE&SW | 24W-14N | 22 |
| Hilltop Rd. N&S | 24W-12N | 22 |
| Holbrook Ln.* NE&SW | 24W-14N | 22 |
| Holly Ln. E&W | 22W-11N | 33 |
| Hudson Dr. NE&SW | 24W-15N | 22 |
| Hunters Ridge Ct. E&W | 30W-12N | 20 |
| Hunters Ridge, E. N&S | 30W-12N | 20 |

| | Grid | Page |
|---|---|---|
| Hunters Ridge, W. N&S | | |
| | 30W-12N | 20 |
| Huntington Blvd. N&S | | |
| | 25W-12N,25W-15N | 22 |
| Huttner Ct. NW&SE | | |
| | 26W-12N | 21 |
| Ida Rd. NE&SW .... 24W-12N | | 22 |
| Illinois Blvd. NE&SW | | |
| | 24W-10N,23W-11N | 32 |
| Interstate 90 E&W | | |
| | 31W-12N,24W-12N | 20 |
| Islandview Ct. N&S | | |
| | 25W-12N | 22 |
| Jade Ln. NE&SW .. 24W-15N | | 22 |
| Jamestown Cir. NS&EW | | |
| | 25W-12N | 22 |
| Jamison Ln. E&W .. 24W-12N | | 22 |
| Jefferson Rd. NW&SE | | |
| | 24W-12N | 22 |
| Jenifer Ln. E&W ....25W-12N | | 22 |
| Jody Ln. N&S .... 24W-11N | | 32 |
| John Dr. E&W | | |
| | 25W-11N,24W-11N | 32 |
| Jones Rd. N&S | | |
| | 24W-11N,24W-12N | 32 |
| Juniper Tree Ct. N&S | | |
| | 23W-11N | 32 |
| Kelly Dr. N&S ...... 30W-12N | | 20 |
| Kenilworth Cir. NS&EW | | |
| | 25W-12N | 22 |
| Kensington Ln. NE&SW | | |
| | 25W-12N | 22 |
| Kent Rd. N&S .... 23W-12N | | 22 |
| Kenwood Rd. N&S 25W-12N | | 22 |
| Kettering Rd.* E&W | | |
| | 24W-13N | 22 |
| Kingman Ln. E&W | | |
| | 24W-11N,23W-11N | 32 |
| Kingsdale Rd. N&S | | |
| | 25W-11N,25W-12N | 32 |
| Kingston Dr. N&S .. 24W-16N | | 12 |
| Knoll Ln. N&S .... 24W-11N | | 32 |
| Laburnum Rd. E&W | | |
| | 24W-14N | 22 |
| Lafayette Ln. E&W | | |
| | 24W-12N,23W-12N | 22 |
| Lafleur Ln. N&S .... 24W-14N | | 22 |
| Lake Ct. NW&SE .. 24W-12N | | 22 |
| Lake Edge Ct. E&W | | |
| | 25W-15N | 22 |
| Lakeside Plaza NS&EW | | |
| | 24W-12N | 22 |
| Lakeview Ln. E&W 24W-11N | | 32 |
| Lakewood Blvd. E&W | | |
| | 25W-13N | 22 |
| Lancaster Ct. E&W | | |
| | 24W-12N | 22 |
| Lancaster Ln. NE&SW | | |
| | 25W-12N,24W-12N | 22 |
| Landers Dr. NS&EW | | |
| | 30W-12N | 20 |
| Langdon Pl. E&W .. 26W-12N | | 21 |
| Larchmont Rd. NE&SW | | |
| | 23W-12N | 22 |
| Latour Ct. NE&SW 24W-14N | | 22 |
| Leather Leaf Ct. E&W | | |
| | 25W-14N | 22 |
| Leather Leaf Ln. NE&SW | | |
| | 25W-14N | 22 |
| Legend Ln. E&W . 25W-12N | | 22 |
| Lexington Dr. NS&EW | | |
| | 24W-14N,23W-14N | 22 |
| Liberty Pl.* E&W ...24W-13N | | 22 |
| Lichfield Dr. NS&EW | | |
| | 24W-16N | 12 |
| Lincoln Dr. N&S .. 23W-11N | | 32 |
| Lincoln St. N&S .. 23W-10N | | 32 |
| Lincolnshire Ln. E&W | | |
| | 24W-11N | 32 |
| Lombardy Ct. N&S 24W-15N | | 22 |
| Lombardy Ln. NS&EW | | |
| | 24W-15N | 22 |
| London Sq. E&W .. 24W-11N | | 32 |
| Londondery Ct. N&S | | |
| | 23W-14N | 22 |
| Ludington Ct. N&S..25W-15N | | 22 |
| Mallard Ln. NW&SE | | |
| | 30W-12N | 20 |
| Manchester Dr. N&S | | |
| | 25W-12N | 22 |
| Maple Ln. NW&SE..24W-11N | | 32 |
| Maricopa Ln. N&S .. 23W-11N | | 32 |
| Marquette Ln.* N&S | | |
| | 24W-13N | 22 |
| Mason Dr. N&S .. 23W-15N | | 22 |
| Mayfield Ln. N&S | | |
| | 26W-12N,25W-12N | 21 |
| Maywood Ln. E&W | | |
| | 24W-11N | 32 |
| McDonough Rd. N&S | | |
| | 30W-12N | 20 |
| Meadow Ln. N&S .. 24W-11N | | 32 |
| Mesa Dr. E&W .. 24W-11N | | 32 |
| Meyer Rd. N&S .. 25W-12N | | 22 |
| Michael Ct. NW&SE | | |
| | 24W-15N | 22 |
| Micheline Ct. NW&SE | | |
| | 24W-14N | 22 |
| Milan Ln. E&W .. 24W-11N | | 32 |
| Milton Ln. E&W .. 24W-11N | | 32 |
| Mohave Ln. N&S | | |
| | 23W-10N,23W-11N | 32 |
| Monarch Ln. N&S | | |
| | 24W-15N | 22 |
| Monterey Ct. NE&SW | | |
| | 25W-12N | 22 |
| Monticello Rd. N&S | | |
| | 23W-12N | 22 |

| | Grid | Page |
|---|---|---|
| Moon Lake Blvd. NW&SE | | |
| | 24W-12N,29W-12N | 21 |
| Morgan Ln. E&W .. 24W-10N | | 32 |
| Morton St. N&S .. 24W-10N | | 32 |
| Moulin Ln. NW&SE | | |
| | 24W-14N | 22 |
| Mumford Ct. NW&SE | | |
| | 24W-15N | 22 |
| Mumford Dr. N&S.. 24W-15N | | 22 |
| N. Bluebonnet Rd. N&S | | |
| | 23W-11N | 32 |
| N. Dexter Ln. N&S..25W-11N | | 32 |
| N. Dovington Dr. N&S | | |
| | 25W-11N | 32 |
| N. Firestone Dr. N&S | | |
| | 23W-14N,24W-15N | 22 |
| N. Oakmont Rd. N&S | | |
| | 25W-12N | 22 |
| N. Sapphire Dr. N&S | | |
| | 24W-15N | 22 |
| N. Tamarack Dr. N&S | | |
| | 24W-16N | 12 |
| N. Victoria Ln. N&S | | |
| | 25W-12N | 22 |
| Nantucket Ct. E&W | | |
| | 24W-15N | 22 |
| Nantucket Ct. NW&SE | | |
| | 24W-15N | 22 |
| Navajo Ln. E&W ...23W-10N | | 32 |
| New Britton Dr. NS&EW | | |
| | 24W-15N | 22 |
| New Castle Ln. E&W | | |
| | 25W-12N | 22 |
| New Sutton Rd. N&S | | |
| | 28W-13N | 21 |
| Newark Ln. E&W | | |
| | 24W-10N,23W-10N | 32 |
| Newman Pl. N&S .. 23W-15N | | 22 |
| Newport Rd. NS&EW | | |
| | 24W-12N,23W-12N | 22 |
| Newton St. NE&SW | | |
| | 24W-10N | 32 |
| Nicholson Dr. NS&EW | | |
| | 30W-12N | 20 |
| Nogales St. N&S .. 23W-10N | | 32 |
| Norman Dr. E&W | | |
| | 24W-14N,23W-14N | 22 |
| Norridge Ln. E&W .. 24W-10N | | 32 |
| Northview Ln. NW&SE | | |
| | 24W-12N | 22 |
| Northwest Tollway E&W | | |
| | 31W-12N,24W-12N | 20 |
| Nottingham Ln. E&W | | |
| | 26W-12N,25W-12N | 21 |
| O'Hare Dr. N&S .. 24W-15N | | 22 |
| Oak Knoll Ln. NW&SE | | |
| | 25W-15N | 22 |
| Oak Tree Ln. E&W..23W-11N | | 32 |
| Oakdale Rd. N&S .. 25W-12N | | 22 |
| Old Barrington Rd. N&S | | |
| | 25W-13N | 22 |
| Old Higgins Rd. E&W | | |
| | 26W-12N | 21 |
| Old Sutton Rd. N&S | | |
| | 28W-13N | 21 |
| Old Timber Ct. NW&SE | | |
| | 24W-15N | 22 |
| Old Timber Ln. N&S | | |
| | 24W-15N | 22 |
| Olive St. N&S ...... 24W-11N | | 32 |
| Olmstead Dr. N&S .. 24W-15N | | 22 |
| Olmstead Dr. NE&SW | | |
| | 24W-15N | 22 |
| Opal Dr. NS&EW .. 24W-15N | | 22 |
| Orange Ln. E&W .. 24W-10N | | 32 |
| Osage Ln. E&W .. 24W-10N | | 32 |
| Oxford Ln.* N&S .. 24W-13N | | 22 |
| Pacific Av. N&S .... 26W-11N | | 31 |
| Paige Dr. NE&SW .. 24W-10N | | 32 |
| Paisly Ct. E&W .... 24W-16N | | 12 |
| Palatine Rd. E&W .. 24W-16N | | 12 |
| Paris Ln. E&W .... 24W-10N | | 32 |
| Park Ln. E&W .... 23W-15N | | 22 |
| Parkside Dr. NS&EW | | |
| | 25W-15N | 22 |
| Parkview Cir. N&S ..25W-13N | | 22 |
| Partridge Hill Dr. NS&EW | | |
| | 24W-11N | 32 |
| Patriot Ct. NE&SW 24W-14N | | 22 |
| Patriot Ln. E&W ....24W-14N | | 22 |
| Payson Dr. N&S .. 24W-10N | | 32 |
| Pebble Beach Ct. NW&SE | | |
| | 25W-12N | 22 |
| Pebble Beach Dr. NS&EW | | |
| | 25W-12N | 22 |
| Pebblewood Ln. NW&SE | | |
| | 25W-15N | 22 |
| Pembroke Av. NS&EW | | |
| | 26W-12N | 21 |
| Perry Ln. E&W .... 24W-10N | | 32 |
| Pheasant Trail Ct. NS&EW | | |
| | 30W-12N | 20 |
| Picardy Ln. NW&SE | | |
| | 24W-14N | 22 |
| Pierce Rd. N&S .. 23W-12N | | 22 |
| Pleasant St. N&S | | |
| | 24W-10N | 32 |
| Plymouth Rd. NE&SW | | |
| | 24W-14N | 22 |
| Ponderosa Ln. E&W | | |
| | 24W-16N | 12 |
| Poplar Creek Dr. NE&SW | | |
| | 26W-12N | 21 |
| Port Arthur Ct. E&W | | |
| | 25W-15N | 22 |
| Portage Ln. N&S .. 24W-15N | | 22 |
| Portshire Ct. N&S .. 23W-14N | | 22 |

| | Grid | Page |
|---|---|---|
| Prairie Stone Pkwy. E&W | | |
| | 30W-13N,29W-13N | 20 |
| Pratum Av. NW&SE | | |
| | 29W-13N | 20 |
| Preswick Pl. NS&EW | | |
| | 24W-16N | 12 |
| Princeton St. N&S .. 24W-10N | | 32 |
| Quail Run Ln. E&W ..30W-12n | | 20 |
| Queensbury Cir. N&S | | |
| | 25W-12N | 22 |
| Raleigh Ln.* E&W .. 24W-13N | | 22 |
| Raleigh Pl.* E&W .. 24W-13N | | 22 |
| Randi Ln. N&S .... 24W-11N | | 32 |
| Rebecca Dr. NE&SW | | |
| | 25W-12N | 22 |
| Regent Dr. E&W | | |
| | 23W-14N | 22 |
| Ridgewood Ln. E&W | | |
| | 25W-15N | 22 |
| Robin Cir. N&S .... 25W-12N | | 22 |
| Robin Ln. E&W .... 25W-12N | | 22 |
| Rochelle Ct. N&S .. 24W-15N | | 22 |
| Rochester Dr. N&S | | |
| | 24W-16N | 12 |
| Rock Cove Ct. E&W | | |
| | 25W-15N | 22 |
| Rock Cove Dr. N&S | | |
| | 24W-15N | 22 |
| Rolling Prairie Ct. E&W | | |
| | 24W-15N | 22 |
| Rosedale Ln. E&W | | |
| | 25W-12N,24W-12N | 22 |
| Roselle Rd. N&S .. 23W-11N | | 32 |
| Rt. 58 E&W .... 26W-12N | | 21 |
| Rt. 59 N&S .... 28W-13N | | 21 |
| Rt. 62 E&W .... 23W-14N | | 22 |
| Rt. 72 NW&SE | | |
| | 30W-14N,22W-11N | 20 |
| Rubin Ln. N&S .. 25W-12N | | 22 |
| Salem Dr. N&S | | |
| | 24W-11N,24W-12N | 32 |
| Salem Dr. N&S .. 24W-11N | | 32 |
| Sandlewood Ln. NS&EW | | |
| | 24W-15N | 22 |
| Scarbrough Cir. E&W | | |
| | 24W-11N | 32 |
| Sears Pkwy. NS&EW | | |
| | 29W-13N | 20 |
| Seaver Ln. E&W .. 26W-12N | | 21 |
| Sessions Walk E&W | | |
| | 24W-15N | 22 |
| Shagbark Ct. E&W 24W-15N | | 22 |
| Shephard Rd. N&S 24W-12N | | 22 |
| Shoe Factory Rd. E&W | | |
| | 31W-12N,27W-12N | 20 |
| Shorewood Ct. N&S | | |
| | 25W-15N | 22 |
| Shorewood Dr. N&S | | |
| | 25W-15N | 22 |
| Silver Pine Dr. NE&SW | | |
| | 24W-16N | 12 |
| Smethwick Ln.* E&W | | |
| | 24W-13N | 22 |
| Somersworth Pl. NW&SE | | |
| | 26W-12N | 21 |
| Somerton Dr. N&S ..24W-16N | | 12 |
| Spring Mill Dr. N&S | | |
| | 24W-11N | 32 |
| Stockton Dr.* NW&SE | | |
| | 24W-13N | 22 |
| Stone Harbor Ct. E&W | | |
| | 25W-15N | 22 |
| Stonington Av. NE&SW | | |
| | 26W-12N | 21 |
| Stratham Pl. N&S | | |
| | 26W-12N | 21 |
| Sturbridge Ct. E&W | | |
| | 25W-15N | 22 |
| Sturbridge Dr. NE&SW | | |
| | 24W-15N | 22 |
| Sudbury Dr.* E&W ..24W-13N | | 22 |
| Suffolk Ct. NW&SE | | |
| | 23W-15N | 22 |
| Suffolk Ln. N&S | | |
| | 23W-14N,23W-15N | 22 |
| Sumac Tr. NW&SE | | |
| | 24W-15N | 22 |
| Sundance Cir. NE&SW | | |
| | 24W-15N | 22 |
| Sundance Ct. NE&SW | | |
| | 24W-15N | 22 |
| Sunflower Ln. NS&EW | | |
| | 24W-15N | 22 |
| Sussex Walk E&W..25W-12N | | 22 |
| Sutherland Pl.* E&W | | |
| | 24W-13N | 22 |
| Swindon Pl. N&S .. 26W-12N | | 21 |
| Sycamore Ct. NW&SE | | |
| | 24W-14N | 22 |
| Tamarack Ct. N&S..24W-16N | | 12 |
| Tarrington Dr. N&S | | |
| | 24W-16N | 12 |
| Teal Ct. N&S ...... 30W-12N | | 20 |
| Terrace Ct. N&S .. 26W-12N | | 21 |
| Thacker St. E&W .. 22W-11N | | 33 |
| Thornbark Ct. E&W | | |
| | 24W-15N | 22 |
| Thornbark Dr. E&W | | |
| | 24W-15N,24W-16N | 22 |
| Tolouse Ct. NW&SE | | |
| | 24W-14N | 22 |
| Topaz Ln. N&S .... 24W-15N | | 22 |
| Trailside Ct. N&S .. 24W-15N | | 22 |
| Treaty Ct. N&S .... 23W-14N | | 22 |
| Treaty Ln. N&S .... 23W-14N | | 22 |
| Trillium Blvd. E&W | | |
| | 30W-13N,29W-13N | 20 |

| | Grid | Page |
|---|---|---|
| Turnberry Dr. NW&SE | | |
| | 24W-16N | 12 |
| Valley Ln. N&S ... 24W-11N | | 32 |
| Versailles Rd. N&S 24W-14N | | 22 |
| Victoria Dr. NS&EW | | |
| | 24W-12N | 22 |
| Vista Ln. E&W ... 25W-12N | | 22 |
| Volid Dr. NE&SW .. 25W-12N | | 22 |
| W. Berkley Ln. E&W | | |
| | 23W-11N | 32 |
| W. Dexter Ln. E&W | | |
| | 25W-11N | 32 |
| W. Dovington Dr. E&W | | |
| | 25W-11N,24W-11N | 32 |
| W. Firestone Dr. E&W | | |
| | 24W-15N,23W-15N | 22 |
| Cir. ............ 24W-15N | | 22 |
| W. Oakmont Rd. E&W | | |
| | 25W-12N | 22 |
| W. Tamarack Dr. E&W | | |
| | 24W-16N | 12 |
| W. Thacker St. E&W | | |
| | 23W-11N | 32 |
| Wainsford Dr. NS&EW | | |
| | 25W-11N | 32 |
| Warington Ln. NS&EW | | |
| | 24W-11N | 32 |
| Warwick Cir., N. E&W | | |
| | 24W-11N | 32 |
| Warwick Cir., S. E&W | | |
| | 24W-11N | 32 |
| Washington Blvd. N&S | | |
| | 24W-10N,24W-11N | 32 |
| Wellington Pl.* N&S | | |
| | 24W-13N | 22 |
| Westbridge Ct. N&S | | |
| | 24W-15N | 22 |
| Westbury Dr. E&W 25W-15N | | 22 |
| Western St. N&S .. 24W-11N | | 32 |
| Westhaven Ct. N&S | | |
| | 24W-16N | 12 |
| Westview St. N&S | | |
| | 24W-10N,24W-11N | 32 |
| Whispering Trails Ct. E&W | | |
| | 25W-15N | 22 |
| Whispering Trails Dr. NS&EW | | |
| | 25W-14N,25W-15N | 22 |
| Whitepine Ct. N&S..24W-16N | | 12 |
| Whitingham Ln.* E&W | | |
| | 24W-13N | 22 |
| Wildwood Ct. NE&SW | | |
| | 24W-15N | 22 |
| William Ct. N&S .... 23W-15N | | 22 |
| Williamsburg Dr. E&W | | |
| | 26W-12N | 21 |
| Willow Tree Ct. E&W | | |
| | 23W-11N | 32 |
| Wilmington Ln. NS&EW | | |
| | 24W-11N | 32 |
| Wilshire Dr. NW&SE | | |
| | 23W-14N | 22 |
| Winding Trail Ln. N&S | | |
| | 25W-14N | 22 |
| Winston Cir. NE&SW | | |
| | 23W-14N | 22 |
| Winston Cove E&W | | |
| | 23W-14N | 22 |
| Winston Dr. N&S | | |
| | 23W-14N,23W-15N | 22 |
| Winston Ln. E&W .. 23W-14N | | 22 |
| Winston Pl. N&S .. 23W-14N | | 22 |
| Wood Dr. NW&SE .. 24W-11N | | 32 |
| Woodhollow Ct. E&W | | |
| | 24W-15N | 22 |
| Woodlawn St. N&S | | |
| | 24W-11N | 32 |
| Worthington Dr. E&W | | |
| | 24W-11N | 32 |
| Yardley Ct. E&W .. 25W-11N | | 32 |
| Yardley Ln. N&S ....25W-11N | | 32 |
| Yorkshire Ct. N&S.. 23W-14N | | 22 |

## Hometown

| | Grid | Page |
|---|---|---|
| Beck Pl. NE&SW .... 5W-10S | | 66 |
| Cicero Av. N&S....... 5W-10S | | 66 |
| Co-op Ln. N&S .... 5W-10S | | 66 |
| Corcoran Rd. NE&SW | | |
| | 5W-10S | 66 |
| Duffy Av. NW&SE .... 5W-10S | | 66 |
| Keating Av. N&S .... 5W-10S | | 66 |
| Keating Ln. N&S .... 5W-10S | | 66 |
| Keeler Av. N&S .... 5W-10S | | 66 |
| Kenneth Av. N&S .. 5W-10S | | 66 |
| Kenton Ln. N&S .... 5W-10S | | 66 |
| Kilbourn Av. N&S .... 5W-10S | | 66 |
| Kildare Av. N&S .... 5W-10S | | 66 |
| Kilpatrick Ln. N&S .. 5W-10S | | 66 |
| Knox Av. N&S .... 5W-10S | | 66 |
| Knox Ln. N&S .... 5W-10S | | 66 |
| Kolin Av. N&S .... 5W-10S | | 66 |
| Kolmar Av. N&S .... 5W-10S | | 66 |
| Komensky Av. N&S .. 5W-10S | | 66 |
| Kostner Av. N&S .... 5W-10S | | 66 |
| Main St. NE&SW .... 5W-10S | | 66 |
| Merrion Ln. N&S .... 5W-10S | | 66 |
| Pulaski Rd. N&S .... 5W-10S | | 66 |
| Rt. 50 N&S .... 5W-10S | | 66 |
| Rt. 7 NE&SW ...... 5W-10S | | 66 |
| Ryan Rd. NE&SW .. 5W-10S | | 66 |
| South Buckley Rd. N&S | | |
| | 5W-10S | 66 |
| Southwest Hwy. NE&SW | | |
| | 5W-10S | 66 |
| Staycoff Ln.* NE&SW | | |
| | 5W-10S | 66 |
| 87th Pl. E&W....... 5W-10S | | 66 |
| 87th St. E&W ........ 5W-9S | | 66 |

| | Grid | Page |
|---|---|---|
| 88th Pl. E&W........ 5W-10S | | 66 |
| 88th St. E&W........ 5W-10S | | 66 |
| 89th Pl. E&W........ 5W-10S | | 66 |
| 89th St. E&W........ 5W-10S | | 66 |
| 90th Pl. E&W........ 5W-10S | | 66 |
| 90th St. E&W........ 5W-10S | | 66 |
| 91st St. E&W........ 5W-10S | | 66 |

## Homewood

| | Grid | Page |
|---|---|---|
| Aberdeen St. N&S | | |
| | 1W-22S,1W-21S | 88 |
| Alexander Rd. E&W .. 3W-22S | | 87 |
| Alexander Ter. E&W 2W-22S | | 87 |
| Argyle Av. N&S | | |
| | 3W-22S,3W-21S | 87 |
| Armitage Pl. N&S .. 1W-21S | | 88 |
| Ashland Av. N&S .... 2W-21S | | 87 |
| Birch Rd. E&W | | |
| | 3W-22S,1W-21S | 88 |
| Boulder Ct. N&S .. 1W-22S | | 88 |
| Bowling Green Rd. E&W | | |
| | 1W-22S | 88 |
| Bretz Dr. N&S .... 0W-21S | | 88 |
| Briar Av. NE&SW .. 2W-21S | | 87 |
| Burr Oak Rd. E&W | | |
| | 2W-21S,1W-21S | 87 |
| California Av. N&S | | |
| | 3W-22S,3W-21S | 87 |
| Capenter St. N&S...1W-22S | | 88 |
| Caroline Dr. E&W .. 3W-21S | | 87 |
| Carson Ct. E&W .. 2W-22S | | 88 |
| Carson Dr. N&S .... 2W-22S | | 87 |
| Castle Rd. N&S...1W-22S | | 88 |
| Cedar Rd. E&W .... 2W-22S | | 87 |
| Center Av. N&S | | |
| | 1W-22S,1W-21S | 88 |
| Center Ct. E&W .... 1W-23S | | 88 |
| Chayes Park Dr. E&W | | |
| | 3W-22S | 87 |
| Cherry Creek Dr. N&S | | |
| | 3W-22S | 87 |
| Cherry Ln. E&W .. 2W-22S | | 87 |
| Cherrywood Ct. E&W | | |
| | 3W-21S | 87 |
| Cherrywood Ln. N&S | | |
| | 3W-21S | 87 |
| Chestnut Rd. NW&SE | | |
| | 2W-21S | 87 |
| Clyde Rd. NE&SW .. 3W-22S | | 87 |
| Clyde Ter. E&W .... 3W-22S | | 87 |
| Coach Rd. E&W .... 1W-22S | | 88 |
| Cowing Av. N&S .. 2W-22S | | 87 |
| Debra Ln. E&W......3W-22S | | 87 |
| Delta Rd. N&S .... 1W-22S | | 88 |
| Dixie Hwy. N&S | | |
| | 2W-22S,2W-21S | 87 |
| Dixmoor Dr. N&S .. 2W-21S | | 87 |
| Dolphin Lake Dr. NS&EW | | |
| | 3W-21S | 87 |
| Downey Rd. E&W .. 2W-22S | | 87 |
| Dundee Av. N&S | | |
| | 3W-22S,3W-21S | 87 |
| Elder Rd. E&W .... 1W-21S | | 88 |
| Elliot Ln. E&W ....... 2W-22S | | 87 |
| Elm Rd. NW&SE .... 2W-21S | | 87 |
| Evergreen Rd. E&W | | |
| | 2W-22S,1W-22S | 87 |
| Francis Rd. E&W .. 2W-22S | | 87 |
| Francisco Av. N&S .. 3W-22S | | 87 |
| Fresno Ln. NS&EW .. 3W-22S | | 87 |
| Gladville Av. N&S | | |
| | 2W-22S,2W-21S | 87 |
| Golfview Av. N&S | | |
| | 2W-22S,2W-21S | 87 |
| Gottschalk Av. N&S | | |
| | 2W-22S,2W-21S | 87 |
| Governors Hwy. N&S | | |
| | 3W-21S | 87 |
| Halsted St. N&S | | |
| | 1W-23S,1W-21S | 88 |
| Hart Dr. N&S .... 1W-21S | | 88 |
| Harwood Av. NE&SW | | |
| | 2W-22S,2W-21S | 87 |
| Hawthorne Rd. E&W | | |
| | 3W-21S,3W-10S | 87 |
| Heather Ct. E&W .. 1W-22S | | 88 |
| Heather Rd. E&W .. 1W-22S | | 88 |
| Hedgerow Ln. E&W .. 3W-22S | | 87 |
| Hickory Rd. E&W | | |
| | 3W-21S,1W-21S | 87 |
| Highland Av. N&S | | |
| | 2W-22S,2W-21S | 87 |
| Hillside Av. N&S .... 1W-21S | | 87 |
| Hillview Rd. E&W .. 1W-21S | | 87 |
| Holbrook Rd. E&W .. 1W-23S | | 88 |
| Hollydale Dr. E&W .. 3W-21S | | 87 |
| Homewood Av. N&S | | |
| | 2W-22S,2W-21S | 87 |
| Homewood Av. N&S | | |
| | 3W-22S | 87 |
| Hood Av. N&S | | |
| | 1W-22S,1W-21S | 88 |
| Howe Av. N&S ...... 2W-21S | | 87 |
| Idlewild Ln. E&W .. 1W-22S | | 88 |
| Jamie Ct. N&S ...... 1W-22S | | 88 |
| Jamie Ln. E&W...... 1W-22S | | 88 |
| Jefferey Ct. E&W .. 1W-22S | | 88 |
| Jefferey Dr. N&S .. 1W-22S | | 88 |
| Jill Ct. E&W ...... 1W-22S | | 88 |
| Jill Ter. E&W .... 1W-22S | | 88 |
| Jodi Ter. N&S .... 1W-22S | | 88 |
| Jonathan Ln. N&S .. 1W-22S | | 88 |
| Juhlin Dr. N&S .... 2W-22S | | 88 |
| Kathleen Ct. E&W .. 1W-22S | | 87 |
| Kings Rd. N&S .... 1W-22S | | 88 |
| Klimm Av. N&S...2W-22S | | 87 |
| Knollwood Ln. E&W .. 4W-22S | | 87 |

| | Grid | Page |
|---|---|---|
| Kroner Dr. N&S | 0W-21S | 88 |
| L.A. Ct., N. NE&SW | 3W-21S | 87 |
| L.A. Ct., S. SE&NW | 3W-21S | 87 |
| Lahaigh Rd. N&S | 1W-21S | 88 |
| Larkspur Ln. N&S | 3W-21S | 87 |
| Lexington Av. N&S | 2W-22S | 87 |
| Lincoln Av. N&S | 3W-21S | 87 |
| Linden Rd. E&W | | |
| | 3W-21S,1W-21S | 87 |
| Locust Rd. E&W | 3W-21S | 87 |
| Loomis Av. N&S | | |
| | 1W-22S,1W-21S | 88 |
| Loomis Ct. N&S | 1W-23S | 88 |
| Loomis Dr. N&S | | |
| | 1W-23S,1W-22S | 88 |
| Los Angeles Av. N&S | | |
| | 3W-21S | 87 |
| Lyn Ct. N&S | 1W-22S | 88 |
| Magnolia Rd. E&W | 2W-22S | 87 |
| Maple Av. E&W | 1W-22S | 88 |
| Maple Rd. E&W | | |
| | 3W-21S,2W-21S | 87 |
| Marlin Ln. N&S | 3W-21S | 87 |
| Marshfield Av. | 2W-22S | 87 |
| Martin Av. N&S | | |
| | 2W-22S,2W-21S | 87 |
| Matthew Ln. E&W | 3W-22S | 87 |
| May Av. N&S | 1W-22S | 88 |
| Morgan Av. N&S | | |
| | 1W-22S,1W-21S | 88 |
| Morris Av. N&S | 2W-22S | 87 |
| Mueller Ct. E&W | 2W-21S | 87 |
| Oak Rd. E&W | 2W-21S | 87 |
| Olive Rd. E&W | | |
| | 3W-21S,1W-21S | 87 |
| Page Av. N&S | 2W-22S | 87 |
| Page Ct. N&S | 2W-22S | 87 |
| Palmer Av. N&S | 2W-22S | 87 |
| Palmer Rd. NW&SE | 2W-22S | 87 |
| Park Av. NE&SW | 2W-21S | 87 |
| Patricia Ln. E&W | 3W-21S | 87 |
| Perth Av. N&S | | |
| | 3W-22S,3W-21S | 87 |
| Pierce Av. N&S | 1W-22S | 88 |
| Pierce St. N&S | 1W-23S | 88 |
| Pierce Ter. N&S | 1W-22S | 88 |
| Pine Rd. E&W | 2W-21S | 87 |
| Pine St. E&W | 2W-21S | 87 |
| Poplar Av. NW&SE | 1W-22S | 88 |
| Presidents Dr. NE&SW | | |
| | 1W-21S | 88 |
| Queens Rd. N&S | 1W-21S | 88 |
| Reigel Rd. NW&SE | | |
| | 1W-23S,1W-21S | 88 |
| Ridge Rd. E&W | | |
| | 2W-21S,1W-21S | 87 |
| Riegel Oaks Ln. E&W | | |
| | 1W-22S | 88 |
| Robin Ln. NE&SW | 3W-22S | 87 |
| Roosevelt Av. N&S | 2W-21S | 87 |
| Royal Rd. N&S | 1W-22S | 88 |
| Sacramento Av. N&S | | |
| | 3W-22S,3W-21S | 87 |
| Sailfish Rd. E&W | 3W-21S | 87 |
| San Diego Av. N&S | 3W-21S | 87 |
| Spruce Rd. E&W | | |
| | 3W-21S,1W-21S | 87 |
| Stedhall Rd. N&S | 3W-22S | 87 |
| Stewart Av. N&S | | |
| | 3W-22S,3W-21S | 87 |
| Stockton Av. N&S | 3W-22S | 87 |
| Sycamore Ct. E&W | 2W-21S | 87 |
| Sycamore Dr. N&S | 2W-21S | 87 |
| Tarpon Ct. N&S | 1W-21S | 87 |
| Terrace Rd. E&W | 2W-22S | 87 |
| Thomas St. E&W | 1W-22S | 88 |
| Tipton Av. N&S | 2W-21S | 87 |
| Turtle Creek Dr. N&S | | |
| | 3W-21S | 87 |
| Virginia Pl. E&W | 3W-21S | 87 |
| Walnut Rd. E&W | 3W-21S | 87 |
| Walton Ln. NW&SE | 1W-21S | 88 |
| Washington Av. N&S | | |
| | 2W-21S | 87 |
| Willow Rd. E&W | | |
| | 3W-22S,1W-21S | 87 |
| 175th St. E&W | 1W-21S | 88 |
| 178th St. E&W | 3W-21S | 87 |
| 182nd Pl.* E&W | 2W-22S | 87 |
| 183rd Pl.* E&W | 1W-22S | 88 |
| 183rd St. E&W | | |
| | 3W-21S,1W-21S | 87 |
| 184th Pl. E&W | 1W-22S | 88 |
| 184th St. E&W | | |
| | 4W-22S,1W-22S | 87 |
| 185th Pl. E&W | 1W-22S | 88 |
| 185th St. E&W | | |
| | 4W-22S,1W-22S | 87 |
| 186th Pl. E&W | 1W-22S | 88 |
| 186th St. E&W | | |
| | 4W-22S,1W-22S | 87 |
| 187th St. E&W | | |
| | 2W-22S,1W-22S | 87 |
| 188th St. E&W | 2W-22S | 87 |
| 190st St. E&W | 1W-22S | 88 |
| 191st St. E&W | 1W-22S | 88 |

### Indian Head Park

| | Grid | Page |
|---|---|---|
| Acacia NS&EW | 13W-7S | 58 |
| Algonquin N&S | 14W-7S | 58 |
| Apache E&W | 14W-7S | 58 |
| Arrowhead* N&S | 14W-6S | 58 |
| Big Bear Dr. E&W | 14W-7S | 58 |
| Blackhawk Dr. N&S | 14W-7S | 58 |
| Briarwood Ln. E&W | 13W-7S | 58 |
| Button Wood N&S | 13W-7S | 58 |
| Cascade E&W | 13W-7S | 58 |
| Cherokee E&W | 14W-7S | 58 |
| Cherrywood NE&SW | | |
| | 13W-7S | 58 |
| Cochise E&W | 14W-7S | 58 |
| Deercrest E&W | 13W-7S | 58 |
| East E&W | 14W-7S | 58 |
| Elmwood Ct.* E&W | 14W-6S | 58 |
| Elmwood Square* N&S | | |
| | 14W-6S | 58 |
| Hawthorne Sq.* E&W | | |
| | 13W-7S | 58 |
| Heatherwood Ct.* N&S | | |
| | 14W-6S | 58 |
| Hiawatha Ln. E&W | 14W-6S | 58 |
| Howard N&S | 13W-7S | 58 |
| I-294 N&S | 14W-7S | 58 |
| Indian Head Ct.* N&S | | |
| | 14W-6S | 58 |
| Indian Head Tr.* N&S | | |
| | 14W-6S | 58 |
| Joliet SW&NE | 14W-7S | 58 |
| Keokok N&S | 14W-7S | 58 |
| Laurel N&S | 13W-7S | 58 |
| Mohawk Ct. NW&SE | | |
| | 14W-7S | 58 |
| Nacona Ln.* E&W | 13W-7S | 58 |
| Osceola NE&SW | 14W-7S | 58 |
| Pontiac NW&SE | 14W-7S | 58 |
| Potawatomie N&S | 13W-7S | 58 |
| Sauk E&W | 13W-7S | 58 |
| Sequoya Ln. E&W | 14W-6S | 58 |
| Cir. | 14W-7S | 58 |
| Shawnee E&W | 13W-7S | 58 |
| Sioux N&S | 14W-7S | 58 |
| Square E&W | 13W-7S | 58 |
| Stonehearth Ln. E&W | | |
| | 13W-7S | 58 |
| Stratford Pl.* N&S | 13W-7S | 58 |
| Sweetwood E&W | 13W-7S | 58 |
| Tanglewood Ct.* N&S | | |
| | 13W-7S | 58 |
| Tecumseh E&W | 14W-7S | 58 |
| Thunderbird E&W | 14W-7S | 58 |
| Timber Ridge Rd. N&S | | |
| | 14W-6S | 58 |
| Vine N&S | 14W-7S | 58 |
| Waubanse NE&SW | 14W-7S | 58 |
| Westwood Ct.* E&W | | |
| | 14W-6S | 58 |
| Westwood Square* N&S | | |
| | 14W-6S | 58 |
| Wood N&S | 14W-6S | 58 |
| 65th St. E&W | 13W-7S | 58 |
| 65th Pl. E&W | 13W-7S | 58 |

### Inverness

| | Grid | Page |
|---|---|---|
| Abbotsford Dr. NS&EW | | |
| | 25W-16N,24W-16N | 12 |
| Aberdeen Rd. E&W | | |
| | 22W-16N | 13 |
| Aberdour Ln.* N&S | | |
| | 23W-16N | 12 |
| Afton Cir. NW&SE | 24W-17N | 12 |
| Alexander Ct. NW&SE | | |
| | 25W-16N | 12 |
| Alnwick Ct. NW&SE | | |
| | 25W-16N | 12 |
| Appleby Rd. NE&SW | | |
| | 23W-15N,22W-15N | 22 |
| Applecross Rd. NW&SE | | |
| | 25W-16N | 12 |
| Ardmore Av. N&S | | |
| | 24W-15N,23W-15N | 22 |
| Arlington Rd. N&S | | |
| | 23W-15N,23W-16N | 22 |
| Ayshire Ln. N&S | 23W-16N | 12 |
| Baldwin Rd. E&W | 24W-16N | 12 |
| Balmoral Cir. NE&SW | | |
| | 22W-14N | 23 |
| Balmoral Dr. E&W | 22W-14N | 23 |
| Balmoral Ln. N&S | | |
| | 22W-14N,22W-15N | 23 |
| Banbury Rd. E&W | | |
| | 23W-17N,22W-17N | 12 |
| Bannockburn E&W | 23W-14S | 22 |
| Barclay Cir. NS&EW | | |
| | 24W-17N | 12 |
| Barra Ln. NE&SW | 22W-16N | 13 |
| Beaver Pond Rd. E&W | | |
| | 23W-15N | 22 |
| Bedlington Dr. N&S | | |
| | 24W-17N | 12 |
| Berwick E&W | 23W-14N | 22 |
| Betty Dr. NW&SE | 23W-17N | 12 |
| Bishop Ct. NE&SW | | |
| | 25W-16N | 12 |
| Blackburn Rd. NS&EW | | |
| | 23W-17N | 12 |
| Blair Ln.* E&W | 23W-16N | 12 |
| Blythe Ct. NW&SE | 24W-16N | 12 |
| Bonne Ln. NW&SE | 22W-16N | 13 |
| Bonny Glen Gates E&W | | |
| | 23W-14N | 22 |
| Bordeaux Ct. N&S | 24W-17N | 12 |
| Borthwick Ln. E&W | | |
| | 22W-16N | 13 |
| Bradwell Ct. E&W | | |
| | 25W-16N,23W-16N | 12 |
| Braeburn Rd. N&S | | |
| | 23W-16N,23W-17N | 12 |
| Braymore Ct. NE&SW | | |
| | 25W-16N | 12 |
| Braymore Dr. E&W | | |
| | 25W-16N | 12 |
| Braymore Dr., S. NS&EW | | |
| | 25W-16N | 12 |
| Brodick Ln. NW&SE | | |
| | 22W-16N | 13 |
| Burleigh Ln. E&W | 22W-16N | 13 |
| Camphill Cir E&W | 23W-15N | 22 |
| Canterbury Ln. NW&SE | | |
| | 23W-16N,23W-17N | 12 |
| Carberry Cir. NS&EW | | |
| | 24W-17N | 12 |
| Carlisle Dr. NS&EW | | |
| | 24W-17N | 12 |
| Cawdor Dr. NE&SW | | |
| | 22W-16N | 13 |
| Cheviot Dr. NS&EW | 24W-16N | 12 |
| Chimney Rock N&S | 23W-14N | 22 |
| Clover Dr. NE&SW | | |
| | 23W-14N,22W-15N | 22 |
| Colonial Pkwy. NS&EW | | |
| | 23W-14N | 22 |
| Colony Dr. NE&SW | 23W-14N | 22 |
| Common Ridings Way N&S | | |
| | 25W-16N | 12 |
| Cornell Av. E&W | 22W-16N | 13 |
| Country Oak Ln. N&S | | |
| | 23W-15N | 22 |
| Courtbridge Rd. N&S | | |
| | 24W-17N | 12 |
| Craigie Ln. E&W | 22W-16N | 13 |
| Crichton Ln. E&W | 22W-16N | 13 |
| Cumnock Rd. NS&EW | | |
| | 23W-16N | 12 |
| Dairy Ln. N&S | 23W-17N | 12 |
| Dewey Rd. NW&SE | | |
| | 23W-16N | 12 |
| Dirleton Ln.* E&W | 23W-16N | 12 |
| Dover Cir. NE&SW | 23W-15N | 22 |
| Drummond Cir. NW&SE | | |
| | 24W-17N | 12 |
| Dublin Ct. NE&SW | 22W-15N | 23 |
| Dumfries Ct. NE&SW | | |
| | 22W-15N | 23 |
| Dunbar Rd. E&W | | |
| | 23W-17N,22W-17N | 12 |
| Dunbarton Dr. E&W | | |
| | 25W-16N | 12 |
| Dunheath Dr. NW&SE | | |
| | 24W-17N | 12 |
| Duntrone Ln.* E&W | | |
| | 23W-16N | 12 |
| Durham Dr. E&W | 23W-16N | 12 |
| Edinburgh Ct. NS&EW | | |
| | 24W-16N | 12 |
| Ela Rd. N&S | | |
| | 23W-14N,23W-17N | 22 |
| Fairway N&S. NS&EW | | |
| | 23W-16N | 12 |
| Fife Ct. N&S | 24W-16N | 12 |
| Fincharn Ln. E&W | 22W-16N | 13 |
| Firth Rd. NS&EW | 23W-15N | 22 |
| Florence Av. E&W | | |
| | 24W-16N,23W-16N | 12 |
| Fox Trail NW&SE | 22W-14N | 23 |
| Freeman Ct. E&W | 24W-15N | 22 |
| Freeman Rd. E&W | 23W-15N | 22 |
| Gaelic Ct. E&W | 23W-16N | 12 |
| Cir. | 24W-16N | 12 |
| Glamis Ln. NW&SE | | |
| | 22W-16N | 13 |
| Glen Eagles Ct. NW&SE | | |
| | 22W-16N | 13 |
| Glencrest Dr. NS&EW | | |
| | 24W-17N | 12 |
| Glenmore Ct. N&S | 24W-17N | 12 |
| Grayfriars Ln. N&S | 22W-16N | 13 |
| Great Glen E&W | 24W-16N | 12 |
| Greenock NS&EW | 23W-14N | 22 |
| Guthrie Ct. N&S | 24W-17N | 12 |
| Guthrie Dr. NE&SW | | |
| | 24W-17N | 12 |
| Halbert Ln. NW&SE | | |
| | 25W-16N | 12 |
| Halkirk Cir. E&W | 22W-15N | 23 |
| Haman Rd. N&S | | |
| | 24W-17N,24W-16N | 12 |
| Hamilton Ct. N&S | 25W-16N | 12 |
| Harmening Av. E&W | | |
| | 23W-15N | 22 |
| Harrow Gate Dr. N&S | | |
| | 25W-16N | 12 |
| Heather Ln. N&S | 23W-16N | 12 |
| Highland Rd. N&S | 23W-16N | 12 |
| Hillshire Ct. E&W | 25W-17N | 12 |
| Hillshire Ln. NS&EW | | |
| | 25W-17N | 12 |
| Huntley E&W | 23W-16N | 12 |
| Inverray Rd. E&W | 23W-15N | 22 |
| Jules Rd. N&S | 23W-16N | 12 |
| Julie Dr. N&S | 24W-17N | 12 |
| Keise Glen Ct. (Pvt.) E&W | | |
| | 23W-16N | 12 |
| Kilchurn Ln.* E&W | 23W-16N | 12 |
| Kilrenny N&S | 23W-14N | 22 |
| Kirkwall Ct. E&W | 23W-16N | 12 |
| Kirkwood Dr. NE&SW | | |
| | 23W-17N | 12 |
| Kitson Cir. NE&SW | | |
| | 23W-17N | 12 |
| Knockderry Ln. E&W | | |
| | 22W-16N | 13 |
| Knox Ct. NS&EW | 25W-16N | 12 |
| Lanark Ln. NW&SE | | |
| | 23W-17N | 12 |
| Lancaster Ct. N&S | 24W-17N | 12 |
| Lauder NS&EW | | |
| | 23W-15N | 22 |
| Lillian Av. E&W | | |
| | 24W-16N,23W-16N | 12 |
| Livingston Ct. E&W | | |
| | 25W-16N | 12 |
| Livingston Ln. E&W | | |
| | 25W-16N | 12 |
| Loch Lomond Dr. NS&EW | | |
| | 22W-16N | 13 |
| Lochleven Ln.* NW&SE | | |
| | 23W-16N | 12 |
| Lomond Dr. NE&SW | | |
| | 23W-16N | 12 |
| Cir. | 25W-16N | 12 |
| MacAlpin Ct. NW&SE | | |
| | 23W-16N | 12 |
| MacAlpin Dr. NS&EW | | |
| | 23W-16N | 12 |
| Macbain Way N&S | 24W-16N | 12 |
| Marie Dr. E&W | 23W-17N | 12 |
| Midmar Ln.* E&W | 23W-16N | 12 |
| Milton Rd. NE&SW | | |
| | 23W-16N,23W-17N | 12 |
| Muirfield Rd. NW&SE | | |
| | 24W-17N | 12 |
| Mulguy Ct. NW&SE | | |
| | 23W-16N | 12 |
| Mulguy Dr. NE&SW | | |
| | 23W-16N | 12 |
| Newcastle Ct. NW&SE | | |
| | 24W-17N | 12 |
| Newport Ln. E&W | 25W-17N | 12 |
| Newport St. N&S | 25W-17N | 12 |
| Northwest Highway NW&SE | | |
| | 24W-17N,22W-16N | 12 |
| Old Wick Ln. NW&SE | | |
| | 22W-16N | 13 |
| Palatine Rd. E&W | | |
| | 25W-16N,22W-16N | 12 |
| Peregrine Dr. E&W | 22W-14N | 23 |
| Pheasant Tr. NW&SE | | |
| | 23W-15N,22W-15N | 22 |
| Plymouth Ct. NE&SW | | |
| | 23W-15N | 22 |
| Plymouth Dr. N&S | 23W-15N | 22 |
| Port Center Dr. NE&SW | | |
| | 22W-14N,23W-14N | 22 |
| Poteet Av. N&S | | |
| | 23W-15N,23W-16N | 22 |
| Prestwick Dr. NS&EW | | |
| | 23W-15N | 22 |
| Quail Run N&S | 23W-14N | 22 |
| Ravenscraig Ln. N&S | | |
| | 23W-16N | 13 |
| Rob Roy Ct. NW&SE | | |
| | 22W-16N | 13 |
| Roberts Rd. N&S | | |
| | 24W-15N,24W-17N | 22 |
| Roselle Rd. N&S | | |
| | 22W-14N,22W-16N | 23 |
| Rosemary Av. E&W | | |
| | 24W-16N | 12 |
| Rosslyn Ln.* NE&SW | | |
| | 23W-16N | 12 |
| Rt. 68 SW&NE | 25W-17N | 12 |
| Sanday Ln. E&W | 23W-16N | 12 |
| Scots Ct. N&S | 22W-16N | 13 |
| Selkirk Ct. NS&EW | | |
| | 24W-16N | 12 |
| Shetland Rd. NW&SE | | |
| | 25W-16N | 12 |
| Shire Cir. NW&SE | 24W-16N | 23 |
| Skye Ln. E&W | 24W-16N | 12 |
| St. Andrews Ln. N&S | | |
| | 22W-16N | 13 |
| Sterling Rd. N&S | | |
| | 23W-16N,23W-17N | 12 |
| Stonefield Ct. NE&SW | | |
| | 23W-17N | 12 |
| Stonehaven Ct. E&W | | |
| | 23W-14N | 22 |
| Stratford Ln. NE&SW | | |
| | 23W-16N,23W-17N | 12 |
| Strome Ln.* E&W | 23W-16N | 12 |
| Stuart Ln. E&W | 23W-16N | 12 |
| Summer Isle Ln. E&W | | |
| | 25W-16N | 12 |
| Sunset Dr. E&W | 23W-16N | 12 |
| Tantallon Ln.* E&W | 23W-16N | 12 |
| Tarbat Ct. NS&EW | 23W-16N | 12 |
| Thompson's Way N&S | | |
| | 23W-14N | 22 |
| Thompsons Cir. E&W | | |
| | 23W-14N | 22 |
| Thor Dr. E&W | 23W-14N | 22 |
| Thornhill Rd. E&W | 23W-16N | 12 |
| Thos Atkinson Rd. E&W | | |
| | 23W-14N | 22 |
| Thyra Ln. N&S | 23W-14N | 22 |
| Turkey Ct. NE&SW | | |
| | 23W-14N | 22 |
| Turkey Trail E&W | | |
| | 23W-14N,22W-14N | 22 |
| Tweed Rd. NS&EW | | |
| | 23W-17N | 12 |
| Tyne Ct. N&S | 24W-16N | 12 |
| Valley Lake Ln. NE&SW | | |
| | 22W-14N | 23 |
| Versailles Ct. NS&EW | 24W-17N | 12 |
| Warkworth Ln.* N&S | | |
| | 23W-16N | 12 |
| Warren Av. E&W | 23W-15N | 22 |
| Waterford Ln. E&W | | |
| | 24W-17N | 12 |
| Whispering Pines Ct. E&W | | |
| | 25W-17N | 12 |
| Williams Rd. N&S | | |
| | 24W-15N,24W-17N | 22 |
| Willow St. E&W | | |
| | 24W-16N,23W-16N | 12 |
| Windsor Cir. NW&SE | | |
| | 23W-15N | 22 |
| Windsor Rd. NE&SW | | |
| | 23W-15N | 22 |
| Winfield Ln. E&W | 25W-16N | 12 |
| Withorn Ln. E&W | 22W-16N | 13 |
| Wood St. E&W | | |
| | 24W-16N,23W-16N | 12 |
| Woodburn Ct. E&W | | |
| | 23W-17N | 12 |

### Justice

| | Grid | Page |
|---|---|---|
| Archer SW&NE | 11W-8S | 58 |
| Archer Av. NE&SW | | |
| | 11W-9S,10W-8S | 64 |
| Banks N&S | 11W-8S | 58 |
| Blackstone SW&NE | 10W-8S | 59 |
| Blazer N&S | 11W-8S | 58 |
| Christeen Dr. NS&EW | | |
| | 10W-9S | 65 |
| Cork Av. N&S | 11W-8S | 58 |
| Cronin N&S | 11W-8S | 58 |
| Deer Path N&S | 11W-9S | 64 |
| Fawn Tr. N&S | 11W-9S | 64 |
| Figura N&S | 11W-8S | 58 |
| Garden Ln. N&S | 11W-8S | 58 |
| Heather Tr. NW&SE | 10W-9S | 59 |
| Huntington E&W | 10W-8S | 59 |
| Indian NW&SE | 11W-8S | 58 |
| Interstate 294 SE&NW | | |
| | 10W-9S | 65 |
| Jocare Av. N&S | 11W-8S | 58 |
| Madison N&S | 11W-8S | 58 |
| Maple NW&SE | 10W-9S | 59 |
| Maplewood Dr. NS&EW | | |
| | 10W-8S | 59 |
| Marion Dr. E&W | 10W-9S | 65 |
| Marisa E&W | 10W-8S | 59 |
| Mary E&W | 11W-8S | 58 |
| Moisan Av. N&S | 11W-9S | 64 |
| Murray E&W | 11W-8S | 58 |
| Oak Grove N&S | 11W-8S | 58 |
| Oak Ridge Dr. E&W | 11W-9S | 64 |
| Pawtrail Rd. N&S | 11W-9S | 59 |
| Rose SW&NE | 11W-8S | 59 |
| Rt. 171 NE&SW | | |
| | 11W-9S,11W-8S | 64 |
| Skyline Dr. NS&EW | 10W-8S | 59 |
| Thomas St. E&W | 10W-9S | 65 |
| Tri State Tollway SE&NW | | |
| | 10W-9S | 65 |
| Willow NW&SE | 10W-8S | 59 |
| 72nd E&W | 10W-8S | 59 |
| 72nd Pl. NW&SE | 10W-9S | 59 |
| 73rd E&W | 10W-8S | 59 |
| 73rd Pl. E&W | 10W-8S | 59 |
| 74th E&W | 10W-8S | 59 |
| 75th E&W | 11W-8S | 58 |
| 78th E&W | 9W-8S | 59 |
| 78th Ct. N&S | 11W-8S | 58 |
| 79th E&W | 10W-9S | 65 |
| 79th Av. N&S | 9W-9S | 65 |
| 79th Ct. N&S | 10W-9S | 65 |
| 79th Pl. E&W | 11W-9S | 64 |
| 79th St. E&W | | |
| | 11W-8S,10W-8S | 58 |
| 80th Av. N&S | 10W-9S | 65 |
| 80th Ct. N&S | 10W-9S | 65 |
| 81st Av. N&S | 10W-9S | 65 |
| 81st St. E&W | | |
| | 11W-9S,10W-9S | 64 |
| 82nd Av. N&S | 10W-9S | 65 |
| 82nd Ct. N&S | 10W-9S | 65 |
| 82nd St. E&W | 10W-9S | 65 |
| 83rd Av. N&S | 10W-9S | 65 |
| 83rd Ct. N&S | 10W-9S | 65 |
| 83rd Pl. E&W | | |
| | 11W-9S,10W-9S | 64 |
| 83rd St. E&W | | |
| | 11W-9S,10W-9S | 64 |
| 84th Av. N&S | 11W-9S | 64 |
| 84th Ct. N&S | 10W-9S | 65 |
| 84th Pl. E&W | | |
| | 11W-9S,10W-9S | 64 |
| 84th St. E&W | | |
| | 11W-9S,9W-9S | 64 |
| 85th Av. N&S | 11W-9S | 64 |
| 85th Ct. N&S | 10W-9S | 65 |
| 85th Pl. E&W | | |
| | 11W-9S,10W-9S | 64 |
| 85th St. E&W | | |
| | 11W-9S,9W-9S | 64 |
| 86th Av. N&S | | |
| | 10W-9S,10W-8S | 65 |
| 86th Ct. N&S | 10W-9S | 65 |
| 86th St. E&W | | |
| | 11W-9S,9W-9S | 64 |
| 87th Ct. N&S | 10W-9S | 65 |
| 87th St. N&S | | |
| | 10W-9S,10W-9S | 65 |
| 88th Ct. N&S | 11W-9S | 58 |
| 90th Av. N&S | 11W-9S | 64 |

### Kenilworth

| | Grid | Page |
|---|---|---|
| Abbotsford Rd. NW&SE | | |
| | 4W-14N | 29 |
| Abingdon Av. NE&SW | | |
| | 3W-14N | 29 |
| Brier St. N&S | 4W-14N | 29 |
| Cumberland Av. N&S | | |
| | 4W-14N | 29 |
| Cummings Av. | 4W-14N | 29 |
| Cumnor Rd. NW&SE | | |
| | 4W-14N | 29 |
| Devonshire Ln. N&S | 3W-14N | 29 |

|  | Grid | Page |
|---|---|---|
| Earlston Rd. NE&SW | 4W-14N | 29 |
| Essex Rd. NW&SE | 4W-14N | 29 |
| Exmoor Rd. N&S | 4W-14N | 29 |
| Glendening Rd. N&S | 4W-14N | 29 |
| Green Bay Rd. NW&SE | 4W-14N | 29 |
| Greenwood Av. E&W | 4W-14N | 29 |
| Ivy Ct. E&W | 4W-14N | 29 |
| Kenilworth Av. NE&SW | 4W-14N | 29 |
| Kenilworth Ter. E&W | 4W-14N | 29 |
| Kent Rd. E&W | 4W-14N | 29 |
| Leicester Rd. NW&SE | 3W-14N | 29 |
| McLean Av. NE&SW | 4W-14N | 29 |
| Melrose Av. NE&SW | 4W-14N | 29 |
| Oxford Rd. NW&SW | 3W-14N | 29 |
| Park Dr. E&W | 4W-14N | 29 |
| Raleigh Rd. NW&SE | 3W-14N | 29 |
| Richmond Rd. N&S | 4W-14N | 29 |
| Ridge Rd. NW&SE | 4W-14N | 29 |
| Robsart Pl. E&W | 3W-14N | 29 |
| Robsart Rd. E&W | 3W-14N | 29 |
| Rogers Av. E&W | 4W-14N | 29 |
| Roslyn Rd. NW&SE | 4W-14N | 29 |
| Sterling Rd. N&S | 4W-14N | 29 |
| Tudor Pl. E&W | 3W-14N | 29 |
| Warwick Ln. E&W | 3W-14N | 29 |
| Warwick Rd. NW&SE | 4W-14N,3W-14N | 29 |
| Wayland Av. E&W | 4W-14N | 29 |
| Woodstock Av. NE&SW | 4W-14N,3W-14N | 29 |
| 10th St. N&S | 3W-14N | 29 |

**La Grange**

|  | Grid | Page |
|---|---|---|
| Arlington E&W | 12W-4S | 52 |
| Ashland N&S | 12W-4S | 52 |
| Bassford N&S | 13W-4S | 52 |
| Beaco N&S | 12W-4S | 52 |
| Bell E&W | 13W-4S,12W-4S | 52 |
| Benton E&W | 12W-4S | 52 |
| Birchwood N&S | 13W-5S | 58 |
| Birks E&W | 13W-5S | 58 |
| Blackstone N&S | 13W-4S | 52 |
| Bluff N&S | 12W-4S | 52 |
| Brighton N&S | 13W-5S | 58 |
| Burlington SW&NE | 12W-4S | 52 |
| Calendar E&W | 12W-4S | 52 |
| Calendar SW&NE | 12W-4S | 52 |
| Calle View E&W | 12W-5S | 58 |
| Carriage E&W | 13W-5S | 58 |
| Catherine N&S | 12W-4S | 52 |
| Cossitt N&S | 13W-4S,12W-4S | 52 |
| Country Club E&W | 12W-5S | 58 |
| Drexel N&S | 13W-4S | 52 |
| Eberly N&S | 12W-4S | 52 |
| Edgewood N&S | 13W-4S | 52 |
| Elder N&S | 12W-4S | 52 |
| Elm E&W | 13W-4S,12S-4S | 52 |
| Franklin St. NE&SW | 12W-4S | 52 |
| Glenwood N&S | 13W-5S | 58 |
| Goodman E&W | 13W-4S,12W-4S | 52 |
| Haris SW&NE | 12W-4S | 52 |
| Hayes N&S | 12W-4S | 52 |
| Hazel N&S | 12W-4S | 52 |
| Hill Grove SW&NE | 12W-4S | 52 |
| Hillberry N&S | 13W-5S | 58 |
| Kensington N&S | 12W-5S,12W-4S | 58 |
| LaGrange N&S | 12W-5S | 58 |
| Leitch N&S | 13W-4S | 52 |
| Linklater E&W | 12W-5S | 58 |
| Locust N&S | 12W-4S | 52 |
| Madison N&S | 12W-4S | 52 |
| Maple E&W | 13W-4S,12W-4S | 52 |
| Mason N&S | 13W-5S | 58 |
| Mason Dr. E&W | 13W-5S | 58 |
| Ogden E&W | 12W-4S | 52 |
| Park N&S | 13W-4S | 52 |
| Peck N&S | 12W-4S | 52 |
| Plainfield NE&SW | 12W-6S | 52 |
| Poplar N&S | 13W-4S | 52 |
| Sawyer N&S | 12W-4S | 52 |
| Shawmut N&S | 12W-4S | 52 |
| Spring N&S | 12W-5S,12W-4S | 58 |
| Stone N&S | 12W-4S | 52 |
| Sunset N&S | 13W-4S | 52 |
| Tilden N&S | 12W-4S | 52 |
| Waiola N&S | 12W-4S | 52 |
| Washington N&S | 12W-4S | 52 |
| 6th N&S | 12W-5S,12W-4S | 58 |
| 7th N&S | 12W-4S | 52 |
| 8th N&S | 12W-4S | 52 |
| 9th N&S | 12W-5S,12W-4S | 58 |
| 10th N&S | 12W-5S,12W-4S | 58 |
| 11th N&S | 12W-4S | 52 |
| 12th N&S | 12W-4S | 52 |
| 41st E&W | 13W-4S | 52 |
| 47th E&W | 13W-4S | 52 |
| 48th E&W | 12W-5S | 58 |
| 49th E&W | 12W-4S | 52 |
| 50th E&W | 13W-5S,12W-4S | 58 |
| 51st E&W | 13W-5S | 58 |
| 51st N&S | 13W-5S | 58 |
| 52nd E&W | 12W-4S | 52 |
| 52nd Pl. E&W | 13W-5S | 58 |
| 53rd E&W | 12W-4S | 52 |
| 54th E&W | 12W-5S | 58 |

|  | Grid | Page |
|---|---|---|
| **La Grange Park** | | |
| Alma N&S | 11W-2S | 53 |
| Ashland N&S | 12W-3S | 52 |
| Barnsdale St. N&S | 12W-3S | 52 |
| Beach N&S | 12W-3S,12W-2S | 52 |
| Blanchan N&S | 11W-2S | 53 |
| Brainard N&S | 12W-3S | 52 |
| Brewster N&S | 12W-3S | 52 |
| Catherine N&S | 12W-3S | 52 |
| Cleveland N&S | 11W-2S | 53 |
| Community N&S | 12W-3S | 52 |
| Deerpath N&S | 12W-2S | 52 |
| Dover N&S | 13W-3S | 52 |
| Edgewood N&S | 13W-3S | 52 |
| Elmwood E&W | 12W-3S | 52 |
| Finsbury E&W | 12W-3S | 52 |
| Forest N&S | 12W-3S,12W-2S | 52 |
| Garfield E&W | 12W-3S | 52 |
| Harding E&W | 12W-3S | 52 |
| Harrison N&S | 11W-2S | 53 |
| Homestead N&S | 12W-3S,12W-2S | 52 |
| Huntington E&W | 12W-3S | 52 |
| Jackson E&W | 12W-3S | 52 |
| Kemman N&S | 12W-3S,12W-2S | 52 |
| Kensington N&S | 12W-3S | 52 |
| Kings N&S | 12W-2S | 52 |
| Lincoln N&S | 12W-3S | 52 |
| Logan E&W | 11W-3S | 53 |
| Malden N&S | 13W-3S | 52 |
| Maple N&S | 11W-3S | 52 |
| Monroe E&W | 12W-3S | 52 |
| Morgan N&S | 11W-2S | 53 |
| Newberry N&S | 12W-3S,12W-2S | 52 |
| Oak E&W | 12W-3S | 52 |
| Ostrander N&S | 11W-2S | 53 |
| Park N&S | 13W-3S | 52 |
| Pine N&S | 12W-3S | 52 |
| Pine Tree E&W | 12W-2S | 52 |
| Raymond N&S | 11W-2S | 53 |
| Richmond E&W | 12W-3S | 52 |
| Robinhood N&S | 12W-3S,12W-2S | 52 |
| Scotdale Dr. E&W | 12W-2S | 52 |
| Spring N&S | 12W-3S | 52 |
| Stone N&S | 12W-3S | 52 |
| Stonegate E&W | 12W-2S | 52 |
| Thorpe N&S | 12W-2S | 52 |
| Timber E&W | 12W-3S | 52 |
| U.S. Rt. 12 N&S | 12W-2W | 52 |
| U.S. Rt. 40 N&S | 12W-2S | 52 |
| U.S. Rt. 45 N&S | 12W-2S | 52 |
| Waiola N&S | 12W-3S | 52 |
| Woodlawn E&W | 13W-3S,12W-3S | 52 |
| Woodside N&S | 12W-2S | 52 |
| 26th E&W | 12W-2S | 52 |
| 28th E&W | 12W-2S | 52 |
| 29th E&W | 12W-2S | 52 |
| 30th E&W | 12W-2S | 52 |
| 31st E&W | 13W-2S,12W-2S | 52 |

**Lansing**

|  | Grid | Page |
|---|---|---|
| Ada St. N&S | 4E-22S,4E-21S | 89 |
| Adams St. E&W | 4E-21S | 89 |
| Ann St. E&W | 4E-21S | 89 |
| Arcadia Av. N&S | 3E-21S,3E-20S | 89 |
| Barb Ct. N&S | 4E-22S | 89 |
| Bensley Av. N&S | 2E-20S | 89 |
| Bernadine Ln. N&S | 4E-22S | 89 |
| Bernadine St. N&S | 4E-22S,4E-20S | 89 |
| Bernice Av. N&S | 3E-20S,4E-20S | 89 |
| Bernice Rd. E&W | 2E-20S,4E-20S | 89 |
| Bock Rd. N&S | 2E-21S | 89 |
| Burnham Av. N&S | 3E-22S,3E-20S | 89 |
| Burnham Ct. N&S | 3E-21S,3E-20S | 89 |
| Calhoun Av. N&S | 2E-20S | 89 |
| Calhoun St. N&S | 2E-20S | 89 |
| Carriage Ln. N&S | 2E-21S | 89 |
| Central St. E&W | 4E-21S | 89 |
| Cherry N&S | 3E-22S | 89 |
| Chicago Av. N&S | 3E-22S,3E-19S | 89 |
| Christina Dr. N&S | 2E-21S | 89 |
| Clyde N&S | 2E-21S | 89 |
| Columbian Dr. NW&SE | 3E-20S | 89 |
| Commercial Av. N&S | 3E-21S | 89 |
| Community St. N&S | 4E-20S | 89 |
| Dash St. N&S | 3E-20S | 89 |
| De Jong Ln. N&S | 2E-21S | 89 |
| Decker Av. N&S | 3E-21S | 89 |
| Escanaba Av. N&S | 3E-21S | 89 |
| Exchange Av. N&S | 3E-21S,3E-19S | 89 |
| Forest Ct. E&W | 2E-21S | 89 |
| Forest Ln. N&S | 3E-22S | 89 |
| Fred St. N&S | 3E-21S | 89 |
| Fritz Dr. N&S | 3E-20S | 89 |
| Glen Oak Av. N&S | 3E-21S,3E-20S | 89 |
| Glen Ter. N&S | 3E-21S | 89 |
| Glenwood Lansing Rd. E&W | 3E-22S | 89 |
| Grant St. N&S | 4E-22S,4E-20S | 89 |
| Greenbay Av. N&S | 3E-22S,3E-20S | 89 |

|  | Grid | Page |
|---|---|---|
| Hearth Cir. E&W | 2E-21S | 89 |
| Henry Ct. N&S | 4E-22S | 89 |
| Henry St. N&S | 4E-22S,4E-21S | 89 |
| Hickory Av. N&S | 2E-21S | 89 |
| Holiday Ter. E&W | 2E-20S | 89 |
| Hoxie Av. N&S | 2E-20S | 89 |
| Illi-Indy Dr. NW&SW | 4E-21S | 89 |
| Illinois St. E&W | 4E-21S | 89 |
| Indiana Av. E&W | 3E-20S | 89 |
| Industrial Dr. NW&SE | 3E-20S,4E-20S | 89 |
| Jackson St. E&W | 3E-20S | 89 |
| Keegan Av. N&S | 2E-21S,3E-21S | 89 |
| Kettle Ct. E&W | 2E-21S | 89 |
| Kingery Expwy. E&W | 4E-21S | 89 |
| Lake St. E&W | 4E-21S | 89 |
| Lange St. N&S | 4E-21S,4E-22S | 89 |
| Lee Av. N&S | 3E-20S | 89 |
| Locust Av. N&S | 2E-21S,2E-20S | 89 |
| Lorenz Av. N&S | 2E-21S,3E-21S | 89 |
| Louise Ct. NE&SW | 4E-22S | 89 |
| Louise St. N&S | 4E-22S | 89 |
| Luna Dr. N&S | 4E-20S | 89 |
| Madison St. E&W | 4E-21S | 89 |
| Maple Av. NW&SE | 4E-20S | 89 |
| Maple Ct. NE&SW | 4E-20S | 89 |
| Maple St. N&S | 4E-20S | 89 |
| Marble Av. N&S | 3E-20S | 89 |
| Marble Av. N&S | 3E-20S | 89 |
| Miller Dr. N&S | 4E-21S | 89 |
| Monroe St. E&W | 4E-22S | 89 |
| N. Manor Dr. E&W | 4E-22S | 89 |
| Oak Av. N&S | 3E-21S,3E-20S | 89 |
| Oak St. N&S | 3E-21S,3E-23S | 89 |
| Oakley Av. N&S | 3E-21S,3E-20S | 89 |
| Oakley Av. N&S | 3E-21S,3E-20S | 89 |
| Oakwood Av. N&S | 3E-22S,3E-21S | 89 |
| Old Farm Rd. N&S | 2E-21S | 89 |
| Otto St. E&W | 3E-20S | 89 |
| Park Av. N&S | 3E-20S | 89 |
| Park Av. N&S | 3E-22S,3E-20S | 89 |
| Park Blvd. NW&SE | 3E-20S | 89 |
| Paxton Av. N&S | 2E-20S | 89 |
| Railroad Av. NW&SE | 3E-20S | 89 |
| Randolph St. E&W | 3E-22S,4E-22S | 89 |
| Ridge Rd. E&W | 2E-21S,3E-21S | 89 |
| Ridgewood Av. N&S | 3E-22S,3E-21S | 89 |
| River Rd. E&W | 4E-20S | 83 |
| Riviera Rd. NE&SW | 4E-19S | 89 |
| Rose Av. N&S | 3E-21S | 89 |
| Rosewood Dr. N&S | 2E-20S | 89 |
| Roy St. N&S | 4E-22S,4E-20S | 89 |
| Rt. 94-80 E&W | 2E-20S,4E-20S | 89 |
| Sailor Ln. N&S | 3E-21S | 89 |
| School St. N&S | 3E-21S | 89 |
| Schultz Av. E&W | 3E-20S | 89 |
| Schultz Dr. E&W | 4E-21S | 89 |
| Schultz Dr., N. E&W | 4E-21S | 89 |
| Schultz Dr., S. E&W | 4E-21S | 89 |
| Sharon Ct. N&S | 4E-22S | 89 |
| Sherman St. N&S | 4E-22S,4E-21S | 89 |
| Shirley Dr. N&S | 4E-20S | 89 |
| South Manor Dr. E&W | 4E-22S | 89 |
| State Line Rd. N&S | 4E-21S,4E-20S | 89 |
| Stewart Av. NW&SE | 4E-21S | 89 |
| Terrace Dr. E&W | 4E-21S | 89 |
| Ton Av. N&S | 3E-20S | 89 |
| Torrence Av. N&S | 2E-22S,2E-20S | 89 |
| Violet Av. N&S | 2E-21S | 89 |
| Violet Rd. N&S | 2E-21S | 89 |
| Vollbrecht Rd. N&S | 1E-20S | 89 |
| Walter St. N&S | 4E-22S,4E-20S | 89 |
| Ward St. N&S | 3E-21S | 89 |
| Washington St. E&W | 4E-21S | 89 |
| Wentworth Av. N&S | 4E-22S,4E-20S | 89 |
| West Lake Dr. E&W | 3E-20S | 89 |
| West Louise Dr. N&S | 4E-22S | 89 |
| West St. NW&SE | 4E-22S | 89 |
| Wildwood Av. N&S | 3E-22S,3E-21S | 89 |
| William St. N&S | 4E-22S,4E-20S | 89 |
| Willow Ln. N&S | 4E-21S | 89 |
| Wright St. N&S | 4E-20S | 89 |
| Yates Av. N&S | 3E-21S,3E-19S | 89 |
| 169th Ct. E&W | 4E-19S | 83 |
| 170th Pl. E&W | 4E-20S | 89 |
| 170th St. E&W | 3E-19S,4E-20S | 83 |
| 171st St. E&W | 3E-21S,3E-20S | 89 |
| 172nd St. E&W | 2E-20S,4E-20S | 89 |
| 173rd Pl. E&W | 3E-20S,4E-20S | 89 |
| 173rd St. E&W | 2E-20S,4E-20S | 89 |
| 174th Pl. E&W | 2E-20S | 89 |

|  | Grid | Page |
|---|---|---|
| 175th Pl. E&W | 3E-20S | 89 |
| 175th St. E&W | 2E-20S,4E-20S | 89 |
| 176th Av. E&W | 3E-20S | 89 |
| 176th Pl. E&W | 4E-20S | 89 |
| 176th St. E&W | 2E-20S,4E-20S | 89 |
| 177th Pl. E&W | 2E-20S,4E-20S | 89 |
| 177th St. E&W | 2E-20S,4E-20S | 89 |
| 178th St. E&W | 3E-20S,4E-20S | 89 |
| 179th St. E&W | 2E-21S,3E-21S | 89 |
| 180th St. E&W | 4E-21S,2E-20S | 89 |
| 181st Pl. E&W | 4E-21S | 89 |
| 181st St. E&W | 4E-21S,2E-20S | 89 |
| 182nd Pl. E&W | 2E-21S,3E-21S | 89 |
| 182nd St. E&W | 3E-21S | 89 |
| 183rd Pl. E&W | 2E-21S,3E-21S | 89 |
| 183rd St. E&W | 2E-21S,3E-21S | 89 |
| 184th Pl. E&W | 2E-21S | 89 |
| 184th St. E&W | 2E-21S,3E-21S | 89 |
| 185th Pl. E&W | 2E-21S | 89 |
| 185th St. E&W | 2E-21S,3E-21S | 89 |
| 186th Pl. E&W | 3E-22S | 89 |
| 186th St. E&W | 2E-21S,3E-21S | 89 |
| 187th Pl. E&W | 3E-22S | 89 |
| 187th St. E&W | 3E-22S,3E-22S | 89 |
| 188th Pl. E&W | 3E-22S | 89 |
| 188th St. E&W | 3E-22S,4E-22S | 89 |
| 189th Pl. E&W | 3E-22S | 89 |
| 189th St. E&W | 3E-22S,4E-22S | 89 |
| 190th Pl. E&W | 3E-22S | 89 |
| 190th St. E&W | 3E-22S,4E-22S | 89 |
| 191st Pl. E&W | 3E-22S,4E-22S | 89 |
| 191st St. E&W | 3E-22S,4E-22S | 89 |
| 192nd Pl. E&W | 3E-22S,4E-22S | 89 |
| 192nd St. E&W | 3E-22S,4E-22S | 89 |
| 193rd Pl. E&W | 3E-22S,4E-22S | 89 |
| 193rd St. E&W | 3E-22S | 89 |
| 194th Pl. E&W | 3E-23S | 89 |
| 194th St. E&W | 3E-22S | 89 |
| 195th Ct. E&W | 3E-23S | 89 |

**Lemont**

|  | Grid | Page |
|---|---|---|
| Acorn St. N&S | 19W-15S | 70 |
| Alpine Av. N&S | 19W-14S | 70 |
| Aspen Ct. NE&SW | 20W-14S | 70 |
| Brady St. NW&SE | 19W-13S | 70 |
| Brown Dr. NW&SW | 20W-14S | 70 |
| Canal Av. N&S | 19W-13S | 70 |
| Cass St. NE&SW | 19W-13S | 70 |
| Catherine St. NW&SE | 19W-13S | 70 |
| Cedar St. N&S | 20W-14S | 70 |
| Cherokee Pl. N&S | 19W-14S | 70 |
| Chestnut St. N&S | 19W-14S | 70 |
| Connacht St. E&W | 19W-15S | 70 |
| Country Ct. N&S | 18W-14S | 70 |
| Country Ln. E&W | 18W-14S | 70 |
| Crestview Dr. N&S | 19W-14S | 70 |
| Crestview Rd. NW&SE | 19W-14S | 70 |
| Custer St. E&W | 19W-14S | 70 |
| Czacki St. N&S | 19W-14S,19W-13S | 70 |
| Deer Ln. E&W | 19W-15S | 70 |
| Derby Rd. NW&SE | 19W-13S,18W-13S | 70 |
| Division St. N&S | 19W-13S | 70 |
| Eaglecrest N&S | 19W-15S | 70 |
| East St. N&S | 19W-14S | 70 |
| Edgewood Ct. N&S | 19W-14S | 70 |
| Emil St. N&S | 19W-13S | 70 |
| Eureka Av. E&W | 19W-14S | 70 |
| Eureka Dr. N&S | 19W-14S | 70 |
| Evergreen Dr. NW&SE | 20W-14S | 70 |
| Evergreen Pl. NW&SE | 20W-14S | 70 |
| Florence St. N&S | 19W-13S | 70 |
| Forest Ln. N&S | 19W-13S | 70 |
| Freehauf St. E&W | 19W-13S | 70 |
| Fremont St. NW&SE | 19W-13S | 70 |
| Gillian St. N&S | 19W-13S | 70 |
| Glenview Av. N&S | 19W-14S | 70 |
| Glenys Dr. NS&EW | 19W-13S,4E-20S | 70 |
| Grant St. N&S | 19W-13S | 70 |
| Grove St. NE&SW | 19W-13S | 70 |
| Harasek St. N&S | 18W-14S | 70 |
| Hermes St. N&S | 18W-14S | 70 |
| Hickory St. N&S | 19W-14S | 70 |
| Hilltop St. N&S | 18W-13S | 70 |
| Hilltop Dr. E&W | 18W-13S | 70 |
| Hillview Ct. NE&SW | 19W-14S | 70 |

|  | Grid | Page |
|---|---|---|
| Hillview Dr. N&S | 19W-14S | 70 |
| Holmes St. NW&SE | 19W-13S | 70 |
| Houston St. N&S | 19W-14S | 70 |
| Illinois St. NE&SW | 19W-13S | 70 |
| Jacqueline Ct. N&S | 19W-14S | 70 |
| Jands Ln. NW&SE | 18W-14S | 70 |
| Jane Av. NW&SE | 18W-15S | 70 |
| John St. N&S | 19W-14S | 70 |
| Joliet St. NW&SE | 19W-13S | 70 |
| Julia St. N&S | 19W-13S | 70 |
| Keepotaw Ct. E&W | 19W-14S | 70 |
| Keepotaw Dr. E&W | 19W-14S | 70 |
| Keepotaw Ln. E&W | 19W-14S | 70 |
| Kettering Ln. E&W | 19W-14S | 70 |
| Kim Pl. N&S | 19W-14S | 70 |
| Kimball St. NE&SW | 19W-13S | 70 |
| Kip Pl. N&S | 19W-14S | 70 |
| Kromray Rd. N&S | 18W-14S | 70 |
| Kruz St. NS&EW | 18W-14S | 70 |
| Ledochowski St. N&S | 19W-14S | 70 |
| Lemont St. NW&SE | 19W-13S | 70 |
| Lenox Ct. E&W | 18W-13S | 70 |
| Lenox St. E&W | 18W-13S | 70 |
| Lincoln St. NE&SW | 19W-13S | 70 |
| Lindsay Ct. E&W | 18W-13S | 70 |
| Lintz St. E&W | 19W-14S | 70 |
| Lockport St. E&W | 19W-14S | 70 |
| Logan St. NS&EW | 20W-14S,19W-14S | 70 |
| Losey St. E&W | 19W-14S | 70 |
| Luna Av. E&W | 19W-14S | 70 |
| Luxemburg Av. N&S | 19W-14S | 70 |
| Main St. E&W | 19W-14S,19W-13S | 70 |
| Margret St. N&S | 19W-14S | 70 |
| Marian Dr. NS&EW | 18W-15S | 70 |
| Mayfair Ct. NW&SE | 18W-15S | 70 |
| McCarthy St. N&S | 19W-14S,19W-13S | 70 |
| Meagan Ln. NS&EW | 19W-14S | 70 |
| Cir. | 18W-14S | 70 |
| Moczygemba St. E&W | 19W-14S | 70 |
| Norton Av. E&W | 19W-14S | 70 |
| Norton Dr. NW&SE | 19W-14S | 70 |
| Oak St. NE&SW | 19W-14S | 70 |
| Oak Ln. NS&EW | 19W-14S | 70 |
| Para Maria St. N&S | 18W-14S | 70 |
| Park Pl. N&S | 19W-14S | 70 |
| Peiffer Av. E&W | 20W-14S,19W-14S | 70 |
| Porter St. N&S | 19W-13S | 70 |
| Povalish Ct. N&S | 20W-13S | 70 |
| Pruyne St. NW&SE | 19W-13S | 70 |
| Przewolki St. N&S | 18W-14S | 70 |
| Pulawski St. E&W | 19W-14S | 70 |
| Ridge Rd. NS&EW | 19W-14S | 70 |
| River St. N&S | 19W-13S | 70 |
| Roberta St. N&S | 19W-15S,19W-14S | 70 |
| Rosehill Dr. E&W | 19W-14S | 70 |
| S. Canal Av. NE&SW | 19W-13S | 70 |
| Sara St. N&S | 19W-14S | 70 |
| Schultz St. E&W | 18W-14S | 70 |
| Short St. E&W | 19W-14S | 70 |
| Singer Av. N&S | 19W-14S | 70 |
| Sobieski St. E&W | 19W-14S | 70 |
| Spruce Ct. E&W | 20W-14S | 70 |
| State St. N&S | 19W-14S | 70 |
| Stephen St. NW&SE | 19W-13S | 70 |
| Talcott Av. NE&SW | 19W-13S | 70 |
| Timberline Ct. NW&SE | 20W-14S | 70 |
| Timberline Dr. N&S | 20W-14S | 70 |
| Timberline Pl. E&W | 20W-14S | 70 |
| Tomasezwski St. N&S | 18W-14S | 70 |
| Una Dr. E&W | 19W-4S | 70 |
| Walnut St. N&S | 19W-14S | 70 |
| Walter St. N&S | 19W-14S | 70 |
| Warner Av. N&S | 19W-14S | 70 |
| Weimer Av. E&W | 18W-13S | 70 |
| Wend St. E&W | 19W-15S,19W-14S | 70 |
| Wexford Ct. N&S | 18W-13S | 70 |
| Wexford Dr. N&S | 18W-13S | 70 |
| Wheeler Ct. N&S | 18W-13S | 70 |
| Wheeler Dr. NW&SE | 18W-13S | 70 |
| Woodcrest Ln. N&S | 18W-14S | 70 |
| Young St. N&S | 18W-14S | 70 |
| 2nd St. N&S | 18W-14S | 70 |
| 4th St. N&S | 18W-14S | 70 |
| 6th St. N&S | 18W-14S | 70 |
| 127th St. E&W | 18W-14S | 70 |
| 128th St. E&W | 19W-15S,18W-15S | 70 |

## Lemont Township

| | Grid | Page |
|---|---|---|
| Angelico E&W | 18W-15S | 70 |
| Apple Av. E&W | 17W-14S | 71 |
| Archer Av. NE&SW | 18W-15S,15W-11S | 70 |
| Arctic Ct. N&S | 16W-15S | 71 |
| Arctic Ln. E&W | 16W-15S | 71 |
| Artesian St. N&S | 16W-13S | 71 |
| Baltic Cir. N&S | 17W-15S | 71 |
| Bell Oak Ln. NE&SW | 15W-14S | 71 |
| Bell Rd. N&S | 16W-15S,16W-14S | 71 |
| Birch Ct. NW&SE | 17W-15S | 71 |
| Black Fox Ln. N&S | 17W-15S | 71 |
| Bluff Rd. E&W | 20W-13S | 70 |
| Boyer St. N&S | 17W-14S | 71 |
| Briar Patch Ln. E&W | 16W-15S | 71 |
| Bridle Path NE&SW | 15W-13S | 71 |
| Brookside Dr. N&S | 15W-13S | 71 |
| Buckskin NW&SE | 15W-13S | 71 |
| Campbell St. E&W | 16W-13S | 71 |
| Carriage Ln. E&W | 15W-14S | 71 |
| Cedar Rd. N&S | 15W-13S | 70 |
| Center Dr. N&S | 18W-14S | 70 |
| Chestnut N&S | 15W-14S | 71 |
| Clear View E&W | 15W-13S | 71 |
| Connacht St. E&W | 19W-15S | 70 |
| Crestwood Ln. E&W | 18W-14S | 70 |
| DaVinci N&S | 18W-15S | 70 |
| David Ln. N&S | 18W-15S | 70 |
| Derby Rd. N&S | 17W-15S,17W-14S | 71 |
| Dineff Rd. N&S | 15W-13S | 71 |
| Dixon Way Dr. E&W | 17W-15S | 71 |
| El Grecco E&W | 18W-15S | 70 |
| Elm Ct. NE&SW | 17W-15S | 71 |
| Emerald Dr. N&S | 19W-15S | 70 |
| Emily Ln. NS&EW | 19W-15S | 70 |
| Equestrian Way N&S | 15W-14S | 71 |
| Fairway Dr. N&S | 20W-15S | 70 |
| Fox Burrow Ln. E&W | 17W-15S | 71 |
| Fox Hollow E&W | 18W-15S | 70 |
| Fox Ln. N&S | 18W-15S | 70 |
| Fox Tail N&S | 16W-15S | 71 |
| Foxhill Ct. E&W | 16W-15S | 71 |
| Foxhill Dr. N&S | 16W-15S | 71 |
| Fr. Linkus Dr. (Pvt) N&S | 15W-14S | 71 |
| Franciscan Dr. E&W | 18W-13S | 70 |
| Galway Ct. NE&SW | 16W-14S | 71 |
| Galway Ln. E&W | 16W-14S | 71 |
| Galway Rd. N&S | 16W-14S | 71 |
| Golden Spur NE&SW | 15W-13S | 71 |
| Gordon Ln. N&S | 20W-15S | 70 |
| Gray Ln. E&W | 16W-15S | 71 |
| Hawthorne Dr. NS&EW | 17W-15S | 71 |
| Hickory Av. E&W | 18W-15S | 70 |
| Hillcrest Dr. N&S | 18W-14S,18W-13S | 70 |
| Hillcrest Rd. E&W | 17W-13S | 71 |
| Horseshoe Ln. NE&SW | 15W-13S | 71 |
| Hunt Master Ln. E&W | 16W-15S | 71 |
| Huntsman Ln. N&S | 15W-13S | 71 |
| Katie Rd. N&S | 19W-15S | 70 |
| King Rd. N&S | 18W-15S | 71 |
| Kit Ln. E&W | 17W-15S | 71 |
| Klotz Av. NW&SE | 17W-14S | 71 |
| Lakeview NE&SE | 15W-13S | 71 |
| Lariat Ct. NW&SE | 15W-13S | 71 |
| Leinster Dr. NS&EW | 19W-15S | 70 |
| Lemont Rd. NW&SE | 19W-15S | 70 |
| Lemont St. N&S | 19W-15S | 70 |
| Liberty Dr. E&W | 16W-13S | 71 |
| Longwood Way E&W | 20W-15S | 70 |
| Main St. E&W | 16W-12S | 71 |
| Maley Rd. N&S | 16W-12S | 71 |
| Maple St. N&S | 18W-15S | 70 |
| Martin Ct. N&S | 19W-15S | 71 |
| McCarthy Rd. N&S | 17W-14S,15W-14S | 71 |
| Meadow Hill Ln. NS&EW | 16W-15S | 71 |
| Melissa Dr. E&W | 19W-15S | 70 |
| Moorefield Ct. E&W | 16W-15S | 71 |
| Munster Rd. E&W | 19W-15S | 70 |
| N. Red Coat Dr. N&S | 16W-15S | 71 |
| Nordic Ln. N&S | 17W-15S | 71 |
| North Trail N&S | 15W-13S | 71 |
| Oak Av. E&W | 17W-14S | 71 |
| Oak Ct. NE&SW | 17W-15S | 71 |
| Oak Tree Ct. NE&SW | 17W-14S | 71 |
| Oak Tree Ln. NS&EW | 17W-14S | 71 |
| Oakmont Ct. NE&SW | 20W-15S | 70 |
| Oakmont Dr. N&S | 20W-15S | 70 |
| Paddock N&S | 15W-13S | 71 |
| Parker Rd. N&S | 17W-15S,17W-13S | 71 |
| Paso Fino N&S | 15W-13S | 71 |
| Pine Av. N&S | 17W-14S | 71 |
| Prairie Av. N&S | 17W-14S | 71 |
| Raphael N&S | 18W-15S | 70 |
| Red Dr. NS&EW | 17W-15S | 71 |
| Red Fox Ct. N&S | 16W-15S | 71 |
| Riva Ridge NW&SE | 15W-15S | 71 |
| Roy Ln. N&S | 18W-15S | 70 |
| Rusty Rd. NS&EW | 15W-13S | 71 |
| S. Red Coat Dr. N&S | 16W-15S | 71 |
| Saddlebrook Ln. N&S | 16W-14S | 71 |
| Shannon Ct. E&W | 19W-15S | 70 |
| Silver Spur N&S | 15W-13S | 71 |
| Silverfox N&S | 17W-15S,16W-15S | 71 |
| Smitty Av. NW&SE | 17W-14S | 71 |
| Sorrel Ct. E&W | 15W-13S | 71 |
| Split Rail NW&SE | 15W-13S | 71 |
| Spruce Ct. NW&SE | 17W-15S | 71 |
| St. Anne Ct.* N&S | 17W-13S | 70 |
| St. Anthony Ct.* E&W | 17W-13S | 70 |
| St. Bonaventure Ct.* E&W | 17W-13S | 70 |
| St. Colette Ct.* N&S | 17W-13S | 70 |
| St. Joseph Ct.* E&W | 17W-13S | 70 |
| State St. N&S | 19W-15S | 70 |
| Stone Creek Dr. N&S | 15W-13S | 71 |
| Sunhill Ln. E&W | 16W-14S | 71 |
| Surrey E&W | 15W-14S | 71 |
| Sylvan Woods Dr. NW&SE | 17W-15S | 71 |
| Timber View N&S | 15W-13S | 71 |
| Valley View Ct. N&S | 20W-15S | 70 |
| Valley View Dr. E&W | 20W-15S | 70 |
| Village Dr. NE&SW | 18W-13S | 70 |
| W. 113th St. E&W | 15W-13S | 71 |
| W. 115th St. E&W | 15W-13S | 71 |
| W. Red Coat Dr. N&S | 16W-15S | 71 |
| Waitkus Dr. E&W | 15W-13S | 71 |
| Walker Rd. N&S | 18W-14S,18W-13S | 70 |
| Walnut St. N&S | 19W-15S | 70 |
| Wild Oak Ct. E&W | 18W-14S | 70 |
| Wildplum Ct. E&W | 18W-14S | 70 |
| Wildwood Dr. NW&SE | 18W-14S | 70 |
| Will Cook Rd. N&S | 15W-15S,15W-13S | 71 |
| Willow N&S | 18W-15S | 70 |
| Woodcrest Ct. N&S | 18W-14S | 70 |
| Woodcrest Ln. N&S | 18W-14S,18W-13S | 70 |
| Woodland Dr. E&W | 18W-15S | 70 |
| Woodlawn N&S | 16W-13S | 71 |
| Woodview Ln. N&S | 15W-13S | 71 |
| 107th St. E&W | 15W-12S | 71 |
| 111th St. E&W | 15W-12S | 71 |
| 117th Pl. E&W | 18W-13S | 70 |
| 117th St. E&W | 18W-13S,17W-13S | 70 |
| 117th St. E&W | 17W-13S | 71 |
| 118th St. E&W | 18W-13S | 70 |
| 119th St. E&W | 18W-13S,15W-13S | 70 |
| 121st St. E&W | 18W-14S | 70 |
| 127th St. E&W | 20W-14S,18W-14S | 70 |
| 127th St. E&W | 17W-14S | 71 |
| 129th St. E&W | 19W-15S | 70 |
| 130th Pl. E&W | 19W-15S | 70 |
| 131st St. E&W | 19W-15S | 70 |
| 131st St. E&W | 18W-15S,15W-15S | 70 |
| 132nd St. E&W | 19W-15S | 70 |
| 133rd Ct. E&W | 19W-15S | 70 |
| 133rd St. E&W | 18W-15S | 70 |

## Leyden Township

| | Grid | Page |
|---|---|---|
| Access Rd. N. N&S | 14W-5S | 40 |
| Access Rd. S. N&S | 14W-5S | 40 |
| Alcoa N&S | 13W-3N | 40 |
| Alta N&S | 13W-3N | 40 |
| Altgeld E&W | 13W-3N | 40 |
| Armitage E&W | 12W-2N | 46 |
| Atlantic N&S | 12W-2N | 46 |
| Bank Dr. N&S | 14W-3N | 40 |
| Barry E&W | 14W-3N | 40 |
| Behrns Dr. E&W | 14W-3N | 40 |
| Belden E&W | 12W-2N | 46 |
| Bellwood N&S | 13W-3N | 40 |
| Calwagner N&S | 14W-5N | 40 |
| Cargo Rd. NW&SE | 14W-5N | 40 |
| Castello N&S | 13W-3N | 40 |
| Charles N&S | 13W-3N | 40 |
| Derrough N&S | 14W-3N | 40 |
| Dickens E&W | 12W-2N | 46 |
| Diversey E&W | 13W-3N | 40 |
| Dora N&S | 12W-2N | 46 |
| Drummond Pl. E&W | 13W-3N | 40 |
| Emerson N&S | 12W-2N | 46 |
| Fairfield N&S | 12W-2N | 46 |
| Fullerton N&S | 13W-3N | 40 |
| Geneva N&S | 13W-3N | 40 |
| Granville N&S | 13W-3N | 40 |
| Gustave N&S | 12W-2N | 46 |
| Haber N&S | 13W-3N | 40 |
| Harold N&S | 13W-3N | 40 |
| Hawthorne N&S | 12W-2N | 46 |
| Hyde Park N&S | 13W-3N | 40 |
| Inland N&S | 14W-3N | 40 |
| Joyce N&S | 13W-3N | 40 |
| Laporte N&S | 13W-3N | 40 |
| Lee N&S | 13W-3N | 40 |
| Louis N&S | 12W-2N,12W-3N | 46 |
| Lyndale E&W | 13W-2N,12W-2N | 46 |
| Mac Arthur Dr. E&W | 13W-3N | 40 |
| Marion N&S | 14W-3N | 40 |
| Martin N&S | 14W-3N | 40 |
| McDonough Rd. N&S | 14W-5N | 40 |
| McKay E&W | 13W-3N | 40 |
| McLean E&W | 12W-2N | 46 |
| Medill E&W | 12W-2N | 46 |
| Melrose E&W | 13W-3N | 40 |
| Montana E&W | 13W-3N | 40 |
| Nevada E&W | 13W-3N | 40 |
| Old Irving Park Rd. E&W | 14W-5N | 40 |
| Palmer E&W | 13W-2N,12W-2N | 46 |
| Parker E&W | 13W-3N,13W-3N | 40 |
| Pearl N&S | 14W-3N | 40 |
| Post Office Rd. NW&SE | 14W-5N | 40 |
| Prater N&S | 14W-3N | 40 |
| Rhodes N&S | 14W-3N | 40 |
| Rowlet N&S | 13W-3N | 40 |
| Roy N&S | 13W-3N | 40 |
| Ruby N&S | 12W-2N | 46 |
| Sandra N&S | 14W-3N | 40 |
| Schubert E&W | 13W-3N | 40 |
| Scott N&S | 12W-2N,12W-2N | 46 |
| Wellington E&W | 13W-3N | 40 |
| Winters Dr. E&W | 13W-3N | 40 |
| Wolf N&S | 14W-3N | 40 |
| Wrightwood E&W | 13W-3N | 40 |

## Lincolnwood

| | Grid | Page |
|---|---|---|
| Albion Av. E&W | 6W-8N,4W-8N | 38 |
| Arthur Av. E&W | 5W-8N,4W-8N | 38 |
| Avers Av., N. N&S | 4W-8N | 38 |
| Carpenter Rd. N&S | 6W-8N | 38 |
| Central Park Av. N&S | 4W-8N | 38 |
| Chase Av. E&W | 5W-8N,4W-9N | 38 |
| Cherry Av. N&S | 4W-8N | 38 |
| Christiana Av. N&S | 4W-8N | 38 |
| Cicero Av. N&S | 5W-8N | 38 |
| Columbia Av. E&W | 5W-8N,4W-8N | 38 |
| Crawford Av. N&S | 5W-8N | 38 |
| Devon Av. E&W | 4W-8N | 38 |
| Dowagiac Av. NW&SE | 6W-8N | 38 |
| Drake Av. N&S | 4W-8N | 38 |
| Estes Av. E&W | 5W-8N | 38 |
| Farwell Av. E&W | 4W-8N | 38 |
| Fitch Av. E&W | 5W-8N,4W-8N | 38 |
| Greenleaf Av. E&W | 5W-8N,4W-8N | 38 |
| Hamlin Av., N. N&S | 4W-8N | 38 |
| Harding Av., N. N&S | 4W-8N | 38 |
| Interstate 94 N&S | 6W-8N | 38 |
| Ionia Av. NW&SE | 6W-8N | 38 |
| Jarlath Av. E&W | 4W-9N | 38 |
| Karlov Av., N. N&S | 5W-8N | 38 |
| Keating Av. N&S | 6W-8N,5W-8N | 38 |
| Kedvale Av., N. N&S | 5W-8N | 38 |
| Keeler Av., N. N&S | 5W-8N | 38 |
| Kenneth Av. N&S | 5W-8N | 38 |
| Kenton Av. N&S | 5W-8N | 38 |
| Keystone Av., N. N&S | 5W-8N | 38 |
| Kilbourn Av. N&S | 5W-8N | 38 |
| Kildare, Av., N. N&S | 5W-8N | 38 |
| Kilpatrick Av. N&S | 5W-8N | 38 |
| Kimball Av. N&S | 4W-8N | 38 |
| Knox Av. N&S | 5W-8N | 38 |
| Kolmar Av. N&S | 5W-8N | 38 |
| Kostner Av., N. N&S | 5W-8N | 38 |
| LaPorte Av. N&S | 6W-8N | 38 |
| Lawndale Av. N. N&S | 4W-8N | 38 |
| Legett NE&SW | 6W-8N | 38 |
| Lemai Av. N&S | 6W-8N | 38 |
| Leroy Av. N&S | 6W-8N | 38 |
| Lincoln Av. NW&SE | 5W-8N | 38 |
| Longmeadow Av. N&S | 6W-8N | 38 |
| Lowell Av. N&S | 5W-8N | 38 |
| Loyola Av. E&W | 5W-8N | 38 |
| Lunt Av. N&S | 5W-8N | 38 |
| McCormick Blvd. N&S | 4W-8N | 38 |
| Minnehaha Av. NE&SW | 6W-8N | 38 |
| Monticello Av. N&S | 4W-8N | 38 |
| Morse Av. E&W | 5W-8N,4W-8N | 38 |
| Navajo Av. NE&SW | 6W-8N | 38 |
| Nokomis Av. NE&SW | 6W-8N | 38 |
| North Shore Av. E&W | 6W-8N,4W-8N | 38 |
| Prairie Rd., E. N&S | 4W-8N | 38 |
| Pratt Av. E&W | 4W-8N | 38 |
| Private Rd. NE&SW | 4W-8N | 38 |
| Proesel Av., N. N&S | 4W-8N | 38 |
| Ramona Av. NE&SW | 6W-8N | 38 |
| Rance Ter. E&W | 4W-8N | 38 |
| Ridgeway Av. N&S | 4W-8N | 38 |
| Rt. 50 N&S | 5W-8N | 38 |
| Sauganash Av. NW&SE | 6W-8N | 38 |
| Schreiber Av. E&W | 4W-8N | 38 |
| Sherwin Av. E&W | 4W-9N | 38 |
| Spaulding Av. N&S | 4W-8N | 38 |
| Spokane Av. NE&SW | 6W-8N | 38 |
| Springfield Av. N&S | 4W-8N | 38 |
| St. Louis Av. N&S | 4W-8N | 38 |
| Touhy Av. E&W | 5W-9N | 38 |
| Tower Cir., W. N&S | 6W-8N | 38 |
| Tower Ct. NE&SW | 6W-8N | 38 |
| Tripp Av., N. N&S | 5W-8N | 38 |
| Trumbull Av. N&S | 4W-8N | 38 |
| U.S. Route 41 SE&NW | 5W-8N,4W-8N | 38 |
| Wallen Av. E&W | 4W-8N | 38 |

## Lynwood

| | Grid | Page |
|---|---|---|
| Alanna Ln. N&S | 4E-25S | 95 |
| Arbon Ct.* NW&SE | 3E-25S | 95 |
| Arroyo Av. N&S | 3E-23S | 95 |
| Bensley Av. N&S | 2E-24S | 95 |
| Berrine Ct.* N&S | 3E-25S | 95 |
| Bozard Ct.* E&W | 3E-25S | 95 |
| Bregenz Ct.* E&W | 3E-25S | 95 |
| Brenner Ct.* E&W | 3E-25S | 95 |
| Brentwood Dr. E&W | 4E-24S | 95 |
| Brentz Ct.* E&W | 3E-25S | 95 |
| Brook Av. N&S | 3E-23S | 89 |
| Burnham Av. N&S | 3E-24S,3E-23S | 95 |
| Catalpa Av. N&S | 3E-25S | 95 |
| Chilton Dr.* NS&EW | 3E-25S | 95 |
| Crescent Av. N&S | 3E-23S | 89 |
| Cypress Av. N&S | 3E-23S | 89 |
| Daron Dr. NS&EW | 4E-25S | 95 |
| Deborah Ct. NE&SW | 4E-25S | 95 |
| Dewey Av. N&S | 2E-23S | 89 |
| Dolphin Av. N&S | 3E-23S | 89 |
| Driftwood Av. N&S | 3E-25S | 95 |
| Duke Dr.* N&S | 3E-25S | 95 |
| Geneva Dr. N&S | 4E-25S | 95 |
| Glarus Ln.* N&S | 3E-25S | 95 |
| Glenwood Dyer Rd. NW&SE | 2E-23S,3E-24S | 95 |
| Joe Orr Rd. E&W | 3E-24S | 95 |
| Juniper Av. N&S | 4E-25S | 95 |
| Kruse Rd. N&S | 4E-24S | 95 |
| Lake Lynwood Dr. N&S | 3E-23S | 89 |
| Lake Park Ct. NE&SW | 3E-23S | 89 |
| Lake Park Dr. NS&EW | 3E-23S | 89 |
| Lake Shore Dr. N&S | 3E-23S | 89 |
| Lakewood Av. N&S | 3E-23S | 89 |
| Laurelwood Cir. N&S | 4E-24S | 95 |
| Lighthouse Ct. NE&SW | 3E-23S | 89 |
| Linda Dr. E&W | 4E-25S | 95 |
| Linda Ln. N&S | 4E-25S | 95 |
| Lisa Ln. NS&EW | 4E-25S | 95 |
| Mariner Ct. N&S | 3E-23S | 89 |
| Marlin Ct. N&S | 3E-23S | 89 |
| Marquette Av. N&S | 3E-24S | 95 |
| Maureen Ct. NE&SW | 3E-23S | 89 |
| Monterey Av. N&S | 3E-23S | 89 |
| Muskegon Av. N&S | 3E-23S | 89 |
| Oakwood Av. N&S | 3E-23S | 89 |
| Orchard Av. N&S | 3E-23S | 89 |
| Park Av. N&S | 3E-23S | 89 |
| Pattie Ln. NW&SE | 3E-23S | 89 |
| Redwood Av. N&S | 3E-23S | 89 |
| Redwood Cir. N&S | 3E-23S | 89 |
| Redwood Ct. N&S | 4E-25S | 95 |
| Rose St. N&S | 2E-23S | 89 |
| Rt. 83 SE&NW | 2E-23S,4E-25S | 89 |
| Sandridge Ct. N&S | 2E-24S | 95 |
| Sandridge Rd. N&S | 2E-24S | 95 |
| Sequoia Av. N&S | 3E-23S | 89 |
| Cir. | 3E-25S | 95 |
| Stony Island Av. N&S | 1E-24S | 95 |
| Surf Ct. E&W | 4E-25S | 95 |
| Terrace Av. NS&EW | 3E-23S | 89 |
| Todd Ter. N&S | 4E-25S | 95 |
| Torrence Av. N&S | 3E-23S | 89 |
| Vale Ct.* N&S | 3E-25S | 95 |
| Vollmer St. E&W | 1E-24S | 95 |
| Westwood Ln. E&W | 4E-25S | 95 |
| Willow Dr. N&S | 4E-25S | 95 |
| Wind Point Ct. E&W | 3E-23S | 89 |
| Zurich Dr. N&S | 4E-25S | 95 |
| 195th Pl. E&W | 2E-23S | 89 |
| 195th St. E&W | 3E-23S | 89 |
| 196th St. E&W | 2E-23S | 89 |
| 197th St. E&W | 2E-23S | 89 |
| 198th Pl. E&W | 2E-23S | 89 |
| 198th St. E&W | 2E-23S,3E-23S | 89 |
| 199th St. E&W | 2E-23S | 89 |
| 200th Pl. E&W | 2E-23S | 89 |
| 200th St. E&W | 3E-23S,4E-23S | 89 |
| 201st Pl. E&W | 3E-23S | 89 |
| 201st St. E&W | 3E-23S,4E-24S | 89 |
| 207th Pl. E&W | 2E-24S | 95 |
| 207th St. E&W | 2E-24S | 95 |
| 208th St. E&W | 4E-25S | 95 |

## Lyons

| | Grid | Page |
|---|---|---|
| Amelia N&S | 9W-4S | 54 |
| Anna N&S | 10W-4S | 53 |
| Cech E&W | 9W-4S | 53 |
| Center N&S | 9W-4S | 54 |
| Clyde N&S | 10W-4S | 53 |
| Collins E&W | 9W-4S | 54 |
| Columbus N&S | 9W-3S | 54 |
| Cracow N&S | 10W-4S | 53 |
| Egandale N&S | 9W-4S | 53 |
| Elm N&S | 9W-4S | 54 |
| Fern N&S | 10W-4S | 53 |
| Fishermans N&S | 9W-4S | 54 |
| Gage N&S | 9W-4S | 54 |
| Harlem N&S | 9W-4S | 53 |
| Hawthorne N&S | 10W-4S | 53 |
| Joliet E&W | 9W-4S | 54 |
| Joliet Av. N&S | 10W-4S | 53 |
| Joliet Rd. N&S | 9W-4S | 53 |
| Kenwood E&W | 10W-4S | 53 |
| Konrad N&S | 10W-4S | 53 |
| Lafayette E&W | 9W-3S | 54 |
| Leland N&S | 10W-4S | 53 |
| Lincoln E&W | 10W-4S | 53 |
| Maple N&S | 9W-4S | 54 |
| Oak N&S | 9W-4S | 54 |
| Oakwind E&W | 10W-4S | 54 |
| Patricia E&W | 10W-4S | 53 |
| Powell N&S | 9W-4S | 54 |
| Prescott N&S | 9W-4S | 54 |
| Pulaski N&S | 10W-4S | 53 |
| Rose N&S | 10W-4S | 53 |
| Salisbury St. N&S | 10W-4S | 53 |
| U.S. Rt. 34 E&W | 10W-4S | 53 |
| Warsaw N&S | 10W-4S | 53 |
| White E&W | 9W-4S | 54 |
| Winchester N&S | 10W-4S | 53 |
| 38th Pl. E&W | 9W-4S | 54 |
| 39th E&W | 9W-3S | 54 |
| 40th E&W | 10W-4S,9W-4S | 53 |
| 41st Ct. E&W | 9W-4S | 54 |
| 41st Pl. E&W | 9W-4S | 54 |
| 42nd E&W | 10W-4S | 53 |
| 42nd Ct. E&W | 9W-4S | 53 |
| 43rd E&W | 9W-4S | 53 |
| 43rd Pl. E&W | 9W-4S | 53 |
| 44th E&W | 10W-4S,9W-4S | 53 |
| 44th Pl. E&W | 9W-4S | 53 |
| 45th E&W | 9W-4S | 53 |
| 45th Ct. E&W | 9W-4S | 53 |
| 46th Pl. E&W | 9W-4S | 53 |
| 47th E&W | 10W-4S | 53 |

## Lyons Township

| | Grid | Page |
|---|---|---|
| Bielby Av. N&S | 13W-9S | 64 |
| Blackstone N&S | 13W-6S | 58 |
| Buege Ln. E&W | 14W-9S | 64 |
| Burr Oak N&S | 12W-8S | 58 |
| Coronet E&W | 14W-9S | 64 |
| Deerpath Tr. NS&EW | 14W-9S | 64 |
| Degener N&S | 14W-1S | 52 |
| Dickens E&W | 14W-1S | 52 |
| Dory Ln. N&S | 14W-9S | 64 |
| Edgewood N&S | 13W-6S | 58 |
| Edgewood View N&S | 13W-8S | 58 |
| Franklin N&S | 13W-6S | 58 |
| Hamilton N&S | 14W-1S | 52 |
| Howard N&S | 13W-6S | 58 |
| Howard Av. N&S | 13W-9S | 64 |
| Interstate 294 N&S | 14W-1S | 52 |
| Jann E&W | 13W-6S | 58 |
| Laurel E&W | 13W-6S | 58 |
| Lincoln E&W | 13W-6S | 58 |
| Linden N&S | 13W-6S | 58 |
| Linn E&W | 13W-6S | 58 |
| Locust N&S | 13W-6S | 58 |
| Lorraine St. N&S | 13W-8S | 58 |
| Marian N&S | 14W-1S | 52 |
| Maridon N&S | 12W-8S | 58 |
| Mt. Lored Ct. E&W | 14W-9S | 64 |
| Northeast Ct. E&W | 13W-5S | 58 |
| Northwest Ct. E&W | 13W-5S | 58 |
| Oak Knoll NE&SW | 14W-9S | 64 |
| Parkside E&W | 13W-6S | 58 |
| Peck N&S | 13W-6S | 58 |
| Sanders N&S | 13W-6S | 58 |
| Southwest Ct. E&W | 13W-6S | 58 |
| Sunset N&S | 13W-6S | 58 |
| Tri-State Tollway N&S | 14W-1S | 52 |
| Tri-State Tollway NW&SE | 12W-8S | 58 |
| Turner N&S | 14W-1S | 52 |
| Vial N&S | 13W-6S | 58 |
| Willow Springs N&S | 13W-6S | 58 |
| 53rd E&W | 13W-5S | 58 |
| 54th E&W | 13W-5S | 58 |
| 54th Pl. E&W | 13W-6S | 58 |
| 55th E&W | 13W-6S | 58 |
| 56th E&W | 13W-6S | 58 |
| 57th E&W | 13W-6S | 58 |
| 58th E&W | 13W-6S | 58 |
| 58th Pl. E&W | 13W-6S | 58 |

| | Grid | Page |
|---|---|---|
| 59th E&W | 13W-6S | 58 |
| 59th Pl. E&W | 13W-6S | 58 |
| 60th E&W | 13W-6S | 58 |
| 61st E&W | 13W-6S | 58 |
| 61st Pl. E&W | 13W-6S | 58 |
| 62nd E&W | 13W-6S | 58 |
| 62nd Pl. E&W | 13W-6S | 58 |
| 63rd Pl. E&W | 13W-7S | 58 |
| 64th E&W | 13W-7S | 58 |
| 74th E&W | 13W-8S | 58 |
| 79th E&W | 13W-8S | 58 |
| 79th St. E&W | 13W-8S,12W-8S | 58 |
| 80th Pl. E&W | 13W-9S | 64 |
| 87th St. E&W | 14W-9S | 64 |

## Maine Township

| | Grid | Page |
|---|---|---|
| Acres Ln. N&S | 12W-10N | 36 |
| Alexis Ct. N&S | 9W-12N | 27 |
| Allison Ct. E&W | 9W-12N | 27 |
| Apple Creek Ln. N&S | 12W-10N | 36 |
| Ashley Ct. E&W | 10W-12N | 27 |
| Aspen Dr. N&S | 11W-11N | 26 |
| Aspen Ln. N&S | 11W-11N | 26 |
| Barberry Ln. E&W | 11W-11N | 26 |
| Bay Colony E&W | 11W-11N | 26 |
| Bianco Ter. N&S | 11W-12N | 26 |
| Bobbie Ln. E&W | 11W-11N | 26 |
| Burton Ln. E&W | 11W-10N | 36 |
| Busse Hwy. NW&SE | 12W-10N | 36 |
| Canavan Rd. N&S | 10W-12N | 27 |
| Cedar Ln. N&S | 11W-11N | 26 |
| Cherry Cir. E&W | 11W-12N,10W-12N | 26 |
| Cherry Ct. NE&SW | 10W-12N | 27 |
| Cherry Ln. NW&SE | 10W-12N | 27 |
| Clancy Dr. N&S | 11W-11N | 26 |
| Crawford Ln. N&S | 11W-12N | 26 |
| Crescent Dr. N&S | 10W-12N | 27 |
| Culver St. N&S | 11W-12N | 26 |
| David Pl. N&S | 11W-12N | 26 |
| Decook Ct., N. E&W | 11W-10N | 36 |
| Decook Ct., S. E&W | 11W-10N | 36 |
| Decook Ln. E&W | 11W-10N | 36 |
| Dee Rd. N&S | 11W-10N,11W-12N | 26 |
| Delphia Av. N&S | 10W-11N | 27 |
| Diane Rd. N&S | 16W-10N | 34 |
| Donald Ct. E&W | 9W-12N | 27 |
| Donald Ter. N&S | 9W-12N | 27 |
| East River Rd. N&S | 12W-10N | 26 |
| Elder Ct. N&S | 10W-12N | 27 |
| Elder Ln. N&S | 10W-12N | 27 |
| Elm Dr. E&W | 10W-11N | 27 |
| Elm Rd. N&S | 15W-8N | 34 |
| Emerson St. E&W | 11W-11N | 26 |
| Fairlawn Dr. E&W | 10W-12N | 27 |
| Farwell Av. E&W | 13W-8N | 35 |
| Fenton Ln. E&W | 11W-10N | 36 |
| Fern Ln. N&S | 11W-11N | 26 |
| Fernwood Dr. NS&EW | 9W-12N | 27 |
| Forest Pl. E&W | 11W-12N | 26 |
| Gayle Ct. N&S | 9W-12N | 27 |
| Greenwood Dr., E. N&S | 10W-11N | 27 |
| Greenwood Dr., W. N&S | 10W-11N | 27 |
| Greenwood Rd. N&S | 10W-11N | 27 |
| Gregory Ln. NW&SE | 10W-12N | 27 |
| Hamilton Dr. E&W | 11W-12N | 26 |
| Hamlin Av. N&S | 11W-11N | 26 |
| Harrison St. E&W | 11W-12N | 26 |
| Hazelwood N&S | 10W-12N | 27 |
| Helen Ct. N&S | 10W-12N | 27 |
| Helen Dr. N&S | 10W-12N | 27 |
| Hollyberry Av. E&W | 11W-11N | 26 |
| Home Av. N&S | 11W-11N | 26 |
| Home Cir. N&S | 11W-11N | 26 |
| Home Ct. N&S | 11W-11N | 26 |
| Home Ter. N&S | 11W-11N | 26 |
| Ironwood Ln. N&S | 11W-11N | 26 |
| James Ct. N&S | 9W-12N | 27 |
| James St. N&S | 9W-12N | 27 |
| Josephine St. E&W | 10W-12N | 27 |
| Judy Dr. E&W | 11W-12N | 26 |
| Julie Dr. N&S | 9W-12N | 27 |
| Kathy Ct. N&S | 11W-12N | 26 |
| Kathy Ln. E&W | 11W-11N | 26 |
| Kenneth Dr. E&W | 11W-12N | 26 |
| Knight Av. N&S | 10W-11N | 27 |
| Lee Ln. N&S | 16W-9N | 34 |
| Leslie Ln. N&S | 11W-12N | 26 |
| Lincoln Av. N&S | 10W-11N | 27 |
| Linda Ct. N&S | 9W-12N | 27 |
| Linnea Ln. E&W | 11W-12N | 26 |
| Lois Dr. N&S | 11W-12N | 27 |
| Lunt Av. E&W | 13W-8N | 35 |
| Lyman Av. N&S | 11W-12N | 26 |
| Lyons St. E&W | 11W-11N,10W-11N | 26 |
| Manor Dr. N&S | 11W-10N | 36 |
| Maple Ln. N&S | 11W-11N | 26 |
| Maple Rd. N&S | 15W-8N | 34 |
| Marcus Ct., E. N&S | 11W-10N | 36 |

| | Grid | Page |
|---|---|---|
| Marcus Ct., W. N&S | 11W-10N | 36 |
| Margail St. N&S | 11W-11N | 26 |
| Margaret St. N&S | 13W-8N | 35 |
| Maynard Ter. E&W | 10W-12N | 27 |
| Meadow Ln. N&S | 11W-11N,11W-12N | 26 |
| Memory Ln. E&W | 10W-12N | 27 |
| Michael Manor N&S | 10W-12N | 27 |
| Morse Av. E&W | 13W-8N | 35 |
| Nellie Ct. N&S | 9W-12N | 27 |
| Noel Av. E&W | 11W-11N | 26 |
| Norma Ct. E&W | 10W-12N | 27 |
| North Shore Dr. E&W | 11W-12N | 26 |
| Oak Ln. N&S | 11W-12N | 26 |
| Oak Pl. N&S | 11W-12N | 26 |
| Oaks Av. E&W | 11W-11N | 26 |
| Park Ln. N&S | 11W-11N | 26 |
| Parkside Dr. N&S | 11W-11N | 26 |
| Pauline Av. E&W | 10W-12N | 27 |
| Poplar Ln. N&S | 10W-12N | 27 |
| Potter Rd. N&S | 11W-12N | 26 |
| Pratt Av. E&W | 13W-8N | 35 |
| Rancho Ln. N&S | 11W-12N | 26 |
| Redling Cir. NS&EW | 11W-12N | 26 |
| Robin Dr. N&S | 11W-11N | 26 |
| Ronald Rd. NS&EW | 10W-12N | 27 |
| Roppollo Dr. N&S | 16W-9N | 34 |
| Sanders Dr. N&S | 11W-11N | 26 |
| Sell Rd. N&S | 15W-8N | 34 |
| Sherry Ln. N&S | 11W-11N | 26 |
| Stacy Ct. N&S | 9W-12N | 27 |
| Stacy St. N&S | 9W-12N | 27 |
| Stevens Dr. N&S | 11W-12N | 26 |
| Sumac Rd. N&S | 11W-11N | 26 |
| Teela Ln. E&W | 12W-12N | 26 |
| Terrace Dr. E&W | 11W-12N | 26 |
| Terrace Pl. N&S | 11W-11N | 26 |
| Thornberry E&W | 10W-12N | 27 |
| Tri-state Tollway N&S | 12W-9N | 36 |
| Twin Oak Ln. N&S | 11W-11N | 26 |
| Tyrell Av. N&S | 11W-10N | 36 |
| Valerie Ct. N&S | 9W-12N | 27 |
| Victor Av. N&S | 9W-12N | 27 |
| Western Av. N&S | 10W-11N | 27 |
| William Av. E&W | 9W-12N | 27 |

## Markham

| | Grid | Page |
|---|---|---|
| Afton Dr. NW&SE | 3W-18S | 81 |
| Albany Av. N&S | 3W-19S,3W-17S | 81 |
| Alta Rd. N&S | 4W-18S | 81 |
| Artesian Av. N&S | 3W-19S | 81 |
| Arthur Ter. E&W | 4W-19S | 81 |
| Ashland Av. N&S | 2W-19S | 81 |
| Belleplaine Dr. NW&SE | 4W-19S | 81 |
| Berkshire Dr. N&S | 4W-19S | 81 |
| Bibb Ln. N&S | 3W-18S | 81 |
| Birch Rd. N&S | 4W-18S | 81 |
| Blackstone Av. E&W | 4W-19S | 81 |
| California Av. N&S | 3W-19S,3W-18S | 81 |
| Calitonia Dr. NW&SE | 3W-18S | 81 |
| Cambridge Ct. N&S | 3W-19S | 81 |
| Cambridge Dr. N&S | 3W-19S | 81 |
| Campbell Av. N&S | 3W-19S | 81 |
| Central Park Av. N&S | 4W-19S,4W-18S | 81 |
| Cherry Ln. N&S | 4W-18S | 81 |
| Cir. | 3W-19S | 81 |
| Clifton Park Av. N&S | 4W-19S,4W-18S | 81 |
| Country Aire Dr. E&W | 4W-18S | 81 |
| Crawford Av. N&S | 4W-19S | 81 |
| Crockett Ln. NW&SE | 3W-18S | 81 |
| Cypress Rd. N&S | 4W-18S | 81 |
| Dan Ryan Expwy. NE&SW | 3W-18S,3W-17S | 81 |
| Dixie Hwy. N&S | 2W-19S | 81 |
| Firestone Dr. N&S | 3W-18S | 81 |
| Francisco Av. N&S | 3W-19S,3W-18S | 81 |
| Grange Dr. NW&SE | 3W-18S | 81 |
| Hamlin Av. N&S | 4W-19S | 81 |
| Harding Av. N&S | 4W-18S | 81 |
| Heather Dr. E&W | 4W-18S | 81 |
| Hermitage Av. N&S | 2W-19S | 81 |
| Hillcrest Dr. NW&SE | 4W-19S | 81 |
| Homan Av. N&S | 4W-19S,4W-17S | 81 |
| Honore St. N&S | 2W-19S | 81 |
| Hoyne Av. N&S | 2W-19S | 81 |
| Interstate 294 N&S | 4W-18S | 81 |
| Interstate 57 NE&SW | 4W-18S | 81 |
| Justine Av. N&S | 1W-19S | 82 |
| Kedvale Av. N&S | 5W-19S | 80 |
| Kedzie Av. N&S | 4W-19S,4W-17S | 81 |
| Kenner Av. N&S | 1W-19S | 82 |
| Laflin St. N&S | 1W-19S | 82 |
| Lancaster Dr. N&S | 4W-19S | 81 |
| Lathop Av. N&S | 1W-19S | 82 |
| Lawndale Av. N&S | 4W-19S,4W-18S | 81 |

| | Grid | Page |
|---|---|---|
| Leavitt Av. N&S | 2W-19S | 81 |
| Lincoln Dr. NE&SW | 3W-18S | 81 |
| Magnolia Dr. E&W | 4W-18S | 81 |
| Maple Ln. NS&EW | 4W-18S | 81 |
| Maplewood Av. N&S | 3W-19S | 81 |
| Marshfield Av. N&S | 3W-19S | 81 |
| Meade Ln. NE&SW | 3W-18S | 81 |
| Millard Av. N&S | 4W-18S | 81 |
| Mozart Av. N&S | 3W-20S,3W-18S | 87 |
| Nottingham Av. E&W | 3W-19S | 81 |
| Oakley Av. N&S | 2W-19S | 81 |
| Oxford Dr., N. NS&EW | 3W-19S | 81 |
| Oxford Dr., S. NS&EW | 3W-19S | 81 |
| Park Av. NE&SW | 1W-19S | 82 |
| Parkside Dr. NW&SE | 3W-18S | 81 |
| Paulina Av. N&S | 2W-19S | 81 |
| Plainview Dr. E&W | 4W-19S | 81 |
| Plymouth Dr. N&S | 3W-19S | 81 |
| Richmond Av. N&S | 3W-20S,3W-18S | 87 |
| Ridgeway Av. N&S | 4W-18S | 81 |
| Rockwell Av. N&S | 3W-19S | 81 |
| Rockwell St. N&S | 3W-19S | 81 |
| Roesner Av. E&W | 4W-18S | 81 |
| Rose Manor Ter. E&W | 4W-19S | 81 |
| Sacramento Av. N&S | 3W-18S,3W-17S | 81 |
| Sawyer Av. N&S | 3W-19S | 81 |
| Sherwood Av. E&W | 3W-19S | 81 |
| Spaulding Av. N&S | 4W-19S,4W-17S | 81 |
| Springfield Av. N&S | 4W-19S | 81 |
| St. Louis Av. N&S | 4W-19S,4W-17S | 81 |
| Stafford Av. N&S | 3W-19S | 81 |
| Sunset Av. E&W | 4W-19S | 81 |
| Sussex Av. NS&EW | 3W-19S | 81 |
| Sussex Ct. NW&SE | 3W-19S | 81 |
| Tri-State Tollway N&S | 3W-19S,3W-18S | 81 |
| Troy Av. N&S | 3W-18S,3W-17S | 81 |
| Trumbull Av. N&S | 4W-19S,4W-17S | 81 |
| Turner Av. N&S | 4W-19S,4W-17S | 81 |
| Washington Dr. NE&SW | 3W-18S | 81 |
| Washtenaw Av. N&S | 3W-18S | 81 |
| Wassel Dr. NW&SE | 3W-18S | 81 |
| Wedgewood Dr. NW&SE | 4W-19S | 81 |
| Western Av. N&S | 3W-19S | 81 |
| Whipple Av. N&S | 3W-18S,3W-17S | 81 |
| Willow Ln. N&S | 4W-18S | 81 |
| Wilshire Av. N&S | 4W-18S | 81 |
| Winchester Av. N&S | 2W-19S | 81 |
| Wolcott Av. N&S | 2W-19S | 81 |
| Wood St. N&S | 2W-19S | 81 |
| 145th Ct. E&W | 6W-17S | 80 |
| 149th St. E&W | 4W-17S | 81 |
| 150th St. E&W | 4W-17S | 81 |
| 151st St. E&W | 3W-17S | 81 |
| 152nd Ct. E&W | 4W-18S | 81 |
| 152nd St. E&W | 4W-18S | 81 |
| 153rd St. E&W | 4W-18S | 81 |
| 154th Pl. E&W | 4W-18S | 81 |
| 154th St. E&W | 4W-18S | 81 |
| 154th Ter. E&W | 4W-18S | 81 |
| 155th St. E&W | 4W-18S,3W-18S | 81 |
| 156th St. E&W | 4W-18S,3W-18S | 81 |
| 157th Pl. E&W | 2W-18S | 81 |
| 157th St. E&W | 4W-18S,3W-18S | 81 |
| 158th St. E&W | 4W-18S,2W-18S | 81 |
| 159th Pl. E&W | 4W-19S | 81 |
| 159th St. E&W | 4W-18S,3W-18S | 81 |
| 160th St. E&W | 4W-19S | 81 |
| 161st Pl. E&W | 2W-19S | 81 |
| 161st St. E&W | 5W-19S,2W-19S | 80 |
| 162nd Pl. E&W | 4W-19S | 81 |
| 162nd St. E&W | 4W-19S,2W-19S | 81 |
| 163rd Pl. E&W | 3W-19S,2W-19S | 81 |
| 163rd St. E&W | 4W-19S,2W-19S | 81 |
| 164th St. E&W | 4W-19S,1W-19S | 81 |
| 165th St. E&W | 4W-19S,2W-19S | 81 |
| 166th St. E&W | 4W-19S,3W-19S | 81 |
| 167th St. E&W | 4W-19S,2W-19S | 81 |
| 168th St. E&W | 3W-20S | 87 |

## Matteson

| | Grid | Page |
|---|---|---|
| Academy Av. N&S | 5W-24S | 92 |
| Allemong Dr. E&W | 7W-24S | 91 |
| Amherst Pl. E&W | 7W-25S | 91 |

| | Grid | Page |
|---|---|---|
| Apple Hill Ln. E&W | 7W-24S | 91 |
| Applewood Ln. E&W | 5W-25S | 92 |
| Aspen Ln. E&W | 7W-24S | 91 |
| Basswood Rd. E&W | 6W-24S | 91 |
| Beaver Dam Rd. E&W | 7W-24S | 91 |
| Beechwood Ct. NE&SW | 6W-24S | 91 |
| Beechwood Rd. E&W | 7W-24S,6W-24S | 91 |
| Birchwood Dr. N&S | 6W-24S | 91 |
| Bradley Av. N&S | 6W-25S | 91 |
| Briarwood Ct. N&S | 7W-24S,6W-24S | 91 |
| Bridgewood Ct. E&W | 6W-24S | 91 |
| Bridgewood Rd. N&S | 6W-24S | 91 |
| Butterfield Pkwy. N&S | 4W-25S | 92 |
| Cambridge Av. N&S | 6W-25S | 91 |
| Campus Av. N&S | 5W-25S | 92 |
| Carnation Ln. N&S | 5W-25S | 92 |
| Cedarwood Ln. E&W | 5W-25S | 92 |
| Central Av. N&S | 7W-26S,6W-24S | 91 |
| Charles St. N&S | 4W-26S | 92 |
| Charleston Rd. E&W | 5W-26S | 92 |
| Churn Rd. NW&SE | 7W-24S | 91 |
| Cicero Av. N&S | 6W-26S,6W-24S | 91 |
| Cloverleaf Rd. N&S | 7W-24S | 91 |
| Colgate Ln. N&S | 7W-25S | 91 |
| College Av. N&S | 5W-25S | 92 |
| Columbine Ln. NS&EW | 5W-24S | 92 |
| Cornell Way E&W | 7W-25S | 91 |
| Cornfield Rd. N&S | 7W-25S | 91 |
| Corporate Lakes Dr. N&S | 6W-25S,6W-24S | 91 |
| Crawford Av. N&S | 5W-26S,5W-25S | 92 |
| Crestwood Ct. NW&SE | 7W-24S | 91 |
| Crestwood Rd. NE&SW | 7W-24S | 91 |
| Dartmouth Av. N&S | 7W-25S | 91 |
| Deerpath Rd. N&S | 4W-25S | 92 |
| Dettmering Dr. N&S | 4W-25S | 92 |
| Drake Ln. E&W | 6W-25S | 91 |
| Duke Dr. E&W | 6W-25S | 91 |
| Edgewood Rd. N&S | 7W-24S | 91 |
| Elm Ln. E&W | 7W-24S | 91 |
| Elmwood Ln. E&W | 5W-25S | 92 |
| Fernwood Ct. E&W | 7W-25S | 91 |
| Fox Run Rd. E&W | 7W-24S | 91 |
| Front St. E&W | 4W-25S | 92 |
| Georgetown Dr. E&W | 6W-25S | 91 |
| Goldenrod Cir. N&S | 5W-24S | 92 |
| Hanson Ln. N&S | 6W-25S | 91 |
| Harvard Ln. N&S | 6W-25S | 91 |
| Highland Av. N&S | 5W-25S | 92 |
| Highland Rd. N&S | 7W-24S | 91 |
| Holiday Plaza Dr. NE&SW | 6W-26S | 91 |
| Homeland Rd. N&S | 5W-25S | 92 |
| Huntingwood Rd. N&S | 7W-24S | 91 |
| Interstate 57 N&S | 6W-26S,6W-24S | 91 |
| Jean Av. N&S | 4W-25S | 92 |
| Jeffrey Dr. N&S | 4W-25S | 92 |
| Keeler Av. N&S | 5W-25S,5W-24S | 92 |
| Kildare Av. N&S | 5W-25S | 92 |
| Kildare Ct. E&W | 5W-25S | 92 |
| Kostner Av. N&S | 5W-26S,5W-25S | 92 |
| Larkspur Ln. NS&EW | 5W-24S | 92 |
| Lincoln Hwy. E&W | 6W-25S,4W-25S | 91 |
| Lincoln Mall Dr. NS&EW | 5W-25S | 92 |
| Lindenwood Dr. E&W | 5W-25S | 92 |
| Locust St. N&S | 4W-26S,4W-25S | 92 |
| Macon Rd. N&S | 5W-26S | 92 |
| Main St. N&S | 4W-26S,4W-25S | 92 |
| Maple St. N&S | 4W-26S,4W-25S | 92 |
| Marsh Ln. E&W | 7W-24S | 91 |
| Mary Todd Cir. E&W | 5W-26S | 92 |
| McClellan Dr. NE&SW | 5W-26S | 92 |
| Morning Glory Dr. E&W | 5W-24S | 92 |
| Notre Dame Dr. N&S | 6W-25S | 91 |
| Oak St. N&S | 4W-26S,4W-25S | 92 |
| Oakhurst Ln. N&S | 7W-24S | 91 |
| Oakhurst Rd. N&S | 7W-24S | 91 |
| Oakview N&S | 7W-24S | 91 |
| Oakwood Ln. N&S | 5W-24S | 92 |
| Old Creek Ln. E&W | 5W-26S | 92 |
| Old Farm Rd. N&S | 7W-24S | 91 |
| Old Meadow Rd. N&S | 7W-24S | 91 |

| | Grid | Page |
|---|---|---|
| Old Mill Rd. NW&SE | 7W-24S | 91 |
| Olympian Way NE&SW | 4W-25S | 92 |
| Oriole Rd. N&S | 7W-24S | 91 |
| Oxford Av. N&S | 6W-25S | 91 |
| Partridge Rd. N&S | 7W-24S | 91 |
| Pheasant Rd. N&S | 7W-24S | 91 |
| Phlox Cir. NW&SE | 5W-25S | 92 |
| Pinewood Ln. E&W | 5W-25S | 92 |
| Post Av. N&S | 6W-25S | 91 |
| Primrose Cir. E&W | 5W-25S | 92 |
| Primrose Ln. NS&EW | 5W-24S | 92 |
| Princeton Av. N&S | 7W-25S | 91 |
| Purdue Ln. N&S | 6W-25S | 91 |
| Quail Run Rd. N&S | 7W-24S | 91 |
| Quinn Av. N&S | 4W-25S | 92 |
| Red Barn Rd. N&S | 7W-24S | 91 |
| Richmond Ct. E&W | 5W-26S | 92 |
| Richmond Rd. N&S | 5W-26S | 92 |
| Richton Rd. N&S | 4W-26S | 92 |
| Ridgeland Av. N&S | 7W-24S | 91 |
| Rose Ln. NW&SE | 5W-25S | 92 |
| Rt. 50 N&S | 6W-26S,6W-24S | 91 |
| School Av. N&S | 5W-25S | 92 |
| Southwick Dr. E&W | 6W-26S | 91 |
| Spring Ln. E&W | 7W-24S | 91 |
| Sprucewood Ln. E&W | 5W-25S | 92 |
| St. Lawrence Av. E&W | 5W-25S | 92 |
| Streamwood Ln. E&W | 7W-24S | 91 |
| Sumter Dr. E&W | 5W-26S | 92 |
| Sunflower Rd. E&W | 7W-24S | 91 |
| Timberlane Dr. NS&EW | 7W-24S | 91 |
| Tower Av. N&S | 4W-25S | 92 |
| U.S. Route 30 E&W | 6W-25S,4W-25S | 91 |
| University Av. N&S | 5W-25S | 92 |
| Violet Ln. N&S | 5W-25S | 92 |
| Vollmer Rd. E&W | 7W-23S,6W-23S | 86 |
| Washington Av. E&W | 5W-25S | 92 |
| Wedgewood Ct. E&W | 7W-24S | 91 |
| Wheatfield N&S | 7W-24S | 91 |
| White Birch Ln. E&W | 7W-24S | 91 |
| White Oaks Rd. N&S | 7W-24S | 91 |
| Willow Ct. E&W | 7W-24S | 91 |
| Willow Rd. N&S | 7W-24S | 91 |
| Wolf Rd. N&S | 7W-24S | 91 |
| Woodgate Rd. E&W | 7W-24S | 91 |
| Yale Ln. E&W | 6W-24S | 91 |
| 205th Pl. E&W | 6W-24S | 91 |
| 207th St. E&W | 5W-24S | 92 |
| 211th Pkwy. E&W | 7W-25S | 91 |
| 211th Pl. E&W | 4W-25S | 92 |
| 212th Pl. E&W | 4W-25S | 92 |
| 213th Pl. E&W | 4W-25S | 92 |
| 213th St. E&W | 4W-25S | 92 |
| 214th Pl. E&W | 4W-25S | 92 |
| 214th St. E&W | 4W-25S | 92 |
| 215th St. E&W | 4W-25S | 92 |
| 216th Pl. E&W | 4W-26S | 92 |
| 216th St. E&W | 5W-26S,4W-26S | 92 |
| 217th St. E&W | 4W-26S | 92 |
| 218th Pl. E&W | 4W-26S | 92 |
| 218th St. E&W | 4W-26S | 92 |
| 219th St. E&W | 4W-26S | 92 |

## Maywood

| | Grid | Page |
|---|---|---|
| Adams E&W | 11W-0S | 47 |
| Augusta Ln. E&W | 10W-1N | 47 |
| Bataan E&W | 11W-0S | 47 |
| Congress E&W | 10W-0S | 47 |
| DesPlaines N&S | 10W-0N | 47 |
| Dwight D. Eisenhower Expwy. E&W | 11W-0S,10W-0S | 47 |
| Erie E&W | 10W-0N | 47 |
| Fillmore E&W | 11W-0S | 47 |
| Green E&W | 10W-0S | 47 |
| Greenwood N&S | 10W-0S | 47 |
| Harrison E&W | 10W-0S | 47 |
| Harvard E&W | 11W-0S,10W-0S | 47 |
| Huron E&W | 10W-0N | 47 |
| Iowa E&W | 10W-1N | 47 |
| Lexington E&W | 11W-0S,11W-0S | 47 |
| Madison E&W | 11W-0N | 47 |
| Main E&W | 10W-0N | 47 |
| Maple E&W | 10W-0N | 47 |
| Maybrook Dr. E&W | 10W-0S | 47 |
| Maybrook Dr. E&W | 10W-0S | 48 |
| Maywood Dr. E&W | 11W-0S | 47 |
| Monroe E&W | 10W-0S | 47 |
| Oak E&W | 11W-0N | 47 |
| Ohio E&W | 10W-0N | 47 |
| Orchard N&S | 10W-0S | 47 |
| Pine E&W | 10W-0S | 47 |
| Quincy E&W | 10W-0S | 47 |
| Railroad E&W | 11W-0N | 47 |
| Randolph E&W | 10W-1N | 47 |
| Rice E&W | 10W-1N | 47 |
| School E&W | 11W-0N | 47 |
| South Maywood Dr. E&W | 11W-0S | 47 |
| St. Charles Rd. E&W | 11W-0N | 47 |
| Superior E&W | 10W-0N | 47 |

| | Grid | Page |
|---|---|---|
| Van Buren E&W | 11W-0S | 47 |
| Walnut E&W | 10W-0N | 47 |
| Walton E&W | 10W-1N | 47 |
| Warren E&W | 10W-0N | 47 |
| Washington Blvd. E&W | 11W-0N | 47 |
| Wilcox E&W | 10W-0S | 47 |
| 1st N&S | 10W-0S | 47 |
| 2nd N&S | 10W-0S,10W-1N | 47 |
| 3rd N&S | 10W-0S,10W-1N | 47 |
| 4th N&S | 10W-0S | 47 |
| 4th N&S | 10W-0S,10W-1N | 47 |
| 5th N&S | 10W-0S,10W-1N | 47 |
| 6th N&S | 10W-0S,10W-1N | 47 |
| 7th N&S | 10W-0S,10W-1N | 47 |
| 8th N&S | 10W-0S,10W-1N | 47 |
| 9th N&S | 11W-0S,10W-0N | 47 |
| 10th N&S | 11W-0S | 47 |
| 11th N&S | 11W-0S | 47 |
| 12th N&S | 11W-0S | 47 |
| 17th N&S | 11W-0S | 47 |
| 18th N&S | 11W-0S | 47 |
| 19th N&S | 11W-0S | 47 |
| 20th N&S | 11W-0S | 47 |
| 21st N&S | 11W-0S | 47 |

## McCook

| | Grid | Page |
|---|---|---|
| Clyde N&S | 10W-5S | 59 |
| Egandale N&S | 10W-5S | 59 |
| Grand N&S | 10W-5S | 59 |
| Joliet SW&NE | 11W-6S | 58 |
| Lawndale N&S | 10W-5S | 59 |
| Riverside N&S | 10W-5S | 59 |
| 49th E&W | 10W-5S | 59 |
| 50th E&W | 10W-5S | 59 |
| 53rd E&W | 10W-5S | 59 |
| 55th E&W | 11W-5S | 58 |

## Melrose Park

| | Grid | Page |
|---|---|---|
| Andy Dr. E&W | 10W-1N | 47 |
| Armitage E&W | 10W-2N | 47 |
| Augusta E&W | 11W-1N | 47 |
| Bloomingdale E&W | 12W-1N,11W-2N | 46 |
| Braddock E&W | 10W-1N | 47 |
| Broadway N&S | 11W-1N | 47 |
| Cary N&S | 13W-1N | 46 |
| Channing Ct. N&S | 10W-1N | 47 |
| Charleston Ct. N&S | 10W-1N | 47 |
| Chicago E&W | 11W-1N | 47 |
| Clay Ct. N&S | 10W-1N | 47 |
| Clinton Ct. N&S | 10W-1N | 47 |
| Concord E&W | 10W-1N | 47 |
| Cornell N&S | 12W-2N | 46 |
| Cortez E&W | 11W-1N | 47 |
| Davis E&W | 10W-1N | 47 |
| Division E&W | 12W-1N,11W-1N | 46 |
| Doris St. E&W | 10W-1N | 47 |
| Elsie Dr. E&W | 11W-2N | 47 |
| George N&S | 11W-2N | 47 |
| Grant N&S | 11W-1N | 47 |
| Haddon E&W | 11W-1N | 47 |
| Harold N&S | 13W-1N | 46 |
| Hawthorne N&S | 12W-2N | 46 |
| Helen Dr. E&W | 11W-1N | 47 |
| Hirsch E&W | 12W-1N,11W-1N | 46 |
| Indian Boundary Dr. N&S | 12W-2N | 46 |
| Iowa E&W | 11W-1N | 47 |
| James Pl. E&W | 13W-2N | 46 |
| Janice N&S | 13W-2N | 46 |
| Lake E&W | 11W-1N | 47 |
| Le Moyne E&W | 11W-1N | 47 |
| Lee N&S | 11W-1N | 47 |
| Main E&W | 11W-0N | 47 |
| Mannheim N&S | 13W-2N | 46 |
| Nichols Ln. E&W | 10W-1N | 47 |
| North Av. E&W | 11W-2N | 47 |
| Norwood E&W | 11W-1N | 47 |
| Park Dr. N&S | 11W-1N | 47 |
| Porter St. E&W | 11W-1N | 47 |
| Rice E&W | 11W-1N | 47 |
| Roberta N&S | 13W-1N | 46 |
| Rose St. E&W | 11W-1N | 47 |
| Rt. 64 E&W | 12W-2N | 46 |
| Ruby E&W | 12W-2N | 46 |
| Sherman E&W | 10W-1N | 47 |
| Silver St. E&W | 11W-1N | 47 |
| Thomas E&W | 11W-1N | 47 |
| Walton E&W | 11W-1N | 47 |
| Winston Dr. NS&EW | 11W-1N,10W-1N | 47 |
| 9th N&S | 11W-1N | 47 |
| 10th N&S | 11W-1N | 47 |
| 11th N&S | 11W-1N | 47 |
| 12th N&S | 11W-1N | 47 |
| 13th E&W | 12W-1N | 46 |
| 13th N&S | 11W-1N | 47 |
| 14th N&S | 11W-1N | 47 |
| 15th N&S | 11W-1N,11W-2N | 47 |
| 16th N&S | 11W-1N | 47 |
| 17th N&S | 11W-1N,11W-2N | 47 |
| 18th N&S | 11W-1N,11W-2N | 47 |
| 19th N&S | 11W-2N | 47 |
| 20th N&S | 11W-1N | 47 |
| 21st N&S | 11W-1N | 47 |
| 22nd N&S | 11W-0N,11W-1N | 47 |
| 23rd N&S | 11W-0N,11W-1N | 47 |
| 24th N&S | 11W-0N,11W-1N | 47 |
| 25th N&S | 12W-1N | 46 |
| 30th N&S | 12W-1N | 46 |
| 31st N&S | 12W-1N | 46 |
| 32nd N&S | 12W-1N | 46 |
| 33rd N&S | 12W-1N | 46 |
| 34th N&S | 12W-1N | 46 |
| 35th N&S | 12W-1N | 46 |
| 36th N&S | 12W-1N | 46 |
| 46th N&S | 13W-1N | 46 |
| 47th N&S | 13W-1N | 46 |

## Merrionette Park

| | Grid | Page |
|---|---|---|
| Albany Dr. N&S | 3W-13S | 75 |
| Central Park Av. N&S | 4W-14S | 75 |
| Homan Av. N&S | 4W-13S | 75 |
| Kedzie Av. N&S | 4W-13S | 75 |
| Mahoney Dr. N&S | 3W-13S | 75 |
| Meadowlane Dr. E&W | 3W-13S | 75 |
| Merrion Ln. NS&EW | 4W-13S | 75 |
| Morgan Park Av. E&W | 3W-13S | 75 |
| Palisades Dr. E&W | 3W-13S | 75 |
| Park Lane Dr. E&W | 3W-13S | 75 |
| Sacramento Dr. N&S | 3W-13S | 75 |
| Troy Dr. N&S | 3W-13S | 75 |
| Whipple Dr. N&S | 3W-13S | 75 |
| Whipple St. N&S | 3W-13S | 75 |
| 113th Pl. E&W | 3W-13S | 75 |
| 113th St. E&W | 3W-13S | 75 |
| 114th Pl. E&W | 3W-13S | 75 |
| 114th St. E&W | 3W-13S | 75 |
| 115th St. E&W | 3W-13S | 75 |
| 116th Pl. E&W | 3W-13S | 75 |
| 118th St. E&W | 3W-13S | 75 |
| 119th St. E&W | 4W-13S,3W-13S | 75 |

## Midlothian

| | Grid | Page |
|---|---|---|
| Abbottsford Rd. NE&SW | 4W-17S | 81 |
| Avers Av. N&S | 4W-18S,4W-17S | 81 |
| Central Av. N&S | 7W-17S | 80 |
| Central Park Av. N&S | 4W-17S | 81 |
| Cicero Av. N&S | 5W-17S | 80 |
| Clifton Park Av. N&S | 4W-17S | 81 |
| Concordia Ct. E&W | 5W-17S | 80 |
| Country Club Dr. NW&SE | 6W-17S | 80 |
| Crawford Av. N&S | 5W-17S | 80 |
| Hamlin Av. N&S | 4W-18S,4W-17S | 81 |
| Harding Av. N&S | 4W-18S | 81 |
| Homan Av. N&S | 4W-17S | 81 |
| Interstate 294 E&W | 4W-17S | 81 |
| Karlov Av. N&S | 5W-17S | 80 |
| Keating Av. N&S | 5W-17S | 80 |
| Kedvale Av. N&S | 5W-17S | 80 |
| Kedzie Av. N&S | 4W-17S | 81 |
| Keeler Av. N&S | 5W-17S | 80 |
| Kenneth Av. N&S | 5W-17S | 80 |
| Kenton Av. N&S | 5W-17S | 80 |
| Keystone Av. N&S | 5W-17S | 80 |
| Kilbourn Av. N&S | 5W-18S,5W-17S | 80 |
| Kildare Av. N&S | 5W-17S | 80 |
| Kilpatrick Av. N&S | 5W-17S | 80 |
| Knox Av. N&S | 5W-17S | 80 |
| Kolin Av. N&S | 5W-17S | 80 |
| Kolmar Av. N&S | 5W-17S | 80 |
| Kostner Av. N&S | 5W-17S | 80 |
| Lacrosse Av. N&S | 6W-17S | 80 |
| Lamon Av. N&S | 6W-17S | 80 |
| Laporte Av. N&S | 6W-17S | 80 |
| Lawndale Av. N&S | 4W-18S,4W-17S | 81 |
| Linder Av. N&S | 6W-17S | 80 |
| Long Av. N&S | 6W-17S | 80 |
| Maple Ln. NS&SE | 6W-17S | 80 |
| Midlothian Turnpike NE&SW | 6W-16S | 74 |
| Millard Av. N&S | 4W-18S,4W-17S | 81 |
| Raday Dr. N&S | 4W-18S | 81 |
| Rexford Rd. NE&SW | 4W-17S | 81 |
| Ridgeway Av. N&S | 4W-18S,4W-17S | 81 |
| Rt. 50 N&S | 5W-17S | 80 |
| Rt. 83 N&S | 5W-17S | 80 |
| Saint Louis Av. N&S | 4W-17S | 81 |
| Sawyer Av. N&S | 4W-17S | 81 |
| Spaulding Av. N&S | 4W-17S | 81 |
| Springfield Av. N&S | 4W-18S,4W-17S | 81 |
| Terrace Ln. NE&SW | 5W-17S | 80 |
| Tri State Tollway E&W | 4W-17S | 81 |
| Tripp Av. N&S | 5W-17S | 80 |
| Trumbull Av. N&S | 4W-17S | 81 |
| Turner Av. N&S | 4W-17S | 81 |
| Waverly Av. N&S | 5W-18S,4W-18S | 80 |
| 143rd Pl. E&W | 6W-17S | 80 |
| 143rd St. E&W | 5W-16S | 74 |
| 144th St. E&W | 6W-17S,4W-17S | 80 |
| 145th St. E&W | 6W-17S,4W-17S | 80 |
| 146th St. E&W | 5W-17S,4W-17S | 80 |
| 147th Ct. E&W | 6W-17S | 80 |
| 147th Pl. E&W | 6W-17S | 81 |
| 147th St. E&W | 6W-17S,4W-17S | 80 |
| 148th Ct. E&W | 6W-17S | 80 |
| 148th Pl. E&W | 4W-17S | 81 |
| 148th St. E&W | 5W-17S,4W-17S | 80 |
| 149th St. E&W | 5W-17S,4W-17S | 80 |
| 150th St. E&W | 5W-17S,4W-17S | 80 |
| 151st Ct. E&W | 5W-18S | 80 |
| 151st St. E&W | 5W-17S,4W-17S | 80 |
| 152nd Pl. E&W | 4W-18S | 81 |
| 152nd St. E&W | 5W-18S,4W-18S | 80 |
| 153rd Pl. E&W | 4W-18S | 81 |
| 153rd St. E&W | 4W-18S | 81 |
| 154th St. E&W | 4W-18S | 81 |

## Morton Grove

| | Grid | Page |
|---|---|---|
| Albert Av. E&W | 8W-11N | 27 |
| Arcadia Av. E&W | 9W-11N | 27 |
| Austin Av. N&S | 7W-10N,7W-11N | 37 |
| Beckwith Rd. E&W | 9W-11N,8W-11N | 27 |
| Belleforte Av. N&S | 8W-11N | 27 |
| Birch Av. N&S | 8W-11N | 27 |
| Callie Av. N&S | 7W-10N | 37 |
| Cameron Ln. NW&SE | 9W-11N | 27 |
| Capri Ln. E&W | 7W-11N | 28 |
| Capulina Av. E&W | 7W-11N | 37 |
| Carol Av. E&W | 7W-10N | 37 |
| Central Av. N&S | 7W-10N,7W-11N | 37 |
| Cherry Av. N&S | 8W-11N | 27 |
| Chestnut St. E&W | 8W-10N | 37 |
| Church St. E&W | 9W-11N,7W-11N | 27 |
| Church Ter. E&W | 9W-11N | 27 |
| Churchill Av. N&S | 8W-11N | 27 |
| Churchill St. E&W | 8W-11N | 27 |
| Cleveland St. E&W | 7W-10N | 37 |
| Crain St. E&W | 7W-10N | 37 |
| Davis St. E&W | 9W-11N,7W-11N | 27 |
| Dempster St. E&W | 9W-11N,7W-11N | 27 |
| Edens Expy. N&S | 7W-10N | 37 |
| Eldorado Dr. E&W | 8W-11N | 27 |
| Elm St. E&W | 8W-10N,7W-10N | 37 |
| Emerson St. E&W | 9W-11N | 27 |
| Enfield Av. N&S | 9W-11N,8W-11N | 27 |
| Fernald Av. N&S | 7W-10N | 37 |
| Ferris Av. N&S | 7W-11N | 37 |
| Forest Dr. E&W | 7W-11N | 28 |
| Foster Av. E&W | 9W-11N | 27 |
| Georgiana Av. N&S | 7W-10N | 37 |
| Golf Rd. E&W | 9W-11N | 27 |
| Greenwood Av. E&W | 9W-11N,7W-11N | 27 |
| Gross Point Rd. NE&SW | 6W-10N | 38 |
| Grove St. E&W | 7W-10N | 37 |
| Hamilton N&S | 6W-10N | 38 |
| Harms Rd. NW&SE | 6W-11N | 28 |
| Hazel St. E&W | 8W-11N | 27 |
| Henning Ct. N&S | 7W-10N | 37 |
| Hoffman Av. N&S | 8W-11N | 27 |
| Hoffman Ct. N&S | 8W-11N | 27 |
| Ida Ln. N&S | 8W-11N | 27 |
| Interstate 94 N&S | 7W-10N | 37 |
| Keeney Ct. N&S | 7W-10N | 37 |
| Keeney St. E&W | 7W-10N,6W-10N | 37 |
| Kirk St. E&W | 7W-9N | 37 |
| Lake St. E&W | 9W-11N,7W-11N | 27 |
| Launa Av. N&S | 9W-11N | 27 |
| Lee St. E&W | 7W-10N | 37 |
| Lehigh Av. NW&SE | 8W-11N,7W-10N | 27 |
| Lillibet Ter. NE&SW | 7W-10N | 37 |
| Lincoln Av. E&W | 7W-11N | 37 |
| Linder Av. N&S | 6W-9N | 38 |
| Long Av. N&S | 6W-10N | 38 |
| Lotus Av. N&S | 6W-9N | 38 |
| Luna Av. N&S | 6W-9N,6W-11N | 38 |
| Lyons Av. N&S | 6W-10N | 28 |
| Lyons St. E&W | 9W-11N,6W-11N | 27 |
| Madison Ct. E&W | 7W-10N | 37 |
| Madison St. E&W | 7W-10N | 37 |
| Main St. E&W | 7W-10N | 37 |
| Major Av. N&S | 7W-10N,7W-11N | 37 |
| Mango Av. N&S | 7W-10N,7W-11N | 37 |
| Mansfield Av. N&S | 7W-10N,7W-11N | 37 |
| Maple Dr. E&W | 9W-11N | 27 |
| Maple St. E&W | 9W-11N,8W-11N | 27 |
| Marion Av. N&S | 8W-11N | 27 |
| Marmora Av. N&S | 7W-10N | 37 |
| Mason Av. N&S | 7W-10N,7W-11N | 37 |
| McVicker Av. N&S | 7W-10N | 37 |
| Meade Av. N&S | 7W-11N | 28 |
| Menard Av. N&S | 7W-10N,7W-11N | 37 |
| Merrill N&S | 9W-11N | 27 |
| Michael Av. E&W | 9W-11N | 27 |
| Michael Ct. N&S | 9W-11N | 27 |
| Monroe Ct. E&W | 7W-10N | 37 |
| Monroe St. E&W | 7W-10N | 37 |
| Moody Av. N&S | 7W-11N | 28 |
| Morton N&S | 7W-10N | 37 |
| Mulford St. E&W | 6W-9N | 38 |
| Murray Ct. N&S | 9W-11N | 27 |
| Nagle Av. N&S | 8W-9N | 37 |
| Narragansett Av. N&S | 7W-10N,7W-11N | 37 |
| Nashville Av. N&S | 8W-11N | 27 |
| Natchez N&S | 8W-11N | 27 |
| Natchez Av. N&S | 8W-9N | 37 |
| National Av. N&S | 8W-11N | 27 |
| Natoma Av. N&S | 8W-11N | 27 |
| Neenah Av. N&S | 8W-11N | 27 |
| New England Av. N&S | 8W-11N | 27 |
| Newcastle Av. N&S | 8W-11N | 27 |
| Normandy Av. N&S | 8W-11N | 27 |
| Oak Park Av. N&S | 8W-11N | 27 |
| Oak St. E&W | 8W-10N | 37 |
| Oakton St. E&W | 9W-11N | 27 |
| Oconto Av. N&S | 9W-11N | 27 |
| Octavia Av. N&S | 9W-11N | 27 |
| Odell Av. N&S | 9W-11N | 27 |
| Oketo Av. N&S | 9W-11N | 27 |
| Olcott N&S | 9W-11N | 27 |
| Oleander N&S | 9W-11N | 27 |
| Oliphant Av. N&S | 9W-11N | 27 |
| Oriole Av. N&S | 9W-11N | 27 |
| Osceola Av. N&S | 9W-11N | 27 |
| Oswego St. N&S | 9W-11N | 27 |
| Ottawa Av. N&S | 9W-11N | 27 |
| Overhill Av. N&S | 9W-11N | 27 |
| Ozanam Av. N&S | 9W-11N | 27 |
| Ozark Av. N&S | 9W-11N | 27 |
| Palma Ln. E&W | 9W-11N,8W-11N | 27 |
| Park Av. N&S | 7W-10N | 37 |
| Park Av., S. E&W | 7W-10N | 37 |
| Parkside Av. N&S | 7W-10N,7W-11N | 37 |
| Ponto St. E&W | 9W-11N | 27 |
| Reba Ct. N&S | 7W-10N | 37 |
| Reba St. E&W | 7W-10N | 37 |
| River Dr. NS&EW | 7W-10N | 37 |
| Rt. 43 N&S | 8W-11N | 27 |
| Rt. 58 E&W | 8W-11N,7W-11N | 27 |
| Sayre Av. N&S | 8W-11N | 27 |
| School St. N&S | 7W-10N | 37 |
| Shermer Rd. NW&SE | 8W-11N | 27 |
| Smithwood Dr. E&W | 7W-10N | 37 |
| Suffield Ct. E&W | 9W-11N | 27 |
| Suffield St. E&W | 9W-11N | 27 |
| Theobald Rd. NE&SW | 7W-10N | 37 |
| U.S. Route 14 E&W | 9W-11N | 27 |
| Warren Ct. E&W | 7W-10N | 37 |
| Warren St. E&W | 7W-10N | 37 |
| Washington St. E&W | 7W-10N,6W-10N | 37 |
| Waukegan Rd. N&S | 8W-11N | 27 |
| Wilson Ter. E&W | 9W-11N,8W-11N | 27 |

## Mt. Prospect

| | Grid | Page |
|---|---|---|
| Addison Ct. E&W | 16W-10N | 34 |
| Albert St. N&S | 15W-11N,15W-12N | 25 |
| Albion Ln. E&W | 14W-14N | 25 |
| Alder Ln. E&W | 14W-14N | 25 |
| Algonquin Rd. NW&SE | 17W-11N,16W-10N | 24 |
| Algonquin Tr. N&S | 17W-11N | 24 |
| Almond Ln. E&W | 13W-14N | 26 |
| Althea Dr. N&S | 13W-14N | 26 |
| Andoa Ln. N&S | 13W-15N | 16 |
| Ann Marie N&S | 17W-10N | 34 |
| Apache Ln. E&W | 13W-14N | 26 |
| Apple Ct. N&S | 16W-14N | 25 |
| Apricot Ct. NW&SE | 16W-14N | 25 |
| Aralia Dr. N&S | 13W-15N | 16 |
| Arbor Ct. N&S | 17W-11N | 24 |
| Ardyce Ln. E&W | 14W-13N | 25 |
| Ash Dr. E&W | 16W-11N | 25 |
| Aspen Dr. E&W | 13W-15N | 16 |
| Audrey Ln. N&S | 17W-12N | 24 |
| Autumn Ln. NW&SE | 14W-13N | 25 |
| Azalea Ln. E&W | 13W-14N | 26 |
| Azalea Pl. E&W | 13W-14N | 26 |
| Aztec Ln. E&W | 13W-15N | 16 |
| Badger Rd. N&S | 16W-10N | 34 |
| Barberry Ln. N&S | 14W-14N | 25 |
| Basswood Ln. N&S | 13W-14N | 26 |
| Beech Rd. N&S | 13W-15N | 16 |
| Beechwood Dr. N&S | 17W-11N | 24 |
| Belaire St. N&S | 16W-11N | 25 |
| Bershire Ln. E&W | 15W-13N | 25 |
| Beverly Ln. E&W | 14W-13N | 25 |
| Birch Dr. N&S | 16W-11N | 25 |
| Bittersweet E&W | 13W-14N | 26 |
| Blackhawk Dr. E&W | 16W-10N | 25 |
| Bob-o-link Rd. E&W | 15W-14N | 25 |
| Bobby Ln. N&S | 16W-12N | 25 |
| Bonita Av. E&W | 17W-12N,16W-12N | 24 |
| Boro Ln. N&S | 13W-14N | 26 |
| Boulder Dr. E&W | 13W-14N | 26 |
| Boxwood Dr. N&S | 15W-14N | 25 |
| Brentwood Ln. N&S | 14W-14N | 25 |
| Briarwood Dr., E. N&S | 17W-10N | 34 |
| Bridgeport Dr. N&S | 15W-14N | 25 |
| Brighton Pl. E&W | 15W-14N | 25 |
| Brownstone Ct. N&S | 17W-11N | 24 |
| Buckthorn Dr. N&S | 13W-15N | 16 |
| Bunting Ln. E&W | 14W-14N | 25 |
| Burning Bush Ln. N&S | 13W-14N,13W-15N | 26 |
| Burr Oak Dr. E&W | 13W-14N | 26 |
| Business Center Ct. E&W | 14W-13N | 25 |
| Business Center Dr. N&S | 14W-13N | 25 |
| Busse Av. E&W | 16W-12N,15W-12N | 25 |
| Busse Rd. N&S | 17W-10N,17W-12N | 34 |
| Butternut Ln. NS&EW | 16W-14N | 25 |
| Byron Ct. N&S | 15W-14N | 25 |
| Callero Cir. E&W | 13W-14N | 25 |
| Camp McDonald Rd. E&W | 13W-15N | 16 |
| Candota Rd. N&S | 16W-11N | 25 |
| Cannon Dr. N&S | 16W-10N | 34 |
| Carboy Rd. N&S | 16W-10N | 34 |
| Cardinal Ln. E&W | 14W-13N | 25 |
| Carib Ln. E&W | 13W-14N | 26 |
| Carol Ln. N&S | 17W-11N,17W-12N | 24 |
| Catalpa Ln. E&W | 17W-11N,16W-11N | 25 |
| Cathy Ln. N&S | 16W-12N | 25 |
| Catino Ct. N&S | 14W-13N | 25 |
| Cayuga Ln. NW&SE | 13W-15N | 16 |
| Cedar Glen N&S | 17W-11N | 24 |
| Cedar Ln. E&W | 14W-14N | 25 |
| Centenial Dr. E&W | 14W-13N | 25 |
| Central Rd. E&W | 16W-13N,14W-13N | 25 |
| Chapel E&W | 17W-11N | 24 |
| Chariot Ct. E&W | 17W-10N | 34 |
| Charlotte Rd. E&W | 17W-10N | 34 |
| Cherrywood Dr. N&S | 17W-11N | 24 |
| Chestnut Dr. N&S | 16W-11N | 25 |
| Chinkapin Oak Dr. E&W | 13W-14N | 26 |
| Chold Ln. N&S | 13W-14N | 26 |
| Chris Ln. N&S | 17W-12N | 24 |
| Church Rd. N&S | 16W-11N | 25 |
| Circle Dr. E&W | 16W-12N | 25 |
| Clevin Av. N&S | 16W-12N | 25 |
| Clove Ct. NE&SW | 16W-14N | 25 |
| Colony Dr. N&S | 16W-10N | 34 |
| Columbine Dr. N&S | 13W-14N | 26 |
| Connie Ln. E&W | 17W-12N | 24 |
| Corktree Ln. E&W | 13W-14N | 26 |
| Cottonwood Ln. E&W | 16W-11N | 25 |
| Council Tr. E&W | 16W-12N,15W-12N | 25 |
| Country Ln. N&S | 15W-11N | 25 |
| Coventry Pl. E&W | 15W-14N | 25 |
| Crabtree Ln. N&S | 14W-14N | 25 |
| Craig Ct. N&S | 17W-12N | 24 |
| Cree Ln. NS&EW | 13W-14N | 26 |
| Crestwood Dr. N&S | 17W-12N | 24 |
| Crystal Ln. N&S | 17W-10N | 34 |
| Cypress Ct. NW&SE | 13W-15N | 16 |
| Cypress Dr. N&S | 16W-11N | 25 |
| Dale Av. N&S | 16W-13N | 25 |
| Debbie Dr. N&S | 14W-14N | 25 |
| Deborah Ln. N&S | 17W-11N,17W-12N | 24 |
| Delaware Dr. N&S | 16W-10N | 34 |
| Dempster St. E&W | 15W-11N | 25 |
| Deneen Ln. N&S | 14W-13N | 25 |
| Dennis Dr. E&W | 17W-10N | 34 |
| Des Plaines River Rd. N&S | 13W-14N | 26 |
| Diane Rd. N&S | 16W-10N | 34 |
| Dogwood Ln. E&W | 15W-14N,14W-14N | 25 |
| Dove Ct. N&S | 16W-11N | 25 |
| Dover Pl. E&W | 15W-14N | 25 |
| Dresser Dr. NS&EW | 16W-14N | 25 |
| East Dr. N&S | 15W-14N | 25 |
| Eastman Ct. N&S | 15W-13N | 25 |
| Eastman Dr. N&S | 15W-13N | 25 |
| Eastwood Av. N&S | 15W-13N | 25 |
| Edgewood Ln. N&S | 16W-11N,16W-12N | 25 |
| Edward St. N&S | 15W-11N,15W-12N | 25 |
| Elderberry Ln. E&W | 14W-14N | 25 |
| Elm St. N&S | 15W-11N,15W-13N | 25 |
| Elmhurst Av. N&S | 16W-12N,16W-13N | 25 |

| Name | Grid | Page |
|---|---|---|
| Elmhurst Rd. N&S | 16W-10N | 34 |
| Elyane Ct. N&S | 17W-10N | 34 |
| Emerson Ct. NW&SE | 15W-11N | 25 |
| Emerson Ln. N&S | 14W-13N | 25 |
| Emerson St. | 15W-11N,15W-13N | 25 |
| Enterprise Dr. | 16W-10N | 34 |
| Eric Av. N&S | 14W-13N | 25 |
| Eric Ct. N&S | 14W-13N | 25 |
| Estates Dr. E&W | 17W-12N | 24 |
| Euclid Av. E&W | 13W-14N | 26 |
| Eva Ln. E&W | 16W-11N | 25 |
| Evergreen Av. E&W | 16W-12N,15W-12N | 25 |
| Fairmont Pl. N&S | 15W-14N | 25 |
| Fairview St. N&S | 15W-13N | 25 |
| Falcon Dr. E&W | 17W-11N | 24 |
| Feehanville Dr. NS&EW | 14W-13N | 25 |
| Fern Dr. N&S | 16W-13N | 25 |
| Forest Av. N&S | 16W-13N | 25 |
| Forest Cove Dr. E&W | 17W-10N | 34 |
| Foster St. E&W | 17W-10N | 24 |
| Foundry Rd. E&W | 14W-13N | 25 |
| Franklin Dr. N&S | 16W-10N | 34 |
| Frediani Ct. E&W | 17W-12N | 24 |
| Freedom Ct. E&W | 13W-14N | 26 |
| Frost Dr. E&W | 16W-11N | 25 |
| Garwood Av. E&W | 15W-13N | 25 |
| George St. N&S | 15W-11N,15W-12N | 25 |
| Glendale Ln. N&S | 16W-12N | 25 |
| Glenn Ln. E&W | 16W-11N | 25 |
| Go-Wan-Do Av. E&W | 16W-12N | 25 |
| Golf Rd. E&W | 17W-11N,15W-11N | 24 |
| Golfhurst Av. E&W | 15W-11N | 25 |
| Golfview Dr. N&S | 15W-11N | 25 |
| Golfview Pl. N&S | 15W-11N | 25 |
| Grace Dr. N&S | 16W-11N | 25 |
| Green Acres Ln. N&S | 16W-11N | 25 |
| Green Ln. N&S | 14W-13N | 25 |
| Greenbriar Dr. E&W | 16W-12N | 25 |
| Greenfield Ln. N&S | 14W-14N | 25 |
| Greenwood Dr. E&W | 14W-14N | 25 |
| Gregory Ln. E&W | 14W-13N | 25 |
| Gregory St. E&W | 16W-13N,15W-13N | 25 |
| Grindel Dr. E&W | 17W-12N | 24 |
| Grove Dr. N&S | 17W-11N | 24 |
| Hackberry Ln. E&W | 14W-14N | 25 |
| Hampshire Pl. E&W | 15W-14N | 25 |
| Hanover Pl. E&W | 15W-14N | 25 |
| Harvest Ln. N&S | 14W-13N | 25 |
| Hatherleigh Ct. E&W | 17W-11N | 24 |
| Hatlen Av. N&S | 17W-12N | 24 |
| Haven St. E&W | 17W-12N | 24 |
| Hawthorn NS&EW | 16W-10N | 34 |
| Hazelhill N&S | 17W-10N | 34 |
| Helena Av. N&S | 17W-12N | 24 |
| Hemlock Ln. N&S | 14W-14N | 25 |
| Henry St. E&W | 16W-13N,14W-13N | 25 |
| Heritage Dr. N&S | 13W-14N | 26 |
| Hi-lusi Av. N&S | 16W-11N,16W-13N | 25 |
| Hiawatha N&S | 16W-12N,15W-12N | 25 |
| Hiawatha Pl. N&S | 15W-12N | 25 |
| Hiawatha Tr. E&W | 15W-12N | 25 |
| Hickory Dr. N&S | 16W-11N | 25 |
| Highland Av. N&S | 15W-13N | 25 |
| Hill St. E&W | 15W-13N | 25 |
| Holly Av. N&S | 15W-13N | 25 |
| Holly Ct. E&W | 15W-13N | 25 |
| Hopi Ln. E&W | 13W-14N | 26 |
| Horner Ln. N&S | 14W-13N | 25 |
| Hunt Club Dr. N&S | 15W-11N | 25 |
| Huntington Commons Rd. E&W | 16W-11N | 25 |
| I-oka Av. N&S | 16W-11N,16W-12N | 25 |
| Ida Ct. N&S | 16W-11N | 25 |
| Imperial Ct. N&S | 16W-10N | 34 |
| Independence Ct. E&W | 13W-14N | 26 |
| Indigo Ct. N&S | 13W-14N | 26 |
| Inner Circle Dr. N&S | 15W-12N | 25 |
| Interstate 90 NW&SE | 17W-10N | 34 |
| Ironwood Dr. E&W | 14W-14N | 25 |
| Ironwood Pl. N&S | 14W-14N | 25 |
| Isabella St. E&W | 16W-13N,15W-13N | 25 |
| Ivanhoe E&W | 16W-11N | 25 |
| Ivy Ln. E&W | 13W-14N | 26 |
| Jeffrey Dr. N&S | 14W-13N | 25 |
| Jerry Dr. N&S | 14W-13N | 25 |
| Jody Ct. E&W | 17W-12N | 24 |
| Judith Ann Dr. E&W | 15W-13N | 25 |
| Juniper Ln. NS&EW | 14W-14N | 25 |
| Kenilworth Av. N&S | 16W-12N,16W-13N | 25 |
| Kennicott Pl. N&S | 17W-11N | 24 |
| Kensington Rd. E&W | 15W-14N | 25 |
| Kim Av. E&W | 17W-12N | 24 |
| Kingston Ct. N&S | 14W-13N | 25 |
| Kiowa Ln E&W | 13W-14N | 26 |
| Knights Bridge E&W | 17W-11N | 24 |
| La Vergne Dr. N&S | 17W-11N | 24 |
| LaSalle St. E&W | 16W-10N | 34 |
| Lakeview Ct. N&S | 14W-13N | 25 |
| Lama Ln. N&S | 13W-14N | 26 |
| Lams Ct. N&S | 14W-13N | 25 |
| Lancaster Av. N&S | 16W-11N,16W-13N | 25 |
| Larch Dr. NS&EW | 13W-15N | 16 |
| Larkdale Ln. E&W | 15W-14N | 25 |
| Laurel Dr. N&S | 13W-15N | 16 |
| Leonard Ln. N&S | 17W-12N | 24 |
| Lexington Dr. N&S | 16W-10N | 34 |
| Liberty Ct. N&S | 13W-14N | 26 |
| Lincoln St. E&W | 17W-12N,15W-12N | 24 |
| Linden Ln. E&W | 14W-14N | 25 |
| Linneman Rd. N&S | 16W-10N,16W-13N | 34 |
| Locust Ln. E&W | 17W-11N | 24 |
| Lois Ct. N&S | 17W-12N | 24 |
| Lonnquist Blvd. E&W | 16W-12N | 25 |
| Louis St. N&S | 15W-11N,15W-12N | 25 |
| Lowden Ln. E&W | 14W-13N | 25 |
| Lynn Ct. N&S | 17W-10N | 34 |
| MacArthur Dr. N&S | 16W-13N | 25 |
| Magnolia Ct. N&S | 16W-12N | 24 |
| Main St. N&S | 15W-13N | 25 |
| Mallard N&S | 16W-11N | 25 |
| Malmo Rd. N&S | 16W-10N | 34 |
| Mamiya Dr. N&S | 16W-13N | 25 |
| Manawa Tr. E&W | 16W-12N | 25 |
| Mansard Ln. NS&EW | 17W-10N | 34 |
| Maple St. N&S | 15W-11N,15W-13N | 25 |
| Marcella Rd. N&S | 14W-13N | 25 |
| Mark Dr. E&W | 14W-13N | 25 |
| Mark Ter. E&W | 17W-12N | 24 |
| Martha Ln. E&W | 17W-12N | 24 |
| Martin Ln. E&W | 17W-12N | 24 |
| Maya Ln. E&W | 13W-15N | 16 |
| Meadow Ln. NW&SE | 15W-14N | 25 |
| Meier Rd. N&S | 17W-12N | 24 |
| Memory Ln. E&W | 16W-13N,15W-13N | 25 |
| Michael St. N&S | 17W-10N | 24 |
| Midway Dr. E&W | 16W-10N | 34 |
| Milburn Av. E&W | 16W-12N,15W-12N | 25 |
| Mitchell Dr. E&W | 14W-13N | 25 |
| Moehling Ln. E&W | 15W-12N | 25 |
| Mohawk Ln. E&W | 13W-15N | 16 |
| Moki Ln. N&S | 13W-14N | 26 |
| Montgomery St. E&W | 16W-10N | 34 |
| Morrishill* N&S | 16W-10N | 34 |
| Mt. Prospect Rd. N&S | 15W-8N,14W-12N | 34 |
| Mulberry Ln. N&S | 14W-14N | 25 |
| Mura Ln. N&S | 13W-15N | 16 |
| Myrtle Dr. E&W | 17W-12N | 24 |
| Na-wa-ta Av. N&S | 16W-11N,16W-13N | 25 |
| Neil Av. N&S | 14W-13N | 25 |
| Newberry N&S | 14W-14N | 25 |
| Noah Ter. N&S | 17W-12N | 24 |
| Nordic Rd. N&S | 16W-10N | 34 |
| North Ln. E&W | 17W-11N | 24 |
| Northwest Hwy. NW&SE | 16W-13N,15W-12N | 25 |
| Northwest Tollway NW&SE | 17W-10N | 34 |
| Nutmeg Ct. NW&SE | 16W-14N | 25 |
| Oak Av. N&S | 16W-13N | 25 |
| Oak Dr. E&W | 13W-14N | 26 |
| Oakwood Dr. N&S | 17W-11N | 24 |
| Ojibwa Tr. N&S | 16W-12N | 25 |
| Ojibwa Tr. N&S | 16W-12N | 25 |
| Ojibway Ter. N&S | 16W-12N | 25 |
| Oneida Ln. N&S | 13W-15N | 16 |
| Orchard Pl. N&S | 15W-11N | 25 |
| Oriole Ln. E&W | 15W-14N | 25 |
| Owen St. N&S | 15W-11N,15W-13N | 25 |
| Oxford Pl. E&W | 15W-14N | 25 |
| Palm Dr. E&W | 17W-11N,16W-11N | 24 |
| Park Dr. N&S | 13W-14N,13W-15N | 26 |
| Parliament Pl. E&W | 16W-14N | 25 |
| Partridge E&W | 16W-11N | 25 |
| Pawnee Ln. E&W | 13W-15N | 16 |
| Peachtree Ln. N&S | 16W-14N | 25 |
| Peartree Ln. N&S | 13W-14N | 26 |
| Pecos Ln. N&S | 13W-14N | 26 |
| Pendleton Pl. E&W | 17W-12N | 24 |
| Persimmon Ln. N&S | 16W-14N | 25 |
| Pheasant Tr. E&W | 17W-11N | 24 |
| Phillip* N&S | 16W-10N | 34 |
| Picadilly Cir. N&S | 15W-14N | 25 |
| Pima Ln. N&S | 13W-14N | 26 |
| Pin Oak Dr. E&W | 13W-14N | 26 |
| Pine St. N&S | 15W-12N,15W-13N | 25 |
| Plum Ct. NW&SE | 16W-14N | 25 |
| Prairie Av. N&S | 17W-12N | 24 |
| Prendegast Ln. E&W | 17W-12N | 24 |
| Prospect Av. NW&SE | 16W-13N,16W-12N | 25 |
| Prospect Manor Av. N&S | 15W-13N | 25 |
| Quail Walk N&S | 16W-11N | 25 |
| Quince Ct. E&W | 13W-14N | 26 |
| Quince Ln. N&S | 13W-14N | 26 |
| Raleigh Pl. E&W | 15W-14N | 25 |
| Rand Rd. NW&SE | 16W-14N,14W-13N | 25 |
| Redwood Av. N&S | 16W-11N | 25 |
| Redwood Dr. N&S | 16W-11N | 25 |
| Regency Ct. E&W | 13W-14N | 26 |
| Ridge Av. N&S | 15W-13N | 25 |
| Rob Rd. N&S | 16W-12N | 25 |
| Robbie Ln. E&W | 17W-12N | 24 |
| Robert Dr. N&S | 16W-11N | 25 |
| Robin Ln. E&W | 16W-11N | 25 |
| Rosetree Ln. NW&SE | 13W-15N | 16 |
| Rt. 58 E&W | 16W-11N | 25 |
| Rt. 62 N&SW | 16W-10N | 34 |
| Rt. 83 N&S | 15W-13N | 25 |
| Russel St. N&S | 15W-13N | 25 |
| Rusty Rd. E&W | 17W-12N | 24 |
| Sable Ln. N&S | 17W-10N | 34 |
| Sanford Cliffs N&S | 17W-11N | 24 |
| Santee Ln. E&W | 13W-14N | 26 |
| Sauk Ln. N&S | 13W-14N | 26 |
| School St. N&S | 15W-11N,15W-13N | 25 |
| Scott Ter. E&W | 17W-12N | 24 |
| See-gwun Av. N&S | 16W-11N,16W-12N | 25 |
| Seneca Ln. E&W | 13W-15N | 16 |
| Shabonne Tr. E&W | 16W-12N,15W-12N | 25 |
| Sioux Ln. N&S | 16W-11N | 25 |
| Sir Galahad N&S | 16W-11N | 25 |
| Sir Lancelot N&S | 16W-11N | 25 |
| Sitka Ln. N&S | 13W-14N | 26 |
| Sivic St. N&S | 17W-12N | 24 |
| Slawin Ct. NW&SE | 14W-13N | 25 |
| Small Ln. N&S | 17W-12N | 25 |
| South Ln. E&W | 17W-11N | 24 |
| Sprucewood Dr. N&S | 17W-11N | 24 |
| St. Cecilia Dr. N&S | 17W-12N | 24 |
| Stevenson Ln. N&S | 14W-13N | 25 |
| Stratford Pl. E&W | 15W-14N | 25 |
| Stratton N&S | 14W-13N | 25 |
| Sullivan Ct. E&W | 17W-12N | 24 |
| Sumac Ln. N&S | 13W-14N | 26 |
| Sunset Rd. E&W | 16W-11N,15W-11N | 25 |
| Susan Dr. E&W | 16W-12N | 25 |
| Sycamore Ln. N&S | 14W-14N | 25 |
| Tamarack Dr. N&S | 17W-11N | 24 |
| Tano Ln. E&W | 13W-14N | 26 |
| Terminal Dr. E&W | 16W-10N | 34 |
| Thackery Rd. E&W | 15W-14N | 25 |
| Thayer St. E&W | 15W-13N,14W-13N | 25 |
| Thornwood Ln. E&W | 17W-11N | 24 |
| Tower Dr. N&S | 15W-11N | 25 |
| Tower Ln. N&S | 15W-11N | 25 |
| Verde Dr. E&W | 17W-12N | 24 |
| Victoria Dr. E&W | 17W-10N | 34 |
| W. Briarwood Dr. NW&SE | 17W-10N | 34 |
| Wall St. N&S | 16W-10N | 34 |
| Walnut St. E&W | 15W-13N | 25 |
| Wapella Av. N&S | 16W-11N,16W-12N | 25 |
| Waverly Av. N&S | 16W-11N | 25 |
| Waverly Pl. N&S | 16W-12N,16W-13N | 25 |
| We-go Tr. N&S | 16W-11N,16W-12N | 25 |
| Wedgewood NE&SE | 15W-14N | 25 |
| Weller Ln. N&S | 16W-12N | 25 |
| Westgate Rd. N&S | 14W-14N | 25 |
| Wheeling N&S | 14W-13N,15W-14N | 25 |
| White E&W | 17W-11N | 24 |
| White Oak St. E&W | 17W-12N | 24 |
| Whitegate Dr. E&W | 16W-12N | 25 |
| Whithorn Ln. E&W | 16W-12N | 25 |
| Wigwam Tr. E&W | 16W-12N | 25 |
| Wildwood Dr. E&W | 14W-13N | 25 |
| Wille St. N&S | 15W-12N,15W-13N | 25 |
| William St. N&S | 15W-11N,15W-13N | 25 |
| Willow Ln. E&W | 17W-11N,16W-11N | 24 |
| Willow Rd. N&S | 13W-15N | 16 |
| Wilshire Dr. N&S | 15W-13N | 25 |
| Wimbolton Pl. E&W | 15W-14N | 25 |
| Windsor Dr. N&S | 16W-12N | 25 |
| Wintergreen Av. E&W | 13W-15N | 16 |
| Wistoria Ct. N&S | 13W-14N | 26 |
| Wolf Rd. N&S | 14W-14N | 25 |
| Wood Ln. N&S | 13W-14N | 26 |
| Woodview Dr. E&W | 13W-15N | 16 |
| Yarmouth Pl. N&S | 15W-14N | 25 |
| Yates St. N&S | 14W-13N | 25 |
| Yuma Ln. E&W | 13W-15N | 16 |

## New Trier Township

| Name | Grid | Page |
|---|---|---|
| Colton Ln. N&S | 6W-14N | 28 |
| Forest Way Dr. N&S | 6W-16N,6W-15N | 18 |
| Golf Rd. N&S | 5W-14N | 28 |
| Holly Ln. E&W | 6W-16N | 18 |
| Indian Hill Rd. E&W | 5W-15N | 28 |
| Locust Rd. N&S | 5W-14N | 28 |
| Long Meadow Rd. N&S | 8W-14N | 27 |
| Woodley Manor N&S | 5W-14N | 28 |
| Woodley Rd. NE&SW | 5W-14N | 28 |
| Woodley Way N&S | 5W-14N | 28 |
| Woodley Woods N&S | 5W-14N | 28 |

## Niles

| Name | Grid | Page |
|---|---|---|
| Albion Av. E&W | 8W-8N | 37 |
| Amelia Dr. E&W | 10W-10N | 36 |
| Ashland Av. N&S | 10W-11N | 27 |
| Austin Av. N&S | 7W-8N | 37 |
| Belleforte Pl. N&S | 8W-10N | 37 |
| Betty Ter. E&W | 10W-10N | 36 |
| Birchwood Av. E&W | 8W-9N | 37 |
| Breen St. E&W | 9W-10N | 37 |
| Bruce Dr. E&W | 10W-10N | 36 |
| Callero Dr. NW&SE | 10W-11N | 27 |
| Canavan Ct. N&S | 10W-12N | 27 |
| Canavan Rd. N&S | 10W-12N | 27 |
| Carol Av. N&S | 8W-10N | 37 |
| Carol Ct. NW&SE | 8W-10N | 37 |
| Carol St. | 10W-9N,10W-10N | 36 |
| Catino NE&SW | 10W-11N | 27 |
| Cedar Ln. N&S | 10W-10N | 36 |
| Cherry Av. NE&SW | 8W-8N | 37 |
| Chester Av. N&S | 10W-10N,10W-11N | 36 |
| Church St. E&W | 10W-11N | 27 |
| Churchill Cir. NW&SE | 10W-11N | 27 |
| Clara Ct. E&W | 10W-10N | 36 |
| Clara Dr. N&S | 10W-10N | 36 |
| Cleveland St. E&W | 10W-9N,8W-10N | 37 |
| Clifton Av. N&S | 10W-10N,10W-11N | 36 |
| Concord Ln. NW&SE | 7W-8N | 37 |
| Conrad St. E&W | 9W-10N | 37 |
| Courte Dr. E&W | 10W-11N | 27 |
| Courtland Dr. NE&SW | 10W-11N | 27 |
| Crain Av. E&W | 8W-10N | 37 |
| Crain St. E&W | 10W-9N,10W-10N | 36 |
| Croname Rd. N&S | 7W-9N | 37 |
| Cumberland Av. N&S | 10W-10N | 36 |
| Davis St. E&W | 10W-11N | 27 |
| Days Ter. NW&SE | 8W-8N | 37 |
| Dempster St. E&W | 10W-11N | 27 |
| Dobson St. E&W | 8W-9N | 37 |
| Doreen Ln. E&W | 9W-10N | 37 |
| Ebinger Dr. NE&SW | 8W-8N | 37 |
| Elizabeth Av. E&W | 10W-11N | 27 |
| Elmore St. N&S | 9W-10N,9W-11N | 37 |
| Elmwood Dr. E&W | 11W-12N | 26 |
| Fargo Av. E&W | 8W-9N | 37 |
| Farnsworth Dr. N&S | 10W-10N | 36 |
| Field Dr. NE&SW | 10W-10N | 36 |
| Forestview Ln. NE&SW | 8W-8N | 37 |
| Foster Ln. E&W | 10W-11N | 27 |
| Fox Glen Dr. N&S | 11W-12N | 26 |
| Franks Av. NW&SE | 8W-8N | 37 |
| Georgia Dr. E&W | 8W-10N | 37 |
| Glendale Rd. N&S | 10W-12N | 27 |
| Grace Av. N&S | 10W-12N | 27 |
| Grand Ct. E&W | 10W-10N | 36 |
| Grand St. N&S | 10W-10N | 36 |
| Greendale St. N&S | 10W-10N | 36 |
| Greenleaf Av. E&W | 8W-10N | 37 |
| Greenleaf Dr. E&W | 8W-8N,7W-8N | 37 |
| Greenleaf St. E&W | 9W-10N | 37 |
| Greenwood Blvd. E&W | 10W-11N | 27 |
| Greenwood Rd. N&S | 10W-10N,10W-11N | 36 |
| Grennan Pl. E&W | 10W-9N,8W-10N | 37 |
| Gross Point Rd. SW&NE | 8W-9N,7W-9N | 37 |
| Hamilton Dr. E&W | 8W-10N | 37 |
| Harlem Av. N&S | 9W-10N | 37 |
| Harts Rd. NE&SW | 8W-8N | 37 |
| Harvard St. E&W | 8W-9N | 37 |
| Heathwood Dr. E&W | 11W-12N | 26 |
| Howard St. E&W | 9W-9N,7W-9N | 37 |
| Huber Oval NW&SE | 10W-12N | 27 |
| Jarvis Av. E&W | 8W-9N,7W-9N | 37 |
| Jarvis St. E&W | 8W-9N | 37 |
| Joey Dr. NW&SE | 10W-11N | 27 |
| Johanna Dr. E&W | 10W-10N | 36 |
| Jonquil Ter. E&W | 9W-9N,8W-9N | 37 |
| Kay St. E&W | 10W-11N | 27 |
| Kedzie St. E&W | 9W-10N | 37 |
| Keeney St. E&W | 9W-10N,8W-10N | 37 |
| Kirk Dr. E&W | 9W-9N | 37 |
| Kirk Ln. E&W | 9W-9N | 37 |
| Kirk St. E&W | 9W-8N,9W-9N | 37 |
| Lake St. E&W | 10W-11N | 27 |
| Lauren Ln. NE&SW | 10W-12N | 27 |
| Lawler Av. N&S | 9W-9N | 37 |
| Lee St. E&W | 9W-10N,8W-9N | 37 |
| Lehigh Av. NW&SE | 7W-8N | 37 |
| Lexington Ln. NW&SE | 7W-8N | 37 |
| Lill Ct. E&W | 9W-10N | 37 |
| Lill St. E&W | 9W-10N,8W-10N | 37 |
| Loras Ln. NW&SE | 10W-11N | 27 |
| Lyons St. NW&SE | 9W-11N | 27 |
| Madison Av. N&S | 10W-10N | 36 |
| Madison Ct. N&S | 10W-10N | 36 |
| Madison Dr. N&S | 10W-10N | 36 |
| Madison St. E&W | 9W-10N,8W-10N | 37 |
| Main St. E&W | 9W-10N,8W-10N | 37 |
| Maryland St. N&S | 10W-11N | 27 |
| Maynard Dr. N&S | 10W-12N | 27 |
| Maynard Oval NE&SW | 10W-13N | 27 |
| Maynard Rd. E&W | 10W-12N | 27 |
| Maynard Ter. N&S | 10W-12N | 27 |
| McVicker Av. N&S | 7W-9N | 37 |
| Meacham Ct. N&S | 10W-10N | 36 |
| Meade Av. N&S | 7W-9N | 37 |
| Melvina Av. N&S | 7W-9N | 37 |
| Merard Av. N&S | 7W-9N | 37 |
| Merrill St. N&S | 9W-10N,9W-11N | 37 |
| Merrimac Av. N&S | 7W-9N | 37 |
| Milwaukee Av. NE&SW | 10W-11N,8W-8N | 27 |
| Monroe Ct. E&W | 8W-10N | 37 |
| Monroe St. E&W | 10W-10N,8W-10N | 36 |
| Mulford Dr. E&W | 9W-10N | 37 |
| Mulford St. E&W | 9W-9N,7W-9N | 37 |
| Natchez Av. N&S | 8W-10N | 37 |
| National Av. N&S | 8W-10N | 37 |
| Neva Av. N&S | 8W-9N,8W-10N | 37 |
| New England Av. N&S | 8W-10N | 37 |
| Newark Av. N&S | 8W-8N | 37 |
| Newcastle N&S | 8W-10N | 37 |
| Newland Av. N&S | 8W-10N | 37 |
| Nieman NE&SW | 8W-8N | 37 |
| Niles Av. NE&SW | 8W-10N | 37 |
| Niles Ter. E&W | 8W-9N | 37 |
| Nora Av. N&S | 8W-9N,8W-10N | 37 |
| Nordica Av. N&S | 8W-9N | 37 |
| Norma Ct. NE&SE | 10W-12N | 27 |
| Normal Av. N&S | 10W-10N | 36 |
| Normal Ct. E&W | 10W-10N | 36 |
| North Av. E&W | 10W-10N | 36 |
| Nottingham St. N&S | 8W-9N | 37 |
| Oak Av. N&S | 10W-11N | 27 |
| Oak Ln. E&W | 10W-10N | 36 |
| Oak Park Av. N&S | 8W-9N | 37 |
| Oakton Ct. E&W | 8W-10N | 37 |
| Oakton St. E&W | 9W-10N,8W-10N | 37 |
| Oconto Av. N&S | 9W-9N | 37 |
| Octavia Av. N&S | 10W-10N | 37 |
| Odell Av. N&S | 9W-9N,9W-10N | 37 |
| Oketo Av. N&S | 9W-9N,9W-10N | 37 |
| Olcott Av. N&S | 9W-10N | 37 |
| Oleander Av. N&S | 9W-9N,9W-10N | 37 |
| Oriole N&S | 9W-10N | 37 |
| Osceola Av. N&S | 9W-10N | 37 |
| Ottawa Av. N&S | 9W-10N | 37 |
| Overhill Av. N&S | 9W-10N | 37 |
| Ozanam Av. N&S | 9W-10N | 37 |
| Ozark Av. N&S | 9W-10N | 37 |
| Park Av. E&W | 10W-11N,9W-11N | 27 |
| Park Av. N&S | 10W-10N | 36 |
| Peter Ter. E&W | 10W-10N | 36 |
| Prospect Ct. E&W | 10W-10N | 36 |
| Prospect St. N&S | 10W-11N | 27 |
| Riverside Dr. NE&SW | 8W-8N | 37 |
| Riverview Av. NE&SW | 8W-8N | 37 |
| Robin Rd. NE&SW | 10W-10N | 27 |
| Root Ct. N&S | 10W-10N | 36 |
| Root St. N&S | 10W-11N | 27 |
| Rosemary Dr. NW&SE | 8W-8N | 37 |
| Roseview Dr. E&W | 10W-10N | 36 |
| Rt. 21 SE&NW | 9W-9N | 37 |
| Rt. 43 N&S | 9W-9N | 37 |
| School St. N&S | 8W-9N | 37 |

| Street | Grid | Page |
|---|---|---|
| Seward St. E&W | 9W-10N,8W-10N | 37 |
| Sherwin Av. E&W | 7W-9N | 37 |
| Stolting Rd. E&W | 10W-10N | 36 |
| Sunset Rd. E&W | 10W-10N | 36 |
| Susan Ct. N&S | 10W-10N | 36 |
| Touhy Av. E&W | 8W-9N,7W-9N | 37 |
| Vapor Ln. N&S | 8W-9N | 37 |
| Warren Oval E&W | 10W-12N | 27 |
| Washington St. N&S | 10W-10N | 36 |
| Waukegan Rd. N&S | 8W-9N | 37 |
| Wendy Way NE&SW | 10W-12N | 27 |
| Willow Ln. N&S | 10W-11N | 27 |
| Wisner St. N&S | 9W-10N,9W-11N | 37 |
| Wood River Dr. NE&SW | 8W-9N | 37 |
| Woodland Dr. NE&SW | 10W-11N | 27 |
| Wright Ter. E&W | 8W-10N | 37 |

### Norridge

| Street | Grid | Page |
|---|---|---|
| Agatite E&W | 10W-5N,8W-5N | 41 |
| Ainslie E&W | 10W-6N | 41 |
| Argyle E&W | 10W-6N,9W-6N | 41 |
| Belle Plaine E&W | 10W-6N | 42 |
| Berteau E&W | 9W-5N | 42 |
| Berwyn E&W | 10W-6N | 41 |
| Canfield Rd. N&S | 10W-5N,10W-6N | 41 |
| Carmen E&W | 10W-6N,9W-6N | 41 |
| Charmaine E&W | 10W-6N | 41 |
| Chester N&S | 10W-6N | 41 |
| Clifton N&S | 10W-6N | 41 |
| Coral E&W | 10W-5N | 41 |
| Courtland N&S | 10W-5N,10W-6N | 41 |
| Crescent N&S | 10W-6N | 41 |
| Cullom E&W | 9W-5N | 42 |
| Delphia N&S | 10W-6N | 41 |
| Denal N&S | 10W-6N | 41 |
| Eastwood E&W | 10W-5N | 41 |
| Elm E&W | 10W-5N | 41 |
| Executive E&W | 10W-6N | 41 |
| Foster E&W | 10W-6N | 41 |
| Frank Pkwy. N&S | 9W-6N | 42 |
| Giddings E&W | 10W-5N,9W-5N | 41 |
| Gunnison E&W | 10W-6N,9W-6N | 41 |
| Knight Av. N&S | 10W-6N | 41 |
| Leland E&W | 10W-5N | 41 |
| Leonard Dr. N&S | 10W-6N | 41 |
| Lincoln N&S | 10W-6N | 41 |
| Maple E&W | 10W-5N | 41 |
| Mission Dr. N&S | 9W-6N | 42 |
| Monterey N&S | 9W-6N | 42 |
| Montrose E&W | 9W-5N,8W-5N | 42 |
| Moreland Dr. N&S | 9W-6N | 42 |
| Neva N&S | 8W-5N | 42 |
| Nordica N&S | 10W-5N | 42 |
| Norridge E&W | 9W-6N | 42 |
| North Chester N&S | 10W-6N | 41 |
| North Plainfield N&S | 10W-6N | 41 |
| Nottingham N&S | 8W-5N | 42 |
| Oak E&W | 10W-5N | 41 |
| Octavia N&S | 9W-5N | 42 |
| Odell N&S | 9W-5N | 42 |
| Oketo N&S | 9W-5N | 42 |
| Olcott N&S | 9W-5N | 42 |
| Oleander N&S | 9W-5N | 42 |
| Oneida N&S | 9W-6N | 42 |
| Opal N&S | 9W-5N,9W-6N | 42 |
| Orange N&S | 9W-5N,9W-6N | 42 |
| Oriole N&S | 9W-5N | 42 |
| Osage N&S | 9W-5N | 42 |
| Osceola N&S | 9W-5N | 42 |
| Ottawa N&S | 9W-5N | 42 |
| Overhill N&S | 9W-5N,9W-6N | 42 |
| Ozanam N&S | 9W-5N,9W-6N | 42 |
| Ozark N&S | 9W-5N,9W-6N | 42 |
| Paris N&S | 10W-5N | 41 |
| Pensacola E&W | 9W-5N | 42 |
| Philips N&S | 9W-5N | 42 |
| Pittsburgh N&S | 10W-6N | 41 |
| Plainfield N&S | 10W-5N | 41 |
| Pontiac N&S | 10W-5N,10W-6N | 41 |
| Prospect N&S | 10W-6N | 41 |
| Redwood Dr. N&S | 10W-5N | 41 |
| Ridge N&S | 10W-5N | 41 |
| Sayre N&S | 8W-5N | 42 |
| Strong E&W | 10W-6N,9W-6N | 41 |
| Sunnyside E&W | 9W-5N,8W-5N | 42 |
| Sunrise N&S | 9W-6N | 42 |
| Thatcher N&S | 10W-5N | 41 |
| Vine N&S | 10W-5N | 41 |
| Wilson E&W | 10W-5N | 41 |
| Windsor E&W | 9W-5N,8W-5N | 42 |
| Winnemac E&W | 10W-6N | 41 |
| Winona E&W | 10W-6N,9W-6N | 41 |
| 82nd N&S | 10W-5N | 41 |

### North Riverside

| Street | Grid | Page |
|---|---|---|
| Burroak N&S | 9W-2S | 54 |
| Country Club E&W | 10W-2S | 53 |
| Des Plaines N&S | 10W-2S | 53 |
| Edgewater E&W | 10W-2S | 53 |
| Elm N&S | 11W-2S | 53 |
| Forest E&W | 11W-2S | 53 |
| Forest N&S | 9W-2S | 54 |
| Golfview N&S | 10W-2S | 53 |
| Groveland N&S | 10W-2S | 53 |
| Hainsworth N&S | 9W-2S | 54 |
| Keystone N&S | 9W-2S | 54 |
| Lathrop N&S | 9W-2S | 54 |
| Lewe N&S | 10W-2S | 53 |
| Lincoln N&S | 10W-2S | 53 |
| Madison N&S | 11W-2S | 53 |
| Northgate N&S | 9W-2S | 54 |
| Park N&S | 9W-2S | 54 |
| Prairie N&S | 11W-2S | 53 |
| Seegers N&S | 11W-2S | 53 |
| Traube N&S | 9W-2S | 54 |
| Westover N&S | 9W-2S | 54 |
| 1st N&S | 10W-2S | 53 |
| 2nd N&S | 10W-2S | 53 |
| 3rd N&S | 10W-2S | 53 |
| 4th N&S | 10W-2S | 53 |
| 5th N&S | 10W-2S | 53 |
| 6th N&S | 10W-2S | 53 |
| 7th N&S | 10W-2S | 53 |
| 8th N&S | 10W-2S | 53 |
| 9th N&S | 11W-2S | 53 |
| 10th N&S | 10W-2S | 53 |
| 11th N&S | 11W-2S | 53 |
| 12th N&S | 11W-2S | 53 |
| 22nd Pl. E&W | 11W-2S | 53 |
| 23rd E&W | 11W-2S | 53 |
| 23rd Pl. E&W | 11W-2S | 53 |
| 24th E&W | 11W-2S,9W-2S | 53 |
| 24th Pl. E&W | 11W-2S | 53 |
| 25th E&W | 11W-2S,9W-2S | 53 |
| 26th E&W | 9W-2S | 54 |
| 27th E&W | 10W-2S | 53 |
| 28th E&W | 10W-2S | 53 |
| 30th E&W | 10W-2S | 53 |

### Northbrook

| Street | Grid | Page |
|---|---|---|
| Academy Dr. N&S | 11W-18N | 16 |
| Acorn Ln. E&W | 11W-17N | 16 |
| Adelaide N&S | 10W-17N | 17 |
| Adirondack Dr. N&S | 11W-17N | 16 |
| Alice Rd. N&S | 11W-18N | 16 |
| Alleghany Ln. N&S | 11W-17N | 16 |
| Allen Dr. NW&SE | 10W-15N | 17 |
| Ancient Tree Rd. NS&EW | 11W-17N | 16 |
| Angle Av. NW&SE | 9W-17N | 17 |
| Anjou Dr. N&S | 12W-18N | 16 |
| Antelope Springs Rd. E&W | 11W-17N | 16 |
| Anthony Trail N&S | 11W-18N | 16 |
| Antique Ln. E&W | 8W-18N | 18 |
| Appletree Ct. N&S | 10W-17N | 17 |
| Appletree Ln. E&W | 10W-17N | 17 |
| Applewood Ln. NS&EW | 12W-18N | 16 |
| Arbeleda Ln. NE&SW | 10W-15N | 17 |
| Arnold Ln. E&W | 11W-18N | 16 |
| Arrowood Dr. N&S | 13W-18N | 16 |
| Asbury Rd. E&W | 10W-17N | 17 |
| Ash Ln. NW&SE | 10W-17N | 17 |
| Aspen Dr. E&W | 11W-16N | 16 |
| Astor Pl. NE&SW | 7W-16N | 18 |
| Atlanta Av. N&S | 8W-18N | 18 |
| Auburn Ln. N&S | 11W-15N,11W-16N | 16 |
| Bach St. N&S | 10W-17N | 17 |
| Ballantrae Dr. N&S | 8W-18N | 18 |
| Banyan Dr. N&S | 11W-16N | 16 |
| Bar Harbor Ter. N&S | 10W-17N | 17 |
| Barberry Ln. N&S | 11W-16N | 16 |
| Barnsley Pl. NE&SW | 8W-18N | 18 |
| Bay View* E&W | 11W-17N | 16 |
| Bayberry Dr. E&W | 11W-18N | 16 |
| Beaver Av. E&W | 7W-17N | 18 |
| Beckwith Ct. N&S | 11W-17N | 16 |
| Beechnut Rd. NE&SW | 10W-17N | 17 |
| Bellevue Rd. E&W | 10W-16N | 17 |
| Berglund Pl. E&W | 8W-17N | 18 |
| Bermuda Dunes Pl. N&S | 12W-17N | 16 |
| Bernay Dr. E&W | 12W-18N | 16 |
| Big Oak Cir. E&W | 9W-17N | 17 |
| Big Oak Ln. E&W | 10W-17N,9W-17N | 17 |
| Bindle Ct. E&W | 11W-17N | 16 |
| Birch Rd. N&S | 10W-16N | 17 |
| Birchwood Cir. N&S | 10W-18N | 17 |
| Bittersweet, E. N&S | 9W-17N | 17 |
| Bittersweet, S. E&W | 9W-17N | 17 |
| Bittersweet, W. N&S | 9W-17N | 17 |
| Blackthorn Ln. N&S | 10W-17N | 17 |
| Blue Hill Ter. NW&SE | 10W-16N | 17 |
| Bob-o-link Ln. E&W | 10W-16N | 17 |
| Bordeaux N&S | 12W-18N | 16 |
| Bordeaux Dr. NE&SW | 12W-18N | 16 |
| Brairwood Ln. N&S | 10W-17N | 17 |
| Brees Way Ln. N&S | 9W-17N | 17 |
| Brentwood Rd. E&W | 10W-16N | 17 |
| Brian Dr. E&W | 10W-15N | 17 |
| Briarwood Ln. N&S | 8W-17N | 18 |
| Bridlewood Ln. (Pvt.) N&S | 8W-17N | 18 |
| Bridlewood Rd. (Pvt.) E&W | 8W-17N | 18 |
| Brighton Ct. E&W | 10W-16N | 17 |
| Brindle Ct. E&W | 11W-16N | 16 |
| Bristol Ct. E&W | 12W-17N | 16 |
| Brittany Ct. NW&SE | 12W-18N | 16 |
| Brittany Rd. E&W | 12W-18N | 16 |
| Brookside Ln. N&S | 10W-17N | 17 |
| Buckland Ln. NE&SW | 10W-18N | 17 |
| Buckthorn Cir. NS&EW | 13W-18N | 16 |
| Burgundy Ln.* NE&SW | 9W-16N | 17 |
| Butternut N&S | 10W-16N,10W-17N | 17 |
| Buttonwood Dr. E&W | 8W-17N | 18 |
| Cambridge Dr. N&S | 11W-16N | 16 |
| Campden Dr. E&W | 10W-17N | 17 |
| Candlewood Hill Rd. N&S | 10W-17N | 17 |
| Canterbury Dr. E&W | 11W-16N | 16 |
| Cargill Dr. N&S | 10W-16N | 17 |
| Caribou Crossing NS&EW | 13W-18N | 16 |
| Carlson Dr. N&S | 9W-16N | 17 |
| Carlyle Ct. N&S | 10W-18N | 17 |
| Carol Ct. NW&SE | 9W-17N | 17 |
| Carriage Ln. E&W | 9W-18N | 17 |
| Carter Ct. E&W | 7W-16N | 18 |
| Caryn Ter. N&S | 9W-17N | 17 |
| Catherine St. E&W | 10W-17N | 17 |
| Cayuga Dr. N&S | 11W-16N | 16 |
| Cedar Ct. N&S | 11W-18N | 17 |
| Cedar Ln. NW&SE | 10W-17N | 17 |
| Center Av. E&W | 10W-17N | 17 |
| Chapel Ct. NE&SW | 9W-17N | 17 |
| Chapel Wood* E&W | 11W-17N | 16 |
| Charlemagne Dr. N&S | 12W-18N | 16 |
| Charles Dr. NE&SW | 12W-17N | 16 |
| Charlwood* E&W | 11W-17N | 16 |
| Chartres Dr. NW&SE | 10W-18N | 17 |
| Chedworth Ct. E&W | 10W-18N | 17 |
| Cherry Ln. E&W | 11W-17N,9W-17N | 16 |
| Chesapeake Ln. E&W | 10W-17N | 17 |
| Chestnut Rd. N&S | 10W-18N | 17 |
| Chestnut St. E&W | 10W-17N | 17 |
| Chewton Glen (Pvt.) E&W | 8W-18N | 18 |
| Chipili Dr. N&S | 7W-17N | 18 |
| Christina Ln. N&S | 11W-17N | 16 |
| Church N&S | 9W-17N | 17 |
| Clover Ct. NE&SW | 11W-16N | 16 |
| Clover Rd. N&S | 11W-16N | 16 |
| Coachmaker Dr. N&S | 8W-18N | 18 |
| Cobblestone Ct. E&W | 8W-18N | 18 |
| Cobblestone*. N&S | 11W-17N | 16 |
| Cobblestone* Dr. E&W | 10W-15N | 17 |
| Colonade Dr. N&S | 8W-18N | 18 |
| Colony Ct. E&W | 10W-17N | 17 |
| Commercial Dr. E&W | 12W-18N,11W-18N | 36 |
| Concord Ct. E&W | 11W-17N | 16 |
| Connecticut Av. E&W | 8W-18N | 18 |
| Constance Ln. N&S | 12W-18N | 16 |
| Cornflower Trail E&W | 11W-16N | 16 |
| Cotswolds Ct. NW&SE | 11W-16N | 16 |
| Cotswolds Way N&S | 11W-16N | 16 |
| Cottonwood Rd. N&S | 9W-18N | 17 |
| Country Ln. E&W | 9W-17N | 17 |
| County Line Rd. N&S | 8W-18N | 18 |
| Coventry Ln. N&S | 11W-17N | 16 |
| Crabtree Ln. NS&EW | 11W-17N,10W-17N | 16 |
| Cresson Av. N&S | 7W-17N | 18 |
| Crestwood Dr. N&S | 11W-17N | 16 |
| Crimson Ct. E&W | 11W-17N | 16 |
| Cuyler Av. N&S | 7W-17N | 18 |
| Cypress Ln. N&S | 10W-16N | 17 |
| Dalton Pl. E&W | 8W-17N | 18 |
| Dana Ct. N&S | 9W-17N | 17 |
| Daryl Ln. N&S | 9W-17N | 17 |
| Dauphine Av. NS&EW | 12W-18N | 16 |
| Dauphine Ct. N&S | 11W-18N | 16 |
| Deer Trail E&W | 13W-18N | 16 |
| Deer Trail Ct. N&S | 13W-18N | 16 |
| Dehne Rd. E&W | 10W-16N | 17 |
| Dell Rd. NW&SE | 8W-17N | 18 |
| Dennis Dr. NW&SE | 8W-18N | 18 |
| Devonshire Ct. N&S | 11W-16N | 16 |
| Division St. N&S | 10W-17N | 17 |
| Donegal Ln. N&S | 11W-17N | 16 |
| Donovan Glen Ct. E&W | 11W-16N | 16 |
| Doolittle Dr. E&W | 11W-18N | 16 |
| Doriann Ct. E&W | 11W-15N | 16 |
| Dorset Dr. N&S | 12W-17N | 16 |
| Downing St. N&S | 12W-17N | 16 |
| Driftwood Ln. NS&EW | 8W-16N | 18 |
| Dundee Rd. E&W | 11W-18N | 16 |
| Cir. | 10W-18N | 17 |
| East Wind Ct. E&W | 12W-17N | 16 |
| Eastwood Ln. E&W | 9W-17N | 17 |
| Echo Ln. E&W | 11W-16N | 16 |
| Edens Expwy N&S | 7W-17N | 18 |
| Edgewood Ln. NS&EW | 8W-17N | 18 |
| Elcid Ct. N&S | 9W-17N | 17 |
| Elder Ct. E&W | 11W-17N | 16 |
| Ellendale Dr. NS&EW | 10W-16N | 17 |
| Elm Av. E&W | 9W-17N | 17 |
| Elm Ct. N&S | 10W-18N | 17 |
| Elm Ridge Dr. N&S | 10W-16N | 17 |
| Era Dr. N&S | 12W-18N | 16 |
| Erin Ln. N&S | 7W-16N | 18 |
| Essex Dr.* E&W | 9W-16N | 17 |
| Estate Ct. N&S | 12W-18N | 16 |
| Evert Ct. N&S | 12W-17N | 16 |
| Fair Ln. NW&SE | 11W-17N | 16 |
| Fairford Ln. E&W | 11W-17N | 16 |
| Fairview Ln. E&W | 12W-18N | 16 |
| Fairway E&W | 8W-18N | 18 |
| Farmington Rd. E&W | 11W-15N,10W-15N | 16 |
| Farnsworth Ln. E&W | 10W-16N | 17 |
| Fern Av. E&W | 11W-16N | 16 |
| Ferndale Av. E&W | 9W-17N | 17 |
| Fieldwood Dr. N&S | 10W-16N | 17 |
| First St. NW&SE | 10W-17N | 17 |
| Floral Dr. E&W | 11W-16N | 16 |
| Forest Rd. N&S | 9W-18N | 17 |
| Forestview Dr. E&W | 13W-18N | 16 |
| Forestway Dr., E. E&W | 7W-17N | 18 |
| Foxdale Dr. E&W | 11W-17N | 16 |
| Foxrun Dr. N&S | 9W-18N | 17 |
| Galway Ct. N&S | 11W-17N | 16 |
| Glen Oak Ln. E&W | 9W-17N | 17 |
| Glendale Av. N&S | 9W-17N | 17 |
| Grace Rd. E&W | 10W-17N | 17 |
| Grand Rd. N&S | 11W-16N | 16 |
| Grant Rd. N&S | 8W-17N | 18 |
| Greenacre Dr. E&W | 12W-17N | 16 |
| Greenbriar Ln. N&S | 10W-17N | 17 |
| Greenview Dr. E&W | 10W-15N | 17 |
| Greenview Rd. N&S | 10W-16N | 17 |
| Greenway* NE&SW | 11W-17N | 16 |
| Greenwood Rd. N&S | 10W-18N,10W-15N | 16 |
| Gregg Rd. E&W | 8W-17N | 18 |
| Hampton Ln. N&S | 11W-15N,11W-16N | 16 |
| Harbinger Falls* E&W | 11W-17N | 16 |
| Harbor Ln. E&W | 11W-16N | 16 |
| Harborside N&S | 11W-17N | 16 |
| Harris Dr. E&W | 11W-18N | 16 |
| Hawthorne Ln. N&S | 10W-17N | 17 |
| Hazelwood Av. N&S | 11W-18N | 16 |
| Heather Ct. NE&SW | 11W-16N | 16 |
| Heather Ln. NW&SE | 11W-16N | 16 |
| Helen Rd. N&S | 11W-18N | 16 |
| Hemlock Knoll Ter. N&S | 11W-16N | 16 |
| Hemlock Ln. E&W | 11W-16N | 16 |
| Henrici Dr. NW&SE | 8W-18N | 18 |
| Heritage Dr. E&W | 12W-17N | 16 |
| Hickory Ct. N&S | 9W-18N | 17 |
| Hickory Ln. NE&SW | 9W-18N | 17 |
| Hidden Bay* E&W | 11W-17N | 16 |
| Hiddenwells* NE&SW | 11W-17N | 16 |
| High Point Dr. N&S | 11W-17N | 16 |
| Highland Dr. E&W | 11W-18N | 16 |
| Hillcrest Ln. NW&SE | 10W-15N | 17 |
| Hillside N&S | 9W-17N | 16 |
| Holly Ct. E&W | 8W-17N | 18 |
| Holly Ct. N&S | 11W-15N | 17 |
| Holste Rd. E&W | 9W-15N | 17 |
| Honeysuckle Dr. N&S | 13W-18N | 16 |
| Horizon Ln. N&S | 12W-17N | 16 |
| Huckleberry Ln. N&S | 10W-17N | 17 |
| Huehl Rd. N&S | 10W-16N | 16 |
| Huntington Ln. E&W | 11W-16N | 16 |
| Illinois Rd. E&W | 10W-17N,9W-17N | 17 |
| Indian Wells Ln. E&W | 11W-16N | 16 |
| Interstate 294 N&S | 12W-16N | 16 |
| Interstate 94 E&W | 11W-18N,8W-18N | 16 |
| Iris Ct. E&W | 11W-16N | 16 |
| Island Point* N&S | 11W-17N | 16 |
| Ivy Ln. N&S | 11W-16N | 16 |
| Janke Dr. E&W | 9W-16N | 17 |
| Jefferson Pl. NW&SE | 8W-17N | 18 |
| Jeffrey Ct., N. N&S | 9W-17N | 17 |
| Jeffrey Ct., S. N&S | 9W-17N | 17 |
| Jeffrey Ct., W. N&S | 9W-17N | 17 |
| Jeffrey Ln. E&W | 9W-17N | 17 |
| Juli-lyn Ct. N&S | 12W-17N | 16 |
| Juli-lyn Ln. N&S | 12W-17N | 16 |
| Juniper Ln. N&S | 10W-17N | 17 |
| Kay Jay Dr. E&W | 11W-15N | 16 |
| Keystone Av. N&S | 9W-17N | 17 |
| Keystone Cir. N&S | 9W-17N | 17 |
| Keystone Rd. E&W | 11W-16N | 16 |
| Kiest Av. E&W | 10W-17N,9W-17N | 17 |
| Killarney Ln. NW&SE | 7W-18N | 18 |
| Kingsport Ct. N&S | 11W-17N | 16 |
| Kingston Ct. E&W | 10W-17N | 17 |
| Koehling Rd. E&W | 9W-18N,8W-18N | 17 |
| Koepke Rd. E&W | 11W-16N | 16 |
| Laburnun Dr. N&S | 12W-18N | 16 |
| Lagoon View* E&W | 11W-16N | 16 |
| Cir. | 11W-16N | 16 |
| Lake Placid Ln. E&W | 11W-16N | 16 |
| Lake-Cook Rd. E&W | 9W-18N,8W-18N | 17 |
| Lakeside Av. E&W | 11W-16N | 16 |
| Landwehr Rd. N&S | 11W-17N,11W-18N | 16 |
| Lane Winchester E&W | 11W-17N | 16 |
| Larkdale Rd. N&S | 10W-17N | 17 |
| Larrabee Ln. E&W | 9W-17N | 17 |
| Laurel Rd. N&S | 9W-17N | 17 |
| Lavigne Ln. N&S | 11W-16N | 16 |
| Lawrence Ln. (Pvt.) NS&EW | 8W-18N | 18 |
| Lee Rd. N&S | 9W-18N,8W-18N | 17 |
| Lexington Ct. N&S | 11W-17N | 16 |
| Lilac Ln. E&W | 8W-17N | 18 |
| Lincoln Av. E&W | 9W-17N | 17 |
| Lindberg Ln. N&S | 11W-18N | 16 |
| Linden Rd. E&W | 9W-17N | 17 |
| Linden Rd. NS&EW | 9W-18N | 17 |
| Lindenwood Ln. E&W | 12W-18N | 16 |
| Lisa Ct. N&S | 10W-15N | 17 |
| Little Ln. E&W | 11W-17N | 16 |
| Long Meadow N&S | 8W-18N | 18 |
| Long Valley Dr. NS&EW | 11W-16N | 16 |
| Longaker Ln. NW&SE | 8W-17N | 18 |
| Longmeadow Rd. E&W | 10W-17N | 17 |
| Lorete Ln. N&S | 11W-17N | 16 |
| Lori-lyn Ln. NE&SW | 12W-17N | 16 |
| Mallard NS&EW | 10W-17N | 17 |
| Manor Dr. NW&SE | 11W-16N | 16 |
| Maple Av. E&W | 10W-17N,9W-17N | 17 |
| Maplewood Rd. E&W | 10W-18N,9W-18N | 17 |
| Marcee Ln. N&S | 9W-17N | 17 |
| Marden Ct. E&W | 10W-17N | 17 |
| Margo Ln. E&W | 11W-16N | 16 |
| Maria Av. E&W | 11W-16N | 16 |
| Marshall Rd. E&W | 8W-17N | 18 |
| Mayapple Ct. NS&EW | 10W-16N | 17 |
| Mayapple Ln. NE&SW | 10W-16N | 17 |
| McArthur Blvd. E&W | 11W-16N | 16 |
| Meadow Rd. NW&SE | 10W-17N | 17 |
| Cir. | 10W-17N | 17 |
| Melvin Dr. N&S | 11W-18N | 16 |
| Micheline Ln. NS&EW | 12W-18N | 16 |
| Midfield Ct. E&W | 8W-16N | 18 |
| Midway Rd. NW&SE | 8W-17N | 18 |
| Miller Rd. N&S | 11W-16N | 16 |
| Milton Av. E&W | 10W-17N,9W-17N | 17 |
| Moon Hill Rd. E&W | 11W-16N | 16 |
| Mt. Vernon Ter. NW&SE | 10W-17N | 17 |
| Muirwood* N&S | 11W-17N | 16 |

| | Grid | Page |
|---|---|---|
| Mulberry Ln. E&W .. 10W-16N | | 17 |
| New England Av. N&S | | |
| ........................8W-18N | | 18 |
| New Hampshire E&W | | |
| ........................8W-18N | | 18 |
| New Jersey E&W ...... 8W-18N | | 18 |
| Newport Rd. NW&SE | | |
| ........................10W-15N | | 17 |
| Norfolk Rd. NS&EW  7W-16N | | 18 |
| Normandy Ln. E&W | | |
| ........................12W-18N | | 16 |
| North Corner NE&SW | | |
| ........................11W-17N | | 16 |
| North Ln. N&S ...... 8W-16N | | 18 |
| Northbrook Av. NE&SW | | |
| ........................8W-17N | | 18 |
| Northmoor Ct. N&S | | |
| ........................10W-17N | | 17 |
| Norway Pine Ln. N&S | | |
| ........................11W-16N | | 16 |
| Oak Av. E&W | | |
| ........................10W-17N,9W-17N | | 17 |
| Oak Knoll Ct. E&W | | |
| ........................12W-18N | | 16 |
| Oak Knoll Ter. N&S | | |
| ........................12W-18N | | 16 |
| Oak Leaf Ter. N&S .. 9W-17N | | 17 |
| Oakwood Rd. E&W | | |
| ........................10W-18N,9W-18N | | 17 |
| Old Hunt Rd. E&W .. 8W-16N | | 18 |
| Old Mill Rd. NS&EW | | |
| ........................11W-16N | | 16 |
| Old Post Rd. N&S .. 8W-18N | | 17 |
| Orchard Ln. N&S .... 9W-17N | | 17 |
| Otis Pl. NE&SW ...... 9W-17N | | 18 |
| Overlook Bluff E&W | | |
| ........................11W-17N | | 16 |
| Oxford Ln. E&W....11W-16N | | 16 |
| Palm Canyon Dr. NS&EW | | |
| ........................12W-17N | | 16 |
| Palm Ln. E&W....11W-16N | | 16 |
| Pamella Ln. E&W . 12W-18N | | 16 |
| Park Dr. E&W ...... 7W-17N | | 18 |
| Partridge Ln. E&W . 10W-17N | | 17 |
| Pawtucket Rd. E&W | | |
| ........................11W-17N | | 16 |
| Peachtree Ln. N&S | | |
| ........................10W-17N | | 17 |
| Pebble Beach Rd. E&W | | |
| ........................11W-16N | | 16 |
| Pebblebrook Rd. E&W | | |
| ........................8W-16N | | 18 |
| Penfold Pl N&S .. 10W-16N | | 17 |
| Pfingsten Rd. N&S..11W-16N | | 16 |
| Pheasant Creek Dr. N&S&SW | | |
| ........................11W-17N | | 16 |
| Phillips Av. N&S .... 10W-16N | | 16 |
| Phyllis Ln. NW&SE  12W-18N | | 16 |
| Picardy Dr. E&W .. 12W-18N | | 16 |
| Picardy Dr. NS&EW | | |
| ........................12W-18N | | 16 |
| Pine Tree Rd. N&S . 9W-18N | | 17 |
| Pinto Ln. E&W ...... 12W-17N | | 16 |
| Pleasant St. E&W . 11W-17N | | 16 |
| Plum Island Dr. E&W | | |
| ........................11W-17N | | 16 |
| Plymouth Ln. E&W  10W-16N | | 17 |
| Pondside Dr. N&S . 8W-16N | | 17 |
| Poplar Ct. NW&SE..13W-18N | | 16 |
| Portsmouth Ct. E&W | | |
| ........................9W-17N | | 17 |
| Powderhorn Dr. N&S | | |
| ........................9W-18N | | 17 |
| Prestbury Ct. NS&EW | | |
| ........................10W-18N | | 17 |
| Prestwick Ln. E&W | | |
| ........................11W-17N | | 16 |
| Prince St. E&W .... 10W-15N | | 17 |
| Quail Ln. N&S ...... 10W-15N | | 17 |
| Queens Way N&S . 10W-15N | | 17 |
| Radcliffe Dr. E&W .. 12W-17N | | 16 |
| Raintree Ln. E&W . 12W-17N | | 16 |
| Raliegh Ct. E&W .. 8W-17N | | 18 |
| Raymond Dr. E&W . 9W-16N | | 17 |
| Red Coach Ln. N&S  9W-18N | | 17 |
| Red Oak Ln. N&S .. 9W-18N | | 17 |
| Redhaw Rd. N&S....9W-17N | | 17 |
| Redwood Ln. E&W | | |
| ........................10W-17N,9W-17N | | 17 |
| Regent Dr. N&S .. 12W-17N | | 16 |
| Rennes Ct. E&W .. 11W-17N | | 16 |
| Revere Dr. NW&SE..9W-18N | | 17 |
| Ridge Rd. E&W ...... 9W-18N | | 17 |
| Ridge Rd. N&S...... 8W-17N | | 18 |
| Ridgeland Av. E&W | | |
| ........................12W-17N | | 16 |
| Ridgewood Dr. E&W | | |
| ........................9W-17N | | 17 |
| Ring Rd. N&S ...... 9W-18N | | 17 |
| Riverdale E&W ...... 7W-16N | | 18 |
| Riverfalls Dr. E&W..11W-17N | | 16 |
| Riviera Ct. E&W .. 12W-17N | | 16 |
| Robincrest Dr. E&W | | |
| ........................11W-16N | | 16 |
| Rosemary Ln. E&W | | |
| ........................11W-17N | | 16 |
| Rosewood Ct. E&W .. 7W-17N | | 18 |
| Royal Dr. N&S ...... 9W-17N | | 17 |
| Rt. 43 NW&SE ...... 9W-16N | | 17 |
| Rt. 68 E&W | | |
| ........................10W-18N,8W-18N | | 17 |
| Rudolph Dr. N&S .. 9W-18N | | 17 |
| Russet Ct. NE&SW | | |
| ........................12W-17N | | 16 |
| Russet Ln. E&W.... 12W-17N | | 16 |
| Rutgers Ln. N&S . 12W-17N | | 16 |
| Salceda Dr. N&S | | |
| ........................10W-15N,9W-15N | | 17 |

| | Grid | Page |
|---|---|---|
| Sanders Rd. N&S | | |
| ........................12W-17N,12W-18N | | 16 |
| Saranec N&S .. 10W-17N | | 17 |
| School Dr. E&W ... 10W-16N | | 17 |
| Scotch Pine Ln. N&S | | |
| ........................11W-16N | | 16 |
| Scott Rd. E&W .. 10W-16N | | 17 |
| Second St. (Pvt.) N&S | | |
| ........................10W-16N | | 17 |
| Seville Ct. E&W ... 9W-15N | | 17 |
| Shagback Ln. E&W . 9W-17N | | 17 |
| Shannon Ct. E&W . 11W-17N | | 16 |
| Shannon Rd. E&W | | |
| ........................11W-17N,10W-17N | | 16 |
| Shawnee Tr. N&S . 11W-16N | | 16 |
| Shermer Av. N&S | | |
| ........................10W-16N,9W-17N | | 17 |
| Silverpine Dr. NS&EW | | |
| ........................11W-16N | | 16 |
| Skokie Blvd. NW&SE | | |
| ........................8W-18N | | 18 |
| Sleepy Hollow N&S | | |
| ........................11W-16N | | 16 |
| Smith Rd. N&S .. 11W-16N | | 16 |
| Snowbird Ln. E&W  12W-17N | | 16 |
| Somerset Ln. N&S.. 10W-17N | | 17 |
| Sorrel Dr. E&W .... 11W-18N | | 16 |
| South Bridge Ln. E&W | | |
| ........................10W-16N | | 17 |
| South Ln. N&S .... 8W-16N | | 18 |
| South Wind Dr. N&S | | |
| ........................10W-16N | | 16 |
| Southgate Dr. E&W ..7W-17N | | 18 |
| Spring Hill Dr. NS&EW | | |
| ........................11W-17N | | 16 |
| Spruce Rd. N&S .. 9W-18N | | 17 |
| Spruce St. N&S .... 9W-17N | | 17 |
| Spyglass Ln. NE&SW | | |
| ........................12W-17N | | 16 |
| Stanley St. E&W .. 9W-16N | | 17 |
| Stephens Green E&W | | |
| ........................10W-17N | | 17 |
| Stone Creek* NW&SE | | |
| ........................10W-17N | | 17 |
| Stonebridge Ln. E&W | | |
| ........................10W-16N | | 17 |
| Stonegate Ln. E&W | | |
| ........................11W-17N | | 16 |
| Stowe Ct. NE&SW..10W-18N | | 17 |
| Stratford Pl. N&S .. 11W-17N | | 16 |
| Suffield Ter. NS&EW | | |
| ........................12W-17N | | 16 |
| Sugarpine Ln. N&S | | |
| ........................11W-16N | | 16 |
| Summerfield Rd. NS&EW | | |
| ........................7W-16N | | 18 |
| Summerton Pl. N&S | | |
| ........................10W-17N | | 17 |
| Sunburst Ln. N&S . 12W-17N | | 16 |
| Sunnyside Cir. N&S | | |
| ........................10W-16N | | 17 |
| Sunset Ct. E&W . 7W-16N | | 18 |
| Sunset Ln. E&W .. 12W-16N | | 16 |
| Sunset Ridge Rd. N&S | | |
| ........................8W-16N,8W-17N | | 18 |
| Surrey Ln. N&S....9W-17N | | 17 |
| Sussex Dr. N&S .. 11W-17N | | 16 |
| Sutton Dr. N&S .. 12W-17N | | 16 |
| Sycamore Ln. N&S . 9W-17N | | 17 |
| Tamarind Dr. E&W..11W-18N | | 16 |
| Techny Rd. E&W | | |
| ........................11W-16N,8W-16N | | 16 |
| Terri-lyn Ln. NS&EW | | |
| ........................12W-17N | | 16 |
| The Mews E&W..10W-18N | | 17 |
| The Strand NE&SW | | |
| ........................10W-15N | | 17 |
| Thornapple Ln. NS&EW | | |
| ........................9W-17N | | 17 |
| Thornwood Ln. E&W | | |
| ........................10W-17N,9W-17N | | 17 |
| Thornwood Ln. N&S | | |
| ........................9W-18N | | 17 |
| Timber Ln. N&S .. 9W-17N | | 17 |
| Toulon Dr. NS&EW | | |
| ........................12W-17N | | 16 |
| Touraine Ter. N&S . 12W-18N | | 16 |
| Trailwood Ct. NW&SE | | |
| ........................12W-18N | | 16 |
| Trailwood Ln. NW&SE | | |
| ........................12W-18N | | 16 |
| Tri-state Tollway N&S | | |
| ........................12W-17N | | 16 |
| Tyron Wood* N&S..11W-17N | | 16 |
| Valencia Dr. E&W . 10W-15N | | 17 |
| Valley Rd. N&S .. 11W-16N | | 16 |
| Vermont Av. E&W . 8W-18N | | 18 |
| Versailles Dr. N&S | | |
| ........................12W-18N | | 16 |
| Vicki Ln. E&W .... 11W-15N | | 17 |
| Violet Ln. N&S .. 11W-16N | | 16 |
| Vista Ct.* E&W .... 9W-15N | | 17 |
| Voltz Ct. N&S .... 9W-18N | | 17 |
| Voltz Rd. E&W | | |
| ........................8W-17N,7W-17N | | 18 |
| Wainwright Dr. N&S | | |
| ........................11W-18N | | 16 |
| Walnut Cir. NE&SW | | |
| ........................12W-17N | | 16 |
| Walnut Ln. N&S .. 10W-17N | | 17 |
| Walters Av. E&W | | |
| ........................12W-17N,9W-17N | | 17 |
| Water Edge Ct. N&S | | |
| ........................9W-18N | | 17 |
| Water Edge Ln. NW&SE | | |
| ........................9W-18N | | 17 |
| Waukegan Rd. NW&SE | | |
| ........................8W-16N,10W-18N | | 18 |
| Weber Dr. N&S .. 12W-18N | | 16 |

| | Grid | Page |
|---|---|---|
| Weller Ln. NE&SW..11W-17N | | 16 |
| Wendy Dr. N&S .... 9W-17N | | 17 |
| Wescott Rd. N&S .. 10W-17N | | 17 |
| Wessling Dr. N&S .. 12W-17N | | 16 |
| Western Av. N&S | | |
| ........................10W-16N,10W-17N | | 17 |
| Westwood Ct. N&S | | |
| ........................10W-17N | | 17 |
| Whisperwoods Ct. E&W | | |
| ........................11W-16N | | 16 |
| White Mountain Dr. N&S | | |
| ........................11W-17N | | 16 |
| White Oak Dr. N&S | | |
| ........................11W-16N | | 16 |
| White Pine Dr. E&W | | |
| ........................11W-16N | | 16 |
| Whitehall Dr. NS&EW | | |
| ........................9W-17N | | 17 |
| Whitfield Rd. NW&SE | | |
| ........................8W-17N | | 18 |
| Wildwood Ln. (Pvt.) NS&EW | | |
| ........................8W-17N | | 18 |
| Williamsburg Dr. N&S | | |
| ........................9W-18N | | 17 |
| Willow Ln. N&S .... 8W-17N | | 18 |
| Willow Rd. E&W | | |
| ........................10W-15N,8W-15N | | 17 |
| Wilshire Ln. E&W .. 10W-16N | | 17 |
| Windrush Ln. NS&EW | | |
| ........................10W-18N | | 17 |
| Windsor Ln.* NW&SE | | |
| ........................9W-16N | | 17 |
| Wintercrescent Cir. E&W | | |
| ........................10W-16N | | 17 |
| Wood Dr. N&S .. 10W-16N | | 17 |
| Woodbine Ln. N&S | | |
| ........................10W-16N | | 17 |
| Woodhead Dr. E&W | | |
| ........................12W-18N | | 16 |
| Woodhill Dr. E&W....9W-17N | | 17 |
| Woodland Dr. N&S | | |
| ........................11W-16N,10W-16N | | 16 |
| Woodlark Dr. N&S .. 8W-17N | | 18 |
| Woodlawn Rd. N&S | | |
| ........................10W-17N | | 17 |
| Woodlawn St. E&W | | |
| ........................10W-16N | | 17 |
| Woodmere Ct. N&S | | |
| ........................11W-16N | | 16 |
| Woodmere Dr. E&W | | |
| ........................11W-16N | | 16 |
| York Ct. E&W .... 8W-17N | | 18 |
| Yorkshire Ln. E&W  12W-17N | | 16 |

## Northfield

| | Grid | Page |
|---|---|---|
| Abbot Ct. E&W ...... 7W-15N | | 18 |
| Alice Pl. E&W ...... 7W-15N | | 18 |
| Ash E&W ...... 6W-15N | | 18 |
| Avon Av. N&S ...... 7W-15N | | 18 |
| Balmoral Av., E. N&S | | |
| ........................7W-14N | | 28 |
| Balmoral Av., W. N&S | | |
| ........................7W-14N | | 28 |
| Birchwood Ln. (Pvt.) E&W | | |
| ........................7W-15N | | 18 |
| Bosworth Ln. E&W . 7W-15N | | 18 |
| Bracken Ln. (Pvt.) NS&EW | | |
| ........................7W-15N | | 18 |
| Brandon Rd. N&S....7W-14N | | 28 |
| Briar Ln. (Pvt.) .. 7W-15N | | 18 |
| Bridlegate Ln. NW&SE | | |
| ........................7W-16N | | 18 |
| Bridlewood Ln. NS&EW | | |
| ........................7W-14N | | 28 |
| Bristol Rd. N&S ...... 7W-15N | | 18 |
| Bristol St. N&S ...... 7W-15N | | 18 |
| Brookhill Dr. NE&SW | | |
| ........................7W-16N | | 18 |
| Burr Oak E&W .... 8W-15N | | 18 |
| Camden Ln. E&W....7W-16N | | 18 |
| Canterbury Ln. E&W | | |
| ........................7W-14N | | 28 |
| Central Av. N&S .... 7W-15N | | 18 |
| Chapel Hill Ln. N&S . 7W-15N | | 18 |
| Cherry E&W .... 6W-15N | | 18 |
| Churchill St. N&S .. 7W-15N | | 18 |
| Clover Ln. (Pvt.) E&W | | |
| ........................7W-15N | | 18 |
| Coach Rd. (Pvt.) N&S | | |
| ........................8W-15N | | 18 |
| Colonial Ln. E&W....6W-15N | | 18 |
| Country Ln. E&W....7W-16N | | 18 |
| Courts of Regentwood | | |
| NS&EW ........ 8W-15N | | 18 |
| Coventry Rd. N&S .. 7W-14N | | 28 |
| Crooked Creek E&W | | |
| ........................7W-15N | | 18 |
| Dickens Rd. N&S .. 7W-15N | | 18 |
| Dickens St. N&S .. 7W-15N | | 18 |
| Dorina Dr. E&W .. 8W-15N | | 18 |
| Drury Ln. (Pvt.) E&W | | |
| ........................7W-15N | | 18 |
| Earl Dr. N&S ...... 7W-15N | | 18 |
| Eaton St. N&S ...... 7W-15N | | 18 |
| Eddy Ln. N&S ...... 7W-15N | | 18 |
| Edens Expwy. N&S | | |
| ........................7W-16N,6W-15N | | 18 |
| Edens Ln. N&S ...... 7W-15N | | 18 |
| Edgewood Ln. N&S.. 8W-15N | | 18 |
| Elder St. E&W ...... 7W-15N | | 18 |
| Elm E&W ...... 7W-15N | | 18 |
| Enid Ln. N&S ...... 7W-15N | | 18 |
| Frontage Rd. N&S .. 6W-15N | | 18 |
| Graemere St. N&S .. 7W-15N | | 18 |
| Grove E&W ...... 7W-15N | | 18 |
| Happ Rd. N&S | | |
| ........................7W-16N,6W-15N | | 18 |

| | Grid | Page |
|---|---|---|
| Harding Rd. E&W ....6W-15N | | 18 |
| Heather Ter. E&W .. 7W-15N | | 18 |
| Hedge Row (Pvt.) E&W | | |
| ........................8W-15N | | 18 |
| Holder Ln. E&W .... 6W-15N | | 18 |
| Hoyt Ln. N&S ...... 7W-14N | | 28 |
| Ingram St. N&S.....7W-15N | | 18 |
| Jeffrey St. N&S.....7W-15N | | 18 |
| Lagoon Dr. N&S .... 6W-15N | | 18 |
| Lagoon Ln. N&S .... 6W-14N | | 28 |
| Latrobe Av. N&S .... 6W-15N | | 18 |
| Laurie Ln. N&S ...... 7W-15N | | 18 |
| Linder Av. N&S....6W-15N | | 18 |
| Lockwood Av. N&S .. 6W-15N | | 18 |
| Maple E&W .... 6W-15N | | 18 |
| Maple Row E&W .... 7W-16N | | 18 |
| Martin Ln. E&W .. 6W-15N | | 18 |
| Meadow Lark Ln. N&S | | |
| ........................8W-15N | | 18 |
| Meadowbrook Dr. E&W | | |
| ........................7W-16N | | 18 |
| Meadowview Rd. N&S | | |
| ........................6W-14N | | 28 |
| Meadowwood Ln. N&S | | |
| ........................7W-14N | | 28 |
| Middle Fork Rd. (Pvt.) E&W | | |
| ........................7W-16N | | 18 |
| Mt. Pleasant St. E&W | | |
| ........................6W-15N | | 18 |
| Norfork Rd. N&S .... 7W-15N | | 18 |
| Northfield Rd. N&S .. 7W-15N | | 18 |
| Northfield Sq. N&S .. 7W-15N | | 18 |
| Northgate Rd. NE&SW | | |
| ........................7W-16N | | 18 |
| Oak E&W .... 7W-15N | | 18 |
| Oak Tree Ln. E&W .. 7W-15N | | 18 |
| Old Farm Rd. E&W . 7W-16N | | 18 |
| Old Willow Rd. E&W | | |
| ........................7W-15N | | 18 |
| Orchard Ln. E&W....6W-15N | | 18 |
| Pebble Fork E&W .... 8W-15N | | 18 |
| Pine St. E&W......7W-16N | | 18 |
| Pleasant View Ln. N&S | | |
| ........................7W-15N | | 18 |
| Pvt. Ln. E&W ...... 7W-15N | | 18 |
| Red Barn Ln. N&S . 7W-15N | | 18 |
| Ridge Rd. N&S .... 7W-15N | | 18 |
| Riverside Dr. N&S .. 7W-15N | | 18 |
| Robinhood Ln. NW&SE | | |
| ........................7W-15N | | 18 |
| Rolling Ridge Rd. E&W | | |
| ........................8W-16N | | 18 |
| Rt. 43 N&S........ 8W-15N | | 18 |
| Shadowood Ln. E&W | | |
| ........................7W-16N | | 18 |
| Somerset Ln. (Pvt.) N&S | | |
| ........................7W-15N | | 18 |
| South Ridge Ter. NW&SE | | |
| ........................7W-16N | | 18 |
| Southgate Rd. NE&SW | | |
| ........................7W-16N | | 18 |
| Sterling Ln. NE&SW  7W-15N | | 18 |
| Stockton Dr. N&S .. 7W-15N | | 18 |
| Suffolk Rd. NE&SW.. 7W-16N | | 18 |
| Sunset Dr. E&W .. 7W-16N | | 18 |
| Sunset Rd. E&W .. 6W-15N | | 18 |
| Sunset Ridge Rd. N&S | | |
| ........................8W-16N | | 18 |
| Thackerary St. N&S .. 7W-15N | | 18 |
| Thornwood Ln. (Pvt.) N&S | | |
| ........................7W-15N | | 18 |
| Valley View Rd. NW&SE | | |
| ........................7W-16N | | 18 |
| Wagner Rd. N&S .. 7W-15N | | 18 |
| Walnut N&S ...... 7W-15N | | 18 |
| Westfield Ln. E&W .. 8W-15N | | 18 |
| Whittier Ln. (Pvt.) N&S | | |
| ........................7W-15N | | 18 |
| Willow Hill Ct. N&S . 7W-15N | | 18 |
| Willow Rd. E&W .... 7W-15N | | 18 |
| Willow Ter. E&W .... 7W-15N | | 18 |
| Winfield Ct. N&S .. 6W-14N | | 28 |
| Winfield Dr. E&W .. 6W-14N | | 28 |
| Winnetka Ct. N&S .. 8W-15N | | 18 |
| Winnetka Rd. E&W .. 8W-15N | | 18 |
| Woodland Ln., S. N&S | | |
| ........................7W-15N | | 18 |

## Northfield Township

| | Grid | Page |
|---|---|---|
| Anets Dr. NW&SE .. 9W-16N | | 17 |
| Applegate Ct. N&S  10W-13N | | 27 |
| Applegate Ln. N&S | | |
| ........................10W-13N | | 27 |
| Applegate Rd. E&W | | |
| ........................10W-13N | | 27 |
| Beach Ln. N&S .. 12W-16N | | 16 |
| Central Av. N&S.... 11W-16N | | 16 |
| Central Rd. E&W .. 11W-13N | | 26 |
| Constance Ln. N&S | | |
| ........................12W-18N | | 16 |
| Countryside Ln. E&W | | |
| ........................11W-13N,10W-13N | | 26 |
| Cumberland Dr. N&S | | |
| ........................12W-17N | | 16 |
| East Circle N&S .. 8W-16N | | 18 |
| Elmdale Rd. N&S .. 10W-13N | | 27 |
| Euclid Av. E&W .. 12W-14N | | 26 |
| Evergreen Ln. NW&SE | | |
| ........................12W-16N | | 16 |
| Forest Dr. N&S .. 12W-14N | | 26 |
| Forest Way Dr. N&S | | |
| ........................7W-17N | | 18 |
| Garden St. E&W....11W-16N | | 16 |
| Glendale Rd. N&S .. 10W-13N | | 27 |
| Glenshire Rd. N&S.. 10W-13N | | 27 |
| Glenwood Ln. N&S | | |
| ........................10W-13N | | 27 |

| | Grid | Page |
|---|---|---|
| Greendale Rd. NE&SW | | |
| ........................10W-13N | | 27 |
| Greenleaf Av. E&W | | |
| ........................12W-14N | | 26 |
| Greenwood Rd. N&S | | |
| ........................10W-13N | | 27 |
| Grove Ln. N&S .. 12W-15N | | 16 |
| Grove St. E&W .. 10W-13N | | 27 |
| Henley St. E&W .. 10W-13N | | 27 |
| Highland Av. N&S .. 11W-16N | | 16 |
| Highland Ct. N&S .. 10W-13N | | 27 |
| Hillside Rd. N&S.... 10W-13N | | 27 |
| Holly Av. N&S .... 11W-16N | | 16 |
| Holly Ln. N&S ...... 10W-13N | | 27 |
| Huber Ln. N&S .... 10W-13N | | 27 |
| Knollwood Ln. E&W | | |
| ........................10W-13N | | 27 |
| Landreth Ln. NW&SE | | |
| ........................8W-16N | | 18 |
| Landwehr Rd. N&S | | |
| ........................11W-13N | | 26 |
| Larch Av. E&W .. 12W-14N | | 26 |
| Laurel Av. E&W .. 12W-14N | | 26 |
| Liberty Ln. E&W .. 10W-13N | | 27 |
| Lilac Av. E&W .. 12W-14N | | 26 |
| Linden Av. E&W .. 12W-14N | | 26 |
| Linneman St. E&W  10W-13N | | 27 |
| Locust Av. E&W .. 12W-14N | | 26 |
| Long Meadow Ln. N&S | | |
| ........................10W-13N | | 27 |
| Longview Rd. N&S  11W-16N | | 16 |
| Magnolia St. N&S .. 12W-14N | | 26 |
| Maple Av. E&W .. 12W-17N | | 16 |
| Maple St. N&S .. 12W-14N | | 26 |
| Meadow Ln. NS&EW | | |
| ........................10W-13N | | 27 |
| Meadow St. N&S .. 11W-16N | | 16 |
| Milton St. N&S .. 12W-14N | | 26 |
| Milwaukee Av. NW&SE | | |
| ........................12W-15N,11W-13N | | 16 |
| Oak Av. E&W .. 12W-17N | | 16 |
| Pamela Ln. E&W .. 12W-18N | | 16 |
| Peachgate Ct. N&S | | |
| ........................10W-13N | | 27 |
| Peachgate Ln. N&S | | |
| ........................10W-13N | | 27 |
| Peachgate Rd. E&W | | |
| ........................10W-13N | | 27 |
| Pensive Ln. N&S .. 10W-16N | | 16 |
| Pfingston N&S .. 11W-13N | | 26 |
| Pfingston Rd. N&S.. 11W-13N | | 26 |
| Phyllis Rd. E&W .. 12W-18N | | 16 |
| Post Rd. N&S .. 12W-16N | | 16 |
| Prairie Av. N&S .. 12W-16N | | 16 |
| Revere Rd. N&S.... 10W-13N | | 27 |
| Ridge Dr. N&S ...... 11W-16N | | 16 |
| Riverdale E&W ...... 7W-16N | | 18 |
| Rolling Ridge Rd. E&W | | |
| ........................8W-16N | | 18 |
| Rosedale Rd. N&S.. 10W-13N | | 27 |
| Steeplechase E&W | | |
| ........................8W-16N | | 18 |
| Sunset Trail E&W .. 11W-16N | | 16 |
| Sunshine Ln. N&S .. 12W-18N | | 16 |
| Techny Rd. E&W .. 12W-16N | | 16 |
| Timberlane Dr. E&W | | |
| ........................12W-16N | | 16 |
| Tri-state Tollway N&S | | |
| ........................11W-13N,12W-17N | | 26 |
| Valley Way E&W .. 8W-16N | | 18 |
| Vogay Ln. N&S .. 12W-15N | | 16 |
| Wedel Ln. N&S .. 10W-13N | | 27 |
| Western Av. N&S.. 12W-16N | | 16 |
| Whirlaway Dr. NS&EW | | |
| ........................12W-16N,11W-16N | | 16 |
| Winkleman Rd. NW&SE | | |
| ........................12W-15N | | 16 |

## Northlake

| | Grid | Page |
|---|---|---|
| Alvin N&S .......... 13W-2N | | 46 |
| Armitage E&W ...... 13W-2N | | 46 |
| Ashbel N&S ........ 14W-1N | | 46 |
| Bell Dr. E&W ...... 13W-2N | | 46 |
| Bernice E&W ...... 13W-2N | | 46 |
| Caryl N&S .......... 13W-2N | | 46 |
| Charles E&W ...... 13W-2N | | 46 |
| Country Club Dr. E&W | | |
| ........................13W-2N | | 46 |
| Dewey E&W ...... 13W-2N | | 46 |
| Dickens E&W......13W-2N | | 46 |
| Diversey E&W .... 14W-3N | | 40 |
| Dodd N&S .......... 13W-1N | | 46 |
| East Dr. N&S...... 13W-2N | | 46 |
| Edward N&S ........ 13W-2N | | 46 |
| Elm N&S............ 14W-1N | | 46 |
| Franklin Dr. E&W .. 14W-2N | | 46 |
| Gail N&S .......... 13W-1N | | 46 |
| Geneva N&S ........ 13W-2N | | 46 |
| Golfview Dr. E&W .. 14W-2N | | 46 |
| Haber Ct. N&S .... 13W-2N | | 46 |
| Harold N&S ........ 13W-2N | | 46 |
| Harvard N&S ...... 14W-1N | | 46 |
| Hayes E&W ...... 13W-3N | | 40 |
| Hillside N&S ...... 14W-1N | | 46 |
| Hirsch E&W ...... 13W-2N | | 46 |
| Irving N&S ........ 14W-1N | | 46 |
| Jerome Dr. N&S .. 13W-2N | | 46 |
| Lakewood N&S...... 13W-1N | | 46 |
| Laporte E&W ...... 13W-2N | | 46 |
| Lavergne N&S | | |
| ........................14W-1N,14W-2N | | 46 |
| Le Moyne E&W | | |
| ........................14W-1N,13W-1N | | 46 |
| Lind N&S .......... 14W-1N | | 46 |
| Longfield E&W .... 14W-2N | | 46 |
| Lyndale E&W ...... 13W-2N | | 46 |
| Major Dr. E&W ...... 13W-2N | | 46 |

| | Grid | Page |
|---|---|---|
| Marilyn N&S | | |
| | 13W-1N,13W-2N | 46 |
| McLean N&S | 13W-2N | 46 |
| Medill E&W | 13W-2N | 46 |
| Morse E&W | 13W-1N | 46 |
| Palmer N&S | 13W-2N | 46 |
| Park View Dr. E&W | 13W-2N | 46 |
| Prater N&S | 13W-1N,13W-2N | 46 |
| Railroad Av. N&S | 14W-2N | 46 |
| Rhodes N&S | 14W-3N | 40 |
| Roberta N&S | 13W-2N | 46 |
| Romans N&S | 14W-2N | 46 |
| Roy N&S | 13W-1N,13W-2N | 46 |
| Rt. 16 N&S | 14W-3N | 40 |
| Sandra N&S | 13W-2N | 46 |
| Soffel E&W | 14W-1N,13W-1N | 46 |
| Tri-State Tollway N&S | | |
| | 14W-3N | 40 |
| U.S. Rt. 12 N&S | 13W-1N | 46 |
| U.S. Rt. 20 E&W | 13W-1N | 46 |
| U.S. Rt. 45 N&S | 13W-2N | 46 |
| Victoria Dr. E&W | 13W-1N | 46 |
| Victoria N&S | 13W-1N | 46 |
| Village Dr. E&W | 13W-1N | 46 |
| Wagner Dr. E&W | 13W-3N | 40 |
| West Dr. E&W | 14W-2N | 46 |
| West Dr. N&S | 13W-2N | 46 |
| Westward Ho Dr. E&W | | |
| | 14W-2N | 46 |
| Whitehall E&W | 13W-2N | 46 |
| Whittier E&W | 13W-2N | 46 |
| William N&S | 13W-2N | 46 |
| 44th N&S | 13W-1N | 46 |
| 45th N&S | 13W-1N | 46 |

**Norwood Park Township**

| | Grid | Page |
|---|---|---|
| Balmoral E&W | 10W-6N | 41 |
| Bryn Mawr E&W | 10W-6N | 41 |
| Courtland N&S | 10W-7N | 41 |
| Fairview N&S | 10W-7N | 41 |
| Gregory E&W | 10W-6N | 41 |
| Linden N&S | 9W-6N | 41 |
| Manor Ln. N&S | 10W-7N | 41 |
| Olive E&W | 10W-7N | 41 |
| Prospect N&S | 10W-7N | 41 |
| Redwood N&S | 10W-7N | 41 |
| Seminole E&W | 10W-7N | 41 |
| Summerdale E&W | 10W-6N | 41 |
| Vine N&S | 10W-7N | 41 |
| Washington N&S | 10W-6N | 41 |

**Oak Forest**

| | Grid | Page |
|---|---|---|
| Adele Ln. E&W | 6W-19S | 80 |
| Adeline Pl. E&W | 6W-18S | 80 |
| Aimee Ct. E&W | 6W-19S | 80 |
| Alameda Av. NS&EW | | |
| | 7W-18S | 80 |
| Albert Dr. NW&SE | 7W-18S | 80 |
| Aldersyde Rd. E&W | 6W-20S | 86 |
| Ann Marie Dr. N&S | 6W-18S | 80 |
| Ann Marie Ln. N&S | 6W-18S | 80 |
| Anne Ct. N&S | 6W-18S | 80 |
| Arroyo Dr. N&S | 7W-18S | 80 |
| Avalon E&W | 7W-18S | 80 |
| Babette Ct. E&W | 6W-19S | 80 |
| Barry Ln. E&W | 6W-18S | 80 |
| Barton Ln. N&S | 5W-19S | 80 |
| Becky Ct. N&S | 6W-17S | 80 |
| Bellaire Rd. E&W | 6W-20S | 86 |
| Belle St. N&S | 6W-20S | 86 |
| Beth Ct. N&S | 6W-19S | 80 |
| Betty Ann Ln. N&S | 6W-18S | 80 |
| Blair Ln. N&S | 6W-18S | 80 |
| Boca Rio Dr. N&S | 7W-18S | 80 |
| Bonnie Tr. NS&EW | 6W-20S | 86 |
| Brenden Ln. N&S | 5W-19S | 80 |
| Bret Dr. E&W | 7W-18S | 80 |
| Brianne Ln. N&S | 6W-18S | 79 |
| Briar Ln. N&S | 7W-18S | 80 |
| Brockton Ln. N&S | 5W-19S | 80 |
| Brookwood Dr. E&W | | |
| | 7W-18S | 80 |
| Caletta Ter. E&W | 7W-17S | 80 |
| Carol Belle Tr. E&W | 6W-18S | 80 |
| Carolyn E&W | 6W-18S | 80 |
| Carriage Way E&W | 7W-17S | 80 |
| Catalina Av. E&W | 7W-18S | 80 |
| Cedar Rd. E&W | 8W-18S | 79 |
| Central Av. N&S | | |
| | 7W-18S,7W-17S | 80 |
| Charles E&W | 7W-18S | 80 |
| Charleston St. E&W | 8W-18S | 79 |
| Chaucer Dr. NS&EW | | |
| | 7W-18S | 80 |
| Cherry Rd. N&S | 8W-18S | 79 |
| Chestnut N&S | 8W-18S | 79 |
| Church Ln. N&S | 8W-18S | 79 |
| Cicero Av. N&S | | |
| | 6W-20S,6W-17S | 86 |
| Colina Av. N&S | 7W-18S | 80 |
| Concha Ct. NW&SE | 7W-18S | 80 |
| Condado Dr. N&S | 7W-18S | 80 |
| Corey Ln. E&W | 7W-18S | 80 |
| Coulter Rd. E&W | 6W-20S | 86 |
| Courtney Dr. E&W | 8W-18S | 79 |
| Craig Dr. N&S | 5W-19S | 80 |
| Creekside Dr. NE&SW | | |
| | 6W-18S | 80 |
| Crescent Green Ln. NS&EW | | |
| | 6W-18S | 80 |
| Crescent Ln. E&W | 6W-18S | 80 |
| Cromwell Ln. E&W | 6W-18S | 80 |
| Cypress Ct. E&W | 6W-20S | 86 |
| Dan Ryan Expwy. NE&SW | | |
| | 5W-19S | 80 |

| | Grid | Page |
|---|---|---|
| Daniel Ln. E&W | 7W-17S | 80 |
| David Ln. N&S | 7W-18S | 80 |
| Debbie Ct. NE&SW | 6W-19S | 80 |
| Debra Dr. N&S | 6W-19S | 80 |
| Deerpath Rd. E&W | 6W-20S | 86 |
| Diamond Dr. E&W | 6W-18S | 80 |
| Diane Ct. E&W | 6W-18S | 80 |
| Dolores Dr. E&W | 7W-18S | 80 |
| Dover Rd. NW&SE | 7W-18S | 80 |
| Duncan Rd. N&S | 7W-18S | 80 |
| Edgewood Ct. E&W | 7W-17S | 80 |
| Edward Dr. E&W | 7W-17S | 80 |
| El Morro Ct. E&W | 7W-18S | 80 |
| El Morro Ln. N&S | 7W-18S | 80 |
| El Vista Av. N&S | 6W-17S | 80 |
| Elderwood Ct. E&W | 7W-17S | 80 |
| Elizabeth Ct. NW&SE | | |
| | 6W-20S | 86 |
| Ellen Ct. E&W | 6W-19S | 80 |
| Elm Ln. N&S | 8W-18S | 79 |
| Elmwood Rd. E&W | 6W-20S | 86 |
| Essex Rd. E&W | 7W-18S | 80 |
| Fairfax Rd. E&W | 7W-18S | 80 |
| Farmsley Ct. NW&SE | | |
| | 6W-20S | 86 |
| Fawn Ct. E&W | 6W-18S | 80 |
| Fern Av. E&W | | |
| | 7W-17S,6W-17S | 80 |
| Fieldcrest Dr. E&W | 5W-19S | 80 |
| Forest Ave. N&S | | |
| | 6W-20S,6W-19S | 86 |
| Forest Ct. E&W | 6W-20S | 86 |
| Forest Edge Ln. E&W | | |
| | 6W-17S | 80 |
| Forest Tr. E&W | 6W-17S | 80 |
| Forestview Dr. E&W | | |
| | 8W-18S,7W-18S | 79 |
| Geoffrey Rd. N&S | 7W-18S | 80 |
| George Dr. N&S | 5W-19S | 80 |
| Grange Av. E&W | | |
| | 7W-17S,6W-17S | 80 |
| Greentree Rd. E&W | 6W-19S | 80 |
| Grove Av. N&S | 6W-19S | 80 |
| Harbor Dr. N&S | 7W-17S | 80 |
| Harold St. N&S | 5W-19S | 80 |
| Hawthorne Rd. E&W | | |
| | 6W-20S | 86 |
| Henry St. N&S | 5W-19S | 80 |
| Heron Dr. E&W | 7W-18S | 80 |
| Hickory Ln. N&S | 8W-18S | 79 |
| Hickory Rd. N&S | 8W-18S | 79 |
| Hillside Av. N&S | 7W-18S | 80 |
| Independence Av. E&W | | |
| | 7W-18S | 80 |
| Independence Ct. N&S | | |
| | 6W-17S | 80 |
| Interstate 57 NE&SW | | |
| | 5W-19S | 80 |
| James Dr. NW&SE | 7W-18S | 80 |
| Jamie Ct. E&W | 6W-19S | 80 |
| Jamie Ln. N&S | 6W-19S | 80 |
| Janet Ct. NW&SE | 6W-19S | 80 |
| Jean Ct. N&S | 6W-19S | 80 |
| Jessica Dr. E&W | 6W-20S | 86 |
| Jill Ann Dr. E&W | 7W-18S | 80 |
| Joann Ln. N&S | 7W-18S | 80 |
| Jon Rd. N&S | 7W-18S | 80 |
| Jones Ct. E&W | 6W-17S | 80 |
| Judy Ct. E&W | 6W-20S | 86 |
| Kara Ct. N&S | 6W-20S | 86 |
| Keating N&S | 5W-18S | 80 |
| Kedvale Av. N&S | 5W-18S | 80 |
| Kenneth Av. N&S | 5W-18S | 80 |
| Kenton Av. N&S | 5W-18S | 80 |
| Kilbourn Av. N&S | | |
| | 5W-20S,5W-18S | 86 |
| Kilpatrick Av. N&S | 5W-18S | 80 |
| Kimberly Ct. E&W | 6W-20S | 86 |
| Knollwood Dr. E&W | 7W-17S | 80 |
| Knox Av. N&S | 5W-18S | 80 |
| Kolmar N&S | 5W-18S | 80 |
| La Grange Ct. E&W | 7W-18S | 80 |
| La Palm Ct. E&W | 6W-17S | 80 |
| La Palm Dr. NS&EW | | |
| | 7W-17S | 80 |
| La Paz Ct. N&S | 7W-18S | 80 |
| La Paz Dr. E&W | 7W-18S | 80 |
| Lacrosse Av. N&S | 6W-18S | 80 |
| Lamon Av. N&S | | |
| | 6W-18S,6W-17S | 80 |
| Lancaster Ln. NE&SW | | |
| | 7W-18S | 80 |
| Landings Ln. N&S | 7W-18S | 80 |
| Langley Ct. NW&SE | 6W-20S | 86 |
| Laporte Av. N&S | 6W-18S | 80 |
| Laramie Av. N&S | | |
| | 6W-19S,6W-18S | 80 |
| Laramie Ct. E&W | 6W-18S | 80 |
| Laramie Rd. N&S | 6W-20S | 80 |
| Las Flores Ln. N&S | 7W-18S | 80 |
| Las Robles Ct. NW&SE | | |
| | 7W-18S | 80 |
| Las Robles St. N&S | 7W-18S | 80 |
| Latrobe Av. N&S | | |
| | 6W-19S,6W-18S | 80 |
| Laura Ln. N&S | 5W-19S | 80 |
| Lavergne Av. N&S | | |
| | 6W-19S,6W-17S | 80 |
| Lawler Av. N&S | 6W-17S | 80 |
| Leclaire Av. N&S | | |
| | 6W-20S,6W-17S | 86 |
| Leslie Ln. E&W | 6W-19S | 80 |
| Liberty Square E&W | 7W-18S | 80 |
| Linden Dr. NE&SW | 8W-18S | 79 |
| Linder Av. N&S | 6W-18S | 80 |
| Lisa Ln. N&S | 5W-19S | 80 |
| Lockwood Dr. N&S | | |
| | 6W-19S,16W-18S | 80 |

| | Grid | Page |
|---|---|---|
| Long Av. N&S | | |
| | 6W-19S,6W-17S | 80 |
| Loran Ln. E&W | 6W-17S | 80 |
| Lorel Av. N&S | | |
| | 6W-19S,6W-18S | 80 |
| Lynne Ct. N&S | 6W-18S | 80 |
| Mann St. E&W | 5W-19S | 80 |
| Maple Ct. NW&SE | 8W-18S | 79 |
| Maple Dr. N&S | 8W-18S | 79 |
| Margie Ln. E&W | 6W-19S | 80 |
| Martha Ln. E&W | 6W-20S | 86 |
| Mary Ann Ct. E&W | 6W-19S | 80 |
| Massasoit Av. N&S | 7W-17S | 80 |
| Meadowdale Dr. N&S | | |
| | 6W-20S | 86 |
| Menard Av. N&S | 7W-17S | 80 |
| Merlin Ct. E&W | 6W-18S | 80 |
| Michaele Dr. N&S | 6W-18S | 80 |
| Mission Av. N&S | 6W-18S | 80 |
| Moorings Ct. N&S | 7W-17S | 80 |
| Natalie Dr. NS&EW | 6W-18S | 80 |
| Newport Dr. NE&SW | | |
| | 6W-20S | 86 |
| Oak Park Av. N&S | 8W-18S | 79 |
| Oak Rd. NE&SW | 8W-18S | 79 |
| Oak St. N&S | 8W-18S | 79 |
| Oakland E&W | 7W-18S | 80 |
| Oakwood Ct. NW&SE | | |
| | 6W-20S | 86 |
| Orange Ln. E&W | 8W-18S | 79 |
| Orchard Rd. N&S | 8W-18S | 79 |
| Orogrande Ct. NW&SE | | |
| | 7W-18S | 80 |
| Orogrande St. N&S | 7W-18S | 80 |
| Oxford Ct. N&S | 6W-18S | 80 |
| Pamela Ct. NW&SE | 6W-19S | 80 |
| Park Av. N&S | 7W-17S | 80 |
| Parkside Av. N&S | 7W-17S | 80 |
| Parkwood Ct. E&W | 7W-17S | 80 |
| Peggy Ln. E&W | 7W-18S | 80 |
| Pine Ct. N&S | 8W-18S | 79 |
| Pine Rd. N&S | 8W-18S | 79 |
| Reynolds Ln. N&S | 7W-18S | 80 |
| Richard Av. N&S | 5W-19S | 80 |
| Ridgeland Av. N&S | 8W-18S | 79 |
| Ridgewood Dr. N&S | 7W-17S | 80 |
| Rio Verde Dr. N&S | 7W-18S | 80 |
| Rob Roy Cir. NW&SE | | |
| | 7W-18S | 80 |
| Rob Roy Dr. NS&EW | | |
| | 7W-18S | 80 |
| Roy St. N&S | 7W-18S | 80 |
| Sara Ann Ln. NW&SE | | |
| | 6W-17S | 80 |
| Scarborough Ln. NW&SE | | |
| | 6W-17S | 80 |
| School E&W | 7W-18S | 80 |
| Scott St. E&W | 5W-19S | 80 |
| Sequoia St. N&S | 7W-18S | 80 |
| Sierra Dr. N&S | 7W-18S | 80 |
| Spruce Ln. N&S | 8W-18S | 79 |
| Stuart Ln. E&W | 7W-18S | 80 |
| Sunset Av. N&S | 6W-17S | 80 |
| Sunset Ct. N&S | 6W-17S | 80 |
| Sussex Ct. N&S | 6W-17S | 80 |
| Sycamore Ln. NE&SW | | |
| | 6W-20S | 86 |
| Temple St. N&S | 5W-19S | 80 |
| Terrace Dr. N&S | 7W-18S | 80 |
| Terry Ln. N&S | 5W-19S | 80 |
| Thackery Av. N&S | 6W-20S | 86 |
| Timber Ct. E&W | 6W-20S | 86 |
| Tudor Rd. N&S | 7W-18S | 80 |
| Ventura St. N&S | 7W-18S | 80 |
| Vera Ct. N&S | 6W-19S | 80 |
| Victoria Ct. N&S | 7W-18S | 80 |
| Victoria Dr. E&W | | |
| | 8W-18S,7W-17S | 79 |
| Vine St. E&W | | |
| | 7W-17S,6W-17S | 80 |
| Vista Ct. N&S | 7W-18S | 80 |
| Wagman St. E&W | 7W-18S | 80 |
| Walnut Rd. NE&SW | 8W-18S | 79 |
| Waverly Av. NE&SW | | |
| | 5W-18S | 80 |
| Westview Dr. NS&EW | | |
| | 8W-18S | 79 |
| Willow Ln. N&S | 8W-18S | 79 |
| Willowick Dr. N&S | 5W-19S | 80 |
| Woodland Dr. E&W | 8W-18S | 79 |
| 69th Ct. E&W | 8W-18S | 79 |
| 147th St. E&W | | |
| | 7W-17S,6W-17S | 80 |
| 149th St. E&W | 6W-17S | 80 |
| 150th Pl. E&W | 7W-17S | 80 |
| 150th St. E&W | | |
| | 7W-17S,6W-17S | 80 |
| 151st St. E&W | | |
| | 8W-17S,6W-17S | 79 |
| 152nd Pl. E&W | 8W-18S | 79 |
| 152nd St. E&W | | |
| | 8W-18S,5W-18S | 79 |
| 153rd St. E&W | | |
| | 6W-18S | 80 |
| 154th Pl. E&W | 8W-18S | 79 |
| 154th St. N&S | 8W-18S | 79 |
| 155th Pl. E&W | 8W-18S | 79 |
| 155th St. N&S | 8W-18S | 79 |
| 156th St. E&W | 6W-18S | 80 |
| 157th Pl. E&W | 7W-18S | 80 |
| 157th St. E&W | | |
| | 8W-18S,6W-18S | 79 |
| 158th St. E&W | 6W-18S | 80 |
| 159th St. E&W | | |
| | 8W-18S,6W-18S | 79 |
| 160th St. E&W | 6W-19S | 80 |
| 161st St. E&W | 6W-19S | 80 |
| 162nd St. E&W | 6W-19S | 80 |

| | Grid | Page |
|---|---|---|
| 163rd St. E&W | 6W-19S | 80 |
| 165th St. E&W | 5W-19S | 80 |
| 166th St. E&W | 5W-19S | 80 |
| 167th St. E&W | | |
| | 7W-19S,6W-19S | 80 |
| 169th Pl. E&W | 6W-20S | 86 |
| 169th St. E&W | 6W-20S | 86 |
| 170th Pl. E&W | 6W-20S | 86 |
| 170th St. E&W | 6W-20S | 86 |

**Oak Lawn**

| | Grid | Page |
|---|---|---|
| Adeline Dr. E&W | 5W-12S | 66 |
| Alexander Pl. E&W | 6W-11S | 66 |
| Alice Ct. N&S | 6W-11S | 66 |
| Arnold Pl. NE&SW | 5W-12S | 66 |
| Austin Av. N&S | | |
| | 7W-11S,7W-10S | 66 |
| Avery Pl. E&W | 6W-11S | 66 |
| Avon Av. NW&SE | 8W-11S | 65 |
| Brandt Av. N&S | 6W-11S | 66 |
| Buell Av. N&S | 6W-11S | 66 |
| Burns Av. N&S | 6W-11S | 66 |
| Campbell N&S | 6W-11S | 66 |
| Cass St. E&W | 6W-10S | 66 |
| Central Av. N&S | | |
| | 6W-12S,6W-10S | 66 |
| Cicero Av. N&S | | |
| | 5W-12S,6W-10S | 66 |
| Columbus Dr. NE&SW | | |
| | 6W-10S | 66 |
| Cook Av. N&S | | |
| | 6W-12S,6W-11S | 66 |
| Crescent Ln. N&S | 6W-10S | 65 |
| David Ct. E&W | 7W-11S | 66 |
| Dean Dr. NE&SW | 5W-12S | 66 |
| Deblin Ln. N&S | 6W-12S | 66 |
| Drury Ln. E&W | 6W-11S | 66 |
| Dumke Dr. E&W | 6W-10S | 66 |
| East Shore Dr. NE&SW | | |
| | 6W-11S | 66 |
| Edison Av. N&S | | |
| | 7W-11S,6W-11S | 66 |
| Elm Circle Dr. NE&SW | | |
| | 6W-11S | 66 |
| Fairfax St. E&W | 5W-12S | 66 |
| Franklin Av. NE&SW | | |
| | 6W-11S | 66 |
| Georgia Ln. N&S | 6W-11S | 66 |
| Grant St. E&W | 5W-12S | 66 |
| Harnew Rd., E. N&S | | |
| | 6W-11S | 66 |
| Harnew Rd., S. E&W | | |
| | 6W-11S | 66 |
| Harnew Rd., W. NE&SW | | |
| | 6W-11S | 66 |
| Hilton Dr. N&S | 5W-10S | 66 |
| Jodan Ln. N&S | 6W-10S | 66 |
| Karlov Av. N&S | | |
| | 5W-12S,5W-10S | 66 |
| Kathleen Ln. E&W | 5W-12S | 66 |
| Keating Av. N&S | | |
| | 5W-12S,5W-10S | 66 |
| Kedvale Av. N&S | | |
| | 5W-12S,5W-10S | 66 |
| Keeler Av. N&S | | |
| | 5W-12S,5W-10S | 66 |
| Kenneth Av. N&S | | |
| | 5W-12S,5W-11S | 66 |
| Kenton Av. N&S | | |
| | 5W-12S,5W-11S | 66 |
| Kilbourn Av. N&S | | |
| | 5W-12S,5W-11S | 66 |
| Kildare Av. N&S | | |
| | 5W-12S,5W-11S | 66 |
| Kilpatrick Av. N&S | | |
| | 5W-12S,5W-11S | 66 |
| Kimball Pl. E&W | 6W-11S | 66 |
| Knox Av. N&S | | |
| | 5W-12S,5W-10S | 66 |
| Knox Ct. N&S | 5W-11S | 66 |
| Kolin Av. N&S | | |
| | 5W-12S,5W-11S | 66 |
| Kolmar Av. N&S | | |
| | 5W-12S,5W-10S | 66 |
| Komensky Av. N&S | | |
| | 5W-12S,5W-10S | 66 |
| Kostner Av. N&S | | |
| | 5W-12S,5W-10S | 66 |
| La Crosse Av. N&S | | |
| | 6W-12S,6W-11S | 66 |
| La Porte Av. N&S | 6W-12S | 66 |
| Lamb Dr. E&W | 6W-11S | 66 |
| Lamon Av. N&S | 6W-12S | 66 |
| Laramie Av. N&S | | |
| | 6W-12S,6W-11S | 66 |
| Lavergne Av. N&S | 6W-12S | 66 |
| Lawler Av. N&S | 6W-12S | 66 |
| Lawrence Ct. N&S | 6W-11S | 66 |
| Lawton Dr. NE&SW | 6W-11S | 66 |
| Le Claire Av. N&S | 6W-12S | 66 |
| Linder Av. N&S | 6W-12S | 66 |
| Linus Ln. E&W | 6W-11S | 66 |
| Lockwood Av. N&S | 6W-12S | 66 |
| Long Av. N&S | 6W-12S | 66 |
| Longwood Ln. N&S | 6W-12S | 66 |
| Lorel Av. N&S | 6W-12S | 66 |
| Lynwood Dr. NS&EW | | |
| | 7W-10S | 66 |
| Major Av. N&S | | |
| | 7W-11S,7W-10S | 66 |
| Mansfield Av. N&S | | |
| | 7W-12S,7W-11S | 66 |
| Maple Av. N&S | 7W-11S | 66 |
| Marion Av. N&S | 7W-11S | 66 |
| Mason Av. N&S | | |
| | 7W-12S,7W-11S | 66 |

| | Grid | Page |
|---|---|---|
| Massasoit Av. N&S | | |
| | 7W-11S,7W-10S | 66 |
| Mayfield Av. N&S | | |
| | 7W-12S,7W-10S | 66 |
| Meade Av. N&S | | |
| | 7W-11S,7W-10S | 66 |
| Melvina Av. N&S | | |
| | 7W-11S,7W-10S | 66 |
| Menard Av. N&S | | |
| | 7W-12S,7W-10S | 66 |
| Merrimac Av. N&S | | |
| | 7W-11S,7W-10S | 66 |
| Merton Av. N&S | 7W-11S | 66 |
| Minnick Av. N&S | 6W-11S | 66 |
| Mobile Av. N&S | 7W-10S | 66 |
| Monitor Av. N&S | 7W-10S | 66 |
| Moody Av. N&S | | |
| | 7W-11S,7W-10S | 66 |
| Msgr. Mc Nichols Dr. E&W | | |
| | 7W-10S,7W-9S | 66 |
| Mulberry Av. N&S | 6W-11S | 66 |
| Mulligan Dr. N&S | 7W-10S | 66 |
| Nashville Av. N&S | | |
| | 8W-11S,8W-10S | 65 |
| Natchez Av. N&S | 8W-11S | 65 |
| Natoma Av. N&S | | |
| | 8W-11S,8W-10S | 65 |
| Neva Av. N&S | 8W-10S | 65 |
| New England Av. N&S | | |
| | 8W-11S,8W-10S | 65 |
| Newland Av. N&S | 8W-11S | 65 |
| Nora Av. N&S | 8W-11S | 65 |
| Nordica Av. N&S | 8W-11S | 65 |
| Normandy Av. N&S | | |
| | 8W-11S | 65 |
| North St. E&W | 6W-10S | 66 |
| Nottingham Av. N&S | | |
| | 8W-11S | 65 |
| Oak Center Dr. E&W | | |
| | 6W-11S | 66 |
| Oak Park Av. N&S | | |
| | 8W-11S,8W-10S | 65 |
| Oak St. E&W | 6W-10S | 66 |
| Oakdale Dr. E&W | 6W-11S | 66 |
| Otto Pl. E&W | 6W-10S | 66 |
| Pacific NE&SW | 7W-11S | 66 |
| Pacific SW&NE | 7W-11S | 66 |
| Parke Av. N&S | 7W-11S | 66 |
| Parkside Av. N&S | | |
| | 7W-12S,7W-10S | 66 |
| Paxton Rd. NE&SW | 6W-11S | 66 |
| Pulaski Rd. N&S | | |
| | 5W-12S,5W-10S | 66 |
| Ridgeland Av. N&S | | |
| | 8W-11S,8W-10S | 65 |
| Robertson Av. N&S | 6W-11S | 66 |
| Rt. 7 E&W | 8W-11S,5W-10S | 65 |
| Ruby St. E&W | 6W-10S | 66 |
| Rumsey Av. NE&SW | | |
| | 5W-10S | 66 |
| Rutherford Av. N&S | 8W-11S | 65 |
| Sayre Av. N&S | | |
| | 8W-11S,8W-10S | 65 |
| Scott Ln. E&W | 6W-11S | 66 |
| Southwest Hwy. E&W | | |
| | 7W-11S,5W-10S | 66 |
| Spring Rd. NE&SW | 6W-11S | 66 |
| Sproat Av. N&S | 6W-10S | 66 |
| St. James Ct. N&S | | |
| | 7W-10S | 66 |
| Stillwell Pl. E&W | 5W-12S | 66 |
| Stone Circle E&W | 6W-11S | 66 |
| Stony Creek Dr. NW&SE | | |
| | 6W-12S | 66 |
| Tomcin Tr. E&W | 6W-12S | 66 |
| Tripp Av. N&S | | |
| | 5W-12S,5W-10S | 66 |
| Tulley Av. N&S | | |
| | 6W-11S,6W-10S | 66 |
| W. 107th St. NW&SE | | |
| | 6W-12S | 66 |
| W. 108th Pl. NS&EW | | |
| | 6W-12S | 66 |
| W. 108th St. E&W | 6W-12S | 66 |
| Wabash Av. NE&SW | | |
| | 6W-11S | 66 |
| Wainwright Pl. NE&SW | | |
| | 5W-12S | 66 |
| Warren Av. N&S | 6W-11S | 66 |
| Washington St. N&S | | |
| | 6W-11S | 66 |
| West Shore Dr. NE&SW | | |
| | 6W-11S | 66 |
| Wick Dr. NW&SE | 6W-11S | 66 |
| William Pl. E&W | 5W-11S | 66 |
| Wolfe Dr. NE&SW | 6W-11S | 66 |
| 48th Ct. N&S | 6W-10S | 66 |
| 49th Av. E&W | | |
| | 6W-11S,6W-10S | 66 |
| 49th Ct. N&S | 6W-10S | 66 |
| 50th Av. N&S | 6W-11S | 66 |
| 50th Ct. N&S | 6W-11S | 66 |
| 51st Av. N&S | | |
| | 6W-11S,6W-10S | 66 |
| 51st Ct. N&W | 6W-12S | 66 |
| 52nd Av. N&S | | |
| | 6W-11S,6W-10S | 66 |
| 52nd Ct. N&S | 6W-10S | 66 |
| 53rd Av. N&S | | |
| | 6W-11S,6W-10S | 66 |
| 53rd Ct. E&W | 6W-10S | 66 |
| 54th Av. N&S | | |
| | 6W-11S,6W-10S | 66 |
| 54th Ct. N&S | 6W-10S | 66 |
| 55th Av. N&S | | |
| | 6W-11S,6W-10S | 66 |
| 55th Ct. N&S | 6W-10S | 66 |
| 68th Ct. N&S | 8W-10S | 65 |

Grid Page

69th Av. N&S........8W-10S 65
69th Ct. N&S........8W-10S 65
87th Pl. E&W
........8W-10S,7W-10S 65
87th St. E&W
........8W-10S,6W-10S 65
88th Pl. E&W
........8W-10S,6W-10S 65
88th St. E&W
........8W-10S,6W-10S 65
89th Pl. E&W
........8W-10S,7W-10S 65
89th St. E&W
........7W-10S,6W-10S 66
90th Pl. E&W......7W-10S 66
90th St. E&W
........8W-10S,6W-10S 65
91st Pl. E&W
........8W-10S,6W-10S 65
91st St. E&W
........8W-10S,6W-10S 65
92nd Pl. E&W .... 7W-10S 66
92nd St. E&W
........8W-10S,5W-10S 65
93rd Pl. E&W
........8W-10S,5W-10S 65
93rd St. E&W
........8W-10S,5W-10S 65
94th Pl. E&W
........8W-10S,5W-10S 65
94th St. E&W
........8W-10S,5W-10S 65
95th Pl. E&W
........8W-10S,5W-11S 65
95th St. E&W
........8W-0N,5W-11S 65
96th Pl. E&W
........8W-11S,5W-11S 65
96th St. E&W
........8W-11S,5W-11S 65
97th Pl. E&W
........6W-11S,5W-11S 66
97th St. E&W
........8W-11S,5W-11S 65
98th Pl. E&W
........7W-11S,5W-11S 66
98th St. E&W
........8W-11S,5W-11S 65
99th Pl. E&W
........7W-11S,5W-11S 66
99th St. E&W
........8W-11S,5W-11S 65
100th Pl. E&W
........7W-11S,5W-11S 66
100th St. E&W
........7W-11S,5W-11S 66
101st Pl. E&W
........7W-11S,5W-11S 66
101st St. E&W
........7W-11S,5W-11S 66
102nd Pl. E&W ...... 5W-11S 66
102nd St. E&W
........7W-11S,5W-11S 66
103rd Pl. E&W .... 6W-12S 66
103rd St. E&W
........7W-11S,5W-11S 66
104th Ln. E&W ..... 5W-12S 66
104th Pl. E&W ..... 5W-12S 66
104th St. E&W
........7W-12S,5W-12S 66
105th Pl. E&W
........6W-12S,5W-12S 66
105th St. E&W
........7W-12S,5W-12S 66
106th Pl. E&W
........6W-12S,15W-12S 66
106th St. E&W
........6W-12S,5W-12S 66
107th Pl. E&W
........6W-12S,5W-12S 66
107th St. E&W
........6W-12S,5W-12S 66
108th Pl. E&W
........6W-12S,5W-12S 66
108th St. E&W
........6W-12S,5W-12S 66
109th Pl. E&W
........6W-12S,5W-12S 66
110th Pl. E&W .... 5W-12S 66
110th St. E&W
........6W-12S,5W-12S 66
111th St. E&W
........6W-12S,5W-12S 66

**Oak Park**

Adams E&W.........8W-0S 48
Augusta E&W........7W-1N 48
Austin Blvd. N&S
........7W-0S,7W-1N 48
Belleforte N&S......8W-1N 48
Berkshire E&W......8W-1N 48
Carpenter N&S......8W-1N 48
Clarence N&S........8W-0S 48
Clinton N&S .. 8W-0S,8W-1N 48
Columbian N&S......8W-1N 48
Cuyler N&S....7W-0S,7W-1N 48
East N&S ........ 8W-1N 48
Edmer N&S........8W-1N 48
Elizabeth Ct. E&W....8W-0N 48
Elmwood N&S
........8W-0S,8W-1N 48
Erie E&W .. 8W-0N,7W-0N 48
Euclid N&S ...... 8W-1N 48
Fair Oaks N&S ...... 8W-1N 48
Fillmore E&W........8W-0S 48
Flournoy E&W........7W-0S 48
Forest N&S........8W-1N 48
Garfield E&W .. 8W-0S,7W-0S 48
Greenfield E&W....8W-1N 48
Grove N&S....8W-0S,8W-1N 48

Grid Page

Gunderson N&S ...... 8W-0S 48
Harlem Ct. N&S ...... 8W-0N 48
Harrison E&W ........ 7W-0S 48
Harvard E&W ........ 8S-0S 48
Harvey N&S .. 7W-0S,7W-1N 48
Hayes N&S ...... 7W-1N 48
Highland N&S ...... 8W-0N 48
Holly Ct. E&W ...... 8W-0N 48
Home N&S ........ 8W-0S 48
Humphrey N&S
........7W-0S,7W-1N 48
Iowa E&W............8W-1N 48
Jackson Blvd. E&W....8W-0S 48
Kenilworth N&S
........8W-0S,8W-1N 48
Le Moyne Pkwy. E&W
........8W-1N 48
Lenox E&W .........8W-1N 48
Linden N&S .........8W-1N 48
Lombard N&S 7W-0S,7W-1N 48
Lyman N&S .........7W-0S 48
Madison E&W........8W-0N 48
Maple N&S .... 8W-0S,8W-0N 48
Mapleton N&S......7W-1N 48
Marion N&S .. 8W-0N,8W-1N 48
Miller E&W .........8W-0S 48
Monroe E&W ........ 8W-0S 48
North Blvd. E&W....8W-0N 48
Oak Park N&S
........8W-0S,8W-1N 48
Ontario E&W .........8W-0N 48
Paulina N&S .........8W-1N 48
Pleasant E&W
........8W-0N,7W-0N 48
Pleasant Pl. E&W ....8W-0N 48
Randolph E&W
........8W-0N,7W-0N 48
Ridgeland N&S
........8W-0S,8W-1N 48
Roosevelt E&W......8W-0S 48
Rossell N&S.........8W-1N 48
Schneider E&W......8W-1N 48
Scoville N&S .. 8W-0S,8W-0N 48
South Blvd. E&W ....8W-0N 48
Superior E&W........8W-0N 48
Taylor N&S....7W-0S,7W-1N 48
Thomas E&W .........8W-1N 48
Van Buren E&W......8W-0S 48
Washington E&W....8W-0N 48
Wenonah N&S........8W-0S 48
Wesley N&S .. 8W-0S,8W-0N 48
Westgate E&W .......8W-1N 48
Wisconsin N&S........8W-0S 48
Woodbine N&S ......8W-1N 48

**Olympia Fields**

Achilles Av. N&S ... 4W-24S 92
Alexander St. NW&SE
........3W-25S 92
Apollo Cir. E&W ... 3W-25S 92
Arcadian Dr. NE&SW
........4W-24S 92
Athens Rd. E&W ... 3W-25S 92
Attica Rd. N&S ... 4W-24S 92
Birch Ln. N&S ...... 4W-24S 92
Bristol Ln. N&S ... 3W-25S 92
Brookside Blvd. N&S
........4W-25S 92
Brookwood Dr. NS&EW
........3W-25S,3W-24S 92
Brookwood Ter. N&S
........3W-24S 92
Byron Ct. NE&SW . 4W-25S 92
Cambridge Ln. N&S .. 3W-25S 92
Chariot Ln. E&W ... 3W-24S 92
Chelsea Ct. E&W ...3W-25S 92
Corinth Rd. N&S
........3W-25S,3W-24S 92
Country Club Rd. NE&SW
........3W-24S 92
Crawford Av. N&S
........4W-25S,4W-24S 92
Cumberland Tr. NW&SE
........4W-24S 92
Cumnock Rd. N&S .. 4W-25S 92
Danube Way N&S . 4W-25S 92
Dartmouth Ln. E&W ..3W-25S 92
Doria Ln. NE&SW .. 4W-24S 92
Dutra N&S........ 2W-24S 93
Elliott Ct. NS&EW....4W-25S 92
Evergreen Cir. N&S .. 4W-25S 92
Exmoor Rd. N&S ... 4W-25S 92
Fairfield Av. N&S .. 4W-24S 92
Gardner Av. N&S
........2W-25S,2W-24S 93
Gleneagles Dr. E&W 3W-24S 92
Governors Dr. NE&SW
........4W-24S 92
Governors Hwy. NE&SW
........4W-25S,4W-24S 92
Graymoor Ln. NS&EW
........2W-24S 93
Greenwood Cen. Ct. N&S
........4W-25S 92
Greenwood Ct. E&W
........4W-25S 92
Greenwood Dr. E&W
........4W-25S 92
Harding Av. N&S .. 4W-25S 92
Harding St. N&S .. 3W-25S 92
Hellenic Dr. N&S .. 3W-24S 92
Hutchinson Av. N&S
........2W-25S,2W-24S 93
Ionia Av. N&S .... 4W-24S 92
Ithaca Rd. NE&SW .. 4W-24S 92
Joe Orr Rd. E&W....2W-24S 93

Grid Page

Kedzie Av. N&S ...... 92
Lincoln Hwy. E&W
........4W-25S,4W-24S 92
London Dr. E&W ... 3W-25S 92
Marathon Ct. N&S .. 4W-24S 92
Maros Ln. E&W.....3W-25S 92
Mellett Ct. E&W .. 4W-24S 92
Mohawk Tr. NE&SW
........4W-24S 92
Oakwood Dr. E&W .. 3W-24S 92
Oakwood Ter. NE&SW
........3W-25S 92
Olympian Way NE&SW
........3W-24S 92
Olympic Cir. E&W .. 4W-24S 92
Orchard Dr., N. N&S
........3W-25S 92
Oregon Tr. NE&SW .. 4W-24S 92
Overland Trail NE&SW
........4W-24S 92
Paris Rd. E&W ..... 3W-25S 92
Parthenon Way E&W
........4W-24S 92
Pine Av. E&W .... 4W-25S 92
Platte Tr. E&W .... 4W-24S 92
Promethian Way N&S
........3W-24S 92
Reigler Dr. N&S....3W-25S 92
Roslyn Rd. N&S ... 4W-25S 92
Santa Fe Trail NW&SE
........4W-24S 92
Sheffield Cir. NE&SW
........3W-25S 92
Sparta Ct. NE&SW .. 3W-25S 92
Sparta Ln. N&S.....3W-25S 92
St. Andrews Ct. N&S
........3W-24S 92
St. Andrews Dr. E&W
........3W-24S 92
Strauss Ln. N&S .. 4W-24S 92
Tenata Ct. N&S.....3W-24S 92
Thaxted Cir. NE&SW
........4W-25S 92
Thornwood Dr. E&W .. 4W-25S 92
Trails Dr. NW&SE .... 4W-24S 92
Travers Av. N&S
........2W-25S,2W-24S 93
Troy Cir. N&S .... 3W-25S 92
U.S. Rt. 30 E&W
........4W-25S,3W-24S 92
Vollmer Rd. E&W
........4W-24S,2W-24S 92
Warren Ct. N&S .. 3W-25S 92
Washington St. N&S
........3W-25S 92
Western Av. N&S
........3W-25S,3W-24S 92
Wilderness Tr. N&S .. 4W-24S 92
Wingate Rd. N&S .. 4W-25S 92
Woodland Ct. E&W .. 4W-25S 92
Woodland Dr. E&W . 4W-25S 92
Woodstock Rd. N&S
........4W-25S 92
203rd St. E&W
........4W-24S,3W-24S 92
204th St. E&W
........4W-24S,3W-24S 92
205th St. E&W .... 4W-24S 92
206th St. E&W .... 4W-24S 92
207th St. E&W .... 4W-24S 92

**Orland Hills**

Applewood Ln. N&S
........11W-19S 78
Beacon Ct. E&W .. 11W-19S 78
Beacon Ln. N&S....11W-19S 78
Birch Ct. N&S......11W-19S 78
Birchwood Dr. E&W
........11W-19S 78
Brigitte Ct. N&S .. 11W-19S 78
Cedarwood Dr. NW&SE
........11W-19S 78
Christopher Av. N&S
........11W-19S 78
Dwight Ct. E&W .. 11W-19S 78
Elm Pl. E&W ..... 11W-19S 78
Fox Ct. E&W ..... 11W-19S 78
Haven Av. N&S .. 11W-20S 85
Haven Av. NE&SW 11W-19S 78
Herbert Ct. NW&SE
........11W-19S 78
Hickory Ln. N&S ...11W-20S 85
Hickory Dr. E&W .. 11W-20S 85
Highview Av. N&S .. 11W-20S 85
Hilltop Av. N&S .... 11W-20S 85
Hobart Av. N&S .. 11W-20S 85
Hunter's Ct. E&W .. 11W-19S 78
Leslie Dr. E&W .... 11W-19S 78
Marigold Pl. N&S .. 11W-19S 79
Marilyn E&W .... 11W-19S 78
Marshfield Ln. E&W
........11W-19S 79
Meadowview Dr. E&W
........11W-19S 79
Pepperwood Ln. N&S
........11W-19S 78
Pristine Pl. N&S .. 11W-19S 79
Quail Ct. N&S .... 11W-19S 78
Redwood Ct. N&S .. 11W-19S 85
Rioge Ln. N&S .... 11W-19S 78
Rosebud Pl. N&S .. 11W-19S 79
Sharon Ct. N&S .. 11W-19S 78
Vicky Ln. N&S....11W-20S 85
Westwood Ct. N&S
........11W-20S 85

Grid Page

Westwood Dr. E&W
........11W-20S 85
Willow Terrace Dr. E&W
........11W-19S 78
88th Ct. N&S .... 11W-20S 85
88th St. N&S
........11W-20S,11W-19S 85
89th Av. N&S .. 11W-20S 85
89th Ct. N&S .... 11W-20S 85
90th Av. N&S .. 11W-20S 85
90th Ct. N&S .. 11W-19S 78
91st Av. N&S
........11W-20S,11W-19S 85
92nd Av. N&S
........11W-20S,11W-19S 85
93rd Av. N&S .. 11W-20S 85
94th Av. N&S
........11W-20S,11W-19S 85
159th Pl. E&W .. 11W-19S 78
160th Pl. E&W .. 11W-19S 78
161st Pl. E&W ..11W-19S 78
161st St. E&W .. 11W-19S 78
162nd St. E&W .. 11W-19S 78
163rd St. E&W .. 11W-19S 78
167th Pl. E&W .. 11W-20S 85
167th St. E&W .. 11W-19S 78
169th Pl. E&W .. 11W-20S 85
169th St. E&W .. 11W-20S 85
170th Pl. E&W .. 11W-20S 85
170th St. E&W .. 11W-20S 85
171st St. E&W .. 11W-20S 85

**Orland Park**

Abbey Ln. E&W ....11W-18S 78
Acacia Dr. N&S .... 10W-18S 79
Addison Ln. N&S ... 13W-21S 84
Adria Ct. N&S....10W-15S 73
Alabama Ct.* NE&SW
........13W-22S 84
Alaska Ct.* NE&SW
........13W-22S 84
Aldwych Dr. N&S ...9W-16S 79
Alice Dr. N&S .. 13W-21S 84
Alpine Dr. N&S .. 14W-18S 78
Alveston St. E&W .. 12W-17S 78
Andrea Ct. E&W ....13W-21S 84
Andrea Dr. NS&EW
........13W-21S 84
Anne Ct. NE&SW .. 10W-18S 79
Anne Dr. E&W .. 10W-18S 79
Apache Ln. N&S .. 9W-16S 79
Apache Pl. E&W .. 9W-16S 79
Arbor Dr. E&W .. 14W-18S 78
Arbor Ridge Ln. NW&SE
........11W-18S 78
Aris Ct. NW&SE .. 11W-18S 78
Arizona Ct. N&S....13W-22S 84
Arkansas Ct. NE&SW
........13W-22S 84
Arrowhead Ct. N&S
........10W-16S 79
Arrowhead Ln. E&W
........10W-16S 79
Arthur Ct. E&W .. 13W-21S 84
Arthur Dr. N&S .. 13W-21S 84
Ascot Ct. E&W .. 11W-18S 78
Ash St. N&S .. 11W-17S 78
Ashford Ct. NS&EW
........13W-16S 78
Ashley Ct. N&S .. 10W-17S 79
Ashley Dr. E&W .. 10W-17S 79
Ashton Ln. SW&NE
........13W-16S 78
Ashwood Ln. NW&SE
........14W-20S 84
Aspen St. N&S .. 11W-17S 78
Aster Ln. N&S .. 9W-16S 79
Atwood Ct. E&W .. 13W-16S 78
Aubrieta Ct. N&S .. 9W-18S 79
Aubrieta Ln. E&W....9W-18S 79
Auburn Ct. E&W .. 12W-16S 78
Avenida Del Este N&S
........12W-17S 78
Avenida Del Norte E&W
........12W-17S 78
Baltuscrol Dr. N&S
........11W-18S,10W-18S 78
Barleycorn Ct. E&W
........11W-18S 78
Bayberry Ct. N&S .. 10W-18S 79
Bayhill Ct. E&W .. 10W-18S 79
Beacon Av. N&S...12W-17S 78
Bedford Ln. N&S .. 11W-18S 78
Beech St. N&S .. 11W-17S 78
Begonia Ct. N&S .. 9W-18S 79
Berkhansted Ct. E&W
........10W-16S 79
Bernard Dr. EW&NS
........13W-21S 84
Beth Dr. E&W .. 13W-21S 84
Beverly Ln. E&W .. 10W-15S 73
Billinary Ct. E&W .. 14W-21S 84
Biloba Ln. E&W .. 11W-17S 78
Biltmore Dr. E&W .. 10W-18S 79
Binford Dr. E&W .. 10W-16S 79
Birch St. NS&EW .. 11W-17S 78
Birchbark Ct. N&S .. 11W-17S 78
Blackhawk Ln. N&S ..9W-16S 79
Blue Heron Dr. NE&SW
........13W-20S 84
Bluejay Dr. E&W .. 13W-20S 84
Bob-o-link Rd. N&S
........10W-18S 79
Bonbury Ln. N&S .. 10W-16S 79
Bos Dr. EW&NS .. 13W-21S 84
Boyne Ct. NW&SE .. 14W-21S 84
Bradford Ln. E&W .. 11W-17S 78

Grid Page

Bradley Ct. E&W .. 14W-21S 84
Braeburn Ln. E&W .. 10W-18S 79
Bramlett Ct. .. 14W-17S 78
Brassie Ct. N&S .... 10W-18S 79
Brassie Dr. N&S....10W-18S 79
Brentwood Av. N&S
........11W-17S 78
Briarwood Ln. E&W
........11W-15S 72
Brighton Ct. NS&EW
........10W-16S 79
Brigitte Ter. E&W .. 14W-16S 78
Bromley St. E&W .. 10W-17S 79
Brook Crossing Ct. NE&SW
........14W-20S 84
Brook Crossing Dr. NE&SW
........14W-20S 84
Brook Hill Ct. E&W 14W-21S 84
Brook Hill Dr. NS&EW
........14W-21S,14W-20S 84
Brook St. N&S .... 12W-17S 78
Brookdale Ct. E&W
........14W-20S 84
Brookfield Dr. NS&EW
........14W-20S 84
Brookgate Dr. N&S
........14W-20S 84
Brookshire Dr. E&W
........14W-20S 84
Brookwood Ct. N&S
........14W-20S 84
Brookwood Dr. NS&EW
........14W-20S 84
Brushwood Ln. NW&SE
........14W-20S 84
Bunker Dr. NS&EW
........10W-18S 79
Butler Ct. N&S .... 10W-18S 79
Butterfield Ln. E&W
........11W-15S,10W-15S 72
Byron Dr. N&S .. 11W-19S 78
Caddy Ct. E&W .. 11W-17S 78
California Ct.* NW&SE
........13W-22S 84
Calypso Ln. N&S .. 9W-18S 79
Cambridge Dr. E&W
........10W-16S,9W-16S 79
Camden Dr. N&S .. 10W-16S 79
Camelia Ln. NS&EW
........10W-18S 79
Cameron Pkwy. NS&EW
........14W-21S 84
Canterbury Ln. N&S
........10W-18S 79
Cardinal Dr. N&S .. 13W-20S 84
Carlisle Ln. N&S .. 11W-17S 78
Carnoustie Dr. E&W
........11W-18S,10W-18S 78
Carol Ct. N&S....10W-18S 79
Carolina Ln. N&S .. 11W-16S 79
Carolyn Ct. N&S .. 13W-18S 78
Cascade Ct. E&W .. 9W-17S 79
Cashew Dr. E&W .. 10W-18S 79
Castlebar Ln. N&S ..11W-17S 78
Catalina Ct. N&S .. 9W-18S 79
Catalina Dr. N&S .. 10W-18S 79
Cathrine Ct.* E&W .. 12W-16S 78
Cathrine Dr. N&S .. 12W-16S 78
Cedar St. N&S .. 10W-16S 79
Centennial Ct. N&S
........12W-18S 78
Centennial Dr. N&S
........12W-18S 78
Chadburn Dr. E&W 11W-19S 78
Chapel Hill Rd. N&S
........10W-16S 79
Charleston Dr. N&S
........11W-16S 79
Chateau Ct. E&W .. 9W-17S 79
Chauser Dr. N&S .. 13W-20S 84
Cherry Hills Ct. N&S
........10W-16S 79
Cherry Ln. N&S .. 10W-16S 79
Cherrywood Ct. N&S
........10W-18S 79
Chertsey E&W .. 10W-17S 79
Chesterfield Ln. N&S
........11W-18S 78
Chestnut Dr. N&S .. 9W-18S 79
Cheswick Dr. N&S .. 10W-16S 79
Christine Ct. E&W .. 11W-16S 79
Churchview Dr. N&S
........11W-19S 78
Clairmont Ct.* E&W
........10W-17S 79
Claridge Ct. N&S .. 9W-17S 79
Clearview Dr. N&S
........11W-17S,11W-16S 78
Coghill Ln. N&S .. 11W-16S 79
Coleman Dr. N&S .. 13W-18S 78
Colette Ct. E&W .. 10W-18S 79
Colorado Ct.* E&W
........13W-22S 84
Concord Dr. N&S .. 11W-17S 78
Connecticut Ct.* NE&SW
........13W-22S 84
Constitution Ct. E&W
........12W-18S 78
Constitution Dr. E&W
........12W-18S 78
Cordoba Ct. N&S .. 12W-18S 78
Cottonwood Ct. N&S
........14W-18S 78
Country Club Ln. N&S
........10W-18S 79
Country Ct. NW&SE
........10W-18S 79
Coventry Ct. N&S .. 10W-18S 79

| | Grid | Page |
|---|---|---|
| Cranna Ct. E&W | 14W-21S | 84 |
| Creek Crossing Dr. NE&SW | | |
| | 14W-16S | 78 |
| Creekside Dr. NW&SE | | |
| | 14W-16S | 78 |
| Cressmoor Ct. E&W | | |
| | 10W-18S | 79 |
| Crestview Ct. NW&SE | | |
| | 14W-21S | 84 |
| Crestview Dr. NS&EW | | |
| | 14W-21S | 84 |
| Crestwood Dr. E&W | | |
| | 14W-16S | 78 |
| Cristina Av. NS&EW | | |
| | 10W-16S | 79 |
| Croydon Ln. E&W | 11W-18S | 78 |
| Crystal Ridge Ct. E&W | | |
| | 13W-17S | 78 |
| Crystal Springs Ln. NS&EW | | |
| | 13W-17S | 78 |
| Crystal Tree Dr. E&W | | |
| | 13W-17S | 78 |
| Cypress Ct. NE&SW | | |
| | 11W-17S | 78 |
| Dakota Ln. E&W | 9W-16S | 78 |
| Danbury Ln. E&W | 11W-18S | 78 |
| Davids Ln. N&S | 13W-21S | 84 |
| Dear Island Av. E&W | | |
| | 13W-19S | 78 |
| Deer Run Dr. N&S | 13W-20S | 84 |
| Deerfield Ct. N&S | 10W-18S | 79 |
| Deerpath Dr. N&S | 10W-16S | 79 |
| Delaware Ct.* NE&SW | | |
| | 13W-22S | 84 |
| Devonshire Ln. N&S | | |
| | 11W-18S | 78 |
| Dewberry Ln. E&W | | |
| | 11W-18S | 78 |
| Dexter Ct. E&W | 11W-17S | 78 |
| Dogwood Dr. NW&SE | | |
| | 11W-17S | 78 |
| Doral Ln. E&W | 11W-16S | 78 |
| Dorstep Ln. E&W | 10W-17S | 79 |
| Dublin St. E&W | 11W-17S | 78 |
| Eagle Ridge Dr. NS&EW | | |
| | 13W-21S | 84 |
| Edgewood Dr. N&S | | |
| | 10W-18S | 79 |
| Eileen Ct. NW&SE | 11W-16S | 78 |
| El Cameno Ct. E&W | | |
| | 12W-18S | 78 |
| El Cameno Ct. E&W | | |
| | 12W-18S | 78 |
| El Cameno Re'al N&S | | |
| | 12W-18S,12W-17S | 78 |
| El Cameno Ter. N&S | | |
| | 12W-18S | 78 |
| Elizabeth Av. NS&EW | | |
| | 10W-16S | 79 |
| Elm St. N&S | 11W-16S | 78 |
| Equestrian Tr. NS&EW | | |
| | 13W-18S | 78 |
| Esther N&S | 13W-21S | 84 |
| Evergreen Av. N&S | 9W-18S | 79 |
| Evergreen Dr. N&S | 9W-18S | 79 |
| Eynsford Dr. E&W | 10W-17S | 79 |
| Fairmont Ct.* NE&SW | | |
| | 10W-17S | 79 |
| Fairway Dr. E&W | 14W-20S | 84 |
| Fane Ct. E&W | 14W-20S | 84 |
| Farm Hill Dr. NE&SW | | |
| | 10W-18S | 79 |
| Fawn Creek Ln. E&W | | |
| | 14W-18S | 78 |
| Fawn Ct. NE&SW | 10W-15S | 73 |
| Feather Ct. NE&SW | | |
| | 10W-15S | 73 |
| Fernwood Ct. NW&SE | | |
| | 11W-17S | 78 |
| Fir St. N&S | 10W-16S | 79 |
| Firestone Dr. N&S | 11W-16S | 72 |
| Flamingo Cir. E&W | 10W-18S | 79 |
| Flint Ln. N&S | 10W-15S | 73 |
| Florida Ct.* NE&SW | | |
| | 13W-22S | 84 |
| Foxbend Ct. N&S | 10W-18S | 79 |
| Frances Ln. N&S | 11W-18S | 78 |
| Franchesca Ct. E&W | | |
| | 12W-18S | 78 |
| Franklin Ct. E&W | 11W-17S | 78 |
| Garden View Ct. N&S | | |
| | 9W-18S | 79 |
| Garrett Dr. E&W | 13W-21S | 84 |
| Georgia Ct.* N&S | 13W-22S | 84 |
| Ginger Creek Ln. E&W | | |
| | 14W-18S | 78 |
| Glen Oak Rd. E&W | | |
| | 10W-18S | 79 |
| Gleneagle Ln. N&S | 11W-16S | 78 |
| Glenlake Dr. N&S | 13W-18S | 78 |
| Glenwoody Ct. E&W | | |
| | 10W-16S | 79 |
| Golf Rd. NS&EW | 13W-17S | 78 |
| Golfview Dr. E&W | 10W-17S | 79 |
| Grace Rd. E&W | 10W-18S | 79 |
| Grandview Dr. N&S | | |
| | 14W-18S | 78 |
| Grange Dr. N&S | 14W-20S | 84 |
| Grants Tr. N&S | 13W-19S | 84 |
| Great Egret Dr. E&W | | |
| | 13W-20S | 84 |
| Green Valley Dr. N&S | | |
| | 14W-16S | 84 |
| Green View Rd. N&S | | |
| | 13W-17S | 78 |
| Greencastle Ln. E&W | | |
| | 11W-17S | 78 |
| Greenfield Ct. N&S | 14W-21S | 84 |
| Greenfield Dr. E&W | | |
| | 14W-21S | 84 |
| Greenland Av. N&S | | |
| | 12W-17S | 78 |
| Hackney Dr. N&S | 12W-19S | 78 |
| Hale Dr. N&S | 11W-17S | 78 |
| Halesia Ct. E&W | 9W-18S | 79 |
| Harbor Town Dr. N&S | | |
| | 9W-18S | 79 |
| Harlem Av. N&S | 9W-18S | 79 |
| Hartwood Ct.* E&W | | |
| | 12W-16S | 78 |
| Harvest Crossing E&W | | |
| | 14W-17S | 78 |
| Harvest Hill Ct. NW&SE | | |
| | 14W-21S | 84 |
| Harvest Hill Dr. NW&SE | | |
| | 14W-20S | 84 |
| Haverhill Ln. N&S | 14W-16S | 78 |
| Hawaii Ct.* N&S | 13W-22S | 84 |
| Hawthorne Dr. E&W | | |
| | 12W-17S | 78 |
| Hazel Ct. NW&SE | 12W-17S | 78 |
| Heather Ct. N&S | 9W-18S | 79 |
| Helen Ct. N&S | 11W-18S | 78 |
| Helen Ln. E&W | 11W-18S | 78 |
| Hemlock Dr. E&W | | |
| | 9W-18S,10W-16S | 79 |
| Hempstead Ln. N&S | 9W-16S | 78 |
| Henry St. E&W | 10W-18S | 79 |
| Hiawatha Trail NS&EW | | |
| | 12W-18S | 78 |
| Hibiscus Dr. E&W | 12W-17S | 78 |
| Hidden Brook Ct. NE&SW | | |
| | 14W-20S | 84 |
| Highbrush Rd. N&S | | |
| | 13W-20S | 84 |
| Highgate Ct. E&W | 10W-17S | 79 |
| Highland Av. N&S | | |
| | 12W-18S,12W-17S | 78 |
| Highwood Ct. NW&SE | | |
| | 14W-20S | 84 |
| Highwood Dr. NW&SE | | |
| | 14W-20S | 84 |
| Hill Creek Ct. N&S | 14W-20S | 84 |
| Hillcrest Dr. E&W | 12W-19S | 78 |
| Hilltop Ct. E&W | 12W-18S | 78 |
| Hilltop Dr. N&S | 12W-18S | 78 |
| Holiday Ct. N&S | 12W-17S | 78 |
| Hollow Tree Ct. NW&SE | | |
| | 13W-17S | 78 |
| Hollow Tree Rd. NS&EW | | |
| | 13W-17S | 78 |
| Holly Ct. N&S | 12W-17S | 78 |
| Hollyhock Ct. N&S | 9W-18S | 79 |
| Hollywood Dr. N&S | | |
| | 10W-18S | 79 |
| Hopkins Ct. N&S | 12W-17S | 78 |
| Horn Rd. N&S | 10W-18W | 79 |
| Huguelet Pl. E&W | 11W-17S | 78 |
| Hummingbird Hill Dr. E&W | | |
| | 12W-19S | 78 |
| Huntington Ct. N&S | | |
| | 12W-18S,12W-17S | 78 |
| Huntington Pl. NW&SE | | |
| | 12W-17S | 78 |
| Hyacinth Dr. E&W | 12W-17S | 78 |
| Idaho Ct.* NE&SW | 13W-22S | 84 |
| Idlewild Dr. N&S | 11W-16S | 78 |
| Indiana Ct.* NE&SW | | |
| | 13W-22S | 84 |
| Innsbrook Dr. N&S | 14W-18S | 79 |
| Innshmor Ct. E&W | 14W-21S | 84 |
| Inverness Dr. N&S | 11W-16S | 78 |
| Iowa Ct.* NE&SW | 13W-22S | 84 |
| Irving Av. N&S | 12W-17S | 78 |
| Ishnala Dr. N&S | 9W-16S | 79 |
| Jean Creek Dr. N&S | | |
| | 11W-15S | 73 |
| Jefferson Av. N&S | 12W-17S | 78 |
| Jennifer Dr. N&S | 13W-21S | 84 |
| Jenny Ln. N&S | 13W-18S | 78 |
| Jillian Rd. NS&EW | 13W-18S | 78 |
| John Charles Dr. NW&SE | | |
| | 13W-21S | 84 |
| John Humphrey Dr. N&S | | |
| | 11W-17S | 78 |
| Juniper Ct. E&W | 11W-17S | 78 |
| Kansas Ct.* NE&SW | | |
| | 13W-22S | 84 |
| Karley Ln. N&S | 14W-21S | 84 |
| Kathy Ct. E&W | 11W-16S | 78 |
| Katy Ln. N&S | 10W-17S | 79 |
| Kelsey Ln. N&S | 14W-21S | 84 |
| Kemper Dr. N&S | 11W-18S | 78 |
| Kennedy Ct. E&W | 11W-17S | 78 |
| Kensington Way E&W | | |
| | 11W-18S | 78 |
| Kiley Ln. E&W | 14W-21S | 84 |
| Kingsport Rd. N&S | 13W-19S | 78 |
| Kingston Ln. E&W | 11W-18S | 78 |
| Kingswood Dr. E&W | | |
| | 14W-16S | 78 |
| Knightsbridge Ln. E&W | | |
| | 11W-18S | 78 |
| Knollwood Ln. E&W | | |
| | 10W-18S | 79 |
| Kropp Ct. N&S | 14W-20S | 84 |
| La Grange Rd. N&S | | |
| | 12W-18S,12W-16S | 78 |
| La Reina Ct. E&W | 12W-17S | 78 |
| La Reina Re'al N&S | | |
| | 12W-18S,12W-17S | 78 |
| Laguna Ln. E&W | 9W-18S | 79 |
| Lake Brook Dr. NE&SW | | |
| | 14W-20S | 84 |
| Lake Hills Dr. N&S | 10W-18S | 79 |
| Lake Lawn Ln. NE&SW | | |
| | 14W-18S | 78 |
| Lake Ridge Rd. NE&SW | | |
| | 13W-17S | 78 |
| Lakebrook Ct. N&S | | |
| | 14W-20S | 84 |
| Lakebrook Dr. NE&SW | | |
| | 14W-20S | 84 |
| Lakeside Dr. NS&EW | | |
| | 13W-18S | 78 |
| Lakeview Dr. NS&EW | | |
| | 11W-17S | 78 |
| Lancaster Ct. N&S | 11W-18S | 78 |
| Landings Dr. E&W | 13W-20S | 84 |
| Larkspur Ln. N&S | 9W-18S | 79 |
| Laurel Dr. N&S | 10W-19S | 79 |
| Laurel Hill Dr. E&W | | |
| | 13W-20S | 84 |
| Lawrence Ct. NE&SW | | |
| | 10W-18S | 79 |
| Lee St. N&S | 13W-20S | 84 |
| Legend Ln. E&W | 10W-16S | 79 |
| Leicester Ct. N&S | 10W-16S | 79 |
| Lexington Cir. E&W | | |
| | 10W-16S | 79 |
| Liberty Ct. N&S | 12W-18S | 78 |
| Lilac Ct. N&S | 9W-18S | 79 |
| Lincoln Ct. E&W | 11W-17S | 78 |
| Lincolnshire Dr. N&S | | |
| | 11W-16S | 78 |
| Lindsay Dr. N&S | 10W-16S | 79 |
| Lisa Ct. N&S | 10W-18S | 79 |
| Lissp Annon Ct. E&W | | |
| | 14W-20S | 84 |
| Lori Ln. NW&SE | 11W-16S | 78 |
| Louetta Ln. E&W | 13W-21S | 84 |
| Lunar Ct. E&W | 11W-17S | 78 |
| Lynn Dr. E&W | 13W-21S | 84 |
| Magarita Av. N&S | 9W-16S | 79 |
| Magnolia Ct. E&W | 11W-17S | 78 |
| Mallard Cir. NW&SE | | |
| | 10W-18S | 79 |
| Maple E&W | 11W-17S | 78 |
| Maple Av. N&S | 10W-16S | 79 |
| Marilyn Ct. E&W | 13W-16S | 78 |
| Marilyn Ter. N&S | 13W-16S | 78 |
| Marley Brook Ct. N&S | | |
| | 14W-20S | 84 |
| Mary Dr. NE&SW | 11W-18S | 78 |
| Mason Ln. N&S | 11W-17S | 78 |
| Maude Dr. N&S | 13W-21S | 84 |
| Maycliff Dr. N&S | 10W-17S | 79 |
| Mayfair Ln. E&W | 11W-18S | 78 |
| Mayflower Ln. NS&EW | | |
| | 13W-16S | 78 |
| Mayo Dr. N&S | 11W-17S | 78 |
| Meadowbrook Ln. E&W | | |
| | 10W-18S | 79 |
| Meadowview Ct. N&S | | |
| | 10W-18S | 79 |
| Medina Dr. N&S | 11W-15S | 72 |
| Melissa Dr. N&S | 13W-21S | 84 |
| Merion Dr. E&W | 11W-18S | 78 |
| Micheal Dr. N&S | 11W-16S | 78 |
| Michelle Ct. N&S | 9W-17S | 79 |
| Millbank Dr. NS&EW | | |
| | 10W-18S | 79 |
| Mimosa Dr. E&W | 9W-18S | 79 |
| Mission Hill Ct. N&S | | |
| | 10W-16S | 79 |
| Misty Hill Rd. NE&SW | | |
| | 13W-17S | 78 |
| Mohawk Ln. N&S | 9W-16S | 79 |
| Montgomery Dr.* E&W | | |
| | 10W-17S | 79 |
| Morningside Rd. N&S | | |
| | 13W-17S | 78 |
| Narcissus Ct. N&S | 9W-18S | 79 |
| Narcissus Ln. N&S | 9W-18S | 79 |
| Nelson Ln. E&W | 9W-18S | 79 |
| Newgate Ct. N&S | 10W-16S | 79 |
| Nicole Ct. N&S | 11W-18S | 78 |
| Oak N&S | 12W-17S | 78 |
| Oak St. E&W | 11W-17S | 78 |
| Oakdale Ct. E&W | 11W-17S | 78 |
| Oakland Dr. N&S | 11W-18S | 78 |
| Oakley Av. N&S | 12W-17S | 78 |
| Old Orchard Dr. N&S | | |
| | 10W-18S | 79 |
| Olivia Ln. N&S | 13W-21S | 84 |
| Orchid Ct. N&S | 9W-18S | 79 |
| Orchid Ln. N&S | 9W-18S | 79 |
| Orenia Ct. E&W | 9W-18S | 79 |
| Oriole Ct. E&W | 10W-18S | 79 |
| Orlan Brook Dr. N&S | | |
| | 10W-18S | 79 |
| Orland Ct. E&W | 11W-18S | 78 |
| Orland Cir. | 11W-17S | 78 |
| Orland Woods Ln. N&S | | |
| | 14W-20S | 84 |
| Oxford Ln. N&S | 11W-18S | 78 |
| Paddock Ct. E&W | 13W-18S | 78 |
| Palm Ct. N&S | 9W-18S | 79 |
| Palm Dr. E&W | 9W-18S | 79 |
| Palos Springs Dr. E&W | | |
| | 11W-15S | 73 |
| Paradise Ln. E&W | 8W-18S | 79 |
| Park Hill Dr. N&S | 11W-18S | 78 |
| Park Ln. N&S | 12W-17S | 78 |
| Parkview Dr. N&S | 10W-16S | 79 |
| Patricia Ln. NW&SE | | |
| | 11W-18S | 78 |
| Patrick Ct. NW&SE | | |
| | 11W-18S | 78 |
| Patty Ln. NE&SW | 11W-15S | 73 |
| Paul Ct. N&S | 13W-20S | 84 |
| Pawnee Rd. N&S | 9W-18S | 79 |
| Peachtree Dr. N&S | 11W-18S | 78 |
| Pebble Beach Ln. E&W | | |
| | 11w-16S | 79 |
| Pembrooke Ln. E&W | | |
| | 11W-18S | 78 |
| Persimmon Ct. E&W | | |
| | 13W-16S | 78 |
| Persimmon Dr. NS&EW | | |
| | 13W-16S | 78 |
| Pine Grove Dr. E&W | | |
| | 14W-16S | 78 |
| Pine St. E&W | 11W-16S,10W-16S | 78 |
| Pine Tree Rd. N&S | 13W-17S | 78 |
| Plum Tree Dr. N&S | | |
| | 10W-18S | 79 |
| Pluskota Dr. E&W | 10W-18S | 79 |
| Ponderosa Ct. E&W | 9W-18S | 79 |
| Poplar Creek Ct. N&S | | |
| | 10W-18S | 79 |
| Poplar Creek Ln. NS&EW | | |
| | 14W-18S | 78 |
| Poplar Ct. NE&SW | 11W-17S | 78 |
| Poplar Rd. NS&EW | | |
| | 11W-17S | 78 |
| Prestwick Ln. E&W | | |
| | 11W-15S | 72 |
| Primrose Ct. N&S | 9W-18S | 79 |
| Primrose Ln. N&S | 9W-18S | 79 |
| Putney Pl. N&S | 10W-16S | 79 |
| Quail Hollow Dr. N&S | | |
| | 10W-18S | 79 |
| Raccoon Curve E&W | | |
| | 13W-20S | 84 |
| Raintree Dr. N&S | 10W-18S | 79 |
| Raintree Ln. E&W | 11W-18S | 78 |
| Raney's Ln. N&S | 12W-17S | 78 |
| Ravinia Av. N&S | | |
| | 12W-18S,12W-17S | 78 |
| Ravinia Ct. N&S | 12W-17S | 78 |
| Ravinia Ln. E&W | 12W-17S | 78 |
| Red Oak Ln. E&W | 10W-16S | 79 |
| Redondo Ln. E&W | 9W-16S | 79 |
| Redwood Av. N&S | 10W-16S | 79 |
| Regent Dr. N&S | 11W-16S | 78 |
| Revell Ct. E&W | 10W-17S | 79 |
| Ridge Av. N&S | 12W-17S | 78 |
| Riviera Ln. E&W | 11W-17S | 78 |
| Rob Roy Dr. E&W | 10W-18S | 79 |
| Robin Ct. N&S | 13W-20S | 84 |
| Robinhood Dr. NS&EW | | |
| | 10W-20S,10W-19S | 85 |
| Royal Creek Ln. N&S | | |
| | 14W-18S | 78 |
| Royal Foxhunt Rd. N&S | | |
| | 11W-18S | 78 |
| Royal Glen Ct. N&S | | |
| | 14W-18S | 78 |
| Royal Glen Dr. E&W | | |
| | 13W-18S | 78 |
| Rt. 43 N&S | 9W-18S | 79 |
| Rt. 7 E&W | | |
| | 12W-17S,11W-16S | 78 |
| Rutherford Ln. NE&SW | | |
| | 11W-18S | 78 |
| Ryan Ln. N&S | 13W-21S | 84 |
| Ryehill Cir. N&S | 13W-19S | 78 |
| Salvatori Ct. E&W | 9W-16S | 79 |
| Sandlewood Dr. N&S | | |
| | 10W-16S | 79 |
| Sandpiper Ct.* N&S | | |
| | 10W-17S | 79 |
| Sawgrass Ct. E&W | | |
| | 10W-18S | 79 |
| Sayre Av. N&S | 8W-18S | 79 |
| Sean Ln. N&S | 13W-21S | 84 |
| Seapines Rd. E&W | 9W-18S | 79 |
| Seminole Ct. E&W | 10W-18S | 79 |
| Sequoia Ct. E&W | 9W-18S | 79 |
| Seton Pl. NS&EW | 11W-19S | 78 |
| Shade Cove Ct. E&W | | |
| | 14W-18S | 78 |
| Shady Ln. E&W | 12W-18S | 78 |
| Shagbark Ct. E&W | 10W-18S | 79 |
| Shaker Ln. E&W | 14W-18S | 78 |
| Shannon Ct. E&W | 14W-21S | 84 |
| Sheffield Ln. N&S | 11W-18S | 78 |
| Shenandoah Dr. NS&EW | | |
| | 11W-18S | 78 |
| Sheri Ct. NW&SE | 11W-16S | 78 |
| Sheri Lane West E&W | | |
| | 11W-16S | 78 |
| Sheri Ln. E&W | 11W-16S | 78 |
| Sheridans Tr. N&S | 13W-20S | 84 |
| Sherwood Dr. N&S | 10W-19S | 78 |
| Shipston St. E&W | 10W-16S | 79 |
| Shire Dr. N&S | 13W-18S | 78 |
| Silo Ridge Dr. N&S | 14W-17S | 78 |
| Silo Ridge Rd. E. N&S | | |
| | 14W-17S | 78 |
| Silo Ridge Rd. N. E&W | | |
| | 14W-18S | 78 |
| Silo Ridge Rd. S. E&W | | |
| | 14W-18S | 78 |
| Silo Ridge Rd. W. N&S | | |
| | 14W-17S | 78 |
| Silverdale Dr. E&W | 11W-17S | 78 |
| Singletree Rd. NE&SW | | |
| | 14W-18S | 78 |
| Sioux Rd. N&S | 9W-16S | 79 |
| Sir Raleigh Dr. E&W | | |
| | 13W-20S | 84 |
| Somerset Ct.* NS&EW | | |
| | 10W-17S | 79 |
| Somerset Dr. E&W | | |
| | 14W-16S | 78 |
| Southwest Hwy. SW&NE | | |
| | 11W-16S | 78 |
| Spicebrush Ln. N&S | | |
| | 13W-20S | 84 |
| Spring Creek Ln. E&W | | |
| | 14W-18S | 78 |
| Spring Ln. N&S | 13W-16S | 78 |
| Springbrook Ct. E&W | | |
| | 14W-20S | 84 |
| Springview Ln. N&S | | |
| | 14W-16S | 78 |
| Spruce Dr. E&W | 10W-16S | 79 |
| Spyglass Cir. E&W | 10W-18S | 79 |
| St. Andrews Ct. N&S | | |
| | 10W-18S | 79 |
| St. Andrews Dr. N&S | | |
| | 10W-18S | 79 |
| St. James Ct. E&W | | |
| | 10W-18S | 79 |
| St. James Dr. N&S | | |
| | 10W-18S | 79 |
| St. Mary Cir. N&S | 10W-16S | 79 |
| Stonegate Ln. N&S | | |
| | 14W-16S | 78 |
| Stonehenge E&W | | |
| | 10W-16S | 79 |
| Stonewall E&W | 10W-16S | 79 |
| Stradford Ln. N&S | 11W-18S | 78 |
| Strawberry Ln. N&S | | |
| | 10W-15S | 73 |
| Streamstown Ct. E&W | | |
| | 9W-16S | 79 |
| Suffield Dr. E&W | 9W-16S | 79 |
| Sunflower Ct. N&S | 9W-18S | 79 |
| Sunny Ln. N&S | 10W-17S | 79 |
| Sunrise Ln. NS&EW | | |
| | 11W-18S | 78 |
| Sunset Ridge Ct. E&W | | |
| | 10W-18S | 79 |
| Sunset Ridge Dr. N&S | | |
| | 10W-18S | 79 |
| Sunshine Ln. E&W | 10W-15S | 73 |
| Susan Ln. N&S | 13W-19S | 84 |
| Sussex Dr. N&S | 10W-19S | 79 |
| Sutton Ct.* N&S | 10W-17S | 79 |
| Swallow Ln. N&S | 13W-20S | 84 |
| Swilly Ct. E&W | 14W-21S | 84 |
| Sycamore Ct. N&S | 9W-18S | 79 |
| Sycamore Dr. N&S | 9W-18S | 79 |
| Tally Ho Ln. E&W | 11W-18S | 78 |
| Tamarack Ln. N&S | 10W-16S | 79 |
| Teakwood Ct. E&W | | |
| | 10W-18S | 79 |
| Tee Brook Dr. N&S | | |
| | 10W-18S | 79 |
| Terry Ct. NW&SE | 11W-18S | 78 |
| Terry Dr. N&S | 11W-16S | 78 |
| Teton Ct. N&S | 9W-16S | 79 |
| Teton Rd. E&W | 9W-16S | 79 |
| Therese Ct.* E&W | 12W-16S | 78 |
| Thistlewood Dr. N&S | | |
| | 10W-18S | 79 |
| Thistlewood Ln. E&W | | |
| | 11W-18S | 78 |
| Thomas Dr. N&S | 11W-16S | 78 |
| Thorngate Ct. E&W | | |
| | 10W-18S | 79 |
| Thorngate Dr. N&S | | |
| | 10W-18S | 79 |
| Tiffany Dr. E&W | 9W-18S | 79 |
| Timber Edge Ln. E&W | | |
| | 14W-18S | 78 |
| Timber Trail Rd. N&S | | |
| | 11W-16S | 78 |
| Timberidge Ct. N&S | | |
| | 14W-18S | 78 |
| Timberline Ct. NW&SE | | |
| | 13W-17S | 78 |
| Timothy Ct. E&W | 11W-16S | 78 |
| Timothy Dr. N&S | 11W-16S | 78 |
| Tod William Dr. N&S | | |
| | 14W-18S | 78 |
| Torrey Pines Dr. N&S | | |
| | 13W-19S | 78 |
| Touchstone Pl. N&S | | |
| | 13W-19S | 78 |
| Tower Dr. E&W | 13W-20S | 84 |
| Trafalgar Ct. E&W | 10W-16S | 79 |
| Treetop Dr. NS&EW | | |
| | 12W-18S | 78 |
| Trenton Dr. N&S | 11W-18S | 78 |
| Tulip Ct. N&S | 9W-18S | 79 |
| Union St. N&S | 12W-16S | 78 |
| Uxbridge Dr. E&W | 10W-16S | 79 |
| Vail Ct. NW&SE | 14W-18S | 78 |
| Valentina Ln. N&S | 10W-18S | 79 |
| Valley Brook Dr. E&W | | |
| | 14W-20S | 84 |
| Valley Ct. N&S | 13W-17S | 78 |
| Virginia Ct.* E&W | 12W-16S | 78 |
| Vista Dr. E&W | 10W-16S | 79 |
| Vivian Ct. N&S | 13W-21S | 84 |
| Voss Dr. N&S | 13W-21S | 84 |
| Walnut St. E&W | 10W-16S | 79 |
| Warbler Ln. N&S | 13W-20S | 84 |
| Waterford Ln. E&W | | |
| | 11W-18S | 78 |
| West Av. N&S | | |
| | 12W-18S,12W-17S | 78 |
| Westbrook Dr. N&S | | |
| | 14W-21S,14W-20S | 84 |
| Westgate Ct. N&S | 11W-15S | 72 |
| Westminster Dr. N&S | | |
| | 11W-18S | 78 |
| Westwood Dr. N&S | | |
| | 12W-18S | 78 |
| Wexford Ln. E&W | 10W-18S | 79 |
| Wheeler Dr. E&W | | |
| | 11W-18S,9W-18S | 78 |
| Wherry Ln. E&W | 11W-18S | 78 |

| | Grid | Page |
|---|---|---|
| Whispering Hill Dr. E&W | 14W-21S | 84 |
| Whitehall Ln. N&S | 11W-18S | 78 |
| Wildflower Rd. E&W | 13W-17S | 78 |
| Will Cook Rd. N&S | 14W-21S,14W-20S | 84 |
| William Ct.* E&W | 12W-16S | 78 |
| William Dr. N&S | 11W-16S | 78 |
| Willow Creek Ln. E&W | 14W-18S | 78 |
| Willow St. N&S | 11W-17S | 78 |
| Willowood Ct. E&W | 9W-18S | 79 |
| Wilrose Ct. N&S | 13W-16S | 78 |
| Wilrose Ln. N&S | 13W-16S | 78 |
| Wind Mill Rd. E&W | 14W-17S | 78 |
| Winding Creek Ct. NE&SW | 14W-20S | 84 |
| Winding Creek Dr. NW&SE | 14W-20S | 84 |
| Windmill Turn N&S | 14W-17S | 78 |
| Windsor Dr. EW&NS | 11W-18S,11W-17S | 78 |
| Wittington Ct. N&S | 9W-16S | 79 |
| Woburn Ct. E&W | 12W-17S | 78 |
| Wood Duck Ln. E&W | 13W-20S | 84 |
| Woodbury Ct.* E&W | 12W-16S | 78 |
| Wooded Path N&S | 10W-17S | 79 |
| Woodland Av. N&S | 12W-17S | 78 |
| Woodmar Dr. N&S | 10W-18S | 79 |
| Woodridge Ln. N&S | 11W-16S | 78 |
| Woodruff Dr. E&W | 9W-18S | 79 |
| Woodstock Dr. E&W | 13W-16S | 78 |
| Woodward Dr. N&S | 10W-16S | 79 |
| Yearling Crossing NS&EW | 13W-20S | 84 |
| Yorkshire Ln. N&S | 11W-18S | 78 |
| Yorktown Ct. NE&SW | 11W-16S | 78 |
| Yorktown Dr. N&S | 11W-16S | 78 |
| 1st Av. N&S | 12W-17S | 78 |
| 2nd Av. N&S | 12W-17S | 78 |
| 3rd Av. N&S | 12W-17S | 78 |
| 70th Ct. N&S | 8W-18S | 79 |
| 71st Ct. N&S | 8W-18S | 79 |
| 73rd Av. N&S | 9W-18S | 79 |
| 73rd Ct. N&S | 9W-18S | 79 |
| 74th Av. N&S | 9W-18S | 79 |
| 74th Ct. N&S | 9W-18S | 79 |
| 75th Ct. N&S | 9W-18S | 79 |
| 77th Av. N&S | 9W-18S | 79 |
| 80th Av. N&S | 10W-18S,10W-16S | 79 |
| 81st Av. N&S | 10W-17S | 79 |
| 81st Ct. N&S | 10W-17S | 79 |
| 82nd Av. N&S | 10W-18S,10W-16S | 79 |
| 82nd Ct. N&S | 10W-16S | 79 |
| 83rd Av. N&S | 10W-16S | 79 |
| 83rd Ct. N&S | 10W-16S | 79 |
| 84th Av. N&S | 10W-17S,10W-16S | 79 |
| 85th Av. N&S | 10W-17S,10W-16S | 79 |
| 86th Av. N&S | 10W-18S,10W-16S | 79 |
| 87th Av. N&S | 10W-17S | 79 |
| 88th Av. N&S | 10W-18S,11W-15S | 79 |
| 88th St. N&S | 11W-19S | 78 |
| 89th Av. N&S | 11W-19S | 78 |
| 89th Ct. N&S | 11W-19S | 78 |
| 91st Av. N&S | 11W-16S | 78 |
| 92nd Av. N&S | 11W-16S | 78 |
| 92nd Ct. N&S | 11W-17S | 78 |
| 94th Av. N&S | 11W-19S,11W-17S | 78 |
| 96th Av. N&S | 12W-19S | 78 |
| 97th Av. N&S | 12W-19S | 78 |
| 104th Av. N&S | 13W-20S,13W-19S | 84 |
| 105th Ct. N&S | 13W-19S | 78 |
| 106th Ct. N&S | 13W-19S | 78 |
| 107th Pl. N&S | 13W-19S | 78 |
| 108th Av. N&S | 13W-20S,13W-21S | 84 |
| 108th Av. N&S | 13W-21S,13W-19S | 84 |
| 110th Av. N&S | 13W-21S,13W-19S | 84 |
| 131st St. E&W | 11W-15S | 72 |
| 135th St. E&W | 11W-15S,10W-15S | 72 |
| 135th St. E&W | 11W-15S | 79 |
| 137th St. E&W | 11W-16S,10W-16S | 78 |
| 138th Pl. E&W | 10W-16S | 79 |
| 138th St. E&W | 11W-16S,10W-16S | 78 |
| 139th St. E&W | 14W-16S,10W-16S | 78 |
| 139th St. E&W | 9W-16S | 79 |
| 140th St. E&W | 13W-16S,10W-16S | 78 |
| 141st St. E&W | 10W-16S | 79 |
| 142nd St. E&W | 13W-16S,11W-16S | 78 |
| 143rd Pl. E&W | 12W-17S,10W-17S | 78 |
| 143rd St. E&W | 13W-16S,10W-16S | 78 |
| 144th Pl. E&W | 12W-17S,10W-17S | 78 |
| 144th St. E&W | 12W-17S,10W-17S | 78 |
| 145th Pl. E&W | 12W-17S,10W-17S | 78 |
| 145th St. E&W | 12W-17S,10W-17S | 78 |
| 146th St. E&W | 12W-17S | 78 |
| 147th St. E&W | 12W-17S,11W-17S | 78 |
| 149th St. E&W | 12W-17S | 78 |
| 151st St. E&W | 14W-17S,9W-17S | 78 |
| 152nd St. E&W | 10W-18S,8W-18S | 79 |
| 153rd Pl. E&W | 12W-18S,9W-18S | 78 |
| 153rd St. E&W | 13W-18S,9W-18S | 78 |
| 154th Pl. E&W | 9W-18S | 79 |
| 154th St. E&W | 9W-18S | 79 |
| 155th St. E&W | 9W-18S | 79 |
| 156th St. E&W | 8W-18S | 79 |
| 157th Pl. E&W | 9W-18S | 79 |
| 157th St. E&W | 10W-18S,8W-18S | 79 |
| 158th Ct. E&W | 9W-18S | 79 |
| 158th St. E&W | 8W-18S | 79 |
| 159th St. E&W | 12W-18S,9W-18S | 78 |
| 160th St. E&W | 13W-19S | 78 |
| 161st Pl. E&W | 12W-19S | 79 |
| 161st Pl. E&W | 10W-19S | 79 |
| 161st St. E&W | 13W-19S | 79 |
| 162nd St. E&W | 10W-19S | 79 |
| 163rd Pl. E&W | 10W-19S | 79 |
| 163rd St. E&W | 12W-19S,10W-19S | 78 |
| 164th Pl. E&W | 13W-19S,11W-19S | 78 |
| 164th St. E&W | 11W-19S,10W-19S | 78 |
| 165th St. E&W | 13W-19S,10W-19S | 78 |
| 166th Pl. E&W | 11W-19S | 78 |
| 166th St. E&W | 10W-19S | 79 |
| 166th St. E&W | 10W-19S | 78 |
| 167th Pl. E&W | 13W-20S | 84 |
| 167th Pl. E&W | 10W-20S | 85 |
| 167th St. E&W | 13W-19S,10W-19S | 78 |
| 168th St. E&W | 13W-20S | 84 |
| 168th St. E&W | 10W-20S | 85 |
| 169th St. E&W | 10W-20S | 85 |
| 170th Pl. E&W | 10W-20S | 85 |
| 170th St. E&W | 10W-20S | 85 |
| 171st St. E&W | 11W-20S | 85 |
| 179th St. E&W | 13W-21S | 84 |
| 183rd St. E&W | 13W-21S | 84 |

### Orland Township

| | Grid | Page |
|---|---|---|
| Beech Av. N&S | 13W-19S | 78 |
| Brook View Ln. N&S | 14W-17S | 78 |
| California Tr. E&W | 14W-16S | 78 |
| Camelot Ct. N&S | 14W-16S | 78 |
| Camelot Ln. E&W | 14W-16S | 78 |
| Cedar Av. N&S | 13W-19S | 78 |
| Chisholm Tr. E&W | 14W-16S | 78 |
| Circle Dr. N&S | 11W-16S | 78 |
| Creek Crossing Ct. NE&SW | 14W-17S | 78 |
| Creek Crossing Dr. N&S | 14W-17S | 78 |
| Creekview Dr. N&S | 14W-17S | 78 |
| Creekwood Dr. NE&SW | 14W-17S | 78 |
| Crescent Dr. N&S | 11W-16S | 78 |
| Crestline Dr. E&W | 14W-16S | 78 |
| Crestwood Dr. E&W | 14W-16S | 78 |
| Dusty Tr. NE&SW | 14W-16S | 78 |
| E. Hazel Pl. N&S | 13W-19S | 78 |
| Fenview Ct. NE&SW | 14W-17S | 78 |
| Fenwood Ct. NE&SW | 14W-17S | 78 |
| Forest View Dr. E&W | 10W-17S,9W-17S | 79 |
| Glenview Dr. E&W | 14W-17S | 78 |
| Grange Rd. N&S | 12W-21S | 84 |
| Hancock St. E&W | 13W-19S | 78 |
| Hastings Dr. E&W | 9W-16S | 79 |
| Hazel Av. N&S | 13W-19S | 78 |
| Howe Dr. N&S | 11W-16S | 78 |
| Juanita Dr. E&W | 14W-19S | 78 |
| Kaup Ln. E&W | 14W-16S | 78 |
| Kristoffer Av. N&S | 14W-16S | 78 |
| Kristoffer Ct. E&W | 14W-16S | 78 |
| Kristoffer Ln. E&W | 14W-16S | 78 |
| Lago Ln. N&S | 14W-16S | 79 |
| Lagrange Rd. E&W | 12W-21S | 84 |
| Lakewood Ln. N&S | 14W-17S | 78 |
| Logan Ct. E&W | 14W-16S | 78 |
| Logan Dr. N&S | 14W-16S | 78 |
| Logan Dr. N&S | 14W-16S | 78 |
| Lynch Dr. N&S | 14W-17S | 78 |
| Maple Dr. N&S | 14W-16S | 78 |
| Mark Ln. E&W | 14W-16S | 78 |
| Mayflower Ct. N&S | 13W-16S | 78 |
| McCabe Ct. N&S | 13W-16S | 78 |
| McCabe Dr. N&S | 14W-16S | 78 |
| Meade St. E&W | 13W-19S | 78 |
| Meadow Ln. N&S | 9W-19S | 79 |
| Mesquite Dr. N&S | 14W-17S | 78 |
| Minetz Ct. E&W | 14W-16S | 78 |
| Natchez Trail N&S | 14W-16S | 78 |
| Newbury Dr. N&S | 9W-16S | 79 |
| Oak Ct. NW&SE | 14W-17S | 78 |
| Old Post Rd. N&S | 14W-16S | 78 |
| Old Spanish Ct. N&S | 14W-16S | 78 |
| Old Spanish Tr. E&W | 14W-16S | 78 |
| Old Tamarack Ln. N&S | 13W-16S | 78 |
| Orange Av. N&S | 13W-19S | 78 |
| Oregon Tr. E&W | 14W-16S | 78 |
| Overland Trial N&S | 14W-16S | 78 |
| Palm Av. N&S | 13W-19S | 78 |
| Park Ln. N&S | 13W-19S | 79 |
| Paw Paw Av. N&S | 13W-19S | 78 |
| Pine St. N&S | 10W-16S | 79 |
| Pinecreek Dr., N. E&W | 14W-17S | 78 |
| Pinecreek Dr., S. E&W | 14W-17S | 78 |
| Pineview St. E&W | 14W-17S | 78 |
| Pineview Dr. E&W | 14W-17S | 78 |
| Pinewood Ct. NE&SW | 14W-17S | 78 |
| Pinewood Dr. NS&EW | 14W-17S | 78 |
| Ridge Rd. N&S | 9W-16S | 79 |
| Rt. 43 N&S | 9W-17S,9W-16S | 79 |
| Rt. 45 N&S | 12W-21S,12W-20S | 84 |
| Rt. 6 NE&SW | 14W-21S,13W-19S | 84 |
| Ruggles Ct. E&W | 14W-16S | 78 |
| Sante Fe Trail N&S | 14W-16S | 78 |
| Scott Ln. N&S | 9W-16S | 79 |
| Selva Ln. N&S | 9W-16S | 79 |
| Sherman St. E&W | 13W-19S | 78 |
| Silver Ct. E&W | 9W-17S | 79 |
| Silver Lake Dr. E&W | 10W-17S | 79 |
| Spruce Ln. NS&EW | 14W-17S | 78 |
| Stagecoach Dr. E&W | 14W-16S | 78 |
| Streamwood Dr. NE&SW | 14W-17S | 78 |
| Touchstone Pl. N&S | 13W-19S | 78 |
| Valley View Ct. NW&SE | 14W-17S | 78 |
| Valley View Dr. NE&SW | 14W-17S | 78 |
| W. Hazel Pl. E&W | 13W-19S | 78 |
| Will Cook Rd. N&S | 14W-18S,14W-16S | 78 |
| Willow Av. N&S | 13W-19S | 78 |
| Wolf Rd. N&S | 14W-21S,14W-16S | 84 |
| Woodlake Ln. N&S | 14W-17S | 78 |
| 80th Av. N&S | 10W-21S,10W-17S | 85 |
| 81st Av. N&S | 10W-17S | 79 |
| 81st Ct. N&S | 10W-17S | 79 |
| 84th Av. N&S | 10W-21S | 85 |
| 94th Av. N&S | 11W-21S,11W-20S | 85 |
| 94th Ct. N&S | 11W-20S | 85 |
| 96th Av. N&S | 12W-20S | 84 |
| 104th Av. N&S | 13W-20S,13W-19S | 84 |
| 108th Av. N&S | 13W-21S,13W-16S | 84 |
| 109th Ct. N&S | 13W-18S | 84 |
| 110th Av. N&S | 13W-20S,13W-16S | 84 |
| 110th Ct. N&S | 13W-20S | 84 |
| 112th Ct. N&S | 13W-20S | 84 |
| 113th Av. N&S | 14W-18S | 78 |
| 113th Ct. N&S | 14W-18S | 78 |
| 114th Av. N&S | 14W-18S | 78 |
| 114th Ct. N&S | 14W-18S | 85 |
| 115th Av. N&S | 14W-18S | 78 |
| 115th Ct. N&S | 14W-18S | 78 |
| 116th Av. N&S | 14W-18S | 78 |
| 116th Ct. N&S | 14W-18S | 78 |
| 117th Av. N&S | 14W-18S | 78 |
| 117th Ct. N&S | 14W-18S | 78 |
| 118th Av. N&S | 14W-19S,14W-18S | 78 |
| 135th St. E&W | 14W-15S,10W-15S | 72 |
| 136th St. E&W | 11W-16S | 78 |
| 139th St. E&W | 14W-16S,9W-16S | 78 |
| 143rd St. E&W | 14W-16S,9W-16S | 78 |
| 144th St. E&W | 11W-17S | 78 |
| 145th Pl. E&W | 10W-17S | 79 |
| 151st St. E&W | 14W-17S | 78 |
| 152nd St. E&W | 14W-18S | 78 |
| 155th St. E&W | 13W-18S | 78 |
| 156th St. E&W | 14W-18S | 78 |
| 157th St. E&W | 14W-18S | 78 |
| 158th St. E&W | 14W-18S | 78 |
| 159th St. E&W | 14W-18S,12W-18S | 78 |
| 167th St. E&W | 14W-19S,9W-19S | 78 |
| 169th St. E&W | 13W-20S | 84 |
| 171st St. E&W | 13W-20S,11W-20S | 84 |
| 172nd St. E&W | 13W-20S | 84 |
| 173rd St. E&W | 13W-20S | 84 |
| 175th St. E&W | 13W-20S,11W-20S | 84 |
| 179th St. E&W | 12W-21S | 84 |
| 183rd St. E&W | 13W-21S,10W-21S | 84 |

### Palatine

| | Grid | Page |
|---|---|---|
| Abbey Hill Ln. N&S | 22W-15N | 23 |
| Aldridge Av. E&W | 21W-14N | 23 |
| Alex Ct. E&W | 21W-16N | 13 |
| Alex Ln. (Pvt.) E&W | 21W-16N | 13 |
| Alison Dr. E&W | 19W-16N | 14 |
| Amherst St. E&W | 20W-17N | 13 |
| Anderson Dr. NW&SE | 19W-16N,18W-16N | 14 |
| Arbor Ct. N&S | 23W-17N | 12 |
| Arbor Ln. N&S | 23W-17N | 12 |
| Arlene NS&EW | 19W-16N | 14 |
| Arrowhead Dr. N&S | 20W-17N | 13 |
| Ash St. N&S | 21W-15N | 23 |
| Ashland Av. N&S | 20W-15N,20W-14N | 23 |
| Auburn Woods Ct. E&W | 21W-17N | 13 |
| Auburn Woods Dr. NS&EW | 21W-16N,21W-14N | 13 |
| Aurelia Ct. N&S | 21W-16N | 13 |
| Austin Ln. NS&EW | 22W-15N | 23 |
| Babcock Dr. NS&EW | 19W-16N | 14 |
| Baldwin Rd. E&W | 22W-17N | 13 |
| Baldwin Rd. NW&SE | 20W-16N,19W-16N | 13 |
| Balsam Ln. E&W | 20W-17N | 13 |
| Baronet Ln. E&W | 19W-17N | 14 |
| Baybrook Dr. N&S | 19W-15N | 14 |
| Beacon Dr. NS&EW | 19W-16N | 14 |
| Bedford Dr. E&W | 22W-15N | 23 |
| Bel Air Ter. N&S | 20W-16N | 13 |
| Belle Av. N&S | 19W-15N | 14 |
| Bennett Av. N&S | 21W-15N | 23 |
| Benton St. N&S | 20W-15N,20W-14N | 23 |
| Bishop Ct. NW&SE | 22W-15N | 23 |
| Bissell Dr. NS&EW | 19W-16N | 14 |
| Bon Aire Dr. NS&EW | 20W-16N | 13 |
| Borders Dr. E&W | 22W-15N | 23 |
| Bothwell St. N&S | 21W-15N,19W-16N | 23 |
| Boynton Dr. N&S | 19W-16N | 14 |
| Brandon Ct. NS&EW | 21W-16N | 13 |
| Brighton Ct. NE&SW | 22W-15N | 23 |
| Brighton Ln. N&S | 22W-15N | 23 |
| Bristol Ct. N&S | 22W-15N | 23 |
| Broadwalk Ct. N&S | 21W-14N | 23 |
| Broadwalk Dr. E&W | 21W-14N | 23 |
| Brockway St. N&S | 19W-16N | 14 |
| Bryant Av. E&W | 21W-14N | 23 |
| Burno Dr. NS&EW | 21W-14N | 23 |
| Cady Dr. N&S | 19W-16N | 14 |
| Cambridge Dr. N&S | 22W-16N | 13 |
| Cardinal NS&EW | 19W-17N | 14 |
| Cardinal Dr. N&S | 19W-17N | 14 |
| Carmel Dr. N&S | 20W-17N | 13 |
| Carolyn Dr. E&W | 22W-15N | 23 |
| Carpenter Dr. E&W | 20W-17N,19W-17N | 13 |
| Carriageway Ct. NW&SE | 21W-14N | 23 |
| Carriageway Ln. N&S | 21W-14N | 23 |
| Carter St. N&S | 21W-16N | 13 |
| Cedar St. N&S | 21W-14N,21W-16N | 23 |
| Charlotte Av. E&W | 20W-16N | 13 |
| Chatham Dr. E&W | 22W-15N | 23 |
| Cherrywood Dr. NW&SE | 21W-17N | 13 |
| Cheryl Ln. E&W | 21W-15N | 23 |
| Chesapeake Ct. N&S | 19W-17N | 14 |
| Chesapeake Ln. N&S | 19W-17N | 14 |
| Chestnut St. N&S | 21W-16N | 13 |
| Chewink Ct. NW&SE | 20W-16N | 13 |
| Chivalry Ct. NW&SE | 19W-16N | 14 |
| Church St. E&W | 19W-16N | 14 |
| Churchill Dr. N&S | 19W-16N | 14 |
| Citadel Ct. NW&SE | 19W-16N | 14 |
| Clark Dr. N&S | 19W-16N,19W-17N | 14 |
| Clearwater Ct. N&S | 22W-17N | 13 |
| Clinton Ct. N&S | 22W-15N | 23 |
| Club House Dr. N&S | 19W-17N | 14 |
| Colfax St. NS&EW | 21W-16N,20W-16N | 13 |
| Comfort Ln. NS&EW | 20W-16N | 13 |
| Comfort St. E&W | 21W-16N | 13 |
| Concord Way E&W | 21W-14N | 23 |
| Consumers Av. N&S | 19W-15N | 14 |
| Coolidge Av. N&S | 22W-17N | 13 |
| Cooper Dr. N&S | 19W-17N | 14 |
| Cornell Av. E&W | 21W-16N | 13 |
| Cottonwood Ln. N&S | 19W-15N | 14 |
| Countryside Dr. NS&EW | 22W-17N | 13 |
| Creekside Dr. NE&SW | 19W-15N | 14 |
| Creekwood Dr. E&W | 21W-18N | 13 |
| Crestview Dr. N&S | 20W-17N | 13 |
| Crooked Willow Ln. E&W | 22W-14N | 23 |
| Crown Ct. N&S | 19W-15N | 14 |
| Cunningham Dr. E&W | 21W-17N | 13 |
| Daniels Rd. E&W | 20W-15N | 23 |
| David Dr. N&S | 19W-16N | 14 |
| Dean Dr. N&S | 19W-16N | 14 |
| Deer Run Dr. (Pvt.) N&S | 21W-16N | 13 |
| Delgado Dr. NW&SE | 20W-17N | 13 |
| Dorest Av. E&W | 21W-15N | 23 |
| Dorothy Dr. E&W | 19W-16N | 14 |
| Drovers Ln. NW&SE | 22W-15N | 23 |
| DuPont Av. E&W | 21W-14N | 23 |
| Dundee Rd. E&W | 21W-18N | 13 |
| E. Castle Ct. E&W | 19W-16N | 14 |
| Eagle Ln. N&S | 20W-16N | 13 |
| East Meadow Lake Dr. NS&EW | 19W-17N | 14 |
| Easy St. N&S | 21W-16N | 13 |
| Eaton Ct. N&S | 22W-15N | 23 |
| Echo Ln. NS&EW | 21W-15N | 23 |
| Edgewater Ct. N&S | 23W-17N | 12 |
| Edgewater Ln. N&S | 23W-17N,22W-17N | 12 |
| Eisenhower Av. E&W | 20W-16N | 13 |
| Eisenhower Ct. N&S | 20W-16N | 13 |
| Elizabeth Av. NW&SE | 19W-15N | 14 |
| Elizabeth Ct. NE&SW | 19W-15N | 14 |
| Elm Ct. NW&SE | 21W-14N | 23 |
| Elm St. E&W | 22W-17N | 13 |
| Elm St. N&S | 21W-14N,21W-15N | 23 |
| Elmwood Av. N&S | 20W-15N,20W-16N | 23 |
| Eric Dr. N&S | 21W-16N | 13 |
| Euclid Av. E&W | 22W-14N,21W-14N | 23 |
| Everett Dr. N&S | 19W-16N | 14 |
| Evergreen Ct. E&W | 21W-15N | 23 |
| Evergreen Dr. NS&EW | 19W-17N | 14 |
| Exner Ct. NW&SE | 22W-15N | 23 |
| Fairway Ct. NW&SE | 20W-17N | 13 |
| Fairway Dr. NE&SW | 20W-17N | 13 |
| Falmore Dr. N&S | 22W-14N | 23 |
| Fern Cir. E&W | 19W-16N | 14 |
| Fern Ct. E&W | 21W-14N | 23 |
| First Bank Dr. NS&EW | 20W-16N | 13 |
| Flake Dr. NS&EW | 19W-16N | 14 |
| Forest Av. N&S | 20W-15N,20W-16N | 23 |
| Forest Ct. N&S | 20W-16N | 13 |
| Forest Knolls Dr. E&W | 20W-18N | 13 |
| Forestview Cir. NW&SE | 22W-17N | 13 |
| Fosket Dr. NE&SW | 19W-16N | 14 |
| Fremont St. N&S | 20W-16N | 13 |
| Frontage Rd. NS&EW | 19W-15N,19W-16N | 14 |
| Gary Dr. N&S | 21W-16N | 13 |
| Geri Av. E&W | 21W-16N | 13 |
| Geri St. N&S | 21W-16N | 13 |
| Gilbert Av. E&W | 21W-16N | 13 |
| Gilbert Av. N&S | 21W-15N | 23 |
| Gilbert Rd. E&W | 21W-15N,20W-15N | 23 |
| Gilbert St. E&W | 21W-15N | 23 |
| Glade Av., E. E&W | 20W-15N | 23 |
| Glade Av., W. E&W | 21W-15N | 23 |
| Glencoe Rd. E&W | 20W-17N | 13 |
| Glencoe Rd. E&W | 21W-15N | 23 |
| Glencoe St. E&W | 23W-17N | 13 |
| Glencoe St. N&S | 20W-15N,19W-15N | 23 |
| Glenn Dr. N&S | 19W-16N,19W-17N | 14 |
| Glennwood St. N&S | 20W-15N,20W-16N | 23 |
| Gloria Dr. N&S | 19W-16N | 14 |
| Golfview Ter. E&W | 21W-17N | 13 |
| Goodwin E&W | 19W-18N | 14 |
| Greeley Av. N&S | 21W-15N,21W-16N | 23 |
| Greenwood Ct. E&W | 20W-16N | 13 |

| | Grid | Page |
|---|---|---|
| Greenwood Dr. N&S | | |
| | 20W-16N | 13 |
| Grissom Ct. E&W | 19W-17N | 14 |
| Groh Ct. E&W | 22W-15N | 23 |
| Gull Ct. NE&SW | 22W-14N | 23 |
| Haddington Ct. E&W | | |
| | 22W-15N | 23 |
| Hale St. N&S | | |
| | 20W-15N,20W-16N | 23 |
| Hampton Ct. N&S | 22W-15N | 23 |
| Hampton Pl. E&W | 22W-15N | 23 |
| Hamstead Ct. N&S | 22W-15N | 23 |
| Harrison Av. N&S | 22W-15N | 23 |
| Harrison St. N&S | 22W-15N | 23 |
| Hart St. N&S | | |
| | 21W-15N,21W-16N | 23 |
| Harvard St. N&S | 22W-14N | 23 |
| Hawk Ct. N&S | 20W-16N | 13 |
| Heatherlea Dr., E. N&S | | |
| | 20W-17N | 13 |
| Hedgewood Dr. N&S | | |
| | 20W-17N | 13 |
| Helen Rd. E&W | | |
| | 21W-15N,20W-15N | 23 |
| Heron Dr. E&W | 20W-16N | 13 |
| Hickory St. N&S | 21W-16N | 23 |
| Hicks Pl. NW&SE | 20W-16N | 13 |
| Hicks Rd. N&S | | |
| | 20W-15N,20W-17N | 23 |
| Hill Av. N&S | 22W-16N | 13 |
| Hunting Ct. NW&SE | | |
| | 22W-15N | 23 |
| Hunting Dr. NE&SW | | |
| | 22W-15N | 23 |
| Illinois Av. E&W | | |
| | 22W-15N,21W-15N | 23 |
| Imperial Ct. NE&SW | | |
| | 21W-15N | 23 |
| Inverary E&W | 19W-18N | 14 |
| Jane Addams Dr. E&W | | |
| | 19W-17N | 14 |
| Jennifer Ln. NS&EW | | |
| | 21W-16N | 13 |
| Jewel Ct. N&S | 19W-15N | 14 |
| Joan Dr. E&W | 19W-16N | 14 |
| Johnson St. E&W | 21W-16N | 23 |
| Jonathan Dr. E&W | 19W-16N | 14 |
| Joyce Av. E&W | 19W-15N | 14 |
| Juniper Dr. E&W | 20W-17N | 13 |
| Karen Ln. NE&SW | 19W-16N | 13 |
| Kathleen Dr. E&W | 22W-15N | 23 |
| Kelly Ann Dr. E&W | 22W-15N | 23 |
| Kenilworth Av. E&W | | |
| | 22W-15N,19W-15N | 23 |
| Kenilworth Rd. E&W | | |
| | 20W-15N | 23 |
| Kensington Ct. NE&SW | | |
| | 22W-15N | 23 |
| Kerry Ct. NS&EW | 21W-14N | 23 |
| Kerwood St. N&S | | |
| | 20W-16N,20W-15N | 13 |
| Kimball Dr. N&S | 21W-15N | 23 |
| King Edward Ct. N&S | | |
| | 21W-17N,21W-18N | 13 |
| Kitson Dr. NS&EW | 19W-16N | 14 |
| Knox St. E&W | 20W-17N | 13 |
| Krista Ct. E&W | 19W-15N | 14 |
| Krista Ln. N&S | 19W-15N | 14 |
| Lake Dr. E&W | 19W-15N | 14 |
| Lake Louise Dr. E&W | | |
| | 19W-16N | 14 |
| Lakeshore Dr. N&S | | |
| | 22W-15N | 13 |
| Lalonde Av. N&S | 21W-14N | 23 |
| Lanark Ln. N&S | 22W-15N | 23 |
| Lanark St. E&W | | |
| | 22W-15N,21W-15N | 23 |
| Leonard Dr. N&S | 19W-15N | 14 |
| Lincoln St. E&W | 20W-16N | 13 |
| Linden Av. N&S | | |
| | 20W-15N,20W-17N | 23 |
| Linden St. N&S | | |
| | 20W-15N,20W-16N | 23 |
| Longview Ln. E&W | | |
| | 21W-15N | 23 |
| Louise Ln. N&S | 22W-15N | 13 |
| Lynn Dr. NS&EW | 21W-16N | 13 |
| Lytle Dr. N&S | 19W-16N | 14 |
| Mac Arthur Dr. N&S | | |
| | 20W-16N | 13 |
| Malibou Ln. E&W | 20W-16N | 13 |
| Mallard Ct. NW&SE | | |
| | 22W-14N | 23 |
| Mallard Dr. NE&SW | | |
| | 22W-14N | 23 |
| Maple Ct. N&S | 21W-15N | 23 |
| Maple St. N&S | | |
| | 21W-15N,21W-16N | 23 |
| Marion St. N&S | 20W-16N | 13 |
| Marsha Dr. N&S | 20W-17N | 13 |
| Mart Ct. N&S | 20W-16N | 13 |
| Meadow Ln. E&W | 20W-16N | 13 |
| Medford Dr. E&W | 21W-14N | 23 |
| Merril Av. N&S | | |
| | 21W-15N,21W-16N | 23 |
| Michele Dr. E&W | 19W-16N | 14 |
| Michigan Av. E&W | | |
| | 21W-15N,20W-15N | 23 |
| Middleton Av. NW&SE | | |
| | 22W-15N | 23 |
| Middleton Ct. NE&SW | | |
| | 22W-15N | 23 |
| Mill Valley Rd. E&W | | |
| | 20W-17N | 13 |
| Minnesota Av. E&W | | |
| | 21W-16N | 13 |
| Monterey Rd. E&W | | |
| | 20W-17N | 13 |

| | Grid | Page |
|---|---|---|
| Morris Dr. E&W | | |
| | 20W-16N,19W-16N | 13 |
| Morrison Av. E&W | | |
| | 22W-16N,22W-17N | 13 |
| Mozart St. N&S | 20W-16N | 13 |
| Myrtle St. E&W | 22W-17N | 13 |
| N. Hamilton Ct. N&S | | |
| | 21W-17N | 13 |
| N. Mullgan Ct. N&S | | |
| | 21W-17N | 13 |
| N. Newkirk Ln. N&S | | |
| | 19W-16N | 14 |
| N. Victoria Dr. NS&EW | | |
| | 19W-16N | 14 |
| N. Westminster Dr. N&S | | |
| | 22W-16N | 13 |
| Nightingale Dr. N&S | | |
| | 22W-14N | 23 |
| Norman Dr. E&W | 19W-16N | 14 |
| North Court N&S | 20W-16N | 13 |
| Northwest Hwy. NW&SE | | |
| | 21W-16N,19W-15N | 13 |
| Oak Ridge Rd. N&S | | |
| | 20W-18N | 13 |
| Oak St. N&S | | |
| | 20W-15N,20W-16N | 23 |
| Old Northwest Highway | | |
| | NW&SE 22W-16N,21W-16N | 13 |
| Old Virginia Ct. N&S | | |
| | 19W-17N | 14 |
| Old Virginia Rd. NS&EW | | |
| | 19W-17N | 14 |
| Olive St. E&W | 19W-15N | 14 |
| Oxford Ct. NW&SE | | |
| | 22W-15N | 23 |
| Paddock Dr. E&W | 19W-16N | 14 |
| Palatine Rd. E&W | | |
| | 22W-15N,19W-15N | 23 |
| Palmer E&W | 19W-18N | 14 |
| Panorama Dr. NS&EW | | |
| | 20W-15N | 23 |
| Parallel St. N&S | | |
| | 20W-15N | 23 |
| Park Lane N&S | 19W-15N | 14 |
| Park Pl. N&S | 21W-14N | 23 |
| Park Ter. E&W | 21W-14N | 23 |
| Parkside Dr. NS&EW | | |
| | 21W-14N | 23 |
| Parkwood E&W | 21W-14N | 23 |
| Partridge Ct. N&S | 22W-14N | 23 |
| Partridge Dr. N&S | 22W-14N | 23 |
| Patricia Ct. E&W | 19W-15N | 14 |
| Patricia Ln. NE&SW | | |
| | 19W-15N | 14 |
| Patten Dr. E&W | 19W-16N | 14 |
| Pebble Creek Rd. NS&EW | | |
| | 20W-15N | 13 |
| Pebbles Dr. N&S | 22W-15N | 23 |
| Peder Ln. E&W | 21W-16N | 13 |
| Peregrine Ct. NE&SW | | |
| | 22W-14N | 23 |
| Pine St. N&S | 21W-15N | 23 |
| Pintail Ct. N&S | 22W-14N | 23 |
| Plate Dr. E&W | 19W-16N | 14 |
| Pleasant Hill Blvd. E&W | | |
| | 21W-15N | 23 |
| Plum Grove Rd. N&S | | |
| | 21W-16N,21W-17N | 23 |
| Plum Tree Ct. NW&SE | | |
| | 21W-14N | 23 |
| Plum Tree Ln. N&S | | |
| | 21W-14N | 23 |
| Pompano Ln. E&W | 20W-16N | 13 |
| Poplar St. E&W | 22W-17N | 13 |
| Potomac Ct. N&S | 19W-17N | 14 |
| Potomac Dr. N&S | 19W-17N | 14 |
| Prairie Brook Dr. E&W | | |
| | 19W-17N | 14 |
| Pratt Dr. E&W | 19W-16N | 14 |
| Princeton St. E&W | 20W-17N | 13 |
| Providence Rd. E&W | | |
| | 20W-16N | 13 |
| Quail Hollow Ln., W. NE&SW | | |
| | 22W-14N | 23 |
| Quentin Rd. N&S | | |
| | 22W-14N,22W-17N | 23 |
| Rand Rd. NW&SE | 19W-17N | 14 |
| Raven Ln. E&W | 22W-15N | 23 |
| Ravine Hills Ct., W. NW&SE | | |
| | 22W-14N | 23 |
| Reading Ct. E&W | 21W-14N | 23 |
| Reseda Ct. N&S | 20W-17N | 13 |
| Reseda Pkwy. E&W | | |
| | 20W-17N | 13 |
| Revere Ln. E&W | 21W-14N | 23 |
| Reynolds Dr. E&W | 19W-16N | 14 |
| Richards Dr. N&S | 19W-16N | 14 |
| Richmond St. N&S | | |
| | 21W-16N | 13 |
| Ridge Trail E&W | 21W-17N | 13 |
| Rimini St. NE&SW | 20W-16N | 13 |
| Roanoke Ct. E&W | 21W-15N | 23 |
| Robertson St. N&S | | |
| | 21W-16N | 13 |
| Robinson Dr. N&S | 19W-16N | 14 |
| Rohlwing Rd. N&S | | |
| | 20W-15N,20W-17N | 23 |
| Rose St. N&S | | |
| | 21W-15N,21W-16N | 23 |
| Rosita Dr. N&S | 19W-16N | 14 |
| Route 68 Rd. E&W | 23W-17N | 12 |
| Royal Ct. NE&SW | 21W-15N | 23 |
| Russet Way E&W | 21W-15N | 23 |
| S. Hidden Brook Trail NS&EW | | |
| | 22W-14N | 23 |
| S. Windhill Dr. N&S | | |
| | 22W-14N | 23 |

| | Grid | Page |
|---|---|---|
| Saddle Ridge Ct., S. N&S | | |
| | 22W-14N | 23 |
| Salem Ct. NW&SE | 20W-16N | 13 |
| Sanborn Dr. NS&EW | | |
| | 19W-16N,19W-17N | 14 |
| Sandpiper Ct. E&W | | |
| | 22W-14N | 23 |
| Saratoga Dr. N&S | 20W-17N | 13 |
| Sayles Dr. E&W | 19W-16N | 14 |
| Schiller St. N&S | 20W-16N | 13 |
| Schirra Dr. E&W | 19W-17N | 14 |
| Schubert St. N&S | 20W-16N | 13 |
| Sellstrom Dr. NW&SE | | |
| | 20W-15N | 23 |
| Shady Ln. E&W | 21W-18N | 13 |
| Sherman St. E&W | | |
| | 21W-16N,20W-16N | 13 |
| Sherwood Ct. E&W | | |
| | 23W-17N | 12 |
| Sherwood Ln. NS&EW | | |
| | 23W-17N | 12 |
| Skylark Ct. N&S | 22W-14N | 23 |
| Skylark Dr. E&W | 22W-14N | 23 |
| Slade St. E&W | | |
| | 20W-16N | 13 |
| Slayton Dr. E&W | 19W-16N | 14 |
| Smith Rd. N&S | 21W-17N | 13 |
| Smith St. N&S | | |
| | 21W-15N,21W-16N | 23 |
| Sparrow Ct. N&S | 22W-15N | 23 |
| Spring Willow Bay E&W | | |
| | 22W-15N | 23 |
| St. James Ct. E&W | | |
| | 22W-15N | 23 |
| Stark Dr. N&S | | |
| | 20W-16N,20W-17N | 13 |
| Steeplechase Ln., W. E&W | | |
| | 22W-14N | 23 |
| Stephen Dr. N&S | 21W-16N | 13 |
| Sterling Dr. E&W | 22W-17N | 13 |
| Stonebridge Ct. E&W | | |
| | 19W-15N | 14 |
| Stonehedge Ln. N&S | | |
| | 21W-14N | 23 |
| Stonington Dr. N&S | | |
| | 19W-15N | 14 |
| Stuart Ln. N&S | 21W-15N | 23 |
| Sunset Ln. E&W | 22W-17N | 13 |
| Sutherland Dr. N&S | | |
| | 19W-17N | 14 |
| Tahoe Tr. E&W | 20W-16N | 13 |
| Teal E&W | 22W-15N | 23 |
| Tern Dr. E&W | 22W-14N | 23 |
| Terrace Dr. NS&EW | | |
| | 21W-16N | 13 |
| Thomas St. E&W | 19W-15N | 14 |
| Three Willow Ct. N&S | | |
| | 22W-14N | 23 |
| Thurston Dr. E&W | 19W-16N | 14 |
| Topanga Dr. N&S | 20W-17N | 13 |
| Tymore Ct. N&S | 22W-14N | 23 |
| U.S. Route 14 N&S | | |
| | 23W-17N,19W-14N | 12 |
| Valley Ln. NE&SW | 21W-14N | 23 |
| Valor Ct. N&S | 19W-17N | 14 |
| Ventura Dr. N&S | 20W-17N | 13 |
| Vermont St. N&S | 20W-17N | 13 |
| Virginia Dr. E&W | 19W-16N | 14 |
| Virginia Lake Ct. N&S | | |
| | 19W-17N | 14 |
| W. Bombay Way E&W | | |
| | 22W-16N | 13 |
| W. Crescent Dr. E&W | | |
| | 22W-16N | 13 |
| W. Hamilton Dr. E&W | | |
| | 21W-17N | 13 |
| W. Hidden Hill Ln. N&S | | |
| | 22W-16N | 13 |
| W. Windhill Dr. E&W | | |
| | 22W-14N | 23 |
| Walnut St. N&S | 21W-15N | 23 |
| Wanda Ln. NE&SW | | |
| | 19W-16N | 13 |
| Warren Av. N&S | 19W-15N | 14 |
| Warwick Rd. E&W | 20W-16N | 13 |
| Washington Ct. E&W | | |
| | 21W-15N | 23 |
| Washington St. E&W | | |
| | 20W-15N | 23 |
| Wente N&S | 19W-17N | 14 |
| West Ct. E&W | 20W-16N | 13 |
| Westminster Dr. N&S | | |
| | 22W-16N | 13 |
| Whippoorwill Ln. NE&SW | | |
| | 22W-14N | 23 |
| Whitcomb Dr. NW&SE | | |
| | 19W-16N | 14 |
| White Willow Bay N&S | | |
| | 22W-14N,22W-15N | 23 |
| Whitehall Dr. N&S | 22W-15N | 23 |
| Whytecliff Rd. E&W | | |
| | 22W-15N | 23 |
| Wilke Rd. N&S | | |
| | 19W-15N,19W-16N | 23 |
| Williams Av. N&S | 19W-15N | 14 |
| Williams Dr. N&S | | |
| | 19W-16N,19W-17N | 14 |
| Willmette Av. E&W | 19W-16N | 14 |
| Willow Ct. NW&SE | 20W-16N | 13 |
| Willow Walk Dr. N&S | | |
| | 22W-14N | 23 |
| Willow Wood Dr. N&S | | |
| | 22W-16N | 13 |
| Wilmette Rd. N&S | | |
| | 20W-15N,19W-15N | 23 |
| Wilshire St. N&S | 20W-16N | 13 |
| Wilson St. E&W | | |
| | 21W-16N,20W-16N | 13 |

| | Grid | Page |
|---|---|---|
| Wilton Ct. NE&SW | 20W-16N | 13 |
| Winnetka St. E&W | 22W-17N | 13 |
| Winslowe Dr. NE&SW | | |
| | 19W-17N | 14 |
| Winston Dr. N&S | | |
| | 19W-15N,19W-16N | 14 |
| Wood St. E&W | | |
| | 21W-16N,20W-16N | 13 |
| Woodwork Ln. N&S | | |
| | 21W-16N | 13 |
| Wren Av. N&S | 20W-16N | 13 |
| Yale Ct. NW&SE | 22W-14N | 23 |

## Palatine Township

| | Grid | Page |
|---|---|---|
| Abbeywood Ct.* NS&EW | | |
| | 20W-20N | 47 |
| Aldridge Av. E&W | 21W-14N | 23 |
| Algonquin Rd. NW&SE | | |
| | 23W-14N,20W-13N | 22 |
| Almond Ct. N&S | 19W-18N | 14 |
| Alva St. E&W | 22W-16N | 13 |
| Anna Ct. E&W | 23W-18N | 12 |
| Apple Tree Ct. N&S | | |
| | 20W-17N | 13 |
| Arlington Dr. NS&EW | | |
| | 24W-18N | 12 |
| Ashbury Ln. NS&EW | | |
| | 23W-14N | 22 |
| Aster Av. E&W | 19W-18N | 14 |
| Azalea Ln.* E&W | 20W-20N | 47 |
| Baldwin Ct. N&S | 19W-17N | 14 |
| Baldwin Ln. N&S | | |
| | 19W-17N,19W-18N | 14 |
| Baldwin Rd. N&S | 19W-18N | 14 |
| Baldwin Way NW&SE | | |
| | 19W-18N | 14 |
| Banberry E&W | 19W-18N | 14 |
| Barrington Woods Rd. N&S | | |
| | 23W-18N | 12 |
| Bayer Dr. E&W | 21W-17N | 13 |
| Bayside Dr. NS&EW | | |
| | 19W-17N | 14 |
| Beaumont Ln. E&W | | |
| | 23W-18N | 12 |
| Benton St. N&S | | |
| | 20W-14N,20W-15N | 23 |
| Big Oaks Rd. N&S | 21W-18N | 13 |
| Birchwood Av.* E&W | | |
| | 21W-18N | 13 |
| Bloomington Av. N&S | | |
| | 19W-18N | 14 |
| Blossom Tr. NE&SW | | |
| | 21W-13N | 23 |
| Bonhill Dr. NW&SE | 19W-18N | 14 |
| Bradley Ct. NS&EW | | |
| | 19W-18N | 14 |
| Brentwood Dr. E&W | | |
| | 21W-18N | 13 |
| Briar Pl. NE&SW | 24W-18N | 12 |
| Briarwood Ln. E&W | | |
| | 20W-13N | 23 |
| Brise Ct.* N&S | 19W-18N | 14 |
| Broadmore Ct.* NW&SE | | |
| | 21W-18N | 13 |
| Brookdale Ct. N&S | 20W-13N | 23 |
| Brookdale Ln. N&S | | |
| | 20W-13N | 23 |
| Brookdale Ln., N. E&W | | |
| | 20W-13N | 23 |
| Brookdale Ln., S. E&W | | |
| | 20W-13N | 23 |
| Brookside St. E&W | | |
| | 22W-15N | 23 |
| Brookview Ln. N&S | | |
| | 21W-13N | 23 |
| Bryant Av. E&W | 21W-14N | 23 |
| California Av. N&S | | |
| | 20W-13N,20W-14N | 23 |
| Cambridge Ct. NW&SE | | |
| | 19W-18N | 14 |
| Candlenut Ln. E&W | | |
| | 19W-18N | 14 |
| Canterbury Ln.* N&S | | |
| | 19W-20N | 47 |
| Canterbury Ter.* | 19W-20N | 47 |
| Capri Dr. N&S | | |
| | 20W-18N,19W-18N | 13 |
| Carol Ct. NS&EW | 19W-17N | 14 |
| Carolyn Dr. E&W | 22W-15N | 23 |
| Carriage Ln. NS&EW | | |
| | 19W-18N | 14 |
| Cascade Ln.* N&S | 19W-18N | 14 |
| Castle Ct. E&W | 19W-18N | 14 |
| Cedarwood Ct. E&W | | |
| | 20W-17N | 13 |
| Center Rd. E&W | 21W-18N | 13 |
| Central Rd. E&W | | |
| | 23W-13N,22W-13N | 22 |
| Chelsea Av.* N&S | 19W-18N | 13 |
| Cherry Wood Dr. NW&SE | | |
| | 20W-17N | 13 |
| Circle Ct. E&W | 21W-12N | 23 |
| Circle Ln. N&S | 20W-14N | 23 |
| Clear Creek Bay* E&W | | |
| | 19W-18N | 14 |
| Club Ct. N&S | 20W-17N | 13 |
| Clyde Av. N&S | 22W-15N | 23 |
| Coach Rd. NE&SW | | |
| | 20W-18N | 13 |
| Constitution Dr. E&W | | |
| | 20W-18N | 13 |
| Conway Bay* N&S | 19W-18N | 14 |
| Coolidge Av. N&S | | |
| | 22W-17N | 13 |
| County Line Rd. E&W | | |
| | 23W-18N,21W-18N | 12 |

| | Grid | Page |
|---|---|---|
| Creekwood Dr. E&W | | |
| | 21W-18N | 13 |
| Crescent Ln. N&S | | |
| | 22W-15N,22W-16N | 23 |
| Crimson Ln. NE&SW | | |
| | 19W-17N | 14 |
| Crooked Creek Tr. NS&EW | | |
| | 23W-18N | 12 |
| Crystal Ln. NE&SW | | |
| | 19W-18N | 14 |
| Cumnor Rd. E&W | 23W-17N | 12 |
| Cunningham Rd. E&W | | |
| | 21W-17N | 13 |
| Cypress Ct. NE&SW | | |
| | 20W-17N | 13 |
| Daniels Rd. E&W | 21W-15N | 23 |
| Dartmoor Av.* E&W | | |
| | 21W-18N | 13 |
| Dee Ln. N&S | 21W-18N | 13 |
| Deer Av. N&S | 22W-17N | 13 |
| Deerpath Rd. N&S | 22W-18N | 13 |
| Del Mar Dr. N&S | 20W-17N | 13 |
| Denise Dr. NE&SW | | |
| | 20W-18N | 13 |
| Denton Av. NS&EW | | |
| | 21W-18N | 13 |
| Diane Dr. NE&SW | 20W-18N | 13 |
| Diane Ln. NS&EW | 20W-18N | 13 |
| Doe Rd. N&S | 23W-17N | 12 |
| Doral Ct. E&W | 22W-18N | 13 |
| Dorchester St. E&W | | |
| | 22W-15N | 23 |
| Dorset Av. E&W | 22W-15N | 23 |
| Dresden Av.* E&W | 21W-18N | 13 |
| Driftwood Av. N&S | 21W-18N | 13 |
| Dundee Qtr. NS&EW | | |
| | 19W-18N | 14 |
| Dundee Rd. E&W | | |
| | 24W-17N,19W-18N | 12 |
| Dunegal Bay* N&S | 19W-18N | 14 |
| Dupont Av. N&S | 21W-14N | 23 |
| Eastbrook E&W | 19W-18N | 14 |
| Echo Ln. N&S | 21W-17N | 13 |
| Edgebrook E&W | 19W-18N | 14 |
| Ela Rd. N&S | | |
| | 23W-13N,23W-18N | 22 |
| Ellis St. E&W | 22W-15N | 23 |
| Elm St. NS&EW | | |
| | 22W-17N,20W-17N | 13 |
| Elmwood Av. NE&SW | | |
| | 20W-17N | 13 |
| Elmwood Ct. NW&SE | | |
| | 20W-13N | 23 |
| Elmwood Ln., N. NS&EW | | |
| | 20W-13N | 23 |
| Elmwood Ln., S. NS&EW | | |
| | 20W-13N | 23 |
| Emerald Ln. NW&SE | | |
| | 19W-18N | 14 |
| Emerson Av. E&W | 21W-14N | 23 |
| Enlund Dr. N&S | 19W-18N | 14 |
| Evergreen Ln. N&S | | |
| | 19W-18N | 14 |
| Fairfax Av. E&W | 20W-18N | 14 |
| Fairfield Ct.* E&W | 21W-18N | 13 |
| Farmgate* N&S | 20W-17N | 13 |
| Fern Cir. E&W | 21W-14N | 23 |
| Fern Ct. E&W | 21W-14N | 23 |
| Fielding Pl. NW&SE | | |
| | 23W-18N | 12 |
| Fielding Place Ct. NW&SE | | |
| | 23W-18N | 12 |
| Forest Av. N&S | 22W-17N | 13 |
| Forest Ln. N&S | 20W-13N | 23 |
| Fox Chase Ct. N&S | | |
| | 24W-18N | 12 |
| Fox Glove Ln.* E&W | | |
| | 20W-20N | 47 |
| Foxwood Ln. E&W | 23W-18N | 12 |
| Frances Ln. E&W | 23W-18N | 12 |
| Franklin Av. N&S | | |
| | 22W-16N,22W-17N | 13 |
| Frontage Rd. N&S | 19W-17N | 14 |
| Frost Rd. E&W | 23W-13N | 22 |
| Galena Av. N&S | 19W-18N | 14 |
| Galesburg Av. N&S | | |
| | 19W-18N | 14 |
| Garden Av. E&W | | |
| | 21W-17N,20W-17N | 13 |
| Garden Ct. N&S | 21W-17N | 13 |
| Gardenia Ln. E&W | 19W-18N | 14 |
| Garfield Av. E&W | 20W-14N | 23 |
| Gary Dr. N&S | | |
| | 19W-16N,21W-17N | 13 |
| Gatewood Av. N&S | | |
| | 21W-17N | 13 |
| Glavin Cir. E&W | 19W-18N | 14 |
| Glencoe Av. N&S | | |
| | 23W-17N,20W-18N | 12 |
| Glencoe Rd. E&W | 22W-15N | 23 |
| Glencoe St. E&W | 22W-15N | 13 |
| Goodwin E&W | 19W-18N | 14 |
| Grace Ln. N&S | 24W-18N | 12 |
| Grandview Ter. NS&EW | | |
| | 24W-18N | 12 |
| Greenbrier Ln.* E&W | | |
| | 20W-20N | 47 |
| Greenview Av. N&S | | |
| | 23W-17N | 12 |
| Grove Av. N&S | 22W-17N | 13 |
| Grove Ln. N&S | 23W-18N | 12 |
| Haig Ct. E&W | 19W-18N | 14 |
| Hancock Dr. NS&EW | | |
| | 20W-20N | 47 |
| Harrison Av. N&S | | |
| | 22W-15N,22W-16N | 23 |
| Hawk Dr. E&W | 24W-18N | 12 |

| Street | Grid | Page |
|---|---|---|
| Hawthorne Dr. NE&SW | 24W-18N | 12 |
| Heatherlea Dr., W. NS&EW | 20W-17N | 13 |
| Helen Rd. N&S | 22W-15N | 23 |
| Heritage Cir.* NS&EW | 20W-18N | 14 |
| Heritage Dr.* E&W | 20W-18N | 14 |
| Hickory Ln. E&W | 23W-13N | 22 |
| Hicks Rd. N&S | 20W-17N,20W-18N | 13 |
| Cir. | 20W-18N | 14 |
| Hidden Oaks Dr. N&S | 23W-18N | 12 |
| High Grove Ln. N&S | 19W-18N | 14 |
| High Rd. SW&NE | 24W-18N | 12 |
| Hill Av. N&S | 22W-16N | 13 |
| Hill Rd. E&W | 21W-17N | 13 |
| Hillcrest E&W | 21W-18N | 13 |
| Hillcrest St. N&S | 24W-18N | 12 |
| Hillcrest Dr. NW&SE | 24W-18N,23W-18N | 12 |
| Hillside Rd. E&W | 24W-18N,24W-18N | 12 |
| Hillside St. E&W | 22W-15N | 23 |
| Holly Way E&W | 19W-18N | 14 |
| Home Av. E&W | 20W-17N | 13 |
| Howe Ter. NW&SE | 24W-18N | 14 |
| Hudson Bay* E&W | 19W-18N | 14 |
| Independence Dr. NE&SW | 20W-18N | 13 |
| Irene Dr. N&S | 21W-18N | 13 |
| Iris Dr. N&S | 19W-18N | 14 |
| Isle Royal Ln.* N&S | 19W-18N | 14 |
| Ivy Pl. N&S | 19W-18N | 14 |
| Jamestown Dr.* N&S | 20W-20N | 47 |
| Jarvis Ct. N&S | 20W-18N | 13 |
| Jennifer Ln. NW&SE | 19W-18N | 14 |
| Joan Dr. N&S | 23W-18N | 12 |
| Kenilworth Av. N&S | 22W-15N,21W-15N | 23 |
| Kennedy Dr. (Pvt.) N&S | 19W-18N | 14 |
| Kevin Cir. E&W | 19W-18N | 14 |
| King Arthur Dr. N&S | 21W-17N | 13 |
| King Charles Ct. N&S | 21W-17N | 13 |
| King George Dr. NS&EW | 21W-17N | 13 |
| King Henry Ct. E&W | 21W-17N | 13 |
| King: Row NS&EW | 19W-18N | 14 |
| Knollwood N&S | 20W-13N | 23 |
| Knoxboro Ln. E&W | 23W-18N | 12 |
| Kuhl Rd. N&S | 21W-18N | 13 |
| Lakeside Dr. NE&SW | 21W-17N | 13 |
| Laurel Rd. N&S | 19W-18N | 14 |
| Lee Ct. N&S | 20W-18N | 13 |
| Lenwood Dr. N&S | 21W-18N | 13 |
| Leonard Rd. E&W | 22W-15N | 23 |
| Lexington Dr.* N&S | 20W-18N | 14 |
| Lilac Ln. E&W | 19W-18N | 14 |
| Lilac Pl. N&S | 19W-18N | 14 |
| Lilly Ln. E&W | 19W-18N | 14 |
| Linden Ln. N&S | 20W-13N | 23 |
| Linder Ln. E&W | 24W-18N | 12 |
| Little City Dr. N&S | 23W-14N | 22 |
| Long Acres Ln. NS&EW | 20W-13N | 23 |
| Long Ln. E&W | 20W-13N | 23 |
| Long Valley Ln. NW&SE | 19W-17N | 14 |
| Lorelei Ln. EW&NS | 24W-18N | 12 |
| Louise Ln. N&S | 21W-17N | 13 |
| Lynda Dr. NW&SE | 20W-18N | 13 |
| Maple Av. N&S | 22W-16N,22W-17N | 13 |
| Marshall Ct. E&W | 19W-18N | 14 |
| Martin Dr. E&W | 21W-17N | 13 |
| Meacham Rd. N&S | 21W-13N,21W-14N | 23 |
| Meadow Ln. NW&SE | 20W-13N | 23 |
| Middleton Av. N&S | 22W-15N,22W-16N | 13 |
| Morrison Av. N&S | 22W-16N | 13 |
| Myrtle St. E&W | 22W-17N | 13 |
| N. Circle Dr. N&S | 20W-13N | 23 |
| Nantucket Ln. N&S | 23W-18N | 12 |
| New Haven Av. N&S | 19W-18N | 14 |
| Nichols Rd. E&W | 19W-18N | 14 |
| North Rd. N&S | 19W-18N | 14 |
| North St. E&W | 22W-17N | 13 |
| Norway Ln. NS&EW | 19W-17N | 14 |
| Oak Ct. N&S | 24W-18N | 12 |
| Oak Ridge Rd. N&S | 20W-18N | 13 |
| Oak St. N&S | 20W-17N | 13 |
| Oaksbury Ln. E&W | 20W-13N | 23 |
| Oakwood N&S | 20W-13N | 23 |
| Old Bridge Rd. NS&EW | 20W-17N | 13 |
| Old Hicks Rd. NS&EW | 19W-18N | 14 |
| Old Mill Dr. N&S | 20W-17N | 13 |
| Osage NW&SE | 20W-18N | 13 |
| Palm Dr. N&S | 23W-18N | 12 |
| Palos Av. N&S | 22W-17N | 13 |
| Panorama Dr. NS&EW | 22W-17N | 13 |
| Park Av. N&S | 22W-17N | 13 |
| Park Dr. NE&SW | 20W-14N | 23 |
| Pennsylvannia Dr. NW&SE | 20W-18N | 13 |
| Pepper Tree Dr. N&S | 20W-17N | 13 |
| Perry Dr. N&S | 21W-17N | 13 |
| Pheasant Ln. N&S | 24W-18N | 12 |
| Pheasant Ter. N&S | 24W-18N | 12 |
| Pine Dr. E&W | 21W-17N | 13 |
| Plum Grove Rd. N&S | 21W-13N,21W-17N | 23 |
| Poplar St. E&W | 22W-17N | 13 |
| Port Center Dr. N&S | 22W-14N,23W-14N | 22 |
| Portage Av. N&S | 22W-17N | 13 |
| Ports 'O' Call Dr. N&S | 19W-17N | 14 |
| Prescon N&S | 19W-17N | 14 |
| Private Dr. NS&EW | 19W-18N | 14 |
| Prospect Dr. E&W | 24W-18N | 12 |
| Public St. N&S | 21W-18N | 13 |
| Queens Ct. NW&SE | 19W-18N | 14 |
| Queensburg Cir.* NS&EW | 20W-20N | 47 |
| Queensburg Ln.* E&W | 20W-20N | 47 |
| Quentin Rd. N&S | 22W-15N,22W-17N | 23 |
| Rainbow Bay* N&S | 19W-18N | 14 |
| Rand Ct. NW&SE | 20W-18N | 13 |
| Rand Grove Village N&S | 20W-18N | 13 |
| Rand Rd. NW&SE | 20W-18N,19W-17N | 13 |
| Randall Ln. NE&SW | 19W-18N | 14 |
| Randville Dr. E&W | 19W-17N | 14 |
| Ridgewood Ln. N&S | 20W-17N | 13 |
| Rosalie Ln. E&W | 21W-18N | 13 |
| Rose Av. NW&SE | 19W-18N | 14 |
| Rosiland Rd. E&W | 21W-18N | 13 |
| Roslyn Rd. N&S | 24W-18N | 12 |
| Roth Av. N&S | 24W-18N | 12 |
| Rt. 53 NW&SE | 20W-18N,19W-17N | 13 |
| Rt. 68 E&W | 23W-17N,20W-17N | 12 |
| S. Circle Dr. E&W | 21W-12N | 23 |
| Shadow Lake Ter.* N&S | 19W-20N | 47 |
| Shady Dr. E&W | 20W-14N | 23 |
| Shady Lane E&W | 21W-18N | 13 |
| Shady Pine Ct. E&W | 20W-17N | 13 |
| Shagbark Ct. NW&SE | 23W-18N | 12 |
| Shannon Bay* E&W | 19W-18N | 14 |
| Silver Ln. NS&EW | 19W-17N | 14 |
| Silver Strand Cir.* N&S | 19W-20N | 47 |
| Smith Rd. N&S | 21W-17N | 13 |
| Smith St. N&S | 21W-14N,21W-15N | 23 |
| Spruce NW&SE | 20W-18N | 13 |
| Sue Ln. E&W | 21W-13N | 23 |
| Sunset Dr. E&W | 21W-13N | 23 |
| Sunset Rd. N&S | 21W-13N | 23 |
| Suthers Ln. N&S | 21W-18N | 13 |
| Tall Trees Ln. E&W | 23W-18N | 12 |
| Tanglewood Av.* NS&EW | 21W-18N | 13 |
| Thackeray Dr. N&S | 19W-18N | 14 |
| Thorntree Ln. N&S | 20W-13N | 23 |
| Timber Ln. E&W | 20W-17N | 13 |
| Timberlea Dr. N&S | 20W-17N | 13 |
| Trail Ridge E&W | 19W-18N | 14 |
| Tulip Dr. N&S | 19W-18N | 14 |
| Turtle Creek Dr. N&S | 19W-17N | 14 |
| Vermillion Ln.* E&W | 19W-18N | 14 |
| Vermont St. N&S | 21W-14N | 23 |
| Wainwright Ct. N&S | 19W-18N | 14 |
| Waterford Ln. NE&SW | 19W-18N | 14 |
| Wedgewood Dr. N&S | 23W-18N | 12 |
| West Frontage Rd. N&S | 20W-13N | 23 |
| Westmoreland Dr. N&S | 19W-18N | 14 |
| Westwood Ln. N&S | 20W-13N,21W-18N | 23 |
| Wheatherstone Rd. NS&EW | 23W-18N | 12 |
| Whispering Oaks Ln. NS&EW | 19W-18N | 14 |
| Whispering Springs* NW&SE | 19W-20N | 47 |
| White Gate Ct. NW&SE | 23W-18N | 12 |
| White Sands Bay* N&S | 19W-18N | 14 |
| Whitewater Bay* N&S | 19W-18N | 14 |
| Willamsburg Dr.* NS&EW | 20W-20N | 47 |
| Willow St. E&W | 22W-16N | 13 |
| Wilmette Av. E&W | 20W-14N | 23 |
| Wilson St. E&W | 22W-16N | 13 |
| Winchester Hills Dr. NS&EW | 19W-18N | 14 |
| Wind River Ter.* N&S | 19W-18N | 14 |
| Winnetka Av. | 20W-14N | 23 |
| Winnetka St. E&W | 22W-17N | 13 |
| Wood St. N&S | 22W-16N,22W-17N | 13 |
| Woodbury Dr. NE&SW | 19W-17N | 14 |
| Woodland Ct. N&S | 20W-13N | 23 |
| Woodland St. E&W | 21W-18N | 13 |
| Zinnia Ln. E&W | 19W-18N | 14 |

## Palos Heights

| Street | Grid | Page |
|---|---|---|
| Aberdeen Ct. E&W | 10W-15S | 73 |
| Aberdeen Dr. E&W | 10W-15S | 73 |
| Arbor Tr. N&S | 7W-14S | 74 |
| Arquilla Dr. N&S | 9W-15S | 73 |
| Auburn Av. N&S | 8W-15S | 73 |
| Briar Ln. N&S | 8W-15S | 73 |
| Burris Ct. E&W | 8W-14S | 73 |
| Canterberry Ct. E&W | 9W-13S | 73 |
| Carmicheal Dr. E&W | 9W-14S | 73 |
| Carol Ln. N&S | 7W-14S | 74 |
| Carriage Trail NE&SW | 9W-19S | 79 |
| Cedar Creek N&S | 8W-14S | 73 |
| Cedar Ln. N&S | 9W-15S | 73 |
| Cheyenne Dr. N&S | 8W-14S | 73 |
| Chippewa Dr. E&W | 8W-14S | 73 |
| Choctaw Rd. E&W | 8W-14S | 73 |
| Coach Rd. NS&EW | 9W-15S | 73 |
| College Dr. E&W | 9W-14S,9W-13S | 73 |
| Comanche Dr. E&W | 9W-15S | 73 |
| Country Club Ct. N&S | 9W-15S | 73 |
| Country Squire Ct. NE&SW | 9W-14S | 73 |
| Country Squire Rd. N&S | 9W-14S | 73 |
| Cypress Ln. N&S | 9W-15S | 73 |
| Deer Ln. E&W | 8W-15S | 73 |
| Diane Dr. N&S | 9W-14S | 73 |
| Dogwood Ln.* N&S | 7W-14S | 74 |
| Edgewood Rd. E&W | 8W-15S | 73 |
| Edinburgh Dr. N&S | 10W-15S | 73 |
| Elm Ct. NW&SE | 9W-15S | 73 |
| Evergreen Av. E&W | 8W-15S | 73 |
| Feldner Dr. N&S | 9W-15S | 73 |
| Flambeau Dr. N&S | 8W-14S | 73 |
| Forest Hill Ct. NS&EW | 9W-15S | 73 |
| Forest Hill Ln. E&W | 9W-15S | 73 |
| Forestview Rd. N&S | 9W-15S | 73 |
| Fox Ln. N&S | 8W-15S | 73 |
| Golf Dr. E&W | 9W-15S | 73 |
| Golfview Ln. E&W | 8W-15S | 73 |
| Harlem Av. N&S | 9W-15S,9W-14S | 73 |
| Harold Av. N&S | 8W-15S | 73 |
| Highland Dr. E&W | 8W-15S | 73 |
| Ishnala Dr. NE&SW | 9W-15S | 73 |
| Kiowa Ln. NE&SW | 9W-15S | 73 |
| Kirkcaldy Dr. E&W | 10W-15S | 73 |
| Lakeview Ct. N&S | 9W-15S | 73 |
| Linden Dr. E&W | 8W-15S | 73 |
| Manitoba Ct. N&S | 9W-15S | 73 |
| Maple Ln. N&S | 8W-14S | 73 |
| McCarthy Rd. NW&SE | 9W-14S | 73 |
| McIntosh Dr. E&W | 9W-15S | 73 |
| Melvina Av. N&S | 7W-14S | 74 |
| Menominee Pkwy. E&W | 8W-14S | 73 |
| Misty Meadow Dr. N&S | 10W-15S | 73 |
| Nagle Av. N&S | 9W-15S | 73 |
| Nashville Av. N&S | 8W-14S | 73 |
| Natchez Av. N&S | 8W-14S | 73 |
| Natoma Av. N&S | 8W-14S | 73 |
| Navaho Dr. N&S | 8W-14S | 73 |
| Navajo Ct., E. N&S | 8W-14S | 73 |
| Navajo Ct., W. NE&SW | 8W-14S | 73 |
| Navajo Dr., E. N&S | 8W-14S | 73 |
| Navajo Dr., W. N&S | 8W-14S | 73 |
| Oak N&S&SE | 9W-15S | 73 |
| Oak Hills Ct. E&W | 9W-15S | 73 |
| Oak Hills Pkwy. N&S | 9W-15S | 73 |
| Oak Ln. N&S | 9W-15S | 73 |
| Oak Park Av. N&S | 8W-15S,8W-14S | 73 |
| Oak Ridge Dr. E&W | 9W-15S | 73 |
| Oak Ridge Trail N&S | 9W-15S | 73 |
| Oak Trail Ct. E&W | 9W-14S | 73 |
| Oakview St. N&S | 9W-15S | 73 |
| Old George's Way NS&EW | 9W-15S | 73 |
| Old Oak Trail N&S | 9W-14S | 73 |
| Onekema Dr. E&W | 8W-14S | 73 |
| Orchard Dr. E&W | 7W-14S | 74 |
| Palos Av. E&W | 9W-15S | 73 |
| Park Ln. E&W | 8W-15S | 73 |
| Parliament Dr., E. N&S | 9W-13S | 73 |
| Parliament Dr., W. N&S | 9W-13S | 73 |
| Pheasant N&S | 8W-15S | 73 |
| Pine Pl.* NS&EW | 7W-14S | 74 |
| Ponderosa Dr. NS&EW | 9W-15S | 73 |
| Pottawatami Ct. NE&SW | 9W-15S | 73 |
| Pottawatami Dr. E&W | 9W-15S | 73 |
| Pueblo Dr. N&S | 9W-15S | 73 |
| Pueblo Ln. NE&SW | 9W-15S | 73 |
| Quail Ct. N&S | 8W-15S | 73 |
| Raleigh Ct. E&W | 9W-15S | 73 |
| Richard Av. N&S | 9W-14S | 73 |
| Ridgeland Av. N&S | 8W-15S,8W-14S | 73 |
| Seneca Rd. N&S | 9W-15S | 73 |
| Sequoia Dr. NE&SW | 9W-15S | 73 |
| Shawnee Rd. N&S | 9W-15S | 73 |
| Shiawassie Dr. E&W | 8W-14S | 73 |
| Shoshone Rd. N&S | 9W-15S | 73 |
| Sioux Ln. N&S | 9W-15S | 73 |
| Sorrento Dr. N&S | 8W-14S | 73 |
| Spruce Pl.* NS&EW | 7W-14S | 74 |
| Squire Pl. E&W | 9W-14S | 73 |
| Surrey Hill Ct. NW&SE | 9W-14S | 73 |
| Surrey Hill Rd. NE&SW | 9W-14S | 73 |
| Sycamore Ln. N&S | 9W-13S | 73 |
| Tennyson Ct. E&W | 9W-13S | 73 |
| Turtle Pond Ln. N&S | 9W-15S | 73 |
| Ute Ln. E&W | 9W-15S | 73 |
| Westgate Av. N&S | 8W-15S | 73 |
| Westview N&S | 9W-15S | 73 |
| White Oak Ct. NE&SW | 9W-14S | 73 |
| White Pine N&S | 9W-15S | 73 |
| Willow Wood Dr. E&W | 7W-14S | 74 |
| Winnebago Rd. N&S | 9W-15S | 73 |
| Wolf Rd. N&S | 14W-15S,14W-14S | 72 |
| Wyandot Dr. E&W | 8W-14S | 73 |
| 68th Ct. N&S | 8W-14S | 73 |
| 69th Av. N&S | 8W-14S | 73 |
| 69th Ct. N&S | 8W-15S,8W-14S | 73 |
| 70th Av. N&S | 8W-15S,8W-14S | 73 |
| 70th Ct. N&S | 8W-15S,8W-14S | 73 |
| 71st Av. N&S | 8W-15S,8W-14S | 73 |
| 71st Ct. N&S | 8W-15S,8W-14S | 73 |
| 72nd Ct. N&S | 9W-14S | 73 |
| 73rd Av. N&S | 9W-14S | 73 |
| 73rd Ct. N&S | 9W-14S | 73 |
| 74th Av. N&S | 9W-14S | 73 |
| 75th Av. N&S | 9W-14S | 73 |
| 76th Ct. N&S | 9W-15S,9W-14S | 73 |
| 77th Pl. N&S | 9W-15S | 73 |
| 78th Ct. N&S | 9W-15S | 73 |
| 79th Av. N&S | 9W-15S | 73 |
| 80th Av. N&S | 9W-15S | 73 |
| 96th Av. N&S | 11W-14S | 72 |
| 119th Pl. E&W | 9W-14S | 73 |
| 120th St. E&W | 9W-14S,8W-14S | 73 |
| 121st St. E&W | 9W-14S,8W-14S | 73 |
| 122nd St. E&W | 9W-14S,8W-14S | 73 |
| 123rd Pl. E&W | 9W-14S | 73 |
| 123rd St. E&W | 9W-14S,8W-14S | 73 |
| 124th Pl. E&W | 9W-14S,7W-14S | 73 |
| 124th St. E&W | 9W-14S,8W-14S | 73 |
| 125th Pl. E&W | 7W-14S | 74 |
| 125th St. E&W | 9W-14S,8W-14S | 73 |
| 126th Pl. E&W | 8W-14S | 73 |
| 126th St. E&W | 9W-14S,8W-14S | 73 |
| 127th St. E&W | 9W-14S,8W-14S | 73 |
| 128th St. E&W | 9W-15S | 73 |
| 129th St. E&W | 9W-15S | 73 |
| 130th St. E&W | 9W-15S | 73 |
| 131st St. E&W | 9W-15S,8W-15S | 73 |

## Palos Hills

| Street | Grid | Page |
|---|---|---|
| Alta Dr. N&S | 10W-12S | 65 |
| Amee Ct. (Pvt.) E&W | 10W-12S | 65 |
| Aspen N&S | 10W-12S | 65 |
| Aum Ridge Dr. (Pvt.) E&W | 10W-12S | 65 |
| Avon Ct. N&S | 10W-12S | 65 |
| Bennett Dr. (Pvt.) E&W | 10W-12S | 65 |
| Boulder Ct. E&W | 10W-13S | 73 |
| Breckenridge Dr. E&W | 10W-12S | 65 |
| Broadmoor Dr. N&S | 10W-12S | 65 |
| Brookledge Dr. N&S | 9W-12S | 65 |
| Cambridge Ct. N&S | 10W-11S | 65 |
| Carlton Hide Dr. E&W | 10W-12S | 65 |
| Catherine Ln.* N&S | 10W-13S | 73 |
| Center Rd. E&W | 11W-13S | 72 |
| Chamonieux Dr. N&S | 10W-12S | 65 |
| Charles Av. NE&SW | 10W-11S | 65 |
| Cherry Ct. N&S | 10W-13S | 73 |
| Chestnut Dr. N&S | 10W-13S | 73 |
| Cinnamon Creek Dr. E&W | 11W-11S | 64 |
| Circle Ct. N&S | 10W-12S | 65 |
| Circle Dr. E&W | 10W-12S | 65 |
| Cobblestone Ct.* E&W | 10W-13S | 73 |
| College Dr. N&S | 10W-12S | 65 |
| Cottonwood Dr. N&S | 10W-13S | 73 |
| Cour Caravelle E&W | 10W-13S | 73 |
| Cour D'Alene N&S | 10W-13S | 73 |
| Cour De La Reide N&S | 10W-13S | 73 |
| Cour Deauville N&S | 10W-13S | 73 |
| Cour La Salle E&W | 10W-13S | 73 |
| Cour Leroux N&S | 10W-13S | 73 |
| Cour Madeleine N&S | 10W-13S | 73 |
| Cour Marquis E&W | 10W-13S | 73 |
| Cour Masson E&W | 10W-13S | 73 |
| Cour Michele E&W | 10W-13S | 73 |
| Cour Monnet N&S | 10W-13S | 73 |
| Cour Montreal N&S | 10W-13S | 73 |
| Cour Saint Tropez N&S | 10W-13S | 73 |
| Cour Versaille E&W | 10W-13S | 73 |
| Crista Ct. N&S | 10W-12S | 65 |
| Dartmouth Dr. E&W | 10W-12S | 65 |
| Deerpath Ln. N&S | 11W-13S | 72 |
| Del Prado Dr. E&W | 11W-11S | 64 |
| Devon Shire Ln. E&W | 11W-11S | 64 |
| Doric Cir. N&S | 10W-12S | 65 |
| East Rd. N&S | 11W-13S | 72 |
| Eastwood Dr. N&S | 9W-12S | 65 |
| Eleanor Av. NE&SW | 10W-11S | 65 |
| Erin Dr. E&W | 10W-11S | 65 |
| Granada Ln. N&S | 10W-11S | 65 |
| Green Valley Dr. NS&EW | 10W-12S | 65 |
| Gruener Ct. (Pvt.) E&W | 10W-12S | 65 |
| Gruener Ct.* E&W | 10W-13S | 73 |
| Harlem Av. N&S | 10W-12S | 65 |
| Helena Dr. N&S | 11W-13S | 72 |
| Heritage Hills Dr. N&S | 11W-13S | 72 |
| Hickory Crest N&S | 11W-11S | 64 |
| Holly Ct. E&W | 10W-13S | 73 |
| Interlochen Ct. NE&SW | 10W-12S | 65 |
| Interlochen Dr. NW&SE | 10W-13S | 73 |
| Juniper Ct. E&W | 10W-13S | 73 |
| Kathy Ct. N&S | 9W-12S | 65 |
| Kean Av. N&S | 11W-13S,11W-11S | 72 |
| Kingsbury Ct. N&S | 10W-11S | 65 |
| Lori Ln. N&S | 9W-12S | 65 |
| Los Palos Ln. NE&SW | 11W-11S | 64 |
| Loveland Ln. E&W | 10W-12S | 65 |
| Lucas Dr. (Pvt.) NS&EW | 11W-13S,10W-13S | 72 |
| Maple Crest N&S | 11W-11S | 64 |
| Meadow Ln. N&S | 10W-12S | 65 |
| Mehta Ct. (Pvt.) E&W | 10W-12S | 65 |
| Meryton Ct. N&S | 10W-11S | 65 |
| Michael Dr. N&S | 10W-12S | 65 |
| Millstone Ct.* E&W | 10W-13S | 73 |
| Moraine Dr. E&W | 10W-13S | 73 |
| Moraine Valley Golf Range E&W | 10W-12S | 65 |
| Mullberry Ct. N&S | 10W-13S | 73 |
| North Rd. E&W | 11W-13S | 72 |
| Northwest Rd. NW&SE | 11W-13S | 73 |
| O'Gorman Dr. E&W | 10W-13S | 73 |
| O'Gorman N&S | 10W-13S | 73 |
| Oak Crest NW&SE | 11W-11S | 64 |
| Olympic Cir. N&S | 10W-12S | 65 |
| One Executive Dr. N&S | 9W-13S | 73 |
| Palos Dr. N&S | 9W-13S | 73 |
| Paxos Dr. E&W | 9W-13S | 73 |
| Peak Dr. NW&SE | 9W-13S | 73 |
| Pebble Ct.* E&W | 10W-13S | 73 |
| Pemberly Ct. N&S | 10W-11S | 65 |

|  | Grid | Page |
|---|---|---|
| Poplar Ct. E&W .... | 10W-13S | 73 |
| Possum Dr. N&S .. | 11W-13S | 72 |
| Roberts Rd. E&W | | |
| ............. | 10W-12S,10W-11S | 65 |
| Sand Castle E&W (Pvt.) N&S | 11W-11S | 64 |
| Sheffield Rd. N&S .. | 9W-12S | 65 |
| Sierra Ln. E&W .... | 11W-11S | 64 |
| South 84th Ter. N&S | | |
| ............. | 10W-11S | 65 |
| South 86th Ter. N&S | | |
| ............. | 10W-11S | 65 |
| South Rd. E&W .. | 11W-13S | 72 |
| Spathis Dr. N&S .... | 10W-13S | 73 |
| Stonebridge Ct.* N&S | | |
| ............. | 10W-13S | 73 |
| Stoney Creek Dr. (Pvt.) N&S | | |
| ............. | 10W-12S | 65 |
| Stony Creek Dr. N&S | | |
| ............. | 10W-12S | 65 |
| Stowe Ct. N&S | 10W-12S | 65 |
| Stratford Ln. E&W . | 11W-11S | 64 |
| Sun Valley Ct. N&S | | |
| ............. | 10W-12S | 65 |
| Sun Valley Dr. E&W | | |
| ............. | 10W-12S | 65 |
| Surray Pk. E&W .... | 10W-11S | 65 |
| Sycamore Ct. N&S.. | 10W-13S | 73 |
| Sycamore Ln. N&S | 10W-13S | 73 |
| Taos Dr. E&W .... | 10W-12S | 65 |
| Terry Dr. N&S ...... | 9W-12S | 65 |
| Theresa Cir. NE&SW | | |
| ............. | 10W-12S | 65 |
| Todd Dr. N&S ...... | 9W-12S | 65 |
| Tuttle E&W ........ | 10W-13S | 73 |
| Urmi Ct. (Pvt.) E&W | | |
| ............. | 10W-12S | 65 |
| Vail Dr. E&W ...... | 10W-12S | 65 |
| Valley Ct. N&S .... | 10W-12S | 65 |
| Valley Dr. E&W ... | 10W-12S | 65 |
| Vickey Ln. N&S...... | 9W-12S | 65 |
| Walnut Ter. N&S .. | 10W-11S | 65 |
| West 102nd Ter. N&S | | |
| ............. | 10W-11S | 65 |
| West 103rd Ter. E&W | | |
| ............. | 10W-11S | 65 |
| West 99th Ter. E&W | | |
| ............. | 10W-11S | 65 |
| Westwood Dr. N&S | | |
| ............. | 9W-13S,9W-12S | 73 |
| Willow Dr. E&W ... | 10W-13S | 73 |
| Windsor Dr. E&W .. | 11W-11S | 64 |
| Winter Park Dr. NW&SE | | |
| ............. | 10W-12S | 65 |
| Wood Ln. NE&SW .. | 10W-11S | 65 |
| Wooded Path Dr. NE&SW | | |
| ............. | 11W-11S | 64 |
| Zermatt Dr. E&W .. | 10W-12S | 65 |
| 73rd Av. N&S .... | 9W-12S | 65 |
| 73rd Ct. N&S...... | 9W-12S | 65 |
| 74th Av. N&S...... | 9W-12S | 65 |
| 75th Av. N&S .... | 9W-12S | 65 |
| 75th Ct. N&S ...... | 9W-12S | 65 |
| 76th Av. N&S...... | 9W-12S | 65 |
| 78th Av. N&S...... | 9W-12S | 65 |
| 79th Ct. N&S...... | 9W-12S | 65 |
| 80th Ct. N&S | | |
| ........ | 10W-12S,10W-11S | 65 |
| 81st Av. N&S | | |
| ............. | 10W-12S,10W-11S | 65 |
| 81st Ct. N&S | | |
| ............. | 10W-12S,10W-11S | 65 |
| 82nd Av. N&S | | |
| ............. | 10W-12S,10W-11S | 65 |
| 82nd Ct. N&S | | |
| ............. | 10W-12S,10W-11S | 65 |
| 83rd Av. N&S ...... | 10W-12S | 65 |
| 83rd Ct. N&S | | |
| ............. | 10W-12S,10W-11S | 65 |
| 84th Av. N&S | | |
| ............. | 10W-13S,10W-11S | 73 |
| 85th Av. N&S | | |
| ............. | 10W-13S,10W-12S | 73 |
| 86th Av. N&S | | |
| ............. | 10W-13S,10W-12S | 73 |
| 86th Ct. N&S ...... | 10W-11S | 65 |
| 87th Av. N&S...... | 10W-11S | 65 |
| 87th Ct. N&S ...... | 10W-11S | 65 |
| 88th Ct. N&S | | |
| ............. | 10W-12S,11W-11S | 65 |
| 89th Av. N&S | | |
| ............. | 11W-12S,11W-11S | 64 |
| 90th Av. N&S | | |
| ............. | 11W-12S,11W-11S | 64 |
| 96th Pl. E&W .... | 10W-11S | 65 |
| 96th St. E&W .... | 11W-11S | 65 |
| 97th Pl. E&W .... | 11W-11S | 64 |
| 97th St. E&W | | |
| ............. | 11W-11S,10W-11S | 64 |
| 98th Pl. E&W | | |
| ............. | 11W-11S,10W-11S | 64 |
| 98th St. E&W | | |
| ............. | 11W-11S,10W-11S | 64 |
| 99th Pl. E&W | | |
| ............. | 11W-11S,9W-11S | 64 |
| 99th St. E&W | | |
| ............. | 11W-11S,10W-11S | 64 |
| 100th Pl. E&W | | |
| ............. | 11W-11S,9W-11S | 64 |
| 100th St. E&W | | |
| ............. | 11W-11S,9W-11S | 64 |
| 101st Pl. E&W | | |
| ............. | 11W-11S,10W-11S | 64 |
| 101st St. E&W | | |
| ............. | 10W-11S,9W-11S | 65 |
| 101st Ter. E&W .. | 10W-11S | 65 |
| 102nd Pl. E&W .. | 11W-11S | 64 |
| 102nd St. E&W | | |
| ............. | 11W-11S,9W-11S | 64 |

|  | Grid | Page |
|---|---|---|
| 103rd Pl. E&W .... | 11W-12S | 64 |
| 103rd St. E&W | | |
| ............. | 11W-11S,9W-11S | 64 |
| 104th St. E&W | | |
| ............. | 11W-12S,10W-12S | 64 |
| 105th St. E&W | | |
| ............. | 11W-12S,9W-12S | 64 |
| 106th St. E&W .... | 10W-12S | 65 |
| 107th St. E&W | | |
| ............. | 10W-12S,9W-12S | 65 |
| 108th St. E&W .... | 9W-12S | 65 |
| 109th St. E&W .... | 9W-12S | 65 |
| 111th Pl. E&W .... | 9W-13S | 73 |
| 111th St. E&W | | |
| ............. | 11W-12S,9W-12S | 64 |
| 112th Pl. E&W .... | 9W-13S | 73 |
| 112th St. E&W .... | 9W-13S | 73 |
| 113th Pl. E&W .... | 9W-13S | 73 |
| 113th St. E&W .... | 9W-13S | 73 |

### Palos Park

| Algoma Dr. E&W .. | 10W-14S | 73 |
| Alpine Av. (Pvt.) N&S | | |
| ............. | 10W-13S | 73 |
| Autobahn Dr. (Pvt.) NW&SE | | |
| ............. | 10W-13S | 73 |
| Autobahn Dr., E. (Pvt.) N&S | | |
| ............. | 10W-13S | 73 |
| Autobahn Dr., S. E&W | | |
| ............. | 10W-13S | 73 |
| Autobahn Dr., W. NW&SE | | |
| ............. | 10W-13S | 73 |
| Black Forest Ln. (Pvt.) | | |
| NW&SE...... | 10W-13S | 73 |
| Brand Av. NE&SW .. | 9W-14S | 73 |
| Brien Av. N&S....10W-14S | 73 |
| Brookside Dr. N&S | 10W-13S | 73 |
| Calumet Sag. Rd. E&W | | |
| ............. | 11W-13S,10W-13S | 72 |
| Cherokee Rd. E&W | | |
| ............. | 10W-14S | 73 |
| Danmar Trail E&W . | 14W-15S | 72 |
| Edelweiss Dr. (Pvt.) N&S | | |
| ............. | 10W-13S | 73 |
| Eldridge Av. N&S . | 10W-13S | 73 |
| Elm St. N&S ...... | 11W-14S | 73 |
| Forest Av. N&S .... | 9W-14S | 73 |
| Forest Glen Blvd. E&W | | |
| ............. | 11W-14S | 72 |
| Forest View Ln. N&S | | |
| ............. | 10W-14S | 73 |
| Fox Ln. N&S ...... | 13W-14S | 72 |
| Fox Ln., N. E&W .. | 13W-14S | 72 |
| Fox Ln., S. E&W .. | 13W-14S | 72 |
| Highwood Dr. N&S..10W-13S | 73 |
| Hillcrest Ln. E&W .. | 11W-14S | 72 |
| Hillside Cir. NE&SW | | |
| ............. | 10W-14S | 73 |
| Hillside Dr. NS&EW | | |
| ............. | 10W-14S | 73 |
| Hobart Av. N&S .... | 11W-14S | 72 |
| Holmes Av. N&S....10W-13S | 73 |
| Huntleigh Rd. E&W | | |
| ............. | 13W-14S | 72 |
| Iroqois Rd. N&S .... | 10W-14S | 73 |
| Kean Av. N&S......11W-14S | 73 |
| Kimber Ln. NW&SE | | |
| ............. | 10W-13S | 73 |
| Kinvarra Dr. N&S . | 12W-14S | 72 |
| Knollwood Dr. E&W | | |
| ............. | 10W-14S | 73 |
| Laurie Av. N&S .... | 10W-14S | 73 |
| Matterhorn Cir. (Pvt.) N&S | | |
| ............. | 10W-13S | 73 |
| Mc Kinley Av. N&S | 11W-14S | 72 |
| McCarthy Rd. E&W | | |
| ............. | 14W-14S,9W-14S | 72 |
| Meadow Rd. NE&SW | | |
| ............. | 14W-14S | 72 |
| Mohawk Rd. NE&SW | | |
| ............. | 10W-14S | 73 |
| Oak Ln. N&S ...... | 11W-14S | 72 |
| Oak Ridge Dr. E&W..9W-14S | 73 |
| Old Creek Rd. N&S | | |
| ............. | 14W-15S,14W-14S | 72 |
| Old Prague Path (Pvt.) N&S | | |
| ............. | 10W-13S | 73 |
| Old Timber Ln. E&W | | |
| ............. | 13W-14S | 72 |
| Palos Av. E&W ...... | 9W-14S | 73 |
| Park Lane Dr. E&W | | |
| ............. | 12W-14S | 72 |
| Partridge Ln. E&W . | 14W-15S | 72 |
| Pawnee Rd. NS&EW | | |
| ............. | 10W-14S | 73 |
| Post Rd. N&S ...... | 13W-14S | 72 |
| Rail Ln. NS&EW .... | 13W-14S | 72 |
| Ramsgate Dr. E&W | | |
| ............. | 14W-14S | 72 |
| Regina Ln. N&S .... | 9W-14S | 73 |
| Ridge Av. NE&SW ..11W-14S | 72 |
| Roma Rd. NW&SE ..10W-14S | 73 |
| Romiga Ln. NS&EW | | |
| ............. | 14W-15S | 72 |
| Rosewood Av. NW&SE | | |
| ............. | 11W-14S | 72 |
| Rt. 7 SW&NE | | |
| ............. | 11W-15S,10W-14S | 72 |
| Rt. 83 SE&NW | | |
| ............. | 11W-13S,10W-13S | 72 |
| Seminole Rd. N&S .. | 10W-14S | 73 |
| Somerset Ln. E&W | 12W-14S | 72 |
| South St. E&W | | |
| ............. | 11W-14S,10W-14S | 72 |
| Southwest Hwy. E&W | | |
| ............. | 11W-15S,10W-14S | 72 |
| Spring Rd. N&S .... | 11W-14S | 72 |

|  | Grid | Page |
|---|---|---|
| St. Moritz Dr. NS&EW | | |
| ............. | 10W-13S | 73 |
| Sunny Slope Ln. N&S | | |
| ............. | 13W-14S | 72 |
| Timber Dr. N&S .... | 10W-14S | 73 |
| Timber Ln. N&S .... | 10W-14S | 73 |
| Vienna Av. (Pvt.) N&S | | |
| ............. | 10W-13S | 73 |
| Virgil Av. N&S .... | 9W-14S | 73 |
| Walnut Ridge Dr. N&S | | |
| ............. | 10W-13S | 73 |
| Wild Cherry Ln. E&W | | |
| ............. | 12W-14S | 72 |
| Wild Wood Tr. E&W | | |
| ............. | 10W-14S | 73 |
| Williams Av. N&S .. | 10W-14S | 73 |
| Windsor Dr. N&S .. | 12W-14S | 72 |
| Winslow Rd. N&S .. | 12W-14S | 72 |
| Woodland Trail E&W | | |
| ............. | 10W-14S | 73 |
| Woodland Trail, S. N&S | | |
| ............. | 10W-14S | 73 |
| 79th Av. N&S........9W-14S | 73 |
| 80th Av. N&S......10W-14S | 73 |
| 81st Av. N&S ...... | 10W-14S | 73 |
| 82nd Av. N&S | | |
| ............. | 10W-14S,10W-13S | 73 |
| 82nd Ct. N&S | | |
| ............. | 10W-14S,10W-13S | 73 |
| 83rd Av. N&S | | |
| ............. | 10W-14S,10W-13S | 73 |
| 84th Av. N&S ...... | 10W-14S | 73 |
| 85th Av. N&S | | |
| ............. | 10W-14S,10W-13S | 73 |
| 86th St. N&S ...... | 10W-14S | 73 |
| 87th Av. N&S .... | 10W-14S | 73 |
| 88th Av. N&S .... | 11W-14S | 72 |
| 89th Av. N&S .... | 11W-14S | 72 |
| 89th Ct. N&S...... | 11W-14S | 72 |
| 90th Av. N&S .... | 11W-14S | 72 |
| 90th St. N&S ...... | 11W-14S | 72 |
| 91st St. N&S ...... | 11W-14S | 72 |
| 92nd St. N&S .... | 11W-14S | 72 |
| 93rd St. N&S...... | 11W-14S | 72 |
| 94th St. N&S .... | 11W-14S | 72 |
| 114th Av. N&S .... | 14W-14S | 72 |
| 115th Av. N&S .... | 14W-14S | 72 |
| 116th Av. N&S .... | 14W-14S | 72 |
| 116th Ct. E&W .... | 10W-13S | 73 |
| 118th St. N&S .... | 10W-13S | 73 |
| 119th Pl. E&W .... | 10W-14S | 73 |
| 119th St. E&W | | |
| ............. | 11W-13S,10W-13S | 72 |
| 120th St. E&W | | |
| ............. | 11W-14S,9W-14S | 72 |
| 121st St. E&W | | |
| ............. | 14W-14S,10W-14S | 73 |
| 122nd St. E&W | | |
| ............. | 14W-14S,10W-14S | 72 |
| 123rd Pl. E&W .... | 14W-14S | 72 |
| 123rd Pl. E&W .... | 9W-14S | 73 |
| 123rd St. E&W | | |
| ............. | 11W-14S,10W-14S | 72 |
| 124th St. E&W | | |
| ............. | 11W-14S,10W-14S | 72 |
| 125th St. E&W | | |
| ............. | 11W-14S,10W-14S | 72 |
| 126th St. E&W | | |
| ............. | 11W-14S,10W-14S | 72 |
| 127th St. E&W | | |
| ............. | 14W-14S,9W-14S | 72 |
| 131st St. E&W .... | 10W-15S | 73 |

### Palos Township

| Adsit Rd. N&S......13W-15S | 72 |
| Archer Av. NE&SW | | |
| ............. | 14W-11S,14W-10S | 64 |
| Arlington Ct. E&W . | 13W-15S | 72 |
| Arlington Ln. E&W .. | 13W-15S | 72 |
| Barberry Ct. N&S . | 13W-14S | 72 |
| Bernice Dr. E&W .. | 13W-15S | 72 |
| Birchwood Dr. E&W | | |
| ............. | 13W-14S | 72 |
| Bishop Ct. NE&SW | | |
| ............. | 12W-15S | 72 |
| Black Walnut Tr. NS&EW | | |
| ............. | 11W-15S,11W-14S | 72 |
| Bloomfield Dr. E&W | | |
| ............. | 13W-15S | 72 |
| Blue Heron Dr. N&S | | |
| ............. | 13W-15S | 72 |
| Brian Pl. N&S .... | 13W-15S | 72 |
| Brittany Dr. N&S...13W-15S | 72 |
| Brodt Dr. NW&SE . | 13W-15S | 72 |
| Buege Ln. E&W .. | 14W-9S | 64 |
| Carriage House Ln. NS&EW | | |
| ............. | 13W-15S | 72 |
| Charlotte Ct. NE&SW | | |
| ............. | 13W-15S | 72 |
| Cherrywood Dr. E&W | | |
| ............. | 13W-14S | 72 |
| Circle Pkwy. NS&EW | | |
| ............. | 12W-15S | 72 |
| Cornell Ln. N&S .. | 10W-15S | 73 |
| Creek Rd. E&W .... | 13W-15S | 72 |
| Deerwood Dr. E&W ..9W-15S | 73 |
| E. Tanglewood Cir. N&S | | |
| ............. | 12W-15S | 72 |
| Edgewater Ln. N&S | | |
| ............. | 12W-15S | 72 |
| Elm Av. N&S ...... | 14W-10S | 64 |
| Farm Hill Av. E&W | 10W-15S | 73 |
| Farm Hill Ln. N&S .. | 10W-15S | 73 |
| Fitzsimmons Dr. E&W | | |
| ............. | 13W-15S | 72 |
| Flavin Rd. N&S .... | 13W-11S | 64 |

|  | Grid | Page |
|---|---|---|
| Ford Rd. NW&SE | | |
| ............. | 14W-14S,14W-13S | 72 |
| Forest Woods Dr. NE&SW | | |
| ............. | 13W-10S | 64 |
| Frances Ct. N&S . | 13W-15S | 72 |
| Georgetown Dr. N&S | | |
| ............. | 13W-15S | 72 |
| Glen Rd. N&S ...... | 14W-13S | 72 |
| Grandview Dr. E&W | | |
| ............. | 13W-14S | 72 |
| Haas Dr. NE&SW .. | 13W-14S | 72 |
| Hampton Ct. N&S . | 13W-15S | 72 |
| Hampton Rd. E&W | 13W-15S | 72 |
| Hillcrest Dr. E&W | | |
| ............. | 13W-15S,10W-15S | 72 |
| Indian Trail Dr. NS&EW | | |
| ............. | 12W-14S | 72 |
| Joseph Dr., S. N&S | | |
| ............. | 12W-15S | 72 |
| Joseph Dr., W. E&W | | |
| ............. | 12W-15S | 72 |
| Kean Av. N&S | | |
| ............. | 11W-13S,11W-10S | 72 |
| Kindling Ct. E&W .. | 12W-14S | 72 |
| Kinvarra Dr. N&S . | 12W-14S | 72 |
| Knightbridge Rd. NW&SE | | |
| ............. | 11W-12S | 64 |
| Laflin Ct. E&W .... | 12W-15S | 72 |
| Lake Trail Dr. N&S .. | 12W-15S | 72 |
| Lakeland Dr. E&W . | 12W-14S | 72 |
| Lakeview Ct. NW&SE | | |
| ............. | 12W-15S | 72 |
| Longwood Ct. N&S | | |
| ............. | 10W-15S | 73 |
| Lucille Ln. N&S .... | 13W-14S | 72 |
| Maple Av. N&S .... | 14W-10S | 64 |
| McCarthy Dr. N&S | | |
| ............. | 14W-14S,12W-14S | 72 |
| Meadowlark Dr. N&S | | |
| ............. | 10W-15S | 73 |
| Mill Rd. N&S ...... | 12W-15S | 72 |
| Mission Dr. NE&SW | | |
| ............. | 12W-15S | 72 |
| Newport Dr. N&S .. | 12W-15S | 72 |
| Northbridge Ct. E&W | | |
| ............. | 13W-15S | 72 |
| Northbridge Ln. E&W | | |
| ............. | 13W-15S | 72 |
| Oakgrove Av. N&S..14W-10S | 64 |
| Oakwood Dr. E&W | 13W-14S | 72 |
| Orchard Dr. NS&EW | | |
| ............. | 14W-10S | 64 |
| Paloma Dr. E&W....10W-15S | 73 |
| Palos West Dr. NS&EW | | |
| ............. | 13W-14S | 72 |
| Park Lane Dr. E&W | | |
| ............. | 12W-15S | 72 |
| Parkside Dr. N&S .. | 12W-15S | 72 |
| Parkview Dr. E&W .. | 12W-15S | 72 |
| Parkview Rd. N&S..14W-15S | 64 |
| Pauline St. N&S .... | 10W-15S | 73 |
| Peace Memorial Dr. N&S | | |
| ............. | 12W-15S | 72 |
| Pebble Dr. NS&EW | | |
| ............. | 12W-15S | 72 |
| Powell Rd. E&W .. | 12W-14S | 72 |
| Prarie View Dr. E&W | | |
| ............. | 12W-14S | 72 |
| Public St. E&W .... | 14W-10S | 64 |
| Railroad Av. NE&SW | | |
| ............. | 14W-10S | 64 |
| Regent Dr. N&S....11W-12S | 64 |
| Richmond Ct. E&W | | |
| ............. | 13W-15S | 72 |
| Ridgewood Dr. NS&EW | | |
| ............. | 13W-15S | 72 |
| Rt. 171 NE&SW | | |
| ............. | 14W-11S,13W-10S | 64 |
| Rt. 45 N&S | | |
| ............. | 12W-15S,11W-10S | 72 |
| Sandburg Ct. N&S.. | 12W-15S | 72 |
| Sedgewick Dr. NS&EW | | |
| ............. | 13W-14S | 72 |
| Sheffield Ct. N&S .. | 13W-15S | 72 |
| Somerset Ln. E&W . | 13W-15S | 72 |
| Stark Dr. N&S......14W-10S | 64 |
| Stephen Dr. N&S . | 13W-15S | 72 |
| Suffield Dr. N&S .. | 13W-15S | 72 |
| Surrey Ct. N&S .. | 12W-15S | 72 |
| Tanglewood Cir., W. N&S | | |
| ............. | 12W-15S | 72 |
| Tanglewood Ct. NW&SE | | |
| ............. | 12W-15S | 72 |
| Timber Edge Ln. E&W | | |
| ............. | 12W-14S | 72 |
| Walter Dr. E&W .. | 13W-15S | 72 |
| Westminster Ct. E&W | | |
| ............. | 11W-12S | 64 |
| Westport Dr. N&S . | 12W-15S | 72 |
| Whispering Lake Dr. E&W | | |
| ............. | 12W-14S | 72 |
| Wild Cherry Ln. E&W | | |
| ............. | 12W-14S | 72 |
| Wildwood Dr. NS&EW | | |
| ............. | 13W-14S | 72 |
| Will Cook Rd. N&S | | |
| ............. | 14W-14S,14W-13S | 72 |
| Willow St. NW&SE..13W-10S | 64 |
| Windsor Dr. N&S .. | 12W-14S | 72 |
| Windward Trail N&S | | |
| ............. | 10W-15S | 73 |
| Wisteria Ct. N&S .. | 13W-14S | 72 |
| Wolf Rd. N&S .... | 14W-15S | 72 |
| 76th Av. N&S......9W-15S | 73 |
| 80th Av. N&S...... | 10W-15S | 73 |
| 81st Av. N&S ...... | 10W-15S | 73 |
| 82nd Av. N&S ...... | 10W-15S | 73 |
| 82nd Ct. N&S ...... | 10W-15S | 73 |

|  | Grid | Page |
|---|---|---|
| 83rd Av. N&S .... | 10W-15S | 73 |
| 83rd Ct. N&S .... | 10W-15S | 73 |
| 84th Av. N&S .... | 10W-15S | 73 |
| 84th Ct. N&S .... | 10W-15S | 73 |
| 85th Av. N&S .... | 10W-15S | 73 |
| 85th Ct. N&S .... | 10W-15S | 73 |
| 86th Av. N&S .... | 10W-15S | 73 |
| 87th Av. N&S .... | 10W-15S | 73 |
| 87th St. E&W | | |
| ............. | 14W-10S,11W-10S | 64 |
| 91st St. E&W .... | 14W-10S | 64 |
| 95th Av. N&S | | |
| ............. | 12W-15S,12W-14S | 72 |
| 95th St. E&W | | |
| ............. | 13W-11S,11W-11S | 64 |
| 100th Av. N&S | | |
| ............. | 12W-12S,12W-10S | 64 |
| 104th Av. N&S | | |
| ............. | 13W-15S,13W-10S | 72 |
| 107th St. E&W | | |
| ............. | 14W-12S,11W-12S | 64 |
| 108th Av. N&S | | |
| ............. | 13W-15S | 72 |
| 111th St. E&W | | |
| ............. | 14W-12S,11W-12S | 64 |
| 118th St. E&W ... | 14W-13S | 72 |
| 126th St. E&W .... | 12W-14S | 72 |
| 127th St. E&W | | |
| ............. | 10W-15S,9W-15S | 73 |
| 128th Pl. E&W .... | 10W-15S | 73 |
| 129th Pl. E&W .... | 10W-15S | 73 |
| 129th St. N&S .... | 10W-15S | 73 |
| 130th St. E&W | | |
| ............. | 12W-15S,10W-15S | 72 |
| 131st Pl. E&W ....11W-15S | 72 |
| 131st St. E&W | | |
| ............. | 14W-15S,10W-15S | 72 |
| 132nd St. E&W .. | 10W-15S | 73 |
| 133rd St. E&W | | |
| ............. | 13W-15S,10W-15S | 72 |
| 134th St. E&W .... | 13W-15S | 72 |
| 135th St. E&W | | |
| ............. | 14W-15S,10W-15S | 72 |

### Park Forest*
(Also see Will County)

| Algonquin Ct. E&W . | 2W-26S | 93 |
| Allegheny Ct. E&W . | 2W-26S | 93 |
| Allegheny St. E&W . | 2W-26S | 93 |
| Antietam St. E&W .. | 4W-25S | 92 |
| Antioch Pl. N&S . | 2W-26S | 93 |
| Apache St. E&W .. | 2W-26S | 93 |
| Apple Ct. NE&SW . | 3W-27S | 92 |
| Apple Ln. NW&SE . | 3W-27S | 92 |
| Arcadia St. E&W .. | 2W-26S | 93 |
| Arrowhead St. E&W | 2W-26S | 93 |
| Arrowhead St. E&W . | 2W-26S | 93 |
| Ash St. E&W ...... | 2W-26S | 93 |
| Bailey Rd. E&W......2W-26S | 93 |
| Bender Rd. E&W .. | 2W-26S | 93 |
| Berry St. E&W .... | 3W-27S | 92 |
| Bertoldo Rd. NW&SE | | |
| ............. | 2W-26S | 93 |
| Bigelow Rd. NW&SE | | |
| ............. | 2W-26S | 93 |
| Birch St. N&S ...... | 2W-26S | 93 |
| Blackhawk Dr. NW&SE | | |
| ............. | 4W-27S,3W-27S | 92 |
| Blair St. E&W......4W-25S | 92 |
| Cedar St. N&S .... | 2W-27S | 93 |
| Central Park Av. N&S | | |
| ............. | 4W-27S | 92 |
| Chase St. E&W....4W-25S | 92 |
| Cherry St. N&S .... | 3W-27S | 92 |
| Chestnut Ct. NW&SE | | |
| ............. | 2W-27S | 93 |
| Chestnut St. NS&EW | | |
| ............. | 2W-27S | 93 |
| Choate Rd. NW&SE..2W-26S | 93 |
| Cromwell St. E&W .. | 2W-26S | 93 |
| Davis St. E&W .... | 4W-25S | 92 |
| Dogwood St. N&S .. | 2W-27S | 93 |
| Douglas St. N&S .. | 3W-27S | 92 |
| Dunham Rd. N&S...2W-27S | 93 |
| Dunlap St. E&W .. | 2W-26S | 93 |
| Early St. E&W .... | 3W-25S | 92 |
| Elm St. N&S ...... | 3W-26S | 93 |
| Farragut St. E&W .. | 4W-25S | 92 |
| Fir St. E&W ...... | 3W-26S | 93 |
| Forest Bl. | | |
| ............. | 3W-27S,3W-26S | 92 |
| Garman Rd. NW&SE | | |
| ............. | 2W-27S | 93 |
| Gentry St. E&W .... | 3W-25S | 92 |
| Gerstung St. E&W . | 3W-25S | 92 |
| Gettysburg St. N&S..4W-25S | 92 |
| Gibson Rd. N&S .... | 2W-27S | 93 |
| Gold St. E&W .... | 3W-27S | 92 |
| Grant St. E&W .... | 3W-25S | 92 |
| Green St. E&W .... | 3W-27S | 92 |
| Hamlin St. E&W .. | 3W-25S | 92 |
| Hay St. E&W ...... | 3W-25S | 92 |
| Hemlock St. N&S ....3W-27S | 92 |
| Herndon St. N&S ....3W-25S | 92 |
| Hickory Ct. E&W .. | 4W-25S | 92 |
| Hickory St. E&W .. | 3W-26S | 93 |
| Holly St. N&S......3W-26S | 93 |
| Homan Av. NE&SW..4W-25S | 92 |
| Homan St. E&W .. | 4W-25S | 92 |
| Horwood Blvd. E&W | | |
| ............. | 3W-26S | 93 |
| Huron St. E&W .... | 3W-25S | 92 |
| Illinois Ct. NE&SW . | 3W-25S | 92 |
| Illinois St. N&S | | |
| ............. | 4W-25S,3W-25S | 92 |
| Indiana St. NS&EW | | |
| ............. | 4W-25S,3W-25S | 92 |

|  | Grid | Page |
|---|---|---|
| Indianwood Blvd. NE&SW | 3W-27S | 92 |
| Iroquois St. NW&SE | 3W-27S | 92 |
| Jackson St. N&S | 4W-25S | 92 |
| Juniper St. N&S | 3W-25S | 92 |
| Kentucky Ct. E&W | 3W-25S | 92 |
| Kentucky St. E&W | 3W-25S | 92 |
| Krotiak Rd. E&W | 3W-26S | 92 |
| Lakewood Blvd. E&W | 4W-26S,3W-26S | 92 |
| Lakewood Ct. N&S | 3W-27S | 92 |
| Larue St. E&W | 3W-25S | 92 |
| Lee St. E&W | 3W-25S | 92 |
| Leims Rd. E&W | 3W-27S | 92 |
| Lester Rd. N&S | 3W-27S | 92 |
| Main St. N&S | 4W-26S | 92 |
| Manitowac St. NE&SW | 3W-27S | 92 |
| Mantua Ct. NE&SW | 4W-27S | 92 |
| Mantua St. NW&SE | 4W-27S,3W-27S | 92 |
| Marquette Pl. NE&SW | 3W-27S | 92 |
| Marquette St. NW&SE | 4W-27S,3W-27S | 92 |
| McCarthy Rd. E&W | 3W-27S | 92 |
| McGarity Rd. NE&SW | 3W-27S | 92 |
| Meota St. N&S | 3W-25S | 92 |
| Merrimac St. NE&SW | 3W-27S | 92 |
| Miami St. NW&SE | 4W-27S | 92 |
| Michael Rd. E&W | 2W-27S | 93 |
| Minocqua Ct. E&W | 4W-27S | 92 |
| Minocqua St. N&S | 4W-27S | 92 |
| Mohawk St. NW&SE | 4W-27S | 92 |
| Monitor St. N&S | 3W-27S | 92 |
| Nashua St. E&W | 4W-27S,3W-27S | 92 |
| Nassau St. NE&SW | 3W-27S | 92 |
| Neola St. NE&SW | 3W-27S | 92 |
| New Salem St. N&S | 3W-25S | 92 |
| Nokomis St. NE&SW | 3W-27S | 92 |
| North St. E&W | 3W-26S | 92 |
| Norwood Bl. E&W | 3W-26S | 93 |
| Oak Ln. E&W | 3W-25S | 92 |
| Oakwood St. NE&SW | 3W-27S | 92 |
| Onarga St. N&S | 3W-27S | 92 |
| Orchard Dr., N. N&S | 3W-25S | 92 |
| Orchard Dr., S. N&S | 3W-27S,3W-26S | 92 |
| Osage St. N&S | 3W-25S | 92 |
| Oswego St. N&S | 3W-25S | 92 |
| Ottawa St. NW&SE | 3W-27S | 92 |
| Park St. N&S | 3W-26S | 92 |
| Peach St. NE&SW | 3W-27S | 92 |
| Rich Ct. E&W | 4W-27S | 92 |
| Rich Rd. E&W | 4W-27S | 92 |
| Rocket Cir., E. N&S | 3W-27S | 92 |
| Rocket Cir., W. N&S | 3W-27S | 92 |
| Rockwell St. N&S | 3W-25S | 92 |
| Rutledge St. N&S | 3W-25S | 92 |
| Saginaw Pl. N&S | 3W-25S | 92 |
| Sandburg St. N&S | 3W-25S | 92 |
| Sangamon Ct. N&S | 3W-25S | 92 |
| Sangamon St. NW&SE | 4W-25S | 92 |
| Sassabee St. NE&SW | 4W-25S | 92 |
| Sauganash St. E&W | 4W-27S | 92 |
| Saugatuck St. N&S | 4W-27S | 92 |
| Sauk Ct. NE&SW | 3W-27S | 92 |
| Sauk Trail NW&SE | 3W-27S | 92 |
| Seminole St. N&S | 4W-27S | 92 |
| Seneca St. E&W | 4W-27S | 92 |
| Seward St. E&W | 3W-25S | 92 |
| Shabbona Dr. N&S | 4W-27S | 92 |
| Shawnee St. N&S | 4W-27S | 92 |
| Sheridan St. E&W | 3W-25S | 92 |
| Sherman St. E&W | 3W-25S | 92 |
| Sioux St. E&W | 4W-27S | 92 |
| Somonauk Ct. N&S | 4W-27S | 92 |
| Somonauk St. E&W | 4W-27S | 92 |
| South St. E&W | 3W-26S | 92 |
| Springfield St. NS&EW | 3W-25S | 92 |
| Stanton St. N&S | 3W-25S | 92 |
| Suwanee St. E&W | 4W-27S | 92 |
| Thomas St. E&W | 3W-25S | 92 |
| Todd St. N&S | 3W-25S | 92 |
| U.S. 30 E&W | 3W-25S | 92 |
| Victory Bl. E&W | 3W-27S | 92 |
| Waldmann Dr. E&W | 4W-26S | 92 |
| Walnut St. NE&SW | 4W-26S | 92 |
| Warwick Ct. E&W | 3W-26S | 92 |
| Warwick St. NE&SW | 3W-26S | 92 |
| Washington Ct. E&W | 4W-26S | 92 |
| Washington St. N&S | 4W-26S | 92 |
| Water St. N&S | 3W-26S | 92 |
| Watseka St. E&W | 4W-27S | 92 |
| Waverly Ct. N&S | 4W-26S | 92 |
| Waverly St. E&W | 4W-26S | 92 |
| Wayne Ct. N&S | 4W-26S,3W-26S | 92 |
| Wayne St. E&W | 4W-26S | 92 |
| Well Ct. E&W | 3W-26S | 92 |
| Well St. E&W | 3W-26S | 92 |
| Western Av. N&S | 3W-27S,3W-25S | 92 |
| Westgate Dr. E&W | 4W-26S | 92 |

|  | Grid | Page |
|---|---|---|
| Westwood Ct. E&W | 3W-26S | 92 |
| Westwood Dr. NS&EW | | 92 |
| Wildwood Dr. NE&SW | 4W-26S | 92 |
| Willow St. NE&SW | 3W-26S | 92 |
| Wilshire St. E&W | 4W-26S | 92 |
| Wilson Ct. NE&SW | 4W-26S | 92 |
| Wilson St. NE&SW | 4W-26S | 92 |
| Windsor St. N&S | 4W-27S | 92 |
| Winnebago St. NS&EW | | 92 |
| Winnemac St. E&W | 4W-26S | 92 |
| Winona St. E&W | 4W-26S | 92 |
| Winslow St. E&W | 3W-26S | 92 |
| 26th St. E&W | 2W-26S | 93 |

## Park Ridge

|  | Grid | Page |
|---|---|---|
| Albion Av. E&W | 11W-8N,9W-8N | 36 |
| Aldine Av. N&S | 11W-8N,11W-9N | 36 |
| Archbury Ln. NW&SE | 11W-8N | 36 |
| Arthur St. E&W | 11W-8N,9W-8N | 36 |
| Ascot Dr. NS&EW | 11W-8N | 36 |
| Ashbury Cir.* E&W | 11W-8N | 36 |
| Ashland Av. N&S | 10W-7N,10W-9N | 36 |
| Astoria Way* NE&SW | 11W-8N | 36 |
| Austin Av. E&W | 10W-9N | 36 |
| Avondale Av. NW&SE | 11W-9N,9W-8N | 36 |
| Babetta Ln. N&S | 11W-9N | 36 |
| Ballard Rd. E&W | 11W-11N | 26 |
| Beau Dr. NS&EW | 10W-10N | 36 |
| Belle Plaine Av. N&S | 11W-8N,10W-8N | 36 |
| Berry Pkwy. N&S | 9W-8N | 37 |
| Birch St. NE&SW | 11W-10N | 36 |
| Boardwalk Pl.* E&W | 11W-8N | 36 |
| Bonita Dr. E&W | 10W-9N | 36 |
| Bonnie Dr. E&W | 10W-7N | 36 |
| Bouterse St. E&W | 11W-9N | 36 |
| Broadway Av. N&S | 11W-8N,11W-9N | 36 |
| Brookline Av. NW&SE | 10W-9N | 36 |
| Brophy Av. E&W | 11W-9N | 36 |
| Burton Ln. E&W | 11W-10N | 36 |
| Busse Hwy. NW&SE | 11W-9N,11W-10N | 36 |
| Canfield Av. N&S | 9W-7N | 37 |
| Carol St. E&W | 10W-10N | 36 |
| Carolyn Ln. N&S | 11W-9N | 36 |
| Castle E&W | 10W-7N | 36 |
| Cedar St. E&W | 11W-9N,10W-9N | 36 |
| Cherry St. E&W | 11W-9N,10W-9N | 36 |
| Chester Av. N&S | 10W-7N,10W-9N | 36 |
| Cleveland Av. N&S | 9W-8N | 37 |
| Clifton Av. N&S | 10W-7N,10W-9N | 36 |
| Clinton Av. N&S | 10W-9N | 36 |
| Columbia Av. N&S | 9W-8N | 37 |
| Courtland Av. N&S | 10W-7N,10W-8N | 36 |
| Crain St. E&W | 10W-10N | 36 |
| Crescent Av. N&S | 11W-8N,10W-8N | 36 |
| Cumberland Av. N&S | 10W-8N | 36 |
| Cuttriss St. E&W | 10W-9N | 36 |
| Cynthia Av. NW&SE | 10W-9N | 36 |
| Davis St. E&W | 11W-11N | 26 |
| DeCook Av. E&W | 11W-10N | 36 |
| Dee Rd. N&S | 11W-8N,11W-10N | 36 |
| Delphia Av. N&S | 10W-8N,10W-9N | 36 |
| Des Plaines Av. E&W | 11W-8N | 36 |
| Devon Av. E&W | 10W-8N | 36 |
| East Av. N&S | 9W-8N | 37 |
| Edgemont Ln. E&W | 11W-9N,9W-9N | 36 |
| Edna Av. E&W | 11W-10N | 36 |
| Elliot Av. N&S | 11W-10N | 36 |
| Elm St. E&W | 11W-9N,10W-9N | 36 |
| Elmore St. N&S | 10W-9N | 36 |
| Engel Blvd. NE&SW | 11W-8N | 36 |
| Evergreen Ln. E&W | 11W-10N | 36 |
| Fairview Av. N&S | 10W-7N,10W-9N | 36 |
| Farrell Av. E&W | 11W-10N | 36 |
| Fenton Ln. E&W | 11W-10N | 36 |
| Florence Dr. N&S | 11W-9N | 36 |
| Forestview Av. N&S | 11W-9N | 36 |
| Fortuna Av. NE&SW | 11W-10N | 36 |
| Frances Pkwy. E&W | 10W-7N | 36 |
| Gables Av. N&S | 11W-10N | 36 |
| Garden Av. NW&SE | 10W-8N | 36 |
| Garden St. E&W | 11W-8N,10W-8N | 36 |
| Gillick St. E&W | 11W-8N,10W-9N | 36 |
| Glenlake Av. E&W | 10W-7N,9W-7N | 36 |

|  | Grid | Page |
|---|---|---|
| Glenview Av. E&W | 11W-10N | 36 |
| Good Av. N&S | 11W-10N | 36 |
| Goodwin Dr. N&S | 11W-9N | 36 |
| Grace Av. N&S | 10W-7N,10W-9N | 36 |
| Grand Blvd. E&W | 10W-9N | 36 |
| Grant Pl. E&W | 10W-9N | 36 |
| Granville Av. E&W | 10W-7N,9W-7N | 36 |
| Greendale Av. E&W | 11W-10N | 36 |
| Greenwood Av. N&S | 10W-7N,10W-8N | 36 |
| Greenwood Rd. N&S | 10W-9N | 36 |
| Grove Av. N&S | 9W-7N | 37 |
| Habberton St. N&S | 11W-10N | 36 |
| Halien Ter.* N&S | 11W-8N | 36 |
| Hamlin Av. N&S | 11W-8N,11W-10N | 36 |
| Hamlin Ct. NE&SW | 11W-8N | 36 |
| Hansen Pl. E&W | 11W-10N | 36 |
| Harrison St. N&S | 9W-8N | 37 |
| Hastings St. E&W | 11W-9N | 36 |
| Helen St. N&S | 11W-10N | 36 |
| Higgins Rd. NW&SE | 10W-7N | 36 |
| Hoffman Av. N&S | 11W-10N | 36 |
| Home Av. N&S | 11W-8N,11W-11N | 36 |
| Imperial St. E&W | 9W-8N | 37 |
| Interstate 294 N&S | 12W-10N | 36 |
| Irwin Av. E&W | 10W-10N | 36 |
| Irwin St. E&W | 11W-9N | 36 |
| Joyce Pl. E&W | 9W-9N | 37 |
| Kathleen Dr. E&W | 9W-9N | 36 |
| Kent Av. E&W | 10W-7N | 36 |
| Knight Av. N&S | 10W-7N,10W-10N | 36 |
| Lahon St. E&W | 11W-9N,9W-9N | 36 |
| Lake Av. NE&SW | 10W-8N | 36 |
| Laverne Av. E&W | 11W-9N,10W-9N | 36 |
| Leonard St. N&S | 10W-9N | 36 |
| Lincoln Av. N&S | 10W-7N,10W-10N | 36 |
| Linden Av. N&S | 9W-7N | 37 |
| Lois Av. E&W | 10W-7N | 36 |
| Lois Ct. N&S | 10W-7N | 36 |
| Lundergan Av. N&S | 12W-10N | 36 |
| Luther Ln. N&S | 10W-10N | 36 |
| Main St. NW&SE | 10W-8N | 36 |
| Manor Ln. E&W | 11W-10N | 36 |
| Marguerite St. E&W | 11W-10N | 36 |
| Marlowe E&W | 11W-8N | 36 |
| Marvin Pkwy. NW&SE | 11W-9N | 36 |
| Mary Jane Ln. E&W | 11W-9N | 36 |
| Mayfield Av. N&S | 11W-10N | 36 |
| Meacham Av. N&S | 10W-9N | 36 |
| Merrill St. N&S | 9W-8N,9W-9N | 37 |
| Michael John Dr. E&W | 10W-9N,9W-9N | 36 |
| Milton Av. N&S | 11W-10N | 36 |
| Morris St. N&S | 10W-9N | 36 |
| Murphy Lake Ln.* E&W | 11W-8N | 36 |
| Murphy Lake Rd. E&W | 11W-9N | 36 |
| Newton Av. N&S | 9W-7N | 37 |
| Norman Blvd. E&W | 11W-8N | 36 |
| Northwest Hwy. NW&SE | 10W-9N | 36 |
| Oak St. NE&SW | 10W-8N | 36 |
| Oakton St. E&W | 11W-10N | 36 |
| Oaktree Ln. E&W | 11W-10N | 36 |
| Oriole Av. N&S | 9W-8N | 37 |
| Ottawa Av. N&S | 9W-7N | 37 |
| Park Ln.* E&W | 11W-8N | 36 |
| Park Pl. NE&SW | 11W-8N | 36 |
| Park Plaine Av. N&S | 11W-8N | 36 |
| Park Ridge Blvd. NE&SW | 11W-8N | 36 |
| Parkside Av. N&S | 11W-10N | 36 |
| Parkside Dr. N&S | 11W-11N | 26 |
| Parkwood Av. N&S | 11W-9N | 36 |
| Peale Av. N&S | 9W-8N | 37 |
| Peterson Av. E&W | 10W-7N | 36 |
| Poplar St. NW&SE | 11W-10N | 36 |
| Potter Rd. N&S | 11W-10N | 36 |
| Prairie Av. NS&EW | 11W-8N,10W-8N | 36 |
| Prospect Av. N&S | 10W-7N,10W-9N | 36 |
| Rabe Ct. NE&SW | 10W-9N | 36 |
| Redfield Ln. E&W | 10W-9N | 36 |
| Redfield Rd. N&S | 11W-9N | 36 |
| Renaissance Dr. NW&SE | 11W-10N | 36 |
| Rene Ct. E&W | 10W-8N | 36 |
| Ridge Ter. NE&SW | 10W-8N | 36 |
| Riverside Dr. N&S | 11W-9N | 36 |
| Root St. N&S | 10W-9N | 36 |
| Rose Av. N&S | 11W-8N,10W-7N | 36 |
| Rosemont Av. E&W | 10W-7N | 36 |
| Rowe Av. NE&SW | 11W-9N | 36 |
| Ruth Av. E&W | 11W-10N | 36 |
| Scottlynne Dr. NW&SE | 11W-9N | 36 |
| Seeley Av. NE&SW | 11W-9N | 36 |

|  | Grid | Page |
|---|---|---|
| Seminary Av. N&S | 11W-8N,11W-9N | 36 |
| Shibley Av. NE&SW | 11W-9N | 36 |
| Shore Line Dr. N&S | 11W-9N | 36 |
| Sibley St. E&W | 11W-9N,9W-9N | 36 |
| Spring St. NE&SW | 11W-9N | 36 |
| St. James Pl. E&W | 10W-8N | 36 |
| Stanley Av. E&W | 11W-8N,9W-8N | 36 |
| Stewart Av. E&W | 11W-8N,10W-8N | 36 |
| Summit Av. N&S | 10W-8N,10W-9N | 36 |
| Sylviawood Av. N&S | 11W-9N | 36 |
| Talcott Pl. NW&SE | 10W-7N | 36 |
| Talcott Rd. NW&SE | 9W-7N | 37 |
| Thames E&W | 10W-7N | 36 |
| Thames Pkwy. N&S | 11W-9N | 36 |
| Thorndale Av. E&W | 10W-7N | 36 |
| Tomawadee Dr. N&S | 10W-9N | 36 |
| Touhy Av. E&W | 11W-9N | 36 |
| Tri-State Tollway N&S | 12W-10N | 36 |
| Tyrell Av. N&S | 11W-10N | 36 |
| U.S. Route 14 E&W | 10W-7N,10W-8N | 36 |
| Vernon Av. N&S | 11W-10N | 36 |
| Vine Av. NS&EW | 10W-7N,10W-8N | 36 |
| Virginia St. E&W | 11W-9N | 36 |
| Walnut St. NE&SW | 11W-10N | 36 |
| Warren NE&SW | 11W-8N | 36 |
| Washington Av. N&S | 10W-7N,10W-9N | 36 |
| Washington Pl. N&S | 9W-7N | 37 |
| Weeg Way E&W | 11W-10N | 36 |
| Wesley Dr. N&S | 11W-9N | 36 |
| Western Av. N&S | 11W-9N,11W-11N | 36 |
| Wilkinson Pkwy. N&S | 11W-9N | 36 |
| Wilma Pl. E&W | 9W-9N | 37 |
| Windsor Mall E&W | 11W-8N | 36 |
| Wisnen St. N&S | 9W-9N | 37 |
| Woodland Av. E&W | 11W-10N | 36 |
| Woodview Ln. N&S | 11W-11N | 26 |
| Yost Av. N&S | 9W-7N | 37 |
| 1st St. N&S | 10W-8N | 36 |
| 3rd St. NE&SW | 10W-8N | 36 |

## Phoenix

|  | Grid | Page |
|---|---|---|
| Belle Ct. E&W | 0W-18S | 82 |
| Frances St. E&W | 0W-18S | 82 |
| Halsted St. N&S | 1W-18S | 82 |
| Miller Pl. E&W | 0W-18S | 82 |
| Vincennes Av. NW&SE | 0W-18S | 82 |
| Wallace Av. N&S | 0W-18S,0W-17S | 82 |
| Walton St. NW&SE | 0W-18S | 82 |
| 1st Av. N&S | 0W-18S,0W-17S | 82 |
| 2nd Av. N&S | 0W-18S,0W-17S | 82 |
| 3rd Av. N&S | 0W-18S,0W-17S | 82 |
| 4th Av. N&S | 0W-18S | 82 |
| 5th Av. N&S | 0W-18S | 82 |
| 6th Av. N&S | 0W-18S | 82 |
| 7th Av. N&S | 0W-18S | 82 |
| 8th Av. N&S | 0W-18S | 82 |
| 9th Av. N&S | 0W-18S | 82 |
| 149th St. E&W | 0W-17S | 82 |
| 151st Pl. E&W | 0W-18S | 82 |
| 151st St. E&W | 0W-18S | 82 |
| 152nd Pl. E&W | 0W-18S | 82 |
| 152nd St. E&W | 0W-18S | 82 |
| 153rd St. E&W | 0W-18S | 82 |
| 154th Pl. E&W | 0W-18S | 82 |
| 154th St. E&W | 0W-18S | 82 |
| 155th Ct. E&W | 0W-18S | 82 |
| 155th Pl. E&W | 0W-18S | 82 |
| 155th St. E&W | 0W-18S | 82 |

## Posen

|  | Grid | Page |
|---|---|---|
| Albany Av. N&S | 3W-17S | 81 |
| Albert Av. N&S | 3W-17S | 81 |
| Blaine Av. N&S | 3W-17S,3W-16S | 81 |
| California Av. N&S | 3W-17S,3W-16S | 81 |
| Campbell Av. N&S | 3W-17S | 81 |
| Cleveland Av. N&S | 3W-17S,3W-16S | 81 |
| Division St. N&S | 3W-17S | 81 |
| Elm St. E&W | 3W-16S | 75 |
| Fairfield Av. NW&SE | 3W-17S | 81 |
| Francisco Av. N&S | 3W-17S | 81 |
| Grove St. E&W | 2W-17S | 81 |
| Harrison Av. N&S | 3W-17S,3W-16S | 81 |
| Kedzie Av. N&S | 3W-17S | 81 |
| Maple St. E&W | 3W-16S | 75 |
| Mc Kinley Av. N&S | 3W-17S | 81 |
| Mozart Av. N&S | 3W-17S | 81 |
| Palmer Av. N&S | 3W-17S,3W-16S | 81 |
| Richmond Av. N&S | 3W-17S | 81 |
| Sacramento Av. N&S | 3W-17S | 81 |

|  | Grid | Page |
|---|---|---|
| Sherman Av. N&S | 3W-17S | 81 |
| Short St. N&S | 2W-17S | 81 |
| Tri State Tollway SE&NW | 3W-17S | 81 |
| Troy St. N&S | 3W-17S | 81 |
| Utica Av. N&S | 3W-17S | 81 |
| Western Av. N&S | 2W-17S | 75 |
| Whipple St. N&S | 3W-17S | 81 |
| 139th Pl. E&W | 3W-16S | 75 |
| 139th St. E&W | 3W-16S | 75 |
| 140th St. E&W | 3W-16S | 75 |
| 141st St. E&W | 3W-16S | 75 |
| 142nd St. E&W | 3W-16S | 75 |
| 143rd St. E&W | 3W-16S | 75 |
| 144th St. E&W | 3W-17S | 81 |
| 145th St. E&W | 3W-17S | 81 |
| 146th St. E&W | 3W-17S | 81 |
| 147th St. E&W | 3W-17S | 81 |
| 148th St. E&W | 3W-17S | 81 |
| 149th St. E&W | 4W-17S | 81 |

## Prospect Heights

|  | Grid | Page |
|---|---|---|
| Aberdeen Ln.* E&W | 14W-15N | 15 |
| Alderman Av. E&W | 13W-15N | 16 |
| Alton Rd. N&S | 14W-14N | 25 |
| Andover Dr. E&W | 15W-16N | 15 |
| Anne Ct. E&W | 15W-16N | 15 |
| Apple Dr. E&W | 13W-15N | 16 |
| Blossom Ln. N&S | 13W-15N | 16 |
| Bonniebrook Ct. E&W | 14W-15N | 15 |
| Break St. E&W | 14W-14N | 25 |
| Brian Ln. N&S | 14W-15N | 15 |
| Brook Rd. NW&SE | 15W-14N | 25 |
| Burning Bush Ln. N&S | 13W-15N | 16 |
| Burr Oak Ln.* E&W | 14W-15N | 15 |
| Calway E&W | 14W-15N | 15 |
| Camp McDonald Rd. E&W | 16W-15N,14W-15N | 15 |
| Carl Ct. NW&SE | 15W-15N | 15 |
| Carrbridge Ln.* NE&SW | 14W-15N | 15 |
| Center Ln. NE&SW | 16W-15N | 15 |
| Chester Ln. N&S | 15W-14N | 25 |
| Cider Ln. N&S | 13W-15N | 16 |
| Circle Av., E. N&S | 15W-15N | 15 |
| Circle Av., W. N&S | 15W-15N | 15 |
| Claire Ln. E&W | 14W-15N | 15 |
| Clarendon St. E&W | 16W-15N,15W-15N | 15 |
| Coldren Dr. N&S | 14W-15N | 15 |
| Compton Ln. N&S | 15W-14N | 25 |
| Country Club Dr. NS&EW | 14W-14N | 25 |
| Countryside Ln. E&W | 15W-16N | 15 |
| Court St. E&W | 15W-15N | 15 |
| Cove Dr. N&S | 13W-15N | 16 |
| Crabapple Dr. E&W | 13W-15N | 16 |
| Creek Ct. E&W | 15W-15N | 15 |
| Crest Hill Dr. E&W | 16W-16N | 15 |
| Crimson Ct. N&S | 13W-15N | 16 |
| Dale Av. N&S | 16W-15N | 15 |
| DeCook Ln. E&W | 11W-10N | 36 |
| Delicious Ct. N&S | 13W-14N,13W-15N | 26 |
| Derbyshire Ct. NE&SW | 15W-16N | 15 |
| Des Plaines River Rd. N&S | 13W-15N | 16 |
| Dorset St. E&W | 16W-15N | 15 |
| Drake Av. N&S | 15W-16N | 15 |
| Drake Ter. E&W | 15W-16N | 15 |
| Drury Ln. N&S | 16W-16N | 15 |
| Duchess Ct. N&S | 13W-15N | 16 |
| East Kenilworth Av. E&W | 15W-15N | 15 |
| Edinburgh Ln. NE&SW | 14W-14N | 25 |
| Edward Cul De Sac N&S | 14W-14N | 25 |
| Edward Rd. E&W | 14W-14N | 25 |
| Elaine Cir., E. N&S | 14W-15N | 15 |
| Elaine Cir., W. N&S | 14W-15N | 15 |
| Eleanor Dr. E&W | 15W-16N | 15 |
| Elm St. N&S | 15W-15N | 15 |
| Elmhurst Rd. N&S | 15W-14N,15W-16N | 25 |
| Essex St. N&S | 15W-16N | 15 |
| Etowah Av. N&S | 16W-15N | 15 |
| Euclid Av. E&W | 14W-14N | 25 |
| Fairway Ct. E&W | 14W-14N | 25 |
| Fairway Dr. N&S | 14W-14N | 25 |
| Ferndale Ct. NW&SE | 14W-14N | 25 |
| Ferndale Ln. NE&SW | 14W-14N | 25 |
| Frankie Ct. E&W | 16W-15N | 15 |
| Gail Ct., N. N&S | 16W-15N | 15 |
| Gail Ct., S. N&S | 16W-15N | 15 |
| Garden Ct. N&S | 16W-15N | 15 |
| Garden Ln. E&W | 16W-15N | 15 |
| Glasgow Ln.* N&S | 14W-15N | 15 |
| Glenbrook Dr. E&W | 15W-16N | 15 |
| Glendale Dr. E&W | 15W-15N | 15 |
| Golfview Cir. E&W | 14W-14N | 25 |
| Green Bridge Ln. N&S | 14W-14N | 25 |
| Greening Ct. N&S | 13W-15N | 16 |

| | Grid | Page |
|---|---|---|
| Grego Ct. E&W | 14W-15N | 15 |
| Greystone Ln. NW&SE | 14W-14N | 25 |
| Grove Pl. NE&SW | 15W-14N | 25 |
| Hawthorne Pl. E&W | 15W-14N | 25 |
| Highland Dr. N&S | 15W-16N | 15 |
| Hill Ct. NW&SE | 15W-15N | 15 |
| Hillcrest Dr. N&S | 15W-15N | 15 |
| Hillside Av. NE&SW | 15W-15N | 15 |
| Jonathan Ct. E&W | 13W-15N | 16 |
| Kenilworth Av. E&W | 15W-15N | 15 |
| Kenilworth Ct. E&W | 15W-15N | 15 |
| Kenneth Av. E&W | 15W-16N | 15 |
| Kerry Ct. E&W | 16W-16N | 15 |
| Kewaunee Ct. N&S | 16W-15N | 15 |
| Kingsmill Ln.* NW&SE | 14W-15N | 15 |
| Lancaster Av. N&S | 16W-15N | 15 |
| Lanford Ln. E&W | 15W-14N | 25 |
| Leon Ln., E. N&S | 14W-15N | 15 |
| Leon Ln., W. N&S | 14W-15N | 15 |
| Lewis Isle Ln.* NW&SE | 14W-15N | 15 |
| Linden N. N&S | 16W-15N | 15 |
| Linden S. N&S | 16W-15N | 15 |
| Loch Lomond Ln.* NE&SW | 14W-15N | 15 |
| Lonsdale Rd. E&W | 15W-14N | 25 |
| Love Dr. E&W | 13W-15N | 16 |
| Lynnbrook Dr. E&W | 15W-16N | 15 |
| Mandel Ln. N&S | 13W-15N | 16 |
| Manor Av. N&S | 15W-15N | 15 |
| Maple Av. N&S | 15W-15N | 15 |
| Maple Ln. N&S | 15W-14N,15W-16N | 25 |
| Maple St. N&S | 15W-15N,15W-16N | 15 |
| Marberry Dr. E&W | 15W-14N | 25 |
| Margate Ln.* E&W | 14W-15N | 15 |
| Marion Av. E&W | 15W-15N | 15 |
| Marion St. E&W | 16W-15N,15W-15N | 15 |
| Mars Pl. E&W | 15W-14N | 25 |
| McIntosch Ct. E&W | 13W-15N | 16 |
| Meadow Ridge Ln. E&W | 16W-16N | 15 |
| Minnaqua Dr. E&W | 16W-15N | 15 |
| Natawa Pl. E&W | 16W-15N | 15 |
| Newcastle E&W | 14W-15N | 15 |
| Newgate Ln.* N&S | 14W-15N | 15 |
| North Pkwy. E&W | 15W-15N | 15 |
| Oak Av. N&S | 15W-16N | 15 |
| Oakwood Dr. E&W | 15W-16N | 15 |
| Olive Av. E&W | 15W-15N | 15 |
| Olive St. E&W | 16W-15N | 15 |
| Owen Ct. E&W | 15W-15N | 15 |
| Owen Pl. N&S | 15W-14N | 25 |
| Owen St. N&S | 15W-15N | 15 |
| Palatine Rd. E&W | 13W-15N | 16 |
| Parkview West NE&SW | 13W-15N | 16 |
| Patricia Ln. NW&SE | 14W-15N | 15 |
| Pembridge Ln.* N&S | 14W-15N | 15 |
| Phelps Av. N&S | 16W-15N | 15 |
| Pin Oak Dr. N&S | 16W-16N | 15 |
| Pin Oak Ln. N&S | 16W-16N | 15 |
| Pine Forest Ln. E&W | 14W-14N | 25 |
| Pine St. N&S | 15W-15N | 15 |
| Pinecrest Dr. N&S | 13W-15N | 16 |
| Piper Cir. N&S | 13W-15N | 16 |
| Piper Ln. E&W | 13W-15N | 16 |
| Plaza Dr. N&S | 13W-15N | 16 |
| Prospect Ct. N&S | 15W-15N | 15 |
| Prospect Dr. E&W | 15W-16N | 15 |
| Quaker Ln. N&S | 13W-15N | 16 |
| Rand Rd. NW&SE | 16W-14N | 25 |
| Regent Ln.* N&S | 14W-15N | 15 |
| Ridge Av. E&W | 15W-15N | 15 |
| Riley Av. N&S | 14W-15N | 15 |
| Roberts Ln. E&W | 13W-15N | 16 |
| Robyn Ct. E&W | 14W-15N | 15 |
| Rose Av. E&W | 14W-15N | 15 |
| Royal Ct. N&S | 16W-15N | 15 |
| Rt. 83 N&S | 15W-16N | 15 |
| Saunders Rd. E&W | 12W-15N | 16 |
| School Ln. NS&EW | 15W-14N | 25 |
| Shannon Dr. N&S | 14W-15N | 15 |
| Shawn Ln. E&W | 14W-15N | 15 |
| Sherwood Dr. N&S | 15W-16N | 15 |
| South Pkwy. E&W | 15W-15N | 15 |
| Spruce Dr. N&S | 15W-15N,15W-16N | 15 |
| Stirling Ln.* N&S | 14W-15N | 15 |
| Stonegate Dr., E. NE&SW | 15W-16N | 15 |
| Stonegate Dr., W. NW&SE | 15W-16N | 15 |
| Sussex Corner Ln. N&S | 14W-14N | 25 |
| Sutherland Ln.* E&W | 14W-15N | 15 |
| Thierry Ln. N&S | 14W-15N | 15 |
| Thistle Ln. NW&SE | 14W-14N | 25 |
| Tomah Av. N&S | 16W-15N | 15 |
| Tree Ln. N&S | 13W-15N | 16 |
| Tully Pl. NW&SE | 15W-14N | 25 |
| Viola Ln. E&W | 15W-15N | 15 |
| Cir. | 13W-15N | 16 |
| Walden Ln. E&W | 16W-16N | 15 |
| Waterford Dr. N&S | 14W-15N | 15 |
| Waterman Av. N&S | 16W-15N | 15 |
| Wheeling Rd. N&S | 15W-15N | 15 |
| Wildwood Dr., E. E&W | 15W-16N | 15 |
| Wildwood Dr., N. E&W | 15W-16N | 15 |
| Wildwood Dr., S. N&S | 15W-16N | 15 |
| Wildwood Dr., W. N&S | 15W-16N | 15 |
| Williamsburg Ln.* E&W | 14W-15N | 15 |
| Willow Hills Ln. E&W | 14W-14N | 25 |
| Willow Rd. E&W | 15W-15N | 15 |
| Wimbledon Cir. E&W | 13W-15N | 16 |
| Windsor Dr. N&S | 16W-15N | 15 |
| Winesap Ct. E&W | 13W-15N | 16 |
| Winkelman Rd. NW&SE | 12W-15N | 16 |
| Wolf Rd. N&S | 14W-15N | 15 |
| Woodview Dr. N&S | 16W-16N | 15 |
| Wurtz Ct. E&W | 15W-15N | 15 |

## Proviso Township

| | Grid | Page |
|---|---|---|
| Buck Rd. N&S | 14W-0S | 46 |
| Concord St. E&W | 14W-0S | 46 |
| Des Plaines N&S | 9W-1S | 54 |
| Harvard St. E&W | 14W-0S | 46 |
| 18th E&W | 9W-1S | 54 |
| 19th E&W | 9W-1S | 54 |

## Rich Township

| | Grid | Page |
|---|---|---|
| Blackstone Av. N&S | 5W-24S | 92 |
| Blackthorn Rd. NS&EW | 8W-26S | 90 |
| Briar Ln. E&W | 5W-24S | 92 |
| Briarbranch Ter. NS&EW | 8W-26S | 90 |
| Brushwood Dr. E&W | 8W-26S | 90 |
| Burlwood Ct. E&W | 8W-26S | 90 |
| Candlegate Ct. NS&EW | 8W-26S | 90 |
| Central Av. N&S | 7W-26S,7W-22S | 91 |
| Central Park Av. N&S | 4W-23S | 87 |
| Chapparal Ter. NS&EW | 8W-26S | 90 |
| Cicero Av. N&S | 6W-23S | 86 |
| Davis Av. E&W | 5W-27S | 92 |
| Dewey Av. E&W | 5W-27S | 92 |
| Elmwood Ln. E&W | 5W-25S | 92 |
| Flossmorr Rd. E&W | 7W-22S,4W-22S | 86 |
| Green Sward Way N&S | 8W-26S | 90 |
| Hearthemeade Rd. NW&SE | 8W-26S | 90 |
| Heartside Rd. NS&EW | 8W-26S | 90 |
| Hedgewick Ct. E&W | 8W-26S | 90 |
| Hickory Glen NW&SE | 8W-26S | 90 |
| Homan Av. N&S | 4W-23S | 87 |
| Homeland Rd. N&S | 5W-25S | 92 |
| Huntsbridge Rd. NS&EW | 8W-26S | 90 |
| Interstate 57 N&S | 6W-23S,6W-22S | 86 |
| Ivvlog Terr. NS&EW | 8W-26S | 90 |
| Keeler Av. N&S | 5W-24S | 92 |
| Keystone Av. N&S | 5W-24S | 92 |
| Knollwood Cir. NS&EW | 8W-26S | 90 |
| Kostner Av. N&S | 5W-27S,5W-24S | 92 |
| Leclaire Av. N&S | 6W-22S | 86 |
| Lincoln Hwy. E&W | 7W-25S | 91 |
| Maple Av. E&W | 5W-26S | 92 |
| Maplewood Ln. E&W | 5W-25S | 92 |
| Moorfield Rd. NS&EW | 8W-26S | 90 |
| N. Windmere Cir. NS&EW | 8W-26S | 90 |
| Orchard Ln. E&W | 5W-24S | 92 |
| Pleasant Ter. NS&EW | 8W-26S | 90 |
| Polk Av. E&W | 5W-27S | 92 |
| Poplar Av. E&W | 5W-26S | 92 |
| Prairie Rd. NW&SE | 8W-26S | 90 |
| Ridgeland Av. N&S | 8W-27S,8W-22S | 90 |
| Rt. 43 N&S | 8W-25S,8W-23S | 90 |
| Sauk Trail E&W | 8W-26S | 90 |
| Sprucewood Ln. E&W | 5W-25S | 92 |
| Steger Rd. E&W | 8W-27S,4W-28S | 90 |
| Sunset Rd. E&W | 5W-24S | 92 |
| Tanglewood Rd. E&W | 8W-26S | 90 |
| Thistle Ct. E&W | 8W-26S | 90 |
| Thorntree Ter. NS&EW | 8W-26S | 90 |
| Thornwood Av. E&W | 5W-24S | 92 |
| Timber Ridge Rd. NW&SE | 8W-26S | 90 |
| Tullamore Ter. NS&EW | 8W-26S | 90 |
| Vollmer Rd. E&W | 8W-23S,5W-23S | 85 |
| Wildrock Ter. NS&EW | 8W-26S | 90 |
| Woodbine Ter. NS&EW | 8W-26S | 90 |
| 66th Av. N&S | 8W-22S | 85 |
| 192nd St. E&W | 4W-23S | 87 |
| 194th St. E&W | 4W-23S | 87 |
| 196th St. E&W | 4W-23S | 87 |
| 197th St. E&W | 4W-23S | 87 |
| 198th St. E&W | 4W-23S | 87 |
| 204th St. E&W | 5W-24S | 92 |
| 205th St. E&W | 5W-24S | 92 |
| 206th Pl. E&W | 5W-24S | 92 |
| 206th St. E&W | 5W-24S | 92 |

## Richton Park

| | Grid | Page |
|---|---|---|
| Adams Dr. N&S | 5W-27S | 92 |
| Amy Dr. N&S | 6W-27S | 91 |
| Andover Dr. NW&SE | 5W-26S | 92 |
| Appleby Ln. E&W | 4W-26S | 92 |
| Arlington Dr. E&W | 5W-26S | 92 |
| Arquilla Dr. NS&EW | 6W-27S | 91 |
| Ascot Ct. E&W | 5W-26S | 92 |
| Balmoral Dr. N&S | 5W-26S | 92 |
| Belmont Rd. NE&SW | 5W-26S | 92 |
| Birchwood Rd. E&W | 5W-26S,4W-26S | 92 |
| Bretz Dr. E&W | 5W-27S | 92 |
| Brighton Ln. E&W | 4W-26S | 92 |
| Bruce Dr. N&S | 6W-27S | 91 |
| Butterfield Rd. N&S | 5W-27S | 92 |
| Camden Ct. E&W | 5W-26S | 92 |
| Carlborg Ct. E&W | 6W-27S | 91 |
| Carol Anne Ct. E&W | 5W-27S | 92 |
| Cedar Rd. E&W | 4W-26S | 92 |
| Central Av. N&S | 7W-26S | 91 |
| Central Park Av. N&S | 4W-27S | 92 |
| Cherie Ct. E&W | 6W-26S | 91 |
| Churchill Dr. NS&EW | 5W-26S | 92 |
| Cicero Av. N&S | 6W-27S | 91 |
| Clarendon Av. N&S | 5W-27S | 92 |
| Clark Dr. NW&SE | 5W-26S | 92 |
| Crawford Av. N&S | 5W-26S | 92 |
| Cresent Way E&W | 5W-27S | 92 |
| Cypress Ct. E&W | 6W-27S | 91 |
| Davis Av. E&W | 4W-27S | 92 |
| Dewey Av. E&W | 4W-27S | 92 |
| East Dr. N&S | 6W-27S | 91 |
| Elm Rd. E&W | 4W-26S | 92 |
| Euclid Ln. NS&EW | 4W-26S | 92 |
| Farmington Av. NW&SE | 5W-27S | 92 |
| Franklin Dr. N&S | 5W-27S | 92 |
| Governors Hwy. N&S | 5W-27S | 92 |
| Grant Av. E&W | 4W-27S | 92 |
| Greenbriar Ln. E&W | 5W-26S | 92 |
| Hamilton Dr. N&S | 5W-27S | 92 |
| Hawthorne Way N&S | 5W-26S | 92 |
| Heartland Dr. N&S | 5W-27S | 92 |
| Hillside Dr. N&S | 6W-26S | 91 |
| Imperial Ct. NE&SW | 6W-27S | 91 |
| Imperial Dr. NS&EW | 6W-27S,5W-27S | 91 |
| Jackson Av. E&W | 4W-27S | 92 |
| Jefferson Dr. E&W | 5W-27S | 92 |
| Kara Ln. E&W | 6W-27S | 91 |
| Karlov Av. N&S | 5W-26S | 92 |
| Keenehand Ct. E&W | 5W-26S | 92 |
| Keith Dr. E&W | 6W-27S | 91 |
| Kings Ct. E&W | 6W-27S | 91 |
| Kolin Av. N&S | 5W-27S | 92 |
| Kostner Av. N&S | 5W-26S | 92 |
| Lake Shore Dr. N&S | 6W-27S | 91 |
| Latonia Ct. NW&SE | 5W-27S | 92 |
| Latonia Ln. N&S | 5W-27S | 92 |
| Laurel Dr. E&W | 5W-26S | 92 |
| Lawndale Av. N&S | 4W-27S | 92 |
| Lee Av. E&W | 4W-27S | 92 |
| Lee Ct. E&W | 5W-26S | 92 |
| Linden Rd. E&W | 4W-26S | 92 |
| Lioncrest Dr. E&W | 4W-26S | 92 |
| Lorraine Ct. N&S | 6W-27S | 91 |
| Main St. N&S | 4W-26S | 92 |
| Maple Av. E&W | 5W-26S | 92 |
| Millard Av. N&S | 4W-27S,4W-26S | 92 |
| Mission Dr. N&S | 6W-27S | 91 |
| Monterey Dr. E&W | 6W-27S | 91 |
| Parkview Dr. NE&SW | 5W-27S | 92 |
| Patterson Ct. N&S | 4W-26S | 92 |
| Pleasant Dr. N&S | 6W-27S | 91 |
| Polk Av. E&W | 4W-27S | 92 |
| Poplar Av. E&W | 5W-26S | 92 |
| Poplar St. E&W | 5W-26S | 92 |
| Redwood Dr. N&S | 6W-27S | 91 |
| Richton Pl. N&S | 4W-26S | 92 |
| Richton Rd. N&S | 4W-26S | 92 |
| Richton Square N&S | 4W-27S | 92 |
| Ridgeway Av. N&S | 4W-27S,4W-26S | 92 |
| Riverside Dr. NS&EW | 6W-27S | 91 |
| Roberta Ln. E&W | 6W-27S | 91 |
| Rockingham Rd. NE&SW | 5W-26S | 92 |
| Salem Ct. E&W | 5W-26S | 92 |
| Saratoga Rd. E&W | 5W-26S | 92 |
| Sauk Trail E&W | 4W-26S | 92 |
| Schaff Ct. E&W | 6W-26S | 91 |
| Scott Dr. N&S | 6W-26S | 91 |
| St. Ives Ln. E&W | 4W-26S | 92 |
| Steger Rd. E&W | 6W-27S | 91 |
| Taylor Av. E&W | 4W-27S | 92 |
| Thomas Ct. E&W | 4W-26S | 92 |
| Thomas Dr. E&W | 6W-27S | 91 |
| Tyler Dr. E&W | 5W-27S | 92 |
| Valley Dr. N&S | 6W-27S | 91 |
| Washington Dr. E&W | 5W-27S | 92 |
| Windsor Ct. E&W | 5W-26S | 92 |
| 219th St. E&W | 4W-26S | 92 |

## River Forest

| | Grid | Page |
|---|---|---|
| Ashland N&S | 9W-0N,9W-1N | 48 |
| Augusta E&W | 9W-1N | 48 |
| Auvergne N&S | 10W-0N | 47 |
| Berkshire E&W | 9W-1N | 48 |
| Bonnie Brae N&S | 9W-0N,9W-1N | 48 |
| Central E&W | 10W-0N,9W-0N | 47 |
| Chicago E&W | 9W-1N | 48 |
| Clinton Pl. N&S | 9W-0N,9W-1N | 48 |
| Division E&W | 9W-1N | 48 |
| Edgewood Pl. N&S | 10W-0N | 47 |
| Forest N&S | 9W-0N,9W-1N | 48 |
| Franklin N&S | 9W-0N,9W-1N | 48 |
| Gale N&S | 10W-0N | 47 |
| Garden E&W | 9W-0N | 48 |
| Greenfield E&W | 9W-1N | 48 |
| Hawthorne E&W | 9W-0N | 48 |
| Holly E&W | 9W-0N | 48 |
| Iowa E&W | 9W-1N | 48 |
| Jackson N&S | 9W-0N,9W-1N | 48 |
| Keystone N&S | 9W-0N,9W-1N | 48 |
| Lake E&W | 9W-0N | 48 |
| Lathrop N&S | 9W-0N,9W-1N | 48 |
| Le Moyne E&W | 9W-1N | 48 |
| Linden E&W | 9W-0N | 48 |
| Monroe N&S | 9W-0N,9W-1N | 48 |
| Oak E&W | 9W-0N | 48 |
| Park N&S | 9W-0N,9W-1N | 48 |
| Park Dr. E&W | 9W-0N | 48 |
| Quick E&W | 9W-0N | 48 |
| River Oaks NE&SW | 10W-0N | 47 |
| River Oaks NE&SW | 10W-0N | 47 |
| Rt. 64 E&W | 9W-1N | 48 |
| Thatcher N&S | 10W-0N,10W-1N | 47 |
| Thomas E&W | 9W-1N | 48 |
| Vine E&W | 9W-0N | 48 |
| Vinson N&S | 10W-1N,9W-1N | 47 |
| William N&S | 9W-0N,9W-1N | 48 |

## River Grove

| | Grid | Page |
|---|---|---|
| Arnold E&W | 10W-3N | 41 |
| Auxplaines N&S | 10W-3N | 41 |
| Belden E&W | 10W-2N | 47 |
| Beulah N&S | 11W-3N | 41 |
| Boyle St. N&S | 10W-3N | 41 |
| Budd N&S | 10W-3N | 41 |
| Carey E&W | 10W-3N | 41 |
| Center E&W | 10W-3N | 41 |
| Clark N&S | 11W-3N | 41 |
| Clinton N&S | 10W-3N | 41 |
| Davisson N&S | 10W-3N | 41 |
| Des Plaines River Rd. NW&SE | 11W-3N,10W-2N | 41 |
| Elm N&S | 11W-2N | 47 |
| Enger St. E&W | 10W-3N | 41 |
| Erie N&S | 10W-3N | 41 |
| Forest N&S | 10W-3N | 41 |
| Forest View N&S | 10W-3N | 41 |
| Fullerton E&W | 11W-3N | 41 |
| Greenwood Ter. E&W | 10W-3N | 41 |
| Grove N&S | 10W-3N | 41 |
| Haymond N&S | 10W-3N | 41 |
| Herrick E&W | 11W-3N,10W-3N | 41 |
| Hessing N&S | 10W-3N | 41 |
| Indian Rd. NE&SW | 10W-3N | 41 |
| Julian Ter. N&S | 10W-3N | 41 |
| Leyden N&S | 11W-3N | 41 |
| Lyndale E&W | 10W-2N | 47 |
| Maple N&S | 10W-3N | 41 |
| Marwood N&S | 10W-3N | 41 |
| O'Conner E&W | 10W-3N | 41 |
| Oak N&S | 10W-3N | 41 |
| Pacific E&W | 11W-3N | 41 |
| Palmer E&W | 10W-2N | 47 |
| Paris N&S | 10W-3N | 41 |
| Park N&S | 10W-3N | 41 |
| Rhodes N&S | 11W-3N | 41 |
| Richard E&W | 11W-3N | 41 |
| Ridge E&W | 10W-3N | 41 |
| River N&S | 10W-3N | 41 |
| River Grove E&W | 10W-3N | 41 |
| Roosevelt Ln. E&W | 10W-3N | 41 |
| Smith St. E&W | 10W-3N | 41 |
| Spruce N&S | 11W-3N | 41 |
| Struckmann N&S | 10W-3N | 41 |
| Thatcher Rd. N&S | 10W-3N,10W-2N | 41 |
| Trumbull N&S | 10W-2N | 47 |
| Walsh St. E&W | 10W-3N | 41 |
| West N&S | 11W-2N,11W-3N | 47 |
| Wood N&S | 10W-3N | 41 |
| Wrightwood E&W | 11W-3N,10W-3N | 41 |
| 1st N&S | 10W-2N | 47 |
| 9th N&S | 11W-2N | 47 |
| 80th N&S | 10W-3N | 41 |

## Riverdale

| | Grid | Page |
|---|---|---|
| Acme Av. E&W | 0W-15S | 76 |
| Ashland Av. N&S | 1W-16S,1W-15S | 82 |
| Atlantic Av. N&S | 0W-16S,0W-15S | 82 |
| Basic Steel Dr. N&S | 1W-16S | 82 |
| Blue Island-Riverdale Rd. E&W | 1W-16S,0W-15S | 82 |
| Charles Dr. E&W | 1W-15S | 76 |
| Clark St. N&S | 0W-16S | 82 |
| Dearborn St. N&S | 0W-16S | 82 |
| Edbrook Av. N&S | 0W-16S | 82 |
| Eggleston N&S | 0W-16S,0W-15S | 82 |
| Emerald Av. N&S | 1W-17S,1W-16S | 82 |
| Forest View Av. E&W | 0W-15S | 76 |
| Fritz Blvd. N&S | 1W-15S | 76 |
| Glen Ln. E&W | 0W-16S | 82 |
| Halsted St. N&W | 1W-16S,1W-15S | 82 |
| Highlawn Av. NE&SW | 0W-16S | 82 |
| Illinois St. NE&SW | 0W-16S,0W-15S | 82 |
| Indiana Av. N&S | 0W-16S | 82 |
| Industrial Dr. N&S | 1W-15S | 76 |
| Ivanhoe Ct. E&W | 0W-16S | 82 |
| Jackson St. E&W | 1W-15S | 76 |
| La Salle St. N&S | 0W-16S | 82 |
| Lotz Dr. N&S | 1W-16S | 82 |
| Lowe Av. N&S | 1W-16S | 82 |
| Michigan Av. N&S | 0W-16S,0W-15S | 82 |
| Normal Av. N&S | 0W-16S,0W-15S | 82 |
| Pacesetter Pkwy. E&W | 1W-15S,0W-15S | 76 |
| Parnell Av. N&S | 0W-16S,0W-15S | 82 |
| Perry Av. N&S | 0W-15S | 76 |
| Rt. 1 N&S | 1W-16S | 82 |
| School Ln. N&S | 0W-16S,0W-15S | 82 |
| State St. N&S | 0W-16S | 82 |
| Stewart Av. N&S | 0W-16S,0W-15S | 82 |
| Tracy Av. N&S | 0W-16S,0W-15S | 82 |
| Union Av. N&S | 1W-17S,1W-16S | 82 |
| Wabash Av. N&S | 0W-16S,0W-15S | 82 |
| Wallace St. N&S | 0W-16S,0W-15S | 82 |
| Wentworth Av. N&S | 0W-16S,0W-15S | 82 |
| 135th Pl. E&W | 0W-15S | 76 |
| 136th Pl. E&W | 0W-15S | 76 |
| 136th St. E&W | 0W-15S | 76 |
| 137th Pl. E&W | 0W-15S | 76 |
| 137th St. E&W | 0W-15S | 76 |
| 138th St. E&W | 1W-15S,0W-15S | 76 |
| 139th St. E&W | 0W-16S | 82 |
| 140th Ct. E&W | 0W-16S | 82 |
| 140th Pl. E&W | 0W-16S | 82 |
| 140th St. E&W | 0W-16S | 82 |
| 141st St. E&W | 0W-16S | 82 |
| 142nd St. E&W | 1W-16S,0W-16S | 82 |
| 143rd St. E&W | 1W-16S,0W-16S | 82 |
| 144th St. E&W | 1W-16S,0W-16S | 82 |
| 145th Pl. E&W | 0W-16S | 82 |
| 145th St. E&W | 1W-16S,0W-16S | 82 |
| 146th St. E&W | 1W-16S,0W-16S | 82 |

## Riverside

| | Grid | Page |
|---|---|---|
| Addison E&W | 9W-3S | 54 |
| Akenside N&S | 9W-3S | 54 |
| Arlington N&S | 9W-2S | 54 |
| Audubon N&S | 9W-2S | 54 |
| Barry Point N&S | 9W-3S | 54 |
| Bartram N&S | 9W-2S | 54 |
| Berkeley E&W | 9W-2S | 54 |
| Blackhawk E&W | 9W-3S | 54 |
| Blooming Bank N&S | 10W-3S | 53 |
| Blythe E&W | 9W-3S | 54 |
| Burling E&W | 9W-3S | 54 |
| Burlington E&W | 10W-3S,9W-3S | 53 |
| Byrd N&S | 9W-2S | 54 |
| Cowley N&S | 9W-3S | 54 |
| Cir. | 9W-3S | 54 |
| Downing N&S | 9W-2S | 54 |

**Grid Page**

E. Longcommon E&W
.......... 9W-3S 54
Cir. .......... 9W-3S 54
Evelyn E&W .......... 9W-2S 54
Fairbank N&S .... 10W-3S 53
Forbes N&S .... 10W-3S 53
Forest E&W .... 10W-3S 53
Forest N&S....10W-3S 53
Gage E&W .......... 9W-3S 54
Gatesby E&W ...... 9W-2S 54
Groveland N&S .... 10W-3S 53
Haas N&S .......... 9W-3S 54
Harris St. N&S.......9W-3S 54
Herbert N&S.......9W-3S 54
Herrick E&W.......9W-3S 54
Kent E&W.......9W-2S 54
Kimbark N&S .... 10W-3S 53
Lawton E&W.......9W-3S 54
Leesley N&S.......20W-2S 54
Lincoln N&S .... 10W-3S 53
Lindberg E&W ...... 9W-3S 54
Lionel E&W .......9W-3S 54
Longcommon E&W ...9W-2S 54
Loudoun E&W.......9W-3S 54
Maplewood N&S .... 10W-3S 53
Michavy N&S ...... 9W-3S 54
Millbridge E&W
..........10W-3S,9W-3S 53
Northgate Ct. N&S......9W-2S 54
Northgate Rd. E&W ...9W-2S 54
Northwood N&S
..........9W-3S,9W-2S 54
Nuttail N&S.......9W-3S,9W-2S 54
Ogden E&W.......9W-3S 54
Olmstead E&W ...... 9W-3S 54
Park E&W .......... 10W-3S 53
Parkway N&S ...... 9W-3S 54
Pine E&W .......... 10W-3S 53
Quincy N&S ..10W-3S,9W-3S 53
Repton N&S.......9W-3S 54
Ridgewood E&W .... 10W-3S 53
Riverside N&S ...... 9W-3S 54
Robinson E&W ...... 9W-3S 54
Scottswood Dr. N&S
..........10W-3S 53
Scottswood Rd. N&S
..........10W-3S 53
Selbourne E&W ...... 9W-3S 54
Shenstone E&W ...... 9W-3S 54
Southcote E&W ...... 9W-2S 54
Uvedale E&W ...... 9W-2S 54
Uvedale Ct. NW&SE .. 9W-2S 53
Waubansee E&W .... 10W-3S 53
West N&S .......... 10W-3S 53
Wood Side N&S ...... 9W-3S 54
York E&W .......... 9W-3S 54
1st Av. N&S .... 10W-3S 53

**Riverside Township**
Bismarck E&W.......9W-3S 54
Columbus N&S ...... 9W-3S 54
Gladstone N&S ...... 9W-3S 54
Shakespeare N&S ...9W-3S 54
Stanley N&S..........9W-3S 54
Washington N&S.......9W-3S 54
39th E&W .......... 9W-3S 54

**Robbins**
Albany Av. N&S .... 3W-16S 75
Avers Av. N&S
..........4W-16S,4W-15S 75
Broadway NE&SW .. 3W-15S 75
Central Park Av. N&S
..........4W-16S,4W-15S 75
Clifton Park Av. N&S
..........4W-16S,4W-15S 75
Emery Ln. E&W .... 4W-16S 75
Finley Av. NE&SW .. 4W-16S 75
Francisco Av. N&S . 3W-15S 75
Glenn Av. NW&SE .. 4W-16S 75
Grace Av. N&S .... 4W-16S 75
Hamlin Av. N&S
..........4W-16S,4W-15S 75
Harding Av. N&S .. 4W-15S 75
Hendricks Rd. NW&SE
..........4W-16S 75
Homan Av. N&S
..........4W-16S,4W-15S 75
Karlov Av. N&S.....5W-15S 74
Kedvale Av. N&S
..........5W-16S,5W-15S 74
Kedzie Av. N&S
..........4W-16S,4W-15S 75
Keystone Av. N&S . 5W-16S 74
Kildare Av. N&S .... 5W-15S 74
Kinne Rd. E&W .... 4W-16S 75
Kolin Av. N&S ...... 5W-15S 74
Komensky Av. N&S . 5W-15S 74
Kostner Av. N&S .... 5W-15S 74
Lawndale Av. N&S
..........4W-16S,4W-15S 75
Lincoln Ln., E. E&W . 4W-15S 75
Lincoln Ln., W. E&W
..........5W-15S,4W-15S 74
Lydia Av. NE&SW .. 4W-16S 75
Maxey Ct. E&W .... 4W-16S 75
Mcbreen Av. NW&SE
..........4W-16S 75
Midlothian Turnpike NE&SW
..........4W-16S 75
Monticello Av. N&S
..........4W-16S,4W-15S 75
Nelson Av. N&S .. 4W-16S 75
Pulaski Rd. N&S .. 5W-16S 74
Reeves Rd. NE&SW 4W-16S 75

Rexford Rd. NE&SE
..........4W-16S 75
Richardson Av. NW&SE
..........4W-16S 75
Richmond St. N&S . 3W-15S 75
Ridgeway Av. N&S
..........4W-16S,4W-15S 75
Sacramento Av. N&S
..........3W-16S 75
Sawyer Av. N&S
..........4W-16S,4W-15S 75
Spaulding Av. N&S . 4W-16S 75
Springfield Av. N&S . 4W-15S 75
St. Louis Av. N&S
..........4W-16S,4W-15S 75
Tripp Av. N&S .... 5W-15S 74
Troy St. N&S...... 3W-16S 75
Trumbull Av. N&S .. 4W-16S 75
Turner Av. N&S
..........4W-16S,4W-15S 75
Utica Av. N&S ...... 3W-16S 75
Woodlawn Av. N&S .. 3W-15S 75
134th Pl. E&W .... 4W-15S 75
134th St. E&W
..........5W-15S,4W-15S 74
135th Pl. E&W
..........5W-16S,4W-16S 74
135th St. E&W
..........5W-15S,3W-15S 74
136th Pl. E&W
..........5W-16S,4W-16S 74
136th St. E&W
..........5W-16S,3W-16S 74
137th Pl. E&W .... 5W-16S 74
137th St. E&W
..........5W-16S,3W-16S 74
138th St. E&W
..........5W-16S,3W-16S 74
139th Pl. E&W
..........4W-16S,3W-16S 75
139th St. E&W
..........4W-16S,3W-16S 75
140th Pl. E&W .... 4W-16S 75
140th St. E&W .... 4W-16S 75
141st St. E&W .... 4W-16S 75
142nd St. NE&SW .. 4W-16S 75

**Rolling Meadows**
Adams St. NW&SE
..........20W-14N 23
Adler Ct.* N&S .... 21W-14N 23
Algonquin Pkwy. NS&EW
..........19W-12N 24
Algonquin Rd. NW&SE
..........20W-12N,19W-12N 23
Alton E&W ...... 19W-11N 33
Amanda Ct. NS&EW
..........21W-13N 23
Anseline Ct. E&W .. 20W-14N 23
Apollo Dr. N&S .... 20W-12N 23
Apple Jack Rd. NS&EW
..........20W-13N 23
Arbor Dr. N&S.....21W-12N 23
Arlingdale Ct. NE&SW
..........22W-14N 23
Arlingdale Dr. NW&SE
..........22W-14N 23
Arrowood Ln. N&S 21W-14N 23
Asbury E&W ...... 20W-13N 23
Ashland Av. N&S .. 20W-14N 23
Astor Ln. N&S...... 19W-12N 24
Attleboro E&W .... 19W-10N 33
Auburn E&W ...... 20W-13N 23
Barker Av. N&S
..........20W-12N,19W-13N 23
Barrow NW&SE .. 20W-11N 33
Belford Ln. E&W .. 20W-11N 33
Bent Creek Ct. NS&EW
..........21W-13N 23
Benton St. N&S .. 20W-14N 23
Berdnick St. E&W 4W-15N 23
Bethel N&S ...... 19W-11N 33
Birch Ln. E&W .... 19W-12N 24
Black Twig N&S .. 20W-13N 23
Blackhawk Dr. E&W
..........20W-15N 23
Bluebird Ln. NS&EW
..........19W-13N,19W-14N 24
Bob White Ln. N&S
..........20W-13N 23
Bob-o-Link Ln. NS&EW
..........20W-13N 23
Bobwhite Ln. E&W 20W-13N 23
Bridgeton N&S .... 19W-11N 33
Brookmeade Dr. NW&SE
..........20W-12N,20W-13N 23
Brookton NW&SE . 19W-11N 33
Brookwood Way Dr. N&S
..........20W-14N 23
Bryant Av. NS&EW
..........20W-14N 23
Burning Trees N&S
..........20W-13N 23
Butterfield Ct. N&S
..........21W-14N 23
Calchester E&W ... 19W-11N 33
California Av. N&S 20W-13N 23
California Ct. E&W . 20W-13N 23
California St. N&S . 20W-14N 23
Calvert Dr. N&S .. 21W-12N 24
Campbell St. E&W
..........20W-14N,19W-14N 23
Cardinal Dr. NS&EW
..........19W-13N,19W-14N 24
Carlisle NW&SE .... 20W-11N 33
Carnegie St. N&S . 20W-15N 23
Carr St. N&S ...... 19W-15N 14

Carriageway Dr. NW&SE
..........19W-12N 24
Cedar Glen Dr. N&S
..........20W-13N 23
Cedar St. E&W .... 19W-12N 24
Central Rd. E&W
..........20W-13N,19W-13N 23
Chapman Ct. N&S. 20W-14N 23
Chas Dr. N&S .... 20W-14N 23
Chelsea N&S ...... 19W-11N 33
Cheshire Dr. E&W . 19W-12N 24
Cheviot NW&SE .. 20W-11N 33
Chichester N&S .... 19W-11N 33
Chicory Ct. N&S .. 21W-14N 23
Cold Springs Ct. E&W
..........21W-13N 23
Coleen Ct. N&S .... 20W-13N 23
College Crossing NW&SE
..........21W-13N 23
Comstock N&S .... 19W-11N 33
Coventry NW&SE . 20W-11N 33
Crane Ct. E&W .... 19W-13N 24
Creekside Dr. E&W
..........20W-13N 23
Creekside Dr. N&S 21W-13N 23
Crestwood Dr. N&S
..........20W-13N 23
Croftwood Ct. N&S
..........21W-14N 23
Cross Rds. Of Commerce Dr.
E&W ..........20W-12N 23
Crossing Ct. NE&SW
..........21W-13N 23
Croydon NW&SE .. 20W-11N 33
Cyndi Ct. E&W .... 18W-13N 24
Dahlia Ct. N&S .. 21W-14N 23
Davis Ct. NW&SE . 20W-13N 23
Dawngate Ct. N&S 20W-13N 23
Dawngate Ln. N&S
..........20W-13N 23
Debra Ct. E&W .... 20W-13N 23
Deepwood Ln. E&W
..........21W-13N 23
Deerfield E&W
..........21W-13N,21W-14N 23
Denny Ct. N&S .... 20W-14N 23
Dogwood Rd. E&W
..........20W-13N 23
Donegal E&W .... 20W-11N 33
Dove Ct. NW&SE . 19W-13N 24
Dove St. N&S
..........19W-13N,19W-14N 24
Dunbar E&W .... 20W-11N 33
Duxbury N&S ...... 20W-14N 23
Eagle Ln. N&S .... 19W-13N 24
Ealing NW&SE .. 20W-11N 33
East Frontage Rd. N&S
..........20W-13N 23
Eastman St. E&W . 19W-14N 24
Eaton NW&SE .... 20W-11N 33
Edgar St. N&S .... 20W-13N 23
Edgewood Ct. N&S
..........21W-14N 23
Edison Pl. NW&SE. 20W-15N 23
Eleanore Ct. N&S . 20W-13N 23
Elk Grove Rd. NE&SW
..........18W-11N 24
Emerson Av. E&W . 20W-11N 33
Essex Way N&S....19W-12N 24
Euclid E&W
..........20W-14N,19W-14N 23
Exeter NW&SE .... 20W-11N 33
Fairfax Av. E&W ... 20W-14N 23
Falcon Ct., N. NS&EW
..........20W-13N 23
Falcon Ct., S. E&W
..........20W-13N 23
Falkirk N&S ...... 20W-11N 33
Falmouth NW&SE . 20W-11N 33
Farmington Ct. N&S
..........21W-14N 23
Fieldstone N&S .. 20W-13N 23
Finch Ct. E&W .... 20W-13N 23
Flicker Ln. N&S .. 20W-14N 23
Forest Av. N&S .... 20W-14N 23
Fox Av. N&S ...... 21W-13N 23
Foxcroft E&W .... 19W-11N 33
Fremont St. E&W
..........20W-14N,19W-13N 23
Fulle St. E&W ...... 19W-13N 24
George Ct. NW&SE
..........19W-13N 24
George St. E&W ... 19W-13N 24
Gettysburg E&W .. 20W-14N 23
Ginger Ct. E&W ... 21W-14N 23
Golf Place E&W .. 19W-13N 24
Golf Rd. E&W
..........20W-12N,18W-12N 23
Green Meadow Ct. N&S
..........21W-13N 23
Greenwich Ct. E&W
..........21W-13N 23
Grimsby NW&SE .. 20W-11N 33
Grouse Ct. N&S .. 19W-13N 24
Grouse Ln. E&W .. 19W-13N 24
Grove St. E&W .... 19W-13N 24
Groveside E&W
..........21W-13N 23
Gull Ct. NE&SW .. 19W-13N 24
Hampton E&W .... 19W-10N 33
Hartung Rd. E&W . 21W-13N 23
Haverhill E&W .... 19W-11N 33
Hawk Ct. NE&SW . 19W-14N 24
Hawk Ln. N&S .... 19W-14N 24
Hawthorne Ln. N&S
..........20W-12N 23
Heather Ct. E&W . 21W-14N 23

Heron Ct. N&S .... 19W-14N 24
Hicks Rd. N&S .... 20W-14N 23
Highland Dr. NS&EW
..........22W-14N 23
Holliston NE&SW . 19W-11N 33
Holly Ln. E&W ..... 20W-13N 23
Holyoke E&W .... 19W-10N 33
Honeysuckle Ln. NE&SW
..........21W-14N 23
Hoover Ct. N&S .. 20W-13N 23
Hoover St. N&S
..........20W-14N 23
Huron Ct. N&S .... 19W-14N 24
Industrial Av. E&W
..........20W-15N,20W-14N 23
Interstate 290 N&S
..........20W-12N,20W-14N 23
Interstate 90 NW&SE
..........20W-12N 23
Ironwood Ct. E&W . 21W-14N 23
Jasmine E&W . 21W-14N 23
Jay Ln. N&S
..........19W-13N,19W-14N 24
Jessica E&W . 21W-14N 23
Jill Ct. N&S ...... 20W-14N 23
Jody Ct. NS&EW . 20W-13N 23
Jonquil E&W .... 21W-14N 23
Juniper Rd. NE&SW
..........20W-13N 23
Kendal N&S...... 20W-11N 33
Kenilworth Ct. N&S
..........21W-13N 23
Kettering N&S.... 20W-13N 23
Kevin Ln. N&S .... 21W-14N 23
Keystone Ct. N&S . 19W-12N 24
Kieth Ct. NW&SE . 20W-14N 23
Killarney Ct. N&S . 19W-14N 24
Kimball Hill Dr. N&S
..........19W-12N 24
Kimberry Ct. E&W . 21W-14N 23
King's Walk Dr. N&S
..........20W-14N 23
Kingfisher E&W .. 20W-13N 23
Kingfisher Ct. NE&SW
..........20W-13N 23
Kingfisher Ln., E. NW&SE
..........19W-13N 24
Kirchoff Rd. E&W
..........20W-14N,19W-14N 23
Kittery E&W ...... 19W-11N 33
Knoll Ridge Rd. N&S
..........20W-13N 23
Lark Ct. NW&SE . 19W-14N 24
Lilac Ct. N&S ...... 21W-14N 23
Lincoln Av. E&W . 20W-14N 23
Lincoln Ct. N&S .. 20W-14N 23
Linden Ln. N&S
..........19W-12N,19W-13N 24
Lisa Ct. N&S ...... 21W-13N 23
Lois Dr. NW&SE .. 19W-12N 24
Magnolia Dr. N&S . 20W-12N 23
Mallard Ct. N&S .. 20W-13N 23
Mallory Ct. N&S .. 21W-14N 23
Manomet E&W .. 19W-10N 33
Maple Ct. N&S .... 19W-12N 24
Maple E&W ...... 19W-12N 24
Margate NW&SE . 20W-11N 33
Martin Ct. N&S .. 19W-14N 24
Martin Ln. N&S .. 19W-14N 24
Mayberry Ct. E&W . 21W-14N 23
McKone Ct. N&S .. 19W-14N 24
Meacham Rd. N&S
..........21W-13N 23
Meadow Dr. NE&SW
..........19W-13N,19W-14N 24
Meadow Edge Dr. N&S
..........21W-14N 23
Meadowbrook Ct. E&W
..........19W-12N 24
Meadowbrook-Industrial Ct.
N&S ..........19W-12N 24
Michael Ct. E&W . 21W-14N 23
Mill Creek Ln. N&S
..........21W-13N 23
Millstone Ln. NW&SE
..........19W-13N 23
New Castle Ct. E&W
..........21W-14N 23
Newport Dr. NW&SE
..........19W-12N 24
North Carona N&S
..........22W-13N,22W-14N 23
North Hampton Dr. N&S
..........19W-12N 24
Northwest Tollway NW&SE
..........20W-15N,19W-15N 23
Norwood Ct. N&S . 19W-12N 24
Oak Ln. E&W .... 19W-12N 24
Oaksbury Ct. E&W 20W-13N 23
Oaksbury E&W
..........20W-13N 23
Old Creek Rd. E&W
..........20W-13N 23
Old Hickory Rd. N&S
..........20W-13N 23
Old Mill N&S
..........21W-13N,21W-14N 23
Old Saybrook E&W
..........19W-10N 33
Old Valley N&S .. 20W-13N 23
Oriole Ln. N&S
..........19W-13N,19W-14N 24
Owl Dr. N&S
..........20W-13N,19W-13N 23
Owl Ln. NE&SW
..........20W-13N,19W-14N 23
Oxford NS&EW .... 20W-14N 23

Park Ct. N&S .... 19W-13N 24
Park St. NW&SE .. 19W-13N 24
Peacock Ct. NE&SW
..........19W-13N 24
Peacock Dr. N&S
..........20W-12N,19W-13N 23
Peacock Ln. NW&SE
..........19W-13N 24
Pebblebrook Ln. N&S
..........21W-13N,21W-14N 23
Pembroke N&S .... 20W-11N 33
Pepperell N&S .... 19W-11N 33
Pheasant Dr. N&S . 19W-13N 24
Pine Valley N&S .... 20W-13N 23
Piper Ct. E&W .... 20W-13N 23
Plum Grove Dr. NW&SE
..........20W-12N 23
Plum Grove Rd. N&S
..........21W-14N 23
Plum Tree Ln. N&S
..........21W-13N,21W-14N 23
Pocassett N&S .... 19W-11N 33
Polk Av. N&S .... 20W-14N 23
Prarie Ln. E&W .... 22W-14N 23
Prestwick E&W .. 20W-11N 33
Pride Ct. E&W
..........21W-14N,20W-14N 23
Quail Ct. NE&SW . 19W-13N 24
Quail Ln. E&W .... 19W-13N 24
Quentin Rd. N&S
..........21W-13N,21W-18N 23
Raven Ln. N&S .. 19W-13N 24
Red Haw N&S....20W-13N 23
Redbud Rd. NW&SE
..........20W-13N 23
Redwing Ct. NE&SW
..........20W-13N 23
Rhiannon Ct. E&W . 21W-14N 23
Richnee Ln. N&S . 20W-13N 23
Robin Ln. N&S .... 19W-14N 24
Rohlwing Rd. N&S
..........20W-14N,20W-15N 23
Rose Wood Dr. N&S
..........20W-13N 23
Rt. 53 N&S
..........20W-13N,20W-14N 23
Rt. 58 E&W
..........20W-12N,18W-12N 23
Rt. 62 NW&SE
..........20W-12N,18W-12N 23
Rumford N&S .... 19W-11N 33
Rywick Dr. E&W...20W-13N 23
Saint George Dr. NS&EW
..........20W-14N 23
Salt Creek N&S
..........20W-14N,19W-14N 23
Scarborough N&S . 20W-11N 33
School Dr. NE&SW
..........19W-14N 24
School St. NW&SE
..........19W-13N,19W-14N 24
Shady St. NE&SW 20W-13N 23
Shagbark N&S .... 20W-13N 23
Shannon N&S .... 20W-11N 33
Sigwalt St. E&W
..........19W-14N,19W-13N 24
Silent Brook Ln. NS&EW
..........21W-14N 23
Smith St. N&S ....21W-14N 23
South Corona Dr. E&W
..........22W-13N 23
South Ct. N&S .. 19W-13N 24
South Hampton Dr. E&W
..........19W-12N 24
South St. E&W .. 19W-13N 24
Spruce Ct. NW&SE
..........20W-14N 23
Squibb Av. E&W...20W-12N 23
St. Alban's N&S .. 20W-11N 33
St. James St. E&W
..........19W-14N 24
Starling Ln. E&W . 19W-13N 24
Stirling E&W .... 20W-11N 33
Stoneridge Rd. N&S
..........20W-13N 23
Stork Ct. E&W .... 19W-14N 24
Stuart N&S ...... 20W-11N 33
Swallow Ln. E&W . 19W-13N 24
Swan Ln. N&S .... 19W-14N 24
Sycamore Av. N&S
..........20W-12N 23
Taft Av. N&S .... 20W-14N 23
Tall Oaks Ln. E&W 20W-13N 23
Teal Ct. E&W ...... 20W-13N 23
Teonia Woods Rd. E&W
..........20W-13N 23
Tern Ct. N&S .... 20W-14N 23
Theda Ln. N&S .. 20W-14N 23
Thorntree Ln. N&S. 20W-12N 23
Thrush Ct. N&S .. 19W-13N 24
Thrush Ln. E&W
..........20W-13N,19W-13N 23
Tollview Dr. NW&SE
..........20W-12N,19W-12N 23
Troy E&W........20W-11N 33
Upton N&S ...... 19W-11N 33
Vermont Ct. N&S . 20W-14N 23
Vermont St. NS&EW
..........20W-14N 23
Villa Cir. NS&EW . 21W-13N 23
Viola Ct. N&S .... 21W-14N 23
Walnut Dr. N&S .. 20W-13N 23
Weber Dr. N&S .. 19W-12N 24
West Frontage Rd. N&S
..........20W-13N 23
Wildwood Dr. N&S. 20W-13N 23
Wilke Rd. N&S
..........19W-12N,19W-14N 24

| | Grid | Page |
|---|---|---|
| Williamsburg Ct. E&W | 20W-14N | 23 |
| Willow Ln. E&W | 19W-12N | 24 |
| Wilmette Av. E&W | 20W-14N | 23 |
| Wilson Av. NW&SE | 20W-14N | 23 |
| Windemere N&S | 20W-11N | 33 |
| Wing St. E&W | 19W-14N | 24 |
| Winnetka Av. NE&SW | 20W-14N,20W-15N | 23 |
| Winnetka Cir. N&S | 20W-14N | 23 |
| Winterport NW&SE | 19W-11N | 33 |
| Wiscassett N&S | 19W-11N | 33 |
| Woodbine N&S | 20W-13N | 23 |
| Woodcliff Ct. E&W | 21W-13N | 23 |
| Woodcliff Ln. E&W | 20W-13N | 23 |
| Woodland Ct. E&W | 20W-13N | 23 |
| Woods Chapel N&S | 20W-13N | 23 |
| Wren Ct. NE&SW | 19W-13N | 24 |
| Wren Ln. NS&EW | 19W-13N,19W-14N | 24 |
| Yarrow Ct. N&S | 21W-14N | 23 |
| Yarrow Ln. N&S | 21W-14N | 23 |

## Roselle*
**(Also see Du Page County)**

| | Grid | Page |
|---|---|---|
| Acadia Bay * E&W | 23W-8N | 32 |
| Acadia Ct. N&S | 22W-8N | 33 |
| Acadia Tr. E&W | 22W-8N | 33 |
| Bryce Tr. E&W | 22W-8N | 33 |
| Canterbury Tr.* NE&SW | 23W-8N | 32 |
| Carlsbad Tr. E&W | 22W-8N | 33 |
| Chisolm Tr. E&W | 22W-8N | 33 |
| Conway Bay* NE&SW | 23W-8N | 32 |
| Cross Creek Ct. E&W | 22W-8N | 33 |
| Cross Creek Dr. E&W | 22W-8N | 33 |
| Cumberland Rd. N&S | 22W-8N | 33 |
| Glacier Bay* N&S | 23W-8N | 32 |
| Glacier Ct.* NW&SE | 23W-8N | 32 |
| Glacier Tr. E&W | 22W-8N | 33 |
| Isle Royal Bay E&W | 22W-8N | 33 |
| Nerge Rd. E&W | 22W-8N | 33 |
| Oregon Tr. E&W | 22W-8N | 33 |
| Overland Ct. E&W | 22W-8N | 33 |
| Sequoia Bay N&S | 22W-8N | 33 |
| Sequoia Tr. NW&SE | 22W-8N | 33 |
| Shadow Lake Bay* NE&SW | 23W-8N | 32 |
| Shawnee Tr. E&W | 22W-8N | 33 |
| White Sands Bay NE&SW | 22W-8N | 33 |
| Woodfield Tr. NS&EW | 22W-8N | 33 |
| Yosemite Ct. N&S | 22W-8N | 33 |
| Yosemite Tr. E&W | 22W-8N | 33 |

## Rosemont

| | Grid | Page |
|---|---|---|
| Allen St. Ext. E&W | 11W-6N | 41 |
| Anne Ct. E&W | 13W-8N | 35 |
| Ardmore St. E&W | 12W-7N | 36 |
| Balmoral Av. E&W | 12W-6N | 40 |
| Barry St. N&S | 13W-8N | 35 |
| Betty Ct. E&W | 13W-8N | 35 |
| Bryn Mawr Av. E&W | 12W-7N | 36 |
| Byron St. N&S | 12W-7N | 36 |
| Carol Ct. E&W | 13W-8N | 35 |
| Chestnut St. N&S | 13W-8N | 35 |
| Devon Av. E&W | 12W-8N | 36 |
| Devon Ct. E&W | 12W-7N | 36 |
| Doris Ct. E&W | 13W-8N | 35 |
| Emerson St. N&S | 12W-7N | 36 |
| Estelle Dr. E&W | 12W-7N | 36 |
| Ethel Ct. E&W | 13W-8N | 35 |
| Evenhouse Av. E&W | 11W-7N | 36 |
| Foster Av. E&W | 12W-6N,11W-6N | 40 |
| Gage St. N&S | 11W-7N | 36 |
| Graff Dr. E&W | 12W-7N | 36 |
| Granville St. E&W | 12W-7N | 36 |
| Hawthorne St. N&S | 12W-7N | 36 |
| Higgins Rd. NW&SE | 13W-8N | 35 |
| Hirschman St. E&W | 11W-7N | 41 |
| Hope Dr. E&W | 12W-7N | 36 |
| Kirschoff St. N&S | 12W-7N | 36 |
| Lunt St. E&W | 13W-8N | 35 |
| Lyman St. N&S | 11W-7N | 41 |
| Lyndon St. N&S | 13W-8N | 35 |
| Mannheim Rd. N&S | 13W-8N | 35 |
| Michigan St. N&S | 12W-6N | 40 |
| Milton Ct. N&S | 12W-6N | 41 |
| Milton Parkway N&S | 12W-6N | 40 |
| Morse Av. E&W | 13W-8N | 35 |
| Northwest Tollway NW&SE | 12W-7N,11W-7N | 36 |
| Norwood St. E&W | 12W-7N | 36 |
| Otto Av. N&S | 12W-6N | 40 |
| Pearl St. N&S | 12W-6N | 40 |
| Pine St. N&S | 13W-8N | 35 |
| River Rd. N&S | 11W-6N | 41 |
| River Rose St. E&W | 11W-7N | 36 |
| Rose St. N&S | 11W-6N | 41 |
| Rosemont St. E&W | 12W-7N | 36 |
| Ruby St. N&S | 12W-7N | 36 |
| Scott St. N&S | 12W-7N | 36 |
| Thorndale Av. E&W | 12W-7N | 36 |
| Wesley Ter. N&S | 11W-6N | 41 |
| William St. E&W | 11W-6N | 41 |
| Willow Creek Dr. N&S | 11W-7N | 36 |
| 60th St. E&W | 12W-6N | 40 |
| 61st St. E&W | 12W-6N | 40 |
| 62nd St. E&W | 12W-6N | 40 |

## Sauk Village

| | Grid | Page |
|---|---|---|
| Apache Dr. E&W | 2E-26S | 95 |
| Arlene Ct. E&W | 2E-27S | 95 |
| Astor St. E&W | 2E-25S | 95 |
| Barry Ln. NE&SW | 2E-25S | 95 |
| Brookwood Av. N&S | 3E-27S | 95 |
| Calumet Expwy. N&S | 1E-27S,1E-26S | 94 |
| Carol Av. N&S | 2E-26S | 95 |
| Carole Ln. E&W | 2E-26S | 95 |
| Carolina Dr. E&W | 2E-27S | 95 |
| Cedar Ln. NE&SW | 2E-25S | 95 |
| Chappel Av. N&S | 2E-27S,2E-26S | 95 |
| Charlotte Ct. NW&SE | 2E-26S | 95 |
| Chestnut Av. N&S | 2E-25S | 95 |
| Clyde Av. N&S | 2E-26S | 95 |
| Constance Av. E&W | 2E-26S | 95 |
| Cornell Av. N&S | 2E-27S | 95 |
| Cynthia Av. N&S | 2E-26S | 95 |
| Eastbrook Ct. NW&SE | 2E-27S | 95 |
| Eastbrook Dr. N&S | 2E-27S | 95 |
| Evergreen Ln. E&W | 2E-25S | 95 |
| Galine Av. N&S | 2E-26S | 95 |
| Grand St. E&W | 2E-25S | 95 |
| Jeffery Av. N&S | 2E-27S,2E-26S | 95 |
| Joshua Dr. N&S | 1E-27S | 95 |
| Kalvelage Dr. E&W | 3E-26S | 95 |
| Kathy Dr. N&S | 2E-27S | 95 |
| Katz-Corner Rd. E&W | 3E-26S | 95 |
| Lincoln Hwy. E&W | 2E-25S | 95 |
| Locust Av. N&S | 2E-25S | 95 |
| Luella Ct. N&S | 2E-26S | 95 |
| Maple Ct. N&S | 2E-25S | 95 |
| Maple Ln. NE&SW | 2E-25S | 95 |
| Merrill Av. N&S | 2E-27S,2E-26S | 95 |
| Merrill Ct. N&S | 2E-26S | 95 |
| Murphy Av. N&S | 3E-27S | 95 |
| Navaho Av. N&S | 2E-26S | 95 |
| Nichols Av. N&S | 3E-27S | 95 |
| Nichols Dr. E&W | 3E-27S | 95 |
| Oak St. E&W | 2E-25S | 95 |
| Oakbrook Ct. E&W | 2E-27S | 95 |
| Oakbrook Ln. E&W | 2E-27S | 95 |
| Olivia Av. N&S | 2E-26S | 95 |
| Orion Av. N&S | 2E-26S | 95 |
| Paxton Av. N&S | 2E-26S | 95 |
| Peach Tree Av. N&S | 3E-26S | 95 |
| Penrose Av. E&W | 2E-25S | 95 |
| Peterson Av. N&S | 2E-26S | 95 |
| Pine Av. N&S | 2E-25S | 95 |
| Pomo Ct. E&W | 2E-26S | 95 |
| Poplar Ln. E&W | 2E-25S | 95 |
| Prairie Av. N&S | 2E-26S | 95 |
| Reichert Av. E&W | 2E-27S | 95 |
| Ross Ct. E&W | 2E-27S | 95 |
| Rt. 394 N&S | 2E-26S | 95 |
| Sauk Pointe Dr. N&S | 1E-27S,1E-26S | 95 |
| Sauk Trail E&W | 2E-26S | 95 |
| Scott Dr. NW&SE | 2E-25S | 95 |
| Shirley Av. N&S | 2E-26S | 95 |
| Southbrook Dr. NE&SW | 2E-27S | 95 |
| Spencer Av. N&S | 3E-27S | 95 |
| Steger Rd. E&W | 2E-27S | 95 |
| Strassburg Av. NE&SW | 2E-27S | 95 |
| Talandis Dr. N&S | 2E-26S | 95 |
| Theisen Av. N&S | 3E-27S | 95 |
| Theodore Av. N&S | 3E-27S | 95 |
| Torrence Av. N&S | 2E-27S,2E-26S | 95 |
| U.S. Rt. 30 E&W | 2E-25S | 95 |
| Walton Pl. NW&SE | 2E-25S | 95 |
| Westbrook Ct. NW&SE | 2E-27S | 95 |
| Westbrook Dr. N&S | 2E-27S | 95 |
| Westbrook Tr. N&S | 2E-27S | 95 |
| Willow Tree Ln. N&S | 3E-26S | 95 |
| Yates Av. NE&SW | 2E-27S,2E-26S | 95 |
| 30th St. E&W | 3E-27S | 95 |
| 215th Pl. E&W | 2E-26S | 95 |
| 216th Ct. E&W | 2E-26S | 95 |
| 216th Pl. E&W | 2E-26S | 95 |
| 216th St. E&W | 2E-26S | 95 |
| 217th Pl. E&W | 2E-26S | 95 |
| 217th St. E&W | 2E-26S | 95 |
| 218th Pl. E&W | 2E-26S | 95 |
| 218th St. E&W | 2E-26S | 95 |
| 219th Pl. E&W | 2E-26S | 95 |
| 219th St. E&W | 2E-26S | 95 |
| 220th St. NE&SW | 2E-26S | 95 |
| 221st St. E&W | 2E-26S | 95 |
| 222nd Pl. E&W | 2E-26S | 95 |
| 222nd St. E&W | 2E-26S | 95 |
| 223rd Pl. E&W | 2E-27S,3E-27S | 95 |
| 223rd St. E&W | 2E-26S,1E-27S | 95 |
| 224th Ct. E&W | 2E-27S | 95 |
| 224th Pl. E&W | 3E-27S | 95 |
| 224th St. E&W | 2E-27S,3E-27S | 95 |
| 225th Pl. E&W | 2E-27S,3E-27S | 95 |
| 225th St. E&W | 2E-27S,3E-27S | 95 |
| 226th St. E&W | 3E-27S | 95 |
| 227th St. E&W | 1E-27S | 95 |

## Schaumburg*
**(Also see Du Page County)**

| | Grid | Page |
|---|---|---|
| Abbington Pl. N&S | 24W-11N | 32 |
| Aberdeen Ct. N&S | 26W-10N | 31 |
| Academy Ct.* N&S | 24W-13N | 22 |
| Acorn Ct. N&S | 23W-10N | 32 |
| Adams Ct. NW&SE | 27W-10N | 31 |
| Adler Ct. N&S | 26W-11N | 31 |
| Aegaean Dr. N&S | 24W-9N | 32 |
| Aimee Ln. E&W | 26W-10N | 31 |
| Aimee Way N&S | 26W-10N | 31 |
| Aimtree Pl. E&W | 24W-10N | 32 |
| Akron Ct. E&W | 25W-9N | 32 |
| Albany Ct. NS&EW | 25W-8N | 32 |
| Albion Av. E&W | 24W-8N,23W-8N | 32 |
| Alcott Ct. E&W | 25W-9N | 32 |
| Alden Ln. N&S | 24W-10N | 32 |
| Alder Ct. N&S | 24W-10N | 32 |
| Alexandra Ct. E&W | 24W-9N | 32 |
| Algonquin Rd. NW&SE | 22W-13N | 23 |
| Allcott Ct. E&W | 25W-9N | 32 |
| Allison Ln. E&W | 25W-11N | 32 |
| Allonby Dr. NW&SE | 24W-11N | 32 |
| Alpine Dr. N&S | 25W-10N | 32 |
| Altoona Ct. E&W | 25W-11N | 32 |
| Amanda Ln. E&W | 23W-12N | 22 |
| Amber Ct. NW&SE | 27W-10N | 31 |
| Amboy Ln. N&S | 25W-10N | 32 |
| American Ln. E&W | 22W-11N,21W-11N | 33 |
| Amherst Dr. NE&SW | 25W-10N | 32 |
| Andover Ct.* E&W | 24W-14N | 22 |
| Andrew Ct. E&W | 24W-9N | 32 |
| Andrew Ln. N&S | 24W-8N,24W-9N | 32 |
| Andria Ct. E&W | 26W-11N | 31 |
| Angus Ct.* E&W | 23W-13N | 22 |
| Apple Dr. N&S | 25W-11N | 32 |
| Arbor Dr. NS&EW | 21W-12N,20W-12N | 23 |
| Arbor Sq. N&S | 21W-12N | 23 |
| Ardmore Ct. E&W | 24W-9N | 32 |
| Argyll Ln. N&S | 24W-11N | 32 |
| Arklow Pl. E&W | 26W-10N | 31 |
| Arleen Ct. NW&SE | 26W-10N | 31 |
| Arlington Ln. E&W | 25W-10N | 32 |
| Arrowwood Ct.* NE&SW | 21W-9N | 33 |
| Arthur Av. E&W | 23W-8N | 32 |
| Asbury Ln. N&S | 23W-9N | 32 |
| Ascot Cir. NS&EW | 23W-10N | 32 |
| Ash Ct. N&S | 24W-9N | 32 |
| Ashburn Ct NW&SE | 27W-10N | 31 |
| Ashcroft Ln. N&S | 23W-10N | 32 |
| Ashley Ln. N&S | 25W-11N | 32 |
| Ashling Ct. E&W | 27W-10N | 31 |
| Ashton Ct. N&S | 23W-9N | 32 |
| Ashwood Ct. N&S | 24W-9N | 32 |
| Ashwood Dr. NE&SW | 24W-9N,23W-9N | 32 |
| Aspen Ct. E&W | 25W-10N | 32 |
| Aspen Dr. N&S | 25W-10N | 32 |
| Aster Dr. N&S | 21W-10N | 33 |
| Athena Ct. E&W | 24W-9N | 32 |
| Attleboro Ct. N&S | 24W-9N | 32 |
| Auburn Cir. E&W | 25W-9N | 32 |
| Auburn Ln. N&S | 25W-9N | 32 |
| Austin Ln. NS&EW | 23W-12N | 22 |
| nw&se | 25w-8n | 32 |
| Avon Ct. E&W | 25W-8N | 32 |
| Azalea Dr.* NS&EW | 20W-10N | 33 |
| Bahama Ct. N&S | 24W-9N | 32 |
| Bahama Ln. N&S | 24W-9N | 32 |
| Balboa Ct. NE&SW | 24W-9N | 32 |
| Baldwin Ct. E&W | 26W-10N | 31 |
| Balsam Ct. E&W | 24W-10N,23W-10N | 32 |
| Banbury Ct. NW&SE | 26W-11N | 31 |
| Bank Dr. NS&EW | 21W-11N | 33 |
| Bar Harbour Rd. N&S | 21W-10N | 33 |
| Barcliffe Ln. N&S | 24W-10N | 32 |
| Bardsey Dr. N&S | 25W-10N | 32 |
| Bark Wood Rd. NE&SW | 21W-13N | 23 |
| Barrett Ln. E&W | 23W-9N | 32 |
| Barrington Rd. N&S | 27W-10N | 31 |
| Barton Cir. NS&EW | 23W-10N | 32 |
| Basswood Rd. N&S | 22W-12N | 23 |
| Bates Ct. N&S | 25W-9N | 32 |
| Bates Ln. E&W | 25W-9N | 32 |
| Bayshore Dr. NE&SW | 24W-11N | 32 |
| Bayview Pt. E&W | 22W-10N | 33 |
| Beach Comber Dr. N&S | 24W-9N | 32 |
| Beacon Dr. N&S | 24W-9N | 32 |
| Beckett Ln. E&W | 21W-10N | 33 |
| Bedford Ct. N&S | 24W-9N | 32 |
| Beech Ct. NE&SW | 23W-9N | 32 |
| Beech Dr. E&W | 23W-10N,22W-10N | 32 |
| Beechmont Ct. N&S | 27W-10N | 31 |
| Beechwood Ct. SW&NE | 21W-10N | 33 |
| Belinder Ln. E&W | 21W-13N | 23 |
| Belmont Ct.* E&W | 23W-14N | 22 |
| Bent Tree Ln. E&W | 23W-12N | 22 |
| Bentley Ln. E&W | 23W-9N | 32 |
| Benwick Ct. NW&SE | 23W-9N | 32 |
| Berkley Ct. E&W | 22W-10N | 33 |
| Berkshire Ct. E&W | 22W-9N | 33 |
| Berkshire Ln. E&W | 22W-9N | 33 |
| Berry Ct. E&W | 26W-11N | 31 |
| Beverly Ct. E&W | 23W-9N | 32 |
| Birch Pl. E&W | 21W-12N | 23 |
| Birdsong Ct. E&W | 26W-11N | 31 |
| Bishop Ct.* N&S | 23W-13N | 22 |
| Bittersweet Ct. NW&SE | 23W-10N | 32 |
| Blackhawk Ct. N&S | 22W-9N | 33 |
| Bladon Rd. N&S | 24W-12N | 22 |
| Blaine Ct. NW&SE | 21W-13N | 23 |
| Blandford Ct. E&W | 21W-10N | 33 |
| Blenheim Dr. NW&SE | 24W-12N | 22 |
| Bode Rd. E&W | 26W-11N,25W-11N | 31 |
| Bonded Pkwy. N&S | 27W-10N | 31 |
| Cir. | 22W-9N | 33 |
| Bourne Ln. NW&SE | 24W-9N | 32 |
| Boxwood Dr. NS&EW | 24W-9N | 32 |
| Bradford Ct. N&S | 24W-9N | 32 |
| Bradford Ln. E&W | 24W-9N | 32 |
| Braintree Ct. NE&SW | 25W-10N | 32 |
| Braintree Dr. N&S | 25W-9N,25W-10N | 32 |
| Bramble Ct. NW&SE | 24W-10N | 32 |
| Bramble Ln. NE&SW | 24W-10N | 32 |
| Branchwood Ct. E&W | 23W-10N | 32 |
| Branchwood Dr. NE&SW | 23W-10N | 32 |
| Breakers Pt. E&W | 22W-10N | 33 |
| Brendon Dr. N&S | 26W-11N | 31 |
| Brent Ct. E&W | 26W-10N | 31 |
| Brentwood Ct. N&S | 24W-9N | 32 |
| Brewster Ln. N&S | 25W-9N | 32 |
| Brian Av. N&S | 26W-11N | 31 |
| Briar Hill Dr. E&W | 26W-11N | 31 |
| Briar Trail N&S | 21W-13N | 23 |
| Briarwood Ct. N&S | 24W-10N | 32 |
| Bridgeport Dr. N&S | 22W-8N | 33 |
| Bridgeview Pt. E&W | 22W-10N | 33 |
| Bridle Ln. N&S | 21W-11N | 33 |
| Bridlewood Ct.* NW&SE | 20W-10N | 33 |
| Bright Ridge Dr. NS&EW | 22W-10N | 33 |
| Brighton Ct. NW&SE | 24W-9N | 32 |
| Brightridge Dr. E&W | 22W-10N | 33 |
| Bristol Ln. N&S | 24W-11N | 32 |
| Brittany Ct.* E&W | 23W-13N | 22 |
| Brixham Pl. N&S | 25W-10N | 32 |
| Broadway Ln. NS&EW | 26W-10N | 31 |
| Brockton Ln. NS&EW | 25W-9N | 32 |
| Bromley Ct.* E&W | 23W-13N | 22 |
| Brookhill Ct. E&W | 23W-9N | 32 |
| Brookside Ln. N&S | 21W-13N | 23 |
| Brookston Ct.* N&S | 21W-9N | 33 |
| Brookston Dr. N&S | 21W-10N | 33 |
| Brown Ct. N&S | 25W-9N | 32 |
| Brunswick Cir. NW&SE | 23W-9N | 32 |
| Brunswick Harbor* N&S | 22W-9N | 33 |
| Brush Rd. N&S | 21W-13N | 23 |
| Bryn Mawr Ct.* E&W | 24W-13N | 22 |
| Buccaneer Dr. E&W | 21W-13N | 23 |
| Buckingham Ct.* N&S | 21W-9N | 33 |
| Burberry Cir.* NW&SE | 20W-10N | 33 |
| Burberry Ln.* E&W | 20W-10N | 33 |
| Burgess Ct.* N&S | 24W-13N | 22 |
| Burke Ct. N&S | 22W-10N | 33 |
| Burnley Cir. E&W | 22W-10N | 33 |
| Burr Oak Ln. NW&SE | 23W-10N | 32 |
| Buttercup Ln. N&S | 21W-11N | 33 |
| Buttonwood Cir.* NS&EW | 20W-9N | 33 |
| Cable Ct. NW&SE | 25W-9N | 32 |
| Cabot Ln. E&W | 25W-9N | 32 |
| Cambia Dr. E&W | 23W-8N | 32 |
| Cambourne Ln. E&W | 25W-10N | 32 |
| Cambridge Dr. N&S | 25W-9N,24W-9N | 32 |
| Camden Ct. NW&SE | 26W-10N | 31 |
| Camellia Ln. E&W | 21W-11N | 33 |
| Cannon Ct. NW&SE | 25W-9N | 32 |
| Canterbury Dr. NW&SE | 24W-12N | 22 |
| Cape Ln. N&S | 25W-9N | 32 |
| Capital Ct. NW&SE | 25W-9N | 32 |
| Capri Ln. NW&SE | 25W-9N | 32 |
| Cardiff Ct.* E&W | 23W-13N | 22 |
| Cardinal Ct.* E&W | 24W-13N | 22 |
| Carlisle Ct.* E&W | 23W-13N | 22 |
| Carlton Ct. N&S | 24W-10N | 32 |
| Carlton Ln. NW&SE | 24W-10N | 32 |
| Carmelhead Ln. E&W | 23W-10N | 32 |
| Carnaby Ct.* N&S | 23W-13N | 22 |
| Carolina Ct. N&S | 25W-8N | 32 |
| Caron Ct. N&S | 25W-9N | 32 |
| Carr Ct. N&S | 25W-9N | 32 |
| Carriage Ct. E&W | 22W-9N | 33 |
| Carriage Ln. N&S | 22W-9N | 33 |
| Carson Ct. E&W | 25W-9N | 32 |
| Carver Ln. N&S | 25W-10N | 32 |
| Caryville Ln. N&S | 26W-10N | 31 |
| Casa Dr. E&W | 22W-11N | 33 |
| Case Ct. NE&SW | 25W-9N | 32 |
| Casey Ct. E&W | 21W-13N | 23 |
| Cedar Ct. N&S | 24W-10N | 32 |
| Cedarcrest Dr. NS&EW | 24W-9N,24W-10N | 32 |
| Center Ct. NS&EW | 23W-12N | 22 |
| Century Ct. E&W | 23W-10N | 32 |
| Chalfront Dr. E&W | 25W-11N | 32 |
| Champlaine Ct. N&S | 22W-8N | 33 |
| Charlene Ln. NW&SE | 24W-10N | 32 |
| Charleston Ct.* NE&SW | 27W-10N | 31 |
| Charleston Dr. E&W | 26W-10N | 31 |
| Charlotte Ct.* NE&SW | 27W-10N | 31 |
| Chartwell Rd. N&S | 24W-12N | 22 |
| Chatham Ct. N&S | 25W-10N | 32 |
| Chatham Ln. E&W | 25W-10N | 32 |
| Chatsworth Cir. NS&EW | 23W-10N,22W-10N | 32 |
| Chaucer Ct. E&W | 24W-9N | 32 |
| Chelsea Ln. E&W | 24W-9N | 32 |
| Cheltenham Pl. E&W | 25W-11N | 32 |
| Cherry Ct. N&S | 25W-11N | 32 |
| Cherry Dr. N&S | 25W-11N | 32 |
| Cherrywood Dr. N&S | 23W-10N | 32 |
| Chesapeake Ln. E&W | 25W-8N | 32 |
| Chesterfield Ct. N&S | 27W-10N | 31 |
| Chestnut Ct. NE&SW | 24W-9N | 32 |
| Cheswick Ct. NW&SE | 26W-10N | 31 |
| Chilmark Ln. N&S | 26W-10N | 31 |
| Chopin Ct. E&W | 24W-9N | 32 |
| Churchill Rd. N&S | 24W-12N | 22 |
| Civic Dr. N&S | 25W-10N | 32 |
| Claredon Springs Ct.* N&S | 23W-13N | 22 |
| Claridge Ct. NE&SW | 26W-11N | 31 |
| Classic Rd. E&W | 23W-9N | 32 |
| Clayton Cir.* NE&SW | 24W-13N | 22 |
| Clearbrook Ct. E&W | 23W-9N | 32 |
| Clearwater Ln. N&S | 22W-10N | 33 |
| Clematis Dr. NW&SE | 27W-10N | 31 |
| Cleveland Ct. N&S | 23W-10N | 32 |
| Clifton Ct. E&W | 24W-9N | 32 |
| Clipper Dr. N&S | 21W-13N | 23 |
| Cloud Ct. N&S | 25W-9N | 32 |
| Clover Ln. N&S | 25W-9N | 32 |
| Cloverdale Ln. NE&SW | 25W-10N | 32 |
| Cobbler Ln. NS&EW | 22W-10N | 33 |
| Cobblestone Ct.* SE&NW | 20W-10N | 33 |
| Colby Ln. NW&SE | 25W-9N | 32 |
| Cole Ct. NW&SE | 25W-9N | 32 |
| College Dr. NE&SW | 22W-13N | 23 |
| College Hill Cir. NS&EW | 22W-13N | 23 |
| Colony Lake Dr. NS&EW | 24W-11N | 32 |
| Columbia Ct.* N&S | 27W-10N | 31 |
| Columbine Cir. NW&SE | 21W-11N | 33 |
| Columbine Rd. NS&EW | 21W-11N | 33 |
| Colwyn Dr. E&W | 25W-11N,25W-10N | 32 |
| Commerce Dr. NS&EW | 23W-12N,22W-12N | 22 |

| Name | Grid | Page |
|---|---|---|
| Commodore Ct. E&W | 25W-8N | 32 |
| Commodore Ln. N&S | 25W-8N | 32 |
| Commons Dr. N&S | 22W-11N | 33 |
| Compton Ln. NW&SE | 25W-10N | 32 |
| Concord Ln. E&W | 25W-9N | 32 |
| Concordia Ln. NW&SE | 25W-9N | 32 |
| Continental Ln. NS&EW | 26W-10N | 31 |
| Cooper Ct. E&W | 22W-12N | 23 |
| Copperfield Ln. N&S | 23W-9N | 32 |
| Coral Ct. N&S | 25W-9N | 32 |
| Cornell Ln. N&S | 25W-9N | 32 |
| Corporate Crossing NE&SW | 21W-10N | 33 |
| Cottington Dr. E&W | 25W-11N | 32 |
| Cottington Ct. NE&SW | 25W-11N | 32 |
| Cottonwood Ct. E&W | 23W-9N | 32 |
| Cottonwood Ln. N&S | 23W-9N | 32 |
| Cotuit Ct. N&S | 25W-10N | 32 |
| Cougar Trail N&S | 22W-10N | 33 |
| Country Club Ln. N&S | 23W-9N | 32 |
| County Farm Ln. NS&EW | 26W-10N | 31 |
| Courtenay Ln. E&W | 23W-9N | 32 |
| Courtland Ct. N&S | 24W-9N | 32 |
| Cove Pt. N&S | 22W-10N | 33 |
| Covehill Ct. NE&SW | 24W-10N | 32 |
| Coventry Rd. N&S | 24W-12N | 22 |
| Coveside Ln. E&W | 24W-9N | 32 |
| Covington Pl. | 25W-10N | 32 |
| Crabtree Ln. N&S | 23W-8N | 32 |
| Cranbrook Ct. NS&EW | 24W-8N,24W-9N | 32 |
| Crandell Ln. E&W | 23W-9N | 32 |
| Crandon Ln. E&W | 23W-9N | 32 |
| Creek Bend Rd. N&S | 21W-13N | 23 |
| Creighton Ln. N&S | 23W-9N | 32 |
| Crescent Ln. NE&SW | 27W-10N | 31 |
| Crest E&W | 25W-8N | 32 |
| Crest Ct. N&S | 23W-8N,23W-9N | 32 |
| Crest St. N&S | 23W-8N | 32 |
| Crest Wood Ct. NE&SW | 23W-12N | 22 |
| Crooked Creek Rd. N&S | 21W-13N | 23 |
| Crown Ct. N&S | 23W-9N | 32 |
| Crystal Ct. N&S | 22W-9N | 33 |
| Crystal Ct., N. NW&SE | 22W-9N | 33 |
| Crystal Ct., S. NW&SE | 22W-9N | 33 |
| Cumberland Dr. N&S | 25W-10N | 32 |
| Cutters Mill Ct. N&S | 25W-11N | 32 |
| Cutters Mill Ln. N&S | 25W-11N | 32 |
| Cypress Ct. NW&SE | 23W-9N | 32 |
| Dana Ct. E&W | 23W-9N | 32 |
| Danbury Ct. E&W | 23W-9N | 32 |
| Daniels Ct. E&W | 24W-11N | 32 |
| Dansforth Dr. E&W | 23W-9N | 32 |
| Dante Ct. E&W | 24W-9N | 32 |
| Danvers Ct.* E&W | 23W-14N | 22 |
| Dartford Ln. N&S | 25W-10N | 32 |
| Dartmouth Ln. NS&EW | 25W-9N | 32 |
| Debbie Ln. NW&SE | 27W-10N | 31 |
| Deborah Ct. N&S | 23W-9N | 32 |
| Dedham Ct. E&W | 25W-9N | 32 |
| Deerfield Ct. E&W | 24W-13N | 22 |
| Deerpath Ct.* N&S | 21W-9N | 33 |
| Del Lago Dr. N&S | 22W-11N | 33 |
| Delaware Ct. NE&SW | 27W-10N | 31 |
| Denham Pl. E&W | 25W-11N | 32 |
| Dennis Ct. N&S | 25W-9N | 32 |
| Denton Ct.* E&W | 24W-14N | 22 |
| Derby Ct. E&W | 23W-9N | 32 |
| Derry Ct. E&W | 23W-9N | 32 |
| Desmond Dr. E&W | 24W-9N,23W-9N | 32 |
| Devon Av. E&W | 23W-8N | 32 |
| Devonshire Ct.* NE&SW | 20W-10N | 33 |
| Dickens Way N&S | 23W-9N | 32 |
| Dighton Ln. N&S | 22W-11N | 33 |
| Discovery Dr. E&W | 26W-11N | 31 |
| Dixie Ct. NW&SE | 25W-8N | 32 |
| Dogwood Ct.* E&W | 24W-13N | 22 |
| Donna Ct. N&S | 23W-9N | 32 |
| Dorchester Ct.* N&S | 24W-13N | 22 |
| Dorset Ln. E&W | 23W-9N | 32 |
| Dorshire Ct.* N&S | 27W-10N | 31 |
| Dover Ct. N&S | 23W-9N | 32 |
| Downing Dr. E&W | 24W-12N | 22 |
| Dracut Ln. NS&EW | 22W-11N | 33 |
| Drake Cir. E&W | 22W-9N | 33 |
| Drake Ct. NW&SE | 22W-9N | 33 |
| Driftwood Ln.* N&S | 21W-9N | 33 |
| Drummer Dr. E&W | 21W-12N | 23 |
| Dublin Ln. NW&SE | 26W-10N | 31 |
| Dumont Ln. E&W | 25W-11N | 32 |
| Dunbar Ct.* N&S | 23W-13N | 22 |
| Dunlap Pl. N&S | 25W-10N | 32 |
| Dunsford Ct.* E&W | 23W-13N | 22 |
| Durham Ct. N&S | 22W-9N | 33 |
| Duxbury Ct. NW&SE | 24W-9N | 32 |
| Duxbury Ln. E&W | 24W-9N | 32 |
| Eagle Ct.* N&S | 24W-13N | 22 |
| East Point Rd. N&S | 22W-9N | 33 |
| East Wood Ct. SW&NE | 23W-12N | 22 |
| Eastham Ct. N&S | 25W-10N | 32 |
| Eastham Ln. E&W | 25W-10N | 32 |
| Eastview Ct. E&W | 22W-10N | 33 |
| Eaton Ct. NW&SE | 23W-9N | 32 |
| Ebbtide Pt. E&W | 22W-10N | 33 |
| Eden Dr. E&W | 24W-12N | 22 |
| Edgelake Pt.* E&W | 22W-10N | 33 |
| Effingham Ct. NE&SW | 27W-10N | 31 |
| Elgin Ln. N&S | 25W-11N | 32 |
| Ellington Dr. N&S | 25W-10N | 32 |
| Ellisville Ln. E&W | 25W-10N | 32 |
| Elm Dr. NE&SW | 25W-10N | 32 |
| Elmhurst Ln. NW&SE | 25W-11N | 32 |
| Elmont Ct. NE&SW | 22W-10N | 33 |
| Elmwood Ln.* N&S | 21W-10N | 33 |
| Emerald Dr. E&W | 22W-11N | 33 |
| Emerson Dr. N&S | 25W-10N | 32 |
| Epping Pl. E&W | 25W-11N | 32 |
| Essex Ct. N&S | 25W-10N | 32 |
| Estes Av. E&W | 24W-8N | 32 |
| Estes Ct. E&W | 24W-8N | 32 |
| Evening Song Ct. N&S | 26W-11N | 31 |
| Evergreen Ct. E&W | 23W-10N | 32 |
| Exeter Ct. N&S | 23W-9N | 32 |
| Exmore Dr. E&W | 25W-10N | 32 |
| Fabish Ct. E&W | 26W-10N | 31 |
| Fairbanks Ct. E&W | 22W-10N | 33 |
| Fairfield Ct. N&S | 23W-10N | 32 |
| Fairfield Ln. N&S | 25W-10N | 32 |
| Fairhaven Ln. E&W | 25W-11N | 32 |
| Fairlane Ct. N&S | 24W-10N | 32 |
| Fairlane Dr. N&S | 25W-8N,25W-9N | 32 |
| Fairview Ln. N&S | 24W-9N | 32 |
| Falbrook Ct. NW&SE | 27W-10N | 31 |
| Falmouth Ln. NW&SE | 25W-9N | 32 |
| Farmgate Dr. E&W | 23W-9N | 32 |
| Farnham Ct. E&W | 25W-11N | 32 |
| Featherstone Ct. E&W | 26W-10N | 31 |
| Fennel Ct. N&S | 22W-9N | 33 |
| Fennel Ln. E&W | 22W-9N | 33 |
| Fenwick Ct.* E&W | 23W-13N | 22 |
| Fermi Ct. N&S | 24W-10N | 32 |
| Fern Ct. N&S | 23W-9N | 32 |
| Ferndale Ct.* N&S | 21W-9N | 33 |
| Fieldstone Ct. E&W | 24W-11N | 32 |
| Finchley Ct.* E&W | 23W-13N | 22 |
| Fiskeville Ln.* E&W | 23W-14N | 22 |
| Fleming Ln. E&W | 23W-9N | 32 |
| Flintshire Dr. N&S | 25W-11N | 32 |
| Flower Ct.* E&W | 24W-13N | 22 |
| Forest Ct. N&S | 23W-10N | 32 |
| Forest Ln. E&W | 24W-10N,23W-10N | 32 |
| Forestdale Ct. E&W | 23W-9N | 32 |
| Foxboro Ct. N&S | 24W-9N | 32 |
| Foxboro Ln. N&S | 24W-9N | 32 |
| Foxwood Ct. NW&SE | 24W-11N | 32 |
| Fremont Ct. NW&SE | 27W-10N | 31 |
| Gareth Ct. N&S | 24W-10N | 32 |
| Garnet Cir. NW&SE | 23W-9N | 32 |
| Gayton Ln. N&S | 24W-9N | 32 |
| Geneva Ct. E&W | 23W-9N | 32 |
| Georgean Ln. E&W | 24W-10N | 32 |
| Georgia Ct. E&W | 25W-8N | 32 |
| Gilcrest Ct. N&S | 27W-10N | 31 |
| Glasgow Ct. N&S | 26W-10N | 31 |
| Glasgow Ln. N&S | 26W-10N | 31 |
| Glastonbury Ln.* E&W | 23W-13N | 22 |
| Glen Bryn Ct. NE&SW | 27W-10N | 31 |
| Glen Laven Ct. E&W | 27W-10N | 31 |
| Glengary Ct. N&S | 26W-10N | 31 |
| Glenn Ct. N&S | 23W-9N | 32 |
| Glenridge Ln. N&S | 26W-10N | 31 |
| Glenview Ct. E&W | 23W-14N | 22 |
| Glouchester Cir. NW&SE | 23W-9N | 32 |
| Glouchester Harbor* N&S | 22W-9N | 33 |
| Golf Rd. E&W | 26W-11N,21W-11N | 31 |
| Good Speed Ln. NE&SW | 26W-11N | 31 |
| Governor's Dr. N&S | 23W-9N | 32 |
| Grace Ct. E&W | 24W-9N | 32 |
| Grace Ln. N&S | 24W-9N | 32 |
| Grand Central Ln. NW&SE | 24W-10N | 32 |
| Gray Ct. N&S | 25W-8N | 32 |
| Green Briar Dr. E&W | 21W-10N | 33 |
| Green Bridge Ct. NE&SW | 26W-10N | 31 |
| Green River Ct. NW&SE | 25W-11N | 32 |
| Green River Dr. NS&EW | 25W-11N | 32 |
| Greenhill Ln. NS&EW | 22W-10N | 33 |
| Greenview Ct. N&S | 23W-8N | 32 |
| Gregory Ct. E&W | 23W-9N | 32 |
| Gregory Ln. N&S | 24W-9N,23W-9N | 32 |
| Greystone Ct.* N&S | 21W-9N | 33 |
| Groen Ct. E&W | 22W-9N | 33 |
| Groen Ln. E&W | 22W-9N | 33 |
| Groton Ct.* E&W | 23W-13N | 22 |
| Grove Av. E&W | 25W-8N | 32 |
| Grovenor Dr. E&W | 23W-9N | 32 |
| Hackberry Ct. N&S | 23W-10N | 32 |
| Hadley Run Ln. E&W | 22W-10N | 33 |
| Halifax Ct. N&S | 24W-9N | 32 |
| Hamilton Cir.* E&W | 24W-13N | 22 |
| Hamilton Pl.* E&W | 24W-13N | 22 |
| Hammond Dr. NE&SW | 22W-12N,21W-13N | 23 |
| Hampshire Ct. N&S | 22W-9N | 33 |
| Hampton Cir. N&S | 22W-9N | 33 |
| Hampton Ln. E&W | 22W-9N | 32 |
| Hanley Ct.* E&W | 23W-13N | 22 |
| Hanover Ct. E&W | 23W-9N | 32 |
| Hanscom Ct. E&W | 26W-10N | 31 |
| Harbour Ct. NW&SE | 25W-8N | 32 |
| Hartford Ct. NE&SW | 23W-9N | 32 |
| Hartford Dr. E&W | 23W-9N,22W-9N | 32 |
| Hartley Rd. E&W | 21W-12N | 23 |
| Hartmann Dr. E&W | 25W-9N | 32 |
| Harvard Cir. E&W | 25W-9N | 32 |
| Harvard Ln. NS&EW | 25W-9N | 32 |
| Harwich Ln. E&W | 24W-10N | 32 |
| Hastings Ct.* E&W | 23W-14N | 22 |
| Haverford Ct.* NW&SE | 20W-10N | 33 |
| Haverhill Ln. N&S | 26W-10N | 31 |
| Hawk Ct. N&S | 27W-10N | 31 |
| Hawthorne Ct.* N&S | 21W-9N | 33 |
| Hazel Dr. N&S | 23W-9N,23W-10N | 32 |
| Heather Ct.* N&S | 21W-9N | 33 |
| Heatherstone Dr. NE&SW | 22W-11N | 33 |
| Heatherwood Ct. E&W | 27W-10N | 31 |
| Heatherwood Dr. E&W | 27W-10N | 31 |
| Helene Ln. E&W | 24W-10N | 32 |
| Hemlock Pl. N&S | 21W-12N | 23 |
| Heron Av. NE&SW | 25W-8N | 32 |
| Heron Ct. NW&SE | 25W-8N | 32 |
| Hickory Ct. N&S | 23W-10N | 32 |
| Hickory Ln. E&W | 24W-10N,23W-10N | 32 |
| Higgins Rd. N&S | 22W-11N,21W-11N | 33 |
| Highland Ct. NE&SW | 26W-10N | 31 |
| Highpoint Ct. N&S | 22W-9N | 33 |
| Hillside Ct. E&W | 23W-9N | 32 |
| Hilltop Ct. E&W | 24W-10N | 32 |
| Hilltop Dr. N&S | 24W-10N | 32 |
| Hillwick Ln. N&S | 22W-10N | 33 |
| Hingham Ct. E&W | 24W-9N | 32 |
| Hingham Ln. NE&SW | 24W-9N | 32 |
| Hinkle Ct. E&W | 24W-10N | 32 |
| Hinkle Ln. N&S | 24W-10N | 32 |
| Hitching Post Ln. NS&EW | 26W-10N,26W-11N | 31 |
| Holliston Ct.* N&S | 23W-13N | 22 |
| Holmes Way E&W | 26W-10N | 31 |
| Holmes Way NE&SW | 27W-10N | 31 |
| Holyoke Ct. NE&SW | 23W-9N | 32 |
| Houlton Ct. NW&SE | 23W-9N | 32 |
| Howard Dr. N&S | 23W-9N | 32 |
| Hunt Wyck Ct.* E&W | 20W-10N | 33 |
| Hunterdon Ct. NE&SW | 27W-10N | 31 |
| Hunters Ct. E&W | 23W-9N | 32 |
| Huntington Ln. N&S | 23W-9N | 32 |
| Huntly Ct.* N&S | 24W-14N | 22 |
| Hyannis Ct. E&W | 24W-10N | 32 |
| Hyde Ct.* E&W | 24W-13N | 22 |
| Idle Wild Ct. N&S | 22W-11N | 33 |
| Idlestone Ln. N&S | 25W-10N | 32 |
| Illinois Av. E&W | 23W-10N | 32 |
| Indian Hill Dr. N&S | 23W-8N | 32 |
| Interstate 290 N&S | 21W-10N,20W-12N | 33 |
| Interstate 90 E&W | 23W-12N,21W-12N | 22 |
| Ironwood Ct.* E&W | 21W-9N | 33 |
| Irving Park Rd. NW&SE | 25W-8N,24W-8N | 32 |
| Island Ct. N&S | 27W-10N | 31 |
| Islington Ln. N&S | 26W-10N | 31 |
| Iverson Ct. N&S | 25W-11N | 32 |
| Ivy Ct. E&W | 26W-10N | 31 |
| James Ct. NE&SW | 25W-11N | 32 |
| Jamestown Ct. N&S | 23W-9N | 32 |
| Janine Ln. E&W | 24W-9N | 32 |
| Jeffrey Ct. N&S | 24W-10N | 32 |
| Jeffrey Ln. E&W | 24W-10N | 32 |
| Jessica Ln. N&S | 21W-13N | 23 |
| John Ct. N&S | 23W-9N | 32 |
| John Rolfe Dr. E&W | 26W-11N | 31 |
| John Smith Dr. E&W | 26W-11N | 31 |
| Jones Rd. N&S | 24W-11N,24W-12N | 32 |
| Juli Ct. E&W | 23W-9N | 32 |
| Juli Ln. N&S | 23W-9N | 32 |
| Juniper Ln. E&W | 24W-9N | 32 |
| Kavalier Ct.* E&W | 24W-13N | 22 |
| Keats Ct. E&W | 24W-9N | 32 |
| Kemah Ct. NE&SW | 24W-10N | 32 |
| Kemah Ln. NS&EW | 24W-10N | 32 |
| Kendall Ct.* N&S | 24W-13N | 22 |
| Kendrick Ct. N&S | 24W-9N | 32 |
| Kenilworth Dr. E&W | 22W-10N | 33 |
| Kenmore Ct. E&W | 26W-10N | 31 |
| Kensington Ct. E&W | 26W-11N | 31 |
| Kent Ct. E&W | 24W-9N | 32 |
| Kern Dr. E&W | 21W-11N | 33 |
| Killarney Ct. N&S | 23W-9N | 32 |
| Kimberly Dr. E&W | 21W-11N | 33 |
| Kings Mill Ct. NW&SE | 24W-12N | 22 |
| Kingsbury Dr. N&S | 26W-10N | 31 |
| Kingsley Dr. E&W | 25W-11N | 32 |
| Kingsport Ln. E&W | 23W-9N | 32 |
| Kingston Ct. N&S | 25W-9N | 32 |
| Kingston Dr. E&W | 25W-9N | 32 |
| Kingston Ln. E&W | 25W-9N | 32 |
| Kirkwall Ln. E&W | 24W-10N | 32 |
| Knightsbridge Ln. NW&SE | 24W-12N | 22 |
| Knollwood Ct.* E&W | 24W-13N | 22 |
| Knollwood Dr. N&S | 26W-10N,26W-11N | 31 |
| Knottingham Ct. N&S | 22W-8N | 33 |
| Knottingham Dr. NE&SW | 22W-8N | 33 |
| Kristin Cir. E&W | 23W-12N | 22 |
| Kristin Dr. E&W | 23W-12N | 22 |
| La Ron Ct. NE&SW | 25W-11N | 32 |
| Laconia Ln. E&W | 24W-10N | 32 |
| Lakeland Ct. NE&SW | 22W-10N | 33 |
| Lakeland Dr. E&W | 22W-10N | 33 |
| Lakeview Pt. E&W | 22W-10N | 33 |
| Lambert Dr. E&W | 23W-10N | 32 |
| Lamorak Ct. N&S | 22W-10N | 33 |
| Lamorak Dr. N&S | 22W-10N | 33 |
| Lamorak Ln. E&W | 22W-10N | 33 |
| Lancashire Ct.* E&W | 23W-13N | 22 |
| Langley Ct. N&S | 23W-9N | 32 |
| Langley Dr. E&W | 23W-9N | 32 |
| Larch Ct. E&W | 27W-10N | 31 |
| Largo Ct.* E&W | 23W-13N | 22 |
| Laurel Ln. N&S | 23W-9N | 32 |
| Laurette Ct. N&S | 22W-9N | 33 |
| Lawn Ct. E&W | 26W-10N | 31 |
| Lawson Rd. | 26W-11N,25W-11N | 31 |
| Lear Ct. E&W | 24W-13N | 22 |
| Leeds Pass NW&SE | 25W-11N | 32 |
| Lela Ct. NW&SE | 24W-10N | 32 |
| Lela Ln. NE&SW | 24W-10N | 32 |
| Lengl Dr. E&W | 23W-9N | 32 |
| Lenox Ct. N&S | 26W-10N | 31 |
| Leonard Dr. NE&SW | 23W-8N | 32 |
| Leslie Ct. N&S | 26W-11N | 31 |
| Lewis Ct. E&W | 26W-11N | 31 |
| Lexington Cir. E&W | 21W-10N | 33 |
| Lexington Ln. | 21W-11N | 33 |
| Liberty Ct.* E&W | 24W-13N | 22 |
| Library Ct. N&S | 23W-10N | 32 |
| Library Ln. N&S | 23W-10N | 32 |
| Lighthouse Dr. N&S | 24W-9N | 32 |
| Lilac Ct. NW&SE | 25W-9N | 32 |
| Lily Ct. N&S | 23W-9N | 32 |
| Limerick Ln. N&S | 23W-9N | 32 |
| Lincoln Meadows Ct. NS&EW | 20W-10N | 33 |
| Lincoln Meadows Dr.* NE&SW | 20W-10N | 33 |
| Lincoln St. N&S | 23W-8N,23W-10N | 32 |
| Lincolnshire Ct. NW&SE | 23W-10N | 32 |
| Linsey Av. N&S | 26W-11N | 31 |
| Linton Ct. E&W | 25W-8N | 32 |
| Linwood Ln. E&W | 24W-10N | 32 |
| Lippitt Ct. NE&SW | 24W-9N | 32 |
| Locust Pl. E&W | 21W-12N | 23 |
| Long Boat Ct. N&S | 24W-11N | 32 |
| Long Boat Ln. E&W | 24W-11N | 32 |
| Long Meadow Dr. NS&EW | 23W-9N | 32 |
| Longtree Ct. E&W | 21W-12N | 23 |
| Lorelei Dr. E&W | 24W-9N | 32 |
| Lowell Cir. N&S | 24W-9N | 32 |
| Lowell Ln. E&W | 24W-9N | 32 |
| Lundy Ln. N&S | 23W-10N | 32 |
| Lunt Av. E&W | 24W-8N,23W-8N | 32 |
| Luther Dr. E&W | 23W-10N | 32 |
| Lynnfield Ln. N&S | 26W-10N | 31 |
| Magnolia Ct. N&S | 23W-10N | 32 |
| Maidstone Ct. N&S | 27W-10N | 31 |
| Malden Ct. N&S | 23W-9N | 32 |
| Mall Dr. N&S | 22W-11N | 33 |
| Mallard Cir. E&W | 22W-9N | 33 |
| Mallard Ct. NW&SE | 22W-9N | 33 |
| Mallow Ct. E&W | 26W-10N | 31 |
| Manchester Rd. N&S | 23W-9N | 32 |
| Manomet Ct. E&W | 22W-11N | 33 |
| Manomet Ln. E&W | 22W-11N | 33 |
| Manor Cir.* N&S | 24W-13N | 22 |
| Mansfield Ct. NW&SE | 25W-11N | 32 |
| Maple Pl. N&S | 21W-12N | 23 |
| Maplebrook Ct. E&W | 23W-10N | 32 |
| Maplewood Ct.* N&S | 21W-9N | 33 |
| Marble Hill Ct. N&S | 23W-10N | 32 |
| Margate Ct. N&S | 23W-10N | 32 |
| Maribel Ct. N&S | 27W-10N | 31 |
| Marie Ln. N&S | 24W-9N,24W-10N | 32 |
| Mariner Pt. N&S | 22W-10N | 33 |
| Martingale Rd. N&S | 21W-10N,21W-11N | 33 |
| Mashpee Ln. N&S | 24W-10N | 32 |
| Matfield Ct.* E&W | 23W-13N | 22 |
| Mayfair Ln.* N&S | 21W-9N | 33 |
| Maywood Ln. N&S | 26W-11N | 31 |
| McConnor Pkwy. E&W | 21W-12N | 23 |
| Meacham Rd. N&S | 21W-9N,21W-11N | 33 |
| Meadow Lane Ct. NW&SE | 27W-10N | 31 |
| Meadow Ln. N&S | 27W-10N | 31 |
| Medford Cir. N&S | 23W-9N | 32 |
| Melody Ct. N&S | 26W-11N | 31 |
| Mendon Ct. N&S | 26W-10N | 31 |
| Mercury Ct. N&S | 26W-9N | 32 |
| Mercury Dr. N&S | 25W-8N,25W-9N | 32 |
| Merlin Dr. NS&EW | 22W-9N | 33 |
| Mermaid Ct. NW&SE | 24W-9N | 32 |
| Middlebury Ct.* N&S | 21W-9N | 33 |
| Milan Ct. E&W | 23W-9N | 32 |
| Milford Ct. E&W | 24W-9N | 32 |
| Millbrook Ct. E&W | 25W-10N | 32 |
| Millbrook Ln. N&S | 25W-10N | 32 |
| Millis Ln. N&S | 26W-10N | 31 |
| Milton Ln. E&W | 25W-9N | 32 |
| Mistic Harbour Ln. E&W | 24W-9N | 32 |
| Mitchell Blvd. N&S | 24W-8N | 32 |
| Mohawk Ct. N&S | 22W-8N | 33 |
| Mohegan Ln.* N&S | 23W-13N | 22 |
| Monet Ct. N&S | 24W-9N | 32 |
| Monson Ct. N&S | 21W-10N | 33 |
| Monterey Av. E&W | 23W-8N | 32 |
| Mora Ct. E&W | 25W-8N | 32 |
| Morning Song Ct. N&S | 26W-11N | 31 |
| Morse Av. E&W | 24W-8N | 32 |
| Mullingar Ln. E&W | 23W-9N | 32 |
| N. Brookdale Dr. E&W | 25W-11N | 32 |
| Nantucket Harbor E&W | 23W-9N | 32 |
| National Pkwy. NS&EW | 22W-11N,23W-12N | 33 |
| Natwick Ln. N&S | 26W-10N | 31 |
| Nauset Ln. N&S | 24W-10N | 32 |
| Neal Ct. N&S | 22W-9N | 33 |
| New Mills Ct. N&S | 23W-10N | 32 |
| Newbury Ct. NW&SE | 22W-11N | 33 |
| Newbury Ln. NS&EW | 22W-11N | 33 |
| Newgate Ct. E&W | 23W-10N | 32 |
| Newport Harbor* NS&EW | 22W-9N | 33 |
| Newton Ct.* E&W | 24W-13N | 22 |
| Niagara Av. E&W | 23W-8N,22W-8N | 32 |
| Night Song Ct. NS&EW | 26W-11N | 31 |
| Norman Ct. E&W | 23W-9N | 32 |
| North Brookdale Rd. E&W | 25W-11N | 32 |
| North Point Dr. E&W | 22W-9N | 33 |

| Street | Grid | Page |
|---|---|---|
| Northbury Ct. E&W | 21W-10N | 33 |
| Northway Dr. N&S | 26W-10N | 31 |
| Northwest Tollway NW&SE | 23W-12N,21W-12N | 22 |
| Northwind Cir. E&W | 26W-11N | 31 |
| Norwell Ct. N&S | 25W-9N | 32 |
| Norwell Ln. E&W | 25W-9N | 32 |
| Norwood Ln. NE&SW | 24W-9N | 32 |
| Notis Ct. NS&EW | 24W-9N | 32 |
| Oak Creek Cir. NW&SE | 23W-10N | 32 |
| Oak Ct. NW&SE | 27W-10N | 31 |
| Oak Knoll Ct.* N&S | 21W-9N | 33 |
| Oak Lawn Ct. NS&EW | 23W-12N | 22 |
| Oak Meadow Ct. E&W | 21W-10N | 33 |
| Oakmont Ln. N&S | 22W-11N | 33 |
| Oakview Ct. E&W | 24W-10N | 32 |
| Oakwood Ct. NW&SE | 24W-9N | 32 |
| Odlum Ct. NW&SE | 27W-10N | 31 |
| Odlum Dr. NS&EW | 27W-10N | 31 |
| Office Sq. N&S | 21W-12N | 23 |
| Old Farm Rd. E&W | 21W-13N | 23 |
| Old Kings Ct.* N&S | 24W-13N | 22 |
| Old Mills Dr. N&S | 23W-9N | 32 |
| Old Schaumburg Rd. E&W | 21W-10N | 33 |
| Olde Oaks Rd. E&W | 21W-13N | 23 |
| Oleander Dr. NS&EW | 21W-11N | 33 |
| Oliver Ct. E&W | 23W-9N | 32 |
| Omni Dr. E&W | 23W-9N | 32 |
| Onyx Ct.* N&S | 24W-13N | 22 |
| Orchard Av. NW&SE | 25W-8N | 32 |
| Orleans Ln. N&S | 25W-9N,25W-10N | 32 |
| Orrington Ct. N&S | 22W-10N | 33 |
| Osage Ln. E&W | 24W-10N | 32 |
| Oxford Ct. NW&SE | 26W-11N,25W-11N | 31 |
| Oxhill Ct.* E&W | 24W-13N | 22 |
| Palace Ct.* E&W | 24W-13N | 22 |
| Palisades Pt. N&S | 22W-10N | 33 |
| Palmer Dr. NE&SW | 21W-13N | 23 |
| Park Dr. NW&SE | 25W-10N | 32 |
| Park Trail Ct.* N&S | 20W-10N | 33 |
| Parker Dr. E&W | 24W-11N | 32 |
| Parkville Rd. E&W | 26W-11N | 31 |
| Partridge Dr. E&W | 22W-8N | 33 |
| Patricia Ct. NW&SE | 24W-10N | 32 |
| Patricia Dr. N&S | 24W-10N | 32 |
| Patuxet Ct. N&S | 24W-10N | 32 |
| Paxton Ln. N&S | 25W-10N | 32 |
| Payne Rd. N&S | 22W-12N | 23 |
| Peach Ln. E&W | 25W-11N | 32 |
| Pebble Ct. E&W | 22W-9N | 33 |
| Pembridge Ln. NE&SW | 23W-10N | 32 |
| Pembroke Ct.* NE&SW | 27W-10N | 31 |
| Pembroke Dr. N&S | 26W-10N | 31 |
| Pennsbury Ct. E&W | 26W-10N | 31 |
| Pennview Ln. NW&SE | 26W-11N | 31 |
| Penny Ln. NS&EW | 22W-12N | 23 |
| Penrith Pl. E&W | 25W-10N | 32 |
| Penwood Ct. NE&SW | 21W-10N | 33 |
| Perimeter Dr. NS&EW | 21W-11N | 33 |
| Persimmon Ct. NW&SE | 25W-8N | 32 |
| Perth Dr. E&W | 24W-10N | 32 |
| Petersham Ln. E&W | 21W-10N | 33 |
| Pheasant Walk Dr. N&S | 23W-9N | 32 |
| Pickwick Dr. NW&SE | 23W-9N | 32 |
| Pine Valley Dr. N&S | 21W-13N | 23 |
| Pinehurst Ln. N&S | 24W-9N | 32 |
| Pinetree Ln.* N&S | 21W-9N | 33 |
| Pirates Cove N&S | 21W-13N | 23 |
| Plaza Dr. N&S | 21W-11N | 33 |
| Pleasant Dr. NS&EW | 23W-10N | 32 |
| Plum Grove Rd. N&S | 21W-13N | 23 |
| Plum Grove Rd. N&S | 22W-8N,22W-12N | 33 |
| Plum Tree Ct.* E&W | 21W-9N | 33 |
| Plumrose Ct. N&S | 23W-10N | 32 |
| Plumrose Ln. NS&EW | 23W-10N | 32 |
| Plumwood Ct. N&S | 22W-11N | 33 |
| Plumwood Dr. E&W | 22W-11N | 33 |
| Plymouth Ln. E&W | 25W-9N | 32 |
| Pocasset Ct. N&S | 25W-10N | 32 |
| Pochet Ct. NE&SW | 24W-10N | 32 |
| Pochet Ln. NW&SE | 24W-10N | 32 |
| Pond View Ct. NE&SW | 24W-10N | 32 |
| Popular Pl. N&S | 21W-12N | 23 |
| Portland Dr. N&S | 25W-11N | 32 |
| Portsmouth Ct. N&S | 25W-10N | 32 |
| Portsmouth Ln. E&W | 25W-10N | 32 |
| Post Oak Pl. N&S | 21W-12N | 23 |
| Prairie Sq. N&S | 21W-12N | 23 |
| Prairie Wind Ln. E&W | 21W-12N | 23 |
| Pratt Av., N. E&W | 24W-8N | 32 |
| Pratt Av., S. E&W | 24W-8N | 32 |
| Presidio Ct. E&W | 23W-12N | 22 |
| Preston Ln. E&W | 22W-9N | 33 |
| Primrose Ln. N&S | 26W-11N | 31 |
| Prince Charles Ct. E&W | 24W-12N | 22 |
| Prince Charles Ln. NW&SE | 24W-12N | 22 |
| Prince Edward Cir. NE&SW | 22W-9N | 33 |
| Prince Edward Dr. E&W | 22W-9N | 33 |
| Princeton Ct. N&S | 25W-9N | 32 |
| Princeton Ln. NS&EW | 25W-9N | 32 |
| Putnam Ln. E&W | 24W-9N | 32 |
| Pvt. Rd. NW&SE | 23W-12N | 22 |
| Quanset Ct. E&W | 24W-10N | 32 |
| Queen's Ct. N&S | 23W-9N | 32 |
| Quentin Rd. N&S | 22W-13N,21W-13N | 23 |
| Quincy Ct. E&W | 23W-9N | 32 |
| Quindel Av. E&W | 23W-10N | 32 |
| Radcliffe Ln. NE&SW | 25W-9N | 32 |
| Raleigh Ct.* NW&SE | 27W-10N | 31 |
| Ramsey Cir.* NS&EW | 24W-13N | 22 |
| Raymond Ct. N&S | 22W-9N | 33 |
| Rebecca Ct. E&W | 24W-9N | 32 |
| Redwood Ln. N&S | 24W-9N | 32 |
| Reedham Pass NE&SW | 25W-10N | 32 |
| Regal Ct. E&W | 25W-11N | 32 |
| Regatta Pt. NW&SE | 22W-10N | 33 |
| Regency Ct. N&S | 24W-8N | 32 |
| Regency Dr. NS&EW | 24W-8N | 32 |
| Regent Cir. N&S | 23W-10N | 32 |
| Remington Cir. NS&EW | 23W-12N | 22 |
| Remington Rd. E&W | 22W-12N,21W-12N | 23 |
| Republic Ct. N&S | 23W-9N | 32 |
| Revere Cir. NS&EW | 25W-10N | 32 |
| Richmond Ct.* E&W | 23W-13N | 22 |
| Ridge Ct. N&S | 22W-9N | 33 |
| Ridgeway Ct. NE&SW | 24W-11N | 32 |
| Ripplebrook Ct.* N&S | 20W-10N | 33 |
| Rob Roy Ct. NE&SW | 26W-10N | 31 |
| Rochester Ct. E&W | 26W-11N | 31 |
| Rockne Ct. NW&SE | 26W-10N | 31 |
| Rodenburg Rd. N&S | 24W-8N | 32 |
| Romm Ct. E&W | 26W-10N | 31 |
| Rose Ct. E&W | 26W-11N | 31 |
| Roselle Rd. N&S | 23W-8N,23W-10N | 32 |
| Rosewood Ct. E&W | 21W-10N | 33 |
| Roslyn Ln. E&W | 24W-11N | 32 |
| Rothbury Ct. N&S | 22W-9N | 33 |
| Routh Ct. NS&EW | 23W-12N | 22 |
| Roxbury Ln. NW&SE | 24W-11N | 32 |
| Royal Ct. E&W | 24W-9N | 32 |
| Rt. 19 NW&SE | 24W-8N | 32 |
| Rt. 58 E&W | 25W-12N,21W-12N | 22 |
| Rt. 72 NW&SE | 26W-12N,21W-11N | 21 |
| Rugby Pl. N&S | 24W-10N | 32 |
| Ruskin Ct.* N&S | 23W-13N | 22 |
| Russelwood Ct. NE&SW | 26W-10N | 31 |
| Russett Ct. N&S | 23W-9N | 32 |
| Rutland Ct.* E&W | 20W-10N | 33 |
| Rutland Ln. E&W | 21W-10N | 33 |
| Sagamore Ct. N&S | 24W-10N | 32 |
| Sagamore Dr. NS&EW | 24W-10N | 32 |
| Salado Ct. NS&EW | 23W-12N | 22 |
| Salem Ct. N&S | 24W-10N | 32 |
| Salem Dr. N&S | 24W-9N,24W-10N | 32 |
| Salford Dr. N&S | 22W-8N | 33 |
| Samoset Ct. E&W | 24W-10N | 32 |
| Samoset Ln. N&S | 24W-10N | 32 |
| Sandalwood Ln. NW&SE | 21W-10N | 33 |
| Sandburg Dr.* E&W | 20W-10N | 33 |
| Sandhurst Ct.* NW&SE | 21W-9N | 33 |
| Sandpebble Dr. NE&SW | 24W-9N | 32 |
| Sandy Ct. N&S | 24W-9N | 32 |
| Santuit Ct. E&W | 24W-10N | 32 |
| Sarah Constant Ln. N&S | 26W-11N | 31 |
| Sarahs Grove Ln. NS&EW | 23W-10N | 32 |
| Saugus Ln. N&S | 21W-10N | 33 |
| Savannah Ln. NS&EW | 25W-8N | 32 |
| Savoy Ct. N&S | 24W-9N | 32 |
| Saylesville Ln.* E&W | 23W-13N | 22 |
| Scarsdale Ct.* N&S | 21W-9N | 33 |
| Schaumburg Ct. NW&SE | 22W-10N | 33 |
| Schaumburg Rd. E&W | 26W-10N,22W-10N | 31 |
| Schreiber Av. E&W | 23W-8N | 32 |
| Scott Dr. E&W | 22W-8N | 33 |
| Scully Ct. N&S | 23W-10N | 32 |
| Scully Dr. E&W | 23W-10N | 32 |
| Seafarer Dr. E&W | 24W-9N | 32 |
| Seaside Ct. NW&SE | 24W-9N | 32 |
| Seaton Ln. E&W | 25W-10N | 32 |
| Seaview Ct. N&S | 24W-9N | 32 |
| Sedgfield Ct. E&W | 26W-10N | 31 |
| Selkirk Dr. N&S | 25W-11N | 32 |
| Sequoia Ct. N&S | 23W-9N | 32 |
| Serenade Ct. E&W | 23W-9N | 32 |
| Seven Pines Rd. E&W | 21W-10N | 33 |
| Seville Ct. NW&SE | 25W-8N | 32 |
| Shady Ln. E&W | 21W-10N | 33 |
| Shagbark Ct. N&S | 23W-10N | 32 |
| Shakespeare Ct. E&W | 25W-10N | 32 |
| Shannock Ln.* N&S | 23W-13N | 22 |
| Sharon Ln. E&W | 25W-10N,24W-10N | 32 |
| Shattuck Ct. N&S | 24W-10N | 32 |
| Shattuck Ln. E&W | 24W-10N | 32 |
| Shaw Ct.* N&S | 24W-13N | 22 |
| Sheffield Dr. NW&SE | 27W-10N | 31 |
| Shell Ct. NE&SW | 24W-9N | 32 |
| Sherborn Ln. E&W | 26W-10N | 31 |
| Sheridan Ln. N&S | 23W-9N | 32 |
| Sherwood Ln. E&W | 22W-10N | 33 |
| Shore Ct. N&S | 23W-9N | 32 |
| Shore Dr. NS&EW | 23W-9N | 32 |
| Shoreline Cir. NW&SE | 22W-10N | 33 |
| Sienna Ct. NW&SE | 23W-9N | 32 |
| Sienna Dr. NS&EW | 23W-9N | 32 |
| Silverwood Ct. N&S | 21W-9N | 33 |
| Sky Water Dr. NW&SE | 21W-12N | 23 |
| Skyvue Ln. N&S | 26W-10N | 31 |
| Sleepy Hollow Ct. N&S | 23W-12N | 22 |
| Slingerland Dr. SW&NE | 25W-9N | 32 |
| Small Dr. E&W | 27W-10N | 31 |
| Somerset Ct. NW&SE | 25W-10N | 32 |
| Somerset Ln. E&W | 25W-10N | 32 |
| Song Sparrow Ct. E&W | 21W-12N | 23 |
| South Point Ct. N&S | 22W-8N | 33 |
| South Point Dr. E&W | 22W-8N | 33 |
| Southbridge Ct. E&W | 25W-11N | 32 |
| Southbridge Ln. NS&EW | 25W-11N | 32 |
| Southbury Ct.* E&W | 21W-9N | 33 |
| Southwick Ln. N&S | 21W-10N | 33 |
| Southwind Cir E&W | 26W-11N | 31 |
| Spinnaker Pt. E&W | 22W-10N | 33 |
| Spring Cove Dr. N&S | 24W-9N | 32 |
| Spring Creek Cir.* NE&SW | 20W-10N | 33 |
| Spring Valley Ct. NS&EW | 22W-10N | 33 |
| Springinsguth Rd. N&S | 25W-8N,25W-10N | 32 |
| Springwood Ct. E&W | 23W-8N | 32 |
| Springwood Dr. NW&SE | 23W-8N | 32 |
| Springwood Dr. NW&SE | 21W-10N | 33 |
| Spruce Ct. N&S | 24W-10N | 32 |
| Spruce Dr. NW&SE | 24W-10N | 32 |
| Squanto Ct. N&S | 24W-10N | 32 |
| Staffire Dr. N&S | 26W-10N | 31 |
| Staffmark Ln. N&S | 23W-10N | 32 |
| Stamford Ct. N&S | 23W-9N | 32 |
| Standish Ln. N&S | 25W-10N | 32 |
| Stanley Ct. NS&EW | 26W-11N | 31 |
| Stanton Ct. N&S | 23W-10N | 32 |
| Starboard Pt. E&W | 22W-10N | 33 |
| State Parkway NS&EW | 22W-11N,23W-12N | 33 |
| Steeplechase Ct.* NW&SE | 20W-10N | 33 |
| Stevens Dr. N&S | 21W-10N | 33 |
| Stirling Ln. NS&EW | 26W-10N | 31 |
| Stock Port Ln. NE&SW | 23W-10N | 32 |
| Stockbridge Ct.* N&S | 23W-14N | 22 |
| Stone Circle Ct. E&W | 22W-10N | 33 |
| Stone Gate Cir. NS&EW | 23W-9N | 32 |
| Stonefield Ct.* NE&SW | 20W-10N | 33 |
| Stonehedge Dr. N&S | 24W-11N | 32 |
| Stonehill Ln. E&W | 23W-10N | 32 |
| Stonington Ct.* NW&SE | 23W-14N | 22 |
| Stormy Ct. E&W | 25W-8N | 32 |
| Stoughton Ct. E&W | 24W-10N | 32 |
| Stratford Dr. E&W | 22W-9N | 33 |
| Stratham Ct. NW&SE | 24W-9N | 32 |
| Stratton Pond Ln. NE&SW | 25W-11N | 32 |
| Sturnbridge Ct. N&S | 22W-11N | 33 |
| Sturnbridge Ln. E&W | 22W-11N | 33 |
| Sudbury Ct.* E&W | 23W-13N | 22 |
| Suffield Ter. N&S | 23W-9N | 32 |
| Sumac Ct. NE&SW | 23W-10N | 32 |
| Sumac Ln. N&S | 23W-10N | 32 |
| Summer Song Ct. E&W | 26W-11N | 31 |
| Summit Ct. E&W | 23W-9N | 32 |
| Summit Dr. N&S | 23W-8N,23W-10N | 32 |
| Sunfish Pt. E&W | 22W-10N | 33 |
| Superior Ct. E&W | 23W-10N | 32 |
| Surf Dr. E&W | 22W-11N | 33 |
| Surfside Pt. E&W | 22W-10N | 33 |
| Surrey Ln. NS&EW | 22W-8N | 33 |
| Susan Ct. N&S | 22W-9N | 33 |
| Sussex Cir. N&S | 23W-10N | 32 |
| Sutton Ln. E&W | 25W-10N | 32 |
| Swansea Ct.* E&W | 23W-14N | 22 |
| Swartmore Ct. N&S | 25W-9N | 32 |
| Sycamore Pl. E&W | 21W-12N | 23 |
| Syracuse Ln. NW&SE | 25W-9N | 32 |
| Tadmore Ct. NW&SE | 25W-11N | 32 |
| Tall Timbers Rd. NS&EW | 21W-13N | 23 |
| Tamworth Pl. N&S | 25W-10N | 32 |
| Tarpon Ct. NW&SE | 24W-9N | 32 |
| Taunton Ct.* N&S | 23W-14N | 22 |
| Teal Ct. E&W | 23W-9N | 32 |
| Tebay Pl. N&S | 26W-11N,25W-11N | 31 |
| Terrace Ct. N&S | 22W-9N | 33 |
| Thacker Dr. E&W | 22W-11N | 33 |
| Thacker St. E&W | 22W-11N | 33 |
| Thacker St., E. E&W | 22W-11N | 33 |
| Thames Cir. N&S | 22W-9N | 33 |
| Thames Dr. NW&SE | 22W-9N | 33 |
| Thistle Ct. N&S | 26W-10N | 31 |
| Thoreau Ct. E&W | 25W-9N | 32 |
| Thoreau Dr., N. NS&EW | 21W-12N | 23 |
| Thorney Lea Ter. E&W | 24W-9N | 32 |
| Thornhill Ct.* N&S | 21W-9N | 33 |
| Thornton Ct. E&W | 22W-8N | 33 |
| Thornwood Dr. N&S | 23W-8N | 32 |
| Ticknor Ct. E&W | 25W-8N | 32 |
| Tiffany Dr. E&W | 26W-10N | 31 |
| Tilipi Ct. NE&SW | 24W-9N | 32 |
| Tilipi Ln. NW&SE | 24W-10N | 32 |
| Timbercrest Dr. N&S | 23W-10N | 32 |
| Timberwood Ct. NS&EW | 21W-10N | 33 |
| Timothy Ct. N&S | 22W-9N | 33 |
| Tipperary Ct. N&S | 23W-9N | 32 |
| Tisbury Ln. E&W | 24W-9N | 32 |
| Tiverton Ct. N&S | 24W-9N | 32 |
| Tobey Ct. E&W | 24W-10N | 32 |
| Tonset Ct. N&S | 25W-10N | 32 |
| Tonset Ln. E&W | 25W-10N | 32 |
| Tower Rd. E&W | 22W-12N,21W-12N | 23 |
| Tracy Ct. N&S | 23W-9N | 32 |
| Trails Dr. NE&SW | 22W-10N | 33 |
| Tralee Ct. N&S | 23W-9N | 32 |
| Travis Ct. E&W | 23W-12N | 22 |
| Treebark Ct. E&W | 24W-10N | 32 |
| Treebark Dr. NW&SE | 24W-10N | 32 |
| Trent Ln. NS&EW | 22W-9N | 33 |
| Trenton Ct. N&S | 22W-10N | 33 |
| Truro Ct. N&S | 24W-10N | 32 |
| Tudor Ln. N&S | 23W-10N | 32 |
| Tulip Ct. N&S | 26W-10N | 31 |
| Tullamore Ct. N&S | 23W-9N | 32 |
| Tyburn Dr. E&W | 25W-10N | 32 |
| Tyler Dr. N&S | 23W-9N | 32 |
| Vada Ct. E&W | 25W-8N | 32 |
| Valley Lake Dr. NS&EW | 23W-12N | 22 |
| Valley View Dr. E&W | 25W-8N | 32 |
| Vasser Ct. NE&SW | 25W-9N | 32 |
| Vasser Ln. NW&SE | 25W-9N | 32 |
| Venice Ct. N&S | 24W-9N | 32 |
| Verde Dr. N&S | 22W-11N | 33 |
| Verona Ct. N&S | 24W-9N | 32 |
| Victoria Ln. E&W | 24W-10N | 32 |
| Viola Ct. NW&SE | 26W-11N | 31 |
| Vista Ct. E&W | 25W-8N | 32 |
| W. Remington Cir. N&S | 23W-12N | 22 |
| W. Remington Ln. E&W | 23W-12N | 22 |
| Waban Ct. N&S | 25W-10N | 32 |
| Waban Ln. NE&SW | 25W-10N | 32 |
| Wakeby Ln. E&W | 25W-10N | 32 |
| Wakefield Ln. NS&EW | 24W-10N | 32 |
| Walden Ct. N&S | 25W-9N | 32 |
| Walden Office Square N&S | 21W-12N | 23 |
| Walnut Ln. NS&EW | 26W-10N,26W-11N | 31 |
| Walpole Ln.* N&S | 23W-13N | 22 |
| Wapoos Ct. N&S | 24W-10N | 32 |
| Wareham Ln. N&S | 25W-10N | 32 |
| Warwick Ct. NE&SW | 26W-11N | 31 |
| Warwick Ln. E&W | 26W-10N,25W-10N | 31 |
| Washington St. N&S | 23W-8N | 32 |
| Waterbury Ln. N&S | 23W-10N | 32 |
| Waterford Dr. N&S | 22W-10N | 33 |
| Waterford Dr. NS&EW | 23W-9N | 32 |
| Waterfront Dr. N&S | 22W-11N | 33 |
| Waterville Ln. E&W | 25W-11N | 32 |
| Waverly Ln. N&S | 25W-10N | 32 |
| Wax Wing Ct. E&W | 21W-12N | 23 |
| Wayland Ct. N&S | 25W-10N | 32 |
| Wayland Ln. E&W | 25W-10N | 32 |
| Weathersfield Way N&S | 26W-10N,22W-9N | 31 |
| Webley Ct. E&W | 22W-9N | 33 |
| Webley Ln. N&S | 22W-9N | 33 |
| Webster Ct. N&S | 25W-10N | 32 |
| Webster Ln. N&S | 25W-9N,25W-10N | 32 |
| Wedgewood Ln. E&W | 25W-10N | 32 |
| Wellesly Ln. NE&SW | 25W-10N | 32 |
| Wellington Rd. E&W | 23W-12N | 22 |
| West Brookdale Rd. NE&SW | 25W-11N | 32 |
| West Frontage Rd. N&S | 21W-11N | 33 |
| West Minster Ct. N&S | 27W-10N | 31 |
| West Point Dr. N&S | 22W-9N | 33 |
| West Remington Cir. NS&EW | 23W-12N | 22 |
| Westbridge Ct. E&W | 25W-11N | 32 |
| Westbridge Ln. E&W | 25W-11N | 32 |
| Westchester Cir. N&S | 22W-9N | 33 |
| Westchester Rd. E&W | 22W-9N | 33 |
| Westfield Ln. E&W | 24W-9N | 32 |
| Weston Ln. E&W | 25W-10N | 32 |
| Westover Ct. N&S | 25W-10N | 32 |
| Westover Ln. NS&EW | 25W-9N,25W-10N | 32 |
| Weyers Ct. NW&SE | 25W-8N | 32 |
| Weymouth Ct. E&W | 25W-10N | 32 |
| Weymouth Ln. E&W | 25W-10N | 32 |
| Whalom Ln. E&W | 22W-11N | 33 |
| Whidah Ct. NS&EW | 24W-10N | 32 |
| White Branch Ct., N. NE&SW | 26W-10N | 31 |
| White Branch Ct., S. NE&SW | 26W-10N | 31 |
| White Oak Ct. E&W | 23W-12N | 22 |
| White Oak Ln. N&S | 23W-12N | 22 |
| White Pine Dr. NS&EW | 23W-10N | 32 |
| Whitehall Ct. N&S | 25W-11N | 32 |
| Whitesail Dr. E&W | 22W-10N | 33 |
| Whitheger Dr. N&S | 23W-12N | 22 |
| Whitman Ct.* E&W | 20W-10N | 33 |
| Whitman Dr. NE&SW | 21W-10N | 33 |
| Whittier Ct. N&S | 25W-10N | 32 |
| Whittier Ln. NS&EW | 25W-10N | 32 |
| Wianno Ln. N&S | 24W-10N | 32 |
| Wickham Dr. N&S | 25W-10N | 32 |
| Wildberry Ct.* N&S | 21W-9N | 33 |
| Wildflower Ln. NE&SW | 21W-10N | 33 |

| | Grid | Page |
|---|---|---|
| Wiley Rd. E&W | 22W-12N,21W-12N | 23 |
| Wilkening Ct. N&S | 23W-12N | 22 |
| Wilkening Rd. N&S | 23W-12N | 22 |
| Williams Ct. E&W | 24W-10N | 32 |
| Williams Dr. N&S | 24W-10N | 32 |
| Williamsburg Dr. E&W | 21W-10N | 33 |
| Willington Rd. E&W | 21W-11N | 32 |
| Willoby Ct.* E&W | 20W-10N | 33 |
| Willow Brook Ct. SE&NW | 23W-12N | 22 |
| Willow Rd. E&W | 21W-10N | 33 |
| Wilmette Ct. NW&SE | 21W-9N | 33 |
| Wilmslow Ln. N&S | 25W-10N | 32 |
| Wilton Ln. N&S | 25W-10N | 32 |
| Wiltshire St. E&W | 23W-9N | 32 |
| Winchester Ct. NW&SE | 25W-10N | 32 |
| Winchester Ln. E&W | 25W-10N | 32 |
| Windemere Cir. N&S | 26W-11N | 31 |
| Windsong Ct. E&W | 26W-11N | 31 |
| Windsong Dr. NE&SW | 26W-11N | 31 |
| Windsor Dr. N&S | 23W-9N | 32 |
| Windward Dr. N&S | 22W-10N | 33 |
| Winfall Dr. NE&SW | 23W-10N | 33 |
| Winfield St. N&S | 27W-10N | 31 |
| Wingate Dr. N&S | 22W-9N,22W-10N | 33 |
| Winsboro Ct. N&S | 27W-10N | 31 |
| Winston Ln. NS&EW | 25W-10N | 32 |
| Winthrop Ct. N&S | 25W-10N | 32 |
| Winthrop Ln. E&W | 25W-10N | 32 |
| Wise Rd. E&W | 25W-9N,22W-9N | 32 |
| Wisteria Ct.* NW&SE | 20W-9N | 33 |
| Wisteria Ln.* NW&SE | 20W-9N | 33 |
| Woburn Ln. N&S | 21W-10N | 33 |
| Wolcott Ct. E&W | 23W-10N | 32 |
| Wood Creek Rd. N&S | 21W-13N | 23 |
| Woodbury Ct. N&S | 21W-10N | 33 |
| Woodcroft Ct. NE&SW | 22W-11N | 33 |
| Woodcroft Ln. N&S | 22W-11N | 33 |
| Woodfield Office Ct. E&W | 22W-11N | 33 |
| Woodfield Rd. E&W | 22W-11N,21W-11N | 33 |
| Woodland Dr. E&W | 21W-12N | 23 |
| Woodside Ct. NE&SW | 21W-10N | 33 |
| Woodville Ln. N&S | 23W-10N | 32 |
| Woonsocket Ct.* N&S | 23W-14N | 22 |
| Worcester Ct. E&W | 24W-9N | 32 |
| Wright Blvd. N&S | 24W-8N | 32 |
| Wyoma Ln. N&S | 26W-10N | 31 |
| Yale Ln. E&W | 25W-9N | 32 |
| Yardley Ln. NW&SE | 26W-10N | 31 |
| Yarmouth Ct. E&W | 25W-10N | 32 |
| Yarmouth Ln. N&S | 25W-10N | 32 |
| Yorkshire Ln. E&W | 25W-10N | 32 |

## Schaumburg Township

| | Grid | Page |
|---|---|---|
| Algonquin Dr. N&S | 22W-8N | 33 |
| Blackhawk Dr. E&W | 23W-8N | 32 |
| Bulrush Dr. E&W | 25W-11N | 32 |
| Circle Ct. E&W | 21W-12N | 23 |
| Circle Dr. NE&SW | 21W-12N | 23 |
| Council Ct. E&W | 23W-8N | 32 |
| Crest Av. E&W | 25W-8N | 32 |
| Crest St. N&S | 23W-8N | 32 |
| Crowfoot Cir, N. E&W | 25W-11N | 32 |
| Crowfoot Cir, S. E&W | 25W-11N | 32 |
| Elmwood Ln. NE&SW | 21W-12N | 23 |
| Fenz Rd. E&W | 25W-8N | 32 |
| Grant St. N&S | 23W-8N | 32 |
| Greenbriar Ln. N&S | 22W-8N | 33 |
| Greenview Ct. N&S | 23W-8N | 32 |
| Half Ln. E&W | 23W-8N | 32 |
| Harmon Rd. N&S | 25W-11N | 32 |
| Hillcrest St. E&W | 22W-8N | 33 |
| Home Av. N&S | 21W-8N | 33 |
| Indian Hill Dr. N&S | 23W-8N | 32 |
| Irving Park Rd. NW&SE | 25W-8N | 32 |
| Larson Ln. N&S | 23W-8N | 32 |
| Lincoln St. N&S | 23W-8N | 32 |
| Lincoln St. N&S | 20W-8N | 33 |
| Logan St. N&S | 23W-8N | 32 |
| Long Av. N&S | 25W-8N | 32 |
| Marion St. N&S | 23W-8N | 32 |
| Martha St. N&S | 20W-8N | 33 |
| May St. N&S | 23W-8N | 32 |
| Meadow Ln. N&S | 25W-8N | 32 |
| Mitchell St. N&S | 23W-8N | 32 |
| Mohawk Dr. N&S | 23W-8N | 32 |
| Monterey Av. NS&EW | 22W-8N | 33 |
| Morse Av. E&W | 23W-8N | 32 |
| Myrtle St. N&S | 23W-8N | 32 |
| Nerge Rd. E&W | 25W-8N,21W-8N | 32 |
| Northshore Av. E&W | 25W-8N | 32 |
| Northwest Tollway NW&SE | 22W-12N | 23 |
| Omaha Cir. N&S | 21W-8N | 33 |
| Oneida Dr. E&W | 22W-8N | 33 |
| Park Av. N&S | 25W-8N | 32 |
| Park St. N&S | 23W-8N | 32 |
| Parkview Dr. N&S | 25W-8N | 32 |
| Pleasant Dr. N&S | 25W-8N | 32 |
| Plum Grove Rd. N&S | 22W-8N | 33 |
| Pratt Av. N&S | 23W-8N | 32 |
| Rodenburg Rd. E&W | 25W-8N | 32 |
| Roselle Rd. N&S | 23W-8N | 32 |
| Roslyn Ln. N&S | 23W-8N | 32 |
| Roslyn Rd. N&S | 23W-8N | 32 |
| Rucks St. E&W | 21W-8N | 33 |
| Seward St. N&S | 23W-8N | 32 |
| Sunset Dr. N&S | 22W-8N | 33 |
| Valleyview Dr. E&W | 25W-8N | 32 |
| Wise Rd. E&W | 25W-8N | 32 |

## Schiller Park

| | Grid | Page |
|---|---|---|
| Agatite Ct. E&W | 12W-5N | 40 |
| Ainsiee E&W | 11W-6N | 41 |
| Atlantic N&S | 12W-5N | 40 |
| Belle Plaine E&W | 12W-5N | 40 |
| Bernice E&W | 11W-4N | 41 |
| Berteau E&W | 12W-5N | 40 |
| Bobby Ln. N&S | 11W-4N | 41 |
| Byron E&W | 11W-4N | 41 |
| Cary Av. E&W | 12W-5N | 40 |
| Cora N&S | 12W-6N | 40 |
| Cullom E&W | 12W-5N | 40 |
| Denley N&S | 12W-4N | 40 |
| Des Plaines River Rd. N&S | 11W-6N,11W-4N | 41 |
| Eastwood Ct. E&W | 12W-5N | 40 |
| Eden Av. E&W | 12W-4N | 40 |
| Emerson N&S | 12W-4N,12W-5N | 40 |
| Florence Av. E&W | 11W-6N | 41 |
| Foster N&S | 12W-6N | 40 |
| Garden Ct. E&W | 12W-5N | 40 |
| Grace N&S | 12W-5N | 40 |
| Gremley N&S | 11W-5N | 41 |
| Gross N&S | 12W-5N | 40 |
| Harold E&W | 12W-6N | 40 |
| Harold N&S | 12W-6N | 40 |
| Hartford E&W | 12W-4N | 40 |
| Interstate 294 N&S | 12W-5N | 40 |
| Ivanhoe N&S | 12W-4N | 40 |
| Ivanhoe Cir. N&S | 12W-4N | 40 |
| Ivanhoe St. E&W | 11W-4N | 41 |
| Jill Ln. E&W | 11W-4N | 41 |
| Judd N&S | 12W-5N | 40 |
| Kelvin E&W | 11W-6N | 41 |
| Kolze N&S | 12W-5N | 41 |
| Lawrence N&S | 11W-5N | 41 |
| Lawrence Ct. E&W | 12W-5N | 40 |
| Linn E&W | 12W-6N | 40 |
| Lucy E&W | 11W-5N | 41 |
| Marie E&W | 11W-5N | 41 |
| Michigan N&S | 12W-6N | 40 |
| Montrose E&W | 12W-5N,11W-5N | 40 |
| Moore Ln. E&W | 12W-5N | 40 |
| Pace E&W | 12W-4N | 40 |
| Panoramic Dr. E&W | 12W-4N | 40 |
| Prairie N&S | 12W-5N | 40 |
| River St. E&W | 12W-4N,12W-5N | 40 |
| Rose N&S | 12W-4N,12W-5N | 40 |
| Ruby N&S | 12W-5N | 40 |
| Sally Ln. N&S | 11W-5N | 41 |
| Sarah E&W | 12W-4N | 40 |
| Scott Av. N&S | 12W-4N,12W-5N | 40 |
| Scott St. N&S | 12W-5N | 40 |
| Seymour E&W | 12W-5N | 40 |
| Sod Line Ter. N&S | 11W-5N | 41 |
| Soreng E&W | 12W-5N | 40 |
| South E&W | 12W-6N | 40 |
| Sterling Ln. E&W | 12W-4N | 40 |
| Sunnyside E&W | 12W-5N,11W-5N | 40 |
| Wagner N&S | 12W-5N | 40 |
| Waveland E&W | 12W-4N | 40 |
| Wehrman Pl. E&W | 12W-4N | 40 |
| Wesley N&S | 11W-6N,11W-5N | 41 |
| Wesley Ter. N&S | 11W-5N | 41 |
| Willow E&W | 11W-4N | 41 |
| Winona E&W | 11W-6N | 41 |
| 5th N&S | 12W-6N | 40 |
| 9th N&S | 12W-6N | 40 |
| 25th N&S | 12W-4N,12W-5N | 40 |

## Skokie

| | Grid | Page |
|---|---|---|
| Arcadia St. E&W | 6W-11N,4W-11N | 28 |
| Austin Av. NW&SE | 7W-9N | 37 |
| Avers Av. N&S | 4W-10N,4W-11N | 38 |
| Babb Av. NE&SW | 6W-9N | 38 |
| Bennett Av. N&S | 4W-10N,4W-11N | 38 |
| Beverly Dr. N&S | 5W-12N | 28 |
| Birchwood Av. E&W | 9N,4W-9N | 38 |
| Bobolink Ter. E&W | 5W-10N | 38 |
| Brandess Ter. E&W | 6W-11N | 28 |
| Bronx Av. N&S | 6W-12N | 38 |
| Bronx Pl. (Pvt.) N&S | 6W-11N | 28 |
| Brown St. E&W | 6W-10N | 38 |
| Brummel St. E&W | 4W-9N,4W-9N | 38 |
| Capitol St. E&W | 4W-10N | 38 |
| Carol St. E&W | 6W-10N,4W-10N | 38 |
| Central Av. N&S | 7W-12N | 28 |
| Central Av. N&S | 6W-9N | 38 |
| Central Park Av. | 4W-9N,4W-11N | 38 |
| Chase Av. E&W | 6W-9N,4W-9N | 38 |
| Cherry Pkwy. (Pvt.) N&S | 5W-12N | 28 |
| Christiana Av. N&S | 4W-10N | 38 |
| Church St. E&W | 5W-12N | 28 |
| Clark St. E&W | 5W-11N | 28 |
| Cleveland St. E&W | 6W-10N,4W-10N | 38 |
| Clifford Ter. E&W | 5W-10N | 38 |
| Colfax Pl. N&S | 6W-12N | 38 |
| Colfax St. E&W | 6W-12N,5W-12N | 28 |
| Concord Ln. E&W | 5W-10N | 38 |
| Conrad St. E&W | 6W-10N | 38 |
| Coyle Av. E&W | 6W-8N | 38 |
| Crain St. E&W | 6W-10N,4W-10N | 38 |
| Crawford Av. N&S | 4W-11N | 28 |
| Culver St. E&W | 5W-12N | 28 |
| Dahlin Dr. (Pvt.) E&W | 7W-9N | 37 |
| Dartmoth Pl. E&W | 4W-11N | 28 |
| Davis St. E&W | 6W-11N,4W-11N | 28 |
| Dobson St. N&S | 6W-9N,4W-9N | 38 |
| Drake Av. N&S | 4W-10N,4W-11N | 38 |
| East Prairie Rd. NE&SW | 4W-9N,4W-11N | 38 |
| Edens Expwy. N&S | 6W-12N | 28 |
| Elgin St. NW&SE | 4W-11N | 29 |
| Elm St. E&W | 6W-10N | 38 |
| Elm Ter. E&W | 6W-10N | 38 |
| Elmwood St. NE&SW | 6W-10N | 38 |
| Emerson St. E&W | 6W-11N,4W-11N | 28 |
| Enfield St. E&W | 6W-11N,4W-11N | 28 |
| Estes Av. E&W | 6W-8N | 38 |
| Ewing Av. N&S | 4W-11N | 29 |
| Fairview St. E&W | 6W-8N | 38 |
| Fargo Av. E&W | 6W-9N,6W-8N | 38 |
| Farwell Av. E&W | 6W-8N | 38 |
| Fitch Av. E&W | 6W-8N | 38 |
| Floral Av. N&S | 6W-10N | 38 |
| Forestview Rd. N&S | 4W-11N | 29 |
| Foster St. E&W | 6W-11N,4W-11N | 28 |
| Four Winds Way N&S | 4W-11N | 29 |
| Galitz St. E&W | 6W-9N | 38 |
| George St. E&W | 6W-9N | 38 |
| Golf Rd. E&W | 7W-12N,5W-12N | 28 |
| Grant St. E&W | 6W-12N,5W-12N | 28 |
| Greenleaf St. E&W | 6W-10N,4W-10N | 38 |
| Greenwood St. E&W | 6W-11N,4W-11N | 28 |
| Gross Point Rd. NE&SW | 6W-11N,5W-12N | 28 |
| Grove St. E&W | 6W-11N,4W-11N | 28 |
| Hamlin Av. N&S | 4W-9N,4W-11N | 38 |
| Harding Av. N&S | 4W-10N,4W-11N | 38 |
| Harms Rd. NW&SE | 7W-12N,6W-©0N | 28 |
| Harmswood Ter. E&W | 6W-11N | 28 |
| Harvard Ter. E&W | 6W-9N,4W-9N | 38 |
| Harvest Ln. E&W | 5W-10N | 38 |
| Hipple St. E&W | 5W-11N | 28 |
| Hoffman St. E&W | 6W-10N | 38 |
| Howard St. E&W | 6W-9N,5W-9N | 38 |
| Hull St. E&W | 6W-9N,4W-9N | 38 |
| Interstate 94 E&W | 6W-12N | 28 |
| Isabel St. E&W | 4W-10N | 38 |
| James Dr. E&W | 5W-10N | 38 |
| Jarlath St. E&W | 6W-9N | 38 |
| Jarvis Av. E&W | 6W-9N,4W-9N | 38 |
| Jerome Av. E&W | 6W-9N,4W-9N | 38 |
| Jonathan Ln. (Pvt.) E&W | 5W-12N | 28 |
| Karlov Av. N&S | 5W-9N,5W-12N | 38 |
| Keating Av. N&S | 5W-10N,5W-11N | 38 |
| Kedvale Av. N&S | 5W-9N,5W-12N | 38 |
| Kedzie Av. N&S | 4W-9N | 38 |
| Keeler Av. N&S | 5W-9N,5W-12N | 38 |
| Keeney St. E&W | 5W-10N,4W-10N | 38 |
| Kellen Av. E&W | 6W-9N | 38 |
| Kenneth Av. N&S | 5W-9N,5W-11N | 38 |
| Kenneth Ter. N&S | 5W-11N | 28 |
| Kenton Av. N&S | 5W-9N,5W-12N | 38 |
| Keystone Av. N&S | 5W-9N,5W-12N | 38 |
| Kilbourn Av. N&S | 5W-9N,5W-11N | 38 |
| Kildare Av. N&S | 5W-9N,5W-11N | 38 |
| Kilpatrick Av. NW&SE | 5W-9N,5W-11N | 38 |
| Kimball N&S | 4W-10N | 38 |
| Kirk St. E&W | 6W-9N,4W-9N | 38 |
| Klehm Ct. E&W | 6W-10N | 38 |
| Knox Av. N&S | 5W-10N,5W-12N | 38 |
| Kolmar N&S | 5W-9N,5W-12N | 38 |
| Kostner Av. N&S | 5W-9N,5W-12N | 38 |
| Kostner Ter. N&S | 5W-11N | 28 |
| LaCrosse Av. N&S | 6W-9N,6W-12N | 38 |
| Lake St. E&W | 6W-12N | 28 |
| Lamon Av. N&S | 6W-8N,6W-12N | 38 |
| Lamon Av. (Pvt.) N&S | 6W-11N | 28 |
| Laramie Av. N&S | 6W-8N,6W-12N | 38 |
| Latrobe Av. N&S | 6W-8N,6W-11N | 38 |
| Lavergne Av. N&S | 6W-8N,6W-12N | 38 |
| Lawler Av. N&S | 6W-11N | 28 |
| Lawndale Av. N&S | 4W-9N,4W-11N | 38 |
| LeClaire Av. N&S | 6W-8N,6W-12N | 38 |
| Lee St. E&W | 6W-10N,4W-10N | 38 |
| Lemington Av. N&S | 6W-12N | 28 |
| Lewis Ter. N&S | 5W-11N | 28 |
| Lincolnwood Dr. N&S | 4W-11N | 29 |
| Linder Av. N&S | 6W-9N | 38 |
| Little Elm Bend N&S | 4W-11N | 29 |
| Little One Path N&S | 4W-11N | 29 |
| Lockwood Av. N&S | 6W-12N | 28 |
| Lockwood Av. N&S | 6W-8N,6W-12N | 38 |
| Long Av. N&S | 6W-9N,6W-12N | 38 |
| Lorel Av. N&S | 6W-9N,6W-12N | 38 |
| Lotus Av. N&S | 6W-9N,6W-12N | 38 |
| Louise St. E&W | 6W-9N,4W-9N | 38 |
| Lowell Av. N&S | 5W-9N,5W-11N | 38 |
| Lowell Ter. N&S | 5W-11N | 38 |
| Lunt Av. E&W | 6W-8N | 38 |
| Lyons Av. N&S | 6W-11N,4W-11N | 28 |
| Madison St. E&W | 6W-10N,4W-10N | 38 |
| Main St. E&W | 6W-10N | 38 |
| Major Av. N&S | 7W-9N,7W-12N | 37 |
| Mango Av. N&S | 7W-9N | 37 |
| Manor Ct. E&W | 4W-11N | 29 |
| Marmora Av. N&S | 7W-9N | 37 |
| McCormick Blvd. N&S | 4W-9N,4W-10N | 38 |
| Menard Av. N&S | 7W-9N | 37 |
| Monroe St. E&W | 6W-10N | 38 |
| Monticello Av. N&S | 4W-9N,4W-11N | 38 |
| Morgan N&S | 4W-11N | 29 |
| Morse Av. E&W | 6W-8N | 38 |
| Mulford St. E&W | 6W-9N,5W-7N | 38 |
| Murphy Ln. N&S | 4W-11N | 29 |
| New Gross Point Rd. N&S | 7W-9N | 37 |
| Niles Av. N&S | 6W-9N | 38 |
| Niles Center Rd. N&S | 6W-9N,6W-11N | 38 |
| Oakton St. E&W | 6W-10N | 38 |
| Old Orchard Rd. N&S | 6W-12N,5W-12N | 28 |
| Palma Pl. E&W | 6W-11N,6W-12N | 28 |
| Park Av. NE&SW | 6W-9N | 38 |
| Parkside Av. N&S | 7W-9N,7W-12N | 37 |
| Payne St. E&W | 6W-12N,5W-12N | 28 |
| Peach Pkwy. (Pvt.) N&S | 5W-12N | 28 |
| Pottawattami Dr. N&S | 4W-11N | 29 |
| Pratt Av. E&W | 6W-8N | 38 |
| Railroad Av. N&S | 6W-11N | 28 |
| Ridgeway Av. N&S | 4W-9N,4W-11N | 38 |
| Ridgeway Ter. N&S | 4W-10N,4W-11N | 38 |
| Roth Ter. E&W | 4W-10N | 38 |
| Russet Ln. (Pvt.) E&W | 5W-12N | 28 |
| Salem Ln. NS&EW | 4W-11N | 29 |
| Samoset Blvd. N&S | 4W-11N | 29 |
| Searle Pkwy. E&W | 6W-10N | 38 |
| Sherwin Av. N&S | 6W-9N | 38 |
| Skokiana Ter. E&W | 5W-11N | 28 |
| Skokie Blvd. N&S | 6W-9N,6W-11N | 38 |
| Sleeping Bear Rd. N&S | 4W-11N | 29 |
| Springfield Av. N&S | 4W-10N,4W-11N | 38 |
| St. Louis Av. N&S | 4W-9N,4W-10N | 38 |
| Suffield Ct. E&W | 6W-11N,5W-11N | 28 |
| Suffield Ter. E&W | 6W-11N | 28 |
| Sugarloaf Ln. E&W | 4W-11N | 29 |
| Tamora Ter. N&S | 4W-11N | 29 |
| Terminal Av. NW&SE | 6W-11N,6W-12N | 28 |
| Tierney Dr. N&S | 7W-9N | 37 |
| Touhy Av. E&W | 6W-9N | 38 |
| Tower Cir. E&W | 5W-11N | 28 |
| Tripp Av. N&S | 5W-9N,5W-11N | 38 |
| Trumbull Av. N&S | 4W-10N | 38 |
| Turner Av. E&W | 4W-11N | 29 |
| U.S. Route 41 N&S | 6W-12N | 28 |
| Warren St. E&W | 6W-11N,4W-10N | 38 |
| Washington St. E&W | 6W-10N,5W-10N | 38 |
| Weber Ln. E&W | 6W-8N | 28 |
| Whitecloud Dr. E&W | 4W-11N | 38 |
| Wilder St. E&W | 4W-10N | 38 |
| Williamsburg Cir. N&S | 4W-11N | 29 |
| Williamsburg Ct. N&S | 4W-11N | 29 |
| Williamsburg Ln. N&S | 4W-11N | 29 |
| Williamsburg Ter. N&S | 4W-11N | 29 |
| Wilson Ter. E&W | 5W-11N | 28 |
| Wright Ter. E&W | 6W-10N,4W-10N | 38 |

## South Barrington

| | Grid | Page |
|---|---|---|
| Algonquin Rd. NW&SE | 27W-15N,25W-14N | 21 |
| Ambrose Ln. N&S | 26W-13N | 21 |
| Ashford Ct. NW&SE | 25W-15N | 22 |
| Avon Ln. N&S | 24W-14N | 22 |
| Back Bay NE&SW | 26W-14N | 21 |
| Barrington Rd. N&S | 26W-13N,25W-15N | 21 |
| Bartlett Rd. N&S | 27W-13N,27W-15N | 21 |
| Bay-Reef Dr. E&W | 27W-13N | 21 |
| Beacon Hill Dr. E&W | 27W-15N | 21 |
| Beechnut Dr. NS&EW | 27W-15N | 21 |
| Berkshire Ct. N&S | 27W-13N | 21 |
| Blanchard Cir. N&S | 26W-13N | 21 |
| Blossom Ct. NE&SW | 27W-13N | 21 |
| Brackley Ln. NW&SE | 25W-15N | 22 |
| Brandywine Rd. NS&EW | 27W-14N | 21 |
| Bridlewood Trail N&S | 26W-14N,26W-15N | 21 |
| Brookhaven Cir. NE&SW | 27W-15N | 21 |
| Buckthorn Rd. NS&EW | 26W-15N | 21 |
| Butera Ln. NW&SE | 26W-14N | 21 |
| Campden Dr. N&S | 25W-15N | 22 |
| Canterbury Ct. NW&SE | 24W-14N | 22 |
| Champlain Rd. NE&SW | 27W-15N | 21 |
| Chipping Dr. E&W | 25W-15N | 22 |
| Concord Ct. NE&SW | 27W-14N | 21 |
| Corey Dr. N&S | 26W-13N | 21 |
| Covered Bridge Rd. E&W | 26W-14N | 21 |
| Creet Ln. N&S | 26W-13N | 21 |
| Cutter's Run NS&EW | 27W-13N | 21 |
| Deveaux NW&SE | 26W-15N | 21 |
| East Cove NE&SW | 26W-14N | 21 |
| Easting Way NE&SW | 27W-15N | 21 |
| Eton Ct. N&S | 24W-14N | 22 |
| Evergreen Pkwy. E&W | 26W-14N | 21 |
| Forest Ln. NS&EW | 25W-14N,25W-15N | 22 |
| Foxshire Ct. NE&SW | 26W-14N | 21 |
| Gibbs Dr. N&S | 26W-13N | 21 |
| Gregory Ln. N&S | 26W-13N | 21 |
| Hackney Cir. NE&SW | 27W-13N | 21 |
| Headwater Cove N&S | 27W-14N | 21 |
| Heath Way NS&EW | 26W-15N | 21 |

| | Grid | Page |
|---|---|---|
| Higgins Rd. NW&SE | 27W-13N | 21 |
| Kitson Dr. E&W | 26W-13N | 21 |
| Knoll Ct. E&W | 25W-15N | 22 |
| Lake Adalyn Dr. NS&EW | 26W-13N | 21 |
| Lakeside Ct. N&S | 27W-15N | 21 |
| Lakeside Dr. NS&EW | 27W-15N | 21 |
| Lexington Rd. NW&SE | 27W-14N | 21 |
| Liberty Dr. NS&EW | 27W-14N | 21 |
| Loch Ln. E&W | 26W-15N | 21 |
| McGlashen Dr. N&S | 26W-13N | 21 |
| Midlands Dr. E&W | 26W-13N | 21 |
| Mohawk Ct. E&W | 25W-13N | 22 |
| Mohawk Dr. N&S | 25W-13N | 22 |
| Morgan Ln. E&W | 27W-14N | 21 |
| Mundhank Rd. NS&EW | 27W-13N,25W-13N | 21 |
| North Meadow Ct. N&S | 27W-13N | 21 |
| Old Barrington Rd. N&S | 26W-13N | 21 |
| Old Coach Dr. N&S | 26W-14N | 21 |
| Overbrook Rd. NS&EW | 26W-14N | 21 |
| Pacer Tr. NS&EW | 27W-14N | 21 |
| Palatine Rd. E&W | 27W-15N,25W-15N | 21 |
| Pembury Way NW&SE | 25W-15N | 22 |
| Penny Rd. E&W | 27W-15N,26W-15N | 21 |
| Pentwater Dr. NS&EW | 27W-13N | 21 |
| Polo Dr. NS&EW | 26W-14N | 21 |
| Quincy Cir. SE&NW | 27W-15N | 21 |
| Red Ridge Cir. E&W | 27W-15N | 21 |
| Revere Dr. N&S | 27W-14N | 21 |
| Rose Blvd. E&W | 26W-13N | 21 |
| Rt. 59 N&S | 28W-13N | 21 |
| Rt. 62 NW&SE | 27W-15N,25W-14N | 21 |
| Rt. 72 NW&SE | 27W-13N | 21 |
| Saucer Cir. N&S | 27W-13N | 21 |
| Shire Tr. NW&SE | 27W-13N | 21 |
| Shirebrook Way E&W | 25W-15N | 22 |
| Shoreside Dr. NS&EW | 27W-15N | 21 |
| Somerset Ct. N&S | 24W-14N | 22 |
| South Cove E&W | 26W-14N | 21 |
| South Meadow Ct. NE&SW | 27W-13N | 21 |
| Spring Creek Dr. N&S | 27W-15N | 21 |
| Squire Ct. N&S | 26W-14N | 21 |
| Stannington Way N&S | 25W-15N | 22 |
| Star Ln. NW&SE | 27W-13N | 21 |
| Stellata Ct. E&W | 27W-13N | 21 |
| Stonebrook Ct. N&S | 27W-13N | 21 |
| Stoneridge Dr. NS&EW | 26W-15N | 21 |
| Taynton Ln. E&W | 25W-15N | 22 |
| Tennis Club Ln. E&W | 26W-13N | 21 |
| Tewkesbury Ln. E&W | 25W-15N | 22 |
| Tiffany Cir. N&S | 27W-13N | 21 |
| Trenton Ct. NE&SW | 27W-14N | 21 |
| Turning Shore NE&SW | 27W-14N,26W-14N | 21 |
| Upper Pond Rd. NS&EW | 27W-14N | 21 |
| Vandenbergh Dr. E&W | 26W-13N | 21 |
| Walnut Ln. NE&SW | 27W-15N | 21 |
| Watercrest Ct. NE&SW | 27W-13N | 21 |
| Watergate Rd. NS&EW | 27W-14N,26W-14N | 21 |
| Wellingborough Ct. E&W | 25W-15N | 22 |
| Wescott Dr. NS&EW | 26W-13N | 21 |
| Westlake Dr. NS&EW | 27W-15N | 21 |
| Willow Bay Dr. NS&EW | 27W-13N | 21 |
| Willowmere Dr. N&S | 25W-14N,25W-15N | 22 |
| Windemere Ln. NE&SW | 24W-14N | 22 |
| Windridge Dr. NS&EW | 27W-15N | 21 |
| Windsor Ct. N&S | 26W-14N,26W-15N | 21 |
| Witt Rd. N&S | 26W-14N | 21 |
| Woodbury Ct. NE&SW | 27W-15N | 21 |
| Woodhaven Dr. NS&EW | 27W-13N | 21 |
| Wynchwood Ln. N&S | 25W-15N | 22 |
| Yorktown Ct. E&W | 27W-14N | 21 |

## South Chicago Heights

| | Grid | Page |
|---|---|---|
| Aberdeen St. N&S | 1W-26S | 93 |
| Benton Av. E&W | 1W-27S | 93 |
| Butler Av. N&S | 0W-27S | 94 |
| Campbell Av. N&S | 1W-27S | 93 |
| Cappelletti Ln. N&S | 1W-27S | 93 |
| Cherry Ln. E&W | 1W-27S | 93 |
| Chestnut Av. E&W | 1W-27S | 93 |
| Chicago & Vincennes Rd. N&S | 1W-26S | 93 |
| Chicago Pl. N&S | 1W-27S | 93 |
| Commercial Av. N&S | 1W-26S | 93 |
| Courtney Ln. N&S | 1W-27S | 94 |
| Crescenzo Dr. N&S | 1W-27S | 93 |
| Deer Path N&S | 1W-27S | 94 |
| Dornell Dr. N&S | 1W-27S | 93 |
| East End Av. N&S | 0W-26S | 94 |
| Enterprise Park Av. N&S | 1W-27S | 93 |
| Euclid Av. N&S | 1W-27S | 93 |
| Euclid Dr. N&S | 1W-27S | 93 |
| Fairview Av. N&S | 1W-27S | 93 |
| Forest Dr. E&W | 1W-27S | 93 |
| Helfred Av. N&S | 1W-27S | 93 |
| Holeman Av. N&S | 0W-27S | 94 |
| Interocean Av. E&W | 1W-26S | 93 |
| Jackson Av. N&S | 1W-26S | 93 |
| Lawrence Av. N&S | 1W-27S | 93 |
| Lynnwood Dr. N&S | 1W-27S | 93 |
| Magnolia Plaza NS&EW | 1W-27S | 93 |
| Maple Av. E&W | 1W-27S | 93 |
| Miller Av. N&S | 1W-27S | 93 |
| Park Terr. E&W | 1W-27S | 93 |
| Paulsen St. E&W | 1W-26S,0W-26S | 93 |
| Rennine-Smith Dr. N&S | 0W-27S | 94 |
| Rosiclaire Ct. N&S | 1W-27S | 94 |
| Rt. 1 N&S | 1W-27S | 93 |
| Sauk Trial E&W | 0W-27S | 94 |
| State St. N&S | 0W-27S | 94 |
| Vincennes Rd. N&S | 1W-27S,0W-27S | 93 |
| Willow Rd. N&S | 1W-27S | 93 |
| 26th St. E&W | 1W-26S | 93 |
| 27th Pl. E&W | 1W-26S | 93 |
| 27th St. E&W | 1W-26S | 93 |
| 28th Pl. E&W | 1W-26S | 93 |
| 28th St. E&W | 1W-26S | 93 |
| 29th Pl. E&W | 1W-26S | 93 |
| 29th St. E&W | 1W-26S | 93 |
| 30th Pl. E&W | 1W-27S | 93 |
| 30th St. E&W | 1W-26S | 93 |
| 31st St. E&W | 1W-27S | 93 |
| 33rd St. E&W | 1W-27S,0W-27S | 93 |
| 34th St. E&W | 1W-27S | 93 |

## South Holland

| | Grid | Page |
|---|---|---|
| Armory Dr. E&W | 0W-19S | 82 |
| Avalon Av. N&S | 1E-19S,1E-18S | 82 |
| Bennett Av. NE&SW | 2E-20S | 89 |
| Bernice Rd. E&W | 2E-20S | 89 |
| Betty Ln. N&S | 0E-19S | 82 |
| Calumet Expwy. N&S | 1E-18S | 82 |
| Canal St. N&S | 0W-20S,0W-19S | 88 |
| Champlain St. N&S | 0E-18S | 82 |
| Cherry St. N&S | 0E-18S | 82 |
| Church Dr. NW&SE | 0E-18S | 82 |
| Claire Ln. N&S | 0E-19S | 82 |
| Clark St. N&S | 0W-17S | 82 |
| Clyde Av. N&S | 2E-20S,20E-19S | 89 |
| Constance Av. NE&SW | 2E-20S | 89 |
| Cornell Av. N&S | 1E-20S | 89 |
| Cottage Grove Av. N&S | 0E-19S,0E-18S | 82 |
| Cregier Av. N&S | 1E-20S | 89 |
| Dante Dr. N&S | 1E-18S | 82 |
| Dearborn St. N&S | 0W-18S,0W-17S | 82 |
| Debbie Ln. N&S | 1E-18S | 82 |
| Dobson Av. N&S | 1E-20S,1E-17S | 89 |
| Dobson Ct. N&S | 1E-19S | 82 |
| Dorchester Av. N&S | 1E-18S | 82 |
| Drexel Av. N&S | 1E-20S,1E-17S | 89 |
| Ellis Av. N&S | 1E-19S,1E-17S | 82 |
| Ellis Ct. N&S | 1E-20S,1E-19S | 89 |
| Elm Ct. N&S | 0E-19S | 82 |
| Elm St. N&S | 0E-19S,0E-18S | 82 |
| Evans Av. N&S | 0E-20S,0E-18S | 88 |
| Evans Ct. NW&SE | 0E-20S,0E-19S | 88 |
| Evans Dr. NW&SE | 0E-20S | 88 |
| Everett Av. N&S | 1E-20S | 89 |
| Gouwens Ln. NE&SW | 0E-18S | 82 |
| Greenwood Av. N&S | 1E-20S,1E-19S | 89 |
| Holland Av. NW&SE | 0E-19S | 82 |
| Indiana Av. N&S | 0W-19S | 82 |
| Ingleside Av. N&S | 1E-20S,1E-17S | 89 |
| Ingleside Ct. NE&SW | 1E-19S | 82 |
| Ingleside Dr. NW&SE | 1E-19S | 82 |
| Interstate 294-80 E&W | 0E-20S | 88 |
| Interstate 94 N&S | 1E-20S,1E-19S | 89 |
| Jeffrey St. N&S | 2E-20S | 89 |
| Joyce Cir. E&W | 0E-19S | 82 |
| Joyce Ct. E&W | 0E-19S | 82 |
| Kenwood Av. N&S | 1E-20S,1E-18S | 89 |
| Kenwood Ct. NE&SW | 1E-19S | 82 |
| Kenwood Dr. NW&SE | 1E-19S | 82 |
| Kimbark Av. N&S | 1E-20S,1E-18S | 89 |
| Kimbark Ct. N&S | 1E-19S | 82 |
| King Av. NW&SE | 1E-18S | 82 |
| King Cir. NE&SW | 1E-18S | 82 |
| La Salle St. N&S | 0W-18S,0W-17S | 82 |
| Langley Av. N&S | 0E-20S,0E-18S | 88 |
| Louis Av. N&S | 0E-20S,0E-18S | 88 |
| Louis Ct. N&S | 0E-20S,0E-19S | 88 |
| Lowell Av. N&S | 0E-19S | 82 |
| Luella Av. N&S | 2E-19S | 83 |
| Maple Ct. N&S | 0E-19S | 82 |
| Maple St. N&S | 0E-19S,0E-18S | 82 |
| Marie Dr. E&W | 0E-19S | 82 |
| Marion Dr. N&S | 1E-18S | 82 |
| Maryland Av. N&S | 1E-20S,1E-19S | 89 |
| Merrill Av. N&S | 2E-19S | 83 |
| Michigan Av. N&S | 0E-19S,0E-18S | 82 |
| Michigan Av. N&S | 0W-17S | 82 |
| Minerva Av. N&S | 1E-18S | 82 |
| Mutual Ter. NW&SE | 0E-18S | 82 |
| Naughton Av. N&S | 1E-17S | 82 |
| Orchid Dr. NE&SW | 0E-18S | 82 |
| Park Ln. NE&SW | 0E-18S | 82 |
| Park Plaza E&W | 0E-18S | 82 |
| Parkside Av. N&S | 1E-19S,1E-18S | 82 |
| Parkside St. N&S | 0E-20S | 88 |
| Paxton Av. N&S | 2E-20S | 89 |
| Perry Av. N&S | 0W-17S | 82 |
| Prairie Av. N&S | 0E-19S,0E-18S | 82 |
| Prince Dr. NW&SE | 1E-18S | 82 |
| Reitveldt Rd. N&S | 2E-19S | 83 |
| Riverside Dr. NW&SE | 0E-17S | 82 |
| Riverside St. E&W | 0E-18S | 82 |
| Riverview Dr. NW&SE | 1E-18S | 82 |
| Rose Dr. NE&SW | 0E-18S | 82 |
| Rt. 83 E&W | 0W-17S | 82 |
| School St. N&S | 0E-20S,0E-19S | 88 |
| Cir. | 1E-18S | 82 |
| Shirley Ct. N&S | 0E-19S | 82 |
| Sibley Blvd. E&W | 0E-17S | 82 |
| South Park Av. N&S | 0E-20S,0E-18S | 88 |
| State St. E&W | 0W-18S,0W-17S | 82 |
| Sun Tone Dr. N&S | 0W-18S | 82 |
| Taft Dr. E&W | 0W-19S | 82 |
| Thornton Av. NW&SE | 0E-19S | 82 |
| Thornwood Ct. NW&SE | 0E-20S | 88 |
| Thornwood Dr. NW&SE | 0E-20S | 88 |
| Union Av. N&S | 0W-20S | 88 |
| Univeristy Av. N&S | 1E-20S,1E-18S | 89 |
| Univeristy Ct. N&S | 1E-19S | 82 |
| Van Drunen Rd. N&S | 0W-18S | 82 |
| Vincennes Av. NW&SE | 0W-18S,0E-20S | 82 |
| Volbrecht Ct. E&W | 2E-20S | 89 |
| Volbrecht Dr. N&S | 2E-20S | 89 |
| Volbrecht Rd. N&S | 1E-20S | 89 |
| Wabash Av. N&S | 0E-19S,0E-17S | 82 |
| Wabash Ct. NE&SW | 0E-18S | 82 |
| Wallace Av. N&S | 0W-20S | 88 |
| Waterman Ct. NE&SW | 1E-17S | 82 |
| Waterman Dr. NW&SE | 1E-17S | 82 |
| Wausau Av. N&S | 0E-20S,0E-18S | 88 |
| Wausau Ct. N&S | 0E-20S,0E-19S | 88 |
| Wentworth Av. N&S | 0W-18S | 82 |
| Westview Av. N&S | 0W-20S | 88 |
| Woodlawn Av. N&S | 0E-19S,0E-18S | 82 |
| Woodlawn Av., E. N&S | 1E-19S,1E-18S | 82 |
| Woodlawn Ct. N&S | 1E-19S | 82 |
| Woodlawn Dr., E. E&W | 1E-18S | 82 |
| Woodlawn Rd. West N&S | 0E-17S | 82 |
| Yates Av. N&S | 2E-20S | 89 |
| 148th St. E&W | 0W-17S,0E-17S | 82 |
| 149th St. E&W | 0W-17S,0E-17S | 82 |
| 150th Pl. E&W | 0W-17S,1E-17S | 82 |
| 152nd St. E&W | 1E-17S | 82 |
| 153rd Pl. E&W | 1E-17S | 82 |
| 153rd St. E&W | 1E-17S | 82 |
| 154th Pl. E&W | 0E-18S | 82 |
| 154th St. E&W | 0W-17S,0E-17S | 82 |
| 155th Pl. E&W | 0E-18S,1E-18S | 82 |
| 155th St. E&W | 0W-18S,0E-18S | 82 |
| 156th Pl. E&W | 0E-18S | 82 |
| 156th St. E&W | 0E-18S | 82 |
| 157th Pl. E&W | 0E-18S | 82 |
| 157th St. E&W | 0E-18S | 82 |
| 158th Pl. E&W | 0E-18S | 82 |
| 158th St. E&W | 0E-18S | 82 |
| 159th Ct. E&W | 0E-18S,1E-18S | 82 |
| 159th Pl. E&W | 0E-18S,1E-18S | 82 |
| 159th St. E&W | 0E-18S,1E-18S | 82 |
| 160th Ct. E&W | 0E-18S | 82 |
| 160th Pl. E&W | 0E-18S,1E-18S | 82 |
| 160th St. E&W | 0E-18S,1E-18S | 82 |
| 161st Pl. E&W | 0E-18S,1E-18S | 82 |
| 161st St. E&W | 1E-18S | 82 |
| 162nd Pl. E&W | 0E-19S,1E-19S | 82 |
| 162nd St. E&W | 0W-18S,1E-18S | 82 |
| 163rd Ct. E&W | 0E-19S | 82 |
| 163rd Pl. E&W | 0E-19S,1E-19S | 82 |
| 163rd St. E&W | 0E-19S,1E-19S | 82 |
| 164th Cir. E&W | 0E-19S | 82 |
| 164th Ct. E&W | 1E-19S | 82 |
| 164th Pl. E&W | 0E-19S,1E-19S | 82 |
| 164th St. E&W | 0E-19S,1E-19S | 82 |
| 165th Pl. E&W | 0E-19S,1E-19S | 82 |
| 165th St. E&W | 0E-19S,1E-19S | 82 |
| 166th Pl. E&W | 0E-19S,2E-19S | 82 |
| 166th St. E&W | 0W-19S,2E-19S | 82 |
| 167th Pl. E&W | 0E-19S,1E-19S | 82 |
| 167th St. E&W | 0W-19S,1E-19S | 82 |
| 168th Ct. E&W | 0E-19S | 82 |
| 168th Pl. E&W | 0E-19S,1E-19S | 82 |
| 168th St. E&W | 0W-19S,2E-19S | 82 |
| 169th Pl. E&W | 1E-19S,2E-19S | 82 |
| 169th St. E&W | 0W-19S,1E-19S | 82 |
| 170th Pl. E&W | 0E-20S,2E-20S | 88 |
| 170th St. E&W | 0W-19S,2E-19S | 82 |
| 171st Pl. E&W | 0E-20S,2E-20S | 88 |
| 171st St. E&W | 0E-20S,2E-20S | 88 |
| 172nd St. E&W | 0W-20S,2E-20S | 88 |
| 173rd Pl. E&W | 0E-20S,2E-20S | 88 |
| 173rd St. E&W | 0E-20S,2E-20S | 88 |

## Steger*
**(Also see Will County)**

| | Grid | Page |
|---|---|---|
| Adair Rd. N&S | 0E-27S | 94 |
| Butler Av. N&S | 0W-27S | 51 |
| Carpenter St. N&S | 1W-27S | 51 |
| Cottage Grove Av. N&S | 1E-27S | 94 |
| Dorchester Av. N&S | 1E-27S | 94 |
| Emerald Av. N&S | 1W-27S | 51 |
| Florence Av. N&S | 0W-27S | 51 |
| Frederick Rd. N&S | 0E-27S | 94 |
| George St. NW&SE | 0E-27S | 94 |
| Green St. N&S | 1W-27S | 51 |
| Halsted St. N&S | 1W-27S | 51 |
| Holeman Av. N&S | 0W-27S | 51 |
| Hopkins Av. N&S | 0W-27S | 51 |
| Keeney Av. N&S | 0W-27S | 94 |
| Lahon Rd. N&S | 0E-27S | 94 |
| Lewis Av. N&S | 0W-27S | 51 |
| Lisa Ln. E&W | 0E-27S | 94 |
| Loverock Av. N&S | 0W-27S | 51 |
| Mach Dr. N&S | 0E-27S | 94 |
| Michigan Av. N&S | 0E-27S | 94 |
| Miller Rd. N&S | 0E-27S | 94 |
| Morgan St. N&S | 1W-27S | 51 |
| Oakland Dr. N&S | 0E-27S | 94 |
| Patricia Rd. N&S | 0E-27S | 94 |
| Peoria St. N&S | 1W-27S | 51 |
| Phillips Av. N&S | 0W-27S | 51 |
| Route 1 N&S | 1W-27S | 51 |
| Sangamon St. N&S | 1W-27S | 51 |
| Sherman Rd. N&S | 0E-27S | 94 |
| State St. N&S | 0W-27S | 94 |
| Steger Rd. E&W | 0E-27S | 94 |
| Stewart Av. N&S | 0W-27S | 94 |
| Union Av. N&S | 0W-27S | 51 |
| Wallace Av. N&S | 0W-27S | 51 |
| Wentworth Av. N&S | 0W-27S | 94 |
| Woodlawn Av. N&S | 1E-27S | 94 |
| 30th Pl. E&W | 1W-27S,0W-27S | 93 |
| 30th St. E&W | 1W-26S,0W-26S | 93 |
| 30th St. E&W | 1E-27S | 94 |
| 31st Pl. E&W | 1W-27S,0W-27S | 93 |
| 31st St. E&W | 1W-27S,0W-27S | 93 |
| 32nd Pl. E&W | 1W-27S | 93 |
| 32nd St. E&W | 1W-27S,0W-27S | 93 |
| 32nd St. E&W | 1E-27S | 94 |
| 33rd Pl. E&W | 1W-27S,0W-27S | 93 |
| 33rd St. E&W | 1W-27S,0W-27S | 93 |
| 33rd St. E&W | 0E-27S | 94 |
| 34th Pl. E&W | 0E-27S | 94 |
| 34th St. E&W | 1W-27S,0W-27S | 93 |
| 34th St. E&W | 0E-27S | 94 |

## Stickney

| | Grid | Page |
|---|---|---|
| Clarence N&S | 8W-4S | 54 |
| East N&S | 8W-4S | 54 |
| Elmwood N&S | 8W-4S | 54 |
| Euclid N&S | 8W-4S | 54 |
| Gunderson N&S | 8W-4S | 54 |
| Kenilworth N&S | 8W-4S | 54 |
| Lorraine E&W | 8W-4S | 54 |
| Pershing E&W | 8W-4S,7W-4S | 54 |
| Scoville N&S | 8W-4S | 54 |
| Wenonah N&S | 8W-4S | 54 |
| Wesley N&S | 8W-4S | 54 |
| Wisconsin N&S | 8W-4S | 54 |
| 40th E&W | 8W-4S | 54 |
| 40th Pl. E&W | 8W-4S | 53 |
| 41st E&W | 8W-4S | 54 |
| 42nd E&W | 8W-4S | 54 |
| 43rd E&W | 8W-4S | 54 |
| 44th E&W | 8W-4S | 54 |
| 45th E&W | 8W-4S | 54 |

## Stickney Township

| | Grid | Page |
|---|---|---|
| Central N&S | 6W-5S | 60 |
| Laramie N&S | 6W-5S | 60 |
| Latrobe N&S | 6W-5S | 60 |
| 48th E&W | 6W-5S | 60 |
| 49th E&W | 6W-5S | 60 |
| 50th E&W | 6W-5S | 60 |
| 51st E&W | 6W-5S | 60 |

## Stone Park

| | Grid | Page |
|---|---|---|
| Soffel E&W | 12W-1N | 46 |
| 37th N&S | 12W-1N | 46 |
| 38th N&S | 12W-1N | 46 |
| 39th N&S | 12W-1N | 46 |
| 40th N&S | 12W-1N | 46 |
| 43rd N&S | 13W-1N | 46 |

## Streamwood

| | Grid | Page |
|---|---|---|
| Abbeywood Cir. NE&SW | 28W-11N | 31 |
| Abington Ct. N&S | 29W-9N,29W-10N | 30 |
| Acorn Dr. E&W | 27W-10N | 31 |
| Adams Ct. NW&SE | 29W-10N | 30 |
| Alexander Av. N&S | 28W-9N | 31 |
| Alexander Ct. NW&SE | 28W-9N | 31 |
| Alexander Ln. N&S | 28W-9N | 31 |
| Alexander Pl. E&W | 28W-9N | 31 |
| Andover Ct. NW&SE | 28W-9N | 31 |
| Apple Hill Ln. NE&SW | 28W-11N | 31 |
| Arabian Ct. E&W | 30W-10N | 30 |
| Arbor Ct. E&W | 30W-10N | 30 |
| Arbor Dr. N&S | 30W-10N | 30 |
| Arnold Av. E&W | 28W-9N | 31 |
| Arrowood Ct.* E&W | 24W-13N | 22 |
| Arthur Ct. N&S | 28W-10N | 31 |
| Ascot Ln. NS&EW | 29W-11N | 30 |
| Ash Ct. E&W | 27W-10N | 31 |
| Ashton Ct. NS&EW | 29W-9N,28W-9N | 30 |
| Aspen Ct. E&W | 27W-10N | 31 |
| Attleboro Ln. E&W | 29W-9N | 30 |
| Audubon Rd. E&W | 28W-10N | 31 |
| Autumn Ln. NS&EW | 29W-9N | 30 |
| Azalea Cir. NS&EW | 27W-10N | 31 |
| Barrington Rd. N&S | 27W-9N,27W-11N | 31 |
| Bartlett Rd. N&S | 29W-9N,28W-11N | 30 |
| Bayberry Ct. NE&SW | 27W-10N | 31 |
| Beaver Dr. N&S | 28W-10N | 31 |
| Beebe Ct. E&W | 28W-9N | 31 |
| Berkely Pl. E&W | 28W-10N | 31 |
| Berkshire Ct. N&S | 29W-9N | 30 |
| Beverley Ct. E&W | 29W-9N | 30 |

| | Grid | Page |
|---|---|---|
| Beverley Ln. N&S | 29W-9N | 30 |
| Big Oaks Ct. N&S | 28W-10N | 31 |
| Big Oaks Rd. NW&SE | 28W-10N | 31 |
| Birchwood Ct.* N&S | 24W-13N | 22 |
| Bittersweet Ln. N&S | 30W-10N | 30 |
| Blackberry Ct. E&W | 30W-10N | 30 |
| Bluff Ct. E&W | 29W-10N | 30 |
| Bode Rd. E&W | 29W-11N,26W-11N | 30 |
| Bonded Pkwy. N&S | 27W-10N | 31 |
| Borris Cir. NS&EW | 28W-11N | 31 |
| Bourbon Pkwy. N&S | 27W-10N | 31 |
| Boxwood Ct.* E&W | 24W-13N | 22 |
| Brandy Pkwy. E&W | 27W-10N | 31 |
| Briarwood Dr. E&W | 28W-9N | 31 |
| Bristol Ct. NE&SW | 29W-9N | 30 |
| Brittany Dr. NS&EW | 29W-9N | 30 |
| Brooks Dr. NE&SW | 27W-11N | 31 |
| Brookstone Ct. N&S | 29W-10N | 30 |
| Brookstone Dr. NS&EW | 29W-10N | 30 |
| Brunswick Ct. NW&SE | 28W-9N | 31 |
| Buchanan Ln. E&W | 29W-10N | 30 |
| Burgundy Pkwy. E&W | 27W-10N | 31 |
| Bussey Ct. E&W | 27W-9N | 31 |
| Butternut Ln. E&W | 27W-10N | 31 |
| Buttitta Dr. E&W | 27W-9N | 31 |
| Cahill Rd. E&W | 29W-10N | 30 |
| Cambridge Av. E&W | 28W-9N | 31 |
| Canterbury Ct. E&W | 28W-11N | 31 |
| Canton Ln. NS&EW | 29W-11N | 30 |
| Carey Ln. NE&SW | 28W-11N | 31 |
| Carlson Dr. NS&EW | 28W-9N | 31 |
| Carol Ann Dr. E&W | 28W-11N | 31 |
| Castlewood Dr. N&S | 30W-10N | 30 |
| Cedar Cir. NS&EW | 28W-10N | 31 |
| Cedar Ct. NW&SE | 28W-10N | 31 |
| Cedarcrest Dr. N&S | 28W-10N | 31 |
| Center Rd. N&S | 29W-10N | 30 |
| Chase Ct. NW&SE | 28W-10N | 31 |
| Chase Ter. NW&SE | 28W-10N | 31 |
| Chaucer Ln. E&W | 28W-11N | 31 |
| Cherry Ln. NW&SE | 28W-10N | 31 |
| Chestnut Dr. NS&EW | 28W-10N | 31 |
| Chrisman Dr. E&W | 28W-11N | 31 |
| Claridge Ct.* NW&SE | 24W-13N | 22 |
| Clearwater Ct. N&S | 29W-10N | 30 |
| Clematis Dr. E&W | 27W-10N | 31 |
| Club Tree Dr. NS&EW | 28W-9N | 31 |
| Colony Ct. E&W | 29W-9N,28W-9N | 30 |
| Columbine Ct. E&W | 30W-10N | 30 |
| Concord Ct. N&S | 28W-10N | 31 |
| Coolidge Ct. NW&SE | 29W-10N | 30 |
| Corrington Ct. E&W | 27W-11N | 31 |
| Country Ln. NW&SE | 28W-10N | 31 |
| Creekside Ct. NW&SE | 29W-10N | 30 |
| Crestwood Ct. NE&SW | 28W-9N | 31 |
| Crestwood Dr. NW&SE | 28W-9N | 31 |
| Cypress Dr. NE&SW | 28W-10N | 31 |
| Dana Ln. E&W | 28W-11N | 31 |
| Dartmouth Ct. E&W | 29W-9N | 30 |
| Dato Ct. E&W | 27W-10N | 31 |
| Dato Dr. N&S | 27W-11N | 31 |
| David Dr. N&S | 28W-10N | 31 |
| Debbie Ln. N&S | 27W-11N | 31 |
| Deerfield Dr. E&W | 29W-10N | 30 |
| Diane Dr. E&W | 29W-10N | 30 |
| Dogwood Ct.* E&W | 24W-13N | 22 |
| Dorchester Ct. E&W | 29W-9N | 30 |
| Dorman Dr. N&S | 28W-9N,28W-10N | 31 |
| Dover Dr. N&S | 29W-11N | 30 |
| Driftwood Ct.* E&W | 24W-13N | 22 |
| Dunbar Ct. E&W | 28W-9N | 31 |
| Duxbury Ct. E&W | 28W-10N | 31 |
| E. Bartlett Rd. E&W | 28W-9N | 31 |
| E. Oltendorf Rd. E&W | 28W-9N | 31 |
| E. Pine St. E&W | 28W-10N | 31 |
| E. Shagbark Lane E&W | 28W-11N | 31 |
| E. Streamwood Blvd. NS&EW | 28W-10N | 31 |
| E. Valley Ln. E&W | 28W-9N | 31 |
| East Av. N&S | 27W-9N,27W-10N | 31 |
| Edgewood Dr. NW&SE | 28W-9N | 31 |
| Egan Ct. E&W | 27W-11N | 31 |
| Egan Ct. N&S | 27W-11N | 31 |
| Eliasek Ct. NW&SE | 27W-11N | 31 |
| Elm Ln. NE&SW | 28W-10N | 31 |
| Essex Ct. E&W | 28W-9N | 31 |
| Evans Ct. NE&SW | 28W-9N | 31 |
| Evergreen Dr. NS&EW | 29W-9N | 30 |
| Exmoor Dr. N&S | 28W-9N | 31 |
| Fairview Ln. E&W | 28W-9N | 31 |
| Fallstone Dr. NW&SE | 28W-11N | 31 |
| Falmouth Ct. E&W | 28W-10N | 31 |
| Fernwood Ct.* E&W | 24W-13N | 22 |
| Field Ln. NW&SE | 28W-10N | 31 |
| Filbert Dr. NS&EW | 27W-10N | 31 |
| Fillmore Ln. E&W | 29W-10N | 31 |
| Finch Ct. SW&NE | 30W-10N | 30 |
| Fir Ct. E&W | 27W-10N | 31 |
| Flowers Av. E&W | 27W-8N | 31 |
| Forest Dr. NE&SW | 28W-9N | 31 |
| Foxboro Ct. N&S | 29W-9N | 30 |
| Foxglove Ct. E&W | 30W-10N | 30 |
| Frances Dr. N&S | 27W-9N | 31 |
| Franklin Ct. E&W | 28W-11N | 31 |
| Frederick Av. NE&SW | 28W-9N | 31 |
| Freeman Av. NE&SW | 28W-9N | 31 |
| Fulton Dr. N&S | 29W-9N | 30 |
| Fulton St. N&S | 29W-9N | 30 |
| Gant Cir. NS&EW | 28W-11N | 31 |
| Garden Cir. NS&EW | 27W-11N | 31 |
| Garfield Ln. E&W | 29W-10N | 30 |
| Gayle Ct. E&W | 27W-11N | 31 |
| Genauldi Av. N&S | 28W-8N | 31 |
| Glendale Ct. N&S | 27W-11N | 31 |
| Golf Keys Rd. (Pvt.) NS&EW | 30W-9N | 30 |
| Green Ct. N&S | 27W-11N | 31 |
| Green Knoll Ln. N&S | 26W-11N | 31 |
| Greenbriar Ln. E&W | 29W-9N | 30 |
| Greenwood Ct. E&W | 28W-9N | 31 |
| Gregg Ct. N&S | 27W-11N | 31 |
| Grey Fox Ct. N&S | 30W-10N | 30 |
| Greystone Ct.* NW&SE | 24W-13N | 22 |
| Grow Ln. NW&SE | 28W-10N | 31 |
| Hackberry Dr. NS&EW | 27W-10N | 31 |
| Halick Dr. N&S | 29W-11N | 30 |
| Hampton Ct. E&W | 28W-9N | 31 |
| Harrison Ln. NE&SW | 28W-10N | 30 |
| Hartwood Dr. NS&EW | 27W-9N | 31 |
| Harvest Dr. E&W | 29W-9N | 31 |
| Hastings Mill Rd. N&S | 28W-11N | 31 |
| Hawthorne Ln NW&SE | 28W-10N | 31 |
| Hayward Av. NW&SE | 29W-8N,27W-8N | 31 |
| Hazelnut Dr. N&S | 27W-10N | 31 |
| Heath Ct. NE&SW | 28W-9N | 31 |
| Heather Ct. E&W | 27W-11N | 31 |
| Heather Ln. | 27W-11N | 31 |
| Hecht Rd. N&S | 27W-9N | 31 |
| Heine Ct. E&W | 27W-11N | 31 |
| Heine Dr. N&S | 27W-11N | 31 |
| Helen Ct. N&S | 29W-9N | 30 |
| Hickory Av. NE&SW | 28W-10N | 31 |
| Hillside Ct. NS&EW | 28W-11N | 31 |
| Hillside Dr. NE&SW | 28W-10N,27W-10N | 31 |
| Hise Ct. E&W | 27W-11N | 31 |
| Holly Ct. N&S | 28W-10N | 31 |
| Holly Dr. N&S | 28W-10N | 31 |
| Hoover Ct. NW&SE | 28W-10N | 31 |
| Hummingbird Ct. E&W | 30W-10N | 30 |
| Hummingbird Ln. NS&EW | 30W-10N | 30 |
| Huntington Dr. N&S | 28W-11N | 31 |
| Innsbrook Dr. E&W | 29W-9N | 30 |
| Iris Dr. NS&EW | 27W-10N | 31 |
| Ironwood Ct.* N&S | 24W-13N | 22 |
| Irving Park Rd. NW&SE | 29W-10N,27W-10N | 30 |
| Ivy Ct. E&W | 27W-10N | 31 |
| Jackson Ln. E&W | 29W-10N | 30 |
| Jamestown Ct. N&S | 28W-9N | 31 |
| Janet Av. N&S | 29W-10N | 30 |
| Jefferson Ct. NW&SE | 29W-10N | 30 |
| Jefferson Ln. N&S | 29W-10N,28W-10N | 30 |
| Jill Ln. NW&SE | 27W-10N | 31 |
| Jonquil Ct. E&W | 30W-10N | 30 |
| Joyce Ln. N&S | 29W-10N | 30 |
| Judy Ln. NE&SW | 27W-11N | 31 |
| Juniper Ct. NS&EW | 27W-10N | 31 |
| Kennedy Dr. NW&SE | 27W-11N | 31 |
| Kensington Ct. NW&SE | 29W-11N | 30 |
| Kensington Dr. NS&EW | 29W-11N | 30 |
| Kevin Morris Ct. N&S | 27W-11N | 31 |
| Kimberley Ln. E&W | 27W-10N | 31 |
| King Dr. N&S | 27W-9N | 31 |
| Kingston Ct. NW&SE | 28W-9N | 31 |
| Klafter Ct. N&S | 27W-11N | 31 |
| Klein Dr. E&W | 27W-11N | 31 |
| Kosan Cir. NS&EW | 27W-11N | 31 |
| Krause Av. E&W | 28W-9N,27W-9N | 31 |
| LaSalle Ct. N&S | 28W-9N | 30 |
| LaSalle Rd. E&W | 29W-9N | 30 |
| Lacy Av. E&W | 28W-9N,27W-9N | 31 |
| Lake St. N&S | 29W-9N,28W-8N | 31 |
| Lancaster Ct. E&W | 29W-9N | 30 |
| Larkspur Ln. NS&EW | 30W-10N | 30 |
| Larsen Av. N&S | 28W-9N,27W-9N | 31 |
| Laurel Ct. NW&SE | 28W-10N | 31 |
| Laurel Ln. E&W | 28W-10N | 31 |
| Lee Ct. N&S | 28W-9N | 31 |
| Lexington Ct.* E&W | 24W-13N | 22 |
| Library Ln. E&W | 28W-9N | 31 |
| Lincoln Av. NE&SW | 28W-9N | 31 |
| Lincoln Ct. NW&SE | 27W-9N | 31 |
| Lincolnwood Dr. N&S | 28W-10N | 31 |
| Linda Ln. N&S | 29W-10N | 30 |
| Lisa Ln. N&S | 29W-10N | 30 |
| Little Creek Dr. NS&EW | 30W-10N | 30 |
| Longboat Key Ln. E&W | 30W-10N | 30 |
| Madison Dr. N&S | 29W-10N | 30 |
| Magnolia Ct., W. E&W | 30W-10N | 30 |
| Magnolia Dr. NS&EW | 30W-10N | 30 |
| Manchester Ct. E&W | 29W-11N | 31 |
| Manor Dr. N&S | 28W-9N | 31 |
| Marion Ln. E&W | 28W-11N | 31 |
| Mark Ln. N&S | 27W-11N | 31 |
| Marrayat Pl. E&W | 29W-10N | 30 |
| Maxon Ln. NS&EW | 28W-10N | 31 |
| Mayfield Dr. N&S | 28W-10N | 31 |
| Mc Cabe Dr. N&S | 28W-10N | 31 |
| Mc Kool Av. N&S | 27W-10N | 31 |
| McKinley Ln. NS&EW | 29W-10N | 30 |
| Meadow Ct. N&S | 28W-9N | 31 |
| Meadow Ln. E&W | 28W-9N,27W-9N | 31 |
| Medford Ct. N&S | 28W-9N | 31 |
| Merryoaks Rd. N&S | 29W-9N | 30 |
| Meyer Ct. N&S | 27W-11N | 31 |
| Middlebury Ct.* NS&EW | 24W-14N | 22 |
| Miller Av. NW&SE | 28W-9N,27W-9N | 31 |
| Monroe Ct. N&S | 28W-10N | 31 |
| Moore Av. N&S | 28W-9N | 31 |
| Mulberry Ln. NW&SE | 28W-9N | 31 |
| Mustang Ct. E&W | 30W-10N | 30 |
| Myrtle Ln. N&S | 30W-10N | 30 |
| N. Green Meadow Blvd. E&W | 27W-11N | 31 |
| N. Kennedy Dr. NS&EW | 27W-11N | 31 |
| N. Oltendorf Rd. N&S | 28W-11N | 31 |
| N. Victoria Ln. NS&EW | 28W-11N | 31 |
| N. Walnut St. N&S | 28W-11N | 30 |
| Newberry Dr. N&S | 28W-10N | 31 |
| Nippert Ct. NW&SE | 28W-9N | 31 |
| Nippert Dr. N&S | 28W-9N | 31 |
| Norwood Ct. N&S | 28W-9N | 31 |
| Oak Knoll Ct.* E&W | 24W-14N | 22 |
| Oak Meadow Ct.* E&W | 24W-13N | 22 |
| Oak Ridge Dr. NS&EW | 29W-9N | 30 |
| Oakland Dr. NW&SE | 28W-10N | 31 |
| Oakmont Ct.* N&S | 24W-13N | 22 |
| Old Church Rd. E&W | 27W-11N | 31 |
| Old Oak Ln. E&W | 28W-10N | 31 |
| Oltendorf Rd. N&S | 28W-11N,28W-10N | 31 |
| Oriole Dr. NS&EW | 28W-9N,27W-9N | 31 |
| Oxford Ct. N&S | 28W-9N | 31 |
| Park Blvd. N&S | 29W-9N,28W-11N | 31 |
| Parkside Cir. NS&EW | 28W-9N,28W-10N | 31 |
| Parkside Ct. N&S | 28W-9N | 31 |
| Parkwood Ct. E&W | 27W-9N | 31 |
| Parkwood Dr. N&S | 27W-9N | 31 |
| Patricia Pkwy. E&W | 28W-10N | 30 |
| Pembroke Ct. N&S | 29W-11N | 30 |
| Pepperidge Cir. NS&EW | 27W-10N | 31 |
| Petrie Cir. NE&SW | 27W-11N | 31 |
| Phillippi Creek Dr. NS&EW | 30W-9N | 30 |
| Pinto Ct. E&W | 30W-10N | 30 |
| Pleasant Pl. E&W | 28W-9N | 31 |
| Plum Tree Ct.* N&S | 24W-13N | 22 |
| Plymouth Dr. N&S | 28W-11N | 31 |
| Polk Ct. N&S | 29W-10N | 30 |
| Poplar Creek Ct. N&S | 28W-10N | 31 |
| Post Ln. NW&SE | 28W-9N | 31 |
| Post Pl. NW&SE | 27W-10N | 31 |
| Princeton Ct. N&S | 28W-9N | 31 |
| Quacker Hollow Ln. E&W | 26W-11N | 31 |
| Quarterhorse Ct. E&W | 30W-10N | 30 |
| Quincy Ct. N&S | 28W-9N | 31 |
| Rambler Ct. N&S | 28W-10N | 31 |
| Rambler Ln. N&S | 28W-10N | 31 |
| Rambler Pl. N&S | 28W-10N | 31 |
| Ramblewood Ct. | 27W-9N | 31 |
| Red Cedar Dr. NS&EW | 27W-10N | 31 |
| Redwood Ct. E&W | 27W-10N | 31 |
| Regency Ct. E&W | 29W-10N | 30 |
| Ridge Cir. NS&EW | 28W-10N,27W-10N | 31 |
| Ridge Ct. E&W | 28W-10N | 31 |
| Ridge Ct. N&S | 27W-10N | 31 |
| Ridge Pl. E&W | 27W-10N | 31 |
| Ridgewood Rd. NE&SW | 29W-10N | 30 |
| Robinhood Ct. N&S | 28W-10N | 31 |
| Robinhood Dr. E&W | 28W-10N | 31 |
| Robinson Av. NS&EW | 27W-9N | 31 |
| Roder Ct. N&S | 28W-9N | 31 |
| Romajean Pkwy. NS&EW | 28W-9N | 31 |
| Rowley Ct. NS&EW | 28W-9N | 31 |
| Rt. 19 E&W | 29W-10N,27W-9N | 30 |
| Rt. 59 N&S | 29W-10N,29W-11N | 30 |
| Russet Ln. N&S | 27W-10N | 31 |
| S. Green Meadow Blvd. E&W | 27W-11N | 31 |
| S. Oltendorf Rd. N&S | 28W-10N | 31 |
| S. Pine St. N&S | 28W-10N | 31 |
| Sandalwood Ct.* E&W | 24W-13N | 22 |
| Sandhurst Ct.* E&W | 24W-14N | 22 |
| Sarasota Dr. E&W | 28W-11N | 31 |
| Saybrook Ct. E&W | 28W-9N | 31 |
| Schaumburg Rd. E&W | 29W-11N,27W-10N | 30 |
| Seneca Ct. N&S | 29W-10N | 30 |
| Seton Ct. E&W | 27W-10N | 31 |
| Seton Pl. N&S | 27W-10N | 31 |
| Shadywood Ct. N&S | 29W-10N | 30 |
| Sheffield Ct. E&W | 29W-11N | 30 |
| Sherwood Dr. NE&SW | 28W-10N,29W-10N | 31 |
| Shirley Av. N&S | 28W-9N | 31 |
| Short Av. N&S | 27W-9N | 31 |
| Short St. E&W | 27W-9N | 31 |
| Siesta Key Ln. NW&SE | 30W-9N | 30 |
| Sieverwood Ct.* NW&SE | 24W-13N | 22 |
| Smith Ct. N&S | 27W-11N | 31 |
| Somerset Dr. N&S | 28W-11N | 31 |
| Southbury Ct.* N&S | 24W-13N | 22 |
| Southwood Cir. NS&EW | 27W-9N | 31 |
| Spring Valley Ln. E&W | 28W-10N | 31 |
| Spruce Dr. E&W | 28W-8N,27W-9N | 31 |
| Spur Ct. E&W | 30W-10N | 30 |
| Stowell Av. E&W | 28W-9N,27W-9N | 31 |
| Stowell Pl. NE&SW | 28W-9N | 31 |
| Stratford Cir. NS&EW | 28W-9N | 31 |
| Stratford Ct. NW&SE | 28W-9N | 31 |
| Stratford Ln. NE&SW | 28W-9N | 31 |
| Streamwood Blvd. EW&NS | 29W-10N,28W-10N | 30 |
| Suffolk Ct. N&S | 28W-10N | 31 |
| Suffolk Pl. N&S | 28W-10N,27W-10N | 31 |
| Summac Dr. NS&EW | 28W-9N | 31 |
| Sunnydale Blvd. N&S | 27W-9N | 31 |
| Sunset Cir. NS&EW | 27W-10N | 31 |
| Surrey Ct. E&W | 28W-9N | 31 |
| Surrey Dr. E&W | 28W-9N,27W-9N | 31 |
| Sutton Rd. N&S | 30W-10N,29W-11N | 30 |
| Taft Ct. N&S | 29W-10N | 30 |
| Tall Tree Rd. N&S | 28W-9N | 31 |
| Tanglewood Dr. NS&EW | 29W-10N | 30 |
| Taylor Ct. E&W | 29W-10N | 30 |
| Teak Ln. NE&SW | 27W-10N | 31 |
| Thorndale Ct. NW&SE | 29W-10N | 30 |
| Timber Ct. NE&SW | 28W-10N | 31 |
| Timber Tr. E&W | 28W-10N | 31 |
| Tinnerella Av. NW&SE | 27W-9N | 31 |
| Troy Ct. E&W | 28W-9N | 31 |
| Truman Ct. NW&SE | 29W-10N | 30 |
| Truman Ln. E&W | 29W-10N | 30 |
| Twilight Tr. E&W | 28W-9N | 31 |
| Tyler Ct. E&W | 29W-10N | 30 |
| Uxebridge Ct.* | 28W-9N | 31 |
| Valley Ln. N&S | 28W-9N | 31 |
| Victoria Ln. N&S | 28W-10N | 31 |
| Villa Rd. N&S | 28W-10N,27W-10N | 31 |
| Vine St. N&S | 28W-9N | 31 |
| Vinton Ct. N&S | 28W-9N | 31 |
| Virginia Ct. NS&EW | 29W-10N | 30 |
| W. Green Meadow Blvd. NE&SW | 27W-11N | 31 |
| W. Streamwood Blvd. E&W | 28W-10N,28W-10N | 30 |
| Walden Tr. E&W | 28W-11N | 31 |
| Walker Av. N&S | 28W-9N | 31 |
| Walnut Dr. N&S | 29W-10N,28W-10N | 30 |
| Warwick Ct.* NW&SE | 24W-13N | 22 |
| Washington Av. NE&SW | 29W-10N | 30 |
| Washington Ct. NW&SE | 28W-10N | 31 |
| Waverley Av. NE&SW | 28W-10N,27W-10N | 31 |
| Wellington Dr. E&W | 28W-11N | 31 |
| Westgate Ct. E&W | 27W-10N | 31 |
| Westgate Ter. NS&EW | 27W-10N | 31 |
| Weston Ct. E&W | 29W-11N | 30 |
| Whispering Ct. NW&SE | 29W-10N | 30 |
| Whispering Dr. NS&EW | 29W-10N | 30 |
| White Fence Tr. E&W | 30W-10N | 30 |
| Whitehall Ct.* NW&SE | 24W-13N | 22 |
| Whitewood Dr. NS&EW | 27W-10N | 31 |
| Wicker Av. NW&SE | 28W-9N,27W-9N | 31 |
| Wildflower Way NS&EW | 30W-10N | 30 |
| Wildrose Ct. E&W | 29W-9N | 30 |
| Wildwood Ct. E&W | 27W-9N | 31 |
| Wildwood Ln. NS&EW | 28W-9N | 31 |
| Williamsburg Dr. NS&EW | 28W-11N | 31 |
| Willow Ct. NE&SW | 27W-10N | 31 |
| Willow Rd. N&S | 27W-10N | 31 |
| Wilshire Ct. NE&SW | 29W-10N | 30 |
| Winchester Dr. NS&EW | 29W-9N | 30 |
| Winding Run Ln. N&S | 26W-11N | 31 |
| Windsor Ct. E&W | 27W-11N | 31 |
| Wingate Ct. E&W | 27W-11N | 31 |
| Wisteria Dr. E&W | 27W-10N | 31 |
| Woodbury Ct.* NW&SE | 24W-13N | 22 |
| Woodcrest Ct. N&S | 28W-10N | 31 |
| Woodland Hts. Blvd. E&W | 28W-10N,27W-10N | 31 |
| Woodmar Ct. E&W | 27W-11N | 31 |
| Woodridge Ln. NE&SW | 28W-10N | 31 |
| Woodview Ct. NE&SW | 27W-9N | 31 |
| Woodview Dr. N&S | 27W-9N | 31 |
| Yorkshire Dr. E&W | 27W-9N | 31 |

### Summit

| | Grid | Page |
|---|---|---|
| Archer N&S | 9W-6S | 59 |
| Ashton EW&NS | 13W-2S | 52 |
| Center N&S | 9W-5S | 59 |
| Douglas E&W | 9W-5S | 59 |
| Hanover E&W | 9W-5S | 59 |
| Harlem N&S | 9W-6S | 59 |
| Hunt N&S | 9W-5S | 59 |
| Lawndale Rd. NW&SE | 10W-5S | 59 |
| Park N&S | 9W-5S | 59 |
| Rt. 171 E&W | 9W-6S | 59 |
| Rt. 43 N&S | 9W-6S,9W-5S | 59 |
| 55th E&W | 9W-5S | 59 |

**Grid   Page**

55th Pl. E&W ........ 9W-6S 59
56th Pl. E&W ........ 9W-6S 59
57th Pl. E&W ........ 9W-6S 59
58th Pl. E&W ........ 9W-6S 59
59th St. E&W ........ 9W-6S 59
60th E&W ............ 9W-6S 59
61st E&W ............ 9W-6S 59
61st Pl. E&W ........ 9W-6S 59
62nd E&W ............ 9W-6S 59
62nd Pl. E&W ........ 9W-6S 59
63rd E&W ............ 9W-6S 59
63rd Pl. E&W ........ 9W-7S 59
64th E&W ............ 9W-7S 59
64th Pl. E&W ........ 9W-7S 59
72nd Ct. N&S ........ 9W-6S 59
73rd N&S ............ 9W-6S 59
73rd Ct. N&S ........ 9W-5S 59
74th N&S ...... 9W-6S,9W-5S 59
75th N&S ............ 9W-6S 59
76th N&S ............ 9W-6S 59

### Thornton

Anne Ct. E&W .... 0E-20S 88
Apache Dr. E&W ... 0E-20S 88
Arapaho Dr. N&S .... 0E-20S 88
Armory Dr. E&W ... 0W-19S 82
Arrowhead Dr. NS&EW
............... 0E-20S 88
Blackhawk Dr. NS&EW
............... 0E-20S 88
Blackstone St. N&S
...........0E-21S,0E-20S 88
Bonnie Ct. E&W .... 0E-20S 88
Brown Derby Rd. N&S
............... 0W-21S 88
Brownell Av. N&S .... 0E-21S 88
Canal St. N&S .... 0W-20S 88
Cherry Ln. E&W .... 0E-21S 88
Chicago Rd. N&S ... 0E-20S 88
Chippewa Dr. NE&SW
............... 0E-20S 88
Clark St. N&S .... 0E-20S 88
Cora Ct. E&W ....... 0E-20S 88
Dorie Ct. E&W ...... 0E-20S 88
Eleanor St. E&W .... 0E-21S 88
Evans Av. N&S ... 0W-17S 82
Forest Ln. E&W .... 0E-21S 88
Francis St. E&W .... 0E-21S 88
Harriet St. E&W .... 0E-21S 88
Highland Av. N&S ... 0E-20S 88
Hubbard St. N&S ... 0E-21S 88
Hunter St. N&S .... 0E-21S 88
Indianwood Dr. NS&EW
............... 0E-20S 88
Interstate 294-80 E&W
............ 0W-20S,0E-20S 88
Julian St. N&S
...........0E-21S,0E-20S 88
Juliette St. E&W .... 0E-20S 88
Kinzie Pl. N&S ..... 0E-20S 88
Kinzie St. N&S ..... 0E-21S 88
La Salle St. N&S ... 0W-20S 88
Laura Ln. E&W .... 0E-20S 88
Leavenworth St. N&S
............... 0W-21S 88
Leverette St. N&S ... 0E-21S 88
Malette St. N&S .... 0E-21S 88
Maple Ln. N&S .... 0E-21S 88
Margaret St. N&S .. 0W-21S 88
Maria St. E&W ..... 0E-21S 88
Marion St. E&W .... 0E-21S 88
Michigan Av. N&S ... 0W-20S 88
Mohawk Dr. E&W ... 0E-20S 88
Park Av. N&S ...... 0E-20S 88
Parnell Av. N&S ... 0W-20S 88
Pawnee Dr. E&W ... 0E-20S 88
Queens Ln. E&W ... 0E-21S 88
Ridge Rd. E&W .... 0W-21S 88
Rt. 294-80 E&W
.......... 0W-20S,0E-20S 88
Schwab St. N&S .... 0E-21S 88
Sunnyside Av. N&S .. 0E-20S 88
Tahoe St. N&S ..... 0E-20S 88
Thorncreek Rd. NW&SE
............... 0E-21S 88
Thornton Rd. E&W .. 0E-21S 88
Vincennes Rd. N&S
.......... 0W-20S,0E-20S 88
Wabash Av. N&S ... 0W-20S 88
Water St. N&S ..... 0E-21S 88
Wentworth Av. N&S ..0W-20S 88
Williams St. N&S ... 0E-21S 88
Wolcott St. N&S .....0E-21S 88
168th St. E&W ..... 0W-20S 88
169th St. E&W ..... 0W-20S 88
170th St. E&W ..... 0W-20S 88
171st St. E&W ..... 0E-20S 88
172nd St. E&W ..... 0E-20S 88
175th St. E&W ..... 0E-20S 88

### Thornton Township

Beaubien St. E&W ....1E-21S 89
Blackstone Av. N&S .. 1E-21S 89
Blitz St. E&W ...... 1E-21S 89
Bock Av. N&S ... 2E-21S 89
Calumet Expwy. N&S
...........1E-21S,1E-20S 89
Chappel Av. N&S .... 2E-18S 83
Chappell Av. N&S .... 2E-21S 89
Claremont Av. N&S .. 2W-19S 81
Clyde Av. N&S
.......... 2E-21S,2E-18S 89
Cornell Av. N&S .... 2E-21S 89
Cottage Grove Av. N&S
............... 0E-20S 88
Country Ln. N&S .. 2E-21S 89

**Grid   Page**

Dante Av. N&S ...... 1E-21S 89
East End Av. N&S .... 2E-21S 89
Elizabeth Av. N&S ... 2E-21S 89
Eustace St. E&W .... 1E-21S 89
Fern St. NW&SE .... 2E-21S 89
Greenwood Rd. NW&SE
............... 2E-18S 89
Hamilton Av. N&S .. 2W-19S 81
Harper Av. N&S .... 1E-21S 89
Hoyne Av. N&S .... 2W-19S 81
Indiana Av. NW&SE .. 2E-21S 89
Irving Av. N&S .... 2W-19S 81
Jason Ln. N&S ..... 2E-21S 89
Jeffrey Av. N&S ..... 2E-21S 89
Keegan St. E&W .... 1E-20S 89
Lansing Rd. E&W ... 2E-21S 89
Leavitt St. N&S ... 2W-19S 81
Locust Av. N&S .... 2E-21S 89
Merrill Av. N&S .... 2E-18S 83
Oakley Av. N&S ... 2W-19S 81
Olde Farm Rd. N&S .. 2E-21S 89
Paxton Av. N&S
............2E-21S,2E-18S 89
Ridge Rd. E&W .... 2E-21S 89
Ridgeland Av. N&S .. 2E-21S 89
Saginaw Av. N&S .... 3E-18S 83
St. Andrews St. E&W
............... 1E-21S 89
Stony Island Av. N&S
............... 1E-21S 89
Whitman Ln. N&S ... 2E-21S 89
158th St. E&W
............3E-18S,2E-18S 83
159th St. E&W ..... 3E-18S 83
160th St. E&W ..... 2W-19S 81
161st St. E&W ..... 2W-19S 81
177th St. E&W ..... 1E-21S 89
178th St. E&W ..... 1E-21S 89
180th Pl. E&W ..... 2E-21S 89
181st St. E&W ..... 2E-21S 89
183rd St. E&W ..... 2E-21S 89
185th St. E&W ..... 2E-21S 89

### Tinley Park

Alexandria Dr. N&S
............... 10W-19S 79
Almond Ln. E&W .. 11W-21S 85
Amherst St. N&S ... 9W-20S 85
Andres Av. E&W ... 7W-20S 86
Anne-Marie Av. N&S
............... 7W-20S 86
Anvil Pl. E&W .... 10W-19S 79
Apache Tr. E&W .. 10W-21S 85
Apple Ln. N&S ... 10W-19S 79
Arcadia Dr. N&S ... 7W-20S 86
Arlington St. E&W .. 9W-19S 79
Ash St. N&S ..... 11W-21S 85
Ashford Ct. N&S ... 9W-19S 79
Ashley Ln. E&W ... 10W-19S 79
Aspen Ln. E&W ... 10W-19S 79
Aster Ln. N&S .... 10W-21S 85
Autumn Dr. N&S ... 7W-20S 86
Avon Ln. N&S .... 10W-20S 85
Barbara E&W ..... 7W-20S 86
Barbara Ln. N&S ... 7W-20S 86
Barton Ct. E&W .. 11W-21S 85
Bayberry Ln. NS&EW
............... 11W-21S 85
Bedford Ln. E&W .. 10W-20S 85
Belle Rive Ct. E&W . 9W-20S 85
Berwick Dr. E&W .. 11W-21S 85
Bethany Ln. E&W .. 10W-20S 85
Birchwoode Ct. E&W
............... 8W-19S 79
Blackwater Ct. N&S .9W-19S 79
Blossom Ln. N&S .. 10W-19S 79
Blue Spruce Ct. E&W
............... 10W-19S 79
Bluebird Dr. E&W . 11W-21S 85
Bormet Dr. N&S ... 10W-19S 79
Brementowne Dr. NS&EW
............... 8W-19S 79
Brementowne Rd. NS&EW
............... 8W-19S 79
Briar Dr. N&S .... 11W-20S 84
Briarwood Dr. N&S 11W-20S 84
Bridalwood Ln. N&S
............... 11W-20S 85
Bristol Ln. E&W ... 10W-19S 79
Bristol Park Dr. EW&NS
............... 9W-21S 85
Brittney Ln. E&W .. 7W-20S 86
Brixton Ct. NW&SE
............... 11W-21S 85
Brixton Rd. N&S .. 11W-21S 85
Brunswick Ct. E&W
............... 11W-21S 85
Brunswick Ln. E&W
............... 11W-21S 85
Budingen Ln. E&W .10W-20S 85
Cambridge Pl. N&S
.......... 8W-20S,7W-20S 85
Cardinal Dr. N&S .. 11W-21S 85
Carlsbad Dr. N&S .. 11W-20S 86
Carriage Ln. E&W .. 10W-20S 85
Cartier Av. E&W ... 9W-21S 85
Castle Dr. NE&SW
..........11W-21S,10W-20S 85
Catalpa Ct. NW&SE
............... 11W-20S 85
Caxton Ct. N&S ... 11W-21S 85
Cedar Ln. N&S .... 9W-21S 85
Centennial Cir. NS&EW
............... 8W-19S 79
Centennial Ln. E&W 8W-19S 79
Champlain Av. NE&SW
............... 9W-21S 85

**Grid   Page**

Charnswood Ct.* N&S
............... 9W-19S 79
Charnswood Dr.* N&S
............... 9W-19S 79
Chelsea Rd. N&S .. 8W-19S 79
Cherokee Tr. E&W .10W-21S 85
Cherry Creek Av. N&S
............... 10W-20S 85
Cherry Hill Av. N&S
............... 10W-19S 79
Cherry Stone Pl. NW&SE
............... 10W-19S 79
Chestnut Dr. NE&SW
............... 11W-20S 85
Chippewa Tr. E&W 10W-21S 85
Christopher Ct. N&S
............... 7W-20S 86
Circle Dr. N&S .... 10W-20S 85
Claremont Dr. E&W .9W-20S 85
Clark Ln. N&S .... 8W-19S 79
Clifton Ct. N&S ... 11W-21S 85
Clifton Ln. N&S ... 11W-21S 85
Clover Av. N&S ... 10W-19S 79
Cloverview Dr. NS&EW
............... 10W-21S 85
Coachwood Tr. E&W
............... 8W-19S 79
Cobbler Ct. NE&SW
............... 11W-20S 85
Cobblestone Ct. NS&EW
............... 10W-19S 79
Cottage Ct. N&S .. 10W-20S 85
Cranberry Ct. N&S 10W-19S 79
Creekside Av. N&S
............... 10W-20S 85
Crescent Av. N&S .. 9W-19S 79
Crown Ln. E&W ... 8W-19S 79
Currant Av. N&S ... 10W-19S 79
Cynthia Ct.* N&S . 10W-20S 85
Cypress Ct. NE&SW
............... 11W-21S 85
Debra Av. E&W ... 7W-20S 86
Dee Ct. E&W ..... 10W-20S 85
Derwent Ln. N&S .. 10W-20S 85
Desiree Dr. E&W .. 10W-19S 79
Desota Av. NE&SW . 9W-21S 85
Doneen Av. NS&EW 9W-20S 85
Dooneen Av. NS&EW
............... 10W-20S 85
Dooneen Dr. N&S .. 9W-20S 85
Dorothy Ln. E&W .. 9W-20S 85
Dover Ct. N&S ... 11W-21S 85
Drummond Dr. NS&EW
............... 11W-21S 85
Duvan Dr. N&S ... 9W-21S 85
Eagle Ridge Dr. N&S
............... 10W-19S 79
Edgewood Ct. NE&SW
............... 11W-21S 85
Elm Lane Dr. N&S .. 8W-20S 85
Elmwood Dr. N&S . 11W-21S 85
Everdon Dr. N&S ... 9W-19S 79
Evergreen Dr. N&S 10W-19S 79
Fairfax Dr. N&S ... 8W-19S 79
Farm View Ct. N&S
............... 10W-20S 85
Flamingo Dr. E&W . 11W-21S 85
Forest View Dr. N&S
............... 8W-20S 85
Fox Grove Ln. NW&SE
............... 10W-20S 85
Funsburry Ct. NE&SW
............... 11W-21S 85
Gaynelle Rd. N&S .. 7W-20S 86
Gentry Ln. N&S ... 7W-20S 86
Glen Swilly Cir. NS&EW
............... 8W-21S 85
Glenview Dr. E&W .. 9W-20S 85
Golden Pheasant Dr. EW&NS
............... 11W-21S 85
Goswell Ln. E&W .. 11W-21S 85
Greenwood Dr. E&W
............... 11W-21S 85
Grissom Dr. N&S .. 10W-20S 85
Hamilton Av. N&S ..9W-19S 79
Hanover Dr. E&W .. 9W-20S 85
Harlem Av. N&S
.......... 9W-20S,8W-23S 85
Heather Ct. N&S .. 10W-21S 85
Heather Ln. NW&SE
............... 10W-21S 85
Helen Sandidge Ct. N&S
............... 7W-20S 86
Henry St. N&S .... 10W-19S 79
Hickory St. NE&SW . 9W-19S 79
Highland Av. N&S .. 7W-20S 86
Hillcrest Ct. E&W .. 10W-19S 79
Hillcrest Ln. E&W .. 10W-19S 79
Hillside Pl. N&S ... 7W-20S 86
Holly Ct. NW&SE .. 11W-21S 85
Honey Lane Dr. E&W
.......... 8W-20S,7W-20S 85
Horsehoe Dr. N&S . 10W-19S 79
Hubbard Lane Dr. E&W
............... 8W-20S 85
Humber Ln. SE&NW
..........11W-21S,10W-20S 85
Hummingbird Dr. N&S
............... 10W-21S 85
Hunter Tr. N&S ... 8W-19S 79
Interstate 80 E&W . 8W-22S 85
Inverness Dr. N&S . 10W-20S 85
Ironwood Dr. N&S . 10W-19S 79
Iroquois Trace NS&EW
............... 10W-21S 85
Jacquelin Ct. N&S .. 7W-20S 86
Jean Ln. N&S .... 8W-19S 79
Jeanette Ct. E&W .. 8W-21S 85

**Grid   Page**

Jennifer Av. E&W ....7W-20S 86
Jessica Ln. E&W .. 10W-19S 79
Joliet Dr. EW&NS .. 9W-21S 85
Juniper Ct. NE&SW
............... 11W-20S 85
Justin Ct. E&W ... 10W-19S 79
Kathleen Ln. E&W . 10W-19S 79
Kensington Av. N&S 9W-19S 79
Kingston Ct. NW&SE
............... 8W-19S 79
Kingston Rd. E&W . 8W-19S 79
Lake Bluff Dr. NE&SW
............... 7W-20S 86
Lake Villa Av. N&S . 9W-19S 79
Lakeside Pl. NE&SW
............... 7W-20S 86
Lakeview Ct. N&S . 8W-22S 86
Lakewood Dr. N&S . 7W-20S 86
Laura Ln. NW&SE .. 7W-20S 86
Laverne Ln. E&W .. 8W-19S 79
Lilac Ln. N&S .... 10W-21S 85
Linden St. NS&EW . 11W-21S 85
Lindsay St. E&W .. 12W-20S 84
Live Oak Ct. N&S .. 8W-21S 85
Locust Dr. N&S ... 11W-20S 85
Magnolia Ln. E&W . 11W-21S 85
Mallard Rd. E&W ... 8W-19S 79
Manchester St. N&S 8W-19S 79
Maple Creek Dr. E&W
............... 9W-22S 85
Maple Ln. N&S ... 8W-20S 85
Maplewoode Ct. N&S
............... 9W-19S 79
Marquette Av. EW&NS
............... 9W-21S 85
Meadow Ct. NW&SE
............... 10W-19S 79
Meadow Ln. N&S .. 10W-19S 79
Meadowlark Dr. E&W
............... 11W-21S 85
Michelle Ln. E&W . 10W-19S 79
Milford Av. N&S .. 9W-20S 85
Mockingbird Ln. N&S
............... 11W-21S 85
Mulberry Av. N&S
..........11W-21S,11W-20S 85
Mulberry St. E&W .. 11W-20S 85
Navajo Trace N&S . 10W-21S 85
New England Av. N&S
............... 8W-20S 85
Normandy Ln. NE&SW
............... 8W-20S 85
North Creek Dr. N&S
............... 9W-22S 85
North St. NS&EW .. 9W-20S 85
Nottingham Ct. NW&SE
............... 9W-19S 79
Nottingham Dr. E&W
............10W-19S,9W-19S 79
Oak Forest Av. NE&SW
............... 8W-20S 85
Oak Park Av. N&S
.......... 8W-22S,8W-19S 85
Oakwood Dr. N&S . 11W-21S 85
Oconto Av. N&S ... 9W-20S 85
Odell Av. N&S .... 9W-20S 85
Oketo Av. N&S ... 9W-20S 85
Olcott Av. N&S
.......... 9W-20S,9W-19S 85
Olcott Ct. NW&SE
.......... 9W-20S,9W-19S 85
Old Barn Ct. N&S .. 10W-20S 85
Olde Gatehouse Rd. NS&EW
............... 8W-19S 79
Oleander Av. N&S .. 9W-20S 85
Orchard Av. E&W .. 10W-19S 79
Oriole Av. N&S ... 9W-20S 85
Osceola Av. N&S .. 9W-20S 85
Ottawa Av. N&S .. 9W-20S 85
Overhill Av. N&S .. 9W-20S 85
Oxford Dr. N&S ... 8W-19S 79
Ozark Av. N&S
.......... 9W-20S,9W-19S 85
Park Central Dr. EW&NS
............... 9W-21S 85
Parkside Dr. E&W .. 8W-20S 85
Parkview Av. N&S .. 9W-19S 79
Parliament Av. N&S 9W-19S 79
Paxton Av. N&S
.......... 9W-20S,9W-19S 85
Peacock N&S .... 11W-21S 85
Pecan Ln. N&S ... 11W-21S 85
Pelican Ln. N&S .. 11W-21S 85
Pheasant Lake Dr. N&S
............... 11W-21S 85
Pheasant Ln. N&S . 11W-21S 85
Pin Oak Ln. N&S .. 8W-21S 85
Pine Dr. N&S .... 10W-19S 79
Pine Dr. NW&SE .. 8W-22S 86
Pine Lake Dr. N&S . 8W-22S 86
Pine Point Dr. N&S . 8W-20S 85
Pinewood Av. N&S . 8W-20S 85
Piute Tr. E&W .... 10W-21S 85
Plum Ct. E&W .... 10W-20S 85
Pond View Ct. NW&SE
............... 8W-22S 86
Pond View Dr. NW&SE
............... 8W-22S 86
Poplar St. N&S ... 11W-20S 85
Pottawattomi Tr. E&W
............... 10W-21S 85
Prairie Ln. E&W ... 10W-19S 79
Prairie Dr. N&S ... 10W-19S 79
Prestwick Dr. N&S . 10W-20S 85
Princess Elizabeth Ct. N&S
............... 11W-21S 85
Princeton Av. N&S 9W-19S 79
Quail Cross E&W . 11W-21S 85

**Grid   Page**

Queen Ann Ln. N&S
............... 10W-20S 85
Queen Elizabeth Ln. N&S
............... 10W-20S 85
Queen Mary Ln. N&S
............... 10W-20S 85
Queen Victoria Ln. E&W
............... 10W-20S 85
Radcliffe Ct. N&S . 11W-21S 85
Radcliffe Rd. E&W . 11W-21S 85
Raintree Ln. E&W .. 8W-20S 85
Ravinia Dr. E&W ... 8W-20S 85
Redwood Ln. NW&SE
............... 11W-21S 85
Richards Ct. NW&SE
............... 11W-21S 85
Richards Dr. N&S
..........10W-20S,10W-19S 85
Ridgeland Av. N&S
.......... 8W-24S,8W-19S 90
Riverside Dr. NS&EW
............... 8W-20S 85
Rosewood Ln. NW&SE
............... 11W-21S 85
Rossmore Ct. N&S 11W-21S 85
Rossmore Rd. NE&SW
............... 11W-21S 85
Royal Oak Ct. N&S . 8W-21S 85
Rt. 43 N&S ..9W-22S,8W-22S 85
S. Pointe Dr. N&S
............... 8W-22S 86
Salem Ct. N&S ... 9W-21S 85
Sandalwood Dr. E&W
............... 9W-21S 85
Sandridge Ct. E&W . 9W-19S 79
Sandy Ln. NW&SE . 8W-20S 85
Sayre Av. N&S ... 8W-20S 85
Schuldt St. N&S .. 11W-21S 85
Scott Ct. N&S .... 7W-20S 86
Shannon Ct. N&S . 10W-20S 85
Shetland Dr. N&S . 11W-20S 85
Shoshone Tr. E&W 10W-21S 85
Skyline Dr. N&S .. 8W-19S 79
South St. NE&SW
.......... 8W-20S,7W-20S 85
Spring Creek Dr. N&S
............... 9W-22S 85
Spruce Ln. E&W .. 11W-20S 85
Steeple Dr. NE&SW
............... 10W-20S 85
Steven Pl. NW&SE . 10W-19S 79
Stone Bridge Walk* NE&SW
............... 9W-19S 79
Surrey Dr. N&S ... 10W-19S 79
Sussex Rd. E&W .. 8W-19S 79
Sycamore Ct. E&W
............... 11W-20S 85
Tamar Ln. N&S ... 10W-20S 85
Tanbark Dr. NS&EW
............... 10W-19S 79
Tayside Ln. E&W .. 11W-20S 85
Teakwood Dr. N&S
............... 11W-20S 85
Terrace Dr. E&W ... 10W-20S 85
Theresa Ln. E&W .. 8W-19S 79
Thornwood Dr. E&W
............... 11W-20S 85
Timber Ct. E&W .. 10W-20S 85
Tinley Park Dr. NE&SW
............... 8W-20S 85
Tower Ln. N&S ... 10W-19S 79
Trent Ct. E&W .... 10W-21S 85
Tudor Ln. NS&EW . 10W-20S 85
Tulip Ln. N&S .... 10W-21S 85
Turnberry Ln. E&W
............... 11W-20S 85
Valley Forge Dr. N&S
............... 10W-20S 85
Valleyview Ct. NW&SE
............... 10W-20S 85
Valleyview Dr. NS&EW
............... 10W-20S 85
Vogt St. E&W .... 10W-20S 85
Warwick Rd. N&S . 11W-21S 85
Waterford Dr. E&W
............... 10W-20S 85
Wentworth Dr. E&W 9W-20S 85
West Creek Dr. E&W
............... 9W-22S 85
Westbury Ln. N&S
............... 10W-19S 79
Westbridge Ct. N&S
............... 11W-21S 85
Westbridge Rd. E&W
............... 11W-21S 85
Westwind Ct. NW&SE
............... 8W-20S 85
White Eagle Dr. NS&EW
............... 8W-21S 85
White Tailed Ln. E&W
............... 8W-21S 85
Whittington Dr. E&W
............... 9W-19S 79
Willow Ln. N&S .....8W-20S 85
Windsor Pkwy. E&W
............... 11W-21S 85
Winston Dr. E&W .. 10W-19S 79
Witham Ct. E&W .. 9W-16S 79
Wittington St. N&S .. 9W-19S 79
Woburn Rd. N&S . 11W-21S 85
Woodland Dr. E&W
............... 10W-19S 79
Woodstock Av. E&W
............... 9W-22S 85
64th Ct. N&S
.......... 8W-20S,8W-19S 85
65th Av. N&S
.......... 8W-21S,8W-19S 85

| | Grid | Page |
|---|---|---|
| 65th Ct. N&S | | |
| | 8W-21S,8W-19S | 85 |
| 66th Av. N&S | | |
| | 8W-21S,8W-19S | 85 |
| 66th Ct. N&S | | |
| | 8W-21S,8W-20S | 85 |
| 67th Av. N&S | | |
| | 8W-21S,8W-20S | 85 |
| 67th Ct. N&S | | |
| | 8W-22S,8W-19S | 85 |
| 68th Ct. N&S | | |
| | 8W-21S,8W-20S | 85 |
| 69th Av. N&S | 8W-20S | 85 |
| 70th Av. N&S | 8W-20S | 85 |
| 70th Ct. N&S | 8W-21S | 85 |
| 71st Av. N&S | | |
| | 8W-21S,8W-20S | 85 |
| 71st Ct. N&S | | |
| | 8W-21S,8W-20S | 85 |
| 75th Av. N&S | 9W-19S | 85 |
| 76th Av. N&S | 9W-19S | 79 |
| 78th Av. N&S | 9W-19S | 79 |
| 78th Ct. N&S | 9W-19S | 85 |
| 79th Av. N&S | 9W-20S | 85 |
| 80th Av. N&S | 10W-20S | 85 |
| 81st Av. N&S | 10W-20S | 85 |
| 81st Ct. N&S | 10W-20S | 85 |
| 82nd Av. N&S | 10W-20S | 85 |
| 82nd Ct. N&S | 10W-20S | 85 |
| 83rd Ct. N&S | 10W-20S | 85 |
| 84th Av. N&S | | |
| | 10W-20S,10W-19S | 85 |
| 84th Ct. N&S | 10W-19S | 79 |
| 84th Pl. N&S | 10W-19S | 79 |
| 85th Av. N&S | 10W-19S | 79 |
| 85th Ct. N&S | 10W-19S | 79 |
| 87th Ct. N&S | 10W-20S | 85 |
| 88th Ct. N&S | | |
| | 11W-21S,11W-20S | 85 |
| 92nd Av. N&S | | |
| | 11W-22S,11W-20S | 85 |
| 94th Ct. N&S | 11W-20S | 84 |
| 159th Pl. E&W | 9W-19S | 79 |
| 159th St. E&W | | |
| | 10W-19S,9W-19S | 79 |
| 160th Pl. E&W | | |
| | 10W-19S,9W-19S | 79 |
| 160th St. E&W | 9W-19S | 79 |
| 161st Pl. E&W | | |
| | 10W-19S,9W-19S | 79 |
| 161st St. E&W | | |
| | 10W-19S,9W-19S | 79 |
| 162nd Pl. E&W | | |
| | 10W-19S,9W-19S | 79 |
| 162nd St. E&W | 9W-19S | 79 |
| 163rd Pl. E&W | 9W-19S,8W-19S | 79 |
| 163rd St. E&W | | |
| | 10W-19S,8W-19S | 79 |
| 164th Ct. E&W | 10W-19S | 79 |
| 164th Pl. E&W | | |
| | 10W-19S,8W-19S | 79 |
| 164th St. E&W | | |
| | 10W-19S,8W-19S | 79 |
| 165th Pl. E&W | 9W-19S,8W-19S | 79 |
| 165th St. E&W | | |
| | 10W-19S,8W-19S | 79 |
| 166th Pl. E&W | 9W-19S | 79 |
| 166th St. E&W | | |
| | 9W-19S,8W-19S | 79 |
| 167th Ct. N&S | 8W-21S | 86 |
| 167th Pl. E&W | 10W-20S | 85 |
| 167th St. E&W | | |
| | 10W-19S,8W-19S | 79 |
| 168th Pl. E&W | | |
| | 10W-20S,9W-20S | 85 |
| 168th St. E&W | 10W-20S | 85 |
| 169th Pl. E&W | 10W-20S | 85 |
| 169th St. E&W | | |
| | 10W-20S,8W-20S | 85 |
| 170th Pl. E&W | | |
| | 10W-20S,9W-20S | 85 |
| 170th St. E&W | | |
| | 10W-20S,8W-20S | 85 |
| 171st Pl. E&W | | |
| | 10W-20S,9W-20S | 85 |
| 171st St. E&W | | |
| | 11W-20S,8W-20S | 85 |
| 172nd Pl. E&W | 9W-20S | 85 |
| 172nd St. E&W | | |
| | 11W-20S,8W-20S | 85 |
| 173rd Pl. E&W | | |
| | 9W-20S,8W-20S | 85 |
| 173rd Rd. NW&SE | 11W-20S | 85 |
| 173rd St. E&W | | |
| | 9W-20S,8W-20S | 85 |
| 174th Pl. E&W | | |
| | 10W-20S,8W-20S | 85 |
| 174th St. E&W | | |
| | 11W-20S,8W-20S | 85 |
| 175th Pl. E&W | 8W-21S | 85 |
| 175th St. E&W | | |
| | 11W-20S,7W-20S | 85 |
| 175th St. E&W | | |
| | 9W-21S,9W-20S | 85 |
| 176th Pl. E&W | 8W-21S | 85 |
| 176th St. E&W | | |
| | 11W-21S,8W-20S | 85 |
| 177th Pl. E&W | 8W-21S | 85 |
| 177th St. E&W | | |
| | 11W-21S,8W-21S | 85 |
| 178th St. E&W | | |
| | 11W-21S,8W-21S | 85 |
| 179th Av. N&S | 9W-21S | 85 |
| 179th St. E&W | 8W-21S | 85 |
| 180th Pl. E&W | 8W-21S | 85 |

| | Grid | Page |
|---|---|---|
| 180th St. E&W | 8W-21S | 85 |
| 181st Pl. E&W | 8W-21S | 85 |
| 181st St. E&W | 8W-21S | 85 |
| 182nd Pl. E&W | 8W-21S | 85 |
| 182nd St. E&W | 8W-21S | 85 |
| 183rd St. E&W | | |
| | 11W-21S,8W-21S | 85 |

**Westchester**

| Alexandria St. NS&EW | | |
| | 14W-2S | 52 |
| Ashley Woods Ln. NE&SW | | |
| | 14W-2S | 52 |
| Balmoral N&S | | |
| | 13W-2S,12W-1S | 52 |
| Becket N&S | 13W-2S | 52 |
| Bedford E&W | 13W-2S | 52 |
| Belleview E&W | 13W-2S | 52 |
| Berkshire E&W | 13W-1S | 52 |
| Boeger N&S | 13W-1S | 52 |
| Boeger Ct. SW&NE | | |
| | 13W-2S,13W-1S | 52 |
| Bond E&W | 12W-1S | 52 |
| Brighton Ct. N&S | 13W-1S | 52 |
| Bristol N&S | 12W-1S,12W-0S | 52 |
| Buckingham N&S | 13W-2S | 52 |
| Cir. | 13W-1S | 52 |
| Burton Dr. E&W | 14W-2S | 52 |
| Cambridge E&W | 12W-1S | 52 |
| Camelot E&W | 13W-1S | 52 |
| Canterbury E&W | | |
| | 13W-1S,12W-1S | 52 |
| Carlisle E&W | 13W-2S | 52 |
| Carlton N&S | 13W-1S | 52 |
| Charles E&W | 13W-1S | 52 |
| Chaucer E&W | 12W-1S | 52 |
| Chesapeake St. NS&EW | | |
| | 14W-2S | 52 |
| Claridge E&W | 13W-2S | 52 |
| Concord N&S | 13W-1S | 52 |
| Crestwood St. E&W | 12W-1S | 52 |
| Cromwell N&S | 12W-0S | 46 |
| Denton N&S | 13W-1S | 52 |
| Derby Ln. NW&SE | 12W-1S | 52 |
| Devonshire E&W | 12W-0S | 46 |
| Devonshire Ln. NW&SE | | |
| | 12W-0S | 46 |
| Dickens E&W | | |
| | 13W-1S,12W-1S | 52 |
| Dorchester E&W | 13W-1S | 52 |
| Dover E&W | 12W-1S | 52 |
| Downing N&S | | |
| | 13W-2S,13W-1S | 52 |
| Drake St. N&S | 14W-2S | 52 |
| Drury Ln. NW&SE | 12W-1S | 52 |
| Eaton E&W | 13W-2S | 52 |
| Elizabeth E&W | 12W-1S | 52 |
| Enterprise St. N&S | 14W-2S | 52 |
| Essex E&W | 13W-2S | 52 |
| Evers N&S | 12W-1S | 52 |
| Fairfield E&W | 13W-2S | 52 |
| Fielding E&W | | |
| | 14W-1S,13W-1S | 52 |
| Fleet E&W | 13W-2S | 52 |
| Forest St. N&S | 14W-2S | 52 |
| Gardner N&S | 12W-1S | 52 |
| Gladstone E&W | 12W-0S | 46 |
| Haas N&S | 13W-1S | 52 |
| Halifax N&S | 13W-2S | 52 |
| Hastings N&S | 13W-2S | 52 |
| Hawthorne N&S | 13W-2S | 52 |
| Heidorn N&S | 13W-1S | 52 |
| Highridge N&S | 13W-1S | 52 |
| Hull N&S | 12W-1S,12W-0S | 52 |
| Interstate 290 E&W | 12W-0S | 46 |
| Kensington N&S | | |
| | 13W-2S,13W-1S | 52 |
| Kent E&W | 12W-1S | 52 |
| Kingston E&W | 13W-2S | 52 |
| Kipling E&W | 12W-1S | 52 |
| Kitchener E&W | 12W-0S | 46 |
| LaGrange Rd. N&S | 13W-2S | 52 |
| Lancaster E&W | 13W-2S | 52 |
| Manchester N&S | | |
| | 12W-1S,12W-0S | 52 |
| Mandel N&S | 13W-1S | 52 |
| Mannheim Rd. N&S | 13W-1S | 52 |
| Martindale E&W | 13W-2S | 52 |
| Mayfair N&S | | |
| | 13W-2S,13W-1S | 52 |
| Milford N&S | 12W-1S | 52 |
| Nelson E&W | 13W-2S | 52 |
| Nelson Sq. N&S | 13W-2S | 52 |
| Newberry N&S | 13W-2S | 52 |
| Newcastle N&S | | |
| | 12W-1S,12S-0S | 52 |
| Norfolk N&S | | |
| | 12W-1S,12W-0S | 52 |
| Oxford E&W | 13W-1S | 52 |
| Park St. N&S | 14W-2S | 52 |
| Pelham E&W | 12W-1S | 52 |
| Pell E&W | 12W-1S | 52 |
| Plymouth N&S | 13W-2S | 52 |
| Portsmouth N&S | | |
| | 12W-1S,12W-0S | 52 |
| Prescott Ln. NS&EW | | |
| | 14W-2S | 52 |
| Preston E&W | 13W-2S | 52 |
| Raleigh E&W | 13W-2S | 52 |
| Robin Hood E&W | 13W-2S | 52 |
| Rt. 38 E&W | 13W-1S | 52 |
| Shakespeare E&W | 13W-1S | 52 |
| Shaw SW&NE | 13W-1S | 52 |
| Shelly N&S | 13W-2S | 52 |
| Sherwood N&S | 13W-2S | 52 |
| Somerset N&S | 13W-2S | 52 |
| Stratford N&S | 13W-2S | 52 |

| | Grid | Page |
|---|---|---|
| Suffolk N&S | 12W-1S,12S-0S | 52 |
| Sunnyside N&S | 13W-2S | 52 |
| The Strand E&W | 12W-0S | 46 |
| U.S. Rt. 12 N&S | 13W-1S | 52 |
| U.S. Rt. 20 N&S | 13W-1S | 52 |
| U.S. Rt. 45 N&S | 13W-1S | 52 |
| Wakefield E&W | 13W-2S | 52 |
| Waterford Dr. E&W | 13W-1S | 52 |
| Waverly N&S | 13W-1S | 52 |
| Wellington N&S | 13W-2S | 52 |
| Westchester Blvd. N&S | | |
| | 12W-1S,12W-0S | 52 |
| Westminster E&W | 13W-2S | 52 |
| Windsor E&W | 13W-2S | 52 |
| Woodland St. N&S | 14W-2S | 52 |
| Worcester E&W | 14W-2S | 46 |
| Wright E&W | 12W-1S | 52 |
| 26th St. E&W | 14W-2S | 52 |
| 28th St. E&W | 14W-2S | 52 |
| 29th St. E&W | 13W-2S | 52 |
| 30th St. E&W | 14W-2S | 52 |

**Western Springs**

| Birch E&W | 14W-6S | 58 |
| Burlington SW&NE | 14W-4S | 52 |
| Caroline E&W | 14W-4S | 58 |
| Central N&S | | |
| | 14W-5S,14W-4S | 58 |
| Chestnut E&W | 14W-4S | 52 |
| Clausen N&S | | |
| | 13W-5S,13W-4S | 58 |
| Commonwealth N&S | | |
| | 14W-5S | 58 |
| Courtland E&W | 13W-5S | 58 |
| Crest N&S | 14W-6S | 58 |
| Crestview Dr. N&S | 14W-4S | 58 |
| Crestview Pl. E&W | 14W-4S | 58 |
| Dierks E&W | 13W-5S | 58 |
| Ellington N&S | | |
| | 13W-5S,13W-4S | 58 |
| Elm SW&NE | 13W-4S | 52 |
| Ernst E&W | 13W-4S | 58 |
| Fairels N&S | 14W-5S | 58 |
| Forest N&S | 14W-4S | 52 |
| Franklin N&S | | |
| | 13W-5S,13W-4S | 58 |
| Garden N&S | 14W-4S | 58 |
| Gilbert N&S | 13W-4S | 52 |
| Grand N&S | 14W-6S,13W-4S | 58 |
| Grove N&S | 14W-4S | 52 |
| Hampton N&S | 14W-4S | 58 |
| Harvey N&S | | |
| | 13W-5S,13W-4S | 58 |
| Hill Grove SW&NE | 14W-4S | 52 |
| Howard N&S | | |
| | 13W-5S,13W-4S | 58 |
| Johnson N&S | | |
| | 13W-5S,13W-4S | 58 |
| Kirkland E&W | 13W-5S | 58 |
| Lawn N&S | 14W-5S,15W-4S | 58 |
| Lawn Cir. E&W | 14W-6S | 58 |
| Lawn Ct. E&W | 14W-6S | 58 |
| Lawn Dr. N&S | 14W-6S | 58 |
| Linden N&S | 13W-4S | 52 |
| Linden Cir. NE&SW | 14W-6S | 58 |
| Linden Cir. NS&EW | 14W-6S | 58 |
| Linden Ct. NW&SE | 14W-6S | 58 |
| Longmeadow E&W | 14W-6S | 58 |
| Maple E&W | 14W-4S | 58 |
| Maple N&S | 14W-4S | 58 |
| Oak E&W | 14W-4S | 58 |
| Oak N&S | 14W-6S | 58 |
| Ogden E&W | 14W-4S | 58 |
| Park Ln. E&W | 14W-6S | 58 |
| Park Pl. E&W | 14W-6S | 58 |
| Prospect N&S | 14W-4S | 52 |
| Race E&W | 14W-4S | 52 |
| Reed E&W | 13W-4S | 52 |
| Ridge E&W | 14W-4S | 52 |
| Ridgewood N&S | 14W-6S | 58 |
| Ridgewood Oaks Dr. NS&EW | | |
| | 14W-6S | 58 |
| Rose N&S | 14W-4S | 52 |
| Rugeley E&W | 13W-4S | 52 |
| Sping N&S | 14W-4S | 52 |
| Sunset E&W | 14W-4S | 52 |
| U.S. Rt. 34 E&W | 13W-3S | 52 |
| Walker E&W | 14W-4S | 52 |
| Walnut E&W | 14W-4S | 52 |
| Western N&S | 14W-4S | 52 |
| Willow E&W | 14W-4S | 52 |
| Wolf N&S | 14W-5S | 58 |
| Woodland N&S | | |
| | 14W-5S,14W-4S | 58 |
| 39th E&W | 13W-3S | 52 |
| 40th E&W | 13W-4S | 52 |
| 41st E&W | 13W-4S | 52 |
| 42nd E&W | 13W-4S | 52 |
| 43rd E&W | 13W-4S | 52 |
| 45th E&W | 13W-4S | 52 |
| 46th E&W | 13W-4S | 52 |
| 47th E&W | 14W-4S | 52 |
| 48th E&W | 14W-5S,13W-5S | 58 |
| 49th E&W | 14W-5S | 58 |
| 50th E&W | 14W-4S | 58 |
| 50th Pl. E&W | 13W-5S | 58 |
| 51st E&W | 14W-5S | 58 |
| 51st Pl. E&W | 13W-5S | 58 |
| 52nd E&W | 14W-5S | 58 |
| 52nd Pl. E&W | 14W-5S | 58 |
| 53rd E&W | 14W-5S,13W-5S | 58 |
| 54th E&W | 14W-5S | 58 |
| Cir. | 13W-5S | 58 |
| 55th E&W | 14W-5S | 58 |

**Wheeling**

| | Grid | Page |
|---|---|---|
| Abbey Ct.* NW&SE | | |
| | 13W-18N | 16 |
| Abbott Dr. E&W | 14W-16N | 15 |
| Abourndale Ct. E&W | | |
| | 16W-16N | 15 |
| Acco Plaza Dr. N&S | | |
| | 14W-17N | 15 |
| Acorn Ct.* N&S | 13W-17N | 16 |
| Albert Ter. NE&SW | | |
| | 15W-17N | 15 |
| Alder Dr. N&S | 13W-17N | 16 |
| Alderman Av. E&W | | |
| | 14W-15N | 15 |
| Aldgate Ct.* E&W | 13W-17N | 16 |
| Alice St. NW&SE | 14W-16N | 15 |
| Allen Ct. N&S | 14W-17N | 15 |
| Allendale Dr. E&W | 15W-17N | 15 |
| Alpine Ct.* E&W | 16W-18N | 15 |
| Amy Ct.* NW&SE | 14W-16N | 15 |
| Ande Av. N&S | 14W-16N | 15 |
| Ander Ct. E&W | 15W-16N | 15 |
| Anita Pl. N&S | 14W-17N | 15 |
| Anne Ter. N&S | 15W-17N | 15 |
| Anthony Rd. E&W | 15W-17N | 15 |
| Apache Tr.* N&S | 16W-17N | 15 |
| Aptakisic Rd. NE&SW | | |
| | 16W-18N | 15 |
| Arbour E&W | 14W-18N | 15 |
| Arlene Ct. NE&SW | 14W-17N | 15 |
| Arlington Dr.* NS&EW | | |
| | 13W-18N | 16 |
| Armand Ln. N&S | 15W-18N | 15 |
| Armand St. E&W | 15W-18N | 15 |
| Arrow Tr. N&S | 16W-17N | 15 |
| Ash Ln.* N&S | 16W-18N | 15 |
| Ashton Ct.* N&S | 13W-17N | 16 |
| Audrey Ct. E&W | | |
| | 15W-17N | 15 |
| Baldwin Ct.* N&S | 13W-17N | 16 |
| Barberry Ln.* N&S | 16W-16N | 15 |
| Barnaby Pl.* NE&SW | | |
| | 15W-18N | 15 |
| Bayside Ct.* N&S | 13W-17N | 16 |
| Bayside Dr.* E&W | 15W-18N | 15 |
| Bayside Ln.* E&W | 16W-18N | 15 |
| Beech Dr.* NW&SE | | |
| | 13W-16N | 16 |
| Berkshire Dr. N&S | 16W-18N | 15 |
| Bernice Ct. NE&SW | | |
| | 15W-17N | 15 |
| Beverly Dr. E&W | 15W-18N | 15 |
| Bina Ct. N&S | 14W-17N | 15 |
| Birch Tr. N&S | 16W-17N | 15 |
| Blackfoot Tr.* N&S | 16W-17N | 15 |
| Blackhawk Tr.* E&W | | |
| | 16W-17N | 15 |
| Blaze Tr. E&W | 15W-16N | 15 |
| Boehmer Av. N&S | 14W-17N | 15 |
| Bow Tr.* E&W | 16W-17N | 15 |
| Boxwood E&W | | |
| | 15W-18N | 15 |
| Braeburn Dr. N&S | 13W-17N | 16 |
| Brandon Pl. E&W | 15W-17N | 15 |
| Braver Ct.* N&S | 13W-17N | 16 |
| Brian Ln. NS&EW | 14W-17N | 15 |
| Briarwood Dr. N&S | | |
| | 15W-17N | 15 |
| Bridgeport Pl.* E&W | | |
| | 15W-18N | 15 |
| Bridget Pl. E&W | 15W-18N | 15 |
| Bridgeview Ct.* NS&EW | | |
| | 16W-16N | 15 |
| Bridle Tr. E&W | 15W-16N | 15 |
| Brighton Pl.* N&S | 15W-18N | 15 |
| Brittany Ct.* N&S | 13W-17N | 16 |
| Broadway Ct.* E&W | | |
| | 13W-17N | 16 |
| Brougham Dr. E&W | | |
| | 15W-18N | 15 |
| Buckboard Dr. E&W | | |
| | 16W-16N | 15 |
| Buckeye Dr. N&S | 13W-17N | 16 |
| Buckingham Ct.* E&W | | |
| | 15W-18N | 15 |
| Buffalo Grove Rd. N&S | | |
| | 16W-16N | 15 |
| Buffalo Tr. N&S | 16W-17N | 15 |
| Buxton Ct.* E&W | 13W-17N | 16 |
| Cambridge Pl., W. N&S | | |
| | 15W-18N | 15 |
| Camden Ct.* NW&SE | | |
| | 14W-15N | 15 |
| Camp McDonald Rd. E&W | | |
| | 14W-15N | 15 |
| Canbury Ct.* N&S | 13W-17N | 16 |
| Candlewood Ct.* E&W | | |
| | 16W-16N | 15 |
| Capitol Dr. NS&EW | | |
| | 14W-16N | 15 |
| Capri Ter. E&W | 14W-18N | 15 |
| Captains Ln.* N&S | 15W-17N | 15 |
| Cardinal Ct.* NW&SE | | |
| | 13W-18N | 16 |
| Carpenter Av. E&W | | |
| | 14W-17N | 15 |
| Carriage Hill Rd. N&S | | |
| | 16W-18N | 15 |
| Catherine Ct. E&W | 14W-17N | 15 |
| Cedar Dr. NW&SE | 15W-18N | 15 |
| Cedar Run Dr. N&S | | |
| | 16W-18N | 15 |
| Cedarwood Ct.* N&S | | |
| | 16W-16N | 15 |
| Cedarwood Ln.* N&S | | |
| | 16W-16N | 15 |
| Center Av. E&W | 14W-17N | 15 |

| | Grid | Page |
|---|---|---|
| Century Dr. E&W | 14W-17N | 15 |
| Chaddick Dr. NS&EW | | |
| | 14W-17N | 15 |
| Charabanc Ln. E&W | | |
| | 15W-18N | 15 |
| Chariot Ct.* N&S | 14W-18N | 15 |
| Chariot Rd.* N&S | 14W-18N | 15 |
| Chelsea St.* N&S | 15W-18N | 15 |
| Cherrywood Dr. N&S | | |
| | 15W-17N | 15 |
| Chestnut Lane N&S | | |
| | 15W-18N | 15 |
| Cheswick Ct.* E&W | | |
| | 13W-17N | 16 |
| Chippewa Tr. NS&EW | | |
| | 16W-17N | 15 |
| Chukker Ct.* E&W | 15W-16N | 15 |
| Cindy Ln. N&S | 15W-17N | 15 |
| Clearwater Ct.* N&S | | |
| | 16W-16N | 15 |
| Clearwater Dr.* E&W | | |
| | 16W-16N | 15 |
| Clearwater Ln.* E&W | | |
| | 16W-16N | 15 |
| Cleo Ct.* NW&SE | 14W-16N | 15 |
| Coach Rd.* E&W | 14W-18N | 15 |
| Cobbler Ln.* E&W | 13W-18N | 16 |
| Colonial Dr. NW&SE | | |
| | 15W-18N | 15 |
| Commanche Tr. NS&EW | | |
| | 16W-17N | 15 |
| Commercial Dr. E&W | | |
| | 14W-17N | 15 |
| Coral Ln. N&S | 16W-16N | 15 |
| Corey Ln. E&W | 16W-16N | 15 |
| Cornell Av. N&S | 16W-17N | 15 |
| Cottonwood Ct. N&S | | |
| | 16W-16N | 15 |
| Coventry Pl.* E&W | 15W-18N | 15 |
| Creekside Ct. NE&SW | | |
| | 16W-16N | 15 |
| Crescent Dr. NW&SE | | |
| | 14W-17N | 15 |
| Crimson Dr. N&S | 15W-18N | 15 |
| Crow Tr.* N&S | 16W-17N | 15 |
| Curricle Rd.* N&S | 14W-18N | 15 |
| Custer Tr.* N&S | 16W-17N | 15 |
| Cypress Dr.* E&W | 16W-18N | 15 |
| Cyrille St. E&W | 14W-18N | 15 |
| Dakota Tr. NE&SW | | |
| | 16W-17N | 15 |
| Deborah Ln. E&W | 14W-18N | 15 |
| Deerpath Ct.* N&S | 14W-18N | 15 |
| Delaware Tr.* E&W | | |
| | 16W-17N | 15 |
| Denniston Ct. E&W | | |
| | 15W-18N | 15 |
| Denoyer Tr. E&W | 15W-18N | 15 |
| Denoyer Trail N&S | 15W-18N | 15 |
| Derby St. N&S | 15W-18N | 15 |
| Diens Dr. N&S | 15W-18N | 15 |
| Donna Ct. NE&SW | 14W-17N | 15 |
| Dorset Cir.* E&W | 15W-18N | 15 |
| Dorset Ct. E&W | 15W-18N | 15 |
| Dover Pl.* N&S | 15W-18N | 15 |
| Drae Ct.* NW&SE | 16W-18N | 15 |
| Driftwood Dr.* N&S | | |
| | 15W-18N | 15 |
| Dundee Rd. E&W | | |
| | 15W-18N,14W-18N | 15 |
| Eagle Grove Ct.* N&S | | |
| | 13W-18N | 16 |
| East Dennis Rd. N&S | | |
| | 15W-17N | 15 |
| East Dr. E&W | 14W-16N | 15 |
| East Norman Ln. N&S | | |
| | 15W-17N | 15 |
| Eastchester Rd. N&S | | |
| | 13W-17N | 16 |
| Easton Ct.* E&W | 13W-17N | 16 |
| Edgewood Dr. E&W | | |
| | 14W-18N | 15 |
| Egidi Dr. E&W | 14W-18N | 15 |
| Elden Ct.* N&S | 16W-16N | 15 |
| Elizabeth Ln. N&S | 16W-16N | 15 |
| Elm Dr. E&W | 13W-17N | 16 |
| Elmwood Ln.* N&S | | |
| | 15W-18N | 15 |
| Equestrian Dr. E&W | | |
| | 15W-16N | 15 |
| Exchange Ct. NS&EW | | |
| | 14W-17N | 15 |
| Exeter Ct.* E&W | 16W-18N | 15 |
| Fairfield Ct.* E&W | 13W-17N | 16 |
| Fairway View Dr. NS&EW | | |
| | 16W-18N | 15 |
| Fall Ct. NW&SE | 16W-18N | 15 |
| Fernak Ct. N&S | 15W-18N | 15 |
| Ferndale Ct.* N&S | 15W-18N | 15 |
| Ferne Dr. E&W | 13W-17N | 16 |
| Fletcher Dr. N&S | 15W-17N | 15 |
| Fore Ct.* E&W | 16W-18N | 15 |
| Forestway Ln.* N&S | | |
| | 15W-18N | 16 |
| Forums Ct. N&S | 15W-16N | 15 |
| Foster Av. N&S | 14W-15N | 15 |
| Fox Ln. E&W | 14W-16N | 15 |
| Foxboro Dr. NW&SE | | |
| | 14W-18N | 15 |
| Garden E&W | 15W-16N | 15 |
| Garth Rd. N&S | 15W-18N | 15 |
| Gayle Ct. NE&SW | 14W-17N | 15 |
| Gee Ct.* NW&SE | 16W-18N | 15 |
| George Rd. N&S | 15W-17N | 15 |
| Gilman Av. E&W | 14W-16N | 15 |
| Glendale St.* N&S | 14W-16N | 15 |
| Glengary Ct.* NW&SE | | |
| | 13W-17N | 16 |

| | Grid | Page |
|---|---|---|
| Glengary Ln.* NE&SW | 13W-17N | 16 |
| Glenn Av. N&S | 14W-17N | 15 |
| Gray Ct.* E&W | 16W-18N | 15 |
| Greenview Ln. E&W | 15W-18N | 15 |
| Gregor Ln. E&W | 15W-17N | 15 |
| Greystone Ln.* N&S | 15W-18N | 15 |
| Haben Ln. E&W.. NW&SE | 13W-18N | 16 |
| Hadley Ct.* N&S | 15W-18N | 15 |
| Hansom Ct. N&S | 15W-18N | 15 |
| Hansom Dr. E&W | 15W-18N | 15 |
| Harbour Ct. N&S | 16W-16N | 15 |
| Harbour Dr. E&W | 16W-16N | 15 |
| Harmony Dr. N&S | 13W-17N | 16 |
| Harms Ct.* N&S | 16W-18N | 15 |
| Harvester Ct. E&W | 15W-17N | 15 |
| Hastings Ct. E&W | 15W-18N | 15 |
| Hastings Rd. E&W | 15W-17N | 15 |
| Hawthorne Ct.* E&W | 15W-18N | 15 |
| Heather Ct. E&W | 16W-17N | 15 |
| Henley Ct.* N&S | 13W-17N | 16 |
| Hickory Dr. | 13W-17N | 15 |
| High Goal Dr. NS&EW | 15W-16N | 15 |
| Highland Av. E&W | 14W-17N,13W-17N | 15 |
| Hintz Ln. E&W | 16W-17N | 15 |
| Hintz Rd. E&W | 14W-17N | 15 |
| Holbrook Dr. NS&EW | 15W-16N,14W-16N | 15 |
| Holly Ct. E&W | 16W-18N | 15 |
| Honey Locust Dr. N&S | 13W-17N | 16 |
| Honey Suckle Dr. NW&SE | 15W-16N | 15 |
| Hopi Ter.* E&W | 16W-17N | 15 |
| Hunter Dr. E&W | 16W-17N | 15 |
| Huntington Ln.* N&S | 16W-18N | 15 |
| Inwood Dr. E&W | 14W-15N | 15 |
| Iota Ct.* E&W | 16W-18N | 15 |
| Ironwood Ct.* E&W | 15W-18N | 15 |
| Irvine Ct. N&S | 16W-17N | 15 |
| Isa Dr. NE&SW | 15W-17N | 15 |
| Ivy Ct.* N&S | 16W-16N | 15 |
| Jackson N&S | 16W-17N | 15 |
| Janice Ct. E&W | 15W-16N | 15 |
| Jaspen Ct.* E&W | 16W-18N | 15 |
| Jeanne Ter. | 14W-17N | 15 |
| Jefferson Ct. E&W | 15W-16N | 15 |
| Jeffrey Av. E&W | 13W-17N | 16 |
| Jeffrey Ln. N&S | 14W-17N | 15 |
| Jenkins Ct. E&W | 15W-17N | 15 |
| Jerome Pl. N&S | 13W-17N | 16 |
| Kenilworth E&W | 16W-18N,15W-18N | 15 |
| King Ct. N&S | 15W-18N | 15 |
| Kingsport Dr. E&W | 15W-17N | 15 |
| Kingswood Ln.* N&S | 13W-18N | 16 |
| Kiowa Tr.* N&S | 14W-18N | 15 |
| Kranse Ln. E&W | 14W-18N | 15 |
| Kristy Ln. E&W | 15W-17N | 15 |
| Laguna Ct.* NW&SE | 16W-17N | 15 |
| Lakeland Ct. N&S | 16W-16N | 15 |
| Lakeside Dr. N&S | 16W-17N | 15 |
| Lakeview N&S | 16W-17N | 15 |
| Lakeview Dr. E&W | 16W-17N | 15 |
| Landau Ln. E&W | 15W-18N | 15 |
| Larkin Dr. E&W | 14W-16N | 15 |
| Laurel Ct. NW&SE | 15W-17N | 15 |
| Laurel Tr. N&S | 16W-18N | 15 |
| Lee St. E&W | 15W-17N | 15 |
| Lenox Ct.* NS&EW | 13W-17N | 16 |
| Leslie Ln. N&S | 14W-17N | 15 |
| Lexington Dr. N&S | 15W-18N | 15 |
| Lilac Ln. N&S | 14W-17N | 15 |
| Lincoln Rd. N&S | 14W-17N | 15 |
| Linda Ter. NE&SW | 15W-17N | 15 |
| Linden Ln. | 13W-18N | 16 |
| Locust Dr. NS&EW | 16W-18N | 15 |
| London Pl.* N&S | 15W-18N | 15 |
| Longacre Ln. NE&SW | 15W-16N | 15 |
| Longbow Ct.* N&S | 13W-17N | 16 |
| Longtree Dr. N&S | 15W-17N | 15 |
| Longtree Dr. E&W | 15W-17N | 15 |
| Lotus Ct.* E&W | 16W-18N | 15 |
| Lynn Ln. E&W | 14W-16N | 15 |
| Mae Ct.* E&W | 16W-18N | 15 |
| Mallard Ln. N&S | 16W-17N | 15 |
| Manchester Dr. E&W | 14W-17N,13W-17N | 15 |
| Manda Ln. NS&EW | 16W-18N | 15 |
| Maple Dr. N&S | 13W-17N | 16 |
| Marcy Ln. E&W | 16W-17N,15W-17N | 15 |
| Marion Ct. NE&SW | 15W-17N | 15 |
| Mark Ln. E&W | 16W-16N | 15 |
| Marquardt Dr. E&W | 15W-17N | 15 |
| Marvin Pl. N&S | 13W-17N | 16 |
| Maureen Dr. NE&SW | 15W-17N | 15 |
| Mayer Av. E&W | 14W-18N | 15 |
| McHenry Rd. NW&SE | 15W-18N | 15 |

| | Grid | Page |
|---|---|---|
| Meadow Brook Ln. N&S | 14W-17N | 15 |
| Meadow Ln. E&W | 14W-18N | 15 |
| Melvin Pl. N&S | 14W-17N | 15 |
| Mercantile Ct. NS&EW | 15W-17N | 15 |
| Merle Ln. N&S | 15W-17N | 15 |
| Merle Ln., N. E&W | 15W-17N | 15 |
| Messner Dr. E&W | 14W-16N | 15 |
| Middlebury Ln.* NE&SW | 15W-18N | 15 |
| Milwaukee Av. NW&SE | 14W-18N,13W-17N | 15 |
| Mockingbird Ln. N&S | 16W-18N | 15 |
| Mohawk Tr.* N&S | 16W-17N | 15 |
| Molly Ct. NE&SW | 16W-18N | 15 |
| Mors Av. E&W | 14W-17N,13W-17N | 15 |
| Muriel Ln. E&W | 15W-16N | 15 |
| Nancy Ln. N&S | 15W-17N | 15 |
| Navajo Tr.* N&S | 16W-17N | 15 |
| Newburn Ct.* E&W | 13W-18N | 16 |
| Noel Av. N&S | 14W-16N | 15 |
| North Dennis Rd. E&W | 15W-17N | 15 |
| North Green Dr. N&S | 15W-17N | 15 |
| North Norman Ln. E&W | 15W-17N | 15 |
| North Wayne Pl. E&W | 15W-17N | 15 |
| Northbury Ln.* E&W | 15W-18N | 15 |
| Northgate Pkwy. N&S | 15W-18N,14W-18N | 15 |
| Nottingham Ct.* NW&SE | 13W-17N | 16 |
| Nova Ct.* E&W | 16W-18N | 15 |
| Oak Dr. NW&SE | 16W-18N | 15 |
| Oak St. N&S | 14W-17N | 15 |
| Oakmeadow Ct.* NW&SE | 13W-18N | 16 |
| Oakmont Ln.* N&S | 15W-18N | 15 |
| Oakwood Ln.* N&S | 13W-18N | 16 |
| Oboe Ct.* E&W | 16W-18N | 15 |
| Old McHenry Rd. NW&SE | 16W-18N | 15 |
| Orrington Ct.* E&W | 13W-17N | 16 |
| Osage Tr. NE&SW | 16W-17N | 15 |
| Ottawa Tr.* N&S | 16W-17N | 15 |
| Oxford Pl. N&S | 15W-18N | 15 |
| Oxley Ct.* N&S | 13W-17N | 16 |
| Pacific Ct. N&S | 16W-17N | 15 |
| Paddock Dr. NS&EW | 15W-18N | 15 |
| Palatine Rd. E&W | 14W-16N | 15 |
| Palm Dr. E&W | 16W-17N,15W-17N | 15 |
| Palwaukee N&S | 14W-17N | 15 |
| Pam Ct.* N&S | 16W-18N | 15 |
| Park Av. NW&SE | 15W-17N | 15 |
| Partridge Ln.* E&W | 13W-18N | 16 |
| Peace Dr. N&S | 15W-16N | 15 |
| Pear Tree Ln. NE&SW | 15W-16N | 15 |
| Pebble Dr. N&S | 15W-18N | 15 |
| Pennsbury Ct.* NW&SE | 13W-18N | 16 |
| Peterson Dr. N&S | 14W-16N | 15 |
| Phaeton Dr. E&W | 15W-18N | 15 |
| Pleasant Run Dr. E&W | 15W-16N | 15 |
| Plumtree Ct.* N&S | 15W-18N | 15 |
| Poplar Dr.* N&S | 13W-16N | 16 |
| Portsmouth Pl.* E&W | 15W-18N | 15 |
| Pueblo Tr.* N&S | 16W-18N | 15 |
| Quad Ct.* N&S | 16W-18N | 15 |
| Quail Hollow Dr. E&W | 15W-18N | 15 |
| Queens Ct.* E&W | 15W-18N | 16 |
| Quincy Ct.* E&W | 16W-18N | 15 |
| Railroad Av. N&S | 15W-17N | 15 |
| Ransom Ct.* E&W | 14W-18N | 15 |
| Redwood Tr. N&S | 15W-17N | 15 |
| Reef Ct. N&S | 15W-16N | 15 |
| Regent Ln.* E&W | 14W-16N | 15 |
| Regent Ln.* N&S | 13W-18N | 16 |
| Renee Ter. NS&EW | 13W-18N | 16 |
| Ridgefield Ln. N&S | 15W-16N | 15 |
| Robert Av. N&S | 15W-16N | 15 |
| Rose Ln. E&W | 15W-16N | 15 |
| Roth Ct.* E&W | 16W-18N | 15 |
| Rt. 68 E&W | 16W-18N,13W-18N | 15 |
| Rt. 83 N&S | 13W-18N | 16 |
| Russettwood Ct. E&W | 15W-17N | 15 |
| Rustic Dr.* E&W | 13W-17N | 16 |
| Salvington Pl. E&W | 16W-18N,16W-17N | 15 |
| Sandalwood Ln. E&W | 14W-18N | 15 |
| Sandpebble Dr. N&S | 15W-16N | 15 |
| Sandra Ln. E&W | 15W-17N | 15 |
| Sandstone Dr. N&S | 15W-16N | 15 |
| Sarah Ct. NW&SE | 15W-18N | 15 |
| Sarasota Dr. E&W | 15W-18N | 15 |

| | Grid | Page |
|---|---|---|
| Schoenbeck Rd. N&S | 15W-17N | 15 |
| Scott St. N&S | 16W-17N | 15 |
| Seton Ct. N&S | 15W-17N | 15 |
| Seville Ct.* N&S | 13W-17N | 16 |
| Shawn Ct. E&W | 15W-16N | 15 |
| Shay Ct.* N&S | 14W-18N | 15 |
| Sheldrake Dr. E&W | 16W-17N | 15 |
| Shelly Ct. NW&SE | 14W-17N | 15 |
| Sheppard Av. E&W | 15W-17N | 15 |
| Sheridan Ct.* NE&SW | 13W-17N | 16 |
| Shore Ct.* N&S | 13W-17N | 16 |
| Shoshone Tr.* E&W | 16W-17N | 15 |
| Silverwood Ct.* E&W | 15W-18N | 15 |
| South Dennis Rd. E&W | 15W-17N | 15 |
| South Dr. N&S | 14W-15N | 15 |
| South Fletcher Dr. E&W | 15W-17N | 15 |
| South Merle Ln. E&W | 15W-17N | 15 |
| South Pine St. N&S | 15W-17N | 15 |
| South Wayne Pl. E&W | 15W-17N | 15 |
| Southbury Ln.* E&W | 15W-18N | 15 |
| Springview Ct. E&W | 15W-18N | 15 |
| Spruce Dr. N&S | 16W-18N | 15 |
| Spur Ct.* E&W | 16W-18N | 15 |
| Stafford Ln.* N&S | 13W-18N | 16 |
| Stone Pl. N&S | 14W-17N | 15 |
| Stonehedge Ct.* E&W | 13W-18N | 16 |
| Stratford Ct.* N&S | 13W-18N | 16 |
| Strong Av. E&W | 14W-18N | 15 |
| Summerhill Ln.* N&S | 13W-18N | 16 |
| Sunrise Dr. E&W | 15W-17N | 15 |
| Sunset Ln. N&S | 14W-17N | 15 |
| Surf Ct. N&S | 16W-17N | 15 |
| Surrey Rd.* N&S | 14W-17N | 15 |
| Sutton Ct.* E&W | 16W-18N | 15 |
| Sycamore Ln. N&S | 15W-17N | 15 |
| Tahoe Cir. Dr. E&W | 16W-18N | 15 |
| Tanglewood Dr. N&S | 15W-16N | 15 |
| Teal Ln. E&W | 16W-17N | 15 |
| Thelma Ct. E&W | 15W-17N | 15 |
| Thorndale Ct.* E&W | 15W-18N | 15 |
| Thornhill Ln.* NS&EW | 15W-18N | 15 |
| Thyne Ct.* E&W | 16W-18N | 15 |
| Tide Ct. N&S | 15W-16N | 15 |
| Tilbury Ln. NW&SE | 15W-18N | 15 |
| Tulip Ct.* N&S | 13W-17N | 16 |
| Twilight Ln. E&W | 15W-16N | 15 |
| Union Ct.* E&W | 16W-18N | 15 |
| Vail Ct.* N&S | 16W-18N | 15 |
| Valley Stream Dr. N&S | 16W-18N,15W-18N | 15 |
| Virginia Pl. N&S | 14W-17N | 15 |
| Vita Dr.* NE&W | 13W-16N | 16 |
| Walnut Av. E&W | 14W-17N,13W-17N | 15 |
| Waltz Dr. E&W | 14W-17N | 15 |
| Warwick Ct.* E&W | 13W-17N | 16 |
| Wayne Pl. N&S | 15W-17N | 15 |
| Weeping Willow Dr. NE&SW | 15W-16N | 15 |
| West Green Dr. N&S | 15W-17N | 15 |
| West Lodge Ter.* N&S | 16W-17N | 15 |
| West Pine St. E&W | 15W-17N | 15 |
| West Wayne Pl. N&S | 15W-17N | 15 |
| Westwood Ct.* NE&SW | 16W-16N | 15 |
| Wetumka Tr.* N&S | 16W-17N | 15 |
| Wheeling Av. N&S | 14W-17N | 15 |
| Wheeling Rd. N&S | 15W-16N,14W-17N | 15 |
| Whippletree Rd. N&S | 15W-18N | 15 |
| White Hall Ct.* NW&SE | 13W-18N | 16 |
| Widgeon Dr. N&S | 16W-17N | 15 |
| Wildberry Ct.* N&S | 15W-17N | 15 |
| Wille Av. N&S | 14W-17N | 15 |
| Williamsburg Ct.* N&S | 15W-18N | 15 |
| Willis Av. N&S | 14W-16N | 15 |
| Willow Rd. E&W | 14W-15N | 15 |
| Willow Tr. N&S | 15W-17N | 15 |
| Willowbrook Dr. NW&SE | 15W-18N | 15 |
| Wilshire Dr. E&W | 15W-18N | 15 |
| Wolf Rd. N&S | 14W-15N,13W-18N | 15 |
| Wood Creek Dr. E&W | 14W-15N | 15 |
| Wood Duck St. N&S | 16W-17N | 15 |
| Woodbury Ln.* E&W | 14W-18N | 15 |

| | Grid | Page |
|---|---|---|
| Woodlake Rd. NS&EW | 14W-15N | 15 |
| Woodland Dr. E&W | 15W-18N | 15 |
| Woodmere Ln.* N&S | 13W-18N | 16 |
| Wye Ct.* E&W | 16W-18N | 15 |
| Wynn Ct.* N&S | 16W-18N | 15 |
| Yorkshire Pl.* E&W | 16W-18N | 15 |
| Zee Ct.* E&W | 16W-18N | 15 |
| 1st St. N&S | 14W-18N | 15 |
| 2nd St. N&S | 14W-18N | 15 |
| 3rd St. N&S | 14W-18N | 15 |
| 4th St. N&S | 14W-18N | 15 |
| 5th St. N&S | 14W-18N | 15 |
| 6th St. N&S | 14W-18N | 15 |
| 7th St. N&S | 14W-18N | 15 |
| 8th St. N&S | 14W-18N | 15 |
| 9th St. N&S | 14W-18N | 15 |
| 10th St. N&S | 14W-18N | 15 |
| 11th St. N&S | 14W-18N | 15 |
| 12th St. N&S | 14W-18N | 15 |

## Wheeling Township

| | Grid | Page |
|---|---|---|
| Ande Av. N&S | 14W-16N | 15 |
| Anita Av. E&W | 13W-13N | 26 |
| Betty Dr. N&S | 16W-17N | 15 |
| Carol Av. N&S | 14W-16N | 15 |
| Chestnut Av. N&S | 18W-16N | 14 |
| Chicago Av. N&S | 18W-16N | 14 |
| Cindy Ln. E&W | 14W-16N | 15 |
| Darryl Dr. E&W | 16W-17N | 15 |
| Dean Av. N&S | 16W-17N | 15 |
| Debra Ln. E&W | 14W-16N | 15 |
| Des Plaines River Rd. N&S | 13W-13N,13W-14N | 26 |
| Dryden Av. N&S | 17W-15N | 14 |
| Dun-lo Av. E&W | 16W-17N | 15 |
| Edward St. E&W | 15W-17N | 15 |
| Ellen Dr. N&S | 16W-17N | 15 |
| Elm Ln. N&S | 17W-17N | 14 |
| Fernandez Av. N&S | 18W-16N | 14 |
| Foundry Rd. E&W | 14W-13N | 25 |
| Graylynn Dr. N&S | 13W-13N | 26 |
| Gregory St. E&W | 13W-13N | 26 |
| Harold St. E&W | 18W-16N | 14 |
| Hill St. E&W | 13W-13N | 26 |
| Industrial Ln. E&W | 13W-16N | 16 |
| Island Dr. E&W | 13W-17N | 16 |
| Jane Av. N&S | 17W-15N | 14 |
| LaSalle St. E&W | 18W-16N | 14 |
| Lee St. N&S | 13W-13N | 26 |
| Lillian Av. E&W | 18W-15N,17W-15N | 14 |
| Lynwood Av. E&W | 18W-15N | 14 |
| Maude Av. E&W | 18W-15N | 14 |
| Morrison Av. E&W | 13W-13N | 26 |
| Norman St. E&W | 18W-16N | 14 |
| Park Pl. E&W | 16W-17N | 15 |
| Phelps Av. N&S | 16W-15N | 15 |
| Plant Rd. N&S | 13W-16N | 16 |
| Plum Creek Dr. E&W | 13W-17N | 16 |
| Ridge Av. N&S | 18W-16N | 14 |
| Russell St. N&S | 15W-17N | 15 |
| Salk Rd. N&S | 16W-17N | 15 |
| South St. E&W | 15W-17N | 15 |
| Stavros Rd. N&S | 13W-16N | 16 |
| Stratford Rd. N&S | 16W-15N | 15 |
| Vera Ln. E&W | 15W-17N | 15 |
| Verde Av. N&S | 18W-15N | 14 |
| Vista Rd. N&S | 17W-17N | 14 |
| Wilson Ln. NS&EW | 18W-15N | 14 |
| Woodland Dr. N&S | 13W-13N | 26 |
| Yale Av. N&S | 18W-15N | 14 |
| Yale Ct. E&W | 18W-15N | 14 |

## Willow Springs

| | Grid | Page |
|---|---|---|
| Abbot St. N&S | 12W-9S | 64 |
| Archer Av. NE&SW | 12W-9S,11W-9S | 64 |
| Arizona Trail N&S | 14W-9S | 64 |
| Beech St. N&S | 12W-9S | 64 |
| Beverly Ln. N&S | 11W-9S | 64 |
| Blackstone Av. NW&SE | 12W-9S | 64 |
| Buck Ln. N&S | 13W-9S | 64 |
| Buckingham Ct. NW&SE | 13W-9S | 64 |
| Candlelight Dr. NS&EW | 13W-9S | 64 |
| Cedar St. N&S | 12W-9S | 64 |
| Charleston Av. NW&SE | 12W-9S | 64 |
| Chaucer Dr. NS&EW | 13W-9S | 64 |
| Chelsea Ln. N&S | 13W-9S | 64 |
| Cliff St. N&S | 12W-9S | 64 |
| Cliffside Cir. N&S | 12W-9S | 64 |
| Colonel St. N&S | 13W-9S | 64 |
| Columbia Woods Dr. NW&SE | 13W-9S | 64 |
| Crescent Ct. NS&EW | 12W-9S | 64 |
| Crestview Dr. N&S | 14W-9S | 64 |
| Crown Ct. N&S | 13W-9S | 64 |
| Doogan Av. E&W | 13W-9S | 64 |
| Dunbar St. N&S | 13W-9S | 64 |
| Elm St. N&S | 12W-9S | 64 |
| Fieldcrest Av. N&S | 14W-9S | 64 |
| Flag Av. N&S | 14W-9S | 64 |
| Forest Av. N&S | 12W-9S | 64 |

| | Grid | Page |
|---|---|---|
| German Church Rd. E&W | 13W-9S | 64 |
| Glenwood St. NW&SE | 12W-9S | 64 |
| Grove St. NW&SE | 13W-9S | 64 |
| Hess Av. N&S | 13W-9S | 64 |
| High St. E&W | 12W-9S | 64 |
| Hill St. E&W | 12W-9S | 64 |
| Hilton St. NW&SE | 12W-9S | 64 |
| Independence Dr. N&S | 14W-9S | 64 |
| Interstate 294 NW&SE | 11W-9S | 64 |
| Joyce Av. E&W | 14W-9S | 64 |
| La Grange Rd. NW&SE | 12W-8S | 58 |
| Lake Av. NE&SW | 12W-9S | 64 |
| Liberty Grove Dr. NE&SW | 13W-9S | 64 |
| Louis Dr. E&W | 11W-9S | 64 |
| Maple Av. N&S | 13W-9S | 64 |
| Mona St. NS&EW | 12W-9S | 64 |
| Mound St. NW&SE | 12W-9S | 64 |
| Nolton Av. NW&SE | 12W-9S | 64 |
| Nueport Ct. NE&SW | 14W-9S | 64 |
| Nueport St. N&S | 14W-9S | 64 |
| Oakwood Av. NW&SE | 12W-9S | 64 |
| Orlak Dr. N&S | 14W-9S | 64 |
| Park St. NW&SE | 12W-9S | 64 |
| Pearl St. NW&SE | 12W-9S | 64 |
| Pine St. N&S | 12W-9S | 64 |
| Pleasant View Av. N&S | 14W-9S | 64 |
| Poston Rd. NW&SE | 12W-9S | 64 |
| Prospect Av. E&W | 12W-9S | 64 |
| Providence Ct. N&S | 13W-9S | 64 |
| Rainford Ln. E&W | 13W-9S | 64 |
| Ravine Av., E. N&S | 12W-9S | 64 |
| Ravine Av., W. N&S | 12W-9S | 64 |
| Regency Ct. N&S | 13W-9S | 64 |
| Ridge Ct. N&S | 12W-9S | 64 |
| Rosemere Ct. E&W | 14W-9S | 64 |
| Rt. 171 NE&SW | 13W-10S,12W-9S | 64 |
| Rust St. N&S | 12W-9S | 64 |
| Rust Trail NE&SW | 12W-9S,11W-9S | 64 |
| Scenic Dr. N&S | 14W-9S | 64 |
| School Av. N&S | 13W-9S | 64 |
| Sherwood St. NE&SW | 12W-9S | 64 |
| Spring St. NE&SW | 13W-9S | 64 |
| Spring St. NW&SE | 12W-9S | 64 |
| Stradford Dr. E&W | 13W-9S | 64 |
| Tec-Air Rd. NW&SE | 12W-9S | 64 |
| Tower Rd. N&S | 11W-9S | 64 |
| Tri-State Tollway E&W | 12W-8S,11W-9S | 58 |
| Tudor Cir. N&S | 13W-9S | 64 |
| U.S. Route 45 N&S | 11W-9S | 64 |
| Union St. N&S | 12W-9S | 64 |
| Ursula Dr. NE&SW | 13W-9S | 64 |
| Vana Dr. N&S | 11W-9S | 64 |
| Vinewood Av. NE&SW | 12W-9S | 64 |
| Wadsworth Rd. N&S | 13W-9S | 64 |
| Walnut St. E&W | 12W-9S | 64 |
| Wentworth NW&SE | 13W-9S | 64 |
| Willow Springs Rd. N&S | 13W-9S | 64 |
| Willow West Dr. N&S | 13W-9S | 64 |
| Willows Edge Ct. NW&SE | 13W-10S | 64 |
| 79th St. E&W | 13W-8S | 58 |
| 83rd St. E&W | 14W-9S | 64 |
| 84th Pl. E&W | 14W-9S,13W-9S | 64 |
| 85th Pl. E&W | 14W-9S | 64 |
| 85th St. E&W | 14W-9S,13W-9S | 64 |
| 86th St. E&W | 14W-9S,13W-9S | 64 |
| 87th St. E&W | 14W-9S,12W-9S | 64 |

## Wilmette

| | Grid | Page |
|---|---|---|
| Alison Ln. E&W | 5W-13N | 28 |
| Alpine Ln. N&S | 4W-13N | 29 |
| Amhurst Ln. N&S | 4W-14N | 29 |
| Appletree Ln. N&S | 5W-13N | 28 |
| Ashland Av. | 3W-14N | 29 |
| Ashland Ln. N&S | 4W-14N | 29 |
| Avondale Ct. E&W | 4W-13N | 29 |
| Avondale Dr. E&W | 4W-13N | 29 |
| Beechwood Av. E&W | 5W-14N | 28 |
| Beverly Dr. N&S | 5W-13N | 28 |
| Big Tree Ln. N&S | 6W-13N | 28 |
| Birchwood Av. E&W | 5W-13N,4W-13N | 29 |
| Birchwood Av. | 5W-13N | 28 |
| Birchwood Ln. N&S | 5W-13N | 28 |
| Blackhawk Rd. E&W | 5W-14N | 28 |
| Briar Dr. N&S | 6W-13N | 28 |
| Broadway N&S | 5W-13N | 29 |
| Brookside Dr. N&S | 5W-13N | 28 |
| Bunker Ln. N&S | 7W-14N | 28 |
| Cambridge Ln. N&S | 4W-14N | 29 |
| Canterbury Ct. E&W | 2W-13N | 29 |
| Cardinal Ln. E&W | 5W-13N | 28 |

|  | Grid | Page |
|---|---|---|

Carriage Way N&S .. 5W-12N 28
Catalpa Pl. N&S ... 3W-13N 29
Cedar Ln. N&S .... 4W-13N 29
Central Av. E&W
............ 6W-13N,3W-13N 28
Central Park Av. N&S
.................... 4W-13N 29
Cherokee Rd. N&S .. 5W-14N 28
Chestnut Av. E&W
.......... 4W-14N,3W-14N 29
Chilton Ln. N&S .. 5W-13N 28
Chippewa N&S .... 5W-14N 28
Cleveland St. N&S . 5W-14N 28
Colgate St. N&S ... 5W-14N 28
Columbus Av. N&S . 4W-14N 29
Concord Ln. E&W .. 5W-13N 28
Cornell St. N&S .... 4W-14N 29
Country Ln. E&W .. 6W-14N 28
Cove Ln. N&S .... 5W-13N 28
Crabtree Ln. E&W .. 5W-13N 28
Cranston Ct. E&W .. 6W-14N 28
Crescent Pl. E&W ..3W-13N 29
Crestview Ln. NE&SW
.................... 4W-13N 29
Dartmouth St. N&S .. 5W-14N 28
Dupee Pl. N&S .... 2W-13N 29
Edgewood Ct. NW&SE
.................... 6W-14N 28
Electric Pl. N&S . 3W-13N 29
Elmwood Av. E&W
.......... 6W-14N,3W-14N 28
Fairway Dr. N&S ... 7W-14N 28
Forest Av. E&W
.......... 6W-14N,3W-14N 28
Garrison Av. N&S ..2W-13N 29
Girard Av. N&S .. 2W-13N 29
Glenview Rd. E&W .. 4W-13N 29
Golf Ter. N&S ... 2W-13N 29
Grant St. N&S .... 5W-14N 28
Greenbay Rd. NW&SE
.................... 4W-14N 29
Greenleaf Av. E&W
.......... 6W-13N,3W-13N 28
Greenwood Av. E&W
.......... 6W-14N,3W-14N 28
Gregory Av. E&W
.......... 5W-13N,3W-13N 28
Hartzell St. E&W .... 5W-13N 28
Harvard Ln. N&S
.......... 4W-13N,4W-14N 29
Harvard St. N&S .. 4W-13N 29
Hawthorne Ln. E&W
.......... 5W-13N,4W-13N 28
Heather Ln. N&S .. 6W-13N 28
Hibbard Rd. N&S .. 6W-13N 28
Highcrest E&W .. 4W-13N 29
Highland Av. E&W
.......... 5W-13N,4W-13N 28
Hill Ln. E&W .... 6W-13N 28
Hill St. E&W .... 6W-13N 28
Hollywood Ct. NS&EW
.................... 4W-13N 29
Hunter Ct. E&W .. 5W-13N 28
Hunter Rd. N&S .. 5W-13N 28
Illinois Rd. NW&SE .. 5W-14N 28
Indian Hill Rd. E&W .. 5W-14N 28
Indianwood Rd. E&W
.................... 5W-14N 28
Iroquois Rd. N&S
.......... 5W-14N,4W-14N 28
Karey Ct. N&S .... 5W-13N 28
Kenilworth Av. E&W
.......... 5W-14N,4W-14N 28
Kilpatrick Av. N&S . 5W-13N 28
Kin Ct. N&S .... 4W-13N 29
Knoll Ln. E&W .... 4W-14N 29
Knox Ct. .. 5W-13N,5W-14N 28
Koerper Ct. N&S .. 6W-13N 28
LaCrosse Ct. N&S .. 6W-13N 28
LaPorte Av. N&S .. 6W-13N 28
Lacrosse Av. N&S .. 6W-13N 28
Lake Av. E&W
.......... 5W-14N,3W-14N 28
Lamon Av. N&S .... 6W-13N 28
Laramie Av. N&S
.......... 6W-13N,6W-14N 28
Laurel Av. E&W
.......... 3W-13N,2W-13N 29
Lavergne Av. N&S .. 6W-13N 28
Lawler Av. N&S ... 6W-13N 28
Lawndale Av. N&S .. 4W-13N 29
LeClaire Av. N&S .. 6W-13N 28
Leamington Av. N&S
.................... 6W-13N 28
Leydon Ln. N&S .. 6W-13N 28
Lilac Ln. E&W .. 6W-13N 28
Lincoln Ln. E&W .. 5W-13N 28
Linden Av. E&W
.......... 3W-13N,2W-13N 29
Lockerbie Ln. N&S .. 6W-13N 28
Locust Rd. N&S ... 5W-13N 28
Manor Dr. N&S ... 6W-14N 28
Maple Av. E&W
.......... 4W-13N,3W-13N 29
Marian Ln. E&W .. 5W-13N 28
Meadow Dr., E. N&S
.................... 5W-13N 28
Meadow Dr., S. N&S
.................... 5W-13N 28
Meadow Dr., W. N&S
.................... 5W-13N 28
Meadows Dr., N. N&S
.................... 5W-13N 28
Melrose Ct. E&W .. 6W-14N 28
Miami Rd. N&S .. 5W-14N 28
Michigan Av. NW&SE
.................... 3W-14N 29
Middlebury Ln. N&S..5W-14N 28

Millbrook Ln. N&S .. 6W-13N 28
Mohawk Rd. NS&EW
.................... 5W-14N 28
New Trier Ct. N&S .. 6W-14N 28
Nina Av. E&W .. 6W-13N 28
North Branch Rd. N&S
.................... 6W-14N 28
Oak Cir. Dr. E&W .. 3W-13N 29
Oakwood Av. E&W .. 3W-13N 29
Old Glenview Rd. NE&SW
.................... 5W-14N 28
Osage Ln. N&S .... 5W-14N 28
Ottawa N&S .... 5W-14N 28
Oxford Ln. N&S .. 5W-14N 28
Park Av. NW&SE .. 3W-13N 29
Parkview Ct. NW&SE
.................... 4W-13N 29
Pawnee Rd. N&S...5W-14N 28
Pin Oak Dr. E&W .. 5W-14N 28
Pine Manor Dr. N&S
.................... 4W-13N 29
Pine St. N&S .... 5W-14N 28
Pinecrest Ln. N&S .. 4W-13N 29
Pioneer Ln. E&W .. 4W-13N 29
Plum Tree Ln. N&S .. 5W-12N 28
Pomona Ln. E&W .. 5W-13N 28
Pontiac Rd. NW&SE
.................... 5W-14N 28
Poplar St. NW&SE .. 4W-13N 29
Prairie Av. NW&SE . 4W-13N 29
Princeton St. N&S .. 5W-14N 28
Red Bud Ln. N&S .. 5W-14N 28
Richmond Ln. NW&SE
.................... 4W-14N 29
Ridge Rd. N&S ...... 4W-13N 29
Riverside Dr. E&W .. 4W-14N 29
Romona Ct. E&W .. 5W-14N 28
Romona Rd. N&S .. 5W-14N 28
Sandy Ln. N&S .... 4W-13N 29
Schiller Av. E&W .. 4W-13N 29
Seger St. E&W .... 5W-14N 28
Seminole Rd. N&S .. 5W-14N 28
Seneca Rd. N&S .. 5W-14N 28
Shabona Ln. N&S .. 5W-14N 28
Sheridan Rd. NW&SE
.................... 3W-14N 29
Skokie Rd. N&S .... 5W-13N 28
Skokie Rd. NW&SE . 6W-13N 28
Spencer Av. E&W .. 4W-13N 29
Sprucewood Ln. NW&SE
.................... 5W-14N 28
Sprucewood Rd. E&W
.................... 6W-14N 28
Sterling Ln. N&S .. 4W-13N 29
Sunset Dr. N&S .. 5W-14N 28
Temple Ln. E&W .. 6W-13N 28
Thelin Ct. N&S ...... 5W-13N 28
Thornwood Av. E&W
.......... 6W-14N,5W-14N 28
Timber Ln. N&S .. 4W-14N 29
Valley View Ct. E&W
.................... 5W-13N 28
Valley View Dr. N&S
.................... 5W-13N 28
Vine Ct. E&W .... 5W-13N 28
Vine St. N&S .... 5W-13N 28
Virginia Ln. N&S .. 5W-13N 28
Vista Ct. N&S .... 5W-13N 28
Vista Dr. N&S .... 5W-13N 28
Walden Ln. E&W .. 6W-13N 28
Walnut Av. E&W
.......... 6W-14N,4W-14N 28
Washington Av. E&W
.......... 6W-13N,3W-13N 28
Washington Ct. E&W
.................... 3W-13N 29
Westerfield Dr. E&W
.................... 3W-14N 29
Westmoreland Dr. N&S
.................... 5W-13N 28
Westwood Ln. NS&EW
.................... 5W-13N 28
Wilmette Av. E&W
.......... 5W-13N,3W-13N 28
Wilshire Dr., E. N&S  5W-13N 28
Wilshire Dr., W. N&S
.................... 5W-13N 28
Wood St. N&S .... 5W-14N 28
Woodbine Av. N&S .. 3W-13N 29
Yale St. N&S .... 4W-14N 29
3rd St. N&S .... 2W-13N 29
4th St. N&S .... 3W-13N 29
5th St. N&S .... 3W-13N 29
6th St. N&S .... 3W-13N 29
7th St. N&S
.......... 3W-13N,3W-14N 29
8th St. N&S
.......... 3W-13N,3W-14N 29
9th St. N&S
.......... 3W-13N,3W-14N 29
10th St. N&S
.......... 3W-13N,3W-14N 29
11th St. N&S
.......... 3W-13N,3W-14N 29
12th St. N&S ...3W-13N 29
13th St. N&S
.......... 3W-13N,3W-14N 29
14th St. N&S .. 3W-14N 29
15th St. N&S
.......... 4W-13N,4W-14N 29
16th St. N&S
.................... 4W-14N 29
17th St. N&S
.......... 4W-13N,4W-14N 29
18th St. N&S .. 4W-14N 29
20th St. N&S .. 4W-14N 29
21st St. N&S .. 4W-14N 29

21st St. N&S
.......... 4W-13N,4W-14N 29
25th St. N&S ..... 5W-14N 28
36th Pl. N&S ...... 6W-14N 28

## Winnetka

Alles Rd. E&W .. 5W-15N 19
Appletree Rd. N&S .. 5W-15N 19
Arbor Vitae N&S .... 4W-15N 19
Ardsley Rd. N&S .. 5W-16N 19
Asbury Av. N&S .... 6W-16N 18
Asbury Ct. N&S .... 6W-16N 18
Asbury Ln. N&S .... 6W-16N 18
Ash Av. E&W
.......... 5W-15N,4W-15N 19
Auburn Av. N&S .. 5W-15N 19
Auburn Rd. N&S .. 5W-15N 19
Bell Ln. N&S ...... 6W-15N 19
Berkeley Av. N&S... 5W-16N 19
Bertling Ln. N&S .. 4W-15N 19
Beverly Av. N&S .. 5W-15N 19
Birch St. N&S ...... 5W-15N 19
Blackthorn Rd. N&S  5W-16N 19
Boal Pkwy. N&S .. 6W-16N 18
Briar Ln. NE&SW .. 4W-15N 19
Broadmeadow Rd. E&W
.................... 5W-15N 19
Bryant Av. N&S ....5W-15N 19
Burr Av. N&S......5W-15N 19
Cedar St. N&S .... 5W-15N 19
Chatfield Rd. E&W . 5W-16N 19
Cherry St. E&W
.......... 5W-15N,4W-15N 19
Chestnut Ct. E&W .. 5W-15N 19
Chestnut St. N&S... 5W-15N 19
Church Rd. N&S .. 4W-15N 19
Compton St. N&S .. 6W-15N 19
DeWindt Rd. E&W . 5W-15N 19
Dinsmore Rd. E&W .. 5W-15N 19
Edgewood Ln. E&W  6W-16N 18
Elder Ln. E&W .... 4W-15N 19
Eldorado St. NE&SW
.................... 5W-16N 19
Elm St. E&W
.......... 5W-15N,5W-15N 19
Essex Rd. N&S......5W-15N 19
Euclid N&S .... 5W-15N 19
Fairview Av. N&S .. 5W-15N 19
Fisher Cres. N&S .. 5W-16N 19
Fisher Ln. E&W ..... 5W-16N 19
Forest Glen Dr., E. N&S
.................... 5W-16N 19
Forest Glen Dr., N. E&W
.......... 6W-16N,5W-16N 19
Forest Glen Dr., S.
.......... 6W-16N,5W-16N 18
Forest Glen Dr., W. N&S
.................... 6W-16N 18
Forest St. N&S .... 5W-15N 19
Fox Ln. N&S .... 5W-14N 28
Foxdale Av. NW&SE
.................... 5W-16N 19
Fuller Ln. NW&SE .. 4W-15N 19
Gage St. E&W .... 5W-16N 19
Garland Av. N&S .. 5W-15N 19
Glen Oak Dr. E&W . 5W-16N 19
Glendale Av. N&S .. 5W-15N 19
Golf Rd. N&S........5W-14N 28
Gordon Ter. N&S .. 5W-16N 19
Green Bay Rd. NW&SE
.................... 5W-16N 19
Hackberry Ln. E&W .. 6W-16N 18
Hamptondale Av. NE&SW
.................... 5W-16N 19
Hawthorn Ln. E&W . 4W-15N 19
Hazel Ln. E&W .... 6W-16N 18
Heather Ln. N&S .. 6W-16N 18
Hibbard Rd. N&S .. 6W-16N 18
Hickory Ln. E&W .. 6W-16N 18
Higginson Ln. N&S .. 5W-15N 19
High St. N&S...... 4W-14N 29
Hill Rd. E&W
.......... 5W-15N,4W-15N 19
Hill Ter. E&W........ 4W-15N 19
Holly Ln. E&W .... 6W-16N 18
Hoyt Ln. NW&SE .. 4W-15N 19
Hubbard Pl. E&W... 5W-16N 19
Humboldt Av. E&W . 5W-16N 19
Indian Hill Rd. NE&SW
.................... 5W-14N 28
Indian Mill Rd. E&W . 5W-16N 19
Indian Way Rd. NS&EW
.................... 5W-14N 28
Kent E&W ........ 5W-16N 19
Lake Ln. E&W .... 5W-16N 19
Lamson Dr. E&W .. 5W-16N 19
Laurel Av. E&W .... 5W-16N 19
Lincoln Av. NW&SE
.......... 6W-15N,5W-15N 18
Linden St. N&S .... 5W-15N 19
Lindenwood Dr. E&W
.................... 5W-15N 19
Lloyd Pl. E&W .... 5W-16N 19
Locust Rd. N&S .. 5W-15N 19
Locust St. N&S
.......... 5W-15N,4W-15N 19
Maple St. N&S .... 4W-15N 19
Meadow Ln. E&W .. 5W-15N 19
Meadow Rd. E&W . 4W-14N 29
Merrill St. E&W ...... 5W-16N 19
Mt. Pleasant Ln. E&W
.................... 5W-15N 19
Myrtle St. N&S ...... 4W-15N 19
Oak E&W
.......... 5W-15N,4W-15N 19
Oak St. E&W
.......... 6W-15N,4W-15N 19

Oakley Av. E&W .... 5W-16N 19
Old Green Bay Rd. N&S
.................... 5W-16N 19
Orchard Ln. NS&EW
.................... 4W-15N 19
Park Ln. N&S .... 4W-15N 19
Pelham Rd. (Pvt.) E&W
.................... 5W-16N 19
Pine Ln. (Pvt.) N&S . 5W-16N 19
Pine St. E&W
.......... 6W-16N,4W-16N 19
Pine St. E&W
.......... 5W-16N,4W-16N 19
Pine Tree Ln. NS&EW
.................... 6W-16N 18
Plum Tree Ln. E&W . 6W-16N 18
Poplar St. N&S .... 5W-16N 19
Private Rd., S. E&W 5W-16N 19
Prospect Av. NW&SE
.................... 5W-16N 19
Provident Av. N&S . 5W-16N 19
Ravine Rd. E&W .. 5W-16N 19
Ridge Av. N&S .... 5W-15N 19
Rosewood Av. N&S
.................... 5W-16N 19
Scott Av. E&W .... 6W-16N 18
Sheridan Rd. NW&SE
.................... 4W-16N 19
Smith St. N&S .... 6W-15N 19
Spring Ln. N&S .... 5W-15N 19
Spruce Ln. NE&SW . 4W-15N 19
Spruce St. E&W
.......... 6W-15N,4W-16N 19
Spruce St. E&W
.......... 5W-15N,4W-15N 19
Starr Rd. E&W .... 6W-16N 18
Stockton St. E&W .. 6W-15N 19
Sumac Ln. N&S .... 5W-16N 19
Summit St. NE&SW .5W-16N 19
Sunset Rd. E&W
.......... 5W-15N,4W-15N 19
Sunview Ln. N&S .. 6W-16N 18
Swinton St. N&S .. 6W-15N 18
Taylorsport Ln. N&S
.................... 5W-17N 19
Thorn Tree Ln. (Pvt.) N&S
.................... 5W-16N 19
Tower Manor N&S .. 5W-16N 19
Tower Rd. E&W .... 6W-16N 18
Trapp Ln. E&W .... 6W-16N 18
Vernon St. N&S .... 6W-16N 18
Vine St. E&W ...... 5W-16N 19
Walden Rd. N&S .. 5W-16N 19
Walnut St. N&S....4W-15N 19
Warwick Rd. E&W . 4W-14N 29
Westmoor Rd. E&W . 5W-16N 19
Westmoor Trail E&W
.................... 6W-16N 18
Westview Rd. N&S . 6W-16N 18
White Oak Ln. N&S .. 5W-15N 19
Whitebridge Hill St. E&W
.................... 5W-16N 19
Whitebridge Ln. NW&SE
.................... 5W-17N 19
Willow Rd. E&W
.......... 5W-15N,4W-15N 19
Wilson St. NW&SE . 5W-15N 19
Winnetka Rd. E&W . 4W-15N 19
Woodland Av. N&S . 4W-15N 19

## Worth

Autullo Dr. E&W .. 9W-12S 65
Beloit Av. N&S
.......... 9W-13S,9W-12S 73
Columbus Dr. NE&SW
.................... 9W-13S 73
Crandall Av. E&W...8W-12S 65
Depot St. N&S
.......... 8W-13S,8W-12S 73
Harlem Av. N&S
.......... 9W-13S,9W-12S 73
Highland Rd. N&S .. 8W-12S 65
Home Av. NW&SE .. 8W-13S 73
Lloyd Dr. N&S .... 8W-12S 65
Lode Dr. NE&SW ... 8W-12S 65
Nagle Av. N&S
.......... 8W-13S,8W-12S 73
Nashville Av. N&S
.......... 8W-13S,8W-12S 73
Natchez Av. N&S
.......... 8W-13S,8W-12S 73
Natoma Av. N&S .. 8W-13S 73
Neenah Av. N&S
.......... 8W-13S,8W-12S 73
New England Av. N&S
.................... 8W-12S 65
New England Av. N&S
.......... 8W-13S,8W-12S 73
Nordica Av. N&S .. 8W-12S 65
Normandy Av. N&S
.......... 8W-13S,8W-12S 73
Oak Park Av. N&S
.......... 8W-13S,8W-12S 73
Oak Tree Dr. N&S .. 9W-12S 65
Oconto Ct. N&S .... 9W-12S 65
Octavia Av. N&S
.......... 9W-13S,9W-12S 73
Odell Ct. N&S ...... 9W-12S 65
Oketo Av. N&S
.......... 9W-13S,9S-12S 73
Pacific Dr. NE&SW .. 9W-13S 73
Plahm Ct. NE&SW .. 9W-12S 65
Preller Av. N&S .... 9W-13S 73
Ridgeland Av. N&S .. 8W-12S 65
Rt. 43 N&S........8W-12S 65
Rutherford Av. N&S .. 8W-12S 65

Southwest Hwy. NE&SW
.................... 8W-12S 65
Tri-State Tollway SE&NW
.......... 8W-13S,8W-12S 73
Wabash Dr. N&S .. 8W-12S 65
Wood Av. N&S....8W-13S 73
Worth Av. N&S
.......... 8W-13S,8W-12S 73
71st Ct. N&S .... 8W-12S 65
105th Pl. E&W .... 8W-12S 65
106th Pl. E&W .... 8W-12S 65
107th Pl. E&W .... 8W-12S 65
107th St. E&W
.......... 9W-12S,8W-12S 65
108th Pl. E&W .... 9W-12S 65
108th St. E&W
.......... 9W-12S,8W-12S 65
109th Pl. E&W
.......... 9W-12S,8W-12S 65
109th St. E&W
.......... 9W-12S,8W-12S 65
110th Pl. E&W .... 9W-12S 65
110th St. E&W
.......... 9W-12S,8W-12S 65
111th Pl. E&W
.......... 9W-12S,8W-12S 65
111th St. E&W
.......... 9W-12S,8W-12S 65
112th Pl. E&W
.......... 9W-13S,8W-13S 73
112th St. E&W
.......... 9W-13S,8W-13S 73
113th Pl. E&W
.......... 9W-13S,8W-13S 73
113th St. E&W
.......... 9W-13S,8W-13S 73
114th Pl. E&W
.......... 9W-13S,8W-13S 73
114th St. E&W
.......... 9W-13S,8W-13S 73
115th Pl. E&W .... 8W-13S 73
115th St. E&W
.......... 9W-13S,8W-13S 73
116th St. E&W .... 8W-13S 73

## Worth Township

Austin Av. N&S
.......... 7W-15S,7W-14S 74
Brayton St. N&S .. 3W-15S 75
Francisco Av. N&S .. 3W-15S 75
Major Av. N&S .... 7W-14S 74
Mason Av. N&S .... 7W-14S 74
Massasoit Av. N&S . 7W-14S 74
McVicker Av. N&S
.......... 7W-15S,7W-14S 74
Meade Av. N&S
.......... 7W-15S,7W-14S 74
Melvina Av. N&S .... 7W-15S 74
Moblie Av. N&S .... 7W-15S 74
Monitor Av. N&S .. 7W-15S 74
Moody Av. N&S
.......... 7W-15S,7W-14S 74
Parkside Av. N&S .. 7W-14S 74
Ridgeland Av. N&S
.......... 8W-17S,8W-15S 79
Sacramento Av. N&S
.................... 3W-15S 75
Sheridan Av. N&S .. 3W-15S 75
123rd St. E&W .... 7W-14S 74
124th St. E&W .... 7W-14S 74
125th St. E&W .... 7W-14S 74
127th Pl. E&W .... 7W-15S 74
127th St. E&W .... 7W-15S 74
128th Pl. E&W .... 7W-15S 74
128th St. E&W .... 7W-15S 74
129th Pl. E&W .... 7W-15S 74
129th St. E&W .... 7W-15S 74
130th Pl. E&W .... 7W-15S 74
131st Pl. E&W .... 3W-15S 75
131st St. E&W .... 7W-15S 74
132nd St. E&W .... 3W-15S 75
135th St. E&W .... 7W-15S 74

# RAND McNALLY

# DuPage
## County

## StreetFinder®

page    **Contents**

**A**    Using the StreetFinder

**B**    PageFinder Map

**C**    Vicinity Map

**1**    Contents

**2**    Quick Reference Guide

**4**    StreetFinder Maps

**37**    StreetFinder Index

Photo credit: Amoco Building, DuPage County Development Department

PageFinder™ Map U.S. Patent No. 5,419,586.

Information included in this publication has been checked for accuracy prior to publication. Since changes do occur, the publisher cannot be responsible for any variations from the information printed.

## DuPage County Municipal Offices

| | Location | Page |
|---|---|---|
| Addison Village Hall | 18W-3N | 14 |
| 130 Army Trail Road; 543-4100 | | |
| Bensenville Village Hall | 16W-5N | 19 |
| 700 W Irving Park Rd; 766-8200 | | |
| Bloomingdale Village Hall | 23W-5N | 7 |
| 201 S Bloomingdale Rd; 893-7000 | | |
| Carol Stream Village Hall | 25W-2N | 12 |
| 500 N Gary Ave; 665-7050 | | |
| Clarendon Hills Village Hall | 16W-5S | 27 |
| 1 N Prospect Ave; 323-3500 | | |
| Darien City Hall | 18W-8S | 32,33 |
| 1702 Plainfield Rd; 852-5000 | | |
| Downers Grove Village Hall | 19W-5S | 26 |
| 801 Burlington Ave; 964-0300 | | |
| Elmhurst City Hall | 15W-1N | 15 |
| 119 Schiller; 530-3000 | | |
| Glendale Heights Village Hall | 23W-3N | 13 |
| 300 E Fullerton Ave; 260-6000 | | |
| Glen Ellyn Village Hall | 22W-0N | 13 |
| 535 Duane; 469-5000 | | |
| Hinsdale Village Hall | 15W-4S | 27 |
| 19 E Chicago Ave; 789-7000 | | |
| Itasca Village Hall | 19W-6N | 8 |
| 100 N Walnut; 773-0835 | | |
| Lisle Village Hall | 23W-5S | 24,25 |
| 1040 Burlington Ave; 968-1200 | | |
| Lombard Civic Center | 19W-0S | 20 |
| 255 E Wilson Ave; 620-5700 | | |
| Naperville City Hall | 27W-6S | 23 |
| 175 W Jackson Ave; 420-6111 | | |
| Oak Brook Village Hall | 16W-2S | 21 |
| 1200 Oak Brook Rd; 624-2220 | | |
| Roselle Village Hall | 23W-7N | 6,7 |
| 31 S Prospect Ave; 980-2000 | | |
| Villa Park Village Hall | 18W-0N | 14,15 |
| 20 S Ardmore Ave; 834-8500 | | |
| Warrenville City Hall | 28W-3S | 17 |
| 28 W 630 Stafford Pl; 393-9427 | | |
| Wayne Village Hall | 32W-5N | 4 |
| 5 N 430 Railroad; 584-3031 | | |
| Westmont Village Hall | 18W-5S | 26 |
| 31 W Quincy; 968-0560 | | |
| West Chicago Village Hall | 29W-0N | 10,11 |
| 475 Main St; 231-3322 | | |
| Wheaton City Hall | 24W-0S | 18 |
| 214 N Wheaton; 260-2000 | | |
| Winfield Village Hall | 27W-0S | 17 |
| 27 W 465 Jewell Rd; 665-1778 | | |
| Wood Dale City Hall | 18W-6N | 8 |
| 404 N Wood Dale Rd; 766-4900 | | |
| Woodridge Village Hall | 20W-8S | 32 |
| 1900 W 75th; 852-7000 | | |

## Cemeteries

| | Location | Page |
|---|---|---|
| Allerton Ridge | 20W-2S | 19 |
| Arlington Cem | 15W-2N | 15 |
| Assumption Cem | 28W-1S | 17 |
| Blodgetts Cem | 21W-5S | 25 |
| Bloomingdale Cem | 22W-5N | 7 |
| Bronswood Cem | 16W-3S | 21 |
| Chapel Hills Garden Cem | 17W-1S | 21 |
| Clarendon Hills Cem | 18W-7S | 26 |
| Elm Lawn Cem | 15W-2N | 15 |
| Forest Hill Cem | 22W-1N | 13 |
| Fullersburg Cem | 15W-4S | 27 |
| Glen Oak Cem | 30W-1N | 10 |
| Hinsdale Animal Cem | 17W-7S | 27 |
| Illinois Pet Cem | 27W-6N | 5 |
| Mt Emblem Cem | 15W-3N | 15 |
| Naperville Cem | 27W-7S | 23 |
| Oakwood Cem | 29W-1N | 10 |
| Pet Haven Cem | 20W-7N | 7,8 |
| Resthaven Cem | 15W-5N | 9 |
| Roselle Cem | 23W-7N | 6,7 |
| SS Peter and Paul Cem | 26W-6S | 24 |
| St Bernard Cem | 21W-6S | 25 |
| St Johannes Cem | 15W-6N | 9 |
| St John Cem | 15W-3S | 21 |
| St Johns Cem | 17W-7S | 27 |
| St Marys Cem | 16W-1N | 15 |
| St Michaels Cem | 25W-1S | 18 |
| St Stevens Cem | 24W-1N | 12 |
| Wayne Center Cem | 29W-4N | 5 |
| Wheaton Cem | 25W-1S | 18 |
| York Twp Cem | 15W-1S | 21 |
| Zion Cem | 15W-3S | 21 |

## Colleges & Universities

| | Location | Page |
|---|---|---|
| Col of DuPage | 22W-2S | 19 |
| DeVry Inst of Tech | 20W-1S | 19,20 |
| Illinis Benedictine Col | 24W-2N | 12 |
| Midwest Col of Engineering | 20W-0N | 13,14 |
| National Col of Education | 20W-2S | 20 |
| National Col of Chiropractic | 20W-0S | 19 |
| North Central Col | 26W-6S | 24 |
| Northern Ill Univ Col of Law | 21W-1S | 19 |
| Wheaton Col | 24W-0S | 18 |

## Forest Preserves

| | Location | Page |
|---|---|---|
| Belleau Woods FP | 26W-1S | 18 |
| Churchill Woods FP | 21W-0N | 13 |
| Cricket Creek FP | 17W-3N | 15 |
| Danada FP | 25W-3S | 18 |
| East Branch FP | 21,22W-2,3N | 13 |
| Egerman Woods | 24W-7S | 30 |
| Fischer Woods FP | 17W-4N | 8,9 |

| | Location | Page |
|---|---|---|
| Fullersburg FP | 15W-3S | 21 |
| Fullerton FP | 19W-2N | 14 |
| Green Valley FP | 23W-9S | 31 |
| Herrick Lake FP | 26W-3S | 17,18 |
| Hidden Lake FP | 17W-3N | 15 |
| Mallard Lake FP | 26W-5, 6N | 6 |
| Maple Grove FP | 20W-5S | 26 |
| McDowell Grove FP | 28W-4S | 23 |
| Meacham Grove FP | 23W-6N | 6,7 |
| Pratts Wayne Woods FP | 31W-6N | 4 |
| Roy C. Blackwell FP | 28,29W-2,3S | 17 |
| Salt Creek FP | 19W-5N | 8 |
| Salt Creek Park FP | 18W-5N | 8 |
| Spring Brook Prairie FP | 27,29W-8, 9S | 29 |
| Timber Ridge FP | 28W-1, 2N | 11 |
| Warrenville Grove FP | 28W-3S | 17 |
| Waterfall Glen FP | 18W-10,12S | 34 |
| Wayne Grove FP | 29W-7N | 5 |
| West Branch Reservoir FP | 28W-4,6N | 5 |
| West Chicago Prairie FP | 30,31W-1N | 10 |
| West DuPage FP | 28,29W-0S | 17 |
| Willowbrook FP | 22W-2S | 19 |
| Winfield Mounds FP | 27N-0N | 11 |
| Wood Dale Grove FP | 17W-4N | 8,9 |
| York Woods FP | 15W-1S | 21 |

## Golf Courses & Country Clubs

| | Location | Page |
|---|---|---|
| Addison GC | 19W-3N | 14 |
| Apple Orchard GC | 29W-7N | 5 |
| Arrowhead GC | 26W-3S | 18 |
| Black Horse GC | 18W-7S | 26 |
| Butler National GC | 16W-1,2S | 21 |
| Butterfield CC | 18W-2S | 21 |
| Carrieage Greens GC | 19W-10S | 32 |
| Chicago GC | 25W-1S | 18 |
| Country Lakes GC | 30W-5S | 22 |
| Cress Creek CC | 28W-5S | 23 |
| Downers Grove GC | 21W-4S | 25 |
| Elmhurst GC | 18W-4N | 8 |
| Glendale GC | 22W-5N | 7 |
| Glen Oak CC | 21W-0N | 13,14 |
| Hinsdale GC | 17W-4S | 27 |
| Indian Lakes Resort | 24W-5N | 6 |
| Itasca CC | 19W-6N | 8 |
| Ken Loch Links | 20W-1S | 20 |
| Klein Creek GC | 26W-1N | 12 |
| Medinah CC | 21W-6N | 7 |
| Naperville CC | 25W-6S | 24 |
| Nordic Hills Resort GC | 21W-5N | 7 |
| Oak Meadows GC | 18W-4,5N | 8 |
| Old Wayne GC | 29W-3N | 10,11 |
| Pheasant Run Resort | 32W-3N | 10 |
| Prairie Landing GC | 32W-1N | 10 |

| | Location | Page |
|---|---|---|
| River Forest CC | 15W-4N | 9 |
| Ruth Lake CC | 16W-6S | 27 |
| Salt Creek GC | 18W-7N | 8 |
| St Andrews GC | 29,30W-3N | 10,11 |
| Springbrook GC | 29W-9S | 29 |
| Sugar Creek GC | 17W-0S | 20,21 |
| The Village Green Park | 23W-1S | 19 |
| Twin Lakes GC | 18W-6S | 26 |
| Village Green GC | 20W-8S | 32 |
| Village Links of Glen Ellyn | 22,23W-1S | 19 |
| Western Acres GC | 21W-2S | 19 |
| White Eagle GC | 30W-9S | 28 |
| White Pines GC | 16W-4N | 9 |
| Woodbridge GC | 23W-7S | 24,25 |

## Shopping Centers

| | Location | Page |
|---|---|---|
| Bloomingdale Plaza | 23W-4N | 6, 7 |
| Brush Hill Mall | 28W-6S | 23 |
| Courtyard SC | 18W-0S | 20 |
| Cress Creek SC | 27W-5S | 23 |
| Downers Park SC | 19W-8S | 29 |
| Eastgate SC | 18W-0S | 20 |
| Finley Sq Mall | 20W-2S | 19 |
| Fox Run Square SC | 25W-8S | 30 |
| Fox Valley SC | 30W-7S | 28 |
| Geneva Plaza SC | 24W-1N | 12 |
| Gina's Plaza SC | 24W-1N | 12 |
| Georgetown Sq SC | 18W-6N | 18 |
| Glendale Heights SC | 22W-1, 2N | 13 |
| Greenbrook Shopping Plaza | 26W-7N | 6 |
| Greenknolls SC | 19W-6S | 26 |
| Green Meadow SC | 18W-3N | 14 |
| Hawthorne Square SC | 26W-9S | 30 |
| Hobson West Commons SC | 27W-8S | 29 |
| Lombard Pines SC | 20W-0S | 20 |
| Main Plaza SC | 24W-0N | 12 |
| Market Meadows SC | 25W-8S | 30 |
| Meadowbrook SC | 21W-7S | 25 |
| Naper Plaza SC | 26W-8S | 30 |
| Naper West Plaza SC | 29W-7S | 23 |
| North Park Shopping Mall | 18W-2N | 14 |
| Oakbrook SC | 16W-1S | 21 |
| Ogden Mall SC | 25W-5S | 24 |
| Ogden Place SC | 26W-5S | 24 |
| Plaza Westlake | 23W-4N | 6, 7 |
| Springbrook SC | 23W-5N | 7 |
| Stratford Square SC | 25W-5N | 6 |
| Twin Ctrs SC | 26W-5S | 24 |
| Villa DuPage SC | 18W-1N | 14 |
| Villa Oaks SC | 18W-0S | 20 |
| Woodgrove Festival SC | 20W-8S | 32 |
| Yorktown SC | 19W-2S | 20 |

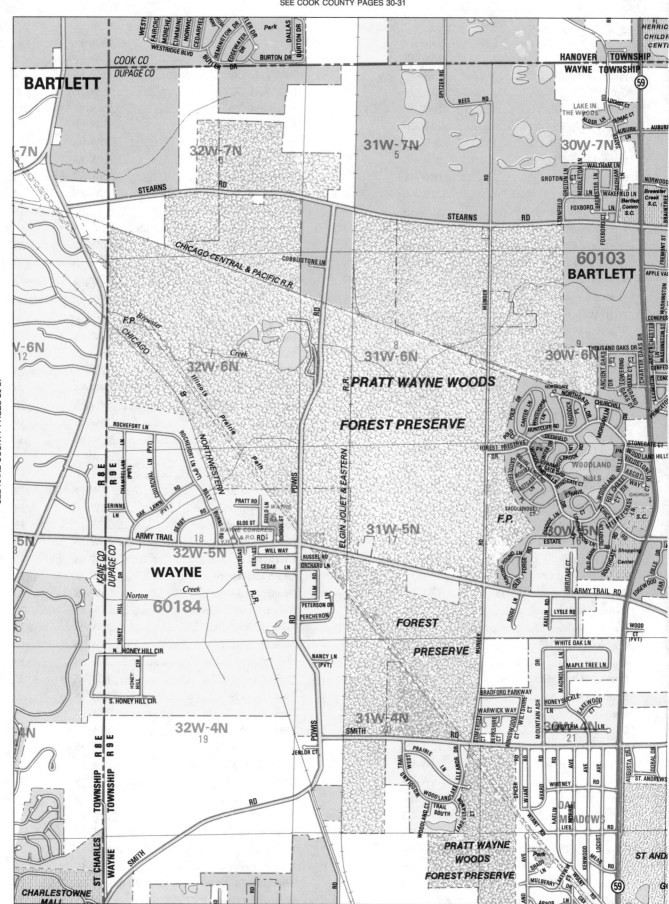

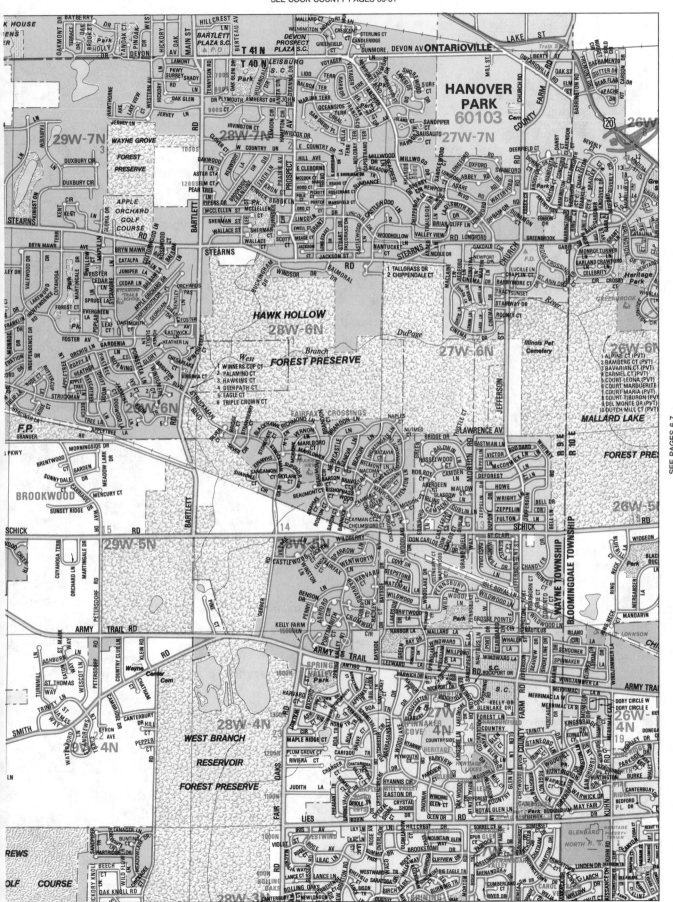

SEE COOK COUNTY PAGES 32-33

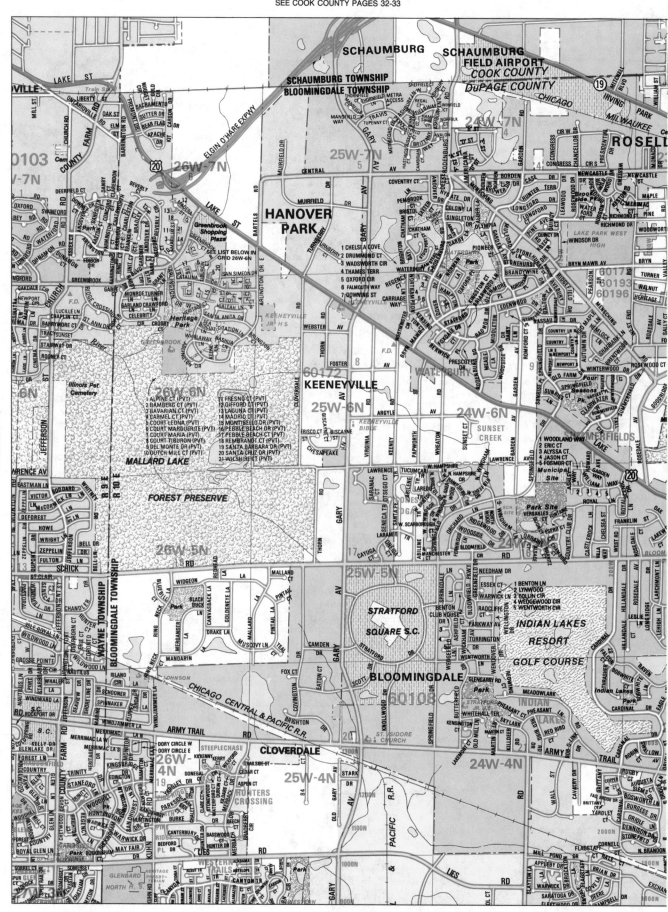

SEE PAGES 4-5

SEE COOK COUNTY PAGES 32-33

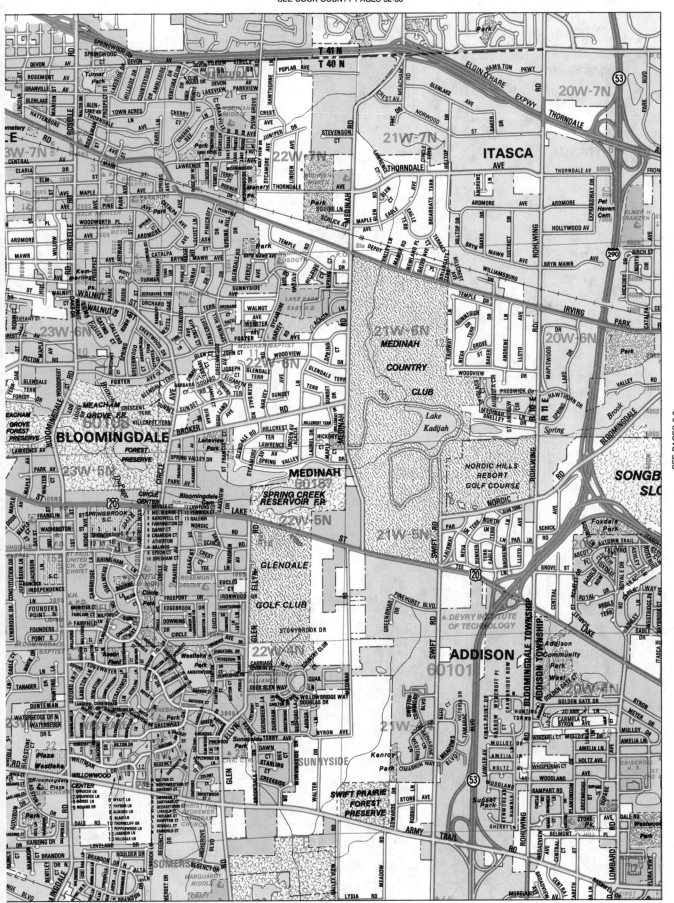

SEE PAGES 8-9

SEE PAGES 12-13

SEE COOK COUNTY PAGES 34-35

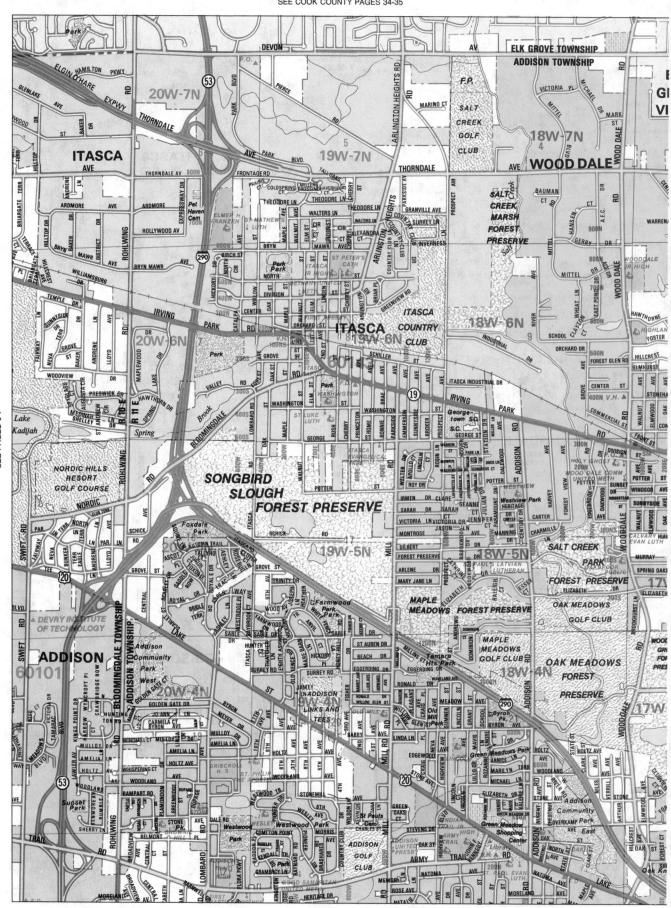

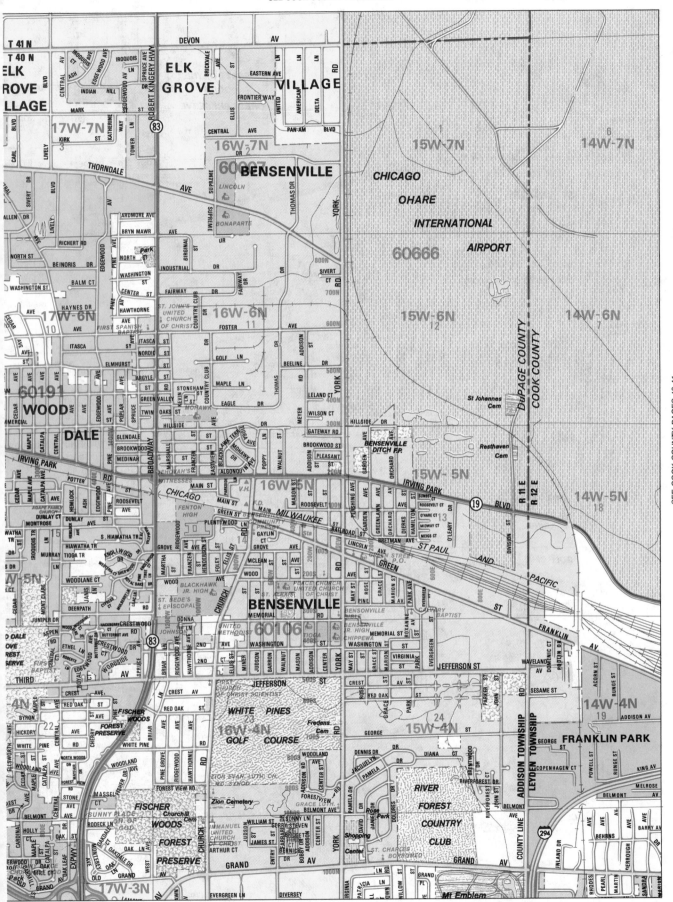

SEE COOK COUNTY PAGES 40-41

SEE PAGES 4-5

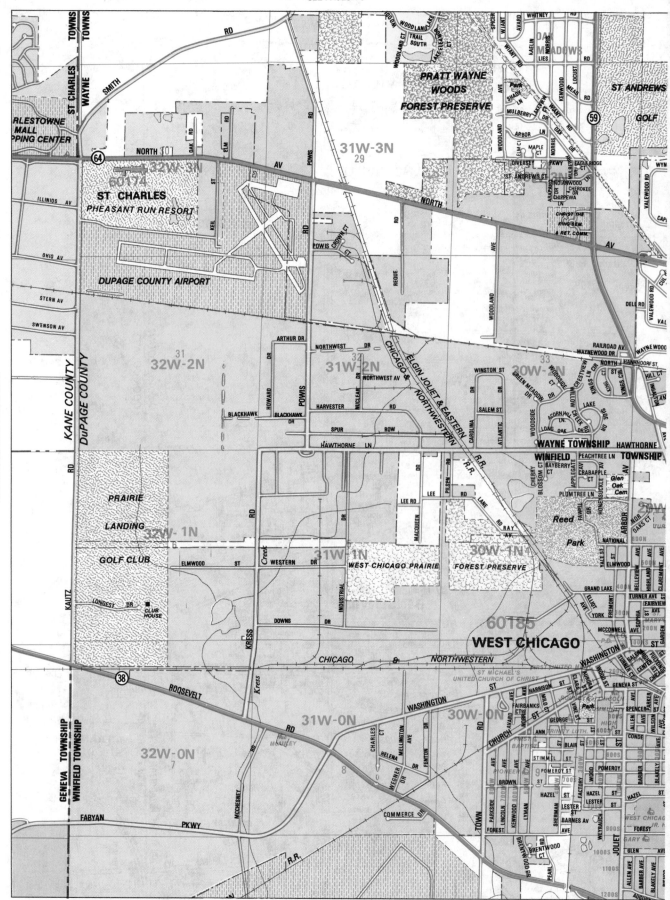

SEE KANE COUNTY PAGES 32-33

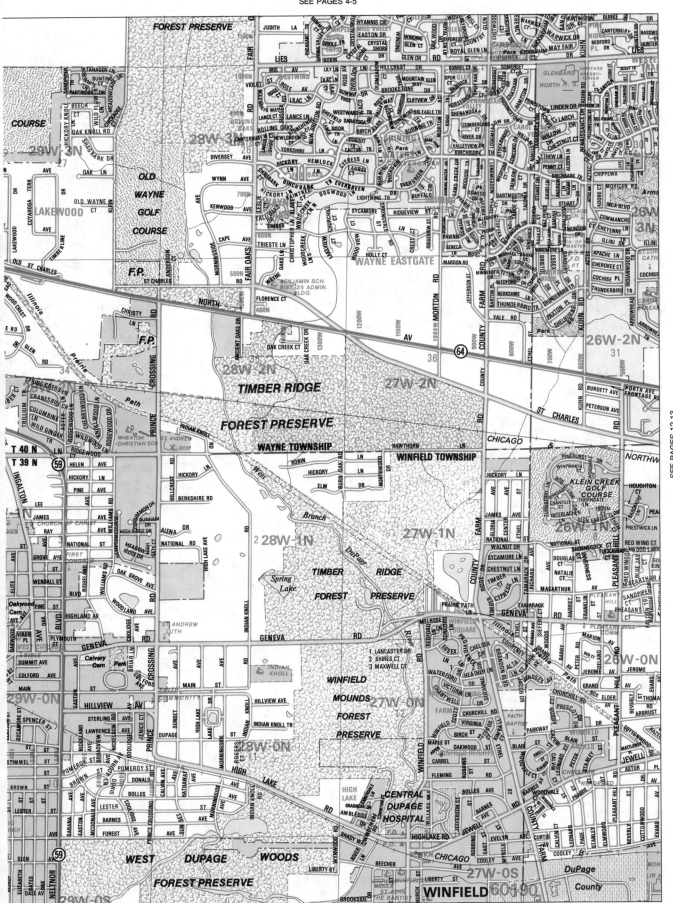

SEE PAGES 12-13

SEE PAGES 6-7

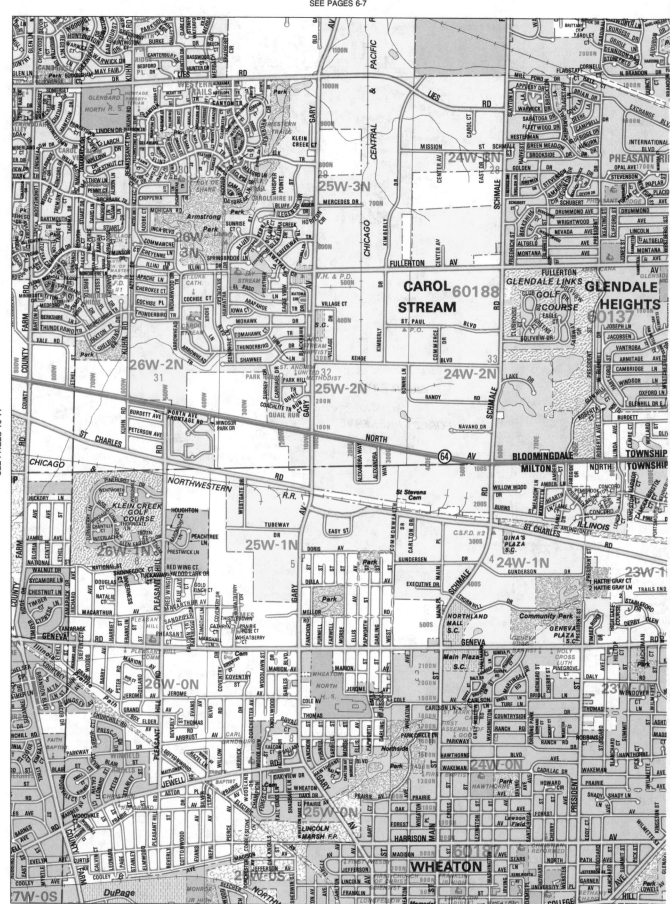

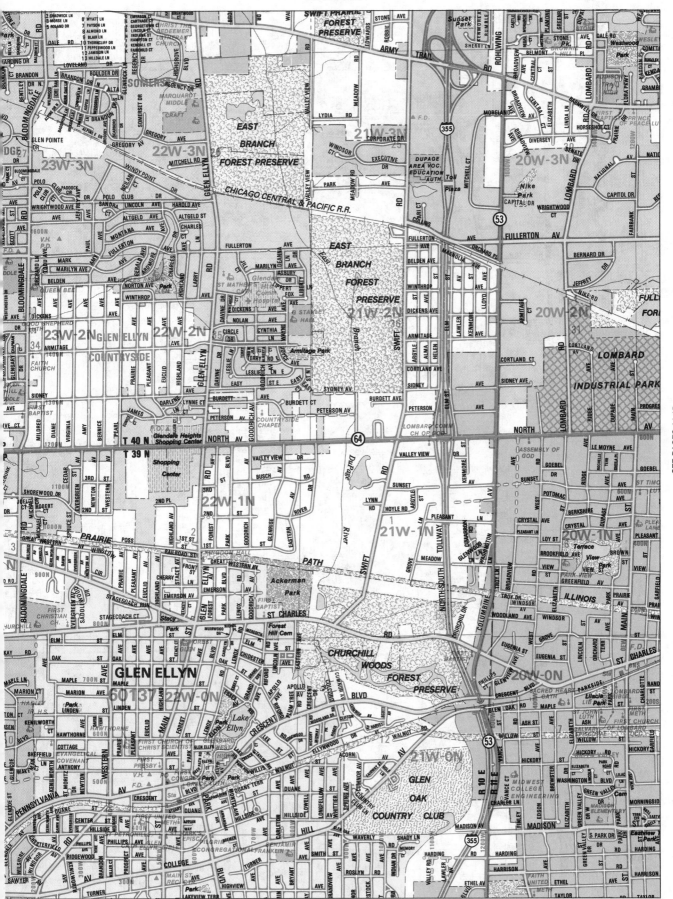

SEE PAGES 14-15

SEE PAGES 8-9

SEE PAGES 12-13

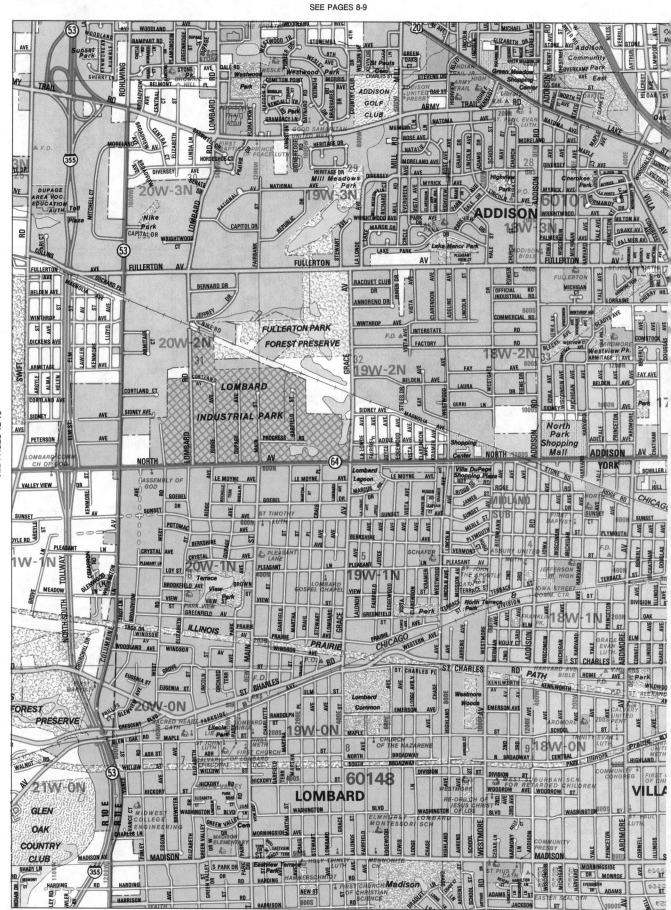

SEE PAGES 8-9

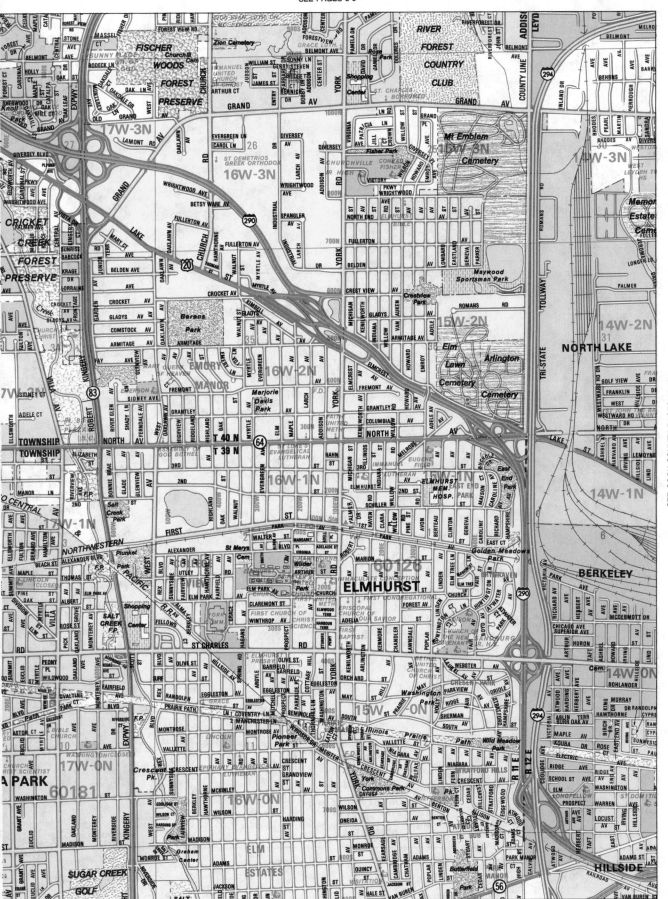

SEE COOK COUNTY PAGES 46-47

SEE PAGES 20-21

# 16 DU PAGE COUNTY

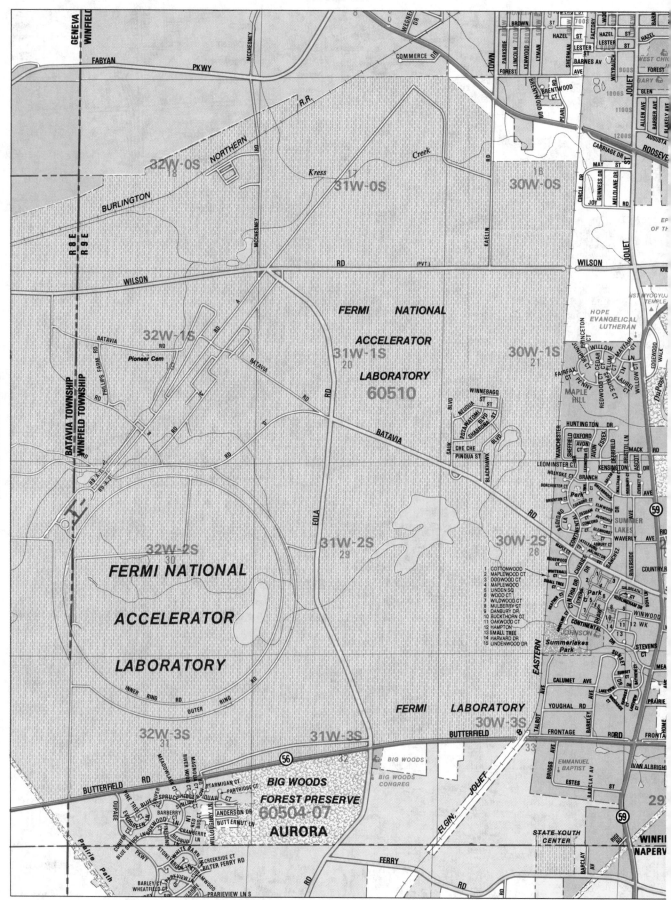

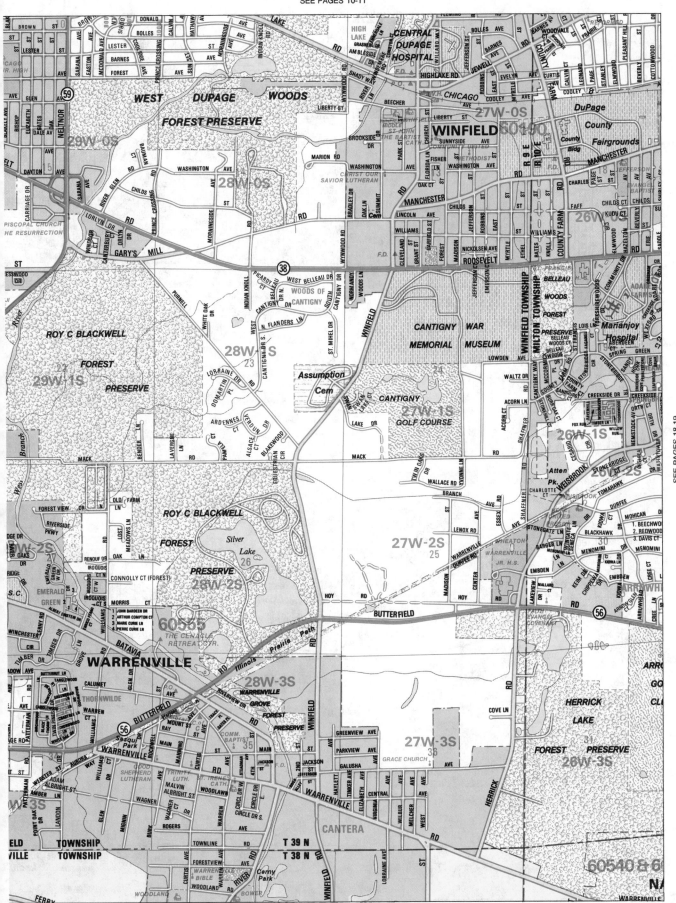

SEE PAGES 18-19

SEE PAGES 12-13

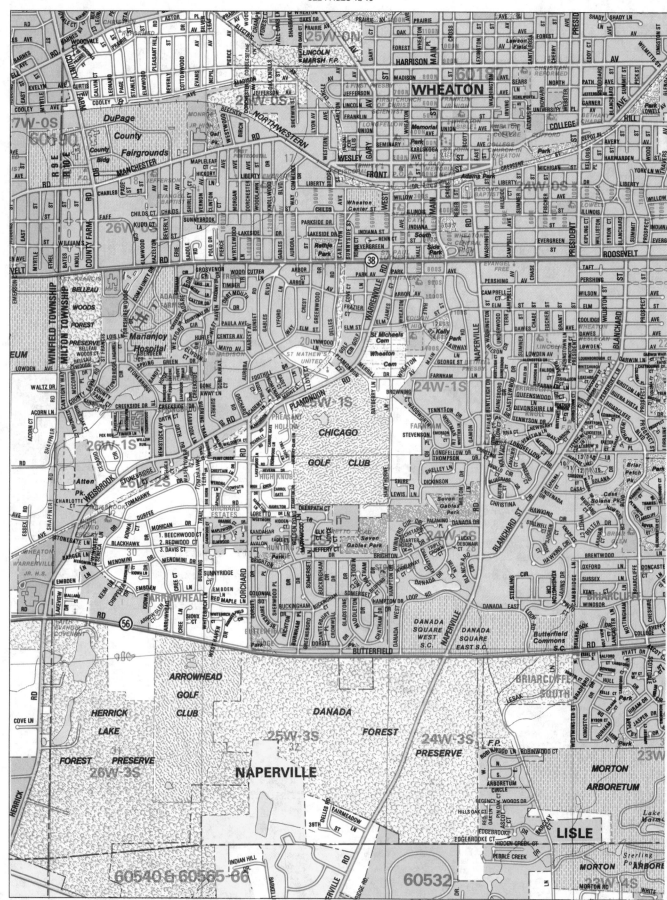

SEE PAGES 12-13

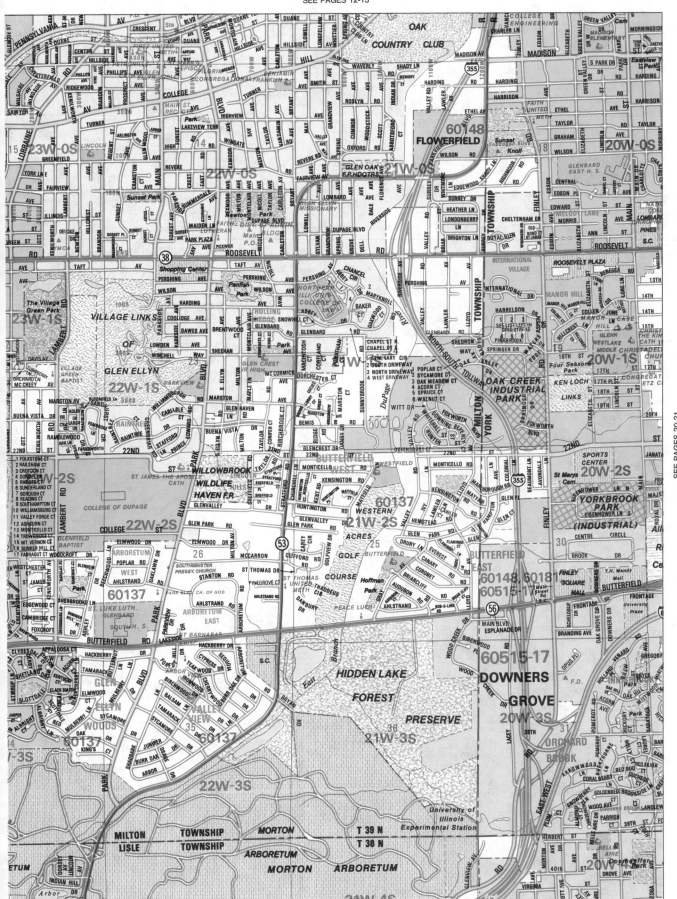

SEE PAGES 20-21

SEE PAGES 14-15

SEE PAGES 18-19

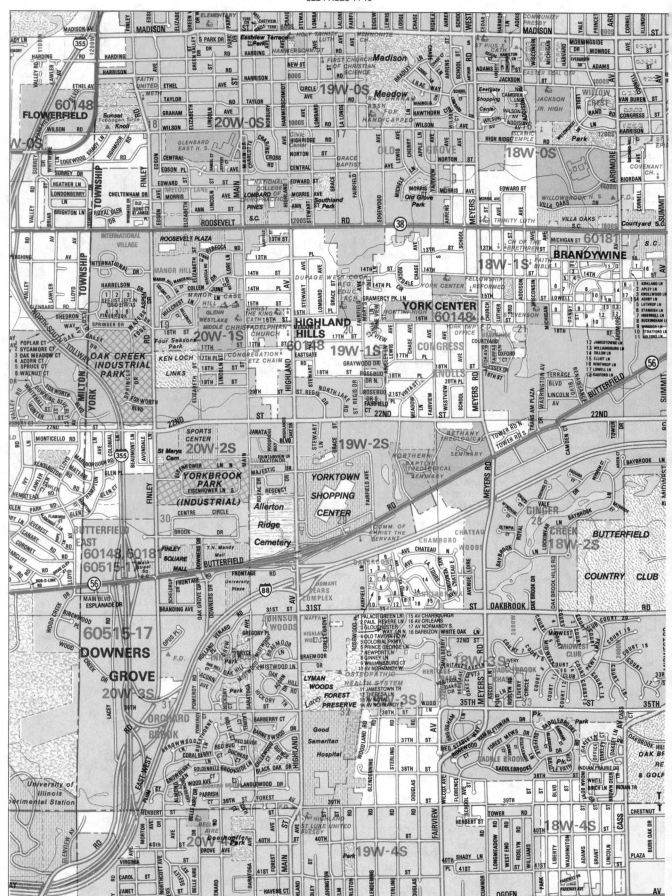

SEE PAGES 14-15

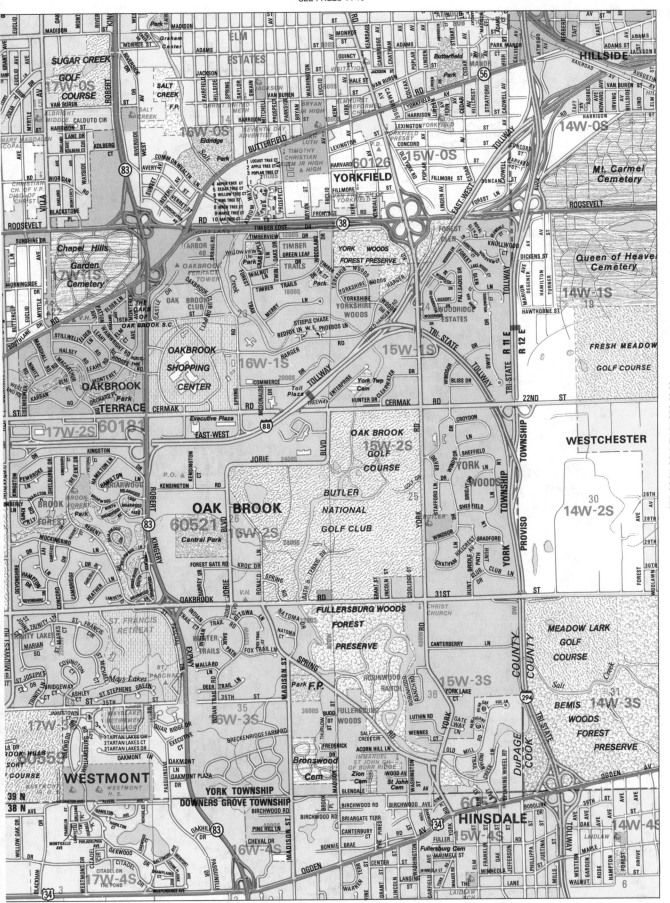

SEE PAGES 26-27

SEE COOK COUNTY PAGES 52-53

SEE PAGES 16-17

BIG WOODS

FOREST PRESERVE

BUTTERFIELD

BUTTERFIELD

ELGIN

FERRY

STATE YOUTH CENTER

STATE YOUTH CENTER

WINF

NAPER

Prairie Path

1 FIELDSTONE CT
2 CROSS CREEK CT
3 STUBBLEFIELD CT
4 WATERFORD CT
5 STANTON CT
6 DEVONSHIRE CT

60504-07

AURORA

31W-4S
5

30W-4S

32W-4S

EAST-WEST TOLLWAY

EAST-WEST

1

6

EAST-WEST TOLLWAY

FISHER DR
COUNTRY FARM DR

NAL

DIEHL RD.

DIEHL RD

WHITE OAK CIR

DIEHL RD.

WHITE OAK CIR

COUNTRY LAKES

PEBBLEWOOD PLAZA S.C.

LASALLE

CHANDLER CT

32W-5S

31W-5S
8

GOLFVIEW RD

COUNTRY LAKES GOLF COURSE

30W-5S

MANOR

PEBBLEWOOD EAST

BROOKDALE

WITCHWOOD

WALNUT BEND

12

R 8 E

R 9 E

STONEBRIDGE

STONEBRIDGE COUNTRY CLUB

INDIAN PLAINS

BAUER RD.

WILLOWBEND WEST

INDIAN TRAIL RD.

NO. AURORA RD VENTURE

WOODEWIND DR.

WHISPERING WINDS DR.

NORTH AURORA RD.

WESTON RIDGE

EOLA

60519

INDUSTRIAL DR

WESTON RIDGE

R.R. STA.

13

EOLA

BURLINGTON

NORTHERN

30W-6S
16

32W-5S

31W-6S
17

ENTERPRISE

COMMONS

MERIDIAN PKWY

GLACIER

PARK AVE

HIGH

SUSSEX AV

COMMERCE ST

R.R.

LIBERTY

ST

LIBERTY

JEFFERS

KANE CO.

DuPAGE CO.

LIBERTY

ENTERPRISE ST

EXCHANGE

COMMONS DR

West Ridge Court S.C.

ELGIN JOLIET & EASTERN

EXCHANGE AV

Yorkshire S.C.

24

32W-7S
19

NEW YORK ST

EOLA ST

20

31W-7S

30W-7S
21

NEW YORK ST

AURORA

Naper West Plaza S.C.

Fox River Commons S.C.

OAKHURST FOREST PRESERVE

CHESHIRE DR

BEAUMONT

60504-07

AURORA

DIAMOND BAY

Spring Lake

Fox Valley Shopping Center

THE WILLOWS

McCOY DR

Fox Valley Center

LAFOX AV

25

Creek

AMBERWOOD
28

ST. JAMES LUTHER

SEE PAGES 16-17

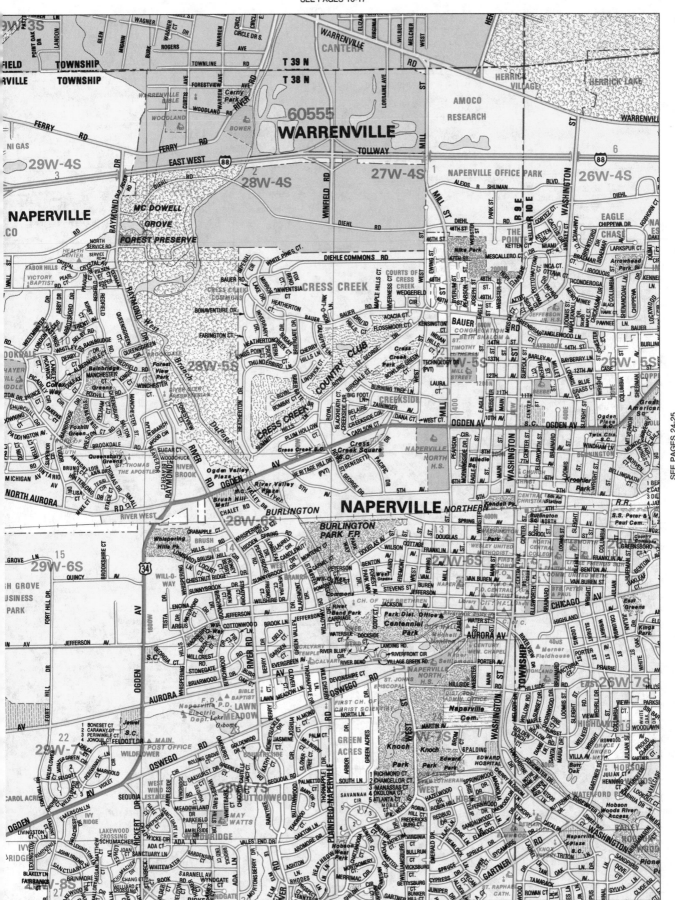

SEE PAGES 24-25

SEE PAGES 18-19

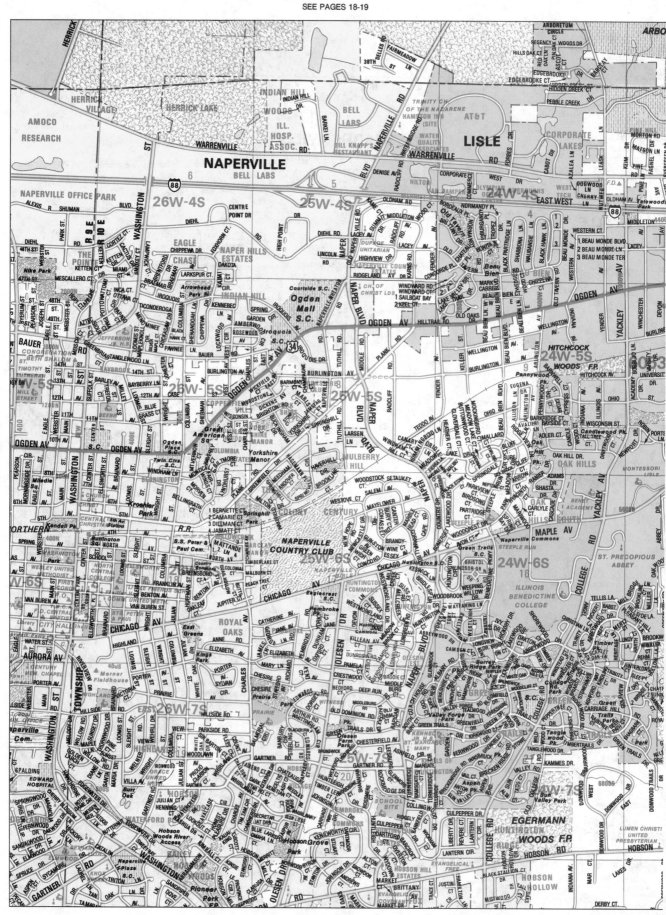

SEE PAGES 22-23

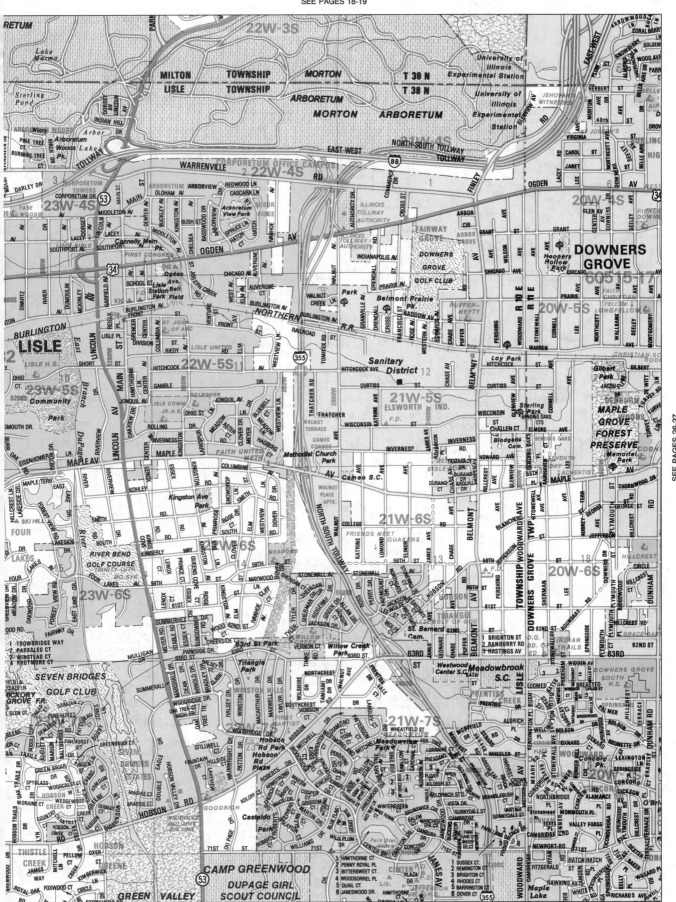

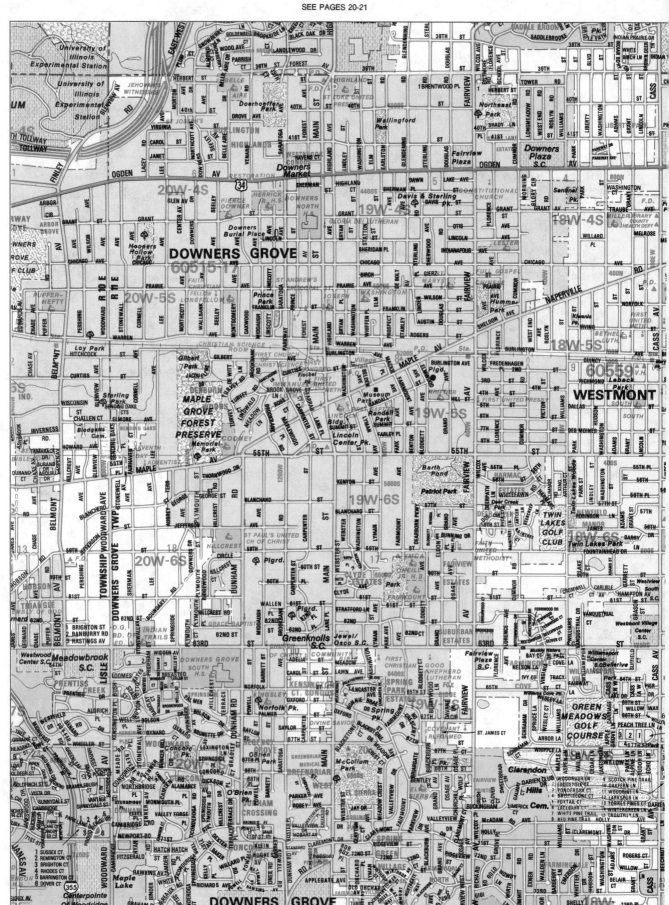

SEE PAGES 20-21

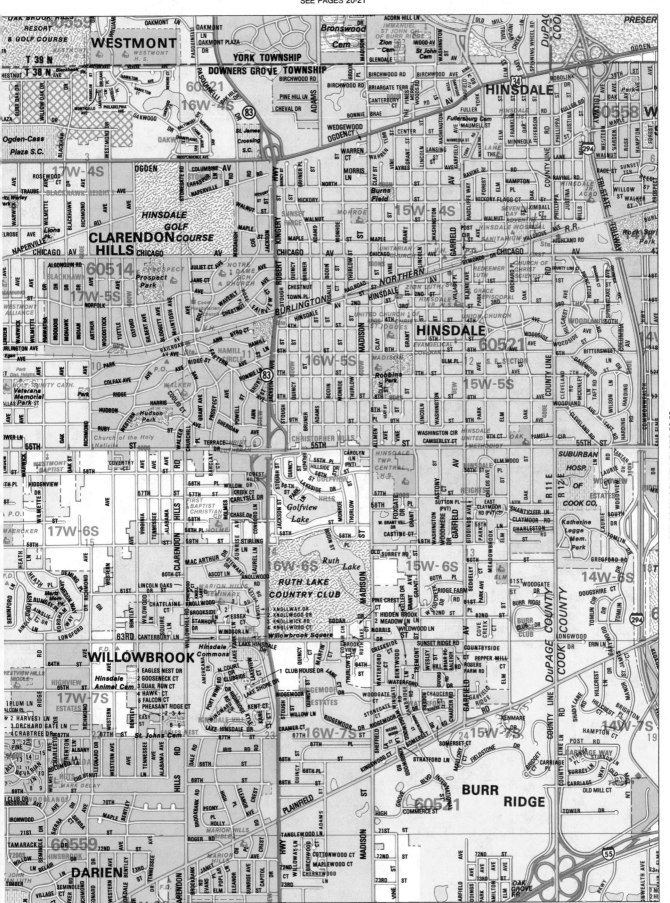

SEE PAGES 22-23

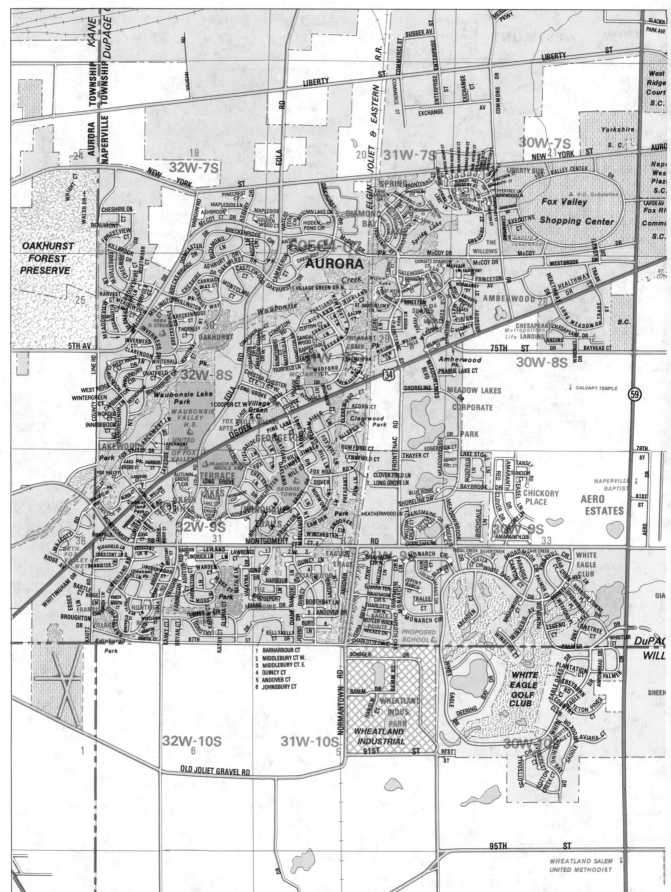

SEE KANE COUNTY PAGES 50-51

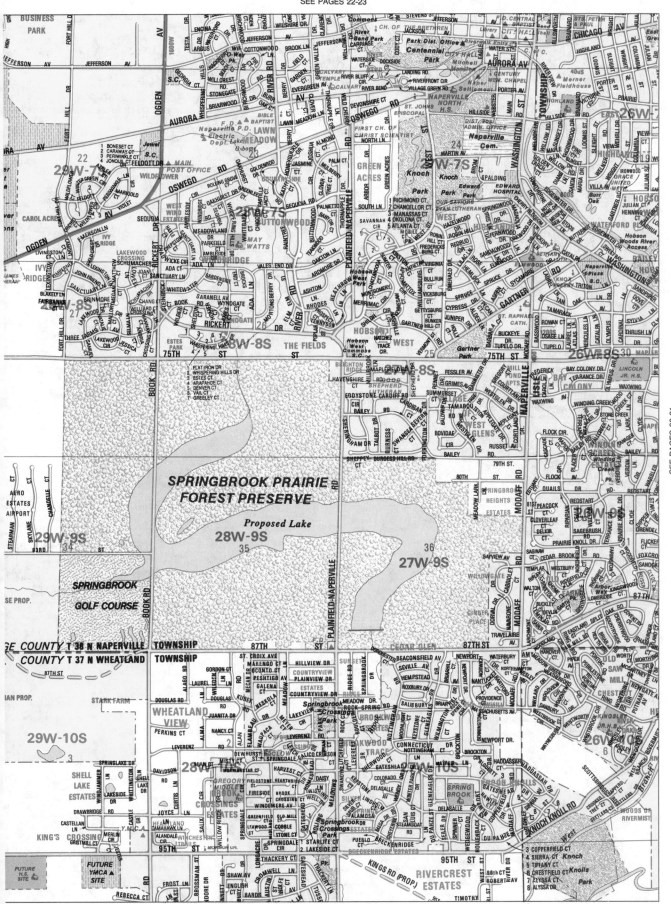

SEE PAGES 24-25

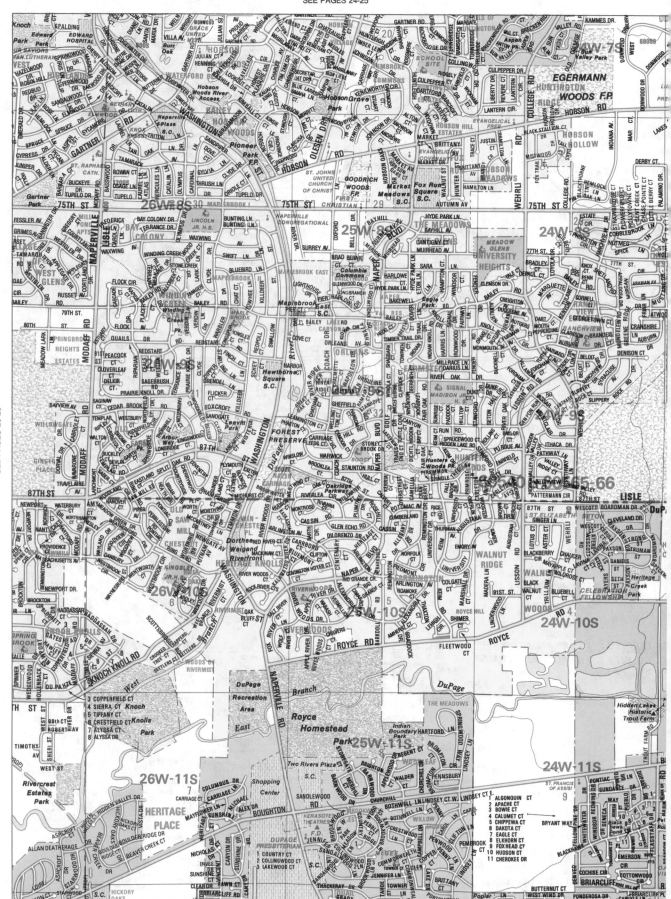

SEE PAGES 24-25

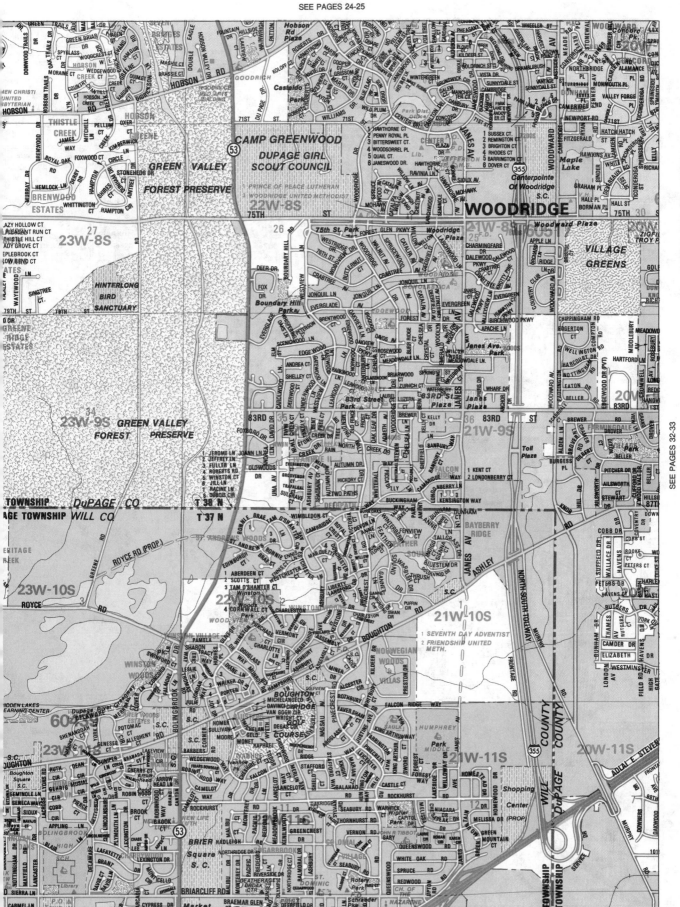

SEE WILL COUNTY PAGES 6-7

SEE PAGES 32-33

SEE PAGES 26-27

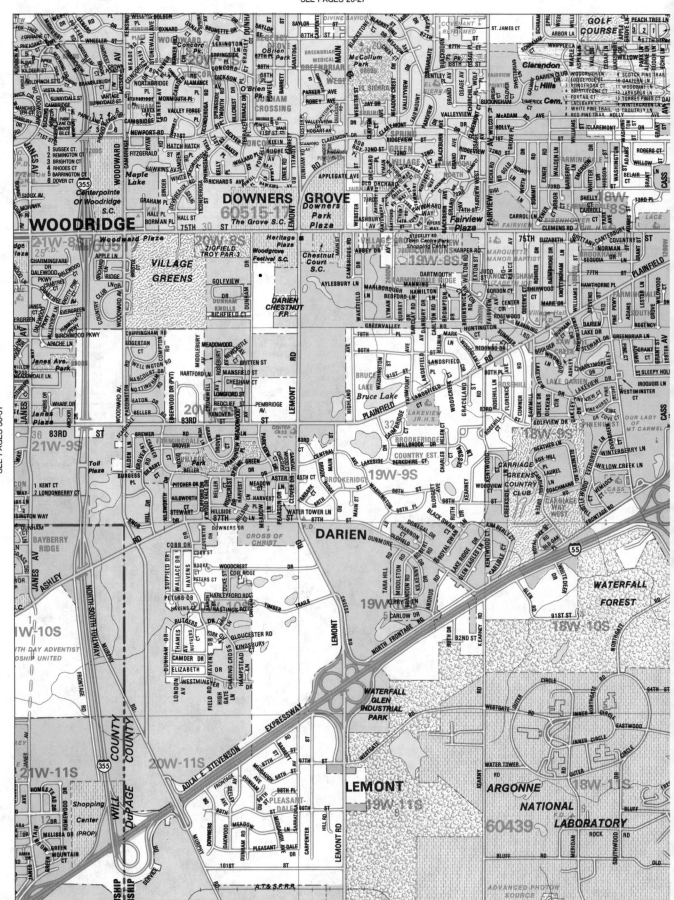

SEE PAGES 30-31

SEE PAGES 34-35

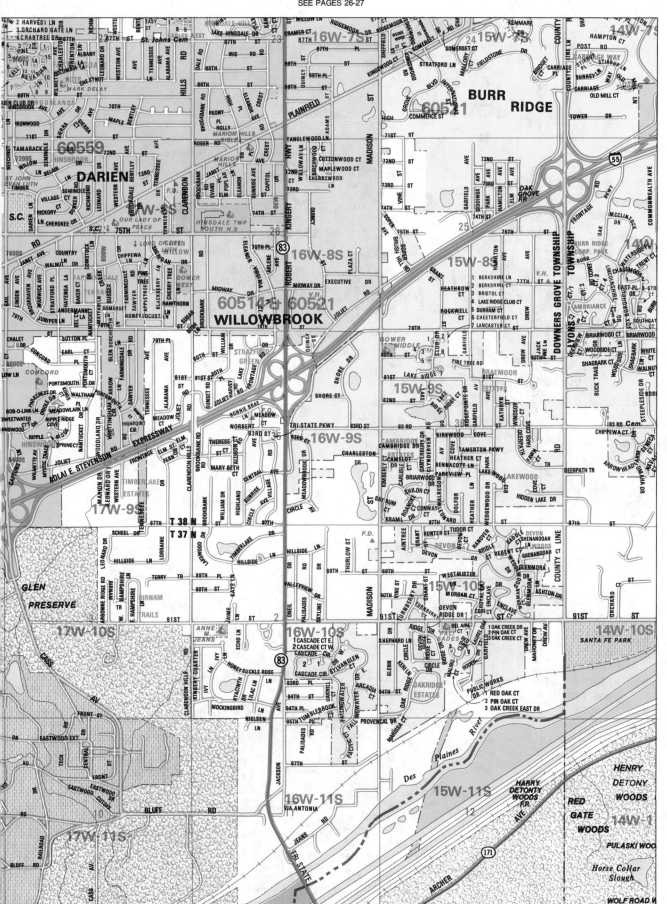

SEE COOK COUNTY PAGES 64-65

WATERFALL FOREST

18W-10S

19W-10S

SEE WILL COUNTY PAGES 6-7

WATERFALL GLEN INDUSTRIAL PARK

LEMONT
19W-11S

21W-11S

20W-11S

ARGONNE NATIONAL LABORATORY

18W-11S

60439

ADLAI E. STEVENSON EXPRESSWAY

PLEASANTDALE

ADVANCED PHOTON SOURCE

St. Patricks Cem.

WOODRIDGE

DuPAGE TOWNSHIP
DOWNERS GROVE TOWNSHIP
WILL COUNTY
DuPAGE COUNTY

INTERNATIONALE CENTRE

WOODRIDGE F.P.

19W-12S

WATERFALL GLEN FOREST PRESERVE

18W-12S

20W-12S

BROMBEREK

HILLCREST LN

LEMONT

19W-12S

A.T. & S.F.R.R.

BLACK PARTRIDGE FOREST PRESERVE

Goose Lake

LEMONT
DuPAGE COUNTY
COOK COUNTY

HINDU TEMPLE

19W-13S

1 ST. BONAVENTURE CT
2 ST. ANTHONY CT
3 ST. JOSEPH CT
4 ST. COLETTE CT
5 ST. ANNE CT

20W-13S

KEEPATAH FOREST PRESERVE

HISTORIC DOWNTOWN LEMONT

18W-13S

FRANCISCAN VILLAGE

McCARTHY POINTE

OUR LADY OF VICTORY CONVENT

CARRIAGE RIDGE

CHAMBER OF COMM. IN THE TRAIN STATION
GENERAL LANDING
HISTORICAL SOCIETY MUSEUM
COOKIE JAR MUSEUM

LEMONT FIRE STATION

INDUSTRIAL PARK DR

21W-14S

20W-14S

LEMONT AIRPORT

19W-14S

1 PANNA MARIA ST

18W-14S

LEMONT
60439

LITHUANIAN WORLD CENTER MONTESSORI

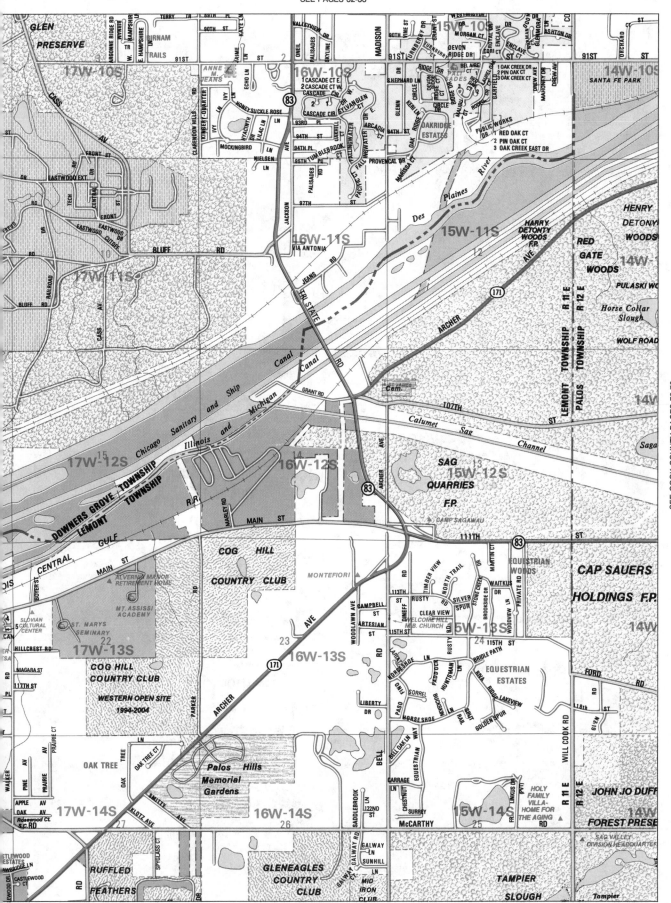

SEE COOK COUNTY PAGES 72-73

# DuPage
# County

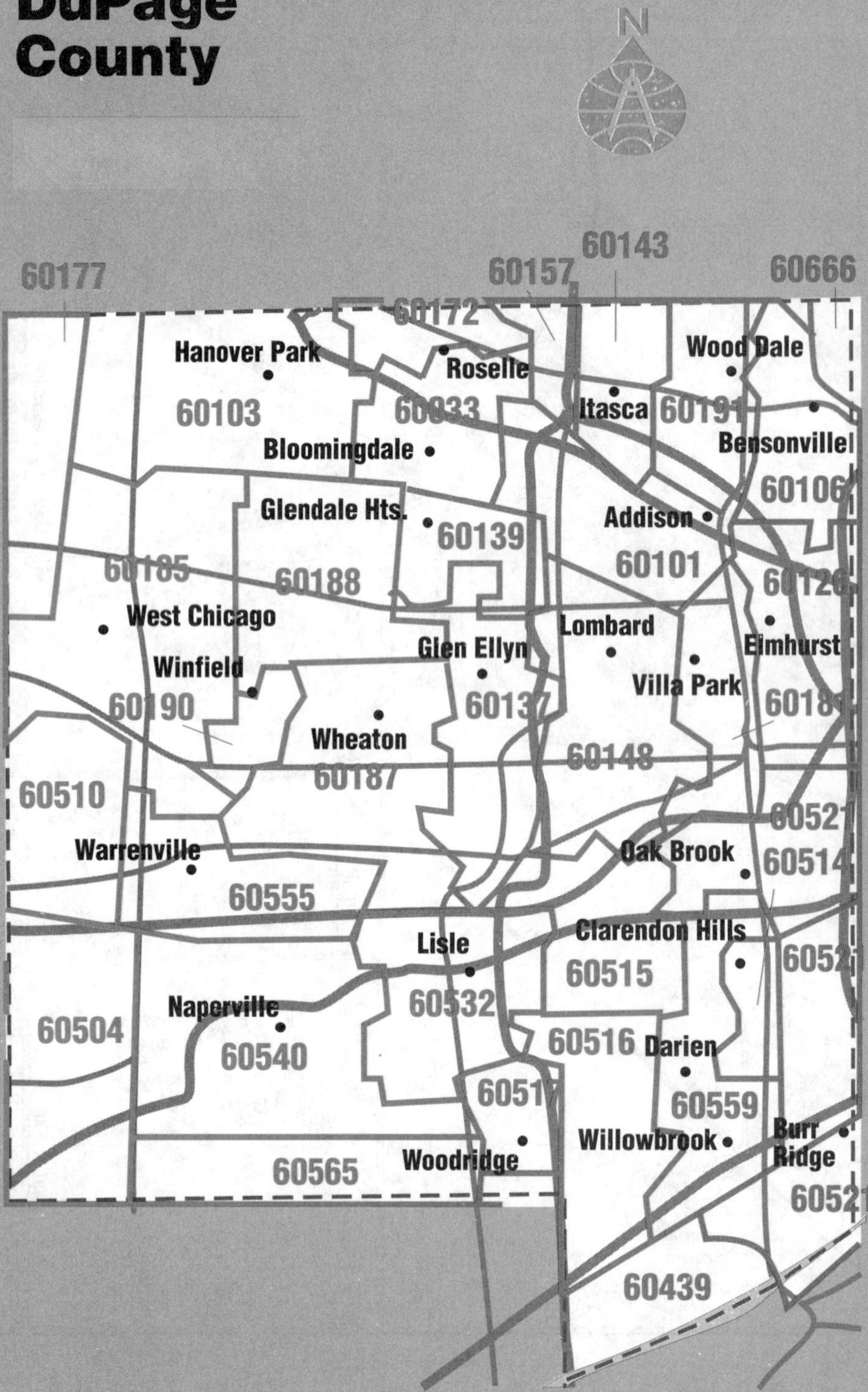

N

60177    60157  60143    60666

60172

Hanover Park    Roselle    Wood Dale

60103    60033    Itasca  60191

Bloomingdale    Bensonville

60106

Glendale Hts.    Addison

60139

60185    60188    60101    60126

West Chicago    Lombard    Elmhurst

Winfield    Glen Ellyn    Villa Park

60190    60137    60189

Wheaton    60148

60187    60527

60510    60514

Warrenville    Oak Brook

60555    Clarendon Hills

Lisle    60515    60521

Naperville    60532

60504    60516  Darien

60540    60517

60559

Woodridge    Willowbrook    Burr
Ridge

60565    60521

60439

DU PAGE COUNTY 37

# Street Index


Grid Page

## Addison

Adams Dr. N&S .... 18W-3N 14
Addison Rd. N&S .......... 18W-2N,18W-4N 14
Adeline Av. N&S .......... 18W-2N,19W-3N 14
Adobe Dr. NE&SW .. 21W-4N 7
Alden Dr. E&W ...... 18W-3N 14
Amelia Ln. E&W .......... 21W-4N,20W-4N 7
Annoreno Dr. E&W .. 19W-2N 14
Anvil Ct. NW&SE .......... 19W-4N,19W-5N 8
Ardmore Av. N&S .... 18W-3N 14
Ardmore Ter. NE&SW .......... 18W-2N 14
Ari Ct. N&S ........ 21W-3N 13
Armitage Av. E&W .. 18W-2N 14
Armitage Ct. N&S .... 20W-2N 14
Army Trail Rd. E&W .......... 21W-3N,18W-3N 13
Ascot Pl. E&W ...... 20W-5N 8
Ashley Ln. NW&SE .. 20W-5N 8
Ashwood Ct. N&S .......... 19W-4N,19W-5N 8
Aspen Way E&W .... 20W-5N 8
Autumn Tr. E&W .... 20W-5N 8
Babbit Av. N&S ...... 19W-4N 8
Barbara Ct. NE&SW .......... 20W-4N 8
Barnwell Dr. NW&SE .......... 20W-3N 14
Baybrook Ct. N&S .......... 20W-5N,19W-5N 8
Baynard Rd. N&S .... 19W-3N 14
Beach Dr. E&W ...... 19W-4N 8
Belden Av. E&W .... 19W-2N 14
Belmont Av. E&W .... 17W-4N 9
Bernard Dr. E&W .... 20N-2N 14
Beverly Av. N&S .......... 17W-2N,17W-3N 14
Blecke Av. NE&SW .. 18W-2N 14
Brashares Dr. N&S .. 19W-3N 14
Byron Av. E&W .......... 20W-4N,18W-4N 8
Capitol Dr. E&W .... 20W-3N 14
Cardinal Av. N&S .......... 17W-3N,17W-4N 14
Carmela Ct. N&S .... 20W-4N 8
Castle Rd. N&S ...... 20W-4N 8
Catalpa Ct. N&S .... 17W-3N 14
Cedar St. N&S ...... 17W-4N 9
Central Av. N&S .... 17W-4N 9
Chatham Av. N&S .......... 17W-2N,17W-3N 14
Cherry Hill Ct. N&S .. 17W-2N 14
Cherry Hill Dr. N&S .. 17W-2N 14
Chestnut St. N&S .... 18W-3N 14
Church St. N&S .... 18W-3N 14
Cimarron Way NS&EW .......... 21W-4N 7
Circle Dr. N&S .... 19W-3N 14
Clarendon Av. N&S .......... 19W-2N,19W-3N 14
Clover Ct. N&S .... 20W-5N 8
Clubview Ct. NW&SE .......... 17W-4N 9
Collins Av. NW&SE .. 21W-3N 13
Commercial Rd. E&W .......... 18W-2N 14
Compton Point E&W .......... 19W-3N 14
Comstock Av. E&W .. 18W-2N 14
Congress Av. NW&SE .......... 17W-3N 14
Corporate Dr. E&W .. 21W-3N 13
Cortland Ct. E&W .. 20W-2N 14
Country Club Dr. N&S .......... 19W-3N,19W-4N 14
Craig Pl. N&S ...... 19W-4N 8
Crawbridge Row N&S .......... 21W-4N 7
Crocket Av. E&W .... 17W-2N 14
Dale Rd. E&W ...... 20W-4N 8
Denise Ct. N&S ...... 18W-4N 8
Diversey Av. E&W .......... 19W-3N,18W-3N 14
Diversey Blvd. E&W .. 17W-3N 14
Douglas Av. N&S .... 17W-2N 14
Drake Av. E&W ...... 18W-3N 14
DuPage Av. N&S .... 20W-4N 8
DuPage Ct. E&W .... 20W-4N 8
Edgewood Av. E&W .......... 19W-4N 8
Eggerding Dr. E&W .. 19W-4N 8
Eighth Av. N&S ...... 19W-4N 8
Elizabeth Dr. E&W .. 18W-4N 8
Ellsworth Av. N&S .......... 17W-2N,17W-4N 14
Evergreen Av. N&S .. 19W-3N 14
Executive Dr. E&W .. 21W-3N 13
Factory Rd. E&W .......... 19W-2N,18W-2N 14
Fairbank St. N&S .... 20W-3N 14
Farmwood Dr. E&W .. 19W-5N 8
Fay Av. E&W ........ 18W-2N 14
Fiene Dr. N&S ...... 18W-2N 14
Fisher Dr. N&S .......... 19W-4N,19W-5N 8
Flora Pkwy. N&S .... 20W-3N 14
Forest Ct. N&S ...... 17W-3N 14
Forest Dr. E&W .... 17W-4N 9
Friars Ct. N&S ...... 19W-3N 14
Fullerton Av. E&W .......... 21W-3N,17W-3N 13
Gerri Ln. E&W ...... 18W-2N 14
Gladys Av. NE&SW .......... 18W-2N,17W-2N 14
Golden Gate Dr. E&W .......... 20W-4N 8
Grace Av. N&S ...... 19W-2N 14
Gramercy Ln. E&W .. 19W-3N 14
Grant Dr. N&S ...... 18W-3N 14
Grant St. N&S ...... 18W-4N 8
Green Meadow Dr. E&W .......... 18W-4N 8
Green Oaks Ct. E&W .......... 19W-4N 8
Greenbriar Dr. N&S .. 21W-5N 7
Greenridge St. N&S .. 20W-4N 8
Haddon Pl. N&S .... 19W-3N 14
Hale St. N&S ...... 18W-3N 14
Harrow Ct. N&S .... 21W-4N 7
Harvard Av. N&S .......... 18W-2N,18W-3N 14
Heather Ct. N&S .... 19W-5N 8
Cir. .......... 19W-3N 14
Hickory Pl. E&W .... 19W-4N 8
Hickory Tr. N&S .... 19W-5N 8
Highview Av. N&S .......... 19W-3N,18W-4N 14
Hilton Av. E&W ...... 18W-3N 14
Holly Ct. E&W ...... 17W-3N 14
Holtz Av. E&W .......... 21W-4N,18W-4N 7
Honey Hill Rd. N&S .......... 19W-4N,19W-5N 8
Horseshoe Ct. E&W 20W-3N 14
Howard Av. N&S .... 19W-4N 8
Hunter Ct. E&W .... 19W-4N 8
Huntington Rd. E&W .......... 21W-4N 7
Industrial Rd. E&W .. 18W-2N 14
Interstate Rd. E&W .......... 19W-2N,18W-2N 14
Iowa Av. N&S .......... 18W-2N,18W-3N 14
Irmen Dr. N&S ...... 19W-2N 14
Itasca Rd. NW&SE .. 20W-5N 8
Jamey Ln. NS&EW .. 19W-4N 8
Janice Ln. E&W .... 18W-4N 8
Jefferey Dr. NE&SW .......... 20W-2N 14
John F. Kennedy Dr. N&S .......... 18W-3N 14
Joseph Ln. N&S .... 19W-5N 8
Joyce Ln. N&S ...... 18W-3N 14
Justin Ct. NS&EW .. 20W-5N 8
Katherine Ln. N&S .. 21W-4N 7
Kay Av. N&S ........ 19W-2N 14
Keebie Ct. N&S ...... 19W-5N 8
Kendall Tr. E&W .... 19W-3N 14
Kenmore Av. N&S .. 21W-4N 7
Kings Point Dr. N&S 21W-4N 7
Kingston Dr. N&S .... 19W-3N 14
Krage Dr. E&W ...... 17W-2N 15
La Londe Av. N&S .. 19W-3N 14
Lake Manor Dr. E&W .......... 19W-3N 14
Lake Park Dr. E&W .......... 19W-3N,18W-3N 14
Lake St. NW&SE .......... 21W-5N,17W-3N 7
Lancers Dr. N&S .... 20W-4N 8
Laporte Ct. N&S .... 18W-3N 14
Laporte Dr. E&W .... 18W-3N 14
Laura Dr. E&W ...... 18W-2N 14
Lawler Av. N&S .... 21W-4N 7
Lenmore St. N&S .... 18W-4N 8
Lilac Ln. NE&SW .... 20W-5N 8
Lincoln Av. E&W .......... 18W-3N,18W-4N 14
Lincoln Ct. N&S .... 18W-4N 8
Lincoln St. N&S .......... 18W-2N,18W-4N 14
Linda Ln. E&W ...... 19W-4N 8
Lois Av. N&S ........ 19W-4N 8
Lombard Rd. N&S .......... 20W-2N,20W-4N 14
Lorraine Av. E&W .......... 19W-2N,17W-2N 14
Macie Ct. N&S ...... 18W-4N 8
Maple Av. NE&SW .. 18W-3N 14
Maple Ct. N&S ...... 18W-3N 14
Maple St. N&S ...... 17W-4N 9
Mare Barn Ln. N&S .. 19W-4N 8
Marilyn Ter. E&W .... 18W-4N 8
Massel Ct. E&W .... 17W-4N 9
Mavis Ln. N&S ...... 18W-4N 8
May St. N&S ........ 18W-3N 14
Meadow Av. E&W .. 18W-4N 8
Meadows Blvd. N&S .......... 21W-4N 7
Memory Ln. E&W .... 19W-3N 14
Meyer Dr. NW&SE .. 20W-4N 8
Michael Ln. E&W .... 18W-4N 8
Michigan Av. N&S .......... 18W-2N,18W-3N 14
Michigan Ct. E&W .. 18W-2N 14
Mill Meadows Ln. N&S .......... 19W-3N 14
Mill Rd. N&S .......... 19W-3N,19W-4N 14
Millins Ct. NW&SE .. 19W-4N 8
Millins Ln. N&S ...... 19W-4N 8
Mitchell Ct. N&S .... 21W-3N 13
Monarch Ln. N&S .... 20W-4N 8
Moreland Av. E&W .......... 19W-3N,18W-3N 14
Morris Av. E&W .... 19W-3N 14
Mulloy Dr. E&W .......... 21W-4N,20W-4N 7
Myrick Av. E&W .......... 19W-3N,18W-3N 14
Natalie Ln. NS&EW .. 19W-3N 14
National Av. NE&SW .......... 20W-3N,19W-3N 14
Natoma Av. E&W .......... 19W-3N,18W-3N 14
Neva Av. N&S ...... 19W-4N 8
Nike Rd. NW&SE .... 20W-2N 14
Normandy Dr. NS&EW .......... 18W-3N 14
North Av. NW&SE .. 18W-3N 14
North-South Tollway N&S .......... 21W-2N,21W-3N 13
Oak Leaf Dr. N&S .. 17W-3N 14
Oak Mill Ct. E&W .... 17W-3N 14
Oak Mill St. N&S .... 17W-3N 14
Oak St. E&W .......... 18W-3N,17W-3N 14
Official Rd. E&W .... 18W-2N 14
Old Fence Rd. N&S .. 19W-4N 8
Old Grand Av. E&W .. 17W-3N 15
Palmer Av. E&W .... 18W-3N 14
Park Av. E&W .......... 19W-3N,18W-3N 14
Park Pl. NW&SE .... 19W-4N 8
Parkview Dr. NW&SE .......... 18W-3N 14
Pinehurst Blvd. E&W .......... 21W-5N 7
Pioneer Dr. N&S .......... 19W-3N,19W-4N 14
Plamondon Dr. N&S .. 20W-4N 8
Pleasant Av. N&S .... 19W-4N 8
Pleasant View Ct. E&W .......... 18W-3N 14
Power Ct. N&S ...... 18W-2N 14
Prairie Dr. N&S ...... 20W-3N 14
Princeton St. N&S .. 18W-3N 14
Racquet Club Dr. E&W .......... 19W-2N 14
Rampart Rd. E&W .. 20W-4N 8
Reed Ct. N&S ...... 21W-4N 7
Regal Ct. N&S ...... 20W-4N 8
Republic Dr. NE&SW .......... 19W-3N 14
Richard Ct. N&S .... 19W-3N 14
Rohlwing Rd. N&S .. 21W-4N 7
Ronald Dr. E&W .... 19W-4N 8
Rose Av. NS&EW .... 19W-3N 14
Rosebud NW&SE .... 20W-5N 8
Royal Dr. E&W ...... 20W-5N 8
Rozanne Dr. N&S .... 18W-4N 8
Rugeley Ct. E&W .... 19W-3N 14
Rumble Ln. N&S .... 21W-4N 7
Sable Dr. E&W .......... 20W-5N,19W-5N 8
School St. N&S .......... 18W-3N,18W-4N 14
Senate Dr. NW&SE .. 20W-3N 14
Sharon Dr. N&S .... 19W-4N 8
Sherry Ln. E&W .... 21W-4N 7
Sidney Av. E&W .......... 21W-2N,18W-2N 13
Squire Ln. E&W .... 20W-5N 8
St. Auben Dr. E&W .. 19W-4N 8
State St. NE&SW .... 18W-3N 14
Stevens Dr. E&W .... 19W-3N 14
Stewart Av. N&S .... 19W-3N 14
Stiles Dr. N&S ...... 19W-2N 14
Stone Av. E&W .......... 20W-4N,18W-4N 8
Stonehedge Rd. N&S .......... 19W-3N 14
Sumner St. N&S .... 18W-4N 8
Surrey Rd. E&W .... 19W-4N 8
Swift Rd. N&S .......... 21W-3N,21W-5N 13
Swifton Commons Blvd. N&S .......... 21W-4N 7
Tallyho Ct. E&W .... 20W-5N 8
Tamarac Blvd. N&S .. 21W-4N 7
Trinity Dr. E&W ...... 19W-5N 8
Valerie Ln. N&S .... 18W-4N 8
Victoria Dr. N&S .... 21W-4N 7
Villa Av. NW&SE .......... 17W-2N,17W-3N 14
Vista Av. N&S .......... 19W-2N,19W-3N 14
Waveland Av. E&W .. 18W-4N 8
Wesley Dr. NS&EW .......... 19W-3N,19W-4N 14
Western Ln N&S .... 21W-4N 7
Westgate Dr. N&S .. 18W-2N 14
Westridge Pl. N&S .. 20W-5N 8
Westview Ct. E&W .. 18W-2N 14
Westwood Av. N&S .. 19W-2N 14
Westwood Tr. E&W .. 19W-4N 8
Whispering Ct. E&W .......... 20W-4N 8
White Fence Ln. NW&SE .......... 19W-5N 8
Willow Glen St. E&W .......... 19W-4N 8
Wilson Ln. N&S ...... 19W-4N 8
Windmill Ct. E&W .......... 21W-4N,20W-4N 7
Windsor Ct. E&W .... 21W-3N 13
Winthrop Av. E&W .......... 19W-2N,18W-2N 14
Wisconsin Av. N&S .......... 18W-2N,18W-3N 14
Wood Av. E&W ...... 19W-5N 8
Woodland Av. E&W .......... 21W-4N,17W-4N 7
Wrightwood Ct. E&W .......... 20W-3N 14
Wyncroft Pl. N&S .... 21W-4N 7
Yale Av. N&S .......... 18W-2N,18W-3N 14
9th Av. N&S .......... 19W-4N,19W-5N 8
10th Av. N&S ...... 19W-4N 8
11th Av. NE&SW .... 19W-4N 8

## Addison Township

Addison Rd. N&S .... 18W-4N 8
Adele Av. E&W ...... 19W-2N 14
Ann Ct. N&S ........ 20W-4N 8
Ardmore Av. E&W .. 17W-7N 9
Arlington Heights Rd. N&S .......... 19W-7N 8
Armitage Av. E&W .. 17W-2N 14
Arthur Av. N&S ...... 18W-4N 8
Arthur Ct. E&W ...... 16W-3N 15
Belmont Av. E&W .......... 17W-4N,15W-4N 9
Belmont Pl. E&W .... 20W-3N 14
Bloomingdale Rd. NE&SW .......... 20W-5N 8
Briar Ln. N&S .......... 17W-4N,16W-4N 9
Broadview Av. N&S .. 20W-3N 14
Bryn Mawr Av. E&W .......... 17W-7N 9
Byron Av. E&W .......... 20W-4N,17W-4N 8
Catalpa Av. N&S .... 17W-6N 9
Catalpa St. N&S .... 17W-4N 9
Cedar Av. N&S ...... 17W-6N 9
Cedar St. N&S ...... 17W-4N 9
Center St. E&W .... 17W-6N 9
Central Av. N&S .......... 17W-2N,17W-6N 14
Chatham Av. N&S .. 17W-2N 14
Cherry St. N&S ...... 17W-4N 9
Chestnut St. N&S .... 18W-4N 8
Church Rd. N&S .... 16W-4N 9
Clarendon Av. N&S .. 19W-2N 14
Clark St. N&S ...... 18W-4N 8
County Line Rd. N&S .......... 15W-3N 15
Crest Av. E&W .......... 17W-4N,16W-4N 9
Crown Rd. N&S .... 15W-3N 15
Diversey Av. E&W .......... 20W-3N,15W-3N 14
Diversey Pl. NW&SE .......... 15W-3N 15
Donna Ln. E&W .... 16W-4N 9
Edgewood Av. N&S .. 17W-2N 14
Elizabeth St. N&S .... 20W-3N 14
Ellis St. N&S ........ 16W-4N 9
Ellsworth Av. N&S .......... 17W-2N,17W-4N 14
Elmhurst St. E&W .. 17W-6N 9
Elmwood Av. N&S .. 17W-4N 9
Emroy Av. N&S ...... 15W-3N 15
Fairfield Av. N&S .... 19W-2N 14
Fay Av. E&W ........ 17W-2N 14
Fisher Dr. NE&SW .. 17W-4N 9
Forest View Rd. E&W .......... 17W-4N,16W-4N 9
Foster Av. E&W .... 17W-6N 9
George St. E&W .... 15W-4N 9
Grand Av. E&W .......... 17W-3N,15W-3N 14
Grand Pl. E&W ...... 15W-3N 15
Granville Av. E&W .. 19W-7N 8
Grove St. E&W .......... 20W-5N,19W-5N 8
Hawthorne Av. N&S .. 16W-4N 9
Hickory Av. E&W .... 17W-4N 9
Hillcrest Av. N&S .... 17W-3N 14
Holtz Av. E&W .......... 19W-4N,18W-4N 8
Howard Av. N&S .... 15W-3N 15
Itasca Rd. N&S .......... 20W-4N,20W-5N 8
Itasca St. E&W ...... 17W-6N 9
Jill Ct. N&S .......... 15W-3N 15
Jo-Ann Ln. E&W .... 20W-4N 8
John St. N&S ........ 15W-4N 9
Joyce Av. N&S ...... 19W-2N 14
Kramer Av. N&S .... 19W-2N 14
La Londe Av. N&S .. 19W-2N 14
Linda Ln. N&S .......... 20W-3N,20W-4N 14
Lombard Rd. N&S .. 20W-3N 14
Lorraine Av. E&W .... 17W-2N 14
Magnolia Av. NW&SE .......... 19W-2N 14
Maple Av. N&S ...... 17W-6N 9
Maple St. N&S ...... 17W-4N 9
Marino Ct. E&W .... 19W-7N 8
Massel Ct. E&W .... 17W-4N 9
Mayfair Dr. N&S .... 17W-4N 9
Mill Rd. N&S .......... 19W-4N,19W-5N 8
Monterey Av. N&S .. 17W-3N 14
Niles Av. N&S ...... 18W-4N 8
North Av. E&W .......... 20W-2N,18W-2N 14
North St. E&W ...... 17W-6N 9
North Woods Dr. E&W .......... 17W-4N 9
Nugent Av. N&S .... 18W-4N 8
Oak Leaf Dr. N&S .. 17W-3N 14
Oak Ln. E&W ...... 17W-3N 14
Oak St. E&W .......... 19W-3N,17W-3N 14
Oakdale Dr. NW&SE .......... 17W-3N 14
Parker St. N&S ...... 15W-4N 9
Parkside Av. N&S .... 19W-7N 8
Patricia Ln. E&W .... 15W-3N 15
Pierce Rd. NW&SE .. 19W-7N 8
Pine Av. N&S .......... 17W-6N,17W-7N 9
Pine Grove Av. N&S 16W-4N 9
Pine St. N&S ........ 17W-4N 9
Plfund Av. E&W .... 17W-3N 14
Potter St. E&W ...... 19W-5N 8
Prospect Av. N&S .. 19W-7N 8
Red Oak St. E&W .......... 17W-4N,16W-4N 9
Ridgewood Av. N&S .......... 16W-4N 9
Robert Kingery Hwy. N&S .......... 17W-6N,17W-7N 9
Rodeck Ln. E&W .... 17W-3N 14
Schick Rd. E&W .......... 20W-5N,19W-5N 8
Sherwood Dr. E&W .. 17W-3N 14
Sidney Av. E&W .... 19W-2N 14
Spruce Av. N&S .... 17W-6N 9
State St. N&S ...... 18W-4N 8
Stone Av. E&W .......... 18W-4N,17W-4N 8
Stonemill Av. E&W .. 19W-4N 8
Third Av. E&W ...... 17W-4N 9
Thorndale Av. E&W .......... 19W-7N,18W-7N 8
Verrill Av. N&S ...... 18W-4N 8
Victory Pkwy E&W .......... 17W-3N,15W-3N 14
Virginia Ln. E&W .... 15W-3N 15
Vista Av. N&S ...... 19W-2N 14
Walnut St. N&S ...... 19W-5N 8
Washington St. E&W .......... 17W-6N 9
West Av. N&S ...... 17W-3N 14
White Pine Rd. E&W .......... 17W-4N,16W-4N 9
Willow St. N&S ...... 15W-3N 15
Wilson St. N&S ...... 15W-3N 15
Wood Dale Rd. N&S .......... 18W-4N,17W-4N 8
Woodland Av. E&W .......... 19W-4N,17W-3N 8
Wrightwood Av. E&W .......... 17W-3N,15W-3N 14
1st Av. N&S ........ 19W-4N 8
2nd Av. E&W ........ 16W-4N 9
2nd Av. N&S ........ 19W-4N 8
2nd Ct. E&W ........ 16W-4N 9
4th Av. N&S ........ 19W-4N 8
5th Av. N&S ........ 19W-4N 8
6th Av. N&S ........ 19W-4N 8
7th Av. N&S ........ 19W-4N 8

| Street | Grid | Page |
|---|---|---|
| 8th Av. N&S | 19W-4N | 8 |
| 9th Av. N&S | 19W-4N | 8 |

## Aurora*
### (Also see Kane County)

| Street | Grid | Page |
|---|---|---|
| Aberdeen Ct. (Pvt.) N&S | 30W-9S | 28 |
| Acorn Ct. E&W | 31W-8S | 28 |
| Alder Ct. E&W | 32W-9S | 28 |
| Allspice Ct. SW&NE | 31W-8S | 28 |
| Amaranth Dr. NS&EW | 30W-9S | 28 |
| Andover Cir. NS&EW | 31W-9S | 28 |
| Andover Ct.* E&W | 31W-10S | 28 |
| Andover Dr. NS&EW | 31W-9S | 28 |
| Anton Dr. NS&EW | 31W-8S | 28 |
| Arlington Ct. E&W | 31W-8S | 28 |
| Arrowwood Ct. N&S | 32W-9S | 28 |
| Asbury Dr. NE&SW | 32W-8S,32W-7S | 28 |
| Ashbrook Ct. N&S | 32W-7S | 22 |
| Ashford Ln. NE&SW | 32W-5S | 22 |
| Ashton Ct. N&S | 32W-9S | 28 |
| Autumn Grove Cir. NS&E | 32W-9S | 28 |
| Autumn Grove Ct. NW&SE | 32W-9S | 28 |
| Autumn Lake Dr. E&W | 31W-7S | 22 |
| Bangor Ln. N&S | 31W-9S | 28 |
| Bannister Ln. E&W | 32W-9S | 28 |
| Bar Harbour Ct.* E&W | 31W-10S | 28 |
| Bar Harbour Rd. NS&EW | 31W-9S | 28 |
| Barberry Ct. N&S | 32W-3S | 16 |
| Barley Ct. NW&SE | 32W-4S | 22 |
| Baybrook Dr. NS&EW | 30W-9S,31W-9S | 28 |
| Bayhead Ct. E&W | 30W-8S | 28 |
| Bear Creek Ct. NW&SE | 30W-9S | 28 |
| Benjamin Franklin Ct. E&W | 30W-7S | 22 |
| Betsy Ross Ct. E&W | 30W-7S | 22 |
| Bilter Ferry Rd. NE&SW | 32W-4S,31W-4S | 22 |
| Bilter Rd. E&W | 32W-4S,31W-4S | 22 |
| Birchdale Ln. NS&EW | 30W-9S | 28 |
| Birmingham Dr. N&S | 32W-5S | 22 |
| Blaine Ct., E* NW&SE | 31W-8S | 28 |
| Blaine Ct., W* NW&SE | 31W-8S | 28 |
| Bloomfield Ct. E&W | 31W-8S | 28 |
| Bloomfield Ln E&W | 31W-8S | 28 |
| Blue Ridge Ct. E&W | 31W-9S | 28 |
| Blue Spruce Ln. E&W | 32W-3S | 16 |
| Boothbay Ln. E&W | 31W-9S | 28 |
| Boxwood Ct. E&W | 32W-3S | 16 |
| Breckenridge Cir. E&W | 32W-7S | 28 |
| Breckenridge Ct. E&W | 32W-8S | 28 |
| Breckenridge Dr. N&S | 32W-8S | 28 |
| Breckenridge Dr. NE&SW | 32W-8S,32W-7S | 28 |
| Bremerton Ct.* E&W | 31W-8S | 28 |
| Bremerton Ln. N&S | 31W-8S | 28 |
| Bridgeport Ln. NS&EW | 31W-9S | 28 |
| Bridle Path Ln. NS&EW | 32W-5S | 22 |
| Bristol Ct. E&W | 32W-9S | 28 |
| Brittany Ct. E&W | 32W-9S | 28 |
| Broadmoor Cir. NS&EW | 30W-9S | 28 |
| Brockton Ct. NE&SW | 31W-9S | 28 |
| Brook Ct. NE&SW | 32W-9S | 28 |
| Brook Ln. NE&SW | 32W-9S | 28 |
| Brookshire Ct. N&S | 32W-8S | 28 |
| Brookshire Ln. NS&EW | 32W-8S | 28 |
| Brookside Ct. NE&SW | 32W-5S | 22 |
| Brookwood Ct. NE&SW | 32W-6S | 22 |
| Brunswick Ln. NE&SW | 31W-9S | 28 |
| Bryan Ct. N&S | 32W-9S | 28 |
| Bunker Hill Cir. E&W | 31W-7S,30W-7S | 22 |
| Burnham Ct. | 32W-6S | 22 |
| Butterfield Rd. E&W | 32W-3S,30W-3S | 16 |
| Cadella Cir. NS&EW | 30W-9S | 28 |
| Camden Ln. N&S | 31W-9S | 28 |
| Cameron Ct. NE&SW | 31W-8S | 28 |
| Candlewood Ct. NS&EW | 31W-6S | 22 |
| Carriage Way NS&EW | 32W-8S | 28 |
| Carriage Way Ct. E&W | 32W-8S | 28 |
| Casper Ct. NE&SW | 32W-8S | 28 |
| Casper Ln., N. N&S | 32W-8S | 28 |
| Casper Ln., S. N&S | 32W-8S | 28 |
| Castlewood Ct. E&W | 32W-8S | 28 |
| Cave Creek Ct. NW&SE | 30W-9S | 28 |
| Chadwick Ct. NS&EW | 32W-6S | 22 |
| Chandler Ct. NE&SW | 32W-5S | 22 |
| Charlemaine Ct. E&W | 31W-9S | 28 |
| Chasewood Ct. E&W | 32W-6S | 22 |
| Chatfield Ct. E&W | 32W-8S | 28 |
| Chelsea Ct. NW&SE | 32W-9S | 28 |
| Chesapeake Dr. E&W | 30W-8S | 28 |
| Cheshire Dr. E&W | 32W-8S | 28 |
| Chicory Ln. NS&EW | 30W-9S | 28 |
| Churchill Ln. N&S | 31W-8S | 28 |
| Cimarron Ct. NE&SW | 32W-8S | 28 |
| Clairmont Ct. NE&SW | 31W-7S | 22 |
| Clara Av. E&W | 32W-5S | 22 |
| Clara Ct. E&W | 32W-5S | 22 |
| Clarendon Ln. E&W | 32W-8S | 28 |
| Clearwood Ct. N&S | 31W-8S | 28 |
| Clifton Ct. E&W | 31W-8S | 28 |
| Clover Field Ln. NW&SE | 31W-9S | 28 |
| Commerce St. N&S | 31W-7S,31W-6S | 22 |
| Commons Dr. N&S | 30W-7S,30W-6S | 22 |
| Commons Dr. N&S | 30W-8S,30W-7S | 22 |
| Compton Rd. NS&EW | 31W-8S | 28 |
| Cooper Ct., E. NE&SW | 31W-8S | 28 |
| Cooper Ct., W.* E&W | 32W-8S | 28 |
| Cooper Ln. N&S | 32W-8S,31W-8S | 28 |
| Copperfield Ct. NE&SW | 31W-9S | 28 |
| Corvalis Ct., S. N&S | 31W-8S | 28 |
| Country Oaks Ct. E&W | 32W-4S | 22 |
| County Line Rd. N&S | 32W-8S | 28 |
| Courtland Ct.* E&W | 32W-6S | 22 |
| Cove Ct. E&W | 32W-9S | 28 |
| Coventry Ct. E&W | 32W-9S | 28 |
| Cranberry Ln. E&W | 32W-3S | 16 |
| Cranbrook Cir. NS&EW | 32W-5S | 22 |
| Creekside Ct. E&W | 32W-4S | 22 |
| Crescent Ln., N. E&W | 32W-9S | 28 |
| Crescent Ln., S. E&W | 32W-9S | 28 |
| Cross Creek Ct.* E&W | 32W-4S | 22 |
| Cumberland Rd. N&S | 32W-9S | 28 |
| Dan Haven Ct. NS&EW | 32W-4S | 22 |
| Devonshire Ct.* N&S | 32W-4S | 22 |
| Diane Dr. E&W | 32W-9S,31W-9S | 28 |
| Diane Dr. NS&EW | 31W-9S | 28 |
| Diehl Rd. E&W | 32W-4S,32W-5S | 22 |
| Dogwood Ln. NE&SW | 32W-9S | 28 |
| Doncaster Dr. E&W | 32W-8S,32W-7S | 28 |
| Dorothy Dr. E&W | 32W-9S | 28 |
| Dover Ln. E&W | 31W-9S | 28 |
| Downing Ct. E&W | 32W-5S | 22 |
| Driftwood Ln. NS&EW | 30W-7S | 22 |
| Dunbarton Dr. NS&EW | 31W-5S,31S-6S | 22 |
| East West Tollway E&W | 32W-4S,31W-4S | 22 |
| Echo Ln. N&S | 31W-8S | 28 |
| Edgebrook Ct. E&W | 30W-8S,30W-9S | 28 |
| Edinburgh Ct. N&S | 32W-9S | 28 |
| Edinburgh Ln. E&W | 32W-9S | 28 |
| Emma Cir. EW&NS | 32W-9S | 28 |
| Enterprise St. N&S | 31W-7S,31W-6S | 22 |
| Eola Rd. N&S | 32W-9S,31W-9S | 28 |
| Essex Ct. E&W | 30W-8S | 28 |
| Estling Ct. N&S | 31W-5S,31W-6S | 22 |
| Eugene Ln. N&S | 31W-8S | 28 |
| Exchange Av. E&W | 31W-7S,30W-7S | 22 |
| Exchange St. N&S | 30W-7S | 22 |
| Executive Ct. NS&EW | 30W-7S | 22 |
| Fairfax Ct., E. E&W | 31W-8S | 28 |
| Fairfax Ct., W. NS&EW | 31W-8S | 28 |
| Fairmount Ct. E&W | 30W-8S | 28 |
| Farington Ct. N&S | 32W-8S | 28 |
| Farington Ln. N&S | 32W-8S | 28 |
| Ferry Rd. E&W | 31W-4S,30W-4S | 22 |
| Fieldside Ln. N&S | 32W-9S,32W-8S | 28 |
| Flanders Ct. NE&SW | 32W-6S | 22 |
| Forest Dr. E&W | 32W-7S | 22 |
| Forestview Ct. NS&EW | 32W-7S | 22 |
| Forestview Ln. NS&EW | 32W-8S | 28 |
| Fossil Creek Ct. NW&SE | 30W-9S | 28 |
| Fox Hill Ln. N&S | 32W-9S | 28 |
| Fox Hill Rd. E&W | 31W-8S,31W-9S | 28 |
| Fox Valley Ct. E&W | 32W-9S | 28 |
| Fox Valley Ctr. Dr. NE&SW | 30W-7S | 22 |
| Fox Valley Dr. NS&EW | 32W-9S | 28 |
| Foxworth Ct. N&S | 32W-8S | 28 |
| Frontenac Rd. N&S | 31W-9S,31W-8S | 28 |
| Frontenac St. NS&EW | 31W-8S,31W-7S | 28 |
| Gloria Ct. N&S | 31W-8S | 28 |
| Goldenwood Ct. N&S | 32W-9S | 28 |
| Grafton Ln. NS&EW | 31W-5S | 22 |
| Graystone Dr. N&S | 32W-5S | 22 |
| Greenbriar Pl. NW&SE | 30W-9S | 28 |
| Greenlake Dr. E&W | 30W-9S | 28 |
| Greenlake Dr. E&W | 32W-5S,31W-5S | 22 |
| Gregory St. NS&EW | 30W-8S,30W-7S | 28 |
| Gresham Ln., E. N&S | 31W-8S | 28 |
| Hackney Dr. NE&SW | 32W-5S | 22 |
| Harbor Ct. E&W | 32W-9S | 28 |
| Harbour Towne Pl. NW&SE | 30W-9S | 28 |
| Harg Ct. N&S | 32W-9S | 28 |
| Harris Dr. NE&SW | 31W-5S,32W-5S | 22 |
| Harvest Ct. NW&SE | 32W-8S | 28 |
| Haverhill Dr. E&W | 31W-9S | 22 |
| Heatherwood Ln. N&S | 31W-9S | 28 |
| Hedgerow Dr. | 32W-3S | 16 |
| Hidden Pond Cir. NS&EW | 31W-7S | 22 |
| Highfield Ct. E&W | 32W-9S | 28 |
| Highfield Ln. E&W | 32W-9S | 28 |
| Horseshoe Ct. N&S | 32W-5S | 22 |
| Hull Ct. N&S | 32W-5S | 22 |
| Humphreys Ct. N&S | 31W-8S | 28 |
| Interstate 88 E&W | 32W-4S,31W-4S | 22 |
| Inverness Dr. E&W | 32W-8S | 28 |
| Inverness Dr. N&S | 32W-8S | 28 |
| Isleworth St. NE&SW | 30W-9S,30W-9S | 28 |
| Jeremy Ranch Ct. E&W | 31W-9S | 28 |
| Jernel Ln. E&W | 32W-5S | 22 |
| John Hancock Ct. E&W | 30W-7S | 22 |
| Johnsbury Ct.* E&W | 31W-10S | 28 |
| Johnsbury Ln. NS&EW | 31W-9S | 28 |
| Jono Dr. E&W | 32W-9S,31W-9S | 28 |
| Juniper Ct. N&S | 32W-3S | 16 |
| Kaimy Ct. N&S | 32W-9S | 28 |
| Karen Ct. N&S | 32W-9S | 28 |
| Kathy Ct. N&S | 32W-9S | 28 |
| Kautz Rd. N&S | 32W-9S | 28 |
| Kelly Ct. E&W | 31W-9S | 28 |
| Kelly Dr. E&W | 31W-9S | 28 |
| Kenyon Ct. E&W | 32W-6S | 22 |
| Killbrook Dr. NW&SE | 32W-7S | 22 |
| Kimberly Ct. NE&SW | 31W-9S | 28 |
| Kingshill Cir. NS&EW | 31W-8S | 28 |
| Kirkwood Ln. N&S | 30W-7S | 22 |
| Knightsbridge Ct. NW&SE | 32W-8S | 28 |
| Laconia Ln. N&S | 31W-9S | 28 |
| Lake Dr. N&S | 32W-9S | 28 |
| Lake Shore Ct. N&S | 31W-8S,30W-8S | 28 |
| Lake Stone Ln. E&W | 32W-9S | 28 |
| Lakeridge Ct. N&S | 32W-6S | 22 |
| Lakeside Dr. E&W | 32W-9S,32W-8S | 28 |
| Landing Dr. E&W | 30W-8S | 28 |
| Lansburgh Ct. NW&SE | 32W-6S | 22 |
| Larchmont Ct. NW&SE | 32W-8S | 28 |
| Lawrence Ct. E&W | 32W-9S | 28 |
| Legacy Dr. NS&EW | 32W-5S | 22 |
| Legacy Dr. NW&SE | 32W-5S | 22 |
| Legend Ct. E&W | 30W-9S | 28 |
| Leyland Ln. E&W | 32W-9S | 28 |
| Liberty St. E&W | 30W-6S | 22 |
| Lindrick Ln. E&W | 32W-9S | 28 |
| Lonetree Ct. E&W | 30W-9S | 28 |
| Long Grove Dr. N&S | 32W-9S,32W-8S | 28 |
| Long Grove Ln. N&S | 31W-9S | 28 |
| Longmeadow Dr. NS&EW | 30W-8S | 28 |
| Lynnfield Ct. E&W | 31W-9S | 28 |
| Magnolia Ct. N&S | 32W-3S | 16 |
| Malmesbury Ct. NE&SW | 32W-9S | 28 |
| Mapleside Ct. E&W | 32W-7S | 22 |
| Mapleside Ln. E&W | 32W-7S | 22 |
| Mayfair Dr. E&W | 30W-8S | 28 |
| Mayfair Ln. E&W | 30W-8S | 28 |
| McCoy Dr. E&W | 32W-8S,30W-7S | 28 |
| Meadow Brook Dr. N&S | 30W-9S | 28 |
| Meadow Lakes Blvd. N&S | 31W-9S | 28 |
| Meadowlark Ct. NW&SE | 32W-3S | 16 |
| Meadowridge Dr. NS&EW | 30W-8S,31W-9S | 28 |
| Meadowview Ln. NS&EW | 32W-8S | 28 |
| Medford Ct. E&W | 31W-8S | 28 |
| Merle Dr. N&S | 32W-5S | 22 |
| Middlebury Ct., E.* E&W | 31W-10S | 28 |
| Middlebury Ct., W.* E&W | 31W-10S | 28 |
| Middlebury Ln. N&S | 31W-9S | 28 |
| Millington Ct. E&W | 32W-8S | 28 |
| Millington Ln. NS&EW | 32W-8S | 28 |
| Monarch Cir. NS&EW | 31W-9S,30W-9S | 28 |
| Montclare Ct. NW&SE | 32W-8S | 28 |
| Montgomery Rd. E&W | 32W-9S,30W-9S | 28 |
| Moss Ct. NW&SE | 32W-9S | 28 |
| Moss Ln. NE&SW | 32W-9S | 28 |
| Natalie Ln. N&S | 32W-9S | 28 |
| Newport Ln. NW&SE | 31W-9S | 28 |
| Normandy Ct. E&W | 30W-9S | 28 |
| Normantown Rd. N&S | 31W-9S | 28 |
| North Aurora Rd. E&W | 31W-6S | 22 |
| Norwalk Ct. E&W | 32W-9S | 28 |
| Norwood Ln. NW&SE | 31W-9S | 28 |
| Oak Shire Ct. SW&NE | 32W-4S | 22 |
| Oakdale Ct. NW&SE | 32W-9S | 28 |
| Oakhurst Dr. N&S | 31W-7S | 28 |
| Oakhurst Dr. NS&EW | 32W-8S | 28 |
| Oakland Ln. N&S | 31W-9S | 28 |
| Old Eola Rd. N&S | 31W-5S,31W-6S | 22 |
| Oxford Ct. E&W | 32W-5S | 22 |
| Palmer Ct. N&S | 30W-9S | 28 |
| Palomino Dr. N&S | 32W-5S | 22 |
| Paradise Canyon Ct. NW&SE | 30W-9S | 28 |
| Park Ridge Ct. NW&SE | 31W-8S | 28 |
| Parkwood Ln. E&W | 32W-8S | 28 |
| Partridge Ct. N&S | 32W-3S | 16 |
| Patrick Henry Ct.* E&W | 30W-7S | 22 |
| Paul Revere Ct. E&W | 30W-7S | 22 |
| Pennsbury Ln. E&W | 31W-5S,31W-6S | 22 |
| Peppertree Ln. E&W | 30W-7S | 22 |
| Pheasant Run Ln. N&S | 31W-9S | 28 |
| Pine Lake Dr. NS&EW | 30W-9S | 28 |
| Pine Tree Ct. N&S | 32W-3S | 16 |
| Pinecone Ct. N&S | 32W-3S | 16 |
| Pinecrest Ct. NS&EW | 32W-7S | 28 |
| Pinegrove Ct. N&S | 32W-9S | 28 |
| Portland Ct. NE&SW | 31W-8S | 28 |
| Ports Mouth Ct. E&W | 32W-9S | 28 |
| Prairie Lake Ct. E&W | 31W-8S,30W-8S | 28 |
| Preston Ct. E&W | 32W-4S | 22 |
| Primrose Ct. E&W | 31W-7S | 22 |
| Princeton Av. E&W | 31W-8S,30W-8S | 28 |
| Ptarmigan Ct. E&W | 32W-3S | 16 |
| Quail Ct. N&S | 32W-3S | 16 |
| Quaker Hill Ct. E&W | 30W-7S | 22 |
| Quincy Ct.* N&S | 31W-10S | 28 |
| Quincy Ln. NS&EW | 31W-9S | 28 |
| Radcliff Ln. NS&EW | 32W-5S | 22 |
| Radford Dr. E&W | 32W-6S,32W-5S | 22 |
| Raintree Ln. E&W | 32W-9S | 22 |
| Red Clover Dr. NS&EW | 30W-9S | 28 |
| Redbud Ct. N&S | 32W-3S | 16 |
| Reddington Dr. NS&EW | 30W-6S | 22 |
| Regency Ct. NE&SW | 30W-8S | 28 |
| Reserve Ct. E&W | 32W-5S | 22 |
| Richland Ct. NE&SW | 31W-8S | 28 |
| Richmond Ln. NS&EW | 32W-8S,32W-7S | 28 |
| Ridge Ln. N&S | 32W-9S | 28 |
| Ridge Rd. E&W | 32W-9S | 28 |
| River Wood Ct. N&S | 32W-3S | 16 |
| Rosefield Ln. N&S | 30W-9S | 28 |
| Rosegate Ct. N&S | 32W-9S | 28 |
| Rumford Ct. E&W | 31W-8S | 28 |
| Salem Ct. E&W | 31W-8S | 28 |
| Sandpebble Ln. NW&SE | 31W-7S | 22 |
| Sandpiper Ct. N&S | 30W-7S | 22 |
| Sandpiper Dr. NW&SE | 32W-6S | 22 |
| Sandstone Ct. N&S | 32W-6S | 22 |
| Scheffer Rd. E&W | 32W-6S | 22 |
| Shadybrook Ln. NS&EW | 31W-7S | 22 |
| Sheffer Rd. E&W | 32W-6S,31W-6S | 22 |
| Sheffield Ct. N&S | 32W-9S | 28 |
| Shoreline Dr. NS&EW | 31W-9S,31W-8S | 28 |
| Silver Creek Ct. NE&SW | 30W-9S | 28 |
| Society Hill Ln. NE&SW | 30W-9S | 28 |
| Society Hill Way NE&SW | 30W-9S | 28 |
| Southgate Ct. NW&SE | 32W-9S | 28 |
| Spur Ln. N&S | 32W-5S | 22 |
| St. Barthelemy Ln. NS&EW | 31W-8S | 28 |
| St. Croix Ct. NS&EW | 31W-8S | 28 |
| St. Kitts Ct. E&W | 31W-8S | 28 |
| Stanton Ct.* NW&SE | 32W-4S | 22 |
| Stockton Ln.* NS&EW | 32W-6S | 22 |
| Stone Bridge Blvd. E&W | 32W-5S,31W-5S | 22 |
| Stratford Ct. N&S | 30W-8S | 28 |
| Streamwood Ct. NW&SE | 32W-4S | 22 |
| Stubblefield Ct.* NE&SW | 32W-4S | 22 |
| Sun Tree Ct. N&S | 31W-9S | 28 |
| Sundew Ct. E&W | 30W-9S | 28 |
| Sunlight Ct. NE&SW | 32W-3S | 16 |
| Sussex Av. E&W | 31W-6S | 22 |
| Sutton Ln. NE&SW | 32W-6S | 22 |
| Sycamore Ln. N&S | 32W-9S | 28 |
| Tansey Rd. E&W | 32W-9S | 28 |
| Teasel Ln. NS&EW | 30W-9S | 28 |
| Terrace Lake Dr. NS&EW | 32W-9S | 28 |
| Terrace View Dr. NS&EW | 32W-9S | 28 |
| Thayer Ct. E&W | 31W-9S | 28 |
| Thomas Jefferson Ct. E&W | 30W-7S | 22 |
| Thomas Paine Ct. E&W | 30W-7S | 22 |
| Thornley Ct. N&S | 32W-8S | 28 |
| Thurston Ct. E&W | 32W-5S | 22 |
| Timber Hill Ct. NE&SW | 31W-9S | 28 |
| Timber Hill Ln. E&W | 31W-9S | 28 |
| Trade St. N&S | 30W-9S | 28 |
| Tralee Ct. E&W | 31W-9S | 28 |
| Trefalgar NS&EW | 32W-9S | 28 |
| Trenton Ct. E&W | 30W-7S | 22 |
| Valayna Dr. N&S | 32W-9S | 28 |
| Valley Forge Ct. E&W | 30W-7S | 22 |
| Vaughan Rd. N&S | 32W-8S,32W-6S | 22 |
| Village Ct. NW&SE | 32W-9S | 28 |
| Village Green Ct. N&S | 31W-8S | 28 |
| Village Green Dr. NE&SW | 32W-8S,31W-8S | 28 |
| Village Green Dr., N. N&S | 31W-8S | 28 |
| Walcott Rd. E&W | 32W-9S | 28 |
| Warden Ct. E&W | 32W-9S | 28 |
| Waterbury Cir. NE&SW | 32W-8S | 28 |
| Waterbury Ct. NS&EW | 32W-8S,32W-8S | 28 |
| Watersedge Cir. NS&EW | 31W-7S | 22 |
| Waterside Ct. N&S | 31W-7S | 22 |
| Waverly Ct. NW&SE | 32W-6S | 22 |
| Wedgefield Ct. E&W | 32W-6S | 22 |

**Grid / Page**

Wentworth Ln. NW&SE
..........32W-5S  22
West Hampton Ct. N&S
..........30W-8S  28
West Ridge Ct. NE&SW
..........32W-8S  28
Westbrook Dr. E&W  30W-8S  28
Westleigh Ct. E&W . 32W-9S  28
Westmoor Ct. N&S .. 32W-8S  28
Wexford Pl. NW&SE
..........30W-9S  28
Wheatfield Ct. E&W . 32W-4S  22
Wheatland Ln. N&S
..........31W-8S,31W-9S  28
White Barn Ln. E&W
..........32W-4S  22
White Eagle Dr. NS&EW
..........30W-9S  28
White Eagle Dr., W. N&S
..........30W-9S  28
White Oak Cir. NS&EW
..........32W-4S,32W-5S  28
Whitehall Ct. E&W . 32W-8S  28
Whiteway Ct. E&W . 32W-8S  28
Willow Ct. NE&SW .. 32W-9S  28
Willowcrest N&S .... 31W-9S  28
Willowfalls Ct. E&W . 31W-8S  28
Willowview Ln. E&W
..........31W-8S  28
Wilshire Ct. NE&SW .32W-4S  22
Winberie Ct. NW&SE
..........30W-9S  28
Winchester Ct., E. E&W
..........31W-9S  28
Winchester Ct., W. E&W
..........31W-9S  28
Windemere Ln. N&S  32W-9S  28
Windrift Dr. N&S ... 30W-8S  28
Windy Hill Ct. E&W . 30W-9S  28
Wingate Ct. N&S ... 32W-4S  22
Woodcrest N&S NS&EW
..........32W-5S  22
Worchester Ln. NE&SW
..........32W-9S,31W-9S  28
Wyndham Ct. NE&SW
..........32W-8S  28
Yorkshire Ct. E&W . 32W-4S  22
Yorktown Ct. E&W . 30W-7S  22

**Bartlett***

**(Also see Cook County)**

Abbey Rd. E&W .... 27W-7N  5
Adare Rd. E&W .... 27W-7N  5
Amherst Dr. E&W...28W-7N  5
Anchor Ct. NW&SE .28W-7N  5
Ancient Oaks Ct. E&W
..........30W-6N  4
Ancient Oaks Dr. N&S
..........30W-6N  4
Anita Dr. N&S .... 28W-7N  5
Apple Orchard Dr. NE&SW
..........29W-6N  5
Apple Valley Dr. E&W
..........30W-6N  4
Appletree Ct. E&W . 29W-6N  5
Appletree Ln. N&S . 29W-6N  5
Arbor St. E&W .... 29W-6N  5
Army Trail Rd. E&W
..........30W-5N,28W-4N  5
Aron Ct. NW&SE .. 28W-7N  5
Ascot Way NW&SE ..30W-5N  4
Asder St. E&W .... 27W-6N  5
Ashford Cir. NS&EW
..........28W-5N  5
Aster Ct. E&W .... 28W-7N  5
Auburn Ln. E&W
..........30W-7N,29W-7N  4
Balboa Ter. E&W ... 28W-7N  5
Balmoral Dr. NW&SE
..........28W-6N  5
Balsam Ln. NE&SW . 29W-6N  5
Bartlett Rd. N&S
..........29W-6N,29W-7N  5
Batavia Ct. N&S ... 27W-5N  5
Bay Ct. NE&SW ... 28W-7N  5
Beechtree Ln. N&S . 29W-6N  5
Belmont Ln. E&W
..........27W-5N,28W-5N  5
Bragg Ln. E&W.....28W-7N  5
Bragg St. E&W .... 28W-7N  5
Braintree Ln. N&S
..........30W-7N,29W-7N  4
Branden Ln. NE&SW
..........28W-7N  5
Briar Cliff Ln. E&W . 27W-7N  5
Brighton Ct. N&S .. 29W-6N  5
Brookside Dr. NE&SW
..........28W-7N  5
Bryn Mawr Av. E&W
..........29W-6N  5
Buckingham Dr. NE&SW
..........28W-6N  5
Burnside Ct. N&S .. 28W-7N  5
Buttercup Ln. N&S . 29W-6N  5
Camberly Ct. NE&SW
..........28W-5N  5
Camdon Ct. N&S .. 28W-7N  5
Capistrano Ter. N&S
..........28W-7N  5
Castlewood Ln. NW&SE
..........27W-7N  5
Catalpa Ln. N&S ... 28W-5N  5
Cayman Ct. N&S .... 28W-5N  5

Cedar Ln. E&W......29W-6N  5
Charter Oaks Ct. E&W
..........30W-6N  4
Charter Oaks Dr. N&S
..........30W-6N  4
Chatsford Ct. N&S . 27W-5N  5
Chelmsford Ct. N&S
..........27W-5N  5
Cherry Ln. E&W ... 27W-7N  5
Chesapeake Ct. NW&SE
..........29W-6N  5
Chippendale Ct.* E&W
..........27W-6N  5
Chippendale Dr. N&S
..........27W-6N  5
Church Rd. N&S ... 28W-6N  5
Circle Ct. NW&SE . 29W-6N  5
Clover Ct. NE&SW . 29W-7N  5
Cobblestone Ln. E&W
..........31W-6N  4
Cobler Ct. N&S ... 28W-5N  5
Colfax St. E&W ... 28W-5N  5
Columbia Cir. NS&EW
..........27W-5N,28W-5N  5
Concord Dr. E&W
..........30W-6N,29W-6N  4
Confederation Dr. E&W
..........30W-6N,29W-6N  4
Congress Dr. E&W . 30W-6N  4
Coral Av. E&W .... 29W-6N  5
Cottonwood Ln. N&S
..........29W-6N  5
Cromwell Cir. E&W . 28W-5N  5
Cuyahoga Ter. N&S ..29W-7N  5
Deanna Dr. N&S ... 28W-7N  5
Deerpath Ct. E&W . 28W-5N  5
Devon Av. E&W
..........29W-7N,28W-7N  5
Dogwood Ln. NW&SE
..........29W-6N  5
Dorchester Ln. N&S..30W-6N  4
Driftwood Ln. N&S . 29W-6N  5
Dunamon Ct. NW&SE
..........27W-7N  5
Dunamon Rd. E&W ..27W-7N  5
Cir. ..........29W-7N  5
E. Cleborne Dr. E&W
..........28W-7N  5
E. Country Dr. E&W  28W-7N  5
E. Sheridan Dr. E&W
..........28W-7N  5
Eagle Ct. N&S .... 28W-6N  5
Eastgate Ln. NE&SW
..........30W-5N  4
Edgewood E&W ... 30W-5N  4
Elm Ct. E&W ..... 29W-6N  5
Evergreen Av. E&W .29W-6N  5
Evergreen Ln. E&W  29W-6N  5
Ewell Ct. E&W .... 29W-7N  5
Fairfax Ln. NW&SE . 28W-5N  5
Fairview Ln. N&S ... 29W-7N  5
Faith Ln. NE&SW .. 28W-7N  5
Far Hills Dr. N&S .. 28W-5N  5
Fieldstone Ct. N&S . 30W-5N  4
Fieldstone Ln. NW&SE
..........30W-5N  4
Forest Ct. E&W.....29W-6N  5
Forest Preserve Dr. N&S
..........30W-5N  4
Foster Av. E&W ... 29W-6N  5
Fox Chase Ct. NE&SW
..........30W-5N  4
Fox Chase Dr. NE&SW
..........30W-5N  4
Francine Dr. NE&SW
..........28W-7N  5
Franklin Dr. E&W
..........30W-6N,29W-6N  4
Fremont St. N&S ... 28W-7N  4
Garden St. NE&SW . 29W-6N  5
Gardenia Ln. E&W . 29W-6N  5
Ginger Brook Ln. E&W
..........28W-7N  5
Gloria Dr. N&S .... 29W-7N  5
Grand Oak Ct. NW&SE
..........30W-6N  4
Grandview Av. E&W  29W-6N  5
Granger Rd. E&W .. 29W-6N  5
Grant N&S . 28W-6N,28W-7N  5
Groton Ct. E&W ... 30W-7N  4
Hadley Ct. N&S ... 28W-5N  5
Hampton Cir. N&S . 28W-7N  5
Harbor Ter. N&S .. 28W-7N  5
Harbor Tr. NE&SW . 27W-7N  5
Harvard Ct. N&S .. 28W-7N  5
Harvard Ln. NW&SE
..........28W-5N  5
Hawkins Ct. NW&SE
..........28W-7N  5
Hawthorne Av. N&S ..29W-7N  5
Heather Ct. E&W .. 29W-6N  5
Hickory Ln. N&S ... 28W-7N  5
Hill Av. E&W ..... 28W-7N  5
Hillandale St. E&W . 28W-7N  5
Hillside Ct. N&S ... 27W-7N  5
Honeysuckle Ln. N&S
..........29W-6N  5
Hood St. E&W .... 28W-7N  5
Hyacinth Ln. E&W . 29W-6N  5
Independence Dr. N&S
..........29W-6N  5
Independence Rd. NE&SW
..........29W-6N  5
Irvington Ct. E&W .. 28W-7N  5

Island Ct. E&W .... 27W-7N  5
Ivy Ct. NW&SE ... 29W-6N  5
Jackson Ct. N&S .. 28W-6N  5
Jackson St. E&W .. 28W-6N  5
Jasmine Ln. NW&SE
..........29W-6N  5
Jervey Ln. E&W ... 29W-7N  5
John Dr. E&W .... 28W-7N  5
Juniper Ln. E&W .. 29W-6N  5
Kelly Farm Ln. N&S . 28W-4N  5
Kent Cir. E&W .... 29W-7N  5
Kingston Ln. N&S .. 29W-7N  5
La Jolla Ter. N&S .. 28W-7N  5
Ladysmith Rd. E&W  27W-7N  5
Lakeside Dr. NW&SE
..........27W-7N  5
Lakeview Ct. NE&SW
..........27W-7N  5
Lakewood Dr. N&S .. 29W-6N  5
Lamont Pkwy. E&W .29W-7N  5
Leaf Ct. E&W .... 29W-6N  5
Lee St. N&S ...... 28W-7N  5
Lenox Ct. NE&SW . 28W-5N  5
Lexington Dr. N&S . 30W-6N  4
Lido Ter. E&W .... 28W-7N  5
Lincoln Dr. E&W .. 28W-7N  5
Longford Ct. E&W . 27W-7N  5
Longford Rd. NE&SW
..........27W-7N  5
Longstreet Dr. N&S .28W-7N  5
Mansfield Ct. E&W . 28W-7N  5
Maple Ct. N&S
..........29W-6N,29W-7N  5
Maple Ln. N&S .... 29W-6N  5
Marlboro Ct. N&S .. 28W-5N  5
Martingale Dr. N&S . 29W-6N  5
Mayflower Ln. NS&EW
..........27W-5N,28W-5N  5
McClellen Ct. N&S . 28W-7N  5
McClellen St. E&W . 28W-7N  5
McCook Ct. E&W .. 28W-7N  5
Meade Ct. E&W ... 28W-7N  5
Meadow Trail E&W . 28W-7N  5
Meridian St. E&W
..........27W-5N  5
Millwood Dr. E&W . 27W-7N  5
Mission Ct. E&W .. 27W-5N  5
Monroe Dr. N&S .. 29W-6N  5
Montauk Ct. NE&SW
..........29W-7N  5
Morning Glory Ln. E&W
..........29W-7N  5
Munger Rd. N&S
..........31W-5N,31W-7N  4
Nacoma Ct. NW&SE
..........27W-5N  5
Nantucket Ct. E&W . 28W-6N  5
Naples St. NE&SW . 27W-6N  5
Newcastle Ln. NS&EW
..........28W-5N,27W-5N  5
Newport Blvd. NW&SE
..........28W-7N,27W-6N  5
Nicole Dr. NS&EW . 27W-6N  5
Nightingale Ln. NE&SW
..........27W-6N,28W-5N  5
Nolobay Ter. N&S . 28W-7N  5
Normandy Ln. N&S . 27W-5N  5
Northbridge Ct. NS&EW
..........30W-6N  4
Northgate Ct. N&S . 30W-6N  4
Northgate Dr. NW&SE
..........30W-6N  4
Norwood Ln. E&W . 30W-7N  4
Nutmeg Ct. E&W .. 27W-5N  5
Oak Glen Dr. E&W . 29W-6N  5
Oakwood Ln. E&W . 28W-7N  5
Oceanside Ter. E&W
..........28W-7N  5
Orchid Ln. E&W ... 29W-6N  5
Ord Ct. E&W ..... 28W-7N  5
Oxford Rd. E&W .. 27W-7N  5
Paddock Pl. N&S .. 30W-6N  4
Palamino Ct. N&S...28W-6N  5
Pear Tree Ln. NS&EW
..........28W-7N  5
Penny Ln. NE&SW . 28W-4N  5
Petersdorf Rd. N&S .29W-4N  5
Pickett Ct. E&W ... 28W-7N  5
Pinetree Ln. N&S .. 29W-6N  5
Pipers Dr. E&W ... 28W-7N  5
Plymouth Ct. E&W . 28W-7N  5
Poinsetta Ln. NW&SE
..........29W-6N  5
Polk Ct. N&S ..... 28W-7N  5
Poplar Ln. N&S ... 29W-6N  5
Poppy Ct. N&S ... 29W-6N  5
Porter Ct. N&S ... 28W-7N  5
Portsmouth Ct. N&S
..........28W-4N  5
Powis Rd. N&S
..........31W-6N,31W-7N  4
Prairie Av. N&S.....28W-7N  5
Princeton Dr. N&S . 30W-6N  4
Prospect Av. N&S
..........28W-7N,28W-8N  5
Redwood Ln. NE&SW
..........28W-7N  5
Rees Rd. E&W .... 31W-7N  4
Richmond Ln. E&W . 28W-6N  5
Ridgefield Ln. N&S . 30W-6N  4
Rose Ct. NE&SW .. 29W-6N  5
Rosecrans Ct. E&W ..28W-7N  5
Rosewood Ln. E&W . 29W-6N  5

S. Sheridan Dr. N&S
..........28W-7N  5
Saddleridge Ct. N&S
..........30W-5N  4
Saddleridge Pl. NS&EW
..........30W-5N  4
San Diego Pl. NW&SE
..........28W-7N  5
San Francisco N&S . 28W-7N  5
Sandlewood Ct. N&S
..........27W-7N  5
Sandpiper Ct. E&W .27W-7N  5
Sausalito Ct. E&W . 27W-7N  5
Schick Rd. E&W
..........30W-5N,29W-5N  4
Schick Rd. NW&SE . 30W-5N  4
Scott Ct. E&W .... 28W-7N  5
Seacrest Ln. N&S .. 28W-7N  5
Shady Ln. E&W ... 29W-7N  5
Sherman Ct. E&W . 28W-7N  5
Sherman St. E&W . 28W-7N  5
Shorewood Ct. NW&SE
..........27W-7N  5
Shorewood Dr. NW&SE
..........27W-7N  5
Sparrow Ln. E&W . 28W-5N  5
Spitzer Rd. N&S ... 31W-7N  4
Spruce Ln. E&W .. 29W-6N  5
Squire Ln. N&S . 30W-5N  4
Stearns Rd. E&W
..........32W-7N,27W-7N  4
Steeplechase Ln. NE&SW
..........30W-5N  4
Stockton Ct. E&W . 28W-5N  5
Stonegate Ct. E&W .30W-5N  4
Struckman Blvd. E&W
..........29W-6N  5
Stuart Dr. N&S ... 28W-7N  5
Sundance Dr. .. 28W-7N  5
Sundance Dr. NW&SE
..........27W-7N  5
Surf Ct. E&W.....27W-7N  5
Surrey Rd. E&W ... 29W-7N  5
Swinford Rd. E&W . 27W-7N  5
Sycamore Ln. N&S . 29W-6N  5
Tallgrass Dr. E&W . 28W-6N  5
Tennyson Rd. E&W . 28W-7N  5
Thousand Oaks Dr. E&W
..........30W-6N  4
Towering Oaks Ct. N&S
..........30W-6N  4
Trailside Ln. E&W . 27W-7N  5
Trenton Ln. N&S ... 27W-5N  5
Triple Crown Ct. N&S
..........28W-6N  5
Tulip Ct. N&S ..... 29W-6N  5
Valewood Dr. N&S . 29W-6N  5
Valley View Dr. E&W
..........27W-7N  5
Vernon St. NE&SW . 28W-5N  5
Village Ln. NE&SW . 28W-5N  5
Virginia Ct. E&W .. 29W-6N  5
Voyager Dr. NW&SE
..........28W-7N  5
W. Country Dr. E&W
..........28W-7N  5
Wallace Ct. N&S .. 28W-7N  5
Wallace St. E&W .. 28W-7N  5
Washington Ct. N&S
..........30W-6N  4
Washington St. N&S
..........30W-6N  4
Waterford Rd. N&S .27W-7N  5
Webster St. E&W . 29W-6N  5
Wentworth Ln. E&W
..........28W-5N  5
White Fence Rd. NS&EW
..........30W-5N  4
Wilcox Dr. E&W ... 28W-7N  5
Wildberry Ln. E&W . 28W-5N  5
Wildwood Ct. NW&SE
..........27W-7N  5
Willow Ct. E&W ... 28W-7N  5
Winchester Ct. NW&SE
..........28W-7N  5
Windemere Ct. N&S  29W-6N  5
Windsor Dr. E&W....28W-6N  5
Winner's Cup Ct. NW&SE
..........28W-6N  5
Winston Ln. NW&SE
..........28W-5N  5
Wood Creek Tr. NW&SE
..........30W-5N,29W-5N  4
Woodhollow Ln. E&W
..........28W-7N,27W-6N  5
Woodland Hills Dr. NS&EW
..........30W-5N,30W-6N  4
Woodland Hills Pkwy. E&W
..........30W-5N  4

**Bensenville**

Addison Rd. N&S
..........16W-3N,16W-4N  15
Addison St. N&S
..........16W-4N,16W-5N  9
Algonquin Av. N&S . 16W-5N  9
Argyle St. E&W
..........17W-6N,16W-6N  9
Ash Av. NE&SW .... 17W-7N  9
Barron St. N&S
..........16W-4N,16W-5N  9
Beeline Dr. N&S ... 16W-4N  9
Belmont Av. E&W....16W-4N  9

Bernice Dr. E&W .... 16W-3N  15
Birginal St. N&S ... 16W-6N  9
Blackhawk Ter. NE&SW
..........16W-5N  9
Bobby Dr. N&S .... 16W-3N  15
Brentwood Dr. N&S . 15W-4N  9
Bretman Av. E&W .. 15W-5N  9
Bridget Ct. E&W ... 16W-3N  15
Broadway N&S .... 17W-5N  9
Brookwood St. E&W
..........17W-5N,16W-5N  9
Bryn Mawr Av. E&W
..........16W-7N  9
Center St. N&S
..........16W-3N,16W-5N  15
Central Av. E&W ... 16W-5N  9
Central Av. N&S ... 17W-7N  9
Church Rd. N&S
..........16W-4N,16W-5N  9
Country Club Dr. N&S
..........16W-6N  9
Crest Ave. E&W ... 15W-4N  9
Daniel Dr. N&S
..........15W-3N,15W-4N  15
David Dr. NE&SW
..........15W-3N,15W-4N  15
Dennis Dr. E&W .... 15W-4N  9
Devon Av. E&W
..........17W-7N,16W-7N  9
Diana Ct. E&W .... 15W-4N  9
Dierks St. N&S .... 15W-5N  9
Division St. N&S ... 15W-5N  9
Dolores Dr. N&S
..........15W-3N,15W-4N  15
Donna Ln. E&W ... 16W-4N  9
Eagle Dr. E&W .... 16W-6N  9
Eastview Av. N&S . 16W-5N  9
Edgewood Av. NE&SW
..........17W-7N  9
Ellis St. N&S
..........16W-4N,16W-7N  9
Elmhurst St. E&W
..........17W-6N,16W-6N  9
Entry St. N&S .... 16W-3N  15
Evergreen Av. N&S . 16W-7N  9
Evergreen St. N&S . 15W-4N  9
Farrari Dr. N&S .... 16W-3N  15
Foley St. N&S ..... 16W-5N  9
Forestview Rd. E&W
..........16W-4N  9
Foster Av. E&W ... 16W-6N  9
Franzen St. N&S ... 16W-5N  9
Frontier Way E&W .. 16W-5N  9
Garden Av. N&S ... 15W-5N  9
Gateway Rd. E&W .. 16W-5N  9
Gaylin Ct. E&W .... 16W-5N  9
Glendale St. E&W
..........17W-5N,16W-5N  9
Golf Ln. E&W ..... 16W-6N  9
Grace St. N&S
..........15W-4N,15W-5N  9
Grand Av. N&S ... 15W-3N  15
Green St. NW&SE
..........16W-5N,15W-5N  9
Greenlawn Av. N&S . 15W-5N  9
Grove Av. E&W .. 16W-5N  9
Hamilton St. N&S . 15W-5N  9
Henderson St. N&S . 16W-5N  9
Hillside Dr. E&W
..........16W-6N,15W-6N  9
Indian Hill Dr. E&W . 17W-7N  9
Industrial Dr. E&W .. 16W-6N  9
Iroquois Ct. NW&SE
..........17W-7N  9
Iroquois Ln. E&W .. 17W-7N  9
Irving Park Blvd. E&W
..........16W-5N,15W-5N  9
Itasca St. E&W
..........17W-6N,16W-6N  9
Jacquelyn Dr. E&W . 15W-4N  9
James St. E&W....16W-3N  15
Jefferson St. E&W
..........16W-4N,16W-4N  9
John St. N&S........15W-4N  9
Judson St. N&S
..........16W-3N,16W-5N  15
Kevin Ln. E&W ..... 16W-6N  9
Leland Ct. E&W ... 16W-6N  9
Lincoln Av. NW&SE . 15W-5N  9
Main St. NW&SE .. 16W-5N  9
Maple Ln. E&W......16W-6N  9
Marion St. N&S
..........15W-4N,15W-5N  9
Marshall Rd. N&S
..........16W-5N,16W-6N  9
Martha St. N&S ... 16W-5N  9
Mason St. N&S
..........16W-4N,16W-5N  9
May St. N&S
..........15W-4N,15W-5N  9
McClean Av. E&W . 16W-5N  9
Medinah St. E&W
..........17W-5N,16W-5N  9
Meigs Ct. E&W .... 15W-5N  9
Memorial Rd. E&W . 15W-5N  9
Meyer Rd. N&S....16W-6N  9
Midway St. N&S ... 15W-5N  9
Miner St. N&S
..........16W-4N,16W-5N  9
Mohawk Dr. NW&SE
..........16W-5N  9
Nordic St. N&S .... 16W-5N  9
..........17W-6N,16W-6N  9

|  | Grid | Page |
|---|---|---|
| O'Hare Ct. E&W .... | 15W-5N | 9 |
| O'Leary Dr. N&S .... | 15W-5N | 9 |
| Orchard Av. N&S ... | 15W-5N | 9 |
| Pamela Dr. N&S .... | 15W-4N | 9 |
| Park St. N&S ...... | 15W-4N | 9 |
| Parkside Ln. N&S .. | 16W-5N | 9 |
| Pershing Av. N&S.... | 15W-5N | 9 |
| Pine Av. N&S...... | 15W-5N | 9 |
| Pleasant St. E&W .. | 16W-5N | 9 |
| Plentywood Ln. E&W | | |
| .......... | 16W-5N | 9 |
| Poppy Ln. N&S .... | 16W-5N | 9 |
| Railroad St. NW&SE | | |
| .......... | 16W-5N,15W-5N | 9 |
| Ridgewood Av. N&S | | |
| .......... | 16W-5N | 9 |
| Riverforest Ct. N&S..15W-4N | | 9 |
| Robert Kingery Hwy. N&S | | |
| ..........16W-7N,17W-7N | | 9 |
| Roosevelt Av. E&W | | |
| .......16W-5N,15W-5N | | 9 |
| Roosevelt Ct. E&W . | 15W-5N | 9 |
| Rose St. N&S | | |
| ..........15W-4N,15W-5N | | 9 |
| Roxanne Av. N&S .. | 15W-4N | 9 |
| Rt. 19 E&W | | |
| .......16W-5N,15W-5N | | 9 |
| Rt. 83 N&S  16W-5N,16W-7N | | 9 |
| Sivert Ct. E&W .... | 16W-6N | 9 |
| Sonny Ln. E&W .. | 16W-3N | 15 |
| Spruce Av. N&S | | |
| ..........17W-5N,17W-7N | | 9 |
| Stoneham St. E&W | | |
| ..........17W-6N,16W-6N | | 9 |
| Sunset Ct. N&S ... | 15W-5N | 9 |
| Supreme Dr. NS&EW | | |
| .......... | 16W-6N | 9 |
| Thomas Dr. N&S | | |
| ..........16W-6N,16W-7N | | 9 |
| Tioga Av. N&S ... | 16W-5N | 9 |
| Tower Ln. N&S......17W-7N | | 9 |
| Twin Oaks St. E&W | | |
| ..........17W-6N,16W-6N | | 9 |
| Virginia St. N&S .. | 15W-4N | 9 |
| Walnut St. N&S | | |
| ..........16W-4N,16W-5N | | 9 |
| Washington St. E&W | | |
| ..........16W-4N,15W-4N | | 9 |
| William St. E&W .. | 16W-3N | 15 |
| Wilson Ct. N&S .... | 16W-6N | 9 |
| Wood Av. E&W | | |
| .......16W-5N,15W-5N | | 9 |
| Woodland Av. E&W.16W-4N | | 9 |
| York Rd. N&S | | |
| .......16W-3N,16W-7N | | 15 |

### Bloomingdale

|  | Grid | Page |
|---|---|---|
| Alsace Ct. N&S ... | 24W-5N | 6 |
| Alyssa Ct.* N&S ... | 24W-6N | 6 |
| Amberwood Ct. N&S | | |
| .......... | 22W-4N | 7 |
| Amherst Ct. E&W .. | 22W-4N | 7 |
| Applewood Ln. E&W | | |
| .......... | 22W-4N | 7 |
| Arbor Ln. N&S ... | 22W-4N | 7 |
| Army Trail Rd. NW&SE | | |
| .......25W-4N,22W-4N | | 6 |
| Ashfield Ct. NS&EW | | |
| .......... | 24W-5N | 6 |
| Atherton Ct. N&S .. | 23W-5N | 6 |
| Bayview Ct. E&W ..22W-4N | | 7 |
| Bedford Ln. N&S ... | 22W-4N | 7 |
| Benton Ln. E&W ... | 24W-5N | 6 |
| Benton Ln. NS&EW ..22W-4N | | 6 |
| Biarritz St. N&S ... | 24W-5N | 6 |
| Billings E&W ...... | 23W-5N | 6 |
| Birchwood Ln. NW&SE | | |
| .......... | 22W-4N | 7 |
| Bloomfield Cir. E&W  24W-5N | | 6 |
| Bloomfield Pkwy. N&S | | |
| .......... | 24W-5N | 6 |
| Bloomingdale Rd. N&S | | |
| .......23W-4N,23W-6N | | 6 |
| Bob-o-link Dr. NE&SW | | |
| .......... | 24W-4N | 6 |
| Bobwhite Ct. N&S . | 23W-4N | 6 |
| Bobwhite Ln. N&S . | 23W-4N | 6 |
| Bourne Ln. NE&SW ..23W-5N | | 6 |
| Bradley Ct. N&S ... | 22W-4N | 7 |
| Braintree Dr. N&S .. | 23W-5N | 6 |
| Brentwood Ct. E&W | | |
| .......... | 22W-4N | 7 |
| Brewster Ct. N&S .. | 23W-5N | 6 |
| Briarwood Ln. E&W ..22W-4N | | 7 |
| Bridgewater Ln. NE&SW | | |
| .......... | 23W-4N | 6 |
| Brighton Dr. E&W ..25W-4N | | 6 |
| Broker Rd. NE&SW ..22W-6N | | 7 |
| Brookdale Dr. N&S . | 22W-4N | 7 |
| Bunting Ln. N&S ... | 23W-4N | 6 |
| Butterfield Dr. N&S . | 24W-4N | 6 |
| Byron Av. E&W .... | 22W-4N | 7 |
| Cambridge Ln. N&S.23W-5N | | 6 |
| Camden Dr. E&W ...25W-5N | | 6 |
| Cardinal Dr. N&S | | |
| .......24W-5N,23W-4N | | 6 |
| Carlton St. E&W ... | 22W-4N | 7 |
| Carriage Way E&W ..22W-4N | | 7 |
| Carthage Ct. E&W | | |
| .......... | 22W-4N | 7 |
| Castlerock Ln. N&S..24W-5N | | 6 |
| Cayuga Ct. NE&SW..25W-5N | | 6 |

|  | Grid | Page |
|---|---|---|
| Chambord Ct. NW&SE | | |
| .......... | 24W-5N | 6 |
| Chatham Ct. NW&SE | | |
| .......... | 23W-5N | 6 |
| Chelsea St. N&S ... | 24W-5N | 6 |
| Circle Av. N&S ... | 22W-5N | 7 |
| Clearbrook Ln. NE&SW | | |
| .......... | 22W-4N | 7 |
| Club House Dr. E&W | | |
| .......... | 24W-5N | 6 |
| College Dr. NE&SW .. | 22W-4N | 7 |
| Colony Ct. E&W ... | 22W-4N | 7 |
| Colony Green Dr. NS&EW | | |
| .......... | 22W-4N | 7 |
| Constitution Dr. N&S | | |
| .......... | 23W-5N | 6 |
| Country Club Ct. NE&SW | | |
| .......... | 22W-4N | 7 |
| Country Club Dr. N&S | | |
| .......... | 24W-5N | 6 |
| Coventry Ct. N&S ..22W-4N | | 7 |
| Covington Dr. N&S | | |
| .......25W-4N,25W-5N | | 6 |
| Crandon Ct. N&S ... | 23W-5N | 6 |
| Creekside Dr. NW&SE | | |
| .......... | 22W-4N | 7 |
| Crest Ct. N&S ... | 22W-4N | 7 |
| Crestwood Ln. N&S..22W-4N | | 7 |
| Cunningham Dr. E&W | | |
| .......... | 23W-4N | 6 |
| Cunningham Ln. N&S | | |
| .......... | 23W-4N | 6 |
| Darby Ct. N&S ..... | 23W-5N | 6 |
| Dartmouth Ct. NE&SW | | |
| .......... | 22W-4N | 7 |
| Dawn Ct. E&W ... | 22W-4N | 7 |
| Day St. N&S ...... | 23W-5N | 6 |
| Dee Ct. N&S ..... | 22W-4N | 7 |
| Deeke Ct. N&S ...25W-7N | | 6 |
| Deer Glen Way E&W | | |
| .......... | 22W-4N | 7 |
| Dijon Ct. N&S ... | 24W-5N | 6 |
| Douglas Dr. E&W ..22W-4N | | 7 |
| Dover Ct. NW&SE .. | 22W-4N | 7 |
| Downing Dr. E&W . | 22W-5N | 7 |
| Driftwood Ln. NE&SW | | |
| .......... | 22W-4N | 7 |
| Durham Ln. N&S .. | 22W-4N | 7 |
| Duxbury Ct. NE&SW | | |
| .......... | 23W-5N | 6 |
| Eagle Ct. N&S .... | 23W-4N | 6 |
| Eagle Ln. NE&SW . | 23W-4N | 6 |
| Eaton Ct. N&S ... | 25W-4N | 6 |
| Edgebrook Dr. E&W | 22W-5N | 7 |
| Edgewater Ct. N&S..23W-4N | | 6 |
| Edgewater Dr. E&W | | |
| .......23W-4N,22W-4N | | 6 |
| Elmwood Ln. N&S ..22W-4N | | 7 |
| Emerson Ct. NE&SW | | |
| .......... | 22W-4N | 7 |
| Epson Ct. N&S ....23W-5N | | 6 |
| Eric Ct.* E&W .... | 24W-6N | 6 |
| Esprit Ct. E&W .... | 24W-5N | 6 |
| Essex Ct. N&S .... | 24W-5N | 6 |
| Euclid Av. N&S ......22W-4N | | 7 |
| Euclid Ct. N&S ... | 22W-4N | 7 |
| Evergreen Ln. N&S ..23W-4N | | 7 |
| Fairchild Ct. NW&SE | | |
| .......... | 22W-4N | 7 |
| Fairfield Ct. N&S ... | 23W-5N | 6 |
| Fairfield Way NS&EW | | |
| .......... | 23W-5N | 6 |
| Fairlane Ct. E&W ..23W-5N | | 6 |
| Falcon Ct. NW&SE .. | 24W-5N | 6 |
| Farrington Ct. N&S .. | 23W-5N | 6 |
| Fernwood Ln. E&W ..23W-5N | | 6 |
| Fontaine Ct. N&S .. | 24W-5N | 6 |
| Forest Dr. E&W .... | 23W-5N | 6 |
| Fosmor Ct. N&S ...22W-4N | | 7 |
| Foster Av. E&W ... | 23W-5N | 6 |
| Cir. ................ | 23W-5N | 6 |
| Cir. ................ | 23W-5N | 6 |
| Fox Ct. E&W ...... | 25W-5N | 6 |
| Franklin St. E&W | | |
| .......24W-5N,23W-5N | | 6 |
| Freeport Dr. E&W ..22W-5N | | 7 |
| Fremont Ct. N&S .. | 22W-4N | 7 |
| Garden Way NW&SE | | |
| .......... | 24W-5N | 6 |
| Gary Av. N&S | | |
| .......25W-4N,25W-6N | | 6 |
| Georgetown Ct. NW&SE | | |
| .......... | 22W-4N | 7 |
| Ghingham Ln. E&W ..23W-5N | | 6 |
| Glen Ellyn Rd. N&S | | |
| .......22W-4N,22W-5N | | 7 |
| Glengarry Rd. E&W ..24W-4N | | 6 |
| Greenfield Dr. N&S . | 24W-5N | 6 |
| Greenway Dr. E&W | | |
| .......23W-4N,22W-4N | | 6 |
| Gresham Ct. N&S ..23W-5N | | 6 |
| Hampton Ct. N&S .. | 23W-4N | 7 |
| Hancock E&W ... | 23W-5N | 6 |
| Harbor Ct. N&S ...22W-4N | | 7 |
| Harvard Ct. N&S .. | 22W-4N | 7 |
| Hawthorne Dr. E&W | 22W-4N | 7 |
| Hearthside Dr. E&W  22W-4N | | 7 |
| Hedgerow Ln. E&W | | |
| .......... | 22W-4N | 7 |
| Hempstead Dr. NW&SE | | |
| .......... | 23W-5N | 6 |
| Hempstead Ln. NE&SW | | |
| .......... | 23W-5N | 6 |
| Hillandale Ct. N&S . | 23W-5N | 6 |

|  | Grid | Page |
|---|---|---|
| Hillandale Dr. N&S . | 23W-5N | 6 |
| Hillcrest Ter. E&W . | 23W-6N | 6 |
| Independence Ln. E&W | | |
| .......... | 23W-5N | 6 |
| Indiana Ct. NW&SE.22W-4N | | 7 |
| Ironwood Dr. E&W . | 22W-5N | 7 |
| Ivy Ln. N&S ...... | 22W-5N | 7 |
| Jackson Ln. N&S .. | 23W-5N | 6 |
| Jason Ct.* E&W ... | 24W-6N | 6 |
| Jefferson Ln. N&S .. | 23W-5N | 6 |
| Juniper Ln. N&S ... | 23W-5N | 6 |
| Karswell Ct. N&S ..23W-5N | | 6 |
| Kendall Ct. E&W ... | 22W-4N | 7 |
| Kensington Ct. E&W | | |
| .......... | 24W-4N | 6 |
| Killdeer Rd. N&S ...24W-4N | | 6 |
| Kingston Ln. N&S ..22W-5N | | 7 |
| Knollwood Dr. N&S . | 25W-4N | 6 |
| Lake St. NW&SE | | |
| .......24W-6N,22W-5N | | 6 |
| Lakemont Ct. NE&SW | | |
| .......... | 24W-4N | 6 |
| Lakeshore Ln. NW&SE | | |
| .......... | 22W-4N | 7 |
| Lakeview Ct. NW&SE | | |
| .......... | 22W-4N | 7 |
| Lakeview Dr. N&S .. | 22W-5N | 7 |
| Lakeview Ln. NE&SW | | |
| .......23W-4N,22W-4N | | 6 |
| Lakewoods Ct. N&S. | 23W-5N | 6 |
| Langton Ct. N&S ... | 23W-4N | 6 |
| Langton Ln. N&S .. | 23W-4N | 6 |
| Larchmont Ln. N&S . | 23W-4N | 6 |
| Laurel Ln. NE&SW . | 22W-4N | 7 |
| Lawford Ct.* N&S .. | 22W-5N | 7 |
| Lawrence Av. E&W | | |
| .......25W-5N,23W-6N | | 6 |
| Lehigh Ln. N&S ...23W-5N | | 6 |
| Leslie Ln. E&W ....23W-5N | | 6 |
| Lincoln Ct. N&S ... | 22W-5N | 7 |
| Lockwood Ln N&S . | 22W-5N | 7 |
| Log Lodge Dr. NE&SW | | |
| .......... | 23W-6N | 6 |
| Long Ridge Dr. N&S | | |
| .......... | 22W-5N | 7 |
| Lorraine Cir. NS&EW | | |
| .......... | 24W-5N | 6 |
| Lynbrook Dr. E&W . | 23W-5N | 6 |
| Manor Ln. N&S.....22W-5N | | 7 |
| Maple Av. N&S ... | 23W-5N | 6 |
| Maple Ct. NE&SW . | 23W-5N | 6 |
| Martin Ct. N&S ....24W-4N | | 6 |
| Martin Ln. N&S ... | 24W-4N | 6 |
| Meadowlark Rd. NW&SE | | |
| .......... | 24W-4N | 6 |
| Melbourne Ct. N&S .. | 23W-5N | 6 |
| Millcreek Ln. NE&SW | | |
| .......... | 22W-4N | 7 |
| Millford Ct. N&S ...23W-5N | | 6 |
| Millford Ln. N&S ...23W-5N | | 6 |
| Milton Ct. N&S ...22W-5N | | 7 |
| Morningside Dr. N&S | | |
| .......... | 22W-4N | 7 |
| N. Bristol Dr. N&S .. | 25W-5N | 6 |
| N. Hampshire Cir. NE&SW | | |
| .......... | 24W-5N | 6 |
| N. Manchester Ct. E&W | | |
| .......... | 25W-5N | 6 |
| N. Sherwood NE&SW | | |
| .......... | 24W-5N | 6 |
| N. Windham Ln. N&S | | |
| .......... | 24W-5N | 6 |
| N. Windsor NE&SW..24W-5N | | 6 |
| Needham Dr. E&W . | 24W-5N | 6 |
| Neville Ct. N&S ...23W-5N | | 6 |
| Nordic Rd. E&W ...22W-5N | | 7 |
| Northwestern Ct. N&S | | |
| .......... | 22W-4N | 7 |
| Northwood Ln. N&S  24W-5N | | 6 |
| Norton Dr. NW&SE .. | 23W-5N | 6 |
| Norton Ln. N&S ... | 23W-5N | 6 |
| Oak St. N&S ..... | 23W-5N | 6 |
| Oakwood Ct. E&W . | 22W-4N | 7 |
| Old Mill Ln. N&S .. | 24W-4N | 6 |
| Oneida Ct. NW&SE.25W-5N | | 6 |
| Orchard Ln. NE&SW | | |
| .......... | 24W-5N | 6 |
| Oriole St. N&S .... | 23W-4N | 6 |
| Otsego Ct. N&S ...23W-5N | | 6 |
| Oxford Ct. N&S ... | 23W-4N | 6 |
| Oxford Ln. N&S ...23W-4N | | 6 |
| Oxford Pl. NW&SE ..23W-4N | | 6 |
| Park Av. E&W | | |
| .......23W-5N,22W-5N | | 7 |
| Parkway N&S E&W . | 23W-5N | 6 |
| Pebble Creek Dr. N&S | | |
| .......... | 22W-4N | 7 |
| Penwick Ct.* N&S .. | 24W-5N | 6 |
| Pheasant Ct. NW&SE | | |
| .......... | 24W-4N | 6 |
| Pheasant Ln. E&W . | 24W-4N | 6 |
| Picton Rd. E&W ...23W-6N | | 6 |
| Pinewood Ln. E&W ..22W-4N | | 7 |
| Pleasant Av. N&S ..22W-5N | | 7 |
| Plymouth Ln. NE&SW | | |
| .......... | 23W-4N | 6 |
| Prairie Av. N&S ... | 22W-5N | 7 |
| Quail Ln. E&W ....22W-5N | | 7 |
| Quincy Ct. E&W ... | 22W-4N | 7 |
| Radcliffe Ct. E&W ..24W-5N | | 6 |
| Raleigh* E&W .... | 23W-5N | 6 |
| Raven Ln. E&W ...22W-4N | | 6 |

|  | Grid | Page |
|---|---|---|
| Red Bird Ct. NE&SW | | |
| .......... | 24W-4N | 6 |
| Red Bird Rd. NW&SE | | |
| .......... | 24W-4N | 6 |
| Redwing Dr. E&W ..24W-4N | | 6 |
| Regency Dr. NS&EW | | |
| .......... | 22W-4N | 7 |
| Ridge Av. N&S ... | 23W-5N | 6 |
| Ridgewood Dr. NW&SE | | |
| .......... | 24W-5N | 6 |
| Robin Ct. N&S . | 23W-4N | 6 |
| Rosedale Av. N&S .. | 23W-4N | 6 |
| Rosedale Ct. N&S .. | 23W-4N | 6 |
| Royal Ln. E&W ... | 24W-5N | 6 |
| Royce Ct. NW&SE . | 23W-4N | 6 |
| Royce Dr. E&W.....23W-4N | | 6 |
| Salem Ct. NE&SW . | 23W-5N | 6 |
| Saranac Ct. N&S .. | 25W-5N | 6 |
| Schick Rd. E&W | | |
| .......25W-5N,22W-5N | | 6 |
| Scott Dr. E&W ....25W-5N | | 6 |
| Seneca Tr. N&S ... | 25W-5N | 6 |
| Signature Dr. E&W . | 22W-5N | 7 |
| Skylark Dr. NW&SE.24W-5N | | 6 |
| Spring Ct. NE&SW ..22W-4N | | 7 |
| Spring Valley Dr. E&W | | |
| .......... | 22W-5N | 7 |
| Springbrook Dr. E&W | | |
| .......... | 23W-5N | 6 |
| Springdale Ln. NS&EW | | |
| .......... | 24W-5N | 6 |
| Springfield Dr. NE&SW | | |
| .......25W-4N,24W-6N | | 6 |
| St. Francis Ct. N&S.22W-5N | | 7 |
| Stanton Ct. N&S ... | 22W-5N | 7 |
| Stanyon Ct. N&S .. | 22W-4N | 7 |
| Starling Ct. NW&SE.22W-5N | | 7 |
| Sterling Ct. N&S ... | 23W-4N | 6 |
| Sterling Dr. E&W .. | 23W-4N | 6 |
| Sterling Ln. N&S ...23W-4N | | 6 |
| Stonybrook Dr. NS&EW | | |
| .......... | 22W-5N | 7 |
| Cir. ................ | 25W-7N | 6 |
| Strathmore Ct. N&S . | 23W-4N | 6 |
| Strathmore Ln. N&S  23W-4N | | 6 |
| Surrey Dr. NW&SE . | 23W-4N | 6 |
| Surrey Ln. N&S ... | 23W-4N | 6 |
| Sutherland Ln. N&S . | 23W-4N | 6 |
| Sutton Ct. N&S ...22W-4N | | 7 |
| Swallow Av. E&W . | 23W-4N | 6 |
| Tamarack Dr. E&W . | 22W-5N | 7 |
| Tanager Dr. E&W ..22W-4N | | 7 |
| Tee Ln. E&W......22W-5N | | 7 |
| Terry Av. E&W ..... | 24W-4N | 6 |
| Thrasher St. N&S ..24W-4N | | 6 |
| Torrington Dr. E&W  24W-5N | | 6 |
| U.S. Route 20 NW&SE | | |
| .......24W-6N,22W-5N | | 6 |
| Versailles Ct. N&S ..24W-5N | | 6 |
| Villa Way N&S ... | 24W-5N | 6 |
| W. Bristol NE&SW ..24W-5N | | 6 |
| W. Hampshire Dr. NW&SE | | |
| .......... | | |
| W. Hampshire Ln. E&W | | |
| .......... | 24W-5N | 6 |
| W. Scarborough Ct. E&W | | |
| .......... | 25W-5N | 6 |
| W. Sheffield Dr. E&W | | |
| .......... | 24W-5N | 6 |
| W. Windsor Dr. N&S | | |
| .......25W-5N,24W-5N | | 6 |
| Walter Ct. N&S ...23W-5N | | 6 |
| Warren Av. N&S ...22W-5N | | 7 |
| Warwick Ln. N&S .. | 24W-5N | 6 |
| Washington St. E&W | | |
| .......... | 23W-5N | 6 |
| Wedgefield Ln. N&S  24W-5N | | 6 |
| Wellington Dr. N&S . | 24W-5N | 6 |
| Wendover Dr. N&S ..24W-5N | | 6 |
| Wentworth Ln. E&W | | |
| .......... | 24W-5N | 6 |
| West Rd. N&S ... | 24W-4N | 6 |
| Whitehall Ter. E&W.24W-4N | | 6 |
| Wickham Av. N&S . | 24W-4N | 6 |
| Willow Ln. NE&SW .22W-4N | | 7 |
| Willowbridge Way N&S | | |
| .......... | 22W-4N | 7 |
| Winston Ln. N&S ...23W-4N | | 6 |
| Woodcrest Ct. N&S.23W-6N | | 6 |
| Woodland Way* E&W | | |
| .......... | 24W-5N | 6 |
| Woodside Dr. NW&SE | | |
| .......... | 24W-5N | 6 |
| Wren Dr. NE&SW ..23W-4N | | 6 |
| 1st St. N&S ...... | 23W-5N | 6 |
| 3rd St. N&S ...... | 23W-5N | 6 |

### Bloomingdale Township

|  | Grid | Page |
|---|---|---|
| Abilene Tr. N&S ... | 25W-5N | 6 |
| Acacia Ln. NE&SW . | 22W-6N | 7 |
| Alma Av. N&S ...... | 21W-2N | 13 |
| Amy Av. N&S ..... | 23W-2N | 12 |
| Andrene Ln. N&S | | |
| .......21W-5N,21W-6N | | 7 |
| Ardmore Av. E&W .. | 23W-7N | 6 |
| Argyle Av. E&W ... | 25W-6N | 6 |
| Argyle Av. N&S ... | 21W-2N | 13 |
| Armitage Av. E&W | | |
| .......23W-2N,21W-2N | | 12 |
| Army Trail Rd. NW&SE | | |
| .......26W-4N,21W-4N | | 6 |
| Baker Dr. N&S ..... | 21W-6N | 7 |

|  | Grid | Page |
|---|---|---|
| Barbara Ct. E&W ..22W-6N | | 7 |
| Bartels Rd. N&S ... | 26W-7N | 6 |
| Belden Av. E&W ... | 21W-2N | 13 |
| Bernice Av. N&S ... | 23W-2N | 12 |
| Biscayne Ct. N&S ..25W-6N | | 6 |
| Biscayne St. N&S . | 25W-6N | 6 |
| Blackduck Ln. E&W.26W-5N | | 6 |
| Bluebill Ct. NW&SE . | 26W-5N | 6 |
| Briargate Ter. E&W | | |
| .......21W-6N,21W-7N | | 7 |
| Broker Rd. NE&SW ..22W-6N | | 7 |
| Bryn Mawr Av. E&W | | |
| .......... | 23W-7N | 6 |
| Bunker Ter. N&S ...21W-5N | | 7 |
| Burdett Av. E&W | | |
| .......26W-2N,21W-2N | | 12 |
| Byron Av. E&W ...22W-4N | | 7 |
| Canvasback Ln. N&S | | |
| .......... | 26W-5N | 6 |
| Cavalry Ct. N&S ...24W-4N | | 6 |
| Central Av. E&W ... | 25W-7N | 6 |
| Chesapeake Ln. NS&EW | | |
| .......... | 25W-6N | 6 |
| Circle Av. N&S ...22W-6N | | 7 |
| Circle Ter. N&S ...21W-7N | | 7 |
| Claire Ct. N&S ... | 23W-2N | 12 |
| Cloverdale Rd. N&S..25W-6N | | 6 |
| Club Ter. NE&SW .. | 21W-5N | 7 |
| Cortland Av. E&W ..21W-2N | | 13 |
| Crescent Ter. N&S ..22W-4N | | 7 |
| Crest Av. E&W | | |
| .......22W-7N,21W-7N | | 7 |
| Depot Pl. NW&SE . | 21W-6N | 7 |
| Diane Av. N&S ... | 23W-2N | 12 |
| Dickens Av. E&W | | |
| .......23W-2N,21W-2N | | 12 |
| Dinah Ct. E&W ...22W-6N | | 7 |
| Dinah Rd. N&S ...22W-6N | | 7 |
| Drake Ln. E&W ... | 26W-5N | 6 |
| Eagle Av. NE&SW . | 21W-7N | 7 |
| Eagle Ter. NS&EW | | |
| .......21W-5N,21W-7N | | 7 |
| Edwards St. N&S ...21W-7N | | 7 |
| Elgin O'Hare Expwy. NE&SW | | |
| .......... | 26W-7N | 6 |
| Elizabeth Ct. NW&SE | | |
| .......... | 22W-6N | 7 |
| Elm St. N&S ..... | 21W-2N | 13 |
| Euclid Av. N&S ... | 22W-2N | 13 |
| Fairway Ln. | | |
| .......21W-5N,21W-6N | | 7 |
| Ferrari Ct. N&S ... | 22W-6N | 7 |
| Foster Av. E&W | | |
| .......25W-6N,22W-6N | | 6 |
| Frisco Ct. N&S ... | 25W-6N | 6 |
| Frisco St. E&W ... | 25W-6N | 6 |
| Fullerton Av. E&W | | |
| .......24W-3N,21W-3N | | 12 |
| Garden Av. N&S ...24W-6N | | 6 |
| Gary Av. N&S | | |
| .......25W-3N,25W-6N | | 12 |
| Gates Av. NE&SW . | 21W-6N | 7 |
| Glen Ct. NE&SW | | |
| .......22W-6N,21W-7N | | 7 |
| Glen Ellyn Rd. N&S.22W-4N | | 7 |
| Glen Rd. N&S .... | 21W-7N | 7 |
| Glendale Rd. N&S . | 22W-6N | 7 |
| Glendale Ter. NE&SW | | |
| .......23W-6N,22W-6N | | 6 |
| Goldeneye Ln. N&S..26W-5N | | 6 |
| Goodridge Ter. NE&SW | | |
| .......... | 23W-6N | 6 |
| Greenwood Av. N&S | | |
| .......... | 22W-6N | 7 |
| Grove St. E&W ... | 21W-6N | 7 |
| Harvey Rd. N&S ...22W-6N | | 7 |
| Hawthorne Ln. N&S..22W-7N | | 7 |
| Helen St. N&S ...21W-2N | | 13 |
| Hickory Ct. E&W .. | 22W-6N | 7 |
| Highland Av. N&S | | |
| .......22W-2N,22W-6N | | 13 |
| Hill St. N&S | | |
| .......23W-6N,23W-7N | | 6 |
| Hillcrest Ct. N&S ..22W-6N | | 7 |
| Hillcrest Ter. E&W .. | 22W-6N | 7 |
| Hillside Ct. N&S ...22W-6N | | 7 |
| Hilltop Dr. N&S ...21W-7N | | 7 |
| James St. N&S ...22W-6N | | 7 |
| John Ct. E&W ...22W-6N | | 7 |
| Joseph Ct. E&W ....21W-6N | | 7 |
| Juniper Dr. NE&SW ..23W-7N | | 7 |
| Keeney Rd. N&S ...25W-6N | | 6 |
| Kenmore St. N&S ..21W-2N | | 13 |
| Kuhn Rd. N&S | | |
| .......26W-2N,26W-4N | | 12 |
| Lake St. NW&SE | | |
| .......26W-7N,21W-7N | | 6 |
| Laramie Tr. N&S ...25W-5N | | 6 |
| Laredo Tr. E&W ...25W-5N | | 6 |
| Laurel Dr. N&S | | |
| .......22W-5N,22W-6N | | 7 |
| Lawler Av. N&S ... | 21W-2N | 13 |
| Lawrence Av. E&W | | |
| .......25W-6N,22W-6N | | 6 |
| Lawrence Ln. NW&SE | | |
| .......... | 21W-7N | 7 |
| Lies Rd. E&W | | |
| .......28W-4N,25W-4N | | 5 |
| Lincoln St. N&S ...23W-7N | | 6 |
| Linda Av. N&S ... | 23W-2N | 12 |
| Linden Av. N&S | | |
| .......22W-6N,22W-7N | | 7 |
| Lloyd Av. N&S | | |
| .......21W-2N,21W-6N | | 13 |

Grid Page

Lydia Rd. E&W ...... 21W-3N 13
Magnolia Av. NW&SE ...... 21W-2N 13
Mallard Ct. E&W ...... 25W-5N 6
Mallard Ln. N&S ...... 26W-5N,25W-5N 6
Mandarin Ln. E&W ...... 26W-5N 6
Manor Rd. NE&SW ...... 21W-6N 7
Maple Av. E&W ...... 23W-7N,21W-7N 6
Maple Ct. N&S ...... 22W-5N 7
Meacham Rd. N&S ...... 21W-7N 7
Meadow Rd. N&S ...... 21W-3N 13
Medinah Rd. N&S ...... 22W-7N,21W-4N 7
Mensching Rd. NW&SE ...... 24W-6N 6
Merganser Ln. N&S ...... 26W-5N 6
Mildred Av. N&S ...... 23W-2N 12
Muscovy Ln. E&W ...... 26W-5N,25W-5N 6
Neva Ter. N&S ...... 21W-5N,21W-6N 7
Newland Pl. NE&SW ...... 21W-6N 7
Nordic Rd. NE&SW ...... 21W-5N 7
North Av. E&W ...... 26W-2N,21W-2N 12
North Ln. E&W ...... 21W-5N 7
North-South Tollway N&S ...... 21W-2N 13
Oak St. N&S ...... 23W-6N 6
Old Gary Av. N&S ...... 25W-4N 6
Olive Ct. E&W ...... 23W-2N 12
Papworth St. N&S ...... 25W-6N 6
Par Ln. E&W ...... 21W-5N 7
Park Av. E&W ...... 21W-3N 13
Pearl Av. N&S ...... 23W-2N 12
Pearson Dr. N&S ...... 24W-6N 6
Peterson Av. E&W ...... 26W-2N,21W-2N 12
Pine Av. E&W ...... 23W-7N 6
Pintail Ct. NE&SW ...... 25W-5N 6
Pleasant Av. N&S ...... 22W-2N 13
Poplar Av. E&W ...... 22W-7N 7
Prairie Av. N&S ...... 22W-2N 13
Redhead Ln. N&S ...... 26W-5N 6
Ring Neck Ct. NE&SW ...... 26W-5N 6
Ring Neck Ln. N&S ...... 26W-5N 6
Robbie Ln. N&S ...... 21W-4N 7
Robert Ct. N&S ...... 22W-6N 7
Roberta Av. N&S ...... 23W-2N 12
Rohlwing Rd. N&S ...... 21W-3N,21W-7N 13
Rosedale Av. N&S ...... 23W-6N 6
Santa Fe Tr. N&S ...... 25W-5N 6
Schick Rd. E&W ...... 26W-5N,25W-5N 6
Schlick Av. E&W ...... 22W-7N 7
Schmale Rd. N&S ...... 24W-3N,24W-4N 12
Shelley Dr. E&W ...... 21W-6N 7
Sidney Av. E&W ...... 23W-2N,21W-2N 12
Sodard Rd. E&W ...... 22W-6N 7
Spring Ct. N&S ...... 22W-6N 7
Squire Ln. E&W ...... 22W-7N 7
St. Charles Rd. NW&SE ...... 26W-2N 12
Stone Av. E&W ...... 21W-4N 7
Sunnyside Dr. NE&SW ...... 21W-6N 7
Sunset Ct. N&S ...... 24W-6N 6
Sunset Ter. E&W ...... 22W-6N 7
Swift Rd. N&S ...... 21W-2N,21W-5N 13
Sycamore Av. N&S ...... 22W-5N,22W-7N 7
Teal Ct. NW&SE ...... 25W-5N 6
Tee Ln. E&W ...... 21W-5N 7
Temple Dr. NW&SE ...... 22W-7N,21W-6N 7
Terrace Ct. NW&SE ...... 21W-7N 7
Thorn Rd. N&S ...... 25W-5N 6
Tucumcari Tr. E&W ...... 25W-5N 6
Turner Av. E&W ...... 23W-6N 6
Valley Ln. NE&SW ...... 21W-6N 7
Valley Rd. N&S ...... 23W-6N,23W-7N 6
Valley View Rd. N&S ...... 22W-3N 13
Virginia Av. N&S ...... 23W-2N 12
Virginia Rd. N&S ...... 25W-6N 6
Walnut Av. E&W ...... 22W-6N 7
Walnut St. NW&SE ...... 23W-6N 6
Walter Dr. N&S ...... 22W-4N 7
Webster Av. E&W ...... 22W-6N 7
West End Rd. N&S ...... 24W-6N 6
Wheaton Rd. N&S ...... 25W-6N 6
Whispering Ct. E&W ...... 21W-4N 7
Widgeon Ln. E&W ...... 26W-5N 6
Willard St. N&S ...... 23W-2N 12
William St. N&S ...... 23W-7N 6
Willow St. N&S ...... 23W-7N 6
Winthrop Av. E&W ...... 21W-2N 13
Woodview Dr. E&W ...... 22W-6N,21W-6N 7
Woodworth Pl. E&W ...... 23W-7N 6
84th Ct. N&S ...... 25W-4N 6

## Bolingbrook*

**(Also see Will County)**

Banbury Ct. NE&SW ...... 21W-9S 31
Bent Tree Ct. N&S ...... 22W-9S 31
Buckingham Way E&W ...... 21W-9S 31
Cambridge Way E&W ...... 22W-10S,21W-9S 13
Everington Ct. E&W ...... 22W-9S 31
Grosvernor Ct. E&W ...... 22W-9S 31
Janes Av. N&S ...... 21W-9S 31
Kensington Way E&W ...... 21W-9S 31
Kent Ct. N&S ...... 21W-9S 31
Londonberry Ct. N&S ...... 21W-9S 31
Londonberry Ln. NS&EW ...... 21W-9S 31
Nelson Ct. NW&SE ...... 22W-9S 31
Piccadilly Ln. NS&EW ...... 21W-9S 31
Rain Tree Dr. NS&EW ...... 22W-9S 31
Sheffield Ln. NS&EW ...... 21W-9S 31
Stone Creek Dr. E&W ...... 22W-9S 31
Sulgrave Ct. E&W ...... 22W-9S 31
Tangly Ct. N&S ...... 22W-9S 31
Trafalgal Ct. E&W ...... 22W-9S 31
Twin Creek Ct. N&S ...... 22W-9S 31
Twin Creek Dr. NS&EW ...... 22W-9S 31
Whitehall Ct. N&S ...... 21W-9S 31

## Burr Ridge*

**(Also see Cook County)**

Arcadia Ct. E&W ...... 16W-10S 33
Ashton Dr. E&W ...... 15W-10S 33
Bel Aire Ct. E&W ...... 15W-10S 33
Bennacott Ln. E&W ...... 15W-9S 33
Berkshire Ct.* E&W ...... 15W-8S 33
Berkshire Ln.* E&W ...... 15W-8S 33
Briarwood Dr. E&W ...... 15W-9S 33
Bridle Ct. NE&SW ...... 15W-10S 33
Bristol Ct.* N&S ...... 15W-8S 33
Burr Ridge Club Dr. NS&EW ...... 15W-6S 27
Cambridge Dr. E&W ...... 15W-9S 33
Camelot Dr. E&W ...... 15W-9S 33
Canterbury Dr. N&S ...... 15W-9S 33
Carlisle Ct. N&S ...... 15W-9S 33
Cascade Cir. NS&EW ...... 16W-10S 33
Cascade Ct., E. E&W ...... 16W-10S 33
Cascade Ct., W. E&W ...... 16W-10S 33
Charleston Dr. E&W ...... 16W-9S 33
Chesterfield Ct.* E&W ...... 15W-8S 33
Circle Ridge Ct. N&S ...... 15W-10S 33
Circle Ridge Dr. NS&EW ...... 15W-10S 33
Clynderven Rd. N&S ...... 15W-9S 33
Conway Ct. E&W ...... 15W-9S 33
Countryside Ct. E&W ...... 15W-7S 27
County Line Creek Dr. E&W ...... 15W-10S 33
County Line Rd. N&S ...... 15W-10S,15W-6S 33
Cove Creek Ct. N&S ...... 15W-6S 27
Deerpath Tr. NS&EW ...... 15W-9S 33
Devon Ct. N&S ...... 15W-10S 33
Devon Dr. E&W ...... 15W-10S 33
Devon Ridge Dr. N&S ...... 15W-10S 33
Dolfor Cove N&S ...... 15W-9S 33
Drew Av. N&S ...... 15W-9S,15W-8S 33
Durham Ct.* E&W ...... 15W-8S 33
Elm Av. N&S ...... 15W-8S 33
Enclave Ct. NW&SE ...... 15W-10S 33
Fallingwater Dr., E. N&S ...... 16W-10S 33
Fallingwater Dr., W N&S ...... 16W-10S 33
Fawn Ct. NE&SW ...... 15W-9S 33
Fieldstone Dr. NE&SW ...... 15W-7S 27
Garfield Av. N&S ...... 15W-9S,15W-8S 33
Glenmora Ln. N&S ...... 15W-10S 33
Glenn Dr. N&S ...... 15W-10S 33
Grant St. NW&SE ...... 15W-10S,15W-8S 33
Hanover Ct. NE&SW ...... 15W-10S 33
Heather Ct. N&S ...... 15W-9S 33
Heather Ln. N&S ...... 15W-9S 33
Hunter Ct. E&W ...... 15W-10S 33
Jack Pine Ln. N&S ...... 15W-9S 33
Joy Ct. E&W ...... 15W-10S 33
Kathryn Ct. NS&EW ...... 15W-9S 33
Keller Dr. N&S ...... 15W-6S 27
Kenmare Dr. NS&EW ...... 15W-7S 27
Keri Ln. NW&SE ...... 15W-10S 33
Kimberly Ct. N&S ...... 15W-9S 33
Kirkwood Cove E&W ...... 15W-9S 33
Lake Ridge Club Ct.* E&W ...... 15W-8S 33
Lake Ridge Club Dr. NS&EW ...... 15W-9S 33
Lake Ridge Ct. NE&SW ...... 15W-9S 33
Lake Ridge Dr. N&S ...... 15W-9S 33
Lakewood Cir. NS&EW ...... 15W-9S 33
Lancaster Ct.* E&W ...... 15W-8S 33
Laurel Oak Ct. N&S ...... 15W-10S 33
Laurel Oak Ct. NE&SW ...... 15W-10S 33
Leonard Ln. NW&SE ...... 15W-9S 33
Linden Ct. NE&SW ...... 15W-10S 33
Madison St. N&S ...... 15W-9S,15W-8S 33
Marissa Ct. NE&SW ...... 15W-11S 15
Morgan Ct. E&W ...... 15W-10S 33
Norman Ct. N&S ...... 15W-10S 33
Norris Dr. E&W ...... 15W-6S 27
Oak Creek Ct. E&W ...... 15W-10S 33
Oak Creek Ct. NS&EW ...... 15W-10S 33
Oak Creek Dr. E&W ...... 15W-10S 33
Oak Creek Dr. N&S ...... 15W-10S 33
Oak Creek East Dr. E&W ...... 15W-10S 33
Oak Ct. N&S ...... 15W-10S 33
Oak Ridge Dr. NE&SW ...... 15W-10S 33
Old Surrey Rd. E&W ...... 15W-6S 27
Pacific St. N&S ...... 16W-11S 35
Park Av. N&S ...... 15W-9S,15W-6S 33
Parkview Pl. E&W ...... 15W-9S 33
Pepper Mill Ct. E&W ...... 15W-7S 27
Pin Oak Ct. N&S ...... 15W-10S 33
Pine Tree Rd. E&W ...... 15W-9S 33
Prairie Dr. N&S ...... 15W-10S 33
Provencal Dr. E&W ...... 15W-10S 33
Red Oak Ct. NW&SE ...... 15W-10S 33
Regent Ct. E&W ...... 15W-10S 33
Ridge Farm Rd. NS&EW ...... 15W-6S 27
Ridgepointe Dr. N&S ...... 15W-9S 33
Rodeo Dr. NE&SW ...... 15W-10S 33
Royal Dr. N&S ...... 15W-10S 33
Saddle Ct. NE&SW ...... 15W-10S 33
Sedgeley Ct. N&S ...... 15W-6S 27
Shenandoah Ct. E&W ...... 15W-10S 33
Shenandoah Ln. N&S ...... 15W-10S 33
Shepherd Ln. E&W ...... 15W-10S 33
Shore Ct. E&W ...... 16W-9S 33
Shore Dr. N&S ...... 16W-9S 33
Soper Av. NW&SE ...... 15W-8S 33
Sylvan Glen Ct. NE&SW ...... 16W-10S 33
Tamarack Dr. N&S ...... 15W-10S 33
Tamerton Pkwy. E&W ...... 15W-9S 33
Tori Ct. E&W ...... 15W-10S 33
Tudor Ct. E&W ...... 15W-10S 33
Tumblebrook Ct. E&W ...... 16W-10S 33
Turnberry Ct. NW&SE ...... 15W-10S 33
Turnberry Dr. NE&SW ...... 15W-10S 33
Walredon Av. N&S ...... 15W-9S 33
Wedgewood Dr. N&S ...... 15W-10S,15W-9S 33
Westmister Dr. E&W ...... 15W-10S 33
White Oak Ct. E&W ...... 15W-10S 33
Windsor Ct. N&S ...... 15W-9S 33
Woodcreek Dr. NS&EW ...... 15W-6S 27
60th Pl. E&W ...... 15W-6S 27
60th St. E&W ...... 15W-6S 27
61st Pl. E&W ...... 15W-6S 27
61st St. E&W ...... 15W-6S 27
62nd St. E&W ...... 15W-6S 27
71st St. E&W ...... 15W-7S 27
72nd St. E&W ...... 15W-8S 33
73rd St. E&W ...... 15W-8S 33
74th St. E&W ...... 15W-8S 33
75th St. E&W ...... 15W-8S 33
77th St. E&W ...... 15W-8S 33
79th St. E&W ...... 15W-8S 33
80th St. E&W ...... 15W-9S 33
83rd St. E&W ...... 15W-9S,14W-9S 33
87th St. E&W ...... 15W-9S 33
91st St. E&W ...... 15W-10S 33
94th St. E&W ...... 15W-10S 33

## Carol Stream

Adam Ln. NS&EW ...... 26W-3N 12
Adobe Ct. N&S ...... 26W-3N 12
Alabama Tr. E&W ...... 26W-3N,25W-3N 12
Alamo Ct. N&S ...... 25W-3N 12
Aleut Tr. E&W ...... 26W-3N 12
Alexandra Way NS&EW ...... 25W-1N,25W-2N 12
Alison Ln. N&S ...... 26W-3N 12
Allegheny Ct. E&W ...... 27W-3N 11
Allegro Ln. NW&SE ...... 25W-3N 12
Alton Ct. NE&SW ...... 27W-3N 11
Amber Ct. N&S ...... 24W-1N 12
Amber Ln. E&W ...... 24W-1N 12
Andrew Ln. N&S ...... 26W-3N 12
Antelope Tr. E&W ...... 26W-3N,25W-3N 12
Antigo Tr. E&W ...... 28W-4N 5
Apache Ln. E&W ...... 26W-2N 12
Appaloosa Ct. N&S ...... 26W-3N 12
Appomattox Tr. NE&SW ...... 28W-4N 5
Arapahoe Tr. E&W ...... 25W-2N 12
Arbor Dr. E&W ...... 25W-3N 12
Arlington Ct. E&W ...... 24W-1N 12
Army Trail Rd. E&W ...... 28W-4N,25W-4N 5
Arrowhead Tr. N&S ...... 26W-2N 12
Ash Ct. N&S ...... 28W-4N 5
Aspen Ct. E&W ...... 26W-4N 6
Aztec Dr. N&S ...... 26W-2N,26W-3N 12
Barton Pl. N&S ...... 27W-2N 11
Basswood Ct. E&W ...... 26W-4N 6
Bear Paw Ct. E&W ...... 27W-3N 11
Bedford Dr. N&S ...... 26W-4N 6
Beech Ct E&W ...... 26W-4N 6
Belair Ct. NE&SW ...... 25W-3N 12
Bennington Dr. N&S ...... 27W-4N 5
Berkshire Ln. E&W ...... 27W-2N 11
Big Eagle Tr. E&W ...... 27W-3N 11
Big Horn Tr. E&W ...... 28W-4N 5
Biloxie Ct. E&W ...... 27W-2N 11
Birchbark Tr. E&W ...... 28W-3N,26W-3N 11
Bison Tr. E&W ...... 28W-3N 11
Blackhawk Dr. N&S ...... 25W-2N 12
Blake Ct. N&S ...... 28W-3N 11
Bluff St. N&S ...... 25W-3N 12
Boa Tr. NE&SW ...... 28W-4N 5
Bonnie Ln. N&S ...... 25W-2N 12
Boone Dr. N&S ...... 25W-3N 12
Bowie Dr. N&S ...... 25W-3N 12
Bowstring Ct. NW&SE ...... 28W-4N 5
Bradbury Cir. N&S ...... 26W-4N 6
Brave Ct. N&S ...... 28W-4N 5
Brighton Dr. N&S ...... 27W-4N 5
Bristol Dr. N&S ...... 26W-2N 12
Brompton Ct. NE&SW ...... 23W-1N,24W-1N 12
Brookstone Dr. E&W ...... 27W-3N 11
Buckskin Ln. NE&SW ...... 27W-3N 11
Buffalo Cir. N&S ...... 27W-3N 11
Burke Dr. E&W ...... 26W-4N 6
Burning Tr. N&S ...... 27W-3N 11
Burns St. E&W ...... 24W-1N 12
Cactus Tr. N&S ...... 27W-3N 11
Camelot Ln. E&W ...... 25W-3N 12
Canterbury Ct. E&W ...... 28W-3N 11
Canterbury Dr. E&W ...... 26W-4N 6
Canyon Tr. E&W ...... 26W-3N,25W-3N 12
Caribou Tr. E&W ...... 28W-4N 5
Carleton Dr. N&S ...... 24W-1N 12
Carol Ct. N&S ...... 24W-3N 12
Carriage Dr. N&S ...... 25W-2N 12
Carson Ct. NE&SW ...... 25W-3N 12
Cedar Ct. E&W ...... 26W-4N 6
Center Av. N&S ...... 24W-3N 12
Chadsford Ct. N&S ...... 27W-2N 11
Chalet Dr. N&S ...... 26W-4N 6
Charger Ct. E&W ...... 28W-4N 5
Chattanooga Tr. E&W ...... 28W-4N 5
Cherokee Ct. E&W ...... 26W-2N 12
Chestnut Ct. E&W ...... 26W-3N 12
Cheyenne Tr. E&W ...... 26W-3N 12
Chippewa Tr. E&W ...... 26W-3N 12
Christopher Ln. NE&SW ...... 28W-3N 11
Cimarron Dr. N&S ...... 27W-3N 11
Clare Ct. E&W ...... 26W-4N 6
Clearwater Ct. N&S ...... 26W-3N,25W-3N 12
Cliff Ct. N&S ...... 26W-3N 12
Cliffview Dr. E&W ...... 27W-3N 11
Coachlite Tr. E&W ...... 25W-2N 12
Cochise Ct. E&W ...... 26W-2N 12
Cochise Pl. E&W ...... 26W-2N 12
Colorado Ct. E&W ...... 27W-2N 11
Columbia Ct. NE&SW ...... 25W-3N 12
Commanche Ct. E&W ...... 26W-3N 12
Commanche Ln. E&W ...... 26W-3N 12
Commerce Dr. N&S ...... 24W-2N 12
Commonwealth Dr. N&S ...... 25W-1N 12
Concord Ct. N&S ...... 23W-1N 12
Concord Dr. N&S ...... 27W-3N 11
Concord Ln. NS&EW ...... 23W-1N,24W-1N 12
Country Glen Ln. N&S ...... 27W-4N 5
Countryside Ln. E&W ...... 27W-4N 5
County Farm Rd. N&S ...... 27W-2N,27W-4N 11
Creekwood Ct. N&S ...... 26W-3N 12
Crystal Shore Ct. NE&SW ...... 27W-4N 5
Crystal Shore Dr. NS&EW ...... 27W-4N 5
Cumberland Ct. E&W ...... 27W-3N 11
Cypress Ln. E&W ...... 28W-3N,27W-3N 11
Dakota Ct. N&S ...... 27W-2N 11
Danbury Dr. N&S ...... 26W-2N 12
Dancing Water Ct. NE&SW ...... 25W-3N 12
Dartmouth Dr. E&W ...... 27W-3N 11
David Ln. N&S ...... 26W-3N 12
Daybreak Ln. NE&SW ...... 25W-3N 12
Dearborn Cir. N&S ...... 25W-3N 12
Deerskin Tr. E&W ...... 26W-3N 12
Delaware Tr. E&W ...... 26W-3N 12
Dodge Ct. N&S ...... 25W-3N 12
Dogwood Ln. N&S ...... 28W-3N 11
Donegal Ct. NS&EW ...... 26W-4N 6
Dorchester Dr. N&S ...... 27W-3N 11
Doris Av. E&W ...... 25W-1N 12
Dublin Ct. NW&SE ...... 26W-4N 6
Dugout Tr. E&W ...... 27W-3N 11
Eagle View Dr. N&S ...... 25W-2N 12
East Dr. N&S ...... 24W-3N 12
Easton Dr. NS&EW ...... 27W-4N 5
Easy St. E&W ...... 25W-1N 12
Eclipse Dr. NW&SE ...... 25W-3N 12
Edgebrook Ct. NE&SW ...... 25W-3N 12
Edington Ct. N&S ...... 26W-4N 6
Edington Ln. N&S ...... 26W-4N 6
El Paso Ln. E&W ...... 25W-2N 12
Elk Tr. E&W ...... 25W-3N 12
Erie Ct. E&W ...... 26W-3N 12
Esselen Ct. E&W ...... 27W-2N 11
Essex Pl. N&S ...... 26W-2N 12
Evergreen Dr. E&W ...... 28W-3N,27W-3N 11
Executive Dr. E&W ...... 24W-1N 12
Fair Oaks Rd. N&S ...... 28W-3N,28W-4N 11
Fairfield Ln. N&S ...... 23W-1N 12
Farm Glen Ln. NW&SE ...... 27W-4N 5
Fawn Ct. E&W ...... 26W-3N 12
Feather Ct. E&W ...... 26W-3N 12
Fireside Dr. N&S ...... 24W-1N 12
Flame Ct. E&W ...... 24W-1N 12
Flame Dr. N&S ...... 24W-1N 12
Flint Tr. E&W ...... 26W-3N 12
Forest Ct. E&W ...... 27W-4N 5
Forest Ln. E&W ...... 27W-4N 5
Fox Ct. NW&SE ...... 27W-3N 11
Frontage Rd. E&W ...... 26W-2N 12
Fullerton Av. E&W ...... 25W-4N,25W-3N 6
Gary Av. N&S ...... 25W-1N,25W-4N 12
Geneva Rd. E&W ...... 24W-1N 12
Georgetown Dr. N&S ...... 28W-4N 5
Glen Ct. NE&SW ...... 27W-4N 5
Glen Flora Dr. NE&SW ...... 25W-3N 12
Glenlake Dr. E&W ...... 27W-4N 5
Gloucester Cir. N&S ...... 27W-4N 5
Greenway Tr. NE&SW ...... 25W-3N 12
Gundersen Dr. E&W ...... 24W-1N 12
Gunsmoke Ct. NE&SW ...... 27W-3N 11
Hampton Ct. N&S ...... 26W-4N 6
Hampton Dr. N&S ...... 27W-3N 11
Harbor Pt. NW&SE ...... 27W-4N 5
Harwich Dr. E&W ...... 27W-4N 5
Hawk Ln. N&S ...... 27W-3N 11
Hearth Ln. NE&SW ...... 24W-1N 12
Heather Ln. N&S ...... 25W-2N 12
Hemlock Ln. N&S ...... 28W-3N 11
Heritage Dr. N&S ...... 27W-4N 5
Hiawatha Dr. NE&SW ...... 25W-2N,25W-3N 12
Hickory Ln. E&W ...... 28W-3N 11
Highridge Pass N&S ...... 27W-3N 11
Hoover Dr. N&S ...... 25W-3N 12
Hopi Ct. NW&SE ...... 25W-3N 12
Horizon Cir. NS&EW ...... 25W-3N 12
Horseshoe Ct. NE&SW ...... 27W-3N 11

| Street | Grid | Page |
|---|---|---|
| Hunter Dr. NS&EW | 26W-4N | 6 |
| Huntington Ct. N&S | 26W-4N | 6 |
| Huron Ct. N&S | 25W-3N | 12 |
| Hyannis Cir. NS&EW | 27W-4N | 5 |
| Idaho St. N&S | 25W-3N | 12 |
| Illini Dr. E&W | 26W-3N | 12 |
| Inca Blvd. E&W | 26W-3N | 12 |
| Indianwood Dr. N&S | 26W-2N | 12 |
| Iowa Ct. E&W | 25W-2N | 12 |
| Iris Av. E&W | 28N-3N | 11 |
| Ironhawk Ct. NW&SE | 25W-3N | 12 |
| Iroquois Tr. N&S | 27W-3N | 11 |
| Juniper Ct. NW&SE | 26W-3N | 12 |
| Kalamazoo Ct. N&S | 26W-3N | 12 |
| Kamiah Ct. N&S | 26W-3N | 12 |
| Kansas St. N&S | 26W-3N | 12 |
| Kehoe Blvd. E&W | 25W-2N,24W-2N | 12 |
| Kelly Dr. E&W | 27W-4N | 5 |
| Kerry Ct. NS&EW | 26W-4N | 6 |
| Kildare Ct. NS&EW | 26W-4N | 6 |
| Kilkenny Ct. NW&SE | 26W-4N | 6 |
| Kimberly Dr. N&S | 25W-2N,25W-3N | 12 |
| Klein Creek Ct. E&W | 25W-3N | 12 |
| Knollwood Dr. N&S | 27W-4N | 5 |
| Kuhn Rd. N&S | 26W-2N,26W-4N | 12 |
| Lacrosse St. N&S | 26W-3N | 12 |
| Laguna Ct. N&S | 26W-3N | 12 |
| Lakeside Ln. N&S | 27W-4N | 5 |
| Lance Ct. E&W | 28W-3N | 11 |
| Lance Ln. E&W | 28W-3N | 11 |
| Laurel Ct. E&W | 27W-3N | 11 |
| Legends Dr. E&W | 25W-3N | 12 |
| Lenox Ct. N&S | 23W-1N | 12 |
| Leslie Ct. N&S | 28W-3N | 11 |
| Lies Rd. E&W | 28W-4N,24W-3N | 5 |
| Lightning Tr. E&W | 27W-3N | 11 |
| Lilac Ct. N&S | 27W-3N | 11 |
| Lilac Ln. E&W | 28W-3N | 11 |
| Lincolnshire Ct. N&S | 28W-3N | 11 |
| Longmeadow Dr. NE&SW | 27W-3N | 11 |
| Ludington Ct. N&S | 27W-5N | 5 |
| Main Pl. N&S | 24W-1N | 12 |
| Malibu Ct. N&S | 26W-3N | 12 |
| Mantle Ln. N&S | 24W-1N | 12 |
| Maple Ridge Ct. E&W | 28W-4N | 5 |
| Matthew Ln. NS&EW | 26W-3N | 12 |
| Meadow Ln. N&S | 24W-1N | 12 |
| Medford Dr. E&W | 27W-2N | 11 |
| Merbach Dr. N&S | 26W-4N | 6 |
| Mercedes Dr. E&W | 25W-3N | 12 |
| Mesa Verde Ct. N&S | 26W-3N | 12 |
| Minnesota Cir. E&W | 27W-2N | 11 |
| Mission St. E&W | 24W-3N | 12 |
| Moccasin Ct. N&S | 26W-3N | 12 |
| Mohawk Dr. E&W | 25W-2N | 12 |
| Mohican Rd. E&W | 26W-3N | 12 |
| Morton Rd. N&S | 27W-3N | 11 |
| Mountain Glen Way E&W | 27W-3N | 11 |
| Munson Dr. E&W | 27W-3N,26W-3N | 11 |
| Nantucket Ct. N&S | 27W-4N | 5 |
| Napa St. N&S | 26W-3N | 12 |
| Narragansett Dr. N&S | 27W-4N | 5 |
| Natoma Cir. E&W | 25W-2N | 12 |
| Navajo St. N&S | 26W-3N | 12 |
| Nebraska Cir. NE&SW | 27W-2N | 11 |
| Nekoma Dr. N&S | 27W-3N | 11 |
| New Britton Rd. N&S | 28W-3N | 11 |
| New London Ct. NE&SW | 28W-3N | 11 |
| Nez Perce Ct. N&S | 26W-3N | 12 |
| Niagara St. N&S | 26W-3N | 12 |
| North Av. E&W | 26W-2N,24W-2N | 12 |
| Oak Wood Dr. NS&EW | 27W-4N | 5 |
| Ohio Ct. N&S | 26W-3N | 12 |
| Old Gary Ave. N&S | 25W-4N | 6 |
| Old Meadow Ct. N&S | 27W-3N | 11 |
| Omaha Ct. N&S | 26W-3N | 12 |
| Oneida Ct. N&S | 26W-3N | 11 |
| Oriole Tr. E&W | 28W-4N | 5 |
| Osage Cir. NW&SE | 27W-3N | 11 |
| Oswego Dr. NS&EW | 27W-3N | 11 |
| Ottawa Ct. N&S | 26W-3N | 12 |
| Overlook Ln. NS&EW | 27W-3N | 11 |
| Oxford St. N&S | 28W-4N | 5 |
| Paddock Dr. E&W | 27W-3N | 11 |
| Palomino St. N&S | 26W-3N | 12 |
| Papoose Ct. N&S | 26W-3N | 12 |
| Park Hill Tr. E&W | 25W-2N | 12 |
| Parkside Ct. NW&SE | 26W-4N | 6 |
| Parkside Dr. NE&SW | 26W-4N | 6 |
| Parkview Cir. NS&EW | 27W-4N | 5 |
| Parkview Ct. NE&SW | 27W-4N | 5 |
| Pawnee Dr. E&W | 27W-3N | 11 |
| Paxton Pl. NE&SW | 26W-2N | 12 |
| Pebble Creek Tr. E&W | 25W-3N | 12 |
| Pembrook Ct. NE&SW | 24W-1N | 12 |
| Pennsboro Ct. NW&SE | 28W-4N | 5 |
| Penny Ct. E&W | 26W-3N | 12 |
| Peoria Ct. NE&SW | 27W-3N | 11 |
| Petersburg Ct. N&S | 28W-4N | 5 |
| Pheasant Tr. NS&EW | 28W-4N | 5 |
| Plains Ct. NE&SW | 27W-3N | 11 |
| Pleasant Hill Rd. N&S | 26W-2N | 12 |
| Plymouth Ct. E&W | 27W-4N | 5 |
| Pocahontas Tr. N&S | 26W-3N | 12 |
| Pontiac Ln. N&S | 27W-3N | 11 |
| Portchester Cir. N&S | 27W-4N | 5 |
| Portsmouth Ct. NE&SW | 28W-4N | 5 |
| Potomac Ct. E&W | 28W-4N | 5 |
| Prairie Ct. NW&SE | 27W-3N | 11 |
| President St. NS&EW | 24W-1N | 12 |
| Princetown Ct. NW&SE | 27W-3N | 11 |
| Provincetown Dr. NW&SE | 27W-3N | 11 |
| Quail Run Ct. NE&SW | 25W-2N | 12 |
| Raintree Ct. E&W | 28W-3N | 11 |
| Randy Rd. E&W | 24W-2N | 12 |
| Redhill Tr. N&S | 25W-3N | 12 |
| Ridge Tr. N&S | 27W-3N | 11 |
| River Dr. NS&EW | 27W-3N | 11 |
| Rockport Dr. E&W | 27W-4N | 5 |
| Rocky Valley Way NS&EW | 27W-3N | 11 |
| Rolling Oaks Dr. E&W | 28W-3N | 11 |
| Rose Av. E&W | 28W-3N | 11 |
| Rose Ct. NE&SW | 28W-3N | 11 |
| Royal Glen Ln. NS&EW | 27W-4N | 5 |
| Rt. 64 NW&SE | 26W-2N,24W-2N | 12 |
| Saginaw Ct. N&S | 26W-3N | 12 |
| Sand Creek Dr. N&S | 27W-3N | 11 |
| Santa Fe Ct. N&S | 26W-3N | 12 |
| Saratoga Dr. NS&EW | 27W-3N | 11 |
| Sauk Ct. N&S | 26W-3N | 12 |
| Schmale Rd. N&S | 24W-1N,24W-3N | 12 |
| Seabury Cir. NS&EW | 27W-4N | 5 |
| Seminole Ln. N&S | 25W-2N | 12 |
| Seneca Dr. N&S | 27W-5N | 5 |
| Seneca Ln. E&W | 27W-3N | 11 |
| Sequoia Ct. N&S | 26W-3N | 12 |
| Shagbark Ct. NW&SE | 28W-3N | 11 |
| Shawnee Dr. E&W | 25W-2N | 12 |
| Sheffield Ct. E&W | 28W-3N | 11 |
| Shelburne Dr. NE&SW | 26W-2N | 12 |
| Shenandoah Dr. E&W | 27W-3N | 11 |
| Shining Water Dr. N&S | 27W-4N | 5 |
| Silverleaf Blvd. N&S | 26W-2N | 12 |
| Sioux Ln. N&S | 26W-2N | 12 |
| Somerset Dr. NS&EW | 27W-3N | 11 |
| Sorrel Ct. E&W | 27W-3N | 11 |
| Split Rail Dr. N&S | 27W-3N | 11 |
| Spring Valley Ct. NW&SE | 28W-4N | 5 |
| Spring Valley Dr. N&S | 28W-4N | 5 |
| Springbrook Ln. E&W | 25W-3N | 12 |
| Spur Ct. NW&SE | 27W-3N | 11 |
| St. Charles Rd. E&W | 25W-1N,24W-1N | 12 |
| St. Paul Blvd. E&W | 25W-2N,24W-2N | 12 |
| Stark Dr. E&W | 25W-4N | 6 |
| Stockbridge Dr. N&S | 27W-3N | 11 |
| Stonehenge Ct. E&W | 28W-3N | 11 |
| Stonewood Cir. N&S | 26W-4N | 6 |
| Stuart Dr. NS&EW | 26W-3N | 12 |
| Summit Pass E&W | 27W-3N | 11 |
| Sundance Ct. N&S | 27W-3N | 11 |
| Sunrise Ct. N&S | 25W-3N | 12 |
| Surrey Dr. N&S | 25W-2N | 12 |
| Sussex Rd. N&S | 28W-3N | 11 |
| Tacoma Dr. N&S | 27W-3N | 11 |
| Tahoe Ct. N&S | 27W-3N | 11 |
| Tall Oaks Dr. E&W | 28W-3N | 11 |
| Tama Ct. NW&SE | 26W-3N | 12 |
| Teton Cir. NS&EW | 27W-2N,27W-3N | 11 |
| Texas Ct. NE&SW | 27W-2N | 11 |
| Thornhill Dr. E&W | 24W-1N | 12 |
| Thunderbird Tr. E&W | 27W-2N,25W-2N | 11 |
| Timber Ridge Dr. N&S | 23W-1N | 12 |
| Tioga Ct. N&S | 26W-3N | 12 |
| Tomahawk Ct. E&W | 25W-2N | 12 |
| Tonto Ct. N&S | 26W-3N | 12 |
| Topeka Cir. N&S | 27W-3N | 11 |
| Topeka Ct. N&S | 27W-3N | 11 |
| Trailside Ct. E&W | 26W-4N | 6 |
| Tremont Ct. N&S | 27W-3N | 11 |
| Tubeway Dr. E&W | 25W-1N | 12 |
| Ute Ln. N&S | 26W-3N | 12 |
| Vale Rd. E&W | 27W-2N | 11 |
| Valleyview Dr. NS&EW | 27W-3N | 11 |
| Village Ct. E&W | 25W-2N | 12 |
| Village Dr. N&S | 25W-2N | 12 |
| Violet St. E&W | 28W-3N | 11 |
| Wabash Ct. N&S | 26W-3N | 12 |
| Waco Dr. NS&EW | 27W-3N | 11 |
| Walnut Cir. E&W | 28W-4N | 5 |
| Wampum Ct. N&S | 26W-3N | 12 |
| Waterford Ct. E&W | 26W-4N | 6 |
| Westgate Dr. N&S | 25W-1N | 12 |
| Westward Tr. NS&EW | 27W-3N | 11 |
| Wexford Ct. N&S | 26W-4N | 6 |
| Whisper Pointe N&S | 25W-3N | 12 |
| Williamstown Dr. N&S | 27W-3N | 11 |
| Willow Dr. NE&SW | 26W-3N | 12 |
| Willow Wood Dr. E&W | 24W-1N | 12 |
| Winchester Ct. NW&SE | 27W-3N | 11 |
| Winding Glen Ct. E&W | 27W-4N | 5 |
| Winding Glen Dr. NS&EW | 27W-4N | 5 |
| Windmere Ln. E&W | 26W-3N | 12 |
| Cir. | 26W-2N | 12 |
| Woodcrest Ct. NE&SW | 25W-3N | 12 |
| Woodhill Dr. E&W | 27W-4N,26W-4N | 5 |
| Yardley Dr. E&W | 26W-4N | 6 |
| Yellowstone St. N&S | 26W-3N | 12 |
| Yorkshire Ln. E&W | 28W-3N | 11 |
| Yuma Ln. NW&SE | 25W-2N | 12 |

## Clarendon Hills

| Street | Grid | Page |
|---|---|---|
| Algonquin Rd. E&W | 17W-5S | 27 |
| Ann Byrd Ct. E&W | 16W-5S | 27 |
| Arthur Av. N&S | 17W-5S | 27 |
| Barclay Ct. N&S | 16W-6S | 27 |
| Blodgett Av. N&S | 17W-5S | 27 |
| Bonnie Ln. E&W | 16W-5S | 27 |
| Burlington Av. E&W | 17W-5S | 27 |
| Chestnut Av. NE&SW | 16W-5S | 27 |
| Churchill Pl. N&S | 16W-5S | 27 |
| Coe Rd. N&S | 16W-4S | 27 |
| Colfax Av. E&W | 17W-5S | 27 |
| Columbine Dr. NS&EW | 16W-4S | 27 |
| Coolid Ct. NW&SE | 17W-5S | 27 |
| Coventry Ct. E&W | 17W-6S | 27 |
| Eastern Av. E&W | 16W-5S | 27 |
| Fairview Ct. E&W | 16W-5S | 27 |
| Forest Hills Dr. E&W | 16W-6S | 27 |
| Gilbert Av. N&S | 17W-5S | 27 |
| Golf Av. NE&SW | 16W-5S | 27 |
| Grant Av. N&S | 16W-5S | 27 |
| Hamill Ln. E&W | 16W-5S | 27 |
| Harris Av. E&W | 17W-5S,16W-5S | 27 |
| Hiawatha Dr. N&S | 17W-5S | 27 |
| Hickory St. E&W | 16W-4S | 27 |
| Hudson Av. E&W | 17W-5S | 27 |
| Indian Dr. N&S | 17W-5S | 27 |
| Iroquois Dr. N&S | 17W-5S | 27 |
| Jackson St. N&S | 16W-4S | 27 |
| Jane Ct. E&W | 16W-5S | 27 |
| Jane Rd. E&W | 17W-5S | 27 |
| Juliet Ct. E&W | 16W-5S | 27 |
| Larkspur Ln. E&W | 16W-4S | 27 |
| Maple St. E&W | 16W-4S | 27 |
| McIntosh Av. N&S | 17W-5S | 27 |
| Middaugh Rd. N&S | 16W-4S | 27 |
| Mohawk Dr. N&S | 17W-5S | 27 |
| Naperville Rd. NE&SW | 17W-4S | 27 |
| Norfolk Av. E&W | 17W-5S,16W-5S | 27 |
| Oxford Av. N&S | 17W-5S,17W-4S | 27 |
| Park Av. E&W | 17W-5S | 27 |
| Powell St. N&S | 16W-5S | 27 |
| Prospect Av. N&S | 16W-5S | 27 |
| Railroad Av. E&W | 17W-5S | 27 |
| Ridge Av. E&W | 17W-5S | 27 |
| Ridge St. E&W | 16W-5S | 27 |
| Rose Pl. NW&SE | 16W-5S | 27 |
| Ruby St. E&W | 17W-5S | 27 |
| Sheridan Av. NW&SE | 16W-5S | 27 |
| Short St. NE&SW | 16W-5S | 27 |
| Stonegate Rd. N&S | 16W-4S | 27 |
| Terrace Dr. E&W | 16W-5S | 27 |
| Tuttle Av. N&S | 17W-5S | 27 |
| Walker Av. N&S | 17W-5S,16W-5S | 27 |
| Walnut St. E&W | 16W-4S | 27 |
| Waverly Av. NE&SW | 16W-5S | 27 |
| Western Av. NE&SW | 17W-5S,16W-5S | 27 |
| Willow Creek Ct. E&W | 16W-6S | 27 |
| Woodstock Av. N&S | 17W-5S,17W-4S | 27 |

## Darien

| Street | Grid | Page |
|---|---|---|
| Adams St. N&S | 18W-9S,18W-8S | 32 |
| Adlai E. Stevenson Expwy. NE&SW | 18W-9S,17W-9S | 32 |
| Alabama Av. N&S | 17W-7S | 27 |
| Albany Ln. E&W | 17W-7S | 27 |
| Andermann Ln. E&W | 17W-8S | 33 |
| Arbor Ct. N&S | 18W-8S | 32 |
| Arrow Ln. N&S | 17W-9S | 33 |
| Ashley Ct. NE&SW | 18W-9S | 32 |
| Aylesbury Ln. E&W | 19W-8S | 32 |
| Bailey Rd. N&S | 18W-9S,18W-8S | 32 |
| Baker Ct. N&S | 17W-8S | 33 |
| Barclay Rd. N&S | 19W-8S | 32 |
| Barrymore Dr. E&W | 18W-9S | 32 |
| Bavarian Ln. E&W | 17W-7S | 27 |
| Bedford Ln. E&W | 19W-8S | 32 |
| Beechnut Ln. N&S | 17W-8S,17W-7S | 33 |
| Belair Dr. NE&SW | 17W-8S | 33 |
| Bentley Av. N&S | 17W-8S,17W-7S | 33 |
| Black Swan Ct. NW&SE | 19W-10S | 32 |
| Bobolink Ln. E&W | 17W-9S | 33 |
| Boulder Dr. E&W | 18W-9S | 32 |
| Bristlecone Ct.* NS&EW | 18W-7S | 26 |
| Brompton Dr. N&S | 19W-8S | 32 |
| Brookbank Rd. N&S | 16W-8S,16W-7S | 33 |
| Brookhaven Av. N&S | 17W-8S | 33 |
| Brunswick Rd. N&S | 19W-8S | 32 |
| Bunker Rd. N&S | 17W-8S | 33 |
| Cambridge Rd. N&S | 19W-8S | 32 |
| Capitol Dr. N&S | 16W-8S | 33 |
| Carriage Green Dr. N&S | 18W-9S | 32 |
| Carrol Ct. E&W | 18W-8S | 32 |
| Carrol Ln. E&W | 18W-8S | 32 |
| Cass Av. N&S | 18W-9S,17W-7S | 32 |
| Center Cir. E&W | 18W-8S | 32 |
| Chalet Dr. E&W | 17W-9S | 33 |
| Cherokee Dr. E&W | 17W-8S | 33 |
| Chestnut Ln. E&W | 17W-7S | 27 |
| Chippewa Ln. E&W | 17W-8S | 33 |
| Clarendon Hills Rd. N&S | 17W-8S,17W-7S | 33 |
| Clemens Rd. E&W | 18W-8S | 32 |
| Coachmans Rd. NE&SW | 18W-9S | 32 |
| Columbia La. NE&SW | 17W-7S | 27 |
| Comstock Ln. N&S | 17W-8S | 33 |
| Country Ln. E&W | 17W-8S | 33 |
| Creekside Ln. N&S | 18W-9S | 32 |
| Crest Rd. N&S | 16W-8S,16W-7S | 33 |
| Dale Rd. N&S | 16W-7S | 27 |
| Danbury Dr. N&S | 19W-8S | 32 |
| Darien Lake Dr. NS&EW | 18W-8S,18W-9S | 32 |
| Darien Ln. N&S | 17W-8S | 33 |
| Del Ct. N&S | 17W-8S | 33 |
| Dickens Cir. N&S | 18W-9S | 32 |
| Dorchester Ln. N&S | 17W-8S | 33 |
| Durham Ct. NE&SW | 18W-9S | 32 |
| Eleanor Pl. NW&SE | 16W-8S,16S-7S | 33 |
| Eleanor Rd. N&S | 16W-8S | 33 |
| Elm St. E&W | 16W-8S | 33 |
| Emerson Dr. N&S | 18W-8S | 32 |
| Evans Pl. N&S | 16W-8S | 33 |
| Evergreen Ct. N&S | 18W-9S | 32 |
| Evergreen Ln. NE&SW | 18W-9S | 32 |
| Exner Rd. N&S | 18W-8S | 32 |
| Fairview Av. N&S | 18W-8S | 32 |
| Farmingdale Dr. N&S | 17W-9S,17W-8S | 33 |
| Fox Hill Pl. E&W | 18W-9S | 32 |
| Foxtail Ct.* NS&EW | 18W-7S | 26 |
| Frontage Rd. NE&SW | 18W-10S,18W-9S | 32 |
| Gail Av. N&S | 17W-8S | 33 |
| Glen Eagles Ln. NE&SW | 19W-10S | 32 |
| Glen Ln. NS&EW | 17W-9S | 33 |
| Glenerye Rd. N&S | 18W-9S | 32 |
| Golfview Dr. E&W | 18W-9S | 32 |
| Gordon Ct. E&W | 18W-8S | 32 |
| Grant Ct. E&W | 18W-9S | 32 |
| Grant St. N&S | 18W-9S,18W-8S | 32 |
| Greenbriar Ln. E&W | 18W-9S | 32 |
| Greenvalley Rd. E&W | 19W-8S | 32 |
| Grove Dr. NS&EW | 18W-8S | 32 |
| Hayenga Ln. N&S | 17W-8S | 33 |
| Heather Ln. E&W | 18W-9S | 32 |
| Hemlock Ct. NE&SW | 18W-9S | 32 |
| Hickory Ln. E&W | 17W-8S | 33 |
| High Rd. N&S | 16W-7S,16W-8S | 27 |
| Highpoint Cir. NS&EW | 17W-9S | 33 |
| Hinsbrook Av. E&W | 17W-7S | 27 |
| Hinswood Dr. NE&SW | 17W-9S | 33 |
| Holly Av. E&W | 18W-7S,16W-7S | 26 |
| Huntington Ct. NS&EW | 19W-8S | 32 |
| Iris Rd. E&W | 16W-7S | 27 |
| Ironwood Av. E&W | 17W-7S | 27 |
| Iroquois Ln. E&W | 18W-9S | 32 |
| Janet Av. NE&SW | 17W-8S,16W-8S | 33 |
| Juniper Ln. E&W | 17W-8S | 33 |
| Kentwood Ct. N&S | 18W-10S,18W-9S | 32 |
| Kimberly Ct. NW&SE | 18W-10S | 32 |
| Knottingham Cir. NW&SE | 18W-9S,18W-8S | 32 |
| Lacebark Ct.* NE&SW | 18W-7S | 26 |
| Lake Ridge Dr. NE&SW | 19W-10S | 32 |
| Lakeview Dr. NS&EW | 18W-9S | 32 |
| Larkspur Ln.* NS&EW | 18W-7S | 26 |
| Laurel Ln. E&W | 18W-9S | 32 |
| Leonard Dr. N&S | 17W-8S,17W-7S | 33 |
| Lester Ct. N&S | 18W-9S | 32 |
| Lester Ln. N&S | 18W-8S | 32 |
| Linden Av. N&S | 17W-8S | 33 |
| Lodgepole Ct.* E&W | 18W-7S | 26 |
| Lyman Av. N&S | 19W-8S | 32 |
| Maple Ln. E&W | 17W-7S | 27 |
| Marlborough Ln. E&W | 19W-8S | 32 |
| Mayfair Ln. N&S | 17W-8S | 33 |
| McAdam Rd. E&W | 18W-7S | 26 |
| Meadowlark Ln. E&W | 17W-9S | 33 |
| Nantucket Dr. N&S | 17W-8S | 33 |
| Norman Dr. NS&EW | 18W-9S | 32 |
| Oakfern Ln.* NE&SW | 18W-7S | 26 |
| Oakley Dr. N&S | 18W-9S | 32 |
| Old Oak Pl. NE&SW | 18W-10S | 32 |
| Oriole Dr. NE&SW | 17W-9S | 33 |
| Park Av. N&S | 18W-8S | 32 |
| Parkcrest Dr. NE&SW | 17W-9S | 33 |
| Peony Pl. E&W | 16W-7S | 27 |
| Pine Bluff Ct. N&S | 18W-9S | 32 |
| Pine Cove Ct. E&W | 18W-9S | 32 |
| Pine Ct. N&S | 18W-9S | 32 |
| Pine Pkwy. N&S | 18W-8S | 32 |
| Pine View Ct. E&W | 18W-9S | 32 |
| Pinehurst Dr. NS&EW | 18W-9S | 32 |
| Plainfield Rd. NE&SW | 18W-9S,16W-8S | 32 |
| Ponderosa Ct.* N&S | 18W-7S | 26 |
| Poplar Ln. N&S | 16W-8S | 33 |
| Portsmouth Dr. NW&SE | 17W-9S | 33 |
| Red Pine Trail* E&W | 18W-7S | 26 |
| Redondo Dr. E&W | 18W-9S | 32 |
| Regency St. E&W | 18W-8S | 32 |
| Richmond Av. N&S | 17W-8S,17W-7S | 33 |
| Ridge Rd. N&S | 17W-7S | 27 |
| Ripple Ridge Cove E&W | 18W-9S,17W-9S | 32 |
| Robert Kingery Hwy. N&S | 16W-8S,16W-7S | 33 |
| Roger Rd. E&W | 16W-8S | 33 |
| Rosewood Ct. E&W | 18W-8S | 32 |
| Royal Oak Rd. NE&SW | 18W-10S | 32 |
| Royal Swan Ln. NE&SW | 19W-10S | 32 |
| Sawmill Creek Dr. N&S | 18W-9S | 32 |
| Sawyer Ct. NW&SE | 17W-9S | 33 |
| Sawyer Rd. N&S | 17W-9S,17W-8S | 33 |
| Scotch Pine Trail* N&S | 18W-7S | 26 |
| Seminole Dr. NS&EW | 17W-8S | 33 |
| Sequoia Ln. E&W | 18W-8S | 32 |

| Street | Grid | Page |
|---|---|---|
| Shelly Ct. E&W | 18W-8S | 32 |
| Sierra Ct. NW&SE | 17W-7S | 27 |
| Sleepy Hollow Ln. E&W | 18W-9S,17W-9S | 32 |
| Somerset Ln. E&W | 17W-8S | 33 |
| Spring Ct. E&W | 18W-9S,17W-9S | 32 |
| Stevens St. N&S | 18W-8S | 32 |
| Stewart Dr. E&W | 18W-9S | 32 |
| Stratford Pl. N&S | 17W-8S | 33 |
| Summit Rd. N&S | 18W-8S | 32 |
| Sunrise Av. N&S | 16W-8S | 33 |
| Surrey Dr. N&S | 19W-8S | 32 |
| Sussex Creek N&S | 17W-8S | 33 |
| Sweetbriar Ln. N&S | 18W-7S | 26 |
| Sweetwater Ct. E&W | 18W-9S,17W-9S | 32 |
| Tamarack Dr. E&W | 17W-8S | 33 |
| Tennessee Dr. N&S | 17W-8S,17W-7S | 33 |
| Thistlewood Ct. NS&EW | 18W-9S | 32 |
| Timber Ln. E&W | 17W-8S | 33 |
| Torrey Pines Ct.* NE&SW | 18W-7S | 26 |
| Troutilly Ln.* NS&EW | 18W-7S | 26 |
| Village Ct. E&W | 17W-8S | 33 |
| Wakefield Dr. N&S | 19W-8S | 32 |
| Walden Ln. N&S | 18W-8S | 32 |
| Walnut Dr. E&W | 17W-8S | 33 |
| Westminister Ct. NS&EW | 18W-9S | 32 |
| White Pine Trail* NE&SW | 18W-7S | 26 |
| Whitter Dr. N&S | 18W-8S | 32 |
| Wilcox Av. N&S | 18W-7S | 26 |
| Wildwood Ct. N&S | 18W-8S | 32 |
| Wildwood Ln. NW&SE | 18W-9S | 32 |
| Willow Creek Ln. E&W | 18W-9S | 32 |
| Willow Ln. E&W | 17W-8S | 33 |
| Wilmette Av. N&S | 17W-9S,17W-7S | 33 |
| Winterberry Ln. E&W | 18W-9S | 32 |
| Wintergreen Ln.* N&S | 18W-7S | 26 |
| Woodbine Ln.* N&S | 18W-7S | 26 |
| Woodrush Ln.* E&W | 18W-7S | 26 |
| Woodview Ct. E&W | 18W-9S | 32 |
| 63rd St. E&W | 17W-7S | 27 |
| 64th St. E&W | 17W-7S | 27 |
| 65th St. E&W | 17W-7S | 27 |
| 67th St. E&W | 17W-7S,17W-6S | 27 |
| 68th St. E&W | 16W-7S | 27 |
| 69th St. E&W | 17W-7S,16W-7S | 27 |
| 71st St. E&W | 17W-7S | 27 |
| 72nd St. E&W | 17W-8S | 33 |
| 73rd St. E&W | 18W-8S,17W-8S | 32 |
| 74th St. E&W | 16W-8S | 33 |
| 75th St. E&W | 18W-8S,17W-8S | 32 |
| 77th St. E&W | 18W-8S | 32 |
| 79th St. E&W | 17W-8S,17W-7S | 33 |

## Downers Grove

| Street | Grid | Page |
|---|---|---|
| Abbey Dr. E&W | 19W-8S | 32 |
| Acorn Av. E&W | 20W-3S | 20 |
| Acorn Dr. NE&SW | 19W-3S | 20 |
| Acorn Dr. N&S | 20W-3S | 20 |
| Alamance Pl. E&W | 20W-7S | 26 |
| Aldrich Pl. E&W | 21W-7S | 25 |
| Almond Ct. N&S | 20W-3S | 20 |
| Andrus Av. E&W | 20W-7S | 26 |
| Applegate Av. E&W | 19W-8S | 32 |
| Arbor Circle NS&EW | 21W-4S | 25 |
| Arquilla Dr. E&W | 21W-6S | 25 |
| Ashbury Av. E&W | 19W-8S | 32 |
| Aspen Av. N&S | 21W-6S | 25 |
| Aubrey Ter. N&S | 20W-6S | 26 |
| Austin St. E&W | 19W-5S | 26 |
| Baimbridge Dr. N&S | 18W-8S | 32 |
| Baker Pl. NW&SE | 20W-8S | 32 |
| Banburry Rd. N&S | 21W-6S | 25 |
| Barclay Ct. N&S | 20W-7S | 26 |
| Barrett St. N&S | 20W-7S | 26 |
| Bateman St. NS&EW | 20W-8S | 32 |
| Bates Pl. NE&SW | 20W-7S | 26 |
| Baybury Rd. N&S | 19W-8S | 32 |
| Belden Av. NW&SE | 19W-5S | 26 |
| Belle Aire Dr. N&S | 20W-4S,20W-3S | 26 |
| Belmont Av. N&S | 21W-6S,21W-5S | 25 |
| Bending Oaks Ct. E&W | 20W-5S | 26 |
| Bending Oaks Pl. N&S | 20W-5S | 26 |
| Bentley Pl. E&W | 19W-7S | 26 |
| Benton Av. N&S | 19W-5S | 26 |
| Binder Rd. N&S | 20W-8S | 32 |
| Birch Av. E&W | 19W-5S | 26 |
| Birchwood Pl. E&W | 21W-3S | 19 |
| Black Oak Dr. E&W | 19W-3S | 20 |
| Blackburn Av. N&S | 19W-8S,19W-7S | 32 |
| Blackburn Ct. NE&SW | 19W-8S | 32 |
| Blackburn Pl. N&S | 19W-7S | 26 |
| Blackstone Ct. NE&SW | 19W-7S | 26 |
| Blackstone Dr. NW&SE | 19W-7S | 26 |
| Blanchard St. E&W | 20W-6S,19W-6S | 26 |
| Blodgett Av. N&S | 19W-7S,19W-5S | 26 |
| Bolson Dr. E&W | 20W-7S | 26 |
| Bonnie Brae Dr. E&W | 19W-7S | 26 |
| Borman Pl. E&W | 20W-8S | 32 |
| Bradley Ct. NS&EW | 20W-7S | 26 |
| Braemoor Dr. E&W | 19W-3S | 20 |
| Breasted E&W | 20W-7S | 26 |
| Brentwood Pl.* E&W | 19W-4S | 26 |
| Briargate Dr. N&S | 19W-7S | 26 |
| Brighton St. NS&EW | 21W-6S | 25 |
| Brook Dr. E&W | 20W-2S | 20 |
| Brookbank Rd. N&S | 20W-6S,20W-5S | 26 |
| Brookwood Dr. E&W | 20W-7S | 26 |
| Brunette Dr. E&W | 20W-7S | 26 |
| Bryan Pl. N&S | 19W-5S | 26 |
| Buckingham Pl. E&W | 19W-7S | 26 |
| Buckthorn Ln. N&S | 20W-3S | 20 |
| Bunker Hill Cir. N&S | 20W-7S | 26 |
| Bunning Dr. E&W | 19W-6S | 26 |
| Burlington Av. E&W | 20W-5S,18W-5S | 26 |
| Bush N&S | 20W-7S | 26 |
| Butterfield Rd. NE&SW | 20W-2S | 20 |
| Camden Ct. N&S | 20W-7S | 26 |
| Camden Pl. NW&SE | 20W-7S | 26 |
| Camden Rd. NS&EW | 20W-8S,20W-7S | 32 |
| Candlewood Dr. E&W | 20W-3S,19W-3S | 20 |
| Carol St. E&W | 20W-4S | 26 |
| Carpenter St. N&S | 19W-7S,19W-5S | 26 |
| Center Av. N&S | 20W-4S | 26 |
| Centre Circle E&W | 20W-2S | 20 |
| Challen Ct. E&W | 21W-5S | 25 |
| Chase Av. N&S | 21W-6S,21W-5S | 25 |
| Chicago Av. E&W | 21W-4S,19W-4S | 25 |
| Churchill Pl. N&S | 19W-7S | 26 |
| Claremont Ct. NE&SW | 19W-7S | 26 |
| Claremont Dr. E&W | 19W-8S,19W-7S | 32 |
| Clayton Ct. N&S | 19W-7S | 26 |
| Clyde Av. E&W | 19W-6S | 26 |
| Commerce Dr. N&S | 21W-4S | 25 |
| Concord Ct. NE&SW | 20W-7S | 26 |
| Concord Dr. E&W | 20W-7S | 26 |
| Concord Pl. N&S | 20W-7S | 26 |
| Coralberry Ln. E&W | 20W-3S | 20 |
| Cornell Av. N&S | 20W-5S | 26 |
| Country Creek Way NE&SW | 19W-8S | 32 |
| Creekside Rd. N&S | 19W-7S | 26 |
| Creekwood Ct. NE&SW | 19W-3S | 20 |
| Crescent Dr. NW&SE | 19W-7S | 26 |
| Cumnor Rd. N&S | 18W-5S,18W-4S | 26 |
| Curtiss St. E&W | 21W-5S,19W-5S | 25 |
| Davis St. E&W | 19W-4S | 26 |
| Dawn Pl. E&W | 19W-4S | 26 |
| De Bolt Av. N&S | 19W-5S | 26 |
| De Witt Ln. N&S | 20W-5S | 26 |
| Dearborn Pkwy. N&S | 19W-6S | 26 |
| Deerpath Ln. N&S | 18W-6S | 26 |
| Devereaux Rd. NE&SW | 20W-8S | 32 |
| Dexter Rd. NW&SE | 20W-8S,20W-7S | 32 |
| Dickson Av. E&W | 20W-7S | 26 |
| Douglas Rd. N&S | 19W-5S,19W-4S | 26 |
| Downers Dr. N&S | 20W-4S,20W-2S | 26 |
| Drew St. NE&SW | 20W-3S | 20 |
| Drove Av. E&W | 20W-4S | 26 |
| Duchess Ct. N&S | 20W-3S | 20 |
| Dunham Rd. N&S | 20W-8S,19W-8S | 32 |
| Durand Ct. E&W | 21W-6S | 25 |
| Durand Dr. NS&EW | 21W-6S | 25 |
| Earlston Rd. N&S | 19W-4S | 26 |
| East-West Tollway NE&SW | 21W-4S,20W-3S | 25 |
| Eldon Pl. N&S | 19W-6S | 26 |
| Elizabeth Ln. E&W | 18W-8S | 32 |
| Elm St. N&S | 19W-5S,19W-4S | 26 |
| Elmore Av. E&W | 21W-5S,20W-5S | 25 |
| Elmwood Av. NW&SE | 19W-5S | 26 |
| Esplanade Dr. E&W | 20W-2S | 20 |
| Essex Pl. E&W | 20W-7S | 26 |
| Fairhaven Ct. N&S | 20W-6S | 26 |
| Fairmount Av. N&S | 19W-8S,19W-5S | 32 |
| Fairview Av. N&S | 19W-8S,19W-4S | 32 |
| Fairview West N&S | 19W-8S | 32 |
| Farley Pl. E&W | 19W-5S | 26 |
| Farrah Ct. NW&SE | 20W-5S | 26 |
| Finley Rd. N&S | 21W-4S,20W-2S | 25 |
| Florence Av. N&S | 18W-8S,18W-4S | 32 |
| Forest Av. N&S | 19W-5S,19W-4S | 26 |
| Foster Pl. N&S | 19W-7S,19W-8S | 26 |
| Franklin St. E&W | 20W-5S,19W-5S | 26 |
| Frontage Rd. E&W | 20W-2S,19W-2S | 20 |
| George St. E&W | 20W-6S | 26 |
| Gierz St. E&W | 19W-5S,18W-5S | 26 |
| Gilbert Av. E&W | 20W-5S | 26 |
| Glen Av. E&W | 20W-4S | 26 |
| Glendenning Rd. N&S | 19W-4S | 26 |
| Glenview Av. N&S | 21W-5S | 25 |
| Golden Bell Ct. E&W | 20W-3S | 20 |
| Goldenbell Ct. E&W | 20W-3S | 20 |
| Grace Ct. E&W | 20W-7S | 26 |
| Graham Pl. E&W | 20W-8S | 32 |
| Grand Av. N&S | 19W-8S,19W-5S | 32 |
| Grand Ct. NE&SW | 19W-8S | 32 |
| Grant St. E&W | 20W-4S,18W-4S | 26 |
| Granville Av. N&S | 21W-5S | 25 |
| Gregory Pl. E&W | 20W-3S | 20 |
| Grove St. E&W | 19W-5S | 26 |
| Haddow Av. E&W | 21W-5S | 25 |
| Hall Pl. E&W | 20W-8S | 32 |
| Harmarc Pl. NW&SE | 18W-6S | 26 |
| Hartford Rd. N&S | 19W-8S | 32 |
| Hastings Av. E&W | 21W-6S | 25 |
| Hatch Pl. E&W | 20W-8S | 32 |
| Hatch St. E&W | 20W-8S | 32 |
| Hathaway Ln. N&S | 20W-7S | 26 |
| Havens Ct. E&W | 19W-4S | 26 |
| Hawkins Av. E&W | 20W-8S | 32 |
| Hawthorne Ln. NE&SW | 20W-5S | 26 |
| Herbert St. E&W | 20W-4S,18W-4S | 26 |
| Hickory Ct. N&S | 20W-3S | 20 |
| Hickory Tr. NW&SE | 19W-3S | 20 |
| Hickory Trail E&W | 19W-3S | 20 |
| Highland Av. N&S | 19W-5S,19W-3S | 26 |
| Highland Ct. E&W | 19W-4S | 26 |
| Hill St. E&W | 19W-5S | 26 |
| Hillcrest Ct. NS&EW | 20W-6S | 26 |
| Hillcrest Dr. N&S | 20W-7S | 26 |
| Hillcrest Rd. NS&EW | 20W-6S | 26 |
| Hitchcock Av. E&W | 21W-5S | 25 |
| Hitchcock St. E&W | 21W-5S,20W-5S | 25 |
| Hobart Av. NS&EW | 19W-8S,19W-7S | 32 |
| Holland Pl. NE&SW | 20W-3S | 20 |
| Holly Ct. N&S | 20W-3S | 20 |
| Hughes Av. E&W | 20W-8S | 32 |
| Indianapolis Av. E&W | 19W-4S | 26 |
| Interstate 88 E&W | 20W-3S | 20 |
| Inverness Rd. E&W | 21W-5S | 25 |
| Jacqueline Dr. NS&EW | 20W-5S | 26 |
| Janes Av. N&S | 21W-6S,21W-5S | 25 |
| Janet St. E&W | 20W-4S | 26 |
| Jay Dr. E&W | 19W-7S | 26 |
| Jefferson Av. E&W | 20W-6S | 26 |
| Katrine Av. N&S | 21W-5S | 25 |
| Kelly Pl. N&S | 20W-8S | 32 |
| Kensington Pl. NS&EW | 20W-7S | 26 |
| Kenyon St. E&W | 19W-6S | 26 |
| Kidwell Rd. N&S | 20W-8S | 32 |
| Knottingham Ln. N&S | 18W-8S | 32 |
| Lacey Rd. N&S | 20W-4S,20W-3S | 26 |
| Lake Av. E&W | 19W-4S | 26 |
| Lamb Ct. N&S | 20W-7S | 26 |
| Lancaster Av. E&W | 19W-7S | 26 |
| Lancaster Pl. N&S | 19W-7S | 26 |
| Lane Pl. N&S | 19W-6S,19W-5S | 26 |
| Laurel Ct. N&S | 20W-3S | 20 |
| Lee Av. N&S | 20W-6S,20W-4S | 26 |
| Lee St. N&S | 20W-4S | 26 |
| Lemont Rd. N&S | 20W-8S,19W-8S | 32 |
| Leonard Av. N&S | 21W-6S | 25 |
| Lexington Ln. E&W | 20W-7S | 26 |
| Lincoln Av. E&W | 19W-4S,18W-4S | 26 |
| Lincoln St. E&W | 20W-4S,19W-4S | 26 |
| Linden Pl. N&S | 19W-5S | 26 |
| Lindley St. N&S | 19W-4S | 26 |
| Lindwald NE&SW | 20W-5S | 26 |
| Linscott Av. N&S | 20W-5S,20W-4S | 26 |
| Longmeadow Rd. N&S | 18W-4S | 26 |
| Loomes NW&SE | 20W-7S | 26 |
| Lyman Av. N&S | 19W-8S,19W-5S | 32 |
| Mackie Pl. NW&SE | 19W-5S | 26 |
| Main Blvd. E&W | 20W-2S | 20 |
| Main St. N&S | 19W-7S,19W-4S | 26 |
| Maplewood Pl. NW&SE | 20W-5S,19W-5S | 26 |
| Marie Dr. E&W | 18W-8S | 32 |
| Meade Rd. N&S | 20W-7S | 26 |
| Meadow Crest Ct. NW&SE | 19W-7S | 26 |
| Meadow Crest Dr. N&S | 19W-7S | 26 |
| Meadow Ln. NE&SW | 20W-5S | 26 |
| Middaugh Av. N&S | 20W-6S,20W-4S | 26 |
| Midhurst Rd. NW&SE | 21W-7S | 25 |
| Mistwood Ct. N&S | 19W-3S | 20 |
| Mistwood Ln. E&W | 19W-3S | 20 |
| Mistwood Pl. NE&SW | 20W-3S | 20 |
| Monmouth Pl. E&W | 20W-7S | 26 |
| Montgomery Av. N&S | 20W-5S | 26 |
| Morton Av. N&S | 20W-4S | 26 |
| Nash St. N&S | 20W-7S | 26 |
| Newport Rd. E&W | 20W-7S | 26 |
| Norfolk St. E&W | 20W-7S | 26 |
| Northcott Av. N&S | 20W-5S,20W-4S | 26 |
| Northgate Way N&S | 19W-8S | 32 |
| Oak Grove Dr. N&S | 20W-2S | 20 |
| Oak Grove Rd. N&S | 20W-2S | 20 |
| Oak Hill Ct. E&W | 20W-3S | 20 |
| Oak Hill Ct. NW&SE | 20W-3S | 20 |
| Oak Hill Rd. E&W | 20W-3S,19W-3S | 20 |
| Oakwood Av. N&S | 20W-5S | 26 |
| Ogden Av. E&W | 20W-4S,18W-4S | 26 |
| Old Orchard Av. E&W | 19W-8S | 32 |
| Oneil Rd. N&S | 19W-8S | 32 |
| Opus Pl. N&S | 20W-3S | 20 |
| Orchard Pl. N&S | 19W-8S | 32 |
| Osage Av. N&S | 19W-8S,19W-6S | 32 |
| Otis Av. E&W | 19W-4S | 26 |
| Otto N&S | 20W-7S | 26 |
| Oxford St. NW&SE | 19W-7S | 26 |
| Oxnard Ct. NW&SE | 20W-7S | 26 |
| Oxnard Dr. NW&SE | 21W-7S,20W-7S | 25 |
| Palmer St. NW&SE | 20W-7S | 26 |
| Park Av. N&S | 19W-6S,19W-5S | 26 |
| Parker Av. E&W | 19W-7S | 26 |
| Parkview Dr. NE&SW | 19W-7S | 26 |
| Parrish Ct. E&W | 20W-3S | 20 |
| Penner Ave. N&S | 20W-7S | 26 |
| Pershing Av. N&S | 21W-5S,21W-4S | 25 |
| Pinewood Dr. N&S | 19W-8S | 32 |
| Pinewood Pl. E&W | 19W-8S | 32 |
| Pipers Way NE&SW | 19W-8S | 32 |
| Plum Ct. NS&EW | 20W-3S | 20 |
| Plymouth Ct. N&S | 20W-6S | 26 |
| Plymouth Pl. N&S | 20W-6S | 26 |
| Plymouth Rd. N&S | 20W-7S | 26 |
| Plymouth St. N&S | 20W-6S | 26 |
| Pomeroy Ct. N&S | 20W-3S | 20 |
| Pomeroy Rd. N&S | 20W-3S | 20 |
| Powell Ct. E&W | 20W-7S | 26 |
| Powell Pl. NE&SW | 20W-8S | 32 |
| Powell St. N&S | 20W-8S,20W-7S | 32 |
| Prairie Av. E&W | 21W-5S,18W-5S | 25 |
| Prentiss Ct. N&S | 20W-7S | 26 |
| Prentiss Dr. E&W | 21W-7S,20W-7S | 25 |
| Prideham St. N&S | 20W-7S | 26 |
| Prince St. N&S | 19W-5S,19W-4S | 26 |
| Prospect Av. N&S | 19W-5S | 26 |
| Puffer Rd. N&S | 21W-7S,21W-5S | 25 |
| Queens Ct. N&S | 18W-8S | 32 |
| Quince Ct. NW&SE | 19W-3S | 20 |
| Railroad St. NW&SE | 22W-5S,21W-5S | 25 |
| Randall St. NE&SW | 19W-5S | 26 |
| Red Bud Ct. E&W | 20W-3S | 20 |
| Red Silver Ct. E&W | 20W-3S | 20 |
| Revere Rd. NW&SE | 20W-7S | 26 |
| Richards Av. E&W | 20W-8S | 32 |
| Ridgeview St. E&W | 19W-8S | 32 |
| Ridgewood Circle NS&EW | 20W-6S | 26 |
| Rob Roy Pl. NW&SE | 19W-8S | 32 |
| Robey Av. E&W | 19W-7S | 26 |
| Roe Ct. NE&SW | 19W-8S | 32 |
| Rogers St. E&W | 19W-5S | 26 |
| Rohrer Dr. N&S | 18W-8S | 32 |
| Rosewood Ln. N&S | 19W-3S | 20 |
| Roslyn Rd. N&S | 18W-4S | 26 |
| Ross Ct. NE&SW | 20W-5S | 26 |
| Saratoga Av. N&S | 20W-7S,20W-3S | 26 |
| Saylor St. E&W | 20W-7S | 26 |
| Scheldrup Dr. N&S | 20W-2S | 20 |
| Seeley Av. N&S | 20W-5S,20W-4S | 26 |
| Selig NW&SE | 20W-8S | 32 |
| Shady Ln. E&W | 18W-4S | 26 |
| Sheldon Av. NE&SW | 18W-5S | 26 |
| Sheridan Pl. E&W | 19W-4S | 26 |
| Sherman St. E&W | 19W-4S | 26 |
| Sherwood Av. N&S | 19W-4S | 26 |
| Sherwood Ct. E&W | 18W-8S | 32 |
| Snowberry Ct. NW&SE | 20W-3S | 20 |
| Snowberry Ln. NE&SW | 20W-3S | 20 |
| Springside Av. N&S | 20W-8S,20W-7S | 32 |
| Springside Pl. E&W | 20W-7S | 26 |
| Stair St. NW&SE | 20W-7S | 26 |
| Stanford Av. E&W | 19W-2S | 32 |
| Stanley Av. N&S | 19W-5S | 26 |
| Sterling Rd. N&S | 19W-4S | 26 |
| Stockley Rd. E&W | 19W-8S | 32 |
| Stonewall Av. N&S | 20W-7S,20W-4S | 26 |
| Stratford Ln. E&W | 19W-6S | 26 |
| Sturbridge Pl. E&W | 20W-7S | 26 |
| Summit St. E&W | 19W-5S | 26 |
| Tamarack Dr. E&W | 21W-6S | 25 |
| Taylor St. E&W | 20W-7S | 26 |
| Terrace Dr. N&S | 20W-7S | 26 |
| Terrace Pl. N&S | 20W-7S | 26 |
| Thatcher Rd. NS&EW | 22W-5S | 25 |
| Thornwood Dr. E&W | 20W-6S | 26 |
| Ticonderoga Pl. N&S | 20W-8S | 32 |
| Ticonderoga Rd. N&S | 20W-7S | 26 |
| Ticonderoga St. NS&EW | 20W-8S | 32 |
| Tomicek Rd. N&S | 22W-5S | 25 |
| Tower Ct. NE&SW | 19W-8S | 32 |
| Tower Rd. E&W | 18W-4S | 26 |
| Trent Rd. N&S | 19W-8S | 32 |
| Turvey Ct. N&S | 20W-5S | 26 |
| Turvey Rd. NE&SW | 20W-5S | 26 |
| Valley Forge Pl. E&W | 20W-7S | 26 |
| Valleyview Dr. E&W | 20W-7S,19W-7S | 26 |
| Venard Rd. NE&SW | 20W-4S,20W-3S | 26 |
| Victor St. N&S | 18W-5S | 26 |
| Virginia St. E&W | 20W-4S | 26 |
| Wall Pl. N&S | 19W-6S | 26 |
| Wallbank Av. N&S | 20W-5S | 26 |
| Wallen Pl. E&W | 20W-6S | 26 |
| Walnut Av. N&S | 22W-6S,22W-5S | 25 |
| Wanda Pl. N&S | 19W-6S | 26 |
| Warren Av. E&W | 20W-5S,19W-5S | 26 |
| Washington St. N&S | 19W-7S,19W-4S | 26 |
| Waterfall Pl. NE&SW | 19W-7S | 26 |
| Weatherbee Av. E&W | 19W-7S | 26 |
| Weatherbee Pl. N&S | 19W-7S | 26 |
| Webster Pl. NW&SE | 19W-6S | 26 |
| Webster St. N&S | 19W-6S | 26 |
| Webster St. N&S | 19W-7S,19W-6S | 26 |
| Wellington Pl. NS&EW | 20W-7S | 26 |
| Wells St. N&S | 20W-7S | 26 |
| Westend Rd. N&S | 18W-4S | 26 |
| Westfield Dr. NE&SW | 21W-7S | 25 |
| Whiffen Pl. N&S | 19W-5S | 26 |
| White Pl. E&W | 20W-8S | 32 |
| Whitefawn Rd. E&W | 18W-6S | 26 |
| Widden Av. E&W | 20W-7S | 26 |
| Wilcox Av. N&S | 18W-6S,18W-5S | 26 |
| Willard Pl. NE&SW | 20W-8S | 32 |
| Williams St. N&S | 18W-8S,18W-4S | 32 |
| Wilson Av. N&S | 21W-4S | 25 |
| Wilson St. E&W | 19W-5S | 26 |
| Windsor Ct. E&W | 20W-7S | 26 |
| Winthrop Ct. NW&SE | 19W-8S | 32 |
| Winward Way NE&SW | 19W-8S | 32 |

| Street | Grid | Page |
|---|---|---|
| Wisconsin St. E&W | 21W-5S | 25 |
| Wolf Pl. N&S | 19W-7S | 26 |
| Wood Av. E&W | 20W-3S | 20 |
| Wood Creek Dr. N&S | 21W-3S,21W-2S | 19 |
| Woodcreek Dr. NS&EW | 21W-2S,20W-3S | 19 |
| Woodward Av. N&S | 21W-5S,21W-4S | 25 |
| York Rd. NE&SW | 19W-8S | 32 |
| 2nd St. E&W | 18W-5S | 26 |
| 4th St. E&W | 18W-5S | 26 |
| 5th St. E&W | 18W-5S | 26 |
| 6th St. E&W | 18W-5S | 26 |
| 7th St. E&W | 18W-5S | 26 |
| 8th St. E&W | 18W-5S | 26 |
| 31st St. E&W | 19W-2S | 20 |
| 35th St. E&W | 20W-3S,19W-3S | 20 |
| 36th St. E&W | 19W-3S | 20 |
| 39th Ct. NW&SE | 20W-4S | 26 |
| 39th St. E&W | 20W-3S,18W-3S | 20 |
| 39th St. E&W | 20W-3S | 20 |
| 40th Pl. E&W | 18W-4S | 26 |
| 40th St. E&W | 20W-4S,19W-4S | 26 |
| 41st St. E&W | 20W-4S,18W-4S | 26 |
| 55th Pl. E&W | 18W-6S | 26 |
| 55th St. E&W | 20W-5S,19W-5S | 26 |
| 56th Ct. NE&SW | 18W-6S | 26 |
| 56th St. E&W | 18W-6S | 26 |
| 59th Pl. E&W | 19W-6S | 26 |
| 59th St. E&W | 20W-6S,19W-6S | 26 |
| 60th Pl. E&W | 20W-6S,19W-6S | 26 |
| 60th St. E&W | 21W-6S,19W-6S | 25 |
| 61st St. E&W | 19W-6S | 26 |
| 62nd Ct. E&W | 19W-6S | 26 |
| 62nd Pl. NE&SW | 19W-6S | 26 |
| 62nd St. E&W | 21W-6S,19W-6S | 25 |
| 63rd St. E&W | 20W-7S,19W-7S | 26 |
| 64th St. E&W | 21W-7S | 25 |
| 65th St. E&W | 19W-7S | 26 |
| 67th Pl. E&W | 20W-7S | 26 |
| 67th St. E&W | 20W-7S,19W-7S | 26 |
| 68th Pl. E&W | 20W-7S | 26 |
| 68th St. E&W | 20W-7S,19W-7S | 26 |
| 71st St. E&W | 20W-8S,19W-7S | 32 |
| 71st Ter. NW&SE | 20W-8S | 32 |
| 72nd Ct. E&W | 19W-8S | 32 |
| 72nd St. E&W | 19W-8S | 32 |
| 73rd St. E&W | 19W-8S | 32 |
| 74th St. E&W | 19W-8S | 32 |
| 75th St. E&W | 20W-8S,19W-8S | 32 |


## Downers Grove Township


| Street | Grid | Page |
|---|---|---|
| Adams St. N&S | 18W-8S,18W-4S | 32 |
| Adelia St. E&W | 19W-7S | 26 |
| Ailsworth Ct. E&W | 20W-9S | 32 |
| Ailsworth Dr. N&S | 20W-9S | 32 |
| Alabama Av. N&S | 17W-9S,17W-6S | 33 |
| Alden Ln. N&S | 20W-9S | 32 |
| Allison Ct. N&S | 16W-9S | 33 |
| Andrus Rd. N&S | 19W-10S | 32 |
| Argonne Ridge Rd. N&S | 17W-10S | 33 |
| Barrett St. NW&SE | 20W-11S | 34 |
| Bay Rum Ct. NW&SE | 15W-9S | 33 |
| Belair Ct. E&W | 18W-8S | 32 |
| Beller Ct. N&S | 20W-9S | 32 |
| Beller Dr. E&W | 20W-9S | 32 |
| Berkshire Ct. E&W | 19W-9S | 32 |
| Birnam Tr. NS&EW | 17W-10S | 33 |
| Blancherd St. E&W | 20W-6S | 26 |
| Blodgett Av. N&S | 19W-9S | 32 |
| Bluff Rd. E&W | 19W-12S,16W-11S | 34 |
| Bonnie Brae Ln. NE&SW | 16W-9S | 33 |
| Boundary Rd. NE&SW | 20W-6S | 26 |
| Brewer Rd. E&W | 20W-9S | 32 |
| Brook Ridge Rd. N&S | 19W-9S | 32 |
| Brook View Ct. NS&EW | 16W-6S | 27 |
| Brookbank Rd. N&S | 16W-9S | 33 |
| Burgess Pl. E&W | 20W-9S | 32 |
| Caimbridge Ct. NE&SW | 19W-9S | 32 |
| Camder Dr. E&W | 20W-10S | 32 |
| Carl Ct. N&S | 19W-9S | 32 |
| Carol St. E&W | 19W-7S | 26 |
| Carpenter St. N&S | 19W-12S,19W-7S | 34 |
| Cass Av. N&S | 17W-11S,17W-8S | 35 |
| Central Av. E&W | 19W-9S,16W-9S | 32 |
| Central Dr. N&S | 17W-11S | 35 |
| Cessna Ln. N&S | 19W-9S | 32 |
| Charles Ct. N&S | 19W-9S | 32 |
| Circle Av. NE&SW | 16W-9S | 33 |
| Claremont Dr. E&W | 18W-7S | 26 |
| Clarendon Hills Rd. N&S | 17W-10S,17W-6S | 33 |
| Cobb Dr. E&W | 20W-10S | 32 |
| Cobb St. E&W | 20W-10S | 32 |
| Concord Pl. NW&SE | 17W-9S | 33 |
| Cramer Ln. NW&SE | 20W-9S | 32 |
| Cumnor Rd. N&S | 18W-9S,18W-6S | 32 |
| Darien Club Dr. E&W | 18W-7S | 26 |
| Deerpath Ln. E&W | 19W-12S | 34 |
| Dixon Ct. N&S | 20W-9S | 32 |
| Don Ct. E&W | 19W-9S | 32 |
| Downers Dr. N&S | 20W-11S,20W-6S | 34 |
| Drew Av. N&S | 15W-10S | 33 |
| Drover Ct. N&S | 20W-9S | 32 |
| Drover Ln. E&W | 20W-9S | 32 |
| Drover Rd. N&S | 20W-9S | 32 |
| Dunham Dr. N&S | 20W-10S | 32 |
| Dunham Rd. N&S | 20W-11S,20W-9S | 34 |
| Dystrup Av. E&W | 19W-12S | 34 |
| E. Hampshire Ln. N&S | 17W-10S | 33 |
| Earl Ct. E&W | 17W-9S | 33 |
| Eastwood Cutoff E&W | 17W-11S | 35 |
| Eastwood Dr. E&W | 18W-11S,17W-11S | 34 |
| Echo Ln. N&S | 16W-10S | 33 |
| Edgewood Dr. (Pvt.) N&S | 20W-9S | 32 |
| Elizabeth Dr. E&W | 20W-10S | 32 |
| Elm Ct. NE&SW | 17W-9S | 33 |
| Elm St. NE&SW | 17W-9S | 33 |
| Fairmount Av. N&S | 19W-9S | 32 |
| Fern St. NE&SW | 17W-9S,16W-9S | 33 |
| Florence Av. N&S | 18W-9S,18W-7S | 32 |
| Freud Rd. NE&SW | 18W-11S,17W-11S | 34 |
| Front St. NS&EW | 17W-11S,17W-10S | 35 |
| Frontage Rd. NE&SW | 18W-9S,16W-9S | 32 |
| Gilbert Ct. NE&SW | 20W-9S | 32 |
| Godair Cir. N&S | 16W-6S | 27 |
| Graceland St. N&S | 19W-9S | 32 |
| Grandview Ln. NW&SE | 20W-9S | 32 |
| Grandview Pl. N&S | 20W-9S | 32 |
| Grant Av. E&W | 18W-4S | 26 |
| Grant St. N&S | 18W-8S,18W-4S | 32 |
| Harvest Ln. N&S | 20W-9S | 32 |
| Harvest Pl. E&W | 20W-9S | 32 |
| Harvey Rd. N&S | 16W-9S | 33 |
| Havens Ct. E&W | 20W-10S | 32 |
| Helen Ct. N&S | 19W-9S | 32 |
| Helix Rd. E&W | 19W-12S | 34 |
| Highland Av. N&S | 19W-9S | 32 |
| Highland Rd. N&S | 16W-9S | 33 |
| Hill Rd. N&S | 19W-12S | 34 |
| Hillcrest Dr. N&S | 20W-9S | 32 |
| Hillcrest Ln. E&W | 19W-12S | 34 |
| Hillside Ct. NE&SW | 20W-9S | 32 |
| Hillside Ln. E&W | 17W-10S,16W-10S | 33 |
| Honeysuckle Rose Ln. E&W | 16W-10S | 33 |
| Hyacinth Dr. NE&SW | 16W-10S | 33 |
| Inner Circle E&W | 18W-11S | 34 |
| Ivy Ln. N&S | 16W-10S | 33 |
| Jackson Av. N&S | 16W-11S,16W-10S | 35 |
| Jackson St. N&S | 16W-6S | 27 |
| Jaime Ln. N&S | 16W-10S | 33 |
| Jeans Rd. NE&SW | 16W-11S | 35 |
| Jefferson St. E&W | 20W-6S | 26 |
| Joliet Rd. NE&SW | 17W-9S,16W-9S | 33 |
| Kearney Rd. N&S | 19W-11S,19W-10S | 34 |
| Kingery Quarter N&S | 16W-10S | 33 |
| Kings Ct. NW&SE | 17W-9S | 33 |
| Kraml Dr. NS&EW | 15W-9S | 33 |
| Lake Dr. NE&SW | 16W-9S | 33 |
| Lakeside Dr. E&W | 19W-9S,16W-6S | 32 |
| Landsfield Av. N&S | 19W-9S | 32 |
| Landsfield Ct. NE&SW | 19W-9S | 32 |
| Landsfield Pl. E&W | 19W-9S | 32 |
| Lemont Rd. N&S | 19W-12S,19W-9S | 34 |
| Leonard Dr. N&S | 17W-10S,17W-9S | 33 |
| Lilac Ln. NE&SW | 16W-10S | 33 |
| Lincoln St. N&S | 18W-4S | 26 |
| Linda Ln. E&W | 19W-9S | 32 |
| London Av. N&S | 20W-10S | 32 |
| Lorraine Dr. N&S | 17W-10S,17W-9S | 33 |
| Main St. N&S | 19W-9S,19W-7S | 32 |
| Mark Ln. E&W | 19W-9S | 32 |
| Mary Beth Ct. E&W | 16W-9S | 33 |
| Meadow Ct. E&W | 20W-9S,16W-9S | 32 |
| Meadow Lawn Av. E&W | 19W-7S | 26 |
| Meadow Ln. E&W | 20W-11S,20W-9S | 34 |
| Meridan Rd. N&S | 18W-11S | 34 |
| Middaugh Av. NW&SE | 20W-11S | 34 |
| Millbrook Dr. E&W | 19W-9S | 32 |
| Mockingbird Ln. E&W | 16W-10S | 33 |
| Nantucket Dr. N&S | 17W-9S | 33 |
| Nielsen Ln. E&W | 17W-10S | 33 |
| Northgate Rd. N&S | 18W-10S | 32 |
| Oakhill Ct. N&S | 16W-10S | 33 |
| Oakwood Av. N&S | 20W-11S | 34 |
| Old Bluff Rd. E&W | 18W-11S,17W-11S | 34 |
| Oneil Dr. N&S | 16W-10S | 33 |
| Orchard Rd. N&S | 20W-12S,20W-11S | 34 |
| Oxford St. E&W | 19W-7S | 26 |
| Palisades Rd. N&S | 16W-11S,16W-10S | 35 |
| Parkview Dr. N&S | 20W-9S | 32 |
| Peters Ct. E&W | 20W-10S | 32 |
| Peters Dr. E&W | 20W-10S | 32 |
| Pine Crest Ct. N&S | 16W-6S | 27 |
| Pitcher Dr. E&W | 20W-9S | 32 |
| Pleasant Dale Dr. E&W | 20W-11S | 34 |
| Plymouth St. N&S | 20W-6S | 26 |
| Portsmouth Ct. N&S | 17W-9S | 33 |
| Portsmouth Dr. E&W | 17W-9S | 33 |
| Quincy Ct. N&S | 16W-7S | 27 |
| Quincy St. N&S | 16W-9S,16W-6S | 33 |
| Railroad Dr. N&S | 17W-11S | 35 |
| Roanoke Ct. NE&SW | 15W-9S | 33 |
| Rock Rd. E&W | 18W-11S | 34 |
| Rogers Ct. E&W | 18W-8S | 32 |
| Rooke Ct. E&W | 20W-10S | 32 |
| Rosehill Ct. NE&SW | 18W-9S | 32 |
| Rosehill Ln. N&S | 18W-9S | 32 |
| Rutgers Ct. N&S | 20W-10S | 32 |
| Rutgers Dr. E&W | 20W-10S | 32 |
| Ruth Dr. N&S | 19W-10S,19W-9S | 32 |
| Ruth Lake Ct. N&S | 16W-6S | 27 |
| Scheel Dr. E&W | 17W-10S | 33 |
| Seeley Av. N&S | 20W-11S | 34 |
| Shiloh Dr. E&W | 15W-9S | 33 |
| Skyline Dr. N&S | 16W-10S | 33 |
| Spring Green Dr. E&W | 20W-9S | 32 |
| Springside Av. N&S | 20W-6S | 26 |
| St. Patrick Rd. E&W | 18W-11S | 34 |
| Stewart Dr. E&W | 20W-9S | 32 |
| Stonewall Av. N&S | 20W-6S | 26 |
| Stough St. N&S | 16W-6S | 27 |
| Suffield Dr. N&S | 20W-10S | 32 |
| Summer Ct. NW&SE | 18W-9S | 32 |
| Sunrise Av. N&S | 16W-6S | 27 |
| Sunset Rd. N&S | 16W-9S | 33 |
| Sutton Pl. E&W | 17W-9S | 33 |
| Tanbark Ct. NE&SW | 19W-9S | 32 |
| Tennessee Av. N&S | 17W-9S,17W-6S | 33 |
| Terry Tr. E&W | 17W-10S | 33 |
| Thames Av. N&S | 20W-10S | 32 |
| Therese Ct. E&W | 16W-9S | 33 |
| Thurlow St. N&S | 16W-10S,16W-6S | 33 |
| Timber Trails E&W | 20W-10S | 32 |
| Tolios Dr. N&S | 19W-12S | 34 |
| Vail Ct. NE&SW | 20W-10S | 32 |
| Valleyview Dr. E&W | 16W-10S | 33 |
| Village Rd. N&S | 16W-9S | 33 |
| Vine St. N&S | 15W-10S | 33 |
| Virginia Av. N&S | 17W-6S | 27 |
| Wallace Dr. N&S | 20W-10S | 32 |
| Waltham Pl. E&W | 17W-9S | 33 |
| Washington St. N&S | 19W-9S,18W-4S | 32 |
| Water Tower Rd. E&W | 18W-11S | 34 |
| Webster St. N&S | 19W-8S | 32 |
| Western Av. N&S | 17W-9S,17W-6S | 33 |
| Westgate Rd. E&W | 19W-10S,18W-11S | 32 |
| Westminster Dr. E&W | 20W-10S | 32 |
| White Deer Dr. N&S | 18W-10S | 32 |
| William Dr. N&S | 16W-9S | 33 |
| Willow Ln. E&W | 18W-8S | 32 |
| Winter Cir. NS&EW | 19W-9S | 32 |
| Wood Vale Dr. N&S | 20W-9S | 32 |
| Woodcreek Ct. N&S | 19W-9S | 32 |
| Woodcrest Dr. E&W | 20W-10S,19W-10S | 32 |
| Woodglen Ln. NW&SE | 19W-9S | 32 |
| York Ln. NW&SE | 20W-10S | 32 |
| 1st St. E&W | 20W-11S,19W-11S | 34 |
| 3rd St. E&W | 20W-11S | 34 |
| 9th St. E&W | 19W-12S | 34 |
| 40th St. E&W | 18W-4S | 26 |
| 41st St. E&W | 18W-4S | 26 |
| 55th Pl. E&W | 20W-6S | 26 |
| 56th Pl. E&W | 16W-6S | 27 |
| 56th St. E&W | 17W-6S,16W-6S | 27 |
| 57th St. E&W | 17W-6S,16W-6S | 27 |
| 58th Pl. E&W | 16W-6S | 27 |
| 58th St. E&W | 17W-6S,16W-6S | 27 |
| 59th St. E&W | 20W-6S,17W-6S | 26 |
| 61st St. E&W | 20W-6S,17W-6S | 26 |
| 62nd St. E&W | 20W-6S | 26 |
| 64th St. E&W | 16W-7S | 27 |
| 67th Ct. E&W | 18W-7S | 26 |
| 72nd St. E&W | 18W-8S,15W-8S | 32 |
| 73rd Pl. E&W | 18W-8S | 32 |
| 73rd St. E&W | 15W-8S | 33 |
| 74th St. E&W | 15W-8S | 33 |
| 75th St. E&W | 15W-8S | 33 |
| 79th Pl. E&W | 19W-9S,17W-9S | 32 |
| 80th St. E&W | 19W-9S,16W-9S | 32 |
| 81st St. E&W | 19W-9S,15W-9S | 32 |
| 82nd St. E&W | 15W-9S | 33 |
| 83rd Ct. E&W | 19W-9S | 32 |
| 83rd St. E&W | 20W-9S,15W-9S | 32 |
| 85th Ct. E&W | 19W-9S | 32 |
| 86th Pl. E&W | 19W-9S | 32 |
| 86th St. E&W | 19W-9S | 32 |
| 87th St. E&W | 20W-9S,16W-9S | 32 |
| 89th Pl. E&W | 16W-10S | 33 |
| 89th St. E&W | 16W-10S,15W-10S | 33 |
| 90th St. E&W | 16W-10S,15W-10S | 33 |
| 91st St. E&W | 18W-10S,14W-10S | 32 |
| 92nd St. E&W | 19W-10S | 32 |
| 93rd Pl. E&W | 16W-10S | 33 |
| 94th Pl. E&W | 16W-10S | 33 |
| 94th St. E&W | 18W-10S,16W-10S | 32 |
| 95th Pl. E&W | 16W-11S | 35 |
| 97th St. E&W | 20W-11S,16W-11S | 34 |
| 98th Pl. NE&SW | 20W-11S | 34 |
| 99th St. E&W | 20W-11S,19W-11S | 34 |


## Elk Grove Village*
**(Also see Cook County)**


| Street | Grid | Page |
|---|---|---|
| American Ln. N&S | 16W-7N | 9 |
| Brickvale Av. N&S | 16W-7N | 9 |
| Carl Blvd. N&S | 17W-7N | 9 |
| Central Av. N&S | 17W-7N | 9 |
| Delta Ln. N&S | 16W-7N | 9 |
| Devon Av. E&W | 17W-7N,16W-7N | 9 |
| Eastern Av. E&W | 16W-7N | 9 |
| Katherine Way N&S | 17W-7N | 9 |
| Kirk St. E&W | 17W-7N | 9 |
| Lively Blvd. N&S | 17W-7N | 9 |
| Mark St. E&W | 17W-7N | 9 |
| Pan Am Blvd. E&W | 16W-7N | 9 |
| Robert Kingery Hwy. N&S | 16W-7N | 9 |
| Thorndale Av. E&W | 17W-7N | 9 |
| United Ln. N&S | 16W-7N | 9 |
| York Rd. N&S | 16W-7N | 9 |


## Elmhurst


| Street | Grid | Page |
|---|---|---|
| Aberdeen Ct. N&S | 15W-0S | 21 |
| Adams Ct. N&S | 15W-0S | 21 |
| Adams St. E&W | 16W-0S,15W-0S | 21 |
| Addison Av. N&S | 16W-2N,16W-3N | 15 |
| Adelaide St. E&W | 16W-1N | 15 |
| Adele Av. N&S | 15W-2N,15W-3N | 15 |
| Adelia St. E&W | 15W-1N | 15 |
| Adell Pl. N&S | 16W-1N | 15 |
| Alben Av. N&S | 16W-1N | 15 |
| Albert St. E&W | 17W-1N | 14 |
| Alexander Blvd. E&W | 17W-1N,16W-1N | 14 |
| Allison St. NW&SE | 15W-0N | 15 |
| Alma Av. NW&SE | 16W-1N | 15 |
| Apple Tree Ct. N&S | 16W-0S | 21 |
| Arbor Dr. NE&SW | 16W-0S | 21 |
| Argyle N&S | 16W-0N | 15 |
| Arlington Av. N&S | 15W-0N,15W-1N | 15 |
| Armitage Av. E&W | 17W-2N,15W-2N | 14 |
| Arthur St. E&W | 16W-1N | 15 |
| Aspen Tree Ct. E&W | 16W-0S | 21 |
| Atwater Av. NE&SW | 15W-1N | 15 |
| Atwood Ct. E&W | 15W-1N | 15 |
| Avery St. NW&SE | 16W-0S | 21 |
| Avon Rd. N&S | 15W-1N | 15 |
| Babcock Av. E&W | 17W-2N | 14 |
| Barclay Ct. N&S | 15W-0N | 15 |
| Belden Av. E&W | 17W-2N,15W-2N | 14 |
| Benton Av. NW&SE | 15W-0N | 15 |
| Benton Ct. E&W | 15W-0N | 15 |
| Berkley Av. N&S | 16W-0S,16W-1N | 21 |
| Berteau Av. N&S | 15W-1N | 15 |
| Betsy Ware Av. E&W | 16W-3N | 15 |
| Beverly Av. NE&SW | 16W-0S | 21 |
| Birch Tree Ct. E&W | 16W-0S | 21 |
| Bonnie Brae Av. N&S | 17W-1N | 14 |
| Boyd Av. N&S | 15W-1N | 15 |
| Bryan St. N&S | 16W-0S,16W-0N | 21 |
| Bucholz Dr. NE&SW | 15W-1N | 15 |
| Butterfield Rd. NE&SW | 16W-0S,15W-0S | 21 |
| Cadwell Av. N&S | 15W-0S | 21 |
| Cambridge Av. N&S | 15W-0S,15W-0N | 21 |
| Carol Ln. E&W | 16W-3N | 15 |
| Caroline Av. N&S | 15W-1N | 15 |
| Cayuga Av. E&W | 15W-0N | 15 |
| Cedar Av. N&S | 15W-0S,15W-0N | 21 |
| Cedar Tree Ct. E&W | 16W-0S | 21 |
| Chandler Av. N&S | 15W-1N | 15 |
| Chatham Av. N&S | 15W-0S,15W-0N | 21 |
| Cherry St. N&S | 15W-0N | 15 |
| Church St. E&W | 16W-1N,15W-1N | 15 |
| Clara Pl. N&S | 15W-1N | 15 |
| Claremont St. E&W | 16W-1N | 15 |
| Clinton Av. N&S | 15W-1N | 15 |
| Colfax Av. N&S | 15W-0S,15W-0N | 21 |
| Colombia Av. E&W | 15W-2N | 15 |
| Commonwealth Ln. NW&SE | 16W-0S | 21 |
| Comstock Av. E&W | 17W-2N | 14 |
| Coolidge St. E&W | 16W-0N | 15 |
| Cottage Hill Av. N&S | 16W-0N,16W-1N | 15 |
| Coventry Ln. N&S | 16W-0N | 15 |
| Crescent Av. E&W | 16W-0N,15W-0N | 15 |
| Crescent St. E&W | 16W-0N | 15 |
| Crest View Av. E&W | 15W-2N | 15 |
| Crockett Av. E&W | 17W-2N,16W-2N | 14 |
| Diversey Av. E&W | 16W-3N | 15 |
| Division St. N&S | 15W-0N | 15 |
| Dorchester Av. NW&SE | 16W-0S | 21 |
| East Ct. E&W | 15W-1N | 15 |
| Eastland St. N&S | 15W-2N,15W-3N | 15 |
| Eaton Ct. N&S | 16W-0N | 15 |
| Edgewood Av. N&S | 15W-0N | 15 |
| Eggleston Av. E&W | 16W-0N | 15 |
| Elizabeth St. E&W | 17W-1N | 14 |
| Elm Av. N&S | 16W-1N,16W-2N | 15 |
| Elm Park Av. E&W | 17W-1N,16W-1N | 14 |
| Elm Tree Ln. N&S | 15W-1N | 15 |
| Elmcrest Av. NW&SE | 15W-2N | 15 |
| Elmhurst Av. E&W | 15W-1N | 15 |
| Elmwood Ter. E&W | 16W-1N | 15 |
| Emery Ln. N&S | 16W-2N | 15 |
| Emroy Av. N&S | 15W-2N,15W-3N | 15 |
| Euclid Av. N&S | 16W-0S,16W-0N | 21 |
| Evergreen Av. N&S | 16W-1N,16W-2N | 15 |
| Evergreen Ln. E&W | 16W-3N | 15 |
| Fair Av. N&S | 15W-0N,15W-1N | 15 |
| Fairfield Av. N&S | 16W-0S,16W-1N | 21 |
| Fay Av. E&W | 17W-2N | 14 |
| Fellows Ct. NW&SE | 16W-1N | 15 |
| Fern Av. N&S | 15W-0S,15W-0N | 21 |
| Fern Ct. N&S | 15W-0N | 15 |
| Ferndale Av. N&S | 17W-2N | 14 |
| First St. E&W | 17W-1N,15W-1N | 14 |
| Forest Av. E&W | 15W-1N | 15 |
| Fremont Av. E&W | 16W-2N,15W-2N | 15 |

DU PAGE COUNTY 45


| Street | Grid | Page |
|---|---|---|
| Fullerton Av. E&W | 16W-3N,15W-3N | 15 |
| Garfield Av. E&W | 16W-0N | 15 |
| Geneva Av. N&S | 15W-1N,15W-3N | 15 |
| Glade Av. N&S | 17W-1N | 14 |
| Gladys Av. E&W | 17W-2N,15W-2N | 14 |
| Glenview Av. N&S | 17W-1N,17W-2N | 14 |
| Grace Av. N&S | 16W-1N | 15 |
| Grand Av. NE&SW | 17W-3N,15W-3N | 14 |
| Grandview St. E&W | 16W-0N | 15 |
| Grantley Av. E&W | 16W-2N,15W-2N | 15 |
| Hagans Av. N&S | 16W-1N | 15 |
| Hahn St. E&W | 16W-1N | 15 |
| Hale St. E&W | 15W-0S | 21 |
| Hampshire Av. N&S | 15W-0N,15W-1N | 15 |
| Harbour Ter. E&W | 16W-1N | 15 |
| Harding St. E&W | 16W-0N | 15 |
| Harrison St. E&W | 16W-0S,15W-0S | 21 |
| Haven Rd. N&S | 15W-1N | 15 |
| Hawthorne Av. N&S | 16W-0N,16W-2N | 15 |
| High St. N&S | 15W-0S | 21 |
| Highland Av. N&S | 16W-1N,16W-2N | 15 |
| Highview Av. N&S | 16W-2N | 15 |
| Hill Av. N&S | 15W-0N | 15 |
| Hillcrest Av. N&S | 15W-0S,15W-0N | 21 |
| Hillside Av. N&S | 16W-0S,16W-0N | 21 |
| Howard Av. N&S | 15W-2N,15W-3N | 15 |
| Huntington Ln. NE&SW | 15W-1N | 15 |
| Ida Ln. N&S | 16W-2N | 15 |
| Illinois St. N&S | 15W-1N | 15 |
| Indiana St. N&S | 15W-1N,15W-3N | 15 |
| Industrial Dr. NS&EW | 16W-2N,16W-3N | 15 |
| Interstate 290 NW&SE | 17W-3N,15W-0N | 14 |
| Jackson St. E&W | 16W-0S,15W-0S | 21 |
| Junior Ter. N&S | 17W-2N | 14 |
| Kearsage Av. N&S | 15W-0S,15W-0N | 21 |
| Kenilworth Av. N&S | 15W-0N,15W-3N | 15 |
| Kenmore Av. N&S | 15W-1N | 15 |
| Kent Av. N&S | 15W-0S | 21 |
| Killarny Ct. N&S | 15W-0N | 15 |
| Kimbell Av. NW&SE | 16W-2N | 15 |
| Kirk Av. N&S | 15W-0S | 21 |
| Lake St. NW&SE | 17W-3N,16W-2N | 14 |
| Lamont Rd. E&W | 17W-3N | 14 |
| Larch Av. N&S | 16W-1N,16W-3N | 15 |
| Laurel Av. NW&SE | 15W-0N | 15 |
| Lawndale Av. N&S | 15W-1N | 15 |
| Linden Av. N&S | 15W-0S,15W-1N | 21 |
| Linden Dr. N&S | 15W-0S | 21 |
| Locust Tree Ct. NW&SE | 16W-0S | 21 |
| Lombard St. N&S | 15W-2N,15W-3N | 15 |
| Lorraine Av. E&W | 17W-2N | 14 |
| Madison Ct. N&S | 15W-0S | 21 |
| Madison St. E&W | 16W-0N,15W-0N | 15 |
| Manchester Ln. N&S | 16W-0N | 15 |
| Maple Av. N&S | 16W-1N,16W-2N | 15 |
| Maple Tree Ct. NW&SE | 16W-0S | 21 |
| Margaret Pl. E&W | 16W-1N | 15 |
| Marion St. E&W | 15W-1N | 15 |
| Mary Ct. NW&SE | 17W-3N | 14 |
| May St. E&W | 15W-0N | 15 |
| Mckinley Av. E&W | 16W-0N | 15 |
| Meister Av. NW&SE | 16W-0N | 15 |
| Melrose Av. NE&SW | 15W-1N,15W-2N | 15 |
| Michigan St. N&S | 15W-1N,15W-3N | 15 |
| Mitchell Av. N&S | 16W-0S,16W-0N | 21 |
| Monroe St. E&W | 16W-0S,15W-0S | 21 |
| Monterey Av. N&S | 17W-1N | 14 |
| Montrose Av. E&W | 16W-0N | 15 |
| Myrtle Av. E&W | 16W-1N,16W-2N | 15 |
| Niagara Av. E&W | 15W-0N | 15 |
| North Av. E&W | 17W-2N,15W-2N | 14 |
| North End Av. E&W | 15W-3N | 15 |
| Oak St. N&S | 16W-1N,16W-2N | 15 |
| Oak Tree Ct. N&S | 16W-0S | 21 |
| Oakland Grove Av. N&S | 17W-1N | 14 |
| Oaklawn Av. N&S | 16W-1N,16W-3N | 15 |

| Street | Grid | Page |
|---|---|---|
| Olive St. E&W | 16W-0N | 15 |
| Oneida Av. E&W | 15W-0N | 15 |
| Orchard St. E&W | 15W-0N | 15 |
| Oriole Av. E&W | 15W-0N | 15 |
| Park Av. E&W | 16W-1N,15W-1N | 15 |
| Park Manor Ct. E&W | 15W-0S | 21 |
| Parker St. N&S | 15W-2N,15W-3N | 15 |
| Parkside Av. N&S | 16W-0S,16W-0N | 21 |
| Parkview Av. NS&EW | 15W-0N | 15 |
| Pick Av. N&S | 17W-1N | 14 |
| Pine St. N&S | 15W-1N | 15 |
| Pine Tree Ct. E&W | 16W-0S | 21 |
| Poplar Av. N&S | 15W-0S,15W-1N | 21 |
| Poplar Tree Ct. NW&SE | 16W-0S | 21 |
| Prairie Av. N&S | 15W-0N | 15 |
| Prairie Path Ln. E&W | 16W-0N | 15 |
| Prospect Av. N&S | 16W-0S,16W-1N | 21 |
| Quincy St. E&W | 15W-0S | 21 |
| Randolph St. NW&SE | 16W-0N | 15 |
| Rex Blvd. N&S | 16W-0N,16W-1N | 15 |
| Richard Av. N&S | 15W-1N | 15 |
| Ridge Av. E&W | 15W-0N | 15 |
| Ridgeland Av. N&S | 16W-2N | 15 |
| River Glen Av. N&S | 17W-2N | 14 |
| Riverside Dr. N&S | 17W-0S,17W-0N | 21 |
| Robert Kingery Expwy. N&S | 17W-0S,17W-3N | 21 |
| Robert T. Palmer Dr. N&S | 15W-1N | 15 |
| Roosevelt Rd. E&W | 16W-0S | 21 |
| Rose St. E&W | 17W-1N | 14 |
| Rt. 38 E&W | 16W-0S | 21 |
| Rt. 64 E&W | 17W-2N,15W-2N | 14 |
| Rt. 83 N&S | 17W-0S,17W-3N | 21 |
| Saylor Av. N&S | 16W-0S,16W-0N | 21 |
| Schiller St. E&W | 15W-1N | 15 |
| Scott St. N&S | 17W-0N | 14 |
| Seminole Av. NW&SE | 16W-0N | 15 |
| Shady Ln. N&S | 17W-2N | 14 |
| Sherman Av. E&W | 15W-0N | 15 |
| Sidney Av. E&W | 17W-2N | 14 |
| Smith Av. N&S | 16W-1N | 15 |
| South St. E&W | 15W-0N | 15 |
| Spangler Av. E&W | 16W-3N | 15 |
| Spring Rd. N&S | 16W-0S,16W-0N | 21 |
| St. Charles Rd. E&W | 17W-1N,15W-1N | 14 |
| Stratford Av. N&S | 15W-0S,15W-0N | 21 |
| Stuart Av. N&S | 15W-0S | 21 |
| Stuart Ct. N&S | 15W-0N | 15 |
| Sturges Pkwy. N&S | 16W-1N | 15 |
| Sunnyside Av. N&S | 16W-0N,16W-1N | 15 |
| Sunrise Rd. E&W | 17W-3N | 14 |
| Sunset Av. NE&SW | 16W-0S | 21 |
| Surf St. E&W | 17W-0N | 14 |
| Swain Av. N&S | 16W-0S,16W-0N | 21 |
| Thomas St. NW&SE | 16W-2N | 15 |
| Thornhill Ln. N&S | 16W-0N | 15 |
| U.S. Route 20 NW&SE | 17W-3N,16W-2N | 14 |
| Utley Rd. E&W | 16W-1N | 15 |
| Vallette St. E&W | 16W-0N,15W-0N | 15 |
| Van Auken St. N&S | 15W-2N,15W-3N | 15 |
| Van Buren St. E&W | 16W-0S,15W-OS | 21 |
| Verret St. NW&SE | 16W-0S | 21 |
| Virginia Ln. N&S | 15W-3N | 15 |
| Virginia St. E&W | 16W-1N | 15 |
| Walnut St. N&S | 16W-1N,16W-2N | 15 |
| Walter St. E&W | 16W-1N | 15 |
| Washington St. N&S | 16W-0S,16W-0N | 21 |
| Webster Av. E&W | 15W-0N | 15 |
| West Av. N&S | 16W-0S | 21 |
| West Av. N&S | 17W-0N,17W-2N | 14 |
| Willow Rd. N&S | 15W-1N,15W-3N | 15 |
| Willow Tree Ct. E&W | 16W-0S | 21 |
| Wilson St. E&W | 16W-0N,15W-0N | 15 |
| Windsor Dr. NW&SE | 16W-0N | 15 |
| Winthrop Av. E&W | 16W-1N | 15 |
| Wrightwood Av. E&W | 16W-3N,15W-3N | 15 |
| York Rd. N&S | 15W-0S,16W-3N | 21 |
| Yorkfield Av. NE&SW | 15W-0S | 21 |

| Street | Grid | Page |
|---|---|---|
| 2nd St. E&W | 17W-1N,15W-1N | 14 |
| 3rd St. E&W | 17W-1N,15W-1N | 14 |


## Glen Ellyn


| Street | Grid | Page |
|---|---|---|
| Abbey Dr. E&W | 21W-1S | 19 |
| Abbotsford Ct. N&S | 21W-0S | 19 |
| Adler Ln. E&W | 23W-1S | 18 |
| Annandale Av. NW&SE | 22W-0N | 13 |
| Anthony St. E&W | 23W-0N,22W-0N | 12 |
| Apollo Av. NE&SW | 22W-0N | 13 |
| Appian Way E&W | 22W-0N | 13 |
| Arbor Ct. E&W | 22W-0S | 19 |
| Arlington Av. E&W | 22W-0S | 19 |
| Ash Ln. E&W | 23W-1S | 18 |
| Baker Ct. E&W | 21W-1S | 19 |
| Bloomfield Ln. E&W | 23W-1S | 18 |
| Brandon Av. N&S | 23W-0S | 18 |
| Bremer Ct. E&W | 22W-0S | 19 |
| Briar St. N&S | 21W-0S | 19 |
| Brighton Ln. E&W | 21W-0S | 19 |
| Bryant Av. N&S | 22W-0S,22W-0N | 19 |
| Carleton Av. N&S | 22W-0S,22W-0N | 19 |
| Carlisle Ct. E&W | 22W-1S | 19 |
| Carolyn Dr. N&S | 22W-0N | 13 |
| Center St. E&W | 23W-0N | 12 |
| Chancel Cir. NW&SE | 21W-1S | 19 |
| Chapel Ct., N. E&W | 21W-1S | 19 |
| Chapel Ct., S. E&W | 21W-1S | 19 |
| Cheltenham Dr. E&W | 20W-0S | 20 |
| Chesterfield Av. E&W | 23W-0S | 18 |
| Chidester Av. E&W | 22W-0N | 13 |
| Clifton Av. E&W | 21W-0N | 13 |
| Colcord Pl. N&S | 21W-0N | 13 |
| College Hill Av. NE&SW | 23W-0S,21W-0N | 19 |
| College St. E&W | 22W-2S | 19 |
| Coolidge Av. E&W | 21W-1S | 19 |
| Cottage Av. E&W | 23W-0N,22W-0N | 12 |
| Country Club Ln. NW&SE | 21W-0N | 13 |
| Cranston Ct. N&S | 22W-0S | 19 |
| Crescent Blvd. NE&SW | 22W-0N,21W-0N | 13 |
| Crescent Ct. E&W | 22W-0N | 13 |
| Crescent Dr. N&S | 21W-0N | 13 |
| Crest Rd. N&S | 22W-0S | 19 |
| Cumnor Av. N&S | 21W-0S | 19 |
| Davis Av. E&W | 23W-1S | 19 |
| Davis Ter. N&S | 23W-0N | 12 |
| Dawes Av. E&W | 22W-1S | 19 |
| Dawn Av. N&S | 23W-0N | 12 |
| Deer Ct. NE&SW | 22W-0N | 13 |
| Deer Path Rd. N&S | 22W-0N | 13 |
| Deicke Dr. E&W | 23W-0S | 18 |
| Dorset Av. E&W | 22W-0S | 19 |
| Dorset Ct. N&S | 22W-0S | 19 |
| Dorset Pl. E&W | 22W-0S | 19 |
| DuPage Blvd. E&W | 22W-0S,21W-0S | 19 |
| Duane St. E&W | 23W-0N,21W-0N | 12 |
| Duane Ter. NE&SW | 22W-0N | 13 |
| East Rd. N&S | 22W-0S | 19 |
| Edgewood Dr. E&W | 22W-0N | 13 |
| Ellyn Av. NE&SW | 22W-0N | 13 |
| Ellyn Ct. E&W | 22W-0N | 13 |
| Ellynwood Dr. NE&SW | 21W-0N | 13 |
| Elm St. E&W | 23W-1N,22W-1N | 12 |
| Essex Ct. NE&SW | 22W-0N | 13 |
| Essex Rd. NW&SE | 22W-0N | 13 |
| Euclid Av. N&S | 22W-0N | 13 |
| Evergreen Av. N&S | 23W-0N,23W-1N | 12 |
| Exmoor Av. N&S | 22W-0S | 19 |
| Fairview Av. E&W | 23W-0S,22W-0S | 18 |
| Fairview Av. E&W | 23W-0S,21W-0S | 19 |
| Farnsworth Ct. E&W | 23W-1S | 18 |
| Finley Rd. N&S | 20W-0S | 20 |
| Fir Ct. E&W | 23W-1S | 18 |
| Fir Ln. N&S | 23W-1S | 18 |
| Forest Av. N&S | 22W-0S,22W-0N | 19 |
| Geneva Rd. E&W | 23W-0N,23W-1N | 12 |
| Glen Ellyn Pl. E&W | 22W-0N | 13 |
| Glen Haven Ln. E&W | 22W-1S | 19 |
| Glen Oak Av. E&W | 21W-0N | 13 |
| Glenbard Rd. E&W | 22W-1S,21W-1S | 19 |
| Glenwood Av. N&S | 22W-0S | 19 |
| Grand Av. NE&SW | 22W-0N | 13 |
| Grandview Av. N&S | 21W-0S | 19 |
| Greenbriar Rd. N&S | 22W-1S | 19 |
| Greenfield Av. E&W | 23W-0S,22W-0S | 18 |
| Greenwood Ct. N&S | 22W-0S | 19 |

| Street | Grid | Page |
|---|---|---|
| Grove Av. N&S | 21W-0S | 19 |
| Harding Av. E&W | 22W-1S | 19 |
| Hawthorne St. E&W | 23W-0N,22W-0N | 12 |
| Heather Ln. E&W | 21W-0S | 19 |
| Hedge Ct. N&S | 22W-1S | 19 |
| Hickory Rd. N&S | 21W-0N | 13 |
| High Rd. E&W | 22W-0S | 19 |
| Highland Av. N&S | 22W-0N | 13 |
| Highview Av. E&W | 22W-0S,21W-0S | 19 |
| Hill Av. E&W | 23W-0S,21W-0N | 18 |
| Hillcrest Av. N&S | 23W-0S | 18 |
| Hillside Av. E&W | 23W-0N,21W-0N | 12 |
| Illinois St. E&W | 23W-0S | 18 |
| Indian Dr. N&S | 21W-0S | 19 |
| Joyce Ct. N&S | 22W-0S | 19 |
| Kenilworth Av. N&S | 23W-0S,23W-0N | 18 |
| Kenilworth Ct. E&W | 23W-0N | 12 |
| Lake Rd. NW&SE | 22W-0N | 13 |
| Lakeview Ter. E&W | 22W-0S | 19 |
| Lambert Av. N&S | 23W-0S | 18 |
| Lambert Rd. N&S | 23W-1S | 18 |
| Larch Ln. E&W | 23W-1S | 18 |
| Lawrence Av. N&S | 23W-0N | 12 |
| Lee St. NW&SE | 22W-0N | 13 |
| Lenox Rd. NE&SW | 22W-0N,22W-1N | 13 |
| Lincoln Av. N&S | 22W-0N | 13 |
| Linden St. E&W | 23W-0N,22W-0N | 12 |
| Lombard Av. E&W | 21W-0S | 19 |
| Londonberry Ln. E&W | 21W-0S | 19 |
| Longfellow Av. N&S | 21W-0N | 13 |
| Lorraine Rd. NE&SW | 23W-0S | 18 |
| Lowden Av. E&W | 22W-1S | 19 |
| Lowell Av. N&S | 21W-0S,21W-0N | 19 |
| Maiden Ln. E&W | 22W-0S | 19 |
| Main St. N&S | 22W-0S,22W-0N | 19 |
| Maple St. E&W | 23W-0N,22W-0N | 12 |
| Marion Av. E&W | 23W-0N | 12 |
| Marston Av. E&W | 23W-1S,22W-1S | 18 |
| Cir. | 21W-1S | 19 |
| May Av. N&S | 21W-0S | 19 |
| Melrose Av. N&S | 22W-0N | 13 |
| Memory Ct. E&W | 21W-0S | 19 |
| Meredith Pl. NW&SE | 22W-1N | 13 |
| Merton Av. N&S | 22W-0S | 19 |
| Midway Pk. N&S | 21W-0N | 13 |
| Miller Ct. N&S | 23W-0S | 18 |
| Milton Av. N&S | 22W-1S,22W-0S | 19 |
| Montclair Av. N&S | 22W-1S,22W-0N | 19 |
| Muirwood Dr. N&S | 22W-1N | 13 |
| Newton Av. N&S | 23W-0S,23W-0N | 18 |
| Nichol Pl. E&W | 22W-1N | 13 |
| Nicoll Av. N&S | 22W-1S,22W-0S | 19 |
| North Driveway NW&SE | 21W-1S | 19 |
| Oak St. E&W | 23W-0N,22W-0N | 12 |
| Oakwood Ct. N&S | 21W-1S | 19 |
| Old Bond Ct. E&W | 20W-0S | 20 |
| Orchard Ln. NS&EW | 23W-1S | 19 |
| Ott Av. N&S | 23W-0S | 18 |
| Oxford Rd. E&W | 21W-0S | 19 |
| Park Blvd. N&S | 22W-2S,22W-0N | 19 |
| Park Plaza Av. E&W | 22W-0S | 19 |
| Park Row NW&SE | 22W-0N | 13 |
| Parkside Av. N&S | 22W-1S,22W-0S | 19 |
| Pembroke Ln. E&W | 23W-1S | 18 |
| Pennsylvania Av. E&W | 23W-0N,22W-0N | 12 |
| Pershing Av. E&W | 22W-1S,21W-1S | 19 |
| Phillips Av. E&W | 23W-0S,22W-0S | 18 |
| Pickwick Pl. E&W | 22W-0S | 19 |
| Pleasant Av. N&S | 22W-0N | 13 |
| Plum Tree Rd. NE&SW | 22W-0N | 13 |
| Prairie Av. N&S | 22W-0N | 13 |
| Prince Edward Rd. NE&SW | 22W-1S | 19 |
| Prospect Av. N&S | 22W-0S,22W-0N | 19 |
| Raintree Ct. NS&EW | 22W-1S | 19 |
| Raintree Dr. E&W | 22W-1S | 19 |
| Ramblewood Dr. E&W | 23W-1S | 18 |
| Regent St. N&S | 22W-0S | 19 |
| Revere Rd. E&W | 22W-0S,21W-0S | 19 |
| Ridgewood Av. E&W | 23W-0S,22W-0S | 18 |
| Riford Rd. N&S | 22W-0N | 13 |

| Street | Grid | Page |
|---|---|---|
| Roger Rd. N&S | 21W-0N | 13 |
| Roscomden Ct. N&S | 23W-1S | 19 |
| Roslyn Rd. E&W | 21W-0S | 19 |
| Royal Glen Dr. E&W | 20W-0S | 20 |
| Rt. 38 E&W | 23W-0S,20W-0S | 18 |
| Rt. 53 N&S | 21W-1S,21W-0S | 19 |
| S. Ellyn Av. N&S | 22W-1S | 19 |
| Cir. | 23W-1N | 13 |
| Sandhurst Cir. N&S | 23W-1S | 18 |
| Scott Av. N&S | 21W-0S | 19 |
| Seminary Cir. NW&SE | 21W-1S | 19 |
| Shadblow Dr. N&S | 23W-1S | 18 |
| Sheehan Av. E&W | 21W-1S | 19 |
| Sheffield Ln. E&W | 23W-0N | 12 |
| Smith St. E&W | 21W-0S | 19 |
| Snowhill Ct. E&W | 21W-1S | 19 |
| South Driveway E&W | 21W-1S | 19 |
| Spaulding Av. NE&SW | 22W-0N | 13 |
| Spring Av. N&S | 21W-0S | 19 |
| Spruce Ln. N&S | 23W-1S | 18 |
| St. Charles Rd. E&W | 23W-1N,22W-1N | 12 |
| St. James Pl. E&W | 20W-0S | 20 |
| St. Moritz Dr. N&S | 23W-0N | 12 |
| Stacy Ct. N&S | 22W-0N | 13 |
| Stafford Ln. NE&SW | 22W-1S | 19 |
| Stagecoach Ct. E&W | 22W-1N | 13 |
| Stagecoach Run E&W | 22W-1N | 13 |
| Stephanie Ln. N&S | 22W-0S | 19 |
| Stonegate Ct. N&S | 22W-1S | 19 |
| Stuart Av. NE&SW | 22W-0N | 13 |
| Summerdale Av. NE&SW | 22W-0S | 19 |
| Sunset Av. N&S | 22W-0S | 19 |
| Sunset Ct. E&W | 22W-0S | 19 |
| Surrey Dr. N&S | 21W-0S | 19 |
| Sylvan Av. N&S | 21W-0S | 19 |
| Taft Av. E&W | 23W-1S,22W-1S | 18 |
| Taylor Av. N&S | 22W-0S,22W-0N | 19 |
| Turnberry Ln. NW&SE | 23W-1S | 19 |
| Turner Av. E&W | 23W-0S,22W-0S | 18 |
| Valley Av. E&W | 21W-0S | 19 |
| Vandamin Av. N&S | 22W-0S | 19 |
| Vine Av. N&S | 23W-0S | 18 |
| Walnut St. E&W | 22W-0N | 13 |
| Waverly Rd. E&W | 21W-0S | 19 |
| West Driveway N&S | 21W-1S | 19 |
| Western Av. N&S | 23W-0N | 12 |
| Whittier Av. N&S | 21W-0N | 13 |
| Williamsburgh Rd. E&W | 22W-1S | 19 |
| Willis St. NE&SW | 22W-0N | 13 |
| Wilson Av. E&W | 22W-1S | 19 |
| Winchell Way E&W | 22W-1S | 19 |
| Windemere Dr. N&S | 20W-0S | 20 |
| Windsor Av. NE&SW | 23W-0S | 18 |
| Wingate Rd. E&W | 22W-0S | 19 |
| Woodland Dr. NE&SW | 21W-0N | 13 |
| Woodstock Av. N&S | 21W-0S | 19 |
| 22nd St. E&W | 22W-2S | 19 |


## Glendale Heights


| Street | Grid | Page |
|---|---|---|
| Alberta Ct. N&S | 22W-2N | 13 |
| Almond Ln. NW&SE | 23W-4N | 6 |
| Alpine Dr., N. NE&SW | 23W-3N | 12 |
| Alpine East Dr. E&W | 23W-3N | 12 |
| Alta Ln. E&W | 23W-3N | 12 |
| Altgeld Av. E&W | 24W-3N,22W-3N | 12 |
| Altgeld St. E&W | 22W-3N | 13 |
| Amhurst Cir. E&W | 24W-3N | 12 |
| Amy Av. N&S | 23W-2N,23W-3N | 12 |
| Appleby Dr. E&W | 24W-3N | 12 |
| Ardmore Av. NE&SW | 22W-2N,22W-3N | 13 |
| Armitage Av. E&W | 23W-2N,22W-2N | 12 |
| Army Trail Rd. E&W | 24W-4N,22W-4N | 6 |
| Asbury Dr. E&W | 22W-2N | 13 |
| Aspen Ln. N&S | 23W-3N | 12 |
| Auburn Dr. NE&SW | 24W-3N | 12 |
| Audubon Dr. N&S | 23W-4N | 6 |
| Baldwin Ct. N&S | 23W-4N | 6 |
| Barclay Dr. E&W | 23W-4N | 6 |
| Basswood Ln. N&S | 23W-3N | 12 |
| Belden Av. E&W | 23W-2N | 12 |
| Bell Ln. N&S | 23W-4N | 6 |
| Bentley Ct. N&S | 23W-3N | 12 |
| Berkshire Ct. NW&SE | 24W-3N | 12 |
| Berkshire St. NE&SW | 24W-3N | 12 |
| Blair Ln. N&S | 23W-4N | 6 |

| | Grid | Page |
|---|---|---|
| Bloomingdale Rd. N&S | | |
| | 23W-1N,23W-4N | 12 |
| Blueridge Dr. NE&SW | | |
| | 24W-3N | 12 |
| Boulder Dr. E&W | 23W-3N | 12 |
| Brahms St. E&W | 23W-4N | 6 |
| Brandon Ct. N&S | 23W-3N | 12 |
| Brandon Dr., N. E&W | | |
| | 23W-3N | 12 |
| Brandon Dr., S. E&W | | |
| | 23W-3N | 12 |
| Brian Dr. NW&SE | 24W-3N | 12 |
| Brittany Ct. E&W | 24W-4N | 6 |
| Brittany Ln. N&S | 24W-4N | 6 |
| Brockton Ln. N&S | 23W-3N | 12 |
| Brookside Dr. E&W | 24W-3N | 12 |
| Burdett Ct. NE&SW | 22W-2N | 13 |
| Burgess Dr. E&W | 23W-4N | 6 |
| Burr Oak Ln. N&S | 23W-3N | 12 |
| Cambridge Ln. E&W | | |
| | 23W-2N | 12 |
| Camden Ct. NE&SW | | |
| | 23W-1N | 12 |
| Campbell Dr. NE&SW | | |
| | 24W-3N | 12 |
| Cardinal Dr. N&S | 24W-4N | 6 |
| Cedar St. N&S | 23W-1N | 12 |
| Chadwick Ln. N&S | 23W-3N | 6 |
| Chapman Ct. E&W | 23W-3N | 12 |
| Charles Ct. E&W | 23W-3N | 12 |
| Charles Dr. N&S | 22W-2N | 13 |
| Chaucer Ln. N&S | 23W-4N | 6 |
| Chippendale Ln. N&S | | |
| | 24W-3N | 12 |
| Circle Dr. E&W | 22W-2N | 13 |
| Clifford St. N&S | 23W-3N | 12 |
| Club Dr. NS&EW | 24W-3N | 12 |
| Clubhouse Ct. N&S | 24W-4N | 6 |
| Copper Ct. E&W | 24W-4N | 6 |
| Cornell Ct. E&W | 24W-4N | 6 |
| Cove Ln. NE&SW | 24W-3N | 12 |
| Cynthia Ln. E&W | 22W-2N | 13 |
| Dale Rd. E&W | 23W-4N | 6 |
| Darlene Ln. E&W | 22W-2N | 13 |
| Davine Dr. N&S | 22W-2N | 13 |
| Deanna Ln. N&S | 22W-2N | 13 |
| Deere Ln. NE&SW | 23W-4N | 6 |
| Dennison Dr. E&W | 23W-4N | 6 |
| Devon Dr. N&S | 23W-3N | 12 |
| Dickens Av. E&W | 22W-2N | 13 |
| Drummond Av. E&W | | |
| | 24W-3N,23W-3N | 12 |
| Dunteman Dr. E&W | 23W-4N | 6 |
| Eagle Ct. NE&SW | 24W-2N | 12 |
| Easy Ct. NW&SE | 22W-2N | 13 |
| Easy St., E. E&W | 22W-2N | 13 |
| Easy St., N. N&S | 22W-2N | 13 |
| Elizabeth Av. N&S | 23W-2N | 12 |
| English Dr. N&S | 24W-3N | 12 |
| Eunice Ct. NE&SW | 22W-2N | 13 |
| Evergreen Ln. N&S | 24W-1N | 12 |
| Exchange Blvd. NW&SE | | |
| | 23W-3N | 12 |
| Fairway Dr. N&S | 24W-2N | 12 |
| Fallbrook Dr. E&W | 24W-4N | 6 |
| Flagstaff Ct. N&S | 24W-3N | 12 |
| Flagstaff Ln. N&S | 24W-3N | 12 |
| Fleetwood Dr. E&W | 24W-3N | 12 |
| Fox Av. E&W | 22W-2N | 13 |
| Frank Ct. N&S | 23W-3N | 12 |
| Friedrich St. N&S | 24W-3N | 12 |
| Fullerton Av. E&W | | |
| | 24W-3N,22W-3N | 12 |
| Garland Ct. NE&SW | 23W-4N | 6 |
| Gerald Av. NE&SW | 22W-2N | 13 |
| Gilberto St. N&S | 23W-3N | 12 |
| Gladstone Ct. N&S | 23W-4N | 6 |
| Glen Ellyn Rd. N&S | | |
| | 22W-1N,22W-4N | 13 |
| Glen Point Dr. N&S | 23W-3N | 12 |
| Glengary Dr. N&S | 23W-3N | 12 |
| Glenhill Ct. NE&SW | 23W-2N | 12 |
| Glenhill Dr., E. E&W | 23W-2N | 12 |
| Glenrock Ln. N&S | 23W-3N | 12 |
| Golfview Dr. NS&EW | | |
| | 24W-3N | 12 |
| Goodrich Av. N&S | 22W-2N | 13 |
| Green Meadow Dr. E&W | | |
| | 24W-3N | 12 |
| Greens Ct. E&W | 24W-2N | 12 |
| Gregory Av. NS&EW | | |
| | 23W-3N,22W-3N | 12 |
| Hale Ct. E&W | 24W-3N | 12 |
| Harding Ct. E&W | 23W-4N | 6 |
| Harding Dr. E&W | 23W-4N | 6 |
| Harold Av. E&W | 22W-2N | 13 |
| Hartford St. N&S | 23W-2N | 12 |
| Harvest Ln. N&S | 24W-3N | 12 |
| Hemlock Ct. NE&SW | 23W-3N | 12 |
| Hemlock Ln. NE&SW | | |
| | 24W-3N | 12 |
| Hesterman Dr. E&W | 23W-4N | 6 |
| Hickory Ln. N&S | 23W-3N | 12 |
| Highgrove Blvd. N&S | | |
| | 22W-3N,22W-4N | 13 |
| Highland Av. N&S | | |
| | 22W-2N,22W-3N | 13 |
| Hilldale Ln. N&S | 23W-4N | 6 |
| Hilton Dr. E&W | 24W-4N | 6 |
| International Blvd. E&W | | |
| | 23W-3N | 12 |
| Jacobsen Av. N&S | 23W-2N | 12 |
| James Ct. E&W | 22W-2N | 13 |
| Jamison Ct. E&W | 23W-4N | 6 |

| | Grid | Page |
|---|---|---|
| Jeffrey Av. N&S | 23W-3N | 12 |
| Jill Ct. NW&SE | 22W-2N | 13 |
| Joel Ct. E&W | 23W-1N | 12 |
| John St. N&S | 24W-3N | 12 |
| Jones St. N&S | 23W-3N | 12 |
| Joseph Ln. E&W | 23W-2N | 12 |
| Joyce Av. NW&SE | 22W-2N | 13 |
| Keating St. N&S | 23W-3N | 12 |
| Kennebunk Ct. N&S | 23W-1N | 12 |
| Lake Dr. E&W | 24W-3N | 12 |
| Larry Ln. N&S | | |
| | 22W-2N,22W-3N | 13 |
| Leslie Av. N&S | 22W-2N | 13 |
| Leslie Ln., E. E&W | 22W-2N | 13 |
| Liberty Dr. N&S | 22W-2N | 13 |
| Lincoln Av. E&W | | |
| | 23W-3N,22W-3N | 12 |
| Lippert Ln. E&W | 22W-2N | 13 |
| Lombard Ln. N&S | 23W-3N | 12 |
| London Dr. N&S | 23W-4N | 6 |
| Loveland Dr. N&S | 23W-3N | 12 |
| Lynne Ct. E&W | 22W-2N | 13 |
| Marilyn Av. E&W | | |
| | 23W-2N,22W-2N | 12 |
| Mark Av. E&W | 23W-2N | 12 |
| Michael Ct. E&W | 23W-1N | 12 |
| Michael Dr. N&S | 23W-1N | 12 |
| Mill Pond Dr. E&W | 24W-3N | 12 |
| Mimosa Ct. N&S | 23W-3N | 12 |
| Mitchell Rd. E&W | 22W-3N | 13 |
| Montana Av. E&W | | |
| | 24W-3N,23W-3N | 12 |
| Morse Ln. N&S | 23W-4N | 6 |
| N. Brandon Dr. E&W | | |
| | 23W-3N | 12 |
| Neilan Ct. NE&SW | 22W-3N | 13 |
| Nevada Av. E&W | 24W-3N | 12 |
| Newport St. NE&SW | | |
| | 23W-2N | 12 |
| Niess Ct. NW&SE | 23W-2N | 12 |
| Nolan Av. N&S | 22W-2N | 13 |
| North Av. E&W | | |
| | 24W-2N,22W-2N | 12 |
| Norton Av. E&W | 23W-3N | 12 |
| Opal Av. E&W | 23W-3N | 12 |
| Orchard Ln. N&S | 23W-3N | 12 |
| Oriole Ln. NS&EW | 23W-4N | 6 |
| Oxford Ln. N&S | 23W-3N | 12 |
| Paddock Cir. E&W | 23W-3N | 12 |
| Park Ct. E&W | 23W-3N | 12 |
| Paul Av. N&S | 23W-3N | 12 |
| Payson Ln. NE&SW | 23W-4N | 6 |
| Pepperwood Ln. N&S | | |
| | 23W-4N | 6 |
| Peterson Av. E&W | 21W-2N | 13 |
| Placid Av. E&W | 23W-3N | 12 |
| Polo Club Ct. NE&SW | | |
| | 23W-3N | 12 |
| Polo Club Dr. E&W | | |
| | 23W-3N,22W-3N | 12 |
| Poplar St. E&W | 23W-3N | 12 |
| Portsmouth Ct. N&S | | |
| | 23W-1N | 12 |
| President Dr. E&W | 23W-1N | 12 |
| President St. N&S | 24W-3N | 12 |
| Quincy Ct. N&S | 23W-3N | 12 |
| Reeves Dr. N&S | 24W-3N | 12 |
| Regency Dr. NS&EW | | |
| | 22W-3N,22W-4N | 13 |
| Ringneck Ln. E&W | 23W-4N | 6 |
| Robert Ct. E&W | 23W-1N | 12 |
| Roberta Ct. E&W | | |
| | 24W-2N,23W-2N | 12 |
| Roland Dr. E&W | 23W-4N | 6 |
| Rugby Ct. E&W | 23W-4N | 6 |
| Sandburg Ct. N&S | 23W-4N | 6 |
| Sandra Ct. E&W | 23W-3N | 12 |
| Saratoga Dr. E&W | 23W-3N | 12 |
| Scarboro Dr. N&S | 23W-3N | 12 |
| Schmale Ct. E&W | 24W-3N | 12 |
| Schubert Av. E&W | | |
| | 24W-3N,23W-3N | 12 |
| Schubert Ct. N&S | 24W-3N | 12 |
| Scott St. N&S | 23W-3N | 12 |
| Shorewood Dr. E&W | | |
| | 23W-1N | 12 |
| Sidney Av. N&S | 22W-2N | 13 |
| Siems Dr. E&W | 23W-4N | 25 |
| Slayton Ln. N&S | 23W-3N | 12 |
| Somerset Dr. N&S | 22W-3N | 13 |
| Spruce St. N&S | 23W-1N | 12 |
| Stevenson Dr. E&W | | |
| | 24W-3N,23W-3N | 12 |
| Sydney Av. E&W | 21W-2N | 13 |
| Terry Rd., E. E&W | 23W-3N | 12 |
| Terry Rd., N. N&S | 23W-3N | 12 |
| Thorncliff Dr. E&W | 23W-4N | 6 |
| Timber Ln. N&S | 23W-3N | 12 |
| Todd Av. N&S | 23W-3N | 12 |
| Towner Av. N&S | 23W-3N | 12 |
| Vail Ln. N&S | 23W-3N | 12 |
| Vanmeter Ct. N&S | 23W-3N | 12 |
| Vanmeter St. N&S | | |
| | 23W-2N,23W-3N | 12 |
| Vantroba Dr. E&W | 23W-3N | 12 |
| Vista Ct. E&W | 23W-4N | 6 |
| W. Glenhill Dr. N&S | 23W-2N | 12 |
| Wall St. N&S | 23W-4N | 6 |
| Warwick Dr. E&W | 24W-3N | 12 |
| Watersedge Dr., N. E&W | | |
| | 23W-4N | 6 |
| Wayne Av. N&S | 22W-3N | 13 |
| Westberg St. N&S | 23W-3N | 12 |

| | Grid | Page |
|---|---|---|
| Westchester Dr. N&S | | |
| | 23W-2N | 12 |
| Whitman Dr. E&W | 23W-4N | 6 |
| Wildwood Cir. N&S | 23W-3N | 12 |
| Windsor Ln. E&W | 23W-2N | 12 |
| Windy Point Dr. NW&SE | | |
| | 22W-3N,23W-3N | 13 |
| Winthrop Av. E&W | 22W-2N | 13 |
| Winthrop Ct. N&S | 22W-2N | 13 |
| Woodside Ln. N&S | 23W-3N | 12 |
| Wren Ct. E&W | 23W-4N | 6 |
| Wrightwood Av. E&W | | |
| | 24W-3N,23W-3N | 12 |
| Wyatt Ln. N&S | 23W-4N | 6 |
| Yardley Ct. E&W | 24W-4N | 6 |

**Hanover Park***
**(Also see Cook County)**

| | Grid | Page |
|---|---|---|
| Aberdeen Ct. N&S | 27W-5N | 5 |
| Alpine Ct. (Pvt.) NE&SW | | |
| | 26W-7N | 6 |
| Amarillo St. N&S | 26W-7N | 6 |
| Andover Dr. N&S | | |
| | 27W-7N,26W-7N | 6 |
| Apache Dr. E&W | 26W-7N | 6 |
| Arlington Cir. NS&EW | | |
| | 26W-6N | 6 |
| Arlington Ct. E&W | 26W-6N | 6 |
| Arlington Dr., E. N&S | | |
| | 26W-6N,25W-7N | 6 |
| Arlington Dr., W. N&S | | |
| | 26W-6N,26W-7N | 6 |
| Arlington Rd. E&W | 27W-7N | 5 |
| Army Trail Rd. E&W | 27W-4N | 5 |
| Baldwin Ln. NS&EW | | |
| | 27W-5N | 5 |
| Bamberg Ct. (Pvt.) NE&SW | | |
| | 26W-7N | 6 |
| Barr Ct. N&S | 26W-7N | 6 |
| Barrington Rd. N&S | | |
| | 27W-7N,26W-7N | 5 |
| Barrymore Ct. E&W | 26W-7N | 6 |
| Bavarian Ct. E&W | 26W-7N | 6 |
| Bayside Dr. N&S | | |
| | 27W-4N,27W-5N | 5 |
| Bear Flag Dr. E&W | 26W-7N | 6 |
| Bedford Ct. N&S | 26W-7N | 6 |
| Bell Dr. E&W | 27W-5N | 5 |
| Bell Ln. N&S | 27W-5N | 5 |
| Beverly Cir. N&S | 26W-7N | 6 |
| Beverly Ct. E&W | 26W-7N | 6 |
| Bradley Ct., N. & S. N&S | | |
| | 26W-7N | 6 |
| Brookbank Dr. N&S | 27W-4N | 5 |
| Camden Ln. E&W | 27W-5N | 5 |
| Carmel Dr. N&S | 26W-6N | 6 |
| Castlebar Ct. E&W | 27W-5N | 5 |
| Castlebar Ln. N&S | 27W-5N | 5 |
| Catalina Dr. E&W | 26W-6N | 6 |
| Cir. | 26W-6N | 6 |
| Chandler Dr. NS&EW | | |
| | 27W-5N | 5 |
| Chaplin Ct. E&W | 27W-5N | 5 |
| Charleston Ct. N&S | 26W-7N | 6 |
| Chatsworth Ct. N&S | | |
| | 26W-7N | 6 |
| Church Rd. N&S | | |
| | 27W-6N,27W-7N | 5 |
| Cinema Dr. E&W | 27W-6N | 5 |
| Citation Ln. E&W | 26W-7N | 6 |
| Clarendon Ct. N&S | 27W-5N | 5 |
| Clipper Dr. N&S | 26W-4N | 5 |
| Concord Ct. N&S | 27W-7N | 5 |
| Cooper Ct. N&S | 26W-7N | 6 |
| County Farm Rd. NE&SW | | |
| | 27W-5N | 5 |
| Cove Dr. NW&SE | 27W-5N | 5 |
| Crawford Ln. E&W | 26W-7N | 6 |
| Crosby Ct. NW&SE | 27W-5N | 5 |
| Ct. 'A' E&W | 26W-6N | 6 |
| Ct. 'B' E&W | 26W-6N | 6 |
| Ct. 'C' E&W | 26W-6N | 6 |
| Ct. 'D' E&W | 26W-6N | 6 |
| Ct. 'E' E&W | 26W-6N | 6 |
| Ct. 'F' N&S | 26W-6N | 6 |
| Ct. 'G' E&W | 26W-6N | 6 |
| Ct. 'H' E&W | 26W-6N | 6 |
| Ct. 'I' NE&SW | 26W-7N | 6 |
| Ct. 'J' N&S | 26W-7N | 6 |
| Ct. 'O' E&W | 26W-7N | 6 |
| Ct. 'P' N&S | 26W-7N | 6 |
| Ct. 'Q' N&S | 26W-7N | 6 |
| Ct. Leona NS&EW | 26W-7N | 6 |
| Ct. Marguerite NE&SW | | |
| | 26W-7N | 6 |
| Ct. Maria NS&EW | 26W-7N | 6 |
| Ct. Tiburon NE&SW | 26W-7N | 6 |
| Curtis Ln. N&S | 26W-7N | 6 |
| Danby Ct. N&S | 27W-7N | 5 |
| Danforth Ct. N&S | 27W-7N | 5 |
| Deerfield Ct. E&W | 27W-5N | 5 |
| Deforest Ct. E&W | 27W-5N | 5 |
| Del Monte Dr. N&S | 26W-7N | 6 |
| Devon Av. E&W | 27W-7N | 5 |
| Don Carlos Ct. N&S | 27W-5N | 5 |
| Don Carlos Dr. E&W | | |
| | 27W-5N | 5 |
| Dory Circle N&S | 26W-4N | 5 |
| Downey Ct. NW&SE | | |
| | 27W-5N | 5 |
| Driftwood Ln. E&W | 27W-5N | 5 |
| Dublin Ct. N&S | 27W-5N | 5 |
| Dublin Ln. E&W | 27W-5N | 5 |

| | Grid | Page |
|---|---|---|
| Dupont Dr. N&S | 27W-5N | 5 |
| Dutch Mill Ct. NE&SW | | |
| | 26W-7N | 6 |
| Eastman Ln. N&S | 27W-5N | 5 |
| Easton Ct. N&S | 27W-7N | 5 |
| Edinburg Ln. N&S | 27W-5N | 5 |
| Edison Cir. E&W | 27W-7N | 5 |
| Elgin O'Hare Expwy. NE&SW | | |
| | 25W-7N | 6 |
| Elm St. E&W | 27W-7N | 5 |
| Erie Ct. NE&SW | 27W-7N | 5 |
| Essex Ct. N&S | 27W-7N | 5 |
| Farmington Ct. N&S | 27W-7N | 5 |
| Farnham Ct., E. N&S | | |
| | 26W-7N | 6 |
| Fonda Ln. N&S | 27W-5N | 5 |
| Franklin Ct., E. N&S | 26W-7N | 6 |
| Fremont Dr. NW&SE | | |
| | 26W-7N | 6 |
| Fresno Ct. NS&EW | 26W-7N | 6 |
| Fulton Ln. N&S | 27W-5N | 5 |
| Gable Ct. NW&SE | 26W-6N | 6 |
| Garbo Ln. N&S | 27W-5N | 5 |
| Gardner Ct. N&S | 26W-7N | 6 |
| Garland Ln. E&W | 26W-6N | 6 |
| Gifford Ct. NE&SW | 26W-7N | 6 |
| Glasgow Ct. NW&SE | | |
| | 27W-5N | 5 |
| Glengary Ct. N&S | 27W-5N | 5 |
| Goddard Ln. E&W | 27W-5N | 5 |
| Gold Cir. N&S | 26W-7N | 6 |
| Grand Duell Way N&S | | |
| | 27W-5N | 5 |
| Grant Ln. N&S | 26W-6N | 6 |
| Green Bay Dr. E&W | 27W-4N | 5 |
| Greenbridge Dr. NS&EW | | |
| | 27W-5N | 5 |
| Greenbrook Blvd. NE&SW | | |
| | 26W-6N | 6 |
| Greenbrook Ct. NW&SE | | |
| | 26W-7N | 6 |
| Grosse Pointe Cir., W & E NS&EW | | |
| | 26W-7N | 6 |
| Hanover Ct. NE&SW | | |
| | 26W-7N | 6 |
| Harbor Pt. NW&SE | 27W-4N | 5 |
| Hardwood Ct. N&S | 27W-5N | 5 |
| Hardy Dr. NW&SE | 26W-7N | 6 |
| Heritage Ct. E&W | 26W-6N | 6 |
| Hialeah Ln. NS&EW | 26W-6N | 6 |
| Howe Ln. E&W | 27W-5N | 5 |
| Hunter Ct. E&W | 27W-5N | 5 |
| Island Cir. E&W | 26W-4N | 5 |
| Isle Royal Ln. NW&SE | | |
| | 27W-5N | 5 |
| Jefferson St. N&S | | |
| | 27W-4N,27W-6N | 5 |
| Keene Ln. N&S | 26W-6N | 6 |
| Kit Carson Dr. N&S | 26W-7N | 6 |
| Kuhn Rd. N&S | 26W-4N | 6 |
| Ladd Ln. N&S | 27W-6N | 5 |
| Laguna Ct. NE&SW | 26W-7N | 6 |
| Lake St. NW&SE | | |
| | 26W-7N,25W-6N | 6 |
| Lakeside Dr. N&S | 27W-5N | 5 |
| Lapoloma Ct. NE&SW | | |
| | 26W-7N | 6 |
| Leeward Ln. E&W | 27W-4N | 5 |
| Lemon Ln. N&S | 27W-6N | 5 |
| Liberty St. E&W | 27W-7N | 5 |
| Maclaine Ln. E&W | 27W-5N | 5 |
| Madera St. N&S | 26W-7N | 6 |
| Madrid Ct. N&S | 26W-7N | 6 |
| Mallard Ln. E&W | 27W-5N | 5 |
| Mallow Ct. E&W | 27W-5N | 5 |
| Marine Dr. N&S | 27W-4N | 5 |
| McCormick Ln. E&W | | |
| | 27W-5N | 5 |
| Merrimac Ln., N. E&W | | |
| | 26W-4N | 6 |
| Mill St. N&S | 27W-7N | 5 |
| Millpond Ln. E&W | 27W-5N | 5 |
| Monitor Dr. N&S | 27W-4N | 5 |
| Monroe Ln. E&W | 26W-6N | 6 |
| Montibello Dr. N&S | 26W-7N | 6 |
| Morton Rd. E&W | 27W-5N | 5 |
| Muirfield Dr. NS&EW | | |
| | 27W-5N | 5 |
| Nashua Ln. E&W | 26W-6N | 6 |
| Nautilus Ln. N&S | 27W-5N | 5 |
| Niven Ln. N&S | 27W-5N | 5 |
| Nugget Cir. NW&SE | 26W-7N | 6 |
| Oak St. E&W | 27W-7N | 5 |
| Ontarioville Rd. NW&SE | | |
| | 27W-7N,26W-7N | 5 |
| Pastoral Ln. NS&EW | | |
| | 27W-5N | 5 |
| Pebble Beach Ct. E&W | | |
| | 26W-7N | 6 |
| Pebble Beach Dr. N&S | | |
| | 26W-7N | 6 |
| Pennsbury Ct. N&S | 27W-5N | 5 |
| Pennsbury Ln. E&W | 27W-5N | 5 |
| Pondview Dr. N&S | 27W-4N | 5 |
| Port Dr. N&S | 27W-4N | 5 |
| Redford Ln. N&S | 27W-5N | 5 |
| Rembrant Ct. E&W | 26W-7N | 6 |
| Ridge Crossing NS&EW | | |
| | 27W-6N | 5 |
| Ring Ct. N&S | 26W-7N | 6 |
| Rob Roy Ct. E&W | 27W-5N | 5 |
| Rooney Ct. E&W | 27W-6N | 5 |
| Russelwood Ct. N&S | | |
| | 27W-5N | 5 |

| | Grid | Page |
|---|---|---|
| Sacramento E&W | 26W-7N | 6 |
| San Simeon Dr. | | |
| | 26W-7N,26W-6N | 6 |
| Sandpiper Ln. N&S | 27W-4N | 5 |
| Santa Anita Dr. E&W | | |
| | 26W-6N | 6 |
| Santa Barbara Dr. N&S | | |
| | 26W-6N,26W-7N | 6 |
| Santa Cruz Cir. N&S | 26W-7N | 6 |
| Santa Cruz Dr. N&S | 26W-7N | 6 |
| Schick Rd. N&S | 27W-5N | 5 |
| Schooner Ln. E&W | | |
| | 27W-4N,26W-4N | 5 |
| Sea Biscuit Ln. E&W | | |
| | 26W-6N | 6 |
| Seaview Dr. N&S | 27W-4N | 5 |
| Shoal Ln. N&S | 26W-4N | 5 |
| Shoreline Dr. N&S | 26W-4N | 5 |
| Sinatra Ln. N&S | 27W-6N | 5 |
| Spinnaker Ln. E&W | | |
| | 27W-4N,26W-4N | 5 |
| Springlake Dr. N&S | 27W-4N | 5 |
| St. Ann Dr. E&W | 27W-4N | 5 |
| St. Claire Ct. E&W | 27W-5N | 5 |
| Stairway Dr. E&W | 27W-4N | 5 |
| Star Dr. N&S | 26W-7N | 6 |
| Starboard Dr. N&S | 27W-4N | 5 |
| Stearns Rd. E&W | 27W-6N | 5 |
| Stepstone Ln. NW&SE | | |
| | 27W-5N | 5 |
| Stirling Ct. E&W | 27W-5N | 5 |
| Sutter Dr. E&W | 26W-7N | 6 |
| Thistle Ct. NE&SW | 27W-5N | 5 |
| Tiburon Ct. N&S | 26W-7N | 6 |
| Toronto Ct. N&S | 27W-5N | 5 |
| Tracy Ct. E&W | 27W-5N | 5 |
| Turnberry Ct. NW&SE | | |
| | 25W-7N | 6 |
| Turnberry Dr. N&S | 25W-7N | 6 |
| Turner Ln. E&W | 26W-6N | 6 |
| U.S. Route 20 NW&SE | | |
| | 26W-7N,25W-6N | 6 |
| Unit Ct. N&S | 26W-7N | 6 |
| Victor Ln. E&W | 27W-5N | 5 |
| Waterfall Ln. NW&SE | | |
| | 27W-5N | 5 |
| Whaler Ln. E&W | 27W-5N | 5 |
| Whirlaway Ln. E&W | 26W-7N | 6 |
| Whitney Dr. NW&SE | | |
| | 27W-5N | 5 |
| Wildwood Ln. N&S | 27W-5N | 5 |
| Wildwood Ln. NW&SE | | |
| | 27W-5N | 5 |
| Wilshire Ct. N&S | 26W-7N | 6 |
| Windjammer Ln. NS&EW | | |
| | 27W-4N,26W-4N | 5 |
| Windmill Dr. NS&EW | | |
| | 27W-5N | 5 |
| Windward Ln. E&W | 27W-4N | 5 |
| Woodlake Rd. N&S | 27W-5N | 5 |
| Wright Ln. E&W | 27W-5N | 5 |
| Zeppelin Dr. NS&EW | | |
| | 27W-5N | 5 |

**Hinsdale***
**(Also see Cook County)**

| | Grid | Page |
|---|---|---|
| Adams St. N&S | | |
| | 16W-5S,16W-4S | 27 |
| Allmen Av. N&S | 15W-5S | 27 |
| Astony Ct. N&S | 15W-6S | 27 |
| Ayres Av. E&W | 15W-4S | 27 |
| Birchwood Av. E&W | 15W-4S | 27 |
| Birchwood Rd. E&W | | |
| | 16W-5S,15W-4S | 27 |
| Blaine Av. N&S | 15W-5S | 27 |
| Bodin St. N&S | 16W-5S | 27 |
| Bonnie Brae Rd. E&W | | |
| | 16W-4S,15W-4S | 27 |
| Briargate Ter. E&W | 15W-4S | 27 |
| Brook Pl. N&S | 16W-4S | 27 |
| Bruner St. N&S | | |
| | 16W-5S,16W-4S | 27 |
| Burr Oak Rd. NS&EW | | |
| | 15W-3S | 21 |
| Canterbury Ct. E&W | | |
| | 15W-4S | 27 |
| Carolyn Ln. (Pvt.) E&W | | |
| | 16W-6S | 27 |
| Castine Ct. E&W | 15W-6S | 27 |
| Center St. E&W | 15W-4S | 27 |
| Chanticleer Ln. E&W | | |
| | 15W-6S | 27 |
| Chestnut St. E&W | 16W-4S | 27 |
| Chicago Av. E&W | | |
| | 16W-4S,14W-4S | 27 |
| Childs Av. N&S | 15W-6S | 27 |
| Clay St. N&S | | |
| | 15W-5S,15W-4S | 27 |
| Claymoor Rd. N&S | 15W-6S | 27 |
| County Line Rd. N&S | | |
| | 14W-5S,14W-4S | 27 |
| East Claymoor Rd. (Pvt.) E&W | | |
| | 15W-6S | 27 |
| Elm St. N&S | | |
| | 15W-6S,15W-4S | 27 |
| Elmwood Pl. E&W | 15W-5S | 27 |
| Flagg St. E&W | 15W-4S | 27 |
| Forest Rd. N&S | 15W-4S | 27 |
| Fox Ln. E&W | 15W-3S | 21 |
| Foxgate Dr. N&S | 15W-4S | 27 |
| Franklin St. N&S | 15W-4S | 27 |
| Fuller Rd. E&W | | |
| | 15W-4S,14W-4S | 27 |

| | Grid | Page |
|---|---|---|
| Garfield Av. N&S | | |
| | 15W-6S,15W-4S | 27 |
| Giddings Av. N&S | 15W-4S | 27 |
| Glendale Av. N&S | 15W-4S | 27 |
| Grant St. N&S | | |
| | 15W-6S,15W-4S | 27 |
| Grason St. N&S | 18W-6S | 26 |
| Hampton Pl. E&W | 15W-4S | 27 |
| Hawthorne Cir. NS&EW | | |
| | 15W-3S | 21 |
| Hickory St. E&W | | |
| | 16W-4S,15W-4S | 27 |
| Hillgrove Av. NE&SW | | |
| | 15W-4S | 27 |
| Hinsdale Av. E&W | | |
| | 16W-5S,15W-5S | 27 |
| Indian Trail N&S | 15W-3S | 21 |
| Jackson Av. N&S | 16W-5S | 27 |
| Jefferson St. N&S | 15W-4S | 27 |
| Kimball Ct. E&W | 15W-4S | 27 |
| King Pl. NE&SW | 15W-4S | 27 |
| Lansing St. E&W | 15W-4S | 27 |
| Lincoln St. N&S | | |
| | 15W-5S,15W-4S | 27 |
| Madison St. N&S | | |
| | 16W-5S,16W-4S | 27 |
| Maple St. N&S | | |
| | 16W-4S,15W-4S | 27 |
| Maumell St. N&S | 15W-4S | 27 |
| Meadowbrook Ln. NS&EW | | |
| | 15W-6S | 27 |
| Merrill Woods Dr. N&S | | |
| | 15W-4S | 27 |
| Mills St. N&S | 15W-4S | 27 |
| Minneola St. E&W | | |
| | 15W-4S,14W-4S | 27 |
| Monroe St. N&S | | |
| | 16W-5S,16W-4S | 27 |
| Morris Ln. E&W | 16W-4S | 27 |
| North St. E&W | | |
| | 16W-4S,15W-4S | 27 |
| Oak St. N&S | | |
| | 15W-6S,15W-4S | 27 |
| Oakwood Ter. N&S | 15W-4S | 27 |
| Ogden Av. E&W | | |
| | 16W-4S,15W-4S | 27 |
| Old Mill Rd. E&W | 15W-3S | 21 |
| Orchard Pl. N&S | 15W-5S | 27 |
| Pamela Cir. E&W | | |
| | 15W-5S,14W-5S | 27 |
| Park Av. N&S | 15W-4S | 27 |
| Post Cir. NS&EW | 15W-4S | 27 |
| Quincy St. N&S | | |
| | 16W-5S,16W-4S | 27 |
| Radcliffe Way N&S | 15W-4S | 27 |
| Railroad St. E&W | 16W-5S | 27 |
| Ravine Rd. E&W | | |
| | 15W-4S,14W-4S | 27 |
| Rosalie Ln. E&W | 16W-5S | 27 |
| Salt Creek Ln. N&S | 15W-3S | 21 |
| Salt Creek Ln. N&S | | |
| | 15W-4S,15W-3S | 27 |
| Spinning Wheel Rd. N&S | | |
| | 15W-3S | 21 |
| Spinning Wheel Rd. N&S | | |
| | 15W-4S,15W-3S | 27 |
| Stough St. N&S | | |
| | 16W-5S,16W-4S | 27 |
| Sutton Pl. (Pvt.) N&S | | |
| | 15W-6S | 27 |
| Symonds Dr. E&W | 15W-5S | 27 |
| The Lane E&W | | |
| | 15W-4S,14W-4S | 27 |
| Thurlow St. N&S | 16W-5S | 27 |
| Town Pl. E&W | 16W-5S | 27 |
| Tri State Tollway N&S | | |
| | 15W-5S,15W-4S | 27 |
| U.S. Route 34 NE&SW | | |
| | 16W-4S,15W-4S | 27 |
| Ulm Pl. E&W | 15W-5S | 27 |
| Village Pl. N&S | 15W-5S | 27 |
| Vine St. N&S | | |
| | 15W-5S,15W-4S | 27 |
| W. Grant Village Dr. E&W | | |
| | 15W-6S | 27 |
| Walker Rd. N&S | 15W-4S | 27 |
| Walnut St. E&W | | |
| | 16W-4S,15W-4S | 27 |
| Warren Ct. E&W | 16W-4S | 27 |
| Warren Ter. NS&EW | | |
| | 15W-4S | 27 |
| Washington St. N&S | | |
| | 15W-6S,15W-4S | 27 |
| Wedgewood Ct. E&W | | |
| | 16W-4S | 27 |
| Wildwood Ln. NS&EW | | |
| | 17W-6S | 27 |
| Woodmere Dr. NS&EW | | |
| | 15W-6S | 27 |
| Woodside Av. E&W | 15W-4S | 27 |
| York Rd. N&S | 15W-4S | 27 |
| 1st St E&W | | |
| | 16W-5S,14W-5S | 27 |
| 2nd St. E&W | | |
| | 16W-5S,15W-5S | 27 |
| 3rd St. E&W | 15W-5S | 27 |
| 4th Av. E&W | 15W-5S | 27 |
| 5th St. E&W | 15W-5S | 27 |
| 6th Av. E&W | 15W-5S | 27 |
| 6th St. E&W | | |
| | 16W-5S,14W-5S | 27 |
| 7th Av. E&W | 15W-5S | 27 |

| | Grid | Page |
|---|---|---|
| 7th St. E&W | | |
| | 16W-5S,15W-5S | 27 |
| 8th Av. E&W | 15W-5S | 27 |
| 8th Pl. E&W | 15W-5S | 27 |
| 8th St. E&W | 16W-4S | 27 |
| 9th Av. E&W | 15W-5S | 27 |
| 9th St. E&W | | |
| | 16W-5S,15W-5S | 27 |
| 55th St. E&W | | |
| | 15W-5S,14W-5S | 27 |
| 56th St. E&W | 15W-6S | 27 |
| 57th St. E&W | 15W-6S | 27 |
| 58th Pl. E&W | 15W-6S | 27 |
| 58th St. E&W | 15W-6S | 27 |

## Itasca

| | Grid | Page |
|---|---|---|
| Alexandra Ct. E&W | 19W-7N | 8 |
| Ardmore Av. E&W | | |
| | 21W-7N,20W-7N | 7 |
| Arlington Heights Rd. NE&SW | | |
| | 19W-6N,19W-7N | 8 |
| Arlington Rd. N&S | 19W-6N | 8 |
| Augusta Cir. N&S | 21W-6N | 7 |
| Baker Dr. N&S | 21W-7N | 7 |
| Birch St. E&W | 19W-6N | 8 |
| Bloomingdale Rd. NE&SW | | |
| | 20W-6N,19W-6N | 8 |
| Bonnie Brae Av. N&S | | |
| | 19W-6N | 8 |
| Briar Pl. N&S | 19W-6N | 8 |
| Broker Av. N&S | 19W-6N | 8 |
| Bryn Mawr Av. N&S | | |
| | 21W-6N,19W-6N | 7 |
| Catalpa Av. N&S | 20W-6N | 8 |
| Center St. E&W | | |
| | 20W-6N,19W-6N | 8 |
| Cherry Cir. N&S | 19W-7N | 8 |
| Cherry Ct. E&W | 19W-7N | 8 |
| Cherry St. N&S | | |
| | 19W-6N,19W-7N | 8 |
| Coldspring Ct. E&W | 19W-7N | 8 |
| Country Club Dr. N&S | | |
| | 19W-6N,19W-7N | 8 |
| Country Club Ln. NW&SE | | |
| | 19W-6N,19W-7N | 8 |
| Crest Av. NS&EW | 21W-7N | 7 |
| Devon Av. E&W | | |
| | 20W-7N,19W-7N | 8 |
| District Dr. N&S | | |
| | 21W-6N,21W-7N | 7 |
| Division St. E&W | | |
| | 20W-6N,19W-6N | 8 |
| Elgin O'Hare Expwy. NW&SE | | |
| | 21W-7N | 7 |
| Elm Cir. N&S | 19W-7N | 8 |
| Elm Ct. E&W | 19W-7N | 8 |
| Elm St. N&S | | |
| | 19W-6N,19W-7N | 8 |
| Emmerson Av. N&S | 19W-6N | 8 |
| Expressway Dr. N&S | | |
| | 20W-7N | 8 |
| FMC Dr. N&S | 21W-7N | 7 |
| Forest Av. N&S | 19W-6N | 8 |
| Frontage Rd. NW&SE | | |
| | 19W-7N,20W-7N | 8 |
| George St. E&W | | |
| | 19W-6N,18W-6N | 8 |
| Glenlake Av. NW&SE | | |
| | 21W-7N | 7 |
| Greenview Rd. NE&SW | | |
| | 19W-6N | 8 |
| Grove St. E&W | 19W-6N | 8 |
| Hamilton Pkwy. E&W | | |
| | 21W-7N | 7 |
| Haverhill Ct. E&W | 19W-7N | 8 |
| Hawthorn Dr. E&W | 20W-6N | 8 |
| Hickory Dr. N&S | 20W-6N | 8 |
| Hillcrest Av. NW&SE | | |
| | 21W-6N | 7 |
| Hilltop Dr. N&S | 19W-7N | 7 |
| Hollywood Av. E&W | 20W-7N | 8 |
| Home Av. N&S | 19W-6N | 8 |
| Industrial Dr. NW&SE | | |
| | 18W-6N | 8 |
| Interstate 290 N&S | | |
| | 20W-6N,20W-7N | 8 |
| Inverness Ln. NS&EW | | |
| | 19W-7N | 8 |
| Irving Park Rd. E&W | | |
| | 21W-6N,18W-6N | 7 |
| Itasca Industrial Dr. E&W | | |
| | 18W-6N | 8 |
| Linden Cir. E&W | 19W-7N | 8 |
| Linden Ct. E&W | 19W-7N | 8 |
| Linden St. N&S | | |
| | 19W-6N,19W-7N | 8 |
| Line St. E&W | 19W-6N | 8 |
| Lombard Rd. N&S | 20W-6N | 8 |
| Maple Av. N&S | | |
| | 19W-6N,19W-7N | 8 |
| Maple St. N&S | 19W-6N | 8 |
| Maplewood Dr. NS&EW | | |
| | 20W-6N | 8 |
| Meacham Rd. N&S | 21W-7N | 7 |
| Medinah Ln. E&W | 21W-6N | 7 |
| Mill Rd. N&S | 19W-5N | 8 |
| Millers Crossing NS&EW | | |
| | 19W-7N | 8 |
| North Cir. N&S | 20W-6N | 8 |
| Norwood St. N&S | 21W-7N | 7 |
| Oak St. N&S | 19W-6N | 8 |
| Orchard St. E&W | 19W-6N | 8 |
| Park Blvd. N&S | 20W-7N | 8 |

| | Grid | Page |
|---|---|---|
| Parkside Av. N&S | 19W-6N | 8 |
| Pierce Rd. NW&SE | 19W-7N | 8 |
| Prairie Rd. N&S | 19W-7N | 8 |
| Preswick Dr. E&W | 21W-6N | 7 |
| Princeton Av. N&S | 19W-6N | 8 |
| Prospect Av. E&W | | |
| | 19W-6N,18W-6N | 8 |
| Rohlwing Rd. N&S | | |
| | 21W-6N,21W-7N | 7 |
| Rt. 19 NW&SE | | |
| | 21W-6N,18W-6N | 7 |
| Rush St. N&S | 19W-6N | 8 |
| Schiller St. NW&SE | 19W-6N | 8 |
| Spring Lake Dr. NS&EW | | |
| | 20W-6N | 8 |
| Spyglass Ct. N&S | 21W-6N | 8 |
| St. Andrew's Cir. N&S | | |
| | 21W-6N | 7 |
| Sunnyside Av. N&S | 19W-6N | 8 |
| Surrey Ln. N&S | 19W-7N | 8 |
| Tall Oaks Ln. NS&EW | | |
| | 25W-7N | 8 |
| Theodore Ln. E&W | 19W-7N | 8 |
| Thorndale Av. E&W | | |
| | 21W-7N,18W-7N | 7 |
| Walnut Av. N&S | 19W-6N | 8 |
| Walnut St. N&S | 19W-6N | 8 |
| Walters Ln. N&S | 19W-7N | 8 |
| Washington St. E&W | | |
| | 19W-6N | 8 |
| Willow St. N&S | 20W-6N | 8 |
| 1st Av. N&S | 19W-6N | 8 |
| 2nd St. N&S | 19W-6N | 8 |

## Lisle

| | Grid | Page |
|---|---|---|
| Abbey Dr. N&S | 23W-5S | 25 |
| Abbeywood Dr. NW&SE | | |
| | 24W-6S | 24 |
| Academy Dr. N&S | 23W-5S | 25 |
| Acorn Hill Ln. E&W | 24W-7S | 24 |
| Adams Dr. E&W | 24W-6S | 24 |
| Adler Ct. N&S | 24W-5S | 24 |
| Alta Ct. NW&SE | 24W-7S | 24 |
| Angel Ln. N&S | 24W-6S | 24 |
| Anton Ct. NW&SE | 24W-7S | 24 |
| Arborview Dr. N&S | 22W-4S | 25 |
| Ascot Ct. N&S | 24W-3S | 18 |
| Ashford Ct. NW&SE | 24W-7S | 24 |
| Aspen Rd. N&S | 24W-7S | 24 |
| Aster Ct. N&S | 22W-5S | 25 |
| Auvergne Av. N&S | 22W-4S | 25 |
| Auvergne Ct. E&W | 22W-5S | 25 |
| Azalea Ln. N&S | 24W-4S | 24 |
| Babst Ct. E&W | 24W-6S | 24 |
| Bannister Ct. NW&SE | | |
| | 23W-7S | 25 |
| Barclay Ct. NE&SW | 24W-3S | 18 |
| Barnwell Ct. NW&SE | | |
| | 24W-5S | 24 |
| Basswood Dr. N&S | 22W-4S | 25 |
| Bayside Ct. E&W | 24W-5S | 24 |
| Beau Bien Blvd. N&S | | |
| | 25W-5S,25W-4S | 24 |
| Beau Bien Dr. E&W | 24W-4S | 24 |
| Beau Monde Blvd. E&W | | |
| | 24W-4S | 24 |
| Beau Monde Dr. N&S | | |
| | 24W-4S | 24 |
| Beau Monde Ln. E&W | | |
| | 24W-4S | 24 |
| Beau Monde Ter. E&W | | |
| | 24W-4S | 24 |
| Benedictine Pkwy. N&S | | |
| | 24W-6S | 24 |
| Bentley Ln. E&W | 24W-7S | 24 |
| Berkshire Ct. N&S | 24W-7S | 24 |
| Black Hawk Ln. N&S | | |
| | 24W-4S | 24 |
| Black Oak Ct. E&W | 24W-4S | 24 |
| Black Partridge Ln. N&S | | |
| | 24W-4S | 24 |
| Bloomfield Dr. NS&EW | | |
| | 24W-7S | 24 |
| Bluebell Ct. E&W | 22W-5S | 25 |
| Bobbi Jo Ln. N&S | 23W-5S | 25 |
| Bonita Ct. N&S | 24W-4S | 24 |
| Bordeaux Pl. NW&SE | | |
| | 24W-4S | 24 |
| Breckenridge Rd. NE&SW | | |
| | 24W-7S | 24 |
| Briarcliff Ln. N&S | 24W-7S | 24 |
| Brighton Ct. NE&SW | | |
| | 24W-6S | 24 |
| Bristol Dr. NS&EW | 24W-6S | 24 |
| Brittany Dr. NW&SE | 24W-6S | 24 |
| Brookline Ct. N&S | 23W-6S | 25 |
| Brookwood Rd. E&W | | |
| | 23W-6S | 25 |
| Brunswick Ct. E&W | 24W-6S | 24 |
| Buckley Av. N&S | 22W-4S | 25 |
| Burgundy Pl. N&S | 24W-4S | 24 |
| Burlington Av. E&W | | |
| | 23W-5S,22W-5S | 25 |
| Burning Tree Ct. E&W | | |
| | 24W-4S | 24 |
| Burr Oak Rd. NW&SE | | |
| | 23W-4S | 25 |
| Bush St. E&W | 22W-5S | 25 |
| Cabot Ct. N&S | 24W-4S | 24 |
| Camden Ct. E&W | 24W-6S | 24 |
| Candle Wood Ct. N&S | | |
| | 24W-5S | 24 |
| Cape Cod Ct. N&S | 25W-7S | 24 |

| | Grid | Page |
|---|---|---|
| Carriage Hill Rd. E&W | | |
| | 24W-7S,23W-7S | 24 |
| Cascade Dr. N&S | | |
| | 24W-6S,24W-5S | 24 |
| Cascara Ln. E&W | 22W-4S | 25 |
| Cedar Ct. NW&SE | 24W-5S | 24 |
| Center Av. N&S | | |
| | 23W-5S,22W-4S | 25 |
| Chateau Pl. NE&SW | 24W-4S | 24 |
| Chatfield Ln. NS&EW | | |
| | 23W-7S | 24 |
| Chelsea Av. N&S | 22W-4S | 25 |
| Cherry Ln. E&W | 24W-4S | 24 |
| Chicago Av. E&W | 22W-5S | 25 |
| Chippewa Ct. E&W | 24W-5S | 24 |
| Christian Ln. NW&SE | | |
| | 24W-6S | 25 |
| Clover Dr. N&S | 22W-5S | 25 |
| Coach House Rd. NS&EW | | |
| | 23W-7S | 24 |
| College Rd. NE&SW | | |
| | 24W-7S,24W-6S | 24 |
| Columbia Av. N&S | 22W-5S | 25 |
| Commerce St. N&S | 24W-4S | 24 |
| Concorde Pl. NE&SW | | |
| | 24W-4S | 24 |
| Corporate West Dr. E&W | | |
| | 24W-4S | 24 |
| Corporetum Dr. E&W | 23W-4S | 25 |
| Cypress Ct. N&S | 24W-5S | 24 |
| Darley Dr. E&W | 23W-4S | 25 |
| Deer Path Ct. NE&SW | | |
| | 24W-7S | 24 |
| Devon Av. N&S | | |
| | 23W-5S,23W-4S | 25 |
| Division St. E&W | | |
| | 23W-5S,22W-5S | 25 |
| Dogwood Ln. E&W | 24W-4S | 24 |
| Dorset Av. N&S | 22W-4S | 25 |
| Driftwood Ct. N&S | 24W-5S | 24 |
| Dry Bridge Ct. NE&SW | | |
| | 23W-7S | 25 |
| Dumoulin Av. N&S | 23W-5S | 25 |
| Edgebrook Ct. N&S | 24W-3S | 18 |
| Edgebrook Ct. E&W | 24W-3S | 18 |
| Eisenhower Ln. E&W | | |
| | 23W-5S | 25 |
| Elm Av. N&S | 22W-5S | 25 |
| Fernwood Dr. NW&SE | | |
| | 24W-6S | 24 |
| Forbes Dr. N&S | 24W-4S | 24 |
| Forest View Rd. N&S | | |
| | 23W-6S | 25 |
| Front St. E&W | | |
| | 23W-5S,22W-5S | 25 |
| Gamble Dr. E&W | 24W-4S | 24 |
| Garden Dr. N&S | 24W-4S | 24 |
| Garfield Av. N&S | 22W-5S | 25 |
| Glenbrook Ct. N&S | 25W-7S | 24 |
| Golfview Dr. N&S | | |
| | 24W-7S,23W-6S | 24 |
| Green Trails Dr. E&W | | |
| | 25W-7S,23W-7S | 24 |
| Greenfield Dr. E&W | 24W-7S | 24 |
| Grenoble Ct. N&S | | |
| | 24W-7S | 24 |
| Hagberg Ct. NW&SE | | |
| | 22W-5S | 25 |
| Hampshire Ct. NE&SW | | |
| | 24W-7S | 24 |
| Hanover Ct. N&S | 24W-7S | 24 |
| Harth Ct. N&S | 23W-6S | 25 |
| Hastings Ln. N&S | 24W-7S | 24 |
| Hatch Ct. NE&SW | 22W-4S | 25 |
| Hatch St. N&S | 22W-4S | 25 |
| Hawthorne Ln. N&S | 23W-5S | 25 |
| Heritage Ln. N&S | 24W-6S | 24 |
| Hickory Dr. NE&SW | 24W-6S | 24 |
| Hidden Creek Ct. E&W | | |
| | 24W-4S | 24 |
| Hills Oak Ln. N&S | 24W-3S | 18 |
| Hillside Ln. NW&SE | 23W-6S | 25 |
| Hilltrail Rd. E&W | 24W-7S | 24 |
| Hinterlong Ct. N&S | 24W-6S | 24 |
| Hitchcock Av. E&W | | |
| | 24W-5S,22W-5S | 24 |
| Holly Ct. NW&SE | 24W-5S | 24 |
| Illinois Av. N&S | 24W-5S | 24 |
| Indiana Av. N&S | 24W-5S | 24 |
| Innsbruck Ct. NE&SW | | |
| | 24W-4S | 24 |
| Inverness Rd. E&W | 22W-5S | 25 |
| Ivanhoe Av. N&S | 22W-4S | 25 |
| Ivy Dr. NS&EW | 22W-5S | 25 |
| Jonquil Av. E&W | | |
| | 23W-5S,22W-5S | 25 |
| Keel Ct.* N&S | 24W-5S | 24 |
| Keller Ct. N&S | 24W-6S | 24 |
| Kent Ct. N&S | 24W-6S | 24 |
| Kindling Ct. NE&SW | 24W-7S | 24 |
| Kingston Av. N&S | | |
| | 22W-5S,22W-4S | 25 |
| Kirkwood Ct. N&S | | |
| | 24W-7S | 24 |
| Knollwood Ct. N&S | | |
| | 24W-7S | 24 |
| Lacey Av. E&W | 23W-4S | 25 |
| Lake Trail Dr. NS&EW | | |
| | 23W-4S,22W-4S | 25 |
| Lake Valley Dr. NE&SW | | |
| | 24W-4S | 24 |

| | Grid | Page |
|---|---|---|
| Lakewood Dr. NE&SW | | |
| | 24W-6S | 24 |
| Larkspur Ln. N&S | 22W-5S | 25 |
| Lexington Dr. N&S | | |
| | 24W-7S,24W-6S | 24 |
| Lincoln Av. N&S | | |
| | 23W-5S,23W-4S | 25 |
| Lisle Pl. E&W | 23W-5S | 25 |
| Longview Dr. E&W | 24W-6S | 24 |
| Lundy Ln. E&W | | |
| | 24W-6S,23W-6S | 24 |
| Main St. NS&EW | | |
| | 23W-5S,23W-4S | 25 |
| Maple Av. E&W | | |
| | 24W-6S,22W-5S | 25 |
| Mark Carre E&W | 24W-4S | 24 |
| Mckinley Av. N&S | 23W-5S | 25 |
| Meadow Ln. NE&SW | | |
| | 22W-5S | 25 |
| Mertz Ct. NE&SW | 24W-6S | 24 |
| Meyer Dr. N&S | 22W-5S | 25 |
| Middleton Av. NW&SE | | |
| | 23W-4S,22W-4S | 25 |
| Mill Bridge Ln. NE&SW | | |
| | 23W-6S | 25 |
| Miller Ln. N&S | 23W-6S | 25 |
| Muirwood Ct. N&S | 24W-7S | 24 |
| Neff Ct. NE&SW | 24W-6S | 24 |
| New Albany Rd. NE&SW | | |
| | 24W-7S,24W-6S | 24 |
| Newport Dr. NE&SW | | |
| | 23W-5S | 25 |
| Normandy Dr. N&S | 24W-4S | 24 |
| Normandy Pl. E&W | | |
| | 24W-4S | 24 |
| North-South Tollway N&S | | |
| | 22W-4S,22W-5S | 25 |
| Nutmeg Ln. N&S | 24W-5S | 24 |
| Oak Hill Dr. E&W | 24W-5S | 24 |
| Oakton Ct. E&W | 24W-6S | 24 |
| Oakview Dr. N&S | 23W-5S | 25 |
| Oakwood Dr. NS&EW | | |
| | 23W-6S | 25 |
| Ogden Av. NE&SW | | |
| | 24W-5S,22W-5S | 24 |
| Ohio St. E&W | | |
| | 22W-5S,22W-5S | 25 |
| Old College Rd. N&S | | |
| | 24W-7S | 24 |
| Old Oaks Dr. NW&SE | | |
| | 24W-5S | 24 |
| Old Tavern Rd. NW&SE | | |
| | 24W-5S,24W-5S | 24 |
| Oldham Av. E&W | | |
| | 23W-4S,22W-4S | 25 |
| Parksleg Ct.* NE&SW | | |
| | 24W-5S | 24 |
| Patton Dr. N&S | 23W-5S | 25 |
| Pebble Creek Dr. E&W | | |
| | 24W-4S | 24 |
| Pennywood Dr. N&S | | |
| | 24W-4S | 24 |
| Peppertree Ct. NE&SW | | |
| | 24W-7S | 24 |
| Pin Oak Ct. N&S | 24W-3S | 18 |
| Pine Tree Ct. E&W | 23W-4S | 25 |
| Pinehurst Ct. N&S | 24W-7S | 24 |
| Pleasant Hill Ln. NW&SE | | |
| | 23W-6S | 25 |
| Portsmouth Dr. E&W | | |
| | 23W-5S | 25 |
| Prutmore Ct.* NE&SW | | |
| | 24W-7S | 24 |
| Raintree Ct. NW&SE | | |
| | 24W-7S | 24 |
| Ranier Dr. NE&SW | | |
| | 24W-6S,24W-5S | 24 |
| Red Oak Ln. N&S | 24W-3S | 18 |
| Redwood Ln. E&W | 22W-4S | 25 |
| Regency Woods Dr. E&W | | |
| | 24W-3S | 18 |
| Regency Woods Ln. E&W | | |
| | 24W-3S | 18 |
| Rehm Ct. E&W | 23W-6S | 25 |
| Reilly Pl. N&S | 23W-5S | 25 |
| Rickert Ct. N&S | 24W-6S | 24 |
| Ridgewood Rd. N&S | | |
| | 24W-7S | 24 |
| Riedy Rd. N&S | | |
| | 23W-5S,22W-5S | 25 |
| River Dr. N&S | | |
| | 23W-5S,23W-4S | 25 |
| Riverview Dr. N&S | 23W-5S | 25 |
| Robin Ln. NW&SE | 23W-5S | 25 |
| Rolling Dr. E&W | | |
| | 23W-5S,22W-5S | 25 |
| Royal Glen Ct. N&S | 23W-7S | 25 |
| Sailboat Bay* NW&SE | | |
| | 24W-5S | 24 |
| Scarlet Oak Ln. E&W | | |
| | 24W-6S | 24 |
| School St. N&S | 23W-5S | 25 |
| Shabbona Ln. N&S | 24W-4S | 24 |
| Shagbark Ct. NE&SW | | |
| | 23W-7S | 25 |
| Shasta Dr. E&W | 24W-6S | 24 |
| Shellingham Dr. NS&EW | | |
| | 24W-6S | 24 |
| Shorewood Ct. NW&SE | | |
| | 24W-5S | 24 |
| Short St. E&W | 23W-5S | 25 |
| Sleepy Hollow Ln. N&S | | |
| | 23W-7S,23W-6S | 25 |

**Grid / Page**

Southbury Ct. NE&SW .......... 25W-7S — 24
Southport Av. E&W . 23W-4S — 25
Spencer Av. N&S ... 23W-5S — 25
Spruce Ln. NE&SW .. 22W-4S — 25
St. Joseph Creek Rd. NW&SE .. 22W-4S,22W-5S — 25
Stonehaven Way .......... 24W-7S — 24
Stowe Ct. NE&SW .. 24W-7S — 24
Sun Valley Rd. NE&SW .......... 24W-7S — 24
Sunnydale Ln. NS&EW .......... 23W-7S — 24
Surrey Ridge Rd. NW&SE ... 24W-6S,24W-5S — 24
Tall Tree Ct. E&W .. 24W-5S — 24
Tanglewood Dr. E&W .......... 24W-7S — 24
Taos Ct. N&S .... 24W-7S — 24
Tealwood Dr. E&W . 24W-7S — 24
Tellis Ln. E&W .... 24W-6S — 24
Telluride Ct. N&S .. 24W-7S — 24
Timbertrails Dr. E&W .......... 24W-7S — 24
Timberview Dr. NW&SE .......... 24W-6S — 24
Torey Pine Ln. N&S . 24W-6S — 24
Tory Ct. N&S ..... 24W-6S — 24
Trinity Dr. NS&EW .. 24W-6S — 24
Trowbridge Way* NE&SW .......... 23W-6S — 25
Twin Oaks Ln. NS&EW .......... 24W-7S — 24
Tyrnbury Dr. N&S .. 24W-6S — 24
University Dr. E&W . 23W-5S — 25
Vail Ct. E&W ...... 24W-7S — 24
Valley Forge Rd. E&W .......... 24W-7S — 24
Varsity Dr. N&S .... 23W-5S — 25
Venture St. N&S ... 22W-5S — 25
Walnut Creek Ln. E&W .......... 22W-5S — 25
Warrenville Rd. E&W .......... 22W-4S — 25
Waterbridge Rd. N&S .......... 25W-4S — 24
Waubansie Ln. N&S. 24W-4S — 24
Wayfaring Ln. E&W . 24W-4S — 24
Wedgewood Ct. N&S .......... 24W-4S — 24
Weeping Willow Dr. E&W .......... 24W-6S — 24
Wellington Av. E&W .24W-5S — 24
West Av. N&S .... 22W-5S — 25
Western Av. N&S....24W-4S — 24
Western Ct. E&W ..24W-4S — 24
Westleigh Ct. N&S . 24W-4S — 24
Westview Ln. N&S .. 22W-5S — 25
White Birch Dr. NS&EW .......... 23W-4S — 25
White Oak La. E&W. 24W-7S — 24
Wildwood Ct. N&S .. 24W-7S — 24
Winchester Av. N&S ..... 23W-5S,23W-4S — 25
Windsor Dr., N. E&W .......... 24W-6S — 24
Windsor Dr., S. E&W .......... 24W-6S — 24
Windward Ct.* NE&SW .......... 25W-5S — 24
Windward Rd.* NE&SW .......... 25W-5S — 24
Winkler Ct. N&S .. 23W-6S — 25
Winstead Ct.* NW&SE .......... 25W-5S — 24
Wisconsin St. E&W . 24W-5S — 24
Woodbriar Ct. NE&SW .......... 24W-7S — 24
Woodcliff Ct. E&W . 24W-7S — 24
Yackley Av. N&S ..... 24W-6S,24W-4S — 24
Yender Av. N&S ..... 24W-5S,24W-4S — 24
Yorkshire Dr. NE&SW .......... 24W-7S — 24

### Lisle Township

Aintree Dr. N&S .. 23W-8S — 31
Allison Av. N&S.... 24W-5S — 24
Arguilla Dr. E&W .. 21W-6S — 25
Arlington Av. N&S .. 24W-5S — 24
Arrow Ct. NE&SW .. 24W-6S — 24
Augusta N&S........23W-7S — 25
Avalieri Av. N&S.... 24W-5S — 24
Avon Ct. N&S .... 24W-6S — 24
Baltusroll Rd. N&S .. 23W-7S — 25
Beau Bien Blvd. N&S .......... 24W-5S — 24
Bell Dr. N&S ........ 25W-8S — 30
Birdsong Ct. N&S .. 24W-6S — 24
Black Oak Dr. N&S. 23W-4S — 25
Black Stone Ct. N&S .......... 24W-6S — 24
Blackthorne Ln. N&S .......... 24W-8S — 30
Blanchard St. NE&SW .......... 24W-5S — 24
Bluff Ct. NE&SW .. 24W-5S — 24
Bluff Ln. E&W .... 24W-5S — 24
Boundary Hill Rd. N&S .......... 22W-8S — 31

Brandywine Ct. E&W .......... 25W-6S — 24
Brenwood Dr. N&S . 23W-8S — 31
Bridlespur Dr. NS&EW .......... 25W-6S — 24
Burlington Av. E&W ..... 25W-5S,24W-5S — 24
Buttonwood Ct. N&S .......... 24W-5S — 24
Canary Ct. E&W .... 25W-5S — 24
Canterbury Ct. NW&SE .......... 25W-6S — 24
Cape Rd. NS&EW .. 25W-6S — 24
Cardinal Ct. NW&SE .......... 24W-5S — 24
Carlyle Ct. NS&EW . 24W-6S — 24
Case St. E&W ...... 26W-5S — 24
Chantilly Ct. E&W ...23W-7S — 25
Charles St. N&S ... 25W-5S — 24
Chase Av. N&S...... 21W-6S — 25
Chicago Av. E&W ..... 25W-6S,24W-6S — 24
Cliff Ct. E&W ..... 24W-5S,22W-6S — 24
Clover Dr. N&S .... 22W-6S — 25
Cloverdale Ct. N&S . 24W-5S — 24
Cohasset Rd. N&S .. 24W-5S — 24
College Rd. NS&EW ..... 24W-8S,21W-6S — 30
Columbine Av. E&W 22W-6S — 25
Concord Rd. NE&SW .......... 25W-6S — 24
Cornwall Rd. NW&SE .......... 25W-6S — 24
Country Ct. E&W .. 23W-7S — 25
Country Dr. N&S ... 24W-6S — 24
Creek Ct. E&W .... 23W-7S — 25
Creek Dr. N&S ..... 23W-8S,23W-7S — 31
Cross St. N&S ..... 21W-5S,21W-4S — 25
Derby Ct. E&W .... 24W-8S — 30
Derby Dr. NE&SW .. 23W-8S — 31
Devon Av. N&S..... 23W-4S — 25
Donwood Dr. N&S .. 24W-7S — 24
Donwood Dr., E. NE&SW .......... 24W-7S — 24
Donwood Dr., W. N&S .......... 24W-7S — 24
Donwood Trails Dr. N&S .......... 23W-7S — 25
Dorset Av. N&S....23W-4S — 25
Dover Dr. N&S ...... 22W-6S — 25
Drendall Rd. N&S ..... 21W-5S,21W-4S — 25
Dunham Dr. NW&SE .......... 23W-8S — 31
Dupage Dr. N&S .. 22W-7S — 25
East Lake Dr. NS&EW .......... 23W-6S — 25
Elinor Av. N&S .... 21W-6S — 25
Elm St. N&S ...... 22W-6S — 25
Essex Rd. N&S .... 24W-6S — 24
Eugena Dr. NE&SW..24W-5S — 24
Evergreen Dr. N&S .. 23W-6S — 25
Fairway Dr. E&W .. 23W-6S — 25
Fender Av. N&S ..... 24W-5S,24W-4S — 24
Forest View Rd. N&S .......... 23W-6S — 25
Four Lakes Av. E&W .......... 23W-6S — 25
Foxwood Ct. NW&SE .......... 23W-8S — 31
Francisco St. N&S . 21W-5S — 25
Glenview Av. N&S ..... 21W-6S,21W-5S — 25
Green Briar Ct. E&W .......... 23W-7S — 25
Green Briar Dr. E&W .......... 23W-7S — 25
Green Trails Dr. E&W .......... 23W-7S — 25
Greene Rd. N&S ..... 23W-9S,23W-7S — 31
Greenview Rd. . 23W-6S — 25
Greenwich Ct. NW&SE .......... 25W-6S — 24
Greenwood Ct. N&S .......... 24W-6S — 24
Gunston Av. NW&SE .......... 25W-6S — 24
Hampton Cir. NS&EW .......... 23W-8S — 31
Heather Ct. E&W .. 24W-5S — 24
Hemlock Ln. E&W ..... 24W-8S,23W-8S — 30
Highview Dr. E&W .. 25W-4S — 24
Hillcrest Av. N&S .. 21W-6S — 25
Hillcrest Ln. N&S .. 23W-6S — 25
Hillside Dr. E&W .. 26W-7S — 24
Hobson Rd. E&W ..... 25W-8S,23W-7S — 30
Hobson Trails Dr. N&S .......... 23W-7S — 25
Howard Av. E&W .. 21W-5S — 25
Hummingbird Ln. NE&SW ..... 25W-5S,24W-5S — 24
Hyacinth Ct. NE&SW .......... 24W-6S — 24
Indian Hill Dr. N&S . 23W-4S — 25
Iris Ln. N&S ...... 22W-6S — 25
Ivanhoe Av. N&S .. 22W-6S — 25
James Way E&W .. 23W-8S — 31

Janes Av. N&S .. 21W-6S — 25
Jefferson St. NE&SW .......... 21W-6S — 25
Julian St. N&S .... 26W-7S — 24
Kame Ct. NW&SE .. 25W-4S — 24
Kammes Dr. E&W .. 24W-7S — 24
Karns Rd. N&S .... 24W-7S — 24
Katrine Av. N&S .. 21W-6S — 25
Keim Dr. N&S .... 23W-4S — 25
Kimberly Way E&W . 22W-6S — 25
Kimberwick Ln. E&W .......... 23W-8S — 31
Kings Cove N&S .. 23W-8S — 31
Kingston Av. N&S...22W-6S — 25
Kohley Rd. E&W ..... 23W-6S,22W-6S — 25
Lacey Av. N&S...... 25W-4S — 24
Lakeside Dr. N&S .. 24W-6S — 24
Lakewood Dr. N&S . 24W-6S — 24
Leask Ln. N&S.... 24W-6S — 24
Lenox Ct. N&S .... 22W-6S — 25
Lenox Rd. N&S ..... 23W-6S,22W-6S — 25
Lincoln Av N&S ..... 23W-6S,23W-4S — 25
Lomond Av. N&S ..... 21W-6S,21W-5S — 25
Longreen Rd. N&S .......... 25W-6S5S — 25
Lyn Dr. N&S .... 23W-7S — 25
Malibu Ct. NE&SW ..... 24W-6S,24W-4S — 24
Malibu Ln. E&W ... 24W-6S — 24
Mallard Ct. E&W .. 24W-5S — 24
Maple Ter. E&W .. 23W-6S — 25
Marble Head Ct. NE&SW .......... 25W-6S — 24
Marion N&S ...... 24W-7S — 25
Mariwood Ct. NW&SE .......... 24W-6S — 24
Matson Ln. E&W .. 23W-4S — 25
Mayflower Av. NE&SW .......... 25W-6S — 24
Maywood Ln. E&W . 22W-6S — 25
Mcintyre Rd. N&S .. 21W-4S — 25
Meadow Dr. N&S .. 23W-6S — 25
Meadow Lake Dr. N&S ..... 25W-5S,24W-5S — 24
Meadowbrook Ct. NE&SW .......... 25W-6S — 24
Middle Rd. N&S .... 25W-5S — 24
Middleton Av. E&W ..... 25W-4S,23W-4S — 24
Millcreek Ct. N&S .. 25W-6S — 24
Millcreek Ln. N&S...25W-6S — 24
Mitchell Ln. N&S ..... 23W-8S,23W-7S — 31
Mockingbird Ct. N&S .......... 24W-5S — 24
Moraine Ct. N&S .. 23W-7S — 25
Morton Rd. E&W .. 23W-4S — 25
Murray Dr. N&S .. 23W-8S — 31
Neptune Ct. E&W .. 24W-6S — 24
New Hope Rd. NW&SE .......... 23W-6S — 25
Newcastle Dr. NE&SW .......... 24W-6S — 24
Northcrest Dr. E&W ..22W-7S — 25
Oak Trails Dr. N&S . 23W-7S — 25
Ohio St. E&W .... 24W-5S — 24
Oldham Rd. E&W .. 25W-4S — 24
Oldwoods Dr. E&W .. 22W-9S — 31
Oriole Ln. NW&SE ..... 25W-5S,24W-5S — 24
Oxer Ct. E&W .... 23W-8S — 31
Oxford Ln. N&S ... 24W-8S — 30
Palamino Dr. N&S...24W-8S — 30
Park Meadow Dr. N&S ..... 24W-6S,24W-5S — 24
Parkside Av. E&W .. 26W-7S — 24
Parkview Ct. N&S .. 24W-6S — 24
Partridge Ct. E&W .. 24W-6S — 24
Pellum Ct. N&S .... 23W-8S — 31
Pershing Av. N&S...21W-6S — 25
Pin Oak Ln. E&W .. 24W-8S — 30
Pine Ln. N&S .... 23W-4S — 25
Pine Rd. E&W .... 23W-4S — 25
Pinehurst Ct. N&S .. 23W-7S — 25
Pinehurst Ln. E&W . 23W-7S — 25
Plank Rd. NE&SW ..... 26W-6S,25W-5S — 24
Prairie Av. E&W .. 21W-5S — 25
Prentiss Dr. NW&SE .......... 21W-7S — 25
Primrose Av. N&S .. 21W-5S — 25
Prince Ct. E&W .. 22W-6S — 25
Queens Cove N&S .. 22W-6S — 25
Radcliff Rd. N&S .......... 24W-5S — 24
Ridge View Ln. NW&SE .......... 24W-5S — 24
Ridgeland Av. E&W . 25W-4S — 24
River Dr. N&S ...... 25W-8S — 30
River Rd. N&S ...... 23W-6S — 25
Riverview Dr. N&S .. 23W-6S — 25
Rose Av. N&S .... 21W-5S — 25
Rose Av. E&W .... 22W-6S — 25
Royal Oak Rd. E&W .......... 23W-8S — 31
Salem Av. N&S .. 25W-6S — 24
Setauket Av. E&W ..... 25W-6S,25W-5S — 24
Shires Ln. N&S .... 23W-8S — 31
Sierra Ln. NE&SW .. 24W-5S — 24

Singtree Ct. N&S .... 23W-8S — 31
Smith Rd. E&W ..... 23W-6S,22W-6S — 25
Snowdrop Ln. N&S .. 22W-6S — 25
Somerset Ct. NE&SW .......... 24W-6S — 24
South Rd. E&W ..... 23W-6S,22W-6S — 25
Southcrest Dr. E&W ..... 22W-7S,21W-7S — 25
Spring Bay Dr. NW&SE .......... 24W-6S — 24
Springdale Dr. NW&SE ..... 24W-6S,24W-5S — 24
Spyglass Ct. E&W .. 23W-7S — 25
Starling Ct. NW&SE ..24W-5S — 24
Steeple Run Dr. N&S ..... 24W-6S,24W-5S — 24
Stonehedg Ct. E&W . 23W-8S — 31
Stonehedg Dr. E&W. 23W-8S — 31
Summit Dr. NE&SW . 25W-4S — 24
Surf Ct. E&W .... 24W-5S — 24
Surrey Av. E&W .. 25W-8S — 30
Tamiami Ct. N&S .. 22W-7S — 25
Teddo Av. NE&SW ..... 25W-5S,24W-5S — 24
Tuthill Rd. N&S .... 25W-4S — 24
Una Av. N&S...... 22W-9S — 31
Vale Ct. NW&SE .. 21W-7S — 25
Vest St. N&S .... 26W-5S — 24
Walnut Av. N&S .. 24W-7S — 25
Wayewood Ln. NS&EW .......... 23W-8S — 31
Wedgewood Ct. E&W .......... 23W-7S — 25
Wellington Av. NE&SW .......... 24W-5S — 24
Westove Ct. E&W .. 24W-5S — 24
Westview Ln. N&S ..... 22W-6S,22W-5S — 25
White Oak Dr. N&S .. 26W-7S — 24
Whittington Ct. NE&SW .......... 23W-8S — 31
Wilshire Dr. N&S .. 22W-7S — 25
Windham Hill Ct. NW&SE .......... 25W-5S — 24
Wood Ct. N&S ..... 25W-4S,22W-6S — 24
Woodbrook Dr. E&W .......... 24W-6S — 24
Woodcrest Ct., E. E&W .......... 23W-7S — 25
Woodcrest Ct., W. E&W .......... 23W-7S — 25
Woodlawn Av. E&W ..26W-7S — 24
Woodstock Ct. E&W .......... 25W-6S — 24
Woodward Av. N&S..21W-6S — 25
Yackley Av. N&S .. 24W-8S — 30
59th St. E&W ..... 22W-6S,21W-6S — 25
61st St. E&W ..... 22W-6S,21W-6S — 25
62nd St. E&W ..... 22W-6S,21W-6S — 25
63rd St. E&W ..... 22W-7S,21W-7S — 25
75th St. E&W ..... 24W-8S,22W-8S — 30
79th St. E&W...... 23W-8S — 31

### Lombard

Acorn Ct.* N&S...21W-1S — 19
Adams Av. N&S .. 18W-0S — 20
Addison Av. N&S .. 18W-0N — 14
Addison Av. NS&EW .......... 18W-0S — 20
Ahrens Av. N&S ..... 18W-0S,18W-1N — 20
Ahrens Ct. N&S .. 18W-0N — 14
Ainsley Ln. N&S .. 19W-1S — 20
Ann St. E&W ..... 20W-0S,19W-0S — 20
Apple Ln. N&S .. 19W-0S — 20
Arthur Dr. N&S .. 18W-0S — 20
Ash St. E&W........20W-0N — 14
Berkshire Av. E&W ..... 20W-1N,19W-1N — 14
Beverly Ct. N&S .. 21W-1S — 19
Bradley Ln. NE&SW .19W-0S — 20
Brewster Av. N&S .. 20W-0N — 14
Broadview Av. N&S .. 20W-1N — 14
Brookfield Av. E&W..20W-1N — 14
Brown St. E&W......20W-1N — 14
Cambria Ln., N. NS&EW .......... 18W-0S — 20
Cambria Ln., S. NS&EW .......... 18W-0S — 20
Cedar Ln. N&S .. 18W-0N — 14
Central Av. E&W ..... 20W-0S,19W-0S — 20
Charing Cross Rd. N&S .......... 19W-0S — 20
Charles Ln. E&W .. 20W-0N — 14
Charlotte St. E&W ..... 19W-1S,19W-1N — 20
Chase Av. N&S ..... 19W-0N,19W-1N — 14
Chase Ct. NE&SW .. 18W-0S — 20
Chase Ln. N&S .. 19W-0S — 20
Cherry Ln. N&S...19W-0S — 20
Circle Av. N&S .. 19W-0S — 20
Circle Ter. N&S......19W-0N — 14

Clarendon Av. N&S . 19W-1N — 14
Collen Ct. NW&SE .. 20W-1S — 20
Collen Dr. N&S .... 20W-1S — 20
Colony Ct. NW&SE . 20W-1S — 20
Columbine Av. N&S .. 21W-1N — 13
Concord Ln. N&S .. 18W-0S — 20
Cortland Av. E&W .. 20W-2N — 14
Craig Pl. E&W ..... 19W-0N,19W-1N — 14
Crescent Blvd. E&W .......... 20W-0N — 14
Crystal Av. E&W .. 20W-1N — 14
Daniel Ct. N&S .. 20W-0S — 20
Division St. E&W ..... 19W-0N,18W-0N — 14
Downing St. NW&SE .......... 21W-1S — 19
DuPage Av. N&S ..... 20W-1N,20W-2N — 14
East West Tollway E&W .......... 19W-2S — 20
Eastview Ter. E&W .. 19W-0N — 14
Edgewood Av. N&S ..... 19W-0S,19W-1N — 20
Edson Dr. N&S ..... 20W-0S,20W-0N — 20
Edson Pl. E&W .. 20W-0S — 20
Edward St. E&W ..... 20W-0S,20W-0S — 20
Eisenhower Ln., N. E&W .......... 20W-2S — 20
Eisenhower Ln., S. E&W .......... 20W-2S — 20
Elizabeth Ct. N&S . 20W-0N — 14
Elizabeth Dr. N&S .. 20W-0N — 14
Elizabeth St. N&S ..... 20W-1S,20W-1N — 20
Elm St. E&W .... 19W-0N — 14
Emerson Av. N&S ..... 19W-0N,18W-0N — 20
Ethel Av. E&W .. 20W-0S — 20
Eugenia St. E&W .. 20W-0N — 14
Fairfield Av. N&S ..... 19W-2S,19W-1N — 20
Fairview Av. N&S .... 18W-0S — 20
Finley Rd. N&S ..... 20W-2S,20W-0N — 20
Fountainview Ln. E&W .......... 20W-2S — 20
Foxworth Blvd. NE&SW ..... 21W-1S,20W-1S — 19
Garfield St. N&S ..... 19W-1S,19W-2N — 20
Garfield Ter. N&S .... 19W-0N — 14
Glen Oak Rd. E&W .. 20W-0N — 14
Glenview Av. NE&SW .......... 20W-0N — 14
Glenwood Ln. NW&SE .......... 21W-1N — 13
Goebel Dr. E&W ..... 20W-1N,19W-1N — 14
Grace Av. N&S .... 19W-1N — 14
Grace St. N&S ..... 19W-2S,19W-0N — 20
Graham Av. E&W .. 20W-0S — 20
Graywood Dr. N&S .. 19W-1S — 20
Green Valley Dr. NS&EW ..... 20W-0S,20W-0N — 20
Green Valley Dr., W. E&W .......... 20W-0N — 14
Greenfield Av. E&W .. 20W-1N — 14
Grove St. E&W...... 20W-0N — 14
Hamilton Ln. E&W .. 18W-0S — 20
Hammerschmidt Av. N&S .......... 19W-0S — 20
Harding Rd. E&W ..... 20W-0S,19W-0S — 20
Harmony Ln. N&S .. 18W-0N — 14
Harrelson Dr. E&W . 20W-1S — 20
Harrison Rd. E&W ..... 20W-0S,19W-0S — 20
Hawthorn Cir. E&W ..... 19W-0S,18W-0S — 20
Hickory Rd. E&W ....20W-0N — 14
Hickory St. E&W ..... 20W-0N,19W-0N — 14
High Ridge Rd. E&W ..... 19W-0S,18W-0S — 20
Highland Av. E&W ..... 19W-2S,19W-0S — 20
Highlands Lake Dr. N&S .......... 20W-2S — 20
Hillcrest Ct. NW&SE 20W-1S — 20
Hillcrest Ln. NE&SW .. 20W-1S — 20
Hunter St. E&W .... 21W-1S — 19
International Dr. E&W .......... 20W-1S — 20
Interstate 88 NE&SW .......... 19W-1S — 20
Jackson St. E&W .. 18W-0S — 20
Janata Blvd. E&W .. 20W-2S — 20
Jeffrey Ct. N&S......20W-0S — 20
Joyce Av. N&S .. 19W-1N — 14
June Ln. E&W .... 20W-1S — 20
Kaplan Ct. E&W .. 19W-1N — 14
Kelly Ct. N&S...... 18W-0N — 14
Kenilworth Av. E&W  19W-1N — 14
Kramer Av. N&S .. 19W-1N — 14
Lalonde Av. N&S ..... 19W-0S,18W-1N — 20
Lalonde St. N&S .. 19W-0N — 14
LeMoyne Av. E&W ..... 20W-1N,19W-1N — 14

| | Grid | Page |
|---|---|---|
| Lewis Av. N&S | | |
| | 19W-0S,19W-1N | 20 |
| Liberty Ln. N&S | 18W-0S | 20 |
| Lilac Ln. E&W | 20W-0N | 14 |
| Lilac Way E&W | | |
| | 19W-0S,18W-0S | 20 |
| Lincoln Ct. N&S | 20W-0N | 14 |
| Lincoln St. N&S | | |
| | 20W-1S,20W-1N | 20 |
| Lloyd Av. N&S | 21W-1S | 19 |
| Lodge Av. N&S | 19W-0N | 14 |
| Lodge Ln. N&S | 19W-0S | 20 |
| Lombard Av. E&W | | |
| | 19W-0S,19W-1N | 20 |
| Lombard Cir. NW&SE | | |
| | 18W-0S | 20 |
| Lombard Rd. N&S | 20W-2N | 14 |
| Lore Ln. E&W | 20W-1N | 14 |
| Loy St. E&W | 20W-1N | 14 |
| Lynne Ln. E&W | 20W-1S | 20 |
| Madison St. E&W | | |
| | 20W-0S,18W-0S | 20 |
| Magnolia Cir. E&W | 19W-0S | 20 |
| Main Dr. N&S | 19W-0S | 20 |
| Main St. N&S | | |
| | 20W-2S,20W-2N | 20 |
| Majestic Dr. E&W | 19W-2S | 20 |
| Manor Hill Ct. E&W | 20W-1S | 20 |
| Manor Hill Ln. | 20W-1S | 20 |
| Maple St. E&W | | |
| | 20W-0N,18W-0N | 14 |
| Marcus Dr. E&W | 19W-1N | 14 |
| Martha St. N&S | | |
| | 19W-0N,19W-1N | 14 |
| Meadow Ln. E&W | 19W-1S | 14 |
| Meadow Ln. E&W | 20W-0N | 14 |
| Michele Ln. NE&SW | 19W-0S | 20 |
| Morningside Av. E&W | | |
| | 19W-0N | 14 |
| Morris Av. E&W | | |
| | 20W-0S,18W-0S | 20 |
| Morris Ct. E&W | 19W-0S | 20 |
| New St. E&W | 19W-0S | 20 |
| Norbury Av. N&S | 19W-0S | 20 |
| North Av. E&W | 20W-2N | 14 |
| North Broadway E&W | | |
| | 19W-0N,19W-1N | 14 |
| North Lake Rd. NS&EW | | |
| | 19W-1S | 20 |
| North-South Tollway N&S | | |
| | 21W-0N,20W-1S | 13 |
| Norton St. E&W | | |
| | 19W-0S,18W-0S | 20 |
| Oak Creek Dr. E&W | | |
| | 21W-0S,20W-0S | 19 |
| Oak Meadow Ct.* N&S | | |
| | 21W-1S | 19 |
| Oakton Dr. E&W | 20W-2S | 20 |
| Orchard Ter. N&S | 20W-0N | 14 |
| Park Av. N&S | | |
| | 20W-0N,20W-1N | 14 |
| Park Dr. E&W | 20W-0S | 20 |
| Park Rd. N&S | 20W-0N | 14 |
| Park Road Ct. E&W | 20W-0N | 14 |
| Parker Dr. E&W | 19W-1N | 14 |
| Parkside Av. NE&SW | | |
| | 20W-0N,19W-0N | 14 |
| Parkview Blvd. N&S | 21W-0S | 19 |
| Phillips Ct. E&W | 21W-0N | 14 |
| Pinebrook Dr. E&W | 20W-1S | 20 |
| Pleasant Ln. E&W | | |
| | 20W-1N,19W-1N | 14 |
| Poplar Ct.* N&S | 21W-1S | 19 |
| Potomac Av. E&W | 20W-1N | 14 |
| Prairie Av. E&W | | |
| | 20W-1N,19W-1N | 14 |
| Progress Rd. E&W | 19W-2N | 14 |
| Queensbury Ct. E&W | | |
| | 21W-1S | 19 |
| Randolph St. E&W | 19W-0N | 14 |
| Rebecca Rd. NS&EW | | |
| | 20W-1S | 20 |
| Regency Rd. E&W | 19W-2S | 20 |
| Reskin Rd. E&W | 19W-1N | 14 |
| Revere Ct. E&W | 18W-0S | 20 |
| Ridge Av. N&S | | |
| | 20W-1N,20W-2N | 14 |
| Rochelle Ter. N&S | 20W-1N | 14 |
| Roosevelt Rd. E&W | | |
| | 20W-0S,19W-0S | 20 |
| Royal Dr. N&S | 19W-2S | 20 |
| Rt. 38 E&W | | |
| | 20W-0S,19W-0S | 20 |
| Rt. 64 E&W | | |
| | 20W-2N,19W-2N | 14 |
| School Ct. E&W | 18W-0S | 20 |
| School St. N&S | | |
| | 18W-0S,18W-0N | 20 |
| Shedron Way E&W | 21W-1S | 19 |
| Sheila Pl. N&S | 20W-1N | 14 |
| South Broadway E&W | | |
| | 19W-0N | 14 |
| Springer Dr. NS&EW | | |
| | 20W-1S | 20 |
| Spruce Ct.* N&S | 21W-1S | 19 |
| St. Charles Pl. E&W | 19W-0N | 14 |
| St. Charles Rd. NE&SW | | |
| | 20W-0N,18W-0N | 14 |
| St. Regis Dr. N&S | 19W-1S | 20 |
| Stewart Av. N&S | | |
| | 19W-0S,19W-1N | 20 |
| Stewart Ln. E&W | 19W-2S | 20 |
| Sunset Av. E&W | | |
| | 20W-1N,19W-1N | 14 |

| | Grid | Page |
|---|---|---|
| Sycamore Ct.* N&S | 21W-1S | 19 |
| Taylor Rd. E&W | | |
| | 20W-0S,19W-0S | 20 |
| Troy Dr. E&W | 20W-1N | 14 |
| Troy Ln. N&S | 20W-1N | 14 |
| Valley Rd. NS&EW | 21W-1S | 19 |
| Vance Ct. N&S | 20W-0N | 14 |
| Vance St. N&S | 20W-0N | 14 |
| View Av. N&S | 19W-0N | 14 |
| View St. E&W | | |
| | 20W-1N,19W-1N | 14 |
| Vista Av. N&S | 19W-1N | 14 |
| Walnut Ct.* N&S | 21W-1S | 19 |
| Washington Blvd. E&W | | |
| | 20W-0N,18W-0N | 14 |
| Waters Edge NE&SW | | |
| | 20W-1S | 20 |
| West Rd. N&S | | |
| | 20W-0N,20W-1N | 14 |
| Western Av. NE&SW | | |
| | 19W-1N | 14 |
| Westmore Av. N&S | | |
| | 18W-0N,18W-1N | 14 |
| Westwood Av. N&S | 19W-1N | 14 |
| Whitehall St. NW&SE | | |
| | 21W-1S | 19 |
| Willow St. E&W | 20W-0N | 14 |
| Wilson Av. E&W | | |
| | 19W-0S,18W-0S | 20 |
| Wilson Av. NS&EW | 18W-0S | 20 |
| Wilson Ct. N&S | 18W-0S | 20 |
| Windsor Av. E&W | | |
| | 20W-1N,19W-1N | 14 |
| Witt Dr. NW&SE | 21W-1S | 19 |
| Woodland Av. E&W | 20W-1N | 14 |
| Woodridge Way N&S | | |
| | 20W-2S | 20 |
| Woodrow Av. E&W | 18W-0N | 14 |
| 2nd Av. N&S | 18W-0N | 14 |
| 3rd Av. N&S | 18W-0N | 14 |
| 13th St. E&W | 19W-1N | 14 |
| 16th St. E&W | | |
| | 20W-1S,19W-1S | 20 |
| 17th Pl. E&W | 20W-1S | 20 |
| 17th St. E&W | 20W-1S | 20 |
| 18th St. E&W | 20W-1S | 20 |
| 19th St. E&W | 20W-1S | 20 |
| 22nd St. E&W | | |
| | 20W-1S,19W-1S | 20 |

## Milton Township

| | Grid | Page |
|---|---|---|
| Acorn Av. E&W | 21W-0N | 13 |
| Ahlstrand Rd. E&W | | |
| | 22W-2S,21W-2S | 19 |
| Apache Dr. E&W | 25W-2S | 18 |
| Arbor Ln. NE&SW | 22W-3S | 19 |
| Arboretum Cir. E&W | | |
| | 24W-3S | 18 |
| Arboretum Rd. E&W | | |
| | 22W-3S,22W-2S | 19 |
| Arbrust Av. E&W | 26W-0N | 12 |
| Argyle St. N&S | 23W-1N | 12 |
| Arnold Av. N&S | 23W-1N | 12 |
| Arrow Glen Ct. NS&EW | | |
| | 26W-2S | 18 |
| Arrowhead Dr. N&S | 26W-2S | 18 |
| Ashley Dr. NE&SW | 23W-2S | 18 |
| Astor Pl. E&W | 26W-0N | 12 |
| Audubon Ct. NE&SW | | |
| | 21W-2S | 19 |
| Audubon Rd. NW&SE | | |
| | 21W-2S | 19 |
| Balsam Ln. NW&SE | 22W-3S | 19 |
| Bancroft Ct. N&S | 23W-2S | 18 |
| Barclay Pl. N&S | 23W-2S | 18 |
| Barry Av. N&S | 26W-0N | 12 |
| Bayberry Ln. N&S | 25W-1S | 18 |
| Beechwood Ln. N&S | | |
| | 22W-2S | 19 |
| Bemis Rd. E&W | 23W-1N | 19 |
| Beverly St. N&S | | |
| | 26W-0S,26W-0N | 18 |
| Big Horn Dr. N&S | 25W-2S | 18 |
| Birch Av. N&S | 26W-0N | 12 |
| Birchwood Dr. NW&SE | | |
| | 22W-3S | 19 |
| Birchwood Pl. E&W | 21W-3S | 19 |
| Blackcherry Ln. N&S | | |
| | 23W-3S | 18 |
| Blackhawk Dr. E&W | 26W-2S | 18 |
| Blenheim Ct. N&S | 23W-2S | 18 |
| Bloomingdale Rd. N&S | | |
| | 23W-1N | 12 |
| Blue Jay Ct. N&S | 26W-1N | 12 |
| Bob-o-Link Rd. N&S | 21W-2S | 19 |
| Box Elder Av. E&W | 26W-0N | 12 |
| Briarcliff Ct. NE&SW | | |
| | 21W-2S | 19 |
| Briarcliff Rd. NW&SE | | |
| | 21W-2S | 19 |
| Brook Ct. NE&SW | 21W-1S | 19 |
| Bryan Rd. N&S | 22W-3S | 19 |
| Bud Ct. NW&SE | 26W-0N | 12 |
| Buena Vista Dr. E&W | | |
| | 23W-1S,22W-1S | 18 |
| Burning Trail N&S | 26W-2S | 18 |
| Burr Oak Ln. E&W | | |
| | 22W-3S | 19 |
| Busch Rd. E&W | 22W-1N | 13 |
| Butternut Ln. N&S | 22W-3S | 19 |
| Calvin St. E&W | 26W-0S | 18 |
| Cambridge Ct. E&W | 23W-2S | 18 |
| Canary Rd. NW&SE | 21W-3S | 19 |

| | Grid | Page |
|---|---|---|
| Carey Cir. N&S | 23W-2S | 19 |
| Carrol Gate NS&EW | | |
| | 25W-2S,26W-1S | 18 |
| Cathryn Ct. E&W | 25W-1N | 12 |
| Cesario Cir. NS&EW | | |
| | 26W-2S,26W-1S | 18 |
| Cheiftain Ln. E&W | 25W-2S | 18 |
| Cherry Ln. E&W | 22W-1N | 13 |
| Cherrywood Dr. NW&SE | | |
| | 22W-3S | 19 |
| Chippewa Dr. NE&SW | | |
| | 26W-2S | 18 |
| Churchill Ln. N&S | 23W-1N | 12 |
| Clifford Rd. E&W | 21W-2S | 19 |
| Cole Av. E&W | 25W-0N | 12 |
| Conifer Ct. N&S | 22W-1S | 19 |
| Cooley Av. N&S | 26W-0S | 18 |
| Coronet Rd. NW&SE | | |
| | 21W-2S | 19 |
| Cottonwood Dr. N&S | | |
| | 26W-0S,26W-0N | 18 |
| Cotuit Ct. NE&SW | 21W-1S | 19 |
| Country Club Ln. N&S | | |
| | 25W-2S,25W-1S | 18 |
| Coventry Ct. NE&SW | | |
| | 25W-0N | 12 |
| Coventry Dr. N&S | | |
| | 25W-0N,25W-1N | 12 |
| Coventry St. E&W | 25W-1N | 12 |
| Cree Ct. N&S | 26W-2S | 18 |
| Crest Ct. N&S | 21W-1S | 19 |
| Cumnor Av. NW&SE | | |
| | 21W-0N | 13 |
| Curtis Av. E&W | 26W-0S | 18 |
| Cypress Dr. NW&SE | | |
| | 22W-3S | 19 |
| Daly Rd. N&S | 23W-0N | 12 |
| Danbury Dr. N&S | 21W-2S | 19 |
| Danby Dr. N&S | 21W-1S | 19 |
| Darling St. N&S | | |
| | 25W-0N,25W-1N | 12 |
| Dawn Av. N&S | 23W-1N | 12 |
| Delano St. N&S | 26W-0N | 12 |
| Della Av. E&W | 25W-1N | 12 |
| Delles Rd. N&S | 25W-3S | 18 |
| Derby Glen Dr. E&W | | |
| | 23W-1N | 12 |
| Devonshire Ln. N&S | 23W-2S | 18 |
| Dorchester Av. N&S | 25W-0N | 12 |
| Dorchester Ct. E&W | 21W-1S | 19 |
| Dorchester Rd. N&S | | |
| | 25W-0N | 12 |
| Douglas Ct. N&S | 26W-1N | 12 |
| Drury Ln E&W | 21W-2S | 19 |
| Durfee Rd. E&W | | |
| | 26W-2S,25W-2S | 18 |
| Eastern Av. N&S | 22W-1N | 13 |
| Eddy Rd. N&S | 22W-1S | 19 |
| Edgebrook Pl. E&W | 21W-3S | 19 |
| Edgewood Ct. E&W | 23W-2S | 18 |
| Edgewood Rd. E&W | | |
| | 21W-0N | 13 |
| Electric Av. NW&SE | 25W-0N | 12 |
| Ellis Av. N&S | | |
| | 25W-0N,25W-1N | 12 |
| Ellynwood Dr. NE&SW | | |
| | 21W-0N | 13 |
| Elmwood Ct. E&W | 23W-3S | 18 |
| Elmwood Dr. E&W | | |
| | 25W-2S,22W-2S | 18 |
| Elmwood St. N&S | | |
| | 26W-0S,26W-0N | 18 |
| Embden Ln. E&W | | |
| | 26W-2S,25W-2S | 18 |
| Emerson Av. E&W | 22W-1N | 13 |
| Ethel Av. E&W | 21W-0S | 19 |
| Euclid Av. N&S | 22W-1N | 13 |
| Evans Av. N&S | | |
| | 26W-0S,26W-0N | 18 |
| Everest Rd. NW&SE | | |
| | 21W-2S | 19 |
| Evergreen Av. N&S | 23W-1N | 12 |
| Fairmeadow Ln. NW&SE | | |
| | 23W-3S | 18 |
| Fairway St. N&S | 21W-0N | 13 |
| Falcon Tr. N&S | 26W-1N | 12 |
| Fanchon St. N&S | | |
| | 25W-0N,25W-1N | 12 |
| Farwell St. N&S | | |
| | 25W-0N,25W-1N | 12 |
| Fetzer Rd. E&W | 25W-2S | 18 |
| Flamingo Ct. NE&SW | | |
| | 21W-2S | 19 |
| Flamingo Ln. NE&SW | | |
| | 21W-2S | 19 |
| Flint Creek Rd. E&W | | |
| | 25W-2S | 18 |
| Forest Av. N&S | 22W-1N | 13 |
| Forest Hill Dr. NS&EW | | |
| | 22W-3S | 19 |
| Foxcroft Dr. E&W | 23W-2S | 18 |
| Franklin St. N&S | 26W-1N | 12 |
| Front St. N&S | 22W-1N | 13 |
| Gables Blvd. N&S | 25W-0N | 12 |
| Glen Av. NE&SW | 21W-2S | 19 |
| Glen Park Rd. E&W | | |
| | 22W-2S,21W-2S | 19 |
| Glenbard Rd. E&W | 21W-1S | 19 |
| Glencrest Dr. E&W | 22W-1S | 19 |
| Glenrise Av. N&S | 23W-2S | 18 |
| Glenvalley Dr. E&W | | |
| | 22W-2S | 19 |
| Gold Finch Ct. | 26W-1N | 12 |
| Golf Ln. NW&SE | 21W-0N | 13 |

| | Grid | Page |
|---|---|---|
| Golfview Dr. N&S | 21W-2S | 19 |
| Goodrich Av. N&S | 22W-1N | 13 |
| Grand Av. N&S | 26W-0N | 12 |
| Grange Ct. E&W | 25W-2S | 18 |
| Gray Av. NE&SW | 23W-2S | 19 |
| Great Western Av. | | |
| | 23W-1N,22W-1N | 12 |
| Greenview Dr. N&S | 21W-1S | 19 |
| Grove Ln. NE&SW | 21W-1N | 13 |
| Hackberry Dr. E&W | | |
| | 23W-3S,22W-3S | 18 |
| Hamilton Dr. E&W | 25W-2S | 18 |
| Hamilton Ln. NW&SE | | |
| | 25W-2S | 18 |
| Hampton Ct. NE&SW | | |
| | 21W-2S | 19 |
| Harding Rd. E&W | 21W-0S | 19 |
| Harriet St. N&S | 26W-1N | 12 |
| Harvey St. E&W | 21W-0N | 13 |
| Hattie Gray Ct. E&W | | |
| | 23W-2S | 12 |
| Hattie Gray Ln. E&W | | |
| | 23W-2S | 12 |
| Hawthorne Ln. N&S | | |
| | 25W-2S,25W-1S | 18 |
| Hazel Ln. N&S | 26W-0N | 12 |
| Hemstead Rd. E&W | 21W-2S | 19 |
| Herrick Dr. N&S | 25W-0N | 12 |
| Hevern Dr. E&W | 25W-2S | 18 |
| High Knob Dr. N&S | 25W-2S | 18 |
| Highland Av. N&S | 22W-1N | 13 |
| Hill Av. NE&SW | 21W-0N | 13 |
| Hills Oak Ct. E&W | 24W-3S | 18 |
| Hoyle Rd. E&W | 21W-1N | 13 |
| Huntington Ct. N&S | 21W-2S | 19 |
| Huntington Pl. N&S | 21W-2S | 19 |
| Huntington Rd. E&W | | |
| | 21W-2S | 19 |
| Ironwood Ln. N&S | | |
| | 25W-2S,25W-1S | 18 |
| Ivy Ln. N&S | 21W-2S | 19 |
| Jerome Av. E&W | | |
| | 26W-0N,25W-0N | 12 |
| Jewell Rd. N&S | | |
| | 26W-0N,25W-0N | 12 |
| Jewell Rd. NW&SE | 26W-0N | 12 |
| Juniper Ln. NE&SW | 22W-3S | 19 |
| Keim Dr. NE&SW | 26W-2S | 18 |
| Kenilworth Av. N&S | | |
| | 23W-2S,23W-1N | 18 |
| Kenmore St. N&S | 21W-1N | 13 |
| Kensington Rd. E&W | | |
| | 21W-2S | 19 |
| Kent Rd. N&S | 21W-2S | 19 |
| King's Ct. N&S | | |
| | 23W-3S,22W-3S | 18 |
| Kiowa Ct. N&S | 26W-2S | 18 |
| Kiowa Dr. N&S | 26W-2S | 18 |
| Kiowa Ln. E&W | 26W-2S | 18 |
| Knollwood Dr. N&S | 25W-0N | 12 |
| Lakeview Dr. N&S | 26W-2S | 18 |
| Lakewood Ln. N&S | 25W-2S | 18 |
| Lambert Rd. N&S | 23W-2S | 18 |
| Lawler Av. N&S | | |
| | 21W-1S,21W-0S | 19 |
| Lawler Ln. N&S | 21W-2S | 19 |
| Lenox Rd. N&S | 22W-1N | 13 |
| Leonard St. N&S | | |
| | 26W-0S,26W-0N | 18 |
| Lloyd Av. N&S | | |
| | 21W-2S,21W-1S | 19 |
| Lorry Ct. NE&SW | 22W-1S | 19 |
| Lynn Rd. E&W | 21W-1N | 13 |
| Macarthur Av. E&W | | |
| | 26W-1N,26W-2S | 12 |
| Madison Av. E&W | 21W-0N | 13 |
| Mallard Ct. E&W | 26W-2S | 18 |
| Maple Ln. N&S | 22W-1S | 19 |
| Marion Av. NW&SE | | |
| | 22W-2S | 19 |
| Marlborough Rd. E&W | | |
| | 21W-2S | 19 |
| Marshall Ln. E&W | | |
| | 25W-1N,26W-1N | 12 |
| Marston St. N&S | 21W-1S | 19 |
| Mayfair Rd. E&W | 21W-2S | 19 |
| Mayfield Ct. E&W | 21W-2S | 19 |
| Mayfield St. N&S | | |
| | 21W-2S | 19 |
| Mayflower Pl. NE&SW | | |
| | 26W-0N | 12 |
| McCarron Rd. E&W | 22W-2S | 19 |
| McCormick Av. E&W | | |
| | 22W-1S | 19 |
| McCreey Av. E&W | 23W-1S | 12 |
| Meadow Ln. E&W | 21W-1N | 13 |
| Mellor Rd. E&W | 25W-1N | 12 |
| Menomini Ct. N&S | 26W-2S | 18 |
| Menomini Dr. N&S | 26W-2S | 18 |
| Menomini Ln. E&W | 26W-2S | 18 |
| Midwest Rd. N&S | | |
| | 17W-1S,17W-3S | 21 |
| Mildred Av. N&S | 23W-1N | 12 |
| Milton Av. N&S | 22W-1N | 13 |
| Milton Rd. N&S | 22W-1S | 19 |
| Mohican Dr. E&W | 26W-2S | 18 |
| Monticello Ct. N&S | 21W-2S | 19 |
| Monticello Rd. E&W | 21W-2S | 19 |
| Morse St. N&S | | |
| | 25W-0N,25W-1N | 12 |
| Mulberry Ln. NE&SW | | |
| | 25W-3S,24W-3S | 18 |
| Naperville Rd. NE&SW | | |

| | Grid | Page |
|---|---|---|
| Natalie Ct. E&W | 26W-1N | 12 |
| National St. E&W | 26W-1N | 12 |
| Nepil Av. N&S | | |
| | 25W-0S,25W-0N | 18 |
| Newton Av. N&S | 26W-1N | 12 |
| North-South Tollway N&S | | |
| | 21W-1S,21W-1N | 19 |
| Oaklawn Dr. NE&SW | | |
| | 22W-2S | 19 |
| Oakwood Ct. N&S | 25W-2S | 18 |
| Orchard Rd. N&S | 25W-2S | 18 |
| Osage Dr. NW&SE | 22W-3S | 19 |
| Ott Av. N&S | 23W-1S | 18 |
| Page St. N&S | | |
| | 26W-0S,26W-0N | 18 |
| Papworth St. N&S | | |
| | 26W-0N,25W-1N | 12 |
| Park Blvd. NE&SW | | |
| | 22W-3S,22W-1N | 19 |
| Parkway Dr. E&W | 26W-0N | 12 |
| Partridge Dr. N&S | 26W-1N | 12 |
| Pershing Av. E&W | 21W-1S | 19 |
| Peter Rd. N&S | 26W-0N | 12 |
| Pheasant Ct. E&W | 26W-1N | 12 |
| Picadilly Rd. NE&SW | | |
| | 25W-1S | 18 |
| Pierce Av. N&S | 25W-0N | 12 |
| Pin Oak Ct. N&S | 24W-3S | 18 |
| Pine Dr. E&W | 23W-1N | 12 |
| Pinegrove Ct. N&S | 24W-0N | 12 |
| Plamondon Rd. NE&SW | | |
| | 25W-1S | 18 |
| Pleasant Av. N&S | 22W-1N | 13 |
| Pleasant Hill Rd. N&S | | |
| | 26W-0N,26W-1N | 12 |
| Pleasant Ln. E&W | 21W-1N | 13 |
| Poplar Rd. N&S | 22W-2S | 19 |
| Poss St. E&W | 22W-1N | 13 |
| Prairie Av. E&W | | |
| | 22W-0N,25W-0N | 12 |
| Prairie Av. E&W | 22W-1N | 13 |
| Prairie St. E&W | 26W-0N | 12 |
| Prairie Rose Ct. E&W | | |
| | 25W-1N | 12 |
| President St. N&S | 23W-1N | 12 |
| Purnell St. N&S | | |
| | 25W-0N,25W-1N | 12 |
| Railroad St. NW&SE | | |
| | 22W-1N | 13 |
| Red Maple Ln. E&W | | |
| | 25W-2S | 12 |
| Red Oak Dr. E&W | | |
| | 23W-3S,22W-3S | 18 |
| Red Oak Ln. N&S | 24W-3S | 18 |
| Red Wing Ct. N&S | 26W-1N | 12 |
| Red Wing Dr. N&S | 26W-1N | 12 |
| Richard Av. N&S | 26W-1N | 12 |
| Ridge Rd. N&S | 21W-2S | 19 |
| River Dr. NE&SW | | |
| | 22W-1N,21W-1N | 13 |
| Riverside Av. N&S | 21W-1S | 19 |
| Robinwood Ln. E&W | | |
| | 24W-3S | 18 |
| S. Ellyn Rd. N&S | 25W-1S | 19 |
| Sandpiper Ct. E&W | 26W-1N | 12 |
| Scott Av. N&S | 21W-0N | 13 |
| Seneca Dr. N&S | 26W-2S | 18 |
| Sequoia Dr. NW&SE | | |
| | 24W-3S | 19 |
| Shagbark Ln. NE&SW | | |
| | 22W-3S | 19 |
| Sheffield Ct. E&W | 22W-2S | 19 |
| Sheffield Pl. E&W | 22W-2S | 19 |
| Sherbrooke Ln. E&W | | |
| | 23W-2S | 18 |
| Silverleaf Blvd. N&S | 25W-0N | 12 |
| Sioux Ct. N&S | 26W-2S | 18 |
| Spring Av. N&S | 21W-0N | 13 |
| St. Charles Rd. E&W | | |
| | 24W-1N,21W-1N | 12 |
| St. James Ct. E&W | 23W-2S | 18 |
| St. Thomas Dr. N&S | | |
| | 22W-2S | 19 |
| Stableford Dr. E&W | 23W-1N | 12 |
| Stacey Av. N&S | 22W-1N | 13 |
| Stacey Ct. N&S | 22W-1N | 13 |
| Stanley St. N&S | | |
| | 26W-0S,26W-0N | 18 |
| Stanton Rd. E&W | 22W-2S | 19 |
| Stoddard Av. N&S | 23W-0N | 12 |
| Stratford Ct. N&S | 22W-2S | 19 |
| Stratford Rd. N&S | 22W-2S | 19 |
| Stuarton Dr. N&S | 25W-2S | 18 |
| Summerfield Cir. E&W | | |
| | 25W-2S | 18 |
| Summerhill Pl. NW&SE | | |
| | 23W-2S | 18 |
| Sunnybrook Rd. N&S | | |
| | 21W-1S | 19 |
| Sunset Av. E&W | 21W-1N | 13 |
| Swift Rd. N&S | 21W-1N | 13 |
| Sycamore Dr. NW&SE | | |
| | 23W-3S,22W-3S | 18 |
| Tamarack Dr. NW&SE | | |
| | 23W-3S,22W-3S | 18 |
| Taylor Rd. E&W | | |
| | 22W-2S,22W-1S | 19 |
| Teakwood Dr. E&W | 22W-3S | 19 |
| Thaddeus Cir. E&W | 21W-2S | 19 |
| Thistledown Ct. E&W | | |
| | 25W-1N | 12 |
| Thomas Rd. E&W | | |
| | 26W-0N,25W-0N | 12 |
| Timothy Ln. N&S | 26W-1N | 12 |

| | Grid | Page |
|---|---|---|
| Tomahawk Dr. NE&SW ........ 26W-2S | | 18 |
| Tomahawk Ter. N&S ........ 26W-2S | | 18 |
| Towpath Ct. E&W .. 25W-2S | | 18 |
| Trails End Rd. E&W ..23W-1N | | 12 |
| Tree Tops Ln. N&S ........ 25W-2S,25W-1S | | 18 |
| Valley View Dr. E&W ........ 22W-1N,21W-1N | | 13 |
| Waldorth E&W .. 25W-1S | | 18 |
| Walnut Rd. NE&SW ..21W-0N | | 13 |
| Washington Ln. NE&SW ........ 21W-1N | | 13 |
| Weisbrook Rd. NE&SW ........ 26W-2S | | 18 |
| Wenona Ln. E&W ...25W-2S | | 18 |
| West Haven Dr. N&S ........ 25W-2S | | 18 |
| West St. N&S  25W-1N | | 12 |
| Westchester Ct. E&W ........23W-2N | | 12 |
| Western Av. N&S ...23W-1N | | 12 |
| Wheatbury Ct. E&W  25W-1N | | 12 |
| Wheatbury Dr. N&S ..25W-1N | | 12 |
| Whitebirch Ct. N&S ..25W-2N | | 12 |
| Whitebirch Ln. N&S ..25W-2N | | 12 |
| Whitmore Ln. N&S .. 21W-0S | | 19 |
| Willow Rd. N&S  25W-0N | | 12 |
| Wilson Rd. N&S ....21W-0S | | 19 |
| Woodcreek Dr. N&S ........21W-3S,21W-2S | | 19 |
| Woodcroft Dr. E&W ..23W-2S | | 18 |
| Woodland Dr. N&S .. 25W-0N | | 12 |
| Woodlark Dr. E&W .. 26W-1N | | 12 |
| Woodlawn St. N&S .. 25W-0N | | 12 |
| Woods Av. N&S ........ 26W-0N,26W-1N | | 12 |
| Woodvale Ct. E&W .. 26W-0N | | 12 |
| Woodvale St. NW&SE ........ 26W-0N | | 12 |
| 1st St. E&W ....... 22W-1N | | 13 |
| 2nd Pl. E&W ...... 22W-1N | | 13 |
| 2nd St. E&W ........23W-1N,22W-1N | | 12 |
| 3rd St. E&W ........23W-1N,22W-1N | | 12 |
| 22nd St. E&W ........ 23W-1S,21W-2S | | 18 |
| 39th St. E&W........25W-3S | | 18 |

## Naperville*
### (Also see Will County)

| | Grid | Page |
|---|---|---|
| Abbotsford Dr. NS&EW ........ 29W-5S | | 23 |
| Abby Dr. N&S ...... 29W-5S | | 23 |
| Abrahamson Ct. NE&SW ........ 26W-8S | | 30 |
| Acacia Ct. N&S.....27W-5S | | 23 |
| Ada Ct. E&W ......28W-8S | | 29 |
| Ada Ln. E&W.......28W-8S | | 29 |
| Albermarle Ct. N&S ..29W-5S | | 23 |
| Alder Ln. NE&SW....27W-8S | | 29 |
| Alexis R Shuman Blvd. E&W ........ 27W-4S,26W-4S | | 23 |
| Almond Ct. NE&SW ..28W-7S | | 23 |
| Alton Ct. E&W .... 25W-8S | | 30 |
| Amberwood Cir. NE&SW ........ 26W-5S,25W-5S | | 24 |
| Ambleside Cir. NS&EW ........ 28W-7S | | 23 |
| Andover Ct. NE&SW ........ 25W-6S | | 24 |
| Andrews Ct. NW&SE ........ 28W-8S | | 30 |
| Anne Rd. E&W .. 26W-6S | | 24 |
| Anthony Ct. NW&SE ........ 29W-6S | | 23 |
| Antietam Ct. E&W .. 29W-6S | | 23 |
| Apache Dr. NE&SW ........ 27W-5S,26W-4S | | 23 |
| Appaloosa Dr. NS&EW ........ 24W-8S | | 30 |
| Appleby Ct. N&S .. 25W-7S | | 24 |
| Applegate Ct. NE&SW ........ 28W-8S | | 29 |
| Applegate Dr. NW&SE ........ 28W-8S | | 29 |
| Appomattox Ct. N&S ........ 27W-8S | | 29 |
| Arabian Av. E&W ..24W-8S | | 30 |
| Ardmore Dr. NE&SW ........28W-8S,28W-7S | | 29 |
| Argus E&W........28W-8S | | 23 |
| Ashfield Rd. NW&SE ........ 25W-7S | | 24 |
| Aspen Ct. E&W .. 28W-8S | | 29 |
| Atlanta Ct. NW&SE .. 27W-7S | | 23 |
| Atlas Ln. N&S ...... 26W-8S | | 30 |
| Atwood Cir. NS&EW ........ 24W-9S | | 30 |
| Auburn Dr. NE&SW ..24W-8S | | 30 |
| Augusta Dr. N&S .. 30W-5S | | 22 |
| Aurora Av. E&W ........ 29W-7S,29W-6S | | 23 |
| Autumn Av. N&S .. 25W-8S | | 23 |
| Aztec Cir. NE&SW ........ 27W-5S,26W-5S | | 23 |
| Bailey Rd. N&S ........ 27W-8S,24W-8S | | 29 |
| Bainbridge Dr. N&S ..29W-5S | | 23 |
| Bakewell Ln. E&W .. 25W-8S | | 30 |
| Baldwin Dr. N&S .... 27W-8S | | 29 |
| Balmoral Cir. NS&EW ........ 25W-7S | | 24 |
| Balton Ct. N&S .... 29W-5S | | 23 |
| Banbury Cir. NW&SE ........ 25W-7S | | 24 |
| Bankfield Ct. NE&SW ........ 25W-7S | | 24 |
| Bannister Dr. N&S ........ 27W-8S | | 29 |
| Banyon Ct. NS&EW ..28W-7S | | 23 |
| Barbara Ct. NE&SW  27W-8S | | 29 |
| Barcroft Ct. NW&SE ........ 25W-7S | | 24 |
| Barkei Rd. N&S......25W-4S | | 24 |
| Barley Av. E&W .. 26W-5S | | 24 |
| Basswood Dr. N&S .. 26W-8S | | 30 |
| Bauer Rd. E&W ........ 28W-5S,26W-5S | | 23 |
| Bay Colony Dr. E&W ........ 26W-8S | | 30 |
| Bay Ct. N&S .. 26W-9S | | 30 |
| Bayberry Ln. E&W .. 26W-5S | | 24 |
| Bayhill Av. E&W .. 25W-8S | | 30 |
| Baylor Ct. E&W .....24W-9S | | 30 |
| Bayview Ct. E&W .. 27W-9S | | 29 |
| Bedford Ct. NE&SW  25W-7S | | 24 |
| Beech Ct. NE&SW .. 28W-8S | | 23 |
| Belaire Ct. N&S .. 28W-7S | | 23 |
| Bellingrath Ct. NW&SE ........ 26W-6S | | 24 |
| Beloit Ct. N&S .. 24W-9S | | 30 |
| Beloit Ct. E&W .. 24W-9S | | 30 |
| Benedetti Dr. NE&SW ........27W-6S,27W-5S | | 23 |
| Bent Creek Ct.* N&S ........23W-9S | | 31 |
| Benton Av. E&W ........27W-6S,26W-6S | | 23 |
| Berkley Ct. N&S .... 26W-9S | | 30 |
| Bernie Ct. E&W .. 26W-9S | | 30 |
| Berry Dr. N&S ........ 28W-7S,28W-6S | | 23 |
| Big Foot Ln. N&S ..27W-5S | | 23 |
| Biltmore Ct. N&S .. 26W-6S | | 24 |
| Birchwood Dr. N&S ........ 28W-7S,28W-6S | | 23 |
| Birkdale Ct. NE&SW ........ 27W-5S | | 23 |
| Black Hawk Ct. E&W ........ 26W-5S | | 24 |
| Black Stallion Ct. E&W ........ 24W-8S | | 30 |
| Black Stallion Dr. NE&SW ........ 24W-8S | | 30 |
| Blackburn Ct. NE&SW ........ 25W-7S | | 24 |
| Blue Grass Ct. E&W ........ 26W-5S | | 24 |
| Blue Larkspur Ln. E&W ........ 25W-7S | | 24 |
| Bluebird Ln. E&W .. 26W-9S | | 30 |
| Bob-o-Link Ln. N&S..28W-5S | | 23 |
| Bonaventure Dr. N&S ........ 28W-5S | | 23 |
| Bond St. N&S .. 29W-5S | | 23 |
| Book Rd. E&W .. 28W-8S | | 29 |
| Bourbon Ct. N&S .. 29W-5S | | 30 |
| Bovidae Cir. NS&EW ........ 27W-8S | | 29 |
| Boweset Ct. E&W .. 29W-7S | | 29 |
| Bowling Green Ct. NE&SW ........ 27W-5S | | 23 |
| Brad Ct. E&W .. 25W-8S | | 30 |
| Bradley Ct. E&W .. 25W-8S | | 30 |
| Braemar Av. NS&EW ........26W-5S,26W-4S | | 24 |
| Braemar Dr. E&W .. 26W-5S | | 24 |
| Brainard St. N&S .. 26W-7S | | 24 |
| Brainard St. N&S ........ 26W-6S,26W-5S | | 24 |
| Brandeis Ct. E&W .. 24W-9S | | 30 |
| Brandy Cir. NS&EW ........ 28W-5S,24W-8S | | 30 |
| Brentford Dr. NE&SW ........ 26W-4S | | 24 |
| Brestal Ct. N&S......25W-9S | | 30 |
| Briarheath Cir. NW&SE ........ 26W-9S | | 30 |
| Briarwood Dr. E&W ..28W-7S | | 23 |
| Bridgewater Ct. E&W ........ 26W-9S | | 30 |
| Briergate Ct. N&S....28W-5S | | 23 |
| Brighton Rd. E&W .. 25W-5S | | 24 |
| Bristlecone Ct. N&S..25W-9S | | 30 |
| Bristol Ct. NW&SE .. 26W-9S | | 30 |
| Brittany Av. E&W ........ 25W-8S,24W-8S | | 30 |
| Brom Ct. N&S .. 27W-7S | | 23 |
| Brook Ln. E&W.....28W-6S | | 23 |
| Brookdale Rd. NS&EW ........ 29W-5S,28W-5S | | 23 |
| Brooklea Ct. NE&SW ........ 29W-6S | | 30 |
| Brookline Ct. N&S ........ 25W-6S | | 24 |
| Brookshire Ct. N&S .. 29W-6S | | 23 |
| Bruno Ct. E&W .. 29W-6S | | 23 |
| Brunswick Ct. E&W .. 25W-7S | | 24 |
| Brush Hill Cir. NS&EW ........ 28W-8S | | 23 |
| Buckeye Ct. E&W .. 27W-8S | | 29 |
| Buckingham Dr. N&S ........ 25W-6S | | 24 |
| Buckley Ct. N&S .. 26W-9S | | 30 |
| Bucknell Ct. N&S .. 24W-9S | | 30 |
| Bullrun Ct. E&W .... 27W-8S | | 29 |
| Burke Ct. N&S .... 30W-5S | | 22 |
| Burning Tree Ln. E&W ........ 27W-5S | | 23 |
| Burr Oak Ct. NW&SE ........ 28W-7S | | 23 |
| Butler Ct. N&S .. 24W-9S | | 30 |
| Butte Ct. N&S .. 26W-6S | | 24 |
| Butternut Dr. N&S ........ 28W-7S | | 23 |
| Buttonwood Cir. N&S ........ 28W-7S | | 23 |
| Byron Ct. NE&SW .. 25W-8S | | 30 |
| Cabriolet Ct. N&S....27W-9S | | 29 |
| Cactus Dr. NE&SW .. 24W-9S | | 30 |
| Calcutta Ln. N&S .. 28W-5S | | 23 |
| Camellia Ct. N&S .. 25W-9S | | 30 |
| Candlenut Dr. E&W .. 28W-6S | | 23 |
| Canonero Dr. NE&SW ........ 26W-7S,25W-7S | | 24 |
| Cantigny Ct. NS&EW ........ 28W-5S | | 30 |
| Canyon Run Rd. E&W ........ 25W-9S | | 30 |
| Cardiff Rd. E&W .. 27W-8S | | 29 |
| Cardigan Ct. NW&SE ........ 27W-8S | | 29 |
| Cardinal Ln. N&S .. 26W-8S | | 30 |
| Carleton Av. E&W .. 24W-9S | | 30 |
| Carleton Cir. NS&EW ........ 24W-9S | | 30 |
| Carlson Ct. N&S .. 27W-5S | | 23 |
| Carmel Ct. N&S .. 28W-6S | | 23 |
| Carnegie Ct. NE&SW ........ 24W-9S | | 30 |
| Carol Ln. N&S .. 26W-8S | | 30 |
| Carriage Ct. E&W .. 27W-6S | | 23 |
| Carriage Hill Rd. E&W ........ 25W-9S | | 30 |
| Carriage Way Dr. NE&SW ........ 25W-7S | | 24 |
| Carthage Ct. NE&SW ........ 24W-9S | | 30 |
| Castillejact Ct. N&S .. 28W-7S | | 23 |
| Catalpa Ln. NW&SE ........ 26W-8S,26W-7S | | 30 |
| Catherine Av. E&W .. 25W-6S | | 24 |
| Cavalcade Cir. NE&SW ........ 26W-7S | | 23 |
| Ceals Ct. N&S .. 26W-9S | | 30 |
| Cedarbrook Rd. NS&EW ........ 26W-9S | | 30 |
| Celtic Ash Ct. N&S .. 25W-7S | | 23 |
| Center St. N&S ........ 26W-6S,26W-5S | | 24 |
| Central Park Rd. N&S ........ 26W-6S | | 24 |
| Centre Point Dr. NS&EW ........ 26W-4S | | 24 |
| Chadwicke Cir. EW&NS ........ 28W-7S | | 23 |
| Chalet Rd. E&W .. 28W-6S | | 23 |
| Challdon Ct. NW&SE ........ 26W-7S | | 24 |
| Chalmette Ct. NS&EW ........ 25W-9S | | 30 |
| Chancellor Ct. NW&SE ........ 27W-7S | | 23 |
| Charles St. N&S ........ 26W-7S,25W-5S | | 24 |
| Chat Ct. N&S......26W-8S | | 30 |
| Chateaugay Av. NS&EW ........ 25W-7S | | 24 |
| Chatham Ct. N&S .. 25W-9S | | 30 |
| Chattanooga Ct. N&S ........ 27W-8S | | 29 |
| Chepstow Ct. NE&SW ........ 28W-7S | | 23 |
| Cherry Blossom Ln. NW&SE ........ 27W-7S,26W-7S | | 23 |
| Cherry Hills Ln. E&W ........ 28W-5S | | 23 |
| Cherrywood Cir. NW&SE ........ 26W-9S | | 30 |
| Chesire Av. E&W .. 25W-7S | | 24 |
| Chesterfield Av. E&W ........ 27W-7S | | 24 |
| Chestnut Ridge Dr. E&W ........ 28W-6S | | 23 |
| Chicago Av. E&W ........ 26W-6S,25W-6S | | 24 |
| Chickasaw Dr. N&S .. 25W-8S | | 23 |
| Chicory Ct. N&S .. 28W-7S | | 23 |
| Chippewa Dr. N&S ........ 26W-5S,26W-4S | | 24 |
| Churchill Dr. NW&SE ........ 29W-5S | | 23 |
| Citadel Dr. NE&SW .. 24W-9S | | 30 |
| Claremont Ct. N&S .. 28W-6S | | 23 |
| Clarissa Ct. NE&SW  25W-8S | | 30 |
| Clarkson Ct. E&W .. 24W-9S | | 30 |
| Clemson Dr. NS&EW ........ 24W-8S | | 30 |
| Cliffside Ct. N&S .. 25W-9S | | 30 |
| Cloverleaf Ct. N&S .. 26W-9S | | 30 |
| Clovertree Ct. N&S .. 28W-7S | | 23 |
| Clyde Dr. NE&SW ........ 26W-9S,26W-8S | | 30 |
| Coach Dr. N&S .. 25W-9S | | 30 |
| Cody Ct. N&S .. 27W-6S | | 23 |
| Colfax Ct. E&W .. 29W-5S | | 23 |
| Collingwood Dr. NS&EW ........ 25W-7S | | 24 |
| Colonial Ct. E&W .. 26W-6S | | 24 |
| Columbia St. N&S ........ 26W-7S,26W-5S | | 24 |
| Cornell Ct. E&W .. 24W-8S | | 30 |
| Cortez Ct. NE&SW .. 26W-4S | | 24 |
| Cottage Av. E&W ....27W-6S | | 23 |
| Cottonwood Ln. E&W ........ 28W-6S | | 23 |
| Count Fleet Ct. N&S ........ 26W-7S | | 24 |
| Country Farm Dr. N&S ........ 30W-4S | | 22 |
| Countryside Cir. NW&SE ........ 26W-8S | | 30 |
| Court Pl. N&S .. 26W-6S | | 24 |
| Courtland Dr. N&S .. 27W-8S | | 29 |
| Cove Ct. NE&SW .. 26W-9S | | 30 |
| Coventry Ct. E&W .. 26W-8S | | 30 |
| Crabapple Ct. N&S .. 28W-6S | | 23 |
| Cranberry Ct. N&S .. 25W-9S | | 30 |
| Cranshire Ln. E&W .. 24W-9S | | 30 |
| Creekside Cir. NS&EW ........ 27W-5S | | 23 |
| Creighton Av. E&W .. 24W-8S | | 30 |
| Crestwood Ct. E&W  25W-7S | | 24 |
| Crossing Ct. NS&EW ........ 29W-8S | | 29 |
| Crossing Ln. ........ 29W-8S | | 29 |
| Culpepper Dr. NE&SW ........ 25W-7S,24W-7S | | 24 |
| Cypress Dr. E&W .. 27W-8S | | 29 |
| Dakota Cir. NE&SW ..26W-4S | | 24 |
| Dana Ct. E&W .... 27W-5S | | 23 |
| Darius Ln. E&W .. 25W-9S | | 30 |
| Dark Star Rd. NW&SE ........ 26W-7S | | 24 |
| Dartford Ct. N&S .. 25W-7S | | 24 |
| Dartmoor Ct. N&S .. 25W-7S | | 24 |
| Dartmouth Ct. NE&SW ........ 24W-9S | | 30 |
| DePaul Ct. E&W .. 24W-8S | | 30 |
| Deep Run Rd. E&W ..25W-7S | | 24 |
| Deepwood Ct. NW&SE ........ 26W-8S | | 30 |
| Deerpath Ct. N&S....25W-9S | | 30 |
| Delkir Ct. E&W .. 26W-9S | | 30 |
| Denison Ct. E&W .. 24W-9S | | 30 |
| Denisport Dr. E&W .. 25W-8S | | 30 |
| Derby Ct. E&W .... 29W-5S | | 23 |
| Devlin Ct. NW&SE .. 26W-9S | | 30 |
| Devon Ln. E&W .. 25W-6S | | 24 |
| Devonshire Ct. E&W ........ 27W-6S | | 23 |
| Diane Ln. NE&SW .. 26W-7S | | 24 |
| Dichtl Ct. N&S .. 25W-9S | | 30 |
| Dickens Dr. NW&SE ........ 26W-5S,25W-5S | | 24 |
| Diehl Rd. E&W ........ 29W-4S,25W-4S | | 23 |
| Dockside Ct. N&S .. 27W-9S | | 30 |
| Dorset Ct. NE&SW .. 25W-7S | | 24 |
| Dorval Dr. N&S ...... 27W-9S | | 29 |
| Douglas Av. NE&SW ........ 27W-6S | | 23 |
| Dove Ct. NW&SE .. 26W-8S | | 30 |
| Dover Ln. N&S .. 27W-9S | | 30 |
| Downing Ct. NE&SW ........ 29W-5S | | 23 |
| Drake Ct. E&W .. 24W-9S | | 30 |
| Drendel Ln. E&W .. 26W-9S | | 30 |
| Druid Hills Ct. NW&SE ........ 27W-5S | | 23 |
| Duke Ct. E&W .. 24W-9S | | 30 |
| Duke Dr. E&W .. 24W-9S | | 30 |
| Duquesne Av. E&W ..24W-9S | | 30 |
| Durham Ct. N&S .. 26W-6S | | 24 |
| Durness Ct. N&S .. 27W-8S | | 29 |
| Eagle St. N&S ........ 27W-6S,27W-5S | | 23 |
| East Av. NE&SW .. 25W-5S | | 24 |
| East West Tollway E&W ........ 30W-4S,25W-4S | | 22 |
| Eastland Ct. N&S ........ 26W-9S | | 30 |
| Eddystone Cir. NS&EW ........ 27W-8S | | 29 |
| Edgewater Dr. NW&SE ........ 26W-7S | | 24 |
| Edwards Rd. NE&SW ........ 25W-7S | | 24 |
| Elizabeth Av. E&W ........ 26W-6S,25W-5S | | 24 |
| Ellsworth St. N&S ........ 26W-6S,25W-6S | | 24 |
| Elm Ct. N&S .. 28W-8S | | 29 |
| Elm St. N&S .. 28W-8S | | 29 |
| Elmwood Dr. NE&SW ........ 27W-8S,26W-7S | | 23 |
| Emerald Dr. N&S ........ 27W-8S,27W-7S | | 29 |
| Encina Ct. N&S .. 28W-6S | | 23 |
| Estate Cir. E&W .. 24W-8S | | 30 |
| Estuary Ct. NE&SW..26W-9S | | 30 |
| Eton Ln. N&S......25W-8S | | 30 |
| Evergreen Av. E&W ..28W-7S | | 23 |
| Ewing St. N&S .. 27W-6S | | 23 |
| Fair Oak Rd. N&S....25W-9S | | 30 |
| Fair Oaks Ct. N&S ........ 30W-5S | | 22 |
| Fairway N&S ........ 30W-6S,30W-5S | | 22 |
| Fairway Ln. N&S .... 25W-9S | | 30 |
| Fairwinds Ct. N&S ........ 26W-6S | | 24 |
| Fall Brook Ct. N&S .. 26W-9S | | 30 |
| Fallcreek Ct. N&S .. 26W-8S | | 30 |
| Farington Ct. N&S .. 25W-5S | | 24 |
| Feldott Dr. NS&EW .. 29W-7S | | 29 |
| Fender Rd. N&S ........ 25W-9S,25W-8S | | 30 |
| Ferncroft Ct. NW&SE ........ 28W-5S | | 23 |
| Fernwood Dr. E&W ..27W-7S | | 23 |
| Ferry Rd. E&W ........ 30W-4S,29W-4S | | 22 |
| Fessler Av. E&W .. 27W-8S | | 29 |
| Field Ct. NE&SW .. 28W-6S | | 30 |
| Finch Ct. NW&SE .. 26W-9S | | 30 |
| Fir Ct. NW&SE .... 26W-9S | | 30 |
| Fisher Dr. E&W .... 30W-4S | | 22 |
| Flicker Ct. E&W .. 26W-9S | | 30 |
| Flock Av. E&W .. 26W-9S | | 30 |
| Flock Cir. NS&EW .. 26W-8S | | 30 |
| Floret Ct. E&W .. 24W-9S | | 30 |
| Flossmoor Ct. NW&SE ........ 27W-5S | | 23 |
| Flowerfield Ct.* N&S ........23W-9S | | 31 |
| Fordham Ct. NE&SW ........ 24W-9S | | 30 |
| Forest Av. N&S......27W-6S | | 23 |
| Forestview Ct. NW&SE ........ 28W-5S | | 23 |
| Fort Hill Dr. N&S ........ 29W-7S,29W-6S | | 23 |
| Fox Bend Ct. N&S .. 28W-5S | | 23 |
| Fox Trail Ct. N&S .. 24W-8S | | 30 |
| Foxcroft Rd. E&W .. 26W-9S | | 30 |
| Foxhill Rd. E&W .. 29W-5S | | 23 |
| Foxhorn Ct. NE&SW ........ 26W-4S | | 24 |
| Franklin Av. E&W ........ 27W-6S,26W-6S | | 23 |
| Frederick Ln. E&W .. 26W-8S | | 30 |
| Fredericksburg Ct. E&W ........ 27W-7S | | 23 |
| Fresno Ct. N&S .. 28W-6S | | 23 |
| Friar Ln. N&S ........ 24W-9S,24W-8S | | 30 |
| Furman Av. E&W .. 24W-9S | | 30 |
| Garaway Ct. E&W .. 29W-7S | | 29 |
| Garden Ct. NW&SE .. 28W-5S | | 23 |
| Gardenside Ct. E&W ........ 28W-8S | | 29 |
| Garth Ct. NE&SW .. 26W-9S | | 30 |
| Gartner Rd. E&W ........ 27W-8S,26W-7S | | 23 |
| George Ln. NS&EW ..25W-6S | | 24 |
| Georgetown Ct. E&W ........ 24W-9S | | 30 |
| Georgia Ct. NW&SE  28W-9S | | 23 |
| Gettysburg Ct. E&W ........ 27W-8S | | 29 |
| Glencoe Ct. NW&SE ........ 26W-9S | | 30 |
| Glenmore Ct. NW&SE ........ 25W-7S | | 24 |
| Goldenrod Dr. NE&SW ........ 28W-7S | | 23 |
| Golf Dr. N&S........25W-9S | | 30 |
| Golfview Rd. NE&SW  31W-5S | | 22 |
| Gowdey Rd. E&W ........ 29W-6S,29W-5S | | 23 |
| Great Oak Ct. N&S ........ 24W-9S | | 30 |
| Green Ridge Dr. NS&EW ........ 24W-8S | | 30 |
| Green Trails Dr. E&W ........ 25W-7S | | 24 |
| Greenlee Ct. E&W .. 28W-7S | | 23 |
| Greensboro Ct. E&W ........ 26W-6S | | 24 |
| Greensfield Dr. E&W ........ 25W-6S,25W-5S | | 24 |
| Gregory Ct. NW&SE ........ 27W-8S | | 29 |
| Grimes Av. E&W .. 27W-8S | | 29 |
| Hackberry Ct. NE&SW ........ 28W-7S,28W-6S | | 23 |
| Hagemann Pl. NW&SE ........ 25W-6S,25W-5S | | 24 |
| Hamilton Ln. NS&EW ........ 25W-8S,24W-8S | | 30 |
| Hampton Ct. N&S.... 25W-8S | | 30 |
| Hansom Ct. N&S .. 25W-9S | | 30 |
| Harbor Ct. N&S .. 26W-9S | | 30 |
| Harlowe Ct. N&S .. 25W-9S | | 30 |
| Harris Ln. N&S .. 25W-9S | | 30 |
| Harvard Av. NW&SE ........ 24W-9S | | 30 |
| Hastings St. N&S .. 29W-5S | | 23 |
| Haverhill Cir. NE&SW ........ 25W-5S | | 24 |
| Hawthorne Dr. NW&SE ........ 27W-9S,26W-7S | | 23 |
| Hayle Ct. NW&SE...28W-7S | | 23 |
| Hazelwood Dr. E&W ........ 27W-7S | | 23 |
| Heatherton Ct. NW&SE ........ 28W-6S | | 23 |
| Heatherton Dr. NS&EW ........ 28W-5S | | 23 |
| Heathrow Ln. NE&SW ........ 28W-8S,27W-8S | | 29 |
| Hedg Ct. NE&SW....25W-9S | | 30 |

| | Grid | Page |
|---|---|---|
| Hemlock Ln. NW&SE | 27W-8S | 29 |
| Henning Ct. NW&SE | 26W-7S | 24 |
| Hercules Ln. N&S | 26W-8S | 30 |
| Heritage Hill Dr. (Pvt.) E&W | 28W-6S | 23 |
| Hickory Ln. NW&SE | 26W-7S | 24 |
| Hidden Bay Ct. N&S | 25W-9S | 30 |
| Hidden Lake Rd. E&W | 25W-9S | 30 |
| Hidden Spring Rd. E&W | 28W-6S | 23 |
| Hidden Valley Dr. E&W | 24W-9S | 30 |
| High Grove Ln. NS&EW | 29W-6S | 23 |
| High Point Dr. NS&EW | 25W-4S | 24 |
| Highland Av. E&W | 26W-6S | 24 |
| Hillside Rd. E&W | 27W-7S,26W-6S | 23 |
| Hilltop Ct. N&S | 25W-9S | 30 |
| Hilton Head Dr. N&S | 30W-5S | 22 |
| Hinterlong Dr. E&W | 29W-6S | 23 |
| Hobson Hollow Dr. N&S | 24W-8S | 30 |
| Hobson Mill Dr. E&W | 26W-8S,25W-8S | 30 |
| Hobson Oaks Ct. NW&SE | 25W-8S | 30 |
| Hobson Oaks Dr. N&S | 25W-8S | 30 |
| Hobson Rd. E&W | 26W-8S,24W-8S | 30 |
| Holly Ct. NW&SE | 27W-8S | 29 |
| Hollytowne Ct.* N&S | 23W-9S | 31 |
| Honest Pleasure Dr. NE&SW | 26W-7S | 24 |
| Honey Berry Ct. N&S | 28W-6S | 23 |
| Honeysuckle Dr. N&S | 28W-7S | 23 |
| Hopi Ct. N&S | 27W-5S | 23 |
| Huffman St. N&S | 26W-6S | 24 |
| Hull Ct. N&S | 25W-9S | 30 |
| Hunter St. N&S | 25W-8S | 30 |
| Huntington Cir. NS&EW | 24W-6S | 24 |
| Huntleigh Dr. NW&SE | 25W-7S | 24 |
| Hyde Park Ln. NS&EW | 25W-8S | 30 |
| I-88 Tollway E&W | 30W-4S,25W-4S | 22 |
| Imperial Cir. NE&SW | 28W-5S | 23 |
| Inca Ct. E&W | 26W-5S | 24 |
| Indian Hills Ct. NW&SE | 27W-5S | 23 |
| Indian Knoll Rd. N&S | 29W-5S | 30 |
| Indian Trail Dr. N&S | 25W-9S | 30 |
| Industrial Dr. N&S | 30W-6S | 22 |
| Inland Cir. NS&EW | 30W-6S,30W-5S | 22 |
| Inverness Ct. N&S | 27W-5S | 23 |
| Inverrary Dr. N&S | 28W-5S | 23 |
| Iona Ct. E&W | 24W-9S | 30 |
| Iona Dr. N&S | 24W-9S | 30 |
| Iris Ln. N&S | 27W-7S | 23 |
| Iron Liege Ct. E&W | 25W-7S | 24 |
| Ironwood N&S | 26W-7S | 24 |
| Iroquois Av. E&W | 26W-5S,25W-5S | 24 |
| Ishnala Dr. N&S | 25W-9S | 30 |
| Jackson Av. N&S | 27W-6S | 23 |
| Jaipur Av. N&S | 25W-7S | 24 |
| James Ln. NE&SW | 25W-6S | 24 |
| Jane Av. E&W | 26W-6S | 24 |
| Jasmine Ct. E&W | 28W-7S | 23 |
| Jefferson Av. E&W | 29W-6S,27W-6S | 23 |
| John Friend Dr. NW&SE | 29W-8S | 29 |
| Johnson Dr. NW&SE | 25W-8S,25W-7S | 30 |
| Johoull Ct. E&W | 29W-7S | 29 |
| Joshua Ct. E&W | 28W-7S | 23 |
| Julian St. N&S | 26W-7S,26W-6S | 24 |
| Juniper Ct. E&W | 27W-8S | 29 |
| Jupiter Ct. E&W | 26W-6S | 24 |
| Justin Ct. E&W | 24W-8S | 30 |
| Kaimi Ct. N&S | 26W-4S | 24 |
| Kathy Ct. N&S | 28W-7S | 23 |
| Kauai King Ct. E&W | 26W-7S | 24 |
| Keim Ct. N&S | 25W-9S | 30 |
| Keim Dr. NW&SE | 25W-9S | 30 |
| Kemper Dr. N&S | 30W-5S | 22 |
| Kennebec Ln. E&W | 26W-5S | 24 |
| Kennesaw Ct. N&S | 27W-8S | 29 |
| Kensington Ct. E&W | 27W-5S | 23 |
| Kent Ct. E&W | 25W-7S | 24 |
| Kenyon Dr. NE&SW | 24W-9S,24W-8S | 30 |
| Kerria Ct. N&S | 25W-9S | 30 |
| Kesick Ct. E&W | 25W-6S | 23 |
| Ketten Ct. E&W | 26W-4S | 24 |
| Ketten Dr. N&S | 26W-4S | 24 |
| Killdeer Ln. N&S | 26W-9S,26W-8S | 30 |
| Kimball Ct. NW&SE | 26W-8S,26W-7S | 30 |
| Kinglet Ct. NW&SE | 26W-9S | 30 |
| Kings Ct. NE&SW | 29W-5S | 23 |
| Kings Point Ct. E&W | 28W-5S | 23 |
| Kingswood Ct. E&W | 26W-9S | 30 |
| Kinsie Ct. NW&SE | 26W-8S | 30 |
| Kinston Ct. NW&SE | 27W-7S | 23 |
| Kiowa Dr. N&S | 29W-5S | 30 |
| Kirby Ct. N&S | 29W-5S | 23 |
| Knoll Dr. N&S | 25W-10S,25W-9S | 12 |
| Knox Ct. E&W | 24W-8S | 30 |
| Laird St. N&S | 27W-6S | 23 |
| Lakeview Ct. NW&SE | 29W-5S | 30 |
| Lambsgate Dr. N&S | 28W-8S | 29 |
| Lampwick Ct. N&S | 26W-4S | 24 |
| Lancaster Cir. NS&EW | 26W-9S | 30 |
| Lancaster Ct. NE&SW | 26W-9S | 30 |
| Langley Cir. NS&EW | 29W-5S | 23 |
| Lantern Cir. NS&EW | 24W-7S | 24 |
| Larchmont Ct. N&S | 26W-9S | 30 |
| Lark Ln. N&S | 26W-9S | 30 |
| Larkspur Ct. E&W | 26W-4S | 24 |
| Larsen Ln. NE&SW | 25W-5S | 24 |
| Laura Ct. E&W | 27W-5S | 23 |
| Laurel Ln. N&S | 26W-8S | 30 |
| Laurei Cir. E&W | 28W-6S | 23 |
| Le Province Av. NS&EW | 26W-8S | 30 |
| Leabrook Ln. N&S | 25W-9S | 30 |
| Leamington Ct. NW&SE | 25W-9S | 30 |
| Leeds Ct. E&W | 25W-9S | 30 |
| Leesburg Ct. N&S | 25W-7S | 24 |
| Lexington Ln. E&W | 29W-7S | 29 |
| Liberty Dr. N&S | 25W-7S | 24 |
| Lighthouse Dr. N&S | 25W-8S | 30 |
| Lilac Ln. NE&SW | 27W-8S,27W-7S | 29 |
| Lincoln Rd. E&W | 25W-4S | 24 |
| Linden Ct. N&S | 28W-6S | 23 |
| Lindrick Ct. NE&SW | 28W-5S | 23 |
| Lisa Ct. E&W | 29W-6S | 23 |
| Lisson Rd. NE&SW | 24W-9S | 30 |
| Lockwood Cir. NS&EW | 26W-5S | 24 |
| Locust Ln. E&W | 28W-6S | 23 |
| Lois Ann Dr. NE&SW | 29W-6S | 23 |
| Lombardy Ln. NW&SE | 28W-6S | 23 |
| London Ct., S. NE&SW | 29W-5S | 23 |
| Longleaf Dr. N&S | 28W-6S | 23 |
| Longridge Ct. E&W | 29W-5S | 30 |
| Longspur Ct. NE&SW | 26W-9S | 30 |
| Lookout Ct. NW&SE | 26W-7S | 24 |
| Loomis St. N&S | 26W-7S,26W-6S | 24 |
| Loyola Dr. N&S | 24W-8S | 30 |
| Lynchburg Ct. NE&SW | 25W-7S | 24 |
| Lyndhurst Ct. NS&EW | 26W-6S | 24 |
| Magnolia Ln. N&S | 27W-7S | 23 |
| Main St. N&S | 27W-7S,27W-6S | 23 |
| Manassas Ct. NE&SW | 27W-7S | 23 |
| Manchester Ct. NW&SE | 29W-5S | 23 |
| Manchester St. N&S | 29W-5S | 23 |
| Maple Hills Ct. N&S | 27W-5S | 23 |
| Maple Ln. E&W | 26W-7S | 24 |
| Mapleknoll Dr. N&S | 26W-5S | 24 |
| Maplewood Cir. E&W | 30W-5S | 22 |
| Margate Ct. E&W | 24W-7S | 24 |
| Market Av. NE&SW | 25W-8S | 30 |
| Market Ct. N&S | 25W-8S | 30 |
| Market Dr. E&W | 25W-8S | 30 |
| Marls Ct. NW&SE | 24W-7S | 24 |
| Marquette Av. NE&SW | 24W-8S | 30 |
| Martin Av. E&W | 27W-8S | 29 |
| Mary Ln. E&W | 25W-6S | 24 |
| Masters Ct. N&S | 30W-5S,30W-4S | 22 |
| Mattande Dr. E&W | 26W-6S | 24 |
| Mcdowell Rd. E&W | 29W-5S | 23 |
| Meadow Green Dr. NW&SE | 26W-10S | 30 |
| Meadowland Dr. E&W | 28W-7S | 23 |
| Meander Dr. N&S | 28W-8S | 29 |
| Meisch Ct. N&S | 27W-5S | 23 |
| Meisenger Ln. NE&SW | 26W-7S | 24 |
| Melody Ln. N&S | 26W-7S | 24 |
| Menominee Ln. E&W | 26W-5S | 24 |
| Merrimac Cir. NS&EW | 27W-8S | 29 |
| Merritt Ct. NE&SW | 25W-8S | 30 |
| Mescallero Ct. E&W | 26W-4S | 24 |
| Miami Ct. N&S | 26W-4S | 24 |
| Michele St. N&S | 24W-8S | 30 |
| Michigan Av. E&W | 29W-6S | 23 |
| Middleburg Ct. NE&SW | 25W-7S | 24 |
| Middleburg Rd. NE&SW | 25W-7S | 24 |
| Mike Ct. NE&SW | 29W-6S | 23 |
| Mill St. N&S | 27W-6S,27W-4S | 23 |
| Millburn Ct. E&W | 26W-6S,25W-6S | 24 |
| Millet St. N&S | 26W-5S | 24 |
| Millrace Ln. E&W | 25W-9S | 30 |
| Milton Dr. E&W | 25W-6S | 24 |
| Mirror Lake Dr. E&W | 28W-5S | 23 |
| Mistwood Dr. NS&EW | 24W-8S | 30 |
| Misty Ct. NW&SE | 28W-10S | 29 |
| Mobile Ct. NW&SE | 27W-7S | 23 |
| Monmouth Av. E&W | 24W-9S | 30 |
| Montclair Dr. NW&SE | 24W-8S | 30 |
| Monterey Ct. N&S | 28W-6S | 23 |
| Montgomery Ct. NE&SW | 27W-8S | 29 |
| Monticello Dr. NE&SW | 26W-6S | 24 |
| Morgan Cir. NS&EW | 24W-8S | 30 |
| Morningside Dr. N&S | 27W-5S | 23 |
| Mortonsberry Dr. N&S | 28W-8S | 29 |
| Morven Ct. NW&SE | 26W-6S | 24 |
| Mountain Ct. N&S | 26W-6S | 24 |
| Mt. Vernon Ct. N&S | 26W-6S,26W-5S | 24 |
| Muirhead Av. E&W | 25W-8S | 30 |
| Muirhead Ct. N&S | 25W-8S | 30 |
| Mulberry Ct. NW&SE | 28W-7S | 23 |
| Mulligan Dr. N&S | 30W-5S,30W-4S | 22 |
| Mundelein Rd. NS&EW | 24W-9S | 30 |
| Murostone Ct. NE&SW | 25W-9S | 30 |
| Mustang Dr. NS&EW | 24W-8S | 30 |
| Naper Blvd. N&S | 25W-9S,25W-4S | 30 |
| Naperville Rd. N&S | 25W-4S | 24 |
| Naperville-Wheaton Rd. NE&SW | 25W-5S | 24 |
| Napoleon Dr. N&S | 25W-9S | 30 |
| Nashua Dr. NE&SW | 26W-7S | 24 |
| Nashville Ct. NW&SE | 27W-8S | 29 |
| Natchez Trace Cir. E&W | 27W-8S | 29 |
| Navarone Dr. N&S | 27W-9S | 29 |
| Needham Rd. NE&SW | 25W-6S,25W-5S | 24 |
| Needles Ct. E&W | 25W-5S | 24 |
| North Av. E&W | 26W-6S | 24 |
| North Service Rd. E&W | 29W-4S | 23 |
| Northfield Ct. N&S | 26W-9S | 30 |
| Northfield Dr. N&S | 26W-9S | 30 |
| Norwood Av. NE&SW | 25W-8S | 30 |
| Notre Dame Dr. NE&SW | 26W-7S | 24 |
| Oak Ct. NE&SW | 25W-9S | 30 |
| Oakhurst Dr. NS&EW | 28W-7S | 23 |
| Oakleaf Ct. E&W | 26W-6S | 24 |
| Oakton Ln. NE&SW | 28W-8S,28W-7S | 29 |
| Oakwood Dr. N&S | 27W-7S | 23 |
| Ogden Av. E&W | 28W-6S,25W-5S | 23 |
| Okolona Ct. NE&SW | 27W-7S | 23 |
| Old Dominion Ct. E&W | 25W-7S | 24 |
| Old Dominion Rd. E&W | 25W-7S | 24 |
| Old Naperville Rd. N&S | 25W-4S | 24 |
| Olesen Dr. NE&SW | 25W-8S,25W-6S | 30 |
| Olympus Dr. N&S | 26W-8S | 30 |
| Omaha Ct. NW&SE | 25W-7S | 24 |
| Ontario Av. E&W | 29W-6S | 23 |
| Oriole Ct. NE&SW | 26W-8S | 30 |
| Orleans Av. E&W | 25W-9S | 30 |
| Osage Ln. E&W | 26W-8S | 30 |
| Oswego Rd. SW&NE | 28W-7S,22W-7S | 23 |
| Ottawa St. N&S | 26W-5S | 24 |
| Overstreet Ct. N&S | 25W-9S | 30 |
| Overton Ct. NW&SE | 25W-7S | 24 |
| Oxford Ct. NW&SE | 27W-6S | 23 |
| Pacific Dr. N&S | 27W-8S | 23 |
| Paddington Av. E&W | 29W-5S | 23 |
| Paddock Ct. N&S | 25W-9S | 30 |
| Page Ct. E&W | 27W-6S | 23 |
| Palm Ct. E&W | 28W-7S | 23 |
| Palmetto Ct. E&W | 28W-7S | 23 |
| Pamela Ct. E&W | 25W-7S | 24 |
| Papago Ct. NW&SE | 26W-5S | 24 |
| Park St. N&S | 27W-4S | 23 |
| Park Way Dr. N&S | 27W-6S | 23 |
| Parkfield Ct. E&W | 28W-7S | 23 |
| Pas Ct. N&S | 29W-6S,29W-5S | 23 |
| Pathway Ln. N&S | 24W-9S | 30 |
| Pattermann Ct. NS&EW | 24W-9S | 30 |
| Pawnee Ln. E&W | 26W-5S | 24 |
| Peachtree Ct. E&W | 25W-6S,25W-5S | 24 |
| Peacock Ct. E&W | 26W-9S | 30 |
| Pearson Cir. NS&EW | 27W-6S,25W-5S | 23 |
| Pecan Ct. NW&SE | 27W-8S | 29 |
| Pelham Ct. N&S | 29W-5S | 23 |
| Pemberton Ct. N&S | 25W-8S | 30 |
| Pembroke Rd. N&S | 25W-6S | 24 |
| Penn Ct. E&W | 24W-8S | 30 |
| Pepperdine Ct. E&W | 24W-9S | 30 |
| Pepperidge Rd. N&S | 28W-6S | 23 |
| Periwinkle Ct. E&W | 29W-7S | 29 |
| Persimmon Ct. N&S | 25W-9S | 30 |
| Peterson Ct. E&W | 27W-6S | 23 |
| Phaeton Ct. NW&SE | 25W-9S | 30 |
| Picadilly Cir. N&S | 29W-5S | 23 |
| Pickwick Ct. NW&SE | 29W-5S | 23 |
| Pier Av. E&W | 25W-8S | 30 |
| Pier Ct. E&W | 25W-8S | 30 |
| Pima Ct. NW&SE | 26W-5S | 24 |
| Pine Ct. NW&SE | 26W-7S | 24 |
| Pinetree Dr. N&S | 27W-8S | 29 |
| Placer Ct. N&S | 26W-9S,26W-8S | 30 |
| Plainfield-Naperville Rd. N&S | 27W-8S,27W-7S | 29 |
| Plank Rd. E&W | 26W-6S,25W-5S | 24 |
| Plum Hollow Ct. NE&SW | 28W-5S | 23 |
| Pomona Ct. E&W | 28W-6S | 23 |
| Poplar St. N&S | 28W-8S | 29 |
| Porter Av. E&W | 26W-7S | 24 |
| Pottowattomi Ct. N&S | 26W-5S | 24 |
| Prague Ct. N&S | 29W-5S | 23 |
| Prairie Knoll Dr. NS&EW | 26W-9S | 30 |
| Prairie St. E&W | 26W-7S | 24 |
| Prairieview Ct. N&S | 30W-5S | 22 |
| Preston Rd. E&W | 29W-5S | 23 |
| Prestwick Dr. N&S | 30W-5S | 22 |
| Primrose Ln. N&S | 25W-9S | 30 |
| Prince Ct. E&W | 29W-5S | 23 |
| Princeton Cir. NE&SW | 24W-8S | 30 |
| Proud Clarion Ct. NE&SW | 26W-7S | 24 |
| Purdue Av. E&W | 24W-9S | 30 |
| Quail Hollow Ct. N&S | 26W-6S | 24 |
| Quails Dr. E&W | 26W-9S | 30 |
| Queen Ct. NW&SE | 29W-5S | 23 |
| Queensbury Ct. N&S | 29W-5S | 23 |
| Queensgreen Cir. E&W | 29W-5S | 23 |
| Queensgreen Ct. N&S | 29W-5S | 23 |
| Quin Ct. N&S | 29W-6S,29W-5S | 23 |
| Quincy Ave. E&W | 29W-6S | 23 |
| Raintree Dr. N&S | 28W-7S | 23 |
| Rampart Cir. N&S | 25W-9S | 30 |
| Ranchview Dr. N&S | 24W-9S,24W-8S | 30 |
| Rapidan Ct. N&S | 25W-9S | 24 |
| Rapids Ct. NW&SE | 26W-8S | 30 |
| Raymond Dr. N&S | 28W-6S,29W-4S | 23 |
| Redbud Dr. E&W | 27W-7S | 23 |
| Redfield Rd. NS&EW | 29W-5S | 23 |
| Redpoll Ct. N&S | 26W-9S | 30 |
| Redstart Rd. NW&SE | 26W-9S | 30 |
| Rennet Dr. N&S | 27W-8S | 29 |
| Revere Ct. N&S | 27W-8S | 29 |
| Rhodes Dr. E&W | 28W-8S | 29 |
| Richard Rd. N&S | 25W-7S,25W-6S | 24 |
| Richmond Ct. N&S | 27W-7S | 23 |
| Rickert Dr. N&S | 29W-7S,28W-7S | 23 |
| Ridgefield Ln. E&W | 26W-9S | 30 |
| Ridgely Ct. E&W | 25W-7S | 24 |
| Rill Ct. N&S | 26W-9S | 30 |
| Ring Rd. N&S | 26W-10S,26W-9S | 30 |
| Riparian Ct. NE&SW | 26W-9S | 30 |
| Ripley Ct. NE&SW | 26W-9S | 30 |
| Riva Ridge Ct. N&S | 25W-7S | 24 |
| River Bluff Cir. NS&EW | 27W-7S | 23 |
| River Oak Ct. N&S | 25W-9S,24W-9S | 30 |
| River Rd. N&S | 28W-8S,28W-5S | 29 |
| River Ridge Cir. NS&EW | 25W-9S | 30 |
| Riverfront Cir. NS&EW | 27W-7S | 23 |
| Riverlea Ct. E&W | 25W-9S | 30 |
| Riverridge Ct. E&W | 25W-9S | 30 |
| Riverview Ln. NW&SE | 26W-7S | 24 |
| Robin Hill Ct. E&W | 27W-7S | 23 |
| Robin Hill Dr. E&W | 27W-7S | 23 |
| Rockbridge Dr. NS&EW | 25W-7S | 24 |
| Rolling Grove Ct. E&W | 28W-7S | 23 |
| Rollins Ct. N&S | 24W-9S | 30 |
| Rose Ln. NW&SE | 27W-7S,27W-8S | 23 |
| Rosewood Ln. E&W | 26W-5S,25W-5S | 24 |
| Rossmere Ct. N&S | 25W-9S | 30 |
| Rowan Ct. E&W | 26W-8S | 30 |
| Royal Blackheath Ct. N&S | 28W-5S,27W-5S | 23 |
| Royal Bombay Ct. NE&SW | 28W-5S | 23 |
| Royal St. George Dr. NE&SW | 25W-5S,27W-5S | 23 |
| Russet Av. E&W | 27W-8S | 29 |
| Rutgers Ct. NS&EW | 24W-9S | 30 |
| Saber Ct. N&S | 26W-9S | 30 |
| Sagebrush Rd. E&W | 26W-9S | 30 |
| Saginaw Ct. E&W | 26W-9S | 30 |
| Samstag Ct. NE&SW | 25W-5S | 24 |
| Sanctuary Ln. EW&NS | 28W-8S,28W-7S | 29 |
| Sandalwood Dr. NE&SW | 27W-7S | 23 |
| Sandgate Ct. NW&SE | 26W-9S | 30 |
| Sandpiper Ln. NW&SE | 26W-9S | 30 |
| Sara Ln. N&S | 26W-9S | 30 |
| Saranell Av. E&W | 28W-8S | 29 |
| Savannah Cir. NS&EW | 29W-7S | 23 |
| Schey Ct. N&S | 26W-9S | 30 |
| School St. E&W | 26W-7S | 24 |
| Scott Ct. N&S | 26W-7S | 24 |
| Secretariat Dr. N&S | 25W-7S | 24 |
| Selby Rd. E&W | 29W-5S | 23 |
| Sequoia Ct. N&S | 28W-7S | 23 |
| Sequoia Rd. E&W | 28W-7S | 23 |
| Service Rd. NS&EW | 29W-4S,29W-5S | 23 |
| Seton Hall Dr. N&S | 24W-9S | 30 |
| Severn Ct. NE&SW | 27W-8S | 29 |
| Shanahan St. N&S | 25W-9S | 24 |
| Sheffield Rd. E&W | 25W-9S | 30 |
| Shenandoah Ln. N&S | 26W-5S | 24 |
| Shepherd Dr. N&S | 28W-7S | 29 |
| Sheppey Ct. N&S | 27W-8S | 29 |
| Sheringham Dr. NS&EW | 27W-8S | 29 |
| Sherman Av. N&S | 26W-5S | 24 |
| Shetland Rd. NW&SE | 28W-8S | 30 |
| Shiloh Cir. E&W | 27W-8S | 29 |
| Shome Ct. NW&SE | 26W-9S | 30 |
| Signal Dr. N&S | 25W-9S | 30 |
| Silver Maple St. N&S | 26W-5S | 24 |
| Sir Barton Ct. NW&SE | 26W-7S | 24 |
| Sleepy Hollow Ct. E&W | 24W-9S | 30 |
| Sleight St. N&S | 26W-7S,26W-5S | 24 |
| Slippery Rock Ct. NE&SW | 24W-9S | 30 |
| Slippery Rock Dr. NE&SW | 24W-9S | 30 |
| Small Ct. E&W | 29W-6S | 23 |
| Smokey Ct. N&S | 26W-4S | 24 |
| Snowdon Ct. NW&SE | 25W-9S | 30 |
| Spalding Dr. E&W | 27W-7S | 23 |
| Spindle Tree Av. E&W | 25W-9S | 30 |
| Split Oak Rd. NE&SW | 26W-9S | 30 |
| Spring Garden Ct. E&W | 25W-5S | 24 |
| Spring St. E&W | 27W-6S | 23 |
| Spring Valley Rd. E&W | 24W-9S | 30 |
| Springhill Cir. NS&EW | 25W-6S,25W-5S | 24 |
| Springside Cir. NS&EW | 26W-9S | 30 |
| Springwood Dr. NE&SW | 27W-7S | 23 |
| Spruce Dr. E&W | 27W-8S | 29 |
| Sprucewood Ct. E&W | 25W-9S | 30 |

| | Grid | Page |
|---|---|---|
| Stacie Ct. N&S | 29W-6S | 23 |
| Stafford Av. N&S | 25W-7S | 24 |
| Standish Ct. NE&SW | | |
| | 26W-8S | 23 |
| Stanford Dr. N&S | 24W-9S | 30 |
| Stanhope Ct. NE&SW | | |
| | 25W-9S | 30 |
| Stanton Dr. NE&SW | 25W-8S | 30 |
| Starling Ln. NW&SE | 26W-9S | 30 |
| Stauffer Dr. N&S | 28W-6S | 23 |
| Staunton Rd. E&W | 25W-9S | 30 |
| Steinbeck Ct. N&S | 28W-9S | 29 |
| Sterling Ct. N&S | 27W-8S | 24 |
| Stevens St. E&W | 27W-6S | 23 |
| Stone Creek Ct. E&W | | |
| | 28W-8S | 30 |
| Stone Ct. NE&SW | 25W-5S | 24 |
| Stonegate Rd. E&W | 28W-7S | 23 |
| Stonehenge Ct. NW&SE | | |
| | 29W-5S | 23 |
| Stoney Brook Dr. E&W | | |
| | 25W-9S | 30 |
| Stoos Ln. NW&SE | 26W-7S | 24 |
| Stratford Ct. N&S | 28W-6S | 23 |
| Strawbridge Ct. N&S | | |
| | 23W-9S | 31 |
| Stuart Ct. N&S | 27W-5S | 24 |
| Suffolk St. N&S | 26W-5S | 24 |
| Sugar Creek Ct. NW&SE | | |
| | 28W-5S | 23 |
| Summerset Ct. N&S | 27W-8S | 29 |
| Summit Hills Dr. NE&SW | | |
| | 28W-5S | 23 |
| Sumter Ct. N&S | 27W-8S | 29 |
| Sunderland Ct. N&S | 26W-9S | 30 |
| Sunrise Ct. N&S | 25W-9S | 30 |
| Sunset Dr. NS&EW | 26W-7S | 24 |
| Surrey Av. N&S | 25W-8S | 30 |
| Sussex Ct. NW&SE | 25W-6S | 24 |
| Sussex Rd. N&S | 25W-6S | 24 |
| Swallow St. N&S | | |
| | 26W-9S,26W-8S | 30 |
| Swansea Ct. NE&SW | | |
| | 27W-8S | 29 |
| Sweetbay Ct. NW&SE | | |
| | 26W-7S | 24 |
| Swift Ln. E&W | 26W-8S | 30 |
| Sycamore Dr. NE&SW | | |
| | 27W-8S,26W-7S | 29 |
| Sylvan Cir. NW&SE | 26W-7S | 24 |
| Sylvia Ln. E&W | 26W-9S | 30 |
| Syracuse Av. NE&SW | | |
| | 24W-9S | 30 |
| Talbot Dr. N&S | 27W-8S | 29 |
| Tall Oaks Ct. NW&SE | | |
| | 24W-8S | 30 |
| Tamarack Av. E&W | 26W-8S | 30 |
| Tan Oak Ln. E&W | 26W-8S | 30 |
| Tanager Ct. E&W | 26W-8S | 30 |
| Tanglewood Ln. E&W | | |
| | 26W-5S | 24 |
| Teakwood Ct. NE&SW | | |
| | 28W-7S | 23 |
| Technology Dr. (Pvt.) E&W | | |
| | 27W-5S | 23 |
| Templar Rd. N&S | 26W-9S | 30 |
| Tennyson Ln. EW&NS | | |
| | 28W-8S,27W-8S | 29 |
| Terrance Dr. NS&EW | | |
| | 26W-9S,26W-8S | 30 |
| Terri Cir. NS&EW | 29W-6S | 23 |
| Testa Ct. N&S | 28W-6S | 23 |
| Teton Ct. NW&SE | 27W-8S | 29 |
| Thomas Dr. N&S | 29W-6S | 23 |
| Thornwood Dr. N&S | 26W-7S | 24 |
| Thrush Ln. E&W | 26W-8S | 30 |
| Thunderbird Ln. E&W | | |
| | 28W-5S | 23 |
| Ticonderoga Ln. E&W | | |
| | 26W-5S | 24 |
| Tim Tam Cir. NS&EW | | |
| | 26W-7S | 24 |
| Timber Lee Ct. N&S | 25W-7S | 24 |
| Timber Trail Dr. E&W | | |
| | 25W-9S | 30 |
| Timberlake Ct. E&W | | |
| | 26W-6S,25W-5S | 24 |
| Torrington Dr. N&S | 27W-8S | 29 |
| Towhee Ln. N&S | 26W-8S | 30 |
| Towpath Ct. N&S | 25W-9S | 30 |
| Trace Cir. N&S | 25W-9S | 30 |
| Trails End Ct. N&S | 25W-9S | 30 |
| Travelaire Av. E&W | 27W-9S | 29 |
| Trefoil Ct. E&W | 26W-5S | 24 |
| Trent Av. E&W | 29W-5S | 23 |
| Triton Ln. E&W | 26W-8S | 30 |
| Tudor Dr. N&S | | |
| | 29W-5S,29W-6S | 23 |
| Tufts Ct. NE&SW | 24W-8S | 30 |
| Tulane Dr. N&S | 24W-8S | 30 |
| Tulip Ln. E&W | 27W-7S | 23 |
| Tupelo Dr. E&W | | |
| | 27W-8S,26W-8S | 29 |
| Tumbridge Cir. NS&EW | | |
| | 25W-7S | 24 |
| Turtle Cove Ct. N&S | | |
| | 25W-9S | 30 |
| Union Ct. N&S | 30W-5S | 22 |
| University Ct. N&S | 25W-10S | 30 |
| University Dr. N&S | | |
| | 25W-10S,24W-9S | 30 |
| Vales End Dr. NE&SW | | |
| | 28W-8S | 29 |
| Valley Dr. NW&SE | 28W-6S | 23 |

| | Grid | Page |
|---|---|---|
| Valley Ridge Ct. E&W | | |
| | 24W-9S | 30 |
| Van Buren Av. E&W | 27W-6S | 23 |
| Van Buren St. E&W | 26W-6S | 24 |
| Vanderbilt Ct. N&S | 24W-9S | 30 |
| Vassar Dr. NW&SE | 24W-9S | 30 |
| Venetian Ct. E&W | 25W-7S | 24 |
| Ventura Ct. N&S | 28W-6S | 23 |
| Vermont Ct. NE&SW | | |
| | 27W-8S | 29 |
| Vest Dr. N&S | 26W-5S | 24 |
| Vest St. N&S | 26W-5S | 24 |
| Vicksburg Ct. E&W | 27W-8S | 29 |
| Victoria Ct. NE&SW | 26W-7S | 24 |
| View Ct. E&W | 26W-7S | 24 |
| Villa Av. E&W | 26W-7S | 24 |
| Village Green Rd. E&W | | |
| | 27W-7S | 23 |
| Villanova Dr. NW&SE | | |
| | 24W-9S | 30 |
| Violet Cir. NE&SW | 29W-7S | 29 |
| Virginia Ct. E&W | 27W-7S | 23 |
| Wakefield Ct. N&S | 25W-6S | 24 |
| Wall St. N&S | | |
| | 29W-5S,29W-4S | 23 |
| Walnut St. N&S | 25W-8S | 30 |
| Walton Ct. N&S | 26W-9S | 30 |
| Warbler Ln. N&S | | |
| | 26W-9S,26W-8S | 30 |
| Warrenville Rd. E&W | | |
| | 27W-4S,25W-4S | 23 |
| Warwick Dr. E&W | 25W-9S | 30 |
| Washington St. N&S | | |
| | 26W-10S,26W-4S | 23 |
| Water St. E&W | 27W-6S | 23 |
| Watercress Dr. NE&SW | | |
| | 26W-7S | 24 |
| Waterford Ct. N&S | 28W-6S | 23 |
| Waterside Ct. NW&SE | | |
| | 27W-6S | 23 |
| Waverly Ct. N&S | 26W-6S | 24 |
| Waxwing Av. E&W | 26W-8S | 30 |
| Webster St. N&S | | |
| | 27W-7S,27W-5S | 23 |
| Wedgefield Cir. NS&EW | | |
| | 27W-5S | 23 |
| Wehrli Dr. N&S | 26W-7S | 24 |
| Wehrli Rd. N&S | 24W-9S | 30 |
| Wellington Ct. N&S | 25W-9S | 30 |
| Welner Rd. N&S | 26W-7S | 24 |
| Welton Ct. N&S | 26W-9S | 30 |
| West Ct. N&S | 27W-5S | 23 |
| West St. N&S | | |
| | 27W-8S,27W-4S | 29 |
| Westbury Ct. E&W | 26W-9S | 30 |
| Westglen Dr. NS&EW | | |
| | 27W-8S | 29 |
| Westminster Dr. N&S | | |
| | 29W-5S | 23 |
| Westmoreland Ct. NW&SE | | |
| | 25W-6S | 24 |
| Westmoreland Dr. N&S | | |
| | 25W-6S | 24 |
| Weston Ridge Dr. N&S | | |
| | 30W-6S | 22 |
| Westwind Ct. NE&SW | | |
| | 25W-9S | 30 |
| Wexford Ct. NE&SW | | |
| | 25W-7S | 24 |
| Whirlaway Av. NW&SE | | |
| | 26W-7S,25W-7S | 24 |
| Whispering Hills Ct. E&W | | |
| | 28W-6S | 23 |
| Whispering Hills Rd. NS&EW | | |
| | 28W-8S,28W-6S | 29 |
| White Oak Dr. N&S | | |
| | 26W-7S,26W-6S | 24 |
| White Pines Ct. E&W | | |
| | 28W-6S | 23 |
| Whitebark Ct. N&S | 28W-7S | 23 |
| Whitewater Ct. E&W | | |
| | 28W-8S | 29 |
| Whitley Rd. E&W | 29W-5S | 23 |
| Cir. | 25W-7S | 24 |
| Wickfield Ct. NE&SW | | |
| | 25W-7S | 24 |
| Wickham Ct. N&S | | |
| | 25W-7S | 24 |
| Wildflower Cir. NE&SW | | |
| | 29W-9S | 29 |
| Wildflower Ct. N&S | 29W-7S | 29 |
| Willcrest Rd. E&W | 28W-7S | 23 |
| Williamsburg Dr. N&S | | |
| | 27W-8S,27W-7S | 29 |
| Williard Ct. N&S | 29W-8S | 29 |
| Willow Rd. NW&SE | 26W-7S | 24 |
| Willoway Dr. N&S | 28W-6S | 23 |
| Wilshire Dr. E&W | 28W-6S | 23 |
| Wilson Av. E&W | 27W-6S | 23 |
| Winchester Ct. E&W | | |
| | 28W-5S | 23 |
| Windham Ln. N&S | 26W-5S | 24 |
| Winding Creek Dr. NS&EW | | |
| | 26W-8S | 30 |
| Windridge Ct. N&S | 28W-7S | 23 |
| Windsor Dr. N&S | 25W-8S | 30 |
| Winola Ct. N&S | 25W-9S | 30 |
| Winslow Ct. E&W | 25W-9S | 30 |
| Wisconsin St. N&S | 26W-9S | 24 |
| Wisteria Ct. NE&SW | | |
| | 26W-9S | 30 |
| Wood Creek Ct. E&W | | |
| | 26W-8S | 30 |

| | Grid | Page |
|---|---|---|
| Woodfield Ct. NW&SE | | |
| | 26W-9S | 30 |
| Wright St. N&S | | |
| | 27W-7S,26W-5S | 24 |
| Wydown Ct. NW&SE | | |
| | 28W-5S | 30 |
| Wyndgate Ct. E&W | 28W-9S | 29 |
| Yale Ct. NE&SW | 24W-8S | 30 |
| Yellow Daisy Ct. E&W | | |
| | 30W-5S | 22 |
| York Ct. N&S | 26W-5S | 24 |
| Yorkshire Dr. E&W | 25W-5S | 24 |
| Zaininger Av. NW&SE | | |
| | 27W-5S | 23 |
| 4th Av. E&W | 26W-6S | 24 |
| 5th Av. E&W | | |
| | 28W-6S,26W-6S | 23 |
| 6th Av. E&W | | |
| | 27W-6S,26W-6S | 23 |
| 7th Av. E&W | 26W-6S | 24 |
| 8th Av. E&W | | |
| | 27W-6S,26W-6S | 23 |
| 10th Av. E&W | 27W-6S | 23 |
| 11th Av. E&W | | |
| | 27W-5S,26W-5S | 23 |
| 12th Av. E&W | | |
| | 27W-5S,26W-5S | 23 |
| 13th Av. E&W | 27W-5S | 23 |
| 14th St. E&W | | |
| | 27W-5S,26W-5S | 23 |
| 75th St. E&W | | |
| | 27W-8S,25W-8S | 29 |
| 77th St. E&W | 24W-8S | 30 |
| 79th St. E&W | 24W-8S | 30 |
| 81st St. E&W | 26W-9S | 30 |
| 87th St. E&W | | |
| | 28W-9S,24W-9S | 29 |

### Naperville Township

| | Grid | Page |
|---|---|---|
| Aero Dr. N&S | 29W-9S | 29 |
| Allister Ct. NW&SE | 30W-5S | 22 |
| Allister Ln. E&W | 30W-5S | 22 |
| Arbor Dr. N&S | 29W-7S | 23 |
| Argyll Ln. E&W | 30W-5S | 22 |
| Aurora Av. E&W | | |
| | 29W-7S,28W-7S | 23 |
| Bailey Rd. E&W | 27W-9S | 29 |
| Bauer Rd. E&W | 27W-9S | 29 |
| Berry Ct. N&S | 28W-7S | 23 |
| Bonnie Ct. NE&SW | 30W-5S | 22 |
| Book Rd. N&S | | |
| | 29W-9S,29W-8S | 29 |
| Briar Ln. E&W | 30W-5S | 22 |
| Bruce Ln. E&W | 30W-5S | 22 |
| Bunker Cir. E&W | 30W-5S | 22 |
| Byerum St. N&S | 27W-5S | 23 |
| Campbell Dr. N&S | 30W-5S | 22 |
| Chandelle Ct. N&S | 29W-9S | 29 |
| Claymore Ln. E&W | 30W-5S | 22 |
| Clover Ct. N&S | 28W-7S | 23 |
| Country Club Blvd. N&S | | |
| | 30W-5S | 22 |
| Country Glen Dr. N&S | | |
| | 30W-6S | 22 |
| Country Lakes Dr. E&W | | |
| | 30W-5S | 22 |
| Diehl Rd. E&W | | |
| | 31W-4S,28W-4S | 22 |
| Doral Dr. E&W | 30W-5S | 22 |
| Eagle St. N&S | 27W-5S | 23 |
| Eola Rd. N&S | | |
| | 31W-7S,31W-5S | 22 |
| Estuary Ct. NW&SE | 26W-9S | 30 |
| Ewing St. N&S | 27W-5S | 23 |
| Fairway Dr. N&S | | |
| | 30W-6S,30W-5S | 22 |
| Ferry Rd. E&W | | |
| | 31W-4S,30W-4S | 22 |
| Firestone Ct. N&S | 30W-5S | 22 |
| Flamenco Ct. NW&SE | | |
| | 30W-5S | 22 |
| Frontenac Rd. N&S | 31W-5S | 22 |
| Glenoban Dr. N&S | 30W-5S | 22 |
| Gordon Terrace Rd. N&S | | |
| | 30W-5S | 22 |
| Granada Ct. NW&SE | | |
| | 30W-5S | 22 |
| Green Acres Dr. N&S | | |
| | 27W-7S | 23 |
| Hacienda Ct. NW&SE | | |
| | 30W-5S | 22 |
| Huntington Ct. NE&SW | | |
| | 30W-6S | 24 |
| Innisbrook Dr. E&W | 30W-5S | 22 |
| Joseph St. N&S | 27W-5S | 23 |
| Kautz Rd. N&S | 32W-5S | 22 |
| Kirk Ct. N&S | 30W-5S | 22 |
| Lawn Meadow Ln. E&W | | |
| | 28W-7S | 23 |
| Liberty St. N&S | | |
| | 32W-7S,31W-7S | 22 |
| McGregor Ln. N&S | 30W-5S | 22 |
| Meadow Lark Ln. N&S | | |
| | 27W-9S | 29 |
| Meadow Rd. N&S | 30W-4S | 22 |
| Medinah Ct. N&S | 30W-5S | 22 |
| Medinah Dr. N&S | 30W-5S | 22 |
| Mill St. N&S | 27W-5S | 23 |
| Modaff Rd. E&W | 29W-9S | 29 |
| Molitor Rd. E&W | 32W-5S | 22 |
| Monterrey Ct. NE&SW | | |
| | 30W-5S | 22 |

| | Grid | Page |
|---|---|---|
| New York St. E&W | | |
| | 32W-7S,30W-7S | 22 |
| North Aurora Rd. E&W | | |
| | 31W-6S,29W-6S | 22 |
| North Ln. E&W | 27W-7S | 23 |
| Northfield Ct. N&S | 26W-9S | 30 |
| Ogden Av. NE&SW | 29W-8S | 29 |
| Oswego Rd. NE&SW | | |
| | 28W-7S | 23 |
| Paxton Dr. E&W | 30W-5S | 22 |
| Pearson St. N&S | 27W-5S | 23 |
| Pebble Beach Ln. N&S | | |
| | 30W-5S | 22 |
| Pebblewood Ln. N&S | | |
| | 30W-5S,30W-4S | 22 |
| Pebblewood Trail NS&EW | | |
| | 30W-5S,30W-4S | 22 |
| Pinehurst Dr. N&S | 30W-5S | 22 |
| Pioneer Ct. E&W | 26W-9S | 30 |
| Poss Rd. N&S | | |
| | 32W-6S,31W-6S | 22 |
| Ramona Ct. NW&SE | | |
| | 30W-5S | 22 |
| Reid Pl. E&W | 31W-6S | 22 |
| River Rd. NW&SE | 28W-6S | 23 |
| Rt. 59 N&S | 29W-9S,29W-6S | 29 |
| Scheffer Rd. E&W | 32W-6S | 22 |
| Schooner Ct. E&W | 26W-9S | 30 |
| Scotts Dr. N&S | 30W-5S | 22 |
| Skylane Ct. N&S | 29W-9S | 29 |
| South Ln. E&W | 27W-7S | 23 |
| Spyglass Ct. N&S | 30W-5S | 22 |
| St. Andrews Ct. N&S | | |
| | 30W-5S | 22 |
| Stearman Ct. N&S | 29W-9S | 29 |
| Stewart Dr. N&S | 30W-5S | 22 |
| Stone Creek Ct. E&W | | |
| | 26W-8S | 30 |
| Stonebridge Blvd. NE&SW | | |
| | 32W-6S | 22 |
| Tartan Ln. N&S | 30W-5S | 22 |
| Thornapple Dr. N&S | 28W-7S | 23 |
| Timberlane Ct. N&S | | |
| | 30W-6S,30W-5S | 22 |
| Valencia Ct. NE&SW | | |
| | 30W-5S | 22 |
| Vista Ct. N&S | 30W-5S | 22 |
| Wagon Wheel Ct. E&W | | |
| | 26W-9S | 30 |
| Webster St. N&S | 27W-5S | 23 |
| Westwind Dr. N&S | | |
| | 30W-6S,30W-5S | 22 |
| Whispering Winds Dr. E&W | | |
| | 30W-6S | 22 |
| Wild Cherry Ln. N&S | | |
| | 28W-7S | 23 |
| Woodwind Dr. E&W | | |
| | 30W-6S,30W-5S | 22 |
| 4th St. N&S | 31W-6S | 22 |
| 5th St. N&S | 32W-6S | 22 |
| 7th St. N&S | 32W-6S | 22 |
| 46th St. E&W | 27W-4S | 23 |
| 47th St. E&W | 27W-4S | 23 |
| 48th St. E&W | 27W-5S | 23 |
| 49th St. E&W | 27W-5S | 23 |
| 75th St. E&W | | |
| | 30W-8S,28W-8S | 28 |
| 79th St. E&W | 27W-9S | 29 |
| 80th St. E&W | 27W-9S | 29 |
| 81st St. E&W | 29W-9S | 29 |
| 82nd Ct. E&W | 27W-9S | 29 |
| 82nd Pl. E&W | 27W-9S | 29 |
| 83rd St. E&W | 27W-9S | 29 |
| 87th St. E&W | | |
| | 28W-9S,24W-9S | 29 |

### Oak Brook

| | Grid | Page |
|---|---|---|
| Abbeywood Ct. NW&SE | 15W-1S | 21 |
| Acorn Hill Ln. E&W | 15W-3S | 21 |
| Arden Ct. N&S | 18W-2S | 20 |
| Ascot Ln. N&S | 18W-3S | 20 |
| Ashley Ct. NW&SE | 17W-3S | 21 |
| Avenue Loire N&S | 18W-2S | 20 |
| Bath & Tennis Dr. N&S | | |
| | 16W-2S,15W-2S | 21 |
| Baybrook Ct. NW&SE | | |
| | 18W-2S | 20 |
| Baybrook Ln. E&W | | |
| | 18W-2S,17W-2S | 20 |
| Berseem Ct. NE&SW | | |
| | 18W-2S | 20 |
| Birchwood Rd. E&W | | |
| | 16W-4S | 27 |
| Bliss Dr. N&S | 15W-1S | 21 |
| Bluegrass Ct. N&S | 18W-3S | 20 |
| Bradford Ln. NS&EW | | |
| | 15W-2S | 21 |
| Breckenridge Farm Rd. E&W | | |
| | 16W-3S | 21 |
| Briarwood Av. E&W | 17W-2S | 21 |
| Briarwood Central N&S | | |
| Cir. | 17W-2S | 21 |
| Briarwood Dr. E&W | 17W-2S | 21 |
| Briarwood Ln. E&W | 17W-2S | 21 |
| Briarwood Loop E&W | | |
| | 17W-2S | 21 |
| Briarwood North E&W | | |
| | 17W-2S | 21 |
| Briarwood Pass E&W | | |
| | 17W-2S | 21 |

| | Grid | Page |
|---|---|---|
| Briarwood South N&S | | |
| | 17W-2S | 21 |
| Bridgeway Ct. NW&SE | | |
| | 17W-3S | 21 |
| Bridle Path Cir. NS&EW | | |
| | 18W-3S | 20 |
| Brighton Ln. N&S | 15W-2S | 21 |
| Brougham Ln. N&S | 18W-3S | 20 |
| Burr Oak Ct. N&S | 15W-1S | 21 |
| Butterfield Rd. NE&SW | | |
| | 18W-2S | 20 |
| Cambridge Dr. N&S | 17W-2S | 21 |
| Camden Ct. N&S | 18W-2S | 20 |
| Camelot Dr. NE&SW | | |
| | 17W-2S | 21 |
| Canterberry Ln. E&W | | |
| | 15W-3S | 21 |
| Carlisle Dr. N&S | 17W-2S | 21 |
| Carriage Ct. NW&SE | | |
| | 18W-3S | 20 |
| Cass Ct. N&S | | |
| | 18W-3S,17W-3S | 20 |
| Castle Dr. N&S | 16W-1S | 21 |
| Cermak Rd. E&W | | |
| | 16W-1S,15W-1S | 21 |
| Charleton Pl. E&W | 17W-2S | 21 |
| Cheval Dr. N&S | 16W-4S | 27 |
| Cochise Ct. NE&SW | 18W-2S | 20 |
| Commerce Dr. E&W | 16W-1S | 21 |
| Concord Ct. N&S | 17W-2S | 21 |
| Coolidge St. N&S | 15W-2S | 21 |
| Court 1 N&S | 18W-3S | 20 |
| Court 10 N&S | 18W-3S | 20 |
| Court 11 N&S | 18W-3S | 20 |
| Court 12 N&S | 18W-3S | 20 |
| Court 13 N&S | 18W-3S | 20 |
| Court 14 N&S | 18W-3S | 20 |
| Court 15 N&S | 18W-3S | 20 |
| Court 16 N&S | 18W-1S | 20 |
| Court 17 N&S | 17W-3S | 21 |
| Court 18 E&W | 17W-3S | 21 |
| Court 19 E&W | 18W-3S | 20 |
| Court 2 N&S | 18W-3S | 20 |
| Court 20 N&S | 18W-3S | 20 |
| Court 3 N&S | 18W-3S | 20 |
| Court 4 N&S | 18W-3S | 20 |
| Court 5 N&S | 18W-3S | 20 |
| Court 6 N&S | 18W-3S | 20 |
| Court 7 E&W | 18W-3S | 20 |
| Court 8 E&W | 18W-3S | 20 |
| Court 9 N&S | 18W-3S | 20 |
| Covington Ct. NS&EW | | |
| | 17W-3S | 21 |
| Crab Apple Ln. N&S | 16W-1S | 21 |
| Croydon Ln. E&W | 15W-2S | 21 |
| Deer Trail Ln. E&W | 16W-3S | 21 |
| Derby Ct. N&S | 18W-3S | 20 |
| Devonshire Dr. NS&EW | | |
| | 17W-2S | 21 |
| Dover Dr. E&W | 15W-2S | 21 |
| East-West Freeway E&W | | |
| | 18W-2S,15W-1S | 20 |
| Enterprise NE&SW | 15W-1S | 21 |
| Fairview Av. N&S | 18W-3S | 20 |
| Forest Gate Rd. E&W | | |
| | 16W-2S | 21 |
| Forest Glen Ln. NW&SE | | |
| | 15W-1S | 21 |
| Forest Mews Dr. E&W | | |
| | 18W-3S | 20 |
| Forest Trail N&S | 16W-1S | 21 |
| Fox Trail Ct. N&S | 16W-3S | 21 |
| Fox Trail Ln. E&W | 16W-3S | 21 |
| Fox Trail Rd. E&W | 16W-3S | 21 |
| Foxiana Ct. NW&SE | 18W-2S | 21 |
| Frederick Dr. E&W | 16W-3S | 21 |
| Gateway Ln. E&W | 15W-3S | 21 |
| Glendale Av. E&W | 15W-3S | 21 |
| Golf Dr. NS&EW | 15W-2S | 21 |
| Green Leaf Dr. E&W | | |
| | 16W-1S | 21 |
| Hambletonian Dr. E&W | | |
| | 18W-3S | 20 |
| Hamilton Ln. E&W | 17W-2S | 21 |
| Hampton Dr. E&W | 17W-2S | 21 |
| Harger Rd. E&W | | |
| | 16W-1S,15W-1S | 21 |
| Heather Ln. NE&SW | | |
| | 17W-2S | 21 |
| Heritage Oaks Cir. E&W | | |
| | 18W-3S | 20 |
| Heritage Oaks Ct. N&S | | |
| | 18W-3S | 20 |
| Heritage Oaks Ln. (Pvt.) E&W | | |
| | 18W-3S | 20 |
| Hickory Dr. E&W | 15W-1S | 21 |
| Hunt Club Dr. N&S | 15W-2S | 21 |
| Hunt Club Rd. N&S | 15W-2S | 21 |
| Hunter Dr. E&W | 15W-1S | 21 |
| Indian Trail Ct. N&S | 16W-3S | 21 |
| Indian Trail Dr. N&S | 16W-3S | 21 |
| Indian Trail Rd. NS&EW | | |
| | 16W-3S | 21 |
| Interstate 294 N&S | | |
| | 15W-2S,15W-1S | 21 |
| Interstate 88 E&W | | |
| | 18W-2S,15W-1S | 20 |
| Ivy Ln. N&S | 17W-2S | 21 |
| Jorie Blvd. N&S | | |
| | 16W-2S,16W-3S | 21 |
| Kensington Ct. N&S | 16W-2S | 21 |
| Kensington Rd. E&W | | |
| | 16W-2S | 21 |
| Cir. | 17W-2S | 21 |

| Name | Grid | Page |
|---|---|---|
| Kimberly Ln. E&W .. 17W-2S | | 21 |
| Kingsbury Ct. N&S .. 17W-2S | | 21 |
| Kingston Dr. E&W .. 17W-2S | | 21 |
| Lakewood Dr. E&W .. 15W-1S | | 21 |
| Lambeth Ct. E&W .. 17W-2S | | 21 |
| Lincoln St. N&S.....15W-2S | | 21 |
| Livery Circle N&S...18W-3S | | 20 |
| Livery Ct. E&W ... 18W-3S | | 20 |
| Lockinvar Ln. N&S .. 18W-2S | | 20 |
| Luthin Rd. E&W ... 15W-3S | | 21 |
| Madison St. N&S ... 16W-3S | | 21 |
| Mallard Ln. E&W .. 16W-3S | | 21 |
| Marian Sq. E&W ... 17W-3S | | 21 |
| McDonalds Dr. N&S..16W-1S | | 21 |
| Meadowood Dr. N&S .........15W-1S | | 21 |
| Merry Ln. E&W .... 16W-1S | | 21 |
| Meyers Rd. N&S .......18W-3S,18W-2S | | 20 |
| Cir. ...... 18W-3S | | 20 |
| Midwest Rd. N&S ....17W-3S,17W-2S | | 21 |
| Mockingbird Ln. E&W .........17W-2S | | 21 |
| Monterey Av. N&S .. 17W-1S | | 21 |
| Mulberry Ct. N&S...18W-3S | | 20 |
| Oak Brook Dr. N&S.. 18W-2S | | 20 |
| Oak Brook Hills Rd. N&S ............18W-2S | | 20 |
| Oak Brook Rd. E&W .....18W-2S,16W-2S | | 20 |
| Old Harger Rd. NE&SW .........15W-1S | | 21 |
| Olympia Ct. N&S ... 18W-2S | | 20 |
| Ottawa Ln. E&W ... 16W-3S | | 21 |
| Palisades Dr. N&S .. 15W-1S | | 21 |
| Pembroke Ln. E&W.. 17W-2S | | 21 |
| Phoebos Ln. E&W .. 16W-1S | | 21 |
| Pine Hill Ln. E&W .. 16W-4S | | 27 |
| Polo Ln. N&S.....18W-3S | | 20 |
| Red Stable Way E&W .........18W-3S | | 20 |
| Redfox Ln. E&W ... 16W-1S | | 21 |
| Regent Ct. NE&SW .. 17W-2S | | 21 |
| Regent Dr. N&S ... 17W-3S | | 21 |
| Ridgewood Ct. E&W .........18W-3S | | 20 |
| Robert Kingery Expwy. N&S .........16W-3S,16W-1S | | 21 |
| Robinhood Ranch Rd. NS&EW ..... 15W-3S | | 21 |
| Roslyn Rd. N&S ... 18W-3S | | 20 |
| Royal Glen Ct. N&S..15W-1S | | 21 |
| Royal Vale Dr. NE&SW .........18W-2S | | 20 |
| Saddlebrooke Dr. NS&EW .........18W-3S | | 20 |
| Salt Creek Cir. E&W .........15W-3S | | 21 |
| Sauk Path N&S.....16W-3S | | 21 |
| Sheffield Ln. NS&EW .........15W-2S | | 21 |
| Shelburne Dr. N&S .. 17W-2S | | 21 |
| Spring Rd. N&S .........16W-1S,15W-2S | | 21 |
| Cir. .......17W-3S | | 21 |
| St. Johns Ct. NW&SE .........17W-3S | | 21 |
| St. Joseph's Ct. NS&EW .........17W-3S | | 21 |
| St. Joseph's Dr. E&W .........17W-3S | | 21 |
| St. Marks Ct. N&S .. 17W-3S | | 21 |
| St. Michael Ct. N&S.. 17W-3S | | 21 |
| St. Stephen's Green E&W .........17W-3S | | 21 |
| Stafford Ln. N&S ... 15W-2S | | 21 |
| Steeplechase West E&W .........16W-1S | | 21 |
| Steepleridge Ct. N&S .........18W-3S | | 20 |
| Suffolk Ln. N&S ... 18W-3S | | 20 |
| Surrey Dr. N&S ... 18W-2S | | 20 |
| Swaps Ct. NW&SE .. 18W-2S | | 20 |
| Swift Dr. N&S ..... 15W-1S | | 21 |
| Thurlow St. N&S ... 16W-3S | | 21 |
| Timber Edge Dr. E&W .........16W-1S | | 21 |
| Timber Trails Ct. NW&SE .........16W-1S | | 21 |
| Timber Trails Dr. E&W .........16W-1S | | 21 |
| Timberview Dr. E&W .........16W-1S | | 21 |
| Tower Dr. N&S ..... 18W-2S | | 20 |
| Tri-State Tollway N&S .........15W-2S,15W-1S | | 21 |
| Trinity Ct. E&W .... 17W-3S | | 21 |
| Trinity Ln. N&S .... 17W-3S | | 21 |
| Twin Oaks Dr. N&S..16W-1S | | 21 |
| Victoria Ct. N&S ... 17W-2S | | 21 |
| Walnut Ln. E&W ... 16W-1S | | 21 |
| Wennes Ct. N&S ... 15W-3S | | 21 |
| White Oak Ln. E&W..18W-3S | | 20 |
| Wildwood Ct. N&S .. 15W-1S | | 21 |
| Willow View Ln. E&W .........16W-1S | | 21 |
| Windsor Dr. N&S .........15W-2S,15W-1S | | 21 |
| Wood Av. E&W.....15W-3S | | 21 |
| Woodglen Ln. NE&SW .........15W-1S | | 21 |
| Woodland Dr. N&S .. 16W-1S | | 21 |
| Woodridge Dr. E&W .. 15W-1S | | 21 |

| Name | Grid | Page |
|---|---|---|
| Woodside Dr. E&W .. 15W-1S | | 21 |
| Woodview Ct. N&S .. 15W-1S | | 21 |
| Wyndham Ct. E&W .. 18W-2S | | 20 |
| York Rd. N&S .......15W-3S,15W-1S | | 21 |
| Cir. ......15W-1S | | 21 |
| 22nd St. E&W .......18W-1S,15W-1S | | 20 |
| 31st St. E&W .....15W-2S | | 21 |
| 33rd St. E&W ... 17W-3S | | 21 |
| 35th St. E&W .......18W-3S,16W-3S | | 20 |
| 38th St. E&W......18W-3S | | 20 |

### Oakbrook Terrace

| Name | Grid | Page |
|---|---|---|
| Ardmore Av. N&S...18W-1S | | 20 |
| Astor Av. N&S .... 18W-1S | | 20 |
| Butterfield Rd. NE&SW .......18W-1S,17W-1S | | 21 |
| Castle Dr. N&S ... 16W-1S | | 21 |
| Courtyard Dr. E&W .. 18W-1S | | 20 |
| Eisenhower Rd. N&S .........17W-1S | | 21 |
| Elder Ln. NE&SW ... 17W-1S | | 21 |
| Elm Ct. NE&SW .... 17W-1S | | 21 |
| Elm Pl. E&W ...... 17W-1S | | 21 |
| Essex Dr. E&W ... 18W-1S | | 20 |
| Fairfax Ln. N&S ... 18W-1S | | 20 |
| Halsey Rd. E&W ... 17W-1S | | 21 |
| Hodges Rd. E&W ... 17W-1S | | 21 |
| Karban Rd. E&W ... 17W-1S | | 21 |
| Leahy Rd. N&S.....17W-1S | | 21 |
| Lincoln Av. E&W ... 18W-1S | | 20 |
| MacArthur Dr. N&S .. 17W-1S | | 21 |
| Marshall Rd. NW&SE .........17W-1S | | 21 |
| Monterey Av. NE&SW .........17W-1S | | 21 |
| Nimitz Rd. NW&SE .. 17W-1S | | 21 |
| Oakland Av. N&S ... 17W-1S | | 21 |
| Orchard Pl. E&W ... 17W-1S | | 21 |
| Oxford Ct. E&W ... 18W-1S | | 20 |
| Patton Av. N&S.....17W-1S | | 21 |
| Renaissance Blvd. N&S .........18W-1S | | 20 |
| Robert Kingery Expwy. N&S .........17W-1S | | 21 |
| Roosevelt Rd. E&W .. 17W-0S | | 21 |
| Spring Rd. N&S.....16W-1S | | 21 |
| Stillwell Rd. E&W ... 17W-1S | | 21 |
| Terrace Blvd. E&W .. 18W-1S | | 20 |
| Wainwright Rd. NW&SE .........17W-1S | | 21 |
| Washington Av. N&S .........18W-1S | | 20 |
| West End Rd. E&W .. 17W-1S | | 21 |
| 16th St. E&W......17W-1S | | 21 |

### Roselle*
(Also see Cook County)

| Name | Grid | Page |
|---|---|---|
| Acacia Ln. N&S.....22W-6N | | 7 |
| Alder Ln. N&S ... 24W-7N | | 6 |
| Ambleside Dr. NE&SW .........23W-7N | | 6 |
| Americana Ct. N&S .. 24W-7N | | 6 |
| Andover Dr. N&S .. 25W-7N | | 6 |
| Ardmore Av. E&W .. 23W-7N | | 6 |
| Ash St. E&W ..... 22W-7N | | 7 |
| Ashbury Ct. N&S...25W-7N | | 6 |
| Ashbury Ln., E. N&S .........25W-7N | | 6 |
| Ashbury Ln., W. N&S .........25W-7N | | 6 |
| Ashley Ct. NW&SE .. 24W-7N | | 6 |
| Autumn Dr. N&S ... 24W-6N | | 6 |
| Avalon Ct. N&S ... 24W-6N | | 6 |
| Avebury Ct. N&S ... 24W-6N | | 6 |
| Avebury Ln. NW&SE .........24W-6N | | 6 |
| Banbury Ct. N&S ... 23W-6N | | 6 |
| Banbury Ter. N&S .. 23W-6N | | 6 |
| Berkshire Ter. N&S .. 23W-6N | | 6 |
| Berwick Pl. E&W .......25W-6N,24W-6N | | 6 |
| Birch Ct. NW&SE ... 22W-6N | | 7 |
| Birmingham Ct. N&S .........25W-7N | | 6 |
| Bokelman St. NE&SW .........23W-7N | | 6 |
| Borden Ct. N&S ... 24W-7N | | 6 |
| Borden Dr. N&S ... 24W-7N | | 6 |
| Brandywine Dr. E&W .........24W-6N | | 6 |
| Briarwood Ln. N&S..24W-6N | | 6 |
| Brighton Bay N&S .. 25W-7N | | 6 |
| Bristol Ct. E&W ... 25W-7N | | 6 |
| Brittany Way E&W .. 25W-7N | | 6 |
| Brookside Dr. N&S .. 24W-7N | | 6 |
| Brookwood Ter. N&S .........23W-6N | | 6 |
| Brower Dr. N&S ... 23W-7N | | 6 |
| Bryn Mawr Av. E&W .......25W-6N,22W-6N | | 6 |
| Butternut Ct. N&S .. 23W-6N | | 6 |
| Callero Ct. NW&SE .. 23W-6N | | 6 |
| Cambrian Ct. N&S .. 25W-7N | | 6 |
| Carriage Way E&W .. 25W-6N | | 6 |
| Case Dr. N&S ..... 24W-7N | | 6 |
| Catalpa Av. NW&SE .......23W-7N,22W-7N | | 6 |
| Catino Ct. N&S .... 23W-6N | | 6 |

| Name | Grid | Page |
|---|---|---|
| Central Av. E&W .......24W-7N,23W-7N | | 6 |
| Century Dr. N&S ... 22W-7N | | 7 |
| Chancellor Dr. N&S .. 24W-7N | | 6 |
| Chatfield Ct. E&W .. 25W-7N | | 6 |
| Chatham Ct. N&S .. 25W-7N | | 6 |
| Chatham Ln. N&S .. 25W-7N | | 6 |
| Chelsea Cove* E&W .........25W-7N | | 6 |
| Cherry Ct. E&W ... 22W-7N | | 7 |
| Cherry St. E&W ... 22W-7N | | 7 |
| Churchill Ct. E&W...25W-7N | | 6 |
| Circle Dr. E&W .... 22W-7N | | 7 |
| Claria Dr. E&W .... 23W-7N | | 6 |
| Clearwater N. E&W .. 24W-6N | | 6 |
| Clearwater S. NW&SE .........24W-6N | | 6 |
| Club House Dr. NE&SW .........22W-7N | | 7 |
| Colony Ln. E&W ... 24W-6N | | 6 |
| Congress Cir., S. E&W .........24W-7N | | 6 |
| Congress Cir., W. NS&EW .........24W-7N | | 6 |
| Country Ln., E. N&S .........24W-6N | | 6 |
| Country Ln., N. E&W .........24W-6N | | 6 |
| Country Ln., S. E&W .........24W-6N | | 6 |
| Countryside Dr. NE&SW .........23W-7N | | 6 |
| Coventry Ct. E&W .. 25W-7N | | 6 |
| Crestwood Dr. NW&SE .........23W-6N | | 6 |
| Cypress Ct. N&S ... 23W-6N | | 6 |
| Daisy Ln. N&S.....24W-6N | | 6 |
| Dalton Ln. N&S.....24W-6N | | 6 |
| Darby Ln. NE&SW .. 24W-6N | | 6 |
| Dee Ln. NE&SW ... 22W-7N | | 7 |
| Devon Av. E&W .......23W-7N,22W-7N | | 6 |
| Dinah Rd. N&S .... 23W-6N | | 7 |
| Dover Dr. N&S .... 25W-6N | | 6 |
| Downing St. E&W .. 25W-6N | | 6 |
| Drummond Ct.* E&W .........25W-7N | | 6 |
| Edenwood Dr. E&W..24W-6N | | 6 |
| Elm St. E&W .....23W-7N | | 6 |
| Exeter Ct. N&S .... 25W-7N | | 6 |
| Fall Cir. NW&SE ... 24W-6N | | 6 |
| Falmouth Way NW&SE .........25W-6N | | 6 |
| Fordham Pl. NE&SW .........24W-6N | | 6 |
| Forest Av. E&W ... 23W-6N | | 6 |
| Forum Dr. E&W ... 22W-7N | | 7 |
| Foster Av. E&W .......23W-6N,22W-6N | | 6 |
| Foxdale Ct. NE&SW .........25W-6N,24W-6N | | 6 |
| Garden Av. N&S ... 24W-6N | | 6 |
| Garden Rd. N&S ... 24W-7N | | 6 |
| Gary Av. N&S .......25W-7N,25W-6N | | 6 |
| Glendale Ter. E&W .. 23W-6N | | 6 |
| Glenlake Av. E&W .. 23W-7N | | 6 |
| Glenmore Pl. NE&SW .........24W-6N | | 6 |
| Golf View Dr. E&W .. 22W-7N | | 7 |
| Granville Av. E&W .........25W-6N | | 6 |
| Greenwood Ct. N&S .........23W-6N | | 6 |
| Hampshire Ct. E&W..25W-7N | | 6 |
| Hampton Ln. NW&SE .........25W-6N | | 6 |
| Hamstead Ct. NE&SW .........25W-7N | | 6 |
| Harvest Ln. N&S ... 24W-6N | | 6 |
| Harvest Pl. NE&SW..24W-6N | | 6 |
| Hastings Ct. N&S...25W-7N | | 6 |
| Hattendorf Av. NW&SE .........23W-7N | | 6 |
| Hazel Ct. E&W ... 22W-6N | | 6 |
| Hemlock Ln. NW&SE .........24W-6N | | 6 |
| Heritage Dr. E&W .. 23W-6N | | 6 |
| High Pointe Ct. NE&SW .........22W-7N | | 7 |
| High Ridge Rd. E&W .........22W-7N | | 7 |
| Hill St. N&S .......23W-6N,23W-7N | | 6 |
| Hillside Dr. NE&SW .. 23W-7N | | 6 |
| Howard Av. N&S ... 24W-7N | | 6 |
| Hudson Ct. N&S ... 24W-7N | | 6 |
| Hunter Ter. E&W ... 24W-7N | | 6 |
| Hygate Dr. E&W ... 22W-6N | | 6 |
| Imansfield Ct. NW&SE .........25W-7N | | 6 |
| Imansfield Way N&S .........25W-7N | | 6 |
| Irving Park Rd. NW&SE .......24W-7N,22W-7N | | 6 |
| Kensington Ct. NW&SE .........25W-6N | | 6 |
| Kingston Ct. N&S...24W-6N | | 6 |
| Kipling Ct. N&S ... 22W-7N | | 7 |
| Lake Pointe Ct. N&S .........22W-7N | | 7 |
| Lake Shore Dr. N&S .........22W-7N | | 7 |
| Lake St. NW&SE ... 24W-6N | | 6 |

| Name | Grid | Page |
|---|---|---|
| Lakeside Dr. NE&SW .........23W-7N | | 6 |
| Lakeview Dr. E&W .. 22W-7N | | 7 |
| Lawrence Av. E&W .. 22W-7N | | 7 |
| Leawood Dr. N&S .. 24W-7N | | 6 |
| Lexington Av. N&S .. 22W-6N | | 7 |
| Lincoln St. N&S.....23W-7N | | 6 |
| Locust Ln. N&S ... 22W-7N | | 7 |
| Longford Ct. N&S...24W-7N | | 6 |
| Longford Dr. E&W .. 24W-7N | | 6 |
| Main St. NW&SE ... 23W-7N | | 6 |
| Maple Av. N&S.....23W-7N | | 6 |
| Marion St. N&S.....23W-7N | | 6 |
| Meade Ln. N&S ... 24W-6N | | 6 |
| Mensching Rd. NW&SE .......24W-7N,23W-6N | | 6 |
| Merimac Ct. N&S...24W-7N | | 6 |
| Merriford Ct. N&S .. 25W-7N | | 6 |
| Metra Access N&S .. 25W-7N | | 6 |
| Middleton Dr. N&S .. 24W-6N | | 6 |
| Monaco Dr. N&S ... 23W-7N | | 6 |
| Morningside Ct. E&W .........22W-7N | | 7 |
| Morningside Dr. N&S .........22W-7N | | 7 |
| Mulford Ct. N&S ... 24W-7N | | 6 |
| Nassau Dr. N&S ... 24W-6N | | 6 |
| Newcastle Ct. E&W .. 24W-7N | | 6 |
| Newcastle Dr. E&W .. 24W-6N | | 6 |
| Newport N. E&W ... 24W-6N | | 6 |
| Newport S. E&W ... 24W-6N | | 6 |
| Newport W. N&S ... 24W-6N | | 6 |
| Norfolk Ct. N&S ... 25W-7N | | 6 |
| Norman Ln. NE&SW .........24W-6N | | 6 |
| Northhampton Ln. N&S .........25W-6N | | 6 |
| Oak St. N&S ..... 23W-6N | | 6 |
| Old Farm Dr. E&W .. 24W-6N | | 6 |
| Olympia Ln. E&W .. 24W-7N | | 6 |
| Orchard Ct. E&W ... 22W-7N | | 7 |
| Orchard Ter. E&W .......23W-6N,22W-6N | | 6 |
| Oxford Cir. E&W ... 25W-6N | | 6 |
| Oxford Pl. NE&SW .. 24W-6N | | 6 |
| Park Ln. N&S .....23W-6N | | 6 |
| Park St. N&S .....23W-6N | | 6 |
| Parkview Ct. E&W .. 22W-7N | | 7 |
| Pembrook Ct. E&W .. 25W-7N | | 6 |
| Picton Rd. E&W ... 23W-6N | | 6 |
| Pierce Av. N&S .... 22W-7N | | 7 |
| Pine Av. E&W .......24W-7N,23W-7N | | 6 |
| Pinecroft Dr. N&S .........22W-6N,22W-7N | | 7 |
| Pioneer Ct. NW&SE..24W-7N | | 6 |
| Plum Grove Rd. N&S .......24W-7N,23W-6N | | 6 |
| Plumtree Ln. NW&SE .........22W-7N | | 7 |
| Portwine Rd. N&S .. 22W-7N | | 7 |
| Prescott Dr. N&S...24W-7N | | 6 |
| Presidential Dr. N&S .........24W-7N | | 6 |
| Prospect St. N&S...23W-7N | | 6 |
| Quincy Ct. N&S....24W-7N | | 6 |
| Quincy Dr. N&S ... 24W-7N | | 6 |
| Radnor Dr. N&S ... 24W-6N | | 6 |
| Red Maple Ln. N&S..24W-6N | | 6 |
| Regal Ct. NW&SE .. 25W-7N | | 6 |
| Regency Ct. N&S .. 25W-6N | | 6 |
| Reston St. NE&SW .. 24W-7N | | 6 |
| Richmond Ct. N&S .. 24W-7N | | 6 |
| Richmond Dr. E&W .. 24W-7N | | 6 |
| Ridge Ct. N&S ....22W-6N | | 7 |
| Ridge Rd. N&S .......22W-6N,22W-7N | | 7 |
| Ridgefield Dr. N&S .. 24W-7N | | 6 |
| Robin Ct. N&S ....23W-6N | | 6 |
| Rodenburg Rd. N&S .......25W-7N,24W-7N | | 6 |
| Rose Dr., E. N&S...22W-7N | | 7 |
| Rose Dr., W. N&S .. 22W-7N | | 7 |
| Rosedale Av. N&S .. 23W-6N | | 6 |
| Roselle Rd. N&S .......23W-6N,23W-7N | | 6 |
| Rosemont Av. E&W .. 23W-7N | | 6 |
| Rosewood Ct. NE&SW .........24W-6N | | 6 |
| Rosewood Dr. N&S .. 24W-7N | | 6 |
| Rosner Dr. E&W ... 24W-7N | | 6 |
| Royce Ln. NE&SW .. 24W-7N | | 6 |
| Rt. 19 NW&SE .......23W-7N,22W-7N | | 6 |
| Rush St. N&S ....23W-6N | | 6 |
| Sally Ct. N&S.....23W-6N | | 6 |
| Salt Creek Rd. N&S..22W-7N | | 7 |
| Scott Ct. NE&SW .. 23W-6N | | 6 |
| Shagbark Ln. NE&SW .........24W-6N | | 6 |
| Sheffield Ct. N&S .. 25W-7N | | 6 |
| Siems Cir. E&W ... 23W-6N | | 6 |
| Singleton Ct. E&W .. 24W-7N | | 6 |
| Spring Av. N&S ... 23W-7N | | 6 |
| Spring Ct. NE&SW .. 23W-7N | | 6 |
| Spring Hill Dr. N&S .........22W-6N,22W-7N | | 7 |
| Spring St. N&S .........23W-6N | | 6 |
| Springfield Dr. N&S..24W-6N | | 6 |
| Springfield St. N&S .. 24W-6N | | 6 |
| Stafford Dr. NE&SW .........25W-6N,24W-6N | | 6 |

| Name | Grid | Page |
|---|---|---|
| Stevenson Ct. E&W..22W-7N | | 7 |
| Stockport Ct. N&S .. 25W-7N | | 6 |
| Stonefield Pl. N&S .. 24W-6N | | 6 |
| Stonehurst Dr. E&W .........24W-7N | | 6 |
| Stonehurst Ln. E&W .........24W-7N | | 6 |
| Summerdale Ln. N&S .........24W-6N | | 6 |
| Summerfield Ct. NW&SE .........24W-6N | | 6 |
| Summerfield Dr. NE&SW .........24W-6N | | 6 |
| Sunnyside Rd. E&W..22W-6N | | 7 |
| Sunrise Ln. E&W ... 24W-6N | | 6 |
| Sunrise Pl. N&S ... 24W-6N | | 6 |
| Sussex Ct. N&S ... 25W-7N | | 6 |
| Terry Ct. E&W ... 22W-7N | | 7 |
| Terry Dr. N&S .... 22W-7N | | 7 |
| Thames Ter.* E&W .. 25W-7N | | 6 |
| Thorndale Av. E&W .. 23W-7N | | 6 |
| Thornfield Ct. N&S .. 25W-7N | | 6 |
| Thornfield Ln. E&W .. 25W-7N | | 6 |
| Tiffany St. E&W ... 23W-6N | | 7 |
| Town Acres Ln. E&W .........23W-7N | | 7 |
| Travis Pkwy. NS&EW .........25W-7N | | 6 |
| Tupenny Ct. N&S...25W-7N | | 6 |
| Turner Av. E&W .......23W-6N,22W-6N | | 6 |
| Ventura Club Dr. NE&SW .........22W-7N | | 7 |
| Wadsworth Cir. E&W .........25W-6N | | 6 |
| Walnut Ct. E&W ... 23W-6N | | 6 |
| Walnut St. E&W ... 23W-6N | | 6 |
| Walter Dr. N&S ... 23W-7N | | 6 |
| Waterbury Ln. NW&SE .........25W-7N,24W-6N | | 6 |
| Waterford Ct. E&W .. 24W-7N | | 6 |
| West End Rd. N&S .........24W-7N,23W-6N | | 6 |
| Westminster Cir. N&S .........25W-6N | | 6 |
| White Oak Dr. N&S .. 25W-6N | | 7 |
| Wildwood Dr. N&S .. 24W-7N | | 6 |
| Willow St. N&S ... 23W-7N | | 6 |
| Windsor Dr. N&S .. 24W-7N | | 6 |
| Winfield Ct. N&S .. 25W-7N | | 6 |
| Winfield Way E&W .. 25W-7N | | 6 |
| Winterwood Ct. N&S .........24W-6N | | 6 |
| Winterwood Dr. E&W .........24W-6N | | 6 |
| Woodside Dr. N&S .. 24W-6N | | 6 |
| Woodworth Pl. E&W .........23W-7N | | 6 |
| York Ln. NE&SW ... 22W-6N | | 7 |

### Schaumburg*
(Also see Cook County)

| Name | Grid | Page |
|---|---|---|
| Mitchell Blvd. NE&SW .........24W-7N | | 6 |

### St. Charles*
(Also see Kane County)

| Name | Grid | Page |
|---|---|---|
| North Av. E&W......32W-3N | | 10 |
| Oak Rd. N&S.......32W-3N | | 10 |

### Villa Park

| Name | Grid | Page |
|---|---|---|
| Adams St. E&W .........18W-0S,18W-0N | | 20 |
| Addison Rd. N&S ... 18W-1N | | 14 |
| Adele Av. E&W ... 18W-2N | | 14 |
| Adele Ct. E&W ... 17W-2N | | 14 |
| Ardmore Av. N&S .........18W-0S,18W-1N | | 20 |
| Armitage Av. E&W .. 18W-2N | | 14 |
| Astor Ct. E&W ... 17W-0N | | 14 |
| Beach St. E&W ... 17W-1N | | 14 |
| Belden Way E&W ... 18W-2N | | 14 |
| Beverly Av. N&S .........17W-1N,17W-2N | | 14 |
| Bierman Av. E&W .. 18W-1N | | 14 |
| Blackstone Pl. E&W..17W-0S | | 21 |
| Calduto Ct. N&S ... 17W-0S | | 21 |
| Central Blvd. NE&SW .......18W-0N,17W-0N | | 14 |
| Charles Av. N&S ... 17W-1N | | 14 |
| Chatham Av. N&S .........17W-1N,17W-2N | | 14 |
| Congress St. N&S .. 17W-0S | | 21 |
| Cornell Av. N&S .........17W-0S,17W-1N | | 21 |
| Crescent Dr. NE&SW .........17W-0N | | 14 |
| Cross St. NW&SE .. 17W-0S | | 21 |
| Division St. E&W .........18W-1N,17W-1N | | 14 |
| Douglas Av. N&S .........17W-1N,17W-2N | | 14 |
| Ellsworth Av. N&S .........17W-1N,17W-2N | | 14 |
| Elm St. E&W .........18W-1N,17W-1N | | 14 |
| Euclid Av. E&W .........17W-0S,17W-1N | | 21 |
| Evergreen Pl. E&W .. 18W-0S | | 20 |
| Fairfield Av. E&W ... 17W-0N | | 14 |
| Frank St. E&W ... 17W-0S | | 21 |

| Street | Grid | Page |
|---|---|---|
| Fulton Av. N&S | 17W-1N,17W-2N | 14 |
| Gerard Av. N&S | 17W-1N | 14 |
| Grant Av. N&S | 17W-0S,17W-0N | 21 |
| Hamilton Av. N&S | 17W-1N | 14 |
| Harrison St. E&W | 17W-0S | 21 |
| Harvard Av. N&S | 18W-0S,18W-2N | 20 |
| Highland Av. E&W | 17W-0N | 14 |
| Holly Ct. E&W | 18W-1N | 14 |
| Home Av. E&W | 18W-0N,17W-0N | 14 |
| Hugo Ct. NW&SE | 18W-1N | 14 |
| Illinois Av. N&S | 17W-0N,17W-1N | 14 |
| Iowa Av. N&S | 18W-1N | 14 |
| Jackson St. E&W | 18W-0S,17W-0S | 20 |
| James St. E&W | 18W-1N | 14 |
| Julia Dr. NE&SW | 17W-0S | 21 |
| Kenilworth Av. E&W | 18W-0N,17W-0N | 14 |
| Kolberg Ct. E&W | 17W-0S | 21 |
| Lane Dr. E&W | 17W-0S | 21 |
| Leslie Ln. N&S | 18W-0S | 20 |
| Lincoln Av. N&S | 18W-1N | 14 |
| Madison St. E&W | 18W-0N,17W-0N | 14 |
| Main St. E&W | 17W-0N | 14 |
| Maple St. E&W | 17W-1N | 14 |
| Merle St. E&W | 18W-1N | 14 |
| Michigan Av. N&S | 18W-0S,18W-1N | 20 |
| Michigan St. E&W | 18W-1S | 20 |
| Mission Av. N&S | 18W-1N | 14 |
| Monroe St. E&W | 18W-0S,17W-0S | 20 |
| Monterey Av. N&S | 17W-0S,17W-0N | 21 |
| Morningside Dr. E&W | 18W-0S | 20 |
| Myrtle Av. N&S | 17W-0S,17W-0N | 21 |
| North Av. E&W | 18W-2N,17W-2N | 14 |
| Oak Ct. E&W | 17W-1N | 14 |
| Oak St. E&W | 17W-1N | 14 |
| Oakland Av. N&S | 17W-0S,17W-0N | 21 |
| Orchard Hill Ct. N&S | 17W-0S | 21 |
| Ovaltine Ct. E&W | 17W-0N | 14 |
| Park Blvd. E&W | 18W-0N,17W-0N | 14 |
| Peony Pl. E&W | 17W-0N | 14 |
| Pine St. E&W | 17W-1N | 14 |
| Pleasant Av. E&W | 18W-1N | 14 |
| Plymouth St. E&W | 18W-1N,17W-1N | 14 |
| Princeton Av. N&S | 18W-0N,18W-2N | 14 |
| Rand Rd. NS&EW | 18W-0S | 20 |
| Ridge Rd. E&W | 18W-1N | 14 |
| Riordan Rd. NW&SE | 17W-0S | 21 |
| Riverside Ct. E&W | 17W-0N | 14 |
| Riverside Dr. N&S | 17W-0N | 14 |
| Robert Kingery Expwy. N&S | 17W-0S,17W-0N | 21 |
| Roosevelt Rd. E&W | 18W-0S,17W-0S | 20 |
| Roy Dr. E&W | 18W-1N | 14 |
| Rt. 38 E&W | 18W-0S,17W-0S | 20 |
| Rt. 64 E&W | 18W-2N,17W-2N | 14 |
| Rt. 83 N&S | 17W-0S,17W-0N | 21 |
| Salt Creek Dr. NW&SE | 16W-0S | 21 |
| School St. E&W | 18W-0N | 14 |
| Sidney Av. E&W | 18W-2N | 14 |
| Sidney Ct. E&W | 17W-2N | 14 |
| St. Charles Rd. E&W | 18W-1N,17W-1N | 14 |
| Stone Rd. NW&SE | 18W-1N | 14 |
| Summit Av. N&S | 17W-0S,17W-1N | 21 |
| Sunset Ct. E&W | 18W-1N | 14 |
| Sunset Dr. E&W | 18W-1N,17W-1N | 14 |
| Terrace St. E&W | 18W-1N | 14 |
| Terry Ln. NE&SW | 17W-0S | 21 |
| Van Buren St. E&W | 17W-0S | 21 |
| Vermont St. E&W | 18W-1N,17W-1N | 14 |
| Villa Av. N&S | 17W-0S,17W-2N | 21 |
| Washington St. E&W | 18W-0N,17W-0N | 14 |
| Wayside Dr. N&S | 17W-0S | 21 |
| Westmore Av. N&S | 18W-1N | 14 |
| Westwood Av. N&S | 19W-1N | 14 |
| Wildwood St. E&W | 17W-0N | 14 |
| Willowcrest Dr. NE&SW | 18W-0S | 20 |
| Wisconsin Av. N&S | 18W-1N,18W-0S | 14 |
| Woodrow St. E&W | 18W-0N | 14 |
| Yale Av. N&S | 18W-0N,18W-2N | 14 |
| 2nd Av. N&S | 18W-1N | 14 |
| 3rd Av. N&S | 18W-1N | 14 |

## Warrenville

| Street | Grid | Page |
|---|---|---|
| Albert Einstein Dr. E&W | 29W-2S | 16 |
| Albright St. NW&SE | 29W-3S,28W-3S | 16 |
| Amber Ln. E&W | 29W-3S | 16 |
| Angeline Ct. N&S | 30W-2S | 16 |
| Arbury Ct. E&W | 30W-2S | 16 |
| Arlington Ct. NW&SE | 30W-2S | 16 |
| Arthur Compton Ct. N&S | 29W-2S | 16 |
| Ascot N&S | 29W-1S,29W-2S | 16 |
| Attleboro Ct. NW&SE | 30W-2S | 16 |
| Aurora Way NE&SW | 29W-3S | 16 |
| Avon Ct. E&W | 30W-1S | 16 |
| Avondale Ct. E&W | 30W-2S | 16 |
| Barclay Av. N&S | 30W-3S,30W-4S | 16 |
| Barkley Av. N&S | 30W-3S | 16 |
| Batavia Rd. NW&SE | 30W-2S,28W-3S | 16 |
| Bayview Ct. N&S | 29W-3S | 16 |
| Bedford Ln. N&S | 30W-2S | 16 |
| Birchwood Ln. N&S | 29W-3S | 16 |
| Blackthorn Ln. N&S | 29W-3S | 16 |
| Branch Av. E&W | 30W-2S | 16 |
| Briarwood Dr. N&S | 29W-3S | 16 |
| Briggs Av. N&S | 30W-3S | 16 |
| Brighton Ct. E&W | 30W-2S | 16 |
| Bristol Ln. N&S | 30W-1S,30W-2S | 16 |
| Brookside Ct. NW&SE | 30W-3S | 16 |
| Buckthorn Ct. E&W | 30W-2S | 16 |
| Burk Av. NE&SW | 29W-3S,28W-3S | 16 |
| Butterfield Rd. E&W | 30W-3S,28W-3S | 16 |
| Calumet Av. E&W | 30W-3S,28W-3S | 16 |
| Candlewood Ln. E&W | 29W-3S | 16 |
| Cedar Ct. N&S | 30W-1S | 16 |
| Central Av. E&W | 27W-3S | 17 |
| Cerny Rd. N&S | 29W-2S | 16 |
| Cherice Dr. N&S | 30W-2S | 16 |
| Circle Dr., E. N&S | 28W-3S | 17 |
| Circle Dr., S. E&W | 28W-3S | 17 |
| Circle Dr., W. N&S | 28W-3S | 17 |
| Concord Ct. E&W | 30W-2S | 16 |
| Continental Dr. N&S | 30W-2S | 16 |
| Cottonwood * NE&SW | 30W-2S | 16 |
| Country Ridge Dr.* NW&SE | 29W-2S | 16 |
| Crabtree Ln. NE&SW | 29W-3S | 16 |
| Curtis Av. N&S | 28W-4S,28W-3S | 23 |
| Cynthia Ct. N&S | 30W-2S | 16 |
| Cynthia Dr. N&S | 30W-2S | 16 |
| Danbury Dr.* E&W | 30W-2S | 16 |
| Dedham Ct. E&W | 30W-2S | 16 |
| Deerfield N&S | 30W-1S,30W-2S | 16 |
| Diehl Rd. E&W | 28W-4S,27W-4S | 23 |
| Dogwood Ct.* NE&SW | 30W-2S | 16 |
| Dorchester Ct. E&W | 30W-2S | 16 |
| East-West Tollway E&W | 29W-4S,28W-4S | 23 |
| Elizabeth Av. N&S | 27W-3S | 17 |
| Elmwood Ct. E&W | 30W-2S | 16 |
| Emerald Green Dr. N&S | 29W-2S | 16 |
| Essex N&S | 30W-1S | 16 |
| Estes St. E&W | 30W-3S | 16 |
| Everett Ct. N&S | 29W-2S | 16 |
| Fairfax Ct. E&W | 30W-1S | 16 |
| Ferry Rd. E&W | 29W-4S,28W-4S | 23 |
| Forestview Av. E&W | 28W-4S | 23 |
| Forestview Dr., N. E&W | 29W-2S | 16 |
| Foxboro Ct. E&W | 30W-2S | 16 |
| Frontage Rd. E&W | 30W-3S,29W-3S | 16 |
| Galbreath E&W | 30W-2S,29W-2S | 16 |
| Galusha Av. E&W | 27W-3S | 17 |
| Gates Pl. NE&SW | 28W-3S | 17 |
| Glen Dr. NE&SW | 29W-3S | 16 |
| Glenhurst Ct. E&W | 30W-2S | 16 |
| Greenbriar Ln. E&W | 29W-3S | 16 |
| Greenbrook Ct. NW&SE | 30W-2S | 16 |
| Greenview Av. E&W | 27W-3S | 17 |
| Grove Ln. NS&EW | 29W-2S,29W-3S | 16 |
| Hampton * N&S | 30W-2S | 16 |
| Harvard Dr. N&S | 30W-2S | 16 |
| Hawthorne Ln. N&S | 29W-3S | 16 |
| Haylett Av. N&S | 28W-3S | 17 |
| Heather Ct. NE&SW | 30W-2S | 16 |
| Herrick Rd. N&S | 27W-3S | 17 |
| Home Av. N&S | 29W-3S | 16 |
| Huntington Dr. E&W | 30W-1S | 16 |
| Hurlingham Ct. N&S | 29W-2S | 16 |
| Hurlingham Dr. E&W | 30W-2S,29W-2S | 16 |
| Interstate 88 E&W | 28W-4S,27W-4S | 23 |
| Iroquois Ct., N. E&W | 29W-2S | 16 |
| Jackson St. E&W | 28W-3S | 17 |
| Jefferson St. E&W | 28W-3S | 17 |
| John Bardeen Dr. N&S | 29W-2S | 17 |
| Juniper Ct. N&S | 30W-1S | 16 |
| Kensington Dr. E&W | 30W-2S | 16 |
| Lakeview Ct. N&S | 29W-3S | 16 |
| Lakeview Dr. E&W | 30W-3S,29W-3S | 16 |
| Landon Av. N&S | 29W-3S | 16 |
| Laurel Ct. NW&SE | 30W-1S | 16 |
| Leominster Ct. E&W | 30W-2S | 16 |
| Lexington Ct. N&S | 30W-2S | 16 |
| Linden Sq.* NS&EW | 30W-2S | 16 |
| Lindenwood Dr.* NW&SE | 30W-2S | 16 |
| Lorraine Av. N&S | 27W-4S,27W-3S | 23 |
| Lynn Ct. N&S | 30W-2S | 16 |
| Mack Rd. E&W | 30W-1S,29W-1S | 16 |
| Main St. E&W | 28W-3S | 17 |
| Manchester N&S | 30W-1S | 16 |
| Manning Av. NE&SW | 28W-3S | 17 |
| Maple Ct. NW&SE | 30W-2S | 16 |
| Maplewood * NW&SE | 30W-2S | 16 |
| Maplewood Ct.* NE&SW | 30W-2S | 16 |
| Marie Curie Ln. E&W | 29W-2S | 16 |
| Mayfair Ct. NE&SW | 30W-1S | 16 |
| Meadow Av. E&W | 29W-3S | 16 |
| Melcher Av. N&S | 27W-3S | 17 |
| Melvin Albright St. E&W | 28W-3S | 17 |
| Middleton Av. E&W | 27W-4S | 23 |
| Mignin Dr. N&S | 29W-3S | 16 |
| Mill St. N&S | 27W-4S | 23 |
| Mount St. NW&SE | 28W-3S | 17 |
| Mulberry Ct.* E&W | 30W-2S | 16 |
| Oakwood Ct.* E&W | 30W-2S | 16 |
| Oxford E&W | 30W-1S | 16 |
| Parkview Av. E&W | 27W-3S | 17 |
| Patterman Rd. NE&SW | 29W-3S | 16 |
| Penny Ln. E&W | 30W-1S | 16 |
| Pierre Curie Ln. NE&SW | 29W-2S | 16 |
| Plum Ct. NE&SW | 30W-1S | 16 |
| Point Oak Dr. N&S | 29W-3S | 16 |
| Prairie Av. E&W | 29W-3S | 16 |
| Princeton Ct. N&S | 30W-1S | 16 |
| Ray St. NW&SE | 28W-3S | 17 |
| Raymond Dr. N&S | 29W-4S | 23 |
| Redwood Ct. N&S | 30W-1S | 16 |
| Ridge Dr. E&W | 29W-2S | 16 |
| Ridgewood Ct. E&W | 30W-2S | 16 |
| Rigi Rd. (Pvt.) NE&SW | 30W-3S | 16 |
| River Alley NE&SW | 28W-3S | 17 |
| River Oaks Dr. NS&EW | 29W-2S | 16 |
| River Rd. NE&SW | 28W-3S,28W-4S | 17 |
| Riverside Av. N&S | 29W-2S | 16 |
| Riverside Pkwy. NS&EW | 29W-2S | 16 |
| Riverview Dr. NW&SE | 28W-3S | 17 |
| Rockwell St. NE&SW | 29W-3S,28W-3S | 16 |
| Rogers Av. E&W | 28W-3S | 17 |
| Route 56 E&W | 30W-3S,28W-3S | 16 |
| Route 59 N&S | 29W-1S,29W-3S | 16 |
| Roxbury Ct. N&S | 30W-2S,29W-2S | 16 |
| Salem Ct. NE&SW | 30W-2S | 16 |
| Sanchez Dr. N&S | 30W-2S | 16 |
| Shaw Dr. N&S | 30W-2S | 16 |
| Sheffield N&S | 30W-1S | 16 |
| Small Trees Ct. NW&SE | 30W-2S | 16 |
| Sova Ln. N&S | 29W-2S | 16 |
| Spruce Ct. NW&SE | 30W-1S | 16 |
| Stafford Pl. NE&SW | 28W-3S | 17 |
| Steadman Av. N&S | 28W-3S | 17 |
| Stevens Ct. E&W | 29W-2S | 16 |
| Sunset Ct. E&W | 30W-3S | 16 |
| Sunset Dr. N&S | 30W-3S | 16 |
| Talbot Av. N&S | 30W-3S | 16 |
| Tanglewood Ln. E&W | 29W-3S | 16 |
| Thornwood Ln. NE&SW | 29W-3S | 16 |
| Timber Dr. NE&SW | 29W-3S,28W-3S | 16 |
| Tinker Av. N&S | 27W-3S | 17 |
| Townline Rd. E&W | 29W-3S,28W-3S | 16 |
| Townline Rd. E&W | 29W-4S,28W-4S | 23 |
| Tracy Pl. NE&SW | 28W-3S | 17 |
| Virginia Av. N&S | 27W-3S | 17 |
| Wagner Ct. N&S | 28W-3S | 17 |
| Wagner Dr. E&W | 29W-3S,28W-3S | 16 |
| Wagner Rd. E&W | 28W-3S | 17 |
| Waltham Ct. N&S | 30W-2S | 16 |
| Warren Av. N&S | 28W-4S,28W-3S | 23 |
| Warren Ct. E&W | 29W-3S | 16 |
| Warrenville Rd. E&W | 28W-3S,27W-3S | 17 |
| Waverly Av. E&W | 30W-2S,29W-2S | 16 |
| Webster St. NE&SW | 29W-3S | 16 |
| West Av. N&S | 27W-3S | 17 |
| White Oak Dr. NE&SW | 29W-3S | 16 |
| Whitehall Ct. E&W | 30W-2S | 16 |
| Wilbur Av. N&S | 28W-3S,27W-3S | 17 |
| Wildwood Ct.* NE&SW | 30W-2S | 16 |
| Williams Ct. NE&SW | 29W-3S | 16 |
| Williams Rd. N&S | 29W-3S,29W-2S | 16 |
| Willow Ln. E&W | 30W-1S,29W-1S | 16 |
| Winchester Cir. E&W | 29W-2S | 16 |
| Winfield Rd. N&S | 28W-3S | 17 |
| Winwood Wk. E&W | 29W-2S | 16 |
| Wood Ct.* NW&SE | 30W-2S | 16 |
| Woodland Rd. E&W | 28W-4S | 23 |
| Woodlawn Av. E&W | 28W-3S | 17 |
| Youghal Rd. E&W | 30W-3S | 16 |
| 2nd St. N&S | 28W-3S | 17 |
| 4th St. N&S | 28W-3S | 17 |

## Wayne*

**(Also see Kane County)**

| Street | Grid | Page |
|---|---|---|
| Army Trail Rd. E&W | 32W-5N,30W-5N | 4 |
| Berkshire Ct. N&S | 30W-4N | 4 |
| Billy Burns Rd. NW&SE | 32W-5N | 4 |
| Bradford Pkwy. E&W | 30W-4N | 4 |
| Cedar Ln. E&W | 32W-5N | 4 |
| Chambellan Ln. N&S | 32W-5N | 4 |
| Courcval Ln. NW&SE | 32W-5N | 4 |
| Derby Rd. NE&SW | 32W-5N | 4 |
| Elm Rd. N&S | 31W-5N | 4 |
| Forsynthia Ln. E&W | 30W-4N | 4 |
| Glos St. E&W | 32W-5N | 4 |
| Guild Ln. N&S | 32W-5N | 4 |
| Heritage Ct. N&S | 30W-5N | 4 |
| Honey Hill Cir. NS&EW | 32W-4N | 4 |
| Honey Hill Dr. N&S | 32W-5N | 4 |
| Honeysuckle Ln. E&W | 30W-4N | 4 |
| Kaelin Rd. N&S | 30W-5N | 4 |
| Keil St. N&S | 32W-5N | 4 |
| Kingswood Ct. N&S | 30W-4N | 4 |
| Lakewood Ct. NE&SW | 30W-4N | 4 |
| Lysle Rd. E&W | 30W-5N | 4 |
| Magnolia Ln. N&S | 30W-4N | 4 |
| Maple Tree Ln. E&W | 30W-4N | 4 |
| Mountain Ash Dr. N&S | 30W-4N | 4 |
| Oak Lawn Rd. NE&SW | 32W-5N | 4 |
| Orchard Ln. E&W | 31W-5N | 4 |
| Percheron Ln. NS&EW | 31W-5N | 4 |
| Peterson Dr. E&W | 31W-5N | 4 |
| Powis Rd. N&S | 32W-5N,31W-4N | 4 |
| Pratt Rd. E&W | 32W-5N | 4 |
| Railroad N&S | 32W-5N | 4 |
| Ridge Ln. N&S | 30W-5N | 4 |
| Rochefort Ln. E&W | 32W-6N | 4 |
| Russel Rd. E&W | 31W-5N | 4 |
| School St. N&S | 32W-5N | 4 |
| Serinne Ln. E&W | 32W-5N | 4 |
| Somerset Ct. N&S | 30W-4N | 4 |
| Warwick Way E&W | 30W-4N | 4 |
| White Oak Ln. E&W | 30W-4N | 4 |
| Will Way E&W | 32W-5N | 4 |
| Wiltshire Ct. N&S | 30W-4N | 4 |

## Wayne Township

| Street | Grid | Page |
|---|---|---|
| Ancient Oaks Dr. N&S | 28W-2N | 11 |
| Arbor Ln. E&W | 30W-3N | 10 |
| Army Trail Rd. E&W | 29W-5N | 5 |
| Ashburn Ln. E&W | 29W-4N | 5 |
| Augusta Dr. N&S | 30W-4N | 4 |
| Avard Rd. N&S | 30W-4N | 4 |
| Bartlett Rd. N&S | 29W-5N,29W-7N | 5 |
| Beech Ct. E&W | 29W-3N | 11 |
| Brentwood Ct. E&W | 29W-5N | 5 |
| Byron Av. E&W | 29W-4N | 5 |
| Cambridge Dr. NW&SE | 29W-4N | 5 |
| Canterbury Dr. E&W | 29W-4N | 5 |
| Cape Av. E&W | 29W-3N,29W-4N | 11 |
| Carriage Way Dr. NW&SE | 29W-5N | 5 |
| Chatham Ct. NW&SE | 29W-4N | 5 |
| Christy Ln. E&W | 29W-2N | 11 |
| Churchill Ct. N&S | 28W-3N | 11 |
| Country Club Ln. N&S | 29W-4N | 5 |
| County Farm Rd. N&S | 27W-2N | 11 |
| Crest Ct. N&S | 27W-3N | 11 |
| Cul De Sac NE&SW | 29W-2N | 11 |
| Cuyahoga Ter. N&S | 29W-3N,29W-5N | 11 |
| Dell Rd. E&W | 29W-2N | 11 |
| Diversey Av. E&W | 28W-3N | 11 |
| Diversey Pkwy. E&W | 30W-3N | 10 |
| Doral Dr. N&S | 30W-4N | 4 |
| Eaton Way N&S | 29W-4N | 5 |
| Elm Ct. N&S | 30W-3N | 10 |
| Elm Rd. N&S | 32W-3N | 10 |
| Ethel St. N&S | 27W-2N | 11 |
| Fair Oaks Rd. N&S | 28W-2N,28W-4N | 11 |
| Florence Ct. E&W | 28W-2N | 11 |
| Garden Dr. E&W | 29W-5N | 5 |
| Gerber Rd. NE&SW | 28W-5N | 5 |
| Glen Rd. NW&SE | 29W-2N | 11 |
| Hawthorn Ln. E&W | 27W-2N | 11 |
| Hickory Knoll Ln. N&S | 29W-3N | 11 |
| Hill Ct. E&W | 29W-4N | 5 |
| Holly Ct. E&W | 27W-3N | 11 |
| Indian Knoll Rd. NW&SE | 28W-2N | 11 |
| Ingalton Av. NW&SE | 29W-2N | 11 |
| Jefferson St. N&S | 27W-2N | 11 |
| Jenlor Ct. E&W | 31W-4N | 4 |
| Judith Ln. E&W | 28W-4N | 5 |
| Keil St. N&S | 32W-3N | 10 |
| Kenwood Av. E&W | 28W-3N | 11 |
| Klein Rd. N&S | 29W-3N,29W-4N | 11 |
| Lake Eleanor Ct. N&S | 31W-4N | 4 |
| Lake Eleanor Dr. N&S | 31W-4N | 4 |
| Lakeview Ct. N&S | 28W-3N | 11 |
| Lakewood Dr. N&S | 29W-3N | 11 |
| Lawrence Av. E&W | 27W-6N | 5 |
| Lies Rd. E&W | 30W-4N | 4 |
| Locust Av. N&S | 30W-3N,30W-4N | 10 |
| Maple Ct. N&S | 30W-3N | 10 |
| Mardon Rd. E&W | 27W-2N | 11 |
| Martingale Dr. N&S | 29W-5N | 5 |
| Mead Rd. NW&SE | 30W-3N | 10 |
| Meadow Lark Dr. N&S | 29W-5N | 5 |
| Mercury Ct. E&W | 29W-5N | 5 |
| Morningside Av. N&S | 28W-2N,28W-3N | 11 |
| Morningside Dr. E&W | 29W-5N | 5 |
| Morton Rd. N&S | 27W-2N | 11 |
| Mulberry Dr. E&W | 30W-3N | 10 |
| Munger Rd. N&S | 31W-4N,31W-7N | 4 |
| Norris Av. N&S | 30W-3N,30W-4N | 10 |
| North Av. E&W | 32W-3N,27W-2N | 10 |
| Oak Creek Ct. E&W | 28W-2N | 11 |
| Oak Creek Dr. N&S | 28W-2N | 11 |
| Oak Dr. NW&SE | 30W-3N | 10 |
| Oak Knoll Rd. E&W | 29W-3N | 11 |
| Oak Ln. E&W | 29W-3N | 11 |
| Oak Rd. N&S | 32W-3N | 10 |
| Old St. Charles Rd. NW&SE | 29W-2N | 11 |
| Old Wayne Ct. E&W | 29W-3N | 11 |
| Orchard Ln. E&W | 29W-5N | 5 |
| Pepper Ct. E&W | 29W-4N | 5 |
| Petersdorf Rd. N&S | 29W-4N,29W-5N | 5 |
| Pine Ct. NW&SE | 28W-5N | 5 |
| Powis Rd. N&S | 31W-3N,31W-7N | 10 |
| Prairie Ln. NW&SE | 31W-4N | 4 |
| Prince Crossing Rd. N&S | 29W-2N | 11 |
| Reque Rd. N&S | 31W-2N,31W-3N | 10 |
| Ridgeview St. NS&EW | 27W-3N | 11 |
| Riviera Ct. E&W | 28W-4N | 5 |
| Sayer Rd. N&S | 30W-7N | 4 |
| Schick Rd. E&W | 31W-4N | 4 |
| Shady Ln. E&W | 30W-3N | 10 |
| Shagbark Dr. E&W | 29W-3N | 11 |
| Smith Rd. E&W | 31W-4N,29W-4N | 4 |
| Spicer Rd. N&S | 30W-4N | 4 |
| Springvale Rd. N&S | 27W-3N | 11 |

| | Grid | Page |
|---|---|---|
| St. Andrews Ln. E&W | | |
| | 30W-4N | 4 |
| St. Andrews Trace Ln. N&S | | |
| | 29W-4N | 5 |
| St. Charles Rd. E&W | | |
| | 29W-2N,27W-2N | 11 |
| St. James Way NW&SE | | |
| | 29W-4N | 5 |
| St. Mark Way N&S .. 29W-4N | | 5 |
| St. Thomas Way E&W | | |
| | 29W-4N | 5 |
| Stearns Rd. E&W | | |
| | 32W-7N,28W-6N | 4 |
| Sunnydale Ct. E&W .. 29W-5N | | 5 |
| Sunset Ridge Dr. E&W | | |
| | 29W-5N | 5 |
| Sycamore St. E&W .. 27W-3N | | 11 |
| Timber Ln. E&W | | |
| | 28W-3N,27W-3N | 11 |
| Timberline R. N&S .. 28W-3N | | 11 |
| Trieste Ln. E&W .. 28W-3N | | 11 |
| Trinity N&S E&W .. 29W-4N | | 5 |
| Turnmill N&S .. 29W-4N | | 5 |
| Vale Rd. E&W ...... 29W-2N | | 11 |
| Valewood Rd. N&S | | |
| | 29W-2N,29W-3N | 11 |
| Waterford Ln. N&S . 29W-4N | | 5 |
| Wayne Oaks Ln. N&S | | |
| | 28W-2N | 11 |
| Waynewood Dr. E&W | | |
| | 29W-2N | 11 |
| Wescot Ln. N&S .. 29W-4N | | 5 |
| Whitney Rd. E&W .. 30W-4N | | 4 |
| Wiant Rd. N&S | | |
| | 30W-3N,30W-4N | 10 |
| Wild Flower Ln. N&S | | |
| | 29W-3N | 11 |
| Wood Ct. E&W .... 30W-5N | | 4 |
| Woodcreek Ln., N. N&S | | |
| | 28W-3N | 11 |
| Woodcreek Ln., S. N&S | | |
| | 28W-3N | 11 |
| Woodcrest Dr. NW&SE | | |
| | 29W-2N | 11 |
| Woodland Av. N&S | | |
| | 30W-2N,30W-3N | 10 |
| Woodland Ct. N&S .. 31W-4N | | 4 |
| Woodland Trail S. E&W | | |
| | 31W-4N | 4 |
| Woodland Trail W. E&W | | |
| | 31W-4N | 4 |
| Woodview Ct. N&S .. 27W-3N | | 11 |
| Wynn Av. E&W | | |
| | 29W-3N,28W-3N | 11 |

## West Chicago

| | Grid | Page |
|---|---|---|
| Acorn Hill Ln. NS&EW | | |
| | 30W-2N | 10 |
| Allen Av. N&S | | |
| | 29W-0S,29W-0N | 16 |
| Amber Ct. NS&EW .. 29W-2N | | 11 |
| Ann St. E&W ...... 30W-0N | | 10 |
| Applegate Av. N&S .. 30W-1N | | 10 |
| Arapako Ct. N&S .. 30W-3N | | 10 |
| Arbor Av. N&S .... 30W-1N | | 10 |
| Arthur Ct. E&W .... 31W-2N | | 10 |
| Aster Ln. N&S .... 30W-2N | | 11 |
| Atlantic Dr. N&S .. 30W-2N | | 10 |
| Augusta Av. N&S....29W-0S | | 16 |
| Aurora St. NW&SE .. 30W-0N | | 10 |
| Avard Av. N&S .... 30W-0N | | 10 |
| Barber Av. N&S | | |
| | 29W-0S,29W-0N | 16 |
| Bayberry Ct. E&W .. 30W-1N | | 10 |
| Belleview St. N&S .. 29W-1N | | 10 |
| Bishop St. N&S | | |
| | 29W-0S,29W-0N | 16 |
| Blackhawk Dr. E&W | | |
| | 32W-2N,31W-2N | 10 |
| Blair St. E&W | | |
| | 30W-0N,29W-0N | 10 |
| Blakeley Av. N&S | | |
| | 29W-0S,29W-0N | 16 |
| Bobwhite Ln. NS&EW | | |
| | 29W-3N | 11 |
| Brentwood Ct. E&W 30W-0S | | 16 |
| Brentwood St. N&S . 30W-0S | | 16 |
| Brown St. E&W | | |
| | 30W-0N,29W-0N | 10 |
| Bunting Ct. E&W .. 29W-3N | | 11 |
| Canterbury Ct. N&S..29W-0S | | 16 |
| Carolina St. N&S .. 30W-2N | | 10 |
| Carriage Dr. N&S .. 29W-0S | | 16 |
| Carriage Dr. NW&SE | | |
| | 30W-0S | 16 |
| Center St. N&S .. 29W-0N | | 10 |
| Charles Ct. N&S .. 31W-0N | | 10 |
| Cherokee Rd. N&S .. 30W-0N | | 10 |
| Cherry Blossom Ct. N&S | | |
| | 30W-1N | 10 |
| Cherrywood Ln. N&S | | |
| | 29W-2N | 11 |
| Chicago St. NE&SW | | |
| | 29W-0N | 11 |
| Chippewa Ln. E&W . 30W-3N | | 10 |
| Church St. NE&SW .. 30W-0N | | 10 |
| Clara St. N&S .... 30W-0N | | 10 |
| Claremont Av. N&S . 29W-1N | | 11 |
| Clayton St. N&S .. 29W-0N | | 11 |
| Colford Ct. E&W .. 29W-0N | | 11 |
| Columbine Ln. NW&SE | | |
| | 29W-2N | 11 |
| Commerce Dr. E&W 31W-0N | | 10 |
| Conde St. NW&SE .. 29W-0N | | 11 |
| Coolidge Av. N&S .. 29W-0N | | 11 |
| Crabapple Ct. E&W . 30W-1N | | 10 |
| Cranesbill Dr. NW&SE | | |
| | 29W-2N | 11 |
| Crestview Ln. N&S .. 30W-2N | | 10 |
| Crown Ct. NE&SW . 31W-3N | | 10 |
| Dale Av. E&W .... 29W-0S | | 16 |
| Dayton Av. N&S .. 29W-0S | | 16 |
| Downs Dr. E&W .. 31W-1N | | 10 |
| Dunham Dr. E&W .. 29W-1N | | 11 |
| Eagle Ridge Ct. E&W | | |
| | 30W-3N | 10 |
| Easton Av. N&S .. 29W-0N | | 11 |
| Elite Av. N&S .... 29W-1N | | 11 |
| Elizabeth St. N&S | | |
| | 29W-0S,29W-0N | 16 |
| Elliot Av. NW&SE .. 30W-1N | | 10 |
| Elmwood St. E&W | | |
| | 30W-1N,29W-1N | 10 |
| Fabyan Pkwy E&W .. 32W-0N | | 10 |
| Factory St. N&S .. 30W-0N | | 10 |
| Fairbanks Ct. N&S . 30W-0N | | 10 |
| Fairview Av. E&W...29W-1N | | 11 |
| Fawell Dr. N&S .. 30W-1N | | 10 |
| Fenton Dr. S .. 31W-0N | | 10 |
| Forest Av. E&W | | |
| | 30W-0N,29W-0N | 10 |
| Fremont St. N&S .. 30W-1N | | 10 |
| Fulton St. NW&SE .. 29W-0N | | 11 |
| Galena NE&SW ... 29W-0N | | 11 |
| Garden St. N&S .. 29W-1N | | 11 |
| Garys Mill Rd. E&W . 29W-0S | | 16 |
| Gates St. N&S | | |
| | 29W-0S,29W-0N | 16 |
| Geneva Rd. E&W .. 29W-0N | | 11 |
| Geneva St. E&W | | |
| | 30W-0N,29W-0N | 11 |
| George St. E&W .. 30W-0N | | 10 |
| Glen Av. E&W .... 29W-0S | | 16 |
| Grand Lake Blvd. E&W | | |
| | 30W-1N,29W-1N | 10 |
| Green Meadow Dr. NW&SE | | |
| | 30W-2N | 10 |
| Grove Av. E&W .... 29W-1N | | 11 |
| Hahndorf St. NW&SE | | |
| | 29W-2N,29W-0N | 10 |
| Hampton Course NS&EW | | |
| | 29W-1N | 11 |
| Harrison St. NE&SW | | |
| | 30W-0N | 10 |
| Harvester Rd. E&W . 31W-2N | | 10 |
| Hawthorne Ln. E&W | | |
| | 29W-2N | 10 |
| Hazel St. E&W | | |
| | 30W-0N,29W-0N | 10 |
| Helena Dr. NW&SE . 31W-0N | | 10 |
| High Gate Ct. N&S . 29W-1N | | 11 |
| High Ridge Dr. E&W | | |
| | 29W-1N | 11 |
| High St. NW&SE .. 29W-0N | | 11 |
| Highland Av. E&W .. 29W-1N | | 11 |
| Highland Av. N&S....29W-1N | | 11 |
| Hill Ct. E&W .... 29W-1N | | 11 |
| Hillview Av. E&W .. 29W-1N | | 11 |
| Honeysuckle Av. N&S | | |
| | 30W-1N | 10 |
| Howard Dr. N&S .. 31W-2N | | 10 |
| Indianwood Ln. E&W | | |
| | 30W-3N | 10 |
| Industrial Dr. N&S...31W-1N | | 10 |
| Ingalton Av. E&W .. 29W-0N | | 11 |
| Joliet St. N&S | | |
| | 30W-0S,30W-0N | 16 |
| Kenwood Av. N&S .. 30W-0N | | 10 |
| King Ct. NW&SE .... 30W-2N | | 10 |
| Cir. | 30W-2N | 10 |
| Knollwood Ln. N&S .. 29W-2N | | 11 |
| Kress Rd. N&S | | |
| | 32W-0N,32W-1N | 10 |
| Kresswood Dr. N&S...29W-1S | | 17 |
| Lake Side Dr. NS&EW | | |
| | 30W-2N | 10 |
| Lawrence Av. E&W .. 29W-0N | | 10 |
| Lester St. E&W | | |
| | 30W-0N,29W-0N | 10 |
| Lincoln Av. N&S .... 30W-0N | | 10 |
| Long Oak Dr. E&W . 30W-2N | | 10 |
| Longest Dr. E&W .. 32W-1N | | 10 |
| Lorlyn Dr. NW&SE . 29W-0S | | 16 |
| Lyman Av. N&S .. 30W-0N | | 10 |
| Main St. E&W .... 29W-0N | | 11 |
| McChesney Rd. N&S | | |
| | 32W-0N | 10 |
| McConnell Av. E&W | | |
| | 30W-1N,29W-1N | 10 |
| Meadow Ridge Dr. NW&SE | | |
| | 29W-1N | 11 |
| Meadowlark Dr. NS&EW | | |
| | 29W-3N | 11 |
| Mellington Av. N&S .. 31W-0N | | 10 |
| Milo Ct. E&W .... 30W-0N | | 10 |
| Mulberry Dr. N&S .. 30W-1N | | 10 |
| National St. E&W | | |
| | 30W-1N,29W-1N | 10 |
| Neltnor Blvd. N&S | | |
| | 29W-0S,29W-1N | 16 |
| Nickelson Rd. N&S .. 30W-0N | | 10 |
| Norris Av. N&S .... 30W-0N | | 10 |
| North St. E&W .... 29W-1N | | 11 |
| Northwest Av. E&W . 31W-2N | | 10 |
| Northwest Av. E&W . 30W-1N | | 10 |
| Nuclear Dr. N&S .. 31W-2N | | 10 |
| Oak Av. N&S........29W-1N | | 11 |

| | Grid | Page |
|---|---|---|
| Oak St. N&S | | |
| | 29W-0S,29W-0N | 16 |
| Oakwood Av. N&S | | |
| | 29W-0N,29W-1N | 11 |
| Orlyn Dr. N&S ...... 29W-0S | | 16 |
| Parker Av. N&S.....29W-0N | | 11 |
| Parkside Av. N&S....30W-0N | | 10 |
| Peachtree Ln. E&W . 30W-1N | | 11 |
| Perrimmon Dr. N&S . 29W-1N | | 11 |
| Pine St. E&W......29W-1N | | 10 |
| Plumtree Ln. E&W . 30W-1N | | 10 |
| Plymouth St. E&W .. 29W-1N | | 11 |
| Pomeroy St. E&W | | |
| | 30W-0N,29W-0N | 10 |
| Powis Ct. N&S | | |
| | 31W-2N,31W-3N | 10 |
| Powis Rd. N&S | | |
| | 31W-2N,31W-3N | 10 |
| Railroad Av. N&S .. 30W-2N | | 10 |
| Ridgewood Ct. E&W | | |
| | 29W-2N | 11 |
| Ridgewood Ln. N&S | | |
| | 29W-2N | 11 |
| Roosevelt Rd. E&W | | |
| | 32W-0N,29W-0S | 16 |
| Rosewood Dr. NS&EW | | |
| | 29W-2N | 11 |
| Salem St. E&W .... 29W-2N | | 11 |
| Sarana Av. N&S .. 29W-0S | | 16 |
| Sherman St. N&S....30W-0N | | 10 |
| Sophia St. N&S.....29W-1N | | 11 |
| Spencer St. E&W .. 29W-0N | | 11 |
| Spring Cress Ln. NW&SE | | |
| | 29W-2N | 11 |
| Spur Row E&W....31W-2N | | 10 |
| St. Andrew's Ct. E&W | | |
| | 30W-3N | 10 |
| Sterling Av. E&W .. 29W-0N | | 10 |
| Stimmel St. E&W | | |
| | 30W-0N,29W-0N | 10 |
| Summit Av. N&S .. 29W-0N | | 11 |
| Sycamore St. N&S .. 29W-0N | | 11 |
| Tanager Ln. N&S .. 29W-3N | | 11 |
| Town Rd. N&S .... 30W-0N | | 10 |
| Trillium Tr. N&S....29W-2N | | 11 |
| Turner Av. N&S .... 29W-1N | | 11 |
| Turner Ct. NW&SE | | |
| | 30W-0N,29W-0N | 10 |
| Vine St. NW&SE .... 30W-0N | | 10 |
| Virgie Pl. E&W ...... 29W-1N | | 11 |
| Washington St. NE&SW | | |
| | 30W-0N,31W-0N | 10 |
| Waynewood Dr. N&S | | |
| | 30W-2N | 10 |
| Wegner Dr. NE&SW . 30W-2N | | 10 |
| Wendall St. E&W .. 29W-1N | | 11 |
| Western Dr. E&W....31W-1N | | 10 |
| Weyrauch St. N&S . 30W-0N | | 10 |
| Wild Ginger Tr. NW&SE | | |
| | 29W-2N | 11 |
| Wildwood Ln. E&W . 29W-2N | | 11 |
| Willow Creek Rd. N&S | | |
| | 30W-2N | 10 |
| Wilson Av. N&S .... 29W-0N | | 11 |
| Windsor St. E&W .. 29W-0S | | 16 |
| Winston St. E&W .. 30W-0N | | 10 |
| Wood St. N&S .... 30W-0N | | 10 |
| Woodland Av. N&S | | |
| | 30W-2N,30W-3N | 10 |
| Woodside Ct. NW&SE | | |
| | 30W-2N | 10 |
| Woodside Dr. NW&SE | | |
| | 30W-2N | 10 |
| Yale St. N&S........30W-1N | | 10 |
| York Av. E&W | | |
| | 30W-1N,29W-1N | 10 |

## Westmont

| | Grid | Page |
|---|---|---|
| Adams St. N&S | | |
| | 18W-6S,18W-5S | 26 |
| Ainslie Dr. NW&SE .. 17W-6S | | 27 |
| Alpine Ln. N&S .... 18W-7S | | 26 |
| Antler Ln. N&S .... 18W-6S | | 26 |
| Arbor Ln. N&S .... 18W-6S | | 26 |
| Arlington Av. E&W . 17W-4S | | 27 |
| Ashford Ln. NS&EW | | |
| | 17W-6S | 27 |
| Aspen Ln., S. N&S . 18W-7S | | 26 |
| Baltimore Av. NE&SW | | |
| | 16W-4S | 27 |
| Barry Ln. N&S .... 18W-6S | | 26 |
| Bay Ct. E&W........18W-7S | | 26 |
| Beechwood Ct. NE&SW | | |
| | 18W-6S | 26 |
| Beechwood Dr. E&W | | |
| | 18W-6S | 26 |
| Beninford Ln. N&S . 17W-6S | | 27 |
| Blackhawk Dr. N&S | | |
| | 17W-4S,17W-3S | 27 |
| Brookside Dr. E&W . 18W-6S | | 26 |
| Brown Deer Dr. N&S | | |
| | 18W-3S | 20 |
| Brown Deer Tr. N&S | | |
| | 18W-3S | 20 |
| Buck Ct. N&S .... 18W-6S | | 26 |
| Burr Oak Dr. N&S . 17W-4S | | 27 |
| Buttonwood Dr. N&S | | |
| | 18W-6S | 26 |
| Carlisle Ln. NS&EW . 18W-6S | | 26 |
| Carriage Ln. N&S...18W-7S | | 26 |
| Cass Av. N&S | | |
| | 18W-7S,18W-4S | 26 |
| Cass Ln., W. N&S . 18W-7S | | 26 |

| | Grid | Page |
|---|---|---|
| Cedar Ln. N&S .... 18W-7S | | 26 |
| Champlaine Av. N&S | | |
| | 16W-4S | 27 |
| Chestnut Av. E&W . 17W-4S | | 27 |
| Chicago Av. E&W | | |
| | 18W-5S,17W-5S | 26 |
| Citadel Cir. NS&EW . 17W-4S | | 27 |
| Citadel Dr. NS&EW . 17W-4S | | 27 |
| Cove Ct. E&W .... 18W-7S | | 26 |
| Creekwood Ct. N&S 18W-6S | | 26 |
| Cromwell Ct. NE&SW | | |
| | 18W-6S | 26 |
| Cumnor Rd. NW&SE | | |
| | 18W-6S | 26 |
| Dallas St. N&S | | |
| | 18W-5S,17W-5S | 26 |
| Deercreek Ln. N&S . 18W-6S | | 26 |
| Deming Pl. NW&SE . 17W-6S | | 27 |
| Des Moines St. N&S | | |
| | 18W-5S,17W-5S | 26 |
| Doe Cir. N&S .... 18W-6S | | 26 |
| Echo Ln. N&S .... 18W-7S | | 26 |
| Elmwood Ct. NE&SW | | |
| | 18W-6S | 26 |
| Executive Ct. NE&SW | | |
| | 16W-3S | 21 |
| Fairway Ln. N&S .. 18W-7S | | 26 |
| Fernwood Ct. N&S | | |
| | 18W-6S | 26 |
| Fernwood Dr. NS&EW | | |
| | 18W-6S | 26 |
| Fordham Way NE&SW | | |
| | 17W-6S | 27 |
| Fountainhead Dr. E&W | | |
| | 18W-6S | 26 |
| Franklin St. N&S .. 17W-4S | | 27 |
| Garrett St. NS&EW . 18W-6S | | 26 |
| Grant St. N&S | | |
| | 18W-6S,18W-5S | 26 |
| Hamilton Av. E&W . 17W-4S | | 27 |
| Hamilton Ct. E&W .. 17W-4S | | 27 |
| Hampton Av. E&W . 18W-6S | | 26 |
| Heath Ln. N&S .... 18W-6S | | 27 |
| Heath Pl. NW&SE...17W-6S | | 27 |
| Hiddenview Dr. E&W | | |
| | 17W-6S | 27 |
| Honeywood Dr. N&S | | |
| | 18W-6S | 26 |
| Hudson St. N&S .. 18W-5S | | 26 |
| Independence Av. E&W | | |
| | 16W-4S | 27 |
| Indian Bdry Dr. N&S 18W-3S | | 20 |
| Indian Prairie Dr. E&W | | |
| | 18W-3S | 20 |
| Indian Tr. E&W .. 18W-3S | | 20 |
| Irving St. E&W | | |
| | 18W-5S,17W-5S | 26 |
| Ivy Ct. E&W ........ 18W-7S | | 26 |
| James Dr. E&W .... 18W-6S | | 26 |
| Jameson Way NW&SE | | |
| | 17W-6S | 27 |
| Jamestown Ct. E&W | | |
| | 17W-3S | 21 |
| King Arthur Ct. NS&EW | | |
| | 18W-6S | 26 |
| Lafayette Av. E&W . 17W-4S | | 27 |
| Lake Ct. N&S .... 18W-6S | | 26 |
| Lake Dr. N&S .... 18W-7S | | 26 |
| Lincoln St. N&S | | |
| | 18W-5S,18W-4S | 26 |
| Linden Av. N&S | | |
| | 17W-6S,17W-5S | 27 |
| Lindley St. N&S .. 18W-6S | | 26 |
| Longford Dr. NE&SW | | |
| | 18W-7S | 26 |
| Maple N&S .... 18W-7S | | 26 |
| Maple Av. N&S .. 18W-5S | | 26 |
| Melrose Av. E&W | | |
| | 18W-4S,17W-4S | 26 |
| Monticello Av. E&W . 17W-4S | | 27 |
| Morning Glory Cir. N&S | | |
| | 18W-4S | 26 |
| Naperville Rd. NE&SW | | |
| | 18W-5S,17W-4S | 26 |
| Nelson Dr. N&S .. 18W-6S | | 26 |
| New Port Av. N&S . 16W-4S | | 27 |
| Norfolk St. E&W | | |
| | 18W-5S,17W-5S | 26 |
| Oak Av. N&S........17W-5S | | 27 |
| Oak Hill Dr. E&W .. 17W-5S | | 27 |
| Oak St. N&S...... 17W-6S | | 27 |
| Oakbrook Hills Dr. E&W | | |
| | 17W-3S | 21 |
| Oakley Ct. N&S..... 18W-3S | | 20 |
| Oakley Dr. N&S .. 18W-3S | | 20 |
| Oakley Ln. N&S .. 18W-3S | | 20 |
| Oakmont Ln. E&W | | |
| | 17W-3S,16W-3S | 21 |
| Oakmont Plaza Dr. E&W | | |
| | 16W-3S | 21 |
| Oakwood Ct. NE&SW | | |
| | 17W-3S | 21 |
| Oakwood Dr. N&S | | |
| | 17W-4S,17W-3S | 20 |
| Office Dr. N&S .. 18W-3S | | 20 |
| Oliver Ct. E&W .. 18W-6S | | 26 |
| Orleans Ct. E&W .. 18W-6S | | 26 |
| Park Ln. N&S......18W-7S | | 26 |
| Park St. N&S | | |
| | 18W-6S,18W-4S | 26 |
| Parkway Av. N&S.. 18W-4S | | 26 |
| Parkway Dr. NE&SW | | |
| | 18W-4S | 26 |

| | Grid | Page |
|---|---|---|
| Pasquinelli Dr. NW&SE | | |
| | 16W-4S,16W-3S | 27 |
| Philadelphia Av. E&W | | |
| | 17W-4S | 27 |
| Pier Dr. E&W........18W-7S | | 26 |
| Plaza Dr. E&W...... 17W-4S | | 27 |
| Quail Ridge Dr. E&W | | |
| | 16W-3S | 21 |
| Quebec Pl. N&S .... 17W-4S | | 27 |
| Quincy Av. E&W | | |
| | 18W-5S,17W-5S | 26 |
| Raintree Ct. NW&SE | | |
| | 18W-6S | 26 |
| Raintree Ln. N&S .. 18W-6S | | 26 |
| Revere Av. E&W | | |
| | 17W-4S,16W-4S | 27 |
| Revere Ct. N&S .. 17W-4S | | 27 |
| Richmond Av. N&S | | |
| | 17W-6S,17W-4S | 27 |
| Richmond St. E&W | | |
| | 18W-5S,17W-5S | 26 |
| Robinson Ct. E&W . 18W-6S | | 26 |
| Rosewood Ct. E&W . 17W-4S | | 27 |
| Roslyn Rd. N&S | | |
| | 18W-5S,18W-4S | 26 |
| Rumsey Pl. N&S...17W-6S | | 27 |
| Schramm Ct. NE&SW | | |
| | 18W-7S | 26 |
| Schramm Dr. N&S . 18W-7S | | 26 |
| Spruce Ln. N&S .. 18W-7S | | 26 |
| Suffield Ct. N&S .. 18W-7S | | 26 |
| Tartan Lakes Cir. NS&EW | | |
| | 17W-3S | 21 |
| Tartan Lakes Ct. NS&EW | | |
| | 17W-3S | 21 |
| Tartan Lakes Dr. N&S | | |
| | 17W-3S | 21 |
| Tartan Lakes Way N&S | | |
| | 17W-3S | 21 |
| Tower Ln. E&W .. 17W-5S | | 27 |
| Tracy Ct. E&W .. 18W-7S | | 26 |
| Traube Av. E&W | | |
| | 18W-4S,17W-4S | 26 |
| Tudor Ln. N&S .... 18W-7S | | 26 |
| Vail Dr. N&S .... 18W-7S | | 26 |
| Vandustrial Dr. E&W | | |
| | 18W-6S | 26 |
| Vandustrial Dr. N&S . 18W-6S | | 26 |
| Virginia Dr. N&S .. 18W-7S | | 26 |
| Warwick Av. N&S | | |
| | 17W-6S,17W-4S | 27 |
| Washington St. N&S | | |
| | 18W-6S,18W-4S | 26 |
| Wesley Ct. N&S .. 18W-7S | | 26 |
| Wesley Ln. N&S...18W-7S | | 26 |
| West End Av. N&S . 18W-5S | | 26 |
| Westmont Dr. N&S . 17W-4S | | 27 |
| Whipple Ln. E&W . 18W-7S | | 26 |
| White Birch Ln. E&W | | |
| | 18W-3S | 20 |
| Willard Pl. E&W......18W-4S | | 26 |
| Williams St. N&S | | |
| | 18W-7S,18W-5S | 26 |
| Williamsburg Dr. N&S | | |
| | 17W-3S | 21 |
| Williamsport Dr. NE&SW | | |
| | 18W-7S | 26 |
| Willow Ln. N&S......18W-6S | | 26 |
| Willow Oak Dr. 17W-4S | | 27 |
| Willow Way E&W .. 18W-7S | | 26 |
| Wilmette Av. N&S | | |
| | 17W-6S,17W-4S | 27 |
| 35th St. N&S ...... 17W-3S | | 21 |
| 55th Pl. E&W .... 18W-6S | | 26 |
| 55th St. E&W | | |
| | 18W-6S,17W-6S | 26 |
| 56th Pl. E&W | | |
| | 18W-6S,17W-6S | 26 |
| 56th St. E&W | | |
| | 18W-6S,17W-6S | 26 |
| 57th St. E&W | | |
| | 18W-6S,17W-6S | 26 |
| 58th St. E&W | | |
| | 18W-6S,17W-6S | 26 |
| 60th St. E&W | | |
| | 18W-6S,17W-6S | 26 |
| 61st St. E&W .... 18W-6S | | 26 |
| 64th St. E&W .... 18W-7S | | 26 |
| 65th St. E&W ....18W-7S | | 26 |
| 66th St. E&W....18W-7S | | 26 |

## Wheaton

| | Grid | Page |
|---|---|---|
| Aberdeen Ct. N&S .. 26W-1S | | 18 |
| Academy Ln. NE&SW | | |
| | 25W-1S | 18 |
| Acorn Ct. NE&SW .. 23W-3S | | 18 |
| Adare Dr. N&S .... 26W-1S | | 18 |
| Albright Ct. NW&SE . 23W-3S | | 18 |
| Albright Ln. NW&SE 23W-3S | | 18 |
| Alchester Dr. N&S . 24W-1S | | 18 |
| Appaloosa Ct., E. E&W | | |
| | 23W-3S | 18 |
| Appaloosa Ct., W. E&W | | |
| | 23W-3S | 18 |
| Appleby Ct. N&S .. 23W-3S | | 18 |
| Appleby Dr. NS&EW | | |
| | 23W-3S | 18 |
| Arbor Av. E&W | | |
| | 25W-1S,24W-1S | 18 |
| Arbor Ct. E&W .... 25W-1S | | 18 |
| Ardmore Ln. E&W . 26W-1S | | 18 |
| Ascot Ct. NW&SE .. 23W-3S | | 18 |
| Ashburn Ct. N&S .. 23W-2S | | 18 |

| | Grid | Page |
|---|---|---|
| Ashford Ct. NE&SW | 23W-1S | 18 |
| Ashton Ct. E&W | 23W-0N | 12 |
| Aurora Way N&S | 25W-1S,25W-0S | 18 |
| Avalon Ct. N&S | 25W-2S | 18 |
| Avery Av. N&S | 23W-0S | 18 |
| Barger Ln. E&W | 26W-2S | 18 |
| Bates St. N&S | 26W-0S | 18 |
| Beecher NW&SE | 25W-0S | 18 |
| Beechwood Ct.* E&W | 26W-2S | 18 |
| Belleau Woods Dr. E&W | 26W-1S | 18 |
| Berkshire Pl. N&S | 25W-2S | 18 |
| Birch N&S | 25W-0S | 18 |
| Blackburn St. NE&SW | 24W-1S | 18 |
| Blacksmith Dr. NS&EW | 23W-3S | 18 |
| Blanchard Dr. N&S | 23W-0N | 12 |
| Blanchard St. N&S | 24W-2S,23W-0S | 18 |
| Borough Ct.* E&W | 23W-2S | 18 |
| Bradford Dr. NE&SW | 23W-3S | 18 |
| Brandon Dr. N&S | 24W-1S | 18 |
| Brentwood Ct. NW&SE | 23W-2S | 18 |
| Brentwood Dr. NS&EW | 23W-2S | 18 |
| Briar Cove N&S | 26W-1S | 18 |
| Briarbrook Dr. NS&EW | 23W-2S | 18 |
| Briarcliffe Blvd. N&S | 23W-2S,24W-1S | 18 |
| Bridge St. N&S | 25W-0S | 18 |
| Bridle Ln. E&W | 24W-0N | 12 |
| Brighton Dr. E&W | 25W-2S,24W-2S | 18 |
| Bristol Ct. N&S | 23W-3S | 18 |
| Brittany Ct. N&S | 24W-1S | 18 |
| Brookside Cir. NE&SW | 24W-0N | 12 |
| Browning Ct. E&W | 24W-1S | 18 |
| Buckingham Dr. NS&EW | 25W-2S | 18 |
| Buena Vista Dr. NW&SE | 23W-1S | 18 |
| Bunker Hill Ct. NW&SE | 25W-2S | 18 |
| Burnham Pl. N&S | 25W-2S | 18 |
| Burning Trail N&S | 26W-1S | 18 |
| Burning Trail Ct. N&S | 25W-1S | 18 |
| Burr Oak Ct. NE&SW | 26W-1S | 18 |
| Butterfield Rd. E&W | 26W-2S,23W-2S | 18 |
| Byron Ct. N&S | 23W-0S | 18 |
| Cadillac Dr. E&W | 24W-0N | 12 |
| Cambridge Ln. N&S | 24W-2S,23W-2S | 18 |
| Campbell Av. N&S | 24W-1S,24W-0S | 18 |
| Campbell Ct. E&W | 24W-1S | 18 |
| Canterbury Pl. N&S | 25W-2S | 18 |
| Cantigny Way N&S | 25W-1S | 18 |
| Carlson Ln. E&W | 24W-0N | 12 |
| Carlton Av. N&S | 25W-0S,25W-0N | 18 |
| Casa Solana Dr. NE&SW | 23W-2S | 18 |
| Castbourne Ct. E&W | 24W-1S | 18 |
| Castlewood Dr. N&S | 24W-1S | 18 |
| Caxton Dr. E&W | 26W-1S | 18 |
| Center Av. N&S | 25W-1S | 18 |
| Charles St. E&W | 26W-0S | 18 |
| Charlotte Ct. NW&SE | 26W-2S | 18 |
| Chase St. N&S | 24W-1S,24W-0N | 18 |
| Chatham Dr. N&S | 25W-2S | 18 |
| Chelsea Ct. N&S | 26W-2S | 18 |
| Cherry Ct. N&S | 24W-0N | 12 |
| Cherry St. N&S | 24W-0N | 12 |
| Cheshire Ct. NW&SE | 23W-2S | 18 |
| Cheshire Ln. N&S | 23W-2S | 18 |
| Chesterfield Av. NW&SE | 23W-0S | 18 |
| Childs Ct. E&W | 26W-0S | 18 |
| Childs St. N&S | 26W-0S,25W-0S | 18 |
| Circle Av. N&S | 25W-0S | 18 |
| Clifden Ct. NW&SE | 26W-1S | 18 |
| Clinton Ct. N&S | 25W-0S | 18 |
| Clydesdale Dr. NS&EW | 23W-3S | 18 |
| Cole Av. N&S | 24W-0N | 12 |
| College Av. NE&SW | 24W-0S,23W-0S | 18 |
| College Hill Av. E&W | 24W-0S,23W-0S | 18 |
| College Ln. N&S | 23W-0S | 18 |
| Coloma Ct. N&S | 23W-1S | 18 |
| Coloma Pl. N&S | 23W-1S | 18 |
| Colonial Sq. E&W | 25W-2S | 18 |
| Community Dr. NE&SW | 26W-1S | 18 |
| Coolidge Ct. E&W | 23W-1S | 18 |
| Cordova Ct. E&W | 24W-2S,23W-2S | 18 |
| Countryside Dr. E&W | 24W-0N | 12 |
| County Farm Rd. N&S | 26W-1S,26W-0S | 18 |
| Courtenay Dr. NE&SW | 25W-1S | 18 |
| Cove Ct. N&S | 25W-1S | 18 |
| Creekside Cove N&S | 26W-1S | 18 |
| Creekside Dr. NS&EW | 26W-1S | 18 |
| Crescent St. E&W | 24W-0S | 18 |
| Crest St. N&S | 25W-1S,25W-0S | 18 |
| Cromwell Dr. N&S | 25W-2S | 18 |
| Cross St. N&S | 24W-0N | 18 |
| Croydon Ct.* E&W | 23W-2S | 18 |
| Culham Ct. NE&SW | 23W-3S | 18 |
| Daly Rd. E&W | 24W-0N,23W-0N | 12 |
| Darling St. N&S | 25W-0N | 12 |
| Dartmouth Dr. NS&EW | 25W-1S | 18 |
| Darwin Ct. NE&SW | 23W-1S | 18 |
| Darwin Ln. E&W | 23W-1S | 18 |
| Davis Ct.* E&W | 26W-2S | 18 |
| Dawes Av. E&W | 24W-1S,23W-1S | 18 |
| Delles Rd. N&S | 25W-1S | 18 |
| Depot Pl. NE&SW | 23W-0S | 18 |
| Derby Ct. N&S | 23W-3S | 18 |
| Devonshire Ln. E&W | 24W-1S | 18 |
| Dickinson Dr. NS&EW | 24W-0N | 12 |
| Doncaster Ct. E&W | 23W-2S | 18 |
| Dorchester Av. N&S | 25W-0S | 18 |
| Dorset Dr. NS&EW | 23W-1S | 18 |
| Downing Ct. E&W | 23W-3S | 18 |
| Driving Park Rd. N&S | 24W-0N | 12 |
| Dundee Dr. N&S | 23W-2S | 18 |
| Dunlay N&S | 23W-3S | 18 |
| Durham Dr. NS&EW | 23W-3S | 18 |
| Eagle Ct. E&W | 25W-2S | 18 |
| East St. N&S | 24W-0S | 18 |
| Eaton Ct. N&S | 23W-1S | 18 |
| Eddy Ct. N&S | 23W-0N | 12 |
| Edgewood Av. N&S | 25W-0S | 18 |
| Edinburgh Ct. E&W | 23W-1S | 18 |
| Ellis Av. N&S | 25W-0S,25W-0N | 18 |
| Elm St. E&W | 25W-1S,23W-1S | 18 |
| Elmwood St. N&S | 26W-0S | 18 |
| Emerson Ct. E&W | 24W-1S | 19 |
| Enis Ln. E&W | 26W-1S | 18 |
| Ensenada Dr. NW&SE | 24W-2S | 18 |
| Erie St. N&S | 26W-0S | 18 |
| Essel Ct., E. E&W | 23W-3S | 18 |
| Essel Ct., W. E&W | 23W-3S | 18 |
| Evergreen St. N&S | 25W-0S,23W-0S | 18 |
| Exeter Ct. N&S | 23W-1S | 18 |
| Faff Cir. NS&EW | 26W-0S | 18 |
| Faganel Ct. N&S | 26W-1S | 18 |
| Fairway Ln. E&W | 24W-1S | 18 |
| Falson Ct. E&W | 24W-1S | 18 |
| Fanchon St. N&S | 25W-0N | 12 |
| Farnham Ln. E&W | 24W-1S | 18 |
| Farragut Ct. E&W | 23W-2S | 19 |
| Farragut Ct. N&S | 23W-2S | 18 |
| Farwell St. N&S | 25W-0N | 12 |
| Fischer St. N&S | 24W-1S,24W-0S | 18 |
| Folkstone Ct.* E&W | 23W-2S | 18 |
| Foothill Ct. NW&SE | 25W-1S | 18 |
| Foothill Dr. NE&SW | 25W-1S | 18 |
| Forest Av. E&W | 24W-0N,23W-0N | 12 |
| Fox Run E&W | 26W-1S | 18 |
| Franklin St. N&S | 25W-0S,24W-0S | 18 |
| Frazier Ct. N&S | 25W-1S | 18 |
| Friars Ct. N&S | 24W-1S | 18 |
| Front St. E&W | 25W-1S,25W-0S | 18 |
| Gables Blvd. N&S | 25W-1S,25W-0S | 18 |
| Gainesboro Ct. N&S | 24W-1S | 18 |
| Gainesboro Dr. N&S | 24W-1S | 18 |
| Gamon Rd. N&S | 24W-0S | 18 |
| Garner Av. E&W | 23W-0S | 18 |
| Gary Av. N&S | 25W-0S,25W-0N | 18 |
| Gary St. N&S | 25W-0N | 12 |
| Geneva Pl. E&W | 24W-0N | 12 |
| Geneva Rd. E&W | 24W-1N,23W-1N | 12 |
| George St. E&W | 24W-0N | 12 |
| Gladstone Dr. N&S | 25W-2S | 18 |
| Glencoe St. N&S | 23W-0N | 12 |
| Glendale Av. NE&SW | 23W-0S | 18 |
| Golden Pond Ln. N&S | 25W-2S | 18 |
| Golf Cir. N&S | 25W-1S | 18 |
| Golf Ln. N&S | 25W-1S | 18 |
| Golf View Ct. N&S | 23W-2S | 18 |
| Gone Away Ct. N&S | 25W-1S | 18 |
| Gone Away Ln. E&W | 26W-1S,25W-1S | 18 |
| Grant St. N&S | 24W-1S | 18 |
| Greensboro Dr. N&S | 25W-2S | 18 |
| Greenwood Dr. N&S | 25W-1S | 18 |
| Gresham Cir. N&S | 26W-1S | 18 |
| Grey Willow Rd. N&S | 24W-0N | 12 |
| Grosvenor Cr. E&W | 26W-1S,25W-1S | 18 |
| Groton Ct. E&W | 23W-1S | 18 |
| Groton Ln. NW&SE | 23W-1S | 18 |
| Hailshaw Ct.* E&W | 23W-2S | 18 |
| Hale St. N&S | 24W-1S,24W-0S | 18 |
| Harrison Av. E&W | 25W-0N,23W-0N | 12 |
| Harwarden St. E&W | 23W-0S | 18 |
| Haverhill Dr. N&S | 24W-1S | 18 |
| Hawthorne Blvd. E&W | 24W-0N,23W-0N | 12 |
| Hazelton Av N&S | 26W-0S | 18 |
| Heatherbrook Ct. E&W | 24W-1S | 18 |
| Heathrow Ct. E&W | 23W-1S | 18 |
| Hemstock Av. N&S | 26W-1S | 18 |
| Heritage Lake Dr. E&W | 24W-2S,23W-2S | 18 |
| Hertford Ct. E&W | 23W-1S | 18 |
| Hickory Ln. E&W | 25W-0S | 18 |
| Hidden Ct. N&S | 25W-2S | 18 |
| Hill Av. E&W | 25W-0S | 18 |
| Hillside Ct. N&S | 24W-0S | 18 |
| Hiram Ct. N&S | 23W-3S | 18 |
| Hiram Dr. NE&SW | 23W-3S | 18 |
| Howard Ct. E&W | 24W-0N | 12 |
| Howard Ct. N&S | 24W-0N | 12 |
| Howard St. N&S | 24W-0S,24W-0N | 18 |
| Hull Dr. E&W | 23W-3S | 18 |
| Huntleigh Ct. N&S | 24W-1S | 18 |
| Huntleigh Dr. N&S | 24W-1S | 18 |
| Hurley Dr. E&W | 26W-1S,25W-1S | 18 |
| Hyatt Dr. N&S | 23W-3S | 18 |
| Illinois St. E&W | 25W-0S,23W-0S | 18 |
| Indiana St. E&W | 25W-0S,23W-0S | 18 |
| Irving Av. N&S | 24W-0S,24W-0N | 18 |
| Ivy Ct., E. E&W | 23W-3S | 18 |
| Ivy Ct., W. E&W | 23W-3S | 18 |
| James Ct. N&S | 25W-1S,24W-1S | 18 |
| Jasper Ct. E&W | 23W-3S | 18 |
| Jasper Dr. NE&SW | 23W-3S | 18 |
| Jefferson Av. E&W | 25W-0S,23W-0S | 18 |
| Jewell Rd. E&W | 25W-0N | 12 |
| Johnstown Ln. N&S | 24W-1S | 18 |
| Joyce Ct. N&S | 25W-2S | 18 |
| Kandahar Ct. E&W | 25W-2S | 18 |
| Karlskoga Av. E&W | 24W-0S | 18 |
| Kay Rd. E&W | 24W-0N | 12 |
| Kelle Ct. E&W | 23W-3S | 18 |
| Kellogg Pl. N&S | 23W-0S | 18 |
| Kenilworth Av. E&W | 24W-0S | 18 |
| Kensington Cir. N&S | 24W-2S | 18 |
| Kensington Cir. NS&EW | 24W-2S | 18 |
| Kent Ct. E&W | 23W-3S | 18 |
| Kentucky Ct. E&W | 23W-3S | 18 |
| Kilkenny Dr. N&S | 25W-1S | 18 |
| Kingston Dr. N&S | 23W-3S | 18 |
| Kingston St. N&S | 23W-0N | 12 |
| Kipling Ct. N&S | 23W-3S | 18 |
| Knoll St. N&S | 26W-0S | 18 |
| Knollwood Dr. N&S | 25W-0S | 18 |
| Kudu Ct. E&W | 26W-0S | 18 |
| LaPalma Ct. N&S | 24W-2S | 18 |
| Lakeside Dr. E&W | 24W-1S | 18 |
| Lancaster Ln. N&S | 23W-2S | 18 |
| Langford Ct. NW&SE | 23W-3S | 18 |
| Langford Ln. N&S | 23W-3S | 18 |
| Leabrook Ln. N&S | 26W-1S | 18 |
| Leafbrook Cove N&S | 26W-1S | 18 |
| Leask Ln. NW&SE | 23W-3S | 18 |
| Leeds Ct. N&S | 23W-3S | 18 |
| Leicester Ct. N&S | 23W-3S | 18 |
| Lewis Ln. E&W | 24W-0S | 18 |
| Lexington St. N&S | 24W-0N | 12 |
| Leystone Ln. NE&SW | 23W-1S | 18 |
| Liberty Dr. E&W | 25W-0S,25W-0S | 18 |
| Lincoln Av. N&S | 25W-0S,24W-0S | 18 |
| Liskeard Ct. E&W | 23W-1S | 18 |
| Lloyd Ct. N&S | 23W-3S | 18 |
| Lois Ln. E&W | 26W-1S | 18 |
| Lorraine St N&S | 23W-1S,23W-0S | 18 |
| Loughborough Ct. E&W | 23W-1S | 18 |
| Lowden Av. E&W | 24W-1S,24W-1S | 18 |
| Lowell Av. E&W | 23W-0S | 18 |
| Lyford Ln. N&S | 25W-1S | 18 |
| Lynwood Ln. E&W | 25W-1S | 18 |
| Lyon Av. N&S | 25W-0S | 18 |
| Madera Dr. NW&SE | 23W-2S | 18 |
| Madison Av. E&W | 25W-0S,24W-0S | 18 |
| Madsen Ct. E&W | 23W-0N | 12 |
| Main St. N&S | 24W-1S,24W-0N | 18 |
| Manchester Rd. E&W | 26W-0S,25W-0S | 18 |
| Maple Ln. E&W | 23W-0N | 12 |
| Mapleleaf Ct. E&W | 25W-0S | 18 |
| Maplewood Dr. E&W | 25W-2S | 18 |
| Marcey Av. N&S | 25W-1S | 18 |
| Martingale Rd. NE&SW | 24W-0N | 12 |
| Mayo Av. E&W | 25W-1S | 18 |
| Merrill Dr. E&W | 25W-1S | 18 |
| Michigan St. E&W | 24W-0S | 18 |
| Middleton Ct. N&S | 25W-2S | 18 |
| Middleton Dr. N&S | 25W-2S | 18 |
| Milton Ln. N&S | 25W-2S | 18 |
| Monticello Ct. N&S | 23W-2S | 18 |
| Morgan Av. N&S | 25W-0S | 18 |
| Morse St. N&S | 25W-0N | 12 |
| Mt. Vernon Ct. E&W | 23W-2S | 18 |
| Myrtlewood Ln. N&S | 25W-0S | 18 |
| Nachtman Ct. N&S | 25W-2S | 18 |
| Naperville Rd. N&S | 24W-2S,23W-2S | 18 |
| Nelson Cir. E&W | 24W-1S | 18 |
| Newberry Ln. N&S | 24W-1S | 18 |
| North Path Av. E&W | 24W-0S,23W-0S | 18 |
| Nottingham Ln. N&S | 23W-2S | 18 |
| Oak Av. E&W | 24W-0N | 12 |
| Oak Knolls St. N&S | 25W-0S | 18 |
| Oak View Dr. N&S | 25W-0N | 12 |
| Orchard Rd. N&S | 25W-2S | 18 |
| Orchard Rd. NW&SE | 25W-1S | 18 |
| Orth Ct. E&W | 26W-1S | 18 |
| Orth Dr. NW&SE | 26W-1S | 18 |
| Ott Av. N&S | 23W-0S | 18 |
| Oxford Ln. E&W | 23W-2S | 18 |
| Paddock Ct. NE&SW | 24W-0N | 12 |
| Paddock Ln. N&S | 24W-0N | 12 |
| Page St. N&S | 26W-0S | 18 |
| Papworth St. N&S | 26W-0S | 12 |
| Park Av. E&W | 25W-1S,24W-1S | 18 |
| Park Circle Dr. E&W | 24W-0N | 12 |
| Parkside Dr. N&S | 25W-0S | 18 |
| Parkway Dr. N&S | 25W-0N | 12 |
| Paula Av. N&S | 24W-1S | 18 |
| Pebblestone Cove N&S | 25W-1S | 18 |
| Pembroke Ln. NE&SW | | 18 |
| Pershing Av. E&W | 24W-1S,23W-1S | 18 |
| Pick Ct. N&S | 23W-0N | 18 |
| Pick St. N&S | 23W-0N | 18 |
| Pierce Av. N&S | 24W-1S | 18 |
| Pinto Ct. NW&SE | 24W-2S | 18 |
| Plamondon Ct. NW&SE | 25W-1S | 18 |
| Plamondon Rd. NE&SW | 25W-1S | 18 |
| Prairie Av. E&W | 25W-0N,23W-0N | 12 |
| President St. N&S | 24W-1S,24W-0N | 18 |
| Princeton Ct. N&S | 24W-1S | 18 |
| Prospect Ct. NE&SW | 23W-1S | 18 |
| Prospect St. N&S | 23W-1S,23W-0S | 18 |
| Purnell St. N&S | 25W-0N | 12 |
| Queenswood Ct. E&W | 24W-1S | 18 |
| Ralph Ct. E&W | 25W-0N | 12 |
| Ranch Rd. E&W | 24W-1S | 18 |
| Ravenhill N&S | 26W-1S | 18 |
| Reading Ct.* E&W | 23W-2S | 18 |
| Reber St. N&S | 24W-0S | 18 |
| Redwood Ct.* E&W | 26W-2S | 18 |
| Renn Ct. N&S | 26W-2S | 18 |
| Rhodes Ct.* NW&SE | 23W-2S | 18 |
| Richmond Dr. N&S | 23W-3S | 18 |
| Richton Dr. N&S | 25W-2S | 18 |
| Robinwood Ct. E&W | 24W-3S | 18 |
| Robinwood Ln. E&W | 24W-3S | 18 |
| Roosevelt Rd. E&W | 26W-0S,23W-0S | 18 |
| Royal Ct. E&W | 25W-0N | 12 |
| Ryson Ct. E&W | 23W-3S | 18 |
| Salford Ct. E&W | 23W-3S | 18 |
| Sandy Hook N&S | 26W-1S | 18 |
| Santa Rosa Av. N&S | 24W-0N | 12 |
| Scott St. N&S | 24W-0S,24W-0N | 18 |
| Scottdale Cir. NS&EW | 23W-3S | 18 |
| Scottdale Ct. NW&SE | 23W-3S | 18 |
| Sears Ln. E&W | 24W-0S | 18 |
| Seminary Av. N&S | 25W-0S,24W-0S | 18 |
| Shady Ln. E&W | 23W-0N | 12 |
| Shaffner Rd. N&S | 26W-2S,26W-1S | 18 |
| Shagbark Ln. N&S | 25W-0N | 12 |
| Sheffield Ln. N&S | 23W-2S | 18 |
| Sheldon Ct. N&S | 24W-1S | 18 |
| Shelley Ln. E&W | 24W-2S | 18 |
| Sherwin St. N&S | 25W-0S | 18 |
| Sherwood Pl. N&S | 25W-2S | 18 |
| Shetland Dr. E&W | 23W-3S | 18 |
| Shire Ct. E&W | 24W-2S | 18 |
| Shirley Ct. N&S | 26W-0S | 18 |
| Somerset Ln. NS&EW | 25W-2S | 18 |
| Southampton Ct.* N&S | 23W-2S | 18 |
| Spring Green Dr E&W | 26W-1S | 18 |
| St. Francis Ct. N&S | 26W-1S | 18 |
| Stallion Ct. NW&SE | 23W-3S | 18 |
| Stanley St. N&S | 26W-0S | 18 |
| Stevenson Pl. E&W | 24W-1S | 18 |
| Stirrup Ln. NS&EW | 23W-3S | 18 |
| Stoddard Av. N&S | 23W-0S,23W-0N | 18 |
| Stonebridge Cir. N&S | 26W-1S | 18 |
| Stonebridge Ct. NE&SW | 26W-2S | 18 |
| Stonebridge Tr. NW&SE | 26W-1S | 18 |
| Stonegate Ln. E&W | 26W-1S | 18 |
| Stonehill Ct. N&S | 26W-1S | 18 |
| Summit St. N&S | 23W-0S,23W-0N | 18 |
| Sumner St. N&S | 24W-1S,24W-0S | 18 |
| Sunderland Ct.* NW&SE | 23W-2S | 18 |
| Sunnybrook Ln. E&W | 26W-0S,25W-0S | 18 |
| Sunnyside St. N&S | 25W-0S | 18 |
| Sunset Rd. N&S | 25W-1S | 18 |
| Surrey Dr. N&S | 25W-1S | 18 |
| Surrey Rd. E&W | 24W-0N | 12 |
| Sussex Ln. E&W | 23W-2S | 18 |
| Taft Av. N&S | 23W-1S | 18 |
| Tall Oaks Ln. N&S | 25W-0N | 12 |
| Tennyson Dr. E&W | 24W-1S | 18 |
| Thomas Ln. E&W | 23W-0N | 12 |
| Thompson Dr. E&W | 24W-2S | 18 |
| Thornwood N&S | 26W-1S | 18 |
| Timber Ln. E&W | 26W-1S | 18 |
| Timber Tr. NS&EW | 25W-1S | 18 |
| Trent Ct. E&W | 23W-1S | 18 |
| Trowbridge Ct. NW&SE | 23W-2S | 18 |
| Turf Ln. E&W | 24W-0N | 12 |
| Underwood Ter. N&S | 24W-1S | 18 |
| Union Av. E&W | 25W-0S,24W-0S | 18 |
| University Pl. E&W | 24W-0S | 18 |
| Valley Forge Ct.* NE&SW | 23W-2S | 18 |
| Wadham Ct. E&W | 23W-1S | 18 |
| Wadham Pl. N&S | 23W-1S | 18 |
| Wadsworth Rd. NW&SE | 24W-1S | 18 |
| Wakeman Av. E&W | 24W-0N,23W-0N | 12 |
| Wakeman Ct. E&W | 23W-0N | 12 |
| Wales Dr. N&S | 24W-1S | 18 |
| Walnut Ct. NW&SE | 25W-1S | 18 |
| Warrenville Rd. N&S | 25W-1S | 18 |
| Warwick Ct. N&S | 23W-1S | 18 |
| Washington St. N&S | 24W-1S,24W-0N | 18 |
| Watertower Ct. N&S | 26W-1S | 18 |
| Webster Av. N&S | 24W-0S,24W-0N | 18 |
| Weisbrook Rd. NE&SW | 26W-2S,25W-1S | 18 |
| Wesley St. E&W | 25W-0S,24W-0S | 18 |
| West St. N&S | 25W-0S | 18 |
| Western Av. N&S | 25W-0S | 18 |
| Westhaven Dr. N&S | 25W-1S | 18 |
| Westminister St. N&S | 23W-3S | 18 |
| Westwood N&S | 25W-0S | 18 |
| Wexford Cir. NE&SW | 26W-1S | 18 |
| Wheaton Av. N&S | 24W-1S,24W-0N | 18 |
| Wheaton Oaks Ct. N&S | 25W-0N | 12 |
| Wheaton Oaks Dr. E&W | 25W-0N | 12 |
| Wheaton Pl. N&S | 24W-0N | 12 |
| Whitchurch Ct. E&W | 23W-1S | 18 |
| Whitman Ln. NW&SE | 24W-1S | 18 |
| Whitt Ct. N&S | 23W-2S | 18 |
| Whittier Ln. N&S | 24W-1S | 18 |

| | Grid | Page |
|---|---|---|
| Wigtown Ct. NW&SE | 23W-1S | 18 |
| Williams St. E&W | 26W-0S | 18 |
| Williamsburg Ct.* NE&SW | 23W-2S | 18 |
| Williston St. N&S | 23W-1S,23W-0S | 18 |
| Willow Av. E&W | 24W-0S,23W-0S | 18 |
| Willow Run E&W | 26W-1S | 18 |
| Wilmette St. N&S | 23W-0N | 12 |
| Wilshire Av. NE&SW | 23W-0S | 18 |
| Wilson Av. E&W | 23W-1S | 18 |
| Windsor Dr. E&W | 23W-2S | 18 |
| Wingate Ln. N&S | 26W-2S | 18 |
| Wood St. N&S | 23W-0S | 18 |
| Woodcutter Ln. E&W | 25W-1S | 18 |
| Woodhaven N&S | 26W-1S | 18 |
| Woodlawn St. N&S | 25W-0S,25W-0N | 18 |
| York Ln., E. E&W | 23W-0S | 18 |
| York Ln., W. E&W | 23W-0S | 18 |
| Yorkshire Woods Ct. N&S | 26W-1S | 18 |

## Willowbrook

| | Grid | Page |
|---|---|---|
| Adams St. N&S | 16W-8S,16W-7S | 33 |
| Americana Dr. N&S | 16W-7S | 27 |
| Appletree Ln. N&S | 17W-8S | 33 |
| Arlene Av. N&S | 16W-8S | 33 |
| Ascot Ln. E&W | 16W-6S | 27 |
| Birchwood Ct. N&S | 16W-8S | 33 |
| Blackberry Ln. N&S | 17W-8S | 33 |
| Briar Rd. N&S | 15W-7S | 27 |
| Brookbank Rd. N&S | 16W-8S | 33 |
| Brookside Ln. E&W | 16W-6S | 27 |
| Cambridge Rd. N&S | 15W-7S | 27 |
| Canterbury Ln. N&S | 16W-7S | 27 |
| Chatelaine Ct. E&W | 17W-6S | 27 |
| Chaucer Ct. E&W | 15W-7S | 27 |
| Chaucer Rd. N&S | 15W-7S | 27 |
| Cherry Tree Ln. N&S | 17W-8S | 33 |
| Cherrywood Ln. E&W | 16W-8S | 33 |
| Clarendon Hills Rd. N&S | 16W-7S,16W-6S | 27 |
| Clubside Dr. E&W | 16W-7S | 27 |
| Cottonwood Ct. E&W | 16W-8S | 33 |
| Cramer Ct. E&W | 16W-7S | 27 |
| Eagles Nest Dr. E&W | 17W-7S | 27 |
| Easy St. E&W | 17W-7S | 27 |
| Eleanor Pl. N&S | 16W-8S | 33 |
| Essex Ct. N&S | 16W-6S | 27 |
| Executive Dr. E&W | 16W-8S | 33 |
| Falcon Ct. N&S | 17W-7S | 27 |
| Garfield Ridge NS&EW | 15W-7S | 27 |
| Gooseneck Ct. N&S | 17W-7S | 27 |
| Hawk Ct. N&S | 17W-7S | 27 |
| Hawthorn Ln. E&W | 17W-8S | 33 |
| Hidden Brook Ln. E&W | 15W-6S | 27 |
| Highridge Rd. NW&SE | 16W-7S | 27 |
| Hill Rd. E&W | 15W-7S | 27 |
| Honey Locust Ln. E&W | 17W-8S | 33 |
| Joliet Rd. NE&SW | 16W-8S | 33 |
| Kane Ct. N&S | 16W-7S | 27 |
| Kent Ct. E&W | 16W-7S | 27 |
| Kingswood Ct. NE&SW | 15W-7S | 27 |
| Kingswood Rd. NW&SE | 15W-7S | 27 |
| Knoll Lane Ct. N&S | 16W-6S | 27 |
| Knoll Valley Dr. N&S | 16W-6S | 27 |
| Knollwick Rd. N&S | 16W-6S | 27 |
| Knollwood Dr. N&S | 16W-6S | 27 |
| Knollwood Rd. E&W | 16W-6S | 27 |
| Kyle Ct. E&W | 16W-7S | 27 |
| Lake Hinsdale Dr. E&W | 16W-7S | 27 |
| Lake Park Ln. N&S | 16W-7S,16W-6S | 27 |
| Lake Shore Dr. NE&SW | 16W-7S | 27 |
| Lakeview Ct. N&S | 16W-7S | 27 |
| Lane Ct. NW&SE | 16W-7S | 27 |
| Laurel Ln. N&S | 16W-6S | 27 |
| Lincoln Oaks Dr. E&W | 17W-6S | 27 |
| Mac Arthur Dr. NS&EW | 16W-6S | 27 |
| Madison St. N&S | 16W-8S,16W-7S | 33 |
| Maplewood Ct. E&W | 16W-8S | 33 |
| Martin Ct. NE&SW | 16W-7S | 27 |
| Meadow Ln. N&S | 15W-6S | 27 |
| Midway Dr. E&W | 16W-8S | 33 |
| N. Court Dr. NE&SW | 16W-7S | 27 |
| Oxford Rd. N&S | 15W-7S | 27 |
| Pine Tree Ln. E&W | 17W-8S | 33 |
| Pinewood Ct. N&S | 16W-6S | 27 |
| Plainfield Rd. NE&SW | 16W-7S | 27 |
| Plaza Ct. N&S | 16W-8S | 33 |
| Port Wine Rd. N&S | 16W-7S | 27 |
| Quail Run Ct. N&S | 17W-7S | 27 |
| Quincy St. N&S | 16W-8S,16W-7S | 33 |
| Raleigh Rd. N&S | 15W-7S | 27 |
| Ridgemoor Ct. NW&SE | 15W-7S | 27 |
| Ridgemoor Dr. E&W | 16W-7S,15W-7S | 27 |
| Rogers Ct. E&W | 15W-7S | 27 |
| Rogers Dr. N&S | 15W-7S | 27 |
| Rogers Farm Rd. E&W | 15W-7S | 27 |
| Sheffield Ln. N&S | 15W-7S | 27 |
| Sheridan Dr. NW&SE | 17W-8S | 33 |
| Somerset Rd. NE&SW | 15W-7S | 27 |
| Squire Ln. N&S | 17W-6S | 27 |
| Stanhope Dr. E&W | 16W-6S | 27 |
| Stewart Dr. NW&SE | 16W-6S | 27 |
| Stirling Ln. E&W | 16W-6S | 27 |
| Stonegate Ct. NE&SW | 15W-7S | 27 |
| Stough St. N&S | 16W-7S | 27 |
| Stratford Ln. E&W | 15W-7S | 27 |
| Sugar Bush Ln. NE&SW | 17W-8S | 33 |
| Sunset Ridge Rd. E&W | 15W-7S | 27 |
| Tanglewood Ln. E&W | 16W-8S | 33 |
| Virginia Ct. N&S | 16W-8S | 33 |
| Waterford Dr. E&W | 15W-7S | 27 |
| Wedgewood Ct. NE&SW | 15W-7S | 27 |
| Wedgewood Ln. NW&SE | 15W-7S | 27 |
| Willow Ln. E&W | 16W-7S | 27 |
| Willoway Ln. N&S | 16W-8S | 33 |
| Windsor Ln. E&W | 16W-6S | 27 |
| Windward Cir. NS&EW | 16W-7S | 27 |
| Wingate Rd. N&S | 15W-7S | 27 |
| Woodgate Ct. NS&EW | 15W-7S | 27 |
| 67th Pl. E&W | 16W-7S | 27 |
| 67th St. E&W | 16W-7S | 27 |
| 68th Pl. E&W | 16W-7S | 27 |
| 68th St. E&W | 16W-7S | 27 |
| 69th St. E&W | 16W-7S | 27 |
| 72nd Ct. E&W | 16W-8S | 33 |
| 73rd Ct. E&W | 16W-8S | 33 |

## Winfield

| | Grid | Page |
|---|---|---|
| Alta Ln. E&W | 27W-0N | 11 |
| Ambleside Dr. E&W | 27W-0N | 11 |
| Arbor Ct. N&S | 26W-0N | 12 |
| Aspen Ct. NE&SW | 27W-0N | 11 |
| Bardmore Ln. NS&EW | 26W-1N | 12 |
| Barnes Av. NE&SW | 27W-0N,26W-0N | 11 |
| Barnes Ct. NE&SW | 26W-0N | 12 |
| Beecher Av. E&W | 27W-0S | 17 |
| Birch St. E&W | 27W-0N | 11 |
| Birkdale Ct. NE&SW | 26W-1N | 12 |
| Blair St. E&W | 27W-0N,26W-0N | 11 |
| Bob-O-Link Dr. NW&SE | 26W-1N | 12 |
| Bolles Av. E&W | 27W-0N | 11 |
| Bradley Dr. N&S | 27W-0S | 17 |
| Brandon Blvd. N&S | 27W-0N | 11 |
| Brookside Dr. E&W | 27W-0S | 17 |
| Calvin Ct. N&S | 26W-0N | 12 |
| Carrel St. E&W | 27W-0N | 11 |
| Chantilly Ct. E&W | 26W-1N | 12 |
| Chartwell Dr. E&W | 27W-0N | 11 |
| Chelsea Cir. E&W | 27W-0N | 11 |
| Chestnut Ln. E&W | 27W-1N | 11 |
| Childs St. E&W | 27W-0S | 17 |
| Church St. N&S | 27W-0S | 17 |
| Churchill Rd. E&W | 27W-0N,26W-0N | 11 |
| Cleveland St. N&S | 27W-0S | 17 |
| Cloos Ct. N&S | 27W-0N | 11 |
| Concord Ln. N&S | 27W-0N | 11 |
| Conniston Ct. N&S | 27W-0N | 11 |
| Cooley Av. E&W | 27W-0S | 17 |
| County Farm Rd. NW&SE | 27W-0N,27W-1N | 11 |
| Courtney NW&SE | 27W-0N | 11 |
| Cypress Ln. NE&SW | 27W-1N | 11 |
| East St. N&S | 27W-0S | 17 |
| Emerson Ct. N&S | 27W-1S | 17 |
| Ennerdale Ln. N&S | 27W-0N | 11 |
| Essex Ln. E&W | 27W-0N | 11 |
| Ethel St. N&S | 27W-0S,27W-0N | 17 |
| Evelyn Av. E&W | 27W-0S | 17 |
| Fisher Ln. E&W | 27W-0S | 17 |
| Fleming Rd. E&W | 27W-0N | 11 |
| Florida Ln. N&S | 27W-0S | 17 |
| Forest St. N&S | 27W-0S | 17 |
| Garfield St. N&S | 27W-0S | 17 |
| Glen Eagles Dr. E&W | 26W-1N | 12 |
| Grant St. N&S | 27W-0S | 17 |
| Grasnere Dr. E&W | 27W-0N | 11 |
| Heather Ln. E&W | 27W-0N | 11 |
| Highlake Rd. E&W | 27W-0S | 11 |
| Interlachen Ln. E&W | 26W-1N | 12 |
| Jacob Dr. N&S | 27W-0N | 11 |
| Jefferson Ct. N&S | 27W-1S,27W-0S | 17 |
| Jefferson St. N&S | 27W-0S,27W-0N | 17 |
| Jewell Rd. NE&SW | 27W-0S | 11 |
| Kimball Ct. N&S | 27W-0N | 11 |
| Knoll Ct. NE&SW | 26W-0N | 12 |
| Kytham Ct. E&W | 26W-1N | 12 |
| Lancaster Dr. NS&EW | 27W-0N | 11 |
| Leonard St. N&S | 26W-0N | 12 |
| Liberty St. E&W | 27W-0S | 17 |
| Lincoln Av. E&W | 27W-0S | 17 |
| Lindsey Av. E&W | 27W-0N,26W-0N | 11 |
| Lytham Ct. N&S | 26W-1N | 12 |
| Madison St. N&S | 27W-0S | 17 |
| Manchester Rd. E&W | 27W-0S | 17 |
| Maple St. E&W | 27W-0N | 11 |
| Melrose Ln. E&W | 27W-1N | 11 |
| Myrtle St. N&S | 27W-0S | 17 |
| Nickolsen Av. E&W | 27W-0S | 17 |
| Oak Ct. E&W | 27W-0S | 17 |
| Oak Ln. N&S | 27W-0S | 17 |
| Oakwood St. E&W | 27W-0N | 11 |
| Park St. N&S | 27W-0S | 17 |
| Peter Rd. N&S | 26W-0N | 12 |
| Pleasant Hill Rd. N&S | 26W-1N | 12 |
| Prairie Path Ln. N&S | 27W-1N | 11 |
| Prescott Dr. NS&EW | 26W-0N | 12 |
| Prestwick Ln. E&W | 26W-1N | 12 |
| Providence Ln. E&W | 27W-0N | 11 |
| Redford Ln. N&S | 27W-0N,27W-1N | 11 |
| River Ln. NE&SW | 27W-0S | 17 |
| Robbins St. N&S | 27W-0S,27W-0N | 17 |
| Scott Dr. NE&SW | 27W-0N | 11 |
| Shady Way NW&SE | 27W-0S | 17 |
| Shires Ct. N&S | 27W-0N | 11 |
| Siefert Ct. N&S | 26W-1N | 12 |
| St. John Av. E&W | 27W-0N,26W-0N | 11 |
| Summit Dr. N&S | 27W-0S | 17 |
| Sunnyside Av. E&W | 27W-0S | 17 |
| Suzanne Dr. N&S | 27W-0N | 11 |
| Sycamore Ln. E&W | 27W-1N | 11 |
| Tamarack Ct. NW&SE | 27W-1N | 11 |
| Tamarack Dr. NS&EW | 27W-1N | 11 |
| Thorngate Ln. N&S | 26W-1N | 12 |
| Timber Ct. NE&SW | 27W-1N | 11 |
| Timber Ridge Dr. N&S | 27W-1N | 11 |
| Troon Ct. E&W | 26W-1N | 12 |
| Turnberry Pinehurst Dr. E&W | 26W-1N | 12 |
| Turnberry Pinhurst Ln. N&S | 26W-1N | 12 |
| Victoria Ln. NS&EW | 27W-0N | 11 |
| Virginia St. E&W | 27W-0N | 11 |
| Walnut Dr. E&W | 27W-1N | 11 |
| Washington Av. E&W | 27W-0S | 17 |
| Waterford Dr. E&W | 27W-0N | 11 |
| Wentworth Ct. N&S | 26W-1N | 12 |
| Williams St. E&W | 27W-0S | 17 |
| Windemere Rd. NE&SW | 27W-0N | 11 |
| Winfield Rd. N&S | 27W-0S,27W-0N | 17 |
| Woodhall Ct. N&S | 26W-1N | 12 |
| Woodvale Ct. N&S | 27W-0N,26W-0N | 11 |
| Wynwood Rd. N&S | 28W-0S | 17 |

## Winfield Township

| | Grid | Page |
|---|---|---|
| Acorn Av. NE&SW | 29W-0N | 11 |
| Acorn Ct. N&S | 27W-1S | 17 |
| Acorn Ln. E&W | 27W-1S | 17 |
| Alena Dr. E&W | 28W-1N | 11 |
| Alsace Ct. N&S | 28W-1S | 17 |
| Anderson Dr. E&W | 32W-3S | 16 |
| Ardennes Ct. E&W | 28W-1S | 17 |
| Barnes Av. E&W | 30W-0N,28W-0N | 10 |
| Batavia Rd. NW&SE | 32W-1S,30W-2S | 16 |
| Bauman Ct. NW&SE | 29W-0S | 16 |
| Belleau Dr., N. N&S | 28W-1S | 17 |
| Bender Ln. N&S | 29W-1S | 16 |
| Berkshire Rd. E&W | 28W-1N | 11 |
| Blackhawk Blvd. N&S | 30W-2S,30W-1S | 16 |
| Bolles Av. E&W | 29W-0N,28W-0N | 11 |
| Branch Av. E&W | 27W-2S | 17 |
| Briar Ln. N&S | 29W-0N | 11 |
| Broadview Av. N&S | 29W-0N | 11 |
| Brown St. E&W | 29W-0N | 11 |
| Burr Oak Rd. N&S | 28W-1N | 11 |
| Butterfield Rd. E&W | 32W-3S,27W-2S | 16 |
| Butternut Ln. E&W | 32W-3S | 16 |
| Calvin Av. N&S | 28W-0N | 11 |
| Cantigny Dr., S. N&S | 28W-1S | 17 |
| Center Av. N&S | 27W-2N,27W-1N | 11 |
| Che Che Pinqua St. E&W | 30W-1S | 16 |
| Childs St. E&W | 29W-0S,28W-0S | 16 |
| Circle Dr. N&S | 30W-0S | 16 |
| Colford Av. NW&SE | 29W-0N | 11 |
| Connolly Ct. E&W | 29W-2S | 16 |
| Coolidge Av. N&S | 29W-0N,29W-1N | 11 |
| County Farm Rd. N&S | 27W-1N | 11 |
| Cove Ln. E&W | 27W-3S | 17 |
| Domartin Pl. NE&SW | 28W-1S | 17 |
| Donald Av. E&W | 29W-0N,28W-0N | 11 |
| Doris Ln. N&S | 29W-0N | 11 |
| DuPage St. E&W | 28W-0N | 11 |
| Easton Av. N&S | 29W-0N | 11 |
| Edgewood Walk N&S | 29W-1S | 16 |
| Elm Dr. E&W | 28W-1N,27W-1N | 11 |
| Elmwood St. E&W | 32W-1N | 10 |
| Eola Rd. N&S | 31W-3S,31W-1S | 16 |
| Essex Rd. N&S | 27W-2S | 17 |
| Ethel St. N&S | 27W-1N | 11 |
| Fabyan Pkwy. E&W | 32W-0N | 10 |
| Forest Av. E&W | 29W-0N,28W-0N | 11 |
| Gary's Mill Rd. E&W | 29W-0S,28W-0S | 16 |
| Geneva Rd. E&W | 29W-1N,27W-1N | 11 |
| Gloria Av. N&S | 27W-1N | 11 |
| Guiness Dr. N&S | 30W-0S | 16 |
| Hathaway Av. N&S | 28W-0N | 11 |
| Helen Av. E&W | 29W-1N | 11 |
| Herrick Rd. N&S | 27W-3S | 17 |
| Hickory Ln. E&W | 29W-1N,27W-1N | 11 |
| High Lake Av. N&S | 28W-0N,28W-1N | 11 |
| High Lake Rd. NW&SE | 28W-0N | 11 |
| Hillcrest Rd. N&S | 28W-1N | 11 |
| Hillview Av. E&W | 28W-0N | 11 |
| Home Av. N&S | 29W-3S | 16 |
| Hoy Rd. E&W | 28W-2S,27W-2S | 17 |
| Indian Knoll Rd. N&S | 28W-1S,28W-1N | 17 |
| Indian Knoll Tr. E&W | 28W-0N | 11 |
| Ingalton Av. NW&SE | 29W-1N,29W-2N | 11 |
| Cir. | 32W-3S | 16 |
| James Av. E&W | 29W-1N,27W-1N | 11 |
| Joliet St. N&S | 30W-0S | 16 |
| Joy Rd. E&W | 30W-0S | 16 |
| Kaelin Rd. N&S | 30W-1S,30W-0S | 16 |
| Kautz Rd. N&S | 32W-1N | 10 |
| Kress Rd. N&S | 32W-1N | 10 |
| Lake Dr. N&S | 28W-0N | 11 |
| Lane Rd. NW&SE | 30W-1N | 10 |
| Lavergne Ln. N&S | 28W-1S | 17 |
| Lee Rd. E&W | 31W-1N,29W-1N | 10 |
| Lenox Rd. E&W | 27W-2S | 17 |
| Lester St. E&W | 30W-0N,28W-0N | 10 |
| Liberty St. E&W | 28W-0S | 17 |
| Lorraine Dr. E&W | 28W-1S | 17 |
| Lost Meadows Ln. N&S | 29W-2S | 16 |
| Lowden Av. E&W | 27W-1S | 17 |
| Mack Rd. E&W | 29W-1S,27W-1S | 16 |
| Macqueen Dr. N&S | 31W-1N | 10 |
| Madison St. N&S | 27W-2S | 17 |
| Main St. E&W | 28W-0N | 11 |
| Marion Rd. E&W | 28W-0S | 17 |
| May St. E&W | 30W-0S | 16 |
| McChesney Rd. N&S | 32W-0S | 16 |
| McDonald Av. N&S | 29W-0N | 11 |
| Melolane Dr. N&S | 30W-0S | 16 |
| Morningside Av. N&S | 28W-0S,28W-0N | 17 |
| Morris Ct. E&W | 29W-2S | 16 |
| N. Flanders Ln. E&W | 28W-1S | 17 |
| National Rd. E&W | 28W-1N | 11 |
| National St. E&W | 29W-1N,27W-1N | 11 |
| Neuqua St. E&W | 30W-1S | 16 |
| Northwood Dr. N&S | 27W-1N | 11 |
| Oak Grove Av. E&W | 29W-1N | 11 |
| Oak Ln. E&W | 29W-2S | 16 |
| Old Farm Ln. E&W | 29W-2S | 16 |
| Cir. | 32W-3S | 16 |
| Pamela Ct. N&S | 28W-1S | 17 |
| Pearl Rd. N&S | 30W-0S | 16 |
| Phillips Farm Rd. N&S | 32W-1S | 16 |
| Picardy Ct. NW&SE | 28W-1S | 17 |
| Pilsen Rd. N&S | 30W-1N | 10 |
| Pine Av. E&W | 29W-1N | 11 |
| Pomeroy St. E&W | 30W-0N,29W-0N | 10 |
| Potawatomi Blvd. NE&SW | 30W-1S | 16 |
| Prairie Av. E&W | 29W-3S | 16 |
| Prince Crossing Rd. N&S | 29W-0S,29W-1N | 16 |
| Purnell Rd. NW&SE | 28W-1S | 17 |
| Ray Av. E&W | 30W-1N,29W-1N | 10 |
| Rd. A NE&SW | 32W-1S,31W-0S | 16 |
| Rd. B NW&SE | 32W-1S | 16 |
| Rd. C NE&SW | 32W-1S | 16 |
| Rd. D NE&SW | 32W-1S,31W-1S | 16 |
| Rd. L NW&SE | 32W-1S | 16 |
| Renouf Dr. E&W | 29W-2S | 16 |
| Ridgeland Av. N&S | 29W-0N,29W-1N | 11 |
| River Glen Rd. NE&SW | 29W-0S | 16 |
| Robin Ln. E&W | 28W-1N,27W-1N | 11 |
| Rogers Ct. N&S | 28W-0N | 11 |
| Roosevelt Rd. NW&SE | 32W-0N,28W-0S | 10 |
| Sarana Av. N&S | 29W-0N | 11 |
| Sauk Blvd. N&S | 30W-1S | 16 |
| Shabbona St. NE&SW | 30W-1S | 16 |
| Shaffner Rd. N&S | 27W-2S,27W-1S | 17 |
| Sherman St. N&S | 30W-0N | 10 |
| South Cantigny Dr. N&S | 28W-1S | 17 |
| St. Mihel Dr. N&S | 28W-1S | 17 |
| Sunset Av. N&S | 28W-0N | 11 |
| Swan Lake Ct. NE&SW | 27W-1S | 17 |
| Swan Lake Dr. N&S | 27W-1S | 17 |
| Twin Oaks Dr. N&S | 27W-2S | 17 |
| Verdun Dr. NS&EW | 28W-1S | 17 |
| Wallace Rd. E&W | 27W-2S | 17 |
| Waltz Dr. E&W | 27W-1S | 17 |
| Warrenville Av. NE&SW | 27W-2S | 17 |
| Washington Av. E&W | 28W-0S | 17 |
| West Belleau Dr. E&W | 28W-1S | 17 |
| West Cantigny Dr. E&W | 28W-1S | 17 |
| White Oak Dr. N&S | 28W-1S | 17 |
| Williams Rd. N&S | 29W-1N | 11 |
| Willoughby Ln. N&S | 32W-3S | 16 |
| Wilson Rd. E&W | 32W-1S,31W-0S | 16 |
| Wilson St. E&W | 30W-0S,29W-0S | 16 |
| Winfield Rd. N&S | 28W-2S,27W-1S | 17 |
| Winnebago St. E&W | 30W-1S | 16 |
| Woodland Av. E&W | 29W-1N | 11 |
| Wynwood Rd. N&S | 28W-0S | 17 |
| Yvonne Ln. N&S | 27W-2S | 17 |

## Wood Dale

| | Grid | Page |
|---|---|---|
| A.E.C. Dr. N&S | 18W-7N | 8 |
| Abbotsford Rd. E&W | 18W-5N | 8 |
| Ace Dr. N&S | 18W-6N | 8 |
| Addison Rd. N&S | 18W-4N,18W-6N | 8 |
| Apollo Ct. N&S | 19W-5N | 8 |
| Arlene Dr. E&W | 19W-5N | 8 |
| Ash Av. N&S | 17W-5N,17W-6N | 9 |
| Aspen Rd. E&W | 17W-4N | 9 |
| Balm Ct. E&W | 17W-6N | 9 |
| Bauman Ct. E&W | 18W-7N | 8 |
| Beinoris Dr. E&W | 17W-6N | 9 |
| Brookhurst Ln. N&S | 17W-5N | 9 |
| Brookwood Dr. N&S | 18W-5N | 8 |
| Brookwood Pl. N&S | 18W-5N | 8 |
| Butternut Av. E&W | 17W-4N | 9 |
| Butternut Dr. N&S | 17W-4N | 9 |
| Carter Av. E&W | 18W-5N | 8 |
| Carter Dr. E&W | 18W-5N | 8 |
| Catalpa Av. N&S | 17W-5N,17W-6N | 9 |
| Catherine Ct. NW&SE | 18W-5N | 8 |
| Cedar Av. N&S | 17W-5N,17W-6N | 9 |
| Cedar St. N&S | 17W-5N | 9 |
| Center St. E&W | 18W-6N | 8 |
| Central Av. N&S | 17W-5N,17W-7N | 9 |
| Central Ct. NS&EW | 17W-4N | 9 |
| Century Dr. N&S | 18W-5N | 8 |
| Charmille Ln. E&W | 18W-5N | 8 |
| Clare Ct. NS&EW | 18W-5N | 8 |
| Clayton Ct. NE&SW | 18W-6N | 8 |

| Street | Grid | Page |
|---|---|---|
| Commercial St. E&W | 18W-6N,17W-6N | 8 |
| Crestwood Ct. E&W | 17W-4N | 9 |
| Crestwood Rd. E&W | 17W-4N | 9 |
| Cypress Ct. NW&SE | 17W-5N | 9 |
| Dalewood Av. N&S | 18W-5N,18W-6N | 8 |
| Deerpath Rd. E&W | 17W-5N | 9 |
| Division St. E&W | 18W-5N,17W-5N | 8 |
| Dominion Ct. E&W | 18W-5N | 8 |
| Dominion Dr. N&S | 18W-4N,18W-5N | 8 |
| Duck Ln. E&W | 18W-5N | 8 |
| Dunlay Ct. E&W | 17W-5N | 9 |
| Dunlay St. E&W | 17W-5N | 9 |
| East Pond Dr. N&S | 18W-6N | 8 |
| Edgebrook Rd. N&S | 18W-5N | 8 |
| Edgewood Av. N&S | 17W-4N,17W-7N | 9 |
| Elizabeth Ct. E&W | 17W-5N | 9 |
| Elizabeth Dr. E&W | 18W-5N | 8 |
| Elmhurst St. E&W | 17W-6N | 9 |
| Elmwood Av. N&S | 17W-5N,17W-6N | 9 |
| Essex Ct. NE&SW | 18W-5N | 8 |
| Ethel Ln. E&W | 17W-4N | 9 |
| Fishing Ln. N&S | 18W-5N | 8 |
| Forest Glen Rd. E&W | 18W-6N | 8 |
| Forest Preserve Dr. E&W | 19W-5N,18W-5N | 8 |
| Forest View Av. N&S | 18W-5N | 8 |
| Frederick Pl. N&S | 18W-5N | 8 |
| Front St. NW&SE | 17W-5N | 9 |
| Gay St. N&S | 18W-5N | 8 |
| Geanne Ct. E&W | 18W-5N | 8 |
| George St. E&W | 18W-6N | 8 |
| Gerry Dr. E&W | 18W-7N | 8 |
| Gilbert Dr. E&W | 19W-5N,18W-5N | 8 |
| Green Ct. N&S | 18W-5N | 8 |
| Grove Av. N&S | 18W-6N | 8 |
| Hackberry Ct. E&W | 17W-4N | 9 |
| Hansen Ct. NE&SW | 18W-7N | 8 |
| Harvey Av. N&S | 18W-5N | 8 |
| Haynes Dr. E&W | 17W-6N | 9 |
| Hemlock Av. N&S | 17W-5N,17W-6N | 9 |
| Heritage Dr. E&W | 18W-5N | 8 |
| Hiawatha Tr. E&W | 17W-5N | 9 |
| Homestead St. E&W | 18W-5N | 8 |
| Hoover Dr. N&S | 18W-5N | 8 |
| Irmen Dr. E&W | 19W-5N | 8 |
| Iroquois Tr. N&S | 17W-5N | 9 |
| Irving Park Rd. E&W | 18W-6N,17W-5N | 8 |
| Jason Ln. E&W | 18W-5N | 8 |
| Jefferson Ln. N&S | 18W-5N | 8 |
| Jennifer Ct. E&W | 18W-5N | 8 |
| Julian Dr. N&S | 18W-5N | 8 |
| Juniper Dr. E&W | 17W-5N | 9 |
| Knollwood Ct. E&W | 17W-5N | 9 |
| Knollwood Dr. E&W | 17W-5N | 9 |
| Lafayette St. N&S | 18W-5N | 8 |
| Lilac Ln. N&S | 17W-5N | 9 |
| Lincoln Ct. N&S | 19W-5N | 8 |
| Lively Blvd. N&S | 17W-7N | 9 |
| Manning Dr. E&W | 18W-5N | 8 |
| Maple Av. N&S | 17W-5N,17W-6N | 9 |
| Mark St. E&W | 18W-7N,17W-7N | 8 |
| Mary Jane Ln. E&W | 19W-5N | 8 |
| Michael Dr. N&S | 18W-7N | 8 |
| Miller Ln. N&S | 18W-5N | 8 |
| Mittel Blvd. N&S | 18W-7N | 8 |
| Mittel Dr. E&W | 18W-6N | 8 |
| Mittel Rd. N&S | 18W-6N,18W-7N | 8 |
| Monroe Pl. E&W | 18W-5N | 8 |
| Mont Clare Ln. N&S | 17W-5N | 9 |
| Montrose Av. E&W | 19W-5N,17W-5N | 8 |
| Mulberry Ln. NE&SW | 17W-5N | 9 |
| Murray Dr. E&W | 17W-5N | 9 |
| Murray Ln. E&W | 17W-5N | 9 |
| North St. E&W | 17W-6N | 9 |
| Oak Av. N&S | 17W-5N,17W-6N | 9 |
| Oakwood Dr. N&S | 18W-5N | 8 |
| Orchard Dr. E&W | 18W-6N | 8 |
| Paramount Dr. N&S | 18W-5N | 8 |
| Park Ln. E&W | 18W-5N | 8 |
| Pine Av. N&S | 17W-5N,17W-6N | 9 |
| Pine Tree Ln. N&S | 17W-5N | 9 |
| Poplar Av. N&S | 17W-6N | 9 |
| Potter St. E&W | 19W-5N,17W-5N | 8 |
| Prospect Av. N&S | 18W-5N | 8 |
| Raleigh Ct. N&S | 18W-5N | 8 |
| Richert Rd. E&W | 17W-6N | 9 |
| River Av. N&S | 18W-6N | 8 |
| Robert Kingery Hwy. N&S | 17W-4N,17W-7N | 9 |
| Roberts Ln. NW&SE | 17W-4N | 9 |
| Robin Ln. N&S | 19W-5N | 8 |

| Street | Grid | Page |
|---|---|---|
| Roosevelt Av. E&W | 17W-5N | 9 |
| Roy Dr. E&W | 19W-5N | 8 |
| Royal Oaks Dr. E&W | 17W-5N | 9 |
| Royal St. N&S | 17W-4N | 9 |
| S. Hiawatha Tr. E&W | 17W-5N | 9 |
| Sarah Ct. E&W | 18W-5N | 8 |
| Sarah Dr. E&W | 19W-5N | 8 |
| School E&W | 18W-6N | 8 |
| Sherwood Dr. NE&SW | 17W-5N | 9 |
| Sivert Ct. N&S | 16W-6N | 9 |
| Sivert Dr. N&S | 17W-7N | 9 |
| Spring Oaks Dr. E&W | 17W-5N | 9 |
| St. Andrews Dr. N&S | 18W-4N,18W-5N | 8 |
| Station Dr. N&S | 18W-5N,18W-6N | 8 |
| Stoneham St. E&W | 17W-6N | 9 |
| Sunnyside Av. E&W | 17W-5N | 9 |
| Sunset Dr. E&W | 18W-5N | 8 |
| Thorndale Av. E&W | 18W-7N,17W-7N | 8 |
| Tioga Tr. E&W | 17W-5N | 9 |
| Victoria Dr. E&W | 18W-5N | 8 |
| Victoria Ln. E&W | 19W-5N | 8 |
| Victoria Pl. E&W | 18W-7N | 8 |
| Walnut Av. N&S | 17W-5N,17W-6N | 9 |
| Warren Ct. E&W | 18W-5N | 8 |
| Warrenallen Dr. E&W | 17W-7N | 9 |
| Washington Sq. E&W | 18W-5N | 8 |
| Welter Dr. N&S | 19W-5N | 8 |
| Westeria Ct. NW&SE | 17W-5N | 9 |
| Wheat Ln. N&S | 18W-6N | 8 |
| Windsor Av. E&W | 17W-5N | 9 |
| Woodbine Ct. NE&SW | 17W-4N | 9 |
| Woodbine Dr. E&W | 17W-4N | 9 |
| Wooddale Rd. N&S | 18W-7N,17W-5N | 8 |
| Woodside Dr. NE&SW | 17W-4N | 9 |


## Woodridge*

**(Also see Will County)**


| Street | Grid | Page |
|---|---|---|
| Adbeth Av. N&S | 21W-9S | 31 |
| Allan Dr. NW&SE | 22W-6S | 25 |
| Anchor Dr. N&S | 21W-9S | 31 |
| Andover Ct. E&W | 21W-7S | 25 |
| Andrea Ct. E&W | 22W-9S | 31 |
| Andrea Ln. N&S | 22W-9S | 31 |
| Apache Ln. NW&SE | 21W-9S | 31 |
| Apple Ln. E&W | 21W-8S | 31 |
| Armour Ct. E&W | 23W-7S | 25 |
| Armstrong Ct. NE&SW | 22W-7S | 25 |
| Arnold Dr. N&S | 22W-7S | 25 |
| Audubon Av. N&S | 21W-7S | 25 |
| Autumn Dr. NS&EW | 22W-9S | 31 |
| Baron St. N&S | 20W-10S | 32 |
| Barrington Ct.* N&S | 21W-8S | 31 |
| Beller Rd. NS&EW | 20W-9S | 32 |
| Bern Ct. N&S | 21W-9S | 31 |
| Birchwood Pkwy. E&W | 21W-9S | 31 |
| Bittersweet Ct.* E&W | 21W-8S | 31 |
| Blue Flag Av. N&S | 22W-7S | 25 |
| Bobby Jones Ln. N&S | 23W-7S | 25 |
| Bonnie Ct. N&S | 21W-8S | 31 |
| Bradley Dr. N&S | 22W-7S | 25 |
| Bramblebush Ct. E&W | 21W-7S | 25 |
| Brassie Ct. E&W | 23W-7S | 25 |
| Brentwood Ct. E&W | 22W-9S | 31 |
| Brewer Ln. E&W | 21W-9S | 31 |
| Briarwood Ct. E&W | 21W-9S | 31 |
| Brighton Ct.* NE&SW | 21W-8S | 31 |
| Bristol Ct. N&S | 20W-8S | 32 |
| Britten St. E&W | 20W-9S | 32 |
| Brook Ct. N&S | 21W-7S | 25 |
| Brunswick Cir. E&W | 21W-7S | 25 |
| Buckingham Cir. NS&EW | 21W-7S | 25 |
| Burke Ct. NE&SW | 22W-7S | 25 |
| Burr Ridge Ct. N&S | 21W-9S | 31 |
| Butternut Ct. NE&SW | 22W-8S | 31 |
| Cambridge N&S | 20W-8S | 32 |
| Cambridge Dr. E&W | 21W-7S | 25 |
| Canterbury Ln. N&S | 21W-9S | 31 |
| Cardinal Ct. N&S | 21W-7S | 25 |
| Carlton Dr. NE&SW | 21W-8S,21W-7S | 31 |
| Carolwood Ln. N&S | 22W-9S | 31 |
| Carpenter Ct. N&S | 22W-7S | 25 |
| Catalpa Av. NW&SE | 21W-8S | 31 |
| Catalpa Ct. NW&SE | 21W-8S | 31 |
| Charmingfare Dr. E&W | 21W-8S | 31 |
| Chelsea Dr. N&S | 21W-9S | 31 |
| Chelsea Ln. N&S | 21W-9S | 31 |
| Cherry Tree Av. N&S | 21W-7S | 25 |

| Street | Grid | Page |
|---|---|---|
| Cherry Tree Ct. E&W | 21W-7S | 25 |
| Chesham Ct. E&W | 20W-9S | 32 |
| Chestnut Av. N&S | 21W-8S | 31 |
| Chick Evans Ln. N&S | 23W-7S | 25 |
| Chippingham Rd. E&W | 20W-9S | 32 |
| Church Ct. NE&SW | 22W-7S | 25 |
| Clarendon Ln. E&W | 21W-9S | 31 |
| Clark Dr. NE&SW | 22W-7S | 25 |
| Cole Ridge Ct. E&W | 20W-10S | 32 |
| Compton Rd. N&S | 20W-9S | 32 |
| Concord Dr. E&W | 21W-7S | 25 |
| Cooper Ct. E&W | 22W-7S | 25 |
| Country Club Dr. NS&EW | 21W-8S | 31 |
| Crabtree Av. E&W | 22W-8S,21W-8S | 31 |
| Crabtree Ct. NE&SW | 21W-8S | 31 |
| Creekside Ct. E&W | 22W-6S | 25 |
| Cromwell Av. N&S | 20W-9S | 32 |
| Crown Point St. E&W | 21W-7S | 25 |
| Crystal Ct. N&S | 21W-9S | 31 |
| Dalewood Ct. NE&SW | 21W-8S | 31 |
| Dalewood Pkwy. NS&EW | 21W-9S | 31 |
| Danbury Dr. NW&SE | 21W-7S | 25 |
| David Dr. N&S | 22W-9S | 31 |
| Davos Av. NW&SE | 21W-9S | 31 |
| Dean Dr. N&S | 22W-7S | 25 |
| Deer Dr. NS&EW | 22W-8S | 31 |
| Deerfield Av. N&S | 21W-8S | 31 |
| Deerwood Ct. N&S | 22W-9S | 31 |
| Demaret Ct. NE&SW | 23W-7S | 25 |
| Diamond Ct. NE&SW | 22W-7S | 25 |
| Didrickson Ln. N&S | 23W-7S | 25 |
| Double Eagle Dr. E&W | 23W-7S | 25 |
| Dove St. N&S | 21W-7S | 25 |
| Dover Ct.* NS&EW | 21W-8S | 31 |
| Dryden St. N&S | 20W-10S | 32 |
| Duke St. N&S | 20W-10S | 32 |
| Dunham Dr. N&S | 20W-9S,20W-8S | 32 |
| Eastgate Ct. NW&SE | 21W-6S | 25 |
| Eastside Av. N&S | 21W-7S | 25 |
| Eastwood Ln. N&S | 22W-9S | 31 |
| Eaton Dr. NS&EW | 20W-9S | 32 |
| Edgerton Ct. E&W | 20W-9S | 32 |
| Edgewood Ct. N&S | 22W-9S | 31 |
| Edgewood Pkwy. E&W | 22W-9S | 31 |
| Elm St. N&S | 22W-9S | 31 |
| Emerald Ct. N&S | 21W-9S | 31 |
| Essex Ct. N&S | 22W-6S | 25 |
| Everglade Av. NE&SW | 22W-9S,21W-8S | 31 |
| Evergreen Ct. E&W | 21W-8S | 31 |
| Evergreen Ln. E&W | 21W-8S | 31 |
| Fairmount Dr. N&S | 21W-6S | 25 |
| Field Rd. N&S | 20W-10S | 32 |
| Fitzgerald E&W | 20W-8S | 32 |
| Forest Dr. E&W | 21W-9S | 31 |
| Forest Glen Pkwy. E&W | 22W-8S,21W-8S | 31 |
| Fountain Dr. NE&SW | 22W-7S | 25 |
| Fox Dr. E&W | 22W-8S | 31 |
| Fox Tree Av. NS&EW | 21W-7S | 25 |
| Foxboro Dr. NW&SE | 22W-9S | 31 |
| Foxglove St. NW&SE | 21W-7S | 25 |
| Frost Ct. NE&SW | 21W-9S | 31 |
| Gatewood Ln. N&S | 22W-9S | 31 |
| Geneva St. N&S | 21W-9S | 31 |
| Glenn Ct. N&S | 22W-7S | 25 |
| Goldfinch St. E&W | 21W-7S | 25 |
| Golfview Dr. NS&EW | 20W-8S | 32 |
| Green Dr. NE&SW | 22W-6S | 25 |
| Greene Rd. NS&EW | 23W-7S | 25 |
| Greenleaf St. NW&SE | 21W-7S | 25 |
| Grissom Ct. E&W | 22W-7S | 25 |
| Hagen Ct. E&W | 23W-7S | 25 |
| Halsey Ct. NW&SE | 22W-7S | 25 |
| Halsey Dr. N&S | 22W-7S | 25 |
| Harcourt Dr. E&W | 20W-9S | 32 |
| Harleyford Rd. E&W | 20W-10S | 32 |
| Hartford Ln. E&W | 20W-9S | 32 |
| Harvest Av. N&S | 21W-7S | 25 |
| Hastings Rd. E&W | 20W-10S | 32 |
| Hawthorne Av. N&S | 21W-8S | 31 |
| Hiawatha Pkwy. NE&SW | 21W-9S | 31 |
| Hickory Ct. E&W | 22W-9S | 31 |
| High Gate Ln. N&S | 20W-10S | 32 |
| High Tr. NE&SW | 22W-7S | 25 |
| Highland Ct. NW&SE | 21W-8S | 31 |
| Hillside Ct. E&W | 22W-7S | 25 |
| Hobson Ct. E&W | 22W-7S | 25 |

| Street | Grid | Page |
|---|---|---|
| Hobson Rd. NE&SW | 23W-7S,22W-7S | 25 |
| Hobson Valley Dr. N&S | 22W-7S | 25 |
| Iroquois Ct. N&S | 22W-9S | 31 |
| Jackson Ct. N&S | 22W-6S | 25 |
| Jackson Dr. NE&SW | 22W-6S,21W-6S | 25 |
| Janes Ct. E&W | 21W-8S | 31 |
| Janeswood Dr.* NS&EW | 21W-7S | 25 |
| Jo Ann Ln. E&W | 22W-9S | 31 |
| Jonquil Ln. E&W | 22W-8S,21W-8S | 31 |
| Juneberry Av. NE&SW | 21W-7S | 25 |
| Kelly Ct. N&S | 21W-9S | 31 |
| Kelly Dr. E&W | 21W-9S | 31 |
| Kildeer St. E&W | 21W-7S | 25 |
| Kimball Ct. NW&SE | 22W-7S | 25 |
| Kincaid Ct. NW&SE | 22W-7S | 25 |
| Kincaid Dr. NE&SW | 22W-7S | 25 |
| Knob Hill Dr. N&S | 20W-10S,20W-9S | 32 |
| Knotty Pine Ct. NE&SW | 21W-8S | 31 |
| Koloff Ct. NE&SW | 22W-7S | 25 |
| Lakeview Ct. N&S | 22W-7S | 25 |
| Langley Ct. NW&SE | 21W-7S | 25 |
| Larchwood Av. N&S | 21W-8S | 31 |
| Larchwood Ln. NW&SE | 21W-8S | 31 |
| Larkspur Ln. NE&SW | 21W-7S | 25 |
| Laurel Ct. E&W | 21W-9S | 31 |
| Leawood Ct. NW&SE | 22W-9S | 31 |
| Leawood Ln. N&S | 22W-9S | 31 |
| Lee St. NW&SE | 21W-6S | 25 |
| Lindenwood Ln. N&S | 22W-9S | 31 |
| Longford St. E&W | 20W-9S | 32 |
| Lorraine Ct. E&W | 21W-7S | 25 |
| Luzern Ct. E&W | 21W-9S | 31 |
| Macarthur Dr. N&S | 22W-7S | 25 |
| Manchester Ct. E&W | 21W-7S | 25 |
| Mansfield St. E&W | 20W-9S | 32 |
| Marshall Dr. N&S | 22W-7S | 25 |
| Martin Ct. NW&SE | 22W-7S | 25 |
| Martin Dr. NW&SE | 22W-7S | 25 |
| Mashie Ct. N&S | 22W-7S,23W-7S | 25 |
| Meadowdale Ln. E&W | 21W-9S | 31 |
| Meadowood Av. NW&SE | 20W-9S | 32 |
| Mendingwall Dr. N&S | 22W-9S | 31 |
| Meyer Rd. N&S | 22W-6S | 25 |
| Middlebury Av. N&S | 20W-9S | 32 |
| Middlecoff Ct. N&S | 23W-7S | 25 |
| Mitchell Dr. NE&SW | 22W-7S,21W-7S | 25 |
| Mohawk Av. E&W | 21W-8S | 31 |
| Mulligan Dr. NS&EW | 23W-7S | 25 |
| Nelson Ct. E&W | 23W-7S | 25 |
| Newcastle Ct. NE&SW | 20W-9S | 32 |
| Newport Ct. E&W | 21W-7S | 25 |
| Newport Dr. N&S | 21W-7S | 25 |
| North Creek Dr. E&W | 22W-9S,21W-9S | 31 |
| North-South Tollway N&S | 21W-9S,21W-6S | 31 |
| Northgate Ct. NW&SE | 21W-6S | 25 |
| Norwood Ct. N&S | 22W-9S | 31 |
| Nottingham Rd. E&W | 20W-9S | 32 |
| O'Hare Ct. NW&SE | 22W-7S | 25 |
| Oak Leaf Ct. N&S | 21W-9S | 31 |
| Oak Tree Ct. E&W | 22W-7S | 25 |
| Oak Tree Tr. N&S | 22W-7S | 25 |
| Oakview Ct. E&W | 22W-9S | 31 |
| Oakview Ln. N&S | 22W-9S | 31 |
| Old Fence Ct. N&S | 22W-9S | 31 |
| Orchard Ln. N&S | 21W-8S | 31 |
| Orchard Rd. N&S | 20W-12S,20W-11S | 34 |
| Oriole Ct. N&S | 21W-7S | 25 |
| Ouimet Ct. E&W | 23W-7S | 25 |
| Paddington Rd. N&S | 20W-9S | 32 |
| Park Lane Ct. E&W | 21W-7S | 25 |
| Park Lane Dr. NW&SE | 21W-7S | 25 |
| Parkside Dr. E&W | 22W-6S | 25 |
| Parkwood Ln. NW&SE | 22W-9S | 31 |
| Patterson Ct. NW&SE | 21W-7S | 25 |
| Patton Dr. N&S | 22W-7S | 25 |
| Patty Berg Ct. NE&SW | 23W-7S | 25 |
| Pembridge Av. N&S | 20W-9S | 32 |
| Penny Royal Pl.* E&W | 21W-8S | 31 |
| Perry Dr. N&S | 21W-6S | 25 |
| Pershing Ct. NW&SE | 22W-7S | 25 |
| Peterson Ct. NE&SW | 22W-9S | 31 |

| Street | Grid | Page |
|---|---|---|
| Pheasant St. E&W | 21W-7S | 25 |
| Piers Dr. N&S | 21W-9S | 31 |
| Plover Ct. E&W | 21W-7S | 25 |
| Prairieview Av. N&S | 21W-7S | 25 |
| Providence Dr. NE&SW | 21W-7S | 25 |
| Quail Ct.* N&S | 21W-8S | 31 |
| Ravinia Ln. E&W | 21W-8S | 31 |
| Red Bud Ln. NE&SW | 21W-7S | 25 |
| Redcliff St. E&W | 20W-9S | 32 |
| Redwing Ct. NW&SE | 21W-7S | 25 |
| Redwing Dr. NW&SE | 21W-7S | 25 |
| Remington Ct.* N&S | 21W-8S | 31 |
| Rhodes Ct.* N&S | 21W-8S | 31 |
| Richfield Ct. E&W | 20W-8S | 32 |
| Ridge Ln. E&W | 21W-8S | 31 |
| Ridgeway Dr. NE&SW | 22W-6S | 25 |
| Roberts Ct. NE&SW | 22W-7S | 25 |
| Roberts Dr. N&S | 22W-7S | 25 |
| Rosebury Av. N&S | 20W-9S | 32 |
| Rosewood Ct. E&W | 21W-9S | 31 |
| Ross Dr. N&S | 21W-6S | 25 |
| Ryan N&S | 20W-8S | 32 |
| Salem Ct. NE&SW | 21W-7S | 25 |
| Sarazen Ct. E&W | 23W-7S | 25 |
| Scarsdale Ct. NE&SW | 20W-9S | 32 |
| Scenicwood Ln. E&W | 22W-9S | 31 |
| Seminole Ct. N&S | 21W-8S | 31 |
| Shagbark Ct. N&S | 22W-9S | 31 |
| Shelley Ct. E&W | 22W-9S | 31 |
| Shepherd Ct. E&W | 22W-7S | 25 |
| Sheridan Ct. NW&SE | 22W-6S | 25 |
| Sheridan Dr. NE&SW | 22W-6S | 25 |
| Sherman Dr. NE&SW | 22W-6S | 25 |
| Sioux Av. NE&SW | 21W-8S | 31 |
| Slayton Ct. N&S | 22W-7S | 25 |
| Snead Ct. NS&EW | 23W-7S | 25 |
| Spring St. E&W | 21W-9S | 31 |
| Sprucewood Av. NW&SE | 21W-8S | 31 |
| Stable Rd. N&S | 22W-6S | 25 |
| Steven Ct. N&S | 21W-9S | 31 |
| Stevenson Expressway NE&SW | 20W-11S | 34 |
| Stillwell Ct. E&W | 22W-7S | 25 |
| Stonewall Av. E&W | 22W-6S,21W-6S | 25 |
| Stonewall Ct. NW&SE | 21W-6S | 25 |
| Sumac St. NW&SE | 21W-7S | 25 |
| Summerall N&S | 22W-7S | 25 |
| Summerhill Dr. E&W | 22W-6S | 25 |
| Sun Drop Av. N&S | 21W-7S | 25 |
| Sundowner Rd. N&S | 22W-6S | 25 |
| Sunnydale St. E&W | 21W-7S | 25 |
| Sussex Ct.* E&W | 21W-8S | 31 |
| Swallow Ct. N&S | 21W-7S | 25 |
| Taylor Dr. N&S | 22W-7S | 25 |
| Timke Rd. N&S | 22W-6S | 25 |
| Two Paths E&W | 22W-9S | 31 |
| Tyler Ct. NE&SW | 22W-6S | 25 |
| Tyler Dr. N&S | 22W-6S | 25 |
| Vail Ln. NE&SW | 20W-10S | 32 |
| Valleyview Ln. N&S | 21W-9S,21W-8S | 31 |
| Vantage St. E&W | 21W-7S | 25 |
| Vardon Ct. E&W | 23W-7S | 25 |
| Vernon Ct. E&W | 22W-6S | 25 |
| Vista Dr. E&W | 21W-7S | 25 |
| Wainwright Dr. N&S | 22W-7S | 25 |
| Wake Robin Ct. NW&SE | 21W-7S | 25 |
| Walnut Av. NW&SE | 21W-8S | 31 |
| Waterbury Ct. NE&SW | 21W-9S | 31 |
| Waterbury Dr. E&W | 21W-9S | 31 |
| Wellington Rd. E&W | 20W-9S | 32 |
| Westgate Ct. NW&SE | 21W-6S | 25 |
| Westmoreland Dr. NW&SE | 22W-7S,21W-7S | 25 |
| Westridge Dr. NW&SE | 22W-8S | 31 |
| Westview Ln. N&S | 22W-9S,22W-8S | 31 |
| Wharf Dr. E&W | 21W-9S | 31 |
| Wheatfield St. E&W | 21W-7S | 25 |
| Wheeler St. E&W | 21W-7S | 25 |
| Whispering Oaks Ln. NW&SE | 22W-9S | 31 |
| White Ct. NE&SW | 22W-7S | 25 |
| White Dr. E&W | 22W-7S | 25 |
| Wild Plum Dr. E&W | 22W-7S,21W-7S | 25 |
| Williams Dr. NE&SW | 22W-7S | 25 |
| Willow Av. N&S | 21W-8S | 31 |
| Willow Ct. NE&SW | 21W-8S | 31 |
| Willow Ln. NW&SE | 21W-8S | 31 |
| Willow Wood Dr. NE&SW | 21W-9S | 31 |
| Winston Dr. N&S | 22W-7S | 25 |

| | Grid | Page |
|---|---|---|
| Wintergreen Ct. E&W | | |
| ................. 21W-7S | 25 |
| Wolfe Ct. NE&SW .. 21W-6S | 25 |
| Wolfe Dr. NE&SW .. 21W-6S | 25 |
| Woodlyn Dr. N&S.... 21W-9S | 31 |
| Woodridge Dr. NW&SE | | |
| .......... 21W-9S,22W-7S | 31 |
| Woodsorrel Pl.* E&W | | |
| ................. 21W-8S | 31 |
| Woodview Dr. NE&SW | | |
| ................. 22W-8S | 31 |
| Woodward Av. N&S | | |
| .......... 21W-9S,21W-7S | 31 |
| Wren Ct. E&W ...... 21W-7S | 25 |
| Yellow Star St. N&S  21W-7S | 25 |
| York Ct. E&W ...... 21W-7S | 25 |
| Young Ct. N&S ...... 22W-7S | 25 |
| Zurich Ct. E&W .... 21W-9S | 31 |
| 63rd St. E&W | | |
| .......... 22W-7S,21W-6S | 25 |
| 71st St. E&W | | |
| .......... 22W-7S,21W-7S | 25 |
| 76th St. NW&SE .... 22W-8S | 31 |
| 83rd St. E&W | | |
| .......... 22W-9S,21W-9S | 31 |

## York Township

| | Grid | Page |
|---|---|---|
| Adams St. N&S ...... 18W-4S | 20 |
| Addison Av. N&S .... 18W-1S | 20 |
| Ahrens Av. N&S .... 18W-0S | 20 |
| Apley Ln.* E&W .... 17W-1S | 21 |
| Ardmore Av. N&S... 18W-1S | 20 |
| Ashby Ln.* NW&SE . 17W-1S | 21 |
| Ave. Barbizon* E&W | | |
| ................. 19W-3S | 20 |
| Ave. Chateau E. N&S | | |
| ................. 18W-2S | 20 |
| Ave. Chateau N. E&W | | |
| ................. 19W-2S | 20 |
| Ave. Cherburg* NE&SW | | |
| ................. 19W-3S | 20 |
| Ave. LaTours N&S .. 19W-2S | 20 |
| Ave. Normande* E&W | | |
| ................. 19W-3S | 20 |
| Ave. Orleans* NW&SE | | |
| ................. 19W-3S | 20 |
| Ave. Royal* NW&SE | | |
| ................. 19W-3S | 20 |
| Avondale Ln. N&S .. 20W-2S | 20 |
| Barbara Ln.* E&W .. 19W-3S | 20 |
| Beaumont Ln. N&S .. 20W-2S | 20 |
| Bryan St. N&S ...... 16W-0S | 21 |
| Buckingham Ln.* E&W | | |
| ................. 17W-1S | 21 |
| Buttercup Ln. N&S .. 17W-1S | 21 |
| Cadwell Av. N&S .... 15W-0S | 21 |
| Cedar Av. N&S ...... 15W-0S | 21 |
| Charlotte Ln.* E&W . 19W-3S | 20 |
| Chase Av. N&S ...... 19W-1S | 20 |
| Church St. N&S .... 18W-1S | 20 |
| Clara Ct.* E&W ...... 19W-3S | 20 |
| Colonial Ln. N&S .... 20W-2S | 20 |
| Concord St. E&W .... 15W-0S | 21 |
| Cornell Av. N&S .... 17W-0S | 21 |
| Danby St. N&S ...... 18W-1S | 20 |
| Dillon Ln. N&S ...... 18W-1S | 20 |
| Douglas Rd. N&S .... 19W-3S | 20 |
| Duncan St. E&W .... 15W-0S | 21 |
| Eastgate Rd. E&W .. 19W-1S | 20 |
| Edgewood Av. N&S .. 19W-0S | 20 |
| Edgewood Rd. E&W | | |
| ................. 20W-2S | 20 |
| Edward St. E&W .... 18W-0S | 20 |
| Elliot Ln.* N&S ...... 18W-1S | 20 |
| Euclid Av. N&S | | |
| .......... 17W-1S,17W-0S | 21 |
| Fairfield Av. N&S | | |
| .......... 19W-0S,19W-1S | 20 |
| Fairfield Ln. N&S .... 19W-2S | 20 |
| Fillmore St. E&W .... 15W-0S | 21 |
| Florence Av. N&S.... 18W-3S | 20 |
| Forest Grove Ln. N&S | | |
| ................. 19W-3S | 20 |
| Forest Ln. NE&SW .. 15W-0S | 21 |
| Formento Ct.* E&W . 19W-3S | 20 |
| Frontage Rd. E&W | | |
| .......... 16W-0S,15W-0S | 21 |
| Ginger Brook Dr.* E&W | | |
| ................. 19W-3S | 20 |
| Ginny Ln.* E&W .... 19W-3S | 20 |
| Glen Av. N&S ...... 20W-2S | 20 |
| Glen Ct. E&W ...... 20W-2S | 20 |
| Glen Pl. E&W........ 20W-2S | 20 |
| Glendenning Rd. N&S | | |
| ................. 19W-3S | 20 |
| Gloria Ln.* E&W .. 19W-3S | 20 |
| Grace St. N&S ...... 19W-1S | 20 |
| Gramercy Park Ln. E&W | | |
| ................. 19W-3S | 20 |
| Grant St. N&S ...... 18W-4S | 20 |
| Hampton Ln. N&S .. 20W-2S | 20 |
| Harding Rd. E&W.... 20W-0S | 20 |
| Harvard St. E&W .... 15W-0S | 21 |
| Highland Av. N&S.... 19W-1S | 20 |
| Highmoor Rd. NE&SW | | |
| ................. 20W-0S | 20 |
| Hill St. E&W ........ 17W-1N | 14 |
| Holyoke Ln.* N&S.... 17W-1S | 21 |
| Ingersoll Ln.* N&S .. 17W-1S | 21 |
| Ingrid Ln.* E&W .... 19W-3S | 20 |
| Jamestowne Ln. E&W | | |
| ................. 18W-1S | 20 |
| Karlin Dr.* N&S ...... 19W-3S | 20 |

| | Grid | Page |
|---|---|---|
| Kendall Av. N&S .... 15W-0S | 21 |
| Kirk Av. N&S ........ 15W-0S | 21 |
| Kirkland Ln.* E&W .. 17W-1S | 21 |
| Knollwood Ln.* E&W | | |
| ................. 17W-1S | 21 |
| Lathrop Ln.* E&W .. 17W-1S | 21 |
| Lewis Av. N&S ...... 19W-1S | 20 |
| Lexington St. NE&SW | | |
| ................. 15W-0S | 21 |
| Liberty Blvd. N&S.... 18W-4S | 20 |
| Lincoln St. N&S...... 18W-4S | 20 |
| Linden Av. N&S...... 15W-0S | 21 |
| Lombard Av. N&S .. 19W-1S | 20 |
| Lowell Ln.* E&W .... 18W-1S | 20 |
| Luther Av. N&S...... 18W-1S | 20 |
| Manor Ln. E&W .... 17W-1N | 14 |
| Margaret Ln.* E&W . 19W-3S | 20 |
| Marion Ln.* E&W .... 19W-3S | 20 |
| Marlborough Rd. E&W | | |
| ................. 20W-2S | 20 |
| Mary's Ln. N&S...... 19W-1S | 20 |
| Mayfair Rd. E&W .... 20W-2S | 20 |
| Meadow Ln. N&S.... 19W-1S | 20 |
| Michigan Av. N&S.... 18W-1S | 20 |
| Morningside Dr. E&W | | |
| ................. 17W-1S | 21 |
| Morris Av. E&W .... 18W-0S | 20 |
| Myrtle Av. E&W .... 17W-1S | 21 |
| Oakbrook Club Dr. N&S | | |
| ................. 16W-1S | 21 |
| Old York Rd. N&S .. 15W-0S | 21 |
| Park St. N&S........ 18W-4S | 20 |
| Pine Ln. N&S........ 19W-1S | 20 |
| Pine View Ct. N&S .. 19W-1S | 20 |
| Pine View St. N&S .. 19W-1S | 20 |
| Poplar Av. N&S...... 15W-0S | 21 |
| Prospect Av. N&S .. 16W-0S | 21 |
| Radford Ln. N&S .... 18W-1S | 20 |
| Riordan Rd. E&W.... 17W-0S | 21 |
| Riverview Av. N&S .. 17W-1N | 14 |
| Rochdale Cir. NS&EW | | |
| ................. 19W-1S | 20 |
| Rosebud Dr., N. NS&EW | | |
| ................. 19W-1S | 20 |
| Rosebud Dr., S. N&S | | |
| ................. 19W-1S | 20 |
| Schiller St. E&W .... 17W-1N | 14 |
| School Av. N&S | | |
| .......... 18W-0S,18W-1S | 20 |
| School St. N&S...... 18W-3S | 20 |
| Shady Ln. NE&SW .. 20W-0S | 20 |
| Southlane Dr. NE&SW | | |
| ................. 17W-1S | 21 |
| Standish Ln. E&W .. 17W-1S | 21 |
| Sterling Rd. N&S .... 19W-3S | 20 |
| Stewart Av. N&S .... 19W-1S | 20 |
| Stratford Ln.* N&S .. 17W-1S | 21 |
| Summit Av. N&S .... 17W-0S | 21 |
| Sunshine Dr. E&W .. 17W-1S | 21 |
| Theresa Ln.* E&W .. 19W-3S | 20 |
| Tower Rd., N. E&W.. 18W-2S | 20 |
| Tower Rd., S. E&W .. 18W-2S | 20 |
| Villa Av. N&S........ 17W-0S | 21 |
| Vista St. NE&SW .... 19W-1S | 20 |
| Vivian Ln.* E&W .... 19W-3S | 20 |
| Washington St. N&S | | |
| ................. 18W-4S | 20 |
| Westview Av. N&S .. 18W-1S | 20 |
| Wilcox Av. N&S...... 18W-3S | 20 |
| Williams St. N&S .... 18W-4S | 20 |
| Williamsburg Ln. E&W | | |
| ................. 18W-1S | 20 |
| Windsor Ln.* N&S .. 17W-1S | 21 |
| Winthrop Ln.* N&S .. 18W-1S | 20 |
| Wisconsin Av. N&S .. 18W-1S | 20 |
| Woodland Ln. N&S .. 19W-3S | 20 |
| Woodland Rd. N&S .. 19W-3S | 20 |
| 2nd St. E&W ........ 17W-1N | 14 |
| 3rd St. N&S ........ 18W-1S | 20 |
| 13th Pl. E&W........ 19W-1S | 20 |
| 13th St. E&W | | |
| .......... 19W-1S,18W-1S | 20 |
| 14th Pl. E&W........ 19W-1S | 20 |
| 14th St. E&W | | |
| .......... 19W-1S,17W-1S | 20 |
| 15th Pl. E&W........ 19W-1S | 20 |
| 15th St. E&W | | |
| .......... 19W-1S,18W-1S | 20 |
| 16th St. E&W | | |
| .......... 19W-1S,18W-1S | 20 |
| 17th Pl. E&W........ 19W-1S | 20 |
| 17th St. E&W ...... 19W-1S | 20 |
| 18th St. E&W | | |
| .......... 19W-1S,18W-1S | 20 |
| 20th Pl. E&W........ 18W-1S | 20 |
| 20th St. E&W ...... 19W-1S | 20 |
| 21st Pl. E&W........ 18W-1S | 20 |
| 22nd St. E&W | | |
| .......... 20W-2S,18W-1S | 20 |
| 31st St. E&W........ 19W-2S | 20 |
| 36th St. E&W........ 19W-3S | 20 |
| 37th St. E&W........ 19W-3S | 20 |
| 38th St. E&W........ 19W-3S | 20 |
| 39th St. E&W | | |
| .......... 19W-3S,18W-3S | 20 |

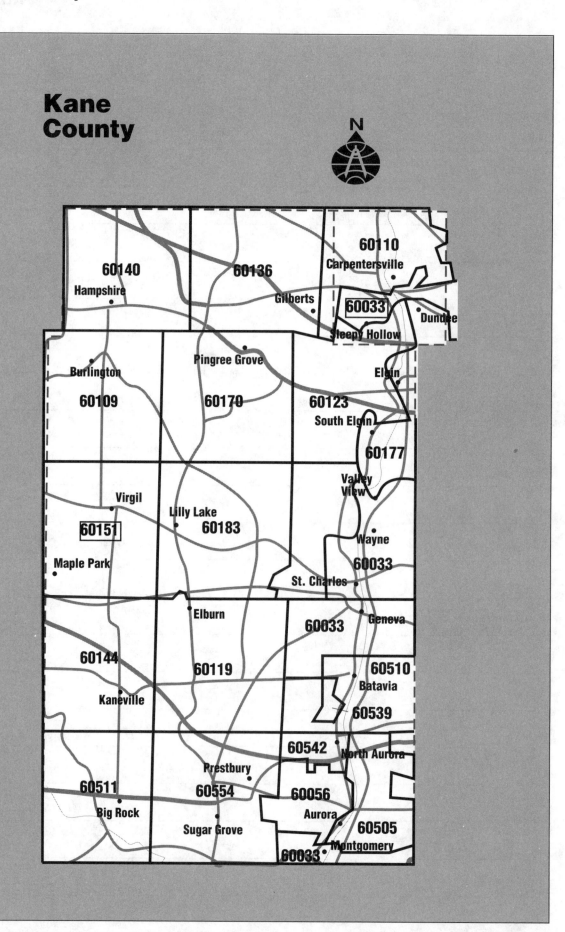

# Kane County

N

60140
Hampshire

60136
Gilberts

60110
Carpentersville

60033

Dundee

Sleepy Hollow

Burlington

Pingree Grove

Elgin

60109

60170

60123
South Elgin

60177

Valley
View

Virgil

Lilly Lake

60151

60183

Wayne

Maple Park

60033

St. Charles

Elburn

Geneva

60033

60144

60510
Batavia

60119

Kaneville

60539

60542
North Aurora

Prestbury

60511

60554

60056

Big Rock

Aurora

60505

Sugar Grove

Montgomery

60033

# RAND McNALLY

# Kane
# County

## StreetFinder®

Photo credit: Geneva Dam, Kane County Development Department

## Kane County Municipal Offices

| | Location | Page |
|---|---|---|
| Aurora City Hall | 35W-7S | 51 |
| 44 E Downer Pl; 892-8811 | | |
| Batavia City Hall | 35W-1S | 39 |
| 101 N Island Ave; 879-1424 | | |
| Carpentersville Village Hall | 32W-16N | 51 |
| 1200 L W Besinger Dr; 426-3439 | | |
| East Dundee Village Hall | 32W-15N | 15 |
| 120 Barrington Ave; 426-2822 | | |
| Elgin City Hall | 34W-11N | 21 |
| 150 Dexter Ct; 695-6500 | | |
| Geneva City Hall | 35W-1N | 33 |
| 21 S 1st; 232-0854 | | |
| Gilberts Village Hall | 38W-16N | 13 |
| Montgomery Village Hall | 36W-9S | 50,51 |
| 1300 S Broadway Ave; 896-8080 | | |
| North Aurora Village Hall | 36W-4S | 44 |
| 25 E State; 897-8228 | | |
| St. Charles City Hall | 35W-3N | 33 |
| 2 E Main; 377-4446 | | |
| Sleepy Hollow Village Hall | 34W-14N | 15 |
| Thoroughbred Lane & Sleepy Hollow Rd; 426-6700 | | |
| South Elgin Village Hall | 34W-8N | 27 |
| 10 N Water; 742-5780 | | |
| West Dundee Village Hall | 33W-15N | 15 |
| 102 S Second; 426-6161 | | |

## Cemeteries

| | Location | Page |
|---|---|---|
| Baker Cem | 44W-8N | 24 |
| Blackberry Cem | 43W-1N | 30 |
| Bluff City Cem | 32W-10N | 21 |
| Burlington Union Cem | 48W-11W | 16 |
| Calvary Cem | 35W-6S | 44,45 |
| Dundee Twp Cem | 31W-14N | 17 |
| East Aurora Cem | 35W-7S | 51 |
| Eastside Cem | 35W-0S | 39 |
| Fowler Grove Cem | 48W-9S | 46 |
| French Cem | 36W-9S | 50,51 |
| Gardner Cem | 49W-1N | 28 |
| Hampshire Center Cem | 46W-16N | 11 |
| Jericho Cem | 43W-9S | 48 |
| Lily Lake Cem | 44W-5N | 24 |
| Little Woods Cem | 33W-7N | 27 |
| Mt. Hope Cem | 32W-10N | 21 |
| Mt. Olivet Cem | 36W-8S | 50 |
| New Hampshire Cem | 44W-4N | 30 |
| North Cem | 35W-4N | 33 |
| Oak Hill Cem | 34W-1N | 33 |
| Old St. Mary's Cem | 48W-0N | 34 |
| Resurrection Cem | 37W-0S | 38 |
| Riverside Cem | 36W-9S | 50,51 |
| River Valley Mem Gardens | 33W-13N | 21 |
| Spring Lake Cem | 36W-8S | 50 |
| St. Joseph Cem | 35W-5S | 45 |

| | Location | Page |
|---|---|---|
| St. Michael Cem | 35W-6S | 45 |
| St. Nicholas Cem | 34W-7S | 51 |
| St. Paul's Cem | 35W-9S | 51 |
| Sts. Peter & Paul Cem | 47W-4N | 28,29 |
| South Burlington Cem | 49W-8N | 22 |
| Sugar Grove Cem | 42W-4S | 42 |
| Thatcher Cem | 48W-3N | 28 |
| Union Cem | 35W-4N | 33 |
| Welch Cem | 47W-8S | 46,47 |
| West Aurora Cem | 35W-6S | 44,45 |
| West Big Rock Cem | 50W-6S | 40 |
| Westside Cem | 35W-2S | 39 |

## Colleges & Universities

| | Location | Page |
|---|---|---|
| Aurora Univ | 37W-7S | 50 |
| Elgin Comm Col | 36W-10N | 20 |
| Judson Col | 34W-12N | 21 |
| Waubonsee Comm Col | 43W-4S | 42 |
| Waubonsee Comm Col D T Campus | 35W-7S | 51 |

## Forest Preserves

| | Location | Page |
|---|---|---|
| Aurora West | 39, 40W-5S | 43 |
| Binnie | 37W-17N | 8 |
| Blackhawk | 34W-7N | 27 |
| Bliss Woods | 42W-5S | 42 |
| Buffalo Park | 34W-19N | 9 |
| Burnidge | 37W-13N | 20 |
| Campton | 41W-4N | 31 |
| Elburn | 45W-2N | 30 |
| Fabyan | 35W-0N | 39 |
| Fox River Shores | 33W-17N | 9 |
| Glenwood Park | 35W-2S | 39 |
| Gunar Anderson | 35W-0N | 39 |
| Hampshire | 43W-16N | 12 |
| Helm Woods | 31W-17N | 11 |
| Johnson's Mound | 41W-0N | 37 |
| Leroy Oaks | 37W-4N | 32 |
| Les Arends | 36W-3S | 44 |
| Lone Grove | 48W-1S | 34 |
| Nelson Lake | 39W-2S | 38 |
| Oakhurst | 33W-8S | 51 |
| Rutland | 40W-15N | 12,13 |
| Tekakwitha Woods | 35W-6N | 27 |
| Tyler Creek | 34W-12N | 21 |
| Voyageurs Landing | 32W-13N | 15 |

## Golf & Country Clubs

| | Location | Page |
|---|---|---|
| Aurora CC | 37W-8S | 50 |
| Bonnie Dundee CC | 31W-16N | 11 |
| Burr Hill CC | 38W-5N | 26 |
| Eagle Brook CC | 36W-0N | 38 |
| Elgin CC | 37W-11N | 19 |
| Fox Chase GC | 34W-4N | 33 |
| Fox Mill GC | 39W-0N | 38 |

| | Location | Page |
|---|---|---|
| Fox Valley CC | 35W-3S | 44,45 |
| Geneva GC | 35W-1N | 33 |
| Phillips Park & GC | 34W-9S | 51 |
| Prestbury GC | 41W-6S | 49 |
| Randall Oaks GC | 36W-16N | 14 |
| Royal Fox GC | 33W-4N | 33 |
| St. Charles CC | 35W-4N | 33 |
| Spartan Meadows GC | 36W-10N | 20 |
| Valley Green GC | 36W-4S | 44 |

## Hospitals

| | Location | Page |
|---|---|---|
| Copley Mem Hosp | 35W-7S | 51 |
| Copley Hosp | 35W-8S | 51 |
| Marion Joy Rehab. Ctr. | 35W-3N | 32,33 |
| Mercy Center for Health | | |
| Care Services | 36W-5S | 44 |
| St. Josephs Hosp | 36W-11N | 20 |
| Sherman Hosp | 33W-12N | 21 |

## Shopping Centers

| | Location | Page |
|---|---|---|
| Ashland Plaza SC | 35W-9S | 51 |
| Charlestowne Mall SC | 33W-3N | 33 |
| Clock Tower Plaza SC | 33W-10N | 21 |
| Eastgate Plaza SC | 35W-6S | 44,45 |
| Fox River Business Plaza SC | 33W-13N | 21 |
| Huntley Factory Shops | 41W-17N | 6 |
| Indian Trail SC | 35W-6S | 44,45 |
| Indian Trail Court SC | 35W-5S | 45 |
| Meadowdale SC | 32W-16N | 15 |
| Midland SC | 37W-4S | 44 |
| Northgate SC | 35W-6S | 44,45 |
| South Ctr SC | 36W-9S | 50,51 |
| Spring Hill Mall SC | 33W-15N | 15 |
| Town & Country Plaza SC | 35W-10N | 20,21 |
| Tyler Creek Plaza SC | 35W-12N | 20 |
| Valley Creek SC | 36W-12N | 14 |
| Village Mart SC | 34W-6S | 45 |
| West Aurora Plaza SC | 38W-7S | 50 |
| Wing Park Manor SC | 35W-12N | 20 |

## Kane County Close-up

### Elgin Public Museum
225 Grand Blvd., Elgin
This natural history museum features rotating exhibits in the fields of geology, Native American history and endangered species studies. Discovery Room features hands-on exhibits for children. Closed during January.

### Beith House
8 Indiana St., St. Charles
Constructed in 1850 by stonemason William Beith, this preservation study house remains one of the few riverstone homes with its original design features. Those who appreciate fine architecture will appreciate its masonry, woodwork and unusual decorative details. This fully restored dwelling includes a research library and exhibits. Touch-It Table displays fabrics, tools, maps and other artifacts. Listed on National Register of Hisoric Places. Open June-Nov. or by appointment.

### Aurora Historical Society
corner of Cedar St. and Oak Ave., Aurora
Dedicated to preserving Aurora's history, this site features 2 exhibition facilities: the 18-room William Tanner house, built in 1857, is a fully furnished Victorian home open to the public; the History Center is a multi-use exhibition space that houses artifacts relating to the history of this once big "railroad town": furniture, musical instruments, motor cycles, a railway hand car and even locally found Mastodon bones. Open mid-April to mid-December.

### Blackberry Farm Village
corner of Barnes Rd. and Galena Blvd., Aurora
This 54-acre historical farm village features a carriage house, a 19th century farm museum, Huntoon House and a one-room schoolhouse. Blacksmiths, potters, weavers and other artisans give frequent craft demonstrations. Visitors can enjoy pony rides, hay rides, fishing and train rides. Open from mid-April to Labor Day.

### SciTech
18 W. Benton, Aurora
This interactive museum, with its hands-on exhibits, lets visitors experience the wonders of science. Changing exhibits feature experiments in light, sound and electricity. Comprehensive programs for children. Auditorium, activity room, concessions and gift shop. Open daily.

### Kane County Flea Market
Kane County Fairgrounds, Randall Rd., between Rtes. 64 & 38, St. Charles
Not just another flea market! Since its founding in 1967, this flea market has grown into a major event with fans the world over. Unique merchandise includes antiques and other collectibles. Country breakfasts available. Open the first Sunday of every month and the preceding Saturday, all year.

### Garfield Farm Museum
5 miles W of Geneva, IL, off Rt. 38 on Garfield Rd., LaFox
This historically intact farm features a homestead and teamster's inn constructed in the 1840's. Resting on 250 acres, this unique site has undergone substantial prairie restoration and includes an 1842 hay barn, an 1849 horse barn and heirloom-variety vegetable and flower gardens. Rare animal breeds include Devon oxen and Marino sheep. Open by appointment all year.

### Schingoethe Center for Native American Cultures
347 S. Gladstone Ave., Aurora
Located on the campus of Aurora University, Schingoethe Center displays artifacts relating to America's first inhabitants. Its collection of 10,000 objects include Kachinas, pottery, musical instruments, pipes and textiles. Many of its artifacts are touchable objects. Also, workshops, lectures and demonstrations.

### Red Oak Nature Center
Rte. 25, 1 mile N of Rte. 56, N. Aurora
This site covers 40 acres of oak and maple forest on the east bank of the Fox River. This beautiful region includes a visitor's center, an observation deck, hiking trails and separate biking trails. Also, one of the few limestone caves in northeast Illinois is on the premises. Abundant wildlife.

# 4  KANE COUNTY

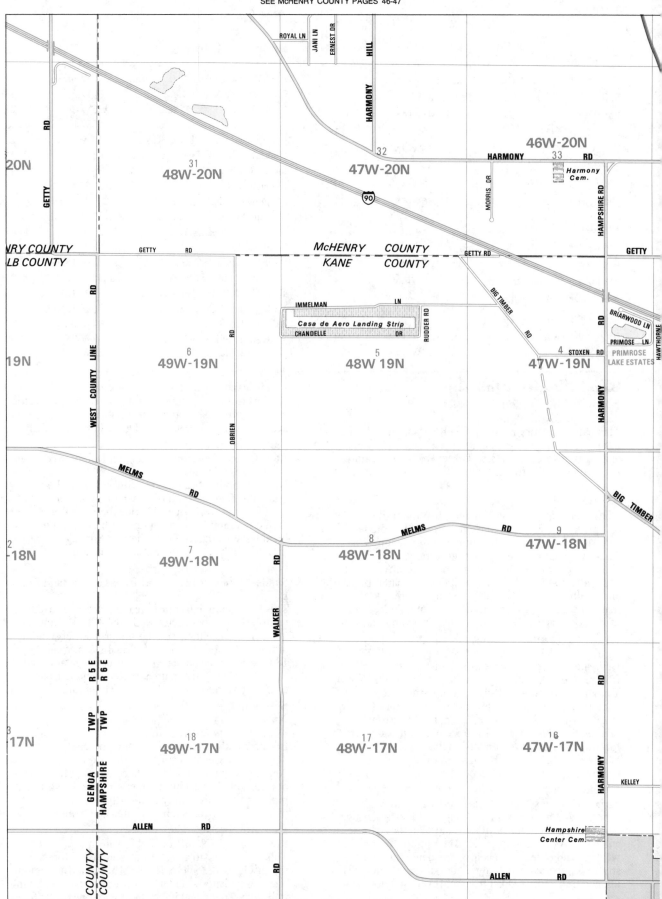

ROYAL LN

JANI LN

ERNEST DR

HARMONY HILL

HARMONY

46W-20N

20N

GETTY RD

48W-20N

31

47W-20N

HARMONY 33 RD

MORRIS DR

Harmony Cem.

HAMPSHIRE RD

NRY COUNTY
LB COUNTY

GETTY RD

McHENRY COUNTY
KANE COUNTY

Getty Rd

GETTY

BIG TIMBER RD

RD

BRIARWOOD LN

HAWTHORNE

WEST COUNTY LINE RD

RD

IMMELMAN LN

Casa de Aero Landing Strip

CHANDELLE DR

RUDDER RD

PRIMOSE LN

PRIMROSE
LAKE ESTATES

19N

6

49W-19N

OBRIEN

5

48W 19N

4 STOXEN RD

47W-19N

HARMONY

MELMS RD

2

-18N

7

49W-18N

WALKER RD

8

MELMS

48W-18N

MELMS RD

9

47W-18N

BIG TIMBER

R 5 E
R 6 E

TWP
TWP

GENOA
HAMPSHIRE

3

-17N

18

49W-17N

RD

17

48W-17N

16

47W-17N

HARMONY RD

KELLEY

ALLEN RD

Hampshire
Center Cem.

COUNTY
COUNTY

RD

ALLEN RD

PEBBLE DR

ARBOR LN

BURR OAK

WINDWOOD LN

OVERLOOK LN

HILLSBORO DR

SEEMAN RD

CORAL

GRAFTON

BORHART RD

HILLSBORO COVE

**HARMONY**

34

35

HARMONY

36

31

45W-20N

44W-20N

43W-20N

42W-2

HARMONY TRAIL ESTATES

PEREGRINE

MANDA DR

DR

TR

CAMP

BEALL LN

CONDOR LN

HERON DR

CT

TRAIL

PINOAK

RD

BRIER HILL RD

CORAL TWP    T 43 N

HAMPSHIRE TWP    T 42 N

RD

CLANYARD    RD

NORTHWEST

LN

3    TOLLWAY

DIETRICH    2

RD    1

6

46W-19N

45W-19N

44W-19N

43W-1

WOODVIEW

GREEN MEADOWS LN

PKWY

HAMPSHIRE OAKS ESTATES

WOODVIEW

PKWY

HILLCREST DR

FELSMITH

RD

HENNIG RD

HIGGINS    RD

River

AHREN'S

43W-1

10    RD

11

12

7

46W-18N

45W-18N

44W-18N

43W-1

RD    RD

**HAMPSHIRE**

WIDMAYER

GAST

Kishwaukee

BRIER HILL

HENNIG    RD

BIG    TIMBER

RD

15    RD

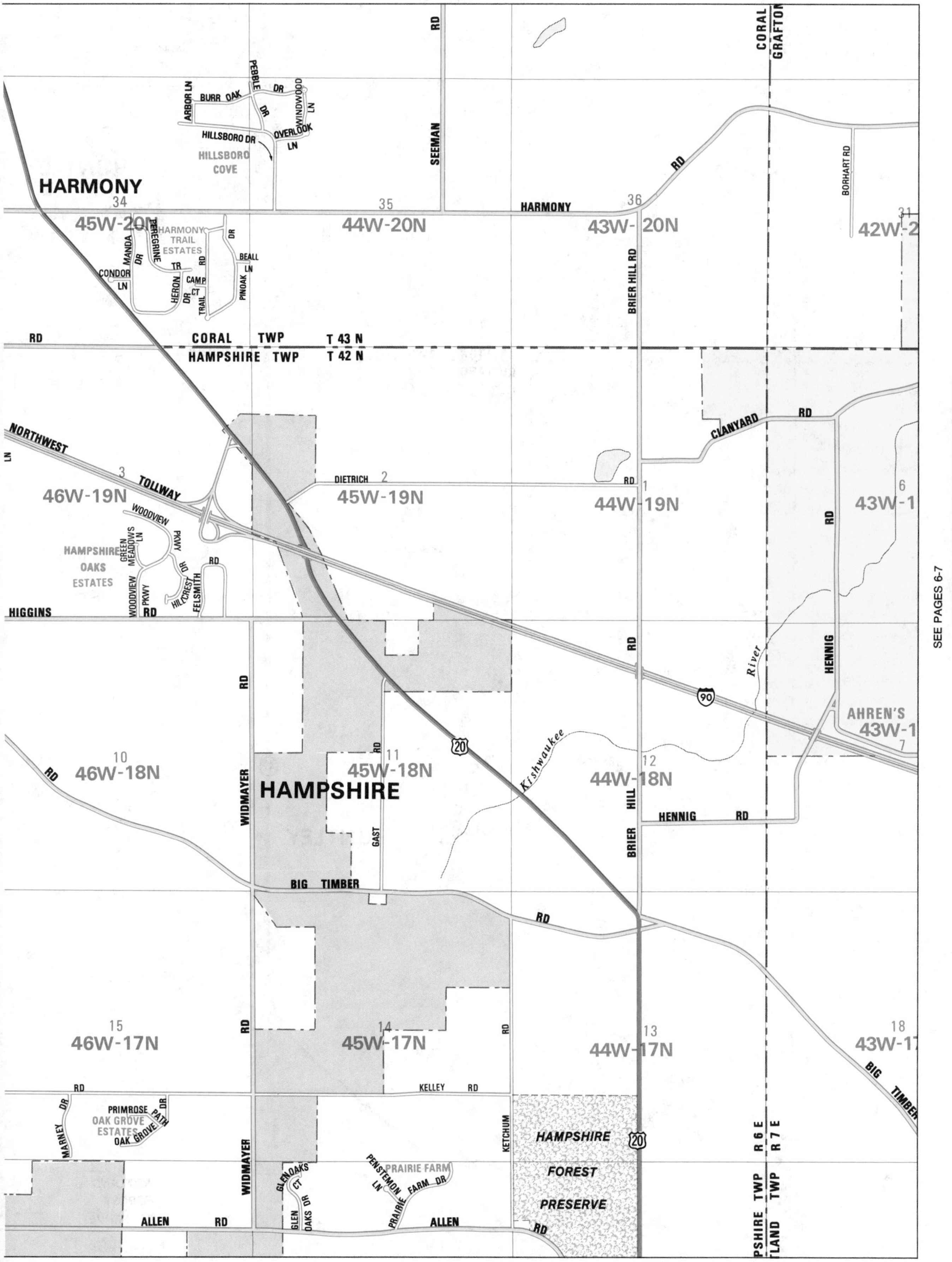

14

13

18

46W-17N

45W-17N

44W-17N

43W-17

WIDMAYER

RD

KELLEY    RD

R 6 E

R 7 E

MARNEY DR

PRIMROSE PATH

OAK GROVE DR

KETCHUM

HAMPSHIRE

20

OAK GROVE ESTATES

OAK GROVE DR

GLENOAKS CT

PRAIRIE FARM

FOREST

PENSTEMON LN

PRAIRIE FARM DR

PRESERVE

WIDMAYER RD

GLEN OAKS DR

PSHIRE TWP

LAND TWP

ALLEN    RD

PRAIRIE

ALLEN

RD

SEE PAGES 6-7

SEE McHENRY COUNTY PAGES 48-49

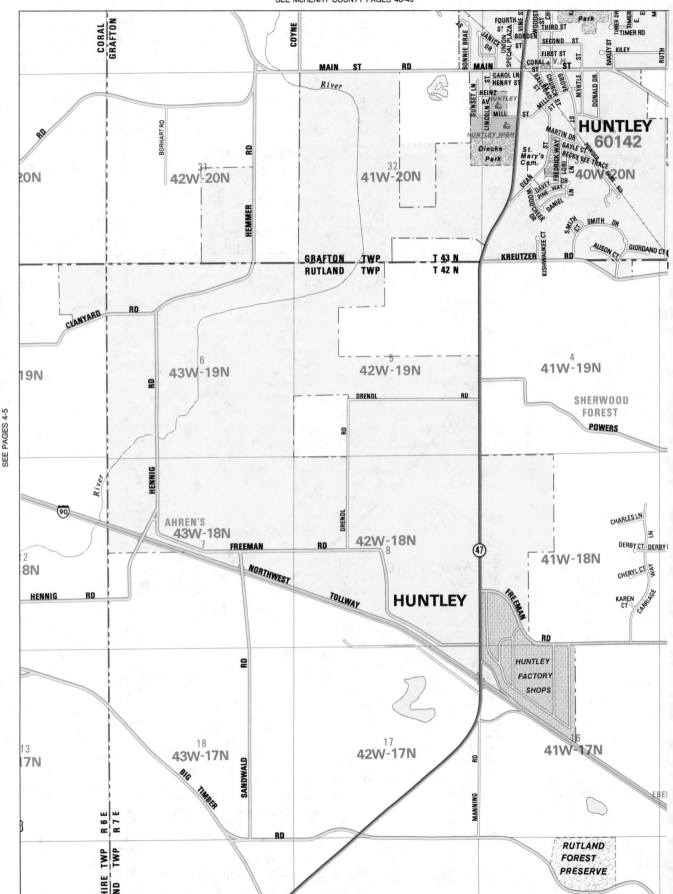

SEE PAGES 4-5

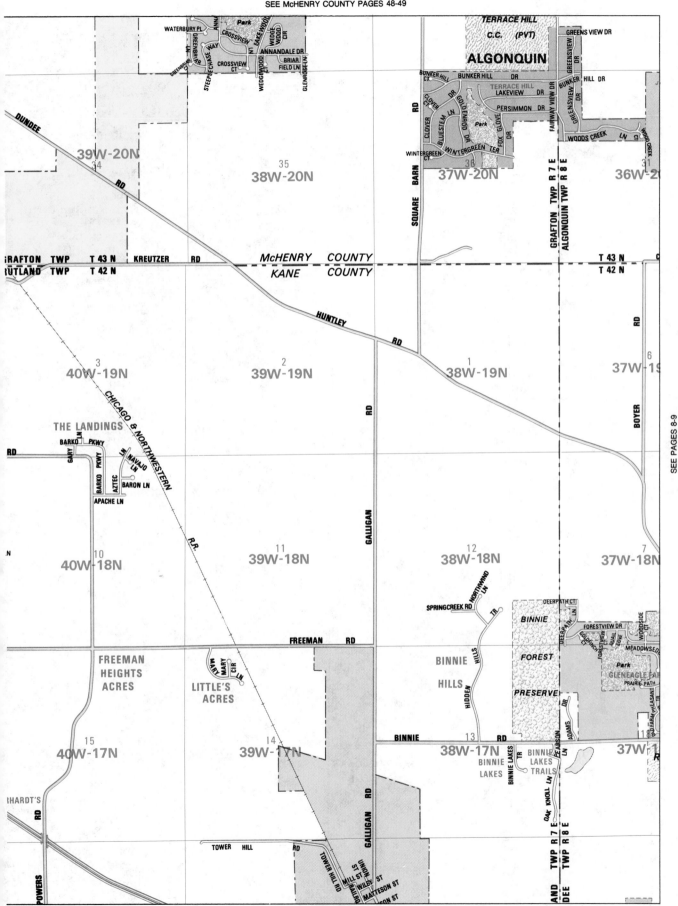

SEE PAGES 8-9

SEE McHENRY COUNTY PAGES 50-51

SEE PAGES 6-7

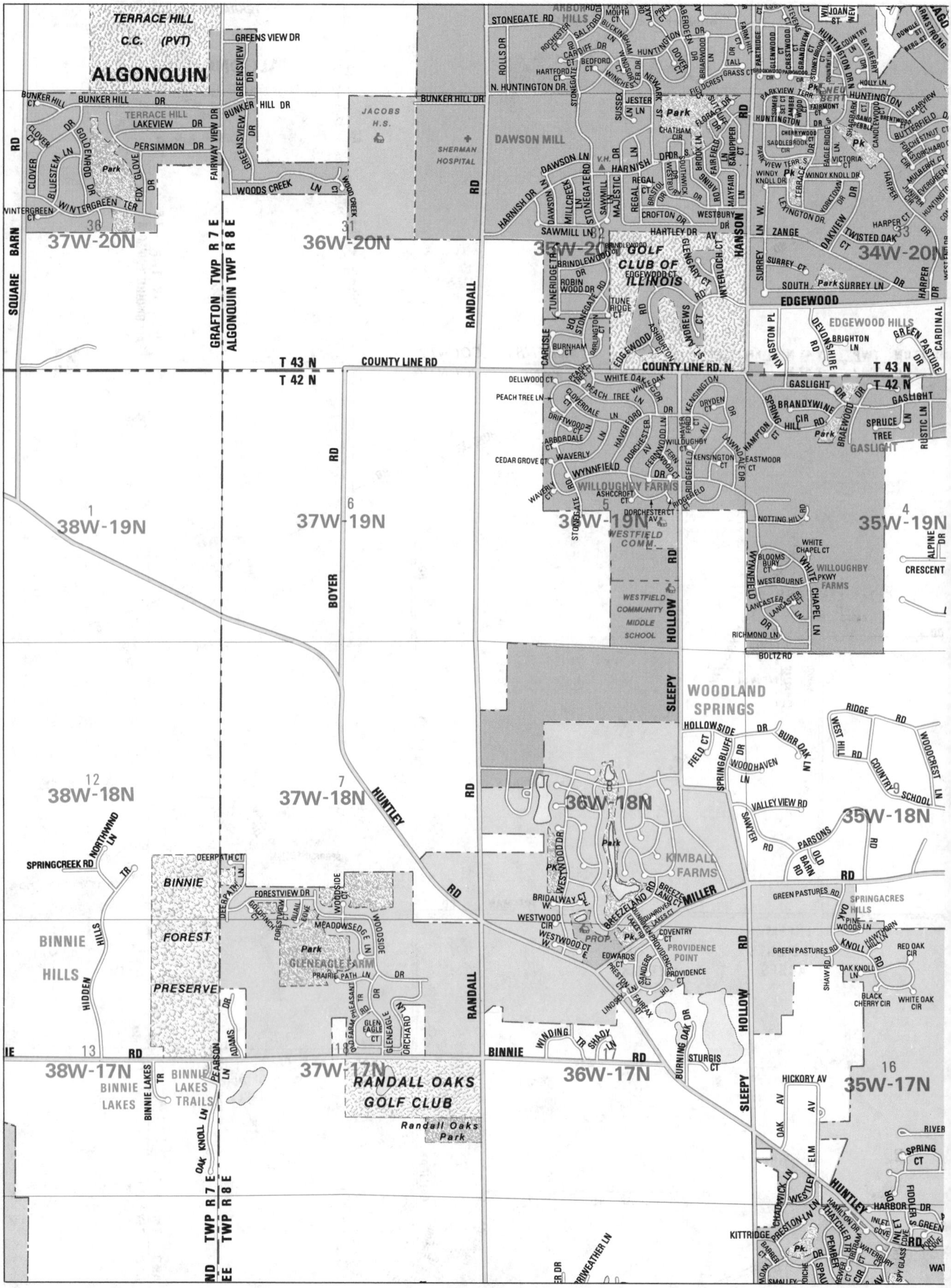

TERRACE HILL C.C. (PVT)

**ALGONQUIN**

GREENS VIEW DR

STONEGATE RD

BUNKER HILL CT
BUNKER HILL
BUNKER HILL DR
TERRACE HILL LAKEVIEW DR
GREENSVIEW DR
FAIRWAY VIEW DR
PERSIMMON DR
CLOVER CT
CLOVER LN
GOLDENWOOD DR
BLUESTEM LN
WINTERGREEN TER
FOX GLOVE DR
Park
WINTERGREEN CT

JACOBS H.S.
SHERMAN HOSPITAL
DAWSON MILL

WOODS CREEK LN

SQUARE BARN RD

GRAFTON TWP R 7 E
ALGONQUIN TWP R 8 E

RANDALL RD

37W-20N
36W-20N
35W-20N

GOLF CLUB OF EDGEWOOD
ILLINOIS

EDGEWOOD
EDGEWOOD HILLS

34W-20N

HANSON RD

COUNTY LINE RD
T 43 N
T 42 N

COUNTY LINE RD. N.

GASLIGHT DR
GASLIGHT

38W-19N
37W-19N
38W-19N
35W-19N

BOYER RD

WILLOUGHBY FARMS

WYNNFIELD

WESTFIELD COMM.

WHITE CHAPEL LN

WILLOUGHBY FARMS

CRESCENT
ALPINE DR

WESTFIELD COMMUNITY MIDDLE SCHOOL

HOLLOW RD

BOLTZ RD

SLEEPY

WOODLAND SPRINGS

38W-18N
37W-18N
36W-18N
35W-18N

HUNTLEY RD

SPRINGCREEK RD

BINNIE FOREST PRESERVE

BINNIE HILLS

KIMBALL FARMS

MILLER RD

SANDER

RANDALL RD

GLENEAGLE FARM

PRAIRIE PATH DR

PROVIDENCE POINT

SLEEPY HOLLOW RD

38W-17N
37W-17N
36W-17N
35W-17N

BINNIE LAKES
BINNIE LAKES TRAILS

RANDALL OAKS GOLF CLUB

Randall Oaks Park

BINNIE RD

HUNTLEY RD

TWP R 7 E
TWP R 8 E

SEE PAGES 14-15

SEE McHENRY COUNTY PAGES 50-51

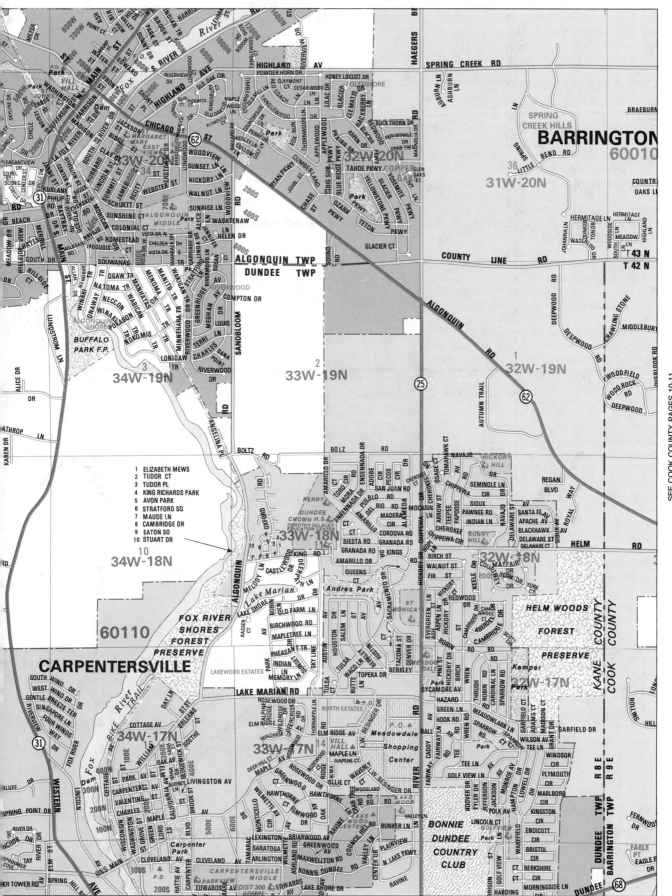

SEE COOK COUNTY PAGES 10-11

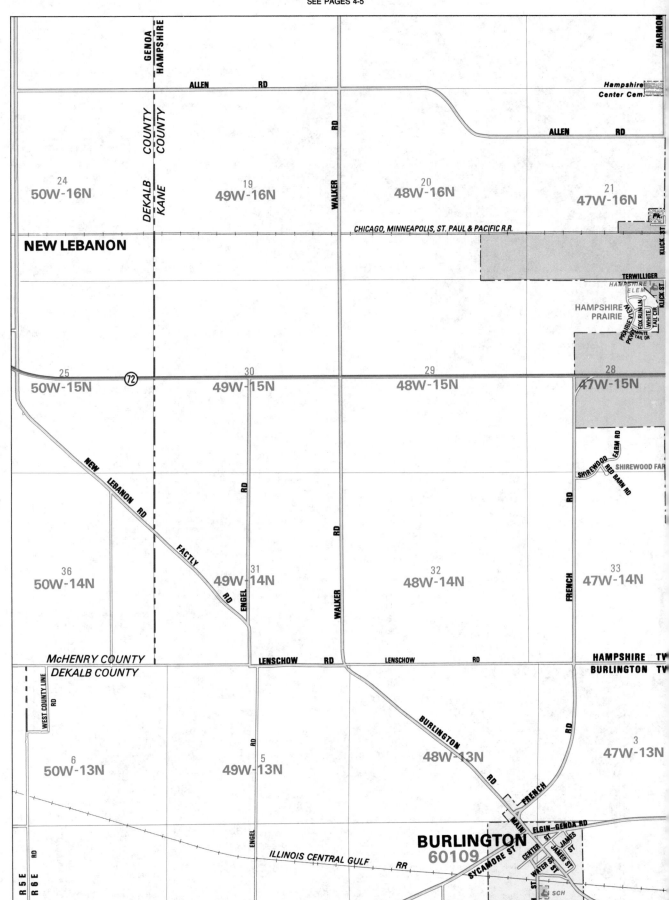

GENOA
HAMPSHIRE

HARMON

ALLEN        RD

Hampshire
Center Cem.

DEKALB    COUNTY
COUNTY

WALKER        RD

ALLEN       RD

24
50W-16N

19
49W-16N

20
48W-16N

21
47W-16N

Pk.

KLICK ST

DEKALB
KANE

CHICAGO, MINNEAPOLIS, ST. PAUL & PACIFIC R.R.

**NEW LEBANON**

TERWILLIGER

HAMPSHIRE
ELEM.

PRAIRIE VIEW PKWY
FOX RUN LN
WHITE
TAIL DR
KLICK ST

HAMPSHIRE
PRAIRIE

WHITE
TAIL CR

72

25
50W-15N

30
49W-15N

29
48W-15N

28
47W-15N

FARM RD

NEW LEBANON RD

FACTLY
RD

RD

WALKER        RD

SHIREWOOD
RED BARN RD

SHIREWOOD FARM

RD

36
50W-14N

31
49W-14N

ENGEL

32
48W-14N

33
47W-14N

FRENCH

McHENRY COUNTY
DEKALB COUNTY

LENSCHOW       RD

LENSCHOW       RD

HAMPSHIRE    TW
BURLINGTON    TW

WEST COUNTY LINE
RD

6
50W-13N

RD

5
49W-13N

BURLINGTON

48W-13N

3
47W-13N

RD

FRENCH     RD

ILLINOIS CENTRAL GULF

ENGEL     RD

RR

ELGIN—GENOA RD

**BURLINGTON**
**60109**

SYCAMORE ST

MAIN

CENTER
ST

JAMES
ST

JAMES ST

WATER ST

R 5 E
R 6 E

RD

ST

SCH

SEE PAGES 4-5

KELLEY RD

KELLEY RD

MARNEY DR

PRIMROSE PATH DR

OAK GROVE ESTATES

OAK GROVE DR

WIDMAYER

GLENOAKS CT

GLEN OAKS DR

PENSTEMON LN

PRAIRIE FARM

PRAIRIE FARM DR

KETCHUM

**HAMPSHIRE**

**FOREST**

**PRESERVE**

20

HAMPSHIRE TWP R 6 E

RUTLAND TWP R 7 E

ALLEN RD

ALLEN RD

**HAMPSHIRE 46W-16N**

**60140**

ST

22

INDUSTRIAL DR

23

**45W-16N**

24

**44W-16N**

WEST ST

CENTER ST

EAST ST

MILL ST

KEYES AV

MAPLE ST

ST. CHARLES BORR/CEO SCH.

ST

RINN AV

WASHINGTON ST

STL

JEFFERSON ST

V.H. ST

ST

ST

JACKSON ST

GROVE

ASH ST

WALNUT

WARNER

MADISON ST

PARKSIDE ST

GRACE ST

ST

STATE

PRAIRIE

OAK

PARK

Hampshire Pl.

SOUTH ST

EDGEWOOD AV

PANAMA

SMITH RD

HAMPSHIRE HIGH

HIGHLAND AV

HILLCREST AV

ELM

JAKE LN

JULIE AV

OLD MILL AV

CENTENNIAL DR

BROOKEDGE DR

TIMBER LN

DUCHESS LN

OAK

72

KNOLL

27 DR

**46W-15N**

26

**45W-15N**

25

**44W-15N**

GETZELMAN RD

Cem.

RD

RD

OAKSHIRE LN

WHITE PINES LN

VOLKENING CIR

SUNSET DR

WHISPERING TRAIL

LITTLEWOOD TR

BRIER HILL

DEER PATH LN

WHISPERING TRAIL

**BRIER PINES**

34

**46W-14N**

35

BERNER RD

**45W-14N**

ROMKE

36

**44W-14N**

GETZELMAN

/P T 42 N

/P T 41 N

LENSCHOW RD

2

**46W-13N**

RD

1

**45W-13N**

6

**44W-13N**

43

RD

ROMKE

GREEN HILL

BRIER HILL RD

PLANK RD

HARTJE'S

BRIER HILL

SEE PAGES 12-13

SEE PAGES 16-17

TIMBER

SAN

MANNING

EBERHARDT

RD

R 6 E
R 7 E

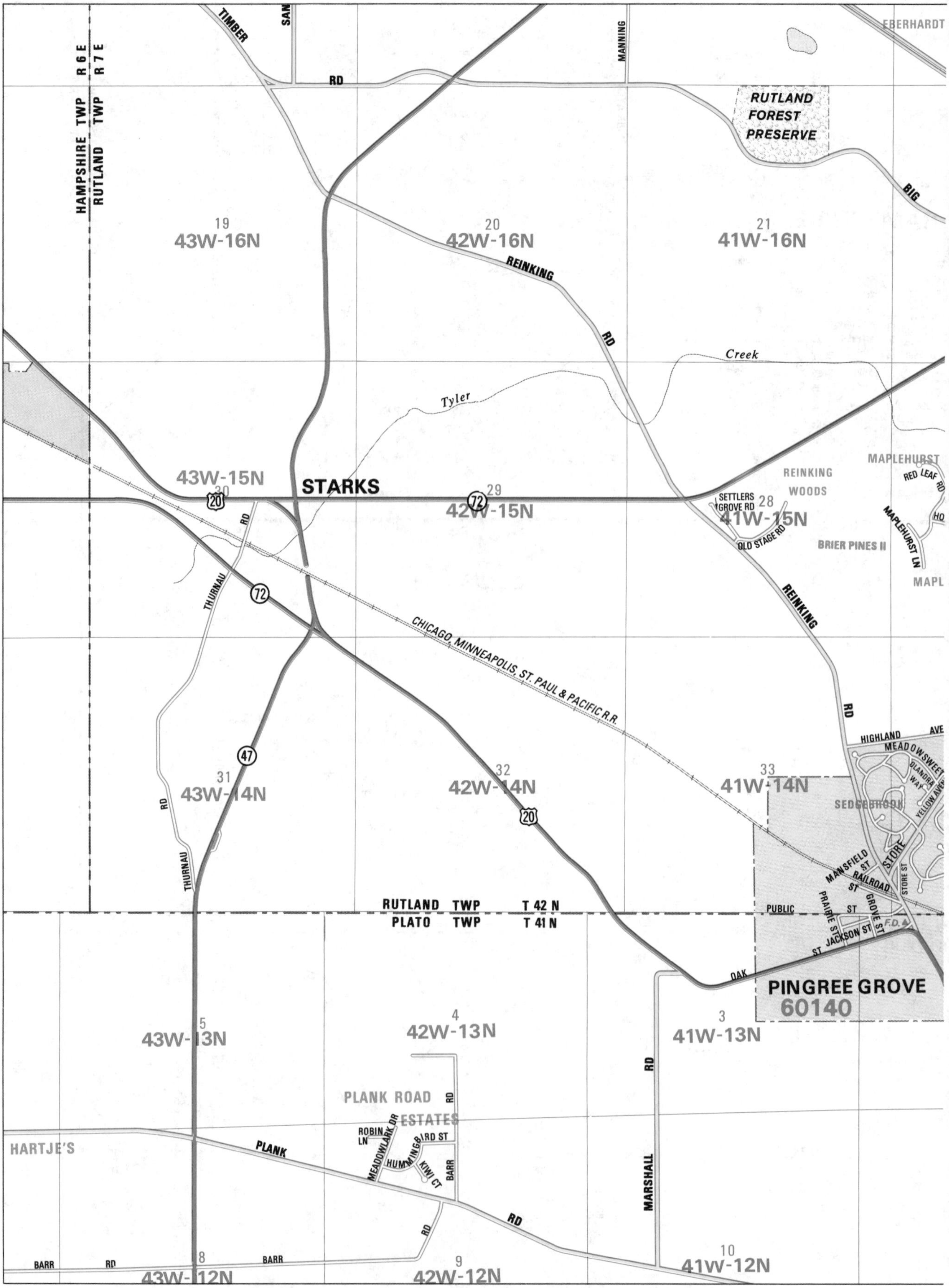

HAMPSHIRE TWP
RUTLAND TWP

**RUTLAND FOREST PRESERVE**

BIG

19
43W-16N

20
42W-16N

21
41W-16N

REINKING

RD

Creek

Tyler

MAPLEHURST

RED LEAF RD

REINKING WOODS

43W-15N

**STARKS**

20

72

29
42W-15N

SETTLERS GROVE RD

28
41W-15N

MAPLEHURST LN

BRIER PINES II

MAPL

OLD STAGE RD

THURNAU

72

CHICAGO, MINNEAPOLIS, ST. PAUL & PACIFIC R.R.

REINKING

RD

HIGHLAND AVE

MEADOWSWEET

47

RD

31
43W-14N

32
42W-14N

20

33
41W-14N

SEDGEBROOK

BLANDRA WAY

YELLOW AVE

THURNAU

MANSFIELD ST

STORE

RAILROAD

STORE ST

ST

GROVE ST

PUBLIC

PRAIRIE ST

ST

RUTLAND TWP T 42 N
PLATO TWP T 41 N

JACKSON ST

F.D.

OAK

**PINGREE GROVE**
**60140**

5
43W-13N

4
42W-13N

3
41W-13N

RD

PLANK ROAD ESTATES

RD

HARTJE'S

PLANK

ROBIN LN

MEADOWLARK DR

HUMMINGBIRD ST

KIWI CT

BARR

MARSHALL

RD

RD

BARR RD BARR

8
43W-12N

9
42W-12N

10
41W-12N

SEE PAGES 10-11

SEE PAGES 14-15

GILBERTS

60136

BURNIDGE

FOREST
WILDWOOD
VALLEY
PRESERVE

BIG TIMBER ACRES

TRIPLE OAKS FARM

HEMMINGFORD HILLS

LYNCHMOORE

WILDWOOD WEST

HADEN'S

HIGHLAND ACRES

WEST HIGHLAND ACRES

HIGHLAND HAVEN

HIGHLAND GLEN

DUNDEE MIDDLE

40W-16N   39W-16N   38W-16N   37W-16N
40W-15N   39W-15N   38W-15N   37W-15N
40W-14N   39W-14N   38W-14N   37W-14N
40W-13N   39W-13N   38W-13N   37W-13N
40W-12N   39W-12N   38W-12N   37W-12N

RUTLAND TWP R 7 E
DUNDEE TWP R 8 E

TYRRELL R 7 E
R 8 E

T 42 N
T 41 N

NORTHWEST TOLLWAY

NORTHWESTERN

CHICAGO & NORTH

CHICAGO MINNEAPOLIS ST. PAUL

POWERS RD

TIMBER RD

GALLIGAN RD

TOWER HILL RD

MCCORNACK RD

COOMBS RD

TYRRELL RD

CHICAGO RD

BIG TIMBER RD

HIGHLAND AVE

SWITZER RD

DAMISCH RD

72

90

20

TOWER HILL

MILL ST
WILBY ST
RAILROAD ST
MATTESON ST
JACKSON ST
TURNER
GALLIGAN
UNION ST

TYLER CREEK

TOLLVIEW TER
TOLLVIEW CT
PARK ST
S PARK ST
WINDMILL
WEST END DR

ELGIN ST

CENTER RD
SOLA DR
EAST DR

ARROWHEAD DR
ARROWHEAD DR
WHITE FEATHER DR
RED HAWK DR
SLEEPING BEAR DR
SHINING MOON PATH
RUNNING DEER LN
TOWNE
PIERCE ST
JOAN CT
SANDRA CT
JEAN ST
PAMELA ST
TOWNE CT
DEBORAH ST
SUZANNE ST
PAULINE CT

KILKENNY CT
KILDARE ST
WELCH CT
KERRY ST
TIPPERARY
HENNESSY CT
MASON ST
MASON RD

TIMBER RIDGE DR
GRAND AV
OLIVER DR
BONNIE LN
PLEASANT DR

CASTLE KNOLL
KNOLL
GUNPOWDER CT
GUNPOWDER TR
HIDDEN CT
ABILENE

CHISOLM LN
CHISOLM TR
HIGH
CHAPPAREL
WESTERN AV
CHEYENNE CT
BRINDLEWOOD CT
RIDGEWOOD LN
AMBERWOOD DR
WEDGEWOOD DR

BRECHIN TRAIL
GLENDOWER TERR
GLENMORE LN
STONEHAVEN DR
STONEHAVEN CT
BLENMORE CT
ELMER DR
LINDA LN

TRIPLE OAKS FARM RD
FARM VIEW CT
PHEASANT CT
FIELD LN
HARPER CT
GUTHRIE DR
ATCHISON RD
HOMESTEAD DR

LIMERICK LN

POLLITT DR

ALFT

OAK KNOLL

INDUSTRIAL DR

SEE PAGES 8-9

SEE PAGES 12-13

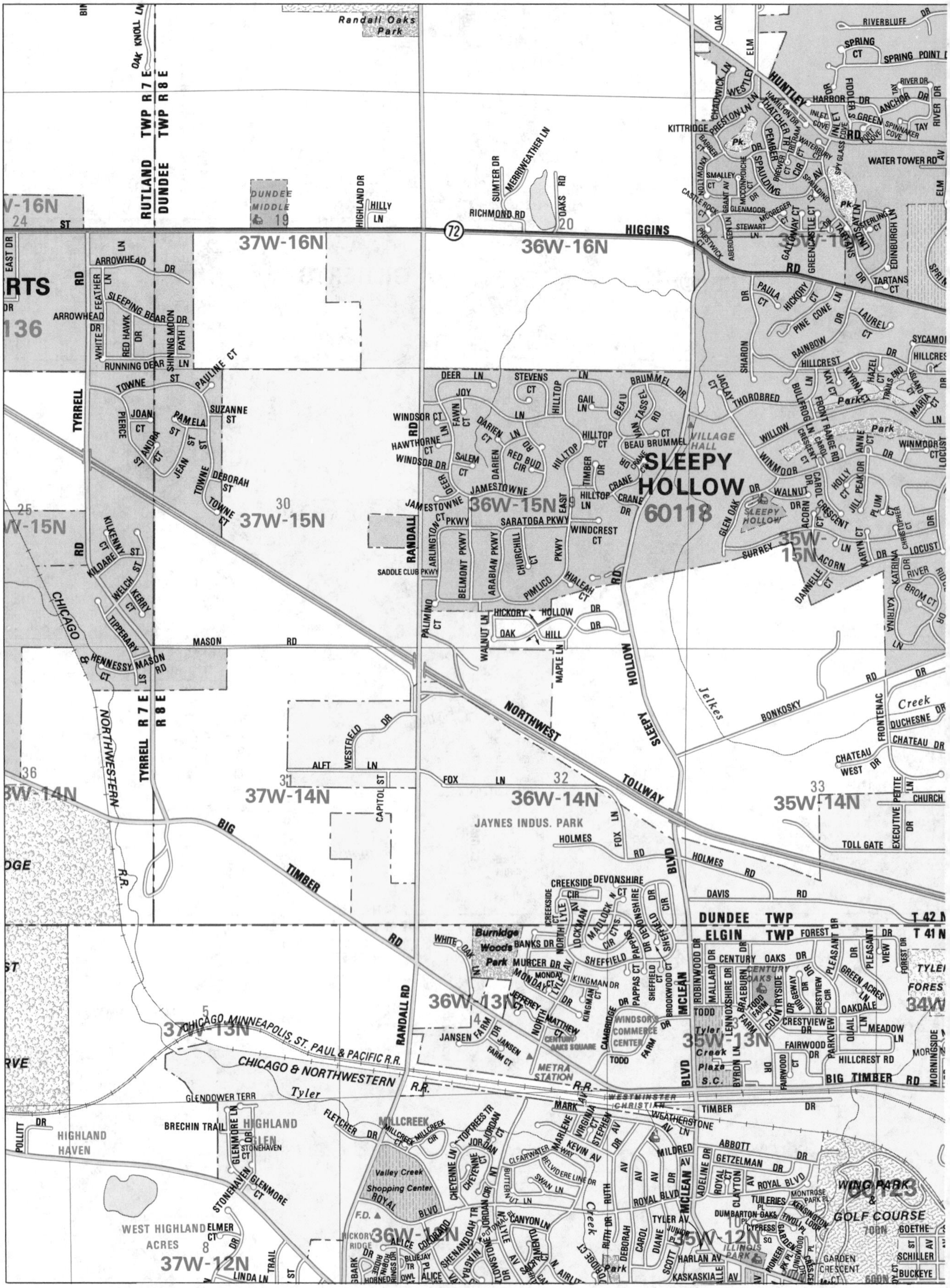

SLEEPY HOLLOW 60118

VILLAGE HALL

Randall Oaks Park

DUNDEE MIDDLE

RUTLAND TWP R 7 E
DUNDEE TWP R 8 E

RICHMOND RD

HIGGINS RD

37W-16N
36W-16N
37W-15N
36W-15N
35W-15N
37W-14N
36W-14N
35W-14N
36W-13N
35W-13N
37W-13N
37W-12N
36W-12N
35W-12N

V-16N 24
V-15N 25
36

RTS 136

JAYNES INDUS. PARK

NORTHWEST TOLLWAY

Jelkes Creek

Frontenac Creek

DUNDEE TWP
ELGIN TWP
T 42 N
T 41 N

TYRRELL R 7 E
TYRRELL R 8 E

CHICAGO, MINNEAPOLIS, ST. PAUL & PACIFIC R.R.

CHICAGO & NORTHWESTERN R.R.

METRA STATION

Burnidge Woods Park

WINDSOR COMMERCE CENTER

Windsor Oaks Square

WEST HIGHLAND ACRES

HIGHLAND GLEN

HIGHLAND HAVEN

Valley Creek Shopping Center

Millcreek

WING PARK & GOLF COURSE 60123

BIG TIMBER RD

RANDALL RD

CHICAGO ST

NORTHWESTERN R.R.

Century Oaks Farm

33

32

31

30

20

19

8

5

4

SEE PAGES 8-9

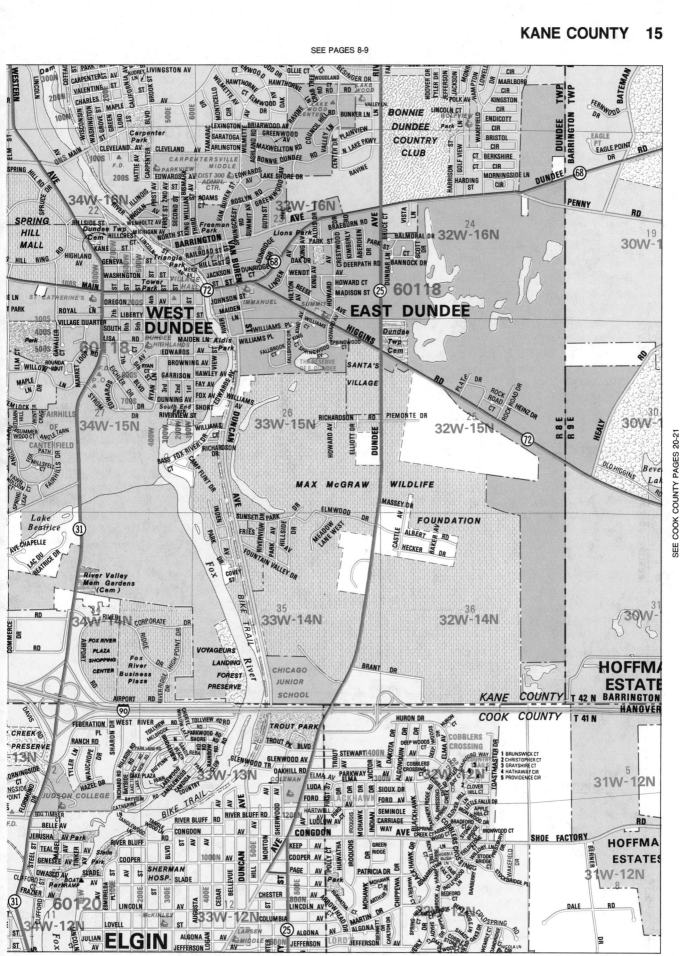

SEE COOK COUNTY PAGES 20-21

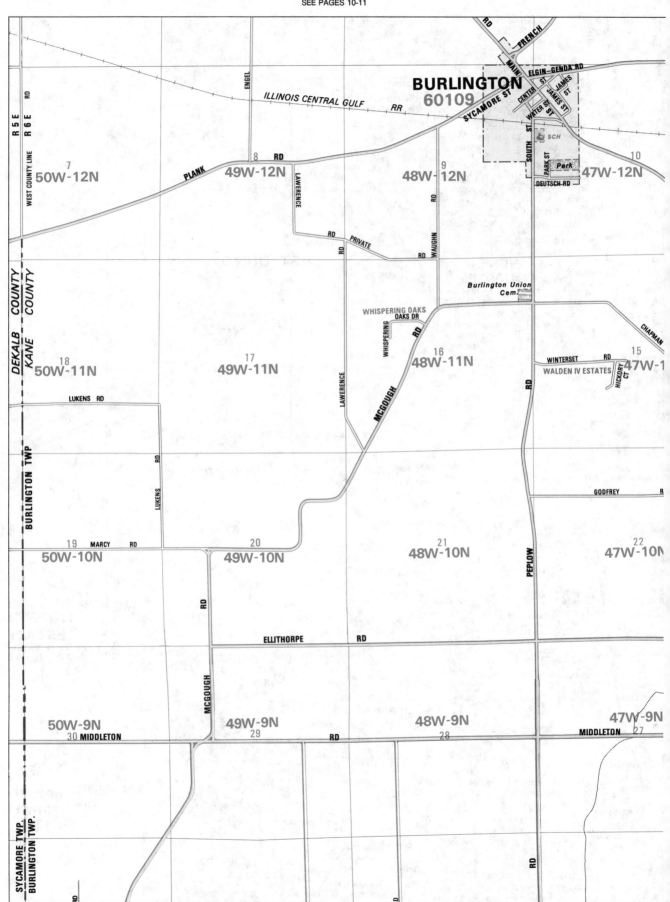

**BURLINGTON**
**60109**

ILLINOIS CENTRAL GULF RR

FRENCH RD

ENGEL

R 5 E
R 6 E
RD

WEST COUNTY LINE

PLANK RD

8 RD
**49W-12N**

7
**50W-12N**

LAWERENCE

RD
RD PRIVATE

WAUGHN RD

9
**48W-12N**

RD

SYCAMORE ST

MAIN

ELGIN-GENDA RD

CENTER ST
JAMES ST
JAMES ST

WATER ST
SOUTH ST

SCH

PARK ST
Park

DEUTSCH-RD

10
**47W-12N**

DEKALB COUNTY
KANE COUNTY

BURLINGTON TWP

LUKENS RD

18
**50W-11N**

17
**49W-11N**

LAWERENCE

WHISPERING OAKS
OAKS DR

WHISPERING RD

MCGOUGH

16
**48W-11N**

Burlington Union
Cem.

RD

PEPLOW

WINTERSET RD
WALDEN IV ESTATES
HICKORY
CT

CHAPMAN

15
**47W-1**

LUKENS RD

19 MARCY RD
**50W-10N**

RD

20
**49W-10N**

21
**48W-10N**

GODFREY R

22
**47W-10N**

ELLITHORPE RD

MCGOUGH

MCGOUGH

50W-9N
30 MIDDLETON

**49W-9N**
29

RD

**48W-9N**
28

MIDDLETON

**47W-9N**
27

SYCAMORE TWP.
BURLINGTON TWP.

RD

RD

RD

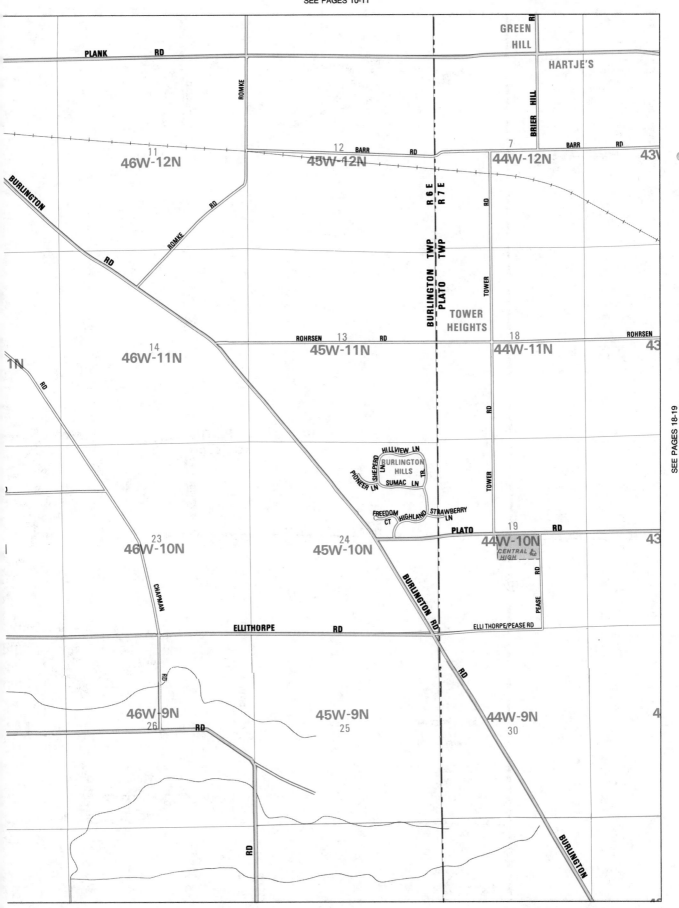

SEE PAGES 18-19

SEE PAGES 12-13

SEE PAGES 16-17

PLANK ROAD

HARTJE'S

PLANK

ESTATES

ROBIN LN

MEADOWLARK DR

HUMMINGBIRD ST

KIWI CT

BARR

MARSHALL

BRIER HILL

BARR RD

8

BARR

RD

9

10

**12N**

**43W-12N**

**42W-12N**

**41W-12N**

ILLINOIS CENTRAL GULF RR

ROHRSEN RD

17

RD

16

ROHRSEN

15

RD

**11N**

**43W-11N**

**42W-11N**

**41W-11N**

RD

**PLATO CENTER**

F.D.

CHICAGO ST

RUSSELL RD

SCH

WOODROW LN

LAKESIDE CT

HID

LAKE

RIPPBURGER RD

MUIRHEAD

CHIPPEWA

CHIPPEWA

MOHAWK TR

PASS

RD

20

PLATO

21

RD

22

WILDB.

**43W-10N**

**42W-10N**

**41W-10N**

47

PEASE RD

RD

DITTMAN

RD

SILENT MEADOW

MEADOW DR

MUIRHEAD LN

TRIBUTARY LN

HIGHBANK

BOWES

DR BEND

LN

GREENFIELD RD

MUIRHEAD CT

BOWES BEND

CT

CURRENT

CHANNEL CT

KENDALL RD

MUIRHEAD RD

BOWES BEND

WINGOVER PARK

CARLETTA LN

SOUTH GATE RD

CREEKWOOD

CREEKWOOD CT

**43W-9N**

29

**42W-9N**

28

TAMARA DR

TAMARA HEIGHTS

MUIRHEAD RD

**41W-9N**

27

PLATO RIDGE DR

CREEKVIEW DR

MUIRHEAD RD

SILVANA DR

LILLY ST

OAK BLUFF DR

OAK BLUFF

CONNORS RD

LENZ

RD

47

BURLINGTON

THE WOODLANDS

STEEPLE CIR

LN

CIR

EDGEWOOD RD

RD

WOODBRIDGE

SEE PAGES 24-25

CHICAGO & NO

GLENDOWER TERR

Tyle

BRECHIN TRAIL HIGHLAND

POLLITT DR

HIGHLAND HAVEN

GLENMORE LN
GLENMORE DR
CT

STONEHAVEN GLENMORE

AVE
W

PRESERVE

SWITZER RD

20

**40W-12N** 11

**39W-12N** 12

COOMBS RD

**38W-12N** 7

WEST HIGHLAND ACRES

ELMER DR

STONEHAVEN CT

JACKSON
CHARLOTTE CT
TINA
LINDA LN
WEST VIEW ST
OLWIN
WEST VIEW RD
AV
TERR

**37W-12N** 8

HILLTOP
ALMORA

PLANK RD

**UDINA**

F.D.

ORCHARD LN

ORCHARD HIDDEN HILL TR

OATWIND

MARSHFIELD
HIDDEN
MASON
AVALON
WINCHESTER
COLONIAL
SARAH
RANDALL RIDGE CT
NEWBERRY CT

ALMORA HEIGHTS

BROOKSIDE
HOWARD

RANDALL RIDGE

WINHAVEN DR

COLONIAL DR

**40W-11N** 14

**39W-11N** 13

RUSSELL RD

MONTAGUE FOREST

CLIFF DR

ROMEO CIR

VERONA DR

JULIET DR

CAPULET CT

JULIET DR

CAPULET

ROMEO CIR

SAIGUN DR

CENTRAL DR

PLATO TWP
ELGIN TWP

R 7 E
R 8 E

NESTLER RD

**38W-11N** 18

RALEIGH

WILLIAMSBURG GREEN

WILLIAMSBURG DR

JOHNSTON
MARYHILL CT
LAMONT

WELD RD

WELD RD

STRATFORD LN

BURGESS DR

JAGUAR CT

OXFORD

YORK LN

NEWPORT CT

FLAGPOLE CT

ELGIN COUNTRY CLUB

LEITH CT

WELDWOOD

Fitchie

WOODEN
LAKES

GREENVIEW LN

OAK RIDGE FARM

PRAIRIE CROSS LN

OAK RIDGE LN

LONG LN

**40W-10N** 23

**39W-10N** 24

Creek

NESTLER RD

WATER RD

**38W-10N** 19

WILLIAMSBURG DR

MANCHESTER LN

**37W-10N** 20

WOODBR
NO
COVERE

BRIAR LN

TRAILS END

RED CLOUD LN

HOGAN HILL

KOSHARE CIR

HOPI TR

LELAND CT
S
N

BECKMAN LN

APACHE RUN

HOGAN HILL

TIMBER LANE
W LORI

LORI LN

PUEBLO PEAK

SANTA FE TR

**CATATOGA**

KOSHARE

ARROW

**38W-9N**

MAKER

PARK PATH

TIPI LN

TIPI

THUNDER GAP

**37W-9N** 29

WEATHERINGTON CT RD

WHISPERING SPRINGS LN

**SADDLEBROOK**

CORRON RD

OAK TREE LN

**40W-9N** 26

NESTLER RD

ADOBE RIDGE RD

**39W-9N** 25

BOWES RD

NOKOMIS LN

30

HEARTLAN

SUNFLOWER LN

CROSS CT

CREEK

SAVANNA LAKES DR

SAVANNA LAKES CT

NOLAN RD

Bowes

STURBRIDGE WAY

BRIMFIELD DR

RD

HOPPS RD

BITTERSWEET LN

PASEO PL

BITTERSWEET LN

**38W-8N**

RICHARD DR
DR
LN
SA

ACORN LN

WOOD
LN
KRISTEN

NING DEER TRAIL

HOPPS RD

ILLINOI

Creek

SEE PAGES 20-21

SEE PAGES 14-15

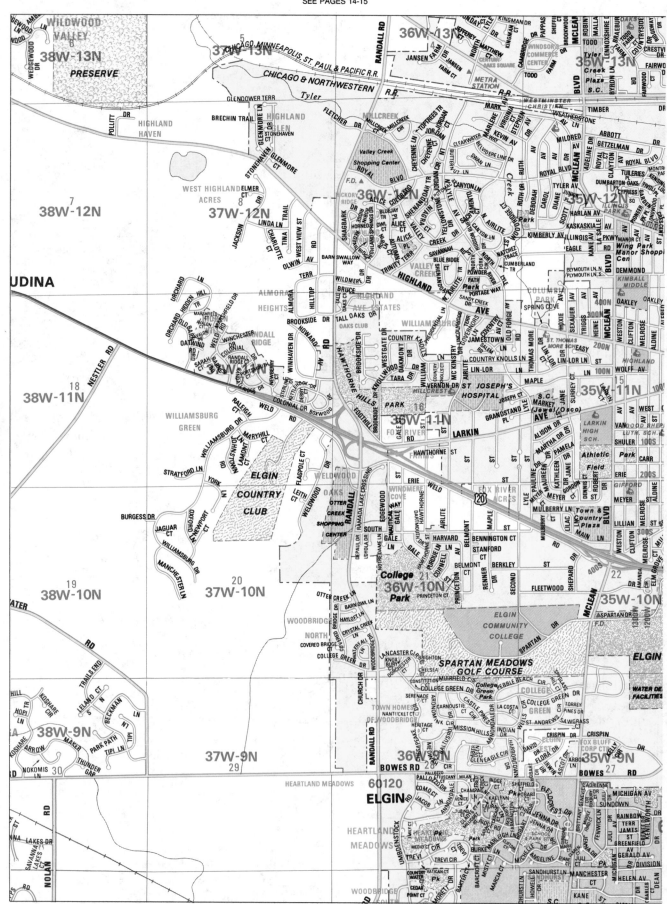

SEE PAGES 14-15

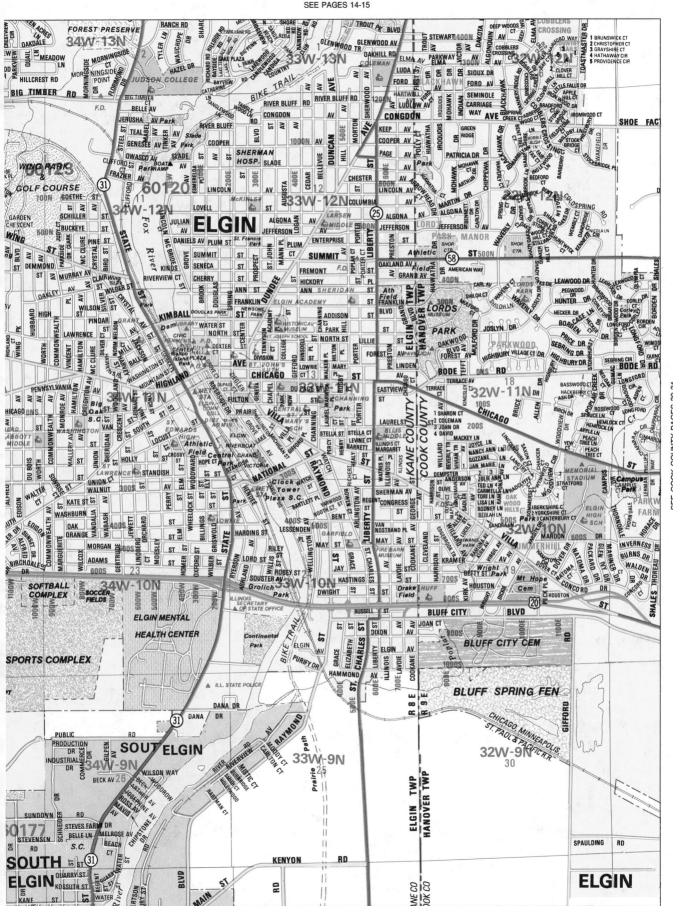

ELGIN

SEE COOK COUNTY PAGES 30-31

SEE PAGES 26-27

SEE PAGES 16-17

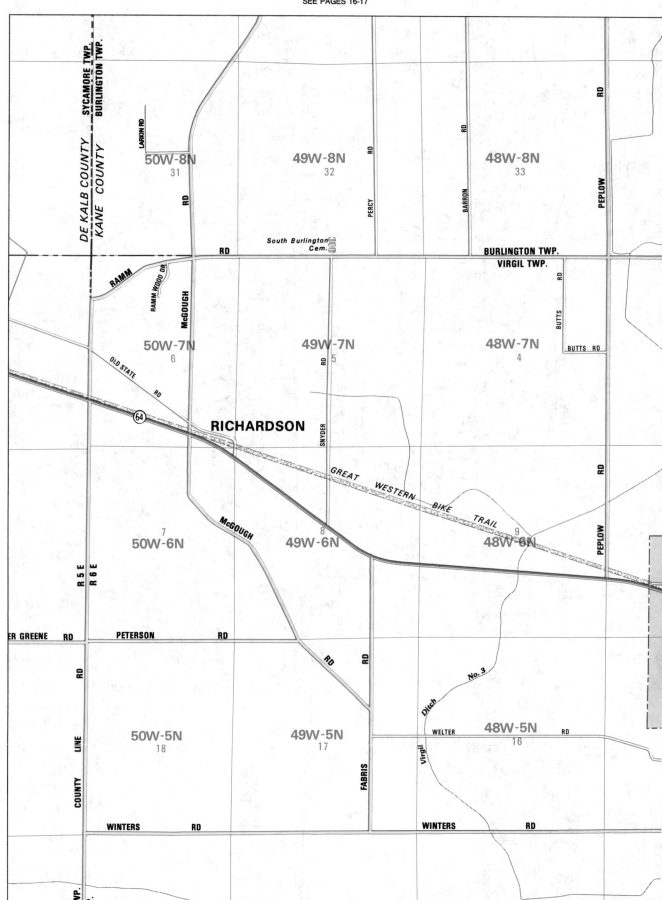

SYCAMORE TWP.
BURLINGTON TWP.

DE KALB COUNTY
KANE COUNTY

LARKIN RD

50W-8N
31

49W-8N
32

48W-8N
33

RD

PERCY

RD

BARRON

PEPLOW

RD

South Burlington Cem.

RD

BURLINGTON TWP.
VIRGIL TWP.

RAMM

RAMM WOOD DR

McGOUGH

RD

BUTTS

RD

50W-7N
6

49W-7N
5

48W-7N
4

BUTTS RD

OLD STATE

RD

RD

64

RICHARDSON

SNYDER

GREAT WESTERN BIKE TRAIL

RD

McGOUGH

7
50W-6N

8
49W-6N

9
48W-6N

PEPLOW

R 5 E
R 6 E

ER GREENE RD

PETERSON RD

RD

RD

RD

Ditch No. 3

RD

COUNTY LINE

50W-5N
18

49W-5N
17

FABRIS

WELTER

Virgil

48W-5N
16

RD

WINTERS RD

WINTERS RD

WP.

SEE PAGES 28-29

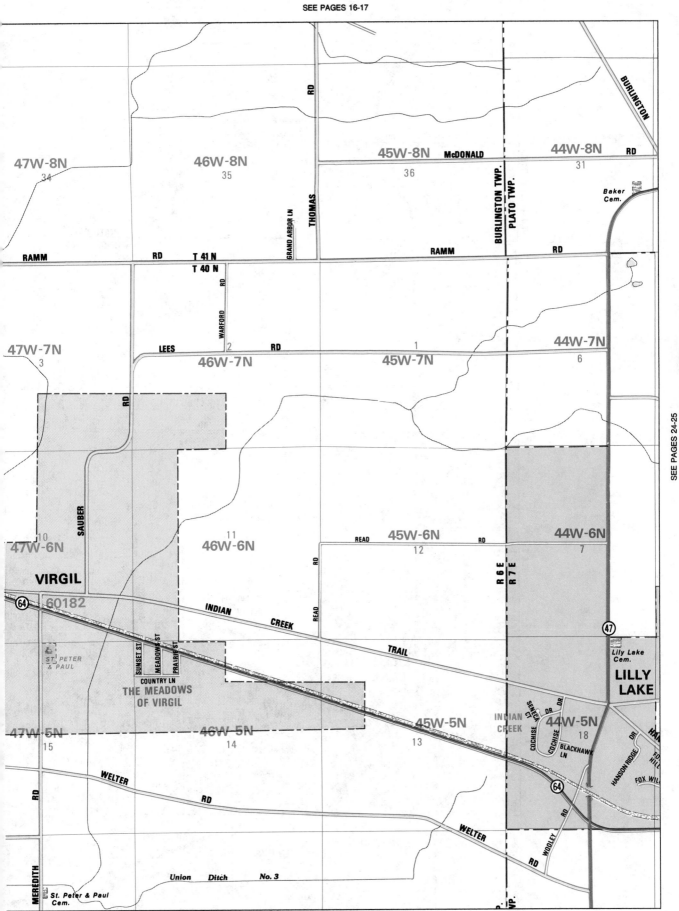

SEE PAGES 24-25

47W-8N
34

46W-8N
35

45W-8N   McDONALD
36

44W-8N
31

BURLINGTON

RD

THOMAS

GRAND ARBOR LN

Baker
Cem.

BURLINGTON TWP.
PLATO TWP.

RAMM          RD          T 41 N
              T 40 N

WARFORD   RD

RAMM          RD

47W-7N
3

LEES       RD
46W-7N          2

45W-7N

44W-7N
6

SAUBER   RD

47W-6N
10

46W-6N
11

READ      RD
45W-6N
12

R 6 E
R 7 E

44W-6N
7

**VIRGIL**

(64)  **60182**

INDIAN      CREEK      TRAIL

READ   RD

(47)

Lily Lake
Cem.

**LILLY
LAKE**

ST. PETER
& PAUL

SUNSET ST   MEADOW ST   PRAIRIE ST

COUNTRY LN
**THE MEADOWS
OF VIRGIL**

INDIAN
CREEK

44W-5N
18

COCHISE CT   SENECA DR   COCHISE DR

BLACKHAWK
LN

HANSON RIDGE DR

FOX
HILL

FOX WIL

47W-5N
15

46W-5N
14

45W-5N
13

(64)

WELTER      RD

WELTER

MEREDITH   RD

St. Peter & Paul
Cem.

Union   Ditch   No. 3

WOOLEY   RD

HAN

SEE PAGES 18-19

SEE PAGES 22-23

CONNORS RD

BURLINGTON

47

THE WOODLANDS

WOODBRIDGE

STEEPLE CIR
STEEPLE CIR
EDGEWOOD RD
HILL CIR
KENDALL
ANNIS
TALL PINES
WOODBRIDGE LN

45W-8N McDONALD RD
36

44W-8N RD
31

43W-8N
32

42W-8N
33

Baker Cem.

RD

BRIERWOOD

BRIERWOOD

ICKENHAM

PLATO TWP.
CAMPTON TWP.

BURLINGTON TWP.
PLATO TWP.

RAMM RD

DITTMAN RD

45W-7N
1

44W-7N
6

43W-7N
5

42W-7N
4

GLI

No. 2

SILVER

GLEN

RD

EVENING PRAIRIE DR
NANCY LN
GARY CT

Virgil Ditch

VEI

45W-6N RD
12

44W-6N
7

43W-6N
8

42W-6N
9

H

R 6 E
R 7 E

BUCK CT

GOPHER CT

VALLEY DR

BADGER CT

OTTER LN

PRAIRIE VALLEY

BEAVER LN
BEAVER

PRAIRIE

CREEKSIDE CT

SWANBERG RD

THE KNOLLS

EMPIR

47

TRAIL

Lily Lake Cem.

LILLY LAKE

60151

EMPIRE RD

KETTLEHOOK CT
TIMBER TR
RAVINE

KINGSWOOD
AUDUBON CT
IRONWOOD CT
ARBORETUM
FOREST
GLEN LN

CRANBERRY LN
RANGER LN
JENS JENSON
MEADOWLARK CT
SYLVAN

QUAIL CT

JENS JENSON CT
EAGLE LN
LOST LN

WINDIN

STEEPLE CHASE

COPP

45W-5N
13

INDIAN CREEK

COCHISE DR
SENECA CT

44W-5N
18

BLACKHAWK LN
COCHISE

HANSON RIDGE DR

HANSON

MEADOWVIEW LN

HEATHER LN
CLOVER CT
FESCUE CT

CORNWALL DR

LESLIE CT
COLEMAN LN

43W-5N
17

HAZELWOOD

HAZELWOOD TRAIL

FOXMOOR DR

HARVEST LN
PADDOCK LN
BRIDLE CT

42W-5N
16

FERSON

HIDDEN

SPRINGS CT

RETREAT CT

FOX HUNT

FOX HILL CT
FOX WILDS DR
FOX WILDS CT

CAMPTON

SANCTUARY

CAMPTON MEADOWS

EERSON CT

HAZELWOOD

GREAT WESTERN

BIKE Ferson TRAIL

RETREAT CT

WINDIN

TRAIL

64

WOOLEY RD

RD

MARY MEADOWS

W. MARY DR
CAROL
MARY CT
MARY E. MARY DR

WEST WOODS
HUNTERS HILL
WESTWOOD DR

WEST DR

TWP.
TWP.

WELTER RD

OAK OPENINGS

PATHFINDER
HAWKEYE
KILDEER LN
MOHICAN LN
FENMORE LN
DEERSLAYER DR
BLUE LARKSPUR LN
JUNCUS

CHALLEDON DR

WHIRLAWAY DR

COUNCIL

HAWK

FOXFIELD DR

FORES

CHAFFIELD

CHAFFIELD

SEE PAGES 30-31

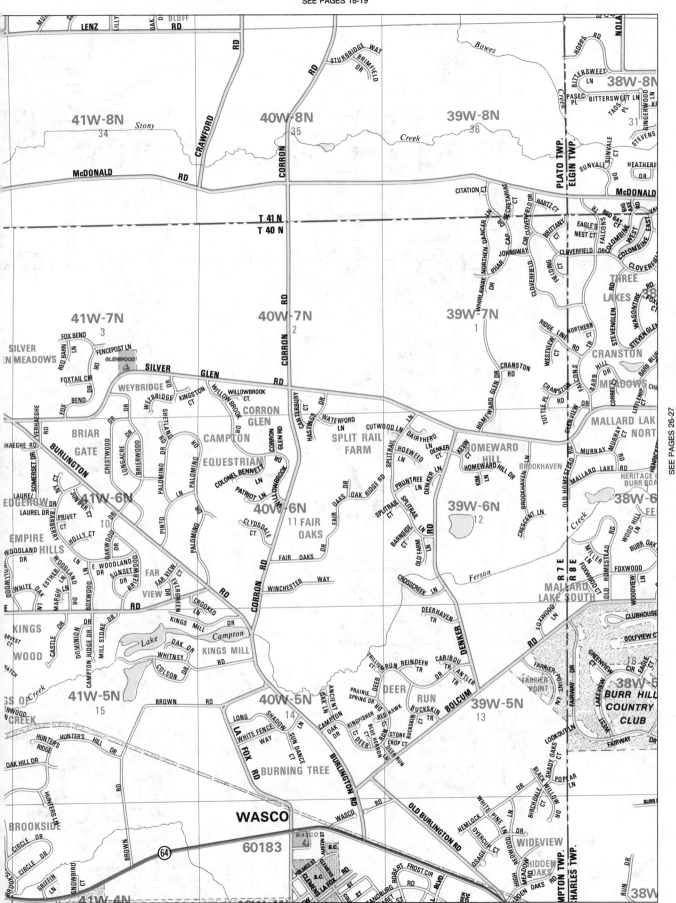

SEE PAGES 26-27

SEE PAGES 30-31

SEE PAGES 20-21

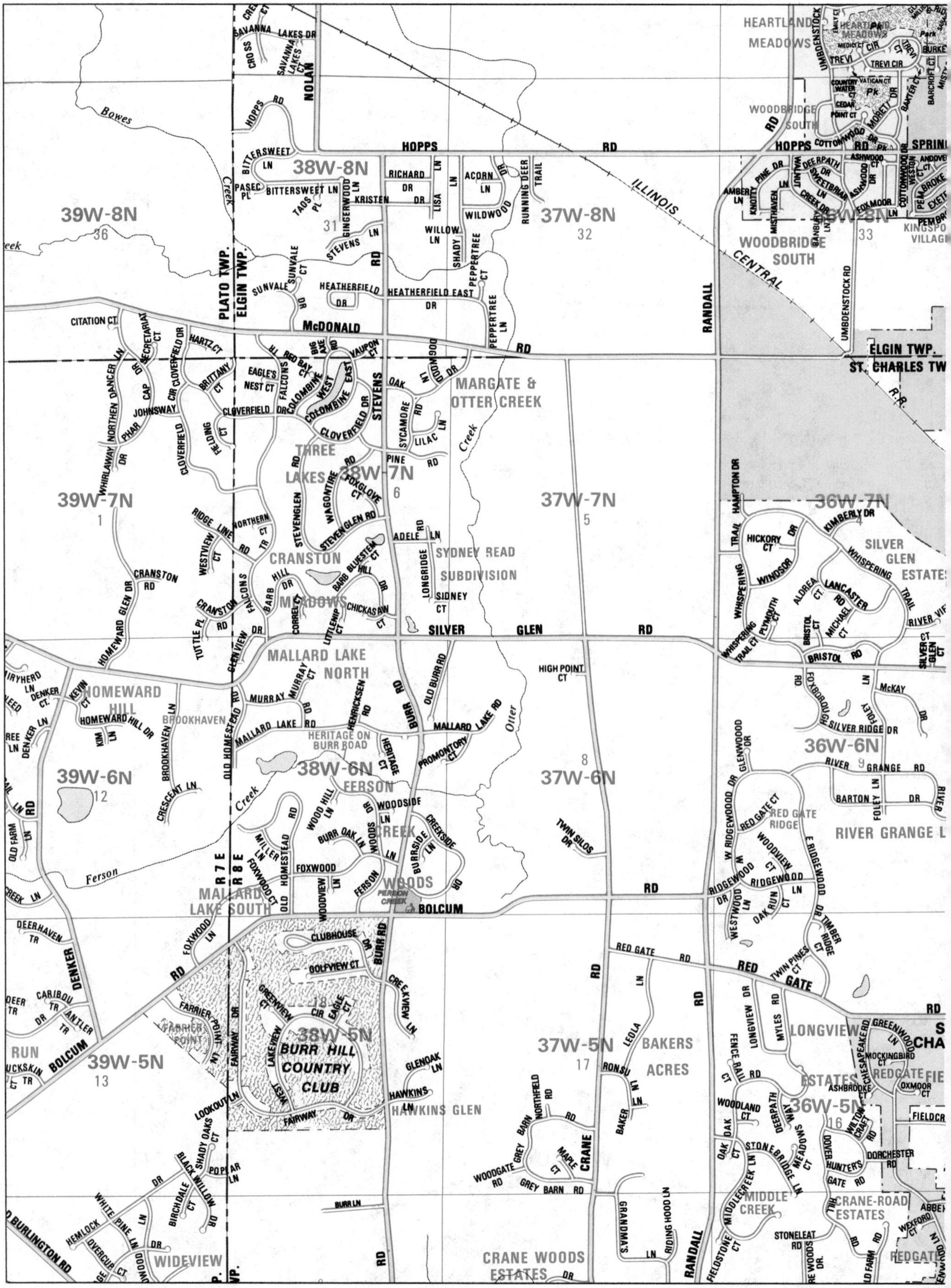

HEARTLANDS MEADOWS

WOODBRIDGE SOUTH

HOPPS RD

ILLINOIS

39W-8N
36

38W-8N
31

37W-8N
32

38W-8N
33

WOODBRIDGE SOUTH

RANDALL

CENTRAL

ELGIN TWP.
ST. CHARLES TWP.

PLATO TWP.
ELGIN TWP.

McDONALD RD

MARGATE & OTTER CREEK

THREE LAKES

39W-7N
1

38W-7N
6

37W-7N
5

36W-7N
4

SILVER GLEN ESTATES

CRANSTON MEADOWS

SYDNEY READ SUBDIVISION

SILVER GLEN RD

MALLARD LAKE NORTH

HOMEWARD HILL

HERITAGE ON BURR ROAD

39W-6N
12

38W-6N

37W-6N
8

36W-6N
9

RIVER GRANGE L

MALLARD LAKE SOUTH

FERSON CREEK WOODS

BOLCUM

RED GATE RIDGE

RD

RED GATE RD

BOLCUM RD

39W-5N
13

38W-5N
BURR HILL COUNTRY CLUB

37W-5N
17

BAKERS ACRES

LONGVIEW ESTATES

REDGATE FIE

36W-5N
16

CRANE

MIDDLE CREEK

CRANE-ROAD ESTATES

WIDEVIEW

BURR LN

CRANE WOODS ESTATES

RANDALL

SEE PAGES 24-25

SEE PAGES 20-21

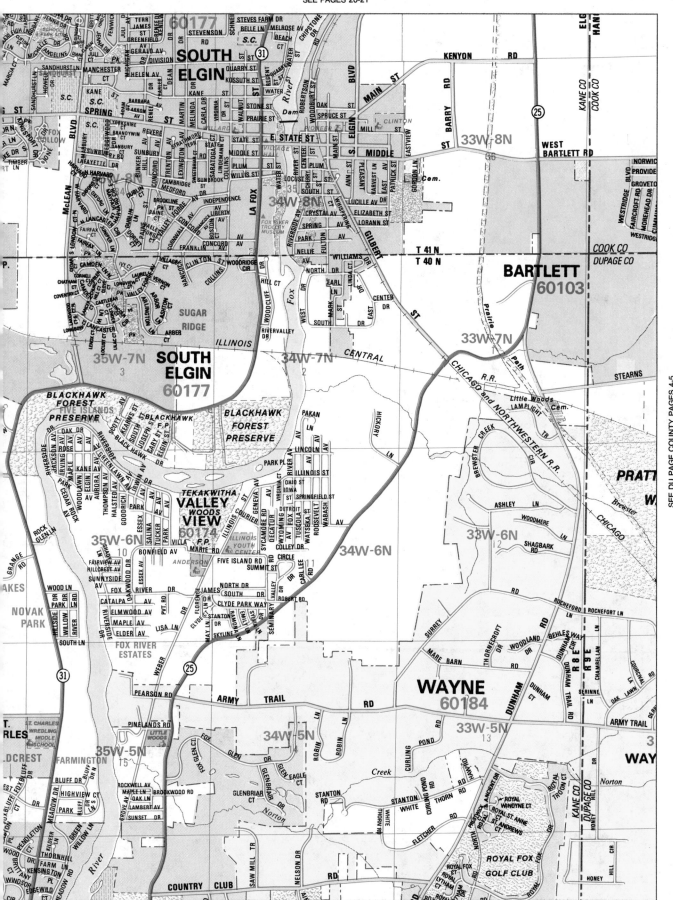

SEE PAGES 32-33

SEE DU PAGE COUNTY PAGES 4-5

SEE PAGES 22-23

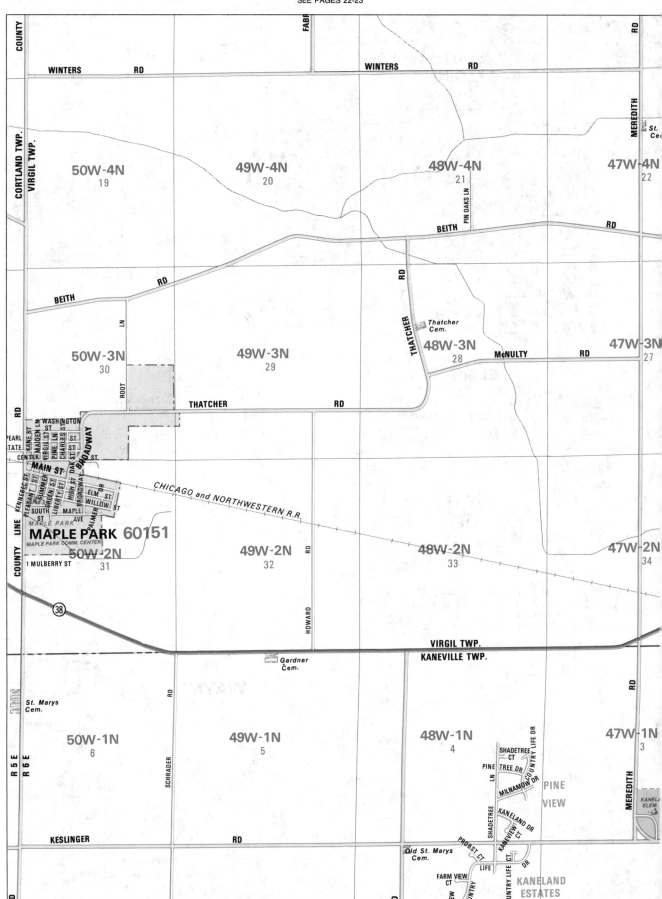

SEE PAGES 34-35

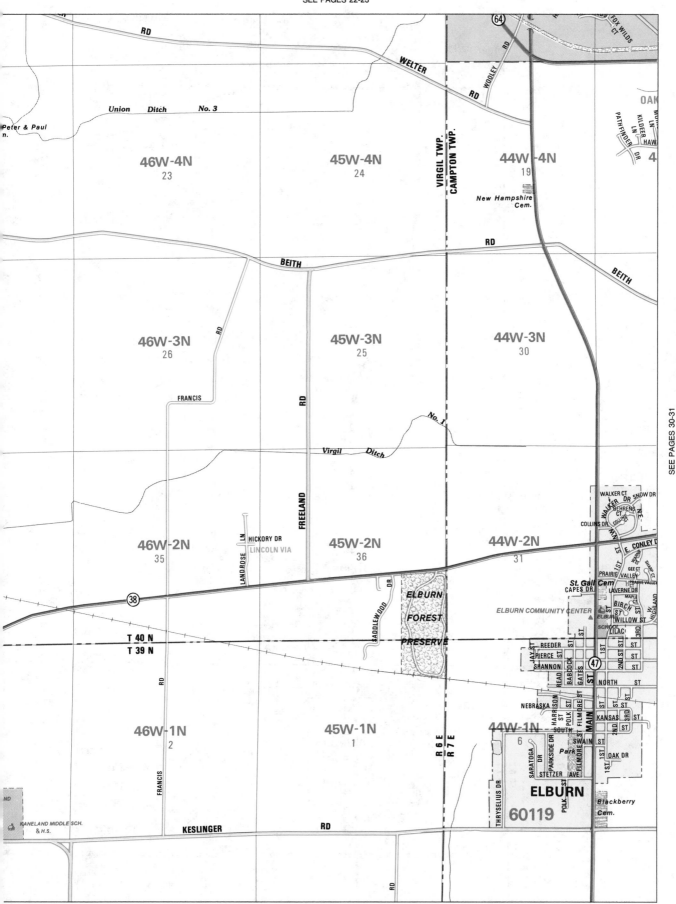

RD

WELTER RD

Union Ditch No. 3

Peter & Paul
n.

OAK

64

WOOLEY RD

PATHFINDER LN
KILDEER LN
HAW

**46W-4N**
23

**45W-4N**
24

VIRGIL TWP.
CAMPTON TWP.

**44W-4N**
19

New Hampshire
Cem.

RD

BEITH

BEITH

**46W-3N**
26

RD

**45W-3N**
25

RD

**44W-3N**
30

FRANCIS

No. 1

Virgil Ditch

FREELAND

WALKER CT
SNOW DR
BEHRENS
CT

WALKER DR
N.E.

COLLINS DR

E. CONLEY D

**46W-2N**
35

LANDROSE LN
HICKORY DR
LINCOLN VIA

**45W-2N**
36

**44W-2N**
31

1ST ST

GEE CT
SILVER CT

PRAIRIE VALLEY

St. Gall Cem
CAPES DR
LAVERNE DR
MAPLE CT
BIRCH ST
HIGHLAND

38

SADDLEWOOD DR

**ELBURN
FOREST
PRESERVE**

ELBURN COMMUNITY CENTER
ELBURN
SCH.
WILLOW ST
LILAC

3RD ST

T 40 N
T 39 N

REEDER ST
PIERCE ST
SHANNON

MAX ST
READ
BABCOCK
GATES

ST
ST

1ST

2ND ST
ST

47

NORTH ST

RD

NEBRASKA
HARRISON ST
POLK ST
FILMORE ST

KANSAS ST
2ND ST
3RD ST

**46W-1N**
2

FRANCIS

**45W-1N**
1

R 6 E
R 7 E

SOUTH

MAIN ST

**44W-1N**
6

SARATOGA DR
PARKSIDE DR
STETZER AVE

Park

SWAIN ST
FILMORE ST

1ST ST
OAK DR

ND

KANELAND MIDDLE SCH.
& H.S.

THRYSELIUS DR

**ELBURN
60119**

POLK ST

Blackberry
Cem.

KESLINGER RD

RD

SEE PAGES 30-31

SEE PAGES 24-25

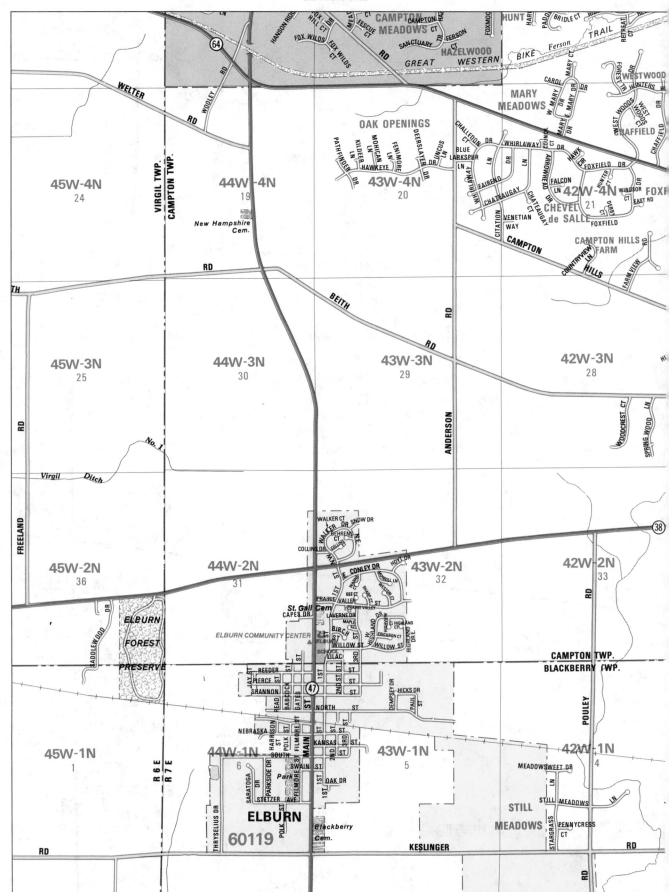

SEE PAGES 28-29

SEE PAGES 36-37

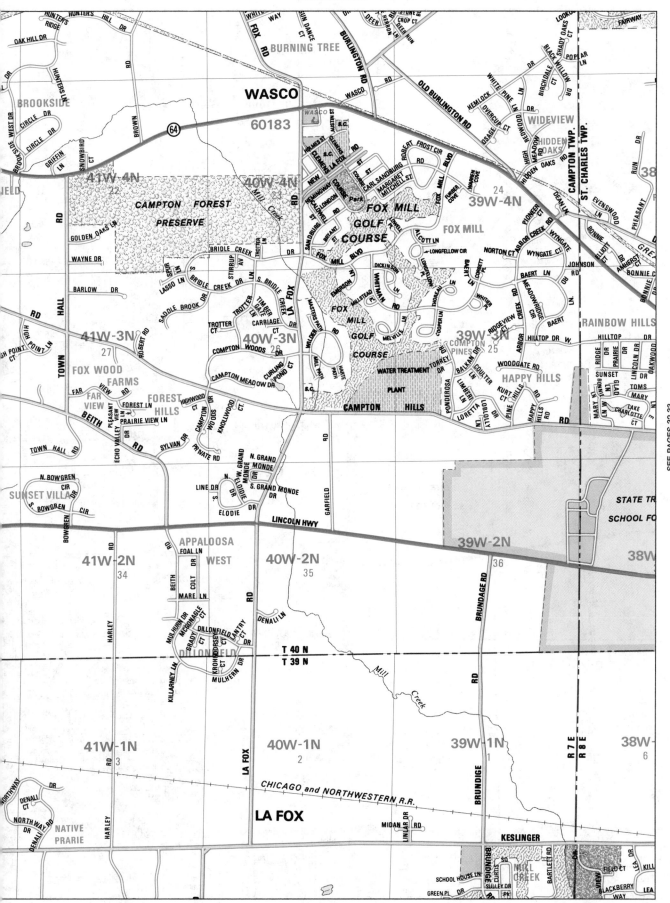

SEE PAGES 26-27

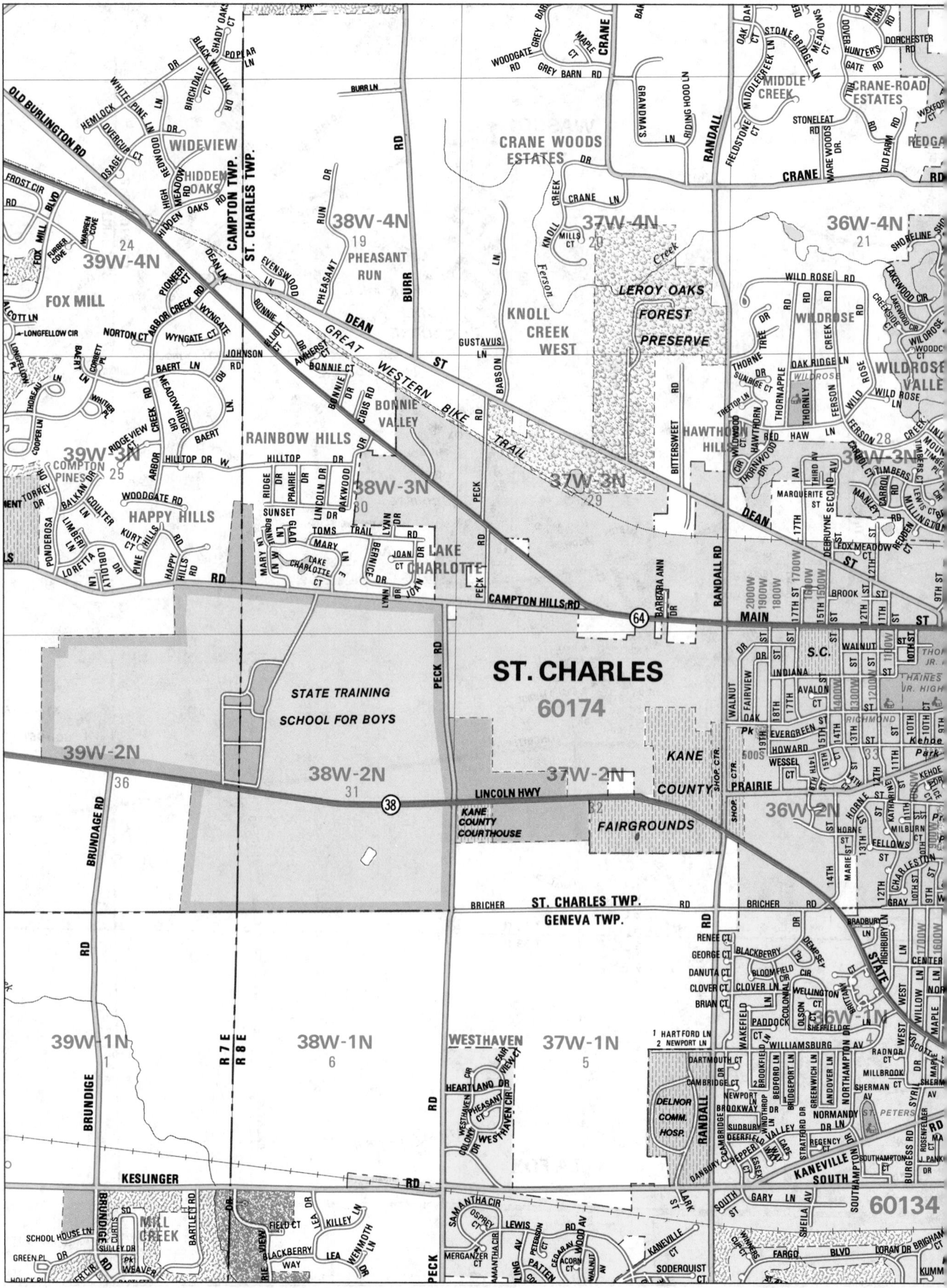

SEE PAGES 30-31

**ST. CHARLES**

**60174**

STATE TRAINING
SCHOOL FOR BOYS

KANE
COUNTY

KANE
COUNTY
FAIRGROUNDS

KANE
COUNTY
COURTHOUSE

LINCOLN HWY

ST. CHARLES TWP.
GENEVA TWP.

CRANE WOODS
ESTATES

KNOLL
CREEK
WEST

LEROY OAKS
FOREST
PRESERVE

HAWTHORN
HILLS

MIDDLE
CREEK

CRANE-ROAD
ESTATES

WILDROSE

WILDROSE
VALLE

WIDEVIEW

HIDDEN
OAKS

FOX MILL

COMPTON
PINES

HAPPY HILLS

RAINBOW HILLS

BONNIE
VALLEY

LAKE
CHARLOTTE

PHEASANT
RUN

GREAT WESTERN BIKE TRAIL

DEAN ST.

OLD BURLINGTON RD

WESTHAVEN

DELNOR
COMM.
HOSP.

MILL
CREEK

KESLINGER RD

60134

39W-4N
24

38W-4N
19

37W-4N
20

36W-4N
21

39W-3N
25

38W-3N
30

37W-3N
29

36W-3N

39W-2N
36

38W-2N
31

37W-2N
32

36W-2N
33

39W-1N
1

38W-1N
6

37W-1N
5

36W-1N
4

R 7 E
R 8 E

CAMPTON HILLS RD

CAMPTON TWP.
ST. CHARLES TWP.

RANDALL RD

PECK RD

BRUNDAGE RD

BRUNDIGE RD

SEE PAGES 38-39

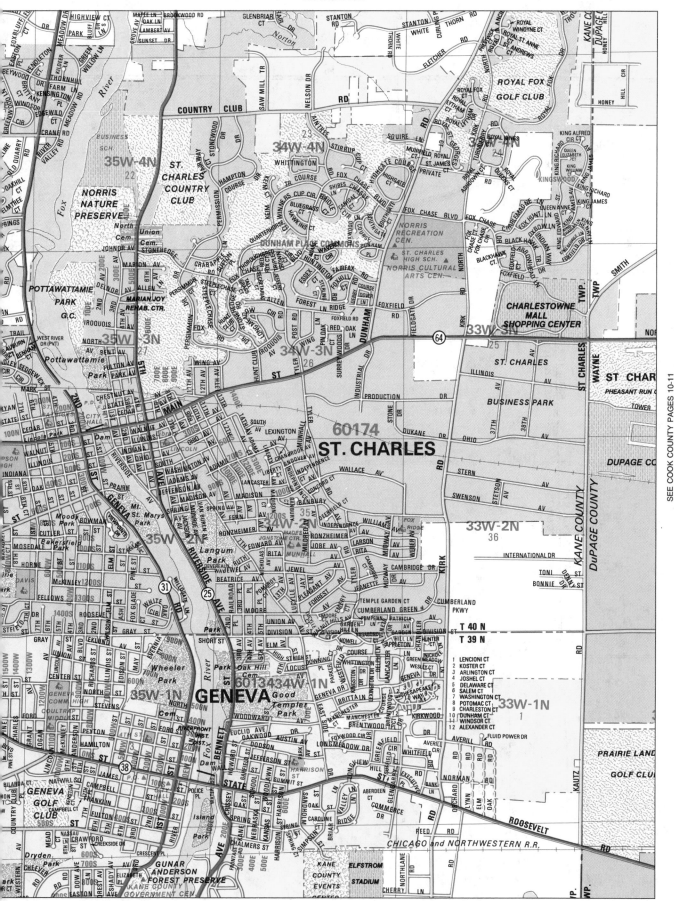

SEE PAGES 28-29

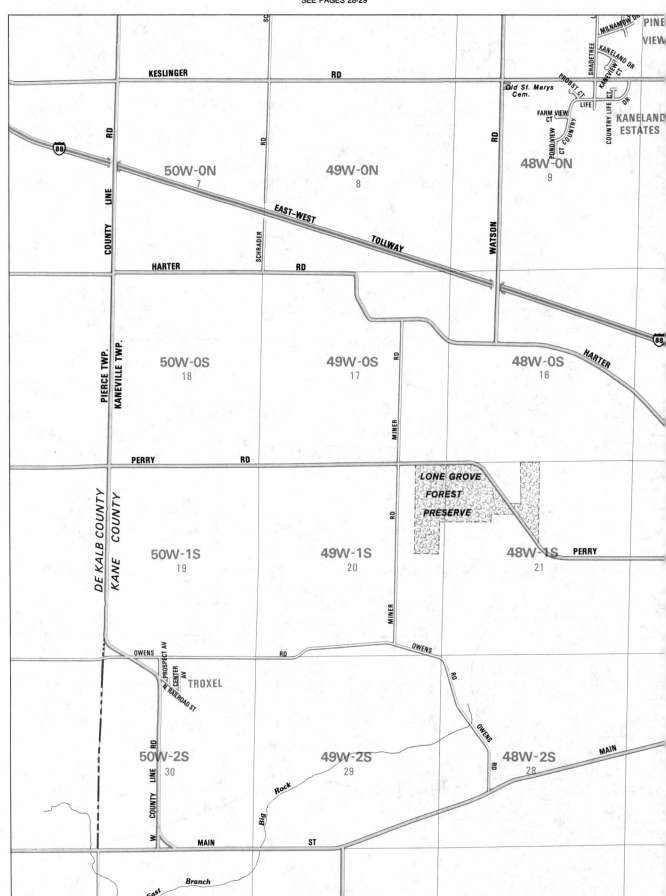

SEE PAGES 40-41

SEE PAGES 28-29

SEE PAGES 36-37

MEREDIT

KANELAND ELEM.

KANELAND MIDDLE SCH. & H.S.

FRANC

KESLINGER RD

THRYSELIUS DR

STETZER

**ELBU**

**60119**

**47W-0N**
10

**46W-0N**
11

**45W-0N**
12

**44W-0N**
7

RD

SCHNEIDER

**47W-0S**
15

**46W-0S**
14

**45W-0S**
13

ROWE RD

**44W-0S**
18

RD

Creek

ROWE

RD

**KANEVILLE TWP.**
**BLACKBERRY TWP.**

BATEMAN

RD

Bateman

RD

EAST–WEST

DAUBERMAN

RD

Welch

TOLLWAY

RD

**47W-1S**
22

**46W-1S**
23

BATEMAN

**45W-1S**
24

LORANG

CONCORD CT

GREENBRIER DR

**44W-1S**
19

**BLACKBERRY ACRES**

ST

MAIN

Cem

SOUTH LORANG RD

LORANG RD

SCHOOL ST

LOVELL ST

MERRIL AV

LOCUST CT

ELM CT

LOCUST ST

LOCUST ST

ELM

ST

PINE ST

MAPLE ST

ELM ST

CEDAR CT

HARTER

**KANEVILLE**
**60144**

**45W-2S**
25

88

**47W-2S**
27

**46W-2S**
26

RD

SEAVEY RD

LORANG

**44W-2S**
30

SHIP

SEE PAGES 40-41

SEE PAGES 30-31

60119

KESLINGER RD

RD

**45W-0N**
12

**44W-0N**
7

OAKWOOD DR

ROMBURY OAKS

**43W-0N**
8

HUGHES RD

CAROLYN CT

SPRING VALLEY DR

**42W-0N**
9

POULEY RD

STARG CT

THRYSE

POL

Bluebbery Cem.

SCHNEIDER RD

KENMAR

WINDENOAK

SURREY DR

ROWE

KENMAR DR

KENMAR CT

KENMAR LN

KENMAR LN

KENMAR DR

Creek

HUGHES

RD

**45W-0S**
13

KANEVILLE TWP.

BLACKBERRY TWP.

**44W-0S**
18

ROWE RD

WHISPERING OAKS DR

WHISPERING OAKS

AUTUMN LN

TIMBER CREST DR

TIMBERCREST

**43W-0S**
17

Blackberry

**42W-0S**
16

GREEN RD

Creek

ROWE

SMITH

DONNY HILL DR

NORTHERN VIEW CT

RIDGE DR

CLOVER HILL LN

BATEMAN RD

BATEMAN RD

THORNDON

DONNY HILL MEADOWS

SEE PAGES 34-35

**45W-1S**
24

TOLLWAY

LORANG RD

CONCORD CT

GREENBRIER DR

**44W-1S**
19

BLACKBERRY ACRES

47

MAIN

**43W-1S**
20

BLACKBERRY HILL RD

ST

GREEN RD

**42W-1S**
21

SOUTH LORANG RD

TALL OAKS TRAIL

WOODHILL ESTATES

WILLOW CREEK

WILLOW CREEK DR

WILLOW CREEK CT

PINE ROW

WILLOW CREEK DR

GREEN ST

GREEN

CREEKSIDE CT

**45W-2S**
25

LORANG RD

88

**44W-2S**
30

NOTTINGHAM WOODS

THE OLD MIDLOTHIAN TURNPIKE

NOTTINGHAM

MILL RD

OAKLEAF

DEBUSSEY DR

OAKWOOD TERR

RED OAK DR

**43W-2S**
29

**42W-2S**
28

SEAVEY RD

SEAVEY RD

SEAVEY RD

TOWNSHIP

TOWNSHIP

EAST-WEST

88

33

SEE PAGES 30-31

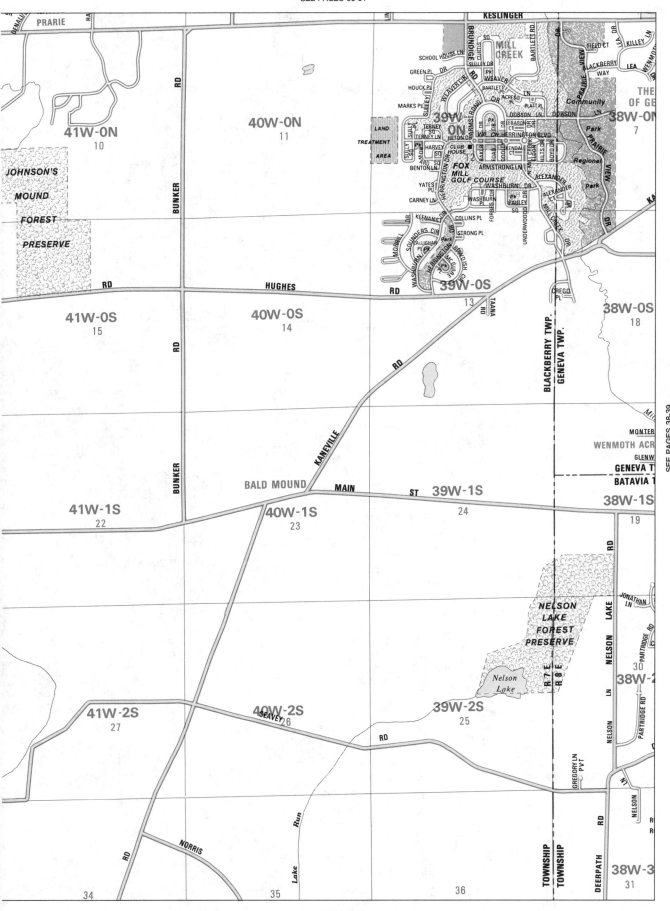

SEE PAGES 38-39

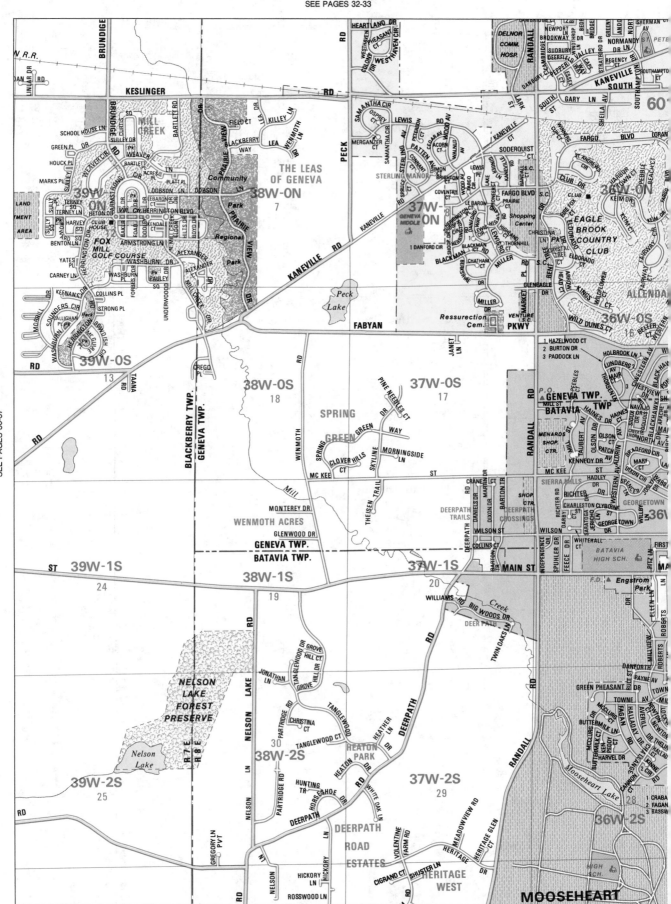

SEE PAGES 32-33

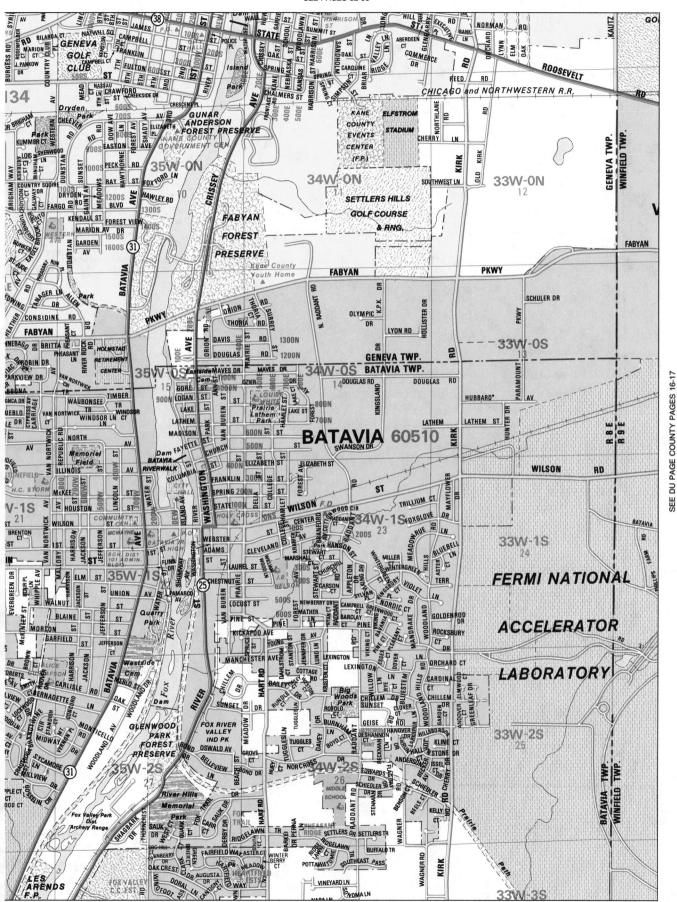

# BATAVIA 60510

# FERMI NATIONAL ACCELERATOR LABORATORY

SEE DU PAGE COUNTY PAGES 16-17

SEE PAGES 44-45

# 40 KANE COUNTY

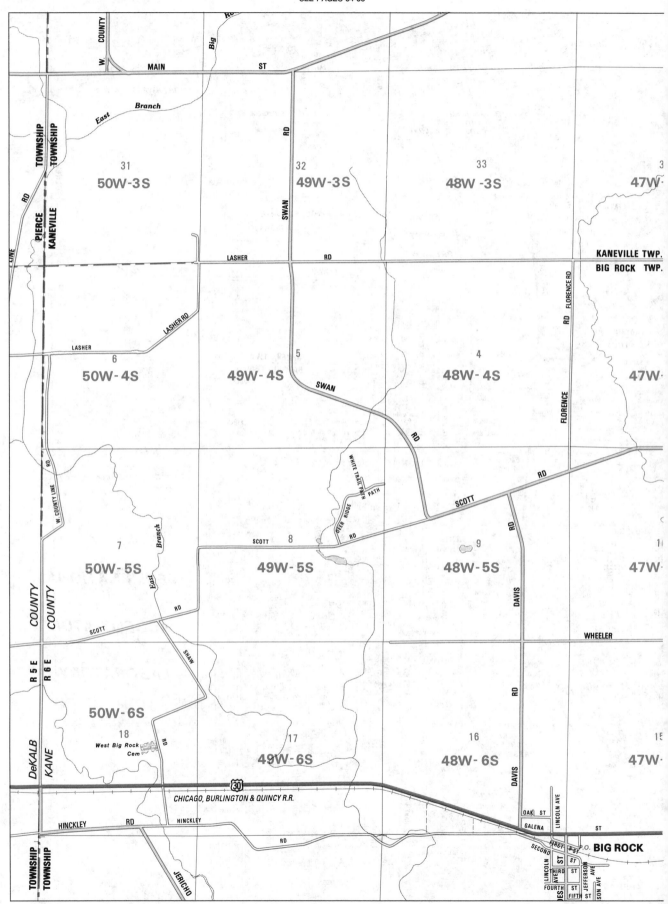

SEE PAGES 34-35

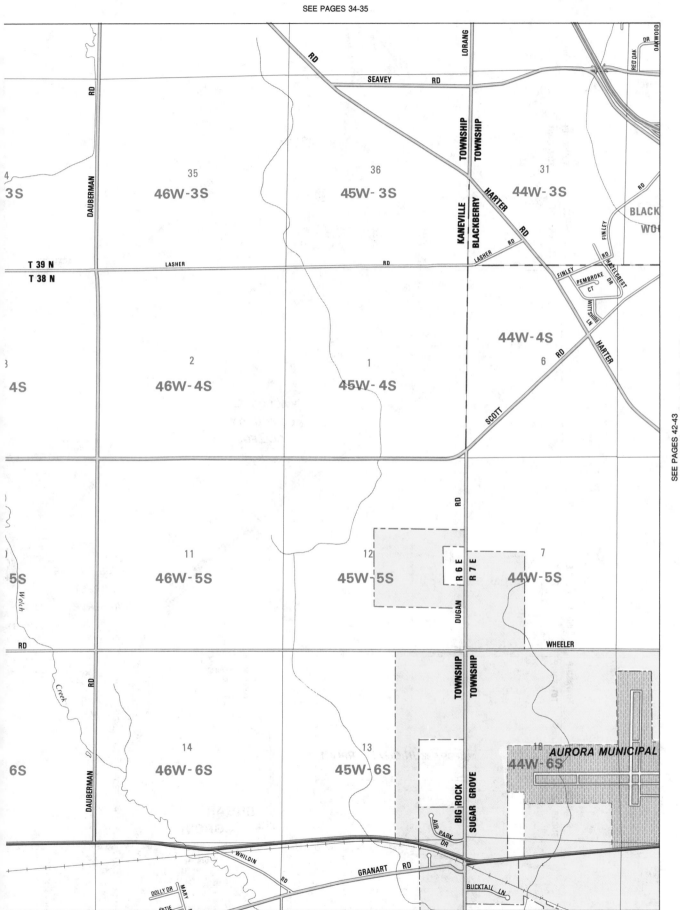

SEE PAGES 42-43

SEE PAGES 40-41

LORANG

SEAVEY RD

SEAVEY RD

RED OAK DR

OAKWOOD DR

EAST-WEST

**88**

TOWNSHIP

TOWNSHIP

KANEVILLE

BLACKBERRY

HARTER RD

36

3S

31

**44W-3S**

MARIAN LA

MARIAN CIR

FINLEY RD

NORTH RD

THORNAPPLE TREE

SCOTT RD

**47**

32

**43W-3S**

LAKEWOOD DR

TOLLWAY

33

**42W-3S**

BLACKBERRY WOODS

LASHER RD

RD

FINLEY RD

PEMBROKE CT

HAZELCREST DR

WITTSHIRE LN

THORNAPPLE TREE RD

MERRILL RD

BLACKBERRY

SUGAR GROVE

**44W-4S**

HARTER RD

6

SCOTT RD

**43W-4S**

OLD OAK RD

5

MERRILL RD

**42W-4S**

RD

4

4S

4S

WAUBONSEE COMMUNITY COLLEGE

Sugar Grove Cem

WINDSTONE LN

COURTNEY CIR

HAVERHILL CT

STAFFORD WOODS

WINDSOR RD

FAIRLEE RD

RD

R 6 E

R 7 E

DUGAN RD

2

5S

7

**44W-5S**

8

**43W-5S**

LINDSEY DR

RD

KA-DE-KA RD

9

**42W-5S**

SMELBURNE CT

HANOVER LN

BRIAR GATE CIR

DOUGLAS

LYNCH

**BLISS WOODS FOREST PRESERVE**

MAY RD

BLISS RD

FOREST PRESER

JASON

STAYNER RD

WHEELER RD

CARRIAGE HILL LN

CARRIAGE HILL CT

JODY LN

PARK DR

CAPITOL RD

TOWNSHIP

TOWNSHIP

BIG ROCK

SUGAR GROVE

AIR PARK DR

18

19

**AURORA MUNICIPAL AIRPORT**

**44W-6S**

**43W-6S**

DIVISION DR

PARK AV

16

**47**

**42W-6S**

3

6S

6S

**SUGAR GROVE**

ANART RD

**30**

BUCKTAIL LN

**60554**

MEADOWS DR

MEADOWS CT

BASTIN DR

YOLANE CT

V.H. & P.D.

TERRY RD

MONNA ST

YOLANE DR ST

SNOW ST

ICIA LA

CALKINS DR

NNON ST

P.O.

RICHARD ST

NEIL STANLEY

JOY ST

CROSS ARBOR AV

JOY CT

**56**

SEE PAGES 48-49

SEE PAGES 36-37

GREGORY LN PVT

NELSON LN

HICKO

ROSSWO
ROSEWO

NORRIS RD

Lake Run

DEERPATH RD

**38W-3S**
31

34

35

**40W-3S**

36

**39W-3S**

TERRACE DR

TANNER
WOODS

BLACKBERRY TOWNSHIP

BATAVIA TOWNSHIP

**41W-3S**

BLISS RD

TANNER

OAKLAND LN

RD

DEER OAKS RD

DEERPATH RD

ORCHARD RD

ORCHARD

**TOWNSHIP**
**TOWNSHIP**

T 39 N
T 38 N

HEALY

NORRIS RD

RD

OAK

**41W-4S**

**40W-4S**

2

1

**39W-4S**

**38W-4S**

3

DENNY RD

SEE PAGES 44-45

EAST-WEST

88

56

NORRIS RD

NORTH INDIAN TR

SEQUOIA DR

CROFT

**39W-5S**

12

R 7 E R 8 E

SULLIVAN RD 7

**38W-5S**

BOWMAN DR

JOYCE DR

LAKEVI

11

**40W-5S**

**AURORA**
**WEST**
**FOREST**
**PRESERVE**

PRESTBURY
ELEM

Park

NORTH BUCKINGHAM

HANKES RD

**PRESTBURY**
**GOLF CLUB**

GOLFVIEW RD

HANKES RD

WEST RIDGE DR

DEERPATH RD

INDIAN TRAIL RD

INDIAN TRAIL RD

SUGAR GROVE TOWNSHIP

AURORA TOWNSHIP

IRONWOOD

FOXCROFT

OAKLEAF CT RD

SAPPHIRELA

1 MARIGOLD CT
2 BUTTERCUP CT
3 GOLDENROD CT
4 SUNFLOWER CT
5 GREENFIELD CT

**ORCHARD**
**VALLEY**
**G.C.**

ALMOND DR

ing Stable

**41W-6S**

15

Blackberry

Nature Trail

Creek

14

DENSMORE

WILDWOOD DR

SHAGBARK LA

HANKES RD

**39W-6**

13

**38W 6S**

**40W-6S**

GALENA

BLVD

Pioneer
Park

**WEST**
**AURORA**
**PLAZA**
**SHOPPING CENT**

BLACKBERRY
HISTORICAL VILLAGE

CHATHAM CIR

CAMBRIDGE

SEE PAGES 48-49

SEE PAGES 38-39

SEE PAGES 42-43

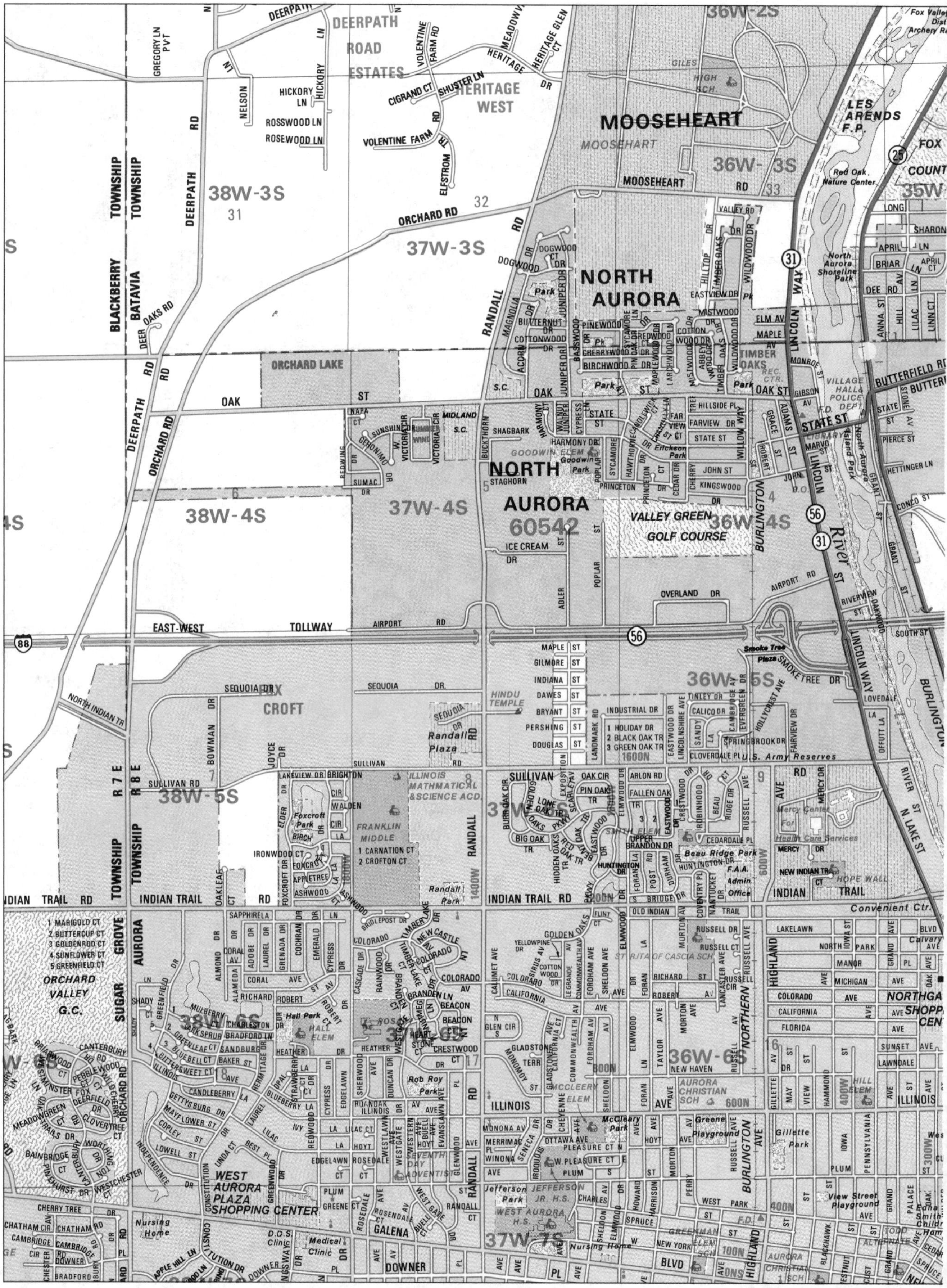

**MOOSEHEART**
*Mooshart*

**NORTH AURORA**

**NORTH AURORA 60542**

**LES ARENDS F.P.**

**FOX COUNT**

DEERPATH ROAD ESTATES

HERITAGE WEST

ORCHARD LAKE

VALLEY GREEN GOLF COURSE

EAST-WEST TOLLWAY

AIRPORT RD

HINDU TEMPLE

ILLINOIS MATHMATICAL & SCIENCE ACAD.

FRANKLIN MIDDLE

Foxcroft Park

Randall Plaza

Randall Park

U.S. Army Reserves

Mercy Center for Health Care Services

ORCHARD VALLEY G.C.

WEST AURORA PLAZA SHOPPING CENTER

NORTHGA SHOPP CEN

BLACKBERRY TOWNSHIP

BATAVIA TOWNSHIP

SUGAR GROVE TOWNSHIP

AURORA TOWNSHIP

38W-3S

37W-3S

38W-4S

37W-4S

36W-4S

38W-5S

37W-5S

36W-5S

38W-6S

37W-6S

36W-6S

37W-7S

35W

36W-2S

36W-3S

INDIAN TRAIL RD

ORCHARD RD

DEERPATH RD

RANDALL RD

BURLINGTON AVE

LINCOLN WAY

ILLINOIS

GALENA

DOWNER

SEE PAGES 38-39

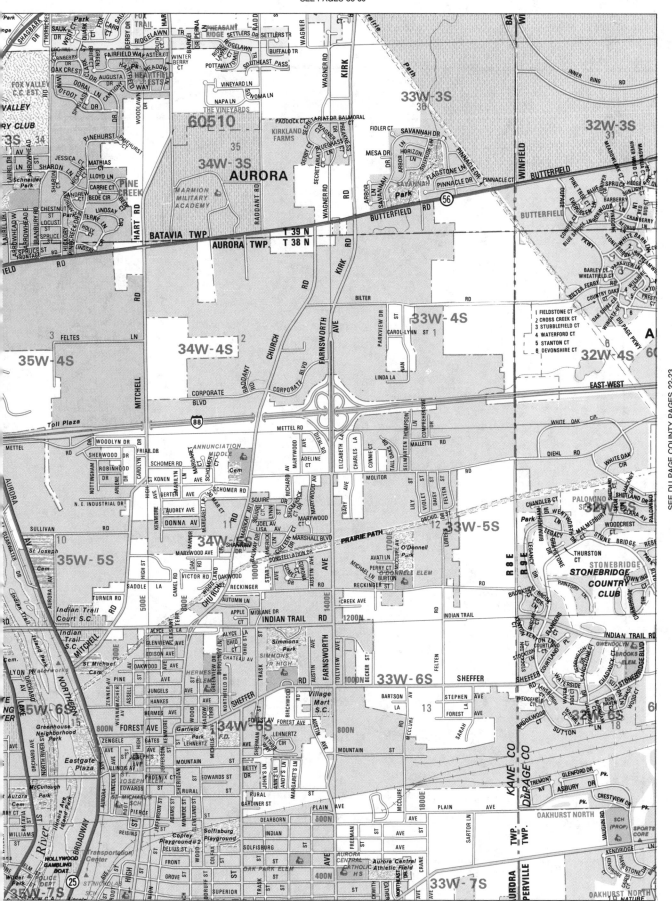

SEE DU PAGE COUNTY PAGES 22-23

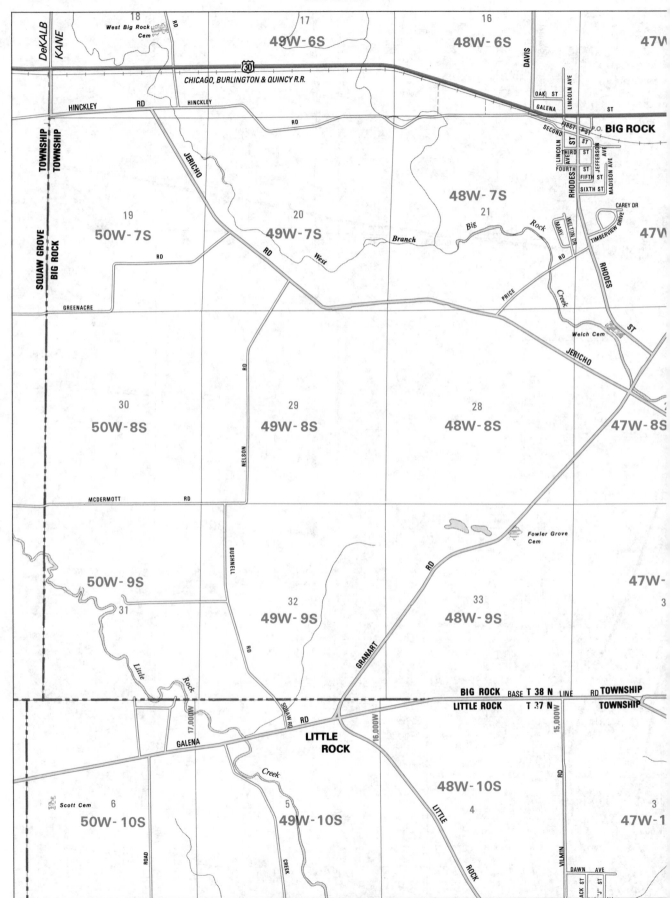

DeKALB
KANE

West Big Rock Cem

**49W-6S**
17

**48W-6S**
16

**47W**

DAVIS

CHICAGO, BURLINGTON & QUINCY R.R.
30

HINCKLEY RD
HINCKLEY RD

RD

OAK ST
GALENA

LINCOLN AVE

ST

**P.O. BIG ROCK**

TOWNSHIP
TOWNSHIP

JERICHO

SECOND ST
FIRST ST

SQUAW GROVE
BIG ROCK

**50W-7S**
19

**49W-7S**
20

RD

West

Branch

Big

**48W-7S**

21

Rock

LINCOLN AVE
THIRD ST
FOURTH ST
FIFTH ST
SIXTH ST

RHODES ST

JEFFERSON AVE
MADISON AVE

CAREY DR

**47W**

MARY
WELTON DR

TIMBERVIEW DRIVE

RD

RHODES

RD

GREENACRE

Price

Creek

Welch Cem

ST

JERICHO

**50W-8S**
30

**49W-8S**
29

**48W-8S**
28

**47W-8S**

NELSON RD

McDERMOTT RD

BUSHNELL

RD

Fowler Grove Cem

**50W-9S**

31

**49W-9S**
32

GRANART

RD

**48W-9S**
33

**47W-**

Little

Rock

17,000W

SQUAW RD

RD

16,000W

15,000W

**BIG ROCK** BASE T 38 N LINE RD **TOWNSHIP**
**LITTLE ROCK** T 37 N **TOWNSHIP**

GALENA

**LITTLE ROCK**

Creek

**48W-10S**

LITTLE

4

VILMIN RD

RD

3

Scott Cem
6

**50W-10S**

5

**49W-10S**

CREEK

ROCK

DAWN AVE
ACK ST "J" ST

**47W-1**

3

SEE PAGES 40-41

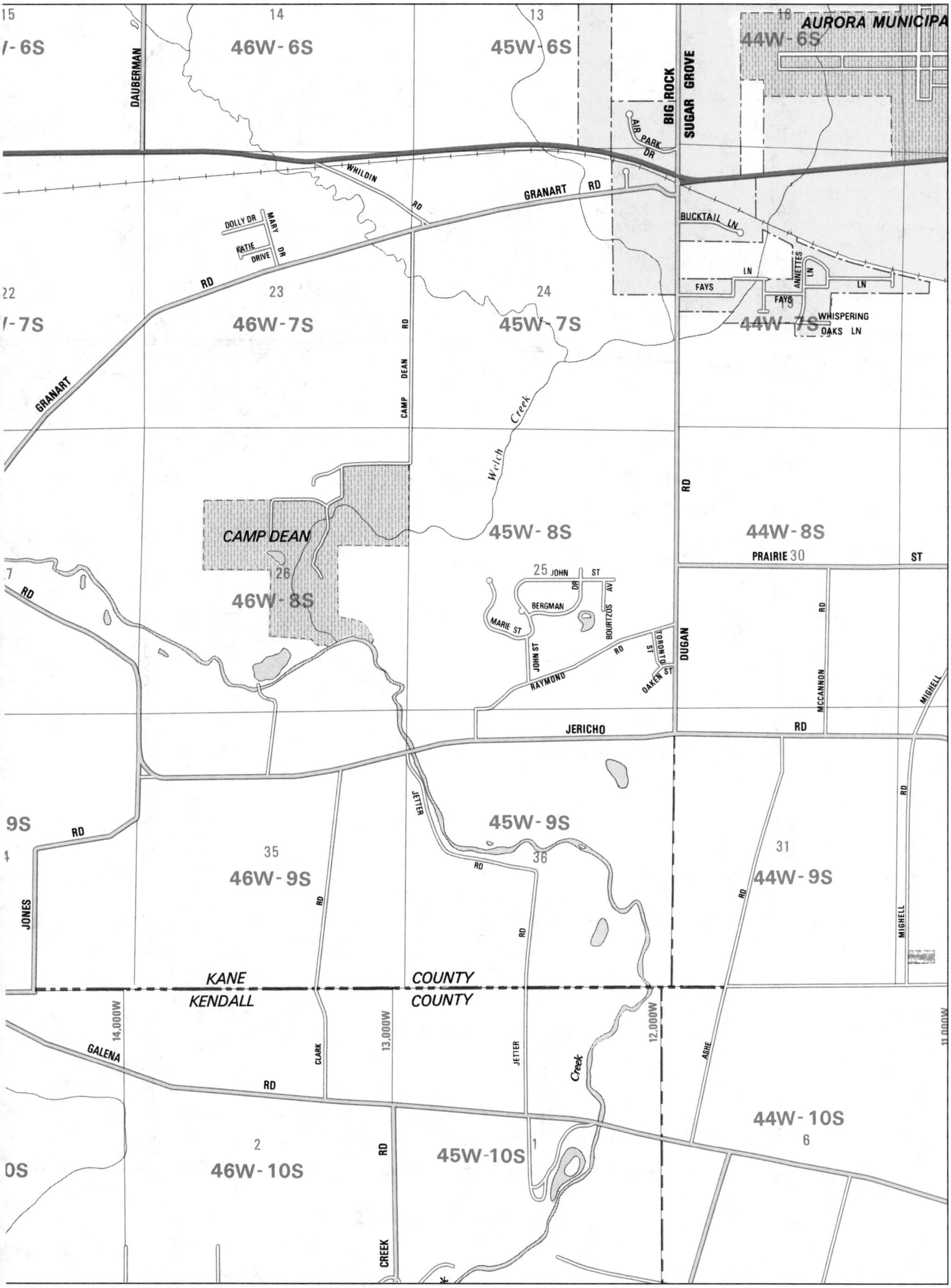

15    14    13    18    **AURORA MUNICIPA**

**/-6S**    **46W-6S**    **45W-6S**    **44W-6S**

DAUBERMAN

BIG ROCK

SUGAR GROVE

AIR PARK DR

WHILDIN    GRANART  RD

RD

BUCKTAIL  LN

DOLLY DR    MARY  DR

KATIE DRIVE

RD    23    24

**/-7S**    **46W-7S**    **45W-7S**    **44W-7S**

FAYS    LN

ANNETTES  LN

LN

FAYS

WHISPERING OAKS  LN

22

GRANART

CAMP DEAN  RD

Welch Creek

RD

RD

**/-8S**    **45W-8S**    **44W-8S**

PRAIRIE 30    ST

CAMP DEAN    25  JOHN  ST    ST

26    JOHN  DR

BERGMAN    BOURTZOS  AV

**46W-8S**    MARIE  ST

JOHN ST    RD

RD

TORONTO ST

OAKEN ST

DUGAN

MCCANNON

MIGHELL

RAYMOND

RD

JERICHO    RD

7

RD

JETTER

**9S**    RD    **45W-9S**

35    RD    36

**46W-9S**    RD    **44W-9S**

4

RD

JONES

MIGHELL

**KANE**    **COUNTY**

**KENDALL**    **COUNTY**

14,000W

13,000W

12,000W

11,000W

GALENA    CLARK    JETTER    ASHE

RD    Creek

2    1    6

**46W-10S**    RD    **45W-10S**    **44W-10S**

0S

CREEK

SEE PAGES 48-49

SEE PAGES 42-43

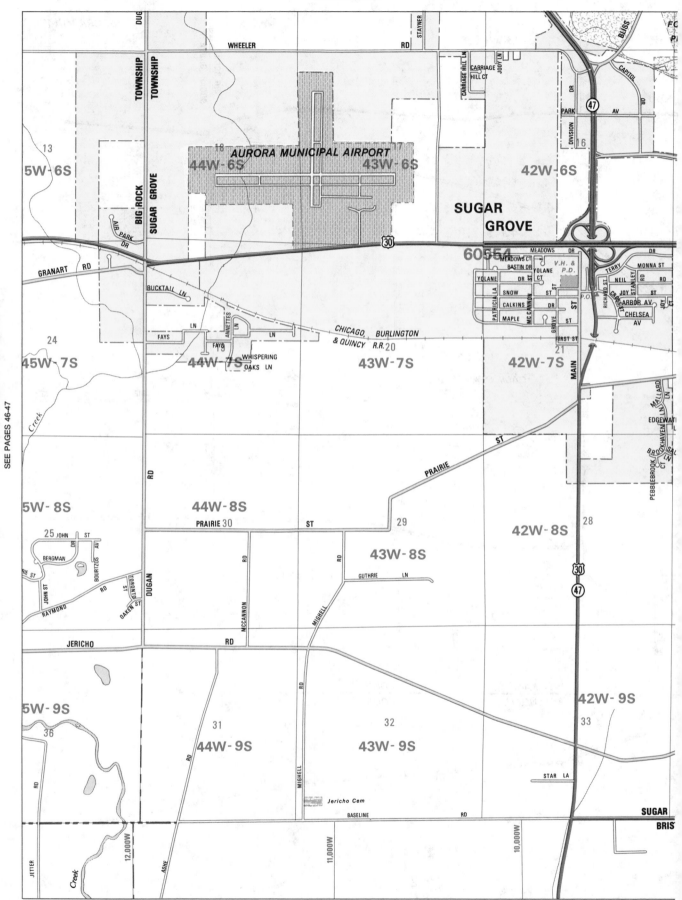

SEE PAGES 46-47

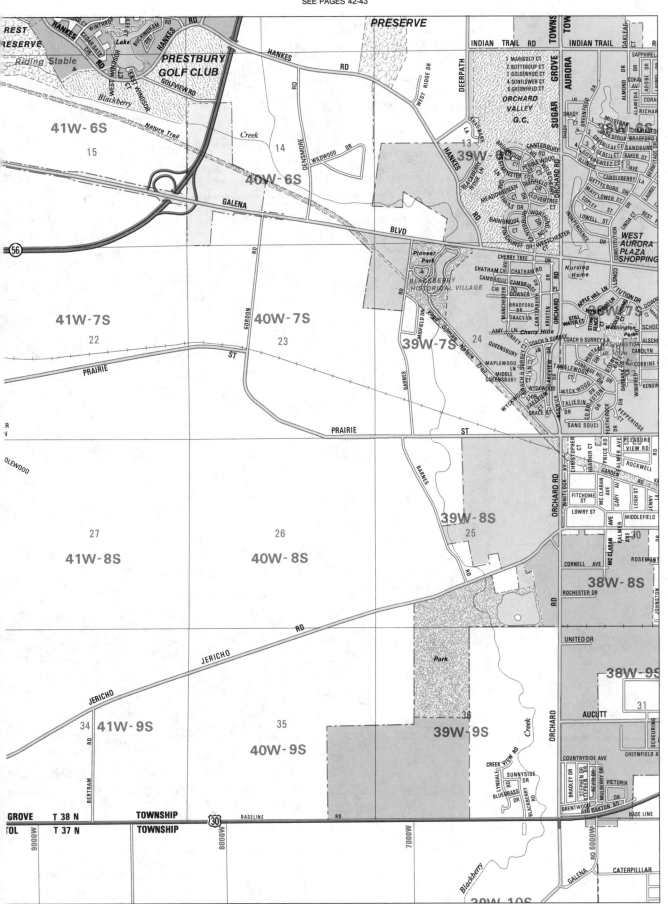

SEE PAGES 42-43

SEE PAGES 50-51

SEE PAGES 44-45

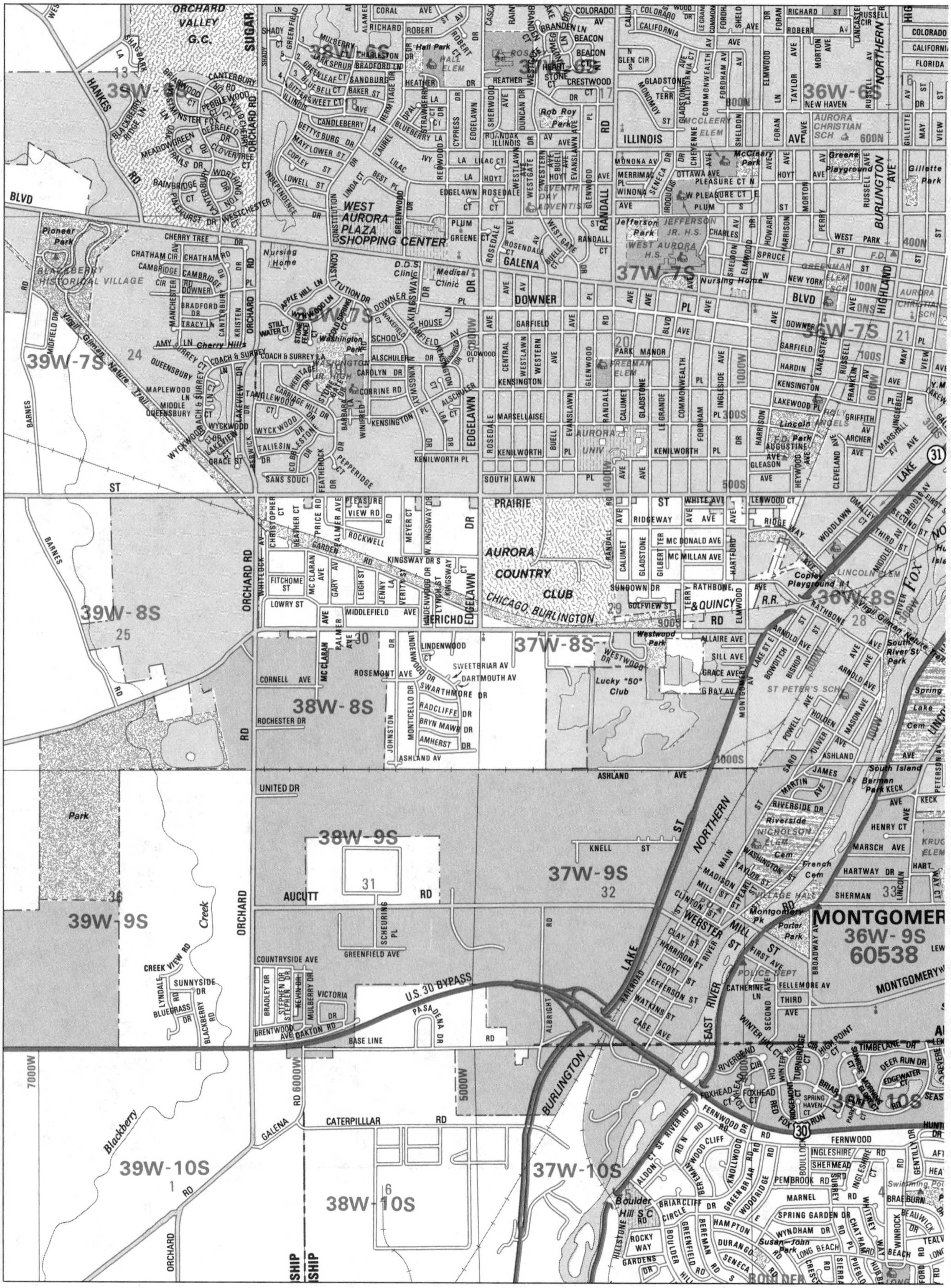

ORCHARD VALLEY G.C.
SUGAR
39W-6S
38W-6S
37W-6S
36W-6S
Hall Park
HALL ELEM
Rob Roy Park
ILLINOIS
McCLEERY ELEM
McCleery Park
AURORA CHRISTIAN SCH
Greene Playground
Gillette Park
NORTHERN
BURLINGTON AVE
BLVD
Pioneer Park
BLACKBERRY HISTORICAL VILLAGE
WEST AURORA PLAZA SHOPPING CENTER
Nursing Home
D.D.S. Clinic
Medical Clinic
GALENA
JEFFERSON JR. H.S.
WEST AURORA H.S.
Jefferson Park
37W-7S
38W-7S
36W-7S
39W-7S
Nursing Home
GREENMAN ELEM SCH
HIGHLAND
DOWNER
Cherry Hills
Washington Park
WASHINGTON JR. HIGH
Virgil Gilman Nature Trail
FREEMAN ELEM
AURORA UNIV
EDGELAWN
RANDALL
Lincoln Park
HOLY ANGELS
F.D. Park
AUGUSTINE
ORCHARD RD
AURORA COUNTRY CLUB
CHICAGO BURLINGTON & QUINCY R.R.
PRAIRIE
Copley Playground #1
LINCOLN ELEM
36W-8S
39W-8S
38W-8S
37W-8S
Westwood Park
Lucky "50" Club
ST PETER'S SCH
South River St Park
Fox River
Spring Lake Cem
South Island
Berman Park
Riverside Cem
NICHOLSON ELEM
French Cem
VILLAGE HALL
Montgomery Pk
Porter Park
POLICE DEPT
MONTGOMERY
36W-9S
60538
Park
38W-9S
37W-9S
39W-9S
AUCUTT RD
Creek
U.S. 30 BYPASS
BASE LINE RD
BURLINGTON
LAKE ST
NORTHERN
CATERPILLAR RD
Blackberry
39W-10S
38W-10S
37W-10S
36W-10S
Boulder Hill S C
Susan-John Park
FOXHEAD
FERNWOOD
ASHLAND AVE
7000W
6000W
5000W

SEE PAGES 48-49

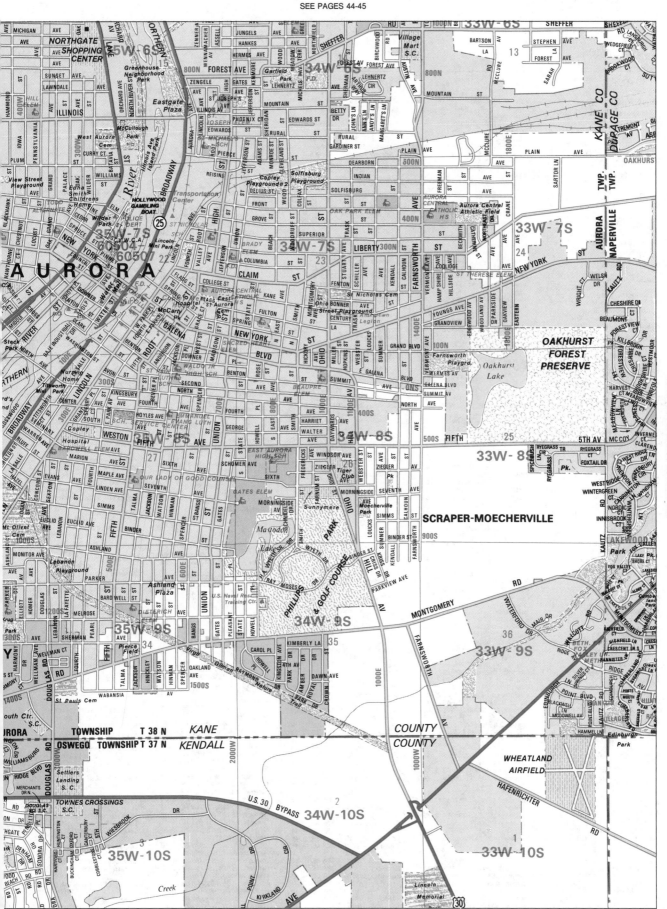

SEE DU PAGE COUNTY PAGES 28-29

## Street Index

**Algonquin***
(Also see McHenry County)

| | Grid | Page |
|---|---|---|
| Arbordale Ct. E&W | 36W-19N | 8 |
| Arbordale Ln. NS&EW | | |
| .......... | 36W-19N | 8 |
| Ashcroft Ct. NE&SW | | |
| .......... | 36W-19N | 8 |
| Boltz Rd. E&W | | |
| ....35W-19N, | 36W-19N | 8 |
| Braewood Dr. N&S | | |
| .......... | 35W-19N | 8 |
| Brandywine Cir. E&W | | |
| .......... | 35W-19N | 8 |
| Cedar Grove Ct. N&S | | |
| .......... | 36W-19N | 8 |
| Charles St. E&W | 34W-19N | 9 |
| Cloverdale Ct. NW&SE | | |
| .......... | 36W-19N | 8 |
| Cloverdale Ln. NW&SE | | |
| .......... | 36W-19N | 8 |
| Compton Ct. E&W | 34W-19N | 9 |
| Dana Point NW&SE | | |
| .......... | 34W-19N | 9 |
| Dellwood Ct. NW&SE | | |
| .......... | 36W-19N | 8 |
| Dorchester Av. NS&EW | | |
| .......... | 36W-19N | 8 |
| Dorchester Ct. NW&SE | | |
| .......... | 36W-19N | 8 |
| Driftwood Ct. NW&SE | | |
| .......... | 36W-19N | 8 |
| Dryden Ct. E&W | 36W-19N | 8 |
| Eastmoor Ct. E&W | 36W-19N | 8 |
| Fernwood Ct. E&W | | |
| .......... | 36W-19N | 8 |
| Fernwood Ln. N&S | | |
| .......... | 36W-19N | 8 |
| Gaslight Dr. E&W | 35W-19N | 8 |
| Greenridge Av. N&S | | |
| .......... | 34W-19N | 9 |
| Hampton Ct. NE&SW | | |
| .......... | 35W-19N | 8 |
| Hanson Rd. E&W | 35W-19N | 8 |
| Haverford Ct. N&S | 36W-19N | 8 |
| Haverford Dr. NS&EW | | |
| .......... | 36W-19N | 8 |
| Hillside Ct. NW&SE | | |
| .......... | 35W-19N | 8 |
| Kensington Ct. E&W | | |
| .......... | 36W-19N | 8 |
| Kensington Dr. NS&EW | | |
| .......... | 36W-19N | 8 |
| Lawndale Av. N&S | 36W-19N | 8 |
| Louis Av. E&W | 34W-19N | 9 |
| Meghan Av. N&S | 34W-19N | 9 |
| Minnehaha Tr. N&S | | |
| .......... | 34W-19N | 9 |
| Peach Tree Ct. N&S | | |
| .......... | 36W-19N | 8 |
| Peach Tree Ln. NW&SE | | |
| .......... | 36W-19N | 8 |
| Ridgefield Av. NS&EW | | |
| .......... | 36W-19N | 8 |
| Ridgefield Ct. E&W | | |
| .......... | 36W-19N | 8 |
| Riverwood Dr. N&S | | |
| .......... | 34W-19N | 9 |
| Riverwood Ln. N&S | | |
| .......... | 34W-19N | 9 |
| Rustic Ln. E&W | 35W-19N | 8 |
| Sleepy Hollow Rd. N&S | | |
| ....36W-18N, | 36W-19N | 8 |
| Spring Hill Dr. NE&SW | | |
| .......... | 35W-19N | 8 |
| Spruce Tree Ln. N&S | | |
| .......... | 35W-19N | 8 |
| Stonegate Rd. N&S | | |
| .......... | 36W-19N | 8 |
| Stratford Ln. NE&SW | | |
| .......... | 34W-19N | 9 |
| Terri St. E&W | 34W-19N | 9 |
| Waverly Ct. N&S | 36W-19N | 8 |
| Waverly Ln. NS&EW | | |
| .......... | 36W-19N | 8 |
| White Oak Ct. NE&SW | | |
| .......... | 36W-19N | 8 |
| White Oak Dr. NS&EW | | |
| .......... | 36W-19N | 8 |
| Willoughby Ct. E&W | | |
| .......... | 36W-19N | 8 |
| Winfield Dr. E&W | 36W-19N | 8 |

**Aurora***
(Also see Du Page County)

| | Grid | Page |
|---|---|---|
| Adams St. N&S | 34W-6S | 45 |
| Adobe Dr. N&S | 38W-6S | 44 |
| Alameda Dr. N&S | 38W-6S | 44 |
| Allaire Dr. E&W | 37W-8S | 50 |
| Almond Dr. N&S | 38W-6S | 44 |
| Alschuler Ct. E&W | 38W-7S | 50 |
| Alschuler Dr. NS&EW | | |
| .......... | 38W-7S | 50 |
| Alyce Ln. E&W | 34W-6S | 45 |
| Amy Ln. E&W | 39W-7S | 49 |
| Anderson St. NE&SW | | |
| ....35W-8S, | 35W-7S | 51 |
| Apple Ct. E&W | 34W-5S | 45 |
| Apple Hill Ln. SW&NE | | |
| .......... | 38W-7S | 49 |
| Appletree Ln. E&W | 38W-5S | 44 |
| Archer Av. E&W | 36W-7S | 50 |
| Arlene Dr. N&S | 35W-5S | 45 |
| Arlon Rd. E&W | 36W-5S | 44 |
| Arnold Av. NW&SE | 36W-8S | 50 |
| Arthur Way NW&SE | 34W-6S | 45 |
| Ashland Av. E&W | | |
| ....36W-9S, | 35W-9S | 50 |
| Ashland Ct. N&S | 36W-9S | 50 |
| Ashwood Ct. NW&SE | | |
| .......... | 35W-5S | 44 |
| Ashwood Ln. NS&EW | | |
| .......... | 38W-5S | 44 |
| Assel Av. N&S | 35W-6S | 45 |
| Augustine Av. E&W | 36W-7S | 50 |
| Aurora Av. N&S | | |
| ....35W-6S, | 35W-5S | 45 |
| Austin Av. NW&SE | | |
| ....34W-6S, | 34W-5S | 45 |
| Autumn Ln. E&W | 34W-5S | 45 |
| Avati Ln. E&W | 33W-5S | 45 |
| Avon St. E&W | 35W-8S | 51 |
| Baje Industrial Dr. NE&SW | | |
| .......... | 36W-7S | 50 |
| Baker St. E&W | 38W-6S | 44 |
| Balmoral Ct. E&W | 33W-3S | 45 |
| Bangs St. N&S | | |
| ....35W-9S, | 35W-8S | 51 |
| Barbara Ln. N&S | 38W-7S | 50 |
| Bardwell St. E&W | 35W-9S | 51 |
| Barnes Rd. N&S | 39W-7S | 49 |
| Bartle Rd. E&W | 33W-9S | 51 |
| Batavia St. N&S | 35W-6S | 45 |
| Beach St. N&S | 34W-7S | 51 |
| Beau Ridge Ct. NW&SE | | |
| .......... | 36W-3S | 44 |
| Beau Ridge Dr. N&S | | |
| .......... | 36W-5S | 44 |
| Beckwith St. N&S | 33W-7S | 51 |
| Benton St. NE&SW | | |
| ....35W-7S, | 34W-8S | 51 |
| Berwick Dr. N&S | 39W-7S | 49 |
| Best Pl. NW&SE | 38W-6S | 44 |
| Beverly Dr. N&S | 33W-3S | 45 |
| Bevier Pl. N&S | 35W-8S | 51 |
| Bilter Rd. E&W | | |
| ....34W-4S, | 33W-4S | 45 |
| Binder St. NE&SW | | |
| ....35W-8S, | 35W-9S | 51 |
| Birch Ln. E&W | 38W-5S | 44 |
| Bishop St. N&S | 36W-8S | 50 |
| Bittersweet Ct. NW&SE | | |
| .......... | 38W-6S | 44 |
| Blackhawk St. N&S | 36W-7S | 50 |
| Blackwell St. NE&SW | | |
| .......... | 33W-9S | 28 |
| Bluebell Ct. E&W | 38W-6S | 44 |
| Blueberry Ln. NW&SE | | |
| .......... | 38W-6S | 44 |
| Bluegrass Ln. E&W | | |
| ....34W-3S, | 33W-3S | 45 |
| Bluff St. NW&SE | 36W-8S | 50 |
| Bonner Av. E&W | 34W-7S | 51 |
| Bowditch St. NE&SW | | |
| .......... | 36W-8S | 50 |
| Bowman Dr. N&S | 38W-5S | 44 |
| Bradford Dr. E&W | 39W-7S | 49 |
| Bradford Ln. E&W | 38W-6S | 44 |
| Bridlepost Dr. E&W | 37W-6S | 44 |
| Brighton Cir. NS&EW | | |
| .......... | 38W-5S | 44 |
| Broadway NE&SW | | |
| ....36W-8S, | 35W-6S | 50 |
| Broughton Dr. N&S | 33W-9S | 51 |
| Buell Av. N&S | 37W-7S | 50 |
| Buell Ct. NE&SW | 37W-7S | 50 |
| Burgundy Ln. N&S | 34W-6S | 45 |
| Burton St. E&W | 33W-5S | 45 |
| Buttercup Ct.* NW&SE | | |
| .......... | 39W-6S | 43 |
| Butterfield Rd. N&S | | |
| ....33W-3S, | 34W-4S | 45 |
| Calhoun St. N&S | | |
| ....34W-8S, | 34W-7S | 51 |
| Calico Dr. E&W | 36W-5S | 44 |
| California Av. E&W | | |
| ....37W-6S, | 35W-6S | 44 |
| California St. | 37W-6S | 44 |
| Calumet Av. N&S | | |
| ....37W-7S, | 37W-6S | 50 |
| Cambridge Av. N&S | 36W-5S | 44 |
| Cambridge Cir. E&W | | |
| .......... | 39W-7S | 49 |
| Cambridge Rd. E&W | | |
| .......... | 39W-7S | 49 |
| Candleberry Ln. E&W | | |
| .......... | 38W-6S | 44 |
| Canterbury Rd. N&S | | |
| .......... | 39W-7S | 49 |
| Carnation Ct.* N&S | 37W-5S | 44 |
| Carolyn Dr. E&W | 39W-7S | 50 |
| Carriage Hill Dr. NW&SE | | |
| .......... | 37W-6S | 44 |
| Cascade Dr. N&S | 37W-6S | 44 |
| Cedar St. NW&SE | | |
| ....36W-7S, | 35W-7S | 50 |
| Cedardale Pl. E&W | 36W-5S | 44 |
| Center Av. E&W | 35W-8S | 51 |
| Central Av. N&S | 37W-7S | 50 |
| Century Ln. E&W | 34W-7S | 51 |
| Charles St. NW&SE | | |
| ....37W-7S, | 37W-6S | 50 |
| Charleston Dr. E&W | 38W-6S | 44 |
| Chateau Av. E&W | 34W-6S | 45 |
| Chatham Cir. E&W | 39W-7S | 49 |
| Chatham Rd. E&W | 39W-7S | 49 |
| Cherry Tree Dr. E&W | | |
| .......... | 39W-7S | 49 |
| Chestnut St. NE&SW | | |
| .......... | 39W-7S | 49 |
| Cheyenne Av. N&S | 37W-6S | 44 |
| Church Rd. NE&SW | | |
| .......... | 36W-7S | 50 |
| ....34W-6S, | 34W-4S | 45 |
| Claim St. E&W | | |
| ....35W-7S, | 34W-7S | 51 |
| Clark St. NW&SE | | |
| ....35W-8S, | 35W-7S | 51 |
| Clearwater Dr. NW&SE | | |
| .......... | 35W-5S | 45 |
| Cleveland Av. N&S | 36W-7S | 50 |
| Cleveland St. N&S | 34W-6S | 45 |
| Cloverdale Pl. E&W | 36W-5S | 44 |
| Coach & Surrey Ln. E&W | | |
| ....39W-7S, | 38W-7S | 49 |
| Cobblestone Dr. NE&SW | | |
| .......... | 38W-7S | 50 |
| Cochran St. E&W | 38W-6S | 44 |
| Cold Spring Ct. N&S | | |
| .......... | 38W-7S | 49 |
| Colfax St. N&S | 34W-7S | 51 |
| College St. N&S | 35W-7S | 51 |
| Colorado Av. E&W | | |
| ....37W-6S, | 35W-6S | 44 |
| Columbia St. E&W | | |
| ....35W-7S, | 34W-7S | 51 |
| Comet Dr. NS&EW | 34W-5S | 45 |
| Commonwealth Av. N&S | | |
| ....37W-7S, | 37W-6S | 50 |
| Comprehensive Dr. N&S | | |
| ....33W-5S, | 33W-4S | 45 |
| Concord St. N&S | 36W-8S | 50 |
| Constellation Dr. NE&SW | | |
| .......... | 34W-5S | 45 |
| Constitution Dr. N&S | | |
| .......... | 38W-7S | 49 |
| Constitution Dr. N&S | | |
| ....38W-7S, | 38W-6S | 50 |
| Coolidge Av. E&W | 33W-7S | 51 |
| Copley St. N&S | 38W-6S | 44 |
| Coral Av. E&W | 38W-6S | 44 |
| Corona Ct. N&S | 34W-5S | 45 |
| Corporate Blvd. E&W | | |
| .......... | 34W-4S | 45 |
| Corporate Blvd. NE&SW | | |
| .......... | 34W-4S | 45 |
| Corrine Rd. E&W | 38W-7S | 50 |
| Cottonwood Dr. E&W | | |
| .......... | 37W-6S | 44 |
| Council St. NW&SE | 35W-7S | 51 |
| Coventry Pl. NS&EW | | |
| .......... | 36W-5S | 44 |
| Crestwood Ct. E&W | 37W-6S | 44 |
| Crestwood Dr. N&S | 36W-5S | 44 |
| Crofton Ct.* NW&SE | | |
| .......... | 37W-5S | 44 |
| Cross St. N&S | 36W-7S | 50 |
| Curry Ct. E&W | 35W-6S | 45 |
| Cypress Dr. E&W | 38W-6S | 44 |
| Daisy St. N&S | 38W-6S | 44 |
| Daywards Ct. N&S | 34W-8S | 51 |
| Dearborn Av. E&W | 34W-7S | 51 |
| Deerpath Rd. N&S | 39W-6S | 43 |
| Delius St. E&W | 34W-7S | 51 |
| Derby Ct. N&S | 34W-3S | 45 |
| Donna Av. E&W | 34W-5S | 45 |
| Douglas Av. N&S | | |
| ....34W-9S, | 36W-8S | 50 |
| Downer Pl. E&W | | |
| ....39W-7S, | 34W-8S | 49 |
| Downer Pl. E&W | 38W-7S | 50 |
| Duncan Dr. N&S | 37W-6S | 44 |
| Durham Dr. N&S | 36W-5S | 44 |
| E. Galena Blvd. NW&SE | | |
| .......... | 34W-8S | 51 |
| E. Park Av. N&S | 35W-8S | 51 |
| E. Park Pl. N&S | | |
| ....35W-8S, | 35W-7S | 51 |
| E. Pleasure Ct. E&W | | |
| .......... | 36W-6S | 44 |
| East-West Tollway E&W | | |
| ....38W-5S, | 33W-4S | 44 |
| Eastern Av. N&S | 35W-7S | 51 |
| Eastwood Ct. N&S | 36W-5S | 44 |
| Eastwood Dr. N&S | 37W-5S | 44 |
| Edgelawn Ct. E&W | 38W-6S | 44 |
| Edgelawn Dr. N&S | | |
| ....38W-7S, | 38W-6S | 50 |
| Edgewood Av. N&S | 33W-5S | 51 |
| Edinburgh Ln. N&S | 33W-9S | 28 |
| Edison Av. E&W | | |
| ....36W-6S, | 34W-6S | 45 |
| Edwards St. E&W | | |
| ....35W-6S, | 34W-6S | 45 |
| Elder Dr. N&S | 38W-5S | 44 |
| Elliot Av. N&S | 36W-9S | 50 |
| Elm St. N&S | 35W-7S | 51 |
| Elmwood Dr. N&S | | |
| ....37W-6S, | 36W-5S | 44 |
| Emerald Dr. N&S | 38W-6S | 44 |
| Essex Ln. N&S | 33W-9S | 51 |
| Euclid Av. E&W | | |
| ....36W-8S, | 35W-8S | 50 |
| Evans Av. E&W | | |
| ....36W-8S, | 35W-8S | 50 |
| Evanslawn Av. N&S | | |
| ....37W-7S, | 37W-6S | 50 |
| Evergreen Dr. N&S | 38W-6S | 44 |
| Farnsworth Av. N&S | | |
| ....34W-7S, | 34W-4S | 51 |
| Farnum St. E&W | 34W-8S | 51 |
| Featherock Ct. N&S | 38W-7S | 50 |
| Felten St. N&S | 33W-5S | 45 |
| Fenton St. E&W | 34W-7S | 51 |
| Fifth Av. E&W | | |
| ....35W-8S, | 33W-8S | 51 |
| Fifth St. N&S | | |
| ....35W-9S, | 35W-8S | 51 |
| First St. NW&SE | 36W-8S | 50 |
| Flagg St. NW&SE | 35W-7S | 51 |
| Flint Ct. E&W | 37W-6S | 44 |
| Florida Av. N&S | | |
| ....36W-6S, | 35W-6S | 44 |
| Foran Ln. N&S | | |
| ....36W-6S, | 36W-5S | 44 |
| Fordham St. N&S | | |
| ....37W-7S, | 37W-6S | 50 |
| Forest Av. E&W | | |
| ....36W-6S, | 34W-6S | 45 |
| Fourth Av. E&W | | |
| ....36W-8S, | 34W-8S | 51 |
| Fourth St. N&S | | |
| ....35W-9S, | 35W-7S | 51 |
| Foxcroft Dr. NS&EW | | |
| .......... | 38W-5S | 44 |
| Foxtail Dr. NS&EW | 33W-8S | 51 |
| Franklin Av. N&S | 36W-7S | 50 |
| Frazier Ct. NW&SE | 36W-7S | 50 |
| Fredericks Av. N&S | 34W-8S | 51 |
| Front St. E&W | | |
| ....35W-7S, | 34W-7S | 51 |
| Fulton St. E&W | | |
| ....35W-7S, | 34W-7S | 51 |
| Gale St. NW&SE | 36W-7S | 50 |
| Galena Blvd. NW&SE | | |
| ....39W-6S, | 34W-8S | 43 |
| Garfield Av. E&W | | |
| ....37W-7S, | 37W-6S | 50 |
| Gates Av. E&W | | |
| ....36W-6S, | 34W-6S | 45 |
| Gates St. N&S | 35W-8S | 51 |
| George Av. E&W | | |
| ....36W-8S, | 34W-8S | 51 |
| Gettysburg Dr. NW&SE | | |
| .......... | 38W-6S | 44 |
| Gillette Av. N&S | 36W-6S | 44 |
| Gladstone Av. E&W | | |
| ....37W-7S, | 37W-6S | 50 |
| Gladstone Ter. E&W | | |
| .......... | 37W-6S | 44 |
| Gleason Av. E&W | 36W-7S | 50 |
| Glenview Av. E&W | 34W-6S | 45 |
| Glenwood Pl. N&S | | |
| ....37W-7S, | 37W-6S | 50 |
| Golden Oaks Pkwy. N&S | | |
| .......... | 37W-5S | 44 |
| Golden Oaks Pkwy. NS&EW | | |
| .......... | 37W-5S | 44 |
| Goldenrod Ct.* NW&SE | | |
| .......... | 39W-6S | 43 |
| Grace Av. E&W | 37W-8S | 50 |
| Grace Ct. N&S | 35W-7S | 51 |
| Grace St. E&W | 39W-7S | 49 |
| Grand Av. N&S | | |
| ....35W-6S, | 35W-5S | 51 |
| Grand Blvd. E&W | | |
| ....39W-7S, | 33W-7S | 51 |
| Grandview Dr. E&W | 33W-7S | 51 |
| Grant Pl. NW&SE | 35W-8S | 51 |
| Gray Av. E&W | 37W-8S | 50 |
| Greene Ct. E&W | 37W-7S | 50 |
| Greenfield Ct.* E&W | 39W-6S | 43 |
| Greenfield Dr. N&S | 38W-6S | 44 |
| Greenleaf Ct. E&W | 38W-6S | 44 |
| Greenview Dr. N&S | 34W-6S | 45 |
| Greenwood Dr. N&S | | |
| .......... | 38W-6S | 44 |
| Grenada Dr. N&S | 38W-6S | 44 |
| Griffith Av. E&W | 36W-7S | 50 |
| Grove St. E&W | | |
| ....35W-7S, | 33W-7S | 51 |
| Hamilton St. NE&SW | | |
| .......... | 36W-8S | 50 |
| Hammond Av. N&S | 36W-6S | 44 |
| Hampshire Av. N&S | 33W-7S | 51 |
| Hamuel Ln. N&S | 33W-9S | 28 |
| Hankes Av. N&S | | |
| ....35W-6S, | 34W-6S | 45 |
| Hankes Rd. NW&SE | | |
| .......... | 39W-6S | 43 |
| Hardin Av. E&W | 36W-7S | 50 |
| Harriet Av. E&W | 34W-8S | 51 |
| Harrison Av. N&S | | |
| ....36W-7S, | 36W-6S | 50 |
| Hart Rd. N&S | 34W-3S | 39 |
| Hartford Av. N&S | 37W-8S | 50 |
| Hawthorne Ct. N&S | 36W-7S | 50 |
| Hazel Av. NW&SE | 36W-8S | 50 |
| Heartstone Ct. NS&EW | | |
| .......... | 37W-6S | 44 |
| Heather Dr. E&W | | |
| ....38W-6S, | 37W-6S | 44 |
| Heritage Dr. NE&SW | | |
| .......... | 38W-7S | 50 |
| Hermes Av. E&W | 34W-6S | 45 |
| Hermitage Dr. N&S | 38W-6S | 44 |
| Heywood Av. N&S | 36W-7S | 50 |
| Hickory Av. N&S | 34W-8S | 51 |
| High St. NE&SW | | |
| ....35W-7S, | 35W-6S | 51 |
| Highland Av. N&S | | |
| ....36W-7S, | 36W-6S | 50 |
| Hill Av. N&S | 34W-8S | 51 |
| Hillside Av. N&S | 33W-7S | 51 |
| Hinman St. NE&SW | | |
| ....35W-9S, | 35W-8S | 51 |
| Holden Av. NW&SE | 36W-5S | 50 |
| Holiday Dr. E&W | 36W-5S | 44 |
| Hollycrest Av. N&S | 36W-5S | 44 |
| Homer Av. N&S | 36W-9S | 50 |
| Hopkins St. N&S | 34W-8S | 51 |
| Howard Av. N&S | | |
| ....36W-7S, | 36W-6S | 51 |
| Howell Pl. N&S | 34W-8S | 51 |
| Hoyles Av. E&W | 35W-8S | 51 |
| Hoyt Av. E&W | | |
| ....37W-6S, | 36W-6S | 44 |
| Hoyt Pl. NE&SW | 35W-7S | 51 |
| Huntington Dr. E&W | 36W-5S | 44 |
| Huntington Dr. | 37W-5S | 44 |
| Illinois Av. E&W | | |
| ....36W-6S, | 35W-6S | 44 |
| Independence Dr. NS&EW | | |
| .......... | 38W-5S | 44 |
| Indian Av. E&W | 34W-7S | 51 |
| Indian Trail Rd. N&S | | |
| ....38W-5S, | 34W-5S | 44 |
| Industrial Dr. E&W | | |
| ....37W-5S, | 36W-5S | 44 |
| Ingleside Av. N&S | 37W-7S | 50 |
| Iowa St. N&S | | |
| ....36W-7S, | 36W-6S | 50 |
| Ironwood Ct. NE&SW | | |
| .......... | 38W-5S | 44 |
| Iroquois Dr. N&S | 37W-6S | 44 |
| Ivy Ln. E&W | 38W-6S | 44 |
| Jackson Pl. NE&SW | | |
| ....35W-8S, | 35W-7S | 51 |
| Jackson St. N&S | | |
| ....35W-9S, | 35W-8S | 51 |
| Jefferson St. NE&SW | | |
| ....35W-7S, | 34W-6S | 51 |
| Jericho Rd. E&W | | |
| ....39W-8S, | 36W-8S | 49 |
| Jinglebell Ln. N&S | 36W-7S | 50 |
| Joel Av. E&W | 34W-5S | 45 |
| Joyce Dr. N&S | 38W-5S | 44 |
| Jungels Av. E&W | | |
| ....35W-6S, | 34W-6S | 45 |
| Kane St. E&W | 34W-7S | 51 |
| Kautz Rd. N&S | 33W-9S | 51 |
| Keck Av. E&W | 36W-9S | 50 |
| Kendall St. N&S | | |
| ....34W-8S, | 34W-7S | 51 |
| Kenilworth Pl. E&W | | |
| ....38W-7S, | 37W-7S | 50 |
| Kenmore Av. N&S | | |
| ....34W-6S, | 34W-5S | 45 |
| Kensington Ct. NW&SE | | |
| .......... | 38W-7S | 50 |
| Kensington Pl. E&W | | |
| ....38W-7S, | 36W-7S | 50 |
| Kingsbury Av. E&W | 35W-8S | 51 |
| Kingsway Dr. N&S | 38W-7S | 50 |
| Kirk Rd. N&S | | |
| ....33W-4S, | 33W-3S | 45 |
| Kristen Dr. N&S | 39W-7S | 49 |
| Lafayette St. N&S | | |
| ....35W-9S, | 35W-8S | 51 |
| Lake St. N&S | | |
| ....36W-8S, | 35W-6S | 50 |
| Lake St. E. NE&SW | 36W-8S | 50 |
| Lakelawn Blvd. E&W | | |
| .......... | 38W-6S | 44 |
| Lakeview Ct. NE&SW | | |
| .......... | 39W-7S | 49 |
| Lakeview Ct. E&W | 38W-5S | 44 |
| Lakeview Dr. N&S | 39W-7S | 49 |
| Lakeview Dr. NE&SW | | |
| .......... | 37W-6S | 44 |
| Lakewood Ct. NW&SE | | |
| .......... | 36W-7S | 50 |
| Lakewood Pl. E&W | 36W-7S | 50 |
| Lancaster Av. N&S | | |
| ....36W-8S, | 35W-7S | 50 |
| Landmark Rd. N&S | 37W-5S | 44 |
| Larkspur Ct. E&W | 38W-6S | 44 |
| Lasalle St. N&S | | |
| ....36W-8S, | 35W-7S | 50 |
| Laurel Dr. N&S | 38W-6S | 44 |

| | Grid | Page |
|---|---|---|
| Lawndale Av. E&W . . | 35W-6S | 45 |
| Le Grande Av. N&S . . | 37W-6S | 45 |
| Le Grande Blvd. N&S | | |
| . . . . . . . . . . . | 37W-7S | 50 |
| Lebanon St. N&S | | |
| . . . . . . . . 35W-9S,35W-8S | | 51 |
| Legrande Av. N&S . . | 37W-6S | 44 |
| Lehnertz Av. NS&EW | | |
| . . . . . . . . . . . | 34W-6S | 45 |
| Lehnertz Cir. E&W . . | 34W-6S | 45 |
| Lenwood Ct. E&W . . | 36W-8S | 50 |
| Liberty St. E&W . . . | 34W-7S | 51 |
| Lilac Ct. E&W . . . . . | 34W-7S | 44 |
| Lilac Ln. NW&SE . . . | 38W-6S | 44 |
| Lily St. N&S . . . . . . | 33W-5S | 45 |
| Lincoln Av. NE&SW | | |
| . . . . . . . 36W-8S,35W-6S | | 50 |
| Lincolnshire Av. N&S | | |
| . . . . . . . . . . . | 36W-5S | 44 |
| Linda Ct. NE&SW . . . | 34W-4S | 44 |
| Linda Ln. E&W . . . . | 33W-4S | 45 |
| Linden Av. E&W . . . . | 35W-8S | 51 |
| Locust St. NE&SW . . | 36W-7S | 50 |
| Logan St. N&S . . . . . | 36W-8S | 50 |
| Loreen Dr. N&S . . 33W-5S | | 45 |
| Loucks St. N&S | | |
| . . . . . . . . 34W-8S,34W-7S | | 51 |
| Lowell St. E&W . . . . | 38W-6S | 44 |
| Lra Dr. N&S . . . . . . | 38W-7S | 50 |
| Lynn St. N&S . . . . . . | 34W-5S | 45 |
| Lyon Pl. E&W . . . . . | 35W-6S | 45 |
| Madison St. NE&SW | | |
| . . . . . . . . . . . | 35W-8S | 51 |
| Mair Dr. NE&SW . . . | 33W-9S | 51 |
| Mallette Rd. E&W . . 33W-5S | | 45 |
| Manchester Av. N&S | | |
| . . . . . . . . . . . | 39W-7S | 49 |
| Manor Pl. E&W | | |
| . . . . . . . 36W-6S,35W-6S | | 44 |
| Maple Av. E&W . . . . | 35W-8S | 51 |
| Maplewood Ln. E&W | | |
| . . . . . . . . . . . | 39W-7S | 49 |
| Margaret Ct. N&S . . 34W-5S | | 45 |
| Margaret Ln. N&S . . 34W-5S | | 45 |
| Marigold Ct.* NW&SE | | |
| . . . . . . . . . . . | 39W-6S | 43 |
| Marikay Dr. NE&SW . | 34W-5S | 45 |
| Marion Av. E&W . . . | 35W-8S | 51 |
| Marseillaise Pl. E&W . | 37W-7S | 50 |
| Marshall Av. NE&SW | | |
| . . . . . . . . . . . | 36W-7S | 50 |
| Marshall Blvd. E&W . | 34W-5S | 45 |
| Marywood Av. N&S . . | 34W-5S | 45 |
| Mason Av. N&S . . | 36W-8S | 50 |
| May St. N&S | | |
| . . . . . . . 36W-7S,36W-6S | | 44 |
| Mayflower St. NW&SE | | |
| . . . . . . . . . . . | 38W-6S | 44 |
| McClure Av. N&S . . . 33W-6S | | 45 |
| McDowell Av. E&W . . | 33W-9S | 28 |
| Meadow Ter. N&S . . . | 34W-6S | 45 |
| Melrose Av. E&W . . . | 35W-9S | 51 |
| Merrimac Pl. E&W . . | 37W-7S | 50 |
| Mettle Dr. E&W . . . . | 35W-5S | 45 |
| Michael Ln. NW&SE . . | 33W-5S | 45 |
| Michels Av. N&S . . . | 34W-6S | 45 |
| Michigan Av. E&W | | |
| . . . . . . . 36W-6S,35W-6S | | 44 |
| Middle Av. NE&SW | | |
| . . . . . . . 36W-8S,35W-7S | | 50 |
| Middle Queensbury Ct. E&W | | |
| . . . . . . . . . . . | 39W-7S | 49 |
| Midlane Dr. E&W . . . | 34W-5S | 45 |
| Miller St. N&S . . . . . | 34W-8S | 51 |
| Mitchell Rd. N&S . . 34W-5S | | 45 |
| Mitchell Rd. NE&SW | | |
| . . . . . . . 35W-6S,34W-4S | | 45 |
| Molitor Rd. E&W . . . | 33W-9S | 45 |
| Monitor Av. E&W . . . | 36W-9S | 50 |
| Monomoy St. NW&SE | | |
| . . . . . . . . . . . | 37W-6S | 44 |
| Monona Av. E&W . . . | 37W-6S | 44 |
| Monroe St. N&S . . . | 34W-6S | 45 |
| Montgomery Av. N&S | | |
| . . . . . . . . . . . | 37W-8S | 50 |
| Montgomery Rd. NE&SW | | |
| . . . . . . . . . . . | 33W-9S | 51 |
| Montgomery St. N&S | | |
| . . . . . . . . . . . | 34W-7S | 51 |
| Morningside Av. E&W | | |
| . . . . . . . . . . . | 34W-8S | 51 |
| Morton Av. N&S | | |
| . . . . . . . 36W-7S,36W-6S | | 50 |
| Mountain St. E&W | | |
| . . . . . . . 34W-6S,33W-6S | | 45 |
| Mulberry Ct. E&W . . | 38W-6S | 44 |
| N. East Av. N&S . . . . | 34W-7S | 51 |
| N. Glen Cir. E&W . . . | 37W-6S | 44 |
| N. Kingsway Dr. N&S | | |
| . . . . . . . . . . . | 38W-7S | 50 |
| N. Lake St. NW&SE | | |
| . . . . . . . 35W-5S,36W-5S | | 45 |
| N. Smith St. N&S . . 34W-7S | | 51 |
| N.E. Industrial Dr. E&W | | |
| . . . . . . . . . . . | 35W-5S | 45 |
| Nantucket Dr. N&S | | |
| . . . . . . . 36W-6S,36W-5S | | 44 |
| New Haven Dr. E&W | | |
| . . . . . . . 37W-6S,36W-6S | | 44 |
| New Indian Trail Ct. NS&EW | | |
| . . . . . . . . . . . | 36W-5S | 44 |
| New York St. E&W | | |
| . . . . . . . 35W-7S,33W-7S | | 50 |
| North Av. E&W | | |
| . . . . . . . 36W-7S,34W-8S | | 50 |
| North Park Av. E&W | | |
| . . . . . . . 36W-6S,35W-6S | | 44 |
| Northfield Dr. N&S . . | 34W-6S | 45 |

| | Grid | Page |
|---|---|---|
| Nottingham Dr. N&S | 35W-5S | 45 |
| O'Malley Ct. NE&SW | | |
| . . . . . . . . . . . | 36W-8S | 50 |
| Oak Av. N&S | | |
| . . . . . . . 35W-7S,35W-6S | | 51 |
| Oak St. E&W . . . . . . | 38W-4S | 44 |
| Oakleaf Ct. N&S . . . | 38W-6S | 44 |
| Oakview Av. N&S . . 33W-7S | | 51 |
| Oakwood Av. E&W | | |
| . . . . . . . 35W-6S,34W-6S | | 45 |
| Ogden Av. SW&NE | | |
| . . . . . . . 33W-8S,36W-9S | | 51 |
| Ohio Ct. E&W . . . . . | 34W-6S | 45 |
| Ohio St. N&S | | |
| . . . . . . . 34W-8S,34W-7S | | 51 |
| Old Indian Trail E&W | | |
| . . . . . . . 36W-6S,35W-6S | | 44 |
| Oldwood Ct. E&W . . | 38W-7S | 50 |
| Oliver Av. NE&SW . . | 36W-8S | 50 |
| Opal Ln. NE&SW . . . | 38W-6S | 44 |
| Orchard Av. N&S . . . | 35W-6S | 45 |
| Orchard Rd. N&S . . . | 38W-7S | 50 |
| Orchid St. E&W . . . . | 33W-5S | 45 |
| Ottawa Av. E&W . . . | 37W-6S | 44 |
| Paddock Ct. NW&SE | | |
| . . . . . . . . . . . | 34W-3S | 45 |
| Palace St. N&S | | |
| . . . . . . . 35W-7S,35W-6S | | 51 |
| Park Manor E&W . . . | 37W-7S | 50 |
| Parker Av. E&W | | |
| . . . . . . . 36W-9S,35W-9S | | 50 |
| Parkside Av. N&S . . 33W-7S | | 51 |
| Pearl St. N&S | | |
| . . . . . . . . . . . | 33W-8S | 51 |
| Pennsylvania Av. N&S | | |
| . . . . . . . 36W-7S,36W-6S | | 50 |
| Pepperidge Ct. NW&SE | | |
| . . . . . . . . . . . | 38W-7S | 50 |
| Perry Av. N&S | | |
| . . . . . . . 36W-7S,36W-6S | | 50 |
| Perry Ct. E&W . . . . . | 33W-5S | 45 |
| Peterson Av. N&S . . | 36W-9S | 50 |
| Phoenix St. E&W . . | 34W-6S | 45 |
| Pierce St. E&W | | |
| . . . . . . . 35W-6S,34W-6S | | 45 |
| Pine Av. E&W | | |
| . . . . . . . 36W-8S,35W-8S | | 50 |
| Pinney St. NW&SE . . | 35W-7S | 51 |
| Plain Av. E&W | | |
| . . . . . . . 34W-6S,33W-6S | | 45 |
| Pleasant Ter. N&S . . | 34W-6S | 45 |
| Pleasant Ct., N. E&W | | |
| . . . . . . . . . . . | 37W-6S | 44 |
| Plum St. E&W | | |
| . . . . . . . 38W-7S,35W-7S | | 50 |
| Post Rd. N&S . . . . . | 36W-5S | 44 |
| Powell Av. NE&SW . . | 36W-8S | 50 |
| Prairie Path NW&SE | | |
| . . . . . . . . . . 33W-2S3S | | 39 |
| Prairie St. E&W | | |
| . . . . . . . 39W-8S,36W-8S | | 49 |
| Preakness Ct. N&S . . 33W-3S | | 45 |
| Preakness Dr. N&S . . 33W-3S | | 45 |
| Queensbury Ct. NW&SE | | |
| . . . . . . . . . . . | 39W-7S | 49 |
| Raddant Rd. N&S . . 34W-4S | | 45 |
| Rainwood Dr. N&S . . | 37W-6S | 44 |
| Randall Ct. N&S . . . . | 37W-7S | 50 |
| Randall Rd. N&S | | |
| . . . . . . . 37W-7S,37W-5S | | 50 |
| Rathbone Av. NW&SE | | |
| . . . . . . . . . . . | 36W-8S | 50 |
| Ray Moses Dr. E&W | | |
| . . . . . . . . . . . | 34W-9S | 51 |
| Reckinger Rd. N&S | | |
| . . . . . . . 34W-5S,33W-5S | | 45 |
| Redwood Dr. N&S . . | 38W-6S | 44 |
| Reising St. E&W | | |
| . . . . . . . 35W-7S,34W-7S | | 51 |
| Richard St. E&W | | |
| . . . . . . . 38W-6S,36W-6S | | 44 |
| Ridge Rd. NW&SE . . 33W-9S | | 28 |
| Ridgeway Av. NW&SE | | |
| . . . . . . . . . . . | 36W-8S | 50 |
| River St. NE&SW | | |
| . . . . . . . 36W-8S,35W-8S | | 50 |
| Roanoak Av. E&W . . 37W-6S | | 44 |
| Robert Av. E&W . . . | 38W-6S | 44 |
| Robert Ct. NW&SE . . 38W-6S | | 44 |
| Robinhood Dr. NS&EW | | |
| . . . . . . . 36W-5S,35W-5S | | 44 |
| Root St. N&S | | |
| . . . . . . . 35W-7S,35W-6S | | 51 |
| Rose St. N&S . . . . . 34W-8S | | 51 |
| Rosedale Av. N&S | | |
| . . . . . . . 37W-7S,37W-6S | | 50 |
| Rosedale St. E&W . . 37W-6S | | 44 |
| Rosedale Ct. E&W . . 37W-7S | | 50 |
| Rosewood Av. NE&SW | | |
| . . . . . . . . . . . | 36W-8S | 50 |
| Rt. 25 N&S . 36W-8S,35W-5S | | 50 |
| Rt. 31 N&S . . 35W-8S,35W-5S | | 50 |
| Rural St. N&S | | |
| . . . . . . . 35W-6S,34W-6S | | 45 |
| Russell Av. N&S | | |
| . . . . . . . 36W-7S,36W-6S | | 50 |
| Russell Cir. E&W . . . | 36W-6S | 44 |
| Russell Ct. E&W . . . | 36W-6S | 44 |
| Russell Dr. E&W . . . | 36W-6S | 44 |
| Ryegrass Cir. E&W . . 33W-8S | | 51 |
| Ryegrass Dr. E&W . . 33W-8S | | 51 |
| Ryegrass Tr. EW&NS | | |
| . . . . . . . . . . . | 33W-8S | 51 |
| S. Bridge Dr. E&W . . 36W-5S | | 44 |
| S. East Av. N&S . . 34W-8S | | 51 |
| S. Glen Cir. E&W . . 37W-6S | | 44 |
| S. Pleasure Ct. E&W | | |
| . . . . . . . . . . . | 37W-6S | 44 |

| | Grid | Page |
|---|---|---|
| Sandburg St. E&W . . 38W-6S | | 44 |
| Sandy Ln. N&S . . . . 36W-5S | | 44 |
| Sans Souci Dr. NS&EW | | |
| . . . . . . . . . . . | 38W-7S | 50 |
| Sapphire Ln. E&W . . 38W-6S | | 44 |
| Saro Av. NE&SW . . 36W-8S | | 50 |
| Scheffer Rd. E&W . . 34W-5S | | 45 |
| Schiller Av. N&S . . . | 34W-8S | 51 |
| Schnidel Dr. N&S . . 34W-8S | | 51 |
| Schomer Av. E&W | | |
| . . . . . . . 35W-8S,34W-8S | | 51 |
| Schomer Ct. N&S . . 34W-8S | | 45 |
| Schomer Rd. E&W . . 34W-5S | | 45 |
| School House Ln. EW&NS | | |
| . . . . . . . . . . . | 38W-7S | 50 |
| Second Av. E&W | | |
| . . . . . . . 35W-8S,34W-8S | | 51 |
| Second St. NW&SE . 36W-8S | | 50 |
| Secretariat Ct. N&S . 34W-3S | | 45 |
| Secretariat Dr. E&NS | | |
| . . . . . . . 34W-3S,33W-3S | | 45 |
| Selmarten Rd. N&S . 33W-5S | | 45 |
| Seminary Av. E&W | | |
| . . . . . . . 36W-8S,35W-8S | | 50 |
| Seneca Dr. NE&SW . 37W-6S | | 44 |
| Sequoia Dr. N&S | | |
| . . . . . . . 38W-5S,37W-5S | | 44 |
| Seventh Av. NW&SE | | |
| . . . . . . . . . . . | 35W-8S | 51 |
| Sexton St. N&S . . . . 35W-8S | | 51 |
| Shady Ct. NW&SE . . 38W-6S | | 44 |
| Shady Ln. NS&EW . . 38W-6S | | 44 |
| Shamrock Ct. N&S . . 34W-5S | | 45 |
| Shannon Dr. E&W . . 34W-5S | | 45 |
| Sheldon Av. N&S | | |
| . . . . . . . 37W-7S,37W-6S | | 50 |
| Sheridan St. E&W . . 34W-8S | | 45 |
| Sherman Av. E&W . . 35W-9S | | 51 |
| Sherman St. N&S . . . | 34W-6S | 45 |
| Sherwood Av. N&S . . | 37W-6S | 44 |
| Sherwood Dr. E&W . . | 34W-5S | 45 |
| Sill Av. E&W . . . . . . | 37W-8S | 50 |
| Silver Springs Ct. E&W | | |
| . . . . . . . . . . . | 33W-9S | 28 |
| Simms St. E&W | | |
| . . . . . . . 36W-8S,35W-8S | | 50 |
| Sirus Av. N&S . . . . . | 37W-6S | 44 |
| Sivas Rd. E&W . . . . | 36W-5S | 44 |
| Sixth Av. E&W | | |
| . . . . . . . 35W-8S,34W-8S | | 51 |
| Smith St. N&S | | |
| . . . . . . . 34W-8S,34W-7S | | 51 |
| Solfisburg Av. E&W . 34W-7S | | 51 |
| South Av. E&W . . . . 34W-8S | | 50 |
| South Lawn Pl. E&W | | |
| . . . . . . . . . . . | 37W-7S | 50 |
| Spencer St. N&S | | |
| . . . . . . . 35W-8S,35W-7S | | 51 |
| Sperry Ct. N&S . . . . 35W-8S | | 51 |
| Spicebush Ln. NS&EW | | |
| . . . . . . . . . . . | 33W-8S | 51 |
| Spring St. NW&SE | | |
| . . . . . . . 35W-7S,34W-7S | | 51 |
| Springbrook Dr. E&W | | |
| . . . . . . . . . . . | 36W-5S | 44 |
| Spruce St. NW&SE | | |
| . . . . . . . 37W-7S,36W-7S | | 50 |
| Squire Ct. N&S . . . . 34W-5S | | 45 |
| Squire Dr. E&W . . . . 34W-5S | | 45 |
| St. Joseph's Av. E&W | | |
| . . . . . . . . . . . | 35W-6S | 45 |
| Star Av. N&S . . . . . . | 34W-5S | 45 |
| State St. N&S | | |
| . . . . . . . 38W-5S,35W-5S | | 44 |
| Stillwater Ct. N&S . . 38W-7S | | 49 |
| Stolp Av. NE&SW . . 35W-7S | | 51 |
| Stone Fence Ct. N&S | | |
| . . . . . . . . . . . | 38W-7S | 49 |
| Stone Gate Dr. NE&SW | | |
| . . . . . . . . . . . | 38W-7S | 50 |
| Strawberry Ct. N&S . 38W-6S | | 44 |
| Stuart Av. N&S . . . . 34W-7S | | 51 |
| Sullivan Rd. N&S | | |
| . . . . . . . 38W-5S,35W-5S | | 44 |
| Summit Av. E&W | | |
| . . . . . . . 34W-8S,33W-8S | | 51 |
| Sumner Av. N&S | | |
| . . . . . . . 34W-8S,33W-8S | | 51 |
| Sunflower Ct. NW&SE | | |
| . . . . . . . . . . . | 38W-6S | 44 |
| Sunset Av. E&W | | |
| . . . . . . . 36W-6S,35W-6S | | 44 |
| Superior St. E&W | | |
| . . . . . . . 35W-7S,33W-7S | | 51 |
| Surrey Ct. NW&SE . . 39W-7S | | 49 |
| T St. N&S . . . . . . . . 35W-8S | | 51 |
| Taliesin Dr. E&W . . . 37W-7S | | 50 |
| Tall Oaks Dr. N&S . . 33W-5S | | 45 |
| Talma St. NE&SW | | |
| . . . . . . . 35W-9S,35W-8S | | 51 |
| Tanglewood Ct. N&S | | |
| . . . . . . . . . . . | 38W-7S | 50 |
| Tanglewood Dr. NW&SE | | |
| . . . . . . . . . . . | 38W-7S | 50 |
| Taylor Av. N&S . . . . 36W-8S | | 44 |
| Third St. NW&SE . . . 36W-8S | | 50 |
| Thompson Ln. N&S | | |
| . . . . . . . 33W-5S,33W-4S | | 45 |
| Timber Lake Ct. N&S | | |
| . . . . . . . . . . . | 37W-6S | 44 |
| Tinley Dr. N&S . . . . 36W-5S | | 44 |
| Titsworth Ct. NW&SE | | |
| . . . . . . . . . . . | 36W-8S | 50 |
| Tollview Av. N&S . . . | 34W-6S | 45 |
| Tracy Ln. N&S . . . . . | 39W-7S | 49 |
| Trask St. N&S | | |
| . . . . . . . 34W-7S,34W-6S | | 51 |

| | Grid | Page |
|---|---|---|
| Union St. N&S | | |
| . . . . . . . 35W-9S,34W-7S | | 51 |
| Upper Brandon Dr. E&W | | |
| . . . . . . . . . . . | 36W-5S | 44 |
| Valley Av. N&S . . . . | 35W-7S | 51 |
| Vermont Av. N&S | | |
| . . . . . . . 33W-7S,33W-8S | | 51 |
| View St. N&S | | |
| . . . . . . . 36W-7S,36W-6S | | 50 |
| Vine St. NW&SE . . . | 35W-7S | 51 |
| Violet St. N&S . . . . 33W-5S | | 45 |
| W. New York St. N&S | | |
| . . . . . . . . . . . | 36W-7S | 50 |
| W. Park Pl. NE&SW . . 35W-7S | | 51 |
| W. Pleasure Ct. E&W | | |
| . . . . . . . . . . . | 37W-6S | 44 |
| Wagner Ct. NW&SE | | |
| . . . . . . . . . . . | 34W-3S | 45 |
| Wagner Rd. N&S | | |
| . . . . . . . 34W-3S,33W-3S | | 45 |
| Wakefield Ct. NW&SE | | |
| . . . . . . . . . . . | 38W-7S | 50 |
| Walden Av. E&W . . . | 34W-8S | 51 |
| Walter Av. E&W . . . 34W-8S | | 51 |
| Warren Av. N&S . . 36W-8S | | 50 |
| Washington St. NW&SE | | |
| . . . . . . . . . . . | 35W-8S | 51 |
| Water St. N&S . . . . . | 35W-7S | 51 |
| Waterford Dr. NW&SE | | |
| . . . . . . . . . . . | 33W-9S | 51 |
| Watson St. NE&SW | | |
| . . . . . . . 35W-9S,35W-8S | | 51 |
| Webster St. N&S . . 34W-8S | | 51 |
| Welsh Dr. N&S . . . . 33W-7S | | 51 |
| Wennamacher Av. N&S | | |
| . . . . . . . . . . . | 35W-6S | 45 |
| West Park Av. E&W | | |
| . . . . . . . 36W-7S,35W-7S | | 50 |
| West St. N&S | | |
| . . . . . . . 35W-8S,35W-7S | | 51 |
| Western Av. N&S | | |
| . . . . . . . 37W-7S,37W-6S | | 50 |
| Westgate Dr. N&S | | |
| . . . . . . . 37W-7S,37W-6S | | 50 |
| Westlawn Av. N&S | | |
| . . . . . . . 37W-7S,37W-6S | | 50 |
| Weston Av. E&W . . . 35W-8S | | 51 |
| Westwood Dr. NS&EW | | |
| . . . . . . . . . . . | 37W-8S | 50 |
| White Av. E&W . . . . 37W-8S | | 50 |
| Whitingham Dr. NE&SW | | |
| . . . . . . . . . . . | 33W-9S | 51 |
| Wilder St. N&S | | |
| . . . . . . . 35W-7S,35W-6S | | 51 |
| Williams St. E&W . . 35W-7S | | 51 |
| Windsor Av. E&W . . 34W-8S | | 51 |
| Winifred Dr. NE&SW | | |
| . . . . . . . . . . . | 38W-7S | 50 |
| Winifred Rd. N&S . . 38W-7S | | 50 |
| Winona Av. N&S . . 37W-6S | | 44 |
| Wood St. N&S | | |
| . . . . . . . 34W-7S,34W-6S | | 51 |
| Woodlawn Av. N&S . . 33W-7S | | 51 |
| Woodlawn Av. NE&SW | | |
| . . . . . . . 36W-8S,36W-7S | | 50 |
| Woodruff St. N&S . . 34W-7S | | 51 |
| Wright Ct. N&S . . . . 33W-7S | | 51 |
| Wyckwood Ct. NE&SW | | |
| . . . . . . . . . . . | 39W-7S | 49 |
| Wyckwood Dr. E&W | | |
| . . . . . . . 39W-7S,38W-7S | | 49 |
| Wyeth Dr. NW&SE . . 34W-9S | | 51 |
| Wynwood Ln. SW&NE | | |
| . . . . . . . . . . . | 38W-7S | 49 |
| Yellowpine Dr. E&W . 37W-6S | | 44 |
| Youngs Av. NE&SW . 33W-7S | | 51 |
| Zengele Av. E&W . . 35W-6S | | 45 |
| Zenner Av. N&S . . . 35W-6S | | 45 |
| Ziegler Av. E&W . . 34W-8S | | 51 |

## Aurora Township

| | Grid | Page |
|---|---|---|
| Adeline Ct. E&W . . . 34W-5S | | 45 |
| Amherst Dr. E&W . . 38W-8S | | 50 |
| Andy's Ln. N&S . . . . 34W-6S | | 45 |
| Ann's Ln. N&S . . . . 34W-6S | | 45 |
| Ashland Av. E&W . . 38W-9S | | 50 |
| Aucutt Rd. E&W . . . 38W-9S | | 50 |
| Audrey Av. E&W . . . 34W-5S | | 45 |
| Austin Av. NW&SE . 34W-6S | | 45 |
| Bangs St. N&S . . . . 35W-9S | | 51 |
| Bartson Ln. E&W . . 33W-6S | | 45 |
| Base Line Rd. N&S | | |
| . . . . . . . 38W-9S,37W-9S | | 50 |
| Becker St. N&S . . . 33W-6S | | 45 |
| Beckwith St. N&S . . 33W-7S | | 51 |
| Bilter Rd. E&W . . . . 33W-4S | | 45 |
| Binder St. E&W | | |
| . . . . . . . 34W-9S,34W-8S | | 51 |
| Birchwood Rd. N&S . 34W-6S | | 45 |
| Bradley Dr. N&S . . 38W-9S | | 50 |
| Brentwood Av. E&W | | |
| . . . . . . . . . . . | 38W-9S | 50 |
| Bryant St. E&W . . . 37W-5S | | 44 |
| Bryn Mawr Dr. E&W | | |
| . . . . . . . . . . . | 38W-8S | 50 |
| Calhoun St. N&S | | |
| . . . . . . . 34W-9S,34W-8S | | 51 |
| Calumet Av. N&S . . 37W-5S | | 50 |
| Camel Rd. N&S . . . 34W-5S | | 45 |
| Carol-Lynn St. N&S . 33W-4S | | 45 |
| Carolyn Dr. N&S . . . 35W-5S | | 45 |
| Catherine St. N&S . . 33W-7S | | 51 |
| Charles Ln. N&S . . . 33W-5S | | 45 |
| Christopher Ct. N&S | | |
| . . . . . . . . . . . | 38W-8S | 50 |
| Church Rd. NE&SW | | |
| . . . . . . . 34W-5S,34W-4S | | 45 |

| | Grid | Page |
|---|---|---|
| Connie Ct. N&S . . . . 33W-5S | | 45 |
| Coolidge Av. E&W . . 33W-7S | | 51 |
| County Line Rd. N&S | | |
| . . . . . . . . . . . | 33W-8S | 51 |
| Crane St. N&S . . . . 33W-7S | | 51 |
| Creek Av. E&W . . . . 33W-5S | | 45 |
| Criss Dr. NW&SE . . 34W-9S | | 51 |
| Dartmouth Av. NE&SW | | |
| . . . . . . . . . . . | 38W-8S | 50 |
| Dawes St. E&W . . . 37W-5S | | 44 |
| Dearborn Av. E&W . . 33W-7S | | 51 |
| Deerpath Rd. NE&SW | | |
| . . . . . . . . . . . | 38W-4S | 44 |
| Diehl Rd. NW&SE . . 34W-5S | | 45 |
| Douglas St. E&W . . 37W-5S | | 44 |
| East-West Tollway N&S | | |
| . . . . . . . 38W-4S,33W-4S | | 44 |
| Eastern Av. N&S . . . 33W-7S | | 51 |
| Edgelawn Dr. N&S . . 38W-8S | | 50 |
| Elizabeth Ln. N&S . . 33W-5S | | 45 |
| Elmwood Dr. N&S . . 37W-8S | | 50 |
| Exposition Av. N&S . 37W-5S | | 44 |
| Farnsworth Av. N&S | | |
| . . . . . . . 34W-8S,33W-9S | | 51 |
| Felten Rd. N&S | | |
| . . . . . . . 33W-6S,33W-5S | | 45 |
| Fifth Av. E&W | | |
| . . . . . . . 34W-8S,33W-8S | | 51 |
| Fifth St. N&S . . . . . 33W-8S | | 51 |
| Fitchome St. E&W . . 38W-8S | | 50 |
| Forest Av. E&W | | |
| . . . . . . . 34W-6S,33W-6S | | 45 |
| Freeman St. N&S . . 33W-7S | | 51 |
| Friar Dr. E&W . . . . 35W-5S | | 45 |
| Galena Blvd. E&W . . 33W-8S | | 51 |
| Garden Rd. NW&SE . 38W-8S | | 50 |
| Gardiner Av. E&W . . 34W-6S | | 45 |
| Gary Av. N&S . . . . 33W-5S | | 45 |
| Gary Av. N&S . . . . 38W-8S | | 50 |
| Gates St. N&S . . . . 35W-9S | | 51 |
| Gerten Av. E&W . . 34W-5S | | 45 |
| Gilbert Ter. N&S . . 37W-5S | | 44 |
| Gilmore St. E&W . . 37W-5S | | 44 |
| Gladstone Av. N&S . 37W-8S | | 50 |
| Golfview St. E&W . . 37W-8S | | 50 |
| Grand Blvd. E&W . . 33W-8S | | 51 |
| Hartford Av. N&S . . 37W-8S | | 50 |
| Heather Ct. N&S . . 38W-8S | | 50 |
| High St. N&S . . . . . 35W-5S | | 45 |
| Hinman St. N&S . . . 35W-9S | | 51 |
| Howell Pl. N&S . . . . 34W-9S | | 51 |
| Indian Av. E&W . . . 33W-7S | | 51 |
| Indian Trail E&W . . 33W-5S | | 45 |
| Indiana St. E&W . . 37W-5S | | 44 |
| Jenny Ln. N&S . . . . 38W-8S | | 50 |
| Jericho Rd. E&W | | |
| . . . . . . . 38W-8S,37W-8S | | 50 |
| Jo Mar Ct. NW&SE . 34W-6S | | 45 |
| John's Ln. N&S . . . . 34W-6S | | 45 |
| Johnston Dr. N&S . . 38W-8S | | 50 |
| Kendall St. N&S | | |
| . . . . . . . 34W-9S,34W-8S | | 51 |
| Kevin Dr. E&W . . . . 38W-9S | | 50 |
| Kingsway Ct. N&S . . 38W-8S | | 50 |
| Kingsway Dr., S. E&W | | |
| . . . . . . . . . . . | 38W-8S | 50 |
| Konen Av. E&W | | |
| . . . . . . . 35W-5S,34W-5S | | 45 |
| Kriss Dr. NW&SE . . 34W-9S | | 51 |
| Leigh St. N&S . . . . 38W-8S | | 50 |
| Liberty St. E&W . . . 33W-7S | | 51 |
| Lindenwood Ct. E&W | | |
| . . . . . . . . . . . | 38W-8S | 50 |
| Lindenwood Dr. N&S | | |
| . . . . . . . . . . . | 38W-8S | 50 |
| Loucks St. N&S . . . 34W-8S | | 51 |
| Lowry St. E&W . . . . 38W-8S | | 50 |
| Lynch St. N&S . . . . 38W-8S | | 50 |
| Maple St. E&W . . . . 37W-5S | | 44 |
| Margaret Ln. N&S . . 34W-6S | | 45 |
| Margaret's Ln. N&S . 34W-6S | | 45 |
| Marilyn Ln. N&S . . . 34W-5S | | 45 |
| Marywood Av. N&S . 34W-5S | | 45 |
| McClaran Av. N&S . . 38W-8S | | 50 |
| McClure Av. N&S . . 33W-6S | | 45 |
| McClure Rd. N&S | | |
| . . . . . . . 33W-7S,33W-6S | | 51 |
| McDonald Av. N&S . 37W-8S | | 50 |
| McMillan Av. E&W . . 37W-8S | | 50 |
| Melrose Av. E&W . . 35W-9S | | 51 |
| Mettel Rd. E&W | | |
| . . . . . . . 35W-4S,34W-5S | | 45 |
| Meyer Ct. N&S . . . . 38W-8S | | 50 |
| Middlefield Av. E&W . 38W-8S | | 50 |
| Montgomery Rd. | | |
| . . . . . . . 35W-9S,33W-9S | | 51 |
| Monticello Dr. N&S . 38W-8S | | 50 |
| Morningside Av. E&W | | |
| . . . . . . . . . . . | 34W-8S | 51 |
| Nan St. N&S . . . . . 33W-4S | | 45 |
| North Av. E&W | | |
| . . . . . . . 34W-8S,33W-8S | | 51 |
| Oak St. N&S . . . . . 34W-5S | | 45 |
| Oakland Av. E&W . . 35W-9S | | 51 |
| Oakview Av. N&S . . 33W-7S | | 51 |
| Oakwood St. E&W . . 34W-5S | | 45 |
| Ohio St. N&S . . . . . 34W-9S | | 51 |
| Palmer Av. N&S . . . 38W-8S | | 50 |
| Parkside Av. N&S . . 33W-7S | | 51 |
| Parkview Av. NE&SW | | |
| . . . . . . . . . . . | 34W-9S | 51 |
| Parkview Dr. N&S . . 33W-4S | | 45 |
| Pasadena Dr. NS&EW | | |
| . . . . . . . . . . . | 38W-9S | 50 |
| Pershing St. E&W . . 37W-5S | | 44 |
| Plain Av. E&W | | |
| . . . . . . . 34W-6S,33W-6S | | 45 |
| Pleasant Pl. N&S . . 35W-9S | | 51 |

| Name | Grid | Page |
|---|---|---|
| Pleasure View Rd. E&W | 38W-8S | 50 |
| Price Rd. N&S | 38W-8S | 50 |
| Radcliffe Dr. E&W | 38W-8S | 50 |
| Randall Rd. N&S | 37W-8S | 50 |
| Rathbone Av. E&W | 37W-8S | 50 |
| Reckinger Rd. E&W | 34W-5S | 45 |
| Richard Av. N&S | 34W-5S | 45 |
| Ridgeway Av. E&W | 37W-8S | 50 |
| Rockwell Rd. NS&EW | 38W-8S | 50 |
| Rosemont Av. E&W | 38W-8S | 50 |
| Rural St. E&W | 34W-6S | 45 |
| Saddle Ln. E&W | 35W-5S,34W-5S | 45 |
| Sarah Ln. N&S | 33W-6S | 45 |
| Sartor Ln. N&S | 33W-7S | 51 |
| Schomer Rd. E&W | 34W-5S | 45 |
| Seventh Av. E&W | 34W-8S | 51 |
| Sheffer Rd. E&W | 33W-8S | 45 |
| Sherman Av. E&W | 35W-9S | 51 |
| Simms St. E&W | 34W-8S | 51 |
| Spencer St. N&S | 35W-9S | 51 |
| State St. N&S | 34W-9S | 51 |
| Stephen Av. E&W | 33W-6S | 45 |
| Stephen Dr. N&S | 38W-9S | 50 |
| Summit Av. E&W | 34W-8S,33W-8S | 51 |
| Sumner St. N&S | 34W-7S,34W-8S | 51 |
| Sundown Dr. E&W | 37W-8S | 50 |
| Swarthmore Dr. E&W | 38W-8S | 50 |
| Sweetbriar Av. NE&SW | 38W-8S | 50 |
| Talma St. N&S | 35W-9S | 51 |
| Terry Av. N&S | 37W-8S | 50 |
| Turner Rd. E&W | 35W-5S | 45 |
| U. S. 30 Bypass NE&SW | 38W-9S,37W-9S | 50 |
| Union St. N&S | 35W-9S | 51 |
| Verity St. N&S | 38W-8S | 50 |
| Victor Rd. E&W | 34W-5S | 45 |
| W. Kingsway Dr. N&S | 38W-8S | 50 |
| Wabansia Av. N&S | 35W-9S | 51 |
| Watson St. N&S | 35W-9S | 51 |
| Webster St. N&S | 34W-8S | 51 |
| Wermes Av. N&S | 33W-8S | 51 |
| White Av. N&S | 37W-8S | 50 |
| Whitlock Av. N&S | 38W-8S | 50 |
| Woodland Dr. NE&SW | 34W-5S | 45 |
| Woodlyn Dr. E&W | 35W-5S | 45 |
| Ziegler Ln. E&W | 34W-8S | 51 |

**Barrington Hills***
(Also see Cook, Lake and McHenry Counties)

| Name | Grid | Page |
|---|---|---|
| Algonquin Rd. (Rt. 62) NW&SE | 32W-19N | 9 |
| Autumn Trail NS&EW | 32W-19N | 9 |
| Deepwood Rd. NW&SE | 32W-19N | 9 |
| Helm Rd. E&W | 32W-18N | 9 |
| Regan Blvd. NS&EW | 32W-18N | 9 |
| Royal Way N&S | 32W-18N | 9 |

**Batavia***
(Also see Du Page County)

| Name | Grid | Page |
|---|---|---|
| Adams St. E&W | 35W-1S | 39 |
| Anderson Dr. NW&SE | 34W-2S,33W-2S | 39 |
| Andover Ct. N&S | 33W-2S | 39 |
| Ann St. N&S | 35W-0S | 39 |
| Apache Dr. N&S | 36W-0S | 38 |
| Appleton Dr. N&S | 34W-1S | 39 |
| Aster Ct. N&S | 33W-1S | 39 |
| Averill St. NW&SE | 36W-2S | 38 |
| Bailey Dr. E&W | 34W-2S | 39 |
| Barclay Ct. E&W | 34W-1S | 39 |
| Barkei Dr. N&S | 34W-2S | 39 |
| Barton Tr. N&S | 37W-1S,37W-0S | 38 |
| Basswood Ct. NW&SE | 36W-2S | 38 |
| Batavia Av. N&S | 35W-2S,35W-0S | 39 |
| Beach St. N&S | 35W-2S | 39 |
| Becker Av. E&W | 34W-2S | 39 |
| Beckman Ln. N&S | 37W-1S,37W-0S | 39 |
| Belleview Ln. NW&SE | 35W-2S | 39 |
| Bernadette Ln. NW&SE | 36W-2S,35W-2S | 38 |
| Big Woods Dr. NW&SE | 37W-1S | 38 |
| Birch St. N&S | 36W-0S | 38 |
| Blackhawk Dr. NS&EW | 36W-0S | 38 |
| Blaine St. E&W | 36W-1S,35W-1S | 38 |
| Blair Ln. EW&NS | 36W-1S | 38 |
| Blair Pl. EW&NS | 36W-1S | 38 |
| Bluebell Ln. E&W | 33W-1S | 39 |
| Bluestem Ln. NS&EW | | |
| Bond Dr. NW&SE | 35W-2S | 39 |
| Boyd Ct. N&S | 34W-2S | 39 |
| Bradford Cir. NW&SE | 36W-0S | 38 |
| Brandywine Cir. NS&EW | 36W-2S,35W-2S | 38 |
| Brenton St. E&W | 36W-1S | 39 |
| Britta Ln. N&S | 36W-0S | 38 |
| Brown Ct. N&S | 36W-2S | 38 |
| Buffalo Tr. EW&NS | 34W-3S,34W-2S | 39 |
| Burnham Ln. NW&SE | 34W-2S | 39 |
| Burton Dr. E&W | 36W-0S | 38 |
| Buttermilk Ct. N&S | 36W-2S | 38 |
| Buttermilk Ln. E&W | 36W-2S | 38 |
| Campbell Ct. E&W | 34W-1S | 39 |
| Cannon Ct. N&S | 34W-1S | 39 |
| Cardinal Ct. E&W | 34W-2S,33W-2S | 39 |
| Carlisle Rd. NW&SE | 36W-2S,35W-2S | 38 |
| Carlson Ct. E&W | 34W-1S | 39 |
| Carr Ct. NW&SE | 35W-2S | 39 |
| Carriage Dr. N&S | 36W-0S | 38 |
| Center Av. NE&SW | 34W-1S | 39 |
| Challange Rd. NE&SW | 36W-2S | 38 |
| Charleston St. E&W | 36W-1S | 38 |
| Cherry Dr. N&S | 33W-2S | 39 |
| Chestnut St. N&S | 35W-1S,34W-1S | 39 |
| Chillem Dr. E&W | 34W-2S,33W-2S | 39 |
| Church St. N&S | 35W-0S,34W-0S | 39 |
| Churchill Ct. NE&SW | 34W-1S | 39 |
| Clark St. N&S | 35W-2S | 39 |
| Cleveland Av. NE&SW | 34W-1S | 39 |
| Clover Ct. E&W | 34W-2S | 39 |
| College St. N&S | 34W-1S,34W-0S | 39 |
| Collins Ct. E&W | 34W-2S | 39 |
| Columbia St. NE&SW | 35W-1S | 39 |
| Concord Ct. NE&SW | 35W-2S | 39 |
| Cottage Rd. E&W | 34W-2S | 39 |
| Cottonwood Cir. NE&SW | 34W-1S | 39 |
| Crane Ct. E&W | 36W-0S | 38 |
| Creek Dr. E&W | 36W-0S | 38 |
| Creek Ln. E&W | 36W-0S | 38 |
| Crestview Dr. NW&SE | 36W-0S | 38 |
| Cypress Av. N&S | 36W-0S | 38 |
| Danforth Dr. E&W | 36W-2S | 38 |
| Daniels Dr. N&S | 36W-1S | 38 |
| Darby Ct. N&S | 36W-1S | 39 |
| Davey Dr. N&S | 34W-2S | 39 |
| Davis Rd. E&W | 34W-0S,34W-2S | 39 |
| Deerpath Rd. N&S | 37W-0S | 39 |
| Delia St. N&S | 34W-1S,34W-1S | 39 |
| Derby Dr. N&S | 35W-2S | 39 |
| Deshannon Ct. E&W | 34W-2S | 39 |
| Dixon Cir. NW&SE | 36W-1S,36W-0S | 38 |
| Dixon Dr. N&S | 37W-0S | 38 |
| Douglas Rd. E&W | 35W-0S,34W-0S | 39 |
| Dover Ct. N&S | 34W-2S | 39 |
| Edwards Dr. E&W | 34W-2S | 39 |
| Elizabeth St. E&W | 34W-1S | 39 |
| Elm St. E&W | 35W-1S | 39 |
| Elmwood Ct. N&S | 33W-2S | 39 |
| Essex Ct. N&S | 34W-2S | 39 |
| Fabyan Pkwy. E&W | 36W-0S,33W-2S | 39 |
| Fagan Ct. NW&SE | 36W-2S | 38 |
| Fagan Rd. NW&SE | 36W-2S | 38 |
| Fayette St. NE&SW | 35W-0S | 39 |
| Feece Dr. N&S | 36W-1S | 38 |
| Finley Ct. NE&SW | 34W-2S | 39 |
| First St. E&W | 36W-1S | 38 |
| Flag Day Rd. N&S | 34W-2S | 39 |
| Flinn Dr. E&W | 35W-1S | 39 |
| Forest Av. N&S | 34W-1S,34W-0S | 39 |
| Fox Trail Dr. NS&EW | 35W-2S | 39 |
| Foxglove Dr. E&W | 34W-1S,33W-1S | 39 |
| Franklin St. E&W | 35W-1S,34W-1S | 39 |
| Garden Ct. N&S | 33W-2S | 39 |
| Garfield St. E&W | 36W-1S,35W-1S | 38 |
| Geise Rd. E&W | 34W-2S | 39 |
| Goldenrod Dr. E&W | 33W-1S | 39 |
| Gore St. E&W | 35W-1S | 39 |
| Green Pheasant Dr. E&W | 36W-2S | 38 |
| Greenleaf Dr. N&S | 33W-2S | 39 |
| Greenwood Ct. NW&SE | 34W-1S | 39 |
| Grove Ct. NS&EW | 34W-2S | 39 |
| Hadley Dr. EW&NS | 36W-1S | 38 |
| Hall Ct. E&W | 34W-2S | 39 |
| Halladay Ct. NW&SE | 36W-2S | 38 |
| Halladay Dr. N&S | 36W-2S | 38 |
| Hamlet St. N&S | 35W-2S,35W-1S | 39 |
| Hanover Dr. E&W | 34W-2S | 39 |
| Hanson St. NW&SE | 34W-1S | 39 |
| Harrison St. N&S | 35W-2S,35W-1S | 39 |
| Harvel Dr. E&W | 36W-2S | 38 |
| Hazelwood Ct. E&W | 36W-0S | 38 |
| Hillsboro Dr. NS&EW | 34W-2S,33W-2S | 39 |
| Holbrook Ln. N&S | 36W-0S | 38 |
| Hollister Dr. N&S | 36W-0S | 39 |
| Houston St. N&S | 36W-1S,35W-1S | 38 |
| Hubbard Av. E&W | 33W-0S | 39 |
| Huey Ct. NE&SW | 34W-2S | 39 |
| Hunter Dr. N&S | 33W-0S | 39 |
| Illinois Av. E&W | 35W-1S | 39 |
| Independence Dr. NE&SW | 35W-1S | 38 |
| Iroquois Dr. NE&SW | 36W-0S | 38 |
| Island Av. N&S | 35W-1S | 39 |
| Issel Ct. E&W | 33W-2S | 39 |
| Jackson St. N&S | 35W-2S,35W-1S | 39 |
| Jefferson Ct. E&W | 35W-1S | 39 |
| Jefferson St. N&S | 35W-2S,35W-0S | 39 |
| Jennifer St. N&S | 35W-2S,34W-1S | 39 |
| Johnston Dr. NS&EW | 34W-2S,33W-2S | 39 |
| Joslyn St. N&S | 36W-1S | 38 |
| K.P.K. Dr. N&S | 34W-0S | 39 |
| Ken Peddy Ct. N&S | 36W-2S | 38 |
| Kickapoo Av. E&W | 36W-0S | 38 |
| Kingsbury Ct. NE&SW | 34W-1S | 39 |
| Kingsland Dr. N&S | 34W-0S | 39 |
| Kirk Rd. N&S | 33W-2S,33W-0S | 39 |
| Kline Ct. E&W | 34W-2S | 39 |
| Kramer Ct. N&S | 34W-1S | 39 |
| Kristen Ct. N&S | 34W-1S | 39 |
| Lake Ct. N&S | 34W-0S | 39 |
| Lake St. E&W | 35W-0S,34W-0S | 39 |
| Landfield Rd. N&S | 36W-1S | 39 |
| Larkspur Ln. N&S | 34W-2S | 39 |
| Lathem St. E&W | 35W-0S,33W-0S | 39 |
| Laurel St. E&W | 35W-1S,34W-1S | 39 |
| Lexington E&W | 34W-2S | 39 |
| Lexington Ln. E&W | 34W-2S | 39 |
| Lincoln St. N&S | 35W-1S,35W-0S | 39 |
| Lockwood Ct. NE&SW | 36W-2S | 38 |
| Lockwood Ln. NW&SE | 36W-2S | 38 |
| Locust St. E&W | 35W-1S,34W-1S | 39 |
| Logan St. N&S | 35W-0S | 39 |
| Lund Ln. N&S | 34W-2S,34W-1S | 39 |
| Lundberg Av. N&S | 36W-0S | 38 |
| Lyon Rd. E&W | 34W-0S | 39 |
| Madison St. N&S | 35W-0S,34W-0S | 39 |
| Main St. E&W | 36W-1S,35W-1S | 38 |
| Mair Ct. N&S | 36W-0S | 38 |
| Mallory Av. N&S | 35W-1S | 39 |
| Manchester Av. NS&EW | 35W-2S,34W-1S | 39 |
| Mandrake Dr. N&S | 34W-1S | 39 |
| Maple Ln. E&W | 36W-0S,35W-0S | 38 |
| Marshall Ct. E&W | 34W-0S | 39 |
| Martin St. N&S | 37W-0S | 38 |
| Mary Ct. E&W | 34W-0S | 38 |
| Mather Ln. E&W | 34W-1S | 39 |
| Maves Dr. E&W | 34W-2S | 39 |
| Mayflower Dr. N&S | 33W-1S | 39 |
| McClurg Ct. NW&SE | 36W-2S | 38 |
| McClurg Dr. N&S | 36W-2S | 38 |
| McKee St. E&W | 36W-1S,36W-0S | 38 |
| Meadowrue Ln. NS&EW | 34W-1S,33W-1S | 39 |
| Midway Dr. NW&SE | 36W-2S,35W-2S | 38 |
| Mill St. NS&EW | 36W-2S | 38 |
| Miller Ct. E&W | 34W-1S | 39 |
| Millview Ct. NE&SW | 36W-2S | 38 |
| Millview Dr. NS&EW | 35W-2S,36W-1S | 38 |
| Monticello Rd. NW&SE | 35W-2S | 39 |
| Morton St. E&W | 36W-1S,35W-0S | 38 |
| Mt. Vernon Pl. NE&SW | 35W-2S | 39 |
| N. Raddant Rd. NW&SE | 34W-0S | 39 |
| Navajo Dr. N&S | 36W-0S | 38 |
| Newton Av. NW&SE | 36W-2S | 38 |
| Norcross Dr. E&W | 34W-2S | 39 |
| Nordic Ct. E&W | 34W-2S | 39 |
| North Av. E&W | 36W-0S,35W-0S | 38 |
| Olympic Dr. E&W | 34W-2S | 39 |
| Orchard Ct. E&W | 33W-1S | 39 |
| Orion Rd. NS&EW | 35W-0S,34W-0S | 39 |
| Oswald Av. E&W | 35W-2S | 39 |
| Ozier Ct. N&S | 35W-0S | 39 |
| Paddock Ln. E&W | 35W-1S | 39 |
| Pamarco Av. N&S | 35W-1S | 39 |
| Paramount Pkwy. N&S | 33W-0S | 39 |
| Park St. N&S | 35W-0S | 39 |
| Parkview Dr. E&W | 36W-0S | 38 |
| Payne Av. E&W | 36W-2S | 38 |
| Peebles Ct. N&S | 36W-0S | 38 |
| Perna Ct. N&S | 34W-2S | 39 |
| Pheasant Ct. N&S | 35W-0S | 39 |
| Pheasant Ln. E&W | 35W-0S | 39 |
| Pine Ct. NE&SW | 34W-1S | 39 |
| Pine Dr. E&W | 34W-1S | 39 |
| Pine St. E&W | 35W-1S,34W-1S | 39 |
| Pitz Ln. N&S | 36W-1S | 38 |
| Pleasant Ct. NE&SW | 34W-1S | 39 |
| Ponca Dr. E&W | 36W-0S | 38 |
| Pontiac Dr. NE&SW | 36W-0S | 38 |
| Pottawatomie Tr. EW&NS | 34W-3S | 39 |
| Prairie St. N&S | 35W-1S,34W-0S | 39 |
| Pueblo Dr. E&W | 36W-0S | 38 |
| Quark Ct. N&S | 35W-2S | 39 |
| Raddant Rd. N&S | 34W-1S | 39 |
| Randall Rd. N&S | 37W-1S,36W-1S | 38 |
| Ravania St. NE&SW | 34W-1S | 39 |
| Republic Rd. N&S | 35W-1S,35W-0S | 39 |
| Richter Ct. N&S | 36W-1S | 38 |
| Richter Rd. N&S | 36W-1S | 38 |
| Ridgelawn Ct. N&S | 34W-3S,34W-2S | 39 |
| Ridgelawn Tr. N&S | 34W-2S,35W-2S | 39 |
| River Rock Rd. N&S | 35W-0S | 39 |
| River St. N&S | 35W-2S,35W-0S | 39 |
| Roberts Ct. E&W | 35W-2S | 38 |
| Roberts Ln. N&S | 36W-2S,36W-1S | 38 |
| Robin Dr. E&W | 36W-0S | 38 |
| Rocksbury Ct. N&S | 33W-1S | 39 |
| Rotolo Ct. E&W | 34W-2S | 39 |
| Rt. 25 N&S | 35W-2S,35W-0S | 39 |
| Rt. 31 N&S | 35W-2S,35W-0S | 39 |
| Rule N&S | 36W-1S | 38 |
| Ryan Ct. N&S | 34W-1S | 39 |
| Rye Ct. N&S | 34W-1S | 39 |
| Saratoga Dr. N&S | 36W-1S | 38 |
| Sauk Dr. NS&EW | 35W-2S | 39 |
| Schiedler Dr. E&W | 34W-2S | 39 |
| Schuler Dr. E&W | 33W-0S | 39 |
| Schumway Av. N&S | 34W-1S | 39 |
| Settlers Dr. E&W | 34W-2S | 39 |
| Settlers Tr. E&W | 34W-2S | 39 |
| Shabbona Tr. N&S | 36W-0S,35W-0S | 38 |
| Sioux Dr. NE&SW | 36W-0S | 38 |
| Smith Ct. NE&SW | 36W-0S | 38 |
| South Ct. N&S | 34W-1S | 39 |
| Southeast Pass E&W | 34W-3S | 38 |
| Spencer Ln. E&W | 36W-1S | 38 |
| Spring St. E&W | 35W-1S,34W-1S | 39 |
| Spruce St. N&S | 34W-2S,34W-1S | 39 |
| Spuhler Dr. N&S | 36W-1S | 38 |
| Standish St. N&S | 35W-0S | 39 |
| Stanton St. N&S | 35W-1S,34W-0S | 39 |
| State St. E&W | 35W-1S,34W-1S | 39 |
| Stenman Dr. N&S | 34W-2S | 39 |
| Stewart Ct. NW&SE | 34W-2S,34W-1S | 39 |
| Stewart Dr. NE&SW | 34W-1S | 39 |
| Sunset Dr. E&W | 34W-2S,34W-0S | 39 |
| Surrey St. NE&SW | 34W-0S | 39 |
| Sylvan Pl. NE&SW | 34W-1S | 39 |
| Thoria Ct. NE&SW | 34W-0S | 39 |
| Thoria Rd. NS&EW | 35W-0S,34W-0S | 39 |
| Thorn Ct. N&S | 34W-2S | 39 |
| Thorsen Ln. NW&SE | 36W-0S | 38 |
| Thrun Dr. NS&EW | 34W-0S | 39 |
| Timber Tr. E&W | 36W-0S | 39 |
| Towne Av. E&W | 36W-0S | 38 |
| Trillium Ct. E&W | 34W-1S,33W-1S | 39 |
| Tuggles Ct. N&S | 34W-2S | 39 |
| Tuggles Ln. N&S | 34W-2S | 39 |
| Twin Oaks Ln. N&S | 37W-1S | 38 |
| Union Av. E&W | 35W-1S | 39 |
| Van Buren St. N&S | 35W-1S,35W-0S | 39 |
| Van Nortwick Av. N&S | 35W-2S | 39 |
| Van Nortwick Cir. NW&SE | 35W-0S | 39 |
| Van Nortwick Ct. E&W | 36W-0S | 38 |
| Viking Ct. N&S | 34W-1S | 39 |
| Viking Dr. N&S | 34W-1S | 39 |
| Violet Ln. NW&SE | 34W-1S | 39 |
| Wagner Rd. N&S | 34W-2S | 39 |
| Walnut St. E&W | 36W-1S,35W-1S | 38 |
| Ward Rd. N&S | 34W-2S | 39 |
| Washington Av. N&S | 35W-1S,35W-0S | 39 |
| Water St. N&S | 35W-1S | 39 |
| Waubonsee Tr. E&W | 35W-0S | 39 |
| Webster St. E&W | 35W-1S,34W-1S | 39 |
| West Ct. NE&SW | 35W-2S | 39 |
| Western Av. N&S | 36W-0S | 38 |
| Weston Ct. N&S | 34W-2S | 39 |
| Whitehall Ct. E&W | 36W-1S | 38 |
| Willby Ln. N&S | 36W-1S | 38 |
| Williams Rd. E&W | 37W-1S | 39 |
| Willow Ln. N&S | 34W-2S | 39 |
| Wilson Rd. E&W | 33W-1N | 33 |
| Wilson St. E&W | 36W-1S,33W-1S | 38 |
| Windsor Ln. E&W | 35W-0S | 39 |
| Winnebago Tr. NS&EW | 36W-0S | 38 |
| Wintergreen Ct. NW&SE | 34W-1S | 39 |
| Wintergreen Ter. E&W | 34W-1N | 33 |
| Woodland Hills Rd. N&S | 34W-2S,33W-1S | 39 |
| Young Av. N&S | 35W-1S | 39 |
| 1st St. NE&SW | 35W-1S | 39 |

**Batavia Township**

| Name | Grid | Page |
|---|---|---|
| Arbor Ln. NS&EW | 33W-3S | 45 |
| Arrowhead St. N&S | 35W-3S | 45 |
| Banbury Rd. N&S | 35W-3S,35W-2S | 45 |
| Chillem Dr. NE&SW | 35W-2S,34W-2S | 39 |
| Christina Ct. E&W | 38W-3S | 38 |
| Cigrand Ct. NE&SW | 37W-3S | 44 |
| Deer Oaks Rd. N&S | 38W-3S | 44 |
| Deerpath Rd. E&W | 38W-3S,37W-1S | 44 |
| Eastview Dr. E&W | 36W-3S | 44 |
| Elfstrom Tr. N&S | 37W-3S | 44 |
| Ellen Ln. N&S | 36W-1S | 38 |
| Evergreen Dr. N&S | 36W-1S | 38 |
| Fidler Ct. N&S | 33W-3S | 45 |
| Flagstone Ln. NS&EW | 33W-3S | 45 |
| Geise Rd. E&W | 34W-2S | 39 |
| Gregory Ln. E&W | 38W-3S | 44 |
| Grove Hill Dr. NW&SE | 38W-3S | 38 |
| Hart Rd. N&S | 34W-3S,34W-2S | 45 |
| Heather Ln. N&S | 37W-2S | 38 |
| Heaton Dr. E&W | 38W-2S,37W-2S | 38 |
| Heritage Dr. NW&SE | 37W-3S,37W-2S | 44 |
| Heritage Glen Ct. NE&SW | 37W-2S | 38 |
| Hickory Ln. NS&EW | 38W-3S | 44 |
| Hilltop Dr. N&S | 36W-3S | 44 |
| Horizon Ln. E&W | 33W-3S | 45 |
| Horseshoe Dr. NS&EW | 38W-2S | 38 |
| Hunting Tr. E&W | 38W-2S | 38 |
| Jonathan Ln. E&W | 38W-2S | 38 |
| Kirk Rd. N&S | 33W-3S,33W-2S | 45 |
| Long Av. E&W | 36W-3S,35W-3S | 44 |
| Main St. E&W | 38W-1S,36W-1S | 38 |
| McKee St. E&W | 36W-0S | 38 |
| McKinley St. N&S | 36W-1S | 38 |
| Meadow Dr. N&S | 34W-3S | 39 |
| Meadowview Rd. NE&SW | 37W-2S | 38 |
| Mesa Dr. E&W | 33W-3S | 38, 44 |
| Morton St. E&W | 36W-1S | 38 |
| Napa Ln. EW&NS | 34W-3S | 45 |
| Nelson Lake Rd. N&S | 38W-2S,38W-1S | 38 |
| Nelson Ln. N&S | 38W-3S,38W-1S | 44 |
| Oak St. NW&SE | 34W-3S | 39 |
| Orchard Rd. N&S | 38W-3S,37W-3S | 44 |
| Partridge Rd. NS&EW | 38W-2S | 38 |
| Pinnacle Ct. N&S | 33W-3S | 45 |
| Pinnacle Dr. NS&EW | 33W-3S | 45 |
| Raddant Rd. N&S | 34W-3S,34W-2S | 45 |
| Randall Rd. NE&SW | 37W-3S,36W-1S | 44 |
| Roberts Ln. N&S | 36W-1S | 38 |
| Rosewood Ln. E&W | 38W-3S | 44 |
| Rt. 25 NE&SW | 36W-3S,35W-2S | 44 |
| Rt. 31 NE&SW | 36W-3S,35W-2S | 44 |
| Savannah Cir. E&W | 33W-3S | 45 |
| Savannah Dr. EW&NS | 33W-3S | 45 |
| Sawgrass Dr. NS&EW | 33W-3S | 45 |
| Shagbark Dr. NE&SW | | 39 |
| Shuster Ln. N&S | 37W-3S | 44 |
| Solitude Ln. NS&EW | 33W-3S | 45 |
| Sonoma Ln. NW&SE | 34W-3S | 45 |
| Sunset Dr. E&W | 34W-2S | 39 |

KANE COUNTY 55


| | Grid | Page |
|---|---|---|
| Tanglewood Ct. E&W | 38W-2S | 38 |
| Tanglewood Dr. NW&SE | 38W-1S,37W-2S | 38 |
| Thorncrest N&S | 35W-2S | 39 |
| Valley Rd. E&W | 36W-3S | 44 |
| Vineyard Ln. EW&NS | 34W-3S | 45 |
| Volintine Farm Rd. N&S | 37W-3S | 44 |
| Wagner Rd. N&S | 34W-3S,34W-2S | 45 |
| Western Av. NE&SW | 36W-0S | 38 |
| Whipple Av. N&S | 36W-1S | 38 |
| White Oak Ln. NW&SE | 37W-2S | 38 |
| Wilson Rd. E&W | 33W-1S | 39 |
| Woodland Av. NE&SW | 35W-2S | 39 |
| Woodland Dr. NE&SW | 35W-2S | 39 |

## Big Rock Township

| | Grid | Page |
|---|---|---|
| Base Line Rd. E&W | 48W-9S | 46 |
| Bergman Dr. NS&EW | 45W-8S | 47 |
| Bourtzos Av. N&S | 45W-8S | 47 |
| Bushnell Rd. NW&SE | 49W-9S | 46 |
| Camp Dean Rd. N&S | 46W-8S,46W-7S | 47 |
| Carey Dr. E&W | 47W-7S | 47 |
| Clark Rd. NE&SW | 46W-9S | 47 |
| Dauberman Rd. N&S | 47W-6S,47W-4S | 41 |
| Davis Rd. N&S | 48W-6S,48W-5S | 40 |
| Deer Ridge Path NE&SW | 49W-5S | 40 |
| Dolly Dr. NE&SW | 46W-7S | 47 |
| Dugan Rd. N&S | 45W-5S | 41 |
| Fifth St. E&W | 47W-7S | 47 |
| First St. NW&SE | 48W-7S,47W-7S | 46 |
| Florence Rd. N&S | 48W-5S,48W-4S | 40 |
| Fourth St. E&W | 48W-7S,47W-7S | 46 |
| Galena St. E&W | 48W-6S,47W-6S | 40 |
| Granart Rd. NE&SW | 49W-9S,45W-7S | 46 |
| Greenacre Rd. NS&EW | 50W-7S,49W-7S | 46 |
| Hinckley Rd. E&W | 50W-6S,48W-6S | 40 |
| Jefferson Av. N&S | 47W-7S | 47 |
| Jericho Rd. NW&SE | 50W-7S,45W-9S | 46 |
| Jetter Rd. NS&EW | 45W-9S | 47 |
| John St. NS&EW | 45W-8S | 47 |
| Jones Rd. NS&EW | 47W-9S | 47 |
| Katie Dr. NE&SW | 46W-7S | 47 |
| Lasher Rd. NS&EW | 50W-4S,49W-4S | 40 |
| Lincoln Av. N&S | 48W-7S,48W-6S | 46 |
| Madison Av. N&S | 47W-7S | 47 |
| Marie St. NS&EW | 45W-8S | 47 |
| Mary Dr. NW&SE | 46W-7S | 47 |
| Mary St. NW&SE | 48W-7S | 46 |
| McDermott Rd. E&W | 50W-8S | 46 |
| Nelson Rd. N&S | 49W-8S,49W-7S | 46 |
| Oak St. E&W | 48W-6S | 40 |
| Oaken St. NE&SW | 45W-8S | 47 |
| Price Rd. NE&SW | 48W-7S,47W-7S | 46 |
| Raymond Rd. NE&SW | 45W-9S,45W-8S | 47 |
| Rhodes St. NW&SE | 47W-8S,48W-7S | 47 |
| Scott Rd. NE&SW | 50W-5S,47W-5S | 40 |
| Second St. NW&SE | 48W-7S,47W-7S | 46 |
| Shaw Rd. NS&EW | 50W-6S,50W-5S | 40 |
| Sixth St. E&W | 47W-7S | 47 |
| Swan Rd. NS&EW | 48W-5S,49W-4S | 40 |
| Third St. E&W | 48W-7S,47W-7S | 46 |
| Timberview Dr. NE&SW | 47W-7S | 47 |
| Toronto St. N&S | 45W-8S | 47 |
| U.S. Route 30 E&W | 50W-6S,45W-6S | 40 |
| W. County Line Rd. N&S | 50W-5S,50W-4S | 40 |
| Welton Dr. NW&SE | 48W-7S | 46 |
| Wheeler Rd. E&W | 48W-5S,49W-5S | 40 |
| Whildin Rd. NW&SE | 46W-7S,45W-7S | 47 |
| White Trail Path NW&SE | 49W-5S | 40 |

## Blackberry Township

| | Grid | Page |
|---|---|---|
| Acres Pl. NS&EW | 39W-0N | 37 |
| Alexander Dr. E&W | 39W-0N | 37 |
| Armstrong Cir. NS&EW | 39W-0N | 37 |
| Armstrong Ln. E&W | 39W-0N | 37 |
| Autumn Ln. N&S | 43W-0S | 36 |
| Baker Dr. N&S | 39W-0N | 37 |
| Bartlett Pl. NS&EW | 39W-0N | 37 |
| Bartlett Rd. N&S | 39W-0S,39W-0N | 37 |
| Bateman Rd. E&W | 44W-0S | 36 |
| Benton Ln. E&W | 39W-0N | 37 |
| Blackberry Hill Rd. N&S | 42W-1S | 36 |
| Bliss Rd. NE&SW | 41W-3S,40W-1S | 43 |
| Boyd Dr. N&S | 39W-0N | 37 |
| Brundige Rd. N&S | 39W-1N | 31 |
| Bunker Rd. N&S | 41W-1S,41W-0N | 37 |
| Callighan Pl. NS&EW | 39W-0S | 37 |
| Carney Ln. E&W | 39W-0N | 37 |
| Collins Pl. NS&EW | 39W-0S | 37 |
| Concord Ct. NW&SE | 44W-1S | 36 |
| Creekside Ct. NE&SW | 43W-2S | 36 |
| Curtis Sq. NS&EW | 39W-0N | 37 |
| Denali Ct. E&W | 41W-1N | 31 |
| Denali Rd. NE&SW | 41W-1N | 31 |
| Derussey Rd. N&S | 43W-2S | 36 |
| Dobson Ln. E&W | 39W-0N | 37 |
| Donny Hill Dr. N&S | 43W-1S,43W-0S | 36 |
| Dooley Dr. N&S | 39W-0N | 37 |
| East West Tollway NW&SE | 44W-2S,42W-3S | 36 |
| Eldon Dr. N&S | 39W-0N | 37 |
| Finley Rd. NE&SW | 44W-3S,43W-3S | 42 |
| Foad Dr. N&S | 39W-0N | 37 |
| Forbes Dr. N&S | 39W-0N | 37 |
| Green Pl. NS&EW | 39W-0N | 37 |
| Green Rd. NE&SW | 43W-2S,42W-0S | 36 |
| Green St. EW&NS | 43W-2S | 36 |
| Greenbriar Dr. NE&SW | 44W-1S | 36 |
| Harley Rd. N&S | 41W-1N | 31 |
| Harvey Sq. NS&EW | 39W-0N | 37 |
| Herrington Blvd. E&W | 39W-0N | 37 |
| Heton Dr. E&W | 39W-0N | 37 |
| Hilts Dr. N&S | 39W-0N | 37 |
| Houck Pl. NS&EW | 30W-0N | 37 |
| Howard Sq. NS&EW | 39W-0N | 37 |
| Hughes Rd. E&W | 43W-0N,39W-0S | 36 |
| Interstate 88 NW&SE | 44W-2S,43W-3S | 36 |
| Kaneville Rd. NE&SW | 40W-1S,39W-0S | 37 |
| Keenan Ct. E&W | 39W-0S | 37 |
| Kendall Ct. NS&EW | 39W-0N | 37 |
| Kenmar Ct. NE&SW | 43W-0S | 36 |
| Kenmar Dr. NW&SE | 43W-0S | 36 |
| Kenmar Ln. NE&SW | 43W-0S | 36 |
| Keslinger Rd. E&W | 44W-1N,39W-1N | 30 |
| Killarney Ln. N&S | 41W-1N | 31 |
| Krohn Ct. N&S | 40W-1N | 37 |
| La Fox Rd. N&S | 40W-1N | 37 |
| Lakewood Dr. NW&SE | 43W-3S | 42 |
| Lasher Rd. NE&SW | 44W-3S | 42 |
| Lebaron Ct. NS&EW | 39W-0N | 37 |
| Linlar Dr. N&S | 39W-1N | 31 |
| Lorang Rd. N&S | 44W-3S,44W-1S | 42 |
| Main St. E&W | 44W-1S,39W-1S | 36 |
| Marian Cir. NS&EW | 43W-3S | 42 |
| Marian Ln. N&S | 43W-3S | 42 |
| Marks Pl. NS&EW | 39W-0N | 37 |
| Meadowsweet Dr. E&W | 42W-1N | 30 |
| Midan Rd. E&W | 39W-1N | 31 |
| Mill Rd. NE&SW | 44W-2S | 36 |
| Morrill Dr. N&S | 39W-0S | 37 |
| Mulhern Dr. NE&SW | 41W-1N | 31 |
| N. Mill Creek Dr. N&S | 39W-0N | 37 |
| Norris Rd. NW&SE | 41W-3S,40W-3S | 43 |
| North Dr. NW&SE | 43W-3S | 42 |
| Northern View Ct. N&S | 43W-0S | 36 |
| Northway Dr. NS&EW | 42W-1N,41W-1N | 30 |
| Nottingham Dr. E&W | 43W-2S | 36 |
| Oakland Ln. N&S | 40W-3S | 43 |
| Oakleaf Dr. E&W | 44W-2S,43W-2S | 36 |
| Oakwood Dr. NS&EW | 43W-0N | 36 |
| Oakwood Ter. N&S | 43W-2S | 36 |
| Pauley Sq. NS&EW | 39W-0N | 37 |
| Pennycress Ct. E&W | 42W-1N | 30 |
| Pine Row Ct. N&S | 43W-2S | 36 |
| Platt Pl. NS&EW | 39W-0N | 37 |
| Pouley Rd. N&S | 42W-0N,42W-1N | 36 |
| Preston Ct. NS&EW | 39W-0S | 37 |
| Red Oak Dr. NS&EW | 43W-2S | 36 |
| Ridge Dr. NE&SW | 42W-0S | 36 |
| Rowe Rd. NE&SW | 44W-0S,43W-0S | 36 |
| Rt. 47 N&S | 43W-3S,43W-0N | 42 |
| School House Ln. E&W | 39W-0N | 37 |
| Scott Rd. NE&SW | 43W-3S | 42 |
| Seavey Rd. E&W | 44W-3S,39W-2S | 42 |
| Smith Rd. NE&SW | 43W-0S,42W-0S | 36 |
| Sounders Cr. NS&EW | 39N-0S | 37 |
| Stargrass Ln. N&S | 42W-1N | 30 |
| Still Meadows Ln. E&W | 42W-1N | 30 |
| Strong Pl. NS&EW | 39W-0S | 37 |
| Sulley Dr. NS&EW | 39W-0N | 37 |
| Sulley Pl. N&S | 39W-0N | 37 |
| Sulley Sq. NS&EW | 39W-0N | 37 |
| Surrey Dr. NW&SE | 43W-0S | 36 |
| Taana Rd. N&S | 39W-0S | 37 |
| Tall Oaks Trail E&W | 43W-1S | 36 |
| Tanner Rd. E&W | 40W-3S,39W-3S | 43 |
| Terney Ln. E&W | 39W-0N | 37 |
| Terney Sq. E&W | 39W-0N | 37 |
| Terrace Dr. N&S | 40W-3S | 43 |
| The Old Midlothian Turnpike E&W | 43W-2S | 36 |
| Thorn Apple Tree Rd. NS&EW | 43W-3S | 42 |
| Thorndon Ridge Dr. NS&EW | 43W-1S,42W-0S | 36 |
| Timber Crest Dr. NW&SE | 43W-0S | 36 |
| Underwood Dr. N&S | 39W-0N | 37 |
| Washburn Dr. NS&EW | 39W-0N | 37 |
| Washburn Pl. NS&EW | 39W-0N | 37 |
| Weaver Cir. NS&EW | 39W-0N | 37 |
| Weaver Ln. E&W | 39W-0N | 37 |
| Whispering Oaks Dr. E&W | 43W-0S | 36 |
| Willow Creek Ct. NW&SE | 43W-2S | 36 |
| Willow Creek Dr. NS&EW | 43W-2S | 36 |
| Yates Pl. NS&EW | 39W-0N | 37 |

## Burlington

| | Grid | Page |
|---|---|---|
| Burlington Rd. NW&SE | 48W-13N,47W-12N | 10 |
| Center St. NE&SW | 48W-12N | 16 |
| Deutsch Rd. E&W | 47W-12N | 16 |
| Elgin-Genoa Rd. E&W | 47W-12N | 16 |
| French Rd. NE&SW | 48W-13N,47W-13N | 10 |
| James St. NE&SW | 47W-12N | 16 |
| James St. NW&SE | 47W-12N | 16 |
| Main St. NW&SE | 48W-12N,47W-12N | 16 |
| Park St. N&S | 47W-12N | 16 |
| South St. N&S | 48W-12N | 16 |
| Sycamore St. NE&SW | 48W-12N | 16 |
| Water St. NE&SW | 47W-12N | 16 |

## Burlington Township

| | Grid | Page |
|---|---|---|
| Barr Rd. E&W | 45W-12N | 17 |
| Barron Rd. N&S | 48W-8N,48W-9N | 22 |
| Burlington Rd. NW&SE | 48W-13N,45W-10N | 10 |
| Chapman Rd. NW&SE | 47W-11N,46W-10N | 16 |
| Ellithorpe Rd. E&W | 49W-10N,45W-10N | 16 |
| Engel Rd. N&S | 49W-12N,49W-13N | 16 |
| Freedom Ct. E&W | 45W-10N | 17 |
| Godfrey Rd. E&W | 47W-10N | 16 |
| Grand Arbor Ln. N&S | 46W-8N | 23 |
| Hickory Ct. N&S | 47W-11N | 16 |
| Highland Tr. N&S | 45W-10N | 17 |
| Hillview Ln. E&W | 45W-10N | 17 |
| Indian Creek Tr. NW&SE | 46W-6N | 23 |
| Larkin Rd. N&S | 50W-8N | 22 |
| Lawrence Rd. N&S | 49W-11N,49W-12N | 16 |
| Lukens Rd. NS&EW | 50W-10N,50W-11N | 16 |
| Marcy Rd. E&W | 50W-10N | 16 |
| Mc Gough Rd. E&W | 49W-9N,48W-11N | 16 |
| McDonald Rd. E&W | 45W-8N | 23 |
| McGough Rd. NE&SW | 50W-8N,49W-9N | 22 |
| Middleton Rd. E&W | 50W-9N,47W-9N | 16 |
| Peplow Rd. N&S | 48W-8N,48W-10N | 22 |
| Percy Rd. N&S | 49W-8N,49W-9N | 22 |
| Pioneer Ln. NW&SE | 45W-10N | 17 |
| Plank Rd. E&W | 49W-12N | 16 |
| Private Rd. E&W | 48W-12N | 16 |
| Ramm Rd. E&W | 50W-8N,45W-8N | 22 |
| Read Rd. E&W | 45W-6N | 23 |
| Rohrsen Rd. E&W | 45W-11N | 17 |
| Romke Rd. N&S | 46W-12N | 17 |
| Shepherds Ln. N&S | 45W-10N | 17 |
| Strawberry Ln. E&W | 45W-10N | 17 |
| Sumac Ln. E&W | 45W-10N | 17 |
| Thomas Rd. N&S | 46W-8N,46W-9N | 23 |
| Waughn Rd. N&S | 48W-12N | 16 |
| West County Line Rd. N&S | 50W-12N,50W-13N | 16 |
| Whispering Oaks Dr. E&W | 48W-11N | 16 |
| Winterset Rd. E&W | 47W-11N | 16 |

## Campton Township

| | Grid | Page |
|---|---|---|
| Alcott Ln. E&W | 39W-4N | 31 |
| Ancient Oak Ln. NW&SE | 40W-5N | 25 |
| Anderson Rd. N&S | 43W-2N,43W-4N | 30 |
| Antler Tr. NW&SE | 39W-5N | 25 |
| Arbor Creek Rd. N&S | 39W-3N | 31 |
| Arboretum Ln. N&S | 42W-5N | 24 |
| Arrowhead Dr. NS&EW | 42W-4N | 30 |
| Audubon Ct. E&W | 42W-5N | 24 |
| Austin St. N&S | 40W-4N | 31 |
| Badger Ct. E&W | 43W-6N | 24 |
| Baert Ln. E&W | 39W-3N | 31 |
| Balkan Dr. NE&SW | 39W-3N | 31 |
| Barberry Ln. NW&SE | 41W-6N | 25 |
| Barlow Dr. E&W | 41W-3N | 31 |
| Barnside Ct. NE&SW | 39W-6N | 25 |
| Beaver Ct. NW&SE | 43W-5N | 24 |
| Beaver Ln. E&W | 43W-5N | 24 |
| Beith Rd. NW&SE | 44W-4N,41W-2N | 30 |
| Birchdale Ct. NE&SW | 39W-4N,39W-5N | 31 |
| Black Willow Dr. NW&SE | 39W-4N,39W-5N | 31 |
| Blue Heron Ct. NW&SE | 40W-5N | 25 |
| Blue Larkspur Ln. E&W | 43W-4N | 30 |
| Bolcum Rd. NE&SW | 40W-5N,39W-5N | 25 |
| Bowgren Dr. N&S | 41W-2N | 31 |
| Boxwood Ln. N&S | 41W-6N | 25 |
| Bridle Creek Dr. E&W | 40W-4N | 31 |
| Bridle Ct. E&W | 42W-5N | 24 |
| Brierwood Dr. N&S | 41W-6N,41W-7N | 25 |
| Brittany Ct. NE&SW | 39W-7N | 25 |
| Brookhaven Ln. N&S | 39W-6N | 25 |
| Brookside West Dr. N&S | 42W-4N,41W-4N | 30 |
| Brown Rd. NS&EW | 41W-4N,40W-5N | 31 |
| Brundage Rd. N&S | 39W-2N | 31 |
| Bryant St. NE&SW | 40W-4N | 31 |
| Buck Ct. NE&SW | 43W-6N | 24 |
| Buckskin Ct. N&S | 39W-5N | 25 |
| Buckskin Tr. NS&EW | 39W-5N | 25 |
| Burlington Rd. NW&SE | 43W-7N | 24 |
| Campton Hills Rd. NW&SE | 43W-4N,39W-3N | 30 |
| Campton Meadow Dr. E&W | 40W-3N | 31 |
| Campton Oak Dr. NE&SW | 40W-5N | 25 |
| Campton Ridge Dr. N&S | 41W-5N | 25 |
| Campton Woods Dr. N&S | 41W-3N | 31 |
| Canterbury Ct. N&S | 40W-6N,40W-7N | 25 |
| Caribou Tr. E&W | 39W-5N | 25 |
| Carl Sandburg Rd. NS&EW | 40W-4N,39W-4N | 31 |
| Carol Dr. NW&SE | 42W-4N | 30 |
| Carriage Ct. E&W | 40W-3N | 31 |
| Castle Dr. NE&SW | 41W-5N | 25 |
| Chaffield Dr. N&S | 42W-4N | 30 |
| Challedon Ct. NW&SE | 43W-4N | 30 |
| Chateaugay Ct. NW&SE | 42W-4N | 30 |
| Chateaugay Ln. NS&EW | 43W-4N,42W-4N | 30 |
| Circle Dr. NE&SW | 41W-4N | 31 |
| Citation Ln. N&S | 43W-4N,42W-4N | 30 |
| Clemens Course NE&SW | 40W-4N | 31 |
| Cloverfield Cir. NS&EW | 39W-7N | 25 |
| Cloverfield Dr. NW&SE | 39W-7N | 25 |
| Clydsdale Ct. NW&SE | 40W-6N | 25 |
| Colonel Bennett Ln. NE&SW | 40W-6N | 25 |
| Colson Dr. NS&EW | 41W-5N | 25 |
| Colt Dr. N&S | 41W-2N | 31 |
| Compton Woods Dr. E&W | 40W-3N | 31 |
| Cooper Ln. N&S | 39W-3N | 31 |
| Copperwood Ln. NW&SE | 42W-5N | 24 |
| Corbett Pl. NE&SW | 39W-3N | 31 |
| Corron Glen Rd. N&S | 40W-6N | 25 |
| Corron Rd. N&S | 40W-5N,40W-7N | 25 |
| Coulter Ln. NW&SE | 39W-3N | 31 |
| Council Ct. N&S | 42W-4N | 30 |
| Countryview Ln. NE&SW | 42W-4N | 30 |
| Cranberry Ln. NW&SE | 42W-5N | 24 |
| Cranston Rd. E&W | 39W-7N | 25 |
| Creekside Ct. E&W | 43W-5N | 24 |
| Crescent Ln. E&W | 39W-6N | 25 |
| Crestwood Dr. N&S | 41W-6N | 25 |
| Crooked Ln. NW&SE | 41W-6N,40W-5N | 25 |
| Crosscreek Ln. E&W | 39W-6N | 25 |
| Curling Pond Ct. NE&SW | 40W-3N | 31 |
| Cutwood Ln. E&W | 39W-6N | 25 |
| Dairyherd Ln. E&W | 39W-6N | 25 |
| Deer Run Dr. NS&EW | 40W-5N,39W-5N | 25 |
| Deer Run Ln. NW&SE | 39W-5N | 25 |
| Deerhaven Tr. NW&SE | 39W-5N | 25 |
| Deerslayer Dr. NW&SE | 43W-4N | 30 |
| Denali Ln. E&W | 40W-2N | 31 |
| Denker Rd. N&S | 39W-5N,39W-6N | 25 |
| Derby Ct. NW&SE | 42W-4N | 30 |
| Dickinson Ln. E&W | 40W-4N,40W-3N | 31 |
| Dillonfield Dr. NW&SE | 41W-2N,40W-2N | 31 |
| Dittman Rd. N&S | 42W-7N | 24 |
| Dominion Dr. NS&EW | 41W-5N | 25 |
| Dorsey Ct. N&S | 40W-2N | 31 |
| E. Mary Dr. NE&SW | 42W-4N | 30 |
| E. Woodland Dr. E&W | 41W-6N | 25 |
| Eagle Ct. E&W | 42W-5N | 24 |
| East Rd. E&W | 42W-4N | 30 |
| Echo Valley Dr. N&S | 41W-3N | 31 |
| Emerson N&S | 40W-3N | 31 |
| Empire Rd. NE&SW | 44W-5N,40W-6N | 24 |
| Esther Ln. NE&SW | 41W-6N | 25 |
| Evening Prairie Dr. N&S | 42W-7N | 24 |
| Evergreen Dr. N&S | 41W-6N | 25 |
| Fair Oaks Dr. NE&SW | 40W-6N | 25 |
| Fairend Dr. NE&SW | 43W-4N,42W-4N | 30 |
| Falcon Ln. E&W | 42W-4N | 30 |
| Far View Ct. NE&SW | 41W-6N | 25 |
| Far View Rd. E&W | 41W-3N | 31 |
| Farmview Rd. NE&SW | 42W-3N,42W-4N | 30 |
| Farrier Point Ln. N&S | 39W-5N | 25 |
| Fencepost Ln. E&W | 41W-7N | 25 |
| Fenimore Ln. N&S | 43W-4N | 30 |
| Fielding Ct. NW&SE | 39W-7N | 25 |
| Foal Ln. E&W | 41W-2N | 31 |
| Forest Glen Ln. NW&SE | 42W-5N | 24 |
| Forest Ln. E&W | 41W-3N | 31 |
| Forest Tr. N&S | 42W-5N | 24 |
| Fox Bend Dr. NS&EW | 41W-7N | 25 |
| Fox Mill Blvd. SW&NE | 40W-4N,39W-4N | 31 |
| Foxfield Dr. NS&EW | 42W-4N | 30 |
| Foxtail Cir. E&W | 41W-7N | 25 |
| Foxwood Ln. NE&SW | 39W-5N | 25 |
| Furber Cove NE&SW | 39W-4N | 31 |
| Garfield Rd. N&S | 40W-2N,40W-3N | 31 |
| Gary Ct. N&S | 42W-7N | 24 |
| Golden Oaks Ln. E&W | 41W-4N | 31 |
| Gopher Ct. NW&SE | 43W-6N | 24 |
| Grady Ct. NE&SW | 41W-2N | 31 |
| Griffin Ln. NE&SW | 41W-4N | 31 |
| Hanson Rd. NW&SE | 44W-5N,43W-5N | 24 |
| Happy Hills Rd. NE&SW | 39W-3N | 31 |
| Harley Rd. N&S | 41W-2N | 31 |
| Harte Path NE&SW | 40W-3N | 31 |
| Harvest Ct. NW&SE | 42W-5N | 24 |
| Harvest Ln. N&S | 42W-5N | 24 |
| Hastings Dr. N&S | 40W-6N,40W-7N | 25 |
| Hawk Cir. NE&SW | 42W-4N | 30 |
| Hawkeye Dr. E&W | 43W-4N | 30 |
| Hazelwood Ct. N&S | 43W-5N | 24 |
| Hazelwood Trail NS&EW | 43W-5N | 24 |
| Hemingway St. NE&SW | 40W-4N | 31 |
| Hemlock Dr. NE&SW | 39W-4N,39W-5N | 31 |

**Grid / Page**

Hidden Oaks Rd. NE&SW
................39W-4N 41
Hidden Springs Dr. NE&SW
................42W-5N 24
High Meadow Rd. N&S
................39W-4N 31
High Point Ct. E&W
...........42W-3N,41W-3N 30
High Point Ln. NW&SE
................41W-3N 31
Highwood Ct. E&W .. 41W-3N 31
Hilltop Dr. E&W ... 39W-3N 31
Hilltop Dr. W. E&W . 39W-3N 31
Hoeweed Ln. NW&SE
................39W-6N 25
Holly Ct. NE&SW .... 41W-6N 25
Holmes St. NE&SW . 40W-6N 31
Homeward Glen Dr. N&S
...........39W-6N,39W-7N 25
Homeward Hill Dr. E&W
................39W-6N 25
Hunter Ct. N&S .. 42W-4N 30
Hunter's Hill Dr. E&W
................41W-5N 25
Hunter's Ridge NW&SE
................41W-5N 25
Indian Creek Tr. NW&SE
................44W-5N 24
Ironwood Ct. N&S . 42W-5N 24
Ivy Ct. N&S ... 41W-6N 25
Jens-Jenson Ln. NS&EW
................42W-5N 24
Johnson Rd. E&W .. 39W-3N 31
Johnsway E&W....39W-7N 25
Juniper Ct. NW&SE . 41W-6N 25
Kettlehook Ct. E&W..42W-5N 24
Kevin Ct. E&W.... 39W-6N 25
Kildeer Ln. NE&SW . 43W-4N 30
Killarney Ln. N&S .. 41W-1N 25
Kim Ln. N&S ........ 39W-6N 25
Kingfisher Ct. NE&SW
................40W-5N 25
Kings Mill Dr. E&W
...........41W-5N,40W-5N 25
Kingston Ct. NE&SW
................41W-7N 25
Kingswood Dr. N&S..42W-5N 24
Knollwood Dr. NW&SE
...........42W-6N,41W-6N 24
Kurt Ct. NW&SE ... 39W-3N 31
La Fox Rd. N&S
...........40W-2N,40W-5N 31
Lantry Ct. NE&SW .. 41W-2N 31
Lasso Ct. NW&SE .. 41W-3N 31
Laurel Dr. E&W ... 41W-6N 25
Limberi Ln. NW&SE . 39W-3N 31
Line Dr. E&W.... 40W-2N 31
Loblolly Ln. N&S ... 39W-3N 31
London St. NE&SW . 40W-4N 31
Long Shadow Ln. N&S
................40W-5N 25
Longacre Dr. NS&EW
................41W-6N 25
Longfellow Cir. NS&EW
................39W-4N 31
Longfellow Pl. NW&SE
................39W-4N 31
Loretta Dr. E&W ... 39W-3N 31
Lost View Ln. NW&SE
................42W-5N 24
Lowell Pl. NW&SE
...........40W-4N,39W-4N 31
Mare Ln. E&W .... 41W-2N 31
Margaret Mitchell St. NE&SW
...........40W-4N,39W-4N 31
Margie Ln. NE&SW . 41W-6N 25
Mary Ct. N&S .... 42W-5N 24
Mary Dr. NE&SW ... 42W-4N 30
Masters Path NW&SE
................40W-3N 31
McGonagle Ct. NE&SW
................41W-2N 31
Meadowlark Ln. NE&SW
................42W-5N 24
Meadowridge Cir. N&S
................39W-3N 31
Meadowview Ln. N&S
................43W-5N 24
Melville Ln. N&S
...........40W-3N,39W-3N 31
Mill Path NW&SE .. 40W-3N 31
Millstead Pl. E&W....40W-3N 31
Millstone Dr. NE&SW
................41W-5N 25
Mohican Ln. N&S
................43W-4N 30
Mulhurn Dr. NW&SE
................41W-2N 31
N. Bowgren Cir. E&W
................41W-2N 31
N. Elodie Dr. NW&SE
................40W-2N 31
N. Grand Monde Dr. E&W
................40W-2N 31
Nancy Ln. N&S....42W-7N 24
New La Fox Rd. N&S
................40W-4N 31
Norton Ct. E&W ... 39W-4N 31
Nut Hatch Ct. NW&SE
................42W-5N 24
Oak Dr. NS&EW ... 41W-5N 25
Oak Ridge Rd. N&S
................40W-6N 25
Oakwood Dr. N&S .. 41W-6N 25
Old Burlington Rd. NW&SE
...........40W-5N,39W-4N 31
Old Farm Ln. N&S .. 39W-6N 31
Osage Dr. NE&SW .. 39W-4N 31

Otter Ln. E&W ...... 43W-6N 24
Overcup Ln. NW&SE
................39W-4N 31
Paddock Ln. N&S....42W-5N 24
Palomino Dr. NS&EW
...........41W-6N,40W-6N 25
Pathfinder Dr. NW&SE
................39W-4N 30
Patriot Hill Ln. E&W .40W-6N 25
Pine Hills Rd. NE&SW
................39W-3N 31
Pinto Ln. E&W....41W-6N 25
Pioneer Ct. N&S .. 39W-4N 31
Pleasant View Ln. NW&SE
................41W-3N 31
Ponderosa Dr. N&S . 39W-3N 31
Poplar Ln. E&W ... 39W-5N 25
Pouley Rd. N&S .... 42W-2N 30
Praire View Ln. E&W
................41W-3N 31
Prairie Spring Dr. NW&SE
................40W-5N 25
Prairie Valley Dr. N&S
...........43W-5N,43W-6N 24
Private Rd. N&S
...........41W-3N,40W-3N 31
Privey Ct. E&W......41W-6N 25
Pruntree Ln. NE&SW
................39W-6N 25
Quail Ct. N&S .... 42W-5N 24
Ravine Dr. NS&EW .. 42W-5N 24
Red Barn Ln. N&S .. 41W-7N 25
Red Hawk Ct. E&W
...........40W-5N,39W-5N 25
Red Line Ct. N&S
................39W-7N 25
Redwood Ln. N&S .. 39W-4N 31
Reindeer Tr. E&W .. 39W-5N 25
Retreat Ct. N&S ... 42W-5N 24
Ridge Line Rd. NW&SE
................39W-7N 25
Ridgeview Ct. E&W . 39W-3N 31
Robert Frost Cir. NS&EW
................39W-4N 31
Robert Rd. N&S ... 41W-3N 31
Rt. 38 E&W
...........44W-2N,39W-2N 30
Rt. 47 N&S 44W-2N,44W-7N 30
Rt. 64 E&W
...........44W-5N,39W-4N 24
S. Bowgren Cir. NW&SE
................41W-2N 31
S. Bridle Creek Dr. NW&SE
...........41W-4N,40W-3N 31
S. Elodie Dr. NS&EW
................40W-2N 31
S. Grand Monde Dr. E&W
................40W-2N 31
Saddle Brook Dr. NW&SE
................41W-3N 31
Sandburg Rd. N&S
...........40W-4N,39W-4N 31
Shady Oaks Ct. NE&SW
................39W-5N 25
Shetland Ln. N&S .. 41W-6N 25
Silver Glen Rd. E&W
...........44W-7N,39W-6N 24
Snowbird Ln. N&S .. 41W-4N 31
Somerset Dr. N&S .. 42W-6N 25
Somerset Rd. N&S .. 42W-6N 25
Splitrail Ct. NE&SW . 39W-6N 25
Splitrail Ln. NW&SE . 39W-6N 25
Springwood Ln. N&S
................42W-3N 30
Spur Ln. NW&SE
...........41W-3N,41W-4N 31
Steeple Chase E&W 42W-5N 24
Stirrup Ct. N&S .... 40W-4N 31
Stone Crop Ct. E&W
................39W-5N 25
Sun Dance Ct. NW&SE
................40W-5N 25
Sunset Dr. N&S .... 41W-6N 25
Swanberg Rd. N&S
...........42W-5N,42W-6N 24
Sylvan Dr. NE&SW . 41W-3N 31
Sylvan Ln. NE&SW . 42W-5N 24
Tanager Ct. NE&SW
................42W-5N 24
Thoreau Ln. N&S ... 39W-3N 31
Timber Tr. NW&SE .. 42W-5N 24
Torrey Dr. NE&SW . 39W-3N 31
Town Hall Rd. NS&EW
...........41W-3N,41W-4N 31
Trillium Ct. NW&SE . 40W-5N 25
Trotter Ct. E&W ... 40W-3N 31
Trotter Ln. N&S
...........40W-3N,40W-4N 31
Tuttle Pl. N&S .... 39W-7N 25
Uncus Ln. NE&SW . 39W-6N 25
Venetian Way E&W . 42W-4N 30
Verhaeghe Rd. N&S 41W-6N 25
W. Grand Monde Dr. N&S
................40W-2N 31
W. Mary Dr. NE&SW
................42W-4N 30
Warren Cove N&S .. 39W-4N 31
Wasco Rd. NE&SW
...........40W-4N,39W-4N 31
Waterford Ln. E&W . 40W-6N 25
Wayne Dr. E&W ... 41W-4N 31
Welter Rd. NW&SE . 44W-4N 30
West Woods Ct. N&S
................42W-4N 30
West Woods Dr. N&S
................42W-4N 30
Westview Ct. N&S .. 39W-7N 25

Weybridge Dr. NS&EW
................41W-7N 25
Whirlaway Dr. NS&EW
...........43W-4N,42W-4N 30
White Fence Way NE&SW
................40W-5N 25
White Oak Ln. NS&EW
................41W-6N 25
White Pine Ln. NW&SE
................39W-4N 31
Whitier Pl. NE&SW .. 39W-3N 31
Whitman Rd. N&S
...........40W-3N,39W-3N 31
Whitney Rd. E&W
...........41W-5N,40W-5N 25
Wilder Rd. NE&SW .. 40W-3N 31
Willowbrook Ct. E&W
................40W-6N 25
Willowbrook Dr. NW&SE
................40W-6N 25
Winchester Way E&W
................40W-6N 25
Windsor Ct. E&W... 42W-4N 30
Woodcrest Ct. N&S .. 42W-3N 30
Woodgate Rd. E&W 39W-3N 31
Woodland Dr. N&S
...........42W-6N,41W-6N 24
Wooley Rd. N&S
...........44W-4N,44W-5N 30
Wyngate Ct. E&W .. 39W-4N 31
Wyngate Rd. NW&SE
................39W-4N 31

## Carpentersville

Aberdeen Dr. NS&EW
................32W-18N 9
Adams Ct. N&S....32W-17N 9
Adobe Cir. N&S ... 33W-18N 9
Alameda Dr. N&S .. 33W-18N 9
Algonquin Rd. N&S
................33W-18N 9
Alma N&S.........32W-17N 9
Alpine Ridge N&S . 33W-17N 9
Amarillo Ct. E&W .. 33W-18N 9
Amarillo Dr. N&S
................33W-18N 9
Anchor Dr. E&W .. 35W-16N 14
Apache Av. E&W .. 32W-18N 9
Arlington E&W .... 33W-16N 15
Arrow St. N&S .... 32W-18N 9
Ash St. N&S ..... 32W-17N 9
Aspen Ln. N&S ... 32W-18N 9
Audrey Ln. E&W...34W-17N 9
Austin Av. NS&EW 33W-17N 9
Avon Park* E&W .. 34W-18N 9
Ball Av. E&W .... 32W-17N 9
Berkley St. NS&EW
................33W-17N 9
Berkshire Cir. NS&EW
................32W-16N 15
Berkshire Dr. ..32W-15N 15
Birch St. NS&EW
...........32W-17N,32W-18N 9
Bismark Av. .. 34W-16N 15
Blackhawk Av. E&W
................32W-18N 9
Briarwood Av. E&W
................33W-17N 9
Bristol Cir. NS&EW
................32W-16N 15
Bristol Ct. E&W .. 32W-15N 15
Bristol Ln. N&S ... 32W-15N 15
Brook St. N&S ... 34W-17N 9
Bunker Ln. E&W .. 33W-17N 9
Butte Ln. N&S....33W-18N 9
Caddy Av. N&S ... 32W-17N 9
California Av. E&W . 34W-17N 9
Cambridge Ct. E&W
................32W-18N 9
Cambridge Dr. N&S
...........32W-18N,34W-18N 9
Cambridge Dr.* N&S
................34W-18N 9
Cardinal Ln. N&S . 32W-17N 9
Carpenter Blvd. N&S
................34W-16N 15
Carpenter St. E&W
................34W-17N 9
Center Dr. N&S .. 33W-16N 15
Charles St. E&W .. 34W-17N 9
Cherokee Ct. NE&SW
................32W-18N 9
Cherokee Rd. NS&EW
................32W-18N 9
Cir................32W-18N 9
Cleveland Av. E&W
................34W-16N 15
Cordova Rd. E&W . 33W-18N 9
Cottage Av. NS&EW
................34W-17N 9
Courtney Dr. EW&NS
................32W-18N 9
Day Ln. N&S....34W-17N 9
Deer Hill Ct. NE&SW
................33W-17N 9
Deercreek Rd. N&S
...........34W-17N,33W-17N 9
Deerpath Ct. E&W . 37W-18N 8
Deerpath Ln. N&S . 37W-18N 8
Del Rio Rd. E&W . 33W-18N 9
Delaware Ct. NE&SW
................32W-17N 9
Delaware St. NS&EW
................32W-18N 9
Deleware Ct. N&S 32W-18N 9
Denver St. N&S .. 32W-18N 9
Eaton Sq.* E&W .. 34W-18N 9

Edwards Av. E&W .. 34W-16N 15
Elizabeth Mews* E&W
................34W-18N 9
Elm Ridge Av. E&W
................33W-17N 9
Elm St. N&S .... 35W-16N 14
Elmwood Dr. E&W . 33W-17N 9
Endicott Cir. NS&EW
................32W-17N 9
Ensennada Ct. E&W
................34W-18N 9
Ensennada Dr. NE&SW
................34W-18N 9
Evergreen Ln. N&S
...........32W-17N,32W-18N 9
Fairway Ln. N&S .. 32W-17N 9
Fairway Rd. NE&SW
................32W-17N 9
Fiddler's Green NS&EW
................35W-16N 14
Fir St. E&W .... 32W-18N 9
First Av. N&S .. 34W-16N 15
Forestview Ct. N&S
................37W-18N 8
Forestview Dr. E&W
................37W-18N 8
Four Winds Way NW&SE
................34W-17N 9
Fox River Dr. N&S..34W-17N 9
Garfield Ct. N&S...32W-17N 9
Garfield Dr. E&W .. 32W-17N 9
Gentle Breeze Ter. E&W
................34W-17N 9
Gleneagle Ct. E&W
................37W-17N 8
Gleneagle Dr. N&S .37W-17N 8
Goethe St. NE&SW
................34W-17N 9
Goldfinch Ct. NW&SE
................37W-18N 8
Golf View Ln. E&W
................32W-17N 9
Golf View Ln. N&S..32W-16N 15
Granada Rd. E&W . 33W-18N 9
Grant Dr. N&S....32W-17N 9
Green Ln. E&W .. 32W-17N 9
Green St. N&S ... 34W-17N 9
Greenwood Av. NW&SE
................33W-17N 9
Greenwood Ct. E&W
................33W-17N 9
Grove St. N&S ... 34W-17N 9
Hampton Dr. N&S . 32W-17N 9
Harbor Dr. NE&SW
................35W-16N 14
Harding St. E&W .. 32W-16N 15
Harrison St. N&S .. 33W-16N 15
Hattie Av. N&S ... 33W-16N 15
Hawthorne Ct. E&W
................33W-17N 9
Hawthorne Ln. E&W
................33W-17N 9
Hazard Rd. E&W .. 32W-17N 9
Helm Rd. E&W ... 32W-18N 9
Hickory Ct. NE&SW
................32W-18N 9
Hickory Dr. N&S
...........32W-17N,32W-18N 9
Hillside St. E&W...34W-17N 9
Hook Rd. E&W ... 32W-17N 9
Hoover Dr. N&S .. 32W-17N 9
Hopi Ln. NE&SW .. 32W-18N 9
Houston Dr. N&S .. 33W-17N 9
Huntley Rd. E&W
...........35W-17N,35W-16N 8
Huntley Rd. NW&SE
...........34W-16N,37W-18N 8
Illinois St. N&S ... 34W-16N 15
Indian Ln. E&W ... 32W-18N 9
Inlet Cove Av. NW&SE
................35W-16N 14
Inlet Dr. N&S .... 35W-16N 14
Ivarene Ct. E&W...33W-17N 9
Jackson Av. N&S .. 32W-17N 9
Jefferson Av. NS&EW
................32W-17N 9
Keele Dr. N&S....32W-18N 9
King Rd. E&W ... 33W-18N 9
King Richards Park* E&W
................34W-18N 9
Kingston Cir. E&W .32W-17N 9
Kingston Cir. NE&SW
................32W-16N 15
L.W. Besinger Dr. NS&EW
................33W-17N 9
Lake Marian Rd. N&S
................33W-17N 9
Lexington E&W ... 33W-17N 9
Lincoln Av. N&S .. 34W-17N 9
Lincoln Ct. E&W....32W-17N 9
Livingston Av. NS&EW
................34W-17N 9
Lord St. N&S ... 32W-18N 9
Lowell Dr. N&S ... 32W-17N 9
Madera Ct. E&W .. 33W-18N 9
Madison Ct. N&S .. 32W-17N 9
Main St. E&W .... 34W-16N 15
Maple Av. E&W
...........34W-17N,33W-17N 9
Maple Ln. N&S....33W-17N 9
Marlboro Cir. NS&EW
................32W-17N 9
Maude Ln.* N&S .. 34W-18N 9
Mayfair Dr. N&S .. 34W-18N 9
Meadowlark Ln. NW&SE
................32W-17N 9
Meadowsedge Ln. NS&EW
................37W-17N 8
Miller Rd. NE&SW .. 36W-18N 8

Mocasin Ln. E&W .. 32W-18N 9
Monroe Av. N&S .. 32W-17N 9
Monticello Cir. N&S
................33W-18N 9
Mora Rd. NS&EW .. 33W-18N 9
Cir................32W-16N 15
Morningside Ln. E&W
................32W-16N 15
Navajo Dr. NS&EW
................32W-18N 9
North Lake Pkwy.
................33W-16N 15
Oak Av. N&S .... 34W-17N 9
Oak Ridge Rd. N&S
................37W-17N 9
Ollie Ct. E&W ... 33W-17N 9
Orchard Ln. NS&EW
................37W-17N 9
Orleans St. NE&SW
................34W-17N 9
Osage Ct. N&S .. 32W-18N 9
Oxford Rd. N&S...33W-18N 9
Papoose Rd. N&S . 32W-18N 9
Park Av. E&W ... 34W-17N 9
Pawnee Rd. E&W . 32W-18N 9
Pecos Cir. N&S .. 32W-18N 9
Pheasant Tr. N&S . 37W-17N 9
Pine St. N&S .... 32W-18N 9
Plainview E&W ... 33W-16N 15
Plymouth Cir. NS&EW
................32W-17N 9
Polk Av. E&W .... 32W-17N 9
Port Cove NE&SW .. 35W-16N 14
Prairie Path Ln. E&W
................37W-17N 8
Pueblo Rd. E&W . 33W-18N 9
Quail Cove N&S .. 37W-18N 8
Queens Ct. E&W . 33W-18N 9
Randall Rd. N&S . 37W-17N 9
Ravine Ln. NS&EW
................33W-16N 15
Redwood Dr. N&S 32W-18N 9
River Rd. N&S ... 33W-17N 9
River St. NE&SW . 34W-16N 15
Riverbluff Dr. E&W 35W-17N 9
Riverview Dr. N&S
...........35W-17N,34W-17N 8
Robin Rd. N&S
...........32W-17N,32W-18N 9
Rosewood Ct. NE&SW
................33W-17N 9
Rosewood Dr. E&W
................32W-18N 9
Rosewood Dr. NW&SE
................33W-17N 9
Rt. 25 N&S
...........33W-16N,33W-19N 15
Rt. 31 N&S .... 35W-17N 8
Rt. 68 E&W
...........33W-16N,32W-16N 15
Sacramento Ct. E&W
................33W-18N 9
Sacramento Dr. N&S
................33W-18N 9
Salem Ln. N&S .. 33W-18N 9
San Juan Rd. E&W
................33W-18N 9
Santa Fe Av. E&W .32W-18N 9
Saratoga E&W ... 33W-16N 15
Scott Cir. NW&SE . 32W-18N 9
Second St. N&S .. 34W-16N 15
Sedgewick St. N&S
................34W-17N 9
Seminole Ln. E&W . 32W-18N 9
Siesta Ct. N&S ... 33W-18N 9
Siesta Rd. N&S ... 33W-18N 9
Singapore Ln. NW&SE
...........35W-17N,34W-17N 8
Sioux Av. NS&EW . 32W-18N 9
Sleepy Hollow Rd. N&S
................36W-17N 8
South Wind Dr. NW&SE
...........35W-17N,34W-17N 8
Sparrow Ct. NW&SE
................32W-17N 9
Sparrow Rd. NS&EW
................32W-17N 9
Spinnare Cove E&W
................35W-16N 14
Spring Ct. E&W .. 35W-17N 8
Spring Hill Rd. E&W
................32W-16N 15
Spring Point Dr. E&W
................35W-17N 9
Spruce Dr. NE&SW
................35W-16N 14
Spy Glass Cove N&S
................35W-16N 14
Stanford Cir. N&S . 32W-18N 9
Stratford Sq.* N&S 34W-18N 9
Stuart Dr.* N&S .. 34W-18N 9
Sycamore Av. E&W
................32W-17N 9
Tacoma St. N&S .. 33W-17N 9
Tamarac Dr. N&S . 33W-16N 15
Tay River Dr. N&S
...........35W-16N,35W-17N 14
Tee Ln. NE&SW .. 32W-17N 9
Tee Rd. E&W ... 32W-17N 9
Tepee Av. N&S ... 32W-18N 9
Thornapple Ln. N&S
................32W-17N 9
Thrush Rd. NS&EW
................32W-17N 9
Thrush St. N&S ... 32W-16N 15

| | Grid | Page |
|---|---|---|
| Tomahawk Ct. N&S | 32W-18N | 9 |
| Topeka Dr. E&W | 33W-17N | 9 |
| Toro Cir. NS&EW | 33W-18N | 9 |
| Tudor Ct.* N&S | 34W-18N | 9 |
| Tudor Pl.* E&W | 34W-18N | 9 |
| Tulsa Av. NE&SW | 33W-17N | 9 |
| Tulsa Ct. E&W | 33W-17N | 9 |
| Tyler Dr. N&S | 32W-17N | 9 |
| Valentine Av. E&W | 34W-17N | 9 |
| Valley Ln. E&W | 33W-17N | 9 |
| Van Buren St. N&S | 33W-16N | 15 |
| Vana Ct. N&S | 34W-17N | 9 |
| Vista Ln. N&S | 32W-16N | 15 |
| Waco Ln. NE&SW | 33W-17N | 9 |
| Wakefield Dr. N&S | 32W-16N,32W-17N | 15 |
| Walnut St. E&W | 32W-18N | 9 |
| Washington St. N&S | 34W-17N | 9 |
| Waverly Ct. NE&SW | 33W-17N | 9 |
| West Wind Dr. NW&SE | 35W-17N,34W-17N | 8 |
| Western Av. N&S | 34W-17N | 9 |
| Wildrose Dr. N&S | 33W-17N | 9 |
| William St. NE&SW | 34W-17N | 9 |
| Wilmette Av. NW&SE | 33W-17N | 9 |
| Wilson Av. E&W | 32W-17N | 9 |
| Windham Tr. NS&EW | 33W-17N | 9 |
| Windsor Cir. NS&EW | 32W-17N | 9 |
| Wisconsin St. N&S | 34W-17N | 9 |
| Woodland Ct. E&W | 33W-17N | 9 |
| Woodside Ct. N&S | 37W-18N | 8 |
| Woodside Dr. NS&EW | 37W-18N | 8 |
| Wren Rd. NS&EW | 32W-17N | 9 |
| York Ct. NW&SE | 32W-18N | 9 |
| York Dr. NW&SE | 32W-18N | 9 |
| 2nd Av. N&S | 34W-16N | 15 |

## Dundee Township

| | Grid | Page |
|---|---|---|
| Adams Dr. N&S | 37W-17N | 8 |
| Airport Rd. E&W | 34W-14N | 15 |
| Albert Rd. E&W | 32W-14N | 15 |
| Alice Dr. N&S | 35W-19N | 8 |
| Allan Dr. N&S | 34N-19N | 9 |
| Alpine Dr. N&S | 35W-19N | 8 |
| Angelina Pl. NW&SE | 34W-19N | 9 |
| Arbor Ln. N&S | 34W-19N | 9 |
| Ave Chapelle E&W | 34W-14N | 15 |
| Baker Av. N&S | 32W-14N | 15 |
| Bass Ct. NE&SW | 34W-15N | 15 |
| Big Timber Rd. NW&SE | 37W-14N | 14 |
| Binnie Rd. E&W | 36W-17N | 8 |
| Birchwood Rd. E&W | 33W-18N | 9 |
| Bolz Rd. E&W | 33W-19N | 9 |
| Bonkosky Rd. NE&SW | 35W-14N | 14 |
| Boyer Rd. N&S | 37W-19N | 8 |
| Brandt Dr. E&W | 33W-14N | 15 |
| Burning Oak Dr. N&S | 36W-17N | 8 |
| Burr Oak Ln. NW&SE | 35W-18N | 8 |
| Camp Flint Dr. N&S | 33W-15N | 15 |
| Castle Av. N&S | 32W-14N | 15 |
| Castlewood Dr. NE&SW | 33W-18N | 9 |
| Chateau Dr. E&W | 35W-14N | 14 |
| Chateau West Dr. E&W | 35W-14N | 14 |
| Commerce Dr. E&W | 34W-14N | 15 |
| Country School Rd. NW&SE | 35W-18N | 8 |
| Cover St. E&W | 33W-14N | 15 |
| Crescent Dr. E&W | 35W-19N | 8 |
| Deerpath Ln. NS&EW | 33W-18N | 9 |
| Duchesne Dr. E&W | 35W-14N | 14 |
| Duncan Av. N&S | 33W-15N | 15 |
| Dundee Av. N&S | 33W-15N | 15 |
| Edwards Av. NE&SW | 33W-15N | 15 |
| Elliot Dr. N&S | 33W-15N | 15 |
| Elm Av. N&S | 35W-16N | 14 |
| Elm Av. N&S | 34W-16N | 8 |
| Elmwood Dr. E&W | 33W-15N | 15 |
| Field Ct. N&S | 36W-18N | 8 |
| Fountain Valley Dr. NW&SE | 33W-14N | 15 |
| Fox River Dr. NE&SW | 34W-15N | 15 |
| Fries Av. E&W | 33W-14N | 15 |
| Frontenac Dr. NS&EW | 35W-14N | 14 |
| Hecker Dr. E&W | 32W-14N | 15 |
| Hickory Av. NS&EW | 35W-17N | 8 |
| Hickory Hollow Dr. E&W | 36W-15N | 14 |
| Higgins Rd. E&W | 36W-16N | 14 |
| High Point Dr. N&S | 34W-14N | 15 |
| Highland Dr. N&S | 37W-16N | 14 |
| Hillside Dr. N&S | 33W-14N | 15 |
| Hilly Ln. E&W | 37W-16N | 14 |
| Hollowside Dr. E&W | 36W-18N | 8 |
| Howard Av. N&S | 33W-15N | 15 |
| Huntley Rd. NW&SE | 37W-18N,35W-17N | 8 |
| Indian Ln. E&W | 33W-17N | 9 |
| Karen Dr. N&S | 35W-18N,35W-19N | 8 |
| Kasser Ct. N&S | 33W-18N | 9 |
| Lac Du Beatrice Dr. NE&SW | 34W-14N | 15 |
| Lake Shore Dr. E&W | 33W-18N | 9 |
| Lathrop Ln. E&W | 35W-19N | 8 |
| Linden Av. N&S | 33W-15N,33W-14N | 15 |
| Lonidaw Tr. E&W | 34W-19N | 9 |
| Lundstrom Ln. NW&SE | 34W-19N | 9 |
| Manhatas Tr. NW&SE | 34W-19N | 9 |
| Manito Tr. NW&SE | 34W-19N | 9 |
| Maple Ln. N&S | 36W-14N | 14 |
| Mapletree Ln. E&W | 33W-18N | 9 |
| Mason Rd. E&W | 37W-15N | 14 |
| Massey Dr. E&W | 32W-15N | 15 |
| Meadow Lane W. NW&SE | 33W-14N | 15 |
| Melody Ln. NE&SW | 33W-18N | 9 |
| Memory Ln. E&W | 33W-17N | 9 |
| Menoma Tr. NW&SE | 34W-19N | 9 |
| Merriweather Ln. NE&SW | 36W-16N | 14 |
| Miller Rd. E&W | 36W-18N | 8 |
| Minnehaha Tr. N&S | 34W-19N | 9 |
| Natoma Tr. E&W | 34W-19N | 9 |
| Neccon Tr. NW&SE | 34W-19N | 9 |
| Nokomis Tr. NE&SW | 34W-19N | 9 |
| Northwest Tollway NW&SE | 36W-14N | 14 |
| Oak Av. N&S | 34W-16N | 8 |
| Oak Hill Dr. E&W | 36W-15N | 14 |
| Oaks Rd. N&S | 36W-16N | 14 |
| Ogaw Tr. E&W | 34W-19N | 9 |
| Old Barn Rd. NW&SE | 35W-18N | 8 |
| Old Farm Ln. E&W | 33W-18N | 9 |
| Onaway Tr. N&S | 34W-19N | 9 |
| Park Av. N&S | 33W-14N | 15 |
| Park Av. N&S | 33W-17N | 9 |
| Park Dr. N&S | 33W-14N | 15 |
| Parsons Rd. NS&EW | 35W-18N | 8 |
| Petite Ln. N&S | 35W-14N | 14 |
| Pheasant Tr. E&W | 33W-17N | 9 |
| Piemonte Dr. E&W | 32W-15N | 15 |
| Pokagon Dr. NE&SW | 34W-19N | 9 |
| Randall Rd. N&S | 37W-15N,37W-17N | 14 |
| Richardson Dr. E&W | 33W-15N | 15 |
| Richardson Rd. E&W | 33W-15N | 15 |
| Richmond Rd. E&W | 36W-16N | 14 |
| Ridge Rd. E&W | 35W-18N | 8 |
| River Ridge Rd. NW&SE | 34W-14N | 15 |
| Riverview Dr. N&S | 33W-14N | 15 |
| Robin Ln. N&S | 33W-18N | 9 |
| Rock Ridge Ct. NW&SE | 32W-15N | 15 |
| Rock Ridge Dr. NE&SW | 32W-15N | 15 |
| Rt. 31 N&S | 34W-14N,35W-17N | 15 |
| Rt. 72 E&W | 36W-16N,32W-15N | 14 |
| Sawyer Rd. NW&SE | 35W-18N | 8 |
| Shady Ln. N&S | 36W-17N | 8 |
| Skyline Dr. N&S | 33W-17N | 9 |
| Sleepy Hollow Rd. N&S | 36W-14N,36W-19N | 14 |
| Cir. | 35W-16N,34W-16N | 14 |
| Springbluff Dr. N&S | 36W-18N | 8 |
| Sturgis Ct. E&W | 36W-17N | 8 |
| Sumter Dr. N&S | 36W-16N | 14 |
| Sunset Dr. N&S | 33W-17N | 9 |
| Sunset Park Dr. E&W | 33W-14N | 15 |
| Tyrrell Rd. N&S | 38W-14N | 13 |
| Valley View Rd. E&W | 35W-18N | 8 |
| Wabican Tr. NW&SE | 34W-19N | 9 |
| Wakigan Tr. NW&SE | 34W-19N | 9 |
| Walnut Ln. N&S | 36W-15N | 14 |
| West Hill Rd. NS&EW | 35W-18N | 8 |
| Williams Av. E&W | 33W-15N | 15 |
| Williams Ct. E&W | 33W-15N | 15 |
| Winaki Tr. NS&EW | 34W-19N | 9 |
| Winding Tr. NS&EW | 36W-17N | 8 |
| Woodcrest Ln. N&S | 35W-18N | 8 |
| Woodhaven Ln. E&W | 36W-18N,35W-18N | 8 |

## East Dundee

| | Grid | Page |
|---|---|---|
| Aberdeen Dr. N&S | 33W-16N | 15 |
| Adams Ct. E&W | 33W-16N | 15 |
| Alois Dr. N&S | 33W-16N | 15 |
| Ashland Rd. N&S | 33W-16N | 15 |
| Balmoral Dr. E&W | 32W-16N | 15 |
| Bannock Ct. N&S | 32W-16N | 15 |
| Bannock Dr. E&W | 32W-16N | 15 |
| Bannock Rd. E&W | 32W-15N | 15 |
| Barrington Av. E&W | 34W-16N,33W-16N | 15 |
| Bonnie Dundee Rd. E&W | 33W-16N | 15 |
| Braeburn Rd. E&W | 33W-16N | 15 |
| Bruce Ct. E&W | 32W-16N | 15 |
| Council Hill Rd. NE&SW | 33W-16N,33W-17N | 15 |
| Crabtree Rd. N&S | 33W-17N | 9 |
| Crestwood Dr. N&S | 33W-16N | 15 |
| Dawn Ct. NE&SW | 32W-15N | 15 |
| Deerpath Rd. E&W | 33W-16N | 15 |
| Dunbar Ln. N&S | 32W-16N | 15 |
| Dundee Av. N&S | 33W-15N | 15 |
| Dunridge Cir. NS&EW | 33W-16N | 15 |
| Dunridge Ct. E&W | 33W-16N | 15 |
| Edwards Av. E&W | 33W-16N | 15 |
| First St. N&S | 34W-16N | 15 |
| Fourth St. N&S | 33W-16N | 15 |
| Fox River Dr. NE&SW | 33W-15N | 15 |
| Greenwood Av. N&S | 33W-16N | 15 |
| Guth St. N&S | 33W-16N | 15 |
| Hawthorne Ln. E&W | 33W-17N | 9 |
| Heinz Dr. NW&SE | 32W-15N | 15 |
| Higgins Rd. NW&SE | 33W-15N | 15 |
| Hill St. E&W | 33W-16N | 15 |
| Hilton Av. N&S | 33W-16N | 15 |
| Howard Av. N&S | 33W-16N | 15 |
| Howard Ct. E&W | 33W-16N | 15 |
| Jackson St. E&W | 33W-16N | 15 |
| Johnson St. E&W | 33W-16N | 15 |
| Kimberly Rd. N&S | 33W-16N | 15 |
| King Av. N&S | 33W-16N | 15 |
| King William St. N&S | 34W-16N | 15 |
| Lake Shore Dr. E&W | 33W-16N | 15 |
| Lincoln Av. E&W | 34W-16N | 15 |
| Linden Av. NE&SW | 33W-16N | 15 |
| Madison St. E&W | 33W-16N | 15 |
| Maiden Ln. E&W | 33W-16N | 15 |
| Main St. E&W | 33W-16N | 15 |
| Maxwellton Rd. E&W | 33W-16N | 15 |
| Meier Av. N&S | 34W-16N | 15 |
| Michigan Av. E&W | 34W-16N | 15 |
| North St. E&W | 34W-16N | 15 |
| Oak Dr. E&W | 33W-16N | 15 |
| Onie Ct. N&S | 33W-16N | 15 |
| Park St. E&W | 33W-16N | 15 |
| Plate Dr. NS&EW | 32W-15N | 15 |
| Railroad St. E&W | 33W-16N | 15 |
| Ravine Rd. NE&SW | 33W-17N | 9 |
| Reese Av. NW&SE | 33W-16N | 15 |
| River St. N&S | 33W-15N,34W-16N | 15 |
| Rock Ridge Ct. NW&SE | 32W-15N | 15 |
| Rock Ridge Dr. NE&SW | 32W-15N | 15 |
| Roslyn Rd. NE&SW | 33W-16N | 15 |
| Rt. 25 N&S | 32W-16N | 15 |
| Rt. 68 E&W | 33W-16N | 15 |
| Rt. 72 NW&SE | 33W-16N,32W-15N | 15 |
| Scott Dr. N&S | 33W-16N | 15 |
| Second St. N&S | 34W-16N | 15 |
| Springcrest Rd. N&S | 33W-16N | 15 |
| Summit Av. N&S | 33W-16N | 15 |
| Third St. N&S | 34W-16N | 15 |
| Valley Ln. N&S | 33W-16N | 15 |
| Van Buren St. N&S | 33W-16N | 15 |
| Wendt Av. E&W | 33W-16N | 15 |
| Wenholtz Av. E&W | 34W-16N | 15 |
| Williams Ct. E&W | 33W-15N | 15 |
| Williams Pl. E&W | 33W-15N | 15 |
| Wilmette Av. N&S | 33W-16N | 15 |

## Elburn

| | Grid | Page |
|---|---|---|
| Babcock St. N&S | 44W-1N | 30 |
| Behrens Ct. E&W | 43W-2N | 30 |
| Birch St. E&W | 43W-2N | 30 |
| Capes Dr. E&W | 44W-2N | 30 |
| Carolyn Ct. E&W | 43W-0N | 36 |
| Collins Ct. E&W | 43W-2N | 30 |
| Collins Dr. E&W | 43W-2N | 30 |
| Dempsey Dr. N&S | 43W-1N | 30 |
| E. Conley Dr. EW&NS | 43W-2N | 30 |
| Ericson Ct. N&S | 43W-2N | 30 |
| Filmore St. N&S | 44N-1N | 30 |
| Gates St. N&S | 44W-1N,44W-2N | 30 |
| Gee Ct. N&S | 43W-2N | 30 |
| Harrison St. N&S | 44W-1N | 30 |
| Highland Ct. E&W | 43W-2N | 30 |
| Highland Dr. E. NS&EW | 43W-2N | 30 |
| Highland Dr. W. NS&EW | 43W-2N | 30 |
| Highview Ct. N&S | 43W-2N | 30 |
| Hoyt Dr. N&S | 43W-2N | 30 |
| Jay St. N&S | 44W-1N | 30 |
| Kansas St. E&W | 43W-1N | 30 |
| Keslinger Rd. E&W | 44W-1N | 30 |
| Laverne Dr. E&W | 43W-2N | 30 |
| Lilac E&W | 43W-2N | 30 |
| Main St. N&S | 44W-1N,44W-2N | 30 |
| Maple Ct. E&W | 43W-2N | 30 |
| Merrill Ln. SE&NW | 43W-2N | 30 |
| Nebraska St. E&W | 44W-1N,43W-1N | 30 |
| North St. E&W | 44W-1N,43W-1N | 30 |
| Oak Dr. E&W | 43W-1N | 30 |
| Pierce St. E&W | 44W-1N,43W-1N | 30 |
| Polk St. N&S | 44W-1N | 30 |
| Prairie Valley Ct. N&S | 43W-2N | 30 |
| Prairie Valley St. E&W | 43W-2N | 30 |
| Read St. N&S | 44W-1N | 30 |
| Reeder St. E&W | 44W-1N,43W-1N | 30 |
| Rt. 47 N&S | 44W-1N,44W-2N | 30 |
| Saratoga Dr. N&S | 44W-1N | 30 |
| Shannon St. E&W | 44W-1N,43W-1N | 30 |
| Sharp Ct. NW&SE | 43W-2N | 30 |
| Snow Dr. E&W | 43W-2N | 30 |
| South St. E&W | 44W-1N,43W-1N | 30 |
| Spring Valley Dr. NW&SE | 43W-0S,42W-0N | 30 |
| Stetzer Av. E&W | 44W-1N | 30 |
| Swain St. E&W | 44W-1N,43W-1N | 30 |
| Thryselius Dr. N&S | 44W-1N | 30 |
| Walker Ct. NW&SE | 43W-2N | 30 |
| Walker Dr. N.E. NS&EW | 43W-2N | 30 |
| Walker Dr. N.W. NS&EW | 43W-3N | 30 |
| Warne Ct. N&S | 43W-2N | 30 |
| Weston Ct. NW&SE | 43W-2N | 30 |
| Willow St. E&W | 43W-2N | 30 |
| 1st St. N&S | 43W-1N | 30 |
| 2nd St. N&S | 43W-1N | 30 |
| 3rd St. N&S | 43W-3N,43W-1N | 30 |

## Elgin*

**(Also see Cook County)**

| | Grid | Page |
|---|---|---|
| Abbot Dr. E&W | 35W-12N | 20 |
| Aberdeen Ct. N&S | 36W-9N | 20 |
| Academy Pl. N&S | 33W-11N | 21 |
| Adams St. E&W | 34W-10N | 21 |
| Addison St. E&W | 33W-11N | 21 |
| Adelaide Av. E&W | 34W-12N | 21 |
| Adeline Dr. N&S | 35W-12N | 20 |
| Cir. | 36W-9N | 20 |
| Airlite St. N&S | 36W-10N,36W-11N | 20 |
| Airport Rd. N&S | 34W-14N | 15 |
| Aldine St. N&S | 35W-10N,35W-11N | 20 |
| Alfred Av. N&S | 35W-10N,35W-11N | 20 |
| Alft Ln. E&W | 37W-14N | 14 |
| Algona Av. E&W | 33W-12N | 21 |
| Algonquin Dr. N&S | 32W-13N | 15 |
| Alice Ct. E&W | 36W-12N | 20 |
| Alice Pl. NS&EW | 36W-12N | 20 |
| Alison Dr. NE&SW | 35W-11N | 20 |
| Cir. | 35W-10N | 20 |
| Amber Ln. E&W | 36W-8N | 26 |
| Ann St. E&W | 34W-11N,33W-11N | 21 |
| Annondale Dr. N&S | 36W-9N | 20 |
| Arbor Ln. E&W | 35W-9N | 20 |
| Arlington Av. N&S | 33W-10N | 21 |
| Aronomink Cir. N&S | 36W-9N | 20 |
| Ascot Dr. N&S | 35W-9N | 20 |
| Ashland Av. N&S | 33W-10N | 21 |
| Augusta Av. N&S | 33W-12N | 21 |
| Autumn Ct. N&S | 36W-12N | 20 |
| Avalon Ct. E&W | 37W-11N | 20 |
| Avalon Dr. N&S | 37W-11N | 20 |
| Ball St. NE&SW | 34W-11N | 21 |
| Baltusrol Dr. N&S | 36W-9N | 20 |
| Banbury Ln. N&S | 36W-8N | 26 |
| Banks Dr. E&W | 36W-13N | 14 |
| Barn Owl Ln. E&W | 36W-10N | 20 |
| Barn Swallow Way N&S | 36W-12N | 20 |
| Barnes Rd. NW&SE | 37W-11N | 20 |
| Barrett St. E&W | 33W-11N | 21 |
| Bartlett Pl. NE&SW | 33W-10N | 21 |
| Baxter Ct. NW&SE | 36W-9N | 20 |
| Bayside Rd. N&S | 34W-13N | 15 |
| Bayview Rd. E&W | 33W-13N | 15 |
| Bel-Aire Rd. E&W | 33W-13N | 15 |
| Belle Av. E&W | 34W-12N | 21 |
| Bellevue Av. N&S | 33W-12N | 21 |
| Belmont Ct. E&W | 36W-10N | 20 |
| Belmont St. N&S | 36W-10N | 20 |
| Belvidere Line Dr. NW&SE | 36W-12N | 20 |
| Bennington Ct. E&W | 36W-10N | 20 |
| Bent St. E&W | 33W-10N | 21 |
| Berkley St. E&W | 36W-10N | 20 |
| Big Penn E&W | 33W-13N | 15 |
| Big Timber Ct. E&W | 34W-12N | 21 |
| Big Timber Rd. E&W | 35W-13N,34W-13N | 14 |
| Billings St. N&S | 34W-10N | 21 |
| Birchdale Dr. E&W | 35W-10N | 20 |
| Bird St. N&S | 34W-12N | 21 |
| Blue Ridge Ct. E&W | 36W-12N | 20 |
| Cir. | 36W-12N | 20 |
| Booth Ct. NE&SW | 33W-10N | 21 |
| Bowen Ct. N&S | 33W-10N | 21 |
| Bowes Rd. E&W | 36W-9N | 20 |
| Cir. | 37W-11N | 20 |
| Braeburn Dr. N&S | 35W-13N | 14 |
| Brandt Dr. E&W | 33W-14N | 15 |
| Brechin Tr. E&W | 37W-12N | 20 |
| Bridgeview NW&SE | 33W-13N | 15 |
| Brighton Ct. NS&EW | 36W-10N | 26 |
| Brook St. N&S | 34W-11N | 21 |
| Brookside Dr. N&S | 36W-11N | 20 |
| Brookwood Ct. N&S | 35W-13N | 14 |
| Buckeye St. E&W | 34W-12N | 21 |
| Butternut Ln. NS&EW | 36W-12N | 20 |
| Byron Ln. N&S | 35W-13N | 14 |
| Cambridge Dr. NE&SW | 36W-13N | 14 |
| Candida Rd. NE&SW | 33W-13N | 15 |
| Candlewood Rd. NE&SW | 33W-13N | 15 |
| Canyon Ln. NS&EW | 36W-12N | 20 |
| Capitol St. N&S | 37W-14N | 14 |
| Carlsbad Ct. E&W | 36W-9N | 20 |
| Carnoustie Ct. NE&SW | 36W-9N | 20 |
| Carol Av. N&S | 35W-12N | 20 |
| Carr St. E&W | 35W-11N | 20 |
| Castle Pines Cir. NW&SE | 36W-9N | 20 |
| Catherine Ln. NE&SW | 34W-13N | 15 |
| Cedar Av. N&S | 33W-12N | 21 |
| Cedar Point Ct. E&W | 36W-8N | 26 |
| Center St. N&S | 33W-11N | 21 |
| Century Oaks Dr. E&W | 35W-13N | 14 |
| Channing Ct. N&S | 33W-11N | 21 |
| Channing St. N&S | 33W-11N | 21 |
| Chapel N&S | 33W-11N | 21 |
| Charles St. N&S | 33W-10N | 21 |
| Chelsea Ct. NS&EW | 36W-10N | 20 |
| Cherry St. E&W | 34W-12N | 21 |
| Cheryl N&S | 33W-13N | 15 |
| Chesapeake Dr. N&S | 36W-9N | 20 |
| Chester Av. E&W | 33W-12N | 21 |
| Cheyenne Ct. N&S | 36W-12N | 20 |
| Cheyenne Ln. N&S | 36W-12N | 20 |
| Chicago Ct. N&S | 33W-11N | 21 |
| Chicago St. E&W | 33W-11N,32W-11N | 21 |
| Church Dr. N&S | 36W-10N | 20 |
| Church Rd. E&W | 35W-14N | 14 |
| Clair St. E&W | 34W-12N | 21 |
| Clark St. N&S | 34W-12N | 21 |
| Clayton Av. N&S | 35W-12N | 20 |
| Clearwater Way E&W | 36W-12N | 20 |
| Clifford Av. N&S | 34W-12N | 21 |
| Clifford Ct. E&W | 34W-12N | 21 |
| Clifton St. N&S | 35W-10N,35W-11N | 20 |
| College Green Dr. E&W | 36W-9N | 20 |
| College St. N&S | 33W-11N | 21 |
| Colonial Dr. NS&EW | 37W-11N | 20 |
| Colorado NE&SW | 36W-12N | 20 |
| Columbia Av. E&W | 33W-12N | 21 |
| Commerce Dr. N&S | 34W-14N | 15 |
| Commonwealth Av. N&S | 34W-10N,34W-11N | 21 |
| Como Ct. NW&SE | 36W-9N | 20 |
| Congdon Av. E&W | 33W-12N | 21 |
| Congress St. E&W | 33W-10N | 21 |
| Constitution Ct. N&S | 36W-9N | 20 |
| Cookane Av. N&S | 33W-10N | 21 |
| Cooper Av. E&W | 34W-12N,33W-12N | 21 |
| Cornell N&S | 36W-10N | 20 |
| Coronado Ct. E&W | 36W-9N | 20 |
| Corporate Dr. E&W | 34W-14N | 15 |
| Costa Ct. N&S | 36W-9N | 20 |
| Country Club Rd. NE&SW | 33W-13N | 15 |
| Country Knolls Ct. N&S | 36W-11N | 20 |

| Street | Grid | Page |
|---|---|---|
| Country Knolls Ln. NS&EW | 36W-11N | 20 |
| Country Water Ct. E&W | 36W-8N | 26 |
| Countryside Dr. N&S | 35W-13N | 14 |
| Coventry Ct. NE&SW | 36W-11N | 20 |
| Covered Bridge Ct. E&W | 36W-10N | 20 |
| Covered Bridge Dr. N&S | 36W-10N | 20 |
| Creekside Cir. E&W | 36W-14N | 14 |
| Creekside Ct. N&S | 36W-14N | 14 |
| Creighton Av. N&S | 34W-11N | 21 |
| Crescent St. N&S | 36W-11N | 20 |
| Crestview Cir. N&S | 35W-13N | 14 |
| Crestview Dr. E&W | 35W-9N | 20 |
| Crispin Dr. E&W | 35W-9N | 20 |
| Crosby St. E&W | 34W-11N | 21 |
| Crystal Av. N&S | 34W-11N,34W-12N | 21 |
| Crystal Creek Ln. NE&SW | 36W-10N | 20 |
| Cumberland Tr. N&S | 36W-12N | 20 |
| Cypress Ct. E&W | 35W-12N | 20 |
| Dana Dr. E&W | 34W-9N | 21 |
| Daniels Av. E&W | 34W-12N | 21 |
| Dartmonth Dr. NW&SE | 36W-10N | 20 |
| Davis Rd. E&W | 35W-14N | 14 |
| De Paul Dr. N&S | 30W-10N | 20 |
| Deborah Av. N&S | 35W-11N | 20 |
| Deerpath Dr. E&W | 36W-8N | 26 |
| Demmond St. E&W | 35W-12N | 20 |
| Dennis Ct. N&S | 35W-12N | 20 |
| Derby Ct. N&S | 37W-11N | 20 |
| Cir. | 34W-14N | 14 |
| Devonshire Ct. E&W | 36W-14N | 14 |
| Dexter Av. E&W | 34W-11N | 21 |
| Dexter Ct. E&W | 34W-11N | 21 |
| Diane Av. N&S | 35W-12N | 20 |
| Division St. E&W | 33W-11N | 21 |
| Dixon Av. N&S | 34W-10N | 21 |
| Dorchester Ct. NE&SW | 36W-10N | 20 |
| Douglas Av. N&S | 34W-11N | 21 |
| Du Bois Av. N&S | 35W-11N | 20 |
| Du Page Ct. E&W | 34W-11N | 21 |
| Du Page St. E&W | 33W-11N | 21 |
| Dumbarton Oaks E&W | 35W-12N | 20 |
| Duncan Av. N&S | 35W-12N | 20 |
| Dundee Av. NE&SW | 33W-11N | 21 |
| Dwight St. E&W | 33W-10N | 21 |
| Eagle Av. E&W | 35W-12N | 20 |
| Eastview St. E&W | 33W-11N | 21 |
| Easy St. E&W | 35W-11N | 20 |
| Edgewood N&S | 36W-10N | 20 |
| Edison Av. N&S | 35W-10N | 20 |
| Edison St. E&W | 35W-10N | 20 |
| Elgin Av. N&S | 33W-10N | 21 |
| Elizabeth St. N&S | 33W-10N | 21 |
| Elm Grove Dr. N&S | 35W-10N | 20 |
| Elm St. N&S | 34W-10N | 21 |
| Ely St. N&S | 33W-11N | 21 |
| Emily Ct. N&S | 36W-9N | 20 |
| Enterprise St. E&W | 33W-12N | 21 |
| Erie St. E&W | 36W-11N,35W-11N | 20 |
| Esmerelda Pl. N&S | 34W-11N | 21 |
| Executive Ct. N&S | 35W-14N | 14 |
| Fairwood Ct. N&S | 35W-13N | 14 |
| Fairwood Dr. E&W | 35W-13N | 14 |
| Federation Pl. E&W | 34W-13N | 15 |
| Fleetwood Dr. E&W | 35W-10N | 20 |
| Fletcher Dr. NW&SE | 34W-13N | 15 |
| Florimond Dr. NE&SW | 36W-11N | 20 |
| Foothill Rd. NW&SE | 36W-11N | 20 |
| Ford Av. E&W | 33W-13N | 15 |
| Forest Av. N&S | 33W-11N,32W-11N | 21 |
| Forest Dr. NS&EW | 35W-13N | 14 |
| Fountain Square Plaza NW&SE | 34W-11N | 21 |
| Fox Ln. N&S | 36W-14N | 14 |
| Foxmoor Ln. N&S | 36W-8N | 26 |
| Franklin Blvd. E&W | 33W-11N | 21 |
| Franklin St. E&W | 33W-11N | 21 |
| Frazier Av. N&S | 34W-12N | 21 |
| Fremont St. E&W | 33W-12N | 21 |
| Fulton St. E&W | 33W-11N | 21 |
| Gale Ln. N&S | 36W-10N | 20 |
| Gale St. NW&SE | 36W-10N | 20 |
| Garden Crescent N&S | 35W-12N | 20 |
| Genesee Av. E&W | 34W-12N | 21 |
| Geneva N&S | 35W-12N | 20 |
| George St. N&S | 33W-10N | 21 |
| Gertrude St. N&S | 34W-10N,34W-11N | 21 |
| Getzelman Dr. E&W | 35W-12N | 20 |
| Gifford Pl. NE&SW | 33W-11N | 21 |
| Glendower Ter. E&W | 37W-13N | 14 |
| Gleneagle Cir. NS&EW | 36W-9N | 20 |
| Glenmore Ct. NW&SE | 37W-12N | 20 |
| Glenmore Ln. N&S | 37W-12N | 20 |
| Glenwood Av. E&W | 33W-13N | 15 |
| Glenwood Tr. E&W | 33W-13N | 15 |
| Goethe St. E&W | 34W-12N | 21 |
| Gordon Ct. NE&SW | 35W-10N | 20 |
| Governors Ln. NE&SW | 36W-11N | 20 |
| Grace St. N&S | 33W-10N | 21 |
| Grand Av. E&W | 33W-12N | 21 |
| Grand Blvd. N&S | 33W-11N | 21 |
| Grandstand Pl. E&W | 36W-11N | 20 |
| Grant Av. NW&SE | 34W-12N | 21 |
| Green Acres Ln. NW&SE | 35W-13N | 14 |
| Griswold St. N&S | 34W-10N | 21 |
| Grove Av. NW&SE | 33W-11N,33W-12N | 21 |
| Grove Ct. N&S | 34W-11N | 21 |
| Hamilton Av. N&S | 34W-11N | 21 |
| Hamlin Ct. NW&SE | 35W-11N | 20 |
| Hammond Av. E&W | 33W-9N | 21 |
| Harbor Town Dr. N&S | 36W-9N | 20 |
| Harding St. E&W | 33W-10N | 21 |
| Harlan Av. E&W | 35W-12N | 20 |
| Hartwell St. E&W | 33W-12N | 21 |
| Harvard Ln. E&W | 36W-10N | 20 |
| Harvey St. NW&SE | 34W-11N | 21 |
| Hastings St. E&W | 33W-10N | 21 |
| Hawkins St. NW&SE | 34W-11N | 21 |
| Hawthorne Ln. E&W | 36W-11N | 20 |
| Hawthorne St. N&S | 36W-10N | 20 |
| Hayloft Ln. E&W | 36W-10N | 20 |
| Hazel Dr. E&W | 34W-13N | 15 |
| Healy St. N&S | 33W-11N | 21 |
| Heine Av. N&S | 35W-11N | 20 |
| Hendee St. NW&SE | 33W-10N | 21 |
| Henry St. N&S | 33W-11N | 21 |
| Heritage NS&EW | 36W-9N | 20 |
| Hickory Pl. E&W | 33W-12N | 21 |
| Higgins Rd. E&W | 37W-16N | 14 |
| High St. E&W | 33W-11N | 21 |
| Highland Av. NW&SE | 36W-12N,34W-11N | 21 |
| Highland St. N&S | 35W-11N | 20 |
| Highland Springs Dr. N&S | 36W-12N | 20 |
| Hill Av. N&S | 33W-11N,33W-12N | 21 |
| Hillcrest Rd. E&W | 35W-13N | 14 |
| Hillside Rd. NE&SW | 34W-13N | 15 |
| Hilton Pl. E&W | 33W-11N | 21 |
| Hinsdale Pl. N&S | 33W-11N | 21 |
| Holly St. E&W | 34W-11N | 21 |
| Holmes Rd. E&W | 36W-14N,35W-14N | 14 |
| Homer St. N&S | 34W-10N | 21 |
| Hope Ct. E&W | 34W-11N | 21 |
| Horned Owl Ct. E&W | 36W-12N | 20 |
| Howard Av. N&S | 37W-11N | 20 |
| Hoxie Av. N&S | 35W-11N | 20 |
| Hoxie Ct. N&S | 35W-12N | 20 |
| Hubbard Av. N&S | 35W-11N | 20 |
| Hudson Bluff Dr. N&S | 36W-12N | 20 |
| I-90 E&W | 34W-13N | 15 |
| Illinois Pkwy. E&W | 35W-12N | 20 |
| Indian Wells Cir. NS&EW | 36W-9N | 20 |
| Jackson St. NW&SE | 34W-11N | 21 |
| Jacob Ln. E&W.NS | 36W-9N | 20 |
| Jamestown Ln. E&W | 36W-13N | 14 |
| Jansen Farm Ct. NW&SE | 36W-13N | 14 |
| Jansen Farm Dr. NE&SW | 36W-13N | 14 |
| Jay St. E&W | 33W-10N | 21 |
| Jefferey Ct. E&W | 36W-13N | 14 |
| Jefferey Ln. NW&SE | 36W-13N | 14 |
| Jefferson Av. E&W | 33W-12N | 21 |
| Jerusha Av. E&W | 34W-12N | 21 |
| Jewett St. N&S | 34W-10N | 21 |
| Jordan Cir. N&S | 36W-12N | 20 |
| Jordan Ct. NE&SW | 36W-12N | 20 |
| Jordan Ln. NS&EW | 36W-12N | 20 |
| Joseph Ct. E&W | 36W-11N | 20 |
| Judy Ct. N&S | 36W-12N | 20 |
| Julian Av. E&W | 34W-12N | 21 |
| Junior Pl. E&W | 36W-12N | 20 |
| Kane Av. N&S | 35W-12N | 20 |
| Kaskaskia Av. E&W | 35W-12N | 20 |
| Kate St. E&W | 34W-10N | 21 |
| Kathleen Dr. N&S | 35W-11N | 20 |
| Keep Av. E&W | 33W-12N | 21 |
| Kelly Cir. NE&SW | 35W-9N | 20 |
| Kensington Loop N&S | 35W-12N | 20 |
| Kettlehook Dr. NS&EW | 37W-11N | 20 |
| Kevin Dr. NW&SE | 36W-12N | 20 |
| Kimball St. E&W | 34W-11N | 21 |
| Kimberly Av. E&W | 35W-12N | 20 |
| Kinds Riverview Ct. E&W | 34W-12N | 21 |
| Kingman Ct. N&S | 36W-13N | 14 |
| Kingman Dr. N&S | 36W-13N | 14 |
| Knollwood Dr. E&W | 36W-10N | 20 |
| Knotty Pine Dr. NE&SW | 36W-8N | 26 |
| Knoxbury Tr. N&S | 36W-10N | 20 |
| L. Penn E&W | 33W-13N | 15 |
| La Costa Ct. NE&SW | 36W-9N | 20 |
| La Salle N&S | 35W-12N | 20 |
| Lake Plaza E&W | 34W-13N | 15 |
| Lake St. NE&SW | 33W-11N | 21 |
| Lake Ter. N&S | 34W-13N | 15 |
| Lake View N&S | 34W-13N | 15 |
| Lakewood NE&SW | 33W-13N | 15 |
| Lancaster Cir. NS&EW | 36W-10N | 20 |
| Larkin Av. NE&SW | 36W-11N | 20 |
| Laurel Ct. N&S | 33W-11N | 21 |
| Laurel St. N&S | 33W-11N | 21 |
| Lavoie Av. N&S | 33W-10N | 21 |
| Lawrence Av. E&W | 34W-11N | 21 |
| Lennoxshire Dr. N&S | 35W-13N | 14 |
| Leonard St. N&S | 34W-11N | 21 |
| Lessenden Pl. E&W | 33W-10N | 21 |
| Levine Ct. E&W | 33W-11N | 21 |
| Liberty St. N&S | 33W-10N,33W-12N | 21 |
| Lilac Ln. N&S | 35W-10N | 20 |
| Lillian St. E&W | 35W-10N | 20 |
| Lillie St. E&W | 35W-11N | 21 |
| Lin-Lor Ct. NW&SE | 35W-11N | 20 |
| Lin-Lor Ln. E&W | 36W-11N,35W-11N | 20 |
| Lincoln Av. E&W | 36W-11N,33W-12N | 21 |
| Lincoln Mc Bride St. N&S | 34W-12N | 21 |
| Lincolnwood Ter. N&S | 36W-11N | 20 |
| Lindbergh Ct. N&S | 34W-10N | 21 |
| Linden Av. E&W | 33W-11N | 21 |
| Cir. | 36W-13N | 14 |
| Locust St. NE&SW | 34W-11N | 21 |
| Logan Av. N&S | 33W-11N | 21 |
| Longwood Pl. N&S | 35W-12N | 20 |
| Lord St. E&W | 33W-10N | 21 |
| Lovell St. E&W | 34W-11N | 21 |
| Lowrie Ct. E&W | 33W-11N | 21 |
| Loyola Dr. N&S | 30W-10N | 20 |
| Luda St. E&W | 34W-13N | 15 |
| Ludeka Pl. N&S | 34W-11N | 21 |
| Ludlow Av. E&W | 33W-12N | 21 |
| Lyle Av. N&S | 35W-11N | 20 |
| Lyle St. N&S | 35W-10N | 20 |
| Lynch St. N&S | 34W-11N | 21 |
| Mable Av. N&S | 34W-12N | 21 |
| Madlock Ct. N&S | 36W-13N,36W-14N | 14 |
| Main Ln. N&S | 35W-10N | 20 |
| Mallard Dr. N&S | 35W-13N | 14 |
| Mallery Av. N&S | 34W-11N | 21 |
| Mann Pl. N&S | 33W-12N | 21 |
| Manor Ct. N&S | 35W-12N | 21 |
| Maple Ln. E&W | 35W-10N | 20 |
| Maple St. N&S | 36W-10N | 20 |
| Margaret Pl. E&W | 34W-11N | 21 |
| Marguerite St. N&S | 34W-12N | 21 |
| Mark Av. E&W | 36W-12N | 20 |
| Market St. E&W | 35W-11N | 20 |
| Marlene Av. NE&SW | 36W-12N | 20 |
| Marshfield Ct. E&W | 37W-11N | 20 |
| Marshfield Dr. NS&EW | 37W-11N | 20 |
| Martha Dr. NE&SW | 35W-11N | 20 |
| Mary Pl. E&W | 35W-11N | 21 |
| Matthew Ct. NW&SE | 36W-13N | 14 |
| Maureen Dr. N&S | 35W-11N | 20 |
| May St. E&W | 35W-10N | 21 |
| McClure Av. N&S | 34W-11N,34W-12N | 21 |
| McKinstry Dr. N&S | 36W-11N | 20 |
| McLean Blvd. N&S | 35W-10N,35W-13N | 20 |
| Meadow Ln. E&W | 34W-13N | 15 |
| Medici Ct. NW&SE | 36W-9N | 20 |
| Medinah Cir. NS&EW | 36W-9N | 20 |
| Melrose Av. N&S | 35W-10N,35W-13N | 20 |
| Melrose St. N&S | 35W-10N | 20 |
| Mesa Dr. N&S | 36W-9N | 20 |
| Meyer Ct. NE&SW | 35W-10N | 20 |
| Meyer St. E&W | 35W-10N | 20 |
| Michigan St. NW&SE | 33W-11N | 21 |
| Milan Ct. N&S | 36W-9N | 20 |
| Mildred Av. E&W | 35W-12N | 20 |
| Mill St. E&W | 34W-11N | 21 |
| Millbrook Rd. E&W | 33W-13N | 15 |
| Millcreek Ct. NW&SE | 36W-12N | 20 |
| Miller Dr. N&S | 35W-10N | 20 |
| Mission Hills Dr. E&W | 36W-9N | 20 |
| Misthaven Ln. NS&EW | 36W-13N | 14 |
| Monday Ct. NE&SW | 36W-13N | 14 |
| Monday Dr. NW&SE | 36W-13N | 14 |
| Monroe Av. N&S | 34W-11N | 21 |
| Montrose Pl. E&W | 35W-12N | 20 |
| Moreti Dr. N&S | 36W-9N,36W-8N | 26 |
| Morgan Av. E&W | 34W-10N | 21 |
| Morningside Ct. E&W | 34W-13N | 15 |
| Morningside Dr. N&S | 35W-13N | 15 |
| Morningside Point E&W | 34W-13N | 14 |
| Morton Av. N&S | 33W-12N | 21 |
| Mountain St. NE&SW | 34W-11N | 21 |
| Muirfield Cir. N&S | 36W-9N | 20 |
| Mulberry Ct. N&S | 35W-11N | 20 |
| Mulberry Ln. E&W | 35W-11N | 20 |
| Murcer Dr. E&W | 36W-12N | 20 |
| Murray Av. E&W | 34W-11N | 21 |
| N. Airlite St. N&S | 36W-12N | 20 |
| Nantucket Ct. NS&EW | 36W-9N | 20 |
| Natchez Trace E&W | 36W-12N | 20 |
| National St. NE&SW | 33W-10N,33W-11N | 21 |
| Nautical Way N&S | 36W-10N | 20 |
| Newberry Ct. N&S | 37W-11N | 20 |
| Niagra Ct. N&S | 36W-12N | 20 |
| Norm Nelson Ct. N&S | 34W-11N | 21 |
| North Lyle St. N&S | 34W-12N,36W-14N | 21 |
| North Shore Rd. E&W | 33W-13N | 15 |
| North St. E&W | 34W-11N,33W-11N | 21 |
| Northfork Cir. N&S | 36W-12N | 20 |
| Notre Dame Ln. N&S | 36W-10N | 20 |
| Oak St. E&W | 34W-10N | 21 |
| Oakdale Dr. NS&EW | 33W-13N | 14 |
| Oakhill Rd. E&W | 33W-13N | 15 |
| Oakland Av. E&W | 33W-12N | 21 |
| Oakley Av. E&W | 33W-12N | 21 |
| Oakmont Dr. N&S | 36W-11N | 20 |
| Oatwind Rd. E&W | 37W-11N | 20 |
| Old Forge Rd. N&S | 36W-11N | 20 |
| Orange St. E&W | 34W-10N | 21 |
| Orchard St. N&S | 34W-11N | 21 |
| Otter Creek Ln. E&W | 36W-10N | 20 |
| Owasco Av. E&W | 34W-11N | 21 |
| Oxford St. N&S | 34W-11N | 21 |
| Page Av. E&W | 33W-11N | 21 |
| Pallozzo Ct. N&S | 36W-9N | 20 |
| Pallozzo Dr. E&W | 36W-9N | 20 |
| Pam NW&SE | 36W-13N | 15 |
| Pamela Dr. NE&SW | 35W-11N | 20 |
| Pappas Ct. N&S | 35W-13N | 14 |
| Pappas Dr. N&S | 35W-13N | 14 |
| Park Ln. E&W | 34W-13N | 15 |
| Park Row N&S | 33W-11N | 21 |
| Park St. E&W | 33W-11N | 21 |
| Parkside Dr. N&S | 34W-12N | 21 |
| Parkview Dr. N&S | 34W-13N | 14 |
| Parkwood Rd. E&W | 34W-13N | 15 |
| Pauline Dr. N&S | 35W-12N | 20 |
| Pebble Beach Cir. E&W | 36W-9N,35W-9N | 20 |
| Pennsylvania Av. E&W | 34W-11N | 21 |
| Percy N&S | 33W-11N | 21 |
| Perry St. N&S | 34W-11N | 21 |
| Pindar St. E&W | 34W-11N | 21 |
| Pine St. E&W | 34W-11N | 21 |
| Pioneer Pk. Pl. N&S | 36W-13N | 14 |
| Pleasant Dr. N&S | 35W-13N | 14 |
| Pleasant View N&S | 35W-13N | 14 |
| Plum Ct. E&W | 33W-12N | 21 |
| Plum St. E&W | 33W-12N | 21 |
| Plymouth Ct., N. E&W | 36W-10N | 20 |
| Plymouth Ct., S. E&W | 36W-10N | 20 |
| Poplar Ct. N&S | 33W-12N | 21 |
| Portage Rd. E&W | 36W-12N | 20 |
| Porter Ct. N&S | 33W-12N | 21 |
| Porter St. N&S | 33W-11N,33W-12N | 21 |
| Portsmouth Ct. E&W | 37W-11N | 20 |
| Potomac Pl. E&W | 36W-12N | 20 |
| Powder River Path E&W | 36W-12N | 20 |
| Prairie St. E&W | 33W-11N | 21 |
| Preston Av. N&S | 32W-11N,32W-12N | 21 |
| Princeton Av. N&S | 36W-10N | 20 |
| Princeton Ct. E&W | 36W-10N | 20 |
| Prospect Blvd. N&S | 33W-12N | 21 |
| Purdue Ln. N&S | 36W-10N | 20 |
| Purify Dr. NW&SE | 33W-10N | 21 |
| Quail Ln. N&S | 35W-13N | 14 |
| Rainbow Rd. N&S | 33W-13N | 15 |
| Ranch Rd. E&W | 34W-13N | 15 |
| Randall Rd. N&S | 36W-10N | 20 |
| Randall Ridge Ct. NW&SE | 37W-11N | 20 |
| Cir. | 37W-11N | 20 |
| Raymond St. E&W | 33W-10N,33W-11N | 21 |
| Reba E&W | 33W-13N | 15 |
| Red Tail Ridge N&S | 36W-12N | 20 |
| Regent St. E&W | 33W-10N | 21 |
| Renner Dr. N&S | 36W-10N | 20 |
| Richard Rd. N&S | 34W-13N | 15 |
| Rickert Ct. N&S | 33W-11N | 21 |
| Ridgeway Dr. N&S | 35W-13N | 14 |
| Riley St. E&W | 33W-10N | 21 |
| River Bluff Rd. E&W | 34W-12N,33W-12N | 21 |
| River Ridge Dr. E&W | 34W-14N | 15 |
| Riverside Dr. NW&SE | 34W-11N | 21 |
| Robert Dr. N&S | 35W-10N | 20 |
| Robey St. N&S | 33W-10N | 21 |
| Cir. | 36W-12N | 20 |
| Robin Ridge N&S | 36W-12N | 20 |
| Robinwood Dr. N&S | 35W-13N | 14 |
| Route 20 NW&SE | 37W-11N | 20 |
| Royal Blvd. E&W | 36W-12N,35W-12N | 20 |
| Royal Ct. N&S | 35W-12N | 20 |
| Rt. 25 N&S | 33W-12N | 21 |
| Rt. 31 N&S | 34W-12N | 21 |
| Rugby Pl. N&S | 33W-11N | 21 |
| Russel St. E&W | 33W-10N | 21 |
| Ruth Dr. N&S | 35W-12N | 20 |
| Ryerson Av. N&S | 33W-10N | 21 |
| Sacramento Ct. N&S | 36W-12N | 20 |
| Salem Rd. NW&SE | 36W-11N | 20 |
| Sandy Beach NW&SE | 33W-13N | 15 |
| Sarah Ct. N&S | 37W-11N | 20 |
| Savannah Rd. E&W | 36W-12N | 20 |
| Sawgrass Ct. E&W | 35W-9N | 20 |
| Schiller St. E&W | 34W-12N | 21 |
| Schuler St. N&S | 35W-11N | 20 |
| Scott Dr. N&S | 35W-12N | 20 |
| Second St. N&S | 36W-10N | 20 |
| Seneca St. N&S | 34W-12N | 21 |
| Serenade Ct. E&W | 36W-9N | 20 |
| Sexauer Av. N&S | 35W-12N | 20 |
| Shagbark St. N&S | 36W-12N | 20 |
| Sharon Dr. N&S | 34W-13N | 15 |
| Sheffield St. N&S | 35W-13N | 14 |
| Sheffield Dr. NS&EW | 36W-13N,35W-13N | 14 |
| Shenandoah Tr. N&S | 36W-12N | 20 |
| Shepard Dr. N&S | 35W-10N | 20 |
| Sheridan St. N&S | 34W-11N | 21 |
| Sherman Av. N&S | 33W-10N | 21 |
| Sherwood Av. N&S | 33W-12N | 21 |
| Silver Ct. N&S | 34W-11N | 21 |
| Silver St. N&S | 34W-11N | 21 |
| Slade Av. E&W | 34W-12N,33W-12N | 21 |
| Souster Av. N&S | 33W-10N | 21 |
| South St. E&W | 36W-10N | 20 |
| South St. NE&SW | 35W-10N,34W-11N | 20 |
| Spartan Dr. E&W | 35W-10N | 20 |
| Spring Cove E&W | 35W-11N | 20 |
| Spring Creek Ct. E&W | 32W-12N | 21 |
| Spring St. N&S | 34W-11N | 21 |
| Spyglass Hill Ct. N&S | 35W-10N | 20 |
| St. Andrews Cir. NS&EW | 35W-9N | 20 |
| St. Charles St. N&S | 33W-10N | 21 |
| St. John St. N&S | 33W-12N | 21 |
| Standish Ct. E&W | 33W-11N | 21 |
| Standish St. N&S | 34W-11N | 21 |
| Stanford Ct. E&W | 36W-10N | 20 |
| State St. N&S | 34W-10N,34W-12N | 21 |
| Steel St. N&S | 34W-12N | 21 |
| Stella Ct. N&S | 33W-11N | 21 |
| Stella St. E&W | 33W-11N | 21 |
| Stephen Av. NE&SW | 36W-12N | 20 |
| Sterling Ct. N&S | 37W-11N | 20 |
| Stonehaven Ct. E&W | 37W-12N | 20 |
| Stonehaven Dr. NE&SW | 37W-12N | 20 |
| Stratton Ct. N&S | 36W-9N | 20 |

| | Grid | Page |
|---|---|---|
| Summit St. E&W | | |
| | 34W-12N,33W-12N | 21 |
| Sunrise Ct. NW&SE | | |
| | 34W-10N | 21 |
| Sunset Dr. N&S | 35W-10N | 20 |
| Surrey Ct. N&S | 36W-12N | 20 |
| Swan Ln. NW&SE | 36W-12N | 20 |
| Tall Oaks Ct. N&S | 36W-11N | 20 |
| Cir. | 36W-11N | 20 |
| Tanglewood Ln. NS&EW | | |
| | 33W-12N | 21 |
| Tannery Ridge Rd. N&S | | |
| | 32W-12N | 21 |
| Tara Dr. E&W | 36W-11N | 20 |
| Teal Av. E&W | 34W-12N | 21 |
| Tenneyson Ct. N&S | | |
| | 33W-11N | 21 |
| Thomas More Dr. N&S | | |
| | 35W-11N | 20 |
| Timber Dr. E&W | 35W-11N | 20 |
| Times Sq. NW&SE | 33W-10N | 21 |
| Tinker Av. N&S | 34W-11N | 21 |
| Tivoli Pl. E&W | 35W-12N | 20 |
| Todd Farm Ct. NE&SW | | |
| | 35W-13N | 14 |
| Todd Farm Dr. EW&NS | | |
| | 35W-13N | 14 |
| Toftrees Tr. NW&SE | | |
| | 36W-12N | 20 |
| Toll Gate Rd. E&W | 34W-13N | 15 |
| Tollview Rd. E&W | 33W-13N | 15 |
| Torrey Pines Dr. E&W | | |
| | 35W-9N | 20 |
| Tower Ct. NW&SE | 33W-10N | 21 |
| Trevi Cir. EW&NS | 36W-9N | 20 |
| Trevi Ct. N&S | 36W-9N | 20 |
| Triggs Av. N&S | 35W-11N | 20 |
| Trinity Ter. NE&SW | | |
| | 36W-12N | 20 |
| Trout Pk. Blvd. E&W | | |
| | 33W-13N | 15 |
| Tuileries Pl. E&W | 35W-12N | 20 |
| Turino Ct. NW&SE | 36W-9N | 20 |
| Tuscany Ct. E&W | 36W-9N | 20 |
| Tyler Av. E&W | 34W-13N | 15 |
| Tyler Ln. N&S | 34W-13N | 15 |
| U.S. Route 20 E&W | | |
| | 36W-10N,32W-10N | 20 |
| Umdenstock Rd. N&S | | |
| | 36W-8N | 26 |
| Union N&S | 34W-11N | 21 |
| Union Ct. E&W | 34W-11N | 21 |
| Valley Creek Dr. E&W | | |
| | 34W-12N | 20 |
| Van Nostrand Pl. E&W | | |
| | 33W-10N | 21 |
| Van St. E&W | | |
| | 35W-11N,34W-11N | 21 |
| Vandalia St. N&S | 34W-10N | 21 |
| Vatican Ct. N&S | 36W-9N | 20 |
| Venice Ct. E&W | 36W-9N | 20 |
| Verde Vista Ct. E&W | | |
| | 36W-9N | 20 |
| Vernon Dr. E&W | 36W-11N | 20 |
| Villa St. NE&SW | 33W-11N | 21 |
| Villa St. NW&SE | | |
| | 33W-11N,32W-10N | 21 |
| Vincent Pl. N&S | 34W-11N | 21 |
| Vine St. N&S | 34W-11N | 21 |
| Virginia Ct. NE&SW | | |
| | 36W-12N | 20 |
| Wabash Av. N&S | 33W-11N | 21 |
| Walker Pl. E&W | 33W-11N | 21 |
| Walnut Av. E&W | 34W-10N | 21 |
| Walnut Creek Dr. NW&SE | | |
| | 36W-8N | 26 |
| Walter Ct. NE&SW | 35W-10N | 20 |
| Warwick Pl. N&S | 34W-11N | 21 |
| Washburn St. E&W | | |
| | 34W-10N | 21 |
| Washington St. NE&SW | | |
| | 34W-10N | 21 |
| Watch St. NE&SW | 33W-10N | 21 |
| Water St. E&W | 34W-11N | 21 |
| Waterfall Ln. NS&EW | | |
| | 36W-10N | 20 |
| Watres Pl. N&S | 33W-11N | 21 |
| Wauchope Dr. N&S | | |
| | 34W-13N | 15 |
| Weatherstone Av. E&W | | |
| | 33W-10N | 21 |
| Weld Rd. NW&SE | 36W-10N | 20 |
| Wellington Av. N&S | | |
| | 33W-10N | 21 |
| West Chicago St. N&S | | |
| | 35W-11N | 20 |
| West River Rd. N&S | | |
| | 34W-13N,33W-13N | 15 |
| Westfield Dr. NE&SW | | |
| | 37W-14N | 14 |
| Westgate Dr. N&S | 36W-11N | 20 |
| Weston Av. N&S | | |
| | 35W-10N,35W-11N | 20 |
| Wheelock St. N&S | 34W-10N | 21 |
| White Oak Ln. NS&EW | | |
| | 36W-13N | 14 |
| Wilber St. N&S | 36W-11N | 20 |
| Wilcox Av. N&S | 34W-10N | 21 |
| Wilder St. E&W | 34W-12N | 21 |
| Wildmint Tr. EW&NS | | |
| | 36W-8N | 26 |
| William N&S | 36W-11N | 20 |
| Willis St. N&S | 36W-11N | 20 |
| Willow Lake Rd. NW&SE | | |
| | 33W-13N | 15 |
| Wilson St. E&W | 34W-11N | 21 |
| Winchester Dr. E&W | | |
| | 37W-11N | 20 |

| | Grid | Page |
|---|---|---|
| Wing Park Blvd. N&S | 35W-11N | 20 |
| Wing St. NW&SE | 35W-12N | 20 |
| Wolff Av. E&W | 35W-11N | 20 |
| Woodbridge Dr. N&S | | |
| | 36W-10N | 20 |
| Woodland Av. N&S | | |
| | 34W-11N | 21 |
| Woodridge Ct. NE&SW | | |
| | 36W-12N | 20 |
| Woodward St. N&S | 34W-11N | 21 |
| Worth Av. N&S | 35W-11N | 20 |
| Yardwood St. NE&SW | | |
| | 33W-10N | 21 |
| Yellowstone Dr. N&S | | |
| | 34W-12N | 20 |
| Ziegler Ct. NW&SE | | |
| | 33W-11N | 21 |

## Elgin Township

| | Grid | Page |
|---|---|---|
| Acorn Ln. E&W | 37W-8N | 26 |
| Airlite St. N&S | 36W-10N | 20 |
| Almora Ter. N&S | 37W-11N | 20 |
| Amberwood Dr. NE&SW | | |
| | 38W-13N | 13 |
| Arrow Maker NS&EW | | |
| | 38W-9N | 19 |
| Beckman Ln. NS&EW | | |
| | 38W-9N | 19 |
| Belmont St. N&S | 36W-10N | 20 |
| Big Axe Rd. N&S | 38W-8N | 26 |
| Bittersweet Ln. E&W | | |
| | 38W-8N | 26 |
| Bowes Rd. E&W | 36W-9N | 20 |
| Brindlewood Ln. E&W | | |
| | 38W-13N | 13 |
| Brookside Dr. E&W | | |
| | 37W-11N | 20 |
| Bruce Dr. N&S | 36W-12N | 20 |
| Burgess Dr. NE&SW | | |
| | 37W-10N | 20 |
| Charlotte Ct. N&S | 37W-12N | 20 |
| Crispin Dr. E&W | 35W-9N | 20 |
| Cross Creek Ct. N&S | | |
| | 38W-9N | 19 |
| David Dr. E&W | 35W-9N | 20 |
| Elmer Ct. E&W | 37W-12N | 20 |
| Erie St. E&W | 36W-11N | 20 |
| Flagpole Ct. N&S | 37W-11N | 20 |
| Fletcher Dr. E&W | | |
| | 36W-12N,37W-12N | 38 |
| Flora Dr. N&S | 35W-9N | 20 |
| Foothill Rd. E&W | 36W-11N | 20 |
| Gale St. N&S | 36W-10N | 20 |
| Gingerwood Ln. N&S | | |
| | 38W-8N | 26 |
| Gordon Ln. N&S | 33W-8N | 27 |
| Hawthorne Ln. E&W | | |
| | 36W-11N | 20 |
| Hawthorne St. N&S | | |
| | 36W-10N | 20 |
| Heatherfield Dr. NS&EW | | |
| | 38W-8N | 26 |
| Heatherfield East Dr. E&W | | |
| | 38W-8N,37W-8N | 26 |
| Hidden Hill Tr. N&S | | |
| | 37W-11N | 20 |
| Highland Av. NW&SE | | |
| | 36W-12N | 20 |
| Hilltop Rd. N&S | 37W-11N | 20 |
| Hobart Dr. N&S | 35W-9N | 20 |
| Hogan Hill N&S | | |
| | 39W-9N,38W-9N | 19 |
| Hopi Ln. E&W | 38W-9N | 19 |
| Hopps Rd. E&W | | |
| | 38W-8N,36W-8N | 26 |
| Howard Av. N&S | 37W-11N | 20 |
| Hoxie Av. N&S | 35W-11N | 20 |
| Irwin Dr. NW&SE | 35W-9N | 20 |
| Jackson Dr. N&S | 37W-12N | 20 |
| Jaguar Ct. E&W | 37W-10N | 20 |
| Johnstown Rd. N&S | | |
| | 37W-11N | 20 |
| Koshare Cir. NW&SE | | |
| | 38W-9N | 19 |
| Koshare Tr. N&S | 38W-9N | 19 |
| Kristen Dr. E&W | 38W-8N | 26 |
| Lamont Ct. N&S | 37W-11N | 20 |
| Leith Ct. NW&SE | 37W-10N | 20 |
| Leland Ct., N. NE&SW | | |
| | 38W-9N | 19 |
| Leland Ct., S. NE&SW | | |
| | 38W-9N | 19 |
| Linda Ln. E&W | 37W-12N | 20 |
| Lisa Ln. E&W | 38W-8N | 26 |
| Manchester Ln. N&S | | |
| | 37W-10N | 20 |
| Maple St. N&S | 36W-10N | 20 |
| Maryhill Ln. NW&SE | | |
| | 37W-11N | 20 |
| McDonald Rd. NW&SE | | |
| | 38W-8N,37W-8N | 26 |
| McLean Blvd. N&S | | |
| | 35W-8N,35W-9N | 27 |
| Middle St. E&W | 33W-8N | 27 |
| Nestler Rd. SW&NE | | |
| | 38W-11N | 19 |
| Newport Ct. NE&SW | | |
| | 37W-10N | 20 |
| Nokomis Ln. NS&EW | | |
| | 38W-9N | 19 |
| Nolan Rd. N&S | | |
| | 38W-8N,39W-7N | 26 |
| Oatwind Rd. E&W | 37W-11N | 20 |
| Old Barn Rd. N&S | 37W-12N | 20 |
| Olwin Av. E&W | 37W-12N | 20 |

| | Grid | Page |
|---|---|---|
| Orchard Ln. NS&EW | | |
| | 37W-11N,37W-12N | 20 |
| Oxford Ln. N&S | 37W-10N | 20 |
| Park Path E&W | 38W-9N | 19 |
| Pasec Pl. E&W | 38W-9N | 19 |
| Peppertree Ct. N&S | 37W-8N | 26 |
| Peppertree Ln. N&S | 37W-8N | 26 |
| Pollitt Dr. N&S | 38W-12N | 19 |
| Presidential Ln. NE&SW | | |
| | 36W-11N | 20 |
| Raleigh Ct. NW&SE | | |
| | 37W-11N | 20 |
| Randall Rd. N&S | 36W-10N | 20 |
| Raymond St. N&S | | |
| | 33W-9N | 21 |
| Richard Dr. E&W | 38W-8N | 26 |
| Ridgewood Ln. NW&SE | | |
| | 38W-13N | 13 |
| Rt. 25 N&S | | |
| | 33W-9N,33W-12N | 21 |
| Running Deer Trail N&S | | |
| | 37W-8N | 26 |
| Savanna Lakes Ct. N&S | | |
| | 38W-9N | 19 |
| Savanna Lakes Dr. E&W | | |
| | 38W-9N | 19 |
| Second St. N&S | 36W-10N | 20 |
| Sexauer Av. N&S | 35W-11N | 20 |
| Shady Ln. N&S | 37W-8N | 26 |
| South St. E&W | 36W-10N | 20 |
| Stevens Ln. NE&SW | | |
| | 38W-8N | 26 |
| Stevens Rd. N&S | 38W-8N | 26 |
| Stratford Ln. E&W | 37W-11N | 20 |
| Sunvale Ct. NW&SE | 38W-8N | 26 |
| Sunvale Dr. NS&EW | | |
| | 38W-8N | 26 |
| Taos Pl. N&S | 38W-8N | 26 |
| Thunder Gap NW&SE | | |
| | 38W-9N | 19 |
| Tina Trail N&S | 37W-12N | 20 |
| Tipi Ln. NS&EW | 38W-9N | 19 |
| Trails NW&SE | 38W-9N | 19 |
| Trails End N&S | | |
| | 38W-9N,38W-10N | 19 |
| U.S. Route 20 NW&SE | | |
| | 36W-10N | 20 |
| Umdenstock Rd. N&S | | |
| | 36W-8N | 26 |
| Water Rd. NW&SE | 36W-10N | 19 |
| Wedgewood Dr. N&S | | |
| | 38W-13N | 13 |
| Weld Rd. NW&SE | | |
| | 37W-11N,36W-10N | 20 |
| Weldwood Dr. N&S | | |
| | 37W-10N | 20 |
| West View St. N&S | | |
| | 37W-12N | 20 |
| Wildwood Dr. NS&EW | | |
| | 37W-8N | 26 |
| Williamsburg Ct. N&S | | |
| | 37W-10N,37W-11N | 20 |
| Willow Ln. E&W | 37W-8N | 26 |
| Winhaven Dr. NS&EW | | |
| | 37W-8N | 26 |
| York Ln. NS&EW | 37W-11N | 20 |

## Geneva

| | Grid | Page |
|---|---|---|
| Aberdeen Ct. NS&EW | | |
| | 34W-1N | 33 |
| Acorn Ct. E&W | 37W-0N | 38 |
| Allen Dr. NW&SE | | |
| | 34W-0S,35W-0S | 39 |
| Anderson Blvd. N&S | | |
| | 35W-1N | 33 |
| Andover Ln. N&S | 36W-1N | 32 |
| Appleton Ln. N&S | | |
| | 34W-1N,33W-1N | 33 |
| Arrowhead Ct. N&S | 36W-0S | 38 |
| Ashbury Ct. N&S | 36W-0N | 38 |
| Austin Av. N&S | 34W-1N | 33 |
| Averill Cir. E&W | 33W-1N | 33 |
| Averill Rd. E&W | 33W-1N | 33 |
| Bank Ln. E&W | 33W-1N | 33 |
| Batavia Av. NE&SW | | |
| | 35W-0S,35W-0N | 39 |
| Bedford Ln. N&S | 36W-1N | 32 |
| Bennett St. N&S | 33W-1N | 33 |
| Bent Tree Dr. N&S | 36W-0N | 38 |
| Berkshire Dr. NE&SW | | |
| | 37W-0N | 38 |
| Bilarda Ct. E&W | 36W-1N | 32 |
| Blackberry Dr. NS&EW | | |
| | 36W-1N | 32 |
| Blackman Ct. N&S | 37W-0N | 38 |
| Blackman Rd. NW&SE | 37W-0N | 38 |
| Bloomfield Cir. NS&EW | | |
| | 36W-1N | 32 |
| Bradbury Ln. E&W | 36W-1N | 32 |
| Brentwood Ct. N&S | 34W-1N | 33 |
| Brentwood Pl. E&W | 34W-1N | 33 |
| Brian Ct. E&W | 36W-1N | 32 |
| Briar Ln. N&S | 36W-1N | 32 |
| Bridgeport Ln. N&S | 36W-1N | 32 |
| Brigham Ct. NE&SW | | |
| | 36W-0N | 38 |
| Brigham Way N&S | 36W-0N | 38 |
| Brighton Ct. N&S | 36W-0N | 38 |
| Britta Ln. E&W | 34W-1N | 33 |
| Brittany Ct. NS&EW | 36W-1N | 32 |
| Brookfield Ct. N&S | 36W-1N | 32 |
| Brookway Dr. N&S | 36W-1N | 32 |
| Bunker Ct. NW&SE | 34W-0N | 39 |
| Burgess Rd. N&S | 36W-1N | 32 |
| Cambridge Ct. E&W | 36W-1N | 32 |
| Cambridge Dr. N&S | 36W-1N | 32 |
| Campbell Ct. N&S | 35W-1N | 33 |

| | Grid | Page |
|---|---|---|
| Campbell St. NW&SE | 36W-1N | 33 |
| Cape Way NW&SE | 36W-1N | 32 |
| Caroline Ct. E&W | 34W-1N | 33 |
| Cedar Av. NE&SW | 37W-0N | 38 |
| Center St. E&W | | |
| | 36W-1N,35W-1N | 32 |
| Chalmers St. NW&SE | | |
| | 34W-0N | 39 |
| Chandler Av. N&S | 33W-1N | 33 |
| Charles St. N&S | 36W-1N | 32 |
| Chatham Ct. E&W | 37W-0N | 38 |
| Cheever Av. N&S | 36W-0N | 39 |
| Chesapeake Way E&W | | |
| | 33W-1N | 33 |
| Christina Ln. E&W | 36W-0N | 38 |
| Clover Ct. N&S | 36W-1N | 32 |
| Clover Ln. N&S | 36W-1N | 32 |
| Club Dr. E&W | 36W-0N | 38 |
| Colony Dr. N&S | 37W-1N | 32 |
| Commerce Dr. NW&SE | | |
| | 34W-1N | 33 |
| Connant Ct. E&W | | |
| | 37W-0N | 38 |
| Considine Rd. E&W | | |
| | 36W-0S,35W-0S | 39 |
| Country Club Pl. N&S | | |
| | 36W-1N | 32 |
| Country Squire Dr. E&W | | |
| | 36W-0N | 38 |
| Coventry Ct. E&W | 37W-0N | 38 |
| Crawford St. E&W | 35W-0N | 39 |
| Creekside Dr. N&S | 33W-1N | 33 |
| Crescent Pl. E&W | 35W-0N | 39 |
| Crissey N&S | 34W-1N | 33 |
| Crissey Av. N&S | | |
| | 34W-0N,34W-1N | 39 |
| Croydon Ct. N&S | 36W-0N | 39 |
| Crystal Tree Ct. N&S | | |
| | 36W-0N | 38 |
| Danbury Ct. N&S | | |
| | 36W-1N | 32 |
| Danford Ct. E&W | 37W-0N | 38 |
| Danford Way NS&EW | | |
| | 37W-0N | 38 |
| Danuta Ct. E&W | 36W-1N | 32 |
| Dartmouth Ct. E&W | 36W-1N | 32 |
| Deerfield Way NW&SE | | |
| | 36W-1N | 32 |
| Delphi Ln. N&S | 36W-1N | 33 |
| Demsey Pl. NW&SE | 36W-1N | 32 |
| Dodson St. NW&SE | 34W-1N | 33 |
| Dow Av. N&S | 35W-0N | 39 |
| Downing Pl. E&W | 34W-1N | 33 |
| Dryden Rd. E&W | 35W-0N | 39 |
| Dunstan Rd. E&W | 35W-0N | 39 |
| Eagle Brook NE&SW | | |
| | 36W-0N | 39 |
| East Side Dr. NW&SE | | |
| | 34W-1N | 33 |
| Easton Av. E&W | 35W-0N | 39 |
| Edison St. N&S | 35W-1N | 33 |
| Eklund Av. N&S | 35W-1N | 33 |
| Eldorado Ct. E&W | 36W-0N | 38 |
| Eldorado Dr. N&S | 36W-0N | 38 |
| Elizabeth Pl. E&W | 35W-0N | 39 |
| Elm St. N&S | 34W-1N | 33 |
| Essex Ct. NW&SE | 36W-1N | 32 |
| Euclid Av. N&S | 34W-1N | 33 |
| Evernia Ct. NE&SW | 35W-1N | 33 |
| Executive Pl. NW&SE | | |
| | 33W-1N | 33 |
| Fabyan Pkwy E&W | 34W-0S | 39 |
| Fairview Ct. N&S | | |
| | 37W-1N | 32 |
| Fairway Cir. N&S | | |
| | 36W-0N | 38 |
| Fairway Ct. N&S | 36W-0N | 38 |
| Fargo Blvd. E&W | | |
| | 37W-0N,35W-0N | 38 |
| Fargo Cir. N&S | 37W-0N | 38 |
| Fire Fox N&S | | |
| | 36W-0N | 38 |
| Fluid Power Dr. N&S | | |
| | 33W-1N | 33 |
| Ford St. E&W | | |
| | 36W-1N,35W-1N | 32 |
| Forest Av. N&S | 35W-0N | 39 |
| Forest View Dr. E&W | | |
| | 35W-0N | 39 |
| Foxford St. E&W | 35W-0N | 39 |
| Foxwood Cir. E&W | 34W-1N | 33 |
| Franklin St. E&W | 35W-1N | 33 |
| Frontage Rd. NE&SW | | |
| | 34W-0N | 39 |
| Fulton St. NW&SE | | |
| | 35W-1N,35W-0N | 33 |
| Galway Ct. N&S | 36W-0N | 39 |
| Garden Av. E&W | 35W-0N | 39 |
| Garfield St. NE&SW | 34W-1N | 33 |
| Gary Ln. E&W | 36W-1N | 32 |
| Gaunt Av. N&S | 35W-0N | 39 |
| Geneva Dr. E&W | | |
| | 34W-1N,33W-1N | 33 |
| George Ct. E&W | 36W-1N | 32 |
| Ginger Ln. NW&SE | 37W-0N | 38 |
| Gleneagle Dr. N&S | 36W-0N | 38 |
| Glengarry Dr. E&W | | |
| | 34W-1N,33W-1N | 33 |
| Grant Av. N&S | 35W-1N | 33 |
| Gray St. E&W | | |
| | 36W-1N,35W-1N | 32 |
| Greenfield Cir. NS&EW | | |
| | 34W-1N | 33 |
| Greenmeadow Ln. E&W | | |
| | 33W-1N | 33 |
| Greenwich Ln. N&S | 36W-1N | 32 |
| Hamilton Ct. E&W | 35W-1N | 33 |

| | Grid | Page |
|---|---|---|
| Hampton Cir. NW&SE | | |
| | 36W-1N | 32 |
| Harbor Town Ct. N&S | | |
| | 36W-0N | 38 |
| Harrison St. N&S | | |
| | 34W-0N,34W-1N | 39 |
| Hartford Ln. E&W | 36W-1N | 32 |
| Hawthorne Ln. N&S | 35W-0N | 39 |
| Heartland Dr. E&W | 37W-1N | 32 |
| Heather Rd. NE&SW | | |
| | 36W-0S | 39 |
| Herrington Pl. NE&SW | | |
| | 37W-0N | 38 |
| Herrington Rd. NS&EW | | |
| | 37W-0N | 38 |
| High St. E&W | 34W-1N | 33 |
| Highbury Ln. N&S | 36W-1N | 32 |
| Highland Ct. NW&SE | | |
| | 37W-0N | 38 |
| Hill Rd. NW&SE | | |
| | 34W-1N,33W-1N | 33 |
| Howard St. NE&SW | 34W-1N | 33 |
| Howell Dr. E&W | 34W-1N | 33 |
| Hunter Ct. E&W | 33W-1N | 33 |
| Illinois St. N&S | 35W-1N | 33 |
| J. Pankow Dr. E&W | 36W-1N | 32 |
| James St. N&S | 35W-1N | 33 |
| Jefferson St. NW&SE | | |
| | 34W-1N | 33 |
| Kane St. NE&SW | | |
| | 34W-0N,34W-1N | 39 |
| Kaneville Rd. E&W | | |
| | 37W-1N,35W-1N | 32 |
| Kansas St. N&S | | |
| | 34W-0N,34W-1N | 39 |
| Keim Ct. N&S | 36W-0N | 38 |
| Keim Dr. NS&EW | 36W-0N | 38 |
| Kendall St. E&W | 36W-0N | 39 |
| Kenston Ct. NS&EW | | |
| | 35W-1N | 33 |
| Kings Ct. NW&SE | 36W-0S | 38 |
| Kingston Dr. N&S | 34W-1N | 33 |
| Kirkwood Cir. NS&EW | | |
| | 33W-1N | 33 |
| Kummer Ct. E&W | 36W-0N | 38 |
| Lake Ct. N&S | 37W-0N | 38 |
| Lark St. NW&SE | 37W-0N | 38 |
| Le Baron Ct. NW&SE | | |
| | 37W-0N | 38 |
| Lewis Cir. E&W | 37W-0N | 38 |
| Lewis Pl. E&W | 37W-0N | 38 |
| Lewis Rd. N&S | 37W-0N | 38 |
| Lexington Dr. N&S | 34W-1N | 33 |
| Lincoln Av. N&S | 35W-1N | 33 |
| Locust Av. E&W | 34W-1N | 33 |
| Logan Av. N&S | 35W-1N | 33 |
| Lois Ct. E&W | 36W-0N | 38 |
| Long Meadow Dr. NW&SE | | |
| | 34W-1N | 33 |
| Longview Dr. NS&EW | | |
| | 33W-1N | 33 |
| Loran Dr. E&W | 36W-0N | 38 |
| Manchester Course NS&EW | | |
| | 34W-1N | 33 |
| Manchester Ct. NE&SW | | |
| | 36W-1N | 32 |
| Maple Ct. N&S | 36W-1N | 32 |
| Maple Ln. N&S | 36W-1N | 32 |
| Marion Av. E&W | 35W-0N | 39 |
| Marion Ct. E&W | 36W-1N | 32 |
| Market Pl. N&S | 37W-1N | 33 |
| May St. N&S | 35W-1N | 33 |
| McKinley Av. N&S | 35W-1N | 33 |
| Mead St. E&W | 35W-0N | 39 |
| Meadows Rd. N&S | 35W-0N | 39 |
| Merganzer Ct. NW&SE | | |
| | 37W-0N | 38 |
| Millbrook Ct. N&S | 36W-1N | 32 |
| Miller Dr. E&W | 37W-0S | 38 |
| Miller Rd. NE&SW | 37W-0N | 38 |
| Nassau Ln. E&W | 35W-0N | 39 |
| Natwill Sq. E&W | 35W-1N | 33 |
| Nebraska St. N&S | | |
| | 34W-0N,34W-1N | 39 |
| Newport Ln. E&W | 36W-1N | 32 |
| Nichole Ln. E&W | 36W-1N | 32 |
| Normandy Ln. E&W | 36W-1N | 32 |
| North St. E&W | | |
| | 36W-1N,35W-1N | 32 |
| Northampton Dr. N&S | | |
| | 36W-1N | 32 |
| Oak St. N&S | 34W-1N | 33 |
| Oakwood Av. NW&SE | | |
| | 36W-0N | 38 |
| Osprey Ct. NW&SE | 37W-0N | 38 |
| Paddock Ct. N&S | 36W-1N | 32 |
| Park Av. N&S | 34W-1N | 33 |
| Parker Ct. N&S | 34W-1N | 33 |
| Patten Av. NW&SE | 34W-1N | 33 |
| Pebble Beach Ct. N&S | | |
| | 36W-0N | 38 |
| Peck Rd. E&W | 35W-0N | 39 |
| Pepper Valley Dr. E&W | | |
| | 36W-0N | 32 |
| Peterson Ct. N&S | 37W-0N | 33 |
| Peyton St. NW&SE | 35W-1N | 33 |
| Pheasant Ct. E&W | 37W-0N | 38 |
| Pheasant Run Pl. NS&EW | | |
| | 36W-0S,35W-0N | 38 |
| Pine St. N&S | 36W-1N | 32 |
| Pinto Ct. SW&NE | 36W-0N | 39 |
| Pioneer Ct. N&S | 36W-1N | 32 |
| Police Pl. N&S | 35W-1N | 33 |
| Prairie Ct. N&S | 36W-1N | 32 |
| Radnor Ct. N&S | 36W-1N | 32 |
| Randall Ct. N&S | 37W-0N | 38 |
| Randall Rd. N&S | 37W-0N | 38 |

| | Grid | Page |
|---|---|---|
| Ray St. E&W | 35W-0N | 39 |
| Redwing Ct. E&W | 36W-0S,35W-0S | 39 |
| Regency Ct. E&W | 36W-1N | 32 |
| Renee Ct. E&W | 36W-1N | 32 |
| Richards St. N&S | 35W-1N | 33 |
| Ridge Ln. NS&EW | 34W-1N | 33 |
| River Ln. N&S | 35W-0N,35W-1N | 39 |
| Rosenfelder Ct. N&S | 36W-1N | 32 |
| Samantha Cir. EW&NS | 37W-0N | 38 |
| Samantha Cir. N&S | 37W-0N | 38 |
| Sandholm St. N&S | 34W-0N,34W-1N | 39 |
| School St. NE&SW | 34W-1N | 33 |
| Scott Blvd. NW&SE | 36W-1N | 32 |
| Shady Av. N&S | 35W-0N | 39 |
| Sheffield Ln. E&W | 36W-1N | 32 |
| Sheila Av. N&S | 36W-0N | 38 |
| Sherman Av. E&W | 36W-1N | 32 |
| Sherwood Ln. E&W | 36W-0N | 38 |
| Shoop Cir. E&W | 37W-0N | 38 |
| Shoop Dr. N&S | 37W-0N | 38 |
| Short St. NW&SE | 34W-1N | 33 |
| Simon Ct. E&W | 37W-0N | 38 |
| Simpson St. E&W | 34W-0N,34W-1N | 39 |
| Soderquist Ct. E&W | 37W-0N | 38 |
| South St. E&W | 36W-1N,35W-0N | 32 |
| Southampton Ct. NS&EW | 36W-0N | 38 |
| Southhampton Dr. N&S | 36W-1N | 32 |
| Spring Ct. NS&EW | 34W-0N | 39 |
| Spring St. NW&SE | 34W-1N,34W-0N | 33 |
| Spruce Ct. N&S | 37W-0N | 38 |
| Cir. | 36W-0N | 38 |
| St. Jude Ct. NW&SE | 36W-0N | 39 |
| State St. NW&SE | 36W-1N,34W-1N | 32 |
| Sterling Av. N&S | 37W-0N | 38 |
| Stevens St. NW&SE | 35W-1N | 33 |
| Stratford Dr. N&S | 36W-1N | 32 |
| Sudbury Ln. E&W | 36W-1N | 32 |
| Suffield Ct. N&S | 34W-1N | 33 |
| Summit St. NE&SW | 34W-1N | 33 |
| Sunset Rd. N&S | 35W-0N | 39 |
| Syril Dr. N&S | 36W-1N | 32 |
| Tanager Ln. NE&SW | 36W-0S | 39 |
| Thornhill Ct. E&W | 37W-0N | 38 |
| Turnberry Ct. NW&SE | 36W-0N | 38 |
| Union St. NW&SE | 35W-1N | 33 |
| Valley Ln. N&S | 36W-1N | 32 |
| Wakefield Ln. N&S | 36W-1N | 32 |
| Wall St. N&S | 34W-1N | 33 |
| Walnut Av. N&S | 37W-0N | 38 |
| Water St. N&S | 34W-1N | 33 |
| Wesley Ct. E&W | 33W-1N | 33 |
| West Ln. N&S | 36W-1N | 32 |
| West St. N&S | 36W-1N | 32 |
| Western Av. N&S | 36W-0N | 38 |
| Westfield Course NS&EW | 34W-1N | 33 |
| Westhaven Cir. N&S | 37W-1N | 32 |
| Whitfield Dr. NS&EW | 33W-1N | 33 |
| Whittington Dr. E&W | 34W-1N | 33 |
| Wild Dunes Ct. E&W | 36W-0S | 38 |
| Wildflower Ct. N&S | 36W-0S | 38 |
| Williamsburg Av. E&W | 36W-1N | 32 |
| Willow Ln. N&S | 36W-1N | 32 |
| Wilson St. N&S | 35W-1N | 33 |
| Windham Ct. N&S | 36W-0N | 38 |
| Windthrop Ln. N&S | 36W-1N | 32 |
| Winners Cup Ct. NW&SE | 36W-0N | 38 |
| Wood Av. N&S | 37W-0N | 38 |
| Woodlawn St. NE&SW | 33W-1N | 33 |
| Woodward Av. NW&SE | 34W-1N | 33 |
| 1st St. NE&SW | 35W-0N,35W-1N | 39 |
| 2nd St. N&S | 35W-1N | 33 |
| 3rd Av. N&S | 34W-1N | 33 |
| 3rd St. NE&SW | 35W-0N,35W-1N | 39 |
| 4th Av. N&S | 34W-1N | 33 |
| 4th St. NE&SW | 35W-0N,35W-1N | 39 |
| 5th Av. N&S | 34W-1N | 33 |
| 5th St. NE&SW | 35W-0N,35W-1N | 39 |
| 6th Av. N&S | 34W-1N | 33 |
| 6th St. NE&SW | 35W-1N | 33 |
| 7th Pl. N&S | 35W-1N | 33 |
| 7th St. NE&SW | 35W-1N | 33 |
| 8th St. N&S | 35W-0N,35W-1N | 39 |
| 9th St. N&S | 35W-1N | 33 |

**Geneva Township**

| | Grid | Page |
|---|---|---|
| Alexander Ct. NS&EW | 38N-0N | 38 |
| Alexander Dr. N&S | 38W-0N | 38 |

| | Grid | Page |
|---|---|---|
| Armstrong Ln. E&W | 38W-0N | 38 |
| Blackberry Way E&W | 38W-0N | 38 |
| Bricker Rd. E&W | 37W-1N | 32 |
| Cherry Ln. E&W | 34W-0N,38W-0N | 39 |
| Clover Hills Ct. E&W | 38W-0S,37W-0S | 38 |
| Crego Pl. NS&EW | 38W-0N | 38 |
| Deerpath Rd. NE&SW | 37W-2S | 38 |
| Dobson Ln. E&W | 38W-0N | 38 |
| Elm Rd. N&S | 38W-3N | 33 |
| Fabyan Pkwy. E&W | 38W-0S,36W-0S | 38 |
| Field Ct. E&W | 38W-0N | 38 |
| Glenwood Dr. E&W | 38W-1S | 38 |
| Harrison Rd. NW&SE | 33W-1N | 33 |
| Herrington Blvd. E&W | 38W-0N | 38 |
| Janet Ln. N&S | 37W-0S | 38 |
| Kaneville Rd. NE&SW | 38W-0S,38W-0N | 38 |
| Kautz Rd. N&S | 33W-0N,33W-1N | 39 |
| Keslinger Rd. E&W | 38W-1N,37W-1N | 32 |
| Killey Ln. NE&SW | 38W-0N | 38 |
| Kirk Rd. N&S | 33W-0N,33W-1N | 39 |
| Lea Dr. N&S | 38W-0N | 38 |
| Lynn Rd. N&S | 33W-1N | 33 |
| McKee St. E&W | 38W-0S,37W-0S | 38 |
| Millcreek Dr. N&S | 38W-0S | 38 |
| Minor Rd. NE&SW | 38W-0N | 38 |
| Monterey Dr. E&W | 38W-1S | 38 |
| Morningside Ln. NW&SE | 37W-0S | 38 |
| Norman Rd. E&W | 33W-1N | 33 |
| Northlane Rd. N&S | 33W-1N | 39 |
| Oak Rd. N&S | 33W-1N | 33 |
| Old Kirk Rd. N&S | 33W-0N,33W-1N | 39 |
| Orchard Rd. N&S | 33W-1N | 33 |
| Peck Av. N&S | 38W-0N,38W-1N | 38 |
| Pine Needles Ct. NW&SE | 37W-0S | 38 |
| Prairie View N&S | 38W-0N | 38 |
| Randall Rd. N&S | 37W-0S,37W-1N | 38 |
| Reed Rd. E&W | 33W-0N | 39 |
| River Ln. N&S | 35W-0N,35W-1N | 39 |
| Roosevelt Rd. E&W | 33W-0N,33W-1N | 39 |
| Rt. 31 NE&SW | 35W-0N,35W-1N | 39 |
| Rt. 38 NW&SE | 36W-1N,34W-1N | 32 |
| Skyline Dr. NE&SW | 37W-0S | 38 |
| Southwest Ln. E&W | 33W-0N | 38 |
| Spring Green Way NS&EW | 38W-0S,37W-0S | 38 |
| Theisen Trail N&S | 37W-1S | 38 |
| Wenmoth Ln. NE&SW | 38W-0N | 38 |
| Wenmoth Rd. N&S | 38W-1S,38W-0S | 38 |
| Western Av. N&S | 36W-0S,36W-0N | 38 |

**Gilberts**

| | Grid | Page |
|---|---|---|
| Andra Ct. NE&SW | 38W-15N | 13 |
| Arrowhead Dr. E&W | 38W-16N,37W-16N | 13 |
| Big Timber Rd. NW&SE | 38W-14N | 13 |
| Center Dr. N&S | 38W-16N | 13 |
| Deborah St. E&W | 37W-15N | 13 |
| East Dr. N&S | 38W-16N | 13 |
| Elgin St. E&W | 38W-16N | 13 |
| Galligan Rd. N&S | 38W-16N,39W-17N | 13 |
| Hennessy Ct. E&W | 38W-14N | 13 |
| Industrial Dr. NW&SE | 39W-16N | 13 |
| Jackson St. NE&SW | 38W-16N | 13 |
| Jean St. N&S | 37W-15N | 13 |
| Joan Ct. E&W | 38W-15N | 13 |
| Kerry Ct. NW&SE | 38W-15N | 13 |
| Kildare St. E&W | 38W-15N | 13 |
| Kilkenny Ct. N&S | 38W-15N | 13 |
| Mason Rd. E&W | 38W-14N,37W-15N | 13 |
| Matteson St. NE&SW | 39W-16N | 13 |
| McCornack Rd. N&S | 39W-15N | 13 |
| Mill St. N&S | 39W-16N | 13 |
| Northwest Tollway NW&SE | 39W-16N | 13 |
| Pamela St. E&W | 37W-15N | 13 |
| Park St. NE&SW | 39W-16N | 13 |
| Pauline St. N&S | 37W-15N | 13 |
| Pierce St. NW&SE | 38W-15N | 13 |
| Railroad St. NW&SE | 39W-16N | 13 |
| Red Hawk Dr. N&S | 38W-16N | 13 |
| Rt. 72 E&W | 39W-16N | 13 |

| | Grid | Page |
|---|---|---|
| Running Dear Ln. E&W | 38W-16N,37W-16N | 13 |
| Shining Moon Path N&S | 37W-16N | 13 |
| Sleeping Bear Tr. NW&SE | 38W-16N,37W-16N | 13 |
| Sola Dr. E&W | 38W-16N | 13 |
| Suzanne St. E&W | 37W-15N | 13 |
| Tipperary St. N&S | 38W-15N | 13 |
| Tollview Ct. N&S | 39W-16N | 13 |
| Tollview Ter. E&W | 39W-16N | 13 |
| Tower Hill Rd. NW&SE | 39W-16N | 13 |
| Towne Ct. E&W | 37W-15N | 13 |
| Towne St. NE&SW | 38W-15N,39W-16N | 13 |
| Turner St. E&W | 38W-16N | 13 |
| Tyler Creek St. E&W | 39W-16N | 13 |
| Tyrrell Rd. N&S | 38W-15N,37W-14N | 13 |
| Union St. NW&SE | 39W-16N | 13 |
| Welch St. NE&SW | 39W-16N | 13 |
| West End Dr. N&S | 38W-16N | 13 |
| White Feather Ln. N&S | 38W-16N | 13 |
| Wiley St. N&S | 39W-16N | 13 |
| Wind Mill St. E&W | 39W-16N | 13 |
| Windmill Pl. N&S | 39W-16N | 13 |

**Hampshire**

| | Grid | Page |
|---|---|---|
| Allen Rd. E&W | 47W-15N | 11 |
| Ash St. N&S | 46W-16N | 11 |
| Big Timber Rd. E&W | 45W-17N | 5 |
| Brookedge Dr. N&S | 47W-15N | 10 |
| Centennial Dr. N&S | 46W-15N | 11 |
| Center St. N&S | 47W-16N | 10 |
| Dietrich Rd. E&W | 45W-19N | 5 |
| Duchess Ln. E&W | 47W-15N | 10 |
| East St. N&S | 47W-16N | 10 |
| Edgewood Av. E&W | 47W-15N | 10 |
| Elm St. N&S | 46W-15N | 11 |
| French Rd. N&S | 47W-15N | 10 |
| Getzelman Rd. E&W | 46W-15N | 11 |
| Grace St. N&S | 45W-14N | 11 |
| Grove St. E&W | 46W-16N | 11 |
| Higgins Rd. E&W | 45W-18N | 5 |
| High Av. E&W | 46W-15N | 11 |
| Highland Av. E&W | 46W-15N | 11 |
| Hillcrest Av. E&W | 46W-15N | 11 |
| Industrial Dr. E&W | 46W-16N | 11 |
| Jackson St. N&S | 47W-16N | 10 |
| Jake Ln. E&W | 46W-15N | 11 |
| Jefferson St. E&W | 46W-16N | 11 |
| Julie Av. E&W | 46W-15N | 11 |
| Kelley Rd. N&S | 45W-17N | 5 |
| Ketchum Rd. N&S | 45W-17N | 5 |
| Keys Av. N&S | 46W-16N | 11 |
| Klick St. N&S | 47W-15N,47W-16N | 10 |
| Madison St. N&S | 46W-16N | 11 |
| Maple St. E&W | 46W-16N | 11 |
| Mill St. E&W | 47W-16N | 10 |
| Northwest Tollway NW&SE | 44W-18N,45W-19N | 13 |
| Oak Knoll Dr. E&W | 47W-15N | 10 |
| Oak St. N&S | 47W-16N | 10 |
| Old Mill Av. E&W | 46W-16N | 11 |
| Panama St. N&S | 46W-16N | 11 |
| Park St. N&S | 47W-16N | 10 |
| Parkside St. N&S | 46W-16N | 11 |
| Prairie St. N&S | 47W-15N | 10 |
| Rinn Av. E&W | 46W-16N | 11 |
| Rt. 72 E&W | 44W-15N | 11 |
| Smith Rd. N&S | 46W-15N | 11 |
| South St. NE&SW | 46W-16N | 11 |
| State St. N&S | 47W-16N | 10 |
| Terwilliger St. E&W | 47W-16N | 10 |
| Timber Ln. E&W | 47W-16N | 10 |
| U.S. Route 20 NW&SE | 46W-19N | 5 |
| Walnut St. N&S | 46W-16N | 11 |
| Warner St. N&S | 46W-15N | 11 |
| Washington St. E&W | 46W-16N | 11 |
| West St. N&S | 47W-16N | 10 |
| Widmayer rd. N&S | 45W-18N | 5 |

**Hampshire Township**

| | Grid | Page |
|---|---|---|
| Aileron Rd. E&W | 49W-19N | 4 |
| Allen Rd. E&W | 49W-17N,45W-16N | 11 |
| Berner Rd. E&W | 45W-14N | 11 |
| Big Timber Rd. E&W | 47W-19N,45W-18N | 4 |
| Briarwood Ln. N&S | 47W-19N | 4 |
| Brier Hill Rd. N&S | 44W-14N,44W-18N | 11 |
| Chandelle Dr. E&W | 48W-19N | 4 |
| Clanyard Rd. E&W | 44W-19N | 5 |
| Deer Path Ln. E&W | 44W-14N | 11 |
| Dietrich Rd. N&S | 45W-19N | 5 |
| Engle Rd. N&S | 49W-14N | 10 |
| Factly Rd. NW&SE | 49W-14N | 10 |
| Cir. | 46W-19N | 5 |

| | Grid | Page |
|---|---|---|
| Fox Run Ln. NS&EW | 47W-15N | 10 |
| Gast Rd. N&S | 45W-18N | 5 |
| Getty Rd. E&W | 47W-19N | 4 |
| Getzelman Rd. N&S | 47W-14N | 10 |
| Glen Oaks Ct. E&W | 45W-16N | 11 |
| Glen Oaks Dr. N&S | 45W-16N | 11 |
| Green Meadows Ln. N&S | 46W-19N | 5 |
| Harmony Rd. N&S | 47W-17N,47W-19N | 4 |
| Hawthorne Ln. N&S | 46W-19N | 5 |
| Hennig Rd. E&W | 44W-18N | 5 |
| Higgins Rd. E&W | 46W-19N | 5 |
| Hillcrest Dr. N&S | 46W-19N | 5 |
| I-90 NW&SE | 44W-18N | 5 |
| Immelman Ln. E&W | 48W-19N | 4 |
| Kelly Rd. E&W | 47W-17N | 4 |
| Ketchum Rd. N&S | 45W-17N | 5 |
| Lenschow Rd. E&W | 49W-14N,46W-14N | 10 |
| Littlewood Trail E&W | 44W-15N | 11 |
| Marney Rd. N&S | 46W-17N | 5 |
| Melms Rd. E&W | 49W-18N,48W-18N | 4 |
| New Lebanon Rd. NW&SE | 50W-14N | 10 |
| Northwest Tollway NW&SE | 46W-19N | 5 |
| Oak Grove Dr. NE&SW | 46W-17N | 5 |
| Oakshire Ln. E&W | 44W-15N | 11 |
| Obrien Rd. E&W | 49W-19N | 4 |
| Penstemon Ln. NW&SE | 45W-16N | 11 |
| Prairie Farm Rd. NE&SW | 45W-16N | 11 |
| Prairieview Pkwy. N&S | 47W-15N | 10 |
| Primrose Ln. E&W | 47W-19N | 4 |
| Primrose Path E&W | 46W-17N | 5 |
| Red Barn Rd. NW&SE | 47W-14N | 10 |
| Romke Rd. N&S | 45W-14N | 11 |
| Rt. 72 E&W | 46W-15N | 11 |
| Rudder Rd. N&S | 48W-19N | 4 |
| Shirewood Farm Rd. NE&SW | 47W-15N | 10 |
| Stoxen Rd. E&W | 47W-19N | 4 |
| Sunset Dr. NW&SE | 44W-14N | 11 |
| U.S. Rt. 20 NW&SE | 44W-17N,45W-18N | 5 |
| Volkening Cir. E&W | 44W-14N | 11 |
| Walker Rd. N&S | 49W-14N,49W-18N | 10 |
| West County Line Rd. N&S | 49W-19N | 4 |
| Whispering Tr. N&S | 44W-14N | 11 |
| White Pines Ln. N&S | 44W-14N | 11 |
| White Tail Cir. EW&NS | 47W-15N | 10 |
| White Tail Dr. E&W | 47W-15N | 10 |
| Widmayer Rd. N&S | 46W-16N,46W-18N | 11 |
| Woodview Pkwy. NS&EW | 46W-19N | 5 |

**Huntley**

| | Grid | Page |
|---|---|---|
| Clanyard Rd. E&W | 44W-19N,43W-19N | 6 |
| Drendl Rd. N&S | 42W-19N,42W-18N | 6 |
| Freeman Rd. E&W | 41-18N | 6 |
| Hennig Rd. N&S | 43W-19N,43W-18N | 6 |
| Northwest Tollway NW&SE | 43W-18N,41W-17N | 6 |

**Kaneville Township**

| | Grid | Page |
|---|---|---|
| Bateman Rd. NS&EW | 46W-1S,45W-0S | 35 |
| Cedar Ct. N&S | 46W-2S | 35 |
| Center Av. N&S | 50W-2S | 34 |
| Country Life Ct. N&S | 48W-0N | 34 |
| Country Life Dr. NS&EW | 49W-17N,48W-1N | 34 |
| County Line Rd. N&S | 50W-1S,50W-1N | 34 |
| Dauberman Rd. N&S | 48W-0N | 34 |
| East West Tollway NW&SE | 50W-0N,45W-1N | 34 |
| Elm Ct. N&S | 46W-2S | 35 |
| Elm St. N&S | 46W-2S | 35 |
| Farm View Ct. N&S | 48W-0N | 34 |
| Francis Rd. N&S | 46W-0N | 29 |
| Harter Rd. NW&SE | 50W-0N,45W-3S | 34 |
| Interstate 88 NW&SE | 50W-0N,45W-1S | 34 |
| Kaneland Dr. NW&SE | 48W-1N | 28 |

| | Grid | Page |
|---|---|---|
| Kaneview Ct. NE&SW | 48W-1N | 28 |
| Keslinger Rd. E&W | 50W-1N,45W-1N | 28 |
| Lasher Rd. N&S | 46W-3S | 41 |
| Locust Ct. NW&SE | 46W-2S | 35 |
| Locust St. NE&SW | 46W-2S | 35 |
| Lorang Rd. N&S | 45W-2S,45W-1S | 35 |
| Lovell St. NE&SW | 46W-2S | 35 |
| Main St. NE&SW | 50W-2S,45W-1S | 34 |
| Maple St. N&S | 46W-2S | 35 |
| Meredith Rd. N&S | 47W-1N | 28 |
| Merril Av. N&S | 46W-2S | 35 |
| Milnamow Dr. NE&SW | 48W-1N | 28 |
| Miner Rd. N&S | 49W-1S,49W-0S | 34 |
| N. Railroad St. NW&SE | 50W-2S | 34 |
| Owens Rd. N&S | 50W-1S,48W-2S | 34 |
| Perry Rd. N&S | 50W-0S,47W-1S | 34 |
| Pine St. N&S | 46W-2S | 35 |
| Pine Tree Dr. E&W | 48W-1N | 28 |
| Pond View Ct. N&S | 48W-0N | 34 |
| Probst Ct. N&S | 48W-1N | 28 |
| Prospect Av. N&S | 50W-2S | 34 |
| Rowe Rd. NS&EW | 45W-0S | 35 |
| Rt. 38 E&W | 49W-1N,47W-1N | 28 |
| Schneider Rd. N&S | 45W-0S,45W-0N | 35 |
| School St. N&S | 46W-2S | 35 |
| Schrader Rd. N&S | 50W-0N,50W-1N | 34 |
| Seavey Rd. N&S | 45W-3S | 41 |
| Shadetree Ct. N&S | 48W-1N | 28 |
| Shadetree Ln. N&S | 48W-1N | 34 |
| South Lorang Rd. NW&SE | 45W-2S,45W-1S | 35 |
| Swan Rd. N&S | 49W-3S | 40 |
| W. County Line Rd. N&S | 50W-2S | 34 |
| Watson Rd. N&S | 48W-0S,48W-1N | 34 |

**Lilly Lake**

| | Grid | Page |
|---|---|---|
| Blackhawk Ln. E&W | 44W-5N | 24 |
| Campton Ct. N&S | 43W-5N | 24 |
| Clover Ct. E&W | 43W-5N | 24 |
| Cir. | 44W-5N | 24 |
| Coleman Ln. E&W | 43W-5N | 24 |
| Corrwall Dr. E&W | 43W-5N | 24 |
| Empire Rd. E&W | 43W-5N | 24 |
| Ferson Ct. NE&SW | 43W-5N | 24 |
| Fescue Ct. NW&SE | 43W-5N | 24 |
| Fox Hill Ct. NW&SE | 44W-5N | 24 |
| Fox Wilds Ct. NW&SE | 43W-5N | 24 |
| Fox Wilds Dr. EW&NS | 43W-5N | 24 |
| Foxmoor Dr. N&S | 43W-5N | 24 |
| Hanson Rd. NW&SE | 44W-5N | 24 |
| Hanson Ridge Dr. N&S | 44W-5N | 24 |
| Hazelwood Ct. N&S | 43W-5N | 24 |
| Hazelwood Tr. NS&EW | 43W-5N | 24 |
| Heather Ln. NW&SE | 43W-5N | 24 |
| Leslie Ct. N&S | 43W-5N | 24 |
| Meadowview Ln. N&S | 43W-5N | 24 |
| Route 47 (State) N&S | 44W-6N | 24 |
| Route 64 (State) NW&SE | 44W-5N | 24 |
| Sanctuary Tr. E&W | 43W-5N | 24 |
| Seneca Ct. NW&SE | 43W-5N | 24 |
| Wooley Rd. N&S | 44W-4N | 30 |

**Maple Park**

| | Grid | Page |
|---|---|---|
| Broadway St. N&S | 50W-2N,50W-3N | 28 |
| Center St. E&W | 50W-2N | 28 |
| Charles St. N&S | 50W-2N,50W-3N | 28 |
| County Line Rd. N&S | 50W-2N,50W-3N | 28 |
| Elm St. NW&SE | 50W-2N | 28 |
| Green St. NE&SW | 50W-2N | 28 |
| High St. N&S | 50W-2N | 28 |
| Kane St. N&S | 50W-3N | 28 |
| Kennberg St. NE&SW | 50W-2N | 28 |
| Liberty St. N&S | 50W-2N | 28 |
| Maiden Ln. N&S | 50W-3N | 28 |
| Main St. NW&SE | 50W-2N | 28 |
| Maple Av. E&W | 50W-2N | 28 |
| Mulberry St. NE&SW | 50W-2N | 28 |
| Oak St. N&S | 50W-3N | 28 |
| Palmer Dr. N&S | 50W-3N | 28 |
| Pearl St. N&S | 50W-3N | 28 |
| Pine Ln. N&S | 50W-2N | 28 |
| Pleasant St. NE&SW | 50W-2N | 28 |
| Root Ln. N&S | 50W-2N | 28 |
| South St. E&W | 50W-3N | 28 |
| State St. E&W | 50W-3N | 28 |

| | Grid | Page |
|---|---|---|
| Summer St. NE&SW | 50W-2N | 28 |
| Thatcher Rd. E&W | 50W-3N | 28 |
| Virgil St. N&S | 50W-3N | 28 |
| Washington St. E&W | 50W-3N | 28 |
| Willow St. NW&SE | 50W-2N | 28 |

## Montgomery

| | Grid | Page |
|---|---|---|
| Albright Rd. N&S | 37W-9S | 50 |
| Amber Dr. N&S | 34W-9S | 51 |
| Ashland Av. E&W | 37W-9S | 50 |
| Aucutt Rd. E&W | 38W-9S | 50 |
| Baseline Rd. E&W | 37W-9S | 50 |
| Broadway Av. N&S | 36W-9S | 50 |
| Carol Pl. E&W | 34W-9S | 51 |
| Case Av. NW&SE | 37W-9S | 50 |
| Catherine Ln. E&W | 36W-9S | 50 |
| Clay St. NW&SE | 37W-9S | 50 |
| Clinton St. NW&SE | 37W-9S | 50 |
| Cornell Av. E&W | 38W-8S | 50 |
| Countryside Av. E&W | 38W-9S | 50 |
| Crown St. N&S | 34W-9S | 51 |
| Dawn Av. E&W | 34W-9S | 51 |
| Douglas Rd. N&S | 35W-9S,36W-9S | 51 |
| Fellemore Av. E&W | 36W-9S | 50 |
| First Av. N&S | 36W-9S | 50 |
| Greenfield Av. E&W | 38W-9S | 50 |
| Harmony Ct. NE&SW | 36W-9S | 50 |
| Harmony Dr. N&S | 36W-9S | 50 |
| Harrison St. E&W | 37W-9S | 50 |
| Hartway Ct. NS&EW | 36W-9S | 50 |
| Hartway Dr. E&W | 36W-9S | 50 |
| Henry Ct. E&W | 36W-9S | 50 |
| Hinkley St. N&S | 36W-9S | 51 |
| Howell Pl. NW&SE | 34W-9S | 51 |
| Jackson St. N&S | 35W-9S | 51 |
| James St. E&W | 36W-9S | 50 |
| Jefferson St. NW&SE | 37W-9S | 50 |
| Jericho Rd. E&W | 38W-8S | 50 |
| Keck Av. E&W | 36W-9S | 50 |
| Kimberly Ln. E&W | 34W-9S | 51 |
| Kingston Av. N&S | 34W-9S | 51 |
| Knell St. E&W | 37W-9S | 50 |
| Lake St. NE&SW | 37W-9S | 50 |
| Lebanon St. N&S | 35W-9S | 51 |
| Lewis St. E&W | 36W-9S | 50 |
| Lincoln Av. N&S | 36W-9S | 50 |
| Madison St. NW&SE | 37W-9S | 50 |
| Main St. NE&SW | 37W-9S,36W-9S | 50 |
| Marsch Av. E&W | 36W-9S | 50 |
| Martin Av. NE&SW | 36W-9S | 50 |
| Mill St. NW&SE | 37W-9S,36W-9S | 50 |
| Montgomery Rd. NE&SW | 36W-9S,35W-9S | 50 |
| Mulberry Dr. N&S | 38W-9S | 50 |
| Oakton Rd. E&W | 38W-9S | 50 |
| Orchard Rd. N&S | 38W-9S | 50 |
| Park Ct. NE&SW | 36W-10S | 50 |
| Park Dr. N&S | 34W-9S | 51 |
| Parker Ct. E&W | 36W-9S | 50 |
| Pearl St. NE&SW | 37W-9S | 50 |
| Railroad St. NE&SW | 37W-9S | 50 |
| Raymond Dr. NW&SE | 34W-9S | 51 |
| River St. NE&SW | 37W-9S,36W-9S | 50 |
| Riverside Dr. NS&EW | 36W-9S | 50 |
| Rochester Dr. E&W | 38W-8S | 50 |
| Royal Dr. N&S | 34W-9S | 51 |
| Sard Av. NE&SW | 36W-9S,36W-8S | 50 |
| Scheuring Pl. N&S | 38W-9S | 50 |
| Scott St. NW&SE | 37W-9S | 50 |
| Second Av. N&S | 36W-9S | 50 |
| Sherman Av. E&W | 36W-9S | 50 |
| Spring Haven Ct. NE&SW | 36W-10S | 50 |
| Taylor St. E&W | 36W-9S | 50 |
| Third Av. E&W | 36W-9S | 50 |
| United Dr. E&W | 38W-9S | 50 |
| Victoria Dr. NS&EW | 38W-9S | 50 |
| Washington St. NE&SW | 36W-9S | 50 |
| Watkins St. NW&SE | 37W-9S | 50 |
| Webster St. NW&SE | 37W-9S | 50 |
| Wellman Av. N&S | 36W-9S | 50 |
| Wellman Rd. E&W | 36W-9S | 50 |
| 14th Av. E&W | 34W-9S | 51 |

## North Aurora

| | Grid | Page |
|---|---|---|
| Abbeywood Dr. N&S | 36W-4S,36W-3S | 44 |
| Acorn Dr. N&S | 37W-4S,37W-3S | 44 |
| Adams St. N&S | 36W-4S | 44 |
| Adler St. N&S | 37W-4S | 44 |
| Airport Rd. NE&SW | 37W-4S,36W-4S | 44 |
| Andrew Ct. E&W | 35W-3S | 45 |
| Andrew Ln. N&S | 36W-3S | 44 |
| Anna St. N&S | 36W-3S | 44 |
| April Ln. NS&EW | 36W-3S,35W-3S | 44 |
| Arrowhead E. N&S | 35W-3S | 45 |
| Arrowhead N. N&S | 35W-3S | 45 |
| Arrowhead W. N&S | 35W-3S | 45 |
| Aster Ct. E&W | 34W-3S | 45 |
| Augusta Dr. E&W | 35W-3S | 45 |
| Banbury Rd. N&S | 35W-3S | 45 |
| Basswood Dr. N&S | 37W-3S | 44 |
| Bede Cir. E&W | 35W-3S | 45 |
| Bede Ct. NW&SE | 35W-3S | 45 |
| Birchwood Dr. E&W | 37W-4S,36W-4S | 44 |
| Briar Ln. E&W | 36W-3S,35W-3S | 44 |
| Buckthorn N&S | 37W-4S | 44 |
| Bull Ct. N&S | 37W-4S | 44 |
| Butterfield Rd. NE&SW | 36W-4S,35W-4S | 44 |
| Butternut Dr. | 37W-3S | 44 |
| Candlewick Ct. NE&SW | 37W-4S | 44 |
| Cantigny Ct. NE&SW | 35W-3S | 45 |
| Carrie St. E&W | 35W-3S | 45 |
| Cedar Dr. N&S | 36W-4S | 44 |
| Chantilly Ln. N&S | 36W-4S | 44 |
| Cherry Tree Ct. N&S | 36W-4S | 44 |
| Cherrywood Dr. E&W | 37W-4S,36W-4S | 44 |
| Chestnut St. E&W | 35W-3S | 45 |
| Clark St. N&S | 35W-3S | 45 |
| Coghill Ct. NE&SW | 35W-4S | 45 |
| Conco St. NE&SW | 35W-4S | 45 |
| Cottonwood Dr. E&W | 37W-3S,36W-4S | 44 |
| Cypress Ln. N&S | 37W-4S | 44 |
| Dee Rd. E&W | 36W-3S,35W-3S | 45 |
| Derby Dr. N&S | 34W-3S | 45 |
| Dogwood Ct. N&S | 37W-3S | 44 |
| Dogwood Dr. E&W | 37W-3S | 44 |
| Doral Ln. NW&SE | 35W-3S | 45 |
| East-West Tollway E&W | 36W-5S | 44 |
| Eastview Dr. E&W | 36W-3S | 44 |
| Elm Av. E&W | 36W-3S | 44 |
| Fairfield Way NS&EW | 35W-3S | 45 |
| Fairview Dr. NS&EW | 36W-5S | 44 |
| Farview Ct. E&W | 36W-4S | 44 |
| Farview Dr. E&W | 36W-4S | 44 |
| Feltes Ln. E&W | 35W-4S | 45 |
| Frontage Rd. NE&SW | 35W-4S | 45 |
| Geronimo Dr. NW&SE | 37W-4S | 44 |
| Grace St. N&S | 36W-4S | 44 |
| Grant St. NW&SE | 35W-4S,35W-3S | 45 |
| Greenbrier Ct. NS&EW | 35W-3S | 45 |
| Harmony Ct. N&S | 37W-4S | 44 |
| Harmony Dr. E&W | 37W-4S,36W-4S | 44 |
| Hart Rd. N&S | 34W-3S | 45 |
| Hartfield Way NS&EW | 35W-3S,34W-3S | 45 |
| Hawthorne Dr. N&S | 37W-4S | 44 |
| Hettinger Ln. E&W | 35W-4S | 45 |
| Hickory Ct. N&S | 35W-4S | 45 |
| Hickory St. N&S | 35W-4S,35W-3S | 45 |
| Hill Av. N&S | 35W-3S | 45 |
| Hillside Pl. E&W | 36W-4S | 44 |
| Holly Ct. E&W | 36W-4S | 44 |
| Ice Cream Dr. E&W | 37W-4S | 44 |
| Jessica Ct. N&S | 35W-4S | 45 |
| John St. E&W | 36W-4S | 44 |
| Juniper St. N&S | 37W-4S | 44 |
| Kingswood Dr. E&W | 36W-4S | 44 |
| Larchwood Ln. N&S | 36W-4S,35W-4S | 45 |
| Laurel Dr. N&S | 35W-4S | 45 |
| Lilac St. N&S | 36W-4S | 44 |
| Lincoln St. N&S | 36W-4S | 44 |
| Lincoln Way N&S | 36W-5S,36W-4S | 44 |
| Lindsay Cir. E&W | 35W-3S | 45 |
| Linn St. E&W | 35W-3S | 45 |
| Lloyd St. E&W | 35W-3S | 45 |
| Locust St. E&W | 35W-3S | 45 |
| Long Av. E&W | 35W-4S | 44 |
| Lovedale Ln. E&W | 35W-4S | 44 |
| Magnolia Dr. E&W | 37W-4S | 44 |
| Maple Av. E&W | 36W-3S | 44 |
| Mathias St. E&W | 35W-3S | 45 |
| Meadow Ln. NS&EW | 34W-3S | 45 |
| Mistwood Dr. EW&NS | 36W-4S,35W-3S | 44 |
| Monroe St. N&S | 36W-3S | 44 |
| Napa Ct. E&W | 37W-4S | 44 |
| Oak Av. E&W | 36W-3S | 44 |
| Oak Crest Dr. NW&SE | 35W-3S | 45 |
| Oak Ln. N&S | 35W-3S | 44 |
| Oak St. E&W | 38W-4S,36W-4S | 44 |
| Oakwood NW&SE | 36W-4S | 44 |
| Offutt Ln. N&S | 36W-4S | 44 |
| Pierce St. E&W | 36W-4S,35W-4S | 44 |
| Pine Oak Dr. N&S | 36W-4S | 44 |
| Pinecreek Dr. N&S | 35W-3S | 45 |
| Pinehurst Dr. NW&SE | 35W-3S | 45 |
| Pinehurst Dr. NS&EW | 35W-3S | 45 |
| Pinewood Dr. E&W | 36W-3S | 44 |
| Poplar Pl. N&S | 37W-4S | 44 |
| Poplar St. N&S | 37W-4S | 44 |
| Princeton Ct. N&S | 36W-4S | 44 |
| Princeton Dr. E&W | 37W-4S | 44 |
| Randall Rd. N&S | 37W-4S | 44 |
| Redwing Dr. N&S | 38W-4S | 44 |
| Redwood Ct. E&W | 36W-3S | 44 |
| Riverview St. NE&SW | 36W-4S | 44 |
| Robert St. NW&SE | 36W-4S | 44 |
| Rt. 25 NW&SE | 36W-4S | 44 |
| Rt. 31 N&S | 36W-4S,36W-3S | 44 |
| Rt. 56 NW&SE | 36W-4S | 44 |
| Shagbark E&W | 37W-4S | 44 |
| Sharon Ct. N&S | 35W-3S | 45 |
| Sharon Ln. N&S | 36W-3S,35W-3S | 44 |
| Smoke Tree Dr. NW&SE | 36W-5S | 44 |
| South St. E&W | 35W-5S | 45 |
| Spruce St. N&S | 35W-4S | 45 |
| Spyglass Ct. NE&SW | 35W-3S | 45 |
| Staghorn E&W | 37W-4S | 44 |
| State St. E&W | 37W-4S,36W-4S | 44 |
| Stone Av. N&S | 35W-4S | 45 |
| Sumac Dr. E&W | 38W-4S,37W-4S | 44 |
| Sunshine Dr. NE&SW | 37W-4S | 44 |
| Sycamore Ln. N&S | 36W-4S,36W-3S | 44 |
| Terry Ln. E&W | 35W-3S | 45 |
| Timber Oaks Dr. N&S | 36W-4S,36W-3S | 44 |
| Turnberry Dr. E&W | 35W-3S | 45 |
| Victoria Cir. N&S | 37W-4S | 44 |
| Walnut Dr. N&S | 37W-4S | 44 |
| Wildwood Dr. N&S | 36W-4S,36W-3S | 44 |
| Willow Way N&S | 36W-4S | 44 |
| Wingfoot Dr. NW&SE | 35W-3S | 45 |
| Winterberry Ct. N&S | 34W-3S | 45 |
| Woodlawn Dr. N&S | 35W-3S | 45 |

## Pingree Grove

| | Grid | Page |
|---|---|---|
| Grove St. N&S | 40W-13N | 13 |
| Jackson St. E&W | 41W-13N | 12 |
| Mansfield St. N&S | 41W-14N | 12 |
| Meadowsweet Dr. NW&SE | 40W-14N | 13 |
| Oak St. E&W | 41W-13N | 12 |
| Olandra Way NW&SE | 40W-14N | 13 |
| Prairie Ln. E&W | 41W-13N | 12 |
| Public St. E&W | 41W-14N | 12 |
| Railroad St. NW&SE | 41W-14N | 12 |
| Reinking Rd. N&S | 41W-15N | 12 |
| Store St. NW&SE | 41W-14N | 13 |
| U.S. Rt. 20 E&W | 42W-14N,40W-12N | 12 |
| Yellow Avens Ct. NE&SW | 40W-14N | 13 |

## Plato Township

| | Grid | Page |
|---|---|---|
| Adobe Ridge NW&SE | 39W-9N | 19 |
| Apache Run N&S | 39W-9N | 19 |
| Barr Rd. NS&EW | 44W-12N,42W-12N | 17 |
| Bending Ln. E&W | 41W-13N | 19 |
| Bowes Bend Dr. NS&EW | 41W-9N,40W-9N | 18 |
| Bowes Rd. NW&SE | 40W-10N,39W-9N | 19 |
| Brier Hill Rd. N&S | 44W-12N | 17 |
| Brierwood NW&SE | 43W-8N | 24 |
| Brimfield Dr. NW&SE | 40W-8N | 25 |
| Burlington Rd. NW&SE | 45W-10N,44W-9N | 17 |
| Burlington Rd. NW&SE | 43W-8N | 24 |
| Capulet Cir NE&SW | 39W-10N | 19 |
| Capulet Ct. NW&SE | 39W-11N | 19 |
| Carletta Ln. E&W | 43W-9N | 18 |
| Central Dr. NW&SE | 39W-11N | 19 |
| Channel Ct. N&S | 40W-9N | 19 |
| Channel Dr. N&S | 40W-9N | 19 |
| Cheyenne Dr. NE&SW | 39W-13N | 13 |
| Chicago St. E&W | 41W-10N | 18 |
| Chippewa Pass E&W | 41W-10N | 18 |
| Cir. | 39W-13N | 13 |
| Cliff Dr. NW&SE | 39W-11N | 19 |
| Cloverfield Dr. N&S | 39W-8N | 25 |
| Connors Rd. E&W | 39W-9N | 18 |
| Coombs Rd. N&S | 39W-12N | 19 |
| Corron Rd. N&S | 40W-8N,40W-9N | 25 |
| Crawford Rd. N&S | 40W-8N,40W-9N | 25 |
| Creekview Dr. E&W | 41W-9N | 18 |
| Creekwood Ct. N&S | 40W-9N | 19 |
| Creekwood Dr. E&W | 40W-9N | 19 |
| Current Ct. E&W | 41W-9N | 18 |
| Dittman Rd. N&S | 42W-9N | 18 |
| Elli Thorpe/Pease Rd. E&W | 44W-10N | 17 |
| Greenfield Rd. E&W | 41W-9N | 18 |
| Greenview Ln. NE&SW | 40W-9N | 19 |
| Gunpowder Ln. N&S | 39W-13N | 13 |
| Hartz Ct. E&W | 39W-8N | 25 |
| Heatherington Ct. NE&SW | 40W-9N | 19 |
| Hidden Lakes Dr. N&S | 40W-10N | 19 |
| High Chapparel N&S | 39W-13N | 13 |
| Highbank Ct. NW&SE | 41W-9N | 18 |
| Highland Av. NW&SE | 39W-13N | 13 |
| Hogan Hill E&W | 39W-9N | 19 |
| Hummingbird St. E&W | 42W-12N | 18 |
| Ickenham Ln. NS&EW | 43W-8N,42W-8N | 24 |
| Juliet Dr. NS&EW | 39W-11N | 19 |
| Kendall Rd. N&S | 43W-8N,43W-9N | 24 |
| Kiwi Ct. NE&SW | 42W-12N | 18 |
| Lakeside Ct. NE&SW | 40W-10N | 19 |
| Lenz Rd. E&W | 41W-9N,40W-9N | 18 |
| Lilly St. N&S | 41W-9N | 18 |
| Long Ln. NW&SE | 40W-10N | 19 |
| Lori Ln. E&W | 39W-9N | 19 |
| Marshall Rd. N&S | 41W-12N | 18 |
| McDonald Rd. E&W | 44W-8N,39W-8N | 24 |
| Meadow Dr. NW&SE | 41W-9N | 18 |
| Meadowlark Dr. NW&SE | 42W-12N | 18 |
| Mohawk Tr. N&S | 40W-10N | 19 |
| Muirhead Ct. E&W | 41W-9N | 18 |
| Muirhead Ln. NE&SW | 41W-9N | 18 |
| Muirhead Rd. NE&SW | 41W-9N,41W-10N | 18 |
| Nestler Rd. NE&SW | 39W-9N,39W-10N | 19 |
| Oak Bluff Dr. N&S | 41W-9N | 18 |
| Oak Ridge Dr. N&S | 40W-9N | 19 |
| Oak Tree Ln. NW&SE | 40W-9N | 19 |
| Pease Rd. N&S | 44W-10N | 17 |
| Plank Rd. E&W | 43W-12N,40W-12N | 18 |
| Plato Rd. E&W | 44W-10N,42W-10N | 17 |
| Prairie Crossing N&S | 40W-10N | 19 |
| Pueblo Peak NE&SW | 39W-9N | 19 |
| Red Cloud Ln. NW&SE | 39W-10N | 19 |
| Rippburger Rd. N&S | 41W-10N | 18 |
| Robin Ln. E&W | 42W-12N | 18 |
| Rohrsen Rd. E&W | 43W-11N,41W-11N | 18 |
| Romeo Cir. NW&SE | 39W-11N | 19 |
| Romeo Dr. NE&SW | 39W-11N | 19 |
| Route 47 NS&EW | 43W-8N,43W-9N | 24 |
| Russell Rd. E&W | 41W-11N,39W-11N | 18 |
| Saidon Dr. NW&SE | 39W-11N | 19 |
| Santa Fe Tr. NE&SW | 39W-9N | 19 |
| Silvana Dr. NS&EW | 41W-9N | 18 |
| South Gate Rd. E&W | 43W-8N | 18 |
| Steeple Cir. NW&SE | 43W-8N | 24 |
| Sturbridge Way E&W | 40W-8N | 25 |
| Sunflower Ln. E&W | 40W-9N | 19 |
| Switzer Rd. N&S | 40W-12N | 19 |
| Tamara Dr. E&W | 41W-9N | 18 |
| Tower Rd. N&S | 44W-10N,44W-11N | 17 |
| Tributary Ln. N&S | 41W-10N | 19 |
| U.S. Route 20 NW&SE | 40W-10N | 19 |
| Verona Dr. NW&SE | 39W-11N | 19 |
| W. Lori Ln. E&W | 39W-9N | 19 |
| Western Av. NE&SW | 39W-13N | 13 |
| Whispering Springs Ln. NS&EW | 40W-9N | 19 |
| Wildbriar Ln. E&W | 40W-10N | 19 |
| Woodbridge Ln. NS&EW | 43W-8N | 24 |
| Woodrow Ln. NW&SE | 40W-10N | 19 |

## Prestbury

| | Grid | Page |
|---|---|---|
| Alderley Dr. N&S | 41W-5S,40W-5S | 43 |
| Ashwood Ct. N&S | 40W-5S | 43 |
| Birchwood Ct. NE&SW | 40W-5S | 43 |
| Bliss Rd. N&S | 41W-5S | 43 |
| Briar Gate Cir. N&S | 41W-5S | 43 |
| Buckingham Dr. NW&SE | 41W-5S | 43 |
| Bury Ct. N&S | 41W-5S | 43 |
| Cedar Gate Cir. NW&SE | 41W-5S | 43 |
| Dorchester Ct. N&S | 41W-5S | 43 |
| Fernilee Ct. NW&SE | 41W-5S | 43 |
| Hardwick Ct. NE&SW | 41W-5S | 43 |
| Hathaway Cres. NS&EW | 41W-5S | 43 |
| Hatherley Ct. N&S | 41W-5S | 43 |
| Heaton Ct. N&S | 41W-5S | 43 |
| Merrill New Rd. NE&SW | 41W-5S | 43 |
| Mossfield Ct. NW&SE | 40W-5S | 43 |
| N. Windsor Ct. N&S | 41W-5S | 43 |
| New Bond St. E&W | 41W-5S | 43 |
| Normandie Dr. NW&SE | 41W-5S | 43 |
| Norris Old Rd. NE&SW | 41W-5S | 43 |
| Old Farm Ct. N&S | 41W-5S | 43 |
| Rt. 56 NE&SW | 40W-5S | 43 |
| Saddlewood Ct. E&W | 41W-5S | 43 |
| Walnut Cir. N&S | 41W-5S,40W-5S | 43 |
| Windsor Rd. NW&SE | 41W-6S,41W-5S | 43 |
| Windwood Ct. NW&SE | 41W-5S | 43 |
| Windwood Dr. E&W | 41W-5S | 43 |
| Winthrop New Rd. E&W | 41W-4S | 43 |

## Rutland Township

| | Grid | Page |
|---|---|---|
| Abilene Tr. E&W | 39W-14N | 13 |
| Apache Ln. E&W | 40W-18N | 7 |
| Atchison St. E&W | 40W-15N | 13 |
| Aztec Ln. N&S | 40W-18N | 7 |
| Barko Pkwy. NS&EW | 40W-18N,40W-19N | 7 |
| Baron Ln. E&W | 40W-18N | 7 |
| Big Timber Rd. NW&SE | 43W-17N,40W-16N | 6 |
| Binnie Lakes Tr. N&S | 38W-17N | 7 |
| Binnie Rd. E&W | 38W-17N | 7 |
| Bonnie Ln. N&S | 39W-14N | 13 |
| Carriage Way Ln. N&S | 41W-18N | 6 |
| Charles Ln. E&W | 41W-18N | 6 |
| Cheryl Ct. NE&SW | 41W-18N | 6 |
| Cody Ct. N&S | 39W-14N | 13 |
| Coombs Rd. N&S | 39W-14N | 13 |
| Damisch Rd. NE&SW | 40W-15N | 13 |
| Derby Ct. E&W | 41W-18N | 6 |
| Derby Ln. E&W | 40W-18N,41W-18N | 6 |
| Drendl Rd. NS&EW | 42W-19N | 6 |
| Farm View Ct. E&W | 40W-15N | 13 |
| Freeman Rd. E&W | 41W-18N | 6 |
| Freeman Rd. NW&SE | 41W-18N | 7 |
| Galligan Rd. N&S | 39W-18N | 7 |
| Gary Ln. N&S | 40W-19N | 7 |
| Grand Av. E&W | 39W-14N | 13 |
| Gunpowder Ct. N&S | 39W-14N | 13 |
| Guthrie Ct. E&W | 40W-15N | 13 |
| Harper Dr. E&W | 40W-15N | 13 |
| Hennig Rd. N&S | 43W-18N | 6 |
| Hidden Hills Tr. N&S | 38W-17N | 7 |
| Hidden Knoll Rd. N&S | 39W-14N | 13 |
| Highland Av. E&W | 41W-14N | 12 |
| Homestead Dr. NW&SE | 40W-15N | 12 |
| Huntley Rd. NW&SE | 39W-17N | 7 |
| Karen Ct. NW&SE | 41W-18N | 6 |
| Limerick Ln. N&S | 40W-14N | 13 |
| Manning Rd. N&S | 42W-17N | 6 |
| Maplehurst N&S | 40W-15N | 12 |
| Mary Cir. N&S | 39W-17N | 7 |
| Mary Ln. NS&EW | 39W-17N | 7 |
| McCornack Rd. NE&SW | 40W-14N,39W-15N | 13 |
| Navajo Ln. NW&SE | 40W-18N | 7 |
| Northwest Tollway NW&SE | 43W-18N,39W-16N | 6 |
| Northwind Ln. N&S | 38W-17N | 7 |
| Oak Knoll Rd. N&S | 38W-17N | 8 |
| Old Stage Rd. NE&SW | 41W-15N | 12 |
| Oliver Dr. N&S | 39W-14N | 13 |
| Pheasant Field N&S | 40W-15N | 13 |

| | Grid | Page |
|---|---|---|
| Pleasant Dr. E&W | 39W-14N | 13 |
| Powers Rd. NS&EW | 40W-16N,41W-19N | 13 |
| Red Leaf Rd. NW&SE | 40W-15N | 13 |
| Reinking Rd. NW&SE | 41W-15N,42W-16N | 12 |
| Route 47 N&S | 43W-14N,42W-18N | 12 |
| Route 72 E&W | 43W-15N,39W-16N | 12 |
| Sandwald Rd. N&S | 43W-17N | 6 |
| Settlers Grove Rd. NW&SE | 41W-15N | 12 |
| Springcreek Rd. E&W | 38W-18N | 8 |
| Thurnau Rd. N&S | 43W-14N,43W-15N | 12 |
| Timber Ridge Dr. N&S | 39W-14N | 13 |
| Tower Hill Rd. E&W | 39W-16N | 13 |
| Triple Oaks Farm Rd. E&W | 40W-15N | 13 |
| U.S. Route 20 NW&SE | 43W-15N,42W-14N | 12 |

## Sleepy Hollow

| | Grid | Page |
|---|---|---|
| Acorn Ct. N&S | 35W-15N | 14 |
| Acorn Dr. E&W | 35W-15N | 14 |
| Cir. | 35W-15N | 14 |
| Arabian Pkwy. N&S | 36W-15N | 14 |
| Arlington Pkwy. NS&EW | 36W-15N | 14 |
| Beau Brummel Ct. E&W | 36W-15N | 14 |
| Beau Brummel Dr. E&W | 36W-15N | 14 |
| Belmont Pkwy. N&S | 36W-15N | 14 |
| Brom Ct. NW&SE | 35W-15N | 14 |
| Bullfrog Ln. N&S | 35W-15N | 14 |
| Cir. | 35W-15N | 14 |
| Carol Crescent Dr. N&S | 35W-15N | 14 |
| Christopher Ct. N&S | 35W-15N | 14 |
| Churchill Ct. N&S | 36W-15N | 14 |
| Crane Ct. NE&SW | 36W-15N | 14 |
| Crane Dr. NS&EW | 36W-15N | 14 |
| Dannelle Ct. NE&SW | 35W-15N | 14 |
| Darien Ct. NW&SE | 36W-15N | 14 |
| Darien Ln. N&S | 36W-15N | 14 |
| Deer Ln. NS&EW | 36W-15N | 14 |
| East Hilltop Ln. NS&EW | 36W-15N | 14 |
| Elm Ct. N&S | 34W-15N | 15 |
| Fawn Ct. N&S | 36W-15N | 14 |
| Front Range Rd. N&S | 35W-15N | 14 |
| Gail Ln. E&W | 36W-15N | 14 |
| Glen Oak Dr. NE&SW | 35W-15N | 14 |
| Hawthorne Ct. E&W | 36W-15N | 14 |
| Hazel Ct. N&S | 35W-16N | 14 |
| Hemlock Dr. NS&EW | 34W-15N | 15 |
| Hialeah Ct. NW&SE | 36W-15N | 14 |
| Hickory Ct. NE&SW | 35W-16N | 14 |
| Higgins Rd. E&W | 36W-16N | 14 |
| Hillcrest Dr. E&W | 35W-16N | 14 |
| Cir. | 35W-16N | 14 |
| Hilltop Ct. E&W | 36W-15N | 14 |
| Hilltop Ln. E&W | 35W-15N | 14 |
| Holly Ct. NE&SW | 35W-15N | 14 |
| Island Ct. NW&SE | 35W-15N | 14 |
| Jaclay Ct. NW&SE | 35W-15N | 14 |
| Jamestowne Ct. E&W | 36W-15N | 14 |
| Jamestowne Rd. NS&EW | 36W-15N | 14 |
| Jill Peak Dr. N&S | 35W-15N | 14 |
| Joy Ln. E&W | 36W-15N | 14 |
| Karyn Ct. N&S | 35W-15N | 14 |
| Katrina Dr. N&S | 35W-15N | 14 |
| Katrina Ln. N&S | 35W-15N | 14 |
| Kay Ct. N&S | 35W-15N | 14 |
| Laurel Ct. E&W | 35W-16N | 14 |
| Locust Dr. NS&EW | 35W-15N | 14 |
| Maple Ln. E&W | 34W-15N | 15 |
| Maria Ct. NE&SW | 35W-15N | 14 |
| Cir. | 35W-15N | 14 |
| Palimino Ct. NE&SW | 36W-15N | 14 |
| Paula Ct. NW&SE | 35W-16N | 14 |
| Pimlico Pkwy. NS&EW | 36W-15N | 14 |
| Pine Cone Ln. NE&SW | 35W-16N | 14 |
| Plum Ct. N&S | 35W-15N | 14 |
| Rainbow Dr. NE&SW | 35W-16N | 14 |
| Randall Rd. N&S | 37W-15N | 14 |
| Red Bud Cir. E&W | 36W-15N | 14 |
| River Ridge Dr. NS&EW | 35W-15N | 14 |
| Saddle Club Pkwy. E&W | 36W-15N | 14 |
| Salem Ct. E&W | 36W-15N | 14 |
| Saratoga Pkwy. E&W | 36W-15N | 14 |
| Sharon Dr. N&S | 35W-16N | 14 |
| Sleepy Hollow Rd. N&S | 36W-14N | 14 |
| Cir. | 36W-15N | 14 |
| Surrey Ln. E&W | 35W-15N | 14 |
| Sycamore Ln. E&W | 35W-16N | 14 |
| Thorobred Ln. E&W | 35W-15N | 14 |
| Timber Dr. N&S | 36W-15N | 14 |
| Trails End NE&SW | 35W-15N | 14 |
| Van Tassel Rd. N&S | 36W-15N | 14 |
| Walnut Dr. E&W | 35W-15N | 14 |
| Willow Ln. E&W | 35W-15N,34W-15N | 14 |
| Windcrest Ct. E&W | 36W-15N | 14 |
| Windsor Ct. E&W | 36W-15N | 14 |
| Windsor Dr. E&W | 36W-15N | 14 |
| Winmoor Ct. E&W | 35W-15N | 14 |
| Winmoor Dr. NS&EW | 35W-15N | 14 |

## South Elgin

| | Grid | Page |
|---|---|---|
| Adam Av. N&S | 35W-8N | 27 |
| Adrienne Dr. E&W | 35W-9N | 20 |
| Andover Ct. NW&SE | 36W-8N | 26 |
| Angeline Dr. NS&EW | 35W-9N | 20 |
| Ann St. N&S | 34W-8N | 27 |
| Arron Av. E&W | 35W-8N | 27 |
| Arthur Av. NW&SE | 34W-9N | 21 |
| Barbara Av. E&W | 35W-8N | 27 |
| Barcroft Ct. N&S | 36W-9N | 20 |
| Beach Ct. E&W | 34W-8N | 27 |
| Beck Av. NW&SE | 34W-9N | 21 |
| Belle Ln. E&W | 34W-8N | 27 |
| Boston Ct. N&S | 34W-8N | 27 |
| Brandywine Ct. E&W | 35W-8N | 27 |
| Brittany Ct. N&S | 35W-9N | 20 |
| Brookline St. E&W | 35W-8N | 27 |
| Bunker Hill Av. N&S | 35W-8N | 27 |
| Burke Ln. E&W | 36W-9N | 20 |
| Burnridge NW&SE | 33W-9N | 21 |
| Cambridge Rd. E&W | 35W-8N | 27 |
| Camden Ln., N. E&W | 35W-7N | 27 |
| Camden Ln., W. N&S | 35W-7N | 27 |
| Carla Dr. N&S | 35W-8N | 27 |
| Carlton Ct. NW&SE | 33W-9N | 21 |
| Cascade Ct. N&S | 36W-9N | 20 |
| Castlebar Ct.* E&W | 36W-7N | 27 |
| Cedar Ct. N&S | 35W-7N | 27 |
| Center St. N&S | 34W-8N | 27 |
| Champagne Ln. E&W | 36W-9N | 20 |
| Charles Ct. N&S | 35W-8N | 27 |
| Chatham Ct. E&W | 35W-7N | 27 |
| Cherry St. N&S | 34W-8N | 27 |
| Chipstone Dr. NE&SW | 34W-9N | 21 |
| Churchill Ct.* E&W | 36W-7N | 27 |
| Claren Ct. NE&SW | 35W-9N | 20 |
| Clifton Ct. NW&SE | 36W-9N | 20 |
| Clinton St. E&W | 35W-7N,34W-7N | 27 |
| Clove Ct. N&S | 35W-7N | 27 |
| Cobbler Ct. NE&SW | 35W-7N | 27 |
| Collins St. N&S | 35W-7N,35W-8N | 27 |
| Commerce Dr. N&S | 34W-9N | 21 |
| Concord Av. NS&EW | 35W-8N,34W-8N | 27 |
| Cornell Ct. E&W | 35W-7N | 27 |
| Cornwall Av. NE&SW | 35W-8N,34W-8N | 27 |
| Coventry Ct. E&W | 35W-7N | 27 |
| Crystal Av. E&W | 34W-8N | 27 |
| Dana Dr. E&W | 34W-9N | 21 |
| Danbury Ct. E&W | 35W-8N | 27 |
| Dean Dr. N&S | 35W-8N,35W-9N | 27 |
| Diane Ct. E&W | 35W-9N | 20 |
| Division St. E&W | 35W-8N,34W-8N | 27 |
| Dorset Ct. NW&SE | 35W-8N | 27 |
| Dublin Ct. NE&SW | 35W-8N | 27 |
| Dublin Ln. N&S | 35W-8N | 27 |
| E. Harvard Cir. N&S | 35W-8N | 27 |
| Earl Ln. E&W | 34W-7N | 27 |
| East Av. N&S | 34W-8N | 27 |
| Eastview N&S | 34W-8N | 27 |
| Elizabeth St. E&W | 34W-8N | 27 |
| Exeter Ln. NE&SW | 36W-8N | 26 |
| Fairfax Ct. N&S | 35W-8N | 27 |
| Fairfax Ln. NW&SE | 35W-8N | 27 |
| Fairview Ln. N&S | 36W-9N | 20 |
| Fenwick Ln. N&S | 35W-9N | 20 |
| Fieldcrest Dr. NS&EW | 35W-9N | 20 |
| Foxbury Ct. N&S | 35W-9N | 20 |
| Franklin Av. E&W | 35W-8N | 27 |
| Frederick Ct. N&S | 36W-9N | 20 |
| Fulton St. N&S | 34W-7N,34W-8N | 27 |
| Genevieve Dr. N&S | 35W-9N | 20 |
| Gerald Av. E&W | 35W-9N | 20 |
| Gibbons Ct. N&S | 35W-9N | 20 |
| Gilbert St. NW&SE | 34W-8N | 27 |
| Gilpen Av. N&S | 34W-9N | 21 |
| Gladys Ct. E&W | 36W-9N | 20 |
| Greenfield Av. E&W | 35W-9N | 20 |
| Hancock Av. NE&SW | 35W-7N,35W-8N | 27 |
| Hartman Ct. NW&SE | 34W-9N | 21 |
| Harvard Ct. NW&SE | 35W-8N | 27 |
| Harvest Ln. N&S | 34W-8N | 27 |
| Helen Av. E&W | 35W-8N | 27 |
| Hobart Ct. NS&EW | 35W-9N | 20 |
| Hobart Dr. N&S | 35W-9N | 20 |
| Hollywood NW&SE | 34W-9N | 21 |
| Hollywood Ct. NW&SE | 33W-9N | 21 |
| Howell Dr. N&S | 35W-8N | 27 |
| Independence Av. E&W | 35W-8N,35W-7N | 27 |
| Industrial Dr. E&W | 34W-9N | 21 |
| Ione Dr. N&S | 35W-8N | 27 |
| Ivy Ct. E&W | 35W-7N | 27 |
| James St. E&W | 35W-9N | 20 |
| Jenna Ct. E&W | 35W-9N | 20 |
| Jenna Dr. NS&EW | 35W-9N | 20 |
| Josephine Av. NW&SE | 34W-9N | 21 |
| Juli Ct. N&S | 35W-9N | 20 |
| Juli Dr. NS&EW | 35W-9N | 20 |
| Juniper Ln. N&S | 35W-8N | 27 |
| Kaelynn Ct. NS&EW | 36W-9N | 20 |
| Kane St. E&W | 35W-8N,34W-8N | 27 |
| Kenilworth Av. N&S | 35W-9N | 20 |
| Kingsport Dr. N&S | 36W-8N | 27 |
| Kossuth St. E&W | 34W-8N | 27 |
| La Fox St. N&S | 34W-8N,34W-9N | 27 |
| Lafayette Dr. E&W | 35W-8N | 27 |
| Lakewood Ct., N.* E&W | 36W-7N | 27 |
| Lakewood Ct., S.* E&W | 36W-7N | 27 |
| Lancaster Cir., S. NS&EW | 35W-7N | 27 |
| Lancer Ct.* E&W | 36W-7N | 27 |
| Laura Ct. NS&EW | 36W-9N | 20 |
| Laurel Ct.* E&W | 36W-7N | 27 |
| Lenox Ct.* E&W | 36W-7N | 27 |
| Lexington Av. N&S | 35W-8N | 27 |
| Liberty Av. E&W | 35W-8N,35W-7N | 27 |
| Lilac Ct.* E&W | 36W-7N | 27 |
| Lincoln Ct.* E&W | 36W-7N | 27 |
| Linda Ct. N&S | 34W-7N | 27 |
| Lindemann Ct. N&S | 34W-8N | 27 |
| Linden Ct.* E&W | 36W-7N | 27 |
| Locust Ct.* E&W | 36W-7N | 27 |
| Locust St. E&W | 34W-8N | 27 |
| Longbow Ct.* E&W | 36W-7N | 27 |
| Longview Ct.* E&W | 36W-7N | 27 |
| Lorann St. E&W | 34W-8N | 27 |
| Lowell Dr. N&S | 35W-8N | 27 |
| Lucille Av. E&W | 34W-8N | 27 |
| Main St. NE&SW | 34W-8N | 27 |
| Manchester Ct. E&W | 35W-8N | 27 |
| Marbury St. N&S | 35W-8N | 27 |
| Marcia Ct. N&S | 36W-9N | 20 |
| Marie Ct. E&W | 35W-9N | 20 |
| Mark St. N&S | 34W-7N | 27 |
| Marleigh Ln. NE&SW | 36W-9N | 20 |
| Martin Dr. N&S | 34W-8N,34W-9N | 27 |
| Mavis Av. NW&SE | 34W-9N | 21 |
| Mayfair Ln. N&S | 35W-8N | 27 |
| McLean Blvd. N&S | 35W-8N | 27 |
| Medford Av. E&W | 35W-8N | 27 |
| Melinda Dr. N&S | 35W-8N | 27 |
| Melrose Av. E&W | 34W-9N | 21 |
| Michelle Dr. NE&SW | 36W-9N,35W-9N | 20 |
| Michigan Av. N&S | 35W-8N,35W-9N | 27 |
| Middle St. E&W | 34W-8N | 27 |
| Middleford Ct. N&S | 35W-9N | 20 |
| Mill St. E&W | 34W-8N | 27 |
| Millicent Ct. NE&SW | 36W-9N | 20 |
| Mistic Ct. NW&SE | 33W-9N | 21 |
| Misty Ct. N&S | 36W-9N | 20 |
| Moody Ct. NW&SE | 33W-9N | 21 |
| N. Harvard Cir. E&W | 35W-8N | 27 |
| N. Lancaster Cir. NS&EW | 35W-8N | 27 |
| N. London Ct. N&S | 35W-8N | 27 |
| Nellie Av. E&W | 34W-8N | 27 |
| North Dr. E&W | 34W-7N | 27 |
| Oak St. E&W | 34W-8N | 27 |
| Oxford Ct. NE&SW | 35W-8N | 27 |
| Oxford Ln. NW&SE | 35W-8N | 27 |
| Paine Ct. E&W | 35W-8N | 27 |
| Paine St. NE&SW | 35W-8N | 27 |
| Park Av. E&W | 34W-8N | 27 |
| Patrick St. N&S | 34W-8N | 27 |
| Pembroke Dr., N. NE&SW | 36W-8N | 26 |
| Pembroke Dr., S. NE&SW | 36W-8N | 26 |
| Pleasant Dr. NS&EW | 34W-8N | 27 |
| Plum St. E&W | 34W-8N | 27 |
| Prairie St. E&W | 34W-8N | 27 |
| Production Dr. E&W | 34W-9N | 21 |
| Public Rd. E&W | 34W-9N | 21 |
| Quarry St. E&W | 34W-8N | 27 |
| Rainbow Ter. E&W | 35W-9N | 20 |
| Raymond St. NE&SW | 33W-9N | 21 |
| Regent St. N&S | 34W-8N | 27 |
| Renee Dr. N&S | 35W-8N,35W-9N | 27 |
| Revere E&W | 35W-8N | 27 |
| Ridge Ct. N&S | 35W-9N | 20 |
| Ridge Rd. N&S | 35W-9N | 20 |
| River Rd. NE&SW | 34W-9N,33W-9N | 21 |
| River St. N&S | 34W-8N | 27 |
| Riverside Av. NE&SW | 34W-8N | 27 |
| Riverview Av. NE&SW | 33W-9N | 21 |
| Robertson Rd. N&S | 34W-8N,34W-9N | 27 |
| Ross Av. NW&SE | 34W-9N | 21 |
| Rt. 25 N&S | 33W-7N,33W-8N | 27 |
| Rt. 31 NE&SW | 34W-9N | 21 |
| S. Elgin Blvd. N&S | 34W-8N,34W-9N | 27 |
| S. London Ct. N&S | 35W-8N | 27 |
| Sandhurst Ln. NS&EW | 35W-8N | 27 |
| Sara Ct. N&S | 36W-9N | 20 |
| Saratoga Ct. N&S | 35W-8N | 27 |
| Schneider Dr. N&S | 34W-9N | 21 |
| Sheffield Ct. E&W | 35W-9N | 20 |
| Smith Ct. NW&SE | 34W-9N | 21 |
| South St. E&W | 34W-8N | 27 |
| Spring Av. E&W | 34W-8N | 27 |
| Spring St. E&W | 35W-8N | 27 |
| Spruce St. E&W | 34W-8N | 27 |
| State St. E&W | 35W-8N,34W-8N | 27 |
| Stearns Rd. E&W | 32W-7N | 27 |
| Stevenson Rd. E&W | 35W-9N,34W-9N | 20 |
| Steves Farm Rd. E&W | 34W-9N | 21 |
| Stone St. E&W | 34W-8N | 27 |
| Strathmore Ter. N&S | 35W-8N | 27 |
| Sunbrook St. E&W | 35W-8N | 27 |
| Sunbury Rd. E&W | 35W-8N | 27 |
| Sundown Dr. E&W | 35W-9N | 20 |
| Sundown Rd. E&W | 35W-9N,34W-9N | 20 |
| Sweetbriar Ct. N&S | 35W-8N | 27 |
| Timber Ln. E&W | 36W-8N | 27 |
| Trenton Av. N&S | 35W-8N | 27 |
| Valley Forge Av. NE&SW | 35W-8N,34W-8N | 27 |
| Valley Forge Ct. NW&SE | 35W-8N | 27 |
| Vernon Ct. NW&SE | 35W-7N | 27 |
| Village Ct. E&W | 35W-7N | 27 |
| Virginia Dr. N&S | 34W-8N | 27 |
| W. Harvard Cir. N&S | 35W-8N | 27 |
| Walnut St. N&S | 34W-8N | 27 |
| Water St. N&S | 34W-8N,34W-9N | 27 |
| Wedgewood Dr. N&S | 35W-8N | 27 |
| Weston Ct. N&S | 36W-8N | 26 |
| Whispering Ct. NW&SE | 34W-8N | 27 |
| Williams Dr. E&W | 34W-7N | 27 |
| Willis St. E&W | 34W-8N | 27 |
| Wilson Way E&W | 34W-9N | 21 |
| Woodbridge Cir. E&W | 34W-7N | 27 |
| Woodbury St. N&S | 34W-8N | 27 |
| Woodrow NW&SE | 34W-9N | 21 |
| Yorkshire Ct. E&W | 35W-8N | 27 |

## St. Charles*

**(Also see Du Page County)**

| | Grid | Page |
|---|---|---|
| Adams Av. NE&SW | 35W-2N,34W-2N | 33 |
| Adams Ct. NW&SE | 34W-2N | 33 |
| Adare Ct. N&S | 34W-3N | 33 |
| Aintree Rd. NW&SE | 34W-4N | 33 |
| Alice Ct. NW&SE | 36W-2N | 32 |
| Allen Ln. E&W | 35W-3N,34W-3N | 33 |
| Andover Av. NE&SW | 34W-2N | 33 |
| Arrowhead Ln. N&S | 33W-3N | 33 |
| Ash St. N&S | 35W-2N | 33 |
| Ashbrooke Ct. N&S | 36W-5N | 26 |
| Auburn Ct. E&W | 36W-3N | 33 |
| Avalon Ct. E&W | 36W-2N | 32 |
| Banbury Av. NS&EW | 34W-2N | 33 |
| Banbury Ct. N&S | 34W-2N | 33 |
| Beatrice Av. E&W | 34W-2N | 33 |
| Benham Ct. E&W | 36W-3N | 33 |
| Bent Av. E&W | 35W-3N | 33 |
| Blackhawk Ct. E&W | 33W-3N | 33 |
| Blackhawk Tr. E&W | 33W-4N | 33 |
| Bowman St. E&W | 35W-2N | 33 |
| Bradley Cir. E&W | 36W-3N | 32 |
| Brook St. E&W | 36W-3N | 32 |
| Campton Hills Rd. E&W | 37W-3N | 32 |
| Canidae Ct. NE&SW | 34W-4N | 33 |
| Carrol Ct. NW&SE | 36W-3N | 32 |
| Carrol Rd. N&S | 36W-3N | 32 |
| Cedar Av. NE&SW | 35W-3N | 33 |
| Cedar St. NE&SW | 36W-3N,35W-3N | 32 |
| Chandler Av. NS&EW | 33W-2N | 33 |
| Charlemagne Ln. NE&SW | 33W-4N | 33 |
| Charleston Dr. NE&SW | 36W-2N | 32 |
| Chasse Cir. NS&EW | 34W-4N | 33 |
| Chesapeake Rd. N&S | 36W-5N | 26 |
| Chestnut Av. NE&SW | 35W-3N | 33 |
| Concord Ct. NE&SW | 34W-2N | 33 |
| Country Club Rd. E&W | 35W-4N,33W-4N | 33 |
| Crabapple Ln. NS&EW | 35W-3N,34W-4N | 33 |
| Cranbrook Av. NE&SW | 34W-2N | 33 |
| Crane Rd. E&W | 35W-4N | 33 |
| Creekside Ct. N&S | 36W-4N | 32 |
| Cumberland Green Dr. NE&SW | 34W-2N,33W-2N | 33 |
| Cumberland Pkwy. E&W | 33W-2N | 33 |
| Cutler St. E&W | 36W-2N,35W-2N | 32 |
| De Bruyne St. N&S | 36W-3N | 32 |
| Dean St. NW&SE | 36W-3N | 32 |
| Deerfield Ct. NE&SW | 34W-2N | 33 |
| Delnor Av. E&W | 35W-3N | 33 |
| Derby Course NS&EW | 34W-3N | 33 |
| Devereaux Way E&W | 35W-2N | 33 |
| Division Ct. NS&EW | 34W-1N | 33 |
| Division St. E&W | 34W-2N | 33 |
| Dixmoor Ct. E&W | 36W-5N | 26 |
| Dover Ln. E&W | 34W-3N | 33 |
| Dukane Dr. NW&SE | 33W-3N | 33 |
| Dunham Pl. NS&EW | 34W-3N,34W-4N | 33 |
| Dunham Rd. NE&SW | 34W-3N,33W-4N | 33 |
| Edgewild Ct. E&W | 35W-4N | 33 |
| Edward Av. E&W | 34W-2N | 33 |
| Elm St. NE&SW | 35W-2N | 33 |
| Elmtree Ct. NE&SW | 36W-4N | 32 |
| Emery Ct. NE&SW | 34W-2N | 33 |
| Essex Ct. NE&SW | 34W-3N | 33 |
| Evergreen E&W | 36W-2N | 32 |
| Fairfax Rd. E&W | 34W-3N | 33 |
| Fairview Dr. NS&EW | 36W-2N | 32 |
| Fairway Ct. NW&SE | 35W-4N | 33 |
| Fellows St. E&W | 36W-2N,35W-2N | 32 |
| Fern Av. E&W | 34W-2N | 33 |
| Ferson Creek Rd. NE&SW | 36W-3N | 32 |
| Fieldgate Dr. N&S | 33W-3N | 33 |
| Forest Av. NE&SW | 34W-2N | 33 |
| Forest Ridge Rd. NS&EW | 34W-3N | 33 |
| Fox Chase Blvd. NS&EW | 34W-3N,34W-4N | 33 |
| Fox Chase Cir. NE&SW | 33W-4N | 33 |
| Fox Chase Ct. N&S | 33W-4N | 33 |
| Fox Chase Dr. E&W | 33W-4N | 33 |
| Fox Ct. E&W | 35W-3N | 33 |
| Fox Hunt Ln. NE&SW | 33W-4N | 33 |
| Fox Meadow Ct. E&W | 36W-3N | 32 |
| Foxfield Ct. N&S | 33W-3N | 33 |
| Foxfield Dr. NE&SW | 33W-4N,33W-3N | 33 |
| Foxfield Rd. E&W | 34W-3N | 33 |
| Foxglade Ct. N&S | 35W-2N | 33 |
| Foxhill Ct. NS&EW | 34W-3N | 33 |
| Foxwood Ln. NS&EW | 34W-4N | 33 |
| Fulton Av. NE&SW | 35W-3N | 33 |
| Garden Hill Ln. E&W | 34W-2N | 33 |
| Geneva Rd. NW&SE | 35W-2N | 33 |
| Gray St. E&W | 36W-2N,35W-2N | 32 |
| Green Willow Ln. NE&SW | 35W-4N,35W-5N | 33 |
| Greenwood Ln. N&S | 36W-5N,36W-4N | 33 |
| Hampton Course Dr. NE&SW | 34W-4N | 33 |
| Highgate Course NE&SW | 34W-4N,33W-4N | 33 |
| Highgate Ct. E&W | 33W-4N | 33 |
| Horne St. E&W | 36W-2N,35W-2N | 32 |
| Howard St. E&W | 36W-2N | 32 |
| Huntington Rd. NW&SE | 34W-3N | 33 |
| Illinois Av. E&W | 35W-3N,33W-3N | 33 |
| Illinois St. NE&SW | 35W-2N | 33 |
| Independence Av. NS&EW | 34W-2N | 33 |
| Independence Ct. NE&SW | 34W-2N | 33 |
| Indian Way NW&SE | 33W-4N | 33 |
| Indiana Av. NE&SW | 35W-2N,34W-3N | 33 |
| Indiana St. E&W | 36W-2N,35W-2N | 32 |
| Industrial Dr. NE&SW | 34W-3N | 33 |

| | Grid | Page |
|---|---|---|
| Iroquois Av. E&W | 35W-3N,34W-3N | 33 |
| Jackson Av. NW&SE | 35W-2N | 33 |
| Jay Ln. N&S | 34W-2N | 33 |
| Jeanette Av. E&W | 34W-2N | 33 |
| Jefferson Av. NE&SW | 35W-2N | 33 |
| Jeffery Ct. N&S | 34W-3N | 33 |
| Jewel Av. E&W | 34W-2N | 33 |
| Jobe Av. E&W | 34W-2N | 33 |
| Johnor Av. E&W | 35W-4N | 33 |
| Katharine St. N&S | 36W-2N | 32 |
| Kautz Rd. N&S | 33W-2N,33W-3N | 33 |
| Kehoe Dr. NS&EW | 36W-2N | 32 |
| Kellar Pl. NE&SW | 35W-2N | 33 |
| Kensington Pl. E&W | 35W-4N | 33 |
| Kildeer Ln. N&S | 35W-4N | 33 |
| King Alfred Ct. N&S | 33W-4N | 33 |
| King Charles Ln. NE&SW | 33W-4N | 33 |
| King Edward St. N&S | 33W-4N | 33 |
| King George Ln. NE&SW | 33W-4N | 33 |
| King Henry Ln. NW&SE | 33W-4N | 33 |
| King James Av. N&S | 33W-4N | 33 |
| King James Ct. E&W | 33W-4N | 33 |
| King Richard Cir. NS&EW | 33W-4N | 33 |
| King Richard Ct. N&S | 33W-4N | 33 |
| King William Ct. E&W | 33W-4N | 33 |
| Kirk Rd. N&S | 33W-2N | 33 |
| Kirk Rd., N. N&S | 33W-3N,33W-4N | 33 |
| Lakewood Cir. NS&EW | 36W-4N | 32 |
| Lancaster Av. E&W | 34W-2N | 33 |
| Larson Av. E&W | 34W-2N,33W-2N | 33 |
| Lewis Ct. NW&SE | 36W-3N | 32 |
| Liberty Av. N&S | 34W-2N | 33 |
| Liberty Ct. NE&SW | 34W-2N | 33 |
| Lincoln Hwy. E&W | 37W-2N | 32 |
| Long Meadow Cir. NS&EW | 34W-3N | 33 |
| Lucylle Av. N&S | 34W-2N | 33 |
| Lucylle Ct. N&S | 34W-2N | 33 |
| Madison Av. E&W | 35W-2N,34W-2N | 33 |
| Madison Ct. N&S | 34W-2N | 33 |
| Main St. E&W | 36W-3N,33W-3N | 32 |
| Manley Rd. NW&SE | 36W-3N | 32 |
| Maple Av. NW&SE | 35W-2N | 33 |
| Margaret Ct. N&S | 36W-2N | 32 |
| Marie St. N&S | 36W-2N | 32 |
| Marion Av. E&W | 35W-3N | 33 |
| Mark St. E&W | 36W-3N,35W-3N | 32 |
| McKinley St. E&W | 35W-2N | 33 |
| Meadows Rd. NE&SW | 35W-4N | 33 |
| Midway Av. N&S | 34W-2N | 33 |
| Midway Dr. N&S | 34W-2N | 33 |
| Milburn Ct. E&W | 36W-2N | 32 |
| Mildred Av. N&S | 34W-2N | 33 |
| Millington Way NS&EW | 36W-3N | 32 |
| Mockingbird Ct. N&S | 36W-5N | 26 |
| Monroe Av. NW&SE | 35W-2N | 33 |
| Moore Av. E&W | 34W-2N | 33 |
| Moore Ct. NS&EW | 34W-2N | 33 |
| Mosedale St. E&W | 36W-2N,35W-2N | 32 |
| Muirfield Ct. E&W | 33W-4N | 33 |
| Munhall Av. N&S | 34W-2N,34W-3N | 33 |
| Nicholas Av. N&S | 34W-2N | 33 |
| North Av. E&W | 35W-3N,33W-3N | 33 |
| Oak St. NE&SW | 36W-2N,35W-2N | 32 |
| Oakhill Ct. NE&SW | 36W-4N | 32 |
| Ohio Av. E&W | 35W-2N,33W-2N | 33 |
| Oxbow Ln. E&W | 33W-4N | 33 |
| Oxmoor Ct. E&W | 36W-5N | 26 |
| Park Av. NE&SW | 35W-3N | 33 |
| Patricia Av. NS&EW | 34W-2N | 33 |
| Peck Rd. N&S | 38W-2N | 32 |
| Permission Ct. NE&SW | 35W-3N | 33 |
| Permission Dr. NE&SW | 35W-3N,34W-4N | 33 |
| Pine St. N&S | 35W-2N | 33 |
| Pleasant Av. NE&SW | 34W-2N | 33 |
| Pomeroy Ct. NE&SW | 34W-2N | 33 |
| Post Rd. N&S | 34W-3N | 33 |
| Prairie St. NE&SW | 36W-2N,35W-2N | 32 |
| Prestwick Ct. N&S | 33W-5N | 27 |
| Private Rd. NW&SE | 33W-4N | 33 |
| Production Dr. E&W | 34W-3N,33W-3N | 33 |
| Queen Anne Ct. E&W | 33W-4N | 33 |

| | Grid | Page |
|---|---|---|
| Queen Elizabeth Ct. E&W | 33W-4N | 33 |
| Railroad Pl. N&S | 34W-2N | 33 |
| Randall Rd. N&S | 37W-3N | 32 |
| Redden Ct. NE&SW | 36W-3N | 32 |
| Rita Av. E&W | 34W-2N,33W-2N | 33 |
| River Valley Rd. NE&SW | 35W-4N | 33 |
| Riverside Av. NW&SE | 35W-2N | 33 |
| Ronzheimer Av. E&W | 34W-2N | 33 |
| Roosevelt St. E&W | 35W-2N | 33 |
| Royal & Ancient Dr. N&S | 33W-5N | 27 |
| Royal Ashdown Ct. NE&SW | 33W-4N | 33 |
| Royal Fox Ct. E&W | 33W-4N | 33 |
| Royal Fox Dr. N&S | 33W-4N | 33 |
| Royal Kings Ct. E&W | 33W-4N | 33 |
| Royal Lytham Ct. NW&SE | 33W-4N | 33 |
| Royal Lytham Dr. NE&SW | 33W-4N | 33 |
| Royal Queens Ct. NW&SE | 33W-4N | 33 |
| Royal St.Anne Ct. E&W | 33W-5N | 27 |
| Royal St.Georges Ct. NW&SE | 33W-4N | 33 |
| Royal St.James Ct. E&W | 33W-4N | 33 |
| Royal Troon Ct. N&S | 33W-5N | 27 |
| Royal Windyne Ct. E&W | 33W-5N | 27 |
| Rt. 25 N&S | 34W-2N,35W-4N | 33 |
| Rt. 31 N&S | 35W-2N,35W-4N | 33 |
| Rt. 64 NW&SE | 36W-3N,33W-3N | 32 |
| Ruth Av. NE&SW | 34W-2N | 33 |
| Ryan St. NE&SW | 36W-3N | 32 |
| Secretariat Ct. N&S | 34W-3N | 33 |
| Sedgewick Cir. NW&SE | 36W-3N | 32 |
| Shabbona Av. N&S | 35W-3N | 33 |
| Shires Ln. E&W | 34W-4N | 33 |
| Shoreline Ct. NE&SW | 36W-4N | 32 |
| Shoreline Dr. NS&EW | 36W-4N | 32 |
| Short St. E&W | 36W-2N | 32 |
| Smith Rd. E&W | 33W-3N | 33 |
| South Av. NE&SW | 35W-2N,34W-3N | 33 |
| Southgate Course NW&SE | 34W-4N | 33 |
| Southgate Ct. NE&SW | 34W-4N | 33 |
| Spring Av. NE&SW | 35W-2N,34W-2N | 33 |
| Squire Ln. E&W | 34W-4N,33W-4N | 33 |
| St. Andrews Ct. E&W | 33W-5N | 27 |
| State Av. E&W | 35W-3N | 33 |
| State St. E&W | 36W-3N,35W-3N | 32 |
| Sterling Ct. N&S | 34W-3N | 33 |
| Stern Av. NW&SE | 33W-2N | 33 |
| Stetson Av. NE&SW | 33W-2N | 33 |
| Stirrup Cup Ct. NW&SE | 34W-4N | 33 |
| Stone Dr. N&S | 34W-3N | 33 |
| Stonehedge Rd. NW&SE | 35W-3N,34W-3N | 33 |
| Stonewood Dr. N&S | 34W-4N | 33 |
| Swenson Av. NW&SE | 33W-2N | 33 |
| Tall Grass Ct. N&S | 34W-3N | 33 |
| Temple Garden Ct. N&S | 34W-2N | 33 |
| Thornhill Farm Ln. E&W | 35W-4N | 33 |
| Timbers Cir. NW&SE | 36W-3N | 32 |
| Timbers Ct. N&S | 36W-3N | 32 |
| Timbers Pl. NW&SE | 36W-3N | 32 |
| Timbers Trail E&W | 36W-3N | 32 |
| Turnberry Rd. N&S | 33W-4N | 33 |
| Tyler Rd. N&S | 34W-2N,34W-3N | 33 |
| Union Av. E&W | 34W-2N | 33 |
| Van Buren Av. NW&SE | 35W-2N | 33 |
| Via Veneto Dr. N&S | 34W-2N | 33 |
| Walnut Av. NE&SW | 35W-3N | 33 |
| Walnut Dr. NS&EW | 36W-2N | 32 |
| Walnut Hills Av. E&W | 34W-2N | 33 |
| Walnut St. NE&SW | 36W-2N,35W-2N | 32 |
| Washington Av. NE&SW | 35W-2N | 33 |
| Waverly Cir. E&W | 34W-3N | 33 |
| Weber Av. N&S | 33W-2N | 33 |
| Wessel Ct. E&W | 36W-2N | 32 |
| Westfield Dr. NE&SW | 36W-2N | 32 |
| Wexford Ct. E&W | 36W-4N | 33 |
| White Oak Cir. NS&EW | 35W-2N | 33 |
| Whittington Course NS&EW | 34W-4N | 33 |

| | Grid | Page |
|---|---|---|
| Wildrose Springs Dr. NE&SW | 36W-4N | 32 |
| Williams Av. NW&SE | 34W-2N | 33 |
| Wing Av. E&W | 35W-3N,34W-3NW | 33 |
| Wing Ln. NS&EW | 34W-3N | 33 |
| Woodcreek Ct. E&W | 36W-4N | 32 |
| 1st Av. NW&SE | 35W-2N,35W-3N | 33 |
| 1st St. NW&SE | 35W-2N,35W-3N | 33 |
| 2nd Av. NW&SE | 35W-2N,35W-3N | 33 |
| 2nd Pl. N&S | 34W-2N | 33 |
| 2nd St. NW&SE | 35W-2N,35W-3N | 33 |
| 3rd Av. NW&SE | 35W-2N,35W-3N | 33 |
| 3rd Pl. N&S | 34W-2N | 33 |
| 3rd St. NW&SE | 35W-2N,35W-3N | 33 |
| 4th Av. NW&SE | 35W-2N,35W-3N | 33 |
| 4th Pl. N&S | 34W-2N | 33 |
| 4th St. N&S | 35W-2N,35W-3N | 33 |
| 5th Av. NW&SE | 35W-2N,35W-3N | 33 |
| 5th Pl. N&S | 34W-2N | 33 |
| 5th St. NW&SE | 35W-2N,35W-3N | 33 |
| 6th Av. NW&SE | 35W-2N,35W-3N | 33 |
| 6th St. NW&SE | 36W-3N,35W-2N | 32 |
| 7th Av. NW&SE | 34W-2N,35W-3N | 33 |
| 7th Ct. N&S | 35W-2N | 33 |
| 7th St. NW&SE | 36W-3N,35W-2N | 32 |
| 8th Av. NW&SE | 35W-3N | 33 |
| 8th Ct. N&S | 36W-2N | 32 |
| 8th St. N&S | 36W-2N | 32 |
| 9th Av. NW&SE | 34W-2N,35W-3N | 33 |
| 9th St. N&S | 36W-2N,36W-3N | 32 |
| 10th Av. NW&SE | 34W-2N,35W-3N | 33 |
| 10th Ct. N&S | 36W-2N | 32 |
| 10th St. N&S | 36W-2N | 32 |
| 11th Av. NW&SE | 34W-2N,35W-3N | 33 |
| 11th St. N&S | 36W-2N,36W-3N | 32 |
| 12th Av. NW&SE | 34W-2N,35W-3N | 33 |
| 12th St. N&S | 36W-2N,36W-3N | 32 |
| 13th Av. NW&SE | 34W-3N,34W-2N | 33 |
| 13th St. N&S | 36W-2N | 32 |
| 14th Av. NW&SE | 34W-3N | 33 |
| 14th Ct. NW&SE | 36W-2N | 32 |
| 14th St. NS&EW | 36W-2N | 32 |
| 15th Ct. N&S | 36W-2N | 32 |
| 15th St. N&S | 36W-2N,36W-3N | 32 |
| 16th St. N&S | 36W-2N | 32 |
| 17th St. N&S | 36W-2N,36W-3N | 32 |
| 18th St. N&S | 36W-2N | 32 |
| 19th St. N&S | 36W-2N | 32 |
| 37th Av. NE&SW | 33W-3N | 33 |
| 38th Av. NE&SW | 33W-3N | 33 |

## St. Charles Township

| | Grid | Page |
|---|---|---|
| Adele Ln. E&W | 38W-7N | 26 |
| Aldrea Ct. NE&SW | 36W-7N | 26 |
| Amherst Ct. NE&SW | 38W-4N | 32 |
| Aurora Av. N&S | 35W-6N | 27 |
| Babson Ln. N&S | 37W-3N,37W-4N | 32 |
| Baker Ln. NS&EW | 37W-5N | 26 |
| Barb Hill Dr. NS&EW | 38W-7N | 26 |
| Barbara Ann Dr. N&S | 37W-3N | 32 |
| Barton Dr. E&W | 36W-6N | 26 |
| Bernice Dr. NS&EW | 38W-3N | 32 |
| Bittersweet Rd. N&S | 37W-3N | 32 |
| Blackhawk Dr. NW&SE | 35W-6N,35W-7N | 27 |
| Bluestem Ct. N&S | 38W-7N | 26 |
| Bluff Dr. E&W | 35W-5N | 27 |
| Bluff Dr., N. NE&SW | 35W-5N | 27 |
| Bluff Dr., S. N&S | 35W-5N | 27 |
| Bolcum Rd. E&W | 38W-6N,37W-6N | 26 |
| Bonfield Av. E&W | 35W-6N | 27 |
| Bonnie Ct. E&W | 38W-3N | 32 |
| Bonnie Dr. NW&SE | 38W-3N,38W-4N | 32 |
| Bonnie Ln. N&S | 38W-3N | 32 |
| Bonnie St. E&W | 33W-2N | 33 |
| Brewster Creek Ct. NW&SE | 34W-7N | 27 |
| Bricker Rd. E&W | 37W-2N | 32 |
| Bristol Ct. N&S | 36W-6N | 26 |
| Bristol Rd. E&W | 36W-6N | 26 |
| Brookwood Rd. E&W | 35W-5N | 27 |

| | Grid | Page |
|---|---|---|
| Burr Oak Ln. NW&SE | 38W-6N | 26 |
| Burr Rd. N&S | 38W-4N,38W-6N | 32 |
| Burrside Ln. SW&NE | 38W-6N | 26 |
| Carl Lee Rd. N&S | 34W-6N | 27 |
| Cary St. NE&SW | 35W-6N,35W-7N | 27 |
| Catalpa Av. E&W | 35W-6N | 27 |
| Cedar Rock Av. NW&SE | 35W-6N | 27 |
| Center Dr. E&W | 34W-7N | 27 |
| Chickasaw Ct. E&W | 38W-7N | 26 |
| Cibis Rd. NE&SW | 38W-3N | 32 |
| Circle Dr. NE&SW | 34W-6N | 27 |
| Cloverfield Dr. E&W | 38W-7N | 26 |
| Cloverfield Dr. E&W | 38W-7N | 26 |
| Clubhouse Dr. E&W | 38W-5N | 26 |
| Clyde Ct. NE&SW | 35W-6N,34W-6N | 27 |
| Clyde Park Way E&W | 34W-6N | 27 |
| Colley Dr. E&W | 34W-6N | 27 |
| Colombine East NE&SW | 38W-7N | 26 |
| Colombine West NE&SW | 38W-7N | 26 |
| Correl Ct. N&S | 38W-7N | 26 |
| Courier Av. E&W | 34W-6N | 27 |
| Crane Ln. E&W | 37W-4N | 32 |
| Crane Rd. NS&EW | 37W-7N,36W-4N | 26 |
| Creekside Dr. NW&SE | 38W-6N,37W-6N | 26 |
| Creekview Ln. N&S | 38W-5N | 26 |
| Dean St. NW&SE | 38W-4N,36W-3N | 32 |
| Decatur Av. N&S | 34W-6N | 27 |
| Deerpath Way NW&SE | 36W-5N | 26 |
| Denny Dr. NW&SE | 33W-2N | 33 |
| Detroit St. E&W | 34W-6N | 27 |
| Dogwood Ln. NW&SE | 38W-7N | 26 |
| Dorchester Rd. E&W | 36W-5N | 26 |
| Dover Hill Rd. NW&SE | 36W-4N,36W-5N | 32 |
| E. Ridgewood Dr. N&S | 36W-5N,36W-6N | 26 |
| Eagle Ct. NE&SW | 38W-5N | 26 |
| Eagle's Nest Ct. E&W | 38W-7N | 26 |
| East Dr. N&S | 34W-7N | 27 |
| Elder Av. E&W | 35W-6N | 27 |
| Elgin Av. N&S | 35W-6N,35W-7N | 27 |
| Elgin St. NE&SW | 35W-6N,35W-7N | 27 |
| Elliott Ct. NE&SW | 38W-4N | 32 |
| Elmwood Av. E&W | 35W-6N | 27 |
| Emily Ln. NW&SE | 34W-6N | 27 |
| Essex Av. N&S | 35W-6N | 27 |
| Evenswood Ln. NW&SE | 38W-4N | 32 |
| Fairview Av. E&W | 35W-6N | 27 |
| Fairway Dr. NS&EW | 38W-5N | 26 |
| Falcons Tr. N&S | 38W-7N,38W-8N | 26 |
| Fence Rail Ct. NW&SE | 36W-5N | 26 |
| Ferson Creek Rd. NS&EW | 36W-3N,36W-4N | 32 |
| Ferson Woods Dr. NS&EW | 38W-6N | 26 |
| Fieldcrest Dr. NW&SE | 36W-5N,35W-5N | 26 |
| Fieldstone Ct. NE&SW | 36W-4N | 32 |
| Five Island Rd. E&W | 34W-6N | 27 |
| Florence Ln. N&S | 35W-6N | 27 |
| Foley Ln. N&S | 36W-6N | 26 |
| Fox River Av. N&S | 34W-6N | 27 |
| Fox River Dr. E&W | 35W-6N | 27 |
| Foxbluff Ct. NE&SW | 36W-5N | 26 |
| Foxbluff Dr. NE&SW | 36W-5N | 26 |
| Foxglove Ct. N&S | 38W-7N | 26 |
| Foxwood Ct. N&S | 38W-6N | 26 |
| Foxwood Ln. E&W | 38W-6N | 26 |
| Geneva Av. N&S | 34W-6N | 27 |
| Glad Ln. N&S | 38W-3N | 32 |
| Glenoak Ln. NE&SW | 38W-5N | 26 |
| Glenview Dr. NS&EW | 38W-6N | 26 |
| Glenwood Dr. N&S | 36W-6N | 26 |
| Golfview Ct. E&W | 38W-5N | 26 |
| Goodrich Av. N&S | 35W-6N | 27 |
| Grandma's Ln. NS&EW | 37W-4N | 32 |
| Greenlawn Av. NW&SE | 35W-6N | 27 |
| Greenview Ct. NW&SE | 38W-5N | 26 |
| Grey Barn Rd. NS&EW | 37W-5N | 26 |
| Grove Av. NE&SW | 35W-5N | 27 |
| Gustavus Ln. E&W | 37W-4N | 32 |
| Halsted Av. N&S | 35W-6N | 27 |
| Hampton Dr. N&S | 36W-7N | 26 |
| Hawkins Ln. E&W | 38W-5N | 26 |
| Hawthorn Dr. N&S | 36W-3N | 32 |
| Henricksen Rd. N&S | 38W-6N | 26 |

| | Grid | Page |
|---|---|---|
| Heritage Ct. N&S | 38W-6N | 26 |
| Hickory Ct. E&W | 36W-7N | 26 |
| Hickory Ln. NW&SE | 34W-6N,34W-7N | 27 |
| High Point Ct. E&W | 37W-6N | 26 |
| Highview Ct. E&W | 35W-5N | 27 |
| Hill Ct. NW&SE | 34W-7N | 27 |
| Hillcrest Av. E&W | 35W-6N | 27 |
| Hillside Dr. N&S | 35W-6N | 27 |
| Hilltop Dr. E&W | 38W-3N | 32 |
| Hunter's Gate Rd. NS&EW | 36W-5N | 26 |
| Illinois St. NE&SW | 34W-6N | 27 |
| Indian Mound Rd. E&W | 36W-3N | 32 |
| International Dr. E&W | 33W-2N | 33 |
| Iowa St. E&W | 34W-6N | 27 |
| Irving Av. N&S | 35W-6N,35W-7N | 27 |
| Irwin Av. NE&SW | 35W-6N | 27 |
| Jackson Av. N&S | 35W-6N,35W-7N | 27 |
| James Dr. E&W | 35W-6N,34W-6N | 27 |
| Joan Ct. E&W | 38W-3N | 32 |
| Joan Dr. NS&EW | 38W-3N | 32 |
| Joseph St. NE&SW | 35W-7N | 27 |
| Kane Av. E&W | 35W-6N | 27 |
| Kautz Rd. N&S | 33W-2N | 33 |
| Kearns St. NE&SW | 35W-7N | 27 |
| Kimberly Dr. E&W | 36W-7N | 26 |
| Knoll Creek Dr. NS&EW | 37W-4N | 32 |
| Lake Charlotte Ct. NW&SE | 38W-3N | 32 |
| Lambert Av. E&W | 35W-5N | 27 |
| Lancaster Rd. NW&SE | 36W-7N | 26 |
| Landing Dr. N&S | 34W-6N,34W-7N | 27 |
| Leola Ln. NE&SW | 37W-5N | 26 |
| Lilac Ln. NS&EW | 38W-7N | 26 |
| Lincoln Dr. N&S | 38W-3N | 32 |
| Lincoln St. NW&SE | 34W-6N | 27 |
| Lisa Ln. E&W | 35W-6N | 27 |
| Littenip Ct. N&S | 38W-7N | 26 |
| Longridge Rd. N&S | 38W-7N | 26 |
| Longview Dr. NW&SE | 36W-5N | 26 |
| Lookout Ln. NE&SW | 38W-5N | 26 |
| Lynn Dr. N&S | 38W-3N | 32 |
| Mallard Lake Rd. E&W | 38W-6N | 26 |
| Maple Av. E&W | 35W-6N | 27 |
| Maple Ct. NW&SE | 37W-5N | 26 |
| Maple Ln. E&W | 35W-5N | 27 |
| Marquerite St. E&W | 36W-3N | 32 |
| Marre Dr. NW&SE | 34W-7N | 27 |
| Mary Ln., E. NS&EW | 38W-3N | 32 |
| Mary Ln., W. N&S | 38W-3N | 32 |
| May Ln. N&S | 34W-6N | 27 |
| McKay Dr. NW&SE | 36W-6N | 26 |
| McLean Blvd. N&S | 35W-7N | 27 |
| Meadow Dr. NE&SW | 35W-5N | 27 |
| Meadows Ct. NE&SW | 36W-5N | 26 |
| Michael Ct. NE&SW | 36W-7N | 26 |
| Middlecreek Ln. NS&EW | 36W-4N,36W-5N | 32 |
| Miller Ln. NW&SE | 38W-6N | 26 |
| Mills Ct. E&W | 37W-4N | 32 |
| Murray Ct. NE&SW | 38W-6N | 26 |
| Murray Rd. NS&EW | 38W-6N | 26 |
| Myles Rd. N&S | 36W-5N | 26 |
| North Dr. E&W | 34W-6N | 27 |
| Northern Ct. NE&SW | 38W-7N | 26 |
| Northfield Rd. N&S | 37W-5N | 26 |
| Oak Ct. N&S | 36W-5N | 26 |
| Oak Dr. E&W | 35W-7N | 27 |
| Oak Dr. NE&SW | 38W-7N | 26 |
| Oak Ln. E&W | 35W-5N | 27 |
| Oak Rd. NS&EW | 36W-5N | 26 |
| Oak Ridge Ln. E&W | 36W-3N | 32 |
| Oak Run Ct. NE&SW | 36W-6N | 26 |
| Oakwood Dr. N&S | 35W-6N | 27 |
| Oakwood Dr. NE&SW | 38W-3N | 32 |
| Ohio St. E&W | 34W-6N | 27 |
| Old Burr Rd. N&S | 38W-6N,37W-6N | 26 |
| Old Farm Rd. N&S | 36W-4N | 32 |
| Old Homestead Rd. N&S | 38W-6N | 26 |
| Old Quarry Rd. NE&SW | 36W-4N | 32 |
| Pakan Ln. E&W | 34W-7N | 27 |
| Park Av. NW&SE | 35W-6N | 27 |
| Park Ln. E&W | 35W-5N,35W-6N | 27 |
| Park Pl. E&W | 34W-6N | 27 |
| Pearson Rd. E&W | 35W-5N | 27 |
| Peck Rd. N&S | 37W-3N | 32 |
| Pheasant Run Dr. N&S | 38W-4N | 32 |
| Pine Rd. E&W | 38W-7N | 26 |
| Pinelands Rd. E&W | 35W-5N | 27 |
| Plymouth Ct. N&S | 36W-7N | 26 |
| Prairie Dr. N&S | 38W-3N | 32 |
| Private Rd. E&W | 33W-4N | 33 |
| Promontory Ct. NE&SW | 38W-6N,37W-6N | 26 |
| Pvt. Rd. N&S | 35W-6N | 27 |

| Name | Grid | Page |
|---|---|---|
| Ramona Ln. NW&SE | 34W-6N | 27 |
| Randall Rd. N&S | 37W-2N,37W-7N | 32 |
| Red Bay Ct. NW&SE | 38W-7N | 26 |
| Red Gate Ct. E&W | 36W-6N | 26 |
| Red Gate Rd. N&S | 37W-5N,35W-5N | 26 |
| Red Haw Ln. E&W | 36W-7N | 32 |
| Ridge Dr. N&S | 38W-3N | 32 |
| Ridgewood Dr. NE&SW | 36W-6N | 26 |
| Riding Hood Ln. N&S | 37W-4N | 32 |
| River Grange Rd. E&W | 36W-6N,35W-6N | 26 |
| River Rd. N&S | 35W-6N | 27 |
| River Valley Dr. E&W | 34W-7N | 27 |
| River View Ct. E&W | 36W-7N | 26 |
| Riverside Dr. NW&SE | 36W-6N,35W-7N | 27 |
| Robert Rd. E&W | 34W-6N | 27 |
| Rock Glen Ln. E&W | 35W-6N | 27 |
| Rockwell Av. E&W | 35W-5N | 27 |
| Ronsu Ln. NE&SW | 37W-5N | 26 |
| Roosevelt Av. N&S | 34W-6N,34W-7N | 27 |
| Rose Av. E&W | 35W-7N | 27 |
| Rt. 25 NE&SW | 35W-5N,33W-7N | 27 |
| Rt. 31 N&S | 36W-3N,34W-7N | 32 |
| Rt. 38 E&W | 38W-2N,37W-2N | 32 |
| Salina Av. N&S | 35W-6N | 27 |
| Scott Av. NE&SW | 35W-7N | 27 |
| Second Av. N&S | 36W-3N | 32 |
| Seminary Rd. N&S | 34W-6N | 27 |
| Shady Ln. NW&SE | 35W-6N | 27 |
| Sidney Ct. E&W | 38W-7N | 26 |
| Silver Glen Ct. N&S | 36W-6N | 26 |
| Silver Glen Rd. E&W | 38W-7N,36W-6N | 26 |
| Silver Ridge Dr. N&S | 36W-6N | 26 |
| Skyline Dr. N&S | 34W-6N | 27 |
| Smith Rd. E&W | 33W-3N | 33 |
| South Dr. E&W | 34W-6N,34W-7N | 27 |
| South Ln. E&W | 35W-6N | 27 |
| South St. NE&SW | 35W-7N | 27 |
| Springfield St. E&W | 34W-6N | 27 |
| Stanton Ct. E&W | 35W-5N,35W-5N | 27 |
| Steven Glen Rd. N&S | 38W-7N | 26 |
| Stevens Rd. N&S | 38W-7N | 26 |
| Stonebridge Ln. NW&SE | 36W-5N | 26 |
| Stoneleat Rd. E&W | 36W-4N | 32 |
| Summit St. E&W | 34W-6N | 27 |
| Sunnyside Av. E&W | 35W-6N | 27 |
| Sunrise Dr. NW&SE | 36W-3N | 32 |
| Sunset Dr. E&W | 35W-5N | 27 |
| Sunset Dr. E&W | 38W-3N | 32 |
| Sycamore Rd. N&S | 38W-7N,34W-6N | 26 |
| Sylvia Ln. NW&SE | 34W-6N | 27 |
| Third Av. N&S | 36W-3N | 32 |
| Thompson Av. N&S | 35W-6N | 27 |
| Thornapple Rd. N&S | 36W-3N,36W-4N | 32 |
| Thorne Tree Dr. NE&SW | 36W-3N,36W-4N | 32 |
| Thornly Rd. N&S | 36W-3N,36W-4N | 32 |
| Timber Ridge Ct. NW&SE | 36W-5N | 26 |
| Toms Trail Rd. E&W | 38W-3N | 32 |
| Toni St. E&W | 33W-2N | 33 |
| Treetop Ln. NE&SW | 36W-3N | 32 |
| Tucker Av. N&S | 35W-6N | 27 |
| Tuscola Av. N&S | 34W-6N,34W-7N | 27 |
| Twin Pines Ct. NE&SW | 36W-5N | 26 |
| Twin Silos Dr. NW&SE | 37W-6N | 26 |
| Valley Dr. N&S | 34W-7N | 27 |
| Vaupon Ct. E&W | 38W-7N | 26 |
| Villa Marie Rd. N&S | 35W-6N,34W-6N | 27 |
| Virginia Ct. N&S | 34W-6N | 27 |
| W. Ridgewood Dr. N&S | 36W-6N | 26 |
| W. Ridgewood Ln. NS&EW | 36W-6N | 26 |
| Wabash Av. N&S | 34W-6N | 27 |
| Wagon Tire Rd. N&S | 38W-7N | 26 |
| Watseka Av. N&S | 34W-6N | 27 |
| Weber Dr. NE&SW | 35W-5N,35W-6N | 27 |
| West Dr. N&S | 34W-7N | 27 |
| Cir. | 38W-5N | 26 |
| Westwood Ln. N&S | 36W-5N,36W-6N | 26 |
| Whispering Tr. NS&EW | 38W-7N | 26 |
| Whispering Tr. Ct. NE&SW | 36W-7N | 26 |
| Wild Rose Ln. NW&SE | 36W-3N | 32 |
| Wild Rose Rd. NS&EW | 36W-4N | 32 |
| Willow Dr. N&S | 35W-6N | 27 |
| Wilton Craft Rd. NE&SW | 36W-5N | 26 |
| Windsor Dr. NE&SW | 36W-7N | 26 |
| Wood Hill Ln. N&S | 38W-6N | 26 |
| Wood Ln. E&W | 35W-6N | 27 |
| Woodcliff Dr. N&S | 34W-7N | 27 |
| Woodgate Rd. NE&SW | 37W-5N | 26 |
| Woodland Ct. E&W | 36W-5N | 26 |
| Woodlawn Av. N&S | 35W-6N,35W-7N | 27 |
| Woodside Ln. E&W | 38W-6N | 26 |
| Woodview Ct. NW&SE | 36W-6N | 26 |
| Woodview Ln. N&S | 38W-6N | 26 |
| Wyoming Av. N&S | 34W-6N | 27 |
| 17th Av. N&S | 36W-3N | 32 |

## Sugar Grove

| Name | Grid | Page |
|---|---|---|
| Air Park Dr. E&W | 45W-6S | 41 |
| Annettes Ln. NS&EW | 44W-7S | 48 |
| Arbor Av. E&W | 42W-7S | 48 |
| Bastian Dr. E&W | 43W-7S,42W-7S | 48 |
| Bliss Rd. NE&SW | 41W-5S | 43 |
| Bridgestone Ct. N&S | 41W-5S | 43 |
| Brock Dr. N&S | 45W-7S | 47 |
| Brookhaven Ln. N&S | 43W-7S,42W-8S | 48 |
| Bucktail Lane E&W | 44W-7S | 48 |
| Calkins Dr. E&W | 43W-7S,42W-7S | 48 |
| Cardinal Crest Dr. NW&SE | 42W-5S | 42 |
| Carriage Hill Ct. E&W | 43W-6S | 42 |
| Carriage Hill Ln. N&S | 43W-6S | 42 |
| Chelsea Av. E&W | 41W-7S | 48 |
| Cornwall Ct. N&S | 41W-5S | 43 |
| Cross St. NW&SE | 42W-7S | 48 |
| Cyndi Ct. E&W | 45W-7S | 47 |
| Edgewater Ln. E&W | 42W-7S | 48 |
| Fays Ln. E&W | 44W-7S | 48 |
| First St. E&W | 42W-7S | 48 |
| Gordon Sq. NW&SE | 41W-4S | 43 |
| Granart Rd. NE&SW | 45W-7S | 47 |
| Grove St. N&S | 42W-7S | 48 |
| Hampshire Ct. NE&SW | 41W-4S | 43 |
| Jody Ln. N&S | 42W-6S | 42 |
| Jonathan Dr. N&S | 45W-7S | 47 |
| Joy Ct. N&S | 42W-7S | 48 |
| Joy St. E&W | 42W-7S | 48 |
| Kimbery Ct. E&W | 45W-7S | 47 |
| Kingman Cir. NW&SE | 41W-5S | 43 |
| Knightsbridge Dr. NS&EW | 41W-5S | 43 |
| Litchfield Ct. NE&SW | 41W-5S | 43 |
| Main St. N&S | 42W-7S | 48 |
| Mallard Ln. N&S | 42W-7S | 48 |
| Maple St. E&W | 42W-7S | 48 |
| Marybeth Ln. E&W | 45W-7S | 47 |
| McCannon St. N&S | 42W-7S | 48 |
| Meadowlark Run NE&SW | 42W-5S | 42 |
| Meadows Ct. N&S | 42W-7S | 48 |
| Meadows Dr. E&W | 42W-7S | 48 |
| Merrill New Rd. N&S | 41W-5S,41W-4S | 43 |
| Molly Dr. E&W | 45W-7S | 47 |
| Monna St. E&W | 42W-7S | 48 |
| Neil St. E&W | 42W-7S | 48 |
| Orleans Ct. N&S | 41W-5S | 43 |
| Patricia Ln. N&S | 42W-7S | 48 |
| Pebblebrook Ct. N&S | 42W-8S | 48 |
| Queens Gate Cir. NS&EW | 41W-5S,41W-4S | 43 |
| Richard St. N&S | 42W-7S | 48 |
| Rt. 30 E&W | 45W-7S | 47 |
| Rt. 47 N&S | 42W-7S | 48 |
| Saddlewood Ln. NE&SW | 42W-8S | 48 |
| Snow St. E&W | 43W-7S,42W-7S | 48 |
| Stamford Ct. NW&SE | 41W-4S | 43 |
| Stanley Rd. N&S | 42W-7S | 48 |
| Stonehill Cir. N&S | 41W-5S | 43 |
| Terry Dr. E&W | 42W-7S | 48 |
| Tom St. E&W | 45W-7S | 47 |
| Tudor Ct. E&W | 41W-4S | 43 |
| Washford Pl. N&S | 41W-5S | 43 |
| Wheeler Rd. E&W | 43W-6S | 42 |
| Whipporwill Ln. E&W | 42W-5S | 42 |
| Whispering Oaks Ln. E&W | 44W-7S | 48 |
| Windstone Ln. NW&SE | 41W-5S | 43 |
| Woodbury Cir. E&W | 41W-5S | 43 |
| Woodthrush Ln. NE&SW | 42W-5S | 42 |
| Yolane Ct. E&W | 42W-7S | 48 |
| Yolane Dr. E&W | 43W-7S,42W-7S | 48 |

## Sugar Grove Township

| Name | Grid | Page |
|---|---|---|
| Ashe Rd. NE&SW | 44W-9S | 48 |
| Barnes Rd. N&S | 39W-8S,39W-7S | 49 |
| Baseline Rd. E&W | 44W-9S,39W-9S | 48 |
| Bertram Rd. N&S | 41W-9S | 49 |
| Blackberry Rd. N&S | 39W-9S | 49 |
| Bliss Rd. NE&SW | 42W-6S,41W-4S | 42 |
| Bluegrass Dr. E&W | 39W-9S | 49 |
| Creekview Rd. NE&SW | 39W-9S | 49 |
| Deerpath Rd. N&S | 39W-6S,39W-4S | 43 |
| Denny Rd. E&W | 41W-4S,40W-4S | 43 |
| Densmore Rd. N&S | 40W-6S | 43 |
| Dugan Rd. N&S | 44W-9S,44W-5S | 48 |
| East-West Tollway NW&SE | 41W-4S | 43 |
| Finley Rd. N&S | 44W-4S | 42 |
| Galena Blvd. NW&SE | 42W-6S,39W-6S | 42 |
| Gordon Rd. N&S | 40W-9S,40W-6S | 49 |
| Guthrie Ln. E&W | 43W-8S | 48 |
| Hankes Rd. NW&SE | 40W-6S,39W-6S | 43 |
| Harter Rd. NW&SE | 44W-4S,42W-5S | 42 |
| Hazelcrest Dr. NW&SE | 44W-4S | 42 |
| Healy Rd. NW&SE | 41W-4S,40W-4S | 43 |
| Jericho Rd. NE&SW | 42W-5S | 42 |
| Ka-de-ka Rd. E&W | 42W-5S | 42 |
| Lyndale Rd. N&S | 39W-9S | 49 |
| May Rd. NW&SE | 42W-5S,41W-9S | 42 |
| McCannon Rd. N&S | 44W-8S | 48 |
| Merrill Rd. NW&SE | 43W-4S,41W-5S | 42 |
| Midfield Dr. N&S | 39W-7S | 49 |
| Mighell Rd. N&S | 43W-9S,43W-8S | 48 |
| Norris Rd. N&S | 40W-5S,40W-4S | 43 |
| Old Oak Rd. NW&SE | 43W-4S | 42 |
| Orchard Rd. N&S | 39W-9S,39W-5S | 49 |
| Pembroke Ct. E&W | 44W-4S | 42 |
| Prairie St. N&S | 44W-8S,39W-7S | 48 |
| Rt. 47 N&S | 42W-9S | 48 |
| Rt. 56 NE&SW | 42W-6S | 42 |
| Scott Rd. NE&SW | 44W-4S,43W-4S | 42 |
| Shagbark Ln. NW&SE | 39W-6S | 43 |
| Star Ln. N&S | 44W-9S | 48 |
| Sunnyside Dr. E&W | 39W-9S | 49 |
| Thornapple Tree Rd. NW&SE | 43W-4S | 42 |
| U.S. Rt. 30 N&S | 42W-8S | 48 |
| West Ridge Dr. N&S | 39W-6S | 43 |
| Wheeler Rd. N&S | 44W-5S,42W-5S | 42 |
| Wildwood Dr. NW&SE | 40W-6S | 43 |
| Wittshire Ln. N&S | 44W-4S | 42 |

## Virgil Township

| Name | Grid | Page |
|---|---|---|
| Beith Rd. E&W | 50W-3N,45W-3N | 28 |
| Butts Rd. NE&SW | 48W-7N | 22 |
| Country Ln. E&W | 46W-5N | 23 |
| County Line Rd. N&S | 50W-2N,50W-7N | 28 |
| Fabris Rd. N&S | 49W-5N,49W-6N | 22 |
| Francis Rd. NS&EW | 46W-6N,46W-3N | 29 |
| Freeland Rd. N&S | 45W-2N,45W-3N | 29 |
| Hickory Dr. E&W | 46W-2N | 29 |
| Howard Rd. N&S | 49W-2N,49W-3N | 28 |
| Indian Creek Trail NW&SE | 47W-6N,45W-5N | 23 |
| Landrose Rd. N&S | 46W-2N | 29 |
| Lees Rd. E&W | 46W-7N,45W-7N | 23 |
| McGough Rd. NW&SE | 50W-7N,49W-5N | 22 |
| McNulty Rd. N&S | 48W-3N,47W-3N | 28 |
| Meadows Rd. N&S | 46W-5N | 23 |
| Meredith Rd. N&S | 47W-2N,47W-6N | 28 |
| Old State Rd. NW&SE | 50W-7N | 22 |
| Peplow Rd. N&S | 48W-6N,47W-7N | 22 |
| Peterson Rd. N&S | 50W-6N,49W-6N | 22 |
| Pin Oaks Ln. N&S | 48W-4N | 28 |
| Prairie St. N&S | 46W-5N | 23 |
| Ramm Rd. N&S | 50W-7N,49W-7N | 22 |
| Ramm Wood Dr. N&S | 50W-7N | 22 |
| Read Rd. NS&EW | 45W-6N | 23 |
| Root Ln. N&S | 50W-3N | 28 |
| Rt. 38 E&W | 50W-2N,46W-2N | 28 |
| Rt. 64 NW&SE | 50W-7N,45W-5N | 22 |
| Saddlewood Dr. NE&SW | 45W-2N | 29 |
| Sauber Rd. NS&EW | 47W-6N,47W-7N | 23 |
| Snyder Rd. N&S | 49W-6N,49W-7N | 22 |
| Sunset St. N&S | 46W-5N | 23 |
| Thatcher Rd. N&S | 49W-3N,48W-4N | 28 |
| Warford Rd. N&S | 46W-7N | 23 |
| Welter Rd. NW&SE | 49W-5N,45W-4N | 22 |
| Winters Rd. N&S | 50W-5N,47W-5N | 22 |

## Wayne*
### (Also see Du Page County)

| Name | Grid | Page |
|---|---|---|
| Army Trail Rd. E&W | 35W-5N,33W-5N | 27 |
| Ashely Ln. E&W | 33W-6N | 27 |
| Behles Way E&W | 33W-6N | 27 |
| Brewster Creek Cir. NS&EW | 33W-6N,33W-7N | 27 |
| Country Club Rd. E&W | 34W-4N,33W-4N | 33 |
| Curling Pond Rd. NS&EW | 33W-5N | 27 |
| Dunham Cir. NE&SW | 33W-5N | 27 |
| Dunham Ct. NW&SE | 33W-5N | 27 |
| Dunham Rd. NE&SW | 33W-4N,33W-6N | 33 |
| Dunham Trail Rd. NW&SE | 33W-5N | 27 |
| Fletcher Rd. E&W | 33W-5N,33W-4N | 27 |
| Lamplight Tr. NW&SE | 33W-7N | 27 |
| Mare Barn Rd. E&W | 33W-7N | 27 |
| Nelson Dr. N&S | 34W-4N | 33 |
| Robin Ln. NS&EW | 34W-5N | 27 |
| Rocheford Ln. NW&SE | 33W-6N | 27 |
| Saw Mill Tr. N&S | 34W-4N | 33 |
| Shagbark Rd. E&W | 33W-6N | 27 |
| Surrey Rd. NE&SW | 33W-5N,33W-6N | 27 |
| Thorncroft Dr. NE&SW | 33W-5N | 27 |
| White Thorn Rd. EW&NS | 34W-5N,33W-5N | 27 |
| Woodland Dr. E&W | 33W-5N | 27 |
| Woodmere Ln. E&W | 33W-6N | 27 |

## West Dundee

| Name | Grid | Page |
|---|---|---|
| Aberdeen Ln. N&S | 35W-16N | 14 |
| Barber Ct. NW&SE | 35W-16N | 14 |
| Brewer Ct. N&S | 35W-16N | 14 |
| Browning Av. E&W | 34W-15N | 15 |
| Castle Rock Ct. NW&SE | 35W-16N | 14 |
| Cavalier Ct. N&S | 34W-15N | 15 |
| Chadwick Ln. N&S | 35W-16N,35W-17N | 14 |
| Dunning Av. E&W | 34W-15N | 15 |
| Edinburgh Ln. NS&EW | 35W-16N | 14 |
| Edwards Av. NS&EW | 34W-15N | 15 |
| Eichler Dr. NW&SE | 34W-15N | 15 |
| Fay Av. E&W | 33W-15N | 15 |
| Fox Av. E&W | 33W-15N | 15 |
| Galloway Ct. N&S | 35W-16N | 14 |
| Garrison E&W | 34W-15N | 15 |
| Geneva St. E&W | 34W-15N | 15 |
| Glenmoor Dr. E&W | 35W-16N | 14 |
| Grant Av. N&S | 35W-16N | 14 |
| Greencastle Ct. N&S | 35W-16N | 14 |
| Hamilton Dr. NW&SE | 35W-16N | 14 |
| Hawley Av. E&W | 33W-15N | 15 |
| Highland Av. E&W | 34W-15N | 15 |
| Hillcrest Ct. E&W | 34W-15N | 15 |
| Kane St. E&W | 34W-15N | 15 |
| Kitridge Dr. NW&SE | 35W-16N | 14 |
| Knowlton Dr. NS&EW | 35W-16N | 14 |
| Liberty St. E&W | 34W-16N | 15 |
| Lincoln Av. NW&SE | 34W-15N | 14 |
| Lindsay Ln. N&S | 35W-16N | 14 |
| Lisa Rd. E&W | 34W-15N | 15 |
| Maiden Ln. E&W | 34W-15N | 15 |
| Main St. E&W | 35W-15N | 15 |
| Market Loop Rd. N&S | 34W-15N | 15 |
| McConnoiche Ct. N&S | 35W-16N | 14 |
| McGregor Ct. NE&SW | 35W-16N | 14 |
| Oregon Av. E&W | 34W-16N | 15 |
| Pember Cir. NS&EW | 35W-16N | 14 |
| Preston Ln. NE&SW | 35W-16N | 14 |
| Prestwick Ct. NW&SE | 35W-16N | 14 |
| Riverview St. E&W | 34W-16N | 15 |
| Roundabout Cir. EW&NS | 34W-15N | 15 |
| Royal Ln. E&W | 34W-16N | 15 |
| Ryan Ct. E&W | 34W-15N | 15 |
| Ryan Ln. N&S | 34W-15N | 15 |
| Short E&W | 33W-15N | 15 |
| Smalley Ct. E&W | 35W-16N | 14 |
| South E&W | 34W-15N | 15 |
| Spaulding Av. NS&EW | 35W-16N | 14 |
| Spaulding Ct. NW&SE | 35W-16N | 14 |
| Cir. | 35W-16N | 14 |
| Sterling Ct. NE&SW | 35W-16N | 14 |
| Stewart Ln. E&W | 35W-16N | 14 |
| Strom Dr. E&W | 34W-15N | 15 |
| Tartans Ct. E&W | 35W-16N | 14 |
| Tartans Dr. NW&SE | 35W-16N | 14 |
| Thatcher Tr. NW&SE | 35W-16N | 14 |
| Tritram Ct. NE&SW | 35W-16N | 14 |
| View St. N&S | 33W-15N | 15 |
| Village Quarter E&W | 34W-15N | 15 |
| Washington St. E&W | 34W-16N | 15 |
| Water Tower Rd. E&W | 35W-16N | 14 |
| Waterbury Ct. NW&SE | 35W-16N | 14 |
| Westley Ln. NS&EW | 35W-17N | 8 |
| Willow Ln. NW&SE | 34W-15N | 15 |
| 1st St. N&S | 34W-15N | 15 |
| 2nd St. N&S | 34W-15N | 15 |
| 3rd St. N&S | 34W-15N | 15 |
| 4th St. N&S | 34W-15N | 15 |
| 5th Ct. NW&SE | 34W-15N | 15 |
| 5th St. N&S | 34W-15N | 15 |
| 6th St. N&S | 34W-15N | 15 |
| 7th Blvd. NW&SE | 34W-15N | 15 |
| 7th St. N&S | 34W-15N | 15 |

# RAND M<sup>C</sup>NALLY

# Lake
# County

## StreetFinder®

| page | **Contents** |
|------|----------|
| **A** | Using the StreetFinder |
| **B** | PageFinder Map |
| **C** | Vicinity Map |
| **1** | Contents |
| **2** | Quick Reference Guide |
| **4** | StreetFinder Maps |
| **53** | StreetFinder Index |

Photo credit: Shores of Lake Michigan / Lake County Chamber of Commerce

PageFinder™ Map U.S. Patent No. 5,419,586.

Information included in this publication has been checked for accuracy
prior to publication. Since changes do occur, the publisher cannot be
responsible for any variations from the information printed.

## Lake County Municipal Offices

| | Location | Page |
|---|---|---|
| Antioch Village Hall | 23W-42N | 6 |
| 874 Main St; 395-1000 | | |
| Bannockburn Village Hall | 11W-22N | 50 |
| 2165 Telegraph Rd; 945-6080 | | |
| Deerfield Town Hall | 10W-21N | 50 |
| 850 Waukegan Rd; 945-5000 | | |
| Fox Lake Village Hall | 26W-36N | 13 |
| 305 Rt 59; 587-2151 | | |
| Grayslake Village Hall | 20W-33N | 23 |
| 164 Hawley St; 223-8515 | | |
| Gurnee Village Hall | 14W-35N | 25 |
| 4573 Grand Ave; 673-7650 | | |
| Hainesville Village Hall | 22W-33N | 22 |
| 221 E Pine View; 223-2032 | | |
| Highland Park City Hall | 8W-22N | 51 |
| 1707 St Johns; 432-0800 | | |
| Highwood City Hall | 9W-23N | 51 |
| 17 Highwood Ave; 432-1924 | | |
| Island Lake Village Hall | 29W-28N | 28 |
| Rt 176, PO Box 41; 526-8764 | | |
| Lake Bluff City Hall | 10W-28N | 35 |
| 40 E Center; 234-0774 | | |
| Lake Forest City Hall | 10W-26N | 43 |
| 220 E Deerpath; 234-2600 | | |
| Lake Villa Village Hall | 22W-38N | 14 |
| 65 Cedar Ave; 356-6100 | | |
| Lake Zurich Village Hall | 22W-22N | 46 |
| 61 W Main St; 438-5141 | | |
| Libertyville City Hall | 16W-29N | 33 |
| 200 E Cook; 362-2430 | | |
| Lindenhurst Village Hall | 20W-37N | 15 |
| 2301 Sand Lake Rd; 356-8252 | | |
| Mundelein Village Hall | 18W-28N | 32 |
| 440 E Hawley; 566-7070 | | |
| North Chicago City Hall | 11W-31N | 35 |
| 1850 S Lewis Ave; 578-7750 | | |
| Riverwoods Village Hall | 13W-20N | 44 |
| 2300 Portwine Rd; 945-3990 | | |
| Round Lake Village Hall | 23W-33N | 22 |
| 322 W Railroad Ave; 546-5400 | | |
| Round Lake Beach Village Hall | 23W-34N | 22 |
| 1212 N Cedar Lake Rd; 546-3466 | | |
| Round Lake Heights Village Hall | 23W-35N | 22 |
| 629 W Pontiac Ct; 546-1206 | | |
| Tower Lakes Village Hall | 25W-25N | 37 |
| 115 South Dr; 526-2226 | | |
| Vernon Hills Village Hall | 17W-24N | 40 |
| 290 Evergreen Dr; 367-3700 | | |
| Wauconda Hills Village Hall | 26W-27N | 37 |
| 101 N. Main St; 526-8786 | | |
| Waukegan Mun Bldg | 10W-34N | 27 |
| 106 N Utica St; 360-9000 | | |
| Winthrop Harbor City Hall | 9W42N | 11 |
| 830 Sheridan Rd; 872-3846 | | |
| Zion City Hall | 10W-40N | 11 |
| 2828 Sheridan Rd; 872-4546 | | |

## Cemeteries

| | Location | Page |
|---|---|---|
| Angolian Cem | 22W-37N | 14 |
| Ascension Cem | 14W-30N | 33 |
| Avon Center Cem | 21W-35N | 22,23 |
| Benton Greenwood Cem | 12W-39N | 18 |
| Cemetery | 25W-20N | 45 |
| Cemetery | 25,26W-27N | 37 |
| Diamond Lake Cem | 18W-25N | 40 |
| Druce Cem | 19W-34N | 23 |
| Fort Hill Cem | 24W-32N | 22 |
| Fox Lake Cem | 24W-36N | 13,14 |
| Grant Cem | 26W-33N | 21 |
| Grass Lake Cem | 26W-39N | 13 |
| Home Oaks Cem | 21W-39N | 14,15 |
| Knopf Cem | 18W-20N | 47,48 |
| Lakeside Cem | 16W-29N | 33 |
| Lake Forest Cem | 10W-27N | 43 |
| Lake Mound Cem | 9W-39N | 19 |
| Lake Zurich Cem | 23W-23N | 46 |
| Mooney Cem | 9W-21N | 50,51 |
| Mount Oliver Mem Cem | 12W-41N | 10 |
| Mount Rest Cem | 16W-42N | 8 |
| Naval Cem | 10W-30N | 35 |
| Nicholas Dowden Mem Cem | 17W-28N | 32 |
| North Shore Garden of Mem | 12W-32N | 26 |
| Oakdale Cem | 13W-42N | 9 |
| Oakwood Cem | 10W-33N | 27 |
| Orvis Cem | 29W-41N | 4 |
| Pineview Cem | 10W-38N | 19 |
| St Marys Cem | 10W-27N | 43 |
| St Marys Cem | 10W-33N | 27 |
| St Patrick Cem | 12W-24N | 42 |
| St Patricks Cem | 16W-40N | 8,9 |
| Sand Lake Cem | 21W-37N | 14,15 |
| Vernon Cem | 15W-23N | 49 |
| Warren Cem | 16W-35N | 25 |
| White Cem | 26W-21N | 45 |

## Colleges & Universities

| | Location | Page |
|---|---|---|
| Barat Col | 10W-25N | 43 |
| Benedictine Col | 17W-28N | 32 |
| College of Lake County | 19W-34N | 23 |
| Lake Forest Univ | 10W-26N | 43 |
| St Marys of the Lake Sem | 18W-28N | 32 |
| Trinity Sem | 12W-22N | 50 |

## Forest Preserves

| | Location | Page |
|---|---|---|
| Buffalo Creek FP | 19W-20N | 47 |
| Capt Daniel Wright FP | 15,16W-24N | 41 |
| Countryside FP | 20W-27N | 39 |
| Cuba Marsh FP | 24W-21N | 45,46 |
| Duck Farm FP | 21W-37N | 15 |
| Elm Road FP | 14W-24N | 41 |
| Flint Creek FP | 27W-23N | 45 |
| Forest Preserve | 16W-30,31N | 33 |
| | 15W-39,41N | 9 |
| Fox River FP | 28W-25N | 36 |
| Grassy Lake FP | 36W-23N | 45 |
| Fourth Lake Fen FP | 20W-36,37N | 15 |

| | Location | Page |
|---|---|---|
| Grant FP | 25W-36,37N | 13 |
| Greenbelt FP | 12W-32N | 26 |
| Gurnee Woods | 14W-36N | 17 |
| Lake County FP | 13W-20N | 49 |
| Lake Forest Nature Pres | 9W-25N | 43 |
| Lakewood FP | 24W-26,27N | 37,38 |
| MacDonald Woods FP | 19W-38N | 15,16 |
| Middlefork Savanna FP | 12W-26N | 42 |
| Nature And Conservation Area | 9W-38N | 19 |
| Old School FP | 14W-27N | 41,42 |
| Riverhill FP | 15W-33N | 25 |
| Ryerson Conservation Area | 14W-21N | 49 |
| Rollins Savanna FP | 19,20W-35N | 23 |
| Spring Bluff FP | 9W-43N | 11 |
| Sterling Lake FP | 15W-43N | 9 |
| Sun Lake FP | 22W-39N | 14 |
| Van Patten Woods FP | 15W-42N | 9 |
| Wilmont FP | 15W-30N | 34 |
| Wilmot Woods FP | 16W-32N | 25 |

## Golf & Country Clubs

| | Location | Page |
|---|---|---|
| Antioch CC | 24W-40N | 5,6 |
| Arboretum GC | 17W-22N | 48 |
| Barrington Hills GC | 27W-20N | 44,45 |
| Biltmore CC | 25W-23N | 44 |
| Bob O Link GC | 8W-21N | 51 |
| Bonnie Brook Mun GC | 11W-36,37N | 18 |
| Brae Loch CC | 19W-33N | 24 |
| Briarwood CC | 10W-20N | 50 |
| Buffalo Grove GC | 17W-20N | 48 |
| Chevy Chase CC | 15W-20N | 49 |
| Countryside GC | 20W-27N | 39 |
| Deerfield Park Dist GC | 12W-21N | 50 |
| Deerpath Park & GC | 11W-26N | 42,43 |
| Exmoor CC | 9W-22N | 51 |
| Four Winds GC | 23W-27N | 38 |
| Foss Park GC | 12W-31N | 35 |
| Fox Lake CC | 28W-39N | 12 |
| Glen Flora CC | 10W-36N | 19 |
| Great Lakes GC | 10W-30N | 35 |

| | Location | Page |
|---|---|---|
| Greenshire GC | 11W-38N | 18 |
| Highland Park CC | 9W-22N | 51 |
| Hillcrest CC | 19W-21N | 47 |
| Indian Valley CC | 18W-25N | 40 |
| Knollwood CC | 13W-28N | 34,35 |
| Lake Barrington Shores GC | 26W-24N | 37 |
| Lake Bluff GC | 11W-29N | 35 |
| Lake Zurich GC | 23W-23N | 46 |
| Municipal GC | 17W-24N | 40 |
| Northmoor CC | 8W-21N | 51 |
| Old Elm GC | 10W-24N | 43 |
| Orchard Hills GC & CC | 12,13W-38N | 18 |
| Onwentsia GC | 11W-26N | 43 |
| Ravinia Green CC | 12W-21N | 50 |
| Renwood CC | 22W-35N | 22 |
| Seminary GC | 18W-28N | 32 |
| Shiloh Park GC | 10W-40N | 11 |
| Shore Acres CC | 10W-30N | 35 |
| Stonehenge GC | 27W-22N | 45 |
| Sunset Valley GC | 9W-21N | 50,51 |
| Tally Ho CC | 17W-24N | 40 |
| Thorngate CC | 13W-20N | 49 |
| Twin Orchard CC | 18W-22N | 47,48 |
| USN GC | 12W-30N | 35 |
| Village Green GC | 19W-29N | 32 |

## Hospitals

| | Location | Page |
|---|---|---|
| American International Hosp | 10W-40N | 11 |
| Condell Mem Hosp | 16W-28N | 33 |
| County Hosp | 12W-35N | 26 |
| Good Shepherd Hosp | 28W-22N | 44 |
| Great Lakes Training Center Hosps | 10W-30N | 35 |
| Highland Park Hosp | 8W-22N | 51 |
| Lake Forest Hosp | 11W-26N | 43 |
| Round Lake Medical Clinic | 23W-33N | 22 |
| St Theresa Medical Center | 12W-34N | 26 |
| VA Medical Center | 11W-30N | 35 |
| Victory Mem Hosp | 10W-35N | 27 |

## Lake County Close-up

### Ravinia Festival

Lake Cook & Green Bay Rds., Highland Park
Known to music-lovers the world over, Ravinia is the nation's oldest performance arts festival. Its busy summer schedule includes performances by world-class musicians and dancers. Ravinia is also the summer home of Chicago Symphony Orchestra. Rising Star, an indoor chamber music series, runs during the fall and winter months. Also, programs for children.

### Raupp Memorial Museum

901 Dunham Lane, Buffalo Grove
This charming museum honors local history with a number of exhibits and artifacts. Its collection features clothing, farm equipment and household goods dating back to the mid-1800's. Of special interest is a life-sized re-creation of the area's early business district. Open all year.

### Lake County Museum

Lakewood Forest Preserve, 27277 Forest Preserve Dr., Wauconda
This comprehensive museum, with its more than 18,000 objects, celebrates Lake County history. Its exhibits include costumes, paintings, tools and several Native American artifacts. The museum sponsors Civil War Days, a battle reenactment of the war between the states.

### The Power House

100 Shiloh Blvd., Zion
This unusual museum and resource center features more than 50 hands-on exhibits relating to energy. Educational programs explain alternative energy sources, energy principles and energy conservation. Visitors learn about everything from solar panels to wind turbines. Closed Sundays.

STATE LINE RD

BURTON TWP

T 1 N
T 46 N ANTIOC

**GANDER MOUNTAIN**
28W-43N
**FOREST PRESERVE**

27W-43N
3 WIL

BACCUS LN
REIGER CT
VINEYARD
30W-43N
6
5
29W-43N
4

Fox

River

BREEZY LAWN RD

DOLPH CT
POLARIS RD

BREEZY LAWN RD

7

RD

8

173

WILMOT

28W-42N
9

RD PARK
LAWSON AV
SPRING
CONVERSE
RIVERSIDE RD
WOODLAND AV
FOREST LN
BEACH RD

27W-42N
10

30W-42N

29W-42N

SIEDSCHLAG

RD

ENGLISH PRAIRIE RD
WINTERGREEN
PL
PONDER
CHATEAUGAY DR
SPRINGDALE DR
HUNTERS LN
RICHARDSON RD

ENGLISH PRAIRIE RD

*English Prairie Cem.*

**INDUSTRIAL AREA**
**FOX LAKE**
60020

LAKE COUNTY

RD

15

27W-41N

CT
HUNTERS LN
FOX TRAIL
18

JAMES RD
*Orvis Cem.*
17
29W-41N

JAMES RD
16
28W-41N

PUBLIC RD

30W-41N

*Wray-Imeson Cem.*

**SPRING GROVE**

RD

CHAIN

**CHAIN O' LAKES**

**STATE PARK**
28W-40N
21

27W-40N

LAURINE CT
STEEPLE CT
COUNTRY SHIRE LN
20
29W-40N

WILMOT
CARRIAGE LN
COUNTRY SHIRE LN
CHESTNUT RIDGE
SUNDIAL
APPALOOSA LN
HEATHER RIDGE LN
SURREY CT
CARRIAGE LN

BURTON TWP
ANTIOCH TWP

*Turner Lake*

Fox River

30W-40N
19
PADDOCK
MARGARET LN
ST
SCHMIDT
LEE LN
RITA AV
WILLIAM LN
SAGE LN
WILLIAM LN
WILLIAM
BERWYN
BELLEPL
AL SCHMIDT
SPRING CT
ST

OAK ST
LORAINE
EAST ST
MAIN
ST

*Jackson Bay*

CHURCHILL CT
MORGAN CIR
PARK VISTA LN

STATE PARK

RD
DEER RUN

*Mud Lake*

28W-39N
28

27W-39N
27

LINDEN
RIVER RD
WOODLAND
PKWY
BEVERLY WAY
RAINE
DR
CARLETON
PARK
ARLINGTON DR
MELBOURNE
NIPPERSINK
PL

SPRING
GROVE
29
RD
29W-39N

CHELSEY CT

STATE PARK RD
KEEFE PL
EATON PL
SHORE PL
GOLFVIEW DR

**FOX LAKE COUNTRY CLUB**

CHANNAHON
CEDAR ST
ASH ST
HICKORY ST

30W-39N
MAYO CT DR
30

MELROSE DR
KILLARNEY RD
SPRING RD
LINDEN RD
ISLAND

ENGLES
CASS ST
LUBLINER PL
DANNELL PL
VILLA VISTA
BEACON ST
CASPER ST

WATER AV
CUNEO PL

WELLINGTON ST

**SPRING GROVE**

OAK HILL DR

CHERRYWOOD

Nippersink

BARRY
WINDSOR

MADISON AV

GRASS LAKE

CHEST HILL
VILLAGE CT
DUNWOOD CT
CLARENDON AV
SYCAMORE CT
BALSAM CT
EVERGREEN
MAGNOLIA
HICKORY
VISCAYA DR
JACKSON
WEST END DR
RAVINE
HILL RD
MORRAY

EAST LEISURE
ARLINGTON
ABBOTT
REDWOOD CT
WEST GRASS LAKE
LEXINGTON RD
JACKSON CT

SEE McHENRY COUNTY PAGES 10-11

SEE PAGES 6-7

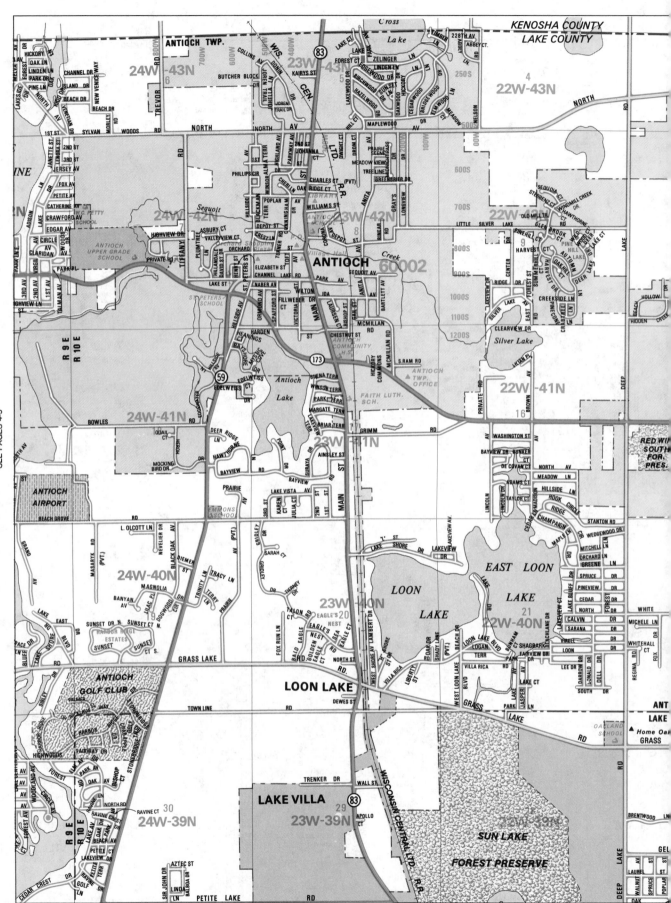

SEE PAGES 4-5

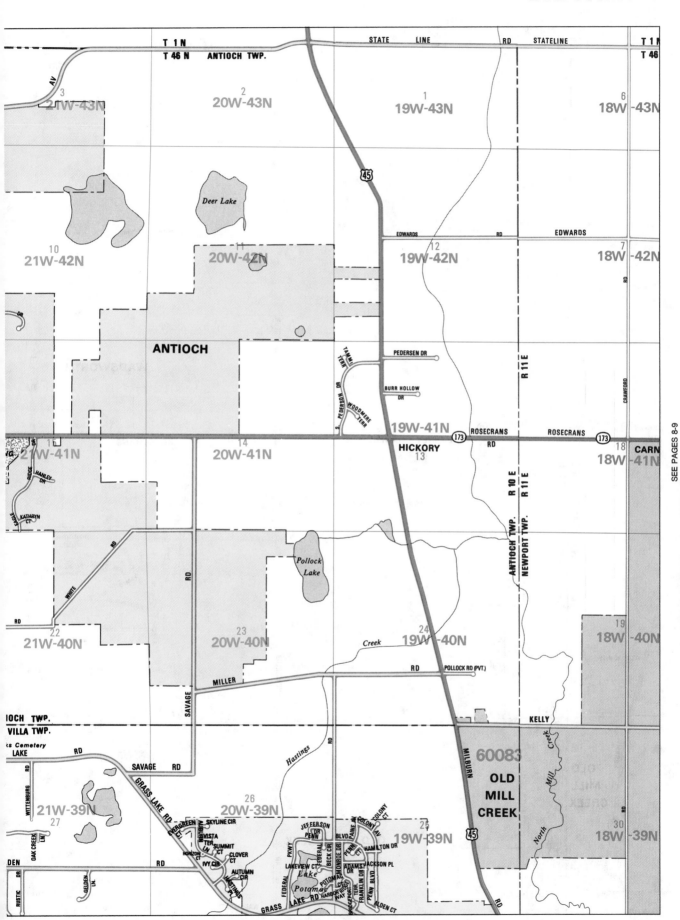

SEE PAGES 8-9

SEE PAGES 14-15

STATELINE RD

**T 1 N**
**T 46 N**

NEWPORT TWP.

94

RD

43N

6
18W -43N

5
17W -43N

4
16W -43N

PUBLIC RD

RD

SHERIDAN OAKS DR

EDWARDS RD

EDWARDS RD

Mount Rest
Cemetery

12
-42N

RD

7
18W -42N

8
17W -42N

9
16W -42N

R 11 E

HUNT CLUB RD

CRAWFORD RD

CERMAK RD

RD

**WADSWORTH**

41N

ROSECRANS RD

ROSECRANS 173

RD

173

18
18W -41N

**CARNEY CORNERS**

17
17W -41N

MILL CREEK

16W -41N

**ROSECRANS**

18

HWY

ANTIOCH TWP.
NEWPORT TWP.

R 10 E
R 11 E

RD

TRI-STATE

HUNT CLUB TR.

SKOKIE

HUNT CLUB RD

PUBLIC RD
THORNE MEADOW CIR.
CHERRYWOOD LN
OLD ORCHARD DR.

St. Patrick's
Cemetery

40N

19
18W -40N

20
17W -40N

NORTH

21
16W -40N

GOLDENROD
FOX GLOVE LN
REED CT.
SEDGE CT.
TRILLIUM LN
CT.

POLLOCK RD (PVT.)

KELLY RD

HUNT CLUB RD

KELLY RD

TOLLWAY

MILL CREEK RD

94

MILBURN

Creek

**60083**

**OLD
MILL
CREEK**

MILL Creek

North

RD

16W -39N

39N

45

30
18W -39N

29
17W -39N

RD

**OLD MILL CREEK**
**60083**

28
16W

BROWNE
SCHOOL

PLAZA LN

▲ THE TEMPEL LIPIZZANS
**WADSWORTH** RD

Tollgate

WISCONSIN
ILLINOIS

KENOSHA COUNTY
LAKE COUNTY

RUSSELL
T 1 N
T 46 N

131

INGRAM DR

STERLING
LAKE
FOREST
PRESERVE

15W-43N

RD

2

14W-43N

RUSSELL

RD

1

13W-43N

LYNN DALE DR

OAKCREST

12W
F
PR

RUSSELL

STERLING LN

GORHAM

VAN PATTON

WOODS

FOREST

PRESERVE

15W-42N

Des Plaines River

SOO LINE R.R.

KILBOURNE

9TH ST

WINTHROP HARBOR

RD

DELANY

RD

ZION

13W-42N

12

Oakdale Cemetery

WINTHROP HARBOR

12W

14W-42N

11

HICKORY RD

RD

NORTHWESTERN R.R.

HIGHLAND
MEADOWS

RD

FOREST

PRESERVE

15W-41N

DELANY

CHICAGO & NORTHWESTERN

BUTTERFIELD LN

HEATH
PRIMR
CT
TALLG

12W-41

4800 W

RD

15

OLD WOODFORD RD

ST

51ST ST

NEWPORT
SCHOOL

14W-41N

14

KILBOURNE

173

13

13W-41N

DUSK DR

MIDWAY DR

DAYBREAK
LN

SUNSHINE LN

SUNS

21ST

21ST ST

ST

21ST

ST

BEACH
PARK

WAVERLY ST

WAVERLY ST

STONEGATE RD

LESTER LN

TIMBERLAND TR

GREENVIEW

FORESTVIEW
DR

NEWPORT TWP. R 11 E
BENTON TWP. R 12 E

CORNELL ST

14W-40N

KAISER RD

RD

23

RD

13W-40N

24

12W

131

DES PLAINES

KAZMER RD

STIEHR RD

27TH ST

RD

27TH PL

28TH ST

AV

SUNSET

28TH AV

AV

PL

29TH ST

RIVER TRAIL

MAUSER

BARTL

BUG

MAPLEWOOD RD

CLARENDON RD

BAYONNE

PEACOCK

GREEN

ADOLPH

RD

FOREST

WEDGEWOOD
CT

PRAIRIEVIEW
DR

ANDOVER RD

PRATUM TERRACE
DR

ADAMS RD

MAJOR AV

PRESERVE

15W-39N

WALDEN

MATURE CT

CONCORD

HARMONY

KT LN

MEL LN

WADSWORTH

32ND ST

HOWE SCHOOL

ILLI

KILBOURNE

JODY LN

14W-39N

HIGHVIEW RD

25

13W-39N

60083

SHERYL LYNN DR

MEADOW LN

OAK KNOLL

RD

WINCHESTER

SHARON ST

Benton
Greenwood
Cemetery

GREEN BAY

PRIM
WAL

WADSWORTH

CAROLINE

R.R.

MARTIN AV

AV AV AV AV

WADSWORTH RD

WADSWORTH RD

SEE PAGES 10-11

SEE PAGES 16-17

WISCONSIN
ILLINOIS
KENOSHA COUNTY
LAKE COUNTY
RUSSELL   T 1 N   RD   RUSSELL
T 46 N
BENTON TWP.

131

13W-43N
1

STATE
LINE
FOREST
PRESERVE

11W-43N
5

ZION

RUSSELL

-43N
RD
2

W

KILBOURNE

WINTHROP HARBOR

13W-42N
12

Oakdale Cemetery

12W-42N
7
WINTHROP HARBOR

NORTH PRAIRIE SCHOOL

11W-42N
8

-42N

HIGHLAND
MEADOWS

WILLOW
FOREST

Mount Oliver
Memorial
Park Cem.

BENTON TWP
ZION TWP
WEST BROADWAY

12W-41N
18

13W-41N
13

-41N

DUSK DR
SUNSHINE LN
MIDWAY DR
DAYBREAK
SUNSHINE LN

HORIZON
VILLAGE

11W-41N
17

Fire Sta.
#2

Ioanna
Park

HORIZON CT

13W-40N
24

Davis
Park

Stella
CT

ZION BENTON TWP
H.S. HORIZON CAMPUS

BEACH
PARK

12W-40N
19

11W-40N
20

Hermon
Park

-40N

WAVERLY ST
WAVERLY ST.

STIEHR RD
27TH ST
27TH PL
28TH ST
28TH AV
29TH PL

27TH ST
HICKORY LN
ASH CT
PINE CT
29TH

WEDGEWOOD CT
PRAIRIEVIEW DR
ANDOVER RD
WALDEN
MATURE LN
CONCOR
HAMMONY
JODY LN

MAPLEWOOD RD
CLARENDON RD
PEACOCK
MAJOR AV

MAUSER
BARTL

30TH ST
31ST ST
32ND ST
33RD ST

ZION   FOREST   PRESERVE

12W-39N

11W-39N

WADSWORTH

13W-39N
25

HOWE SCHOOL
ILLINOIS AV

Benton
Greenwood
Cemetery

-39N
SHERYL LYNN DR
OAK KNOLL

SHARON ST
MARTIN AV

GREEN BAY

WADSWORTH RD

WADSWORTH

ZION TWP

Meadowcreek
Park

SEE PAGES 8-9

SEE PAGES 18-19

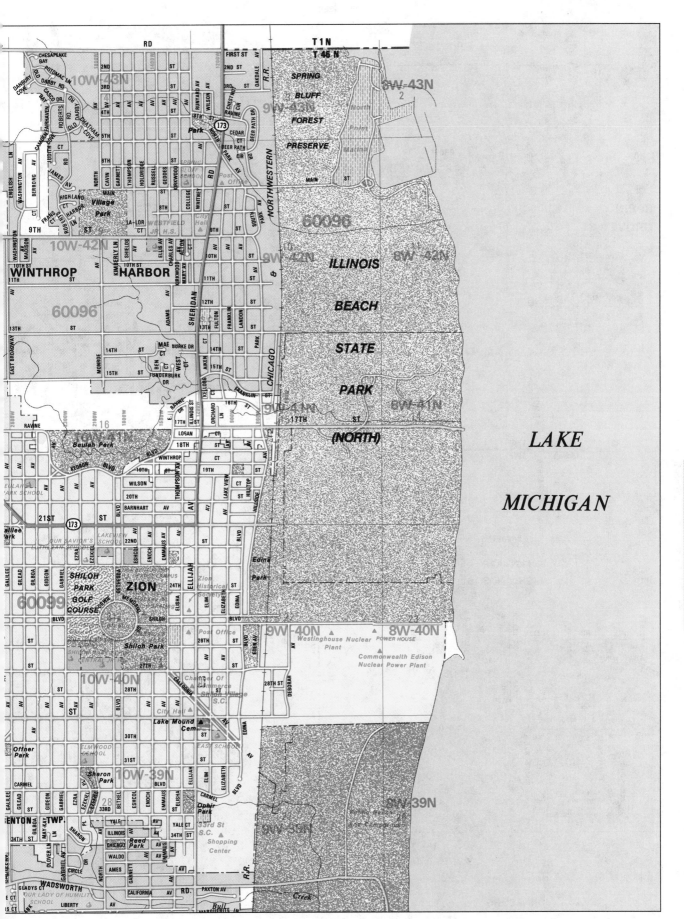

*LAKE*

*MICHIGAN*

SEE PAGES 4-5

SEE McHENRY COUNTY PAGES 18-19

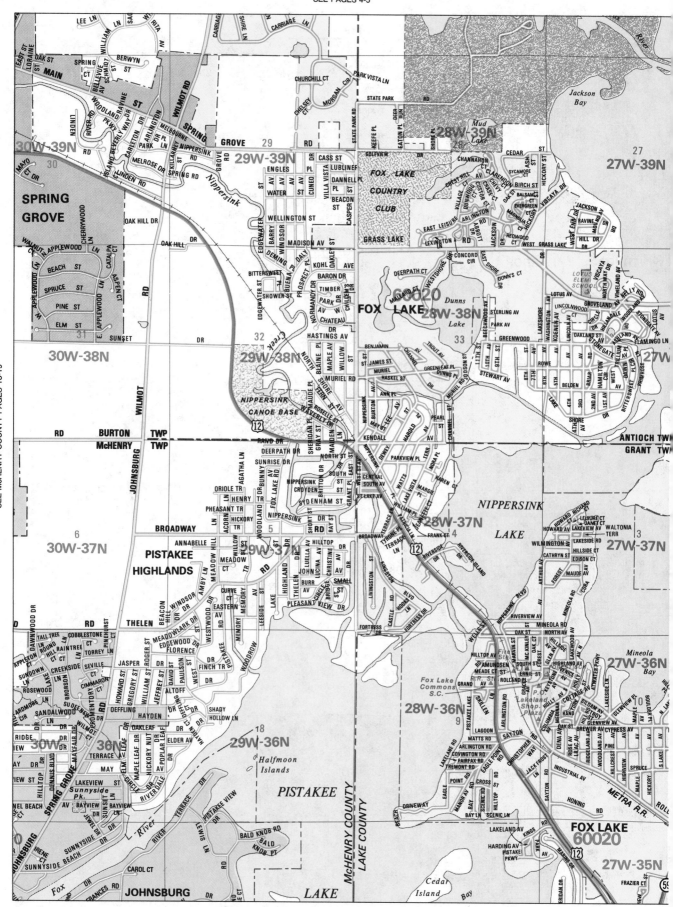

SEE PAGES 20-21

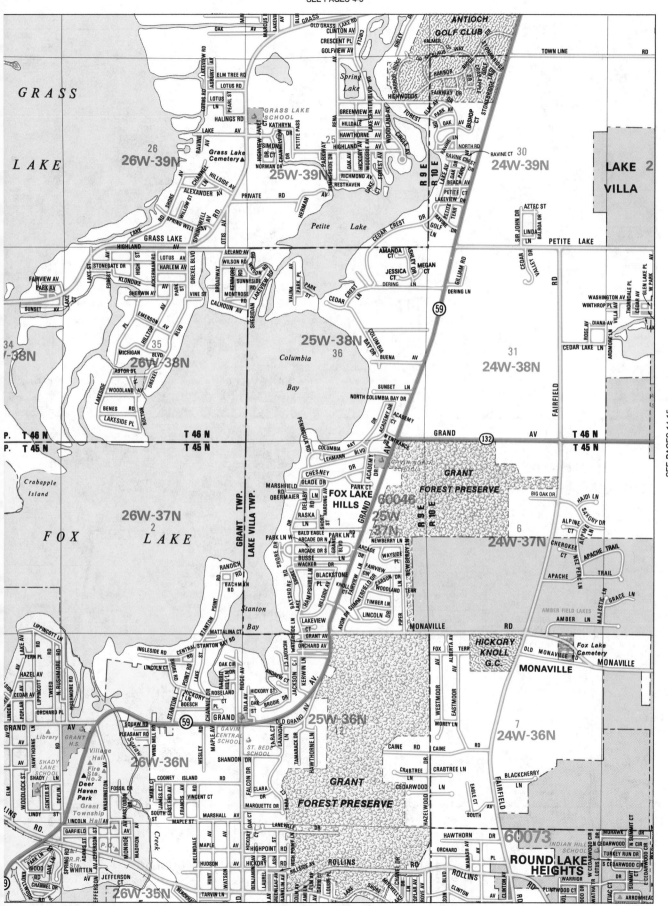

SEE PAGES 4-5

SEE PAGES 14-15

SEE PAGES 20-21

ANTIO
LAKE VI

**LAKE VILLA**
23W-39N
29

TRENKER DR
WALL ST
TOWN LINE RD
DEWES ST
GRASS LAKE
PARK JAS LN
RD
Home Oaks
GRASS

OAKLAND SCHOOL

22W-39N
28

**SUN LAKE FOREST PRESERVE**

Sun Lake

BRENTWOOD LN
GELDI

30
24W-39N
Ravine Ct

R 9 E  R 10 E

PETITE LAKE RD

AZTEC ST
SIR JOHN DR
LINDA
BALBOA DR
CEDAR VALLEY DR

NORTH WAY
NORTH AV
CENTRAL AV

GLEN LAKE PL
LAKEWOOD AV
W PARK
BELMORAL

CEDAR LAKE LN

WASHINGTON AV
WINTHROP AV
DIANA AV
ROSE AV
ROSEMONT LN
LAKE SHORE DR

DEEP LAKE

59

59

AMANDA CT
JESSICA CT
DERING LN
MEGAN CT
GILLIAM RD
DERING LN

LAUREL ST
WALNUT ST
SPRUCE
POPLAR ST

7TH AV
GRATON RD
5TH ST
PIKE ST
EDGEWO
4TH ST
3RD ST
2ND ST
1ST ST

31
24W-38N

CEDAR LAKE LN

**CEDAR LAKE**

32
23W-38N

**DEEP LAKE**

22W-38N
33

Lake Villa

ALLENDALE SCHOOL

**LAKE VILLA**
**60046**

1 BRADFORD CT
SHOSHONI TRAIL
CLAYTON CT
WOODHEAD

BUENA AV
FAIRFIELD

CLEVELAND (PVT)
P.O.
J.J. PLEVIAK SCHOOL
VILLA AV
ARAPAHO TRAIL
WATERS EDGE DR
GRAND AV

SUNSET LN
COLUMBIA BAY DR
ACADEMY DR

**GRAND AV**
132
T 46 N
T 45 N

132
KENZ CT
CREMIN
MONICA DR
ROSELLE CT
Library

PRINCE OF PEACE SCHOOL

60046
25W-37N

**GRANT FOREST PRESERVE**

BIG OAK DR
HAIDI LN
SAXONY DR
ALPINE CT

BURNETT CT
OAK KNOLL DR
WALDEN
LAURIE
OAK KNOLL
WESLEY AV
MC KINLEY
BELMONT AV
BURNETT AV

OAKWOOD AV
OAK
LAKE VILLA INTERMEDIATE SCHOOL

COVENTRY COVE CT
BALSAM AV  BALSAM CT
WHITE PINE LN

Angolian Cemetery
PARK AV
PARK AV

6
24W-37N

CHEROKEE CT
NEZ PERC LN
APACHE TRAIL
TRAIL
APACHE

5
23W-37N

JUNIPER JUNIPER WAY
RED SPRUCE

4
22W-37N
83

NEWBERRY LN
WAYSIDE PL
FAIRVIEW DR
CARSON DR
WOODLAND TERR
AMBER LN
COLN DR
PIPER

GRACE LN
MAJESTIC LN
AMBER LN
AMBER FIELD LAKES

NORTHWIND DR
WINDANCE CT
WINDDANCE DR
MEADOWVIEW CT
OVERLOOK CT
SUMMIT CT

BRIAR RIDGE LN
INDIAN RIDGE LN
FIELDSTONE DR
DAKTON LN
FIELDSTONE DR
MC KINLEY

TERRY DR N
TERRY DR W
MORTON
ROSE CT
MORTON
ENGLE

MONAVILLE

WESTMOOR
EASTMOOR
FOX TERR
ALBERTA AV
MOREY LN

HICKORY KNOLL G.C.
FOX LAKE CEMETERY
OLD MONAVILLE RD
**MONAVILLE**
MONAVILLE RD

REDHEAD CT
WILDFLOWER CT
WILDFLOWER LN
TALL GRASS

22W-36N

BERNICE
NIELSON DR
MARY CT
HELEN CT
SARAH
LAWRENCE CT

7
24W-36N

MONAVILLE RD

8
23W-36N

ACORN CT
BLUEBERRY LN
COVE CT
STUCKTON
STRATFORD
SHAKER CT
LONDON CT

COUNTRY WALK

PENWOOD
HAROLD
PRINCETON CT
LENOX
WESTON
LEXINGTON DR
FOX CHASE

CAINE RD
CAINE
CRABTREE LN
CEDARWOOD LN
EAGLE CT
SOUTH

BIRCHWOOD DR
REDWOOD DR
WILLOW RIDGE DR
SAUK CT

ORCHARD
ROSEWOOD
PEMBROOK
STERLING
PENNSBURY CT
STANTON
SOMERSET

CANTERBURY CT
CLEARVIEW CT
CASTLEMAIN LN
CAMDEN LN

SILVER OAKS

CRABTREE LN
BLACKCHERRY
FAIRFIELD

CIRCUIT CT

STONEBRIDGE
COBBLER

COBBLER
STOCKTON LN

60073
INDIAN HILLS SCHOOL
NORMANDIE LN
TURKEY RUN DR
CEDARWOOD CIR

HAWTHORN DR
ORCHARD AV
WABASH AV

**ROUND LAKE HEIGHTS**
WARRIOR
FLINTWOOD CT
ROLLINS
CLINTON

23W-35N

60073
**ROUND LAKE BEACH**
Medical Clinic
ACRE
22W-35N

24W-35N
PONTIAC CT
HIAWATHA
ARROWHEAD DR
Village Hall
MEADOWBROOK DR
ROLLINS
CIRCLE DR
ROLLINS

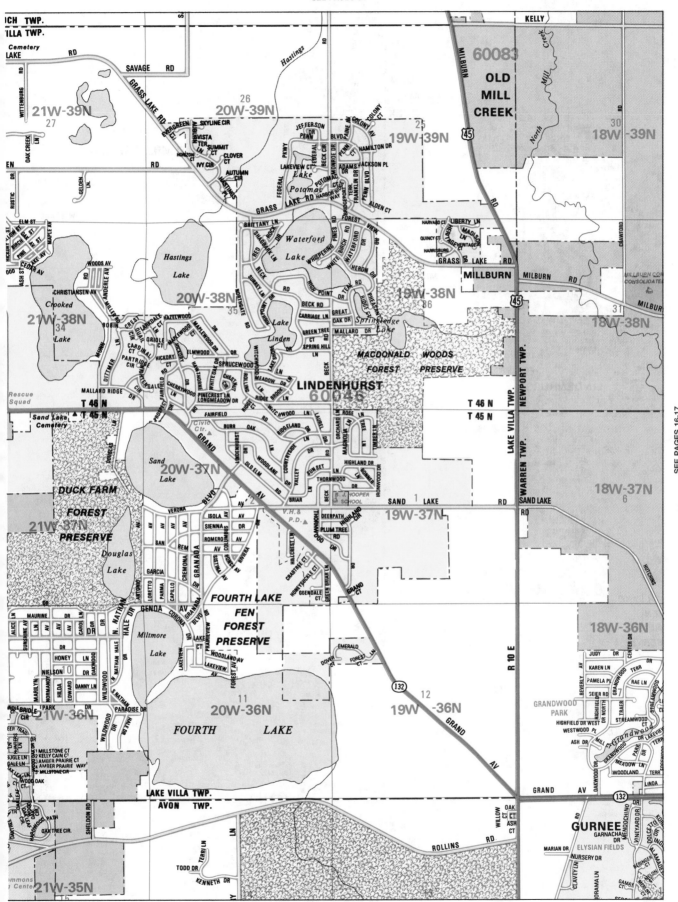

SEE PAGES 16-17

SEE PAGES 8-9

KELLY                    RD

60083
**OLD MILL CREEK**

26

W-39N

19W-39N

18W-39N

17W-39N

**OLD MILL CREEK**
60083

▲ THE TEMPEL LIP

WADSWORTH

GRASS  LAKE  RD

*Lake Potomac*

LIBERTY LN

HERITAGE

*Waterford Lake*

GRASS  LAKE  RD

**MILLBURN**          MILBURN        RD

MILLBURN COMMUNITY
CONSOLIDATED SCHOOL

19W-38N

*Springledge Lake*

MILBURN                RD

31

18W-38N

17W-38N

**MACDONALD  WOODS
FOREST  PRESERVE**

*Lake Linden*

**LINDENHURST**
60046

T 46 N
T 45 N

*Mill              Creek*

19W-37N

SAND  LAKE  RD

18W-37N

SAND   LAKE  RD

17W-37N

V.H. &
P.D.

B. J. HOOPER
SCHOOL

TH LAKE

EN
REST
SERVE

18W-36N

HUNT CLUB
FARMS I

YEARLING    DR

STEARNS SCHOOL

132

12

19W-36N

GRAND

*Grandwood*

GRANDWOOD
PARK

Nature
Pres.

17W-36N

HUNT CLUB
Field & Fenc
Equestion
FARMS

*LAKE*

Nature
Pres.

BRIDLEWOOD

BROOKSIDE

Brookside
Green

ROLLINS        RD

GRAND       AV

132

**GURNEE**

ELYSIAN FIELDS

NURSERY DR

N. STRATTON  LN

STRATTON

SHOPPING
CENTER

**GURNEE**

17
17W-35N

FIRE DEPARTME
SITE

DADA
ROSEWOOD

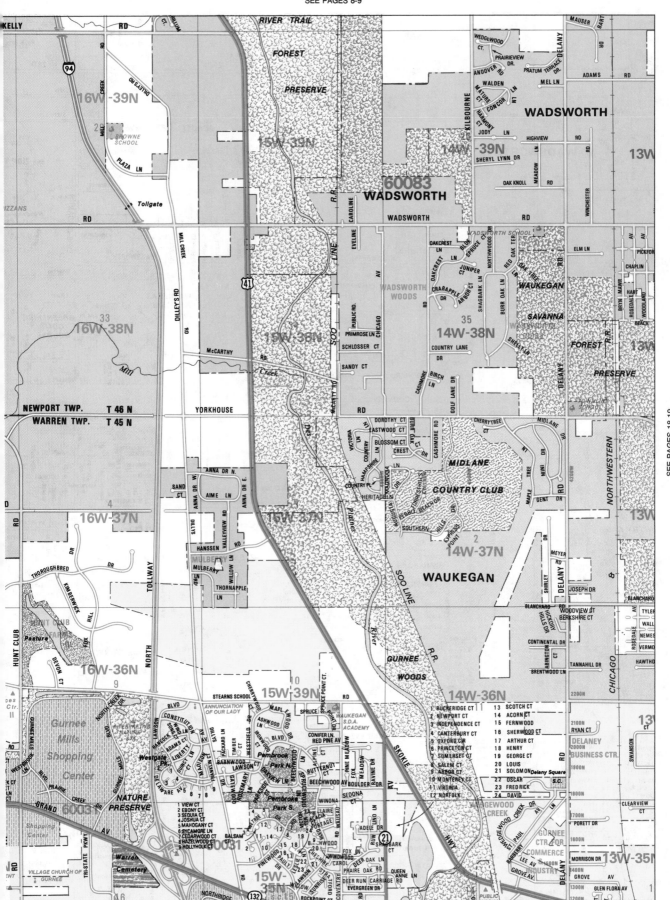

SEE PAGES 18-19

SEE PAGES 10-11

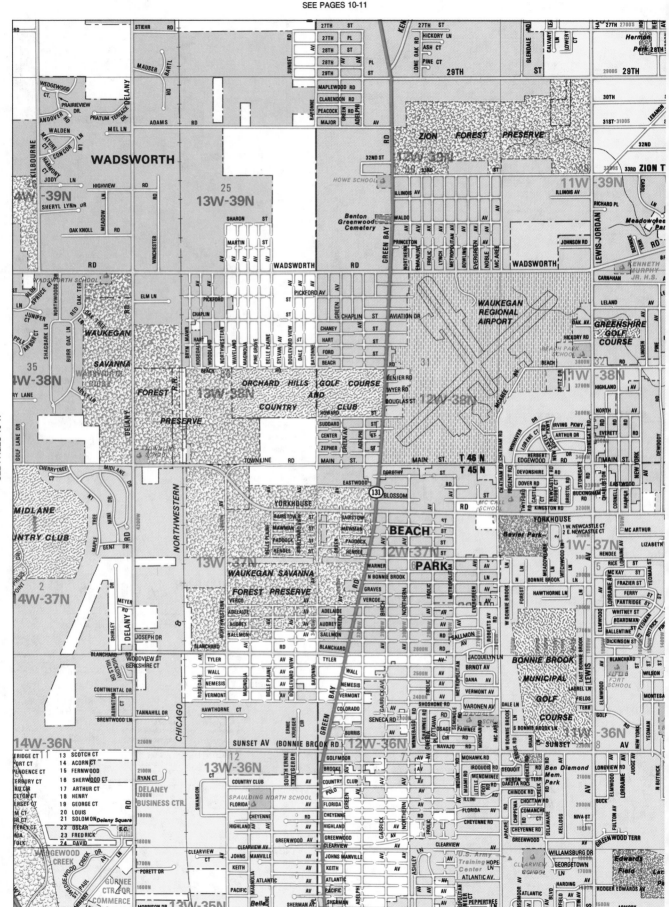

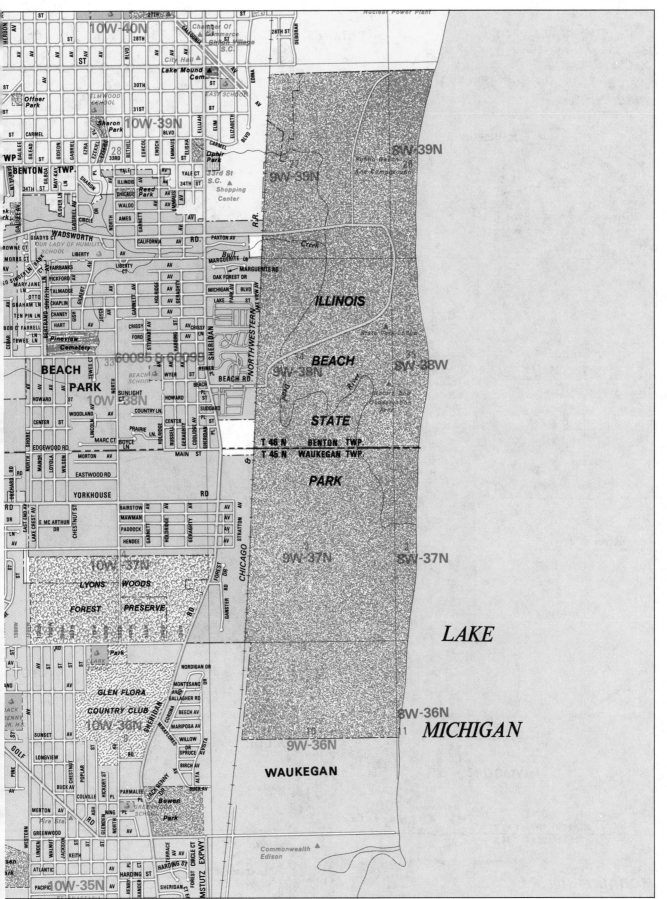

SEE PAGES 12-13

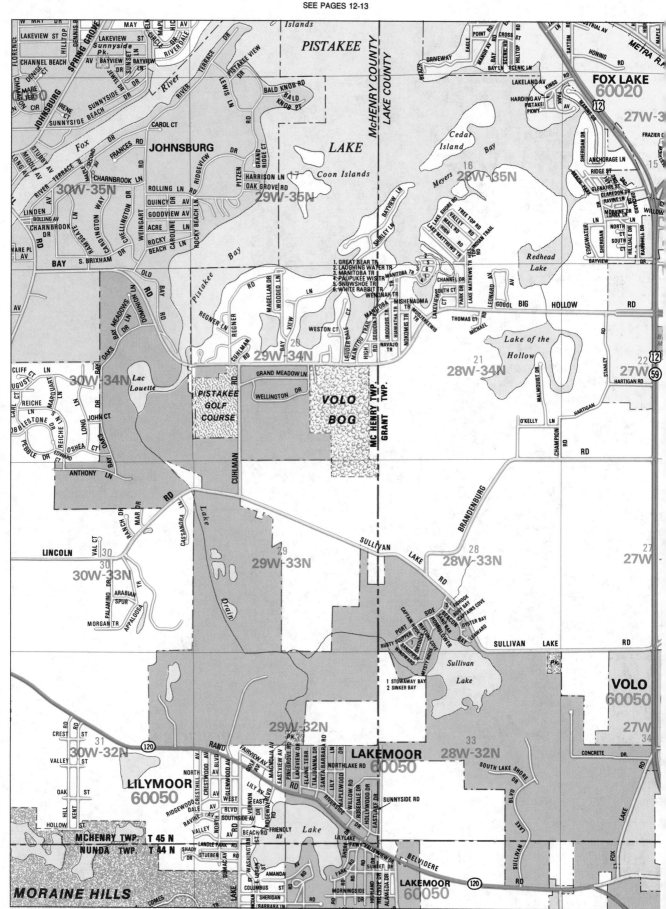

SEE PAGES 28-29

SEE PAGES 12-13

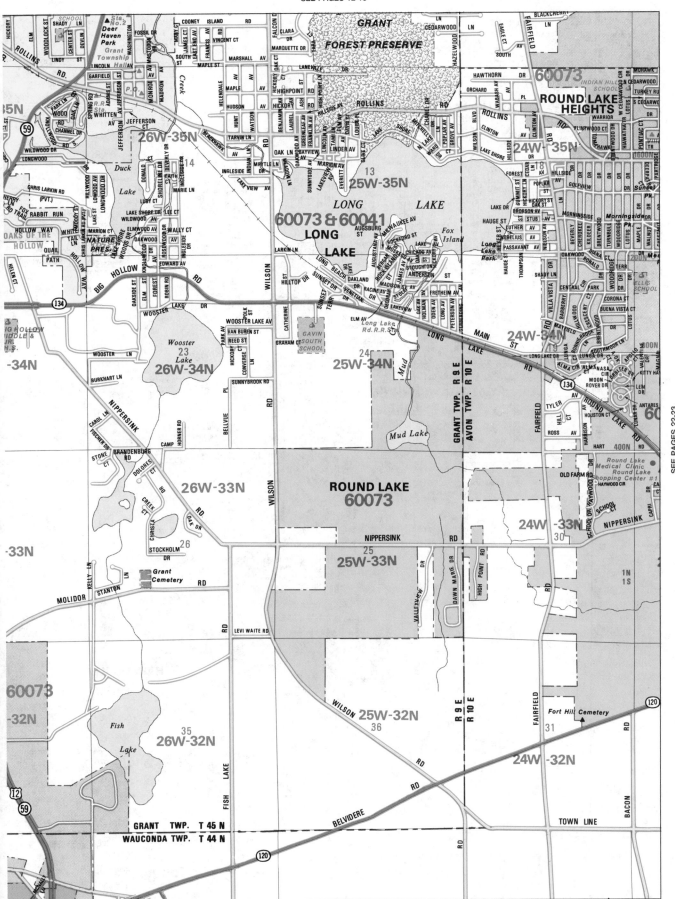

SEE PAGES 22-23

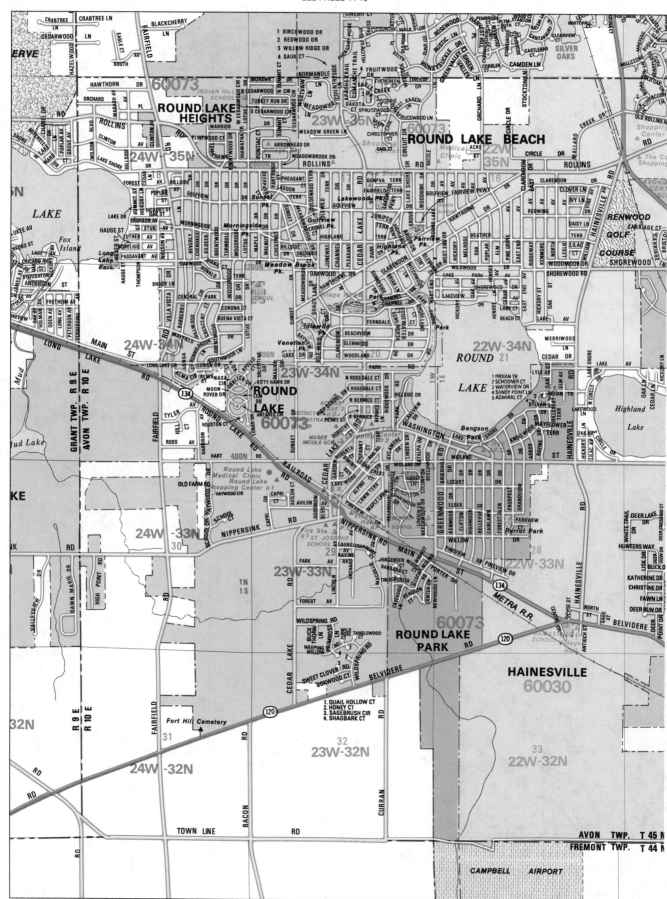

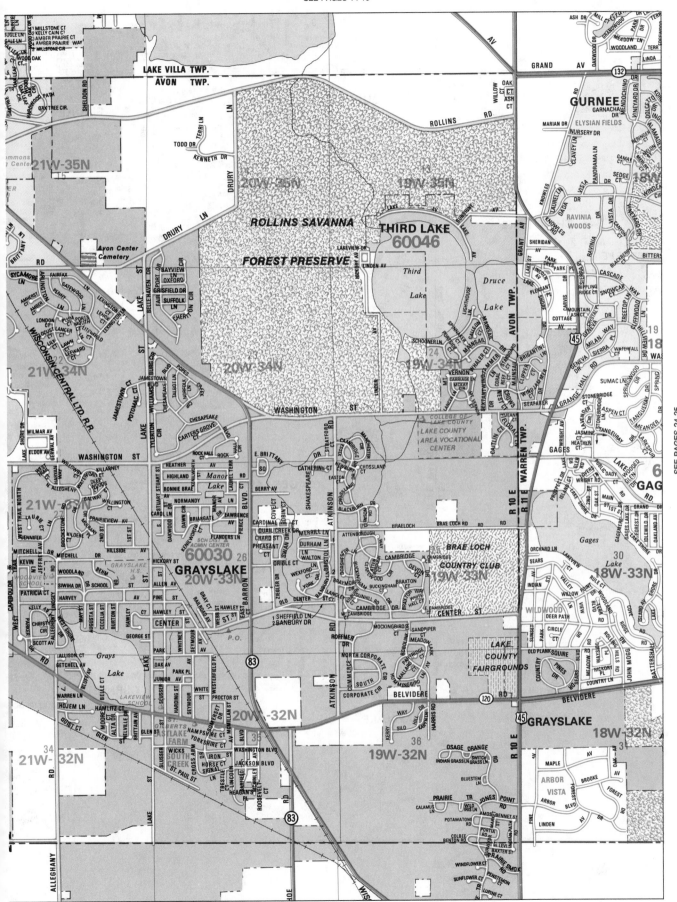

SEE PAGES 24-25

SEE PAGES 22-23

GRAND AV

GURNEE

GURNEE

17W-35N

THIRD LAKE
60046

PRESERVE

SAVANNA

ROLLINS RD

AVON TWP.

WARREN TWP.

19W-35N

19W-34N

18W-35N

ELYSIAN FIELDS

RAVINIA WOODS

GOLF COURSE (U.C.)

OAK KNOLL

17W-34N

18W-34N

WASHINGTON ST

ABERDARE PATRIOT ESTATES

SCHOOL SITE

COLLEGE OF LAKE COUNTY
AREA VOCATIONAL CENTER

WARREN TWP. HOMESTEAD CENTER

TOWNHOMES OF WOODLAND HILLS

60030
GAGES LAKE

GAGES

19W-33N

BRAE LOCH COUNTRY CLUB

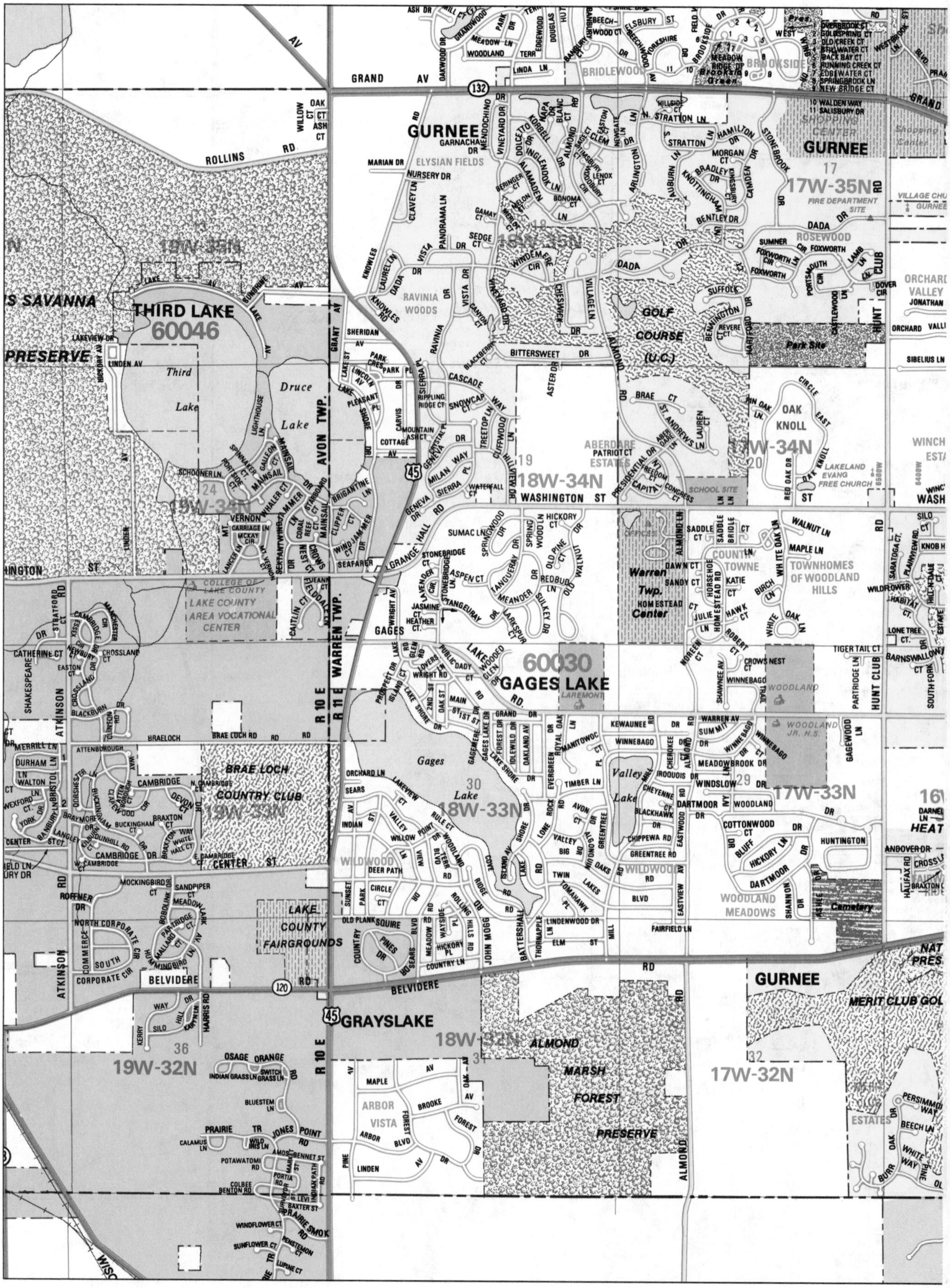

18W-33N

17W-33N

16W

Gages Lake

WILDWOOD

WOODLAND MEADOWS

LAKE COUNTY FAIRGROUNDS

BELVIDERE

GURNEE

GRAYSLAKE

19W-32N

18W-32N

17W-32N

MARSH FOREST PRESERVE

ARBOR VISTA

MERIT CLUB GOL

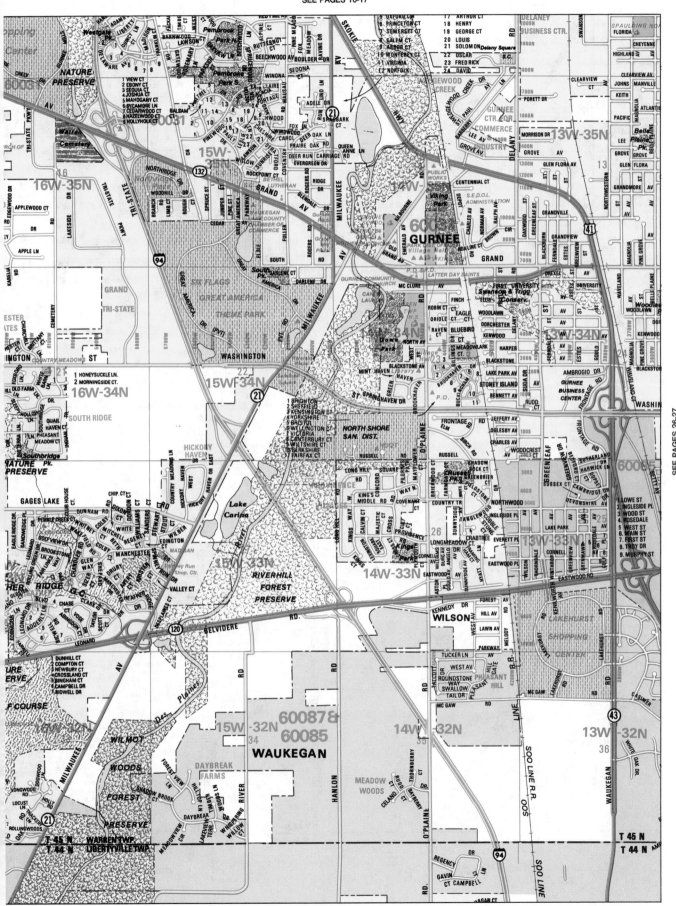

SEE PAGES 26-27

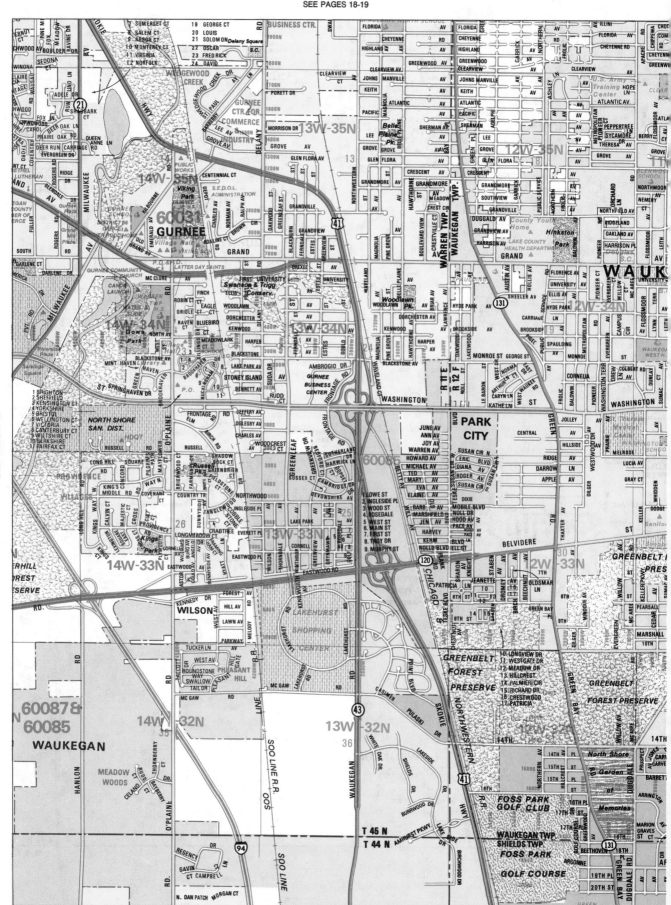

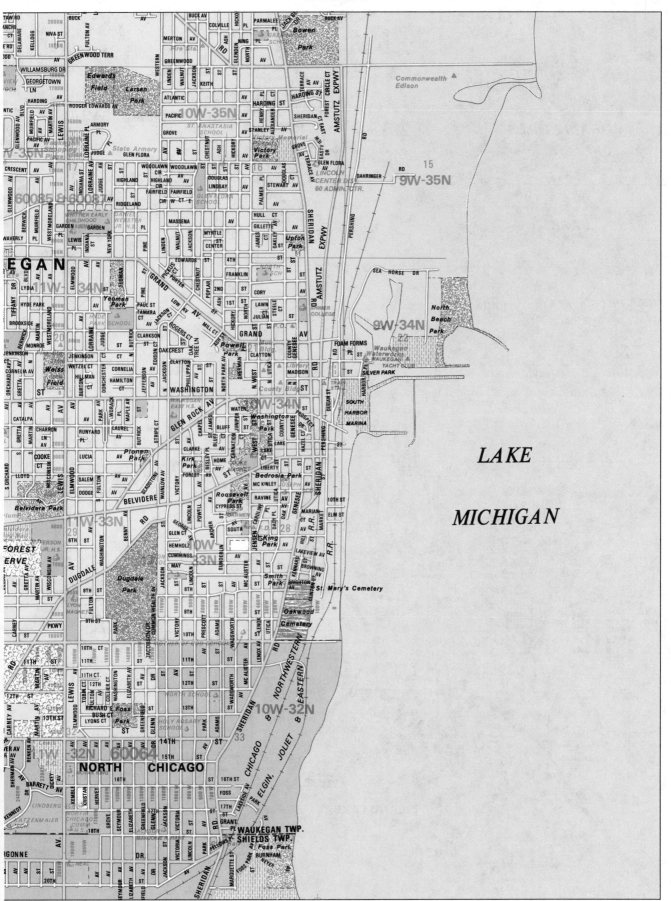

SEE McHENRY COUNTY PAGES 34-35

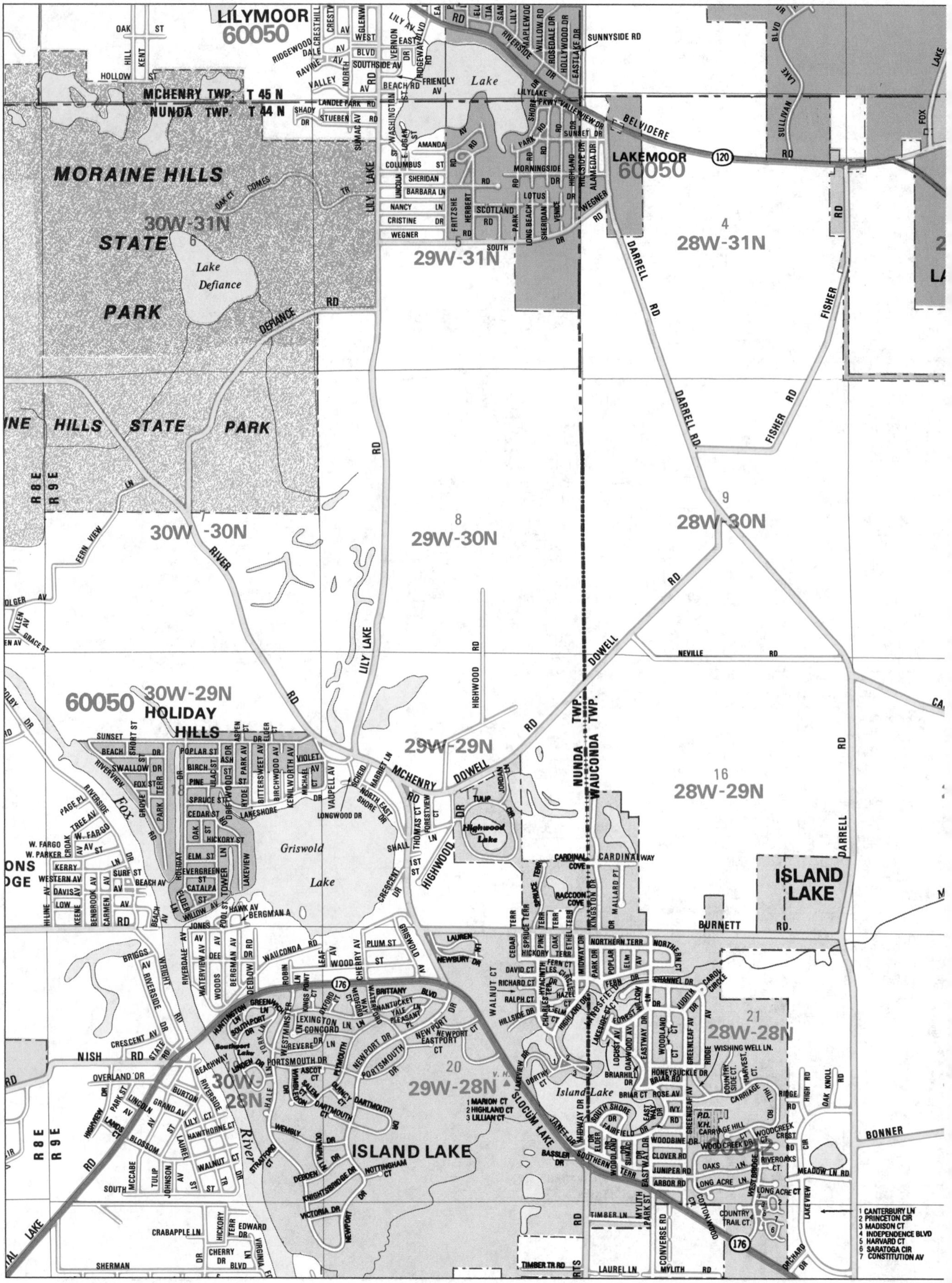

LILYMOOR
**60050**

MCHENRY TWP.  T 45 N
NUNDA TWP.  T 44 N

**MORAINE HILLS**

30W-31N

**STATE**

Lake Defiance

**PARK**

DEFIANCE RD

HILLS  STATE  PARK

30W -30N

30W-29N
**60050**
HOLIDAY HILLS

Fox River

Griswold Lake

LYONS RIDGE

29W-31N

LAKEMOOR
**60050**

4
**28W-31N**

DARRELL RD

FISHER RD

9
**28W-30N**

DOWELL RD
NEVILLE RD

8
**29W-30N**

LILY LAKE RD
HIGHWOOD RD

29W-29N

MCHENRY RD
Highwood Lake

NUNDA TWP.
WAUCONDA TWP.

16
**28W-29N**

ISLAND LAKE

BURNETT RD

18

30W-28N

NISH RD

176

20
**29W-28N**

**ISLAND LAKE**

SLOCUM LAKE

Island Lake

21
**28W-28N**

BONNER RD

176

WISHING WELL LN

1 MARION CT
2 HIGHLAND CT
3 LILLIAN CT

1 CANTERBURY LN
2 PRINCETON CIR
3 MADISON CT
4 INDEPENDENCE BLVD
5 HARVARD CT
6 SARATOGA CIR
7 CONSTITUTION AV

R 8 E
R 9 E

SEE PAGES 20-21

SEE PAGES 30-31

GRANT TWP. T 45 N
WAUCONDA TWP. T 44 N

BELVIDERE RD

TOWN LINE

BACON

MEADOW

120

60

3
7W-31N

2
26W-31N

1
25W-31N

24W-31N
6

LAKEMOOR

RAND RD

GILMER RD

VOLO

FISH LAKE

CALLAHAN RD

WILSON RD

FAIRFIELD RD

CHEROKEE TR

BLACKHAWK TR

MANOR HILL

10
27W-30N

11
26W-30N

12
25W-30N

24W-30N
7

CHARDON RD

CHARDON LN

Monahan Lake

GILMER RD

GOSSELL RD

GARLAND RD

15
27W-29N

14
26W-29N

13
25W-29N

18
24W-29N

Marilyn
Meadow CT

Robin CT

Virginia LN

Timothy TR

Virginia LN

SUNSET CT

BAKER LN

RUSSELL LN

Lake Fairfield

FAIRFIELD RD

Creek

Mutton

RAND RD

CALLAHAN RD

OLD RAND RD

WAUCONDA TWP.
FREMONT TWP.

R 9 E
R 10 E

Lake

LAKE FAIRFIELD LN

WADE ST

Wapa-Siwe

WAUCONDA
1300N

WAUCONDA
INDUSTRIAL PARK

KYLE CT

HOLLOW DR

HITH DR

INDUSTRIAL DR

NORTHVIEW DR

KARL DR

MUTTON DR

JAMES LN

SOUTH DR

BONNER RD

GARDNER RD

MADISON AV

WASHINGTON AV

MONROE AV

JACKSON AV

LAKE PKWY

MACINTOSH

JOHN DR

500E

600E

700E

1100E

25W-28N

24
26W-28N

22
27W-28N

1200N

1100N

DATO LN

BROWN ST

WAUCONDA
60084

APPLE RIDGE

BONNER RD
24W-28N
19

WAUCONDA RD

FAIRFIELD RD

OLD OAK DR

GRANT PL

PERSHING DR

ERICA DR

JESSICA DR

CARDINAL CT

900N

LAUREL AV

OSAGE TERR

AGAR TERR

CRESCENT TERR

CLOVER ROW

WALNUT RD

LARKDALE ROW

MARINE RD

COOK ST

Park

ROBERT CROWN POOL

FARMHILL

COUNTRY RIDGE

PINE ST

700N

600N

WAUCONDA H.S.

MINERVA AV

OSAGE

NORTH AV

Cook Park

GARLAND RD

WEST ZENIR

PLEASANT AV

WELLS ST

FERNE PLAZA

WINDING LANE RD

WEST DR

HACKBERRY

JACKSON CT

DATMORE

ELMWOOD AV

VALENTINE RD

LAKE ST

NORTH SHORE DR

BRANDON LN

PAMELA CT

VAN BUREN AV

SHERIDAN

NORTH SHORE AV

MAIN CT

CARY AV

SHEILA CT

MONROE

MADISON

ADAMS

JACKSON

OAK DR

VIEW AV

WASHINGTON

SUMMIT AV

PLEASANT

EDGEWATER PKWY

OAKDALE DR

WOODLAND

RIDGE AV

PARK PL

LINCOLN AV

PARK DR

BRUNO BLVD

GRAND BLVD

SUMMIT AV

PARKVIEW DR

Lake

EDGE

LAKEPOINTE

SHORE AV

BLVD

SEE PAGES 36-37

SEE PAGES 22-23

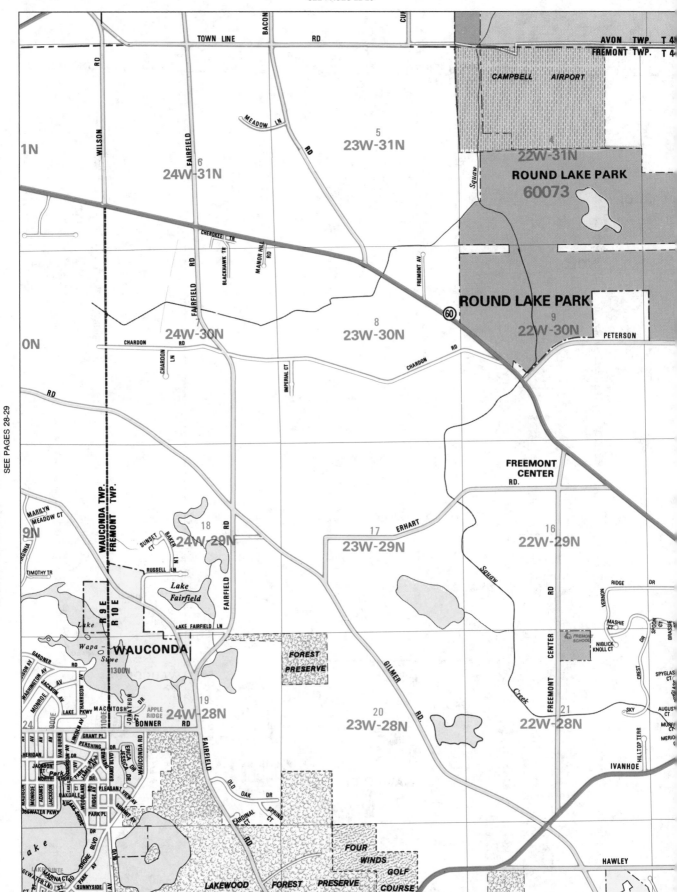

TOWN LINE RD
BACON

AVON TWP. T 4
FREMONT TWP. T 4

CAMPBELL   AIRPORT

MEADOW LN

WILSON RD

FAIRFIELD

1N

24W-31N
6

5
23W-31N

4
22W-31N

Squaw

ROUND LAKE PARK
60073

CHEROKEE TR

FAIRFIELD RD

BLACKHAWK TR

MANOR HILL RD

FREMONT AV

ROUND LAKE PARK

60

ON

CHARDON RD

24W-30N
7

8
23W-30N

CHARDON RD

9
22W-30N
PETERSON

CHARDON LN

IMPERIAL CT

CHARDON RD

RD

SEE PAGES 28-29

FREMONT CENTER RD.

MARILYN
MEADOW CT

9N

WAUCONDA TWP.
FREMONT TWP.

18
24W-29N

SUNSET CT

BAKER LN

17
23W-29N
ERHART

16
22W-29N

RIDGE   DR

VERNON

VIRGINIA

REGINA

TIMOTHY TR

RUSSELL LN

FAIRFIELD

Lake
Fairfield

Squaw

FREMONT
SCHOOL

MASHIE
CT

NIBLICK
KNOLL CT

R 9 E
R 10 E

LAKE FAIRFIELD LN

CREST

SPOON DR

BRASSIE

SPYGLAS

Lake
Wapa-
Stone
1300N

WAUCONDA

FOREST
PRESERVE

GILMER RD

Creek

FREMONT   CENTER   RD

SKY

AUGUSTA
CT

MURFI
CT
MERIO

GARDNER

WASHINGTON AV
JACKSON AV

MONROE
AV

LAKE   RD

HARRISON AV

MACINTOSH DR

JONATHON DR

APPLE
RIDGE

19
24W-28N
BONNER   RD

20
23W-28N

21
22W-28N

IVANHOE

HILLTOP TERR

24

HERIDAN

JACKSON

VAN BUREN

LINCOLN AV

GRANT PL

PERSHING

ERICA DR

WAUCONDA RD

JESSICA DR

BRAND BLVD

PLEASANT

VIEW AV

FAIRFIELD RD

OLD OAK   DR

SPRING CT

MADISON
MONROE
ADAMS
JACKSON

EDGEWATER PKWY

PARK PL

RIDGE RD

WOODLAND

SUNSET AV

CARDINAL CT

FOUR
WINDS

Lake

KEY
LN

MAGINA CT

SHORE BLVD

BRIAR AV

SUNNYSIDE

LAKEWOOD   FOREST   PRESERVE

GOLF
COURSE

HAWLEY

SEE PAGES 38-39

SEE PAGES 22-23

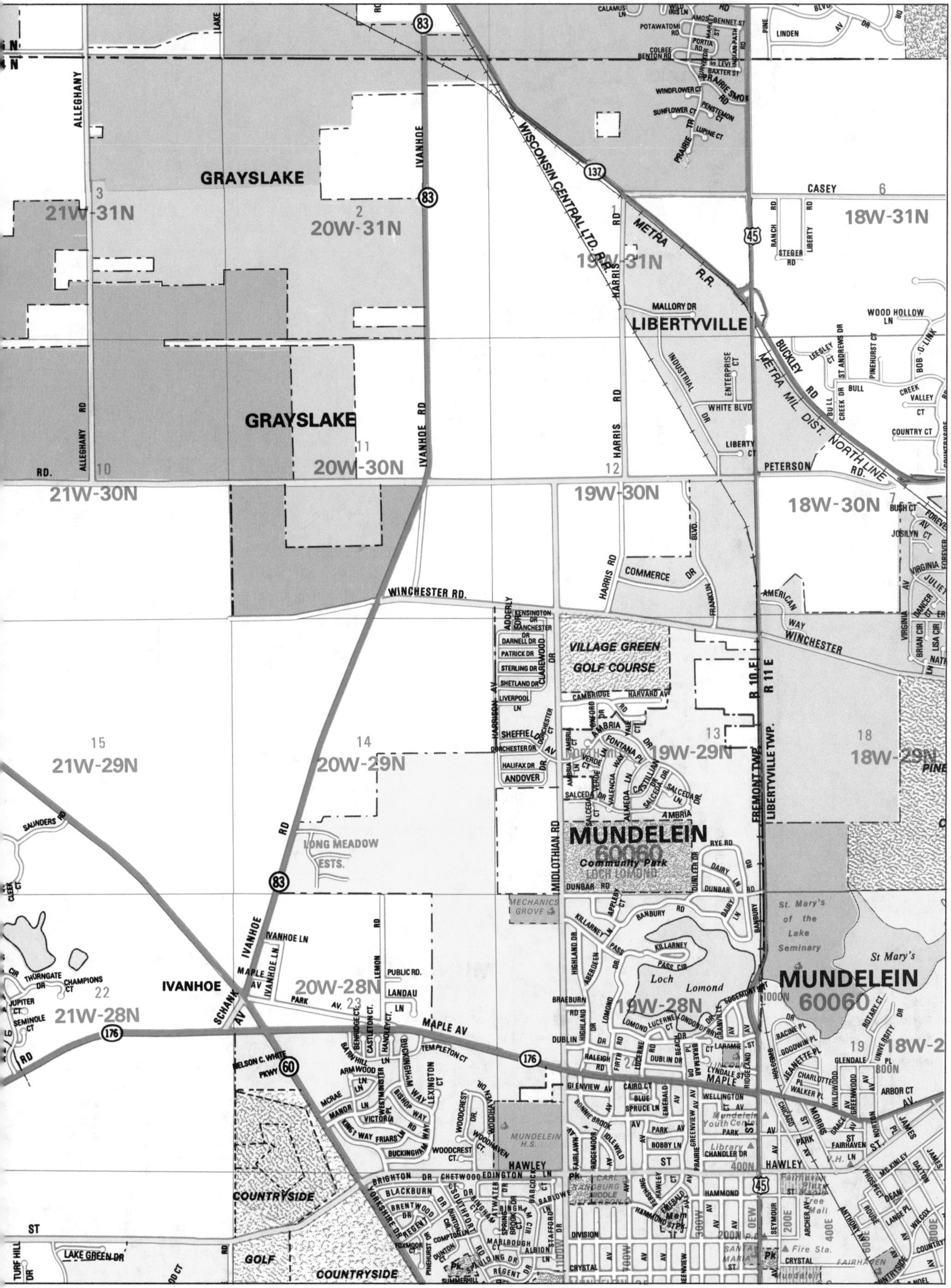

GRAYSLAKE
GRAYSLAKE
LIBERTYVILLE
MUNDELEIN
60060
MUNDELEIN
60060
IVANHOE
21W-31N
20W-31N
19W-31N
18W-31N
21W-30N
20W-30N
19W-30N
18W-30N
21W-29N
20W-29N
19W-29N
18W-29N
21W-28N
20W-28N
19W-28N
ALLEGHANY
ALLEGHANY RD
IVANHOE
IVANHOE RD
WISCONSIN CENTRAL LTD. R.R.
METRA R.R.
METRA MIL. DIST. NORTH LINE
HARRIS RD
CASEY
LINDEN
MALLORY DR
INDUSTRIAL DR
ENTERPRISE CT
WHITE BLVD
LIBERTY CT
PETERSON RD.
BUCKLEY RD
WOOD HOLLOW LN
COUNTRY CT
CREEK VALLEY CT
WINCHESTER RD.
COMMERCE DR
FRANKLIN BLVD.
AMERICAN WAY
WINCHESTER
VILLAGE GREEN GOLF COURSE
HARRISON AV
MIDLOTHIAN RD
FREMONT TWP.
LIBERTYVILLE TWP.
R 10 E
R 11 E
Community Park
LOCH LOMOND
DUNBAR RD
MECHANICS GROVE
St. Mary's of the Lake Seminary
St Mary's
Loch Lomond
LONG MEADOW ESTS.
SAUNDERS RD
IVANHOE LN
MAPLE AV
LEMON RD
PUBLIC RD.
LANDAU LN
PARK AV.
SCHANK AV
MAPLE AV
NELSON C. WHITE PKWY
MUNDELEIN H.S.
HAWLEY
HAWLEY
COUNTRYSIDE
COUNTRYSIDE
GOLF
LAKE GREEN DR
TURF HILL DR
BRIGHTON DR
CHETWOOD
EDINGTON
BLACKBURN
DIVISION
CRYSTAL
HAMMOND
Fire Sta.
FAIRHAVEN
83
137
45
176
60

SEE PAGES 32-33

SEE PAGES 38-39

SEE PAGES 24-25

SEE PAGES 30-31

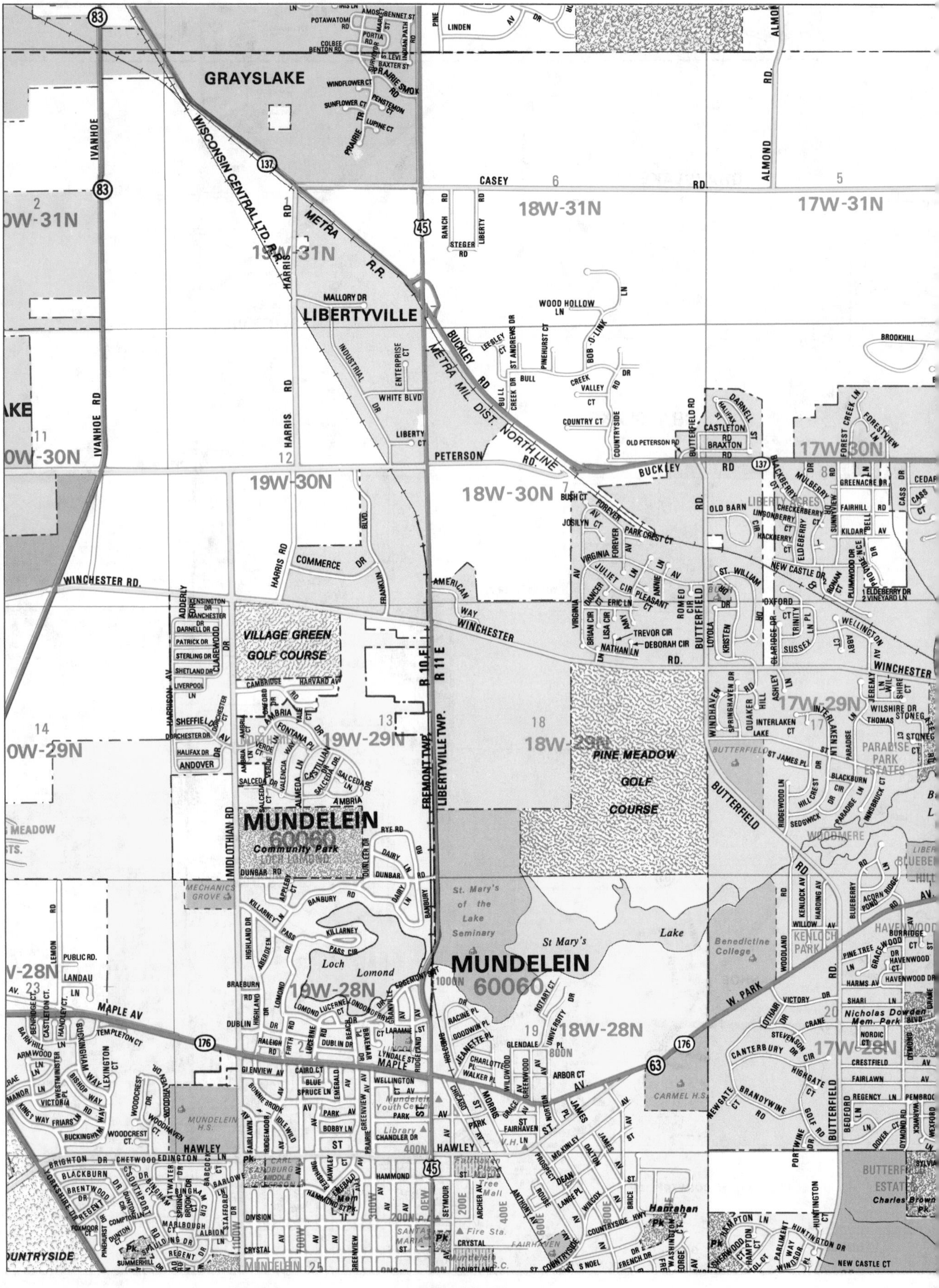
GRAYSLAKE
LIBERTYVILLE
MUNDELEIN
60060
MUNDELEIN
60060
18W-31N
17W-31N
19W-31N
19W-30N
18W-30N
17W-30N
19W-29N
18W-29N
17W-29N
19W-28N
18W-28N
17W-28N
CASEY
RD.
ALMOND
RD.
IVANHOE
IVANHOE RD
WISCONSIN CENTRAL LTD. R.R.
METRA R.R.
METRA MIL. DIST. NORTH LINE
HARRIS RD
MALLORY DR
INDUSTRIAL DR
ENTERPRISE CT
WHITE BLVD
LIBERTY CT
PETERSON RD.
BUCKLEY RD
WOOD HOLLOW LN
BULL CREEK DR
PINEHURST CT
BOB-O-LINK
CREEK VALLEY CT
COUNTRY CT
COUNTRYSIDE
OLD PETERSON RD
BUTTERFIELD RD
CASTLETON
BRAXTON
WINCHESTER RD.
COMMERCE DR
FRANKLIN
AMERICAN WAY
WINCHESTER RD.
VILLAGE GREEN GOLF COURSE
PINE MEADOW GOLF COURSE
FREMONT TWP.
LIBERTYVILLE TWP.
R 10 E
R 11 E
Community Park
St. Mary's of the Lake Seminary
St Mary's Lake
Loch Lomond
Benedictine College
MECHANICS GROVE
MAPLE AV
W. PARK
Nicholas Dowden Mem. Park
MUNDELEIN H.S.
CARMEL H.S.
HAWLEY
Hanrahan Pk
Mundelein Youth Center
Library
Fire Sta.
COUNTRYSIDE HWY
PUBLIC RD.
LEMON
LANDAU
BUTTERFIELD
PARADISE PARK ESTATES
WOODMERE
KENLOCH PARK
HAVENWOOD
BUTTERFIELD ESTATES
Charles Brown Pk
BROOKHILL
MIDLOTHIAN RD
ROLLINS

SEE PAGES 40-41

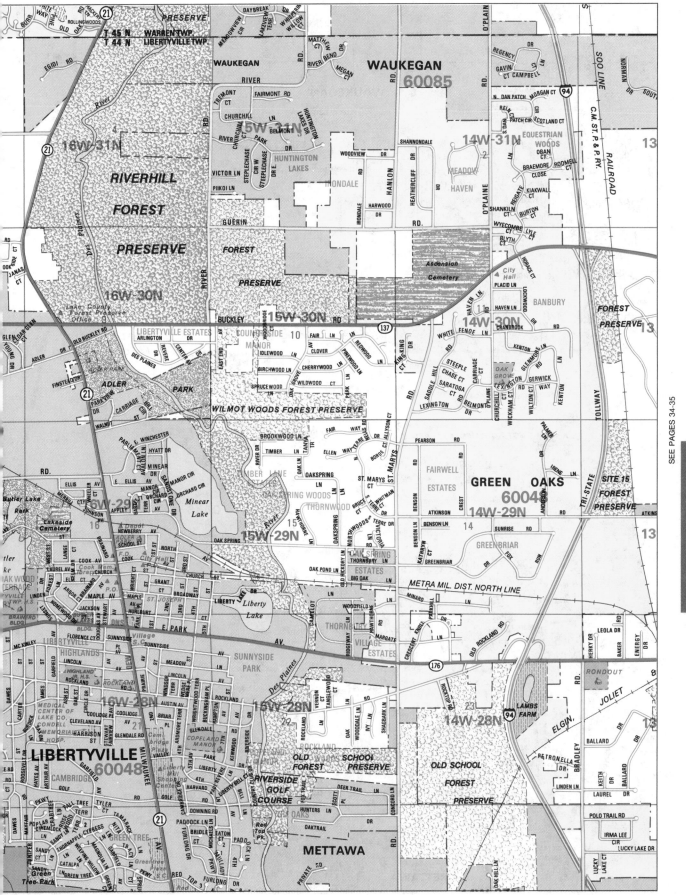

SEE PAGES 26-27

SEE PAGES 32-33

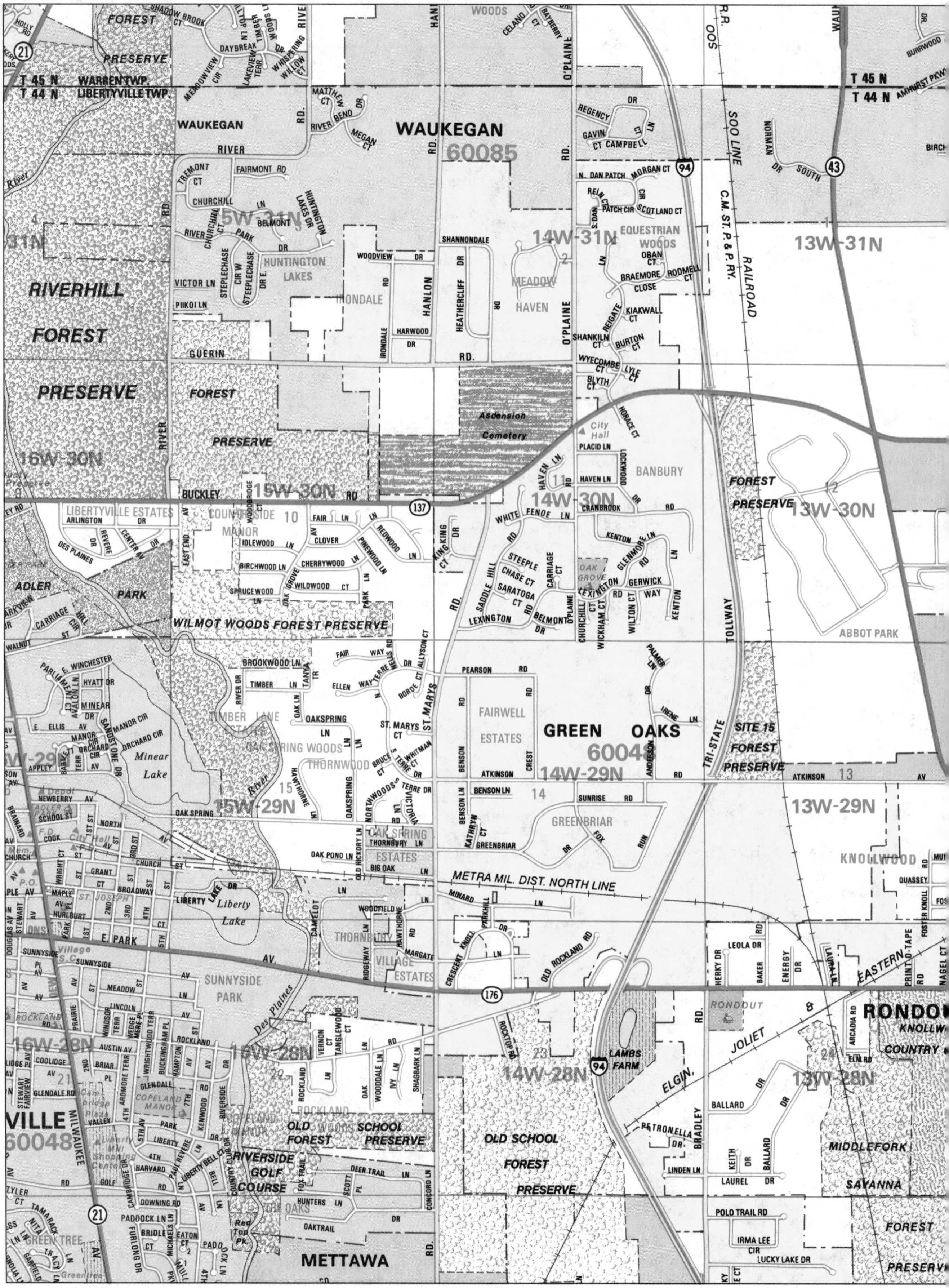

WARREN TWP.
LIBERTYVILLE TWP.
T 45 N
T 44 N

FOREST
PRESERVE

WAUKEGAN

WAUKEGAN
60085

HUNTINGTON LAKES

RIVERHILL

FOREST

PRESERVE

FOREST
PRESERVE

14W-31N

13W-31N

EQUESTRIAN WOODS

SOO LINE
C.M. ST. P. & P. RY.
RAILROAD

16W-30N

15W-30N

14W-30N

13W-30N

Ascension Cemetery

City Hall

BANBURY

FOREST PRESERVE

LIBERTYVILLE ESTATES

COUNTRYSIDE MANOR

WILMOT WOODS FOREST PRESERVE

ADLER

PARK

ABBOT PARK

Minear Lake

OAKSPRING WOODS
THORNWOOD

FAIRWELL ESTATES

GREEN OAKS
60048
14W-29N

SITE 15
FOREST PRESERVE

TRI-STATE    TOLLWAY

15W-29N

13W-29N

KNOLLWOOD

Liberty Lake

METRA MIL. DIST. NORTH LINE

GREENBRIAR

Village S.S.

SUNNYSIDE PARK

THORNBURY
VILLAGE ESTATES

16W-28N

15W-28N

14W-28N

13W-28N

RONDOUT
KNOLL
COUNTRY

JOLIET

LAMBS FARM

VILLE
60048

OLD SCHOOL FOREST PRESERVE

OLD SCHOOL

FOREST

PRESERVE

RIVERSIDE GOLF COURSE

MIDDLEFORK

SAVANNA

FOREST

PRESERVE

METTAWA

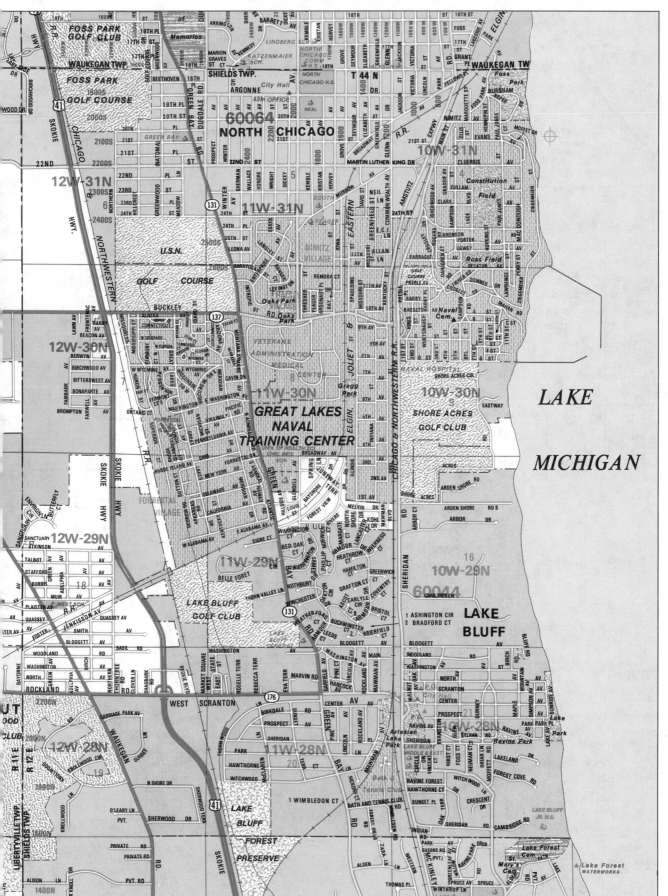

SEE PAGES 28-29

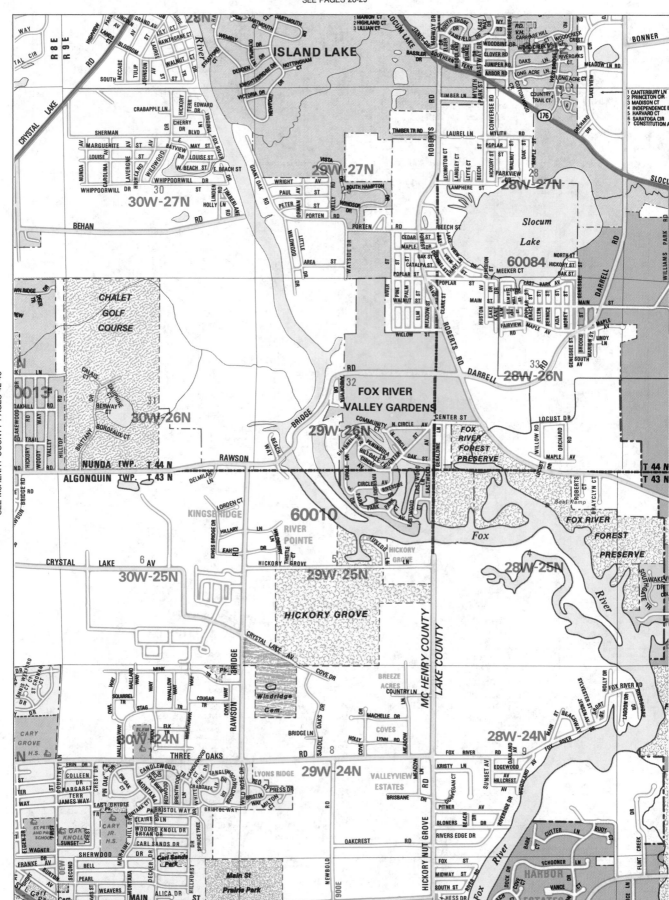

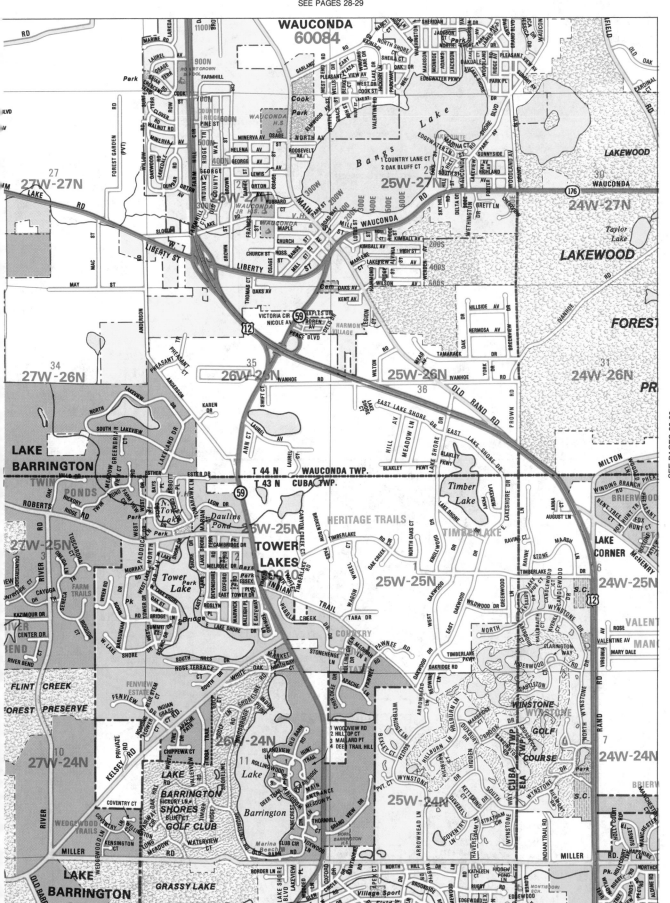

SEE PAGES 30-31

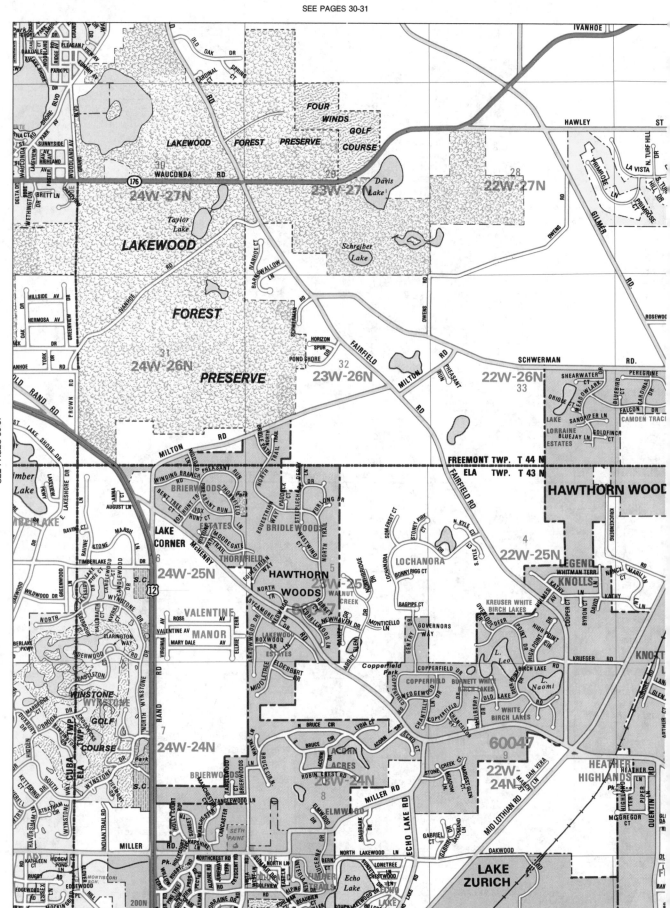

SEE PAGES 36-37

SEE PAGES 30-31

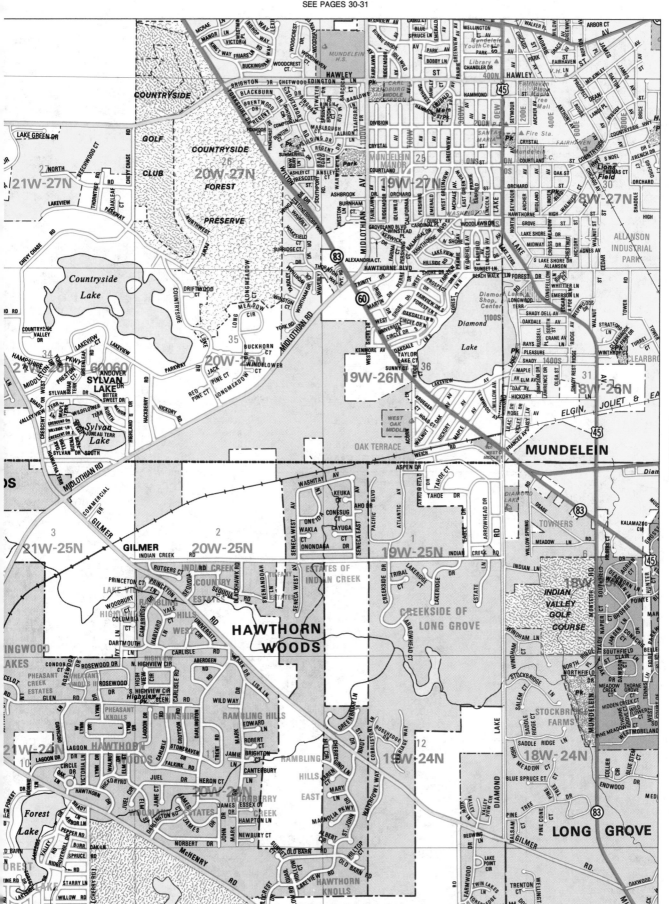

SEE PAGES 40-41

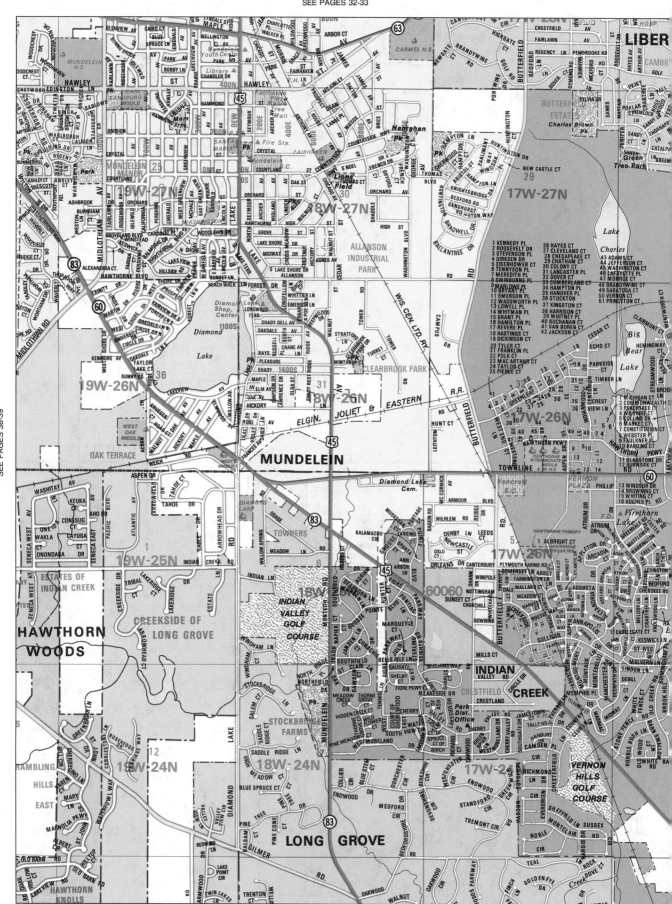

SEE PAGES 32-33

SEE PAGES 42-43

SEE PAGES 48-49

SEE PAGES 34-35

SEE PAGES 40-41

SCHOOL PRESERVE

OLD SCHOOL FOREST PRESERVE

MIDDLEFORK SAVANNA FOREST PRESERVE

PATRONELLA DR
BRAD
KEITH DR
BALLARD
LINDEN LN
LAUREL DR

LIBERTYVILLE TWP
SHIELDS TWP

O'LEARY LN PVT.
KNOLLWOOD
SHERWOOD DR
SHERWOOD TERR

SKOKIE
LAK BL

CONCORD LN
OAK HILL LN
TRAIL LN

POLO TRAIL RD
IRMA LEE CIR
LUCKY LAKE CT
LUCKY LAKE DR

PRIVATE RD
PRIVATE RD
RD
SHERWOOD DR

ALISON LN
OAK KNOLL DR
PVT. RD
GAGE LN

1400N
1200N
PVT. RD
PVT. RD
WINWOOD DR
30

14W-27N
26
13W-27N
12W-27N
31
43

DR
RD
OLD SCHOOL RD
MAUREEN LN

WESTWOODS LN
RITEWAY
MEADOWWOOD CT
MEADOWWOODS

ST. MARYS RD
NORTHWOODS LN

1000N
HOSPITAL DR HWY

HAWTHORNE AV
FORESTHAVEN FOREST DR
OAK AV
ELMWOOD
HAWTHORNE DR
HAWTHORNE DR
HAWTHORNE DR

MIDDLEFORK SAVANNA FOREST PRESERVE

WHITMORE CT
SUMMERFIELD DR
PRIVATE RD
LANE LORRAINE
CASTLEGATE CT
LARCHMONT

IMPERIAL DR
Lake County OASIS
LAKE COUNTY

LAKE FOREST ACADEMY-FERRY HALL

Meadowwood Pk.
CONCORD DR
MEADOWWOOD DR
ASHLAWN
MONTELLO
HALLIGAN
BURTON
RIVERTON RD
Lake Forest Hospital

14W-26N
35
LONGWOOD
INDIAN RIDGE RD
ELM RD
MELLOT LN

36
13W-26N

ACADEMY WOODS
MARQUETT CT
PRINCETON CT
STANFORD CT
HARVARD CT
CORNELL CT
YALE CT
ACADEMY WOODS RD

FOREST
LEXINGTON
FLETCHER
EXETER PL
INVERLIETH
GREENVALE
NATHAWAY CT
INVERLEITH TERR WAY
NORTHCLIFF LN
PARKMEAD LN

DEERPATH
12W-26N
DEERPATH

WEST Lake
EAST Lake

PRESERVE
LONGMEADOW LN
DEERPATH
ARMOUR CIR
WARWICK
VERDA LN
SUSSEX
KENNINGTON TERR
KING
CHILTERN

FIELD DR
FIELD CT
SAVANNA CT
RUE
MELLODY RD
MELLOT
FOGCOTE
RIDGE
ESCOTE

Conway Park Office & Research
MELLODY RUE
FORET
SUFFOLK
ROSCOMMON RD
SUFFOLK RD

60
KENNEDY
HIGH HOLBORN
MELLODY RD

TOWNLINE RD
ON OS

PINECROFT LN
REILLY LN
SUFFOLK LN

14W-25N
2

SAUNDERS RD
WOODLAND LN
NORTH SHORE DR
SOUTH SHORE LN
BROADLAND LN
MEADOW FARM
RIDGEFIELD LN
DUBLIN

200S
LAKE FOREST H.S. WEST CAMPUS
Lake Forest Intermediate

LAKE
6004
FOREST
WALLACE RD
LINDSEY CIR

METTAWA
60044-45

RIVERWOODS
SAUNDERS RD
13W-25N
1
CONWAY

STABLEWOOD LN
400S
12W-25N
6
WESTLEIGH

BARRYS LN
YORKTOWN LN
NEWCASTLE
STABLE LN
NORTH CROFT CT
PRIVATE

SHAGBARK RD
CONWAY FARM RD
OAK KNOLL DR
ABINGTON CAMBS DR
LELAND CT
GAVIN CT
PVT. RD
SHEFFIELD CT
COVENTRY DR
COUNTRY

600S
800S

2300W
2200W
2000W
1800W
1600W
1400W
1200W
LAKEWOOD
FOX TRAIL CT
KNIGHTS BRIDGE LN
GLOUSTER CROSSING
800W

EVERETT RD
EVERETT RD
1000S
EVERETT RD

ST. MARYS RD

CAPT. DANIEL WRIGHT F.P.

Park
BOWLING OLD BARN LN
GREEN
RANDOLPH
FAIRWAY DR
F.D.
Fire CASCADE
SIR WILLIAM RD
BRIDGEVIEW DR
MARLANE DR
FRANZ LN
LYNETTE

14W-24N
11

13W-24N
12
HACKBERRY LN
FARM RD
TRILLIUM LN
ARCADY DR
CASCADE CT N.
CASCADE CT S

JEN FIFER CT
EVERGREEN
CT

CAPT. DANIEL WRIGHT FOREST PRESERVE
TRAIL-WAY
CONCORDIA LN (PVT)
NORTHAMPTON LN
ELM RD
OAK LN
BRIDLE TRAIL

Florsheim Park
WILSON LN
KENNETT LAWRENCE AV LN
KIMMER CT
WOODHILL LN
ESTATE LN E.

1200S
LAWRENCE AV
KAJER CT
FAIRE CT
Everett Park
St. Patrick Cem.
1400S

12W-24N
LAWRENCE
GROVE CT
WILD ROSE LN
43

ELM ROAD FOREST PRESERVE
DANIEL WRIGHT MIDDLE
BRAMPTON CT
STAFFORD CT
BRIARWOOD LN
RIVERWOODS
WHITMORE LN

LITTLE FIELD CT
MINTHAVEN RD
OLD MILL
PVT. RD
ESTATE
OAK KNOLL DR
WHITE OAK
HERITAGE CT
HERITAGE RD

STONELEIGH CT
PARLIAMENT
DEVONSHIRE
ALEXIS CT
DEVONSHIRE LN
LOWELL RD
LARKSPUR LN
GOLDENROD LN
ASPEN DR

River
PLE ORCHARD LN
WIMBLEDON
ASHFORD CT
VALDON RD
WHITE GATE CT
LEEDS CT
DURHAM CT
WIMBLEDON
WEDGEWOOD DR
BIG OAKS LN
ARBOR
BRIDGE DR
TELEGRAPH
SOO

94

SEE PAGES 50-51

SEE PAGES 34-35

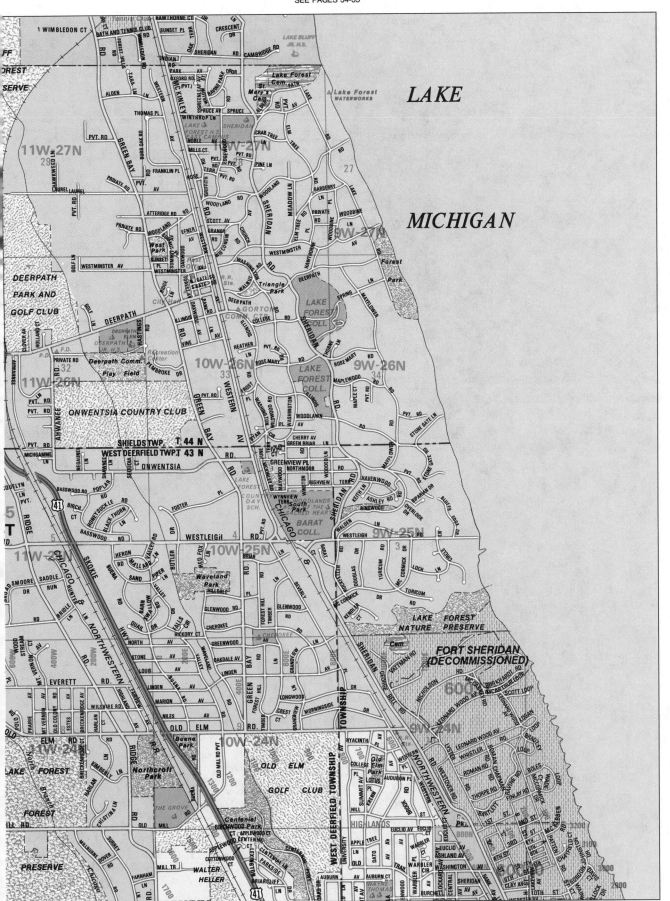

SEE PAGES 36-37

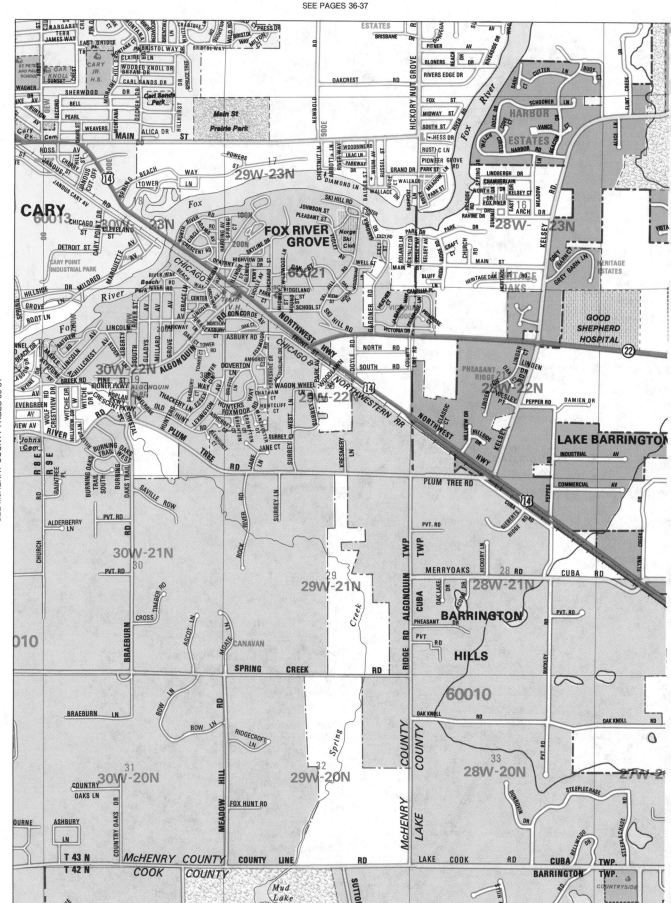

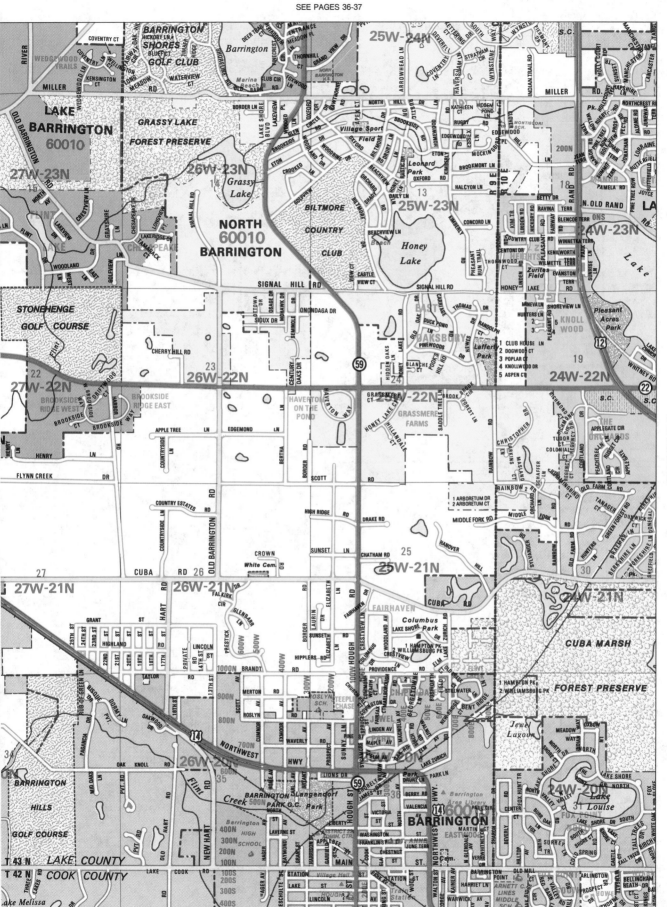

SEE PAGES 46-47

SEE PAGES 38-39

SEE PAGES 44-45

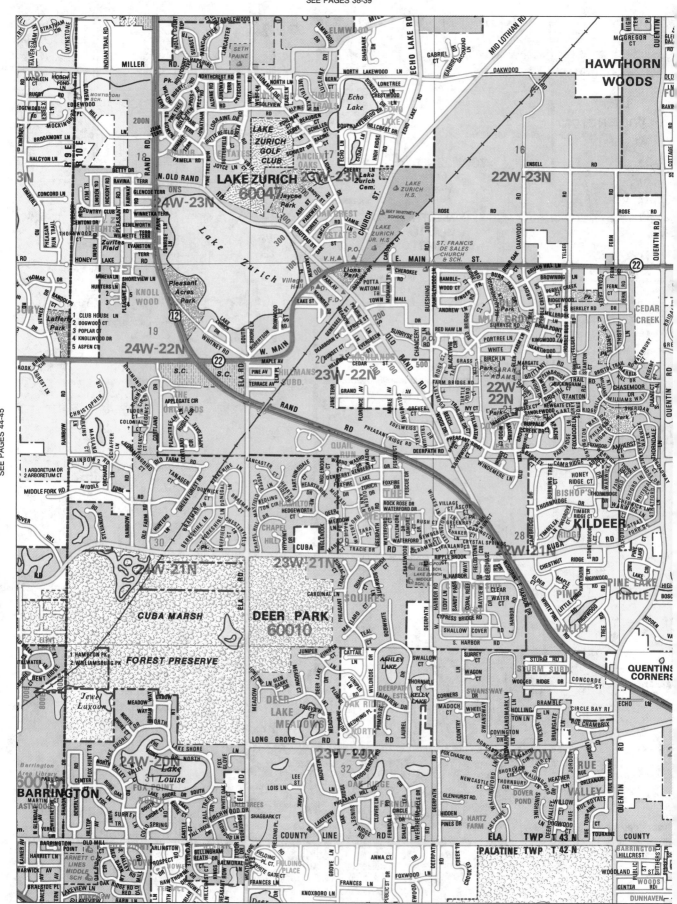

SEE COOK COUNTY PAGES 12-13

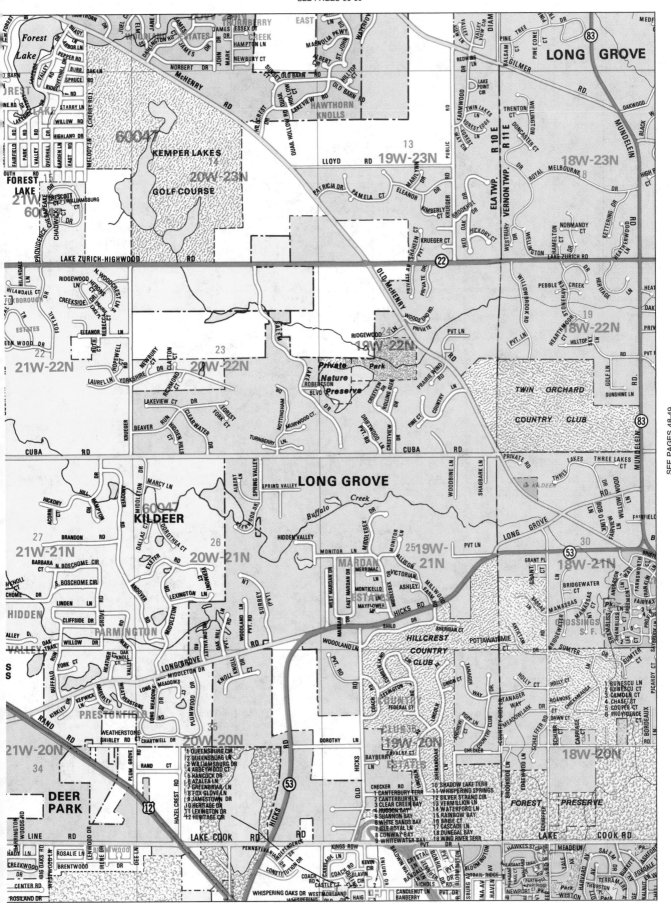

SEE PAGES 48-49

SEE PAGES 46-47

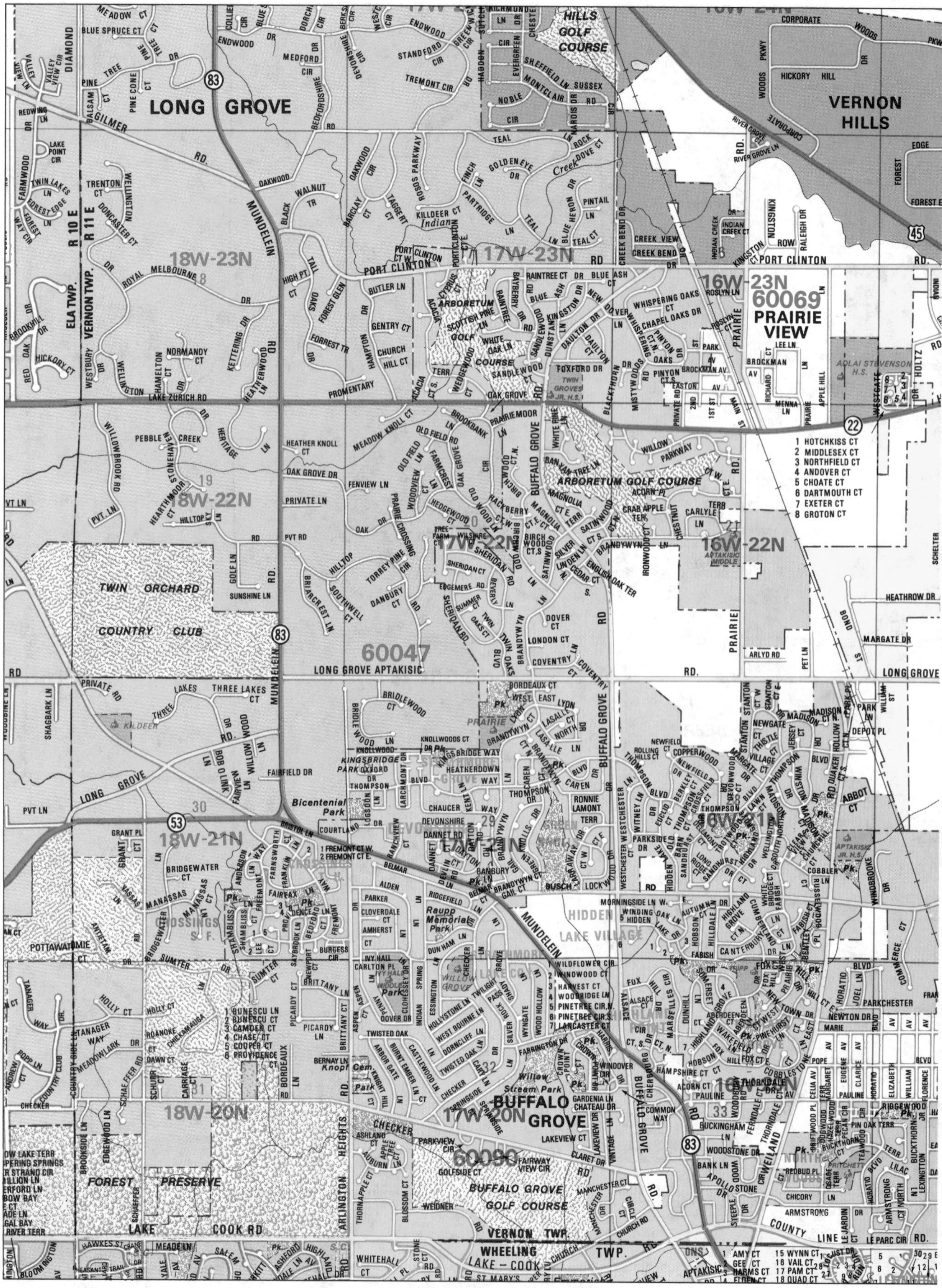

LONG GROVE

VERNON HILLS

PRAIRIE VIEW

60069

16W-23N

MUNDELEIN

HILLS GOLF COURSE

PORT CLINTON

ARBORETUM GOLF COURSE

18W-23N

17W-23N

16W-22N

18W-22N

17W-22N

TWIN ORCHARD COUNTRY CLUB

60047
LONG GROVE APTAKISIC

BUFFALO GROVE

18W-21N

17W-21N

16W-21N

HIDDEN LAKE VILLAGE

18W-20N

17W-20N

60090

FOREST PRESERVE

BUFFALO GROVE GOLF COURSE

NORTHL...

ELA TWP.
VERNON TWP.

R 10 E   R 11 E

1 HOTCHKISS CT
2 MIDDLESEX CT
3 NORTHFIELD CT
4 ANDOVER CT
5 CHOATE CT
6 DARTMOUTH CT
7 EXETER CT
8 GROTON CT

ADLAI STEVENSON H.S.

APTAKISIC MIDDLE

VERNON TWP.
WHEELING TWP.
LAKE-COOK

LAKE COOK RD.

COOK COUNTY LINE

SEE PAGES 40-41

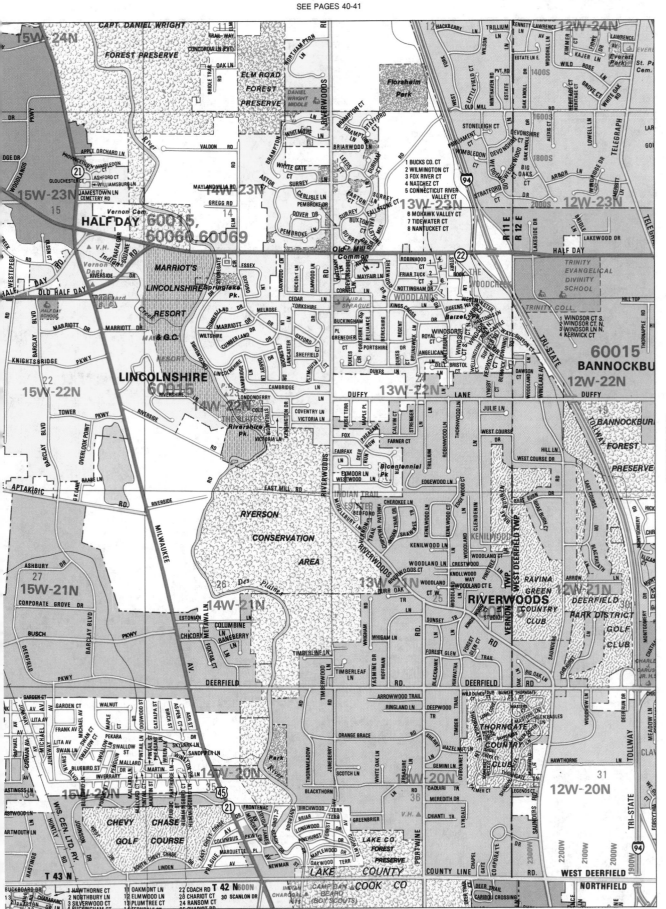

SEE PAGES 50-51

SEE COOK COUNTY PAGES 16-17

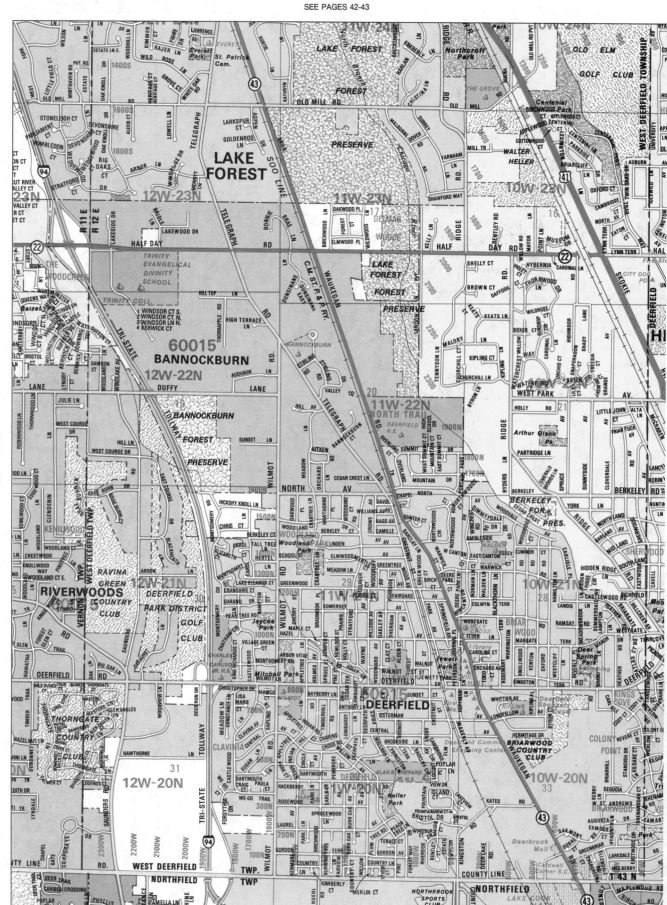

LAKE

MICHIGAN

# Lake
# County

WISCONSIN
ILLINOIS

Antioch

60002

60085

60096

Winthrop
Harbor

60099

Zion

60020

Lake Villa

Old Mill Creek

Wadsworth

60046    Lindenhurst

Fox Lake

60031

60087

Round
Lake

Third Lake

Gurnee

60041    60073    60099

Waukegan

60085

Hainesville    Grayslake    Gages Lake

Park City

60064

North Chicago

LAKE
MICHIGAN

LAKE CO.

60084

Green Oaks

60048

Lake Bluff

Island Lake

60060    Mundelein    Libertyville    60044

60042

Lake Forest

Wauconda

Tower Lakes
Lake Barrington

Indian
Creek    Mettawa
Vernon Hills

60045

60069

60061    Lincolnshire

60037

Highwoood

North Barrington    Lake Zurich

Bannockburn

60035

60047    60089

60015

Riverwoods

Deer Park    Kildeer    Long Grove

60035    Highland Park

60010    Barrington    Buffalo Grove    Deerfield

# Street Index

| | Grid | Page |
|---|---|---|
| **Antioch** | | |
| Abbey Ct. E&W | 22W-43N | 6 |
| Abbey Ln. NS&EW | 22W-43N | 6 |
| Alma Ter. N&S | 23W-42N | 6 |
| Anita Av. N&S | 23W-42N | 6 |
| Asbury Ct. E&W | 24W-42N | 5 |
| Autumn Ln. N&S | 22W-42N | 6 |
| Bartlett Av. N&S | 23W-42N | 6 |
| Bayshore Dr. NW&SE | 24W-41N | 6 |
| Beach Hollow Dr. NS&EW | 21W-42N | 6 |
| Birchwood Dr. NW&SE | 23W-43N | 6 |
| Bishop St. N&S | 23W-42N | 6 |
| Blackman Ter. N&S | 23W-42N | 6 |
| Bowles Rd. E&W | 24W-41N | 5 |
| Bridgewood Dr. N&S | 23W-43N | 6 |
| Buena Ter. E&W | 23W-41N | 6 |
| Butcher Block Dr. E&W | 24W-43N | 5 |
| Cedarwood Ln. N&S | 23W-43N | 6 |
| Channel Lake Rd. E&W | 23W-42N | 6 |
| Charles Ct. (Pvt.) E&W | 23W-42N | 6 |
| Cheri Ln. NW&SE | 23W-42N | 6 |
| Chestnut St. E&W | 23W-41N | 6 |
| Collins Av. NW&SE | 23W-43N | 6 |
| Corona Av. N&S | 23W-42N | 6 |
| Crabtree Ln. N&S | 22W-42N | 6 |
| Creekside Ln. E&W | 22W-42N | 6 |
| Crest Ln. E&W | 23W-42N | 6 |
| Cunningham Dr. N&S | 23W-42N | 6 |
| David St. N&S | 24W-42N | 5 |
| Deep Lake Rd. N&S | 22W-41N,22W-42N | 6 |
| Deer Lake Ct. NE&SW | 22W-42N | 6 |
| Deer Lake Dr. N&S | 22W-42N | 6 |
| Depot St. E&W | 23W-42N | 6 |
| Donin Dr. NW&SE | 23W-43N | 6 |
| Drom Ct. N&S | 23W-42N | 6 |
| Dwight Ct. N&S | 23W-42N | 6 |
| East Rd. N&S | 22W-42N | 6 |
| Edelweiss Ct. E&W | 24W-41N | 5 |
| Edelweiss Dr. E&W | 24W-41N | 5 |
| Edgewood Dr. E&W | 23W-43N | 6 |
| Elizabeth St. E&W | 23W-42N | 6 |
| Elmwood Ln. N&S | 23W-43N,22W-43N | 6 |
| Fillmore Ct. E&W | 23W-42N | 6 |
| Forest Ln. E&W | 23W-43N | 6 |
| Gail St. N&S | 23W-42N | 6 |
| Glen Brook Ct. E&W | 22W-42N | 6 |
| Gray's Dr. N&S | 23W-42N | 6 |
| Greenbrier Dr. E&W | 23W-42N | 6 |
| Harden St. E&W | 23W-41N | 6 |
| Harvest Ct. N&S | 22W-42N | 6 |
| Harvest Rd. N&S | 22W-42N | 6 |
| Hawthorne Ct. NW&SE | 22W-42N | 6 |
| Hazelwood Dr. NW&SE | 23W-43N | 6 |
| Hennings Ct. NW&SE | 24W-41N | 5 |
| Henry St. N&S | 24W-42N | 5 |
| Hickory Commons N&S | 23W-41N | 6 |
| Hickory Ln. N&S | 23W-43N | 6 |
| Hidden Creek Dr. E&W | 21W-42N | 6 |
| Highland Av. N&S | 23W-42N | 6 |
| Highview Dr. E&W | 24W-42N | 5 |
| Hill Ct. NE&SW | 23W-43N | 6 |
| Hillandale Dr. N&S | 24W-42N | 5 |
| Hillside Av. NE&SW | 24W-42N | 6 |
| Ida St. E&W | 23W-42N | 6 |
| Johanna Ct. E&W | 23W-42N | 6 |
| Johella Ln. N&S | 23W-43N | 6 |
| Joren Tr. N&S | 23W-42N | 6 |
| Joren Trail Dr. NS&EW | 23W-43N | 6 |
| Lake Ct. NE&SW | 23W-43N | 6 |
| Lake St. E&W | 24W-42N | 6 |
| Lake St. E&W | 23W-43N | 5 |
| Lakewood Dr. N&S | 23W-43N | 6 |
| Laursen Ct. NW&SE | 23W-42N | 6 |
| Linden Ln. E&W | 23W-43N | 6 |
| | | |
| Little Silver Lake Rd. E&W | 22W-42N | 6 |
| Longview Dr. N&S | 23W-42N | 6 |
| Main St. N&S | 23W-42N | 6 |
| Maplewood Dr. E&W | 23W-43N | 6 |
| McMillan Rd. NS&EW | 23W-41N,23W-42N | 6 |
| Meadow Ct. NW&SE | 22W-43N | 6 |
| Miller Rd. E&W | 20W-40N | 7 |
| Mystic Cove NE&SW | 23W-41N | 6 |
| Naber Av. N&S | 23W-42N | 6 |
| Nelson Rd. N&S | 22W-43N | 6 |
| North Av. E&W | 24W-43N,22W-43N | 5 |
| | 23W-42N | 6 |
| Oak Ridge Ct. E&W | 22W-42N | 6 |
| Oakhill Ct. NW&SE | 23W-43N | 6 |
| Oakwood Dr. N&S | 23W-43N | 6 |
| Old Mill Tr. E&W | 22W-42N | 6 |
| Orchard St. E&W | 24W-42N | 5 |
| Ormond Av. N&S | 23W-42N | 6 |
| Park Av. E&W | 23W-42N | 6 |
| Park Av. N&S | 23W-43N | 6 |
| Parkway Av. N&S | 23W-42N | 6 |
| Phillips Cir. NS&EW | 24W-42N,23W-42N | 5 |
| Pine Cone Ln. NS&EW | 22W-42N | 6 |
| Pinehill Ct. N&S | 22W-42N | 6 |
| Plumtree Ln. N&S | 24W-42N | 5 |
| Poplar Av. E&W | 23W-42N | 6 |
| Private Rd. E&W | 24W-42N | 5 |
| Ram Rd., S. E&W | 23W-41N | 6 |
| Rinear Rd. N&S | 23W-42N | 6 |
| Route 173 E&W | 24W-42N,20W-41N | 5 |
| Route 59 N&S | 24W-41N | 5 |
| Route 83 N&S | 23W-41N,23W-42N | 6 |
| Savage Rd. N&S | 20W-40N | 7 |
| Sequoia Av. E&W | 23W-42N | 6 |
| Sequoia Ct. NW&SE | 22W-42N | 6 |
| Spafford St. N&S | 23W-42N | 6 |
| St. Peters St. N&S | 24W-42N | 5 |
| Sterbenz Ct. NW&SE | 22W-42N | 6 |
| Summerhill Ct. N&S | 22W-42N | 6 |
| Sunset Ln. NE&SW | 23W-43N | 6 |
| Tiffany Rd. N&S | 24W-42N | 5 |
| Timber Ln. E&W | 23W-43N,22W-43N | 6 |
| Toft St. N&S | 23W-42N | 6 |
| Turner Rd. N&S | 23W-42N | 6 |
| U.S. Route 45 N&S | 19W-42N | 7 |
| Valleyview Ct. E&W | 24W-42N | 5 |
| Victoria St. N&S | 23W-42N | 6 |
| White Rd. N&S | 21W-40N | 7 |
| Wildwood Ct. NE&SW | 22W-42N | 6 |
| Williams St. E&W | 23W-42N | 6 |
| Wilton Dr. E&W | 23W-42N | 6 |
| Windmill Creek Dr. NE&SW | 22W-42N | 6 |
| Winsor Dr. E&W | 23W-42N | 6 |
| Winsor Ter. E&W | 23W-41N | 6 |
| Zelinger Ln. E&W | 23W-42N | 6 |
| 1st St. E&W | 23W-42N | 6 |
| 2nd St. E&W | 23W-42N | 6 |
| 228th Av. E&W | 22W-43N | 6 |
| | | |
| **Antioch Township** | | |
| 'H' St. NE&SW | 23W-40N | 6 |
| 'L' St. E&W | 23W-40N | 6 |
| Ackerman Rd. N&S | 26W-38N | 13 |
| Adams Ct. E&W | 22W-41N | 6 |
| Addison Ln. N&S | 25W-42N | 5 |
| Ainsley St. N&S | 23W-41N | 6 |
| Alexander Av. E&W | 26W-39N | 13 |
| Andyville Ln. N&S | 25W-40N | 5 |
| Ann Pl. E&W | 28W-38N | 12 |
| Arbor Ln. N&S | 26W-43N | 5 |
| Asbury Av. N&S | 26W-39N | 13 |
| Ash St. N&S | 26W-42N | 5 |
| Ashland Av. E&W | 27W-38N | 12 |
| Astor St. E&W | 26W-38N | 13 |
| Bald Eagle Rd. N&S | 23W-40N | 6 |
| Banyan Av. E&W | 26W-38N | 5 |
| Bayside Dr. E&W | 25W-41N | 5 |
| Bayview Dr. E&W | 22W-41N | 6 |
| Bayview Rd. E&W | 24W-41N,23W-41N | 5 |
| | | |
| Beach Dr. E&W | 24W-43N | 5 |
| Beach Dr. N&S | 22W-40N | 6 |
| Beach Grove Rd. E&W | 25W-41N | 5 |
| Beach Rd. NE&SW | 27W-42N | 4 |
| Beach St. E&W | 26W-42N | 5 |
| Beachlane Dr. N&S | 22W-40N | 6 |
| Beachview Dr. N&S | 26W-41N,26W-42N | 5 |
| Beechwood Av. N&S | 28W-38N | 12 |
| Belden Av. E&W | 27W-38N | 12 |
| Benes Rd. E&W | 26W-38N | 13 |
| Birch Av. E&W | 26W-42N | 5 |
| Bittersweet Pl. N&S | 27W-38N | 12 |
| Black Oak Av. N&S | 24W-40N | 5 |
| Bluff Dr. N&S | 25W-40N | 5 |
| Bluff Lake Rd. N&S | 25W-40N | 5 |
| Bluff Ln. E&W | 25W-40N | 5 |
| Bolton Pl. N&S | 26W-38N | 13 |
| Bond Rd. NE&SW | 26W-41N | 5 |
| Briar Rd. N&S | 27W-38N | 12 |
| Briar Ter. E&W | 23W-41N | 6 |
| Broadway Av. N&S | 26W-38N | 13 |
| Brown Av. E&W | 26W-38N | 5 |
| Bunham Ct. NE&SW | 24W-40N | 6 |
| Bunker Ct. E&W | 22W-41N | 6 |
| Burr Hollow Dr. E&W | 19W-41N | 7 |
| Burton Av. N&S | 28W-38N | 12 |
| Calhoun Av. E&W | 26W-38N | 13 |
| Calvin Dr. E&W | 22W-40N | 6 |
| Catalpa Rd. E&W | 26W-43N | 5 |
| Catherine Av. E&W | 25W-43N | 5 |
| Catherine Av. N&S | 25W-43N | 5 |
| Cedar Crest Dr. NE&SW | 25W-39N | 13 |
| Cedar Dr. E&W | 22W-40N | 6 |
| Cedar Ln. NE&SW | 22W-40N,22W-41N | 6 |
| Cedar St. E&W | 28W-39N | 12 |
| Cedar St. E&W | 25W-42N | 5 |
| Center Dr. N&S | 22W-42N | 6 |
| Champaign Dr. NW&SE | 22W-40N | 6 |
| Channel Av. E&W | 26W-40N | 5 |
| Channel Dr. E&W | 24W-43N | 5 |
| Channel Ln. NE&SW | 26W-39N | 13 |
| Channel St. N&S | 26W-38N | 12 |
| Channelview Dr. N&S | 25W-39N | 13 |
| Chase Ct. N&S | 26W-42N | 5 |
| Cherry Av. E&W | 26W-42N | 5 |
| Chestnut St. NW&SE | 26W-42N | 5 |
| Cir. | 25W-40N | 5 |
| Circle Av. NW&SE | 25W-39N | 13 |
| Circle Dr. N&S | 26W-41N,25W-40N | 5 |
| Circle Dr. NE&SW | 27W-38N | 12 |
| Clara Av. N&S | 26W-41N | 5 |
| Claridan Av. E&W | 25W-42N | 5 |
| Clark St. E&W | 26W-40N | 5 |
| Clearview Dr. E&W | 22W-41N | 6 |
| Clinton Av. E&W | 25W-40N | 5 |
| Converse Rd. N&S | 28W-42N | 4 |
| Cook Av. E&W | 25W-43N | 5 |
| Country Club Dr. N&S | 26W-41N | 5 |
| Cox Dr. N&S | 25W-43N | 5 |
| Crawford Av. N&S | 25W-42N | 5 |
| Crescent Pl. E&W | 25W-40N | 5 |
| Darrow Av. E&W | 26W-40N | 6 |
| Dawn Cir. SE&NW | 27W-38N | 12 |
| De Coven Ct. E&W | 22W-41N | 6 |
| Deep Lake Rd. N&S | 22W-40N,22W-43N | 6 |
| Deer Ridge Ln. E&W | 24W-41N | 5 |
| Dell Dr. N&S | 22W-40N | 6 |
| Dewes St. E&W | 25W-43N | 5 |
| Diemer St. E&W | 24W-40N | 5 |
| Dogwood Cir. NE&SW | 24W-40N | 5 |
| Donald Dr. N&S | 22W-40N | 6 |
| Dot Pl. N&S | 26W-41N | 5 |
| Douglas Rd. E&W | 25W-40N | 5 |
| Dressels Rd. E&W | 26W-38N | 5 |
| Drexel Blvd. N&S | 26W-38N | 13 |
| Duck Ln. E&W | 26W-41N | 5 |
| Eagle's Nest Rd. E&W | 23W-40N | 6 |
| East Av. E&W | 25W-41N | 5 |
| East Av. N&S | 22W-42N | 6 |
| | | |
| East Dr. NS&EW | 25W-40N | 5 |
| Echo Rd. NW&SE | 25W-40N | 5 |
| Edgar Av. E&W | 25W-42N | 5 |
| Edgewood Av. E&W | 26W-43N | 5 |
| Edwards Rd. E&W | 19W-40N | 7 |
| Elime Rd. N&S | 25W-40N | 5 |
| Elm St. E&W | 28W-39N | 12 |
| Elm St. E&W | 26W-41N | 5 |
| Elm St. E&W | 25W-42N | 5 |
| Elm Tree Rd. E&W | 26W-39N | 13 |
| Emerson Av. NW&SE | 26W-38N | 13 |
| Esther St. N&S | 26W-40N | 5 |
| Evergreen Av. N&S | 26W-42N | 5 |
| Fair Oaks Cir. NE&SW | 26W-42N | 5 |
| Fairview Av. E&W | 27W-38N | 12 |
| Fairview Dr. E&W | 26W-42N | 5 |
| Fairview St. N&S | 25W-40N | 5 |
| Flamingo Ln. E&W | 28W-38N | 12 |
| Florence Av. E&W | 25W-40N | 5 |
| Forest Av. N&S | 26W-38N,25W-39N | 13 |
| Forest Av. NW&SE | 26W-41N | 5 |
| Forest Ct. N&S | 26W-41N | 5 |
| Forest Dr. N&S | 25W-43N | 5 |
| Forest Dr. NW&SE | 25W-39N | 13 |
| Forest Ln. N&S | 26W-40N | 6 |
| Forest Ln. NW&SE | 27W-42N | 4 |
| Forest St. N&S | 22W-42N | 6 |
| Fox Av. E&W | 25W-42N | 5 |
| Fox Dr. N&S | 21W-40N | 7 |
| Fox Run Ln. N&S | 23W-42N | 6 |
| Fredrick Ct. E&W | 25W-42N | 5 |
| Golden Eagle Ct. NE&SW | 23W-40N | 6 |
| Golf Ln. NW&SE | 24W-39N | 13 |
| Golfview Av. N&S | 25W-40N | 5 |
| Golfview Dr. E&W | 28W-39N | 12 |
| Grace Ln. E&W | 25W-40N | 5 |
| Grand Av. N&S | 25W-40N | 5 |
| Grandview Ter. NE&SW | 25W-43N | 5 |
| Grapevine Av. E&W | 26W-42N | 5 |
| Grass Lake Rd. E&W | 27W-38N,22W-40N | 12 |
| Greene Ln. E&W | 22W-40N | 6 |
| Greenleaf Pl. E&W | 28W-38N | 12 |
| Greenview Av. E&W | 25W-39N | 13 |
| Gridley Dr. N&S | 23W-42N | 6 |
| Grimm Rd. E&W | 23W-41N | 6 |
| Groveland Av. E&W | 25W-39N | 13 |
| Gundlach's N&S | 25W-42N | 5 |
| Halings Rd. E&W | 26W-39N | 13 |
| Halverson Rd. E&W | 25W-43N | 5 |
| Hamilton Cir., W. N&S | 27W-38N | 12 |
| Harlem Av. E&W | 26W-38N | 13 |
| Harloff Rd. E&W | 26W-40N,25W-40N | 5 |
| Harold Pl. NE&SW | 28W-38N | 12 |
| Hawthorne Av. E&W | 25W-39N | 13 |
| Hawthorne Ln. E&W | 24W-41N | 5 |
| Heart O Lakes Blvd. E&W | 26W-40N,25W-40N | 5 |
| Henry Pl. NW&SE | 25W-42N | 5 |
| Herman Av. E&W | 25W-39N | 13 |
| Hickory Av. N&S | 25W-39N | 13 |
| Hickory Ln. E&W | 25W-43N | 5 |
| Hickory Rd. E&W | 25W-41N | 5 |
| Hickory St. N&S | 28W-39N | 12 |
| High St. N&S | 26W-43N | 5 |
| Highland Av. E&W | 26W-39N,25W-39N | 13 |
| Highview Dr. N&S | 25W-39N | 13 |
| Highview Ln. E&W | 25W-42N | 5 |
| Highwoods Dr. E&W | 25W-39N | 13 |
| Hill Dr. E&W | 27W-39N | 12 |
| Hill St. N&S | 26W-38N | 5 |
| Hillandale Dr. NS&EW | 27W-38N | 12 |
| Hillcrest Av. E&W | 26W-42N,25W-40N | 5 |
| Hilldale Av. E&W | 25W-39N | 13 |
| Hillside Av. NW&SE | 26W-39N | 13 |
| Hillside Ln. E&W | 22W-41N | 6 |
| Hilltop Av. NE&SW | 26W-38N | 13 |
| Hook Cir. NW&SE | 25W-41N | 5 |
| Island Dr. E&W | 24W-43N | 5 |
| Jackson St. E&W | 27W-39N | 12 |
| James Pl. E&W | 26W-41N | 5 |
| James Rd. E&W | 28W-41N | 4 |
| Janet Ct. N&S | 25W-39N | 13 |
| Janette St. N&S | 25W-42N | 5 |
| | | |
| Jasper Av. N&S | 22W-40N | 6 |
| Jersey Av E&W | 25W-42N | 5 |
| Julia Ct. N&S | 23W-41N | 6 |
| Kairys St. E&W | 23W-43N | 6 |
| Karen Ct. N&S | 23W-41N | 6 |
| Kathryn Dr. E&W | 25W-39N | 13 |
| Kelly Rd. E&W | 27W-38N | 12 |
| Kendall Av. E&W | 28W-38N | 12 |
| Kenmore Rd. N&S | 26W-38N | 13 |
| Kidd Dr. N&S | 25W-43N | 5 |
| Klondike Av. E&W | 26W-38N | 13 |
| Koenen Av. N&S | 27W-38N | 12 |
| Lagoon Ct. N&S | 25W-42N | 5 |
| Lake Av. E&W | 26W-39N | 13 |
| Lake Av. N&S | 25W-41N | 5 |
| Lake Av. N&S | 26W-42N,26W-43N | 5 |
| Lake Av. N&S | 22W-40N | 6 |
| Lake Bluff Rd. N&S | 26W-38N | 6 |
| Lake Blvd. N&S | 25W-40N | 5 |
| Lake Ct. E&W | 22W-40N | 6 |
| Lake Ct. N&S | 26W-38N,25W-39N | 13 |
| Lake Dr. E&W | 25W-42N | 5 |
| Lake Dr. N&S | 22W-40N | 6 |
| Lake Rd. NE&SW | 26W-39N | 13 |
| Lake Shore Dr. E&W | 27W-38N | 12 |
| Lake Shore Dr. N&S | 22W-40N | 6 |
| Lake Shore Dr. N&S | 25W-40N | 5 |
| Lake St. E&W | 26W-42N,25W-42N | 5 |
| Lake St. N&S | 26W-38N | 13 |
| Lake Vista Av. E&W | 23W-41N | 6 |
| Lakes Center Blvd. N&S | 25W-39N | 13 |
| Lakeside Dr. N&S | 25W-43N | 5 |
| Lakeside Pl. E&W | 26W-38N | 13 |
| Lakeview Av. N&S | 25W-40N | 5 |
| Lakeview Av. N&S | 22W-40N | 6 |
| Lakeview Ct. N&S | 22W-40N | 6 |
| Lakeview Dr. E&W | 22W-40N | 6 |
| Lakeview Dr. N&S | 22W-40N | 6 |
| Lakeview Rd. N&S | 26W-39N | 13 |
| Lakeview Ter. N&S | 23W-41N | 6 |
| Lambert Dr. N&S | 23W-40N | 6 |
| Lawson Av. E&W | 27W-42N | 4 |
| Lee Av. NE&SW | 28W-38N | 12 |
| Lee Dr. E&W | 22W-40N | 6 |
| Leland Av. E&W | 26W-38N | 13 |
| Lenora St. N&S | 25W-42N | 5 |
| Liberty St. NE&SW | 23W-40N | 6 |
| Lilac Pl. N&S | 24W-40N | 6 |
| Lillian Av. E&W | 25W-43N | 5 |
| Lillian Pl. NE&SW | 22W-41N | 6 |
| Lincoln Av. N&S | 27W-38N | 12 |
| Lincoln Av. N&S | 22W-41N | 6 |
| Lincoln Dr. N&S | 22W-41N | 6 |
| Linden Av. E&W | 25W-43N | 5 |
| Linden Ln. N&S | 25W-40N | 5 |
| Linden Rd. E&W | 26W-43N | 5 |
| Logan Ter. E&W | 22W-40N | 6 |
| Loon Dr. E&W | 22W-40N | 6 |
| Loon Lake Blvd. E&W | 22W-40N | 6 |
| Lotus Av. E&W | 26W-38N | 13 |
| Lotus Av. N&S | 27W-38N | 12 |
| Lotus Av. NS&EW | 26W-41N | 5 |
| Lotus Ln. E&W | 26W-39N | 13 |
| Lotus Rd. NS&EW | 26W-39N | 13 |
| Madison Av. N&S | 22W-41N | 6 |
| Magnolia Dr. E&W | 24W-40N | 5 |
| Main St. N&S | 23W-41N | 6 |
| Mallard Av. E&W | 26W-40N | 5 |
| Maple Av. E&W | 26W-42N | 5 |
| Maple Dr. N&S | 25W-43N | 5 |
| Maple Ln. N&S | 22W-40N | 6 |
| Marcus Rd. N&S | 26W-40N | 5 |
| Marcus St. N&S | 26W-40N | 5 |
| Margaret St. N&S | 26W-40N | 5 |
| Margate Ter. E&W | 23W-41N | 6 |
| Marie Av. E&W | 26W-41N | 5 |
| Marie Pl. NW&SE | 26W-41N | 5 |
| Mary Av. N&S | 25W-43N | 5 |
| Maryann Rd. E&W | 26W-41N | 5 |
| Masaryk Rd. (Pvt.) N&S | 24W-40N | 5 |
| May St. NW&SE | 28W-38N | 12 |
| Meadow Ln. E&W | 22W-41N | 6 |
| Meadow Ln. N&S | 26W-42N | 5 |
| Melva Av. N&S | 25W-43N | 5 |
| Michele Ln. E&W | 21W-40N | 7 |
| Michigan Blvd. E&W | 26W-38N | 13 |
| Mildred Av. N&S | 25W-40N | 5 |
| Miller Rd. E&W | 20W-40N,19W-40N | 7 |
| Mills St. N&S | 26W-40N | 5 |
| Mineva St. N&S | 25W-40N | 5 |

| | Grid | Page |
|---|---|---|
| Mitchell Ln. E&W .. 22W-40N | | 6 |
| Montrose Rd. E&W | | |
| .............. 26W-38N | | 13 |
| Morley Rd. N&S .... 24W-43N | | 5 |
| Mound Av. N&S .... 27W-39N | | 12 |
| Nevelier Dr. N&S .. 26W-40N | | 5 |
| New Venice Way N&S | | |
| .............. 24W-43N | | 5 |
| Nicklaus Way E&W | | |
| ..... 25W-39N,24W-40N | | 5 |
| Nippersink St. N&S | | |
| .............. 28W-38N | | 12 |
| Norman Dr. E&W .. 24W-43N | | 13 |
| North Av. E&W .... 22W-41N | | 5 |
| North Av. N&S .... 25W-41N | | 5 |
| North Av. NE&SW | | |
| ..... 22W-43N,21W-41N | | 6 |
| North Av. NW&SE .. 25W-43N | | 5 |
| North Dr. E&W .... 22W-40N | | 6 |
| North St. E&W .... 23W-40N | | 6 |
| Northview Ln. E&W | | |
| .............. 26W-42N | | 5 |
| Oak Av. E&W .... 26W-40N | | 5 |
| Oak Av. N&S .... 25W-39N | | 13 |
| Oak Dr. N&S .... 23W-40N | | 6 |
| Oak Ln. N&S .... 25W-42N | | 5 |
| Oak Ln. NS&EW .. 25W-43N | | 5 |
| Oak St. N&S .... 26W-42N | | 5 |
| Oakland St. E&W .. 27W-39N | | 12 |
| Olcott Ln. E&W .. 24W-40N | | 5 |
| Old Grass Lake Rd. E&W | | |
| .............. 25W-40N | | 5 |
| Olive Ct. N&S .... 25W-41N | | 5 |
| Orchard Av. E&W .. 25W-42N | | 5 |
| Orchard Ln. E&W .. 22W-40N | | 6 |
| Orchard Ln. N&S .. 25W-42N | | 5 |
| Otis Av. N&S .... 26W-39N | | 13 |
| Palmer Ct. E&W | | |
| ..... 25W-40N,24W-40N | | 5 |
| Park Av. E&W | | |
| ..... 28W-38N,27W-38N | | 12 |
| Park Av. N&S .... 27W-42N | | 4 |
| Park Av. N&S .... 25W-40N | | 5 |
| Park Dr. E&W .... 25W-43N | | 5 |
| Park Dr. E&W .... 22W-40N | | 6 |
| Park Ln. E&W .... 22W-40N | | 6 |
| Park Ln., E. N&S .. 25W-42N | | 5 |
| Park Ln., W. N&S .. 25W-42N | | 5 |
| Park Pl. E&W | | |
| ..... 26W-42N,25W-42N | | 5 |
| Park St. E&W .... 26W-38N | | 13 |
| Park St. N&S .... 25W-43N | | 5 |
| Park Ter. E&W .... 23W-41N | | 6 |
| Park Ter. N&S .... 25W-43N | | 5 |
| Parkview Dr. NW&SE | | |
| .............. 26W-41N | | 5 |
| Parkway Dr. N&S .. 25W-39N | | 13 |
| Pauline St. N&S .. 25W-41N | | 5 |
| Pearl St. E&W .... 28W-38N | | 12 |
| Pearl St. N&S .... 26W-39N | | 13 |
| Pedersen Dr. E&W .. 19W-41N | | 7 |
| Petite Av. E&W .... 25W-40N | | 5 |
| Petite Pass N&S .. 25W-39N | | 13 |
| Pine Ln. N&S .... 25W-43N | | 5 |
| Pine St. E&W .... 26W-40N | | 5 |
| Pineview Dr. E&W .. 22W-40N | | 6 |
| Point Dr. N&S .... 23W-41N | | 6 |
| Pollock Rd. (Pvt.) E&W | | |
| .............. 19W-40N | | 7 |
| Poplar Av. E&W .. 25W-42N | | 5 |
| Prairie Av. (Pvt.) N&S | | |
| ..... 24W-40N,24W-41N | | 5 |
| Primrose Ln. E&W .. 27W-38N | | 12 |
| Private Rd. E&W | | |
| ..... 26W-39N,25W-39N | | 13 |
| Private Rd. N&S .. 22W-41N | | 6 |
| Prospect Av. E&W .. 26W-42N | | 5 |
| Public Rd. N&S | | |
| ..... 28W-41N,27W-41N | | 4 |
| Rain Tree Rd. N&S | | |
| .............. 25W-43N | | 5 |
| Ravine Dr. E&W .. 26W-39N | | 13 |
| Ravine Dr. E&W .. 27W-39N | | 12 |
| Ravine Dr. NW&SE | | |
| .............. 24W-39N | | 13 |
| Regina Rd. N&S .. 21W-40N | | 7 |
| Rena Av. N&S .... 25W-39N | | 13 |
| Resthaven E&W .. 25W-39N | | 13 |
| Richmond Av. E&W | | |
| .............. 25W-39N | | 13 |
| Ridge Cir. NW&SE | | |
| ..... 22W-40N,22W-41N | | 6 |
| Ridge Dr. E&W .. 22W-42N | | 6 |
| Riverside Rd. E&W | | |
| .............. 27W-42N | | 4 |
| Riverview Av. NE&SW | | |
| .............. 26W-41N | | 5 |
| Riverview Dr. E&W 26W-41N | | 5 |
| Riverview Pl. NW&SE | | |
| .............. 26W-41N | | 5 |
| Rosecrans Rd. E&W | | |
| .............. 19W-41N | | 7 |
| Route 173 E&W | | |
| ..... 28W-42N,19W-41N | | 7 |
| Rowe Av. N&S .... 27W-38N | | 12 |
| S. Pedersen Dr. N&S | | |
| .............. 19W-41N | | 7 |
| Sarah Ct. E&W .. 23W-40N | | 6 |
| Sarana Dr. E&W .. 24W-40N | | 6 |
| Savage Rd. N&S .. 20W-40N | | 7 |
| Scott St. N&S .... 25W-40N | | 5 |
| Sea Eagle Ct. NE&SW | | |
| .............. 23W-40N | | 6 |

| | Grid | Page |
|---|---|---|
| Shady Lane (Pvt.) E&W | | |
| .............. 23W-40N | | 6 |
| Shagbark E&W .. 22W-40N | | 6 |
| Shannon Av. E&W .. 26W-42N | | 5 |
| Sherwin Av. E&W .. 26W-38N | | 13 |
| Shore Av. NE&SW .. 26W-39N | | 13 |
| Shore Dr. NE&SW .. 23W-40N | | 6 |
| Shore Pl. N&S .... 28W-39N | | 12 |
| Sibley Dr. N&S .... 25W-40N | | 5 |
| Silver Lake Av. E&W | | |
| .............. 22W-42N | | 6 |
| Simon Ct. E&W .. 25W-39N | | 13 |
| Smith St. N&S .... 25W-41N | | 5 |
| South Dr. E&W .... 22W-40N | | 6 |
| Spring Av. E&W .... 27W-42N | | 4 |
| Spring Grove Rd. NE&SW | | |
| .............. 27W-42N | | 4 |
| Spring Well Av. NS&EW | | |
| .............. 26W-39N | | 13 |
| Spruce Dr. E&W .. 22W-40N | | 6 |
| Spruce St. E&W .. 26W-42N | | 5 |
| Stanton Rd. E&W .. 22W-40N | | 6 |
| State Line Rd. E&W | | |
| .............. 19W-43N | | 7 |
| State Park Rd. E&W | | |
| .............. 28W-39N | | 12 |
| Sterling Av. E&W .. 28W-38N | | 12 |
| Stewart Av. NW&SE | | |
| .............. 28W-38N | | 12 |
| Stonegate Av. NW&SE | | |
| .............. 27W-38N | | 12 |
| Stonegate Dr. E&W | | |
| .............. 26W-38N | | 13 |
| Summerside Dr. N&S | | |
| .............. 25W-39N | | 13 |
| Sunset E&W .... 24W-40N | | 5 |
| Sunset Av. E&W .. 27W-38N | | 12 |
| Sunset Ct., N. E&W | | |
| .............. 24W-40N | | 5 |
| Sunset Ct., S. E&W | | |
| .............. 24W-40N | | 5 |
| Sunset Dr., N. E&W | | |
| .............. 24W-40N | | 5 |
| Sunset Ln. N&S .. 26W-43N | | 5 |
| Sunset Rd. E&W .. 26W-43N | | 5 |
| Suraya Dr. N&S .. 23W-41N | | 6 |
| Sycamore Av. E&W | | |
| .............. 26W-43N | | 5 |
| Sylvan Dr. E&W .. 25W-43N | | 5 |
| Sylvan Woods Rd. E&W | | |
| .............. 24W-43N | | 5 |
| Talman Av. N&S .. 25W-42N | | 5 |
| Talon Ct. E&W .. 23W-40N | | 6 |
| Tammi Ter. NW&SE | | |
| .............. 19W-41N | | 7 |
| Taylor Ct. E&W .. 22W-41N | | 6 |
| Terry Ln. N&S .... 24W-40N | | 5 |
| Tierney Dr. NE&SW | | |
| .............. 23W-40N | | 6 |
| Tiffany Rd. N&S .. 24W-42N | | 5 |
| Todd St. E&W .... 26W-43N | | 5 |
| Town Line Rd. E&W | | |
| .............. 24W-40N | | 5 |
| Tracy Ln. NW&SE .. 24W-40N | | 5 |
| Trevor Rd. N&S .. 24W-43N | | 5 |
| Trillium Rd. N&S .. 27W-38N | | 12 |
| Trinity Ln. NE&SW .24W-40N | | 5 |
| U.S. Route 45 N&S | | |
| ..... 19W-40N,20W-43N | | 7 |
| Venetian Dr. N&S .. 25W-43N | | 5 |
| Venn Rd. E&W .... 25W-43N | | 5 |
| Villa Rica Rd. E&W | | |
| ..... 23W-40N,22W-40N | | 6 |
| Vine St. E&W .... 26W-38N | | 13 |
| Virell St. E&W .... 22W-40N | | 6 |
| Virgil Av. N&S .... 25W-42N | | 5 |
| Washington Av. N&S | | |
| .............. 27W-38N | | 12 |
| Washington St. E&W | | |
| .............. 22W-41N | | 6 |
| Waters Rd. N&S .. 26W-43N | | 5 |
| Wedgewood Dr. E&W | | |
| .............. 24W-40N | | 6 |
| West E&W .... 25W-40N | | 5 |
| West 'A' St. E&W .. 25W-42N | | 5 |
| West Av. N&S .... 25W-41N | | 5 |
| West End Dr. N&S ..27W-39N | | 12 |
| West Loon Lake Blvd. N&S | | |
| .............. 24W-40N | | 5 |
| West Shore Av. N&S | | |
| .............. 23W-40N | | 6 |
| White Rd. E&W .. 21W-40N | | 7 |
| Whitehall Ct. E&W .. 21W-40N | | 7 |
| Willow Av. N&S .. 25W-43N | | 5 |
| Willow St. NE&SW .26W-39N | | 13 |
| Willow St. NW&SE .. 26W-42N | | 5 |
| Wilmot Rd. E&W | | |
| ..... 27W-43N,26W-43N | | 5 |
| Wilson Rd. E&W .. 26W-38N | | 13 |
| Windsor Dalgaard Jr. Ln. N&S | | |
| .............. 26W-42N | | 5 |
| Winsor Ter. N&S .. 23W-41N | | 6 |
| Witt Rd. N&S .... 25W-42N | | 5 |
| Woodbine Av. NS&EW | | |
| .............. 26W-42N | | 5 |
| Woodland Av. E&W | | |
| .............. 26W-38N | | 13 |
| Woodland Av. N&S | | |
| .............. 26W-38N | | 13 |
| Woodland Av. NE&SW | | |
| .............. 27W-38N | | 12 |
| Woodland Pl. NW&SE | | |
| .............. 27W-42N | | 4 |

| | Grid | Page |
|---|---|---|
| Woodlawn Av. E&W | | |
| .............. 25W-43N | | 5 |
| Woodmere Ter. NW&SE | | |
| .............. 19W-41N | | 7 |
| Woods Dr. N&S .. 25W-42N | | 5 |
| Woodside Av. N&S | | |
| .............. 25W-39N | | 13 |
| 1st Av. N&S ....27W-38N | | 12 |
| 1st Av. N&S ....25W-42N | | 5 |
| 1st St. N&S .... 25W-43N | | 5 |
| 1st St. N&S .... 23W-41N | | 6 |
| 2nd Av. N&S .... 27W-38N | | 12 |
| 2nd Av. N&S .... 25W-42N | | 5 |
| 2nd St. E&W .... 25W-42N | | 5 |
| 2nd St. N&S .... 23W-41N | | 6 |
| 3rd Av. N&S .... 27W-38N | | 12 |
| 3rd Av. N&S .... 25W-42N | | 5 |
| 3rd St. E&W .... 25W-42N | | 5 |
| 3rd St. N&S .... 23W-41N | | 6 |
| 4th Av. N&S .... 27W-38N | | 12 |
| 4th Av. N&S .... 25W-42N | | 5 |
| 5th Av. N&S .... 27W-38N | | 12 |
| 5th Av. N&S .... 25W-42N | | 5 |
| 6th Av. N&S .... 27W-38N | | 12 |
| 6th Av. N&S .... 25W-42N | | 5 |
| 7th Av. N&S .... 28W-38N | | 12 |
| 7th Av. N&S .... 25W-42N | | 5 |
| 8th St. N&S .... 28W-38N | | 12 |
| 9th St. N&S .... 28W-38N | | 12 |
| 10th Av. N&S .... 28W-38N | | 12 |
| 11th St. N&S .... 28W-38N | | 12 |

## Avon Township

| | Grid | Page |
|---|---|---|
| Acre Ct. E&W ...... 22W-35N | | 22 |
| Alleghany Rd. N&S | | |
| ..... 21W-32N,21W-33N | | 23 |
| Ash Ct. E&W .... 19W-35N | | 23 |
| Bacon Rd. N&S .. 24W-32N | | 22 |
| Beach Ct. E&W .. 22W-34N | | 22 |
| Belvidere Rd. E&W | | |
| ..... 24W-32N,19W-32N | | 22 |
| Brorson Av. E&W .. 24W-35N | | 22 |
| Cedar Av. N&S .. 22W-34N | | 22 |
| Cedar Ln. N&S .. 24W-35N | | 22 |
| Cedar Ln. N&S .. 21W-34N | | 23 |
| Center St. E&W .. 19W-33N | | 23 |
| Circle Dr., S. NW&SE | | |
| .............. 22W-34N | | 22 |
| Clinton Av. NS&EW | | |
| .............. 24W-35N | | 22 |
| Curran Rd. N&S .. 23W-32N | | 22 |
| Drury Ln. NW&SE .. 20W-35N | | 23 |
| East End Av. N&S .. 22W-34N | | 22 |
| Eldor Av. E&W .. 21W-34N | | 23 |
| Fairfield Rd. N&S | | |
| ..... 24W-32N,24W-35N | | 22 |
| Forest Av. E&W .. 24W-35N | | 22 |
| Garfield Blvd. N&S .. 20W-32N | | 23 |
| Gerwal Av. N&S .. 21W-34N | | 23 |
| Harris Rd. N&S .. 19W-32N | | 23 |
| Harrison Av. N&S .. 24W-34N | | 22 |
| Hart Rd. E&W .... 24W-34N | | 22 |
| Hauge St. N&S | | |
| ..... 24W-34N,24W-35N | | 22 |
| Hawthorn Dr. E&W | | |
| .............. 24W-35N | | 22 |
| Hendee Av. N&S .. 24W-35N | | 22 |
| Hendee Ln. N&S .. 22W-34N | | 22 |
| Heyer St. N&S .. 24W-35N | | 22 |
| Hickory Ln. N&S .. 22W-34N | | 22 |
| Hickory Rd. N&S | | |
| ..... 19W-34N,19W-35N | | 23 |
| Hickory St. N&S | | |
| ..... 24W-35N,22W-34N | | 22 |
| Hickory St. N&S .. 21W-34N | | 23 |
| Hickory St. E&W ... 24W-35N | | 22 |
| Hill Ct. N&S .... 24W-34N | | 22 |
| Hillside Av. N&S .. 24W-35N | | 22 |
| Indian Trail E&W ..22W-34N | | 22 |
| Ivanhoe Rd. N&S .. 20W-32N | | 23 |
| Kenneth Dr. N&S .. 20W-35N | | 23 |
| Lake Dr. E&W .... 22W-34N | | 22 |
| Lake Dr. E&W .... 24W-35N | | 22 |
| Lake Park Av. E&W | | |
| .............. 22W-34N | | 22 |
| Lake Shore Dr. E&W | | |
| .............. 24W-35N | | 22 |
| Lake Shore Dr. E&W | | |
| .............. 22W-34N | | 22 |
| Lake Shore Dr. E&W | | |
| .............. 21W-34N | | 23 |
| Lake St. N&S | | |
| ..... 21W-32N,21W-34N | | 22 |
| Lakeview Av. E&W | | |
| .............. 22W-34N | | 22 |
| Lakeview Dr. N&S ..22W-34N | | 22 |
| Lakeview Dr. E&W .. 19W-35N | | 23 |
| Lakewood Ln. E&W | | |
| .............. 22W-34N | | 22 |
| Lane Ct. E&W .... 22W-34N | | 22 |
| Lilac Av. N&S ...... 22W-34N | | 22 |
| Linden Av. NS&EW | | |
| ..... 19W-34N,19W-35N | | 23 |
| Luther Av. N&S .. 24W-34N | | 22 |
| Main St. NW&SE .. 24W-34N | | 22 |
| McKinley Av. N&S .. 20W-32N | | 23 |
| Merriwood Ln. E&W | | |
| .............. 22W-34N | | 22 |
| Nielson Av. N&S .. 24W-35N | | 22 |
| Nippersink Rd. E&W | | |
| .............. 24W-33N | | 22 |
| Norelius Av. E&W .. 24W-35N | | 22 |

| | Grid | Page |
|---|---|---|
| Oak Av. E&W .... 22W-34N | | 22 |
| Oak Av. N&S .... 22W-34N | | 22 |
| Oak Ct. E&W .... 19W-35N | | 23 |
| Oak Ln. N&S .... 21W-34N | | 23 |
| Oak St. E&W .... 24W-35N | | 22 |
| Orchard Ln. N&S .. 22W-35N | | 22 |
| Orchard Pl. E&W .. 24W-35N | | 22 |
| Passavant Av. E&W | | |
| .............. 24W-35N | | 22 |
| Poplar St. E&W .. 24W-35N | | 22 |
| Rollins Rd. E&W | | |
| ..... 24W-35N,19W-35N | | 22 |
| Ross Av. N&S .... 24W-34N | | 22 |
| Round Lake Rd. NW&SE | | |
| .............. 24W-34N | | 22 |
| Route 120 E&W | | |
| ..... 24W-32N,19W-32N | | 22 |
| Route 134 NW&SE | | |
| .............. 24W-34N | | 22 |
| Route 45 N&S | | |
| ..... 19W-32N,19W-33N | | 23 |
| Route 83 NW&SE | | |
| ..... 21W-35N,20W-32N | | 23 |
| Sheldon Rd. N&S .. 21W-35N | | 23 |
| Shorewood Dr. E&W | | |
| .............. 22W-34N | | 22 |
| Shorewood Dr. E&W | | |
| ..... 22W-35N,21W-35N | | 22 |
| Stub Av. E&W .... 24W-35N | | 22 |
| Summit St. N&S .. 24W-35N | | 22 |
| Sunshine Av. E&W .. 19W-35N | | 23 |
| Terri Ln. N&S .... 20W-35N | | 23 |
| Thompson St. N&S | | |
| .............. 24W-34N | | 22 |
| Todd Dr. E&W .. 20W-35N | | 23 |
| Town Line Rd. E&W | | |
| ..... 24W-32N,23W-32N | | 22 |
| Tyler Av. N&S .... 24W-34N | | 22 |
| Wabash Av. N&S .. 24W-35N | | 22 |
| Washington St. E&W | | |
| ..... 21W-34N,19W-34N | | 23 |
| Willow Ln. N&S .. 19W-35N | | 23 |
| Wilmar Av. E&W .. 21W-34N | | 23 |
| Wilson Blvd. N&S .. 24W-35N | | 22 |

## Bannockburn

| | Grid | Page |
|---|---|---|
| Aitken Dr. E&W .. 11W-22N | | 50 |
| Audubon Ln. E&W .12W-22N | | 50 |
| Bannockburn Ct. NE&SW | | |
| .............. 11W-22N | | 50 |
| Bridle Ln. NW&SE .. 12W-23N | | 50 |
| Cedar Crest Ln. E&W | | |
| .............. 11W-22N | | 50 |
| Duffy Ln. E&W .. 12W-22N | | 50 |
| Dunsinane East NW&SE | | |
| .............. 11W-23N | | 50 |
| Dunsinane Ln. N&S | | |
| .............. 11W-23N | | 50 |
| Half Day Rd. E&W .. 12W-23N | | 50 |
| High Terrace Ln. E&W | | |
| .............. 12W-23N | | 50 |
| Hill Av. N&S .... 11W-22N | | 50 |
| Hilltop Ln. E&W .. 11W-22N | | 50 |
| Lakeside Dr. N&S .. 12W-23N | | 50 |
| Lakewood Dr. E&W | | |
| .............. 12W-23N | | 50 |
| Meadow Ln. N&S .. 11W-22N | | 50 |
| North Av. E&W .. 11W-22N | | 50 |
| Orchard Ln. E&W .. 11W-22N | | 50 |
| Route 22 E&W | | |
| ..... 12W-23N,11W-23N | | 50 |
| Route 43 N&S | | |
| ..... 11W-22N,11W-23N | | 50 |
| Stirling Rd. NS&EW | | |
| .............. 11W-22N | | 50 |
| Sunset Ln. N&S .. 12W-22N | | 50 |
| Telegraph Rd. NW&SE | | |
| ..... 12W-23N,11W-22N | | 50 |
| Thornapple Rd. N&S | | |
| .............. 12W-22N | | 50 |
| Tri-State Tollway N&S | | |
| .............. 12W-22N | | 50 |
| Valley Rd. N&S 11W-22N | | 50 |
| Waukegan Rd. N&S | | |
| .............. 12W-22N | | 50 |
| Wilmot Rd. N&S .. 12W-22N | | 50 |

## Barrington*
### (Also see Cook County)

| | Grid | Page |
|---|---|---|
| Applebee St. NW&SE | | |
| .............. 25W-20N | | 45 |
| Bellwood Dr. NE&SW | | |
| .............. 28W-20N | | 11 |
| Bent Ridge Ln. NE&SW | | |
| .............. 25W-20N | | 45 |
| Berry Rd. E&W .. 25W-20N | | 45 |
| Beverly Rd. N&S .. 24W-20N | | 46 |
| Birch Rd. N&S .... 25W-20N | | 45 |
| Birchwood Dr. E&W | | |
| .............. 24W-20N | | 46 |
| Bosworth Field N&S | | |
| .............. 25W-20N | | 45 |
| Bryant Av. N&S .. 26W-20N | | 45 |
| Burr Oak Ln. NW&SE | | |
| .............. 24W-20N | | 46 |
| Carl Av. N&S .... 26W-20N | | 45 |
| Castle Ct. N&S .. 24W-20N | | 46 |
| Center Ct. E&W .. 24W-20N | | 46 |
| Chestnut St. E&W .. 25W-20N | | 45 |
| Church Hill Ct. NW&SE | | |
| .............. 25W-20N | | 45 |

| | Grid | Page |
|---|---|---|
| Cold Spring Rd. NS&EW | | |
| .............. 24W-20N | | 46 |
| Commonwealth Ct. N&S | | |
| .............. 25W-20N | | 45 |
| Covington Dr. E&W | | |
| .............. 25W-20N | | 45 |
| Cumnor Av. N&S .. 26W-20N | | 45 |
| Drury Ln. E&W .... 25W-20N | | 45 |
| Ela St. N&S...... 25W-20N | | 45 |
| Elm Av. NE&SW ..25W-20N | | 45 |
| Exmoor Av. N&S .. 26W-20N | | 45 |
| Fairfax Ct. N&S .. 25W-20N | | 45 |
| Fox Hunt Rd. NS&EW | | |
| .............. 24W-20N | | 46 |
| Foxglove Ln. NW&SE | | |
| .............. 24W-20N | | 46 |
| Franklin St. E&W .. 25W-20N | | 45 |
| Garfield St. N&S .. 25W-20N | | 45 |
| Georgetowne Ln. N&S | | |
| .............. 25W-20N | | 45 |
| Grant St. N&S......26W-20N | | 45 |
| Hampton Pk.* E&W | | |
| .............. 24W-20N | | 46 |
| Harrison St. N&S .. 25W-20N | | 45 |
| Hilltop Av. N&S .. 24W-20N | | 46 |
| Home Av. N&S ...26W-20N | | 45 |
| Hough St. N&S ...25W-20N | | 45 |
| Indian Way N&S ...24W-20N | | 46 |
| James St. N&S .. 25W-20N | | 45 |
| June Ter. E&W .... 25W-20N | | 45 |
| Lake Shore Ct. NW&SE | | |
| .............. 24W-20N | | 46 |
| Lake Shore Dr., N. NS&EW | | |
| .............. 24W-20N | | 46 |
| Lake Shore Dr., S. E&W | | |
| .............. 24W-20N | | 46 |
| Lake Zurich Rd. NE&SW | | |
| .............. 25W-20N | | 45 |
| Laverne St. N&S .. 26W-20N | | 45 |
| Liberty St. E&W .. 25W-20N | | 45 |
| Linden Av. N&S ... 25W-20N | | 45 |
| Lions Dr. E&W .... 25W-20N | | 45 |
| Magnolia Av. N&S .. 25W-20N | | 45 |
| Main St. E&W | | |
| ..... 26W-20N,24W-20N | | 45 |
| Maple Av. E&W .. 25W-20N | | 45 |
| Marlborough Rd. N&S | | |
| .............. 25W-20N | | 45 |
| Martin Ct. N&S .. 25W-20N | | 45 |
| Meadow Way E&W | | |
| .............. 24W-20N | | 46 |
| N. Glendale Av. N&S | | |
| .............. 25W-20N | | 45 |
| N. Valley Ct. NE&SW | | |
| .............. 25W-20N | | 46 |
| New Bridge Ct. NE&SW | | |
| .............. 25W-20N | | 45 |
| New Hart Rd. N&S 26W-20N | | 45 |
| North Av. N&S .... 25W-20N | | 45 |
| North Shore Ct. NW&SE | | |
| .............. 24W-20N | | 46 |
| North St. E&W .. 26W-20N | | 45 |
| North Valley Rd. NW&SE | | |
| .............. 24W-20N | | 46 |
| Northwest Highway NW&SE | | |
| ..... 26W-20N,25W-20N | | 45 |
| Oak Rd. NE&SW .. 25W-20N | | 45 |
| Old Creek Ct. SE&NW | | |
| .............. 24W-20N | | 46 |
| Oxbow Ln. NS&EW | | |
| .............. 24W-20N | | 46 |
| Park Ln. NW&SE .. 25W-20N | | 45 |
| Paul Cir. E&W .... 25W-20N | | 45 |
| Pine St. E&W .... 25W-20N | | 45 |
| Ponderosa Ct. N&S | | |
| .............. 24W-20N | | 46 |
| Prospect Av. N&S .. 25W-20N | | 45 |
| Raymond Av. N&S ..26W-20N | | 45 |
| Redwood Ln. NS&EW | | |
| .............. 24W-20N | | 46 |
| Roslyn Rd. E&W | | |
| ..... 26W-20N,25W-20N | | 45 |
| Scott Av. N&S .. 26W-20N | | 45 |
| Sharon Dr. N&S .. 24W-20N | | 46 |
| Shorely Dr. NE&SW | | |
| .............. 24W-20N | | 46 |
| South Shore Ct. NE&SW | | |
| .............. 24W-20N | | 46 |
| Spruce St. N&S .... 25W-20N | | 45 |
| Stillwater Ln. SE&NW | | |
| .............. 25W-20N | | 45 |
| Sunny Ln. N&S .... 25W-20N | | 45 |
| Surrey Ln. NS&EW | | |
| .............. 24W-20N | | 46 |
| Sycamore Av. N&S | | |
| .............. 25W-20N | | 45 |
| Tall Trees Cir. E&W | | |
| .............. 24W-20N | | 46 |
| Tall Trees Dr. NS&EW | | |
| .............. 24W-20N | | 46 |
| Taylor Rd. E&W .. 26W-20N | | 45 |
| The Point N&S .. 24W-20N | | 46 |
| U.S. Route 14 NW&SE | | |
| ..... 26W-20N,25W-20N | | 45 |
| Valencia Av. E&W .. 25W-20N | | 45 |
| Verne Cir. N&S .. 25W-20N | | 45 |
| Victoria Av. E&W .. 25W-20N | | 45 |
| Walnut Rd. NW&SE | | |
| .............. 25W-20N | | 45 |
| Washington St. E&W | | |
| .............. 25W-20N | | 45 |
| Waverly Rd. E&W .. 26W-20N | | 45 |
| White Oak Ct. N&S | | |
| .............. 24W-20N | | 46 |

|  | Grid | Page |
|---|---|---|
| Whitney Dr. N&S . . | 25W-20N | 45 |
| Williamsburg Pk.* E&W | | |
| ............... | 25W-20N | 45 |
| Willow Av. N&S .... | 25W-20N | 45 |
| 16th St. N&S ...... | 26W-20N | 45 |
| 20th St. N&S ...... | 26W-20N | 45 |

**Barrington Hills***
(Also see Cook, Kane and McHenry Counties)

|  | Grid | Page |
|---|---|---|
| Acorn Dr. N&S .. | 28W-21N | 44 |
| Bellwood Dr. NS&EW | | |
| ............... | 28W-20N | 44 |
| Bisque Dr. NW&SE | | |
| ............... | 27W-20N | 44 |
| Buckley Rd. N&S .. | 28W-21N | 44 |
| Cuba Rd. NW&SE .. | 28W-21N | 44 |
| Dormy Ln. (Pvt.) NW&SE | | |
| ............... | 27W-20N | 44 |
| Dunrovin Dr. NW&SE | | |
| ............... | 28W-20N | 44 |
| Hickory Ln. N&S... | 28W-21N | 44 |
| Lake Cook Rd. E&W | | |
| ............... | 26W-20N | 45 |
| Merryoaks Rd. E&W | | |
| ............... | 28W-21N | 44 |
| Mid Oaks Ln. N&S .. | 27W-20N | 44 |
| New Hart Rd. N&S | 26W-20N | 45 |
| Northwest Highway NW&SE | | |
| .......28W-22N, | 26W-20N | 44 |
| Oak Knoll Rd. E&W | | |
| .......28W-20N, | 26W-20N | 44 |
| Oak Lake Dr. N&S.. | 28W-21N | 44 |
| Oakwood Dr. NW&SE | | |
| ............... | 26W-20N | 45 |
| Old Hart Rd. N&S .. | 26W-20N | 45 |
| Pagancia Dr. N&S .. | 27W-20N | 44 |
| Pheasant Dr. N&S .. | 28W-21N | 44 |
| Plum Tree Rd. E&W | | |
| ............... | 28W-21N | 44 |
| ............... | | 44 |
| Private Rd. N&S .. | 26W-20N | 45 |
| Rub-of-Green Ln. N&S | | |
| ............... | 27W-20N | 44 |
| Sieberts Ridge Rd. NE&SW | | |
| ............... | 28W-21N | 44 |
| Steeplechase Rd. NS&EW | | |
| .......28W-20N, | 27W-20N | 44 |

**Beach Park**

|  | Grid | Page |
|---|---|---|
| Adelaide Av. E&W . | 12W-37N | 18 |
| Adelphi Av. N&S | | |
| .......12W-37N, | 12W-40N | 18 |
| Ames Av. E&W .. | 10W-39N | 19 |
| Ash Ct. E&W .... | 12W-40N | 10 |
| Audrey Av. E&W .. | 12W-37N | 18 |
| Bairstow Av. N&S | | |
| ....... 10W-37N, | 9W-37N | 19 |
| Bairstow St. E&W . | 12W-37N | 18 |
| Beach Pl. E&W .. | 10W-38N | 19 |
| Beach Rd. E&W | | |
| ....... 11W-38N, | 9W-38N | 18 |
| Bernice Ter. N&S . | 11W-39N | 18 |
| Birch Av. N&S.... | 11W-39N | 18 |
| Blanchard Rd. E&W | | |
| ............... | 12W-37N | 18 |
| Blossom St. E&W .. | 12W-37N | 18 |
| Bonnie Brook Ln., N. E&W | | |
| ............... | 12W-37N | 18 |
| Bowling Av. N&S . | 12W-39N | 18 |
| Boyce Ln. E&W .. | 10W-38N | 19 |
| California Av. E&W | 10W-39N | 19 |
| Carnahan Av. E&W | | |
| ............... | 11W-38N | 18 |
| Carol Ln. NS&EW .. | 11W-39N | 18 |
| Cedar Av. N&S .. | 11W-38N | 18 |
| Center St. E&W | | |
| .......12W-38N, | 10W-38N | 18 |
| Chaney Av. E&W . | 10W-38N | 19 |
| Chaney St. E&W . | 12W-38N | 18 |
| Chaplin Av. E&W . | 10W-38N | 19 |
| Chaplin St. E&W .. | 12W-38N | 18 |
| Charleston Rd. N&S | | |
| ............... | 11W-38N | 18 |
| Chestnut St. N&S .. | 10W-37N | 19 |
| Chicago Av. E&W . | 10W-39N | 19 |
| Clarendon Rd. E&W | | |
| ............... | 12W-39N | 18 |
| Coolidge Av. N&S . | 10W-38N | 19 |
| Cornell Rd. N&S | | |
| .......11W-37N, | 11W-38N | 18 |
| Cornell St. NW&SE | | |
| ............... | 12W-40N | 10 |
| Country Ln. E&W . | 10W-38N | 19 |
| Crissy Av. E&W ... | 10W-38N | 19 |
| Crissy Ln. E&W .. | 10W-38N | 19 |
| DeWoody Rd. N&S | | |
| .......11W-37N, | 11W-38N | 18 |
| Delores Av. E&W . | 12W-38N | 18 |
| Dorothy St. E&W . | 12W-37N | 18 |
| Douglas St. E&W . | 12W-38N | 18 |
| E. McArthur Dr. E&W | | |
| ............... | 10W-37N | 19 |
| Eastwood Rd. E&W | | |
| .......12W-37N, | 10W-37N | 18 |
| Emanual Av. N&S . | 12W-38N | 18 |
| Emmaus Av. N&S .. | 11W-39N | 18 |
| Everett Rd. E&W .. | 11W-38N | 18 |
| Evergreen Av. E&W | | |
| .......12W-37N, | 12W-38N | 18 |
| Fairbanks Av. E&W | | |
| ............... | 10W-38N | 19 |

|  | Grid | Page |
|---|---|---|
| Ford Av. E&W .... | 10W-38N | 19 |
| Ford St. E&W .... | 12W-38N | 18 |
| Forest Dr. N&S ...... | 9W-37N | 19 |
| Frolic Av. N&S | | |
| .......12W-39N, | 12W-37N | 18 |
| Gabriel Av. N&S .. | 10W-39N | 19 |
| Galilee Av. N&S .. | 11W-39N | 19 |
| Ganster Rd. N&S .... | 9W-37N | 19 |
| Garnett Av. N&S | | |
| .......10W-37N, | 10W-39N | 19 |
| Geneva Ln. N&S.... | 11W-39N | 18 |
| Geraghty Av. N&S | | |
| .......10W-37N, | 10W-39N | 19 |
| Gilbert Av. N&S .. | 10W-38N | 19 |
| Gish Av. E&W ...... | 10W-38N | 19 |
| Glendale Rd. N&S .. | 11W-40N | 10 |
| Graves Av. E&W .. | 12W-37N | 18 |
| Green Av. N&S | | |
| .......12W-38N, | 12W-40N | 18 |
| Green Bay Rd. E&W | | |
| .......12W-37N, | 12W-40N | 18 |
| Griffith Av. N&S .. | 10W-38N | 19 |
| Harding St. N&S.... | 10W-38N | 19 |
| Harper Rd. N&S | | |
| .......11W-37N, | 11W-38N | 19 |
| Hart Av. E&W .... | 10W-38N | 19 |
| Hart St. E&W .... | 12W-38N | 18 |
| Hendee Av. E&W | | |
| ....... 10W-37N, | 9W-37N | 19 |
| Hendee St. E&W .. | 12W-37N | 18 |
| Hickory Ln. .. | 12W-40N | 10 |
| Hickory Rd. E&W .. | 11W-38N | 18 |
| Highland Av. E&W .. | 11W-38N | 18 |
| Holdridge Av. N&S .. | 10W-37N | 19 |
| Holridge Rd. N&S | | |
| .......10W-38N, | 10W-39N | 19 |
| Howard St. E&W | | |
| .......12W-38N, | 10W-38N | 18 |
| Illinois Av. E&W | | |
| .......12W-39N, | 10W-38N | 18 |
| Johnson Rd. E&W .. | 11W-39N | 18 |
| Joyce Av. N&S .... | 10W-38N | 19 |
| Kenosha Rd. NE&SW | | |
| ............... | 12W-40N | 10 |
| Lake Crest Av. N&S | | |
| ............... | 10W-37N | 19 |
| Lake St. E&W .... | 10W-38N | 19 |
| Lake View Av. N&S . | 9W-38N | 19 |
| Lakeside Av. N&S | | |
| ....... 9W-40N, | 9W-41N | 11 |
| Leland Av. E&W .... | 11W-38N | 18 |
| Lewis-Jordan Rd. N&S | | |
| .......11W-38N, | 11W-39N | 18 |
| Liberty Av. E&W | | |
| .......10W-38N, | 10W-39N | 19 |
| Liberty Ct. E&W .. | 10W-38N | 19 |
| Lincoln Av. N&S .. | 10W-38N | 19 |
| Linden Av. N&S .. | 11W-38N | 18 |
| Lone Oak Rd. N&S | | |
| ............... | 12W-40N | 10 |
| Loyola Av. N&S .. | 10W-37N | 19 |
| Lynch Av. N&S .. | 12W-39N | 18 |
| Main St. N&S | | |
| .......11W-38N, | 12W-38N | 18 |
| Main St. E&W ...... | 10W-37N | 19 |
| Major Av. E&W .... | 12W-39N | 18 |
| Manor Av. N&S | | |
| .......10W-37N, | 10W-38N | 19 |
| Maplewood Rd. E&W | | |
| ............... | 12W-39N | 18 |
| Marc Ct. E&W...... | 10W-38N | 19 |
| Marguerite Ln. N&S | 11W-38N | 18 |
| Marguerite Rd. N&S | 9W-38N | 19 |
| Mawman Av. N&S | | |
| ....... 10W-37N, | 9W-37N | 19 |
| Mawman St. E&W . | 12W-37N | 18 |
| McAree Av. N&S .. | 12W-39N | 18 |
| Metropolitan Av. N&S | | |
| ............... | 12W-38N | 18 |
| Michigan Blvd. E&W | 9W-38N | 19 |
| Minturn Av. E&W .. | 12W-38N | 18 |
| Morse Av. N&S .. | 12W-38N | 18 |
| Morton Av. E&W . | 10W-37N | 19 |
| New York Av. N&S | | |
| .......11W-37N, | 11W-38N | 18 |
| Noble Av. N&S .... | 12W-38N | 18 |
| North Av. N&S | | |
| .......11W-38N, | 11W-39N | 18 |
| North Shore Av. N&S | | |
| .......10W-37N, | 10W-38N | 19 |
| Northern Av. N&S .. | 12W-37N | 18 |
| Oak Dr. E&W ...... | 11W-38N | 18 |
| Oak Forest Dr. E&W | | |
| ............... | 9W-38N | 19 |
| Oberg Av. N&S .... | 12W-38N | 18 |
| Orchard Rd. N&S .. | 11W-37N | 18 |
| Paddock Av. N&S | | |
| .......10W-37N, | 9W-37N | 19 |
| Park Av. N&S ...... | 9W-38N | 19 |
| Paxton Av. E&W .. | 9W-39N | 19 |
| Peacock Av. E&W . | 12W-39N | 18 |
| Pickford Av. E&W . | 12W-38N | 18 |
| Pickford St. E&W .. | 12W-38N | 18 |
| Pine Av. N&S .... | 11W-38N | 18 |
| Pine Ct. E&W .... | 12W-40N | 10 |
| Prairie Ln. E&W .. | 10W-38N | 19 |
| Princeton Av. E&W | | |
| ............... | 12W-39N | 18 |
| Renier Pl. E&W .... | 10W-38N | 19 |
| Renier Rd. E&W .. | 12W-38N | 18 |
| Richard Pl. E&W... | 11W-39N | 18 |
| Russell Av. N&S .. | 10W-38N | 19 |
| Ruth Av. N&S .... | 12W-38N | 18 |
| Sallmon Rd. E&W .. | 12W-37N | 18 |

|  | Grid | Page |
|---|---|---|
| Sharon Pl. NW&SE | | |
| ............... | 10W-39N | 19 |
| Sheridan Pl. N&S .. | 9W-38N | 19 |
| Sheridan Rd. N&S | | |
| .......10W-37N, | 10W-39N | 19 |
| Spitz Dr. N&S .... | 11W-38N | 18 |
| Stewart Av. N&S .. | 10W-38N | 19 |
| Stratton Av. N&S ... | 9W-37N | 19 |
| Suddard Pl. E&W | | |
| ....... 9W-38N, | 10W-38N | 19 |
| Sunlight Ct. N&S .. | 10W-38N | 19 |
| Talmadge Av. E&W | | |
| ............... | 10W-38N | 19 |
| Tewes Ct. N&S .. | 10W-38N | 19 |
| Van Ct. NS&EW .. | 12W-40N | 10 |
| Vercoe Av. E&W .. | 12W-37N | 18 |
| Wadsworth Rd. E&W | | |
| .......12W-39N, | 10W-39N | 18 |
| Waldo Av. N&S | | |
| .......12W-39N, | 10W-39N | 18 |
| Warner Av. E&W .. | 12W-37N | 18 |
| Waverly St. E&W .. | 12W-40N | 10 |
| Wilson Av. N&S | | |
| .......10W-37N, | 10W-38N | 18 |
| Woodland Av. E&W | | |
| ............... | 10W-38N | 18 |
| Wyer Rd. E&W .... | 12W-38N | 18 |
| Wyer St. E&W...... | 10W-38N | 18 |
| Yale Av. E&W ...... | 10W-39N | 19 |
| Yorkhouse Rd. E&W | | |
| .......12W-37N, | 10W-37N | 18 |
| Zepher St. E&W .. | 12W-38N | 18 |
| 27th Pl. E&W .... | 12W-40N | 10 |
| 27th St. E&W .... | 12W-40N | 10 |
| 28th Pl. E&W .... | 12W-40N | 10 |
| 28th St. E&W .... | 12W-40N | 10 |
| 29th St. E&W | | |
| .......12W-40N, | 11W-40N | 10 |
| 32nd St. E&W .... | 12W-39N | 18 |
| 33rd St. E&W | | |
| .......12W-39N, | 11W-39N | 18 |
| 34th St. E&W .... | 10W-39N | 19 |

**Benton Township**

|  | Grid | Page |
|---|---|---|
| Barnhart Ct. E&W | | |
| ....... 9W-41N, | 8W-41N | 11 |
| Berrong Av. N&S .. | 10W-42N | 11 |
| Berrong Ct. N&S .. | 10W-42N | 11 |
| Block Ln. E&W .... | 11W-43N | 10 |
| Brockway Av. N&S .. | 9W-40N | 11 |
| Broecker Av. N&S .. | 11W-42N | 10 |
| Burnett Av. N&S | | |
| ....... 8W-40N, | 8W-41N | 11 |
| Dodson Av. N&S .. | 11W-42N | 10 |
| E. Ravine Dr. NE&SW | | |
| ............... | 10W-41N | 11 |
| Edward St. E&W .. | 10W-42N | 10 |
| English Ln. N&S .. | 10W-42N | 11 |
| Fago Av. N&S | | |
| .......11W-42N, | 11W-43N | 10 |
| Forman Dr. E&W | | |
| .......12W-42N, | 11W-42N | 10 |
| Fosslands N&S | | |
| .......11W-42N, | 11W-43N | 10 |
| Fulton Av. N&S | | |
| ....... 8W-40N, | 8W-41N | 11 |
| Green Bay Rd. NW&SE | | |
| ............... | 12W-41N | 10 |
| Hanks Av. N&S | | |
| .......11W-42N, | 11W-43N | 10 |
| Howland Av. N&S... | 9W-40N | 11 |
| Illinois St. N&S .... | 10W-41N | 11 |
| Jensen Av. N&S .. | 11W-43N | 10 |
| Kellogg Ct. N&S ... | 9W-41N | 11 |
| Kenosha Rd. N&S | | |
| .......12W-41N, | 11W-43N | 10 |
| Lake Front Dr. N&S | | |
| ....... 8W-40N, | 8W-41N | 11 |
| Lewis Av. N&S | | |
| .......11W-42N, | 11W-43N | 10 |
| Logan Ct. N&S | | |
| ....... 10W-41N, | 8W-41N | 11 |
| Lynn Dale Dr. N&S | 12W-43N | 10 |
| Mather Av. N&S .. | 11W-42N | 10 |
| Mills Av. N&S........ | 8W-40N | 11 |
| Morse Av. N&S | | |
| ....... 9W-40N, | 9W-41N | 11 |
| Oak Ln. E&W .... | 11W-43N | 10 |
| Oakcrest Ln. N&S . | 12W-43N | 10 |
| Orchard Ln. N&S .. | 9W-41N | 11 |
| Parkview Av. N&S | | |
| ....... 9W-40N, | 9W-41N | 11 |
| Pearsal Av. N&S | | |
| ....... 9W-40N, | 8W-40N | 11 |
| Prairie Av. N&S .. | 11W-43N | 10 |
| Prospect Av. E&W | | |
| ....... 9W-40N, | 8W-40N | 11 |
| Rita Av. E&W | | |
| ....... 9W-40N, | 8W-40N | 11 |
| Russell Rd. E&W | | |
| .......13W-43N, | 10W-43N | 10 |
| Short Av. N&S .... | 9W-40N | 11 |
| Strong Av. N&S .... | 9W-40N | 11 |
| Thorpe Av. N&S .. | 11W-42N | 10 |
| Transportation Av. N&S | | |
| ....... 9W-40N, | 9W-41N | 11 |
| Vista Ln. N&S.... | 12W-42N | 10 |
| Washington Av. N&S | | |
| ............... | 10W-42N | 11 |
| Wilmont Av. N&S .... | 9W-40N | 11 |
| Wilson Ct. E&W | | |
| ....... 9W-41N, | 8W-41N | 11 |

|  | Grid | Page |
|---|---|---|
| Winthrop Ct. E&W | | |
| ....... 10W-41N, | 8W-41N | 11 |
| Winthrop Harbor Rd. E&W | | |
| ............... | 12W-42N | 10 |
| Winthrop Ct. E&W | | |
| .......10W-41N, | 8W-41N | 11 |
| 3rd St. E&W .... | 11W-43N | 10 |
| 4th St. E&W .... | 11W-43N | 10 |
| 5th St. E&W .... | 11W-43N | 10 |
| 9th St. E&W | | |
| .......11W-42N, | 10W-42N | 10 |
| 10th St. E&W .... | 11W-42N | 10 |
| 11th St. E&W .... | 11W-42N | 10 |
| 12th St. E&W .... | 11W-42N | 10 |
| 13th St. E&W .... | 11W-42N | 10 |
| 16th St. E&W ...... | 9W-41N | 11 |
| 17th St. E&W | | |
| ....... 11W-41N, | 8W-41N | 10 |
| 18th St. E&W | | |
| ....... 10W-41N, | 8W-41N | 11 |
| 19th St. E&W | | |
| ....... 10W-41N, | 8W-41N | 11 |
| 20th St. E&W | | |
| ....... 9W-41N, | 8W-41N | 11 |
| 22nd St. E&W | | |
| ....... 9W-40N, | 8W-40N | 11 |
| 23rd St. E&W | | |
| ....... 9W-40N, | 8W-40N | 11 |

**Buffalo Grove***
(Also see Cook County)

|  | Grid | Page |
|---|---|---|
| Aberdeen Ct. E&W | 16W-20N | 48 |
| Aberdeen Ln. N&S.. | 16W-20N | 48 |
| Acacia Ct., S. NE&SW | | |
| ............... | 17W-23N | 48 |
| Acacia Ter. N&S... | 17W-23N | 48 |
| Acorn Ct. E&W .. | 16W-20N | 48 |
| Acorn Pl. E&W .... | 16W-22N | 48 |
| Alden Ct. NS&EW .. | 17W-21N | 48 |
| Alsace Cir. NS&EW | | |
| ............... | 16W-20N | 48 |
| Amherst Ct. E&W .. | 17W-21N | 48 |
| Anderson Ln. N&S .. | 16W-20N | 48 |
| Apollo Dr. NW&SE.. | 16W-20N | 48 |
| Appletree Ct. N&S .. | 17W-20N | 48 |
| Arbor Gate Ln. NW&SE | | |
| ............... | 17W-20N | 48 |
| Arlington Heights Rd. N&S | | |
| .......17W-20N, | 18W-20N | 48 |
| Armstrong Ct., N. N&S | | |
| ............... | 15W-20N | 49 |
| Armstrong Dr. E&W | | |
| ............... | 16W-20N | 48 |
| Ashbury Dr. E&W .. | 15W-21N | 49 |
| Ashland Ct. NE&SW | | |
| ............... | 17W-20N | 48 |
| Aspen Ct. N&S .. | 17W-20N | 48 |
| Aspen Dr. N&S .... | 17W-20N | 48 |
| Auburn Ln. E&W .. | 17W-20N | 48 |
| Autumn Ct. E&W .. | 16W-21N | 48 |
| Banbury Ln. N&S .. | 17W-21N | 48 |
| Bank Ln. E&W .... | 16W-20N | 48 |
| Banyan Tree Ln. E&W | | |
| ............... | 17W-22N | 48 |
| Barclay Blvd. N&S.. | 15W-21N | 49 |
| Bayberry Dr. N&S .. | 17W-23N | 48 |
| Bedford Ct. N&S .. | 18W-21N | 48 |
| Belmar NE&SW | | |
| ............... | 17W-21N | 48 |
| Belmar Ln. NW&SE | | |
| ............... | 17W-21N | 48 |
| Bentley Pl. NS&EW | | |
| ............... | 16W-21N | 48 |
| Berkley Ct. N&S.... | 16W-20N | 48 |
| Beverly Ln. N&S | | |
| ............... | 17W-22N | 48 |
| Birchwood Ct., N. NW&SE | | |
| ............... | 17W-22N | 48 |
| Birchwood Ct., S. E&W | | |
| ............... | 17W-22N | 48 |
| Birchwood Ln. N&S | | |
| ............... | 17W-22N | 48 |
| Blackthorn Dr. NE&SW | | |
| ............... | 16W-23N | 48 |
| Blossom Ct. N&S .. | 17W-20N | 48 |
| Blue Ash Ct. N&S .. | 17W-23N | 48 |
| Blue Ash Dr. E&W .. | 17W-23N | 48 |
| Bordeaux Ct., E. E&W | | |
| ............... | 17W-21N | 48 |
| Bordeaux Ct., W. E&W | | |
| ............... | 17W-21N | 48 |
| Brandwyn Ln. E&W | | |
| ............... | 17W-21N | 48 |
| Brandywyn Ct., N. NW&SE | | |
| ............... | 17W-21N | 48 |
| Brandywyn Ln. NS&EW | | |
| .......17W-22N, | 16W-22N | 48 |
| Bristol Ln. NW&SE | 18W-21N | 48 |
| Buckingham Ln. E&W | | |
| ............... | 16W-20N | 48 |
| Buckthorn Ct. E&W | | |
| ............... | 16W-20N | 48 |
| Buckthorn Ter. NS&EW | | |
| ............... | 16W-20N | 48 |
| Buffalo Grove Rd. N&S | | |
| .......17W-22N, | 16W-20N | 48 |
| Bunescu Ct.* N&S.. | 18W-20N | 48 |
| Bunescu Ln.* E&W | | |
| ............... | 18W-20N | 48 |
| Burgess Cir. E&W .. | 18W-21N | 48 |
| Burnt Ember Ct. E&W | | |
| ............... | 17W-20N | 48 |

|  | Grid | Page |
|---|---|---|
| Burnt Ember Ln. NW&SE | | |
| ............... | 17W-20N | 48 |
| Busch Pkwy. E&W.. | 15W-21N | 49 |
| Busch Rd. E&W | | |
| .......17W-21N, | 16W-21N | 48 |
| Camden Ct.* E&W .. | 18W-20N | 48 |
| Canterbury Ln. E&W | | |
| ............... | 16W-21N | 48 |
| Caren Ct. N&S .... | 17W-21N | 48 |
| Caren Dr. E&W .... | 17W-21N | 48 |
| Carlton Pl. E&W .. | 17W-20N | 48 |
| Carlyle Ln. E&W .. | 16W-22N | 48 |
| Carman Av. N&S .. | 16W-20N | 49 |
| Cary Ln. NW&SE .. | 17W-20N | 48 |
| Castlewood Ln. NW&SE | | |
| ............... | 17W-20N | 48 |
| Cedar Ct., N. NW&SE | | |
| ............... | 17W-22N | 48 |
| Cedar Ct., S. E&W | 17W-22N | 48 |
| Chapel Oaks Dr. E&W | | |
| ............... | 16W-23N | 48 |
| Chase Ct.* E&W ... | 18W-20N | 48 |
| Chateau Dr. E&W .. | 17W-20N | 48 |
| Chaucer Way E&W | | |
| ............... | 17W-21N | 48 |
| Checker Dr. N&S | | |
| .......17W-20N, | 17W-21N | 48 |
| Checker Rd. E&W .. | 17W-20N | 48 |
| Cherbourg Ct., N E&W | | |
| ............... | 16W-20N | 48 |
| Cherbourg Ct., S. E&W | | |
| ............... | 16W-20N | 48 |
| Cherbourg Dr. N&S | | |
| ............... | 16W-20N | 48 |
| Chestnut Ct., E. N&S | | |
| ............... | 16W-22N | 48 |
| Chestnut Ct., W. N&S | | |
| ............... | 16W-22N | 48 |
| Chestnut Ter. NS&EW | | |
| ............... | 16W-22N | 48 |
| Chicory Ln. E&W . | 16W-20N | 48 |
| Church Rd. NE&SW | | |
| ............... | 16W-20N | 48 |
| Churchill Ct. N&S .. | 16W-21N | 48 |
| Circle Ct. NW&SE .. | 16W-20N | 48 |
| Circle Dr. NS&EW .. | 10W-39N | 19 |
| Claret Dr. E&W .... | 17W-20N | 48 |
| Clearview Ct. N&S.. | 16W-21N | 48 |
| Clohessey Dr. N&S | | |
| ............... | 17W-20N | 48 |
| Cloverdale Ct. E&W | | |
| ............... | 17W-21N | 48 |
| Cobbler Ln. E&W .. | 16W-21N | 48 |
| Cobblestone Ct. N&S | | |
| ............... | 16W-20N | 48 |
| Cobblestone Ln. N&S | | |
| ............... | 16W-20N | 48 |
| Commerce Ct. N&S | | |
| .......15W-20N, | 15W-21N | 49 |
| Common Way E&W | | |
| ............... | 16W-20N | 48 |
| Cooper Ct.* E&W .. | 18W-20N | 48 |
| Copperwood Dr. NS&EW | | |
| ............... | 16W-21N | 48 |
| Corporate Grove Dr. E&W | | |
| ............... | 15W-21N | 49 |
| County Line Rd. E&W | | |
| ............... | 16W-20N | 48 |
| Courtland Dr. E&W | | |
| ............... | 17W-21N | 48 |
| Coventry Ct. NW&SE | | |
| ............... | 17W-22N | 48 |
| Coventry Ln. E&W .. | 17W-22N | 48 |
| Crab Apple Ter. E&W | | |
| ............... | 16W-22N | 48 |
| Crossfield Ct. N&S | 16W-21N | 48 |
| Crown Point Ct. N&S | | |
| ............... | 17W-20N | 48 |
| Crown Point Dr. N&S | | |
| ............... | 17W-20N | 48 |
| Cumberland Ct. NE&SW | | |
| ............... | 16W-21N | 48 |
| Cumberland Ln. NW&SE | | |
| ............... | 16W-21N | 48 |
| Cyprus Ct. NE&SW | | |
| ............... | 17W-23N | 48 |
| Dannet Ct. N&S .... | 17W-21N | 48 |
| Dannet Rd. E&W .. | 17W-21N | 48 |
| Dartmouth Ln. E&W | | |
| ............... | 15W-20N | 49 |
| Daulton Ct. NW&SE | | |
| ............... | 17W-23N | 48 |
| Daulton Dr. NE&SW | | |
| ............... | 17W-23N | 48 |
| Dayton Ct. E&W... | 17W-21N | 48 |
| Dayton Rd. N&S.... | 17W-21N | 48 |
| Deerfield Pkwy. NS&EW | | |
| ............... | 15W-21N | 49 |
| Dellwood Ct. N&S .. | 17W-21N | 48 |
| Devlin Rd. N&S .. | 17W-21N | 48 |
| Cir. ............... | 17W-21N | 48 |
| Devonwood Ct. N&S | | |
| ............... | 16W-21N | 48 |
| Dogwood Ter. N&S | | |
| ............... | 16W-20N | 48 |
| Dorncliff Ln. N&S | | |
| ............... | 17W-20N | 48 |
| Dover Ct. NW&SE .. | 17W-22N | 48 |
| Dover Dr. E&W .... | 17W-22N | 48 |
| Driftwood Pl. N&S.. | 16W-20N | 48 |
| Dunham St. NE&SW | | |
| ............... | | 48 |
| Dunhill Dr. NS&EW | 16W-20N | 48 |
| Dunstan Ln. N&S .. | 17W-23N | 48 |

| | Grid | Page |
|---|---|---|
East Chevy Chase Dr.
 NE&SW.........14W-20N  49
Eastwood Ln. E&W
 .............15W-20N  49
Edgemere Rd. E&W
 .............17W-22N  48
English Oak Ter. E&W
 .............17W-22N  48
Essington Rd. N&S ...18W-21N  48
Euclid Ct. N&S  16W-21N  48
Fabish Ct. N&S  16W-21N  48
Fabish Dr. NS&EW  16W-21N  48
Fairfax Ln. E&W ...18W-21N  48
Fairway View Cir. N&S
 .............17W-20N  48
Farnsworth Ct. N&S
 .............18W-21N  48
Farrington Dr. E&W
 .............17W-20N  48
Ferndale Ct. N&S ..17W-20N  48
Fox Hill Ct., E. NW&SE
 .............16W-20N  48
Fox Hill Ct., W. N&S
 .............16W-20N  48
Fox Hill Dr. NS&EW
 .............16W-20N  48
Foxford Dr. NS&EW
 .............17W-23N  48
Franklin Ln. N&S .18W-21N  48
Fremont Ct., E. E&W
 .............18W-21N  48
Fremont Ct., W. E&W
 .............18W-21N  48
Cir. ......18W-21N  48
Gail Ct. NE&SW ...17W-21N  48
Gail Dr. N&S ......17W-21N  48
Gardenia Ln. E&W...17W-20N  48
Golfside Ct. N&S ..17W-20N  48
Green Knolls Dr. E&W
 .............17W-21N  48
Hackberry Ct., E. E&W
 .............17W-22N  48
Hackberry Ct., W. E&W
 .............17W-22N  48
Hampshire Ct. E&W
 .............16W-20N  48
Harris Dr. N&S  17W-20N  48
Harvest Ct.* NE&SW
 .............17W-20N  48
Hastings Ln. N&S
 .............15W-20N  49
Hazelwood Ter. N&S
 .............16W-20N  48
Heatherdown Way E&W
 .............17W-20N  48
Hidden Lake Dr. NS&EW
 .............16W-21N  48
Highland Grove Ct., N.
 NE&SW.........16W-21N  48
Highland Grove Dr. N&S
 ......16W-20N,16W-21N  48
Hill Ct. E. E&W ... 16W-20N  48
Hilldale Ln. N&S ... 16W-21N  48
Hobson Ct. NE&SW
 .............16W-20N  48
Hobson Dr. N&S....16W-21N  48
Hollystone Ln. NE&SW
 .............17W-20N  48
Horatio Blvd. E&W
 ......16W-20N,15W-20N  48
Huntley Rd. NW&SE
 .............15W-20N  49
Indian Spring Ln. N&S
 .............17W-20N  48
Ironwood Ct. N&S .16W-22N  48
Ironwood Rd. E&S..16W-22N  48
Ivy Hall Ln. E&W .. 17W-21N  48
Jersey Ct. N&S .....16W-21N  48
Joel Ln. N&S ......16W-20N  48
Johnson Dr. N&S .. 15W-20N  49
Kent Ln. N&S ......17W-21N  48
Kingsbridge Way E&W
 .............17W-21N  48
Kingston Dr. NE&SW
 .............17W-23N  48
Knight Hill Ct. NW&SE
 .............17W-20N  48
Knollwood Dr. E&W
 .............17W-21N  48
Knollwoods Ct. N&S
 .............17W-21N  48
LaSalle Ct., N. E&W
 .............17W-21N  48
LaSalle Ln. E&W ..17W-21N  48
Lake Cook Rd. E&W
 .............16W-20N  48
Lakeview Ct. E&W .17W-20N  48
Lakeview Dr. NE&SW  18W-21N  48
Lamont Ter. E&W .. 17W-21N  48
Lancaster Ct.* E&W
 .............17W-20N  48
Larchmont Dr. N&S
 .............17W-21N  48
Larraway Dr. N&S .. 17W-21N  48
Lawn Ct. NE&SW .. 16W-20N  48
Cir. ......16W-20N  48
LeJardin Ct. E&W
 .............16W-20N  48
Lee Ct. N&S ......18W-21N  48
Lexington Dr. N&S .15W-20N  49
Lilac Ln. N&S .....15W-20N  49
Linden Av. E&W ...14W-20N  49
Lockwood Ct., E. N&S
 .............17W-21N  48

| | Grid | Page |
|---|---|---|
Lockwood Ct., W. N&S
 .............17W-21N  48
Lockwood Dr. NS&EW
 .............17W-21N  48
Logsdon Ln. N&S ..17W-21N  48
London Ct. E&W .. 17W-22N  48
Long Grove Aptakisic Rd.
 E&W .........17W-22N  48
Long Ridge Ct. NW&SE
 .............16W-21N  48
Lyon Ct. E&W ....17W-21N  48
Lyon Dr. E&W ....17W-21N  48
Madison Ct., N. E&W
 .............16W-21N  48
Madison Ct., S. N&S
 .............16W-21N  48
Madison Dr. NS&EW
 .............16W-21N  48
Magnolia Ct., E. E&W
 .............17W-22N  48
Magnolia Ct., W. E&W
 .............17W-22N  48
Margate Dr. NW&SE
 .............16W-21N  48
Marseilles Cir. N&S
 .............16W-20N  48
Milwaukee Av. NW&SE
 .............14W-21N  49
Mistywoods Rd. N&S
 .............16W-23N  48
Morningside Ln., E. E&W
 .............16W-21N  48
Morningside Ln., W. E&W
 .............16W-21N  48
Mundelein Rd. NW&SE
 .............17W-21N  48
New Dover Ln. E&W
 ......17W-23N,16W-23N  48
New Town Ct., E. N&S
 .............16W-20N  48
New Town Ct., W. NE&SW
 .............16W-20N  48
New Town Dr. NW&SE
 .............16W-20N  48
Newfield Ct. NW&SE
 .............16W-21N  48
Newfield Dr. E&W .16W-21N  48
Newgate Ct. E&W .16W-21N  48
Newman St. E&W ..14W-20N  49
Newport Ct. N&S .. 18W-21N  48
Newton Dr. E&W .. 16W-20N  48
Old Barn N&S ....16W-21N  48
Osage Ter. N&S...16W-20N  48
Oxford Dr. E&W....17W-21N  48
Park Av. E&W ....16W-23N  48
Parkchester E&W ..16W-20N  48
Parker Ln. NS&EW
 .............17W-21N  48
Parkside Dr. E&W .16W-21N  48
Parkview Ct. N&S ..17W-20N  48
Pauline Av. E&W .. 16W-20N  48
Pecan Ct. N&S ....16W-20N  48
Penny Ln. N&S ....17W-20N  48
Pin Oak Ter. E&W .16W-20N  48
Pinehurst Ln. N&S .16W-20N  48
Pinetree Cir., N.* NS&EW
 .............17W-20N  48
Pinetree Cir., S.* NS&EW
 .............17W-20N  48
Pinyon Ct., N. N&S
 .............16W-23N  48
Pinyon Ct., S. N&S
 .............16W-23N  48
Port Clinton Ct., E. N&S
 .............17W-23N  48
Port Clinton Ct., W. N&S
 .............17W-23N  48
Prairie Ln. E&W .. 16W-20N  48
Providence Ct.* N&S
 .............18W-21N  48
Providence Ln. NS&EW
 .............18W-21N  48
Quaker Hollow Ct., N. N&S
 .............16W-21N  48
Quaker Hollow Ct., S. N&S
 .............16W-21N  48
Raintree Ct. E&W ..17W-23N  48
Raintree Rd. N&S .. 17W-23N  48
Ranchview Ct. N&S
 .............17W-21N  48
Raphael Av. N&S .. 15W-20N  49
Redbud Pl. E&W .. 16W-20N  48
Ridgefield Ln. NW&SE
 .............16W-21N  48
Ridgewood N&S...15W-20N  49
Rolling Hills Ct. E&W
 .............16W-21N  48
Ronnie Dr. NS&EW
 .............17W-21N  48
Roslyn Ct. NE&SW
 .............16W-21N  48
Roslyn Ln. E&W...16W-23N  48
Route 21 N&S.....14W-21N  49
Route 83 NW&SE
 ......18W-21N,16W-20N  48
Russelwood Ct. N&S
 .............16W-20N  48
Sandalwood Ct. E&W
 .............17W-23N  48
Sandalwood Rd. N&S
 .............17W-23N  48
Sandhurst Ct. NW&SE
 .............16W-21N  48

| | Grid | Page |
|---|---|---|
Sandhurst Dr. NS&EW
 .............16W-21N  48
Satinwood Ct., N. NE&SW
 .............17W-22N  48
Satinwood Ct., S. E&W
 .............17W-22N  48
Satinwood Ter. NE&SW
 .............17W-22N  48
Saybrook Ln. N&S..18W-21N  48
Scottish Pine Ln. E&W
 .............17W-23N  48
Shady Grove Ln. N&S
 .............17W-20N  48
Shambliss Ct. N&S  18W-21N  48
Shambliss Ln. N&S
 .............18W-21N  48
Sheridan Ct. E&W .. 17W-22N  48
Sheridan rd. NW&SE
 .............17W-22N  48
Silver Linden Ln. NE&SW
 .............17W-22N  48
Silver Rock Ln. N&S
 .............17W-20N  48
Somerset Ln. NE&SW
 .............16W-20N  48
South Chevy Chase Dr. E&W
 .............14W-20N  49
Springside Ct. NW&SE
 .............17W-20N  48
Springside Ln. NE&SW
 .............17W-20N  48
Stanton Ct., E. N&S
 .............16W-21N  48
Stanton Ct., W. N&S
 .............16W-21N  48
Stanton Dr. NS&EW
 .............16W-21N  48
Steeple Dr. NS&EW
 .............16W-20N  48
Summer Ct. NE&SW
 .............17W-22N  48
Teawood Cir. NS&EW
 .............16W-20N  48
Thistle Ct. SW&NE  16W-21N  48
Thompson Blvd. E&W
 ......17W-21N,16W-21N  48
Thompson Ct. N&S
 .............16W-21N  48
Thornapple Ct. NE&SW
 .............17W-20N  48
Thorndale Ct. N&S .16W-20N  48
Thorndale Dr. E&W
 .............16W-20N  48
Tree Farm Ct. N&S
 .............17W-22N  48
Trotwood Ct. N&S .. 16W-21N  48
Twilight Pass NE&SW
 .............17W-20N  48
Twin Oaks Blvd. N&S
 .............17W-22N  48
Twin Oaks Ct. NW&SE
 .............17W-22N  48
Twisted Oak Ln. E&W
 .............17W-20N  48
Village Ct. E&W ....16W-21N  48
Vintage Ln. N&S....17W-20N  48
Wakefield Ct. NW&SE
 .............17W-20N  48
Wakefield Ln. NW&SE
 .............16W-20N  48
Wedgewood Ct. SW&NE
 .............17W-23N  48
Weidner Rd. E&W .. 17W-20N  48
Weiland Rd. N&S
 ......16W-20N,16W-21N  48
Wellington Ct. N&S
 .............16W-21N  48
Wellington North E&W
 ......16W-21N,15W-21N  48
Wellington South E&W
 ......16W-21N,15W-21N  48
West Bourne Ln. NE&SW
 .............17W-20N  48
West Dr. NW&SE .. 14W-20N  49
Westchester Ct. N&S
 .............16W-21N  48
Westchester Ln. N&S
 .............16W-21N  48
Whispering Oaks Ct. E&W
 .............16W-23N  48
Cir. ......16W-23N  48
White Oak Ln. E&W
 .............17W-23N  48
White Pine Ln. N&S
 .............17W-23N  48
Whitebranch Ct. N&S
 .............16W-20N  48
Wildflower Cir. N&S
 .............17W-20N  48
Willow Parkway E&W
 .............16W-22N  48
Wilshire Ct. N&S....17W-22N  48
Windbrooke Dr. N&S
 .............15W-21N  49
Winding Oak Ln. E&W
 .............16W-20N  48
Windover Cir. N&S
 ......17W-20N,16W-20N  48
Windwood Ct.* N&S
 .............16W-20N  48
Winston Dr. N&S .. 16W-21N  48
Witney Ln. N&S....16W-21N  48
Wood Hollow Ln. N&S
 .............17W-20N  48

| | Grid | Page |
|---|---|---|
Woodbury Rd. N&S
 .............16W-20N  48
Woodridge Ln.* N&S
 .............17W-20N  48
Cir. ......16W-20N  48
Woodstone Dr. E&W
 .............16W-20N  48
Wyngate Ln. N&S .. 17W-20N  48

## Cuba Township

Apple Tree Ln. E&W
 .............26W-22N  45
Arch Dr. E&W ....28W-23N  44
Beach Dr. N&S ....28W-24N  36
Beachway NW&SE .28W-24N  36
Bertha Ln. N&S ...26W-22N  45
Bloners Dr. E&W .. 28W-24N  36
Bluff Ln. E&W ....28W-23N  44
Border Rd. N&S
 ......25W-21N,25W-22N  45
Brandt Rd. E&W
 ......26W-21N,25W-21N  45
Broken Bow Pass NW&SE
 ......26W-25N,25W-25N  37
Canyon Creek Ct. N&S
 .............26W-25N  37
Chamberlain Dr. E&W
 .............28W-23N  44
Chatham Rd. N&S .. 25W-21N  45
Church Rd. N&S...28W-23N  44
Columbus Dr. NE&SW
 .............25W-21N  45
Country Estates Rd. E&W
 .............26W-21N  45
Countryside Ln. N&S
 .............26W-22N  45
County Line Rd. N&S
 .............28W-22N  44
Craft Ct. NE&SW . 28W-23N  44
Crestview Ln. NS&EW
 .............25W-21N  45
Crown Rd. NS&EW
 .............26W-21N  45
Cuba Rd. E&W
 ......28W-21N,25W-21N  44
Damien Dr. E&W .. 28W-22N  44
Drake Rd. E&W ...25W-21N  45
E. Lake Shore Dr. N&S
 .............25W-25N  37
East Dr. N&S .... 28W-23N  44
East Oakwood Dr. N&S
 .............25W-25N  37
Edgemond Ln. E&W
 .............26W-22N  45
Edgewood Av. E&W
 .............28W-24N  36
Elizabeth Ln. N&S . 25W-21N  45
Elm Ct. NE&SW . 25W-21N  45
Exmoor Av. N&S . 26W-20N  45
Fairhaven Dr. NE&SW
 .............25W-21N  45
Falkirk Cir. E&W . 26W-21N  45
Flint Creek Dr. N&S
 ......27W-23N,27W-24N  44
Flynn Creek Dr. NS&EW
 .............27W-21N  44
Fox River Dr. NE&SW
 ......28W-23N,28W-24N  44
Fox River Rd. N&S
 ......28W-24N,27W-24N  36
Fox St. E&W ..... 28W-23N  44
Glenbarr Ln. NW&SE
 .............26W-21N  45
Grant St. E&W
 ......27W-21N,26W-21N  44
Grayclyn Ct. N&S . 28W-25N  36
Greenwood Ln. N&S
 .............25W-25N  37
Hanover Hill NW&SE
 .............25W-21N  45
Hart Rd. N&S
 ......26W-20N,26W-21N  45
Heritage Oak Dr. E&W
 .............28W-23N  44
Heritage Tr. N&S .. 28W-23N  44
Hess Dr. N&S ..... 28W-23N  44
Hickory Ln. N&S .. 26W-24N  37
Hickory Nut Grove Rd. N&S
 ......28W-23N,28W-25N  44
High Ridge Rd. E&W
 .............25W-21N  45
High Ridge Rd. N&S
 .............28W-23N  44
Highland Rd. E&W
 ......27W-21N,26W-21N  44
Hillcrest Av. E&W . 28W-24N  36
Hillside Rd. N&S....28W-23N  44
Hipplers Rd. N&S . 25W-21N  45
Holly Dr. N&S .... 28W-24N  36
Hough Rd. N&S
 ......25W-20N,25W-21N  45
Indian Tr. NW&SE
 ......26W-25N,25W-25N  37
Jensen Av. NW&SE
 .............28W-24N  36
Kelsey Av. N&S .... 28W-23N  44
Kelsey Ct. E&W ...28W-23N  44
Kelsey Rd. N&S
 ......28W-22N,28W-23N  44
Knollwood Ln. N&S
 .............25W-25N  37
Kristy Ln. NS&EW . 28W-24N  36
Lagoon Dr. N&S ... 27W-24N  37

| | Grid | Page |
|---|---|---|
Lake Shore Dr. E&W
 .............25W-21N  45
Lake Shore Dr. N&S
 ......25W-25N,25W-21N  37
Lake Zurich Rd. E&W
 .............25W-21N  45
Lakeview Pkwy. NS&EW
 .............25W-25N  37
Laurin Dr. N&S .... 28W-23N  44
Lincoln St. E&W ....26W-21N  45
Lindbergh Dr. E&W
 .............28W-23N  44
Main St. E&W .. 28W-23N  44
Main St. NE&SW . 28W-24N  36
Meadow Ln. NE&SW
 .............28W-23N  44
Merton Rd. E&W . 28W-20N  45
Middle Fork Rd. E&W
 .............25W-21N  45
Midway St. E&W . 28W-23N  44
North Dr. E&W ... 28W-23N  44
North Oaks Ct. N&S
 .............25W-25N  37
Oak Creek Cir. NE&SW
 .............25W-25N  37
Oakland Av. N&S .. 28W-24N  36
Oakridge Rd. E&W  25W-25N  37
Oakwood Dr. N&S
 ......25W-24N,25W-25N  37
Old Barrington Rd. N&S
 .............26W-21N  45
Park Dr. E&W ....28W-23N  44
Park St. NS&EW . 28W-23N  44
Pepper Rd. E&W . 28W-22N  44
Pioneer Grove Rd. E&W
 .............28W-23N  44
Pitner Av. E&W ... 28W-24N  36
Prestick Dr. NS&EW
 .............26W-21N  45
Private Rd. N&S....26W-21N  45
Providence Rd. E&W
 .............25W-21N  45
Ravine Ct. N&S ... 28W-23N  44
River Rd. NE&SW . 28W-23N  44
River St. N&S ..... 28W-23N  44
Rivers Edge Dr. NS&EW
 .............28W-24N  36
Rivershore Dr. N&S
 .............27W-24N  37
Riverside Dr. NE&SW
 .............28W-24N  36
Roberts Ct. N&S .. 28W-25N  36
Roslyn Rd. E&W .. 26W-20N  45
Rustic Dr. N&S .... 25W-21N  45
Rustic Ln. E&W ... 28W-23N  44
Scott Rd. E&W
 ......26W-22N,25W-22N  45
Shoreline Rd. NE&SW
 .............26W-24N  37
Short St. NS&EW . 28W-24N  36
South St. E&W ... 28W-23N  44
Spring Dr. N&S ... 28W-23N  44
Summit Dr. N&S . 28W-23N  44
Sunset Av. N&S ... 28W-24N  36
Sunset Ln. E&W . 25W-21N  45
Sunset Rd. E&W .. 25W-21N  45
Sylvester St. NW&SE
 .............28W-24N  36
Tara Dr. E&W ... 25W-25N  37
Taylor Rd. E&W .. 25W-21N  45
Timberlake Pkwy. E&W
 .............25W-25N  37
Timberlake Rd. N&S
 ......26W-25N,25W-25N  37
Wagon Wheel Ct. N&S
 .............25W-25N  37
Waveland Av. NE&SW
 .............28W-24N  36
West Oakwood Dr. N&S
 .............25W-25N  37
Wildwood Dr. E&W
 .............25W-25N  37
Woodbridge N&S . 26W-25N  37
Woodland Av. N&S
 .............25W-21N  45
13th St. N&S
 ......26W-20N,26W-21N  45
14th St. N&S .... 26W-21N  45
17th St. N&S .... 26W-21N  45
18th St. N&S .... 26W-21N  45
19th St. N&S .... 26W-21N  45
20th St. N&S .... 26W-21N  45
21st St. N&S .... 26W-21N  45
22nd St. N&S .... 27W-21N  44
23rd St. N&S .... 27W-21N  44
24th St. N&S .... 27W-21N  44
25th St. N&S ..... 27W-21N  44

## Deer Park

Bedlington Cir. E&W
 .............23W-21N  46
Bobwhite Ln. N&S . 23W-21N  46
Bramble Ln. N&S .. 22W-20N  46
Briargate Ln. N&S . 22W-20N  46
Cardinal Ln. E&W . 23W-21N  46
Chapel Hill Dr. NS&EW
 .............22W-20N  46
Cheshire Ct. NE&SW
 .............22W-20N  46
Circle Dr. NS&EW . 23W-20N  46
Clover Ln. N&S ... 23W-20N  46
Corners Dr. E&W .. 22W-20N  46

**Grid — Page**

Covington Dr. E&W .... 22W-20N 46
Cuba Rd. E&W .....25W-21N,23W-21N 45
Deer Lake Dr. N&S ................. 23W-20N 46
Deer Valley Dr. N&S ................. 22W-20N 46
Deerpath Rd. N&S .....23W-20N,23W-21N 46
Dogwood Ct. N&S . 23W-20N 46
Doncaster Cir. NW&SE ................. 23W-20N 46
Dover Ct. NS&EW .. 22W-20N 46
Echo Ln. E&W .... 21W-20N 47
Edgeview Ct. NW&SE ................. 23W-20N 46
Ela Rd. N&S .... 24W-21N 46
Fairview Dr. E&W .. 23W-20N 46
Farthingdale Ct. NE&SW ................. 23W-20N 46
Ferndale Rd. N&S .. 23W-20N 46
Foxchase Rd. NW&SE ................. 22W-20N 46
Glen Garry Cir. E&W ................. 23W-20N 46
Glenhurst Rd. E&W ................. 22W-20N 46
Green Forest Rd. NE&SW ................. 23W-20N 46
Hearthside Dr. E&W ................. 23W-20N 46
Heather Ln. E&W .. 22W-20N 46
Hedgeworth Ct. E&W ................. 23W-20N 46
Hidden Pines Dr. N&S ................. 22W-20N 46
Hollington Ln. E&W ................. 22W-20N 46
Hummingbird Ct. NW&SE ................. 24W-21N 46
Hunters Ln. NE&SW ................. 24W-21N 46
Hypoint Dr. N&S...23W-21N 46
Inglenook Ct. N&S.23W-21N 46
Inglenook Ln. N&S..23W-21N 46
Juniper Ct. E&W...23W-20N 46
Juniper Ln. NW&SE ................. 23W-20N 46
Lagrov Ct. N&S .. 22W-20N 46
Lakeview Ct. NE&SW ................. 23W-20N 46
Lancaster Ct. NW&SE ................. 23W-21N 46
Landmark Ln. N&S 22W-20N 46
Laurel Dr. N&S .. 23W-20N 46
Lea Rd. N&S .... 23W-20N 46
Lee St. E&W ...... 23W-20N 46
Lois Ln. E&W .... 23W-20N 46
Lone Pine Ct. NW&SE ................. 23W-20N 46
Long Grove Rd. E&W .......23W-20N,22W-20N 46
Madoch Ct. N&S .. 22W-20N 46
Mallard Ct. NE&SW ................. 23W-21N 46
Mariel Cir. NE&SW 22W-20N 46
Mayfield Ln. NE&SW ................. 23W-21N 46
Meadow Ct. N&S .. 23W-20N 46
Meadow Ln. NS&EW ................. 23W-20N 46
Newcastle Ct. E&W ................. 22W-20N 46
Oak Ridge Ln. N&S ................. 23W-20N 46
Old Farm Rd. NS&EW ................. 24W-21N 46
Park Hill Dr. N&S .. 23W-20N 46
Pheasant Hill Rd. NE&SW ................. 23W-20N 46
Pheasant Trail N&S ................. 23W-21N 46
Primrose Ct. . 23W-20N 46
Quail Ct. NS&EW .. 23W-21N 46
Quentin Rd. N&S .. 22W-20N 46
Rainbow Rd. N&S .. 24W-21N 46
Rand Rd. NW&SE .......22W-20N,21W-20N 46
Regency Ct. N&S .. 24W-22N 46
Route 12 N&S .......21W-20N,20W-20N 47
Rue Chambrix E&W ................. 22W-20N 46
Rue Jordon N&S .. 22W-20N 46
Rue Orleanais E&W ................. 22W-20N 46
Rue Royale E&W .. 22W-20N 46
Rue Tourain N&S .. 22W-20N 46
Shady Ln. .... 22W-20N 46
Shoreham Cir. E&W ................. 22W-20N 46
Sumac Ct. NW&SE ................. 23W-21N 46
Sunset Ridge Rd. NS&EW ................. 23W-20N 46
Sunshine Ln. NS&EW ................. 22W-20N 46
Surrey Ct. E&W .. 22W-20N 46
Swallow Ct. E&W .......23W-20N,22W-20N 46
Swansway N&S .. 22W-20N 46
Sylvander Dr. N&S..24W-21N 46

Tanager Ct. NW&SE ................. 24W-21N 46
Teal Ct. E&W .. 23W-21N 46
Thornbury Cir. E&W ................. 22W-20N 46
Thornhill Ct. E&W .......23W-20N,22W-20N 46
Thrush Ct. NE&SW ................. 23W-21N 46
Touraine Ct. E&W . 22W-20N 46
Vesper Ct. NW&SE ................. 23W-21N 46
Wagon Ct. E&W ...22W-20N 46
Wallingford Ln. NS&EW ................. 22W-20N 46
Wehrheim Rd. N&S ................. 22W-20N 46
Wheel Ct. E&W .. 22W-20N 46
Wicker Dr. N&S .... 22W-20N 46
Willow Ct. E&W .... 22W-20N 46
Woodberry Rd. NE&SW ................. 23W-20N 46

## Deerfield*
### (Also see Cook County)

Alden Ct. N&S .. 11W-20N 50
Ambleside Dr. E&W ................. 10W-20N 50
Anthony Ln. E&W . 11W-20N 50
Appletree Ct. NW&SE ................. 11W-20N 50
Appletree Ln. N&S .......11W-20N,11W-21N 50
Arbor Vitae Rd. E&W ................. 11W-21N 50
Arthur Ct. N&S .... 11W-20N 50
Augusta Ct. E&W . 10W-20N 50
Barclay Ln. NW&SE ................. 11W-21N 50
Bayberry Ln. E&W .11W-20N 50
Bent Creek Ridge N&S ................. 9W-20N 51
Bentley Ct. N&S....11W-20N 50
Berkeley Ct. E&W .......12W-21N,11W-21N 50
Beverly Pl. N&S ... 10W-21N 50
Birch Ct. E&W ....11W-20N 50
Birchwood Av. N&S ................. 11W-20N 50
Blackthorn Ln. N&S ................. 10W-21N 50
Bradmoor Pl. N&S..11W-21N 50
Brand Ln. N&S .. 10W-21N 50
Briarhill Rd. N&S .. 10W-20N 50
Bristol Ct. E&W .... 11W-20N 50
Bristol Dr. E&W .. 11W-20N 50
Brookside Ln. E&W ................. 11W-20N 50
Burning Tree Ln. N&S ................. 11W-20N 50
Burr Oak Av. N&S..11W-20N 50
Burr Oak Ln. N&S..11W-20N 50
Byron Ct. N&S .... 10W-20N 50
Cambridge Cir. NW&SE ................. 11W-20N 50
Camille Av. E&W .. 11W-21N 50
Carlisle Ct. N&S .......10W-20N,9W-20N 50
Carlisle Pl. N&S ... 10W-20N 50
Carol Ct. E&W .. 12W-21N 50
Carol Ln. N&S.....12W-21N 50
Caroline Ct. N&S .. 10W-20N 50
Carriage Way N&S .. 9W-20N 51
Castleworth Ln. N&S .......12W-20N,12W-21N 50
Cedar Crest Dr. NW&SE ................. 10W-20N 50
Cedar Ter. N&S .......11W-20N,11W-21N 50
Central Av. E&W .......12W-20N,11W-20N 50
Chapel Ct. E&W ....11W-20N 50
Charing Cross Rd. E&W ................. 11W-20N 50
Chatham Cir. NE&SE ................. 11W-21N 50
Cherry St. N&S .. 11W-20N 50
Chestnut St. NW&SE .......11W-20N,11W-21N 50
Christopher Dr. E&W ................. 11W-20N 50
Circle Ct. N&S......11W-20N 50
Clavina Av. NE&SW ................. 12W-20N 50
Clay Ct. N&S ...... 11W-20N 50
Cody Ct. NE&SW .. 10W-20N 50
Cody Ln. NE&SW .. 10W-20N 50
Colony Ln. E&W .... 9W-20N 51
Colwyn Ter. E&W .. 10W-21N 50
Constance Ln. N&S ................. 12W-20N 50
Country Ct. N&S .. 11W-20N 50
Country Ln. N&S .. 11W-20N 50
County Line Rd. E&W ................. 10W-20N 50
Crabtree Ln. N&S .. 11W-21N 50
Craig Ct. N&S .... 11W-20N 50
Cranshire Ct. E&W 12W-20N 50
Crestview Dr. N&S.. 9W-20N 51
Crowe Av. N&S .... 11W-20N 50
Cumnor Ct. E&W . 10W-21N 50
Dartmouth Ln. N&S .......12W-20N,11W-20N 50

Davis Av. E&W .... 11W-21N 50
Deer Run Ct. N&S..11W-20N 50
Deere Park Ct. N&S ................. 11W-21N 50
Deere Park Ln. N&S ................. 11W-21N 50
Deerfield Rd. E&W .......11W-21N,10W-20N 50
Deerlake Rd. N&S.. 11W-20N 50
Deerpath Ct. N&S . 11W-20N 50
Deerpath Dr. N&S.. 11W-20N 50
Dimmeydale Dr. E&W ................. 11W-20N 50
Doral Ct. E&W .... 10W-20N 50
Earls Ct. N&S......11W-20N 50
East Canton Ct. E&W ................. 10W-21N 50
East Summit Ct. N&S ................. 11W-22N 50
Eastwood Dr. N&S 10W-20N 50
Elder Ln. N&S .... 11W-20N 50
Elizabeth Ct. NW&SE ................. 12W-21N 50
Ellendale Ct. N&S..11W-20N 50
Elm St. N&S .... 11W-20N 50
Elmwood Av. E&W 11W-20N 50
Essex Ct. N&S .... 11W-20N 50
Estate Dr. E&W .. 11W-20N 50
Estate Rd. N&S .... 11W-20N 50
Evergreen Ct. NW&SE ................. 10W-20N 50
Exmoor Ct. E&W .. 10W-20N 50
Fairoaks Av. E&W .. 11W-21N 50
Fairview Av. N&S .. 11W-21N 50
Ferndale Rd. N&S .. 9W-20N 51
Forest Av. N&S .... 11W-21N 50
Forest Way Dr. N&S ................. 11W-21N 50
Forsythia Dr. N&S .12W-20N 50
Fountainview Ct. N&S ................. 11W-20N 50
Fountainview Dr. E&W ................. 11W-20N 50
Foxhunt Tr. N&S .. 9W-20N 51
Franklin Av. N&S .. 11W-21N 50
Garand Dr. E&W . 12W-20N 50
Gordon Av. N&S .. 11W-21N 50
Gordon Ter. E&W . 11W-20N 50
Green Park Ct. NW&SE ................. 11W-20N 50
Greenbriar Dr. E&W ................. 10W-20N 50
Greentree Av. E&W ................. 11W-20N 50
Greenwood Av. E&W ................. 11W-21N 50
Greenwood Ct. N&S ................. 11W-21N 50
Grove Av. N&S .. 11W-20N 50
Hackberry Rd. E&W ................. 11W-20N 50
Hamilton N&S .. 10W-21N 50
Hampton Ct. N&S . 12W-21N 50
Hawthorne Ln. E&W ................. 12W-20N 50
Hawthorne Pl. N&S ................. 11W-20N 50
Hazel Av. E&W .. 11W-21N 50
Heather Rd. N&S .. 10W-21N 50
Hemlock St. N&S .. 11W-20N 50
Hermitage Dr. E&W ................. 10W-20N 50
Hertel Ln. E&W .. 12W-20N 50
High School Dr. N&S ................. 11W-20N 50
Hillside Av. N&S ... 11W-21N 50
Hoffman Ln. N&S .. 10W-20N 50
Holly Ct. N&S ...... 11W-20N 50
Holly Ln. NW&SE .. 11W-20N 50
Holmes Av. N&S...11W-20N 50
Hunter Ct. N&S .... 11W-20N 50
Hyacinth Ln. N&S . 10W-20N 50
Indian Hill Ct. NW&SE ................. 11W-20N 50
Indian Hill Rd. N&S 11W-20N 50
Interstate 94 N&S .......12W-20N,12W-21N 50
Island Ct. N&S .. 11W-20N 50
Jewett Park Dr. E&W ................. 11W-20N 50
Jonquil Ter. N&S .. 11W-20N 50
Journal Pl. N&S .... 11W-20N 50
Juniper Ct. N&S .. 11W-20N 50
Kates Rd. E&W .... 10W-20N 50
Kenmore Av. N&S .. 11W-21N 50
Kenton Rd. N&S...10W-20N 50
Kerry Ln. N&S......10W-20N 50
Kildare Ct. N&S .. 10W-20N 50
Kildare Ln. E&W .... 9W-20N 51
Kimberly Ct. N&S . 11W-20N 50
King Richards Ct. N&S ................. 12W-21N 50
Kingston Rd. N&S . 11W-20N 50
Kingston Ter. E&W ................. 10W-20N 50
Kipling Dr. N&S .... 11W-20N 50
Knollwood Rd. N&S ................. 10W-20N 50
Lake Cook Rd. E&W .......10W-20N,9W-20N 50
Lake Eleanor Ct. E&W ................. 12W-21N 50
Lakeview Ct. NW&SE ................. 11W-20N 50

Lampton Ln. N&S .. 10W-21N 50
Landis Ln. N&S .... 11W-20N 50
Larkdale Rd. N&S .. 10W-20N 50
Laurel Av. E&W .... 11W-20N 50
Linden Av. E&W....11W-20N 50
Lisa Marie Ct. E&W ................. 12W-20N 50
Locus Pl. N&S...11W-20N 50
Lombardy Ct. N&S 11W-20N 50
Lombardy Ln. N&S ................. 11W-20N 50
Longfellow Av. E&W ................. 10W-20N 50
Mallard Ln. NW&SE ................. 11W-20N 50
Manor Dr. NE&SW..10W-21N 50
Maple Ct. NW&SE..11W-21N 50
Marcie Ct. E&W .. 11W-20N 50
Margate Ter. E&W . 10W-20N 50
Mayer Ct. N&S .... 11W-20N 50
Meadow Ct. E&W .. 11W-21N 50
Meadow Ln. N&S .. 11W-20N 50
Meadowbrook Ln. N&S ................. 10W-21N 50
Merlin Ct. N&S .. 11W-20N 50
Millstone Rd. E&W . 9W-21N 51
Montgomery Ct. NE&SW ................. 12W-20N 50
Montgomery Dr. N&S ................. 12W-20N 50
Montgomery Rd. E&W ................. 12W-20N 50
Mountain Ct. N&S . 11W-22N 50
Mountain Dr. N&S..11W-22N 50
Mulberry Rd. E&W . 10W-20N 50
Myrtle Ct. N&S .. 11W-21N 50
Norman Ln. N&S .. 10W-20N 50
North Av. E&W .... 11W-22N 50
Northwoods Cir. N&S ................. 11W-21N 50
Northwoods Ct. NE&SW ................. 11W-21N 50
Northwoods Rd. N&S ................. 11W-21N 50
Oakley Av. N&S....11W-21N 50
Oakmont Rd. E&W ................. 10W-20N 50
Oakwood Pl. N&S . 11W-20N 50
Orchard Av. N&S .. 10W-21N 50
Osterman Av. E&W ................. 11W-20N 50
Overland Ct. NW&SE ................. 11W-22N 50
Overland Tr. N&S .. 11W-22N 50
Oxford Rd. N&S....10W-21N 50
Park Av. N&S .... 11W-21N 50
Park Ln. N&S .... 11W-20N 50
Parkside Ln. N&S .. 11W-21N 50
Paula Ct. N&S .. 12W-20N 50
Peachtree Ln. NE&SW ................. 11W-20N 50
Pear Tree Rd. E&W ................. 11W-20N 50
Penbroke Ct. N&S . 11W-20N 50
Peterson Ln. N&S .. 11W-21N 50
Pine St. N&S .......11W-20N,11W-21N 50
Plum Tree Rd. N&S ................. 11W-20N 50
Portage Pass N&S . 11W-22N 50
Prairie St. N&S .... 11W-20N 50
Price Ln. N&S .... 11W-20N 50
Princeton Ln. NW&SE ................. 11W-20N 50
Radcliff Cir. NW&SE ................. 11W-20N 50
Rago Av. E&W .... 11W-21N 50
Ramsay Rd. E&W .. 10W-20N 50
Revere Ct. NE&SW ................. 10W-20N 50
River Rd. N&S .... 9W-20N 51
Riverside Dr. N&S .. 11W-20N 50
Robbie Ct. E&W .. 11W-21N 50
Rosemary Ter. N&S ................. 10W-21N 50
Rosewood Av. E&W ................. 11W-20N 50
Route 43 N&S .......11W-21N,10W-20N 50
Sapling Ln. N&S .. 12W-20N 50
School St. E&W .... 11W-21N 50
Sequoia Ln. N&S .. 11W-20N 50
Shagbark Ln. N&S . 9W-20N 51
Shanon Rd. NE&SW ................. 9W-20N 51
Shenandoah Ct. N&S ................. 10W-20N 50
Shenandoah Rd. E&W ................. 9W-20N 51
Sheridan Av. N&S .. 11W-21N 50
Smoke Tree Rd. N&S ................. 9W-20N 51
Somerset Av. E&W ................. 11W-21N 50
Springfield Av. NW&SE ................. 10W-21N 50
Spruce St. N&S .... 11W-20N 50
Sprucewood Ln. N&S ................. 11W-20N 50
St. Andrews Ln. N&S ................. 9W-20N 51
Standish Dr. N&S .. 10W-20N 50
Stratford Rd. N&S .. 11W-20N 50
Summit Dr. E&W .. 11W-22N 50

Sunset Ct. E&W....12W-20N 50
Susan Ln. NE&SW 12W-20N 50
Tall Tree Ln. E&W .. 12W-20N 50
Tamarisk Ln. N&S .. 9W-20N 51
Tanglewood Ct. N&S ................. 9W-20N 51
Terrace Ct. N&S .. 11W-20N 50
Timberhill Rd. N&S 11W-20N 50
Todd Ct. N&S......10W-21N 50
Tri-State Tollway N&S .......12W-20N,12W-21N 50
Village Green Ct. E&W ................. 12W-20N 50
W. Canton Ct. E&W ................. 11W-21N 50
W. St. Andrews Ln. E&W ................. 10W-20N 50
Walden Ln. N&S...10W-21N 50
Walnut St. E&W....11W-21N 50
Warrington Rd. N&S ................. 10W-21N 50
Warwick Ct. NW&SE ................. 11W-21N 50
Warwick Rd. E&W..11W-21N 50
Waukegan Rd. NW&SE .......11W-22N,10W-20N 50
Waverly Av. NW&SE ................. 10W-20N 50
Wayne Av. N&S...11W-21N 50
We-go Ct. NW&SE 12W-20N 50
We-go Trail N&S .. 12W-20N 50
West Summit Ct. N&S ................. 11W-22N 50
Westcliff Ln. N&S .. 10W-21N 50
Westgate Rd. E&W ................. 10W-21N 50
Whittier Av. E&W . 10W-20N 50
Wicklow Ct. N&S....9W-20N 51
Wicklow Rd. NW&SE ................. 9W-20N 51
Williams Av. E&W .. 11W-20N 50
Willow Av. N&S ... 11W-20N 50
Wilmot Ln. E&W .. 12W-21N 50
Wilmot Rd. N&S .......12W-20N,11W-21N 50
Wincanton Dr. N&S ................. 10W-20N 50
Wincrest Rd. N&S .. 10W-21N 50
Windsor Ct. NW&SE ................. 11W-21N 50
Wood Av. N&S .... 11W-21N 50
Woodbine Ct. N&S 11W-21N 50
Woodland Dr. E&W ................. 11W-21N 50
Woodridge Ct. N&S ................. 10W-20N 50
Woodruff Av. N&S..11W-21N 50
Woodvale Av. NW&SE ................. 10W-20N 50
Woodview Ln. N&S ................. 12W-20N 50
Woodward Av. N&S ................. 11W-20N 50

## Deerfield Township

'B' St. NW&SE .........9W-24N,8W-23N 51
'C' St. NW&SE....9W-23N 51
'D' St. NW&SE....9W-23N 51
'F' St. NW&SW....8W-23N 51
'G' St. N&S .... 8W-23N 51
'H' St. N&S ...... 9W-23N 43
Bartlett Ravine Rd. NW&SE ................. 8W-23N 43
Boles Loop NS&EW 8W-24N 51
Bradley Loop NS&EW ................. 9W-24N 43
Bullock Dr. NE&SW..8W-23N 51
Burkhardt Rd. NW&SE ................. 9W-24N 43
Chapman Rd. N&S .. 9W-24N 43
Chatfield Ct. NE&SW ................. 8W-23N 43
Clay Av. E&W .... 9W-23N 43
Davis St. NW&SE....8W-23N 43
Finlay Rd. NE&SW .........9W-24N,8W-24N 43
George Bell Rd. NW&SE ................. 9W-24N 43
Gordon Johnson Dr. NE&SW ................. 8W-23N 43
Leonard Wood Av. NE&SW ................. 9W-24N 43
Logan Loop NS&EW ................. 9W-24N 43
Lyster Rd. NW&SE .. 9W-24N 43
McArthur Loop NE&SW ................. 9W-24N 43
McCaskey Rd. NW&SE ................. 9W-24N 43
McCormick Dr. NE&SW ................. 8W-24N 43
McKibben Rd. NE&SW ................. 8W-23N 43
Nicholson Rd. NE&SW ................. 8W-23N 43
Norman Heck Ct. E&W ................. 8W-23N 51
Patten Rd. NW&SE..8W-23N 43
Roman Rd. NE&SW..9W-24N 43
Scott Loop E&W ....9W-24N 43
Thorpe Rd. NE&SW..9W-24N 43

| | Grid | Page |
|---|---|---|
| Vattman Rd. NE&SW | 9W-24N | 43 |
| Wade Ct. N&S | 8W-24N | 43 |
| Wainwright Ct. NW&SE | 8W-23N | 51 |
| Westover Rd. NW&SW | 9W-24N | 43 |
| Whistler Rd. N&S | 9W-24N | 43 |
| 1st St. NE&SW | 9W-24N,9W-23N | 43 |
| 2nd St. NE&SW | 9W-23N,8W-24N | 51 |
| 3rd St. NE&SW | 9W-23N,8W-24N | 51 |
| 4th St. NE&SW | 8W-23N | 51 |
| 5th St. NE&SW | 8W-23N | 51 |
| 6th St. NE&SW | 8W-23N | 51 |
| 7th St. NE&SW | 8W-23N | 51 |
| 8th St. NE&SW | 8W-23N | 51 |
| 9th St. NE&SW | 9W-23N,8W-23N | 51 |
| 10th St. E&W | 8W-23N | 51 |
| 11th St. E&W | 8W-23N | 51 |

## Ela Township

| | Grid | Page |
|---|---|---|
| Abbey Glen Dr. NW&SE | 23W-25N | 38 |
| Anna Ct. N&S | 24W-25N | 38 |
| Arbor Ln. E&W | 21W-24N | 38 |
| Arrowhead Dr. N&S | 19W-25N | 39 |
| August Ln. E&W | 24W-25N | 38 |
| Bagpipe Ct. E&W | 23W-25N | 38 |
| Berkley Rd. E&W | 22W-22N | 46 |
| Bonnie Ln. N&S | 21W-24N | 38 |
| Bonnyrigg Ct. E&W | 23W-25N | 38 |
| Buckeye Rd. NS&EW | 23W-20N | 46 |
| Bur Oak Ln. E&W | 21W-23N | 47 |
| Cattail Ln. E&W | 23W-20N | 46 |
| Cedar Ln. N&S | 23W-23N | 46 |
| Cedar St. E&W | 23W-22N | 46 |
| Cherry Ln. E&W | 23W-23N | 46 |
| Clover Hill Ln. NS&EW | 24W-23N | 46 |
| Columbia Ct. E&W | 21W-25N | 38 |
| Commercial Dr. NE&SW | 21W-25N | 38 |
| Cottage Rd. N&S | 23W-20N | 47 |
| Crestwood Ln. E&W | 23W-23N | 46 |
| Dan Vera Ln. NE&SW | 22W-24N | 38 |
| Dante Dr. N&S | 23W-25N | 38 |
| Dartmouth Ln. E&W | 21W-25N | 38 |
| Deer Meadow Ln. E&W | 23W-21N | 46 |
| Deerpath Rd. N&S | 23W-21N | 46 |
| Diamond Lake Rd. N&S | 19W-24N,19W-25N | 39 |
| Dorothy Ln. E&W | 20W-20N,19W-20N | 47 |
| Eagle Dr. N&S | 19W-25N | 39 |
| East Ln. N&S | 23W-23N | 46 |
| East Rd. N&S | 21W-23N | 47 |
| Echo Lake Rd. N&S | 23W-23N | 46 |
| Echo Ln. N&S | 23W-23N | 46 |
| Edgewood Pl. E&W | 24W-23N | 46 |
| Ellrie Ter. N&S | 24W-25N | 38 |
| Fairfield Rd. NW&SE | 21W-23N,22W-25N | 47 |
| Florence Ct. N&S | 23W-22N | 46 |
| Forest Dr. NS&EW | 21W-23N,21W-24N | 47 |
| Gabriel Ct. E&W | 22W-24N | 38 |
| Gabriel Dr. N&S | 22W-24N | 38 |
| Garden Ln. N&S | 21W-23N | 47 |
| Gilmer Rd. NW&SE | 21W-25N,19W-24N | 38 |
| Glendale Rd. E&W | 21W-25N | 38 |
| Grand Av. E&W | 23W-22N | 46 |
| Hazel Crest Rd. N&S | 20W-20N | 47 |
| High Ridge Rd. N&S | 23W-23N | 46 |
| Highland Rd. E&W | 21W-23N | 47 |
| Hillcrest Dr. E&W | 23W-23N | 46 |
| Indian Trail Rd. N&S | 24W-24N | 38 |
| Ivy Ln. N&S | 21W-25N | 38 |
| June Ter. N&S | 23W-22N | 46 |
| Juniper Ln. NW&SE | 23W-20N | 46 |
| Kruckenberg Rd. NS&EW | 22W-25N,21W-25N | 38 |
| Lake Zurich-Highwood Rd. E&W | 21W-23N,19W-24N | 47 |
| Lake-Cook Rd. E&W | 20W-20S,19W-20S | 47 |
| Lakeside Dr. NE&SW | 21W-23N,21W-24N | 47 |
| Lloyd Rd. E&W | 20W-23N,19W-23N | 47 |
| Lochanora Dr. E&W | 23W-25N,22W-25N | 38 |
| Lonetree Ln. E&W | 23W-23N | 46 |
| Mable Av. N&S | 23W-23N | 46 |
| March St. NW&SE | 22W-24N | 38 |

| | Grid | Page |
|---|---|---|
| Marilyn Ln. NS&EW | 21W-25N | 38 |
| Mary Dale Av. E&W | 24W-25N | 38 |
| Middle Fork Rd. E&W | 24W-21N | 46 |
| Midlothian Rd. NE&SW | 22W-24N,21W-25N | 38 |
| Millcrest Dr. E&W | 23W-23N | 46 |
| Miller Rd. E&W | 24W-24N,23W-24N | 38 |
| Monticello Ln. E&W | 23W-25N | 38 |
| N. Kyle Ct. NW&SE | 22W-25N | 38 |
| Nancy Ct. E&W | 21W-25N | 38 |
| Newhaven Dr. E&W | 23W-25N | 38 |
| North Lakewood Ln. E&W | 23W-23N | 46 |
| North Ln. E&W | 23W-23N | 46 |
| Northbridge Dr. N&S | 23W-25N | 38 |
| Old Barn Ln. E&W | 21W-23N | 47 |
| Orchard Ln. N&S | 24W-21N | 46 |
| Overhill Dr. NE&SW | 21W-23N,21W-24N | 47 |
| Park Rd. N&S | 21W-23N | 47 |
| Pepper Ln. NW&SE | 21W-24N | 38 |
| Plum Tr. NW&SE | 23W-20N | 46 |
| Public Rd. N&S | 19W-23N,19W-24N | 47 |
| Quentin Rd. N&S | 21W-20N,21W-24N | 47 |
| Rand Ct. E&W | 20W-20N | 47 |
| Rand Rd. N&S | 24W-24N,24W-25N | 38 |
| Ravine Ct. NE&SW | 24W-25N | 38 |
| Ravine Ln. N&S | 24W-25N | 38 |
| Ravine Rd. E&W | 21W-23N | 47 |
| Redwing Pl. NE&SW | 23W-20N | 46 |
| Ridge Rd. E&W | 21W-23N | 47 |
| Rose Av. E&W | 24W-25N | 38 |
| Rose Rd. E&W | 21W-23N | 47 |
| S. Kyle Ct. SE&NW | 22W-25N | 38 |
| Sacomand Ln. NS&EW | 22W-24N | 38 |
| Shady Ln. NW&SE | 21W-24N | 38 |
| Shagbark Dr. N&S | 24W-24N | 38 |
| Shirley Rd. E&W | 21W-20N | 47 |
| Somerset Ct. N&S | 23W-25N | 38 |
| South Lakewood Dr. E&W | 23W-23N | 46 |
| South Rd. E&W | 21W-23N | 47 |
| Spruce Rd. E&W | 21W-23N | 47 |
| Starry Ln. E&W | 21W-23N | 47 |
| Stone Marsh Ln. E&W | 24W-25N | 38 |
| Stoney Kirk Ct. N&S | 22W-25N | 38 |
| Sturm Rd. E&W | 22W-20N | 46 |
| Summit Dr. NW&SE | 23W-23N | 46 |
| Sunset Dr. NW&SE | 23W-23N | 46 |
| Tahoe Ct. NE&SW | 19W-25N | 39 |
| Tahoe Dr. E&W | 19W-25N | 39 |
| Telser Rd. N&S | 22W-22N,22W-23N | 46 |
| Timberlake Dr. E&W | 24W-25N | 38 |
| Valentine Av. E&W | 24W-25N | 38 |
| Valley Rd. NE&SW | 21W-23N,21W-24N | 47 |
| Virginia Av. N&S | 24W-25N | 38 |
| West Ln. N&S | 23W-23N | 46 |
| Wildrose Dr. N&S | 23W-20N | 46 |
| Willow Rd. E&W | 21W-23N | 47 |
| Woodbury Ct. E&W | 21W-25N | 38 |

## Fox Lake*
### (Also see McHenry County)

| | Grid | Page |
|---|---|---|
| Abbott Dr. N&S | 28W-39N | 12 |
| Adam St. N&S | 26W-35N | 21 |
| Amundsen St. E&W | 28W-36N | 12 |
| Arlington Rd. E&W | 28W-39N | 12 |
| Arlington Rd. NE&SW | 28W-36N | 12 |
| Arthur Av. N&S | 28W-37N | 12 |
| Ash St. N&S | 28W-39N | 12 |
| Atwater Pkwy. N&S | 27W-36N | 12 |
| Balsam Ct.* E&W | 27W-38N | 12 |
| Bay Ln. N&S | 28W-36N | 12 |
| Bay Rd. N&S | 28W-36N | 12 |
| Beach Driveway NS&EW | 28W-36N | 12 |
| Benjamin Av. E&W | 28W-38N | 12 |
| Birch St. N&S | 28W-39N | 12 |
| Boulder Dr. N&S | 27W-36N | 12 |
| Brewer E&W | 28W-36N | 12 |
| Castle Rd. N&S | 27W-37N | 12 |
| Cathryn St. E&W | 27W-37N | 12 |
| Cedar Av. E&W | 27W-36N | 12 |
| Cedar St. N&S | 28W-39N | 12 |
| Center St. N&S | 27W-36N | 12 |

| | Grid | Page |
|---|---|---|
| Channahon Ct. N&S | 28W-39N | 12 |
| Channel Dr. E&W | 27W-35N | 20 |
| Channel Dr. NW&SE | 28W-38N | 12 |
| Cherry Ln. E&W | 27W-35N | 21 |
| Chevy Chase Ct. NW&SE | 28W-39N | 12 |
| Christopher Way SW&NE | 28W-36N | 12 |
| Clarendon Ct. NE&SW | 28W-39N | 12 |
| Columbia Av. NE&SW | 27W-36N | 12 |
| Cir. | 28W-38N | 12 |
| Cora Av. N&S | 27W-37N | 12 |
| Cottage Av. NE&SW | 27W-36N | 12 |
| Covington Rd. E&W | 27W-36N | 12 |
| Crest Hill Ct. NE&SW | 28W-39N | 12 |
| Cross St. E&W | 28W-36N | 12 |
| Custor Ct. N&S | 28W-39N | 12 |
| Cypress Av. N&S | 27W-36N | 12 |
| Deerpath E&W | 28W-38N | 12 |
| Dena Av. N&S | 27W-36N | 12 |
| Devlin Rd. N&S | 27W-36N | 12 |
| Dunns Pl. E&W | 27W-36N | 12 |
| Dunwood Ct. N&S | 28W-39N | 12 |
| Eagle Point Rd. NE&SW | 28W-36N | 12 |
| East Leisure Village Av. NE&SW | 28W-39N | 12 |
| East Shore Dr. N&S | 28W-38N | 12 |
| Eaton Pl. N&S | 28W-39N | 12 |
| Edison Ct. E&W | 27W-37N | 12 |
| Elm Av. N&S | 27W-36N | 12 |
| Ernie St. E&W | 28W-36N | 12 |
| Evergreen Ct.* E&W | 27W-38N | 12 |
| Fairfax Rd. E&W | 28W-36N | 12 |
| Fern Pl. E&W | 27W-36N | 12 |
| Forest Av. N&S | 28W-36N,27W-37N | 12 |
| Fortress Dr. NE&SW | 28W-37N | 12 |
| Fossil Dr. E&W | 26W-35N | 13 |
| Fox Trail NW&SE | 27W-35N | 20 |
| Frazier Ct. E&W | 27W-35N | 20 |
| Garfield Av. E&W | 26W-35N | 21 |
| Glen Av. NE&SW | 27W-36N | 12 |
| Glenview Av. | 27W-36N | 12 |
| Glenview Pl. E&W | 27W-36N | 12 |
| Golfview Dr. E&W | 28W-39N | 12 |
| Grace Av. E&W | 27W-36N | 12 |
| Grand Av. E&W | 28W-36N,27W-36N | 12 |
| Grass Lake Rd. E&W | 28W-39N | 12 |
| Greenwood Av. E&W | 28W-38N | 12 |
| Harding Rd. N&S | 28W-35N | 20 |
| Hartigan Rd. E&W | 27W-34N | 20 |
| Haskel St. E&W | 28W-38N | 12 |
| Hawthorne Ln. N&S | 27W-36N | 12 |
| Hazel Av. N&S | 27W-36N | 12 |
| Hickory Av. N&S | 27W-36N | 12 |
| Hickory St. N&S | 28W-39N | 12 |
| Highland Av. E&W | 27W-36N | 12 |
| Highview Av. N&S | 27W-36N | 12 |
| Hill Rd. NE&SW | 27W-36N | 12 |
| Hillcrest Av. N&S | 27W-36N | 12 |
| Hillcrest St. N&S | 27W-35N | 20 |
| Hillside Av. NW&SE | 27W-36N | 12 |
| Hillside Ct. E&W | 27W-37N | 12 |
| Hillside Pl. NW&SE | 27W-36N | 12 |
| Hilltop Av. E&W | 28W-36N | 12 |
| Hilltop Rd. N&S | 27W-36N | 12 |
| Hollow Way NS&EW | 27W-34N,27W-35N | 20 |
| Holly Av., N. N&S | 27W-36N | 12 |
| Holly Av., S. N&S | 27W-36N | 12 |
| Honing Rd NW&SE | 27W-36N | 12 |
| Hooks Ln. NE&SW | 28W-37N | 12 |
| Howard Av. N&S | 27W-36N | 12 |
| Howard Ct. NE&SW | 27W-37N | 12 |
| Industrial Av. NW&SE | 28W-36N | 12 |
| Jack Frost Ln. NE&SW | 28W-36N | 12 |
| Jackson Dr. N&S | 28W-39N | 12 |
| Janet Ct. E&W | 27W-37N | 12 |
| Jefferson Av. N&S | 26W-35N | 21 |
| Jefferson Ct. E&W | 26W-35N | 21 |
| Jefferson St. N&S | 26W-35N | 21 |
| Judson St. N&S | 28W-38N | 12 |
| Keefe Pl. N&S | 28W-39N | 12 |
| Keystone Av. NE&SW | 28W-36N | 12 |
| Kings Rd. NE&SW | 28W-39N | 12 |
| Kingston Blvd. NW&SE | 28W-36N | 12 |
| Knollwood Rd., S. NW&SE | 27W-35N | 20 |
| Lagoon Rd. E&W | 28W-36N | 12 |
| Lake Av. N&S | 27W-36N | 12 |

| | Grid | Page |
|---|---|---|
| Lakeland Av. E&W | 28W-35N | 20 |
| Lakelane Rd. NE&SW | 28W-36N | 12 |
| Lakeshore Dr. N&S | 28W-38N | 12 |
| Lakeside Ln. N&S | 27W-36N | 12 |
| Lakeside Rd. E&W | 27W-37N | 12 |
| Lakeview Av. E&W | 27W-37N | 12 |
| Lakewood Av. N&S | 27W-36N | 12 |
| Leisure Ct. N&S | 27W-37N | 12 |
| Lexington Ln. E&W | 28W-38N | 12 |
| Lilac Av. N&S | 27W-36N | 12 |
| Lincoln Av. N&S | 26W-36N | 13 |
| Linden N&S | 27W-36N | 12 |
| Lindy St. E&W | 27W-36N | 12 |
| Lippencott Ln. NW&SE | 27W-36N | 12 |
| Lippencott N&S | 27W-36N | 12 |
| Livingston St. N&S | 28W-37N | 12 |
| Longwood Dr. E&W | 27W-36N | 20 |
| Lotus Av. E&W | 27W-38N | 12 |
| Madison Av. N&S | 26W-35N | 21 |
| Magnolia Ct.* E&W | 27W-38N | 12 |
| Mallard Ct. NE&SW | 28W-38N | 12 |
| Manor Av. NE&SW | 28W-36N | 12 |
| Maple Av. N&S | 27W-36N | 12 |
| Marvin St. N&S | 28W-36N | 12 |
| Mastodon Dr. N&S | 26W-36N | 13 |
| Matts Rd. E&W | 28W-36N | 12 |
| Maude Av. N&S | 27W-37N | 12 |
| McKinley St. N&S | 28W-36N | 12 |
| Meade Ct. E&W | 28W-36N | 12 |
| Medinah N&S | 27W-36N | 12 |
| Mineola Rd. NS&EW | 27W-37N | 12 |
| Monroe Av. N&S | 26W-35N | 21 |
| Monterrey Ter. N&S | 29W-37N | 12 |
| Muriel Rd. E&W | 28W-36N | 12 |
| N. Lake Av. N&S | 27W-36N | 12 |
| N. Rushmore Rd. N&S | 27W-36N | 12 |
| Nippersink Blvd. NE&SW | 28W-37N | 12 |
| Nippersink St. N&S | 27W-36N | 12 |
| North Av. E&W | 27W-37N | 12 |
| Northway N&S | 27W-36N | 12 |
| Oak Ct. N&S | 28W-36N | 12 |
| Oak Ln. N&S | 27W-35N | 20 |
| Oak St. E&W | 28W-37N,27W-36N | 12 |
| Orchard Pl. E&W | 27W-36N | 12 |
| Park Av. N&S | 28W-35N | 20 |
| Park Ln. NE&SW | 28W-35N | 20 |
| Park Rd. E&W | 28W-39N | 12 |
| Pine Av. E&W | 27W-36N | 12 |
| Pistakee Lake Rd. N&S | 28W-36N | 12 |
| Pistakee Pkwy. E&W | 28W-35N | 20 |
| Poplar Av. N&S | 27W-36N | 12 |
| Quail Path E&W | 27W-34N,27W-35N | 20 |
| Rabbit Run E&W | 27W-35N | 20 |
| Rand E&W | 27W-36N | 12 |
| Richard Ct. NW&SE | 27W-37N | 12 |
| Ridgeland Av. N&S | 27W-36N | 12 |
| Riverside Dr. NE&SW | 28W-37N | 12 |
| Riverside Island Dr. NW&SE | 27W-36N | 12 |
| Riverview Av. E&W | 28W-37N | 12 |
| Rolland Pl. E&W | 28W-36N | 12 |
| Rollins Rd. N&S | 27W-36N,26W-35N | 12 |
| Rose Av. N&S | 27W-36N | 12 |
| Route 59 NE&SW | 27W-35N,26W-36N | 20 |
| Rushmore Rd. N&S | 26W-36N | 13 |
| S. Lake Av. N&S | 28W-36N | 12 |
| Sayton Rd. N&S | 28W-36N | 12 |
| Sayton Rd. N&S | 28W-36N | 12 |
| Scenic Ln. E&W | 28W-36N | 12 |
| Scenic Rd. N&S | 28W-36N | 12 |
| Shady Ln. E&W | 27W-36N | 12 |
| Shore Dr. N&S | 28W-39N | 12 |
| Siloam Av. NW&SE | 28W-36N | 12 |
| Skillen St. E&W | 28W-36N | 12 |
| South St. E&W | 28W-36N | 12 |
| Spring Rd. N&S | 27W-35N | 20 |
| Spruce Rd. N&S | 27W-36N | 12 |
| Squaw Rd. N&S | 26W-36N | 13 |
| St. James St. E&W | 28W-36N | 12 |
| Stanton Point Rd. NE&SW | 26W-36N | 13 |
| State Park Rd. N&S | 28W-38N,28W-39N | 12 |
| Tremont Rd. E&W | 28W-36N | 12 |
| Trout Av. NW&SE | 28W-38N | 12 |

| | Grid | Page |
|---|---|---|
| Troy St. NW&SE | 27W-36N | 12 |
| Tweed Rd. N&S | 27W-36N | 12 |
| U.S. Route 12 N&S | 28W-37N,27W-35N | 12 |
| Venice Av. NW&SE | 27W-36N | 12 |
| Viscaya Dr. NE&SW | 28W-39N,27W-39N | 12 |
| Waltonia Ter. N&S | 27W-37N | 12 |
| Washington Av. N&S | 26W-36N | 13 |
| Wells St. E&W | 28W-37N | 12 |
| West Grass Lake Dr. E&W | 28W-39N,27W-39N | 12 |
| Westshore Dr. N&S | 28W-38N | 12 |
| White Tail Ln. E&W | 27W-35N | 20 |
| Whitten Av. E&W | 26W-35N | 21 |
| Wildwood Dr. E&W | 27W-35N | 20 |
| Willow Rd. E&W | 27W-35N | 21 |
| Wilmington E&W | 27W-37N | 12 |
| Wood Rd. E&W | 27W-35N | 20 |
| Woodland Av. N&S | 27W-36N | 12 |
| Woodlock St. N&S | 27W-36N | 12 |
| York St. N&S | 27W-36N | 12 |

## Fox River Grove

| | Grid | Page |
|---|---|---|
| Camilla Pl. E&W | 28W-22N | 44 |
| Primrose Ln. E&W | 28W-22N | 44 |
| Tiffany Ln. E&W | 28W-22N | 44 |
| Victoria Dr.* E&W | 28W-22N | 44 |

## Fremont Township

| | Grid | Page |
|---|---|---|
| Acorn Ln. N&S | 19W-26N | 39 |
| Alleghany Rd. N&S | 21W-31N,21W-30N | 31 |
| Bacon Rd. SE&NW | 23W-31N | 30 |
| Baker Ln. N&S | 24W-29N | 30 |
| Barnswallow Ln. NE&SW | 23W-26N,23W-27N | 38 |
| Beechwood Ct. NE&SW | 21W-27N | 38 |
| Bitter Sweet Dr. E&W | 21W-26N | 38 |
| Blackhawk Tr. N&S | 24W-30N,24W-31N | 30 |
| Brassie Ct. N&S | 21W-28N,21W-29N | 31 |
| Briar Ter. N&S | 21W-26N | 38 |
| Buckthorn Ct. E&W | 20W-26N | 39 |
| Buena Ter. N&S | 21W-26N | 38 |
| Cambridge Rd. E&W | 19W-29N | 31 |
| Cardinal Ct. NE&SW | 24W-28N | 30 |
| Casey Rd. E&W | 19W-31N | 31 |
| Chardon Ln. N&S | 24W-30N | 30 |
| Chardon Rd. N&S | 24W-30N,22W-30N | 30 |
| Cherokee Tr. E&W | 24W-31N | 30 |
| Chevy Chase Rd. NS&EW | 21W-27N | 38 |
| Circle Dr., N. NW&SE | 19W-26N,18W-26N | 39 |
| Circle Dr., S. E&W | 19W-26N,18W-26N | 39 |
| Countryside Lake Dr. N&S | 20W-26N,20W-27N | 39 |
| Countryside Valley Dr. E&W | 21W-26N | 38 |
| Crescent Dr., E. N&S | 21W-26N | 38 |
| Crescent Dr., N. E&W | 21W-26N | 38 |
| Crescent Dr., S. E&W | 21W-26N | 38 |
| Crescent Dr., W. E&W | 21W-26N | 38 |
| Driftwood Ct. E&W | 20W-26N | 39 |
| Elmwood Av. NW&SE | 19W-26N,18W-26N | 39 |
| Erhart Rd. N&S | 23W-29N,22W-29N | 30 |
| Fairfield Rd. N&S | 24W-31N,23W-26N | 30 |
| Fairview Dr., N. NE&SW | 19W-26N,18W-26N | 39 |
| Fairview Dr., S. NW&SE | 19W-26N,18W-26N | 39 |
| Forest Ln., N. NE&SW | 19W-26N | 39 |
| Forest Ln., S. NW&SE | 19W-26N,18W-26N | 39 |
| Freemont Center Rd. N&S | 22W-28N,22W-29N | 30 |
| Fremont Av. N&S | 23W-30N | 30 |
| Gilmer Rd. NW&SE | 24W-30N,21W-26N | 38 |
| Greeleaf Rd. N&S | 21W-26N | 38 |
| Hackberry Rd. N&S | 20W-26N | 39 |
| Harris Rd. N&S | 19W-30N,19W-31N | 31 |
| Harvard Av. E&W | 19W-29N | 31 |
| Hawley E&W | 22W-27N,21W-27N | 38 |

| | Grid | Page |
|---|---|---|
| Hawthorne Blvd. E&W | | |
| ............... 19W-26N | 39 |
| Hiawatha Ter. N&S | | |
| ............... 21W-26N | 38 |
| Hickory Av. NE&SW | | |
| ........ 19W-26N,18W-26N | 39 |
| Hickory Rd. NW&SE | | |
| ............... 20W-26N | 39 |
| Highland Rd. N&S .. 21W-26N | 38 |
| Hillside Ln. E&W .. 21W-26N | 38 |
| Hilltop Ter. N&S .... 22W-28N | 30 |
| Horizon Spur E&W 23W-26N | 38 |
| Imperial Ct. N&S .. 23W-30N | 30 |
| Iride Dr. NW&SE | | |
| ........ 19W-26N,18W-26N | 39 |
| Ivanhoe Ct. N&S .... 23W-27N | 38 |
| Ivanhoe Ln. NS&EW | | |
| ............... 20W-28N | 31 |
| Ivanhoe Rd. N&S .. 20W-31N | 31 |
| Ivanhoe Rd. NE&SW | | |
| ............... 24W-26N | 38 |
| Jack Pine Ct. NE&SW | | |
| ............... 20W-26N | 39 |
| Kenmore Av. E&W | | |
| ........ 19W-26N,18W-26N | 39 |
| Krueger Ct. NW&SE | | |
| ............... 19W-26N | 39 |
| Lake Fairfield Ln. E&W | | |
| ............... 24W-29N | 30 |
| Lakeview Av. E&W | | |
| ........ 19W-26N,18W-26N | 39 |
| Lakeview Ct. E&W .. 21W-26N | 39 |
| Lakeview Pkwy. E&W | | |
| ........ 21W-27N,20W-26N | 38 |
| Landau Ln. NS&EW | | |
| ............... 20W-28N | 31 |
| Lemon Rd. N&S .... 20W-28N | 31 |
| Longmeadow Cir. NS&EW | | |
| ............... 20W-26N | 39 |
| Longmeadow Ct. N&S | | |
| ............... 20W-26N | 39 |
| Longmeadow Dr. NS&EW | | |
| ............... 20W-26N | 39 |
| Manor Hill Rd. N&S | | |
| ....... 24W-30N,24W-31N | 30 |
| Maple Av. E&W .. 20W-28N | 31 |
| Maple Av. NE&SW | | |
| ........ 19W-26N,18W-26N | 39 |
| Maple Ter. N&S .... 21W-26N | 38 |
| Marion Av. NW&SE | | |
| ............... 21W-26N | 38 |
| Martin Dr. NW&SE | | |
| ........ 19W-26N,18W-26N | 39 |
| Meadow Ln. E&W .. 24W-31N | 30 |
| Midlothian Rd. NE&SW | | |
| ........ 20W-26N,19W-30N | 39 |
| Milton Rd. NE&SW | | |
| ....... 24W-26N,22W-26N | 38 |
| Niblick Knoll Ct. NE&SW | | |
| ............... 22W-28N | 30 |
| North Rd. E&W .. 21W-27N | 38 |
| Northwest Pkwy. NW&SE | | |
| ............... 20W-27N | 39 |
| Oak Av. NE&SW | | |
| ........ 19W-26N,18W-26N | 39 |
| Oak Ter. N&S .... 21W-26N | 38 |
| Oakdale Ln., N. NW&SE | | |
| ....... 19W-26N,18W-26N | 39 |
| Oakdale Ln., S. NE&SW | | |
| ....... 19W-26N,18W-26N | 39 |
| Oakleaf Ct. N&S .. 21W-27N | 38 |
| Old Oak Dr. NW&SE | | |
| ............... 24W-28N | 30 |
| Owens Rd. NS&EW | | |
| ....... 23W-26N,22W-27N | 38 |
| Oxford Dr. N&S .. 19W-29N | 31 |
| Park Av. N&S .. 20W-28N | 31 |
| Peterson Rd. E&W | | |
| ....... 22W-30N,19W-30N | 30 |
| Pheasant Run NW&SE | | |
| ............... 22W-26N | 38 |
| Pierre Dr. NE&SW .. 19W-26N | 39 |
| Pond Shore Dr. NE&SW | | |
| ............... 23W-26N | 38 |
| Prospect Dr. NW&SE | | |
| ............... 19W-26N | 39 |
| Public Rd. E&W .. 20W-28N | 31 |
| Red Pine Ct. NE&SW | | |
| ............... 20W-26N | 39 |
| Ridge Ct. N&S .... 19W-26N | 39 |
| Rosewood Rd. E&W | | |
| ............... 21W-26N | 38 |
| Route 137 NW&SE | | |
| ............... 19W-31N | 31 |
| Route 176 N&S | | |
| ....... 24W-27N,19W-28N | 38 |
| Route 45 N&S ...... 19W-31N | 31 |
| Route 60 NW&SE | | |
| ....... 24W-31N,19W-26N | 30 |
| Route 83 N&S | | |
| ........ 20W-28N,20W-31N | 31 |
| Russell Ln. E&W .. 24W-29N | 30 |
| Schank Rd. NE&SW | | |
| ........ 21W-28N,20W-28N | 31 |
| Schwerman Rd. NW&SE | | |
| ........ 23W-26N,21W-26N | 38 |
| Seminole Ct. E&W .. 21W-28N | 31 |
| Shady Ln. NW&SE 21W-26N | 38 |
| Sky Crest Dr. NS&EW | | |
| ............... 22W-28N | 30 |
| Spring Ct. NE&SW 24W-28N | 30 |
| Spyglass Cir. N&S .. 21W-28N | 31 |
| Spyglass Ct. E&W .. 21W-28N | 31 |
| Sunny Ct. E&W .... 19W-26N | 39 |

| | Grid | Page |
|---|---|---|
| Sunset Ct. NE&SW | | |
| ............... 24W-29N | 30 |
| Sylvan Dr., N. NW&SE | | |
| ............... 21W-26N | 38 |
| Sylvan Dr., S. E&W | | |
| ............... 21W-26N | 38 |
| Taylor Lake Ct. E&W | | |
| ............... 19W-26N | 39 |
| Thorngate Dr. E&W | | |
| ............... 21W-28N | 31 |
| Thorntree Rd. N&S | | |
| ............... 21W-27N | 38 |
| Trinity Dr. N&S | | |
| ........ 19W-26N,18W-26N | 39 |
| University Dr. NE&SW | | |
| ............... 19W-26N | 39 |
| Valley View Ter. NE&SW | | |
| ............... 21W-26N | 38 |
| Vernon Ridge Dr. NS&EW | | |
| ............... 22W-29N | 30 |
| Walnut Av. NE&SW | | |
| ............... 19W-26N | 39 |
| Wauconda Rd. E&W | | |
| ....... 24W-27N,23W-27N | 38 |
| Weich Rd. NE&SW | | |
| ............... 19W-26N | 39 |
| West Shore Rd. E&W | | |
| ........ 19W-26N,18W-26N | 39 |
| Wildflower Ter. E&W | | |
| ............... 21W-26N | 38 |
| Willow Av. N&S | | |
| ........ 19W-26N,18W-26N | 39 |
| Wilson Rd. N&S .. 24W-31N | 30 |
| Winchester Rd. E&W | | |
| ........ 20W-30N,19W-30N | 31 |
| Windflower Ct. E&W | | |
| ............... 20W-26N | 39 |
| Yale Ct. N&S ...... 19W-29N | 31 |

### Grant Township

| | Grid | Page |
|---|---|---|
| Anchorage Ln. E&W | | |
| ............... 27W-35N | 20 |
| Anderson St. E&W .. 25W-34N | 21 |
| Andrew Ct. NW&SE | | |
| ............... 26W-36N | 13 |
| Ash St. N&S ...... 25W-35N | 21 |
| Augsburg St. E&W 25W-35N | 21 |
| Augustana Av. N&S | | |
| ........ 25W-34N,25W-35N | 21 |
| Bachman Rd. E&W | | |
| ............... 26W-37N | 13 |
| Bayview Av. E&W .. 25W-35N | 21 |
| Bayview Av. E&W .. 27W-35N | 20 |
| Bayview Ln. NE&SW | | |
| ............... 28W-35N | 20 |
| Beach Park NW&SE | | |
| ............... 27W-35N | 20 |
| Bellvue Pl. N&S .. 26W-34N | 21 |
| Belvidere Rd. NE&SW | | |
| ............... 25W-32N | 21 |
| Benjamin Av. N&S .. 25W-35N | 21 |
| Bergan St. NE&SW | | |
| ............... 25W-34N | 21 |
| Beverly Dr. N&S .... 26W-35N | 21 |
| Big Hollow Rd. E&W | | |
| ........ 28W-34N,26W-34N | 20 |
| Blackhawk Av. N&S | | |
| ............... 26W-35N | 21 |
| Boesch Pl. E&W .... 26W-36N | 13 |
| Brandenburg Rd. E&W | | |
| ........ 28W-33N,26W-33N | 21 |
| Broadway E&W .. 28W-27N | 36 |
| Brodie Dr. N&S 25W-36N | 13 |
| Burkhart Ln. E&W .. 26W-34N | 21 |
| Caine Rd. E&W .... 25W-36N | 13 |
| Camp Horner Rd. N&S | | |
| ............... 26W-34N | 21 |
| Carol Ln. N&S .... 26W-34N | 21 |
| Catherine St. N&S .. 25W-34N | 21 |
| Cedarwood Ln. E&W | | |
| ............... 25W-36N | 13 |
| Central Av. E&W 28W-37N | 12 |
| Central Rd. N&S | | |
| ............... 26W-36N | 13 |
| Champion Rd. N&S | | |
| ............... 28W-34N | 20 |
| Chanel Dr. N&S .. 25W-35N | 21 |
| Channel Dr. E&W .. 28W-34N | 20 |
| Channel Dr. N&S .. 26W-36N | 13 |
| Chicago Av. E&W .. 25W-35N | 21 |
| Chris Larkin Rd. (Pvt.) | | |
| NS&EW ........ 27W-35N | 20 |
| Christa Dr. N&S .. 26W-33N | 21 |
| Clara Dr. N&S .... 25W-36N | 13 |
| Claredon Dr. E&W .. 27W-35N | 20 |
| Converse Ln. N&S .. 26W-34N | 21 |
| Cooney Island Rd. E&W | | |
| ............... 26W-36N | 13 |
| Crabtree Ln. E&W .. 25W-36N | 13 |
| Creek Ct. NW&SE .. 26W-33N | 21 |
| David Ct. N&S ..... 25W-35N | 21 |
| Decorah Av. N&S .. 25W-34N | 21 |
| Dewey St. N&S | | |
| ............... 28W-37N | 12 |
| Dolores Ct. N&S | | |
| ............... 26W-33N | 21 |
| Donald St. N&S .. 26W-35N | 21 |
| East End Av. N&S .. 26W-36N | 13 |
| Edgewater Ln. N&S | | |
| ............... 27W-35N | 20 |
| Edward Av. E&W .. 26W-34N | 21 |
| Elm Av. E&W .... 25W-35N | 21 |
| Elm Ln. N&S ...... 25W-35N | 21 |

| | Grid | Page |
|---|---|---|
| Elm St. N&S ...... 26W-34N | 21 |
| Elmwood Av. E&W 26W-35N | 21 |
| Everett Av. E&W .. 25W-35N | 21 |
| Faith Ct. E&W ...... 25W-35N | 21 |
| Falcon Dr. N&S .... 25W-36N | 13 |
| Fischer Dr. NW&SE | | |
| ............... 26W-34N | 21 |
| Fish Lake Rd. N&S | | |
| ............... 26W-32N | 21 |
| Forest Av. N&S .... 26W-34N | 21 |
| Fox Lake Rd. NE&SW | | |
| ............... 27W-32N | 20 |
| Francis Av. N&S .. 26W-36N | 13 |
| Frank Ct. E&W .... 28W-37N | 12 |
| Franklin Av. N&S .. 25W-35N | 21 |
| Fretheim Av. E&W .. 25W-34N | 21 |
| Gerberding Av. N&S | | |
| ............... 25W-34N | 21 |
| Glenayre St. E&W .. 27W-35N | 20 |
| Gogol Av. NS&EW .. 25W-34N | 21 |
| Graham Ct. E&W .. 25W-34N | 21 |
| Grand Av. E&W | | |
| ........ 26W-34N,25W-34N | 21 |
| Grant Av. E&W .... 25W-36N | 13 |
| Great Bear Tr. E&W | | |
| ............... 28W-34N | 20 |
| Greenleaf Av. N&S.. 25W-35N | 21 |
| Grove Av. N&S .... 25W-35N | 21 |
| Hartigan Rd. NE&SW | | |
| ............... 27W-34N | 20 |
| Hawthorne Ln. N&S | | |
| ............... 25W-36N | 13 |
| Hazelwood Dr. N&S | | |
| ............... 25W-36N | 13 |
| Helen Ct. N&S .... 27W-34N | 20 |
| Helendale Rd. N&S | | |
| ............... 26W-35N | 21 |
| Hiawatha Tr. N&S .. 28W-34N | 20 |
| Hickory Av. N&S | | |
| ........ 25W-34N,25W-35N | 21 |
| Hickory Ct. N&S.... 25W-36N | 13 |
| Hickory Ct. N&S | | |
| ........ 26W-34N,25W-35N | 21 |
| Hickory Ln. E&W .. 26W-36N | 13 |
| Hickory Rd. E&W .. 25W-36N | 13 |
| Hickory St. E&W .. 25W-36N | 13 |
| High Point Ln. N&S | | |
| ............... 25W-35N | 21 |
| High Rd. NW&SE .. 28W-35N | 20 |
| Highpoint Rd. N&S | | |
| ............... 25W-35N | 21 |
| Hill Top Rd. N&S .. 28W-35N | 20 |
| Hilldale Dr. N&S .... 27W-35N | 20 |
| Hillside Av. E&W .. 25W-34N | 21 |
| Hilltop Dr. N&S .... 25W-34N | 21 |
| Hillwood Av. N&S .. 25W-34N | 21 |
| Holman Av. N&S .. 25W-34N | 21 |
| Hudson Av. E&W .. 26W-35N | 21 |
| Hunt Av. N&S ...... 25W-35N | 21 |
| Indian Ln. N&S .... 26W-35N | 21 |
| Indian Trail NE&SW | | |
| ............... 28W-35N | 20 |
| Ingleside Dr. N&S .. 26W-35N | 21 |
| Ingleside Dr. N&S .. 26W-35N | 21 |
| Ingleside Rd. E&W.. 26W-36N | 13 |
| Iola Av. N&S ...... 25W-36N | 13 |
| Iroquois Tr. N&S.... 28W-34N | 20 |
| Jackson Ct. N&S .. 26W-36N | 13 |
| James Av. N&S .... 25W-34N | 21 |
| James Ct. N&S .... 26W-36N | 13 |
| Jeanette Ct. NE&SW | | |
| ............... 28W-37N | 12 |
| Karen Ct. NW&SE .. 28W-37N | 12 |
| Kelly Ln. N&S ...... 26W-33N | 21 |
| Kerwin Ln. N&S .... 26W-36N | 13 |
| Knollwood Dr. N&S | | |
| ........ 26W-34N,26W-35N | 21 |
| Lake Av. N&S .... 25W-35N | 21 |
| Lake Dr. N&S...... 25W-34N | 21 |
| Lake Mathews Tr. NW&SE | | |
| ........ 28W-34N,28W-35N | 20 |
| Lake Shore Dr. E&W | | |
| ........ 26W-35N,25W-35N | 21 |
| Lake Shore Rd. NE&SW | | |
| ............... 28W-35N | 20 |
| Lake Shore Woods Dr. N&S | | |
| ............... 25W-35N | 21 |
| Lake St. N&S ...... 25W-36N | 13 |
| Lake St. N&S ...... 26W-36N | 13 |
| Lake Vista Ter. NE&SW | | |
| ............... 28W-37N | 12 |
| Lakeview Av. E&W .. 25W-34N | 21 |
| Lakeview Av. E&W | | |
| ........ 26W-35N,25W-35N | 21 |
| Lakeview Ct. N&S .. 25W-34N | 20 |
| Laneville Av. N&S .. 25W-34N | 21 |
| Lannon Ln. N&S.... 26W-36N | 13 |
| Larkin Ln. E&W .... 25W-35N | 21 |
| Laughing Water Tr. N&S | | |
| ............... 28W-35N | 20 |
| Laurel Av. N&S .... 25W-34N | 21 |
| Lee Ct. N&S ...... 26W-33N | 21 |
| Leonard Av. N&S .. 28W-34N | 20 |
| Levi Waite Rd. E&W | | |
| ............... 26W-33N | 21 |
| Lincoln Av. N&S .... 25W-34N | 21 |
| Lincoln St. E&W .... 26W-36N | 13 |
| Linder Av. N&S .... 25W-34N | 21 |
| Long Av. N&S...... 25W-34N | 21 |
| Long Beach Dr. NW&SE | | |
| ............... 25W-34N | 21 |
| Longwood Dr. N&S | | |
| ............... 26W-33N | 21 |
| Louise Pl. N&S .... 25W-35N | 21 |

| | Grid | Page |
|---|---|---|
| Lowood Av. N&S .. 26W-35N | 21 |
| Luana Ln. E&W .... 26W-35N | 20 |
| Luby Ct. N&S ...... 26W-35N | 21 |
| Madison St. E&W .. 25W-34N | 21 |
| Mall Rd. NW&SE .. 28W-35N | 20 |
| Malmquist Dr. N&S | | |
| ............... 28W-35N | 20 |
| Manitoba Tr. NE&SW | | |
| ............... 28W-34N | 20 |
| Maple Av. E&W .... 26W-35N | 21 |
| Maple Av. N&S .... 26W-36N | 13 |
| Maple St. E&W .... 26W-36N | 13 |
| Margie Pl. NW&SE ..28W-37N | 12 |
| Marie Ln. E&W .... 26W-35N | 21 |
| Marine Dr. N&S .... 27W-35N | 20 |
| Marion Av. E&W .... 25W-35N | 21 |
| Marion Ct. E&W .... 26W-35N | 21 |
| Marquette Dr. E&W | | |
| ............... 25W-36N | 13 |
| Marshall Av. N&S .. 25W-35N | 21 |
| Mary Ct. N&S .... 26W-36N | 13 |
| Mattalina Ct. E&W.. 26W-37N | 13 |
| Meadow Ln. N&S .. 25W-35N | 21 |
| Michael Rd. N&S .. 28W-34N | 20 |
| Milwaukee Av. NE&SW | | |
| ............... 25W-35N | 21 |
| Mishenauma Tr. N&S | | |
| ............... 28W-34N | 20 |
| Mitchell Ct. NW&SE | | |
| ............... 25W-35N | 21 |
| Molidor Rd. E&W | | |
| ........ 27W-33N,26W-33N | 20 |
| Moody St. N&S .. 27W-35N | 20 |
| Moraine Dr. E&W .. 25W-35N | 21 |
| Mrytle Ln. E&W .. 26W-35N | 21 |
| Mudjekeewis Tr. NW&SE | | |
| ............... 28W-34N | 20 |
| Muskego Av. NW&SE | | |
| ........ 25W-34N,25W-35N | 21 |
| N. Lake Dr. NE&SW | | |
| ............... 25W-35N | 21 |
| Navajo Tr. N&S .. 28W-34N | 20 |
| Nippersink Pl. NW&SE | | |
| ............... 28W-37N | 12 |
| Nippersink Rd. NW&SE | | |
| ............... 25W-35N | 21 |
| Nokomis Tr. N&S .. 28W-34N | 20 |
| Nora Pl. NE&SW .. 28W-37N | 12 |
| North Ct. E&W .... 27W-35N | 20 |
| O'Kelly Ln. E&W ....28W-34N | 20 |
| Oak Av. N&S ...... 25W-35N | 21 |
| Oak Cir. Dr. E&W .. 26W-36N | 13 |
| Oak Ct. N&S ...... 25W-36N | 13 |
| Oak Dr. N&S ...... 26W-33N | 21 |
| Oak Ln. E&W ...... 25W-36N | 13 |
| Oak St. E&W ...... 25W-36N | 13 |
| Oak St. N&S ...... 25W-35N | 21 |
| Oakland Dr. E&W .. 25W-34N | 21 |
| Oakside St. N&S .. 26W-34N | 21 |
| Oakwood Av. E&W | | |
| ............... 26W-35N | 21 |
| Oakwood Av. N&S .. 26W-35N | 21 |
| Oden Av. N&S .... 25W-34N | 21 |
| Old Grand Av. E&W | | |
| ............... 25W-36N | 13 |
| Olive Ct. N&S ...... 25W-35N | 21 |
| Orchard Av. E&W .. 25W-36N | 13 |
| Orchard Dr. N&S .. 27W-35N | 20 |
| Park Av. N&S ...... 28W-34N | 21 |
| Park Dr. N&S ...... 28W-34N | 20 |
| Parkview Pl. E&W .. 28W-37N | 12 |
| Patricia Ln. NW&SE | | |
| ............... 28W-37N | 12 |
| Paupukkeewis Tr. NW&SE | | |
| ............... 28W-34N | 20 |
| Peterson Av. N&S .. 25W-34N | 21 |
| Pleasant Rd. E&W .. 26W-36N | 13 |
| Polk St. N&S ...... 26W-34N | 21 |
| Poplar Ct. N&S .... 25W-35N | 21 |
| Rabbit Hill Ln. N&S | | |
| ............... 26W-36N | 13 |
| Racine Av. E&W .. 25W-34N | 21 |
| Randhill Dr. N&S .. 27W-35N | 20 |
| Randich Rd. E&W .. 26W-37N | 13 |
| Ravine Ln. E&W.... 27W-35N | 20 |
| Reed St. E&W ...... 26W-34N | 21 |
| Ridge Av. N&S .... 26W-36N | 13 |
| Ridge St. E&W .... 27W-35N | 20 |
| Robin Rd. N&S .... 25W-36N | 13 |
| Rock Island St. NE&SW | | |
| ............... 25W-34N | 21 |
| Rockford St. E&W .. 25W-35N | 21 |
| Rollins St. E&W .... 25W-35N | 21 |
| Roseland Ct. E&W .. 25W-34N | 21 |
| Rosewood Dr. N&S | | |
| ............... 26W-36N | 13 |
| Route 12 N&S | | |
| ........ 27W-35N,28W-37N | 20 |
| Route 134 E&W | | |
| ........ 27W-34N,25W-34N | 20 |
| Route 59 N&S | | |
| ........ 27W-32N,25W-36N | 20 |
| Sequoia Tr. N&S .. 28W-34N | 20 |
| Shandon Dr. E&W | | |
| ........ 26W-36N,25W-36N | 13 |
| Sheridan Dr. N&S .. 27W-35N | 20 |
| Shirley Ln. N&S | | |
| ............... 28W-35N | 20 |
| Shore Rd. N&S .. 26W-36N | 13 |
| Shoreline Ln. E&W.. 25W-35N | 21 |
| Snowshoe Tr. E&W | | |
| ............... 28W-34N | 20 |
| South Av. E&W .. 28W-37N | 12 |

| | Grid | Page |
|---|---|---|
| South Ct. E&W | | |
| ........ 28W-34N,27W-35N | 20 |
| South St. E&W .... 26W-36N | 13 |
| Squaw Rd. N&S .. 26W-36N | 13 |
| Stanley Rd. N&S .. 27W-34N | 20 |
| Stanton Bay Rd. E&W | | |
| ............... 28W-36N | 13 |
| Stanton Ln. NS&EW | | |
| ............... 26W-33N | 21 |
| Stanton Point Rd. NE&SW | | |
| ........ 26W-36N,26W-37N | 13 |
| Stockholm St. E&W | | |
| ............... 26W-33N | 21 |
| Stolaf Av. NS&ED .. 25W-34N | 21 |
| Stoughton Av. E&W | | |
| ............... 25W-34N | 21 |
| Sullivan Lake Rd. E&W | | |
| ............... 28W-33N | 20 |
| Sunnybrook Rd. E&W | | |
| ............... 26W-34N | 21 |
| Sunnyside Av. N&S | | |
| ............... 25W-35N | 21 |
| Sunset Dr. NW&SE | | |
| ............... 25W-34N | 21 |
| Sunset Ter. NE&SW | | |
| ............... 25W-34N | 21 |
| Tamarack Dr. N&S.. 25W-36N | 13 |
| Tami Ln. N&S .... 25W-35N | 21 |
| Tara Ct. N&S ...... 25W-36N | 13 |
| Tarvin Ln. E&W .... 26W-35N | 21 |
| Terrace Ln. NE&SW | | |
| ............... 28W-37N | 12 |
| Thomas Ct. E&W .. 28W-37N | 20 |
| Tree Top Rd. NW&SE | | |
| ............... 28W-35N | 20 |
| Tyrone Pl. NW&SE 28W-37N | 12 |
| Valley Rd. NW&SE 28W-35N | 20 |
| Van Buren St. E&W | | |
| ............... 26W-34N | 21 |
| Venetian Dr. NW&SE | | |
| ............... 25W-34N | 21 |
| Vincent Ct. E&W .. 26W-36N | 13 |
| Wally Ct. E&W .... 26W-35N | 21 |
| Ward Ln. N&S .... 25W-35N | 21 |
| Watson Av. N&S .. 25W-34N | 21 |
| Watts Av. NE&SW .. 28W-37N | 12 |
| Wenonah Tr. E&W .. 28W-34N | 20 |
| Wesley Rd. N&S.... 26W-36N | 13 |
| West Lake Av. E&W | | |
| ............... 28W-37N | 12 |
| West St. N&S...... 28W-37N | 12 |
| White Rabbit Tr. NE&SW | | |
| ............... 28W-34N | 20 |
| Wildwood Av. E&W | | |
| ............... 26W-35N | 21 |
| William Pl. NW&SE 28W-37N | 12 |
| Wilson Rd. N&S | | |
| ........ 26W-36N,25W-32N | 13 |
| Wind Mill Rd. N&S .. 26W-36N | 13 |
| Wooster Lake Av. E&W | | |
| ............... 26W-34N | 21 |
| Wooster Lake Dr. E&W | | |
| ............... 26W-34N | 21 |
| Wooster Ln. E&W .. 26W-34N | 21 |
| 1st Av. NE&SW .... 27W-35N | 20 |
| 2nd Av. NW&SE .. 27W-35N | 20 |
| 3rd Av. NW&SE .... 27W-35N | 20 |

### Grayslake

| | Grid | Page |
|---|---|---|
| Allegheny Rd. N&S | | |
| ........ 21W-31N,21W-32N | 31 |
| Allen Av. E&W .... 20W-33N | 23 |
| Allison Ct. E&W | | |
| ........ 21W-32N,21W-33N | 23 |
| Alta Dr. N&S ...... 21W-32N | 23 |
| Amber Ct. NE&SW 21W-34N | 23 |
| Amherst Ct. NE&SW | | |
| ............... 21W-33N | 23 |
| Amos Bennet St. E&W | | |
| ............... 19W-32N | 23 |
| Arlington Ln. E&W .. 21W-34N | 23 |
| Atkinson Rd. N&S | | |
| ........ 20W-32N,20W-33N | 23 |
| Attenborough Ct. E&W | | |
| ............... 19W-33N | 23 |
| Attenborough Way NS&EW | | |
| ............... 19W-33N | 23 |
| Augusta St. N&S .. 21W-33N | 23 |
| Banbury Dr. E&W .. 20W-33N | 23 |
| Banbury Ln. NE&SW | | |
| ............... 20W-33N | 23 |
| Barron Blvd. N&S .. 20W-33N | 23 |
| Bayview Ln. N&S .. 20W-34N | 23 |
| Behm Dr. NW&SE .. 21W-33N | 23 |
| Belle Ct. N&S .... 21W-32N | 23 |
| Belle Haven N&S .. 20W-34N | 23 |
| Belvidere Rd. E&W | | |
| ........ 21W-32N,18W-32N | 23 |
| Berry Av. E&W .... 20W-33N | 23 |
| Bluestem Ln. N&S .. 19W-32N | 23 |
| Bluff Av. NE&SW .. 21W-32N | 23 |
| Bob-o-link Dr. N&S 19W-32N | 23 |
| Bonnie Brae Av. E&W | | |
| ............... 20W-33N | 23 |
| Brae Loch Rd. E&W | | |
| ............... 19W-33N | 23 |
| Braxton Ct. E&W .. 19W-33N | 23 |
| Braxton Way NE&SW | | |
| ............... 19W-33N | 23 |
| Briargate Dr. E&W .. 20W-33N | 23 |
| Bristol Ln. N&S .... 20W-33N | 23 |
| Brittain Av. N&S .. 21W-32N | 23 |

| | Grid | Page |
|---|---|---|
| Buckingham Ct. NE&SW | | |
| | 19W-33N | 23 |
| Burton St. N&S | 21W-33N | 23 |
| Caitlin Ct. N&S | 19W-34N | 23 |
| Calamus Ln. N&S | 19W-33N | 23 |
| Cambridge Dr. NS&EW | | |
| | 19W-33N | 23 |
| Cambridge Dr. NW&SE | | |
| | 19W-34N | 23 |
| Cardinal Ct. E&W | 20W-33N | 23 |
| Carol Ln. E&W | 20W-33N | 23 |
| Carriage Ln. E&W | 19W-34N | 23 |
| Catherine Ct. E&W | 20W-33N | 23 |
| Cecelia St. N&S | 21W-33N | 23 |
| Center St. E&W | | |
| | 20W-33N,19W-33N | 23 |
| Chard St. E&W | 20W-33N | 23 |
| Chesapeake Blvd. N&S | | |
| | 20W-34N | 23 |
| Christy Cir. E&W | 21W-33N | 23 |
| Clarewood Cir. NS&EW | | |
| | 19W-33N | 23 |
| Colbee Benton Rd. N&S | | |
| | 19W-32N | 23 |
| Commerce N&S | 19W-32N | 23 |
| Country Squire Dr. NS&EW | | |
| | 18W-32N | 23 |
| Cove Ct. N&S | 20W-33N | 23 |
| Cross Arm Dr. N&S | | |
| | 20W-32N | 23 |
| Dawn Cir. N&S | 20W-33N | 23 |
| Deep Woods Ct. E&W | | |
| | 21W-33N | 23 |
| Devon Ct. NW&SE | 19W-33N | 23 |
| Durham Ln. E&W | 20W-33N | 23 |
| Cir. | 20W-33N,20W-34N | 23 |
| E. Cambridge Ct. NW&SE | | |
| | 19W-33N | 23 |
| East St. N&S | 20W-33N | 23 |
| Easton Ct. E&W | 19W-33N | 23 |
| Essex Cir. N&S | 19W-34N | 23 |
| Fair Port Dr. N&S | 20W-34N | 23 |
| Fairfax Ln. E&W | 21W-34N | 23 |
| Fieldale Ln. NW&SE | | |
| | 19W-33N | 23 |
| Flanders Ln. E&W | 20W-33N | 23 |
| Garfield Blvd. N&S | 20W-32N | 23 |
| George St. E&W | 21W-33N | 23 |
| Getchell Av. E&W | 21W-33N | 23 |
| Glen St. E&W | 21W-32N | 23 |
| Gray Ct. E&W | 20W-33N | 23 |
| Greenwood Av. E&W | | |
| | 21W-32N | 23 |
| Grisfield Dr. E&W | 20W-34N | 23 |
| Hamlitz St. E&W | 21W-32N | 23 |
| Hampshire Ct. E&W | | |
| | 20W-32N | 23 |
| Harding St. N&S | 20W-32N | 23 |
| Harris Rd. N&S | 19W-32N | 23 |
| Harvey Av. E&W | 21W-33N | 23 |
| Hawley Ct. NS&EW | | |
| | 21W-33N | 23 |
| Hawley St. E&W | 20W-33N | 23 |
| Heather Av. E&W | 20W-33N | 23 |
| Hickory St. E&W | 20W-33N | 23 |
| Highland Rd. E&W | 20W-33N | 23 |
| Hillside Ct. E&W | 21W-33N | 23 |
| Hojem Ct. N&S | 20W-33N | 23 |
| Hummingbird Ln. NS&EW | | |
| | 19W-32N | 23 |
| Indian Grass Ln. N&S | | |
| | 19W-32N | 23 |
| Indian Pata Rd. N&S | | |
| | 19W-32N | 23 |
| Iron Horse Ct. E&W | | |
| | 20W-32N | 23 |
| Ivanhoe Rd. N&S | | |
| | 20W-31N,20W-32N | 31 |
| Jackson Blvd. E&W | | |
| | 20W-32N | 23 |
| Jamestown Ct. N&S | | |
| | 21W-34N | 23 |
| Jeanne Ct. NE&SW | | |
| | 19W-34N | 23 |
| Jeffrey Av. N&S | 21W-33N | 23 |
| Jennifer Ln. E&W | 21W-33N | 23 |
| Jones Point Rd. E&W | | |
| | 19W-32N | 23 |
| Junior Av. E&W | 20W-32N | 23 |
| Karin Ln. N&S | 19W-32N | 23 |
| Kelly Av. N&S | 21W-33N | 23 |
| Kenilworth Ct. N&S | | |
| | 20W-33N,20W-34N | 23 |
| Kenilworth St. N&S | | |
| | 19W-33N | 23 |
| Kerry Way NS&EW | | |
| | 19W-33N | 23 |
| Kevin Ln. NS&EW | 21W-33N | 23 |
| Kilburn Ct. N&S | 19W-33N | 33 |
| Lake St. N&S | | |
| | 21W-32N,21W-34N | 23 |
| Lancer Ln. NE&SW | | |
| | 19W-33N | 23 |
| Langley Ct. NW&SE | | |
| | 20W-33N | 23 |
| Laurel Ter. N&S | 20W-33N | 23 |
| Laurie Ct. NW&SE | 21W-33N | 23 |
| Lawrence Av. E&W | | |
| | 20W-33N | 23 |
| Levi Baxter St. E&W | | |
| | 19W-31N | 23 |
| Lexington Ln. NE&SW | | |
| | 21W-34N | 23 |
| Lincoln Av. N&S | 20W-32N | 23 |

| | Grid | Page |
|---|---|---|
| Lindsey N&S | 21W-33N | 23 |
| Lupine Ct. NW&SE | | |
| | 19W-31N | 23 |
| Mallard Ct. NE&SW | | |
| | 19W-32N | 23 |
| Manchester Cir. N&S | | |
| | 19W-34N | 23 |
| Manor Av. N&S | 20W-33N | 23 |
| Market St. N&S | 21W-33N | 23 |
| May St. N&S | 21W-33N | 23 |
| McKay Cir. N&S | 19W-34N | 23 |
| McMillan St. N&S | 20W-33N | 23 |
| Meadowlark Av. NS&EW | | |
| | 19W-32N,19W-33N | 23 |
| Merrill Ln. E&W | 20W-33N | 23 |
| Mitchell Dr. E&W | 21W-33N | 23 |
| Moore Ct. N&S | 21W-32N | 23 |
| Mt. Vernon Ct. N&S | | |
| | 19W-34N | 23 |
| Mt. Vernon Dr. NS&EW | | |
| | 19W-34N | 23 |
| N. Allegheny Rd. E&W | | |
| | 21W-33N | 23 |
| N. Cambridge Ct. N&S | | |
| | 19W-33N | 23 |
| Neville Dr. N&S | 21W-32N | 23 |
| Newbury Ct. N&S | 19W-33N | 23 |
| Normandy Ln. E&W | | |
| | 19W-33N | 23 |
| North Corporate Cir. N&S | | |
| | 19W-32N | 23 |
| Oak Av. E&W | 20W-33N | 23 |
| Oakwood Dr. N&S | 20W-33N | 23 |
| Old Center St. E&W | | |
| | 20W-33N | 23 |
| Old Plank Rd. E&W | | |
| | 18W-32N | 24 |
| Oriole Ct. E&W | 20W-33N | 23 |
| Osage Orange Rd. N&S | | |
| | 19W-32N | 23 |
| Oxford Cir. E&W | 20W-34N | 23 |
| Park Av. E&W | 20W-33N | 23 |
| Park Pl. E&W | 20W-33N | 23 |
| Parker Dr. N&S | 21W-33N | 23 |
| Partridge Ct. NE&SW | | |
| | 19W-32N | 23 |
| Patricia Ct. E&W | 21W-33N | 23 |
| Penstemon Ct. NW&SE | | |
| | 19W-31N | 23 |
| Peterson Rd. E&W | 20W-30N | 31 |
| Pheasant Ln. N&S | 20W-33N | 23 |
| Pierce Ct. N&S | 20W-33N | 23 |
| Pine St. E&W | 20W-33N | 23 |
| Pines Dr. NW&SE | 18W-32N | 24 |
| Popes Creek Cir. NW&SE | | |
| | 19W-32N | 23 |
| Portia Rd. E&W | 19W-32N | 23 |
| Potawatomi Rd. N&S | | |
| | 19W-32N | 23 |
| Potomac Ct. N&S | 21W-34N | 23 |
| Prairie Smoke Rd. NW&SE | | |
| | 19W-31N | 23 |
| Prairie Tr. E&W | 19W-32N | 23 |
| Prairie Tr. N&S | 19W-31N | 23 |
| Prairieview Av. E&W | | |
| | 20W-33N | 23 |
| Proctor St. E&W | 20W-33N | 23 |
| Quail Creek Dr. E&W | | |
| | 20W-33N | 23 |
| Quist St. N&S | 20W-33N | 23 |
| Railroad Av. NW&SE | | |
| | 20W-33N | 23 |
| Reagan's Pl. E&W | 20W-32N | 23 |
| Robin Ct. N&S | 20W-33N | 23 |
| Rock Hall Cir. NW&SE | | |
| | 20W-34N | 23 |
| Rock Hall Ct. E&W | 20W-34N | 23 |
| Roffner Dr. E&W | 19W-33N | 23 |
| Rollins Rd. NE&SW | | |
| | 21W-35N | 23 |
| Roosevelt Ct. N&S | 20W-32N | 23 |
| Route 120 E&W | | |
| | 21W-32N,18W-32N | 23 |
| Route 83 N&S | | |
| | 20W-31N,21W-34N | 31 |
| S. Stuart St. N&S | 20W-33N | 23 |
| School St. E&W | 21W-33N | 23 |
| Scott Av. E&W | 21W-33N | 23 |
| Sears Blvd. N&S | 18W-32N | 24 |
| Seymour Av. N&S | | |
| | 20W-32N,20W-33N | 23 |
| Shakespeare Dr. E&W | | |
| | 20W-34N,19W-33N | 23 |
| Sheffield Ln. E&W | 19W-33N | 23 |
| Sheldon Rd. N&S | 19W-35N | 23 |
| Shorewood Rd. E&W | | |
| | 21W-35N | 23 |
| Signal Ln. E&W | 20W-32N | 23 |
| Silo Hill Dr. NE&SW | | |
| | 19W-32N | 23 |
| Silo Rill Ct. E&W | 19W-32N | 23 |
| Siwiha Dr. E&W | 19W-31N | 23 |
| Slusser St. N&S | 20W-33N | 23 |
| Somerset Dr. E&W | 19W-32N | 23 |
| South Corporte Cir. E&W | | |
| | 19W-32N | 23 |
| St. Paul St. NW&SE | | |
| | 19W-32N | 23 |
| Stratford St. N&S | 20W-33N | 23 |
| Stuart St. N&S | 20W-33N | 23 |
| Suffolk Ln. E&W | 20W-34N | 23 |
| Sunflower Ct. E&W | | |
| | 19W-31N | 23 |
| Surveyor St. N&S | 19W-31N | 23 |

| | Grid | Page |
|---|---|---|
| Swan Dr. N&S | 20W-33N | 23 |
| Switchgrass Ln. N&S | | |
| | 19W-31N | 23 |
| Sycamore Ln. E&W | | |
| | 21W-34N | 23 |
| Talbot Ln. N&S | 20W-34N | 23 |
| Trestle Ct. N&S | 20W-32N | 23 |
| Tylerton Cir. N&S | 20W-34N | 23 |
| Vista Ct. N&S | 19W-32N | 23 |
| W. Cambridge Ct. NE&SW | | |
| | 19W-33N | 23 |
| Walton Ln. E&W | 20W-33N | 23 |
| Warren Ln. E&W | 21W-32N | 23 |
| Washington Blvd. N&S | | |
| | 20W-32N | 23 |
| Washington St. E&W | | |
| | 21W-34N,19W-34N | 23 |
| Waterford Dr. NS&EW | | |
| | 21W-33N | 23 |
| Webb St. N&S | 20W-33N | 23 |
| West Shore Dr. NW&SE | | |
| | 21W-33N | 23 |
| West Trail N&S | 21W-33N | 23 |
| West Trail North N&S | | |
| | 21W-33N | 23 |
| Westerfield Pl. N&S | | |
| | 20W-33N | 23 |
| Wexford Ct. E&W | 20W-33N | 23 |
| White St. N&S | 20W-32N | 23 |
| Whitehall Ct. E&W | 19W-33N | 23 |
| Whitney St. N&S | 20W-33N | 23 |
| Wicks St. N&S | 20W-32N | 23 |
| Wild Iris Ln. N&S | 19W-32N | 23 |
| Williamsburg Cir. N&S | | |
| | 20W-34N | 23 |
| Windflower Ct. E&W | | |
| | 19W-31N | 23 |
| Woodland Dr. E&W | | |
| | 21W-33N | 23 |
| York Dr. NE&SW | 20W-33N | 23 |
| Yorkshire Ct. E&W | 20W-33N | 23 |
| Ziegler Dr. N&S | 20W-33N | 23 |
| 1st St. N&S | 21W-33N | 23 |
| 2nd St. N&S | 21W-33N | 23 |

## Great Lakes

| | Grid | Page |
|---|---|---|
| 'A' St. E&W | 10W-30N | 35 |
| 'B' St. E&W | 10W-30N | 35 |
| 'C' St. E&W | 10W-30N | 35 |
| 'D' St. E&W | 10W-30N | 35 |
| 'E' St. N&S | 10W-30N | 35 |
| 'F' St. E&W | 10W-30N | 35 |
| 'G' St. E&W | 10W-30N | 35 |
| Alaska Av. E&W | 12W-30N | 35 |
| Allan Ln. E&W | 11W-31N | 35 |
| Argonaut Pl. N&S | 11W-30N | 35 |
| Arizona Av. N&S | 11W-30N | 35 |
| Arkansas Rd. N&S | 12W-29N | 35 |
| Atlantic Rd. N&S | 11W-29N | 35 |
| Barry Rd. N&S | 10W-30N | 35 |
| Barry Rd. E&W | 10W-30N | 35 |
| Bassett Av. E&W | 10W-30N | 35 |
| Broadway Av. E&W | | |
| | 11W-30N | 35 |
| Bronson Av. E&W | 10W-31N | 35 |
| Buckley Rd. E&W | 12W-30N | 35 |
| Burnham Av. E&W | 10W-30N | 35 |
| California Av. E&W | 11W-29N | 35 |
| Cavin Dr. E&W | 10W-30N | 35 |
| Clark Av. E&W | 10W-30N | 35 |
| Cluerius Av. E&W | 10W-31N | 35 |
| Connecticut Av. E&W | | |
| | 12W-30N | 35 |
| Connecticut Av. E&W | | |
| | 11W-30N | 35 |
| Crosley Dr. N&S | | |
| | 10W-30N,10W-31N | 35 |
| Dahlgren St. N&S | 10W-30N | 35 |
| Decatur Av. E&W | 10W-30N | 35 |
| Delaware Av. E&W | 11W-29N | 35 |
| Depot Dr. N&S | 10W-31N | 35 |
| Dewey Av. E&W | 10W-30N | 35 |
| Downes Av. E&W | 10W-30N | 35 |
| E. Alabama Av. E&W | | |
| | 11W-29N | 35 |
| E. Washington Av. E&W | | |
| | 11W-30N | 35 |
| E. Wyoming Av. E&W | | |
| | 12W-30N | 35 |
| E.C.I. Ct. N&S | 11W-30N | 35 |
| Ellis St. N&S | 10W-30N | 35 |
| Enterprise Av. NE&SW | | |
| | 11W-30N | 35 |
| Erie Ct. N&S | 12W-30N | 35 |
| Essex Av. N&S | 11W-31N | 35 |
| Evans Av. E&W | 10W-30N | 35 |
| Farragut Av. E&W | 10W-30N | 35 |
| Fisher Rd. NE&SW | 10W-30N | 35 |
| Florida Av. E&W | 11W-30N | 35 |
| Forrestal Dr. E&W | 11W-29N | 35 |
| Fullam Av. E&W | 10W-30N | 35 |
| Georgia Rd. N&S | 12W-29N | 35 |
| Grassie Av. N&S | 10W-30N | 35 |
| Great Lakes Dr. N&S | | |
| | 12W-30N | 35 |
| Greenfield St. N&S | 10W-31N | 35 |
| Hawaii Av. N&S | 11W-29N | 35 |
| Hennepin St. N&S | 10W-30N | 35 |
| Hines St. N&S | 10W-30N | 35 |
| Hopkins St. N&S | 11W-30N | 35 |
| Huron St. N&S | 12W-30N | 35 |
| Idaho Ct. N&S | 12W-30N | 35 |
| Idaho St. N&S | 12W-30N | 35 |

| | Grid | Page |
|---|---|---|
| Illinois St. N&S | | |
| | 11W-29N,11W-30N | 35 |
| Indiana St. N&S | 11W-30N | 35 |
| Intrepid St. N&S | 11W-30N | 35 |
| Iowa St. N&S | 11W-31N | 35 |
| Isherwood Av. N&S | | |
| | 10W-31N | 35 |
| Kentucky Ct. N&S | 11W-29N | 35 |
| Kentucky St. N&S | 11W-30N | 35 |
| Langley St. NW&SE | | |
| | 11W-31N | 35 |
| Lawrence St. N&S | 11W-30N | 35 |
| Lexington Av. N&S | 11W-30N | 35 |
| Luce Blvd. N&S | 11W-31N | 35 |
| Mac Donough St. N&S | | |
| | 10W-31N | 35 |
| Mahan Rd. NW&SE | | |
| | 10W-30N | 35 |
| Main St. N&S | 10W-31N | 35 |
| Maine Av. N&S | 11W-30N | 35 |
| Meridian Av. N&S | | |
| | 11W-30N,11W-29N | 35 |
| Michigan St. N&S | 12W-30N | 35 |
| Minnesota Av. N&S | | |
| | 12W-30N | 35 |
| Mississippi St. N&S | | |
| | 12W-30N | 35 |
| Missouri St. N&S | | |
| | 11W-30N,11W-31N | 35 |
| Missouri St. N&S | 12W-30N | 35 |
| Moffet Dr. E&W | 10W-31N | 35 |
| Montana Av. N&S | 11W-30N | 35 |
| N. Admiral Rd. N&S | | |
| | 11W-30N | 35 |
| Nebarska Ct. N&S | 11W-30N | 35 |
| Nevada Ct. N&S | 12W-30N | 35 |
| New York Av. E&W | | |
| | 11W-29N | 35 |
| Neyer St. N&S | 10W-31N | 35 |
| Nimitz Av. E&W | 10W-31N | 35 |
| Ohio Av. E&W | 11W-29N | 35 |
| Ohio St. N&S | | |
| | 11W-29N,11W-30N | 35 |
| Oklahoma Av. N&S | | |
| | 12W-30N | 35 |
| Oklahoma Ct. E&W | 12W-30N | 35 |
| Ontario Ct. E&W | 12W-30N | 35 |
| Oregon Ct. E&W | 12W-30N | 35 |
| Pacific Av. E&W | 11W-30N | 35 |
| Paul Jones Ct. N&S | | |
| | 10W-31N | 35 |
| Paul Jones St. N&S | | |
| | 10W-31N | 35 |
| Pennsylvania Av. E&W | | |
| | 11W-30N | 35 |
| Perry St. N&S | 10W-31N | 35 |
| Porter Av. E&W | 10W-31N | 35 |
| Preble Av. E&W | 10W-30N | 35 |
| Preble Pl. N&S | 10W-30N | 35 |
| Ranger Ct. N&S | 11W-30N | 35 |
| Ray St. N&S | 11W-30N | 35 |
| Remora Ct. E&W | 11W-30N | 35 |
| Rhode Island Av. E&W | | |
| | 12W-29N | 35 |
| Rhode Island Ct. E&W | | |
| | 12W-30N | 35 |
| Rogers St. N&S | 10W-31N | 35 |
| S. Admiral Rd. N&S | | |
| | 11W-29N | 35 |
| Sampson Rd. N&S | 10W-30N | 35 |
| Sampson St. N&S | 10W-31N | 35 |
| Saratoga St. NW&SE | | |
| | 11W-30N | 35 |
| Spaulding St. N&S | 11W-30N | 35 |
| Superior St. N&S | 12W-30N | 35 |
| Sutton St. N&S | 12W-29N | 35 |
| Tennessee Ct. E&W | | |
| | 12W-30N | 35 |
| Texas Ct. E&W | 11W-30N | 35 |
| Thresher St. N&S | 11W-30N | 35 |
| Utah Ct. E&W | 12W-30N | 35 |
| Vermont Ct., N. N&S | | |
| | 12W-30N | 35 |
| Vermont Ct., S. N&S | | |
| | 12W-30N | 35 |
| Virginia Ct. NW&SE | | |
| | 12W-30N | 35 |
| Virginia Rd. E&W | 11W-30N | 35 |
| W. Alabama Av. E&W | | |
| | 12W-29N | 35 |
| W. Colorado Ct. E&W | | |
| | 12W-30N | 35 |
| W. Florida Ct. E&W | | |
| | 12W-30N | 35 |
| W. Wyoming Av. E&W | | |
| | 12W-30N | 35 |
| Washington Av. E&W | | |
| | 12W-30N | 35 |
| Wisconsin Dr., E. NE&SW | | |
| | 12W-30N | 35 |
| Wisconsin Dr., W. NW&SE | | |
| | 12W-30N | 35 |
| Wurtsbaugh St. N&S | | |
| | 10W-30N | 35 |
| Wyoming Ct. E&W | 12W-30N | 35 |
| Yeager St. N&S | 10W-31N | 35 |
| Ziegemeier St. N&S | | |
| | 10W-30N,10W-31N | 35 |
| 1st Av. E&W | 11W-29N | 35 |
| 1st St. N&S | 10W-30N | 35 |
| 2nd Av. E&W | 11W-29N | 35 |
| 2nd St. N&S | 10W-30N | 35 |
| 3rd Av. E&W | 11W-29N | 35 |
| 3rd St. N&S | 10W-30N | 35 |
| 4th Av. E&W | 11W-30N | 35 |

| | Grid | Page |
|---|---|---|
| 4th St. N&S | 10W-30N | 35 |
| 5th Av. E&W | 11W-30N | 35 |
| 5th St. N&S | 10W-30N | 35 |
| 6th Av. E&W | 11W-30N | 35 |
| 6th St. N&S | 10W-30N | 35 |
| 7th Av. E&W | 11W-30N | 35 |
| 7th St. N&S | 11W-30N | 35 |
| 8th Av. E&W | 11W-30N | 35 |
| 8th St. N&S | 10W-30N | 35 |
| 9th Av. E&W | 11W-30N | 35 |
| 9th St. N&S | 10W-30N | 35 |
| 10th Av. E&W | 11W-30N | 35 |
| 10th St. N&S | 10W-30N | 35 |
| 11th Av. E&W | 11W-30N | 35 |
| 11th St. N&S | 10W-30N | 35 |
| 12th Av. E&W | 11W-31N | 35 |
| 24th E&W | 11W-31N | 35 |

## Green Oaks

| | Grid | Page |
|---|---|---|
| Atkinson Av. E&W | | |
| | 14W-29W,13W-19N | 33 |
| Belmont Dr. N&S | 14W-30N | 33 |
| Benson Ln. N&S | 14W-29N | 33 |
| Benson Rd. N&S | 14W-29N | 33 |
| Brentwood Dr. E&W | | |
| | 14W-30N | 33 |
| Buckley Rd. E&W | 14W-30N | 33 |
| Carriage Ct. N&S | 14W-30N | 33 |
| Churchill Ct. N&S | 14W-30N | 33 |
| Cranbrook Rd. E&W | | |
| | 14W-30N | 33 |
| Crescent Knoll Dr. NE&SW | | |
| | 14W-28N | 33 |
| Crest Rd. N&S | 14W-29N | 33 |
| Dan Patch Cir. E&W | | |
| | 14W-31N | 33 |
| Fox Run NS&EW | 14W-29N | 33 |
| Gerwick Way E&W | 14W-30N | 33 |
| Glenmore Rd. E&W | 14W-30N | 33 |
| Greenbriar E&W | | |
| | 14W-29N | 33 |
| Greenbriar Ln. E&W | | |
| | 14W-29N | 33 |
| Gurin Ct. N&S | | |
| | 15W-31N,14W-31N | 33 |
| Hanlon Rd. N&S | 15W-31N | 33 |
| Harwood Dr. E&W | 15W-31N | 33 |
| Haven Ln. NS&EW | 14W-30N | 33 |
| Hawthorne Rd. N&S | | |
| | 15W-28N | 33 |
| Heathercliff Dr. N&S | | |
| | 14W-31N | 33 |
| Horace Ct. NW&SE | | |
| | 14W-30N | 33 |
| Interstate 94 N&S | | |
| | 14W-28N,14W-31N | 33 |
| Irene Ln. E&W | 14W-30N | 33 |
| Irma Lee Cir. E&W | 13W-27N | 41 |
| Irondale Rd. N&S | 15W-31N | 33 |
| Kathryn Ct. N&S | 14W-29N | 33 |
| Kenton Ln. E&W | 14W-30N | 33 |
| King Ct. N&S | 14W-30N | 33 |
| King Dr. N&S | 14W-30N | 33 |
| Lexington Rd. NE&SW | | |
| | 14W-30N | 33 |
| Lockwood Dr. N&S | | |
| | 14W-30N | 33 |
| Lucky Lake Ct. N&S | | |
| | 13W-27N | 41 |
| Lucky Lake Dr. E&W | | |
| | 13W-27N | 41 |
| Margate Ln. E&W | 15W-28N | 33 |
| Minard Ln. E&W | 14W-30N | 33 |
| Morgan Ct. N&S | 14W-31N | 33 |
| N. Dan Patch Cir. E&W | | |
| | 14W-31N | 33 |
| O'Plaine Rd. N&S | | |
| | 14W-30N,14W-31N | 33 |
| Old Rockland Rd. NE&SW | | |
| | 14W-29W | 33 |
| Parkhill N&S | 14W-29W | 33 |
| Pearson Rd. E&W | 14W-29W | 33 |
| Placid Ln. E&W | 14W-30N | 33 |
| Rein Ct. NW&SE | 14W-31N | 33 |
| Rockland Rd. NE&SW | | |
| | 14W-28N | 33 |
| Rocktop Rd. E&W | 14W-28N | 33 |
| Route 137 E&W | | |
| | 14W-30N,15W-30N | 33 |
| S. Dan Patch Cir. NS&EW | | |
| | 14W-31N | 33 |
| Saddle Hill Rd. N&S | | |
| | 14W-30N | 33 |
| Saratoga Ct. E&W | 14W-30N | 33 |
| Scotland Ct. E&W | 14W-31N | 33 |
| Shagbark Ln. N&S | 15W-28N | 33 |
| Shannondale Dr. NS&EW | | |
| | 14W-31N | 33 |
| St. Mary's Rd. N&S | | |
| | 15W-29N,14W-30N | 33 |
| Steeplechase Ct. N&S | | |
| | 14W-30N | 33 |
| Sunrise Rd. E&W | 14W-29N | 33 |
| Thornhill Rd. N&S | 14W-30N | 33 |
| Tri-State Tollway N&S | | |
| | 14W-28N,14W-31N | 33 |
| White Fenoe Ln. E&W | | |
| | 14W-30N | 33 |
| Wickham St. N&S | 14W-30N | 33 |
| Wickham Dr. N&S | 14W-30N | 33 |
| Wilton Ct. N&S | 14W-30N | 33 |
| Wilton Ln. N&S | 14W-30N | 33 |

| | Grid | Page |
|---|---|---|
| Woodview Dr. E&W ...... 15W-31N | | 33 |

## Gurnee

| | Grid | Page |
|---|---|---|
| Aberdare Ln. NE&SW .... 17W-34N | | 24 |
| Abingdon Ct. N&S .. 16W-33N | | 24 |
| Acorn Ct.* NW&SE .... 16W-36N | | 17 |
| Adaline Ct. E&W ....14W-35N | | 25 |
| Adams Ct. NE&SW .... 16W-36N | | 17 |
| Adderly Ln. N&S..16W-33N | | 25 |
| Adele Dr. E&W .... 15W-35N | | 25 |
| Alamaden Ln. NW&SE .... 18W-35N | | 24 |
| Albingdon Ct.* E&W .... 16W-32N | | 25 |
| Almond Rd. N&S ........18W-35N,17W-34N | | 24 |
| Andover Dr. E&W .... 16W-33N | | 24 |
| Angelo Av. N&S .... 14W-33N | | 25 |
| Arbor Ct.* N&S .... 14W-36N | | 17 |
| Arlington Ln. N&S .. 17W-35N | | 24 |
| Arthur* E&W .... 14W-36N | | 17 |
| Ashwood Ln. E&W 15W-36N | | 17 |
| Aster Dr. N&S...... 18W-35N | | 24 |
| Astor Pl. N&S .. 14W-33N | | 25 |
| Atlantic Av. E&W .. 13W-35N | | 26 |
| Auburn Ln. N&S....17W-35N | | 24 |
| Avery Ct. NE&SW .. 16W-33N | | 24 |
| Barberry Ln. NE&SW ....14W-35N | | 25 |
| Barnwood Ct. E&W .... 15W-36N | | 17 |
| Bay Pl. N&S .... 15W-35N | | 26 |
| Beach Ln. E&W .. 16W-32N | | 24 |
| Beechwood Av. E&W .... 15W-36N | | 17 |
| Beechwood Ln. N&S .... 15W-36N | | 17 |
| Belleplaine Av. N&S ..13W-35N,13W-36N | | 26 |
| Belvidere Rd. E&W ......16W-33N,16W-32N | | 24 |
| Bennett Av. E&W .. 14W-34N | | 25 |
| Bennington Ct. N&S .... 17W-35N | | 24 |
| Bentley Dr. E&W .. 17W-35N | | 24 |
| Beringer Ct. NE&SW .... 18W-35N | | 24 |
| Berkshire* NE&SW 14W-34N | | 25 |
| Beth Ct. NW&SE .. 16W-33N | | 24 |
| Bicwell Dr. NW&SE .... 16W-33N | | 24 |
| Big Terra Ln. N&S.. 16W-34N | | 24 |
| Bingham Ct.* E&W .. 16W-32N | | 25 |
| Birch Rd. NW&SE .. 14W-34N | | 25 |
| Birchwood Dr. E&W .... 15W-35N | | 25 |
| Bittersweet Dr. E&W .... 18W-35N | | 24 |
| Blackberry Ct. NE&SW .... 18W-35N | | 24 |
| Blackburn St. N&S..13W-35N | | 26 |
| Blackstone Av. E&W ......14W-35N,13W-35N | | 25 |
| Blanc Ct. N&S......18W-35N | | 24 |
| Bluebird Ct. E&W .. 14W-34N | | 25 |
| Bonoma Ct. E&W .. 18W-35N | | 24 |
| Boulder Dr. E&W .. 15W-36N | | 17 |
| Boulevard View Av. N&S ..13W-35N,13W-36N | | 26 |
| Bradley Dr. E&W .. 17W-35N | | 24 |
| Brae Ct. E&W .... 17W-34N | | 24 |
| Braxton Ct. NW&SE ......16W-33N | | 24 |
| Briar Av. N&S .. 13W-36N | | 26 |
| Brierwood Ct. N&S ......14W-33N | | 25 |
| Brighton* E&W .. 14W-34N | | 25 |
| Bristol* NW&SE .... 14W-34N | | 25 |
| Brittany Ct. NE&SW .... 16W-33N | | 24 |
| Brookhaven Dr. NS&EW ......14W-34N | | 25 |
| Brookstone Ln. NW&SE .... 16W-33N | | 24 |
| Brown Cir. E&W..14W-35N | | 25 |
| Brown Pl. N&S .... 14W-34N | | 25 |
| Buckeridge Ct.* NW&SE ......14W-36N | | 17 |
| Buckingham N&S .. 14W-34N | | 25 |
| Burr Oak Dr. N&S ......17W-32N,16W-32N | | 24 |
| Butternut Av. ..15W-36N | | 17 |
| Calvin Ct. N&S.... 14W-33N | | 25 |
| Camden Dr. N&S .. 17W-35N | | 24 |
| Campbell Dr. NS&EW ......16W-33N | | 24 |
| Campbell Dr.* E&W ......16W-32N | | 25 |
| Canterbury Ct. N&S ......14W-34N | | 25 |
| Canterbury Ct.* E&W ......14W-36N | | 17 |
| Canyon Ct. NW&SE ......18W-35N | | 24 |
| Capital Ln. NE&SW ......17W-34N | | 24 |
| Carol Ln. E&W .. 15W-35N | | 25 |
| Carriage Rd. .. 15W-35N | | 25 |
| Cascade Way E&W ......18W-34N | | 24 |
| Castlewood Ln. E&W ......17W-35N | | 24 |
| Cedar Av. E&W .. 15W-35N | | 25 |
| Cedarwood Ct.* ......16W-35N | | 25 |
| Cemetary Rd. N&S ......16W-34N,16W-35N | | 24 |
| Centennial Ct. E&W ......14W-35N | | 25 |
| Chandler Rd. NE&SW ......16W-33N | | 24 |
| Charles Av. E&W .. 14W-34N | | 25 |
| Charles Av. N&S .. 14W-35N | | 25 |
| Chase Ct. N&S .... 16W-33N | | 24 |
| Chase Ct.* E&W....16W-32N | | 25 |
| Cherrywood Ct. NW&SE ......15W-36N | | 17 |
| Cheshire Rd. E&W..15W-35N | | 25 |
| Cheswick Dr. N&S..18W-35N | | 24 |
| Cheyenne Rd. E&W ......13W-36N | | 18 |
| Chip Ct. NE&SW .. 16W-33N | | 24 |
| Churchill Ln. NW&SE ......16W-34N | | 24 |
| Clark Dr. E&W .. 16W-33N | | 24 |
| Clavey Ln. N&S .. 18W-35N | | 24 |
| Clearview Av. E&W ......13W-35N | | 26 |
| Clearview Ct. E&W ......12W-35N | | 26 |
| Clem Dr. NW&SE .. 18W-35N | | 24 |
| Cliffwood Ln. N&S..18W-34N | | 24 |
| Club House Ct. N&S ......16W-33N | | 24 |
| Colby Ct. N&S .... 16W-33N | | 24 |
| Colby Rd. N&S .... 16W-33N | | 24 |
| Compton Ct.* E&W ......16W-32N | | 24 |
| Concord Sq. NS&EW ......14W-33N | | 25 |
| Concord Square NS&EW ......14W-33N | | 25 |
| Congress Ct. NW&SE ......17W-34N | | 24 |
| Constitution Av. NW&SE ......16W-36N | | 17 |
| Cornell Av. E&W....14W-33N | | 25 |
| Country Club Av. E&W ......13W-36N | | 18 |
| Country Tr. E&W .. 14W-33N | | 25 |
| Covenant Ct. NS&EW ......14W-33N | | 25 |
| Coventry Ln. N&S .. 15W-35N | | 25 |
| Crescent Av. E&W..13W-35N | | 26 |
| Cross Ct. NW&SE .. 14W-33N | | 25 |
| Cross Rd. N&S .... 14W-33N | | 25 |
| Crossland Blvd. E&W ......16W-33N | | 24 |
| Crossland Ct.* E&W ......16W-32N | | 25 |
| Crystal Pl. N&S .... 18W-34N | | 24 |
| Cule Ct. N&S .... 14W-33N | | 25 |
| Dada Dr. E&W ......18W-35N,17W-35N | | 24 |
| Darlene Ct. E&W .. 15W-34N | | 25 |
| Darlene Dr. E&W .. 15W-34N | | 25 |
| Darnell Ln. N&S .. 16W-33N | | 24 |
| David* NW&SE .... 16W-36N | | 17 |
| Delany Rd. N&S ......14W-34N,14W-36N | | 25 |
| Delaware Av. NS&EW ......16W-36N,15W-36N | | 17 |
| Depot Rd. N&S .... 14W-35N | | 25 |
| Desplaines Ct. N&S ......15W-33N | | 25 |
| Dillys Rd. N&S ......15W-35N,16W-37N | | 24 |
| Dixon Ct. NW&SE .. 16W-33N | | 24 |
| Dogwood Ln. N&S.. 16W-32N | | 25 |
| Dolcetto Dr. N&S .. 18W-35N | | 24 |
| Dorchester Av. E&W ......14W-34N,13W-34N | | 25 |
| Dordan Ct. N&S .. 16W-33N | | 24 |
| Dover Cir. E&W .. 17W-35N | | 24 |
| Drexel Dr. E&W .. 13W-34N | | 26 |
| Drury Ct. NW&SE .. 16W-33N | | 24 |
| Dunham Rd. E&W .. 16W-33N | | 24 |
| Eagle Ridge Rd. N&S ......16W-33N | | 24 |
| Easton Ct. N&S .. 17W-35N | | 24 |
| Eastwood Av. E&W ......14W-33N | | 25 |
| Eau Claire E&W .. 15W-35N | | 25 |
| Ebony Ct.* E&W .. 15W-36N | | 25 |
| Edington Ct. N&S .. 15W-35N | | 25 |
| Ellis Av. E&W ......14W-34N,14W-34N | | 25 |
| Elm Rd. NS&EW .. 14W-34N | | 25 |
| Elsie Av. N&S...... 15W-34N | | 25 |
| Emerald Av. .. 14W-35N | | 25 |
| Estate Cir. NW&SE ......16W-34N | | 24 |
| Estes St. N&S ......13W-34N,13W-35N | | 26 |
| Evergreen Dr. E&W ......15W-35N | | 25 |
| Fair Links Way NE&SW ......16W-35N | | 24 |
| Fairfax* N&S......14W-34N | | 25 |
| Farmgate Ct. N&S.. 14W-33N | | 25 |
| Farwell Ct. E&W ......16W-32N,16W-33N | | 25 |
| Farwell Ct. N&S .... 16W-33N | | 24 |
| Ferndale St. N&S ......13W-34N,13W-35N | | 26 |
| Fernwood* NW&SE ......14W-36N | | 17 |
| Fieldstone Ct. NW&SE ......14W-33N | | 25 |
| Finch Ct. E&W .... 14W-34N | | 25 |
| First Pl. E&W ...... 14W-34N | | 25 |
| First St. N&S ...... 14W-34N | | 25 |
| Florida Av. E&W .. 13W-36N | | 18 |
| Formoor Ln. N&S .. 16W-33N | | 25 |
| Fox Ln. NW&SE....15W-35N | | 25 |
| Fox Meadow N&S .. 15W-36N | | 17 |
| Foxboro Ln. NS&EW ......16W-34N | | 24 |
| Framingham Ct. N&S ......14W-33N | | 25 |
| Franklin Ct. N&S .. 15W-36N | | 17 |
| Fredrick* N&S ......14W-36N | | 17 |
| Freedom Ct. NW&SE ......17W-34N | | 24 |
| Fuller Rd. N&S ......15W-35N,15W-36N | | 25 |
| Gages Lake Rd. E&W ......16W-33N | | 25 |
| Gamay Ct. NW&SE ......18W-35N | | 24 |
| Garnacha Dr. E&W 18W-35N | | 24 |
| Gatewood Dr. NS&EW ......15W-36N | | 17 |
| Geneva Dr. NE&SW ......18W-34N | | 24 |
| George Ct.* N&S .. 14W-36N | | 17 |
| Gillings Dr. N&S .... 14W-34N | | 25 |
| Glen Flora Av. E&W ......13W-35N | | 26 |
| Glen Way E&W .... 16W-33N | | 24 |
| Glendale Dr. NW&SE ......15W-35N | | 25 |
| Gloster Ct. E&W....15W-35N | | 25 |
| Golf View Dr. NW&SE ......15W-35N | | 24 |
| Gould Av. N&S .... 14W-33N | | 26 |
| Gould St. N&S .... 14W-33N | | 26 |
| Grace St. N&S .... 13W-34N | | 26 |
| Grand Av. NW&SE ......18W-35N,13W-35N | | 24 |
| Grandmore Av. E&W ......14W-35N | | 26 |
| Grandview Av. E&W ......13W-35N | | 26 |
| Grandville Av. E&W ......13W-35N | | 26 |
| Grange Hall Rd. NE&SW ......18W-34N | | 24 |
| Grass Lake Rd. E&W ......16W-33N,15W-33N | | 24 |
| Great America Parkway N&S ......15W-35N | | 25 |
| Green Haven NS&EW ......14W-34N | | 25 |
| Greenbrier Ct. E&W ......13W-33N | | 26 |
| Greenleaf St. N&S ......13W-34N,13W-35N | | 26 |
| Greenview St. N&S ......13W-35N | | 26 |
| Greenwood Av. E&W ......13W-36N | | 18 |
| Grove Av. E&W ......15W-35N,13W-35N | | 25 |
| Gurnee Mills Blvd. NS&EW ......16W-35N,16W-36N | | 24 |
| Habitat Ct. NW&SE ......16W-34N | | 24 |
| Halifax Rd. N&S....16W-33N | | 24 |
| Hamilton Dr. E&W .. 17W-35N | | 24 |
| Hancock Ln. E&W .. 16W-36N | | 17 |
| Harper Av. E&W ......14W-34N,14W-35N | | 25 |
| Hartford Dr. N&S .. 17W-35N | | 24 |
| Hawthorne Av. N&S ......14W-34N,13W-34N | | 25 |
| Hawthorne St. N&S ......13W-35N | | 26 |
| Hazlewood Ct.* E&W ......15W-35N | | 25 |
| Heather Ridge Dr. E&W ......16W-33N | | 24 |
| Henry* NW&SE .. 14W-36N | | 17 |
| Hickory Haven Dr., E. N&S ......15W-35N | | 25 |
| Hickory Haven Dr., W. NS&EW......15W-35N | | 25 |
| Highland Av. .. 13W-36N | | 18 |
| Hill-n-Dale Ct. N&S .. 16W-34N | | 24 |
| Hillside Ct. E&W....17W-35N | | 24 |
| Hillview Dr. NW&SE ......18W-34N | | 24 |
| Holly Rd. NW&SE .. 16W-32N | | 25 |
| Hollyholk Ct.* E&W ......16W-34N | | 25 |
| Honey Suckle Ln. E&W ......16W-34N | | 24 |
| Hunt Club Ln. E&W ......17W-34N,17W-36N | | 24 |
| Independence Ct.* E&W ......14W-36N | | 17 |
| Indian Tr. E&W .... 16W-34N | | 24 |
| Inglenook Ln. NW&SE ......18W-35N | | 24 |
| Interstate 94 N&S .. 15W-35N | | 25 |
| Ironwood Ct. NW&SE ......15W-36N | | 17 |
| Jeffery Av. E&W....14W-34N | | 25 |
| Johns Manville Av. E&W ......13W-35N | | 26 |
| Joshua Ct.* E&W .. 16W-33N | | 25 |
| Keith Av. E&W .... 13W-35N | | 26 |
| Kensington Ct.* NS&EW ......14W-34N | | 25 |
| Kenwood Av. N&S ......14W-34N,13W-34N | | 25 |
| Kilbourne Rd. NE&SW ......14W-35N | | 25 |
| King's Ct. NW&SE..14W-33N | | 25 |
| King's Way N. E&W ......14W-33N | | 25 |
| King's Way W. N&S ......14W-33N | | 25 |
| Kingsbury Ct. N&S..17W-35N | | 24 |
| Kisten Ct. NE&SW..16W-33N | | 24 |
| Knob Hill Ln. E&W.. 16W-34N | | 24 |
| Knottingham Ln. N&S ......17W-35N | | 24 |
| Knowles Rd. NW&SE ......18W-35N | | 24 |
| Korbell Dr. NW&SE ......18W-35N | | 24 |
| Lake Park Av. E&W ......14W-34N | | 25 |
| Lakeside Dr. NS&EW ......16W-35N | | 24 |
| Laurel Ln. N&S .. 18W-35N | | 24 |
| Lauren Ct. N&S .... 17W-35N | | 24 |
| Lawrence Av. N&S 13W-34N | | 26 |
| Lawson Blvd. NS&EW ......16W-36N,15W-35N | | 17 |
| Lee Av. E&W ......14W-35N,13W-35N | | 25 |
| Lenox Ct. N&S .. 16W-34N | | 24 |
| Leonard Dr. N&S .. 16W-33N | | 24 |
| Leonard Dr. NE&SW ......16W-33N | | 24 |
| Leslie Ln. NS&EW .. 15W-35N | | 25 |
| Lexington Square, E. N&S ......14W-33N | | 25 |
| Liberty Ln. NE&SW ......16W-36N | | 17 |
| Lind Ln. N&S ...... 15W-35N | | 25 |
| Locust Ln. NW&SE ......16W-32N | | 25 |
| Lone Tree Ct. E&W ......16W-34N | | 24 |
| Long Hill Rd. NS&EW ......14W-33N | | 25 |
| Longmeadow Dr. E&W ......14W-33N | | 25 |
| Longwood Rd. NE&SW ......16W-32N | | 25 |
| Louis* NE&SW .. 14W-36N | | 17 |
| Madison Av. N&S .. 16W-36N | | 17 |
| Magnolia Av. N&S ......13W-34N,13W-35N | | 26 |
| Mahogany Ct.* E&W ......15W-35N | | 25 |
| Majestic Ct. N&S .. 14W-33N | | 25 |
| Manchester Ct. E&W ......13W-33N | | 26 |
| Maplewood Dr. NS&EW ......16W-33N,15W-33N | | 24 |
| Mayflower Ct. N&S ......15W-36N | | 17 |
| McClure Av. E&W .. 14W-34N | | 25 |
| Meadow Crest Cir. E&W ......13W-35N | | 26 |
| Meadow Lark Ct. E&W ......14W-34N | | 25 |
| Melon Ct. NE&SW..18W-35N | | 24 |
| Mendochino Rd. N&S ......18W-35N | | 24 |
| Merlot Ct. NW&SE..18W-35N | | 24 |
| Merritt Club Ln. N&S ......16W-32N | | 25 |
| Middle Rd. E&W....14W-33N | | 25 |
| Milan Way NE&SW ......18W-35N | | 24 |
| Milwaukee Av. NE&SW ......18W-35N,16W-35N | | 24 |
| Mint Haven N&S....14W-34N | | 25 |
| Mitchell Ct. NW&SE ......16W-33N | | 24 |
| Monterey Ct.* NW&SE ......14W-36N | | 17 |
| Morgan Ct. E&W .. 17W-35N | | 24 |
| Morningside Ct. E&W ......16W-34N | | 24 |
| Morrison Dr. E&W .. 13W-36N | | 26 |
| Mountain Ash Ct. E&W ......18W-34N | | 24 |
| N. Stratton Ln. E&W ......18W-35N | | 24 |
| Napa Dr. N&S .. 18W-35N | | 24 |
| Newbury Ct.* E&W ......16W-32N | | 25 |
| Newgate Ln. N&S .. 17W-35N | | 24 |
| Newport Ct.* E&W .. 16W-32N | | 25 |
| Norfolk* N&S ...... 14W-36N | | 17 |
| Norman Av. E&W .. 14W-34N | | 25 |
| North Av. E&W .... 14W-34N | | 25 |
| Northwestern Av. E&W ......13W-35N,13W-36N | | 26 |
| Nursery Dr. E&W .. 18W-35N | | 24 |
| O'Plaine Rd. N&S ......14W-33N,14W-34N | | 25 |
| Oak Ln. E&W ...... 15W-35N | | 25 |
| Oakview Ln. NE&SW ......15W-36N | | 17 |
| Oakwood St. N&S.. 13W-35N | | 26 |
| Oglesby Av. E&W .. 14W-34N | | 25 |
| Old Farm Ln. NW&SE ......16W-34N | | 24 |
| Old Grand Av. NW&SE ......14W-35N | | 25 |
| Old Oak Rd. NE&SW ......16W-32N | | 25 |
| Oriole Ct. E&W .. 14W-34N | | 25 |
| Oscar* E&W .... 14W-36N | | 17 |
| Oxford Cir.* NS&EW ......14W-36N | | 17 |
| Pacific Av. E&W .... 13W-35N | | 26 |
| Packard Ln. N&S .. 15W-33N | | 17 |
| Panorama Ln. E&W ......18W-35N | | 24 |
| Par Ct. N&S...... 16W-33N | | 24 |
| Parkside Ct. N&S .. 16W-33N | | 24 |
| Patriot Ct. NW&SE 17W-34N | | 24 |
| Pauly Dr. NW&SE ..15W-35N | | 25 |
| Pebble Creek Ct. E&W ......16W-33N | | 24 |
| Persimmon Way E&W ......16W-32N | | 24 |
| Pheasant Meadow Ct. E&W ......15W-36N | | 17 |
| Pilgrim's Path N&S 14W-33N | | 25 |
| Pine Ct. N&S ...... 15W-36N | | 17 |
| Pine Grove St. N&S ......13W-34N,13W-35N | | 26 |
| Pine Meadow N&S..15W-36N | | 17 |
| Pine Tree Dr. NS&EW ......15W-35N | | 25 |
| Pinewood Rd. NE&SW ......15W-35N | | 25 |
| Plainview Rd..16W-34N | | 24 |
| Plymouth Ln. N&S..14W-33N | | 25 |
| Ponderosa NW&SE ......15W-35N | | 25 |
| Porett St. E&W .... 13W-35N | | 26 |
| Portage Ln. NE&SW ......15W-35N | | 25 |
| Portsmouth Cir. ......17W-35N | | 24 |
| Prairie Creek Dr. NW&SE ......16W-36N,16W-35N | | 17 |
| Prairie Oak Rd. E&W ......15W-35N | | 25 |
| Presidential Dr. NE&SW ......17W-34N | | 24 |
| Princeton Ct.* N&S ......14W-36N | | 17 |
| Providence Rd. E&W ......14W-33N | | 25 |
| Quail Haven Ct. E&W ......16W-34N | | 24 |
| Queen Anne Ln. E&W ......14W-35N | | 25 |
| Quincy Ct. NE&SW ......16W-36N | | 17 |
| Ralph Av. N&S .... 14W-35N | | 25 |
| Raven Ct. E&W .. 14W-34N | | 25 |
| Ravine Dr. N&S .. 15W-36N | | 17 |
| Ravinia Dr. N&S....18W-35N | | 24 |
| Red Pine Av. E&W..15W-36N | | 17 |
| Regency Ct. E&W..16W-33N | | 24 |
| Revere Ct. E&W....17W-35N | | 24 |
| Ridge Dr. E&W .. 15W-35N | | 25 |
| Ridwell Dr.* E&W .. 16W-32N | | 25 |
| Rippling Ridge Ct. E&W ......18W-34N | | 24 |
| Robin Ct. E&W .. 14W-34N | | 25 |
| Rockpoint Ct. E&W ......15W-35N | | 25 |
| Rogers Rd. N&S....15W-35N | | 25 |
| Rolling Green Dr. NE&SW ......16W-33N | | 24 |
| Rolling Woods E&W ......16W-32N | | 25 |
| Rosemary Ln. E&W ......15W-35N | | 17 |
| Route 120 E&W .. 15W-33N | | 25 |
| Route 132 NW&SE ......18W-35N,13W-34N | | 24 |
| Route 21 NE&SW ......15W-34N,14W-35N | | 25 |
| Russell Av. E&W ......14W-33N,14W-34N | | 25 |
| Ryan Ct. E&W .. 13W-35N | | 18 |
| S. Stratton Ln. E&W ......17W-35N | | 24 |
| Sage Ct. N&S .. 18W-35N | | 24 |
| Salem Ct.* E&W .. 14W-36N | | 17 |
| Sanders Ct. N&S .. 16W-33N | | 24 |
| Sandwedge Pl. N&S ......16W-33N | | 24 |
| Saratoga Ct. N&S.. 16W-34N | | 24 |
| Scot Ct. N&S .. 16W-34N | | 24 |
| Scotch Ct.* NE&SW ......14W-36N | | 17 |
| Scott Ct. N&S....16W-33N | | 25 |
| Sedge Ct. E&W .. 18W-35N | | 24 |
| Sedona Ct. E&W .. 15W-39N | | 17 |
| Sequia Ct.* N&S .. 18W-35N | | 24 |
| Shadow Rock Ct. E&W ......14W-35N | | 25 |
| Shagbark Ct. 15W-35N | | 25 |
| Sheffield* E&W .. 14W-34N | | 25 |
| Shepard Ct. N&S.. 16W-33N | | 24 |
| Sherman Av. E&W..13W-35N | | 26 |

| Street | Grid | Page |
|---|---|---|
| Sherwoood Ct.* NW&SE | 14W-36N | 17 |
| Sierra Pl. N&S | 18W-34N | 24 |
| Sizer Ct. E&W | 16W-33N | 24 |
| Skokie Hwy. N&S | 13W-34N,14W-36N | 26 |
| Sleepy Hollow Ln. NS&EW | 16W-34N | 24 |
| Snowcap Ct. E&W | 18W-34N | 24 |
| Solomon* E&W | 14W-36N | 17 |
| Somerset Ct.* N&S | 14W-36N | 17 |
| South Rd. E&W | 15W-34N,15W-35N | 25 |
| Southridge Dr. E&W | 16W-34N | 24 |
| Spinney Run Dr. NE&SW | 16W-33N | 24 |
| Springhaven Dr. E&W | 14W-34N | 25 |
| Spruce St. N&S | 15W-35N | 25 |
| Sprucewood Ln. NE&SW | 15W-36N | 17 |
| St. Andrews Ln. NW&SE | 17W-34N | 24 |
| St. Paul Av. NE&SW | 15W-35N | 25 |
| Stearns School Rd. E&W | 16W-36N,15W-36N | 17 |
| Stewart Ct. N&S | 15W-33N | 25 |
| Stonebrook Dr. N&S | 17W-35N | 24 |
| Stonebrook Dr. N&S | 17W-35N | 24 |
| Stony Island Av. E&W | 14W-34N | 25 |
| Stout Ct. N&S | 15W-33N | 25 |
| Stratford Dr. N&S | 15W-35N | 25 |
| Suda Dr. N&S | 13W-34N | 26 |
| Suffolk Ct. E&W | 17W-34N | 24 |
| Sumner Ct. | 17W-35N | 24 |
| Sunnyside Av. N&S | 14W-33N | 25 |
| Sunrise NE&SW | 15W-35N | 25 |
| Swanson Ct. NS&EW | 13W-36N | 18 |
| Sycamore Ln.* E&W | 16W-35N | 25 |
| Tanglewood Dr. NS&EW | 14W-33N | 25 |
| Taylor Dr. N&S | 16W-33N | 24 |
| Thackery Ln. NW&SE | 16W-32N | 25 |
| Timber Ct. N&S | 15W-36N | 17 |
| Timsbury Ct. NW&SE | 18W-35N | 24 |
| Treetop Ln. N&S | 18W-34N | 24 |
| Tri State North Tollway N&S | 15W-33N,16W-36N | 25 |
| Tri-State Pkwy. NS&EW | 16W-35N | 24 |
| U.S. Route 41 N&S | 13W-35N | 26 |
| U.S. Route 45 N&S | 18W-34N,18W-35N | 24 |
| University Av. N&S | 14W-34N,13W-34N | 25 |
| Valley Ln. N&S | 16W-33N | 24 |
| Victoria* NW&SE | 14W-34N | 25 |
| View Ct.* N&S | 16W-35N | 25 |
| Village Ln. N&S | 18W-35N | 24 |
| Vineyard Dr. N&S | 18W-35N | 24 |
| Virginia* NE&SW | 14W-36N | 17 |
| Vista Dr. E&W | 18W-35N | 24 |
| Vista Dr. N&S | 18W-35N | 24 |
| Vose Dr. N&S | 16W-33N | 24 |
| Wakefield Rd. NW&SE | 16W-33N | 24 |
| Wallace Ln. N&S | 18W-35N | 24 |
| Washington St. E&W | 18W-34N,13W-34N | 24 |
| Waterfall Ct. NW&SE | 18W-34N | 24 |
| Wausau Ln. N&S | 15W-35N,15W-36N | 25 |
| Waveland Av. NW&SE | 13W-34N | 26 |
| Waveland N&S | 13W-34N,13W-35N | 26 |
| Wellington Ct.* N&S | 14W-34N | 25 |
| West St N&S | 14W-34N | 25 |
| Westbrook Ln. NE&SW | 16W-36N | 17 |
| Westfield Dr. N&S | 15W-36N | 17 |
| White Barn Ln. N&S | 16W-34N | 24 |
| White Ct. E&W | 16W-33N | 24 |
| White Oak Ct. N&S | 14W-33N | 25 |
| White Pine Way N&S | 16W-32N | 25 |
| Whitney Ct. NW&SE | 16W-33N | 25 |
| Wilber Ct. NE&SW | 15W-33N | 25 |
| Wild Flower Ln. N&S | 16W-34N | 24 |
| Williams Ct. N&S | 16W-34N | 24 |
| Williamsburg Av. E&W | 14W-33N | 25 |
| Willow Ln. N&S | 15W-35N | 25 |
| Wiltshire Ct.* NE&SW | 14W-34N | 25 |
| Wind Song Ct. NW&SE | 16W-36N | 17 |
| Windemere Cir. E&W | 18W-35N | 24 |
| Windwood E&W | 15W-35N | 25 |
| Winona Ln. E&W | 15W-35N | 25 |
| Woodbury Cir. NW&SE | 18W-35N | 24 |
| Woodhill Dr. N&S | 15W-35N | 25 |
| Woodlawn Av. E&W | 14W-34N,13W-34N | 25 |
| Yorkshire* N&S | 14W-34N | 25 |

## Hainesville

| Street | Grid | Page |
|---|---|---|
| Antioch St. N&S | 22W-33N | 22 |
| Belvidere Rd. E&W | 22W-33N,21W-33N | 22 |
| Buck Dr. E&W | 21W-33N | 22 |
| Caribou Dr. N&S | 21W-33N | 22 |
| Center Dr. NW&SE | 22W-33N | 22 |
| Christine Dr. E&W | 21W-33N | 22 |
| Deer Crossing Ct. N&S | 21W-33N | 22 |
| Deer Lake Dr. E&W | 21W-33N | 22 |
| Deer Point Dr. N&S | 21W-33N | 22 |
| Deer Run Rd. E&W | 21W-33N | 22 |
| Deerview Dr. N&S | 21W-33N | 22 |
| Fawn Ln. E&W | 21W-33N | 22 |
| Gage St. N&S | 22W-33N | 22 |
| Hainesville Rd. N&S | 22W-33N | 22 |
| Hunters Way E&W | 21W-33N | 22 |
| Katherin Dr. E&W | 21W-33N | 22 |
| Lisk Dr. N&S | 21W-33N | 22 |
| North St. E&W | 21W-33N | 22 |
| Pineview Dr. NW&SE | 22W-33N | 22 |
| Route 120 E&W | 22W-33N | 22 |
| Route 134 E&W | 22W-33N | 22 |
| Washington St. E&W | 22W-33N | 22 |
| White Trail Dr. N&S | 21W-33N | 22 |

## Half Day

| Street | Grid | Page |
|---|---|---|
| Andover Ct. E&W | 16W-23N | 48 |
| Cemetery Rd. E&W | 15W-23N | 49 |
| Choate Ct. N&S | 16W-23N | 48 |
| Dartmouth Ct. E&W | 16W-23N | 48 |
| Exeter Ct. E&W | 16W-23N | 48 |
| Groton Ct. E&W | 16W-23N | 48 |
| Hotchkiss Ct. N&S | 16W-23N | 48 |
| Middlesex Ct. E&W | 16W-23N | 48 |
| Northfield Ct. E&W | 16W-23N | 48 |
| Trafalgar Square N&S | 15W-23N | 49 |
| Westgate Dr. NS&EW | 15W-23N | 49 |

## Hawthorn Woods

| Street | Grid | Page |
|---|---|---|
| Aberdeen Rd. E&W | 20W-24N | 39 |
| Acorn Dr. N&S | 23W-24N | 38 |
| Aho Dr. E&W | 19W-25N | 39 |
| Albert Cir. NW&SE | 19W-24N | 39 |
| Arrowwood Dr. N&S | 23W-25N | 38 |
| Arthur Ct. N&S | 22W-24N | 38 |
| Bent Tree Ct. NW&SE | 24W-25N | 38 |
| Birch Lake Rd. E&W | 22W-25N | 38 |
| Bixtone Path NE&SW | 24W-25N | 38 |
| Blackhawk Rd. N&S | 20W-25N | 39 |
| Bluebird Ct. N&S | 19W-26N | 38 |
| Bluejay Ln. E&W | 22W-26N | 38 |
| Boxwood Dr. E&W | 23W-25N | 38 |
| Bridle Path NW&SE | 23W-26N | 38 |
| Brierwoods Ln. NS&EW | 23W-24N | 38 |
| Brighton Ct. E&W | 19W-25N | 39 |
| Bruce Cir., N. NS&EW | 23W-24N | 38 |
| Byron Ct. N&S | 22W-25N | 38 |
| Cambridge Dr. N&S | 20W-25N | 39 |
| Canterbury Ln. E&W | 20W-24N | 39 |
| Cardinal Dr. N&S | 21W-26N | 38 |
| Carlisle Rd. NE&SW | 20W-24N,20W-25N | 39 |
| Cayuga Ct. E&W | 19W-25N | 39 |
| Chancellor Ct. NW&SE | 22W-24N | 38 |
| Chantilly Ln. N&S | 23W-24N,22W-24N | 38 |
| Cherry Hill Cir. N&S | 19W-24N | 39 |
| Cir. | 20W-24N | 38 |
| Cobblewood Ln. NW&SE | 23W-25N | 38 |
| Condor Ct. E&W | 21W-24N | 38 |
| Conesug Ct. E&W | 19W-25N | 39 |
| Cooper St. N&S | 22W-25N | 38 |
| Copperfield Dr. NS&EW | 23W-24N,22W-24N | 38 |
| Croydon Rd. N&S | 20W-25N | 39 |
| Darlington Rd. N&S | 20W-24N | 39 |
| David Ln. N&S | 22W-25N | 38 |
| Deer Point Dr. NS&EW | 22W-24N,22W-25N | 38 |
| Derby Ln. N&S | 23W-25N | 38 |
| Dorset Ct. NW&SE | 23W-25N | 38 |
| E. Lynn Dr. N&S | 21W-24N | 38 |
| Echo Ct. NW&SE | 23W-24N | 38 |
| Edward Ln. E&W | 20W-24N | 38 |
| Elm St. N&S | 21W-24N,20W-24N | 38 |
| Elmwood Dr. NW&SE | 23W-24N | 38 |
| Equestrian Way N&S | 23W-25N | 38 |
| Essex Ct. E&W | 20W-24N | 39 |
| Fairfield Rd. N&S | 22W-25N | 38 |
| Falcon Dr. E&W | 22W-26N,21W-26N | 38 |
| Falkirk Rd. E&W | 20W-24N | 39 |
| Fox Hunt Ct. NW&SE | 24W-25N | 38 |
| Fox Hunt Tr. NE&SW | 24W-25N | 38 |
| Furlong Dr. NE&SW | 23W-25N | 38 |
| Gentry Dr. N&S | 23W-24N,23W-25N | 38 |
| Gilmer Rd. E&W | 19W-24N,19W-26N | 39 |
| Gino Ln. NW&SE | 19W-24N | 39 |
| Glen Rd. E&W | 21W-24N,20W-24N | 38 |
| Goldfinch Ct. E&W | 22W-26N | 38 |
| Govenors Way E&W | 23W-25N | 38 |
| Greenbriar Ln. NS&EW | 19W-25N | 39 |
| Hampton Ln. E&W | 20W-24N | 39 |
| Harvard Ln. N&S | 20W-25N | 39 |
| Harvest Glen Ct. N&S | 22W-24N | 38 |
| Hawthorne Dr. E&W | 21W-24N | 38 |
| Heather Ln. E&W | 20W-24N | 38 |
| Heron Ct. E&W | 20W-24N | 39 |
| Hickory Rd. E&W | 21W-24N | 38 |
| Highland Ter. N&S | 21W-24N | 38 |
| Highpoint Cir. NW&SE | 22W-25N | 38 |
| Highpoint Dr. NE&SW | 22W-25N | 38 |
| Highview Cir. N&S | 20W-24N | 39 |
| Hillcrest Dr. N&S | 20W-25N | 47 |
| Hilltop Ct. NE&SW | 19W-23N | 47 |
| Holmes Av. NE&SW | 22W-25N | 38 |
| Indian Creek Rd. E&W | 20W-25N,19W-25N | 39 |
| James Ct. NW&SE | 20W-24N | 39 |
| James St. N&S | 20W-24N | 39 |
| Jamie Ln. E&W | 20W-24N | 39 |
| Jane Ct. N&S | 20W-24N | 39 |
| John Dr. NS&EW | 20W-24N | 39 |
| Juel Cir. NE&SW | 21W-24N,20W-24N | 38 |
| Juel Ct. E&W | 20W-24N | 39 |
| Karen Ct. N&S | 19W-24N | 39 |
| Kathy Ln. E&W | 22W-25N,21W-25N | 38 |
| Keuka Ct. E&W | 19W-25N | 39 |
| Krueger Rd. E&W | 22W-25N | 38 |
| Lagoon Dr. NS&EW | 21W-24N,20W-24N | 38 |
| Lakeview Rd. NS&EW | 20W-23N,19W-23N | 47 |
| Lancelot Ln. NW&SE | 21W-24N | 38 |
| Lisa Ln. N&S | 20W-24N | 39 |
| Lydia Ct. E&W | 23W-24N | 38 |
| Lynn Dr. N&S | 21W-24N | 38 |
| Magnolia Pkwy. E&W | 19W-24N | 39 |
| Mark Dr. N&S | 20W-24N | 39 |
| Mary Ln. E&W | 19W-24N | 39 |
| McGregor Ct. E&W | 21W-24N | 38 |
| McHenry Rd. NW&SE | 24W-25N,20W-23N | 38 |
| Meadow Ln. N&S | 22W-24N | 38 |
| Meadowlark Dr. NS&EW | 22W-26N | 38 |
| Melody Ln. (Cherry Rd.) N&S | 21W-23N,21W-24N | 47 |
| Midlothian Rd. NE&SW | 22W-24N,21W-25N | 38 |
| Moorgate Trail NW&SE | 24W-25N | 38 |
| Mulberry Dr. NE&SW | 22W-24N | 38 |
| N. Bruce Cir. E&W | 23W-24N | 38 |
| N. Highview Cir. N&S | 20W-24N | 39 |
| Newbury Ct. E&W | 20W-24N | 39 |
| Newhaven Dr. E&W | 23W-25N | 38 |
| Norbert Ct. E&W | 20W-24N | 39 |
| North Trail NS&EW | 23W-25N,23W-26N | 38 |
| Oak Ln. NW&SE | 21W-24N | 38 |
| Old Barn Rd. NS&EW | 20W-23N,19W-23N | 47 |
| Old Lake Rd. NS&EW | 22W-24N | 38 |
| Oneida Ln. NS&EW | 20W-25N | 39 |
| Onondaga Dr. E&W | 20W-25N,19W-25N | 39 |
| Orchard Ln. N&S | 21W-24N | 38 |
| Oriole Ct. NW&SE | 22W-26N | 38 |
| Overlook Dr. SE&NW | 20W-25N | 38 |
| Paddock Ct. N&S | 23W-25N | 38 |
| Peregrine Ln. NS&EW | 21W-26N | 38 |
| Pheasant Run Rd. NS&EW | 24W-25N | 38 |
| Piper Ln. N&S | 21W-24N | 38 |
| Princeton Ct. N&S | 21W-25N | 38 |
| Princeton Ln. NW&SE | 20W-25N | 39 |
| Quail Hollow Ct. N&S | 20W-24N | 47 |
| Quail Hollow Rd. N&S | 20W-23N | 47 |
| Redwood Ln. N&S | 23W-25N | 38 |
| Robert Ct. E&W | 20W-24N | 39 |
| Robin Crest Rd. N&S | 23W-24N | 38 |
| Rosewood Dr. NS&EW | 21W-24N | 38 |
| Rutgers Ct. N&S | 20W-25N | 39 |
| S. Bruce Cir. E&W | 23W-24N | 38 |
| S. Higgins Cir. E&W | 20W-24N | 39 |
| Sandpiper Ln. E&W | 22W-26N | 38 |
| Schrewman Rd. E&W | 22W-26N | 38 |
| Seneca East Av. N&S | 19W-25N | 39 |
| Seneca West Av. N&S | 20W-25N | 39 |
| Sequoia Rd. NS&EW | 20W-25N | 39 |
| Shearwater Ct. E&W | 22W-26N | 38 |
| Shenandoah Ln. N&S | 20W-25N | 39 |
| Squire Rd. NE&SW | 21W-24N | 38 |
| St. John Dr. N&S | 19W-24N | 39 |
| Steeplchase Dr. NS&EW | 23W-25N | 38 |
| Stone Creek Ct. N&S | 23W-24N,22W-24N | 38 |
| Stonehaven Dr. N&S | 20W-24N | 39 |
| Sunset Ct. NW&SE | 20W-23N | 47 |
| Sycamore Dr. NW&SE | 23W-25N | 38 |
| Tanglewood Ct. N&S | 24W-24N | 38 |
| Tanglewood Ln. E&W | 24W-24N | 38 |
| Thornfield Ln. NW&SE | 24W-25N | 38 |
| Trent Rd. N&S | 20W-24N | 39 |
| University Cir. NE&SW | 20W-25N | 39 |
| Victoria Ln. N&S | 21W-24N | 38 |
| W. Lynn Dr. N&S | 21W-24N | 38 |
| Wakla Ct. E&W | 20W-25N | 39 |
| Walnut Dr. N&S | 21W-24N | 38 |
| Washitay Av. NE&SW | 20W-25N,19W-25N | 39 |
| Wayne Ln. N&S | 23W-24N | 38 |
| Wedgewood Dr. NS&EW | 23W-24N,22W-24N | 38 |
| Westwind Ct. E&W | 23W-25N | 38 |
| Whitman Ter. E&W | 22W-25N | 38 |
| Wild Way E&W | 20W-24N | 39 |
| Winding Branch Rd. E&W | 24W-25N | 38 |
| Wooded Ln. N&S | 24W-25N,24W-26N | 38 |
| Yale Ct. E&W | 20W-25N | 39 |

## Highland Park

| Street | Grid | Page |
|---|---|---|
| 'A' St. NW&SE | 8W-23N | 51 |
| 'B' St. NW&SE | 9W-24N,8W-23N | 43 |
| 'F' St. NW&SE | 8W-23N | 51 |
| 'G' St. N&S | 8W-23N | 51 |
| 'H' St. N&S | 8W-23N | 51 |
| Acorn Ln. N&S | 9W-20N | 51 |
| Alta Ln. E&W | 10W-22N | 50 |
| Alvin Pl. NE&SW | 7W-21N | 51 |
| Andean Pl. E&W | 9W-22N | 51 |
| Apple Tree Ln. E&W | 9W-21N | 51 |
| Applewood Ct. E&W | 9W-22N | 51 |
| Arbor Av. N&S | 10W-23N | 50 |
| Arlington Av. N&S | 9W-23N | 51 |
| Ashland Pl. N&S | 7W-20N | 51 |
| Aspen Ln. N&S | 8W-20N | 51 |
| Aster Dr. E&W | 10W-22N | 50 |
| Athletic Field Ln. N&S | 9W-22N | 51 |
| Atlas Ct. N&S | 10W-21N | 50 |
| Auburn Av. E&W | 10W-23N | 50 |
| Auburn Ct. E&W | 9W-23N | 51 |
| Audubon Pl. E&W | 9W-24N | 43 |
| Ava St. NE&SW | 7W-21N | 51 |
| Avignon Ct.* E&W | 9W-21N | 51 |
| Baldwin Rd. NW&SE | 7W-21N | 51 |
| Balsam Rd. E&W | 9W-20N | 51 |
| Barberry Rd. NS&EW | 9W-20N,9W-21N | 51 |
| Barnard Ln. N&S | 9W-21N | 51 |
| Beaupre Ct.* E&W | 9W-21N | 51 |
| Beech Ln. NW&SE | 7W-21N | 51 |
| Beech St. NE&SW | 7W-21N | 51 |
| Belle Av. NE&SW | 8W-22N | 51 |
| Bellevue Pl. NE&SW | 7W-21N | 51 |
| Bentley Rd. N&S | 10W-23N | 50 |
| Berkeley Rd. E&W | 10W-22N | 50 |
| Bertram Ln. E&W | 9W-20N | 51 |
| Beverly Pl. N&S | 9W-21N,9W-22N | 51 |
| Birch Av. E&W | 9W-21N | 51 |
| Birchwood Av. E&W | 9W-22N | 51 |
| Birchwood Ct. E&W | 10W-24N | 43 |
| Blackhawk Rd. NW&SE | 7W-20N | 51 |
| Blackstone Pl. E&W | 7W-20N | 51 |
| Bloom St. NE&SW | 8W-23N | 51 |
| Blossom Ct. NE&SW | 9W-20N | 51 |
| Bob-O-Link Rd. E&W | 9W-21N,8W-21N | 51 |
| Boxer Ct. E&W | 10W-22N | 50 |
| Braeburn Ln. E&W | 7W-20N | 51 |
| Braeside Pl. | 7W-20N | 51 |
| Briar Ln. N&S | 9W-20N | 51 |
| Briarcliff Ln. E&W | 10W-23N | 50 |
| Briargate Dr. NW&SE | 10W-21N | 50 |
| Briarwood Pl. E&W | 7W-20N | 51 |
| Brittany Rd. E&W | 8W-21N | 51 |
| Broadview Av. NW&SE | 8W-21N,7W-20N | 51 |
| Bronson Ln. N&S | 7W-20N | 51 |
| Brook Rd. N&S | 9W-24N | 43 |
| Brown Ct. E&W | 10W-23N | 50 |
| Brownville Rd. E&W | 7W-20N | 51 |
| Burchell Ln. N&S | 9W-23N | 51 |
| Burr Oaks Ln. E&W | 9W-20N | 51 |
| Burton Av. NW&SE | 7W-20N,7W-21N | 51 |
| Byron Ln. N&S | 10W-22N | 50 |
| Calais Dr. N&S | 9W-20N | 51 |
| Cambridge Dr. E&W | 10W-23N | 50 |
| Cardinal Ln. N&S | 10W-23N | 50 |
| Cardinal Ln. N&S | 10W-23N | 50 |
| Carlyle Ter. E&W | 8W-21N | 51 |
| Carol Ct. E&W | 7W-20N | 51 |
| Cary Av. E&W | 7W-21N | 51 |
| Castlewood Rd. E&W | 10W-21N | 50 |
| Cavell Av. N&S | 9W-21N | 51 |
| Cedar Av. E&W | 7W-21N | 51 |
| Centenial Ln. S | 10W-23N | 50 |
| Centenial Ln. NW&SE | 10W-23N | 50 |
| Centennial Pkwy NW&SE | 10W-23N | 50 |
| Centerfield Ct. | 9W-22N | 51 |
| Central Av. NE&SW | 8W-22N | 51 |
| Central Ct. E&W | 8W-22N | 51 |
| Chantilly Blvd. E&W | 9W-20N | 51 |
| Charal Ln. NW&SE | 9W-20N | 51 |
| Chatham Cir. N&S | 7W-20N | 51 |
| Chaucer Ln. N&S | 8W-21N | 51 |
| Cherokee Rd. E&W | 7W-20N | 51 |
| Cherry Ln. E&W | 9W-20N | 51 |
| Chicago Av. E&W | 8W-23N | 51 |
| Churchill Ct. N&S | 11W-22N | 50 |
| Churchill Ln. E&W | 10W-22N | 50 |
| Clavey Ct. N&S | 8W-20N | 51 |
| Clavey Ln. NW&SE | 8W-20N | 51 |
| Clavey Rd. E&W | 9W-20N,8W-20N | 51 |
| Clifton Av. N&S | 9W-22N | 51 |
| Cloverdale Av. N&S | 10W-22N | 50 |
| Cofton Av. N&S | 8W-21N | 51 |
| College Pl. E&W | 9W-24N | 43 |
| Compton Av. N&S | 9W-23N | 51 |
| Comstock Pl. E&W | 7W-20N | 51 |
| Concorde Cir.* E&W | 9W-21N | 51 |
| Concorde Dr. NW&SE | 9W-21N | 51 |
| Conventry Ln. E&W | 9W-21N | 51 |
| Cottonwood Ct. NW&SE | 10W-23N | 50 |
| Country Ln. NE&SW | 9W-21N | 51 |
| County Line Rd. E&W | 8W-20N,8W-21N | 51 |
| Court Av. E&W | 8W-21N | 51 |
| Crawford Pl. NE&SW | 8W-21N,7W-21N | 51 |

| Entry | Grid | Page |
|---|---|---|
| Crescent Ct. NE&SW | 7W-22N | 51 |
| Crofton Av. N&S | 8W-21N | 51 |
| Crofton Ct. N&S | 8W-21N | 51 |
| Daffodil Ct. A | 10W-23N | 50 |
| Dale Av. NW&SE | 8W-22N | 51 |
| Dato Av. N&S | 9W-23N | 51 |
| Dean Av. NE&SW | 7W-20N,7W-21N | 51 |
| Deer Creek Pkwy. N&S | 8W-20N | 51 |
| Deere Park Ln. | 6W-20N | 51 |
| Deerfield Ct. E&W | 9W-21N | 51 |
| Deerfield Pl. N&S | 9W-21N | 51 |
| Deerfield Rd. NS&EW | 9W-21N,8W-21N | 51 |
| Dell Ln. N&S | 7W-20N | 51 |
| Dell Pl. N&S | 7W-20N | 51 |
| Delta Rd. E&W | 7W-20N | 51 |
| Derrick St. N&S | 9W-23N | 51 |
| Detamble Av. NE&SW | 8W-21N | 51 |
| Devonshire Ct. NW&SE | 9W-21N | 51 |
| Division St. E&W | 9W-21N | 51 |
| Driscoll Ct. E&W | 8W-21N | 51 |
| Dryden Ln. E&W | 8W-21N | 51 |
| Eastwood Av. N&S | 10W-21N | 50 |
| Eaton Ct. NE&SW | 10W-23N | 50 |
| Edens Expwy. NW&SE | 8W-20N | 51 |
| Edgecliff Dr. E&W | 8W-23N | 51 |
| Edgewood Ct. N&S | 9W-20N,9W-21N | 51 |
| Edgewood Rd. E&W | 9W-20N,8W-21N | 51 |
| Egandale Rd. NW&SE | 8W-22N | 51 |
| Elder Ln. NW&SE | 6W-20N | 51 |
| Elridge Cir. N&S | 8W-20N | 51 |
| Elm Av. N&S | 8W-22N | 51 |
| Elm Pl. E&W | 8W-22N | 51 |
| Elmwood Dr. N&S | 8W-22N | 51 |
| Emerald Woods Ln. NE&SW | 10W-22N | 50 |
| Euclid Av. E&W | 9W-23N | 51 |
| Euclid Ct E&W | 9W-23N | 51 |
| Exmoor Av. N&S | 9W-22N | 51 |
| Fairview Rd. E&W | 8W-21N | 51 |
| Ferndale Av. N&S | 9W-21N | 51 |
| First St. NW&SE | 9W-22N | 51 |
| Flora Pl. E&W | 7W-20N | 51 |
| Florence Pl. N&S | 8W-21N | 51 |
| Forest Av. N&S | 7W-21N | 51 |
| Fredrickson Pl. NE&SW | 9W-21N | 51 |
| Freesia Ct. E&W | 9W-20N | 50 |
| Friar Tuck Av. E&W | 10W-22N | 50 |
| Ft. Sheridan Av. N&S | 8W-23N | 51 |
| Garland Av. E&W | 10W-21N | 50 |
| Glencoe Av. NW&SE | 8W-21N | 51 |
| Glenview Av. E&W | 8W-22N | 51 |
| Golf Av. E&W | 9W-21N,8W-21N | 51 |
| Grange Av. N&S | 10W-22N | 50 |
| Gray Av. E&W | 8W-21N | 51 |
| Great Elm Ln. E&W | 8W-21N | 51 |
| Green Bay Rd. NW&SE | 8W-23N,7W-20N | 51 |
| Greenwood Av. N&S | 9W-23N | 51 |
| Grove Av. E&W | 9W-21N | 51 |
| Groveland Av. N&S | 7W-20N | 51 |
| Half Day Rd. E&W | 11W-23N,9W-23N | 50 |
| Halsted St. E&W | 8W-21N | 51 |
| Harvard Ct. E&W | 9W-22N | 51 |
| Hastings Av. N&S | 7W-20N | 51 |
| Havenwood Ct. NE&SW | 7W-20N | 51 |
| Hawthorne St. N&S | 7W-21N | 51 |
| Hazel Av. N&S | 8W-22N | 51 |
| Heather Ln. E&W | 9W-21N | 51 |
| Hedge Run E&W | 7W-20N | 51 |
| Hemlock Ln. N&S | 9W-21N | 51 |
| Hiawatha Ct. E&W | 8W-20N | 51 |
| Hiawatha Tr. N&S | 8W-20N | 51 |
| Hickory St. NE&SW | 8W-22N | 51 |
| Hidden Ridge Cir. N&S | 10W-21N | 50 |
| Hidden Ridge Ln. E&W | 10W-21N | 50 |
| Highland Pl. NS&EW | 7W-20N | 51 |
| Highmoor Rd. N&S | 10W-22N | 50 |
| Hill St. E&W | 9W-24N | 43 |
| Hillcrest Av. NE&SW | 10W-21N | 50 |
| Hillside Dr. NW&SE | 7W-20N | 51 |
| Holly Rd. E&W | 10W-22N | 50 |
| Homewood Av. E&W | 8W-22N | 51 |
| Huntington Ln. E&W | 9W-21N | 51 |
| Hyacinth Pl. E&W | 9W-24N | 43 |
| Hybernia Dr. NS&EW | 10W-22N,10W-23N | 51 |
| Idlewild Ln. N&S | 9W-23N | 51 |
| Indian Ln. NW&SE | 7W-20N | 51 |
| Iris Ln. E&W | 7W-20N | 51 |
| Ivy Ln. E&W | 6W-20N | 51 |
| Jasmine Ct. NW&SE | 10W-23N | 50 |
| Johnston Loop NS&EW | 8W-23N | 51 |
| Judson Av. NW&SE | 7W-21N | 51 |
| Keats Ct. N&S | 10W-22N | 50 |
| Keats Ln. E&W | 10W-22N | 50 |
| Kelly Ln. N&S | 11W-23N | 50 |
| Kent Av. E&W | 9W-23N | 51 |
| Kimball Rd. E&W | 8W-21N | 51 |
| Kimballwood Ln. E&W | 8W-21N | 51 |
| Kincaid Av. N&S | 7W-20N | 51 |
| Kipling Ct. E&W | 10W-23N | 50 |
| Kipling Ln. N&S | 10W-23N | 50 |
| Knollwood Ln. NE&SW | 7W-21N | 51 |
| Krenn Av. NE&SW | 9W-24N | 43 |
| Lake Av. NW&SE | 7W-21N | 51 |
| Lake Cook Rd. E&W | 9W-20N | 51 |
| Lakeside Manor Pl. N&S | 6W-20N | 51 |
| Lakeside Pl. N&S | 7W-20N,6W-20N | 51 |
| Lakeview Av. N&S | 8W-23N | 51 |
| Lakeview Ter. E&W | 6W-20N | 51 |
| Lakewood Pl. E&W | 7W-20N | 51 |
| Lambert Tree Av. E&W | 7W-20N | 51 |
| Lancelot Av. E&W | 9W-22N | 51 |
| Larkspur Dr. N&S | 8W-20N | 51 |
| Laurel Av. N&S | 8W-22N | 51 |
| Lauretta Av. N&S | 8W-23N | 51 |
| Lawrence Ln. E&W | 9W-20N | 51 |
| Leslee Ln. NE&SW | 7W-20N | 51 |
| Lewis Ln. E&W | 9W-20N | 51 |
| Lexington Ln. NW&SE | 10W-23N | 50 |
| Lilac Ln. N&S | 9W-21N | 51 |
| Lily Ct. NW&SE | 10W-22N | 50 |
| Lincoln Av. E&W | 8W-21N,7W-21N | 51 |
| Lincoln Pl. E&W | 8W-21N | 51 |
| Lincolnwood Rd. N&S | 7W-20N | 51 |
| Linden Av. N&S | 8W-22N,7W-21N | 51 |
| Linden Park Pl. NE&SW | 8W-22N | 51 |
| Little John Ct. E&W | 10W-23N | 50 |
| Livingston St. E&W | 10W-23N,9W-23N | 50 |
| Llewellyn Av. E&W | 9W-23N | 51 |
| Logan St. NW&SE | 8W-23N | 51 |
| Lorraine Cir.* E&W | 8W-21N | 51 |
| Lotus Pl. E&W | 9W-24N | 43 |
| Lyman Ct. N&S | 7W-20N | 51 |
| Lynn Ter. NS&EW | 10W-23N | 50 |
| Lyons Cir.* E&W | 8W-21N | 51 |
| Magnolia Ln. NW&SE | 9W-20N | 51 |
| Malory Ln. N&S | 11W-23N | 50 |
| Manor Rd. N&S | 10W-22N | 50 |
| Maple Av. NE&SW | 8W-22N | 51 |
| Maple Ln. NW&SE | 8W-22N | 51 |
| Marion Av. E&W | 8W-20N,7W-20N | 51 |
| Marl Oak Dr. N&S | 9W-23N | 51 |
| Marquette Rd. N&S | 8W-20N | 51 |
| Marshman St. NE&SW | 7W-21N | 51 |
| Marvell Ln. E&W | 8W-21N | 51 |
| Mayor Ln. N&S | 10W-23N | 50 |
| McCarn Rd. NW&SE | 9W-23N | 51 |
| McDaniels Av. N&S | 8W-21N | 51 |
| McGovern St. NW&SE | 8W-22N | 51 |
| McKibben Rd NE&SW | 8W-23N | 51 |
| Meadow Ln. E&W | 10W-23N | 50 |
| Melba Av. NW&SE | 8W-23N | 51 |
| Melody Ln. E&W | 7W-20N | 51 |
| Melvin Dr. E&W | 8W-20N | 51 |
| Midland Av. N&S | 10W-21N | 50 |
| Midlothian Av. N&S | 8W-22N | 51 |
| Mill Tr. E&W | 10W-22N | 50 |
| Montgomery Ln. E&W | 8W-23N | 51 |
| Moraine Rd. E&W | 8W-23N | 51 |
| Moseley Rd. E&W | 8W-21N | 51 |
| Mulberry Pl. E&W | 8W-21N | 51 |
| Museum Dr. E&W | 10W-23N | 50 |
| N. Deer Park Dr., E. NW&SE | 6W-20N | 51 |
| N. Deer Park Dr., W. NW&SE | 6W-20N | 51 |
| Naida Ter. E&W | 8W-22N | 51 |
| North Av. E&W | 10W-23N,9W-23N | 50 |
| Northland Av. E&W | 10W-23N | 50 |
| Ny-O-Da Pl. E&W | 8W-23N | 51 |
| Oak Knoll Ter. NS&EW | 6W-20N | 51 |
| Oak St. N&S | 8W-23N | 51 |
| Oakland Dr. NE&SW | 7W-20N | 51 |
| Oakmont Rd. E&W | 7W-21N | 51 |
| Oakvale Rd. E&W | 7W-21N | 51 |
| Oakwood Av. N&S | 8W-21N | 51 |
| Old Barn Ln. N&S | 8W-21N | 51 |
| Old Briar Rd. E&W | 9W-20N | 51 |
| Old Deerfield Rd. NE&SW | 9W-21N | 51 |
| Old Mill Rd. (Pvt.) N&S | 10W-24N | 43 |
| Old Skokie Rd. NW&SE | 9W-21N,9W-22N | 51 |
| Old Trail Rd. E&W | 9W-23N | 51 |
| Onwentsia Av. E&W | 8W-22N | 51 |
| Orchard Ln. E&W | 8W-23N | 51 |
| Orchid Ct. N&S | 10W-23N | 50 |
| Orleans Cir.* N&S | 9W-21N | 51 |
| Orleans Dr. N&S | 9W-21N | 51 |
| Oxford Ct. E&W | 10W-23N | 50 |
| Park Av. NE&SW | 8W-22N | 51 |
| Park Ln. NW&SE | 8W-22N | 51 |
| Parkside Dr. NW&SE | 10W-23N | 50 |
| Partridge Ln. E&W | 10W-23N | 50 |
| Patten St. N&S | 8W-23N | 51 |
| Perennial Ln. N&S | 9W-22N | 51 |
| Picadilly Rd. NW&SE | 9W-21N | 51 |
| Pierce Rd. N&S | 7W-20N | 51 |
| Pine Point Ct. E&W | 6W-20N | 51 |
| Pine Point Dr. | 6W-20N | 51 |
| Pleasant Av. NW&SE | 7W-20N | 51 |
| Point Ln. N&S | 10W-23N | 50 |
| Poplar Rd. N&S | 9W-20N | 51 |
| Port Clinton Rd. N&S | 8W-23N | 51 |
| Pricilla Av. E&W | 9W-23N | 51 |
| Princeton Av. E&W | 9W-23N | 51 |
| Prospect Av. E&W | 8W-22N | 51 |
| Rambler Ln. E&W | 7W-20N | 51 |
| Ravenoaks Ln. NE&SW | 7W-21N | 51 |
| Ravenswood Av. N&S | 9W-23N | 51 |
| Ravine Dr. N&S | 8W-21N | 51 |
| Ravine Ln. NW&SE | 8W-22N | 51 |
| Ravine Ter. NE&SW | 8W-22N | 51 |
| Ravinia Park Rd. N&S | 9W-23N | 51 |
| Ravinia Rd. E&W | 8W-21N,7W-21N | 51 |
| Red Oak Ln. N&S | 9W-20N | 51 |
| Rice St. N&S | 8W-23N | 51 |
| Richfield Av. E&W | 10W-21N | 50 |
| Ridge Rd. NW&SE | 11W-23N,9W-20N | 50 |
| Ridgelee Rd. | 9W-20N | 51 |
| Ridgewood Dr. NW&SE | 8W-21N | 51 |
| Ridgewood Pl. NW&SE | 8W-21N | 51 |
| Ring Ct. NW&SE | 9W-21N | 51 |
| Riparian Av. E&W | 8W-23N | 51 |
| Robin Hood Pl. E&W | 9W-21N | 51 |
| Roger Williams Av. E&W | 7W-20N | 51 |
| Rolling Wood Rd. NS&EW | 8W-21N | 51 |
| Rosemary Rd. E&W | 8W-21N | 51 |
| Rosewood Rd. E&W | 7W-21N | 51 |
| Roslyn Cir. N&S | 8W-23N | 51 |
| Roslyn Ln. N&S | 8W-23N | 51 |
| Route 22 E&W | 10W-23N | 50 |
| Route 41 NW&SE | 10W-23N,8W-20N | 50 |
| Russet Ln. E&W | 9W-20N | 51 |
| Ryders Ln. N&S | 10W-22N | 50 |
| Sandwick Ct. E&W | 9W-22N | 51 |
| Sarabell Ln. (Pvt.) N&S | 7W-20N | 51 |
| Saxony Dr. NW&SE | 8W-21N | 51 |
| Saxony Rd. N&S | 8W-21N | 51 |
| Second St. NW&SE | 8W-22N | 51 |
| Seven Pines Cir. NW&SE | 8W-21N | 51 |
| Shady Ln. N&S | 10W-23N | 50 |
| Sheahen Ct. N&S | 8W-22N | 51 |
| Sheldon Ln. N&S | 7W-20N | 51 |
| Shelly Ct. E&W | 10W-23N | 50 |
| Sheridan Rd. N&S | 8W-22N,6W-20N | 51 |
| Sherwood Rd. N&S | 10W-21N | 50 |
| Skokie Av. N&S | 8W-22N | 51 |
| Skokie Hwy. NW&SE | 10W-23N,8W-20N | 50 |
| Skokie Valley Rd. NE&SW | 8W-20N | 51 |
| Snapdragon Ct. NW&SE | 10W-22N | 50 |
| Cir. | 6W-20N | 51 |
| Southland Av. E&W | 10W-21N | 50 |
| Spruce Av. N&S | 10W-22N | 50 |
| St. Charles Pl. N&S | 7W-20N | 50 |
| St. Johns Av. N&S | 8W-23N,7W-20N | 50 |
| St. Tropez St.* E&W | 9W-21N | 51 |
| Stonegate Dr. E&W | 9W-20N | 51 |
| Stratford Rd. E&W | 9W-20N | 51 |
| Strath Erin E&W | 9W-20N | 51 |
| Sumac Rd. NW&SE | 9W-20N,9W-21N | 51 |
| Summerdale Av. N&S | 10W-21N | 50 |
| Summit Av. N&S | 9W-23N | 51 |
| Sundrop Cir. N&S | 10W-22N | 50 |
| Sunnyside Av. N&S | 10W-21N | 50 |
| Sunset Rd. N&S | 9W-21N,8W-21N | 51 |
| Sycamore Ln. N&S | 7W-21N | 51 |
| Sycamore Pl. E&W | 7W-21N | 51 |
| Sylvester Pl. NW&SE | 7W-22N | 51 |
| Tanglewood Ct. E&W | 9W-20N | 51 |
| Taylor Av. N&S | 9W-22N | 51 |
| Tennyson Ln. N&S | 11W-23N | 50 |
| Thackery Dr. E&W | 9W-21N | 51 |
| Thorntree Ln. E&W | 8W-21N | 51 |
| Thornwood Ln. E&W | 10W-23N | 50 |
| Timber Hill Rd. E&W | 7W-20N | 51 |
| Toulon Ct.* N&S | 8W-21N | 51 |
| Trail Way N&S | 8W-20N | 50 |
| Trailway N&S | 8W-20N | 50 |
| Tree Dr. E&W | 8W-20N | 51 |
| Turnbull Woods Ct. N&S | 7W-20N | 51 |
| Twin Oaks Dr. N&S | 10W-20N | 50 |
| U.S. Route 41 NW&SE | 10W-24N,8W-20N | 43 |
| Underwood Av. E&W | 9W-23N | 51 |
| University Av. N&S | 9W-23N | 51 |
| Valley Rd. N&S | 7W-20N | 51 |
| Vine Av. E&W | 9W-23N | 51 |
| Virginia Rd. NW&SE | 9W-21N | 51 |
| Wade St. NW&SE | 9W-23N | 51 |
| Wahwahtaysee Av. N&S | 8W-20N | 51 |
| Wake Robin Ln. N&S | 7W-20N | 51 |
| Walker Av. E&W | 8W-23N | 51 |
| Walnut St. NE&SW | 8W-22N | 51 |
| Warbler Cir. E&W | 9W-23N | 51 |
| Warbler Ct. NE&SW | 9W-23N | 51 |
| Warbler Pl. N&S | 9W-23N | 51 |
| Washington Ct. NE&SW | 7W-20N | 51 |
| Washington Pl. NE&SW | 7W-20N | 51 |
| Watercrest Way NS&EW | 10W-22N | 50 |
| Waterford Ct. E&W | 10W-22N | 50 |
| Waverly Rd. NE&SW | 7W-21N | 51 |
| West Park Av. E&W | 10W-22N,9W-22N | 50 |
| Wester Pl. N&S | 9W-24N | 43 |
| Western Av. N&S | 9W-22N,9W-24N | 51 |
| Westgate Ter. E&W | 10W-21N | 50 |
| White Oak Ln. (Pvt.) E&W | 8W-21N | 51 |
| Wildrose Ct. NE&SW | 10W-22N | 50 |
| Wildwood Ln. N&S | 7W-21N | 51 |
| Willow Pl. E&W | 10W-23N | 50 |
| Willow Rd. N&S | 10W-22N,10W-23N | 50 |
| Wincanton Av. N&S | 7W-22N | 50 |
| Windsor Rd. N&S | 9W-21N | 51 |
| Windy Hill Ln. E&W | 9W-21N | 51 |
| Winona Rd. N&S | 8W-20N | 51 |
| Winthrop Rd. E&W | 9W-21N | 51 |
| Wood Path NE&SW | 8W-22N | 51 |
| Woodbine Av. N&S | 9W-20N | 51 |
| Woodbine Rd. N&S | 9W-21N | 51 |
| Woodbridge Ln. NE&SW | 8W-23N | 51 |
| Woodland Rd. NE&SW | 7W-20N | 51 |
| Woodleigh Av. E&W | 9W-23N | 51 |
| Yager Av. N&S | 9W-21N | 51 |
| Yale Av. E&W | 9W-22N | 51 |
| York Ln. E&W | 10W-21N | 50 |
| 2nd St. NE&SW | 9W-24N | 43 |
| 3rd St. NE&SW | 8W-23N | 51 |
| 4th St. NE&SW | 8W-23N | 51 |
| 5th St. NE&SW | 8W-23N | 51 |
| 6th St. NE&SW | 8W-23N | 51 |
| 7th St. NE&SW | 8W-23N | 51 |
| 8th St. NE&SW | 8W-23N | 51 |
| 9th St. NE&SW | 8W-23N | 51 |
| 10th St. E&W | 8W-23N | 51 |
| 11th St. E&W | 8W-23N | 51 |

## Highwood

| Entry | Grid | Page |
|---|---|---|
| Ashland Av. N&S | 9W-23N | 51 |
| Bank Ln. N&S | 9W-23N | 51 |
| Burchell Av. N&S | 9W-23N | 51 |
| Burtis Av. E&W | 9W-23N | 51 |
| Central Av. E&W | 9W-23N | 51 |
| Clay Av. E&W | 9W-23N | 51 |
| Euclid Av. E&W | 9W-23N | 51 |
| Euclid Ct. N&S | 9W-23N | 51 |
| Everts Pl. N&S | 9W-23N | 51 |
| Evolution Av. N&S | 9W-23N | 51 |
| Exmoor Ct. N&S | 9W-23N | 51 |
| Funston Av. N&S | 9W-23N | 51 |
| Green Bay Rd. NW&SE | 9W-23N | 51 |
| Grove St. N&S | 9W-23N | 51 |
| H St. N&S | 9W-23N | 51 |
| High St. N&S | 9W-23N | 51 |
| Highwood Av. E&W | 9W-23N | 51 |
| Jeffrey Pl. N&S | 9W-23N | 51 |
| Jocelyn Pl. E&W | 9W-23N | 51 |
| Llewellyn Av. E&W | 9W-23N | 51 |
| Lockard Av. N&S | 9W-23N | 51 |
| Maple St. N&S | 9W-23N | 51 |
| Mears Pl. N&S | 9W-23N | 51 |
| Michigan Av. E&W | 9W-23N | 51 |
| Morgan Pl. N&S | 9W-23N | 51 |
| North Av. N&S | 9W-23N | 51 |
| Oak Av. N&S | 9W-23N | 51 |
| Oak Ter. N&S | 9W-23N | 51 |
| Oakridge Av. E&W | 9W-23N | 51 |
| Palmer Av. N&S | 9W-23N | 51 |
| Pleasant Pl. N&S | 9W-23N | 51 |
| Prairie Av. N&S | 9W-23N | 51 |
| Sheridan Av. E&W | 9W-23N | 51 |
| Sheridan Rd. NW&SE | 9W-23N | 51 |
| Summit Av. E&W | 9W-23N | 51 |
| Washington Av. E&W | 9W-23N | 51 |
| Webster Av. E&W | 9W-23N | 51 |
| Western Av. N&S | 9W-23N,9W-24N | 51 |
| Wrendale Av. E&W | 9W-23N | 51 |
| 3rd St. NE&SW | 9W-23N | 51 |
| 9th St. NE&SW | 9W-23N | 51 |

## Indian Creek

| Entry | Grid | Page |
|---|---|---|
| Circle Dr. NE&SW | 17W-24N | 40 |
| Crestland Rd. E&W | 17W-24N | 40 |
| Mills Ct. E&W | 17W-25N | 40 |
| Shann Dr. N&S | 17W-25N | 40 |
| U.S. Route 45 NW&SE | 17W-24N,17W-25N | 40 |
| Valley Rd. E&W | 17W-24N | 40 |

## Island Lake

| Entry | Grid | Page |
|---|---|---|
| Arbor Rd. E&W | 28W-28N | 28 |
| Briar Ct. E&W | 28W-28N | 28 |
| Briar Hill Dr. NW&SE | 28W-28N | 28 |
| Briar Rd. E&W | 28W-28N | 28 |
| Canterbury Ln.* E&W | 27W-27N | 36 |
| Cardinal E&W | 28W-29N | 28 |
| Carol Cir. NE&SW | 28W-28N | 28 |
| Carriage Hill Ct. E&W | 28W-28N | 28 |
| Carriage Hill Rd. NS&EW | 28W-28N | 28 |
| Channel Dr. E&W | 28W-28N | 28 |
| Clover Rd. E&W | 28W-28N | 28 |
| Constitution Av.* E&W | 27W-27N | 36 |
| Cottonwood Ct. NW&SE | 28W-28N | 28 |
| Country Trail Ct. E&W | 28W-27N | 36 |
| Countryside Ct. N&S | 28W-28N | 28 |
| Eastway Dr. N&S | 28W-28N | 28 |
| Elder Dr. N&S | 28W-28N | 28 |
| Elm Av. N&S | 28W-28N | 28 |
| Fairfield Dr. E&W | 28W-28N | 28 |
| Fern Dr. E&W | 28W-28N | 28 |
| Forest Dr. E&W | 28W-28N | 28 |
| Greenleaf Av. N&S | 28W-28N | 28 |
| Harvard Ct.* E&W | 27W-27N | 36 |
| Harvest Ct. N&S | 28W-28N | 28 |
| Independence Blvd.* E&W | 27W-27N | 36 |
| Ivy Rd. E&W | 28W-28N | 28 |
| Judith Dr. NE&SW | 28W-28N | 28 |
| Juniper Rd. E&W | 28W-28N | 28 |
| Kingston Dr. N&S | 28W-29N | 28 |
| Lakeside Ct. NE&SW | 28W-28N | 28 |
| Landsfield Ct. NE&SW | 28W-28N | 28 |
| Locust Av. N&S | 28W-28N | 28 |
| Longacre Ln. E&W | 28W-28N | 28 |
| Madison Ct.* E&W | 27W-27N | 36 |
| Mallard Pt. N&S | 28W-29N | 28 |
| Mylith Park St. N&S | 28W-28N | 28 |
| Northern Ct. NS&EW | 28W-28N | 28 |
| Northern Ter. E&W | 28W-28N | 28 |
| Oaks Ln. E&W | 28W-28N | 28 |
| Oakwood Av. N&S | 28W-28N | 28 |
| Park Dr. N&S | 28W-28N | 28 |
| Poplar Dr. N&S | 28W-28N | 28 |
| Princeton Cir.* E&W | 27W-27N | 36 |
| Ridge Av. E&W | 28W-28N | 28 |
| River Oaks Ct. E&W | 28W-28N | 28 |
| Rose Av. E&W | 28W-28N | 28 |
| Saratoga Cir.* E&W | 27W-27N | 36 |

|  | Grid | Page |
|---|---|---|
| Slocum Lake Rd. NW&SE | 28W-28N | 28 |
| South Shore Dr. NS&EW | 28W-28N | 28 |
| Southern Ter. NW&SE | 28W-28N | 28 |
| Sumac Dr. N&S | 28W-28N | 28 |
| Timber Ln. | 28W-27N | 36 |
| Westridge Dr. N&S | 28W-27N,28W-28N | 36 |
| Willow Ln. N&S | 28W-28N | 28 |
| Wishing Well Ln. NW&SE | 28W-28N | 28 |
| Woodbine Dr. E&W | 28W-28N | 28 |
| Woodcreek Ct. E&W | 28W-28N | 28 |
| Woodcrest Dr. E&W | 28W-28N | 28 |
| Woodland Ct., N. N&S | 28W-28N | 28 |
| Woodland Ct., S. N&S | 28W-28N | 28 |
| Woodland Dr. N&S | 28W-28N | 28 |

### Kildeer

|  | Grid | Page |
|---|---|---|
| Abbey Ct. NW&SE | 22W-21N | 46 |
| Acorn Ct. N&S | 21W-21N | 47 |
| Amberley Dr. NW&SE | 21W-20N | 47 |
| Andover Rd. NW&SE | 21W-21N,20W-21N | 47 |
| Barbara Ct. E&W | 21W-21N | 47 |
| Barcley Ct. NW&SE | 22W-21N | 46 |
| Boschome Dr. E&W | 21W-21N | 47 |
| Brandon Rd. E&W | 21W-21N | 47 |
| Bridal Tr. NS&EW | 21W-22N | 47 |
| Buffalo Run N&S | 21W-20N,21W-21N | 47 |
| Burning Tree Ct. N&S | 22W-21N | 46 |
| Cambridge Dr. NS&EW | 22W-21N | 46 |
| Chartwell Dr. E&W | 20W-20N | 47 |
| Chesapeake Dr. N&S | 21W-23N | 47 |
| Chestnut Ridge Rd. E&W | 22W-21N | 46 |
| Circle Bay Rd. E&W | 22W-20N | 46 |
| Clayton Ct. N&S | 20W-22N | 47 |
| Cliffside Dr. E&W | 21W-21N | 47 |
| Concorde Ct. E&W | 20W-20N | 46 |
| Creekside Dr. SE&NW | 21W-22N | 47 |
| Cuba Rd. E&W | 22W-21N,20W-21N | 47 |
| Dallas Ct. N&S | 20W-21N | 47 |
| Dorothea Ct. NW&SE | 20W-21N | 47 |
| Elder Ct. NW&SE | 22W-21N | 46 |
| Eleanor Ln. E&W | 21W-22N | 47 |
| Exeter Rd. E&W | 20W-21N | 47 |
| Foxtail Tr. N&S | 21W-22N | 47 |
| Green Wood Dr. E&W | 21W-22N | 47 |
| Grove Rd. N&S | 21W-21N | 47 |
| Hampton Rd. NW&SE | 21W-21N | 47 |
| Hawthorn Ln. N&S | 22W-21N | 46 |
| Heather Ct. N&S | 21W-20N | 47 |
| Herons Ct. NW&SE | 21W-22N | 47 |
| Hickory Hill Dr. E&W | 21W-21N | 47 |
| Hidden Valley Dr. E&W | 21W-21N | 47 |
| Highknoll Dr. | 21W-21N | 47 |
| Highwood Rd. NS&EW | 22W-21N | 46 |
| Hilandale Ct. E&W | 21W-22N | 47 |
| Hilandale Dr. N&S | 21W-22N | 47 |
| Honey Ridge Ct. E&W | 22W-21N | 46 |
| Hopewell Ct. NE&SW | 21W-22N | 47 |
| Kepwick Ln. NE&SW | 21W-20N | 47 |
| Kirkley Dr. E&W | 21W-20N | 47 |
| Krueger Rd. N&S | 21W-22N | 47 |
| Laurel Ln. E&W | 21W-22N | 47 |
| Lexington Ln. E&W | 20W-21N | 47 |
| Linden Ln. E&W | 21W-21N | 47 |
| Little Pond Rd. NE&SW | 22W-21N | 46 |
| Long Grove Rd. N&S | 21W-20N,20W-20N | 47 |
| Long Meadows Ct. NS&EW | 20W-20N | 47 |
| Long Meadows Dr. N&S | 20W-20N | 47 |
| Maple Ct. NW&SE | 22W-21N | 46 |
| Marcy Ln. NW&SE | 21W-21N | 47 |
| Middleton Dr. N&S | 20W-20N,20W-21N | 47 |
| N. Boschome Cir. E&W | 21W-21N | 47 |

|  | Grid | Page |
|---|---|---|
| N. Woodcrest Ln. NW&SE | 21W-22N | 47 |
| Newbury Ct. N&S | 20W-22N | 47 |
| Oak Knoll Ct. E&W | 21W-20N | 47 |
| Oak Trail E&W | 21W-21N | 47 |
| Pine Lake Cir. NS&EW | 21W-21N | 47 |
| Pine Lake Ct. N&S | 21W-21N | 47 |
| Pinegrove Ct. N&S | 22W-21N | 46 |
| Plumwood Dr. N&S | 20W-20N | 47 |
| Prairie Lake Ct. NW&SE | 21W-22N | 47 |
| Prescott Ct. N&S | 21W-22N | 47 |
| Rebecca Ct. N&S | 21W-22N | 47 |
| Richmond Ct. NE&SW | 20W-22N | 47 |
| Ridgewood Ln. N&S | 21W-22N | 47 |
| Ruth Ct. N&S | 21W-22N | 47 |
| S. Boschome Dr. E&W | 21W-21N | 47 |
| S. Woodcrest Ln. N&S | 21W-22N | 47 |
| Stoneybrook Ct. N&S | 22W-21N | 46 |
| Thornridge Dr. E&W | 22W-21N | 46 |
| Timber Ridge Ct. N&S | 22W-21N | 46 |
| Timberlea Ct. NE&SW | 22W-21N | 46 |
| Tree Rd. N&S | 22W-21N | 46 |
| Valley View Rd. NS&EW | 21W-21N | 47 |
| Vermont Ct. N&S | 20W-21N | 47 |
| Weatherstone Rd. NW&SE | 21W-20N | 47 |
| White Pine Rd. NW&SE | 22W-21N | 46 |
| Willow Dr. N&S | 21W-21N | 47 |
| Wooded Ridge Dr. E&W | 22W-20N | 46 |
| York Ct. E&W | 21W-20N | 47 |
| Yorkshire Dr. N&S | 21W-22N,20W-22N | 47 |

### Lake Barrington

|  | Grid | Page |
|---|---|---|
| Alice Ln. N&S | 27W-23N | 44 |
| Apache Ln. NW&SE | 25W-24N | 37 |
| Apache Path NE&SW | 26W-24N | 37 |
| Bark Ct. N&S | 28W-24N | 36 |
| Beacon Dr. N&S | 28W-23N | 44 |
| Bluff Ct. NS&EW | 26W-24N | 37 |
| Brookside Ct. E&W | 27W-22N | 44 |
| Brookside Way NS&EW | 27W-22N,26W-22N | 44 |
| Buoy Ct. NS&EW | 28W-24N | 36 |
| Cayuga Tr. E&W | 27W-25N | 37 |
| Cedar Ridge NE&SW | 26W-24N | 37 |
| Center Dr. E&W | 27W-25N | 37 |
| Cherokee Dr. N&S | 25W-24N | 37 |
| Chesapeake Dr. NS&EW | 26W-23N | 45 |
| Chippewa Ct. E&W | 26W-24N | 37 |
| Classic Ct. NE&SW | 28W-22N | 44 |
| Club Cir. NE&SW | 26W-24N | 37 |
| Commercial Av. E&W | 28W-21N,27W-21N | 44 |
| Countryside Ct. NE&SW | 27W-25N | 37 |
| Countryside Dr. N&S | 27W-25N | 37 |
| Cove Ct. N&S | 28W-23N | 44 |
| Coventry Ct. E&W | 27W-24N | 37 |
| Coventry Ln. NE&SW | 27W-24N | 37 |
| Crestview Ln. NE&SW | 27W-23N | 44 |
| Cutter Ln. E&W | 28W-24N | 36 |
| Darrell Rd. NE&SW | 28W-26N,28W-27N | 36 |
| Deer Trail N&S | 26W-24N | 37 |
| Deer Trail Hill* N&S | 25W-24N | 37 |
| Dock Dr. N&S | 28W-23N | 44 |
| Driftwood Ct. NE&SW | 27W-22N | 44 |
| East Ln. NW&SE | 27W-23N | 44 |
| Fairway Cir. NE&SW | 26W-24N | 37 |
| Farm View Cir. NW&SE | 27W-25N | 37 |
| Flint Dr. NW&SE | 27W-23N | 44 |
| Flynn Creek Dr. N&S | 27W-21N | 44 |
| Foxwood Ln. NW&SE | 26W-24N | 37 |
| Golf Ct. N&S | 26W-24N | 37 |
| Golf Ln. NS&EW | 26W-24N | 37 |
| Golfview Ln. NS&EW | 27W-23N | 44 |
| Grand View Dr. N&S | 25W-24N | 37 |
| Grayshire Ln. N&S | 27W-23N | 44 |

|  | Grid | Page |
|---|---|---|
| Grey Barn Ln. NE&SW | 28W-23N | 44 |
| Harbor Rd. NS&EW | 28W-23N,28W-22N | 44 |
| Henry Ln. NS&EW | 27W-22N | 44 |
| Henry Rd. E&W | 27W-22N | 44 |
| Hickory Ln. N&S | 26W-24N | 37 |
| Hickory Ridge NW&SE | 27W-25N | 37 |
| Hillside Dr. E&W | 28W-22N | 44 |
| Hilltop Ct.* NW&SE | 25W-24N | 37 |
| Hillview Dr. N&S | 28W-22N | 44 |
| Hunt Trail NE&SW | 26W-24N | 37 |
| Indian Point NW&SE | 26W-24N | 37 |
| Industrial Av. E&W | 28W-22N,27W-22N | 44 |
| Iroquois Ct. NW&SE | 27W-25N | 37 |
| Island View Ln. E&W | 26W-24N | 37 |
| Kazimour Dr. E&W | 27W-25N | 37 |
| Kelsey Rd. NE&SW | 28W-23N,27W-24N | 44 |
| Kensington Ct. E&W | 26W-24N | 37 |
| Lakeridge Dr. E&W | 26W-23N | 45 |
| Lakeview Dr. N&S | 27W-23N | 44 |
| Linden Dr. E&W | 28W-22N | 44 |
| Long Meadow NE&SW | 25W-25N | 37 |
| Longview Pt. NE&SW | 26W-23N | 45 |
| Main Entrance E&W | 26W-24N | 37 |
| Main St. E&W | 28W-26N | 36 |
| Mallard Pt.* E&W | 25W-24N | 37 |
| Market Pl. E&W | 26W-25N | 37 |
| Meadow Pl. E&W | 26W-24N | 37 |
| Meadow View Ct. N&S | 27W-25N | 37 |
| Miller Ct. N&S | 27W-24N,26W-24N | 37 |
| North Av. NE&SW | 27W-23N | 44 |
| North Bay Ct. NE&SW | 26W-24N,26W-25N | 37 |
| Northwest Highway NW&SE | 28W-22N,27W-21N | 44 |
| Oak Ct. NW&SE | 28W-22N | 44 |
| Oak Hill Rd. NS&EW | 26W-24N | 37 |
| Oak Hills Rd. NS&EW | 27W-25N | 37 |
| Old Barn Rd. NE&SW | 26W-24N | 37 |
| Old Barrington Rd. NW&SE | 27W-23N | 44 |
| Oneida Ln. N&S | 27W-25N | 37 |
| Pawnee Rd. NE&SW | 25W-24N,25W-25N | 37 |
| Pawnee Rd. N&S | 25W-25N | 37 |
| Pepper Rd. N&S | 28W-21N,28W-22N | 44 |
| Pinecrest Ct. NS&EW | 26W-24N | 37 |
| River Rd. N&S | 27W-24N,27W-25N | 37 |
| Riverbend Ct. N&S | 27W-25N | 37 |
| Roberts Rd. E&W | 27W-25N | 37 |
| Rolling Wood E&W | 26W-24N | 37 |
| Schooner Ln. E&W | 28W-23N | 44 |
| Seneca Tr. NS&EW | 26W-24N | 37 |
| Shoreline Rd. N&S | 26W-24N | 37 |
| Tamarack Ct. NW&SE | 26W-23N | 45 |
| Thornhill Ct. N&S | 26W-24N | 37 |
| Thornhill Ln. E&W | 26W-24N | 37 |
| Timber Ridge N&S | 26W-24N | 37 |
| Tioga Trail N&S | 26W-24N | 37 |
| Tuscarora Ct. N&S | 27W-25N | 37 |
| Twin Pond Ln. E&W | 27W-25N,27W-16N | 37 |
| Valley View Rd. N&S | 26W-24N | 37 |
| Vance Ct. E&W | 28W-23N | 44 |
| Vista Ln. E&W | 27W-23N | 44 |
| W. Brookside Way NS&EW | 27W-22N | 44 |
| Waterview Ct. E&W | 26W-24N | 37 |
| Wedgewood Ln. N&S | 27W-24N | 37 |
| Welch Cir. NS&EW | 28W-23N | 44 |
| Wellington Ct. NW&SE | 27W-22N | 44 |
| West Ln. N&S | 27W-23N | 44 |
| White Oak NE&SW | 27W-23N | 44 |
| White Pine Dr. N&S | 26W-24N | 37 |
| Woodland Dr. N&S | 27W-23N | 44 |
| Woodview Rd.* N&S | 25W-24N | 37 |

### Lake Bluff

|  | Grid | Page |
|---|---|---|
| Arbor Ct. N&S | 10W-29N | 35 |
| Arbor Dr. E&W | 10W-29N | 35 |
| Arden Shore Rd. | 10W-29N | 35 |
| Arden Shore Rd., S. E&W | 10W-29N | 35 |
| Ascot Ct. NE&SW | 11W-29N | 35 |
| Ashington Cir.* E&W | 10W-29N | 35 |
| Bath And Tennis Club Rd. E&W | 11W-28N | 35 |
| Cir. | 11W-29N | 35 |
| Birch Rd. N&S | 10W-28N | 35 |
| Birkdale Rd. E&W | 11W-28N | 35 |
| Blodgett Ln. E&W | 11W-29N,10W-29N | 35 |
| Bluff Rd. N&S | 10W-28N,10W-29N | 35 |
| Bradford Ct.* E&W | 10W-29N | 35 |
| Briar Ln. N&S | 10W-28N | 35 |
| Brierfield Ct. E&W | 11W-29N | 35 |
| Bristol Ct. E&W | 11W-29N | 35 |
| Buckminster Ct. E&W | 11W-29N | 35 |
| Cambridge Rd. E&W | 10W-28N | 35 |
| Carlyle Cir. N&S | 11W-29N | 35 |
| Carriage Park Av. E&W | 12W-28N | 35 |
| Center Av. E&W | 11W-28N,10W-28N | 35 |
| Circle Dr. E&W | 10W-28N | 35 |
| Coventry Ct. E&W | 11W-28N | 35 |
| Crescent Dr. E&W | 11W-29N | 35 |
| Eastway E&W | 10W-30N | 35 |
| Eva Ter. N&S | 11W-28N | 35 |
| Evanston Av. N&S | 10W-28N | 35 |
| Forest Cove Rd. E&W | 10W-28N | 35 |
| Forest Hills Rd. N&S | 11W-28N | 35 |
| Foss Ct. N&S | 10W-28N | 35 |
| Garfield Av. N&S | 11W-28N | 35 |
| Glen Av. N&S | 11W-29N | 35 |
| Grafton Ct. E&W | 11W-29N | 35 |
| Green Bay Rd. N&S | 11W-28N,11W-29N | 35 |
| Greenwich Ct. E&W | 11W-29N | 35 |
| Gurney Av. N&S | 10W-28N | 35 |
| Hamilton Ct. E&W | 11W-29N | 35 |
| Hancock Av. NW&SE | 11W-28N | 35 |
| Hawthorne Ct. N&S | 11W-28N,10W-28N | 35 |
| Heathrow Ct. E&W | 11W-29N | 35 |
| Hickory Ct. N&S | 10W-28N | 35 |
| Hirst Ct. N&S | 11W-29N | 35 |
| Indian Rd. E&W | 11W-28N | 35 |
| Inverness Ct. E&W | 11W-29N | 35 |
| James N&S | 11W-29N | 35 |
| Kohl Dr. E&W | 11W-29N | 35 |
| Lake Av. N&S | 10W-28N | 35 |
| Lakeland Dr. E&W | 11W-28N | 35 |
| Lancaster Ct. E&W | 11W-29N | 35 |
| Leeds Ct. NW&SE | 11W-29N | 35 |
| Lincoln Av. N&S | 11W-28N | 35 |
| Main St. E&W | 10W-28N | 35 |
| Maple Av. N&S | 10W-28N | 35 |
| Margate Ct. N&S | 11W-29N | 35 |
| Market Sq., E. E&W | 11W-28N | 35 |
| Market Sq., W. E&W | 11W-28N | 35 |
| Marvin Rd. E&W | 11W-28N | 35 |
| Mawman Av. NE&SW | 11W-28N | 35 |
| McClaren Ln. N&S | 11W-28N | 35 |
| Moffet Rd. N&S | 10W-28N | 35 |
| Mountain Av. N&S | 11W-28N | 35 |
| N. Shore Dr. E&W | 12W-28N | 35 |
| Neuman Ct. N&S | 11W-28N | 35 |
| North Av. N&S | 10W-28N | 35 |
| Norwich Ct. N&S | 11W-28N | 35 |
| Oak Av. N&S | 10W-28N | 35 |
| Oak Ter. N&S | 10W-28N | 35 |
| Oakton Cir. N&S | 11W-29N | 35 |
| Park Av. E&W | 11W-28N | 35 |
| Park Ln. E&W | 11W-28N | 35 |
| Park Pl. E&W | 10W-28N | 35 |
| Phillip Ct. E&W | 11W-29N | 35 |
| Pine Av. N&S | 11W-28N | 35 |
| Pine Ct. N&S | 11W-28N | 35 |
| Prospect Av. E&W | 11W-29N,10W-29N | 35 |
| Ravine Av. E&W | 10W-29N | 35 |
| Ravine Forest Dr. E&W | 10W-28N | 35 |
| Rebecca Ter. N&S | 11W-28N | 35 |
| Rockland Av. N&S | 11W-28N | 35 |
| Rockland Rd. E&W | 12W-28N | 35 |
| Roselle Ter. N&S | 11W-28N | 35 |
| Rothbury Ct. E&W | 11W-29N | 35 |
| Route 131 N&S | 11W-29N | 35 |
| Route 176 E&W | 11W-29N | 35 |
| Route 43 N&S | 12W-28N | 35 |
| Scranton Av. E&W | 10W-28N | 35 |
| Sheridan Pl. E&W | 11W-28N,10W-28N | 35 |

|  | Grid | Page |
|---|---|---|
| Sheridan Rd. NS&EW | 10W-28N,10W-29N | 35 |
| Sherwood Dr. E&W | 12W-28N | 35 |
| Sherwood Ter. N&S | 12W-28N | 35 |
| Shore Acres Cir. E&W | 10W-30N | 35 |
| Shore Acres Rd. E&W | 10W-29N | 35 |
| Signe Ct. E&W | 11W-29N | 35 |
| Simpson Av. N&S | 10W-28N | 35 |
| Skokie Hwy. N&S | 12W-29N,11W-28N | 35 |
| State St. N&S | 10W-28N | 35 |
| Sunrise Av. N&S | 10W-28N | 35 |
| Sunset Pl. E&W | 11W-28N | 35 |
| Sunset Ter. N&S | 11W-28N | 35 |
| Surrey Ln. NS&EW | 12W-28N | 35 |
| Sylvan Rd. E&W | 10W-28N | 35 |
| Thorn Valley Ln. E&W | 11W-29N | 35 |
| Thornwood Ln. NE&SW | 11W-28N | 35 |
| U.S. Route 41 N&S | 12W-28N,11W-28N | 35 |
| Vincent Ct. N&S | 10W-28N | 35 |
| Walnut Av. N&S | 10W-28N | 35 |
| Warrington Ct. E&W | 11W-29N | 35 |
| Warrington Dr. N&S | 12W-28N | 35 |
| Washington Av. E&W | 11W-28N | 35 |
| Washington St. E&W | 10W-28N | 35 |
| Waukegan Rd. NW&SE | 12W-28N | 35 |
| Weatherford Ct. E&W | 11W-29N | 35 |
| West Scranton Av. E&W | 12W-28N,11W-28N | 35 |
| Wimbledon Ct. N&S | 11W-28N | 35 |
| Wimbleton Rd. N&S | 11W-28N | 35 |
| Winchester Ct. E&W | 11W-29N | 35 |
| Witchwood Ln. E&W | 11W-28N,10W-28N | 35 |
| Woodland Rd. E&W | 10W-28N | 35 |

### Lake Forest

|  | Grid | Page |
|---|---|---|
| Abington Cambs Dr. E&W | 12W-25N | 42 |
| Ahwahnee Ln. N&S | 11W-26N | 43 |
| Ahwanee Rd. N&S | 11W-26N | 43 |
| Alden Ln. E&W | 11W-27N | 43 |
| Alexis Ct. N&S | 12W-25N | 50 |
| Alison Ln. E&W | 12W-27N | 42 |
| Arbor Ln. E&W | 12W-23N | 50 |
| Arcady Dr. E&W | 12W-24N | 42 |
| Armour Cir. E&W | 12W-26N | 42 |
| Ashlawn Ln. E&W | 12W-26N | 42 |
| Ashley Rd. E&W | 9W-25N | 43 |
| Aspen Dr. NW&SE | 12W-23N | 50 |
| Atteridge Rd. E&W | 10W-27N | 43 |
| Bank Ln. N&S | 10W-25N | 43 |
| Barat Ct. N&S | 10W-25N | 43 |
| Barberry Ln. E&W | 10W-27N,10W-26N | 43 |
| Barn Swallow Rd. N&S | 11W-25N | 43 |
| Barrys Ct. E&W | 12W-25N | 42 |
| Basswood Rd. E&W | 11W-25N | 43 |
| Bear Ct. NW&SE | 12W-26N | 42 |
| Beverly Pl. N&S | 11W-25N | 43 |
| Big Oaks Ln. E&W | 12W-23N | 50 |
| Birch Ct. E&W | 11W-25N | 43 |
| Blackthorn Ln. NE&SW | 11W-25N | 43 |
| Bluffs Edge Dr. NW&SE | 9W-25N | 43 |
| Bowling Green Dr. E&W | 13W-24N | 42 |
| Breckenridge Av. N&S | 11W-23N | 50 |
| Breckenridge Ct. N&S | 11W-24N | 43 |
| Bridgeview E&W | 12W-24N | 42 |
| Bridle Ln. E&W | 11W-25N | 43 |
| Brier Ln. E&W | 11W-25N | 43 |
| Broadsmore Dr. NS&EW | 11W-25N | 43 |
| Buena Rd. N&S | 11W-25N,10W-24N | 43 |
| Burr Oak Rd. N&S | 10W-27N | 43 |
| Burton Dr. N&S | 12W-26N | 42 |
| Butler Dr. N&S | 10W-25N | 43 |
| Cascade Ct., N. E&W | 12W-24N | 42 |
| Cascade Ct., S. E&W | 12W-24N | 42 |
| Castlegate Ct. E&W | 12W-24N | 42 |
| Cherokee Rd. E&W | 10W-26N | 43 |
| Cherry Av. E&W | 10W-26N | 43 |
| Chiltern Dr. N&S | 11W-26N | 43 |

| | Grid | Page |
|---|---|---|
| Chistina Ln. NE&SW | | |
| | 11W-24N | 43 |
| Church Rd. NW&SE | | |
| | 10W-27N | 43 |
| Circle Ln. N&S .... 9W-25N | | 43 |
| Clover Av. N&S ..11W-26N | | 43 |
| College Rd. E&W .. 10W-26N | | 43 |
| Conway Farm Rd. NE&SW | | |
| | 13W-25N | 42 |
| Conway Ln. N&S ..12W-25N | | 42 |
| Conway Rd. NW&SE | | |
| | 13W-26N,12W-26N | 42 |
| Country Pl. N&S ..11W-24N | | 43 |
| Coventry Dr. N&S ..12W-25N | | 43 |
| Crab Tree Ln. E&W | | |
| | 10W-27N | 43 |
| Crest Ct. E&W .. 10W-24N | | 43 |
| Deerpath Ln. | | |
| | 12W-26N,10W-26N | 42 |
| Deerpath Sq. N&S ..11W-26N | | 43 |
| Devonshire Ct. NW&SE | | |
| | 12W-23N | 50 |
| Devonshire Ln. NE&SW | | |
| | 13W-23N | 49 |
| Douglas Dr. N&S .. 9W-25N | | 43 |
| Dover Rd. E&W .. 11W-23N | | 50 |
| Edgecote Ln. NW&SE | | |
| | 11W-26N | 43 |
| Edgewood Rd. N&S | | |
| | 10W-27N | 43 |
| Efner Av. E&W .. 10W-27N | | 43 |
| Elder Path N&S | | |
| | 10W-27N | 43 |
| Elm Tree Rd. N&S .. 10W-27N | | 43 |
| Estate Ln. N&S .. 13W-24N | | 42 |
| Estate Ln., E. E&W | | |
| | 12W-24N | 42 |
| Estes Ln. N&S .. 11W-24N | | 43 |
| Everett Rd. E&W | | |
| | 13W-24N,11W-24N | 42 |
| Evergreen Dr. N&S 12W-24N | | 43 |
| Exter Pl. N&S ..12W-26N | | 42 |
| Fairview Av. N&S .. 11W-24N | | 43 |
| Fairway Dr. E&W .. 12W-24N | | 43 |
| Falls Cir. SW&NE .. 10W-25N | | 43 |
| Farm Rd. E&W .. 13W-24N | | 42 |
| Farnham Ln. E&W ..11W-23N | | 50 |
| Field Ct. NS&EW .. 13W-26N | | 42 |
| Field Dr. N&S .. 13W-26N | | 42 |
| Fiore Dr. N&S .. 12W-24N | | 42 |
| Fletcher Cir. N&S .. 12W-26N | | 42 |
| Forest Av. N&S .. 10W-26N | | 43 |
| Forest Hill Rd. N&S | | |
| | 10W-24N,10W-25N | 43 |
| Foster Pl. NE&SW .. 12W-24N | | 43 |
| Fox Trail Ct. N&S .. 12W-24N | | 42 |
| Franklin Pl. E&W .. 10W-27N | | 43 |
| Franz Ct. E&W .. 12W-24N | | 42 |
| Frost Pl. NE&SW .. 10W-26N | | 43 |
| Gage Ln. E&W .. 12W-27N | | 42 |
| Gavin Ct. NS&EW .. 12W-25N | | 42 |
| Glenwood Rd. E&W | | |
| | 10W-25N | 43 |
| Glouchester Crossing NE&SW | | |
| | 12W-24N | 42 |
| Goldenrod Ln. E&W | | |
| | 12W-23N | 50 |
| Golf Ln. N&S .... 11W-26N | | 43 |
| Granby Rd. E&W .. 10W-27N | | 43 |
| Grandview N&S | | |
| | 10W-24N | 43 |
| Green Bay Rd. N&S | | |
| | 10W-24N,11W-27N | 43 |
| Green Briar Ln. E&W | | |
| | 10W-26N | 43 |
| Greenleaf Av. N&S..10W-27N | | 43 |
| Greenvale Rd. N&S | | |
| | 12W-26N | 42 |
| Greenview Pl. E&W | | |
| | 10W-25N | 43 |
| Greenwood Av. E&W | | |
| | 10W-24N | 43 |
| Griffith Rd. N&S ....10W-27N | | 43 |
| Grove Ct. NW&SE ..12W-24N | | 42 |
| Hackberry Ln. E&W | | |
| | 13W-24N | 42 |
| Halligan Cir. N&S .. 12W-26N | | 42 |
| Harlan Ct. N&S .. 11W-24N | | 43 |
| Harlan Ln. N&S .. 11W-24N | | 43 |
| Hastings Ct. N&S .. 11W-26N | | 43 |
| Hathaway Cir. N&S | | |
| | 12W-26N | 42 |
| Havenwood Ln. E&W | | |
| | 9W-25N | 43 |
| Hawkweed Ln. N&S | | |
| | 11W-27N | 43 |
| Hawthorne Ln. E&W | | |
| | 13W-25N | 42 |
| Hawthorne Pl. N&S | | |
| | 10W-26N,10W-27N | 43 |
| Heather Ct. N&S .. 10W-26N | | 43 |
| Heritage Ct. N&S .. 12W-24N | | 43 |
| Heron Rd. E&W .. 11W-25N | | 43 |
| Hickory Ct. E&W .. 10W-26N | | 43 |
| High Holborn N&S .. 12W-26N | | 42 |
| Highland Av. N&S .. 11W-24N | | 43 |
| Highview Ter. E&W | | |
| | 10W-25N | 43 |
| Hilldale Ct. E&W .. 10W-26N | | 43 |
| Holland Ct. N&S....11W-26N | | 43 |
| Honeysuckle Rd. NE&SW | | |
| | 11W-25N | 43 |
| Hospital Dr. NS&EW | | |
| | 12W-27N,11W-27N | 42 |

| | Grid | Page |
|---|---|---|
| Hunter Ln. NW&SE | | |
| | 11W-25N | 43 |
| Illinois Rd. NS&EW 10W-26N | | 43 |
| Inverlieth Rd. E&W ..12W-26N | | 42 |
| Inverlieth Ter. E&W | | |
| | 12W-26N | 42 |
| Ivy Ct. E&W........10W-25N | | 43 |
| Jacquelyn Ln. (Pvt.) E&W | | |
| | 11W-25N | 43 |
| Jennifer Ct. E&W .. 12W-24N | | 43 |
| June Ter. N&S .... 10W-25N | | 43 |
| Kajer Ln. E&W .... 12W-24N | | 43 |
| Kathryn Ln. N&S .. 12W-24N | | 43 |
| Keith Ln. NE&SW .... 9W-25N | | 43 |
| Kendler Ct. NE&SW .. 9W-25N | | 43 |
| Kennedy Rd. E&W ..12W-26N | | 42 |
| Kennett Ln. E&W .. 12W-24N | | 42 |
| Kennington Ter. E&W | | |
| | 11W-26N | 43 |
| Kimberly Ln. E&W .. 11W-24N | | 43 |
| Kimmer Ct. N&S....12W-24N | | 42 |
| King Muir Rd. N&S 12W-26N | | 42 |
| Knight's Bridge Ct. E&W | | |
| | 12W-24N | 42 |
| Knollwood Cir. NE&SW | | |
| | 12W-28N | 35 |
| Knollwood Ln. N&S | | |
| | 12W-28N | 35 |
| Knollwood Rd. NS&EW | | |
| | 12W-28N | 35 |
| Kurtis Ln. NW&SE ..12W-24N | | 42 |
| Lake Rd. NW&SE | | |
| | 10W-27N,9W-27N | 43 |
| Lakewood Dr. NS&EW | | |
| | 12W-24N | 42 |
| Lane Lorraine E&W | | |
| | 12W-26N | 42 |
| Larchmont Ln. E&W | | |
| | 12W-26N | 42 |
| Larkspur Ln. E&W ..12W-23N | | 50 |
| Laurel Av. E&W .... 11W-27N | | 43 |
| Lawrence Av. N&S | | |
| | 12W-26N | 42 |
| Leilly Ln. E&W .... 12W-25N | | 42 |
| Leland Ct. N&S .. 12W-26N | | 42 |
| Lexington Dr. N&S ..12W-26N | | 42 |
| Linden Av. E&W .. 10W-24N | | 43 |
| Lindsey Cir. E&W .. 12W-25N | | 42 |
| Littlefield Ct. N&S .. 13W-24N | | 42 |
| Loch Ln. E&W .... 9W-25N | | 43 |
| Longmeadow Ln. E&W | | |
| | 10W-26N | 42 |
| Longwood Dr. E&W | | |
| | 10W-24N | 43 |
| Louis Av. E&W .... 11W-24N | | 43 |
| Lowell Ln. N&S .. 12W-23N | | 50 |
| Lynette NE&SW ....12W-24N | | 42 |
| Mallard Ln. E&W .. 11W-25N | | 43 |
| Maple Ct. N&S .... 9W-26N | | 43 |
| Maplewood Rd. E&W | | |
| | 10W-25N | 43 |
| Mar-Lane Dr. N&S ..12W-24N | | 42 |
| Marion Av. E&W .. 10W-24N | | 43 |
| Mayflower Rd. N&S | | |
| | 9W-25N,9W-26N | 43 |
| Maywood Rd. N&S | | |
| | 10W-25N | 43 |
| McCormick Dr. NS&EW | | |
| | 9W-25N | 43 |
| McKinley Rd. N&S | | |
| | 10W-25N,10W-27N | 43 |
| Meadow Lake Ln. NW&SE | | |
| | 13W-25N | 42 |
| Meadow Ln. E&W .. 13W-25N | | 42 |
| Meadow Ln. N&S .. 10W-27N | | 43 |
| Meadowood Dr. N&S | | |
| | 13W-25N | 42 |
| Mellody Rd. E&W .. 12W-26N | | 42 |
| Memory Ln. N&S .. 12W-23N | | 50 |
| Michgamme Ln. N&S | | |
| | 11W-25N | 43 |
| Millburne Rd. N&S ..11W-23N | | 50 |
| Mills Ct. E&W ...... 10W-27N | | 43 |
| Minthaven Rd. N&S | | |
| | 13W-24N | 42 |
| Monticello Cir. N&S | | |
| | 12W-26N | 42 |
| Morningside Dr. E&W | | |
| | 10W-24N | 43 |
| Mt. Vernon Av. N&S | | |
| | 11W-24N | 43 |
| Negaunee Ln. N&S | | |
| | 11W-25N | 43 |
| Newcastle Dr. NW&SE | | |
| | 10W-25N | 42 |
| Niles Av. E&W......10W-24N | | 43 |
| Noble Av. E&W .... 10W-27N | | 43 |
| North Av. E&W .... 11W-24N | | 43 |
| North Cliff Way E&W | | |
| | 12W-24N | 43 |
| North Croft Ct. N&S | | |
| | 11W-25N | 43 |
| North Gate Sq. E&W | | |
| | 10W-26N | 43 |
| Northmoor Rd. E&W | | |
| | 10W-25N | 43 |
| O'Leary Ln. (Pvt.) E&W | | |
| | 12W-28N | 35 |
| Oak Knoll Dr. N&S | | |
| | 12W-23N,12W-27N | 50 |
| Oakdale Av. E&W .. 10W-24N | | 43 |
| Oakwood Av. N&S | | |
| | 10W-26N,10W-27N | 43 |
| Old Barn Ln. N&S .. 13W-24N | | 42 |

| | Grid | Page |
|---|---|---|
| Old Colony Rd. N&S | | |
| | 11W-24N | 43 |
| Old Elm Rd. E&W | | |
| | 11W-24N,10W-24N | 43 |
| Old Mill Rd. E&W | | |
| | 13W-24N,11W-24N | 42 |
| Onwentsia Rd. E&W | | |
| | 11W-25N,10W-25N | 43 |
| Orchard Hill Rd. NS&EW | | |
| | 13W-25N | 42 |
| Overlook Dr. NW&SE | | |
| | 9W-25N | 43 |
| Oxford Rd. (Pvt.) E&W | | |
| | 10W-27N | 43 |
| Park Av. E&W......10W-27N | | 43 |
| Parkmead Ln. E&W | | |
| | 12W-26N | 42 |
| Parliament Ct. E&W | | |
| | 13W-23N | 49 |
| Pembroke Dr. E&W | | |
| | 10W-26N | 43 |
| Pine Ln. E&W ...... 10W-27N | | 43 |
| Pinecroft Ln. NE&SW | | |
| | 12W-25N | 42 |
| Polo Dr. N&S .... 11W-24N | | 43 |
| Poplar Rd. E&W .. 11W-25N | | 43 |
| Prairie Av. N&S .. 11W-24N | | 43 |
| Prairie View Ln. E&W | | |
| | 13W-25N | 42 |
| Private Rd. E&W | | |
| | 12W-26N,12W-27N | 42 |
| Private Rd. E&W .. 11W-26N | | 43 |
| Quail Dr. N&S .... 11W-25N | | 43 |
| Ranch Rd. N&S .... 13W-24N | | 42 |
| Ravine Park Dr. E&W | | |
| | 10W-27N | 43 |
| Red Fox Ln. N&S .. 10W-27N | | 43 |
| Reilly Ln. E&W .. 12W-25N | | 42 |
| Ridge Ln. NE&SW .. 10W-26N | | 43 |
| Ridge Rd. N&S | | |
| | 11W-23N,11W-26N | 50 |
| Ridgefield Ln. NW&SE | | |
| | 13W-25N | 42 |
| Ringwood Rd. NS&EW | | |
| | 9W-25N | 43 |
| Riparian Dr. NE&SW | | |
| | 9W-25N | 43 |
| Rockfeller Rd. N&S .. 9W-25N | | 43 |
| Rose Ter. E&W .. 10W-27N | | 43 |
| Rosemary Rd. E&W | | |
| | 10W-26N,9W-26N | 43 |
| Route 43 N&S | | |
| | 12W-24N,12W-27N | 42 |
| Route 60 E&W .... 13W-26N | | 42 |
| Rue Foret NW&SE ..12W-26N | | 42 |
| Ryan Pl. NE&SW .. 12W-26N | | 42 |
| S. Gate Sq. E&W .. 10W-26N | | 43 |
| Saddle Run E&W .. 11W-25N | | 43 |
| Sand Piper Ln. E&W | | |
| | 11W-25N,10W-25N | 43 |
| Saunders Rd. N&S 13W-25N | | 42 |
| Savanna Ct. NW&SE | | |
| | 12W-26N | 42 |
| Scott Av. N&S .... 10W-26N | | 43 |
| Sequoia Ct. N&S .. 11W-26N | | 43 |
| Shawford Way E&W | | |
| | 11W-23N | 50 |
| Shawnee Ln. N&S ..11W-25N | | 43 |
| Sheffield Ct. NW&SE | | |
| | 12W-25N | 42 |
| Sheridan Rd. N&S | | |
| | 10W-27N,9W-24N | 43 |
| Sir William Ln. N&S | | |
| | 12W-24N | 42 |
| Skokie Hwy. N&S | | |
| | 11W-25N,11W-27N | 43 |
| South Shore Ln. NW&SE | | |
| | 9W-26N | 43 |
| Spring Ln. E&W .... 9W-26N | | 43 |
| Spruce Av. E&W .. 10W-27N | | 43 |
| Stable Ln. N&S .. 11W-25N | | 43 |
| Stablewood Ln. E&W | | |
| | 12W-25N | 42 |
| Stone Av. E&W .. 11W-24N | | 43 |
| Stone Gate Ln. NE&SW | | |
| | 9W-26N | 43 |
| Stone Gate Rd. N&S | | |
| | 9W-25N | 43 |
| Stoneleigh Ct. E&W | | |
| | 13W-23N | 49 |
| Stratford Ct. E&W .. 13W-23N | | 49 |
| Suffolk Ln. N&S | | |
| | 12W-25N,12W-26N | 50 |
| Suffolk Ln. N&S | | |
| | 12W-26N,11W-26N | 42 |
| Summerfield Dr. NE&SW | | |
| | 12W-26N,12W-27N | 42 |
| Summit Av. N&S | | |
| | 10W-26N,10W-27N | 43 |
| Summit Pl. NW&SE | | |
| | 10W-26N | 43 |
| Sunset Pl. E&W .. 10W-26N | | 43 |
| Surrey Ln. N&S .. 11W-23N | | 50 |
| Sussex Ln. NE&SW | | |
| | 12W-26N | 42 |
| Tanglewood Ct. N&S | | |
| | 12W-25N | 42 |
| Tara Ln. N&S .... 11W-24N | | 43 |
| Telegraph Rd. N&S | | |
| | 12W-23N | 50 |
| Thomas Pl. E&W .. 10W-27N | | 43 |
| Thorne Ln. NE&SW | | |
| | 10W-26N | 43 |

| | Grid | Page |
|---|---|---|
| Timber Ln. N&S | | |
| | 10W-24N,10W-25N | 43 |
| Tiverton Rd. N&S .. 11W-26N | | 43 |
| Trillium Ln. E&W.. 13W-24N | | 42 |
| Turicum Rd. NS&EW | | |
| | 9W-25N | 43 |
| U.S. Route 41 N&S | | |
| | 11W-24N,11W-27N | 43 |
| Valley Rd. N&S | | |
| | 10W-24N,10W-25N | 43 |
| Verda Ln. E&W .. 12W-26N | | 42 |
| Vine Av. E&W .. 10W-26N | | 43 |
| Walden Ln. E&W .... 9W-25N | | 43 |
| Wallace Rd. N&S .. 12W-25N | | 42 |
| Walnut Rd. NE&SW | | |
| | 10W-26N | 43 |
| Warwick Rd. E&W ..12W-26N | | 42 |
| Washington Cir. N&S | | |
| | 10W-26N | 43 |
| Washington Rd. N&S | | |
| | 10W-26N | 43 |
| Waukegan Rd. N&S | | |
| | 12W-25N | 42 |
| Waveland Rd. N&S | | |
| | 10W-24N | 43 |
| Wedgewood Ct. NE&SW | | |
| | 13W-23N | 49 |
| Wedgewood Dr. NW&SE | | |
| | 13W-23N | 49 |
| West Fork Dr. N&S | | |
| | 13W-25N | 42 |
| Western Av. N&S | | |
| | 10W-25N,10W-27N | 43 |
| Westleigh Rd. E&W | | |
| | 12W-25N,9W-25N | 42 |
| Westminster Av. E&W | | |
| | 11W-26N,10W-27N | 43 |
| Westmoreland Rd. N&S | | |
| | 11W-26N | 43 |
| White Oak Rd. NE&SW | | |
| | 12W-24N | 42 |
| Wild Rose Ln. E&W | | |
| | 12W-24N | 42 |
| Wildwood Rd. N&S | | |
| | 10W-26N | 43 |
| Willow St. N&S .... 10W-27N | | 43 |
| Wilshire Rd. E&W .. 10W-24N | | 43 |
| Wilson Dr. N&S .. 13W-24N | | 42 |
| Wimbledon Ct. E&W | | |
| | 13W-23N | 49 |
| Windhaven E&W....12W-24N | | 42 |
| Windridge Dr. NS&EW | | |
| | 12W-23N | 50 |
| Winston Rd. N&S .. 10W-25N | | 43 |
| Winwood Dr. E&W ..12W-27N | | 42 |
| Wisconsin Av. NE&SW | | |
| | 9W-27N | 43 |
| Woodbine Ln. E&W .. 9W-27N | | 43 |
| Woodbine Pl. N&S .. 10W-27N | | 43 |
| Wooded Ln. N&S .. 10W-25N | | 43 |
| Woodhill Ln. N&S .. 10W-27N | | 43 |
| Woodland Rd. E&W | | |
| | 10W-27N | 43 |
| Woodlawn Av. E&W | | |
| | 10W-26N | 43 |
| Woodstream Ct. N&S | | |
| | 11W-24N | 43 |
| Wynnfield Ter. E&W | | |
| | 10W-25N | 43 |
| Yorktown Ln. NW&SE | | |
| | 12W-25N | 42 |

## Lake Villa

| | Grid | Page |
|---|---|---|
| Amber Ln. E&W | | |
| | 22W-38N | 14 |
| Apache Trail NS&EW | | |
| | 24W-37N,23W-37N | 14 |
| Arapaho Trail E&W | | |
| | 22W-38N | 14 |
| Balsam Av. E&W .. 22W-37N | | 14 |
| Balsam Ct. E&W .. 22W-37N | | 14 |
| Belmont Av. E&W .. 22W-37N | | 14 |
| Bradford Ct. NW&SE | | |
| | 22W-38N | 14 |
| Briar Ridge Ln. NE&SW | | |
| | 22W-37N | 14 |
| Burnett Av. E&W | | |
| | 22W-37N,22W-38N | 14 |
| Cedar Av. NE&SW .. 22W-38N | | 14 |
| Cedar Lake Rd. N&S | | |
| | 23W-36N,23W-37N | 14 |
| Cedar Ln. N&S .... 23W-38N | | 14 |
| Cedar Village Rd. NW&SE | | |
| | 22W-38N | 14 |
| Central Av. NW&SE | | |
| | 22W-38N | 14 |
| Chelsea Cir. N&S .. 22W-37N | | 14 |
| Cherokee Ct. 24W-37N | | 14 |
| Circuit Ct. E&W .... 23W-36N | | 14 |
| Clayton Av. NW&SE | | |
| | 21W-38N | 14 |
| Cleveland Av. (Pvt.) N&S | | |
| | 23W-38N | 14 |
| Coventry Cove Ct. E&W | | |
| | 23W-37N | 14 |
| Coventry Cove Ln. E&W | | |
| | 22W-37N | 14 |
| Cremin Dr. N&S .... 22W-37N | | 14 |
| Deep Lake Rd. N&S | | |
| | 22W-39N,21W-38N | 14 |
| Delwood Av. N&S .. 23W-37N | | 14 |
| Fairfield Rd. N&S .. 24W-37N | | 14 |

| | Grid | Page |
|---|---|---|
| Fieldstone Ct. E&W | | |
| | 22W-36N | 14 |
| Fieldstone Dr. N&S | | |
| | 22W-37N | 14 |
| Grace Ln. E&W .... 23W-37N | | 14 |
| Grand Av. E&W .. 22W-38N | | 14 |
| Grass Lake Rd. NW&SE | | |
| | 22W-39N | 14 |
| Indian Ridge Ln. E&W | | |
| | 22W-37N | 14 |
| Juniper Ct. E&W .. 22W-37N | | 14 |
| Juniper Way E&W ..22W-37N | | 14 |
| Kenz Ct. E&W......22W-37N | | 14 |
| Kevin Av. E&W .... 22W-37N | | 14 |
| Lake Av. NW&SE .. 22W-38N | | 14 |
| Lake Shore Dr. E&W | | |
| | 23W-37N | 14 |
| Laurie Ct. E&W ... 23W-37N | | 14 |
| Majestic Ln. N&S .. 24W-37N | | 14 |
| McKinley Av. N&S .. 22W-37N | | 14 |
| Meadowview Ct. N&S | | |
| | 22W-37N | 14 |
| Milwaukee Av. NW&SE | | |
| | 22W-38N,23W-38N | 14 |
| Monaville Rd. E&W | | |
| | 23W-36N | 14 |
| Monica Dr. N&S .. 22W-37N | | 14 |
| N. Cedar Lake Av. N&S | | |
| | 23W-38N | 14 |
| N. Shore Av. N&S ..23W-38N | | 14 |
| Nez Perc Ln. N&S .. 24W-37N | | 14 |
| Northwind Dr. E&W | | |
| | 23W-37N | 14 |
| Northwind Ln. N&S ..23W-37N | | 14 |
| Oak Knoll Dr. N&S ..23W-37N | | 14 |
| Oak Ln. N&S ...... 23W-37N | | 14 |
| Oakton Ln. E&W .. 22W-37N | | 14 |
| Oakwood Ct. E&W | | |
| | 23W-37N | 14 |
| Overlook Ct. N&S .. 23W-36N | | 14 |
| Park Av. N&S .... 22W-37N | | 14 |
| Petite Lake Rd. E&W | | |
| | 23W-39N | 14 |
| Pineview Pass N&S | | |
| | 22W-37N | 14 |
| Red Spruce Tr. NE&SW | | |
| | 22W-37N | 14 |
| Roselle Ct E&W .. 22W-37N | | 14 |
| Rosemont Ln. E&W | | |
| | 23W-38N | 14 |
| Route 132 E&W | | |
| | 23W-38N,22W-38N | 14 |
| Route 83 NW&SE | | |
| | 22W-37N,23W-38N | 14 |
| Sheehan Dr. N&S .. 22W-37N | | 14 |
| Sherwood Av. N&S | | |
| | 22W-37N | 14 |
| Shoshoni Trail E&W | | |
| | 22W-38N | 14 |
| Summit Ct. NW&SE | | |
| | 23W-36N | 14 |
| Tallgrass Ln. N&S .. 22W-37N | | 14 |
| Trenker Dr. E&W .. 23W-39N | | 14 |
| Twin Oaks Dr. E&W | | |
| | 22W-38N | 14 |
| Villa Av. E&W ...... 22W-38N | | 14 |
| Walden Ln. N&S .. 23W-37N | | 14 |
| Waterbury Cir. N&S | | |
| | 23W-37N | 14 |
| Waters Edge Dr. NE&SW | | |
| | 22W-38N | 14 |
| Wesley Av. N&S | | |
| | 23W-37N,22W-37N | 14 |
| White Pine Ln. E&W | | |
| | 22W-37N | 14 |
| Windance Ct. N&S .. 22W-37N | | 14 |
| Windance Dr. E&W | | |
| | 23W-37N | 14 |
| Woodhead Dr. N&S | | |
| | 21W-38N | 14 |

## Lake Villa Township

| | Grid | Page |
|---|---|---|
| Academy Ct. NW&SE | | |
| | 25W-38N | 13 |
| Academy Dr. NE&SW | | |
| | 25W-37N,25W-38N | 13 |
| Alberta Av. N&S .... 24W-36N | | 13 |
| Alice Ln. N&S .... 21W-36N | | 15 |
| Alpine Ct. E&W .... 24W-37N | | 13 |
| Alpine Ln. NE&SW .. 24W-37N | | 13 |
| Amanda Ct. E&W .. 25W-38N | | 13 |
| Anderle Av. N&S .. 21W-38N | | 15 |
| Antonio Av. N&S .. 21W-37N | | 15 |
| Apollo Ct. E&W .... 23W-39N | | 14 |
| Arcade Dr. E&W .. 23W-37N | | 14 |
| Arcade Dr., N. E&W | | |
| | 25W-37N | 13 |
| Arcade Dr., S. E&W | | |
| | 25W-37N | 13 |
| Ardmore Ln. N&S .. 23W-38N | | 14 |
| Ash St. N&S ...... 21W-38N | | 15 |
| Ashley Dr. N&S .. 25W-38N | | 13 |
| Avon Dr. N&S ...... 25W-37N | | 13 |
| Aztec St. E&W .... 24W-39N | | 13 |
| Balboa Dr. N&S .... 24W-39N | | 13 |
| Bald Eagle Rd. E&W | | |
| | 25W-38N | 13 |
| Bayshore Rd. N&S 25W-37N | | 13 |
| Beach Av. E&W .. 24W-39N | | 13 |
| Beck Rd. N&S | | |
| | 20W-38N,20W-39N | 15 |
| Belmoral Park N&S | | |
| | 23W-38N | 14 |

| | Grid | Page |
|---|---|---|
| Bernice Dr. N&S | 22W-36N | 14 |
| Big Oak Dr. E&W | 24W-37N | 13 |
| Birch St. NE&SW | 21W-38N | 15 |
| Bishop Ct. E&W | 24W-39N | 13 |
| Blackcherry Ln. E&W | 24W-36N | 13 |
| Blackstone Pl. E&W | 25W-37N | 13 |
| Brentwood Ln. E&W | 21W-39N | 15 |
| Buena Av. E&W | 25W-38N | 13 |
| Busse Av. E&W | 25W-37N | 13 |
| Caine Rd. E&W | 24W-36N | 13 |
| Capillo Av. N&S | 20W-37N | 15 |
| Carol Ln. N&S | 21W-36N | 15 |
| Carson Dr. E&W | 25W-37N | 13 |
| Cedar Av. E&W | 21W-38N | 15 |
| Cedar Av. N&S | 23W-38N | 14 |
| Cedar Crest Ln. E&W | 25W-38N | 13 |
| Cedar Lake Ln. E&W | 24W-38N | 13 |
| Cedar Lake Rd. N&S | 23W-37N | 14 |
| Cedar Valley Dr. N&S | 24W-38N | 13 |
| Cedarwood Ln. E&W | 24W-36N | 13 |
| Central Av. NE&SW | 23W-38N | 14 |
| Chesney Dr. E&W | 25W-37N | 13 |
| Christiansen Av. E&W | 21W-38N | 15 |
| Columbia Bay Dr. N&S | 25W-37N,25W-38N | 13 |
| Columbus Av. N&S | 20W-37N | 15 |
| Corona Dr. NW&SE | 20W-36N | 15 |
| Crabapple Dr. N&S | 24W-39N | 13 |
| Crabtree Ln. E&W | 24W-36N | 13 |
| Cremona Av. N&S | 20W-37N | 15 |
| Danny Ln. E&W | 21W-36N | 15 |
| Deep Lake Rd. N&S | 22W-39N,21W-38N | 14 |
| Delaby Ln. N&S | 25W-37N | 13 |
| Dering Ln. E&W | 25W-38N,24W-38N | 13 |
| Diana Av. E&W | 24W-38N | 13 |
| Douglas Ln. N&S | 21W-37N | 15 |
| Eagle Ct. NW&SE | 24W-36N | 13 |
| Eastmore Av. N&S | 24W-36N | 13 |
| Edgewood Av. E&W | 21W-38N | 15 |
| Edgewood Av. N&S | 21W-38N | 15 |
| Edward Av. N&S | 21W-36N | 15 |
| Elizabeth Ct. N&S | 21W-36N | 15 |
| Elizabeth Dr. N&S | 21W-36N | 15 |
| Elm Av. E&W | 24W-39N | 13 |
| Elm St. E&W | 21W-38N | 15 |
| Engle Dr. E&W | 21W-36N | 15 |
| Entrance Dr. NW&SE | 25W-38N | 13 |
| Fairfield Rd. N&S | 24W-36N,24W-38N | 13 |
| Fairview Cir. E&W | 25W-37N | 13 |
| Fairview Ln. NE&SW | 25W-37N | 13 |
| Fairway Dr. NS&EW | 24W-38N | 13 |
| Forest Av. N&S | 20W-36N | 15 |
| Fox Ter. E&W | 24W-36N | 13 |
| Garcia Dr. E&W | 20W-37N | 15 |
| Gelden Rd. E&W | 21W-39N | 15 |
| Genoa Av. E&W | 20W-36N | 15 |
| George Ct. N&S | 20W-37N | 14 |
| Gilliam Rd. NE&SW | 24W-38N | 13 |
| Glade Dr. E&W | 25W-37N | 13 |
| Glen Lake Pl. N&S | 23W-38N | 14 |
| Golf Ln. E&W | 24W-39N | 13 |
| Granada Blvd. NE&SW | 20W-36N,20W-37N | 15 |
| Grand Av. NS&EW | 25W-37N,19W-36N | 13 |
| Grand Blvd. N&S | 25W-37N | 13 |
| Grass Lake Rd. NW&SE | 22W-39N,19W-39N | 14 |
| Graton Rd. N&S | 24W-37N | 13 |
| Haidi Ln. E&W | 24W-37N | 13 |
| Hampshire Ln. N&S | 25W-37N | 13 |
| Harbor Ridge Dr. NS&EW | 25W-39N,24W-39N | 13 |
| Harding Av. N&S | 25W-37N | 13 |
| Harold Ln. E&W | 22W-36N | 14 |
| Hazelwood Dr. N&S | 24W-36N | 13 |
| Helen Ct. N&S | 21W-38N | 15 |
| Helen Dr. N&S | 21W-38N | 15 |
| Hickory St. N&S | 21W-38N | 15 |
| Highwood Av. E&W | 24W-39N | 13 |
| Hilda Av. N&S | 21W-36N | 15 |
| Hillside Av. N&S | 25W-37N | 13 |
| Honey Ln. E&W | 21W-36N | 15 |
| Ironwood Av. N&S | 19W-37N | 15 |
| Isola Av. N&S | 20W-37N | 15 |
| James Ct. N&S | 24W-36N | 13 |
| James Dr. N&S | 22W-36N | 14 |
| Jessica Ct. E&W | 25W-38N | 13 |
| Knoll Ct. N&S | 25W-37N | 13 |

| | Grid | Page |
|---|---|---|
| Lake Av. N&S | 23W-38N | 14 |
| Lake Av. NE&SW | 24W-39N | 13 |
| Lake Av. NE&SW | 21W-38N | 15 |
| Lake Ct. E&W | 20W-36N | 15 |
| Lake Shore Dr. E&W | 23W-38N | 14 |
| Lake Shore Dr. N&S | 23W-38N | 13 |
| Lakeview N&S | 20W-36N | 15 |
| Lakeview Av. NW&SE | 20W-36N | 15 |
| Lakeview Ct. E&W | 25W-37N | 13 |
| Lakeview Dr. E&W | 24W-39N | 13 |
| Lakeview Rd. NE&SW | 25W-38N | 13 |
| Lakewood Av. N&S | 23W-38N | 14 |
| Laurel Ct. N&S | 25W-37N | 13 |
| Lawrence Ct. N&S | 21W-36N | 15 |
| Lawrence Dr. N&S | 21W-36N | 15 |
| Lehmann Blvd. E&W | 25W-37N | 13 |
| Liberty Av. E&W | 23W-38N | 14 |
| Lincoln Dr. E&W | 25W-37N | 13 |
| Linda Ln. E&W | 24W-39N | 13 |
| Loretto Av. N&S | 20W-37N | 15 |
| Maple Av. N&S | 21W-38N | 15 |
| Marilyn Ln. N&S | 21W-36N | 15 |
| Marshfield Rd. E&W | 25W-37N | 13 |
| Mary Ct. N&S | 21W-36N | 15 |
| Mary Dr. N&S | 21W-36N | 15 |
| Maurine Dr. E&W | 21W-36N | 15 |
| Megan Ct. NE&SW | 25W-38N | 13 |
| Milburn Rd. NW&SE | 19W-39N | 15 |
| Miller Rd. NW&SE | 21W-38N | 15 |
| Monaville Rd. E&W | 24W-37N,22W-36N | 13 |
| Morey Ln. E&W | 24W-36N | 13 |
| Morton N&S | 22W-36N | 14 |
| Morton Dr. E&W | 22W-36N,21W-37N | 14 |
| Munn Rd. N&S | 21W-36N | 15 |
| N. Shore Dr. E&W | 23W-38N | 14 |
| Nathan Hale Dr. N&S | 21W-36N | 15 |
| Newberry Ln. NS&EW | 25W-37N | 13 |
| Nielson Dr. E&W | 21W-36N | 15 |
| Normandy Av. N&S | 21W-36N | 15 |
| North Av. NE&SW | 25W-38N | 13 |
| North Columbia Bay Dr. E&W | 25W-38N | 13 |
| North Dr. E&W | 24W-39N | 13 |
| North Rd. E&W | 24W-39N | 13 |
| North St. N&S | 21W-38N | 15 |
| North Way Av. E&W | 23W-38N | 14 |
| Oak Av. E&W | 24W-39N | 13 |
| Oak Av. NW&SE | 21W-38N,21W-39N | 15 |
| Oak Creek Ln. N&S | 21W-39N | 15 |
| Oak Dr. N&S | 24W-39N | 13 |
| Oakwood Dr. N&S | 21W-36N | 15 |
| Obermaier Ln. E&W | 25W-37N | 13 |
| Old Monaville Rd. E&W | 24W-36N | 13 |
| Paradise Ln. E&W | 21W-36N | 15 |
| Park Av. N&S | 24W-39N | 13 |
| Park Av. N&S | 24W-39N | 13 |
| Park Ct. E&W | 25W-37N | 13 |
| Park Dr. E&W | 22W-36N,21W-36N | 14 |
| Park Ln., E. N&S | 25W-37N | 13 |
| Park Ln., W. N&S | 25W-37N | 13 |
| Park Pl. N&S | 25W-38N | 13 |
| Park St. NW&SE | 23W-38N | 14 |
| Parma Av. N&S | 20W-37N | 15 |
| Peninsula Rd. N&S | 25W-37N,25W-38N | 13 |
| Petite Ct. E&W | 24W-39N | 13 |
| Petite Lake Rd. N&S | 24W-39N,23W-39N | 13 |
| Petite Ter. N&S | 24W-39N | 13 |
| Pike St. NE&SW | 21W-39N | 15 |
| Pine St. NE&SW | 21W-38N | 15 |
| Piper Ln. N&S | 25W-37N | 13 |
| Ponce Av. NE&SW | 20W-37N | 15 |
| Poplar St. N&S | 21W-38N,21W-39N | 15 |
| Prairieview Dr. N&S | 20W-36N | 15 |
| Raska Ln. E&W | 25W-37N | 13 |
| Ravine Crest Dr. NW&SE | 24W-39N | 13 |
| Ravine Ct. NW&SE | 24W-39N | 13 |
| Ravine Dr. NW&SE | 24W-39N | 13 |
| Ravine Ln. NE&SW | 24W-39N | 13 |
| Richard Ln. N&S | 22W-36N | 14 |
| Riviera Dr. NE&SW | 20W-37N | 15 |
| Romero Av. E&W | 20W-37N | 15 |
| Rose Av. N&S | 24W-36N | 13 |
| Rose Ct. E&W | 22W-36N | 14 |
| Rosemont Ln. E&W | 23W-38N | 14 |

| | Grid | Page |
|---|---|---|
| Route 132 E&W | 25W-38N,19W-36N | 13 |
| Route 83 N&S | 23W-39N,22W-36N | 14 |
| Rustic Dr. N&S | 21W-39N | 15 |
| S. Nathan Hale Dr. NE&SW | 21W-36N | 15 |
| San Rem Av. E&W | 20W-37N | 15 |
| Sand Lake Rd. E&W | 19W-37N | 15 |
| Sarah Dr. E&W | 21W-36N | 15 |
| Savage Rd. NS&EW | 21W-39N,20W-39N | 15 |
| Saxony Dr. NW&SE | 24W-37N | 13 |
| Sheridan Rd. N&S | 25W-38N | 13 |
| Shore Dr. N&S | 25W-37N | 13 |
| Short St. N&S | 25W-37N | 13 |
| Sienna Dr. E&W | 20W-37N | 15 |
| Sir John Dr. N&S | 24W-39N | 13 |
| Sistina Av. NW&SE | 20W-37N | 15 |
| South Av. E&W | 24W-36N | 13 |
| Spruce St. N&S | 21W-39N | 15 |
| Stonebridge Dr. NW&SE | 24W-36N | 13 |
| Summerfield Dr. NE&SW | 25W-37N | 13 |
| Sunnyside Rd. E&W | 25W-38N | 13 |
| Sunset Ln. E&W | 25W-38N | 13 |
| Sunshine Av. N&S | 21W-36N | 15 |
| Terry Dr., E. NW&SE | 24W-36N | 14 |
| Terry Dr., N. E&W | 22W-37N | 14 |
| Terry Dr., W. E&W | 22W-36N | 14 |
| Thorndale Pl. N&S | 23W-38N | 14 |
| Timber Ln. E&W | 23W-38N | 14 |
| Trenker Dr. E&W | 23W-39N | 14 |
| U.S. Route 45 N&S | 19W-39N,19W-36N | 15 |
| Valina Av. N&S | 25W-38N | 13 |
| Verona Av. E&W | 20W-37N | 15 |
| Villa Av. N&S | 24W-38N | 14 |
| Villa Ct. N&S | 22W-38N | 14 |
| W. Park Av. N&S | 23W-38N | 14 |
| Wacker Dr. E&W | 23W-38N | 14 |
| Wall St. E&W | 23W-39N | 14 |
| Walnut Av. N&S | 21W-39N | 15 |
| Washington Av. E&W | 23W-38N | 14 |
| Wayside Pl. E&W | 25W-37N | 13 |
| West Av. N&S | 23W-38N | 14 |
| Westmoor Av. N&S | 24W-36N | 13 |
| Wildwood Dr. N&S | 21W-36N | 15 |
| Willow St. NE&SW | 21W-38N | 15 |
| Wilson Rd. E&W | 25W-38N | 13 |
| Wilton Av. N&S | 23W-38N | 14 |
| Wilton Way NW&SE | 23W-38N | 14 |
| Winthrop Pl. E&W | 24W-38N,23W-38N | 13 |
| Wittenburg Rd. N&S | 21W-39N | 15 |
| Woodland Av. NW&SE | 20W-36N | 15 |
| Woodland Ter. E&W | 25W-37N | 13 |
| Woods Av. E&W | 21W-38N | 15 |
| 1st St. E&W | 21W-38N | 15 |
| 2nd St. E&W | 21W-38N | 15 |
| 3rd St. E&W | 21W-38N | 15 |
| 4th St. E&W | 21W-38N | 15 |
| 5th St. E&W | 21W-38N | 15 |
| 6th St. E&W | 22W-38N | 14 |
| 7th Av. E&W | 21W-38N | 15 |

## Lake Zurich

| | Grid | Page |
|---|---|---|
| Aldine Rd. N&S | 24W-23N | 46 |
| Alpine Dr. E&W | 23W-23N | 46 |
| Amherst Ct. E&W | 22W-23N | 47 |
| Andrew Ln. E&W | 22W-22N | 46 |
| Apache Ct. N&S | 22W-22N | 46 |
| Applegate Cir. E&W | 24W-22N | 46 |
| Applegate Ln. NW&SE | 24W-22N | 46 |
| Ascot Ct. N&S | 22W-22N | 46 |
| Ash St. NE&SW | 23W-23N | 46 |
| Aspen Ct. N&S | 24W-22N | 46 |
| Bayview Ct. N&S | 22W-21N | 46 |
| Beach Rd. N&S | 22W-22N | 46 |
| Beaubien Ct. E&W | 23W-23N | 46 |
| Beauteau St. NW&SE | 23W-23N | 46 |
| Beechwood Dr. NW&SE | 22W-22N | 46 |
| Berkshire Ln. NS&EW | 24W-21N | 46 |
| Bern Ct. E&W | 23W-23N | 46 |
| Betty Dr. E&W | 23W-23N | 46 |
| Blacktwig Cir. N&S | 22W-22N | 46 |
| Braemar Ct. NW&SE | 24W-21N | 46 |
| Braemar Ln. NE&SW | 24W-21N | 46 |
| Briar Point Ct. E&W | 22W-22N | 46 |
| Bristol Trail Rd. E&W | 22W-22N,21W-22N | 46 |
| Brittany Rd. E&W | 22W-22N | 46 |

| | Grid | Page |
|---|---|---|
| Broadway Ct. NW&SE | 21W-21N | 47 |
| Brookfield Ct. E&W | 22W-22N | 46 |
| Browning Ln. E&W | 22W-22N | 46 |
| Brush Hill Ln. E&W | 22W-22N | 46 |
| Buckingham Ct. NW&SE | 22W-22N | 46 |
| Bueshing Rd. N&S | 23N-22N | 46 |
| Buffalo Creek Dr. E&W | 22W-22N | 46 |
| Burr Oak Ct. NE&SW | 22W-22N | 46 |
| Burr Oak Dr. NS&EW | 22W-22N | 46 |
| Bushrun Ct. NE&SW | 22W-22N | 46 |
| Butterfield Ct. N&S | 23W-23N | 46 |
| Butterfield Rd. E&W | 24W-23N | 46 |
| Carolyn Ct. N&S | 23W-23N | 46 |
| Carriage Ln. E&W | 24W-22N | 46 |
| Cedar Creek Dr. NS&EW | 22W-22N,21W-22N | 46 |
| Centoni Ct. E&W | 24W-23N | 46 |
| Century Ct. N&S | 22W-22N | 46 |
| Chancery Ln. N&S | 23W-22N | 46 |
| Chasemoor Dr. E&W | 21W-22N | 46 |
| Chasewood Dr. N&S | 22W-21N | 46 |
| Cherokee Rd. E&W | 23W-23N | 46 |
| Cherry Ln. E&W | 23W-23N | 46 |
| Chesterfield Ln. NS&EW | 24W-21N | 46 |
| Cheswick Ln. E&W | 21W-21N | 47 |
| Church St. NE&SW | 23W-23N | 46 |
| Clearwater Ct. E&W | 22W-21N | 46 |
| Clubhouse Ln. NW&SE | 24W-22N | 46 |
| Colonial Ct. E&W | 24W-22N | 46 |
| Columbine N&S | 23W-22N | 46 |
| Coral Reef Way E&W | 22W-22N | 46 |
| Cortland Cir. N&S | 24W-22N | 46 |
| Cortland N&S | 24W-22N | 46 |
| Country Club Rd. N&S | 24W-23N | 46 |
| Country Ridge Ct., N. N&S | 22W-22N | 46 |
| Country Ridge Ct., S. N&S | 22W-22N | 46 |
| Craig Ter. NW&SE | 24W-23N | 46 |
| Crescent Rd. NS&EW | 24W-23N | 46 |
| Cromwell Ct. E&W | 22W-21N | 46 |
| Cypress Bridge Rd. E&W | 22W-21N | 46 |
| Dearborn Ct. N&S | 23W-22N | 46 |
| Deerchase Rd. N&S | 22W-22N | 46 |
| Deerpath Rd. NS&EW | 23W-21N,22W-21N | 46 |
| Denberry Ct. E&W | 23W-21N | 46 |
| Denberry Dr. E&W | 23W-21N | 46 |
| Dogwood Ct. E&W | 24W-22N | 46 |
| Donegal Ln. N&S | 24W-22N | 46 |
| Dunwick Ct. E&W | 24W-21N | 46 |
| E. Main St. E&W | 23W-23N,22W-23N | 46 |
| Eddy Ln. N&S | 22W-21N | 46 |
| Edelweiss Dr. E&W | 23W-22N | 46 |
| Ela Rd. N&S | 22W-22N | 46 |
| Elm Pl. N&S | 23W-22N | 46 |
| Ensell Rd. N&S | 22W-23N,21W-22N | 46 |
| Evanston Ter. E&W | 24W-23N | 46 |
| Evergreen St. NE&SW | 23W-23N | 46 |
| Fairway Rd. N&S | 24W-23N | 46 |
| Farm Bridge Rd. E&W | 22W-22N | 46 |
| Fern Ct. E&W | 22W-22N,21W-22N | 46 |
| Fern Rd. N&S | 21W-22N,22W-23N | 47 |
| Ferndale Ct. N&S | 22W-22N | 46 |
| Fescue Ct. N&S | 23W-21N | 46 |
| Fescue Dr. N&S | 23W-21N | 46 |
| Fieldstone Cir. N&S | 22W-21N | 46 |
| Forest Av. NE&SW | 23W-23N | 46 |
| Foxfire Dr. N&S | 23W-21N | 46 |
| Foxmoor Ln. NS&EW | 22W-22N | 46 |
| Garland Ct. E&W | 23W-22N | 46 |
| Genesee St. NE&SW | 23W-23N | 46 |
| Ginger Tr. NE&SW | 23W-22N | 46 |
| Glen Farm Ln. N&S | 22W-22N | 46 |
| Glencoe Ter. E&W | 24W-23N | 46 |
| Golf View Rd. NE&SW | 24W-23N,23W-23N | 46 |
| Greenbay Ct. E&W | 22W-21N | 46 |

| | Grid | Page |
|---|---|---|
| Grever Ct. E&W | 23W-22N | 46 |
| Greystone N&S | 22W-22N | 46 |
| Grove St. NW&SE | 23W-23N | 46 |
| Hapshire Ln. E&W | 24W-24N | 38 |
| Harvest Dr. E&W | 22W-22N | 46 |
| Heartwood Ln. E&W | 22W-22N | 46 |
| Hickory Rd. N&S | 24W-23N | 46 |
| Hillside Ct. NE&SW | 23W-22N | 46 |
| Hobble Bush Dr. N&S | 22W-22N | 46 |
| Holly Court Rd. E&W | 24W-24N | 38 |
| Hollycourt Ter. NE&SW | 22W-22N | 46 |
| Honeylake Rd. E&W | 24W-23N | 46 |
| Huntclub Dr. E&W | 22W-22N,21W-22N | 46 |
| Hunters Ln. E&W | 22W-22N | 46 |
| Huntington Way NS&EW | 22W-22N | 46 |
| Indigo Ct. NE&SW | 22W-22N | 46 |
| Interlaken Dr. N&S | 23W-23N | 46 |
| Ironwood Ct. N&S | 23W-22N | 46 |
| Ivy Ct. E&W | 22W-22N | 46 |
| Jamie Ln. NW&SE | 23W-23N | 46 |
| Jean Ter. E&W | 24W-23N | 46 |
| Jonathan Rd. N&S | 24W-23N | 46 |
| Joyce Ln. E&W | 24W-23N | 46 |
| June Ter. N&S | 23W-23N | 46 |
| Juneway Ter. N&S | 24W-23N | 46 |
| Kenilworth Ter. E&W | 24W-23N | 46 |
| Kim Tr. N&S | 24W-23N | 46 |
| Kincaid Rd. NS&EW | 23W-23N | 46 |
| Kingwood Ln. E&W | 22W-22N | 46 |
| Knollwood Ln. E&W | 24W-22N | 46 |
| Kylemore Dr. N&S | 23W-21N | 46 |
| Lake St. E&W | 23W-22N | 46 |
| Lake Zurich Dr. E&W | 23W-21N | 46 |
| Lake Zurich Dr. NW&SE | 24W-22N | 46 |
| Lakeview Pl. N&S | 23W-22N | 46 |
| Lancaster N&S | 24W-24N | 38 |
| Lexington Ln. NS&EW | 22W-21N | 46 |
| Linden Rd. N&S | 24W-23N | 46 |
| Lions Dr. NW&SE | 23W-23N | 46 |
| Lismore Ct. N&S | 23W-21N | 46 |
| Lorraine Dr. NS&EW | 23W-23N | 46 |
| Lucerne Dr. N&S | 23N-23N,23W-24N | 46 |
| Manchester NE&SW | 24W-24N | 38 |
| Manor Rd. N&S | 24W-23N | 46 |
| Maple Av. E&W | 23W-22N | 46 |
| Marble Hill Dr. E&W | 21W-22N | 47 |
| Margate Ct. E&W | 22W-22N | 46 |
| Maria Ct. N&S | 22W-21N | 46 |
| Meadow Ln. NW&SE | 22W-22N | 46 |
| Meadowbrook Ct. E&W | 22W-22N | 46 |
| Meadowbrook Ln. N&S | 22W-22N | 46 |
| Michael Ct. NW&SE | 23W-21N | 46 |
| Millbrook Ln. E&W | 22W-22N | 46 |
| Miller Rd. E&W | 24W-23N,23W-23N | 46 |
| Minerva Ln. E&W | 24W-22N | 46 |
| Mionske Dr. NW&SE | 23W-23N | 46 |
| Mohawk Rd. N&S | 23W-22N | 46 |
| Mohawk Tr. N&S | 23W-22N | 46 |
| N. Diane Ct. N&S | 21W-22N | 46 |
| N. Harbor Dr. E&W | 22W-21N | 46 |
| N. Old Rand Rd. E&W | 24W-23N | 46 |
| Newberry Ct. E&W | 22W-21N | 46 |
| Newgate Ct. NW&SE | 22W-22N | 46 |
| Northcrest Rd. E&W | 24W-23N | 46 |
| Oak St. NE&SW | 23W-23N | 46 |
| Oakwood Rd. N&S | 23W-23N | 46 |
| Old Mill Grove Rd. N&S | 24W-23N,23W-23N | 46 |
| Orrington Ct. E&W | 22W-21N | 46 |
| Oxford Ct. N&S | 21W-21N | 47 |
| Oxford Ln. N&S | 21W-21N | 47 |
| Pamela Rd. E&W | 22W-22N | 46 |
| Park Av. NW&SE | 22W-22N | 46 |
| Park Ln N&S | 22W-22N | 46 |
| Parkway Av. NE&SW | 23W-23N | 46 |
| Partridge Ln. NS&EW | 22W-22N | 46 |
| Peachtree Ln. N&S | 24W-22N | 46 |
| Pebblecreek Ct. E&W | 22W-22N | 46 |
| Pebblecreek Dr. N&S | 22W-22N | 46 |

| | Grid | Page |
|---|---|---|
| Pembridge Rd. NS&EW | | |
| | 22W-22N | 46 |
| Pheasant Ridge Ct. NE&SW | | |
| | 22W-22N | 46 |
| Pheasant Ridge Dr. E&W | | |
| | 22W-22N,21W-21N | 46 |
| Pheasant Ridge Rd. E&W | | |
| | 23W-22N,21W-21N | 46 |
| Pine Av. E&W | 23W-22N | 46 |
| Pine Tree Row NE&SW | | |
| | 24W-23N | 46 |
| Pleasant Rd. N&S | 24W-23N | 46 |
| Pohlman Ct. E&W | 24W-23N | 46 |
| Poplar Ct. E&W | 24W-22N | 46 |
| Portree Ln. E&W | 22W-22N | 46 |
| Pottawatomi Tr. NS&EW | | |
| | 23W-22N | 46 |
| Prairie Ln. NW&SE | 23W-22N | 46 |
| Prescott Ct. E&W | 21W-23N | 46 |
| Prospect Rd. N&S | 24W-23N | 46 |
| Queen Ann Ln. N&S | | |
| | 23W-21N | 46 |
| Quentin Rd. N&S | | |
| | 21W-21N,21W-23N | 47 |
| Racine Ct. E&W | 23W-23N | 46 |
| Railway St. NE&SW | | |
| | 23W-22N | 46 |
| Ramblewood Ct. E&W | | |
| | 22W-22N | 46 |
| Ramblewood Ln. N&S | | |
| | 22W-22N | 46 |
| Rand Rd. N&S | | |
| | 24W-23N,22W-21N | 46 |
| Ravenswood Ct. N&S | | |
| | 22W-22N | 46 |
| Ravinia Ter. E&W | 24W-23N | 46 |
| Red Bridge Ct. NW&SE | | |
| | 22W-22N | 46 |
| Red Bridge Rd. N&S | | |
| | 22W-22N | 46 |
| Red Haw Ln. E&W | 24W-22N | 46 |
| Regency Dr. N&S | 24W-22N | 46 |
| Regent Ct. NE&SW | | |
| | 21W-22N | 47 |
| Richmond Cir. NE&SW | | |
| | 24W-22N | 46 |
| Richmond Ct. NW&SE | | |
| | 22W-22N | 46 |
| Ridgewood Ct. E&W | | |
| | 22W-22N | 46 |
| Riley Ln. N&S | 22W-22N | 46 |
| Ripple Brook Ct. E&W | | |
| | 22W-21N | 46 |
| Robertson Rd. NE&SW | | |
| | 23W-22N | 46 |
| Rock Rose Dr. E&W | | |
| | 23W-21N | 46 |
| Rose Rd. E&W | 24W-23N | 46 |
| Rugby Rd. NE&SW | | |
| | 24W-23N | 46 |
| Rush Ct. E&W | 22W-21N | 46 |
| Russet Cir. NE&SW | | |
| | 24W-22N | 46 |
| S. Diane Ct. N&S | 21W-22N | 47 |
| S. Harbor Rd. E&W | | |
| | 22W-21N | 46 |
| S. Old Rand Rd. NW&SE | | |
| | 23W-22N | 46 |
| Sandlewood Ct. E&W | | |
| | 22W-22N | 46 |
| Sandy Pass N&S | 22W-21N | 46 |
| Schiller St. E&W | 23W-23N | 46 |
| Schuldt Dr. E&W | 23W-23N | 46 |
| Sebby Ln. NE&SW | 23W-23N | 46 |
| Shaker Ln. NS&EW | | |
| | 22W-21N | 46 |
| Shallow Cover Rd. E&W | | |
| | 22W-21N | 46 |
| Sheffield Ct. N&S | 24W-21N | 46 |
| Sheridan Ct. NW&SE | | |
| | 21W-22N | 47 |
| Shoreview Ln. E&W | | |
| | 24W-22N | 46 |
| Silverwood Ct. NE&SW | | |
| | 22W-22N | 46 |
| South Shore Ln. N&S | | |
| | 23W-22N | 46 |
| Spring Ct. NE&SW | 22W-22N | 46 |
| Spruce St. NE&SW | | |
| | 23W-22N | 46 |
| Stanton Ct. N&S | 22W-22N | 46 |
| Stanton Rd. N&S | | |
| | 22W-22N | 46 |
| Stillwater Ct. N&S | 22W-22N | 46 |
| Stone Av. N&S | 22W-22N | 46 |
| Stratford Ln. E&W | 21W-21N | 47 |
| Summit Ter. NW&SE | | |
| | 23W-23N | 46 |
| Sunrise Ln. N&S | 24W-23N | 46 |
| Sunset Ct. N&S | | |
| | 22W-22N | 46 |
| Sunset Tr. NS&EW | | |
| | 24W-24N | 38 |
| Surryse Rd. E&W | 24W-22N | 46 |
| Sussex Ct. N&S | 23W-22N | 46 |
| Tall Grass Cir. NS&EW | | |
| | 22W-22N | 46 |
| Tara Ct. E&W | 23W-21N | 46 |
| Telser Rd. N&S | | |
| | 22W-22N,24W-23N | 46 |
| Terrace Av. E&W | 23W-22N | 46 |
| Thistle Ln. NS&EW | | |
| | 22W-22N,21W-22N | 46 |

| | Grid | Page |
|---|---|---|
| Thorndale Ct. NW&SE | | |
| | 21W-21N | 47 |
| Thorndale Ln. SW&NE | | |
| | 22W-21N | 47 |
| Thornwood Ct. E&W | | |
| | 24W-23N | 46 |
| Timberwood Dr. N&S | | |
| | 22W-22N | 46 |
| Town Mall Dr. NE&SW | | |
| | 23W-22N | 46 |
| Tracie Dr. NS&EW | 23W-21N | 46 |
| Trailside Dr. NW&SE | | |
| | 22W-22N | 46 |
| Trillium Trail N&S | 23W-22N | 46 |
| Tudor Ct. E&W | 24W-22N | 46 |
| Turtle Pond Ct. NS&EW | | |
| | 22W-22N | 46 |
| Vista Ct. N&S | 24W-23N | 46 |
| Vista Rd. N&S | 24W-23N | 46 |
| W. Harbor Rd. N&S | | |
| | 22W-21N | 46 |
| W. Main St. NE&SW | | |
| | 24W-22N,23W-22N | 46 |
| Warwick Ct. NW&SE | | |
| | 22W-21N | 46 |
| Warwick Ln. NS&EW | | |
| | 21W-21N,21W-22N | 47 |
| Washo Ct. E&W | 23W-21N | 46 |
| Washo Dr. E&W | 23W-21N | 46 |
| Washo Ln. N&S | 23W-21N | 46 |
| Waterbury Ct. NE&SW | | |
| | 21W-22N | 47 |
| Waterford Ct. N&S | 23W-21N | 46 |
| Waterford Dr. NS&EW | | |
| | 23W-21N | 46 |
| White Birch Ln. E&W | | |
| | 22W-22N | 46 |
| Whitehall Ct. N&S | 21W-21N | 47 |
| Whitney Rd. NW&SE | | |
| | 24W-22N | 46 |
| Wilkes Ln. NW&SE | | |
| | 22W-22N | 46 |
| Williams Ct. N&S | 22W-22N | 46 |
| Williams Way E&W | | |
| | 22W-22N,21W-22N | 46 |
| Willow Ter. NW&SE | | |
| | 24W-23N | 46 |
| Wilmette Ter. E&W | | |
| | 24W-23N | 46 |
| Windermere Ln. NW&SE | | |
| | 22W-21N | 46 |
| Winnetka Ter. E&W | | |
| | 24W-23N | 46 |
| Woodbine Cir. NW&SE | | |
| | 22W-22N | 46 |
| Yorkshire Ln. NE&SW | | |
| | 24W-21N | 46 |

### Lakemoor*
**(Also see McHenry County)**

| | Grid | Page |
|---|---|---|
| Beacon Bay NW&SE | | |
| | 28W-33N | 20 |
| Belvidere Rd. E&W | | |
| | 28W-31N,27W-31N | 28 |
| Bouy Bay NW&SE | 28W-33N | 20 |
| Captain Hook NW&SE | | |
| | 28W-33N | 20 |
| Captains Cove NE&SW | | |
| | 28W-33N | 20 |
| Concrete Dr. NS&EW | | |
| | 27W-32N | 20 |
| Drydock NE&SW | 28W-33N | 20 |
| Fishook NE&SW | 28W-33N | 20 |
| Fox Lake Rd. NE&SW | | |
| | 27W-31N,27W-32N | 20 |
| Fox Lake Rd. NE&SW | | |
| | 27W-32N | 20 |
| Gilmer Rd. NW&SE | | |
| | 27W-31N | 29 |
| Hornblower NW&SE | | |
| | 28W-33N | 20 |
| Leaward NE&SW | 28W-33N | 20 |
| Mysty Ridge N&S | 28W-32N | 20 |
| Neptune Cove NW&SE | | |
| | 28W-33N | 20 |
| Oyster Bay E&W | 28W-33N | 20 |
| Port Side NE&SW | 28W-33N | 20 |
| Rand Rd. N&S | 27W-31N | 29 |
| Route 59 N&S | 27W-32N | 20 |
| Rusty Scupper NE&SW | | |
| | 28W-33N | 20 |
| Sand Bar NW&SE | 28W-33N | 20 |
| Sandpiper NW&SE | 28W-33N | 20 |
| Sinker Bay* NW&SE | | |
| | 28W-33N | 20 |
| South Lake Shore Dr. E&W | | |
| | 28W-32N | 20 |
| Stowaway Bay* NE&SW | | |
| | 28W-32N | 20 |
| Sullivan Lake Blvd. N&S | | |
| | 28W-31N,28W-32N | 28 |
| Sullivan Lake Rd. E&W | | |
| | 28W-33N | 20 |
| Sunnyside Rd. E&W | | |
| | 28W-32N | 20 |
| U.S. Route 12 N&S | | |
| | 27W-32N | 20 |
| Windward NW&SE | 28W-32N | 20 |

### Libertyville

| | Grid | Page |
|---|---|---|
| Abby Ct. N&S | 17W-29N | 32 |
| Acorn Ln. N&S | 17W-29N | 32 |
| Adler Dr. E&W | 16W-30N | 33 |
| American Way NS&EW | | |
| | 18W-29N,18W-30N | 32 |
| Ames St. N&S | 16W-28N | 33 |
| Amy N&S | 18W-29N | 32 |
| Amy Ln. N&S | 18W-30N | 32 |
| Annie Ln. N&S | 18W-30N | 32 |
| Apple Tree Ln. N&S | | |
| | 15W-26N | 41 |
| Appley Av. E&W | 16W-29N | 33 |
| Arbor Ct. NW&SE | 16W-29N | 33 |
| Ardmore Ter. N&S | 16W-28N | 33 |
| Artaius Pkwy. N&S | 16W-27N | 41 |
| Arthur Av. N&S | 16W-29N | 33 |
| Ascot Ct.* E&W | 15W-26N | 41 |
| Ash St. N&S | 16W-28N | 33 |
| Ashley Ln. N&S | 17W-29N | 32 |
| Austin Av. N&S | 16W-28N | 33 |
| Avalon Ln. N&S | 16W-29N | 33 |
| Bartlett Ter. N&S | 16W-29N | 33 |
| Bedford Ln. N&S | 17W-28N | 32 |
| Big Oak Ln. E&W | 16W-28N | 33 |
| Blackberry Ct. NW&SE | | |
| | 17W-30N | 32 |
| Blackburn Cir. E&W | | |
| | 17W-29N | 32 |
| Blueberry Rd. N&S | 17W-28N | 32 |
| Brainard Av. N&S | 16W-29N | 33 |
| Brandywine Rd. NW&SE | | |
| | 17W-28N | 32 |
| Braxton Rd. E&W | 17W-28N | 32 |
| Brian Cir. N&S | 18W-29N | 32 |
| Briar Pl. E&W | 16W-28N | 33 |
| Briarwood Ln. E&W | | |
| | 16W-27N | 41 |
| Bridle Ct. E&W | 16W-27N | 41 |
| Broadway E&W | 16W-29N | 33 |
| Buckingham Pl. N&S | | |
| | 16W-28N | 33 |
| Buckley Rd. N&S | 17W-30N | 32 |
| Burdick St. N&S | 16W-28N | 33 |
| Burridge Ct. E&W | 17W-28N | 32 |
| Bush Ct. NW&SE | 18W-30N | 32 |
| Butterfield Rd. N&S | | |
| | 17W-28N,18W-30N | 32 |
| Caliente Ct.* E&W | 15W-26N | 41 |
| Cambridge Dr. N&S | | |
| | 16W-28N | 33 |
| Camelot Ln. N&S | | |
| | 15W-28N,15W-29N | 33 |
| Canterbury Cir. E&W | | |
| | 17W-28N | 32 |
| Carriage Hill Cir. NE&SW | | |
| | 16W-29N | 33 |
| Carter St. N&S | 17W-28N | 32 |
| Cass Ct. N&S | 17W-30N | 32 |
| Cass Dr. N&S | 17W-30N | 32 |
| Castleton Rd. E&W | | |
| | 17W-30N | 32 |
| Catalpa Ln. E&W | 16W-27N | 41 |
| Cedar Glen Ct. NE&SW | | |
| | 17W-30N | 32 |
| Cedar Glen Dr. E&W | | |
| | 17W-30N | 32 |
| Chatham Ct.* N&S | 15W-26N | 41 |
| Checkberry Ct. E&W | | |
| | 17W-28N | 32 |
| Church St. E&W | 16W-29N | 33 |
| Circle Dr. N&S | 16W-28N | 33 |
| Claridge Dr. N&S | 17W-29N | 32 |
| Cleveland Av. E&W | | |
| | 16W-28N | 33 |
| Concord Ln. N&S | | |
| | 15W-27N,15W-28N | 41 |
| Cook Av. N&S | 16W-29N | 33 |
| Coolidge Av. E&W | 16W-28N | 33 |
| Coolidge Pl. E&W | 16W-28N | 33 |
| Country Club Dr. N&S | | |
| | 15W-28N | 33 |
| Crabtree Ln. N&S | 16W-27N | 41 |
| Crane Blvd. E&W | 17W-28N | 32 |
| Crestfield Av. E&W | | |
| | 17W-28N | 32 |
| Cypress Ln. E&W | 16W-27N | 41 |
| Dancer Ct. NE&SW | | |
| | 18W-30N | 32 |
| Darnell St. N&S | 17W-30N | 32 |
| Dawes St. N&S | | |
| | 17W-27N,17W-28N | 40 |
| Deborah Cir. N&S | | |
| | 18W-29N,18W-30N | 32 |
| Deer Trail Ln. E&W | | |
| | 15W-28N | 33 |
| Douglas Av. N&S | 16W-28N | 33 |
| Dover Ct. NE&SW | 17W-28N | 32 |
| Downing Rd. E&W | 16W-27N | 41 |
| Downs Pkwy.* N&S | | |
| | 15W-26N | 41 |
| Drake St. N&S | 17W-28N | 32 |
| Dymond Rd. N&S | 17W-28N | 32 |
| E. Ellis Av. E&W | 16W-29N | 33 |
| E. Park Av. E&W | 16W-29N | 33 |
| E. Winchester E&W | | |
| | 16W-29N | 33 |
| Eaton Ct. N&S | 15W-27N | 41 |
| Eldeberry Dr. N&S | 17W-28N | 32 |
| Ellis Av. N&S | 16W-29N | 33 |
| Elm Ct. N&S | 16W-29N | 33 |
| Elm Dr. N&S | 16W-29N | 33 |

| | Grid | Page |
|---|---|---|
| Emerson Ln.* N&S | 15W-26N | 41 |
| Enterprise Ct. N&S | 19W-30N | 31 |
| Eric Ln. N&S | 18W-29N | 32 |
| Evergreen Ct. E&W | | |
| | 16W-27N | 41 |
| Fairlawn Av. E&W | 17W-28N | 32 |
| Fairview Av. N&S | 16W-28N | 33 |
| Finstead Dr. E&W | 16W-30N | 33 |
| Flamingo Pkwy.* N&S | | |
| | 15W-26N | 41 |
| Florence Ct. E&W | 16W-28N | 33 |
| Florsheim Dr. E&W | | |
| | 16W-27N,15W-27N | 41 |
| Forest Creek Ln. N&S | | |
| | 17W-30N | 32 |
| Forest Ln. N&S | 16W-29N | 33 |
| Forestview Ln. NW&SE | | |
| | 17W-30N | 32 |
| Forever Av. NW&SE | | |
| | 16W-27N | 41 |
| Fox Trail N&S | 15W-28N | 33 |
| Furlong Dr. NS&EW | | |
| | 16W-27N | 41 |
| Garfield Av. NW&SE | | |
| | 16W-29N,16W-28N | 33 |
| Garrison St. E&W | 16W-29N | 33 |
| Glendale Rd. E&W | 16W-28N | 33 |
| Golf Rd. E&W | | |
| | 17W-28N,16W-28N | 32 |
| Gracewood Dr. E&W | | |
| | 17W-28N | 32 |
| Grant Ct. E&W | 17W-28N | 32 |
| Green Tree Pkwy. E&W | | |
| | 16W-27N | 41 |
| Greentree Ct. NW&SE | | |
| | 16W-27N | 41 |
| Gulfstream Pkwy.* E&W | | |
| | 15W-26N | 41 |
| Hackberry Ln. E&W | | |
| | 17W-30N | 32 |
| Halifax St. N&S | 17W-30N | 32 |
| Hampton Av. N&S | 15W-28N | 33 |
| Harding Av. N&S | 17W-28N | 32 |
| Harms Av. E&W | 17W-28N | 32 |
| Harris Rd. N&S | | |
| | 19W-30N,19W-31N | 31 |
| Harrison St E&W | 16W-28N | 33 |
| Harvard Ln. E&W | 16W-28N | 33 |
| Havenwood Ct. N&S | | |
| | 17W-28N | 32 |
| Havenwood Dr. E&W | | |
| | 17W-28N | 32 |
| Hayes Av. N&S | 16W-28N | 33 |
| Hemlock Ln. N&S | 16W-27N | 41 |
| Highgate Ct. NW&SE | | |
| | 17W-28N | 32 |
| Hillcrest Dr. N&S | 17W-29N | 32 |
| Hollister Dr. N&S | 16W-26N | 41 |
| Homewood Dr. NW&SE | | |
| | 16W-29N | 33 |
| Hunters Ln. E&W | 15W-27N | 41 |
| Hurlburt Ct. N&S | 16W-28N | 33 |
| Hyatt Dr. E&W | 16W-29N | 33 |
| Industrial Dr. NW&SE | | |
| | 19W-30N | 31 |
| Innsbruck Ct. N&S | 17W-29N | 32 |
| Interlaken Ct. E&W | | |
| | 17W-29N | 32 |
| Interlaken Ln. NW&SE | | |
| | 17W-29N | 32 |
| Jackson St. E&W | 16W-29N | 33 |
| James Ct.* N&S | 15W-26N | 41 |
| Jeremy Ln.* N&S | 15W-26N | 41 |
| Johnson Av. NW&SE | | |
| | 16W-29N | 33 |
| Josilyn Ct. N&S | 18W-30N | 32 |
| Julie Ln. N&S | 18W-30N | 32 |
| Juliet Cir. NW&SE | 18W-30N | 32 |
| Juniper Pkwy. N&S | | |
| | 16W-27N | 41 |
| Kempton Ln. N&S | 15W-27N | 41 |
| Kenlock Av. N&S | 17W-28N | 32 |
| Kenwood Av. N&S | 15W-28N | 33 |
| Kristen Dr. N&S | 17W-29N | 32 |
| Lake St. E&W | | |
| | 17W-29N,16W-29N | 33 |
| Lange Ct. E&W | 16W-29N | 33 |
| Laurel Av. E&W | 16W-29N | 33 |
| Liberty Bell Ct. NE&SW | | |
| | 15W-28N | 33 |
| Liberty Bell Ln. E&W | | |
| | 16W-28N,15W-28N | 33 |
| Liberty Ct. N&S | 19W-30N | 31 |
| Liberty Lake Dr. E&W | | |
| | 15W-28N | 33 |
| Lilac Ct. N&S | 16W-27N | 41 |
| Lincoln Av. E&W | 16W-29N | 33 |
| Linden Ln. E&W | 16W-29N | 33 |
| Lingonberry Ct. NW&SE | | |
| | 17W-30N | 32 |
| Lisa Cir. N&S | 18W-30N | 32 |
| Loatonia Ct.* N&S | 15W-26N | 41 |
| Lothair Ct. N&S | 17W-28N | 32 |
| Loyola Dr. N&S | 17W-29N | 32 |
| Magnolia Ln. NW&SE | | |
| | 16W-27N | 41 |
| Mallory Dr. E&W | 19W-31N | 31 |
| Manor Cir. E&W | 16W-29N | 33 |
| Maple Av. N&S | 16W-29N | 33 |
| Margate Ln. E&W | 15W-28N | 33 |
| Mayfair Dr. N&S | 17W-27N | 40 |
| Maywood Ct.* E&W | | |
| | 15W-26N | 41 |
| McKinley Av. E&W | 16W-28N | 33 |

| | Grid | Page |
|---|---|---|
| Meadow Ln. E&W | 16W-28N | 33 |
| Merril Ct. N&S | 16W-28N | 33 |
| Michaels Ln. N&S | 16W-27N | 41 |
| Miller Ct. N&S | 16W-30N | 33 |
| Milwaukee Av. NW&SE | | |
| | 16W-28N | 33 |
| Minear Dr. E&W | 16W-29N | 33 |
| Mulberry Dr. NW&SE | | |
| | 17W-30N | 32 |
| Mullady Pkwy. NW&SE | | |
| | 15W-27N | 41 |
| Nathan Ln. E&W | 18W-29N | 32 |
| New Castle Dr. NW&SE | | |
| | 17W-30N | 32 |
| Newberry Av. E&W | | |
| | 16W-29N | 33 |
| Newgate Ct. NE&SW | | |
| | 17W-30N | 32 |
| Nita Ln. E&W | 16W-27N | 41 |
| Nordic Ct. E&W | 17W-28N | 32 |
| North Av. E&W | 16W-29N | 33 |
| Oak Spring Rd. E&W | | |
| | 15W-29N | 33 |
| Oak St. N&S | 16W-28N | 33 |
| Oaktrail Dr. E&W | 15W-27N | 41 |
| Cir. | 17W-30N | 32 |
| Old Buckley Rd. E&W | | |
| | 16W-30N | 33 |
| Old Peterson Rd. E&W | | |
| | 18W-30N | 32 |
| Orchard Cir. NE&SW | | |
| | 16W-29N | 33 |
| Oxford Ct. E&W | 17W-29N | 32 |
| Paddock Ct.* N&S | 15W-26N | 41 |
| Paddock Ln. E&W | | |
| | 16W-27N,15W-27N | 41 |
| Paradise Ln. N&S | 17W-29N | 32 |
| Park Crest E&W | | |
| | 18W-30N | 32 |
| Park Pl. N&S | 16W-28N | 33 |
| Parkview Dr. NE&SW | | |
| | 16W-30N | 33 |
| Parliament Ct. NW&SE | | |
| | 16W-29N | 33 |
| Paul Revere Ln. NE&SW | | |
| | 15W-28N | 33 |
| Pembrooke Rd. E&W | | |
| | 17W-28N | 32 |
| Peterson Rd. E&W | | |
| | 19W-30N,18W-30N | 31 |
| Pimlico Pkwy.* E&W | | |
| | 15W-26N | 41 |
| Pine Tree Ln. NE&SW | | |
| | 17W-28N | 32 |
| Pleasant Ct. E&W | 18W-30N | 32 |
| Pond Ridge Rd. NE&SW | | |
| | 17W-28N | 32 |
| Poplar Ct. E&W | 16W-27N | 41 |
| Portwine Rd. N&S | 17W-28N | 32 |
| Prairie Av. N&S | 16W-28N | 33 |
| Quaker Hill N&S | 17W-29N | 32 |
| Red Top Dr. E&W | 16W-27N | 41 |
| Regency Ln. E&W | 17W-29N | 32 |
| Ridgeway Ln. N&S | 15W-28N | 33 |
| Ridgewood Ln. N&S | | |
| | 17W-29N | 32 |
| Riva Ridge Dr. E&W | | |
| | 15W-27N | 41 |
| Riverside Dr. N&S | 15W-28N | 33 |
| Rockland Ct. E&W | | |
| | 16W-28N,15W-28N | 33 |
| Romeo Cir. N&S | 18W-30N | 32 |
| Ronan St. NE&SW | 17W-30N | 32 |
| Roosevelt Dr. N&S | 17W-28N | 32 |
| Rosewood Ter. N&S | | |
| | 16W-27N | 41 |
| Route 137 E&W | 17W-30N | 32 |
| Route 176 E&W | | |
| | 17W-28N,15W-28N | 32 |
| Route 21 N&S | | |
| | 16W-27N,16W-30N | 41 |
| Route 45 N&S | | |
| | 18W-29N,19W-30N | 32 |
| Ruidoso Ct.* N&S | 15W-26N | 41 |
| Sandstone Dr. N&S | | |
| | 16W-29N | 33 |
| Sandy Ct. E&W | 16W-27N | 41 |
| Sandy Ln. E&W | 16W-27N | 41 |
| Saxon Ln. N&S | 15W-28N | 33 |
| School St. N&S | 16W-29N | 33 |
| Scott Pl. N&S | 15W-28N | 33 |
| Sedgwick Dr. NE&SW | | |
| | 17W-29N | 32 |
| Shari Ln. E&W | 17W-28N | 32 |
| Springhaven Dr. N&S | | |
| | 17W-29N | 32 |
| Spruce Ct. N&S | 16W-27N | 41 |
| St. James Pl. 17W-29N | 32 |
| St. William Dr. NS&EW | | |
| | 17W-29N,17W-30N | 32 |
| Stevenson Dr. NW&SE | | |
| | 17W-28N | 32 |
| Stewart Av. N&S | | |
| | 16W-28N,16W-29N | 33 |
| Stonegate Ct. E&W | | |
| | 17W-29N | 32 |
| Stonegate Rd. N&S | 17W-29N | 32 |
| Suffolk Ct.* E&W | 15W-26N | 41 |
| Sunnyside Av. E&W | | |
| | 16W-28N | 33 |
| Sunnyside Pl. E&W | | |
| | 16W-28N | 33 |
| Sunset Dr. N&S | 16W-29N | 33 |

|  | Grid | Page |
|---|---|---|
| Sussex Ln. N&S | 17W-29N | 32 |
| Sylvia Dr. E&W | 17W-27N | 40 |
| Tall Tree Ter. E&W | | |
| | 16W-28N | 33 |
| Tamarack Ln. NW&SE | | |
| | 16W-27N | 41 |
| Tempel Dr. E&W | 19W-30N | 31 |
| Thomas Ct. E&W | 17W-29N | 32 |
| Thornapple Ln. NE&SW | | |
| | 16W-27N | 41 |
| Thornbury Ln. E&W | | |
| | 15W-29N | 33 |
| Tiffany Ln. N&S | 18W-29N | 32 |
| Tracy Ln. NW&SE | 18W-27N | 41 |
| Trevor Cir. N&S | 18W-29N | 32 |
| Trinity Pl. N&S | 17W-29N | 32 |
| Tyler Ct. E&W | 16W-28N | 33 |
| U.S. Route 45 N&S | | |
| | 18W-29N,19W-29N | 32 |
| Valley Park Dr. E&W | | |
| | 16W-28N | 33 |
| Victory Dr. E&W | 17W-28N | 32 |
| Vineyard Ln. E&W | 17W-30N | 32 |
| Virginia Av. N&S | | |
| | 18W-29N,18W-30N | 32 |
| Virginia Av. NS&EW | 18W-30N | 32 |
| W. Park Av. NE&SW | | |
| | 17W-28N | 32 |
| Walnut St. E&W | 16W-28N | 33 |
| Warwick Ln. N&S | 17W-28N | 32 |
| Wedgemere Pl. N&S | | |
| | 16W-28N | 33 |
| Weeping Willow Ln. NW&SE | | |
| | 16W-27N | 41 |
| Wellington Av. E&W | | |
| | 17W-29N | 32 |
| West St. N&S | 16W-29N | 33 |
| Wexford Ct. N&S | 17W-28N | 32 |
| Wheeler N&S | 15W-29N | 33 |
| White Blvd. N&S | 19W-30N | 31 |
| Willow Av. E&W | 17W-28N | 32 |
| Wilshire Cir. N&S | 17W-29N | 32 |
| Wilshire Dr. E&W | 17W-29N | 32 |
| Wimbledon Ct. NE&SW | | |
| | 15W-23N | 49 |
| Winchester Rd. N&S | | |
| | 18W-29N,16W-29N | 32 |
| Windhaven Rd. N&S | | |
| | 17W-29N | 32 |
| Windsor Ter. N&S | 16W-28N | 33 |
| Winners Cir.* NE&SW | | |
| | 15W-26N | 41 |
| Woodfield Ln. E&W | | |
| | 15W-29N | 33 |
| Woodland Rd. N&S | | |
| | 17W-28N | 32 |
| Wright Ct. N&S | 16W-29N | 33 |
| Wrightwood Ter. N&S | | |
| | 16W-28N | 33 |
| Young Dr. N&S | 17W-30N | 32 |
| 1st St. N&S | | |
| | 16W-28N,16W-29N | 33 |
| 2nd St. N&S | | |
| | 16W-28N,16W-29N | 33 |
| 3rd St. N&S | 16W-29N | 33 |
| 4th Av. N&S | | |
| | 16W-28N,15W-27N | 33 |
| 4th St. N&S | | |
| | 16W-28N,16W-29N | 33 |
| 5th Av. N&S | 16W-28N | 33 |
| 5th St. N&S | 16W-29N | 33 |
| 7th St. N&S | 15W-28N | 33 |

## Libertyville Township

| Allyson Ct. N&S | 15W-29N | 33 |
|---|---|---|
| Almond Rd. N&S | 17W-31N | 32 |
| Arcadia Rd. N&S | 13W-28N | 34 |
| Arlington Dr. E&W | 16W-30N | 33 |
| Atkinson Av. E&W | 13W-29N | 34 |
| Baker Rd. N&S | 13W-28N | 34 |
| Ballard Dr. NS&EW | | |
| | 13W-28N | 34 |
| Bayonne Av. N&S | 13W-28N | 34 |
| Bell Ln. N&S | 17W-30N | 32 |
| Birchwood Ln. E&W | | |
| | 15W-30N | 33 |
| Bob-O-Link Ln. N&S | | |
| | 18W-30N,18W-31N | 32 |
| Borde Ct. N&S | 15W-29N | 33 |
| Bradley Rd. N&S | 14W-28N | 33 |
| Brookhill Rd. E&W | 17W-30N | 32 |
| Brookside Ct. NS&EW | | |
| | 17W-30N | 32 |
| Brookwood Ln. E&W | | |
| | 15W-29N | 33 |
| Bruce Ct. NE&SW | 15W-29N | 33 |
| Buckley Rd. E&W | 15W-30N | 33 |
| Bull Creek Dr. NS&EW | | |
| | 18W-30N | 32 |
| Casey Rd. E&W | 18W-31N | 32 |
| Center Av. NW&SE | | |
| | 16W-30N | 33 |
| Cherrywood Ln. E&W | | |
| | 15W-30N | 33 |
| Clover Ln. E&W | 15W-30N | 33 |
| Country Ct. E&W | 15W-30N | 33 |
| Countryside Rd. N&S | | |
| | 15W-30N | 33 |
| Daisy Ln. N&S | 18W-26N | 40 |
| Des Plaines Dr. E&W | | |
| | 16W-30N | 33 |

|  | Grid | Page |
|---|---|---|
| Diamond Lake Rd. NE&SW | | |
| | 18W-26N | 40 |
| East End Av. N&S | 15W-30N | 33 |
| Ellen Way E&W | 15W-29N | 33 |
| Elm Rd. E&W | 13W-28N | 34 |
| Elmwood Av. N&S | | |
| | 14W-26N,14W-27N | 41 |
| Energy Dr. N&S | 13W-28N | 34 |
| Fair Ln. E&W | 15W-30N | 33 |
| Fair Way E&W | 15W-29N | 33 |
| Fairhill Rd. E&W | 17W-30N | 32 |
| Forest Dr. E&W | 14W-27N | 41 |
| Foster Av. E&W | 13W-29N | 34 |
| Foster Knoll Rd. N&S | | |
| | 13W-29N | 34 |
| Frances Av. NE&SW | | |
| | 18W-26N | 40 |
| Greenacre Dr. E&W | | |
| | 17W-30N | 32 |
| Gurin Rd. E&W | 15W-31N | 33 |
| Hawthorne Av. E&W | | |
| | 14W-27N | 41 |
| Hawthorne Ln. NW&SE | | |
| | 15W-29N | 33 |
| Herky Dr. N&S | 13W-28N | 34 |
| Hickory Ln. E&W | 18W-26N | 40 |
| Idlewood Ln. E&W | 15W-30N | 33 |
| Imperial Dr. E&W | 14W-26N | 41 |
| Ivy Ln. N&S | 15W-28N | 33 |
| Janas Ct. NE&SW | 17W-30N | 32 |
| Keith Dr. N&S | 13W-28N | 34 |
| Kildare Av. E&W | 17W-30N | 32 |
| Laura Ln. NS&EW | 13W-28N | 34 |
| Laurel Dr. E&W | 13W-28N | 34 |
| Leesley Ct. N&S | 18W-30N | 32 |
| Leola Dr. E&W | 13W-28N | 34 |
| Liberty Rd. N&S | 18W-31N | 32 |
| Lilac Dr. N&S | 18W-26N | 40 |
| Linden Ln. E&W | 14W-28N | 33 |
| Longwood Dr. N&S | | |
| | 14W-26N | 41 |
| Melody Ln. NS&EW | | |
| | 14W-26N | 41 |
| Muir Av. E&W | 13W-29N | 34 |
| N. Terre Dr. E&W | 15W-29N | 33 |
| Nagel Ct. N&S | 13W-28N | 34 |
| Nells Rd. N&S | 15W-29N | 33 |
| Northwoods Dr. N&S | | |
| | 15W-29N | 33 |
| Northwoods Dr. NS&EW | | |
| | 15W-29N | 33 |
| Oak Av. E&W | 18W-26N | 40 |
| Oak Av. E&W | 14W-27N | 41 |
| Oak Grove Av. N&S | | |
| | 15W-30N | 33 |
| Oak Ln. N&S | | |
| | 15W-28N,15W-29N | 33 |
| Oak Pond Ln. E&W | | |
| | 15W-29N | 33 |
| Oaksprings Ln. NS&EW | | |
| | 15W-29N | 33 |
| Old Hickory Ln. N&S | | |
| | 15W-29N | 33 |
| Park Ln. N&S | 15W-30N | 33 |
| Peterson Rd. E&W | 18W-30N | 32 |
| Petronella Dr. E&W | | |
| | 14W-28N | 33 |
| Pinehurst Ln. E&W | 18W-30N | 32 |
| Pinewood Ln. NW&SE | | |
| | 15W-30N | 33 |
| Print-O-Tade Rd. N&S | | |
| | 13W-28N | 34 |
| Providence Dr. N&S | | |
| | 17W-30N | 32 |
| Quassey Av. N&S | 13W-29N | 34 |
| Ranch Rd. N&S | 18W-31N | 32 |
| Redwood Ln. NW&SE | | |
| | 15W-30N | 33 |
| Revere Ct. N&S | 16W-30N | 33 |
| River Dr. N&S | 16W-29N | 33 |
| River Rd. N&S | 16W-30N | 33 |
| Rockland Ln. N&S | 16W-30N | 33 |
| Rose Av. E&W | 18W-26N | 40 |
| Route 137 E&W | | |
| | 18W-30N,17W-30N | 32 |
| Route 176 E&W | | |
| | 14W-28N,13W-28N | 33 |
| Route 21 N&S | 16W-31N | 33 |
| Shagbark Ln. N&S | 15W-28N | 33 |
| Sprucewood Ln. E&W | | |
| | 15W-30N | 33 |
| St. Andrew's Dr. N&S | | |
| | 18W-30N | 32 |
| St. Mary's Ct. E&W | | |
| | 15W-29N | 33 |
| St. Mary's Rd. N&S | | |
| | 15W-29N | 33 |
| Steger Rd. N&S | 18W-31N | 32 |
| Sunnyview Rd. N&S | | |
| | 17W-30N | 32 |
| Tanglewood Ct. N&S | | |
| | 15W-28N | 33 |
| Terre Dr., S. E&W | 15W-29N | 33 |
| Timber Ln. E&W | 15W-29N | 33 |
| U.S. Route 45 N&S | | |
| | 18W-30N,18W-31N | 32 |
| Valley Ln. E&W | 18W-30N | 32 |
| Vernon Ct. N&S | 15W-28N | 33 |
| Victor Ln. E&W | 15W-31N | 33 |
| Victoria Ln. NW&SE | | |
| | 15W-29N | 33 |
| Violet Dr. N&S | 18W-26N | 40 |
| Whitman Ct. NE&SW | | |
| | 15W-29N | 33 |

|  | Grid | Page |
|---|---|---|
| Wildwood Ct. E&W | | |
| | 15W-30N | 33 |
| Wood Hollow Ln. E&W | | |
| | 18W-31N | 32 |
| Woodbridge Ct. N&S | | |
| | 15W-30N | 33 |
| Wooddale Ln. N&S | | |
| | 15W-28N | 33 |

## Lincolnshire

| Angelican Ln. E&W | | |
|---|---|---|
| | 13W-22N | 49 |
| Ashford Ct. E&W | 14W-23N | 49 |
| Astor Ct. E&W | 14W-23N | 49 |
| Avon Ln. E&W | 13W-23N | 49 |
| Barclay Blvd. N&S | 15W-22N | 49 |
| Bedford Ct. N&S | 13W-21N | 49 |
| Berkshire Ln. N&S | 13W-22N | 49 |
| Berwick Ct. N&S | 13W-22N | 49 |
| Bond St. N&S | 16W-22N | 48 |
| Brampton Ct. E&W | | |
| | 13W-23N | 49 |
| Brampton Ln. NS&EW | | |
| | 14W-23N,13W-23N | 49 |
| Briarwood Ln. E&W | | |
| | 13W-22N | 49 |
| Bristol Ct. E&W | 13W-22N | 49 |
| Brunswick Ln. N&S | | |
| | 13W-22N | 49 |
| Buckingham Pl. E&W | | |
| | 13W-22N | 49 |
| Bucks Co. Ct.* E&W | | |
| | 13W-22N | 49 |
| Burnham Ct. E&W | 13W-22N | 49 |
| Buxton Ct. N&S | 13W-23N | 49 |
| Cambridge Ln. NS&EW | | |
| | 14W-22N | 49 |
| Camden Ct. E&W | 13W-22N | 49 |
| Canterbury Rd. N&S | | |
| | 13W-22N | 49 |
| Carlisle Ln. E&W | 14W-23N | 49 |
| Cedar Ln. E&W | 14W-23N | 49 |
| Coldstream Cir. NS&EW | | |
| | 14W-22N | 49 |
| Connecticut River Val. Ct. | | |
| E&W | 14W-23N | 49 |
| Cornell Ln. E&W | 13W-23N | 49 |
| Coventry Ln. E&W | 14W-22N | 49 |
| Cumberland Dr. E&W | | |
| | 14W-22N | 49 |
| Darby Ln. N&S | 13W-22N | 49 |
| Deer Run N&S | 13W-22N | 49 |
| Devonshire Ln. E&W | | |
| | 13W-23N | 49 |
| Dover Dr. E&W | 14W-23N | 49 |
| Downing Sq. N&S | 12W-22N | 50 |
| Dukes Cir. N&S | 13W-22N | 49 |
| Dukes Ct. N&S | 13W-22N | 49 |
| Dukes Ln. E&W | 13W-22N | 49 |
| Durham Ct. NE&SW | | |
| | 13W-23N | 49 |
| Elmwood Ln. N&S | 14W-23N | 49 |
| Elsinoor Dr. N&S | 14W-23N | 49 |
| Essex Ln. NS&EW | 14W-23N | 49 |
| Exmoor Ln. E&W | 13W-22N | 49 |
| Fairfax Ln. E&W | 13W-22N | 49 |
| Fallstone Ct. N&S | 13W-23N | 49 |
| Fallstone Dr. N&S | 13W-23N | 49 |
| Fox River Ct. E&W | | |
| | 13W-23N | 49 |
| Fox Tr. E&W | 13W-22N | 49 |
| Friar Truck Ct. E&W | | |
| | 13W-23N | 49 |
| Glouchester Ct. E&W | | |
| | 13W-23N | 49 |
| Grenedier Ct. E&W | | |
| | 13W-22N | 49 |
| Half Day Rd. E&W | 15W-23N | 49 |
| Hampshire Ln. E&W | | |
| | 13W-22N | 49 |
| Heathrow Ln. E&W | | |
| | 15W-22N | 49 |
| Hickory Ln. N&S | 14W-23N | 49 |
| Interstate 94 N&S | 13W-23N | 49 |
| Jamestown Ln. E&W | | |
| | 15W-23N | 49 |
| Kensington Dr. N&S | | |
| | 14W-22N | 49 |
| Kent NE&SW | 13W-22N | 49 |
| Kerwick Ct.* N&S | 12W-22N | 49 |
| Kings Cross Dr. N&S | | |
| | 13W-22N | 49 |
| Knightsbridge Pkwy. E&W | | |
| | 15W-22N | 49 |
| Lancaster Ln. N&S | 14W-22N | 49 |
| Leeds Ct. NW&SE | 13W-23N | 49 |
| Lincolnshire Dr. NS&EW | | |
| | 14W-22N | 49 |
| Londonderry Ln. E&W | | |
| | 14W-22N | 49 |
| Margate Dr. E&W | | |
| | 16W-22N,15W-22N | 48 |
| Marriott Dr. E&W | | |
| | 15W-22N,14W-22N | 49 |
| Mayfair Ln. E&W | 13W-23N | 49 |
| Melrose Ln. NS&EW | | |
| | 14W-22N | 49 |
| Middlebury Ln. N&S | | |
| | 13W-21N | 49 |
| Mohawk Valley Ct. N&S | | |
| | 13W-22N | 49 |
| Nantucket Ct. N&S | | |
| | 13W-23N | 49 |

|  | Grid | Page |
|---|---|---|
| Natchez Ct. E&W | 13W-23N | 49 |
| Northampton Ln. N&S | | |
| | 14W-24N | 41 |
| Nottingham Dr. E&W | | |
| | 13W-23N | 49 |
| Oakwood Ln. N&S | 14W-23N | 49 |
| Overlook Point N&S | | |
| | 15W-22N | 49 |
| Oxford Dr. NW&SE | | |
| | 14W-22N,14W-23N | 49 |
| Park Ln. E&W | 16W-21N | 48 |
| Park Pl. E&W | 16W-21N | 48 |
| Parton Ct. NW&SE | 13W-23N | 49 |
| Pembroke Dr. E&W | | |
| | 14W-23N | 49 |
| Pembroke Ln. E&W | | |
| | 14W-23N | 49 |
| Pheasant Row NE&SW | | |
| | 13W-22N | 49 |
| Plymouth Ct. N&S | 14W-22N | 49 |
| Portshire Dr. NS&EW | | |
| | 13W-22N | 49 |
| Provincetown Ct. NW&SE | | |
| | 15W-23N | 49 |
| Queens Way E&W | 13W-22N | 49 |
| Regent Ln. N&S | 13W-22N | 49 |
| Reliance Ln. E&W | 13W-22N | 49 |
| Rivershire Ln. E&W | | |
| | 14W-22N | 49 |
| Riverside Dr. E&W | 15W-23N | 49 |
| Riverside Rd. NW&SE | | |
| | 15W-22N | 49 |
| Riverwoods Rd. N&S | | |
| | 14W-22N,14W-24N | 49 |
| Robinhood Ct. E&W | | |
| | 15W-22N | 49 |
| Route 21 N&S | 15W-22N | 49 |
| Route 22 E&W | | |
| | 15W-23N,13W-23N | 49 |
| Royal Ct. E&W | 13W-22N | 49 |
| Schelter Rd. N&S | 15W-22N | 49 |
| Sheffield Ct. E&W | 14W-22N | 49 |
| Sherwood Dr. NW&SE | | |
| | 13W-23N | 49 |
| Stafford Ln. N&S | 13W-23N | 49 |
| Stonegate Cir. N&S | | |
| | 14W-22N | 49 |
| Suffield Sq. N&S | 13W-22N | 49 |
| Surrey Ct. E&W | 13W-23N | 49 |
| Surrey Ln. NS&EW | | |
| | 14W-23N,13W-23N | 49 |
| Sutton Ct. NW&SE | 12W-22N | 49 |
| Tidewater Ct. E&W | | |
| | 15W-22N | 49 |
| Tower Pkwy. E&W | 15W-22N | 49 |
| Trafalgar Square N&S | | |
| | 13W-23N | 49 |
| Tri-state Tollway N&S | | |
| | 13W-23N | 49 |
| U.S. Route 45 E&W | | |
| | 13W-23N | 49 |
| Victoria Ln. E&W | 14W-22N | 49 |
| Wellington Ct. N&S | | |
| | 13W-22N | 49 |
| Westminster Way NW&SE | | |
| | 13W-22N | 49 |
| Westwood Ln. E&W | | |
| | 13W-22N | 49 |
| Whitby Ct. N&S | 13W-22N | 49 |
| Whitmore Ln. E&W | | |
| | 14W-22N | 49 |
| Whyte Gate Ln. E&W | | |
| | 14W-22N | 49 |
| William St. N&S | 15W-21N | 49 |
| Williamsburg Ln. N&S | | |
| | 15W-23N | 49 |
| Wilmington Ct. E&W | | |
| | 13W-22N | 49 |
| Wiltshire Ct. E&W | 14W-22N | 49 |
| Wimbledon Ct. NE&SW | | |
| | 15W-23N | 49 |
| Windsor Ct., S. N&S | | |
| | 13W-22N | 49 |
| Windsor Dr. E&W | 14W-22N | 49 |
| Yorkshire Dr. E&W | 14W-22N | 49 |

## Lindenhurst

| Adams Dr. E&W | 19W-39N | 15 |
|---|---|---|
| Alden Ct. NW&SE | 19W-39N | 15 |
| Auburn Ln. NS&EW | | |
| | 20W-39N | 15 |
| Autumn Cir. NE&SW | | |
| | 20W-39N | 15 |
| Beck Cir. N&S | 19W-39N | 15 |
| Beck Rd. NS&EW | | |
| | 20W-37N,20W-38N | 15 |
| Bonner Ln. NW&SE | | |
| | 19W-37N | 15 |
| Briar Ln. E&W | 20W-37N | 15 |
| Bridgeport Ter. N&S | | |
| | 19W-39N | 15 |
| Brittany Ln. N&S | 20W-38N | 15 |
| Brook Ln. NE&SW | 20W-38N | 15 |
| Burr Oak Ln. NW&SE | | |
| | 20W-38N | 15 |
| Cardinal Ct. NW&SE | | |
| | 21W-38N,20W-38N | 15 |
| Carriage Ln. E&W | 20W-38N | 15 |
| Cherrywood Ln. NW&SE | | |
| | 20W-38N | 15 |
| Chestnut Cir. N&S | 20W-38N | 15 |
| Clover Ct. NE&SW | 20W-39N | 15 |

|  | Grid | Page |
|---|---|---|
| Colony Av. NW&SE | | |
| | 19W-39N | 15 |
| Colony Ct. NE&SW | | |
| | 19W-39N | 15 |
| Columbus Av. NW&SE | | |
| | 20W-37N | 15 |
| Countryside Ln. NE&SW | | |
| | 20W-37N | 15 |
| Crabtree Ct. NE&SW | | |
| | 20W-37N | 15 |
| Deep Lake Rd. N&S | | |
| | 21W-38N | 15 |
| Deerpath Dr. NS&EW | | |
| | 20W-37N,19W-37N | 15 |
| Dittmer Ln. N&S | 21W-38N | 15 |
| Dover Ct. N&S | | |
| | 19W-36N,20W-36N | 15 |
| Elmwood Ct. N&S | 20W-39N | 15 |
| Evergreen Ct. N&S | 20W-39N | 15 |
| Fairfield Rd. NS&EW | | |
| | 20W-37N,20W-38N | 15 |
| Federal Ct. N&S | 20W-39N | 15 |
| Federal Pkwy N&S | 20W-39N | 15 |
| Forest View Rd. NS&EW | | |
| | 19W-39N | 15 |
| Franklin Dr. N&S | 19W-39N | 15 |
| Glendale Ct. N&S | 20W-39N | 15 |
| Grand Av. NW&SE | 20W-37N | 15 |
| Grand Ct. NE&SW | 19W-37N | 15 |
| Grass Lake Rd. E&W | | |
| | 20W-39N | 15 |
| Great Oak Dr. E&W | | |
| | 19W-38N | 15 |
| Green Briar Ln. N&S | | |
| | 20W-37N | 15 |
| Green Tree Ct. E&W | | |
| | 20W-38N | 15 |
| Hamilton Dr. E&W | 19W-39N | 15 |
| Harbor Ridge Way NE&SW | | |
| | 19W-38N | 15 |
| Harrisburg Ct. E&W | | |
| | 19W-38N | 15 |
| Harvard Ct. N&S | 19W-38N | 15 |
| Hastings Pl. NW&SE | | |
| | 20W-39N | 15 |
| Hawthorne Dr. N&S | | |
| | 19W-38N | 15 |
| Hazelwood Dr. E&W | | |
| | 20W-38N | 15 |
| Heritage Ct. NE&SW | | |
| | 19W-38N | 15 |
| Heritage Dr. N&S | 19W-38N | 15 |
| Heron Dr. NW&SE | 19W-38N | 15 |
| Hickory Ct. E&W | 20W-38N | 15 |
| Hickory Dr. N&S | 20W-38N | 15 |
| Highland Cir. NE&SW | | |
| | 19W-37N | 15 |
| Highland Dr. E&W | 19W-37N | 15 |
| Highpoint Dr. NS&EW | | |
| | 20W-38N | 15 |
| Hillcrest Ln. N&S | 20W-37N | 15 |
| Honeysuckle Ct. NE&SW | | |
| | 20W-37N | 15 |
| Horizon Ct. E&W | 20W-38N | 15 |
| Ironwood Dr. N&S | 19W-37N | 15 |
| Ivy Cir. E&W | 20W-39N | 15 |
| Jackson Pl. E&W | 19W-39N | 15 |
| Jefferson Dr. N&S | 20W-39N | 15 |
| Lakeshore Dr. N&S | | |
| | 20W-38N | 15 |
| Lakeview Ct. E&W | 20W-39N | 15 |
| Larkdale Ct. NE&SW | | |
| | 20W-38N | 15 |
| Laurel Dr. NW&SE | 20W-37N | 15 |
| Liberty Ln. E&W | 19W-38N | 15 |
| Lindenhurst Dr. N&S | | |
| | 20W-38N | 15 |
| Longmeadow Dr. E&W | | |
| | 20W-38N | 15 |
| Madison Ln. NW&SE | | |
| | 19W-38N | 15 |
| Magnolia Ln. N&S | 19W-37N | 15 |
| Mallard Dr. E&W | 19W-38N | 15 |
| Mallard Ridge Dr. NE&SW | | |
| | 21W-38N | 15 |
| Maplewood Ct. NE&SW | | |
| | 20W-38N | 15 |
| Maplewood Dr. NW&SE | | |
| | 20W-38N | 15 |
| Meadow Dr. E&W | 20W-38N | 15 |
| Monroe Dr. N&S | 19W-38N | 15 |
| Munn Rd. N&S | 21W-38N | 15 |
| Nightengale Ln. NS&EW | | |
| | 21W-38N,20W-38N | 15 |
| Northgate Rd. N&S | | |
| | 20W-38N | 15 |
| Old Elm Rd. NW&SE | | |
| | 20W-37N | 15 |
| Orchard Ln. N&S | 19W-37N | 15 |
| Oriole Ct. E&W | 20W-38N | 15 |
| Paine Av. N&S | 19W-39N | 15 |
| Partridge Cir. E&W | 21W-38N | 15 |
| Penn Blvd. NS&EW | | |
| | 20W-39N,19W-39N | 15 |
| Penn Ct. NE&SW | 19W-39N | 15 |
| Pheasant Ridge Ct. NW&SE | | |
| | 19W-38N | 15 |
| Pinecrest Ln. E&W | 20W-38N | 15 |
| Plum Tree Rd. E&W | | |
| | 20W-37N,19W-37N | 15 |
| Potomac Ct. NE&SW | | |
| | 20W-39N | 15 |
| Prospect Dr. NE&SW | | |
| | 20W-37N,20W-38N | 15 |

|  | Grid | Page |
|---|---|---|
| Quail Cir. N&S | 21W-38N | 15 |
| Quincy Ct. E&W | 19W-38N | 15 |
| Red Rock Dr. NE&SW | 20W-38N | 15 |
| Ridge Ct. NE&SW | 20W-38N | 15 |
| Ridgeland Dr. E&W | 20W-37N | 15 |
| Robin Crest Ln. NS&EW | 21W-38N,20W-38N | 15 |
| Rolling Ridge Ln. NS&EW | 20W-38N | 15 |
| Rose Tree Ln. NS&EW | 20W-37N | 15 |
| Route 132 NW&SE | 21W-38N,20W-37N | 15 |
| Sand Lake Rd. E&W | 20W-37N,19W-37N | 15 |
| Shagbark Ln. NW&SE | 20W-38N | 15 |
| Skyline Cir. E&W | 20W-39N | 15 |
| Spring Hill Ln. E&W | 20W-38N | 15 |
| Sprucewood Ln. E&W | 20W-38N | 15 |
| Summit Ct. N&S | 20W-39N | 15 |
| Sunset Ln. E&W | 20W-37N | 15 |
| Surrey Ln. NW&SE | 20W-38N | 15 |
| Teal Rd. E&W | 19W-38N | 15 |
| Thornwood Dr. NS&EW | 20W-37N,19W-37N | 15 |
| Timber Ln. E&W | 19W-37N | 15 |
| Valley Dr. N&S | 20W-37N | 15 |
| Vista Ter. E&W | 20W-39N | 15 |
| Waterford Dr. NE&SW | 19W-38N | 15 |
| Whispering Pines Rd. NE&SW | 20W-38N,19W-38N | 15 |
| White Birch Rd. NE&SW | 19W-38N | 15 |
| White Oak Dr. N&S | 20W-38N | 15 |
| Witchwood Ln. NE&SW | 20W-37N,20W-38N | 15 |
| Woodlane Dr. NW&SE | 20W-37N | 15 |

### Long Grove

| | Grid | Page |
|---|---|---|
| Albert Ln. NW&SE | 20W-21N | 47 |
| Allison NW&SE | 19W-21N | 47 |
| Andrew Ct. NE&SW | 19W-20N | 47 |
| Antietam Dr. NW&SE | 18W-21N | 48 |
| Arlington Heights Rd. N&S | 18W-20N | 48 |
| Arrowhead Ct. N&S | 19W-25N | 39 |
| Ashley E&W | 19W-21N | 47 |
| Aspen Dr. E&W | 19W-25N | 39 |
| Atlantic Av. N&S | 19W-25N | 39 |
| Barclay Ct. SW&NE | 17W-23N | 48 |
| Bayberry Ln. E&W | 20W-22N | 47 |
| Beaver Run Dr. NS&EW | 18W-24N | 40 |
| Bedfordshire Dr. N&S | 18W-24N | 40 |
| Berkshire Cir. N&S | 18W-24N | 40 |
| Bernay Ln. E&W | 18W-20N | 48 |
| Black Walnut Tr. E&W | 18W-23N | 48 |
| Blue Heron Dr. N&S | 17W-23N | 48 |
| Blue Stem Ct. N&S | 18W-24N | 40 |
| Bob-O-Link Ln. N&S | 18W-21N | 48 |
| Bordeaux Ln. N&S | 18W-20N | 48 |
| Briarcrest Ln. NW&SE | 18W-22N | 48 |
| Bridgewater Ct. E&W | 18W-21N | 48 |
| Bridgewater Ln. N&S | 18W-21N | 48 |
| Bridlewood Ct. NW&SE | 17W-21N | 48 |
| Bridlewood Ln. NS&EW | 17W-21N | 48 |
| Brittany Ct. N&S | 18W-20N | 48 |
| Brittany Ln. E&W | 18W-20N | 48 |
| Brookbank E&W | 17W-22N | 48 |
| Brookhill Dr. NE&SW | 19W-23N | 47 |
| Brookside Ln. N&S | 18W-20N | 48 |
| Butler Ln. E&W | 17W-23N | 48 |
| Carriage Ct. N&S | 18W-20N | 48 |
| Carriage Way N&S | 19W-24N | 39 |
| Cavalry Ct. E&W | 19W-20N | 47 |
| Cedar Ct. N&S | 18W-24N | 40 |
| Checker Rd. E&W | 19W-20N | 47 |
| Chickamauga Ln. N&S | 18W-20N | 48 |
| Chickamuga Ln. NS&EW | 18W-20N | 48 |
| Church Hill Ct. E&W | 17W-23N | 48 |
| Clearwater Dr. NW&SE | 20W-22N | 47 |
| Coach Rd. N&S | 19W-20N | 47 |
| Cobblestone Ln. N&S | 19W-24N | 39 |
| Collier Cir. N&S | 18W-24N | 40 |
| Country Club Dr. N&S | 19W-20N | 47 |
| Country Ln. N&S | 19W-22N | 47 |
| Country Ln. N&S | 19W-22N | 47 |
| Country Side Ln. N&S | 18W-20N | 48 |
| Countryside Ln. N&S | 18W-20N | 48 |
| Creekside Dr. | 19W-25N | 39 |
| Crestview Dr. N&S | 19W-22N | 47 |
| Cuba Rd. E&W | 20W-22N,19W-22N | 47 |
| Cumberland Cir. NS&EW | 19W-20N | 47 |
| Danbury Ct. NE&SW | 17W-22N | 48 |
| Dawn Ct. E&W | 18W-20N | 48 |
| Deerwood Dr. NS&EW | 20W-21N | 47 |
| Devonshire Cir. N&S | 17W-24N | 40 |
| Diamond Lake Rd. N&S | 19W-24N,19W-25N | 39 |
| Doncaster Ct. NW&SE | 18W-23N | 48 |
| Dorchester Cir. N&S | 18W-24N | 40 |
| Driftwood Ln. (Pvt.) NW&SE | 19W-22N | 47 |
| Driftwood Rd. (Pvt.) N&S | 19W-22N | 47 |
| East Mardan Dr. N&S | 19W-21N | 47 |
| Edgewood Ln. N&S | 18W-20N | 48 |
| Eleanor Dr. E&W | 19W-23N | 47 |
| Endwood Dr. NE&SW | 18W-24N,17W-24N | 40 |
| Estate Ln. N&S | 19W-25N | 39 |
| Evergreen Ct. E&W | 18W-24N | 40 |
| Fairfield Dr. E&W | 18W-21N | 48 |
| Fairview Ln. N&S | 18W-21N | 48 |
| Farmcrest Ln. NW&SE | 17W-22N | 48 |
| Farmwood Dr. N&S | 19W-23N,19W-24N | 47 |
| Federal Ct. E&W | 19W-20N | 47 |
| Fenview Ln. E&W | 17W-22N | 48 |
| Finch Ln. NE&SW | 17W-23N | 48 |
| Forest Edge Ln. E&W | 19W-23N | 47 |
| Forest Fork Ct. E&W | 20W-22N | 47 |
| Forest Glen NE&SW | 19W-23N | 48 |
| Forest Way Cir. NW&SE | 19W-23N | 47 |
| Forrest Tr. E&W | 18W-23N | 48 |
| Gentry Ct. E&W | 17W-23N | 48 |
| Gilmer Rd. NW&SE | 18W-24N | 40 |
| Goldeneye Dr. N&S | 17W-23N | 48 |
| Golf Ln. N&S | 18W-22N | 48 |
| Grant Ct. N&S | 18W-21N | 48 |
| Grant Pl. E&W | 18W-21N | 48 |
| Greenwich Ct. NE&SW | 17W-24N | 40 |
| Hamelton Ct. N&S | 18W-23N | 48 |
| Hampton Dr. N&S | 17W-23N | 48 |
| Heather Knoll Ct. NW&SE | 17W-22N | 48 |
| Heatherwood Ln. N&S | 18W-23N | 48 |
| Heathmoor Ct. N&S | 18W-23N | 48 |
| Hedgewood Ct. NW&SE | 17W-22N | 48 |
| Heritage Ln. NS&EW | 18W-22N | 48 |
| Hickory Ct. E&W | 19W-23N | 47 |
| Hicks Rd. SW&NE | 19W-21N | 47 |
| Hidden Hills Ct. N&S | 20W-22N | 47 |
| Hidden Valley NS&EW | 20W-21N | 47 |
| High Meadow Ct. NW&SE | 19W-23N | 47 |
| High Point Ct. NE&SW | 18W-23N | 48 |
| Highland Dr. E&W | 18W-24N | 40 |
| Hilltop Rd. NW&SE | 18W-22N,17W-22N | 48 |
| Holly Ct. E&W | 18W-20N | 48 |
| Holly Ln. NW&SE | 18W-20N | 48 |
| Indian Creek Rd. E&W | 19W-25N | 39 |
| Indian Ln. E&W | 18W-25N | 40 |
| Juniper Ln. E&W | 19W-20N | 47 |
| Kettering Dr. NE&SW | 18W-23N | 48 |
| Killdeer Ct. E&W | 17W-23N | 48 |
| Kimberly Ct. E&W | 19W-23N | 47 |
| Kimberly Ct. NS&EW | 19W-23N | 47 |
| Knoll Ct. N&S | 19W-23N | 47 |
| Knoll Dr. N&S | 20W-20N | 47 |
| Krueger Ct. E&W | 19W-23N | 47 |
| Krueger Ln. E&W | 19W-23N | 47 |
| Krueger Rd. N&S | 19W-23N | 47 |
| Lake Point Cir. NS&EW | 19W-23N | 47 |
| Lake Zurich Rd. E&W | 18W-23N | 48 |
| Lakeridge Ct. NW&SE | 19W-25N | 39 |
| Lakeridge Dr. N&S | 19W-25N | 39 |
| Lakeridge Dr. NS&EW | 19W-25N | 39 |
| Lakeview Ct. E&W | 20W-22N | 47 |
| Lexington Dr. NS&EW | 19W-20N | 47 |
| Lincoln Av. N&S | 19W-20N | 47 |
| Long Grove Aptakisic Rd. E&W | 18W-22N,17W-22N | 48 |
| Manassas Ct. N&S | 18W-21N | 48 |
| Manassas Ln. NW&SE | 18W-21N | 48 |
| Mardan Dr. N&S | 19W-21N | 48 |
| Marilynn Dr. NE&SW | 19W-23N | 48 |
| Mayflower Ln. E&W | 19W-21N | 47 |
| Meadow Knoll Ct. NE&SW | 17W-22N | 48 |
| Meadow Lark Dr. E&W | 18W-20N | 48 |
| Meadow Ln. E&W | 18W-25N | 40 |
| Meadowlark Dr. E&W | 18W-20N | 48 |
| Medford Cir. E&W | 18W-24N | 40 |
| Merrimac Ln. E&W | 19W-21N | 47 |
| Middlesex Dr. N&S | 19W-21N | 47 |
| Millwood Farm Rd. NW&SE | 19W-21N | 47 |
| Moniter Ln. E&W | 19W-21N | 47 |
| Monitor Ln. NS&EW | 19W-21N | 47 |
| Monticello Ln. E&W | 19W-21N | 47 |
| Muirwood Ct. N&S | 20W-22N | 47 |
| Mundelein Rd. N&S | 18W-21N,18W-24N | 48 |
| Normandy Ct. E&W | 18W-23N | 48 |
| North Ridge Pl. E&W | 18W-24N | 40 |
| Nottinghamn Dr. N&S | 20W-20N | 47 |
| Oak Dr. E&W | 17W-22N | 48 |
| Cir. | 17W-22N | 48 |
| Oak Grove Dr. E&W | 18W-22N | 48 |
| Oak Hill Ln. N&S | 20W-21N | 47 |
| Oakwood Cir. NS&EW | 17W-23N | 48 |
| Oakwood Rd. E&W | 18W-23N | 48 |
| Old Field Ln. SW&NE | 17W-22N | 48 |
| Old Field Rd. NW&SE | 17W-22N | 48 |
| Old Hicks Rd. N&S | 19W-20N,19W-21N | 47 |
| Old McHenry Rd. NW&SE | 19W-22N,18W-21N | 47 |
| Old Wood Ln. NW&SE | 19W-22N | 48 |
| Osage Rd. NW&SE | 18W-25N | 40 |
| Pacific Blvd. N&S | 19W-25N | 39 |
| Pamela Ct. N&S | 19W-23N | 47 |
| Pamela Ct. NE&SW | 19W-23N | 47 |
| Partridge Ln. NW&SE | 17W-23N | 48 |
| Patricia Dr. E&W | 19W-23N | 47 |
| Pebble Creek E&W | 18W-20N | 48 |
| Picardy Ct. N&S | 18W-20N | 48 |
| Picardy Ct. E&W | 18W-20N | 48 |
| Pine Cone Ct. N&S | 18W-24N | 40 |
| Pine Ct. NE&SW | 19W-20N | 47 |
| Pine Tree Ct. N&S | 18W-24N | 40 |
| Pintail Ln. E&W | 18W-23N | 48 |
| Popp Ln. NW&SE | 19W-20N | 47 |
| Port Clinton Rd. E&W | 17W-23N | 48 |
| Pottawatomie Ct. E&W | 19W-21N,19W-20N | 47 |
| Prairie Crossing NW&SE | 17W-22N | 48 |
| Prairiemoor Ln. E&W | 19W-23N | 47 |
| Private Dr. N&S | 19W-20N | 47 |
| Private Ln. N&S | 19W-21N,19W-20N | 47 |
| Private Rd. E&W | 18W-21N | 48 |
| Private Rd. N&S | 19W-22N | 47 |
| Private Rd. NW&SE | 19W-23N | 47 |
| Promentary E&W | 17W-23N | 48 |
| Pvt. Ln. NE&SW | 18W-22N | 48 |
| Red Oak Dr. NS&EW | 19W-23N | 47 |
| Redwing Ln. E&W | 19W-24N | 39 |
| Ridgewood Ln. NE&SW | 18W-20N | 48 |
| Roanoke Ct. E&W | 18W-20N | 48 |
| Robert Parker Coffin Rd. NE&SW | 20W-20N,18W-21N | 47 |
| Robertson Blvd. E&W | 20W-22N | 47 |
| Rock Dove Ct. NE&SW | 17W-23N | 48 |
| Rolling Glen Dr. N&S | 19W-22N | 47 |
| Rosehedge Dr. NW&SE | 19W-24N | 39 |
| Rosos Parkway N&S | 17W-23N | 48 |
| Route 22 E&W | 19W-23N,17W-23N | 47 |
| Route 53 E&W | 20W-20N,18W-21N | 47 |
| Route 83 N&S | 18W-21N,18W-25N | 48 |
| Royal Melbourne Dr. E&W | 18W-23N | 48 |
| Saddle Ridge Ct. N&S | 18W-24N | 40 |
| Saddle Ridge Ln. N&S | 18W-24N | 40 |
| Salem Ct. NE&SW | 18W-24N | 40 |
| Salem Lake Dr. N&S | 20W-22N,19W-22N | 47 |
| Schaeffer Rd. N&S | 18W-20N,18W-21N | 48 |
| Schurr Ct. N&S | 19W-21N | 48 |
| Shagbark Ln. N&S | 19W-21N | 47 |
| Shaheen Ct. (Pvt.) N&S | 19W-23N | 47 |
| Shenandoah Ln. N&S | 19W-20N | 47 |
| Sheridan Ct. E&W | 19W-21N | 47 |
| Shilo Dr. E&W | 19W-21N | 47 |
| Sky Ln. N&S | 18W-22N | 48 |
| Southwell Ct. NW&SE | 19W-20N | 48 |
| Spring Valley NS&EW | 20W-21N | 47 |
| Standford Cir. NE&SW | 17W-24N | 40 |
| Stockbridge Ln. NW&SE | 18W-24N | 40 |
| Stonehaven Dr. NE&SW | 18W-22N | 48 |
| Sumter Ct. N&S | 18W-20N | 48 |
| Sumter Dr. E&W | 18W-20N | 48 |
| Sunshine Ln. E&W | 18W-22N | 48 |
| Surrey Ln. (Pvt.) NW&SE | 20W-21N | 47 |
| Taggert Ct. NW&SE | 17W-23N | 48 |
| Tall Oaks Dr. N&S | 18W-23N | 48 |
| Tanager Way NS&EW | 19W-20N,18W-20N | 47 |
| Teal Ct. E&W | 17W-23N | 48 |
| Teal Ln. NS&EW | 17W-23N | 48 |
| Three Lakes Ct. E&W | 18W-21N | 48 |
| Three Lakes Dr. NE&SW | 18W-21N | 48 |
| Tremont Cir. E&W | 17W-24N | 40 |
| Trenton Ct. E&W | 18W-21N | 48 |
| Tribal Ct. E&W | 19W-25N | 39 |
| Turnberry Ln. E&W | 20W-22N | 47 |
| Twin Lakes Dr. E&W | 19W-23N | 47 |
| Union Ct. N&S | 19W-20N | 47 |
| Valley View Cir. NS&EW | 19W-24N | 39 |
| Valley View Ln. NW&SE | 19W-24N | 39 |
| Victorian E&W | 19W-21N | 47 |
| Walnut Ln. E&W | 19W-20N | 47 |
| Waterfowl Way N&S | 19W-24N | 39 |
| Wellington Dr. NS&EW | 18W-23N | 48 |
| West Mardan Dr. N&S | 19W-21N | 47 |
| Westbury Dr. N&S | 18W-23N | 48 |
| Westchester Cir. N&S | 17W-24N | 40 |
| Westmoreland Dr. E&W | 18W-24N | 40 |
| Wildwood Ln. N&S | 18W-24N | 48 |
| Wildwood Ln. N&W | 18W-21N | 48 |
| Willow Brook Rd. N&S | 18W-22N | 48 |
| Willow Spring Rd. N&S | 18W-25N | 40 |
| Willow Valley Rd. N&S | 20W-20N,20W-21N | 47 |
| Willowbrook Rd. N&S | 18W-22N | 48 |
| Windham Ct. N&S | 18W-25N | 40 |
| Windham Ln. NW&SE | 18W-25N | 40 |
| Woodbine Ln. N&S | 19W-22N | 47 |
| Woodland Ln. N&S | 20W-20N | 47 |
| Woods End Rd. N&S | 19W-22N | 47 |
| Woodview Ct. N&S | 17W-22N | 48 |

### Mettawa

| | Grid | Page |
|---|---|---|
| Bradley Rd. N&S | 14W-26N | 41 |
| Everett Rd. E&W | 14W-24N | 41 |
| Hawthorne Dr. E&W | 13W-27N | 42 |
| Indian Ridge Rd. E&W | 14W-26N | 41 |
| Interstate 94 N&S | 13W-27N | 42 |
| Little St. Mary's Rd. NS&EW | 15W-27N | 41 |
| Maureen Ln. E&W | 14W-27N | 41 |
| Meadowood Ln. N&S | 14W-27N | 41 |
| Meadowoods Ct. NW&SE | 14W-27N | 41 |
| Oak Hill Ln. N&S | 14W-27N | 41 |
| Old School Rd. E&W | 15W-27N,14W-27N | 41 |
| Prairie View Ln. E&W | 14W-25N | 41 |
| Private Rd. NS&EW | 15W-27N | 41 |
| Riverwoods Rd. N&S | 13W-25N | 42 |
| Route 60 E&W | 15W-26N,14W-26N | 41 |
| Shagbark Ln. E&W | 14W-25N | 41 |
| St. Mary's Rd. N&S | 15W-25N,15W-27N | 41 |
| Townline Rd. E&W | 14W-26N | 41 |
| Tri-State Tollway N&S | 13W-26N | 42 |
| Westwoods Ln. NS&EW | 14W-27N | 41 |

### Mundelein

| | Grid | Page |
|---|---|---|
| Aberdeen Ln. NE&SW | 19W-28N | 31 |
| Adderly Dr. N&S | 19W-29N | 31 |
| Agnes Av. E&W | 18W-27N | 40 |
| Albion Ln. E&W | 19W-27N | 39 |
| Alexandra Ct. E&W | 19W-27N | 39 |
| Allanson Rd. E&W | 18W-27N | 40 |
| Ambria Ct. N&S | 19W-29N | 31 |
| Ambria Dr. NW&SE | 19W-29N | 31 |
| Ambria Ln. N&S | 19W-29N | 31 |
| Andover Dr. E&W | 19W-29N | 31 |
| Ansley Ct. E&W | 20W-27N | 39 |
| Anthony Av. NW&SE | 18W-27N | 40 |
| Appleby Cir. N&S | 19W-28N | 31 |
| Appleby Ct. N&S | 19W-28N | 31 |
| Arbor Ct. E&W | 18W-28N | 32 |
| Archer Av. N&S | 18W-27N | 40 |
| Armour Blvd. E&W | 17W-25N | 40 |
| Armwood Ln. E&W | 20W-28N | 31 |
| Ashbrook Dr. E&W | 19W-27N | 39 |
| Atwater Dr. N&S | 19W-27N | 39 |
| Babcock Ct. N&S | 19W-27N | 39 |
| Ballantree Dr. E&W | 17W-27N | 40 |
| Balmoral Dr. E&W | 19W-27N | 39 |
| Banbury Rd. NS&EW | 19W-28N | 31 |
| Barlowe Ln. E&W | 19W-27N | 39 |
| Barnhill Ln. NS&EW | 20W-28N | 31 |
| Baskin Rd. N&S | 17W-25N | 40 |
| Beach Pl. N&S | 19W-28N | 31 |
| Bedford Rd. E&W | 17W-27N | 40 |
| Benridge Ct. N&S | 20W-28N | 31 |
| Bingham Cir. NS&EW | 20W-27N,19W-27N | 39 |
| Bingham Ct. NW&SE | 20W-27N | 39 |
| Bishop Way NW&SE | 20W-28N | 31 |
| Blackburn Dr. E&W | 20W-27N | 39 |
| Blue Spruce Ln. E&W | 19W-28N | 31 |
| Bobby Ln. E&W | 19W-28N | 31 |
| Bonnie Brook Av. E&W | 19W-28N | 31 |
| Bradford Ln. N&S | 19W-27N | 39 |
| Bradwell Dr. EW&NS | 17W-27N | 40 |
| Braeburn Dr. E&W | 19W-28N | 31 |
| Braemar Dr. N&S | 19W-28N | 31 |
| Brentwood Dr. E&W | 20W-27N | 39 |
| Brice Av. N&S | 18W-27N | 40 |
| Brighton Dr. E&W | 20W-27N | 39 |
| Bristol Ct. N&S | 17W-27N | 40 |
| Buckingham Way NS&EW | 20W-28N | 31 |
| Burnham Ct. E&W | 19W-27N | 39 |
| Butterfield Rd. N&S | 17W-25N,17W-27N | 40 |
| Cairo Ct. N&S | 19W-28N | 31 |
| California Av. N&S | 19W-27N | 39 |
| Campus Dr. NS&EW | 17W-26N | 40 |
| Canterbury E&W | 17W-25N | 40 |
| Cardinal Pl. E&W | 19W-27N | 39 |
| Castleton Ct. N&S | 20W-28N | 31 |

| | Grid | Page |
|---|---|---|
| Cedar St. N&S | 18W-27N | 40 |
| Chandler Dr. E&W | 19W-28N | 31 |
| Charlotte Pl. E&W | 18W-28N | 32 |
| Chestnut St. N&S | 18W-27N | 40 |
| Chetwood Ct. E&W | | |
| | 20W-27N | 39 |
| Chicago Av. NW&SE | | |
| | 18W-27N,18W-28N | 40 |
| Churchill St. E&W | 17W-25N | 40 |
| Clarewood Dr. N&S | | |
| | | 31 |
| Clearbrook Park Dr. NE&SW | | |
| | 18W-26N | 40 |
| Compton Ln. N&S .. | 20W-27N | 39 |
| Courtland St. E&W | | |
| | 19W-27N,18W-27N | 39 |
| Crane Av. E&W | 18W-26N | 40 |
| Cross Meadow Dr. N&S | | |
| | 18W-27N | 40 |
| Crystal St. N&S | | |
| | 19W-27N,18W-27N | 39 |
| Dairy Ln. N&S | | |
| | 19W-28N,19W-29N | 31 |
| Dalton Av. NW&SE | | |
| | 18W-27N | 40 |
| Darnell Ct. E&W | 19W-29N | 31 |
| Dean Pl. E&W | 18W-27N | 40 |
| Deepwoods Dr. NE&SW | | |
| | 18W-26N | 40 |
| Derby Ln. E&W | 17W-25N | 40 |
| Diamond Lake Rd. N&S | | |
| | 18W-26W | 40 |
| Division St. E&W | 19W-27N | 39 |
| Dorchester Ct. E&W | | |
| | 19W-29N | 31 |
| Dorchester Dr. E&W | | |
| | 19W-29N | 31 |
| Downing E&W | 17W-25N | 40 |
| Dublin Dr. E&W | 19W-28N | 31 |
| Dunbar Rd. E&W | | |
| | 19W-28N,19W-29N | 31 |
| Dunlee Dr. N&S | 19W-29N | 31 |
| Dunton Cir. NS&EW | | |
| | 20W-27N | 39 |
| Dunton Ct. NE&SW | | |
| | 20W-27N | 39 |
| E. Garfield Av. N&S | | |
| | 19W-27N | 39 |
| East Greenview N&S | | |
| | 19W-27N | 39 |
| Edgar A. Poe Ln. N&S | | |
| | 18W-26N | 40 |
| Edgemont St. E&W | | |
| | 19W-28N | 31 |
| Edington Ln. E&W | | |
| | 20W-27N,19W-27N | 39 |
| Elm Av. E&W | 18W-26N | 40 |
| Emerald Av. N&S | | |
| | 19W-27N,19W-28N | 39 |
| Emerson Ln. E&W . 18W-26N | | 40 |
| Eton Way N&S | 17W-27N | 40 |
| Fair Lawn N&S | | |
| | 19W-27N,19W-28N | 39 |
| Fairhaven Ln. E&W | | |
| | 18W-28N | 32 |
| Farina Dr. N&S | 19W-27N | 39 |
| Firth Rd. E&W | 18W-28N | 31 |
| Forest Dr. E&W | 18W-26N | 40 |
| Foxmoor Ct. E&W . 20W-27N | | 39 |
| French Ct. N&S | 20W-27N | 40 |
| French St. E&W | 18W-26N | 40 |
| Friars Ln. E&W | 20W-28N | 31 |
| Garfield Av. N&S . 19W-27N | | 39 |
| George Av. N&S . 18W-27N | | 40 |
| Gifford Ct. NW&SE | | |
| | 18W-27N | 40 |
| Glendale Pl. E&W . 18W-28N | | 32 |
| Glenview Av. E&W . 18W-28N | | 31 |
| Goodwin Pl. NE&SW | | |
| | 18W-28N | 32 |
| Grace Av. NE&SW . 18W-28N | | 32 |
| Granville Av. N&S . 19W-28N | | 31 |
| Greenview Av. N&S | | |
| | 19W-27N,19W-28N | 39 |
| Greenwood Av. N&S | | |
| | 18W-28N | 32 |
| Grove St. E&W . 18W-27N | | 40 |
| Groveland Blvd. E&W | | |
| | 19W-27N | 39 |
| Halifax St. E&W . 19W-29N | | 31 |
| Hammond St. E&W | | |
| | 19W-27N | 39 |
| Hampton Ct. N&S . 17W-27N | | 40 |
| Hampton Ln. E&W . 17W-27N | | 40 |
| Handley Ct. N&S . 20W-28N | | 31 |
| Harrison Av. N&S . 19W-29N | | 31 |
| Hawley Ct. N&S . 19W-27N | | 39 |
| Hawley St. E&W | | |
| | 19W-28N,18W-28N | 31 |
| Hawthorne Blvd. E&W | | |
| | 19W-27N,18W-27N | 39 |
| Hickory St. N&S . 18W-27N | | 40 |
| High St. N&S . 18W-27N | | 40 |
| Highland Dr. N&S . 19W-28N | | 31 |
| Highland Rd. N&S . 19W-28N | | 31 |
| Hilgers Ct. N&S . 18W-25N | | 40 |
| Hillside Rd. E&W . 19W-28N | | 31 |
| Holcomb Rd. N&S . 18W-26N | | 32 |
| Hunt Ct. E&W . 17W-26N | | 40 |
| Huntington Ct. E&W | | |
| | 17W-27N | 40 |
| Huntington Dr. NS&EW | | |
| | 17W-27N | 40 |

| | Grid | Page |
|---|---|---|
| Idlewild Av. N&S | | |
| | 17W-27N,17W-28N | 40 |
| James Av. N&S | | |
| | 19W-27N,18W-28N | 40 |
| James Pl. NW&SE . 18W-28N | | 32 |
| Jeanette Pl. NE&SW | | |
| | 18W-28N | 32 |
| Karl Ct. N&S . 18W-26N | | 40 |
| Kensington Dr. E&W | | |
| | 19W-29N | 31 |
| Killarney Cir. E&W . 19W-28N | | 31 |
| Killarney Pass NW&SE | | |
| | 19W-28N | 31 |
| Killarney Pass Cir. E&W | | |
| | 19W-28N | 31 |
| Kings Way NW&SE | | |
| | 20W-28N | 31 |
| Knightsbridge Dr. E&W | | |
| | 17W-27N | 40 |
| Kreswick Dr. NW&SE | | |
| | 19W-27N | 39 |
| La Vista Dr. E&W . 21W-27N | | 38 |
| Lake Av. N&S | | |
| | 18W-26N,19W-28N | 40 |
| Lake Shore Dr. E&W | | |
| | 18W-27N | 40 |
| Lake St. N&S | | |
| | 18W-26N,19W-27N | 40 |
| Lake Ter. NW&SE . 18W-27N | | 40 |
| Lake View Dr. E&W | | |
| | 19W-27N | 39 |
| Lange St. N&S. 18W-27N | | 40 |
| Laramie St. E&W . 19W-28N | | 31 |
| Lawrence Dr. N&S . 18W-26N | | 40 |
| Leeds Ct. NW&SE . 17W-25N | | 40 |
| Leithton Rd. NS&EW | | |
| | 17W-26N | 40 |
| Lexington Ct. N&S . 20W-28N | | 31 |
| Lincoln Av. N&S . 19W-27N | | 39 |
| Linden Av. N&S . 18W-27N | | 40 |
| Liverpool Ln. E&W . 19W-29N | | 31 |
| Lomond Dr. NS&EW | | |
| | 19W-29N | 31 |
| Londonderry Ct. E&W | | |
| | 19W-29N | 31 |
| Longfellow Ln. N&S | | |
| | 18W-26N | 40 |
| Longwood Ter. E&W | | |
| | 18W-26N | 40 |
| Lucerne St. E&W . 19W-28N | | 31 |
| Lucerne Rd. N&S . 19W-28N | | 31 |
| Lyndale St. E&W . 19W-28N | | 31 |
| Manchester Dr. E&W | | |
| | 19W-29N | 31 |
| Manor Ln. NE&SW . 20W-28N | | 31 |
| Maple Av. NW&SE | | |
| | 19W-28N,18W-28N | 31 |
| Maplewood Av. E&W | | |
| | 18W-26N | 40 |
| Marlbough Ct. E&W | | |
| | 19W-27N | 39 |
| McCormick Av. N&S | | |
| | 17W-25N | 40 |
| McKinley Av. NE&SW | | |
| | 18W-27N,18W-28N | 40 |
| McRae Ln. NE&SW | | |
| | 20W-28N | 31 |
| Michale Av. N&S . 19W-27N | | 39 |
| Midland Av. N&S . 18W-27N | | 40 |
| Midlothian Av. N&S | | |
| | 19W-27N | 39 |
| Midlothian Rd. N&S | | |
| | 19W-28N,19W-29N | 31 |
| Midway Dr. E&W . 18W-27N | | 40 |
| Morris St. E&W . 18W-28N | | 32 |
| N. Shore Dr. E&W . 19W-27N | | 39 |
| New Castle Ct. N&S | | |
| | 17W-27N | 40 |
| Newbury Ln. N&S . 20W-27N | | 39 |
| Newcastle St. NW&SE | | |
| | 17W-27N | 40 |
| North Av. N&S . 18W-27N | | 40 |
| North Shore Dr. E&W | | |
| | 19W-27N | 39 |
| Norton Av. N&S . 18W-28N | | 32 |
| Nottingham E&W . 17W-25N | | 40 |
| Oak St. E&W . 18W-27N | | 40 |
| Oakdale Av. E&W . 18W-26N | | 40 |
| Olga St. N&S . 18W-26N | | 40 |
| Orchard Av. E&W . 18W-27N | | 40 |
| Orchard St. E&W | | |
| | 19W-27N,18W-27N | 39 |
| Orleans Dr. E&W . 17W-25N | | 40 |
| Oslo Ct. E&W . 19W-28N | | 31 |
| Park Av. N&S . 19W-28N | | 31 |
| Park St. E&W . 18W-28N | | 32 |
| Parliment Way N&S | | |
| | 17W-27N | 40 |
| Patrick Dr. E&W . 19W-29N | | 31 |
| Pershing Av. N&S . 19W-27N | | 39 |
| Pershing Dr. NE&SW | | |
| | 19W-27N | 39 |
| Pinehurst Dr. N&S . 20W-27N | | 39 |
| Pleasure Dr. E&W . 18W-26N | | 40 |
| Prairie Av. N&S | | |
| | 19W-27N,19W-28N | 39 |
| Primrose Ln. N&S | | |
| | 22W-27N | 38 |
| Private Rd. N&S . 19W-26N | | 39 |
| Prospect Av. NW&SE | | |
| | 18W-27N | 40 |
| Pymouth Farms Rd. E&W | | |
| | 17W-25N | 40 |
| Quigley Av. E&W . 19W-27N | | 39 |

| | Grid | Page |
|---|---|---|
| Racine Pl. NE&SW . 18W-28N | | 32 |
| Raleigh Rd. E&W . 19W-28N | | 31 |
| Rays Ln. E&W . 18W-26N | | 40 |
| Regent Dr. NS&EW | | |
| | 20W-27N,19W-27N | 39 |
| Reidel Dr. N&S . 17W-25N | | 40 |
| Ridge Av. N&S . 18W-28N | | 31 |
| Ridgeland Av. N&S | | |
| | 19W-28N | 31 |
| Ridgemoor Av. N&S | | |
| | 19W-27N,19W-28N | 39 |
| Rotary Ct. N&S . 18W-28N | | 32 |
| Rouse Av. NW&SE | | |
| | 18W-27N | 40 |
| Route 60 NW&SE . 20W-28N | | 31 |
| Route 63 N&S | | |
| | 19W-27N,19W-29N | 39 |
| Rt. 176 E&W | | |
| | 19W-28N,18W-28N | 31 |
| Russell Pl. N&S . 18W-26N | | 40 |
| Rye Rd. E&W . 19W-28N | | 31 |
| S. Lake Shore Dr. E&W | | |
| | 18W-27N | 40 |
| S. Noel Dr. E&W . 18W-27N | | 40 |
| Salceda Av. NE&SW | | |
| | 19W-29N | 31 |
| Salceda Ln. NW&SE | | |
| | 19W-29N | 31 |
| Sandhurst Rd. E&W | | |
| | 17W-27N | 40 |
| Seymour Av. N&S . 18W-27N | | 40 |
| Shaddle Av. N&S . 18W-27N | | 40 |
| Shady Dell Av. E&W | | |
| | 18W-26N | 40 |
| Shady Ln. E&W . 18W-26N | | 40 |
| Shady Rest Ridge N&S | | |
| | 18W-26N | 40 |
| Sheffield Av. E&W . 19W-29N | | 31 |
| Sherwood St. NE&SW | | |
| | 17W-27N | 40 |
| Shetland Dr. N&S . 19W-29N | | 31 |
| Simpson Dr. N&S . 18W-26N | | 40 |
| South St. N&S . 18W-26N | | 40 |
| Southport Rd. NW&SE | | |
| | 20W-27N | 39 |
| Spaulding Av. E&W | | |
| | 20W-27N,19W-27N | 39 |
| Springbrook Ct.* E&W | | |
| | 20W-27N | 39 |
| Springbrook Dr.* E&W | | |
| | 20W-27N | 39 |
| Stafford Dr. N&S . 19W-29N | | 31 |
| Sterling Dr. N&S . 19W-29N | | 31 |
| Stratford Dr. N&S . 18W-26N | | 40 |
| Summerhill Dr. E&W | | |
| | 20W-27N | 39 |
| Sunset Ln. E&W . 20W-27N | | 39 |
| Surridge Ct. E&W . 20W-27N | | 39 |
| Templeton Ct. E&W | | |
| | 20W-28N | 31 |
| Thomas Blvd. E&W | | |
| | 18W-27N | 40 |
| Thomas Ct. N&S . 18W-27N | | 40 |
| Thornton Way N&S | | |
| | 20W-27N,19W-26N | 39 |
| Tower Rd. N&S . 18W-26N | | 40 |
| Townline Rd. E&W | | |
| | 18W-25N,17W-25N | 40 |
| Trescott St. E&W . 20W-27N | | 39 |
| Turret Dr. N&S . 18W-26N | | 40 |
| U.S. Route 45 N&S | | |
| | 18W-26N,19W-27N | 40 |
| University Av. N&S . 18W-28N | | 32 |
| Verde Ct. N&S . 19W-29N | | 31 |
| Verde Ln. E&W . 19W-29N | | 31 |
| Victoria Rd. E&W . 20W-28N | | 31 |
| W. Garfield Av. N&S | | |
| | 19W-27N | 39 |
| Wakefield Ct. NW&SE | | |
| | 20W-27N | 39 |
| Walker Pl. E&W . 18W-28N | | 32 |
| Walnut Ct. N&S | | |
| | 18W-27N | 40 |
| Walnut St. N&S | | |
| | 18W-26N,18W-28N | 40 |
| Warwick Ln. N&S . 19W-28N | | 39 |
| Washington Blvd. N&S | | |
| | 18W-27N | 40 |
| Washington Ct. N&S | | |
| | 18W-27N | 40 |
| Waverly Dr. N&S | | |
| | 20W-26N,20W-27N | 39 |
| Wellington Av. E&W | | |
| | 19W-28N | 31 |
| Wellington Ct. N&S | | |
| | 19W-28N | 31 |
| West Greenview N&S | | |
| | 19W-27N | 39 |
| Westminister Pl. N&S | | |
| | 20W-28N | 31 |
| Weston Ln. N&S . 19W-27N | | 39 |
| Whitehall Rd. N&S . 17W-25N | | 40 |
| Whittier Ln. E&W . 18W-26N | | 40 |
| Wilcox St. E&W . 19W-27N | | 39 |
| Wildwood Av. N&S . 18W-28N | | 32 |
| Wilhem Rd. E&W . 17W-25N | | 40 |
| Wilton Dr. NW&SE . 20W-27N | | 39 |
| Wimpole E&W . 17W-25N | | 40 |
| Windsor Pl. NE&SW | | |
| | 17W-27N | 40 |
| Wingate Dr. E&W | | |
| | 20W-27N | 39 |
| Winstead Pl. NE&SW | | |
| | 19W-27N | 39 |

| | Grid | Page |
|---|---|---|
| Winston Ct. NW&SE | | |
| | 20W-26N | 39 |
| Winthrop Ct. E&W . 18W-26N | | 40 |
| Woodcrest Cir. E&W | | |
| | 20W-26N | 31 |
| Woodcrest Ct. E&W | | |
| | 20W-28N | 31 |
| Woodcrest Dr. N&S | | |
| | 20W-28N | 31 |
| Woodhaven Ct. NE&SW | | |
| | 20W-28N | 31 |
| Woodhaven Dr. NS&EW | | |
| | 20W-28N | 31 |
| Woodlawn Dr. E&W | | |
| | 19W-27N | 39 |
| Wortham Cir. NW&SE | | |
| | 20W-26N | 39 |
| Wortham Dr. NE&SW | | |
| | 20W-26N | 39 |
| York Rd. NE&SW . 20W-26N | | 39 |
| Yorkshire Dr. NW&SE | | |
| | 20W-27N | 39 |

## Newport Township

| | Grid | Page |
|---|---|---|
| Bayonne Av. N&S | | |
| | 13W-38N,3W-39N | 18 |
| Beach Rd. E&W . 13W-38N | | 18 |
| Belle Plaine Av. N&S | | |
| | 13W-38N,13W-39N | 18 |
| Boulevard View Av. N&S | | |
| | 13W-38N | 18 |
| Browne School Rd. N&S | | |
| | 16W-39N | 17 |
| Chaplin St. E&W . 13W-38N | | 18 |
| Crawford Rd. N&S | | |
| | 18W-38N,18W-43N | 16 |
| Dale Av. N&S . 13W-38N | | 18 |
| Delany Rd. N&S | | |
| | 14W-40N,14W-43N | 9 |
| | 18W-42N,16W-42N | 8 |
| Edwards Rd. E&W | | |
| | 14W-40N | 9 |
| Forestview Rd. N&S | | |
| | 13W-40N | 10 |
| Green Bay Rd. N&S | | |
| | 13W-42N,13W-43N | 10 |
| Greenview Dr. E&W | | |
| | 13W-40N | 10 |
| Hart St. E&W . 13W-38N | | 18 |
| Hickory Rd. E&W | | |
| | 15W-42N,14W-42N | 9 |
| Hunt Club Rd. N&S | | |
| | 17W-41N,17W-43N | 8 |
| Ingram Dr. E&W . 14W-43N | | 9 |
| Kaiser Rd. E&W . 14W-43N | | 9 |
| Kazmer Rd. E&W . 14W-40N | | 9 |
| Kelly Rd. E&W | | |
| | 18W-40N,16W-40N | 8 |
| Kilbourne Rd. E&W | | |
| | 14W-39N,14W-43N | 17 |
| Lester Ln. N&S . 13W-40N | | 10 |
| Magnolia Av. N&S | | |
| | 13W-38N,13W-39N | 18 |
| Martin St. E&W . 13W-38N | | 18 |
| McCarthy Rd. E&W | | |
| | 16W-38N,15W-38N | 17 |
| Mill Creek Rd. N&S | | |
| | 16W-38N,16W-41N | 17 |
| Northwestern Av. N&S | | |
| | 13W-38N,13W-39N | 18 |
| Old Woodford Rd. N&S | | |
| | 15W-41N | 9 |
| Pickford St. E&W . 13W-38N | | 18 |
| Pine Grove Av. N&S | | |
| | 13W-38N,13W-39N | 18 |
| Plaza Ln. NW&SE . 16W-39N | | 17 |
| Rosecrans Rd. E&W | | |
| | 18W-41N,13W-41N | 8 |
| Rosedale Av. N&S . 13W-38N | | 18 |
| Route 131 N&S | | |
| | 13W-42N,13W-43N | 10 |
| Route 173 E&W | | |
| | 18W-41N,13W-41N | 8 |
| Russell Rd. E&W | | |
| | 16W-43N,14W-43N | 8 |
| Sharon St. E&W . 13W-39N | | 18 |
| Sheridan Oaks Dr. N&S | | |
| | 18W-43N | 8 |
| Stateline Rd. E&W | | |
| | 18W-43N,16W-43N | 8 |
| Stonegate Rd. E&W | | |
| | 13W-40N | 10 |
| Sunset Rd. N&S . 13W-40N | | 10 |
| Sylvan Av. N&S . 13W-38N | | 18 |
| Timberland Tr. N&S | | |
| | 13W-40N | 10 |
| Town Line Rd. E&W | | |
| | 13W-38N | 18 |
| Tri State Tollway N&S | | |
| | 16W-38N,16W-43N | 17 |
| Wadsworth Rd. E&W | | |
| | 13W-39N | 18 |
| Waveland Av. N&S 13W-38N | | 18 |
| Waverly St. E&W . 13W-40N | | 10 |
| Winthrop Harbor Rd. E&W | | |
| | 14W-42N,13W-42N | 9 |
| Woodland Av. N&S | | |
| | 13W-38N | 18 |
| Yorkhouse Rd. E&W | | |
| | 15W-38N | 17 |
| 9th St. E&W | | |
| | 15W-42N,14W-42N | 9 |
| 27th Pl. E&W . 13W-40N | | 10 |
| 27th St. E&W . 13W-40N | | 10 |

| | Grid | Page |
|---|---|---|
| 28th Pl. E&W . 13W-40N | | 10 |
| 28th St. E&W . 13W-40N | | 10 |
| 29th St. E&W . 13W-40N | | 10 |

## North Barrington

| | Grid | Page |
|---|---|---|
| Aberdour Ct. N&S . 24W-25N | | 38 |
| Apex Ct. N&S . 25W-23N | | 45 |
| Arboretum Ct.* E&W | | |
| | 25W-21N | 45 |
| Arboretum Dr.* E&W | | |
| | 25W-21N | 45 |
| Arrowhead Ln. N&S | | |
| | 25W-24N | 37 |
| Averill Ct. N&S . 24W-25N | | 38 |
| Beachview Ln. NS&EW | | |
| | 25W-23N | 45 |
| Bexley Ct. N&S | | |
| | 25W-24N | 37 |
| Biltmore Dr. N&S . 25W-23N | | 45 |
| Blanche Ct. E&W . 25W-22N | | 45 |
| Border Ln. E&W . 26W-23N | | 45 |
| Brook Cir. N&S . 25W-23N | | 45 |
| Brook Forest Ln. NW&SE | | |
| | 25W-22N | 45 |
| Brookmont Ln. E&W | | |
| | 25W-23N | 45 |
| Brookside Dr. N&S | | |
| | 26W-23N,25W-23N | 45 |
| Candlewood Ct. NS&EW | | |
| | 24W-25N | 38 |
| Candlewood Dr. N&S | | |
| | 24W-25N | 38 |
| Carriage Rd. N&S . 25W-24N | | 37 |
| Castle View Ct. E&W | | |
| | 25W-23N | 45 |
| Castleton Ct. N&S | | |
| | 25W-24N,24W-25N | 37 |
| Century Oaks Dr. N&S | | |
| | 26W-22N | 45 |
| Cherry Hill Rd. E&W | | |
| | 26W-23N | 45 |
| Christopher Dr. NS&EW | | |
| | 24W-22N | 46 |
| Clarington Way NS&EW | | |
| | 24W-25N | 38 |
| Clover Hill Ln. NS&EW | | |
| | 24W-23N | 46 |
| Concord Ln. E&W . 25W-23N | | 45 |
| Coventry Ln. NE&SW | | |
| | 25W-24N | 37 |
| Crooked Ln. E&W | | |
| | 26W-23N,25W-23N | 45 |
| Crosswicks Ct. NW&SE | | |
| | 24W-24N | 38 |
| Daily Ln. E&W. 25W-23N | | 45 |
| Deverell Dr. NS&EW | | |
| | 24W-24N | 37 |
| Drury Ln. N&S . 25W-23N | | 45 |
| Duck Pond Ln. E&W | | |
| | 25W-22N | 45 |
| Duxbury Dr. NW&SE | | |
| | 24W-24N | 37 |
| Edgewood Rd. E&W | | |
| | 25W-23N | 45 |
| Essex Ln. N&S . 25W-23N | | 45 |
| Eton Dr. NE&SW | | |
| | 26W-23N,25W-23N | 45 |
| Glen Circle Dr. NE&SW | | |
| | 25W-23N | 45 |
| Golfview Dr. N&S | | |
| | 26W-23N,25W-23N | 45 |
| Grassmere Ct. E&W | | |
| | 26W-22N | 45 |
| Halcyon Ln. E&W . 25W-23N | | 45 |
| Hallbraith Ct. N&S . 24W-25N | | 38 |
| Haversham Ln. N&S | | |
| | 25W-24N | 37 |
| Haverton Way NS&EW | | |
| | 25W-23N | 45 |
| Hawthorne Rd. NE&SW | | |
| | 25W,23N | 45 |
| Hewes Dr. N&S . 25W-22N | | 45 |
| Hidden Brook Dr. N&S | | |
| | 25W-24N,24W-24N | 37 |
| Hidden Oaks Ln. NS&EW | | |
| | 25W-22N | 45 |
| Hidden Pond Ln. E&W | | |
| | 25W-23N | 45 |
| Hillandale Ct. NW&SE | | |
| | 25W-22N | 45 |
| Hillburn Ct. N&S . 25W-24N | | 37 |
| Hillburn Ln. N&S . 25W-24N | | 37 |
| Homewood Ln. N&S | | |
| | 25W-23N | 45 |
| Honey Lake Ct. NE&SW | | |
| | 25W-23N | 45 |
| Honey Lake Rd. N&S | | |
| | 25W-22N | 45 |
| Honey Ln. N&S . 25W-23N | | 45 |
| Kathleen Ct. E&W . 25W-23N | | 45 |
| Kensington Dr. NW&SE | | |
| | 25W-24N | 37 |
| Kettering Ct. NW&SE | | |
| | 25W-24N | 37 |
| Kimberly Rd. N&S . 25W-23N | | 45 |
| Lake Shore Blvd. N&S | | |
| | 26W-23N | 45 |
| Lakeside Ct. N&S | | |
| | 24W-25N | 38 |
| Lakeside Dr. NS&EW | | |
| | 24W-25N | 38 |
| Lakeview Pl. N&S . 26W-23N | | 45 |
| Larkins Ln. N&S . 24W-22N | | 46 |

| | Grid | Page |
|---|---|---|
| Marbridge Ct. NE&SW | 25W-24N | 37 |
| Masland Ct. N&S .. | 24W-22N | 46 |
| Miller Rd. E&W | | |
| | 26W-23N,25W-23N | 45 |
| Mockingbird Ln. NS&EW | | |
| | 25W-23N | 45 |
| Mohawk Dr. N&S .. | 26W-22N | 45 |
| North Hill Dr. E&W.. | 25W-23N | 45 |
| North Wynstone Dr. NS&EW | | |
| | 25W-25N,24W-24N | 37 |
| Old Oak Dr. N&S .. | 25W-22N | 45 |
| Onondaga Dr. E&W | | |
| | 26W-22N | 45 |
| Orchard Rd. NW&SE | 25W-23N | 45 |
| Osage Dr. N&S .. | 26W-22N | 45 |
| Ottawa Dr. N&S .... | 26W-22N | 45 |
| Oxford Dr. N&S .... | 25W-23N | 45 |
| Oxford Rd. NW&SE | | |
| | 25W-23N | 45 |
| Pheasant Run Trail N&S | | |
| | 25W-23N | 45 |
| Piermont Dr. N&S .. | 24W-24N | 38 |
| Pinewoods Dr. E&W | | |
| | 25W-22N | 45 |
| Pook's Hill Rd. NE&SW | | |
| | 25W-22N | 45 |
| Private Ct. NS&EW | | |
| | 25W-24N | 37 |
| Rainbow Rd. N&S | | |
| | 25W-22N,24W-21N | 45 |
| Randolph Ct. NW&SE | | |
| | 25W-22N | 45 |
| Redwing Ln. N&S . | 25W-24N | 37 |
| Riderwood Rd. E&W | | |
| | 24W-25N | 38 |
| Rugby Rd. E&W .. | 25W-23N | 45 |
| Rustic Dr. N&S .. | 25W-23N | 45 |
| Saddle Tree Ln. N&S | | |
| | 25W-22N | 45 |
| Schaffer Ln. N&S | | |
| | 25W-21N,24W-22N | 46 |
| Seminole Dr. N&S . | 26W-22N | 45 |
| Shady Ln. NW&SE | 25W-22N | 45 |
| Signal Hill Rd. NE&SW | | |
| | 26W-23N,25W-23N | 45 |
| Sioux Dr. E&W .... | 26W-22N | 45 |
| South Wynstone Dr. NS&EW | | |
| | 25W-24N,24W-24N | 37 |
| Stratham Cir. E&W | 25W-24N | 37 |
| Thomas Dr. E&W .. | 25W-22N | 45 |
| U.S. Route 59 N&S | | |
| | 25W-22N,26W-23N | 45 |
| View Ct. N&S .. | 25W-23N | 45 |
| Weybridge Ln. NW&SE | | |
| | 25W-24N | 37 |
| Williams Park Rd. N&S | | |
| | 27W-27N | 36 |
| Woodbine Pl. NW&SE | | |
| | 25W-23N | 45 |
| Wooded Ln. N&S .. | 26W-23N | 45 |
| Woodland Dr. NW&SE | | |
| | 26W-23N,25W-23N | 45 |
| Wynstone Way N&S | | |
| | 25W-24N | 37 |

## North Chicago

| | | |
|---|---|---|
| Adams St. N&S .... | 10W-32N | 27 |
| Argonne Dr. E&W . | 11W-31N | 35 |
| Arlington Av. NS&EW | | |
| | 11W-31N | 26 |
| Barrett Av. E&W.... | 11W-32N | 26 |
| Barry Av. E&W .... | 12W-30N | 35 |
| Beacon Av. . 12W-30N | | 35 |
| Berwyn Av. E&W .. | 12W-30N | 35 |
| Broadway Av. NE&SW | | |
| | 11W-31N | 35 |
| Brompton Av. E&W | | |
| | 12W-30N | 35 |
| Buckley Rd. E&W . | 12W-30N | 35 |
| Carver Av. . 11W-32N | | 26 |
| Commonwealth Av. N&S | | |
| | 11W-31N | 35 |
| Davis St. N&S .. | 11W-31N | 35 |
| Dickey Av. N&S .. | 11W-31N | 26 |
| Dickey St. N&S .. | 11W-31N | 35 |
| Dugdale Rd. N&S | | |
| | 11W-31N,11W-32N | 35 |
| Elizabeth Av. N&S | | |
| | 11W-31N,11W-32N | 35 |
| Fairbank Av. N&S .. | 12W-30N | 35 |
| Farwell Av. . 12W-30N | | 35 |
| Fellows Pl. NE&SW | | |
| | 10W-31N | 35 |
| Foss Park Av. NS&EW | | |
| | 10W-31N,10W-32N | 35 |
| Frontenac Av. N&S | | |
| | 12W-30N | 35 |
| Glenn Dr. E&W | | |
| | 11W-31N,11W-32N | 35 |
| Golf Course Dr. N&S | | |
| | 12W-31N,12W-32N | 35 |
| Grant Pl. E&W .... | 10W-32N | 27 |
| Green Bay Rd. NW&SE | | |
| | 12W-31N | 35 |
| Greenfield Av. N&S | | |
| | 11W-31N,11W-32N | 35 |
| Greenwood (Natoma) Av. N&S | | |
| | 12W-31N | 35 |
| Grove Av. N&S | | |
| | 11W-31N,11W-32N | 35 |

| | | |
|---|---|---|
| Hervey Av. N&S | | |
| | 11W-31N,11W-32N | 35 |
| Hillcrest Av. N&S | | |
| | 11W-31N,12W-32N | 35 |
| Honore Av. N&S.... | 11W-31N | 35 |
| Honore St. N&S .... | 11W-31N | 35 |
| Jackson St. N&S | | |
| | 10W-31N,10W-32N | 35 |
| Jones Dr. E&W .. | 11W-32N | 26 |
| Kemble Av. N&S | | |
| | 11W-31N,11W-32N | 35 |
| Kennedy Dr. NE&SW | | |
| | 11W-32N | 26 |
| Kristan Av. N&S | | |
| | 11W-31N,11W-32N | 35 |
| Lakeside Av. NE&SW | | |
| | 10W-32N | 27 |
| Lawn Av. N&S . 12W-30N | | 35 |
| Lenox Av. N&S .. | 10W-32N | 27 |
| Leona Av. E&W .. | 11W-31N | 35 |
| Lewis Av. N&S .. | 11W-31N | 35 |
| Lincoln St. N&S .. | 11W-31N | 35 |
| Main St. NE&SW .. | 10W-31N | 35 |
| Marquette St. N&S | 10W-31N | 35 |
| Mc Alister Av. N&S | | |
| | 10W-32N | 27 |
| Meadow Ln. N&S . | 12W-31N | 35 |
| Morrow Av. NE&SW | | |
| | 11W-31N | 35 |
| Natoma (Greenwood) Av. N&S .... | 12W-31N | 35 |
| Neil Ln. E&W .... | 11W-31N | 35 |
| Northern Av. N&S | | |
| | 12W-31N,12W-32N | 35 |
| Park Av. N&S | | |
| | 10W-31N,10W-32N | 35 |
| Prospect Av. N&S | | |
| | 11W-31N,11W-32N | 35 |
| Renken Av. N&S .. | 11W-32N | 26 |
| Route 131 N&S | | |
| | 12W-31N,11W-31N | 35 |
| Route 137 E&W .... | 11W-30N | 35 |
| Seymour Av. N&S | | |
| | 11W-31N,11W-32N | 35 |
| Sheridan Rd. NE&SW | | |
| | 10W-31N,10W-32N | 35 |
| Sherman Av. N&S | | |
| | 11W-31N,11W-32N | 35 |
| U.S. Route 41 N&S | | |
| | 12W-32N | 26 |
| Victoria St. N&S | | |
| | 11W-31N,10W-32N | 35 |
| Wadsworth Av. N&S | | |
| | 10W-32N | 27 |
| Wallace Av. N&S .. | 11W-31N | 35 |
| Wallace St. N&S.... | 11W-31N | 35 |
| Willow Av. N&S .. | 12W-32N | 26 |
| Winter Av. N&S .. | 11W-31N | 35 |
| Wright St. N&S .. | 11W-31N | 35 |
| 11th St. E&W ...... | 10W-32N | 27 |
| 12th St. E&W .... | 10W-32N | 27 |
| 13th St. E&W .... | 10W-32N | 27 |
| 14th Pl. E&W .. | 12W-32N | 26 |
| 14th St. E&W | | |
| | 12W-32N,10W-32N | 26 |
| 15th Pl. E&W .. | 12W-32N | 26 |
| 15th St. E&W | | |
| | 12W-32N,10W-32N | 26 |
| 16th Pl. E&W .. | 10W-32N | 26 |
| 16th St. E&W | | |
| | 12W-32N,10W-32N | 26 |
| 17th Pl. E&W .. | 12W-32N | 26 |
| 17th St. E&W | | |
| | 12W-32N,10W-32N | 26 |
| 18th Pl. E&W .. | 12W-31N | 35 |
| 18th St. E&W | | |
| | 12W-32N,10W-32N | 26 |
| 19th Pl. E&W .. | 12W-31N | 35 |
| 20th Pl. E&W .. | 12W-31N | 35 |
| 20th St. E&W | | |
| | 12W-31N,11W-31N | 35 |
| 21st Pl. E&W .. | 12W-31N | 35 |
| 21st St. E&W | | |
| | 12W-31N,10W-31N | 35 |
| 22nd Pl. E&W .. | 12W-31N | 35 |
| 22nd St. E&W .. | 11W-31N | 35 |
| 23rd Pl. E&W .. | 12W-31N | 35 |
| 23rd St. E&W .. | 11W-31N | 35 |
| 24th Pl. E&W .. | 11W-31N | 35 |
| 24th St. E&W | | |
| | 12W-31N,11W-31N | 35 |
| 25th St. E&WW .. | 11W-31N | 35 |

## Old Mill Creek

| | | |
|---|---|---|
| Brownie Sch. Rd. N&S | | |
| | 16W-39N | 17 |
| Crawford Rd. N&S | | |
| | 18W-38N,18W-40N | 16 |
| Hunt Club Rd. N&S | | |
| | 17W-37N,17W-41N | 16 |
| Hutchins Rd. N&S | | |
| | 18W-36N,18W-37N | 16 |
| Interstate 94 N&S .. | 16W-39N | 17 |
| Kelly Rd. E&W | | |
| | 18W-40N,16W-40N | 8 |
| Milburn Rd. E&W | | |
| | 18W-38N,17W-38N | 16 |
| Rosecrans Rd. E&W | | |
| | 18W-41N,17W-41N | 16 |
| Sand Lake Rd. N&S | | |
| | 17W-37N,16W-37N | 16 |
| Sand Lake Rd. E&W | | |
| | 18W-37N | 16 |

| Tri State North Tollway N&S | Grid | Page |
|---|---|---|
| | 16W-37N,16W-40N | 17 |
| Wadsworth Rd. E&W | | |
| | 17W-39N,16W-39N | 16 |

## Park City

| | | |
|---|---|---|
| Ann Av. E&W ...... | 13W-34N | 26 |
| Barb Av. E&W...... | 13W-33N | 26 |
| Bedford Ct. E&W .. | 13W-33N | 26 |
| Belvidere Rd. E&W | | |
| | 13W-33N,12W-33N | 26 |
| Betty Av. NW&SE . | 13W-33N | 26 |
| Birch Av. N&S...... | 12W-33N | 26 |
| Bryn Mawr Av. N&S | | |
| | 13W-33N | 26 |
| Cambridge Dr. E&W | | |
| | 13W-33N | 26 |
| Cornell Av. E&W | | |
| | 14W-33N,13W-33N | 26 |
| Crestwood* E&W .. | 12W-32N | 26 |
| Devonshire Av. E&W | | |
| | 13W-33N | 26 |
| Diana Av. E&W .. | 13W-33N | 26 |
| Dixie Av. E&W | | |
| | 13W-33N,12W-33N | 26 |
| Dorset Ct. NW&SE | | |
| | 13W-33N | 26 |
| Dromey Av. N&S . | 12W-33N | 26 |
| Eastwood Pl. E&W | 14W-33N | 26 |
| Elaine Av. E&W .. | 13W-33N | 26 |
| Eli St. E&W ........ | 12W-33N | 26 |
| Eric Blvd. E&W .. | 12W-33N | 26 |
| Eva Av. E&W .. | 13W-33N | 26 |
| Everett Pl. E&W .. | 14W-33N | 26 |
| First St. E&W .. | 13W-33N | 26 |
| Greenleaf St. N&S .. | 13W-33N | 26 |
| Greenview Av. N&S | | |
| | 13W-33N | 26 |
| Greenview Dr. N&S | | |
| | 13W-33N | 26 |
| Gulf Pl. N&S .. | 12W-33N | 26 |
| Harvey E&W .. | 13W-33N | 26 |
| Harwick Ln. E&W .. | 13W-33N | 26 |
| Hillcrest* N&S .. | 12W-33N | 26 |
| Hood Av. N&S .. | 13W-33N | 26 |
| Howard Av. E&W .. | 13W-33N | 26 |
| Ingleside Av. N&S | | |
| | 14W-33N,13W-33N | 26 |
| Jeanette Av. E&W .. | 12W-33N | 26 |
| Jen Av. E&W ...... | 13W-33N | 26 |
| Joy Av. E&W .. | 13W-33N | 26 |
| June Av. E&W .. | 13W-34N | 26 |
| Kehm Blvd. E&W | | |
| | 13W-33N,12W-33N | 26 |
| Knight Av. N&S .. | 12W-33N | 26 |
| Lake Park Av. E&W | | |
| | 14W-33N,13W-33N | 26 |
| Longview Dr.* E&W | | |
| | 12W-32N | 26 |
| Lowe St. E&W .. | 13W-33N | 26 |
| Main St. E&W .. | 13W-33N | 26 |
| Marshfield Av. E&W | | |
| | 13W-33N | 26 |
| Mary Av. E&W .. | 13W-33N | 26 |
| Meadow Dr.* E&W | 12W-32N | 26 |
| Michael Av. E&W .. | 13W-33N | 26 |
| Mobile Blvd. E&W .. | 12W-33N | 26 |
| Murphy St. E&W .. | 12W-33N | 26 |
| Noll Dr. E&W .. | 12W-33N | 26 |
| Northwood Av. E&W | | |
| | 14W-33N,13W-33N | 26 |
| Old Plank Rd. NW&SE | | |
| | 13W-33N | 26 |
| Oldsmar Ln. N&S .. | 12W-33N | 26 |
| Pace Av. N&S .. | 12W-33N | 26 |
| Palmori Cir.* N&S .. | 12W-32N | 26 |
| Patricia Ln. E&W .. | 12W-33N | 26 |
| Richard Av.* N&S .. | 12W-32N | 26 |
| Roger Av. E&W .. | 13W-33N | 26 |
| Rollo Blvd. E&W .. | 12W-33N | 26 |
| Rosedale Av. N&S .. | 13W-33N | 26 |
| Rt. 120 E&W .. | 13W-33N | 26 |
| Sharon Av. N&S .. | 12W-33N | 26 |
| Staben Av. N&S .. | 12W-33N | 26 |
| Susan Circle, E. N&S | | |
| | 12W-33N | 26 |
| Susan Circle, N. E&W | | |
| | 12W-33N | 26 |
| Susan Circle, S. E&W | | |
| | 12W-33N | 26 |
| Susan Circle, W. N&S | | |
| | 12W-33N | 26 |
| Sussex Ct. NE&SW | | |
| | 13W-33N | 26 |
| Sutherland Dr. E&W | | |
| | 13W-33N | 26 |
| Ted Av. N&S .... | 13W-33N | 26 |
| Teske Blvd. N&S | | |
| | 13W-33N,12W-33N | 26 |
| Thorndale Av. N&S | | |
| | 13W-33N | 26 |
| Troy Av. E&W .. | 13W-33N | 26 |
| Warren Av. E&W .. | 13W-34N | 26 |
| West St. N&S .. | 13W-33N | 26 |
| Westgate* N&S .. | 13W-32N | 26 |
| Will Av. NW&SE .. | 13W-33N | 26 |
| Wilson Av. N&S .. | 12W-33N | 26 |
| Winthrop Av. N&S .. | 13W-33N | 26 |
| Wood St. N&S .. | 12W-33N | 26 |
| 7th St. E&W ...... | 13W-33N | 26 |
| 8th St. E&W .. | 12W-33N | 26 |
| 9th St. E&W .. | 13W-33N | 26 |

| Riverwoods | Grid | Page |
|---|---|---|
| Arrow Ln. E&W ... | 12W-21N | 49 |
| Arrowwood Tr. E&W | | |
| | 13W-20N | 49 |
| Baneberry Ln. E&W | | |
| | 14W-21N | 49 |
| Big Oak Ln. E&W . | 12W-21N | 49 |
| Blackhawk Ln. N&S | | |
| | 13W-21N | 49 |
| Blackheath Ln. N&S | | |
| | 12W-21N | 49 |
| Blackhorn Rd. E&W | | |
| | 14W-20N | 49 |
| Brae Burn Dr. NS&EW | | |
| | 12W-21N | 49 |
| Brae Burn Ln. N&S | | |
| | 12W-21N | 49 |
| Bunker Ct. N&S .... | 13W-20N | 49 |
| Burr Oak Tr. E&W .. | 14W-21N | 49 |
| Calvin Ct. N&S .. | 13W-22N | 49 |
| Chapel Gate Rd. . | 13W-20N | 49 |
| Cherokee Ln. E&W | | |
| | 13W-21N | 49 |
| Chianti Tr. E&W .. | 13W-20N | 49 |
| Chicory Ln. NS&EW | | |
| | 14W-21N | 49 |
| Chippewa Pathway N&S | | |
| | 13W-21N | 49 |
| Clendenin Ln. N&S | 13W-21N | 49 |
| Columbine Ln. NS&EW | | |
| | 14W-21N | 49 |
| Corporate Dr. NS&EW | | |
| | 13W-20N | 49 |
| County Line Rd. E&W | | |
| | 13W-20N,12W-20N | 49 |
| Crestwood Dr. E&W | | |
| | 13W-20N | 49 |
| Daquiri Dr. E&W.... | 13W-20N | 49 |
| Dawson Ct. N&S .. | 12W-20N | 49 |
| Deepwood Tr. E&W | | |
| | 13W-20N | 49 |
| Deerfield Rd. E&W | | |
| | 14W-21N,12W-21N | 49 |
| Dubonnet Ln. . 13W-20N | | 49 |
| East Course Dr. N&S | | |
| | 12W-21N,12W-20N | 49 |
| Edgewood Ln. E&W | | |
| | 13W-21N,13W-20N | 49 |
| Edgewood Ln. E&W | | |
| | 13W-21N | 49 |
| Farner Ct. E&W .. | 13W-22N | 49 |
| Forest Glen Ct. NE&SW | | |
| | 13W-21N | 49 |
| Forest Glen Trail E&W | | |
| | 13W-20N | 49 |
| Foxtail Ct. N&S .... | 14W-21N | 49 |
| Gemini Ln. E&W .. | 13W-20N | 49 |
| Glen Eagles Ct. E&W | | |
| | 12W-20N | 49 |
| Glen Eagles Ln. E&W | | |
| | 13W-20N | 49 |
| Greenbrier Ln. E&W | | |
| | 13W-20N | 49 |
| Hazel Nut Ln. E&W | | |
| | 14W-21N | 49 |
| Hiawatha Ln. . 13W-21N | | 49 |
| Hill Ln. E&W .. | 12W-22N | 49 |
| Hoffman Ln. N&S .. | 13W-21N | 49 |
| Indian Trail Dr. N&S | | |
| | 13W-21N | 49 |
| Julie Ln. E&W .. | 13W-20N | 49 |
| Juneberry Rd. N&S | | |
| | 14W-20N | 49 |
| Kenilwood Ct. N&S | | |
| | 13W-21N | 49 |
| Kenilwood Ln. NS&EW | | |
| | 13W-21N | 49 |
| Kingswood Ct. NE&SW | | |
| | 13W-21N | 49 |
| Knollwood Way E&W | | |
| | 13W-21N | 49 |
| Legends Ct. E&W .. | 12W-20N | 49 |
| Long Cove N&S .. | 13W-20N | 49 |
| Lyndale Ln. E&W .. | 13W-20N | 49 |
| Lyngby Ln. N&S .. | 13W-22N | 49 |
| Masters Ct. N&S .. | 12W-20N | 49 |
| Masters Ln. NS&EW | | |
| | 12W-20N | 49 |
| Meredith Dr. E&W .. | 13W-20N | 49 |
| Metawa Ln. N&S .. | 14W-21N | 49 |
| Muirfield Ln. N&S .. | 12W-20N | 49 |
| Oak Ln. N&S .. | 12W-21N | 49 |
| Oakhurst Ln. NE&SW | | |
| | 12W-21N | 49 |
| Orange Brace Rd. E&W | | |
| | 13W-20N | 49 |
| Palmer Ct. NW&SE | | |
| | 13W-20N | 49 |
| Pinetree Ln. NE&SW | | |
| | 13W-21N | 49 |
| Portwine Rd. N&S . | 13W-20N | 49 |
| Ringland Ln. E&W . | 13W-20N | 49 |
| Riverwoods Ct. E&W | | |
| | 13W-21N | 49 |
| Riverwoods Rd. NW&SE | | |
| | 13W-21N | 49 |
| Robinhood Ln. N&S | | |
| | 13W-22N | 49 |
| Royal Troon Ct. E&W | | |
| | 13W-20N | 49 |
| Saunders Rd. N&S | 12W-21N | 49 |
| Sawgrass Ct. E&W | | |
| | 12W-20N | 49 |

| | Grid | Page |
|---|---|---|
| Scotch Ln. E&W .. | 13W-20N | 49 |
| Shadow Creek Ct. N&S | | |
| | 12W-20N | 49 |
| Shawnee Tr. N&S .. | 13W-21N | 49 |
| Sherry Ln. NW&SE | | |
| | 13W-20N | 49 |
| Shoal Creek Ct. N&S | | |
| | 12W-20N | 49 |
| Somerset Hills Ct. N&S | | |
| | 13W-20N | 49 |
| Strenger Ln. N&S .. | 13W-22N | 49 |
| Studio Ln. NS&EW | 13W-21N | 49 |
| Sunset Tr. N&S .. | 13W-21N | 49 |
| Thorngate Ct. N&S | | |
| | 12W-20N | 49 |
| Thorngate Ln. N&S | | |
| | 12W-20N | 49 |
| Thorngate Ln. NW&SE | | |
| | 13W-20N | 49 |
| Thornmeadow Rd. N&S | | |
| | 14W-20N | 49 |
| Thornwood Ln. N&S | | |
| | 13W-22N | 49 |
| Timber Trail N&S .. | 13W-20N | 49 |
| Timberleaf Ln. E&W | | |
| | 13W-21N | 49 |
| Timberline Ln. E&W | | |
| | 14W-21N | 49 |
| Timberwood Ln. N&S | | |
| | 14W-21N | 49 |
| Tour Ct. N&S .... | 13W-20N | 49 |
| Treasure Ln. N&S .. | 13W-20N | 49 |
| Trillium Ln. N&S .... | 13W-22N | 49 |
| Vernon Trail N&S .. | 13W-21N | 49 |
| West Course Dr. N&S | | |
| | 13W-22N,12W-22N | 49 |
| Whigam Ln. E&W .. | 13W-21N | 49 |
| Whigam Rd. N&S .. | 13W-21N | 49 |
| White Oak Ln. N&S | | |
| | 13W-20N | 49 |
| Wild Dunes Ct. N&S | | |
| | 13W-20N | 49 |
| Windlake Av. N&S . | 12W-22N | 49 |
| Woodland Ct. E&W | | |
| | 13W-21N | 49 |
| Woodland Ct., E. E&W | | |
| | 13W-21N | 49 |
| Woodland Ct., W. E&W | | |
| | 13W-21N | 49 |
| Woodland Ln. N&S | | |
| | 13W-22N | 49 |
| Woodland Ln. NS&EW | | |
| | 13W-21N | 49 |
| Yasmine Dr. N&S .. | 13W-21N | 49 |

## Round Lake

| | | |
|---|---|---|
| A'Ok Ct. NW&SE .. | 23W-34N | 22 |
| Alma Cir. E&W .. | 24W-34N | 22 |
| Alma Ct. E&W...... | 24W-34N | 22 |
| Alpine Dr. NE&SW .. | 23W-33N | 22 |
| Antares Cir. E&W .. | 23W-34N | 22 |
| Apollo Ct. NE&SW .. | 24W-34N | 22 |
| Avilon Av. E&W .. | 23W-33N | 22 |
| Avilon Ct. N&S .. | 23W-33N | 22 |
| Beechwood Dr. N&S | | |
| | 23W-33N,23W-34N | 22 |
| Belvidere Rd. NE&SW | | |
| | 23W-32N | 22 |
| Bernice Ln. N&S .. | 23W-34N | 22 |
| Biminy Bay NW&SE | | |
| | 23W-33N | 22 |
| Boxwood Ct. E&W | 23W-32N | 22 |
| Buckthorn Ln. N&S | | |
| | 23W-33N | 22 |
| Capri Ct. E&W .. | 23W-33N | 22 |
| Capri Dr. N&S.. | 23W-33N | 22 |
| Catalpa Dr. N&S.. | 23W-34N | 22 |
| Cedar Crest Ct. NW&SE | | |
| | 23W-33N | 22 |
| Cedar Lake Rd. N&S | | |
| | 23W-32N,23W-34N | 22 |
| Cranberry Ct. E&W | | |
| | 23W-33N | 22 |
| Dawn Marie Dr. N&S | | |
| | 25W-33N | 21 |
| Dorothy Ct. NE&SW | | |
| | 23W-34N | 22 |
| Fairfield Rd. N&S | | |
| | 24W-33N,24W-34N | 22 |
| Forest Av. N&S .. | 23W-33N | 22 |
| Garden Ct. N&S.... | 23W-33N | 22 |
| Goodnow Blvd. N&S | | |
| | 23W-33N | 22 |
| Hart Rd. E&W | | |
| | 24W-34N,23W-34N | 22 |
| Haywood Cir. N&S.. | 23W-34N | 22 |
| Haywood Dr. N&S . | 24W-33N | 22 |
| High Point Rd. N&S | | |
| | 24W-33N | 22 |
| High School Dr. NE&SW | | |
| | 23W-34N | 22 |
| Hillandale Dr. N&S . | 23W-33N | 22 |
| Hillside Dr. N&S .... | 23W-33N | 22 |
| Honey Ct. E&W .. | 23W-32N | 22 |
| Houston Ct. N&S .. | 24W-34N | 22 |
| Kitty Hawk Dr. N&S | | |
| | 23W-34N | 22 |
| Lake Dr. E&W.... | 23W-34N | 22 |
| Lakeview Dr. NE&SW | | |
| | 23W-34N | 22 |
| Lakewood Ter. NE&SW | | |
| | 23W-33N,23W-34N | 22 |
| Laurel Av. N&S .... | 23W-33N | 22 |

|  | Grid | Page |
|---|---|---|
| Lawn Ter. NE&SW | 23W-33N | 22 |
| Cir. | 23W-34N | 22 |
| Lincoln Av. N&S | 23W-33N | 22 |
| Linden Dr. N&S | 23W-34N | 22 |
| Long Lake Dr. E&W | 24W-34N | 22 |
| Long Lake Rd. E&W | 25W-34N,24W-34N | 21 |
| Lunar Dr. N&S | 24W-34N | 22 |
| Lunga Ct. N&S | 24W-34N | 22 |
| Lunga Dr. E&W | 24W-34N | 22 |
| MacGillis Dr. N&S | 23W-33N | 22 |
| Magna Dr. N&S | 23W-34N | 22 |
| Maple Lawn NE&SW | | 22 |
| Midland Dr. E&W | 23W-33N | 22 |
| Moon Rover Dr. N&S | 24W-34N | 22 |
| N. Bernice Ct. E&W | 23W-34N | 22 |
| N. Rosedale Ct. E&W | 23W-34N | 22 |
| Cir. | 24W-34N | 22 |
| Nippersink Rd. E&W | 25W-33N,23W-33N | 21 |
| Old Farm Rd. N&S | 24W-33N | 22 |
| Orbiter Dr. E&W | 24W-34N | 22 |
| Orchard Av. N&S | 23W-33N | 22 |
| Park Av. N&S | 23W-33N | 22 |
| Park Rd. NS&EW | 23W-34N | 22 |
| Petite St. N&S | 23W-34N | 22 |
| Pineview Dr. NW&SE | 23W-33N | 22 |
| Primrose Ln. N&S | 23W-33N | 22 |
| Quail Hollow Ct. NW&SE | 23W-33N | 22 |
| Rail Rd. NE&SW | 23W-34N | 22 |
| Railroad Rd. NW&SE | 23W-33N | 22 |
| Ravine Av. N&S | 23W-33N | 22 |
| Ridgewood Dr. N&S | 23W-34N | 22 |
| Roberta St. NE&SW | 23W-34N | 22 |
| Round Lake Rd. NW&SE | 24W-34N | 22 |
| Route 120 E&W | 23W-32N | 22 |
| Route 134 NW&SE | 25W-34N,23W-33N | 21 |
| S. Bernice Ct. E&W | 23W-34N | 22 |
| S. Rosedale Ct. E&W | 23W-32N | 22 |
| Sagebrush Cir. N&S | 23W-32N | 22 |
| School Ct. NE&SW | 24W-33N | 22 |
| School Dr. N&S | 24W-33N | 22 |
| Shagbark Ct. NW&SE | 23W-33N | 22 |
| Spanky Ct. N&S | 23W-34N | 22 |
| Sunset Dr. N&S | 23W-34N | 22 |
| Sweet Clover Rd. E&W | 23W-32N | 22 |
| Sycamore Dr. NE&SW | 23W-34N | 22 |
| Tanglewood Ct. N&S | 23W-33N | 22 |
| Valleyview Dr. N&S | 25W-33N | 21 |
| Washington St. E&W | 23W-34N | 22 |
| Wild Rose Ct. NW&SE | 23W-33N | 22 |
| Wildspring Rd. NS&EW | 23W-33N | 22 |
| Wilson Rd. N&S | 25W-33N | 21 |

### Round Lake Beach

|  | Grid | Page |
|---|---|---|
| Acorn Ct. E&W | 22W-36N | 14 |
| Acorn Dr. N&S | 22W-36N | 14 |
| Acorn Ln. NE&SW | 21W-35N | 23 |
| Amber Prairie Ct.* E&W | 21W-36N | 15 |
| Amber Prairie Way* E&W | 21W-36N | 15 |
| Apache Trail N&S | 23W-35N | 22 |
| Ardmor Dr. N&S | 23W-35N | 22 |
| Aster Pl. NW&SE | 23W-35N | 14 |
| Barberry Ln. N&S | 24W-34N | 22 |
| Bayview Dr. NW&SE | 23W-34N | 22 |
| Beachview Dr. E&W | 23W-34N | 22 |
| Beverly Dr. N&S | 24W-35N | 22 |
| Birchwood Dr.* E&W | 22W-36N | 14 |
| Bluebell Ct. N&S | 22W-36N | 14 |
| Blueberry Ln. NW&SE | 22W-36N | 14 |
| Bonnie Brook Ln. NE&SW | 24W-34N | 22 |
| Brentwood Dr. N&S | 24W-34N,24W-35N | 22 |
| Briar Ln. N&S | 23W-34N | 22 |
| Bridle Cir. NS&EW | 21W-36N | 15 |
| Bridle Ct. NW&SE | 21W-36N | 15 |
| Bristol Ln. N&S | 21W-35N | 23 |
| Brittany Ln. E&W | 21W-35N | 23 |
| Buena Vista Dr. E&W | 24W-34N | 22 |
| Butternut Ct. E&W | 22W-36N | 14 |
| Camden Ln. E&W | 22W-36N | 14 |

|  | Grid | Page |
|---|---|---|
| Canterbury Ln. E&W | 22W-36N | 14 |
| Carl Ct.* E&W | 22W-35N | 22 |
| Carriage Ct. E&W | 21W-35N | 23 |
| Carriage Ln. N&S | 21W-35N | 23 |
| Castlebar Ct. N&S | 22W-36N | 14 |
| Cedar Lake Rd. N&S | 23W-35N | 22 |
| Central Park Dr. E&W | 24W-34N | 22 |
| Cherokee Dr. N&S | 24W-35N | 22 |
| Cherry Cove Ct. NE&SW | 22W-36N | 14 |
| Cherry Cove Ln. NS&EW | 22W-36N | 14 |
| Chestnut Dr. N&S | 23W-35N | 22 |
| Cheswick Ct. N&S | 22W-36N | 14 |
| Chickory Ln.* E&W | 21W-36N | 15 |
| Churchill Ct. N&S | 22W-36N | 14 |
| Circle Dr. N&S | 22W-36N | 14 |
| Circuit Dr. N&S | 23W-35N | 22 |
| Clarendon Dr. NE&SW | 23W-34N,22W-35N | 22 |
| Clarendon East Dr. N&S | 22W-35N | 22 |
| Clearview Ct. E&W | 22W-36N | 14 |
| Clover Ln. E&W | 22W-35N | 22 |
| Cobbler Ct. N&S | 22W-36N | 14 |
| Comanche Trail N&S | 23W-35N | 22 |
| Corona Ct. E&W | 24W-34N | 22 |
| Country Walk Dr. E&W | 23W-34N | 14 |
| Countryside Ln. N&S | 23W-35N | 22 |
| Crescent Ct. N&S | 24W-34N | 22 |
| Dahlia Ln. NE&SW | 23W-36N | 14 |
| Daisy Ln. E&W | 22W-35N | 22 |
| Dakota Ct. E&W | 23W-35N | 22 |
| Deer Tr. E&W | 21W-36N | 15 |
| Deerpath Ct. N&S | 23W-35N | 22 |
| Diana Ct. NW&SE | 24W-34N | 22 |
| Eagle Creek Dr. E&W | 23W-35N | 22 |
| East End Av. N&S | 22W-35N | 22 |
| Edgewater Ct. N&S | 23W-34N | 22 |
| Elm Av. N&S | 22W-35N | 22 |
| Evergreen Ct.* E&W | 22W-35N | 22 |
| Fairfield Rd. N&S | 24W-34N,24W-35N | 22 |
| Fairfield Ter. E&W | 23W-35N | 22 |
| Fairview Pkwy. E&W | 22W-35N | 22 |
| Ferndale Ct. E&W | 23W-34N | 22 |
| Fox Chase Ct. N&S | 22W-36N | 14 |
| Foxchase Dr. E&W | 21W-36N | 14 |
| Fruitwood Dr. E&W | 23W-36N | 14 |
| Geneva Ter. E&W | 23W-35N | 22 |
| Glenview Ct. NW&SE | 23W-35N | 22 |
| Glenwood Dr. E&W | 23W-34N | 22 |
| Goldenwood Ter. N&S | 23W-35N | 22 |
| Golfview Ct. E&W | 23W-35N,22W-35N | 22 |
| Golfview Dr. E&W | 24W-35N,23W-35N | 22 |
| Green Valley Ct. N&S | 22W-36N | 14 |
| Green Valley Ln. NW&SE | 22W-36N | 14 |
| Grove Dr. N&S | 23W-35N | 22 |
| Hainesville Rd. NE&SW | 22W-36N | 22 |
| Hardwood Path NE&SW | 21W-36N | 23 |
| Harvest Hill Pl. N&S | 22W-36N | 14 |
| Hawthorne Dr. NE&SW | 23W-34N,22W-35N | 22 |
| Heather Ter. E&W | 22W-35N | 22 |
| Hickory Av. N&S | 22W-35N | 22 |
| Hickory St. N&S | 22W-34N | 22 |
| Highland Pkwy. N&S | | 22 |
| Highland Ter. E&W | 23W-35N | 22 |
| Hillside Av. N&S | 23W-35N | 22 |
| Hillside Dr. E&W | 23W-35N | 22 |
| Hillwood Ct. N&S | 23W-34N | 22 |
| Honeysuckle Dr. NE&SW | 22W-36N | 14 |
| Hunters Ln. N&S | 21W-36N | 15 |
| Idlewild Dr. N&S | 23W-34N,23W-35N | 22 |
| Ivy Ln. E&W | 22W-35N | 22 |
| Juneway Ter. N&S | 23W-35N | 22 |
| Juniper Ter. E&W | 23W-35N | 22 |
| Kelly Cain Ct. E&W | 21W-36N | 15 |
| Kenilworth Dr. N&S | 23W-34N | 22 |
| Kenmore Av. N&S | 22W-35N | 22 |
| Kildeer Dr. N&S | 24W-35N | 22 |
| Lagoon Ter. N&S | 23W-35N | 22 |
| Laguna Ct. N&S | 22W-36N | 14 |
| Lake Av. E&W | 22W-34N | 22 |

|  | Grid | Page |
|---|---|---|
| Lake Shore Dr. N&S | 23W-34N,23W-35N | 22 |
| Lakewood Pkwy. NE&SW | | 22 |
| Lancaster Ln. N&S | 22W-36N | 15 |
| Laurel Ct. E&W | 23W-35N | 22 |
| Lenox Ct. NW&SE | 22W-36N | 14 |
| Leslie Av. N&S | 22W-35N | 22 |
| Lexington Dr. E&W | 22W-36N | 14 |
| Lilac Ct. E&W | 22W-36N | 14 |
| London Dr. E&W | 22W-36N | 14 |
| Lotus Dr. N&S | 24W-34N,24W-35N | 22 |
| Mallard Creek Dr. NS&EW | 22W-35N | 22 |
| Mallard Ln. N&S | 23W-36N | 14 |
| Maple Dr. N&S | 23W-35N | 22 |
| Martingale Ln. N&S | 21W-36N | 14 |
| Mayfield Dr. NW&SE | 24W-34N | 22 |
| Meadow Green Ln. E&W | 23W-35N | 22 |
| Meadow Ln. N&S | 21W-36N | 14 |
| Meadowbrook Dr. NW&SE | 23W-35N | 22 |
| Meadowhill Ln. N&S | 23W-35N | 22 |
| Melrose Av. N&S | 22W-35N | 22 |
| Millstone Ln. E&W | 21W-33N | 14 |
| Millstone St. E&W | 21W-36N | 15 |
| Millstone Dr. NE&SW | 23W-35N | 22 |
| Morningside Dr. E&W | 24W-35N | 22 |
| N. Channel Dr. NS&EW | 23W-34N,23W-35N | 22 |
| Normandle Ln. E&W | 22W-36N | 14 |
| North Av. N&S | 22W-35N | 22 |
| Oak Av. N&S | 22W-35N | 22 |
| Oak Leaf Cir. NW&SE | 21W-35N | 23 |
| Oak Leaf Ct. NW&SE | 21W-36N | 15 |
| Oak Leaf Ln. N&S | 21W-35N | 23 |
| Oak St. N&S | 22W-34N | 22 |
| Oak Tree Cir. E&W | 21W-35N | 23 |
| Cir. | 21W-35N | 23 |
| Oakwood Dr. E&W | 24W-35N,23W-34N | 22 |
| Old Oak Dr. NW&SE | 21W-35N,21W-36N | 15 |
| Old Oak Dr. NW&SE | 21W-35N | 23 |
| Old Pond Ct. N&S | 23W-36N | 14 |
| Old Rollins Rd. E&W | 21W-35N | 23 |
| Orchard Ct. N&S | 23W-35N | 22 |
| Palm Ct. NW&SE | 22W-36N | 14 |
| Park Dr. N&S | 23W-35N | 22 |
| Partridge Ct. N&S | 23W-35N | 22 |
| Peachtree Ln. NE&SW | 22W-36N | 14 |
| Pembrook Ct. E&W | 22W-36N | 14 |
| Pennsbury Ct. E&W | 22W-36N | 14 |
| Penwood Ct. E&W | 22W-36N | 14 |
| Persimmon Ct. E&W | 22W-36N | 14 |
| Pheasant Ct. N&S | 23W-35N | 22 |
| Pine Grove Av. N&S | 23W-35N | 22 |
| Pleasant Dr. N&S | 23W-35N | 22 |
| Plymouth Ct. E&W | 22W-36N | 14 |
| Poplar Av. N&S | 22W-35N | 22 |
| Princeton Ct. E&W | 22W-36N | 14 |
| Quaker Hollow Ct. E&W | 22W-36N | 14 |
| Redhead Ct. N&S | 23W-36N | 14 |
| Redwing Dr. E&W | 22W-35N | 22 |
| Redwood Dr.* E&W | 22W-36N | 14 |
| Ridgeway Av. N&S | 22W-35N | 22 |
| Rollins Rd. E&W | 24W-35N,21W-35N | 22 |
| Ronald Ter. NW&SE | 24W-34N | 22 |
| Rosewood Ct. NE&SW | 22W-36N | 14 |
| Rosewood Ln. NE&SW | 23W-36N,22W-36N | 14 |
| Round Lake Dr. N&S | 23W-35N | 22 |
| Route 83 N&S | 21W-35N | 23 |
| Rustic Ln. NE&SW | 22W-36N | 14 |
| S. Channel Dr. N&S | 23W-34N | 22 |
| Salem Ln. NW&SW | 23W-35N | 22 |
| Sauk Ct.* E&W | 23W-36N | 14 |
| Sedgefield St. N&S | 22W-36N | 14 |
| Shady Lane Ct. N&S | 23W-35N | 22 |
| Shady Ln. E&W | 24W-34N | 22 |
| Shaker Ct. NW&SE | 22W-36N | 14 |
| Sheffield Ct. N&S | 22W-36N | 14 |
| Shoreland Ct. N&S | 23W-34N | 22 |

|  | Grid | Page |
|---|---|---|
| Shorewood Rd. E&W | 22W-34N | 22 |
| Silver Oaks Dr. N&S | 22W-36N | 14 |
| Somerset Ct. N&S | 22W-36N | 14 |
| Southmoor Ln. E&W | 24W-34N | 22 |
| Springwood Dr. E&W | 22W-36N | 14 |
| Sprucewood Ct.* E&W | 22W-36N | 14 |
| Stanton Ct. E&W | 22W-36N | 14 |
| Sterling Ct. N&S | 22W-36N | 14 |
| Stockton Ct. N&S | 22W-36N | 14 |
| Stockton Ln. N&S | 22W-36N | 14 |
| Stonehedge Ct. NW&SE | 22W-36N | 14 |
| Stratford Ln. E&W | 22W-36N | 14 |
| Sugar Run Ln. N&S | 21W-36N | 14 |
| Sunnyside Dr. NW&SE | 23W-34N | 22 |
| Sunrise Dr. N&S | 23W-36N | 14 |
| Sunset Dr. N&S | 23W-34N,23W-35N | 22 |
| Tall Grass Ct. E&W | 23W-36N | 14 |
| Turnbull Dr. N&S | 24W-35N | 22 |
| Villa Vista Dr. N&S | 23W-35N | 22 |
| Vine Av. NE&SW | 22W-35N | 22 |
| Vineyard Dr. N&S | 22W-36N | 14 |
| Walnut Dr. N&S | 23W-35N | 22 |
| West End Dr. N&S | 23W-34N,23W-35N | 22 |
| Westview Ln. N&S | 23W-35N | 22 |
| White Hall Ct. E&W | 22W-36N | 14 |
| Wildflower Ct. NE&SW | 32W-36N | 14 |
| Wildflower Ln. NW&SE | 22W-36N | 14 |
| Wildwood Dr. E&W | 23W-35N | 22 |
| William Av. NE&SW | 23W-34N | 22 |
| Willow Ridge Dr.* N&S | 22W-36N | 14 |
| Witchwood Ln. NW&SE | 23W-34N | 22 |
| Wood Oak Cir. N&S | 21W-35N | 23 |
| Wood Oak Cir. E&W | 21W-36N | 15 |
| Wood Oak Dr. N&S | 21W-35N,21W-36N | 23 |
| Woodbine Dr. N&S | 23W-35N | 22 |
| Woodland Dr. E&W | 23W-34N | 22 |
| Woodmoor Dr. E&W | 22W-35N | 22 |
| Woodridge Dr. N&S | 24W-34N,24W-35N | 22 |
| Yvonne Ct.* E&W | 22W-35N | 22 |

### Round Lake Heights

|  | Grid | Page |
|---|---|---|
| Arrowhead Dr. E&W | 23W-35N | 22 |
| Brentwood Dr. N&S | 24W-35N | 22 |
| Clinton Av. N&S | 24W-35N | 22 |
| E. Cedarwood Cir. N&S | 23W-35N | 22 |
| Fairfield Rd. N&S | 24W-35N | 22 |
| Flintwood Ct. E&W | 23W-35N | 22 |
| Hiawatha Tr. N&S | 24W-35N | 22 |
| Lotus Dr. N&S | 24W-35N | 22 |
| Meadowbrook Dr. N&S | 23W-35N | 22 |
| Mohawk Dr. E&W | 23W-35N | 22 |
| N. Cedarwood Cir. N&S | 23W-35N | 22 |
| N. Summit Ct. N&S | 23W-35N | 22 |
| Pontiac Ct. N&S | 23W-35N | 22 |
| Rollins Rd. E&W | 24W-35N | 22 |
| S. Cedarwood Cir. N&S | 23W-35N | 22 |
| Summit Ct. N&S | 23W-35N | 22 |
| Tomahawk Tr. NS&EW | 24W-35N | 22 |
| Turkey Run Dr. E&W | 23W-35N | 22 |
| W. Cedarwood Cir. N&S | 23W-35N | 22 |
| Warrior Dr. E&W | 24W-35N | 22 |

### Round Lake Park

|  | Grid | Page |
|---|---|---|
| Alleghany Rd. N&S | 21W-30N,21W-31N | 31 |
| Arbor Dr. N&S | 22W-34N | 22 |
| Barbara Ct. NW&SE | 23W-33N | 22 |
| Beechwood Dr. N&S | 23W-33N | 22 |
| Bellevue Dr. N&S | 22W-33N | 22 |
| Belvidere Rd. E&W | 23W-33N,22W-33N | 22 |
| Bengson Ct. E&W | 23W-33N | 22 |
| Bison Ct. N&S | 23W-33N | 22 |
| Brierhill Dr. N&S | 22W-33N | 22 |
| Cedar Mound Rd. NE&SW | 23W-33N | 22 |

|  | Grid | Page |
|---|---|---|
| Center Dr. N&S | 23W-33N | 22 |
| Clifton Dr. N&S | 23W-33N | 22 |
| Creekside Ln. N&S | 23W-33N | 22 |
| Elder Ct. N&S | 23W-33N | 22 |
| Elm Av. N&S | 23W-33N | 22 |
| Fairlawn Dr. N&S | 22W-33N | 22 |
| Forest Glen Dr. N&S | 23W-33N | 22 |
| Grandview Dr. N&S | 23W-33N | 22 |
| Greenwood Rd. N&S | 22W-33N | 22 |
| Hainesville Rd. N&S | 22W-34N | 22 |
| Highmoor Rd. N&S | 22W-33N | 22 |
| Hillcrest Ter. N&S | 22W-34N | 22 |
| Indian Tr. E&W | 22W-34N | 22 |
| Jorgensen Ct. E&W | 23W-33N | 22 |
| Kenwood Dr. N&S | 23W-33N | 22 |
| Knollwood Dr. NE&SW | 22W-34N | 22 |
| Lake Shore Dr. E&W | 22W-34N | 22 |
| Locust Dr. E&W | 22W-33N | 22 |
| Lyle Av. E&W | 22W-34N | 22 |
| Main St. NE&SW | 23W-33N | 22 |
| Mayflower Ter. E&W | 22W-34N | 22 |
| Midland E&W | 22W-34N | 22 |
| Model Ct. NW&SE | 23W-33N | 22 |
| Newhouse Ln. N&S | 23W-33N | 22 |
| Oak St. N&S | 22W-34N | 22 |
| Parkview Ct. E&W | 22W-33N | 22 |
| Peterson Rd. E&W | 22W-30N,20W-30N | 30 |
| Pineview Dr. NW&SE | 22W-33N | 22 |
| Porter Dr. NW&SE | 22W-33N | 22 |
| Prospect Dr. N&S | 22W-33N | 22 |
| Ravine Dr. N&S | 22W-34N | 22 |
| Route 120 E&W | 23W-33N,22W-33N | 22 |
| Route 134 E&W | 23W-33N,22W-33N | 22 |
| Route 83 N&S | 20W-30N,20W-31N | 31 |
| Sandy Point Ln. E&W | 22W-34N | 22 |
| Schooner Ct. E&W | 22W-34N | 22 |
| Sylvan Dr. E&W | 22W-34N | 22 |
| Timbercreek Dr. E&W | 23W-33N | 22 |
| Washington St. E&W | 22W-34N | 22 |
| Waterview Dr. E&W | 22W-34N | 22 |
| Willow Dr. E&W | 22W-34N | 22 |

### Shields Township

|  | Grid | Page |
|---|---|---|
| Adelphia Av. N&S | 12W-28N,12W-29N | 35 |
| Atkinson Av. E&W | 12W-29N | 35 |
| Basil Rd. E&W | 12W-28N | 35 |
| Bayshore Dr. NE&SW | 11W-29N | 35 |
| Birch Av. N&S | 12W-28N | 35 |
| Birchwood Av. E&W | 12W-30N | 35 |
| Bittersweet Av. E&W | 12W-30N | 35 |
| Blodgett Av. E&W | 12W-29N | 35 |
| Bonaparte Av. E&W | 12W-30N | 35 |
| Brompton Av. E&W | 12W-30N | 35 |
| Burris Av. N&S | 12W-29N | 35 |
| Butterfly Ct. N&S | 12W-29N | 35 |
| Clover Ln. N&S | 12W-29N | 35 |
| Environ Cir. NW&SE | 12W-29N | 35 |
| Fairbank Av. N&S | 12W-29N | 35 |
| Farwell Av. N&S | 12W-30N | 35 |
| Forest View Dr. NE&SW | 11W-29N | 35 |
| Foster Av. NE&SW | 12W-29N | 35 |
| Glendell Av. N&S | 11W-29N | 35 |
| Green Av. N&S | 12W-28N,12W-29N | 35 |
| Hillside Av. N&S | 11W-29N | 35 |
| Jenkisson Av. NE&SW | 12W-29N | 35 |
| Juneway Ter. E&W | 11W-29N | 35 |
| Kohl Dr. E&W | 11W-29N | 35 |
| Louis St. E&W | 11W-29N | 35 |
| Mawman Blvd. N&S | 11W-29N | 35 |
| Melvin Dr. E&W | 11W-29N | 35 |
| Muir Av. E&W | 12W-29N | 35 |
| North Av. E&W | 12W-28N | 35 |
| North Shore N&S | 11W-29N | 35 |
| Northern Av. N&S | 11W-29N | 35 |
| Plaister Av. N&S | 12W-29N | 35 |
| Quassey Av. N&S | 12W-29N | 35 |
| Red Oak Ct. NE&SW | 11W-29N | 35 |
| Rivers Dr. N&S | 11W-29N | 35 |
| Rockland Rd. E&W | 12W-28N | 35 |

|  | Grid | Page |
|---|---|---|
| Sanctuary Ct. E&W | 12W-29N | 35 |
| Sanctuary Ln. E&W | 12W-29N | 35 |
| Shagbark Rd. N&S | 12W-28N | 35 |
| Skokie Blvd. N&S | 12W-28N | 35 |
| Skokie Hwy. N&S | 12W-29N,12W-31N | 35 |
| Smith Av. E&W | 12W-29N | 35 |
| Spring Ln. N&S | 11W-29N | 35 |
| Stafford Av. E&W | 12W-29N | 35 |
| Talbot Av. E&W | 12W-29N | 35 |
| Thorntree Rd. N&S | 12W-28N | 35 |
| Washington Av. E&W | 12W-28N | 35 |
| Woodland Rd. E&W | 12W-28N | 35 |

**Third Lake**

|  | Grid | Page |
|---|---|---|
| Brigantine Ln. E&W | 18W-34N | 24 |
| Clipper Ct. NE&SW | 18W-34N | 24 |
| Coral Reef Ct. N&S | 19W-34N | 23 |
| Crows Nest Ct. N&S | 19W-34N | 23 |
| Galleon Ct. NW&SE | 19W-34N | 23 |
| Grant Av. N&S | 18W-35N | 24 |
| Lake Av. E&W | 19W-35N | 23 |
| Lighthouse Ln. NE&SW | 19W-34N | 23 |
| Mainsail N&S | 18W-34N | 24 |
| Mainsail Dr. NS&EW | 19W-34N | 23 |
| Portside Ct. NW&SE | 19W-34N | 23 |
| Schooner Ln. E&W | 19W-34N | 23 |
| Seafarer Dr. NS&EW | 18W-34N | 24 |
| Sextant Dr. N&S | 19W-34N | 23 |
| Sextant Windjammer NE&SW | 18W-34N | 24 |
| Spinnaker Ct. NW&SE | 19W-34N | 23 |
| Starboard Ct. NW&SE | 19W-34N | 23 |
| Sunshine Av. E&W | 19W-35N | 23 |
| U.S. Route 45 N&S | 18W-34N | 24 |
| Whaler Ct. NE&SW | 19W-34N | 23 |
| Windjammer Ct. NE&SW | 18W-34N | 24 |
| Windjammer Ln. NS&EW | 19W-34N | 23 |

**Tower Lakes**

|  | Grid | Page |
|---|---|---|
| Abbott Pl. N&S | 26W-25N | 37 |
| Barsumian Dr. N&S | 27W-25N | 37 |
| Bays Pl. N&S | 26W-25N | 37 |
| Blue Stem Cr. N&S | 26W-24N | 37 |
| Bridge Ln. E&W | 26W-25N | 37 |
| Cambridge Dr. E&W | 26W-25N | 37 |
| Circle Dr. NS&EW | 26W-25N | 37 |
| Devonshire Rd. N&S | 26W-25N | 37 |
| E. Gateway Dr. N&S | 26W-25N | 37 |
| East Lake Shore Dr. NS&EW | 26W-25N | 37 |
| East Tower Dr. E&W | 26W-25N | 37 |
| Edward Ln. N&S | 26W-25N | 37 |
| Essex Pl. E&W | 26W-25N | 37 |
| Esther Dr. E&W | 26W-25N | 37 |
| Fenview Dr. NW&SE | 27W-24N,26W-24N | 37 |
| Indian Grass Ct. NE&SW | 26W-24N | 37 |
| Indian Trail NW&SE | 26W-25N,25W-25N | 37 |
| Kelsey Rd. NE&SW | 27W-24N,26W-25N | 37 |
| Lake Shore Ter. N&S | 26W-25N | 37 |
| Leon Dr. E&W | 26W-25N | 37 |
| Marian N&S | 26W-25N | 37 |
| Medinah Ln. NW&SE | 25W-25N | 37 |
| Melrose Ct. E&W | 26W-25N | 37 |
| Murray Rd. E&W | 27W-25N,26W-25N | 37 |
| N. Lake Shore Dr. N&S | 26W-25N | 37 |
| Nooding Flower Ct. NE&SW | 26W-24N | 37 |
| North Av. N&S | 26W-25N | 37 |
| Oak St. NW&SE | 26W-25N | 37 |
| Oxford Rd. N&S | 26W-25N | 37 |
| Paddock Ln. N&S | 26W-25N | 37 |
| Pebble Creek Dr. NS&EW | 26W-25N,26W-25N | 37 |
| Raleigh Pl. N&S | 26W-25N | 37 |
| Roberts Rd. E&W | 27W-25N,26W-25N | 37 |

|  | Grid | Page |
|---|---|---|
| Robin Rd. NS&EW | 27W-25N | 37 |
| Rolling Green Dr. N&S | 25W-25N | 37 |
| Rose Terrace Ct. E&W | 26W-24N | 37 |
| Roslyn Pl. E&W | 26W-25N | 37 |
| Scenic Dr. N&S | 26W-25N | 37 |
| South Dr. NE&SW | 26W-24N | 37 |
| South Hills Dr. N&S | 26W-25N | 37 |
| Stonehenge Ln. E&W | 25W-25N | 37 |
| Summit Dr. E&W | 25W-25N | 37 |
| Timber Ct. N&S | 26W-25N | 37 |
| Tomahawk Ln. N&S | 26W-25N | 37 |
| Warwick Rd. N&S | 26W-25N | 37 |
| West Dr. N&S | 26W-25N | 37 |
| West Lake Dr. N&S | 26W-25N | 37 |
| West Lake Shore Dr. NS&EW | 27W-25N,26W-25N | 37 |
| West Tower Dr. N&S | 26W-25N | 37 |
| Wren Rd. N&S | 27W-25N | 37 |

**Vernon Hills**

|  | Grid | Page |
|---|---|---|
| Abbey Ln. E&W | 17W-25N | 40 |
| Abilene Ln. NS&EW | 16W-25N | 41 |
| Adair Ct. E&W | 16W-25N | 41 |
| Adams Ct.* E&W | 17W-27N | 40 |
| Adrian Ct. NE&SW | 18W-25N | 40 |
| Albany Ln. N&S | 17W-25N | 40 |
| Albert Dr. NS&EW | 17W-25N | 40 |
| Albright Ct. NW&SE | 17W-25N | 40 |
| Alexandria Dr. N&S | 17W-25N | 40 |
| Alice Ct. E&W | 16W-25N | 41 |
| Allentown Ct. N&S | 16W-25N | 41 |
| Almond Ct. N&S | 17W-25N | 40 |
| Alpine Dr. E&W | 17W-25N | 40 |
| Altoona Ct. E&W | 16W-25N | 41 |
| Amber Ln. E&W | 17W-25N | 40 |
| Amherst Ct. N&S | 16W-25N | 41 |
| Angela. N&S | 17W-25N | 40 |
| Ann Arbor Ln. E&W | 18W-25N | 40 |
| Ann Ct. E&W | 16W-25N | 41 |
| Annapolis Dr. NW&SE | 17W-25N | 40 |
| Apollo Ct. E&W | 17W-25N | 40 |
| Appian Way NW&SE | 17W-25N | 40 |
| Appleton Dr. N&S | 17W-25N | 40 |
| April Av. N&S | 17W-25N | 40 |
| Aqua Ct. NE&SW | 17W-25N | 40 |
| Arcadia Ct. E&W | 17W-25N | 40 |
| Ardmore Ct. E&W | 17W-25N | 40 |
| Arlington Ct. NW&SE | 17W-25N | 40 |
| Arron Ct. E&W | 17W-25N | 40 |
| Ashland Ct. N&S | 17W-25N | 40 |
| Ashville St. N&S | 16W-25N | 41 |
| Ashwood Ct. NE&SW | 17W-25N | 40 |
| Aspen Dr. N&S | 17W-25N,17W-26N | 40 |
| Astoria Ct. NW&SE | 16W-25N | 41 |
| Athens Ct. E&W | 16W-25N | 41 |
| Atlantic Dr. E&W | 17W-25N | 40 |
| Atrium Dr. NS&EW | 17W-25N | 40 |
| Auburn Ct. N&S | 17W-25N | 40 |
| Augusta Dr. E&W | 17W-25N | 40 |
| Aurora Ct. E&W | 16W-25N | 41 |
| Austin Ct. NE&SW | 17W-25N | 40 |
| Autumn Ln. N&S | 17W-25N | 40 |
| Avon Ct. NW&SE | 17W-25N | 40 |
| Barn Swallow Ln. N&S | 16W-24N | 41 |
| Basswood Dr. NW&SE | 17W-25N | 40 |
| Bedford Rd. E&W | 16W-25N | 41 |
| Belle Isle Ln. E&W | 18W-25N | 40 |
| Birchwood Ct. E&W | 17W-25N | 40 |
| Birmingham Pl. E&W | 16W-25N | 41 |
| Bluewater Ln. N&S | 16W-26N | 41 |
| Brandywine Ct. E&W | 17W-26N | 40 |
| Briarwood Ct. NE&SW | 17W-25N | 40 |
| Brook Hill Ln. N&S | 16W-24N | 41 |
| Brook Ln. E&W | 16W-26N | 41 |
| Brookwood Ct. NW&SE | 17W-25N | 40 |
| Browning Ct.* N&S | 17W-25N | 40 |
| Bryant Pl. NE&SW | 17W-26N | 40 |
| Buchanan Ct. E&W | 17W-26N | 40 |
| Bunker Ct. E&W | 16W-25N | 41 |
| Burnside Ct.* E&W | 17W-26N | 40 |
| Butterfield Rd. N&S | 17W-25N | 40 |
| Camden Pl. E&W | 17W-24N | 40 |

|  | Grid | Page |
|---|---|---|
| Castlegate Ct. E&W | 16W-25N | 41 |
| Cedar Ct. NE&SW | 17W-26N | 40 |
| Center Dr. E&W | 16W-26N | 41 |
| Centurion Ln. N&S | 17W-26N | 40 |
| Chatham Ct.* N&S | 17W-27N | 40 |
| Cherokee Rd. E&W | 16W-25N | 41 |
| Cherry Valley Rd. E&W | 18W-24N,17W-24N | 40 |
| Cherrywood Ct. NE&SW | 17W-25N | 40 |
| Chesapeake Ct. E&W | 17W-27N | 40 |
| Chesterfield Ct. N&S | 17W-24N | 40 |
| Clairmont Ct. NW&SE | 16W-26N | 41 |
| Cleveland Ct.* N&S | 17W-27N | 40 |
| Collins Dr.* E&W | 16W-26N | 41 |
| Colony Ct.* E&W | 17W-27N | 40 |
| Commonwealth Ct.* N&S | 16W-26N | 41 |
| Conachie Ct. NW&SE | 18W-25N | 40 |
| Constitution Ct.* N&S | 16W-26N | 41 |
| Continental Ct. NE&SW | 16W-25N,15W-25N | 41 |
| Corporate Woods Pkwy. NS&EW | 16W-24N,15W-24N | 41 |
| Country Club Ln. NE&SW | 17W-24N | 40 |
| Court Of Ash N&S | 17W-24N | 40 |
| Court Of Birch* N&S | 18W-24N | 40 |
| Court Of Elm NE&SW | 17W-24N | 40 |
| Court Of Shorewood NS&EW | 18W-24N | 40 |
| Court Of Spruce* E&W | 18W-24N | 40 |
| Coventry Cir. NS&EW | 16W-26N | 41 |
| Crabtree Ln. N&S | 16W-25N | 41 |
| Creek Bend Dr. NE&SW | 16W-23N | 48 |
| Creek View Dr. E&W | 16W-23N | 48 |
| Creekside Dr. NW&SE | 17W-25N | 40 |
| Crestview Ln. E&W | 17W-26N | 40 |
| Cromwell Ct. N&S | 16W-26N | 41 |
| Cumberland Ct. N&S | 17W-26N | 40 |
| Dawson Ct. N&S | 18W-24N | 40 |
| Dearborn Ln. NW&SE | 18W-25N | 40 |
| Debill Ct. E&W | 16W-24N | 41 |
| Deerpath Dr. N&S | 16W-24N,16W-25N | 41 |
| Dickinson Ct. NE&SW | 17W-25N | 40 |
| Dirksen Dr.* NW&SE | 17W-27N | 40 |
| Dogwood Ln. NW&SE | 17W-25N | 40 |
| Dover Ct.* N&S | 17W-26N | 40 |
| Echo Ct. E&W | 17W-26N | 40 |
| Edgewood Rd. E&W | 16W-25N | 41 |
| Eisenhower Ct.* NW&SE | 17W-27N | 40 |
| Elm Tree Ln. NE&SW | 16W-25N | 41 |
| Emerson Pl. NW&SE | 17W-26N | 40 |
| Evergreen Dr. N&S | 17W-24N | 40 |
| Executive Way Dr. E&W | 16W-25N,15W-25N | 41 |
| Exeter Pl. NW&SE | 16W-25N | 41 |
| Fairway Dr. N&S | 16W-25N | 41 |
| Farmingdale Cir. N&S | 17W-25N | 40 |
| Farmington Ln. E&W | 17W-25N | 40 |
| Faulkner Pl.* N&S | 17W-25N | 40 |
| Fernwood Ct. NE&SW | 17W-25N | 40 |
| Fiore Parkway N&S | 18W-25N | 40 |
| Forest Edge Dr. NS&EW | 15W-23N | 49 |
| Franklin Pl. NW&SE | 17W-26N | 40 |
| Gladstone Dr.* N&S | 17W-25N | 40 |
| Grant Pl. NW&SE | 17W-26N | 40 |
| Greenbriar Ln. N&S | 17W-24N | 40 |
| Greenleaf Dr. E&W | 17W-26N | 40 |
| Greenvale Rd. NE&SW | 16W-25N | 41 |
| Grosse Pointe Blvd. NE&SW | 18W-25N | 40 |
| Haddon Cir. NS&EW | 17W-24N | 40 |
| Hamilton Pl. E&W | 17W-26N | 40 |
| Hampton Pl. E&W | 17W-26N | 40 |
| Hanover Pl. E&W | 17W-26N | 40 |

|  | Grid | Page |
|---|---|---|
| Harbor Dr. E&W | 16W-25N | 41 |
| Harding Ct.* E&W | 17W-25N | 40 |
| Harrison Ct. E&W | 17W-26N | 40 |
| Harvest Ct. NE&SW | 17W-25N | 40 |
| Hastings Ct. E&W | 17W-26N | 40 |
| Hawthorne Pkwy. E&W | 17W-26N,16W-26N | 40 |
| Hayes Ct.* NW&SE | 17W-27N | 40 |
| Hemingway Ct. E&W | 16W-26N | 41 |
| Hickory Hill Dr. E&W | 16W-24N | 41 |
| Hobble Bush Ln. NE&SW | 16W-24N | 41 |
| Hughes Pl.* N&S | 17W-25N | 40 |
| Hunter Ct. E&W | 18W-25N | 40 |
| Indian Creek Ct. E&W | 16W-23N | 48 |
| Indian Creek Dr. N&S | 16W-23N | 48 |
| Indianwood Dr. N&S | 17W-26N | 40 |
| Jackson Ct. N&S | 17W-26N | 40 |
| Jansen LN. NE&SW | 18W-25N | 40 |
| Jefferson Ct. E&W | 17W-27N | 40 |
| Julie Ln. N&S | 18W-25N | 40 |
| Kalamazoo Cir. NW&SE | 18W-25N | 40 |
| Kennedy Pl.* NE&SW | 17W-27N | 40 |
| Keswick Ln. E&W | 16W-25N | 41 |
| Kingston Ct. N&S | 16W-26N | 41 |
| Knollwood Ct. N&S | 16W-25N | 41 |
| Lafayette Pl.* N&S | 17W-26N | 40 |
| Lakeside Ct. N&S | 17W-24N | 40 |
| Lakeside Dr., E. N&S | 17W-24N | 40 |
| Lakeside Dr., N. E&W | 17W-24N | 40 |
| Lakeview Parkway NS&EW | 16W-26N | 41 |
| Lancaster Pl.* E&W | 17W-26N | 40 |
| Lansing Ct. E&W | 18W-25N | 40 |
| Larchmont Ln. N&S | 16W-25N | 41 |
| Lexington Dr. E&W | 16W-26N | 41 |
| Lindenwood Ct. NW&SE | 17W-25N | 40 |
| Lindon Ln. E&W | 16W-24N | 41 |
| Lowell Pl. NE&SW | 17W-26N | 40 |
| MacArthur Ct. NW&SE | 17W-26N | 40 |
| Mallard Ct. N&S | 17W-25N | 40 |
| Malvern Ln. E&W | 16W-25N | 41 |
| Manchester Ln. N&S | 17W-24N | 40 |
| Marimac Ln. N&S | 17W-24N | 40 |
| Marinewood Dr. NW&SE | 17W-24N | 40 |
| Market Ct.* E&W | 16W-26N | 41 |
| Marlowe Pl. NW&SE | 17W-26N | 40 |
| Marquette Ct. N&S | 18W-25N | 40 |
| Mayflower Rd. NE&SW | 16W-25N | 41 |
| Meadow Ct. E&W | 17W-25N | 40 |
| Melody Ln. N&S | 16W-25N | 41 |
| Memphis Pl. E&W | 17W-24N | 40 |
| Meredith Pl.* NE&SW | 17W-27N | 40 |
| Michigan Ct.* E&W | 16W-26N | 41 |
| Midway Ln. NE&SW | 16W-24N | 41 |
| Milwaukee Av. NW&SE | 15W-25N | 41 |
| Monroe Ct.* E&W | 17W-27N | 40 |
| Montauk Ln. N&S | 17W-24N | 40 |
| Montclair Rd. E&W | 17W-24N | 40 |
| Montebello Dr. N&S | 17W-24N | 40 |
| Monterrey Dr. N&S | 17W-24N | 40 |
| Montgomery Ln. N&S | 17W-25N | 40 |
| Murwood Ct. NE&SW | 17W-25N | 40 |
| Muskegon Ct. NW&SE | 18W-25N | 40 |
| Mystic Ct. NW&SE | 18W-25N | 40 |
| Napier Ct. N&S | 18W-25N | 40 |
| Narois Dr. N&S | 17W-24N | 40 |
| Noble Cir. NS&EW | 17W-24N | 40 |
| Northfield Dr. E&W | 18W-25N | 40 |
| Oakwood Rd. N&S | 17W-24N | 40 |
| Old Creek Rd. N&S | 16W-24N | 41 |
| Old Wood Ct. N&S | 16W-24N | 41 |
| Onwentsia Rd. N&S | 18W-25N | 40 |
| Parkside Ct. E&W | 17W-26N | 40 |
| Peachtree Ct.* E&W | 16W-26N | 41 |
| Phillip Rd. E&W | 17W-26N | 40 |
| Pierce Ct. NE&SW | 17W-26N | 40 |
| Plumwood Ln. NE&SW | 17W-25N | 40 |

|  | Grid | Page |
|---|---|---|
| Plymouth Farms Rd. E&W | 17W-25N | 40 |
| Polk Ct. NW&SE | 17W-26N | 40 |
| Pontiac Ln. NW&SE | 18W-25N | 40 |
| Portage Ct. NE&SW | 18W-25N | 40 |
| Princeton Ct. N&S | 17W-26N | 40 |
| Redwood Ct. NW&SE | 17W-25N | 40 |
| Regency Ln. N&S | 16W-26N | 41 |
| Revere Pl. NW&SE | 17W-26N | 40 |
| Richard Ct. N&S | 17W-24N | 40 |
| Richmond Ct. E&W | 17W-25N | 40 |
| River Grove Ct. NW&SE | 16W-23N | 48 |
| River Grove Ln. E&W | 16W-23N | 48 |
| Roosevelt Ct.* NW&SE | 17W-27N | 40 |
| Route 21 N&S | 16W-27N,15W-24N | 41 |
| Route 60 E&W | 17W-26N,16W-26N | 40 |
| Royal Oak Dr. N&S | 18W-24N,18W-25N | 40 |
| Russet Way NE&SW | 17W-25N | 40 |
| Saddle Back NW&SE | 16W-25N | 41 |
| Saratoga Ct. E&W | 17W-26N | 40 |
| Saugatuck Tr. NS&EW | 18W-24N | 40 |
| Sheffield Ln. N&S | 17W-25N | 40 |
| Sinclair Ct. N&S | 18W-24N | 40 |
| Somerset Ln. E&W | 17W-25N | 40 |
| Southfield Dr. NS&EW | 18W-25N | 40 |
| Southwick Ct. E&W | 16W-26N | 41 |
| Sparta Ct. NW&SE | 18W-25N | 40 |
| Spring Ln. N&S | 16W-25N | 41 |
| St. Clair Ln. NE&SW | 18W-24N | 40 |
| St. Ives Ln. N&S | 16W-25N | 41 |
| Sterling Heights Rd. N&S | 17W-25N | 40 |
| Stevenson Pl.* NE&SW | 17W-27N | 40 |
| Stockton N&S | 17W-26N | 40 |
| Stone Fence Rd. NE&SW | 16W-25N | 41 |
| Streamwood Ln. N&S | 16W-25N | 41 |
| Sullivan Dr. E&W | 17W-25N | 40 |
| Sunset Ct. N&S | 17W-25N | 40 |
| Sussex Cir. NS&EW | 17W-24N | 40 |
| Sutcliffe Cir. NS&EW | 17W-24N | 40 |
| Sutton Ct. N&S | 16W-26N | 41 |
| Swinburne Pl.* NW&SE | 17W-27N | 40 |
| Tally Ho Dr. E&W | 17W-24N | 40 |
| Tanglewood Ct. NE&SW | 17W-25N | 40 |
| Tanwood Ln. NW&SE | 17W-25N | 40 |
| Taylor Ct. NE&SW | 17W-26N | 40 |
| Televista Ct. NE&SW | 17W-24N | 40 |
| Tennis Ln. N&S | 18W-24N | 40 |
| Tennyson Pl.* NW&SE | 17W-27N | 40 |
| Timber Ln. E&W | 17W-26N | 40 |
| Townline Rd. E&W | 17W-26N | 40 |
| Tyler Ct. NE&SW | 17W-26N | 40 |
| U.S. Route 45 NW&SE | 18W-24N,15W-23N | 40 |
| Van Buren Ct. N&S | 17W-26N | 40 |
| Vernon Ct. N&S | 17W-26N | 40 |
| Wadsworth Pl. NW&SE | 17W-26N | 40 |
| Warren Ln. NW&SE | 18W-25N | 40 |
| Warrington Rd. NE&SW | 16W-25N | 41 |
| Washington Ct.* E&W | 17W-27N | 40 |
| Waterview Cir. E&W | 18W-24N | 40 |
| Webster Pl.* E&W | 17W-26N | 40 |
| Wentworth Ct. N&S | 16W-25N | 41 |
| West End Ct. N&S | 17W-26N | 40 |
| West End Ln. NW&SE | 17W-26N | 40 |
| Westmoreland Dr. E&W | 18W-24N,17W-24N | 40 |
| Westwood Ct. NE&SW | 17W-25N | 40 |
| White Barn Rd. E&W | 16W-24N | 41 |
| White Fence Ct. NW&SE | 16W-24N | 41 |
| Whiting Ct.* E&W | 17W-25N | 40 |
| Whitman Pl. NW&SE | 17W-26N | 40 |
| Whitney Pl. N&S | 17W-26N | 40 |
| Wildwood Ct. NE&SW | 17W-25N | 40 |

| | Grid | Page |
|---|---|---|
| Wilshire Ct.* E&W | 16W-26N | 41 |
| Windsor Dr.* E&W | 17W-25N | 40 |
| Wine Ct. N&S | 17W-25N | 40 |
| Woodlands Pkwy. N&S | 15W-23N | 49 |

## Vernon Township

| | Grid | Page |
|---|---|---|
| Apple Hill Ln. N&S | 16W-23N | 48 |
| Apple Orchard Ln. E&W | 15W-23N | 49 |
| Arlyd Rd. E&W | 16W-22N | 48 |
| Ash St. N&S | 14W-20N | 49 |
| Aspen Ct. NW&SE | 14W-20N | 49 |
| Birch St. N&S | 14W-20N | 49 |
| Birchwood Ter. E&W | 14W-20N | 49 |
| Bluebird Ln. N&S | 15W-20N | 49 |
| Bluebird St. E&W | 15W-20N | 49 |
| Brae Burn Ln. N&S | 13W-21N | 49 |
| Briar Ter. E&W | 14W-20N | 49 |
| Bridle Trail Rd. N&S | 14W-24N | 41 |
| Brockman Av. E&W | 16W-23N | 48 |
| Busch Rd. E&W | 17W-21N | 48 |
| Carman Av. N&S | 15W-20N | 49 |
| Catalpa St. N&S | 14W-20N | 49 |
| Celia Av. N&S | 16W-20N | 48 |
| Cemetery Rd. E&W | 15W-23N | 49 |
| Clarice Av. N&S | 16W-20N | 48 |
| Columbus Pkwy E&W | 14W-20N | 49 |
| Concordia Ln. (Pvt.) E&W | 14W-24N | 41 |
| Dell Ln. E&W | 13W-22N | 49 |
| Depot Pl. E&W | 16W-21N | 48 |
| Diamond Lake Rd. N&S | 19W-24N | 39 |
| Dogwood St. N&S | 15W-20N | 49 |
| Duffy Ln. E&W | 13W-22N | 49 |
| East Chevy Chase Dr. NE&SW | 14W-20N | 49 |
| East Mill Rd. E&W | 14W-21N | 49 |
| Easton Av. E&W | 16W-23N | 48 |
| Elizabeth Av. N&S | 15W-20N | 49 |
| Elm Rd. N&S | 14W-23N,14W-24N | 49 |
| Elmwood Av. N&S | 13W-20N | 49 |
| Estonian Ln. E&W | 14W-21N | 49 |
| Eugene Av. N&S | 16W-20N | 48 |
| Florence Av. N&S | 15W-20N | 49 |
| Forest Av. N&S | 14W-20N | 49 |
| Frank Av. E&W | 15W-20N | 49 |
| Frontenac Pl. E&W | 14W-20N | 49 |
| G K Lane N&S | 15W-21N,15W-22N | 49 |
| Garden Ct. E&W | 15W-20N | 49 |
| Gregg Rd. E&W | 14W-23N | 49 |
| Hawthorne Ln. E&W | 13W-25N | 42 |
| Holtz Rd. N&S | 15W-23N | 49 |
| Horatio Blvd. N&S | 15W-20N | 49 |
| Hummingbird Ct. E&W | 14W-20N | 49 |
| Hummingbird Ln. E&W | 14W-20N | 49 |
| Indian Creek Rd. N&S | 15W-23N | 49 |
| Inverrary Ln. E&W | 15W-20N | 49 |
| James Cir. N&S | 14W-20N | 49 |
| Juneway Av. NW&SE | 15W-20N | 49 |
| Kingston Ct. NE&SW | 16W-23N | 48 |
| Kingston Row NS&EW | 16W-23N | 48 |
| Lee Ln. E&W | 16W-23N | 48 |
| Linden Av. E&W | 14W-20N | 49 |
| Lita Av. E&W | 15W-20N | 49 |
| Long Beach Dr. N&S | 14W-20N | 49 |
| Long Grove Aptakistic Rd. E&W | 17W-22N,15W-22N | 48 |
| Longwood Dr. E&W | 14W-20N | 49 |
| Loyola Av. NW&SE | 14W-20N | 49 |
| Main St. NW&SE | 16W-22N,16W-23N | 48 |
| Mallard Ct. E&W | 15W-20N | 49 |
| Mallard Dr. E&W | 15W-20N | 49 |
| Mallard Ln. N&S | 15W-20N | 49 |
| Maple Ct. N&S | 15W-20N | 49 |
| Maple Pl. N&S | 13W-22N | 49 |
| Maplewood Dr. E&W | 14W-20N | 49 |
| Margaret Av. N&S | 16W-20N | 48 |
| Marie Av. E&W | 16W-20N | 48 |
| Marquette Pl. E&W | 14W-20N | 49 |
| Martin Ln. E&W | 14W-20N | 49 |
| Martin St. N&S | 14W-20N | 49 |
| Maryland Villa Rd. E&W | 14W-23N | 49 |
| Menna Ln. E&W | 16W-23N | 48 |
| Mercier Av. NW&SE | 14W-20N | 49 |
| Michael Av. N&S | 15W-20N | 49 |
| Milwaukee Av. NW&SE | 15W-25N,14W-20N | 41 |
| Newman St. E&W | 14W-20N | 49 |
| North Woodbine Cir. E&W | 15W-24N | 41 |
| Oak Ln. E&W | 14W-24N | 41 |
| Oakwood Ter. E&W | 14W-20N | 49 |
| Old Mill Rd. NE&SW | 13W-23N | 49 |
| Olsen Ct. N&S | 15W-23N | 49 |
| Orchard Hill Rd. NE&SW | 13W-25N | 42 |
| Osage Rd. NW&SE | 18W-25N | 40 |
| Park Av. E&W | 16W-23N | 48 |
| Park Pl. NE&SW | 16W-21N | 48 |
| Partridge Ln. N&S | 14W-20N | 49 |
| Pauline Av. E&W | 16W-20N | 48 |
| Pekara Dr. E&W | 15W-20N,14W-20N | 49 |
| Penguin Ln. N&S | 15W-20N | 49 |
| Pet Ln. N&S | 16W-22N | 48 |
| Pheasant Ln. E&W | 14W-20N | 49 |
| Pinehurst Dr. E&W | 14W-20N | 49 |
| Pintail Ct. N&S | 15W-20N | 49 |
| Pintail Ln. N&S | 15W-20N | 49 |
| Pintail St. E&W | 14W-20N | 49 |
| Pope Blvd. E&W | 16W-20N | 48 |
| Port Clinton Rd. E&W | 16W-23N | 48 |
| Prague Av. N&S | 14W-20N | 49 |
| Prairie Ln. N&S | 16W-22N,16W-23N | 48 |
| Prairie Rd. N&S | 16W-22N,16W-23N | 48 |
| Prairie View Ln. E&W | 13W-25N | 42 |
| Private Rd. N&S | 16W-22N,16W-23N | 48 |
| Public St. N&S | 14W-20N,15W-20N | 49 |
| Rabbe Ln. E&W | 15W-22N | 49 |
| Raleigh Dr. N&S | 16W-23N | 48 |
| Raphael Av. N&S | 15W-20N | 49 |
| Richard Ct. N&S | 16W-23N | 48 |
| Riverside Dr. N&S | 14W-20N | 49 |
| Riverside Rd. E&W | 14W-21N | 49 |
| Rose Ter. N&S | 13W-22N | 49 |
| Sandpiper Ln. E&W | 14W-20N | 49 |
| Saunders Rd. N&S | 13W-25N | 42 |
| Schaffer Rd. N&S | 18W-20N | 48 |
| Skylark Ln. NE&SW | 14W-20N | 49 |
| South Woodbine Cir. E&W | 15W-24N | 41 |
| Story Book Ln. N&S | 13W-23N | 49 |
| Strenger Ln. N&S | 13W-22N | 49 |
| Swallow Ct. NE&SW | 15W-20N | 49 |
| Swallow Ln. NE&SW | 15W-20N | 49 |
| Swallow St. E&W | 15W-20N | 49 |
| Swan Blvd. N&S | 15W-20N | 49 |
| Swan Ct. NE&SW | 15W-20N | 49 |
| Swan Ln. E&W | 15W-20N | 49 |
| Trail Way E&W | 14W-24N | 41 |
| Valdon Rd. E&W | 14W-23N | 49 |
| Walnut Dr. E&W | 15W-20N | 49 |
| Weiland Rd. NE&SW | 16W-20N | 48 |
| Westedge N&S | 15W-23N | 49 |
| William Av. N&S | 15W-20N | 49 |
| Winston Dr. NW&SE | 14W-20N | 49 |
| Woodbine Dr. N&S | 15W-24N | 41 |
| Woodland Ln. E&W | 13W-25N | 42 |
| Wren Ln. N&S | 14W-20N | 49 |
| 1st St. N&S | 16W-22N | 48 |
| 2nd St. N&S | 16W-23N | 48 |

## Volo

| | Grid | Page |
|---|---|---|
| Belvidere Rd. E&W | 26W-31N | 29 |
| Fox Lake Rd. NE&SW | 27W-32N,27W-31N | 20 |
| Gilmer Rd. NW&SE | 27W-31N | 29 |
| Rand Rd. N&S | 27W-30N | 20 |
| Sullivan Lake Rd. E&W | 27W-32N | 20 |
| U.S. Route 12 N&S | 27W-32N,27W-31N | 20 |

## Wadsworth

| | Grid | Page |
|---|---|---|
| Adams Rd. E&W | 14W-39N,13W-39N | 17 |
| Aime Ln. E&W | 15W-37N | 17 |
| Andover Rd. E&W | 14W-39N | 17 |
| Anna Dr., E. N&S | 16W-37N | 17 |
| Anna Dr., N. E&W | 15W-37N | 17 |
| Anna Dr., W. N&S | 16W-37N | 17 |
| Arbor Ct. NE&SW | 14W-38N | 17 |
| August Zupec Dr. E&W | 14W-39N,13W-39N | 17 |
| Barth Dr. N&S | 13W-40N | 10 |
| Bartlett Ln. N&S | 13W-40N | 10 |
| Birch Ln. E&W | 14W-38N | 17 |
| Blue Spruce Ct. NE&SW | 14W-38N | 17 |
| Bryn Mawr N&S | 13W-38N | 18 |
| Burr Oak Ln. N&S | 14W-38N | 17 |
| Caroline N&S | 15W-39N | 17 |
| Cashmore Rd. N&S | 14W-38N | 17 |
| Cermak Rd. E&W | 16W-42N | 8 |
| Chaplin St. E&W | 13W-38N | 18 |
| Cherrywood Ln. NW&SE | 16W-40N | 8 |
| Chicago Av. N&S | 15W-38N | 17 |
| Concord Ln. NE&SW | 14W-39N | 17 |
| Country Lane Dr. E&W | 14W-38N | 17 |
| Crabapple E&W | 14W-38N | 17 |
| Delany Rd. N&S | 14W-38N,14W-40N | 17 |
| Delany Rd. N&S | 14W-39N | 9 |
| Dilleys Rd. N&S | 16W-37N,16W-39N | 17 |
| Elm Ln. E&W | 13W-38N | 18 |
| Eveline N&S | 15W-38N | 17 |
| Fox Glove Ln. NW&SE | 16W-40N | 8 |
| Goldenrod Ln. N&S | 16W-40N | 8 |
| Golf Lane Dr. N&S | 14W-38N | 17 |
| Gorham Ln. NW&SE | 15W-42N | 9 |
| Hanssen Rd. E&W | 16W-37N,15W-37N | 17 |
| Harmony Ct. NW&SE | 14W-39N | 17 |
| Hart E&W | 13W-38N | 18 |
| Highview Rd. E&W | 14W-39N | 9 |
| Hunt Club Tr. E&W | 16W-40N | 8 |
| Jody Ln. E&W | 14W-39N | 17 |
| Juniper E&W | 14W-38N | 17 |
| Kilbourne Rd. N&S | 14W-39N,14W-40N | 17 |
| Mature Ct. NW&SE | 14W-39N | 17 |
| Mauser Dr. NS&EW | 13W-39N,13W-40N | 18 |
| McCarthy Rd. E&W | 15W-38N | 17 |
| Meadow Ln. N&S | 14W-39N | 17 |
| Mel Ln. E&W | 14W-39N | 17 |
| Mill Creek Rd. N&S | 16W-40N,16W-41N | 8 |
| Mulberry Ln. E&W | 16W-37N,15W-37N | 17 |
| Nature Ct. NW&SE | 14W-39N | 17 |
| Northwoods Dr. N&S | 14W-38N | 17 |
| Oak Knoll Rd. E&W | 14W-39N | 17 |
| Oak Tree Ln. NW&SE | 14W-38N | 17 |
| Oakcrest Ln. NS&EW | 14W-38N | 17 |
| Old Orchard Dr. NE&SW | 16W-40N | 8 |
| Pickford St. E&W | 13W-38N | 18 |
| Prairie View Dr. N&S | 14W-39N | 17 |
| Pratum Terrace Dr. NE&SW | 14W-39N | 17 |
| Primrose Ln. E&W | 15W-38N | 17 |
| Public Rd. E&W | 15W-38N | 17 |
| Public Rd. NE&SW | 16W-40N | 8 |
| Red Oak Ter. N&S | 14W-38N | 17 |
| Reed St. NE&SW | 16W-40N | 8 |
| Rosedale Av. N&S | 13W-38N | 18 |
| Route 173 E&W | 17W-41N,15W-41N | 8 |
| Sand Ct. E&W | 16W-37N | 17 |
| Sandy Ct. E&W | 15W-38N | 17 |
| Schlosser Ct. E&W | 15W-38N | 17 |
| Sedge Ct. E&W | 16W-40N | 8 |
| Shagbark Ln. N&S | 14W-38N | 17 |
| Shelley Ln. NW&SE | 14W-38N | 17 |
| Shelly Ln. NW&SE | 14W-38N | 17 |
| Sheryl Lynn Dr. E&W | 14W-39N | 17 |
| Skokie Hwy. N&S | 15W-37N,16W-42N | 17 |
| Sterling Ln. NW&SE | 15W-42N | 9 |
| Stiehr Rd. E&W | 13W-40N | 10 |
| Sunset Rd. N&S | 13W-40N | 10 |
| Thorn Meadow Cir. NE&SW | 16W-40N | 8 |
| Thornapple Ln. E&W | 15W-37N | 17 |
| Tri-State North Tollway N&S | 16W-40N,16W-41N | 8 |
| Trillum Ct. NW&SE | 16W-40N | 8 |
| U.S. Route 41 N&S | 15W-37N,16W-42N | 17 |
| Valleyview Rd. N&S | 15W-37N | 17 |
| Wadsworth Rd. E&W | 15W-39N,13W-39N | 17 |
| Walden Ln. NS&EW | 14W-39N | 17 |
| Wedgewood Ct. NW&SE | 14W-39N | 17 |
| Willow Ln. N&S | 15W-37N | 17 |
| Winchester Rd. N&S | 13W-39N | 18 |
| Woodland Av. N&S | 13W-38N | 18 |

## Warren Township

| | Grid | Page |
|---|---|---|
| Adelaide Av. E&W | 12W-37N | 18 |
| Algonquin Dr. N&S | 18W-33N | 24 |
| Almond Ln. N&S | 17W-34N | 24 |
| Almond Rd. N&S | 17W-32N,17W-33N | 24 |
| Apple Ln. E&W | 16W-35N | 24 |
| Applewood Ct. E&W | 16W-35N | 24 |
| Arbor Blvd. E&W | 18W-32N | 24 |
| Ash Dr. E&W | 18W-36N | 16 |
| Ashley Dr. N&S | 17W-33N | 24 |
| Aspen Ct. E&W | 18W-34N | 24 |
| Audrey Av. E&W | 13W-37N | 18 |
| Avon Ct. NW&SE | 18W-33N | 24 |
| Back Bay Ct.* E&W | 17W-35N | 16 |
| Banbury Ct.* E&W | 17W-35N | 16 |
| Banbury Dr. N&S | 18W-36N | 16 |
| Battershall Rd. N&S | 18W-32N,18W-33N | 24 |
| Bayonne Av. N&S | 13W-36N,13W-37N | 18 |
| Beechwood Ct.* E&W | 17W-35N | 16 |
| Belle Plaine Av. N&S | 13W-36N,13W-37N | 18 |
| Belvidere Rd. E&W | 18W-32N,16W-32N | 24 |
| Beverly Av. N&S | 18W-36N | 16 |
| Big Oaks Rd. E&W | 18W-33N,17W-33N | 24 |
| Black Velvet Ln. NS&EW | 17W-37N | 16 |
| Blackhawk Dr. E&W | 17W-33N | 24 |
| Blanchard Rd. E&W | 13W-37N | 18 |
| Blossom St. E&W | 13W-37N | 18 |
| Bluff Dr. NE&SW | 17W-33N | 24 |
| Bough Ct. N&S | 15W-35N | 25 |
| Boulevard View Av. N&S | 13W-36N,13W-37N | 18 |
| Branch Rd. N&S | 15W-35N | 25 |
| Bridle Ct. N&S | 17W-34N | 24 |
| Bridle Ln. N&S | 17W-34N | 24 |
| Bridle Trail Rd. NW&SE | 17W-36N | 16 |
| Brooke Av. E&W | 18W-32N | 24 |
| Brookside Dr. NS&EW | 17W-36N | 16 |
| Carvis Dr. N&S | 18W-34N | 24 |
| Cemetery Rd. N&S | 16W-34N,16W-35N | 24 |
| Center Dr. N&S | 18W-36N | 16 |
| Cherokee Ct. N&S | 17W-33N | 24 |
| Cheyenne Ct. E&W | 17W-33N | 24 |
| Chippewa Rd. E&W | 17W-33N | 24 |
| Circle Ct. E&W | 18W-33N | 24 |
| Circle East SE&NW | 17W-34N | 24 |
| Conifer Ln. NS&EW | 15W-36N | 17 |
| Cottage Av. E&W | 18W-34N | 24 |
| Cottonwood Ct. E&W | 17W-33N | 24 |
| Country Ln. E&W | 18W-33N | 24 |
| Country Ln. N&S | 15W-37N | 17 |
| Cove Rd. NW&SE | 18W-33N | 24 |
| Crows Nest Ct. E&W | 17W-33N | 24 |
| Dady Ct. E&W | 18W-33N | 24 |
| Dartmoor Dr. E&W | 17W-33N | 24 |
| Dawn Ct. E&W | 17W-34N | 24 |
| Deer Path Rd. E&W | 18W-33N | 24 |
| Delany Rd. N&S | 14W-35N,14W-37N | 25 |
| Devon Ct. N&S | 16W-36N | 17 |
| Dillys Rd. N&S | 16W-37N,15W-36N | 17 |
| Douglas Ter. N&S | 18W-36N | 16 |
| Eastview Av. N&S | 17W-33N | 24 |
| Eastwood Av. E&W | 14W-33N | 25 |
| Eastwood Rd. N&S | 17W-33N | 24 |
| Edgewater Ct.* N&S | 17W-35N | 24 |
| Edgewood Dr. N&S | 18W-36N | 16 |
| Edgewood Dr. N&S | 16W-35N | 24 |
| Elizabeth St. E&W | 13W-37N | 18 |
| Elm St. E&W | 18W-32N | 24 |
| Elsbury St. E&W | 17W-36N | 16 |
| Evergreen Dr. N&S | 18W-33N | 24 |
| Fairfield Ln. E&W | 17W-32N | 24 |
| Field View Dr. N&S | 17W-36N | 16 |
| Forest Av. E&W | 14W-33N | 25 |
| Forest Dr. N&S | 18W-32N,18W-33N | 24 |
| Fox Hill Dr. N&S | 16W-36N,16W-37N | 17 |
| Gagemere Dr. N&S | 18W-33N | 24 |
| Gages Lake Dr. N&S | 18W-33N | 24 |
| Gages Lake Rd. E&W | 18W-33N,15W-33N | 24 |
| Gagewood Ln. N&S | 17W-33N | 24 |
| Geier Rd. E&W | 18W-36N | 16 |
| Glen Rd. N&S | 18W-34N | 24 |
| Goldspring Ct.* E&W | 17W-35N | 16 |
| Grand Av. E&W | 17W-36N | 16 |
| Grand Dr. E&W | 18W-33N | 24 |
| Grandwood Dr. NE&SW | 18W-36N | 16 |
| Greentree Pl. N&S | 18W-33N | 24 |
| Greentree Rd. E&W | 17W-33N | 24 |
| Hampshire Ct.* E&W | 17W-35N | 16 |
| Hawk Ct. E&W | 17W-34N | 24 |
| Heather Ct. E&W | 18W-34N | 24 |
| Hendee St. E&W | 13W-37N | 18 |
| Hickory Ct. NW&SE | 18W-34N | 24 |
| Hickory Ln. NE&SW | 17W-33N | 24 |
| Hickory Pl. E&W | 18W-32N | 24 |
| Highfield Dr., N. N&S | 18W-36N | 16 |
| Highfield Dr., W. E&W | 18W-36N | 16 |
| Hill Av. E&W | 14W-33N | 25 |
| Homestead Ct. N&S | 17W-34N | 24 |
| Homestead Rd. NS&EW | 17W-34N | 24 |
| Horseshoe Ln. NS&EW | 17W-34N | 24 |
| Hunt Club Rd. N&S | 17W-33N,17W-36N | 24 |
| Huntington Cir. NS&EW | 17W-33N | 24 |
| Hyatt Ln. N&S | 14W-33N | 25 |
| Idlewild Dr. N&S | 18W-33N | 24 |
| Indian Ln. NW&SE | 18W-33N | 24 |
| Iroquois Dr. E&W | 17W-33N | 24 |
| Island Av. N&S | 18W-33N | 24 |
| Island Ct. N&S | 18W-33N | 24 |
| Ivy Ln. N&S | 17W-33N | 24 |
| Jasmine Ct. E&W | 18W-34N | 24 |
| John Mogg Rd. N&S | 18W-32N,18W-33N | 24 |
| Jonathan Rd. E&W | 16W-35N | 24 |
| Judy Dr. E&W | 18W-36N | 16 |
| Julie Ln. E&W | 17W-34N | 24 |
| Juniper St. N&S | 15W-35N | 25 |
| Karelia Rd. N&S | 16W-34N,16W-35N | 24 |
| Karen Ln. E&W | 18W-36N | 16 |
| Kennedy Dr. E&W | 14W-33N | 25 |
| Kewaunee Dr. E&W | 18W-33N,17W-33N | 24 |
| Kimberwick Ln. NS&EW | 16W-36N,16W-37N | 17 |
| Knowles Rd. NE&SW | 18W-35N | 24 |
| Lake Rd. N&S | 18W-33N | 24 |
| Lake Shore Dr. NW&SE | 18W-33N | 24 |
| Lake St. N&S | 18W-34N | 24 |
| Lakeview Ct. NW&SE | 18W-33N | 24 |
| Lakeview Ter. NE&SW | 18W-36N | 16 |
| Larkspur Ct. NW&SE | 18W-34N | 24 |
| Lavender Cir. NS&EW | 18W-34N | 24 |
| Lawn Av. E&W | 14W-33N | 25 |
| Lee Cir. E&W | 18W-36N | 16 |
| Limb Ct. N&S | 15W-35N | 25 |
| Lincoln Av. NW&SE | 18W-34N | 24 |
| Linda Ln. E&W | 18W-36N | 16 |
| Linden Av. E&W | 18W-32N | 24 |
| Lindenwood Dr. E&W | 18W-33N | 24 |
| Lone Rock Rd. N&S | 18W-33N | 24 |
| Lovers Ln. NE&SW | 18W-33N | 24 |
| Magnolia Av. N&S | 13W-36N,13W-37N | 18 |
| Main St. E&W | 18W-33N | 24 |
| Manitowoc Ct. NE&SW | 18W-33N | 24 |
| Maple Av. E&W | 18W-32N | 24 |
| Maple Ln. E&W | 17W-34N | 24 |
| Marian Dr. E&W | 18W-35N | 24 |
| Mawman St. E&W | 13W-37N | 18 |
| Meadow Ln. E&W | 18W-36N | 16 |
| Meadow Rd. N&S | 18W-33N | 24 |
| Meadow Ridge Dr. E&W | 17W-36N | 16 |
| Meadowbrook Dr. E&W | 17W-33N | 24 |
| Meander Dr. N&S | 18W-34N | 24 |
| Melody Rd. N&S | 14W-33N | 25 |
| Meyer Rd. E&W | 14W-37N | 17 |
| Mill Creek Dr. NE&SW | 17W-36N | 16 |
| Mill Crossing Dr. E&W | 17W-36N | 16 |

| | Grid | Page |
|---|---|---|
| Mill Ct. NW&SE .... | 18W-36N | 16 |
| Mill Rd. N&S | 18W-32N,17W-33N | 24 |
| Nemesis Av. E&W .. | 13W-36N | 18 |
| New Bridge Ct.* NW&SE | 17W-35N | 24 |
| Noreen Ct. NE&SW | 17W-34N | 24 |
| Northwestern Av. N&S | 13W-36N,13W-37N | 18 |
| O'Plaine Rd. N&S . | 14W-32N | 25 |
| Oak Av. N&S ...... | 18W-32N | 24 |
| Oak Knoll NE&SW .. | 17W-34N | 24 |
| Oak St. N&S ...... | 18W-33N | 24 |
| Oakland Av. N&S .. | 18W-33N | 24 |
| Oakwood Dr. N&S .. | 18W-36N | 16 |
| Old Creek Ct.* E&W | 17W-35N | 16 |
| Old Pine Ct. N&S .. | 18W-34N | 24 |
| Old Walnut Dr. N&S | 18W-34N | 24 |
| Old Woods Trail NE&SW | 17W-36N | 16 |
| Orchard Ln. E&W . | 18W-33N | 24 |
| Orchard Valley Dr. E&W | 16W-35N | 24 |
| Overbrook Ct.* E&W | 17W-35N | 16 |
| Paddock St. E&W . | 13W-37N | 18 |
| Pamela Pl. E&W .. | 18W-36N | 16 |
| Park Cres. E&W .. | 18W-34N | 24 |
| Park Dr. E&W .... | 18W-36N | 16 |
| Park Dr. N&S .... | 18W-36N | 16 |
| Park Pl. E&W .... | 18W-34N | 24 |
| Park St. N&S .... | 18W-33N | 24 |
| Parkway Av. E&W . | 14W-32N | 25 |
| Partridge Ln. N&S . | 17W-34N | 24 |
| Pin Oak Ln. E&W . | 17W-34N | 24 |
| Pine Av. N&S ..... | 18W-34N | 24 |
| Pine St. N&S ..... | 15W-35N | 25 |
| Pleasant Pl. E&W . | 18W-34N | 24 |
| Pond Ridge Cir. NS&EW | 18W-32N,17W-36N | 16 |
| Prospect Dr. NE&SW | 18W-33N | 24 |
| Public Rd. NW&SE | 18W-33N | 24 |
| Rae Ln. E&W ...... | 18W-36N | 16 |
| Red Oak St. N&S .. | 18W-34N | 24 |
| Redbud Ln. E&W .. | 18W-34N | 24 |
| Ridge Rd. NW&SE . | 18W-33N | 24 |
| River Rd. N&S .... | 15W-32N | 25 |
| Robert Ct. NW&SE | 17W-34N | 24 |
| Rolling Hills Rd. NW&SE | 18W-32N,18W-33N | 24 |
| Roosevelt Rd. E&W | 18W-35N | 24 |
| Rosedale Av. N&S . | 13W-36N | 18 |
| Route 120 E&W ... | 15W-33N | 25 |
| Route 132 E&W ... | 18W-36N | 16 |
| Royal Oak Ln. N&S | 18W-33N | 24 |
| Rule Ct. NW&SE . | 18W-33N | 24 |
| Running Creek Ct.* E&W | 17W-35N | 16 |
| Saddle Ct. N&S ... | 17W-34N | 24 |
| Saddle Ln. N&S ... | 17W-34N | 24 |
| Salisbury Dr.* E&W | 17W-35N | 16 |
| Salmon Av. E&W .. | 13W-37N | 18 |
| Sandy Ct. E&W ... | 17W-34N | 24 |
| Sears Blvd. NS&EW | 18W-33N | 24 |
| Shannon Dr. N&S . | 17W-33N | 24 |
| Sheridan Av. E&W . | 18W-34N | 24 |
| Shirley Dr. N&S ... | 14W-37N | 17 |
| Sibelius Ln. E&W . | 16W-35N | 24 |
| Skokie Hwy. NW&SE | 14W-35N,14W-35N | 25 |
| Springbrook Ln.* E&W | 17W-35N | 16 |
| Springwood Dr. N&S | 18W-34N | 24 |
| Springwood Ln. NW&SE | 18W-34N | 24 |
| Spruce Point Ct. N&S | 15W-36N | 17 |
| Spruce Point Dr. NW&SE | 15W-36N | 17 |
| Stearns School Rd. E&W | 18W-36N,15W-36N | 16 |
| Stillwater Ct.* E&W | 17W-35N | 16 |
| Stonebridge Ct. E&W | 18W-34N | 24 |
| Streamwood Ct. E&W | 18W-36N | 16 |
| Streamwood Dr. N&S | 18W-36N | 16 |
| Sulkey Dr. N&S ... | 18W-34N | 24 |
| Sumac Ln. E&W ... | 18W-34N | 24 |
| Summit Dr. NE&SW | 17W-33N | 24 |
| Sunnyside Av. N&S | 14W-33N | 25 |
| Sunset Av. N&S .. | 18W-33N | 24 |
| Tangueray Dr. NS&EW | 18W-34N | 24 |
| Telegraph Rd. N&S | 13W-32N | 26 |
| Thornapple Ln. N&S | 18W-32N | 24 |
| Thoroughbred Dr. NS&EW | 17W-36N,16W-37N | 16 |

| | Grid | Page |
|---|---|---|
| Tiger Tail Ct. E&W .. | 17W-33N | 24 |
| Timber Ln. E&W .. | 18W-33N | 24 |
| Tomahawk Pl. NW&SE | 18W-33N | 24 |
| Treaer Ter. NE&SW | 18W-36N | 16 |
| Twin Lakes Blvd. E&W | 18W-33N,17W-33N | 24 |
| Tyler Av. E&W .... | 13W-36N | 18 |
| U.S. Route 41 NW&SE | 14W-35N,15W-37N | 25 |
| U.S. Route 45 N&S | 18W-32N,18W-37N | 24 |
| Valley Dr. E&W ... | 18W-33N | 24 |
| Valley View Dr. NW&SE | 18W-33N | 24 |
| Verco Av. E&W ... | 13W-37N | 18 |
| Vermont Av. E&W . | 13W-36N | 18 |
| Victoria Ln. N&S .. | 15W-37N | 17 |
| Walden Way* E&W | 17W-35N | 16 |
| Wall Av. E&W .... | 13W-36N | 18 |
| Walnut Ln. E&W .. | 17W-34N | 24 |
| Warren Av. E&W .. | 17W-33N | 24 |
| Washington St. E&W | 18W-34N,14W-34N | 24 |
| Wayside Pl. N&S .. | 18W-33N | 24 |
| West Av. N&S .... | 14W-33N | 25 |
| West Wind Dr. NS&EW | 17W-36N | 16 |
| Westwood Pl. E&W | 18W-36N | 16 |
| White Oak Ln. N&S | 17W-34N | 24 |
| Willow Point Dr. E&W | 18W-33N | 24 |
| Windslow Dr. E&W | 17W-33N | 24 |
| Winnebago Ct. NW&SE | 17W-33N | 24 |
| Winnebago Dr. E&W | 17W-33N | 24 |
| Winnebago Trail NS&EW | 17W-33N | 24 |
| Wooded Glen Dr. NE&SW | 18W-33N | 24 |
| Woodland Dr. E&W | 17W-33N | 24 |
| Woodland Ter. E&W | 18W-36N | 16 |
| Woodland Ter. N&S | 18W-33N | 24 |
| Wright Av. N&S ... | 18W-34N | 24 |
| Wright Rd. N&S .. | 18W-33N | 24 |
| Yearling Dr. E&W . | 17W-36N | 16 |
| Yorkhouse Rd. E&W | 15W-37N,13W-37N | 17 |
| Yorkshire Dr.* E&W | 17W-35N | 16 |
| 1st St. E&W ..... | 18W-33N | 24 |
| 2nd St. N&S ..... | 18W-33N | 24 |

## Wauconda

| | Grid | Page |
|---|---|---|
| Adams Av. N&S .... | 25W-28N | 29 |
| Anderson Rd. N&S | 27W-26N,27W-27N | 37 |
| Bangs St. NE&SW .. | 26W-27N | 37 |
| Barbara Ln. NW&SE | 25W-28N | 29 |
| Bonner Rd. E&W | 26W-28N,24W-28N | 29 |
| Brett Ln. E&W .... | 25W-27N | 37 |
| Briar Rd. NW&SE . | 26W-28N | 29 |
| Brown St. N&S | 26W-27N,26W-28N | 37 |
| Buren Av. E&W ... | 26W-26N | 37 |
| Church St. E&W .. | 26W-27N | 37 |
| Clover Rd. E&W .. | 26W-27N | 37 |
| Cook St. E&W ... | 26W-27N | 37 |
| Country Lane Ct. N&S | 25W-27N | 37 |
| Crescent Ter. NW&SE | 26W-28N | 37 |
| Daniel St. N&S ... | 26W-27N | 37 |
| Dato Ln. N&S .... | 26W-28N | 29 |
| Delo Dr. NE&SW . | 26W-26N | 37 |
| Delta Dr. N&S .... | 25W-27N | 37 |
| Dunbar Rd. NS&EW | 26W-27N | 37 |
| Earls Ct. N&S .... | 25W-28N | 29 |
| Edgewater Ln. NW&SE | 25W-27N | 37 |
| Edgewater Pkwy. E&W | 25W-28N | 29 |
| Edward Pl. N&S .. | 25W-28N | 29 |
| Farm Hill Cir. N&S | 26W-27N | 37 |
| Foster Av. N&S ... | 25W-27N | 37 |
| Francis St. N&S ... | 26W-27N | 37 |
| George Av. E&W .. | 26W-27N | 37 |
| Grand Blvd. N&S | 25W-27N,25W-28N | 37 |
| Grant Pl. E&W ... | 25W-28N | 29 |
| Hammond St. N&S | 25W-28N | 29 |
| Harrison Av. N&S . | 25W-28N | 29 |
| Helena Av. E&W .. | 26W-27N | 37 |
| High St. N&S .... | 25W-27N | 37 |
| Highland Av. E&W . | 25W-27N | 37 |
| Hill St. N&S ..... | 25W-27N | 37 |
| Hollow Hill Rd. N&S | 26W-28N | 29 |
| Hubbard Ct. E&W | 26W-27N | 37 |
| Indian Ridge Trail N&S | 26W-27N | 37 |

| | Grid | Page |
|---|---|---|
| Industrial Dr. NS&EW | 26W-28N | 29 |
| Jackson Av. N&S . | 25W-28N | 29 |
| Jackson Ct. E&W . | 25W-28N | 29 |
| Jaime Ln. NS&EW . | 26W-28N | 29 |
| James Av. NE&SW | 25W-28N | 29 |
| Jonathon Ct. N&S . | 24W-28N | 30 |
| Karl Dr. N&S .... | 25W-28N | 29 |
| Kent Av. E&W...... | 25W-26N | 37 |
| Kimball Av. E&W . | 25W-27N | 37 |
| Kyle Ct. N&S .... | 26W-28N | 29 |
| Lake Shore Dr. NW&SE | 25W-28N | 29 |
| Lake St. N&S .... | 25W-27N | 37 |
| Lakeview Av. N&S . | 25W-27N | 37 |
| Larkdale Row N&S | 26W-27N,26W-28N | 37 |
| Laurel Av. N&S ... | 26W-28N | 29 |
| Legion Ct. N&S ... | 25W-26N | 37 |
| Lewis Av. E&W ... | 26W-27N | 37 |
| Liberty St. E&W .. | 26W-27N | 37 |
| Lincoln Av. NE&SW | 25W-28N | 29 |
| Lotus St. N&S...... | 25W-27N | 37 |
| Macintosh Dr. NE&SW | 24W-28N | 30 |
| Madison Av. N&S . | 25W-28N | 29 |
| Main St. N&S | 26W-27N,25W-28N | 37 |
| Maple Av. E&W .. | 25W-27N | 37 |
| Marine Rd. E&W . | 26W-28N | 29 |
| Marlene Av. NE&SW | 25W-27N | 37 |
| Mill St. NE&SW | 26W-27N,25W-27N | 37 |
| Minerva Av. E&W . | 26W-27N | 37 |
| Monroe Av. N&S .. | 25W-28N | 29 |
| Mutton Dr. N&S .. | 26W-28N | 29 |
| Nancy Ct. NE&SW . | 25W-28N | 29 |
| Naples Dr. E&W .. | 25W-26N | 37 |
| Neil Ct. N&S .... | 25W-28N | 29 |
| North Av. E&W .. | 26W-27N | 37 |
| North Shore Ct. NW&SE | 25W-28N | 29 |
| North Shore Dr. NW&SE | 25W-28N | 29 |
| Northview Dr. E&W | 26W-28N | 29 |
| Oak Bluff Ct. E&W | 25W-27N | 37 |
| Oak Dr. E&W ..... | 25W-28N | 29 |
| Oakdale Av. E&W . | 25W-28N | 29 |
| Oaks Av. E&W | 26W-26N,25W-26N | 37 |
| Oakwood Rd. N&S | 26W-27N | 37 |
| Old Country Way N&S | 25W-27N | 37 |
| Old Rand Rd. NW&SE | 26W-28N | 29 |
| Orton Av. NW&SE . | 26W-27N | 37 |
| Osage St. NS&EW . | 26W-27N | 37 |
| Osage Ter. NE&SW | 26W-28N | 29 |
| Pamela Ct. NE&SW | 25W-28N | 29 |
| Park Av. N&S | 25W-27N,25W-28N | 37 |
| Park Pl. E&W .... | 25W-28N | 29 |
| Park St. NE&SW .. | 26W-27N | 37 |
| Peace Blvd. E&W . | 26W-26N | 37 |
| Pershing Dr. E&W . | 25W-28N | 29 |
| Pine St. E&W .... | 26W-27N | 37 |
| Pleasant View Av. E&W | 25W-28N,24W-28N | 29 |
| Ridge Av. N&S ... | 26W-26N | 37 |
| Ridge Ct. E&W ... | 25W-27N | 37 |
| Ridge St. N&S ... | 25W-27N | 37 |
| Road Way NE&SW | 26W-27N,25W-28N | 37 |
| Roosevelt Av. E&W | 26W-27N | 37 |
| Ross St. E&W...... | 26W-27N | 37 |
| Sheila Ct. E&W ... | 25W-28N | 29 |
| Sheridan Dr. E&W . | 25W-28N | 29 |
| Sky Hill Rd. N&S . | 25W-27N | 37 |
| Slocum Lake Rd. E&W | 26W-27N | 37 |
| South Dr. E&W ... | 26W-28N | 29 |
| South St. E&W ... | 25W-27N | 37 |
| Summit Av. NW&SE | 25W-28N,24W-28N | 29 |
| Sunnyside Av. E&W | 25W-27N | 37 |
| Surf Ter. N&S ... | 25W-28N | 29 |
| Thomas Ct. N&S . | 26W-27N | 37 |
| Van Buren Av. N&S | 25W-28N | 29 |
| W. Liberty St. NW&SE | 26W-27N | 37 |
| Walnut Rd. E&W . | 26W-28N | 29 |
| Washington Av. N&S | 25W-28N | 29 |
| Wauconda Rd. N&S | 25W-27N,24W-28N | 37 |
| Wethington Dr. N&S | 25W-28N | 29 |
| Willow Rd. N&S .. | 26W-27N | 37 |
| Woodland Av. N&S | 25W-27N | 37 |
| Woodland Rd. N&S | 25W-28N | 29 |

## Wauconda Township

| | Grid | Page |
|---|---|---|
| Ada St. N&S ...... | 28W-26N | 36 |
| Alameda Dr. N&S . | 28W-31N | 28 |
| Alvinia St. N&S ... | 25W-27N | 37 |
| Ann Ct. N&S ...... | 26W-26N | 37 |
| Ash St. N&S | 28W-26N,25W-27N | 36 |
| Bayview St. NW&SE | 28W-27N | 36 |
| Beech St. N&S ... | 28W-27N | 36 |
| Belvidere Rd. E&W | 28W-31N | 28 |
| Berkely St. N&S .. | 25W-28N | 29 |
| Bernice St. N&S .. | 28W-26N | 36 |
| Blakley Pkwy. E&W | 25W-26N | 37 |
| Bluff St. N&S .... | 25W-27N | 37 |
| Bonner Rd. E&W | 27W-28N,26W-28N | 28 |
| Brooks St. N&S .. | 28W-26N | 36 |
| Brown Rd. N&S ... | 25W-26N | 37 |
| Burnett Rd. E&W . | 28W-28N | 28 |
| Callahan Rd. N&S . | 26W-31N | 29 |
| Callahan Rd. N&S | 26W-29N,26W-31N | 29 |
| Cary Plaza N&S | 25W-28N | 29 |
| Case Rd. NW&SE . | 27W-29N | 28 |
| Channel St. NW&SE | 28W-27N | 36 |
| Clark St. N&S .... | 28W-26N | 36 |
| Converse Rd. N&S | 28W-27N | 36 |
| Cook St. E&W ... | 25W-28N | 29 |
| Crest Rd. E&W ... | 28W-28N | 28 |
| Division St. N&S .. | 28W-27N | 36 |
| Dowell Rd. NE&SW | 28W-29N,28W-30N | 28 |
| East Lake Shore Dr. NW&SE | 25W-26N | 37 |
| East Park Av. E&W | 28W-26N | 36 |
| Ellen St. N&S .... | 28W-26N | 36 |
| Elm St. N&S ..... | 28W-26N | 36 |
| Elmwood Av. NE&SW | 26W-27N | 37 |
| Fairview Rd. E&W . | 28W-27N | 36 |
| Fisher Rd. N&S ... | 28W-31N | 28 |
| Fisher Rd. NS&EW | 28W-30N,28W-31N | 28 |
| Forest Garden Rd. (Pvt.) N&S | 27W-27N | 37 |
| Gardner Rd. NW&SE | 25W-28N | 29 |
| Garland Rd. NS&EW | 26W-28N,25W-29N | 29 |
| Genessee St. N&S | 28W-26N,28W-27N | 36 |
| Geraldine Ln. N&S . | 28W-26N | 36 |
| Gilmer Rd. NW&SE | 26W-31N,25W-30N | 29 |
| Gossell Rd. NW&SE | 25W-30N,25W-29N | 29 |
| Grace St. N&S | 28W-26N,25W-28N | 36 |
| Greenbriar Ct. N&S | 27W-26N | 37 |
| Greenview Dr. N&S | 25W-26N | 37 |
| Harrison Av. N&S . | 25W-29N | 29 |
| Hermosa Av. E&W . | 25W-28N | 29 |
| Hickory Av. N&S .. | 25W-28N | 29 |
| Hickory St. N&S .. | 28W-27N | 36 |
| Hickory St. N&S .. | 28W-27N | 36 |
| High Rd. N&S .... | 28W-28N | 28 |
| Hill Av. N&S ..... | 25W-27N | 37 |
| Hillside Av. N&S ... | 25W-26N | 37 |
| Hillside Dr. N&S .. | 28W-31N | 28 |
| Huston Av. N&S .. | 28W-26N | 36 |
| Ivanhoe Rd. E&W | 26W-26N,25W-28N | 37 |
| Kane St. N&S .... | 26W-27N | 37 |
| Karen Dr. N&S ... | 26W-26N | 37 |
| Lake Dr. N&S .... | 25W-28N | 29 |
| Lake Dr. N&S .... | 28W-26N | 36 |
| Lake Pkwy. E&W .. | 25W-28N | 29 |
| Lake Shore Ct. N&S | 25W-26N | 37 |
| Lake Shore Dr. N&S | 25W-28N | 29 |
| Lake St. E&W .... | 28W-26N | 36 |
| Lakeland Dr. NE&SW | 25W-27N | 37 |
| Lakeview Av. E&W | 26W-26N | 37 |
| Lakeview Cir. NS&EW | 28W-27N,28W-28N | 36 |
| Lakeview Dr. E&W . | 28W-26N | 36 |
| Lakeview Dr. NW&SE | 28W-26N | 36 |
| Lamphere St. E&W | 28W-26N | 36 |
| Langley Ct. N&S... | 28W-27N | 36 |
| Laurel Av. NW&SE | 26W-26N | 37 |
| Laurel Ct. N&S ... | 26W-26N | 37 |
| Laurel Ln. E&W .. | 28W-27N | 36 |
| Lexington Ct. N&S. | 28W-27N | 36 |
| Leyte Ct. N&S ... | 28W-26N | 36 |
| Lindy Ln. E&W ... | 28W-26N | 36 |
| Locust Dr. NS&EW | 28W-26N | 36 |
| Mac St. N&S .... | 27W-27N | 37 |
| Madison Av. N&S | 25W-29N | 29 |

| | Grid | Page |
|---|---|---|
| Maple Av. E&W .... | 28W-26N | 36 |
| Maple St. N&S .... | 28W-27N | 36 |
| Marilyn Meadow Ct. E&W | 25W-29N | 29 |
| Marion St. N&S ... | 28W-26N | 36 |
| May St. E&W .... | 27W-27N | 37 |
| McNally Ln. NE&SW | 27W-31N | 29 |
| Mead Av. N&S .. | 25W-28N | 37 |
| Meadow Lane Rd. E&W | 28W-28N | 28 |
| Meadow Ln. N&S . | 25W-26N | 37 |
| Meeker St. E&W .. | 28W-26N | 36 |
| Monroe Av. NE&SW | 25W-29N | 29 |
| Morey St. N&S ... | 28W-26N | 36 |
| Mylith Rd. N&S .. | 28W-27N | 36 |
| Myrtle St. N&S ... | 28W-26N | 36 |
| Neville Rd. E&W .... | 28W-29N | 28 |
| North Lakeview Dr. | 27W-26N,26W-26N | 37 |
| North St. E&W ... | 28W-27N | 36 |
| Oak Dr. N&S .... | 25W-26N | 37 |
| Oak Knoll Rd. N&S | 28W-28N | 28 |
| Oak St. NS&EW | 28W-26N,28W-28N | 36 |
| Old Rand Rd. NW&SE | 25W-26N | 37 |
| Orchard Dr. NE&SW | 28W-27N | 36 |
| Orchard Rd. N&S . | 28W-26N | 36 |
| Parkview Dr. E&W . | 28W-27N | 36 |
| Pheasant Ct. NW&SE | 26W-26N | 37 |
| Pheasant Trail NS&EW | 26W-26N | 37 |
| Pleasant View Av. E&W | 25W-28N | 29 |
| Poplar St. NS&EW | 28W-26N,28W-27N | 36 |
| Rand Rd. NW&SE | 25W-26N,27W-31N | 37 |
| Ridge Rd. E&W .... | 28W-28N | 28 |
| Ridge St. N&S ... | 25W-27N | 37 |
| Roberts Rd. NS&EW | 28W-26N,28W-29N | 36 |
| Robin Ct. E&W ... | 25W-29N | 29 |
| Shady Ln. N&S ... | 28W-27N | 36 |
| Slocum Lake Rd. E&W | 28W-27N,27W-27N | 36 |
| South Av. E&W ... | 28W-26N | 36 |
| South Lakeview Dr. E&W | 27W-26N,26W-26N | 37 |
| State Hwy. 60 NW&SE | 26W-31N,25W-31N | 29 |
| Sunset Dr. E&W .. | 28W-31N | 28 |
| Swift Ct. N&S .... | 26W-26N | 37 |
| Tamarack Dr. E&W | 25W-26N | 37 |
| Valentine Rd. N&S. | 25W-27N | 37 |
| Virginia Ln. N&S .. | 25W-29N | 29 |
| Wade St. N&S ... | 25W-29N | 29 |
| Walnut St. N&S .. | 28W-26N | 36 |
| Washington Av. NE&SW | 25W-29N | 29 |
| Wegner Rd. NE&SW | 28W-31N | 28 |
| Wells Dr. N&S...... | 25W-29N | 29 |
| Werden Av. N&S .. | 25W-27N | 37 |
| West Dr. N&S .... | 25W-28N | 29 |
| West End Rd. N&S | 26W-28N | 29 |
| Will St. N&S...... | 28W-26N | 36 |
| Willow Rd. N&S .. | 28W-26N | 36 |
| Wilson Av. E&W .. | 25W-27N | 37 |
| Wilson Rd. N&S .. | 25W-31N | 29 |
| Wilton Rd. N&S .. | 25W-26N | 37 |
| Winding Lane Dr. N&S | 25W-28N | 29 |
| York Dr. N&S .... | 25W-26N | 37 |

## Waukegan

| | Grid | Page |
|---|---|---|
| Abington Ct. N&S .. | 14W-36N | 17 |
| Adams St. N&S .... | 10W-33N | 27 |
| Alexander Ct. N&S | 10W-35N | 27 |
| Alta Vista Dr. N&S .. | 10W-36N | 19 |
| Amhurst Pkwy. NE&SW | 13W-32N,13W-31N | 26 |
| Apache Rd. N&S .. | 11W-36N | 18 |
| Apple Av. E&W ... | 12W-33N | 26 |
| Archer Av. N&S ... | 10W-33N | 27 |
| Arizona Av. E&W .. | 12W-36N | 18 |
| Armory Pl. E&W ... | 11W-35N | 26 |
| Arthur Ct. NE&SW . | 12W-34N | 26 |
| Arthur Dr. E&W ... | 11W-38N | 18 |
| Ash St. N&S | 10W-34N,10W-36N | 27 |
| Ashley Ln. N&S ... | 12W-35N | 26 |
| Atlantic Av. E&W | 11W-35N,10W-35N | 26 |
| Atlantic Av. E&W . | 12W-35N | 26 |
| Augusta Dr. N&S .. | 14W-37N | 17 |
| Austin Av. N&S ... | 12W-34N | 26 |
| Avoneida Pl. N&S . | 12W-36N | 18 |
| Baldwin Av. N&S | 12W-34N,12W-35N | 26 |
| Ballentine St. E&W | 11W-38N | 18 |
| Bank NE&SW .... | 10W-38N | 19 |
| Batberry Ct. NE&SW | 14W-32N | 25 |
| Beach Rd. E&W | 12W-38N,10W-38N | 18 |

# 76 LAKE COUNTY

| | Grid | Page |
|---|---|---|
| Beech Av. E&W | 10W-36N | 19 |
| Beechnut Av. N&S | 12W-33N | 26 |
| Belvidere St. E&W | | |
| | 12W-33N,10W-33N | 26 |
| Benny Av. N&S | 11W-33N | 26 |
| Berry Ct. E&W | 11W-35N | 26 |
| Bertrand Ln. E&W | 10W-38N | 19 |
| Berwick Blvd. N&S | | |
| | 10W-34N,11W-35N | 26 |
| Besley Pl. N&S | 10W-33N | 27 |
| Birch Av. E&W | 10W-36N | 19 |
| Birch Av. N&S | 12W-33N | 26 |
| Birchwood Dr. E&W | | |
| | 13W-31N | 35 |
| Birchwood Dr. N&S | 12W-31N | 35 |
| Blanchard Rd. E&W | | |
| | 14W-37N,10W-37N | 17 |
| Blossom Av. E&W | 14W-37N | 17 |
| Bluff Ct. N&S | 10W-34N | 27 |
| Bluff St. E&W | 10W-34N | 27 |
| Boardman St. E&W | 11W-37N | 18 |
| Bob O' Farrell Ln. E&W | | |
| | 10W-38N | 19 |
| Bonnie Brook Ln. N&S | | |
| | 11W-37N | 18 |
| Bonnie Brook Rd. E&W | | |
| | 13W-36N,11W-36N | 18 |
| Brentwood Av. N&S | | |
| | 14W-36N | 17 |
| Briar Ln. N&S | 11W-34N | 18 |
| Brighton Av. E&W | 10W-33N | 27 |
| Bristol Rd. N&S | 11W-37N | 18 |
| Brookside Av. E&W | | |
| | 12W-34N,11W-34N | 26 |
| Browne Ct. E&W | 10W-39N | 19 |
| Browning Av. N&S | | |
| | 10W-33N | 27 |
| Buck Av. E&W | | |
| | 11W-36N,10W-36N | 18 |
| Buckingham Rd. E&W | | |
| | 11W-37N | 18 |
| Burr Oak Dr. N&S | 14W-37N | 17 |
| Burris Av. E&W | 12W-36N | 18 |
| Burwood Dr. NE&SW | | |
| | 13W-32N | 26 |
| Burton Av. N&S | 11W-34N | 26 |
| Bush Ct. N&S | 11W-32N | 26 |
| Butrick St. N&S | 11W-34N | 26 |
| Campbell Ln. NS&EW | | |
| | 14W-31N | 33 |
| Carnation Ct. N&S | 10W-34N | 27 |
| Carney Av. N&S | | |
| | 11W-32N,11W-33N | 26 |
| Caroline Pl. NE&SW | | |
| | 10W-33N | 27 |
| Carriage Ln. E&W | 12W-34N | 26 |
| Caryn Ln. E&W | 12W-34N | 26 |
| Cashmore Rd. N&S | | |
| | 14W-37N | 17 |
| Casimer Pulaski Dr. NW&SE | | |
| | 13W-32N | 26 |
| Castle Ct. N&S | 11W-37N | 18 |
| Catalpa Av. E&W | 11W-34N | 26 |
| Cedar Av. N&S | | |
| | 11W-33N,11W-38N | 26 |
| Celand Dr. NE&SW | | |
| | 14W-32N | 25 |
| Center St. E&W | 10W-35N | 27 |
| Central Av. E&W | 11W-34N | 26 |
| Chaney St. E&W | 12W-38N | 18 |
| Chapel St. E&W | 11W-34N | 27 |
| Chaplin St. E&W | 12W-38N | 18 |
| Charleston St. N&S | | |
| | 11W-37N,11W-38N | 18 |
| Charron Ln. E&W | 11W-34N | 26 |
| Chatham Rd. N&S | 11W-37N | 18 |
| Cherokee Rd. N&S | 11W-36N | 18 |
| Cherry Tree Ct. E&W | | |
| | 14W-37N | 17 |
| Chestnut St. N&S | | |
| | 10W-34N,10W-36N | 27 |
| Cheyenne Rd. N&S | | |
| | 12W-36N,11W-36N | 18 |
| Chinook Rd. N&S | 11W-36N | 18 |
| Chippewa Rd. N&S | | |
| | 11W-36N | 18 |
| Choctaw Rd. E&W | 11W-36N | 18 |
| Churchill Ct. N&S | 15W-31N | 33 |
| Churchill St. N&S | 15W-31N | 33 |
| Circle Ct. N&S | 10W-35N | 27 |
| Clarke Av. N&S | 10W-33N | 27 |
| Clarkson St. N&S | 11W-34N | 26 |
| Clayton St. N&S | | |
| | 10W-34N,9W-34N | 27 |
| Clinton St. N&S | 10W-33N | 27 |
| Colbert Rd. E&W | 12W-36N | 26 |
| Coller Ct. N&S | 11W-32N | 26 |
| Colorado Av. E&W | 12W-36N | 18 |
| Colville Pl. E&W | 10W-36N | 19 |
| Commanche Ct. E&W | | |
| | 11W-36N | 18 |
| Commonwealth Av. N&S | | |
| | 11W-33N,10W-33N | 26 |
| Continental Dr. E&W | | |
| | 14W-36N | 17 |
| Cooke Ct. E&W | 11W-33N | 26 |
| Cornelia Av. N&S | | |
| | 12W-34N,11W-34N | 26 |
| Cornell Rd. E&W | 11W-37N | 18 |
| Corona Rd. NE&SW | | |
| | 10W-36N | 19 |
| Cory Av. E&W | 10W-34N | 27 |
| Country Pl. E&W | 15W-37N | 17 |
| County St. N&S | | |
| | 10W-34N,10W-35N | 27 |
| Creek Rd. N&S | 11W-36N | 18 |
| Crescent Av. N&S | 11W-35N | 26 |
| Crest Ct. E&W | 14W-37N | 17 |
| Cummings Av. E&W | | |
| | 10W-33N | 27 |
| Cypress Point N&S | | |
| | 14W-37N | 17 |
| Cypress St. E&W | 10W-33N | 27 |
| Dady Pl. N&S | 10W-33N | 27 |
| Dahringer Rd. E&W | 9W-35N | 27 |
| Dakota Rd. E&W | 11W-36N | 18 |
| Dale Ln. E&W | 11W-36N | 18 |
| Dana Av. E&W | 12W-36N | 18 |
| Darrow Ln. E&W | 12W-33N | 26 |
| Daybreak Dr. NS&EW | | |
| | 15W-32N | 25 |
| Delany Rd. N&S | | |
| | 14W-36N,14W-37N | 17 |
| Delaware Rd. N&S | | |
| | 11W-35N,11W-36N | 26 |
| Devonshire Rd. E&W | | |
| | 11W-37N | 18 |
| Dickinson St. E&W | 11W-37N | 18 |
| Dilger Av. N&S | | |
| | 12W-33N,12W-34N | 26 |
| Dixie Av. E&W | 12W-33N | 26 |
| Dodge Av. E&W | 11W-33N | 26 |
| Dorchester Av. N&S | | |
| | 12W-34N | 26 |
| Dorchester Ct. N&S | | |
| | 11W-34N | 26 |
| Dorothy Ct. E&W | 14W-37N | 17 |
| Douglas Av. E&W | 10W-35N | 27 |
| Douglas Cir. N&S | 12W-34N | 26 |
| Douglas St. N&S | 10W-35N | 27 |
| Douglas St. E&W | 12W-38N | 18 |
| Dover Rd. E&W | 11W-37N | 18 |
| Dugan St. N&S | 12W-34N | 27 |
| Dugdale Rd. NE&SW | | |
| | 11W-32N,11W-33N | 26 |
| Duggald Av. E&W | 12W-35N | 26 |
| Dunlay Ct. NS&EW | | |
| | 11W-34N | 26 |
| E. Newcastle Ct. E&W | | |
| | 11W-38N | 18 |
| East Bonnie Brook Ln. N&S | | |
| | 11W-36N,11W-37N | 18 |
| East Dr. NW&SE | 12W-34N | 26 |
| East End Av. N&S | 11W-37N | 18 |
| Eastview Dr. N&S | 10W-35N | 27 |
| Eastwood Ct. E&W | | |
| | 14W-37N | 17 |
| Eastwood Rd. E&W | | |
| | 11W-37N | 18 |
| Edison Ct. N&S | | |
| | 11W-34N,10W-34N | 26 |
| Edwards St. E&W | 10W-35N | 27 |
| Egidi Rd. NW&SE | 16W-31N | 33 |
| Elizabeth Av. N&S | 11W-32N | 26 |
| Ellis Av. E&W | 12W-34N | 26 |
| Elm St. E&W | 10W-33N | 27 |
| Elmwood Av. N&S | | |
| | 11W-32N,11W-37N | 26 |
| Emanuel Av. N&S | 12W-38N | 18 |
| Ernie Krueger Cir. N&S | | |
| | 13W-36N | 18 |
| Evergreen Av. N&S | | |
| | 12W-33N,12W-38N | 26 |
| Evergreen Ct. N&S | 12W-34N | 26 |
| Fairfield Cir. E&W | 10W-35N | 27 |
| Fairfield Ct., E. | | |
| | 10W-35N | 27 |
| Fairfield Ct., W. | | |
| | 10W-35N | 27 |
| Ferry St. E&W | 11W-37N | 18 |
| Fields Ter. N&S | 11W-36N | 18 |
| Florence Av. E&W | 12W-34N | 26 |
| Florida Av. E&W | 12W-36N | 18 |
| Flossmoor Av. N&S | | |
| | 11W-34N,11W-35N | 26 |
| Foam Forms Pl. E&W | | |
| | 9W-34N | 27 |
| Ford St. E&W | 12W-38N | 18 |
| Forest Av. E&W | 10W-33N | 27 |
| Forest Av. N&S | 10W-36N | 19 |
| Forest Ln. N&S | 11W-37N | 18 |
| Forest View Ln. NW&SE | | |
| | 15W-32N | 25 |
| Forrest Hills Ct. N&S | | |
| | 14W-37N | 17 |
| Franklin St. E&W | 10W-34N | 27 |
| Frazier St. E&W | 11W-37N | 18 |
| Frolic Av. N&S | | |
| | 12W-34N,12W-38N | 26 |
| Fulton Av. N&S | | |
| | 11W-32N,11W-34N | 26 |
| Gallagher Rd. E&W | | |
| | 10W-36N | 19 |
| Garden Pl. E&W | 11W-35N | 26 |
| Garrick Av. N&S | 12W-36N | 18 |
| Gavin Ct. N&S | 14W-31N | 33 |
| Genessee St. N&S | | |
| | 10W-33N,10W-34N | 27 |
| Gent Dr. E&W | 14W-37N | 17 |
| George Av. NW&SE | | |
| | 10W-33N | 27 |
| George St. E&W | 12W-34N | 26 |
| Georgetown Av. E&W | | |
| | 11W-35N | 26 |
| Gillette Av. E&W | 10W-35N | 27 |
| Gladstone Av. NS&EW | | |
| | 11W-33N | 26 |
| Gladys Ct. E&W | 10W-39N | 19 |
| Glen Ct. E&W | 10W-33N | 27 |
| Glen Flora Av. E&W | | |
| | 12W-35N,10W-35N | 26 |
| Glen Rock Av. N&S | | |
| | 11W-33N,10W-34N | 26 |
| Glendening Pl. NS&EW | | |
| | 10W-36N | 19 |
| Glenn Dr. N&S | 11W-32N | 26 |
| Glenwood Av. N&S | | |
| | 11W-35N | 26 |
| Golf Rd. E&W | | |
| | 11W-36N,10W-36N | 18 |
| Golfmoor Av. N&S | 12W-36N | 18 |
| Grand Av. E&W | | |
| | 12W-35N,10W-34N | 26 |
| Gray Ct. E&W | | |
| | 12W-33N,11W-33N | 26 |
| Green Bay Pl. E&W | | |
| | 12W-33N | 26 |
| Green Bay Rd. N&S | | |
| | 12W-33N,12W-38N | 26 |
| Greenfield Av. N&S | | |
| | 11W-32N | 26 |
| Greenwood Av. N&S | | |
| | 12W-36N,9W-36N | 18 |
| Greenwood Ter. E&W | | |
| | 11W-36N | 18 |
| Gretta Av. N&S | | |
| | 11W-33N,11W-34N | 26 |
| Grove Av. N&S | | |
| | 12W-35N,10W-36N | 26 |
| Grove St. E&W | 10W-35N | 27 |
| Hamilton Ct. E&W | 11W-34N | 26 |
| Hampshire Ln. E&W | | |
| | 15W-37N | 17 |
| Hanlon Rd. N&S | | |
| | 15W-31N,15W-32N | 33 |
| Harbor Pl. N&S | 9W-34N | 27 |
| Harding St. E&W | | |
| | 11W-35N,10W-35N | 26 |
| Harper Rd. N&S | 12W-35N | 26 |
| Harrison Av. E&W | 12W-35N | 26 |
| Hawthorne Ct. E&W | | |
| | 13W-36N | 18 |
| Hawthorne Ln. E&W | | |
| | 11W-37N | 18 |
| Hazel Ct. N&S | 10W-34N | 27 |
| Hemholz Av. N&S | 10W-33N | 27 |
| Hendee Av. E&W | | |
| | 12W-37N,11W-37N | 18 |
| Henry Pl. N&S | 10W-35N | 27 |
| Herbert Dr. E&W | 11W-38N | 18 |
| Heritage Av. E&W | 14W-37N | 17 |
| Hickory Hills Rd. N&S | | |
| | 14W-36N | 17 |
| Hickory St. N&S | | |
| | 10W-34N,10W-36N | 27 |
| Highland Av. E&W | 11W-38N | 18 |
| Highland Av. E&W | | |
| | 11W-35N,10W-35N | 26 |
| Highland Ct. E&W | 10W-35N | 27 |
| Hill St. N&S | 10W-33N | 27 |
| Hillside Av. E&W | 12W-34N | 26 |
| Hilltop Av. N&S | 15W-32N | 25 |
| Hilman Ct. E&W | 11W-34N | 26 |
| Hollis Av. N&S | 12W-34N | 26 |
| Home Av. N&S | 10W-33N | 27 |
| Hope Ln. E&W | 11W-35N | 26 |
| Howard St. E&W | 12W-38N | 18 |
| Hull Ct. E&W | 10W-35N | 27 |
| Huntington Lakes Dr. N&S | | |
| | 15W-31N | 33 |
| Huron Ter. N&S | 11W-36N | 18 |
| Hyde Park Av. E&W | | |
| | 12W-34N,11W-34N | 26 |
| Illini Rd. E&W | 11W-36N | 18 |
| Indian Rd. N&S | 12W-36N | 18 |
| Indiana St. N&S | 11W-35N | 26 |
| Interstate 94 N&S | 14W-31N | 33 |
| Iroquois Rd. N&S | 12W-36N | 18 |
| Irving Pkwy. E&W | 11W-38N | 18 |
| Jackson Ct. NE&SW | | |
| | 10W-34N | 27 |
| Jackson St. N&S | | |
| | 10W-34N,10W-36N | 27 |
| James Ct. N&S | 10W-35N | 27 |
| James St. N&S | 10W-35N | 27 |
| Jaquelyn Ln. E&W | 12W-36N | 18 |
| Jefferson St. N&S | 11W-34N | 26 |
| Jenkinson Ct. E&W | | |
| | 11W-34N | 26 |
| Jensen Ct. N&S | 11W-33N | 27 |
| Jolley Av. E&W | 12W-34N | 26 |
| Judge Av. N&S | | |
| | 11W-34N,11W-36N | 26 |
| Judge Pl. NS&EW | 11W-35N | 26 |
| Julian St. E&W | 10W-35N | 27 |
| Juniper St. N&S | 10W-35N | 27 |
| Kathy Ln. E&W | 12W-34N | 26 |
| Keith Av. E&W | 10W-35N | 27 |
| Keller Av. N&S | | |
| | 11W-33N,11W-34N | 26 |
| Kellogg Av. N&S | 11W-36N | 18 |
| Kennard St. N&S | 10W-33N | 27 |
| Kingston Rd. E&W | 11W-37N | 18 |
| Lake Ct. E&W | 10W-37N | 27 |
| Lake St. E&W | | |
| | 10W-34N,9W-34N | 27 |
| Lakehurst Rd. NS&EW | | |
| | 13W-32N,13W-33N | 26 |
| Lakeside Dr. NW&SE | | |
| | 13W-32N | 26 |
| Lakeview Av. E&W | | |
| | 10W-33N | 27 |
| Lakeview Ter. N&S | | |
| | 15W-32N | 25 |
| Lakewood Av. N&S | | |
| | 12W-34N | 26 |
| Laurel Av. E&W | 11W-34N | 26 |
| Laurel Ln. E&W | 11W-36N | 18 |
| Lawn Ct. E&W | 10W-34N | 27 |
| Le Baron St. N&S | 12W-34N | 26 |
| Leith Av. N&S | | |
| | 11W-34N,11W-35N | 26 |
| Lenox Av. N&S | 10W-33N | 27 |
| Leo Singer Ln. NE&SW | | |
| | 10W-38N | 19 |
| Lewis Av. N&S | | |
| | 11W-32N,11W-38N | 26 |
| Lewis Pl. E&W | 11W-35N | 26 |
| Liberty St. E&W | 10W-33N | 27 |
| Lincoln Av. N&S | | |
| | 10W-33N,10W-34N | 27 |
| Linden Av. N&S | | |
| | 10W-34N,10W-36N | 27 |
| Lindsay Av. E&W | 10W-35N | 27 |
| Little Foot Rd. N&S | | |
| | 12W-36N | 18 |
| Lizabeth Ln. E&W | 11W-37N | 18 |
| Lloyd Av. E&W | 11W-33N | 26 |
| Longview Rd. E&W | | |
| | 11W-34N,11W-36N | 18 |
| Lorene Ct. NE&SW | | |
| | 11W-38N | 18 |
| Lorraine Av. N&S | | |
| | 11W-34N,11W-37N | 26 |
| Lorraine Pl. N&S | 11W-35N | 26 |
| Low Av. NW&SE | 10W-34N | 27 |
| Lucia Av. N&S | | |
| | 12W-34N,12W-35N | 26 |
| Lydia St. N&S | 11W-34N | 26 |
| Lynn Ter. N&S | 11W-34N | 26 |
| Lyons Ct. E&W | 11W-32N | 26 |
| Madison St. E&W | | |
| | 10W-34N,9W-34N | 27 |
| Magnolia Ln. N&S | 14W-37N | 17 |
| Main St. E&W | | |
| | 12W-38N,11W-38N | 18 |
| Maple Av. E&W | 11W-34N | 26 |
| Maple Tree Ln. N&S | | |
| | 14W-37N | 17 |
| Marian Ct. E&W | 10W-33N | 27 |
| Mariposa Av. N&S | 10W-36N | 19 |
| Market St. N&S | | |
| | 10W-33N,10W-34N | 27 |
| Marshall Pkwy. E&W | | |
| | 11W-33N | 26 |
| Martin Av. N&S | | |
| | 11W-32N,11W-35N | 26 |
| Mary Jane Ln. E&W | | |
| | 10W-38N | 19 |
| Massena Av. N&S | 10W-35N | 27 |
| May St. E&W | 10W-33N | 27 |
| McAlister Av. N&S | 10W-33N | 27 |
| McAree Av. N&S | 11W-32N | 18 |
| McAree Rd. N&S | | |
| | 11W-33N,12W-36N | 26 |
| McArthur Dr. E&W | 11W-37N | 18 |
| McGaw Rd. E&W | | |
| | 13W-32N,14W-32N | 26 |
| McKay St. E&W | 11W-37N | 18 |
| McKinley Av. E&W | 10W-33N | 27 |
| Meadowlark Ln. N&S | | |
| | 11W-37N | 18 |
| Meadowview Cir. N&S | | |
| | 15W-32N | 25 |
| Melrose Av. E&W | | |
| | 12W-34N,11W-34N | 26 |
| Menominee Rd. E&W | | |
| | 11W-36N | 18 |
| Merton Av. N&S | 10W-36N | 19 |
| Metropolitan Av. N&S | | |
| | 12W-34N,12W-38N | 26 |
| Miami Rd. N&S | 12W-36N | 18 |
| Midlane Dr. NS&EW | | |
| | 14W-37N | 17 |
| Mill Ct. NW&SE | 10W-34N | 27 |
| Milwaukee Av. NE&SW | | |
| | 16W-32N | 24 |
| Mini Dr. N&S | 14W-37N | 17 |
| Minoque Av. N&S | 12W-33N | 26 |
| Miraflores Av. NW&SE | | |
| | 10W-36N | 19 |
| Mohawk Rd. N&S | 12W-36N | 18 |
| Mohican Rd. N&S | 12W-36N | 18 |
| Monroe St. E&W | | |
| | 12W-34N,11W-34N | 26 |
| Montesano Av. E&W | | |
| | 11W-36N,10W-36N | 18 |
| Morrs Ct. E&W | 10W-38N | 19 |
| Muirfield Av. N&S | 11W-35N | 26 |
| Myrtle St. E&W | 10W-35N | 27 |
| N. Bonnie Brook Ln. E&W | | |
| | 11W-37N | 18 |
| N. Butrick St. N&S | | |
| | 11W-34N,11W-37N | 26 |
| N. Orchard Av. N&S | | |
| Navajo Rd. E&W | 12W-36N | 18 |
| Nemery Ct. N&S | 12W-36N | 18 |
| Nemesis Av. E&W | 12W-36N | 18 |
| New York St. N&S | | |
| | 11W-35N,11W-36N | 26 |
| Newcastle Rd. N&S | | |
| | 11W-37N,11W-38N | 18 |
| Niva St. N&S | 11W-36N | 18 |
| Noble Av. N&S | 12W-38N | 18 |
| Noll St. N&S | 12W-34N | 26 |
| Nordigan Dr. E&W | 10W-36N | 19 |
| Norma Ln. NE&SW | | |
| | 12W-34N | 26 |
| Norman Dr., S. NS&EW | | |
| | 13W-31N | 34 |
| North Av. E&W | 11W-38N | 18 |
| North Av. N&S | | |
| | 10W-34N,10W-37N | 27 |
| North Park Av. N&S | | |
| | 10W-34N | 27 |
| Northern Av. N&S | | |
| | 12W-32N,12W-38N | 26 |
| Northfield Av. E&W | | |
| | 12W-35N | 26 |
| Northmoor Av. E&W | | |
| | 11W-35N | 26 |
| Northwestern Av. N&S | | |
| | 13W-37N | 18 |
| O'Plaine Rd. N&S | | |
| | 14W-32N,14W-33N | 25 |
| O'Plaine Rd. N&S | 14W-31N | 33 |
| Oak Av. E&W | 11W-38N | 18 |
| Oak Crest St. NW&SE | | |
| | 10W-34N | 27 |
| Oak St. N&S | 10W-34N | 27 |
| Oak Tree Ln. E&W | 10W-34N | 27 |
| Oakland Av. E&W | 12W-35N | 26 |
| Oakley Av. N&S | 10W-35N | 27 |
| Oakwood Av. N&S | 12W-34N | 26 |
| Oneida Pl. N&S | 12W-36N | 18 |
| Orchard Ln. N&S | 12W-35N | 26 |
| Osage Cir. E&W | 12W-36N | 18 |
| Otto Graham Ln. E&W | | |
| | 10W-38N | 19 |
| Ottowa Rd. NS&EW | | |
| | 12W-36N | 18 |
| Pacific Av. E&W | 10W-35N | 27 |
| Palmer Pl. N&S | 10W-35N | 27 |
| Parkway Av. E&W | 14W-33N | 25 |
| Parmalee Pl. N&S | 10W-36N | 19 |
| Partridge St. E&W | 11W-37N | 18 |
| Paul St. E&W | 11W-34N | 26 |
| Pawnee Rd. E&W | 12W-36N | 18 |
| Pearsall St. E&W | | |
| | 12W-33N,11W-33N | 26 |
| Pebble Beach Dr. NE&SW | | |
| | 14W-37N | 17 |
| Pershing Rd. N&S | | |
| | 10W-34N,9W-35N | 27 |
| Phillippa Av. N&S | 10W-34N | 27 |
| Piccadilly Ct. N&S | 10W-34N | 27 |
| Pickford St. E&W | 12W-38N | 18 |
| Pickus Ct. NE&SW | 10W-34N | 27 |
| Pigeon Av. NW&SE | | |
| | 12W-34N | 26 |
| Piikoi Ln. E&W | 15W-31N | 33 |
| Pine St. N&S | | |
| | 11W-34N,11W-36N | 26 |
| Pioneer Ct. N&S | 12W-34N | 26 |
| Pioneer Rd. N&S | | |
| | 12W-34N,12W-35N | 26 |
| Pleasant Hill Gate N&S | | |
| | 14W-32N | 26 |
| Poplar St. N&S | | |
| | 10W-34N,10W-36N | 27 |
| Porter St. NW&SE | 10W-34N | 27 |
| Powell Av. N&S | 10W-34N | 27 |
| Prairie Av. N&S | 12W-34N | 26 |
| Prescott St. N&S | 10W-33N | 27 |
| Prospect Ct. NW&SE | | |
| | 10W-34N | 27 |
| Public Service Rd. N&S | | |
| | 12W-34N | 26 |
| Ravine Av. E&W | 10W-33N | 27 |
| Regency Dr. NS&EW | | |
| | 14W-31N | 33 |
| Renier Rd. E&W | 12W-38N | 18 |
| Rice St. E&W | 11W-37N | 18 |
| Richard E. Buch Ct. E&W | | |
| | 11W-32N | 26 |
| Ridge Av. E&W | 12W-33N | 26 |
| Ridgeland Av. N&S | | |
| | 12W-35N,10W-35N | 26 |
| River Park Dr. E&W | | |
| | 15W-31N | 33 |
| River Rd. N&S | | |
| | 15W-31N,15W-32N | 33 |
| Roberts Av. N&S | 12W-37N | 18 |
| Rock Pkwy. NW&SE | | |
| | 11W-38N | 18 |
| Roger Edwards Av. E&W | | |
| | 11W-35N | 26 |
| Roundstone Way E&W | | |
| | 14W-32N | 26 |
| Route 120 E&W | 12W-33N | 26 |
| Route 131 N&S | | |
| | 12W-33N,12W-38N | 26 |
| Route 21 N&S. | 16W-31N | 33 |
| Route 43 N&S | | |
| | 13W-31N,13W-32N | 34 |
| Rudd Ct. NW&SE | 12W-34N | 26 |
| Rugby Ct. N&S | 11W-37N | 18 |
| Runyard Pl. E&W | 11W-34N | 26 |
| S. Bonnie Brook Ln. E&W | | |
| | 11W-36N | 18 |
| S. Orchard N&S | | |
| | 11W-33N,11W-34N | 26 |
| Salem Av. E&W | 11W-33N | 26 |

|  | Grid | Page |
|---|---|---|
| Sea Horse Dr. NS&EW | 9W-34N | 27 |
| Seminole Rd. N&S | 12W-36N | 18 |
| Sequoit Rd. E&W | 11W-36N | 18 |
| Shadow Brook Ct. E&W | 15W-32N | 25 |
| Shawnee Rd. N&S | 12W-36N | 18 |
| Sheeler Av. E&W | 12W-34N | 26 |
| Sheridan Ct., E. E&W | 10W-35N | 27 |
| Sheridan Rd. N&S | 10W-33N,10W-36N | 27 |
| Sherman Pl. N&S | 10W-34N | 27 |
| Shields Dr. N&S | 13W-32N | 26 |
| Shoshone Rd. E&W | 12W-36N | 18 |
| Sioux Rd. N&S | 11W-36N | 18 |
| Skokie Hwy. N&S | 13W-31N | 34 |
| South Av. E&W | 10W-33N | 27 |
| Southern Hills Dr. N&S | 14W-37N | 17 |
| Spaulding Av. E&W | 12W-34N | 26 |
| Spring St. N&S | 10W-34N | 27 |
| Spruce Av. E&W | 10W-36N | 19 |
| St. James St. N&S | 10W-34N | 27 |
| Stanley Av. N&S | 10W-35N | 27 |
| Steele Ct. N&S | 10W-34N | 27 |
| Steeplechase Cir., W. N&S | 15W-31N | 33 |
| Steeplechase Dr., E. N&S | 15W-31N | 33 |
| Stewart Av. E&W | 10W-35N | 27 |
| Stonegate Rd. N&S | 11W-37N,11W-38N | 18 |
| Stripe Ct. N&S | 10W-34N | 27 |
| Sumac Av. N&S | 11W-33N,11W-34N | 26 |
| Sunderlin St.. N&S | 10W-34N | 27 |
| Sunset Av. E&W | 13W-36N,10W-36N | 18 |
| Swallowtail Dr. E&W | 14W-32N | 26 |
| Talcott Dr. N&S | 14W-32N | 26 |
| Tamara Ct. E&W | 11W-34N | 26 |
| Tanahill Dr. E&W | 13W-36N | 18 |
| Telegraph Rd. N&S | 13W-31N,13W-33N | 34 |
| Ten Pin Ln. N&S | 10W-38N | 19 |
| Terrace Av. N&S | 10W-35N | 27 |
| Teske Blvd. N&S | 13W-33N | 26 |
| Tewes Ln. E&W | 10W-38N | 19 |
| Thaxter Av. N&S | 12W-33N | 26 |
| Theresa Av. E&W | 12W-35N | 26 |
| Thornberry Ct. N&S | 14W-32N | 25 |
| Tiffany Dr. N&S | 12W-34N | 26 |
| Timber Woods Ln. N&S | 15W-32N | 25 |
| Tobin Ct. N&S | 11W-32N | 26 |
| Tremont Ct. NS&EW | 15W-31N | 33 |
| Tucker Ln. N&S | 14W-32N | 26 |
| Twyford Rd. N&S | 11W-37N | 18 |
| U.S. Route 41 NW&SE | 12W-31N,12W-32N | 35 |
| University Av. E&W | 12W-34N,11W-34N | 26 |
| Utica St. N&S | 10W-33N,10W-34N | 27 |
| Vermont Av. E&W | 13W-36N | 18 |
| Vernon Av. N&S | 12W-36N | 18 |
| Victory St. N&S | 10W-33N,10W-34N | 27 |
| W. Newcastle Ct. E&W | 11W-37N | 18 |
| Wadsworth Av. N&S | 10W-33N | 27 |
| Wadsworth Rd. E&W | 11W-39N | 18 |
| Wainlow Av. N&S | 10W-33N,11W-33N | 27 |
| Wall Av. E&W | 12W-36N | 18 |
| Walnut St. N&S | 10W-34N,10W-36N | 27 |
| Washington Park N&S | 11W-32N,11W-34N | 26 |
| Washington St. N&S | 12W-34N,10W-34N | 26 |
| Washington Ter. N&S | 12W-34N | 26 |
| Water St. E&W | 10W-34N | 27 |
| Waverly Pl. E&W | 11W-35N | 26 |
| West Av. E&W | 14W-32N | 26 |
| West Dr. N&S | 12W-34N | 26 |
| West St. N&S | 10W-33N,10W-34N | 27 |
| West Waukee Rd. NE&SW | 12W-34N | 26 |
| Western Av. N&S | 10W-35N,10W-36N | 27 |
| Westmoreland Av. N&S | 11W-34N,11W-35N | 26 |
| Wetzel Ct. E&W | 11W-34N | 26 |
| Whidden Av. N&S | 11W-33N,11W-34N | 26 |
| Whispering Willow Ct. NE&SW | 15W-32N | 25 |
| White Oak Dr. NW&SE | 13W-32N | 26 |
| Whitney St. N&S | 11W-37N | 18 |
| Willamsburg Av. E&W | 11W-35N | 26 |
| Willow Av. N&S | 12W-33N | 26 |
| Willow Ct. N&S | 12W-34N | 26 |
| Willow Dr. E&W | 10W-36N | 19 |
| Wilson Av. E&W | 11W-36N | 18 |
| Winhaven Dr. N&S | 11W-37N,11W-38N | 18 |
| Winnebago Rd. N&S | 12W-36N | 18 |
| Wisconsin Av. N&S | 11W-33N,11W-34N | 26 |
| Witchford Ln. N&S | 11W-37N | 18 |
| Witchwood Ln. N&S | 11W-37N | 18 |
| Wood Av. E&W | 12W-33N | 26 |
| Woodlawn Av. E&W | 10W-35N | 27 |
| Woodlawn Cir. E&W | 10W-35N | 27 |
| Worack Pl. N&S | 11W-34N | 26 |
| Wyer St. E&W | 12W-38N | 18 |
| Yeoman St. N&S | 11W-34N,11W-37N | 26 |
| Yorkhouse Rd. N&S | 14W-37N,11W-37N | 17 |
| Zepher St. E&W | 12W-38N | 18 |
| 1st St. E&W | 10W-34N | 27 |
| 2nd St. E&W | 10W-34N | 27 |
| 4th St. E&W | 10W-34N | 27 |
| 6th St. E&W | 12W-33N,11W-33N | 26 |
| 7th St. E&W | 11W-33N | 26 |
| 8th St. E&W | 12W-33N,10W-33N | 26 |
| 9th St. E&W | 12W-33N,10W-33N | 26 |
| 10th Ct. E&W | 11W-32N | 26 |
| 10th St. E&W | 11W-33N,10W-33N | 26 |
| 11th Ct. E&W | 11W-32N | 26 |
| 11th St. E&W | 11W-32N | 26 |
| 12th St. E&W | 11W-32N | 26 |
| 13th St. E&W | 11W-32N | 26 |
| 14th St. E&W | 11W-32N | 26 |

## Waukegan Township

|  | Grid | Page |
|---|---|---|
| Adelphi Av. N&S | 12W-35N,12W-36N | 26 |
| Arizona Av. E&W | 12W-36N | 18 |
| Atlantic Av. E&W | 12W-35N | 26 |
| Austin Av. E&W | 12W-34N | 26 |
| Brooke Av. E&W | 12W-36N | 18 |
| Cheyenne Rd. E&W | 12W-36N | 18 |
| Clearview Av | 12W-35N | 26 |
| Colorado Av. E&W | 12W-35N | 26 |
| Country Club Av. E&W | 12W-36N | 18 |
| Crescent Av. E&W | 12W-35N | 26 |
| Duggald Av. E&W | 12W-35N | 26 |
| Florida Av. E&W | 12W-36N | 18 |
| Frolic Av. N&S | 12W-35N,12W-36N | 26 |
| Garrick Av. N&S | 12W-35N,12W-36N | 26 |
| Glen Flora Av. E&W | 12W-35N | 26 |
| Golfmoor Av. E&W | 12W-36N | 18 |
| Grandmore Av. N&S | 12W-35N | 26 |
| Grandview Av. E&W | 12W-35N | 26 |
| Grandville Av. E&W | 12W-35N | 26 |
| Green Av. N&S | 12W-35N,12W-36N | 26 |
| Green Bay Rd. NE&SW | 12W-35N,12W-36N | 26 |
| Greenwood Av. E&W | 12W-36N | 18 |
| Grove Av. E&W | 12W-35N | 26 |
| Harrison Av. E&W | 12W-35N | 26 |
| Highland Av. E&W | 12W-36N | 18 |
| Johns Manville Av. E&W | 12W-35N | 26 |
| Keith Av. E&W | 12W-35N | 26 |
| Lakewood Av. N&S | 12W-34N | 26 |
| Lee Av. E&W | 12W-35N | 26 |
| Metropolitan Av. N&S | 12W-35N,12W-36N | 26 |
| Nemesis E&W | 12W-36N | 18 |
| North Av. N&S | 10W-37N | 19 |
| Northern Av. N&S | 12W-35N,12W-36N | 26 |
| Northfield Av. E&W | 12W-35N | 26 |
| Pacific Av. E&W | 12W-36N | 26 |
| Paddock St. E&W | 12W-37N | 18 |
| Polo Av. E&W | 12W-36N | 18 |
| Public Service Av. N&S | 12W-35N | 26 |
| Sherman Av. E&W | 12W-35N | 26 |
| Southview Av. E&W | 12W-35N | 26 |
| Tyler Av. E&W | 12W-36N | 18 |
| University Av. E&W | 12W-34N | 26 |
| Vermont Av. E&W | 12W-36N | 18 |
| Wall Av. E&W | 12W-36N | 18 |

## West Deerfield Township

|  | Grid | Page |
|---|---|---|
| Birchwood Ln. N&S | 11W-23N | 50 |
| Carol Ln. N&S | 12W-21N | 50 |
| Chris Ct. E&W | 12W-21N | 50 |
| Elmwood Pl. E&W | 11W-23N | 50 |
| Forest Ct. N&S | 11W-23N | 50 |
| Hickory Knoll Ln. E&W | 12W-21N | 50 |
| London Ln. (Pvt.) N&S | 11W-23N | 50 |
| Montgomery Rd. N&S | 12W-21N | 50 |
| Oakwood Pl. E&W | 11W-23N | 50 |
| Sannders Rd. N&S | 12W-20N | 50 |
| Wildwood Ln. N&S | 11W-23N | 50 |

## Winthrop Harbor

|  | Grid | Page |
|---|---|---|
| Adams Av. N&S | 10W-42N | 11 |
| Aiken Ct. N&S | 9W-41N | 11 |
| Alton Ct. N&S | 10W-41N | 11 |
| Ben Ct. N&S | 10W-41N | 11 |
| Burke Dr. E&W | 10W-41N | 11 |
| Camden Cove NE&SW | 10W-43N | 11 |
| Casco Bay NW&SE | 10W-43N | 11 |
| Cavin Av. N&S | 10W-42N,10W-43N | 11 |
| Cedar Ct. E&W | 10W-42N | 11 |
| Charles Av. N&S | 10W-42N | 11 |
| Chatham Cove NW&SE | 10W-43N | 11 |
| Chestnut Cir. N&S | 9W-43N | 11 |
| Clearview Ct. NE&SW | 11W-43N | 10 |
| College Av. N&S | 10W-42N,10W-43N | 11 |
| Compton Ct. N&S | 11W-42N | 10 |
| Cornerstone Dr. N&S | 11W-42N | 10 |
| Deer Path Cir. N&S | 9W-42N | 11 |
| Deer Path Dr. N&S | 9W-42N,10W-43N | 11 |
| East Broadway Av. N&S | 11W-41N,11W-42N | 10 |
| Ellis Av. N&S | 10W-42N | 11 |
| English Ln. N&S | 10W-42N | 11 |
| Fairhaven Dr. NE&SW | 10W-43N | 11 |
| Franklin Av. N&S | 9W-41N,9W-42N | 11 |
| Franklin St. E&W | 9W-41N | 11 |
| Frans Ct. NE&SW | 10W-42N | 11 |
| Fulton Av. N&S | 9W-41N,9W-42N | 11 |
| Funderburk Dr. N&S | 10W-41N | 11 |
| Garnett Av N&S | 10W-42N,10W-43N | 11 |
| Geddes Av. N&S | 10W-42N,10W-43N | 11 |
| Har-Bar Cir. E&W | 11W-42N | 10 |
| Har-Bar Dr. E&W | 11W-42N | 10 |
| Harbor Ln. NE&SW | 10W-42N | 11 |
| Highland Ct. E&W | 10W-42N | 11 |
| Holdridge Av. N&S | 10W-42N,10W-43N | 11 |
| Ivy Ct. NE&SW | 11W-42N | 10 |
| James Av. NW&SE | 10W-42N | 11 |
| Judith Ct. N&S | 10W-42N | 11 |
| Kenosha Rd. N&S | 11W-42N,10W-43N | 10 |
| Kimberly Ln. N&S | 10W-42N | 11 |
| Kirkwood Av. N&S | 10W-42N | 11 |
| La Lor Ct. E&W | 10W-42N | 10 |
| Landon Av. N&S | 9W-41N,9W-42N | 11 |
| Lewis Av. N&S | 11W-41N,11W-42N | 10 |
| Madison Av. N&S | 10W-42N | 11 |
| Mae Ct. E&W | 10W-41N | 11 |
| Main St. E&W | 10W-42N,9W-42N | 11 |
| Mary Av. N&S | 9W-42N | 11 |
| Meadow Ct. N&S | 11W-42N | 10 |
| Meadow Ln. N&S | 11W-42N | 10 |
| Monroe Av. N&S | 10W-42N | 11 |
| North Ave. N&S | 10W-42N | 11 |
| North Park Av. NW&SE | 9W-42N,9W-43N | 11 |
| Oakdale Av. N&S | 9W-43N | 11 |
| Old Darby Rd. NW&SE | 10W-43N | 11 |
| Park Av. N&S | 9W-41N,9W-42N | 11 |
| Parkview Dr. NW&SE | 11W-42N | 10 |
| Potomac Ln. NW&SE | 11W-42N | 10 |
| Prairie Av. NW&SE | 11W-43N | 10 |
| Ravine Dr. N&S | 9W-42N,9W-43N | 11 |
| Roberts Rd. N&S | 10W-42N,10W-43N | 11 |
| Rose Ct. NW&SE | 11W-42N | 10 |
| Route 173 N&S | 9W-41N,9W-43N | 11 |
| Runyard Av. N&S | 9W-43N | 11 |
| Russell Av. N&S | 10W-42N,10W-43N | 11 |
| Russell Rd. E&W | 10W-43N,9W-43N | 11 |
| Sheridan Rd. E&W | 9W-41N,9W-43N | 11 |
| Shields Av. N&S | 10W-42N | 11 |
| South Park Av. N&S | 9W-42N | 11 |
| Stonegate Dr. E&W | 12W-42N | 10 |
| Thompson Av. N&S | 10W-42N,10W-43N | 11 |
| Valley Rd. NS&EW | 11W-42N | 10 |
| Vista Ln. N&S | 12W-42N | 10 |
| Washington Av. N&S | 11W-41N | 10 |
| West Broadway Av. N&S | 11W-41N,11W-42N | 10 |
| West Ct. N&S | 10W-41N | 11 |
| Whitney Av. N&S | 9W-42N | 11 |
| Wilson Av. N&S | 9W-43N | 11 |
| 2nd St. E&W | 10W-43N,9W-43N | 11 |
| 3rd St. E&W | 10W-43N,9W-43N | 11 |
| 4th St. E&W | 10W-43N,9W-43N | 11 |
| 5th St. E&W | 11W-43N,9W-43N | 11 |
| 6th St. E&W | 10W-42N,9W-42N | 11 |
| 8th St. E&W | 10W-42N,9W-42N | 11 |
| 9th St. E&W | 11W-42N,9W-42N | 11 |
| 10th St. E&W | 10W-42N,9W-42N | 11 |
| 11th St. E&W | 11W-42N,9W-42N | 11 |
| 12th St. E&W | 11W-42N,9W-42N | 11 |
| 13th St. E&W | 11W-41N,9W-42N | 11 |
| 14th St. E&W | 10W-41N,9W-41N | 11 |
| 15th St. E&W | 11W-41N,9W-41N | 10 |

## Zion

|  | Grid | Page |
|---|---|---|
| Barnhart Av. E&W | 10W-41N,9W-41N | 11 |
| Bethel Blvd. N&S | 10W-39N,10W-41N | 19 |
| Bethesda Blvd. N&S | 10W-40N,10W-41N | 11 |
| Bethlehem Av. NW&SE | 11W-41N | 10 |
| Big Highlands Rd. NS&EW | 12W-41N | 10 |
| Brigadoon Dr. NW&SE | 12W-42N | 10 |
| Butterfield Ln. N&S | 12W-41N | 10 |
| Caledonia Av. NW&SE | 11W-41N | 10 |
| Calvary Ln. N&S | 11W-40N | 10 |
| Carmel Blvd. E&W | 10W-39N,9W-39N | 19 |
| Champart St. E&W | 11W-41N | 10 |
| Clover Ln. N&S | 10W-39N | 19 |
| Daybreak Ln. N&S | 12W-41N | 10 |
| Deborah Av. N&S | 10W-40N | 11 |
| Douglas Dr. E&W | 12W-42N | 10 |
| Cir. | 12W-41N | 10 |
| Dusk Dr. E&W | 12W-41N | 10 |
| Eden Av. N&S | 9W-40N | 11 |
| Edina Blvd. N&S | 9W-39N,9W-40N | 19 |
| Elim Av. N&S | 9W-39N,9W-40N | 19 |
| Elisha Av. N&S | 10W-39N,10W-40N | 19 |
| Elizabeth Av. N&S | 9W-39N,9W-40N | 19 |
| Elijah Av. N&S | 10W-39N,10W-41N | 19 |
| Emmaus Av. N&S | 10W-39N,10W-40N | 19 |
| Enoch Av. N&S | 10W-39N,10W-40N | 19 |
| Eshcol Av. N&S | 10W-39N,10W-40N | 19 |
| Ezekiel Av. N&S | 10W-39N,10W-40N | 19 |
| Ezekiel Pl. N&S | 10W-39N | 19 |
| Ezra Av. N&S | 10W-39N,10W-40N | 19 |
| Fleming Av. N&S | 11W-41N | 10 |
| Franklin Ct. NW&SE | 12W-42N | 10 |
| Franklin St. NW&SE | 12W-42N | 10 |
| Gabriel Av. N&S | 10W-39N,10W-40N | 19 |
| Galilee Av. N&S | 11W-39N,11W-40N | 18 |
| Gideon Av. N&S | 10W-39N,10W-41N | 19 |
| Gilboa Av. N&S | 10W-39N,10W-41N | 19 |
| Gilead Av. N&S | 10W-39N,10W-41N | 19 |
| Gregory Dr. NW&SE | 12W-42N | 10 |
| Hampson Ct. N&S | 11W-40N | 10 |
| Harbor Ridge Dr. NE&SW | 11W-41N | 10 |
| Heather Ct. E&W | 12W-41N | 10 |
| Hebron Av. N&S | 11W-40N,11W-41N | 10 |
| Hermon Av. N&S | 11W-40N,11W-41N | 10 |
| Hillside Av. NE&SW | 9W-41N | 11 |
| Hilltop Av. N&S | 9W-41N | 11 |
| Horeb Av. N&S | 11W-40N | 10 |
| Industrial Av. N&S | 11W-41N | 10 |
| Jethro Av. N&S | 11W-40N,11W-41N | 10 |
| Joanna Av. N&S | 11W-40N,11W-41N | 10 |
| Joppa Av. N&S | 11W-40N,11W-41N | 10 |
| Jordan Av. N&S | 11W-39N,11W-40N | 18 |
| Kebron Blvd. E&W | 10W-41N | 11 |
| Kenosha Rd. N&S | 12W-40N,11W-42N | 10 |
| Kensington Ln. E&W | 10W-41N | 11 |
| Lake View Av. N&S | 9W-41N | 11 |
| Leah Av. N&S | 11W-40N | 10 |
| Lebanon Av. NE&SW | 11W-39N | 18 |
| Lewis Av. N&S | 11W-41N | 10 |
| Lorlei Dr. NE&SW | 12W-42N | 10 |
| Lowery Ct. N&S | 11W-40N | 10 |
| Luckie Ct. NW&SE | 12W-42N | 10 |
| Lydia Av. N&S | 11W-40N,11W-41N | 10 |
| Lydia Pl. N&S | 11W-40N | 10 |
| Mary-Kay Ln. N&S | 10W-39N | 19 |
| Midway Dr. N&S | 12W-41N | 10 |
| Primrose Ct. E&W | 12W-41N | 10 |
| Ravine Av. NS&EW | 11W-41N | 10 |
| Ridge Ct. NW&SE | 12W-41N | 10 |
| Route 173 E&W | 12W-41N,10W-41N | 10 |
| Salem Blvd. E&W | 11W-40N,9W-40N | 10 |
| Schooner Ct. N&S | 11W-41N | 10 |
| Sharon Pl. NS&EW | 10W-39N | 19 |
| Shiloh Blvd. E&W | 10W-40N,9W-40N | 11 |
| Southport Ct. E&W | 11W-41N | 10 |
| Stella Ct. E&W | 11W-40N | 10 |
| Sunshine Ln. NW&SE | 12W-41N | 10 |
| Tallgrass Ct. E&W | 12W-42N | 10 |
| Thistle Ln. E&W | 12W-42N | 10 |
| Thompson Av. N&S | 10W-39N | 19 |
| Timothy St. NW&SE | 12W-42N | 10 |
| Wembly Dr. NE&SW | 11W-41N | 10 |
| Willow Ln. E&W | 11W-41N | 10 |
| Wilson Ct. E&W | 10W-41N,9W-41N | 11 |
| Winthrop Ct. E&W | 9W-41N | 11 |
| Winthrop Harbor Rd. E&W | 12W-42N | 10 |
| Yale Ct. E&W | 10W-39N | 19 |
| 15th St. E&W | 11W-41N | 10 |
| 16th St. E&W | 12W-41N,11W-41N | 10 |
| 17th St. E&W | 11W-41N,9W-41N | 10 |
| 18th St. E&W | 11W-41N,9W-41N | 10 |
| 19th St. E&W | 11W-41N,9W-41N | 10 |
| 20th St. E&W | 11W-41N,9W-41N | 10 |
| 21st St. E&W | 11W-41N,9W-41N | 10 |
| 22nd St. E&W | 11W-40N,9W-40N | 10 |
| 23rd St. E&W | 11W-40N,9W-40N | 10 |
| 24th St. E&W | 11W-40N,9W-40N | 10 |
| 25th St. E&W | 11W-40N | 10 |
| 26th St. E&W | 11W-40N,9W-40N | 11 |
| 27th St. E&W | 12W-40N,9W-40N | 10 |
| 28th St. E&W | 10W-40N,9W-40N | 11 |
| 29th St. E&W | 11W-40W,9W-40N | 10 |
| 30th St. E&W | 11W-39N,9W-39N | 18 |
| 31st St. E&W | 11W-39N,9W-39N | 18 |
| 32nd St. E&W | 11W-39N | 18 |
| 33rd St. E&W | 11W-39N,10W-39N | 18 |
| 34th St. E&W | 10W-39N | 19 |

# McHenry County

N

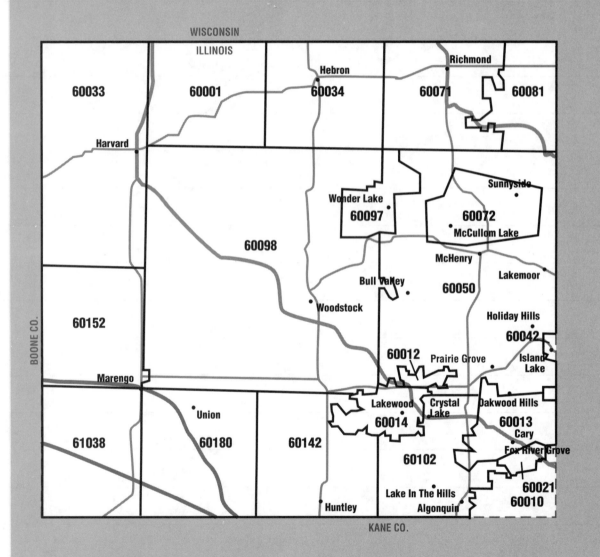

WISCONSIN

ILLINOIS

Richmond

Hebron

60033

60001

60034

60071

60081

Harvard

Sunnyside

Wonder Lake

60097

60072

McCullom Lake

60098

McHenry

Lakemoor

Bull Valley

60050

Woodstock

Holiday Hills

60042

BOONE CO.

60152

60012

Prairie Grove

Island Lake

Marengo

Lakewood

Crystal Lake

Oakwood Hills

Union

60014

60013

60042

Cary

61038

60180

60142

60102

Fox River Grove

Lake In The Hills

60021

60010

Huntley

Algonquin

KANE CO.

# McHenry County

## StreetFinder®

page  **Contents**

A    Using the StreetFinder

B    PageFinder Map

C    Vicinity Map

1    Contents

2    Quick Reference Guide

4    StreetFinder Maps

52    StreetFinder Index

Photo credit: by Don Peasley 388 Lincoln Ave. Woodstock IL

PageFinder™ Map U.S. Patent No. 5,419,586.

Information included in this publication has been checked for accuracy prior to publication. Since changes do occur, the publisher cannot be responsible for any variations from the information printed.

## McHenry County Municipal Offices

| | Location | Page |
|---|---|---|
| Algonquin Village Hall | 33W-20N | 50 |
| Cary Village Hall | 31W-23N | 43 |
| Crystal Lake City Hall | 35W-26N | 42 |
| Grafton Twp Office | 40W-21N | 48 |
| Grafton Twp Village Hall | 37W-25N | 41 |
| Hartland Twp Office | 44W-34N | 23 |
| Lake In The Hills Village Hall | 35W-22N | 50 |
| Marengo Twp Office | 49W-28N | 29 |
| Marengo Village Hall | 49W-26N | 37 |
| McHenry Twp City Hall | 32W-33N | 26,27 |
| Nunda Twp Village Hall | 36W-30N | 33 |
| Nunda Twp Village Hall | 32W-28N | 34 |
| Richmond Village Hall | 34W-41N | 10 |
| Woodstock County Couthouse | 41W-32N | 24 |

## Cemeteries

| | Location | Page |
|---|---|---|
| Alden Cem | 45W-41N | 7 |
| Big Foot Cem | 49W-43N | 6 |
| Brandon Cem | 44W-41N | 7 |
| Calvary Cem | 42W-31N | 24 |
| Cedarvale Cem | 32W-39N | 10,11 |
| Chemung Cem | 52W-38N | 12 |
| Chemung-Dunham Cem | 53W-37N | 12 |
| Christ The King Cem | 36W-36N | 17 |
| Crystal Lake Mem Park Cem | 36W-27N | 33 |
| Eckert Cem | 40W-34N | 24 |
| English Prairie Cem | 29W-41N | 11 |
| First Street Cem | 30W-23N | 43 |
| Greenwood Cem | 38W-35N | 17 |
| Harmony Cem | 46W-20N | 46 |
| Hebron Cem | 40W-41N | 8 |
| Holcombville Cem | 35W-29N | 34 |
| Jerome Cem | 49W-37N | 13 |
| Lawrence Cem | 52W-39N | 4 |
| Linn-Hebron Cem | 42W-43N | 8 |
| Marengo City Cem | 49W-26N | 37 |
| McHenry County Cem | 45W-34N | 23 |
| McMillian Cem | 33W-29N | 34 |
| Mosgrove Cem | 32W-30N | 34,35 |
| Mt Auburn Cem | 49W-37N | 13 |
| Mt Thabor Cem | 39W-26N | 40,41 |
| North Solon Cem | 32W-40N | 10,11 |
| Oakland Cem | 42W-31N | 24 |
| Opfergelt Cem | 43W-32N | 23 |
| Orvis Cem | 29W-41N | 11 |
| Ostend Cem | 35W-34N | 26 |
| Prairie Grove Cem | 31W-27N | 34 |
| Richmond Cem | 34W-42N | 10 |
| Ridgefield Cem | 37W-27N | 33 |
| Ringwood Cem | 34W-36N | 18 |
| Sacred Heart Cem | 50W-27N | 29 |
| Scandinavian Cem | 41W-34N | 24 |
| Scottish Cem | 49W-28N | 30 |
| South Dunham Cem | 50W-33N | 21 |
| St John's Cem | 31W-35N | 19 |
| St John's Cem | 32W-22N | 50,51 |

| | Location | Page |
|---|---|---|
| St Joseph's Cem | 49W-37N | 13 |
| St Joseph's Cem | 34W-43N | 10 |
| St Mary's Cem | 40W-20N | 48 |
| St Mary's Cem | 32W-33N | 26,27 |
| St Patrick's Cem | 43,44W-35N | 15 |
| St Patrick's Countryside Cem | 32W-31N | 26,27 |
| Stewart Cem | 39W-39N | 8,9 |
| Union Cem | 47W-25N | 38 |
| Union Cem | 35W-26N | 42 |
| Unity Church Cem | 54W-34N | 20 |
| Washington Cem | 32W-42N | 10,11 |
| Windridge Cem | 29W-24N | 43 |
| Woodland Cem | 32W-33N | 26,27 |
| Woodstock Mem Cem | 40W-29N | 32 |

## Colleges & Universities

| | Location | Page |
|---|---|---|
| McHenry County Col | 37W-27N | 33 |

## Forest Preserves

| | Location | Page |
|---|---|---|
| Beck Woods FP | 53W-38N | 12 |
| Borrow Woods FP | 49W-36N | 14 |
| Butternut Preserve | 38W-25N | 41 |
| Chain O'Lakes State Park | 29W-40N | 11 |
| Coral Woods FP | 48W-24N | 38 |
| Deep Cut Marsh | 46W-33N | 22,23 |
| Farm Hills Acres | 36W-24N | 41 |
| Harrison Benwell | 35W-35N | 18 |
| Hickory Grove FP | 29W-25N | 43 |
| Indian Ridge FP | 31,32W-29N | 34,35 |
| Lake in the Hills FP | 35W-22N | 50 |
| Marengo Ridge | 49W-29N | 30 |
| Marie Gundstrom Nat Area | 37W-38N | 17 |
| McHenry Co. Cons. District FP | 34W-38N | 18 |
| Moraine Hills State Park | 31,30W-31N | 27 |
| Ryders Woods FP | 41W-30N | 32 |
| The Hollows FP | 32W-24,25N | 42,43 |
| Volo Bog FP | 29W-34N | 27 |
| Weers Nature Area | 42,41W-27N | 32 |

## Golf Courses & Country Clubs

| | Location | Page |
|---|---|---|
| Cary CC | 31W-22N | 51 |
| Chalet Hills GC | 30W-26N | 43 |
| Crystal Lake CC | 36W-24N | 41 |
| Crystal Woods GC | 40W-26,25N | 40 |
| Hunter CC | 34W-42N | 10 |
| Lakewood GC | 38W-24N | 41 |
| McHenry CC | 32W-32N | 26,27 |
| Pinecrest GC | 40W-21N | 48 |
| Pistakee GC | 29W-34N | 27 |
| Twin Ponds GC | 33W24N | 42 |
| Woodstock CC | 39W-30N | 32,33 |

## Shopping Centers

| | Location | Page |
|---|---|---|
| Country Corner Plaza | 35W-25N | 42 |
| Crystal Lake Plaza | 35W-25N | 42 |
| Crystal Point Mall | 34W-25N | 42 |
| Manchester Mall | 33W-33N | 26 |
| McHenry Market Place | 33W-33N | 26 |
| Somerset Mall | 33W-33N | 26 |

# McHenry County Close-up

## Woodstock Opera Company

121 Van Buren Street, Woodstock

Constructed in 1890, this facility offers a mixed program of dance, theater, opera, lectures and art exhibits. It is also home to two resident performance companies, Town Square Players and Woodstock Musical Theater Company. Special events include an annual Mozart Festival. Designed in the architectural style of Steamboat Gothic, this structure is listed with the National Register of Historic Places. Open all year.

## Antique Village Museum & Wild West Town

8512 S. Union Road, Union

This unique site covers 20 acres and consists of a museum and a re-created western town. The museum displays war relics and numerous antique music boxes and phonographs. Wild west town features a replica of a turn-of-the-century street, replete with saloon, blacksmith, sheriff's office and print shop. An old time movie theater shows vintage films. Pony rides and train tours available. Children encouraged to pan for gold.

## McHenry County Historical Museum

6422 Main Street, Union

This comprehensive museum honors the history of McHenry County. On the premises are a one-room schoolhouse built in 1895, a log cabin constructed in 1847, and a tourist cabin built in 1948. Collections include clothing, looms, quilts, toys and farm tools. There is also a research library. Open to the public May through October.

## Illinois Railway Museum

7000 Olson Rd., Union

Visit one of the country's major museums for railway history. Set on 56 acres, this site features a depot constructed in 1851, a restored elevated station, a 1910 signal tower and 300 pieces of historic railway equipment. Vintage trains include several steam and diesel-powered locomotives and a 1936 stainless steel Nebraska Zephyr. Visitors can ride trains and tour the seven large storage barns that house many of the trains. Seasonal.

## Colonel Palmer House

5516 S. Terra Cotta Rd., Crystal Lake

This charming two-story house was built in 1858 for Colonel Gustavus Parker. A fine example of Greek Revival architecture, this dwelling features original furnishings including a vintage piano. Open by appointment.

## Dole Mansion

401 Country Club Rd., Crystal Lake

This handsome dwelling was built for grain merchant Charles Dole in the 1860's. Constructed from imported lumber, this distinctive home includes parquet floors and hand-carved banisters. Open by appointment.

## Moraine Hills State Park

914 S. River Rd., McHenry

This beautiful outdoor getaway covers 1,700 acres of rolling hills and wetlands. The area includes picnic shelters, two nature preserves and several miles of multi-purpose trails. Fox River and three lakes are available for fishing and boating. McHenry Dam is on the premises. No overnight camping. Open all year.

## Chester Gould-Dick Tracy Memorial Museum

101 N. Johnson St., Woodstock

This site honors Chester Gould, creator of one of America's most cherished cartoon characters, Dick Tracy. A Woodstock resident for some fifty years, Gould's syndicated cartoon strip entertained millions of readers. Exhibits includes sketches, storyboards, life-sized figures and other memorabilia. The artist's desk and chair are displayed. Also, the museum holds an annual Dick Tracy Days Parade. Located in historic courthouse building.

## Landmark School

3614 W. Waukegan St., McHenry

Revisit the past at this school building built in 1894. Constructed from local materials, this historic structure remains the area's oldest active school. A registered city landmark.

## Glacial Park

6512 Harts Rd., Ringwood

Nature at its best! Hundreds of acres of glacial sand, wetlands, prairies and marshes. A boardwalk provides visitors with a breathtaking view of the Nippersink valley. Intrepretive staff available for lectures, workshops and nature programs. Abundant wildlife.

## The Hollows

off Rte. 14, between Crystal Lake and Cary,

This unusual terrain, with its large sand and gravel content, features trails for both hiking and cross-country skiing. The area also includes campsites, shelters and play areas for children. Lake Atwood is available for non-motorized boating.

## Rush Creek Conservation Area

Rte. 14 to Harvard, E on McGuire Rd., Harvard

Not just another conservation area, this unique site consists of flood plain, meadows and upland forest. It is available for a wide range of activities including hiking, fishing, cross-country skiing, skating, ice fishing and horseback riding. Campsites and picnic shelters are on the premises.

## America's Cardboard Cup Regatta

Main Beach, 300 Lake Shore Drive, Crystal Lake

This whimsical one-day event delights visitors every year. Crews of up to twelve individuals race in boats made from corrugated cardboard. Proceeds go to charity. June.

## Crystal Lake Gala & Lakeside Festival

401 Country Club Rd., Crystal Lake

This two-weekend festival features a parade, fireworks, live entertainment, a golf touament, beer garden and a carnival. The Cardboard Cup Regatta is the centerpiece event. Proceeds go to charity. June.

## Illinois Storytelling Festival

Spring Grove Village Park, Spring Grove

Experience an art form rich in folk lore. This major one-day event hosts some of America's most accomplished storytellers. Other highlights include old time music. Last weekend in July.

## McHenry County Fair

County Fairgrounds, Woodstock

Fun for all ages! This major event includes carnival rides, special programs for children and various livestock shows. Also, the fair holds a Miss McHenry County Contest. Food and concessions. August.

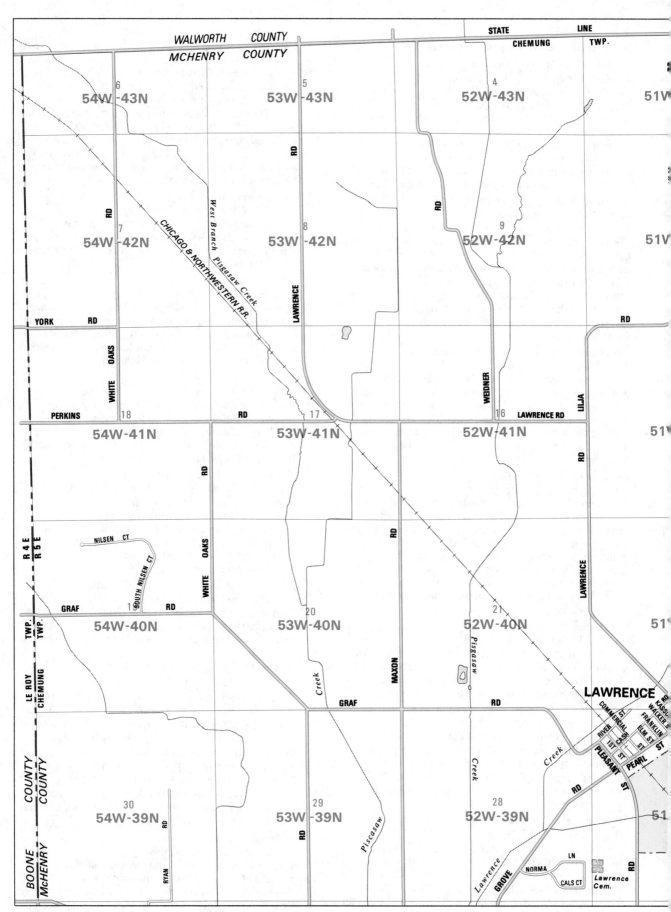

WALWORTH   COUNTY

MCHENRY   COUNTY

STATE   LINE

CHEMUNG   TWP.

6
**54W-43N**

5
**53W-43N**

4
**52W-43N**

**51W**

RD

West Branch Pisgasaw Creek

RD

CHICAGO & NORTHWESTERN R.R.

RD

7
**54W-42N**

8
**53W-42N**

9
**52W-42N**

**51W**

LAWRENCE

YORK   RD

RD

WHITE   OAKS

WEIDNER

LILJA

PERKINS   18   RD   17   16   LAWRENCE RD

**54W-41N**

**53W-41N**

**52W-41N**

**51W**

RD

RD

R 4 E
R 5 E

NILSEN   CT

SOUTH NILSEN CT

WHITE   OAKS

RD

LAWRENCE

GRAF   19   RD   20   RD   21

**54W-40N**

**53W-40N**

**52W-40N**

**51W**

Creek

MAXON

Pisgasaw

LE ROY   TWP.
CHEMUNG   TWP.

GRAF   RD   RD

**LAWRENCE**

Pisgasaw

Creek

COMMERCIAL ST

KASSU
WALKER S

FRANKLIN

RIVER ST

ELM ST

1ST ST

CASH ST

PEARL

Creek

PLEASANT ST

30
**54W-39N**

29
**53W-39N**

28
**52W-39N**

**51**

RYAN   RD

RD

Pisgasaw

GROVE

RD

Lawrence

NORMA   LN

CALS CT

Lawrence
Cem.

BOONE   COUNTY
McHENRY   COUNTY

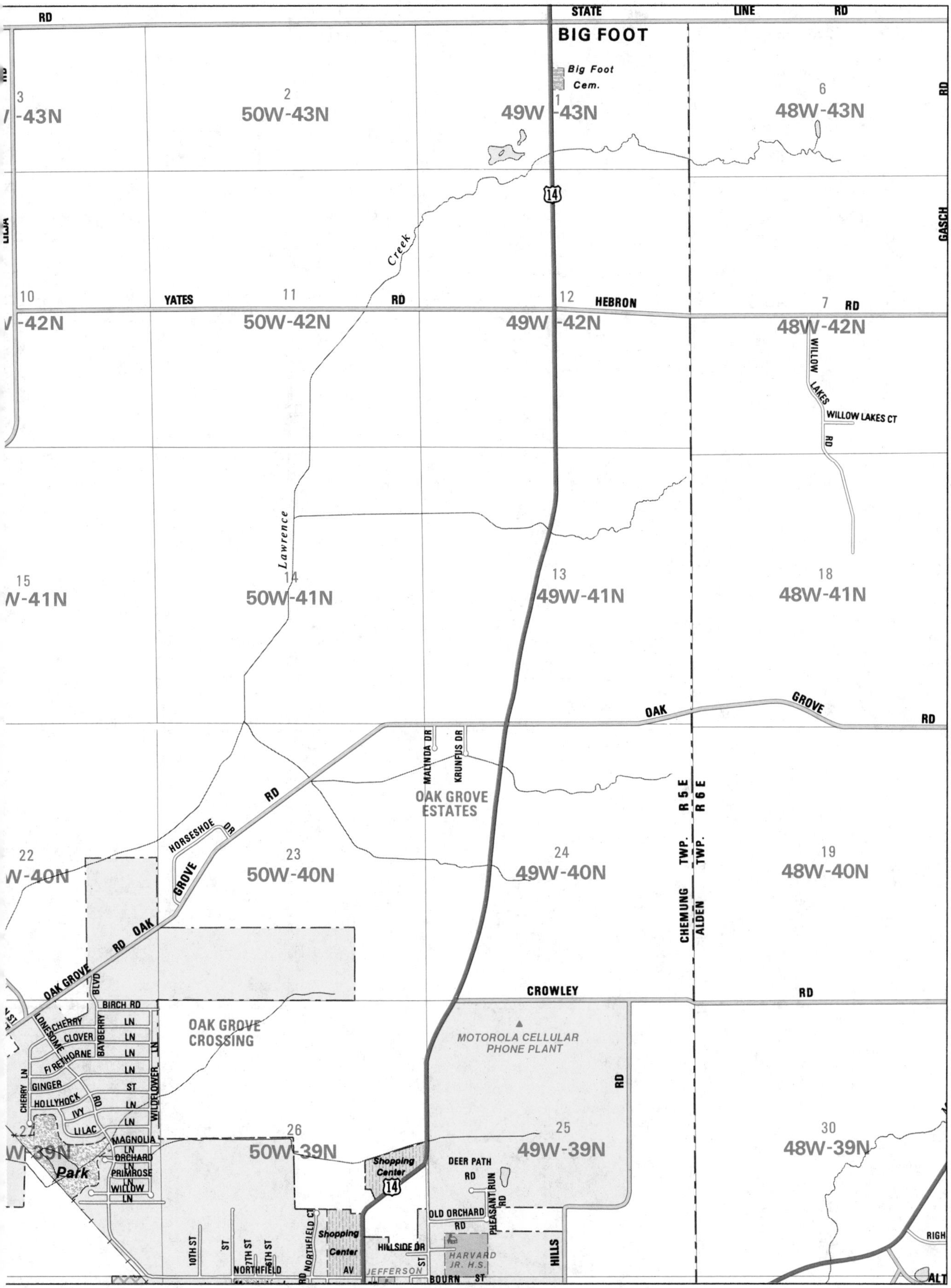

RD

STATE LINE RD

**BIG FOOT**

Big Foot
Cem.

3
-43N

2
50W-43N

1
49W-43N

6
48W-43N

RD

14

GASCH

Creek

10
-42N

YATES

11
50W-42N

RD

12
49W-42N

HEBRON

7 RD
48W-42N

WILLOW LAKES

WILLOW LAKES CT

RD

15
N-41N

Lawrence

14
50W-41N

13
49W-41N

18
48W-41N

OAK GROVE RD

SEE PAGES 6-7

MALINDA DR

KRUNFUS DR

OAK GROVE
ESTATES

HORSESHOE DR

GROVE RD

RD

CHEMUNG TWP. R 5 E
ALDEN TWP. R 6 E

22
W-40N

23
50W-40N

24
49W-40N

19
48W-40N

OAK GROVE RD OAK

BLVD

BIRCH RD

CROWLEY RD

CHERRY LN
LONESOME
CLOVER LN
BAYBERRY LN
FIRETHORNE LN
GINGER ST
HOLLYHOCK LN
IVY LN
LILAC LN
WILDFLOWER LN

OAK GROVE
CROSSING

MOTOROLA CELLULAR
PHONE PLANT

RD

CHERRY LN

MAGNOLIA LN
ORCHARD LN
PRIMROSE LN
WILLOW LN

W-39N

Park

26
50W-39N

Shopping
Center
14

DEER PATH
RD

25
49W-39N

PHEASANT RUN RD

30
48W-39N

10TH ST
7TH ST
6TH ST
NORTHFIELD

NORTHFIELD CT

Shopping
Center
AV
JEFFERSON

HILLSIDE DR

OLD ORCHARD
RD

BOURN ST

HARVARD
JR. H.S.

HILLS

RIGH

ALT

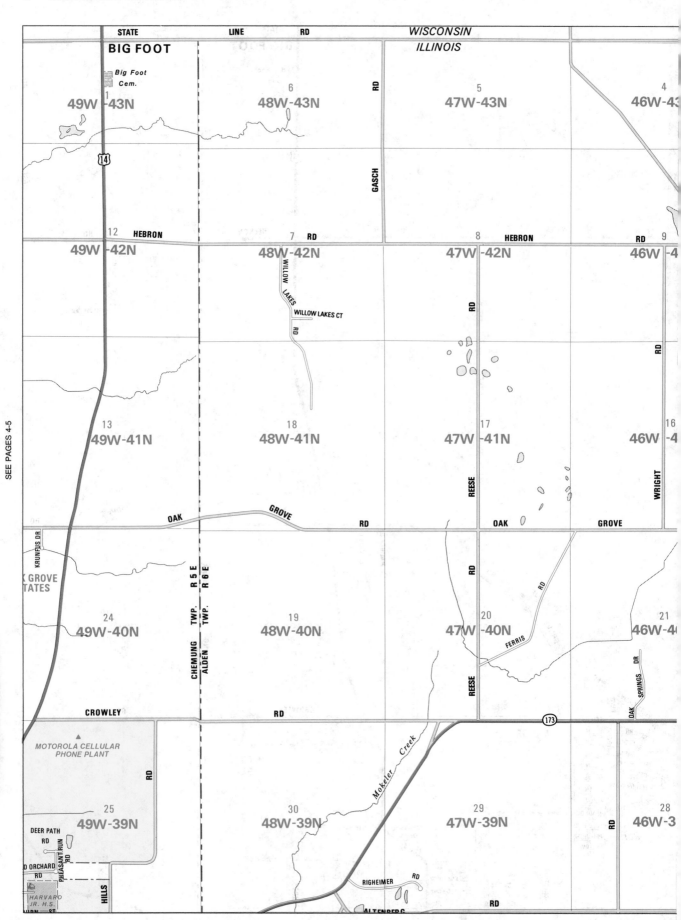

STATE        LINE        RD        WISCONSIN
                                   ILLINOIS

BIG FOOT

Big Foot
Cem.

1
49W -43N

6
48W-43N

RD

5
47W-43N

4
46W-43

U.S. 14

GASCH

12  HEBRON
49W -42N

7  RD
48W-42N

WILLOW  LAKES
WILLOW LAKES CT
RD

8  HEBRON
47W -42N

RD  9
46W-4

RD

13
49W-41N

18
48W-41N

17
47W -41N

16
46W-4

REESE

WRIGHT

SEE PAGES 4-5

OAK        GROVE        RD

OAK        GROVE

KRUNFUS DR

K GROVE
TATES

R 5 E
R 6 E

RD

RD

24
49W-40N

CHEMUNG TWP.
ALDEN TWP.

19
48W-40N

20
47W -40N

FERRIS

21
46W-4

OAK SPRINGS DR

REESE

CROWLEY        RD

RD  173

MOTOROLA CELLULAR
PHONE PLANT

RD

Mokeler Creek

25
49W-39N

DEER PATH
RD

PHEASANT RUN
RD

D ORCHARD
RD

HARVARD
JR. H.S.
URN  ST

HILLS

30
48W-39N

RIGHEIMER        RD

ALTENBERG

29
47W-39N

RD

RD

28
46W-3

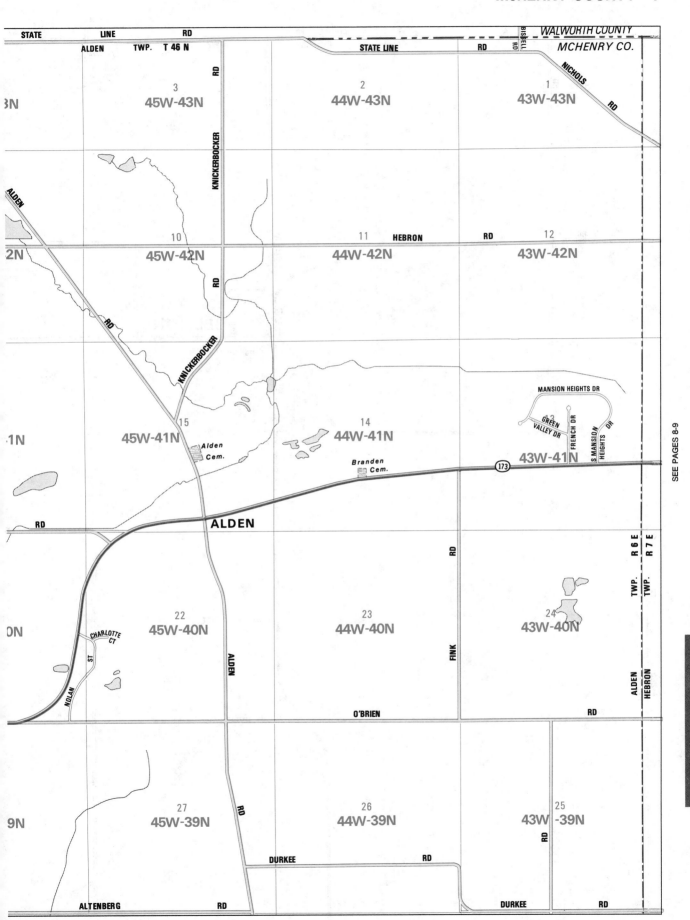

STATE    LINE    RD    WALWORTH COUNTY
ALDEN    TWP.    T 46 N    STATE LINE    RD    MCHENRY CO.

NICHOLS    RD

3
45W-43N

2
44W-43N

1
43W-43N

KNICKERBOCKER    RD

10
45W-42N

11    HEBRON    RD
44W-42N

12
43W-42N

KNICKERBOCKER    RD

MANSION HEIGHTS DR

GREEN VALLEY DR    13
FRENCH DR
S MANSION HEIGHTS DR

15
45W-41N

Alden Cem.

14
44W-41N

Branden Cem.

43W-41N

173

RD    ALDEN

R 6 E    R 7 E
TWP.    TWP.

CHARLOTTE CT
NOLAN ST

22
45W-40N

ALDEN

23
44W-40N

FINK    RD

24
43W-40N

ALDEN
HEBRON

O'BRIEN    RD

27
45W-39N

RD

26
44W-39N

25
43W-39N

RD

DURKEE    RD    RD

ALTENBERG    RD    DURKEE    RD

SEE PAGES 8-9

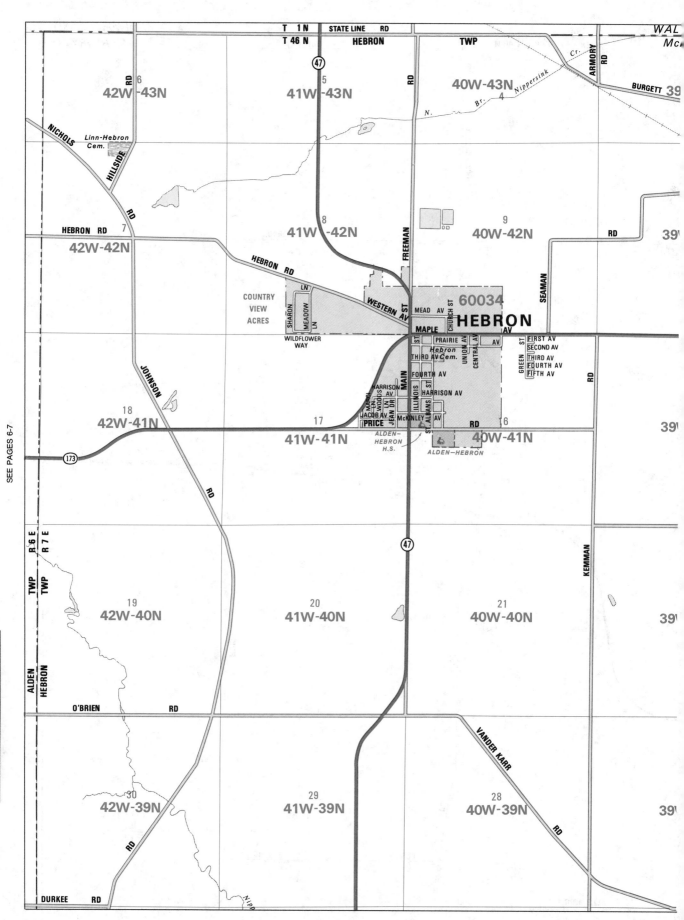

SEE PAGES 6-7

T 1 N  STATE LINE  RD

T 46 N  HEBRON  TWP

WAL
Mc

**42W-43N** 6

**41W-43N** 5

**40W-43N** Nippersink
N. Br. 4 Nippersink

BURGETT 39

ARMORY RD
Cr.

NICHOLS

Linn-Hebron Cem.

HILLSIDE RD

HEBRON RD 7

**42W-42N**

**41W-42N** 8

FREEMAN ST

**40W-42N** 9

SEAMAN

RD

39

HEBRON RD

COUNTRY VIEW ACRES

LN
SHARON
MEADOW LN

WILDFLOWER WAY

WESTERN AV

MEAD AV
CHURCH ST

60034

**HEBRON**

AV

MAPLE ST

PRAIRIE AV
UNION AV
CENTRAL AV

GREEN ST

FIRST AV
SECOND AV
THIRD AV
FOURTH AV
FIFTH AV

RD

JOHNSON RD

Hebron Cem.
THIRD AV

FOURTH AV

MAIN ST

ILLINOIS ST

HARRISON AV

**18**
**42W-41N**

HARRISON AV
MARIE
WOODS LN
JEAN DR
JACOB AV

**17**
**41W-41N**

PRICE
McKINLEY

ST ALBANS AV

ALDEN—
HEBRON
H.S.

16
RD
**40W-41N**

ALDEN—HEBRON

39

173

R 6 E TWP
R 7 E TWP

**19**
**42W-40N**

**20**
**41W-40N**

47

**21**
**40W-40N**

KEMMAN

39

ALDEN
HEBRON

O'BRIEN RD

VANDER KARR RD

**30**
**42W-39N**

**29**
**41W-39N**

**28**
**40W-39N**

RD

39

DURKEE RD

RD

N

SEE PAGES 16-17

WORTH CO  WISCONSIN

HENRY CO  ILLINOIS

| 3 | 2 | 1 | 6 |
|---|---|---|---|
| W-43N | 38W-43N | 37W-43N | 36W-43N |

RD

BURGETT  RD  BURGETT  RD

RD

| 10 | 11 | 12 | 7 |
|---|---|---|---|
| N-42N | 38W-42N | 37W-42N | 36W-42N |

KEYSTONE

*CHICAGO MILWAUKEE ST. PAUL & PACIFIC R.R.*

LANGE

(173)

| 15 | 14 | 13 | 18 |
|---|---|---|---|
| N-41N | 38W-41N | 37W-41N | 36W-41N |

RD

NORGARD  RD

RD

OKESON  RD

| 22 | 23 | 24 | 19 |
|---|---|---|---|
| N-40N | 38W-40N | 37W-40N | 36W-40N |

RD

GREENWOOD

TWP  TWP

HEBRON  RICHMOND

KEYSTONE

REGNIER  RD

R 7 E  R 8 E

| 27 | 26 | 25 | 30 |
|---|---|---|---|
| N-39N | 38W-39N | 37W-39N | 36W-39N |

STEWART

RD

Stewart Cem.

VANDER KARR  RD

TRYON  GROVE  RD

BARNARD

PRIVATE

SEE PAGES 10-11

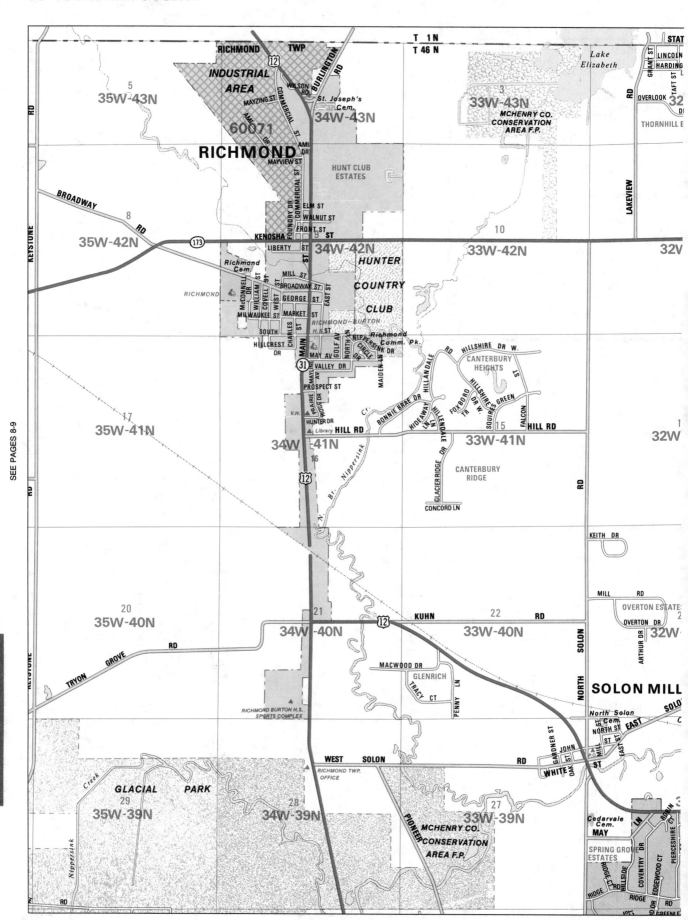

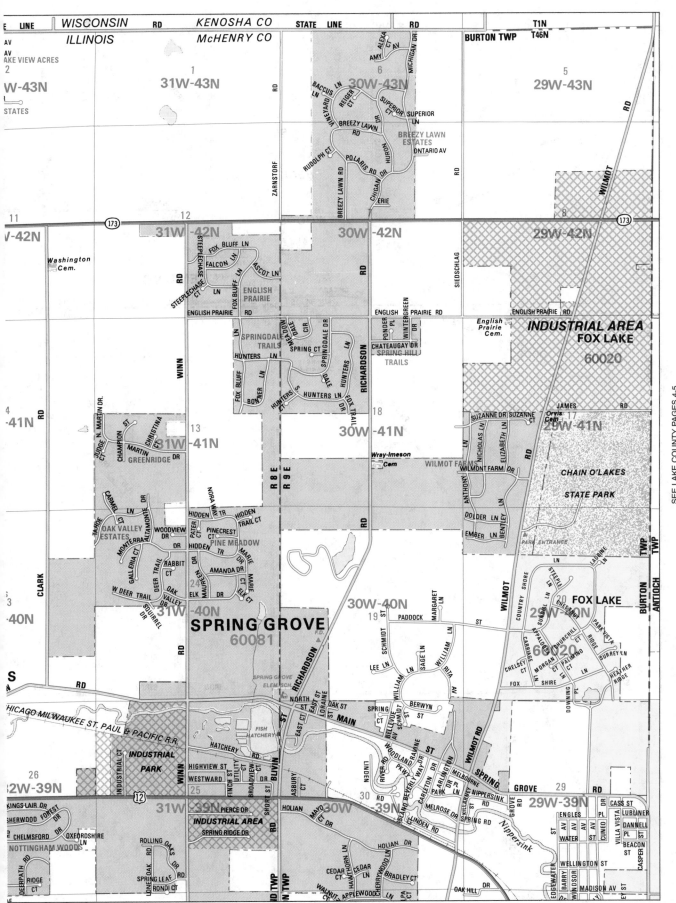

SEE LAKE COUNTY PAGES 4-5

SEE PAGES 4-5

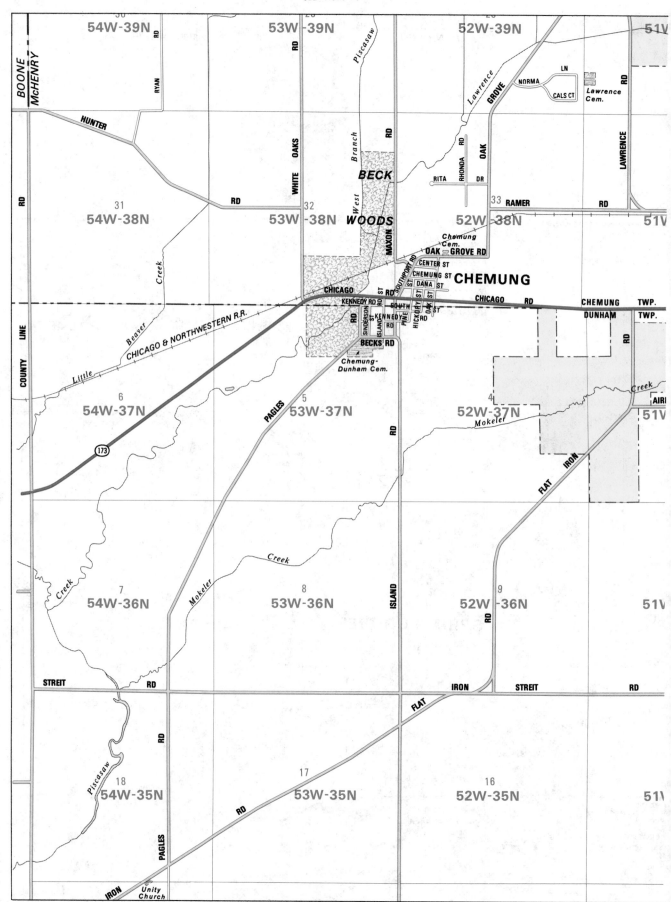

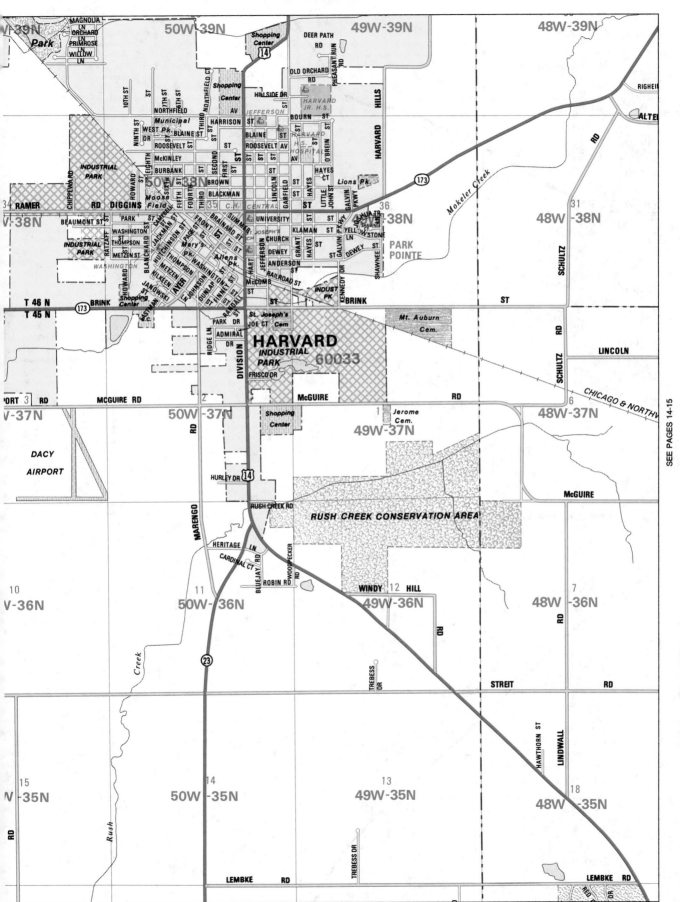

SEE PAGES 6-7

**49W-39N**

**48W-39N**

**47W-39N**

**46W-39**

DEER PATH RD

PHEASANT RUN RD

ORCHARD RD

HARVARD JR. H.S.

RIGHEIMER RD

ALTENBERG

RD

HARVARD HILLS

BURN ST

HARVARD S. SPITAL

O'BRIEN ST

GREEN

SHIELDS

RD

HAYES CT

HAYES ST

LITTLE JOHN ST

GALVIN PKWY

Lions Pk.

173

Mokeler Creek

36

**49W-38N**

SHAWNEE

W STONE

NESHUA TR

**48W-38N**

31

RD

32

**47W-38N**

**46W-38**

33

GREE

AMAN ST

YELL LN

HAYES ST

GALVIN

DEWEY ST

SHAWNEE

**PARK POINTE**

SCHULTZ

KENNEDY DR

INDUST PK

BRINK ST

ST

Mt. Auburn Cem.

**ARD AL**
**60033**

SCHULTZ RD

SCHULTZ

LINCOLN RD

McGUIRE

RD

CHICAGO & NORTHWESTERN R.R.

6

**48W-37N**

5

**47W-37N**

LN

4

**46W-37**

1

Jerome Cem.

**49W-37N**

SEE PAGES 12-13

IRISH

**RUSH CREEK CONSERVATION AREA**

McGUIRE RD

BARTLETT'S COUNTRYSIDE ACRES

COUNTRYSIDE LN

RD

WINDY 12 HILL

**49W-36N**

RD

7

**48W-36N**

RD

8

**47W-36N**

KING

9

**46W-36**

TREBESS DR

STREIT RD

RD

HAWTHORN ST

LINDWALL

13

**49W-35N**

18

**48W-35N**

17

**47W-35N**

RD

16

**46W-35**

TREBESS DR

LEMBKE RD

RED

DR

SEE PAGES 22-23

SEE PAGES 16-17

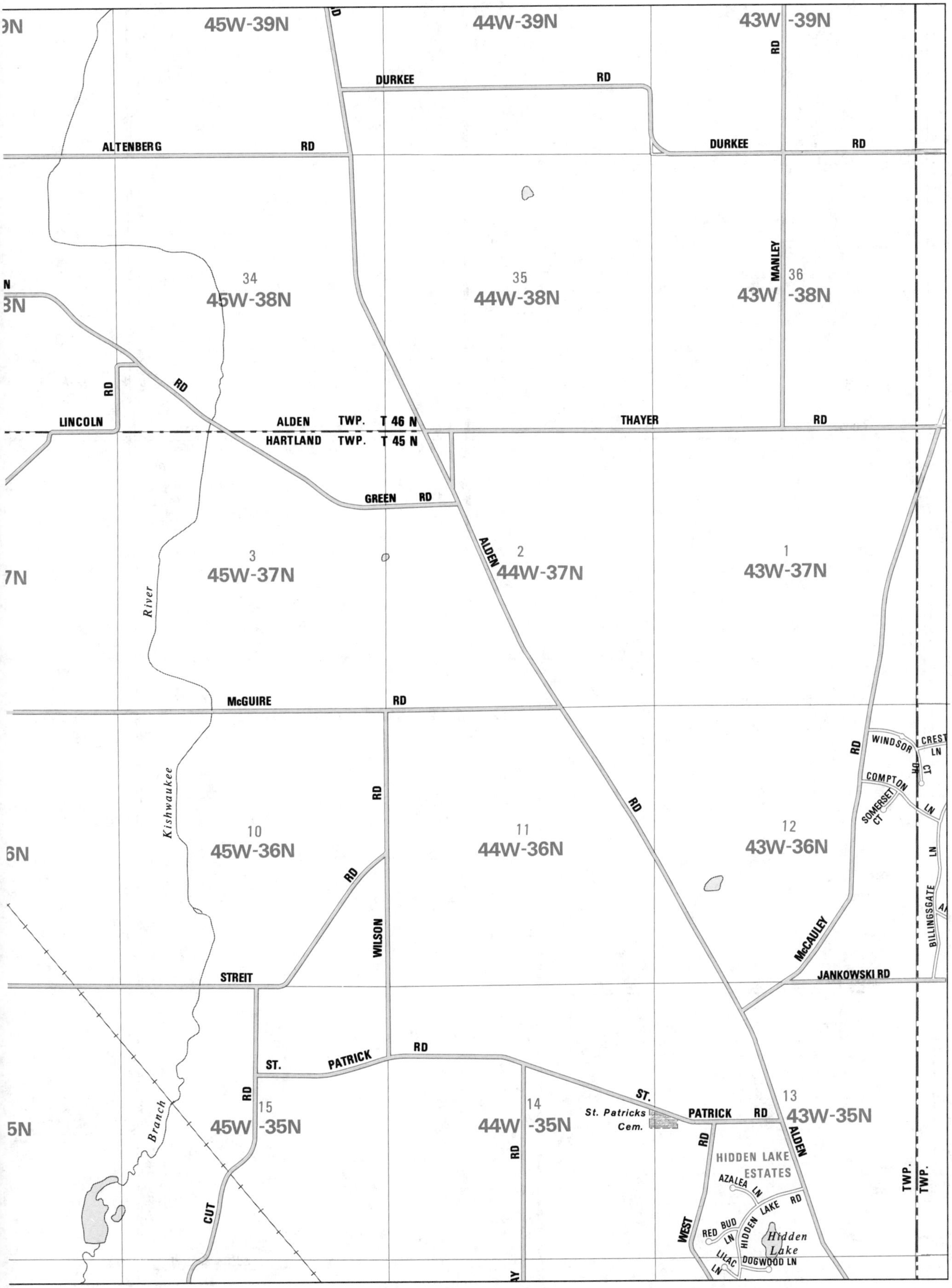

45W-39N

44W-39N

43W-39N

DURKEE RD

ALTENBERG RD

DURKEE RD

MANLEY

34
45W-38N

35
44W-38N

36
43W-38N

RD

RD

LINCOLN

ALDEN TWP. T 46 N

THAYER RD

HARTLAND TWP. T 45 N

GREEN RD

ALDEN

*River*

3
45W-37N

2
44W-37N

1
43W-37N

McGUIRE RD

RD

WINDSOR CREST LN

CT

COMPTON LN

SOMERSET CT

*Kishwaukee*

RD

10
45W-36N

11
44W-36N

12
43W-36N

BILLINGSGATE LN

WILSON

McCAULEY

STREIT

JANKOWSKI RD

ST. PATRICK RD

RD

*Branch*

15
45W-35N

14
44W-35N

ST.

PATRICK RD

St. Patricks Cem.

13
43W-35N

ALDEN

RD

HIDDEN LAKE ESTATES

AZALEA LN

WEST

RED BUD LN

HIDDEN LAKE

LILAC LN

*Hidden Lake*

DOGWOOD LN

CUT

RD

TWP.
TWP.

SEE PAGES 8-9

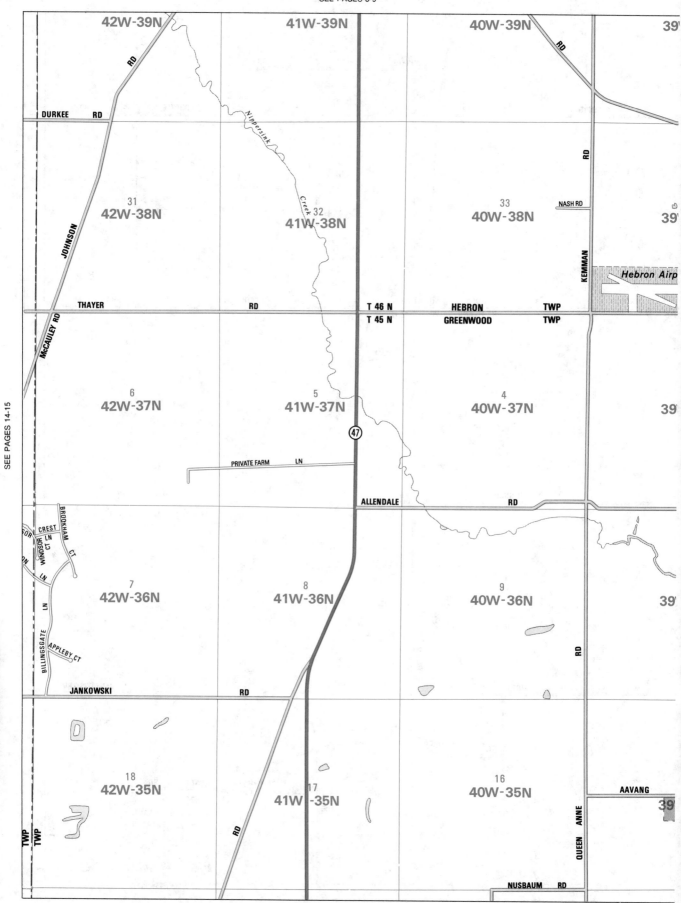

42W-39N

41W-39N

40W-39N

39

RD

DURKEE RD

Nippersink

Creek

JOHNSON

31
42W-38N

32
41W-38N

33
40W-38N

39

NASH RD

KEMMAN

RD

Hebron Airp

THAYER RD

McCAULEY RD

T 46 N
T 45 N

HEBRON TWP
GREENWOOD TWP

6
42W-37N

5
41W-37N

4
40W-37N

39

(47)

PRIVATE FARM LN

SEE PAGES 14-15

ALLENDALE RD

BROOKHAM CT

WINDSOR CREST LN
CT LN

SOR

ON

LN

LN

BILLINGSGATE LN

APPLEBY CT

7
42W-36N

8
41W-36N

9
40W-36N

39

RD

JANKOWSKI RD

18
42W-35N

17
41W-35N

16
40W-35N

AAVANG

39

QUEEN ANNE

RD

TWP
TWP

RD

NUSBAUM RD

SEE PAGES 24-25

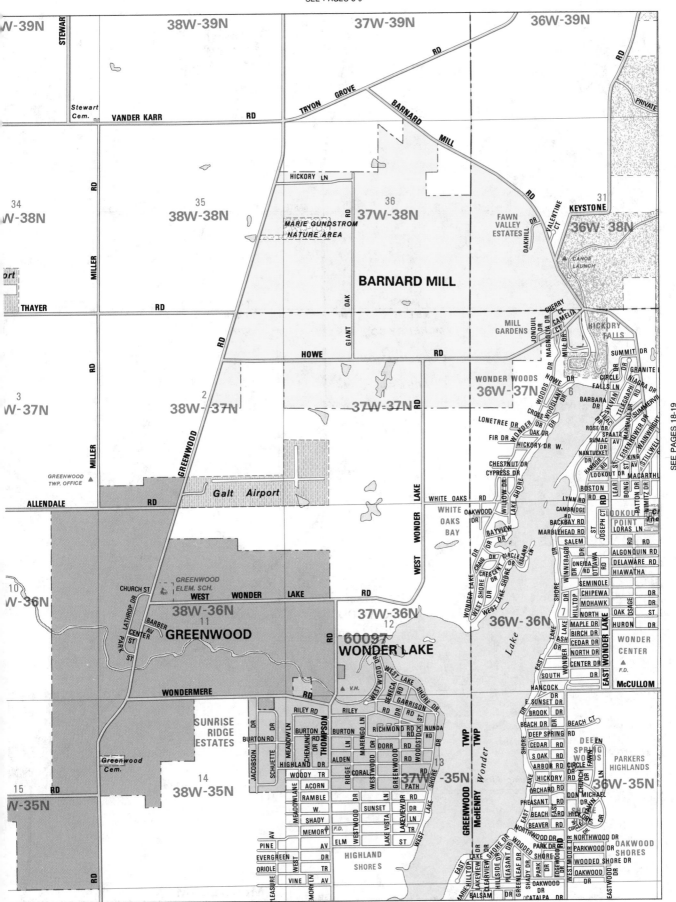

SEE PAGES 10-11

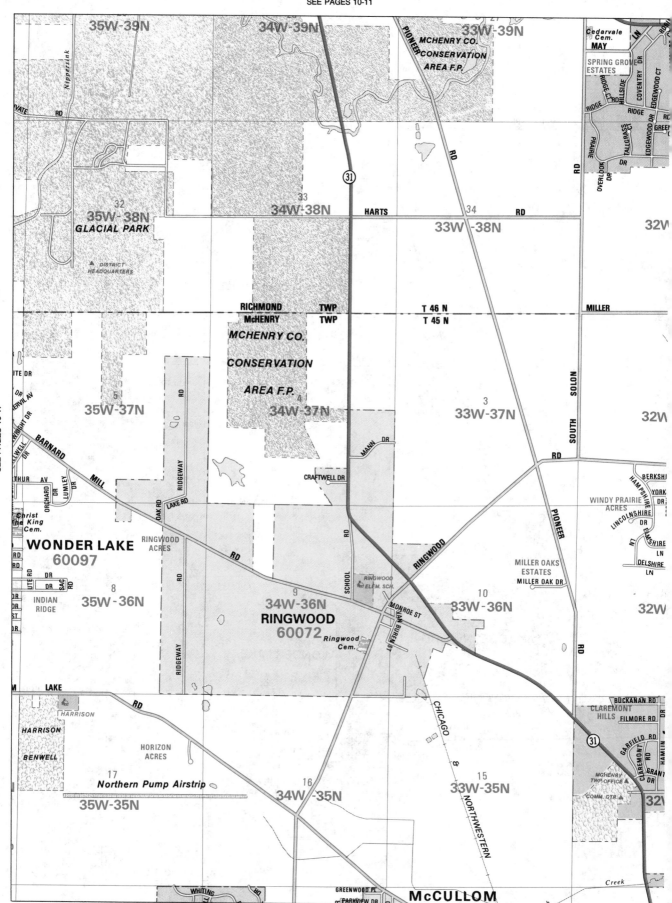

SEE PAGES 16-17

SEE PAGES 10-11

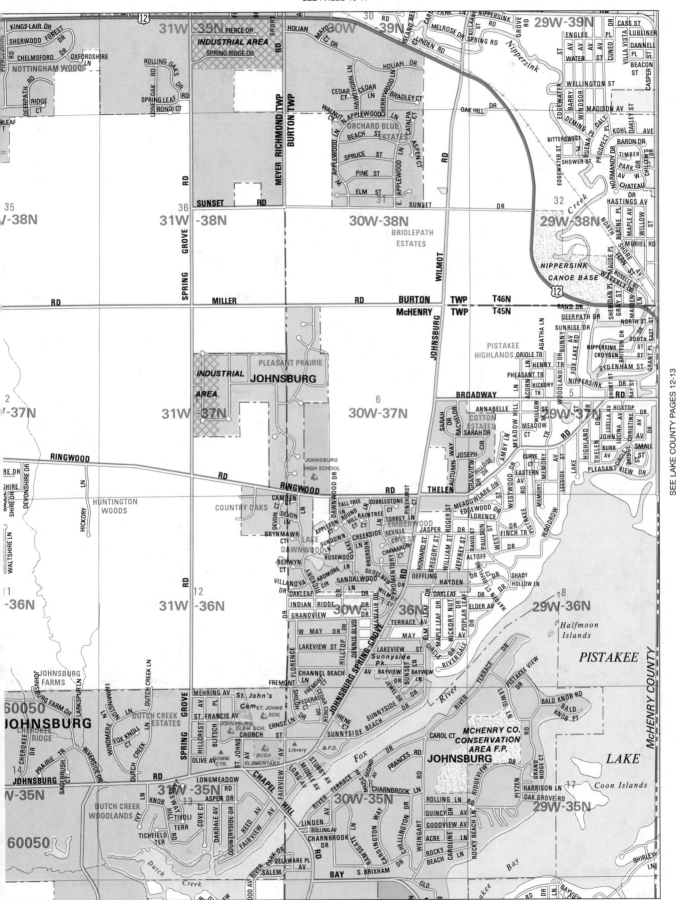

SEE LAKE COUNTY PAGES 12-13

SEE PAGES 12-13

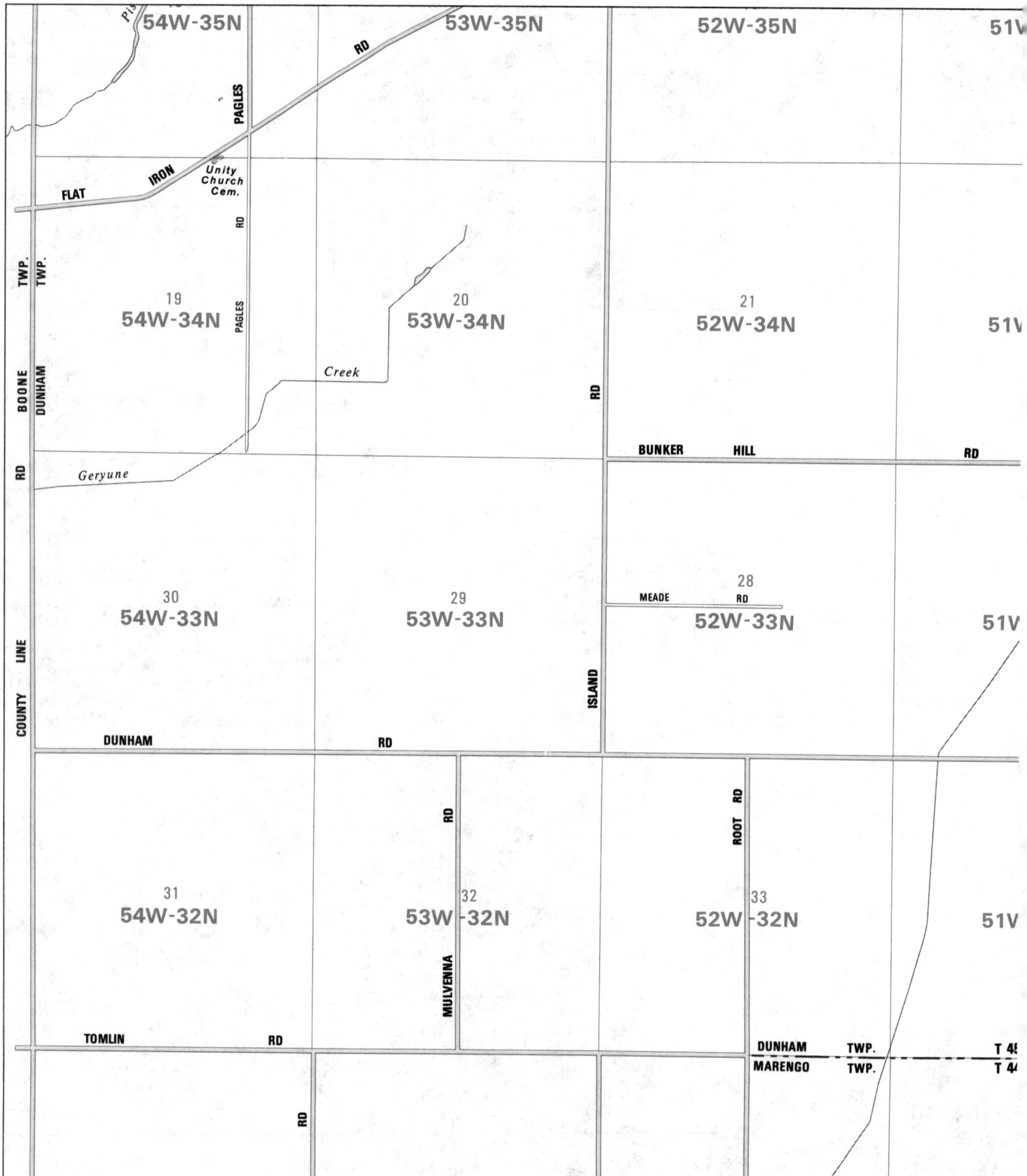

54W-35N

53W-35N

52W-35N

51W

PAGLES RD

IRON

FLAT

Unity
Church
Cem.

19
54W-34N

PAGLES RD

20
53W-34N

21
52W-34N

51W

Creek

RD

BOONE TWP.

DUNHAM TWP.

Geryune

BUNKER HILL RD

RD

COUNTY LINE RD

30
54W-33N

29
53W-33N

28
MEADE RD
52W-33N

51W

ISLAND

DUNHAM RD

RD

ROOT RD

31
54W-32N

32
53W-32N

33
52W-32N

51W

MULVENNA

TOMLIN RD

DUNHAM TWP. T 45
MARENGO TWP. T 44

RD

6
54W-31N

5
53W-31N

RD

4
52W-31N

51W

OLESON RD

ROOT RD

KISHWAUKEE VALLEY RD

KISHWAUKEE

SEE PAGES 28-29

SEE PAGES 12-13

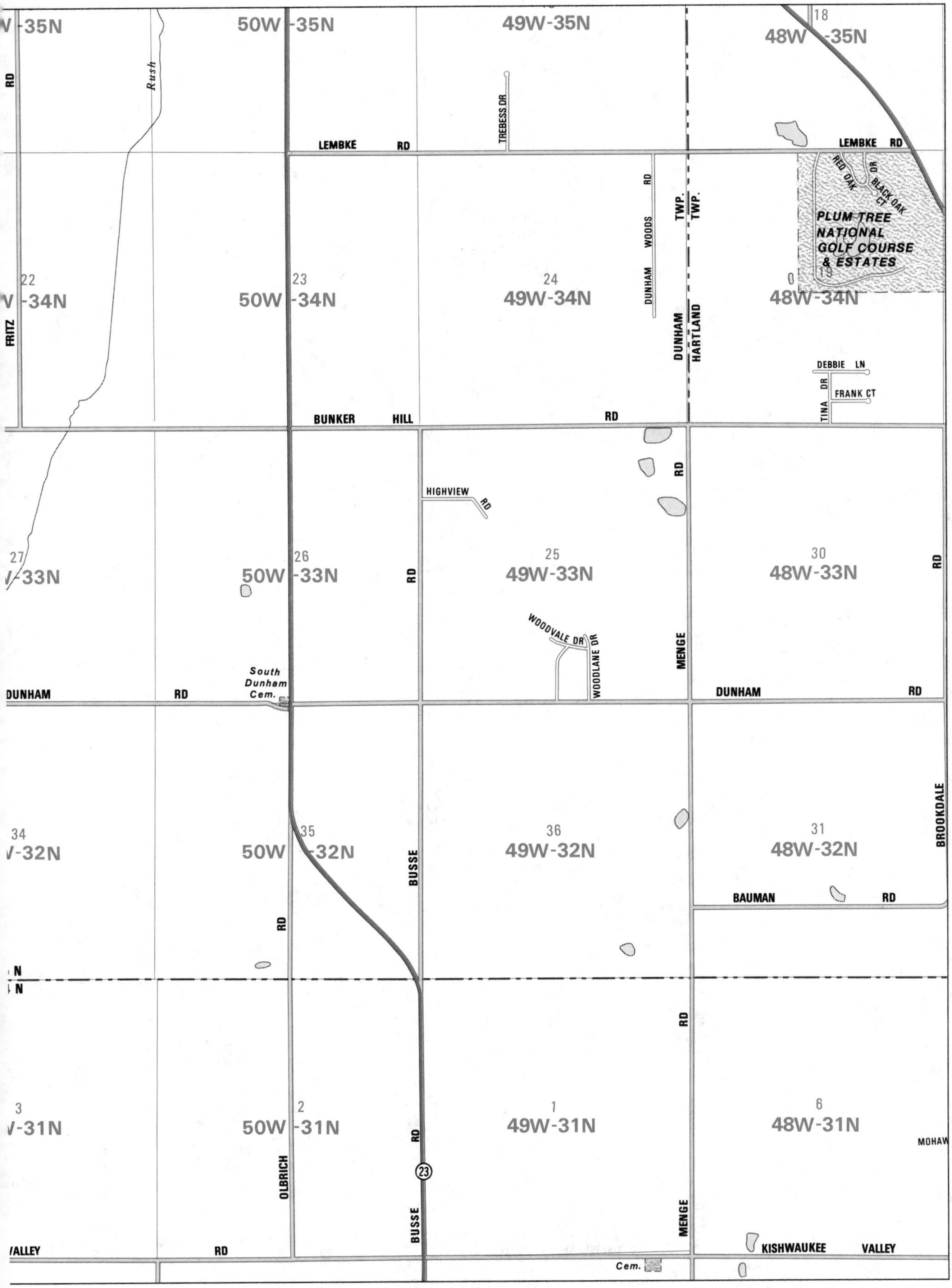

W-35N   50W-35N   49W-35N   48W-35N   18

*Rush*

RD

LEMBKE   RD

TREBESS DR

LEMBKE   RD

RED OAK DR   BLACK OAK CT

PLUM TREE
NATIONAL
GOLF COURSE
& ESTATES

22   23   24   19

W-34N   50W-34N   49W-34N   48W-34N

FRITZ

DUNHAM WOODS RD

TWP.   TWP.

DUNHAM   HARTLAND

DEBBIE LN

TINA DR   FRANK CT

BUNKER   HILL   RD

HIGHVIEW RD

RD

27   26   25   30

W-33N   50W-33N   49W-33N   48W-33N

RD

RD

WOODVALE DR

WOODLANE DR

MENGE

South
Dunham
Cem.

DUNHAM   RD   DUNHAM   RD

BROOKDALE

34   35   36   31

W-32N   50W-32N   49W-32N   48W-32N

RD

BUSSE

BAUMAN   RD

RD

3   2   1   6

W-31N   50W-31N   49W-31N   48W-31N

OLBRICH

BUSSE   RD

(23)

MENGE

MOHAW

BUSSE

VALLEY   RD   KISHWAUKEE   VALLEY

Cem.

SEE PAGES 22-23

SEE PAGES 28-29

SEE PAGES 14-15

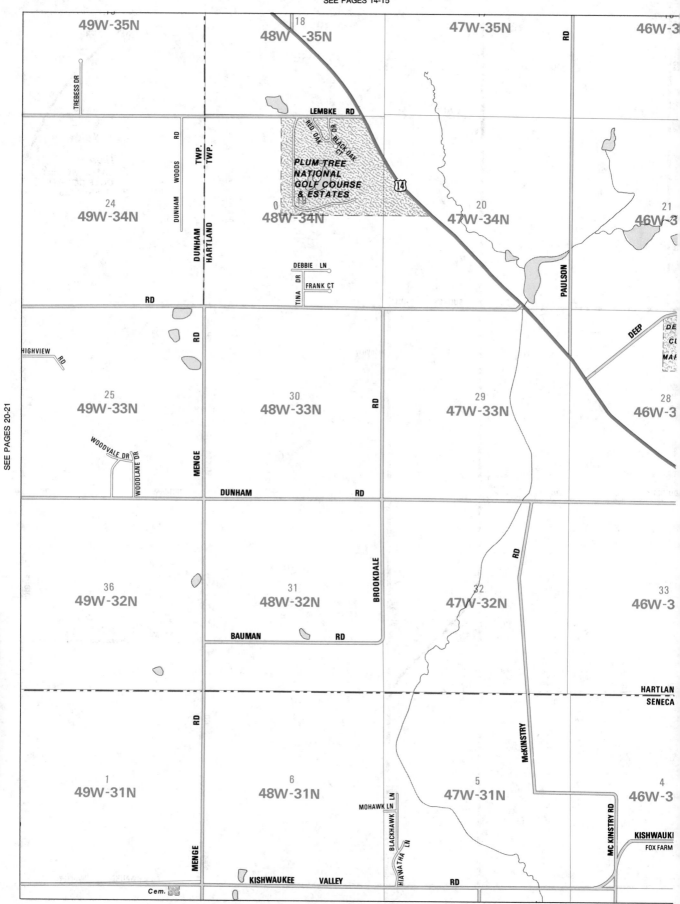

SEE PAGES 20-21

49W-35N

48W-35N

47W-35N

46W-3

TREBESS DR

LEMBKE RD

RED OAK DR

BLACK OAK CT

PLUM TREE NATIONAL GOLF COURSE & ESTATES

14

DUNHAM WOODS RD

TWP. TWP.

DUNHAM HARTLAND

24
49W-34N

18
48W-34N

20
47W-34N

21
46W-3

PAULSON

DEBBIE LN

TINA DR

FRANK CT

RD

HIGHVIEW RD

RD

RD

DEEP

DE
CL
MAR

25
49W-33N

30
48W-33N

29
47W-33N

28
46W-3

WOODVALE DR

WOODLANE DR

MENGE

DUNHAM RD

RD

BROOKDALE

RD

36
49W-32N

31
48W-32N

32
47W-32N

33
46W-3

BAUMAN RD

HARTLAN

SENECA

MCKINSTRY

1
49W-31N

6
48W-31N

5
47W-31N

4
46W-3

MOHAWK LN

BLACKHAWK LN

HIAWATHA LN

MC KINSTRY RD

KISHWAUKI

FOX FARM

MENGE

Cem.

KISHWAUKEE VALLEY RD

SEE PAGES 14-15

45W -35N

44W -35N

St. Patricks Cem.

PATRICK RD

43W -35N

ALDEN

HIDDEN LAKE ESTATES

AZALEA LN

WEST

RED BUD LN

HIDDEN LAKE RD

LILAC LN

DOGWOOD LN

Hidden Lake

HONEYSUCKLE LN

TWP.

TWP.

HARTLAND

GREENWOOD

RD

North

Branch

CUT

DEEP

NELSON

RD

RD

22

MAXWELL ST

HARTLAND

GODDARD ST

COONEY ST

23

NELSON

RD

24

43W -34N

45W -34N

McHenry County Cem.

▲ HARTLAND TWP. OFFICE

**HARTLAND**

**44W -34N**

CHICAGO & NORTHWESTERN R.R.

RD

CUT

DEEP

SH

**LAKOTA**

**BOY SCOUTS**

**OF AMERICA CAMP**

27

**45W -33N**

RD

26

**44W -33N**

WALSH DR

ANTUNA DR

ANTUNA

FARM

25

**43W -33N**

SEE PAGES 24-25

3N

INDUSTRIAL

PARK

**WOODSTOCK**

HILLSIDE LN

PARK LANE DR

HARTLAND

RD

ROSE

Opfergelt Cem.

McGEE RD

S.C.

LAMB RD

PARK LANE

RD

RD

34

**45W -32N**

GREENWAY CROSS

MARAWOOD DR

MAEVE LN

MAEVE LN

SUTTON PL

INDIAN TRACE

35

**MARAWOOD ESTATES**

**44W -32N**

36

**43W - 32N**

120

14

2N

SHAMROCK LN

SHAMROCK LN DR

**GLENGARRY**

MACINTYRE LN

SHANNON

**SHANNON WOODS**

TWP.

TWP.

T 45 N

T 44 N

DIMMEL

3

**45W -31N**

HUGHES RD

2

**44W -31N**

ROSE FARM RD

1

**43W -31N**

1N

VALLEY

RD

RD

KISHWAUKEE VALLEY RD

ALPINE LN

DONAGAL

DOMINION

INFANTA

SEE PAGES 30-31

SEE PAGES 16-17

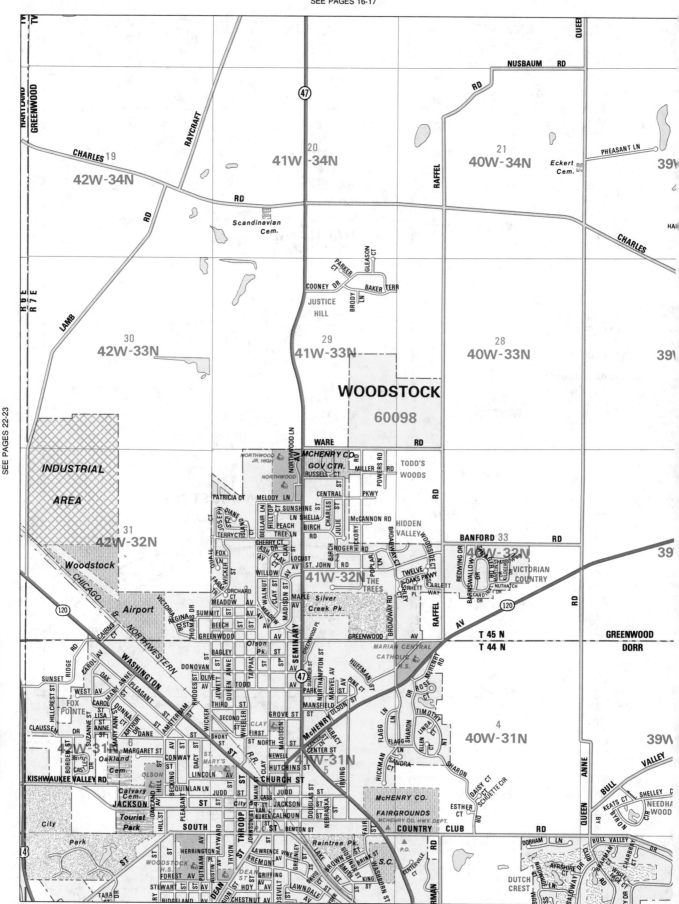

WOODSTOCK
60098

INDUSTRIAL AREA

Woodstock Airport

SEE PAGES 22-23

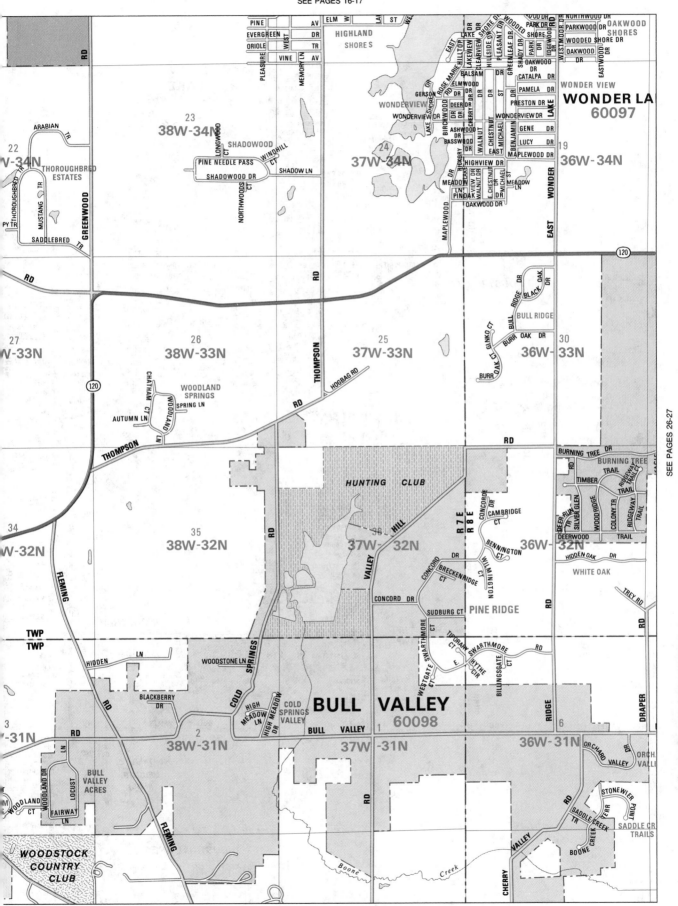

SEE PAGES 26-27

SEE PAGES 18-19

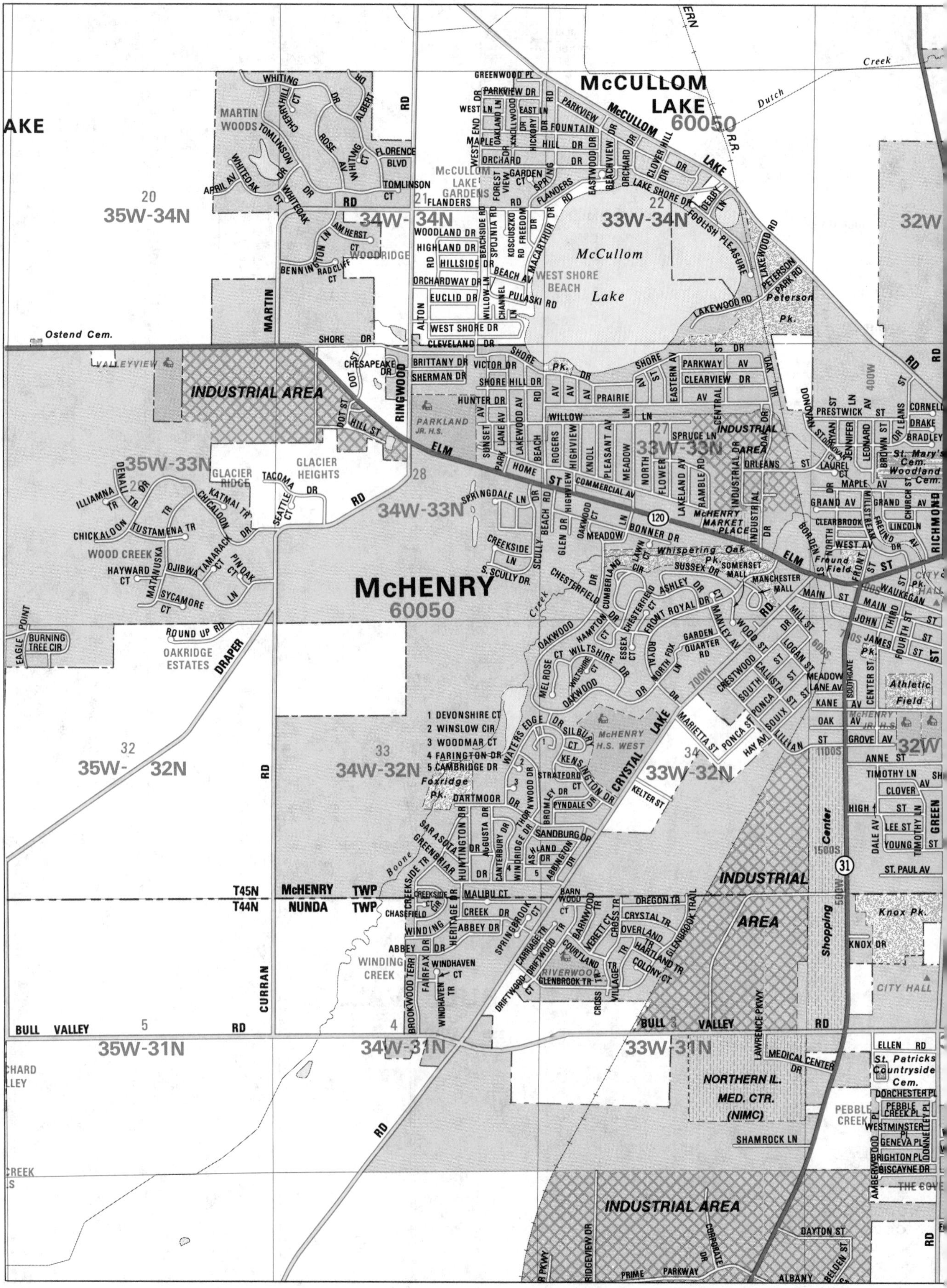

McCULLOM LAKE
60050

LAKE

McCullom Lake

WEST SHORE BEACH

MARTIN WOODS

Ostend Cem.

VALLEYVIEW

**INDUSTRIAL AREA**

20
35W-34N

34W-34N

33W-34N

32W

35W-33N

GLACIER RIDGE

GLACIER HEIGHTS

34W-33N

PARKLAND JR. H.S.

McHENRY MARKET PLACE

INDUSTRIAL AREA

WOOD CREEK

**McHENRY**
60050

1 DEVONSHIRE CT
2 WINSLOW CIR
3 WOODMAR CT
4 FARINGTON DR
5 CAMBRIDGE DR

Foxridge Pk.

OAKRIDGE ESTATES

32
35W- 32N

33
34W-32N

McHENRY H.S. WEST

33W-32N

32W

McHENRY JR. H.S.

Athletic Field

CITY HALL

Knox Pk.

KNOX DR

T45N McHENRY TWP
T44N NUNDA TWP

WINDING CREEK

RIVERWOODS

INDUSTRIAL AREA

BULL VALLEY RD

BULL VALLEY RD

35W-31N

34W-31N

33W-31N

MEDICAL CENTER DR

St. Patricks Countryside Cem.

NORTHERN IL. MED. CTR. (NIMC)

PEBBLE CREEK

SHAMROCK LN

**INDUSTRIAL AREA**

SEE PAGES 24-25

SEE PAGES 34-35

SEE PAGES 18-19

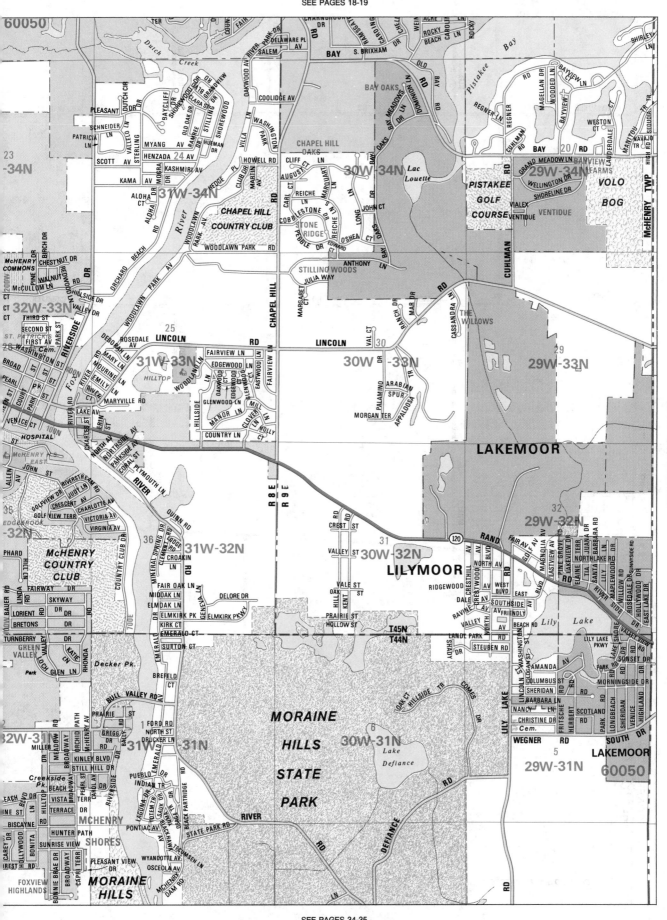

SEE LAKE COUNTY PAGES 20-21

SEE PAGES 20-21

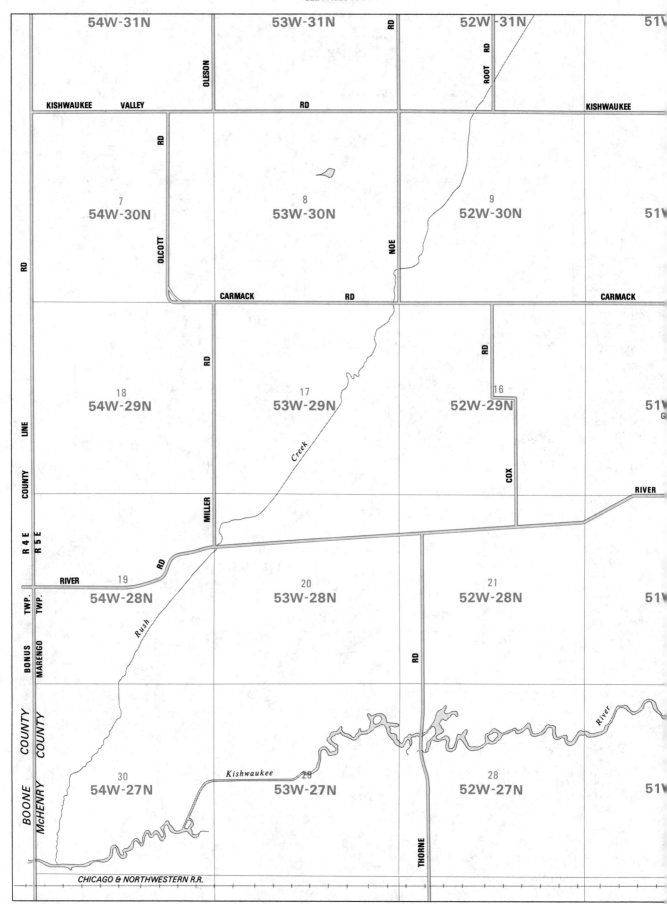

54W-31N
53W-31N
52W-31N
51W

OLESON

ROOT RD

RD

KISHWAUKEE VALLEY RD
RD
KISHWAUKEE

RD

7
54W-30N

8
53W-30N

9
52W-30N

51W

OLCOTT

NOE

CARMACK RD
CARMACK

RD

18
54W-29N

17
53W-29N

16
52W-29N

51W
G

Creek

COUNTY LINE

COX

RIVER

R 4 E
R 5 E

MILLER

RD

TWP. TWP.

RIVER
19
54W-28N

20
53W-28N

21
52W-28N

51W

Rush

RD

BONUS
MARENGO

River

COUNTY
COUNTY

Kishwaukee

30
54W-27N

29
53W-27N

28
52W-27N

51W

BOONE
McHENRY

THORNE

SEE PAGES 36-37

SEE PAGES 20-21

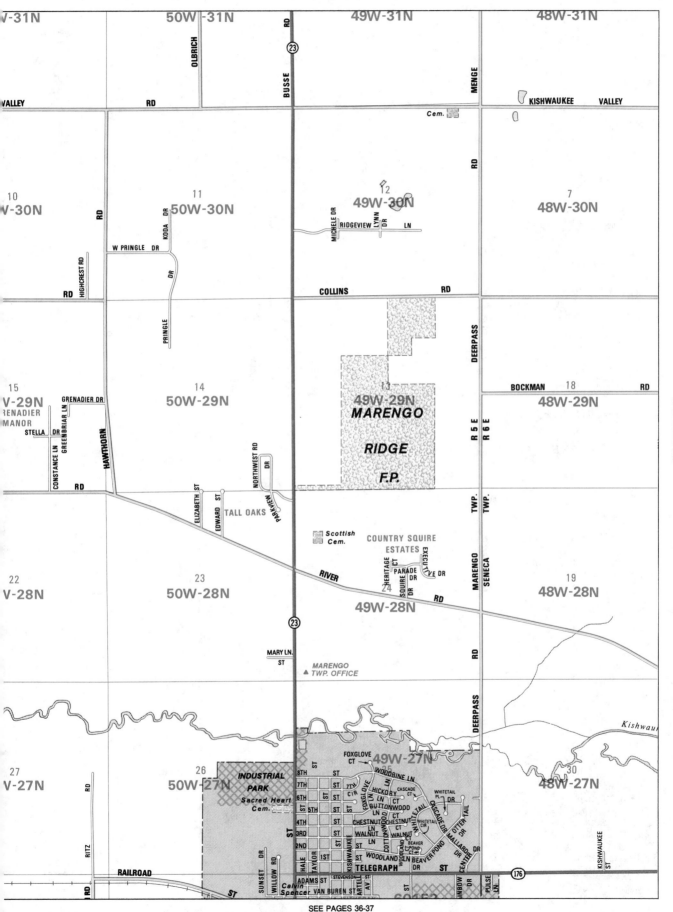

SEE PAGES 30-31

SEE PAGES 36-37

SEE PAGES 22-23

| 49W-31N | 48W-31N | 47W-31N | 46W-31N |

MOHAWK LN

BLACKHAWK LN

HIAWATHA LN

MENGE

MC KINSTRY RD

KISHWAUKEE

FOX FARM

KISHWAUKEE VALLEY RD

RD

Cem.

River

RD

49W-30N

12

MICHELE DR

RIDGEVIEW

LYNN DR

LN

7

48W-30N

8

47W-30N

SULLIVAN

9

46W-30N

Kishwaukee

COLLINS RD

DEERPASS

RD

BOCKMAN

RD

13

49W-29N

**MARENGO**

**RIDGE**

**F.P.**

BOCKMAN 18 RD

48W-29N

17

47W-29N

16

46W-29N

Branch

R 5 E

R 6 E

RD

WOODCLIFF DR

WOODLAND TR

MILLSTREAM RD

DEER PATH TR

ATHY LN

ATHY LN

KILKEE

ATHY CT

Scottish Cem.

COUNTRY SQUIRE ESTATES

TWP.

TWP.

MARENGO

SENECA

EXECUTIVE CT

HERITAGE CT

PARADE DR

SQUIRE DR

EXECUTIVE DR

RIVER

24

RD

19

48W-28N

STANDISH

20

47W-28N

North

VERMONT

21

46W-28N

49W-28N

RD

SANDHILL RD

MARENGO TWP. OFFICE

RD

RIVER RD

NORTH UNION RD

DEERPASS

Kishwaukee

GA

RD

FOXGLOVE CT

49W-27N

WOODBINE LN

H ST

ST

7TH

CIR

FOXGLOVE LN

HICKORY LN

CASCADE CT

CT

WHITETAIL PL

DR

25

30

48W-27N

29 KUNDE

47W-27N

28

46W-27N

H ST

5TH ST

BUTTONWOOD

LN

CT

WHITETAIL

CASCADE DR

CHESTNUT CHESTNUT

LN CT

OTTER TAIL

MALLARD DR

CENTER DR

South

MILLSTREAM

WALNUT LN

WALNUT LN

COTTONWOOD

WHITETAIL CIR

BEAVER POND

WOODLAND

BEAVERPOND DR

KISHWAUKEE

TAYLOR 1ST

ST

WOODLAND DR

**TELEGRAPH** ST

KISHWAUKEE ST

B

ADAMS ST

STEVENSON ST

VAN BUREN ST

ARTELL AV

RAINBOW DR

PULSE LN

176

SEE PAGES 22-23

45W-31N

44W-31N

43W-31N

VALLEY RD

RD

KISHWAUKEE VALLEY RD

ROSE FARM

DOMINION HEIGHTS

WESTWOOD

**WOODSTOCK**

43W-30N

60098

DAKOTA RIDGE

INFANTA CT

ALPINE LN

OONAGAL CT

CASTLE CT

BAR TR

DUBLIN

TRINITY CT

RYAN CT

TERR

SENECA CT

WESTWOOD TR

HILLSIDE

OAKVIEW

MORAINE CT

OAKVIEW CT

MORAINE DR

EDGEWATER

WESTWOOD CT

FIELDCREST AV

RIDGEWAY TER

CREEKWOOD

WESTWOOD ST

CREEKWOOD CT

OSAGE WAY

BRIARWOOD

BLACKFOOT

KIOWA

WINTU CT

DAKOTA DR

SOUTH ST

10

**45W-30N**

11

**44W-30N**

VERMONT

COLLINS RD

SOUTH ST

Pioneer Cem.

SOUTH ST

DAVIS RD

HOBE RD

ROSE FARM RD

RD

15

**45W-29N**

14

**44W-29N**

13

**43W-29N**

FRANKLINVILLE RD

Creek

SECOR RD

SALLY CIR

STIEG DR

SYLVIA LN

CHARLOTTE DR

ELAINE

TWP. TWP.

Franklinville

22 RD

PERKINS 23

RD 24

**45W-28N**

**FRANKLINVILLE**

Cem.

**44W-28N**

**43W-28N**

GARDEN VALLEY RD

GARDEN

VALLEY

RD

SENECA

DORR

RD

RD

RD

KUNDE

RD

River

27

**45W-27N**

FRANKLINVILLE

26

**44W-27N**

GEE

25

**43W-27N**

176

SEE PAGES 32-33

SEE PAGES 38-39

SEE PAGES 24-25

SEE PAGES 30-31

42W-31N

41W-31N

MARGARET ST

CONWAY

KISHWAUKEE VALLEY RD

Oakland Cem.

OLSON

St. MARY'S

NORTH ST

CENTER ST

NEWEL

CLAY

HUTCHINS ST

IRVING

HICKMAN

SANDRA

SHARON

DAISY CT

SCHUETTE CIR

Calvary Cem.

LINCOLN

AV

JUDD

ST

CHURCH ST

JUDD

SCHUETTE CIR

JACKSON

QUINLAN LN

City St

VAN

JACKSON

DOUGLAS ST

McHENRY CO.

FAIRGROUNDS

McHENRY CO. HWY. DEPT.

ESTHER CT

City

Tourist Park

SOUTH

BUREN

CALHOUN

NEBRASKA

BENTON ST

FAIR

COUNTRY    CLUB

DUTCH CREST

(14)

WOODSTOCK H.S. FOREST AV

HERRINGTON

PUTNAM AV

HAYWARD

LAWRENCE

FREMONT

VINE

GREENLEY

BROWN

GOODINGS

BRINK

P.O.

S.C.

Raintree Pk.

CENTERVILLE

PRAIRIE

ZIMMERMAN

DORHAM LN

AYRSHIRE DR

BANOWAY DR

BULL VALLEY

STEWART

RIDGELAND AV

DEAN

GRIFFING

HOY

DAVIS

KING

BLISS

GOLF    CLUB

HIGHLAND

SCHRYVER

CHESTNUT AV

ROOSEVELT

LAWNDALE

OAKDALE

Ryders Woods

OAKLEAF LN

McCONNELL

MAIN LN

TAURUS CT

DEER PA

42W-30N

KIMBALL AV

DIVISION

KIMBALL

JEFFERSON

41W-30N

LAKE

FARM SERVICE

WANDA LN

40W-30N

COURTLAND DR

DILLARD CT

DUNCAN PL

WINSLOW ACRES

DESMOND

BURBANK

LEE ANN

MARK

BARBERRY

WALDEN

MARTHA DR

WINDM CROSS

GERRY

BLAKELY

MURIEL

MITCHELL

RIDGEWOOD

BLUE BONNET

OAK DR

SOUTHVIEW DR

9

APPLEWOOD

HICKORY LN

CLOVER CHASE

VALERIAN

EDGEWOOD

INDUSTRIAL HEIGHTS

KILKENNY CT

APPLEWOOD

PRAIRIE RIDGE

SERBENA LN

ACACIA LN

(47)

CATALPA LN

ASPEN DR

WAGNER LN

OAKWOOD HILLS

DAVIS          RD

DAVIS RD

60098

DAVIS RD

INDUSTRIAL AREA

DAVIS RD

INDUSTRIAL AREA

INDUSTRIAL

WOODSTOCK

Kishwaukee

TECHCOURT

STONELAKE RD

CORPORATE CT

16

39

18

42W-29N

41W-29N

Park

DIECKMAN

S.C. COBBLESTONE

LINDEN LN

40W-29N

Woodstock Mem. Cem.

ARI

POINT RD

CAROL LN

BRIDGEWATER DR

LAKE SHORE

SALLY CIR

NOVEEN PKWY

TWP    TWP

CASTLE

CHARLOTTE DR

HOLLY

CHUKAR PL

HERCULES RD

PERKINS

19

RD

20

21

INDUSTRIAL AREA

39

42W-28N

DEAN

41W-28N

40W-28N

LUCAS

SENECA    DORR

RD

NANCY CT

GAYLE

ST

30

29

28

39W

42W-27N

41W-27N

40W-27N

RD

WEERS NATURE AREA

(47)

(176)

SEE PAGES 40-41

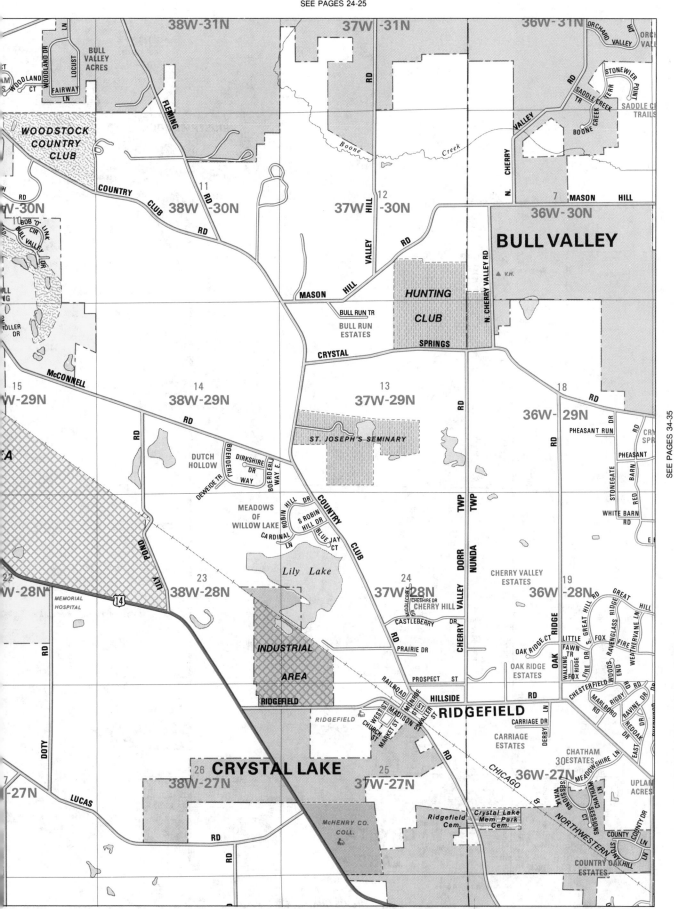

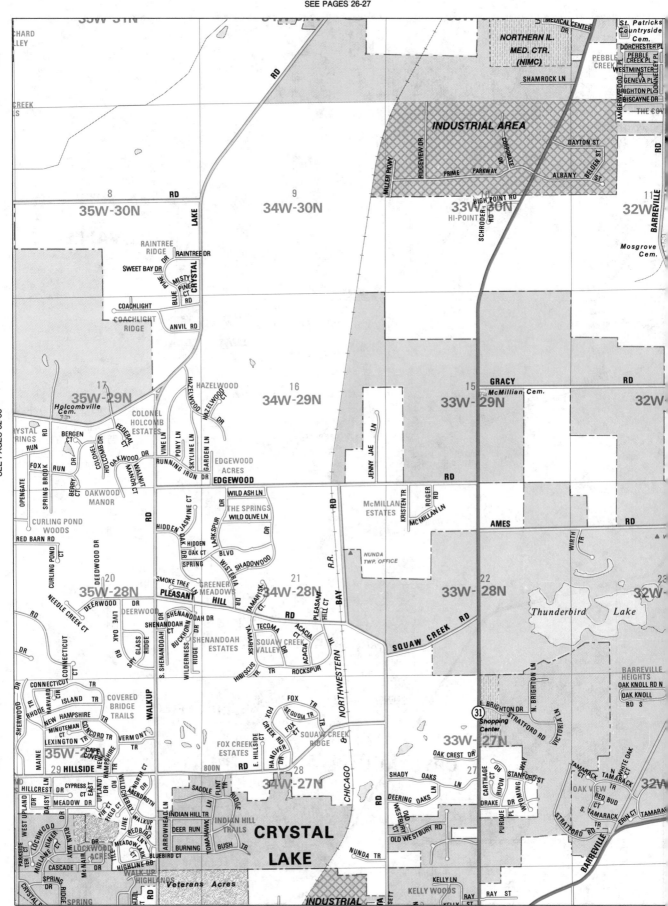

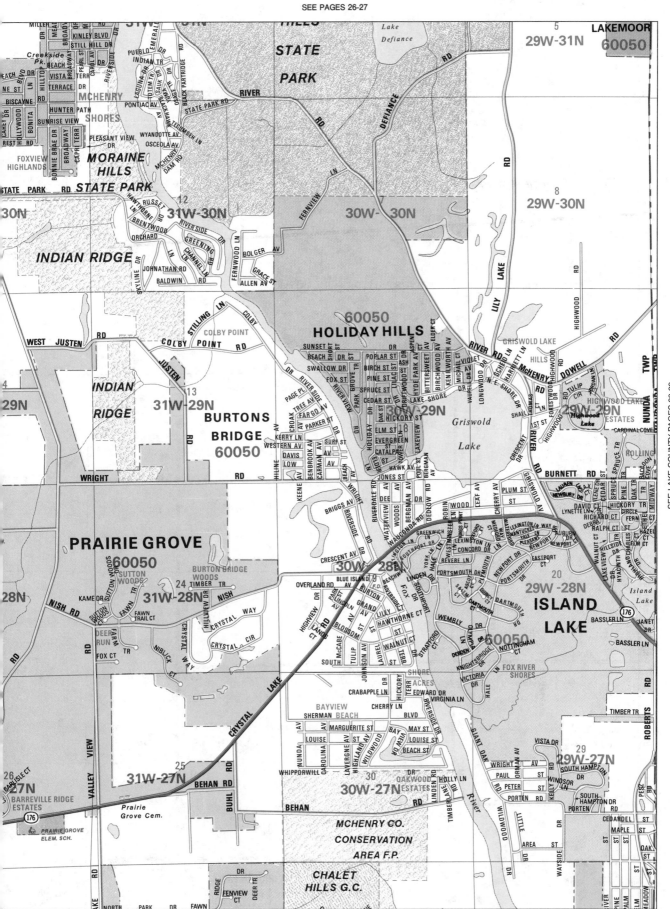

SEE LAKE COUNTY PAGES 28-29

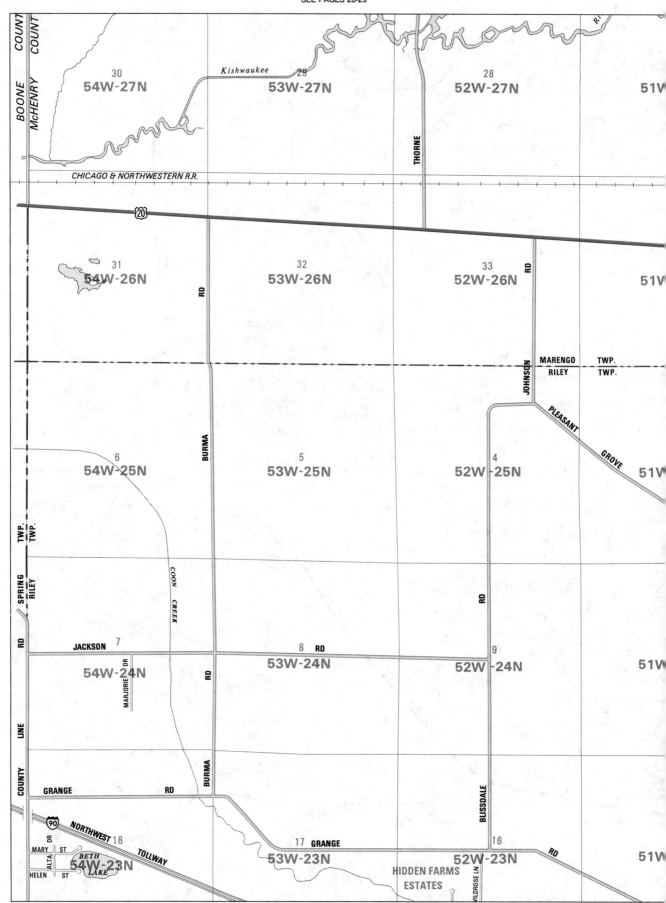

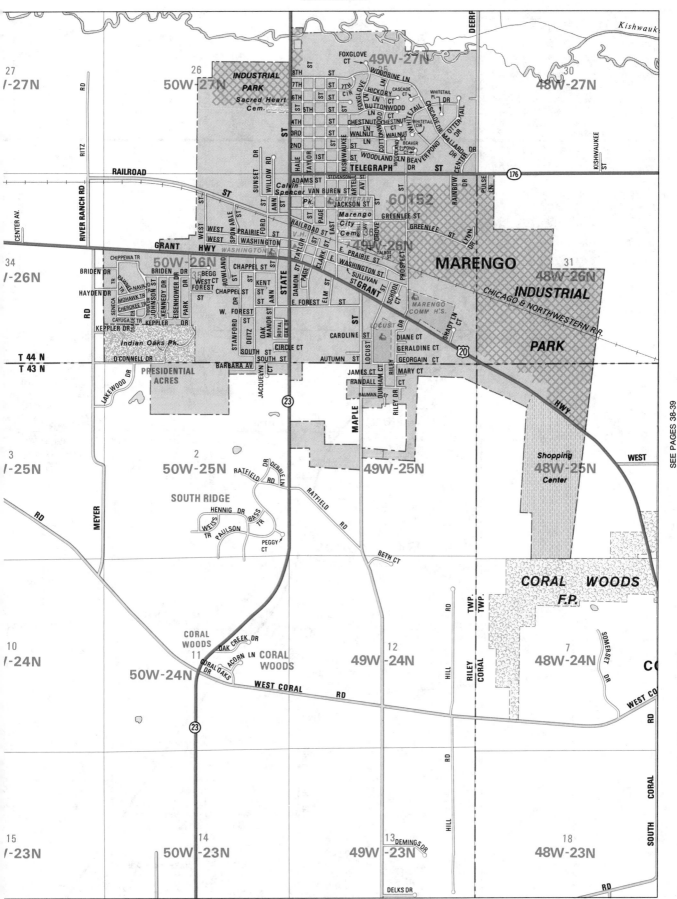

SEE PAGES 38-39

SEE PAGES 30-31

FOXGLOVE CT

49W-27N

WOODBINE LN

CASCADE

HICKORY ST

WHITETAIL DR

BUTTONWOOD

CHESTNUT

WALNUT

COTTONWOOD

WOODLAND

MALLARD DR

BEAVER POND

OTTER CT

CENTER

TELEGRAPH ST

48W-27N

47W-27N

46W-2

30

29 KUNDE

RD

MILLSTREAM

South

Branch

176

STEVENSON

VAN BUREN ST

ARTELL

LUTHERAN

JACKSON ST

PAGE

EAST

60152

Marengo City Cem.

GREENLEE ST

GREENLEE ST

GROVE

LYNN

TALBOT

PROSPECT

RAINBOW DR

PULSE LN

49W-26N

E. PRAIRIE ST

WASHINGTON ST

SULLIVAN

GRANT ST

SCHOOL DR

CLARK

ELM ST

FOREST ST

MARENGO COMM. H.S.

LOCUST

RILEY

MARENGO

INDUSTRIAL

PARK

31

48W-26N

CHICAGO & NORTHWESTERN R.R.

47W -26N

DUNHAM RD

NORTH RD

UNION RD

46W-2

32

33

CAROLINE ST

DIANE CT

GERALDINE CT

GEORGAIN CT

AUTUMN ST

JAMES CT

RANDALL

BAUMAN

DUNHAM DR

RILEY DR

MARY CT

20

HWY

O'CLOCK RD

COUNTRY LN

MEADOW LN

FAIRFIELD DR

PARK ST

ELM ST

Amer Field

SUNVIEW DR

CLARK ST

MALLETT

VINE

INDUSTRIAL PARK

JOHNSON

DEPOT ST

JEFFERSON

WAYNE ST

MAIN ST

DEPO

WASH

MAPLE

Shopping Center

49W-25N

48W-25N

WEST UNION

47W -25N

DUNHAM RD

Union Cem.

JACKSON ST

INDUSTRIAL PARK

SOUTH ST

PRAIRIE ST

RD

ELM

46W-2

5 RD

RATFIELD RD

BETH CT

CORAL WOODS F.P.

TWP.

TWP.

RD

RILEY CORAL

SOMERSET DR

CORAL

NORTHRUP

49W-24N

12

48W-24N

7

WEST CORAL RD

EAST CORAL

47W-24N

8

9

46W-2

HILL RD

RD

SOUTH CORAL RD

SOUTH UNION RD

20

KOA CAMPGROUND

SEVEN ACRES ANTIQUE VILLAGE

13 DEMINGS DR

49W-23N

HILL RD

18

48W-23N

BECK

17 RD

47W- 23N

BECK RD

HARMONY HILL RD

MARENGO RIDGE

GOLF COURSE

16

MARENGO HUNTLE

DELKS DR

RD

RD

SEE PAGES 36-37

SEE PAGES 30-31

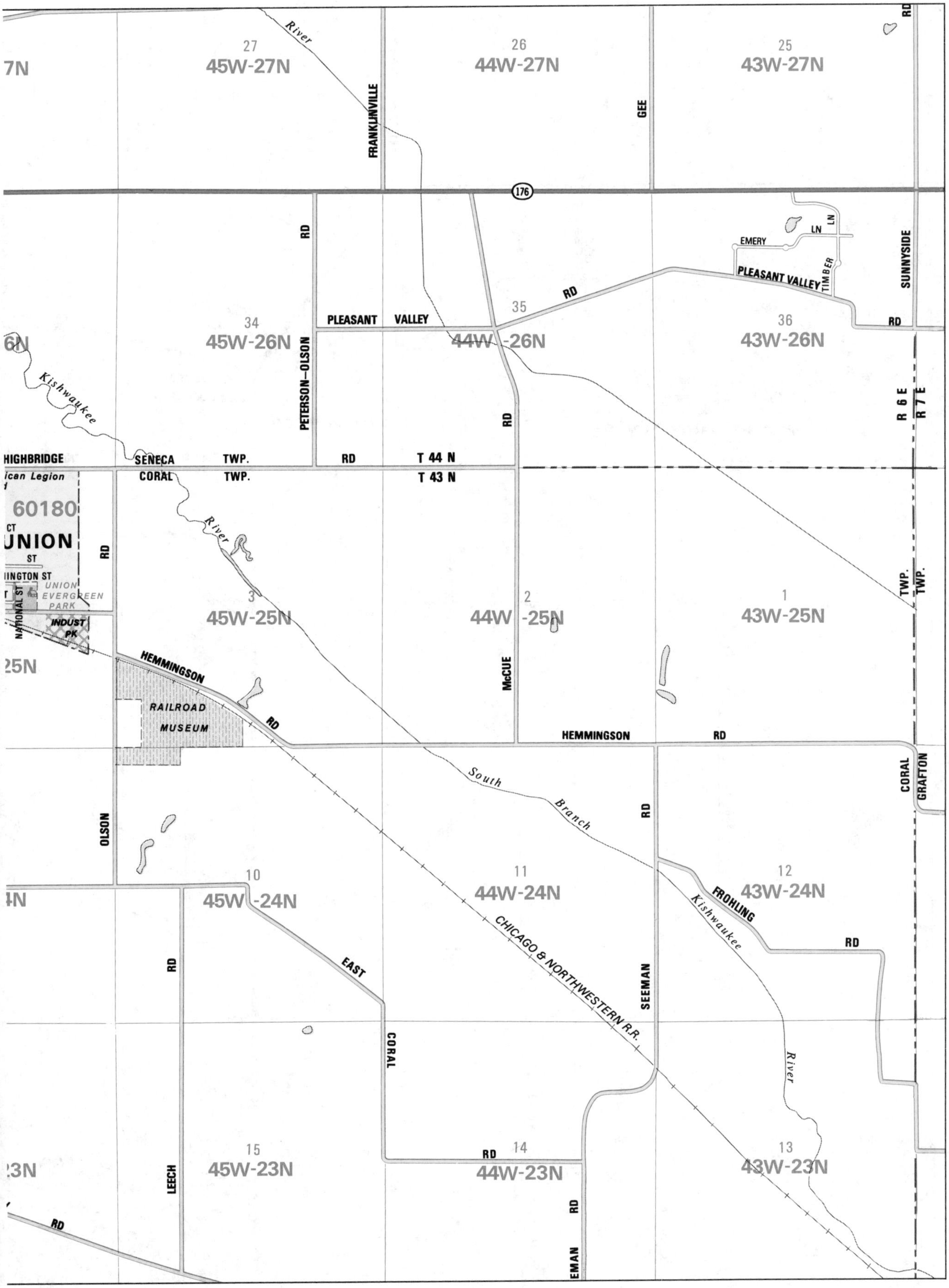

River

7N

45W-27N
27

26
44W-27N

25
43W-27N

FRANKLINVILLE

GEE

176

RD

EMERY

LN

LN

PLEASANT VALLEY

TIMBER

SUNNYSIDE

RD

PLEASANT  VALLEY

PETERSON—OLSON

6N

45W-26N
34

35
44W-26N

36
43W-26N

RD

RD

R 6 E

R 7 E

Kishwaukee

HIGHBRIDGE

SENECA    TWP.

RD

T 44 N

CORAL     TWP.

T 43 N

ican Legion

River

**60180**

CT

RD

**UNION**

ST

INGTON ST

UNION
EVERGREEN
PARK

3
45W-25N

2
44W-25N

1
43W-25N

TWP.

TWP.

SEE PAGES 40-41

NATIONAL ST

INDUST
PK

25N

HEMMINGSON

McCUE

HEMMINGSON

RD

RD

RAILROAD
MUSEUM

RD

South

Branch

CORAL

GRAFTON

OLSON

10
45W-24N

11
44W-24N

RD

12
43W-24N

FROHLING

Kishwaukee

EAST

CHICAGO & NORTHWESTERN R.R.

SEEMAN

RD

RD

CORAL

River

15
45W-23N

RD

14
44W-23N

13
43W-23N

LEECH

RD

EMAN RD

SEE PAGES 46-47

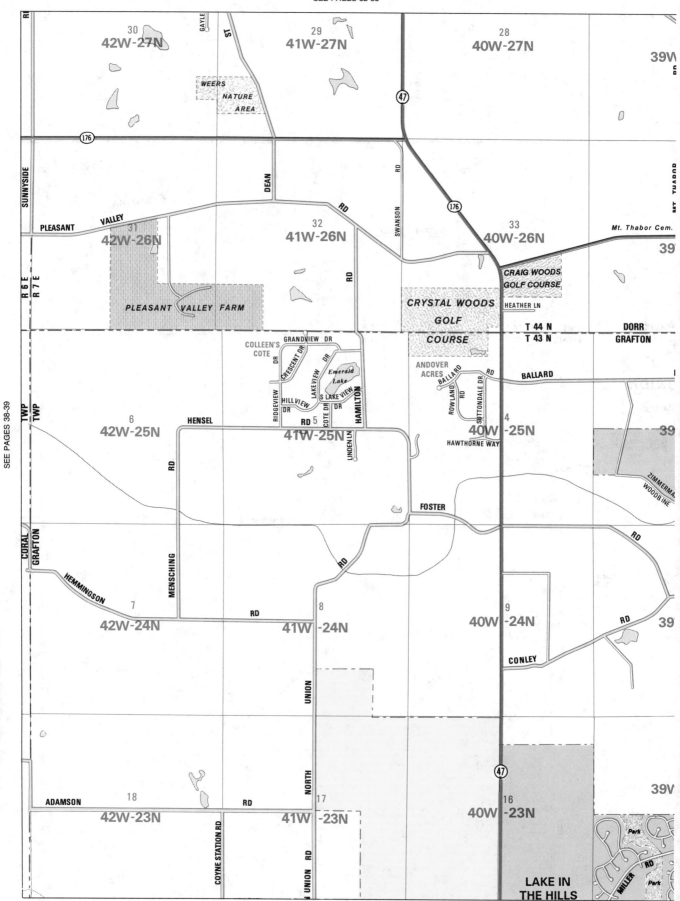

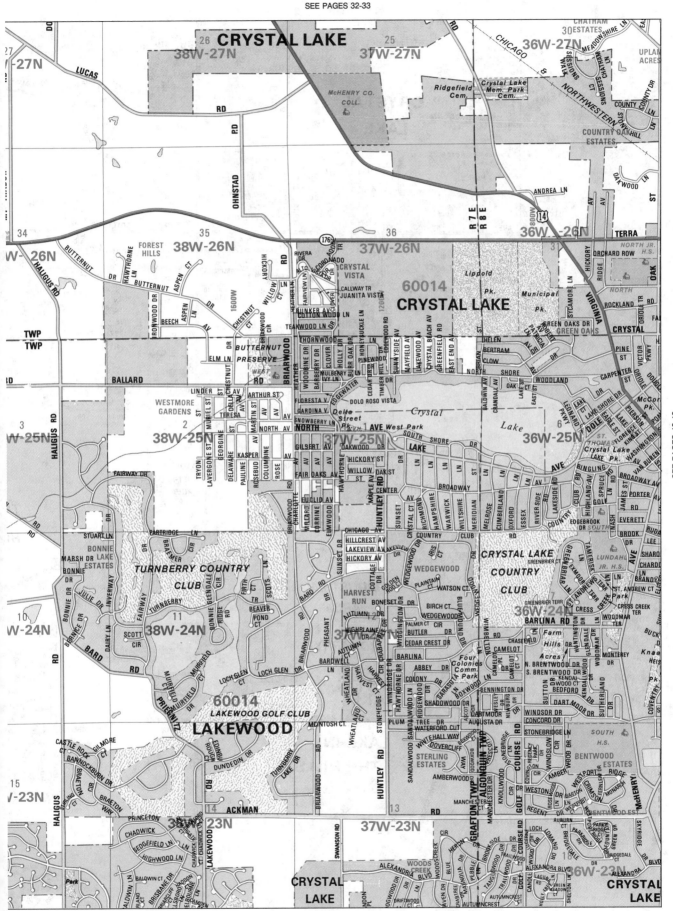

SEE PAGES 34-35

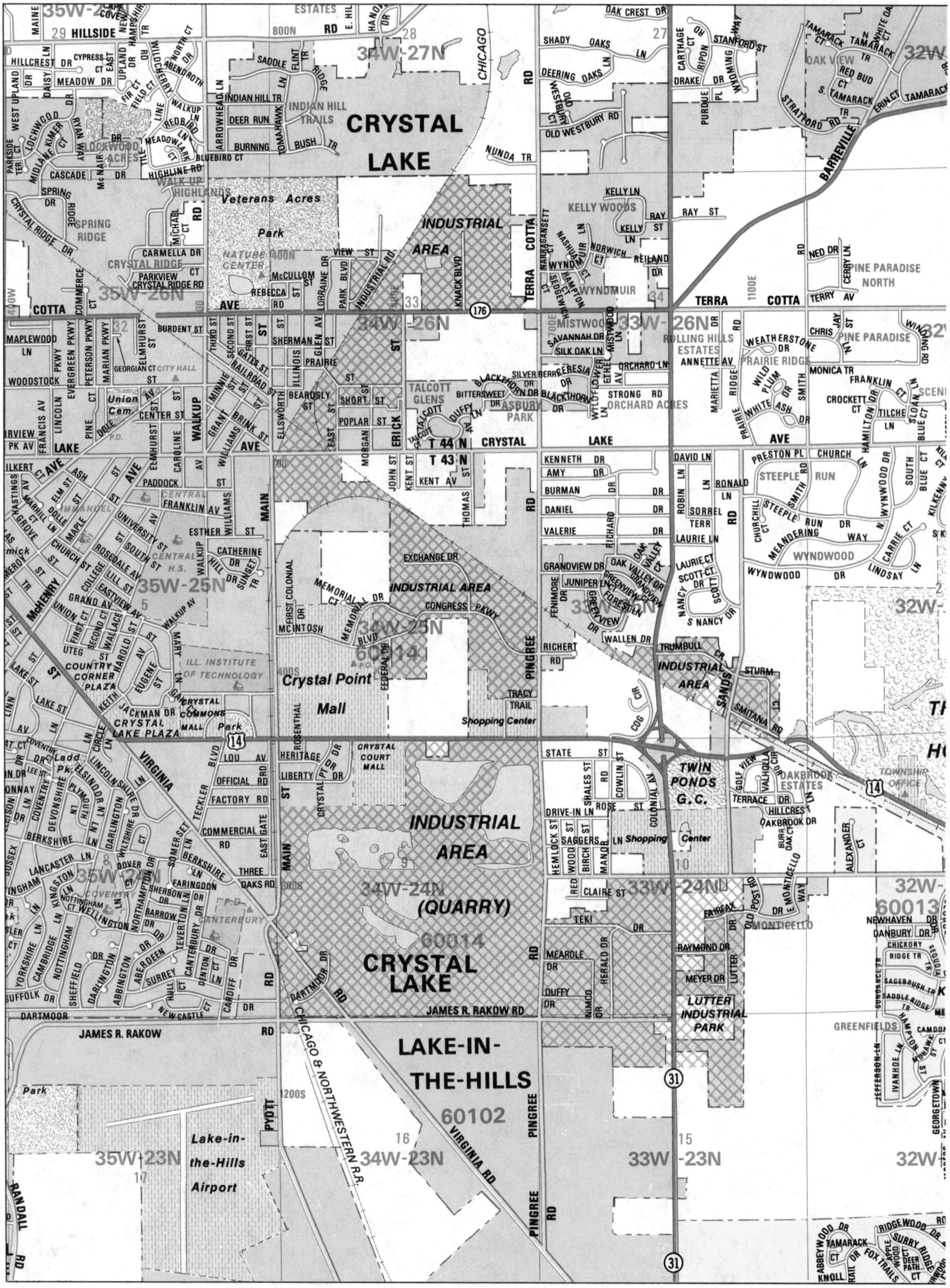

SEE PAGES 40-41

# CRYSTAL LAKE

## INDUSTRIAL AREA

**Veterans Acres Park**

NATURE CENTER

**CRYSTAL LAKE**

Crystal Point Mall

CRYSTAL COURT MALL

## INDUSTRIAL AREA

## INDUSTRIAL AREA (QUARRY)

60014

CRYSTAL LAKE

## LAKE-IN-THE-HILLS

60102

Lake-in-the-Hills Airport

TWIN PONDS G.C.

LUTTER INDUSTRIAL PARK

GREENFIELDS

35W-27N   34W-27N

35W-26N   34W-26N   33W-26N

35W-25N   34W-25N   60014   33W-25N

35W-24N   34W-24N   33W-24N   32W-24N   60013

35W-23N   34W-23N   33W-23N   32W

SEE PAGES 50-51

OAKWOOD HILLS 60013

FOX RIVER VALLEY GARDENS 60021

MCHENRY CO. CONSERVATION AREA F.P.

CHALET HILLS G.C.

OAKWOOD HILLS PARK

MCHENRY CO. CONSERVATION AREA F.P.

HICKORY GROVE

CARY 60013

FOX RIVER GROVE 60021

31W-27N   30W-27N   29W-27N

31W-26N   30W-26N   29W-26N

31W-25N   30W-25N   29W-25N

31W-24N   30W-24N   29W-24N

31W-23N   30W-23N   29W-23N

NUNDA TWP
ALGONQUIN TWP

T44N
T43N

R 8 E
R 9 E

Barreville Ridge Estates
Royal Woods Est
Prairie Grove Cem.
Prairie Grove Elem. Sch.

Lake Killarney
Lake

Lions Pk. North
Lions Pk.
Bright Oaks Pk.
Brittany Woods

Cary-Grove H.S.
Cary Jr. H.S.
St. Peter & Paul
Oaknoll
Northwood Acres Elem. School

Windridge Cem.
First Street Cem.
Carl Sand Park
Main St Prairie Park

Breeze Acres
Coves of Cary
Valley View Estates
Brisbane

Lake Julian
Fox River

Norge Ski Club

Cary Public Works
Cary Point Industrial Park

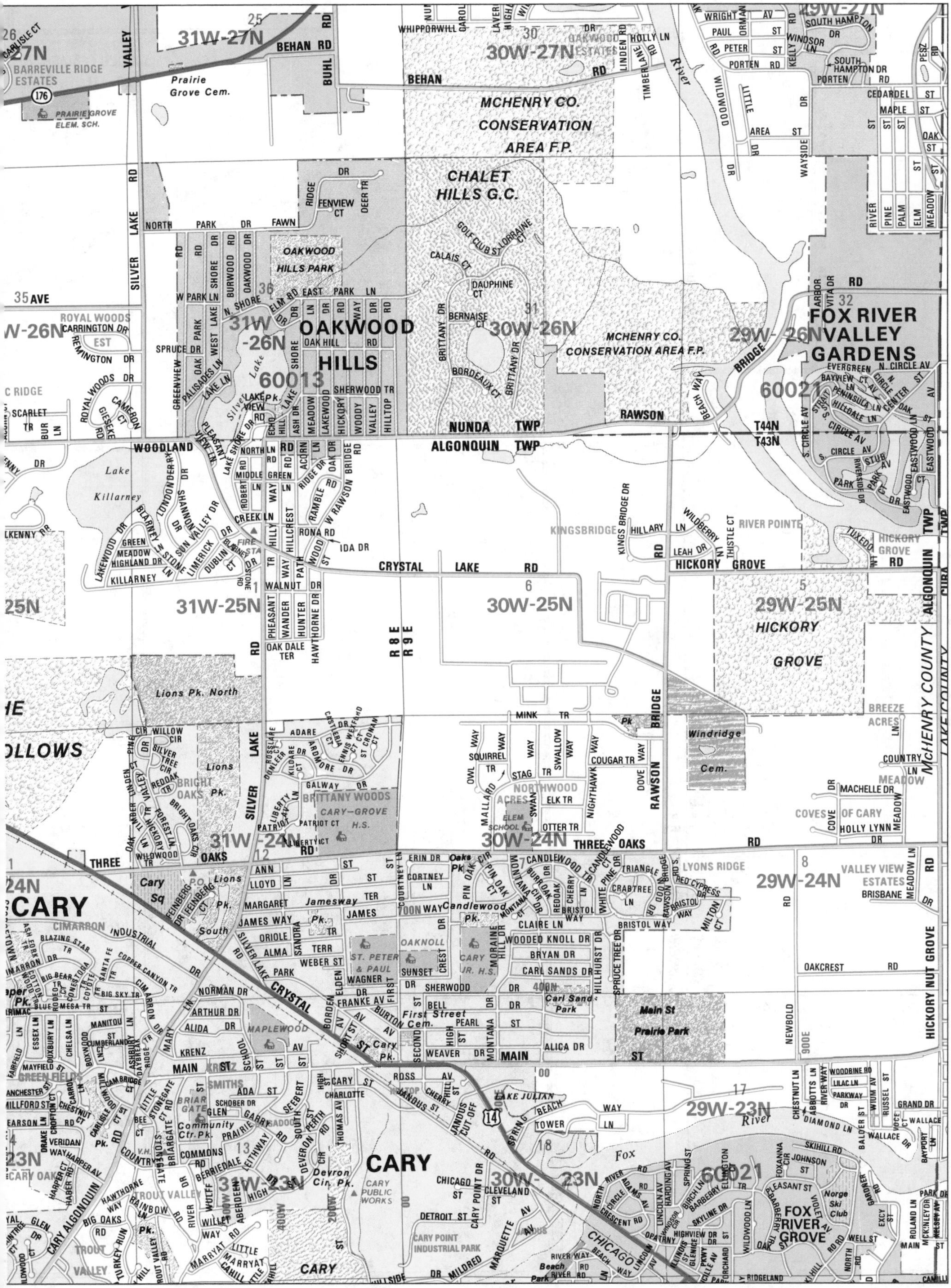

SEE LAKE COUNTY PAGES 36-37

13

18

NORTHWEST TOLLWAY

MARY ST

ALTA DR

HELEN ST

BETH LAKE

**54W-23N**

17 GRANGE

**53W-23N**

52W-2

Coon Creek

**HIDDEN FARMS ESTATES**

WILD ROSE LN

GARDEN PRAIRIE RD

COUNTY LINE RD

ANTHONY RD

Williamson Creek

McKEOWIN RD

ANTHONY

I-90

24

19

**54W-22N**

20

**53W-22N**

21

**52W-2**

HARMONY RD

25

30

**54W-21N**

29

**53W-21N**

28

**52W-**

PINEGER RD

HARTMAN

R 4 E  R 5 E

RD

BOONE COUNTY  McHENRY COUNTY

GENOA RD

RUDOLPH RD

6

31

**54W-20N**

32

**53W-20N**

33

**52W-**

BURROWS RD

DEKALB COUNTY

POPLAR RD

**RILEY TWP**  T

**GENOA TWP**  T

Cem.

NORTH STATE RD

1

6

**55W-19N**

5

**54W-19N**

4

**53W-**

EISENHOWER RD

GENOA RD

MELMS RD

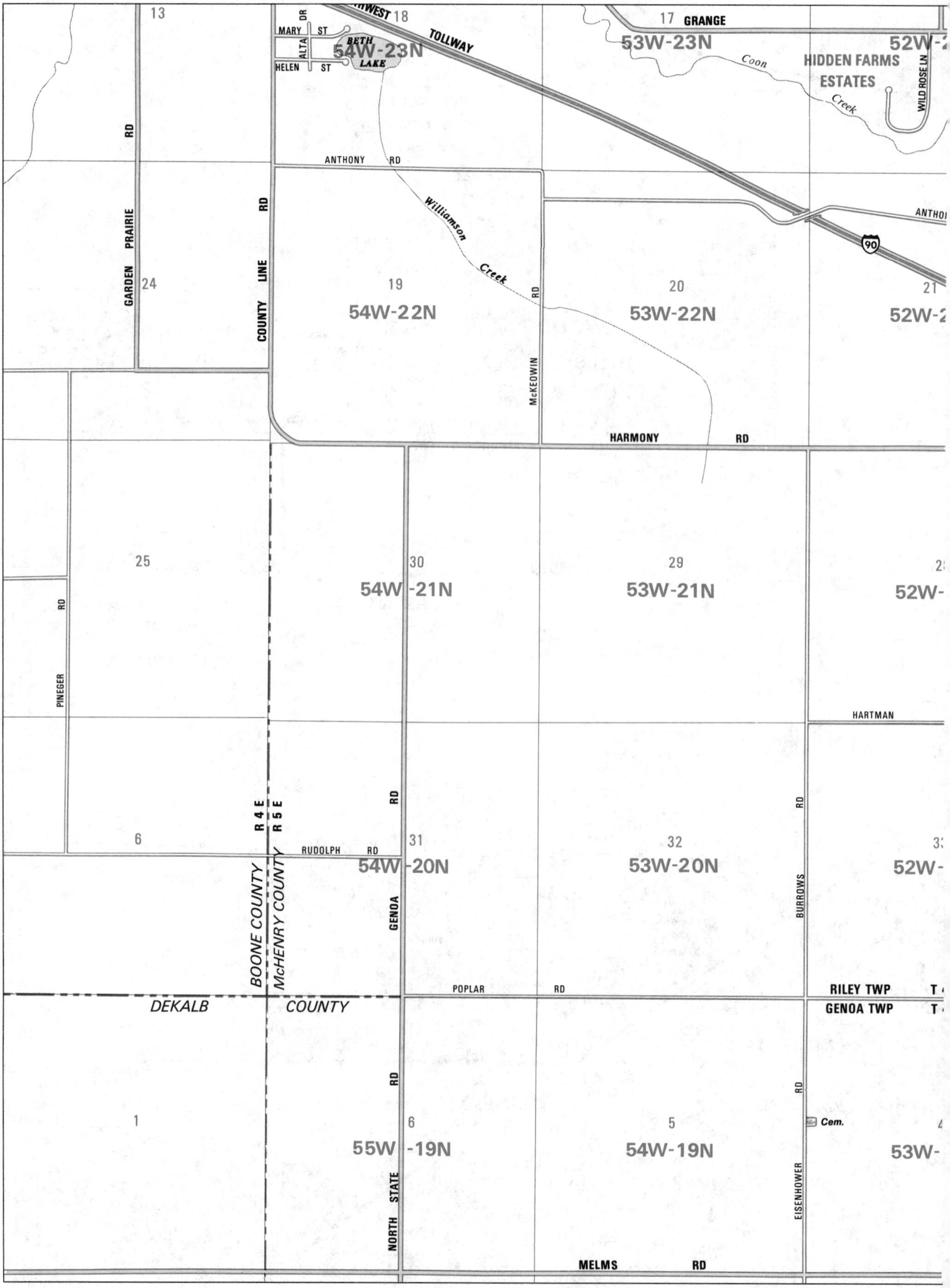

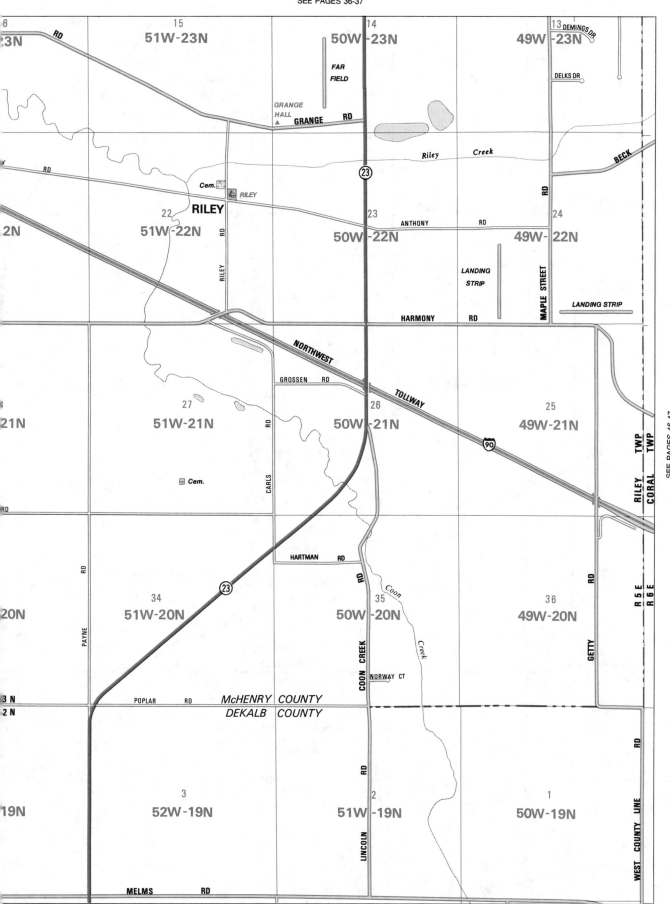

SEE PAGES 46-47

SEE PAGES 38-39

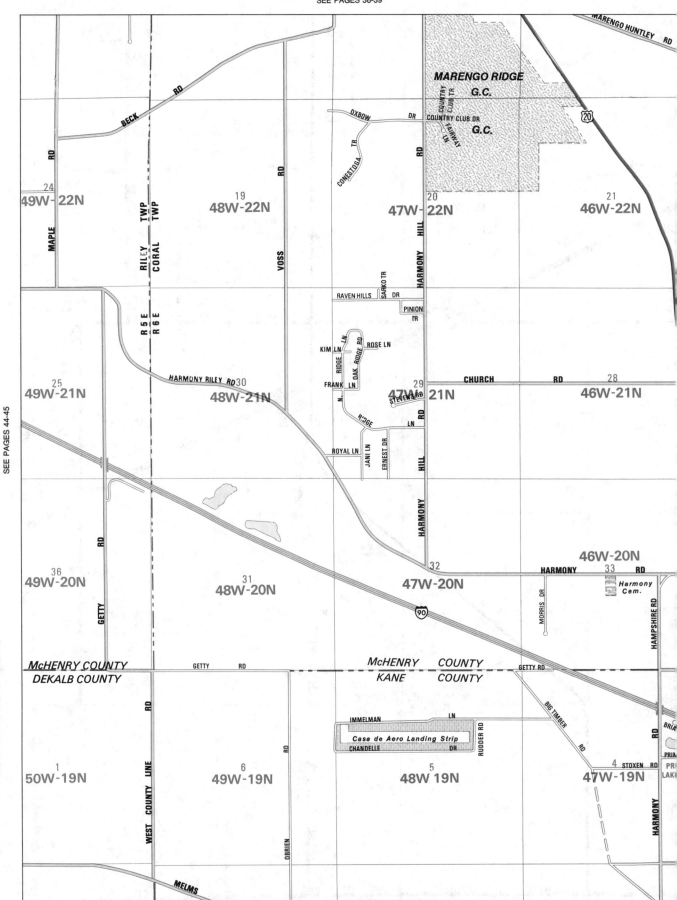

MARENGO HUNTLEY RD

BECK RD

**MARENGO RIDGE G.C.**

COUNTRY CLUB TR

OXBOW DR

CONESTOGA TR

COUNTRY CLUB DR **G.C.**

COUNTRY FAIRWAY LN

20

MAPLE

RILEY TWP
CORAL TWP

VOSS RD

HARMONY HILL RD

| 24 | 19 | 20 | 21 |
|---|---|---|---|
| **49W-22N** | **48W-22N** | **47W-22N** | **46W-22N** |

R 5 E
R 6 E

RAVEN HILLS DR

SARKO TR

PINION TR

KIM LN
ROSE LN

RIDGE LN
OAK RIDGE RD

HARMONY RILEY RD 30

FRANK LN

STEVENS RD

CHURCH RD 28

N

| 25 | 30 | 29 | 28 |
|---|---|---|---|
| **49W-21N** | **48W-21N** | **47W-21N** | **46W-21N** |

RIDGE

LN

ROYAL LN

JANI LN

ERNEST DR

HARMONY HILL RD

HARMONY

SEE PAGES 44-45

46W-20N

32

HARMONY RD 33

Harmony Cem.

MORRIS DR

HAMPSHIRE RD

| 36 | 31 | 32 |  |
|---|---|---|---|
| **49W-20N** | **48W-20N** | **47W-20N** |  |

GETTY RD

90

*McHENRY COUNTY*
*DEKALB COUNTY*

GETTY RD

*McHENRY COUNTY*
*KANE COUNTY*

GETTY RD

BIG TIMBER RD

IMMELMAN LN

**Casa de Aero Landing Strip**

CHANDELLE DR

RUDDER RD

STOXEN RD

BRIA

PRIM

PR
LAK

WEST COUNTY LINE RD

OBRIEN RD

RD

HARMONY

| 1 | 6 | 5 | 4 |
|---|---|---|---|
| **50W-19N** | **49W-19N** | **48W 19N** | **47W-19N** |

MELMS

SEE KANE COUNTY PAGES 4-5

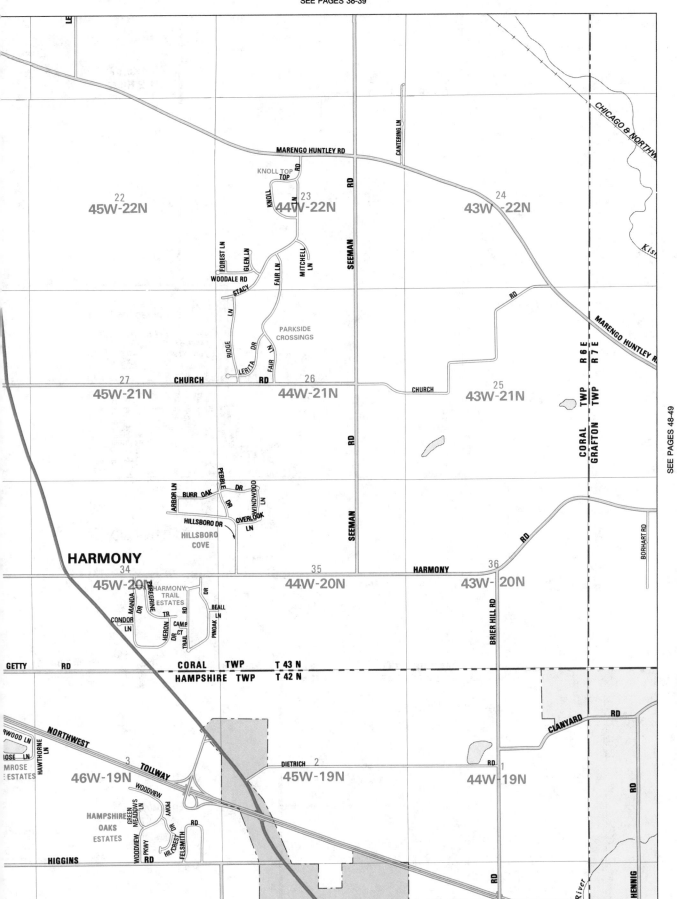

SEE PAGES 48-49

# 48 McHENRY COUNTY

SEE PAGES 40-41

SEE PAGES 46-47

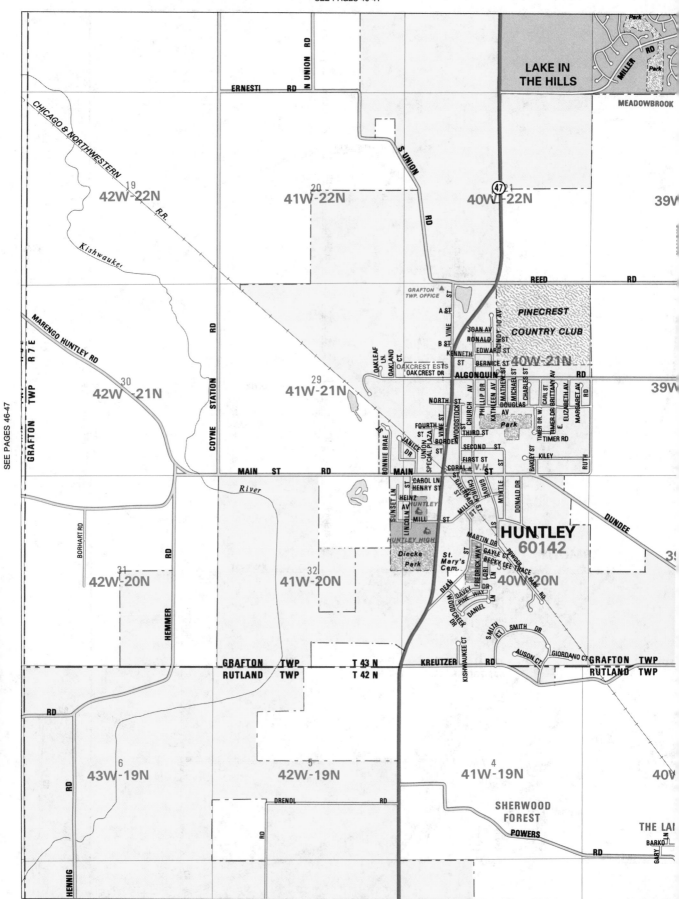

LAKE IN
THE HILLS

MEADOWBROOK

CHICAGO & NORTHWESTERN

42W-22N

41W-22N

40W-22N

39W

Kishwauker

MARENGO HUNTLEY RD

42W-21N

41W-21N

PINECREST
COUNTRY CLUB

40W-21N

39W

GRAFTON TWP R 7 E

COYNE STATION RD

ALGONQUIN

Park

NORTH ST

River

MAIN ST RD

MAIN

UNION
SPECIAL PLAZA

Diecke
Park

Huntley
Mill

HUNTLEY HIGH

St.
Mary's
Cem.

HUNTLEY
60142

DUNDEE

BORHART RD

HEMMER RD

42W-20N

41W-20N

40W-20N

39

GRAFTON TWP
RUTLAND TWP

T 43 N
T 42 N

KREUTZER RD

GRAFTON TWP
RUTLAND TWP

RD

43W-19N

42W-19N

41W-19N

40V

DRENDL RD

SHERWOOD
FOREST

THE LA

POWERS

HENNIG

BARKO LN
GARY LN RD

SEE KANE COUNTY PAGES 6-7

SEE PAGES 40-41

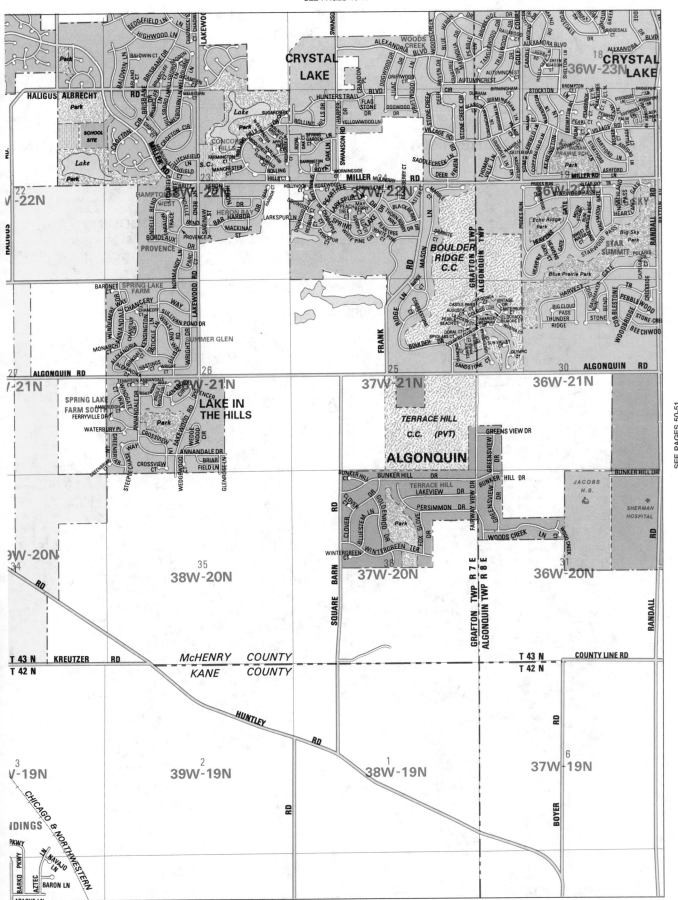

SEE PAGES 50-51

SEE PAGES 42-43

SEE PAGES 48-49

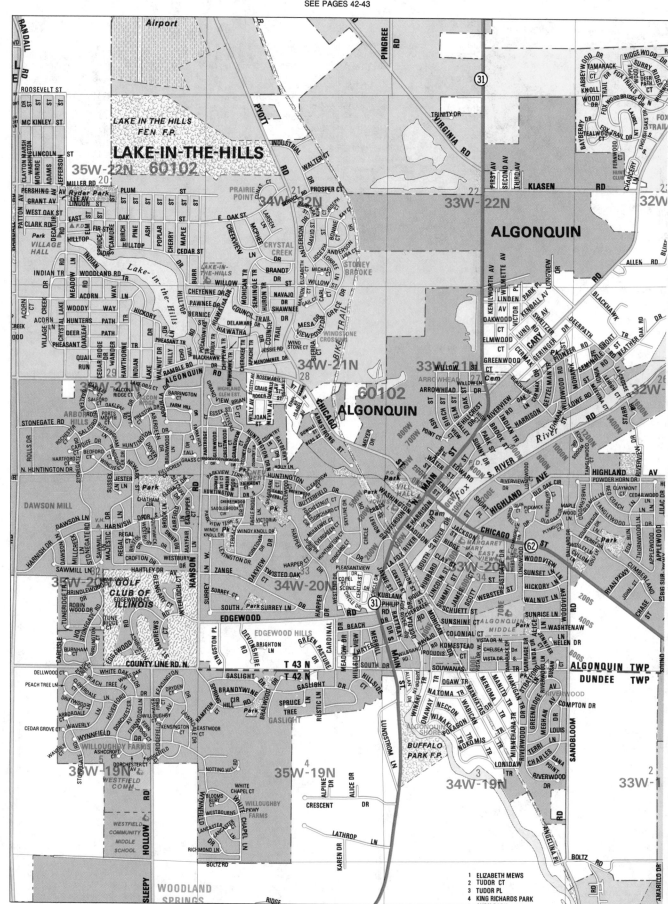

SEE PAGES 42-43

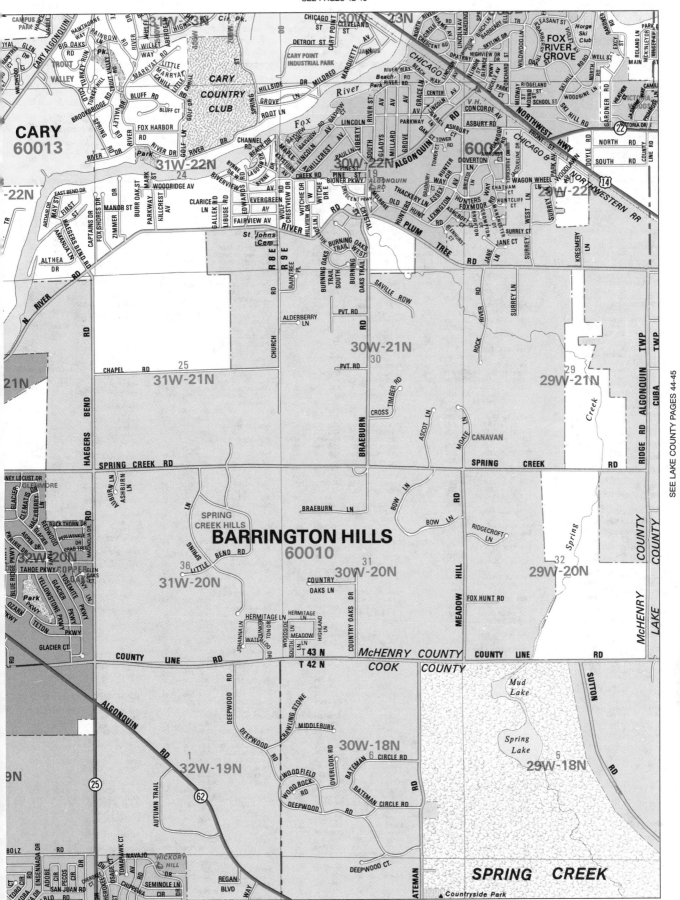

SEE LAKE COUNTY PAGES 44-45

# Street Index

| | Grid | Page |
|---|---|---|

## Alden Township

Alden Rd. NW&SE
...........46W-43N,45W-38N 6
Altenberg Rd. E&W
...........48W-39N,45W-39N 6
Bissell Rd. N&S .... 43W-43N 7
Crowley Rd. E&W .. 48W-40N 6
Durkee Rd. E&W
...........45W-39N,43W-39N 7
Ferris Rd. NE&SW .. 47W-40N 6
Fink Rd. N&S
...........44W-40N,44W-41N 7
French Dr. N&S .. 43W-41N 7
Gasch Rd. N&S
...........48W-42N,48W-43N 6
Green Rd. NS&EW
...........47W-38N,45W-38N 14
Green Valley Dr. NW&SE
...........43W-41N 7
Hebron Rd. E&W
...........48W-39N,43W-42N 6
Knickerbocker Rd. N&S
...........45W-41N,45W-43N 7
Lincoln Rd. N&S .. 46W-38N 14
Manley Rd. N&S
...........43W-38N,43W-39N 15
Mansion Heights Dr. E&W
...........43W-41N 7
Nolan Rd. N&S .... 46W-40N 6
O'Brien Rd. E&W
...........46W-40N,43W-40N 6
Oak Grove Rd. N&S
...........48W-41N,46W-41N 6
Oak Springs Dr. N&S
...........46W-40N 6
Reese Rd. N&S
...........47W-40N,47W-42N 6
Righeimer Rd. E&W
...........48W-39N,47W-39N 6
Rt. 173 NE&SW
...........48W-38N,43W-41N 14
S. Mansion Heights Dr. N&S
...........43W-41N 7
Schultz Rd. N&S . 48W-38N 14
Shields Rd. N&S
...........46W-38N,46W-39N 14
State Line Rd. N&S
...........49W-43N,44W-43N 5
Thayer Rd. E&W
...........44W-38N,43W-38N 15
Willow Lakes Ct. E&W
...........48W-42N 6
Willow Lakes Rd. N&S
...........48W-41N,48W-42N 6
Wright Rd. N&S
...........46W-41N,46W-42N 6

## Algonquin*

### (Also see Kane County)

Aberdeen Dr. N&S . 35W-21N 50
Alice Ln. N&S ...... 33W-20N 50
Amberwood Ct. N&S
...........35W-21N 50
Applewood Ln. N&S
...........32W-20N 50
Arguilla Dr. NS&EW
...........35W-21N 50
Armstrong St. NW&SE
...........34W-21N 50
Arrowhead Dr. N&S
...........33W-21N 50
Ash St. N&S ...... 33W-21N 50
Aspen Dr. E&W .... 32W-20N 50
Ballard Dr. N&S .... 32W-20N 50
Barrington Ct. E&W
...........35W-21N 50
Bayberry Dr., N. N&S
...........34W-21N 50
Beach Dr. E&W .... 34W-20N 50
Beach Way NW&SE
...........33W-21N 50
Bedford Ct. NW&SE
...........35W-21N 50
Berg St. NW&SE . 34W-21N 50
Big Sur Pkwy. N&S
...........32W-20N 50
Birch St. N&S ...... 33W-21N 50
Blue Ridge Pkwy. N&S
...........32W-20N 50
Bluestem Ln. NS&EW
...........37W-20N 49
Brentwood Ct. E&W
...........34W-20N 50
Brian Ct. E&W .... 34W-21N 50
Briarwood Ln. N&S
...........35W-21N 50
Briarwood Ln. NW&SE
...........35W-21N 49
Bridge Ln. E&W .... 29W-24N 43
Brindlewood Ct. N&S
...........35W-20N 50
Brindlewood Dr. E&W
...........35W-20N 50
Bristol Dr. N&S .... 35W-20N 50
Brook St. NW&SE . 33W-21N 50
Brookwood Cir. E&W
...........34W-21N 50
Buck Thorn Dr. E&W
...........32W-20N 50
Bunker Hill Ct. E&W
...........37W-20N 49

Bunker Hill Dr. E&W
...........37W-20N,36W-20N 49
Bunker Hill Dr. E&W
...........36W-20N 49
Burnham Ct. E&W .. 35W-20N 50
Butterfield Dr. E&W
...........34W-20N 50
Candlewood Ct. N&S
...........34W-20N 50
Cardiff Ct. N&S .... 35W-21N 50
Cardiff Dr. E&W .... 35W-21N 50
Carlington Ct. N&S 35W-20N 50
Carlisle St. NS&EW
...........35W-20N 50
Carriage Dr. N&S . 33W-20N 50
Cedarwood Ln. E&W
...........32W-20N 50
Center St. NW&SE 33W-20N 50
Cermak Rd. N&S .. 33W-21N 50
Chase St. NE&SW . 32W-20N 50
Chatham Cir. NS&EW
...........35W-20N 50
Chelsea Dr. E&W .. 35W-20N 50
Cherokee Rd. NE&SW
...........34W-20N 50
Cherrywood Ct. E&W
...........34W-20N 50
Chestnut Ct. NE&SW
...........34W-20N 50
Chicago St. NW&SE
...........34W-21N,33W-20N 50
Clay St. NW&SE ... 33W-20N 50
Cir. ...........32W-21N 50
Clearview Ct. NE&SW
...........34W-20N 50
Clematis Dr. E&W
...........32W-20N 50
Clover Ct. N&S .... 37W-20N 49
Clover Dr. N&S .... 37W-20N 49
Colonial Ct. E&W .. 33W-20N 50
Commerce Ln. N&S
...........33W-20N 50
Concord Ct. NE&SW
...........34W-20N 50
Cornell Ln. N&S .. 33W-20N 50
Country Ln. E&W .. 29W-24N 43
Country Ln. N&S .. 34W-21N 50
Countryside Dr. NE&SW
...........35W-20N 50
Cove Dr. NW&SE . 29W-24N 43
Crabtree Ln. N&S .. 34W-20N 50
Crestwood Ct. N&S
...........34W-21N 50
Crofton Dr. E&W .. 35W-20N 50
Cross St. NW&SE . 34W-20N 50
Cullom Ln. NW&SE
...........33W-20N 50
Cumberland Pkwy. NW&SE
...........32W-20N 51
Darlington Ct. N&S 35W-20N 50
Dawson Ln. NS&EW
...........35W-20N 50
Deer Path Rd. NW&SE
...........32W-21N 50
Division St. NW&SE
...........33W-20N 50
Dover St. N&S .... 35W-21S 50
Dowdle St. NW&SE
...........34W-21N 50
Eagle Ridge Ln. N&S
...........34W-20N 50
Eastgate Dr. N&S . 33W-20N 50
Echo Woods Dr. NS&EW
...........32W-21N 50
Edgewood Ct. N&S
...........35W-20N 50
Edgewood Rd. E&W
...........35W-20N,34W-20N 50
Edward St. NW&SE
...........33W-21N 50
Elm St. N&S ...... 33W-21N 50
Essex St. E&W .... 34W-21N 50
Evergreen Ct. NE&SW
...........34W-20N 50
Fairfield Ln N&S .... 35W-20N 50
Fairmont Ct. N&S .. 34W-20N 50
Fairway View Dr. N&S
...........37W-21N 49
Fairway View Dr. N&S
...........36W-20N 49
Falcon Ridge Ct. N&S
...........35W-21N 50
Farm Hill Ct. NW&SE
...........35W-21N 50
Farm Hill Dr. E&W . 35W-21N 50
Fieldcrest Ct. NE&SW
...........35W-21N 50
Fieldcrest Dr. N&S . 35W-21N 50
Filip Rd. E&W ...... 33W-20N 50
Flora Dr. SW&NE . 35W-20N 50
Forest Ct. NW&SE . 34W-20N 50
Fox Glove Dr. N&S
...........37W-20N 49
Fox River Dr. N&S . 33W-20N 50
Fox Run Ln. N&S .. 33W-20N 50
Front St. NW&SE .. 33W-20N 50
Getzelman Tr. N&S
...........33W-20N 50
Glacier Dr. E&W .. 33W-20N 50
Glacier Pkwy. N&S 32W-20N 50
Glengary Ct. NW&SE
...........35W-20N 50

| | Grid | Page |
|---|---|---|

Glenwood Ct. N&S 34W-21N 50
Goldenrod Dr. N&S
...........37W-20N 49
Golf Ln. NE&SW .. 32W-20N 50
Grandview Ct. N&S
...........34W-20N 50
Greens View Dr. NS&EW
...........36W-20N,36W-21N 49
Greensview Dr. N&S
...........36W-20N 49
Hackberry Ln N&S . 32W-20N 50
Hanson Rd. N&S .. 35W-20N 50
Harnish Dr. SW&NE
...........35W-20N 50
Harper Ct. NW&SE
...........34W-20N 50
Harper Dr. N&S .... 34W-20N 50
Harrison St. NE&SW
...........33W-20N,33W-21N 50
Hartford Ct. E&W . 35W-21N 50
Hartly Dr. E&W .... 35W-20N 50
Hayes E&W ...... 34W-20N 50
Helen Dr. E&W .... 33W-20N 50
Hickory Ln. E&W .. 33W-20N 50
Highland Av. NE&SW
...........33W-20N,32W-20N 50
Hillcrest Dr. NE&SW
...........33W-21N 50
Hillside View N&S
...........35W-19N,34W-21N 50
Holly Ln. E&W .... 34W-21N 50
Homestead Ct. E&W
...........33W-20N 50
Honey Locust Dr. E&W
...........32W-20N 50
Hubbard St. NE&SW
...........33W-20N 50
Huntington Ct. NE&SW
...........34W-20N 50
Huntington Dr. E&W
...........35W-21N 50
Huntington Dr. NW&SE
...........34W-20N 50
Huntington Dr., N. NW&SE
...........34W-21N 50
Inca St. N&S ...... 32W-21N 50
Indian Tr. NW&SE . 33W-21N 50
Interloch Ct. N&S . 35W-20N 50
Ionia Tr. NW&SE .. 32W-21N 50
Ivy Ln. NW&SE .... 32W-20N 50
Jackson St. NW&SE
...........33W-20N 50
James St. N&S 33W-20N 50
Jayne St. NW&SE . 33W-20N 50
Jefferson St. NE&SW
...........33W-20N 50
Jennifer Ct. N&S .. 33W-20N 50
Jester Ln. E&W .... 35W-20N 50
Juniper Ct. NW&SE
...........34W-20N 50
Kingsbury Ct. E&W
...........33W-20N 50
Klasen Rd. E&W
...........32W-22N,33W-22N 50
Kublank E&W ...... 33W-20N 50
La Crosse Ct. N&S
...........32W-21N 50
La Fox River Dr. NE&SW
...........33W-20N 50
Lake Dr., S. N&S .. 35W-21N 50
Lake Dr., S. Ct. N&S
...........35W-21N 50
Lakeview Dr. E&W . 37W-20N 49
Legion Dr. NW&SE
...........32W-21N 50
Lehigh Ct. NW&SE 32W-21N 50
Lehman St. N&S .. 33W-21N 50
Lexington Dr. E&W
...........34W-20N 50
Lilac Dr. N&S ...... 32W-20N 50
Lincoln St. N&S
...........33W-20N 50
Linda Dr. N&S ...... 33W-20N 50
Longwood Ct. N&S
...........35W-20N 50
Longwood Dr. N&S
...........34W-20N 50
Lorden Ct. E&W .. 30W-25N 43
Lowe Rd. NE&SW . 32W-20N 50
Madison St. NW&SE
...........33W-20N 50
Magnolia Dr. E&W . 32W-20N 50
Main St. NE&SW .. 34W-20N 50
Majestic Dr. NS&EW
...........35W-20N 50
Maplewood Ln. E&W
...........33W-20N,32W-20N 50
Mayfair Ln. N&S .... 35W-20N 50
Meadow Dr. N&S .. 34W-20N 50
Melvina Ct. NW&SE
...........32W-21N 50
Merrill Av. N&S .... 34W-20N 50
Meyer Dr. N&S .... 34W-21N 50
Meyer Dr. NW&SE . 34W-11N 50
Millcreek Ln. N&S . 35W-20N 50
Mohawk St. N&S .. 33W-20N 50
Mound St. NE&SW
...........33W-20N,33W-21N 50
Mulberry Ct. NE&SW
...........32W-21N 50
Newark St. N&S .. 35W-20N 50
Oak Ln. NE&SW .. 33W-21N 50
Oak St. N&S ...... 33W-21N 50

| | Grid | Page |
|---|---|---|

Oak Trace E&W .. 32W-20N 50
Oakleaf Ct. E&W .. 35W-21N 50
Oakleaf Rd. NS&EW
...........35W-21N 50
Oakview Dr. NE&SW
...........34W-20N 50
Oceola Dr. N&S .. 33W-20N 50
Old Mill Ln. N&S
...........32W-20N 50
Cir. ...........33W-20N 50
Olin Ct. E&W .... 33W-20N 50
Orchard Ct. NE&SW
...........34W-20N 50
Ozark Pkwy. NW&SE
...........32W-20N 50
Park St. NW&SE .. 33W-21N 50
Parkview Ter. N&S 34W-20N 50
Parkview Ter., S. E&W
...........34W-20N 50
Parkwood Cir. E&W
...........35W-20N 50
Partidge Ct. N&S .. 34W-21N 50
Partridge Ct. N&S . 34W-21N 50
Perry Dr. NW&SE . 32W-20N 50
Persimmon Dr. NS&EW
...........37W-20N 49
Perwinkle Dr. E&W 32W-20N 50
Philip Rd. E&W .... 33W-20N 50
Pickwick Ct. E&W . 33W-20N 50
Pioneer Rd. NE&SW
...........33W-21N 50
Pleasant View Dr. E&W
...........34W-20N 50
Plymouth Ct. N&S . 33W-20N 50
Point Ct. NW&SE . 33W-21N 50
Portsmouth Ct. NW&SE
...........35W-21N 50
Powder Horn Dr. E&W
...........32W-20N 50
Prairie Dr. NW&SE . 33W-20N 50
Preston Ct. N&S .. 35W-21N 50
Preston Dr. E&W .. 35W-21N 50
Randall Rd. N&S
...........35W-20N,36W-20N 49
Rattray Dr. N&S .. 33W-20N 50
Red Coach Ln. E&W
...........34W-20N 50
Redwood Dr. NW&SE
...........32W-20N 50
Regal Ct. E&W .... 35W-20N 50
Regal Ln. N&S .... 35W-20N 50
Ridge Ln. N&S .... 34W-20N 50
Ridge St. NW&SE . 34W-20N 50
River Rd. NE&SW .. 33W-21N 50
Riverview Dr. E&W . 33W-20N 50
Riverview Dr. N&S . 32W-21N 50
Riverview Rd. NE&SW
...........33W-21N 50
Roaring Brook Ln. N&S
...........35W-20N 50
Robinwood Dr. E&W
...........35W-20N 50
Rochester Ct. NE&SW
...........35W-21N 50
Rolls Dr. N&S ...... 35W-20N 50
Rt. 62 NW&SE .... 33W-20N 50
Ryan Pkwy. SW&NE
...........32W-20N 50
Saddle Oaks Dr. N&S
...........29W-24N 43
Saddlebrook Cir. N&S
...........34W-20N 50
Salford Ct. N&S .. 35W-21N 50
Salford Dr. N&S .... 35W-21N 50
Sandbloom Rd. N&S
...........33W-20N 50
Sandpebble Cir. E&W
...........34W-20N 50
Sandpebble Ct. NW&SE
...........34W-20N 50
Sandpiper Ct. N&S 35W-20N 50
Sawmill Ln. NS&EW
...........35W-20N 50
Schuett St. E&W .. 33W-20N 50
Scott St. NE&SW .. 33W-20N 50
Seminole Rd. NE&SW
...........32W-21N 50
Shagbark Ct. N&S . 34W-20N 50
Short Pl. E&W ...... 33W-20N 50
Sioux St. NE&SW .. 33W-20N 50
Skyline Dr. N&S .... 34W-20N 50
Somerset Ct. N&S . 35W-21N 50
Sound Rd. N&S .. 32W-20N 50
South Dr. E&W .... 35W-20N 50
South River Dr. NE&SW
...........33W-20N 50
South Surrey Ln. E&W
...........34W-20N 50
Southwick Dr. N&S
...........35W-20N 50
Souwanas Tr. E&W
...........33W-20N 50
Spring Creek Rd. E&W
...........32W-20N 50
St. Andrews Ct. N&S
...........35W-20N 50
Starr Dr. N&S ...... 34W-21N 50
Stevens Ct. N&S .. 34W-21N 50
Stonegate Dr. N&S
...........35W-20N,35W-21N 50
Stonegate Rd. NS&EW
...........35W-20N 50

| | Grid | Page |
|---|---|---|

Stoneybrook Ct. N&S
...........34W-21N 50
Summit St. NE&SW
...........33W-20N 50
Sunny Dr. NW&SE . 33W-21N 50
Sunrise Ln. E&W .. 33W-20N 50
Sunset Ln. E&W .. 33W-20N 50
Sunshine Ct. E&W . 33W-20N 50
Surrey Ct. E&W .... 34W-20N 50
Surrey Ln. E&W .... 34W-20N 50
Surrey Ln., W. N&S
...........34W-20N 50
Susan Ct. N&S .... 33W-20N 50
Sussex Ln. N&S
...........35W-20N,35W-21N 50
Sutcliff Dr. N&S .. 35W-20N 50
Tahoe Pkwy. E&W . 32W-20N 50
Tallgrass Ct. E&W . 35W-21N 50
Tamarack Dr. N&S . 33W-20N 50
Tanglewood Dr. E&W
...........32W-20N 50
Terrace Dr. N&S .. 34W-20N 50
Thorneapple Ln. N&S
...........32W-20N 50
Thornwood Dr. N&S
...........32W-20N 50
Timberwood Ln. N&S
...........32W-20N 50
Trinity Dr. E&W .... 33W-22N 50
Tuneridge Ct. EW&NS
...........35W-20N 50
Tuneridge Tr. EW&NS
...........35W-20N 50
Twisted Oak Ct. E&W
...........34W-20N 50
Valley View Ct. NW&SE
...........33W-21N 50
Victoria St. E&W .. 34W-20N 50
Vista Dr., N. E&W . 33W-20N 50
Vista Dr., W. E&W . 33W-20N 50
Walnut Ln. E&W ... 33W-20N 50
Washington St. NW&SE
...........33W-20N 50
Washtenaw Ln. E&W
...........33W-20N 50
Water St. NW&SE . 33W-21N 50
Webster Ct. N&S . 33W-20N 50
Webster St. E&W .. 33W-20N 50
Wesley Ln. NW&SE
...........32W-20N 50
West End Dr. N&S . 34W-20N 50
Westbury Dr. E&W . 35W-20N 50
Wilbrandt Rd. E&W
...........33W-20N 50
Wildwood Rd. N&S
...........33W-21N 50
Willow Ln. NW&SE
...........33W-20N 50
Winchester Dr. NS&EW
...........35W-20N 50
Windsor Ct. N&S .. 35W-20N 50
Windy Knoll Dr. E&W
...........34W-20N 50
Wintergreen Ct. E&W
...........37W-20N 49
Wintergreen Ter. E&W
...........37W-20N 49
Woodcreek Ct. NW&SE
...........36W-20N 49
Woods Creek Ln. E&W
...........36W-20N 49
Woodview Ln. E&W
...........33W-20N 50
Yellowstone Pkwy. NW&SE
...........32W-20N 50
Yorktown Dr. NE&SW
...........34W-20N 50
Yosemite Pkwy. N&S
...........32W-20N 50
Zange Dr. E&W .... 34W-20N 50
5 Mile Ct. N&S .... 32W-25N 42

## Algonquin Township

Abbotts Ln. N&S .. 29W-23N 43
Algonquin Rd. E&W
...........36W-21N,35W-21N 49
Algonquin Rd. E&W
...........30W-22N 51
Allen Rd. E&W .... 32W-22N 50
Amy Dr. E&W ...... 32W-25N 42
Arthur Dr. NS&EW . 32W-20N 50
Ashford Ln. NE&SE
...........36W-22N 49
Autumn Ln. E&W .. 32W-23N 50
Balder St. N&S .... 29W-23N 43
Bayport Ln. N&S .. 29W-23N 43
Beach Dr. NE&SW . 31W-22N 51
Becker Ct. N&S .. 36W-22N 49
Big Creek Passe NE&SW
...........36W-22N 49
Big Oaks Rd. NS&EW
...........34W-23N 42
Bioner Pkwy. E&W 30W-22N 51
Birch St. N&S .... 33W-24N 42
Blackhawk Tr. NW&SE
...........35W-20N 50
Blarney Stone Rd. NW&SE
...........31W-25N 43
Bluff Ct. E&W ...... 31W-22N 51
Bluff Rd. E&W .... 31W-22N 51
Bluff Tr. N&S ...... 32W-22N 50

**Grid — Page**

Bridgeport Ln. E&W
..... 36W-22N — 49
Brighton Ln. E&W . 34W-20N — 50
Brisbane Dr. E&W . 29W-24N — 43
Bristol Way E&W . 30W-24N — 43
Brompton Ct. E&W
..... 36W-22N — 49
Brompton Rd. N&S
..... 36W-22N — 49
Brookbridge Rd. NE&SW
.....32W-22N,31W-22N — 50
Burman Dr. E&W ... 32W-25N — 42
Burr Oak Ct. N&S . 33W-24N — 42
Burr Oak St. N&S . 31W-25N — 51
Byrne Dr. NE&SW . 31W-22N — 51
Byrne Dr., W. E&W
..... 31W-22N — 51
Cahill Rd. NW&SE . 31W-23N — 43
Captains Dr. E&W . 32W-22N — 50
Cardinal Dr. N&S . 34W-20N — 50
Carrie Ct. NE&SW . 32W-25N — 42
Cary Rd. NE&SW . 33W-21N — 50
Cary-Algonquin Rd. NE&SW
.....32W-22N,31W-24N — 50
Center St. N&S ... 34W-20N — 50
Cermak Rd. NW&SE
..... 33W-21N — 50
Channel Rd. NE&SW
..... 31W-22N — 51
Chestnut Ln. N&S . 29W-23N — 43
Church Ln. NS&EW
..... 32W-25N — 42
Churchill Ct. N&S . 33W-25N — 42
Circle Dr. N&S....34W-20N — 50
Claire St. E&W ... 33W-24N — 42
Clarice Ln. E&W...31W-22N — 51
Clark St. E&W ....29W-23N — 43
Clear Sky Tr. E&W 36W-22N — 49
Cog Circle N&S . 33W-25N — 42
Cold Spring Rd. NW&SE
.....32W-22N,31W-22N — 50
Colonial Av. N&S . 33W-24N — 42
Cougar Tr. ....30W-24N — 43
Country Ln. E&W . 29W-24N — 43
County Line Rd. E&W
..... 36W-20N — 49
Cove Dr. N&S...29W-24N — 43
Cowlin St. E&W . 33W-24N — 42
Crabtree Ln. E&W . 30W-24N — 43
Craig St. E&W ... 34W-21N — 50
Creek Ln. E&W . 31W-25N — 43
Creek Rd. E&W ... 30W-22N — 51
Crestview Dr. N&S. 29W-25N — 51
Crestview Rd. N&S
..... 30W-22N — 51
Crystal Lake Av. E&W
..... 34W-25N,32W-25N — 42
Crystal Lake Rd. NS&EW
..... 31W-25N,30W-22N — 43
Crystal St. E&W . 30W-22N — 51
Daniel Dr. E&W . 33W-25N — 42
David Ln. E&W ... 33W-25N — 42
Deerpath Rd. NW&SE
..... 32W-21N — 50
Dennis Av. N&S . 34W-21N — 50
Devonshire Rd. N&S
..... 34W-20N — 50
Diamond Ln. E&W ..29W-23N — 43
Dove Way N&S ... 30W-24N — 43
Doyle Rd. N&S ... 29W-22N — 51
Drive-In Ln. E&W .. 33W-24N — 42
Dublin Ct. NE&SW .31W-25N — 43
Dublin Dr. N&S ..31W-25N — 43
E. Monticello Way N&S
..... 33W-24N — 42
Edwards Rd. N&S .31W-22N — 51
Elk Tr. E&W ....30W-24N — 43
Elmwood Ct. E&W .33W-21N — 50
Ethel Av. N&S.....34W-21N — 50
Evergreen Av. E&W
..... 31W-22N — 51
Excy St. N&S ... 29W-23N — 43
Fairfax Dr. E&W .. 33W-24N — 42
Fairview Av. E&W . 31W-22N — 51
First Av. N&S ....33W-22N — 50
First St. NE&SW..32W-22N — 50
Fox Harbor Rd. E&W
..... 31W-22N — 51
Fox River Grove Rd. E&W
..... 29W-22N — 51
Fox Shores Dr. N&S
..... 31W-22N — 51
Gallek Rd. N&S ...31W-22N — 51
Garden Ln. E&W . 32W-22N — 50
Gardner Rd. N&S . 29W-22N — 51
Geringer Dr. NE&SW
..... 33W-21N — 50
Golf Course Rd. N&S
..... 36W-22N — 49
Golf Dr. N&S ...31W-22N — 51
Golf Ln. E&W ...31W-22N — 51
Golf View Dr. NS&EW
..... 33W-24N — 42
Grand Dr. E&W . 29W-23N — 43
Green Ln. E&W . 31W-25N — 43
Green Meadow Ln. N&S
..... 32W-25N,31W-25N — 42
Green Meadow Ln. N&S
..... 32W-25N,31W-25N — 42
Green Pasture Dr. NW&SE
..... 34W-20N — 50
Green Ridge Rd. E&W
..... 31W-25N — 43
Greensview Dr. N&S
..... 36W-21N — 49
Greenwood Ct. E&W
..... 33W-21N — 50
Grove Ln. E&W . 31W-22N — 51
Haegers Bend Rd. N&S
.....32W-20N,32W-22N — 50
Halfmoon Gate N&S
..... 36W-22N — 49

Hartford Ln. NW&SE
..... 36W-22N — 49
Hawthorne Dr. NE&SW
.....32W-23N,31W-25N — 42
Hawthorne Way NE&SW
..... 32W-23N — 42
Heather Dr. NE&SW
..... 32W-21N — 50
Heatland Gate E&W
..... 36w-22N — 49
Heavens Gate NE&SW
..... 36W-22N — 49
Heavens Gate Ct. NW&SE
..... 36W-22N — 49
Hemlock St. N&S . 33W-24N — 42
Hickory Grove Ln. E&W
..... 29W-25N — 43
Hickory Grove Rd. E&W
..... 29W-25N — 43
Highland Dr. E&W
.....32W-25N,31W-25N — 42
Hillary Ln. E&W . 30W-24N — 43
Hillcrest Av. N&S . 31W-22N — 51
Hillcrest Ct. N&S . 33W-24N — 42
Hillcrest Rd. N&S . 31W-25N — 43
Hillside Dr. E&W . 31W-22N — 51
Hilltop Ln. N&S . 30W-22N — 51
Hillview Dr. N&S . 30W-22N — 51
Holly Lynn Dr. E&W
..... 29W-24N — 43
Holly Lynn Rd. E&W
..... 29W-24N — 43
Hunter Path N&S . 31W-25N — 43
Hyinisport Ln. E&W
..... 36W-22N — 49
Ida Dr. NW&SE . 31W-25N — 43
Iroquois E&W ... 33W-20N — 50
Isabel Av. NE&SW . 34W-21N — 50
Joan St. E&W ... 34W-21N — 50
John St. N&S ... 34W-21N — 50
Kendall Av. NE&SW
..... 33W-21N — 50
Kenilworth Av. N&S
..... 33W-21N — 50
Kenneth Dr. E&W .. 33W-25N — 42
Kensington Ln. N&S
..... 36W-22N — 49
Kent Av. N&S....34W-25N — 42
Kent St. N&S ... 34W-25N — 42
Kilkenny Ct. NW&SE
..... 32W-25N — 42
Killarney Dr. E&W
.....32W-25N,31W-25N — 42
Kings Bridge Dr. N&S
..... 30W-25N — 43
Kingsbury Ct. N&S .33W-20N — 50
Kingston Pl. N&S . 34W-20N — 50
Klasen Rd. E&W ..33W-22N — 50
Knoll Dr. N&S ...30W-24N — 43
Lagoon Dr. N&S..29W-23N — 43
Lagoon Dr. NE&SW
..... 31W-22N — 51
Lake Shore Dr. N&S
..... 31W-25N — 43
Lakewood Dr. N&S
.....32W-25N,31W-25N — 42
Laurie Ct. E&W . 33W-25N — 42
Laurie Ln. E&W . 33W-25N — 42
Leah Dr. E&W ...29W-25N — 43
Libuse Rd. N&S...31W-22N — 51
Lilac Ln. E&W ...29W-25N — 43
Limerick Dr. NE&SW
..... 31W-25N — 43
Linden Av. E&W . 34W-21N — 50
Lindsay Ln. NS&EW
..... 32W-25N — 42
Little Cahill N&S
.....31W-22N,31W-23N — 51
Little Marayat E&W
..... 31W-23N — 43
Little Marryat E&W 31W-23N — 43
Little Marryat Ct. E&W
..... 31W-23N — 43
Londonderry Dr. N&S
..... 31W-25N — 43
Longview Dr. N&S . 33W-22N — 50
Lund Av. NE&SW . 33W-21N — 50
Machelle Dr. E&W .29W-24N — 43
Main St. E&W . 29W-23N — 43
Mallard Stag Tr. NS&EW
..... 30W-24N — 43
Manor Rd. N&S . 33W-24N — 42
Manor St. E&W . 31W-22N — 51
Marayat Rd. NE&SW
..... 31W-23N — 43
Marie Av. NE&SW . 34W-21N — 50
Mark St. N&S . 31W-22N — 51
Marryat Rd. E&W
..... 31W-23N — 43
May Av. N&S . 32W-22N — 50
May St. N&S . 32W-22N — 50
McKinley Av. N&S .29W-23N — 43
Meadow Ln. E&W . 29W-24N — 43
Meandering Way E&W
..... 33W-25N,32W-25N — 42
Middle Ln. E&W . 31W-25N — 43
Miller Rd. E&W . 36W-22N — 49
Mink Tr. E&W . 30W-24N — 43
Mohican Dr. NW&SE
..... 33W-20N — 50
Moonstone Run NE&SW
..... 36W-22N — 49
N. Wynwood Dr. N&S
..... 32W-25N — 42
Nancy Dr. NS&EW .33W-25N — 42
Navajo Rd. N&S
..... 33W-20N — 50
Nevin Av. N&S . 34W-21N — 50
Newbold Rd. N&S
.....29W-23N,29W-24N — 43
Newport Ln. E&W . 36W-22N — 49

Nighthawk Way N&S
..... 30W-24N — 43
North Ln. E&W . 31W-25N — 43
North Rd. E&W . 29W-22N — 51
Northlane Rd. E&W
..... 31W-25N — 43
Oak Rd. N&S ... 32W-21N — 50
Oakbrook Dr. E&W
..... 33W-24N — 42
Oakcrest Rd. E&W . 29W-24N — 43
Oakdale Ter. E&W .31W-25N — 43
Oakwood Ct. E&W .33W-21N — 50
Old Post Rd. N&S . 33W-24N — 42
Oscar St. N&S . 34W-21N — 50
Otter Tr. E&W .30W-24N — 43
Owl Way N&S...30W-24N — 43
Park Dr. E&W . 29W-23N — 43
Park Pl. E&W...33W-21N — 50
Parkway N&S . 31W-22N — 51
Parkway Dr. E&W . 29W-23N — 43
Pheasant Dr. . 31W-25N — 43
Pleasant View Ln. NW&SE
..... 31W-25N — 43
Poplar Pkwy. E&W 30W-22N — 51
Poplar Pkwy. NW&SE
..... 30W-22N — 51
Portsmith Rd. N&S 36W-22N — 49
Powers St. N&S . 29W-23N — 43
Preston Pl. NS&EW
..... 33W-25N — 42
Prides Run N&S . 36W-22N — 49
Pringee Rd. N&S
.....33W-24N,33W-25N — 42
Rainbow Ln. E&W . 31W-23N — 43
Ramble Rd. NS&EW
..... 31W-25N — 43
Randall Rd. N&S
.....36W-20N,36W-22N — 49
Rawson Bridge Rd. N&S
.....30W-24N,30W-25N — 43
Raymond Dr. E&W 33W-24N — 42
Redwood St. N&S . 33W-24N — 42
Richard Dr. N&S....33W-25N — 42
Ridge Rd. N&S ... 29W-20N — 51
River Dr. E&W
.....32W-22N,31W-22N — 50
River Ln. E&W . 31W-23N — 43
River Rd. E&W . 30W-22N — 51
River Way N&S . 29W-23N — 43
Riverview Av. E&W
..... 31W-22N — 51
Riverview Dr. N&S.29W-23N — 43
Robert Rd. N&S . 31W-25N — 43
Robin Ln. N&S . 33W-25N — 42
Rodger St. E&W . 34W-21N — 50
Roland Dr. N&S . 29W-23N — 43
Roland Ln. N&S . 29W-23N — 43
Rona Rd. E&W . 29W-24N — 43
Ronald Ln. E&W ..33W-25N — 42
Roosevelt St. E&W
..... 35W-23N — 50
Root Ln. E&W.....33W-25N — 42
Rose St. E&W...33W-24N — 42
Rosemarie St. E&W
..... 34W-21N — 50
Rt. 31 N&S
.....34W-20N,34W-23N — 50
Russel St. N&S . 29W-23N — 43
S. Kilkenny Dr. NS&EW
..... 32W-25N — 42
S. Nancy Dr. E&W .33W-25N — 42
Saggers Ln. E&W . 33W-24N — 42
Sands Rd. N&S
.....33W-24N,33W-25N — 42
Sauwanas Tr. E&W
..... 33W-20N — 50
Scenic Ct. E&W . 34W-20N — 50
Scott Ct. E&W . 33W-25N — 42
Scott Ln. N&S....33W-25N — 42
Scotty Av. N&S . 34W-21N — 50
Second Av. N&S . 33W-22N — 50
Shales St. N&S . 33W-24N — 42
Shannon Dr. N&S . 31W-25N — 43
Short St. E&W . 34W-20N — 50
Short St. NE&SW . 32W-21N — 50
Smith Rd. N&S . 33W-25N — 42
Sorrel Ter. E&W . 33W-25N — 42
South Blue Ct. N&S
..... 33W-25N — 42
South Rd. E&W . 29W-22N — 51
Southlane E&W . 31W-25N — 43
Southport Ln. E&W
..... 36W-22N — 49
Spring Beach Way N&S
..... 30W-23N — 43
Spring Creek Rd. E&W
..... 32W-21N — 50
Spring St. N&S . 32W-21N — 50
Squirrel Tr. . 30W-24N — 43
Starr Dr. N&S . 32W-21N — 50
Starwood Pass E&W
..... 36W-22N — 49
State St. E&W . 33W-24N — 42
Steeple Run E&W
.....33W-25N,32W-25N — 42
Stockport Ln. E&W
..... 36W-22N — 49
Stockton St. NS&EW
..... 36W-22N — 49
Stonegate Rd. N&S
..... 31W-23N — 43
Stratford Dr. N&S
..... 36W-22N — 49
Summer Dr. NE&SW
..... 32W-22N — 50
Sun Valley Dr. NE&SW
..... 31W-25N — 43
Swan Way N&S . 30W-24N — 43
Sweetwater Ct. NE&SW
..... 36W-22N — 49
Sweetwater Ridge N&S
..... 36W-22N — 49

Sweitzer NW&SE . 33W-21N — 50
Teki Dr. E&W . 33W-24N — 42
Terrace Dr. NE&SW
..... 33W-24N — 42
Third St. N&S . 33W-22N — 50
Thistle Ct. N&S . 29W-25N — 43
Thomas St. N&S . 34W-25N — 42
Three Oaks Rd. E&W
.....33W-24N,29W-24N — 42
Topview Rd. NW&SE
..... 31W-25N — 43
Tower Dr. N&S . 30W-23N — 51
Tower Dr. E&W . 30W-23N — 43
Triangle Wood Dr. NE&NS
..... 30W-23N — 43
Trout Valley Rd. N&S
..... 31W-23N — 43
Turkey Hill NE&SW
.....32W-22N,31W-23N — 50
Turkey Run N&S . 32W-22N — 42
Tuxedo Ln. NW&SE
..... 33W-24N — 42
U.S. Route 14 E&W
.....32W-24N,29W-22N — 42
Valerie Dr. E&W ..33W-25N — 42
Valholla Circle NW&SE
..... 33W-24N — 42
Valley Rd. N&S ..31W-22N — 51
Victor Pl. E&W ...33W-21N — 50
Village Ct. N&S . 36W-22N — 49
Village Rd. E&W . 36W-22N — 49
Voce Ct. N&S . 29W-23N — 43
W. Rawson Bridge Rd. N&S
..... 31W-25N — 43
Wallace Dr. E&W . 29W-23N — 43
Wallen Dr. E&W . 33W-25N — 42
Walnut Dr. E&W . 33W-25N — 42
Wander Way N&S . 31W-25N — 43
Warrington Ln. N&S
..... 36W-22N — 49
White Pine Dr. N&S
..... 30W-24N — 43
Wichie Dr., E. N&S 30W-22N — 51
Wichie Dr., W. N&S
..... 30W-22N — 51
Wildberry Ln. N&S .29W-25N — 43
Willet Way E&W . 31W-23N — 43
Willow St. E&W . 33W-21N — 50
Willy Av. N&S . 34W-21N — 50
Wilmette Av. N&S . 34W-21N — 50
Winding Rd. N&S . 32W-26N — 42
Witchie Rd. N&S . 30W-22N — 51
Witchie Dr., E. N&S
..... 30W-22N — 51
Witchie Dr., W. N&S
..... 30W-22N — 51
Wium Av. N&S . 29W-23N — 43
Wolf Rd. N&S . 31W-22N — 51
Wood St. N&S . 31W-25N — 43
Woodbine Rd. E&W
..... 29W-23N — 43
Woodlawn Av. NE&SW
..... 29W-23N — 51
Woodridge Av. E&W
..... 31W-22N — 51
Wyndwood Dr. NS&EW
.....33W-25N,32W-25N — 42
Zimmer Dr. N&S . 31W-22N — 51
1st St. NE&SW . 32W-22N — 50

## Barnard Mill

Barnard Mill Rd. NW&SE
.....36W-38N,37W-38N — 17
Camelia Ct. NE&SW
..... 36W-37N — 17
Cherry Ct. NE&SW
.....36W-37N,36W-38N — 17
Giant Oak Rd. N&S
..... 37W-37N — 17
Giant Oak Rd. N&S
..... 37W-38N — 17
Greenwood Rd. NE&SW
.....38W-37N,38W-38N — 17
Hickory Ln. E&W
.....37W-38N,38W-38N — 17
Howe Dr. E&W . 36W-37N — 17
Howe Rd. E&W
.....37W-37N,38W-37N — 17
Jonquil Dr. N&S ....36W-37N — 17
Magnolia Dr. N&S . 36W-37N — 17
Mill Dr. N&S.....36W-37N — 17
Oak Hill Dr. N&S . 36W-38N — 17
Oakhill Dr. NS&EW
..... 36W-37N — 17
West Wonder Lake Rd. N&S
..... 37W-37N — 17

## Barrington Hills*
### (Also see Cook, Kane and Lake Counties)

Alderberry Ln. E&W
..... 30W-21N — 51
Cir. .....30W-20N — 51
Auburn Ln. N&S . 31W-20N — 51
Barrington Bourne NS&EW
..... 30W-20N — 51
Bow Ln. NW&SE . 30W-20N — 51
Braeburn Ln. E&W .30W-20N — 51
Braeburn Rd. N&S .30W-20N — 51
Burning Oaks Trail NW&SE
..... 30W-20N — 51
Burning Oaks Trail, S.
NW&SE . 30W-20N — 51
Burning Oaks Trail, W. E&W
..... 30W-20N — 51
Chapel Ln. N&S . 31W-20N — 51
Church Rd. N&S . 31W-21N — 51
Country Oaks Dr. N&S
..... 30W-20N — 51

Country Oaks Ln. E&W
..... 30W-20N — 51
County Line Rd. E&W
.....31W-20N,29W-20N — 51
Crescent Pkwy. NW&SE
..... 30W-22N — 51
Cross Timber Rd. NS&EW
..... 30W-21N — 51
Fox Hunt Rd. N&S
..... 29W-20N — 51
Front St. NW&SE . 29W-22N — 51
Haegers Bend Rd. N&S
..... 32W-21N — 51
Jane Ct. E&W . 29W-22N — 51
Jane Ln. NE&SW . 29W-22N — 51
Kresmery Ln. N&S . 29W-22N — 51
Little Bend Rd. NS&EW
..... 31W-20N — 51
Meadow Hill Rd. N&S
..... 30W-20N — 51
N. County Line Rd. E&W
..... 31W-20N — 51
Park Av. N&S . 29W-22N — 51
Phillip Ter. E&W ..30W-21N — 51
Plum Tree Rd. E&W
..... 29W-22N — 51
Pvt. Rd. E&W
.....30W-21N,26W-18N — 51
Pvt. Rd. N&S . 30W-21N — 51
Pvt. Rd. N&S . 29W-21N — 51
Raintree Dr. EW&NS
..... 30W-22N — 51
Raintree Pl. E&W . 30W-22N — 51
Ridge Rd. N&S . 29W-21N — 51
Ridgecroft Ln. NS&EW
..... 29W-20N — 51
Rock Ridge Rd. N&S
..... 29W-21N — 51
Saville Row NW&SE
..... 30W-22N — 51
Spring Creek Rd. E&W
..... 30W-22N — 51
Spring Ln. N&S . 31W-20N — 51
Sunny Meridian N&S
..... 30W-22N — 51
Surrey Ct. E&W . 29W-22N — 51
Surrey Ln. N&S . 29W-21N — 51
Surrey Ln. NS&EW
..... 29W-22N — 51
Surrey West N&S . 29W-22N — 51
Wagon Wheel Ln. E&W
..... 29W-22N — 51

## Bull Valley

Blackberry Dr. NS&EW
..... 38W-31N — 25
Boone Creek Ter. NS&EW
.....36W-30N,36W-31N — 33
Breckenridge Ct. NW&SE
..... 37W-32N — 25
Bull Valley Rd. E&W
.....39W-31N,36W-31N — 24
Cold Springs Rd. N&S
..... 38W-31N,38W-32N — 25
Concord Dr. E&W . 37W-32N — 25
Crystal Springs Rd. E&W
.....39W-29N,35W-29N — 33
Fairway Ln. E&W . 39W-31N — 25
Fleming Rd. E&W
.....39W-31N,38W-31N — 25
High Meadow Dr. NE&SW
..... 38W-31N — 25
High Meadow Ln. E&W
..... 38W-31N — 25
Locust Ln. N&S . 39W-31N — 25
N. Cherry Valley Rd. N&S
.....36W-30N,36W-31N — 33
Orchard Valley Dr. E&W
..... 36W-31N — 25
Ridge Rd. N&S . 36W-31N — 25
Saddle Creek Tr. NW&SE
..... 36W-31N — 25
Sudberg Ct. E&W . 37W-32N — 25
Swarthmore Rd. N&S
.....37W-31N,37W-32N — 25
Valley Hill Rd. N&S
.....37W-31N,37W-32N — 25
Valley Rd. NE&SW
.....36W-30N,36W-31N — 33
Woodland Dr. N&S 39W-31N — 25
Woodstone Ln. E&W
..... 38W-31N — 25

## Burton Township

Ann Pl. E&W . 29W-38N — 19
Arlington Dr. NE&SW
..... 30W-39N — 11
Baron Dr. E&W . 29W-38N — 19
Barry Av. N&S . 29W-39N — 11
Beacon St. E&W . 30W-39N — 11
Bellevue Av. N&S . 30W-39N — 11
Berwyn St. E&W . 30W-39N — 11
Beverly Way NE&SW
..... 30W-39N — 11
Bittersweet Pl. NS&EW
..... 29W-38N — 19
Blaine Pl. N&S...29W-38N — 19
Buena Av. N&S
.....29W-38N,29W-38N — 19
Carleton Ct. N&S . 30W-39N — 11
Casper St. N&S . 29W-38N — 11
Cass St. E&W . 29W-39N — 11
Chateau Dr. E&W . 29W-38N — 19
Coventry Av. N&S . 29W-38N — 19
Cuneo Ct. N&S . 29W-38N — 11
Daly Av. N&S . 29W-38N — 19
Dannell Pl. E&W . 29W-38N — 11
Deming Pl. NW&SE
..... 29W-38N — 19
Edgewater St. N&S
..... 29W-39N — 11

| | Grid | Page |
|---|---|---|
| Engels Pl. E&W .. 29W-39N | | 11 |
| English Prairie Rd. E&W | | |
| ................ 30W-42N | | 11 |
| Fern St. NW&SE .. 29W-38N | | 19 |
| Gray St. N&S ..... 29W-38N | | 19 |
| Grove Rd. N&S .... 29W-39N | | 11 |
| Hastings Av. E&W . 29W-38N | | 19 |
| Island Ct. E&SW .. 30W-39N | | 11 |
| James Rd. E&W .. 29W-41N | | 11 |
| Johnsburg Wilmot Rd. N&S | | |
| ......30W-38N,29W-43N | | 19 |
| Killarney St. N&S .. 29W-38N | | 19 |
| Kohl Av. E&W .... 29W-38N | | 19 |
| Lee Ln. E&W ..... 30W-40N | | 11 |
| Linden Rd. NS&EW | | |
| ................ 30W-39N | | 11 |
| Lubliner St. E&W . 29W-39N | | 11 |
| Madison Av. E&W . 29W-39N | | 11 |
| Maiden Ln. N&S | | |
| ......29W-37N,29W-38N | | 19 |
| Main St. E&W .... 29W-38N | | 11 |
| Maple Av. N&S ... 29W-38N | | 19 |
| Margaret Ln. N&S . 30W-40N | | 11 |
| Maude Pl. N&S ... 29W-38N | | 19 |
| Melbourne Pl. NW&SE | | |
| ................ 30W-39N | | 11 |
| Melrose Dr. E&W | | |
| ................ 30W-39N | | 11 |
| Miller Rd. E&W .. 29W-38N | | 19 |
| Muriel St. E&W .. 29W-38N | | 19 |
| Nippersink Rd. E&W | | |
| ................ 29W-39N | | 11 |
| Normandy Dr. N&S | | |
| ................ 29W-38N | | 19 |
| North Shore Av. NW&SE | | |
| ................ 29W-38N | | 19 |
| Oak Hill Dr. E&W | | |
| ......29W-38N,29W-39N | | 19 |
| Paddock St. E&W . 30W-40N | | 11 |
| Park Ln. E&W .... 30W-39N | | 11 |
| Prospect Pl. N&S .. 29W-38N | | 19 |
| Ravine Dr. NE&SW | | |
| ................ 30W-39N | | 11 |
| Richardson Rd. N&S | | |
| ................ 30W-39N | | 11 |
| Rita Av. N&S .... 30W-40N | | 11 |
| River Rd. N&S ... 30W-39N | | 11 |
| Roselle St. NW&SE | | |
| ................ 29W-38N | | 19 |
| Rt. 173 E&W | | |
| ......30W-42N,30W-40N | | 11 |
| Sage Ln. N&S .... 30W-40N | | 11 |
| Schmidt St. E&W | | |
| ......30W-39N,30W-40N | | 11 |
| Sheridan Pl. N&S . 29W-38N | | 19 |
| Showers St. E&W . 29W-38N | | 19 |
| Siedschlag Rd. N&S | | |
| ................ 30W-42N | | 11 |
| Spring Ct. E&W .. 30W-39N | | 11 |
| Spring Grove Rd. NW&SE | | |
| ......30W-39N,29W-39N | | 11 |
| Spring Rd. E&W .. 29W-39N | | 11 |
| State Park Rd. N&S | | |
| ......29W-38N,29W-39N | | 19 |
| Timber Ln. E&W .. 29W-38N | | 19 |
| U.S. Route 12 E&W | | |
| ......30W-39N,29W-38N | | 11 |
| Valley Rd. NE&SW | | |
| ......36W-29N,36W-31N | | 33 |
| Villa Vista N&S .. 29W-39N | | 11 |
| Vineyard Ln. NS&EW | | |
| ......30W-42N,30W-43N | | 11 |
| Water St. E&W ... 29W-39N | | 11 |
| Waverly Dr. NW&SE | | |
| ................ 29W-38N | | 19 |
| Wellington St. E&W | | |
| ................ 29W-39N | | 11 |
| William Ln. NE&SW | | |
| ................ 30W-40N | | 11 |
| Willow St. N&S .. 29W-38N | | 19 |
| Wilmot Rd. N&S | | |
| ......30W-38N,29W-39N | | 11 |
| Winsor Av. N&S .. 29W-39N | | 11 |
| Woodland Pkwy. NW&SE | | |
| ................ 30W-39N | | 11 |

## Cary

| | Grid | Page |
|---|---|---|
| Abbywood Dr. NS&EW | | |
| ................ 32W-23N | | 42 |
| Aberdeen Rd. N&S . 31W-23N | | 43 |
| Ada St. E&W .... 31W-23N | | 43 |
| Adare Dr. E&W ... 31W-24N | | 43 |
| Alexander Ct. N&S . 32W-24N | | 42 |
| Alica Dr. E&W ...30W-23N | | 43 |
| Alida Dr. E&W ... 31W-24N | | 43 |
| Alma Ter. E&W .. 31W-24N | | 43 |
| Ann St. E&W .... 31W-24N | | 43 |
| Applewood Ct. N&S | | |
| ................ 32W-22N | | 50 |
| Ardmore Dr. NW&SE | | |
| ................ 31W-23N | | 43 |
| Arthur Dr. E&W .. 31W-24N | | 43 |
| Asbury Ln. N&S .. 32W-23N | | 42 |
| Ash Fork Tr. N&S . 32W-24N | | 42 |
| Bayberry Dr. NS&EW | | |
| ................ 32W-22N | | 50 |
| Bee Ct. E&W .... 31W-23N | | 43 |
| Bell Dr. E&W ... 30W-23N | | 43 |
| Berriedale Dr. E&W | | |
| ................ 31W-23N | | 43 |
| Big Bear Tr. E&W . 32W-24N | | 42 |
| Big Sky Tr. E&W | | |
| ......32W-24N,31W-24N | | 42 |
| Blazing Star Tr. NW&SE | | |
| ................ 32W-24N | | 42 |
| Blue Mesa Tr. E&W | | |
| ................ 32W-24N | | 42 |
| Borden Av. N&S .. 31W-23N | | 43 |
| Boxwood Ln. N&S..32W-23N | | 42 |
| Brentwood Ln. N&S | | |
| ................ 30W-24N | | 43 |

| | Grid | Page |
|---|---|---|
| Briargate Rd. N&S ..31W-23N | | 43 |
| Bright Oaks Cir. NW&SE | | |
| ................ 31W-24N | | 43 |
| Bristol Way E&W .. 30W-24N | | 43 |
| Bryan Dr. E&W ... 30W-24N | | 43 |
| Burr Oak Cir. NW&SE | | |
| ................ 30W-24N | | 43 |
| Burton Av. NW&SE | | |
| ................ 31W-23N | | 43 |
| Cambridge Ct. E&W | | |
| ................ 32W-23N | | 42 |
| Camden Ct. E&W .. 32W-23N | | 42 |
| Candlewood Ct. NE&SW | | |
| ................ 30W-24N | | 43 |
| Candlewood Tr. E&W | | |
| ................ 30W-24N | | 43 |
| Carl Sands Dr. E&W | | |
| ................ 30W-24N | | 43 |
| Carlisle Ct. NE&SW | | |
| ................ 32W-23N | | 42 |
| Carrol Ln. N&S ... 32W-23N | | 42 |
| Cary Algonquin Rd. NE&SW | | |
| ................ 32W-22N | | 50 |
| Cary Av. NW&SE .. 30W-23N | | 43 |
| Cary St. E&W .... 31W-23N | | 43 |
| Cary-Algonquin Rd. NE&SW | | |
| ................ 32W-22N | | 50 |
| Casteria Ct. N&S .. 31W-24N | | 43 |
| Charlotte Pl. E&W . 31W-23N | | 43 |
| Chelsea Ln. N&S .. 32W-23N | | 42 |
| Cherry Ln. N&S ... 30W-24N | | 43 |
| Cherry St. NW&SE 30W-23N | | 43 |
| Chestnut Ct. E&W . 32W-23N | | 42 |
| Chicago St. E&W . 30W-23N | | 43 |
| Chickory Ridge Tr. E&W | | |
| ................ 32W-24N | | 42 |
| Cimarron Dr. NE&SW | | |
| ......32W-24N,31W-24N | | 42 |
| Claire Dr. E&W .... 31W-24N | | 43 |
| Cleveland St. E&W 30W-24N | | 43 |
| Colleen Dr. E&W .. 30W-24N | | 43 |
| Conestoga Tr. NE&SW | | |
| ................ 32W-24N | | 42 |
| Copper Canyon Tr. NW&SE | | |
| ......32W-24N,31W-24N | | 42 |
| Cottonwood Tr. N&S | | |
| ................ 32W-24N | | 42 |
| Country Commons Rd. E&W | | |
| ......32W-23N,31W-23N | | 42 |
| Courtney Ln. NS&EW | | |
| ................ 30W-24N | | 43 |
| Coyote Tr. N&S .. 32W-24N | | 42 |
| Crabtree Ln. NS&EW | | |
| ................ 30W-24N | | 43 |
| Crest Dr. N&S ... 30W-24N | | 43 |
| Crofton Ct. N&S ...32W-23N | | 42 |
| Crystal St. NW&SE | | |
| ......32W-24N,31W-23N | | 42 |
| Cumberland Ct. E&W | | |
| ................ 32W-23N | | 42 |
| Danbury Dr. E&W . 32W-24N | | 42 |
| Daybreak Ridge Tr. NS&EW | | |
| ................ 31W-23N | | 43 |
| Decker Dr. N&S | | |
| ......30W-23N,30W-24N | | 43 |
| Deerpath Ct. N&S . 32W-23N | | 42 |
| Detroit St. E&W .. 30W-23N | | 43 |
| Deveron Cir. N&S . 31W-23N | | 43 |
| Drake Ln. N&S ... 32W-23N | | 42 |
| Dunleer Dr. NS&EW | | |
| ................ 31W-24N | | 43 |
| Duxbury Ln. N&S . 32W-23N | | 42 |
| East Oriole Tr. E&W | | |
| ................ 30W-24N | | 43 |
| Elden Dr. N&S....31W-24N | | 43 |
| English Oaks Dr. N&S | | |
| ................ 32W-22N | | 50 |
| Ennis St. E&W .. 31W-24N | | 43 |
| Erin Dr. E&W ... 30W-24N | | 43 |
| Essex Ln. N&S .. 32W-23N | | 42 |
| Fairfield Ln. N&S . 32W-23N | | 42 |
| Feinberg Ct. NE&SW | | |
| ................ 31W-24N | | 43 |
| Feinberg Dr. NE&SW | | |
| ................ 31W-24N | | 43 |
| First St. N&S .... 31W-24N | | 43 |
| Forest Ln. NW&SE 31W-24N | | 43 |
| Fox Trails Dr. | | |
| ......32W-22N,32W-23N | | 50 |
| Fox Trails Dr., N. NW&SE | | |
| ......32W-23N,32W-22N | | 42 |
| Fox Trails Dr., S. NW&SE | | |
| ......32W-23N,32W-22N | | 50 |
| Franke Av. E&W ...31W-23N | | 43 |
| Galway Dr. NS&EW | | |
| ................ 31W-23N | | 43 |
| Georgetown N&S | | |
| ......32W-23N,32W-24N | | 42 |
| Glen Garry Rd. N&S | | |
| ................ 31W-23N | | 43 |
| Grove St. N&S ... 31W-22N | | 51 |
| Haber Rd. NE&SW 32W-22N | | 50 |
| Hampton St. NW&SE | | |
| ................ 32W-23N | | 42 |
| Harper Av. NW&SE | | |
| ................ 32W-23N | | 42 |
| Harper Ct. SW&NE | | |
| ................ 32W-23N | | 42 |
| Hickory Ln. NS&EW | | |
| ................ 31W-24N | | 43 |
| High Av. N&S .... 30W-23N | | 43 |
| High Rd. NS&EW . 31W-23N | | 43 |
| High St. N&S .... 30W-23N | | 43 |
| Hill St. N&S ..... 30W-23N | | 43 |
| Hillhurst Dr. N&S | | |
| ......30W-23N,30W-24N | | 43 |
| Hillside Dr. E&W | | |
| ......31W-22N,30W-22N | | 51 |
| Industrial Dr. NW&SE | | |
| ......32W-24N,31W-24N | | 42 |
| Ivanhoe Ln. N&S .. 32W-24N | | 42 |

| | Grid | Page |
|---|---|---|
| James Way E&W | | |
| ......31W-24N,30W-24N | | 43 |
| Jandus Cary Av. NW&SE | | |
| ................ 30W-23N | | 43 |
| Jandus Cary Rd. NW&SE | | |
| ................ 30W-23N | | 43 |
| Jandus Cut-Off NE&SW | | |
| ................ 30W-23N | | 43 |
| Jefferson Ln. NS&EW | | |
| ................ 32W-24N | | 42 |
| Keith Way NE&SW 31W-23N | | 43 |
| Kildare Ct. N&S .. 31W-24N | | 43 |
| Knollwood Dr. NS&EW | | |
| ......32W-22N,32W-23N | | 50 |
| Krenz Av. E&W .. 31W-23N | | 43 |
| Lake Julian Ln. NE&SW | | |
| ................ 30W-23N | | 43 |
| Laurel Ln. N&S .. 32W-22N | | 50 |
| Leith Way NE&SW ..31W-23N | | 43 |
| Liberty Av. NS&EW | | |
| ................ 31W-23N | | 43 |
| Liberty Ct. N&S .. 31W-24N | | 43 |
| Linden St. N&S ... 31W-24N | | 43 |
| Little Stonegate Ct. NE&SW | | |
| ................ 31W-23N | | 43 |
| Lloyd St. E&W ... 31W-24N | | 43 |
| Main St. N&S ... 30W-23N | | 43 |
| Manchester St. E&W | | |
| ................ 32W-23N | | 42 |
| Manitou Ct. E&W . 32W-23N | | 43 |
| Manitou St. E&W . 32W-23N | | 43 |
| Margaret Ter. E&W | | |
| ......31W-24N,30W-24N | | 43 |
| Marquette Av. NE&SW | | |
| ................ 30W-23N | | 43 |
| Mary Ln. N&S .. 31W-23N | | 43 |
| Mayfield St. E&W . 32W-23N | | 42 |
| Merrimac St. E&W . 32W-23N | | 42 |
| Mildred Av. NE&SW | | |
| ................ 30W-23N | | 43 |
| Milford St. E&W .. 32W-23N | | 42 |
| Millwood St. NW&SE | | |
| ................ 32W-23N | | 42 |
| Milton Ct. N&S .. 29W-24N | | 43 |
| Moders Ave. N&S .. 32W-23N | | 42 |
| Mohawk St. NE&SW | | |
| ................ 32W-23N | | 42 |
| Montana Ct. NE&SW | | |
| ................ 30W-24N | | 43 |
| Montana Dr. N&S | | |
| ......30W-23N,30W-24N | | 43 |
| Moraine Hill Dr. N&S | | |
| ......30W-23N,30W-24N | | 43 |
| Muir Wood Ct. NE&SW | | |
| ................ 32W-23N | | 42 |
| Newhaven Dr. E&W | | |
| ................ 32W-24N | | 42 |
| Norman Dr. E&W . 31W-24N | | 43 |
| Oak Valley Dr. N&S | | |
| ................ 31W-24N | | 43 |
| Oriole Tr. E&W ... 31W-24N | | 43 |
| Park Av. NW&SE | | |
| ......31W-24N,31W-24N | | 43 |
| Patriot Ct. NW&SE 31W-24N | | 43 |
| Patriot Ln. NS&EW | | |
| ................ 31W-24N | | 43 |
| Pearl St. E&W ...30W-23N | | 43 |
| Pearson Rd. NE&SW | | |
| ................ 32W-23N | | 42 |
| Perth Ln. NE&SW . 31W-23N | | 43 |
| Pin Oak Cir. NS&EW | | |
| ................ 30W-24N | | 43 |
| Pin Oak Ct. NW&SE | | |
| ................ 30W-24N | | 43 |
| Pine Cir. NS&EW .. 31W-24N | | 43 |
| Prairie Ln. N&S .. 31W-24N | | 43 |
| Raintree Ct. NE&SW | | |
| ................ 32W-23N | | 42 |
| Rawson Bridge Rd S. N&S | | |
| ................ 29W-24N | | 43 |
| Red Cypress Dr. E&W | | |
| ................ 32W-23N | | 42 |
| Red Oak Dr. N&S . 30W-24N | | 43 |
| Red Oak Tr. N&S . 31W-24N | | 43 |
| Ridgewood Dr. E&W | | |
| ................ 32W-23N | | 42 |
| Rodeo Ct. N&S ... 32W-24N | | 42 |
| Rosewood Ct. N&S | | |
| ......32W-23N,32W-24N | | 50 |
| Ross Av. E&W .... 30W-23N | | 43 |
| Rosslare St. N&S . 31W-24N | | 43 |
| Royal Glen Dr. NS&EW | | |
| ................ 32W-23N | | 42 |
| Rt. 31 N&S | | |
| ......33W-22N,33W-23N | | 42 |
| Saddle Ridge Tr. E&W | | |
| ................ 32W-24N | | 42 |
| Sagebrush Tr. E&W | | |
| ................ 32W-24N | | 42 |
| Sandra Ln. N&S .. 31W-24N | | 43 |
| Santa Fe Tr. N&S . 32W-24N | | 42 |
| Schober Dr. NS&EW | | |
| ................ 31W-23N | | 43 |
| School St. N&S .. 31W-24N | | 43 |
| Second St. N&S .. 30W-23N | | 43 |
| Seebert St. NS&EW | | |
| ................ 31W-23N | | 43 |
| Sequoia Tr. N&S . 32W-24N | | 42 |
| Sherwood Dr. E&W | | |
| ................ 30W-24N | | 43 |
| Short St. NE&SW . 31W-24N | | 43 |
| Silver Lake Rd. N&S | | |
| ................ 31W-24N | | 43 |
| Silver Tree Cir. N&S | | |
| ................ 31W-24N | | 43 |
| South St. N&S ... 31W-24N | | 43 |
| Spring Beach Rd. NE&SW | | |
| ................ 30W-23N | | 43 |
| Spring St. N&S .. 31W-23N | | 43 |
| Spruce Tree Dr. N&S | | |
| ................ 32W-24N | | 43 |

| | Grid | Page |
|---|---|---|
| St. Cronan Ct. N&S | | |
| ................ 31W-24N | | 43 |
| Stonegate Rd. N&S | | |
| ................ 31W-23N | | 43 |
| Sundance Tr. N&S .. 32W-24N | | 42 |
| Sunset Dr. E&W .. 30W-24N | | 43 |
| Surry Ridge Dr. NW&SE | | |
| ................ 32W-23N | | 42 |
| Tamarack Ct. E&W | | |
| ................ 32W-23N | | 42 |
| Tealwood Ct. E&W | | |
| ................ 32W-22N | | 50 |
| Thomas Av. N&S .. 31W-23N | | 43 |
| Three Oaks Rd. E&W | | |
| ......32W-24N,30W-24N | | 42 |
| Timber Ter. N&S . 31W-24N | | 43 |
| Trianglewood Dr. NS&EW | | |
| ................ 30W-24N | | 43 |
| Veridan Way E&W . 32W-23N | | 43 |
| W. Main St. E&W | | |
| ......32W-23N,31W-23N | | 42 |
| Wagner Dr. E&W . 31W-24N | | 43 |
| Weavers Dr. E&W . 30W-23N | | 43 |
| Weber Ct. E&W .. 31W-23N | | 43 |
| Wexford St. N&S . 31W-23N | | 43 |
| Whitepine Dr. N&S .30W-23N | | 43 |
| Wild Rose Dr. N&S | | |
| ................ 29W-24N | | 43 |
| Wildrose Dr. N&S . 30W-24N | | 43 |
| Wildwood Ct. N&S..32W-23N | | 42 |
| Wildwood Tr. 31W-24N | | 43 |
| Willow Cir. NS&EW | | |
| ................ 32W-23N | | 42 |
| Willow Ct. N&S .. 32W-23N | | 42 |
| Winchester St. E&W | | |
| ................ 32W-23N | | 42 |
| Woodbridge Dr. E&W | | |
| ................ 32W-22N | | 50 |
| Wooded Knoll Dr. E&W | | |
| ................ 30W-23N | | 43 |
| Wulff St. N&S......31W-23N | | 43 |

## Chemung Township

| | Grid | Page |
|---|---|---|
| Brink St. E&W......49W-38N | | 13 |
| Cals Ct. E&W ... 52W-39N | | 4 |
| Center St. E&W .. 52W-38N | | 12 |
| Center St. NE&SW | | |
| ......51W-39N,51W-40N | | 4 |
| Chemung St. E&W .. 52W-38N | | 12 |
| Chicago Rd. E&W .. 52W-38N | | 12 |
| Chippewa Rd. N&S | | |
| ................ 51W-38N | | 12 |
| Commercial St. NW&SE | | |
| ................ 51W-39N | | 4 |
| County Line Rd. N&S | | |
| ................ 54W-38N | | 12 |
| Crowley Rd. E&W . 49W-40N | | 5 |
| Dana St. E&W ... 52W-38N | | 12 |
| Elm St. N&S .... 51W-39N | | 4 |
| Franklin NW&SE .. 51W-39N | | 4 |
| Graf Rd. E&W | | |
| ......54W-40N,52W-40N | | 4 |
| Grove Rd. E&W .. 52W-38N | | 12 |
| Harvard Hills Rd. N&S | | |
| ......49W-36N,49W-39N | | 13 |
| Hebron Rd. N. E&W . 49W-42N | | 5 |
| Hickory St. N&S .. 52W-38N | | 12 |
| Horseshoe Dr. NE&SW | | |
| ................ 50W-40N | | 5 |
| Hunter Rd. E&W | | |
| ......54W-38N,53W-38N | | 12 |
| Island Rd. N&S | | |
| ......53W-38N,53W-37N | | 12 |
| Kasson St. NW&SE | | |
| ................ 51W-39N | | 4 |
| Kennedy Dr. N&S . 49W-38N | | 13 |
| Kennedy Rd. E&W | | |
| ......53W-38N,53W-39N | | 12 |
| Krunfus Dr. N&S .. 49W-40N | | 5 |
| Lawrence Rd. NE&SW | | |
| ......53W-43N,51W-38N | | 4 |
| Lilja St. N&S .... 49W-40N | | 5 |
| Malinda St. E&W . 49W-40N | | 5 |
| Maxon Rd. N&S | | |
| ......53W-38N,58W-40N | | 12 |
| Nilsen Ct. N&S ... 54W-40N | | 4 |
| Norma Ln. E&W .. 52W-39N | | 4 |
| Oak Grove Rd. NE&SW | | |
| ......52W-38N,49W-41N | | 12 |
| Oak St. N&S .... 52W-38N | | 12 |
| Pearl St. NE&SW . 51W-39N | | 4 |
| Perkins Rd. E&W | | |
| ......54W-41N,53W-41N | | 4 |
| Pine St. N&S ... 52W-38N | | 12 |
| Pleasant St. NW&SE | | |
| ................ 51W-39N | | 4 |
| Ramer Rd. E&W | | |
| ......52W-38N,51W-38N | | 12 |
| Rhonda Dr. N&S... 52W-38N | | 12 |
| Rita Dr. E&W ... 52W-38N | | 12 |
| River St. NE&SW . 51W-39N | | 4 |
| Rt. 173 NE&SW .. 49W-38N | | 13 |
| Ruhff St. NW&SE . 51W-39N | | 4 |
| Ryan Rd. N&S | | |
| ......54W-38N,54W-39N | | 12 |
| Sinderson St. N&S | | |
| ......53W-37N,53W-38N | | 12 |
| South Nilsen Ct. N&S | | |
| ................ 54W-40N | | 4 |
| Southport Rd. NE&SW | | |
| ................ 52W-38N | | 12 |
| State Line Rd. N&S | | |
| ......54W-43N,49W-43N | | 4 |
| U.S. Route 14 N&S | | |
| ......50W-39N,49W-43N | | 5 |
| Walker St. NW&SE | | |
| ................ 51W-39N | | 4 |
| Weidner Rd. N&S | | |
| ......52W-41N,52W-43N | | 4 |

| | Grid | Page |
|---|---|---|
| White Oaks Rd. N&S | | |
| ......53W-38N,54W-43N | | 12 |
| Yates Rd. E&W | | |
| ......51W-42N,49W-42N | | 4 |
| York Rd. E&W ... 54W-42N | | 4 |

## Coral Township

| | Grid | Page |
|---|---|---|
| Arbor Ln. N&S .... 45W-20N | | 47 |
| Beall Ln. N&S .... 45W-20N | | 47 |
| Beck Rd. E&W | | |
| ......48W-23N,47W-23N | | 38 |
| Brier Hill Rd. N&S . 43W-20N | | 47 |
| Burr Oak Dr. N&S .. 45W-20N | | 47 |
| Camp Ct. E&W ... 45W-20N | | 47 |
| Cantering Ln. N&S..44W-22N | | 47 |
| Church Rd. E&W | | |
| ......47W-21N,43W-21N | | 46 |
| Condor Ln. E&W . 45W-20N | | 47 |
| Conestoga Tr. N&S | | |
| ................ 47W-22N | | 46 |
| Coral East Rd. E&W | | |
| ................ 44W-23N | | 39 |
| Country Club Dr. E&W | | |
| ................ 47W-22N | | 46 |
| Country Club Tr. N&S | | |
| ................ 47W-22N | | 46 |
| Dunham Rd. N&S | | |
| ......47W-25N,47W-26N | | 38 |
| East Coral Rd. E&W | | |
| ......47W-24N,44W-23N | | 38 |
| Ernest Rd. N&S .. 47W-21N | | 46 |
| Fair Ln. N&S .... 44W-22N | | 47 |
| Fairway Ln. N&S . 47W-22N | | 46 |
| Forest Ln. N&S .. 44W-22N | | 47 |
| Frank Ln. E&W .. 47W-21N | | 46 |
| Frohling Rd. N&S | | |
| ......43W-24N,43W-23N | | 39 |
| Glen Ln. N&S ... 44W-22N | | 47 |
| Hampshire Rd. N&S | | |
| ................ 46W-20N | | 47 |
| Harmony Hill Rd. N&S | | |
| ................ 47W-22N | | 38 |
| Harmony Hill Rd. N&S | | |
| ......47W-20N,47W-22N | | 46 |
| Harmony Rd. E&W | | |
| ......46W-20N,43W-20N | | 46 |
| Harmony Riley Rd. NW&SE | | |
| ................ 48W-21N | | 46 |
| Hemmingson Rd. E&W | | |
| ......45W-25N,43W-25N | | 39 |
| Heron Dr. N&S ... 45W-20N | | 47 |
| Highbridge Rd. E&W | | |
| ......46W-25N,44W-25N | | 38 |
| Hill Rd. N&S .... 47W-23N | | 38 |
| Hillsboro Dr. NS&EW | | |
| ................ 44W-20N | | 47 |
| I-90 NW&SE .... 47W-20N | | 46 |
| Jani Ln. N&S .... 47W-21N | | 46 |
| Kim Ln. E&W .... 47W-21N | | 46 |
| Knoll Top Rd. NS&EW | | |
| ................ 44W-22N | | 47 |
| Leech Rd. N&S | | |
| ......45W-23N,45W-24N | | 39 |
| Lerita Dr. NE&SW . 44W-21N | | 47 |
| Manda Dr. N&S .. 45W-20N | | 47 |
| Marengo Rd. NW&SE | | |
| ......45W-22N,43W-22N | | 47 |
| Marengo-Huntley Rd. NW&SE | | |
| ......46W-23N,45W-23N | | 38 |
| McCue Rd. N&S .. 44W-25N | | 39 |
| Mitchell Ln. N&S .. 46W-20N | | 47 |
| Morris Rd. N&S .. 46W-20N | | 47 |
| N. Ridge Ln. NS&EW | | |
| ................ 47W-21N | | 46 |
| Northrup Rd. N&S | | |
| ......46W-24N,46W-25N | | 38 |
| O'Cock Rd. E&W | | |
| ......47W-25N,46W-25N | | 38 |
| Oak Ridge Rd. N&S | | |
| ................ 47W-21N | | 46 |
| Olson Rd. N&S | | |
| ......45W-24N,45W-25N | | 39 |
| Overlook Ln. E&W . 44W-20N | | 47 |
| Oxbow Dr. E&W ... 47W-22N | | 46 |
| Pebble Dr. N&S .. 44W-20N | | 47 |
| Peregrine Tr. NS&EW | | |
| ................ 45W-20N | | 47 |
| Pinion Tr. E&W .. 47W-21N | | 47 |
| Pinoak Dr. N&S .. 45W-20N | | 47 |
| Raven Hills Dr. N&S | | |
| ................ 47W-21N | | 47 |
| Ridge Ln. N&S ... 44W-21N | | 47 |
| Rose Ln. E&W ... 47W-21N | | 46 |
| Royal Ln. E&W ... 47W-21N | | 46 |
| Sarko Tr. N&S ... 47W-21N | | 47 |
| Seeman Rd. N&S | | |
| ......44W-23N,44W-24N | | 39 |
| Seeman Rd. N&S | | |
| ......44W-20N,44W-22N | | 47 |
| Somerset Dr. N&S..48W-24N | | 38 |
| South Coral Rd. N&S | | |
| ......48W-23N,48W-24N | | 38 |
| South Union Rd. N&S | | |
| ......47W-23N,47W-25N | | 38 |
| Stacy Ln. NE&SW . 44W-22N | | 47 |
| Stevens Rd. E&W . 47W-21N | | 46 |
| Trail Rd. N&S .... 45W-20N | | 47 |
| U.S. Route 20 NW&SE | | |
| ......48W-25N,46W-23N | | 38 |
| U.S. Route 20 NW&SE | | |
| ......46W-22N,45W-20N | | 46 |
| Voss Rd. N&S .... 48W-23N | | 38 |
| Voss Rd. N&S .... 48W-23N | | 46 |
| West Coral Rd. E&W | | |
| ......47W-24N,47W-24N | | 38 |
| West Union Rd. N&S | | |
| ................ 48W-25N | | 38 |
| Windwood Ln. N&S | | |
| ................ 44W-20N | | 47 |
| Woodale Rd. E&W .. 44W-22N | | 47 |

| Name | Grid | Page |
|---|---|---|
| Woodwind Dr. N&S | 44W-20N | 47 |

## Crystal Lake

| Name | Grid | Page |
|---|---|---|
| Abbey Dr. E&W | 37W-24N | 41 |
| Abbington Dr. NE&SW | 35W-24N | 42 |
| Aberdeen Dr. NS&EW | 35W-24N | 42 |
| Ackman Rd. E&W | 37W-23N,36W-23N | 41 |
| Adobe Tr. N&S | 37W-26N | 41 |
| Alexandra Blvd. E&W | 37W-23N,36W-23N | 41 |
| Amberwood Dr. EW&NS | 37W-23N,36W-23N | 41 |
| Arrowhead Ln. N&S | 35W-27N | 34 |
| Ascot Dr. N&S | 37W-24N | 41 |
| Ash St. NW&SE | 35W-25N | 42 |
| Ashford Ln. NS&EW | 36W-22N | 49 |
| Auburn Ct. E&W | 36W-23N | 41 |
| Augusta Dr. E&W | 37W-24N,36W-24N | 41 |
| Autumn Ct. E&W | 37W-24N | 41 |
| Autumn Dr. EW&NS | 37W-24N | 41 |
| Autumncrest Ct. NW&SE | 36W-23N | 49 |
| Autumncrest Dr. NS&EW | 36W-23N,37W-23N | 49 |
| Baldwin Av. N&S | 36W-25N | 41 |
| Barberry Dr. N&S | 37W-25N | 41 |
| Bard Rd. NE&SW | 37W-24N | 41 |
| Barlina Rd. E&W | 37W-24N,36W-24N | 41 |
| Barrow Dr. N&S | 35W-24N | 42 |
| Barton Ln. NE&SW | 36W-23N | 41 |
| Beardsly St. E&W | 34W-26N | 42 |
| Becker Ct. N&S | 36W-22N | 49 |
| Bedford Dr. E&W | 36W-24N | 41 |
| Bennington Dr. E&W | 36W-24N | 41 |
| Berkshire Ln. E&W | 35W-24N | 42 |
| Bertram Av. EW&NS | 36W-25N | 41 |
| Birch Dr. NW&SE | 37W-24N | 41 |
| Birmingham Dr. NE&SW | 36W-22N | 49 |
| Birmingham Ln. NS&EW | 36W-22N | 49 |
| Bittersweet Dr. E&W | 34W-26N | 42 |
| Blackthorn Dr. NW&SE | 34W-26N,33W-26N | 42 |
| Blue Heron Dr. NW&SE | 37W-23N | 41 |
| Blue Mound Dr. N&S | 37W-24N | 41 |
| Boneset Dr. E&W | 37W-24N | 41 |
| Boxwood Ct. NE&SW | 37W-23N | 41 |
| Boxwood Ln. NS&EW | 37W-23N,36W-24N | 41 |
| Brandy Dr. E&W | 36W-24N,35W-24N | 41 |
| Brian St. N&S | 37W-25N | 41 |
| Briarwood Cir. NS&EW | 38W-25N | 41 |
| Briarwood Rd. N&S | 37W-25N,37W-26N | 41 |
| Bridgedale Ct. E&W | 36W-23N | 41 |
| Bridgedale Dr. NW&SE | 36W-23N | 41 |
| Bridgeport Ln. NS&EW | 36W-22N | 49 |
| Brigham Ln. NW&SE | 36W-22N | 49 |
| Brink St. NW&SE | 35W-26N | 42 |
| Broadway Av. NW&SE | 36W-25N | 41 |
| Brompton Ct. E&W | 36W-22N | 49 |
| Brompton Rd. N&S | 36W-22N | 49 |
| Brook Dr. E&W | 36W-24N | 41 |
| Brookside Dr. NS&EW | 37W-23N | 41 |
| Buckingham Dr. E&W | 34W-25N | 42 |
| Burdent St. E&W | 35W-26N | 42 |
| Burning Bush Tr. E&W | 35W-27N,34W-27N | 34 |
| Burr Oak Tr. N&S | 36W-25N | 41 |
| Butler Dr. E&W | 37W-24N | 41 |
| Cambridge Ln. NE&SW | 35W-24N | 42 |
| Camelot Ct. N&S | 36W-24N | 41 |
| Camelot Dr. NS&EW | 36W-24N | 41 |
| Camelot Pl. N&S | 36W-24N | 41 |
| Candlewood Dr. N&S | 36W-23N | 41 |
| Canterbury Dr. N&S | 35W-24N | 42 |
| Cardiff Ct. N&S | 35W-24N | 42 |
| Carmella Dr. E&W | 35W-24N | 42 |
| Caroline St. N&S | 35W-25N,35W-26N | 42 |
| Carpenter St. NE&SW | 35W-26N | 41 |
| Cascade Dr. E&W | 35W-27N | 34 |
| Castlefield Ln. E&W | 36W-22N | 49 |
| Catherine St. E&W | 35W-25N | 42 |
| Cedar Crest Dr. E&W | 37W-24N | 41 |
| Cedar Dr. N&S | 37W-25N | 41 |
| Center Av. E&W | 37W-25N | 41 |
| Center St. E&W | 35W-26N | 42 |
| Ceresia Dr. E&W | 33W-26N | 42 |
| Chardonnay Ln. E&W | 36W-24N,35W-24N | 41 |
| Charlotte Av. N&S | 37W-25N | 41 |
| Chasefield Ln. NS&EW | 35W-24N | 41 |
| Church St. NW&SE | 35W-25N | 42 |
| Circle Ln. N&S | 35W-24N,35W-26N | 42 |
| Clover Dr. N&S | 37W-25N,37W-26N | 41 |
| Clow Dr. EW&NE | 36W-25N | 41 |
| College St. NE&SW | 35W-25N | 42 |
| Colony Dr. E&W | 37W-24N | 41 |
| Commerce Ct. N&S | 35W-26N | 42 |
| Commercial Rd. E&W | 35W-24N | 42 |
| Concord Dr. E&W | 36W-23N | 41 |
| Congress Pkwy. E&W | 34W-25N | 42 |
| Copperfield Ln. NE&SW | 36W-22N | 49 |
| Coronado Dr. EW&NS | 36W-26N | 41 |
| Corrine Av. N&S | 37W-25N | 41 |
| Cotton Wood Ln. E&W | 37W-26N | 41 |
| Country Club Rd. NS&EW | 37W-24N,36W-25N | 41 |
| Country Dr. NE&SW | 36W-27N | 33 |
| Coventry Ct. NW&SE | 36W-24N | 42 |
| Coventry Ln. NE&SW | 36W-24N,35W-25N | 41 |
| Covington Cir. NS&EW | 36W-23N | 41 |
| Crabapple Dr. N&S | 37W-24N | 41 |
| Crabtree Dr. N&S | 37W-23N | 41 |
| Crabtree Dr. N&S | 37W-23N | 49 |
| Crandall Av. N&S | 36W-25N | 41 |
| Crandon Pl. N&S | 37W-22N | 49 |
| Cress Creek Ln. NS&EW | 36W-24N | 41 |
| Cress Creek Ter. NE&SW | 36W-24N | 41 |
| Crystal Lake Av. E&W | 36W-26N,34W-26N | 41 |
| Crystal Pt.Dr. N&S | 34W-24N | 42 |
| Crystal Ridge Dr. NW&SE | 35W-26N | 42 |
| Crystal Ridge Rd. E&W | 35W-26N | 42 |
| Cumberland Ln. N&S | 36W-25N | 41 |
| Cunningham Ln. N&S | 36W-22N | 49 |
| Darlington Ln. NE&SW | 35W-24N | 42 |
| Dartmoor Dr. E&W | 36W-24N,34W-24N | 41 |
| Deer Haven Dr. N&S | 37W-22N | 49 |
| Deer Run E&W | 35W-27N,34W-27N | 34 |
| Denton Ct. N&S | 34W-24N | 42 |
| Devonshire Ln. NE&SW | 35W-24N | 42 |
| Dogwood Dr. NS&EW | 37W-23N | 41 |
| Dole Av. N&S | 36W-25N,35W-26N | 41 |
| Dolle Ln. N&S | 35W-26N | 42 |
| Dolo Roso Vista E&W | 37W-23N | 41 |
| Douglas St. NW&SE | 36W-25N,35W-26N | 41 |
| Dover Ct. NS&EW | 35W-24N | 42 |
| Dovercliff Way NS&EW | 37W-23N | 41 |
| Driftwood Ct. E&W | 37W-23N | 41 |
| Driftwood Ct. E&W | 37W-22N | 49 |
| Driftwood Ln. N&S | 37W-23N | 41 |
| Driftwood Ln. N&S | 37W-23N | 49 |
| Duffy Dr. E&W | 33W-24N | 42 |
| Duffy Ln. NW&SE | 34W-26N | 42 |
| Durham Ct. NW&SE | 36W-22N | 49 |
| E. Brighton Dr. E&W | 33W-27N | 34 |
| Eagle St. NW&SE | 36W-25N | 41 |
| East Gate Rd. N&S | 35W-24N | 42 |
| East St. N&S | 36W-26N | 41 |
| East St. N&S | 34W-26N | 42 |
| Eastview Av. NW&SE | 35W-25N | 42 |
| Edgebrook Ln. E&W | 36W-25N | 41 |
| Edgewater Dr. NS&EW | 37W-25N | 41 |
| Edgewood Rd. N&S | 37W-25N | 41 |
| Eletson Dr. NE&SW | 35W-24N | 42 |
| Ellsworth St. N&S | 34W-26N | 42 |
| Elm St. N&S | 35W-25N | 42 |
| Elmhurst St. N&S | 35W-25N | 42 |
| Elmwood St. N&S | 37W-25N | 41 |
| Elsinoor Ln. NW&SE | 36W-22N | 49 |
| Erick St. N&S | 34W-26N | 42 |
| Essex Ln. N&S | 36W-25N | 41 |
| Esther St. E&W | 35W-25N | 42 |
| Euclid Av. E&W | 37W-25N | 41 |
| Eugene St. NE&SW | 35W-25N | 42 |
| Everett Av. E&W | 36W-25N,35W-25N | 41 |
| Evergreen Pkwy. E&W | 35W-26N | 42 |
| Exchange Dr. E&W | 34W-25N | 42 |
| Exmoor Ter. NW&SE | 36W-24N | 41 |
| Factory Rd. E&W | 35W-24N | 42 |
| Fair Oaks Av. E&W | 35W-25N | 41 |
| Fairview Pk. Av. E&W | 36W-26N | 42 |
| Faringdon Dr. E&W | 35W-24N | 42 |
| Federal Dr. N&S | 34W-25N | 42 |
| Fenimore St. N&S | 33W-25N | 42 |
| Fernleaf Dr. N&S | 36W-23N | 41 |
| First Colonial Dr. N&S | 34W-25N | 42 |
| First Ct. NE&SW | 35W-25N | 42 |
| First St. N&S | 35W-26N | 42 |
| Flagstone Dr. E&W | 37W-22N | 49 |
| Flagstone Dr. NS&EW | 37W-22N | 49 |
| Flint Tr. N&S | 34W-27N | 34 |
| Florence St. NE&SW | 35W-25N | 41 |
| Floresta Vista E&W | 37W-25N | 41 |
| Fountain Green Dr. N&S | 36W-23N | 41 |
| Francis Av. N&S | 35W-26N | 42 |
| Franklin Av. E&W | 35W-25N | 42 |
| Gail Ct. NW&SE | 35W-25N | 42 |
| Gardina Vista E&W | 37W-25N | 41 |
| Gates St. NW&SE | 35W-26N | 42 |
| Georgian Ct. E&W | 35W-26N | 42 |
| Gilbert Av. E&W | 35W-25N | 41 |
| Glasgow Ln. E&W | 37W-22N,36W-22N | 49 |
| Glen Av. N&S | 34W-26N | 42 |
| Glendale Dr. N&S | 36W-24N | 41 |
| Golden Rod Ct. SW&NE | 37W-24N | 41 |
| Golf Course Rd. N&S | 36W-22N,36W-24N | 49 |
| Golf Rd. E&W | 36W-25N | 42 |
| Grand Av. NW&SE | 35W-25N | 42 |
| Grandview Ct. NE&SE | 33W-25N | 42 |
| Grant St. NE&SW | 35W-26N | 42 |
| Green Meadow Ct. E&W | 36W-23N | 41 |
| Green Oaks Dr. N&S | 36W-26N | 41 |
| Greenbriar Ln. NS&EW | 36W-24N | 41 |
| Greenbrier Dr. E&W | 36W-24N | 41 |
| Greenbrier Ter. NW&SE | 36W-24N | 41 |
| Greenview Ct. NE&SW | 33W-25N | 42 |
| Grove St. NW&SE | 35W-25N | 42 |
| Hampton Ct. N&S | 35W-26N | 42 |
| Harold St. NE&SW | 35W-25N | 42 |
| Harper Dr. N&S | 37W-22N | 49 |
| Harper Ln. N&S | 37W-22N | 49 |
| Hartford Ln. NW&SE | 36W-22N | 49 |
| Harvest Cir. EW&NS | 37W-24N | 41 |
| Harvest St. N&S | 37W-24N | 41 |
| Hastings Av. N&S | 35W-25N | 42 |
| Hawthorne Dr. N&S | 37W-24N | 41 |
| Heather Ln. N&S | 37W-25N,37W-26N | 41 |
| Heisler Ct. E&W | 35W-25N | 42 |
| Helen Av. NW&SE | 36W-25N | 41 |
| Herald Dr. N&S | 33W-24N | 42 |
| Heritage Dr. E&W | 34W-24N | 42 |
| Hickory Av. N&S | 36W-26N | 41 |
| Highland Av. N&S | 35W-25N | 41 |
| Highplaine Dr. E&W | 37W-24N | 41 |
| Hilkert Ct. E&W | 35W-25N | 42 |
| Hill Dr. NE&SW | 35W-25N | 42 |
| Hillside Rd. E&W | 34W-27N | 42 |
| Holly Dr. N&S | 37W-25N | 41 |
| Holly Tree Ln. N&S | 36W-23N | 41 |
| Honeysuckle Ln. N&S | 37W-25N | 41 |
| Hull Ct. N&S | 35W-24N | 41 |
| Hunters Tr. E&W | 37W-23N | 41 |
| Hunters Tr. NS&EW | 37W-23N | 49 |
| Hunters Trail Blvd. E&W | 37W-22N | 49 |
| Huntington Dr. N&S | 36W-24N | 41 |
| Huntley Rd. N&S | 37W-23N,37W-25N | 41 |
| Hyinisport Ln. N&S | 36W-23N | 49 |
| Illinois St. N&S | 34W-26N | 42 |
| Indian Hill Tr. E&W | 35W-27N,34W-27N | 34 |
| Industrial Rd. NE&SW | 34W-26N | 42 |
| Iris Ct. NE&SW | 37W-24N | 41 |
| Ivy Ln. N&S | 37W-25N | 41 |
| Jackman Dr. E&W | 35W-25N | 41 |
| James St. N&S | 36W-25N | 41 |
| Juniper Dr. E&W | 33W-25N | 42 |
| Keith Av. NE&SW | 35W-25N | 42 |
| Kelly Ln. EW&NS | 33W-26N | 42 |
| Kendallwood Ct. E&W | 36W-24N | 41 |
| Kendallwood Dr. N&S | 36W-24N | 41 |
| Kensington Ln. N&S | 36W-22N | 49 |
| Kimer Ct. N&S | 35W-27N | 34 |
| King St. NE&SW | 36W-25N | 41 |
| Kingston Ln. NS&EW | 36W-22N | 49 |
| Knack Blvd. N&S | 34W-26N | 42 |
| Knollwood Cir. NS&EW | 36W-23N | 41 |
| Laguna Dr. E&W | 36W-23N | 41 |
| Lake Ct. NE&SW | 36W-25N | 41 |
| Lake Shore Dr. NE&SW | 36W-25N | 41 |
| Lake St. NW&SE | 36W-25N,35W-25N | 41 |
| Lakeside Rd. N&S | 36W-25N | 41 |
| Lakeview Dr. E&W | 37W-24N | 41 |
| Lancaster Ln. E&W | 35W-24N | 42 |
| Lee Dr. E&W | 36W-24N,35W-24N | 41 |
| Lee St. NW&SE | 35W-24N | 42 |
| Leonard Pkwy. NW&SE | 36W-25N | 41 |
| Liberty Dr. E&W | 34W-24N | 42 |
| Lilac Dr. NE&SE | 37W-23N | 41 |
| Lill St. NE&SW | 36W-25N | 42 |
| Lincoln Pkwy. N&S | 35W-26N | 42 |
| Lincolnshire Dr. NW&SE | 35W-24N | 42 |
| Linn St. N&S | 35W-25N | 42 |
| Lochwood Dr. N&S | 35W-27N | 34 |
| Lock Lomond Dr. NS&EW | 36W-23N | 41 |
| Lorraine Dr. N&S | 36W-24N | 41 |
| Lou Av. E&W | 35W-24N | 42 |
| Louisville Ln. NW&SE | 36W-22N | 49 |
| Luceme Dr. N&S | 36W-23N | 41 |
| Lutter Dr. N&S | 33W-24N | 42 |
| Magnolia Ct. N&S | 37W-23N | 41 |
| Magnolia Ln. N&S | 37W-23N | 41 |
| Main St. N&S | 34W-24N,34W-26N | 42 |
| Manchester Ct. E&W | 36W-23N | 41 |
| Manchester Dr. N&S | 36W-23N | 41 |
| Maple St. NE&SW | 35W-25N | 42 |
| Maplewood Ln. E&W | 35W-26N | 42 |
| Marhill Ct. NW&SE | 35W-25N | 42 |
| Marian Pkwy. N&S | 35W-25N | 42 |
| Mary Ln. N&S | 35W-25N | 42 |
| McCullom St. E&W | 34W-26N | 42 |
| McHenry Av. N&S | 36W-24N,35W-25N | 41 |
| McIntosh Blvd. E&W | 34W-25N | 42 |
| McNair St. N&S | 35W-27N | 34 |
| Meardle Dr. N&S | 35W-24N | 42 |
| Melrose St. N&S | 36W-25N | 41 |
| Memorial Ct. NW&SE | 34W-25N | 42 |
| Memorial St. NW&SE | 34W-25N | 42 |
| Meyer Dr. E&W | 35W-24N | 42 |
| Michael Ct. N&S | 35W-26N | 42 |
| Midlane Dr. N&S | 35W-27N | 34 |
| Millard Av. N&S | 37W-25N | 41 |
| Miller Rd. E&W | 36W-22N | 49 |
| Minnie St. NE&SW | 35W-26N | 42 |
| Mistwood Ln. N&S | 36W-23N | 41 |
| Monarch NE&SW | 36W-23N | 41 |
| Monterey Dr. E&W | 36W-24N | 41 |
| Morgan St. NW&SE | 34W-26N | 42 |
| Mulberry Ln. N&S | 37W-25N | 41 |
| N.Brentwood Dr. E&W | 36W-24N | 41 |
| Narragansett Ct. N&S | 33W-26N | 42 |
| Nash Rd. N&S | 36W-26N | 41 |
| Nashua Ct. N&S | 33W-26N | 42 |
| Nashville Ln. NW&SE | 36W-22N | 49 |
| Newburg Dr. N&S | 36W-24N | 41 |
| Newcastle Ct. E&W | 35W-24N | 42 |
| Newport Ln. NS&EW | 36W-22N | 49 |
| Nimco Dr. E&W | 35W-24N | 42 |
| North Av. E&W | 37W-25N | 41 |
| North Shore Dr. N&S | 37W-25N,36W-25N | 41 |
| Northampton Dr. NE&SW | 35W-24N | 42 |
| Norwich Ct. N&S | 36W-22N | 49 |
| Nottingham Ct. E&W | 35W-24N | 42 |
| Nottingham Ln. N&S | 35W-24N | 42 |
| Oak Ct. E&W | 36W-25N | 41 |
| Oak Valley Ct. NE&SW | 33W-25N | 42 |
| Oak Valley Dr. NW&SE | 33W-25N | 42 |
| Official Rd. E&W | 35W-24N | 42 |
| Old Westbury Ct. N&S | 33W-27N | 34 |
| Old Westbury Rd. N&S | 33W-27N | 34 |
| Orchard Row E&W | 36W-26N | 41 |
| Oriole Tr. NW&SE | 36W-25N,35W-25N | 41 |
| Oxford Ln. N&S | 36W-25N | 41 |
| Paddock St. E&W | 35W-25N | 42 |
| Palm Ct. N&S | 36W-22N | 49 |
| Palmer Ct. E&W | 37W-24N | 41 |
| Park Blvd. N&S | 34W-26N | 42 |
| Parkridge Ct. E&W | 36W-23N | 41 |
| Parkridge Dr. NE&SW | 36W-23N | 41 |
| Parkside Ct. N&S | 35W-27N | 34 |
| Parkside Dr. E&W | 36W-23N | 41 |
| Parkside Ter. N&S | 35W-27N | 34 |
| Parkview Ct. N&S | 36W-26N | 42 |
| Patricia Ln. NW&SE | 36W-25N | 41 |
| Peachtree Ct., N. N&S | 36W-22N | 49 |
| Peachtree Ct., S. N&S | 36W-22N | 49 |
| Pebble Ln. N&S | 37W-23N | 41 |
| Pebble Ln. N&S | 37W-23N | 41 |
| Pembroke Ct., N. N&S | 36W-22N | 49 |
| Pembroke Ct., S. N&S | 36W-22N | 49 |
| Penny Ln. N&S | 36W-22N | 49 |
| Peterson Pkwy. N&S | 35W-26N | 42 |
| Pierson St. NW&SE | 36W-25N,35W-25N | 41 |
| Pine Ct N&S | 35W-26N | 42 |
| Pine St. E&W | 36W-25N | 41 |
| Pinewood Dr. E&W | 37W-25N | 41 |
| Pingree Rd. N&S | 35W-24N,34W-25N | 42 |
| Plaintain Ct. E&W | 37W-24N | 41 |
| Plum Ct. N&S | 36W-22N | 49 |
| Plum Tree Dr. E&W | 37W-24N | 41 |
| Plymouth Ln. NS&EW | 35W-24N | 42 |
| Pomeroy St. NE&SW | 35W-25N | 42 |
| Poplar St. E&W | 34W-26N | 42 |
| Porter Av. E&W | 35W-25N | 41 |
| Portsmouth Ct. N&S | 36W-22N | 49 |
| Portsmouth Rd. N&S | 36W-22N | 49 |
| Prairie St. E&W | 34W-26N | 42 |
| Prescott Ln. N&S | 36W-23N | 41 |
| Pyott Rd. N&S | 35W-24N | 42 |
| Railroad St. NW&SE | 36W-26N | 42 |
| Ray St. E&W | 33W-26N | 42 |
| Rebecca Rd. E&W | 34W-26N | 42 |
| Regency Park Dr. NS&EW | 36W-23N | 41 |
| Regent Dr. E&W | 36W-23N | 41 |
| Richert Rd. N&S | 33W-25N | 42 |
| Ridge Av. N&S | 36W-26N | 41 |
| Ridgefield Rd. NW&SE | 36W-26N,36W-27N | 41 |
| Ridgewood Dr. N&S | 37W-24N | 41 |
| Ringling Rd. E&W | 36W-25N | 41 |
| Riverside Rd N&S | 36W-25N | 41 |
| Robert Av. NW&SE | 36W-25N | 41 |
| Rockland Rd. E&W | 36W-26N | 41 |
| Rolling Hills Dr. N&S | 37W-22N | 49 |
| Rosedale Av. NW&SE | 35W-25N | 42 |
| Rosenthal Dr. N&S | 34W-24N | 42 |
| Rosewood Ln. N&S | 36W-23N | 41 |
| Rt. 176 (Terra Cotta) E&W | 37W-26N,33W-26N | 41 |
| Rt. 31 N&S | 33W-25N,33W-27N | 42 |
| Rudat Ct. N&S | 36W-24N,25W-24N | 41 |
| Ryan Way N&S | 35W-27N | 34 |
| S.Brentwood Dr. E&W | 36W-24N | 41 |
| Saddle Creek Ln. NE&SW | 37W-22N | 49 |
| Saddle Ridge NS&EW | 34W-27N | 34 |
| Sandlewood Ln. N&S | 37W-23N,37W-24N | 41 |
| Sarasota Ln. NE&SW | 37W-24N | 41 |
| Savannah Dr. E&W | 33W-26N | 42 |
| Second Ct. NE&SW | 35W-25N | 42 |
| Second St. N&S | 35W-26N | 42 |
| Sedgewich Ct. N&S | 35W-24N | 42 |
| Shadowwood Dr. E&W | 37W-24N | 41 |
| Sharon Dr. E&W | 36W-24N,35W-24N | 41 |
| Sheffield Dr. NS&EW | 36W-23N | 41 |
| Shelton Ln. N&S | 36W-23N | 41 |
| Sherbon Dr. E&W | 35W-24N | 42 |
| Sherman St. E&W | 35W-26N,34W-26N | 42 |
| Short St. N&S | 35W-25N | 42 |
| Silk Oak Ln. N&S | 33W-26N | 42 |
| Silver Berry N&S | 34W-26N | 42 |
| Smitana Rd. NW&SE | 33W-25N | 42 |

| | Grid | Page |
|---|---|---|
| Snowberry Ln. E&W | | |
| | 37W-25N | 41 |
| Somerfield Ln. NE&SW | | |
| | 35W-22N | 49 |
| Somerset Ln. NE&SW | | |
| | 35W-24N | 42 |
| South St. NW&SE . 35W-25N | | 42 |
| Southport Ln. E&W | | |
| | 36W-23N | 49 |
| Spring Ridge Dr. EW&NS | | |
| | 35W-26N | 42 |
| Spruce Ln. NS . . 36W-25N | | 41 |
| St.Andrew Ct. NW&SE | | |
| | 36W-24N | 41 |
| St.Andrews Ln. NS&EW | | |
| | 36W-24N | 41 |
| Stockport Ln. NS&EW | | |
| | 35W-22N | 49 |
| Stockton Ln. NW&SE | | |
| | 36W-22N | 49 |
| Stone Creek Cir. NS&EW | | |
| | 37W-22N | 49 |
| Stonebridge Ln. E&W | | |
| | 36W-23N | 41 |
| Stonehedge Dr. N&S | | |
| | 37W-24N | 41 |
| Stony Hill Ln. NS&EW | | |
| | 36W-27N | 33 |
| Stratford Dr. NW&SE | | |
| | 36W-22N | 49 |
| Sturm Ct. NS&EW . 33W-25N | | 42 |
| Suffolk Dr. E&W . 35W-24N | | 42 |
| Summercrest Ct. NW&SE | | |
| | 36W-23N | 49 |
| Summercrest Dr. W&V | | |
| | 36W-23N | 49 |
| Sunset Tr. NE&SW | | |
| | 35W-25N | 42 |
| Surrey Ln. E&W . . . 35W-24N | | 42 |
| Sussex Ln. NE&SW | | |
| | 35W-24N | 42 |
| Sutherland Dr. N&S | | |
| | 36W-24N | 41 |
| Sutton Dr. N&S . . 36W-24N | | 41 |
| Swanson Rd. N&S | | |
| | 37W-22N,37W-23N | 49 |
| Sycamore Ln. N&S 36W-26N | | 41 |
| Talcott Av. NS&EW | | |
| | 34W-26N | 42 |
| Talcott Ct. NS&EW | | |
| | 34W-26N | 42 |
| Tamerisk Ln. N&S . 36W-24N | | 41 |
| Tamerisk Ter. NW&SE | | |
| | 36W-24N | 41 |
| Tanglewood Dr. NE&SW | | |
| | 36W-23N | 41 |
| Teakwood Ln. E&W | | |
| | 37W-26N | 41 |
| Teckler Blvd. NE&SW | | |
| | 35W-24N | 42 |
| Teki Dr. E&W . . . 33W-24N | | 42 |
| Terra Cotta Av. E&W | | |
| | 37W-26N,33W-26N | 41 |
| Teverton Ln. N&S . 35W-24N | | 42 |
| Third St. N&S . . . . 35W-26N | | 42 |
| Thomas St. N&S . . 34W-25N | | 42 |
| Thomasville Ln. N&S | | |
| | 36W-22N | 49 |
| Thornwood Ln. E&W | | |
| | 37W-25N | 41 |
| Three Oaks Rd. E&W | | |
| | 35W-24N | 42 |
| Timber Hill Dr. N&S | | |
| | 37W-25N | 41 |
| Tomahawk Ln. N&S | | |
| | 34W-27N | 34 |
| Tracy Trail NS&EW | | |
| | 34W-24N | 42 |
| Trailwood Ct. E&W | | |
| | 37W-23N | 41 |
| Trailwood Ct. NW&SE | | |
| | 36W-23N | 41 |
| Trailwood Dr. NE&SW | | |
| | 36W-23N | 41 |
| Trumbull Cir. E&W . 33W-25N | | 42 |
| U.S. Route 14 E&W | | |
| | 33W-25N | 42 |
| U.S. Route 14 NW&SE | | |
| | 36W-26N,36W-24N | 41 |
| Union St. NW&SE . 35W-25N | | 42 |
| University St. NW&SE | | |
| | 35W-25N | 42 |
| Uteg St. E&W . . . 35W-25N | | 42 |
| Van Buren St. NE&SW | | |
| | 36W-25N,35W-25N | 41 |
| Victor Pkwy. N&S . 36W-25N | | 41 |
| View St. E&W . . . 34W-26N | | 42 |
| Village Ct. NW&SE 36W-22N | | 49 |
| Village Rd. E&W | | |
| | 37W-22N,36W-22N | 49 |
| Virginia St. E&W | | |
| | 36W-26N,34W-24N | 41 |
| Walkup Av. N&S . .35W-25N | | 42 |
| Walkup Rd. N&S | | |
| | 35W-26N,35W-27N | 42 |
| Wallace Av. NE&SW | | |
| | 35W-25N | 42 |
| Warrington Ln. NW&SE | | |
| | 36W-22N | 49 |
| Washington St. NE&SW | | |
| | 36W-25N | 41 |
| Waterford Cut E&W | | |
| | 37W-23N | 41 |
| Waterford Dr. E&W | | |
| | 37W-23N | 41 |
| Watson Ct. NS&EW | | |
| | 37W-24N | 41 |
| Wedgewood Cir. NS&EW | | |
| | 37W-24N | 41 |
| Wedgewood Ct. N&S | | |
| | 37W-24N | 41 |

| | Grid | Page |
|---|---|---|
| Wedgewood Dr. NS&EW | | |
| | 37W-24N | 41 |
| Wellington Dr. N&S | | |
| | 35W-24N | 42 |
| Wesley Dr. N&S . 36W-24N | | 41 |
| West Porridge Dr. N&S | | |
| | 36W-23N | 41 |
| Weston Dr. E&W . 36W-23N | | 41 |
| Westport Ct. NE&SW | | |
| | 36W-23N | 41 |
| Westport Ridge Dr. NS&EW | | |
| | 36W-23N | 41 |
| Wheatland Dr. N&S | | |
| | 37W-24N | 41 |
| White Pine Ct. E&W | | |
| | 37W-22N | 49 |
| Whitehall Way E&W | | |
| | 37W-23N | 41 |
| Wiggington Dr. N&S | | |
| | 37W-24N | 41 |
| Wildflower Ln. N&S | | |
| | 33W-26N | 42 |
| Williams St. N&S . 35W-25N | | 42 |
| Willow Tree Dr. NS&EW | | |
| | 36W-23N | 41 |
| Wiltshire St. NE&SW | | |
| | 35W-24N | 42 |
| Wimbelton Ln. N&S | | |
| | 36W-24N | 41 |
| Windemere Way NS&EW | | |
| | 38W-21N | 49 |
| Windridge Dr. N&S 37W-24N | | 41 |
| Windsor Dr. E&W . 36W-24N | | 41 |
| Winslow Cir. NS&EW | | |
| | 36W-23N | 41 |
| Wolf Dr. E&W . . . 33W-24N | | 50 |
| Woodbine Dr. N&S 37W-25N | | 41 |
| Woodcreek Cir. NS&EW | | |
| | 37W-23N | 41 |
| Woodhaven Dr. NE&SW | | |
| | 36W-22N | 49 |
| Woodland Dr. E&W | | |
| | 36W-25N | 41 |
| Woodmar Ln. N&S . 36W-24N | | 41 |
| Woodmar Ter. E&W | | |
| | 36W-24N | 41 |
| Woodscreek Cir. NS&EW | | |
| | 37W-23N | 41 |
| Woodstock St. N&S | | |
| | 36W-26N,35W-26N | 41 |
| Wyndmuir Ln. NS&EW | | |
| | 33W-26N | 42 |
| Yellowwood Ln. E&W | | |
| | 37w-22N | 49 |
| Yorkshire Ln. NE&SW | | |
| | 35W-24N | 42 |

## Dorr Township

| | Grid | Page |
|---|---|---|
| Aspen Ct. NE&SW . 38W-26N | | 41 |
| Aspen Ln. N&S . . 38W-26N | | 41 |
| Beech Av. NS&EW | | |
| | 38W-25N,38W-26N | 41 |
| Blue Jay Ct. NW&SE | | |
| | 37W-28N | 33 |
| Boerderij Way NS&EW | | |
| | 38W-29N | 33 |
| Boerderij Way E. N&S | | |
| | 38W-29N | 33 |
| Bryon Cir. NS&EW . 39W-31N | | 24 |
| Bull Valley Rd. NE&SW | | |
| | 39W-31N | 24 |
| Bunker Av. E&W . 37W-26N | | 41 |
| Butternut Dr. NW&SE | | |
| | 39W-26N,38W-26N | 40 |
| Callway Tr. N&S . . 37W-26N | | 41 |
| Cardinal Ln. E&W | | |
| | 38W-28N,37W-28N | 33 |
| Carol Ln. N&S . . 42W-28N | | 32 |
| Castle Rd. N&S | | |
| | 40W-28N,40W-29N | 32 |
| Castleberry Dr. E&W | | |
| | 37W-28N | 33 |
| Charlotte Dr. E&W . 42W-28N | | 32 |
| Cherry Valley Rd. N&S | | |
| | 37W-28N,37W-29N | 33 |
| Cheshire Dr. E&W . 37W-28N | | 33 |
| Chestnut Ct. NE&SW | | |
| | 38W-26N | 41 |
| Chukar Pl. N&S . . 42W-28N | | 32 |
| Church St. NW&SE | | |
| | 37W-27N | 33 |
| Country Club Rd. NW&SE | | |
| | 40W-31N,37W-28N | 24 |
| Crystal Springs Rd. E&W | | |
| | 37W-29N | 33 |
| Daisy Ct. NE&SW . 40W-31N | | 24 |
| Davis Rd. E&W . . 42W-29N | | 32 |
| Dean St. N&S | | |
| | 41W-26N,42W-29N | 40 |
| Deer Path Rd. NS&EW | | |
| | 39W-30N | 32 |
| Deweio Tr. NE&SW | | |
| | 38W-29N | 33 |
| Dirkshire Dr. E&W . 38W-29N | | 33 |
| Doty Rd. N&S | | |
| | 39W-27N,39W-28N | 32 |
| Esther Ct. E&W . . 40W-31N | | 24 |
| Flemming Rd. NW&SE | | |
| | 39W-31N,38W-30N | 24 |
| Gayle Dr. N&S . . 42W-27N | | 32 |
| Haligus Rd. NW&SE | | |
| | 39W-26N | 40 |
| Hamilton Rd. N&S . 41W-26N | | 40 |
| Hawthorne Ln. N&S | | |
| | 38W-26N | 41 |
| Heather Ln. E&W . 40W-26N | | 40 |
| Hercules Rd. E&W . 40W-28N | | 32 |
| Hickory Ln. NS&EW | | |
| | 38W-26N | 41 |
| Hidden Ln. N&S . . 38W-31N | | 25 |
| Hidden Ln. E&W . . 38W-31N | | 25 |

| | Grid | Page |
|---|---|---|
| Hillside Rd. E&W . 37W-27N | | 33 |
| Holly Ln. N&S . . . 42W-28N | | 32 |
| Ironwood Dr. N&S . 38W-26N | | 41 |
| Juanita Vista NW&SE | | |
| | 37W-26N | 41 |
| Keats Ct. E&W . . 39W-31N | | 24 |
| Lily Pond Rd. N&S | | |
| | 38W-28N,38W-29N | 33 |
| Lucas Rd. NW&SE | | |
| | 41W-28N,37W-27N | 32 |
| Madison St. N&S | | |
| | 37W-27N | 33 |
| Market St. NE&SW | | |
| | 37W-27N | 33 |
| Mason Hill Rd. N&S | | |
| | 37W-30N | 33 |
| McConnell Rd. NW&SE | | |
| | 40W-30N,38W-29N | 32 |
| Middlecreek Dr. N&S | | |
| | 37W-28N | 33 |
| Monroe St. NE&SW | | |
| | 37W-27N | 33 |
| Mt. Thabor Rd. N&S | | |
| | 39W-26N,39W-27N | 40 |
| Nancy Ct. NW&SE . 42W-27N | | 32 |
| Noveen Pkwy. E&W | | |
| | 40W-30N | 32 |
| Oakleaf Ln. E&W . 40W-30N | | 32 |
| Ohnstad Rd. N&S | | |
| | 38W-26N,38W-27N | 41 |
| Perkins Rd. E&W . 42W-28N | | 32 |
| Pleasant Valley Rd. E&W | | |
| | 42W-26N,40W-26N | 40 |
| Prairie Dr. E&W . . 37W-28N | | 33 |
| Prospect St. E&W . 37W-27N | | 33 |
| Queen Anne Rd. N&S | | |
| | 39W-31N | 24 |
| Railroad St. NW&SE | | |
| | 37W-27N | 33 |
| Ridgefield Rd. NS&EW | | |
| | 38W-27N,37W-27N | 33 |
| Robin Hill Dr. NS&EW | | |
| | 37W-28N | 33 |
| Rt. 176 E&W | | |
| | 42W-26N,40W-26N | 40 |
| Rt. 47 N&S | | |
| | 41W-27N,41W-29N | 32 |
| S. Robin Hill Rd. NE&SW | | |
| | 37W-28N | 33 |
| Sally Circle E&W . 42W-28N | | 32 |
| Schuette Cir. NE&SW | | |
| | 40W-31N | 32 |
| Sharon Dr. NW&SE | | |
| | 40W-31N | 24 |
| Shelly Ct. E&W . . 39W-31N | | 24 |
| Sunnyside Rd. N&S | | |
| | 42W-26N,42W-28N | 40 |
| Swanson Rd. N&S . 41W-26N | | 40 |
| Tiporary St. NE&SW | | |
| | 37W-31N | 25 |
| U.S. Route 14 NW&SE | | |
| | 42W-30N,38W-28N | 32 |
| Valley Hill Rd. N&S 37W-30N | | 33 |
| Waller St. NE&SW . 37W-27N | | 33 |
| West St. NE&SW . 37W-27N | | 33 |
| Westgate Ct. NE&SW | | |
| | 37W-31N | 25 |
| Willow Ln. N&S . . 38W-26N | | 41 |
| Woodland Ct. E&W | | |
| | 39W-31N | 24 |

## Dunham Township

| | Grid | Page |
|---|---|---|
| Airport Rd. E&W | | |
| | 51W-37N,50W-37N | 12 |
| Becks Rd. E&W . . 53W-37N | | 12 |
| Bluejay Rd. N&S . . 50W-36N | | 13 |
| Bunker Hill Rd. E&W | | |
| | 52W-34N,49W-34N | 20 |
| Busse Rd. N&S | | |
| | 50W-32N,50W-33N | 21 |
| Cardinal Ct. NW&SE | | |
| | 50W-36N | 13 |
| County Line Rd. N&S | | |
| | 54W-32N,54W-37N | 20 |
| Dunham Rd. E&W | | |
| | 54W-33N,49W-33N | 20 |
| Dunham Woods Rd. N&S | | |
| | 49W-34N | 21 |
| Flat Iron Rd. NE&SW | | |
| | 54W-34N,51W-37N | 20 |
| Fritz Rd. N&S | | |
| | 51W-34N,51W-35N | 20 |
| Heritage Ln. E&W . 50W-36N | | 13 |
| Hickory St. N&S . . 52W-37N | | 12 |
| Highview Rd. E&W . 49W-33N | | 21 |
| Hurley Dr. E&W . . 50W-37N | | 13 |
| Island Rd. E&W | | |
| | 53W-37N,52W-37N | 12 |
| Island Rd. N&S . . 53W-37N | | 12 |
| Kennedy Rd. E&W . 53W-37N | | 12 |
| Lembke Rd. E&W | | |
| | 50W-35N,49W-35N | 13 |
| Marengo Rd. N&S | | |
| | 50W-36N,50W-37N | 13 |
| McGuire Rd. E&W | | |
| | 51W-37N,49W-37N | 13 |
| Meade Rd. E&W . . 52W-33N | | 20 |
| Menge Rd. N&S | | |
| | 49W-32N,49W-33N | 21 |
| Mulvenna Rd. N&S 53W-32N | | 20 |
| Olbrich Rd. N&S . . 50W-32N | | 21 |
| Pagles Rd. N&S | | |
| | 54W-34N,53W-37N | 20 |
| Pine St. N&S . . . . 52W-37N | | 12 |
| Ramer Rd. E&W . . 52W-38N | | 12 |
| Robin Rd. N&S . . . 50W-36N | | 13 |
| Root Rd. N&S . . . 52W-32N | | 20 |
| Rt. 173 E&W | | |
| | 54W-37N,51W-37N | 12 |
| Rt. 23 N&S | | |
| | 50W-32N,50W-36N | 21 |

| | Grid | Page |
|---|---|---|
| Rush Creek Rd. E&W | | |
| | 50W-36N | 13 |
| Sinderson St. N&S .53W-37N | | 12 |
| South St. N&S . . . 52W-37N | | 12 |
| Streit Rd. E&W | | |
| | 54W-36N,49W-36N | 12 |
| Tomlin Rd. E&W . . 54W-32N | | 20 |
| Trebess Dr. N&S . 49W-35N | | 13 |
| Trebess Dr. N&S . 49W-36N | | 13 |
| Windy Hill Rd. NS&EW | | |
| | 49W-36N | 13 |
| Woodland Dr. N&S 49W-33N | | 21 |
| Woodpecker Rd. NW&SE | | |
| | 49W-36N,50W-36N | 13 |
| Woodvale Dr. E&W | | |
| | 49W-33N | 21 |

## Fox Lake*
### (Also see Lake County)

| | Grid | Page |
|---|---|---|
| Appaloosa Ln. N&S | | |
| | 29W-40N | 11 |
| Carriage Ln. N&S . 29W-40N | | 11 |
| Chelsey Ct. NE&SW | | |
| | 29W-40N | 11 |
| Chestnut Ridge NW&SE | | |
| | 29W-40N | 11 |
| Churchill Ct. N&S | | |
| | 29W-40N | 11 |
| Country Shore Ln. NS&EW | | |
| | 29W-40N | 11 |
| Downing Pl. N&S . 29W-40N | | 11 |
| English Prairie Rd. E&W | | |
| | 29W-42N | 11 |
| Fox Shire Ln. E&W | | |
| | 29W-40N | 11 |
| Heather Ridge NE&SW | | |
| | 29W-40N | 11 |
| Laurine Ln. NE&SW | | |
| | 29W-40N | 11 |
| Main St. E&W . . . 29W-39N | | 11 |
| Morgan Ct. N&S | | |
| | 29W-40N | 11 |
| Palimino Ln. NE&SW | | |
| | 29W-40N | 11 |
| Park Vista NE&SW 29W-40N | | 11 |
| Steeple Ln. NW&SE | | |
| | 29W-40N | 11 |
| Sundial Ln. NS&EW | | |
| | 29W-40N | 11 |
| Surrey Ln. NE&SW | | |
| | 29W-40N | 11 |
| Wilmot Rd. N&S | | |
| | 29W-40N,29W-41N | 11 |

## Fox River Grove

| | Grid | Page |
|---|---|---|
| Adams Av. NW&SE | | |
| | 30W-23N | 43 |
| Algonquin Rd. NE&SW | | |
| | 30W-22N,29W-22N | 51 |
| Amhurst Ct. E&W . 29W-22N | | 51 |
| Arch Way N&S . . . 30W-22N | | 51 |
| Asbury Av. E&W . 29W-22N | | 51 |
| Asbury Ct. E&W | | |
| | 30W-22N,29W-22N | 51 |
| Asbury Rd. E&W . 29W-22N | | 51 |
| Ashburn Av. E&W . 29W-22N | | 51 |
| Ashbury Ct. E&W . 30W-22N | | 51 |
| Ashcroft Ct. NW&SE | | |
| | 30W-22N | 51 |
| Barberry Tr. NS&EW | | |
| | 29W-22N | 43 |
| Bayview Ct. N&S | | |
| | 30W-22N | 51 |
| Bayview Dr. N&S . 30W-22N | | 51 |
| Bayview Rd. SW&NE | | |
| | 30W-22N | 51 |
| Beach Way NW&SE | | |
| | 30W-22N,30W-23N | 51 |
| Birch Ln. EW&NS . 29W-23S | | 43 |
| Bradbury Ct. N&S . 30W-22N | | 51 |
| Brighton Ct. N&S . 30W-22N | | 51 |
| Bristol Ln. NE&SW 29W-22N | | 51 |
| Cary Rd. NW&SE . 29W-22N | | 51 |
| Center Dr. E&W . . 29W-23N | | 43 |
| Center St. E&W . . 29W-22N | | 51 |
| Chatham Ct. N&S . 29W-22N | | 51 |
| Circle Rd. NE&SW . 30W-23N | | 43 |
| Concorde Av. E&W | | |
| | 29W-22N | 51 |
| Crescent Rd. N&S . 30W-23N | | 43 |
| Crompton Ct. NW&SE | | |
| | 29W-22N | 51 |
| Doverton Ln. E&W . 29W-22N | | 51 |
| Elder Ln. NW&SE . 30W-22N | | 51 |
| Ellington Ct. N&S . 29W-23N | | 43 |
| Essex Rd. NE&SW 30W-22N | | 51 |
| Excy Rd. E&W . . . 29W-22N | | 51 |
| Foxanna Cir. N&S . 29W-23N | | 43 |
| Foxmoor Rd. NE&SW | | |
| | 30W-22N,29W-22N | 51 |
| Gladys Av. N&S . . 30W-22N | | 51 |
| Glenhurst Ct. NW&SE | | |
| | 30W-22N | 51 |
| Glenice Pkwy. N&S | | |
| | 30W-23N | 43 |
| Glenview Ct. N&S | | |
| | 30W-22N | 51 |
| Grace Ln. N&S . . 30W-22N | | 51 |
| Grace Ln. NE&SW .30W-22N | | 51 |
| Grove Av. N&S . . . 29W-22N | | 51 |
| Harding Av. N&S . 29W-23N | | 43 |
| Highview Dr. E&W . 29W-23N | | 43 |
| Hillcrest Av. NE&SW | | |
| | 30W-22N | 51 |
| Huntcliff Ct. NW&SE | | |
| | 29W-22N | 51 |
| Hunter Cir. N&S | | |
| | 30W-22N | 51 |
| Hunters Way NW&SE | | |
| | 30W-22N,29W-22N | 51 |
| Illinois St. NE&SW . 29W-22N | | 43 |
| Johnson St. E&W . 29W-23N | | 43 |

| | Grid | Page |
|---|---|---|
| Keystone Ln. NW&SE | | |
| | 30W-22N | 51 |
| Lexington Av. NE&SW | | |
| | 30W-22N | 51 |
| Liberty Av. N&S . . 30W-22N | | 51 |
| Lily Ln. NE&SW . . 29W-22N | | 43 |
| Lincoln Av. E&W | | |
| | 30W-22N,30W-23N | 43 |
| Lucille Av. E&W | | |
| | 29W-22N,29W-23N | 51 |
| Manchester Ct. NW&SE | | |
| | 29W-22N | 51 |
| Maple Av. NW&SE . 30W-22N | | 51 |
| Melrose Ct. NW&SE | | |
| | 30W-22N | 51 |
| Midway St. N&S . . 29W-22N | | 51 |
| Millard Av. N&S . . 30W-22N | | 51 |
| Mound St. N&S . . 29W-22N | | 51 |
| North Av. N&S . . . 29W-22N | | 51 |
| North Rd. N&S . . . 29W-23N | | 43 |
| North River Rd. NE&SW | | |
| | 30W-23N | 43 |
| North St. NW&SE . 29W-22N | | 51 |
| Northwest Highway NW&SE | | |
| | 30W-23N,29W-22N | 43 |
| Oak Ct. NW&SE . . 30W-22N | | 51 |
| Oak St. E&W . . . 29W-23N | | 43 |
| Old Hunt Rd. NW&SE | | |
| | 30W-22N | 51 |
| Opatrny Dr. E&W | | |
| | 30W-23N,29W-22N | 43 |
| Orchard St. N&S | | |
| | 29W-22N,29W-23N | 51 |
| Park Ct. NW&SE . 29W-22N | | 51 |
| Paul Ln. SW&NE . 29W-22N | | 51 |
| Pine St. N&S . . . 30W-22N | | 51 |
| Pleasant St. E&W . 29W-23N | | 43 |
| Poplar Pkwy. NW&SE | | |
| | 30W-22N | 51 |
| Ridgeland St. E&W | | |
| | 29W-22N | 51 |
| River Way Rd. NE&SW | | |
| | 30W-23N | 43 |
| School Dr. N&S . . 29W-22N | | 51 |
| School St. E&W . . 29W-22N | | 51 |
| Shannon Dr. NW&SE | | |
| | 30W-22N | 51 |
| Ski Hill Rd. NE&SW | | |
| | 29W-22N,29W-23N | 51 |
| Skyline Dr. NE&SW | | |
| | 29W-23N | 43 |
| South River Rd. NS&EW | | |
| | 30W-23N | 43 |
| Spring Ct. N&S . . 29W-23N | | 43 |
| Spring St. N&S . . 29W-23N | | 43 |
| Thackery Ln. NW&SE | | |
| | 30W-22N | 51 |
| Tower Ct. N&S . . . 30W-22N | | 51 |
| Tower Pl. N&S . . . 30W-22N | | 51 |
| Tower Rd. NS&EW | | |
| | 30W-22N | 51 |
| View St. E&W . . . 29W-22N | | 51 |
| Violet Av. NS&EW . 29W-22N | | 43 |
| Well St. E&W . . . 29W-23N | | 43 |
| Wildwood Ln. E&W | | |
| | 29W-23N | 43 |
| Windsor Cir. N&S . 29W-23N | | 43 |
| Woodbine Ln. NE&SW | | |
| | 29W-22N | 51 |
| Yorkshire Dr. N&S . 29W-22N | | 51 |

## Fox River Valley Gardens*
### (Also see Lake County)

| | Grid | Page |
|---|---|---|
| Arbor Vita Dr. N&S . 29w-26N | | 43 |
| Center St. NE&SW | | |
| | 29W-26N,28W-26N | 43 |
| Channel Dr., S. NE&SW | | |
| | 29W-26N | 43 |
| Circle Av. NW&SE . 29W-26N | | 43 |
| Community Ct. E&W | | |
| | 29W-26N | 43 |
| Eastwood Ct. N&S | | |
| | 29W-25N | 43 |
| Eastwood Av. N&S | | |
| | 29W-25N,29W-26N | 43 |
| Eastwood Ln. N&S 29W-26N | | 43 |
| Hilldale Ln. NW&SE | | |
| | 29W-26N | 43 |
| N. Circle Av. NW&SE | | |
| | 29W-26N | 43 |
| Oak St. NW&SE . . 29W-26N | | 43 |
| Park Av. E&W . . . 29W-25N | | 43 |
| Park Ct. NE&SW . 29W-25N | | 43 |
| Park Dr. NW&SE . 29W-25N | | 43 |
| Peninsula NW&SE | | |
| | 29W-26N | 43 |
| Riverside Av. NS&EW | | |
| | 29W-25N | 43 |
| Riverside Dr., S. . 29W-25N | | 43 |
| S. Circle Av. NS&EW | | |
| | 29W-25N,29W-26N | 43 |
| Strait St. NE&SW . 29w-26N | | 43 |

## Grafton Township

| | Grid | Page |
|---|---|---|
| Adamson Rd. E&W | | |
| | 42W-23N,41W-23N | 40 |
| Albrecht Rd. E&W . 39W-23N | | 40 |
| Algonquin Rd. E&W | | |
| | 39W-21N | 48 |
| Arthur St. N&S . . . 38W-25N | | 41 |
| Ballard Rd. E&W | | |
| | 40W-25N,38W-25N | 40 |
| Bard Rd. E&W | | |
| | 39W-24N,37W-24N | 40 |
| Borhart Rd. N&S . . 42W-20N | | 48 |
| Charlotte Av. N&S . 37W-25N | | 41 |
| Chestnut Dr. N&S | | |
| | 38W-25N,38W-26N | 41 |
| Chicago Av. E&W . 37W-24N | | 41 |

|  | Grid | Page |
|---|---|---|

Columbine Av. N&S ........38W-25N 41
Conley Rd. NE&SW ....40W-24N,39W-24N 40
Cote Dr. N&S ... 41W-25N 40
Cottage Dr. N&S .. 37W-24N 41
Coyne Station Rd. N&S ....42W-21N,42W-23N 48
Crescent Dr. NE&SW ........41W-25N 40
Crystal Beach Av. N&S ........37W-25N 41
Crystal Lake Rd. N&S ........38W-22N 49
Delaware St. N&S . 38W-25N 41
Della Av. N&S......38W-25N 41
Dundee Rd. NW&SE ........39W-20N 48
East End Av. N&S . 37W-25N 41
Elm Ln. E&W .... 38W-25N 41
Ernesti Rd. E&W .. 41W-23N 40
Foster Rd. E&W ....40W-25N,39W-24N 40
Frank Rd. N&S .... 37W-21N 49
Georgine St. N&S . 38W-25N 41
Grandview Dr. E&W ........41W-25N 40
Greenfield Rd. N&S ........37W-25N 41
Haligus Rd. N&S ....39W-22N,39W-25N 48
Hamilton Rd. N&S . 41W-25N 40
Hawthorne Way E&W ........40W-25N 40
Hemmer Rd. N&S . 42W-20N 48
Hemmingsen Rd. E&W ....42W-24N,41W-24N 40
Hensel Rd. N&S ....42W-25N,41W-25N 40
Hickory Av. E&W . 37W-24N 41
Hillcrest Av. E&W . 37W-25N 41
Hillview Dr. E&W . 41W-25N 40
Huntley Rd. N&S ....37W-23N,37W-24N 41
Kasper Av. E&W . 38W-25N 41
Kruetzer Rd. E&W . 39W-20N 48
Lakeview Av. E&W ........37W-24N 41
Lakeview Dr. N&S . 41W-25N 40
Lakewood Av. N&S ........37W-25N 41
Lavergone St. N&S ........38W-25N 41
Linder Av. E&W .. 38W-25N 41
Main St. E&W......41W-21N 48
Marengo Rd. NW&SE ........43W-23N 39
Martin St. N&S ... 38W-25N 41
Mayfield Rd. N&S . 37W-25N 41
Mensching Rd. N&S ....42W-24N,42W-25N 40
Miller Rd. E&W .... 38W-22N 49
Muriel St. N&S .... 38W-25N 41
N. Union Rd. N&S ....41W-23N,41W-24N 40
North Av. E&W ... 38W-25N 41
North Union Rd. N&S ....41W-23N,41W-24N 40
Pauline Av. N&S .. 38W-25N 41
Priegnitz Rd. N&S ....38W-22N,38W-20N 49
Reed Rd. E&W .... 40W-22N 48
Ridgeview Dr. N&S ........41W-25N 40
Rose Av. N&S......39W-25N 41
Rosebud Rd. N&S . 38W-25N 41
Rowland Rd. NS&EW ........40W-25N 40
Rt. 47 N&S ...... 40W-22N 48
Ruth Rd. N&S.....40W-21N 48
S. Lakeview Dr. E&W ........41W-25N 40
S. Union Rd. N&S ....40W-22N,41W-23N 48
Square Barn Rd. N&S ........37W-20N 49
Sunnyside Av. N&S ........37W-25N 41
Sunset Dr. N&S .. 37W-24N 41
Suttondale Dr. N&S ........40W-25N 40
Swanson Rd. N&S ....37W-23N,37W-22N 41
Teresa Av. N&S... 38W-25N 41
Tryon St. N&S.....38W-25N 41
Zimmerman Rd. NS&EW ....39W-24N,39W-25N 40

**Greenwood**
Aavang Rd. E&W . 39W-35N 17
Allendale Rd. E&W ....38W-36N,39W-37N 17
Barber Rd. E&W .. 38W-36N 17
Center St. NW&SE 38W-36N 17
Church St. E&W... 38W-36N 17
Greenwood Rd. NE&SW ....38W-35N,39W-37N 17
Lathrop Dr. NE&SW ........38W-36N 17
Miller Rd. N&S ... 38W-37N 17
Park St. NW&SE .. 38W-36N 17
Thompson Rd. N&S ....37W-35N,38W-37N 17
West Wonder Lake Rd. E&W ....37W-36N,38W-36N 17

**Greenwood Township**
Aavang Rd. E&W . 39W-35N 17
Acorn Path E&W . 37W-35N 17
Allendale Rd. E&W ........41W-37N,38W-37N 16

Appleby Ct. NW&SE ........42W-36N 16
Arabian Tr. E&W . 39W-34N 24
Autumn Ln. E&W .. 38W-33N 25
Baker Ter. E&W ... 41W-33N 24
Banford Rd. E&W .. 40W-32N 24
Bennington Ct. NW&SE ........36W-32N 25
Billingsgate Ln. N&S ........42W-36N 16
Birchwood Dr. N&S ........37W-34N 25
Brody Ln. N&S .... 41W-33N 24
Brookham Ct. N&S ........42W-36N 16
Cambridge Ct. E&W ........36W-32N 25
Charles Rd. NW&SE ....42W-34N,39W-33N 24
Chatham Ct. N&S .. 38W-33N 25
Compton Ln. NW&SE ........42W-36N 16
Concorde Dr. N&S . 36W-32N 25
Cooney Dr. E&W .. 41W-33N 24
Crest Ln. E&W .... 42W-36N 16
Deer Dr. E&W .... 37W-34N 25
East Lake Shore Dr. NE&SW ........37W-35N 17
Elm St. N&S .... 37W-35N 17
Elmwood Dr. E&W . 33W-34N 26
Evergreen Dr. E&W ....38W-35N,37W-35N 17
Fleming Rd. N&S .. 39W-32N 24
Gerson Dr. E&W ... 37W-34N 25
Gleason Ct. N&S .. 41W-33N 24
Greenwood Rd. NE&SW ....39W-33N,38W-37N 24
Happy Tr. E&W ... 39W-34N 25
Hickory Dr. N&S... 37W-34N 25
Hilltop Dr. N&S ... 37W-35N 17
Hogbag Rd. NE&SW ........37W-33N 25
Howe Rd. E&W ... 38W-37N 17
Jankowski Rd. E&W ....42W-36N,41W-36N 16
Johnson Rd. NE&SW ........42W-37N 16
Lake Shore Dr. N&S ........37W-34N 25
Lake Vista Ln. N&S ........37W-35N 17
Lamb Rd. N&S ....42W-33N,42W-34N 24
Lathrop Dr. NE&SW ........38W-36N 17
Longwood Ct. N&S ........38W-34N 25
Maplewood Dr. N&S ........37W-34N 25
Marie Dr. NE&SW . 37W-34N 25
McCannon Rd. E&W ........41W-32N 24
McCauley Rd. N&S ........42W-37N 16
Meadow Ln. N&S . 37W-34N 25
Memory Ln. N&S .. 37W-34N 25
Memory Tr. E&W .. 37W-35N 17
Miller Rd. E&W ... 41W-32N 24
Miller Rd. N&S ... 39W-37N 17
Mustang Tr. N&S . 39W-34N 25
Northwoods Ct. N&S ........38W-34N 25
Nusbaum Rd. E&W ........40W-34N 24
Oriole Tr. E&W ....38W-35N,37W-35N 17
Park St. SW&NE . 38W-36N 17
Parker Ct. NW&SE 41W-33N 24
Pheasant Ln. E&W 39W-34N 24
Pine Av. E&W ....38W-35N,37W-35N 17
Pine Needle Pass E&W ........38W-34N 25
Pinoak Ln. E&W .. 37W-34N 25
Pleasure Av. N&S . 38W-35N 17
Powers Rd. N&S .. 41W-32N 24
Private Farm Ln. E&W ....42W-37N,41W-37N 16
Queen Anne Rd. N&S ....40W-32N,40W-37N 24
Raffel Rd. NS&EW ....40W-33N,40W-34N 24
Ramble Rd. E&W .. 37W-35N 17
Raycraft Rd. E&W ....42W-34N,41W-36N 24
Rose Marie Rd. SW&NE ........37W-34N 25
Rose St. N&S .... 37W-34N 25
Rt. 120 NW&SE ....40W-32N,37W-33N 24
Rt. 47 N&S ....41W-33N,41W-37N 24
Saddlebred Tr. E&W ........39W-34N 24
Shadow Ln. E&W . 37W-34N 25
Shadowood Dr. E&W ........38W-34N 25
Shady Ln. E&W ... 37W-35N 17
Spring Ln. E&W .. 38W-33N 25
Thayer Rd. E&W ....42W-37N,38W-37N 16
Thompson Rd. NS&EW ....38W-32N,37W-34N 25
Thoroughbred Tr. N&S ........39W-34N 24
Trey Rd. NW&SE . 36W-32N 25
Valley Hill Rd. E&W ........36W-33N 25
Vine Av. E&W ....38W-35N,37W-35N 17
W. Sunset Dr. E&W ........37W-35N 17

Ware Rd. E&W .... 41W-33N 24
West Lake Shore Dr. NE&SW ........37W-35N 17
West Meadowlane N&S ........37W-35N 17
West Wonder Lake Rd. NS&EW 38W-36N,37W-37N 17
Westwood Dr. N&S ........37W-35N 17
White Oaks Rd. E&W ........37W-37N 17
Wilmington St. N&S ........36W-32N 25
Windhill Ct. NE&SW ........38W-34N 25
Wondermere Rd. E&W ........38W-36N 17
Wonderview Dr. E&W ........37W-34N 25
Woodland Ln. N&S ........38W-33N 25
Woody Tr. E&W .... 37W-35N 17

**Hartland Township**
Alden Rd. NW&SE ....44W-37N,43W-34N 15
Antuna Dr. N&S .. 44W-33N 23
Azalea Ln. NW&SE ........43W-35N 15
Bauman Rd. E&W . 48W-32N 22
Black Oak Ct. NW&SE ........48W-34N 22
Brink St. E&W .... 48W-37N 14
Brookdale Rd. N&S ....48W-32N,48W-33N 22
Bunker Hill Rd. E&W ....48W-34N,47W-34N 22
Compton Ln. NW&SE ........43W-36N 15
Cooney Ln. N&S .. 44W-34N 23
Countryside Ln. N&S ........47W-36N 14
Debbie Ln. E&W ..48W-34N 22
Deep Cut Rd. NE&SW ....46W-33N,45W-35N 22
Dimmel Rd. N&S . 46W-32N 22
Dogwood Ln. E&W ........43W-34N 23
Dunham Rd. E&W ....48W-33N,46W-33N 22
Frank Ct. E&W ... 48W-34N 22
Goddard St. E&W . 44W-34N 23
Green Rd. E&W ....45W-37N,44W-37N 15
Green Rd. N&S ... 44W-37N 15
Green Rd. NW&SE 45W-37N 15
Greenway Cross E&W ........44W-32N 23
Hartland Rd. N&S ....45W-32N,45W-34N 23
Hawthorn St. N&S . 48W-35N 14
Hidden Lake Rd. NE&SW ....43W-34N,43W-36N 23
Hillside Ln. E&W . 45W-33N 23
Honeysuckle Ln. E&W ........43W-34N 23
Indian Trace N&S . 44W-34N 23
Irish Ln. N&S .... 47W-37N 14
Jankowski Rd. E&W ........43W-36N 15
King Rd. N&S .... 47W-36N 14
Lamb Rd. N&S ... 43W-34N 23
Lembke Rd. E&W . 48W-34N 14
Lilac Ln. NW&SE . 43W-34N 23
Lincoln Rd. E&W ....48W-37N,46W-37N 14
Lindwall Rd. E&W ....48W-35N,48W-36N 14
Maeve Ln. NS&EW ........44W-32N 23
Marawood Dr. NW&SE ........44W-32N 23
Maxwell St. N&S . 44W-34N 23
McCauley Rd. E&W ....43W-36N,43W-37N 15
McGee Rd. E&W . 43W-32N 23
McGuire Rd. NE&SW ....48W-37N,44W-37N 14
Menge Rd. N&S ....48W-32N,48W-33N 22
Murray Rd. N&S ....44W-34N,44W-35N 23
Nelson Rd. E&W ....45W-34N,43W-34N 23
Park Lane Dr. N&S ....45W-32N,45W-33N 23
Paulson Rd. N&S ....47W-33N,47W-34N 22
Red Bud Ln. N&S . 43W-35N 15
Red Oak Dr. N&S . 48W-34N 22
Rose Farm Rd. N&S ....44W-32N,44W-34N 23
Rt. 120 E&W .... 43W-32N 23
Schultz Rd. N&S . 48W-37N 14
Shamrock Ln. E&W ....44W-32N,43W-32N 23
Shannon Dr. N&S . 44W-32N 23
Somerset Ln. NE&SW ........43W-36N 15
St.Patrick Rd. E&W ....45W-35N,43W-35N 15
Streit Rd. E&W ....46W-35N,45W-36N 22
Sutton Pl. NS&EW . 44W-32N 23
Thayer Rd. E&W ....44W-37N,43W-37N 15
Tina Rd. N&S ... 48W-34N 22
U.S. Route 14 NW&SE ....48W-35N,43W-31N 14
Walsh Dr. E&W ... 44W-33N 23

West Rd. N&S ....43W-34N,43W-35N 23
Wilson Rd. N&S ....45W-35N,45W-36N 15
Windsor Dr. NS&EW ........43W-36N 15

**Harvard**
Admiral Dr. E&W . 50W-37N 13
Airport Rd. E&W ....50W-37N,51W-37N 12
Anderson St. E&W. 50W-38N 13
Ayer St. NE&SW . 50W-38N 13
Bayberry Blvd. N&S ....51W-39N,51W-40N 5
Beaumont St. E&W ....51W-38N,50W-38N 13
Birch Rd. E&W ... 51W-40N 5
Blackman St. E&W ....50W-38N,49W-38N 13
Blaine St. E&W ....50W-38N,49W-38N 13
Blanchard St. N&S .50W-38N 13
Bourn St. E&W .... 49W-38N 13
Brainard St. N&S ........50W-38N 13
Brink St. E&W ....50W-37N,49W-37N 13
Brown St. E&W ....50W-38N,49W-38N 13
Burbank St. E&W . 50W-38N 13
Campell St. NE&SW ........50W-38N 13
Cash St. SW&NE . 51W-39N 4
Cherry Ln. NS&EW ........51W-39N 5
Chicago Rd. E&W ....51W-38N,52W-37N 12
Church St. E&W ....50W-38N,49W-38N 13
Clover Ln. SW&NE 51W-39N 5
Crowley Rd. E&W . 49W-39N 5
Deer Path Rd. E&W ........49W-39N 13
Dewey St. E&W ....50W-38N,49W-38N 13
Diggins St. E&W ....50W-38N,49W-38N 13
Division St. N&S ....50W-37N,50W-38N 13
Division St. N&S ....49W-36N,49W-39N 13
Dunlap St. NE&SW ........50W-38N 13
Eastman St. NE&SW ........50W-38N 13
Eighth St. N&S ....50W-38N,50W-39N 13
Fifth St. N&S ..... 50W-38N 13
Finney St. NE&SW. 50W-38N 13
Firethorne Ln. SW&NE ........51W-39N 5
First St. N&S .... 50W-38N 13
Flat Iron Rd. SW&NE ........51W-37N 12
Fourth St. N&S ... 50W-38N 13
Frisco Dr. E&W ... 49W-38N 13
Front St. NW&SE . 50W-38N 13
Galvin Pkwy. N&S . 49W-38N 13
Garfield St. E&W ....50W-38N,50W-39N 13
Ginger Ln. EW&NE ........51W-39N 5
Grant St. N&S .... 49W-38N 13
Harrison St. E&W . 50W-38N 13
Hart St. N&S .... 50W-38N 13
Harvard Hills Rd. N&S ....49W-38N,49W-39N 13
Hayes Ct. E&W ... 49W-38N 13
Hayes St. N&S ... 49W-38N 13
Hillside Dr. E&W ..50W-38N 13
Hollyhock St. SW&NE ........49W-38N 13
Howard St. N&S...50W-38N 13
Hutchinson St. NE&SW ........50W-38N 13
Ivy Ln. SW&NE ... 51W-39N 5
Jackman St. NE&SW ........50W-38N 13
Janowski St. NW&SE ........50W-38N 13
Jefferson St. N&S . 50W-38N 13
Joe Ct. N&S .... 49W-38N 13
Johnson St. NE&SW ........50W-38N 13
Joshua Tr. NS&EW ........49W-38N 13
Kennedy Dr. N&S . 49W-38N 13
Kilkeen Ln. NW&SE ........50W-38N 13
Klaman St. E&W . 49W-38N 13
Lawrence Rd. N&S ........51W-39N 4
Lilac Ln. NS&EW . 51W-39N 5
Lincoln St. N&S .. 50W-38N 13
Little John St. N&S ........49W-38N 13
Lonesome St. E&W ....50W-39N,51W-40N 5
Magnolia Ln. N&S . 51W-39N 5
Marengo Rd. N&S . 50W-37N 13
McComb St. E&W . 50W-38N 13
McKinley Av. E&W ........50W-38N 13
Mcguire Rd. E&W . 49W-37N 13
Metzen St. NW&SE ........50W-38N 13
Ninth St. N&S .... 50W-38N 13
Northfield Av. E&W ........50W-38N 13
Northfield Ct. N&S .50W-39N 13

O'Brien St. N&S .. 49W-38N 13
Oak Grove Rd. SW&NE ....51W-39N,51W-40N 5
Old Orchard Rd. E&W ........49W-39N 13
Orchard Ln. E&W . 51W-39N 5
Page St. NE&SW . 50W-38N 13
Park Dr. N&S .... 50W-37N 13
Park St. NW&SE . 50W-38N 13
Pheasant Run Rd. E&W ........49W-39N 13
Pleasant St. NW&SE ........51W-39N 4
Primrose Ln. E&W . 51W-39N 5
Railroad St. NE&SE ........50W-38N 13
Ramer Rd. E&W ....52W-38N,51W-38N 13
Randall St. NE&SW ........50W-38N 13
Ratzaff St. N&S .. 50W-38N 13
Ridge Ln. N&S ... 50W-37N 13
Roosevelt St. E&W ........50W-38N 13
Rt. 173 NE&SW .. 49W-38N 13
Rt. 23 N&S ...... 50W-36N 13
Second St. N&S .. 50W-39N 13
Seventh St. N&S . 50W-39N 13
Shawnee Ct. E&W . 49W-38N 13
Shawnee Ln. N&S . 49W-38N 13
Sixth St. N&S ....50W-38N,50W-39N 13
Summer NW&SE . 50W-38N 13
Tenth St. N&S ... 50W-38N 13
Third St. N&S .... 50W-39N 13
Thompson St. NW&SE ........50W-38N 13
U.S. Rt. 14 N&S ....50W-38N,50W-39N 13
University St. E&W ....50W-38N,49W-38N 13
Washington St. NW&SE ........50W-38N 13
West Dr. E&W ... 50W-38N 13
Wildflower Ln. N&S ........51W-39N 5
Willow Ln. E&W .. 51W-39N 5
Yellowstone Ln. E&W ........49W-38N 13

**Hebron**
Central Av. N&S .. 40W-41N 8
Church St. N&S ... 40W-42N 8
Fourth Av. E&W .. 40W-41N 8
Harrison Rd. E&W ....40W-41N,41W-41N 8
Hebron Rd. E&W . 41W-42N 8
Illinois St. N&S ... 40W-41N 8
Jacob Av. E&W ... 41W-41N 8
Jean Dr. N&S .... 41W-41N 8
Main St. N&S ....41W-41N,41W-42N 8
Maple Av. E&W .. 40W-42N 8
Marci Ln. N&S ... 41W-41N 8
McKinley Av. E&W ....41W-41N,40W-41N 8
Mead Av. E&W ... 40W-42N 8
Meadow Ln. N&S . 41W-42N 8
Prairie Av. E&W .. 40W-41N 8
Price Rd. N&S ....41W-41N,40W-41N 8
Rt. 173 (Maple Av.) NS&EW ........41W-41N 8
Sharon Ln. NS&EW ........41W-41N 8
St. Albans St. N&S ........40W-41N 8
Third Av. E&W ... 40W-41N 8
Union Av. N&S ... 40W-41N 8
Western Av. NW&SE ........41W-42N 8
Wildflower Way E&W ........41W-42N 8
Woods Ln. N&S .. 41W-41N 8

**Hebron Township**
Armory Rd. N&S . 39W-43N 8
Barnard Mill Rd. NW&SE ....37W-39N,37W-38N 9
Burgett Rd. E&W ........38W-43N,37W-43N 9
Durkee Rd. E&W .. 42W-39N 8
Fifth Av. E&W ... 40W-41N 8
First Av. E&W .... 40W-41N 8
Fourth Av. E&W .. 40W-41N 8
Freeman Rd. N&S ........41W-42N,41W-43N 8
Giant Oak Rd. N&S 37W-38N 17
Green St. N&S ... 40W-41N 8
Greenwood Rd. N&S ........38W-38N,38W-41N 17
Hebron Rd. E&W ....42W-42N,41W-42N 8
Hickory Ln. Rd. E&W ........38W-38N,37W-38N 17
Hillside Rd. N&S ....42W-42N,42W-43N 8
Johnson Rd. N&S ....42W-38N,42W-41N 16
Kemman Rd. N&S ....40W-38N,40W-41N 16
Lange Rd. N&S ....38W-42N,38W-43N 9
Miller Rd. N&S ... 39W-38N 17
Nash Rd. N&S ... 40W-38N 16
Nichols Rd. NW&SE ....42W-43N,42W-42N 9
Norgard Rd. E&W . 37W-41N 9
O'Brien Rd. E&W ....42W-40N,40W-40N 8

| | Grid | Page |
|---|---|---|
| Okeson Rd. E&W | | |
| | 39W-41N,38W-41N | 8 |
| Price Rd. E&W | | |
| | 41W-41N,40W-41N | 8 |
| Regnier Rd. E&W . | 37W-40N | 9 |
| Route 173 E&W | | |
| | 42W-41N,37W-41N | 8 |
| Route 47 E&W | | |
| | 41W-38N,41W-43N | 16 |
| Seaman Rd. NS&EW | | |
| | 40W-42N,39W-42N | 8 |
| Second Av. E&W . | 40W-41N | 8 |
| State Line Rd. E&W | | |
| | 41W-43N | 8 |
| Stewart Rd. N&S | | |
| | 39W-39N,39W-40N | 8 |
| Thayer Rd. E&W | | |
| | 42W-38N,38W-38N | 16 |
| Third Av. E&W . | 40W-41N | 8 |
| Tryon Grove Rd. NE&SW | | |
| | 37W-39N | 9 |
| Vander Karr Rd. NW&SE | | |
| | 40W-39N,38W-39N | 8 |

## Holiday Hills

| | Grid | Page |
|---|---|---|
| Ash St. E&W . | 30W-29N | 35 |
| Aspen Ct. N&S . | 30W-29N | 35 |
| Beach Dr. E&W . | 30W-29N | 35 |
| Birch St. E&W | 30W-29N | 35 |
| Birchwood Av. N&S | | |
| | 30W-29N | 35 |
| Bittersweet Av. N&S | | |
| | 30W-29N | 35 |
| Bolger Av. E&W | 30W-30N | 35 |
| Catalpa St. E&W . | 30W-29N | 35 |
| Cedar St. E&W . | 30W-29N | 35 |
| Driftwood Dr. N&S | 30W-29N | 35 |
| Elder Ct. N&S . | 30W-29N | 35 |
| Elder Ln. NS&EW | 30W-29N | 35 |
| Elm St. E&W . | 30W-29N | 35 |
| Evergreen St. E&W | | |
| | 30W-29N | 35 |
| Fernview Ln. NE&SW | | |
| | 30W-30N | 35 |
| Fox St. E&W . | 30W-29N | 35 |
| Grove St. N&S . | 30W-29N | 35 |
| Hickory St. E&W . | 30W-29N | 35 |
| Holiday Dr. N&S . | 30W-29N | 35 |
| Hyde Park Av. N&S | | |
| | 30W-29N | 35 |
| Kenilworth Av. N&S | | |
| | 30W-29N | 35 |
| Lakeshore Dr. E&W | | |
| | 30W-29N | 35 |
| Lakeview Av. E&W | 30W-29N | 35 |
| Lilac St. N&S . | 30W-29N | 35 |
| Michael St. N&S | 30W-29N | 35 |
| Oak St. N&S . | 30W-29N | 35 |
| Park Ter. N&S | 30W-29N | 35 |
| Pine St. E&W . | 30W-29N | 35 |
| Poplar St. E&W . | 30W-29N | 35 |
| River Rd. NW&SE | | |
| | 30W-29N,30W-30N | 35 |
| Riverview Rd. NW&SE | | |
| | 30W-29N | 35 |
| Short St. N&S . | 30W-29N | 35 |
| Spruce St. E&W . | 30W-29N | 35 |
| Sunset Dr. N&S . | 30W-29N | 35 |
| Swallow St. E&W | 30W-29N | 35 |
| Tower Ln. N&S . | 30W-29N | 35 |
| Violet St. E&W . | 30W-29N | 35 |
| Willow Av. NS&EW | | |
| | 30W-29N | 35 |

## Huntley

| | Grid | Page |
|---|---|---|
| A St. E&W . | 40W-21N | 48 |
| Algonquin Rd. E&W | | |
| | 40W-21N | 48 |
| Auson Ct. NW&SE | 40W-20N | 48 |
| B St. E&W . | 40W-21N | 48 |
| Bakley St. N&S . | 40W-21N | 48 |
| Becky Lee Trace E&W | | |
| | 40W-20N | 48 |
| Bernice St. E&W . | 40W-21N | 48 |
| Bonnie Brae St. N&S | | |
| | 41W-21N | 48 |
| Borden St. E&W . | 40W-21N | 48 |
| Brittany Av. N&S . | 40W-21N | 48 |
| Carl St. N&S . | 40W-21N | 48 |
| Carol Ln. E&W . | 40W-20N | 48 |
| Charles St. N&S | 40W-21N | 48 |
| Church Av. N&S . | 40W-21N | 48 |
| Church St. N&S . | 40W-20N | 48 |
| Coral St. E&W . | 40W-21N | 48 |
| Daniel Ln. E&W . | 40W-20N | 48 |
| Davey Dr. E&W . | 40W-20N | 48 |
| Dean St. N&S . | 40W-20N | 48 |
| Donald Dr. N&S . | 40W-20N | 48 |
| Douglas Av. . | 40W-21N | 48 |
| Dundee Rd. NW&SE | | |
| | 39W-20N | 48 |
| Edward St. E&W . | 40W-21N | 48 |
| Elizabeth Av. N&S . | 40W-21N | 48 |
| First St. E&W . | 40W-21N | 48 |
| Fourth St. E&W . | 40W-21N | 48 |
| Fredrick Way N&S . | 40W-20N | 48 |
| Gayle St. N&S . | 40W-20N | 48 |
| Giordano Pl. E&W . | 40W-20N | 48 |
| Grove St. N&S . | 40W-20N | 48 |
| Haugus Rd. N&S . | 39W-22N | 49 |
| Heinz Av. E&W . | 40W-20N | 48 |
| Hemmer Rd. N&S . | 42W-20N | 48 |
| Henry St. E&W . | 40W-21N | 48 |
| Janice Av. N&S . | 40W-21N | 48 |
| Joan Av. N&S . | 40W-20N | 48 |
| Kathleen Av. N&S . | 40W-21N | 48 |
| Kenneth St. E&W . | 40W-20N | 48 |
| Kiley St. E&W . | 40W-21N | 48 |
| Kishwaukee Ct. N&S | | |
| | 40W-20N | 48 |
| Kruetzer Rd. E&W . | 40W-20N | 48 |

| | Grid | Page |
|---|---|---|
| Lincoln St. N&S . | 40W-20N | 48 |
| Lori Ln. N&S . | 40W-20N | 48 |
| Main St. E&W . | 40W-21N | 48 |
| Margaret Av. N&S . | 40W-20N | 48 |
| Martin Dr. NW&SE | 40W-20N | 48 |
| Mathews St. N&S . | 40W-21N | 48 |
| Michael St. N&S . | 40W-21N | 48 |
| Mill St. E&W . | 40W-20N | 48 |
| Miller Rd. E&W | | |
| | 40W-22N,40W-23N | 48 |
| Myrtle St. N&S . | 40W-20N | 48 |
| N. Union Rd. N&S . | 41W-23N | 40 |
| North St. E&W . | 40W-21N | 48 |
| North Union Rd. E&W | | |
| | 41W-23N,41W-24N | 40 |
| Phillip Dr. N&S . | 40W-21N | 48 |
| Pine Way E&W . | 40W-20N | 48 |
| Powder Park Rd. NW&SE | | |
| | 40W-20N | 48 |
| Reed Rd. E&W . | 40W-22N | 48 |
| Ronald St. E&W . | 40W-20N | 48 |
| Rt. 47 N&S | | |
| | 40W-22N,40W-23N | 48 |
| S. Union Rd. E&W | | |
| | 40W-20N,41W-20N | 48 |
| Second St. E&W . | 40W-21N | 48 |
| Cir. | 40W-20N | 48 |
| Smith Dr. NS&EW . | 40W-20N | 48 |
| Sunset Ln. N&S . | 41W-20N | 48 |
| Third St. E&W . | 40W-21N | 48 |
| Timber Dr. E&W . | 40W-21N | 48 |
| Timber Dr., E. N&S | | |
| | 40W-21N | 48 |
| Timer Dr., W. N&S . | 40W-21N | 48 |
| Union Special Plaza N&S | | |
| | 40W-210N | 48 |
| Vine St. N&S . | 40W-21N | 48 |
| Woodcreek Dr. N&S | | |
| | 40W-20N | 48 |
| Woodstock St. N&S | | |
| | 40W-21N | 48 |

## Island Lake*
### (Also see Lake County)

| | Grid | Page |
|---|---|---|
| Ascot Ct. N&S . | 29W-28N | 35 |
| Auburn Dr. N&S . | 29W-28N | 35 |
| Bassler Dr. E&W . | 29W-28N | 35 |
| Bassler Ln. E&W . | 29W-28N | 35 |
| Burnett Rd. E&W | | |
| | 29W-28N,28W-28N | 35 |
| Cardinal Cove E&W | | |
| | 29W-29N | 35 |
| Cedar Ter. N&S . | 29W-28N | 35 |
| Charles St. E&W . | 29W-28N | 35 |
| Cir. | 29W-28N | 35 |
| Concord Dr. E&W | | |
| | 30W-28N,29W-28N | 35 |
| Dartmouth Ct. NW&SE | | |
| | 29W-28N | 35 |
| Dartmouth Dr. NS&EW | | |
| | 30W-28N,29W-28N | 35 |
| David Ct. N&S . | 29W-28N | 35 |
| Debden Dr. SW&NE | | |
| | 30W-28N | 35 |
| Debra Dr. N&S . | 29W-28N | 35 |
| Dorothy Dr. SW&NE | | |
| | 29W-28N | 35 |
| Dorthy Ct. E&W . | 29W-28N | 35 |
| Eastport Ct. E&W . | 29W-28N | 35 |
| Elm Ct. N&S . | 29W-28N | 35 |
| Ethel Ter. N&S . | 29W-28N | 35 |
| Fern Ct. E&W . | 29W-28N | 35 |
| Greenwich Ln. E&W | | |
| | 30W-28N | 35 |
| Hale Ln. N&S . | | |
| | 30W-28N,29W-27N | 35 |
| Hale Ln. N&S . | 30W-28N | 35 |
| Hazel Ct. E&W . | 29W-28N | 35 |
| Hickory Ter. E&W . | 29W-28N | 35 |
| Highland Dr. NE&SW | | |
| | 29W-28N | 35 |
| Hillside Dr. NE&SW | | |
| | 29W-28N | 35 |
| Honeysuckle Dr. E&W | | |
| | 29W-28N | 35 |
| Huntington Ln. NS&EW | | |
| | 29W-28N | 35 |
| Hyacinth Ter. N&S . | 29W-28N | 35 |
| Ilene Dr. N&S . | 29W-28N | 35 |
| Island Dr. NS&EW . | 29W-28N | 35 |
| Janet Dr. E&W . | 29W-28N | 35 |
| Jordan Ln. N&S . | 29W-29N | 35 |
| Kelly Rd. N&S . | 29W-27N | 35 |
| Kings Point Ct. N&S | | |
| | 30W-28N | 35 |
| Knights Bridge Dr. SW&NE | | |
| | 30W-28N | 35 |
| Lakeview Dr. N&S . | 29W-28N | 35 |
| Lauren Ln. NW&SE | | |
| | 29W-29N | 35 |
| Lexington Ln. E&W | | |
| | 30W-28N,29W-28N | 35 |
| Lillian Ct. NW&SE . | 29W-28N | 35 |
| Linden Dr. NS&EW | | |
| | 30W-28N | 35 |
| Lynette Ln. NS&EW | | |
| | 29W-28N | 35 |
| Marion Ct. NW&SE | | |
| | 29W-28N | 35 |
| Max Ct. NS&EW . | 29W-28N | 35 |
| Medford St. N&S . | 29W-28N | 35 |
| Midway Dr. N&S . | 29W-28N | 35 |
| Nantucket Way E&W | | |
| | 29W-28N | 35 |
| Newbury Dr. NW&E | | |
| | 29W-28N | 35 |
| Newport Ct. E&W . | 29W-28N | 35 |
| Newport Dr. NE&SW | | |
| | 29W-28N | 35 |
| Nottingham Ct. N&S | | |
| | 29W-28N | 35 |

| | Grid | Page |
|---|---|---|
| Oak Ter. N&S . | 29W-28N | 35 |
| Olympia Ln. N&S . | 30W-28N | 35 |
| Oxford Ct. SW&NE | | |
| | 29W-28N | 35 |
| Pine Ter. N&S . | 29W-28N | 35 |
| Pleasant Pl. E&W . | 29W-28N | 35 |
| Plymouth Ln. SW&NE | | |
| | 29W-28N | 35 |
| Porten Rd. E&W . | 29W-27N | 35 |
| Portsmouth Dr. E&W | | |
| | 30W-28N,29W-28N | 35 |
| Quiney Ct. E&W . | 29W-28N | 35 |
| Raccoon Cove N&S | | |
| | 29W-29N | 35 |
| Ralph Ct. E&W . | 29W-28N | 35 |
| Revere Ln. E&W | | |
| | 30W-28N,29W-28N | 35 |
| Richard Ct. E&W . | 29W-28N | 35 |
| River St. N&S | | |
| | 29W-26N,29W-27N | 43 |
| Salem Ct. NW&SE | | |
| | 30W-28N,29W-28N | 35 |
| South Hampton Dr. N&S | | |
| | 29W-27N | 35 |
| Southport Dr. NE&SW | | |
| | 30W-28N | 35 |
| Spruce Ter. N&S . | 29W-28N | 35 |
| Spruce Tr. N&S . | 29W-28N | 35 |
| Stafford St. NE&SW | | |
| | 30W-28N | 35 |
| Tulip Cir. SW&NE . | 29W-29N | 35 |
| Victoria Dr. E&W . | 29W-27N | 35 |
| Vista Dr. E&W . | 29W-27N | 35 |
| Walnut Ct. N&S . | 29W-28N | 35 |
| Waterford Way NS&EW | | |
| | 29W-28N | 35 |
| Wayside Dr. N&S . | 29W-27N | 35 |
| Wembly Dr. NW&SE | | |
| | 30W-28N | 35 |
| Westminister Ln. N&S | | |
| | 30W-28N | 35 |
| Windsor Ln. E&W . | 29W-27N | 35 |
| Yale Ln. E&W . | 29W-28N | 35 |
| York Ln. N&S . | 30W-28N | 35 |

## Johnsburg

| | Grid | Page |
|---|---|---|
| Acre Ln. E&W . | 30W-35N | 19 |
| Appleton Ct. NE&SW | | |
| | 30W-36N | 19 |
| Ardmore Cir. NE&SW | | |
| | 30W-36N | 19 |
| Aspen Dr. E&W . | 31W-35N | 19 |
| Autumn Way N&S . | 30W-37N | 19 |
| Bald Knob Pt. E&W | | |
| | 29W-35N | 19 |
| Bald Knob Rd. E&W | | |
| | 29W-35N | 19 |
| Bayview Dr. E&W . | 30W-36N | 19 |
| Bayview Ln. NE&SE | | |
| | 30W-36N | 19 |
| Berwyn Ct. E&W . | 30W-36N | 19 |
| Blitsch Pl. N&S . | 31W-35N | 19 |
| Bolling Av. E&W . | 30W-35N | 19 |
| Broadway Rd. E&W | | |
| | 30W-37N | 19 |
| Brorson Ln. NS&EW | | |
| | 30W-36N | 19 |
| Brynmawr Ct. N&S | | |
| | 30W-36N | 19 |
| Buckanan Rd. E&W | | |
| | 32W-35N | 18 |
| Camden Ct. E&W . | 30W-36N | 19 |
| Cardington Way N&S | | |
| | 30W-35N | 19 |
| Carol Ct. N&S . | 30W-35N | 19 |
| Caroline Dr. N&S . | 30W-35N | 19 |
| Cedar Creek Dr. N&S | | |
| | 30W-35N | 19 |
| Channel Beach Av. E&W | | |
| | 30W-36N | 19 |
| Chapel Hill Rd. NW&SE | | |
| | 31W-35N | 19 |
| Charnbrook Dr. E&W | | |
| | 30W-36N | 19 |
| Charnbrook Ln. E&W | | |
| | 30W-36N | 19 |
| Chellington Dr. N&S | | |
| | 30W-36N | 19 |
| Cherokee Dr. N&S . | 32W-35N | 19 |
| Church St. E&W . | 31W-35N | 19 |
| Cimmaron Cir. NS&EW | | |
| | 30W-36N | 19 |
| Cimmaron Ct. E&W | | |
| | 30W-36N | 19 |
| Claremont Rd. N&S | | |
| | 32W-35N | 18 |
| Cobblestone Ct. E&W | | |
| | 30W-36N | 19 |
| Countryside Dr. N&S | | |
| | 31W-35N | 19 |
| Cove Ct. N&S . | 31W-35N | 19 |
| Creekside Ln. E&W | | |
| | 30W-36N | 19 |
| Dawnwood Dr. N&S | | |
| | 30W-36N | 19 |
| Delaware Pl. E&W | | |
| | 31W-35N,30W-35N | 19 |
| Denise Ct. SW&NE | | |
| | 30W-36N | 19 |
| Dennis Blvd. N&S . | 30W-36N | 19 |
| Devon Dr. N&S . | 31W-35N | 19 |
| Devon Ln. E&W . | 30W-36N | 19 |
| Dutch Creek Ln. N&S | | |
| | 31W-35N | 19 |
| Ernst Ln. SW&NE . | 31W-35N | 19 |
| Fairview Av. N&S . | 31W-35N | 19 |
| Farmington Ln. N&S | | |
| | 30W-36N | 19 |
| Federal Ln. E&W . | 30W-35N | 19 |
| Filmore Rd. E&W . | 32W-35N | 18 |
| Florence Dr. N&S . | 30W-36N | 19 |

| | Grid | Page |
|---|---|---|
| Fox Knoll Ct. E&W . | 31W-35N | 19 |
| Frances Rd. NE&SW | | |
| | 30W-35N | 19 |
| Fremont Ct. E&W | | |
| | 30W-35N,30W-36N | 19 |
| Fremont Ln. E&W | | |
| | 30W-36N,31W-36N | 19 |
| Garfield Rd. NE&SW | | |
| | 32W-35N | 18 |
| Goodview Av. E&W | | |
| | 30W-35N | 19 |
| Grand Ridge Ct. N&S | | |
| | 29W-35N | 19 |
| Grant Dr. E&W . | 32W-35N | 18 |
| Hamblin Dr. N&S . | 32W-35N | 18 |
| Harrison Dr. E&W . | 29W-35N | 19 |
| Hayden Dr. E&W . | 30W-36N | 19 |
| Hickory Ln. N&S . | 30W-36N | 19 |
| Hickory Way N&S . | 30W-36N | 19 |
| Hillcrest Av. N&S . | 31W-35N | 19 |
| Hilltop Dr. N&S . | 30W-36N | 19 |
| Irene Ct. NW&SE . | 30W-36N | 19 |
| Ivy Ln. N&S . | 31W-35N | 19 |
| Jamesway N&S . | 31W-35N | 19 |
| Jewel Dr. NW&SE | | |
| | 30W-35N,30W-36N | 19 |
| Johnsburg Farm Dr. NW&SE | | |
| | 32W-35N,30W-36N | 19 |
| Johnsburg Rd. E&W | | |
| | 32W-35N | 18 |
| Johnsburg Spring Grove Rd | | |
| | NE&SW 30W-35N,30W-36N | 19 |
| Joseph Cir. NS&EW | | |
| | 30W-37N | 19 |
| Knob Hill Rd. NS&EW | | |
| | 30W-36N | 19 |
| Lake Dawnwood Ln. N&S | | |
| | 30W-36N | 19 |
| Lake St. N&S . | 30W-36N | 19 |
| Lakeview St. E&W . | 30W-36N | 19 |
| Larkspur Ln. N&S . | 32W-35N | 19 |
| Lewis Ln. N&S . | 29W-35N | 19 |
| Linden Av. NS&EW | | |
| | 30W-35N | 19 |
| Long Ln. NW&SE . | 30W-35N | 19 |
| Longmeadow Dr. E&W | | |
| | 31W-35N | 19 |
| Maple Av. NW&SE | 30W-35N | 19 |
| Maple Ter. N&S . | 30W-35N | 19 |
| Mayfair Dr. N&S . | 30W-35N | 19 |
| Mehring Av. E&W . | 31W-35N | 19 |
| Middle Av. NW&SE | | |
| | 30W-35N | 19 |
| Oak Grove Rd. E&W | | |
| | 29W-35N | 19 |
| Oak Leaf Dr. N&S . | 30W-36N | 19 |
| Oakdale Av. N&S . | 31W-35N | 19 |
| Oeffling Dr. N&S . | 30W-36N | 19 |
| Old Bay Rd. NW&SE | | |
| | 30W-34N | 27 |
| Olive Av. E&W . | 31W-35N | 19 |
| Pinehurst Ct. N&S . | 30W-36N | 19 |
| Pistakee View Dr. NE&SW | | |
| | 29W-35N | 19 |
| Pitzen Rd. N&S . | 29W-35N | 19 |
| Prairie Tr. SW&NE . | 32W-35N | 19 |
| Promentory Ln. N&S | | |
| | 30W-36N | 19 |
| Quincy Dr. N&S . | 30W-35N | 19 |
| Rachel Dr. N&S . | 30W-37N | 19 |
| Raintree Ct. N&S . | 30W-36N | 19 |
| Ramsgate Ln. N&S | | |
| | 30W-35N | 19 |
| Reed Av. NE&SW . | 31W-35N | 19 |
| Ridgeview Dr. NS&EW | | |
| | 29W-35N | 19 |
| Ringwood Rd. E&W | | |
| | 30W-36N | 19 |
| River Park Dr. NE&SW | | |
| | 31W-35N | 19 |
| River Terrace Dr. NE&SW | | |
| | 30W-35N,29W-36N | 19 |
| Riverside Dr. N&S | | |
| | 32W-34N,32W-35N | 19 |
| Riverview Dr. N&S | | |
| | 30W-35N,29W-35N | 19 |
| Rocky Beach Ln. NS&EW | | |
| | 30W-36N | 19 |
| Rolling Lane Rd. E&W | | |
| | 38W-23N,38W-22N | 19 |
| Rosemarie Dr. E&W | | |
| | 30W-36N | 19 |
| Rosewood Ct. E&W | | |
| | 30W-36N | 19 |
| Rosewood Dr. E&W | | |
| | 30W-36N | 19 |
| Round Hill Ct. NE&SW | | |
| | 30W-36N | 19 |
| S. Brixham Dr. E&W | | |
| | 30W-36N | 19 |
| Sagebrush Ct. N&S | | |
| | 32W-35N | 19 |
| Salem Av. E&W | | |
| | 31W-35N,30W-35N | 19 |
| Sandalwood Ct. E&W | | |
| | 30W-36N | 19 |
| Sandalwood Dr. NW&SE | | |
| | 30W-36N | 19 |
| Sandalwood Ln. N&S | | |
| | 30W-36N | 19 |
| Sarah Dr. NS&EW . | 30W-37N | 19 |
| Second Av. NE&SW | | |
| | 30W-35N | 19 |
| Seville Ct. E&W . | 30W-36N | 19 |
| Shiloh Dr. E&W . | 30W-36N | 19 |
| Spring Grove Rd. N&S | | |
| | 31W-35N | 19 |
| St. Francis Ln. | | |
| | 31W-35N | 19 |
| St. Johns Av. N&S . | 31W-35N | 19 |
| Stubby Av. NW&SE | | |
| | 30W-35N | 19 |

| | Grid | Page |
|---|---|---|
| Sudeenew Dr. E&W | | |
| | 30W-36N | 19 |
| Sundown Ln. E&W . | 30W-36N | 19 |
| Sunnyside Beach Dr. NE&SW | | |
| | 30W-35N | 19 |
| Sunnyside Dr. NE&SW | | |
| | 30W-36N | 19 |
| Sunset Dr. N&S . | 30W-36N | 19 |
| Sunset Ln. N&S . | 30W-36N | 19 |
| Tall Tree Ln. E&W . | 30W-36N | 19 |
| Thelen Rd. E&W . | 30W-37N | 19 |
| Tichfield Ter. E&W . | 31W-36N | 19 |
| Tivoli Ter. N&S . | 31W-35N | 19 |
| Torrey Ln. E&W . | 30W-36N | 19 |
| Villanova Dr. N&S . | 30W-36N | 19 |
| W. Lakeview St. E&W | | |
| | 30W-36N | 19 |
| W. May Dr. E&W . | 30W-36N | 19 |
| Weingart Rd. E&W . | 30W-35N | 19 |
| Wilmot St. NW&SE | | |
| | 30W-36N | 19 |
| Windmere Ln. NS&EW | | |
| | 31W-35N | 19 |

## Lake In The Hills

| | Grid | Page |
|---|---|---|
| Acorn Ct. N&S . | 35W-21N | 50 |
| Acorn Ln. E&W . | 35W-21N | 50 |
| Adams St. N&S . | 35W-22N | 50 |
| Albrecht Rd. E&W . | 39W-23N | 49 |
| Alexandria Ct. NW&SE | | |
| | 38W-21N | 49 |
| Alexandria Dr. E&W | | |
| | 38W-21N | 49 |
| Algonquin Rd. E&W | | |
| | 36W-21N | 49 |
| Amberleigh Ct. E&W | | |
| | 38W-21N | 49 |
| Anderson Dr. NS&EW | | |
| | 34W-22N | 50 |
| Annandale Ct. E&W | | |
| | 38W-21N | 49 |
| Annandale Dr. N&S | | |
| | 38W-21N | 49 |
| Apache Tr. N&S . | 34W-21N | 50 |
| Appletree Ct. NW&SE | | |
| | 38W-22N | 49 |
| Arland Ct. N&S . | 38W-23N | 49 |
| Ash St. N&S . | 35W-22N | 50 |
| Aster Ct. NE&SW . | 37W-22N | 49 |
| Baldwin Ct. N&S . | 38W-23N | 49 |
| Baldwin Ln. N&S . | 38W-23N | 49 |
| Bar Harbor Ct. N&S | | |
| | 38W-22N | 49 |
| Bar Harbor Dr. EW&NS | | |
| | 38W-22N | 49 |
| Barbara St. N&S . | 34W-22N | 50 |
| Baronet Ct. E&W . | 38W-21N | 49 |
| Barrington Ct. N&S | | |
| | 37W-22N | 49 |
| Bauford Ct. NW&SE | | |
| | 38W-23N | 41 |
| Beechwood E&W . | 36W-21N | 49 |
| Bernice St. E&W . | 35W-21N | 50 |
| Big Cloud Pass NS&EW | | |
| | 36W-21N | 49 |
| Birch St. N&S . | 35W-22N | 50 |
| Birkdale Ct. NE&SW | | |
| | 38W-21N | 49 |
| Blackberry Ct. E&W | | |
| | 37W-22N | 49 |
| Blackberry Dr. NS&EW | | |
| | 37W-22N | 49 |
| Blackhawk Dr. E&W | | |
| | 34W-21N | 50 |
| Bonnie Ct. N&S . | 34W-22N | 50 |
| Bordeaux Dr. E&W | | |
| | 38W-22N | 49 |
| Boulder Dr. NS&EW | | |
| | 37W-21N | 49 |
| Brandt Dr. E&W . | 34W-22N | 50 |
| Briarcliff Ct. N&S . | 38W-23N | 41 |
| Briarcliff Ln. N&S . | 38W-22N | 49 |
| Briarfield Ln. EW&NS | | |
| | 38W-21N | 49 |
| Bridlewood Cir. NS&EW | | |
| | 38W-21N | 49 |
| Brisbane Dr. NW&SE | | |
| | 38W-23N,38W-22N | 49 |
| Brittany Bend NS&EW | | |
| | 38W-22N | 49 |
| Burr St. N&S . | 35W-22N | 50 |
| Camden Ct. E&W . | 38W-23N | 41 |
| Capella Ct. N&S . | 36W-22N | 49 |
| Carl Ct. N&S . | 34W-21N | 50 |
| Cedar Ridge Dr. N&S | | |
| | 35W-21N | 50 |
| Cedar St. N&S . | 35W-22N | 50 |
| Chadwick Ct. N&S . | 38W-23N | 41 |
| Chadwick Ln. NS&EW | | |
| | 38W-23N | 41 |
| Chancery Ct. N&S . | 38W-21N | 49 |
| Chancery Way E&W | | |
| | 38W-21N | 49 |
| Chantilly Ct. NS&EW | | |
| | 38W-21N | 49 |
| Cherokee Tr. N&S . | 34W-21N | 50 |
| Cherry St. N&S . | 35W-22N | 50 |
| Clark Rd. E&W . | 34W-22N | 49 |
| Clayton Marsh Dr. N&S | | |
| | 35W-21N | 50 |
| Clear Sky Tr. E&W . | 36W-22N | 49 |
| Cobblestone Ct. N&S | | |
| | 37W-21N | 49 |
| Cobblestone Tr. NS&EW | | |
| | 37W-21N | 49 |
| Coolstone Bend NS&EW | | |
| | 36W-21N | 49 |

| Street | Grid | Page |
|---|---|---|
| Council Tr. NS&EW | 34W-21N | 50 |
| Country Club Dr. NE&SW | 37W-21N | 49 |
| Crabapple Ct. NW&SE | 37W-22N | 49 |
| Creekside N&S | 36W-21N | 49 |
| Creekview Ln. NW&SE | 34W-22N | 50 |
| Crofton Cir. EW&NS | 38W-22N | 49 |
| Crossview Ct. EW&NS | 38W-21N | 49 |
| Crossview Ln. EW&NS | 38W-21N | 49 |
| Crystal Lake Rd. N&S | 35W-21N,35W-22N | 50 |
| Cunat Ct. NS&EW | 34W-22N | 50 |
| David Ct. N&S | 34W-22N | 50 |
| Decatur Av. N&S | 35W-22N | 50 |
| Deer Creek Ct. N&S | 37W-22N | 49 |
| Deer Creek Ln. N&S | 37W-22N | 49 |
| Deer Path E&W | 35W-21N | 50 |
| Delaware Dr. E&W | 34W-21N | 50 |
| Dogwood Ct. E&W | 38W-21N | 49 |
| Dogwood Ln. N&S | 37W-22N | 49 |
| E. Oak St. E&W | 35W-22N | 50 |
| Echo Hill N&S | 35W-21N | 50 |
| Elderberry Ct. NW&SE | 37W-22N | 49 |
| Elizabeth Ct. N&S | 34W-22N | 50 |
| Ellis Rd. N&S | 38W-21N | 49 |
| Elm St. N&S | 35W-22N | 50 |
| Farmington Ct. E&W | 38W-22N | 49 |
| Ferryville Dr. NS&EW | 38W-21N | 49 |
| Fir St. E&W | 35W-22N | 50 |
| Flowerfield Ct. NW&SE | 38W-22N | 49 |
| Gail Ct. E&W | 34W-21N | 50 |
| Glenrose Ln. N&S | 38W-21N | 49 |
| Grace Dr. N&S | 34W-22N | 50 |
| Granite Ct. E&W | 37W-22N | 49 |
| Grant Av. E&W | 35W-22N | 50 |
| Greenbriar Ct. NE&SW | 34W-21N | 49 |
| Greenbriar Ln. N&S | 38W-22N | 49 |
| Greenfield Ln. E&W | 38W-22N | 49 |
| Haddon Ct. NE&SW | 38W-23N | 41 |
| Halfmoon Gate N&S | 36W-22N | 49 |
| Harvest Gate NS&EW | 36W-21N | 49 |
| Hastings Ct. E&W | 38W-21N | 49 |
| Hawthorne Tr. N&S | 35W-21N | 50 |
| Hazelwood Ct. NW&SE | 38W-22N | 49 |
| Heartland Gate E&W | 36W-22N | 49 |
| Heavens Gate NS&EW | 36W-22N | 49 |
| Heavens Gate Ct. NW&SE | | 49 |
| Heron Ct. E&W | 38W-22N | 49 |
| Heron Dr. N&S | 38W-22N | 49 |
| Hiawatha Dr. NS&EW | 34W-21N | 50 |
| Hickory Rd. NW&SE | 35W-21N | 50 |
| Highwood Ln. E&W | 38W-23N | 41 |
| Hillsboro Ln. N&S | 38W-23N,38W-22N | 49 |
| Hilltop Dr. NS&EW | 35W-21N,35W-22N | 50 |
| Hilly Ln. N&S | 35W-21N | 50 |
| Hollyhock Ct. E&W | 37W-22N | 49 |
| Hunters Path E&W | 35W-21N | 50 |
| Huron Tr. N&S | 34W-21N | 50 |
| Immoff Dr. NE&SW | 34W-22N | 50 |
| Indian Tr. N&S | 35W-21N,35W-22N | 50 |
| Industrial Dr. NW&SE | 34W-22N | 50 |
| Jefferson St. N&S | 35W-22N | 50 |
| Jessie Rd. E&W | 34W-21N | 50 |
| Joseph Ct. N&S | 34W-22N | 50 |
| Joseph St. N&S | 34W-22N | 50 |
| Kay Ct. NE&SW | 34W-21N | 50 |
| Kensington N&S | 38W-22N | 49 |
| Kurt Ct. N&S | 38W-22N | 50 |
| Lake Tr. N&S | 35W-21N | 50 |
| Lakewood Rd. N&S | 38W-21N | 49 |
| Lansbury Cir. NS&EW | 38W-21N | 49 |
| Larkspur Ct. NW&SE | 37W-22N | 49 |
| Larkspur Ln. N&S | 37W-22N | 49 |
| Larsen Ln. N&S | 34W-22N | 50 |
| Lee Av. E&W | 35W-22N | 50 |
| Lincoln St. E&W | 35W-22N | 50 |
| Lindon St. E&W | 35W-22N | 50 |
| Lisa Ct. N&S | 34W-22N | 50 |
| Litchfield Ct. E&W | 38W-22N | 49 |
| Litchfield Gate N&S | 38N-22N | 49 |
| Litchfield Ln. N&S | 38N-22N | 49 |
| Lorree Ln. E&W | 38W-22N | 50 |
| MacKinac St. EW&NS | 38W-22N | 49 |
| Manchester Ct. E&W | 38W-22N | 49 |
| Maple St. N&S | 35W-22N | 50 |
| Marble Ct. NW&SE | 37W-22N | 49 |
| Margate Ct. E&W | 38W-23N | 49 |
| Marion Ct. N&S | 34W-21N | 50 |
| Mason Ln. NS&EW | 37W-22N | 49 |
| Mayberry Ct. N&S | 37W-22N | 49 |
| McKinley St. N&S | 35W-22N | 50 |
| McPhee Dr. NW&SE | 34W-22N | 50 |
| Meadow Ln. N&S | 35W-22N | 50 |
| Melbourne Ct. NW&SE | 38W-22N | 49 |
| Melbourne Ln. N&S | 38W-23N | 49 |
| Menominee Dr. E&W | 34W-21N | 50 |
| Michael Ct. E&W | 34W-22N | 50 |
| Middlefield Ct. NW&SE | 38W-22N | 49 |
| Miller Rd. E&W | 39W-23N | 40 |
| Miller Rd. E&W | 38W-23N | 49 |
| Miller Rd. NS&EW | 38W-23N | 49 |
| Mohawk Tr. N&S | 34W-21N | 50 |
| Mohican Tr. N&S | 34W-21N | 50 |
| Monarch Ct. E&E | 34W-21N | 49 |
| Monroe St. N&S | 35W-22N | 50 |
| Moonstone Run NE&SW | 36W-22N | 49 |
| Morningside Ct. NW&SE | 37W-22N | 49 |
| Mulberry Ct. E&W | 38W-21N | 49 |
| Navajo Dr. E&W | 34W-21N | 50 |
| Noelle Bend NS&EW | 38W-22N | 49 |
| Normandy Ln. N&S | 38W-22N | 49 |
| Northland Pass NS&EW | 36W-22N | 49 |
| Oakleaf Rd. N&S | 35W-21N | 50 |
| Parc Ct. NS&EW | 38W-22N | 49 |
| Patton Av. N&S | 35W-22N | 50 |
| Pawnee St. E&W | 35W-21N | 50 |
| Peachtree Ct. | 37W-22N | 49 |
| Peartree Dr. NW&SE | 37W-22N | 49 |
| Pebblewood E&W | 36W-21N | 49 |
| Pershing Av. E&W | 35W-22N | 50 |
| Pheasant Tr. E&W | 35W-21N | 50 |
| Pine St. N&S | 35W-22N | 50 |
| Pingree Rd. N&S | 34W-23N | 42 |
| Plum St. E&W | 35W-22N | 50 |
| Pocahontas Tr. N&S | 34W-21N | 50 |
| Polaris Dr. NS&EW | 36W-22N | 49 |
| Poplar St. N&S | 35W-22N | 50 |
| Prides Run NS&EW | 36W-22N | 49 |
| Princeton Ln. E&W | 38W-23N | 49 |
| Prosper Ct. E&W | 34W-22N | 50 |
| Provence Pl. N&S | 38W-22N | 49 |
| Pyott Rd. NW&SE | 35W-23N,34W-22N | 42 |
| Quail Run E&W | 35W-21N | 50 |
| Rainmaker Run NS&EW | 36W-21N | 49 |
| Ramble Rd. E&W | 35W-21N | 50 |
| Randall Rd. N&S | 36W-22N | 49 |
| Redbud Ct. N&S | 37W-22N | 49 |
| Ridge Ct. NE&SW | 37W-21N | 49 |
| Ridge Ln. NE&SW | 37W-21N | 49 |
| Rolling Hills Ct. E&W | 38W-22N | 49 |
| Rolling Hills Dr. SW&NE | 38W-22N | 49 |
| Roosevelt St. E&W | 35W-23N | 42 |
| Rosewood Ct. N&S | 37W-22N | 49 |
| Royal Oak Ct. N&S | 38W-22N | 49 |
| Royal Oak Ln. N&S | 37W-22N | 49 |
| Rt. 31 N&S | 33W-23N | 42 |
| Saginaw St. N&S | 38W-22N | 49 |
| Sandstone E&W | 37W-21N,36W-22N | 49 |
| Sedgefield Ln. N&S | 38W-23N | 49 |
| Seminole Tr. N&S | 34W-21N | 50 |
| Service Rd. NE&SW | 34W-22N | 50 |
| Shawnee Dr. E&W | 34W-21N | 50 |
| Sioux Tr. N&S | 34W-21N | 50 |
| Spencer Pl. E&W | 38W-21N | 49 |
| Spring Garden Ct. NW&SE | 37W-22N | 49 |
| Springlake Ct. E&W | 37W-22N | 49 |
| Springlake Dr. NS&EW | 37W-22N | 49 |
| Spruce St. N&S | 35W-22N | 50 |
| Starwood Ct. NW&SE | 36W-22N | 49 |
| Starwood Pass E&E | 36W-22N | 49 |
| Steeplechase Way NS&EW | 38W-21N | 49 |
| Stickle Ln. N&S | 38W-21N | 49 |
| Stone Creek NW&SE | 36W-21N | 49 |
| Sugarcreek St. SW&NE | 38W-22N | 49 |
| Sullivan Pond Dr. NW&SE | 38W-21N | 49 |
| Sweet Water Ridge N&S | 36W-22N | 49 |
| Sweet water Ct. NE&SW | 36W-22N | 49 |
| Sycamore St. N&S | 35W-22N | 50 |
| Taralon Trace NS&EW | 38W-22N | 49 |
| Tennyson St. E&W | 38W-21N | 49 |
| Thornberry Way NW&SE | 37W-22N | 49 |
| Village Creek Dr. N&S | 35W-21N,35W-22N | 50 |
| Virginia Rd. NW&SE | 34W-23N,33W-22N | 42 |
| Walnut Dr. N&S | 35W-21N | 50 |
| Walnut Grove Ct. NW&SE | 38W-22N | 49 |
| Walter St. NE&SW | 34W-22N | 50 |
| Wander Way N&S | 35W-21N | 50 |
| Washington St. N&S | 35W-22N | 50 |
| Waterbury Pl. E&W | 38W-21N | 49 |
| Wedgewood Cir. NS&EW | 38W-21N | 49 |
| Wedgewood Ct. N&S | 38W-21N | 49 |
| West Oak St. E&W | 35W-22N | 50 |
| Westminster NE&SW | 38W-22N | 49 |
| White Pine Cir. NS&EW | 37W-22N | 49 |
| Whitmore Way NE&SW | 38W-21N | 49 |
| Willow St. E&W | 34W-22N | 50 |
| Windgate Ct. N&S | 38W-21N | 49 |
| Windgate Way NS&EW | 38N-21N | 49 |
| Woodbridge NE&SW | 36W-21N | 49 |
| Woodland Rd. E&W | 35W-22N | 50 |
| Woody Way E&W | 35W-21N | 50 |
| Wright Ct. E&W | 38W-21N | 49 |
| Wright Dr. N&S | 38W-21N | 49 |

## Lakemoor*
### (Also see Lake County)

| Street | Grid | Page |
|---|---|---|
| Amanda Av. NE&SW | 29W-31N | 27 |
| Anthony Ln. E&W | 30W-33N | 27 |
| Bay Meadows Ln. NE&SW | 30W-34N | 27 |
| Bay Oaks Dr. N&S | 30W-33N,30W-34N | 27 |
| Bay Rd. E&W | 30W-34N | 27 |
| Cuhlman Rd. N&S | 29W-33N,29W-34N | 27 |
| Dominion Dr. NW&SE | 30W-34N | 27 |
| East Lake Dr. N&S | 29W-32N | 27 |
| Edward Ct. N&S | 30W-33N | 27 |
| Elaine Ter. N&S | 29W-32N | 27 |
| Fritsche Rd. N&S | 29W-31N | 27 |
| Grand Meadow Ln. E&W | 29W-34N | 27 |
| Herbert Rd. N&S | 29W-31N | 27 |
| Highland Dr. N&S | 29W-31N | 27 |
| Hollywood Dr. N&S | 29W-32N | 27 |
| Lake Shore Dr. N&S | 29W-31N,29W-32N | 27 |
| Lakeview Rd. N&S | 29W-32N | 27 |
| Lily Lake Pkwy. E&W | 29W-31N | 27 |
| Lily Ln. N&S | 29W-32N | 27 |
| Lincoln Rd. E&W | 30W-33N | 27 |
| Longbeach Rd. N&S | 29W-31N | 27 |
| Lotus Dr. E&W | 29W-31N | 27 |
| Maplewood Dr. N&S | 29W-32N | 27 |
| Morningside Dr. E&W | 29W-31N | 27 |
| Northlake Rd. E&W | 29W-32N | 27 |
| Oshea Ct. E&W | 30W-34N | 27 |
| Park Rd. NS&EW | 29W-32N | 27 |
| Pine Grove Rd. N&S | 29W-32N | 27 |
| Rand Rd. NW&SE | 29W-32N | 27 |
| River Side Dr. NW&SE | 29W-32N | 27 |
| Rosedale Dr. N&S | 29W-32N | 27 |
| Route 120 NW&SE | 30W-32N | 27 |
| Santa Barbara Rd. N&S | 29W-32N | 27 |
| Scotland Rd. N&S | 29W-31N | 27 |
| Sheridan Rd. NS&EW | 29W-31N | 27 |
| Shore Dr. N&S | 29W-31N,29W-32N | 27 |
| Shoreline Dr. NS&EW | 29W-34N | 27 |
| South Dr. E&W | 29W-32N | 27 |
| Sunnyside Rd. E&W | 29W-32N | 27 |
| Sunset Dr. E&W | 29W-31N | 27 |
| Tiajuana St. N&S | 29W-32N | 27 |
| Valley View Dr. NW&SE | 29W-31N | 27 |
| Venice Rd. N&S | 29W-31N | 27 |
| Ventidue E&W | 29W-34N | 27 |
| Vialex E&W | 29W-31N | 27 |
| Wegner Rd. N&S | 29W-31N | 27 |
| Wellington Dr. E&W | 29W-34N | 27 |
| Willow Rd. N&S | 29W-32N | 27 |

## Lakewood

| Street | Grid | Page |
|---|---|---|
| Ackman Rd. E&W | 38W-23N,37W-23N | 41 |
| Ballard Rd. E&W | 38W-25N | 41 |
| Bannockburn Dr. NW&SE | 39W-23N | 41 |
| Bard Rd. N&S | 39W-24N,37W-24N | 41 |
| Bardwell Ln. E&W | 37W-24N | 41 |
| Beaver Pond Ct. E&W | 38W-24N | 41 |
| Bernice Dr. NE&SW | 39W-23N | 41 |
| Bonnie Dr. NS&EW | 38W-24N | 41 |
| Bonnie Ridge Rd. N&S | 39W-23N | 41 |
| Braemer Cir. NS&EW | 38W-24N | 41 |
| Braeton Cir. NS&EW | 39W-23N | 41 |
| Braeton Way NW&SE | 39W-23N | 41 |
| Briarwood Rd. N&S | 37W-24N,37W-23N | 41 |
| Broadway Av. E&W | 37W-24N,36W-25N | 41 |
| Butternut Dr. NW&SE | 38W-26N | 41 |
| Castle Rock Ct. NW&SE | 39W-23N | 41 |
| Center Av. E&W | 37W-25N | 41 |
| Crystal Ct. N&S | 37W-25N | 41 |
| Cumberland Ln. N&S | 36W-25N | 41 |
| Dairy Ln. NS&EW | 38W-24N | 41 |
| Dundedin Dr. SW&NE | 38W-23N | 41 |
| Edinburogh Ct. N&S | 38W-23N | 41 |
| Essex Ln. N&S | 36W-25N | 41 |
| Fairway Dr. N&S | 38W-24N,38W-25N | 41 |
| Firth Ct. NS&EW | 38W-24N | 41 |
| Gilmore Ct. N&S | 39W-23N | 41 |
| Glendale Cir. NS&EW | 38W-24N | 41 |
| Haligus Rd. N&S | 39W-23N,39W-24N | 41 |
| Hampshire Ln. N&S | 37W-25N | 41 |
| Hawthorn St. N&S | 37W-25N | 41 |
| Hickory St. E&W | 37W-25N | 41 |
| Huntley Rd. N&S | 37W-25N | 41 |
| Inverway Dr. NS&EW | 39W-23N,38W-24N | 41 |
| Julie Dr. SE&NW | 39W-24N,38W-24N | 41 |
| Lake Av. NW&SE | 37W-25N,36W-25N | 41 |
| Loch Glen Ct. NE&SW | 38W-24N | 41 |
| Loch Glen Dr. NS&EW | 38W-24N,38W-25N | 41 |
| Marsh Dr. NS&EW | 39W-24N | 41 |
| McIntosh Ct. E&W | 37W-23N | 41 |
| Melrose Ct. N&S | 36W-25N | 41 |
| Meridian St. N&S | 37W-25N | 41 |
| Muirfield Ct. N&S | 38W-24N | 41 |
| Muirfield Dr. NS&EW | 38W-24N | 41 |
| North Av. E&W | 37W-25N | 41 |
| Oak St. E&W | 37W-25N | 41 |
| Oakwood Dr. E&W | 37W-25N | 41 |
| Oxford Ln. N&S | 36W-25N | 41 |
| Partridge Ln. N&S | 37W-24N | 41 |
| Pheasant Dr. N&S | 37W-24N | 41 |
| Priegnitz Rd. N&S | 38W-23N,38W-24N | 41 |
| Richmond St. N&S | 37W-25N | 41 |
| Scots Ln. N&S | 38W-24N | 41 |
| Scott Cir. E&W | 38W-24N | 41 |
| South Shore Dr. N&S | 37W-25N,36W-25N | 41 |
| Stirling Ct. NE&SW | 39W-23N | 41 |
| Stuart Ln. E&W | 39W-24N,38W-24N | 41 |
| Sunset Dr. E&W | 38W-24N | 41 |
| Turnberry Lake Dr. NE&SW | 38W-23N,37W-23N | 41 |
| Turnberry Tr. E&W | 38W-24N | 41 |
| Warwick Ln. N&S | 37W-25N | 41 |
| Willow St. E&W | 37W-25N | 41 |
| Wiltshire Ln. N&S | 37W-25N | 41 |
| Woodbine Rd. NW&SE | 39W-24N,39W-25N | 40 |
| Zimmerman Rd. NW&SE | 39W-24N,39W-25N | 40 |

## Marengo

| Street | Grid | Page |
|---|---|---|
| Adams St. E&W | 49W-26N | 37 |
| Ann St. N&S | 50W-26N | 37 |
| Artell Av. N&S | 49W-26N | 37 |
| Autumn St. E&W | 49W-26N | 37 |
| Barbara Av. E&W | 50W-25N | 37 |
| Bauman St. E&W | 50W-26N | 37 |
| Beaver Pond Ct. N&S | 49W-27N | 29 |
| Beaver Pond Dr. NE&SW | 49W-27N | 29 |
| Begg Ct. E&W | 50W-26N | 37 |
| Briden St. E&W | 50W-26N | 37 |
| Buttonwood Ct. E&W | 49W-27N | 29 |
| Buttonwood Ln. E&W | 49W-27N | 29 |
| Caroline St. E&W | 49W-26N | 37 |
| Cascade Ct. NE&SW | 49W-27N | 29 |
| Cascade Dr. NW&SE | 49W-27N | 29 |
| Cayuga Tr. E&W | 50W-26N | 37 |
| Center Dr. NE&SW | 49W-27N | 29 |
| Chappel St. E&W | 50W-26N | 37 |
| Cherokee Tr. E&W | 50W-26N | 37 |
| Chestnut Ct. E&W | 49W-27N | 29 |
| Chestnut Ln. E&W | 49W-27N | 29 |
| Chippewater E&W | 50W-26N | 37 |
| Circle Ct. E&W | 50W-26N | 37 |
| Clark St. N&S | 49W-27N | 29 |
| Clove Ln. N&S | 49W-27N | 29 |
| Cottonwood Ln. N&S | 49W-27N | 29 |
| Damon St. N&S | 49W-27N | 29 |
| Deerpass Rd. N&S | 49W-27N | 37 |
| Deitz St. N&S | 50W-26N | 37 |
| Diane Ct. E&W | 49W-27N | 37 |
| Dunham Ct. N&S | 49W-25N | 37 |
| East Forest St. N&S | 50W-26N,49W-26N | 37 |
| East Prairie St. E&W | 49W-26N | 37 |
| East St. N&S | 49W-26N,49W-27N | 37 |
| East Washington St. E&W | 49W-26N | 37 |
| Eighth St. E&W | 49W-27N | 29 |
| Eisenhower St. N&S | 50W-26N | 37 |
| Elm St. N&S | 49W-26N | 37 |
| Fifth St. E&W | 49W-27N | 29 |
| First St. E&W | 49W-27N | 29 |
| Ford St. N&S | 50W-26N | 37 |
| Fourth St. E&W | 49W-27N | 29 |
| Foxglove Ct. N&S | 49W-27N | 29 |
| Foxglove Ln. N&S | 49W-27N | 29 |
| Georgain Ct. E&W | 49W-27N | 29 |
| Geraldine Ct. E&W | 49W-26N | 37 |
| Grant Hwy. E&W | 50W-26N,49W-26N | 37 |
| Greenlee St. E&W | 49W-26N | 37 |
| Grove St. N&S | 49W-26N | 37 |
| Hale St. N&S | 49W-27N | 37 |
| Hickory Ct. E&W | 49W-27N | 29 |
| Hickory Ln. E&W | 49W-27N | 29 |
| Jackson St. N&S | 49W-26N | 37 |
| Jacquelyn Ct. N&S | 50W-25N | 37 |
| James Ct. E&W | 49W-26N | 37 |
| Johnson St. N&S | 50W-26N | 37 |
| Kennedy Dr. N&S | 50W-26N | 37 |
| Kent St. E&W | 50W-26N | 37 |
| Keppler Dr. E&W | 50W-26N | 37 |
| Kishwaukee St. N&S | 49W-27N | 29 |
| Locust St. N&S | 49W-26N | 37 |
| Lynn Dr. SW&NE | 49W-26N | 37 |
| Mallard Ct. NW&SE | 49W-27N | 29 |
| Maple St. N&S | 49W-25N,49W-27N | 37 |
| Mary Ct. E&W | 49W-25N | 37 |
| Mohawk Tr. E&W | 50W-26N | 37 |
| Navajo Tr. E&W | 50W-26N | 37 |
| O'Connell Dr. E&W | 50W-25N | 37 |
| Oak Manor St. N&S | 50W-26N | 37 |
| Osage Tr. N&S | 50W-26N | 37 |
| Otter Tail Dr. NE&SW | 49W-27N | 29 |
| Page St. N&S | 49W-26N,49W-27N | 37 |
| Park Dr. N&S | 50W-26N | 37 |
| Pawnee Tr. NW&SE | 50W-26N | 37 |
| Prospect St. N&S | 49W-26N | 37 |
| Pulse Ln. N&S | 48W-26N | 37 |
| Railroad St. NW&SE | 49W-26N | 37 |
| Rainbow St. N&S | 49W-26N | 37 |
| Randall Ct. E&W | 49W-25N | 37 |
| Riley Dr. N&S | 49W-25N,49W-26N | 37 |
| Rowland St. N&S | 50W-26N | 37 |
| Royal Oak Dr. N&S | 50W-26N | 37 |
| Rt. 176 E&W | 49W-26N | 37 |
| Rt. 23 N&S | 50W-26N,50W-27N | 37 |
| School St. NE&SW | 49W-26N | 37 |
| Second St. E&W | 49W-27N | 29 |
| Seneca St. N&S | 50W-26N | 37 |
| Seventh Av. E&W | 49W-27N | 29 |
| Seventh Cir. NS&EW | 49W-27N | 29 |
| Shady Ln. Ct. NE&SW | 49W-27N | 37 |
| Sixth St. E&W | 49W-27N | 29 |
| South St. E&W | 50W-26N | 37 |
| Sponable St. N&S | 50W-26N | 37 |
| Stanford Dr. N&S | 50W-26N | 37 |
| State St. N&S | 50W-26N,50W-27N | 37 |
| Stevenson St. E&W | 50W-26N | 37 |
| Sullivan St. NW&SE | 49W-26N | 37 |
| Sunset Dr. N&S | 50W-26N,50W-27N | 37 |
| Talbot St. E&W | 49W-26N | 37 |
| Taylor St. N&S | 49W-26N,49W-27N | 37 |
| Telegraph St. E&W | 49W-27N | 29 |
| Third St. E&W | 49W-27N | 29 |
| Tioga Tr. N&S | 50W-26N | 37 |
| U.S. Route 20 E&W | 49W-26N | 37 |

Grid Page
Van Buren St. E&W 50W-26N,49W-26N 37
Walnut Ct. E&W 49W-27N 29
Walnut Ln. E&W 49W-27N 29
West Forest St. E&W 50W-26N 37
West Prairie St. E&W 50W-26N 37
West St. N&S 50W-26N 37
West Washington St. E&W 50W-26N 37
Whitetail Cir. NE&SW 49W-27N 29
Whitetail Dr. NS&EW 49W-27N 29
Whitetail Pl. N&S 49W-27N 29
Willow Rd. N&S 50W-26N,50W-27N 37
Woodbine Ln. E&W 49W-27N 29
Woodland Ct. N&S 49W-27N 29
Woodland Ln. E&W 49W-27N 29

## Marengo Township

Briden Dr. E&W 51W-26N 36
Busse Rd. N&S 49W-31N 21
Busse Rd. N&S 50W-31N 29
Carmack Rd. E&W 53W-30N,51W-30N 28
Center Av. N&S 51W-27N 28
Collins Rd. E&W 49W-30N 29
Constance Ln. N&S 51W-29N 28
County Line Rd. N&S 54W-26N,54W-31N 36
Cox Rd. N&S 52W-28N,52W-29N 28
Deerpass Rd. N&S 49W-27N,49W-30N 29
Edward St. N&S 50W-28N 29
Elizabeth St. N&S 50W-28N 29
Executive Dr. N&S 49W-28N 29
Grant Hwy. E&W 54W-26N,50W-26N 36
Greenbriar Ln. N&S 51W-29N 28
Grenadier Dr. E&W 51W-29N 28
Hawthorn Rd. N&S 50W-29N,51W-30N 29
Hayden Dr. E&W 51W-26N 36
Heritage Ct. N&S 49W-28N 29
Highcrest Rd. N&S 51W-30N 28
Johnson Rd. N&S 52W-26N 36
Keppler Dr. E&W 51W-26N 36
Kishwaukee Valley Rd. E&W 54W-31N,49W-31N 20
Koda Dr. N&S 50W-30N 29
Lynn Dr. N&S 49W-30N 29
Mary Ln. St. E&W 50W-28N 29
Menge Rd. N&S 49W-31N 21
Meyer Rd. N&S 51W-26N 36
Michele Dr. N&S 49W-30N 29
Miller Rd. N&S 54W-28N,54W-29N 28
Noe Rd. N&S 53W-30N,53W-31N 28
Northwest Rd. NS&EW 50W-28N,50W-29N 29
O'Connell Dr. E&W 50W-26N 37
Olbrich Rd. N&S 50W-31N 21
Olcott Rd. N&S 54W-30N 28
Oleson Rd. N&S 54W-31N 20
Parade Dr. E&W 49W-28N 29
Parkview Dr. N&S 50W-28N,50W-29N 29
Pringle Dr. N&S 50W-29N,50W-30N 29
Railroad St. E&W 51W-26N,50W-26N 36
Ridgeview Ln. E&W 49W-30N 29
Ritz Rd. N&S 51W-27N 37
River Ranch Rd. N&S 51W-26N 37
River Rd. E&W 54W-28N,49W-28N 28
Root Rd. N&S 52W-31N 20
Rt. 23 N&S 50W-27N,50W-31N 29
Squire Dr. N&S 49W-28N 29
Stella Dr. E&W 51W-29N 28
Thorne Rd. N&S 52W-26N,52W-28N 36
Tomlin Rd. E&W 54W-31N,52W-31N 20
W. Pringle Dr. E&W 50W-30N 29

## McCullom Lake

Beachview Dr. N&S 33W-34N 26
Clover Hill Dr. NE&SW 33W-34N 26
East Ln. E&W 34W-34N 26
Eastwood Dr. N&S 33W-34N 26
Flanders Rd. SW&NE 33W-34N 26
Forest View Dr. N&S 34W-34N 26
Fountain E&W 34W-34N,33W-34N 26
Garden Ct. NW&SE 34W-34N 26
Greenwood Pl. E&W 34W-34N 26
Hickory Dr. N&S 34W-34N 26
Knollwood Dr. N&S 34W-34N 26
Lake Shore Dr. NW&SE 33W-34N 26
Maple Hill Dr. E&W 34W-34N,33W-34N 26
Oakland Ln. N&S 34W-34N 26
Orchard Dr. NS&EW 34W-34N,33W-34N 26
Parkview Dr. E&W 34W-34N 26
Parkview Dr. NW&SE 33W-34N 26
Spring Rd. N&S 33W-34N 26
West End Dr. N&S 34W-34N 26
West Ln. E&W 34W-34N 26

## McHenry

Abbey Dr. E&W 34W-31N 26
Abbington Dr. NE&SW 33W-32N 26
Albany St. E&W 33W-30N,32W-30N 34
Albert Dr. N&S 34W-34N 26
Allen Av. NS&EW 32W-32N 26
Amberwood Pl. N&S 32W-31N 26
Amherst Ct. E&W 34W-34N 26
Anne St. E&W 32W-32N 26
April Av. NE&SW 35W-34N 26
Ashland Dr. E&W 34W-32N,33W-32N 26
Ashley Dr. E&W 33W-33N 26
Augusta Dr. N&S 34W-32N 26
Bally Rd. N&S 31W-31N 27
Barn Wood Ct. E&W 33W-31N 26
Barnwood Tr. NE&SW 33W-31N 26
Bauer Rd. N&S 32W-32N 26
Beach Dr. E&W 32W-31N,31W-31N 26
Beach Rd. N&S 33W-33N,34W-33N 26
Belden St. NE&SW 32W-30N 34
Bennington Ln. NS&EW 34W-34N 26
Birch Dr. N&S 32W-33N 26
Biscayne Dr. E&W 32W-30N 34
Biscayne Rd. E&W 32W-30N 34
Bonita Ln. N&S 32W-30N,32W-31N 34
Bonner Dr. NW&SE 33W-33N 26
Bonnie Brae Dr. N&S 32W-30N 34
Borden St. NW&SE 32W-33N 26
Bradley Ct. E&W 32W-33N 26
Brefeld Ct (Pvt) E&W 31W-31N 27
Bretons Dr. E&W 32W-32N 26
Brighton Pl. E&W 32W-31N 26
Brittany Dr. E&W 34W-33N 26
Broad St. NW&SE 32W-33N 26
Broadway Dr. N&S 32W-30N,32W-31N 34
Bromley Dr. NS&EW 33W-32N 26
Brookwood Tr. N&S 34W-31N 26
Brown St. N&S 32W-33N 26
Bull Valley Rd. E&W 34W-31N,32W-31N 26
Burning Tree Cir. E&W 35W-32N 26
Burning Tree Dr. E&W 36W-32N 25
Callista St. NW&SE 33W-32N 26
Cambridge Dr. E&W 34W-32N,33W-32N 26
Canterbury Dr. N&S 34W-32N 26
Capri Ter. N&S 32W-30N 34
Carey Dr. N&S 32W-30N 34
Carol Av. N&S 31W-31N 27
Carriage Tr. NE&SW 34W-31N 26
Center St. N&S 32W-32N 26
Central St. N&S 33W-33N 26
Charlotte Av. NE&SW 32W-32N,31W-32N 26
Chasefield Circle NS&EW 34W-31N,34W-32N 26
Cherryhill Ct. N&S 34W-34N 26
Chesapeake Dr. EW&NS 34W-33N 26
Chesterfield Ct. NE&SW 33W-32N,33W-33N 26
Chesterfield Dr. NW&SE 33W-32N,33W-33N 26
Chestnut Dr. E&W 32W-33N 26
Chickaloon Dr. NS&EW 35W-33N 26
Church St. N&S 32W-33N 26
Clearbrook Av. E&W 32W-33N 26
Clearview Dr. E&W 33W-33N 26
Clover Av. E&W 32W-32N 26
Colony Ct. NW&SE 33W-31N 26
Colony Tr. N&S 36W-32N 25
Commercial Av. NW&SE 33W-33N 26
Cornell Ct. E&W 32W-33N 26
Corporate Dr. N&S 33W-30N 34
Court St. NE&SW 32W-33N 26
Courtland Tr. NW&SE 33W-31N 26
Creek Dr. E&W 34W-31N 26
Creekside Ct. E&W 34W-31N 26
Creekside Ln. E&W 33W-33N 26
Creekside Tr. NE&SW 34W-31N,34W-32N 26
Crescent Av. E&W 32W-32N 26
Crestwood Dr. NE&SW 33W-32N 26
Cross Tr. N&S 33W-31N 26
Crystal Lake Rd. NE&SW 34W-31N,33W-33N 26
Crystal Trail E&W 33W-31N 26
Cumberland Circle NS&EW 33W-33N 26
Curran Rd. NS&EW 34W-32N,34W-33N 26
Dale Av. N&S 32W-32N 26
Dartmoor Dr. E&W 34W-32N,33W-32N 26
Dayton St. E&W 33W-30N,32W-30N 34
Deer Run Tr. NE&SW 36W-32N 25
Deerwood Tr. E&W 36W-32N 25
Denali Tr. NW&SE 35W-33N 26
Derby Ln. NE&SW 33W-34N 26
Devonshire Ct.* E&W 34W-32N,33W-32N 26
Donnelley Pl. N&S 32W-31N 26
Donovan Ct. NW&SE 32W-33N 26
Donovan St. NW&SE 33W-33N,32W-33N 26
Dorchester Pl. E&W 32W-31N 26
Dot St. N&S 34W-33N 26
Drake Ct. E&W 32W-33N 26
Draper Rd. NE&SW 35W-33N,34W-33N 26
Driftwood Ct. NE&SW 34W-31N 26
Driftwood Tr. NE&SW 33W-31N,33W-31N 26
Eagle Point N&S 35W-32N 26
Eastern Av. N&S 33W-33N 26
Elm St. NW&SE 34W-33N,32W-33N 26
Erin St. N&S 31W-33N 27
Essex Ct. N&S 33W-32N 26
Fairfax Dr. N&S 34W-31N 26
Fairway Dr. E&W 32W-32N 26
Farington Dr. E&W 34W-32N 26
Florence Blvd. E&W 34W-34N 26
Flower St. N&S 33W-33N 26
Foolish Pleasure Dr. NW&SE 33W-34N 26
Forest Rd. E&W 32W-30N 34
Fourth St. NE&SW 32W-32N 26
Foxview Highland Dr. E&W 32W-30N 35
Freund Av. NS&EW 32W-33N 26
Front Royal Dr. NE&SW 33W-32N,33W-33N 26
Front St. NE&SW 32W-33N 26
Garden Quarter Rd. E&W 33W-32N 26
Geneva Pl. E&W 32W-31N 26
Glen Dr. N&S 33W-33N 26
Glenbrook Tr. E&W 34W-31N,33W-31N 26
Golf View Ter. E&W 32W-32N 26
Golfview Dr. SW&NE 32W-32N 26
Grand Av. E&W 32W-33N 26
Green St. N&S 32W-32N,32W-33N 26
Greenbriar Dr. NW&SE 34W-32N 26
Gregg Dr. E&W 31W-31N 27
Grove Av. E&W 32W-32N 26
Hampton Ct. NE&SW 33W-32N 26
Hartland Tr. NW&SE 33W-31N 26
Hayward Ct. E&W 35W-33N 26
Heritage Dr. N&S 34W-31N,34W-32N 26
High St. E&W 32W-32N 26
Highview Av. N&S 33W-33N 26
Hill St. NW&SE 34W-33N 26
Hillside Dr. E&W 32W-33N 27
Hilltop Dr. N&S 32W-30N,32W-31N 34
Hollywood Blvd. N&S 32W-30N,32W-31N 34
Home Av. E&W 34W-33N,33W-33N 26
Hunter Dr. E&W 34W-33N 26
Hunter Path E&W 32W-30N 34
Huntington Dr.. N&S 34W-32N 26
Illiamna Tr. NE&SW 35W-33N 26
Industrial Dr. N&S 33W-33N 26
James St. NW&SE 32W-32N 26
Jennifer Ln. N&S 32W-33N 26
John St. NW&SE 32W-32N 26
Judy Ln. NE&SW 32W-32N 26
Kane Av. E&W 32W-33N 26
Katie Ln. NW&SE 32W-31N 26
Katmai Tr. NW&SE 35W-33N 26
Kensington Dr. NW&SE 33W-32N 26
Kinley Blvd. E&W 32W-31N,31W-31N 26
Knoll Av. N&S 33W-33N 26
Knox Dr. E&W 32W-31N 26
Lakeland Av. N&S 33W-33N 26
Lakewood Av. N&S 34W-33N 26
Lakewood Rd. N&S 33W-34N 26
Laurel Ct. E&W 32W-33N 26
Lawn Ct. N&S 33W-33N 26
Lawrence Pkwy. N&S 33W-31N 26
Lee St. E&W 32W-32N 26
Leonard Av. N&S 32W-33N 26
Lillian St. NW&SE 33W-32N,32W-32N 26
Lincoln St. E&W 32W-33N 26
Linda Rd. N&S 32W-32N 26
Loch Glen Ln. NS&EW 32W-31N 26
Logan St. NW&SE 32W-33N 26
Lorient Dr. E&W 32W-32N 26
Main St. NW&SE 33W-33N,32W-32N 26
Malibu Ct. E&W 34W-31N 26
Manchester Mall NS&EW 33W-33N 26
Manley Av. NW&SE 33W-32N,33W-33N 26
Maple Av. E&W 32W-33N 26
Martin Rd. NS&EW 34W-34N 26
Matanuska Tr. N&S 35W-33N 26
McCullom Lake Rd. NW&SE 32W-33N 26
McCullom Rd. E&W 32W-33N 26
McHenry Av. N&S 32W-31N 26
Meadow Lake Av. E&W 32W-32N 26
Meadow Ln. NS&EW 33W-33N 26
Meadow Rd. N&S 32W-31N 26
Medical Center Dr. NS&EW 33W-31N,32W-31N 26
Melrose Ct. NS&EW 33W-32N 26
Mildred St. E&W 32W-33N 26
Mill St. NW&SE 33W-32N,33W-33N 26
Miller Pkwy. N&S 33W-30N 34
Miller Rd. E&W 32W-31N,31W-31N 26
Millstream Dr. NS&EW 32W-33N 26
North Av. N&S 33W-33N 26
North Dr. N&S 32W-33N 26
North Fox Ln. NE&SW 33W-32N 26
Oak Av. E&W 32W-32N 26
Oak Dr. NW&SE 33W-33N 26
Oakwood Ct. N&S 33W-33N 26
Oakwood Dr. NS&EW 33W-32N,33W-33N 26
Ojibwa Ln. NW&SE 35W-33N 26
Orchid Path N&S 32W-31N 26
Oregon Tr. E&W 33W-31N 26
Orleans St. NS&EW 33W-33N,32W-33N 26
Overland Tr. E&W 33W-31N 26
Park Lane Av. N&S 34W-33N 26
Park St. N&S 32W-33N 26
Parkway Av. E&W 33W-33N 26
Pearl St. NS&EW 32W-31N,32W-33N 26
Pebble Creek Pl. E&W 32W-31N 26
Peterson Park Rd. NE&SW 33W-34N 26
Pine Dr. N&S 33W-33N 26
Pinoak Ct. NW&SE 35W-33N 26
Pleasant Av. N&S 33W-33N 26
Pleasant View Dr. E&W 32W-30N 34
Ponca St. NE&SW 33W-32N 26
Prairie Av. E&W 33W-33N 26
Prairie St. E&W 31W-31N 27
Prestwick St. E&W 32W-33N 26
Prime Parkway E&W 33W-30N 34
Pyndale Dr. E&W 32W-32N 26
Radcliff Ct. E&W 34W-34N 26
Ramble Rd. N&S 33W-33N 26
Redwood Ln. N&S 32W-33N 26
Rhonda Rd. N&S 32W-31N,32W-32N 26
Richmond Rd. N&S 32W-33N 26
Ridgeview Dr. N&S 33W-30N 34
Ridgeway Tr. N&S 36W-32N 25
Ridgeway Trail Ct. N&S 36W-32N 25
Ringwood Rd. N&S 34W-33N,34W-34N 26
River Ct. N&S 32W-33N 27
River Rd. NW&SE 31W-32N,32W-33N 27
Riverside Dr. N&S 31W-31N,32W-33N 27
Riverstream Rd. NE&SW 32W-32N 26
Rogers Av. N&S 33W-32N 26
Rose Av. NW&SE 34W-34N 26
Royal Dr. NW&SE 33W-32N 26
Rt. 120 NW&SE 35W-33N,32W-33N 26
Rt. 31 E&W 33W-30N,32W-34N 34
Ryan St. N&S 32W-33N 26
S. Scully Dr. E&W 34W-33N 26
Sandburg Dr. E&W 33W-32N 26
Sarasota Dr. NW&SE 34W-32N 26
Scully Dr. N&S 34W-33N 26
Shamrock Ln. E&W 33W-31N 26
Shephard Hill Ln. NS&EW 32W-32N 26
Sherman Dr. E&W 34W-33N 26
Shore Dr. E&W 34W-33N,33W-33N 26
Shore Hill Dr. E&W 34W-33N 26
Silbury Ct. NS&EW 33W-32N 26
Silver Glen Rd. N&S 36W-32N 25
Sioux St. NE&SW 33W-32N 26
Skyway Dr. E&W 32W-32N 26
Somerset Mall N&S 33W-33N 26
South St. NE&SW 33W-32N 26
Southgate NS&EW 32W-32N 26
Springbrook Ct. NE&SW 34W-31N 26
Springdale Ln. E&W 34W-33N 26
Spruce Ln. E&W 33W-33N 26
St. Pauls Av. E&W 32W-32N 26
Still Hill Dr. E&W 32W-31N,31W-31N 26
Stratford Ct. E&W 33W-32N 26
Sunrise View E&W 32W-30N 34
Sunset Av. N&S 34W-33N 26
Sussex Dr. E&W 33W-33N 26
Sycamore Ct. E&W 35W-33N 26
Tamarack Ct. NE&SW 35W-33N 26
Terrace Dr. E&W 32W-31N 26
Third St. NE&SW 32W-32N,32W-33N 26
Thornwood Dr. N&S 34W-32N 26
Timber Trail E&W 36W-32N 25
Timothy Ln. NS&EW 32W-32N 26
Tomlinson Ct. E&W 34W-34N 26
Tomlinson Dr. NW&SE 35W-34N,34W-34N 26
Turnberry Dr. E&W 32W-31N 26
Tustamena Tr. E&W 35W-33N 26
Valley Dr. E&W 32W-33N 27
Valley Rd. N&S 32W-32N 26
Venice Ct. E&W 32W-33N 26
Veretta Ct. NE&SW 33W-31N 26
Victor Dr. E&W 34W-33N 26
Victoria Av. E&W 32W-32N,31W-32N 26
Village Tr. N&S 33W-31N 26
Vine St. E&W 32W-31N 26
Virginia Av. E&W 32W-32N,31W-32N 26
Vista Ter. E&W 32W-31N 26
Walnut Ln. E&W 32W-33N 26
Washington St. NW&SE 32W-33N 26
Waters Edge Dr. NE&SW 34W-32N,33W-32N 26
Waukegan St. NW&SE 32W-33N,32W-32N 26
West Av. E&W 32W-33N 26
Westminster Pl. E&W 32W-31N 26
Whiteoak Ct. NW&SE 34W-34N 26
Whiteoak Dr. NS&EW 35W-34N,34W-34N 26
Whiting Ct. N&S 34W-34N 26
Whiting Dr. NW&SE 35W-34N,34W-34N 26
Willow Ln. E&W 34W-33N,33W-33N 26
Wiltshire Ct. NE&SW 33W-32N 26
Wiltshire Dr. NW&SE 33W-32N 26
Windhaven Ct. N&S 34W-31N 26
Windhaven Tr. NS&EW 34W-31N 26
Winding Creek Dr. E&W 34W-31N 26
Windridge Dr. N&S 34W-32N 26
Winslow Circle NW&SE 34W-32N 26
Wood St. NW&SE 33W-32N 26
Woodmar Ct. E&W 34W-32N 26
Woodridge Tr. NS&EW 36W-32N 25
Young St. E&W 32W-32N 26

## McHenry Township

Acorn Ln. N&S 29W-37N 19
Agatha Ln. N&S 29W-37N 19
Algonquin Rd. E&W 36W-36N 17
Aloha Ct. E&W 31W-34N 27
Aloha Dr. N&S 31W-34N 27
Althoff Dr. E&W 29W-36N 19
Altoff Dr. E&W 29W-36N 19
Alton Rd. N&S 34W-34N 26
Amanda Av. E&W 29W-31N 27
Amby Ln. N&S 29W-37N 19
Annabelle St. E&W 29W-37N 19

**Grid Page**

Appaloosa Tr. N&S ........ 30W-33N 27
Arabian Spur E&W .. 30W-33N 27
Arbor Rd. E&W ... 36W-35N 17
Ash Dr. E&W ...... 36W-36N 17
Ashwood Dr. E&W .. 30W-34N 25
August Ln. E&W ... 30W-34N 27
Backbay Rd. E&W .. 36W-36N 17
Balsam Dr. E&W ... 36W-36N 25
Barbara Dr. E&W .. 36W-37N 17
Barnard Mill Rd. NW&SE
........ 35W-37N,33W-36N 18
Basswood Dr. E&W
............... 36W-34N 25
Bay Rd. NW&SE ... 29W-34N 27
Bay View Ln. N&S .. 29W-34N 27
Baycliff Dr. NW&SE . 31W-34N 27
Bayview Ct. NW&SE
............... 29W-34N 27
Bayview Dr. E&W . 36W-36N 17
Bayview Ln. NS&EW
............... 29W-34N 27
Beach Av. N&S ... 34W-34N 26
Beach Dr. E&W ... 36W-36N 17
Beach Rd.
... 29W-35N,36W-35N 19
Beach Rd. E&W ... 29W-32N 27
Beachside Rd. N&S
............... 34W-34N 26
Beaver Rd. E&W .. 36W-34N 25
Benjamin Dr. N&S . 36W-34N 25
Bennington Ct. E&W
............... 36W-32N 25
Berkshire Dr. E&W 32W-37N 18
Birch Dr. E&W ... 36W-36N 17
Black Oak Dr. NE&SW
............... 36W-33N 25
Bong St. N&S .... 36W-37N 17
Boston Rd. E&W .. 36W-37N 17
Bridge St. N&S ... 29W-37N 19
Britton Dr. N&S .. 29W-37N 19
Broadway Rd. E&W
... 30W-37N,29W-37N 19
Brook Dr. E&W ... 36W-35N 17
Brookshire Dr. N&S
... 32W-30N,32W-37N 19
Bull Ridge Dr. NS&EW
............... 36W-33N 25
Bunny Av. N&S ... 29W-37N 19
Burr Av. E&W ..... 29W-37N 19
Burr Oak Ct. NS&EW
............... 36W-33N 25
Burr Oak Dr. .. 36W-33N 25
Cambridge Ct. E&W
............... 36W-32N 25
Cambridge Rd. E&W
............... 36W-36N 17
Carl Ct. N&S ...... 30W-34N 27
Cassandra Ln. N&S
............... 30W-33N 27
Catalpa Dr. E&W .. 36W-34N 25
Cedar Dr. E&W ... 36W-36N 17
Cedar Rd. E&W ... 36W-36N 17
Center Dr. E&W .. 36W-36N 17
Channel Ln. N&S .. 34W-34N 26
Chapel Hill Rd. N&S
............... 31W-32N 27
Charles St. N&S .. 32W-36N 26
Cherry Dr. N&S .. 36W-34N 25
Chestnut Dr. NS&EW
... 36W-34N,36W-36N 25
Chipewa Av. N&S . 36W-36N 17
Christine Av. N&S . 29W-37N 19
Church Dr. N&S .. 36W-35N 17
Circle Av. NE&SW .. 29W-37N 19
Circle Ct. N&S ... 36W-36N 19
Circle Dr. E&W ... 36W-36N 17
Circle Dr. N&S ... 29W-37N 19
Circle Dr. NS&EW .. 36W-37N 17
Circle Dr. N&S ... 36W-36N 19
Clara St. NW&SE .. 31W-34N 27
Clearview Dr. N&S . 36W-37N 17
Clement Rd. N&S .. 31W-32N 27
Cleveland Dr. E&W
............... 34W-34N 26
Cliff Ct. E&W .... 30W-34N 27
Clover Dr. NE&SW 31W-33N 27
Club Dr. N&S .... 29W-37N 19
Cobblestone Dr. NS&EW
............... 30W-36N 27
Concorde Dr. N&S . 36W-32N 25
Coolidge Dr. E&W
... 31W-34N,30W-34N 27
Coral St. N&S .... 31W-32N 27
Country Club Dr. N&S
............... 31W-32N 27
Country Ln. E&W .. 31W-33N 27
Craig Dr. N&S ... 36W-36N 17
Crescent Dr. E&W 36W-36N 17
Crest St. E&W ... 30W-32N 27
Cresthill Av. N&S . 29W-32N 27
Crestwood Av. N&S
............... 29W-32N 27
Croakin Ln. E&W .. 31W-32N 27
Cross Dr. NW&SE .. 36W-37N 17
Croyden St. E&W .. 29W-37N 19
Cuhlman Rd. N&S
... 29W-33N,29W-34N 27
Curve Av. N&S ... 29W-37N 19
Curve Ct. NS&EW .. 29W-37N 19
Cushman Rd. NE&SW
............... 29W-34N 27
Cypress Dr. E&W .. 36W-37N 17
Dale Av. E&W .... 29W-32N 27
David St. N&S ... 29W-37N 19
Deborah Ln. NW&SE
............... 31W-33N 27
Deep Spring Rd. E&W
............... 36W-36N 17
Deerpath Dr. E&W 29W-37N 19
Delaware Rd. E&W
............... 36W-36N 17

Della Pl. E&W ... 30W-35N 19
Delore Dr. E&W ... 31W-32N 27
Delshire Ln. E&W .. 32W-36N 18
Dennis Dr. N&S .. 30W-36N 19
Devonshire Dr. N&S
............... 32W-37N 18
Don Michael Dr. E&W
............... 36W-36N 17
Dot St. N&S .... 34W-33N 26
Draper Rd. NE&SW
............... 35W-32N 26
Dutch Cir. N&S .... 31W-34N 27
E. Chestnut Dr. N&S
............... 36W-34N 25
E. Sunset Dr. E&W
............... 36W-35N 17
East Av. N&S .... 29W-37N 19
East Blvd. NS&EW 29W-32N 27
East Dr. N&S .... 36W-35N 17
East Lake Shore Dr. N&S
... 36W-35N,36W-35N 17
East Maplewood Dr. E&W
............... 36W-34N 25
East St. N&S .... 29W-37N 19
East Wonder Lake Rd. N&S
... 36W-32N,36W-35N 25
Eastern Av. E&W .. 29W-37N 19
Eastview Av. N&S . 29W-32N 27
Eastwood Dr. N&S 36W-36N 17
Eastwood Ln. N&S 31W-33N 27
Edgewood Ct. N&S
............... 31W-33N 27
Edgewood Dr. E&W
............... 29W-36N 19
Edgewood Ln. E&W
............... 36W-35N 17
Edgewood Ln. E&W
............... 31W-33N 27
Edward Ct. N&S ... 30W-34N 27
Eisenhower Dr. NE&SW
............... 36W-37N 17
Elam Av. NE&SW .. 30W-35N 19
Elder Av. E&W ... 29W-36N 19
Elm Leaf Dr. N&S . 30W-36N 19
Elmkirk Pk. E&W .. 31W-32N 27
Elmkirk Pkwy. EW&NS
............... 31W-32N 27
Elmoak Ln. E&W .. 31W-32N 27
Elmshire Ln. NS&EW
............... 32W-36N 18
Emerald Dr. E&W .. 31W-32N 27
Emily Ln. NW&SE .. 31W-33N 27
Euclid Dr. E&W ... 34W-34N 26
Fair Av. NW&SE ... 29W-32N 27
Fair Oak Ln. E&W . 29W-32N 27
Fairview Av. NW&SE
............... 29W-32N 27
Fairview Ln. NS&EW
............... 31W-33N 27
Falls Ln. E&W .... 36W-37N 17
Fawn Ln. N&S ... 36W-35N 17
Finch Tr. E&W ... 29W-36N 19
Fir Dr. E&W .... 36W-37N 17
First Av. E&W ... 32W-33N 26
Flanders Rd. N&S
... 34W-34N,33W-34N 26
Florence Dr. E&W 29W-36N 19
Florence Dr. N&S 30W-36N 19
Fox Lake Rd. N&S 29W-37N 19
Freedom Dr. N&S .. 34W-34N 26
Friendly Av. NS&EW
............... 29W-32N 27
Gene Dr. E&W ... 36W-34N 25
Geneva Ln. N&S .. 31W-32N 27
Ginko Ct. N&S ... 36W-33N 25
Glenwood Av. N&S
............... 29W-32N 27
Glenwood Ct. NW&SE
............... 31W-33N 27
Glenwood Ln. E&W
............... 31W-33N 27
Grandview Dr. E&W
............... 30W-36N 19
Grandview Dr. NE&SW
............... 31W-34N 27
Granite Dr. E&W .. 36W-37N 17
Grant Pl. N&S ... 29W-37N 19
Granview Dr. N&S . 29W-37N 19
Greenleaf Dr. N&S 36W-35N 17
Gregory St. N&S .. 29W-37N 19
Hampshire Ln. N&S
... 32W-36N,32W-37N 18
Hancock Dr. E&W . 36W-35N 17
Harbor Rd. NE&SW
............... 36W-37N 17
Hay Av. NW&SE .. 33W-32N 26
Hayden Ct. NW&SE
............... 29W-36N 19
Hayden Dr. N&S .. 29W-36N 19
Hedge Pl. SW&NE . 31W-34N 27
Henry Tr. E&W ... 29W-37N 19
Henzada Av. E&W 31W-34N 27
Hiawatha Dr. E&W
... 36W-36N,35W-36N 17
Hickman Dr. N&S
... 41W-30N,40W-30N 32
Hickory Dr. NS&EW
............... 36W-35N 17
Hickory Dr., W. E&W
............... 36W-37N 17
Hickory Ln.
... 32W-36N,32W-37N 18
Hickory Rd. E&W . 36W-35N 17
Hickory Tr. E&W .. 29W-37N 19
Hickorynut Dr. N&S
............... 30W-36N 19
Hidden Oak Dr. N&S
............... 36W-36N 17
High Rd. N&S ... 36W-35N 17
Highland Dr. E&W 34W-34N 26
Highland Dr. N&S . 29W-37N 19
Highview Dr. E&W .. 36W-34N 25

Hill Rd. N&S .... 30W-32N 27
Hillside Dr. E&W .. 36W-35N 17
Hillside Dr. NE&SW
............... 29W-37N 19
Hillside Ln. N&S .. 31W-33N 27
Hilltop Dr. E&W .. 29W-37N 19
Hilltop Dr. N&S
... 36W-36N,36W-37N 17
Hilltop Dr. N&S .. 30W-36N 19
Hollow St. E&W .. 30W-36N 27
Holly Ct. E&W ... 31W-33N 27
Howard St. N&S .. 30W-36N 19
Howe Dr. E&W ... 36W-36N 17
Howell Rd. E&W .. 31W-34N 27
Huron Dr. E&W .. 36W-34N 17
Indian Ridge Dr. E&W
............... 30W-36N 19
Island Ln. N&S ... 36W-36N 17
Jasper Dr. N&S ... 30W-36N 19
Jeffery St. N&S ... 30W-36N 19
John Av. E&W ... 29W-37N 19
John Ct. N&S ... 30W-34N 27
Johnsburg Wilmot Rd. N&S
............... 30W-37N 19
Jonquil Dr. N&S .. 36W-37N 17
Joseph Ct. N&S .. 36W-36N 17
Joyce Av. E&W ... 29W-37N 19
Julia Way E&W ... 30W-33N 27
Kama Av. E&W ... 31W-34N 27
Kashmiri Av. E&W . 31W-34N 27
Kelter St. NW&SE . 33W-32N 26
Kent Rd. N&S ... 30W-32N 27
King Av. E&W ... 36W-37N 17
Kirk Ct. E&W .... 31W-34N 27
Kosciuszko Rd. N&S
............... 34W-34N 26
Lake Av. E&W ... 32W-33N 26
Lake Rd. NE&SW .. 35W-37N 18
Lake Shore Dr. NE&SW
... 36W-36N,36W-36N 17
Lake St. N&S .... 29W-37N 19
Lakeview Dr. N&S . 36W-35N 17
Lakeview Dr. N&S . 36W-35N 25
Lauderdale Ct. N&S
............... 29W-34N 27
Lear St. N&S .... 36W-37N 17
Leeside St. N&S .. 29W-37N 19
Lilac Dr. NW&SE .. 36W-36N 17
Lily Av. NW&SE .. 29W-37N 19
Lincoln Rd. E&W
... 31W-33N,30W-34N 27
Lincolnshire Dr. N&S
............... 32W-36N 18
Little St. N&S ... 29W-37N 19
Lodge Rd. NW&SE
............... 31W-32N 27
Lonetree Dr. E&W 36W-37N 17
Long Ln. N&S ... 30W-34N 27
Lookout Dr. E&W .. 36W-37N 17
Loras Ln. E&W ... 36W-36N 17
Louella Av. N&S .. 29W-37N 19
Lucina Av. N&S .. 29W-37N 19
Lucy Dr. E&W ... 36W-34N 25
Luella Av. N&S ... 29W-37N 19
Lumley Dr. N&S .. 35W-37N 18
Lynn Rd. E&W ... 36W-36N 17
Macarthur Av. E&W
... 36W-37N,35W-37N 17
Macarthur Dr. NE&SW
............... 34W-34N 26
Magellan Dr. N&S . 29W-34N 27
Magnolia Ct. N&S . 29W-32N 27
Magnolia Dr. N&S . 36W-37N 17
Manitou Tr. NE&SW
............... 29W-34N 27
Manor Ln. NE&SW 31W-33N 27
Maple Dr. E&W ... 36W-36N 17
Maple Leaf Dr. N&S
............... 30W-36N 19
Mar Dr. N&S .... 30W-33N 27
Marblehead Rd. E&W
............... 36W-36N 17
Margaret Ct. N&S . 30W-36N 27
Marietta St. NW&SE
............... 33W-32N 26
Marquardt Ln. N&S
............... 30W-34N 27
Marquart Ln. N&S . 30W-34N 27
Marshall Dr. N&S . 36W-37N 17
Martin Av. N&S .. 31W-34N 27
Mary Ln. NW&SE . 31W-33N 27
Maryville Rd. E&W . 31W-33N 27
May Av. E&W ... 30W-36N 19
Mayfair Dr. N&S .. 30W-36N 19
McCullom Lake Rd. NW&SE
... 36W-36N,32W-36N 17
Meadow Ct. E&W .. 29W-37N 19
Meadow Hill Ct. E&W
............... 29W-37N 19
Meadow Hill Ln. N&S
............... 29W-37N 19
Meadow Ln. E&W . 36W-36N 25
Meadowlark Dr. NE&SW
... 29W-36N,29W-37N 19
Memory Tr. N&S
... 29W-36N,29W-37N 19
Michael St. N&S .. 36W-34N 25
Midoak Ln. E&W .. 29W-37N 19
Mill Ln. NW&SE .. 31W-33N 27
Miller Oak Dr. E&W
............... 33W-36N 18
Miller Rd. E&W
... 32W-37N,30W-37N 18
Mineral Spring Dr. N&S
............... 31W-32N 27
Mogra St. N&S ... 31W-34N 27
Mohawk Dr. .. 36W-36N 17
Morgan Ter. E&W . 36W-34N 25
Mourine Ln. NW&SE
............... 31W-33N 27
Myang Av. E&W .. 31W-34N 27

N. Brixham Dr. E&W
............... 30W-35N 19
Nantucket Dr. E&W
............... 36W-37N 17
Navajo Tr. E&W .. 29W-34N 27
Niagra Dr. NE&SW 36W-37N 17
Nimitz Dr. N&S .. 36W-37N 17
Nippersink Dr. E&W
............... 29W-37N 19
North Av. E&W ... 29W-32N 27
North Av. NE&SW . 29W-32N 27
North Blvd. N&S .. 29W-32N 27
North Dr. E&W ... 36W-36N 17
North Oak St. E&W
............... 36W-36N 17
North St. E&W ... 29W-37N 19
Northside Av. NE&SW
............... 31W-32N 27
Northwood Dr. E&W
............... 36W-35N 17
O'Shea Ct. E&W .. 30W-34N 27
Oak Dr. E&W .... 30W-34N 27
Oak St. N&S .... 30W-32N 27
Oakleaf Dr. E&W
... 30W-36N,29W-36N 19
Oakwood Av. N&S . 31W-34N 27
Oakwood Ct. N&S . 31W-33N 27
Oakwood Dr. E&W 36W-36N 17
Oakwood Dr. N&S . 36W-34N 25
Oeffling Ct. NW&SE
............... 29W-36N 19
Oeffling Dr. N&S .. 29W-36N 19
Oneida Rd. E&W .. 36W-37N 17
Orchard Beach Rd. N&S
... 31W-33N,31W-34N 27
Orchard Dr. N&S .. 34W-34N 26
Orchard Rd. NE&SW 35W-37N 18
Orchard Rd. E&W .. 36W-35N 17
Orchardway Dr. E&W
............... 34W-34N 26
Oriole Tr. E&W ... 29W-37N 19
Osage Rd. N&S .. 36W-36N 17
Oshea Ct. E&W ... 30W-34N 27
Ottawa Rd. N&S .. 36W-37N 17
Palamino Dr. N&S . 30W-33N 27
Pamela Dr. E&W .. 36W-34N 25
Park Dr. NE&SW .. 36W-35N 17
Parkside Av. NE&SW
............... 31W-32N 27
Parkwood Dr. E&W
............... 36W-35N 17
Patricia Ln. N&S .. 36W-34N 27
Patton St. N&S ... 36W-37N 17
Paulson St. N&S .. 29W-36N 19
Pebble Dr. NW&SE
............... 30W-34N 27
Pheasant Rd. E&W
............... 36W-35N 17
Pheasant Tr. E&W . 29W-37N 19
Pinoak Dr. E&W .. 36W-34N 25
Pioneer Rd. NW&SE
... 32W-35N,33W-37N 18
Pistakee Dr. N&S . 29W-37N 19
Pistakee Rd. N&S
... 29W-36N,29W-37N 19
Pleasant Dr. E&W . 31W-34N 27
Pleasant Rd. N&S . 36W-35N 17
Pleasant View Dr. NS&EW
............... 29W-37N 19
Plymouth Ln. NW&SE
............... 31W-32N 27
Ponca St. NE&SW . 33W-32N 26
Poplar Leaf Dr. N&S
............... 30W-36N 19
Prairie St. E&W ... 29W-32N 27
Preston Dr. E&W .. 36W-34N 25
Pulaski Rd. E&W .. 34W-34N 26
Quinn Rd. N&S ... 31W-32N 27
Ramree Dr. N&S .. 31W-34N 27
Ranch Dr. NW&SE . 30W-33N 27
Rand Dr. E&W ... 29W-37N 19
Ravine Av. E&W
... 30W-32N,29W-32N 27
Ray St. N&S .... 29W-37N 19
Regner Ln. NW&SE
............... 29W-34N 27
Regner Rd. NS&EW
............... 29W-34N 27
Reiche Ln. S&N .. 29W-34N 27
Reiche Ln., S. N&S
............... 29W-34N 27
Ridgeway Rd. N&S
... 35W-36N,35W-37N 18
Ridgeway Rd. N&S
............... 29W-32N 27
Ridgewood Av. E&W
... 30W-32N,29W-32N 27
River Rd. NW&SE
... 31W-33N,31W-33N 27
Riverdale Dr. NE&SW
............... 30W-36N 19
Roger St. N&S ... 30W-36N 19
Rose Ann Ct. N&S . 35W-35N 18
Rose Dr. E&W ... 36W-37N 17
Rosedale Av. E&W 31W-33N 27
Round Up Rd. E&W
............... 35W-32N 26
Rt. 120 E&W
... 36W-34N,30W-32N 25
Rt. 120 E&W .... 30W-32N 27
Rt. 31 N&S
... 32W-34N,34W-37N 26
S. Brixham Ln. E&W
............... 30W-35N 19
S. Circle Dr. NE&SW
............... 30W-35N 19
S.Brixham Dr. E&W
............... 30W-35N 19
S.Oak Rd. N&S .. 36W-35N 17
Sac Rd. N&S .... 36W-37N 17
Salem Rd. E&W .. 36W-36N 17
Schneider Ln. E&W
............... 31W-34N 27

Scott Av. E&W ... 31W-34N 27
Seattle St. N&S ... 34W-33N 26
Second St. E&W .. 32W-33N 26
Seminole Dr.
... 36W-36N,35W-36N 17
Sequoia Tr. N&S .. 29W-34N 27
Shady Dr. N&S ... 36W-35N 17
Shady Dr. NS&EW . 30W-31N 27
Shady Hollow Ln. E&W
............... 29W-37N 19
Shirley Ln. NE&SW
............... 36W-35N 19
Shorewood Dr. SW&NE
............... 31W-34N 27
Shorewood Rd. NS&EW
............... 31W-34N 27
Short St. N&S ... 29W-37N 19
Small St. N&S ... 29W-37N 19
South Dr. E&W ... 36W-36N 17
South Solon Rd. N&S
............... 33W-37N 18
South St. E&W ... 29W-37N 19
Southside Av. E&W
............... 29W-32N 27
Spaatz Av. E&W .. 36W-37N 17
Spojnia Rd. N&S .. 34W-34N 26
Spring Grove Rd. N&S
... 31W-35N,31W-37N 19
Sterling Dr. NS&EW
............... 31W-34N 27
Stilling Blvd. NS&EW
............... 31W-34N 27
Stillwell Dr. NE&SW
... 36W-37N,35W-37N 17
Sumac Dr. E&W .. 36W-37N 17
Summervil Av. NE&SW
............... 36W-37N 17
Summit Dr. E&W .. 36W-37N 17
Sunrise Dr. E&W .. 29W-37N 19
Sydenham St. E&W
............... 29W-37N 19
Sylvan Dr. NE&SW 36W-37N 17
Tacoma Dr. EW&NS
... 34W-33N,35W-33N 26
Telegraph Rd. NE&SW
............... 36W-37N 17
Terrace Av. E&W . 30W-36N 19
Thelen Dr. E&W .. 29W-37N 19
Thelen Rd. NE&SW
... 30W-37N,29W-37N 19
Third St. E&W ... 32W-33N 26
Tichfield Ter. . 31W-35N 19
Trey Rd. NW&SE .. 36W-32N 25
Ute Rd. N&S .... 35W-36N 18
Val Ct. N&S .... 30W-33N 27
Vale St. E&W ... 30W-32N 27
Vallelo Ln. N&S .. 31W-34N 27
Valley Av. E&W .. 29W-32N 27
Valley St. E&W ... 30W-32N 27
Vern St. N&S .... 29W-37N 19
Vernon Dr. N&S .. 29W-32N 27
Villa Ln. NW&SE .. 31W-34N 27
Wainwright Dr. NE&SW
............... 36W-37N 17
Walnut Dr. N&S .. 36W-34N 25
Waltshire Dr. N&S . 32W-36N 18
Washington Park NW&SE
............... 31W-34N 27
Washington St. N&S
............... 29W-32N 27
West Blvd. E&W .. 29W-32N 27
West Lake Shore Dr. NE&SW
............... 36W-36N 17
West Shore Dr. E&W
............... 34W-34N 26
West Shore Dr. N&S
............... 36W-36N 17
West St. N&S .... 29W-37N 19
Westmoor Dr. N&S
............... 36W-35N 17
Westwood Dr. N&S
... 29W-36N,29W-37N 19
White Oaks Rd. E&W
... 37W-37N,36W-37N 19
William St. N&S .. 30W-36N 19
Willow Dr. N&S
... 36W-36N,36W-37N 17
Willow Ln. N&S ... 34W-34N 26
Willow St. N&S ... 29W-37N 19
Wilmington Ct. N&S
............... 36W-32N 25
Winnebago Dr. N&S
............... 36W-36N 17
Wonder Lake Dr. N&S
............... 36W-36N 17
Wonder Woods Dr. NE&SW
............... 36W-37N 17
Wonderview Dr.
... 36W-34N,37W-34N 25
Wooded Ln. N&S .. 29W-34N 27
Wooded Shore Dr. E&W
............... 36W-35N 17
Woodland Dr. E&W
............... 34W-34N 26
Woodland Dr. N&S 29W-37N 19
Woodland Ln. NE&SW
............... 31W-33N 27
Woodlane Dr. NE&SW
............... 34W-34N
Woodlawn Park Av. NE&SW
... 31W-33N,31W-34N 27
Woodrow Av. N&S
............... 29W-37N 19
Yorkshire Dr. E&W 32W-37N 18

## Nunda Township

Abendroth Dr. NW&SE
............... 35W-27N 34
Acacia NS&EW ... 34W-28N 34
Acacia Ct. NW&SE 34W-28N 34

| | Grid | Page |
|---|---|---|
| Acorn Ct. N&S | 32W-26N | 42 |
| Allen Av. NS&EW | 31W-30N | 35 |
| Amanda Av. E&W | 29W-31N | 27 |
| Ames Rd. E&W | 33W-28N | 34 |
| Andrea Ln. E&W | 36W-26N | 41 |
| Annette Av. E&W | 33W-26N | 42 |
| Anvil Rd. E&W | 35W-29N | 34 |
| Area St. E&W | 29W-27N | 35 |
| Baldwin Rd. E&W | 31W-30N | 35 |
| Barbara Ln. E&W | 29W-31N | 27 |
| Barreville Rd. N&S | 32W-27N,32W-31N | 34 |
| Bay Rd. N&S | 34W-28N | 34 |
| Beach Av. NS&EW | 30W-29N | 35 |
| Beach Dr. E&W | 32W-31N | 26 |
| Beach St. E&W | 30W-27N | 35 |
| Beach Way NS&EW | 29W-26N,30W-28N | 43 |
| Behan Rd. E&W | 30W-27N | 35 |
| Benbrook Av. N&S | 30W-29N | 35 |
| Bergen Ct. NW&SE | 35W-29N | 34 |
| Bergman Av. N&S | 30W-28N,30W-29N | 35 |
| Bernaise Ct. E&W | 30W-26N | 43 |
| Berry Ct. NW&SE | 35W-29N | 34 |
| Berway Ct. E&W | 30W-26N | 43 |
| Billingsgate Ct. N&S | 36W-31N | 25 |
| Black Partridge Rd. N&S | 31W-30N,31W-31N | 35 |
| Blackhawk Av. N&S | 31W-30N | 35 |
| Blossom St. NW&SE | 30W-28N | 35 |
| Blue Ct. N&S | 32W-26N | 42 |
| Blue Island Av. E&W | 30W-28N | 35 |
| Blue Pine Dr. N&S | 35W-29N,35W-30N | 34 |
| Bluebird Ct. NE&SW | 35W-27N | 34 |
| Bolger Av. E&W | 31W-30N | 35 |
| Bordeaux Ct. E&W | 30W-26N | 43 |
| Brefeld Ct. E&W | 31W-31N | 27 |
| Brentwood Ln. NW&SE | 31W-30N | 35 |
| Briggs Av. NE&SW | 30W-28N | 35 |
| Brittany Dr. N&S | 30W-26N | 43 |
| Buckhorn Dr. NE&SW | 35W-28N | 34 |
| Bull Valley Rd. E&W | 36W-31N,32W-31N | 25 |
| Bur Ln. N&S | 32W-26N | 42 |
| Burton Ter. NW&SE | 30W-28N | 35 |
| Calais Ct. E&W | 30W-26N | 43 |
| Cameron Ct. N&S | 32W-26N | 43 |
| Cape Cove NW&SE | 35W-27N | 34 |
| Carman Av. N&S | 30W-29N | 35 |
| Carolina Av. N&S | 30W-27N | 35 |
| Carraige Dr. E&W | 36W-27N | 33 |
| Carrington Dr. EW&NS | 32W-26N | 42 |
| Carthage Ct. N&S | 33W-27N | 34 |
| Catalpa St. E&W | 29W-27N | 35 |
| Cedar St. E&W | 29W-27N | 35 |
| Cedardel St. E&W | 29W-27N | 35 |
| Channel Ln. NW&SE | 31W-30N | 35 |
| Chatham Ln. N&S | 36W-27N | 33 |
| Cherry Av. N&S | 29W-28N | 35 |
| Cherry Dr. E&W | 30W-27N | 35 |
| Cherry Ln. E&W | 30W-27N | 35 |
| Cherry Ln. N&S | 32W-26N | 42 |
| Cherry Valley Rd. N&S | 36W-27N,36W-29N | 33 |
| Chesterfield Rd. E&W | 36W-27N | 33 |
| Chris Ln. NS&EW | 32W-26N | 42 |
| Christine Dr. E&W | 29W-31N | 27 |
| Coachlight Rd. E&W | 35W-29N | 34 |
| Colby Dr. NW&SE | 31W-29N,30W-29N | 35 |
| Colby Point Rd. E&W | 31W-29N | 35 |
| Colonel Holcomb Dr. NE&SW | 35W-29N | 34 |
| Columbus St. E&W | 29W-31N | 27 |
| Comes Tr. E&W | 30W-31N,29W-31N | 27 |
| Concord Tr. NW&SE | 35W-27N | 34 |
| Connecticut Ct. N&S | 35W-28N | 34 |
| Connecticut Tr. E&W | 35W-27N | 34 |
| Crabapple Ln. E&W | 30W-27N | 35 |
| Crescent Av. NE&SW | 30W-28N | 35 |
| Crescent Dr. NE&SW | 29W-29N | 35 |
| Cristine Dr. E&W | 29W-31N | 27 |
| Croak Av. N&S | 30W-29N | 35 |
| Crockett Ct. E&W | 32W-26N | 42 |
| Crystal Cir. NS&EW | 31W-28N | 35 |
| Crystal Lake Av. E&W | 34W-26N | 42 |
| Crystal Lake Rd. NE&SW | 31W-27N | 34 |
| Crystal Way NS&EW | 31W-28N | 35 |
| Curling Pond Ct. N&S | 35W-28N | 34 |
| Curran Rd. N&S | 35W-31N | 26 |
| Cypress Ct. E&W | 35W-27N | 34 |
| Daisy Ln. N&S | 35W-27N | 34 |
| Dauphine Ct. N&S | 30W-26N | 43 |
| Davis Av. E&W | 30W-29N | 35 |
| Dedlow Rd. N&S | 30W-28N | 35 |
| Dee Dr. E&W | 30W-28N | 35 |
| Deedwood Dr. N&S | 35W-28N | 34 |
| Deering Oaks Ln. E&W | 33W-27N | 34 |
| Deerwood Dr. E&W | 35W-28N | 34 |
| Defiance Rd. NE&SW | 30W-30N,30W-31N | 35 |
| Delmilar Ln. N&S | 30W-25N | 43 |
| Derby Ln. N&S | 36W-27N | 33 |
| Drake Dr. E&W | 33W-27N | 34 |
| Draper Rd. N&S | 35W-31N | 26 |
| Drucker Ln. E&W | 31W-31N | 27 |
| E. Bayview Dr. E&W | 30W-27N | 35 |
| E. Beach St. E&W | 30W-27N | 35 |
| E. Hillside Ct. N&S | 34W-27N | 34 |
| E. Logan St. N&S | 29W-31N | 27 |
| E. Red Barn Rd. E&W | 36W-28N,35W-28N | 33 |
| E. Swarthmore Rd. E&W | 36W-31N | 25 |
| East Dr. N&S | 36W-27N | 33 |
| East Upland Dr. N&S | 35W-27N | 34 |
| Edgewood Rd. E&W | 35W-29N,33W-29N | 34 |
| Edward Dr. E&W | 30W-27N | 35 |
| Ellen Rd. E&W | 32W-31N | 26 |
| Elm St. N&S | 29W-26N | 43 |
| Emerald Av. N&S | 31W-31N | 27 |
| Emerald Ct. E&W | 31W-31N | 27 |
| Emerald Dr. N&S | 31W-31N | 27 |
| Ethel Av. N&S | 33W-26N | 42 |
| Fargo Av. NE&SW | 30W-29N | 35 |
| Federal Ct. NW&SE | 35W-29N | 34 |
| Fernwood Ln. N&S | 31W-30N | 35 |
| Field Ct. NE&SW | 35W-27N | 34 |
| Fir Ct. NE&SW | 35W-27N | 34 |
| Ford Rd. E&W | 31W-31N | 27 |
| Forest Blvd. NW&SE | 29W-26N,29W-27N | 43 |
| Forestview Ct. N&S | 29W-29N | 35 |
| Forestwood Dr. N&S | 29W-29N | 35 |
| Fox Creek Rd. NW&SE | 34W-27N | 34 |
| Fox Ct. NE&SW | 34W-27N | 34 |
| Fox Fire Dr. NS&EW | 36W-28N,35W-28N | 33 |
| Fox River Dr. NW&SE | 30W-27N | 35 |
| Fox Run E&W | 35W-29N | 34 |
| Fox Tr. NS&EW | 34W-27N | 34 |
| Franklin Ct. E&W | 32W-26N | 42 |
| Garden Ln. N&S | 34W-29N | 34 |
| Giant Oak Rd. N&S | 29W-27N | 35 |
| Gieseke Rd. N&S | 32W-26N | 43 |
| Golf Club St. E&W | 30W-26N | 43 |
| Grace St. NW&SE | 31W-30N | 35 |
| Gracy Rd. E&W | 33W-29N,32W-29N | 34 |
| Grand Av. NW&SE | 30W-28N | 35 |
| Great Hill Rd. E&W | 36W-28N,35W-28N | 33 |
| Greening Rd. NW&SE | 31W-30N | 35 |
| Griswold Av. NW&SE | 29W-28N | 35 |
| Hamilton Dr. N&S | 32W-26N | 42 |
| Hanover Dr. NS&EW | 34W-27N | 34 |
| Harriett Ln. NE&SW | 29W-29N | 35 |
| Harvard Circle N&S | 35W-27N | 34 |
| Hawk Av. E&W | 30W-29N | 35 |
| Hawthorne Ct. NE&SW | 30W-28N | 35 |
| Hawthorne Ln. NW&SE | 31W-30N | 35 |
| Hazelwood Ct. NE&SW | 34W-29N | 34 |
| Hazelwood Dr. NW&SE | 34W-29N,35W-29N | 34 |
| Hibiscus Tr. NE&SW | 34W-28N | 34 |
| Hickory Ter. N&S | 30W-27N | 35 |
| Hidden Oak Ct. E&W | 35W-28N | 34 |
| Hidden Oak Dr. NS&EW | 35W-28N | 34 |
| High Point Rd. E&W | 33W-30N | 34 |
| Highland Av. NE&SW | 30W-27N | 35 |
| Highline Rd. E&W | 35W-27N | 34 |
| Highview Dr. NE&SW | 30W-28N | 35 |
| Highwood Rd. N&S | 29W-29N | 35 |
| Hiline Av. N&S | 30W-29N | 35 |
| Hillcrest Dr. E&W | 35W-27N | 34 |
| Hillside Rd. E&W | 36W-27N,35W-27N | 33 |
| Hillside Tr. E&W | 30W-31N,29W-31N | 27 |
| Holly Ln. E&W | 30W-27N | 35 |
| Hythe Cir. NW&SE | 36W-31N | 25 |
| Indian Tr. E&W | 31W-31N | 27 |
| Jasmine Ct. N&S | 34W-28N | 34 |
| Jenny Jae Ln. N&S | 34W-29N | 34 |
| Johnathan Rd. E&W | 31W-30N | 35 |
| Johnson Av. N&S | 30W-28N | 35 |
| Jones Av. E&W | 30W-28N | 35 |
| Jones St. E&W | 30W-29N | 35 |
| Justen Rd. NS&EW | 32W-29N,31W-29N | 34 |
| Keene Av. N&S | 30W-28N,30W-29N | 35 |
| Keene Av. N&S | 30W-29N | 35 |
| Kenilworth Av. N&S | 30W-29N | 35 |
| Kerry Ln. E&W | 30W-29N | 35 |
| Kirsten Tr. N&S | 33W-28N | 34 |
| Laguna Dr. NE&SW | 31W-31N | 27 |
| Lake View Rd. NS&EW | 31W-26N | 43 |
| Lakeshore Dr. NE&SW | 30W-29N | 35 |
| Landl Park Rd. E&W | 29W-31N | 27 |
| Lands Ct. NW&SE | 30W-28N | 35 |
| Larkspur Dr. N&S | 34W-28N | 34 |
| Laurel St. NW&SE | 30W-28N | 35 |
| Lavergne Av. N&S | 30W-27N | 35 |
| Leaf Av. N&S | 29W-28N | 35 |
| Lexington Tr. E&W | 35W-27N | 34 |
| Lilly Ct. NE&SW | 30W-28N | 35 |
| Lily Lake Rd. N&S | 29W-29N,29W-32N | 35 |
| Lincoln Av. NW&SE | 30W-28N | 35 |
| Lincoln St. N&S | 29W-31N | 27 |
| Linden Rd. N&S | 30W-27N | 35 |
| Little Dr. N&S | 29W-27N | 35 |
| Little Fawn Tr. E&W | 36W-28N | 33 |
| Live Oak Rd. NS&EW | 35W-28N | 34 |
| Logan St. N&S | 29W-31N | 27 |
| Longwood Dr. N&S | 29W-29N | 35 |
| Lorraine Ct. NE&SW | 30W-26N | 43 |
| Louise St. E&W | 30W-27N | 35 |
| Low Av. E&W | 30W-29N | 35 |
| Maine Tr. N&S | 35W-27N | 34 |
| Maple Dr. E&W | 29W-27N | 35 |
| Marguerite St. E&W | 30W-27N | 35 |
| Marietta Dr. N&S | 33W-26N | 42 |
| Marlboro Rd. NW&SE | 36W-27N | 33 |
| Mason Hill Rd. E&W | 36W-30N,35W-30N | 33 |
| May St. E&W | 30W-27N | 35 |
| McCabe Av. N&S | 30W-28N | 35 |
| McHenry Dam Rd. NE&SW | 31W-30N | 35 |
| McHenry Dowell Rd. NE&SW | 29W-29N | 35 |
| McMillan Ln. NE&SW | 33W-28N | 34 |
| Meadow Dr. E&W | 35W-27N | 34 |
| Meadow St. N&S | 29W-26N | 43 |
| Meadowlark Ct. NW&SE | 35W-27N | 34 |
| Meadowshire Ln. NE&SW | 36W-27N | 33 |
| Minuteman Ct. E&W | 35W-27N | 34 |
| Misty Pine Ct. E&W | 35W-30N | 34 |
| Monica Tr. E&W | 32W-26N | 42 |
| N.E. Shore Dr. NW&SE | 29W-29N | 35 |
| Nancy Ln. E&W | 29W-31N | 27 |
| Ned Dr. E&W | 32W-26N | 42 |
| Needle Creek Ct. NW&SE | 35W-28N | 34 |
| New Hampshire Tr. E&W | 35W-27N | 34 |
| Nish Rd. E&W | 30W-28N | 35 |
| North Ct. NE&SW | 35W-27N | 34 |
| North East Shore Dr. NW&SE | 29W-29N | 35 |
| North St. E&W | 31W-31N | 27 |
| Nunda Av. N&S | 30W-27N | 35 |
| Nunda Tr. E&W | 34W-27N | 34 |
| Oak Crest Dr. E&W | 33W-27N | 34 |
| Oak Ct. NE&SW | 30W-31N | 27 |
| Oak Ridge Ct. E&W | 36W-28N | 33 |
| Oak Ridge Rd. N&S | 36W-27N,36W-29N | 33 |
| Oak St. E&W | 29W-27N | 35 |
| Oak St. E&W | 36W-26N,36W-27N | 41 |
| Oakwood Dr. EW&NW | 35W-28N,35W-29N | 34 |
| Oakwood Ln. E&W | 36W-26N | 41 |
| Opengate Rd. N&S | 35W-28N,35W-29N | 34 |
| Orchard Ln. E&W | 33W-26N | 42 |
| Orchard Ln. NS&EW | 31W-30N | 35 |
| Orman Av. N&S | 29W-27N | 35 |
| Osage Dr. N&S | 31W-31N | 27 |
| Osceola Av. E&W | 31W-30N | 35 |
| Overland Rd. E&W | 30W-28N | 35 |
| Page Pl. NE&SW | 30W-29N | 35 |
| Palm St. N&S | 29W-26N | 43 |
| Park St. NE&SW | 30W-28N | 35 |
| Parker St. E&W | 30W-29N | 35 |
| Paul St. E&W | 29W-27N | 35 |
| Pesz Rd. N&S | 29W-27N | 35 |
| Peter St. E&W | 29W-27N | 35 |
| Pheasant Run E&W | 36W-29N,35W-29N | 33 |
| Pine St. N&S | 29W-26N | 43 |
| Pleasant Hill Ct. N&S | 34W-28N | 34 |
| Pleasant Hill Rd. E&W | 35W-28N,34W-28N | 34 |
| Plum St. E&W | 29W-28N | 35 |
| Pontiac Av. E&W | 31W-30N | 35 |
| Pony Ln. N&S | 35W-29N | 34 |
| Pool St. N&S | 30W-29N | 35 |
| Poplar St. E&W | 29W-27N | 35 |
| Porten Rd. E&W | 29W-27N | 35 |
| Prairie Ridge Rd. N&S | 33W-26N | 42 |
| Prairie St. E&W | 31W-30N | 35 |
| Pueblo Dr. E&W | 31W-31N | 27 |
| Pueblo Dr. NW&SE | 31W-31N | 27 |
| Purdue Pl. N&S | 33W-27N | 34 |
| Raintree Dr. E&W | 35W-30N | 34 |
| Ravenglass Ridge N&S | 36W-28N | 33 |
| Ravine Dr. NE&SW | 36W-27N | 33 |
| Rawson Bridge Rd. NE&SW | 30W-26N,29W-26N | 43 |
| Ray St. E&W | 33W-26N | 42 |
| Red Barn Rd. N&S | 36W-28N,36W-29N | 33 |
| Redbird Ln. E&W | 35W-27N | 34 |
| Redoak Dr. NW&SE | 36W-27N | 33 |
| Reiland Dr. E&W | 33W-26N | 42 |
| Remington Dr. NW&SE | 32W-26N,31W-26N | 42 |
| Rhode Island Tr. E&W | 35W-27N | 34 |
| Rigby Rd. NE&SW | 36W-27N | 33 |
| Ripon Rd. N&S | 33W-27N | 34 |
| River Rd. E&W | 31W-30N,29W-29N | 35 |
| River St. N&S | 29W-26N,29W-27N | 43 |
| Riverdale Rd. N&S | 30W-28N | 35 |
| Riverside Dr. NW&SE | 31W-30N,30W-27N | 35 |
| Roberts Rd. N&S | 29W-27N | 35 |
| Robin Ln. N&S | 30W-28N | 35 |
| Rockspur Tr. NS&EW | 34W-28N | 34 |
| Roger Rd. N&S | 33W-28N | 34 |
| Rona Rd. E&W | 31W-25N | 43 |
| Royal Woods Dr. E&W | 32W-26N | 43 |
| Rt. 176 NE&SW | 34N-26N,29W-28N | 42 |
| Rt. 31 N&S | 33W-26N,32W-31N | 42 |
| Running Iron Dr. NW&SE | 35W-29N,34W-29N | 34 |
| Russet Dr. NS&EW | 31W-30N | 35 |
| S. Great Hill Rd. NS&EW | 36W-28N,35W-28N | 33 |
| S. Shenandoah Dr. N&S | 35W-28N | 34 |
| Sauk Dr. N&S | 31W-31N | 27 |
| Sauk Tr. N&S | 31W-31N | 27 |
| Scarlet Tr. E&W | 32W-26N | 42 |
| Scheid Ln. NE&SW | 29W-29N | 35 |
| Schroder Rd. N&S | 33W-30N | 34 |
| Sequoia Tr. E&W | 34W-27N | 34 |
| Sessions Ct. N&S | 36W-27N | 33 |
| Sessions Walk NW&SE | 36W-27N | 33 |
| Shadowood Dr. NS&EW | 34W-28N | 34 |
| Shady Dr. NS&EW | 30W-31N | 27 |
| Shady Oaks Ln. E&W | 33W-27N | 34 |
| Shall Ln. E&W | 29W-29N | 35 |
| Shenandoah Ct. E&W | 35W-28N | 34 |
| Shenandoah Dr. E&W | 35W-28N | 34 |
| Sheridan Rd. E&W | 29W-31N | 27 |
| Sherman Blvd. E&W | 30W-27N | 35 |
| Sherwood Dr. N&S | 35W-27N | 34 |
| Silver Lake Rd. N&S | 31W-26N | 43 |
| Skyline Dr. N&S | 31W-30N | 35 |
| Skyline Ln. N&S | 35W-29N | 34 |
| Sloan Ln. N&S | 32W-26N | 42 |
| Smith Rd. N&S | 33W-26N | 42 |
| Smoke Tree Ln. NW&SE | 35W-28N | 34 |
| South St. E&W | 30W-28N | 35 |
| Spring Blvd. E&W | 35W-28N,34W-28N | 34 |
| Spring Brook Rd. N&S | 35W-28N,35W-29N | 34 |
| Spy Glass Ridge N&S | 35W-28N | 34 |
| Stanford St. N&S | 33W-27N | 34 |
| State Park Rd. E&W | 32W-30N | 34 |
| State Rd. NE&SW | 30W-28N | 35 |
| Steuben Rd. E&W | 29W-31N | 27 |
| Stilling Ln. NE&SW | 31W-29N | 35 |
| Stonegate Dr. N&S | 36W-28N,36W-29N | 33 |
| Stonewier Pt. NS&EW | 36W-31N | 25 |
| Strong Rd. E&W | 33W-26N | 42 |
| Sumac Av. N&S | 29W-31N | 27 |
| Surf St. E&W | 30W-29N | 35 |
| Sutton Ct. E&W | 31W-31N | 27 |
| Sweet Bay Dr. E&W | 35W-30N | 34 |
| Tamarisk Ct. NE&SW | 34W-28N | 34 |
| Tamarisk Tr. NS&EW | 34W-28N | 34 |
| Tecoma Dr. NS&EW | 34W-28N | 34 |
| Tecumseh Av. NW&SE | 31W-30N | 35 |
| Tecumseh Ln. NW&SE | 31W-30N | 35 |
| Terra Cotta Av. E&W | 32W-26N,31W-26N | 42 |
| Terra Cotta Rd. N&S | 34W-26N,34W-28N | 42 |
| Terry Av. E&W | 32W-26N | 42 |
| Thomas Ct. N&S | 29W-29N | 35 |
| Tilche Ln. E&W | 32W-26N | 42 |
| Tile Line Dr. N&S | 35W-27N | 34 |
| Timber Tr. E&W | 29W-27N | 35 |
| Timberlane Rd. N&S | 30W-27N | 35 |
| Totem Tr. N&S | 31W-31N | 27 |
| Tree Av. NE&SW | 30W-29N | 35 |
| Tulip St. N&S | 30W-28N | 35 |
| U.S. Route 14 NW&SE | 36W-26N | 41 |
| Valley Rd. N&S | 36W-29N,36W-30N | 33 |
| Vaupell Av. N&S | 30W-29N,29W-29N | 35 |
| Vermont Tr. E&W | 35W-27N | 34 |
| Vine Ln. N&S | 35W-29N | 34 |
| Virginia Ln. E&W | 30W-27N | 35 |
| W. Beach St. E&W | 30W-27N | 35 |
| W. Fargo Av. NE&SW | 30W-29N | 35 |
| W. Parker St. E&W | 30W-29N | 35 |
| Walking Ridge N&S | 36W-28N | 33 |
| Walkup Ln. E&W | 35W-27N | 34 |
| Walkup Rd. N&S | 35W-27N,35W-29N | 34 |
| Walnut Ct. NE&SW | 30W-28N | 35 |
| Walnut Manor Ct. NW&SE | 35W-29N | 34 |
| Walnut St. E&W | 29W-26N | 43 |
| Waterview Av. N&S | 30W-28N | 35 |
| Wauconda Rd. NE&SW | 30W-28N | 35 |
| Wayside Dr. N&S | 29W-27N | 35 |
| Weatherstone Dr. E&W | 33W-26N | 42 |
| Weathervane Ln. N&S | 36W-28N | 33 |
| Wegner Rd. E&W | 29W-31N | 27 |
| West Justen Rd. E&W | 32W-29N | 34 |
| West Upland Dr. N&S | 35W-27N | 34 |
| Western Av. E&W | 30W-29N | 35 |
| Whipporwill Dr. E&W | 30W-27N | 35 |
| White Ash Dr. E&W | 33W-26N | 42 |
| White Barn Rd. E&W | 36W-28N | 33 |
| Wild Ash Ln. N&S | 34W-28N | 34 |
| Wild Olive Ln. E&W | 34W-28N | 34 |
| Wild Plum Dr. NE&SW | 33W-26N | 42 |
| Wildcherry Rd. N&S | 35W-27N | 34 |
| Wilderness Ridge N&S | 35W-28N | 34 |
| Wildwood Dr. N&S | 29W-27N | 35 |
| Wildwood Dr. NE&SW | 30W-27N | 35 |
| Wisteria Dr. NW&SE | 34W-28N | 34 |
| Wood St. E&W | 30W-28N,29W-28N | 35 |
| Woods Av. N&S | 30W-28N | 35 |
| Woods End N&S | 36W-28N | 33 |
| Wright Av. E&W | 29W-27N | 35 |
| Wright Rd. NW&SE | 31W-29N,30W-28N | 35 |
| Wyandotte Av. E&W | 31W-30N | 35 |
| Wyoming Way N&S | 33W-27N | 34 |
| Yuma Tr. NW&SE | 31W-31N | 27 |
| 1st St. E&W | 29W-29N | 35 |

## Oakwood Hills

| | | |
|---|---|---|
| Acorn Ln. N&S | 31W-25N | 43 |
| Ash Dr. N&S | 31W-26N | 43 |
| Birch Ln. NS&EW | 31W-26N | 43 |
| Burwood Rd. N&S | 31W-26N | 43 |
| Deer Tr. N&S | 31W-26N | 43 |
| East Park Ln. E&W | 31W-26N | 43 |
| Echo Hill Dr. N&S | 31W-26N | 43 |
| Elm Rd. NE&SW | 31W-26N | 43 |
| Fawn Ridge Dr. NS&EW | 31W-26N | 43 |
| Fenview Ct. E&W | 31W-26N | 43 |
| Greenview Rd. N&S | 31W-26N | 43 |
| Hickory Rd. N&S | 31W-26N | 43 |
| Hilltop Rd. N&S | 31W-26N | 43 |
| Lake Ln. NE&SW | 31W-26N | 43 |
| Lake Shore Dr. N&S | 31W-26N | 43 |
| Lakeview NW&SE | 31W-26N | 43 |
| Lakewood Dr. N&S | 31W-26N | 43 |
| Meadow Ln. N&S | 31W-26N | 43 |

| Street | Grid | Page |
|---|---|---|
| North Park Dr. E&W | 31W-26N | 43 |
| North Shore Dr. E&W | 31W-26N | 43 |
| Oak Dr. N&S | 31W-25N | 43 |
| Oak Hill Rd. E&W | 31W-26N | 43 |
| Oak Park Rd. N&S | 31W-26N | 43 |
| Oakwood Dr. N&S | 31W-26N | 43 |
| Palisades Ln. NE&SW | 31W-26N | 43 |
| Sherwood Trail E&W | 31W-26N | 43 |
| Spruce Rd. E&W | 31W-26N | 43 |
| Valley Dr. N&S | 31W-26N | 43 |
| West Lake Shore Dr. N&S | 31W-26N | 43 |
| West Park Ln. E&W | 31W-26N | 43 |
| Woodland Rd. E&W | 31W-25N | 43 |
| Woodland Rd., W. E&W | 31W-26N | 43 |
| Woody Way N&S | 31W-26N | 43 |

## Prairie Grove

| Street | Grid | Page |
|---|---|---|
| Ames Rd. E&W | 33W-28N,32W-28N | 34 |
| Barreville Rd. N&S | 32W-27N,32W-29N | 34 |
| Behan Rd. E&W | 31W-27N | 35 |
| Buhl Rd. N&S | 31W-27N | 35 |
| Carlisle Ct. N&S | 32W-27N | 34 |
| Crystal Cir. NS&EW | 31W-28N | 35 |
| Crystal Lake Rd. E&W | 32W-27N,31W-27N | 34 |
| Crystal Way NS&EW | 31W-28N | 35 |
| Eric St. E&W | 32W-27N | 34 |
| Erin Ct. NE&SW | 32W-27N | 34 |
| Fawn Tr. NS&EW | 31W-28N | 35 |
| Fawn Trail Ct. NW&SE | 31W-28N | 35 |
| Fox Ct. E&W | 31W-28N | 35 |
| Gracy Rd. E&W | 32W-29N | 34 |
| Hillview Dr. N&S | 31W-28N | 35 |
| Kame Dr. E&W | 31W-28N | 35 |
| N. Brighton Ln. N&S | 33W-27N | 34 |
| N. Tamarack Tr. NW&SE | 32W-27N | 34 |
| Niblick Ct. NS&EW | 31W-27N,31W-28N | 35 |
| Nish Rd. E&W | 31W-28N | 35 |
| Oak Knoll North Rd. E&W | 32W-27N | 34 |
| Oak Knoll South Rd. E&W | 32W-27N | 34 |
| Red Bud Ct. NW&SE | 32W-27N | 34 |
| Rt. 176 E&W | 32W-27N | 34 |
| S. Tamarack Tr. NW&SE | 32W-27N | 34 |
| Squaw Creek Rd. NE&SW | 33W-28N | 34 |
| Stratford Rd. NW&SE | 33W-27N,32W-27N | 34 |
| Sutton Woods Ct. E&W | 31W-28N | 35 |
| Sutton Woods Dr. N&S | 31W-28N | 35 |
| Tamarack Cir. NS&EW | 32W-27N | 34 |
| Tamarack Ct. NW&SE | 32W-27N | 34 |
| Tamarack Ct. NW&SE | 32W-27N | 34 |
| Timber Trail Dr. E&W | 31W-28N | 35 |
| Valley View Rd. N&S | 32W-27N,32W-28N | 35 |
| Victoria Ln. N&S | 33W-27N | 34 |
| West Justen Rd. E&W | 32W-29N,31W-29N | 34 |
| White Oak Ct. NW&SE | 32W-27N | 34 |
| Wirth Tr. NS&EW | 32W-28N | 34 |
| Wright Rd. E&W | 32W-29N,31W-29N | 34 |

## Richmond

| Street | Grid | Page |
|---|---|---|
| Ami Dr. NW&SE | 34W-42N,34W-43N | 10 |
| Broadway St. E&W | 34W-42N | 10 |
| Charles St. N&S | 34W-41N,34W-42N | 10 |
| Circle Dr. NW&SE | 34W-41N | 10 |
| Commercial St. NW&SE | 34W-42N,34W-43N | 10 |
| Covell St. N&S | 34W-42N | 10 |
| East St. N&S | 34W-42N | 10 |
| Elm St. E&W | 34W-42N | 10 |
| Foundry Dr. N&S | 34W-42N | 10 |
| Front St. E&W | 34W-42N | 10 |
| George St. E&W | 34W-42N | 10 |
| Golf Av. N&S | 34W-41N | 10 |
| Hillcrest Dr. E&W | 34W-41N | 10 |
| Hunter Dr. E&W | 34W-41N | 10 |
| Kenosha St. E&W | 34W-42N | 10 |
| Liberty St. E&W | 34W-42N | 10 |
| Maiden Ln. N&S | 34W-41N | 10 |
| Main St. N&S | 34W-41N,34W-42N | 10 |
| Market St. E&W | 34W-42N | 10 |
| May Av. E&W | 34W-41N | 10 |
| Mayline Av. N&S | 34W-41N | 10 |
| Mayview St. E&W | 34W-42N | 10 |
| Mayzing St. E&W | 34W-43N | 10 |
| McDonnell Dr. N&S | 34W-42N | 10 |
| Mill St. E&W | 34W-42N | 10 |
| Milwaukee St. E&W | 34W-42N | 10 |
| Nippersink Dr. NW&SE | 34W-41N | 10 |
| North Ln. N&S | 34W-41N | 10 |
| Prairie Ridge Dr. NW&SE | 34W-41N | 10 |
| Rt. 31 N&S | 34W-41N,34W-43N | 10 |
| Rt.173 E&W | 35W-42N,31W-42N | 10 |
| South St. E&W | 34W-42N | 10 |
| Valley Dr. E&W | 34W-41N | 10 |
| Walnut St. E&W | 34W-42N | 10 |
| West St. N&S | 34W-42N | 10 |
| William St. N&S | 34W-42N | 10 |
| Wilson Rd. E&W | 34W-43N | 10 |

## Richmond Township

| Street | Grid | Page |
|---|---|---|
| Arthur Dr. N&S | 32W-40N | 10 |
| Barnard Mill Rd. NW&SE | 36W-38N | 17 |
| Bonnie Brae Dr. NE&SW | 34W-41N,33W-41N | 10 |
| Broadway Rd. NW&SE | 35W-42N,34W-42N | 10 |
| Burgett Rd. E&W | 36W-43N | 9 |
| Burlington Rd. NE&SW | 33W-43N,33W-44N | 10 |
| Clark Rd. N&S | 32W-40N,32W-42N | 10 |
| Concord Ln. E&W | 33W-41N | 10 |
| East Solon Rd. E&W | 32W-39N,31W-39N | 10 |
| East St. N&S | 32W-39N | 10 |
| Falcon St. NS&EW | 33W-41N | 10 |
| Foxboro Tr. NE&SW | 33W-41N | 10 |
| Gardner St. N&S | 33W-39N | 10 |
| Glacier Ridge Dr. N&S | 33W-41N | 10 |
| Grant St. N&S | 32W-43N | 10 |
| Harding Av. E&W | 32W-43N | 10 |
| Harts Rd. E&W | 34W-38N,33W-38N | 18 |
| Hideaway Ln. NE&SW | 33W-41N | 10 |
| Hill Rd. E&W | 34W-41N,33W-41N | 10 |
| Hillandale Rd. NS&EW | 33W-41N | 10 |
| Hillendale Ln. NW&SE | 33W-41N | 10 |
| Hillshire Dr., W. NS&EW | 33W-41N | 10 |
| John St. NE&SW | 33W-39N,32W-39N | 10 |
| Keith Dr. NS&EW | 32W-40N | 10 |
| Keystone Rd. N&S | 36W-38N,36W-43N | 17 |
| Kuhn Rd. E&W | 34W-40N,33W-40N | 10 |
| Lakeview Rd. N&S | 32W-42N,32W-43N | 10 |
| Lincoln Av. E&W | 32W-43N | 10 |
| Macwood Dr. E&W | 34W-40N,33W-40N | 10 |
| May Ln. E&W | 32W-39N | 10 |
| Mayline Av. N&S | 34W-41N | 10 |
| Meyer Rd. N&S | 31W-38N,31W-39N | 19 |
| Mill Rd. E&W | 32W-40N | 10 |
| Mill St. N&S | 32W-39N | 10 |
| Miller Rd. E&W | 32W-38N,31W-38N | 18 |
| Norgard Rd. E&W | 36W-41N | 9 |
| North Solon Rd. N&S | 33W-40N,33W-42N | 10 |
| North St. NE&SW | 32W-39N | 10 |
| Oak St. N&S | 33W-39N | 10 |
| Oakhill Dr. NS&EW | 36W-38N | 17 |
| Overlook Dr. E&W | 32W-43N | 10 |
| Overton Dr. E&W | 32W-40N | 10 |
| Penny Ln. N&S | 33W-40N | 10 |
| Pioneer Rd. NW&SE | 33W-38N,34W-39N | 18 |
| Private Rd. E&W | 36W-39N,35W-39N | 9 |
| Prospect St. E&W | 34W-41N | 10 |
| Rt. 12 NS&EW | 34W-41N,32W-39N | 10 |
| Rt. 31 N&S | 34W-38N,34W-41N | 18 |
| South Solon Rd. N&S | 33W-38N,33W-39N | 18 |
| Spring Grove Rd. N&S | 31W-38N | 19 |
| Squires Green NS&EW | 33W-41N | 10 |
| State Line Rd. E&W | 32W-43N,31W-43N | 10 |
| Sunset Rd. E&W | 31W-38N | 19 |
| Taft St. N&S | 32W-43N | 10 |
| Tracy Ct. NS&EW | 33W-40N | 10 |
| Tryon Grove Rd. NE&SW | 36W-39N,34W-40N | 9 |
| Valentine Ct. NE&SW | 36W-38N | 17 |
| West Solon Rd. E&W | 34W-39N,33W-39N | 10 |
| White St. E&W | 39W-34N,32W-39N | 10 |
| Winn Rd. N&S | 31W-40N,31W-42N | 11 |
| Zarnstorf Rd. N&S | 31W-42N,31W-43N | 11 |

## Riley Township

| Street | Grid | Page |
|---|---|---|
| Acorn Ln. NE&SW | 50W-24N | 37 |
| Alta Dr. N&S | 54W-23N | 44 |
| Anthony Rd. E&W | 52W-22N | 44 |
| Anthony Rd. E&W | 50W-22N | 45 |
| Bass Tr. NE&SW | 50W-25N | 37 |
| Beck Rd. E&W | 49W-22N | 45 |
| Beth Ct. E&W | 49W-25N | 37 |
| Blisdale Rd. N&S | 52W-23N,52W-25N | 45 |
| Burma Rd. N&S | 54W-23N,54W-26N | 44 |
| Burrows Rd. N&S | 53W-20N | 44 |
| Carls Rd. N&S | 51W-21N | 45 |
| Coon Creek Rd. N&S | 50W-20N | 45 |
| Coral Oaks Dr. NW&SE | 50W-24N | 37 |
| County Line Rd. N&S | 54W-20N,54W-25N | 44 |
| Debbie Ln. N&S | 50W-25N | 37 |
| Delks Dr. E&W | 49W-23N | 45 |
| Demings Dr. E&W | 49W-23N | 45 |
| Genoa Rd. N&S | 54W-20N | 44 |
| Getty Rd. N&S | 49W-20N | 45 |
| Grange Rd. E&W | 54W-23N,50W-23N | 44 |
| Grange Rd. E&W | 50W-23N | 45 |
| Grossen Rd. E&W | 50W-21N | 45 |
| Hartman Rd. E&W | 52W-21N | 44 |
| Hartman Rd. E&W | 50W-20N | 45 |
| Helen St. E&W | 54W-23N | 44 |
| Hennig Dr. EW&NS | 50W-25W | 37 |
| Hill Rd. N&S | 49W-23N,49W-24N | 45 |
| Johnson Rd. N&S | 52W-25N | 36 |
| Lakewood Dr. NE&SW | 51W-25N,50W-25N | 36 |
| Maple Rd. N&S | 49W-22N,49W-25N | 45 |
| Maple St. N&S | 49W-25N | 37 |
| Marjorie Dr. N&S | 54W-24N | 36 |
| Mary St. E&W | 54W-23N | 44 |
| McKeowin Rd. N&S | 54W-22N | 44 |
| Meyer Rd. N&S | 51W-25N | 36 |
| Northwest Tollway NW&SE | 54W-23N | 44 |
| Northwest Tollway NW&SE | 50W-21N | 45 |
| Norway Ct. E&W | 50W-20N | 45 |
| O'Connell Dr. E&W | 50W-25N | 37 |
| Oak Creek Dr. E&W | 50W-24N | 37 |
| Paulson Dr. NS&EW | 50W-25N | 37 |
| Payne Rd. N&S | 51W-20N | 45 |
| Peggy Ct. NW&SE | 50W-25N | 37 |
| Pleasant Grove Rd. NW&SE | 52W-25N,50W-24N | 36 |
| Poplar Rd. E&W | 54W-20N | 44 |
| Poplar Rd. E&W | 51W-20N | 45 |
| Ratfield Rd. E&W | 50W-25N | 37 |
| Ratfield Rd. NW&SE | 49W-25N | 37 |
| Riley Dr. N&S | 49W-25N | 37 |
| Riley Harmony Rd. E&W | 53W-22N | 44 |
| Riley Harmony Rd. E&W | 50W-22N | 45 |
| Riley Rd. N&S | 51W-22N | 45 |
| Rt. 23 N&S | 50W-23N,50W-25N | 45 |
| Rudolph Rd. E&W | 54W-20N | 44 |
| Weiss Tr. EW&NS | 50W-25N | 37 |
| West Coral Rd. E&W | 50W-24N,49W-24N | 37 |
| Wildrose Ln. NS&EW | 52W-23N | 44 |

## Ringwood

| Street | Grid | Page |
|---|---|---|
| Barnard Mill Rd. NW&SE | 33W-36N,35W-37N | 18 |
| Craftwell Dr. E&W | 34W-37N | 18 |
| Mann Dr. NE&SW | 34W-37N | 18 |
| Monroe St. NW&SE | 33W-36N | 18 |
| Oak Rd. N&S | 35W-36N,35W-37N | 18 |
| Ridgeway Rd. N&S | 35W-36N,35W-37N | 18 |
| Ringwood Rd. NE&SW | 33W-36N,35W-37N | 18 |
| Route 31 NS&NE | 33W-36N,34W-37N | 18 |
| School Rd. N&S | 34W-36N | 18 |
| Van Buren St. N&S | 33W-36N | 18 |

## Seneca Township

| Street | Grid | Page |
|---|---|---|
| Alpine Ln. NS&EW | 43W-30N,43W-31N | 31 |
| Athy Ct. NW&SE | 47W-28N | 30 |
| Athy Ln. NS&EW | 47W-28N | 30 |
| Blackhawk Ln. N&S | 47W-31N | 22 |
| Bockman Rd. NS&EW | 48W-29N,47W-29N | 30 |
| Charlotte Dr. E&W | 43W-28N | 31 |
| Collins Rd. E&W | 48W-30N,45W-30N | 30 |
| Davis Rd. E&W | 43W-30N | 31 |
| Deer Path Tr. E&W | 47W-29N | 30 |
| Dimmel Rd. N&S | 46W-31N | 22 |
| Dunham Rd. N&S | 47W-26N | 38 |
| Elaine Dr. N&S | 43W-28N | 31 |
| Emery Ln. EW&NS | 43W-26N | 39 |
| Fox Farm Rd. E&W | 46W-31N | 30 |
| Franklinville Rd. N&S | 45W-27N,45W-29N | 31 |
| Garden Valley Rd. E&W | 46W-28N,45W-28N | 31 |
| Gee Rd. N&S | 44W-27N,44W-28N | 31 |
| Hiawatha Ln. N&S | 47W-31N | 22 |
| Highbridge Rd. E&W | 46W-26N | 38 |
| Hobe Rd. N&S | 45W-30N,44W-31N | 31 |
| Hughes Rd. N&S | 45W-31N | 23 |
| Kilkee Ln. NE&SW | 47W-28N | 30 |
| Kishwaukee St. N&S | 48W-27N | 30 |
| Kishwaukee Valley Rd. E&W | 48W-31N,43W-31N | 22 |
| Kunde Rd. E&W | 47W-27N,45W-27N | 30 |
| Macintyre Ln. E&W | 44W-31N | 23 |
| McKinstry Rd. NS&EW | 47W-31N,46W-31N | 22 |
| Millstream Rd. E&W | 47W-29N | 30 |
| Millstream Rd. N&S | 47W-24N,47W-28N | 38 |
| Mohawk Ln. E&W | 47W-31N | 22 |
| North Union Rd. N&S | 46W-26N,46W-28N | 38 |
| O'Clock Rd. E&W | 47W-26N,46W-26N | 38 |
| Perkins Rd. E&W | 44W-28N,43W-28N | 31 |
| Peterson-Olson Rd. N&S | 45W-26N | 39 |
| Pleasant Valley Rd. E&W | 45W-26N,43W-26N | 39 |
| River Rd. NW&SE | 48W-28N,47W-27N | 30 |
| Rose Farm Rd. NE&SW | 44W-30N,43W-31N | 31 |
| Rt. 176 E&W | 48W-27N,44W-27N | 30 |
| Sally Cir. E&W | 43W-28N | 31 |
| Sandhill Rd. E&W | 47W-28N | 30 |
| Secor Rd. E&W | 46W-29N,45W-29N | 30 |
| Shannon Dr. N&S | 43W-31N | 23 |
| South St. E&W | 44W-30N,43W-30N | 31 |
| Standish Rd. N&S | 48W-28N,48W-29N | 30 |
| Steig Rd. N&S | 43W-28N,43W-29N | 31 |
| Stieg Rd. N&S | 43W-28N29N | 31 |
| Sullivan Rd. N&S | 47W-30N | 30 |
| Sunnyside Rd. N&S | 43W-26N,43W-28N | 39 |
| Sylvia Ln. N&S | 43W-29N | 31 |
| Timber Ln. NS&EW | 43W-26N | 39 |
| Vermont Rd. N&S | 46W-28N,46W-30N | 30 |
| Woodcliff Dr. N&S | 47W-29N | 30 |
| Woodland Tr. E&W | 47W-29N | 30 |

## Spring Grove

| Street | Grid | Page |
|---|---|---|
| Alexa Ct. N&S | 30W-43N | 11 |
| Altamonte Dr. N&S | 31W-40N | 11 |
| Amanda Dr. E&W | 31W-40N | 11 |
| Amy Av. NE&SW | 30W-43N | 11 |
| Anthony Ln. N&S | 29W-40N,29W-41N | 11 |
| Asbury Ct. N&S | 30W-39N | 11 |
| Ascot Ln. NS&EW | 31W-42N | 11 |
| Aspen Ct. N&S | 30W-38N | 19 |
| Baccus Ln. NW&SE | 30W-43N | 11 |
| Beach St. E&W | 30W-38N | 19 |
| Belvin St. N&S | 30W-39N | 11 |
| Bentley Ln. N&S | 29W-40N,29W-41N | 11 |
| Blivin St. N&S | 31W-39N,30W-39N | 11 |
| Bradley Ct. E&W | 30W-39N | 11 |
| Breezy Lawn Rd. NS&EW | 30W-43N | 11 |
| Broadview Ct. N&S | 31W-39N | 11 |
| Carmel Ct. NW&SE | 31W-40N,31W-41N | 11 |
| Catalpa Ct. N&S | 30W-38N | 19 |
| Cedar Ct. E&W | 30W-39N | 11 |
| Cedar Ln. E&W | 30W-39N | 11 |
| Champion St. NE&SW | 31W-41N | 11 |
| Chateaugay Dr. E&W | 30W-41N | 11 |
| Chelmsford Dr. E&W | 32W-39N | 10 |
| Cherrywood Ln. N&S | 30W-38N | 19 |
| Christina Ct. NE&SW | 31W-41N | 11 |
| Coventry Dr. N&S | 32W-39N | 10 |
| Dale Ct. NW&SE | 30W-41N | 11 |
| Deer Trail Dr. N&S | 31W-40N | 11 |
| Deerpath Rd. NS&EW | 32W-39N | 11 |
| Dolder Ln. E&W | 29W-40N | 11 |
| E. Applewood Ln. N&S | 30W-38N | 19 |
| East Ct. N&S | 30W-39N | 11 |
| East St. N&S | 30W-39N | 11 |
| Edgewood Ct. NE&SW | 31W-39N | 11 |
| Edgewood Dr. N&S | 32W-38N | 18 |
| Elizabeth Ln. N&S | 29W-41N | 11 |
| Elk Ct. NW&SE | 31W-40N | 11 |
| Elk Dr. E&W | 31W-40N | 11 |
| Elm St. E&W | 30W-38N | 19 |
| Ember Ln. E&W | 29W-40N | 11 |
| English Prairie Rd. E&W | 31W-42N | 11 |
| Erie Av. E&W | 30W-43N | 11 |
| Falcon Ln. NS&EW | 31W-42N | 11 |
| Finch St. N&S | 31W-39N | 11 |
| Fox Bluff Ln. EW&NS | 31W-42N | 11 |
| Fox Trail Dr. N&S | 30W-41N | 11 |
| Galleria Ct. N&S | 31W-40N | 11 |
| Greenleaf Ct. E&W | 32W-38N | 10 |
| Hatchery Rd. NW&SE | 31W-39N | 11 |
| Hawthorn Ln. N&S | 30W-38N,30W-39N | 11 |
| Hidden Tr. E&W | 31W-40N | 11 |
| Hidden Trail Ct. SW&NE | 31W-40N | 11 |
| Highview St. E&W | 31W-39N | 11 |
| Hillside Ridge Rd. NS&EW | 32W-39N | 10 |
| Holian Dr. E&W | 30W-39N | 11 |
| Hunters Ct. NE&SW | 30W-41N | 11 |
| Hunters Ln. EW&NS | 31W-41N,30W-41N | 11 |
| Huron Dr. N&S | 30W-43N | 11 |
| Industrial Ct. N&S | 31W-39N | 11 |
| Judge Ct. NE&SW | 31W-41N | 11 |
| Kings Lair Dr. E&W | 32W-39N | 11 |
| Lair Dr. E&W | 32W-39N | 10 |
| Lone Oak Rd. N&S | 31W-39N | 11 |
| Loraine St. N&S | 30W-39N | 11 |
| Main St. NW&SE | 30W-39N | 11 |
| Marie Ct. N&S | 31W-40N | 11 |
| Marie Dr. N&S | 31W-40N | 11 |
| Martin Dr. E&W | 31W-41N | 11 |
| Maureen Dr. N&S | 31W-40N | 11 |
| May Ln. NE&SW | 32W-39N | 10 |
| Mayo Ct. NE&SW | 30W-39N | 11 |
| Meadowdale Cir. NS&EW | 30W-41N | 11 |
| Meyer Rd. N&S | 31W-39N | 11 |
| Michigan Dr. EW&NS | 30W-43N | 11 |
| Monterra Dr. E&W | 31W-40N | 11 |
| N. Applewood Ln. E&W | 30W-38N | 19 |
| N. Martin Dr. N&S | 31W-41N | 11 |
| Nicholas Ln. EW&NS | 29W-41N | 11 |
| Nora Way N&S | 31W-40N | 11 |
| North St. E&W | 30W-40N | 11 |
| Oak St. E&W | 30W-39N | 11 |
| Oak Valley Dr. NW&SE | 31W-40N | 11 |
| Ontario Av. E&W | 30W-43N | 11 |
| Overlook Dr. N&S | 32W-38N | 18 |
| Oxfordshire Ln. E&W | 32W-39N | 10 |
| Pater Ct. N&S | 31W-40N | 11 |
| Pierce Dr. E&W | 31W-39N | 11 |
| Pierceshire Rd. N&S | 32W-39N | 10 |
| Pine St. E&W | 30W-38N | 19 |
| Pinecrest Ct. E&W | 31W-40N | 11 |
| Polaris Rd. NW&SE | 30W-42N | 11 |
| Ponder Pl. N&S | 30W-41N | 11 |
| Rabbit Ct. E&W | 31W-40N | 11 |
| Reiger Ct. NE&SW | 30W-43N | 11 |
| Richardson Rd. N&S | 30W-40N,30W-41N | 11 |
| Ridge Ct. N&S | 32W-39N | 10 |
| Ridge Rd. E&W | 32W-39N | 10 |
| Robin Ct. NE&SW | 32W-39N | 10 |
| Rolling Oaks Dr. NS&EW | 31W-39N | 11 |
| Rondi Ct. E&W | 31W-39N | 11 |
| Rudolph Ct. NE&SW | 30W-42N | 11 |
| S. Hunters Ln. E&W | 30W-41N | 11 |
| S. Springdale Dr. E&W | 31W-41N,30W-41N | 11 |
| Sherwood Forest Dr. E&W | 32W-39N | 10 |
| Short St. N&S | 31W-39N | 11 |
| Spring Ct. E&W | 30W-41N | 11 |
| Spring Grove Rd. NW&SE | 30W-39N | 11 |
| Spring Leaf Rd. E&W | 31W-39N | 11 |
| Springdale Dr. N&S | 30W-41N | 11 |
| Spruce St. E&W | 30W-38N | 19 |
| Squirrel Dr. NW&SE | 31W-40N | 11 |
| Steeplechase Ct. SW&NE | 31W-42N | 11 |
| Steeplechase Ln. NS&EW | 31W-42N | 11 |
| Sunset Dr. E&W | 30W-38N | 19 |
| Sunset Rd. E&W | 30W-38N | 19 |
| Superior Ct. E&W | 30W-40N | 11 |
| Superior Ln. E&W | 30W-43N | 11 |
| Suzanne Ct. E&W | 29W-41N | 11 |
| Suzanne Dr. E&W | 29W-41N,30W-41N | 11 |
| Tahoe Ln. NE&SW | 31W-40N | 11 |
| Tallgrass Ct. N&S | 32W-38N | 18 |
| U.S. Route 12 E&W | 31W-39N | 11 |

Utility Ct. N&S......31W-39N 11
Vineyard Ln. NS&EW
........30W-43N 11
W. Applewood Ln. N&S
........30W-38N 19
W. Deer Trail. NW&SE
........31W-40N 11
Walnut Ct. NW&SE
........30W-38N 19
Westward Dr. E&W
........31W-39N 11
Wilmont Farm Dr. E&W
........29W-41N,30W-41N 11
Wilmot Rd. N&S ...39W-40N 11
Winn Rd. N&S
........31W-39N,31W-41N 11
Wintergreen Dr. N&S
........30W-41N 11
Woodview Dr. E&W
........31W-40N 11

**Union**
Clark St. E&W...46W-25N 38
Country Ln. N&S ...46W-25N 38
Depot St. E&W ......46W-25N 38
Elm St. N&S ......46W-25N 38
Fairfield Dr. . 46W-25N 38
Highbridge Rd. E&W
........46W-26N 38
Jackson St. E&W ...46W-25N 38
Jefferson St. E&W ..46W-25N 38
Johnson St. E&W ...46W-25N 38
Main St. N&S ......46W-25N 38
Mallett Ct. E&W ...46W-25N 38
Meadow Ln. E&W ...46W-25N 38
Northrup Rd. N&S ..46W-25N 38
O'Clock Rd. E&W ..46W-26N 38
Park St. N&S ......46W-25N 38
Prairie St. E&W ...46W-25N 38
South St. E&W ...46W-25N 38
Sunview Dr. N&S ...46W-25N 38
Vine St. N&S ......46W-25N 38
Washington St. E&W
........46W-25N 38
Wayne St. N&S ......46W-25N 38

**Wonder Lake**
Acorn Path E&W
........38W-35N,37W-35N 17
Alden St. E&W ....37W-35N 17
Beach Ct. E&W ....36W-35N 17
Burton Rd. E&W...37W-35N 17
Burton Rd. E&W....38W-35N 17
Chemung Dr. N&S ..37W-35N 17
Coral Rd. E&W ....37W-35N 17
Dorr Rd. E&W ......37W-35N 17
Garrison Rd. NW&SE
........37W-35N 17
Greenwood Dr. N&S
........37W-35N 17
Highland Dr. E&W
........38W-35N,37W-35N 17
Jacobson Dr. N&S .38W-35N 17
Marengo Ln. N&S ..37W-35N 17
Meadow Ln. N&S ...37W-35N 17
Nunda Rd. E&W....37W-35N 17
Richmond Rd. E&W
........37W-35N 17
Ridge Ln. N&S ...37W-35N 17
Riley Rd. E&W
........38W-35N,38W-35N 17
Riley Rd. E&W ....37W-35N 17
Schuette Dr. NS&EW
........38W-35N 17
Seneca Rd. NE&SW
........37W-35N,37W-36N 17
Thompson Rd. N&S
........37W-35N,37W-36N 17
W. Lake Shore Dr. NW&SE
........37W-35N,37W-36N 17
Westwood Dr. N&S
........37W-35N,37W-36N 17
Wondermere Rd. E&W
........38W-35N,37W-35N 17
Woodstock St. N&S
........37W-35N 17

**Woodstock**
Acacia Ln. N&S ....41W-30N 32
Amber Ct. N&S ....42W-30N 32
Amsterdam St. NE&SW
........42W-31N 24
Ann Ct. E&W ......41W-30N 32
Anne St. E&W....42W-31N 24
Applewood Ln. N&S
........39W-29N 32
Arthur Dr. NE&SW ..42W-31N 24
Ash Av. NW&SE ...41W-32N 24
Ashley Ct. N&S ...41W-30N 32
Aspen Dr. N&S ....39W-29N 32
Austin Av. N&S ...41W-30N 32
Ayrshire Ct. E&W ..40W-30N 32
Bagley St. E&W ...41W-31N 24
Barbary Ln. E&W ..41W-30N 32
Barnswallow Dr. N&S
........40W-32N 24
Becking Av. N&S ..42W-31N 24
Beech Av. E&W ...41W-32N 24
Bellair Ln. N&S ...41W-32N 24
Benton St. N&S ...41W-31N 24
Berltsum Ln. NS&EW
........40W-30N 32
Birch Rd. E&W ....41W-32N 24
Blackfoot Dr. EW&NS
........43W-30N 31
Blakely St. N&S ....42W-30N 32
Bliss Ct. N&S .....40W-30N 32
Blue Bonnet Ln. E&W
........41W-30N 32

Bob 'O' Link Cir. NS&EW
........39W-30N 32
Borden St. N&S...42W-31N 24
Brahman Ct. N&S ..39W-30N 32
Briarwood Ct. N&S
........43W-30N 31
Bridgewater Dr. NW&NE
........40W-29N 32
Brink St. NE&SW ..41W-30N 32
Broadway N&S 40W-32N 24
Broadway Rd. N&S
........41W-32N 24
Brown St. NE&SW..41W-30N 32
Bull Valley Dr. NS&EW
........39W-30N 32
Bunker Av. N&S...41W-30N 32
Burbank Av. E&W ..41W-30N 32
Burbank Ct. E&W ..41W-30N 24
Cairns Ct. NE&SW..42W-32N 24
Calhoun St. E&W ..41W-31N 24
Cardinal Dr. E&W ..40W-32N 24
Carol Av. NE&SW ..42W-31N 24
Carol St. E&W ....42W-31N 24
Cass St. E&W ....41W-31N 24
Castle Bar Tr. NS&EW
........43W-30N 31
Castle Rd. N&S
........40W-28N,40W-29N 32
Castleshire Dr. EW&NS
........42W-31N 24
Catalpa Ln. E&W ..40W-29N 32
Center Ln. NE&SW
........41W-31N 24
Center St. E&W ....41W-31N 24
Centerville Ct. NE&SW
........40W-30N 32
Central Pkwy. E&W
........41W-32N 24
Charbray Ct. N&S ..39W-30N 32
Charles St. N&S....41W-32N 24
Cherry Ct. E&W ...41W-32N 24
Chestnut Av. E&W ..41W-30N 32
Church St. E&W ...41W-31N 24
Claussen Dr. E&W ..42W-31N 24
Clay Ct. NW&SE ..41W-30N 32
Clay St. N&S
........41W-31N,41W-32N 24
Clover Chase Cir. NS&EW
........41W-30N 32
Club Rd. NW&SE ..39W-30N 32
Cobblestone Way E&W
........40W-29N 32
Conway St. E&W ..41W-30N 24
Corporate Ct. N&S 40W-29N 32
Country Club Rd. E&W
........40W-31N 24
Courtland Dr. N&S .40W-30N 32
Creekwood Ct. N&S
........43W-30N 31
Dacy St. N&S ....42W-31N 24
Dakota Dr. NS&EW
........43W-30N 31
Davis St. NE&SW ..40W-30N 32
Davis Rd. NW&SE ..40W-29N 32
Dean St. NE&SW
........41W-29N,41W-30N 32
Desmond Av. E&W
........42W-30N 32
Diane Ct. NW&SE ..41W-32N 24
Dieckman St. E&W ..41W-29N 32
Dillard Ct. NS&EW
........40W-29N,40W-30N 32
Division St. NE&SW
........41W-30N 32
Donagal Ct. NE&SW
........43W-30N 31
Donna Ct. NW&SE 42W-31N 24
Donovan Av. E&W
........42W-31N,41W-31N 24
Dorham E&W ......40W-30N 32
Douglas St. N&S .. 41W-31N 24
Dublin Ct. NS&EW ..43W-30N 31
Duncan Pl. N&S ...40W-30N 32
Duvall Ct. N&S ....40W-30N 32
East St. N&S ......41W-30N 32
Edgewater Dr. E&W
........43W-30N 31
Edgewood Dr. N&S
........41W-29N,40W-30N 32
Ellen Ct. E&W ....40W-31N 24
Fair St. N&S ......41W-30N 32
Farm Service Rd. NW&SE
........40W-30N 32
Farm Tr. NW&SE ..41W-32N 24
Fieldcrest Av. E&W
........43W-30N 31
First St. E&W ....41W-31N 24
Flagg Ln. NS&EW
........41W-31N,40W-31N 24
Forest Av. E&W
........40W-30N,41W-32N 24
Fox Ln. E&W ....41W-32N 24
Fremont Av. NW&SE
........41W-30N 32
Friesian Ct. NS&EW
........40W-30N 32
Galoway Dr. NE&SW
........40W-30N,39W-30N 32
Gerry Ct. N&S....42W-30N 32
Gerry St. E&W ....42W-30N 32
Giddings St. NW&SE
........41W-30N 32
Ginny Ln. N&S ....41W-30N 32
Golden Av. E&W ..42W-30N 32
Gracy St. NW&SE ..41W-30N 24
Greenley St. N&S ..41W-30N 32
Greenwood Av. E&W
........41W-30N 32
Greenwood Pl. NE&SW
........41W-30N 32
Greta Av. E&W ....42W-30N 32
Griffing Av. E&W ..41W-30N 32

Grove St. E&W ....41W-31N 24
Halma Ln. Ct. E&W
........40W-30N 32
Halma Ln., E. E&W
........40W-30N 32
Halma Ln., W. E&W
........40W-30N 32
Harvest Ct. E&W ..42W-30N 32
Hayward St. N&S
........41W-30N,41W-31N 32
Herrington Pl. E&W
........42W-30N,41W-31N 32
Hibbard St. N&S ..41W-30N 32
Hickman Ln. N&S ..41W-31N 24
Hickory Ln. N&S ..42W-30N 32
Hickory Rd. N&S ..41W-32N 24
Highland Av. E&W ..42W-30N 32
Hill St. N&S ......42W-31N 24
Hillcrest St. N&S ..42W-31N 24
Hillside Tr. NE&SW
........43W-30N 31
Hilltop Ln. N&S ..41W-32N 24
Hoy Av. E&W ....41W-30N 32
Hutchins St. E&W ..41W-31N 24
Huffman St. NW&SE
........41W-31N 24
Industrial Heights Dr. NW&SE
........40W-29N 32
Infanta Ct. E&W ..43W-30N 31
Irving Av. N&S....41W-31N 24
Island Ct. N&S ...41W-32N 24
Jackson St. E&W
........42W-31N,41W-31N 24
Jean St. NW&SE ..41W-30N 32
Jefferson St. N&S
........41W-30N,41W-31N 32
Jewett St. N&S
........41W-31N,41W-32N 24
Johnson St. N&S ..41W-31N 24
Joseph St. NS&EW
........41W-32N 24
Judd St. E&W
........42W-31N,41W-31N 24
Julie St. N&S ......41W-32N 24
Kathleen Ct. E&W ..41W-30N 32
Kildeer Dr. N&S ...41W-31N 24
Kilkenny Ct. NW&SE
........41W-30N 32
Kimball Av. E&W
........42W-30N,41W-30N 32
King St. N&S ......41W-30N 32
Lake Av. NW&SE
........41W-30N,40W-29N 32
Lake St. NW&SE .. 41W-30N 32
Lamb Rd. N&S ....43W-32N 23
Laurel Av. N&S ....41W-30N 32
Lawndale Av. E&W
........41W-30N 32
Lawrence Av. E&W
........41W-30N 32
Leah Ln. NS&EW ..40W-30N 32
Lee Ann Ln. NS&EW
........41W-30N 32
Lee St. N&S ......41W-30N 32
Liberty Ln. NW&SE
........41W-30N 32
Lincoln Av. E&W
........42W-31N,41W-31N 24
Linda Ct. E&W ....41W-30N 32
Linden Ln. E&W ..40W-29N 32
Lisa St. E&W ......41W-30N 32
Locust Av. E&W ..41W-32N 24
Lorr Dr. E&W ....42W-30N 32
Madison St. N&S
........41W-31N,41W-32N 24
Main St. N&S ....41W-31N 24
Mansfield St. N&S ..41W-31N 24
Maple Av. E&W ...41W-32N 24
Margaret St. E&W ..41W-30N 32
Mark Ct. E&W......41W-30N 32
Martha Dr. NE&SW
........40W-30N 32
Martin Dr. N&S ...40W-30N 24
Marvel Av. N&S ...41W-30N 24
Mary Ann St. N&S ..42W-31N 24
Mary Anne St. NE&SW
........42W-31N 24
McConnell Rd. NW&SE
........40W-30N,39W-29N 32
McGee Rd. E&W ..43W-32N 23
McHenry Av. NE&SW
........41W-31N,40W-31N 24
McHenry Rd. NE&SW
........40W-31N 24
Meadow Av. E&W ..41W-32N 24
Melody Ln. E&W ..41W-30N 32
Mitchell St. N&S ..42W-30N 32
Moraine Ct. N&S ..43W-30N 31
Moraine Dr. N&S ..43W-30N 31
Muriel St. N&S ...40W-30N 32
Nebraska St. N&S ..41W-31N 24
Newell St. E&W ...41W-30N 24
Nieuwhof Ct. N&S ..40W-30N 32
North St. E&W ....41W-31N 24
Northampton St. N&S
........41W-31N 24
Nuthatch Dr. E&W ..40W-32N 24
Oak St. NW&SE ...42W-30N 24
Oakdale St. NW&SE
........40W-30N 32
Oakland Av. E&W ..42W-31N 24
Oakview Ct. NW&SE
........43W-30N 31
Oakview Ter. NS&EW
........41W-30N 32
Olive Av. E&W ....42W-31N 24
Olson St. N&S ....41W-30N 32
Orchard Ct. NW&SE
........41W-32N 24
Osage Way E&W ..43W-30N 31
Park St. E&W......41W-31N 24

Patricia Ct. E&W ..41W-32N 24
Peach Tree Ln. E&W
........41W-32N 24
Pine Ct. NW&SE ..41W-31N 24
Pinecrest Ct. E&W ..43W-30N 31
Pleasant St. NW&SE
........42W-31N 24
Pond Point Rd. N&S
........40W-29N 32
Poplar Ln. N&S ...41W-32N 24
Portage Ln. N&S ..40W-32N 32
Prairie Ridge Dr. E&W
........41W-30N 32
Prairie View Dr. N&S
........40W-30N 32
Putnam Av. N&S ..42W-30N 32
Quail Ct. N&S ....41W-32N 24
Queen Anne St. N&S
........41W-31N,41W-32N 24
Quinlan Ln. E&W ..42W-31N 24
Raffel Rd. N&S ...40W-32N 24
Ravenwood Ct. N&S
........43W-30N 31
Ravenwood Dr. N&S
........43W-30N 31
Red Barn Ct. SW&NE
........39W-29N 32
Red Barn Rd. NS&EW
........39W-29N 32
Redwing Dr. N&S ..40W-29N 24
Regina St. E&W ...42W-30N 24
Rhett Pl. N&S ....40W-30N 24
Rhodes St. N&S ...42W-31N 24
Ridgeland Av. E&W
........42W-30N 32
Ridgeway Ter. NS&EW
........40W-30N 31
Ridgewood Dr. E&W
........41W-31N 24
Roger Rd. E&W ...41W-32N 24
Roller Dr. E&W ...39W-29N 32
Roosevelt St. N&S ..41W-30N 32
Rose Ct. E&W ....41W-30N 24
Rose Farm Rd. N&S
........44W-30N,44W-33N 31
Rt. 120 E&W
........42W-32N,40W-32N 24
Rt. 47 N&S
........41W-29N,41W-32N 32
Russell Ct. E&W....42W-32N 24
Ryan Ct. N&S .....43W-30N 31
Ryder Dr. NE&SW ..41W-30N 32
Sando Ln. N&S ...42W-30N 32
Sandra Ct. E&W
........40W-31N,41W- 24
Scarlett Way N&S ..40W-30N 24
Schryver Av. E&W ..41W-30N 32
Second St. E&W ..41W-31N 24
Seminary Av. N&S
........41W-31N,41W-32N 24
Seneca Ct. N&S ...43W-30N 31
Sharon Dr. N&S ...40W-31N 24
Shelia St. NS&EW ..41W-32N 24
Short St. E&W ....41W-31N 24
Silver Creek Rd. E&W
........41W-32N 24
Smith St. NW&SE ..41W-30N 32
South St. SW&NE ..43W-30N 31
Southview Dr. NW&SE
........40W-30N 32
Sparrow Dr. E&W ..40W-30N 24
St. John Rd. E&W
........41W-32N,40W-32N 24
Stewart Av. E&W ..42W-30N 32
Stonelake Rd. E&W
........40W-29N 32
Summit Av. E&W
........42W-31N,41W-32N 24
Sunset Ridge Dr. N&S
........42W-31N 24
Sunshine Ln. E&W ..42W-31N 24
Suzanne St. N&S ..42W-31N 24
Tanager Dr. N&S ..40W-32N 24
Tappan St. N&S
........41W-31N,41W-32N 24
Tara Ct. E&W ....42W-30N 32
Tara Dr. N&S ....42W-30N 32
Taurus Ct. E&W ...39W-30N 32
Tech Court N&S ...41W-29N 32
Terry Ct. E&W ....41W-30N 32
Teton Dr. N&S ....43W-30N 31
Third St. E&W ....41W-31N 24
Thomas Dr. N&S ..42W-32N 24
Throop St. N&S ...41W-31N 24
Timothy Ln. NS&EW
........40W-31N 24
Todd Ct. E&W ....41W-30N 32
Trinity Ct. E&W ...43W-30N 31
Tryon St. N&S
........41W-30N,41W-31N 32
Twelve Oaks Pkwy. SW&NE
........40W-32N 24
U.S. Route 14 NW&SE
........42W-30N,39W-28N 32
U.S. Route 14 NW&SE
........41W-29N 32
Valerian Ln. E&W ..41W-30N 32
Van Buren St. E&W
........41W-31N 24
Verbena Ln. E&W ..41W-30N 32
Victoria Dr. NW&SE
........42W-32N 24
Vine St. NS&EW ...41W-30N 32
W. Lake Shore Dr. N&S
........39W-28N,39W-29N 32
Wagner Ln. E&W ..41W-30N 32
Walden Oak Dr. N&S
........40W-30N 32
Walnut Dr. NS&EW
........41W-32N 24

Ware Rd. E&W
........41W-33N,40W-33N 24
Washburn St. NW&SE
........41W-30N 32
Washington St. NW&SE
........42W-31N,41W-31N 24
West Av. E&W ....42W-31N 24
Westwood Ct. NE&SW
........43W-30N 31
Westwood Tr. NS&EW
........43W-30N 31
Wheeler St. N&S
........41W-31N,41W-32N 24
White Face Ct. NW&SE
........39W-30N 32
Wicker St. N&S ...41W-32N 24
Wicker St. N&S ...42W-31N 24
Willow Av. E&W ...41W-32N 24
Winslow Av. E&W ..42W-30N 32
Winslow Cir. EW&NS
........42W-30N 32
Wintu Ct. N&S ...43W-30N 31
Wood Dr. N&S ....41W-30N 32
Woodside Ct. E&W
........40W-32N 24
Yellowhead Ct. NW&SE
........39W-30N 32
Zimmerman Rd. N&S
........40W-30N 32

# Will County

## StreetFinder®

Photo credit: Downtown Joliet, Joliet Region Chamber of Commerce

PageFinder™ Map U.S. Patent No. 5,419,586.

Information included in this publication has been checked for accuracy prior to publication. Since changes do occur, the publisher cannot be responsible for any variations from the information printed.

## Will County Municipal Offices

| | Location | Page |
|---|---|---|
| Crete Village Hall | 1W-29S | 44 |
| 524 Exchange St; 672-5431 | | |
| Frankfort Twp Village Hall | 12W-25S | 32 |
| 123 W Kansas St; 469-2177 | | |
| Joilet City Hall | 24W-23S | 20 |
| 150 W Jefferson St; 740-2220 | | |
| Monee Village Hall | 6W-31S | 42 |
| 500 E Court St; 534-8301 | | |

## Cemeteries

| | Location | Page |
|---|---|---|
| Adem Cem | 1W-29S | 44 |
| Barrett Cem | 20W-20S | 22 |
| Brooks Cem | 17W-17S | 17 |
| County Farm Cem | 27W-24S | 27 |
| Eagle Lake Cem | 3E-32S | 57 |
| Elmhurst Cem | 22W-24S | 29 |
| Frankfort Cem | 11W-25S | 32,33 |
| Hadley Cem | 17W-21S | 23 |
| Hickory Hill Cem | 11W-24S | 24,25 |
| Hills of Rest Cem | 28W-23S | 19 |
| Holy Cross Cem | 26W-21S | 19 |
| Lockport Cem | 22W-19S | 15 |
| Marshall Cem | 15W-23S | 23 |
| Mt Calvary Cem | 22W-21S | 21 |
| Mt Monah Cem | 24W-22S | 20 |
| Mt Olivet Cem | 22W-23S | 21 |
| Pleasant Hill Cem | 12W-25S | 32 |
| Rose Hill Cem | 12W-28S | 40 |
| St Cyril's Cem | 21W-22S | 22 |
| St John's Cem | 24W-22S | 20 |
| St John's Cem | 13W-24S | 32 |
| St Joseph Cem | 24W-22S | 20 |
| St Mary's Cem | 24W-21S | 20 |
| St Patrick's Cem | 24W-23S | 20 |
| St Peter's Cem | 9W-29S | 41 |
| Trinity Cem | 0W-30S | 44 |
| Twining Cem | 13W-30S | 40 |

| | Location | Page |
|---|---|---|
| Union Cem | 10W-30S | 41 |
| Woodland Mem Park Cem | 28W-23S | 19 |
| Zion Cem | 0W-30S | 44 |

## Colleges & Universities

| | Location | Page |
|---|---|---|
| Col of St Francis | 24W-23S | 20 |
| Governors State Univ | 5W-29S | 42 |
| Joilet Jr Col | 23W-24S | 29 |
| Lewis Univ of Science | 23W-18S | 14,15 |

## Forest Preserves

| | Location | Page |
|---|---|---|
| Hammel Woods FP | 29W-23S | 18,19 |
| Higinbotham Woods FP | 19W-23S | 22 |
| Messenger Woods FP | 17W-20S | 23 |
| Van Horn Woods FP | 13W-25S | 32 |

## Golf Courses & Country Clubs

| | Location | Page |
|---|---|---|
| Big Run GC | 21W-16S | 15 |
| Broken Arrow GC | 20W-20S | 22 |
| Boughton Ridge GC | 22W-10S | 7 |
| Green Garden CC | 11W-31S | 40,41 |
| Inwood GC | 27,28W-24S | 27 |
| Joilet CC | 22W-25S | 29 |
| Old Oak CC | 17W-16S | 17 |
| Prestwick CC | 9W-26S | 33 |
| Tamarack GC | 30W-12S | 8 |
| Wedgewood GC | 30W-20S | 18 |
| Willow Run CC | 15W-22S | 23 |
| Woodruff GC | 20W-23S | 22 |

## Hospitals

| | Location | Page |
|---|---|---|
| St Joseph Hosp | 26W-23S | 20 |
| Silver Cross Hosp | 22W-23S | 21 |
| Sunny Acres Sanitarium | 23W-25S | 28,29 |

## Shopping Centers

| | Location | Page |
|---|---|---|
| Hillcrest SC | 26W-21S | 20 |
| Jefferson Square Mall | 27W-24S | 27 |
| Louis Joilet Mall | 28W-20S | 19 |

---

## Will County Close-up

### Rialto Square Theatre
102 N. Chicago St., Joliet

Constructed in 1926, this designated landmark combines several different architectural styles. Its ornate interior boasts gold and silver inlay, a main foyer patterned after the Hall of Versailles and a rotunda inspired by the Parthenon. Known as "the jewel of Joliet," this 1,900-seat theater has hosted the Indianapolis Dance Company, Ruth Page Ballet Company, Hubbard Street Dance Company and Joffrey Ballet Company.

### Jacob Henry Mansion
20 S. Eastern Ave., Joliet

This magnificent 44-room dwelling, built in 1873 for railroad magnet Jacob Henry, remains the largest and best example of Renaissance architecture in Illinois. Its interior of hand-rubbed woods was designed by some of the era's finest German artisans. This one-of-a-kind house features an elaborate staircase with 119 handcarved octagon spindles of burled walnut. Open by appointment.

### Joliet Union Station
50 E. Jefferson, Joliet

Relive Illinois history with a visit to this fully-restored train station. A designated landmark, this structure was

first made possible by Abraham Lincoln who was then a corporate lawyer for Rock Island Railroad. Vintage architecture features a 50-ft. dome ceiling and cast-iron window frames. Buiding materials include Italian marble.

## Isle A La Cache Museum
501 E. Romeo Rd., Romeoville
This unique museum highlights the fur trade of the late 1700's. Museum interpreters, costumed as French Voyageurs, provide demonstrations. Exhibits feature a birch bark canoe and an actual wigwam. Artifacts include pottery and bone tools. Hands-on exhibits. Closed Mondays.

## Will County Historical Society
803 S. State St., Lockport
This site is the location of the Illinois & Michigan Canal Museum and Pioneer Settlement. The I. & M. Canal Museum displays artifacts relating to the canal's history including tools, photographs, shipping rosters and Native American objects. Pioneer Settlement is a living museum staffed by costumed interpreters. It features a smoke house, blacksmith, tinsmith, log cabin, schoolhouse and a mid-19th-century farmhouse.

## Plum Creek Nature Center
27064 S. Dutton Rd., Beecher
Enjoy the outdoors on 689-acres of oak and hickory forest. This region features campsites, picnic shelters and three miles of multi-purpose trails. Available for ice skating and sledding during the winter months.

## Monee Reservoir
27341 Ridgeland Ave., Monee
This public reservoir, surrounded by 195 acres of fields and woods, is an ideal fishing lake. Fish population includes small-mouth bass, large-mouth bass, catfish and bluegill. Free to the public.

## Plainfield Historical Society Museum
217 Main St., Plainfield
Dedicated to the preservation of local history, this museum features an artifact collection that includes tools, farm equipment, toys and several military relics. Also, archives and a research library are on the premises. Open Saturdays.

## Lake Renwick Heron Rookery
23144 W. Renwick Rd., Plainfield
This breeding area for endangered birds rests on a small island. Site features an interpretive staff, a bird viewing area and brief presentations. Spotting scopes provided. Open Wednesdays and Saturdays.

## Illinois State Museum Lockport Gallery
200 W. 8th St., Lockport
This center for visual arts showcases the work of Illinois artists, past and present. Its changing exhibits include paintings, sculpture, photographs and weavings. It also sponsors lectures and educational programs. Open all year.

## Gladys Fox Museum
231 9th St., Lockport
This museum, with its focus on the community of Lockport, is housed in a church constructed from native limestone in 1840. Closed Fridays, Saturdays and Sundays.

## Round Barn Farm Museum and Recreation Area
Rte. 52 South of I-80 (take Briggs St. Exit South), Joliet
Highlights include pony rides, a petting zoo and horse carriage rides. Artifacts include household, agricultural antiques and a barn constructed in 1898.

## Slovenian Union Women's Heritage Museum
431 N. Chicago St., Joliet
This ethnic museum honors Slovenian culture. Exhibits feature clothing, dolls, books and jewelry. Also, video presentations.

## The Herbert Trackman Planetarium
1216 Houbolt Ave., Joliet
Astronomy-lovers enjoy multi-media planetary shows. Several programs for children. Located on the campus of Joliet Junior College. Free admission.

## Bolingbrook Aquatic Center
180 S. Canterbury Lane, Bolingbrook
Enjoy swimming, scuba diving and water aerobics at this indoor wave pool. Swimming and scuba lessons available. Ideal for private parties. Open all year.

## Riegel Mini Farm
580 Farmview Rd., University Park
This small petting zoo covers 7 acres and has a wide variety of farm animals. Highlights include pony rides and hay rides. Special events. Open May thru October.

## Thorn Creek Nature Preserve
247 Monee Rd., Park Forest
Hike some of the most beautiful trails in the region. Experience 180 acres of oak and hickory forest. Variable terrain includes creeks, marshes, flood plains and upland forest. Ideal for bird watching. Interpretive staff available for lectures, workshops and various educational programs.

## Channahon State Park
2 W. Story St., Channahon
Twenty acres of woodlands, ideal for outdoor recreation. This picturesque site includes multi-purpose trails, picnic shelters, horseshoe pits and 75 campsites. Play areas for children. Open all year.

## I & M Canal State Trail
Channahon to LaSalle
This trail of limestone screenings extends 55.5 miles and is available for hiking, jogging, biking and cross-country skiing. Camping and water sports nearby.

## Dellwood Park
State Street, Lockport
Centrally located, this 150-acre park boasts six pavilions, a performance arts center, band shell and an enclosed field house. Play areas for children.

## Gaylord Building
200 W. 8th St., Lockport
Winner of the 1988 President's Award for Historic Preservation. The first of its two wings was constructed in 1838 by the I & M Canal Commission. Currently, it houses a restaurant, art gallery and a visitors center.

# 4  WILL COUNTY

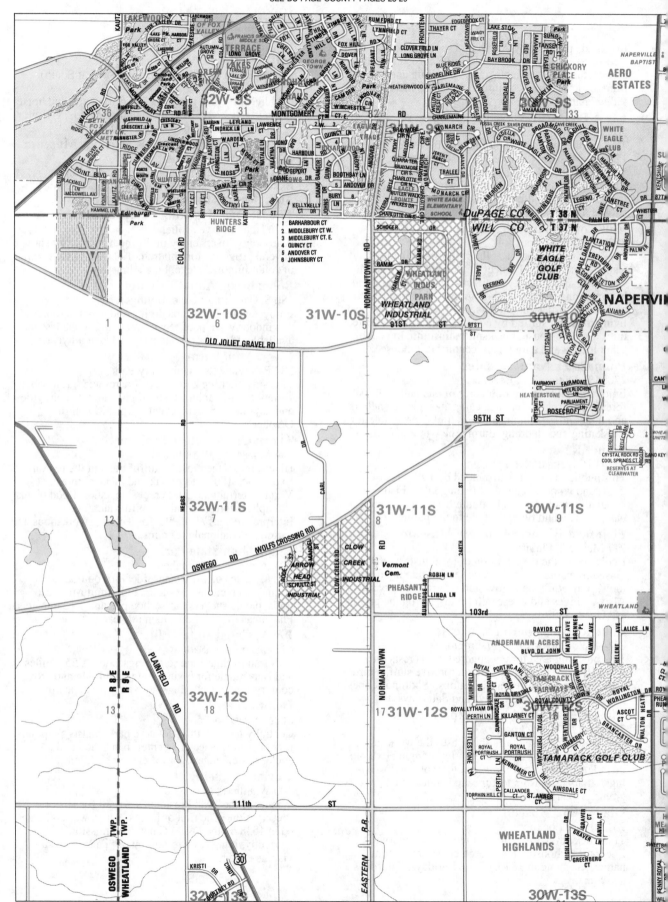

# SPRINGBROOK PRAIRIE FOREST PRESERVE

*Proposed Lake*

28W-9S

29W-9S

27W-9S

**SPRINGBROOK GOLF COURSE**

NAPERVILLE TWP.

WHEATLAND TWP.

MISSION OAKS

STILLWATER

WHEATLAND VIEW

GREGORY MIDDLE SCHOOL

BROOK CROSSINGS ESTATES

Springbrook Crossings Park

ROCKWOOD TRACE

Spring Brook Park

SHELL LAKE ESTATES

KINGS CROSSING

NEQUA VALLEY HIGH SCHOOL

FUTURE JR. HIGH SCHOOL

Y.M.C.A.

95TH ST

KNOCH KNOLL RD

95TH ST

RIVERCREST ESTATES

29W-11S

27W-11S

26W-11S

Rivercrest Estates Park

HERITAGE PLACE

WHEATLAND SOUTH

ASHBURY

ROSE HILL FARM

CLOW CREEK FARM

BOUGHTON

VILLELLA LUTHERAN

WHISPERING LAKES

SADDLE CREEK

29W-12S

28W-12S

27W-12S

26W-12S

NAPERBROOK GOLF COURSE

ZION LUTHERAN

RIVER RUN

HIGH MEADOW ELEMENTARY

YELLOWSTAR

(PROP) F.D.

NAPERBROOK COUNTRY ESTS.

28W-13S

27W-13S

26W

SEE PAGES 6-7

3 COPPERFIELD CT
4 SIERRA CT *Knoch*
5 TIFFANY CT *Knolls*
6 CRESTFIELD CT *Park*
7 ALYSSA CT
8 ALYSSA DR

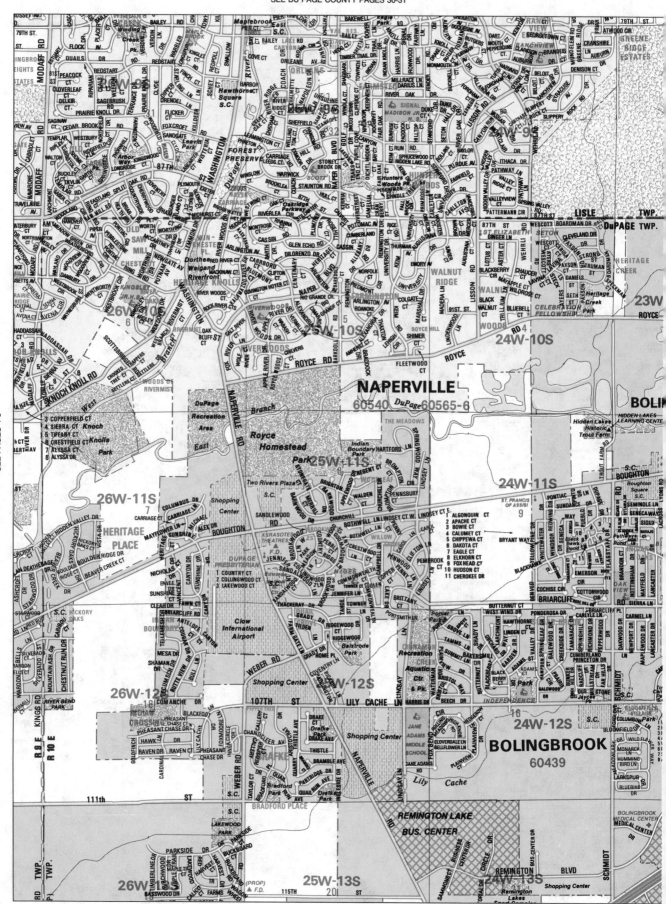

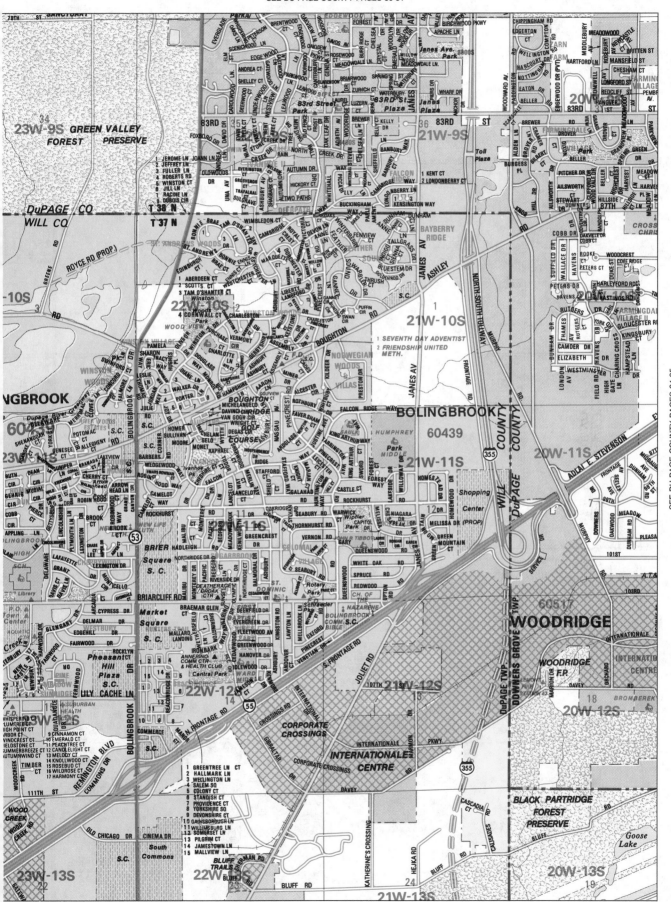

SEE DU PAGE COUNTY PAGES 34-35

# 8 WILL COUNTY

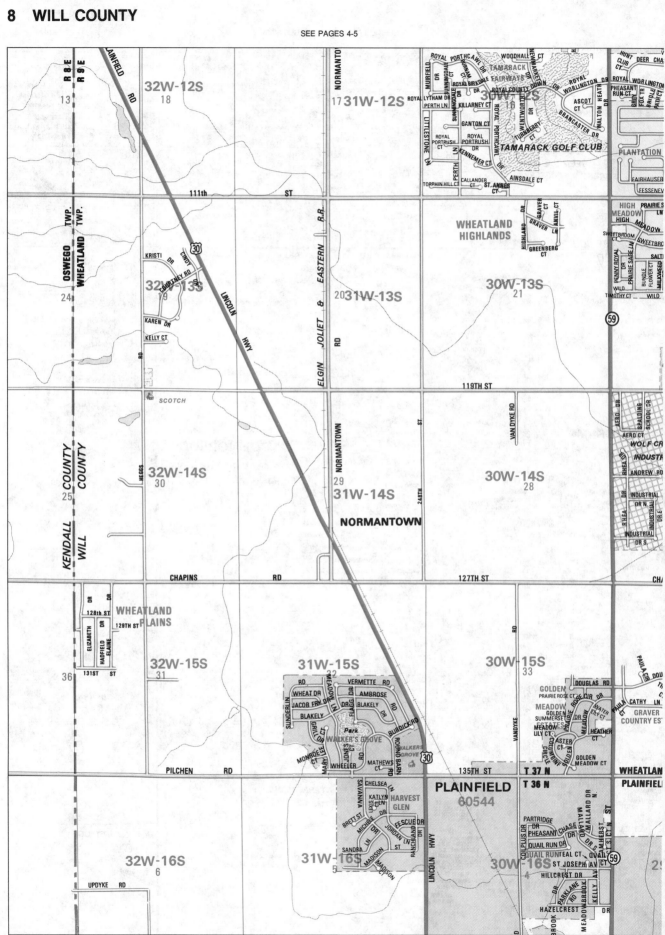

SEE PAGES 4-5

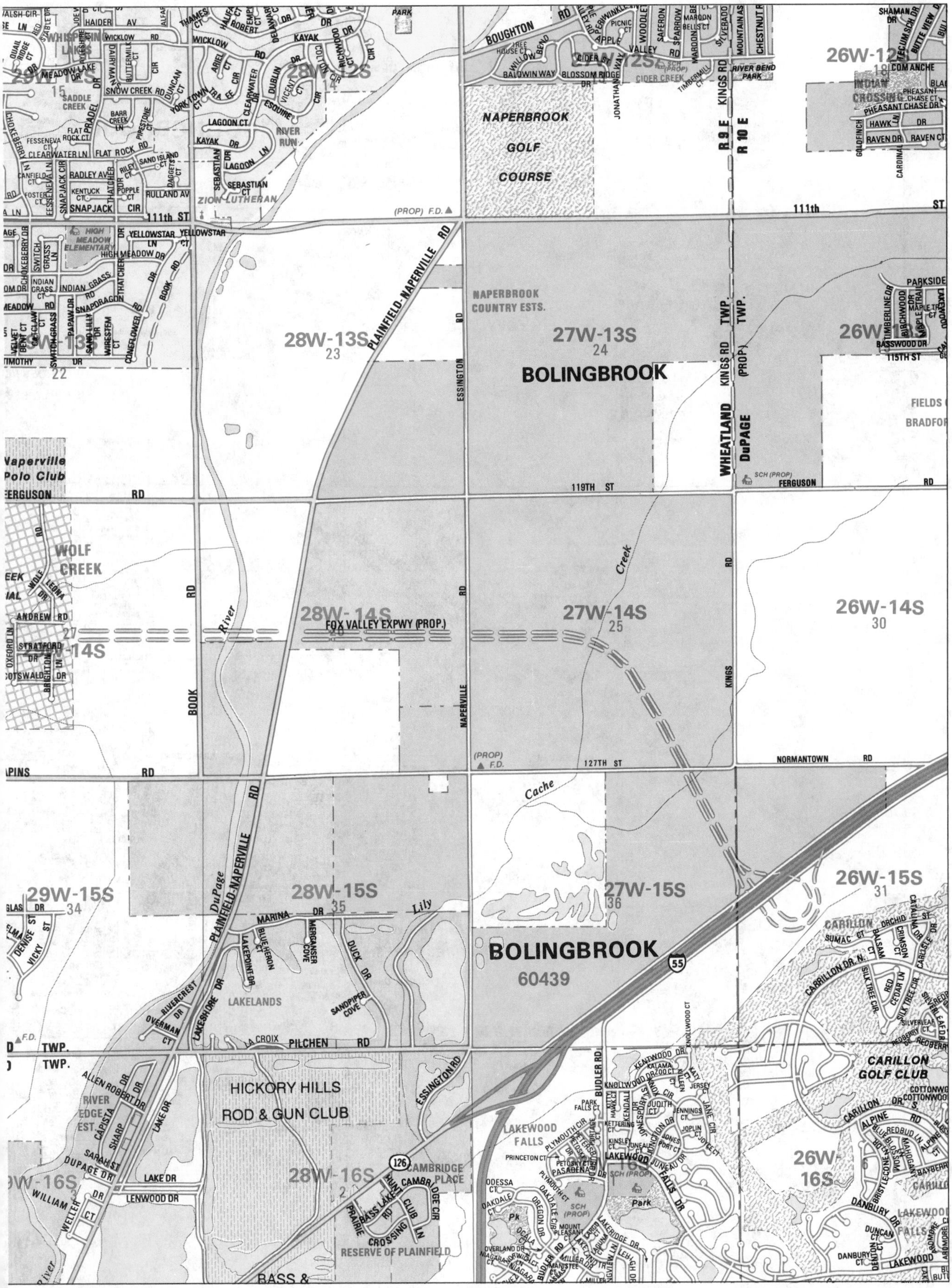

NAPERBROOK GOLF COURSE

NAPERBROOK COUNTRY ESTS.

**BOLINGBROOK**

27W-13S 24

28W-13S 23

26W

WHEATLAND TWP.
DuPAGE TWP.

WOLF CREEK

Naperville Polo Club

28W-14S
FOX VALLEY EXPWY (PROP.)

27W-14S 25

26W-14S 30

119TH ST

127TH ST

NORMANTOWN RD

28W-15S 35

27W-15S 36

26W-15S 31

**BOLINGBROOK**
60439

CARILLON

HICKORY HILLS ROD & GUN CLUB

LAKEWOOD FALLS

CARILLON GOLF CLUB

28W-16S

26W 16S

RESERVE OF PLAINFIELD

SEE PAGES 10-11

**BOLINGBROOK**
60439

26W-12S

24W-12S

25W-13S

24W-13S

26W-13S

26W-14S
30

25W-14S
29

24W-14S
28

26W-15S
31

25W-15S
32

24W-15S

26W-16S

25W-16S
5

24W-16S

WINDHAM LAKES BUSINESS

WINDHAM LAKES BUSINESS PARK

REMINGTON LAKE BUS. CENTER

REMINGTON BLVD

MEADOWDALE ESTATES

LAKEWOOD ESTATES

O'HARA WOODS FOREST PRES.

CARILLON GOLF CLUB

JOLIET JR. COLLEGE

BOLINGBROOK MEDICAL CENTER

CROSS ROADS BUSINESS PARK

ADLAI E. STEVENSON EXPRESSWAY

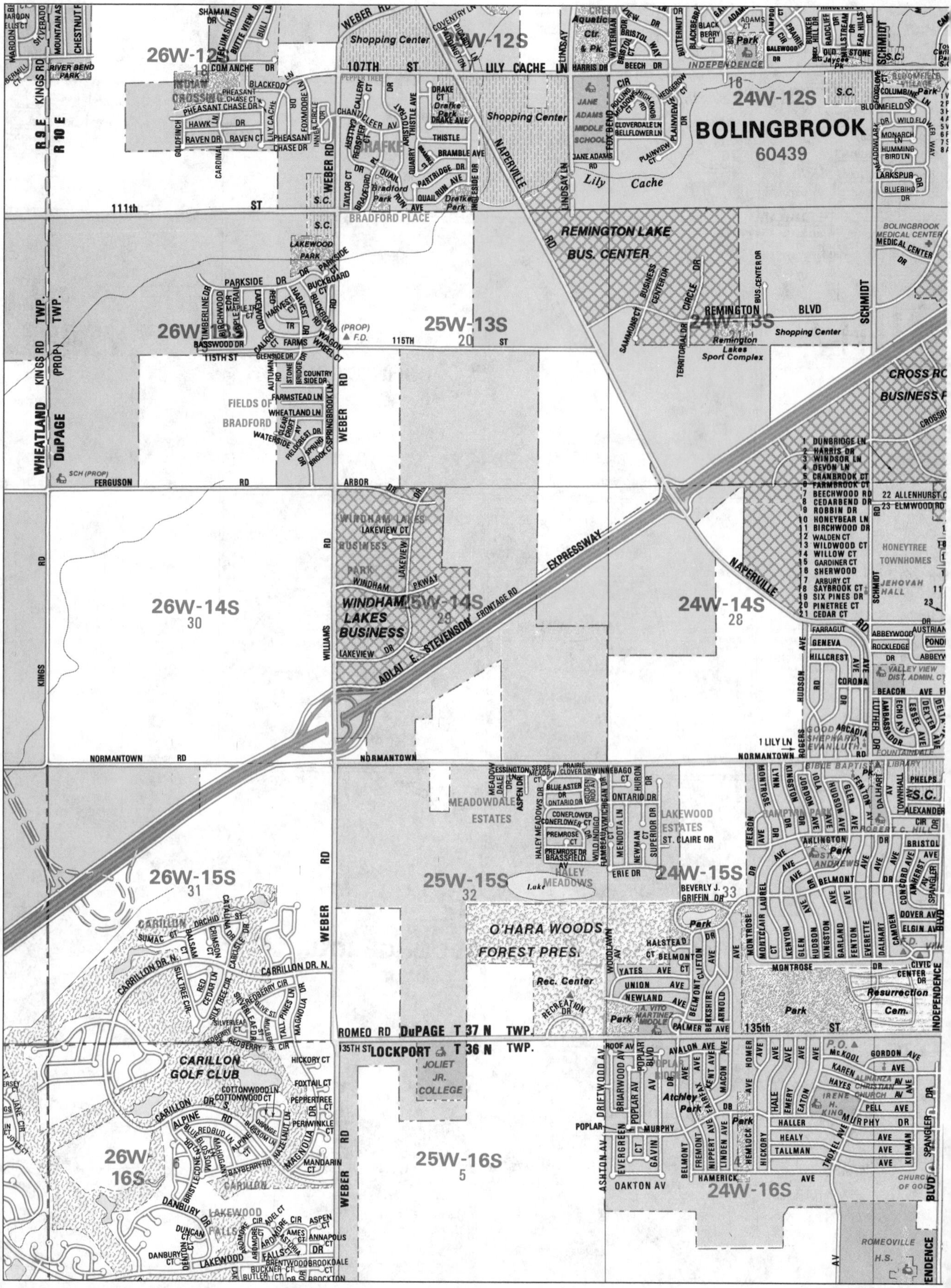

ROMEO RD  DuPAGE T 37 N TWP.
135th ST  LOCKPORT  T 36 N TWP.

ROMEOVILLE H.S.

SEE PAGES 8-9

R 9 E   R 10 E

KINGS RD

WHEATLAND

DuPAGE

WEBER RD

NAPERVILLE RD

NORMANTOWN RD

WILLIAMS RD

FERGUSON RD

ARBOR DR

107TH ST
111th ST
115TH ST
135th ST

WOODRIDGE

WOODRIDGE F.P.

BROMBEREK

20W-12S
18

DuPAGE TWP.
DOWNERS

107TH 21W-12S

JOLIET RD

CORPORATE
CROSSINGS

INTERNATIONALE
CENTRE

INTERNATIONALE PKWY

DAVEY

355

CASCADIA CT

BLACK PARTRIDGE
FOREST
PRESERVE

Goose
Lake

BLUFF RD

20W-13S
19

HILL
Plaza
S.C.

LILY CACHE LN

BOLINGBROOK

22W-12S
14

55

N. FRONTAGE RD

CROSSINGS RD

GIBRALTAR DR

CASCADES

R 10 E    R 11 E

DES PLAINES RIVER RD

NORTH CANAL BANK RD

LEMONT FIRE AV

1 GREENTREE LN CT
2 HALLMARK LN
3 WELLINGTON LN
4 SALEM SQ
5 COLONY CT
6 STANDISH CT
7 PROVIDENCE CT
8 YORKSHIRE SQ
9 DEVONSHIRE CT
10 GAINSBOROUGH LN
11 WILLIAMSBURG LN
12 SOMERSET LN
13 PILGRIM CT
14 JAMESTOWN LN
15 MALLVIEW LN

SHERMAN RD

KATHERINE'S CROSSING

HEJKA RD

BLUFF RD

BLUFF RD

21W-13S

KEEPATAH
FOREST
PRESERVE

River

Des Plaines

INDUSTRIAL PARK DR

23W-13S
22

S.C.

CINEMA DR

OLD CHICAGO DR

South
Commons

BLUFF
TRAILS

22W-13S
BLUFF

PKWY

MARQUETTE

MARQUETTE DR

NAPERVILLE DR

LAKESIDE DR

BUSINESS
PARK

23W-14S

JOLIET RD

VETERANS
WOODS

Rock
Lake

22W-14S
26

R.R.

GULF AV

NEW AV

CENTRAL

21W-14S
25

WILL COUNTY
COOK COUNTY

I-355 PROPOSED (PROP.)

20W-14S
30

EVERGREEN PL

TIMBERLINE PL
TIMBERLINE CT

LEMONT
AIRPORT

INDUSTRIAL
PARK

TIMBERLINE DR

ALBA ST

INDEPENDENCE BLVD

53

FIRST BAPTIST
CHURCH OF HAMPTON PARK

RIDGEWOOD BUS.

HAMPTON
PARK
INDUSTRIAL

ROMEOVILLE
INDUSTRIAL

GREENWOOD AVE

Chicago Sanitary and Ship Canal

Illinois and Michigan Canal

ILLINOIS

127TH

NEW

ST

DuPAGE TWP.
LEMONT TWP.

WILL COUNTY
COOK COUNTY

Danish Ce

ROMEOVILLE
60446 ROMEOVILLE
23W-15S
34

PRAIRIE
NATURE
PRESERVE

HAMPTON
PARK UNITED
PRES.

22W-15S
35

UNO-VEN

21W-15S
36

OLD ORCHARD LN W

FOREST LN

BIG RUN LN

OLD ORCHARD LN E.

20W-15S
31

OAKMONT
CT

LONGWOOD

FAIRWAY DR

BIG RUN
ACRES

VALLEY VIEW DR

355

135TH

JULIET AVE

DEPAUL CT

ISLE A LA
CACHE F.P.

MIKAN LN

ROMEO

ISLE LA CACHE
MUSEUM

RD

NEW AV

135TH ST

WASHINGTON ST
JACKSON ST

HIDDEN RIDGE LN (PVT.)

BIG RUN
GOLF CLUB

SMITH RD

STARR LN

RIDGE HUNTER CT

STERLING DR

BEDFORD LN

138TH ST

ROCK DR

SINDE CIRCLE

LARSON CIR

CALVARY
APOSTOLIC
BAKER CIR

HANSON CIR

23W-16S
3

River

Canal

22W-16S
2

BROADWAY ST

LOCKPORT RD

21W-16S

140TH ST 140TH PL

141ST ST

BASHAM AV

20W-16S

TAMELING DR

SEE COOK COUNTY PAGES 70-71

SEE PAGES 8-9

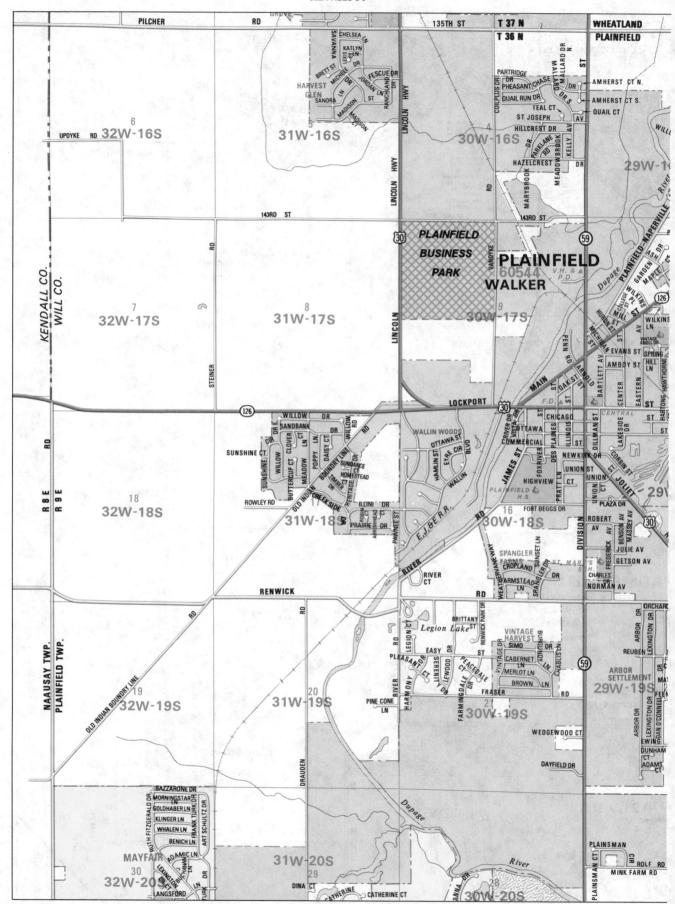

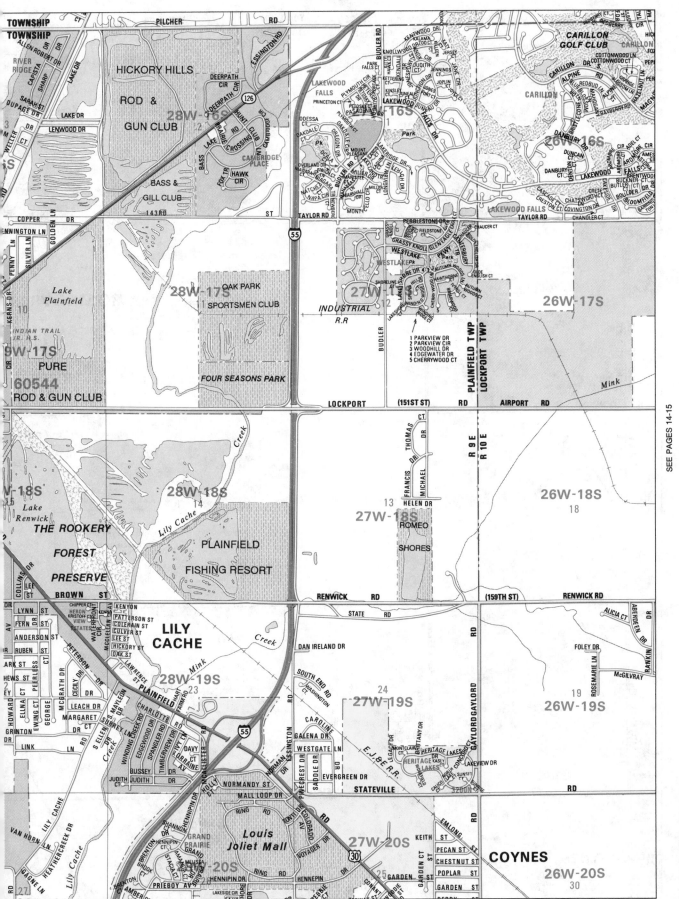

SEE PAGES 10-11

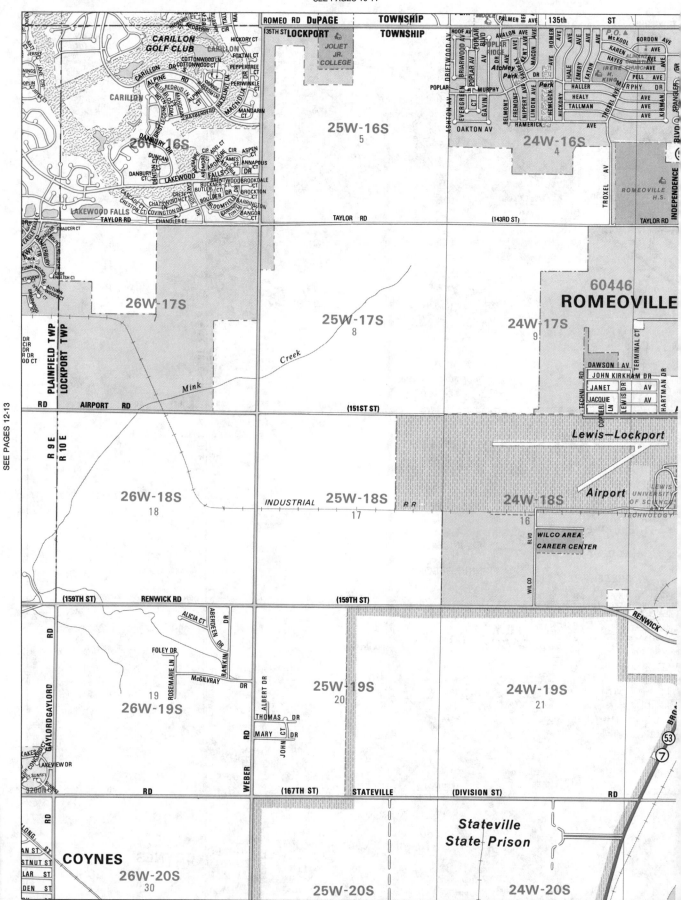

CARILLON GOLF CLUB

CARILLON

26W-16S

25W-16S
5

24W-16S
4

ROMEOVILLE H.S.

TAYLOR RD

(143RD ST)

TAYLOR RD

26W-17S

25W-17S
8

24W-17S
9

60446
**ROMEOVILLE**

PLAINFIELD TWP
LOCKPORT TWP

AIRPORT RD

(151ST ST)

R 9 E
R 10 E

Lewis—Lockport

26W-18S
18

INDUSTRIAL 25W-18S
17

R R

24W-18S
16

Airport

LEWIS UNIVERSITY OF SCIENCE TECHNOLOGY

WILCO AREA CAREER CENTER

(159TH ST) RENWICK RD

(159TH ST)

RENWICK

25W-19S
20

24W-19S
21

26W-19S
19

COYNES

26W-20S
30

(167TH ST) STATEVILLE (DIVISION ST) RD

*Stateville State Prison*

25W-20S

24W-20S

SEE PAGES 12-13

SEE PAGES 20-21

SEE PAGES 10-11

**BIG RUN GOLF COURSE**

ROMEO T 37 N RD

ISLE LA CACHE MUSEUM

ROCK DR
SINDE CIRCLE
LARSON CIR
CALVARY APOSTOLIC BAKER CIR
HANSON CIR CHURCH OF GOD

**23W-16S** 3
**22W-16S** 2
**21W-16S** 1

DEBOER WOODS WEST
STARR
RIDGE HUNTER CT
BEDFORD LN
138TH ST
**20W-16S** 6
140TH ST 140TH PL
ROGER RD
141ST ST
BASHAM AV
BASHAM SUB.
CARRIAGE MANOR ESTATES
TAMELING DR
SHAEFFER DR
RYNBERK

WASHINGTON ST
JACKSON ST
HIDDEN RIDGE LN. (PVT.)

W. 143RD ST
144TH ST
BOULA AV
BOULA SUB.
144TH PL
145TH PL AV
146TH 136TH AV
147TH ST
RIKERMAN RD 135TH
LOCKPORT HEIGHTS
**20W-17S** 7

WOODBROOK LN
LN
145TH ST
SCHOOL HOUSE LN
FOREST LN
**21W-17S**
147TH 12 ST

**22W-17S** 11
**23W-17S** 10

WHITE TAIL WAY
DOE CT
FAWN PATH
BUCK PATH
DEER RUN
PROPOSED
355

171
151ST

Calvary Cem.
THORNDALE
**21W-18S** 13
**22W-18S** 14
**23W-18S** 15

THE FIELDS
MERC AV
OLYMPIC CT
FIELDVIEW
REDWOOD CT
ARBOR TER
WHISPERING PINES
CYPRESS CIR
PRIMROSE
BANBERRY
DOUGLAS
SADDLEWOOD DR
CHESTNUT
BUCKEYE LN
MCDONALD DR
FOREST MANOR
MUIR DR
SCOTT CT
SCOTT
MCKENZIE AV
Fiddyment
**20W-18S** 18

LUDWIG
NORTH BLUFF ST
TIMBERVIEW DR
MEADOW WOOD LN

**LOCKPORT** 60446
159TH

**22W-19S** 23
**21W-18S**

HERITAGE LN
KATHRINE
GLORIA
LOCKPORT CITY CEM.
MILNE GROVE
Central Sq.

7
ASHLEY
JENNIFER CT. N.
MICHAEL
ST. CHARLES DR
CLOVER RIDGE DR
LACOMA DR
PRODEHL DR
**20W-19S** 19
163RD ST.

**23W-19S** 22
7

HOLLY CT
MAPLE CT
KELVIN GROVE
MILNE
MAITLAND
PUTNAM
RUNYAN
LOCKPORT TWP. HIGH SCHOOL EAST
FIELDSTONE DR
WESTWOOD DR
ASH LN

DIVISION ST
DIVISION
STRAWBERRY HILL DR
SUNSHINE CT
PEACHTREE LN
167TH

Fitzpatrick House
INDEPENDENCE BLVD
AIRPORT RD
Des Plaines River
Illinois & Michigan Canal
SANTA FE R.R.
ATCHISON
TOPEKA
Canal
BROADWAY
NEW AV
ARCHER AV
STATE ST

LOCKPORT TWP.
HOMER TWP.

TUSCADORA CT
SHAWNEE DR
SWIFT ARROW DR
WYANDOT CT
CAYUSE DR
MOHAWK
BLACK FOOT DR
MOHICAN
OTTAWA DR
BROKEN ARROW
APACHE DR
PIMA
**20W-20S**

**LOCKPORT**
**23W-20S**
PARKVIEW

SEE PAGES 16-17
SEE PAGES 20-21

SEE PAGES 70-71

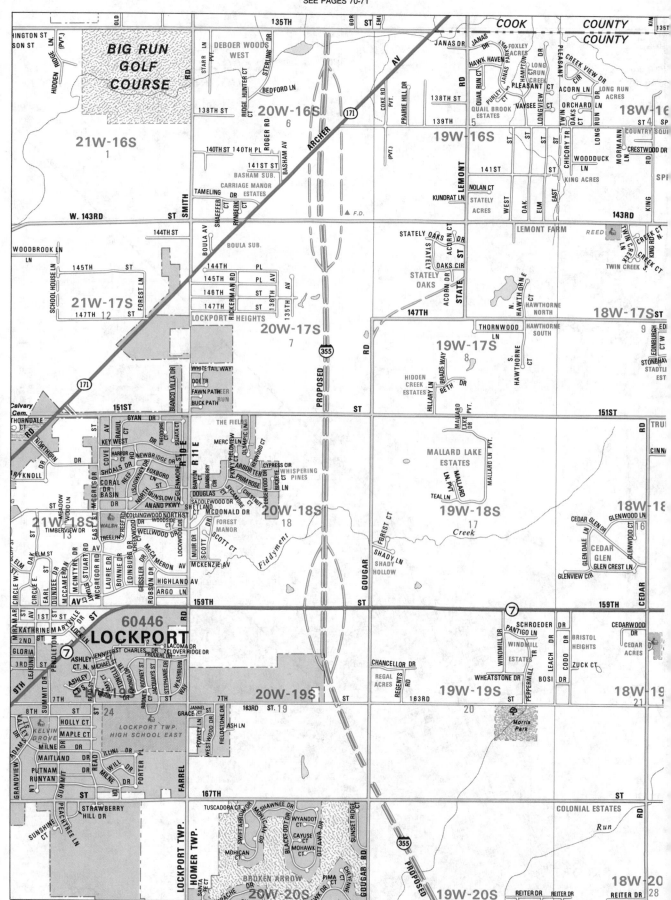

SEE PAGES 14-15

SEE PAGES 22-23

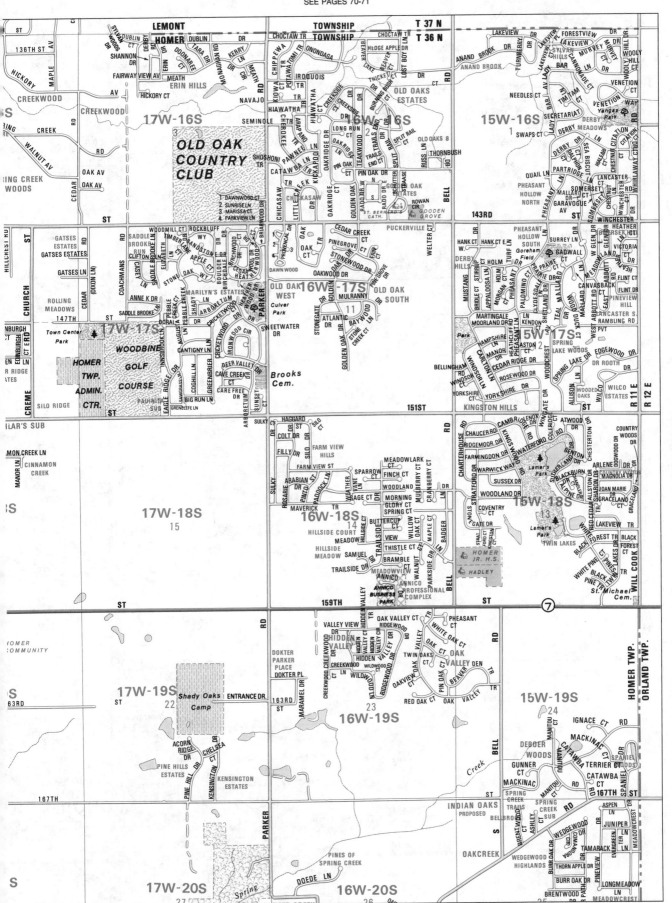

SEE PAGES 78-79

SEE PAGES 12-13

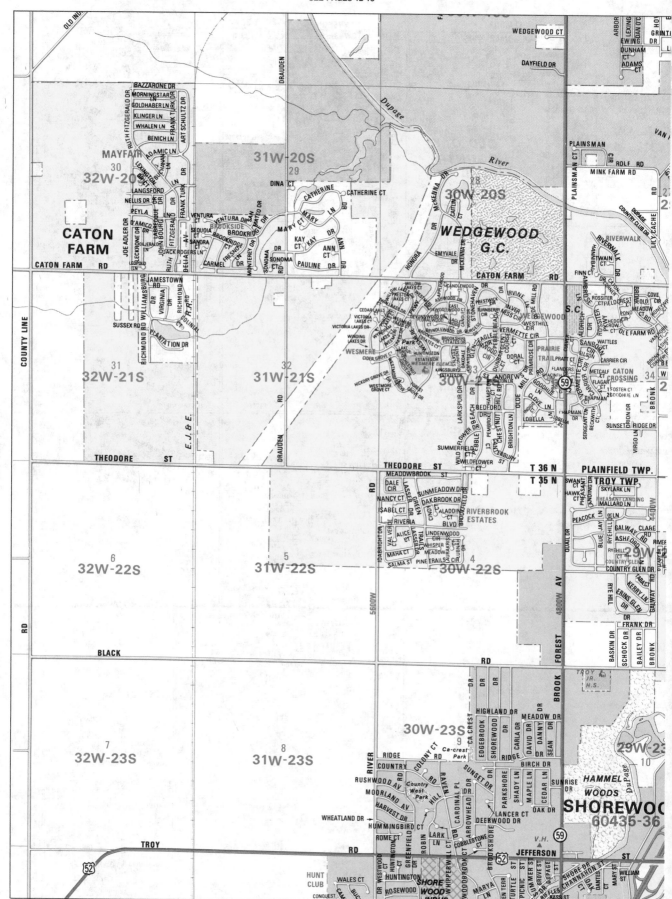

SEE PAGES 26-27

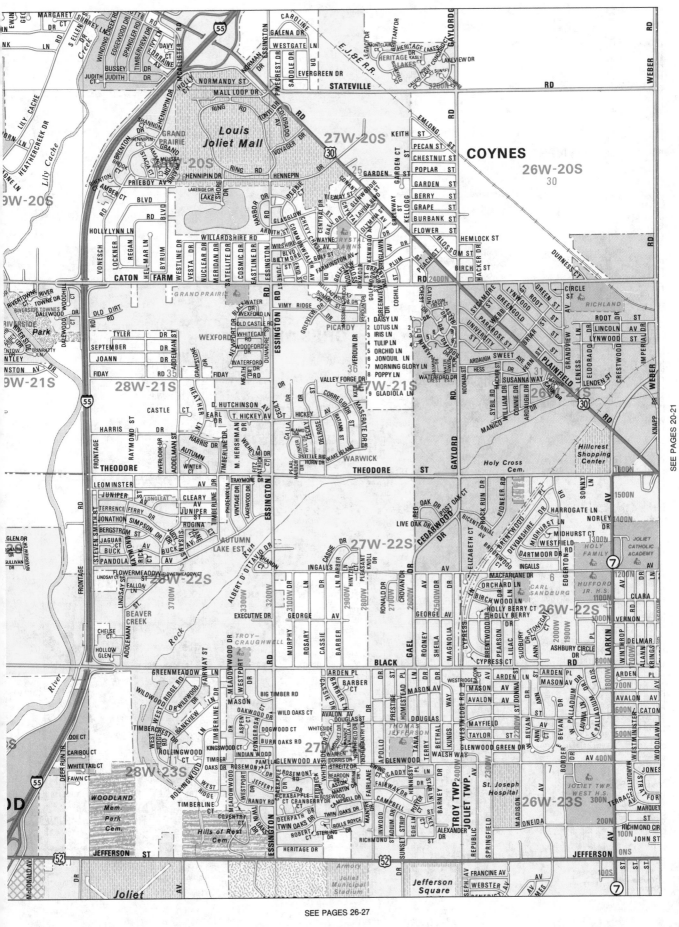

SEE PAGES 14-15

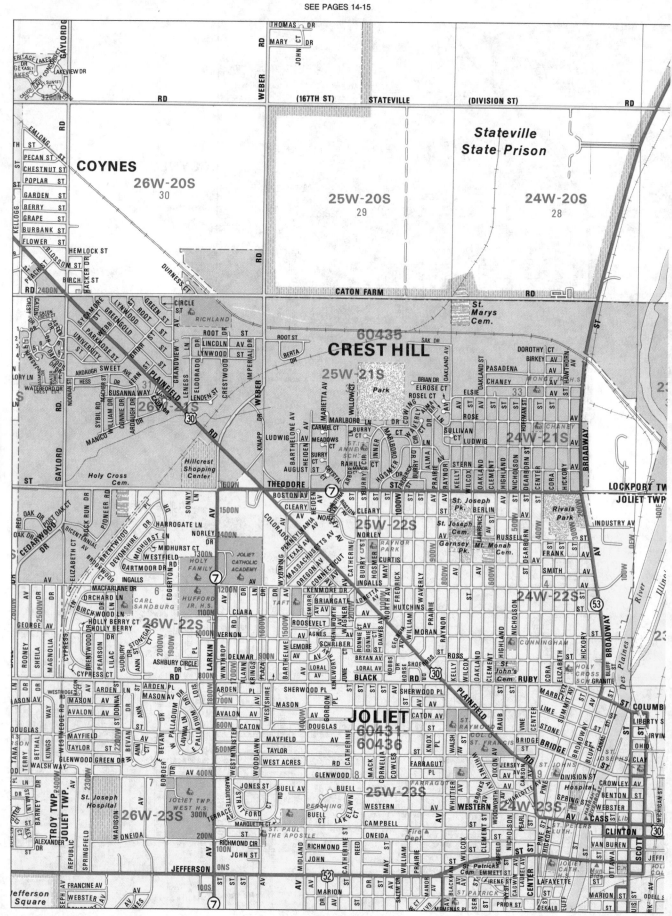

SEE PAGES 18-19

SEE PAGES 28-29

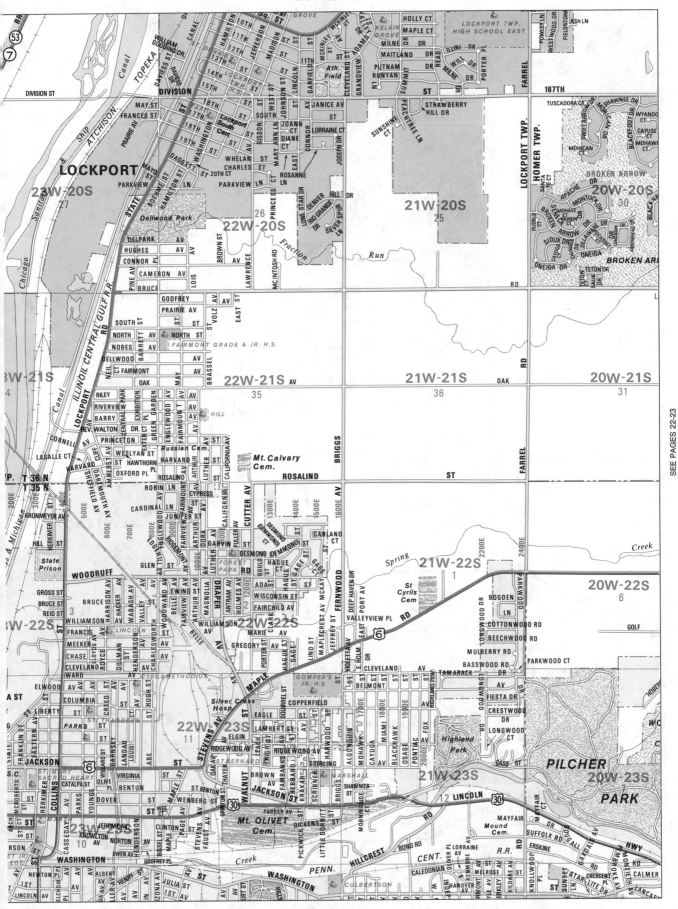

SEE PAGES 16-17

SEE PAGES 20-21

Morris Park

HOLLY CT
MAPLE CT
KELVIN GROVE
MILNE DR
MAITLAND DR
PUTNAM
RUNYAN
GRANDVIEW
SUMMIT
DAM
VALLEY
ILLINI DR
READ
WILL DR
PORTER PL
ST
FARREL

LOCKPORT TWP. HIGH SCHOOL EAST
POWELL LN
WEST WOOD DR
FIELDSTON
ASH LN
167TH

COLONIAL ESTATES
Run
ST
RD

STRAWBERRY HILL DR
SUNSHINE CT
PEACHTREE LN

21W-20S
25

Run
RD

LOCKPORT TWP.
HOMER TWP.

TUSCADORA CT
MOHICAN DR
SWIFTARROW DR
SHAWNEE DR
WYANDOT CT
CAYUSE CT
MOHAWK CT
OTTAWA DR
SUNSET RIDGE
GOUGAR RD

MOHICAN CT
BROKEN ARROW DR
SANTA FE CT
PIMA CT
CHEYENNE
BLACK-FOOT DR

20W-20S
30

APACHE DR
MONTUCK DR
SEMOHAVE
HURON DR
BLACK HAWK DR
COMANCHE CT
OSAGE
RED CLOUD

PUEBLO CT
BROKEN ARROW
SIOUX DR
WINOTA DR
DELAWARE DR
POSSEL
ARROWHEAD DR

CAYUGA
ONEIDA
TETON DR
SAUK
BROKEN ARROW G.C.
ONEIDA DR

Barrett Cem.

355
PROPOSED
Fraction

19W-20S
29

REITER DR  REITER DR
REITER DR

18W-20
28

COLONIAL ACRES
DEER DR
SHELBURNE DR
MCCORMICK CT
RON CT
RON

HERITAGE ESTATES
HERITAGE DR
RON CT
REITER DR
CEDAR CT
CEDAR

LITTLE ACRES
RD

JAMES CT

BRUCE CIR
CEDAR CT

LINSEY LN
CIMARRON RIDGE

PARNELL CIR
MCCARRON RD
MCCARRON

BRUCE CIR
GOMBIS DR
GOMBIS SUB

21W-21S
36
OAK

20W-21S
31
AV

19W-21S
32

ROBERT EMMETT
O'CONNELL DR
KYLEMORE

18W-2
33

ARROWHEAD DR
BLACKHAWK ESTATES
EAGLE BEND
LACROSSE DR

RD
FARREL
ST

GOUGAR

Creek
Spring
21W-22S
1

NEW LENOX
HOM
NEW L

19W-22S
SOUTHWEST
ST

18W-22
4

St Cyrils Cem
VALLEYVIEW PL
EAST HOLM PORT AV
6

2200E
PARKWOOD
LONGWOOD DR
BOGDEN
LN
COTTONWOOD RD
BEECHWOOD RD
MULBERRY RD
BASSWOOD RD
2400E

20W-22S
6

GOLF RD

PARKWOOD CT

DR

WIMBORNE AV
VAIL CT
ALAMOSA ST
ALAMOSA CT
GOLF
CRICKET
AV
SPRINGCREEK ST

CASCADE LN
IVYWILO LN
EDGECREEK
BLANDFORD AVE
BLANDFORD AV

6
CLEVELAND AV
BELMONT
1700E
1800E
1900E
MIAMI
CAYUGA
BLACKHAWK
OSAGE
PONTIAC
2000E
FOX
HIGHLAND PKWY
TAMARACK DR
FIESTA DR
CRESTWOOD DR
LONGWOOD CT
AV
CASS ST

LEWIS LN
WINDSOR LN
COVENTRY
EDGECREEK LN
HICKORY CREEK DR
STEFANIE CT
LAMBETH
PINE GROVE
LAMBETH
IONE DR

HOBERG
WOODRUFF GOLF COURSE

DR

Highland Park

21W-23S

PILCHER
20W-23S
PARK

WOODS

HIGINBOTHAM
FRANCIS
WOODS

19W-23S
8

CLINTON
ABRAHAM DR
MARLA LN
SUNBURST CT
CREEKSIDE

9 BRA
18W-23

MOHAWK
CAYUGA
3200E

MORNINGSIDE
12 LINCOLN
30

MAYFAIR CT
MAYFAIR
Mound Cem.
SUFFOLK RD
DUGALL AV
ERSKINE
TRINITY SCH

ABRAHAM DR
BJORK HILL CIR
SPECTOR RD
CAROL ST
MENNO

HILLCREST
BOND RD
CENT.
OLIVER PL
LORRAINE AV
MELROSE
KENMORE AV
HANOVER AV
KILDARE ST
R.R.
KNOLLWOOD ST
DANDALE AV
STAR-LITE PL
EMBROKEN
MONTE
CRESCENT RD
CALMER RD
LANCAST

BJORK DR
CLINTON ST
GORDON ST
SYCAMORE
GREEN ST
BURHOUSE CRESCENT
WILLOW ST

AS

18W-2

SEE PAGES 30-31

SEE PAGES 16-17

16W-19S

167TH

17W-20S

MESSENGER WOODS

Spring

27

DOEDE LN

DEER CREEK

16W-20S

26

PARKER

Creek

BELL

INDIAN OAKS
PROPOSED

OAKCREEK

PINES OF
SPRING CREEK

OAK MEADOW CT

OAK
MEADOW

HADLEY

LAUFFER RD

ACORN RIDGE DR
PINE HILL DR
CHELSEA CT
KENSINGTON CT
PINE HILLS ESTATES
KENSINGTON ESTATES

IGNACE CT RD

MACKINAC CT

DEBOER WOODS

GUNNER CT

MACKINAC

MANITOU CT

CATAWBA

TERRIER CT

CATAWBA CT

SPANIEL

SPANIEL WOODS

SPR DR

167TH ST

ST

SPRING CREEK TRAILS

SPRING CREEK SUB

BELLBRO

BRENTWOOD CT

MANITOU CT

RD

ASHLEY CT

WEDGEWOOD COMMOR DR

WEDGEWOOD HIGHLANDS

BURR OAK DR

THORN APPLE

BURR OAK DR

DEER PATH

BRENTWOOD DR

ASPEN LN

JUNIPER LN

EVERGREEN TER

TAMARACK CT

PINEVIEW

LONGMEADOW LN

MEADOWCREST

MEADOWCREST DR

15W-20S

25

WILL CO.
COOK CO.

175TH ST

CHICAGO-BLOOMINGTON

RD

(EDMONDS ST)

34

17W-21S

Hadley Cem.

FOXBORO LN

DRIFTWOOD DR

COURT CONNECTION LN

LARKSPUR LN

LARKSPUR CT

GLEN ENTRANCE

ROLLING GLEN

PARKER

179TH ST

LARSEN'S SUB

PARKER WOODS
PROPOSED

RYCON DR

CRYSTAL LAKE DR

CRYSTAL LAKES ESTATES

CRYSTAL LAKE CT

16W-21S

35

Scuds Lake

Rip Slough

BRUCE RD

175TH ST.

MARTI

RD

COUNTRY MANOR

36

179TH ST

15W-21S

SPRING MEADOWS DR

HWY

TEDD RD

DALE RD

SEE PAGES 24-25

ER TWP.
ENOX TWP.

T 36 N
T 35 N

SUMMERFIELD DR

MEADER RD

HILLTOP DR

LARKSPUR DR

MESSENGER MANOR PROPOSED

LEANNE

TRACY

DEBBIE LN

LEANNE LN

CYNTHIA

RACHEL LN

BETTY LN

ELIZABETH LN

ROSS DR

185TH ST

BLODGETT

CONLEE DR

PL

VIRGINIA LN

184TH ST

185TH ST

HASS

SOUTHWEST

MAIN ST

HICKORY ST

VALLEY ST

WILLOW RUN C.C.

MAPLE

80

CASTLE LN

MARLEY ST

HILLS DR

RAYMOND DR

JOSEPHINE

CRAIG CT

MARSHALL CT

THOMAS CT

BRUCE CT

WARREN

RODGER CT

BERNARD CT

WALTER CT

15W-22S

1S

CEDAR HWY

17W-22S

3

355

PROPOSED

80

80

RD

TAMMY DR

TIMOTHY

CARRIE CT

FLORENCE

EDWARD PKWY

RICHARD

LYNN PKWY

RUTH

2

RUTH RD

REGAN

HALEY RD

16W-22S

LAURA LN

TERRYELLEN LN

MICHAEL LN

ELM ST

NCHAW BLVD

BEVERLY BLVD

17W-23S

10

LENOX ST

INNER CT

THOMAS LN

KALARAMA DR

BARBARA LN

MAPLE LN

PINE ST

MARKEV LN

WALLACE ST

JOHN ST

ASPEN DR

KEITHLAND CT

LOCUST LN

HAUSER CT

WALKER WAY

GIBBONS DR

HICKORY CREEK DR

LILA'S CT

REDWOOD AV

WAGON DR

BUCKBOARD DR

LENOX ST

REGAN

LONDON

PARKER RD

FRANCIS

REGAN RD

WOODSIDE DR

LAKESIDE DR

16W-23S

11

HUNTER TRAIL

MARY CT

WOODSIDE DR

REGAN

MARSHALL RD

Marshall Cem.

WOODEDGE

RD

15W-23S

12

MOKENA

SCHOOLHOUSE RD

HILLSIDE DR

PLAZA DR

CARRINGTON RD

SHELLY LN

PICKRAM RD

DONALD

JOEY CT

WALTER DR

ALISON TR

SARRIS SEVAN CT DR

RD

SEE PAGES 30-31

FOREST PRESERVE

FOREST PRESERVE

**14W-20S**

**13W-20S**

**12W-20S**

**14W-21S**

**13W-21S**

**12W-21S**

ORLAND PARK

1 ALASKA CT
2 ARIZONA CT
3 ARKANSAS CT
4 CALIFORNIA CT
5 COLORADO CT
6 CONNECTICUT CT
7 DELAWARE CT
8 FLORIDA CT
9 GEORGIA CT
10 HAWAII CT
11 IDAHO CT
12 INDIANA CT
13 IOWA CT
14 KANSAS CT
15 ALABAMA CT

COOK COUNTY
WILL COUNTY

T 36 N    ORLAND TWP.
T 35 N    FRANKFORT TWP.

Tinley Gardens Tot Lot

**14W-22S**

**13W-22S**

**12W-22S**

MAPLE (MARLEY) RD

187TH ST

**14W-23S  60448**

**13W-23S**

**12W-23S**

MOKENA

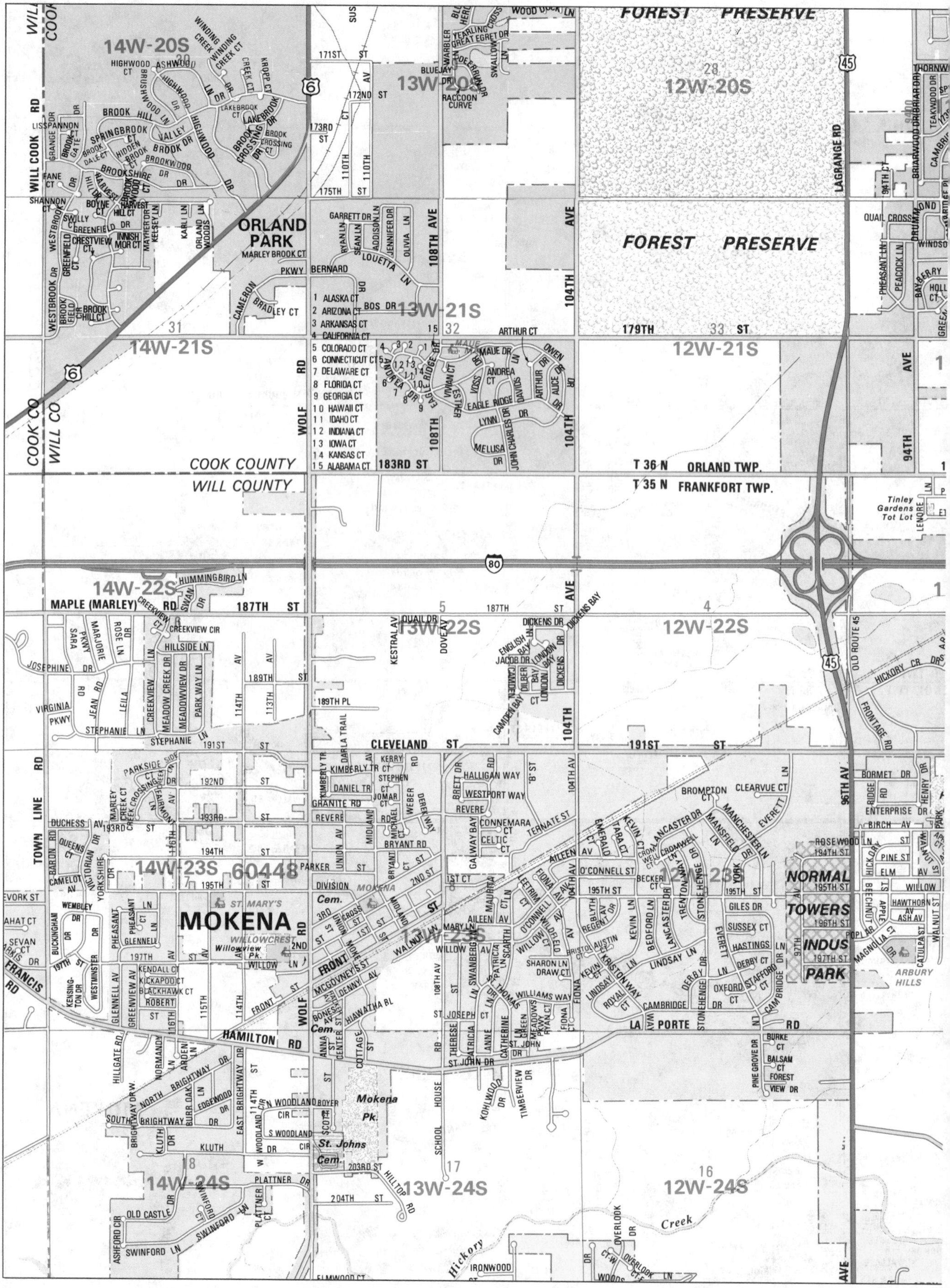

St. Mary's

NORMAL TOWERS INDUS PARK

Arbury Hills

LA PORTE RD

HAMILTON RD

Mokena Pk.

St. Johns Cem.

**14W-24S**

**13W-24S**

**12W-24S**

Creek

Hickory
IRONWOOD

SEE PAGES 22-23

SEE COOK COUNTY PAGES 84-85

SEE COOK COUNTY PAGES 86-87

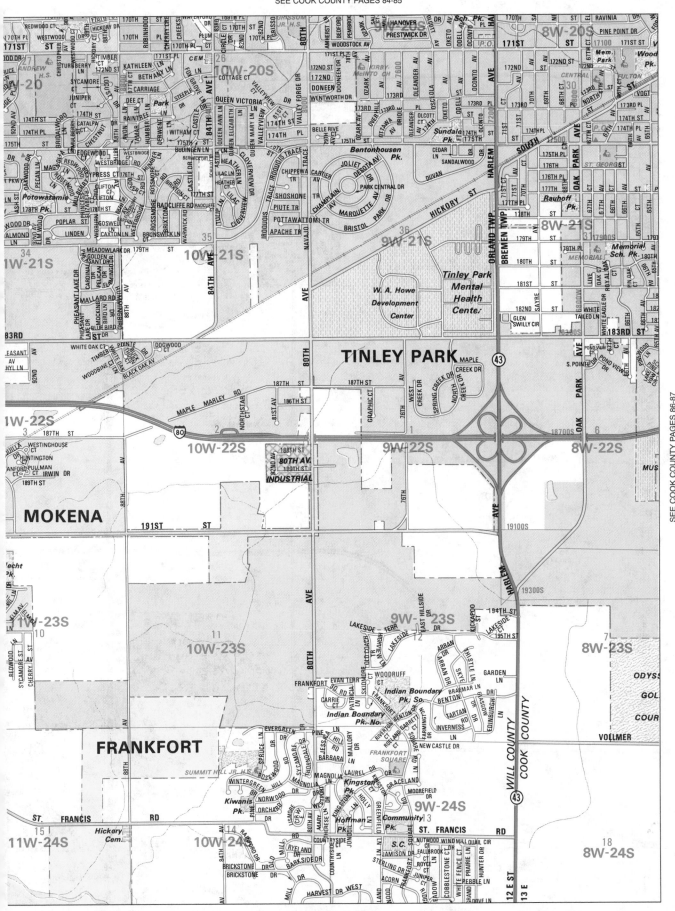

**TINLEY PARK**

**MOKENA**

**FRANKFORT**

SEE PAGES 32-33

SEE PAGES 18-19

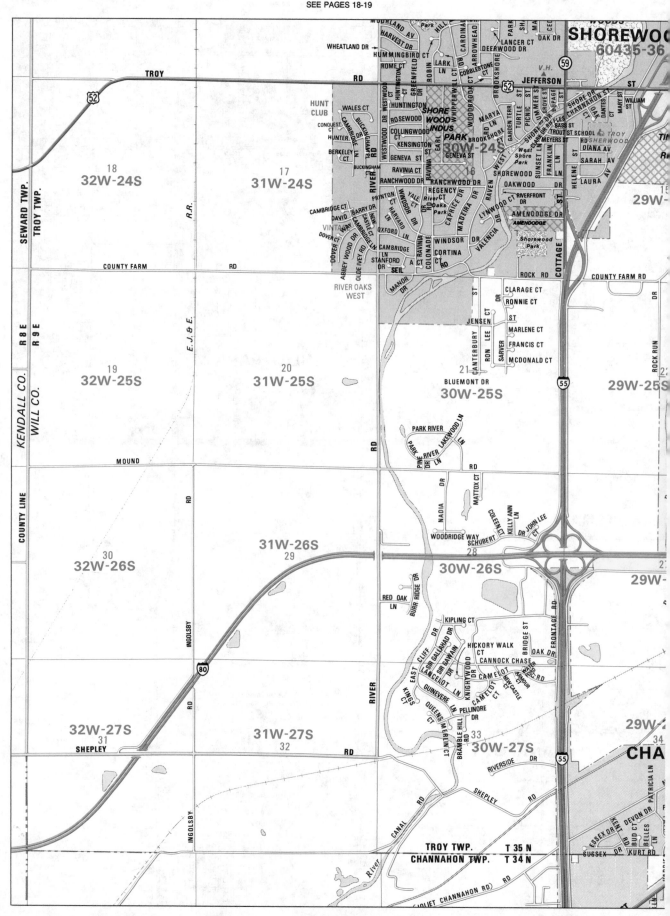

SEE PAGES 34-35

WOODLAND Mem. Park Cem.

TIMBERLINE CT

COVENTRY CT

Hills of Rexl Cem.

RIDGE

ROLL

MEADOW

WES

RANDY RD

CRABAPPLE

DEERPATH DR

TWIN OAKS DR

ROBERT

STERLING DR

HERITAGE DR

MARTIN

ROSEWOOD DR

CRANBERRY DR

TWIN OAKS DR

ROLLS ROYCE

CAMPBELL DR

MAYOR DR

INWOOD

CAMPBELL

EDIE LN

RICHMOND

SUNSET STRIP

STADIUM

ALEXANDER DR

BARNEY

MADISON

POTTER

KEY

ST

JOLIET TWP

TROY TW

WEST H.S.

300N

200N

Hospital

REPUBLIC

SPRINGFIELD

26W-23S

TERRACE

MARQUE

FOR

ONEIDA

WOODLAND

McDONALD AV

LUCIE DR

DR

MBER

DGE

JEFFERSON ST

52

**Joliet Municipal Airport**

ROCK RUN (COUNTY FARM RD) DR

McDONOUGH

14

28W-24S

52

Armory

Joliet Municipal Stadium

**INWOOD GOLF CLUB**

CATERPILLAR DR

13

27W-24S

**Reformatory**

County Farm Cem.

Jefferson Square Mall

MARY CREST

JEFFERSON

FRANCINE AV

WEBSTER AV

BENEDICT AV

MARMION

MADONNA

ST FRANCIS

CAPRI

SAINT JOSEPH AV

ROMAYNE AV

HAMMES AV

ST JUDE AV

KATHLYN PL

NOTRE DAME AV

ST JUDE P.O.

PURDUE

JOYCE

OAK LEAF ST

OAKLEAF CENTER

80

18

BELLARMINE DR W.

BELLARMINE DR E.

ST 400S

500S

ONS

7

W ALLEN ST

EMERY ST

MORRIS ST

MARGARET ST

McDONOUGH

FERRIS PL

IVY PL

LAKEVIEW

KINSIE

STRYKER

OTISER

MORRIS ST

BELL

EMERY

100S

200S

300S

500S

600S

700S

Y.M.C.A.

MULFORD LN

COPLEY LN

MENLO

SHILOH CT

NAT'MA CT

WINDSOR LN

STONEHURST CT

QUINCY CT

PRICE CT

PIONEER CT

LONGFORD CT

MOSBY CT

SURE CT

LEAWOOD DR

LOUISE LN

LOREN DR

CRAIG

CHRISTINE

JERALD DR

LEAWOOD DR

KAREN

KEX CT

CATHY DR

KARAN DR

CATHY DR

60436

**ROCKDALE**

MOEN AV

R 9 E

R 10 E

19

26W-25S

LARKIN

**JOLIET JUNIOR COLLEGE**

JUNIOR COLLEGE DR N

JUNIOR COLLEGE DR S

HOUBOLT

28W-25S

23

RIVERBOAT BLVD

RIVERBOAT CT

27W-25S

24

RD

**ROCKY RUN**

**BUSINESS**

**PARK**

ROCK CREEK BLVD

MOUND

MOUND

80

RD

RD

BUSH RD

CHICAGO, ROCK ISLAND & PACIFIC R.R.

26

28W-26S

CHANNAHON

6

RD

27W-26S

25

EMPRESS DR

TERRY DR

REEVES RD

**CROWN TRYGO INDUSTRIAL**

26W-26S

30

26S

Canal

Illinois & Michigan

MARY LOU AV

KARL AV

DEAL

JOSEPH RD

DONNA RD

CARRIE

CANAL RD

ANDREW AV

28W-27S

EMPRESS RIVERBOAT

Des Plaines River

A.T. & S.F.

I.C.

27W-27S

36

LARAWAY

RD

R.R.

R.R.

31

26W-27S

7S

60410

NNAHON

McCLINTOCK

SHORTLINE RD

PARK PL DR

JONATHON RD

ANNA DR

MICHAEL

WALTA DR

KATHY

GORDO DR

KATHEY CT

PENN LN

McDONALD

FRANCES CT

KATHEY DR

FRANCES WY

ICIA LN

6

6

JOLIET RD

SEE PAGES 28-29

SEE PAGES 20-21

SEE PAGES 26-27

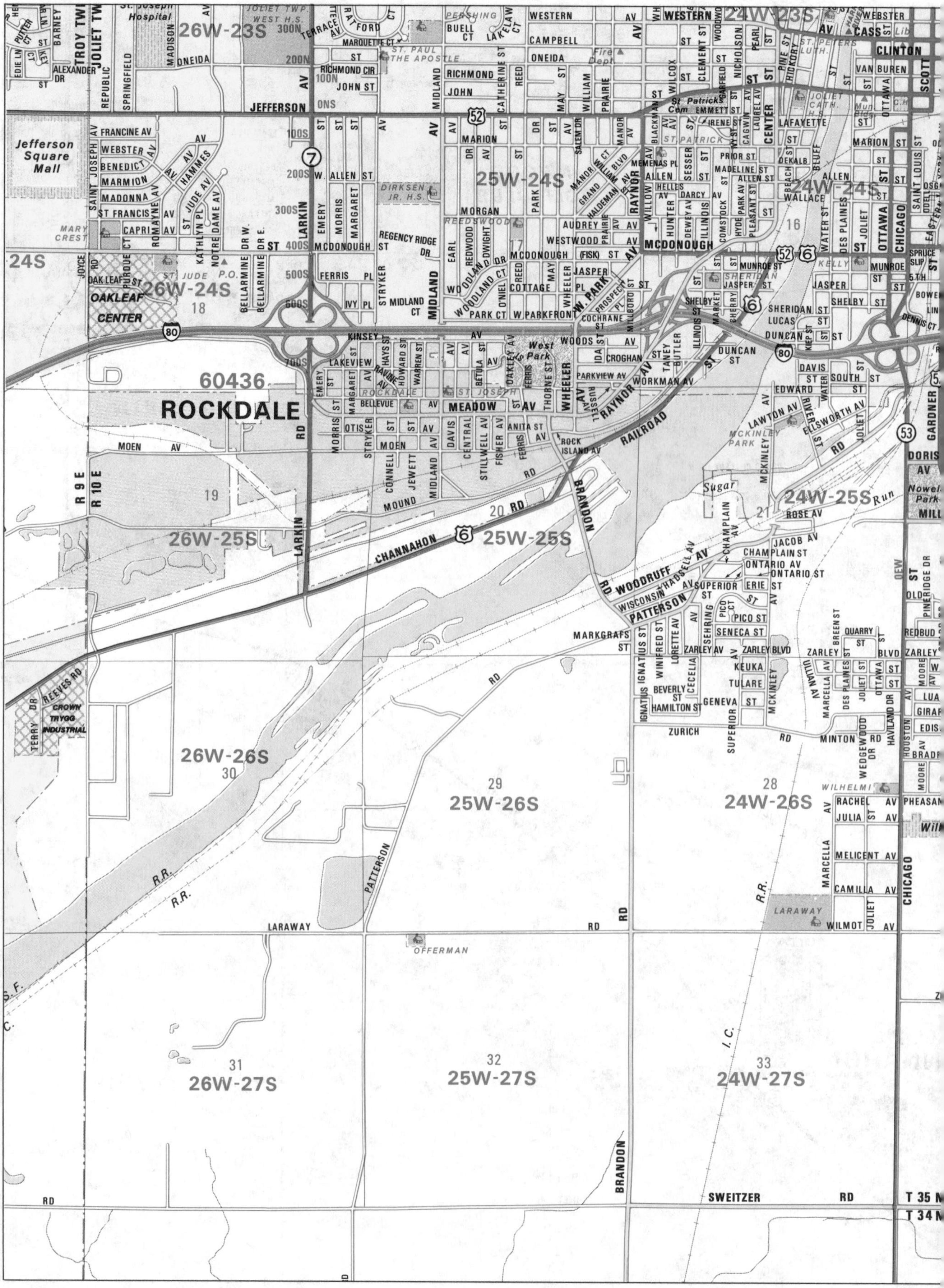

**ROCKDALE**

60436

26W-23S

25W-24S

26W-24S

24W-24S

24S

OAKLEAF CENTER

Jefferson Square Mall

MARY CREST

Jefferson Square

St. Joseph Hospital

Joliet Twp. West H.S.

TROY TWP

JOLIET TW

18

19

20

21

16

17

26W-25S

25W-25S

24W-25S

26W-26S

25W-26S

24W-26S

29

28

30

26W-27S

25W-27S

24W-27S

31

32

33

R 9 E    R 10 E

CROWN TRYGO INDUSTRIAL

McKINLEY PARK

West Park

WEST PARK

Sugar Run

Nowell Park

MILL

LARAWAY

OFFERMAN

SWEITZER          RD

T 35 N
T 34 N

SEE PAGES 36-37

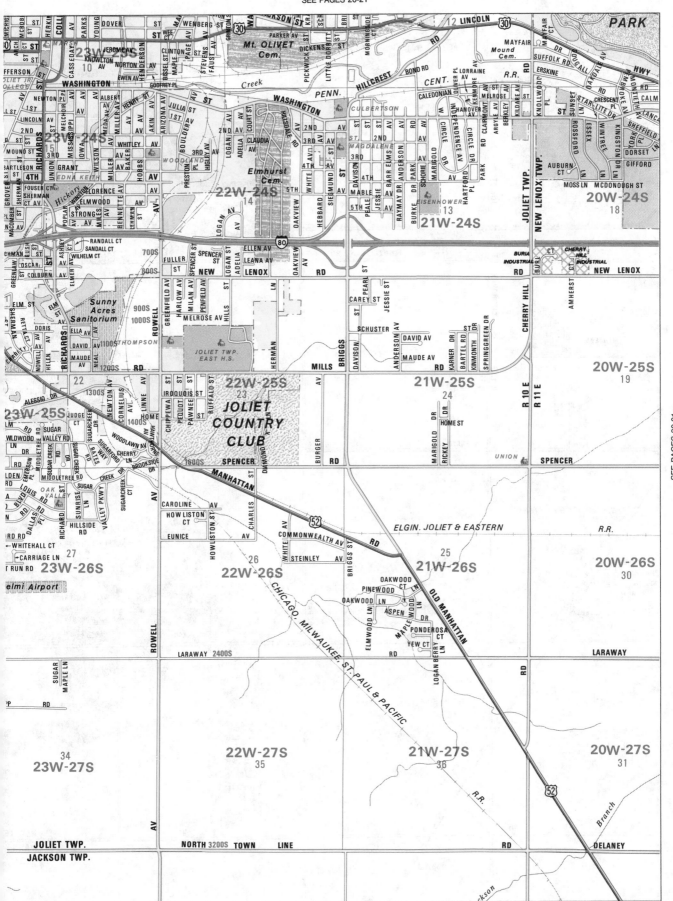

SEE PAGES 30-31

MAYFAIR Mound Cem.

FRANCIS

WOODS

TRINITY SCH.

CENT. R.R.

HILLCREST

BOND RD

MORNINGVIEW CT

OLIVER PL

LORRAINE

KENMORE

MELROSE

CALEDONIAN

HANOVER DR

INDEPENDENCE AV

CIRCLE DR

ARGYLE AV

KILDARE AV

CLAIRMONT

PARK RD

CLAIRMONT RD

SUFFOLK RD

ERSKINE

DOUGALL AV

OAKDALE AV

PEMBROKE AV

MONTIETH AV

LANCASTER

HWY

CALMER RD

KNOLLWOOD

SUNSET ST

STAR-LITE PL

CRESCENT PL

ROSSFORD

ESSEX

WINTREE

KINGSTON DR

SHEFFIELD DR

PARK

DORSET LN

GIFFORD PL

DOXBURY LN

HEMPSTEAD

CHICAGO, ROCK ISLAND & PACIFIC R.R.

PROVIDENCE H.S.

HOLLY HILL CIR

THORNHOUSE

BAMBURG

CRESCENT

BJORK DR

CLINTON

GORDON

SYCAMORE

LN

GREEN

WILLOW ST

WILLOW RD WEST

Hickory

OLD NEW LENOX RD

VINE

19W-24S
17

18W-24

30

HILLSIDE RD

GREENBRIAR DR

PARK LN

MANOR

VINE ST

OLD NEW

ALBERTSON

MAGDALENE

2ND

4TH

PEALE AV

JESSIE AV

NOBLE AV

ST

BARR

ELMS AV

ANDERSON AV

PARK AV

RAYMAY DR

BURKE DR

SHORE

RD

HARTFORD PL

MARIGOLD AV

EISENHOWER
13

21W-24S

JOLIET TWP.

NEW LENOX TWP.

AUBURN CT

MOSS LN

MCDONOUGH ST

20W-24S
18

STONE FERRO DR

FERRO DR

GARNET

FERRO INDUSTRIAL PARK

80

60451

NEW LENOX

BENT TREE LN

BATHILL DR

WINDCREST

BENT TREE CT

TALL GRASS LN

GRAND PRAIRIE

BRITTANY DR

WHITEWATER

ABBEY

VICTORIAN

HONEY

WHISPER CRK DR

FAIRFIELD

KRIS

NELSON RD

GREENBRIAR DR

LIVINGSTON DR

NEW LENOX

PARK LN

JESSIE ST

PEARL ST

BURIA INDUSTRIAL

CHERRY HILL INDUSTRIAL

BURIAL RD

NEW LENOX RD

RD

CHUSTER AV

ANDERSON AV

DAVID AV

MAUDE AV

RD

KARNER DR

BARTEL RD

KINMONTH DR

SPRINGGREEN DR

CHERRY HILL RD

AMHERST ST

R 10 E

R 11 E

20W-25S
19

19W-25S
20

BEECHCRAFT DR

AERONCA CT

JUPITER DR

LEAR LN

CENTRAL RD

MUSTANG LN

MISTY CREEK DR

CORSAIR CT

CESSNA CT

RIDGEFIELD AV

HEARTLAND RD

HARTLAND

BEECH LN

BOEING DR

JOLIET HWY

STAFFORD DR

JOLIET HWY

21W-25S
24

MARIGOLD DR

HOME ST

RICKEY

UNION

SPENCER

RD

JOLIET STAFFORD

ARMSTRONG

WHITE LN

NELSON RD

YOUNG DR

GLENN DR

GRISSOM

CONRAD CT

NORMAN CT

LEXINGTON CT

LEXINGTON DR

WOODLAWN AV

CHURCHILL

NEWCASTLE DR

WILDWOOD DR

WESTERN AV

WISCONSIN

WOOD

18W-25
21

JOLIE

SPENCER

RD

ELGIN, JOLIET & EASTERN

R.R.

19W-26S
29

21W-26S
25

RD

OAKWOOD CT

PINEWOOD LN

WOOD LN

ASPEN

ELMWOOD LN

MAPLEWOOD

PONDEROSA CT

YEW CT

RD

LOGAN BERRY LN

OLD MANHATTAN RD

20W-26S
30

LARAWAY

GOUGAR RD

NELSON RD

CIMARRON

CHERRYWOOD

ANDREA DR

EAGLE VISTA LN

BRIARCREST LN

DELMAR DR

FERNWOOD DR

PORTER

ANDREA DR

COUNTRY CREEK DR

CC CREE CO PAR

18W-2
28

STONEBRIDGE

STONEBRIDGE DR

GRANDVIEW Park

SHAGBARK CT

SHAGBARK

TIMBERWOOD

TIMBER DR

NETHERLAND

WINTER PARK DR

RD

MEADOW RIDGE LN

Park

TIMBER PL

FOXWOOD

RD

PAUL & PACIFIC

RD

RD

SANFORD AV

CARLTON CT

DIGBY DR

JACKSON BRANCH RD

ARGYLE LN Park

DANIEL LEWIS DR

KERRY WINDE DR

GINGER LN

GRAND MESA TR

ARTHURS PASS

PALMER RANCH LN

SWEET WATER TR

CATTLEMEN DR

REITER

21W-27S
36

20W-27S
31

19W-27S
32

18W-27
33

52

Branch

RD

R.R.

DELANEY

KROLL CT

MONARCH AV

PRINCESS AV

KNIGHT LN

DUCHESS AV

CENTURION LN

CENTURION

KINGSWAY

MALIBU DR

AV

RD

NEW LE

MANHA

Jackson

SEE PAGES 28-29

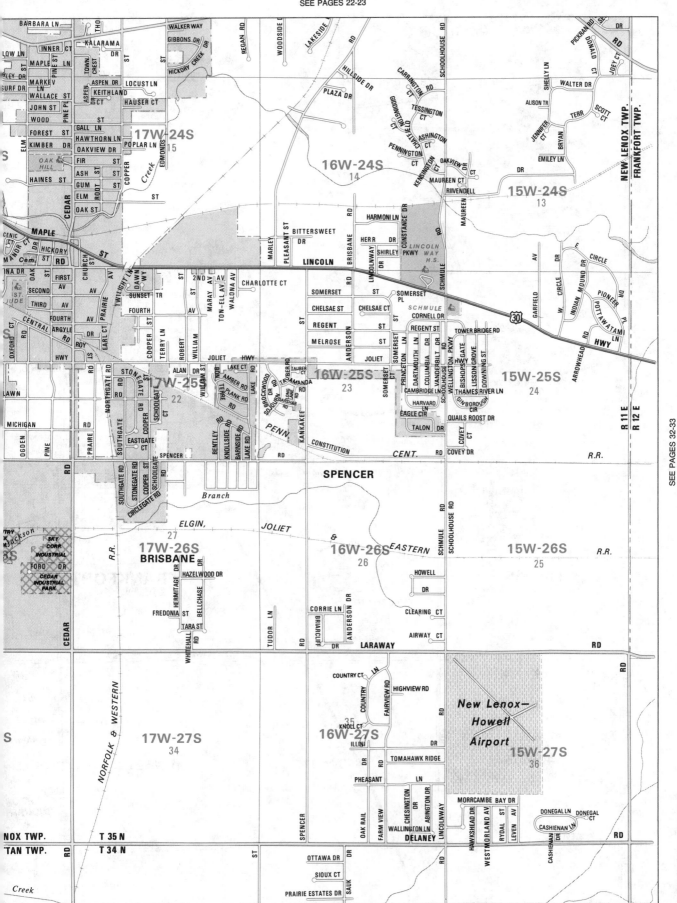

14W-24S    13W-24S    12W-24S

14W-25S    13W-25S    12W-25S

14W-26S    13W-26S    12W-26S

14W-27S    13W-27S    12W-27S

**FRANKFORT**

60423

Mokena Pk.

St. Johns Cem.

VAN HORNE WOODS

Old Plank Road Trail (Under development)

Pleasant Hill Cem.

E. J. & E. RR

INDUSTRIAL PARK

ARBURY HILLS

ABBY WOODS

TOWN CENTER S.C.

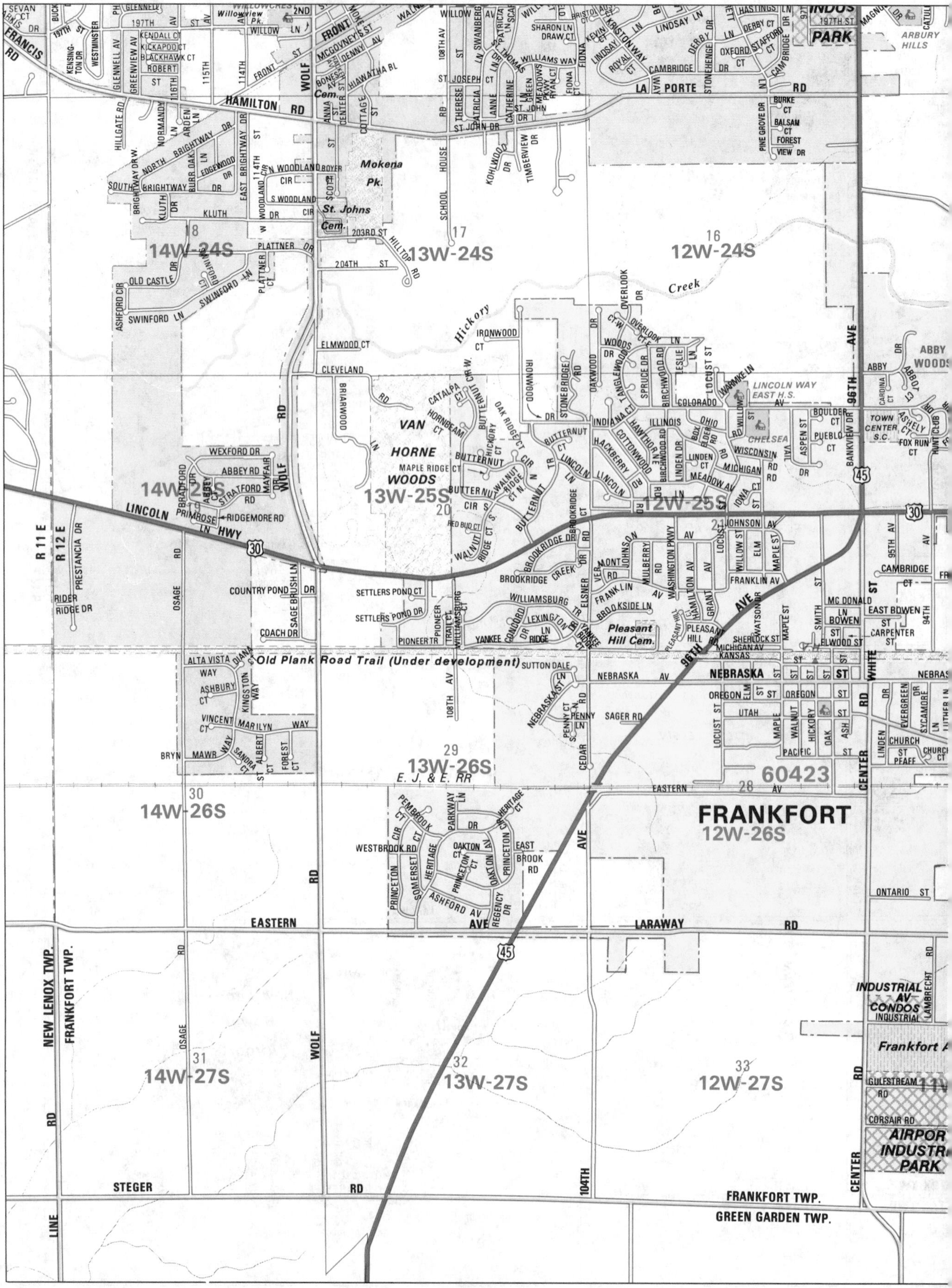

Lincoln Way East H.S.

SEE PAGES 30-31

R 11 E   R 12 E

NEW LENOX TWP.   FRANKFORT TWP.

FRANKFORT TWP.   GREEN GARDEN TWP.

AIRPORT INDUSTRIAL PARK

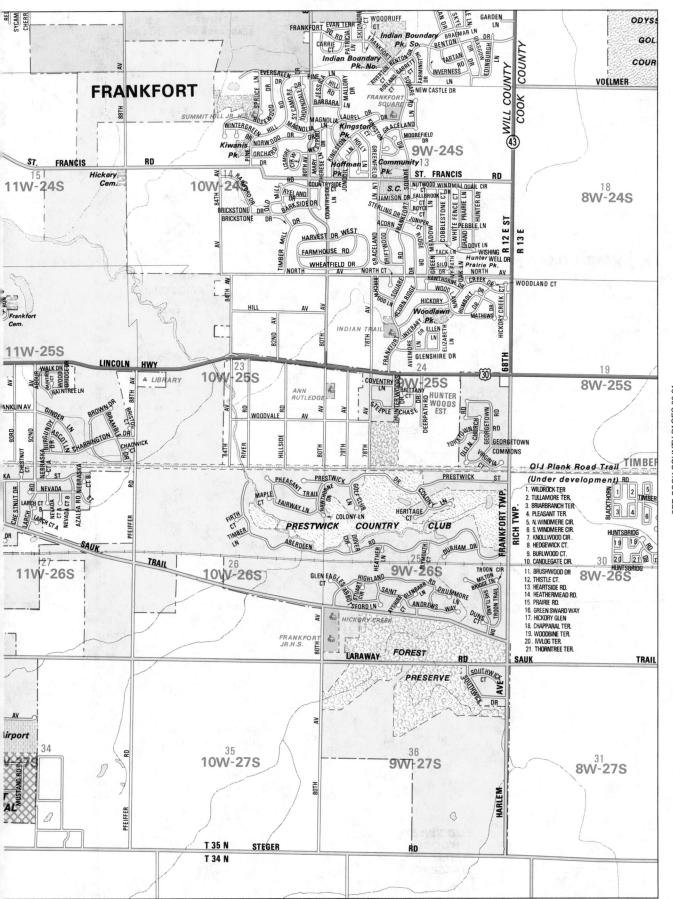

# FRANKFORT

Old Plank Road Trail
(Under development)
1. WILDROCK TER.
2. TULLAMORE TER.
3. BRIARBRANCH TER.
4. PLEASANT TER.
5. N. WINDMERE CIR.
6. S. WINDMERE CIR.
7. KNOLLWOOD CIR.
8. HEDGEWICK CT.
9. BURLWOOD CT.
10. CANDLEGATE CIR.
11. BRUSHWOOD DR.
12. THISTLE CT.
13. HEARTSIDE RD.
14. HEATHERMEAD RD.
15. PRAIRIE RD.
16. GREEN SWARD WAY
17. HICKORY GLEN
18. CHAPPARAL TER.
19. WOODBINE TER.
20. IVVLOG TER.
21. THORNTREE TER.

SEE PAGES 26-27

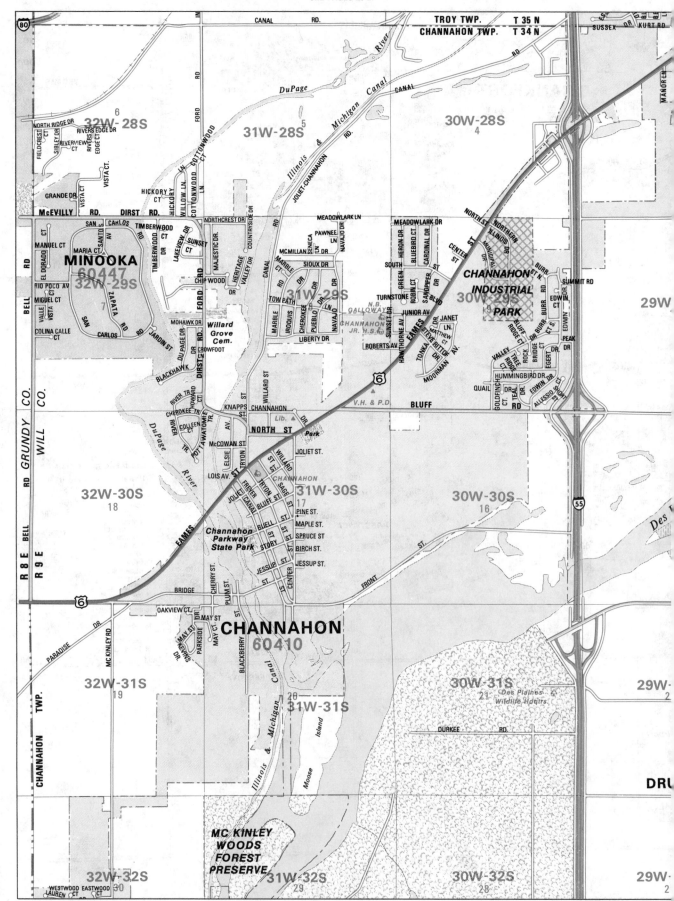

SEE PAGES 46-47

SEE PAGES 26-27

JOLIET                    RD

**60436**

**29W-28S**          2
              **28W-28S**          1
                              **27W-28S**                    6
                                                   **26W-28S**

WILMINGTON          RD

*Troutman Grove Cem.*

CRAIG          RD
MILLSDALE          RD

OLIN          RD

**29S**          **28W-29S**          11
              MILLSDALE          12    RD
              **27W-29S**
                              **26W-29S**          7

PATTERSON          RD.

*Treat    Island*

TORDI LN

MILLSDALE     EXT     RD.          GAS     PLANT     RD.

*Plaines*

*River*

**29W-30S**          15
              **28W-30S**          14
                              **27W-30S**          13
                                             **26W-30S**          18

MILLSDALE RD

R 9 E
R 10 E     MANHATTAN          RD

ARSENAL          RD.

*Jackson*

CHANNAHON  TWP.
JACKSON  TWP.

DIAGONAL          RD.

**31S**          **28W-31S**          23
              *Creek*     **27W-31S**          24
                                       **26W-31S**          19

ST.

**JOLIET ARSENAL
(DE-COMMISSIONED)**

KANKAKEE

*Lloyd C. Er*

**UMMOND**

A & SANTA FE
RR

*Maple
Hill Cem.*

MISSISSIPPI          AV.

LINCOLN          ST.

**32S**          **28W-32S**          26
              **27W-32S**          25
                              **26W-32S**          30

SEE PAGES 36-37

SEE PAGES 46-47

SEE PAGES 28-29

SWEITZER

27W-28S
1

26W-28S
6

25W-28S
5

24W-28S
4

SHARP

BRANDON RD

Troutman Grove Cem.

CRAIG RD

WILMINGTON

CRAIG
MILLSDALE RD

KEITH ALLEN
GARY RAY
GLADYS AV

26W-29S
7

BRANDON RD

25W-29S
8

24W-29S
9

MILLSDALE 12 RD

27W-29S

PATTERSON RD

BRIDGE

G.M. & O.R.R.

SEE PAGES 34-35

TORDI LN

MILLSDALE EXT RD

GAS PLANT RD

NOEL RD

WALNUT ST
SYCAMORE ST
ASH ST

27W-30S
13

26W-30S
18

17 MANHATTAN

25W-30S

BUSH RD

TIMBER DR

Creek

24W-30S
16

R 9 E
R 10 E
MANHATTAN RD

CREEK DR
RONDOREY RD
LOIS LN
TANGLEWOOD DR W.
TANGLEWOOD DR E.

TEHLE RD

Jackson
CHICAGO

CHANNAHON TWP.
JACKSON TWP.

27W-31S
24

26W-31S
19

25W-31S
20

TEHLE RD

24W-31S
21

Creek

KANKAKEE

ST

DIAGONAL RD

TEHLE DR
COBBLESTONE
EAGLE CREEK
DEEPATH LN
ARCHER LN
WYNSTONE DR

AV

TEHLE RD

(NED)

BEATTIE ST

WOODBINE DR

BRIARWOOD CT
LINEBARGO CT

Lloyd C. Erickson
Park

BUSH DR

60421

WOOD

NORTH ST
PARKS
SPENCER ST
Park

CHICAGO
ST

ELWOOD
53

WOOD

Maple Hill Cem.

MISSISSIPPI AV

WOOD ST

P.O.
A.T.H.
& P.D.

MISSISSIPPI AV

GARDNER
MORRIS
JACKSON
SOUTH

CHICAGO
MATTESON ST
DOUGLAS ST
ST. LOUIS ST

LINCOLN

27W-32S
25

26W-32S
30

25W-32S
29

24W-32S
28

SEE PAGES 48-49

SEE PAGES 28-29

RD | T 35 N | JOLIET TWP. | NORTH    TOWN    LINE | RD

T 34 N | JACKSON TWP.

53

Jackson

3

**23W-28S** | **22W-28S** | **21W-28S**

2 | 1

BERNHARD    RD. | STONE    RD

RD

RIDGE

ROWELL

CHERRY HILL

RAYMOND DR

EATON AV

Cem.

**23W-29S** | **22W-29S** | **21W-29S**

10 | 11 | 12

BREEN | RD

RD

53

SPANGLER    RD.

CLAIR CT.

DR.

KINDER RD

HENDREW

ALICE CT.

Jackson

ROB AV.

RICH CT.

MARIAN AV.

BICENTENNIAL DR.

RON CT.

PHEASANT DR.

QUAIL CT.

JEFFREY CT.

MBER DR N.

BER DR S.

TIMBER CT.

15 | 14 | MANHATTAN    RD | 13 | ELWOOD

**23W-30S** | **22W-30S** | **21W-30S**

RD.

RD.

ROWELL

RIDGE

R 10 E | R 11 E

Cem.

Manhattan

Creek

**23W-31S** | **22W-31S** | **21W-31S**

BROWN | 22 | RD. (SWEEDLER) | 23 | BROWN | 24 | RD. (SWEEDLER)

JACKSON TWP.

MANHATTAN TWP.

RD.

RD.

RD.

RD.

**23W-32S** | **22W-32S** | **21W-32S**

27 | 26 | 25

SEE PAGES 38-39

SEE PAGES 48-49

SEE PAGES 30-31

DELANEY
RD
RD
NEW LENO
MANHATTA

52

MALIBU DR

AV

**20W-28S**
6

**19W-28S**
5

**18W-28S**
4

STONE
RD

**21W-28S**

CHERRY HILL
RD

Jackson

Jackson

EASTERN

RD

BAKER

RD

CREEK
DR
KATHRYN AV
WY

DIANE SUSAN LN
WY

**20W-29S**
7

**19W-29S**
8

**18W-29S**
9

**21W-29S**
12

SEE PAGES 36-37

RD

CHERRY HILL

SPANGLER
RD.

SMITH
RD
STAUFFENBURG RD
RIDGEFIELD DR

52
STATE

ROSEWOOD LN
DR
LAKEVIEW
DR

Jackson
ROB AV.

RICH CT.
MARIAN AV.

RON CT.

FOXFORD
DONEGAL DR

EDXFORD
CASHEL BAY RD

RD
ELWOOD MANHATTAN
RD

St. Joseph
Cem.

ED BLACKTHORNE
RD

BLACKTHORNE

**19W-30S**
1

**18W-30S**
16

WESTERN
AV

WATERFORD LN

ST

FAIRVIEW

MORGAN

**60442**

RD

**21W-30S**
13

RD.

SELTZER

WOODROW AV

MARION ST

**MANHATTAN**

R 10 E

R 11 E

**20W-30S**
18

EBERHART ST

PRAIRIE AV
PRAIRIE AV

JULIANNE DR
MANHATTAN M

St. JOSEPH
DR

P.O.

NORTH
ST
ST

BRETT
BRETT
CT.

SHARP
DR

TRASK

MADISON

JESSIE

TERRY
31ST ST
ST

MAY ST

LINCOLN

EASTERN
AV

ST

CENTURY
EAST

COCHRAN ST.

HENRY ST.

FRONT ST.
McCLURE

2ND ST

ST

BRIAN CT.
ANDREA DR

CALLA DR

BROWN
ST.

PARK
Lib. Pk.
F.D.
WHITSON
ST
2ND

FRANCIS
CT

SHEILA RD.

V.H. & P.D.

THELMA
LEE
KAY
JAN

JACKSON TWP.

MANHATTAN TWP.

Creek

**21W-31S**
24

BROWN
RD. (SWEEDLER)

**20W-31S**
19

GOUGAR
RD.

**19W-31S**

ANNA MC DONALD
20

3RD
3RD ST

**18W-31**
21

STATE
ST

GALLAGER
RD.

RD.

RR
RR

KEE ST. PAUL & PACIFIC
OLK & WESTERN

Prairie

**21W-32S**
25

**20W-32S**
30

**19W-32S**
29

**18W-32S**
28

SEE PAGES 50-51

SEE PAGES 30-31

X TWP.

N TWP.

T 35 N

T 34 N

*Creek*

SPE

OA

FAR

**DELANEY**

LINI

HAWKS

WESTMORL

RYD

LEVE

RD

RD

OTTAWA DR

SIOUX CT

PRAIRIE ESTATES DR

SAUK

DR

SCHOOL HOUSE RD

KUSE RD

KUSE RD

**17W-28S**
3

**16W-28S**
2

**15W-28S**
1

HORSESHOE LN

BRIDLE PATH DR

SADDLECREST

HIGHLAND

SCHEER

DR

DR

HIGHLAND

CEDAR

KANKAKEE

ST.

KOEHLER RD

**BAKER**

RD

STUENKEL

RD

HIGHLAND DR

GLEN CT

HEATHER

GLEN

LN

CLOVE CT

HEATHER GLEN

**17W-29S**
10

**16W-29S**
11

**15W-29S**
12

SCHOOL HOUSE

RD.

GREEN GARDEN MANHATTAN RD

CARRIAGE

LN

SMITH

RD

SMITH

RD

SEE PAGES 40-41

CEDAR

RD

KANKAKEE

ST.

**17W-30S**
15

**16W-30S**
14

RD.

KOEHLER

**15W-30S**
13

SCHEER RD

IONEE

RD

KOEHLER

RD.

**MANHATTAN MONEE**

RD

MANHATTAN TWP.  R 11 E

GREEN GARDEN TWP.  R 12 E

**17W-31S**
22

HALEY

23

RD.

**16W-31S**

**15W-31S**
24

GALLAGER RD.   (HALEY RD.)

GALLAGER

RD.

*Creek*

RD.

RD.

**17W-32S**

**16W-32S**

**15W-32S**

SEE PAGES 50-51

SEE PAGES 32-33

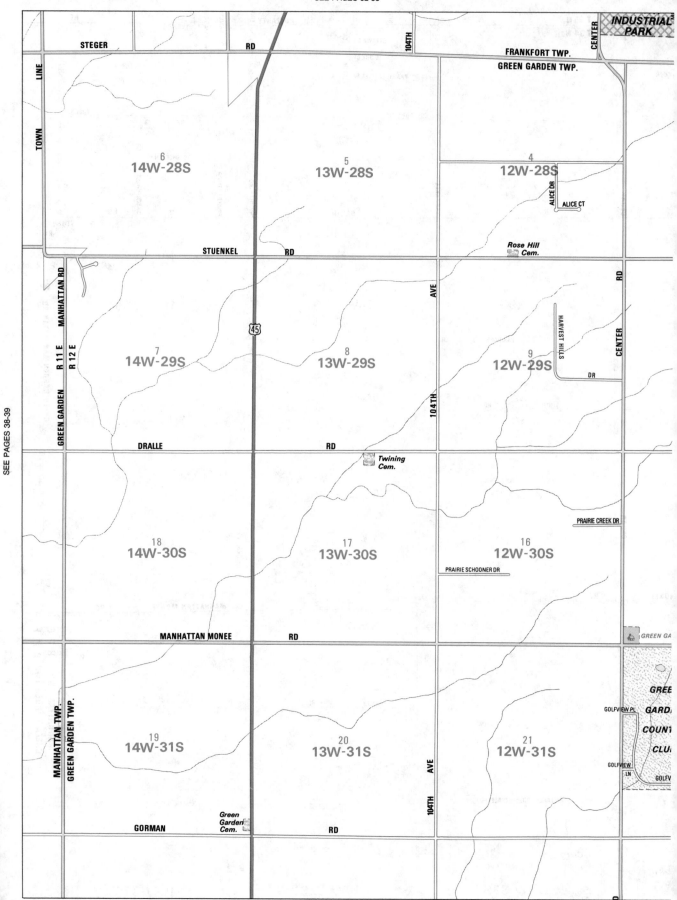

SEE PAGES 38-39

SEE PAGES 32-33

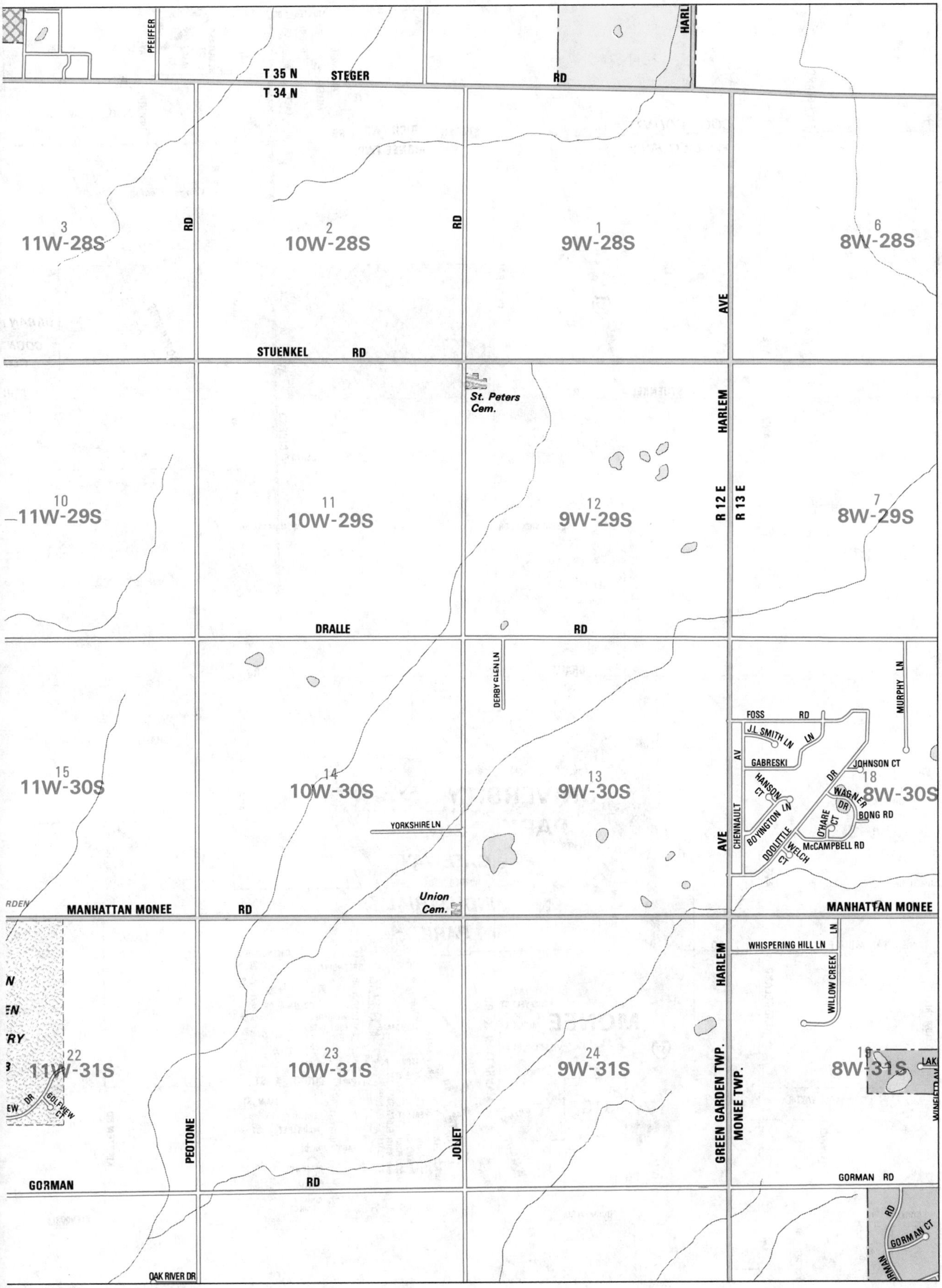

PFEIFFER

T 35 N STEGER RD
T 34 N

RD

RD

HARL

3
11W-28S

2
10W-28S

1
9W-28S

6
8W-28S

STUENKEL RD

AVE

St. Peters Cem.

HARLEM

R 12 E

R 13 E

10
11W-29S

11
10W-29S

12
9W-29S

7
8W-29S

SEE PAGES 42-43

DRALLE RD

DERBY GLEN LN

MURPHY LN

FOSS RD

J.L. SMITH LN

LN

GABRESKI

AV

JOHNSON CT

15
11W-30S

14
10W-30S

13
9W-30S

CHENNAULT

HANSON CT

BOYINGTON LN

WAGNER DR

18
8W-30S

DR

O'HARE CT

BONG RD

DOOLITTLE CT

WELCH

McCAMPBELL RD

YORKSHIRE LN

AVE

RDEN

Union Cem.

MANHATTAN MONEE RD

MANHATTAN MONEE

N
EN
RY

HARLEM

WHISPERING HILL LN

LN

WILLOW CREEK

GREEN GARDEN TWP.

MONEE TWP.

22
11W-31S

23
10W-31S

24
9W-31S

18
8W-31S

LAK

GOLFVIEW CT

EW DR

PEOTONE

JOLIET

WINFIELD AV

GORMAN RD

GORMAN RD

RD

RD

GORMAN CT

OAK RIVER DR

SEE PAGES 52-53

SEE COOK COUNTY PAGES 92-93

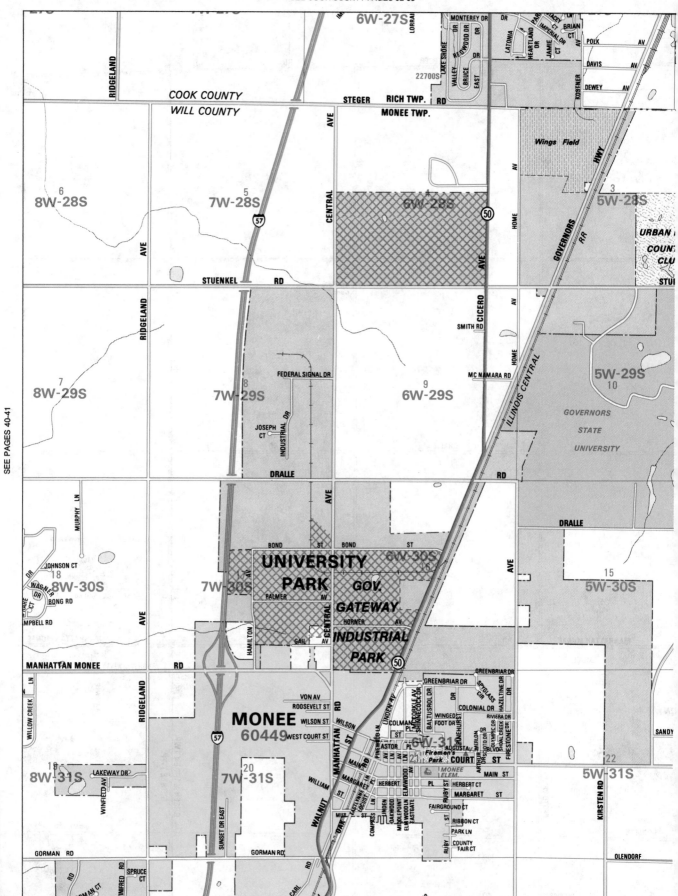

SEE PAGES 40-41

# UNIVERSITY PARK
## 60466

**THORN CREEK WOODS**

**DEER CREEK GOLF COURSE**

1 DRIFTWOOD CT
2 SPRING CT
3 SANDPIPER CT
4 PEBBLE CT
5 REDWOOD CT
6 WILDWOOD CT
7 CYPRESS CT
8 CARMEL CT
9 PACIFICA CT
10 SUNSET CT
11 MARINA CT
12 MONTEREY CT
13 DELMAR CT
14 MENDICINO CT
15 SIERRA CT

1W-27S
4W-28S 3W-28S 2W-28S 1W-28S
4W-29S 3W-29S 2W-29S
4W-30S 3W-30S 2W-30S
4W-31S 3W-31S 2W-31S

R 13 E WESTERN
R 14 E

RICHTON RD
STEGER RD
EXCHANGE ST
HAMILTON RD
CRETE MONEE RD
OLENDORF RD
MONEE RD
CENTRAL PARK AV
KEDZIE AVE
BLACKHAWK
KING RD
WESTERN AVE
OLD MONEE RD
MONEE TWP.
CRETE TWP.

Thorn Creekwoods Nature Center
ST. MARY'S
Park Forest Golf Center
Park Forest Comm. Gardens
Pine Lake Pk
Library
Helgel Rec. Center
Calvary Cem.
DEER CREEK JR. SR. H.S.
CRETE MONEE H.S.
Shabbona Pk
Somonauk Pk
RICHTON SQUARE
Deer Creek Ditch

SEE PAGES 44-45

SEE PAGES 54-55

SEE COOK COUNTY PAGES 94-95

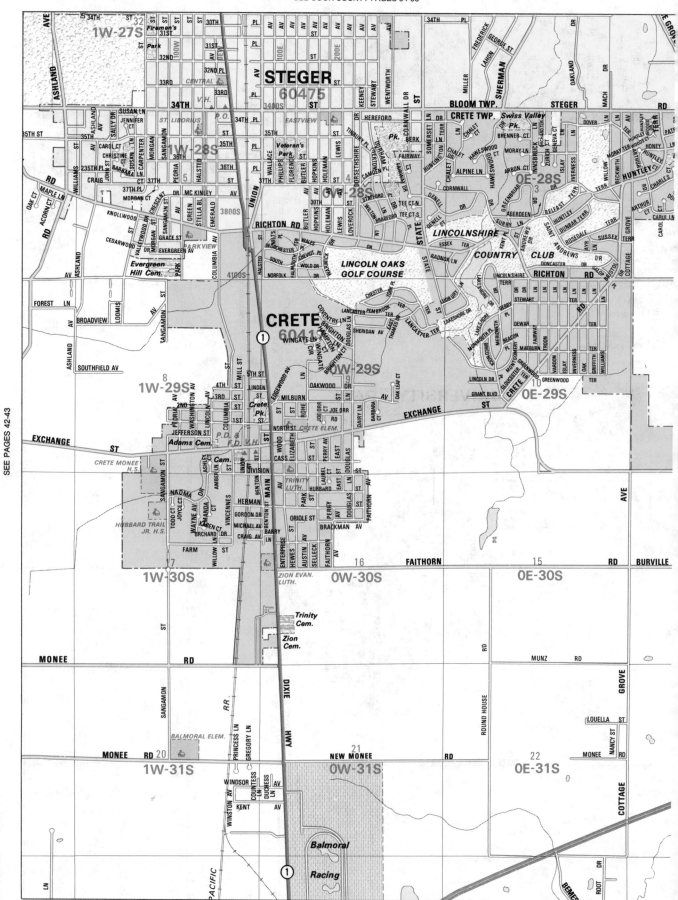

SEE PAGES 42-43

SEE PAGES 56-57

SEE COOK COUNTY PAGES 94-95

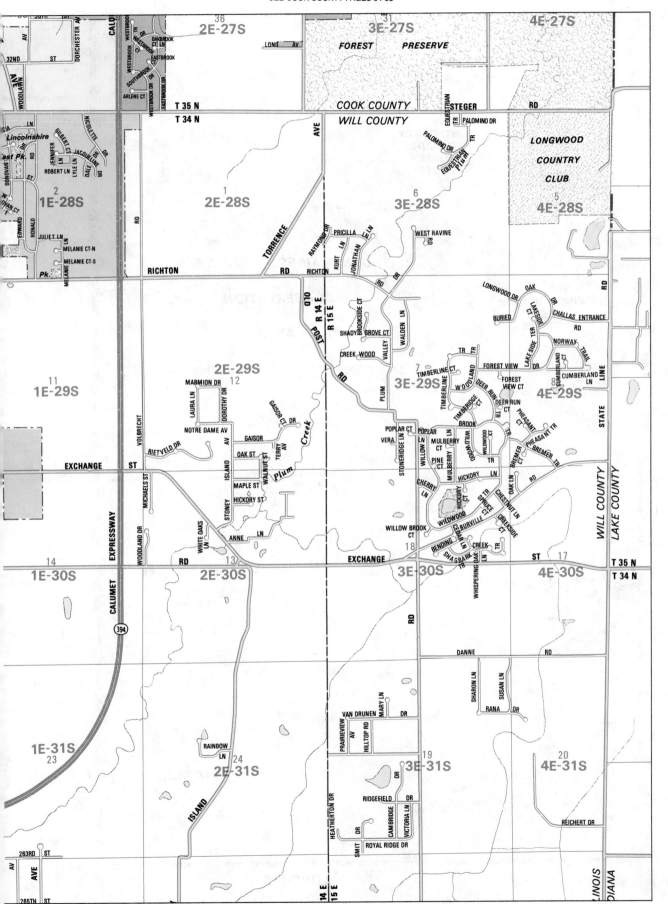

SEE PAGES 34-35

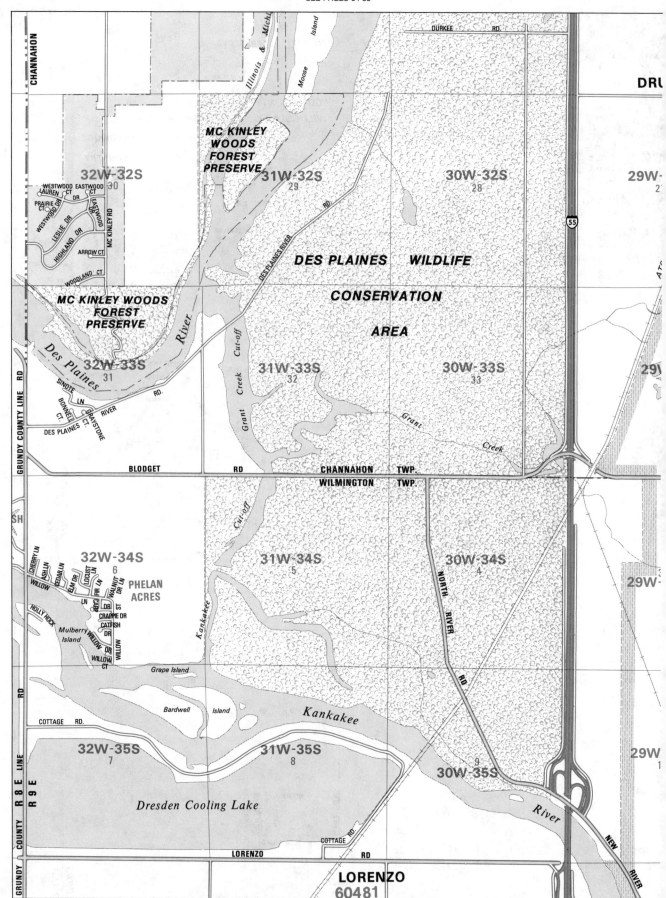

DURKEE RD.

DRU

CHANNAHON

MC KINLEY
WOODS
FOREST
PRESERVE

Illinois & Michi

Moose Island

**32W-32S**
30

**31W-32S**
29

**30W-32S**
28

**29W-**
2

WESTWOOD EASTWOOD CT
LAUREN CT
PRAIRIE CT
WESTWOOD DR
EASTWOOD DR
LESLIE DR
HIGHLAND DR
ARROW CT
WOODLAND CT
MC KINLEY RD

RD.

DES PLAINES RIVER

**DES PLAINES WILDLIFE**

**CONSERVATION**

**AREA**

55

MC KINLEY WOODS
FOREST
PRESERVE

Des Plaines River

**32W-33S**
31

**31W-33S**
32

**30W-33S**
33

**29W**

SINOTE LN
BONNELL CT
GRAYSTONE CT
DES PLAINES RIVER RD.

Grant Creek Cut-off

Grant

Creek

BLODGET RD.

CHANNAHON TWP.
WILMINGTON TWP.

Cut-off

SH

CHERRY LN
ASH LN
CEDAR LN
ELM DR
LOCUST LN
FIR LN
WALNUT DR LN
**32W-34S**
6

**31W-34S**
5

**30W-34S**
4

NORTH RIVER RD.

**29W-**

PHELAN
ACRES

WILLOW LN
RBC DR
ST
CRAPPIE DR
CATFISH DR
WILLOW DR
HOLLY HOCK

Mulberry Island

Kankakee

WILLOW CT

Grape Island

Bardwell Island

Kankakee

COTTAGE RD.

**32W-35S**
7

**31W-35S**
8

**30W-35S**
9

**29W**
1

GRUNDY COUNTY LINE RD.
R 8 E LINE
R 9 E

*Dresden Cooling Lake*

River

NEW RIVER

COTTAGE RD.

LORENZO RD.

## LORENZO
**60481**

SEE PAGES 58-59

SEE PAGES 34-35

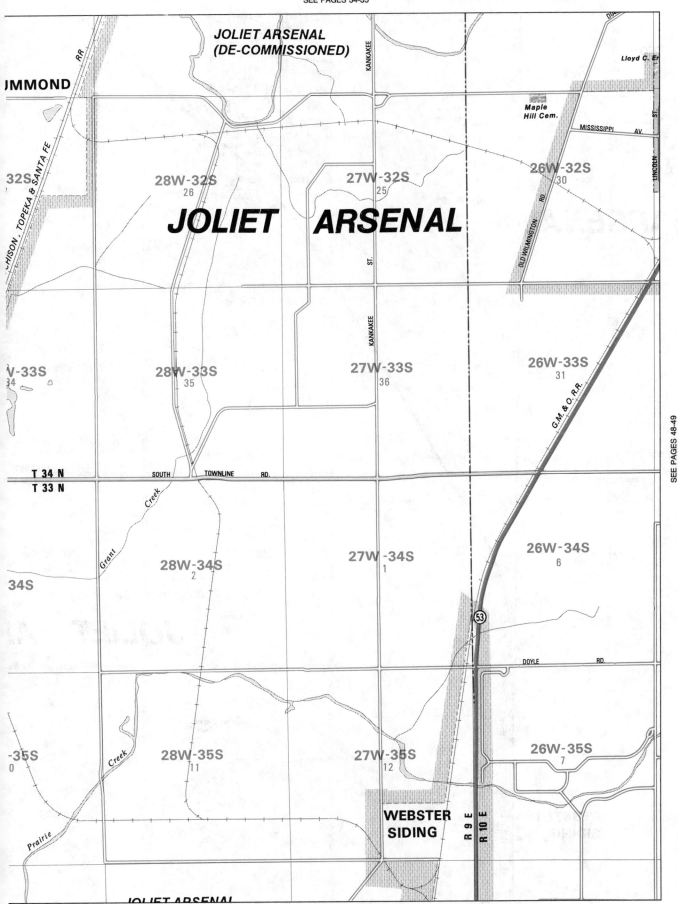

JOLIET ARSENAL
(DE-COMMISSIONED)

UMMOND

Lloyd C. Er

Maple
Hill Cem.

MISSISSIPPI AV.

28W-32S
26

27W-32S
25

26W-32S
30

32S

# JOLIET ARSENAL

ST.

KANKAKEE

V-33S
34

28W-33S
35

27W-33S
36

26W-33S
31

G.M. & O.R.R.

T 34 N
T 33 N

SOUTH TOWNLINE RD.

Creek

Grant

28W-34S
2

27W-34S
1

26W-34S
6

34S

53

DOYLE RD.

35S
0

Creek

28W-35S
11

27W-35S
12

26W-35S
7

Prairie

**WEBSTER
SIDING**

R 9 E
R 10 E

JOLIET ARSENAL

SEE PAGES 48-49

SEE PAGES 58-59

SEE PAGES 36-37

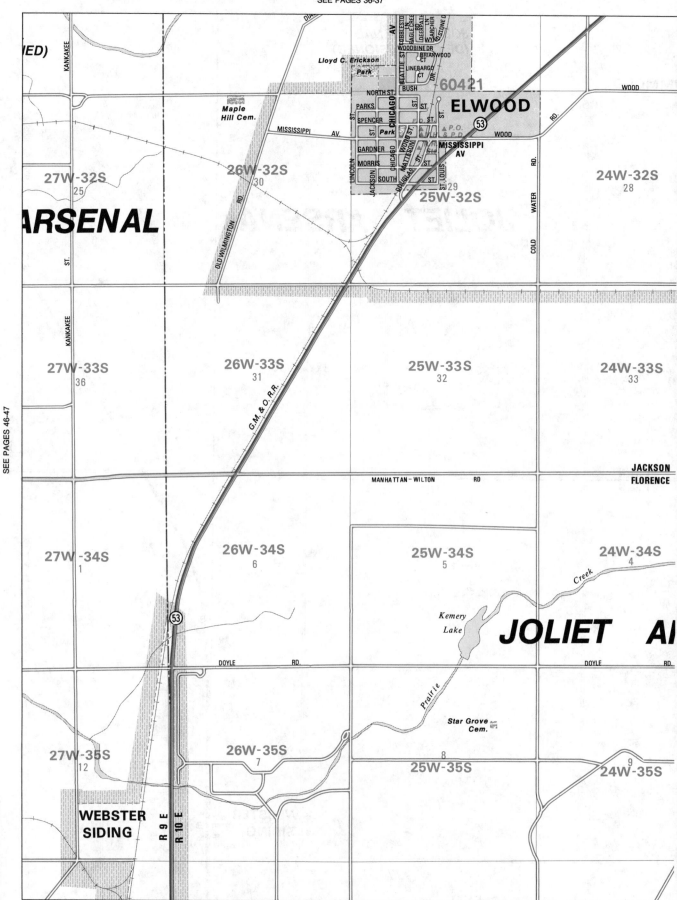

(IED)

KANKAKEE

Lloyd C. Erickson
Park

Maple
Hill Cem.

**ELWOOD**

60421

BUSH

NORTH ST.

PARKS

SPENCER

Park

GARDNER

MORRIS

SOUTH

MISSISSIPPI AV.

MISSISSIPPI
AV.

P.O.
& P.D.

**27W-32S**
25

**26W-32S**
30

**25W-32S**

**24W-32S**
28

**ARSENAL**

ST.

OLD WILMINGTON RD.

SEE PAGES 46-47

**27W-33S**
36

KANKAKEE

**26W-33S**
31

G.M. & O. R.R.

**25W-33S**
32

**24W-33S**
33

**JACKSON**
**FLORENCE**

MANHATTAN – WILTON RD.

**27W-34S**
1

**26W-34S**
6

**25W-34S**
5

Creek

**24W-34S**
4

53

Kemery
Lake

**JOLIET** A

DOYLE RD.

Prairie

Star Grove
Cem.

DOYLE RD.

**27W-35S**
12

**26W-35S**
7

**25W-35S**
8

**24W-35S**
9

**WEBSTER
SIDING**

R 9 E

R 10 E

WOOD

ST. LOUIS RD.

COLD WATER RD.

SEE PAGES 36-37

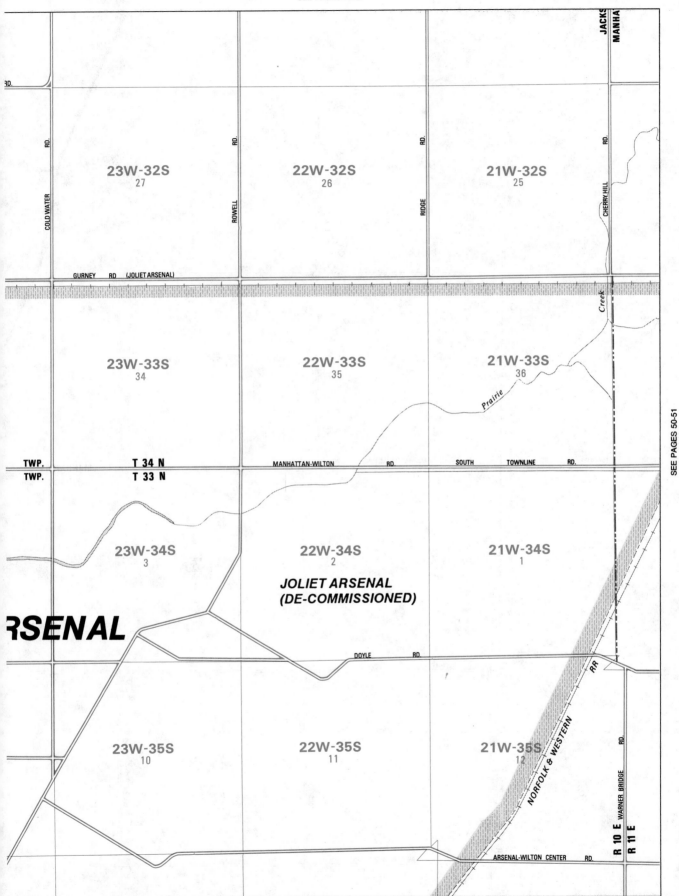

**23W-32S**
27

**22W-32S**
26

**21W-32S**
25

RD.

RD.

RD.

RD.

COLD WATER

ROWELL

RIDGE

CHERRY HILL

GURNEY   RD   (JOLIET ARSENAL)

**23W-33S**
34

**22W-33S**
35

**21W-33S**
36

*Prairie*

*Creek*

TWP.        **T 34 N**

MANHATTAN-WILTON        RD.        SOUTH        TOWNLINE        RD.

TWP.        **T 33 N**

SEE PAGES 50-51

**23W-34S**
3

**22W-34S**
2

**21W-34S**
1

*JOLIET ARSENAL
(DE-COMMISSIONED)*

**RSENAL**

DOYLE        RD.

RR

**23W-35S**
10

**22W-35S**
11

**21W-35S**
12

NORFOLK & WESTERN

WARNER BRIDGE

RD.

R 10 E

R 11 E

ARSENAL-WILTON CENTER        RD.

JACKS

MANHA

SEE PAGES 38-39

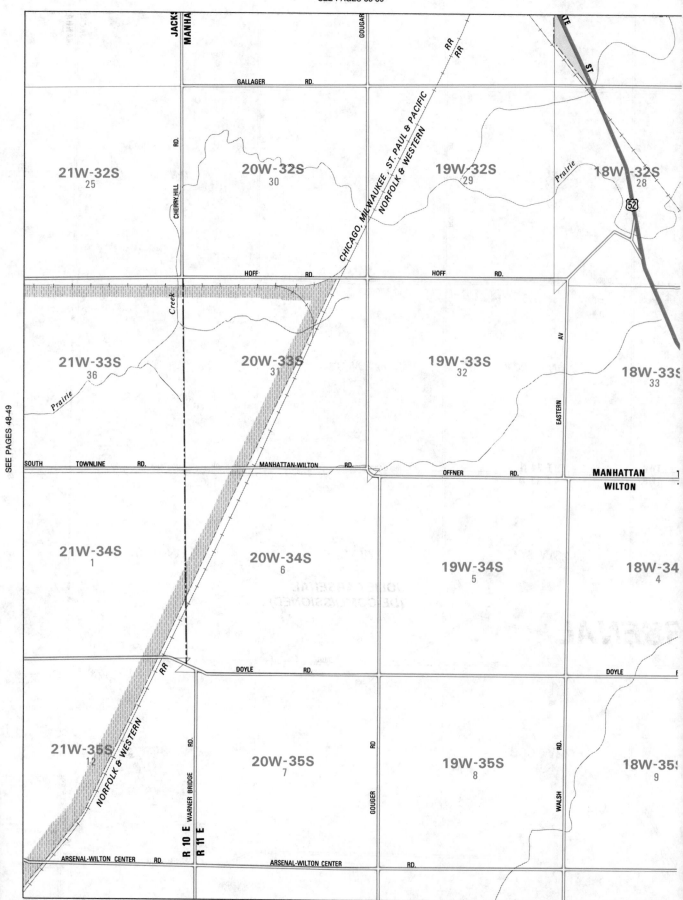

SEE PAGES 48-49

SEE PAGES 62-63

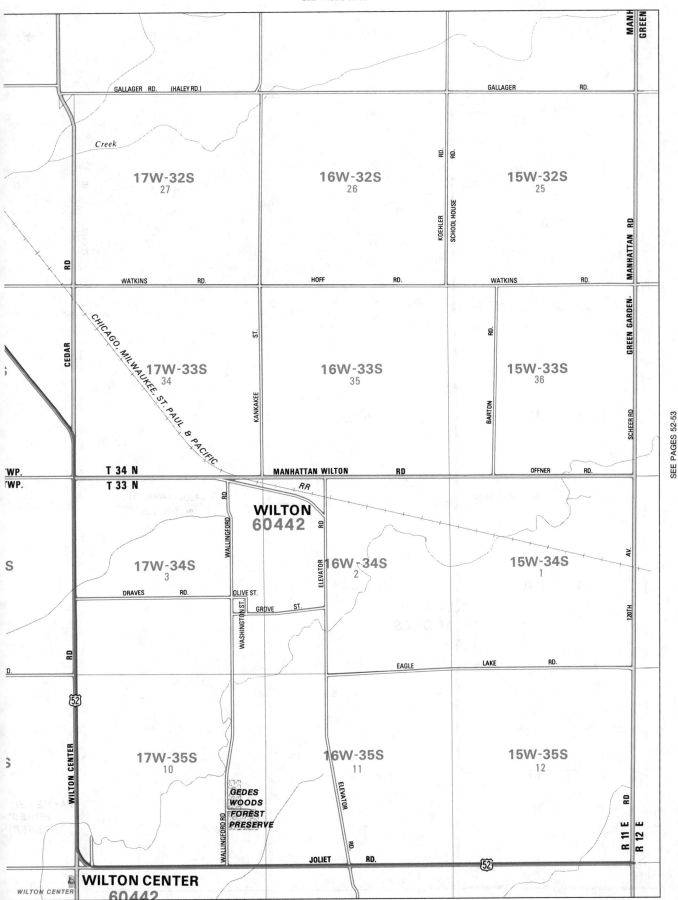

SEE PAGES 40-41

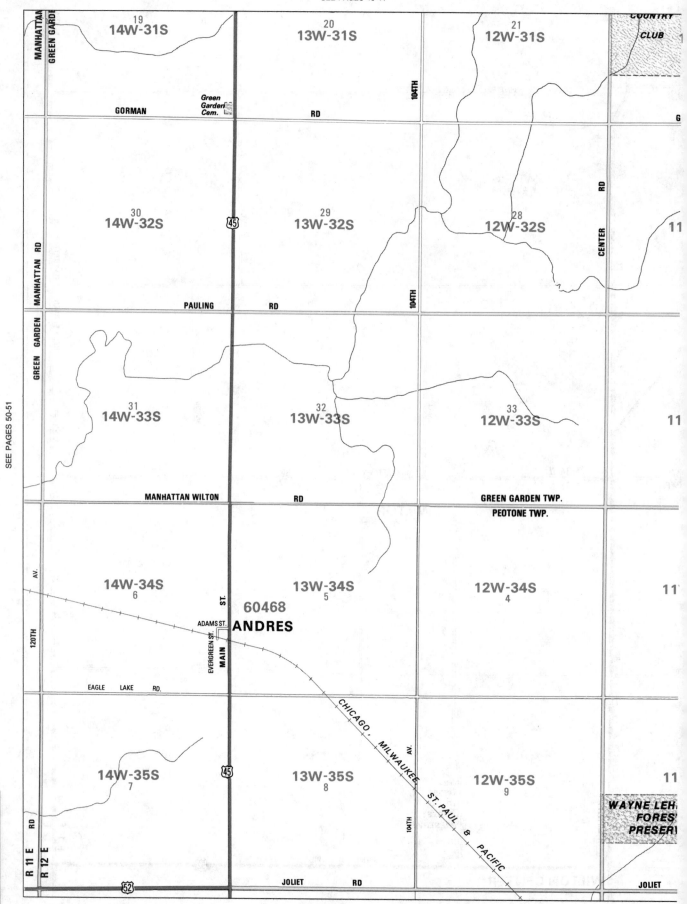

SEE PAGES 50-51

SEE PAGES 64-65

22
**1W-31S**

23
**10W-31S**

24
**9W-31S**

19
**8W-31S**

GREEN GARDEN TWP.

MONEE TWP.

PEOTONE

JOLIET

ORMAN

GORMAN RD

GORMAN

GORMAN RD

WINIFRED RD

GORMAN CT

CEDAR

OAK RIVER DR

OAK RIVER DR

27
**W-32S**

26
**10W-32S**

25
**9W-32S**

30
**8W-32S**

BRADFORD CT

WINIFRED RD

MAPLE CT

BEVERLY DR

COLLEEN CT

PAULING RD

PAULING

AVE

34
**W-33S**

35
**10W-33S**

36
**9W-33S**

31
**8W-33S**

Rest Area

HARLEM

[57]

SEE PAGES 54-55

MANHATTAN WILTON RD

T 34 N

MANHATTAN WILTON

OFFNER RD.

T 33 N

OFFNER RD.

St. Johns Cem.

ST.

AV.

88TH

**W-34S**
3

**10W-34S**
2

RATHJE

**9W-34S**
1

HARLEM AV

[57]

**8W-34S**
6

Creek

EAGLE LAKE RD.

EAGLE LAKE RD.

RR

Rock

RD.

AV.

80TH

Weight Sta.

ILLINOIS CENTRAL GULF

**W-35S**
10

**VERT**
**E**

N. PEOTONE

**10W-35S**
11

**9W-35S**
12

Weight Sta.

**8W-35S**
7

R 12 E

R 13 E

RD

N. PEOTONE RD.

SEE PAGES 42-43

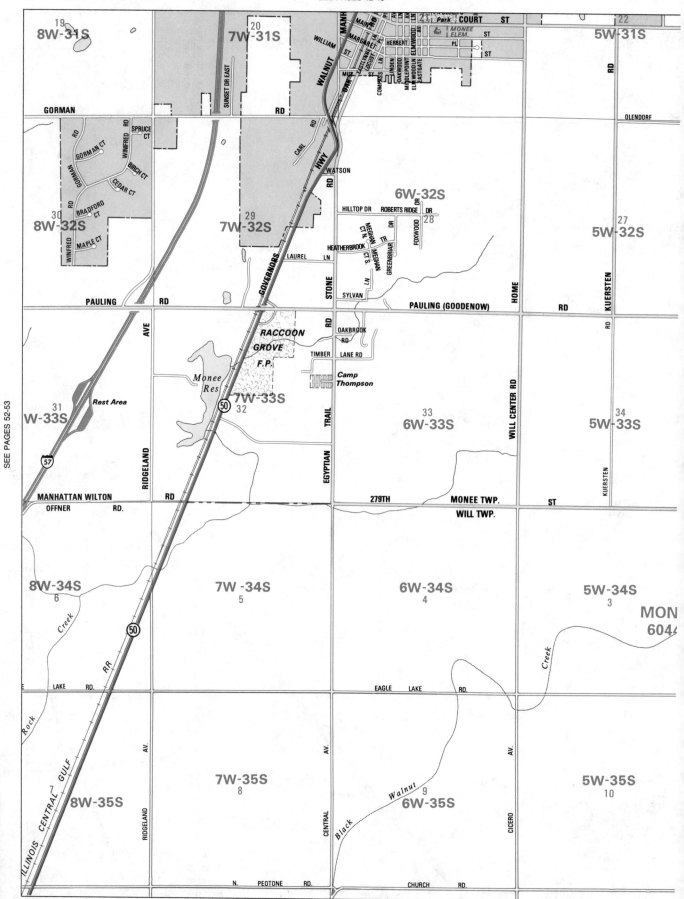

SEE PAGES 52-53

SEE PAGES 66-67

SEE PAGES 42-43

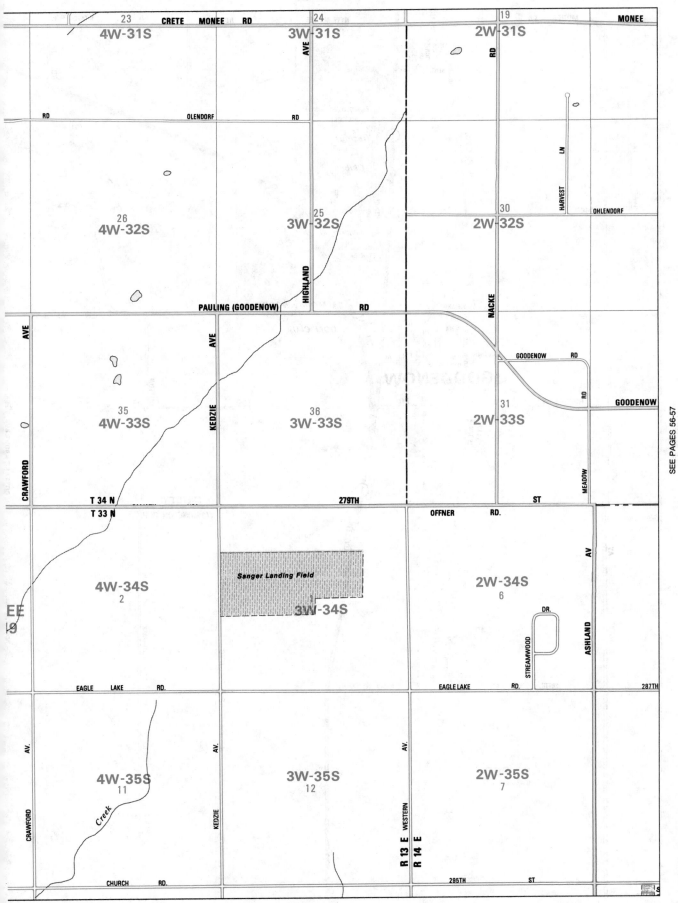

SEE PAGES 56-57

SEE PAGES 66-67

SEE PAGES 44-45

MONEE RD 20
1W-31S

PRIN
GREG

NEW MONEE RD 21
0W-31S

22
MONEE RD
0E-31S

WINDSOR AV
COUNTESS LN
DUCHESS LN AV

KENT AV

COTTAGE

WINSTON AV

UNION PACIFIC

HARVEST LN

Balmoral
Racing
Club

1

BEMES RD

ROOT DR

394

OHLENDORF RD 29
1W-32S

DUNLEITH CT
ELMSCOURT 28
0W-32S

27
0E-32S

RD

ARLINGTON

AUBURN LN
LN
STANTON LN

TAM-O-SHANTER DR
TAM-O-SHANTER CT
BALMORAL DR
WOODS

CALUMET EXPWY

TAM-O-SHANTER DR
BUTLER CT
WOODS

RIDGELAND AV

COLUMBIA

GOODENOW
GLENDALE
ROSEWOOD
HALSTED
GREENVIEW
JANICE
AV
AV
AV
AV
AV
AV

BALMORAL WOODS
GOLF CLUB
PEBBLEBEACH CT

BROADWAY

## GOODENOW

FRANK ST
MAPLE ST

GOODENOW RD 32
1W-33S

CHESTNUT ST
HICKORY ST

GOODENOW RD
0W-33S 33

FOREST VIEW LN

DUTTON 34
0E-33S

GOO

SEE PAGES 54-55

MEADOW

CRETE TWP.
WASHINGTON TWP.

1

HALSTEAD ST

ASHLAND AV

DR.

1W-34S
5

CHICAGO & EASTERN ILLINOIS
LOUISVILLE & NASHVILLE

0W-34S
4

RR

SOUTHPARK AV.

0E-34S 3

CHICAGO, MILWAUKEE, ST. PAUL & PACIFIC

COTTAGE GROVE AVE

287TH ST

EAGLE LAKE RD.

RR

1W-35S
8

0W-35S
9

RD

0E-35S 10

HAHN'S

Creek

CHURCH RD.
295TH ST

St. Pauls

SEE PAGES 44-45

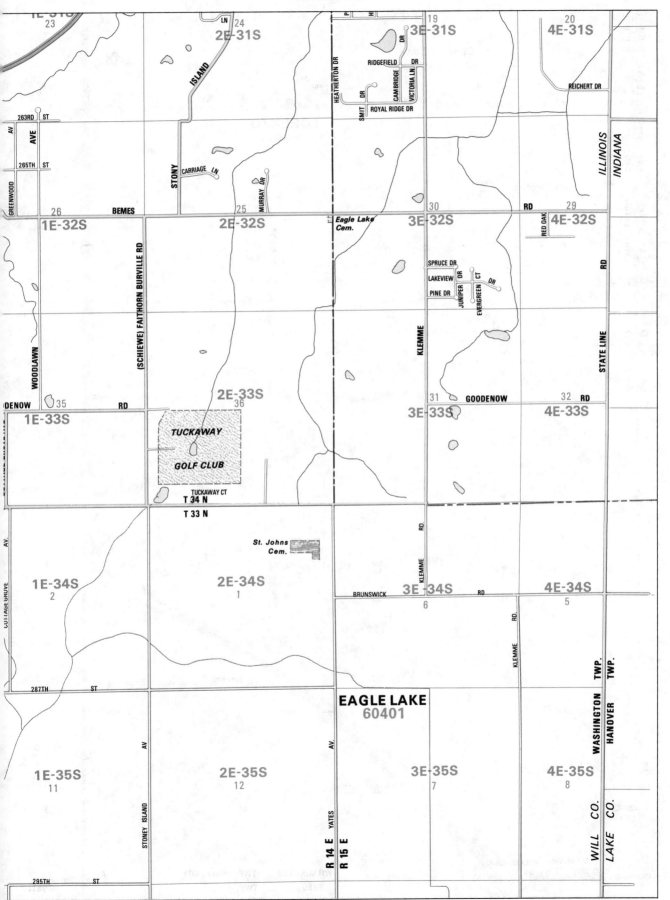

SEE PAGES 68-69

SEE PAGES 46-47

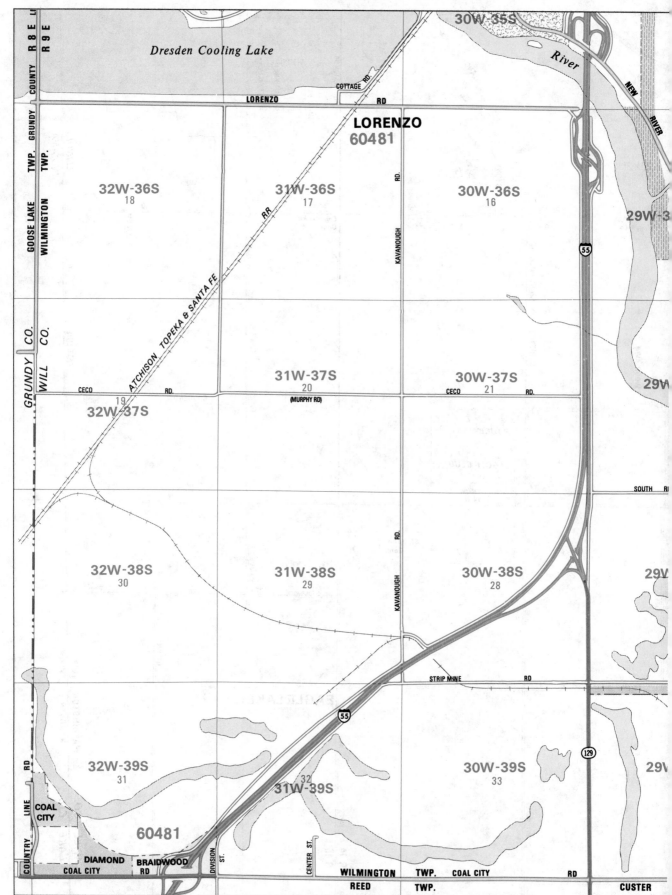

*Dresden Cooling Lake*

30W-35S

New River

LORENZO
60481

COTTAGE RD.

LORENZO RD

R 8 E
R 9 E

GRUNDY COUNTY

GRUNDY TWP.
WILMINGTON TWP.

GOOSE LAKE

32W-36S
18

31W-36S
17

RR

30W-36S
16

29W-3

KAVANOUGH RD.

55

ATCHISON TOPEKA & SANTA FE

GRUNDY CO.
WILL CO.

CECO RD.
19

31W-37S
20
(MURPHY RD)

30W-37S
21

CECO RD.

29W

32W-37S

29W-3

32W-38S
30

31W-38S
29

KAVANOUGH RD.

30W-38S
28

29W

SOUTH RI

STRIP MINE RD

55

32W-39S
31

COAL CITY

31W-39S
32

30W-39S
33

129

29W

LINE RD

COUNTRY

60481

DIAMOND RD
COAL CITY

BRAIDWOOD

DIVISION ST.

CENTER ST.

WILMINGTON TWP.
REED TWP.

COAL CITY RD

CUSTER

SEE PAGES 70-71

SEE PAGES 46-47

**WEBSTER SIDING**

R 9 E

R 10 E

*Prairie*

RD

15

6S

**JOLIET ARSENAL (DE-COMMISSIONED)**

28W-36S
14

27W-36S
13

26W-36S
18

NEW RIVER RD

BOAT HOUSE RD

QUIGLEY RD

G.M. & O. R.R.

TWP.

TWP.

-37S

22

KANKAKEE

28W-37S
23

RIVER DR

27W-37S
24

WILMINGTON

FLORENCE

26W-37S
19

SEE PAGES 60-61

AMBER DR

LINDA LN

MARION ST

JEWELL LN

MARGARETTE ST

CHARLOTTE ST

EULA ST

JOLIET ST

CENTRAL DR

ELWOOD ST

CROSS ST

KANKAKEE RIVER DR

WILMINGTON PEOTONE

VER RD

HAYDEN CT

NORTH OUTER

NORTH CIRCLE DR
Park
SOUTH CIRC.

NORTH WASHINGTON

PARKER CT

ELWOOD ST

SOLDIERS WIDOWS

HOME RD

FIRST ST

River

KANKAKEE ST

SOUTH OUTER DR

NORTH ST

STEWART ST

53

-38S

27

28W-38S
26

STEVENS LN

DAVY LN

R.R. Sta.

CHICAGO ST

CANAL

MILL ST

**WILMINGTON**

*Forked*

27W-38S
25

BALTIMORE ST

JACKSON

26W-38S
30

ALLOTT DR

216TH AV.

North Island Park

VAN BUREN

BEACH ST

JACKSON

MAIN ST

MICHELS ST

MONROE ST

WASHINGTON

JAMES ST

BREWER

*Creek*

FORSYTHE

STRIP MINE RD

SCHOOL ST

**BALTIMORE ST**

53

Hickory Creek Plaza S.C.

CHESTNUT ST

CHERRY

FOURTH ST

THIRD ST

WOOD

MEADOW ST

FIRST

NORTH PARK ST

SOUTH PARK ST

JEFFERSON

LAFAYETTE

LOCUST ST

RIVER ST

KANKAKEE

MANN

BYRON

FULTON

EAST ST

SHAKESPEARE ST

DANIELS ST

WABASH

AV.

WOODS

FOREST

BARR RD

WALNUT ST

WEST ST

South Island Park

Oakwood Cem.

ELIZABETH

VINE ST

WATER ST

LAUREL

RYAN ST

LAUREL AV.

WILMINGTON H.S.

L.J. STEVENS MIDDLE

PRESERVE

Mt. OLIVE Cem.

W. KAHLER RD

WEST ST

OLIVE ST

WILLIAMS ST

RIDGE ST

JOLIET ST

BUCHANNAN

MAE ST

LUTHER

CAMBRIDGE CT.

EAST KAHLER RD

WEST KAHLER 31 RD.

26W-39S

-39S

34

53

28W-39S
35

RD

WEST RIVER (FIFTH ST)

KRISTEN LN

KERRY KOALA CT

KERRY ST

*Kankakee*

TOWPATH LN

DEBBIE DR

LINDY DR

36

27W-39S

102

Winchester Green S.C.

BUCHANNAN

WINCHESTER GREEN DR

JOANN CHANNON

RIDGEWAY

JANET DR

CHESSON LN

JOANN DR

BUTCHER LN

G.M. & O. R.R.

VISTA PARK DR

SUNSET DR

LINDY LN

WILLIDA

BECKY AV.

Christian Living Academy

PHYLLIS DR

ROBERT LN

PRAIRIE LN

COAL CITY RD. **T 33 N**

TWP. **T 32 N**

SEE PAGES 48-49

25W-35S

24W-35S

**WEBSTER SIDING**

R 9 E

R 10 E

**27W-36S**
13

**26W-36S**
18

17

**25W-36S**

WHITE CIR

WHITE CIR

WHITE CIR

**24W-36S**
16

QUIGLEY RD

QUIGLEY RD

JOLIET ARSENAL RD SOUTH

G.M. & O. R.R.

TWP.

TWP.

WILMINGTON

FLORENCE

**26W-37S**
19

RILEY RD.

**25W-37S**
20

INDIAN TRAIL RD.

**24W-37S**
21

SEE PAGES 58-59

24

**27W-37S**

KANKAKEE RIVER DR

WILMINGTON PEOTONE RD

JOLIET ST CENTRAL DR

CROSS ELWOOD ST

ST.

NORTH OUTER
NORTH CIRCLE DR.
Park
SOUTH CUTER
SOUTH OUTER
NORTH
WASHINGTON
STEWART ST.

53

Jordan

SMITH RD

**27W-38S**
**WILMINGTON**
**60481**

**26W-38S**
30

**25W-38S**
29

**24W-38S**
28

BALTIMORE ST.

216TH AV.

BUREN
JACKSON ST.

ALLOTT DR

ALLOTT DR

COUNTY RD.

JEFFERSON
LAFAYETTE
FULTON ST.

Creek

**FORSYTHE**

RIVER
DANIELS
WABASH AV.

**WOODS**

RD

LAUREL AV.

**FOREST**

ELIZABETH ST.
VINE ST.
WILMINGTON
H.S.
LAUREL ST.
BRYAN ST.

L.J. STEVENS
MIDDLE

**PRESERVE**

BARR

(INDIAN TRAIL RD.)

RIDGE ST.
PEARL ST.
Cem.
OLIVE ST.

BUCHANNAN
MAE ST.
LUTHER
CAMBRIDGE
CT.

FAIRCHILD DR

EAST KAHLER RD

WEST KAHLER RD.

31

WEST KAHLER

33

KAHLER

CHRISTIAN
LIVING
ACADEMY

36

Winchester Green
S.C.

**26W-39S**

**25W-39S**

**24W-39S**

**27W-39S**

102

SUNSET DR.
LINDY LN.

WINCHESTER
GREEN DR.
JOANN DR.

RIDGEWAY

JOANN
CHANNON ST.
PHYLLIS DR.

CHESSON CT.
JOANN DR.

BUTCHER LN

FLORE

WES

SEE PAGES 72-73

SEE PAGES 48-49

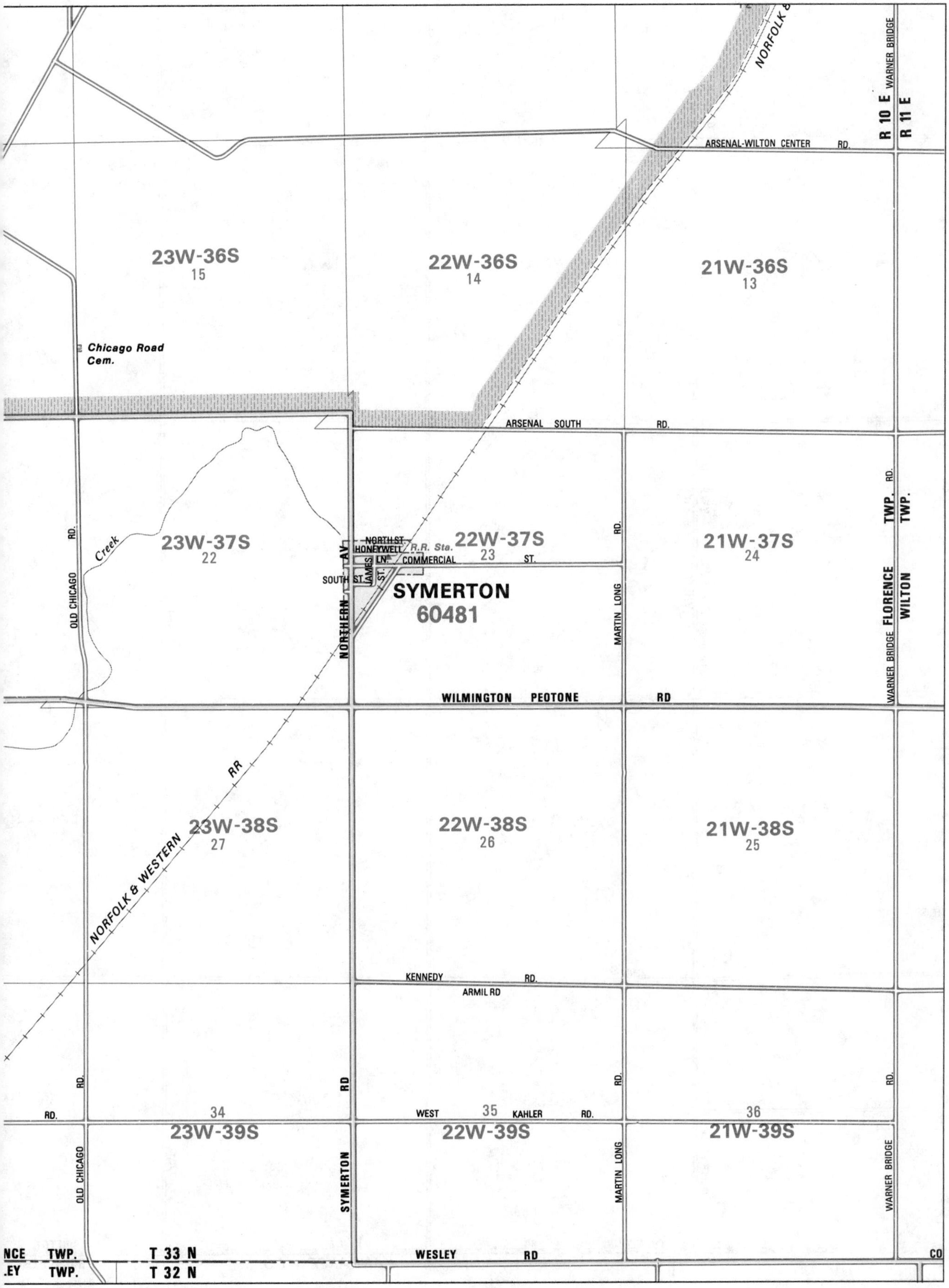

ARSENAL-WILTON CENTER RD.

R 10 E

R 11 E

WARNER BRIDGE

NORFOLK &

**23W-36S**
15

**22W-36S**
14

**21W-36S**
13

Chicago Road
Cem.

ARSENAL SOUTH RD.

OLD CHICAGO RD.

Creek

**23W-37S**
22

NORTH ST.
HONEYWELL
LN.
JAMES
ST.
SOUTH ST.
NORTHERN AV.

R.R. Sta.
COMMERCIAL
ST.

**22W-37S**
23

RD.

MARTIN LONG

**21W-37S**
24

WARNER BRIDGE

FLORENCE TWP.

WILTON TWP.

RD.

SEE PAGES 62-63

**SYMERTON**
**60481**

WILMINGTON PEOTONE RD

NORFOLK & WESTERN RR

**23W-38S**
27

**22W-38S**
26

**21W-38S**
25

KENNEDY RD.
ARMIL RD

RD.

RD.

SYMERTON RD

RD.

WEST 35 KAHLER RD.

34

36

**23W-39S**

**22W-39S**

**21W-39S**

OLD CHICAGO RD.

SYMERTON

MARTIN LONG

WARNER BRIDGE

NCE TWP.
LEY TWP.

**T 33 N**
**T 32 N**

WESLEY RD

CO

SEE PAGES 72-73

SEE PAGES 50-51

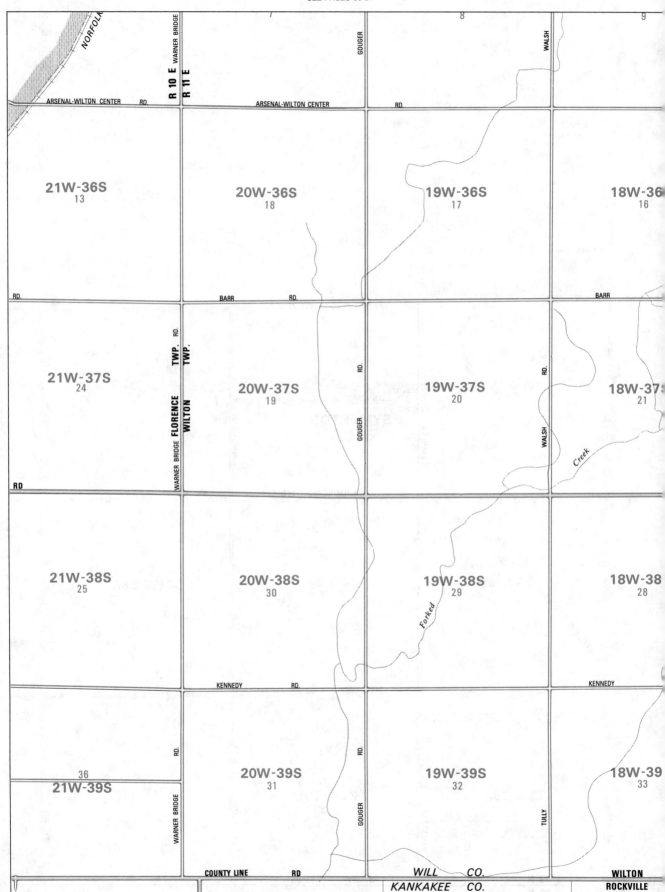

NORFOLK

WARNER BRIDGE

R 10 E

R 11 E

GOUGER

WALSH

ARSENAL-WILTON CENTER    RD.

ARSENAL-WILTON CENTER    RD.

**21W-36S**
13

**20W-36S**
18

**19W-36S**
17

**18W-36**
16

RD.

BARR    RD.

BARR

TWP.    RD.

TWP.

SEE PAGES 60-61

WARNER BRIDGE

FLORENCE

WILTON

**21W-37S**
24

**20W-37S**
19

RD.

GOUGER

**19W-37S**
20

RD.

WALSH

**18W-37**
21

Creek

RD

**21W-38S**
25

**20W-38S**
30

**19W-38S**
29

Forked

**18W-38**
28

KENNEDY    RD.

KENNEDY

RD.

36

**21W-39S**

WARNER BRIDGE

**20W-39S**
31

RD.

GOUGER

**19W-39S**
32

TULLY

**18W-39**
33

COUNTY LINE    RD

*WILL    CO.*

WILTON

*KANKAKEE    CO.*

**ROCKVILLE**

WILTON

R 11 E

R 12 E

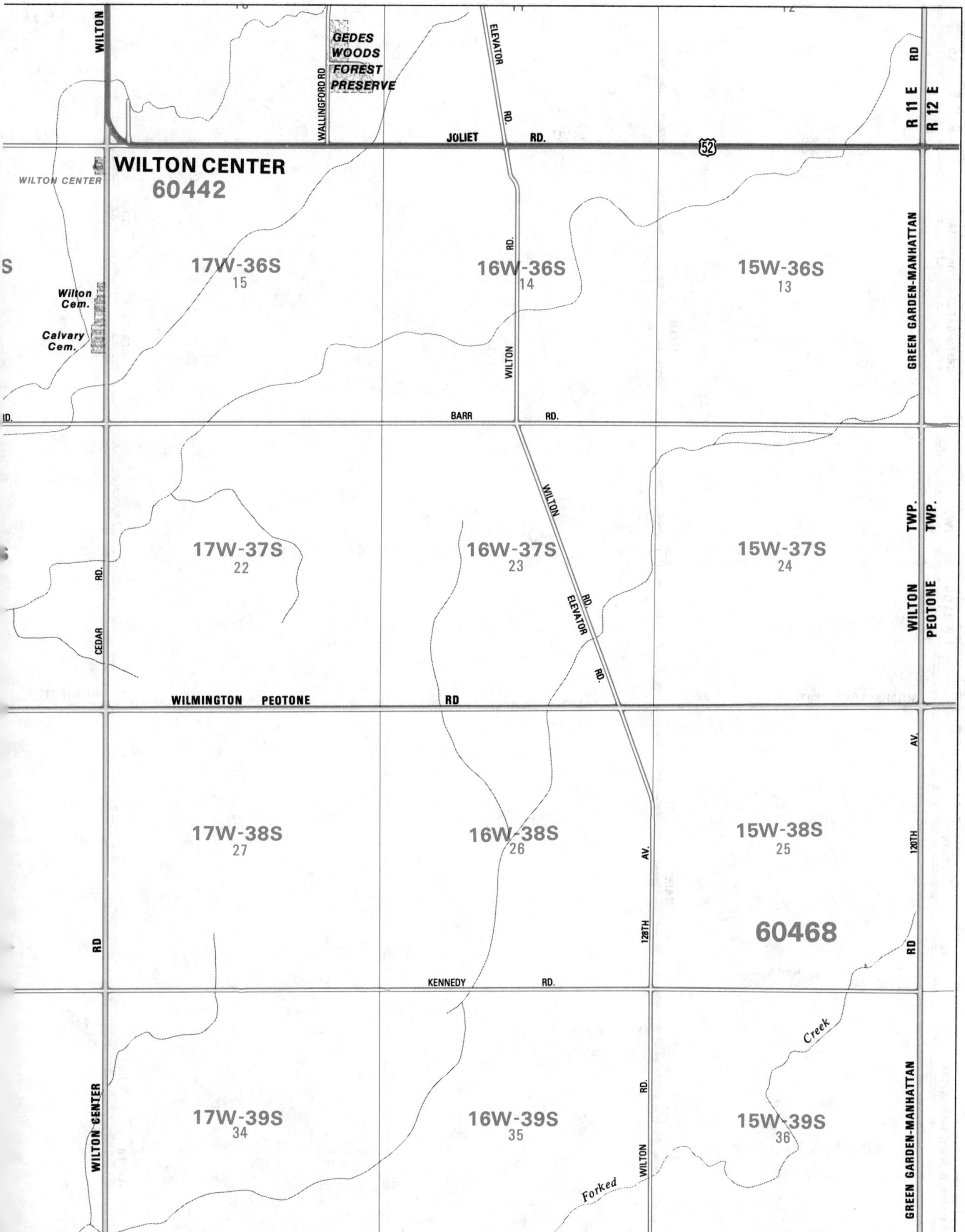

GEDES
WOODS
FOREST
PRESERVE

WALLINGFORD RD.

ELEVATOR    RD.

JOLIET    RD.    52

![map] **WILTON CENTER**
**60442**

WILTON CENTER

Wilton
Cem.

Calvary
Cem.

**17W-36S**
15

**16W-36S**
14

**15W-36S**
13

RD.

WILTON

GREEN GARDEN-MANHATTAN

BARR    RD.

WILTON

**17W-37S**
22

**16W-37S**
23

**15W-37S**
24

CEDAR    RD.

ELEVATOR    RD.

RD.

WILTON  TWP.

PEOTONE  TWP.

SEE PAGES 64-65

WILMINGTON    PEOTONE    RD

AV.

**17W-38S**
27

**16W-38S**
26

**15W-38S**
25

128TH    AV.

120TH

**60468**

RD.

KENNEDY    RD.

Creek

RD

WILTON    CENTER

**17W-39S**
34

**16W-39S**
35

**15W-39S**
36

WILTON    RD.

Forked

GREEN GARDEN-MANHATTAN

P.

P.

**T 33 N**

**T 32 N**

COUNTY LINE    RD

SEE PAGES 52-53

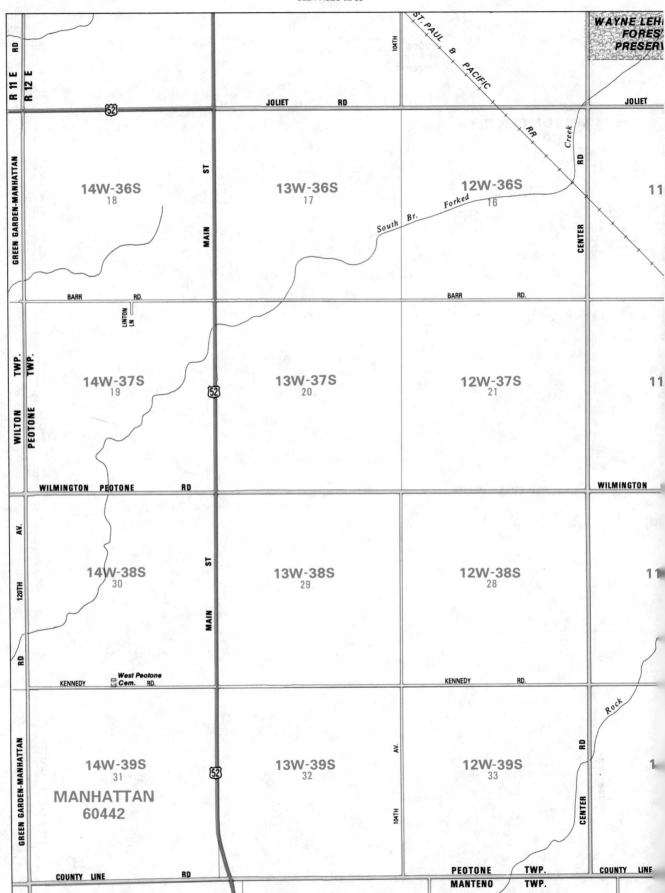

SEE PAGES 66-67

ERT
E

N. PEOTONE

RD

8W-35S

R 12 E
R 13 E

ILLINOIS CENTRAL

Creek

HARLEM AV

V-36S
15

10W-36S
14

9W-36S
13

8W-36S
18

Rock

JOLIET RD

57

JOLIET RD

60468

**PEOTONE**

50

V-37S
22

N. PEOTONE RD

10W-37S
CORNING 23 ST.

9W-37S

H.A. Rathje Mill Hist.
Site

OAK ST. ST.
DIVISION ST.
GLENVIEW
MILL
PEOTONE
PENNY LN.
NORTH
WOOD AV.
CORNING
ST.

SUMMER AV.
LINCOLN
CRAWFORD
Lib
2ND
Pk.
**MAIN ST.**
FIRST
A.V.H. & F.D. & P.D.
WILSON ST.

WASHINGTON ST.
WEST ST.
CONRAD

WALNUT
HAVERT ST.
SIXTH
ST.

BARTON LN.
HAWTHORNE
HICKORY LN.
ST.

CORNING ST.

Cem.

8W-37S

19

8W-37S

GARFIELD AV.

MAPLE ST.
LOCUST LN.
LOUISE LN.
LARK ST.
BONNIE LN.
JEAN
RATHJE
ROYAL LN.
CROWN LN.
DIVISION ST.
MANOR DR.
VAN GOGH CT.
DELFT CT.
HAVERBRINKER DR.
AMSTERDAM BLAINE AV
GARFIELD AV.
PEOTONE H.S.
Park
Will County Fairgrounds
JESSEN ST.
PEOTONE RD. H.S.
4TH ST.
AHLGRIM DR.
SOUTH
3RD
2ND
ORCHARD CT.
TUCKER RD.
SCHROEDER LN.
WEST RD.

OTONE RD

MEADOW
ETHEL ST.

**WILMINGTON RD**

WILMINGTON-PEOTONE RD.

V-38S
27

Creek

10W-38S
26

9W-38S
25

PEOTONE TWP.
WILL TWP.
HARLEM AV

Creek

8W-38S
30

RATHJE ST.

GULF RR

CHICAGO, MILWAUKEE, ST. PAUL

KENNEDY RD.

KENNEDY RD.

ILLINOIS CENTRAL 50

Walnut

HARLEM AV

RD.

V-39S
34

57

10W-39S
35

9W-39S
36

Black

80TH AV.

8W-39S
31

DRECKSLER

RD

T 33 N
T 32 N

COUNTY LINE RD

SEE PAGES 54-55

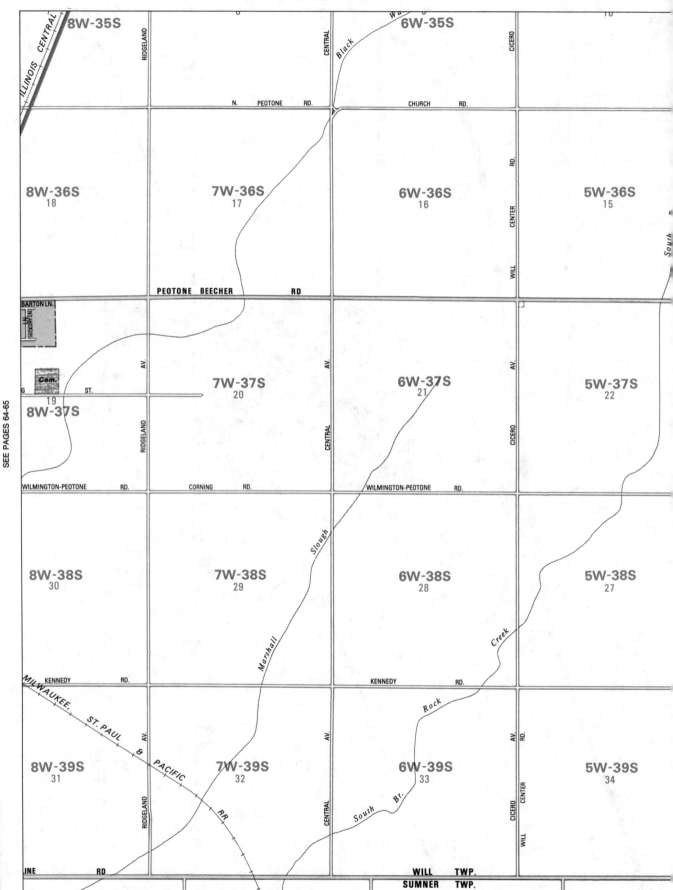

SEE PAGES 64-65

SEE PAGES 54-55

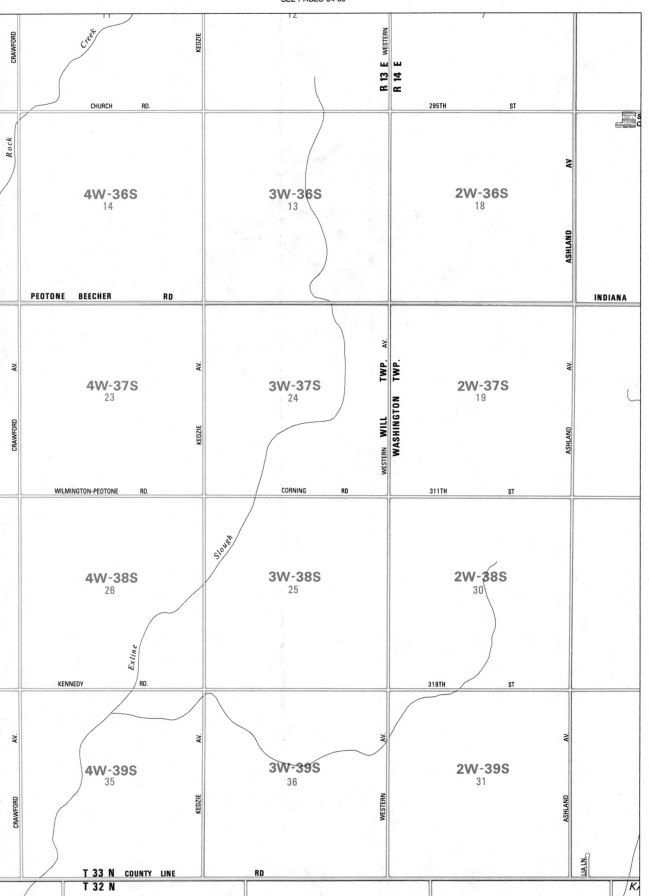

SEE PAGES 68-69

SEE PAGES 56-57

SEE PAGES 66-67

ST

CHURCH RD. 295TH ST

St. Pauls Cem.

CHICAGO, MILWAUKEE

HAHN'S

AV

AV

CATALPA CT.

WILLOW LN.

CHESTNUT ST

OAK DR

LN

HWY

1W-36S
17

60401

**BEECHER**

COUNTRY LN.

MEADOW LN.

ORCHARD LN.

ST.

16

LANGE AV.

CAROLINE AV.

DONOKO AV.

MILLER ST.

OE-36S
15

Trim

RACINE

CATALPA ST.

MILLER

MILLER ST.

OW-36S

① 

ASHLAND

OAK PARK AV.

HODGES ST

ST.

BEECHER H.S.

ST

Fireman's Park

BEECHER ST

PARK DR.

SHADY LAWN GOLF COURSE

ZION LUTHERAN

PENFIELD

REED ST.

P.O.

ST.

F.D.

PARK ST.

CATALPA

PARK DR.

ST.

INDIANA AV

DUNBAR

ELLIOTT

GOULD

RR Sta.

ELM ST

ST.

303RD ST

WOODWARD

V.H. & P.D.

MAXWELL ST.

PASADENA

PRAIRIE AV.

MELROSE LN.

DIXIE

AV.

St. Lukes Cem.

AV.

AV.

1W-37S
20

RACINE

OW-37S
21

OE-37S
22

COTTAGE GROVE

St. Johns Cem.

ST

ST

CHURCH RD

CORNING RD.

Creek

1W-38S
29

OW-38S
28

RR

CHICAGO, MILWAUKEE, ST. PAUL & PACIFIC

OE-38S
27

AV.

Trim

RR RR

319TH ST

KENNEDY RD.

AV

HWY

CHICAGO & EASTERN ILLINOIS

LOUISVILLE & NASHVILLE

DIXIE

COTTAGE GROVE

1W-39S
32

ASHLAND

OW-39S
33

323RD ST

OE-39S
34

LIA LN.

WILL CO.

KANKAKEE CO.

COUNTY LINE

WASHINGTON TWP. RD

YELLOWHEAD TWP.

SEE PAGES 56-57

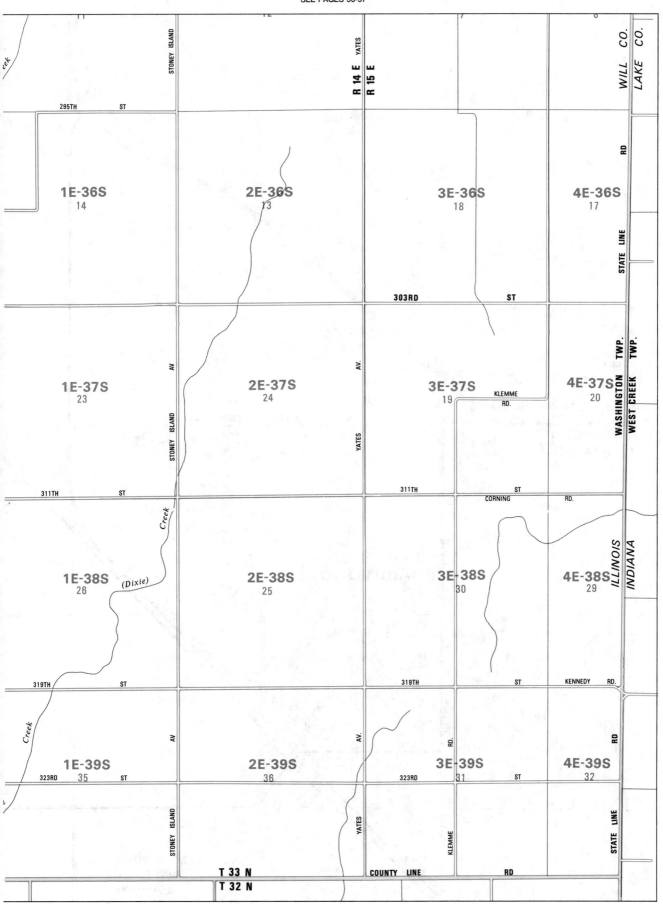

SEE PAGES 58-59

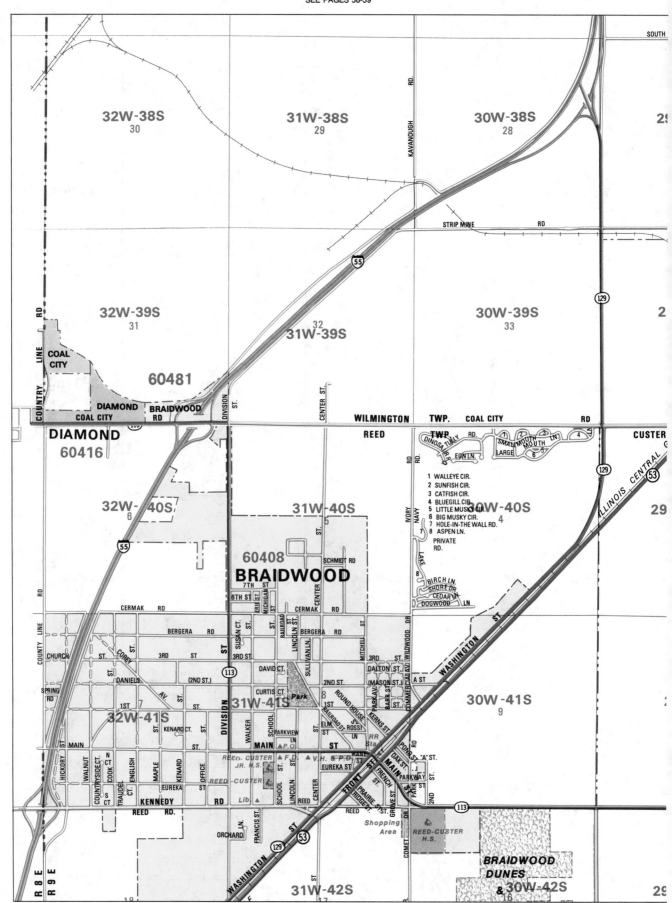

SEE PAGES 74-75

SEE PAGES 58-59

RIVER    RD.

LINDA ST.   MARION ST.   JEWEL

KANKAKEE RIVER DR    WILMINGTON PEOTONE

9W-38S
27

28W-38S
26 LN.

STEVENS

HAYDEN CT.   CHAR   CROSS ST.   NORTH OUTER
NORTH CIRCLE DR.
Park   SOUTH CIRCLE DR.
SOUTH OUTER
NORTH   ST.
STEWART ST.

27W-38S
60481

**WILMINGTON**

53

26W-38S
30

SOLDIERS WIDOWS   HOME RD.   FIRST ST.   DAVY LN.

River

KANKAKEE

R.R. Sta.
CHICAGO ST.
CANAL   MILL   ST.
VAN BUREN   ST.
JACKSON

Forked

JOLIET

BALTIMORE ST.

218TH AV.

ALLOTT   DR

**FORSYTHE**

Creek

**WOODS**

JAMES   ST.   BREMER ST.

STRIP MINE   RD.

Hickory Creek
Plaza S.C.

**BALTIMORE**   ST   53

North
Island
Park

JEFFERSON
LAFAYETTE
RIVER
MAIN

KANKAKEE
FULTON

SHAKESPEARE
EAST ST.
DANIELS   ST.

**FOREST**

WABASH

CHESTNUT   ST.
CHERRY   ST.
MEADOW   LN.

FOURTH ST.
THIRD ST.
SCHOOL ST.
FIRST ST.
WOOD LN.
KOJALA CT.
KRISTEN LN.

North Park St.
SOUTH PARK ST.
WALNUT ST.
South
Island
Park
Oakwood
Cem.

WABASH
WATER
LAUREL

JOLIET ST.
Rose
Laurel   AV.
VINE ST.

WILMINGTON
H.S.

AV.

L.J. STEVENS
MIDDLE

**PRESERVE**

WEST   KAHLER   131 RD.

RD

9W-39S
34

ILLINOIS CENTRAL GULF   RR
53

28W-39S
35

WEST RIVER   (FIFTH ST)

Kankakee

Mt. OLIVE
Cem.
W. KAHLER   RD.

VINE ST.
SULLIVAN ST.
ELIZABETH ST.
West
OLIVE

RIDGE
BUCHANNAN
MAE ST.
LUTHER

EAST KAHLER RD   WEST   KAHLER   131 RD.

CHESSON CT.

RIDGEWAY

26W-39S

Winchester Green
S.C.

CHRISTIAN
LIVING
ACADEMY   36

27W-39S   102

TOWPATH LN.

DEBBIE   DR.   LINDY LN.
VISTA   SUNSET DR.
PARK
BECKY   AV.   WILLIDA

WINCHESTER
GREEN DR.
JOANN
PHYLLIS DR.

JUDY DR.

JANET DR.
JOANN DR.

BUTCHER   LN

COAL   CITY   RD.   T 33 N
GULF   TWP.   T 32 N

KOERNER CT.
DORSET DR.
VISTA DR.

HAMILTON ST.

ALMA
MAPLE ST.
JOHN ST.

MEADOWVIEW LN.

WEST RIVER   RD

Kankakee

CHURCH ST.
ALBERT LN
BASS   ST.

ST.

27W-40S
1

**LAKEWOOD
SHORES**

**60481**

102

W-40S
3

28W-40S
2

26W-40S
6

ROBERT
TROUT   ST.
BRUNING DR.
SUMAC   ST.
BRUNING

BALLOU   RD.

WOOD   ST.
WOODVIEW   GROVE   ST.
DR.
HINTZE   ST.   GROVE   CHARLES   ST.   HINTZE   ST.

LAKEWOOD

Forked

29W-41S
10

28W-41S
11

27W-41S
12

RD

26W-41S
7

SHENK   RD (PVT)

River

ERICKSON LN (PVT)

RIVERSIDE DR.
NORTH
SHORT ST.
GREENWOOD ST.
MAPLE
LAKESIDE

ROSEWOOD DR.
WILDWOOD ST.
WILLOW   DR.
EVERGREEN ST.

ELMWOOD

REST HAVEN   RD

R 9 E   R 10 E

POPLAR ST.
ORCHARD   GRAND
PINE   GROVE AV.
WALNUT   JUNE WAY AV.
STEWART AV.
HICKORY AV.   AV.

OAK ST.

DAVY LN (PVT)

W-42S

28W-42S

27W-42S

26W-42S

SEE PAGES 72-73

SEE PAGES 74-75

SEE PAGES 60-61

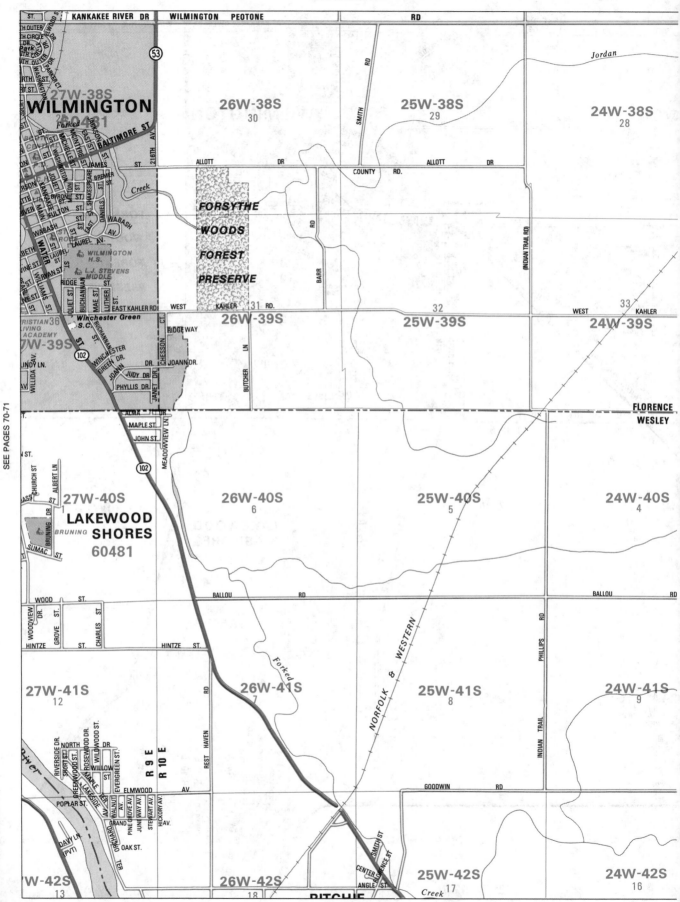

SEE PAGES 70-71

KANKAKEE RIVER DR    WILMINGTON  PEOTONE                    RD

Jordan

27W-38S    26W-38S              25W-38S              24W-38S
WILMINGTON    30                  29                   28
60481

BALTIMORE ST

Creek    ALLOTT    DR    ALLOTT    DR

COUNTY    RD.

FORSYTHE
WOODS
FOREST
PRESERVE

WILMINGTON
H.S.

L.J. STEVENS
MIDDLE

EAST KAHLER RD    WEST    KAHLER    31    RD.              32                   33    WEST    KAHLER
36    Winchester Green                                                                    KAHLER
CHRISTIAN    S.C.    26W-39S              25W-39S              24W-39S
LIVING
ACADEMY
27W-39S

FLORENCE
WESLEY

27W-40S              26W-40S              25W-40S              24W-40S
1    LAKEWOOD              6                    5                    4
SHORES
60481

WOOD    ST.    BALLOU    RD.              BALLOU    RD.

HINTZE    ST.    HINTZE    ST.

27W-41S              26W-41S              25W-41S              24W-41S
12                    7                    8                    9

R 9 E
R 10 E

GOODWIN    RD

W-42S              26W-42S              25W-42S              24W-42S
13                    18    RITCHIE    17                   16
Creek

SEE PAGES 60-61

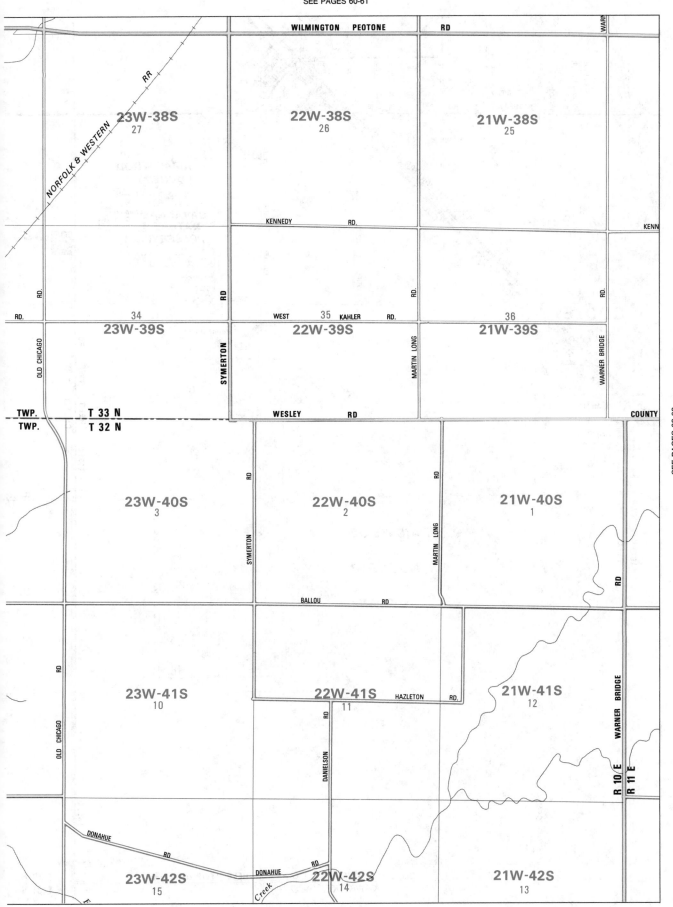

SEE PAGES 62-63

SEE PAGES 76-77

SEE PAGES 70-71

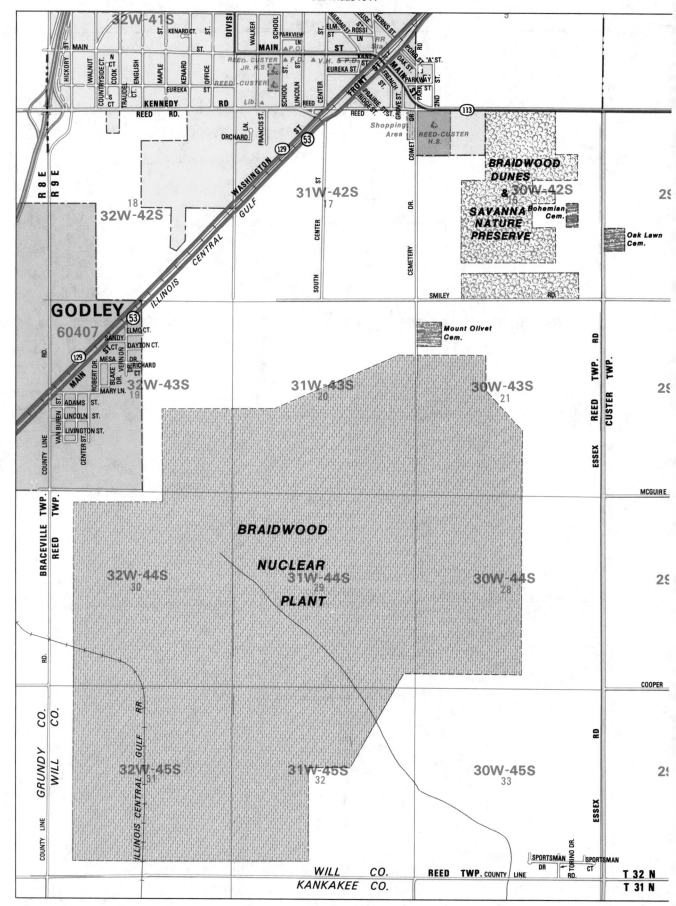

32W-41S

KENARD CT.

DIVISI

WALKER

SCHOOL

PARKVIEW LN.

HOUSE

KERNS ST.

9

MAIN

HICKORY ST.

MAIN

WALNUT

COUNTRYSIDE CT.

COOK

TRAUDEL CT.

ENGLISH

MAPLE

KENARD

OFFICE

REED-CUSTER JR. H.S.

F.D.

P.O.

ST.

ELM ST.

RR Sta.

POPLAR RD.

OAK ST.

FRENCH ST.

MAIN ST.

"A" ST.

PARK ST.

2ND ST.

N CT

S CT

EUREKA

ST.

KENNEDY

RD.

REED-CUSTER School

LINCOLN

CENTER

REED

V.H. & P.D.

EUREKA ST.

KANE

ST.

ROSSI

ST.

RAILROAD ST.

PRAIRIE ST.

GROVE ST.

RIDGE ST.

FRONT ST.

PARKWAY

113

REED RD.

ORCHARD ST.

FRANCIS ST.

129

53

Lib.

Reed

Shopping Area

REED-CUSTER H.S.

COMET DR.

**BRAIDWOOD DUNES & 30W-42S SAVANNA NATURE PRESERVE**

WASHINGTON ST.

ILLINOIS CENTRAL GULF

18

31W-42S

17

CENTER ST.

SOUTH ST.

DR.

CEMETERY DR.

Bohemian Cem.

16

Oak Lawn Cem.

29

32W-42S

R 8 E

R 9 E

SMILEY RD.

Mount Olivet Cem.

**GODLEY**

60407

53

129

ELMO CT.

SANDY ST. CT.

DAYTON CT.

VERNON DR.

RICHARD CT.

MAIN

MESA

BLAKE DR.

DR.

ROBERT DR.

MARY LN.

32W-43S

19

31W-43S

20

30W-43S

21

ESSEX

REED TWP.

CUSTER TWP.

RD.

29

ADAMS

ST.

VAN BUREN

LINCOLN

ST.

CENTER ST.

LIVINGTON ST.

COUNTY LINE

MCGUIRE

RD.

**BRAIDWOOD**

BRACEVILLE TWP.

REED TWP.

**NUCLEAR**

32W-44S

30

31W-44S

29

30W-44S

28

29

**PLANT**

COOPER

RD.

32W-45S

31

ILLINOIS CENTRAL GULF RR

31W-45S

32

30W-45S

33

ESSEX

29

GRUNDY CO.

WILL CO.

COUNTY LINE

SPORTSMAN DR

TORINO DR.

SPORTSMAN

CT

RD.

**WILL CO.**

**KANKAKEE CO.**

**REED TWP.** COUNTY LINE

T 32 N

T 31 N

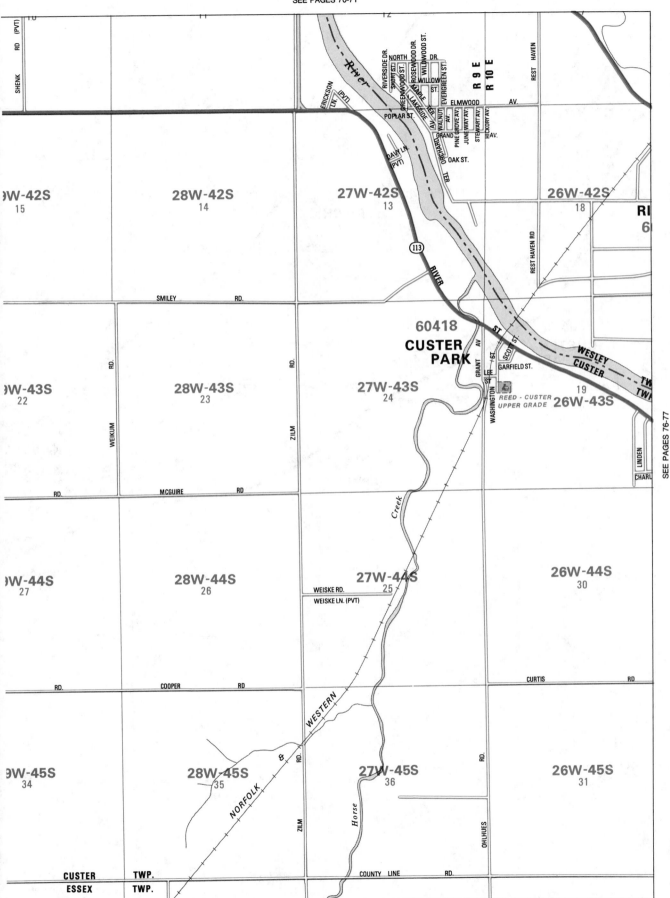

SHENK RD (PVT)

ERICKSON LN. (PVT)

River

RIVERSIDE DR.
SHORT ST.
NORTH
GREENWOOD ST.
ROSEWOOD DR.
WILDWOOD ST.
WILLOW ST.
EVERGREEN ST.
MAPLE
LAKESIDE AV.
WALNUT AV.
POPLAR ST.
ELMWOOD
ORCHARD AV.
PINE GROVE AV.
GRAND
JUNE WAY AV.
STEWART AV.
HICKORY AV.
REST HAVEN AV.

R 9 E
R 10 E

REST HAVEN

DALY LN. (PVT)

OAK ST.

0W-42S
15

28W-42S
14

27W-42S
13

REST HAVEN RD

26W-42S
18

RI
6

113

RIVER

SMILEY RD.

ZILM RD.

RD.

60418

**CUSTER PARK**

GRANT AV
SCOTT ST.
LEE ST.
WASHINGTON
GARFIELD ST.

WESLEY
CUSTER

TWP.
TWP.

0W-43S
22

28W-43S
23

27W-43S
24

REED - CUSTER
UPPER GRADE

26W-43S
19

WEIKUM RD.

LINDEN

CHARL

RD.

MCGUIRE RD.

Creek

0W-44S
27

28W-44S
26

27W-44S
25

WEISKE RD.
WEISKE LN. (PVT)

26W-44S
30

RD.

COOPER RD.

CURTIS RD.

WESTERN

0W-45S
34

28W-45S
35

ZILM

Horse

27W-45S
36

NORFOLK &

RD.

OHLHUES

26W-45S
31

**CUSTER TWP.**
**ESSEX TWP.**

COUNTY LINE RD.

SEE PAGES 76-77

SEE PAGES 72-73

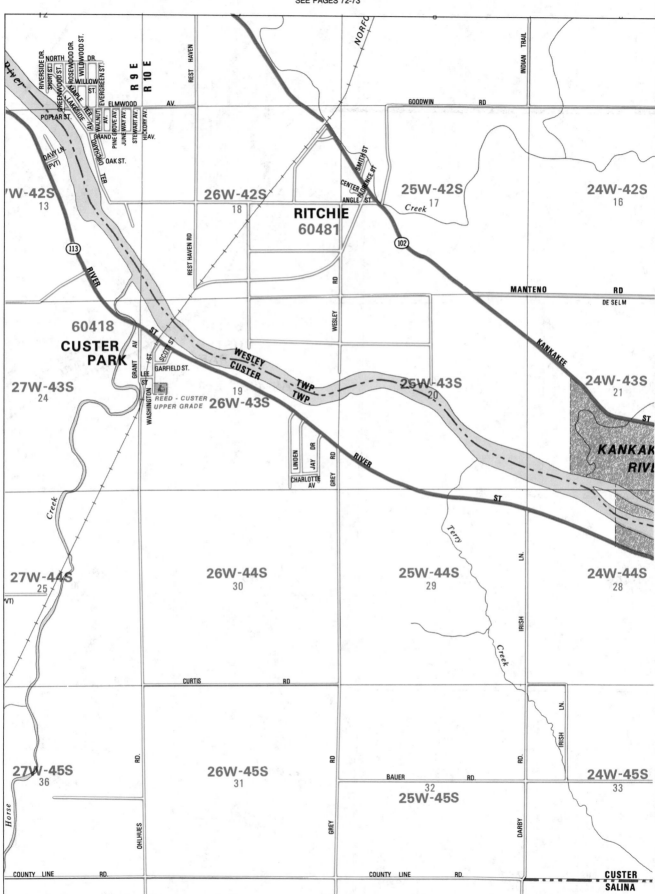

SEE PAGES 74-75

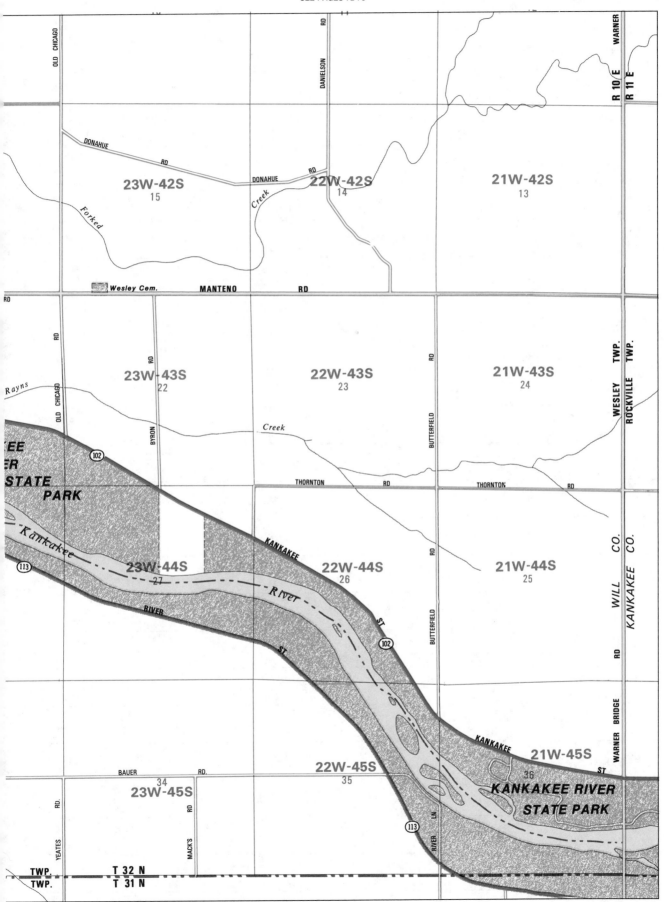

23W-42S
15

22W-42S
14

21W-42S
13

DONAHUE RD

DONAHUE RD

DONAHUE RD

OLD CHICAGO

DANIELSON RD

WARNER

R 10 E

R 11 E

*Forked*

*Creek*

Wesley Cem.   MANTENO   RD

23W-43S
22

22W-43S
23

21W-43S
24

OLD CHICAGO RD

BYRON RD

BUTTERFIELD RD

WESLEY TWP.

ROCKVILLE TWP.

*Rayns*

*Creek*

102

THORNTON   RD

THORNTON   RD

*Kankakee*

STATE

PARK

KANKAKEE

RIVER

STATE PARK

*Kankakee*

113

23W-44S
27

22W-44S
26

21W-44S
25

*River*

RIVER

ST

ST

BUTTERFIELD

102

BUTTERFIELD RD

WILL CO.

KANKAKEE CO.

WARNER BRIDGE

RD

KANKAKEE

ST

BAUER   RD.

22W-45S
35

21W-45S
36

KANKAKEE RIVER

STATE PARK

23W-45S
34

YEATES RD.

MACK'S RD

RIVER LN

113

TWP.   T 32 N
TWP.   T 31 N

# Street Index

## Beecher

| Street | Grid | Page |
|---|---|---|
| Caroline Av. N&S .... 0W-36S | | 68 |
| Catalpa Ct. NW&SE ..0W-36S | | 68 |
| Catalpa St. N&S .... 0W-36S | | 68 |
| Chestnut Ln. E&W .... 0W-36S | | 68 |
| Country Ln. E&W....0W-36S | | 68 |
| Dixie Hwy. N&S ........0W-37S,0W-36S | | 68 |
| Donoko Av. N&S ....0W-36S | | 68 |
| Dunbar St. N&S ....1W-36S | | 68 |
| Elliott St. N&S .... 1W-36S | | 68 |
| Elm St. E&W ......0W-36S | | 68 |
| Gould St. N&S ...... 1W-36S | | 68 |
| Hodges St. E&W ........1W-36S,0W-36S | | 68 |
| Indiana Av. N&S ........1W-36S,0W-36S | | 68 |
| Lange Av. N&S....0W-36S | | 68 |
| Maxwell St. E&W ........0W-37S,0W-36S | | 68 |
| Meadow Ln. E&W .. 0W-36S | | 68 |
| Melrose Ln. E&W .. 0W-37S | | 68 |
| Miller St. E&W ........1W-36S,0W-36S | | 68 |
| Oak Dr. N&S .... 0W-36S | | 68 |
| Oak Park Av. N&S .. 1W-36S | | 68 |
| Orchard Ln. E&W ....0W-36S | | 68 |
| Park Dr. N&S........0W-36S | | 68 |
| Park St. E&W ......0W-36S | | 68 |
| Pasadena Av. N&S ..0W-37S | | 68 |
| Penfield St. E&W ........1W-36S,0W-36S | | 68 |
| Prairie Av. N&S....0W-37S | | 68 |
| Reed St. N&S ........0W-37S,0W-36S | | 68 |
| Route 1 N&S ........0W-37S,0W-36S | | 68 |
| Willow Ln. E&W .... 0W-36S | | 68 |
| Woodward St. N&S ........0W-37S,0W-36S | | 68 |
| 295th St. E&W ........0W-36S,0E-36S | | 68 |
| 303rd St. E&W ........0W-36S,0E-36S | | 68 |

## Bolingbrook*
### (Also see Du Page County)

| Street | Grid | Page |
|---|---|---|
| Aberdeen Ct. N&S ..22W-10S | | 7 |
| Adams St. NE&SW ........24W-12S | | 6 |
| Alcester Cir. E&W .. 24W-10S | | 6 |
| Alex Dr. E&W .... 26W-11S | | 6 |
| Algonquin Ct. N&S..24W-11S | | 6 |
| Allegheny Ct. N&S .. 23W-11S | | 7 |
| Allison Ct. NE&SW ..22W-11S | | 7 |
| Andover Ct. N&S .. 22W-12S | | 7 |
| Anne Ct. NE&SW .. 21W-10S | | 7 |
| Anne Dr. NE&SW .. 21W-10S | | 7 |
| Anne Ln. E&W .... 21W-10S | | 7 |
| Annerino Dr. N&S .. 22W-12S | | 7 |
| Antelope Ct. NW&SE ........26W-12S | | 6 |
| Apache Ct. N&S....24W-11S | | 6 |
| Applewood Dr. NE&SW ........25W-11S | | 6 |
| Appling Ln. E&W .. 23W-11S | | 7 |
| Arcadia Ct. N&S....23W-11S | | 7 |
| Ardglass Ct. NE&SW ........22W-11S | | 7 |
| Aristocrat Dr. N&S .. 25W-12S | | 6 |
| Arrowhead Ln. E&W ........23W-11S | | 7 |
| Ashbury Av. N&S ........22W-12S,22W-9S | | 7 |
| Ashbury Ct. NE&SW ........22W-10S | | 7 |
| Ashbury Ln. N&S ........22W-11S,22W-10S | | 7 |
| Ashley Rd. NE&SW ........21W-10S | | 7 |
| Aspen Dr. NE&SW .. 23W-11S | | 7 |
| Assembly Ct. NW&SE ........22W-10S | | 7 |
| Assembly Dr. E&W .. 22W-10S | | 7 |
| Bakersmill Dr. N&S 24W-12S | | 6 |
| Balewood Dr. N&S.. 24W-12S | | 6 |
| Balmoral Dr. N&S .. 22W-11S | | 7 |
| Barbers Corner Rd. NS&EW ........22W-11S | | 7 |
| Barnwood Dr. NS&EW ........25W-11S | | 6 |
| Beaconridge Dr. N&S ........22W-12S | | 7 |
| Bear Creek Dr. NS&EW ........26W-11S | | 6 |
| Beaver Creek Ct. E&W ........26W-11S | | 6 |
| Bedford Dr. N&S .. 24W-12S | | 6 |
| Beech Dr. E&W .... 24W-12S | | 6 |
| Blackberry Ct. E&W ........24W-12S | | 6 |
| Blackberry Dr. N&S ........24W-12S | | 6 |
| Blackfoot Dr. N&S .. 26W-12S | | 6 |
| Blackhawk Ln. E&W ........24W-11S | | 6 |
| Blair Ln. E&W ...... 23W-11S | | 7 |
| Bolingbrook Dr. N&S ........23W-12S,23W-10S | | 7 |
| Bonnie Brae Ct. NW&SE ........22W-10S | | 7 |
| Bonnie Brae Dr. NS&EW ........22W-10S | | 7 |
| Bothwell Dr. E&W .. 25W-11S | | 6 |
| Boughton Rd. NE&SW ........23W-11S,21W-10S | | 7 |
| Boulder Ridge Ct. E&W ........26W-11S | | 6 |
| Boulder Ridge Dr. E&W ........26W-11S | | 6 |
| Bowie Ct.* N&S .... 24W-11S | | 6 |
| Bowman Ct. N&S .. 22W-11S | | 7 |
| Bradford Pl. N&S .. 25W-12S | | 6 |
| Braemar Glen NS&EW ........22W-12S | | 7 |
| Bramble Av. E&W .. 25W-12S | | 6 |
| Bramble Ct. NW&SE ........25W-12S | | 6 |
| Brandon Ct. N&S .. 23W-11S | | 7 |
| Briarcliff Rd. N&S ........24W-11S,26W-12S | | 6 |
| Brighton Ln. N&S .. 25W-11S | | 6 |
| Bristol Way NW&SE ........24W-12S | | 6 |
| Brittany Ct. E&W .. 25W-11S | | 6 |
| Brompton Cir. NS&EW ........25W-11S | | 6 |
| Brompton Ct. NW&SE ........25W-11S | | 6 |
| Brook Ct. E&W .... 23W-11S | | 7 |
| Brookwood Ln. N&S ........25W-11S | | 6 |
| Brookwood Ln., E. NS&EW ........25W-11S | | 6 |
| Brookwood Ln., W. NS&EW ........23W-11S | | 6 |
| Bryant Way E&W .. 24W-11S | | 6 |
| Buck Eye E&W .... 24W-11S | | 6 |
| Buckboard Ct. NE&SW ........26W-13S | | 10 |
| Buckboard Rd. NW&SE ........26W-13S | | 10 |
| Bunker Hill Dr. N&S ........24W-12S | | 6 |
| Bunting Cir. NW&SE ........21W-10S | | 7 |
| Butte Ln. E&W .... 26W-12S | | 6 |
| Butte View Dr. NE&SW ........26W-12S | | 6 |
| Butternut Ct. N&S ..24W-12S | | 6 |
| Butternut Dr. N&S .. 24W-12S | | 6 |
| Cades Ct. NW&SE ..22W-10S | | 7 |
| Calico Ct. NE&SW .. 26W-13S | | 10 |
| Calisades Rd. N&S 21W-13S | | 11 |
| Callery Ct. N&S .... 25W-11S | | 6 |
| Callery Dr. N&S .... 25W-11S | | 6 |
| Calumet Ct. N&S .. 24W-11S | | 6 |
| Camelot Ct. NE&SW ........22W-11S | | 7 |
| Camelot Way E&W 22W-11S | | 7 |
| Campbell Dr. N&S .. 25W-11S | | 6 |
| Canterbury NE&SW ........22W-12S | | 7 |
| Canyon Dr. N&S ..........26W-12S,26W-11S | | 6 |
| Capitol Dr. N&S ........21W-11S | | 7 |
| Carlyle Ln. E&W ....24W-12S | | 6 |
| Carmel Ln. E&W ....23W-12S | | 7 |
| Carol Ct. N&S .... 25W-11S | | 6 |
| Carol Ln. NE&SW .. 25W-11S | | 6 |
| Carriage Ln. E&W .. 26W-11S | | 6 |
| Cascadia Ct. NW&SE ........21W-13S | | 11 |
| Castle Ct. E&W .... 21W-11S | | 7 |
| Cedarwood Ct. N&S ........22W-12S | | 7 |
| Chantileed Av. E&W ........22W-10S | | 7 |
| Charleston Ct. N&S ........25W-12S | | 6 |
| Charleston Dr. E&W ........25W-12S | | 6 |
| Charlotte Ct. N&S .. 22W-10S | | 7 |
| Charlotte Ln. E&W ..22W-10S | | 7 |
| Chase Ct. N&S .... 22W-11S | | 7 |
| Cherokee Dr. N&S.. 24W-11S | | 6 |
| Cherry Ct. E&W .... 23W-11S | | 7 |
| Chesapeak Dr. NS&EW ........21W-11S | | 7 |
| Cheshire Ct. NE&SW ........22W-11S | | 7 |
| Cheyenne Dr. N&S ........24W-11S | | 6 |
| Chippewa Ct. N&S..24W-11S | | 6 |
| Churchill Dr. E&W .. 25W-11S | | 6 |
| Cinema Dr. E&W .. 22W-13S | | 11 |
| Clear Dr. E&W......26W-12S | | 6 |
| Cleveland Dr. E&W 24W-10S | | 6 |
| Clifton Ln. NE&SW 25W-11S | | 6 |
| Clover Ln. NS&EW 23W-10S | | 7 |
| Cobb Cir. E&W .... 23W-11S | | 7 |
| Cochise Cir. E&W .. 24W-11S | | 6 |
| Collingwood Ln. NW&SE ........25W-11S | | 6 |
| Colony Ct. N&S .... 22W-12S | | 7 |
| Columbus Dr. E&W ........26W-11S | | 6 |
| Comanche Dr. E&W ........26W-12S | | 6 |
| Commonwealth Ct. NE&SW ........25W-11S | | 6 |
| Commonwealth Dr. N&S ........25W-11S | | 6 |
| Concord Ln. NE&SW 23W-10S | | 7 |
| Copper Ct. NE&SW ........25W-11S | | 6 |
| Coral Ct. E&W .... 23W-11S | | 7 |
| Cornwall NW&SE ........22W-10S | | 7 |
| Cortez Dr. N&S .... 23W-11S | | 7 |
| Cottonwood Cir. E&W ........24W-11S | | 6 |
| Cougar Dr. NW&SE ........26W-12S | | 6 |
| Country Ridge Ln. NS&EW ........25W-11S | | 6 |
| Creekside Dr. N&S..24W-12S | | 6 |
| Crestwood Ln. NW&SE ........25W-11S | | 6 |
| Crossing Rd. NE&SW ........22W-12S | | 7 |
| Cumberland Ln. E&W ........24W-12S,23W-12S | | 6 |
| Cypress Dr. E&W .. 23W-12S | | 7 |
| Dakota Ct. N&S .... 24W-11S | | 6 |
| Davinci Dr. E&W .. 22W-11S | | 7 |
| Davis Ct. N&S......23W-11S | | 7 |
| Davis Ln. N&S......23W-11S | | 7 |
| Dean Cir. NE&SW .. 23W-11S | | 7 |
| Deer Crossing Ln. NW&SE ........22W-10S | | 7 |
| Deerfield Ct. E&W .. 22W-12S | | 7 |
| Degas Dr. E&W .... 22W-11S | | 7 |
| Delaware Cir. NS&EW ........23W-11S | | 7 |
| Delaware Ln. E&W .. 23W-11S | | 7 |
| Delmar Dr. E&W...23W-12S | | 7 |
| Denver Yellow Pine Dr. N&S ........24W-11S | | 6 |
| Derbyshire Ct. NE&SW ........22W-10S | | 7 |
| Derbyshire Rd. NE&SW ........22W-10S | | 7 |
| Devon Ct. N&S .... 22W-10S | | 7 |
| Devon Ln. NE&SW 22W-10S | | 7 |
| Devonshire Ct. E&W ........22W-12S | | 7 |
| Diane Ln. NW&SE .. 22W-10S | | 7 |
| Donovan Dr. E&W .. 22W-13S | | 11 |
| Dorchester Ct. N&S ........22W-10S | | 7 |
| Dorchester Dr. N&S ........22W-10S | | 7 |
| Douglass Way NW&SE ........22W-10S | | 7 |
| Drake Av. E&W .... 25W-12S | | 6 |
| Drake Ct. N&S .... 25W-11S | | 6 |
| DuPage Dr. N&S .. 24W-11S | | 6 |
| Dubois Cir.* E&W .. 23W-10S | | 7 |
| Dunham Ct. NE&SW ........21W-10S | | 7 |
| Dunham Ln. N&S .. 21W-10S | | 7 |
| Dunmore Ct. NW&SE ........23W-10S | | 7 |
| Eagle Ct. N&S......24W-11S | | 6 |
| Edgehill Dr. E&W .. 23W-11S | | 7 |
| Edinburgh Ct. E&W ........22W-10S | | 7 |
| Elkhorn Ct. N&S .. 24W-11S | | 6 |
| Elm Ct. N&S ...... 23W-11S | | 6 |
| Emerson Ct. N&S .. 24W-11S | | 6 |
| Ennis Ln. E&W .... 22W-10S | | 7 |
| Eric Way N&S...... 22W-10S | | 7 |
| Essex Ct. E&W .... 24W-12S | | 6 |
| Essington Rd. N&S ........28W-13S | | 9 |
| Evergreen Ct. E&W ........22W-11S | | 7 |
| Fairwood Ct. NE&SW ........23W-12S | | 7 |
| Fairwood Dr. E&W ..23W-12S | | 7 |
| Falcon Ridge Way N&S ........22W-11S,21W-11S | | 7 |
| Falmore Ln. N&S .. 23W-10S | | 7 |
| Far Hills Dr. N&S .. 24W-12S | | 6 |
| Farm Gate Ln. N&S ........25W-12S | | 6 |
| Faversham Ct. E&W ........22W-11S | | 7 |
| Fawn Ct. E&W .... 26W-12S | | 6 |
| Feather Sound Dr. NS&EW ........21W-10S | | 7 |
| Feathersound Dr. NS&EW ........21W-10S | | 7 |
| Fernwood Dr. NS&EW ........23W-11S | | 7 |
| Flagstaff Dr. N&S .. 24W-11S | | 6 |
| Fleetwood Ct. E&W ........22W-12S | | 7 |
| Forest Ct. N&S .... 21W-11S | | 7 |
| Forest Way E&W .. 21W-11S | | 7 |
| Foxhead Ct. E&W .. 24W-11S | | 6 |
| Foxwood Ln. N&S .. 26W-12S | | 6 |
| Friars Ct. NE&SW .. 22W-11S | | 7 |
| Fuller Ln.* NS&EW ..23W-10S | | 7 |
| Galahad Rd. E&W .. 22W-11S | | 7 |
| Gannet Ln. NS&EW ........21W-10S | | 7 |
| Garden Dr. N&S .... 24W-12S | | 6 |
| Gary E&W ........ 21W-11S | | 7 |
| Gehrig Cir. E&W .. 23W-11S | | 7 |
| Genesee Ct. E&W .. 23W-11S | | 7 |
| Gibraltar NW&SE .. 22W-12S | | 7 |
| Glen Lake Dr. NS&EW ........25W-11S | | 6 |
| Glengary Dr. E&W .. 23W-12S | | 7 |
| Grace Ct. N&S .... 23W-11S | | 7 |
| Grady Dr. N&S .... 25W-11S | | 6 |
| Granada Ct. N&S .. 23W-11S | | 7 |
| Grand Canyon E&W ........23W-11S | | 7 |
| Grant Dr. E&W .... 23W-11S | | 7 |
| Green Mountain Ct. E&W ........21W-11S | | 7 |
| Green Mountain Dr. NS&EW ........21W-11S | | 7 |
| Greencrest Dr. E&W ........22W-11S | | 7 |
| Greentree Ct. N&S..22W-12S | | 7 |
| Greentree Ln. N&S 22W-12S | | 7 |
| Greenwood Ct. E&W ........22W-12S | | 7 |
| Grove Ct. NE&SW .. 24W-11S | | 6 |
| Grove Ln. NW&SE .. 24W-11S | | 6 |
| Gull Point Ct. N&S .. 21W-10S | | 7 |
| Hadleigh Rd. E&W .. 22W-11S | | 7 |
| Hallmark Ln. N&S .. 22W-12S | | 7 |
| Hampoon Ct. N&S .. 24W-12S | | 6 |
| Hampshire Ct. E&W ........22W-10S | | 7 |
| Hampshire Ln. NE&SW ........22W-10S | | 7 |
| Hanover Ct. N&S .. 22W-12S | | 7 |
| Harris Dr. E&W .... 24W-12S | | 6 |
| Hartford Ln. E&W .. 25W-11S | | 6 |
| Harvest Ct. NE&SW ........26W-13S | | 10 |
| Harvest Dr. N&S.. 26W-13S | | 10 |
| Harwood Dr. N&S .. 22W-12S | | 7 |
| Hawthorne Ct. E&W ........24W-12S | | 6 |
| Heritage Ct. N&S .. 26W-11S | | 6 |
| Heron Ct. E&W .... 22W-12S | | 7 |
| Hickory Oaks Ct. NW&SE ........26W-11S | | 6 |
| Hickory Oaks Dr. N&S ........26W-11S | | 6 |
| Hidden Valley Ct. E&W ........26W-11S | | 6 |
| Hidden Valley Dr. N&S ........26W-11S | | 6 |
| Home Pl. E&W .... 25W-12S | | 6 |
| Homer E&W........22W-11S | | 7 |
| Homestead Dr. NS&EW ........21W-11S | | 7 |
| Homewood Dr. N&S ........21W-11S | | 7 |
| Hudson Ct. N&S....24W-11S | | 6 |
| Hughes Pl. N&S .. 22W-10S | | 7 |
| Huntington Way N&S ........22W-11S,22W-10S | | 7 |
| Hywood Ct. N&S .. 23W-11S | | 7 |
| Idlewood Ct. N&S .. 22W-12S | | 7 |
| Independence Ct. N&S ........22W-11S | | 7 |
| Independence Dr. N&S ........22W-11S | | 7 |
| Ingleside Dr. N&S .. 22W-12S | | 6 |
| International Dr. NW&SE ........22W-12S,21W-12S | | 7 |
| Ironbark Way NS&EW ........22W-12S | | 7 |
| Jameson Ct. NE&SW ........22W-12S | | 7 |
| Jamestown Ln. E&W ........21W-11S | | 7 |
| Janes Av. N&S ........21W-11S,21W-10S | | 7 |
| Jeffrey Ln.* E&W .. 23W-10S | | 7 |
| Jennifer Ln. NS&EW ........25W-11S | | 6 |
| Jerome Ln.* N&S .. 23W-10S | | 7 |
| Jill Ln.* E&W ...... 23W-10S | | 7 |
| Joliet Rd. N&S .... 21W-10S | | 7 |
| Jordan Way N&S .. 22W-10S | | 7 |
| Joy Dr. N&S ........22W-11S,22W-10S | | 7 |
| Julie Rd. E&W......22W-10S | | 7 |
| Juniper Ln. E&W .. 23W-11S | | 7 |
| Justine Av. NE&SW | | |
| Karen Cir. NS&EW ..21W-11S | | 7 |
| Kedvale Ct. N&S .. 24W-11S | | 6 |
| Kenilworth Dr. NS&EW ........22W-11S | | 7 |
| Kenmore Dr. N&S .. 22W-12S | | 7 |
| Keystone Ct. NE&SW ........22W-10S | | 7 |
| Keystone Dr. N&S.. 22W-10S | | 7 |
| Kildeer Dr. N&S .. 21W-10S | | 7 |
| King Arthur Ct. N&S ........21W-11S | | 7 |
| King Arthur Way E&W ........21W-11S | | 7 |
| Kings Rd. N&S ........27W-14S,27W-13S | | 9 |
| Kingston Rd. N&S .. 22W-12S | | 7 |
| Kirkwood Cir. E&W ........23W-11S | | 7 |
| Knight Ct. N&S .... 22W-11S | | 7 |
| Lacross N&S ...... 23W-11S | | 7 |
| Lafayette Dr. E&W ..23W-11S | | 7 |
| Lakeside Dr. N&S .. 21W-11S | | 7 |
| Lakewood Farms Rd. NS&EW ........26W-13S | | 10 |
| Lancaster Dr. N&S ........23W-11S,23W-12S | | 7 |
| Lancelot Ct. E&W .. 22W-11S | | 7 |
| Lancelot Way N&S ..22W-11S | | 7 |
| Langford Ct. N&S .. 22W-10S | | 7 |
| Langford Dr. E&W .. 22W-10S | | 7 |
| Larchmont N&S .. 24W-12S | | 6 |
| Laurie Cir. NE&SW 21W-11S | | 7 |
| Lavina Ln. NE&SW .24W-10S | | 6 |
| Lawton N&S......22W-12S | | 7 |
| Lee Ln. E&W ...... 23W-11S | | 7 |
| Leicester Ct. NW&SE ........22W-11S | | 7 |
| Leslie Ln. E&W .... 22W-10S | | 7 |
| Lexington Dr. NS&EW ........23W-11S | | 7 |
| Liberty Ct. N&S .... 22W-11S | | 7 |
| Liberty Dr. E&W .. 22W-10S | | 7 |
| Lily Cache Ln. E&W ........25W-12S | | 6 |
| Lincolshire Ct. E&W ........23W-11S | | 7 |
| Linconshire Ln. N&S ........23W-11S | | 7 |
| Linden Ct. E&W .... 24W-12S | | 6 |
| Lindsey Ct., E. E&W ........25W-11S | | 6 |
| Lindsey Ct., W. E&W ........25W-11S | | 6 |
| Lindsey Ln. N&S....25W-11S | | 6 |
| Lyons Rd. N&S .... 22W-11S | | 7 |
| Malibu Ct. E&W .... 22W-11S | | 7 |
| Malibu Dr. N&S .... 22W-11S | | 7 |
| Mallview Ln. N&S .. 21W-12S | | 7 |
| Manor Ct. N&S....22W-12S | | 7 |
| Maplewood Dr. N&S ........23W-12S | | 7 |
| Marian Ct. N&S .. 22W-11S | | 7 |
| Marquette Ct. E&W ........22W-11S | | 7 |
| Mayfield Dr. N&S .. 23W-11S | | 7 |
| Mayflower Ln. N&S ........26W-11S | | 6 |
| Meadowbrook Dr. NS&EW ........22W-11S | | 7 |
| Medical Center Dr. E&W ........23W-13S | | 11 |
| Melissa Dr. NS&EW ........21W-11S | | 7 |
| Mellbrook Ln. N&S..22W-12S | | 7 |
| Merlin Ct. N&S .... 22W-12S | | 7 |
| Merrill Ct. N&S .... 25W-11S | | 6 |
| Mesa Dr. E&W .... 26W-12S | | 6 |
| Michael Dr. NE&SW ........26W-11S | | 6 |
| Michelangelo NE&SW ........22W-11S | | 7 |
| Millstream Dr. N&S 24W-12S | | 6 |
| Miner Dr. E&W .... 22W-11S | | 7 |
| Monet E&W........22W-11S | | 7 |
| Monroe Rd. NW&SE ........22W-10S | | 7 |
| Monterey Dr. N&S .. 22W-11S | | 7 |
| Monticello Cir. NS&EW ........23W-11S | | 7 |
| Moore NW&SE .... 22W-11S | | 7 |
| Musial Cir. N&S....23W-11S | | 7 |
| Mutwood Dr. N&S ........22W-11S | | 7 |
| Naperville Rd. NW&SE ........25W-12S | | 6 |
| Nausau Av. N&S .. 23W-11S | | 7 |
| Navajo Ct. E&W.... 23W-11S | | 7 |
| New Castle Ln. NE&SW ........23W-12S | | 7 |

|  | Grid | Page |
|---|---|---|
| Newberry Ln. NS&EW | 23W-12S | 7 |
| Newport Dr. N&S | 23W-11S | 7 |
| Newton Ct. NE&SW | 22W-11S | 7 |
| Niagara Dr. E&W | 21W-11S | 7 |
| Nicholas Dr. NE&SW | 26W-11S | 6 |
| Norman Way NW&SE | 22W-10S | 7 |
| Northridge Ct. N&S | 22W-11S | 7 |
| Northridge Dr. E&W | 22W-11S | 7 |
| Nottingham Dr. N&S | 23W-11S | 7 |
| Oakwood Dr. N&S | 23W-12S | 7 |
| Old Chicago Dr. E&W | 24W-13S | 11 |
| Old Elm Dr. N&S | 23W-11S | 7 |
| Old Stone Rd. E&W | 24W-12S | 6 |
| Olive Pl. NE&SW | 22W-10S | 7 |
| Olympic Dr. N&S | 22W-11S | 7 |
| Orchard Dr. NW&SE | 24W-12S | 6 |
| Ottawa Dr. N&S | 23W-11S | 7 |
| Overland Dr. N&S | 24W-13S | 10 |
| Oxford Rd. NE&SW | 22W-11S | 7 |
| Ozark Dr. N&S | 23W-11S | 7 |
| Pacific Dr. N&S | 23W-11S | 7 |
| Pamela E&W | 22W-10S | 7 |
| Park Ct. E&W | 21W-11S | 7 |
| Park Lawn Ct. NE&SW | 22W-11S | 7 |
| Park Meadow Ln. NE&SW | 25W-11S | 6 |
| Parkside Ct. NE&SW | 26W-13S | 10 |
| Parkside Dr. E&W | 26W-13S | 10 |
| Parliament N&S | 21W-11S | 7 |
| Partridge Av. E&W | 25W-12S | 6 |
| Pebble Ct. NW&SE | 25W-11S | 6 |
| Pembrook Ct. E&W | 25W-11S | 6 |
| Pennsbury Ct. E&W | 25W-11S | 6 |
| Penny Ct. NW&SE | 25W-11S | 6 |
| Penny Ln. NW&SE | 25W-11S | 6 |
| Penwood Ln. NW&SE | 25W-11S | 6 |
| Pepperwood Dr. N&S | 25W-12S | 6 |
| Pierce Ct. NW&SE | 23W-11S | 7 |
| Pilgrim Ct. N&S | 21W-12S | 7 |
| Pinecrest Ct. NW&SE | 22W-10S | 7 |
| Pinecrest Rd. N&S | 22W-12S,22W-10S | 7 |
| Pinto Dr. E&W | 24W-11S | 6 |
| Planeview Ln. NS&EW | 24W-11S | 6 |
| Plymouth Ln. N&S | 23W-11S | 7 |
| Ponderosa Dr. E&W | 24W-12S | 6 |
| Pontiac Ln. E&W | 24W-11S | 6 |
| Poplar Ln. E&W | 24W-11S | 6 |
| Porter Ln. E&W | 22W-10S | 7 |
| Portsmouth Ln. E&W | 25W-12S | 6 |
| Potomac Ct. E&W | 23W-11S | 7 |
| Prairie Cir. NW&SE | 24W-12S | 6 |
| Preston Dr. N&S | 21W-10S | 7 |
| Princeton Dr. E&W | 24W-12S | 6 |
| Providence Ct. N&S | 22W-12S | 7 |
| Prudential Corp. Cr. NW&SE | 22W-12S | 7 |
| Pueblo Dr. N&S | 24W-11S | 6 |
| Puffin Cir. NW&SE | 21W-10S | 7 |
| Purchase Ct. | 22W-10S | 7 |
| Quadangle Dr. N&S | 22W-12S | 7 |
| Quail Run E&W | 25W-12S | 6 |
| Quarry N&S | 25W-12S | 6 |
| Queenswood Av. NS&EW | 21W-11S | 7 |
| Racine Av.* N&S | 23W-10S | 7 |
| Radcliff Dr. N&S | 24W-11S | 6 |
| Raphael E&W | 22W-11S | 7 |
| Red Tr. NS&EW | 26W-13S | 10 |
| Redspier Ct. N&S | 25W-12S | 6 |
| Redwing Ct. N&S | 24W-11S | 6 |
| Redwood Rd. E&W | 21W-11S | 7 |
| Regent Ct. E&W | 25W-11S | 6 |
| Remington Blvd. NS&EW | 23W-12S,24W-13S | 7 |
| Revere Ct. NW&SE | 22W-10S | 7 |
| Richmond Dr. E&W | 24W-12S | 6 |
| Ridgewood Ct. E&W | 25W-12S | 6 |
| Ridgewood Dr. NS&EW | 25W-12S | 6 |
| Roanoke Ct. E&W | 25W-12S | 7 |
| Roberts Rd.* E&W | 23W-10S | 7 |
| Robinhood Ct. E&W | 23W-11S | 7 |
| Robinhood Way NS&EW | 23W-11S,22W-11S | 7 |
| Rockhurst Rd. E&W | 22W-11S,21W-11S | 7 |
| Rocklyn Ct. E&W | 23W-12S | 7 |
| Roman Cir. NS&EW | 21W-11S | 7 |
| Rose Hill Dr. E&W | 24W-11S | 6 |
| Rothbury Dr. E&W | 22W-10S | 7 |
| Round Hill Ct. NE&SW | 21W-11S | 7 |
| Royal Crest Ct. NW&SE | 22W-10S | 7 |
| Ruth Cir. E&W | 23W-11S | 7 |
| Rye Ct. E&W | 22W-10S | 7 |
| Salem Sq. N&S&EW | 22W-12S | 7 |
| Sandalwood Ct. NE&SW | 25W-11S | 6 |
| Sandalwood Ln. NW&SE | 25W-11S | 6 |
| Scmidt Rd N&S | 24W-13S,24W-11S | 10 |
| Scott Dr. NE&SW | 22W-10S | 7 |
| Seabury Rd. NS&EW | 22W-11S,21W-11S | 7 |
| Seminole Ln. E&W | 23W-11S | 7 |
| Seneca Ct. N&S | 24W-11S | 6 |
| Seneca Ln. E&W | 23W-11S | 6 |
| Seneca Way N&S | 24W-11S | 6 |
| Shady Ln. N&S | 24W-12S | 6 |
| Sharon Dr. NW&SE | 26W-11S | 6 |
| Shawnee N&S | 24W-11S | 6 |
| Shenandoah Ct. N&S | 23W-11S | 7 |
| Sherington Ct. N&S | 22W-12S | 7 |
| Sherwood Ct. N&S | 22W-11S | 7 |
| Shield Ct. N&S | 22W-11S | 7 |
| Shilling Ct. N&S | 22W-10S | 7 |
| Sierra Ln. E&W | 23W-11S | 7 |
| Sioux E&W | 23W-11S | 7 |
| Skokie Ln. E&W | 23W-11S | 7 |
| Somerset Ln. E&W | 22W-12S | 7 |
| Spangler Dr. N&S | 23W-15S | 10 |
| Springhill Dr. N&S | 24W-12S | 6 |
| Springleaf Dr. N&S | 24W-12S | 6 |
| Springwood Way NS&EW | 25W-11S | 6 |
| Spruce Rd. E&W | 21W-11S | 7 |
| St. Andrews Dr. E&W | 22W-10S | 7 |
| Stafford Ct. E&W | 22W-11S | 7 |
| Stafford Way N&S | 22W-11S | 7 |
| Standish Ct. N&S | 22W-12S | 7 |
| Staunton Ct. NW&SE | 22W-11S | 7 |
| Steck Ct. NW&SE | 24W-10S | 6 |
| Stonegate Ln. N&S | 25W-11S | 6 |
| Stoneham Ct. NE&SW | 22W-11S | 7 |
| Sullivan E&W | 22W-11S | 7 |
| Summit Ln. NW&SE | 24W-12S | 6 |
| Sundance Dr. E&W | 24W-11S | 6 |
| Sunset Ln. N&S | 22W-11S | 6 |
| Sunshine Ct. E&W | 26W-11S | 6 |
| Sunshine Dr. N&S | 26W-11S | 6 |
| Sunshine East Dr. E&W | 26W-11S | 6 |
| Swan Cir. N&S | 21W-10S | 7 |
| Swinford Ct. NW&SE | 23W-10S | 7 |
| Sword Way N&S | 21W-11S | 7 |
| Sylvan Rd. N&S | 22W-11S | 7 |
| Tahoe Ct. N&S | 25W-12S | 6 |
| Talcot Ct. NW&SE | 22W-11S | 7 |
| Tam O'Shanter Ct. N&S | 22W-10S | 7 |
| Tam O'Shanter Dr. N&S | 22W-10S | 7 |
| Tamarack Ct. N&S | 24W-12S | 6 |
| Tamms Ln. E&W | 24W-12S | 6 |
| Tarrington Way NW&SE | 21W-11S | 7 |
| Taylor Ct. N&S | 25W-12S | 6 |
| Tecumseh Dr. N&S | 26W-12S | 6 |
| Tellemesh Dr. N&S | 26W-12S | 6 |
| Territorial Ct. | 25W-13S | 10 |
| Thackery Dr. E&W | 25W-12S | 6 |
| Thistle Av. NS&EW | 25W-12S | 6 |
| Thomas Rd. N&S | 24W-11S | 7 |
| Thornhurst Dr. NS&EW | 22W-11S,21W-11S | 7 |
| Tilden Ln. N&S | 24W-12S | 6 |
| Timber Ct. E&W | 23W-12S | 6 |
| Tomahawk Ct. N&S | 24W-11S | 6 |
| Towner Ln. N&S | 25W-12S | 6 |
| Towner Ln. N&S | 25W-12S | 6 |
| Tracy Way NS&EW | 22W-10S | 7 |
| Tudor Ct. N&S | 22W-11S | 7 |
| Tuttle Dr. N&S | 27W-11S | 5 |
| Upton Rd. N&S | 21W-11S | 7 |
| Valley Dr. N&S | 24W-12S | 6 |
| Van Gogh Cir. N&S | 22W-12S | 7 |
| Venetian Dr. NE&SW | 22W-11S | 7 |
| Vermont Cir. E&W | 22W-10S | 7 |
| Vernon Rd. E&W | 22W-11S,21W-11S | 7 |
| Victoria Ct. N&S | 22W-10S | 7 |
| Vigilance Ct. E&W | 22W-10S | 7 |
| Vincent Dr. E&W | 22W-11S | 6 |
| Vista Dr. N&S | 26W-11S | 6 |
| Wagon Wheel Ct. NW&SE | 26W-13S | 10 |
| Walden St. E&W | 25W-11S | 6 |
| Walker Dr. E&W | 22W-10S | 7 |
| Walnut Cir. NS&EW | 23W-11S | 7 |
| Warwick Ct. E&W | 21W-11S | 7 |
| Waterman Dr. N&S | 24W-12S | 6 |
| Weber Rd. NE&SW | 25W-12S | 7 |
| Wedgewood Way E&W | 22W-11S | 7 |
| Wellington Ln. N&S | 22W-12S | 7 |
| West Wind Dr. E&W | 24W-12S | 6 |
| Westchester Ct. NE&SW | 22W-10S | 7 |
| Westchester Ln. N&S | 22W-10S | 7 |
| Wethersfield Ln. N&S | 22W-12S | 7 |
| Whitbury Ct. N&S | 22W-10S | 7 |
| White Oak Rd. E&W | 21W-11S | 7 |
| Whitwater Dr. N&S | 24W-11S | 6 |
| Wildwood Ln. E&W | 23W-11S | 7 |
| Williamsburg N&S | 22W-12S | 7 |
| Willow Ct. N&S | 22W-10S | 7 |
| Willoway Dr. N&S | 21W-11S | 7 |
| Wimbledon Ct. NW&SE | 22W-10S | 7 |
| Windsor Dr. N&S | 24W-11S | 6 |
| Winston Dr. NE&SW | 22W-10S | 7 |
| Wobbler Dr. N&S | 21W-10S | 7 |
| Wood Ct. NE&SW | 25W-11S | 6 |
| Woodcreek Rd. N&S | 23W-13S,23W-12S | 11 |
| Wright Ct. NS&EW | 22W-11S | 7 |
| Wyeth N&S | 22W-11S | 7 |
| Yellow Pine Dr. N&S | 24W-11S | 6 |
| York St. N&S | 23W-11S | 7 |
| Yorkshire Sq. NS&EW | 22W-12S | 7 |
| 107th St. E&W | 25W-12S,21W-12S | 6 |
| 111th St. E&W | 23W-13S,23W-12S | 11 |
| 119th St. E&W | 27W-13S | 9 |

## Braidwood

|  | Grid | Page |
|---|---|---|
| 'A' St. E&W | 30W-41S | 70 |
| 'B' St. N&S | 31W-41S | 70 |
| Barr St. N&S | 31W-41S | 70 |
| Bergera Rd. E&W | 32W-41S,31W-41S | 70 |
| Center St. N&S | 31W-41S,31W-40S | 70 |
| Church St. E&W | 32W-41S,31W-41S | 70 |
| Coal City Rd. E&W | 32W-39S | 70 |
| Commercial Av. N&S | 31W-41S | 70 |
| Cook St. N&S | 32W-41S | 70 |
| Corey St. N&S | 32W-41S | 70 |
| Countryside Ct. N&S | 32W-41S | 70 |
| Curtis Ct. N&S | 31W-41S | 70 |
| Dalton St. N&S | 31W-41S | 70 |
| Daniels (2nd St.) E&W | 32W-41S,31W-41S | 70 |
| David Ct. E&W | 31W-41S | 70 |
| Division St. (Hwy. 113) N&S | 32W-41S,32W-39S | 70 |
| Elm St. E&W | 31W-42S | 74 |
| English St. N&S | 32W-41S | 70 |
| Erie St. N&S | 31W-40S | 70 |
| Eureka St. E&W | 32W-41S,31W-41S | 70 |
| Francis St. N&S | 31W-42S | 74 |
| French St. N&S | 31W-41S | 70 |
| Front St. (Il. 53) NE&SW | 31W-41S | 70 |
| Grove St. N&S | 31W-41S | 70 |
| Hall St. E&W | 32W-41S,31W-41S | 70 |
| Hickory St. N&S | 32W-41S | 70 |
| Highway 113 EW&NS | 32W-39S,30W-41S | 70 |
| Interstate 55 N&S | 32W-41S,32W-39S | 70 |
| Kane St. N&S | 31W-41S | 70 |
| Kenard Ct. E&W | 32W-41S | 70 |
| Kennedy Rd. (Reed Rd.) E&W | 32W-41S,31W-41S | 70 |
| Kerns St. NW&SE | 31W-41S | 70 |
| Lincoln St. N&S | 31W-41S | 70 |
| Main St. E&W | 32W-41S,31W-41S | 70 |
| Maple St. N&S | 32W-41S | 70 |
| Mason (2nd) St. E&W | 31W-41S | 70 |
| Michigan St. N&S | 31W-40S | 70 |
| Mitchell St. N&S | 31W-41S | 70 |
| Oak St. NW&SE | 31W-41S | 70 |
| Office St. N&S | 32W-41S | 70 |
| Orchard Ln. NW&SE | 31W-42S | 74 |
| Park Av. N&S | 31W-41S | 70 |
| Park Rd. N&S | 31W-41S | 70 |
| Parkview Ln. N&S | 31W-41S | 70 |
| Parkway St. E&W | 31W-41S,30W-41S | 70 |
| Pond St. NW&SE | 31W-41S | 70 |
| Prairie St. NW&SE | 31W-41S | 70 |
| Railroad St. NW&SE | 31W-40S | 70 |
| Reed Rd. E&W | 32W-41S | 70 |
| Reed St. E&W | 31W-41S | 70 |
| Ridge St. NW&SE | 31W-41S | 70 |
| Rossi Ln. E&W | 31W-41S | 70 |
| Round House St. NW&SE | 31W-41S | 70 |
| Route 129 NE&SW | 31W-42S,30W-41S | 74 |
| Route 53 NE&SW | 32W-41S,30W-41S | 74 |
| Schmidt Rd. E&W | 31W-41S | 70 |
| School St. N&S | 31W-41S,31W-40S | 70 |
| Small St. E&W | 31W-40S | 70 |
| Spring Rd. E&W | 32W-41S | 70 |
| Sullivan Ln. N&S | 31W-41S | 70 |
| Susan Ct. N&S | 31W-41S | 70 |
| Traudel Ct. N&S | 32W-41S | 70 |
| Walker St. N&S | 31W-41S | 70 |
| Walnut St. N&S | 32W-41S | 70 |
| Washington St. NE&SW | 31W-41S | 70 |
| Wildwood Dr. N&S | 31W-41S | 70 |
| 1st St. N&S | 32W-41S,30W-41S | 70 |
| 2nd St. (Mason St.) E&W | 31W-41S | 70 |
| 3rd St. E&W | 31W-41S | 70 |
| 4th St. E&W | 31W-41S | 70 |
| 6th St. E&W | 31W-40S | 70 |
| 7th St. E&W | 31W-40S | 70 |

## Channahon

|  | Grid | Page |
|---|---|---|
| Alessio Ct. NE&SW | 30W-29S | 34 |
| Andrew Av. E&W | 28W-27S | 27 |
| Arrow Ct. E&W | 32W-32S | 46 |
| Belles Ln. N&S | 29W-27S | 26 |
| Birch St. E&W | 31W-30S | 34 |
| Blackberry St. N&S | 31W-30S | 34 |
| Blackhawk Dr. NS&EW | 32W-32S | 46 |
| Bluebird Ct. N&S | 30W-29S | 34 |
| Bluff Rd. E&W | 31W-29S,30W-29S | 34 |
| Bluff Ridge Ct. NW&SE | 30W-29S | 34 |
| Bluff NE&SW | 31W-30S | 34 |
| Bridge St. E&W | 32W-30S,31W-30S | 34 |
| Bud Ct. N&S | 29W-27S | 26 |
| Buell St. NE&SW | 31W-30S | 34 |
| Burr Ct., N. NW&SE | 30W-29S | 34 |
| Burr Ct., S. NE&SW | 30W-29S | 34 |
| Burr Rd. N&S | 30W-29S | 34 |
| Canal St. N&S | 31W-30S | 34 |
| Cardinal Dr. N&S | 30W-29S | 34 |
| Carrie Av. N&S | 28W-27S | 27 |
| Center St. N&S | 31W-30S | 34 |
| Channahon Dr. E&W | 31W-29S | 34 |
| Cherokee Dr. N&S | 31W-29S | 34 |
| Cherokee Tr. E&W | 32W-30S | 34 |
| Cherry St. N&S | 31W-30S | 34 |
| Chipwood Dr. NS&EW | 31W-29S | 34 |
| Colleen Ct. N&S | 32W-30S | 34 |
| Countryside Dr. N&S | 31W-29S | 34 |
| Crowfoot Ln. E&W | 30W-29S | 34 |
| Deal Av. N&S | 28W-27S | 27 |
| Devon Rd. NE&SW | 29W-27S | 26 |
| Donna Av. N&S | 28W-27S | 27 |
| Dupage Dr. N&S | 32W-29S | 34 |
| Eames St. NE&SW | 32W-30S,29W-28S | 34 |
| Eastwood Ct. N&S | 32W-32S | 46 |
| Eastwood Dr. N&S | 32W-32S | 46 |
| Edwin Ct. N&S | 30W-29S | 34 |
| Edwin Dr. N&S | 30W-29S | 34 |
| Egret Dr. NS&EW | 30W-29S | 34 |
| Elsie Av. N&S | 31W-30S | 34 |
| Essex Dr. NE&SW | 29W-27S | 26 |
| Ford Rd. N&S | 32W-29S | 34 |
| Frances Ct. NE&SW | 29W-27S | 26 |
| Frances Way NW&SE | 29W-27S | 26 |
| Freyer St. NW&SE | 31W-30S | 34 |
| Goldfinch Ct. N&S | 30W-29S | 34 |
| Green Heron Dr. N&S | 30W-29S | 34 |
| Harriet Dr. N&S | 29W-27S | 26 |
| Hawthorne Av. N&S | 30W-29S | 34 |
| Heritage Valley Dr. NE&SW | 31W-29S | 34 |
| Highland Dr. NE&SW | 32W-32S | 46 |
| Howard Ct. N&S | 32W-29S | 34 |
| Hummingbird Dr. E&W | 30W-29S | 34 |
| Interstate 55 N&S | 30W-29S,29W-27S | 34 |
| Iroquois Dr. N&S | 31W-29S | 34 |
| Janet Ln. E&W | 30W-29S | 34 |
| Jessup St. E&W | 31W-30S | 34 |
| Joliet St. N&S | 31W-30S | 34 |
| Joliet-Channahon Rd. NE&SW | 31W-29S,30W-28S | 34 |
| Joseph Av. N&S | 28W-27S | 27 |
| Junior Av. E&W | 30W-29S | 34 |
| Karl Av. E&W | 28W-27S | 27 |
| Kathey Dr. E&W | 29W-27S | 26 |
| Kent Rd. NW&SE | 29W-27S | 26 |
| Kevins Dr. NW&SE | 32W-31S | 34 |
| Knapps St. E&W | 31W-30S | 34 |
| Kurt Rd. E&W | 29W-27S | 26 |
| Lauren Dr. E&W | 32W-32S | 46 |
| Leslie Dr. NE&SW | 32W-32S | 46 |
| Liberty Dr. E&W | 31W-29S | 34 |
| Lois Av. E&W | 31W-30S | 34 |
| Majestic Dr. N&S | 31W-29S | 34 |
| Manor Ln. N&S | 29W-28S | 34 |
| Maple St. E&W | 31W-30S | 34 |
| Marble Ct. NW&SE | 31W-29S | 34 |
| Marble Rd. NE&SW | 31W-29S | 34 |
| Mary Lou E&W | 28W-27S | 27 |
| Matthew Ct. E&W | 30W-29S | 34 |
| May Ct. N&S | 31W-31S | 34 |
| May St. E&W | 32W-31S,31W-31S | 34 |
| McClintock Rd. NE&SW | 29W-27S,28W-27S | 26 |
| McCowan St. E&W | 31W-30S | 34 |
| McKinley Rd. N&S | 32W-32S | 46 |
| Meadowlark Dr. E&W | 30W-29S | 34 |
| Michael Dr. NE&SW | 29W-27S | 26 |
| Mohawk Dr. E&W | 32W-29S | 34 |
| Moorman Av. NE&SW | 30W-29S | 34 |
| Municipal Dr. NW&SE | 30W-29S | 34 |
| North St. E&W | 31W-30S | 34 |
| North St. NW&SE | 30W-29S | 34 |
| Northcrest Dr. E&W | 31W-29S | 34 |
| Northern Illinois Dr. NW&SE | 30W-29S | 34 |
| Oakview Ct. E&W | 32W-31S | 34 |
| Parkside Dr. NW&SE | 32W-31S | 34 |
| Patricia Ln. NW&SE | 29W-27S | 26 |
| Peak Dr. E&W | 30W-29S | 34 |
| Pine St. E&W | 31W-30S | 34 |
| Plum St. N&S | 31W-30S | 34 |
| Pottawatomie Tr. NE&SW | 32W-30S,31W-29S | 34 |
| Prairie Dr. E&W | 32W-32S | 46 |
| Pueblo Dr. NE&SW | 31W-29S | 34 |
| Quail Dr. E&W | 30W-29S | 34 |
| River Tr. NW&SE | 32W-30S,32W-29S | 34 |
| Roberts Av. E&W | 30W-29S | 34 |
| Robin Ct. N&S | 30W-29S | 34 |
| Rock Ridge Ct. N&S | 30W-29S | 34 |
| Sage St. NW&SE | 31W-30S | 34 |
| Sandpiper Dr. N&S | 30W-29S | 34 |
| Short St. NW&SE | 30W-29S | 34 |
| Sioux Dr. E&W | 31W-30S | 34 |
| South St. E&W | 30W-29S | 34 |
| Spruce St. E&W | 31W-30S | 34 |
| Steve Ritoff Dr. NW&SE | 30W-29S | 34 |
| Story St. NE&SW | 31W-30S | 34 |
| Summit Rd. E&W | 30W-29S | 34 |
| Sunset Dr. N&S | 30W-29S | 34 |
| Sussex Dr. E&W | 29W-27S | 26 |
| Teal Dr. NS&EW | 30W-29S | 34 |
| Tonka Dr. NE&SW | 30W-29S | 34 |
| Tow Path Ln. E&W | 31W-29S | 34 |
| Tree Ridge Ct. NW&SE | 30W-29S | 34 |
| Tryon St. N&S | 31W-30S,31W-29S | 34 |
| Turnstone Blvd E&W | 30W-29S | 34 |
| U.S. Route 6 NE&SW | 32W-30S,29W-27S | 34 |
| Valley Dr. NS&EW | 30W-29S | 34 |
| Westwood Ct. N&S | 32W-32S | 46 |
| Westwood Dr. SW&NE | 32W-32S | 46 |
| Willard St. N&S | 31W-30S,31W-29S | 34 |
| Woodland Ct. E&W | 32W-32S | 46 |

| | Grid | Page |
|---|---|---|
| **Channahon Township** | | |
| Arsenal Rd. E&W | | |
| | 30W-31S,27W-30S | 34 |
| Bell Rd. N&S | | |
| | 27W-30S,32W-29S | 34 |
| Blodget Rd. E&W | 32W-33S | 46 |
| Bluff Rd. E&W | | |
| | 31W-30S,29W-30S | 34 |
| Bonnell Ct. NW&SE | | |
| | 32W-33S | 46 |
| Canal Rd. NE&SW | 30W-28S | 34 |
| Center St. NW&SE | 30W-29S | 34 |
| Channahon Rd. NE&SW | | |
| | 30W-28S,29W-28S | 34 |
| Cottonwood Ct. NE&SW | | |
| | 32W-28S | 34 |
| Cottonwood Ln. N&S | | |
| | 32W-28S | 34 |
| Dirst Rd. E&W | | |
| | 32W-28S,32W-29S | 34 |
| Durkee Rd. E&W | 30W-31S | 34 |
| Eames St. E&W | | |
| | 32W-30S,29W-28S | 34 |
| Fieldcrest Ct. N&S | 32W-28S | 34 |
| Ford Rd. N&S | 32W-29S | 34 |
| Front St. E&W | | |
| | 31W-30S,30W-30S | 34 |
| Grande Dr. N&S | 32W-28S | 34 |
| Graystone Ct. NW&SE | | |
| | 32W-33S | 46 |
| Grundy County Line Rd. N&S | | |
| | 32W-33S | 46 |
| Hickory Ct. E&W | 32W-28S | 34 |
| Hickory Ln. N&S | 32W-28S | 34 |
| Ingolsby Rd. N&S | 32W-28S | 34 |
| Interstate 55 N&S | 30W-30S | 34 |
| Joliet Rd. E&W | | |
| | 28W-28S,27W-28S | 35 |
| Joliet-Channahon Rd. NE&SW | | |
| | 28W-28S,30W-28S | 34 |
| Kankakee St. N&S | | |
| | 27W-33S,27W-31S | 47 |
| Lakeview Dr. NS&EW | | |
| | 32W-29S | 34 |
| McEvilly Rd. E&W | 32W-28S | 34 |
| McKinley Rd. N&S | | |
| | 32W-32S,32W-31S | 46 |
| McMillin Dr. E&W | 31W-29S | 34 |
| Meadowlark Ln. E&W | | |
| | 31W-29S | 34 |
| Millsdale Ext. Rd. E&W | | |
| | 28W-29S,27W-29S | 35 |
| Millsdale Rd. EW&NS | | |
| | 27W-29S | 35 |
| Navajo Dr. N&S | | |
| | 31W-29S,28W-30S | 34 |
| North Ridge Dr. E&W | | |
| | 32W-28S | 34 |
| North St. NW&SE | 30W-29S | 34 |
| Olin Rd. NS&EW | 28W-29S | 35 |
| Paradise Dr. NE&SW | | |
| | 32W-31S | 34 |
| Pawnee Ln. E&W | 31W-29S | 34 |
| Pine NW&SE | 32W-29S | 34 |
| Rivers Edge Ct. N&S | | |
| | 32W-28S | 34 |
| Rivers Edge Dr. E&W | | |
| | 32W-28S | 34 |
| Riverview Ct. E&W | 32W-28S | 34 |
| Seneca Ln. N&S | 31W-29S | 34 |
| Sibley Dr. N&S | 32W-28S | 34 |
| Sinote Ln. NS&EW | 32W-33S | 46 |
| Sunset Ct. E&W | 32W-29S | 34 |
| Timberwood Ct. E&W | | |
| | 32W-29S | 34 |
| Timberwood Dr. N&S | | |
| | 32W-29S | 34 |
| Tordi Ln. N&S | 27W-29S | 35 |
| U.S. Route 6 NE&SW | | |
| | 32W-30S,29W-28S | 34 |
| Vista Ct. N&S | 32W-28S | 34 |
| Willow Ln. N&S | 32W-28S | 34 |
| **Crest Hill** | | |
| Alma Dr. N&S | 25W-21S | 20 |
| Arbor Ln. N&S | 25W-21S | 20 |
| Ardaugh Av. E&W | 26W-21S | 20 |
| Ardaugh Dr. N&S | 26W-21S | 20 |
| Aster Dr. N&S | 27W-21S | 19 |
| August St. E&W | 25W-21S | 20 |
| Barthelone Av. N&S | | |
| | 25W-21S | 20 |
| Berta St. N&S&EW | 25W-21S | 20 |
| Bicentennial Av. NW&SE | | |
| | 26W-22S | 20 |
| Birkey Av. E&W | 24W-21S | 20 |
| Brian Dr. E&W | 25W-21S | 20 |
| Broadway St. N&S | 24W-21S | 20 |
| Burry Cir R. NS&EW | | |
| | 25W-21S | 20 |
| Burry Ct. E&W | 25W-21S | 20 |
| Carmel St. E&W | 25W-21S | 20 |
| Caton Crest Ct. E&W | | |
| | 27W-21S | 19 |
| Caton Crest Dr. N&S | | |
| | 27W-21S | 19 |
| Caton Farm Rd. E&W | | |
| | 25W-20S | 20 |
| Cedarwood Dr. NE&SW | | |
| | 27W-22S | 19 |
| Center St. N&S | 24W-21S | 20 |
| Chaney Av. E&W | 24W-21S | 20 |

| | Grid | Page |
|---|---|---|
| Circle St. NW&SE | 26W-21S | 20 |
| Clement St. N&S | 26W-21S | 20 |
| Connie Dr. N&S | 26W-21S | 20 |
| Cora St. N&S | 24W-21S | 20 |
| Cowing Ln. NS&EW | | |
| | 25W-21S | 20 |
| Crestwood Dr. N&S | | |
| | 26W-21S | 20 |
| Crystal Ct. N&S | | |
| | 25W-21S | 20 |
| Daffodil Dr. NW&SE | | |
| | 27W-21S | 19 |
| Daisy Ln.* E&W | 27W-21S | 19 |
| Dearborn St. N&S | 24W-21S | 20 |
| Dorothy Ct. E&W | 24W-21S | 20 |
| Durness Ct. NW&SE | | |
| | 26W-20S | 20 |
| Eldorado St. N&S | 26W-21S | 20 |
| Elrose Ct. E&W | 25W-21S | 20 |
| Elsie Av. E&W | 24W-21S | 20 |
| Fern St. NE&SW | 26W-21S | 20 |
| Frederick St. NE&SW | | |
| | 25W-21S | 20 |
| Garden Dr. NW&SE | | |
| | 27W-21S | 19 |
| Gaylord N&S | 27W-21S | 19 |
| Gladiola Ln.* N&S | 27W-21S | 19 |
| Grandview Av. N&S | | |
| | 26W-21S | 20 |
| Green St. N&S | 26W-21S | 20 |
| Greengold St. NW&SE | | |
| | 26W-21S | 20 |
| Hawthorn Av. N&S | 24W-21S | 20 |
| Heiden Av. N&S | 25W-21S | 20 |
| Hess Dr. N&S | 26W-21S | 20 |
| Hickory St. N&S | 24W-21S | 20 |
| Highland St. N&S | 24W-21S | 20 |
| Hoffman St. N&S | 24W-21S | 20 |
| Hosmer Ln. NS&EW | | |
| | 25W-21S | 20 |
| Imperial St. N&S | 26W-21S | 20 |
| Inner Ct. Dr. NS&EW | | |
| | 25W-21S | 20 |
| Iris Ln.* E&W | 27W-21S | 19 |
| Jasmine Dr. N&S | 27W-21S | 19 |
| Jonquil Ln.* NE&SW | | |
| | 27W-21S | 19 |
| Kelly Av. N&S | 24W-21S | 20 |
| Knapp Dr. NW&SE | | |
| | 26W-21S,25W-21S | 20 |
| Lenden St. E&W | 25W-21S | 20 |
| Leness St. N&S | 26W-21S | 20 |
| Lincoln Av. E&W | 26W-21S | 20 |
| Live Oak Dr. NW&SE | | |
| | 27W-22S | 19 |
| Lotus Ln.* E&W | 27W-21S | 19 |
| Ludwig Av. N&S | | |
| | 25W-21S,24W-21S | 20 |
| Lynwood St. N&S | | |
| | 26W-21S | 20 |
| Macher St. N&S | 26W-21S | 20 |
| Manico Ct. NE&SW | | |
| | 26W-21S | 20 |
| Manico Dr. NE&SW | | |
| | 26W-21S | 20 |
| Manor Ct. E&W | 25W-21S | 20 |
| Marietta Av. N&S | 25W-21S | 20 |
| Marlboro Ln. N&S | 25W-21S | 20 |
| Marlboro St. N&S | 25W-21S | 20 |
| Meadows Ct. E&W | 25W-21S | 20 |
| Morning Glory Ln.* N&S | | |
| | 27W-21S | 19 |
| Nicholson St. N&S | 24W-21S | 20 |
| Noonan St. N&S | 26W-21S | 20 |
| Oakland Av. N&S | | |
| | 25W-21S,24W-21S | 20 |
| Oakland St. N&S | 24W-21S | 20 |
| Orchid Ln.* N&S | 27W-21S | 19 |
| Parkrose St. NW&SE | | |
| | 26W-21S | 20 |
| Pasadena Av. E&W | | |
| | 24W-21S | 20 |
| Pioneer Rd. N&S | 26W-22S | 20 |
| Plainfield Rd. NW&SE | | |
| | 26W-21S | 20 |
| Poppy Ln.* N&S | 27W-21S | 19 |
| Post Oak Ct. NE&SW | | |
| | 27W-22S | 19 |
| Prairie Av. N&S | 25W-21S | 20 |
| Rahill Ct. E&W | 25W-21S | 20 |
| Raynor Av. N&S | 25W-21S | 20 |
| Red Oak Dr. NS&EW | | |
| | 27W-22S | 19 |
| Rock Run Dr. N&S | 26W-22S | 20 |
| Root St. NW&SE | | |
| | 26W-21S,25W-21S | 20 |
| Rose Av. E&W | 24W-21S | 20 |
| Rosel Ct. E&W | 25W-21S | 20 |
| Route 53 N&S | 24W-21S | 20 |
| Route 7 E&W | 25W-21S | 20 |
| Sak Dr. E&W | 25W-21S | 20 |
| Stern Av. E&W | 24W-21S | 20 |
| Sullivan Ct. E&W | 24W-21S | 20 |
| Surry Ct. E&W | 25W-21S | 20 |
| Susanna Way E&W | | |
| | 26W-21S | 20 |
| Sweetbriar St. E&W | | |
| | 26W-21S | 20 |
| Sybil Rd. N&S | 26W-21S | 20 |
| Sycamore St. NE&SW | | |
| | 26W-21S | 20 |
| Theodore St. E&W | 25W-21S | 20 |
| Tulip Ln.* E&W | 27W-21S | 19 |

| | Grid | Page |
|---|---|---|
| U.S. Route 30 NW&SE | | |
| | 26W-21S | 20 |
| University St. NW&SE | | |
| | 26W-21S | 20 |
| Waterford Dr. E&W | | |
| | 27W-21S | 19 |
| Watertower Pl. NS&EW | | |
| | 27W-21S | 19 |
| Waverly Ct. NE&SW | | |
| | 25W-21S | 20 |
| Webb St. NE&SW | 26W-21S | 20 |
| Weber Rd. N&S | 26W-21S | 20 |
| Wilcox St. N&S | 24W-21S | 20 |
| William Dr. N&S | 26W-21S | 20 |
| Willowbridge Rd. N&S | | |
| | 25W-21S | 20 |
| **Crete** | | |
| Aberdeen Dr. E&W | 0E-28S | 44 |
| Alpine Ln. E&W | 0E-28S | 44 |
| Amanda Ct. N&S | 1W-30S | 44 |
| Amber Ln. N&S | 1W-29S | 44 |
| Arbon Ct. E&W | 0E-28S | 44 |
| Arthur Ct. NE&SW | 1E-28S | 45 |
| Arthur Rd. E&W | 1E-28S | 45 |
| Ashley Ct. N&S | 1W-29S | 44 |
| Austin Av. N&S | 0W-30S | 44 |
| Ayr Ln. N&S | 0E-28S | 44 |
| Barbara Ct. N&S | 0E-29S | 44 |
| Barry Ln. E&W | 0W-30S | 44 |
| Beacon Pl. NE&SW | 0E-29S | 44 |
| Beckwith Ln. N&S | 0E-28S | 44 |
| Belfast Ter. NE&SW | 0E-28S | 44 |
| Benton St. N&S | 0W-30S | 44 |
| Berk Ln. E&W | 0E-29S | 44 |
| Brackman Av. E&W | 0W-30S | 44 |
| Bradford Pl. E&W | 0W-28S | 44 |
| Brenner Ct. E&W | 0E-28S | 44 |
| Briconock Pl. E&W | 0E-29S | 44 |
| Brighton Ct. N&S | 0W-29S | 44 |
| Brighton Ln. NW&SE | | |
| | 0W-29S | 44 |
| Bristol Dr. NE&SW | 0E-28S | 44 |
| Carol Ct. N&S | 1E-28S | 45 |
| Carol Ln. E&W | 1E-28S | 45 |
| Cass St. E&W | 0W-29S | 44 |
| Chalet Ct. N&S | 0E-28S | 44 |
| Chalet Dr. E&W | 0E-28S | 44 |
| Chalet Ln. N&S | 0E-28S | 44 |
| Charles Ct. N&S | 1E-28S | 45 |
| Charles St. N&S | 1E-28S | 45 |
| Chester Ter. E&W | 0W-29S | 44 |
| Cheviot St. N&S | 0E-28S | 44 |
| Columbia Av. N&S | 1W-29S | 44 |
| Columbia St. N&S | 1W-29S | 44 |
| Cornwall Dr. N&S | 0E-28S | 44 |
| Cottage Grove Av. N&S | | |
| | 0E-28S | 44 |
| Coventry Ln. NS&EW | | |
| | 0W-29S | 44 |
| Craig Av. E&W | 1W-30S | 44 |
| Crete Rd. NE&SW | 0E-29S | 44 |
| Dairy Ln. N&S | 0W-29S | 44 |
| Dale Dr. N&S | 1E-28S | 45 |
| Denell Ct. NE&SW | 0W-28S | 44 |
| Denell Dr. E&W | 0W-28S | 44 |
| Derby Pl. NE&SW | 0W-29S | 44 |
| Dewar Ter. E&W | 0E-29S | 44 |
| Division St. E&W | | |
| | 1W-29S,0W-29S | 44 |
| Donavan Ct., E. E&W | | |
| | 1E-28S | 45 |
| Donavan Dr. N&S | 1E-28S | 45 |
| Doncaster Dr. E&W | 0E-29S | 44 |
| Donovan Ct., W. NW&SE | | |
| | 1E-28S | 45 |
| Douglas Ln. N&S | | |
| | 0W-30S,0W-29S | 44 |
| Dover Ter. E&W | 0E-28S | 44 |
| Dunbar Ter. NE&SW | 0E-29S | 44 |
| Durham Dr. N&S | 0W-28S | 44 |
| East St. N&S | | |
| | 0W-30S,0W-29S | 44 |
| East Thames Dr. N&S | | |
| | 0W-29S | 44 |
| Edgewood Av. NE&SW | | |
| | 0W-29S | 44 |
| Edward Dr. N&S | 1E-28S | 45 |
| Elizabeth St. N&S | 0W-29S | 44 |
| Enterprize Av. N&S | 0W-30S | 44 |
| Essex Ter. E&W | | |
| | 0W-28S,0E-28S | 44 |
| Exchange St. N&S | | |
| | 1W-29S,0E-29S | 44 |
| Fairway Ct. N&S | 0W-28S | 44 |
| Fairway Dr. N&S | 0W-28S | 44 |
| Fairway Ln. N&S | 0W-28S | 44 |
| Faithorn Av. N&S | 0W-30S | 44 |
| Faithorn Rd. N&S | 0W-30S | 44 |
| Falmouth Ter. N&S | 0E-28S | 44 |
| Farm St. E&W | 1W-30S | 44 |
| Geneva Ct. N&S | 0E-28S | 44 |
| Gilbert Ct. N&S | 1E-28S | 45 |
| Gloucester Dr. N&S | 0E-28S | 44 |
| Gordon Dr. N&S | 1W-30S | 44 |
| Grant Blvd. E&W | 0E-28S | 44 |
| Greenbriar Dr. N&S | 0E-28S | 44 |
| Greenwood Ter. E&W | | |
| | 0E-29S | 44 |
| Griffith Ln. N&S | 0E-29S | 44 |
| Halsted St. N&S | 1W-28S | 44 |
| Hampton Ct. N&S | 0W-29S | 44 |

| | Grid | Page |
|---|---|---|
| Haweswood Ct. E&W | 0E-28S | 44 |
| Haweswood Dr. N&S | | |
| | 0E-28S | 44 |
| Hereford Dr. E&W | 0W-28S | 44 |
| Herman St. E&W | 1W-30S | 44 |
| Hewes St. N&S | 0W-30S | 44 |
| Honey Ln. E&W | 1E-28S | 45 |
| Hubbard St. E&W | 0W-30S | 44 |
| Huntington Ter. N&S | | |
| | 0E-28S | 44 |
| Huntley Ct. NW&SE | 1E-28S | 45 |
| Huntley Ter. NE&SW | | |
| | 0E-28S,1E-28S | 44 |
| Huntley Woods Ct. N&S | | |
| | 1E-28W | 44 |
| Huntley Woods Dr. NS&EW | | |
| | 1E-28W | 44 |
| Innsbruck Ln. N&S | 0E-28S | 44 |
| Inverness Dr. N&S | | |
| | 0E-29S,0E-28S | 44 |
| Islay Ln. N&S | | |
| | 0E-29S,0E-28S | 44 |
| Jaqueline Dr. E&W | 1E-28S | 45 |
| Jefferson St. E&W | 1W-29S | 44 |
| Jennifer Ln. N&S | 1E-28S | 44 |
| Joe Orr Ct. N&S | 0W-29S | 44 |
| Joe Orr Rd. E&W | 0W-29S | 44 |
| Joyce Ct. N&S | 1W-30S | 44 |
| Juliet Ln. E&W | 1E-28S | 45 |
| Karen Ct. NW&SE | 1W-30S | 44 |
| Kent Pl. N&S | 0E-28S | 44 |
| Lakeshore Dr. N&S | 0E-29S | 44 |
| Lancaster Ter. NS&EW | | |
| | 0W-29S | 44 |
| Laurel Ln. N&S | 0E-29S | 44 |
| Lincoln Av. N&S | 1W-29S | 44 |
| Lincoln Dr. N&S | 0E-29S | 44 |
| Lincolnshire Ter. E&W | | |
| | 0E-28S | 44 |
| Linden St. E&W | 1W-29S | 44 |
| Ludbury Ln. NE&SW | 0E-29S | 44 |
| Lyle Ln. N&S | 1E-28S | 45 |
| Maeburn Ter. E&W | 0E-29S | 44 |
| Main St. N&S | | |
| | 0W-30S,0W-29S | 44 |
| Melanie Ct., N. E&W | 1E-28S | 45 |
| Melanie Ct., S. E&W | 1E-28S | 45 |
| Melanie Ln. N&S | 1E-28S | 45 |
| Merioneth Dr. N&S | 0E-29S | 44 |
| Michael Av. E&W | 1W-29S | 44 |
| Milburn Av. E&W | 0W-29S | 44 |
| Mill St. N&S | 1W-29S | 44 |
| Monmouth Pl. NE&SW | | |
| | 0E-29S | 44 |
| Montgomery Dr. N&S | | |
| | 0E-28S | 44 |
| Moray Ln. E&W | 0E-28S | 44 |
| Moray Ter. NE&SW | 0E-28S | 44 |
| Naoma Dr. N&S | 1W-30S | 44 |
| Nicolette Ln. N&S | 1E-28S | 45 |
| Nilts Ct. N&S | 0W-28S | 44 |
| Norfolk Ln. E&W | 0E-28S | 44 |
| North St. E&W | 0W-29S | 44 |
| Oak Leaf Ct. N&S | 0W-28S | 44 |
| Oak Ln. N&S | 0E-29S | 44 |
| Oakwood Dr. E&W | 0W-29S | 44 |
| Old Monee Rd. E&W | | |
| | 1W-30S | 44 |
| Orchard Dr. E&W | 1W-30W | 38 |
| Orchard Ct. N&S | 0E-28S | 44 |
| Oriole St. E&W | 0W-30S | 44 |
| Park St. N&S | 0W-29S | 44 |
| Patricia Ln. E&W | 1E-28S | 45 |
| Pembrook Ter. E&W | | |
| | 0W-29S | 44 |
| Peoria Av. N&S | 1W-29S | 44 |
| Perry Av. N&S | | |
| | 0W-30S,0W-29S | 44 |
| Radnor Ln. E&W | 0W-28S | 44 |
| Richton Rd. E&W | 0E-28S | 44 |
| Robert Ln. E&W | 1E-28S | 45 |
| Rohe Ln. N&S | 0E-28S | 44 |
| Ronald Rd. N&S | 1E-28S | 45 |
| Rosedale Ter. NE&SW | | |
| | 0E-28S | 44 |
| Route 1 N&S | | |
| | 0W-30S,0W-29S | 44 |
| Salop Pl. NW&SE | 0E-28S | 44 |
| Sangamon St. N&S | 1W-30S | 44 |
| Selleck St. N&S | 0W-30S | 44 |
| Sheridan Av. E&W | 0W-29S | 44 |
| Somerset Ln. N&S | 0W-28S | 44 |
| South Wold Dr. E&W | | |
| | 0W-28S | 44 |
| St. Andrews Dr. NS&EW | | |
| | 0E-28S | 44 |
| Stafford Pl. E&W | 0W-28S | 44 |
| State St. N&S | 0W-30S | 44 |
| Stewart Ter. E&W | 0E-28S | 44 |
| Surry Ln. E&W | 0W-28S | 44 |
| Sussex Ter. E&W | 0E-28S | 44 |
| Tee Ct., N. E&W | 0W-28S | 44 |
| Tee Ct., S. E&W | 0W-28S | 44 |
| Tiverton Ln. E&W | 0E-28S | 44 |
| Todd Ct. N&S | 1W-30S | 44 |
| Troon Ct. N&S | 0E-28S | 44 |
| Union St. N&S | | |
| | 1W-30S,1W-29S | 44 |
| Vardon Ln. N&S | 0E-28S | 44 |
| Vincennes St. N&S | 1W-30S | 44 |
| Wales Pl. E&W | 0W-28S | 44 |
| Warwick Dr. N&S | 0W-28S | 44 |

| | Grid | Page |
|---|---|---|
| Washington Av. N&S | 1W-29S | 44 |
| Wayne Dr. N&S | 1W-30S | 44 |
| Williams Ln. N&S | 0E-28S | 44 |
| Willow Ln. N&S | 0E-28S | 44 |
| Willow Ln. N&S | 0W-28S | 44 |
| Wilton Ln. N&S | 0W-28S | 44 |
| Wingate Cir. N&S | 0W-29S | 44 |
| Wingate Ln. E&W | 0W-29s | 44 |
| Wood St. N&S | 0W-29S | 44 |
| Worchester Dr. E&W | | |
| | 0W-28S | 44 |
| York Pl. N&S | 0W-29S | 44 |
| Zurich St. N&S | 0E-28S | 44 |
| 1st St. E&W | 1W-29S | 44 |
| 2nd St. E&W | 1W-29S | 44 |
| 3rd St. E&W | 1W-29S | 44 |
| 4th St. E&W | 1W-29S | 44 |
| 5th St. E&W | 1W-29S | 44 |
| **Crete Township** | | |
| Acorn Ct. NE&SW | 2W-28S | 43 |
| Anne Ln. E&W | 2E-30S | 45 |
| Arlington Ln. E&W | | |
| | 1W-32S,0W-32S | 56 |
| Ashland Av. N&S | | |
| | 2W-29S,1W-28S | 43 |
| Auburn Ln. E&W | 0W-32S | 56 |
| Balmoral Dr. N&S | 0W-32S | 56 |
| Balmoral Woods N&S | | |
| | 0W-32S | 56 |
| Bemes Rd. E&W | | |
| | 0E-32S,4E-32S | 56 |
| Bending Creek Tr. E&W | | |
| | 3E-30S | 45 |
| Bremer Ct. NE&SW | 4E-29S | 45 |
| Bremer Tr. NW&SE | 4E-29S | 45 |
| Broadview Av. E&W | 1W-29S | 44 |
| Broadway Av. E&W | 1W-33S | 56 |
| Brookside Ct. N&S | 3E-29S | 45 |
| Brookview Dr. NS&EW | | |
| | 2W-28S | 43 |
| Buried Oak Dr. E&W | | |
| | 3E-30S,4E-29S | 45 |
| Burville Rd. E&W | | |
| | 1E-30S,3E-30S | 45 |
| Butler Ct. N&S | 0W-32S | 56 |
| Calumet Expwy. NE&SW | | |
| | 0W-33S,1E-29S | 56 |
| Cambridge Dr. N&S | 3E-31S | 45 |
| Carriage Ln. E&W | 2E-32S | 57 |
| Cedar Ln. NW&SE | 3E-30S | 45 |
| Challas Entrance Rd. E&W | | |
| | 4E-29S | 45 |
| Cherry Ln. E&W | 3E-30S | 45 |
| Chestnut Ln. NW&SE | | |
| | 3E-30S | 45 |
| Chestnut St. N&S | 1W-33S | 56 |
| Columbia Av. E&W | 1W-33S | 56 |
| Columbia Av. N&S | 1W-28S | 44 |
| Cottage Grove Av. N&S | | |
| | 1E-33S,0E-31S | 57 |
| Countess Ln. N&S | 1W-31S | 44 |
| Creek Wood Dr. E&W | 3E-29S | 45 |
| Creekside Ct. NW&SE | | |
| | 3E-30S | 45 |
| Cumberland Ct. N&S | 4E-29S | 45 |
| Cumberland Ln. E&W | | |
| | 4E-29S | 45 |
| Danne Rd. E&W | 3E-30S | 45 |
| Deer Run Ct. E&W | 3E-29S | 45 |
| Deer Run Tr. E&W | 3E-29S | 45 |
| Dixie Hwy. N&S | 0W-31S | 44 |
| Dorothy Dr. N&S | 2E-29S | 45 |
| Duchess Ln. N&S | 0W-32S | 56 |
| Dunleith Ct. N&S | 0W-32S | 56 |
| Dutton Rd. N&S | 0E-33S | 56 |
| Elmscourt Dr. N&S | 0W-32S | 56 |
| Equestrian Tr. NE&SW | | |
| | 3E-28S | 45 |
| Evergreen Ct. N&S | 3E-32S | 57 |
| Exchange St. N&S | | |
| | 2W-29S,4E-33S | 43 |
| Faithorn Burville Rd. N&S | | |
| | 1E-33S,1E-32S | 57 |
| Faithorn Rd. E&W | 0W-30S | 44 |
| Forest Ln. E&W | 2W-29S | 43 |
| Forest View Ct. N&S | 3E-29S | 45 |
| Forest View Dr. E&W | | |
| | 3E-29S,4E-29S | 45 |
| Forest View Ln. N&S | | |
| | 0W-33S | 56 |
| Frank St. E&W | 1W-33S | 56 |
| Gaisor Ct. NW&SE | 2E-29S | 45 |
| Gaisor Dr. E&W | 2E-29S | 45 |
| Glendale Av. N&S | 1W-33S | 56 |
| Goodenow Av. N&S | 1W-33S | 56 |
| Goodenow Rd. E&W | | |
| | 2W-33S,4E-33S | 55 |
| Greenview Av. N&S | 0W-33S | 56 |
| Greenwood Av. N&S | 1E-32S | 57 |
| Gregory Ln. N&S | 1W-31S | 44 |
| Halsted Av. N&S | 1W-33S | 56 |
| Harvest Ln. N&S | 2W-32S | 55 |
| Heatherton Dr. N&S | 3E-31S | 45 |
| Hickory Ct. N&S | 3E-30S | 45 |
| Hickory Ln. N&S | 3E-30S | 45 |
| Hickory St. E&W | 2E-30S | 45 |
| Hickory St. N&S | 1W-33S | 56 |
| Hilltop Rd. N&S | 3E-31S | 45 |
| Janice Av. N&S | 0W-33S | 56 |
| Jonathan Ln. N&S | 3E-28S | 45 |
| Juniper Dr. N&S | 3E-32S | 57 |

| | Grid | Page |
|---|---|---|
| Kent Av. E&W ...... | 1W-31S | 44 |
| King Rd. NE&SW ............ | 2W-29S,2W-28S | 43 |
| Klemme Rd. N&S ............ | 3E-33S,3E-30S | 57 |
| Kurt Ln. N&S ........ | 3E-28S | 45 |
| Lakeside Ct. NW&SE ............ | 4E-29S | 45 |
| Lakeside Ter. N&S .. | 4E-29S | 45 |
| Lakeview Dr. E&W . | 3E-32S | 57 |
| Laura Ln. N&S ...... | 3E-29S | 45 |
| Longwood Dr. E&W . | 3E-29S | 45 |
| Loomis St. N&S ............ | 1W-29S,1W-28S | 44 |
| Louella St. E&W ... | 0E-31S | 44 |
| Maple Ln. NW&SE .. | 2W-28S | 43 |
| Maple St. E&W .... | 2E-30S | 45 |
| Maple St. N&S .... | 1W-33S | 56 |
| Marmion Dr. E&W .. | 2E-29S | 45 |
| Mary Ln. N&S........ | 2E-28S | 45 |
| Meadow Rd. N&S .. | 2W-33S | 55 |
| Meadowood Dr. N&S ............ | 2W-29S | 43 |
| Meadowood Rd. N&S ............ | 2W-29S | 43 |
| Michaels St. N&S ... | 2E-30S | 45 |
| Monee Rd. E&W ............ | 2W-31S,0E-31S | 43 |
| Mulberry Ct. E&W .. | 3E-29S | 45 |
| Mulberry Ln. N&S .. | 3E-29S | 45 |
| Munz Rd. E&W .... | 0E-30S | 45 |
| Murray Dr. N&S ... | 2E-32S | 57 |
| Nacke Rd. N&S ............ | 2W-33S,2W-31S | 55 |
| Nancy St. N&S .... | 0E-31S | 44 |
| New Monee Rd. E&W ............ | 0W-31S | 44 |
| Norfolk Av. N&S ... | 2W-28S | 43 |
| Norway Trail NW&SE ............ | 4E-29S | 45 |
| Notre Dame Av. E&W ............ | 2E-29S | 45 |
| Oak Ct. NE&SW ... | 2W-28S | 43 |
| Oak Ln. N&S ........ | 4E-30S | 45 |
| Oak St. E&W ........ | 3E-29S | 45 |
| Offner Rd. E&W ............ | 3E-33S,1E-33S | 57 |
| Ohlendorf Rd. .. | 1W-32S | 56 |
| Old Monee Rd. E&W ............ | 2W-30S | 43 |
| Old Post Rd. NW&SE ............ | 2E-29S,3E-29S | 45 |
| Palamino Dr. NS&EW ............ | 3E-28S | 45 |
| Park Av. N&S .... | 1W-28S | 44 |
| Pebblebeach Ct. N&S ............ | 0W-32S | 56 |
| Pheasant Ct. NW&SE ............ | 4E-29S | 45 |
| Pheasant Tr. NE&SW ............ | 4E-29S | 45 |
| Pine Ct. E&W ....... | 3E-29S | 45 |
| Pine Dr. E&W ....... | 3E-32S | 57 |
| Plum Valley Dr. N&S . | 3E-29S | 45 |
| Poplar Ct. E&W .... | 3W-29S | 43 |
| Poplar Ln. E&W ... | 3E-29S | 45 |
| Prairieview Av. N&S .. | 3W-31S | 43 |
| Pricilla Ln. E&W ... | 3E-28S | 45 |
| Princess Ln. N&S ... | 1W-31S | 44 |
| Rainbow Ln. E&W ... | 2E-31S | 45 |
| Rana Dr. E&W .... | 3E-31S | 45 |
| Raymond Dr. NE&SW ............ | 2E-28S,3E-28S | 45 |
| Red Oak Rd. N&S .... | 4E-32S | 57 |
| Reichert Dr. E&W .. | 4E-31S | 45 |
| Richton Rd. E&W ............ | 2W-28S,2E-28S | 43 |
| Ridgefield Dr. E&W . | 3E-31S | 45 |
| Ridgeland Av. E&W . | 1W-32S | 56 |
| Rietveld Dr. E&W ... | 2E-29S | 45 |
| Root Dr. N&S ...... | 0E-32S | 56 |
| Rosewood Av. N&S .. | 1W-33S | 56 |
| Round House Rd. N&S ............ | 0E-31S,0E-30S | 44 |
| Route 1 N&S ............ | 0W-33S,0W-30S | 56 |
| Royal Ridge Dr. E&W ............ | 3E-31S | 45 |
| Sangamon St. N&S .. | 1W-31S | 44 |
| Schiewe Rd. N&S ............ | 1E-33S,1E-32S | 57 |
| Schultze Rd. N&S.... | 2W-28S | 43 |
| Shady Grove Ct. E&W ............ | 3E-29S | 45 |
| Shagbark Tr. E&W .. | 3E-30S | 45 |
| Sharon Ln. N&S..... | 3E-31S | 45 |
| Smit Dr. N&S ...... | 3E-31S | 45 |
| Southfield Av. E&W .. | 1W-29S | 44 |
| Spruce Ct. NW&SE .. | 3E-30S | 45 |
| Spruce Dr. E&W ... | 3E-32S | 57 |
| Stanton Ct. E&W .... | 0W-32S | 56 |
| State Line Rd. N&S ............ | 4E-33S,4E-29S | 57 |
| Stoneridge Ln. N&S . | 3E-29S | 45 |
| Stoney Island Av. N&S ............ | 2E-32S,2E-29S | 57 |
| Susan Ln. N&S .... | 3E-31S | 45 |
| Tam-O-Shanter Ct. N&S ............ | 0W-32S | 56 |
| Tam-O-Shanter Dr. E&W ............ | 0W-32S | 56 |
| Terry Av. N&S .... | 2E-29S | 45 |
| Thorn Creek Ln. E&W ............ | 2W-29S | 43 |

| | Grid | Page |
|---|---|---|
| Timberidge Ct. NE&SW ............ | 3E-29S | 45 |
| Timberline Ct. E&W . | 3E-29S | 45 |
| Timberline Tr. N&S .. | 3E-29S | 45 |
| Torrence Av. N&S .... | 2E-28S | 45 |
| Tuckaway Ct. N&S .. | 2E-33S | 57 |
| Valleyview Ln. E&W .. | 2W-29S | 43 |
| Van Drunen Dr. E&W ............ | 3E-31S | 45 |
| Vera E&W .......... | 3E-29S | 45 |
| Victoria Ln. N&S..... | 3E-31S | 45 |
| Volbrecht Rd. N&S .. | 1E-29S | 45 |
| Walden Ln. N&S ... | 3E-29S | 45 |
| Walnut St. N&S ............ | 2E-30S,2E-29S | 45 |
| West Ravine Rd. NS&EW ............ | 3E-28S | 45 |
| Whispering Oak Ln. N&S ............ | 3E-30S | 45 |
| White Oaks Ln. N&S .. | 2E-30S | 45 |
| Wildwood Ct. N&S .. | 3E-29S | 45 |
| Wildwood Tr. N&S ............ | 3E-30S,3E-29S | 45 |
| Willow Brook Ct. E&W ............ | 3E-30S | 45 |
| Willow Brook Tr. NS&EW ............ | 3E-29S | 45 |
| Windsor Av. E&W .. | 1W-31S | 44 |
| Winston Av. N&S .... | 1W-31S | 44 |
| Wolpers Rd. E&W .. | 2W-29S | 43 |
| Woodland Dr. N&S .. | 1E-30S | 45 |
| Woodland Tr. N&S ... | 1E-30S | 45 |
| Woodlawn Av. N&S . | 1E-33S | 57 |
| 235th St. E&W .... | 2W-28S | 43 |
| 263rd St. E&W .... | 1E-31S | 57 |
| 265th St. E&W .... | 1E-32S | 57 |

## Custer Township
| | Grid | Page |
|---|---|---|
| Bauer Rd. E&W ............ | 25W-45S,22W-45S | 76 |
| Charlotte Av. E&W .. | 26W-43S | 76 |
| Cooper Rd. E&W ............ | 29W-44S,28W-44S | 74 |
| County Line Rd. N&S ............ | 29W-45S,25W-45S | 74 |
| Curtis Rd. E&W .... | 26W-44S | 76 |
| Darby Rd. N&S .... | 25W-45S | 76 |
| Davy Ln. (Pvt.) NE&SW ............ | 27W-42S | 75 |
| Erickson Ln. (Pvt.) N&S ............ | 27W-41S | 71 |
| Essex Rd. N&S ............ | 29W-45S,29W-42S | 74 |
| Garfield St. E&W .. | 26W-43S | 76 |
| Grant Av. N&S .... | 27W-43S | 75 |
| Grey Rd. N&S ............ | 29W-45S,26W-43S | 76 |
| Irish Ln NS&EW ............ | 25W-44S,24W-45S | 76 |
| Jay Dr. N&S ........ | 26W-43S | 76 |
| Johnson Rd. E&W ............ | 29W-40S,28W-40S | 70 |
| Lee St. N&S ....... | 26W-43S | 76 |
| Linden Rd. N&S .... | 26W-43S | 76 |
| Mack's Rd. N&S ... | 23W-45S | 77 |
| McGuire Rd. E&W ............ | 29W-43S,28W-43S | 74 |
| Ohlhues Rd. N&S ............ | 27W-45S,26W-43S | 75 |
| River Ln. N&S .... | 22W-45S | 77 |
| River St. N&S ............ | 27W-42S,22W-45S | 75 |
| Route 113 NW&SE ............ | 29W-42S,22W-45S | 74 |
| Route 129 N&S .... | 29W-40S | 70 |
| Route 53 NE&SW .. | 29W-40S | 70 |
| Scott St. NE&SW .. | 26W-43S | 76 |
| Shenk Rd. (Pvt.) N&S ............ | 29W-41S | 70 |
| Smiley Rd. N&S ............ | 28W-42S,27W-42S | 75 |
| Washington St. N&S ............ | 26W-43S | 76 |
| Weikum Rd. N&S ... | 29W-43S | 74 |
| Weiske Ln. (Pvt.) E&W ............ | 27W-44S | 75 |
| Weiske Rd. E&W .. | 27W-44S | 75 |
| West River Rd. NW&SE ............ | 28W-40S,27W-41S | 71 |
| Yeates Rd. N&S .... | 24W-45S | 76 |
| Zilm Rd. N&S ............ | 28W-45S,28W-43S | 75 |

## Diamond
| | Grid | Page |
|---|---|---|
| Coal City Rd. E&W | 32W-39S | 58 |
| County Line Rd. N&S ............ | 32W-39S | 58 |

## DuPage Township
| | Grid | Page |
|---|---|---|
| Adlai E. Stevenson Expwy. E&W . | 26W-15S,21W-11S | 10 |
| Arbor Dr. E&W .... | 25W-14S | 10 |
| Balsam Ct. NW&SE ............ | 26W-13S | 10 |
| Big Run Ln. N&S .. | 21W-15S | 11 |
| Carlisle Dr. NE&SW ............ | 23W-10S | 7 |
| Catalina Dr. NW&SE ............ | 23W-10S | 7 |
| Crimson Ct. N&S . | 26W-15S | 10 |
| Donovan Rd. E&W ............ | 22W-13S,21W-13S | 11 |

| | Grid | Page |
|---|---|---|
| Ferguson Rd. E&W ............ | 26W-13S | 10 |
| Forest Ln. N&S .... | 21W-15S | 11 |
| Fox Valley Expwy. NW&SE ............ | 26W-15S | 10 |
| Kings Rd. (proposed) N&S ............ | 25W-13S,26W-12S | 10 |
| Magnolia Dr. N&S . | 26W-15S | 10 |
| Mulberry St. N&S .. | 26W-15S | 10 |
| Naperville Rd. NW&SE ............ | 24W-14S,26W-11S | 10 |
| Normantown Rd. E&W ............ | 26W-15S,24W-15S | 10 |
| North Carrilon Dr. NS&EW ............ | 26W-15S | 10 |
| Old Orchard Ln., E. N&S ............ | 21W-15S | 11 |
| Old Orchard Ln., N. N&S ............ | 21W-15S | 11 |
| Old Orchard Ln., W. N&S ............ | 21W-15S | 11 |
| Orchid St. N&S .. | 26W-15S | 10 |
| Recreation Dr. NS&EW ............ | 25W-15S | 10 |
| Red Cedar Ln. NE&SW ............ | 26W-15S | 10 |
| Redberry Cir. NE&SW ............ | 26W-15S | 10 |
| Redberry Ct. NE&SW ............ | 26W-15S | 10 |
| Remington Blvd. NE&SW ............ | 23W-12S | 7 |
| Royce Rd. E&W ............ | 25W-10S,23W-10S | 6 |
| Royce Rd. (proposed) E&W ............ | 23W-10S,22W-10S | 7 |
| Schmidt Rd. N&S ............ | 24W-13S,24W-12S | 10 |
| Silk Tree Cir. N&S ............ | 26W-15S | 10 |
| Silverleaf Ct. E&W . | 26W-15S | 10 |
| Silverleaf Dr. . | 26W-15S | 10 |
| Smith Rd. N&S ............ | 21W-16S,21W-15S | 15 |
| Sumac Ct. N&S .. | 26W-13S | 10 |
| Tall Pines Ln. N&S . | 26W-15S | 10 |
| Weber Rd. N&S ............ | 26W-15S,26W-12S | 10 |
| Williams Rd. N&S .. | 26W-14S | 10 |
| Windham Pkwy. E&W ............ | 25W-14S | 10 |
| 107th St. E&W ... | 21W-12S | 7 |
| 111th St. E&W ... | 26W-12S | 6 |
| 115th St. E&W ... | 25W-13S | 10 |
| 135th St. E&W ............ | 25W-15S,21W-15S | 10 |

## Elwood
| | Grid | Page |
|---|---|---|
| Archer Ln. N&S .... | 25W-31S | 36 |
| Beattie St. N&S .... | 25W-31S | 36 |
| Briarwood Ct. N&S | 25W-31S | 36 |
| Bush Dr. N&S .... | 25W-31S | 36 |
| Chicago Av. N&S ............ | 25W-32S,25W-31S | 48 |
| Cobblestone Ln. N&S ............ | 25W-31S | 36 |
| Deerpath St. N&S .. | 25W-31S | 36 |
| Douglas St. NE&SW ............ | 25W-32S | 48 |
| Eagle Creek Rd. N&S ............ | 25W-31S | 36 |
| Gardner St. E&W . | 25W-32S | 48 |
| Jackson St. N&S . | 25W-32N | 48 |
| Lincoln St. N&S .. | 25W-32S | 48 |
| Linebarger Ct. N&S ............ | 25W-31S | 36 |
| Manhattan Rd. E&W ............ | 25W-30S | 36 |
| Matteson St. N&S . | 25W-32S | 48 |
| Mississippi Av. E&W ............ | 25W-32S | 48 |
| Morris St. E&W ... | 25W-32S | 48 |
| North St. E&W ... | 25W-32S | 48 |
| Parks St. E&W .. | 25W-32N | 48 |
| Route 53 NW&SE . | 25W-32N | 48 |
| South St. E&W ... | 25W-32S | 48 |
| Spencer St. N&S .. | 25W-32S | 48 |
| St. Louis St. N&S .. | 25W-32S | 48 |
| Tehle Rd. E&W ... | 25W-31S | 36 |
| Wood Rd. N&S .. | 25W-32S | 48 |
| Wood St. NE&SW . | 25W-32S | 48 |
| Woodbine Dr. N&S ............ | 25W-31S | 36 |
| Wyndstone Dr. E&W ............ | 25W-31S | 36 |

## Florence Township
| | Grid | Page |
|---|---|---|
| Allott Dr. E&W ............ | 26W-38S,25W-38S | 60 |
| Armil Dr. E&W .... | 21W-38S | 61 |
| Arsenal South Rd. E&W ............ | 22W-37S,21W-37S | 61 |
| Arsenal-Wilton Center Rd. E&W . | 21W-35S | 49 |
| Barr Rd. N&S ............ | 26W-39S,26W-38S | 60 |
| Butcher Ln. E&W . | 26W-39S | 60 |
| Commercial St. E&W ............ | 22W-37S | 61 |
| County Rd. E&W .. | 25W-38S | 60 |
| Doyle Rd. E&W ............ | 26W-34S,21W-34S | 48 |

| | Grid | Page |
|---|---|---|
| Indian Trail Rd. N&S ............ | 25W-39S,25W-37S | 60 |
| Joliet Aresenal Rd. South E&W .... | 25W-37S | 60 |
| Kennedy Rd. E&W ............ | 22W-38S,21W-38S | 61 |
| Manhattan-Wilton Rd. E&W ............ | 25W-33S,22W-33S | 48 |
| Martin Long Rd. N&S ............ | 22W-39S,22W-37S | 61 |
| Northern Av. N&S ............ | 23W-38S,23W-37S | 61 |
| Old Chicago Rd. ............ | 24W-39S,24W-36S | 60 |
| Quigley Rd. E&W ............ | 26W-36S,23W-36S | 60 |
| Riley Rd. NS&EW ............ | 26W-37S,25W-34S | 60 |
| Route 53 N&S ............ | 26W-39S,26W-34S | 60 |
| Smith Rd. NE&SW . | 25W-38S | 60 |
| South Townline Rd. E&W ............ | 21W-33S | 49 |
| Symerton Rd. N&S | 23W-39S | 61 |
| Warner Bridge Rd. N&S ............ | 21W-39S,21W-35S | 61 |
| Wesley Rd. N&S ............ | 22W-39S,21W-39S | 61 |
| West Kahler Rd. E&W ............ | 26W-39S,21W-39S | 60 |
| White Cir. NS&EW . | 25W-36S | 60 |
| Wilmington-Peotone Rd. E&W ............ | 26W-37S,21W-37S | 60 |

## Frankfort
| | Grid | Page |
|---|---|---|
| Abbotsford Ln. NS&EW ............ | 9W-26S | 33 |
| Aberdeen Rd. E&W ............ | 10W-26S,9W-26S | 33 |
| Abour Walk Dr. NS&EW ............ | 11W-25S | 33 |
| Ascot Ln. NW&SE .. | 11W-25S | 33 |
| Ash St. N&S ..... | 12W-26S | 32 |
| Ashely Ct. NW&SE | 11W-25S | 33 |
| Ashford Av. E&W .. | 13W-26S | 32 |
| Aspen St. N&S .. | 12W-26S | 32 |
| Ayeshire Ct. NE&SW ............ | 9W-26S | 33 |
| Azalea Rd. N&S ... | 11W-26S | 33 |
| Bankview Dr. NS&EW ............ | 12W-25S | 32 |
| Birchwood Rd. N&S ............ | 12W-25S,12W-24S | 32 |
| Boulder Ct. . | 12W-25S | 32 |
| Bowen St. E&W .... | 12W-25S | 32 |
| Box Elder Rd. N&S ............ | 12W-25S | 32 |
| Bramble Dr. NW&SE ............ | 11W-25S | 33 |
| Bristol Ct. N&S .... | 11W-25S | 33 |
| Brittany Ct. N&S .. | 9W-25S | 33 |
| Brookridge Creek Dr. E&W ............ | 13W-25S | 32 |
| Brookridge Ct. N&S ............ | 13W-25S | 32 |
| Brookridge Dr. NE&SW ............ | 13W-25S | 32 |
| Brookside Ln. E&W ............ | 12W-25S | 32 |
| Brown Dr. N&S ... | 11W-25S | 33 |
| Butternut Cir., N. E&W ............ | 13W-25S | 32 |
| Butternut Cir., S. NS&EW ............ | 13W-25S | 32 |
| Butternut Cir., W. N&S ............ | 13W-25S | 32 |
| Butternut NE&SW ............ | 13W-25S | 32 |
| Butternut Tr. N&S . | 13W-25S | 32 |
| California Av. E&W | 12W-26S | 32 |
| Carpenter St. N&S.. | 12W-25S | 32 |
| Cedar Rd. N&S .. | 12W-25S | 32 |
| Center Rd. N&S ... | 12W-25S | 32 |
| Chadwick Ct. E&W | 11W-25S | 33 |
| Charrington Dr. E&W ............ | 11W-25S | 33 |
| Chestnut Ct. N&S .. | 11W-26S | 33 |
| Chestnut Dr. N&S .. | 11W-26S | 33 |
| Church Ct. E&W .. | 11W-26S | 33 |
| Church St. E&W .. | 11W-26S | 33 |
| Colony Ln. NW&SE . | 9W-26S | 33 |
| Colorado Av. E&W | 12W-25S | 32 |
| Concord Dr. N&S . | 13W-26S | 32 |
| Corsair Rd. E&W .. | 11W-27S | 33 |
| Cottonwood Rd. NW&SE ............ | 12W-25S | 32 |
| Coventry Ln. E&W . | 9W-25S | 33 |
| Deerpath Dr. N&S... | 9W-25S | 33 |
| Dover Cir. NW&SE . | 12W-25S | 32 |
| Drummore Ln. E&W . | 9W-26S | 33 |
| Duns Ct. N&S .... | 9W-25S | 33 |
| Durham Ct. E&W .. | 9W-26S | 33 |
| East Brook Rd. E&W ............ | 13W-26S | 32 |
| Eastern Av. N&S .. | 12W-26S | 32 |
| Eisner Rd. N&S .... | 13W-25S | 32 |
| Elm St. N&S ............ | 12W-26S,12W-25S | 32 |
| Elmwood St. E&W.. | 12W-25S | 32 |
| Evergreen Dr. N&S | 11W-26S | 33 |
| Fairway Ln. NW&SE ............ | 10W-26S | 33 |
| Firth Ct. NE&SW .. | 10W-26S | 33 |

| | Grid | Page |
|---|---|---|
| Fox Run Cir. NS&EW ............ | 11W-25S | 33 |
| Fox Run Ct. E&W .. | 11W-25S | 33 |
| Franklin Av. E&W ............ | 12W-25S,11W-25S | 32 |
| Georgetown Commons E&W ............ | 9W-25S | 33 |
| Georgetown Rd. N&S ............ | 9W-25S | 33 |
| Ginger Ln. NW&SE | 11W-25S | 33 |
| Glen Bard Ln. NE&SW ............ | 9W-26S | 33 |
| Glen Eagles Ct. NW&SE ............ | 9W-26S | 33 |
| Golf Club Ln. NW&SE ............ | 9W-26S | 33 |
| Gulfstream Rd. E&W ............ | 11W-27S | 33 |
| Hackberry Rd. NW&SE ............ | 12W-25S | 32 |
| Harlem Av. N&S ............ | 9W-27S,9W-25S | 33 |
| Hawthorne Dr. N&S ............ | 10W-26S | 33 |
| Hawthorne Rd. NW&SE ............ | 12W-25S | 32 |
| Heather Ln. N&S .. | 10W-26S | 33 |
| Heritage Ct. NE&SW ............ | 9W-26S | 33 |
| Heritage Dr. NE&SW ............ | 13W-26S | 32 |
| Hickory Ct. N&S.... | 13W-25S | 32 |
| Hickory St. N&S .. | 12W-26S | 32 |
| Highland Rd. E&W . | 9W-26S | 33 |
| Hornbeam Rd. NW&SE ............ | 13W-25S | 32 |
| Hunt Club Dr. N&S | 11W-25S | 33 |
| Hunterwoods Dr. N&S ............ | 9W-25S | 33 |
| Illinois Rd. E&W .. | 12W-25S | 32 |
| Indiana Ct. E&W .. | 12W-25S | 32 |
| Industry Av. E&W .. | 11W-27S | 33 |
| Iowa Ct. E&W ..... | 12W-25S | 32 |
| Johnson Av. NS&EW ............ | 12W-25S | 32 |
| Kansas St. E&W .. | 12W-26S | 32 |
| Lambrecht Rd. N&S ............ | 11W-27S | 33 |
| Laraway Rd. E&W ............ | 12W-26S,9W-26S | 32 |
| Larch Ct. 'A' E&W .. | 11W-26S | 33 |
| Larch Ct. 'B' E&W .. | 11W-26S | 33 |
| Larch Rd. N&S .... | 11W-26S | 33 |
| Leslie Ln. N&S .. | 12W-24S | 32 |
| Lexington Ln. E&W ............ | 13W-25S | 32 |
| Lincoln Hwy. E&W ............ | 11W-25S,9W-25S | 33 |
| Lincoln Ln. NW&SE ............ | 13W-25S,12W-25S | 32 |
| Linden Ct. N&S .. | 12W-25S | 32 |
| Linden Dr. N&S .. | 12W-25S | 32 |
| Linden Dr. N&S .. | 11W-25S | 33 |
| Locust St. N&S ............ | 12W-26S,12W-25S | 32 |
| Luther Ln. N&S .... | 11W-26S | 33 |
| Maple Ct. E&W ... | 11W-26S | 33 |
| Maple Ridge Ct. NE&SW ............ | 13W-25S | 32 |
| Maple St. N&S ............ | 12W-26S,12W-24S | 32 |
| McDonald Ln. E&W . | 12W-25S | 32 |
| Meadow Av. E&W . | 12W-25S | 32 |
| Michigan Av. E&W . | 12W-25S | 32 |
| Michigan Av. N&S . | 12W-25S | 32 |
| Milton Bridge Tr. NE&SW ............ | 9W-26S | 33 |
| Mulberry Rd. N&S . | 12W-25S | 32 |
| Nebraska Ct. 'A' N&S ............ | 11W-25S | 33 |
| Nebraska Ct. 'B' N&S ............ | 11W-25S | 33 |
| Nebraska St. E&W ............ | 12W-25S,11W-25S | 32 |
| Nevada Ct. 'A' N&S ............ | 11W-25S | 33 |
| Nevada Ct. 'B' N&S ............ | 11W-26S | 33 |
| Nevada St. E&W .. | 11W-26S | 33 |
| North St. E&W .... | 12W-25S | 32 |
| Oak Ridge Ct. N&S ............ | 13W-25S | 32 |
| Oakton Av. NW&SE ............ | 13W-26S | 32 |
| Oakton Ct. E&W ... | 13W-26S | 32 |
| Oakwood Dr. N&S ............ | 12W-25S,12W-24S | 32 |
| Ohio Rd. E&W ..... | 12W-25S | 32 |
| Old N. Church Rd. NS&EW ............ | 9W-25S | 33 |
| Ontario St. E&W .. | 11W-25S | 33 |
| Oregon St. E&W .. | 12W-25S | 32 |
| Overlook Ct., E. E&W ............ | 12W-24S | 32 |
| Overlook Ct., W. NW&SE ............ | 12W-24S | 32 |
| Overlook Dr. N&S .. | 12W-25S | 32 |
| Pacific St. E&W .. | 12W-26S | 32 |
| Parkway Ln. N&S . | 13W-26S | 32 |
| Pembrook Ct. NW&SE ............ | 13W-26S | 32 |
| Pfaff Dr. E&W...... | 11W-26S | 33 |

**Grid / Page**

Pfeiffer Rd. N&S
.........11W-27S,11W-25S  33
Pheasant Trail NW&SE
..............10W-26S  33
Pioneer Trail EW&NS
..............13W-25S  32
Pioneer Trail Ct. E&W
..............13W-25S  32
Plymouth Ct. N&S ..10W-26S  33
Prestwick Dr. E&W
..............10W-26S  33
Princeton Cir. NS&EW
..............10W-26S  32
Princeton Ct. N&S
..............13W-26S  32
Pueblo Ct. E&W ..12W-25S  32
Raintree Ct. N&S .. 11W-25S  33
Raintree Ln. N&S .. 11W-25S  33
Red Bud Ct. E&W .13W-25S  32
Regency Dr. N&S . 13W-26S  32
Route 30 E&W
.........13W-25S,9W-25S  32
Route 45 N&S .......10W-26S  32
Sager Rd. E&W ....12W-26S  32
Sauk Trail Dr. NW&SE
.........11W-26S,9W-26S  33
Settlers Pond Ct. E&W
..............13W-25S  32
Settlers Pond Dr. NS&EW
..............13W-25S  32
Sherlock St. E&W ..12W-25S  32
Smith St. N&S....12W-25S  32
Somerset Ct. N&S .13W-26S  32
Southwick Ct. E&W ..9W-27S  33
Southwick Dr. NS&EW
..............9W-27S  33
Spruce Dr. N&S
.........12W-25S,12W-24S  32
St. Andrew's Way E&W
..............9W-26S  33
Steeplechase Dr. NS&EW
..............9W-26S  33
Steger Rd. E&W .... 9W-27S  33
Stonebridge Rd. N&S
.........13W-25S,13W-24S  32
Stuart Ct. N&S ... 9W-26S  33
Sycamore Ln. N&S 11W-26S  33
Tanglewood Dr. N&S
.........12W-25S,12W-24S  32
Thorn Trail N&S .. 9W-26S  33
Timber Ct. NE&SW
..............10W-26S  33
Troon Ct. N&S ... 9W-26S  33
Utah St. E&W ....12W-26S  32
Vail Dr. N&S .... 12W-25S  32
Vermont Rd. N&S .. 12W-25S  32
Virginia Ct. E&W .... 9W-25S  33
Walnut Ridge Ct. NE&SW
..............13W-25S  32
Walnut Ridge Ct., N. NE&SW
..............13W-25S  32
Walnut Ridge Ct., S. NE&SW
..............13W-25S  32
Walnut St. N&S ... 12W-26S  32
Warmke Ln. NE&SW
..............12W-25S  32
Watson Dr. N&S...12W-25S  32
Westbrook Rd. E&W
..............13W-26S  32
Williamsburg Ct. N&S
..............13W-25S  32
Williamsburg Tr. E&W
..............13W-25S  32
Willow St. N&S ... 12W-25S  32
Wisconsin Rd. E&W
..............12W-25S  32
Woodbridge Dr. N&S
..............11W-25S  33
Woods Dr. E&W....12W-24S  32
Yankee Ridge Ct. NW&SE
..............13W-25S  32
Yankee Ridge Dr. NE&SW
..............13W-25S  32
Yorktown Rd. E&W .. 9W-25S  33
84th Av. N&S ....10W-25S  33
95th Av. N&S ... 11W-25S  33
96th Av. NE&SW
.........13W-26S,12W-24S  32
108th Av. N&S
.........13W-26S,13W-25S  32

## Frankfort Township
Abbotsford Ln. E&W
..............9W-26S  33
Acorn Ridge Dr. N&S
.........9W-25S,9W-24S  33
Apple Ct. N&S.....11W-23S  25
Arden Ln. N&S .. 14W-24S  32
Arran Dr. N&S ... 9W-23S  25
Ash Av. E&W .... 11W-23S  25
Aviemore Ln. N&S . 9W-25S  33
Ayshire Ct. SW&NE..9W-26S  33
Barbara Ln. N&S...9W-24S  33
Barkside Dr. E&W .. 10W-24S  33
Baron Rd. N&S .. 14W-23S  24
Beechnut Dr. N&S . 9W-23S  25
Benton Dr. NE&SW .. 9W-23S  25
Birch Av. E&W ... 11W-23S  25
Birchwood Ln. E&W .. 9W-23S  25
Braemar Ln. N&S .. 9W-23S  25
Briarwood Ln. N&S
..............13W-25S  32

Brickstone Dr. E&W
..............10W-24S  33
Camelot Av. E&W . 14W-23S  24
Carrie Ct. NS&EW .. 9W-23S  25
Catulpa St. N&S....11W-23S  25
Cedar Rd. N&S ... 13W-26S  32
Center Rd. N&S .. 12W-27S  32
Cherry St. N&S .... 11W-23S  25
Cleveland Dr. N&S
.........13W-25S,13W-24S  32
Cobblestone Ct. N&S
..............9W-24S  33
Countryside Ct. E&W
..............10W-24S  33
Countryside Dr. E&W
..............10W-24S  33
Countryside Ln. N&S
..............10W-24S  33
Dove Ln. E&W .... 9W-24S  33
Driftwood N&S .... 9W-24S  33
Drummore Ln. E&W . 9W-26S  33
Duchess Av. E&W .. 14W-23S  24
E. Hillside Dr. N&S . 9W-23S  25
Eastern Av. E&W .. 14W-26S  32
Edinburgh Ln. N&S . 9W-23S  25
Elizabeth Ln. N&S . 9W-25S  33
Ellen Ln. NS&EW ... 9W-23S  25
Elm Av. E&W ..... 11W-23S  25
Elmwood Ct. E&W . 13W-24S  32
Ethyl Ln. E&W.....11W-22S  25
Evan Ter. E&W .... 9W-23S  25
Evergreen Dr. E&W
..............10W-24S  33
Fallbrook Ct. E&W .. 9W-24S  33
Farmhouse Rd. E&W
..............10W-24S  33
Farmington Dr. N&S..9W-23S  25
Francis Rd. NW&SE
..............14W-23S  24
Frankfort Square Rd. NS&EW
.........9W-25S,9W-24S  33
Franklin Av. E&W .. 11W-25S  33
Front St. NE&SW .. 14W-23S  24
Garden Ln. E&W .. 9W-23S  25
Garrett Ct. E&W ... 9W-23S  25
Glasgow Dr. N&S ... 9W-23S  25
Glen Eagles Ct. NW&SE
..............9W-26S  33
Glenbark Ln. NE&SW
..............9W-26S  33
Glenshire Dr. E&W . 9W-25S  33
Graceland Ln. N&S . 9W-24S  33
Grand Prairie Ln. N&S
..............9W-24S  33
Green Meadow Ln. N&S
..............9W-24S  33
Greenfield Ln. N&S . 9W-24S  33
Hamilton Rd. E&W . 14W-24S  32
Harlem Av. N&S
.........9W-27S,9W-26S  33
Harvest Dr., W. E&W
..............10W-24S  33
Hawthorn St. N&S ..11W-23S  25
Hawthorne Dr. E&W . 11W-23S  25
Hickory Creek Ct. N&S
..............9W-25S  33
Hickory Creek Dr. E&W
..............9W-25S  33
Hickory St. N&S....11W-23S  25
Highview Ln. NW&SE
..............9W-23S  25
Hill Av. E&W .... 10W-25S  33
Hillgate Rd. N&S..14W-24S  32
Hillside Rd. N&S .. 10W-25S  33
Hilltop Rd. NW&SE 13W-24S  32
Holly Ln. NW&SE .. 9W-24S  33
Humbolt Dr. NE&SW
..............9W-25S  33
Hunter Dr. N&S .... 9W-25S  33
Interstate 80 E&W
.........13W-22S,10W-22S  24
Inverary Dr. NE&SW 9W-25S  33
Inverness Ln. NS&EW
..............9W-23S  25
Ironwood Ct. E&W . 13W-24S  32
Ironwood Dr. N&S
.........13W-25S,13W-24S  32
Ivy Path N&S.......9W-24S  33
Jamison Dr. E&W .. 9W-24S  33
Jean Rd. N&S .... 14W-22S  24
Jessica Ln. NS&EW . 9W-24S  33
Jonquil St. N&S .... 9W-24S  33
Josephine Dr. E&W
..............14W-22S  24
Juniper Ct. NS&EW . 9W-23S  25
Kingston Ct. NW&SE
..............9W-24S  33
Kingston Dr. NE&SW
..............9W-24S  33
Kohlwood Dr. N&S..13W-24S  32
Lakeside Dr. N&S . 9W-23S  25
Lakeside Ter. N&S . 9W-23S  25
Laraway Rd. E&W
.........12W-26S,9W-26S  32
Laurel Dr. N&S ... 9W-24S  33
Leila Dr. N&S .... 14W-22S  24
Lenore Ln. N&S ... 11W-22S  25
Lismore Cir., E. N&S
..............10W-24S  33
Lismore Cir., W. N&S
..............10W-24S  33
Locust St. N&S
.........12W-25S,12W-24S  32
Magnolia Av. E&W ..11W-23S  25

Magnolia Dr. E&W .10W-24S  33
Magnolia Ln. N&S .. 9W-24S  33
Mallory Dr. N&S ... 9W-24S  33
Maple (Marley) Rd. N&S
..............14W-22S  24
Marjorie Pkwy. N&S
..............14W-22S  24
Marley (Maple) Rd. N&S
..............14W-22S  24
Mary Therese Ln. N&S
..............10W-24S  33
Mathews Dr. NS&EW
..............9W-25S  33
Milton Bridge Tr. E&W
..............9W-26S  33
Moorefield Dr. E&W..9W-26S  33
New Castle Dr. E&W
..............9W-24S  33
Normandy Ln. N&S
..............14W-22S  32
North Av. E&W
.........10W-24S,9W-24S  33
North Ct. N&S ... 9W-24S  33
Norwood Dr. E&W..10W-24S  33
Nutwood Ct. E&W .. 9W-24S  33
Oak Ln. N&S
.........9W-25S,9W-24S  33
Old Coach Tr. N&S . 9W-23S  25
Old Mill Rd. N&S&EW
..............10W-24S  33
Old Route 45 N&S..22W-22S  24
Orchard Dr. E&W .. 10W-24S  33
Osage Rd. N&S
.........14W-27S,14W-25S  32
Patricia Ln. N&S ... 9W-23S  25
Pebble Ln. E&W ... 9W-24S  33
Pfeiffer Rd. N&S
.........11W-27S,11W-25S  33
Pheasant Trail E&W
..............10W-26S  33
Pine Hill Rd. N&S
.........10W-24S,9W-24S  33
Pine St. N&S .... 11W-23S  25
Pleasant Av. E&W .. 11W-22S  25
Poplar St. N&S ... 11W-23S  25
Prestwick St. N&S .. 9W-26S  33
Queens Ct. NW&SE
..............14W-23S  24
Rainford Dr. N&S . 10W-24S  33
Redwood Ln. N&S .. 9W-23S  25
River Rd. N&S....10W-25S  33
Riverton Ct. NE&SW
..............9W-23S  25
Roeland Ct. NE&SW
..............9W-23S  25
Rose Ln. N&S......14W-22S  24
Rosewood Dr. N&S
..............10W-24S  33
Rosewood Ln. E&W
.........12W-23S,11W-23S  24
Route 30 E&W
.........14W-25S,9W-25S  32
Route 45 N&S
.........11W-24S,11W-23S  33
Royce Ct. N&S.....9W-24S  33
Ryeland Dr. E&W .. 9W-24S  33
Saint Andrews Way E&W
..............9W-26S  33
Sara Rd. N&S .. 14W-22S  24
School House Rd. N&S
..............13W-24S  32
Shetland Dr. N&S .. 9W-26S  33
Silo Dr. E&W .... 9W-26S  33
Skidmore Ct. N&S .. 9W-23S  25
Skye Dr. N&S .... 9W-23S  25
Spruce Ln. N&S .. 10W-24S  33
St. Francis Dr. E&W
.........11W-24S,9W-24S  33
Steger Rd. E&W
.........14W-27S,9W-27S  32
Stephaine Ln. E&W
..............14W-22S  24
Sterling Dr. NW&SE..9W-26S  33
Stuart Cir. N&S .... 9W-26S  33
Stuart Dr. N&S ... 10W-24S  33
Sycamore Dr. N&S..10W-24S  33
Sycamore St. N&S..11W-23S  25
Tack Ln. N&S .... 9W-23S  25
Tartan Rd. E&W .. 9W-23S  25
Thistle Ln. N&S ... 9W-23S  25
Thorndale Dr. N&S..10W-24S  33
Timber Mill Dr. N&S
..............10W-24S  33
Timberview Dr. N&S
..............13W-24S  32
Town Line Rd. E&W
.........14W-27S,14W-23S  32
Troon Cir. N&S ... 9W-26S  33
Troon Trail N&S .. 9W-26S  33
Victorian Dr. N&S .. 14W-23S  24
Virginia Pkwy. E&W
..............14W-22S  24
Walnut St. N&S ... 11W-23S  25
Westport Dr. N&S .. 10W-24S  33
Wheatfield Dr. E&W
..............10W-24S  33
White Fence Ct. N&S
..............9W-24S  33
Willow Ln. E&W ... 11W-23S  25
Windmill Dr. E&W ...9W-24S  33
Wintergreen Dr. E&W
..............10W-24S  33
Wishing Well Dr. N&S
..............9W-24S  33

Wolf Rd. N&S
.........14W-27S,14W-24S  32
Woodland Ct. NE&SW
..............8W-25S  33
Woodlawn Dr. E&W..9W-25S  33
Woodruff St. N&S .. 9W-23S  25
Woodvale Av. E&W
..............10W-25S  33
42nd St. N&S ....11W-22S  33
68th Av. N&S.....9W-25S  33
76th Av. N&S ....9W-22S  33
78th Av. N&S ....9W-22S  33
79th Av. N&S ....9W-22S  33
80th Av. N&S
.........10W-27S,10W-22S  33
82nd Av. N&S....10W-25S  33
84th Av. N&S
.........10W-25S,10W-24S  33
88th Av. N&S
.........11W-24S,11W-22S  33
92nd Av. N&S ...11W-25S  33
93rd Av. N&S .. 11W-25S  33
94th Av. N&S ... 11W-25S  33
104th Av. N&S
.........13W-27S,13W-22S  32
108th Av. N&S .. 13W-26S  32
113th Av. N&S .. 14W-22S  24
114th Av. N&S
.........14W-23S,14W-22S  24
115th Av. N&S .. 14W-22S  24
118th Av. N&S .. 14W-22S  24
187th St. N&S
.........14W-22S,10W-22S  24
189th Pl. E&W .. 13W-22S  24
189th St. E&W .. 14W-22S  24
191st St. E&W .. 14W-22S  24
192nd St. E&W .. 14W-23S  24
193rd St. E&W .. 14W-22S  24
194th St. E&W
.........14W-23S,9W-23S  24
195th St. E&W .. 14W-23S  24
203rd St. E&W .. 14W-24S  32
204th St. E&W .. 13W-24S  32

## Godley
Adams St. E&W...32W-43S  74
Blake Dr. N&S.....32W-43S  74
Center St. N&S .. 32W-43S  74
County Line Rd. N&S
.........32W-43S,32W-42S  74
Dayton Ct. E&W...32W-43S  74
Elmo Ct. E&W....32W-43S  74
Lincoln St. E&W ..32W-43S  74
Livington St. E&W .. 32W-43S  74
Main St. NE&SW ..32W-43S  74
Mary Ln. E&W.....32W-43S  74
Mesa Dr. E&W ... 32W-43S  74
Richard Ct. E&W .. 32W-43S  74
Robert Dr. N&S ...32W-43S  74
Route 129 NE&SW
..............32W-43S  74
Route 53 NE&SW .. 32W-43S  74
Sandy Ct. E&W .. 32W-43S  74
Van Buren St. N&S
..............32W-43S  74
Vernon Dr. N&S....32W-43S  74

## Green Garden Township
Alice Ct. E&W ... 12W-28S  40
Alice Dr. N&S.....12W-28S  40
Beverly Dr. NS&EW .. 9W-32S  53
Center Rd. N&S
.........12W-33S,12W-28S  52
Colleen Ct. E&W .. 9W-32S  53
Derby Glen Ln. N&S 9W-30S  41
Dralle Rd. E&W
.........14W-29S,9W-29S  40
Golfview Ct. NW&SE
..............11W-31S  40
Golfview Dr. E&W .. 11W-31S  40
Golfview Ln. E&W .. 11W-31S  40
Golfview Pl. E&W .. 11W-31S  40
Gorman Rd. E&W
.........14W-31S,9W-31S  40
Green Garden Manhattan Rd.
N&S...14W-33S,14W-29S  52
Harlem Av. N&S
.........9W-33S,9W-28S  53
Harvest Hills Dr. NS&EW
..............12W-29S  40
Joliet Rd. N&S
.........10W-33S,10W-28S  53
Manhattan Monee Rd. E&W
.........14W-30S,9W-30S  40
Manhattan Wilton Rd. E&W
.........14W-33S,9W-33S  52
Pauling Rd. E&W
.........14W-32S,9W-32S  52
Peotone Rd. N&S
.........11W-33S,11W-28S  52
Prairie Creek Dr. E&W
..............12W-30S  40
Prairie Schooner Dr. E&W
..............12W-30S  40
Steger Rd. E&W
.........14W-28S,9W-28S  40
Stuenkel Rd. E&W
.........14W-28S,9W-28S  40
Town Line Rd. N&S
..............14W-28S  40

U.S. Route 45 N&S
.........14W-33S,13W-28S  52
Yorkshire Ln. E&W 10W-30S  41
104th Av. N&S .. 13W-32S  52

## Homer Township
Acorn Ct. N&S ... 19W-17S  16
Acorn Dr. N&S ... 19W-17S  16
Acorn Ln. E&W .. 18W-16S  16
Acorn Ridge Dr. E&W
..............17W-19S  17
Allen Ct. N&S ... 15W-16S  17
Allison Ln. N&S .. 15W-17S  17
Allston Dr. N&S .. 15W-18S  17
Alpine Dr. NS&EW ..15W-18S  17
Anand Brook Dr. N&S
.........16W-16S,15W-16S  17
Annico Dr. N&S ... 16W-18S  17
Appaloosa Ln. N&S
..............15W-17S  17
Apple Ct. NW&SE . 17W-17S  17
Arabian Dr. E&W . 16W-18S  17
Arapano Tr. N&S . 16W-16S  17
Arboretum Dr. NS&EW
..............17W-17S  17
Archer Av. NE&SW
.........20W-16S,19W-16S  16
Arlene Dr. N&S ... 16W-18S  17
Arrowhead Dr. E&W
..............19W-21S  22
Ashley Ct. N&S .. 15W-20S  23
Aspen Ln. E&W .. 15W-20S  23
Aston Ct. E&W .. 16W-17S  17
Atlantic Dr. E&W . 16W-17S  17
Atwood Dr. NS&EW
..............15W-18S  17
Augusta Ln. N&S .. 17W-17S  17
Badger Ln. N&S .. 16W-18S  17
Basham Av. N&S .. 20W-16S  16
Baywood Ln. NE&SW
..............16W-17S  17
Beaver Ct. N&S .. 16W-16S  17
Beaver Den Tr. E&W
..............15W-19S  17
Beaver Lake Dr. NS&EW
..............16W-16S  17
Bedford Ln. E&W . 20W-16S  16
Bell Rd. N&S
.........16W-18S,16W-16S  17
Bell Rd. N&S
.........15W-20S,15W-19S  23
Bellingham Rd. E&W
..............15W-17S  17
Benton Dr. N&S .. 15W-18S  17
Beth Dr. NE&SW .. 19W-17S  16
Big Run Ln. E&W . 17W-17S  17
Birchdale Dr. N&S . 17W-17S  17
Birchwood Ct. NW&SE
..............17W-17S  17
Birchwood Dr. E&W
..............16W-17S  17
Black Forest Ct. E&W
..............15W-18S  17
Black Forest Tr. E&W
..............15W-18S  17
Black Pine Tr. NW&SE
..............15W-18S  17
Blackburn Dr. E&W
..............15W-18S  17
Bosi Dr. E&W .... 19W-19S  16
Boula Av. N&S .. 20W-17S  16
Boulder Dr. N&S....17W-17S  17
Brads Way N&S .. 19W-17S  16
Bramble Ct. E&W . 16W-18S  17
Brentwood Dr. E&W
..............15W-20S  23
Briarwood Dr. E&W
..............16W-17S  17
Bridle Ct. N&S....15W-17S  17
Bruce Cir. NS&EW
.........18W-21S,18W-20S  22
Bruce Dr. E&W
.........20W-20S,15W-20S  22
Burning Bush Ct. NE&SW
..............16W-16S  17
Burr Oak Dr. NS&EW
..............15W-20S  23
Buttercup Ct. E&W
..............16W-18S  17
Cambridge Rd. NS&EW
..............15W-18S  17
Cannonade Ct. NW&SE
..............15W-16S  17
Cantigny Ln. E&W . 17W-17S  17
Canvasback Ct. N&S
..............15W-17S  17
Carefree Dr. N&S .. 17W-17S  17
Carlton Ln. N&S .. 15W-17S  17
Casey Ln. NS&EW . 17W-17S  17
Catawba Ct. E&W . 15W-17S  17
Catawba Ln. E&W . 16W-16S  17
Catawba Rd. NW&SE
..............15W-19S  17
Catawba Tr. E&W . 16W-16S  17
Cave Creek Ct. E&W
..............16W-17S  17
Cedar Creek Ct. N&S
..............16W-17S  17
Cedar Ct. N&S ... 18W-20S  22
Cedar Glen Dr. NW&SE
..............18W-18S  16
Cedar Rd. N&S .. 18W-16S  17

| | Grid | Page |
|---|---|---|

Cedar Rd. N&S
..........18W-21S,18W-18S 22
Cedar Ridge Dr. E&W
.............15W-17S 17
Cedarbend Dr. N&S
.............16W-17S 17
Cedarwood Dr. NS&EW
.............18W-19S 16
Chancellor Dr. E&W
.............19W-19S 16
Chandler Ct. N&S .. 15W-18S 17
Charterhouse Rd. N&S
.............15W-18S 17
Chaucer Rd. E&W . 15W-18S 17
Chelsea Ct. N&S
.............17W-19S 17
Cherokee Tr. NW&SE
.............16W-16S 17
Chesterton Dr. N&S
.............15W-18S 17
Chestnut Ct. N&S .. 15W-16S 17
Chestnut Ln. N&S . 15W-16S 17
Chicago-Bloomington Rd.
NE&SW...........17W-21S 23
Chicasaw Tr. N&S.. 16W-16S 17
Chicory Tr. N&S ... 18W-16S 16
Chippewa Tr. N&S .. 16W-16S 17
Choctaw Tr. E&W . 16W-16S 17
Church St. N&S .... 18W-17S 16
Cinnamon Creek Ln. E&W
.............18W-18S 16
Citation Ct. NE&SW
.............15W-16S 17
Cir..............15W-16S 17
Citation Dr. NS&EW
.............15W-16S 17
Clifton Ln. E&W ... 17W-17S 17
Clydesdale Ln. N&S
.............15W-17S 17
Coachman's Rd. N&S
.....17W-17S,17W-16S 17
Codo Dr. N&S ..... 18W-19S 16
Coghill Ln. N&S ... 17W-17S 17
Coke Rd. (Pvt.) N&S
.............19W-16S 16
Coleridge Ct. N&S
.............15W-18S 17
Colt Dr. E&W ...... 16W-18S 17
Comandora Cir. NS&EW
.............15W-20S 23
Country Woods Dr. NW&SE
.............15W-18S 17
Court Connection NW&SE
.............17W-21S 23
Coventry Ct. E&W . 15W-18S 17
Cranberry Ct. N&S..16W-18S 17
Creek Ct., N. NE&SW
.............18W-17S 16
Creek Ct., S. NW&SE
.............18W-17S 16
Creek View Dr. NW&SE
.............18W-16S 16
Creekside Ct. NW&SE
.............16W-16S 17
Creekside Dr. NS&EW
.............16W-16S 17
Creekview Dr. NW&SE
.............18W-16S 16
Creekwood Ct. N&S
.............16W-19S 17
Creekwood Dr. N&S
.............16W-19S 17
Creekwood Ln. E&W
.............16W-19S 17
Creme Rd. N&S .. 18W-17S 16
Crestwood Dr. E&W
.............18W-16S 16
Cricketwood Ct. NE&SW
.............17W-17S 17
Cricketwood Dr. NS&EW
.............17W-17S 17
Crystal Lake Ct. E&W
.............16W-21S 23
Crystal Lake Dr. N&S
.........16W-21S,16S-20S 23
Dale Rd. E&W .... 15W-21S 23
Dalphon Ct. NW&SE
.............15W-17S 17
Deer Dr. N&S ...... 19W-20S 22
Deerpath Dr. N&S . 15W-20S 23
Deervalley Dr. E&W
.............17W-17S 17
Derby Dr. NE&SW .. 15W-16S 17
Derby Ln. NS&EW . 15W-16S 17
Derby Rd. N&S .... 15W-16S 17
Dixon Ln. N&S .... 17W-17S 17
Doede Ln. E&W .. 16W-20S 23
Dogwood Dr. N&S . 15W-18S 17
Dokter Pl. E&W .. 16W-19S 17
Doonaree Ct. NW&SE
.............17W-16S 17
Doral Dr. E&W ... 17W-17S 17
Driftwood Ln. NE&SW
.............17W-16S 17
Dublin Ct. E&W .. 17W-16S 17
Dublin Dr. N&S ... 17W-16S 17
E. Glen Dr. N&S .. 15W-17S 17
Eagle Bend NS&EW
.............19W-21S 22
Eagle Ridge Dr. NS&EW
.............19W-21S 22
East Abbott Rd. N&S
.............15W-17S 17
East St. N&S ...... 19W-16S 16

Edgewood Dr. E&W
.............15W-18S 17
Edinburgh Ct. E&W
.............15W-17S 16
Edinburgh Ct., E. N&S
.............18W-17S 16
Edinburgh Ct., W. N&S
.............18W-17S 16
Edmonds (Meador) St. N&S
.............17W-21S 23
Elizabeth Ln. N&S .. 17W-17S 17
Elm St. N&S .... 19W-16S 16
Erin Ct. N&S ..... 16W-17S 17
Erin Dr. N&S ..... 17W-16S 17
Evergreen Ter. N&S
.............15W-20S 23
Fairway View Av. E&W
.............16W-16S 17
Farmingdon Dr. E&W
.............15W-18S 17
Farmview St. E&W..16W-18S 17
Fieldview Ln. N&S . 20W-18S 16
Filly Dr. E&W .... 16W-18S 17
Finch Ct. E&W .. 16W-18S 17
Flint Ct. E&W .... 15W-17S 17
Flint Dr. E&W .... 15W-17S 17
Forest Ct. N&S .. 19W-18S 16
Forestview Dr. NS&EW
.............15W-16S 17
Foxboro Ln. N&S .. 17W-21S 23
Gadwall Ct. NW&SE
.............17W-17S 17
Garavogue Av. N&S
.............15W-16S 17
Gatses Estates E&W
.......18W-17S,17W-17S 16
Gatses Ln. E&W
.......18W-17S,17W-17S 16
Glen Crest Ln. E&W
.............18W-18S 16
Glen Dale Ln. N&S . 18W-18S 16
Glen Entrance E&W
.............16W-21S 23
Glenview Cir. E&W..18W-18S 16
Glenwood Ct. N&S..18W-18S 16
Glenwood Dr. E&W
.............18W-18S 16
Golden Oak Dr. N&S
.......16W-17S,16W-16S 17
Gombis Dr. E&W .. 18W-21S 22
Gougar Rd. N&S
.....20W-21S,20W-18S 22
Graceland Ct. E&W
.............15W-18S 17
Graceland Dr. N&S 15W-18S 17
Greenbrier Ln. N&S
.............17W-17S 17
Grenelefe Ln. E&W 17W-17S 17
Gunner Ct. E&W ..15W-19S 17
Hadley Rd. NE&SW
.............16W-20S 23
Haggard St. E&W . 16W-18S 17
Hampshire Ln. E&W
.............15W-17S 17
Hampton Ct. N&S.. 19W-16S 16
Hank Ct., E. E&W . 15W-17S 17
Hank Ct., W. E&W..15W-17S 17
Hass Rd. N&S.....16W-21S 23
Hawk Haven E&W . 19W-16S 16
Heathcliff Rd. N&S..15W-17S 17
Heather Ct. N&S .. 15W-17S 17
Heather Ln. N&S .. 15W-17S 17
Heatherwood Ct. N&S
.............17W-17S 17
Heatherwood Dr. NS&EW
.............17W-17S 17
Hedge Apple Dr. N&S
.............16W-18S 17
Heritage Dr. N&S .. 18W-20S 22
Hiawatha Ct. N&S .. 16W-16S 17
Hiawatha Dr. E&W . 16W-16S 17
Hickory Av. NW&SE
.......18W-16S,17W-6S 16
Hickory Ct. E&W .. 17W-16S 17
Hidden Valley Dr. NS&EW
.............16W-19S 17
Hidden Valley Tr. N&S
.............16W-19S 17
Hillary Ln. N&S ... 19W-17S 16
Hillcrest Rd. . 18W-17S 16
Hillside Ct. N&S .. 16W-18S 17
Hilltop Dr. E&W .. 17W-21S 23
Holm Ct. N&S .... 15W-17S 17
Holm Dr. E&W .... 15W-17S 17
Hunter Ct. N&S .. 20W-16S 16
Ignace Ct. NW&SE 15W-19S 17
Innsbrook Ln. N&S..17W-19S 17
Cir..............17W-17S 17
Iroquis Tr. E&W .. 16W-16S 17
Ivy Ct. N&S .... 15W-17S 17
James Ct. E&W .. 19W-21S 22
Janas Ct. N&S .. 19W-16S 16
Joan Marie Dr. E&W
.............15W-18S 17
Juniper Ln. E&W .. 15W-20S 23
Kelly Ct. N&S .... 20W-18S 16
Kendon Ct. E&W . 15W-17S 17
Kensington Dr. N&S
.............17W-19S 17
Kerry Dr. NE&SW .. 17W-16S 17
Kerry Ln. NE&SW .. 17W-16S 17
Kickapoo Tr. N&S . 16W-16S 17
King Rd. N&S
.......18W-17S,18W-16S 16

Kingston Ct. N&S . 15W-18S 17
Kingswood Rd. N&S
.............15W-18S 17
Kiowa Ct. N&S .... 15W-18S 17
Kundrat Ln. N&S .. 19W-16S 17
Lacrosse Dr. N&S . 19W-21S 22
Lady Bar Av. N&S .. 15W-16S 17
Lady Bar Ct. N&S . 15W-16S 17
Lady Bar Dr. N&S . 15W-16S 17
Lakeview Ct. N&S . 15W-16S 17
Lakeview Dr. N&S . 15W-16S 17
Lakeview Pl. N&S . 15W-16S 17
Lakeview Tr. E&W . 15W-18S 17
Lancaster Ct. E&W
.............15W-16S 17
Larkspur Ct. N&S . 16W-21S 23
Larkspur Dr. NE&SW
.............17W-21S 23
Lauffer Rd. NW&SE
.............16W-20S 23
Leach Dr. N&S .... 19W-19S 16
Lemont Rd. N&S .. 19W-16S 16
Lenox Dr. E&W ... 15W-18S 17
Linsey Ln. E&W ... 20W-21S 22
Cir..............16W-16S 17
Little Creek Dr. NS&EW
.............16W-16S 17
Long Run Ct. E&W
.............16W-16S 17
Long Run Dr. N&S..18W-16S 16
Longmeadow Ln. E&W
.............15W-20S 23
Longrun Dr. N&S .. 18W-16S 16
Longview Dr. N&S . 19W-16S 16
Lost Boy Ln. N&S . 16W-16S 17
Mackinac Ct. NW&SE
.............15W-19S 17
Mackinac Rd. NE&SW
.............15W-19S 17
Magnolia Dr. E&W . 15W-18S 17
Mallard Dr. N&S
.......15W-17S,15W-16S 17
Mallard Lake Dr. (Pvt.) N&S
.............19W-18S 16
Mallard Ln. N&S ... 15W-17S 17
Mallard Ln. (Pvt.) NS&EW
.............19W-18S 16
Manitou Ct. NE&SW
.............15W-19S 17
Manitou Rd. NS&EW
.............15W-19S 17
Manor Dr. N&S ... 15W-17S 17
Manor Ln. N&S ... 18W-18S 16
Maple Av. N&S ... 18W-18S 16
Maple Ct. N&S ... 18W-18S 16
Maramel Dr. N&S . 16W-19S 17
Marti Rd. N&S.....15W-21S 23
Martingale Ln. E&W
.............16W-18S 17
Maverick Tr. E&W . 16W-18S 17
McCarron Rd. N&S
.......18W-21S,18W-20S 22
McCormick Ln. N&S
.............19W-20S 22
McDonald Dr. E&W
.............20W-18S 16
McKenzie Av. E&W
.............20W-18S 16
Meador Rd. (Edmonds St.)
N&S ..........17W-21S 23
Meadow View Ln. N&S
.............16W-18S 17
Meadowcrest Dr. N&S
.............15W-20S 23
Meadowland Dr. NE&SW
.............15W-17S 17
Meadowlark Ct. E&W
.............16W-18S 17
Meath Cir. N&S ... 17W-16S 17
Meath Ct. N&S ... 17W-16S 17
Meath Dr. E&W ... 17W-16S 17
Monaghan Dr. N&S
.............17W-16S 17
Monaghan Rd. N&S
.............17W-16S 17
Moorland Dr. E&W..15W-17S 17
Morgan Ct. NE&SW
.............15W-17S 17
Mormann Ln. N&S . 18W-16S 16
Morning Glory Ct. E&W
.............16W-18S 17
Muir Dr. N&S .... 20W-18S 16
Mulberry Ct. N&S . 16W-18S 17
Mulraney Dr. NS&EW
.............16W-17S 17
Murvey Ct. NW&SE
.............15W-16S 17
Murvey Dr. E&W ... 15W-16S 17
Mustang Dr. N&S . 15W-17S 17
N. Hawthorne Ct. N&S
.............15W-17S 16
Navajo Tr. E&W ... 16W-16S 17
Navajo Tr. N&S ... 17W-16S 17
Needles Ct. N&S . 15W-16S 17
Needles Ct. N&S . 15W-16S 17
Nolan Ct. E&W ... 19W-16S 16
O'Connell Dr. E&W 18W-21S 22
Oak Av. E&W ... 17W-16S 17
Oak Ct. E&W .... 16W-17S 17
Oak Ct. NW&SE ... 16W-19S 17
Oak Meadow Ct. NW&SE
.............16W-20S 23
Oak Ridge Ct. NE&SW
.............16W-16S 17

Oak Ridge Dr. N&S
.............16W-16S 17
Oak Ridge Ln. NW&SE
.............16W-16S 17
Oak St. N&S .... 21W-21S 21
Oak St. N&S .... 19W-16S 16
Cir.............16W-17S 17
Oak Valley Ct. E&W
.............16W-19S 17
Oak Valley Tr. NS&EW
.............16W-19S 17
Oakridge Ct. N&S . 16W-16S 17
Oakridge Dr. N&S . 16W-16S 17
Oakridge Ln. NW&SE
.............16W-16S 17
Oakview Ct. N&S . 16W-16S 17
Oakwood Dr. E&W 16W-17S 17
Onondaga NW&SE 16W-16S 17
Orchard Ln. E&W . 18W-16S 16
Paddock Ln. NE&SW
.............16W-18S 17
Palomino Ct. N&S .. 15W-17S 17
Pantigo Ln. E&W .. 19W-19S 16
Parker Rd. N&S
.......16W-21S,17W-17S 23
Parkside Dr. N&S . 15W-18S 17
Parnell Cir. NE&SW
.............18W-21S 22
Partridge Ln. E&W ..15W-16S 17
Pawnee Ln. NE&SW
.............16W-16S 17
Pebble Creek Ct. E&W
.............15W-20S 23
Pebble Creek Dr. N&S
.............17W-17S 17
Peppermill Tr. N&S 19W-19S 16
Pheasant Cir. NS&EW
.............18W-16S 16
Pheasant Ct. N&S . 16W-19S 17
Pheasant Ln. N&S
.......15W-17S,15W-16S 17
Pin Oak Ct. E&W . 15W-17S 17
Pin Oak Ct. N&S .. 16W-19S 17
Pin Oak Dr. N&S .. 16W-16S 17
Pine Grove Dr. NS&EW
.............16W-17S 17
Pine Hill Dr. N&S .. 17W-19S 17
Pinegrove Ct. E&W
.............16W-17S 17
Pineview Dr. N&S . 15W-20S 23
Pinto St. NE&SW .. 18W-16S 16
Cir..............18W-16S 16
Pleasant Dr. E&W . 19W-16S 16
Potawatamie Ct. N&S
.............16W-16S 17
Potawatomi Tr. N&S
.............16W-16S 17
Prairie Ct. E&W .... 15W-17S 17
Prairie Dr. NW&SE..15W-17S 17
Prairie Hill Dr. N&S..19W-16S 16
Purley Ct. NE&SW..19W-16S 16
Quail Ln. E&W.....15W-16S 17
Quail Run Ct. N&S..19W-16S 16
Rado Dr. NE&SW .. 16W-16S 17
Rambling Rd. (Pvt.) E&W
.............15W-17S 17
Red Cedar Tr. N&S
.............15W-18S 17
Red Oak Ct. E&W . 16W-19S 17
Regents Rd. N&S . 19W-19S 16
Reiter Dr. E&W ... 19W-20S 22
Rickerman Rd. N&S
.............20W-17S 16
Ridge Ct. N&S ... 20W-16S 16
Ridgemoor Dr. E&W
.............15W-18S 17
Ridgewood Dr. NS&EW
.............16W-18S 17
Robert Emmett Dr. N&S
.............18W-21S 22
Rockbluff Way NS&EW
.............17W-17S 17
Roger Rd. N&S ... 20W-16S 16
Ron Ct. E&W
.......19W-20S,18W-20S 22
Rosarie Dr. N&S...16W-18S 17
Rosewood Dr. E&W
.............15W-17S 17
Route 171 NE&SW
.............20W-16S 16
Route 355 (proposed) N&S
.......18W-21S,20W-16S 22
Route 7 E&W
.......19W-19S,15W-18S 16
Russ Ln. N&S ... 16W-16S 17
Rycon Dr. E&W ... 16W-21S 23
Rynberk Ct. N&S . 20W-16S 16
S. Bell Rd. N&S .. 15W-19S 17
S. Hawthorne Ct. N&S
.............19W-17S 16
Saddle Brooke Ln. N&S
.............17W-17S 17
Sage Ct. E&W.....16W-17S 17
Samuel Dr. NS&EW
.............16W-18S 17
Sandi Ln. E&W ... 20W-18S 16
Sandstone Dr. E&W
.............19W-19S 16
Sawgrass Ln. N&S..17W-17S 17
Schroeder Dr. E&W
.............19W-19S 16
Scott Ct. NW&SE . 20W-18S 16
Scott Dr. N&S.....20W-18S 16

Sea Biscuit Ct. N&S
.............15W-16S 17
Secretariat Ln. NS&EW
.............15W-16S 17
Seminole Tr. E&W
.......17W-16S,16W-16S 17
Shady Ln. NS&EW..17W-15S 17
Shady Ln. NW&SE..17W-15S 16
Shaeffer Ct. N&S . 20W-16S 16
Shannon Dr. NS&EW
.............17W-16S 17
Sharon Dr. N&S ... 15W-18S 17
Shelburne Rd. N&S..19W-20S 22
Shetland Ct. NE&SW
.............20W-18S 16
Shetland Dr. N&S . 15W-17S 17
Shoshoni Dr. E&W..16W-16S 17
Shoshoni Tr. E&W . 17W-16S 17
Silo Ct. NE&SW ... 16W-18S 17
Silo Dr. N&S .... 16W-18S 17
Somerset Ct. N&S . 15W-16S 17
Somerset Rd. NE&SW
.............15W-16S 17
South Janas Pkwy. NS&EW
.............19W-16S 16
Cir.............15W-19S 17
Sparrow Ct. E&W . 16W-18S 17
Split Rail Ct. NE&SW
.............16W-16S 17
Split Rail Dr. E&W . 16W-16S 17
Spring Creek Rd. E&W
.......18W-16S,17W-16S 16
Spring Ct. E&W ... 16W-16S 17
Spring Lake Dr. NE&SW
.............15W-17S 17
Spring Meadows Dr. N&S
.............15W-21S 23
Starr Ln. (Pvt.) N&S
.............20W-16S 16
State St. N&S .... 19W-17S 16
Stately Oaks Cir. NS&EW
.............19W-17S 16
Stately Oaks Dr. E&W
.............19W-17S 16
Sterling Dr. NE&SW
.............20W-16S 16
Stirrup Ct. N&S ... 15W-17S 17
Stone Creek Ct. NE&SW
.............16W-17S 17
Stone Oak Way E&W
.............17W-17S 17
Stonegate Dr. NS&EW
.............16W-17S 17
Stonehaven Ln. E&W
.............18W-17S 16
Stonewood Dr. E&W
.............16W-17S 17
Stratford Ct. N&S . 15W-18S 17
Stratford Dr. N&S . 15W-18S 17
Sulky Ct. NW&SE . 16W-18S 17
Sulky Dr. N&S....16W-18S 17
Sunset Ct. N&S ... 17W-17S 17
Surrey Ln. E&W ... 15W-17S 17
Sussex Dr. E&W....15W-18S 17
Sutherland NS&EW
.............15W-17S 17
Swaps Ct. E&W ... 15W-16S 17
Sweetwater Dr. E&W
.............15W-17S 17
Tamarack Ln. E&W
.............15W-20S 23
Tameling Dr. E&W . 20W-16S 16
Tara Dr. NW&SE .. 17W-16S 17
Teakwood Dr. N&S
.............16W-17S 17
Teal Dr. N&S .... 15W-17S 17
Teal Ln. N&S .... 19W-18S 16
Tedd Rd. E&W ... 15W-21S 23
Terrier Ct. E&W ... 15W-19S 17
Thicket Ct. N&S...16W-16S 17
Thistle Ct. E&W ... 16W-18S 17
Thorn Apple Dr. E&W
.............15W-20S 23
Thornbush Dr. NS&EW
.............16W-16S 17
Thornwood Ln. E&W
.............19W-17S 16
Tim Tam Ct. NE&SW
.............15W-16S 17
Timber Lane Ct. NW&SE
.............17W-17S 17
Trails End NE&SW
.............16W-16S 17
Trails End Dr. N&S 16W-16S 17
Trailside Dr. N&S . 16W-16S 17
Turf Ln. N&S .... 15W-17S 17
Turnberry Dr. N&S..15W-16S 17
Twin Creek Ln. N&S
.............18W-17S 16
Twin Lakes Dr. N&S
.............15W-18S 17
Twin Oaks Ct. N&S
.............18W-16S 16
Twin Oaks Ct. N&S
.............16W-19S 17
Valley View Dr. N&S
.............16W-19S 17
Vaysee Ct. N&S...19W-16S 16
Venetion Ct. NE&SW
.............15W-16S 17
Venetion Way NS&EW
.............15W-16S 17
Victoria Ct. E&W .. 15W-17S 17

WILL COUNTY 85


| | Grid | Page |
|---|---|---|
| Walnut Av. NW&SE | 18W-16S | 16 |
| Walnut Ct. N&S | 16W-18S | 17 |
| Warwick Way E&W | 15W-18S | 17 |
| Waterford Rd. NS&EW | 15W-18S | 17 |
| Weather Vane Ln. N&S | 16W-18S | 17 |
| Wedgewood Dr. NE&SW | 15W-20S | 23 |
| Welter Ct. N&S | 16W-17S | 17 |
| West Abbott Rd. N&S | 15W-17S | 17 |
| West St. N&S | 19W-16S | 16 |
| Wheatstone Dr. E&W | 19W-19S | 16 |
| Whirlaway Ct. N&S | 15W-16S | 17 |
| White Oak St. NW&SE | 16W-19S | 17 |
| White Pines Ct. NE&SW | 15W-18S | 17 |
| White Pines Tr. NW&SE | 15W-18S | 17 |
| Wilco Dr. NS&EW | 15W-17S | 17 |
| Wildwood Ct. SW&NE | 16W-19S | 17 |
| Wildwood Ln. NS&EW | 16W-19S | 17 |
| Will Cook Rd. N&S | 15W-18S,15W-16S | 17 |
| Willow Oak Ct. N&S | 16W-18S | 17 |
| Winchester Ct. N&S | 15W-16S | 17 |
| Winchester Dr. NS&EW | 15W-16S | 17 |
| Windmill Dr. N&S | 19W-19S | 16 |
| Wingate Dr. N&S | 15W-17S | 17 |
| Wingate Rd. N&S | 15W-18S | 17 |
| Winsor Ct. E&W | 15W-17S | 17 |
| Winsor Ln. N&S | 15W-17S | 17 |
| Wirlway Ct. N&S | 15W-16S | 17 |
| Wood Duck Ct. N&S | 15W-17S | 17 |
| Woodcrest Av. N&S | 15W-17S | 17 |
| Woodduck Ln. E&W | 18W-16S | 16 |
| Woodland Dr. E&W | 16W-18S,15W-18S | 17 |
| Woodmill Ct. E&W | 17W-17S | 17 |
| Wooly Hill Ct. E&W | 15W-16S | 17 |
| Wooly Hill Dr. N&S | 15W-16S | 17 |
| Yorkshire Ct. E&W | 15W-17S | 17 |
| Yorkshire Dr. E&W | 15W-17S | 17 |
| Zuck Ct. E&W | 18W-19S | 16 |
| 7th St. E&W | 20W-19S | 16 |
| 135th Av. N&S | 20W-17S | 16 |
| 135th St. E&W | 18W-16S | 16 |
| 136th Av. N&S | 20W-17S | 16 |
| 136th St. E&W | 18W-16S | 16 |
| 138th St. E&W | 20W-16S,19W-16S | 16 |
| 139th St E&W | 19W-16S,18W-16S | 16 |
| 140th Pl. E&W | 20W-16S | 16 |
| 140th St. E&W | 20W-16S | 16 |
| 141th St. E&W | 20W-16S,19W-16S | 16 |
| 143rd St. E&W | 18W-16S,16W-16S | 16 |
| 144th Pl. E&W | 20W-17S | 16 |
| 145th Pl. E&W | 20W-17S | 16 |
| 146th St. E&W | 20W-17S | 16 |
| 147th St. E&W | 19W-17S,18W-17S | 16 |
| 151st St. E&W | 18W-17S,16W-17S | 16 |
| 159th St. E&W | 20W-18S,16W-18S | 16 |
| 163rd St. E&W | 19W-19S,18W-19S | 16 |
| 167th St. E&W | 20W-19S,15W-19S | 16 |
| 175th St. E&W | 18W-20S | 22 |
| 179th St. E&W | 17W-21S,15W-21S | 23 |


## Jackson Township


| | Grid | Page |
|---|---|---|
| Alice Ct. NE&SW | 22W-30S | 37 |
| Arsenal Rd. E&W | 26W-30S,25W-30S | 36 |
| Ash St. E&W | 24W-30S | 36 |
| Bernhard Rd. E&W | 22W-28S | 37 |
| Bicentennial Dr. NS&EW | 22W-30S | 37 |
| Brandon Rd. NS&EW | 25W-29S,25W-28S | 36 |
| Breen Rd. E&W | 23W-29S,22W-29S | 37 |
| Bridge Rd. N&S | 24W-29S | 36 |
| Brown Rd. (Sweedler) E&W | 23W-31S,21W-31S | 37 |
| Bush Rd. N&S | 25W-30S | 36 |
| Cherry Hill Rd. N&S | 21W-32S,21W-28S | 49 |
| Chicago Rd. N&S | 25W-31S,25W-30S | 36 |
| Clair Ct. NW&SE | 22W-30S | 37 |
| Coldwater Rd. N&S | 24W-32S,24W-30S | 48 |
| Craig Rd. E&W | 26W-29S,24W-28S | 36 |
| Creek Dr. N&S | 24W-30S | 36 |
| Diagonal Rd. NE&SW | 26W-31S,25W-31S | 36 |
| Eaton Av. E&W | 24W-29S | 36 |
| Gary Ray Dr. N&S | 24W-29S | 36 |
| Gas Plant Rd. E&W | 26W-29S,25W-29S | 36 |
| Gladys Av. E&W | 24W-29S | 36 |
| Gurney Rd. (Joliet Arsenal) E&W | 23W-32S,21W-32S | 49 |
| Hemphill Dr. NS&EW | 22W-30S | 37 |
| Jeffrey Ct. N&S | 24W-30S | 36 |
| Keith Allen Dr. NE&SW | 24W-29S | 36 |
| Kinder Rd. E&W | 22W-30S | 37 |
| Lois Ln. N&S | 24W-30S | 36 |
| Manhattan-Wilton Rd. E&W | 25W-33S,22W-33S | 48 |
| Marian Av. N&S | 21W-30S | 37 |
| Millsdale Ext. Rd. E&W | 26W-29S,25W-29S | 36 |
| Millsdale Rd. NE&SW | 26W-29S | 36 |
| Mississippi Av. E&W | 26W-32S | 48 |
| Noel Rd. E&W | 24W-29S | 36 |
| North Town Line Rd. E&W | 23W-28S,21W-28S | 37 |
| Old Wilmington Rd. NE&SW | 26W-32S | 48 |
| Patterson Rd. N&S | 26W-29S | 36 |
| Pheasant Dr. N&S | 24W-30S | 36 |
| Quail Ct. E&W | 24W-30S | 36 |
| Raymond Dr. NS&EW | 24W-29S | 36 |
| Rich Ct. E&W | 21W-30S | 37 |
| Ridge Rd. N&S | 22W-32S,22W-28S | 49 |
| Rob Av. E&W | 21W-30S | 37 |
| Ron Ct. E&W | 21W-30S | 37 |
| Rondorey Rd. N&S | 24W-30S | 36 |
| Route 53 NE&SW | 24W-29S,24W-28S | 36 |
| Rowell Av. N&S | 23W-29S,23W-28S | 37 |
| Rowell Rd. N&S | 23W-32S,23W-30S | 49 |
| Sharp Rd. E&W | 24W-28S | 36 |
| South Townline Rd. E&W | 21W-33S | 49 |
| Spangler Rd. E&W | 21W-29S | 37 |
| Stone Rd. E&W | 21W-28S | 37 |
| Sweitzer Rd. E&W | 26W-28S,24W-28S | 36 |
| Sycamore St. N&S | 24W-30S | 36 |
| Tanglewood Dr., E. E&W | 24W-30S | 36 |
| Tanglewood Dr., W. E&W | 24W-30S | 36 |
| Tehle Rd. NE&SW | 24W-31S,24W-30S | 36 |
| Timber Ct. NW&SE | 24W-30S | 36 |
| Timber Dr. N&S | 24W-30S | 36 |
| Timber Dr., N. E&W | 24W-30S | 36 |
| Timber Dr., S. E&W | 24W-30S | 36 |
| Walnut St. N&S | 24W-30S | 36 |
| Wilmington Rd. N&S | 26W-29S,26W-28S | 36 |
| Wood Rd. E&W | 24W-32S,24W-31S | 48 |


## Joliet


| | Grid | Page |
|---|---|---|
| A Wilhelmi Dr. E&W | 28W-21S | 19 |
| Abe St. N&S | 23W-23S | 21 |
| Ada St. E&W | 22W-22S | 21 |
| Addleman St. N&S | 28W-22S,28W-21S | 19 |
| Adella Av. N&S | 22W-24S | 29 |
| Agnes Av. E&W | 25W-22S | 20 |
| Akin Av. N&S | 23W-24S | 29 |
| Alamo Dr. E&W | 27W-21S | 19 |
| Alamosa Ct. E&W | 19W-22S | 22 |
| Alamosa St. N&S | 19W-22S | 22 |
| Alann Dr. N&S | 26W-22S | 20 |
| Albert Av. E&W | 23W-24S | 29 |
| Albert D'Ottavio Dr. NE&SW | 28W-22S | 19 |
| Aldrich Dr. N&S | 29w-21S | 18 |
| Alessio Dr. E&W | 23W-25S | 29 |
| Alexander Dr. E&W | 27W-23S | 19 |
| Allen St. E&W | 24W-24S | 28 |
| Amber Ct. NW&SE | 28W-20S | 19 |
| Ambrose Ln. N&S | 29W-21S | 18 |
| Ann Ct. N&S | 26W-23S | 20 |
| Ann St. N&S | 26W-23S | 20 |
| Antram Av. N&S | 22W-22S | 21 |
| Apollo Dr. N&S | 27W-23S | 19 |
| Applewood Ct. N&S | 30W-21S | 18 |
| Arch Ct. N&S | 23W-23S | 21 |
| Arden Ln. E&W | 26W-23S | 20 |
| Arden Pl. E&W | 27W-23S,26W-23S | 19 |
| Arizona Av. N&S | 22W-24S | 29 |
| Art Schultz Dr. N&S | 32W-20S | 18 |
| Arthur Av. N&S | 22W-22S | 21 |
| Ashbury Circle Dr. E&W | 26W-22S | 20 |
| Ashwood Dr. NS&EW | 30W-21S | 18 |
| Aspen Ct. N&S | 28W-23S | 19 |
| Audrey Av. E&W | 25W-24S | 28 |
| Avalon Av. E&W | 26W-23S | 20 |
| Baker Av. N&S | 23W-24S | 29 |
| Bankview Ln. NE&SW | 28W-23S | 19 |
| Barber Ct. E&W | 27W-23S | 19 |
| Barber Ln. NE&SW | 27W-22S | 19 |
| Barber Ln. NW&SE | 27W-23S | 19 |
| Barney Dr. N&S | 27W-23S | 19 |
| Barthelme Av. N&S | 25W-22S | 20 |
| Bartleson St. E&W | 23W-24S | 29 |
| Basswood Rd. E&W | 21W-22S | 21 |
| Bataan St. NW&SE | 27W-21S | 19 |
| Bazzarone Dr. E&W | 32W-20S | 18 |
| Beach St. N&S | 24W-24S | 28 |
| Beckwith Ct. N&S | 29W-21S | 18 |
| Bedford Dr. E&W | 30W-21S | 18 |
| Beechwood Rd. E&W | 21W-22S | 21 |
| Bellarmine Dr., E. N&S | 26W-24S | 28 |
| Bellarmine Dr., W. N&S | 26W-24S | 28 |
| Belle Av. NW&SE | 22W-22S | 21 |
| Belmont Av. E&W | 21W-23S | 21 |
| Benedict Av. E&W | 26W-24S | 28 |
| Benich Ln. E&W | 32W-20S | 18 |
| Bennette Av. N&S | 23W-24S | 29 |
| Bentley Dr. E&W | 29W-21S | 18 |
| Benton St. E&W | 24W-23S,22W-23S | 20 |
| Bergstrom St. E&W | 28W-22S | 19 |
| Berlin Av. E&W | 24W-22S | 20 |
| Bethal Dr. N&S | 27W-23S | 19 |
| Betula St. N&S | 25W-24S | 28 |
| Big Timber Dr. E&W | 28W-23S | 19 |
| Birchwood Ln. E&W | 26W-22S | 20 |
| Bissel St. N&S | 22W-23S | 21 |
| Black Rd. E&W | 29W-22S,25W-22S | 18 |
| Blackman Av. N&S | 24W-24S | 28 |
| Blackwater Dr. E&W | 28W-21S | 19 |
| Blandford Av. E&W | 19W-22S | 22 |
| Blue Jay Ln. N&S | 29W-22S | 18 |
| Bluff St. N&S | 24W-24S,24W-22S | 28 |
| Cir. | 21W-22S | 21 |
| Border Dr. N&S | 26W-23S | 20 |
| Boston Av. E&W | 25W-22S | 20 |
| Boulder Av. N&S | 22W-24S | 29 |
| Bowen Pl. E&W | 23W-24S | 29 |
| Brentwood Dr. N&S | 26W-22S | 20 |
| Brentwood Pl. NE&SW | 26W-22S | 20 |
| Briargate Av. E&W | 25W-22S | 20 |
| Bridge St. NW&SE | 24W-23S | 20 |
| Brighton Ln. NE&SW | 30W-21S | 18 |
| Brindlewood Dr. NS&EW | 30W-21S | 18 |
| Brink Dr. N&S | 27W-23S | 19 |
| Brittany Dr. N&S | 27W-19S | 13 |
| Broadway Av. N&S | 24W-23S,24W-22S | 20 |
| Bronk Rd. N&S | 29W-22S,29W-21S | 18 |
| Brookfield Dr. N&S | 30W-22S | 18 |
| Brookridge Ct. E&W | 31W-20S | 18 |
| Brookridge Dr. NS&EW | 31W-20S | 18 |
| Brooks Av. NE&SW | 24W-23S | 20 |
| Brookshire Estates Ct. E&W | 30W-21S | 18 |
| Brookshire Estates Dr. E&W | 30W-21S | 18 |
| Brookwood Ct. NW&SE | 26W-22S | 20 |
| Bruce St. E&W | 23W-22S | 21 |
| Bryan Av. E&W | 25W-22S | 20 |
| Buck Av. E&W | 28W-22S | 19 |
| Buell Av. E&W | 25W-23S | 20 |
| Buell Ct. NW&SE | 25W-23S | 20 |
| Burgess Dr. NS&EW | 30W-21S | 18 |
| Burr Oaks Rd. E&W | 28W-23S | 19 |
| Burry St. N&S | 25W-22S | 20 |
| Bush Rd. NW&SE | 28W-26S | 27 |
| Bush St. N&S | 23W-24S | 29 |
| Caddy Ln. E&W | 27W-23S | 19 |
| Cagwin Av. N&S | 24W-24S | 28 |
| Calico Ct. N&S | 27W-19S | 13 |
| California Av. N&S | 22W-22S | 21 |
| Campbell St. E&W | 27W-23S,24W-23S | 19 |
| Canal Rd. NE&SW | 28W-27S | 27 |
| Canal St. NE&SW | 24W-23S | 20 |
| Candlewood Ct. N&S | 30W-21S | 18 |
| Candlewood Dr. N&S | 30W-21S | 18 |
| Canterbury Ct. N&S | 30W-21S | 18 |
| Canterbury St. E&W | 30W-21S | 18 |
| Capri Av. E&W | 26W-24S | 28 |
| Cardinal Ln. E&W | 22W-22S | 21 |
| Carmel Dr. E&W | 31W-20S | 18 |
| Carrier Cir. NS&EW | 29W-21S | 18 |
| Carson Av. N&S | 24W-23S | 20 |
| Carter Ln. E&W | 32W-20S | 18 |
| Casey Ct. N&S | 27W-19S | 13 |
| Cass St. E&W | 24W-23S,21W-23S | 20 |
| Casseday Av. N&S | 23W-23S | 21 |
| Cassie Dr. NE&SW | 27W-23S | 19 |
| Cassie Dr. NW&SE | 27W-22S | 19 |
| Catalpa St. E&W | 23W-23S | 21 |
| Caterpillar Dr. N&S | 27W-24S | 27 |
| Catherine St. N&S | 25W-23S,25W-22S | 20 |
| Cathy Dr. NS&EW | 28W-25S | 27 |
| Caton Av. E&W | 26W-23S,25W-23S | 20 |
| Caton Farm Rd. E&W | 32W-20S,27W-20S | 18 |
| Cecily Dr. N&S | 27W-21S | 19 |
| Cedar Lakes Ct. E&W | 30W-20S | 18 |
| Center St. N&S | 24W-24S,24W-22S | 28 |
| Central Av. N&S | 25W-24S | 28 |
| Channahon Rd. NE&SW | 28W-27W,27W-26S | 27 |
| Chapman Dr. E&W | 29W-21S | 18 |
| Charlesworth Av. N&S | 23W-22S | 21 |
| Charlotte Av. NE&SW | 24W-23S | 20 |
| Chase Av. E&W | 23W-22S,22W-22S | 21 |
| Cherry St. N&S | 24W-24S | 28 |
| Chestnut Grove Dr. N&S | 30W-21S | 18 |
| Chestnut Hill Rd. NE&SW | 30W-21S | 18 |
| Chicago St. N&S | 24W-24S,24W-23S | 28 |
| Chippewa St. N&S | 22W-25S | 29 |
| Christina Ln. NE&SW | 25W-22S | 20 |
| Christine Ct. N&S | 28W-25S | 27 |
| Cider Grove Ct. E&W | 30W-21S | 18 |
| Clara Av. E&W | 26W-22S,25W-22S | 20 |
| Clark St. N&S | 22W-22S | 21 |
| Claudia Av. E&W | 22W-24S | 29 |
| Clay St. E&W | 23W-23S | 21 |
| Cleary Av. E&W | 25W-22S | 20 |
| Cleary St. E&W | 25W-22S | 20 |
| Clement St. N&S | 24W-23S,24W-22S | 20 |
| Cleveland Av. E&W | 23W-22S | 21 |
| Clinton St. E&W | 24W-23S,22W-23S | 20 |
| Clove Ln. E&W | 30W-21S | 18 |
| Cochrane St. E&W | 25W-24S | 28 |
| Colburn Av. E&W | 23W-24S | 29 |
| Collins St. N&S | 23W-23S,23W-22S | 21 |
| Colorado Av. NW&SE | 25W-22S | 20 |
| Columbia St. E&W | 24W-23S,23W-23S | 20 |
| Comstock St. N&S | 24W-24S | 28 |
| Concord Ct. N&S | 27W-19S | 13 |
| Connecticut Av. NE&SW | 25W-22S | 20 |
| Copley Ln. N&S | 28W-25S | 27 |
| Copperfield Av. E&W | 22W-23S | 21 |
| Cora St. N&S | 24W-22S | 20 |
| Cornelia St. N&S | 25W-23S | 20 |
| Corregidor St. NW&SE | 27W-21S | 19 |
| Cottage Pl. E&W | 25W-24S | 28 |
| Cottonwood Rd. E&W | 21W-22S | 21 |
| Country Glen Dr. E&W | 29W-22S | 18 |
| County Farm Rd. E&W | 28W-24S | 27 |
| Court St. N&S | 22W-24S | 29 |
| Cove Cir. E&W | 29W-21S | 18 |
| Coventry Ct. NE&SW | 28W-23S | 19 |
| Cowles Av. N&S | 25W-23S | 20 |
| Crabapple Ct. N&S | 27W-23S | 19 |
| Crabapple Dr. N&S | 27W-23S | 19 |
| Craig Dr. E&W | 28W-25S | 27 |
| Cranberry Ct. N&S | 27W-23S | 19 |
| Creed St. N&S | 23W-23S | 21 |
| Croghan St. E&W | 25W-24S,24W-24S | 28 |
| Crowley Av. E&W | 24W-23S,23W-23S | 20 |
| Culver Ct. N&S | 29W-21S | 18 |
| Curtis Av. E&W | 25W-22S,24W-22S | 20 |
| Cutter Av. N&S | 22W-22S | 21 |
| Cypress Ct. NE&SW | 26W-22S | 20 |
| Cypress Ln. N&S | 26W-22S | 20 |
| Cypress St. E&W | 22W-22S | 21 |
| D'Amico Dr. E&W | 32W-20S | 18 |
| D. Hutchinson Av. E&W | 28W-21S | 19 |
| Dalewood Ct. N&S | 29W-21S | 19 |
| Dalewood Dr. E&W | 29W-21S | 19 |
| Darcy Av. E&W | 24W-24S | 28 |
| Dartmoor Dr. E&W | 26W-22S | 20 |
| David Av. E&W | 23W-25S | 29 |
| Davis Av. N&S | 25W-24S | 28 |
| Davis St. E&W | 24W-24S | 28 |
| Dawes Av. N&S | 25W-22S | 20 |
| DeKalb St. E&W | 24W-24S | 28 |
| Dearborn St. N&S | 24W-22S | 20 |
| Deerpath Dr. E&W | 27W-23S | 19 |
| Dejerald Ln. E&W | 32W-20S | 18 |
| Delmar Av. E&W | 25W-22S,24W-22S | 20 |
| Delrose St. N&S | 27W-21S | 19 |
| Demmond (Desmond) Ct. E&W | 22W-22S | 21 |
| Dennis Ct. E&W | 23W-24S | 29 |
| Des Plaines St. N&S | 24W-24S,24W-23S | 28 |
| Desmond (Demmond) Ct. E&W | 22W-22S | 21 |
| Devonshire Dr. NE&SW | 26W-22S | 20 |
| Dewey Av. N&S | 24W-24S | 28 |
| Dillman St. N&S | 23W-22S | 21 |
| Division St. E&W | 24W-23S | 20 |
| Dixon Av. N&S | 24W-23S | 20 |
| Dogwood Ct. E&W | 28W-23S | 19 |
| Donna St. N&S | 26W-23S | 20 |
| Donnie Ct. N&S | 25W-22S | 20 |
| Dora Av. N&S | 22W-22S | 21 |
| Doral Ct. E&W | 30W-21S | 18 |
| Doris Av. E&W | 23W-25S | 29 |
| Douglas St. E&W | 27W-23S,25W-23S | 19 |
| Dover St. E&W | 23W-23S | 21 |
| Draper Av. N&S | 22W-22S | 21 |
| Dunbar Ct. N&S | 30W-21S | 18 |
| Duncan St. E&W | 24W-24S | 28 |
| Dunmore St. N&S | 28W-21S | 19 |
| Dwight Av. N&S | 25W-24S | 28 |
| E. Bevan Dr. N&S | 26W-23S | 20 |
| E. Palladium Dr. N&S | 26W-23S | 20 |
| Eagle St. E&W | 22W-23S | 21 |
| Eaglewood Ct. E&W | 30W-21S | 18 |
| Earl Av. N&S | 25W-24S | 28 |
| Eastern Av. NE&SW | 23W-24S,23W-23S | 29 |
| Eastwood Ct. E&W | 30W-21S | 18 |
| Edgecreek Dr. E&W | 19W-23S | 22 |
| Edgehill St. N&S | 22W-22S | 21 |
| Edgerton Dr. N&S | 26W-22S | 20 |
| Edie Ln. N&S | 27W-23S | 19 |
| Edward St. E&W | 24W-25S | 28 |
| Elgin Av. E&W | 22W-23S | 21 |
| Elizabeth Ct. N&S | 26W-22S | 20 |
| Elizabeth St. N&S | 24W-22S | 20 |
| Ella Av. E&W | 23W-25S | 29 |
| Elm St. NE&SW | 23W-25S | 29 |
| Elmwood Av. E&W | 23W-24S | 29 |
| Elwood St. E&W | 23W-23S | 21 |
| Emery St. N&S | 26W-24S | 28 |
| Emmett St. NW&SE | 24W-24S | 28 |
| Empress Dr. N&S | 27W-27S,26W-27S | 27 |
| Englewood Av. N&S | 22W-22S | 21 |
| Erins Glen Dr. NW&SE | 29W-22S | 18 |
| Essington Rd. N&S | 28W-23S,28W-19S | 19 |
| Ewen Av. E&W | 23W-23S | 21 |
| Ewing St. E&W | 22W-22S | 21 |
| Executive Dr. E&W | 28W-22S | 19 |
| F. Pierce Dr. N&S | 32W-20S | 18 |
| Fairbanks N&S | 22W-23S | 21 |
| Fairchild Av. E&W | 22W-22S | 21 |
| Fairlane Dr. N&S | 27W-23S | 19 |
| Fairmont Av. N&S | 22W-22S | 21 |
| Fairview Av. N&S | 22W-22S | 21 |
| Fairway Dr. NW&SE | 27W-23S | 19 |
| Farragut Pl. E&W | 25W-23S | 20 |
| Ferris Pl. E&W | 26W-24S | 28 |
| Ferris St. NW&SE | 25W-24S | 28 |
| Fetz Av. NE&SW | 24W-23S | 20 |
| Fiday Rd. E&W | 28W-21S | 19 |
| Fiesta Dr. E&W | 21W-23S | 21 |
| Finn Ct. SW&NE | 29W-20S | 18 |
| Fitzpatrick Ct. N&S | 28W-21S | 19 |
| Flagar Ct. E&W | 29W-21S | 18 |

| | Grid | Page |
|---|---|---|
| Flanders Ct. E&W .. 29W-21S | | 18 |
| Floralwood Ct. E&W | | |
| .................. 30W-21S | | 18 |
| Florence Av. E&W .. 23W-24S | | 29 |
| Flowermeadow Ct. E&W | | |
| .................. 28W-22S | | 19 |
| Forest Grove Dr. E&W | | |
| .................. 30W-21S | | 18 |
| Foster Ct. E&W .. 29W-21S | | 18 |
| Fouser Ct. E&W .. 23W-24S | | 29 |
| Foxwood Ct. .. 30W-21S | | 18 |
| Francine Av. E&W .. 26W-24S | | 28 |
| Francis St. E&W | | |
| ......... 23W-22S,22W-22S | | 21 |
| Frank Av. E&W .. 24W-22S | | 20 |
| Frank Turk Dr. N&S | | |
| .................. 32W-20S | | 18 |
| Franklin St. N&S .. 23W-23S | | 21 |
| Fredrick St. N&S .. 25W-22S | | 20 |
| Fresno Ln. N&S .... 31W-20S | | 18 |
| Frontage Rd. N&S | | |
| ......... 28W-21S,28W-21S | | 18 |
| Fuller Av. N&S...... 22W-22S | | 21 |
| G.R. Ford Ct. NE&SW | | |
| .................. 32W-20S | | 18 |
| G.R. Ford Ln. NW&SE | | |
| .................. 32W-20S | | 18 |
| Gael Dr. N&S .... 27W-22S | | 19 |
| Gage Ct. NW&SE .. 22W-22S | | 21 |
| Gage St. N&S ...... 22W-22S | | 21 |
| Galway Rd. N&S .. 29W-22S | | 18 |
| Gardner St. N&S | | |
| ......... 23W-25S,23W-24S | | 29 |
| Garfield St. N&S .... 24W-23S | | 20 |
| Garland Ct. E&W .. 22W-22S | | 21 |
| Garnsey Av. N&S .. 23W-23S | | 21 |
| Garvin St. E&W .... 22W-22S | | 21 |
| George Av. N&S | | |
| ......... 27W-22S,26W-22S | | 19 |
| Georgia Av. NE&SW | | |
| .................. 25W-22S | | 20 |
| Gilson Ct. E&W .. 29W-21S | | 18 |
| Glen St. E&W ...... 22W-22S | | 21 |
| Gleneagle Dr. N&S .. 30W-21S | | 18 |
| Glens Course Ct. N&S | | |
| .................. 30W-21S | | 18 |
| Glenwood Av. E&W | | |
| ......... 27W-23S,24W-23S | | 19 |
| Glenwood Green Dr. E&W | | |
| .................. 26W-23S | | 20 |
| Godfrey Pl. E&W .. 23W-23S | | 21 |
| Goldhaber Ln. E&W | | |
| .................. 32W-20S | | 18 |
| Golfview Dr. NE&SW | | |
| .................. 27W-21S | | 19 |
| Goodhue St. NW&SE | | |
| ......... 30W-21S,29W-21S | | 18 |
| Gordon Pl. N&S .... 25W-23S | | 20 |
| Goss Ct. E&W ...... 29W-21S | | 18 |
| Gould St. N&S .... 22W-22S | | 21 |
| Grand Blvd. NE&SW | | |
| .................. 25W-24S | | 28 |
| Granite St. E&W .... 24W-22S | | 20 |
| Grant Av. E&W | | |
| ......... 23W-24S,22W-24S | | 29 |
| Graystone Dr. N&S | | |
| .................. 28W-21S | | 19 |
| Gross St. E&W .... 23W-22S | | 21 |
| Grover St. N&S .... 23W-24S | | 29 |
| H.S. Truman Dr. N&S | | |
| .................. 32W-20S | | 18 |
| Hacker Av. N&S .... 23W-22S | | 21 |
| Hague Ct. E&W .... 22W-22S | | 21 |
| Hague St. N&S .... 22W-22S | | 21 |
| Haldeman Av. NE&SW | | |
| .................. 25W-24S | | 28 |
| Hammes Av. N&S | | |
| ......... 26W-24S,26W-23S | | 28 |
| Hampton Ct. N&S .. 30W-21S | | 18 |
| Hannibal Dr. NS&EW | | |
| .................. 29W-20S | | 18 |
| Harbor Dr. NS&EW | | |
| .................. 28W-20S | | 19 |
| Harrison Av. N&S .. 23W-22S | | 21 |
| Harrogate Ln. E&W | | |
| .................. 26W-22S | | 20 |
| Harwood St. N&S .. 23W-22S | | 21 |
| Hawk Ct. E&W .. 29W-22S | | 18 |
| Hebbard Av. N&S .. 23W-22S | | 21 |
| Hebbard St. N&S .. 22W-22S | | 21 |
| Heiden Av. N&S .. 25W-22S | | 20 |
| Helles Av. E&W .. 24W-24S | | 28 |
| Henderson Av. N&S | | |
| ......... 23W-23S,23W-22S | | 21 |
| Hennepin Dr. N&S | | |
| ......... 28W-20S,27W-20S | | 19 |
| Hennessy Pl. N&S .. 27W-23S | | 19 |
| Henry St. N&S .. 23W-24S | | 29 |
| Heritage Dr. E&W .. 27W-23S | | 19 |
| Heritage Lakes Dr. E&W | | |
| .................. 27W-19S | | 13 |
| Herkimer St. N&S | | |
| ......... 23W-23S,23W-22S | | 21 |
| Hickory Creek Dr. NW&SE | | |
| .................. 19W-23S | | 22 |
| Hickory Grove Dr. E&W | | |
| .................. 30W-21S | | 18 |
| Hickory St. N&S | | |
| ......... 24W-24S,23W-24S | | 29 |
| High St. N&S .. 22W-22S | | 21 |
| Highland Av. N&S .. 25W-22S | | 20 |
| Higley Av. N&S .. 22W-24S | | 29 |
| Hill St. E&W ........ 23W-22S | | 21 |

| | Grid | Page |
|---|---|---|
| Hillside Rd. NW&SE | | |
| .................. 22W-24S | | 29 |
| Hintze Ct. E&W .... 27W-22S | | 19 |
| Hobbs Av. N&S .... 23W-24S | | 29 |
| Hobbs Dr. N&S .... 25W-22S | | 20 |
| Holly Berry Ct. N&S | | |
| .................. 26W-22S | | 20 |
| Holly Berry Dr. N&S | | |
| .................. 26W-22S | | 20 |
| Holly Ct. NE&SW .. 28W-20S | | 19 |
| Holmes Av. N&S....22W-22S | | 21 |
| Home St. E&W | | |
| ......... 23W-25S,22W-25S | | 29 |
| Homestead Pl. N&S | | |
| .................. 27W-23S | | 19 |
| Honeywood Ct. NE&SW | | |
| .................. 29W-21S | | 18 |
| Horseshoe Dr. NS&EW | | |
| .................. 25W-22S | | 20 |
| Hosmer St. N&S .... 25W-22S | | 20 |
| Houbolt St. N&S | | |
| ......... 28W-26S,28W-24S | | 27 |
| Hugh St. N&S .... 23W-23S | | 21 |
| Hunter Av. N&S .... 24W-24S | | 28 |
| Huntington Estates Dr. E&W | | |
| .................. 30W-21S | | 18 |
| Hutchins St. E&W | | |
| ......... 25W-22S,24W-22S | | 20 |
| Hyacinth Ct. NW&SE | | |
| .................. 30W-21S | | 18 |
| Hyde Park Av. N&S | | |
| .................. 24W-24S | | 28 |
| Ida St. N&S .... 25W-24S | | 28 |
| Illinois St. N&S .... 24W-24S | | 28 |
| Indian Wood Ln. E&W | | |
| .................. 28W-23S | | 19 |
| Indigo Ct. NE&SW .. 30W-21S | | 18 |
| Industry Ln. E&W .. 24W-22S | | 20 |
| Ingalls Av. E&W | | |
| ......... 23W-22S,24W-22S | | 19 |
| Interstate 55 N&S | | |
| ......... 29W-24S,28W-19S | | 26 |
| Interstate 80 NE&SW | | |
| ......... 29W-26S,23W-24S | | 26 |
| Inverness Cir. SE&NW | | |
| .................. 30W-21S | | 18 |
| Inwood Dr. NS&EW | | |
| .................. 27W-23S | | 19 |
| Iowa Av. N&S .... 23W-24S | | 29 |
| Irene Av. N&S .... 24W-24S | | 28 |
| Iroquois St. N&S .... 22W-25S | | 29 |
| Irvine Ln. N&S .... 30W-21S | | 18 |
| Irving St. E&W .... 23W-23S | | 21 |
| Ivy Pl. E&W ...... 26W-24S | | 28 |
| Ivy St. N&S ...... 24W-24S | | 28 |
| J. Buchanan Ln. N&S | | |
| .................. 32W-20S | | 18 |
| J.F. Kennedy Dr. N&S | | |
| .................. 32W-20S | | 18 |
| J.K. Polk Dr. E&W .. 32W-20S | | 18 |
| Jackson St. E&W | | |
| ......... 23W-23S,22W-23S | | 21 |
| Jaguar St. E&W .... 28W-22S | | 19 |
| Jane Ct. NW&SE .. 28W-22S | | 19 |
| Jasper St. E&W | | |
| ......... 25W-24S,24W-24S | | 28 |
| Jefferson St. E&W | | |
| ......... 29W-24S,23W-23S | | 26 |
| Jeffery Dr. E&W | | |
| ......... 28W-23S,27W-23S | | 19 |
| Jerald Dr. NE&SW .. 28W-25S | | 27 |
| Jerome Av. E&W .. 23W-23S | | 21 |
| Jersey St. E&W .... 24W-23S | | 20 |
| Joe Adler Dr. N&S .. 32W-20S | | 18 |
| John Bourg Dr. N&S | | |
| .................. 32W-20S | | 18 |
| John St. E&W | | |
| ......... 26W-23S,24W-23S | | 20 |
| Joliet St. N&S | | |
| ......... 24W-25S,24W-23S | | 28 |
| Jonathon Simpson Dr. E&W | | |
| .................. 28W-22S | | 19 |
| Jones St. E&W | | |
| ......... 26W-23S,25W-23S | | 20 |
| Joyce Rd. N&S .. 26W-24S | | 28 |
| Judy Dr. NW&SE .. 28W-22S | | 19 |
| Julia St. NW&SE .. 22W-24S | | 29 |
| June St. N&S .... 25W-22S | | 20 |
| Junie Ct. N&S .... 25W-22S | | 20 |
| Junior College Dr., N. E&W | | |
| .................. 28W-25S | | 27 |
| Junior College Dr., S. E&W | | |
| .................. 28W-25S | | 27 |
| Juniper Av. E&W .. 28W-22S | | 19 |
| Juniper St. E&W .... 22W-22S | | 21 |
| Karen Ct. E&W .. 28W-25S | | 27 |
| Karen Dr. NE&SW .. 28W-25S | | 27 |
| Kathlyn Pl. N&S .. 26W-24S | | 28 |
| Katie Ct. N&S .... 27W-21S | | 19 |
| Kelly Av. N&S .... 24W-22S | | 20 |
| Kenilworth Av. N&S | | |
| .................. 25W-22S | | 20 |
| Kenmore Dr. E&W .. 25W-22S | | 20 |
| Kensington Estates Dr. | | |
| .................. 30W-21S | | 18 |
| Kerry Ln. NW&SE .. 29W-22S | | 18 |
| Key Ct. N&S .... 27W-23S | | 19 |
| Kiep St. N&S .... 24W-24S | | 28 |
| Kingsbury Estates Dr. | | |
| NS&EW........ 30W-21S | | 18 |
| Kingswood Ct. NE&SW | | |
| .................. 28W-23S | | 19 |
| Kinsey Av. N&S .... 25W-24S | | 28 |
| Klinger Ln. E&W .. 32W-20S | | 18 |

| | Grid | Page |
|---|---|---|
| Knowlton Av. E&W .. 23W-23S | | 21 |
| Knox Pl. N&S .... 25W-23S | | 20 |
| Krakar Av. N&S .. 22W-23S | | 21 |
| Krings Ln. N&S .. 26W-22S | | 20 |
| Kronmeyer Av. E&W | | |
| ......... 23W-22S | | 21 |
| Kungs Way N&S .. 27W-23S | | 19 |
| Labrecque Dr. N&S | | |
| .................. 32W-20S | | 18 |
| Lafayette St. E&W .. 24W-24S | | 28 |
| Lakegrove Dr. N&S | | |
| .................. 30W-21S | | 18 |
| Lakelawn St. N&S .. 29W-23S | | 20 |
| Lakeside Cir. EW&NS | | |
| .................. 28W-20S | | 19 |
| Lakeview E&W .... 27W-19S | | 13 |
| Lakeview E&W .... 28W-24S | | 28 |
| Lakewook Dr. N&S | | |
| .................. 28W-22S | | 19 |
| Lambert St. N&S .. 23W-22S | | 21 |
| Lambeth Ln. N&S .. 19W-22S | | 22 |
| Landau Av. N&S .. 23W-23S | | 21 |
| Langsford Ln. E&W | | |
| .................. 32W-20S | | 18 |
| Larkin Av. N&S | | |
| ......... 26W-24S,26W-22S | | 28 |
| Laurel Av. N&S .. 24W-24S | | 28 |
| Lavinia Ln. N&S .. 26W-23S | | 20 |
| Lawrence Av. .24W-22S | | 20 |
| Lawton Av. NE&SW | | |
| .................. 24W-25S | | 28 |
| Leach N&S ...... 22W-23S | | 21 |
| Leawood Ct. NE&SW | | |
| .................. 28W-25S | | 27 |
| Leawood Dr. N&S .. 28W-25S | | 27 |
| Leckrone Dr. N&S .. 32W-20S | | 18 |
| Legacy Dr. N&S .. 27W-19S | | 13 |
| Lehman St. N&S ...23W-24S | | 29 |
| Lemore Av. E&W .. 25W-22S | | 20 |
| Lemorr Av. N&S .. 25W-22S | | 20 |
| Leopold Ln. E&W .. 32W-20S | | 18 |
| Lexington Dr. NE&SW | | |
| .................. 32W-20S | | 18 |
| Liberty St. E&W .. 23W-23S | | 21 |
| Lilac Ln. N&S .... 26W-22S | | 20 |
| Lime St. NW&SE .. 24W-23S | | 20 |
| Lincoln Av. E&W ...23W-24S | | 29 |
| Linden Av. E&W .. 23W-24S | | 29 |
| Lindsay Ct. N&S .. 28W-22S | | 19 |
| Linne Av. N&S......23W-25S | | 29 |
| Little Big Horn Dr. E&W | | |
| .................. 27W-21S | | 19 |
| Lloyds Av. N&S .. 23W-22S | | 21 |
| Lobella Ct. E&W ...30W-21S | | 18 |
| Lobella Ln. EW&NS | | |
| .................. 30W-21S | | 18 |
| Logan Av. N&S .. 22W-24S | | 29 |
| Lois Pl. N&S | | |
| ......... 26W-23S,26W-22S | | 20 |
| Longford Dr. NW&SE | | |
| .................. 28W-25S | | 27 |
| Longwood Dr. N&S | | |
| ......... 21W-23S,21W-22S | | 21 |
| Loral Av. E&W .... 25W-22S | | 20 |
| Loren Dr. N&S .... 28W-25S | | 27 |
| Loretta Av. NE&SW | | |
| .................. 25W-22S | | 20 |
| Louis Ct. N&S .... 23W-23S | | 21 |
| Louise Ln. N&S .. 28W-25S | | 27 |
| Lucas St. E&W .. 24W-24S | | 28 |
| Lucie Dr. N&S .... 29W-24S | | 26 |
| Luther Av. N&S .. 22W-22S | | 21 |
| M. Hershman Dr. N&S | | |
| .................. 28W-21S | | 19 |
| Mack St. N&S......25W-23S | | 20 |
| Macomber St. N&S | | |
| .................. 23W-24S | | 29 |
| Madeline St. E&W .. 24W-24S | | 28 |
| Madison St. N&S .. 25W-24S | | 28 |
| Madonna Av. NE&SW | | |
| .................. 26W-24S | | 28 |
| Magnolia Av. N&S .. 22W-22S | | 21 |
| Magnolia Dr. N&S .. 27W-22S | | 19 |
| Mall Loop Dr. E&W | | |
| .................. 28W-20S | | 19 |
| Mallard Ln. E&W .. 29W-22S | | 18 |
| Manor Av. N&S .. 25W-24S | | 28 |
| Manor Ct. N&S...... 25W-24S | | 28 |
| Maple Rd. NE&SW .. 22W-23S | | 21 |
| Maple St. N&S .... 23W-23S | | 21 |
| Marble St. NW&SE .. 24W-23S | | 20 |
| Margaret St. N&S .. 26W-24S | | 28 |
| Marion St. E&W | | |
| ......... 25W-24S,23W-24S | | 28 |
| Market St. N&S .... 24W-24S | | 28 |
| Marmion Av. NE&SW | | |
| .................. 26W-24S | | 28 |
| Marquette Ct. NW&SE | | |
| .................. 25W-23S | | 20 |
| Marquette Rd. NS&EW | | |
| ......... 26W-23S,25W-23S | | 20 |
| Maserati Dr. NW&SE | | |
| .................. 27W-21S | | 19 |
| Mason Av. E&W | | |
| ......... 28W-23S,24W-23S | | 19 |
| Massachusetts Av. NE&SW | | |
| .................. 25W-22S | | 20 |
| Maude Av. N&S .. 23W-24S | | 29 |
| May St. N&S | | |
| ......... 25W-24S,25W-22S | | 28 |
| Mayfield St. N&S | | |
| ......... 26W-23S,25W-23S | | 20 |
| McDonald Av. N&S | | |
| .................. 29W-24S | | 26 |

| | Grid | Page |
|---|---|---|
| McDonough St. E&W | | |
| ......... 28W-24S,24W-24S | | 27 |
| McFarlane Dr. E&W | | |
| .................. 26W-22S | | 20 |
| McKay St. N&S .... 22W-22S | | 21 |
| McKinley Av. N&S .. 24W-25S | | 28 |
| McRoberts St. N&S | | |
| .................. 23W-23S | | 21 |
| Meadowwood Dr. N&S | | |
| .................. 28W-23S | | 19 |
| Meath Dr. N&S .. 28W-21S | | 19 |
| Meda Av. N&S .. 23W-24S | | 29 |
| Meeker Av. E&W | | |
| ......... 23W-22S,22W-22S | | 21 |
| Melchoir Ct. N&S .. 23W-24S | | 29 |
| Memenas Pl. E&W...24W-24S | | 28 |
| Menlo Ct. N&S .. 28W-25S | | 27 |
| Metcalf St. E&W....29W-21S | | 18 |
| Michigan St. N&S .. 23W-23S | | 21 |
| Midhurst Ct. E&W .. 26W-22S | | 20 |
| Midhurst Ln. NE&SW | | |
| .................. 26W-22S | | 20 |
| Midland Ct. E&W .. 23W-24S | | 29 |
| Midland St. E&W .. 25W-24S | | 28 |
| Midland St. N&S | | |
| ......... 25W-24S,25W-22S | | 28 |
| Miles Av. N&S .... 23W-24S | | 29 |
| Millboro St. N&S .. 25W-24S | | 28 |
| Miller Av. .... 23W-24S | | 29 |
| Mills Rd. E&W | | |
| ......... 23W-25S,22W-25S | | 29 |
| Mississippi Av. N&S | | |
| .................. 23W-24S | | 29 |
| Montclair Ct. N&S .. 27W-19S | | 13 |
| Monterey Dr. N&S .. 31W-20S | | 18 |
| Moran St. E&W | | |
| ......... 25W-22S,24W-22S | | 20 |
| Morgan St. N&S | | |
| ......... 25W-24S,24W-24S | | 28 |
| Morningstar Ln. E&W | | |
| .................. 32W-20S | | 18 |
| Morris St. N&S .. 26W-24S | | 28 |
| Mosby Ct. N&S .. 28W-25S | | 27 |
| Mound Rd. N&S | | |
| ......... 29W-26S,27W-25S | | 26 |
| Mound St. N&S .. 23W-24S | | 29 |
| Mulberry Rd. E&W .. 21W-22S | | 21 |
| Mulford Ln. N&S...28W-25S | | 27 |
| Munroe St. N&S .. 24W-24S | | 28 |
| Nancy Vallela Ln. E&W | | |
| .................. 27W-23S | | 19 |
| Natoma Ct. N&S .. 28W-25S | | 27 |
| Neal Av. N&S .. 23W-25S | | 29 |
| Nellis Dr. N&S .. 32W-20S | | 18 |
| Newport Dr. N&S .. 28W-21S | | 19 |
| Newton St. N&S...23W-24S | | 29 |
| Nicholson St. N&S | | |
| ......... 24W-23S,24W-22S | | 20 |
| Nixon Ln. E&W .. 32W-20S | | 18 |
| Norley Ln. N&S .. 25W-22S | | 20 |
| Norley Dr. N&S .. 26W-22S | | 20 |
| Norman Av. NE&SW | | |
| .................. 28W-19S | | 19 |
| Normandy St. E&W | | |
| .................. 28W-20S | | 19 |
| North Av. N&S .. 25W-22S | | 20 |
| Northlake Ct. N&S .. 27W-19S | | 13 |
| Norton Av. E&W .. 23W-23S | | 21 |
| Notre Dame Av. N&S | | |
| .................. 26W-24S | | 28 |
| O'Donahue Dr. E&W | | |
| .................. 29W-22S | | 19 |
| O'Leary Dr. N&S .. 29W-22S | | 19 |
| O'Niel St. N&S .. 25W-24S | | 28 |
| O'Sullivan Dr. E&W | | |
| .................. 29W-22S | | 19 |
| Oak Leaf St. E&W .. 26W-24S | | 28 |
| Oakdale Estates Dr. N&S | | |
| .................. 30W-21S | | 18 |
| Oakland Av. N&S | | |
| ......... 24W-23S,24W-22S | | 20 |
| Oakley Av. N&S .. 25W-24S | | 28 |
| Oakview Av. N&S .. 22W-24S | | 29 |
| Oakwood Dr. E&W .. 28W-22S | | 19 |
| Odell St. NS&EW .. 23W-24S | | 29 |
| Ohio St. N&S .... 23W-23S | | 21 |
| Old Castle Rd. E&W | | |
| .................. 28W-21S | | 19 |
| Old Meadow Ct. E&W | | |
| .................. 29W-21S | | 18 |
| Olde Mill Rd. N&S .. 30W-21S | | 18 |
| Ole Farm Rd. NE&SW | | |
| .................. 29W-21S | | 18 |
| Olive Pl. E&W......23W-23S | | 21 |
| Oneida St. E&W | | |
| ......... 26W-23S,24W-23S | | 20 |
| Orchard Av. .. 26W-22S | | 20 |
| Oregon Av. NE&SW | | |
| .................. 25W-22S | | 20 |
| Orion Ln. N&S......29W-21S | | 18 |
| Osgood St. . 23W-24S | | 29 |
| Ottawa St. N&S | | |
| ......... 24W-24S,24W-23S | | 28 |
| Overlook Dr. N&S .. 28W-21S | | 19 |
| Page Av. N&S......22W-23S | | 21 |
| Pamela Ct. NE&SW | | |
| .................. 28W-23S | | 19 |
| Pandola Av. E&W .. 28W-22S | | 19 |
| Park Ct. E&W...... 25W-24S | | 28 |
| Park Dr. N&S .... 25W-24S | | 28 |
| Parks Av. N&S .. 23W-23S | | 21 |
| Parkview Av. N&S ...25W-24S | | 28 |
| Parkwood Ct. E&W | | |
| .................. 21W-22S | | 21 |

| | Grid | Page |
|---|---|---|
| Parkwood Dr. N&S | | |
| ......... 21W-23S,21W-22S | | 21 |
| Peacock Ln. NS&EW | | |
| .................. 29W-22S | | 18 |
| Pearl St. N&S .... 24W-23S | | 20 |
| Pearson Dr. N&S .. 26W-22S | | 20 |
| Pebble Beach Dr. N&S | | |
| .................. 30W-21S | | 18 |
| Pembrook Ct. N&S .. 30W-21S | | 18 |
| Pennsylvania Av. NE&SW | | |
| .................. 25W-22S | | 20 |
| Pequot St. N&S .. 22W-25S | | 29 |
| Peyla Ln. E&W .... 32W-20S | | 18 |
| Pheasant Landing Dr. N&S | | |
| .................. 29W-22S | | 18 |
| Pine St. NE&SW....24W-23S | | 20 |
| Pioneer Ct. E&W .. 28W-25S | | 27 |
| Plainfield Rd. NW&SE | | |
| ......... 28W-19S,24W-23S | | 13 |
| Plaza Dr. N&S......25W-22S | | 20 |
| Pleasant Knoll Dr. N&S | | |
| .................. 27W-22S | | 19 |
| Pleasant St. N&S .. 24W-24S | | 28 |
| Ponderosa Ct. N&S | | |
| .................. 28W-23S | | 19 |
| Poplar Av. N&S .. 23W-24S | | 29 |
| Portside Lakes Ct. N&S | | |
| .................. 30W-21S | | 18 |
| Prairie Av. N&S | | |
| ......... 25W-24S,25W-22S | | 28 |
| Prairie Trail Ct. N&S | | |
| .................. 30W-21S | | 18 |
| Pratt Ct. E&W......29W-21S | | 18 |
| Prestige St. N&S .. 27W-23S | | 19 |
| Preston Lakes Ct. N&S | | |
| .................. 30W-21S | | 18 |
| Preston Pl. N&S .. 22W-24S | | 29 |
| Prestwick Cir. E&W | | |
| .................. 30W-21S | | 18 |
| Price Ct. E&W .. 28W-25S | | 27 |
| Prieboy Av. E&W .. 28W-20S | | 19 |
| Primrose Dr. N&S .. 30W-21S | | 18 |
| Prior St. E&W .... 24W-24S | | 28 |
| Prospect Pl. NE&SW | | |
| .................. 25W-24S | | 28 |
| Purdue Ct. N&S .. 26W-24S | | 28 |
| Putter Ct. NE&SW .. 27W-23S | | 19 |
| Quail Dr. N&S .... 29W-22S | | 18 |
| Quincy Ct. E&W .. 28W-25S | | 27 |
| R.B. Hayes Ln. E&W | | |
| .................. 32W-20S | | 18 |
| Railroad St. NE&SW | | |
| .................. 24W-24S | | 28 |
| Randy Rd. E&W .. 28W-23S | | 19 |
| Raub St. N&S .... 24W-23S | | 20 |
| Raymond St. N&S .. 28W-22S | | 19 |
| Raynor Av. N&S | | |
| ......... 25W-24S,25W-22S | | 28 |
| Rebbeca Rd. N&S .. 27W-23S | | 19 |
| Redwood Dr. N&S .. 25W-24S | | 28 |
| Reed St. N&S | | |
| ......... 25W-24S,25W-23S | | 28 |
| Reeves Rd. NE&SW | | |
| .................. 27W-26S | | 27 |
| Regency Ridge Dr. E&W | | |
| .................. 25W-24S | | 28 |
| Reichman St. E&W .. 23W-24S | | 29 |
| Reid St. E&W .. 23W-22S | | 21 |
| Republic Av. N&S .. 26W-23S | | 20 |
| Richards St. N&S | | |
| ......... 23W-25S,23W-24S | | 29 |
| Richmond Cir. E&W | | |
| .................. 26W-23S | | 20 |
| Richmond St. E&W | | |
| ......... 27W-23S,24W-23S | | 19 |
| Rick St. N&S .... 28W-22S | | 19 |
| Ridgefield Ct. N&S ...27W-19S | | 13 |
| Ridgemont Av. NW&SE | | |
| .................. 22W-22S | | 21 |
| Ridgewood Av. E&W | | |
| .................. 22W-23S | | 21 |
| Ring Rd. EW&NS .. 28W-20S | | 19 |
| River Glen Dr. E&W | | |
| .................. 29W-22S | | 19 |
| River Rd. N&S......31W-22S | | 18 |
| River St. N&S | | |
| ......... 25W-24S,24W-24S | | 28 |
| Riverboat Blvd. E&W | | |
| .................. 28W-25S | | 27 |
| Riverboat Ct. SW&NE | | |
| .................. 28W-25S | | 27 |
| Riverboat Dr. N&S .. 28W-25S | | 27 |
| Riverside Dr. NW&SE | | |
| .................. 29W-31S | | 34 |
| Rivertowne Ct. E&W | | |
| .................. 29W-21S | | 19 |
| Rivertowne Dr. NS&EW | | |
| .................. 29W-21S | | 19 |
| Riverview Dr. N&S .. 29W-22S | | 19 |
| Riverwalk Dr. NS&EW | | |
| .................. 29W-20S | | 18 |
| Robert Ct. N&S .. 28W-23S | | 19 |
| Robin Ln. E&W .. 22W-22S | | 21 |
| Rock Creek Blvd. NS&EW | | |
| ......... 28W-26S,28W-25S | | 27 |
| Rock Run Dr. E&W | | |
| ......... 29W-24S,28W-24S | | 26 |
| Rogina Ct. E&W .. 25W-24S | | 28 |
| Romayne Av. .26W-24S | | 28 |
| Ronnie Ct. N&S .. 23W-24S | | 29 |
| Rooney Av. N&S .. 27W-22S | | 19 |
| Roosevelt Av. E&W | | |
| .................. 25W-22S | | 20 |

| | Grid | Page |
|---|---|---|
| Rosemont Dr. E&W | 28W-23S | 19 |
| Rosemont Rd. E&W | 27W-23S | 19 |
| Ross St. E&W | 28W-22S,24W-22S | 20 |
| Rossiter Ct. E&W | 29W-21S | 18 |
| Rossiter Pkwy. N&S | 29W-21S | 18 |
| Route 53 N&S | 24W-25S,24W-22S | 28 |
| Route 59 N&S | 30W-22S,30W-21S | 18 |
| Route 7 N&S | 26W-24S,26W-22S | 28 |
| Royce Av. N&S | 23W-22S | 21 |
| Ruby St. E&W | 24W-22S,23W-22S | 20 |
| Russell St. E&W | 24W-22S | 20 |
| Ruth-Fitzgerald Dr. N&S | 32W-20S | 18 |
| Ryehill Dr. NS&EW | 29W-22S | 18 |
| Saint Joseph Av. N&S | 26W-24S | 28 |
| Saint Louis St. N&S | 23W-24S | 29 |
| Salem Dr. N&S | 25W-24S | 28 |
| San Mateo Dr. N&S | 31W-20S | 18 |
| Sanborn Cir. NW&SE | 29W-21S | 18 |
| Sanora Ct. E&W | 31W-20S | 18 |
| Schriber St. E&W | 25W-22S | 20 |
| Scott St. N&S | 23W-23S | 21 |
| Scribner St. N&S | 22W-23S | 21 |
| Sequoia Ct. E&W | 31W-20S | 18 |
| Sergeant Ln. N&S | 29W-21S | 18 |
| Sesser St. N&S | 24W-24S | 28 |
| Shannon Ct. E&W | 28W-20S | 19 |
| Sharon St. NW&SE | 28W-22S | 19 |
| Sheila Dr. N&S | 27W-22S | 19 |
| Shelby St. E&W | 24W-24S | 28 |
| Sheridan St. E&W | 24W-24S | 28 |
| Sherman Ct. E&W | 23W-24S | 29 |
| Sherman St. N&S | 23W-24S | 29 |
| Sherwood Pl. E&W | 25W-23S | 20 |
| Shiloh St. E&W | 28W-25S | 27 |
| Siegmund St. N&S | 22W-24S | 29 |
| Skylark Ln. E&W | 29W-22S | 18 |
| Smith Av. N&S | 24W-22S | 20 |
| Somerset St. N&S | 19W-22S | 22 |
| Somme Ct. NW&SE | 27W-21S | 19 |
| Somme St. NW&SE | 27W-21S | 19 |
| Sonny Ln. N&S | 26W-22S | 20 |
| Sonoma Ct. E&W | 31W-20S | 18 |
| Sonoma Dr. NS&EW | 31W-20S | 18 |
| South St. E&W | 24W-24S | 28 |
| Spring St. E&W | 24W-23S | 20 |
| Springfield Av. N&S | 26W-23S | 20 |
| Squirrel St. N&S | 22W-23S | 21 |
| St. Andrews EW&NS | 30W-21S | 18 |
| St. Francis Av. E&W | 26W-24S | 28 |
| St. Jude Av. NE&SW | 26W-24S | 28 |
| Stadium Dr. N&S | 27W-23S | 19 |
| Star Ln. N&S | 27W-23S | 19 |
| State St. N&S | 23W-23S | 21 |
| Stateville Rd. E&W | 27W-20S | 19 |
| Stefani St. NE&SW | 19W-23S | 22 |
| Steven Smith St. N&S | 28W-22S | 19 |
| Stevens Av. NE&SW | 22W-23S | 21 |
| Stirling St. E&W | 22W-23S | 21 |
| Stone St. NW&SE | 24W-23S | 20 |
| Stonehaven Dr. NW&SE | 30W-21S | 18 |
| Stonehurst St. E&W | 28W-25S | 27 |
| Stratford Ct. NS&EW | 26W-23S,25W-23S | 20 |
| Strong Av. E&W | 23W-24S | 29 |
| Stryker Av. N&S | 25W-24S,25W-23S | 28 |
| Summit St. N&S | 24W-23S,24W-22S | 20 |
| Sunrise Ct. E&W | 27W-19S | 13 |
| Sunset Ct. N&S | 27W-19S | 13 |
| Sunset Ridge Dr. E&W | 29W-21S | 18 |
| Sunset Strip N&S | 27W-23S | 19 |
| Surrey Ct. NE&SW | 28W-25S | 27 |
| Susan St. N&S | 28W-22S | 19 |
| Sussex Rd. E&W | 32W-21S | 18 |
| Swan Ct. E&W | 29W-22S | 18 |
| Swing St. NW&SE | 27W-23S | 19 |
| T. Hickey St. E&W | 28W-21S,27W-21S | 19 |
| Tamarack Dr. E&W | 21W-23S | 21 |
| Tana St. N&S | 27W-23S | 19 |
| Taney Butler N&S | 24W-24S | 28 |
| Tara Ct. NW&SE | 29W-22S | 18 |
| Taylor St. E&W | 26W-23S,24W-23S | 20 |
| Terrace Av. NE&SW | 26W-23S | 20 |
| Terrence Ferry Dr. E&W | 28W-22S | 19 |
| Terry Dr. N&S | 27W-26S,27W-23S | 27 |
| Texas Av. NE&SW | 25W-22S | 20 |
| Theodore St. N&S | 32W-21S,27W-21S | 18 |
| Timber Oaks Dr. N&S | 28W-23S | 19 |
| Timbercrest Dr. NW&SE | 28W-23S | 19 |
| Tonti NE&SW | 28W-20S,27W-20S | 19 |
| Torwood Cir. NW&SE | 30W-21S | 18 |
| Traymore Dr. E&W | 28W-22S | 19 |
| Turnberry Cir. E&W | 30W-21S | 18 |
| Twain Ct. E&W | 29W-20S | 18 |
| Twin Lakes Ct. NW&SE | 30W-21S | 18 |
| Twin Lakes Dr. NE&SW | 30W-21S | 18 |
| Twin Oaks Dr. NS&EW | 28W-23S,27W-23S | 19 |
| U.S. Route 30 NW&SE | 27W-20S,22W-23S | 19 |
| U.S. Route 52 E&W | 29W-24S,24W-24S | 26 |
| U.S. Route 6 NE&SW | 28W-27S,28W-23S | 27 |
| Union St. N&S | 23W-24S | 29 |
| Vail Ct. E&W | 19W-22S | 22 |
| Valley Av. N&S | 23W-22S | 21 |
| Valley Forge Dr. E&W | 27W-21S | 19 |
| Van Buren St. E&W | 24W-23S,23W-23S | 20 |
| Ventura Ct. E&W | 31W-20S | 18 |
| Ventura Dr. NS&EW | 31W-20S | 18 |
| Verdun Dr. E&W | 27W-21S | 19 |
| Vermette St. E&W | 30W-21S,29W-21S | 18 |
| Vernon Av. E&W | 25W-22S,24W-22S | 20 |
| Victoria Lakes Ct. N&S | 30W-21S | 18 |
| Victoria Lakes Dr. N&S | 30W-21S | 18 |
| Vimy Ridge Dr. E&W | 27W-21S | 19 |
| Vine St. N&S | 24W-23S | 20 |
| Vintage Dr. N&S | 28W-22S | 19 |
| Virginia St. E&W | 23W-23S,22W-23S | 21 |
| Virgo Ln. N&S | 29W-21S | 18 |
| Vonesch Rd. NE&SW | 28W-20S,28W-19S | 19 |
| Voyager Dr. NE&SW | 27W-20S | 19 |
| W. Allen St. E&W | 26W-24S | 28 |
| W. Bevan Dr. N&S | 26W-23S | 20 |
| W. Palladium Dr. N&S | 26W-23S | 20 |
| W. Park Av. NE&SW | 25W-24S | 28 |
| W. Parkfront St. E&W | 25W-24S | 28 |
| Wabash Av. N&S | 23W-22S | 21 |
| Wagner Av. N&S | 25W-22S | 20 |
| Wake Island Dr. NE&SW | 27W-21S | 19 |
| Wallace St. E&W | 24W-24S | 28 |
| Walnut St. NW&SE | 22W-23S | 21 |
| Walsh Av. N&S | 24W-23S | 20 |
| Walsh Way E&W | 27W-23S | 19 |
| Ward Av. E&W | 23W-23S | 21 |
| Washington St. E&W | 23W-24S,22W-24S | 29 |
| Water St. N&S | 24W-25S,24W-24S | 28 |
| Waterford Dr. N&S | 28W-21S | 19 |
| Wattles Ct. E&W | 29W-21S | 18 |
| Waverly St. N&S | 25W-22S | 20 |
| Webster Av. NW&SE | 26W-24S | 28 |
| Webster St. N&S | 24W-23S,23W-23S | 20 |
| Wee Ct. E&W | 22W-23S | 21 |
| Wenberg St. E&W | 22W-23S | 21 |
| Wesmere Lakes Ct. N&S | 30W-21S | 18 |
| Wesmere Lakes Dr. N&S | 30W-21S | 18 |
| West Acres Rd. E&W | 28W-23S,25W-23S | 20 |
| West Ridge Rd. NE&SW | 28W-23S | 19 |
| Western Av. E&W | 25W-23S,24W-23S | 20 |
| Westfield Rd. E&W | 28W-22S | 19 |
| Westhill Cir. SE&NW | 30W-21S | 18 |
| Westmere Dr. E&W | 30W-21S | 19 |
| Westmere Pkwy. N&S | 30W-21S | 18 |
| Westminister Rd. N&S | 26W-23S,26W-22S | 20 |
| Westmore Grove Ct. E&W | 30W-21S | 18 |
| Westmore Grove Dr. N&S | 30W-21S | 18 |
| Westport Dr. N&S | 28W-23S | 19 |
| Westshire Dr. E&W | 25W-23S,25W-22S | 20 |
| Westwood Av. E&W | 25W-24S | 28 |
| Wexford Ln. E&W | 28W-21S | 19 |
| Whalen Ln E&W | 32W-20S | 18 |
| Wheeler Av. N&S | 25W-24S | 28 |
| White Av. N&S | 22W-24S | 29 |
| Whitegate Rd. E&W | 28W-21S | 19 |
| Whitley Av. E&W | 23W-24S | 29 |
| Whitney Av. NW&SE | 24W-23S | 20 |
| Whittier Av. N&S | 24W-23S | 20 |
| Wilcox St. N&S | 24W-24S,24W-22S | 28 |
| Wild Oaks Ct. E&W | 28W-23S | 19 |
| Wildwood Dr. NE&SW | 28W-23S | 19 |
| Willard St. N&S | 23W-23S | 21 |
| William St. N&S | 25W-24S,25W-22S | 28 |
| Williamson Av. N&S | 23W-22S,22W-22S | 21 |
| Willow Av. N&S | 24W-24S | 28 |
| Willow Lakes Ct. N&S | 30W-21S | 18 |
| Willow Lakes Dr. NS&EW | 30W-21S | 18 |
| Wilson Av. N&S | 23W-24S | 29 |
| Winding Lakes Dr. NS&EW | 30W-21S | 18 |
| Windsor Ln. E&W | 28W-25S | 27 |
| Winston Av. NE&SW | 23W-24S | 29 |
| Winthrop Av. N&S | 26W-22S | 20 |
| Wisconsin St. N&S | 22W-22S | 21 |
| Woodford Dr. E&W | 28W-21S | 19 |
| Woodhill St. N&S | 29W-21S | 19 |
| Woodland Ct. NE&SW | 25W-24S | 28 |
| Woodland Dr. NE&SW | 25W-24S | 28 |
| Woodlawn Av. N&S | 25W-23S | 20 |
| Woodruff Rd. E&W | 23W-22S,22W-22S | 21 |
| Woods Av. E&W | 25W-24S | 28 |
| Woodward Av. NS&EW | 22W-22S | 21 |
| Woodworth Av. N&S | 24W-23S | 20 |
| Workman Av. E&W | 24W-24S | 28 |
| Wyndham Lakes Ct. E&W | 30W-21S | 18 |
| Wyoming Av. N&S | 25W-22S | 20 |
| York Av. N&S | 23W-24S | 29 |
| Youngs Av. N&S | 23W-23S | 21 |
| 1st Av. E&W | 23W-24S,22W-24S | 29 |
| 2nd Av. E&W | 23W-24S,22W-24S | 29 |
| 3rd Av. E&W | 23W-24S,22W-24S | 29 |
| 4th Av. E&W | 23W-24S | 29 |
| 5th Av. E&W | 23W-24S | 29 |

## Joliet Township

| | Grid | Page |
|---|---|---|
| Adelia Av. N&S | 22W-24S | 29 |
| Alessio Dr. E&W | 23W-25S | 29 |
| Algonquin St. N&S | 21W-23S | 21 |
| Anderson Av. N&S | 21W-25S | 29 |
| Argyle Av. N&S | 21W-24S,21W-23S | 29 |
| Ashley St. N&S | 21W-24S | 29 |
| Aspen Dr. NW&SE | 21W-26S | 29 |
| Barr Elms Av. N&S | 21W-24S | 29 |
| Bartel Rd. N&S | 21W-25S | 29 |
| Bates Rd. NW&SE | 23W-25S | 29 |
| Belmont Av. N&S | 21W-23S | 21 |
| Berkley Av. N&S | 21W-24S | 29 |
| Beverly St. N&S | 24W-26S | 28 |
| Blackhawk St. N&S | 21W-23S | 21 |
| Bond Rd. NE&SW | 21W-23S | 21 |
| Bradford Rd. E&W | 23W-26S | 29 |
| Brandon Rd. N&S | 25W-27S,25W-25S | 28 |
| Breen St. N&S | 24W-25S | 28 |
| Briggs St. N&S | 22W-26S,22W-23S | 29 |
| Brookside Dr. E&W | 23W-25S | 29 |
| Brown Av. E&W | 23W-23S | 21 |
| Buffalo St. N&S | 22W-25S | 29 |
| Burger Av. N&S | 22W-25S | 29 |
| Burke Dr. N&S | 21W-24S | 29 |
| Caledonian St. N&S | 21W-24S,21W-23S | 29 |
| Camilla St. E&W | 24W-26S | 28 |
| Carey St. E&W | 21W-25S | 29 |
| Caroline Av. N&S | 22W-26S | 29 |
| Carriage Ln. N&S | 23W-26S | 29 |
| Cayuga St. N&S | 21W-23S | 21 |
| Cecelia Av. N&S | 24W-26S,24W-25S | 28 |
| Champlain Av. E&W | 24W-25S | 28 |
| Champlain St. N&S | 24W-25S | 28 |
| Channahon Rd. NE&SW | 26W-25S,25W-25S | 28 |
| Charity Av. NE&SW | 24W-25S | 29 |
| Charles St. N&S | 24W-26S | 29 |
| Cherry Hill Rd. N&S | 21W-27S,21W-23S | 29 |
| Cherry Ln. NE&SW | 23W-25S | 29 |
| Chicago St. N&S | 23W-26S,23W-25S | 29 |
| Clairmont Av. N&S | 21W-24S,21W-23S | 29 |
| Cleveland Av. E&W | 21W-25S | 21 |
| Commonwealth Av. E&W | 22W-26S | 29 |
| Copperfield Av. E&W | 21W-23S | 21 |
| Cornelius St. N&S | 21W-25S | 29 |
| Crestwood Dr. E&W | 21W-23S | 21 |
| Dallas Pl. NE&SW | 23W-26S | 29 |
| David Av. E&W | 21W-25S | 29 |
| Davison St. N&S | 21W-25S | 29 |
| Deep Haven Dr. N&S | 21W-22S | 21 |
| Des Plaines St. N&S | 24W-26S,24W-25S | 28 |
| Diamond 'K' Ln. N&S | 22W-25S | 29 |
| Dickens St. E&W | 22W-23S | 21 |
| Doris Av. E&W | 23W-25S | 29 |
| E. Circle Dr. N&S | 21W-24S | 29 |
| East Holm Dr. N&S | 23W-24S | 29 |
| East Port Av. N&S | 21W-22S | 21 |
| Edison Rd. E&W | 23W-26S | 29 |
| Elgin Av. N&S | 21W-23S | 21 |
| Ellen Av. E&W | 24W-24S | 29 |
| Ellsworth Av. NE&SW | 24W-25S | 28 |
| Elm St. E&W | 23W-25S | 29 |
| Elmer Av. N&S | 23W-24S | 29 |
| Elmwood Ln. N&S | 21W-26S | 29 |
| Emerson Pl. N&S | 23W-26S | 29 |
| Erie St. E&W | 24W-25S | 28 |
| Eunice Av. E&W | 22W-26S | 29 |
| Farrel Rd. N&S | 21W-22S | 21 |
| Faust Av. N&S | 22W-23S | 21 |
| Fernwood Av. N&S | 22W-22S | 21 |
| Fox St. N&S | 21W-23S | 21 |
| Fuller St. E&W | 22W-24S | 29 |
| Gage St. N&S | 22W-22S | 21 |
| Geneva St. E&W | 24W-26S | 28 |
| Girard Blvd. NE&SW | 23W-26S | 29 |
| Greenfield Av. N&S | 22W-25S | 29 |
| Greenlaw St. N&S | 23W-24S | 29 |
| Gregory Av. E&W | 22W-24S | 29 |
| Grinton St. N&S | 22W-23S | 21 |
| Hadsell Av. N&S | 24W-25S | 28 |
| Hamilton St. E&W | 24W-26S | 28 |
| Hanover Av. E&W | 21W-24S | 29 |
| Harlow Av. N&S | 22W-24S | 29 |
| Hartford Pl. N&S | 21W-24S | 29 |
| Haviland Dr. N&S | 24W-26S | 28 |
| Hawthorne Av. NW&SE | 23W-25S | 29 |
| Hebbard Av. N&S | 22W-24S | 29 |
| Helen Av. N&S | 23W-25S | 29 |
| Herman Ln. N&S | 22W-25S | 29 |
| Highland Pkwy. N&S | 21W-23S | 21 |
| Hillcrest Rd. NE&SW | 21W-23S | 21 |
| Hills St. N&S | 22W-25S | 29 |
| Hillside Rd. E&W | 23W-26S | 29 |
| Home St. E&W | 21W-25S | 29 |
| Houston Av. N&S | 23W-26S | 29 |
| Howliston Ct. E&W | 22W-26S | 29 |
| Howliston St. N&S | 22W-26S | 29 |
| Ignatius St. N&S | 24W-26S,24W-25S | 28 |
| Independence Av. N&S | 21W-24S | 29 |
| Industry Av. N&S | 22W-22S | 20 |
| Interstate 80 E&W | 23W-25S,21W-24S | 29 |
| Jackson St. NW&SE | 22W-23S | 21 |
| Jacob Av. E&W | 24W-25S | 28 |
| Jeffrey St. N&S | 22W-25S | 29 |
| Jessie St. N&S | 21W-25S,21W-24S | 29 |
| Joliet Rd. N&S | 26W-27S,25W-27S | 28 |
| Joliet St. N&S | 24W-26S,24W-25S | 28 |
| Judge Ct. E&W | 23W-25S | 29 |
| Julia Av. N&S | 24W-26S | 28 |
| Karner Dr. N&S | 23W-25S | 29 |
| Kenmore Av. N&S | 21W-24S | 29 |
| Keuka St. N&S | 21W-26S | 29 |
| Kildare Av. N&S | 21W-25S | 29 |
| Kinmonth Dr. N&S | 21W-25S | 29 |
| Laraway Rd. E&W | 26W-26S,21W-26S | 29 |
| Leana Av. E&W | 22W-24S | 29 |
| Lincoln Hwy. E&W | 21W-23S | 21 |
| Lind St. N&S | 22W-22S | 21 |
| Little Dorritt St. N&S | 22W-23S | 21 |
| Logan Av. NS&EW | 22W-24S | 29 |
| Logan Berry Ln. N&S | 21W-26S | 29 |
| Longwood Ct. N&S | 23W-23S | 21 |
| Lorette Av. N&S | 24W-25S | 28 |
| Lorraine Av. E&W | 21W-24S | 29 |
| Louis Rd. NW&SE | 23W-26S | 29 |
| Luana Rd. NW&SE | 23W-26S | 29 |
| Mable Av. E&W | 21W-24S | 29 |
| Manhattan Rd. N&S | 23W-25S,22W-26S | 29 |
| Maple Rd. NE&SW | 22W-22S,21W-22S | 21 |
| Maplecrest Av. N&S | 22W-22S | 21 |
| Maplewood Ln. N&S | 21W-26S | 29 |
| Marcella Av. N&S | 24W-26S | 28 |
| Marie Av. E&W | 22W-22S | 21 |
| Marigold Dr. N&S | 21W-25S,21W-24S | 29 |
| Markgrafs St. E&W | 24W-25S | 28 |
| Maude Av. E&W | 24W-26S | 29 |
| McKinley Av. N&S | 24W-26S,24W-25S | 28 |
| Melicent Av. E&W | 24W-26S | 28 |
| Melrose Av. N&S | 22W-25S | 29 |
| Melrose St. E&W | 21W-24S | 29 |
| Miami St. N&S | 21W-23S | 21 |
| Middletree Rd. NS&EW | 23W-26S,23W-25S | 29 |
| Milan Av. N&S | 22W-25S | 29 |
| Mills Rd. E&W | 22W-25S,21W-25S | 29 |
| Minton Rd. E&W | 24W-26S | 28 |
| Moen Av. N&S | 26W-25S | 28 |
| Mohawk St. N&S | 21W-23S | 21 |
| Moore Av. N&S | 23W-26S | 29 |
| Morningside Ct. N&S | 21W-23S | 21 |
| New Lenox Rd. E&W | 22W-24S,21W-24S | 29 |
| Newton Av. N&S | 21W-24S | 29 |
| North Town Line Rd. E&W | 22W-27S,21W-27S | 29 |
| Nowell Av. N&S | 21W-24S | 29 |
| Oak Av. N&S | 22W-23S | 21 |
| Oakview Av. N&S | 22W-24S | 29 |
| Oakwood Ct. NW&SE | 21W-26S | 29 |
| Oakwood Ln. E&W | 21W-26S | 29 |
| Old Elm Rd. E&W | 23W-25S | 29 |
| Old Manhattan Rd. NW&SE | 21W-27S,21W-26S | 29 |
| Oliver Pl. N&S | 21W-24S,21W-23S | 29 |
| Ontario Av. E&W | 24W-25S | 28 |
| Ontario St. E&W | 24W-25S | 28 |
| Osage St. N&S | 21W-23S | 21 |
| Oscar Av. E&W | 23W-24S | 29 |
| Ottawa St. N&S | 24W-26S,24W-25S | 28 |
| Park Rd. N&S | 21W-24S,21W-23S | 29 |
| Parker Av. E&W | 21W-24S | 21 |
| Patterson Rd. NE&SW | 25W-26S,25W-25S | 28 |
| Pawnee St. N&S | 22W-23S | 21 |
| Peale St. N&S | 21W-24S | 29 |
| Pearl St. N&S | 21W-25S | 29 |
| Penfield Av. N&S | 22W-25S | 29 |
| Pheasant Run E&W | 23W-26S | 29 |
| Pickwick St. N&S | 22W-23S | 21 |
| Pico Ct. N&S | 24W-25S | 28 |
| Pico St. E&W | 24W-25S | 28 |
| Pineridge Dr. N&S | 23W-25S | 29 |
| Pinewood Ln. E&W | 21W-26S | 29 |
| Ponderosa Ct. E&W | 21W-26S | 29 |
| Pontiac St. N&S | 21W-23S | 21 |
| Porter St. N&S | 22W-22S | 21 |
| Quarry St. E&W | 24W-25S | 28 |
| Quarry St. NE&SW | 23W-25S | 29 |
| Rachel Av. N&S | 24W-26S | 29 |
| Randall Ct. N&S | 23W-24S | 29 |
| Raymay Dr. N&S | 21W-24S | 29 |
| Red Bud Dr. E&W | 23W-25S | 29 |
| Retta Ct. NW&SE | 23W-25S | 29 |
| Richard St. N&S | 23W-26S | 29 |
| Rickey St. N&S | 21W-24S | 29 |
| River St. N&S | 24W-25S | 28 |
| Rose Av. E&W | 24W-25S | 28 |
| Route 53 N&S | 24W-27S,24W-25S | 28 |
| Rowell Av. N&S | 23W-24S,23W-27S | 29 |
| Sandall St. N&S | 23W-24S | 29 |
| Schorie Av. N&S | 21W-24S | 29 |
| Schuster St. E&W | 21W-25S | 29 |
| Sehring St. NS&EW | 24W-25S | 28 |

| | Grid | Page |
|---|---|---|
| Seneca St. E&S | 24W-25S | 28 |
| Shawnita St. E&W | 21W-23S | 21 |
| Sherman St. NW&SE | | |
| | 23W-25S | 29 |
| Spencer Rd. E&W | | |
| | 22W-25S,20W-25S | 29 |
| Spencer St. NS&EW | | |
| | 22W-24S | 29 |
| Springgreen Dr. N&S | | |
| | 21W-25S | 29 |
| Starr Dr. N&S | 23W-25S | 29 |
| Steinley Av. E&W | 22W-26S | 29 |
| Stirling Av. N&S | | |
| | 22W-23S,21W-23S | 21 |
| Suffolk Rd. NS&EW | | |
| | 21W-23S | 21 |
| Sugar Creek Dr. NS&EW | | |
| | 23W-26S,23W-25S | 29 |
| Sugar Creek Rd. N&S | | |
| | 23W-25S | 29 |
| Sugar Maple Ln. N&S | | |
| | 23W-27S | 29 |
| Sugar Valley Rd. N&S | | |
| | 23W-25S | 29 |
| Sugarcreek Ct. N&S | | |
| | 23W-26S | 29 |
| Sugarford Way NW&SE | | |
| | 23W-25S | 29 |
| Sunrise Ln. N&S .. 23W-26S | | 29 |
| Superior Av. N&S | | |
| | 24W-26S,24W-25S | 28 |
| Superior St. E&W .. 24W-25S | | 28 |
| Sweitzer Rd. E&W | | |
| | 24W-27S,23W-27S | 28 |
| Thayer St. N&S .... 22W-23S | | 21 |
| Tulare St. E&W .... 24W-26S | | 28 |
| U.S. Route 30 E&W | | |
| | 21W-23S | 21 |
| U.S. Route 52 NW&SE | | |
| | 23W-24S,21W-27S | 29 |
| U.S. Route 6 NE&SW | | |
| | 26W-25S,21W-22S | 28 |
| Ullian Av. NW&SE .. 24W-26S | | 28 |
| Valley Plwy. N&S .. 23W-26S | | 29 |
| Valleyview Pl. E&W | | |
| | 22W-22S,21W-22S | 21 |
| Violetta St. N&S ...21W-22S | | 21 |
| Voyager Dr. NE&SW | | |
| | 27W-20S | 19 |
| W. Circle Dr. N&S .. 21W-24S | | 29 |
| Walden Rd. E&W .. 23W-26S | | 29 |
| Walnut St. N&S .... 22W-23S | | 21 |
| Washington St. E&W | | |
| | 21W-24S | 29 |
| Wedgewood Dr. N&S | | |
| | 24W-26S | 28 |
| White Av. N&S .... 22W-26S | | 29 |
| Whitehall Ct. N&S .. 23W-26S | | 29 |
| Wildwood Ln. E&W | | |
| | 23W-25S | 29 |
| Wilhelm Ct. E&W .. 23W-24S | | 29 |
| Wilmot Av. E&W | | |
| | 24W-26S,23W-26S | 28 |
| Winifred St. N&S .. 24W-25S | | 28 |
| Wisconsin Av. NE&SW | | |
| | 25W-25S,24W-25S | 28 |
| Woodlawn Av. E&W | | |
| | 23W-25S | 29 |
| Woodruff Av. NE&SW | | |
| | 25W-25S,24W-25S | 28 |
| Yew Ct. E&W ... 21W-26S | | 29 |
| Zarley Av. E&W .. 24W-25S | | 28 |
| Zarley Blvd. E&W .. 24W-25S | | 28 |
| Zarley Rd. E&W .. 23W-25S | | 29 |
| Zipp Rd. E&W ....23W-27S | | 29 |
| Zurich Rd. E&W .. 24W-26S | | 28 |
| 2nd Av. E&W .... 21W-24S | | 29 |
| 3rd Av. E&W .... 21W-24S | | 29 |
| 4th Av. E&W | | |
| | 22W-24S,21W-24S | 29 |
| 5th Av. E&W | | |
| | 22W-24S,21W-24S | 29 |

**Lockport**

| | Grid | Page |
|---|---|---|
| Adams St. NE&SW | | |
| | 22W-19S,21W-19S | 15 |
| Ames St. E&W .. 22W-19S | | 15 |
| Amy Ct. NW&SE .. 21W-19S | | 15 |
| Apache Dr. E&W .. 20W-20S | | 22 |
| Arbor Ter. NW&SE 20W-18S | | 15 |
| Archer Rd. NE&SW | | |
| | 22W-18S,21W-18S | 15 |
| Arrowhead Dr. N&S | | |
| | 20W-20S | 22 |
| Ash Ln. E&W .. 20W-19S | | 15 |
| Ashley Ct. E&W .. 21W-19S | | 15 |
| Banberry Cir. N&S..20W-18S | | 15 |
| Banyon Ct. N&S....20W-18S | | 15 |
| Basin Dr. E&W .. 21W-18S | | 15 |
| Bianco Villa Dr. N&S | | |
| | 21W-17S | 15 |
| Blackfoot Dr. N&S..20W-20S | | 22 |
| Blackhawk Dr. NS&EW | | |
| | 20W-20S | 22 |
| Boehme St. NE&SW | | |
| | 22W-20S | 21 |
| Broadway St. 23W-18S | | 15 |
| Broadway St. NE&SW | | |
| | 22W-18S,22W-17S | 15 |
| Broken Arrow Dr. E&W | | |
| | 20W-20S | 22 |
| Bruce Ct. N&S .. 22W-20S | | 21 |
| Buck Path E&W ....20W-17S | | 15 |

| | Grid | Page |
|---|---|---|
| Buckeye Ct. N&S .. 20W-18S | | 15 |
| Canal St. E&W .. 22W-19S | | 15 |
| Cayoga Ct. SE&NW | | |
| | 20W-20S | 22 |
| Cayuse Ct. E&W .. 20W-20S | | 22 |
| Charles St. E&W .. 22W-20S | | 21 |
| Chestnut Ct. N&S | | |
| | 20W-18S | 15 |
| Cheyenne Ct. N&S.. 20W-20S | | 22 |
| Chinook Dr. N&S .. 20W-20S | | 22 |
| Cleveland St. N&S ..21W-19S | | 15 |
| Clinton St. NE&SW | | |
| | 22W-19S | 15 |
| Clover Ridge Dr. N&S | | |
| | 21W-19S | 15 |
| Commanche Ct. N&S | | |
| | 20W-20S | 22 |
| Connor Av. N&S .. 22W-20S | | 21 |
| Coral Dr. E&W .. 21W-18S | | 15 |
| Country Ln. N&S .. 20W-18S | | 15 |
| Cove Ct. N&S....21W-18S | | 15 |
| Daggett St. NW&SE | | |
| | 22W-20S | 21 |
| Darin Dr. E&W......21W-19S | | 15 |
| Daviess Dr. NW&SE | | |
| | 22W-19S | 15 |
| Daviess St. NE&SW | | |
| | 22W-19S | 15 |
| Delaware Dr. NE&SW | | |
| | 20W-20S | 22 |
| Delpark Av. E&W | | |
| | 23W-20S,22W-20S | 21 |
| Denver Hill Dr. NE&SW | | |
| | 22W-20S | 21 |
| Diane Ct. E&W .. 22W-20S | | 21 |
| Division St. E&W | | |
| | 22W-19S,21W-19S | 15 |
| Doe Tr. E&W .. 20W-17S | | 15 |
| Douglas Pkwy. NS&EW | | |
| | 20W-18S | 15 |
| Dunslow Ln. E&W .. 21W-18S | | 15 |
| East St. N&S ...... 22W-20S | | 21 |
| Edgewood Dr. N&S | | |
| | 20W-18S | 15 |
| Farrel Rd. N&S | | |
| | 21W-18S,21W-29S | 15 |
| Fawn Path E&W .. 20W-17S | | 15 |
| Fieldstone Pl. N&S..20W-19S | | 15 |
| Fieldview Ct. E&W .. 20W-18S | | 15 |
| Foxboro Ln. E&W .. 21W-18S | | 15 |
| Frances St. E&W .. 23W-20S | | 21 |
| Franklin St. NW&SE | | |
| | 22W-18S | 15 |
| Garfield St. N&S....22W-19S | | 15 |
| Georges St. E&W .. 22W-20S | | 21 |
| Glenmore St. N&S ..21W-19S | | 15 |
| Gloria St. E&W .. 21W-19S | | 15 |
| Grace St. E&W .. 20W-19S | | 15 |
| Grandview St. NE&SW | | |
| | 22W-19S,21W-19S | 15 |
| Hamilton St. NE&SW | | |
| | 22W-20S,22W-18S | 21 |
| Harbor Ct. E&W .. 21W-18S | | 15 |
| Heritage Ln. NW&SE | | |
| | 22W-19S | 15 |
| Holly Ct. E&W....21W-19S | | 15 |
| Huron Ct. NE&SW .. 20W-20S | | 22 |
| Illini Dr. E&W ...... 21W-19S | | 15 |
| Industry Dr. NW&SE | | |
| | 22W-18S | 15 |
| Isabella Av. N&S...21W-19S | | 15 |
| Jacquays St. N&S ..21W-19S | | 15 |
| Janice Av. E&W .. 22W-20S | | 21 |
| Jannel Ct. N&S .. 21W-19S | | 15 |
| Jefferson St. NE&SW | | |
| | 22W-20S,22W-18S | 21 |
| Jennifer Ct. N&S | | |
| | 21W-19S | 15 |
| Joann Ct. E&W .. 22W-20S | | 21 |
| Johnson St. N&S .. 22W-20S | | 21 |
| Joseph Dr. N&S .. 22W-20S | | 21 |
| Kathrine Ct. E&W .. 21W-19S | | 15 |
| Key West Dr. E&W 21W-18S | | 15 |
| Lacoma Ct. N&S .. 21W-19S | | 15 |
| Lawrence Av. N&S ..22W-20S | | 21 |
| Lejeune Av. N&S .. 21W-19S | | 15 |
| Lincoln St. N&S .. 22W-19S | | 15 |
| Lisdowney Dr. E&W | | |
| | 21W-18S | 15 |
| Lock Ln. N&S . 21W-19S | | 15 |
| Lone Star Dr. N&S..22W-20S | | 21 |
| Longbow Dr. NS&EW | | |
| | 20W-20S | 22 |
| Lorraine Ct. E&W .. 22W-20S | | 21 |
| Madison St. N&S | | |
| | 22W-20S,22W-19S | 21 |
| Maitland St. N&S .. 21W-19S | | 15 |
| Maple Ct. E&W .. 21W-19S | | 15 |
| Market St. NW&SE | | |
| | 22W-18S | 15 |
| Mary Ann Ln. N&S..22W-20S | | 21 |
| Maryknoll Dr. NW&SE | | |
| | 22W-18S,21W-18S | 15 |
| May St. E&W .. 23W-20S | | 21 |
| Mayo St. NW&SE .. 22W-20S | | 21 |
| McGregor St. N&S..21W-18S | | 15 |
| McIntosh Rd. N&S..22W-20S | | 21 |
| McKinley Ct. NS&EW | | |
| | 22W-19S | 15 |
| McKinley St. NS&EW | | |
| | 22W-19S | 15 |
| Merc Ln. N&S....20W-18S | | 15 |
| Michael St. E&W .. 21W-19S | | 15 |
| Mikan Ct. E&W .. 22W-20S | | 21 |

| | Grid | Page |
|---|---|---|
| Mikan Dr. E&W .. 22W-20S | | 21 |
| Milne Dr. NS&EW .. 21W-19S | | 15 |
| Milne St. NW&SE .. 22W-19S | | 15 |
| Mohave Ct. NE&SW | | |
| | 20W-20S | 22 |
| Mohawk Ct. E&W .. 20W-20S | | 22 |
| Mohican St. NS&EW | | |
| | 20W-20S | 22 |
| Mohican Dr. N&S | | |
| | 20W-20S | 22 |
| Montuck Dr. N&S .. 20W-20S | | 22 |
| Morgan St. NW&SE | | |
| | 22W-18S | 15 |
| Muehl St. N&S .. 21W-19S | | 15 |
| New Av. NE&SW .. 22W-18S | | 15 |
| Newbridge Dr. E&W | | |
| | 21W-18S | 15 |
| North St. E&W .. 21W-18S | | 15 |
| Northern Dr. NW&SE | | |
| | 21W-18S | 15 |
| Olympic Ln. N&S .. 20W-18S | | 15 |
| Oneida Dr. EW&NS | | |
| | 20W-20S | 22 |
| Osage Ct. NS&EW ..20W-20S | | 22 |
| Ottawa Dr. N&S .. 20W-20S | | 22 |
| Parkview Ln. E&W | | |
| | 23W-20S,22W-20S | 21 |
| Peachtree Ln. NW&SE | | |
| | 21W-20S | 21 |
| Pima Ct. N&S ...... 20W-20S | | 22 |
| Pocasset Ct. SE&NW | | |
| | 20W-20S | 22 |
| Porter Pl. N&S......21W-19S | | 15 |
| | | 15 |
| Prairie St. NE&SW .. 23W-20S | | 21 |
| Primrose Ln. NW&SE | | |
| | 20W-18S | 16 |
| Princess Ct. N&S .. 22W-20S | | 21 |
| Prodehl Dr. E&W .. 21W-19S | | 15 |
| Pueblo Ct. N&S .. 20W-20S | | 22 |
| Putnam Dr. E&W .. 21W-19S | | 15 |
| Read St. N&S ....21W-19S | | 15 |
| Red Cloud Dr. NS&EW | | |
| | 20W-20S | 22 |
| Redwood Ct. N&S | | |
| | 20W-18S | 16 |
| Reef Rd. N&S......21W-18S | | 15 |
| Rhonda Dr. N&S....21W-19S | | 15 |
| Rio Grande Dr. NE&SW | | |
| | 22W-20S | 21 |
| Rodney St. N&S.... 21W-19S | | 15 |
| Rosanne Ln. E&W .. 22W-20S | | 21 |
| Route 53 N&S | | |
| | 23W-19S,23W-18S | 15 |
| Route 7 E&W | | |
| | 23W-19S,21W-19S | 15 |
| Runyan Dr. E&W .. 21W-19S | | 15 |
| Saddlewood Dr. E&W | | |
| | 20W-18S | 15 |
| Santa Fe Ct. N&S .. 20W-20S | | 22 |
| Sauk Dr. N&S......20W-20S | | 22 |
| Seneca Dr. E&W .. 20W-20S | | 22 |
| Shawnee Dr. N&S .. 20W-20S | | 22 |
| Shoals Dr. NE&SW 21W-18S | | 15 |
| Silver Spur Ln. NS&EW | | |
| | 20W-20S | 21 |
| Sioux Dr. EW&NS .. 20W-20S | | 22 |
| Sisson St. N&S .. 22W-20S | | 21 |
| South St. E&W .. 22W-20S | | 21 |
| St. Charles Dr. E&W | | |
| | 21W-19S | 15 |
| State St. NE&SW | | |
| | 22W-20S,22W-18S | 21 |
| Stephanie Dr. N&S..21W-19S | | 15 |
| Strawberry Hill Dr. NS&EW | | |
| | 21W-18S | 15 |
| Sujada Ct. N&S .. 21W-18S | | 15 |
| Summit Dr. N&S | | |
| | 21W-20S,21W-19S | 21 |
| Sunset Ridge Ct. NS&EW | | |
| | 20W-20S | 22 |
| Sunshine Ct. NE&SW | | |
| | 21W-20S | 21 |
| Swift Arrow Dr. E&W | | |
| | 20W-20S | 22 |
| Sycamore Ct. NW&SE | | |
| | 20W-18S | 15 |
| Table St. NE&SW .. 22W-18S | | 15 |
| Teton Ct. N&S .... 20W-20S | | 22 |
| Teton Dr. E&W .. 20W-20S | | 22 |
| Theodore Ct. N&S.. 21W-18S | | 15 |
| Thornton Av. E&W | | |
| | 22W-18S,21W-19S | 15 |
| Tonelli St. NW&SE ..21W-19S | | 15 |
| Tuscadora Ct. NW&SE | | |
| | 20W-20S | 22 |
| Valley Dr. NW&SE ..21W-19S | | 15 |
| Vine St. NE&SW....22W-19S | | 15 |
| Warren St. NW&SE | | |
| | 22W-18S | 15 |
| Washburn Way NS&EW | | |
| | 21W-19S | 15 |
| Washington St. E&W | | |
| | 22W-20S,22W-18S | 21 |
| Water St. NE&SW .. 22W-18S | | 15 |
| West St. N&S......22W-20S | | 21 |
| Westwood Dr. E&W | | |
| | 20W-19S | 15 |
| Whelan St. E&W .. 22W-20S | | 21 |
| White Tail Way NS&EW | | |
| | 20W-17S | 15 |
| Will Dr. E&W .. 21W-19S | | 15 |
| Wyandot Ct. E&W .. 20W-20S | | 22 |

| | Grid | Page |
|---|---|---|
| 2nd St. NW&SE | | |
| | 22W-19S,21W-19S | 15 |
| 3rd St. NW&SE | | |
| | 22W-19S,21W-19S | 15 |
| 4th St. NW&SE .... 22W-19S | | 15 |
| 5th St. NW&SE .... 22W-19S | | 15 |
| 6th St. NW&SE .... 22W-19S | | 15 |
| 7th St. E&W | | |
| | 22W-19S,21W-19S | 15 |
| 8th St. E&W | | |
| | 22W-19S,21W-19S | 15 |
| 9th St. NW&SE | | |
| | 23W-19S,21W-19S | 15 |
| 10th St. NW&SE....22W-19S | | 15 |
| 11th St. NW&SE .. 22W-19S | | 15 |
| 12th St. NW&SE .. 22W-19S | | 15 |
| 13th St. NW&SE .. 22W-19S | | 15 |
| 14th St. NW&SE .. 22W-19S | | 15 |
| 16th St. NW&SE .. 22W-20S | | 21 |
| 15th St. NW&SE | | |
| | 22W-20S,22W-19S | 21 |
| 17th St. E&W .. 22W-20S | | 21 |
| 18th St. NW&SE .. 22W-20S | | 21 |
| 19th St. NW&SE .. 22W-20S | | 21 |
| 20th Ct. E&W .... 22W-20S | | 21 |
| 151st St. E&W .. 21W-18S | | 15 |
| 167th St. E&W .. 20W-20S | | 22 |

**Lockport Township**

| | Grid | Page |
|---|---|---|
| Aberdeen Dr. E&W 26W-19S | | 14 |
| Adel Ct. NE&SW ... 26W-16S | | 13 |
| Airport Rd. E&W | | |
| | 26W-17S,23W-17S | 15 |
| Albert Dr. N&S .. 25W-19S | | 14 |
| Alicia Ct. N&S .. 26W-19S | | 14 |
| Alpine Ct. NE&SW .. 26W-16S | | 14 |
| Alpine Rd. NW&SE 26W-16S | | 14 |
| Ames Ct. E&W .. 26W-16S | | 13 |
| Amherst Av. N&S .. 23W-21S | | 21 |
| Annapolis Ct. N&S 26W-16S | | 13 |
| Archer Rd. NE&SW | | |
| | 26W-18S,21W-17S | 15 |
| Ardmore Cir. NS&EW | | |
| | 26W-16S | 13 |
| Ardmore Ct. N&S .. 26W-16S | | 13 |
| Argo Ln. E&W......21W-18S | | 15 |
| Astoria Ct. NW&SE | | |
| | 26W-16S | 13 |
| Barret St. N&S .. 23W-21S | | 21 |
| Barrington Ct. E&W | | |
| | 26W-16S | 13 |
| Barrington Ln. NS&EW | | |
| | 26W-16S | 13 |
| Barry Av. E&W | | |
| | 23W-21S,22W-21S | 21 |
| Bayberry Rd. NE&SW | | |
| | 26W-16S | 14 |
| Bellwood Av. E&W | | |
| | 23W-21S,22W-21S | 21 |
| Birch St. E&W .. 26W-20S | | 20 |
| Blossom St. E&W .. 26W-20S | | 20 |
| Blue Blossom Ct. NE&SW | | |
| | 26W-16S | 14 |
| Blue Blossom Ln. NW&SE | | |
| | 26W-16S | 14 |
| Bluff St. E&W .. 22W-18S | | 15 |
| Bonnie Dr. N&S .... 21W-18S | | 15 |
| Brassel St. N&S....22W-21S | | 21 |
| Brentwood Ct. E&W | | |
| | 26W-16S | 13 |
| Bristolcone Dr. N&S | | |
| | 26W-16S | 14 |
| Broadway St. NE&SW | | |
| | 24W-21S,23W-19S | 20 |
| Brown St. N&S .... 22W-20S | | 21 |
| Bruce Rd. E&W | | |
| | 23W-20S,21W-20S | 21 |
| Buckner Ct. N&S .. 26W-16S | | 13 |
| Butler Ct. N&S .... 26W-16S | | 13 |
| California Av. N&S ..22W-21S | | 21 |
| Cameron Ct. N&S | | |
| | 23W-20S,22W-20S | 21 |
| Carillon Dr., S. NW&SE | | |
| | 26W-16S | 14 |
| Cascade Ct. NW&SE | | |
| | 26W-16S | 13 |
| Central Park N&S .. 23W-21S | | 21 |
| Chandler Ct. N&S .. 26W-16S | | 13 |
| Chatsworth Ln. NS&EW | | |
| | 26W-16S | 13 |
| Cherry Ln. N&S .. 26W-16S | | 14 |
| Circle E. N&S ...... 21W-18S | | 15 |
| Circle W. N&S .... 21W-18S | | 15 |
| Cliff Av. N&S ...... 23W-21S | | 21 |
| Connor Av. E&W | | |
| | 23W-20S,22W-20S | 21 |
| Cornell Av. E&W .. 23W-21S | | 21 |
| Cottonwood Ln. NE&SW | | |
| | 26W-16S | 14 |
| Country Ln. N&S | | |
| | 23W-20S,22W-17S | 15 |
| Covington Dr. E&W | | |
| | 26W-16S | 13 |
| Creston Ct. E&W .. 26W-16S | | 13 |
| Crete Ct. NW&SE .. 26W-16S | | 13 |
| Dartmouth Av. NW&SE | | |
| | 23W-21S | 21 |
| Dawson Av. E&W .. 24W-17S | | 14 |
| Disposal Rd. E&W .. 23W-16S | | 15 |
| Division St. E&W | | |
| | 25W-19S,21W-19S | 14 |
| Dundee Dr. N&S...21W-18S | | 15 |
| Earl St. N&S ...... 21W-18S | | 15 |

| | Grid | Page |
|---|---|---|
| East Rd. N&S ...... 22W-20S | | 21 |
| East St. N&S | | |
| | 22W-21S,21W-18S | 21 |
| Edinburg Dr. N&S .. 21W-18S | | 15 |
| Elm St. E&W .... 21W-18S | | 15 |
| Englewood Av. N&S | | |
| | 22W-21S | 21 |
| Exhibition Pl. N&S .. 23W-21S | | 21 |
| Exter Ct. N&S .... 23W-21S | | 21 |
| Fairmont Av. E&W | | |
| | 23W-21S,22W-21S | 21 |
| Fairmount Av. N&S | | |
| | 22W-21S | 21 |
| Farrel Rd. N&S | | |
| | 21W-21S,21W-18S | 21 |
| Foley Dr. E&W .. 26W-19S | | 14 |
| Forest Ln. N&S .. 21W-17S | | 15 |
| Gaylord Rd. N&S | | |
| | 26W-20S,26W-19S | 20 |
| Giesler Dr. N&S .. 21W-18S | | 15 |
| Godfrey Av. E&W .. 22W-21S | | 21 |
| Green Garden Pl. N&S | | |
| | 23W-21S,23W-20S | 21 |
| Hacker Dr. N&S .. 26W-20S | | 20 |
| Hartman Dr. N&S .. 23W-17S | | 15 |
| Harvard St. E&W .. 23W-21S | | 21 |
| Hawthorn Pl. N&S .. 23W-21S | | 21 |
| Hazelnut Ln. NS&EW | | |
| | 26W-16S | 14 |
| Hemlock St. E&W .. 26W-20S | | 20 |
| Highland Av. E&W 21W-18S | | 15 |
| Hopkins Rd. N&S .. 24W-18S | | 14 |
| Hughes Av. E&W | | |
| | 23W-20S,22W-20S | 21 |
| Jacquie Av. E&W | | |
| | 24W-17S,23W-17S | 14 |
| Janet Av. E&W | | |
| | 24W-17S,23W-17S | 14 |
| John Ct. N&S ...... 25W-19S | | 14 |
| John Kirkham Dr. E&W | | |
| | 24W-17S,23W-17S | 14 |
| Joliet Rd. N&S | | |
| | 23W-17S,23W-16S | 15 |
| LaSalle Ct. NE&SW | | |
| | 23W-21S | 21 |
| Laurie Dr. N&S .. 21W-18S | | 15 |
| Lawrence Av. N&S..22W-20S | | 21 |
| Lejeune Av. N&S .. 21W-19S | | 15 |
| Lewis Dr. N&S .. 24W-17S | | 14 |
| Lockport Rd. NE&SW | | |
| | 23W-21S,22W-16S | 21 |
| Lois Av. N&S .. 22W-20S | | 21 |
| Luther Av. N&S ....22W-21S | | 21 |
| Magnolia Dr. N&S .. 26W-16S | | 14 |
| Mahogany Ln. NW&SE | | |
| | 26W-16S | 14 |
| Mary Dr. E&W .. 25W-19S | | 14 |
| Maryknoll Dr. NS&EW | | |
| | 21W-18S | 15 |
| Maryville Dr. NE&SW | | |
| | 21W-19S | 15 |
| May St. N&S .. 22W-21S | | 21 |
| McCameron Av. NS&EW | | |
| | 21W-18S | 15 |
| McGilvray Dr. E&W | | |
| | 26W-19S | 14 |
| McGregor Rd. N&S | | |
| | 21W-18S | 15 |
| McGregor St. N&S .. 21W-18S | | 15 |
| McIntosh Rd. N&S..22W-20S | | 21 |
| McIntyre Dr. N&S .. 21W-18S | | 15 |
| Meadow Wood Ln. N&S | | |
| | 21W-18S | 15 |
| Miramor St. N&S .. 21W-19S | | 15 |
| Neil Ct. N&S .. 23W-21S | | 21 |
| Nobes Av. E&W | | |
| | 23W-21S,22W-21S | 21 |
| North Av. E&W .. 23W-21S | | 21 |
| North St. E&W | | |
| | 22W-18S,21W-18S | 15 |
| North St. E&W .. 22W-21S | | 21 |
| Northern Dr. NW&SE | | |
| | 21W-18S | 15 |
| Oak Av. E&W | | |
| | 23W-21S,21W-21S | 21 |
| Oak St. N&S .. 21W-18S | | 15 |
| Orange Blossom Ln. NW&SE | | |
| | 26W-16S | 14 |
| Oxford Pl. E&W .. 23W-21S | | 21 |
| Pendleton St. N&S..21W-19S | | 15 |
| Pilcher Rd. E&W | | |
| | 26W-16S,25W-16S | 14 |
| Pine Av. N&S .. 23W-20S | | 21 |
| Prairie Av. E&W .. 22W-21S | | 21 |
| Princeton St. E&W | | |
| | 23W-21S,23W-20S | 21 |
| Rankin Dr. N&S .. 26W-16S | | 14 |
| Redbud Ln. N&S .. 26W-16S | | 14 |
| Renwick Rd. E&W | | |
| | 26W-18S,23W-19S | 14 |
| Riley Av. E&W | | |
| | 23W-21S,22W-21S | 21 |
| Riverview Av. N&S | | |
| | 23W-21S,22W-21S | 21 |
| Robson Dr. N&S...21W-18S | | 15 |
| Rosalind St. E&W | | |
| | 22W-21S,21W-21S | 21 |
| Rosemarie Ln. N&S | | |
| | 26W-19S | 14 |
| Route 171 NE&SW | | |
| | 21W-17S | 15 |
| Route 53 N&S | | |
| | 23W-19S,23W-16S | 15 |

| | Grid | Page |
|---|---|---|
| S. Carillon Dr. NW&SE | | |
| ............... 26W-16S | 14 |
| School House Ln. N&S | | |
| ............... 21W-17S | 15 |
| Sheffield Av. NW&SE | | |
| ............... 23W-21S | 21 |
| Smith Rd. N&S .... 21W-16S | 15 |
| South St. E&W | | |
| ...... 23W-21S,22W-21S | 21 |
| State St. NE&SW | | |
| ...... 23W-20S,22W-18S | 21 |
| Stateville Rd. E&W | | |
| ...... 26W-19S,23W-19S | 14 |
| Stuart Ct. NW&SE .. 21W-18S | 15 |
| Stuart Rd. N&S .... 21W-18S | 15 |
| Taylor Rd. E&W | | |
| ...... 26W-16S,23W-16S | 14 |
| Terminal St. N&S .. 23W-17S | 15 |
| Thomas Dr. E&W .. 25W-19S | 14 |
| Thorndale Ct. E&W | | |
| ............... 21W-18S | 15 |
| Thornton Av. E&W | | |
| ...... 22W-18S,21W-18S | 15 |
| Timberview Dr. E&W | | |
| ............... 21W-18S | 15 |
| Volz Av. N&S ...... 22W-21S | 21 |
| W. 143rd St. E&W .. 21W-16S | 15 |
| Weber Rd. N&S | | |
| ......... 26W-20S,26W-16S | 20 |
| Weslyan St. E&W .. 23W-21S | 21 |
| West Bluff St. N&S | | |
| ............... 21W-18S | 15 |
| Woodbrook Ln. E&W | | |
| ............... 21W-17S | 15 |
| Yale Av. E&W | | |
| ...... 23W-21S,22W-21S | 21 |
| 1st St. E&W ...... 21W-19S | 15 |
| 135th St. E&W .... 21W-16S | 15 |
| 144th St. E&W .... 21W-17S | 15 |
| 145th St. E&W .... 21W-17S | 15 |
| 147th St. E&W .... 21W-17S | 15 |

## Manhattan

| | | |
|---|---|---|
| Andrea Dr. NE&SW | | |
| ............... 18W-31S | 38 |
| Blackthorne Rd. NE&SW | | |
| ............... 19W-31S | 38 |
| Brett Ct. NE&SW .. 18W-31S | 38 |
| Brett Dr. NS&EW .. 18W-31S | 38 |
| Brian Ct. E&W ....18W-31S | 38 |
| Brynn Dr. N&S .... 18W-31S | 38 |
| Calla Dr. N&S .... 18W-31S | 38 |
| Cashel Bay Rd. N&S | | |
| ............... 19W-30S | 38 |
| Cochran St. E&W .. 19W-31S | 38 |
| Donegal Dr. NW&SE | | |
| ............... 19W-30S | 38 |
| Eastern Av. N&S | | |
| ......... 19W-31S,19W-30S | 38 |
| Eberhart St. NE&SW | | |
| ............... 19W-30S | 38 |
| Edmon Ct. NW&SE | | |
| ............... 19W-30S | 38 |
| Fairview Dr. NS&EW | | |
| ............... 19W-30S | 38 |
| Foxford Dr. NE&SW | | |
| ............... 19W-30S | 38 |
| Francis Ct. E&W .. 18W-31S | 38 |
| Front St. NE&SW .. 19W-31S | 38 |
| Henry St. E&W .... 19W-31S | 38 |
| Jan Av. N&S ...... 18W-31S | 38 |
| Jessie St. E&W | | |
| ......... 19W-31S,18W-31S | 38 |
| Kay Av. N&S ...... 18W-31S | 38 |
| Lakeview Dr. NW&SE | | |
| ............... 19W-30S | 38 |
| Lee St. E&W ...... 18W-31S | 38 |
| Lincoln St. N&S .. 19W-31S | 38 |
| Madison St. N&S .. 19W-31S | 38 |
| Manhattan-Monee Rd. E&W | | |
| ............... 18W-30S | 38 |
| Marion St. NW&SE | 38 |
| May St. NS&EW .... 19W-31S | 38 |
| McClure Av. NE&SW | | |
| ............... 19W-31S | 38 |
| Morgan Ct. NE&SW | | |
| ............... 19W-30S | 38 |
| North St. E&W | | |
| ......... 19W-30S,18W-31S | 38 |
| Park Av. N&S | | |
| ......... 19W-31S,19W-30S | 38 |
| Prairie Av. N&S .. 19W-30S | 38 |
| Ridgefield Dr. E&W | | |
| ............... 19W-30S | 38 |
| Rosewood Ln. NE&SW | | |
| ............... 19W-30S | 38 |
| Sharp Dr. N&S | | |
| ......... 19W-31S,19W-30S | 38 |
| Shelia Rd. N&S .... 19W-31S | 38 |
| Smith Rd. E&W .... 19W-29S | 38 |
| State St. NW&SE | | |
| ......... 18W-31S,19W-30S | 38 |
| Stauffenburg Rd. E&W | | |
| ......... 19W-30S,19W-29S | 38 |
| Terry Ct. E&W .... 18W-31S | 38 |
| Thelma Av. N&S .. 18W-31S | 38 |
| Trask St. E&W .... 19W-31S | 38 |
| U.S. Rt. 52 NW&SE | | |
| ......... 18W-31S,19W-30S | 38 |
| Waterford Ln. NW&SE | | |
| ............... 19W-30S | 38 |
| Western Av. E&W .. 19W-30S | 38 |

| | | |
|---|---|---|
| Whitson St. E&W | | |
| ......... 19W-31S,18W-31S | 38 |
| Woodrow Av. NE&SW | | |
| ............... 19W-30S | 38 |
| 1st Ct. N&S........18W-31S | 38 |
| 1st St. E&W | | |
| ......... 19W-31S,18W-31S | 38 |
| 2nd St. E&W | | |
| ......... 19W-31S,18W-31S | 38 |
| 3rd St. E&W | | |
| ......... 19W-31S,18W-31S | 38 |

## Manhattan Township

| | | |
|---|---|---|
| Baker Rd. E&W | | |
| ......... 20W-28S,15W-28S | 38 |
| Barton Rd. N&S .... 15W-33S | 51 |
| Brett Dr. E&W .... 18W-31S | 38 |
| Bridle Path Dr. N&S | | |
| ............... 15W-28S | 39 |
| Brown St. E&W | | |
| ......... 20W-31S,19W-31S | 38 |
| Carriage Ln. E&W .. 17W-29S | 39 |
| Cedar Rd. N&S | | |
| ......... 18W-33S,18W-28S | 50 |
| Clover Ct. N&S .... 15W-29S | 39 |
| Creek Dr. NE&SW .. 20W-29S | 38 |
| Delaney Rd. E&W | | |
| ......... 20W-28S,15W-28S | 38 |
| Diane Way NS&EW | | |
| ............... 20W-29S | 38 |
| Eastern Av. N&S | | |
| ......... 19W-33S,19W-28S | 50 |
| Elwood Manhattan Rd. E&W | | |
| ............... 20W-30S | 38 |
| Gallager Rd. (Haley Rd.) E&W | | |
| ......... 20W-31S,15W-31S | 38 |
| Gougar Rd. N&S | | |
| ......... 20W-33S,20W-31S | 50 |
| Green Garden-Manhattan Rd | | |
| N&S..... 15W-33S,15W-28S | 51 |
| Haley (Gallager) Rd. EW&NS | | |
| ......... 17W-31S,16W-31S | 39 |
| Heather Glen Ct. N&S | | |
| ............... 15W-29S | 39 |
| Heather Glen Ln. E&W | | |
| ......... 15W-29S,15W-28S | 39 |
| Highland Dr. N&S .. 15W-28S | 39 |
| Hoff Rd. E&W | | |
| ......... 20W-32S,16W-32S | 50 |
| Horseshoe Ln. E&W | | |
| ............... 15W-28S | 39 |
| Julianne Ct. NW&SE | | |
| ............... 18W-31S | 38 |
| Julianne Dr. NS&EW | | |
| ............... 18W-31S | 38 |
| Kankakee St. N&S | | |
| ......... 17W-33S,17W-28S | 51 |
| Kathryn Av. E&W .. 20W-29S | 38 |
| Koehler Rd. N&S | | |
| ......... 16W-32S,16W-28S | 51 |
| Kuse Rd. E&W | | |
| ......... 16W-28S,15W-28S | 39 |
| Malibu Dr. N&S .... 19W-28S | 38 |
| Manhattan-Monee Rd. E&W | | |
| ......... 18W-30S,15W-30S | 38 |
| Nelson Rd. N&S .... 18W-28S | 38 |
| Old Manhattan Rd. NW&SE | | |
| ......... 20W-29S,20W-28S | 38 |
| Ottawa Dr. E&W .... 16W-28S | 39 |
| Prairie Estates Dr. E&W | | |
| ............... 16W-28S | 39 |
| Saddlecreek Dr. N&S | | |
| ............... 15W-28S | 39 |
| Sauk Dr. N&S .... 16W-28S | 39 |
| Scheer Rd. N&S | | |
| ......... 15W-28S,15W-27S | 39 |
| Schoolhouse Rd. N&S | | |
| ............... 16W-28S | 39 |
| Schoolhouse Rd. N&S | | |
| ......... 15W-32S,15W-29S | 51 |
| Seltzer Rd. N&S .. 20W-30S | 38 |
| Sioux Ct. E&W .... 16W-28S | 39 |
| Smith Rd. E&W | | |
| ......... 19W-29S,15W-29S | 38 |
| State St. NW&SE .. 18W-31S | 38 |
| Stuenkel Rd. E&W .. 15W-29S | 39 |
| Susan Ln. E&W .... 20W-29S | 38 |
| U.S. Rt. 52 NW&SE | | |
| ......... 18W-33S,20W-28S | 50 |
| Watkins Rd. N&S | | |
| ......... 18W-32S,15W-32S | 50 |
| 1st St. E&W ...... 18W-31S | 38 |

## Minooka

| | | |
|---|---|---|
| Bell Rd. N&S ...... 32W-29S | 34 |
| Colina Calle Ct. E&W | | |
| ............... 32W-29S | 34 |
| Dirst Rd. NS&EW | | |
| ......... 32W-28S,32W-29S | 34 |
| El Dorado Ct. N&S.. 32W-29S | 34 |
| Grande Dr. E&W....32W-28S | 34 |
| Jardin St. NW&SE .. 32W-29S | 34 |
| Manuel Ct. N&S .. 32W-29S | 34 |
| Maria Ct. E&W .... 32W-29S | 34 |
| McEvilly Rd. E&W .. 32W-29S | 34 |
| Miguel Ct. E&W .. 32W-29S | 34 |
| Rio Roco Av. E&W .. 32W-29S | 34 |
| San Carlos NS&EW | | |
| ............... 32W-29S | 34 |
| San Carlos Rd. NS&EW | | |
| ............... 32W-29S | 34 |
| Santos Av. N&S .. 32W-29S | 34 |

| | | |
|---|---|---|
| Valle Vista Ct. N&S | | |
| ............... 32W-29S | 34 |
| Vista Ct. NS&EW .. 32W-28S | 34 |
| Zapata Rd. NW&SE | | |
| ............... 32W-29S | 34 |
| 96th Av. N&S ...... 12W-23S | 24 |

## Mokena

| | | |
|---|---|---|
| Aileen Av. NE&SW .. 13W-23S | 24 |
| Alta Vista Way E&W | | |
| ............... 14W-26S | 32 |
| Anna St. N&S ...... 13W-24S | 32 |
| Anne Ln. N&S ...... 13W-23S | 24 |
| Anne Ln. N&S | | |
| ......... 13W-24S,13W-23S | 32 |
| April Ct. NW&SE .. 11W-23S | 25 |
| April Ln. N&S ...... 11W-23S | 25 |
| Arahat Ct. N&S .... 13W-23S | 23 |
| Ashbury Ct. E&W .. 14W-26S | 32 |
| Ashford Cir. N&S .. 14W-24S | 32 |
| Austin Ct. NE&SW .. 12W-23S | 24 |
| Becket Ct. E&W .... 12W-23S | 24 |
| Bedford Ln. N&S .. 13W-23S | 24 |
| Blackhawk Ct. E&W | | |
| ............... 14W-23S | 24 |
| Blyth Av. N&S .... 12W-23S | 24 |
| Bones Av. N&S .... 13W-23S | 24 |
| Bormet Dr. E&W .. 11W-23S | 25 |
| Boyer Ct. E&W .... 13W-24S | 32 |
| Brett Dr. N&S ...... 13W-23S | 24 |
| Bristol Ct. NE&SW .. 12W-23S | 24 |
| Brompton Ct. NW&SE | | |
| ............... 12W-23S | 24 |
| Bryant Ct. N&S .... 13W-23S | 24 |
| Bryant Rd. E&W .... 13W-23S | 32 |
| Bryn Mawr Way E&W | | |
| ............... 14W-26S | 32 |
| Burr Oak Ln. N&S .. 14W-24S | 32 |
| Cambridge Dr. NS&EW | | |
| ............... 12W-23S | 24 |
| Camden Bay NW&SE | | |
| ............... 13W-22S | 24 |
| Camden Ct. NS&EW | | |
| ............... 13W-22S | 24 |
| Catherine Ln. N&S | | |
| ......... 13W-24S,13W-23S | 32 |
| Celtic Ct. E&W .... 13W-23S | 24 |
| Center St. N&S | | |
| ......... 13W-24S,13W-23S | 32 |
| Clearvue Ct. E&W .. 12W-23S | 24 |
| Cleveland St. E&W.. 13W-23S | 24 |
| Connemara Ct. E&W | | |
| ............... 13W-23S | 24 |
| Creek Crossing Dr. E&W | | |
| ............... 13W-23S | 24 |
| Creek Side Ln. N&S | | |
| ............... 14W-23S | 24 |
| Creekview Cir. NW&SE | | |
| ............... 14W-22S | 24 |
| Creekview Ct. NW&SE | | |
| ............... 14W-22S | 24 |
| Creekview Ln. N&S | | |
| ............... 14W-22S | 24 |
| Cromwell Ct. NE&SW | | |
| ............... 12W-23S | 24 |
| Cromwell Ln. N&S | | |
| ............... 12W-23S | 24 |
| Cross St. NE&SW .. 13W-23S | 24 |
| Daniel Tr. E&W .... 13W-23S | 24 |
| Darla Trail N&S .... 13W-23S | 24 |
| Denny Av. NE&SW .. 13W-23S | 24 |
| Derby Ct. NE&SW .. 12W-23S | 24 |
| Derby Ln. NE&SW .. 12W-23S | 24 |
| Derek Way NW&SE | | |
| ............... 13W-23S | 24 |
| Diana Ct. NE&SW .. 14W-26S | 32 |
| Dickens Bay NE&SW | | |
| ............... 13W-22S | 24 |
| Dilber Bay N&S .... 13W-22S | 24 |
| Division St. E&W .. 13W-23S | 24 |
| Draw Ct. E&W .... 13W-23S | 24 |
| East Brightway Dr. N&S | | |
| ............... 14W-24S | 32 |
| Edgewood Dr. NE&SW | | |
| ............... 14W-24S | 32 |
| Elm St. NW&SE .... 11W-23S | 25 |
| Emerald Ct. NW&SE | | |
| ............... 12W-23S | 24 |
| English Bay Ln. N&S | | |
| ............... 13W-22S | 24 |
| Enterprise Dr. E&W | | |
| ............... 11W-23S | 25 |
| Everett Ct. N&S .... 12W-23S | 24 |
| Fairmont Ln. NW&SE | | |
| ............... 14W-23S | 24 |
| Fiona Av. N&S .... 13W-23S | 24 |
| Forest Ct. N&S .... 14W-26S | 32 |
| Front St. NE&SW | | |
| ......... 14W-23S,13W-23S | 24 |
| Frontage Rd. NW&SE | | |
| ............... 11W-22S | 25 |
| Galway Bay N&S .. 13W-22S | 24 |
| Giles Dr. E&W ...... 12W-23S | 24 |
| Glennell Av. N&S .. 14W-23S | 24 |
| Glennell Ln. N&S .. 14W-23S | 24 |
| Granite Rd. E&W .. 13W-23S | 24 |
| Greenmeadows Pkwy. N&S | | |
| ............... 13W-23S | 24 |
| Greenview Av. N&S | | |
| ............... 14W-23S | 24 |
| Hacker Ct. N&S .... 13W-23S | 24 |
| Halligan Way E&W .. 13W-23S | 24 |
| Hamilton Rd. E&W .. 14W-24S | 32 |

| | | |
|---|---|---|
| Hastings Ln. E&W .. 12W-23S | 24 |
| Henry Dr. N&S .... 11W-23S | 25 |
| Hiawatha Blvd. N&S | | |
| ............... 13W-23S | 24 |
| Hickory Cr. NS&EW | | |
| ............... 11W-22S | 25 |
| Hillside Ln. E&W .. 14W-22S | 24 |
| Hummingbird Ln. E&W | | |
| ............... 14W-22S | 24 |
| Ibyzar Av. N&S .... 15W-23S | 23 |
| Jacob Dr. E&W .... 13W-23S | 24 |
| Jomar Ct. E&W .... 13W-23S | 24 |
| Kendall Ct. N&S .... 13W-23S | 24 |
| Kerry Ct. E&W .... 13W-23S | 24 |
| Kevin Ct. NE&SW .. 13W-23S | 24 |
| Kevin Ln. N&S .... 12W-23S | 24 |
| Kevork St. N&S .... 15W-23S | 23 |
| Kickapoo Ct. E&W .. 14W-23S | 24 |
| Kimberly Tr. NS&EW | | |
| ............... 13W-23S | 24 |
| Kingston Way N&S .. 14W-26S | 32 |
| Kluth Dr. E&W .... 14W-24S | 32 |
| Kriston Way NW&SE | | |
| ............... 13W-23S | 24 |
| LaPorte Rd. E&W .. 12W-23S | 24 |
| Lancaster Dr. NE&SW | | |
| ............... 12W-23S | 24 |
| Leetrim Ct. NW&SE | | |
| ............... 13W-23S | 24 |
| Lincoln Hwy. E&W .. 14W-25S | 32 |
| Lindsay Ln. NE&SW | | |
| ............... 12W-23S | 24 |
| London Bay NE&SW | | |
| ............... 13W-22S | 24 |
| London Ln. N&S .... 13W-22S | 24 |
| Manchester Ct. N&S | | |
| ............... 12W-23S | 24 |
| Manchester Ln. N&S | | |
| ............... 12W-23S | 24 |
| Mansfield Ln. NW&SE | | |
| ............... 12W-23S | 24 |
| Marilyn Way E&W .. 14W-26S | 32 |
| Marley Creek Ct. N&S | | |
| ............... 13W-23S | 24 |
| Maurita Ct. N&S....13W-23S | 24 |
| McGovney St. NE&SW | | |
| ............... 13W-23S | 24 |
| Meadow Creek Dr. N&S | | |
| ............... 14W-22S | 24 |
| Meadowview N&S | | |
| ............... 14W-22S | 24 |
| Michael Ct. N&S....13W-23S | 24 |
| Midland Av. N&S .. 13W-23S | 24 |
| Mokena St. N&S | | |
| ......... 13W-24S,13W-23S | 32 |
| N. Woodland Cir. N&S | | |
| ............... 14W-24S | 32 |
| North Brightway Dr. NE&SW | | |
| ............... 14W-24S | 32 |
| O'Connell Av. NE&SW | | |
| ............... 13W-23S | 24 |
| O'Connell St. E&W 12W-23S | 24 |
| Old Castle Dr. NE&SW | | |
| ............... 14W-24S | 32 |
| Osage Rd. N&S .... 14W-25S | 32 |
| Oxford Ct. E&W .... 12W-23S | 24 |
| Park Dr. N&S ...... 11W-23S | 25 |
| Park Way Ln. N&S.. 14W-22S | 24 |
| Parker St. E&W .... 13W-23S | 24 |
| Parkside Ct. E&W .. 13W-23S | 24 |
| Patricia Ln. N&S | | |
| ......... 13W-24S,13W-23S | 32 |
| Pheasant Ct. N&S .. 14W-23S | 24 |
| Pheasant Ln. N&S .. 14W-23S | 24 |
| Pickran Rd. NW&SE | | |
| ............... 15W-23S | 23 |
| Plattner Ct. N&S .. 14W-24S | 32 |
| Plattner Dr. NE&SW 14W-24S | 32 |
| Prestan Circle Dr. N&S | | |
| ............... 14W-25S | 32 |
| Regent Dr. N&S....12W-23S | 24 |
| Revere Rd. E&W .. 13W-23S | 24 |
| Rider Ridge Dr. N&S | | |
| ............... 14W-25S | 32 |
| Ridge Rd. N&S .... 11W-23S | 25 |
| Robert St. E&W .... 14W-23S | 24 |
| Route 45 N&S | | |
| ......... 12W-23S,12W-22S | 24 |
| Royal Ct. NE&SW .. 12W-23S | 24 |
| Ryan Ct. N&S ...... 13W-23S | 24 |
| S. Woodland Cir. E&W | | |
| ............... 14W-24S | 32 |
| Sandra Ct. NW&SE | | |
| ............... 14W-26S | 32 |
| Sarris Dr. NW&SE .. 15W-23S | 23 |
| Scarth Ln. N&S .... 13W-23S | 24 |
| Scott St. N&S ...... 14W-23S | 32 |
| Sevan Ct. NW&SE .. 15W-23S | 23 |
| Sharon Ln. E&W .. 13W-23S | 24 |
| South Brightway Dr. E&W | | |
| ............... 14W-24S | 32 |
| St. Albert Ct. N&S .. 14W-26S | 32 |
| St. John Dr. E&W .. 13W-24S | 32 |
| St. Joseph Ct. E&W | | |
| ............... 13W-23S | 24 |
| Stafford Ct. NE&SW | | |
| ............... 12W-23S | 24 |
| Stephan Ct. E&W .. 13W-23S | 24 |
| Stephanie Ln. E&W | | |
| ............... 14W-23S | 24 |
| Stonehenge Dr. N&S | | |
| ............... 12W-23S | 24 |
| Sussex Ct. E&W.... 12W-23S | 24 |
| Swan Dr. N&S......14W-22S | 24 |

| | | |
|---|---|---|
| Swanberg N&S 13W-23S | 24 |
| Swinford Ct. NW&SE | | |
| ............... 14W-24S | 32 |
| Swinford Ln. NE&SW | | |
| ............... 14W-24S | 32 |
| Tara Ct. NW&SE .. 12W-23S | 24 |
| Ternate St. NE&SW | | |
| ............... 13W-23S | 24 |
| Therese St. N&S | | |
| ......... 13W-24S,13W-23S | 32 |
| Thomas Dr. NW&SE | | |
| ............... 13W-23S | 24 |
| Trenton Ln. N&S .. 12W-23S | 24 |
| Union Av. N&S .... 13W-23S | 24 |
| Union St. NW&SE .. 13W-23S | 24 |
| Vincent Ct. E&W .. 14W-26S | 32 |
| W. Brightway Rd. N&S | | |
| ............... 14W-24S | 32 |
| W. Woodland Cir. N&S | | |
| ............... 14W-24S | 32 |
| Walnut St. N&S .... 11W-23S | 24 |
| Weber Ct. N&S .... 13W-23S | 24 |
| Weber Rd. N&S .... 13W-23S | 24 |
| Westport Way E&W | | |
| ............... 13W-23S | 24 |
| Wild Field Ct. NW&SE | | |
| ............... 13W-23S | 24 |
| Willers Way N&S .. 13W-23S | 24 |
| Willow Av. E&W .... 13W-23S | 24 |
| Willow Av. NE&SW | | |
| ............... 13W-23S | 24 |
| Willow Ln. E&W .... 14W-23S | 24 |
| Wolf Rd. N&S | | |
| ......... 14W-24S,14W-22S | 32 |
| York Dr. N&S ...... 12W-23S | 24 |
| 1st Ct. E&W ...... 13W-23S | 24 |
| 1st St. NE&SW .... 13W-23S | 24 |
| 2nd St. NE&SW .. 13W-23S | 24 |
| 3rd St. NE&SW .. 13W-23S | 24 |
| 82nd St. N&S ...... 10W-22S | 25 |
| 96th Av. N&S ...... 12W-23S | 24 |
| 97th St. E&W ...... 12W-23S | 24 |
| 104th Av. N&S | | |
| ......... 13W-22S,12W-23S | 24 |
| 108th Pl. N&S .... 12W-23S | 24 |
| 114th Av. N&S .... 14W-23S | 24 |
| 114th St. N&S..... 14W-24S | 32 |
| 116th Av. N&S .... 14W-23S | 24 |
| 188th St. E&W .... 10W-22S | 25 |
| 189th St. E&W .... 10W-22S | 25 |
| 191st St. E&W | | |
| ......... 14W-22S,10W-22S | 24 |
| 193rd St. E&W .. 14W-22S | 24 |
| 194th St. E&W | | |
| ......... 14W-23S,12W-23S | 24 |
| 195th St. E&W | | |
| ......... 14W-23S,12W-23S | 24 |
| 196th St. E&W .... 12W-23S | 24 |
| 197th St. E&W | | |
| ......... 14W-23S,12W-23S | 24 |

## Monee

| | | |
|---|---|---|
| Anna Ln. N&S ...... 8W-32S | 53 |
| Arthur Dr. N&S ...... 6W-31S | 42 |
| Astor Pl. E&W ...... 6W-31S | 42 |
| Augusta Blvd. E&W .. 6W-31S | 42 |
| Birch Ct. NW&SE .. 8W-32S | 53 |
| Bradford Ct. N&S .. 8W-32S | 53 |
| Carl Rd. NE&SW .... 7W-32S | 54 |
| Cedar Ct. NW&SE .. 8W-32S | 53 |
| Colonial Dr. E&W .. 6W-31S | 42 |
| Compass Ln. N&S .. 6W-31S | 42 |
| County Fair Ct. E&W | | |
| ............... 6W-31S | 42 |
| Court St. E&W ...... 6W-31S | 42 |
| Eastgate Av. N&S .. 6W-31S | 42 |
| Eastlynne Ln. NE&SW | | |
| ............... 6W-31S | 42 |
| Elmwood Ln. N&S .. 6W-31S | 42 |
| Fairground Ct. E&W.. 6W-31S | 42 |
| Firestone Dr. N&S .. 6W-31S | 42 |
| George Tr. E&W .... 8W-32S | 53 |
| Gorman Ct. E&W .. 8W-32S | 53 |
| Gorman Rd. E&W | | |
| ......... 8W-31S,7W-31S | 41 |
| Gorman Rd. N&S .. 8W-32S | 53 |
| Goverors Hwy. NE&SW | | |
| ............... 7W-32S | 54 |
| Greenbriar Dr. N&S .. 6W-31S | 42 |
| Hazeltine Dr. N&S .. 6W-31S | 42 |
| Herbert Ct. E&W .... 6W-31S | 42 |
| Herbert Pl. E&W .... 6W-31S | 42 |
| Home Av. N&S ...... 6W-31S | 42 |
| Interstate 57 N&S....7W-31S | 42 |
| Linden Av. N&S......6W-31S | 42 |
| Locust Pl. NE&SW .. 6W-31S | 42 |
| Main St. E&W ...... 6W-31S | 42 |
| Manhattan Rd. N&S .. 6W-31S | 42 |
| Manhattan-Monee Rd. E&W | | |
| ............... 8W-30S | 41 |
| Maple Ct. E&W .... 8W-32S | 53 |
| Margaret St. E&W .. 6W-31S | 42 |
| Merlon Dr. N&S....6W-31S | 42 |
| Middlepoint Av. N&S | | |
| ............... 6W-31S | 42 |
| Mill St. E&W ...... 6W-31S | 42 |
| Oak Pk. N&S ...... 6W-31S | 42 |
| Oakwood N&S .... 6W-31S | 42 |
| Olympic Ct. E&W .. 6W-31S | 42 |
| Park Ln. E&W ...... 6W-31S | 42 |
| Pinehurst Dr. N&S .. 6W-31S | 42 |
| Pinewood Ln. N&S .. 6W-31S | 42 |
| Ribbon Ct. E&W .... 6W-31S | 42 |

| | Grid | Page |
|---|---|---|
| Ridgleal Av. N&S .. | 8W-31S | 41 |
| Riviera Dr. E&W .... | 6W-31S | 42 |
| Roosevelt St. E&W .. | 7W-31S | 42 |
| Route 50 N&S | | |
| ...... | 7W-32S,6W-31S | 54 |
| Ruby St. N&S ...... | 6W-31S | 42 |
| Scioto Dr. N&S ...... | 6W-31S | 42 |
| Shagcreek Dr. N&S.. | 6W-31S | 42 |
| Shinnecock Dr. N&S | 6W-31S | 42 |
| Spruce Ct. E&W .... | 8W-32S | 53 |
| Spyglass Cir. N&S .. | 6W-31S | 42 |
| Sunset Dr., E. N&S .. | 7W-31S | 42 |
| Tonie Marie Ln. E&W | | |
| ...... | 8W-32S | 53 |
| Von Av. E&W...... | 7W-31S | 42 |
| Walnut St. NE&SW | | |
| ...... | 7W-31S,6W-31S | 42 |
| Watson E&W...... | 7W-32S | 54 |
| West Court St. E&W | | |
| ...... | 7W-31S | 42 |
| William St. NW&SE | | |
| ...... | 7W-31S,6W-31S | 42 |
| Wilson St. E&W | | |
| ...... | 7W-31S,6W-31S | 42 |
| Winfred Rd. N&S .... | 8W-32S | 53 |
| Winged Foot Dr. E&W | | |
| ...... | 6W-31S | 42 |

## Monee Township

| | Grid | Page |
|---|---|---|
| Bong Rd. E&W .... | 8W-30S | 41 |
| Boyington Ln. NE&SW | | |
| ...... | 8W-30S | 41 |
| Central Av. N&S .... | 7W-28S | 42 |
| Central Park Av. N&S | | |
| ...... | 4W-28S | 43 |
| Chennault Av. N&S.. | 8W-30S | 41 |
| Cicero Av. N&S...... | 6W-29S | 42 |
| Colman Pl. E&W .... | 6W-31S | 42 |
| Crawford Av. N&S .. | 5W-33S | 54 |
| Crete Monee Rd. E&W | | |
| ...... | 4W-31S,3W-30S | 43 |
| Doolittle Rd. NE&SW | | |
| ...... | 8W-30S | 41 |
| Dralle Rd. E&W | | |
| ...... | 7W-29S,5W-30S | 42 |
| Egyptian Trail Rd. N&S | | |
| ...... | 7W-33S | 54 |
| Foss Rd. E&W .... | 8W-30S | 41 |
| Foxwood Dr. N&S .. | 6W-32S | 54 |
| Gabreski Ln. E&W .. | 8W-30S | 41 |
| Goodenow (Pauling) Rd. E&W | | |
| ...... | 6W-32S,3W-32S | 54 |
| Gorman Rd. E&W .. | 8W-31S | 41 |
| Governors Hwy. NE&SW | | |
| ...... | 7W-32S | 54 |
| Greenbrier Dr. N&S .. | 6W-32S | 54 |
| Hamilton Av. N&S... | 7W-30S | 42 |
| Hamilton Rd. E&W .. | 4W-30S | 43 |
| Hansan Ct. NW&SE .. | 8W-30S | 41 |
| Hawthorne Ct. E&W | | |
| ...... | 4W-28S | 43 |
| Hawthorne Dr. N&S .. | 6W-32S | 54 |
| Heatherbrook Tr. E&W | | |
| ...... | 6W-32S | 54 |
| Highland Av. N&S | | |
| ...... | 3W-32S,3W-31S | 55 |
| Hilltop Dr. E&W .. | 6W-32S | 54 |
| Home Av. N&S | | |
| ...... | 6W-32S,6W-28S | 54 |
| Interstate 57 NE&SW | | |
| ...... | 8W-33S,7W-28S | 53 |
| J.L. Smith Ln. E&W .. | 8W-30S | 41 |
| Johnson Ct. E&W .... | 8W-30S | 41 |
| Kedzie Av. N&S .... | 4W-33S | 55 |
| Kirsten Rd. N&S | | |
| ...... | 5W-33S,5W-31S | 54 |
| Laurel Ln. E&W .... | 7W-32S | 54 |
| Linden Av. NS&EW .. | 6W-31S | 42 |
| Manhattan Wilton Rd. E&W | | |
| ...... | 8W-33S | 53 |
| Manhatten Monee Rd. E&W | | |
| ...... | 8W-30S | 41 |
| McCampbell Rd. E&W | | |
| ...... | 8W-30S | 41 |
| McCorkle Av. N&S .. | 6W-31S | 42 |
| McNamara Rd. E&W | | |
| ...... | 6W-29S | 42 |
| Meghan Ct., N. N&S | | |
| ...... | 6W-32S | 54 |
| Meghan Ct., S. N&S | 6W-32S | 54 |
| Melissa Ct. N&S .... | 6W-32S | 54 |
| Michelle Ct. N&S .... | 6W-32S | 54 |
| Murphy Ln. N&S .... | 8W-30S | 41 |
| O'Hare Ct. N&S .... | 8W-30S | 41 |
| Oak Dr. E&W .... | 4W-29S | 54 |
| Oakbrook Rd. E&W .. | 6W-33S | 54 |
| Olendorf Rd. E&W | | |
| ...... | 5W-31S,3W-31S | 42 |
| Olivia Ct. N&S .... | 6W-32S | 54 |
| Pauling (Goodenow) Rd. E&W | | |
| ...... | 8W-32S,3W-32S | 53 |
| Pinewood Dr. NE&SW | | |
| ...... | 4W-31S | 43 |
| Pinewood Ln. N&S .. | 4W-31S | 43 |
| Ridgeland Av. N&S | | |
| ...... | 8W-33S,8W-28S | 53 |
| Roberts Rd. E&W .. | 6W-32S | 54 |
| Roberts Ridge Dr. E&W | | |
| ...... | 6W-32S | 54 |
| Route 50 N&S | | |
| ...... | 7W-33S,6W-28S | 54 |
| Sandy Ct. E&W.... | 5W-31S | 42 |
| Smith Rd. E&W.... | 6W-29S | 42 |

| | Grid | Page |
|---|---|---|
| Spear Ruler Ln. E&W | | |
| ...... | 5W-33S | 54 |
| Spurge Av. N&S .... | 4W-28S | 43 |
| Steger Monee Rd. N&S | | |
| ...... | 5W-30S,4W-30S | 42 |
| Stephanie St. NW&SE | | |
| ...... | 6W-32S | 54 |
| Stone Rd. N&S .... | 7W-32S | 54 |
| Stuenkel Rd. E&W | | |
| ...... | 8W-28S,4W-28S | 41 |
| Sylvan Ln. N&S .... | 6W-32S | 54 |
| Timber Lane Rd. N&S | | |
| ...... | 7W-33S,6W-33S | 54 |
| Wagner Dr. E&W .. | 8W-30S | 41 |
| Welch St. NW&SE .. | 8W-30S | 41 |
| Western Av. N&S | | |
| ...... | 3W-29S,3W-28S | 43 |
| Whispering Hill Ln. E&W | | |
| ...... | 8W-31S | 41 |
| Will Center Rd. N&S | 6W-33S | 54 |
| Willow Creek Ln. N&S | | |
| ...... | 8W-31S | 41 |
| 279th St. E&W | | |
| ...... | 6W-33S,3W-33S | 54 |

## Naperville*
### (Also see Du Page County)

| | Grid | Page |
|---|---|---|
| Alamosa Dr. .. | 27W-10S | 5 |
| Albert Hall Ct. E&W | | |
| ...... | 28W-11S | 5 |
| Alexandria Dr. NE&SW | | |
| ...... | 25W-10S | 6 |
| Allegany Dr. NE&SW | | |
| ...... | 25W-10S | 6 |
| Alyssa Ct.* NW&SE | | |
| ...... | 26W-10S | 5 |
| Alyssa Dr.* NW&SE | | |
| ...... | 26W-10S | 6 |
| Amherst Ct. NE&SW | | |
| ...... | 25W-10S | 6 |
| Amy Ct. E&W .... | 26W-10S | 6 |
| Apple River Dr. NS&EW | | |
| ...... | 25W-10S | 6 |
| Ardley Ct. NW&SE.. | 26W-10S | 6 |
| Ariel Ct. E&W .. | 28W-12S | 5 |
| Arlington Av. E&W | | |
| ...... | 26W-10S,25W-10S | 6 |
| Ashbury Dr. N&S .. | 28W-11S | 5 |
| Ashtonlee Ct. N&S.. | 26W-10S | 6 |
| Aster Ct. N&S ...... | 24W-10S | 6 |
| Augustana Ct. N&S | | |
| ...... | 24W-10S | 6 |
| Augustana Dr. E&W | | |
| ...... | 25W-10S,24W-10S | 6 |
| Austin Ln. N&S .. | 28W-11S | 5 |
| Austin St. N&S .. | 28W-11S | 5 |
| Aviara Ct. N&S .. | 30W-10S | 4 |
| Avon Ct. E&W.... | 28W-11S | 5 |
| Bards Av. E&W .. | 28W-11S | 5 |
| Barkdoll Ct. N&S .. | 25W-10S | 6 |
| Barkdoll Rd. N&S .. | 25W-10S | 6 |
| Barnes Ln. N&S .. | 28W-11S | 5 |
| Barth Dr. N&S.... | 25W-10S | 6 |
| Beaconsfield Av. E&W | | |
| ...... | 27W-10S | 5 |
| Becket Rd. E&W .. | 28W-11S | 5 |
| Bennett Dr. N&S .. | 28W-11S | 5 |
| Bennington Ct. N&S | | |
| ...... | 27W-10S | 5 |
| Black Walnut Ct. E&W | | |
| ...... | 24W-10S | 6 |
| Blodgett Dr. NW&SE | | |
| ...... | 27W-10S | 5 |
| Bluebell Ct. E&W .. | 24W-10S | 6 |
| Bluemont Ct. N&S.. | 25W-10S | 6 |
| Book Rd. N&S .. | 29W-13S | 9 |
| Boswell Ln. NE&SW | | |
| ...... | 28W-11S | 5 |
| Boulder Ct. N&S.. | 27W-10S | 5 |
| Braddock Dr. N&S .. | 25W-10S | 6 |
| Branford Ln. NE&SW | | |
| ...... | 28W-11S | 5 |
| Breckenridge Ln. NS&EW | | |
| ...... | 27W-10S | 5 |
| Briarhill Ct. N&S .. | 27W-10S | 5 |
| Briarhill Dr. EW&NS | | |
| ...... | 27W-10S | 5 |
| Brockton Cir. NS&EW | | |
| ...... | 27W-10S | 5 |
| Bronte Av. E&W .. | 28W-11S | 5 |
| Bronte Ct. N&S .. | 28W-11S | 5 |
| Brook Crossing Ct. E&W | | |
| ...... | 28W-10S | 5 |
| Brossman N&S .. | 28W-11S | 5 |
| Brown Ct. N&S .. | 24W-10S | 6 |
| Bundle Flower Ct. N&S | | |
| ...... | 29W-13S | 9 |
| Burbany Ct. N&S .. | 28W-11S | 5 |
| Caine Dr. N&S.... | 28W-11S | 5 |
| Calico Av. E&W .. | 28W-10S | 5 |
| Calvert Ct. NW&SE | | |
| ...... | 25W-10S | 6 |
| Candeur Dr. N&S .. | 28W-11S | 5 |
| Carlyle Rd. E&W .. | 28W-11S | 5 |
| Carrboro Ct. NW&SE | | |
| ...... | 25W-10S | 6 |
| Cassin Rd. E&W .. | 28W-11S | 5 |
| Catclaw Ct. N&S .. | 29W-13S | 9 |
| Celeste Ln. NS&EW | | |
| ...... | 28W-10S | 5 |
| Centenary Ct. N&S | 25W-10S | 6 |
| Chaucer Ct. E&W .. | 24W-10S | 6 |

| | Grid | Page |
|---|---|---|
| Cherokee Ct. NE&SW | | |
| ...... | 28W-12S | 5 |
| Cheyenne Dr. N&S.. | 27W-10S | 5 |
| Chilvers Ct. NE&SW | | |
| ...... | 25W-10S | 6 |
| Cir. .. | 28W-11S | 5 |
| Christie Ct. E&W .. | 28W-11S | 5 |
| Cimarron Ct. N&S .. | 28W-11S | 5 |
| Clearwater Dr. NS&EW | | |
| ...... | 28W-12S | 5 |
| Cobblestone Ct. E&W | | |
| ...... | 28W-10S | 5 |
| Colgate Ct. E&W .. | 25W-10S | 6 |
| Colorado Ct. E&W.. | 27W-10S | 5 |
| Conan Doyle Rd. E&W | | |
| ...... | 28W-11S | 5 |
| Coneflower Dr. NE&SW | | |
| ...... | 29W-13S | 9 |
| Connecticut Dr. E&W | | |
| ...... | 27W-10S | 5 |
| Copperfield Ct.* N&S | | |
| ...... | 26W-10S | 5 |
| Copperfield Dr. N&S | | |
| ...... | 27W-10S | 5 |
| Coralberry Cir. E&W | | |
| ...... | 29W-13S | 9 |
| Cordula Ln. NS&EW | | |
| ...... | 28W-11S | 5 |
| Covington Ct. E&W | | |
| ...... | 25W-10S | 6 |
| Crestfield Ct.* NW&SE | | |
| ...... | 26W-10S | 5 |
| Crimson Ct. E&W .. | 28W-11S | 5 |
| Cromwell Ln. NS&EW | | |
| ...... | 28W-11S | 5 |
| Crooked Tree Ct. NE&SW | | |
| ...... | 26W-10S | 6 |
| Cumberland Ct. E&W | | |
| ...... | 25W-10S | 6 |
| Daisy Ct. N&S .... | 27W-10S | 5 |
| Danbury Dr. E&W .. | 26W-10S | 6 |
| Dandelion Ct. N&S | | |
| ...... | 29W-13S | 8 |
| Darwin St. N&S .. | 28W-11S | 5 |
| DeFoe Ct. N&S | | |
| ...... | 28W-11S,28W-12S | 5 |
| DeLaSalle Av. E&W | | |
| ...... | 27W-10S | 5 |
| Delaware Ct. N&S .. | 28W-12S | 5 |
| Dewhurst St. N&S .. | 28W-11S | 5 |
| Diamond Ct. N&S .. | 28W-12S | 5 |
| Dilorenzo Ct. E&W.. | 25W-10S | 6 |
| Dorchester Ct. E&W | | |
| ...... | 25W-10S | 6 |
| Dryden Ct. E&W .. | 28W-11S | 5 |
| Du Pahze St. N&S | | |
| ...... | 27W-10S,26W-10S | 5 |
| Dublin Dr. NE&SW.. | 28W-12S | 5 |
| Eliot Ln. NS&EW .. | 28W-11S | 5 |
| Emory Av. E&W .. | 25W-10S | 6 |
| Emporia Ct. N&S .. | 28W-11S | 5 |
| English Ct. E&W .. | 28W-11S | 5 |
| Esquire Cir. NS&EW | | |
| ...... | 28W-12S | 6 |
| Falkner Ct. E&W .. | 28W-11S | 5 |
| Fieldstone Ct. E&W | | |
| ...... | 28W-10S | 5 |
| Fireside Ct. N&S .. | 28W-10S | 5 |
| Flambeau Dr. N&S .. | 28W-10S | 5 |
| Fleetwood Ct. NS&EW | | |
| ...... | 25W-10S | 6 |
| Fox River Ct. N&S | 26W-10S | 6 |
| Fox River Dr. N&S | | |
| ...... | 26W-10S,25W-10S | 6 |
| Frost St. N&S .. | 28W-11S | 5 |
| Garnette Ct. N&S | | |
| ...... | 28W-12S,28W-11S | 5 |
| Gateshead Dr. NS&EW | | |
| ...... | 28W-11S,26W-10S | 5 |
| Ginger Ln. E&W .. | 24W-10S | 6 |
| Glen Echo Rd. E&W | | |
| ...... | 25W-10S | 6 |
| Gleneagles Dr. N&S | | |
| ...... | 27W-10S | 5 |
| Goldtown Ct. E&W | 28W-12S | 5 |
| Greenfield Ct. E&W | | |
| ...... | 28W-10S | 5 |
| Haddassah Ct. E&W | | |
| ...... | 27W-10S | 5 |
| Haddassah Dr. NW&SE | | |
| ...... | 26W-10S | 6 |
| Halifax Ct. NE&SW | | |
| ...... | 28W-12S | 5 |
| Hamlet Rd. E&W .. | 28W-11S | 5 |
| Hampshire Ct. E&W | | |
| ...... | 26W-10S | 6 |
| Hanover Ct. N&S .. | 26W-10S | 6 |
| Hartford Ct. N&S.. | 27W-10S | 5 |
| Harvest Ct. E&W .. | 28W-10S | 5 |
| Hawley Ct. NW&SE | | |
| ...... | 27W-10S | 5 |
| Hearthside Ct. E&W | | |
| ...... | 28W-10S | 5 |
| Heirloom Ct. N&S | 28W-12S | 5 |
| Hempstead Av. E&W | | |
| ...... | 27W-10S | 5 |
| Heritage Ct. NE&SW | | |
| ...... | 25W-10S | 5 |
| High Meadow Dr. E&W | | |
| ...... | 29W-13S | 9 |
| Hobbes Dr. N&S.... | 28W-11S | 5 |
| Hollenback Ct. N&S | | |
| ...... | 27W-10S | 5 |

| | Grid | Page |
|---|---|---|
| Hollingswood Av. E&W | | |
| ...... | 28W-11S | 5 |
| Homestead Dr. N&S | | |
| ...... | 28W-10S | 5 |
| Hoyer Ct. NW&SE .. | 25W-10S | 6 |
| Hudson Ct. NE&SW | | |
| ...... | 28W-10S | 5 |
| Jubilant Ct. N&S... | 28W-11S | 5 |
| Junegrass Dr. N&S | 29W-13S | 8 |
| Kalamazoo River Dr. N&S | | |
| ...... | 26W-10S | 6 |
| Kaskaskia Ct. N&S | 26W-10S | 6 |
| Kayak Dr. E&W .. | 28W-12S | 5 |
| Keats Dr. E&W .. | 28W-11S | 5 |
| Keim Rd. N&S.... | 25W-10S | 6 |
| Keystone Ct. N&S .. | 27W-10S | 5 |
| Kingsley Dr. N&S .. | 26W-10S | 6 |
| Knock Knoll Rd. NE&SW | | |
| ...... | 26W-10S | 6 |
| Kubek Rd. E&W .. | 28W-10S | 5 |
| Lagoon Ct. E&W .. | 28W-12S | 5 |
| Lagoon Ln. NE&SW | | |
| ...... | 28W-12S | 5 |
| Lakeside Ct. NW&SE | | |
| ...... | 28W-10S | 5 |
| Landore Dr. N&S .. | 28W-11S | 5 |
| Lawrence St. N&S | | |
| ...... | 28W-12S,28W-11S | 5 |
| Leach Dr. NE&SW .. | 28W-11S | 5 |
| Leawood Ct. E&W.. | 28W-10S | 5 |
| Lehigh Cir. NS&EW | | |
| ...... | 25W-10S | 6 |
| Lemmon Dr. NE&SW | | |
| ...... | 26W-10S | 6 |
| Leverenz Dr. NS&EW | | |
| ...... | 27W-10S | 5 |
| Lindenwood Ln. N&S | | |
| ...... | 24W-10S | 6 |
| Lindholm Ct. NW&SE | | |
| ...... | 27W-10S | 5 |
| Litchfield Ct. N&S .. | 27W-10S | 5 |
| Longacre Dr. N&S .. | 28W-10S | 5 |
| Lotus Ct. N&S...... | 24W-10S | 6 |
| Mackinaw Ct. E&W | | |
| ...... | 26W-10S | 6 |
| Madera Ln. N&S.... | 24W-10S | 6 |
| Magenta Ct. N&S .. | 28W-11S | 5 |
| Malvina Ct. N&S .. | 28W-11S | 5 |
| Mandeville Ct. E&W | | |
| ...... | 28W-12S,28W-11S | 5 |
| Marengo Ct. E&W .. | 28W-11S | 5 |
| Marshall Ct. N&S .. | 25W-10S | 6 |
| Massachusetts Av. EW&NS | | |
| ...... | 27W-10S | 5 |
| Mayapple Ct. N&S | 24W-10S | 6 |
| McCartny Ln. NE&SW | | |
| ...... | 26W-10S | 6 |
| Meadow Green Dr. NE&SW | | |
| ...... | 28W-10S | 5 |
| Mecan Dr. N&S .. | 28W-10S | 5 |
| Mercer Ct. N&S .. | 24W-10S | 6 |
| Mesa Dr. NE&SW .. | 27W-10S | 5 |
| Meyer Ct. NW&SE .. | 28W-10S | 5 |
| Midhurst Ct. E&W .. | 26W-9S | 6 |
| Midland Dr. N&S... | 28W-10S | 5 |
| Milkweed Dr. N&S .. | 29W-13S | 9 |
| Modaff Rd. N&S | | |
| ...... | 27W-10S,27W-8S | 5 |
| Montrose Ct. NE&SW | | |
| ...... | 28W-10S | 5 |
| Morningstar Ct. E&W | | |
| ...... | 28W-10S | 5 |
| Nantucket Dr. NE&SW | | |
| ...... | 27W-10S | 5 |
| Naper Blvd. NE&SW | | |
| ...... | 25W-10S | 6 |
| Neskola Ct. NE&SW | | |
| ...... | 28W-10S | 5 |
| Newgate Av. NW&SE | | |
| ...... | 26W-10S | 6 |
| Newman Ct. E&W .. | 28W-11S | 5 |
| Newport Dr. NS&EW | | |
| ...... | 27W-10S | 5 |
| Norfolk Ct. N&S .. | 25W-10S | 6 |
| Northhampton Ct. E&W | | |
| ...... | 27W-10S | 5 |
| Norwich Ct. N&S .. | 27W-10S | 5 |
| Nottingham Dr. NS&EW | | |
| ...... | 27W-10S | 5 |
| Oak Bluff Ct. NE&SW | | |
| ...... | 26W-10S | 6 |
| Oberlin Ct. N&S .. | 25W-10S | 6 |
| Oconto Ct. E&W .. | 28W-11S | 5 |
| Old Mill Ct. E&W .. | 28W-10S | 5 |
| Old Wehrli Rd. N&S | | |
| ...... | 24W-10S | 6 |
| Orwell Rd. E&W .. | 28W-11S | 5 |
| Othello Dr. N&S .. | 28W-11S | 5 |
| Papaw Dr. N&S .. | 27W-10S | 5 |
| Parador Dr. N&S... | 28W-11S | 5 |
| Pebblestone Rd. NW&SE | | |
| ...... | 27W-10S | 5 |
| Penny Royal Dr. N&S | | |
| ...... | 29W-13S | 8 |
| Peshtigo Av. E&W.. | 28W-10S | 5 |
| Petra Ct. N&S .. | 28W-11S | 5 |
| Petworth Ct. N&S .. | 26W-10S | 6 |
| Piedmont Cir. NS&EW | | |
| ...... | 25W-10S | 6 |
| Piper Av. N&S .. | 26W-10S | 6 |
| Poet Ct. N&S .. | 28W-11S | 5 |
| Pontiac Cir. NE&SW | | |
| ...... | 26W-10S | 6 |
| Potomac Av. E&W.. | 25W-10S | 6 |

| | Grid | Page |
|---|---|---|
| Pradel Dr. N&S .... | 29W-13S | 9 |
| Prairie Sage Dr. N&S | | |
| ...... | 29W-13S | 9 |
| Prairie Dock Rd. E&W | | |
| ...... | 29W-13S | 9 |
| Prelude Ct. N&S .. | 28W-11S | 5 |
| Prestige Ct. N&S .. | 28W-11S | 5 |
| Princess Rd. E&W.. | 28W-12S | 5 |
| Providence Ct. NW&SE | | |
| ...... | 27W-10S | 5 |
| Pueblo Ct. E&W.... | 27W-10S | 5 |
| Putnam Av. NE&SW | | |
| ...... | 26W-10S | 6 |
| Red River Ct. E&W | | |
| ...... | 26W-10S | 6 |
| Relstar Ct. E&W .. | 28W-11S | 5 |
| Remington Dr. N&S | | |
| ...... | 26W-10S | 6 |
| Richwood Ct. N&S.. | 28W-12S | 5 |
| Rio Grande Ct. NE&SW | | |
| ...... | 25W-10S | 6 |
| Rivanna Ct. N&S .. | 25W-10S | 6 |
| River Woods Ct. NE&SW | | |
| ...... | 26W-10S | 6 |
| Rivermist Ct. NS&EW | | |
| ...... | 26W-10S | 6 |
| Roanoke Ct. E&W.. | 25W-10S | 6 |
| Robert Dr. N&S .. | 28W-12S | 5 |
| Rock Ct. N&S...... | 27W-10S | 5 |
| Rock River Ct. E&W | | |
| ...... | 26W-10S | 6 |
| Rock Spring Ct. E&W | | |
| ...... | 27W-10S | 5 |
| Rock Spring Rd. E&W | | |
| ...... | 27W-10S | 5 |
| Rode St. N&S.... | 31W-11S | 4 |
| Rosada Dr. N&S | | |
| ...... | 28W-12S,28W-11S | 5 |
| Rosehill Ct. N&S .. | 25W-10S | 6 |
| Roxbury Ct. E&W.. | 27W-10S | 5 |
| Royce Rd. E&W | | |
| ...... | 25W-10S,24W-10S | 6 |
| Royce Woods Ct. NS&EW | | |
| ...... | 25W-10S | 6 |
| Ryan Ct. N&S .. | 28W-10S | 5 |
| Cir. .. | 30W-10S | 4 |
| Salisbury Dr. NS&EW | | |
| ...... | 27W-10S | 5 |
| Salt River Ct. E&W | | |
| ...... | 26W-10S | 6 |
| Saltmeadow Rd. E&W | | |
| ...... | 29W-13S | 9 |
| San Luis Ct. N&S .. | 27W-10S | 5 |
| Sandlilly Dr. N&S .. | 29W-13S | 9 |
| Saratoga Rd. E&W | 28W-11S | 5 |
| Saw Mill Rd. NE&SW | | |
| ...... | 26W-10S | 6 |
| Saxon Ln. NS&EW | 28W-11S | 5 |
| Scottsbridge Rd. NW&SE | | |
| ...... | 26W-10S | 6 |
| Sebastian Ct. E&W | | |
| ...... | 28W-12S | 5 |
| Sebastian Dr. N&S.. | 28W-12S | 5 |
| Seiler Dr. N&S...... | 27W-10S | 5 |
| Settlers Ct. NE&SW | | |
| ...... | 26W-10S | 6 |
| Settlers Dr. NE&SW | | |
| ...... | 26W-10S | 6 |
| Seville Av. E&W .. | 27W-10S | 5 |
| Shakespeare Ln. E&W | | |
| ...... | 28W-11S | 5 |
| Shaw Av. E&W ... | 28W-11S | 5 |
| Sherwood Ct. NW&SE | | |
| ...... | 27W-10S | 5 |
| Shimer Ct. E&W .. | 25W-10S | 6 |
| Shire Ct. N&S .. | 28W-11S | 5 |
| Sierra Av. NE&SW .. | 26W-10S | 6 |
| Sierra Ct.* NE&SW.. | 26W-10S | 6 |
| Silver Spur Ct. NE&SW | | |
| ...... | 28W-12S | 5 |
| Snapdragon Rd. E&W | | |
| ...... | 29W-13S | 9 |
| Spencer Ct. N&S .. | 28W-11S | 5 |
| Spinner Ct. N&S... | 27W-10S | 5 |
| St. Croix Av. E&W.. | 28W-10S | 5 |
| Starlite Ct. NS&EW | | |
| ...... | 28W-10S | 5 |
| Steamboat Rd. E&W | | |
| ...... | 29W-13S | 9 |
| Stillwater Ct. NE&SW | | |
| ...... | 26W-10S | 6 |
| Sweetbroom Ct. E&W | | |
| ...... | 29W-13S | 9 |
| Sweetbroom Rd. E&W | | |
| ...... | 29W-13S | 8 |
| Switchgrass Dr. N&S | | |
| ...... | 29W-13S | 9 |
| Thackery Ct. E&W.. | 28W-11S | 5 |
| Thackery Ln. NW&SE | | |
| ...... | 28W-11S | 5 |
| Thames Ct. NE&SW | | |
| ...... | 28W-12S | 5 |
| Thatcher Dr. N&S .. | 29W-13S | 9 |
| Thaxton Ct. N&S .. | 25W-10S | 6 |
| Thurman Av. N&S .. | 25W-10S | 6 |
| Tiara Ct. E&W .... | 28W-12S | 5 |
| Tiffany Ct.* NW&SE | | |
| ...... | 26W-11S | 6 |
| Townsend Dr. NE&SW | | |
| ...... | 26W-10S | 5 |
| Cir. .. | 28W-12S | 5 |
| Trappers Ct. NE&SW | | |
| ...... | 26W-10S | 6 |

| | Grid | Page |
|---|---|---|
| Treesdale Ct. NE&SW | | |
| .................. 30W-10S | 4 |
| Trillium Ln. N&S .... 24W-10S | 6 |
| Tuscany Dr. NS&EW | | |
| .................. 28W-11S | 5 |
| Tussell St. N&S ... 28W-11S | 5 |
| University Ct. N&S . 25W-10S | 6 |
| Velvet Bent Ct. N&S | | |
| .................. 29W-13S | 9 |
| Vermillion Ct. NW&SE | | |
| .................. 25W-10S | 6 |
| Vesper Ct. N&S .... 28W-12S | 5 |
| Wabash Ct. NW&SE | | |
| .................. 25W-10S | 6 |
| Waterbury Ct. E&W | | |
| .................. 27W-10S | 5 |
| Watford Dr. NW&SE | | |
| .................. 28W-10S | 5 |
| Watson Av. E&W | | |
| ........ 28W-12S,28W-11S | 5 |
| Waupaca Ct. N&S .. 28W-10S | 5 |
| Wayland Ln. N&S .. 26W-10S | 6 |
| Waynesburg St. N&S | | |
| .................. 26W-10S | 6 |
| Weatherford Ln. NS&EW | | |
| .................. 26W-10S | 6 |
| Wedgewood Dr. N&S | | |
| .................. 27W-10S | 5 |
| Wendy Rd. N&S .... 27W-10S | 5 |
| Wentworth Ct. E&W | | |
| .................. 26W-10S | 6 |
| Wesley Av. NW&SE | | |
| .................. 26W-10S | 6 |
| West Branch Ct. NE&SW | | |
| .................. 26W-10S | 6 |
| Westbrook Cir. NS&EW | | |
| .................. 26W-10S | 6 |
| Wicklow Way Rd. E&W | | |
| .................. 28W-12S | 5 |
| Wild Timothy Dr. E&W | | |
| .................. 29W-13S | 9 |
| Wildrose Ln. E&W .. 24W-10S | 6 |
| Windemere Av. E&W | | |
| .................. 28W-10S | 5 |
| Winter Park Dr. N&S | | |
| .................. 27W-10S | 5 |
| Wirestem Ct. N&S .. 29W-13S | 9 |
| Wishing Well Dr. NW&SE | | |
| .................. 28W-10S | 5 |
| Wolfe Ct. N&S .... 28W-11S | 5 |
| Woodland Cir. NS&EW | | |
| ...... 26W-10S,26W-9S | 6 |
| Woodview Cir. NE&SW | | |
| .................. 26W-10S | 6 |
| Woodview Ct. NE&SW | | |
| .................. 26W-10S | 6 |
| Wooster Ct. N&S .. 24W-10S | 6 |
| Worthing Dr. NS&EW | | |
| .................. 26W-10S | 6 |
| Xavier Ct. N&S .... 24W-10S | 6 |
| Yellowstar Ct. E&W | | |
| .................. 29W-13S | 9 |
| Yellowstar Ln. E&W | | |
| .................. 29W-13S | 9 |
| Cir. .............. 28W-12S | 5 |
| Yorktown Ct. NE&SW | | |
| .................. 28W-12S | 5 |
| 91st St. E&W ...... 24W-10S | 6 |

### New Lenox

| | Grid | Page |
|---|---|---|
| Abbey Ct. N&S ... 19W-24S | 30 |
| Abraham Dr. E&W . 18W-23S | 22 |
| Aeronca Ct. E&W .. 18W-25S | 30 |
| Andrea Dr. NS&EW | | |
| .................. 19W-24S | 30 |
| Argyle Dr. E&W ... 17W-25S | 31 |
| Argyle Ln. E&W .... 19W-27S | 30 |
| Armstrong Ln. E&W | | |
| .................. 18W-25S | 30 |
| Arthurs Pass N&S . 18W-27S | 30 |
| Ash St. E&W ...... 17W-24S | 31 |
| Aspen Dr. NS&EW .17W-24S | 31 |
| Auburn Ct. NE&SW | | |
| .................. 20W-24S | 30 |
| Barbara Ln. E&W .. 18W-23S | 22 |
| Barnside Rd. N&S .. 17W-25S | 31 |
| Bathill Dr. E&W ... 19W-24S | 30 |
| Beech Ln. E&W ... 18W-25S | 30 |
| Beechcraft Dr. N&S | | |
| .................. 18W-25S | 30 |
| Bent Tree Ct. N&S .19W-24S | 30 |
| Bent Tree Ln. N&S 19W-24S | 30 |
| Bentley Rd. E&W .. 17W-25S | 31 |
| Blandford Av. NE&SW | | |
| .................. 19W-22S | 22 |
| Boeing Dr. N&S ... 18W-25S | 30 |
| Bon Terre Rd. NW&SE | | |
| .................. 17W-25S | 31 |
| Borman Ln. N&S .. 18W-25S | 30 |
| Briarcrest Ln. NW&SE | | |
| .................. 19W-26S | 30 |
| Brittany Dr. N&S ... 19W-24S | 30 |
| Carlton Ct. E&W ... 19W-27S | 30 |
| Cattlemen Dr. N&S 18W-27S | 30 |
| Cedar Rd. N&S | | |
| ........ 18W-25S,18W-22S | 30 |
| Central Rd. NW&SE | | |
| .................. 18W-25S | 30 |
| Centurion Ln. E&W | | |
| .................. 19W-27S | 30 |
| Cessna Dr. E&W .. 18W-25S | 30 |
| Cherry Hill Rd. N&S | | |
| .................. 21W-24S | 29 |

| | Grid | Page |
|---|---|---|
| Cherrywood Ln. NE&SW | | |
| .................. 19W-26S | 30 |
| Church St. NS&EW | | |
| .................. 17W-24S | 31 |
| Churchill Dr. N&S . 18W-25S | 30 |
| Cimarron Dr. NW&SE | | |
| .................. 19W-26S | 30 |
| Circlegate Rd. NE&SW | | |
| .................. 17W-26S | 31 |
| Clinton St. N&S | | |
| ........ 18W-23S,18W-22S | 22 |
| Conrad Ln. E&W . 18W-25S | 30 |
| Cooper St. N&S | | |
| ........ 17W-26S,17W-25S | 31 |
| Copper St. N&S ... 17W-24S | 31 |
| Corsair Ct. E&W .. 18W-25S | 30 |
| Country Creek Dr. E&W | | |
| .................. 18W-26S | 30 |
| Coventry Rd. E&W .19W-23S | 22 |
| Cricket Av. NE&SW | | |
| .................. 19W-22S | 22 |
| Daniel Lewis Dr. NE&SW | | |
| .................. 19W-27S | 30 |
| Dawn Way N&S ... 17W-26S | 31 |
| Delmar Dr. NW&SE | | |
| .................. 19W-26S | 30 |
| Digby Dr. NE&SW . 19W-27S | 30 |
| Dorset Ln. E&W ... 20W-24S | 30 |
| Doxbury Ln. N&S .. 19W-24S | 30 |
| Duchess Av. E&W .. 19W-27S | 30 |
| Eagle Vista Dr. NW&SE | | |
| .................. 19W-26S | 30 |
| Earl Ct. N&S ...... 17W-25S | 31 |
| Eastgate Ct. E&W . 17W-25S | 31 |
| Elm St. E&W ..... 17W-24S | 31 |
| Elm St. N&S | | |
| ........ 18W-24S,18W-23S | 30 |
| Essex Ln. N&S .... 20W-24S | 30 |
| Fairfield Dr. N&S .. 19W-24S | 30 |
| Fernwood Ter. N&S | | |
| .................. 19W-26S | 30 |
| Ferro Dr. E&W ... 19W-24S | 30 |
| Fir St. E&W ...... 17W-24S | 31 |
| First Av. E&W .... 18W-25S | 30 |
| Forest St. E&W ... 18W-24S | 30 |
| Fourth Av. E&W | | |
| ........ 18W-25S,17W-25S | 30 |
| Foxwood Dr. N&S .. 18W-26S | 30 |
| Francis Rd. E&W | | |
| ........ 18W-23S,17W-23S | 22 |
| Gall Ln. E&W ..... 17W-24S | 31 |
| Garnet Dr. NS&EW | | |
| .................. 19W-24S | 30 |
| Gear Dr. N&S .... 18W-25S | 30 |
| Gibbons Dr. E&W .. 17W-23S | 31 |
| Gifford Pl. E&W ... 20W-24S | 30 |
| Gina Dr. E&W .... 18W-25S | 30 |
| Ginger Ln. E&W .. 19W-27S | 30 |
| Glenn Dr. N&S ... 19W-25S | 30 |
| Golf Av. NE&SW .. 19W-22S | 22 |
| Gougar Rd. N&S | | |
| ........ 19W-26S,19W-22S | 30 |
| Grand Mesa Tr. E&W | | |
| .................. 19W-27S | 30 |
| Grand Prairie Dr. E&W | | |
| .................. 19W-24S | 30 |
| Grandview Dr. NE&SW | | |
| .................. 19W-26S | 30 |
| Greenbriar Dr. N&S | | |
| .................. 18W-24S | 30 |
| Grissom Ln. E&W . 18W-25S | 30 |
| Grumman Ct. E&W 18W-25S | 30 |
| Gum St. N&S ..... 17W-24S | 31 |
| Haines St. E&W ... 18W-24S | 30 |
| Hauser St. E&W .. 17W-24S | 31 |
| Hawthorn Ln. E&W | | |
| .................. 17W-23S | 23 |
| Heartland Rd. E&W | | |
| .................. 18W-25S | 30 |
| Heatherway Ln. N&S | | |
| .................. 19W-26S | 30 |
| Hickory Creek Dr. EW&NS | | |
| .................. 17W-23S | 31 |
| Hickory Dr. E&W .. 18W-24S | 30 |
| Honey Ln. NS&EW 19W-24S | 30 |
| Inner Ct. E&W .... 18W-23S | 22 |
| Interstate 80 NE&SW | | |
| ........ 19W-24S,18W-23S | 30 |
| Ione Dr. E&W ..... 19W-23S | 22 |
| Jackson Branch Dr. N&S | | |
| .................. 19W-27S | 30 |
| John St. E&W .... 18W-24S | 30 |
| Joliet Hwy. E&W | | |
| ........ 18W-25S,17W-25S | 30 |
| Keithland Ct. E&W .17W-24S | 31 |
| Kerry Winde Dr. N&S | | |
| .................. 19W-27S | 30 |
| Kimber Dr. E&W .. 18W-24S | 30 |
| Kingston Dr. N&S .. 20W-24S | 30 |
| Kingsway N&S .... 19W-27S | 30 |
| Knight Av. E&W ... 19W-27S | 30 |
| Knollside Rd. N&S .. 17W-25S | 31 |
| Kris Dr. N&S | | |
| ........ 19W-24S,18W-24S | 30 |
| Kroll Ct. SW&NE .. 19W-27S | 30 |
| Lake Rd. N&S .... 17W-25S | 31 |
| Lambeth Ln. N&S . 18W-23S | 22 |
| Laraway Rd. E&W | | |
| ........ 19W-26S,18W-26S | 30 |
| Lear Dr. N&S ..... 18W-25S | 30 |
| Lewis Ln. NE&SW . 19W-23S | 22 |
| Lexington Ct. N&S . 18W-25S | 30 |
| Lexington Dr. E&W | | |
| .................. 18W-25S | 30 |

| | Grid | Page |
|---|---|---|
| Lincoln Hwy. E&W ..17W-24S | 31 |
| Livingston Dr. E&W | | |
| .................. 18W-24S | 30 |
| Manor Ct. NE&SW .18W-24S | 30 |
| Manor Dr. NW&SE ..18W-24S | 30 |
| Maple Ln. E&W ... 18W-23S | 22 |
| Maple St. NW&SE | | |
| ........ 18W-24S,17W-24S | 30 |
| Markev Ln. E&W .. 18W-24S | 30 |
| Marla Ln. N&S..... 18W-23S | 22 |
| McDivitt Dr. N&S .. 18W-25S | 30 |
| McDonough St. E&W | | |
| .................. 20W-24S | 30 |
| Meadow Ridge Ln. E&W | | |
| .................. 18W-26S | 30 |
| Michigan Rd. E&W ..18W-25S | 30 |
| Misty Creek Dr. NW&SE | | |
| .................. 18W-25S | 30 |
| Monarch Av. E&W .18W-25S | 30 |
| Moss Ln. E&W .... 20W-24S | 30 |
| Mustang Ln. E&W . 18W-25S | 30 |
| Nelson Rd. N&S | | |
| ........ 19W-26S,19W-24S | 30 |
| New Lenox Rd. E&W | | |
| ........ 19W-24S,18W-24S | 30 |
| Newcastle Rd. E&W | | |
| .................. 18W-25S | 30 |
| Northgate Rd. N&S | | |
| .................. 17W-25S | 31 |
| Oak Dr. N&S ..... 18W-24S | 30 |
| Oak St. E&W ..... 17W-24S | 31 |
| Oakview Dr. E&W .. 17W-24S | 31 |
| Ogden Rd. N&S ... 18W-24S | 30 |
| Old New Lenox Rd. NW&SE | | |
| .................. 18W-24S | 30 |
| Oxford Ct. N&S ... 18W-25S | 30 |
| Palmer Ranch Dr. N&S | | |
| .................. 18W-27S | 30 |
| Park Ln. NW&SE .. 18W-24S | 30 |
| Pine Grove Ln. N&S | | |
| .................. 19W-23S | 22 |
| Pine Pl. N&S ..... 18W-24S | 30 |
| Pine St. N&S | | |
| ........ 18W-25S,18W-23S | 30 |
| Piper Dr. N&S .... 18W-25S | 30 |
| Poplar Ln. E&W ... 17W-24S | 31 |
| Prairie Av. N&S .... 18W-25S | 30 |
| Princess Av. E&W . 19W-27S | 30 |
| Ridgefield Av. E&W | | |
| .................. 18W-25S | 30 |
| Root St. N&S ..... 17W-25S | 31 |
| Rossford Ln. N&S .. 20W-24S | 30 |
| Route 355 (proposed) | | |
| NW&SE ........ 18W-22S | 22 |
| Roy St. NS&EW .... 17W-25S | 31 |
| Sanford Av. NS&EW | | |
| .................. 19W-27S | 30 |
| Scenic Dr. E&W ... 18W-24S | 30 |
| Schoolgate Ct. N&S | | |
| .................. 17W-25S | 31 |
| Schoolgate Rd. N&S | | |
| .................. 17W-26S | 31 |
| Second Av. E&W | | |
| ........ 18W-25S,17W-25S | 30 |
| Shagbark Ct. N&S . 19W-26S | 30 |
| Shagbark Rd. E&W | | |
| ........ 19W-26S,18W-26S | 30 |
| Sheffield Dr. NW&SE | | |
| .................. 20W-24S | 30 |
| Southgate Rd. N&S | | |
| ........ 17W-26S,17W-25S | 31 |
| Southwest Hwy. E&W | | |
| ........ 19W-22S,18W-22S | 22 |
| Spencer Rd. E&W | | |
| ........ 18W-25S,17W-25S | 30 |
| Springcreek St. N&S | | |
| .................. 19W-22S | 22 |
| Stafford Ct. E&W .. 18W-25S | 30 |
| Stafford St. N&S .. 18W-25S | 30 |
| Stone Ct. NW&SE .. 19W-24S | 30 |
| Stonebridge Ct. E&W | | |
| .................. 19W-26S | 30 |
| Stonebridge Dr. NW&SE | | |
| .................. 19W-26S | 30 |
| Stonegate Rd. NE&SW | | |
| ........ 17W-26S,17W-25S | 31 |
| Sunset Tr. E&W ... 17W-25S | 31 |
| Surf Dr. E&W ..... 18W-24S | 30 |
| Sweetwater Tr. E&W | | |
| .................. 18W-27S | 30 |
| Tall Grass Ct. N&S 19W-24S | 30 |
| Third Av. E&W .... 18W-25S | 30 |
| Timber Ct. N&S ... 19W-26S | 30 |
| Timber Pl. E&W | | |
| ........ 19W-26S,18W-26S | 30 |
| Town Crest EW&NS | | |
| .................. 17W-23S | 31 |
| Twilight Ln. NE&SW | | |
| .................. 17W-25S | 31 |
| U.S. Route 30 E&W | | |
| ........ 17W-24S,17W-24S | 30 |
| Victorian Way N&S 19W-24S | 30 |
| Vine St. N&S ..... 18W-25S | 30 |
| Walker Way E&W .. 17W-23S | 31 |
| Wallace St. E&W .. 18W-24S | 30 |
| Warren Av. N&S... 18W-25S | 30 |
| Washington St. E&W | | |
| .................. 20W-24S | 30 |
| Western Av. N&S .. 18W-25S | 30 |
| Whisper Creek Dr. N&S | | |
| .................. 19W-24S | 30 |
| White Ln. N&S .... 18W-25S | 30 |
| Whitewater Ct. N&S | | |
| .................. 19W-24S | 30 |

| | Grid | Page |
|---|---|---|
| Wildwood Dr. NE&SW | | |
| .................. 18W-25S | 30 |
| Willow Ln. E&W ... 18W-23S | 22 |
| Wimborne Av. NW&SE | | |
| .................. 19W-22S | 22 |
| Windcrest Ln. N&S 19W-26S | 30 |
| Winsor Ln. N&S ... 19W-23S | 22 |
| Winter Park Dr. E&W | | |
| .................. 18W-26S | 30 |
| Wintree Ln. N&S .. 20W-24S | 30 |
| Wood St. E&W | | |
| ........ 18W-24S,17W-24S | 30 |
| Woodlawn Rd. E&W | | |
| ........ 18W-25S,17W-25S | 30 |
| York Pl. NE&SW ... 18W-25S | 30 |
| Young St. N&S ... 18W-25S | 30 |

### New Lenox Township

| | Grid | Page |
|---|---|---|
| Abbington Ln. N&S | | |
| .................. 16W-27S | 31 |
| Airway Ct. E&W .. 16W-26S | 31 |
| Alan Dr. E&W .... 17W-25S | 31 |
| Alison Tr. E&W ... 15W-24S | 31 |
| Amanda Rd. E&W . 16W-25S | 31 |
| Amherst Ct. N&S .. 16W-24S | 30 |
| Anderson Ln. N&S . 16W-26S | 31 |
| Anderson Rd. N&S . 16W-25S | 31 |
| Arrowhead Rd. NE&SW | | |
| .................. 15W-25S | 31 |
| Ashington Ct. E&W | | |
| .................. 16W-24S | 31 |
| Banbury Ln. N&S . 19W-24S | 30 |
| Barbara Ln. N&S .. 18W-23S | 22 |
| Bellchase Rd. NS&EW.19W-24S | 30 |
| Bernard Ct. N&S .. 15W-22S | 23 |
| Betty Ln. E&W .... 19W-22S | 23 |
| Beverly Blvd. E&W | | |
| ........ 18W-23S,17W-23S | 22 |
| Bittersweet Dr. E&W | | |
| .................. 16W-24S | 31 |
| Bjork Dr. N&S .... 19W-22S | 23 |
| Blodgett Rd. N&S . 17W-22S | 23 |
| Branchaw Blvd. E&W | | |
| .................. 18W-23S | 22 |
| Briarcliff Dr. NS&EW | | |
| .................. 16W-26S | 31 |
| Brisbane Rd. N&S . 16W-24S | 31 |
| Brockwood Rd. N&S | | |
| .................. 16W-25S | 31 |
| Bruce Ct. N&S .... 15W-22S | 23 |
| Bryan Ter. NS&EW | | |
| .................. 15W-24S | 31 |
| Buckboard Dr. E&W | | |
| .................. 17W-23S | 23 |
| Burl Ct. NS&EW ... 20W-24S | 30 |
| Calmer Rd. E&W .. 20W-24S | 30 |
| Carol Rd. E&W ... 18W-23S | 22 |
| Carrie Ct. NW&SE . 16W-22S | 23 |
| Carrington Ct. NW&SE | | |
| .................. 16W-24S | 31 |
| Cedar Rd. N&S | | |
| ........ 18W-27S,18W-22S | 30 |
| Charlotte Ct. E&W . 17W-25S | 31 |
| Chatfield Rd. NE&SW | | |
| .................. 16W-24S | 31 |
| Chelsae Ct. E&W .. 16W-25S | 31 |
| Chelsae St. E&W .. 16W-25S | 31 |
| Chessington Ln. N&S | | |
| .................. 16W-27S | 31 |
| Clearing Ct. N&S .. 16W-26S | 31 |
| Clinton St. N&S ... 19W-23S | 22 |
| Conlee Dr. N&S ... 16W-22S | 23 |
| Constance Dr. N&S | | |
| .................. 16W-24S | 31 |
| Constitution Rd. E&W | | |
| .................. 16W-25S | 31 |
| Cooper St. N&S ... 17W-25S | 31 |
| Corrie Ln. E&W ... 16W-26S | 31 |
| Country Ct. N&S .. 16W-27S | 31 |
| Country Ln. NS&EW | | |
| .................. 16W-27S | 31 |
| Covey Ct. N&S .... 15W-25S | 31 |
| Covey St. N&S .... 15W-25S | 31 |
| Craig Ct. NW&SE . 15W-22S | 23 |
| Cresent Pl. N&S .. 20W-24S | 30 |
| Cynthia Ln. NS&EW | | |
| .................. 17W-22S | 23 |
| Darshar Rd. E&W . 16W-25S | 31 |
| Debbie Ln. E&W .. 17W-22S | 23 |
| Delaney Rd. E&W | | |
| ........ 20W-27S,15W-27S | 30 |
| Donald Ct. N&S .. 15W-23S | 23 |
| Dougall Rd. NW&SE | | |
| ........ 20W-24S,20W-23S | 30 |
| E. Circle Dr. NW&SE | | |
| ........ 15W-25S,15W-24S | 31 |
| Edmonds Ct. E&W | | |
| ........ 17W-24S,17W-23S | 31 |
| Edward Pkwy. NE&SW | | |
| .................. 16W-22S | 23 |
| Elizabeth Ln. E&W . 17W-22S | 23 |
| Elm St. N&S ..... 15W-23S | 22 |
| Emiley Ln. E&W ... 15W-24S | 31 |
| Erskine Rd. NE&SW | | |
| ........ 20W-24S,20W-23S | 30 |
| Fairview Rd. N&S .. 16W-27S | 31 |
| Farm View Rd. N&S | | |
| .................. 16W-27S | 31 |
| Florence Rd. E&W . 16W-22S | 23 |
| Ford Dr. E&W ..... 18W-26S | 30 |
| Fourth Av. E&W ... 17W-25S | 31 |
| Francis Rd. E&W | | |
| ........ 19W-23S,15W-23S | 22 |

| | Grid | Page |
|---|---|---|
| Fredonia St. E&W .. 17W-26S | 31 |
| Garfield Av. N&S | | |
| ........ 15W-25S,15W-24S | 31 |
| Giddington Ct. NW&SE | | |
| .................. 16W-23S | 31 |
| Golf Rd. E&W ..... 20W-22S | 22 |
| Gordon St. N&S .. 18W-23S | 22 |
| Gougar Rd. N&S | | |
| ........ 20W-26S,20W-22S | 30 |
| Green St. N&S | | |
| ........ 18W-24S,18W-23S | 30 |
| Haley Rd. N&S ... 15W-22S | 23 |
| Harmoni Ln. E&W . 16W-24S | 31 |
| Hass Rd. N&S..... 16W-22S | 23 |
| Hawkshead Dr. N&S | | |
| .................. 15W-27S | 31 |
| Hazelwood Dr. E&W | | |
| .................. 17W-26S | 31 |
| Hempstead Pl. N&S | | |
| .................. 20W-24S | 30 |
| Herr Dr. E&W ..... 16W-24S | 31 |
| Hickory St. N&S ... 15W-25S | 23 |
| Highview Rd. E&W . 16W-27S | 31 |
| Hillside Dr. NW&SE | | |
| .................. 16W-23S | 23 |
| Hillside Rd. E&W .. 18W-24S | 30 |
| Hoberg Dr. NE&SW | | |
| .................. 20W-23S | 22 |
| Holly Hill Cir. N&S . 19W-24S | 30 |
| Howell Dr. NS&EW 16W-26S | 31 |
| Hunter Tr. NS&EW . 16W-23S | 31 |
| Illini Dr. E&W ..... 16W-27S | 31 |
| Indian Mound Dr. NE&SW | | |
| ........ 15W-25S,15W-24S | 31 |
| Interstate 80 NE&SW | | |
| ........ 20W-24S,15W-22S | 30 |
| Jennifer Ct. NE&SW | | |
| .................. 15W-24S | 31 |
| Joey Ct. N&S ..... 15W-23S | 23 |
| Joliet Hwy. | | |
| ........ 17W-25S,15W-25S | 31 |
| Josephine Dr. E&W | | |
| .................. 15W-22S | 23 |
| Kalarama Dr. E&W . 17W-23S | 23 |
| Kankakee St. N&S . 16W-25S | 31 |
| Knoll Ct. SW&NE .. 16W-27S | 31 |
| Knollwood Pl. N&S . 16W-25S | 30 |
| Lakeside Dr. NE&SW | | |
| .................. 16W-23S | 31 |
| Lancaster Dr. NW&SE | | |
| .................. 20W-24S | 30 |
| Laraway Rd. E&W | | |
| ........ 20W-26S,15W-26S | 30 |
| Laura Ln. E&W .... 18W-23S | 22 |
| Leanne Ct. E&W .. 17W-22S | 23 |
| Leanne Ln. N&S ... 17W-22S | 23 |
| Lenox St. E&W ... 17W-23S | 23 |
| Leven Av. N&S .... 15W-27S | 31 |
| Lila's Ct. E&W .... 17W-23S | 23 |
| Lincoln Hwy. NW&SE | | |
| ........ 16W-24S,15W-25S | 31 |
| Lincolnway Dr. N&S | | |
| .................. 16W-24S | 31 |
| Lincolnway Rd. N&S | | |
| .................. 16W-27S | 31 |
| Locust Ln. E&W ... 17W-24S | 31 |
| London Rd. E&W . 16W-23S | 23 |
| Long Lane Rd. N&S | | |
| .................. 16W-25S | 31 |
| Lynn Pkwy. NW&SE | | |
| .................. 16W-22S | 23 |
| Main St. NE&SW .. 15W-22S | 23 |
| Maple St. N&S .... 15W-22S | 23 |
| Maray Av. N&S .... 17W-25S | 31 |
| Marley Rd. NE&SW | | |
| ........ 16W-24S,16W-23S | 31 |
| Marshall Ct. E&W | | |
| .................. 15W-22S | 23 |
| Mary Ct. N&S ..... 16W-23S | 23 |
| Maureen Ct. E&W . 15W-24S | 31 |
| Maureen Dr. N&S . 15W-24S | 31 |
| Mayfair Ct. N&S .. 20W-23S | 22 |
| Mayfair Dr. NW&SE | | |
| .................. 20W-23S | 22 |
| Melrose St. E&W .. 16W-25S | 31 |
| Menno Ct. NW&SE | | |
| .................. 18W-23S | 22 |
| Menno Dr. NE&SW | | |
| .................. 18W-23S | 22 |
| Michael Ln. E&W .. 18W-23S | 22 |
| Michigan Rd. E&W | | |
| ........ 18W-25S,17W-25S | 30 |
| Montieth Av. N&S . 20W-24S | 30 |
| Morccambe Bay Dr. E&W | | |
| .................. 15W-27S | 31 |
| Nelson Rd. N&S | | |
| ........ 19W-27S,19W-23S | 30 |
| Oak Rail Dr. N&S .. 16W-27S | 31 |
| Oakdale Av. NE&SW | | |
| .................. 20W-23S | 22 |
| Oakview Ct. NW&SE | | |
| .................. 15W-24S | 31 |
| Ogden Av. N&S ... 18W-25S | 30 |
| Old New Lenox Rd. NW&SE | | |
| ........ 18W-24S,18W-24S | 30 |
| Parker Rd. N&S | | |
| ........ 16W-23S,16W-22S | 23 |
| Pembroke Av. N&S | | |
| ........ 20W-24S,20W-23S | 30 |
| Pennington Ct. E&W | | |
| .................. 16W-24S | 31 |
| Pheasant Ln. E&W . 16W-27S | 31 |
| Pine St. N&S ..... 18W-25S | 30 |

| | Grid | Page |
|---|---|---|
| Pioneer Pl. NW&SE | | |
| .......... 15W-25S | 31 | |
| Plaza Dr. E&W .... 16W-24S | 31 | |
| Pleasant St. N&S . 16W-24S | 31 | |
| Pottawatamie Ln. NW&SE | | |
| .......... 15W-25S | 31 | |
| Prairie Rd. N&S .... 17W-25S | 31 | |
| Quails Roost Dr. E&W | | |
| .......... 15W-25S | 31 | |
| Rachel Dr. N&S .... 16W-22S | 23 | |
| Raymond Dr. E&W .15W-22S | 23 | |
| Redwood Av. E&W | | |
| .......... 17W-23S | 23 | |
| Regan Rd. N&S .... 17W-23S | 23 | |
| Regan Rd. NE&SE | | |
| .......... 16W-23S,15W-23S | 23 | |
| Regent St. E&W .... 16W-25S | 31 | |
| Richard Av. N&S | | |
| .......... 16W-23S | 23 | |
| Rivendell Dr. E&W .. 15W-24S | 31 | |
| Robert St. N&S .... 17W-25S | 31 | |
| Rodger Ct. NE&SE | | |
| .......... 15W-25S | 23 | |
| Ross Dr. N&S .... 17W-22S | 23 | |
| Route 355 (proposed) | | |
| NW&SE 17W-23S,18W-22S | 23 | |
| Ruth Rd. NS&EW .. 16W-22S | 23 | |
| Rydal St. N&S....15W-27S | 31 | |
| Scheer Rd. N&S....15W-27S | 31 | |
| Schmule Rd. N&S | | |
| .......... 16W-26S,16W-23S | 31 | |
| Scott Ct. NW&SE .. 15W-24S | 31 | |
| Shelly Ln. N&S .... 15W-24S | 31 | |
| Shirley Pkwy. E&W | | |
| .......... 16W-24S | 31 | |
| Sojourn Rd. N&S .. 16W-25S | 31 | |
| Somerset Ct. N&S.. 16W-25S | 31 | |
| Somerset Pl. NE&SW | | |
| .......... 16W-25S | 31 | |
| Somerset St. NS&EW | | |
| .......... 16W-25S | 31 | |
| Southwest Hwy. E&W | | |
| .......... 20W-22S,15W-22S | 22 | |
| Spector Rd. N&S .. 18W-23S | 22 | |
| Spencer Rd. NS&EW | | |
| .......... 19W-25S,16W-27S | 30 | |
| Star-Lite Dr. NW&SE | | |
| .......... 20W-24S | 30 | |
| Suffolk Rd. E&W .. 20W-23S | 22 | |
| Summerfield Dr. E&W | | |
| .......... 17W-22S | 23 | |
| Sunset Ln. N&S .. 20W-24S | 30 | |
| Sycamore Ln. E&W | | |
| .......... 18W-24S | 30 | |
| Tammy Dr. NS&EW | | |
| .......... 16W-22S | 23 | |
| Tara St. E&W .... 17W-26S | 31 | |
| Tauber Ct. N&S.. 16W-25S | 31 | |
| Tauber Rd. N&S.. 16W-25S | 31 | |
| Terry Ln. N&S .... 17W-25S | 31 | |
| Terryellen Ln. E&W | | |
| .......... 18W-23S | 22 | |
| Tessington Ct. NW&SE | | |
| .......... 16W-24S | 31 | |
| Thomas Ct. N&S .. 15W-22S | 23 | |
| Thomas Ln. N&S .. 17W-23S | 23 | |
| Thornhouse Crescent SW&NE | | |
| .......... 19W-24S | 30 | |
| Timothy Ln. NS&EW | | |
| .......... 16W-22S | 23 | |
| Tomahawk Ridge E&W | | |
| .......... 16W-27S | 31 | |
| Ton-Ell Av. N&S .... 17W-25S | 31 | |
| Tower Bridge Rd. N&S | | |
| .......... 15W-25S | 31 | |
| Tracy St. N&S.... 17W-22S | 23 | |
| Tudor Ln. N&S .. 16W-26S | 31 | |
| U.S. Route 30 E&W | | |
| .......... 20W-23S,15W-25S | 22 | |
| U.S. Route 52 NW&SE | | |
| .......... 20W-27S | 30 | |
| U.S. Route 6 E&W | | |
| .......... 20W-22S,15W-22S | 22 | |
| Valley St. E&W .. 15W-22S | 23 | |
| Vine St. N&S | | |
| .......... 18W-24S,18W-23S | 30 | |
| Virginia N&S.... 16W-22S | 23 | |
| W. Circle Dr. N&S | | |
| .......... 15W-25S,15W-24S | 31 | |
| Wagon Dr. E&W .. 17W-23S | 23 | |
| Walona Av. N&S....17W-25S | 31 | |
| Walter Ct. NW&SE.. 15W-22S | 23 | |
| Walter Dr. E&W .. 15W-24S | 31 | |
| Warren Dr. NS&EW | | |
| .......... 15W-22S | 23 | |
| Washington St. E&W | | |
| .......... 20W-24S | 30 | |
| Westmorland Av. N&S | | |
| .......... 15W-27S | 31 | |
| Whitehall Rd. N&S .. 17W-26S | 31 | |
| William St. N&S .. 17W-25S | 31 | |
| Willow Rd., W. E&W | | |
| .......... 19W-24S,18W-24S | 30 | |
| Willow St. N&S .. 18W-24S | 30 | |
| Wisconsin Av. N&S | | |
| .......... 18W-25S | 30 | |
| Woodedge Ln. N&S | | |
| .......... 15W-23S | 23 | |
| Woodlawn Av. E&W | | |
| .......... 18W-23S | 30 | |
| Woodside Dr. N&S..16W-23S | 23 | |
| 2nd. Av. E&W .... 15W-23S | 23 | |
| 184th Pl. E&W .... 16W-22S | 23 | |
| 185th St. E&W .... 16W-22S | 23 | |

## Park Forest*
### (Also see Cook County)

| | Grid | Page |
|---|---|---|
| Abbey Ln. NW&SE .. 2W-28S | 43 | |
| Braeburn Rd. SW&NE | | |
| .......... 3W-28S | 43 | |
| Brook Park Ln. N&S | | |
| .......... 2W-28S | 43 | |
| Brookside Ln. SW&NE | | |
| .......... 3W-28S | 43 | |
| E. Sycamore Dr. E&W | | |
| .......... 2W-28S | 43 | |
| Forest Wood Ln. E&W | | |
| .......... 2W-28S | 43 | |
| Monee Ct. NW&SE .. 3W-28S | 43 | |
| Monee Rd. NE&SW | | |
| .......... 3W-28S,3W-27S | 43 | |
| Nanti St. N&S | | |
| .......... 4W-28S,3W-28S | 43 | |
| Natoma St. N&S .... 4W-28S | 43 | |
| Nauvoo St. E&W .. 4W-28S | 43 | |
| Navajo St. N&S .... 4W-28S | 43 | |
| Neosho N&S ...... 4W-28S | 43 | |
| Niagara N&S | | |
| .......... 3W-28S,3W-27S | 43 | |
| North Arbor Trail N&S | | |
| .......... 4W-28S,3W-28S | 43 | |
| Shabbona E&W .. 4W-28S | 43 | |
| South Arbor Trail N&S | | |
| .......... 2W-28S | 43 | |
| Tahoe St. N&S .. 4W-28S | 43 | |
| Talala St. NS&EW .. 4W-28S | 43 | |
| Tamarack St. E&W .. 4W-28S | 43 | |
| Tampa St. E&W .... 4W-28S | 43 | |
| Thorn Creek Dr. N&S | | |
| .......... 3W-28S | 43 | |
| Tioga St. N&S .... 4W-28S | 43 | |
| Titonka St. N&S .. 4W-28S | 43 | |
| Tomahawk St. N&S .. 4W-28S | 43 | |
| Topeka St. E&W .. 4W-28S | 43 | |
| Towanda Ct. NW&SE | | |
| .......... 4W-28S | 43 | |
| Woodland Ct. N&S . 3W-28S | 43 | |
| Woodland Glen E&W | | |
| .......... 3W-28S | 43 | |

## Peotone

| | Grid | Page |
|---|---|---|
| Ahlborn Dr. NE&SW ..9W-37S | 65 | |
| Amsterdam Ln. E&W | | |
| .......... 9W-37S | 65 | |
| Barton Ln. E&W .. 8W-37S | 65 | |
| Blaine Av. N&S....9W-37S | 65 | |
| Bonnie Ln. E&W ..10W-37S | 65 | |
| Conrad Av. N&S .. 9W-37S | 65 | |
| Corning St. N&S .. 9W-37S | 65 | |
| Crawford St. N&S . 9W-37S | 65 | |
| Crown Ln. E&W .... 9W-37S | 65 | |
| Delfi Ct. N&S....9W-37S | 65 | |
| Division St. N&S .. 9W-37S | 65 | |
| Ethel St. E&W ....10W-37S | 65 | |
| First St. N&S .... 9W-37S | 65 | |
| Garfield Av. E&W | | |
| .......... 10W-37S,9W-37S | 65 | |
| Glenview Ln. NS&EW | | |
| .......... 9W-37S | 65 | |
| Hans Brinker Ct. E&W | | |
| .......... 9W-37S | 65 | |
| Hans Brinker Dr. N&S | | |
| .......... 9W-37S | 65 | |
| Harlem Av. N&S .. 9W-37S | 65 | |
| Havert St. E&W....8W-37S | 65 | |
| Hawthorne Ln. N&S..8W-37S | 65 | |
| Hickory Ln. N&S .. 8W-37S | 65 | |
| Jean Ln. N&S .....10W-37S | 65 | |
| Jessen St. E&W .. 9W-37S | 65 | |
| Joliet Rd. E&W ......9W-37S | 65 | |
| Lark St. E&W ....10W-37S | 65 | |
| Lincoln St. E&W .. 9W-37S | 65 | |
| Louise Ln. E&W ..10W-37S | 65 | |
| Main St. E&W .... 9W-37S | 65 | |
| Manor Dr. N&S .....9W-37S | 65 | |
| Maple St. E&W .... 9W-37S | 65 | |
| Meadow Ln. N&S ..10W-37S | 65 | |
| Mill St. N&S .... 9W-37S | 65 | |
| North St. E&W .... 9W-37S | 65 | |
| Oak St. E&W ....9W-37S | 65 | |
| Orchard St. E&W .. 9W-37S | 65 | |
| Penny Ln. E&W .... 9W-37S | 65 | |
| Peotone-Beecher Rd. E&W | | |
| .......... 8W-37S | 65 | |
| Rathie St. N&S .. 9W-37S | 65 | |
| Route 50 N&S .... 9W-37S | 65 | |
| Royal Ln. E&W .... 9W-37S | 65 | |
| Schroeder Av. NE&SW | | |
| .......... 9W-37S | 65 | |
| Sixth St. N&S .. 8W-37S | 65 | |
| South St. E&W .. 9W-37S | 65 | |
| Summer Av. E&W .. 9W-37S | 65 | |
| Tucker Rd. E&W .. 9W-37S | 65 | |
| Van Gough Ct. N&S 9W-37S | 65 | |
| Walnut St. N&S .. 9W-37S | 65 | |
| West St. N&S .... 9W-37S | 65 | |
| Wilmington Rd. E&W | | |
| .......... 10W-37S,9W-37S | 65 | |
| Wilson St. N&S....9W-37S | 65 | |
| Wood Av. N&S .... 9W-37S | 65 | |
| 2nd St. N&S .... 9W-37S | 65 | |
| 3rd St. N&S .... 9W-37S | 65 | |

## Peotone Township

| | Grid | Page |
|---|---|---|
| Adams St. N&S.... 14W-34S | 52 | |
| Barr Rd. E&W | | |
| .......... 14W-36S,11W-36S | 64 | |
| Center Rd. N&S | | |
| .......... 12W-39S,12W-34S | 64 | |
| Corning St. N&S .. 10W-37S | 65 | |
| County Line Rd. E&W | | |
| .......... 14W-39S,9W-39S | 64 | |
| Eagle Lake Rd. E&W | | |
| .......... 14W-34S,9W-34S | 52 | |
| Evergreen St. N&S.. 14W-34S | 52 | |
| Green Garden-Manhattan Rd | | |
| N&S.... 14W-39S,14W-34S | 64 | |
| Harlem Av. N&S | | |
| .......... 9W-39S,9W-34S | 65 | |
| Interstate 57 NE&SW | | |
| .......... 14W-39S,9W-34S | 64 | |
| Joliet Rd. NS&EW | | |
| .......... 13W-35S,9W-36S | 52 | |
| Kennedy Rd. E&W | | |
| .......... 14W-38S,9W-38S | 64 | |
| Linton Av. N&S .... 14W-37S | 64 | |
| Locust Ln. NE&SW | | |
| .......... 10W-37S | 65 | |
| Main St. N&S | | |
| .......... 14W-38S,14W-34S | 64 | |
| Manhattan-Wilton Rd. E&W | | |
| .......... 14W-34S,9W-34S | 52 | |
| N. Peotone Rd. E&W | | |
| .......... 9W-35S | 53 | |
| N. Peotone Rd. N&S | | |
| .......... 11W-37S,11W-34S | 64 | |
| Offner Rd. E&W | | |
| .......... 11W-34S,9W-34S | 52 | |
| Rathie St. N&S | | |
| .......... 10W-38S,10W-34S | 65 | |
| Route 50 NE&SW | | |
| .......... 10W-39S,9W-38S | 65 | |
| U.S. Route 45 N&S | | |
| .......... 14W-35S,14W-34S | 52 | |
| U.S. Route 52 NS&EW | | |
| .......... 14W-37S,10W-37S | 64 | |
| 80th Av. N&S | | |
| .......... 10W-39S,10W-35S | 65 | |
| 88th Av. N&S .... 11W-34S | 52 | |
| 104th Av. N&S | | |
| .......... 13W-39S,13W-34S | 64 | |
| 120th Av. N&S | | |
| .......... 14W-38S,14W-34S | 64 | |

## Plainfield

| | Grid | Page |
|---|---|---|
| Amboy St. E&W .... 29W-17S | 12 | |
| Amherst Ct., N. N&S | | |
| .......... 30W-16S | 12 | |
| Amherst Ct., S. N&S | | |
| .......... 30W-16S | 12 | |
| Arnold St. N&S .. 30W-17S | 12 | |
| Arrowhead Ct. N&S | | |
| .......... 31W-18S | 12 | |
| Ash St. N&S .... 29W-17S | 12 | |
| Asther Ct. E&W .. 30W-15S | 8 | |
| Bartlett St. N&S .. 29W-17S | 12 | |
| Brett St. E&W .... 31W-16S | 12 | |
| Brown Ln. E&W .. 30W-19S | 12 | |
| Burgundy Ln. N&S.. 30W-19S | 12 | |
| Buttercup Ct. E&W .. 31W-18S | 12 | |
| Cambridge Cir. NS&EW | | |
| .......... 28W-16S | 13 | |
| Center St. N&S .. 29W-17S | 12 | |
| Chablis Ln. N&S....30W-19S | 12 | |
| Chelsea Ln. E&W . 31W-16S | 12 | |
| Chicago St. E&W | | |
| .......... 30W-18S,29W-18S | 12 | |
| Chipper Ct. E&W .. 29W-19S | 13 | |
| Clover Ct. N&S .. 31W-18S | 12 | |
| Coilplus Dr. N&S....30W-16S | 12 | |
| College St. NE&SW | | |
| .......... 29W-17S | 12 | |
| Columbia Cir. E&W | | |
| .......... 30W-15S | 8 | |
| Commercial St. E&W | | |
| .......... 30W-18S | 12 | |
| Corbin St. E&W .. 29W-18S | 12 | |
| Creekside Dr. NW&SE | | |
| .......... 31W-18S | 12 | |
| Cropland Dr. E&W . 30W-18S | 12 | |
| Daisy Ct. N&S....31W-18S | 12 | |
| Dayfield Dr. E&W .. 30W-19S | 12 | |
| DesPlaines St. N&S | | |
| .......... 30W-18S,30W-17S | 12 | |
| Dillman St. N&S .. 29W-18S | 12 | |
| Division St. N&S | | |
| .......... 30W-18S,30W-16S | 12 | |
| DuPage Dr. NW&SE | | |
| .......... 29W-16S | 12 | |
| Eastern Av. N&S .. 29W-17S | 12 | |
| Evans St. E&W .. 29W-17S | 12 | |
| Eyre Cir. NS&EW .. 30W-18S | 12 | |
| Farmstead Ln. E&W | | |
| .......... 30W-18S | 12 | |
| Fescue Dr. E&W ..31W-16S | 12 | |
| Fort Beggs Dr. E&W | | |
| .......... 30W-18S | 12 | |
| Foxriver St. N&S .. 30W-18W | 12 | |
| Fraser Rd. E&W .. 30W-19S | 12 | |
| Golden Meadow Ct. NW&SE | | |
| .......... 30W-15S | 8 | |
| Golden Meadow N&S | | |
| .......... 30W-15S | 8 | |

| | Grid | Page |
|---|---|---|
| Hamlin St. NS&EW 30W-18S | 12 | |
| Hartong St. N&S.. 29W-17S | 12 | |
| Hawthorne Cir. NS&EW | | |
| .......... 29W-17S | 12 | |
| Hazelcrest Dr. E&W | | |
| .......... 30W-16S | 12 | |
| Heather Ct. E&W .. 30W-15S | 8 | |
| Highview Ct. E&W .. 30W-16S | 12 | |
| Hillcrest Dr. E&W . 30W-16S | 12 | |
| Homestead Ct. E&W | | |
| .......... 31W-18S | 12 | |
| Huron St. NW&SE . 29W-17S | 12 | |
| Illini Dr. E&W .... 31W-18S | 12 | |
| Illinois St. N&S | | |
| .......... 30W-18S,30W-17S | 12 | |
| James St. NE&SW .30W-18S | 12 | |
| Joliet Rd. NW&SE .. 29W-18S | 12 | |
| Jordan Ln. SE&NW | | |
| .......... 31W-16S | 12 | |
| Joseph Av. N&S .. 30W-16S | 12 | |
| Judith Ct. E&W .. 28W-19S | 13 | |
| Katlyn Ln. E&W .. 31W-16S | 12 | |
| Kelly Ln. N&S .... 30W-16S | 12 | |
| Kenna Ln. N&S .. 29W-19S | 13 | |
| Kristoff Ct. E&W .. 29W-19S | 13 | |
| Lakeside Dr. N&S . 29W-18S | 12 | |
| Lexis St. N&S....31W-16S | 12 | |
| Lincoln Hwy. N&S . 30W-16S | 12 | |
| Lockport St. N&S | | |
| .......... 30W-17S,29W-17S | 12 | |
| Lynn St. E&W .... 29W-19S | 12 | |
| Madison Ct. SE&NW | | |
| .......... 31W-16S | 12 | |
| Madison St. N&S . 31W-16S | 12 | |
| Main St. NE&SW | | |
| .......... 30W-18S,29W-17S | 12 | |
| Mallard Dr., N. N&S | | |
| .......... 30W-16S | 12 | |
| Mallard Dr., S. N&S | | |
| .......... 30W-16S | 12 | |
| Maple Ct. NE&SW . 29W-17S | 12 | |
| Marybrook Dr. N&S | | |
| .......... 30W-16S | 12 | |
| Meadow Ln. N&S .. 31W-18S | 12 | |
| Meadowbrook N&S | | |
| .......... 30W-16S | 12 | |
| Merlot St. N&S .. 30W-19S | 12 | |
| Michele Dr. EW&NS | | |
| .......... 31W-16S | 12 | |
| Michigan St. NW&SE | | |
| .......... 29W-17S | 12 | |
| Milk Farm Rd. E&W | | |
| .......... 29W-20S | 18 | |
| Mill St. NW&SE .. 29W-17S | 12 | |
| New Kirk Dr. E&W . 30W-18S | 12 | |
| Norman Av. N&S .. 29W-18S | 12 | |
| Oak St. NE&SW .. 30W-17S | 12 | |
| Old Indian Boundary Line | | |
| NE&SW.... 31W-18S | 12 | |
| Ottawa St. E&W | | |
| .......... 30W-18S,29W-18S | 12 | |
| Parklane Rd. NE&SW | | |
| .......... 30W-16S | 12 | |
| Partridge Dr. NW&SE | | |
| .......... 30W-16S | 12 | |
| Pawnees St. N&S .. 31W-18S | 12 | |
| Penn Rd. NW&SE . 30W-17S | 12 | |
| Pheasant Chase Dr. E&W | | |
| .......... 30W-16S | 12 | |
| Plainfield-Naperville Rd. | | |
| NE&SW 29W-17S,28W-15S | 12 | |
| Plainsman Cir. NS&EW | | |
| .......... 29W-20S | 18 | |
| Plainsman Dr. N&S 29W-20S | 18 | |
| Plaza Dr. E&W | | |
| .......... 30W-18S,29W-18S | 12 | |
| Poppy Ln. N&S .. 31W-18S | 12 | |
| Prairie Dr. E&W .. 31W-18S | 12 | |
| Pratt Ln. N&S .... 30W-18S | 12 | |
| Quail Ct. E&W .. 31W-18S | 12 | |
| Quail Ct., N. N&S.. 30W-16S | 12 | |
| Quail Run Dr. NS&EW | | |
| .......... 30W-16S | 12 | |
| Ranchland Dr. N&S | | |
| .......... 31W-16S | 12 | |
| River Dr. N&S .. 30W-18S | 12 | |
| River Rd. NE&SW .. 30W-18S | 12 | |
| Robin Ct. N&S .. 31W-18S | 12 | |
| Rolf Rd. E&W .. 29W-20S | 12 | |
| Route 126 N&S | | |
| .......... 31W-18S,29W-17S | 12 | |
| Route 59 N&S | | |
| .......... 30W-18S,30W-16S | 12 | |
| Sandbank Dr. E&W | | |
| .......... 31W-18S | 12 | |
| Sandra Ln. E&W .. 31W-18S | 12 | |
| Savanna Dr. N&S . 31W-16S | 12 | |
| Simo Dr. E&W .. 30W-19S | 12 | |
| Spangler Dr. N&S .. 30W-18S | 12 | |
| Spring Hill Ln. E&W | | |
| .......... 29W-17S | 12 | |
| St. Joseph Av. E&W | | |
| .......... 30W-16S | 12 | |
| Sundance Ct. E&W | | |
| .......... 31W-18S | 12 | |
| Sunset Ln. N&S .. 30W-16S | 12 | |
| Sunshine Cir. NS&EW | | |
| .......... 31W-18S | 12 | |
| Sunshine Ct. E&W .. 31W-18S | 12 | |
| Teal Ct. N&S .. 30W-16S | 12 | |
| Timber Dr. NW&SE | | |
| .......... 31W-18S | 12 | |
| U.S. Route 30 E&W | | |
| .......... 30W-17S,29W-18S | 12 | |

| | Grid | Page |
|---|---|---|
| Union Ct. N&S......29W-18S | 12 | |
| Union St. N&S | | |
| .......... 30W-18S,29W-18S | 12 | |
| Vandyke Rd. N&S | | |
| .......... 30W-17S,30W-16S | 12 | |
| Vintage Dr. N&S .. 30W-18S | 12 | |
| Vintage Knoll Dr. NS&EW | | |
| .......... 29W-17S | 12 | |
| Vista Dr. N&S .... 30W-18S | 12 | |
| Wallin Blvd. NS&EW | | |
| .......... 30W-18S | 12 | |
| Waterfront Cir. N&S | | |
| .......... 29W-19S | 13 | |
| Weathervane Way E&W | | |
| .......... 30W-18S | 12 | |
| Willow Dr. E&W .. 31W-18S | 12 | |
| Willow Dr., E. N&S .. 31W-18S | 12 | |
| Willow Rd. N&S .. 31W-18S | 12 | |
| 143rd St. E&W | | |
| .......... 32W-16S,30W-16S | 12 | |

## Plainfield Township

| | Grid | Page |
|---|---|---|
| Addelman St. N&S . 28W-21S | 19 | |
| Anderson St. E&W .. 28W-19S | 13 | |
| Ann Ct. E&W ...... 31W-20S | 18 | |
| Ann Dr. N&S .... 31W-20S | 18 | |
| Ardith St. E&W .. 27W-20S | 19 | |
| Ash St. NW&SE .. 29W-17S | 12 | |
| Benson Av. N&S.. 29W-18S | 12 | |
| Bently Dr. E&W .. 29W-21S | 18 | |
| Berry St. E&W .... 27W-20S | 19 | |
| Biltmore St. E&W .. 27W-20S | 19 | |
| Blossom St. NW&SE | | |
| .......... 27W-19S | 13 | |
| Brittany St. E&W .. 30W-19S | 12 | |
| Bronk Rd. N&S .. 29W-21S | 18 | |
| Brown St. E&W | | |
| .......... 29W-18S,28W-18S | 12 | |
| Budler Rd. N&S | | |
| .......... 27W-17S,27W-16S | 13 | |
| Burbank St. E&W .. 27W-20S | 19 | |
| Bussey Dr. E&W...28W-19S | 13 | |
| Byrum Blvd. N&S .. 28W-20S | 19 | |
| Caitlin Ct. N&S .. 30W-20S | 18 | |
| Caroline Dr. NS&EW | | |
| .......... 27W-19S | 13 | |
| Castle Ct. E&W .. 28W-21S | 19 | |
| Catherine Ct. E&W .31W-20S | 18 | |
| Catherine Dr. NS&EW | | |
| .......... 31W-20S | 18 | |
| Caton Farm Rd. E&W | | |
| .......... 32W-20S,27W-20S | 18 | |
| Cecily Dr. N&S .. 29W-19S | 12 | |
| Central Dr. N&S .. 27W-20S | 19 | |
| Charlotte Rd. NW&SE | | |
| .......... 28W-19S | 13 | |
| Chestnut St. E&W .. 27W-20S | 19 | |
| Chevy Chase Dr. NW&SE | | |
| .......... 27W-19S | 13 | |
| Clark St. N&S .. 28W-19S | 13 | |
| Coghill St. N&S .. 27W-20S | 19 | |
| Colerain St. E&W .. 28W-19S | 13 | |
| Colinia Ct. NW&SE 32W-21S | 18 | |
| Collins Dr. NE&SW 29W-18S | 12 | |
| Commonwealth Av. NE&SW | | |
| .......... 27W-20S | 19 | |
| Conant Av. NW&SE | | |
| .......... 27W-20S | 19 | |
| Copper Dr. E&W...29W-17S | 12 | |
| Cosmic Dr. N&S .. 28W-20S | 19 | |
| County Line Rd. N&S | | |
| .......... 32W-21S,32W-18S | 18 | |
| Crystal Dr. NW&SE | | |
| .......... 27W-20S | 19 | |
| Culver St. E&W .. 28W-19S | 13 | |
| Dan Ireland Dr. E&W | | |
| .......... 27W-19S | 19 | |
| Dan O'Connell Dr. N&S | | |
| .......... 29W-19S | 12 | |
| Davy Ct. E&W .. 28W-19S | 13 | |
| Debbie Ct. NE&SW | | |
| .......... 27W-20S | 19 | |
| Delia Av. N&S .. 32W-20S | 18 | |
| Dina Ct. E&W .... 31W-20S | 18 | |
| Division St. N&S | | |
| .......... 30W-18S,30W-16S | 12 | |
| Dixmoor St. N&S . 27W-20S | 19 | |
| Drauden Rd. N&S | | |
| .......... 31W-20S,31W-19S | 18 | |
| DuPage Dr. NW&SE | | |
| .......... 29W-16S | 12 | |
| Dupage Country Club Dr. | | |
| NW&SE.... 29W-20S | 18 | |
| Earl Dr. E&W .. 28W-21S | 19 | |
| Eastline Dr. N&S.. 28W-20S | 19 | |
| Easy St. E&W .... 29W-18S | 12 | |
| Edgewood Dr. NE&SW | | |
| .......... 28W-19S | 13 | |
| Elna Ct. N&S .. 28W-19S | 13 | |
| Emlong St. NW&SE | | |
| .......... 27W-20S | 19 | |
| Emyvale Dr. E&W . 30W-20S | 18 | |
| Enid St. N&S .... 27W-20S | 19 | |
| Essington Rd. N&S | | |
| .......... 28W-20S,27W-20S | 19 | |
| Evergreen Dr. N&S | | |
| .......... 29W-19S | 13 | |
| Ewing Ct. N&S .. 28W-19S | 13 | |
| Ewing Dr. E&W .. 28W-19S | 13 | |
| Farmingdale Dr. E&W | | |
| .......... 30W-19S | 12 | |
| Farmington Av. N&S | | |
| .......... 27W-20S | 19 | |

| | Grid | Page |
|---|---|---|
| Feeney Dr. E&W | 28W-19S | 13 |
| Fern St. E&W | 28W-19S | 13 |
| Fiday Rd. E&W | 28W-21S | 19 |
| Flossmoor St. N&S | 27W-20S | 19 |
| Flower St. E&W | 27W-20S | 19 |
| Francis Dr. N&S | 27W-18S | 13 |
| Fraser Rd. E&W | 30W-19S | 12 |
| Frederick Av. N&S | 29W-18S | 12 |
| Frontage Rd. N&S | 28W-21S | 19 |
| Gael Dr. NE&SW | 27W-20S | 19 |
| Gagne Ln. NW&SE | 29W-20S | 18 |
| Galena Dr. E&W | 27W-19S | 13 |
| Garden Ct. N&S | 27W-20S | 19 |
| Garden Dr. NE&SW | 29W-17S | 12 |
| Garden St. E&W | 27W-20S | 19 |
| Gaylord Rd. N&S | 27W-20S,27W-19S | 19 |
| George Ct. N&S | 28W-19S | 13 |
| Getson Av. E&W | 29W-18S | 12 |
| Glasglow St. E&W | 27W-20S | 19 |
| Glenwoodie St. NE&SW | 27W-20S | 19 |
| Golden Ln. N&S | 29W-17S | 12 |
| Golf St. E&W | 27W-20S | 19 |
| Golfmoor St. N&S | 27W-20S | 19 |
| Golfview Dr. E&W | 27W-20S | 19 |
| Grape St. E&W | 27W-20S | 19 |
| Graystone Dr. N&S | 28W-21S | 19 |
| Greenview Cir. NW&SE | 27W-20S | 19 |
| Greenview Dr. N&S | 27W-21S | 19 |
| Greenway St. N&S | 27W-20S | 19 |
| Greglawn Av. N&S | 27W-20S | 19 |
| Grinton Dr. E&W | 28W-19S | 13 |
| Harmony Dr. NE&SW | 30W-19S | 12 |
| Harris Dr. E&W | 28W-21S | 19 |
| Heather Ln. N&S | 28W-21S | 19 |
| Heathercreek Dr. NE&SW | 29W-20S | 18 |
| Hel-Mar Ln. N&S | 28W-20S | 19 |
| Helen Dr. E&W | 27W-18S | 13 |
| Hickory St. E&W | 28W-19S | 13 |
| Hollylynn Ln. E&W | 28W-20S | 19 |
| Honora Dr. NE&SW | 30W-20S | 18 |
| Howard Av. N&S | 28W-19S | 13 |
| Interstate 55 N&S | 29W-21S,27W-16S | 18 |
| Ivy Ln. NE&SW | 28W-19S | 13 |
| Jamestown Rd. E&W | 32W-21S | 18 |
| Joann Dr. E&W | 28W-21S | 19 |
| Joliet Rd. NW&SE | 29W-18S | 12 |
| Judith Dr. E&W | 28W-19S | 13 |
| Julie Av. E&W | 29W-18S | 12 |
| June St. N&S | 27W-20S | 19 |
| Kay Ct. E&W | 31W-20S | 18 |
| Kay Dr. NE&SW | 31W-20S | 18 |
| Kellog St. N&S | 27W-20S | 19 |
| Kenwood Av. N&S | 27W-20S | 19 |
| Kenyon E&W | 28W-19S | 13 |
| Kerns Dr. N&S | 29W-17S | 12 |
| Keith St. E&W | 27W-20S | 19 |
| Lake Dr. NS&EW | 29W-16S | 13 |
| Lavida Blvd. NE&SW | 27W-20S | 19 |
| Lawrence St. NW&SE | 28W-19S | 13 |
| Leach Dr. E&W | 28W-19S | 13 |
| Lee St. E&W | 29W-18S,28W-19S | 12 |
| Legion Ct. N&S | 30W-19S | 12 |
| Lenwood Dr. E&W | 29W-16S | 13 |
| Lewood Dr. N&S | 30W-19S | 12 |
| Lily Cache Rd. NE&SW | 29W-20S,28W-19S | 18 |
| Lincoln Hwy. N&S | 31W-17S,31W-16S | 12 |
| Link Ln. E&W | 28W-19S | 13 |
| Lockner Blvd. NS&EW | 28W-20S | 19 |
| Lockport Rd. E&W | 28W-17S,27W-17S | 13 |
| Lorraine Av. NW&SE | 28W-19S | 13 |
| Margaret Ct. E&W | 28W-19S | 13 |
| Mary Ct. NE&SW | 31W-20S | 18 |
| Mary Ln. E&W | 31W-20S | 18 |
| Massey Av. N&S | 29W-18S | 12 |
| Mathews St. E&W | 29W-19S | 12 |
| McAllister Rd. N&S | 28W-19S | 13 |
| McClellan Av. N&S | 28W-19S | 13 |
| McGrath Dr. N&S | 28W-19S | 13 |
| McKenna Dr. N&S | 30W-20S | 18 |
| Meridan Dr. N&S | 28W-20S | 19 |
| Michael Dr. N&S | 27W-18S | 13 |
| Mink Farm Rd. E&W | 29W-20S | 18 |
| Nuclear Dr. N&S | 28W-20S | 19 |
| Oak St. E&W | 28W-19S | 13 |
| Old Indian Boundary Line NE&SW | 32W-19S,31W-18S | 12 |
| Olympia St. NE&SW | 27W-20S | 19 |
| Orion Dr. N&S | 29W-21S | 18 |
| Patterson St. E&W | 28W-19S | 13 |
| Pauline Dr. E&W | 31W-20S | 18 |
| Peacedale NW&SE | 30W-19S | 12 |
| Peach St. NE&SW | 27W-20S | 19 |
| Pecan St. E&W | 27W-20S | 19 |
| Peerless Dr. N&S | 28W-19S | 13 |
| Pennington Ln. E&W | 29W-17S | 12 |
| Penny Ln. N&S | 29W-17S | 12 |
| Peterson Dr. NW&SE | 28W-19S | 13 |
| Pilcher Rd. E&W | 32W-16S,27W-16S | 12 |
| Pincrest Dr. N&S | 27W-19S | 13 |
| Pine Cone Ln. E&W | 31W-19S | 12 |
| Plainfield Rd. NW&SE | 28W-19S,27W-20S | 13 |
| Plainfield-Naperville Rd. NE&SW | 29W-17S,29W-16S | 12 |
| Plantation Dr. E&W | 32W-21S | 18 |
| Pleasant Ct. NW&SE | 30W-19S | 12 |
| Plum St. E&W | 27W-20S | 19 |
| Poplar St. E&W | 27W-20S | 19 |
| Raymond St. N&S | 28W-21S | 19 |
| Regan Rd. NS&EW | 28W-20S | 19 |
| Renwick Park Dr. N&S | 30W-19S | 12 |
| Renwick Rd. E&W | 32W-18S,27W-18S | 12 |
| Richmond Rd. NS&EW | 32W-21S | 18 |
| River Ct. NS&EW | 30W-18S | 12 |
| River Rd. N&S | 31W-19S | 12 |
| Robert Av. E&W | 29W-18S | 12 |
| Route 126 E&W | 32W-17S,27W-16S | 12 |
| Route 59 N&S | 29W-21S,30W-19S | 18 |
| Rowley Rd. E&W | 31W-18S | 12 |
| Ruben St. E&W | 29W-19S | 12 |
| S. Mayleon NE&SW | 29W-19S,28W-19S | 12 |
| Saddle Dr. N&S | 27W-19S | 13 |
| Satellite Dr. N&S | 28W-20S | 19 |
| September Dr. E&W | 28W-21S | 19 |
| Serenity Dr. N&S | 30W-19S | 12 |
| Silver Ln. N&S | 29W-17S | 12 |
| South End Rd. NW&SE | 27W-19S | 13 |
| Spangle Rd. NE&SW | 28W-19S | 13 |
| State Rd. E&W | 27W-19S | 13 |
| Stateville Rd. E&W | 27W-19S | 13 |
| Steiner Rd N&S | 32W-17S | 12 |
| Sunset Ridge Dr. E&W | 29W-21S | 18 |
| Surrey Ln. E&W | 32W-21S | 18 |
| Surrey Ln. NW&SE | 28W-19S | 13 |
| Sussex Rd. E&W | 32W-21S | 18 |
| Teeway St. NE&SW | 27W-20S | 19 |
| Thomas Ct. N&S | 27W-18S | 13 |
| Timberview Dr. NE&SW | 28W-19S | 13 |
| Tyler Dr. E&W | 28W-21S | 19 |
| U.S. Route 30 NW&SE | 31W-16S,27W-20S | 12 |
| Updyke Rd. NS&EW | 32W-16S | 12 |
| Vandyke Rd. N&S | 30W-17S,30W-16S | 12 |
| Vanhorn Ln. NW&SE | 29W-20S | 18 |
| Vesta Dr. N&S | 28W-20S | 19 |
| Virginia Dr. E&W | 32W-21S | 18 |
| Virgo Ln. N&S | 29W-21S | 18 |
| Vonesch Rd. NE&SW | 28W-20S | 19 |
| Wattles Ct. E&W | 29W-21S | 18 |
| Wayne Av. E&W | 27W-20S | 19 |
| Wedgewood Ct. E&W | 30W-19S | 12 |
| Weller Dr. NE&SW | 29W-16S | 12 |
| Westgate Ln. E&W | 27W-19S | 13 |
| Westline Dr. N&S | 28W-20S | 19 |
| Wilkins Ln. N&S | 29W-17S | 12 |
| Wilkins Pl. NW&SE | 29W-17S | 12 |
| Willardshire Rd. E&W | 28W-20S | 19 |
| William Ct. NW&SE | 29W-16S | 12 |
| Williamsburg Dr. N&S | 32W-21S | 18 |
| Wilshire Blvd. E&W | 27W-20S | 19 |
| Winding Creek Rd. NE&SW | 28W-19S | 13 |
| Winston Av. E&W | 29W-21S | 18 |
| 143rd St. E&W | 28W-16S,27W-16S | 13 |

## Reed Township

| | Grid | Page |
|---|---|---|
| 'A' St. E&W | 30W-41S | 70 |
| Aspen Ln. E&W | 30W-40S | 70 |
| Big Musky Cir. NE&SW | 30W-40S | 70 |
| Birch Ln. E&W | 30W-40S | 70 |
| Bluegill Cir. NS&EW | 30W-40S | 70 |
| Catfish Cir. NS&EW | 30W-40S | 70 |
| Cedar Ln. NS&EW | 30W-40S | 70 |
| Cemetery Dr. N&S | 31W-42S | 74 |
| Center St. N&S | 31W-42S,31W-40S | 74 |
| Coal City Rd. E&W | 32W-40S,30W-40S | 70 |
| Comet Dr. N&S | 31W-42S | 74 |
| County Line Rd. NS&EW | 32W-40S,30W-45S | 70 |
| Dogwood Ln. NS&EW | 30W-40S | 70 |
| Eon Ln. E&W | 30W-40S | 70 |
| Essex Rd. N&S | 30W-45S,30W-42S | 74 |
| Fifth St. E&W | 32W-40S | 70 |
| Hole-in-the Wall Rd. NS&EW | 30W-40S | 70 |
| Interstate 55 NE&SW | 32W-40S | 70 |
| Ivory Rd. N&S | 30W-40S | 70 |
| Kennedy Rd. E&W | 32W-42S | 74 |
| Lake Shore Dr. NS&EW | 30W-40S | 70 |
| Large Mouth Ln. E&W | 30W-40S | 70 |
| Little Musky Cir. E&W | 30W-40S | 70 |
| Navy Rd. N&S | 30W-40S | 70 |
| Park St. E&W | 30W-41S | 70 |
| Route 113 NS&EW | 32W-40S,30W-41S | 70 |
| Route 129 NE&SW | 32W-42S,30W-40S | 74 |
| Route 53 NE&SW | 32W-42S,30W-40S | 74 |
| Small Mouth Ln. E&W | 30W-40S | 70 |
| Smiley Rd. E&W | 31W-42S,30W-42S | 74 |
| Sportsman Ct. E&W | 30W-45S | 74 |
| Sportsman Dr. E&W | 30W-45S | 74 |
| Sunfish Cir. NS&EW | 30W-40S | 70 |
| Torino Dr. N&S | 30W-45S | 74 |
| Tully Rd. NE&SW | 30W-40S | 70 |
| Walleye Cir. NS&EW | 30W-40S | 70 |
| 1st St. N&S | 30W-41S | 70 |
| 2nd St. N&S | 30W-41S | 70 |

## Rockdale

| | Grid | Page |
|---|---|---|
| Anita St. E&W | 25W-25S | 28 |
| Bellevue Av. E&W | 26W-25S,25W-25S | 28 |
| Brandon Rd. NW&SE | 25W-25S | 28 |
| Central Av. N&S | 25W-25S,25W-24S | 28 |
| Channahon Rd. E&W | 25W-25S | 28 |
| Connell St. N&S | 25W-25S | 28 |
| Davis Av. N&S | 25W-25S,25W-24S | 28 |
| Emery St. N&S | 26W-25S,26W-24S | 28 |
| Ferris St. N&S | 25W-25S | 28 |
| Fisher Av. N&S | 25W-25S | 28 |
| Hays St. N&S | 25W-25S | 28 |
| Howard St. N&S | 25W-25S,25W-24S | 28 |
| Jewett St. N&S | 25W-25S | 28 |
| Kinsey Av. E&W | 26W-25S,25W-25S | 28 |
| Lakeview Av. E&W | 26W-24S,25W-24S | 28 |
| Larkin Rd. N&S | 26W-25S,26W-24S | 28 |
| Margaret St. N&S | 26W-25S,26W-24S | 28 |
| Meadow Av. E&W | 26W-25S,25W-25S | 28 |
| Midland Av. N&S | 25W-25S,25W-24S | 28 |
| Moen Av. E&W | 26W-25S,25W-25S | 28 |
| Morris St. N&S | 26W-25S,26W-24S | 28 |
| Mound Rd. NE&SW | 26W-25S,25W-25S | 28 |
| Otis Av. E&W | 26W-25S,25W-25S | 28 |
| Railroad St. NE&SW | 25W-25S,24W-25S | 28 |
| Ravine Av. NW&SE | 25W-25S,25W-24S | 28 |
| Raynor Av. NE&SW | 25W-25S | 28 |
| Rock Island Av. NE&SW | 25W-25S | 28 |
| Stillwell Av. N&S | 25W-25S | 28 |
| Stryker Av. N&S | 26W-25S,26W-24S | 28 |
| Thorne St. N&S | 25W-25S | 28 |
| Warren St. N&S | 25W-25S,25W-24S | 28 |
| Wheeler Av. N&S | 25W-25S | 28 |

## Romeoville

| | Grid | Page |
|---|---|---|
| Abbeywood Dr. E&W | 23W-14S | 11 |
| Airport Rd. E&W | 24W-17S,23W-18S | 14 |
| Alexander Cir. NS&EW | 24W-15S | 10 |
| Allenhurst Ct.* E&W | 23W-13S | 11 |
| Ambassador Dr. NS&EW | 23W-14S | 11 |
| Amherst Av. N&S | 23W-15S | 11 |
| Anderson Dr. NS&EW | 23W-15S | 11 |
| Anton Dr. E&W | 23W-14S | 11 |
| Arbor Dr. E&W | 25W-14S | 10 |
| Arcadia E&W | 24W-14S | 10 |
| Arlington Dr. E&W | 24W-15S,23W-15S | 10 |
| Arnold Av. N&S | 24W-15S | 10 |
| Arsenal Rd. E&W | 23W-16S | 15 |
| Ashton Av. N&S | 24W-16S | 14 |
| Autumn Woods Ct. E&W | 27W-17S | 13 |
| Autumn Woods Ln. NS&EW | 27W-17S | 13 |
| Avalon Av. E&W | 24W-16S | 14 |
| Cir. | 23W-16S | 15 |
| Beacon Av. E&W | 23W-14S | 11 |
| Beechwood Rd.* E&W | 24W-14S | 10 |
| Belmont Ct. E&W | 24W-15S | 10 |
| Belmont Dr. N&S | 24W-16S,24W-15S | 14 |
| Berkshire Av. N&S | 24W-15S | 10 |
| Beverly J. Griffin Dr. E&W | 24W-15S | 10 |
| Birchwood Dr.* E&W | 24W-14S | 10 |
| Bluff Dr. N&S | 23W-14S | 11 |
| Bluff Rd. E&W | 22W-13S | 11 |
| Briarwood Av. N&S | 24W-16S | 14 |
| Briarwood Ct. N&S | 27W-17S | 13 |
| Bristol Av. E&W | 23W-15S | 11 |
| Broadway St. N&S | 23W-18S | 15 |
| Brookstone Ct. N&S | 27W-17S | 13 |
| Bull Run Dr. E&W | 23W-15S | 11 |
| Camden Av. N&S | 23W-15S | 11 |
| Canterbury Tr. NS&EW | 27W-17S | 13 |
| Cascade Dr. NW&SE | 23W-14S | 11 |
| Caton Farm Rd. E&W | 25W-20S,24W-20S | 20 |
| Cedar Ct.* E&W | 24W-14S | 10 |
| Cedarbend Dr.* E&W | 24W-14S | 10 |
| Chaucer Ct. NE&SW | 27W-17S | 13 |
| Chaucer Dr. NE&SW | 27W-17S | 13 |
| Cherrywood Ct. N&S | 27W-17S | 13 |
| Cherrywood Ln. N&S | 27W-17S | 13 |
| Civic Center Dr. E&W | 23W-15S | 11 |
| Clifton Dr. NS&EW | 24W-15S | 10 |
| Concord Av. N&S | 23W-15S | 11 |
| Corona E&W | 24W-14S | 10 |
| Cranbrook Ct.* E&W | 24W-13S | 10 |
| Dalhart Av. N&S | 23W-15S | 11 |
| DeLaSalle Dr. E&W | 23W-18S | 15 |
| Delta Av. N&S | 23W-14S | 11 |
| Devon Ln.* E&W | 24W-13S | 10 |
| Devonwood Av. E&W | 23W-15S | 11 |
| Dexter Av. N&S | 23W-14S | 11 |
| Disposal Rd. E&W | 23W-16S | 15 |
| Dover Av. E&W | 23W-15S | 11 |
| Driftwood Av. N&S | 24W-16S | 14 |
| Dunbridge Ln.* E&W | 24W-13S | 10 |
| Eaton Av. N&S | 24W-16S | 14 |
| Echo Av. N&S | 23W-14S | 11 |
| Edgewater Dr. NE&SW | 27W-17S | 13 |
| Elgin Av. E&W | 23W-15S | 11 |
| Elmwood Rd.* E&W | 23W-13S | 11 |
| Emery Av. N&S | 24W-16S | 14 |
| Enterprise Dr. N&S | 23W-14S,23W-13S | 11 |
| Erie Dr. E&W | 24W-15S | 10 |
| Essex Av. N&S | 23W-14S | 11 |
| Everette Av. N&S | 24W-15S | 10 |
| Evergreen Ct. N&S | 24W-16S | 14 |
| Fairfax Av. N&S | 24W-16S | 14 |
| Farmbrook Ct.* E&W | 24W-14S | 10 |
| Farragut Av. NS&EW | 24W-14S | 10 |
| Fenton Av. N&S | 24W-15S | 10 |
| Fernwood Ct. N&S | 23W-14S | 11 |
| Fieldstone Ct. NW&SE | 27W-17S | 13 |
| Flambeau Ct. N&S | 24W-15S | 10 |
| Forestwood Dr. NE&SW | 23W-14S | 11 |
| Fremont Av. N&S | 24W-16S | 14 |
| Front St. N&S | 23W-16S,23W-15S | 15 |
| Front St. N&S | 23W-16S | 15 |
| Frontage Rd. E&W | 25W-14S | 10 |
| Gardner Ct.* E&W | 24W-14S | 10 |
| Garland Ave. N&S | 24W-15S | 10 |
| Gavin Av. N&S | 24W-16S | 14 |
| Geneva Av. NS&EW | 24W-14S | 10 |
| Glen Av. N&S | 24W-15S | 10 |
| Gleneagle Ct. N&S | 27W-17S | 13 |
| Gleneagle Dr. NE&SW | 27W-17S | 13 |
| Gordon Av. E&W | 23W-16S | 15 |
| Gordon Dr. E&W | 23W-16S | 15 |
| Grassy Knoll Ct. N&S | 27W-17S | 13 |
| Grassy Knoll Dr. E&W | 27W-17S | 13 |
| Greenwood Av. E&W | 23W-15S | 11 |
| Halde Av. N&S | 24W-16S | 14 |
| Hale Av. N&S | 24W-16S | 14 |
| Haller Av. E&W | 24W-16S,23W-16S | 14 |
| Halstead Ct. E&W | 24W-15S | 10 |
| Hamerick Av. E&W | 24W-16S | 14 |
| Hamrick Av. E&W | 24W-16S | 14 |
| Cir. | 23W-16S | 15 |
| Harris Dr.* E&W | 24W-13S | 10 |
| Hawthorne Ct. E&W | 27W-17S | 13 |
| Hayes Av. E&W | 24W-16S,23W-16S | 14 |
| Healy Av. E&W | 24W-16S,23W-16S | 14 |
| Hemlock Av. N&S | 24W-16S | 14 |
| Hickory Av. N&S | 24W-16S | 14 |
| Hickory Dr. E&W | 23W-14S | 11 |
| High Rd. N&S | 22W-15S | 11 |
| Hillcrest Dr. NS&EW | 24W-14S | 10 |
| Homer Av. N&S | 24W-16S | 14 |
| Honeybear Ln.* E&W | 24W-14S | 10 |
| Honeytree Dr. N&S | 23W-14S | 11 |
| Hopkins Rd. N&S | 24W-18S | 14 |
| Hudson Av. N&S | 24W-15S,24W-14S | 10 |
| Huron Dr. N&S | 24W-15S | 10 |
| Independence Blvd. N&S | 23W-18S,23W-17S | 15 |
| Iola Av. N&S | 24W-15S | 10 |
| Ivyhill Ct. N&S | 27W-17S | 13 |
| Jackson Av. E&W | 22W-16S | 15 |
| Jackson St. E&W | 22W-16S | 15 |
| Joliet Rd. N&S | 23W-17S,23W-14S | 15 |
| Jordon Av. N&S | 24W-15S | 10 |
| Juliet Av. E&W | 23W-15S | 11 |
| Karen Av. E&W | 24W-16S,23W-16S | 14 |
| Kent Av. N&S | 24W-16S | 14 |
| Kenyon Av. N&S | 24W-15S | 10 |
| Kingston Dr. N&S | 24W-15S | 10 |
| Kirman Av. N&S | 23W-16S | 15 |
| Lake Shore Dr. NS&EW | 27W-17S | 13 |
| Lakeshore Ct. SW&NE | 27W-17S | 13 |
| Lakeside Ct. N&S | 23W-14S | 11 |
| Lakeside Dr. N&S | 23W-14S,23W-13S | 11 |
| Lakeview Ct. E&W | 25W-14S | 10 |
| Lakeview Dr. E&W | 25W-14S | 10 |
| Cir. | 23W-16S | 15 |
| Laurel Av. N&S | 24W-15S | 10 |
| Lemont Rd. N&S | 22W-15S | 11 |
| Linden Av. N&S | 24W-16S | 14 |
| Lynn Dr. N&S | 24W-15S | 10 |
| Macon Av. N&S | 24W-16S | 14 |
| Marquette Dr. E&W | 23W-13S | 11 |
| McKool Av. E&W | 24W-16S,23W-16S | 14 |
| Mendota Ln. N&S | 24W-15S | 10 |
| Michigan Dr. N&S | 24W-15S | 10 |
| Mikan Ln. E&W | 23W-15S | 11 |
| Montrose Dr. NS&EW | 24W-15S | 10 |
| Murphy Dr. E&W | 24W-16S | 14 |
| Naperville Dr. NS&EW | 23W-14S,23W-13S | 11 |
| Naperville Rd. N&S | 23W-14S | 11 |
| Nelson Av. N&S | 24W-15S | 10 |
| Newland Av. E&W | 24W-15S | 10 |
| Newman Ct. N&S | 24W-15S | 10 |
| Nippert Av. N&S | 24W-16S | 14 |
| Normantown Rd. E&W | 25W-15S,23W-15S | 10 |
| Oakton Av. E&W | 24W-16S | 14 |
| Olde English Ct. SW&NE | 27W-17S | 13 |
| Olde English Dr. N&S | 27W-17S | 13 |
| Ontario Dr. E&W | 24W-15S | 10 |
| Palmer Av. E&W | 24W-15S | 10 |
| Parkview Cir. EW&NS | 27W-17S | 13 |
| Parkview Dr. N&S | 27W-17S | 13 |
| Parkwood Av. N&S | 23W-15S,23W-14S | 11 |
| Pebblestone Dr. NS&EW | 27W-17S | 13 |
| Pell Av. E&W | 24W-16S,23W-16S | 14 |
| Phelps Av. E&W | 23W-15S | 11 |
| Pinetree Ct.* E&W | 24W-14S | 10 |
| Poplar Av. N&S | 24W-16S | 14 |

|  | Grid | Page |
|---|---|---|
| Poplar Blvd. N&S .. | 24W-16S | 14 |
| Ridgewood Av. E&W ............... | 23W-14S | 11 |
| Riveredge Dr. N&S | 23W-15S | 11 |
| Robbin St.* E&W .. | 24W-14S | 10 |
| Rocbaar Dr. E&W .. | 23W-14S | 11 |
| Rogers Rd. N&S .. | 24W-14S | 10 |
| Romeo Rd. E&W ............... | 23W-16S,22W-16S | 15 |
| Romeoville Rd. E&W ............... | 23W-16S,22W-16S | 15 |
| Roof Av. E&W..... | 24W-16S | 14 |
| Route 53 N&S ............... | 23W-18S,23W-16S | 15 |
| Route 7 N&S ............... | 24W-20S,23W-19S | 20 |
| Saybrook Ct.* E&W ............... | 24W-14S | 10 |
| Scarbury Ct.* E&W ............... | 24W-14S | 10 |
| Sherman Rd. NS&EW ............... | 22W-13S | 11 |
| Sherwood* E&W.... | 24W-14S | 10 |
| Shoreline Ct. E&W .. | 27W-17S | 13 |
| Sinde Cir. NS&EW.. | 23W-16S | 15 |
| Six Pines Dr.* E&W ............... | 24W-14S | 10 |
| Spangler Av. N&S .. | 23W-15S | 11 |
| Spring Hill Ct. NS&EW ............... | 27W-17S | 13 |
| St. Claire Dr. E&W .. | 24W-15S | 10 |
| Stateville Rd. E&W ............... | 25W-19S,23W-19S | 20 |
| Superior Dr. N&S .. | 24W-15S | 10 |
| Tallman Av. E&W ............... | 24W-16S,23W-16S | 14 |
| Techni Rd. N&S .. | 24W-17S | 14 |
| Troxel Av. NE&SW | 24W-16S | 14 |
| Union Av. E&W .. | 24W-16S | 10 |
| Waldon Ct.* E&W .. | 24W-14S | 10 |
| Washington Av. E&W ............... | 22W-16S | 15 |
| Washington St. E&W ............... | 22W-16S | 15 |
| Weber Rd. N&S .. | 25W-20S | 20 |
| Westlake Pkwy. NS&EW ............... | 27W-17S | 13 |
| Wildwood Ct.* E&W ............... | 24W-14S | 10 |
| Willow Ct.* E&W... | 24W-14S | 10 |
| Windham Pkwy. E&W ............... | 25W-14S | 10 |
| Winding Ridge Ct. NW&SE ............... | 27W-17S | 13 |
| Winding Ridge Dr. NS&EW ............... | 27W-17S | 13 |
| Windsor Ln.* E&W.. | 24W-13S | 10 |
| Winnebago Ct. E&W ............... | 24W-15S | 10 |
| Woodhill Dr. NW&SE ............... | 27W-17S | 13 |
| Woodlawn Av. N&S ............... | 25W-15S | 10 |
| Yates Av. E&W .. | 24W-15S | 10 |
| 135th St. E&W .. | 24W-15S | 10 |
| 135th St. E&W .. | 24W-16S | 14 |

## Shorewood

|  | Grid | Page |
|---|---|---|
| 'A' Ct. E&W........ | 30W-24S | 26 |
| 'D' Ct. NS&EW .. | 30W-24S | 26 |
| Abbeywood Dr. N&S ............... | 31W-24S | 26 |
| Amendodge Dr. E&W ............... | 30W-24S | 26 |
| Arrowhead Dr. N&S ............... | 30W-23S | 18 |
| Bass St. E&W.... | 30W-24S | 26 |
| Berkeley Ct. E&W .. | 31W-24S | 26 |
| Birch Dr. E&W.... | 30W-23S | 18 |
| Black Rd. E&W .. | 30W-22S | 18 |
| Brook Forest Av. N&S ............... | 30W-23S,30W-22S | 18 |
| Brookshore Ct. NE&SW ............... | 30W-24S | 26 |
| Brookshore Dr. N&S ............... | 30W-24S,30W-23S | 26 |
| Buckingham Ct. E&W ............... | 31W-24S | 26 |
| Buckingham Pl. E&W ............... | 31W-24S | 26 |
| Ca-Crest Dr. N&S .. | 30W-23S | 18 |
| Cambridge Ct. E&W ............... | 31W-24S | 26 |
| Cambridge Ln. NW&SE ............... | 30W-24S,31W-24S | 26 |
| Caprice Ct. NE&SW ............... | 30W-24S | 26 |
| Cardinal Pl. N&S.... | 30W-23S | 18 |
| Carla Dr. N&S .. | 30W-23S | 18 |
| Cedar Ln. N&S .. | 30W-23S | 18 |
| Channahon St. NE&SW ............... | 29W-24S | 26 |
| Clark Dr. NE&SW .. | 30W-24S | 26 |
| Cobblestone Ct. E&W ............... | 30W-23S | 18 |
| Collingwood Ct. E&W ............... | 30W-24S | 26 |
| Colonade Rd. N&S.. | 30W-24S | 26 |
| Colony Ct. NE&SW ............... | 30W-23S | 18 |
| Conquest Ct. NE&SW ............... | 31W-24S | 26 |
| Cortina Ct. E&W.... | 30W-24S | 26 |
| Cottage St. N&S.... | 30W-24S | 26 |
| Country Rd. NW&SE ............... | 30W-23S | 18 |
| Danny Dr. N&S .. | 30W-23S | 18 |
| Dantes Ct. E&W .... | 29W-24S | 26 |
| David Barry Dr. E&W ............... | 31W-24S | 26 |
| David Dr. N&S.... | 30W-23S | 18 |
| Deerwood Dr. E&W ............... | 30W-23S | 18 |
| Diana Av. E&W .. | 29W-24S | 26 |
| Dover Ct. E&W .... | 31W-24S | 26 |
| Dover Way N&S.... | 30W-24S | 26 |
| DuPage St. N&S .. | 30W-24S | 26 |
| Earl Rd. N&S .... | 30W-24S | 26 |
| Edgebrook Dr. N&S ............... | 30W-23S | 18 |
| Franklin Ln. N&S .. | 30W-24S | 26 |
| Garden Ter. N&S .. | 30W-24S | 26 |
| Geneva St. E&W .. | 30W-24S | 26 |
| Greenfield Rd. N&S ............... | 30W-23S | 18 |
| Grove St. N&S .... | 30W-24S | 26 |
| Harvard Ln. NW&SE ............... | 30W-24S | 26 |
| Harvest Dr. NW&SE ............... | 30W-23S | 18 |
| Helene St. E&W .... | 29W-24S | 26 |
| Highland Dr. E&W .. | 30W-23S | 18 |
| Hummingbird Ct. E&W ............... | 30W-23S | 18 |
| Hunter Dr. E&W .. | 31W-24S | 26 |
| Huntington Ct. N&S ............... | 30W-24S | 26 |
| Huntington Dr. E&W ............... | 30W-24S | 26 |
| Interstate 55 NE&SW ............... | 29W-24S,29W-23S | 26 |
| Jefferson St. E&W ............... | 30W-23S,29W-23S | 18 |
| Kensington St. E&W ............... | 30W-23S | 18 |
| Lancer Ct. E&W .. | 30W-23S | 18 |
| Lark Ln. E&W .... | 30W-23S | 18 |
| Laura Av. NS&EW .. | 29W-24S | 26 |
| Lynwood Ct. NE&SW ............... | 30W-23S | 18 |
| Madeira St. E&W ............... | 30W-23S | 18 |
| Manor Dr. NE&SW. | 30W-25S | 26 |
| Maple Ln. N&S .... | 30W-23S | 18 |
| Mary St. N&S .... | 29W-24S | 26 |
| Marya St. E&W .. | 30W-23S | 18 |
| Meadow Dr. E&W . | 30W-23S | 18 |
| Meyers St. E&W.... | 30W-24S | 26 |
| Moorland Av. NW&SE ............... | 30W-23S | 18 |
| New Castle Ct. SE&NW ............... | 31W-24S | 26 |
| Oak Ct. NW&SE.... | 29W-24S | 26 |
| Oak Dr. E&W .... | 30W-23S | 18 |
| Oakwood Dr. E&W .. | 30W-23S | 18 |
| Olde Ivey Rd. N&S . | 31W-24S | 26 |
| Oxford Ln. E&W.... | 30W-24S | 26 |
| Parkshore Dr. N&S .. | 30W-23S | 18 |
| Picnic St. N&S.... | 30W-24S | 26 |
| Princeton Ct. E&W .. | 30W-24S | 26 |
| Ranchwood Dr. E&W ............... | 30W-24S | 26 |
| Raven Rd. N&S .. | 30W-24S | 26 |
| Ravinia Ct. NE&SW . | 30W-24S | 26 |
| Ravinia Dr. N&S .... | 30W-24S | 26 |
| Regency Ct. NW&SE ............... | 30W-24S | 26 |
| Ridge Dr. E&W .. | 30W-23S | 18 |
| Ridge Rd. E&W .. | 30W-24S | 26 |
| Riffles E&W .... | 30W-24S | 26 |
| River Rd. N&S.... | 31W-23S | 18 |
| Riverfront Dr. N&S.. | 30W-24S | 26 |
| Robin Hill Dr. NS&EW ............... | 30W-23S | 18 |
| Rock Rd. E&W .... | 30W-24S | 26 |
| Rome Ct. E&W .. | 30W-23S | 18 |
| Rosewood St. E&W ............... | 30W-24S | 26 |
| Route 59 N&S ............... | 30W-24S,30W-23S | 26 |
| Rushwood Av. E&W ............... | 30W-23S | 18 |
| Sarah Av. E&W .. | 29W-24S | 26 |
| School Rd. E&W.... | 29W-24S | 26 |
| Sean Dr. N&S .. | 30W-23S | 18 |
| Seil Rd. NE&SW .. | 30W-24S | 26 |
| Shady Ln. N&S .. | 30W-23S | 18 |
| Shore Dr. NE&SW .. | 29W-24S | 26 |
| Shorewood Dr. N&S ............... | 30W-23S | 18 |
| Shorewood Ln. E&W ............... | 30W-24S | 26 |
| Stanford Dr. E&W .. | 30W-24S | 26 |
| Summer St. N&S .. | 30W-24S | 26 |
| Sunrise Dr. E&W .. | 30W-23S | 18 |
| Sunset Dr. NW&SE ............... | 30W-23S | 18 |
| Sunset Ln. N&S .. | 30W-24S | 26 |
| Trout St. E&W.... | 30W-24S | 26 |
| Turtle St. N&S...... | 30W-24S | 26 |
| U.S. Route 52 E&W ............... | 30W-24S,29W-24S | 26 |
| Valencia Dr. NE&SW ............... | 30W-24S | 26 |
| Wales Ct. E&W .. | 30W-24S | 26 |
| West Shore Dr. NE&SW ............... | 30W-24S | 26 |
| Westwood Ct. N&S ............... | 30W-24S | 26 |
| Westwood Dr. N&S ............... | 30W-24S | 26 |
| Wheatland Dr.* NW&SE ............... | 30W-23S | 18 |
| Whipperwill Ct. NW&SE ............... | 30W-23S | 18 |
| William St. E&W .. | 29W-24S | 26 |
| Windsor Dr. NW&SE ............... | 30W-24S | 26 |
| Woodbrook Ct. E&W ............... | 30W-23S | 18 |
| Yale Ct. NW&SE... | 30W-24S | 26 |

## Steger*
### (Also see Cook County)

|  | Grid | Page |
|---|---|---|
| Ashland Av. N&S .. | 1W-28S | 44 |
| Barbara Ln. E&W .. | 0W-28S | 44 |
| Berk Ln. E&W .... | 0W-28S | 44 |
| Butler Av. N&S .... | 0W-28S | 44 |
| Camden Pl. NE&SW | 0W-28S | 44 |
| Carol Ct. E&W ..... | 1W-28S | 44 |
| Carpenter St. N&S .. | 1W-28S | 44 |
| Cedarwood Dr. E&W ............... | 1W-28S | 44 |
| Christine Ct. E&W .. | 1W-28S | 44 |
| Cornwall Dr. N&S .. | 0W-28S | 44 |
| Craig Ct. E&W ..... | 1W-28S | 44 |
| Crescent Dr. NE&SW ............... | 1W-28S | 44 |
| Dorsetshire Dr. N&S | 0W-28S | 44 |
| Durham Dr. N&S .. | 1W-28S | 44 |
| Emerald Av. N&S .. | 1W-28S | 44 |
| Evergreen Av. N&S .. | 0W-28S | 44 |
| Florence Av. N&S.... | 0W-28S | 44 |
| Grace St. N&S .... | 1W-28S | 44 |
| Green St. N&S .... | 1W-28S | 44 |
| Halsted St. N&S .. | 1W-28S | 44 |
| Hereford Dr. E&W .. | 0W-28S | 44 |
| Holeman Av. N&S.... | 0W-28S | 44 |
| Hopkins Av. N&S .. | 0W-28S | 44 |
| Jennifer Ct. N&S .. | 1W-28S | 44 |
| John St. N&S........ | 1W-28S | 44 |
| Knollwood Dr. E&W .. | 1W-28S | 44 |
| Lewis Av. N&S .... | 0W-28S | 44 |
| Loverock Av. N&S .. | 0W-28S | 44 |
| McKinley Av. E&W . | 1W-28S | 44 |
| Morgan Ct. N&S .. | 1W-28S | 44 |
| Morgan St. N&S .. | 1W-28S | 44 |
| Park Av. N&S ...... | 1W-28S | 44 |
| Peoria St. N&S .... | 1W-28S | 44 |
| Phillips Av. N&S .... | 0W-28S | 44 |
| Richton Rd. E&W ............... | 1W-28S,0W-28S | 44 |
| Route 1 N&S........ | 1W-28S | 44 |
| Sally Dr. N&S........ | 1W-28S | 44 |
| Sangamon St. N&S .. | 1W-28S | 44 |
| Stella Bl. N&S .... | 1W-28S | 44 |
| Susan Ln. NS&EW . | 1W-28S | 44 |
| Tinbury Pl. NW&SE .. | 0W-28S | 44 |
| Tiverton Ln. N&S .. | 0W-28S | 44 |
| Union Av. N&S .... | 1W-28S | 44 |
| Valleywood Dr. N&S | 1W-28S | 44 |
| Wallace Av. N&S .. | 0W-28S | 44 |
| Williams St. N&S .. | 1W-28S | 44 |
| 30th St. E&W...... | 0W-28S | 44 |
| 34th Pl. E&W .... | 1W-28S | 44 |
| 34th St. E&W .... | 1W-28S | 44 |
| 35th Pl. E&W .... | 1W-28S | 44 |
| 35th St. E&W ............... | 1W-28S,0W-28S | 44 |
| 36th Pl. E&W .... | 1W-28S | 44 |
| 36th St. E&W ............... | 1W-28S,0W-28S | 44 |
| 37th Pl. E&W .... | 1W-28S | 44 |
| 37th St. E&W ............... | 1W-28S,0W-28S | 44 |

## Symerton

|  | Grid | Page |
|---|---|---|
| Commercial St. E&W ............... | 23W-37S,22W-37S | 61 |
| Honeywell Ln. E&W ............... | 22W-37S | 61 |
| James St. N&S .... | 22W-37S | 61 |
| North St. E&W .. | 22W-37S | 61 |
| Northern Av. N&S .. | 22W-37S | 61 |
| South St. E&W .. | 22W-37S | 61 |
| Traverse St. E&W .. | 22W-37S | 61 |

## Tinley Park*
### (Also see Cook County)

|  | Grid | Page |
|---|---|---|
| East Hillside Dr. N&S ............... | 9W-23S | 25 |
| Interstate 80 E&W .. | 9W-22S | 25 |
| Lakeside Ct. SW&NE ............... | 9W-23S | 25 |
| Maple Creek Dr. E&W ............... | 9W-22S | 25 |
| North Creek Dr. N&S ............... | 9W-22S | 25 |
| Route 43 N&S ...... | 9W-22S | 25 |
| Spring Creek Dr. N&S ............... | 9W-23S | 25 |
| West Creek Dr. E&W ............... | 9W-23S | 25 |
| 76th Av. N&S .... | 9W-22S | 25 |
| 187th St. E&W .. | 10W-22S | 25 |
| 195th St. E&W ...... | 9W-23S | 25 |

## Troy Township

|  | Grid | Page |
|---|---|---|
| Addelman Dr. N&S .. | 28W-22S | 19 |
| Aston Martin Dr. NE&SW ............... | 27W-23S | 19 |
| Bailey Dr. N&S .. | 29W-22S | 18 |
| Bankview Ln. NE&SW ............... | 28W-23S | 19 |
| Barber Ln. N&S .. | 27W-22S | 19 |
| Baskin Dr. N&S .. | 29W-22S | 18 |
| Beckett Dr. N&S.... | 27W-23S | 19 |
| Black Rd. E&W ............... | 32W-22S,27W-22S | 18 |
| Bluemont Dr. E&W . | 30W-25S | 26 |
| Bramble Hill Rd. N&S ............... | 30W-27S | 26 |
| Bridge St. N&S .. | 30W-26S | 26 |
| Bronk Rd. N&S .. | 29W-22S | 18 |
| Burr Ridge Dr. N&S ............... | 30W-26S | 26 |
| Bush Rd. NW&SE .. | 28W-26S | 27 |
| Camelot Ct. NE&SW ............... | 30W-27S | 26 |
| Camelot Rd. E&W .. | 30W-27S | 26 |
| Campbell Dr. E&W.. | 27W-23S | 19 |
| Canal Rd. NE&SW . | 30W-27S | 26 |
| Cannock Chase E&W ............... | 30W-26S | 26 |
| Canterbury St. N&S ............... | 30W-26S | 26 |
| Cassie Dr. E&W .. | 27W-22S | 19 |
| Chancer Dr. E&W .. | 27W-23S | 19 |
| Clarage Ct. E&W . | 30W-26S | 26 |
| Cleary Av. E&W .. | 28W-22S | 19 |
| Colleen Ct. NW&SE ............... | 30W-26S | 26 |
| County Farm Rd. E&W ............... | 32W-24S,29W-24S | 26 |
| County Line Rd. N&S ............... | 32W-27S,32W-26S | 26 |
| Dover Cloud Dr. E&W ............... | 27W-23S | 19 |
| East Cliff Dr. NE&SW ............... | 30W-27S | 26 |
| Fairway St. N&S... | 28W-23S | 19 |
| Fawn Ct. E&W .. | 29W-23S | 19 |
| Francis Ct. E&W .. | 30W-25S | 26 |
| Frank Dr. E&W .. | 29W-22S | 18 |
| Frontage Rd. N&S ............... | 30W-27S,29W-22S | 26 |
| George Av. E&W .. | 27W-22S | 19 |
| Glenwood Av. E&W ............... | 27W-22S | 19 |
| Greenmeadow Ln. E&W ............... | 28W-23S | 19 |
| Guinevere Ln. NW&SE ............... | 30W-27W | 26 |
| Hickory Walk Ct. E&W ............... | 30W-27S | 26 |
| Ingalls Av. E&W .. | 27W-22S | 19 |
| Ingolsby Rd. N&S ............... | 32W-27S,32W-26S | 26 |
| Interstate 55 N&S ............... | 30W-27S,29W-22S | 26 |
| Interstate 80 E&W ............... | 32W-27S,27W-25S | 26 |
| Jensen St. E&W .. | 30W-25S | 26 |
| John Lee Ct. NE&SW ............... | 30W-26S | 26 |
| Joliet Rd. E&W ............... | 28W-27S,27W-27S | 27 |
| Juniper St. E&W .. | 28W-22S | 19 |
| Kelly Ann Ln. N&S .. | 30W-26S | 26 |
| Kings Ct. NW&SE .. | 30W-27S | 26 |
| Kipling Ct. E&W .. | 30W-26S | 26 |
| Knightwood Dr. N&S ............... | 30W-27S | 26 |
| Lakewood Ln. NE&SW ............... | 30W-25S | 26 |
| Lancelot Ln. N&S ............... | 30W-27S | 26 |
| Leominster Av. E&W ............... | 28W-22S | 19 |
| Mantry Dr. N&S .. | 27W-23S | 19 |
| Marlene Ct. E&W .. | 30W-25S | 26 |
| Mattox Ct. E&W .. | 30W-26S | 26 |
| McDonald Ct. E&W ............... | 30W-25S | 26 |
| Merlin St. E&W .. | 30W-27S | 26 |
| Mound Ct. NW&SE ............... | 28W-26S | 27 |
| Mound Rd. E&W ............... | 32W-25S,30W-25S | 26 |
| Murphy Dr. N&S.... | 27W-22S | 19 |
| Nadia Dr. N&S.... | 30W-26S | 26 |
| Oak Dr. E&W .... | 30W-26S | 26 |
| Park River Ln. NS&EW ............... | 30W-26S | 26 |
| Pellinore Ct. E&W .. | 30W-27S | 26 |
| Pine Dr. N&S .... | 30W-25S | 26 |
| Queens Ct. NW&SE ............... | 30W-27S | 26 |
| Red Oak Ln. E&W .. | 30W-26S | 26 |
| River Rd. N&S ............... | 31W-27S,31W-22S | 26 |
| Riverside Dr. E&W .. | 30W-27S | 26 |
| Rock Rd. E&W .... | 30W-24S | 26 |
| Rock Run Dr. NE&SW ............... | 29W-25S,29W-24S | 26 |
| Rollingwood Ct. E&W ............... | 28W-23S | 19 |
| Rollingwood Ln. NE&SW ............... | 28W-23S | 19 |
| Rolls Royce Dr. E&W ............... | 27W-23S | 19 |
| Ron Lee Ct. N&S .. | 30W-25S | 26 |
| Ronnie Ct. E&W .. | 30W-25S | 26 |
| Rosary Ln. N&S .. | 27W-22S | 19 |
| Route 59 N&S..... | 29W-22S | 18 |
| Sarver Dr. N&S .. | 29W-24S | 26 |
| Schock Dr. N&S .. | 29W-22S | 18 |
| Schubert Dr. N&S .. | 30W-26S | 26 |
| Shepley Rd. E&W ............... | 32W-27S,30W-27S | 26 |
| Sir Gallahad Dr. NE&SW ............... | 30W-26S | 26 |
| Sir Gawain Dr. NE&SW ............... | 30W-27S,30W-26S | 26 |
| Sterling Dr. E&W .. | 27W-23S | 19 |
| Theodore St. E&W ............... | 32W-22S,30W-22S | 18 |
| Timberline Ct. N&S | 28W-23S | 19 |
| Timberline Dr. N&S ............... | 28W-23S,28W-22S | 19 |
| Troy Rd. E&W ............... | 32W-23S,31W-23S | 18 |
| Twin Oaks Dr. E&W ............... | 27W-23S | 19 |
| U.S. Route 52 E&W ............... | 32W-24S,29W-23S | 26 |
| West Ridge NW&SE ............... | 28W-23S | 19 |
| Woodridge Way E&W ............... | 30W-26S | 26 |

## University Park

|  | Grid | Page |
|---|---|---|
| Abbott Ln. E&W .... | 3W-30S | 43 |
| Amherst Ln. E&W... | 3W-30S | 43 |
| Ann Ln. E&W .... | 3W-30S | 43 |
| Anvil Ct. N&S .... | 3W-30S | 43 |
| Ashridge Ln. NE&SW ............... | 3W-30S | 43 |
| Barbara Ct. N&S .. | 3W-29S | 43 |
| Barrington Ct. E&W .. | 3W-30S | 43 |
| Barrow Ct. N&S .. | 3W-30S | 43 |
| Blackhawk Dr. N&S . | 3W-30S | 43 |
| Bond St. E&W ............... | 7W-30S,6W-30S | 42 |
| Bradfield Ct. N&S .. | 3W-30S | 43 |
| Brampton Ct. NW&SE ............... | 3W-30S | 43 |
| Brockhurst Ct. N&S .. | 3W-30S | 43 |
| Buckley Ct. E&W .. | 3W-30S | 43 |
| Burnham Dr. N&S .. | 3W-30S | 43 |
| Carmel Ct.* NE&SW | 4W-29S | 43 |
| Carol Ln. E&W .... | 3W-30S | 43 |
| Central Av. N&S .... | 7W-30S | 42 |
| Circle Dr. E&W .... | 3W-29S | 43 |
| Clover Ln. E&W .... | 3W-30S | 43 |
| Cordoba St. N&S.... | 3W-30S | 43 |
| Crawford Av. N&S .. | 5W-29S | 42 |
| Cypress Ct.* E&W .. | 4W-29S | 43 |
| Delmar Ct.* NW&SE | 4W-30S | 43 |
| Doral Ter. NE&SW .. | 2W-30S | 43 |
| Dralle Rd. E&W.... | 7W-29S | 42 |
| Driftwood Ct.* E&W . | 4W-29S | 43 |
| Exchange St. E&W ............... | 4W-29S,3W-29S | 43 |
| Farmview Ct. N&S ............... | 3W-30S | 43 |
| Farmview Rd. E&W . | 3W-30S | 43 |
| Federal Signal Dr. E&W ............... | 7W-29S | 42 |
| Fiesta Dr. E&W .... | 3W-30S | 43 |
| Gail Av. E&W...... | 7W-30S | 42 |
| Gordon Ter. E&W .. | 3W-29S | 43 |
| Governors Hwy. NE&SW ............... | 5W-28S | 42 |
| Hamilton Av. N&S... | 7W-30S | 42 |
| Hamilton Rd. E&W .. | 4W-30S | 43 |
| Harvest Ln. NS&EW . | 3W-30S | 43 |
| Hickock Av. N&S .. | 3W-30S | 43 |
| Hickock Dr. E&W.... | 3W-30S | 43 |
| Home Av. N&S .... | 6W-30S | 42 |
| Horner Av. E&W .. | 6W-30S | 42 |
| Horseshoe Ln. N&S . | 3W-30S | 43 |
| Industrial Dr. N&S... | 7W-29S | 42 |
| Interstate 57 N&S... | 7W-30S | 42 |
| Irving Pl. E&W .... | 3W-30S | 43 |
| Joseph Ct. E&W .... | 7W-29S | 42 |
| Kedzie Av. N&S .. | 4W-30S | 43 |
| King Rd. N&S .... | 2W-30S | 43 |
| Landau Rd. E&W .. | 2W-30S | 43 |
| Love Ln. E&W .... | 2W-29S | 43 |
| Marina Ct.* N&S .. | 4W-30S | 43 |
| Mendicino Ct.* NE&SW ............... | 4W-30S | 43 |
| Mesa Ct. N&S .... | 3W-30S | 43 |
| Mildred Ln. N&S .. | 3W-30S | 43 |
| Mission Dr. E&W .. | 3W-30S | 43 |
| Monterey Ct. N&S .. | 3W-30S | 43 |
| Monterey Ct.* E&W .. | 3W-30S | 43 |
| Morningside Dr. NW&SE ............... | 3W-30S | 43 |
| Nathan Rd. E&W .. | 3W-30S | 43 |
| Oakside Ln. E&W.... | 3W-29S | 43 |
| Old Forge Ct. N&S .. | 3W-30S | 43 |
| Old Monee Rd. E&W ............... | 2W-30S | 43 |
| Pacifica Ct.* NE&SW ............... | 4W-30S | 43 |
| Palmer Av. E&W .. | 7W-30S | 42 |
| Pebble Beach Ct. N&S ............... | 2W-30S | 43 |
| Pebble Ct.* N&S .. | 4W-29S | 43 |

| | Grid | Page |
|---|---|---|
| Pine Oak Ln. NW&SE | | |
| .................. 3W-30S | | 43 |
| Pine Trace Ct. E&W .. 4W-29S | | 43 |
| Pinewood Ct. E&W .. 4W-29S | | 43 |
| Red Oak Ln. N&S ...3W-29S | | 43 |
| Redwood Ct.* NE&SW | | |
| .................. 4W-29S | | 43 |
| Regent Rd. E&W .. 3W-30S | | 43 |
| Reigel Farm Rd. N&S | | |
| .................. 3W-30S | | 43 |
| Route 50 N&S .... 6W-30S | | 42 |
| Samson Ct. E&W .. 3W-30S | | 43 |
| Samson Dr. N&S ... 3W-30S | | 43 |
| Sandpiper Ct.* N&S ..4W-29S | | 43 |
| Sandra Dr. E&W ... 3W-29S | | 43 |
| Sierra Ct.* E&W .. 4W-30S | | 43 |
| Sierra Dr. N&S ... 4W-30S | | 43 |
| Spring Ct.* N&S .... 4W-29S | | 43 |
| Stegar Monee Rd. NW&SE | | |
| .................. 4W-29S | | 43 |
| Stuenkel Rd. E&W .. 5W-28S | | 42 |
| Sullivan Ln. E&W ... 3W-30S | | 43 |
| Sunset Ct.* NW&SE 4W-29S | | 43 |
| Surrey Ln. E&W .. 3W-30S | | 43 |
| Union Dr. N&S .... 3W-30S | | 43 |
| Western Av. N&S ... 2W-30S | | 43 |
| White Oak Ln. E&W .. 3W-30S | | 43 |
| Wildwood Ct.* E&W ..4W-29S | | 43 |
| Wright Rd. N&S .... 3W-29S | | 43 |

## Washington Township

| | Grid | Page |
|---|---|---|
| Ashland Av. N&S | | |
| ............ 2W-39S,2W-34S | | 67 |
| Brunswick Rd. E&W | | |
| ..........3E-34S,4E-34S | | 57 |
| Church Rd. E&W .. 1W-35S | | 56 |
| Church Rd. E&W .. 0W-37S | | 68 |
| Corning Rd. E&W | | |
| ........0E-37S,4E-37S | | 68 |
| Cottage Grove Av. N&S | | |
| ........0E-39S,1E-36S | | 68 |
| County Line Rd. E&W | | |
| ......... 2W-39S,4E-39S | | 67 |
| Dixie Hwy. N&S | | |
| ........0W-39S,0W-36S | | 68 |
| Eagle Lake Rd. E&W | | |
| ......... 2W-34S,0E-34S | | 55 |
| Hahn's Rd. N&S ........0E-35S | | 56 |
| Halstead St. N&S ....0W-34S | | 56 |
| Indiana Av. E&W .. 1W-36S | | 68 |
| Kennedy Rd. N&S | | |
| ........0E-38S,4E-38S | | 68 |
| Klemme Rd. NS&EW | | |
| ..........3E-39S,3E-34S | | 69 |
| Lia Ln. N&S ........ 1W-39S | | 68 |
| Oak Park Av. N&S .. 1W-36S | | 68 |
| Racine Av. N&S | | |
| ........ 1W-37S,1W-36S | | 68 |
| Route 1 N&S | | |
| ........0W-39S,0W-34S | | 68 |
| Southpark Av. N&S .. 0E-34S | | 56 |
| State Line Rd. N&S | | |
| ........4E-39S,4E-34S | | 69 |
| Stony Island Av. N&S | | |
| ......1E-39S,1E-34S | | 69 |
| Streamwood Dr. NS&EW | | |
| .................. 2W-34S | | 55 |
| Yates Av. N&S | | |
| ............2E-39S,2E-34S | | 69 |
| 287th St. E&W | | |
| .......... 1W-34S,2E-34S | | 56 |
| 295th St. E&W | | |
| ......... 2W-35S,1E-35S | | 55 |
| 303rd St. E&W | | |
| ........0E-37S,4E-37S | | 68 |
| 311th St. E&W | | |
| ......... 2W-37S,4E-37S | | 67 |
| 319th St. E&W | | |
| ......... 2W-38S,4E-38S | | 67 |
| 323rd St. E&W | | |
| ........0W-39S,4E-39S | | 68 |

## Wesley Township

| | Grid | Page |
|---|---|---|
| Albert Ln. N&S .... 27W-40S | | 71 |
| Alma Dr. E&W | | |
| ......27W-40S,26W-40S | | 71 |
| Angle St. E&W .. 25W-42S | | 76 |
| Ballou Rd. E&W | | |
| ......26W-40S,21W-40S | | 72 |
| Bass St. E&W ......27W-40S | | 71 |
| Bruning Dr. N&S ....27W-40S | | 71 |
| Butterfield Rd. N&S | | |
| ......25W-45S,22W-40S | | 76 |
| Byron Rd. N&S .. 23W-43S | | 77 |
| Center NW&SE .. 25W-40S | | 76 |
| Charles St. N&S .. 27W-41S | | 71 |
| Church St. N&S .... 27W-40S | | 71 |
| Danielson Rd. E&W | | |
| ..........22W-42S,22W-41S | | 77 |
| De Selm Rd. E&W .. 24W-43S | | 76 |
| Donahue Rd. E&W | | |
| ......23W-42S,22W-40S | | 77 |
| Dorset Dr. E&W ... 27W-40S | | 71 |
| Elmwood Av. N&S | | |
| ......27W-41S,26W-41S | | 71 |
| Evergreen St. N&S.. 27W-41S | | 71 |
| Florence St. NE&SW | | |
| .................. 25W-42S | | 76 |
| Goodwin Rd. E&W | | |
| ......25W-41S,24W-41S | | 72 |
| Grand Av. E&W .... 27W-42S | | 75 |

| | Grid | Page |
|---|---|---|
| Greenwood St. N&S | | |
| .................. 27W-41S | | 71 |
| Grove St. N&S .... 27W-41S | | 71 |
| Hamilton St. E&W .. 27W-40S | | 71 |
| Hazelton Rd. E&W | | |
| ......22W-41S,21W-41S | | 73 |
| Hickory Av. N&S....27W-42S | | 75 |
| Hintze St. E&W | | |
| ......27W-41S,26W-41S | | 71 |
| Indian Trail-Phillips Rd. N&S | | |
| ......25W-41S,25W-40S | | 72 |
| John St. E&W | | |
| ......27W-40S,26W-40S | | 71 |
| Juneway Av. N&S .. 27W-42S | | 75 |
| Kankakee St. NW&SE | | |
| ......24W-43S,22W-44S | | 76 |
| Koerner St. E&W .. 27W-40S | | 71 |
| Lakeside Av. NW&SE | | |
| ......27W-41S,27W-41S | | 75 |
| Lakewood Dr. N&S | | |
| ......27W-41S,27W-40S | | 71 |
| Manteno Rd. E&W | | |
| ......25W-42S,21W-42S | | 76 |
| Maple St. E&W | | |
| ......27W-40S,26W-40S | | 71 |
| Maple Ter. N&S | | |
| ......27W-42S,27W-41S | | 75 |
| Martin Long Rd. N&S | | |
| .................. 22S-40S | | 73 |
| Meadowview Ln. N&S | | |
| .................. 26W-40S | | 72 |
| North Dr. E&W .... 27W-41S | | 71 |
| Oak St. E&W ...... 27W-42S | | 75 |
| Old Chicago Rd. N&S | | |
| ......24W-43S,24W-40S | | 76 |
| Orchard Ter. NW&SE | | |
| .................. 27W-42S | | 75 |
| Pine Grove Av. N&S | | |
| .................. 27W-42S | | 75 |
| Poplar St. NE&SW ..27W-41S | | 71 |
| Rest Haven Rd. N&S | | |
| ......26W-42S,26W-41S | | 76 |
| Riverside Dr. N&S .. 27W-41S | | 71 |
| Robert St. N&S .. 27W-40S | | 71 |
| Rosewood Dr. N&S | | |
| .................. 27W-41S | | 71 |
| Route 102 N&S | | |
| ......27W-40S,22S-44S | | 71 |
| Short St. N&S .... 27W-41S | | 71 |
| Smith St. NE&SW .. 25W-42S | | 76 |
| Stewart Av. N&S .. 27W-42S | | 75 |
| Sumac St. NW&SE 27W-40S | | 71 |
| Symerton Rd. N&S 23W-40S | | 73 |
| Thornton Rd. E&W | | |
| ......22W-43S,21W-43S | | 77 |
| Trout St. N&S ... 27W-40S | | 71 |
| Vista Dr. N&S .... 27W-40S | | 71 |
| Walnut Av. N&S .. 27W-42S | | 75 |
| Warner Bridge Rd. N&S | | |
| ..........21W-45S,21W-40S | | 77 |
| Wesley Rd. N&S | | |
| ......26W-43S,26W-42S | | 76 |
| Wildwood St. N&S.. 27W-41S | | 71 |
| Willow St. E&W .... 27W-41S | | 71 |
| Wood St. N&S .... 27W-40S | | 71 |
| Woodview Dr. N&S | | |
| .................. 27W-41S | | 71 |

## Wheatland Township

| | Grid | Page |
|---|---|---|
| Aero Ct. E&W .... 29W-14S | | 9 |
| Aero Dr. N&S .... 29W-14S | | 9 |
| Ainsdale Ct. E&W . 30W-12S | | 4 |
| Alago Rd. N&S .. 28W-10S | | 5 |
| Alamosa Ct. E&W .. 27W-10S | | 5 |
| Alan Dr. N&S ..... 28W-10S | | 5 |
| Alice Ln. E&W .. 30W-12S | | 4 |
| Alma Ln. N&S......28W-10S | | 5 |
| Andermann Dr. E&W | | |
| .................. 29W-11S | | 5 |
| Andrew Rd. E&W .. 29W-14S | | 9 |
| Anvil Ct. N&S .... 30W-13S | | 8 |
| Arrowhead Dr. N&S | | |
| .................. 30W-10S | | 4 |
| Ascot Ct. N&S .. 30W-12S | | 4 |
| Ashbury Rd. N&S .. 28W-11S | | 5 |
| Asther Ct. E&W .. 30W-15S | | 8 |
| Book Rd. N&S | | |
| ..........29W-14S,29W-11S | | 9 |
| Boughton Rd. NE&SW | | |
| .................. 27W-12S | | 5 |
| Brancaster Dr. NW&SE | | |
| .................. 30W-12S | | 4 |
| Brenner Pl. N&S.. 30W-12S | | 4 |
| Bridle Path Ct. N&S | | |
| .................. 30W-12S | | 4 |
| Burnham Ct. N&S . 30W-12S | | 4 |
| Carl Dr. N&S | | |
| ......31W-11S,31W-10S | | 4 |
| Castellan Ln. NS&EW | | |
| .................. 29W-10S | | 5 |
| Castle Dr. N&S .. 29W-10S | | 5 |
| Cathy Ln. NS&EW .. 29W-15S | | 9 |
| Chapins Rd. E&W | | |
| ......32W-14S,29W-14S | | 8 |
| Charles Ct. N&S .. 27W-10S | | 5 |
| Christine Ct. NE&SW | | |
| .................. 29W-13S | | 9 |
| Cindy Dr. NW&SE .. 32W-13S | | 8 |
| Clow Creek Rd. N&S | | |
| .................. 31W-11S | | 4 |
| Clow Ct. N&S .... 29W-13S | | 9 |
| Columbia Cir. E&W | | |
| .................. 30W-15S | | 8 |

| | Grid | Page |
|---|---|---|
| Condor Dr. N&S | | |
| ..........29W-12S,29W-11S | | 5 |
| Cotswald Dr. E&W .. 29W-14S | | 9 |
| Country Club Dr. NW&SE | | |
| .................. 30W-10S | | 4 |
| Countryview Dr. E&W | | |
| .................. 28W-10S | | 5 |
| Courtney Rd. NE&SW | | |
| .................. 32W-13S | | 8 |
| Curtis Ln. N&S .. 28W-10S | | 5 |
| Darcum Cir. N&S .. 28W-11S | | 5 |
| Davids St. N&S .. 30W-12S | | 4 |
| Davidson Rd. E&W 28W-10S | | 5 |
| Dawn Av. N&S .. 30W-12S | | 4 |
| De John Blvd. E&W | | |
| .................. 30W-12S | | 4 |
| Deer Chase Ln. NS&EW | | |
| .................. 29W-13S | | 5 |
| Denise St. N&S .. 29W-15S | | 9 |
| Dickens St. N&S .. 28W-11S | | 5 |
| Douglas Dr. E&W .. 29W-15S | | 5 |
| Douglas Rd. E&W .. 28W-10S | | 5 |
| Douglas Rd. E&W .. 29W-15S | | 9 |
| Drawbridge Rd. E&W | | |
| .................. 29W-10S | | 5 |
| Elaine Dr. N&S .. 30W-15S | | 8 |
| Elizabeth Dr. N&S .. 32W-15S | | 8 |
| Essington Rd. N&S | | |
| .................. 28W-13S | | 9 |
| Fairview Ct. NW&SE | | |
| .................. 29W-13S | | 9 |
| Falcon Rd. E&W .... 29W-12S | | 5 |
| Ferguson St. E&W | | |
| ..........29W-13S,28W-13S | | 9 |
| Fox Valley Expwy. NW&SE | | |
| ..........28W-14S,27W-14S | | 9 |
| Ganton Ct. E&W....30W-12S | | 4 |
| Giddings Dr. EW&NS | | |
| .................. 29W-13S | | 9 |
| Golden Meadow Ct. NW&SE | | |
| .................. 30W-15S | | 8 |
| Golden Meadow Dr. N&S | | |
| .................. 30W-15S | | 8 |
| Gordon Ct. E&W .. 28W-10S | | 5 |
| Graver Ct. N&S .. 28W-13S | | 9 |
| Graver Ln. E&W....30W-13S | | 9 |
| Greenburg Ct. E&W | | |
| .................. 30W-13S | | 8 |
| Grey Fox Tr. N&S .. 29W-12S | | 5 |
| Gristmill Ct. E&W .. 29W-10S | | 5 |
| Grommon Rd. E&W | | |
| .................. 28W-11S | | 5 |
| Hadfield Dr. N&S .. 30W-15S | | 8 |
| Hanslick Ct. N&S .. 31W-10S | | 4 |
| Hartman Dr. E&W .. 29W-11S | | 5 |
| Heggs Rd. N&S | | |
| ..........32W-14S,32W-10S | | 8 |
| Helene Av. N&S .... 30W-12S | | 4 |
| High Meadow Dr. N&S | | |
| .................. 29W-13S | | 9 |
| Highland Dr. N&S .. 30W-13S | | 8 |
| Hillview Dr. E&W .. 28W-10S | | 5 |
| Honey Locust Dr. NS&EW | | |
| .................. 29W-13S | | 9 |
| Hummingbird St. N&S | | |
| .................. 29W-12S | | 5 |
| Hunt Club Ct. E&W | | |
| .................. 29W-12S | | 5 |
| Industrial Dr., E. N&S | | |
| .................. 29W-14S | | 9 |
| Industrial Dr., N. E&W | | |
| .................. 29W-14S | | 9 |
| Industrial Dr., S. E&W | | |
| .................. 29W-14S | | 9 |
| Jane Ct. E&W ...... 29W-11S | | 5 |
| Jester Ct. E&W .... 29W-10S | | 5 |
| Joyce Ln. E&W .... 28W-10S | | 5 |
| Juanita Dr. E&W .. 29W-10S | | 5 |
| Karen Dr. NS&EW .. 32W-13S | | 8 |
| Kelly Ct. E&W ...... 32W-10S | | 8 |
| Kennemer Ct. E&W | | |
| .................. 30W-12S | | 4 |
| Killarney Ct. E&W .. 30W-12S | | 4 |
| Kings Rd. N&S .... 27W-14S | | 9 |
| Kings Rd. (proposed) NW&SE | | |
| ..........27W-13S,27W-11S | | 9 |
| Kipling Ct. E&W .... 29W-10S | | 5 |
| Kristal Rd. NS&EW 29W-13S | | 9 |
| Kristi Dr. NW&SE .. 32W-13S | | 8 |
| Lakeside Dr. E&W .. 29W-10S | | 5 |
| Lakeview Cir. E&W | | |
| .................. 28W-10S | | 5 |
| Laurel Ln. E&W .. 28W-10S | | 5 |
| Leona Dr. NW&SE .. 29W-14S | | 9 |
| Leverenz Rd. E&W 28W-10S | | 5 |
| Lillian Ct. N&S...... 29W-11S | | 5 |
| Lincoln Hwy. NW&SE | | |
| .................. 32W-13S | | 8 |
| Linda Ln. E&W .. 31W-11S | | 4 |
| Lois Ln. N&S ...... 29W-13S | | 9 |
| Mallard Ln. NS&EW | | |
| .................. 29W-11S | | 5 |
| Marie Ct. E&W .... 29W-13S | | 9 |
| Mark Dr. E&W......29W-11S | | 5 |
| Marquette Av. NE&SW | | |
| .................. 27W-10S | | 5 |
| Marte Ct. N&S .. 28W-10S | | 5 |
| Mayfair Meadows Dr. NS&EW | | |
| .................. 27W-10S | | 5 |
| Mayre Av. N&S .. 30W-12S | | 4 |
| McGrath Ln. N&S .. 29W-11S | | 5 |
| Meadow Dr. E&W .. 29W-10S | | 5 |
| Meadow Lake Dr. E&W | | |
| .................. 29W-12S | | 5 |

| | Grid | Page |
|---|---|---|
| Meadow Lily Ct. NW&SE | | |
| .................. 30W-15S | | 8 |
| Meadow Ln. N&S .. 28W-10S | | 5 |
| Merlin Cir. NE&SW ..29W-10S | | 5 |
| Muirfield Dr. N&S . 30W-12S | | 4 |
| Nancy Ct. E&W .. 28W-10S | | 5 |
| Naperville Rd. N&S | | |
| ..........28W-14S,28W-13S | | 9 |
| Newmarket Dr. N&S | | |
| .................. 30W-12S | | 4 |
| Nighthawk Rd. N&S | | |
| .................. 29W-11S | | 5 |
| Normantown Rd. N&S | | |
| ..........31W-10S,31W-14S | | 4 |
| Old Joliet Gravel Rd. E&W | | |
| ..........32W-10S,31W-10S | | 4 |
| Old Wheaton Dr. E&W | | |
| .................. 27W-10S | | 5 |
| Oswego Rd. NE&SW | | |
| ..........32W-11S,31W-11S | | 4 |
| Overman Ct. NW&SE | | |
| .................. 29W-15S | | 9 |
| Owl Rd. E&W ...... 29W-12S | | 5 |
| Oxford Ln. N&S .... 29W-14S | | 9 |
| Palmer Cir. NS&EW | | |
| .................. 30W-10S | | 4 |
| Park Ln. N&S .... 28W-10S | | 5 |
| Partlow Dr. E&W .. 29W-11S | | 5 |
| Paul Cir. N&S .... 29W-15S | | 9 |
| Paula Ct. NE&SW .. 29W-15S | | 9 |
| Perkins Ct. E&W .. 29W-15S | | 9 |
| Pheasant Run Ct. E&W | | |
| .................. 29W-12S | | 5 |
| Pilchers Rd. E&W | | |
| ..........32W-15S,28W-15S | | 8 |
| Pine Ridge Ct. NW&SE | | |
| .................. 27W-10S | | 5 |
| Plainfield-Naperville Rd. N&S | | |
| ..........28W-15S,28W-13S | | 9 |
| Plainview Dr. E&W .. 29W-13S | | 9 |
| Plantation Ct. E&W | | |
| .................. 30W-10S | | 4 |
| Poet Cir. N&S .. 28W-11S | | 5 |
| Quail Ridge Ct. N&S | | |
| .................. 29W-12S | | 5 |
| Ramm Dr. N&S .... 31W-10S | | 4 |
| Ramm Rd. N&S .... 31W-10S | | 4 |
| Rebecca Ct. E&W . 29W-11S | | 5 |
| Red Oak Rd. NS&EW | | |
| .................. 29W-13S | | 9 |
| Red Stable Dr. NW&SE | | |
| .................. 29W-12S | | 5 |
| Rhea Dr. N&S .... 29W-14S | | 9 |
| Richard St. E&W . 28W-11S | | 5 |
| Ridge Rd. N&S .... 27W-10S | | 5 |
| River Dr. N&S...... 27W-11S | | 5 |
| Rivercrest Dr. NE&SW | | |
| .................. 29W-15S | | 9 |
| Riverside Ct. NW&SE | | |
| .................. 29W-13S | | 5 |
| Robert Av. N&S ....21W-11S | | 7 |
| Robert Dr. N&S | | |
| ..........28W-12S,28W-11S | | 5 |
| Robin Ln. E&W .... 31W-11S | | 4 |
| Royal Birkdale Dr. E&W | | |
| .................. 30W-12S | | 4 |
| Royal County Down Dr. | | |
| NW&SE........30W-12S | | 4 |
| Royal Lytham Dr. N&S | | |
| .................. 30W-12S | | 4 |
| Royal Porthcawl Dr. N&S | | |
| .................. 30W-12S | | 4 |
| Royal Portrush Dr. E&W | | |
| .................. 30W-12S | | 4 |
| Schillinger Dr. NS&EW | | |
| .................. 29W-10S | | 5 |
| Schultz St. N&S....31W-11S | | 4 |
| Sharon Ct. E&W .. 29W-13S | | 9 |
| Sharon Rd. NS&EW | | |
| .................. 29W-13S | | 9 |
| Shell Lake Dr. E&W | | |
| .................. 29W-10S | | 5 |
| Sheri St. N&S .... 27W-11S | | 5 |
| Shoger Dr. NS&EW | | |
| .................. 29W-13S | | 9 |
| Snowbird St. N&S .. 29W-11S | | 5 |
| South Point Rd. N&S | | |
| .................. 29W-13S | | 9 |
| Southfield Dr. N&S .. 29W-13S | | 9 |
| Southpoint Dr. N&S | | |
| .................. 29W-13S | | 9 |
| Spalding School Dr. N&S | | |
| .................. 29W-14S | | 9 |
| Sparrow Ln. E&W .. 29W-12S | | 5 |
| Springbrook Dr. N&S | | |
| .................. 28W-10S | | 5 |
| Springdale Cir. N&S | | |
| .................. 29W-10S | | 5 |
| Springlake Dr. N&S | | |
| .................. 29W-10S | | 5 |
| Staffeldt Av. E&W .. 29W-11S | | 5 |
| Stevenson St. N&S | | |
| .................. 28W-11S | | 5 |
| Stratford Dr. E&W .. 29W-14S | | 9 |
| Sunningdale Ct. N&S | | |
| .................. 30W-12S | | 4 |
| Sunrise Dr. N&S .. 31W-11S | | 4 |
| Swandyke Ct. N&S | | |
| .................. 27W-10S | | 5 |
| Tern Ct. N&S .... 29W-13S | | 9 |
| Thatcher Ct. NW&SE | | |
| .................. 29W-13S | | 9 |
| Thatcher Dr. NW&SE | | |
| .................. 29W-13S | | 9 |

| | Grid | Page |
|---|---|---|
| Thelma Ct. NW&SE | | |
| .................. 29W-15S | | 9 |
| Timothy Av. E&W .. 27W-11S | | 5 |
| Treyburn Rd. NW&SE | | |
| .................. 30W-10S | | 4 |
| Turnberry Ct. NE&SW | | |
| .................. 30W-12S | | 4 |
| Vandyke Rd. N&S .. 30W-15S | | 8 |
| Vicky St. N&S....29W-15S | | 9 |
| Wagner Rd. E&W | | |
| ..........29W-11S,28W-11S | | 5 |
| Walter Ln. NW&SE 29W-11S | | 5 |
| Walton Heath Dr. N&S | | |
| .................. 30W-12S | | 4 |
| Webster Ln. NW&SE | | |
| .................. 29W-11S | | 5 |
| Wentworth Dr. N&S | | |
| .................. 30W-12S | | 4 |
| West St. NS&EW .. 27W-11S | | 5 |
| White Eagle Dr. NE&SW | | |
| .................. 30W-10S | | 4 |
| White Eagle Dr., S.E. NW&SE | | |
| .................. 30W-10S | | 4 |
| Whittington Ln. N&S | | |
| ..........29W-10S,29W-11S | | 5 |
| Wild Flower Dr. N&S | | |
| .................. 29W-13S | | 9 |
| Wilde Av. E&W .. 28W-11S | | 5 |
| Wileden Ln. N&S .. 28W-10S | | 5 |
| Windjammer Ln. N&S | | |
| .................. 29W-10S | | 5 |
| Winter Park Ct. E&W | | |
| .................. 27W-10S | | 5 |
| Wolf Rd. N&S .... 29W-14S | | 9 |
| Wolfs Crossing Rd. NE&SW | | |
| ..........32W-11S,31W-11S | | 4 |
| Woodhall Ct. E&W . 30W-12S | | 4 |
| Worcester Dr. N&S | | |
| .................. 27W-10S | | 5 |
| 91st St. E&W | | |
| ..........31W-10S,30W-10S | | 4 |
| 95th Av. E&W | | |
| ..........30W-11S,27W-11S | | 4 |
| 95th St. E&W | | |
| ..........31W-10S,28W-10S | | 4 |
| 96th Ct. E&W .... 27W-11S | | 5 |
| 103rd St. E&W | | |
| ..........31W-11S,29W-11S | | 4 |
| 104th St. E&W .. 28W-12S | | 5 |
| 111th St. E&W | | |
| ..........32W-12S,26W-12S | | 4 |
| 119th St. E&W | | |
| ..........32W-13S,27W-13S | | 8 |
| 127th St. E&W | | |
| ..........31W-14S,30W-14S | | 8 |
| 128th St. E&W .... 32W-15S | | 8 |
| 129th St. E&W .... 32W-15S | | 8 |
| 131st St. E&W .... 32W-15S | | 8 |
| 135th St. E&W | | |
| ..........30W-15S,29W-15S | | 8 |
| 248th St. N&S | | |
| ..........31W-14S,31W-11S | | 8 |

## Will Township

| | Grid | Page |
|---|---|---|
| Central Av. N&S | | |
| ..........7W-39S,7W-34S | | 66 |
| Church Rd. E&W | | |
| ..........6W-35S,3W-35S | | 54 |
| Cicero Av. N&S | | |
| ..........6W-39S,6W-34S | | 66 |
| Corning Rd. E&W | | |
| ..........7W-37S,3W-37S | | 66 |
| Corning St. E&W | | |
| ..........8W-37S,7W-37S | | 65 |
| County Line Rd. E&W | | |
| ..........3W-39S,3W-39S | | 65 |
| Crawford Av. N&S | | |
| ..........5W-39S,5W-34S | | 66 |
| Drecksler Rd. N&S .. 8W-39S | | 65 |
| Eagle Rd. E&W | | |
| ..........8W-34S,3W-34S | | 53 |
| Harlem Av. N&S | | |
| ..........8W-39S,8W-34S | | 65 |
| Joliet Rd. E&W | | |
| ..........8W-35S,3W-35S | | 53 |
| Kedzie Av. N&S | | |
| ..........4W-39S,4W-34S | | 67 |
| Kennedy Rd. E&W | | |
| ..........8W-38S,3W-38S | | 65 |
| Manhattan-Wilton Rd. E&W | | |
| ..........8W-34S,7W-34S | | 53 |
| N. Peotone Rd. E&W | | |
| ..........8W-35S,7W-35S | | 53 |
| Offner Rd. E&W | | |
| ..........8W-34S,3W-34S | | 53 |
| Peotone-Beecher Rd. E&W | | |
| ..........3W-36S,3W-36S | | 67 |
| Ridgeland Av. N&S | | |
| ..........8W-39S,8W-34S | | 65 |
| Route 50 NE&SW | | |
| ..........8W-37S,7W-34S | | 65 |
| Western Av. N&S | | |
| ..........3W-39S,3W-34S | | 67 |
| Will Center Rd. N&S | | |
| ..........5W-39S,5W-36S | | 66 |
| Wilmington-Peotone Rd. E&W | | |
| ..........8W-37S,3W-37S | | 65 |
| 219th St. E&W | | |
| ..........6W-34S,3W-34S | | 54 |

|  | Grid | Page |
|---|---|---|
| **Wilmington** | | |
| Amber Dr. NW&SE | 28W-37S | 59 |
| Baltimore St. (IL Hwy 53) | | |
| NE&SW | 28W-38S,27W-38S | 59 |
| Becky Av. E&W | 27W-39S | 59 |
| Bremer St. E&W | 27W-38S | 59 |
| Buchannan St. N&S | | |
| | 27W-39N | 59 |
| Byron St. E&W | 27W-38S | 59 |
| Cambridge Ct. E&W | | |
| | 27W-39S | 59 |
| Canal St. NE&SW | 27W-38S | 59 |
| Central Dr. NE&SW | | |
| | 27W-37S | 59 |
| Charlotte St. N&S | 27W-37S | 59 |
| Cherry St. E&W | 28W-39S | 59 |
| Chesson Ct. N&S | 26W-39S | 60 |
| Chestnut St. E&W | 28W-39S | 59 |
| Chicago St. NE&SW | | |
| | 27W-38S | 59 |
| Cross St. E&W | 27W-37S | 59 |
| Daniels St. N&S | | |
| | 27W-39S,27W-38S | 59 |
| Debbie Ln. E&W | | |
| | 28W-39S,27W-39S | 59 |
| E. Park St. N&S | | |
| | 27W-39S,27W-38S | 59 |
| East Kahler Rd. E&W | | |
| | 27W-39S | 59 |
| East St. E&W | | |
| | 27W-39S,27W-38S | 59 |
| Elizabeth St. NE&SW | | |
| | 27W-39S | 59 |
| Elm St. N&S | 27W-39S | 59 |
| Elwood St. NE&SW | | |
| | 27W-38S,27W-37S | 59 |
| Eula St. E&W | 27W-37S | 59 |
| Fairchild Dr. N&S | 27W-39S | 59 |
| Fifth St. (West River Rd.) | | |
| N&S | 28W-39S | 59 |
| First St. N&S | | |
| | 28W-39S,28W-38S | 59 |
| Fourth St. N&S | 28W-39S | 59 |
| Fulton St. NE&SW | | |
| | 27W-39S,27W-38S | 59 |
| Hayden Ct. E&W | 27W-38S | 59 |
| Hwy. 53 NS&EW | | |
| | 28W-39S,27W-38S | 59 |
| Jackson St. NS&EW | | |
| | 27W-38S | 59 |
| James St. E&W | 27W-38S | 59 |
| Janet Dr. N&S | 27W-38S | 59 |
| Jefferson St. NE&SW | | |
| | 27W-38S | 59 |
| Jewel Ln. N&S | 28W-37S | 59 |
| JoAnn Dr. E&W | | |
| | 27W-39S,26W-39S | 59 |
| Joliet St. N&S | | |
| | 27W-39S,27W-38S | 59 |
| Joliet St. NE&SW | 27W-37S | 59 |
| Kankakee River Dr. E&W | | |
| | 27W-37S | 59 |
| Kankakee St. N&S | | |
| | 27W-39S,27W-37S | 59 |
| Kerry Ct. N&S | 28W-39S | 59 |
| Kerry St. E&W | 28W-39S | 59 |
| Kirsten Ln. N&S | 28W-39S | 59 |
| Koala Ct. NE&SW | 28W-39S | 59 |
| Lafayette St. NE&SW | | |
| | 27W-38S | 59 |
| Laurel Av. E&W | 27W-39S | 59 |
| Laurel St. NE&SW | 27W-39S | 59 |
| Linda Ln. N&S | 28W-37S | 59 |
| Lindy Ln. E&W | 27W-39S | 59 |
| Locust St. NE&SW | 27W-39S | 59 |
| Luther St. N&S | 27W-39S | 59 |
| Mae St. N&S | 27W-39S | 59 |
| Main St. NW&SE | | |
| | 27W-39S,27W-38S | 59 |
| Margarette St. E&W | | |
| | 27W-37S | 59 |
| Marion St. E&W | 28W-37S | 59 |
| McIntyre St. NW&SE | | |
| | 27W-38S | 59 |
| Meadow Wood Ln. E&W | | |
| | 28W-39S | 59 |
| Michelle St. NW&SE | | |
| | 27W-38S | 59 |
| Middle St. E&W | 27W-38S | 59 |
| Mill St. NE&SW | 27W-38S | 59 |
| Milton St. N&S | 27W-38S | 59 |
| North Circle Dr. E&W | | |
| | 27W-38S | 59 |
| North Outer Dr. NS&EW | | |
| | 27W-38S | 59 |
| North Park St. NE&SW | | |
| | 27W-39S,27W-38S | 59 |
| North St. E&W | 27W-38S | 59 |
| North St. NS&EW | 27W-38S | 59 |
| Olive St. NE&SW | 27W-39S | 59 |
| Park Dr. N&S | 27W-39S | 59 |
| Parker Ct. NW&SE | 27W-38S | 59 |
| Pearl St. NW&SE | 27W-39S | 59 |
| Phyllis Dr. E&W | 27W-39S | 59 |
| Prairie Ln. E&W | 27W-39S | 59 |
| Ridge St. E&W | 27W-39S | 59 |
| Ridge Way E&W | 26W-39S | 60 |
| River St. NE&SW | 27W-39S | 59 |
| Robert St. N&S | 27W-39S | 59 |
| Route 102 NW&SE | | |
| | 27W-39S,27W-38S | 59 |
| Ryan St. NE&SW | 27W-39S | 59 |
| School St. N&S | 28W-38S | 59 |

|  | Grid | Page |
|---|---|---|
| Shakespeare St. N&S | | |
| | 27W-38S | 59 |
| Soldiers Widows Home Rd. | | |
| NW&SE | 28W-38S | 59 |
| South Circle Dr. NS&EW | | |
| | 27W-38S | 59 |
| South Outer Dr. NS&EW | | |
| | 27W-38S | 59 |
| South Park St. NE&SW | | |
| | 27W-39S | 59 |
| South St. E&W | 27W-38S | 59 |
| Stevens Ln. E&W | 28W-38S | 59 |
| Stewart St. E&W | 27W-38S | 59 |
| Strip Mine Rd. E&W | | |
| | 29W-39S,28W-39S | 58 |
| Sunset Dr. N&S | 27W-39S | 59 |
| Third St. N&S | 28W-39S | 59 |
| Tow Path Ln. NE&SW | | |
| | 28W-39S | 59 |
| Van Buren St. NE&SW | | |
| | 27W-38S | 59 |
| Vine St. NE&SW | 27W-39S | 59 |
| Vista Dr. N&S | 27W-39S | 59 |
| W. Kahler Rd. E&W | | |
| | 27W-39S | 59 |
| Wabash Av. NS&EW | | |
| | 27W-39S | 59 |
| Wabash St. NE&SW | | |
| | 27W-39S | 59 |
| Walnut St. E&W | 27W-39S | 59 |
| Washington St. NW&SE | | |
| | 27W-38S | 59 |
| Water St. NW&SE | | |
| | 27W-39S,27W-38S | 59 |
| West River Rd. (Fifth St.) | | |
| N&S | 28W-39S | 59 |
| West St. NS&EW | 27W-39S | 59 |
| West Water St. N&S | | |
| | 27W-38S | 59 |
| Williams St. NW&SE | | |
| | 27W-39S | 59 |
| Willida Av. N&S | 27W-39S | 59 |
| Winchester Green Dr. NE&SW | | |
| | 27W-39S | 59 |
| 216th Av. N&S | 27W-38S | 59 |

| **Wilmington Township** | | |
|---|---|---|
| Ash Ln. N&S | 32W-34S | 46 |
| Blodgett Rd. E&W | | |
| | 32W-34S,30W-34S | 46 |
| Boat House Rd. N&S | | |
| | 29W-37S,29W-36S | 58 |
| Carp Dr. NS&EW | 32W-34S | 46 |
| Catfish Dr. E&W | 32W-34S | 46 |
| Ceco Rd. (Murphy Rd.) E&W | | |
| | 32W-37S,30W-37S | 58 |
| Cedar Ln. N&S | 32W-34S | 46 |
| Center St. N&S | 31W-39S | 58 |
| Cherry Ln. NE&SW | | |
| | 32W-34S | 46 |
| Coal City Rd. (IL. Hwy 113) | | |
| E&W | 32W-39S,28W-39S | 58 |
| Cottage Rd. NS&EW | | |
| | 32W-35S,30W-35S | 46 |
| County Line Rd. N&S | | |
| | 32W-39S | 58 |
| Crappie Dr. E&W | 32W-34S | 46 |
| Division St. N&S | 32W-39S | 58 |
| Elm Dr. NE&SW | 32W-34S | 46 |
| Fir Ln. N&S | 32W-34S | 46 |
| Grundy County Line Rd. E&W | | |
| | 32W-37S,32W-34S | 58 |
| Holly Hock NW&SE | | |
| | 32W-34S | 46 |
| Hwy 129 N&S | | |
| | 30W-39S,30W-38S | 58 |
| Hwy 53 NE&SW | | |
| | 29W-39S,27W-35S | 58 |
| Interstate 55 N&S | | |
| | 32W-39S,30W-34S | 58 |
| Kankakee River Dr. NW&SE | | |
| | 28W-37S,27W-37S | 59 |
| Kankakee St. N&S | | |
| | 27W-37S,27W-33S | 59 |
| Kavanough Rd. N&S | | |
| | 31W-38S,31W-36S | 58 |
| Locust Ln. NS&EW | | |
| | 32W-34S | 46 |
| Lorenzo Rd. E&W | | |
| | 32W-35S,30W-35S | 46 |
| Murphy Rd. E&W | 31W-37S | 58 |
| New River Rd. NW&SE | | |
| | 29W-35S,27W-37S | 46 |
| North River Rd. NW&SE | | |
| | 30W-35S,30W-34S | 46 |
| School St. N&S | 28W-38S | 59 |
| South River Rd. E&W | | |
| | 29W-37S | 58 |
| Stevens Ln. E&W | 28W-38S | 59 |
| Strip Mine Rd. E&W | | |
| | 30W-38S,28W-38S | 58 |
| Townline Rd. E&W | | |
| | 29W-34S,27W-34S | 46 |
| Walnut Dr. Ln. N&S | | |
| | 32W-34S | 46 |
| Willow Ct. N&S | 32W-34S | 46 |
| Willow Dr. NW&SE | 32W-34S | 46 |
| Willow Ln. NW&SE | 32W-34S | 46 |
| Willow St. N&S | 32W-34S | 46 |

| **Wilton Township** | | |
|---|---|---|
| Arsenal Rd. E&W | | |
| | 20W-36S,15W-36S | 62 |
| Arsenal-Wilton Center Rd. | | |
| E&W | 20W-35S | 50 |
| Cedar Rd. N&S | 18W-37S | 62 |
| County Line Rd. E&W | | |
| | 20W-39S,15W-39S | 62 |
| Doyle Rd. E&W | | |
| | 20W-34S,18W-34S | 50 |
| Draves Rd. E&W | 17W-34S | 51 |
| Eagle Lake Rd. E&W | | |
| | 16W-34S,15W-34S | 51 |
| Eastern Av. N&S | | |
| | 19W-37S,19W-34S | 62 |
| Elevator Rd. N&S | | |
| | 16W-37S,16W-34S | 63 |
| Gouger Rd. N&S | | |
| | 20W-39S,20W-34S | 62 |
| Green Garden-Manhatten Rd. | | |
| N&S | 15W-39S,15W-34S | 63 |
| Grove St. E&W | | |
| | 17W-34S,16W-34S | 51 |
| Hwy 52 NS&EW | | |
| | 18W-34S,15W-35S | 50 |
| Joliet Rd. (St.) N&S | | |
| | 17W-35S,16W-34S | 51 |
| Kennedy Rd. E&W | | |
| | 20W-38S,15W-38S | 62 |
| Manhattan-Wilton Rd. E&W | | |
| | 20W-34S,15W-34S | 50 |
| Offner Rd. E&W | | |
| | 20W-34S,15W-34S | 50 |
| Olive St. E&W | 17W-34S | 51 |
| Tully Rd. N&S | | |
| | 19W-39S,19W-34S | 62 |
| Wallingford Rd. N&S | | |
| | 17W-35S,17W-34S | 51 |
| Washington St. N&S | | |
| | 17W-34S | 51 |
| Wilmington-Peotone Rd. E&W | | |
| | 20W-37S,15W-37S | 62 |
| Wilton Center Rd. N&S | | |
| | 18W-39S,18W-34S | 63 |
| Wilton Rd. N&S | | |
| | 16W-39S,16W-36S | 63 |
| 120th Av. N&S | | |
| | 15W-38S,15W-34S | 63 |
| 128th Av. N&S | 16W-38S | 63 |

| **Woodridge*** | | |
|---|---|---|
| **(Also see Du Page County)** | | |
| Davey Rd. E&W | | |
| | 21W-12S,20W-12S | 7 |
| Marmon Dr. N&S | 21W-12S | 7 |